INFORMATION RIGHTS

LAW AND PRACTICE

Third Edition

INFORMATION RIGHTS
LAW AND PRACTICE

Third Edition

by

Philip Coppel QC

Contributors

Anna Bicarregui
Estelle Dehon
Saima Hanif
Sarah Hannett
Hodge Malek QC
Oliver Sanders
His Honour Judge Shanks
Richard Spearman QC

·HART·
PUBLISHING

OXFORD – PORTLAND OREGON
2010

Published in North America (USA and Canada) by
Hart Publishing
c/o International Specialized Book Services
920 NE 58th Avenue, Suite 300
Portland, OR 97213 – 3786
USA
Tel: +1 503 287 3093 or toll-free (1) 800 944 6190
Fax: +1 503 280 8832
e-mail: orders@isbs.com
Website: http://www.isbs.com

First published 2004
Second edition 2007

Hart Publishing Ltd
16C Worcester Place, Oxford, OX1 2JW
Telephone: +44 (0)1865 517530
Fax: +44 (0)1865 510710
E-mail: mail@hartpub.co.uk
Website: http://www.hartpub.co.uk

British Library Cataloguing in Publication Data
Data Available

ISBN: 978-184946-0118

Printed and bound in Great Britain on acid-free paper by
TJ International Ltd, Padstow, Cornwall

PREFACE

In the two and a half years since publication of the second edition of this work, there have been 300-odd Information Tribunal decisions. From these there have also been a small number of appeals to the Courts. These are, of course, important. However, it is fair to say that it is through the Tribunal's decisions that most of the important principles are being worked out. This is not surprising. The sheer quantity of appeals to the Tribunal provides a wealth of material from which to fashion principles. Moreover, as a merit-review body hearing of the evidence, often from all three parties (applicant, public authority and Information Commissioner), as well as seeing the information in dispute, it has unique insight into the practical consequences of the competing interpretations. Once again, I have striven to incorporate into this edition as much of the jurisprudence of the Tribunal as practicable.

Notwithstanding the increased wealth of domestic authority, I have retained the comparative jurisprudence. It continues to provide a useful normative yardstick, illustrating how other democratic countries with similar legal traditions have addressed the problems to which such legislation inevitably gives rise.

I noted in the Preface to the Second Edition that it was not to be expected that New Year's Day 2005 would be marked by precipitate culture change within government departments or elsewhere. The abortive attempt to amend the Freedom of Information Act so as to exempt everything held by or coming from the Houses of Parliament — the Bill for which was passed by the House of Commons with a comfortable majority — evidences that.[1] The instinctive urge of public authorities to keep private their information gravitates against the concepts that animate the Freedom of Information Act 2000. This cannot realistically be expected to alter. Rather, re-reading the justifications put forward for the Amendment Bill provides a reminder of the ever-present need to examine rigorously claims for exemption, particularly those resulting in weakened public accountability.

The most significant procedural change since the last edition has been the creation of a comprehensive administrative tribunal system in the United Kingdom: the First-tier Tribunal and the Upper Tribunal. In terms of administrative law, their creation — underscored by the stature of their members — stands to be the most important administrative law development in a lifetime. Time will tell whether the opportunity it presents for a general right of independent, merit-review of administrative decisions relating to an individual will be realised. However, so far as appeals against information rights decisions are concerned, that day arrived with the Freedom of Information Act 2000 itself. The effect of the tribunal reform has been to abolish the Information Tribunal, with its jurisdiction being moved into the First-tier and Upper Tribunals. This bifurcation has provided the means to divide the groundbreaking appeals from the more mundane ones. And it enables the judiciary to decide legal principles having heard the evidence and seen the documents.

Once again, I extend my gratitude to the contributors. There have been changes here, with a number of former authors having taken on writing projects of their own. I have not

---

[1] See further §1—036.

sought to distract them. They have allowed me to bring fresh eyes to existing text.

I thank my father for his very considerable assistance in preparing this edition. His support in my faltering moments have seen it through to completion.

And finally, I am indebted to Richard Hart for having taken over this publication. He has improved the quality of production whilst bringing the work within reach of a wider audience. In so doing, he has shown what can be done in legal publishing.

For all the remaining shortcomings in this edition, I take full responsibility.

As far as practicable, I have attempted to state the law in light of the material available to me at 1 May 2010.

Philip Coppel QC
4–5 Gray's Inn Square
London
WC1R 5AH

15 June 2010

PREFACE TO THE FIRST EDITION

The enactment of the Freedom of Information Act 2000 represents the most significant step in the development within the United Kingdom of the right of an individual to elicit information from a public authority. Over the 40 preceding years, a patchwork of legislation had provided the individual with limited rights of access to information held by public authorities. Invariably, these rights were confined in scope by reference to the subject matter of the information, to the identity of the public authority holding the information, to the identity of the person seeking the information, or to any combination of these. While Freedom of Information Act 2000 largely dispenses with these limitations, the patchwork of earlier legislation remains in place. To the extent that a right of access to particular information can be grounded in the earlier legislation, the regime operates to require that that right be used over the right that might otherwise exist under the Freedom of Information Act 2000. Both for the individual seeking to secure information from a public authority and for the public authority responding to a request for information, what is of paramount concern is whether there is a right of access to that information: it is not merely whether there is a right of access to that information under the Freedom of Information Act 2000. This work has therefore sought to treat comprehensively rights of access to information held by public authorities, whatever the source of that right. These have been compendiously termed "information rights". It is, in any event, a term that I consider better describes the reality, with its sharply competing considerations, than does "freedom of information".

The work is a practitioner's text. By this I do not just mean legal practitioners, but all those whose occupation involves seeking or handling requests for official information. Its purpose is not evangelical: that is a purpose that is well served by the material already on offer.

The Freedom of Information Act 2000 is at once both complex and subtle. It is to be hoped that this work will assist in resolving its complexities and in revealing its subtleties. The complexities, which may seem needless at times, are in no small part due to its respect for the earlier evolution of information rights. It is only by simultaneously considering these other information rights that its complexities can begin to be unpicked.

Both during its passage through Parliament and afterwards, considerable criticism was levelled at the range of exemptions provided by the Freedom of Information Act 2000. It is enough for present purposes to make the following observation. It is true that the Act has been cast widely, with an extensive range of public authorities being netted; but it is also true that the mesh of that net is wide in parts. And yet, this is to miss the central feature of the Freedom of Information Act 2000: the role of the public interest and of the Information Commissioner. Together, these result in the ultimate "strength" of the Act lying in the hands of the latter through his conceptualisation of the former.

Inevitably, there has within this work been a certain amount of speculation as to the meaning and operation of the provisions of the Freedom of Information Act 2000. I have sought to found that speculation upon a consideration of cognate branches of the law and by reference to the jurisprudence of comparative jurisdictions. The Freedom of Information Act 2000 will, of course, have to be interpreted according to its own terms and having regard to the circumstances and standards of this jurisdiction. However, in asking and answering the right questions on issues involving complex and sensitive concepts, it is illuminating to consider how other democratic jurisdictions enjoying similar legal traditions have addressed these issues. That a comparable jurisdiction has had to wrestle with these issues is comforting; that that jurisdiction has worked out solutions consistent with its constitutional standards is both invaluable and instructive. Given that freely available databases on the Internet enable sedentary access to most of the comparative authorities cited in this work, it would be wilful to ignore this seam of jurisprudence.

In writing this book, I must first extend my gratitude to the contributors. Having been persuaded or cajoled by me into joining an enterprise that I promised would not materially interfere with their practices, I provided each with piles of material and lists of authorities that I feel reasonably confident none expected. The work has been much enhanced by their expertise and their contributions. For any remaining shortcomings in the book, I take full responsibility.

I am grateful to Mr Justice Richards for making the time to read the proofs and to write his generous Foreword. Finally, I thank my father for his unstinting support for me in this project.

I have attempted to state the law in light of the material available to me at January 1, 2004. It is intended to keep the book updated by the issue of cumulative supplements as appropriate. Comments on the work, critical or otherwise, are generally welcomed.

Philip Coppel
4–5 Gray's Inn Square
London
WC1R 5AH

1 January 2004

CONTENTS

Chapter 1 – Eliciting Official Information

Chapter 2 – The Comparative Jurisdictions

Chapter 3 – The Influence of the European Convention on Human Rights etc

Estelle Dehon

Chapter 4 – Rights of Access under European Union Law

Anna Bicarregui

Chapter 5 – Access to Personal Information under the Data Protection Act 1998

Estelle Dehon

Chapter 6 – Access under the Environmental Information Regulations

Chapter 18 – International and Internal Relations

Oliver Sanders (section 2)

Chapter 19 – Economic and Financial Interests

Chapter 20 – Investigation, Audit, Law Enforcement and the Courts

HHJ Shanks

Chapter 21 – Privilege

Hodge Malek QC (section 2)

Chapter 22 – Policy Formulation and Public Affairs

Sarah Hannett

Chapter 23 – Health and Safety

Chapter 24 – Personal Information

Estelle Dehon

Chapter 25 – Confidential Information

Richard Spearman QC

Materials

Tribunal Rules, Orders and Practice Notes

Statutory Codes of Practice

European Union Directives and Regulations

TABLES OF CASES

United Kingdom

xxii

l

European Union

United States of America

Australia

Canada

New Zealand

Republic of Ireland

TABLES OF PRIMARY LEGISLATION

Freedom of Information Act 2000

Freedom of Information (Scotland) Act 2002

Other UK Primary Legislation

c

TABLES OF SECONDARY LEGISLATION

Environmental Information Regulations 2004

Environmental Information (Scotland) Regulations 2004

Other UK Secondary Legislation

TABLES OF EU LEGISLATION

Regulations

Directives

TABLES OF NATIONAL LEGISLATION

Australia

Australian Secondary Legislation

Canada

New Zealand

Republic of Ireland

United States of America

TABLE OF ABBREVIATIONS

CPR	Civil Procedure Rules 1998
DCA	Department of Constitutional Affairs
DEFRA	Department for Environment, Food and Rural Affairs
DPA	Data Protection Act 1998
DP (Fees) Regs	Data Protection (Subject Access) (Fees and Miscellaneous Provisions) Regulations 2000
EIR	Environmental Information Regulations 2004
EI(S)R	Environmental Information (Scotland) Regulations 2004
FOIA	Freedom of Information Act 2000
FOI (Time) Regs	Freedom of Information (Time for Compliance with Request) Regulations 2004
FOI(S)A	Freedom of Information (Scotland) Act 2002
FOI & DP (Limit & Fees) Regs	Freedom of Information and Data Protection (Appropriate Limit and Fees) Regulations 2004
FTT Rules	Tribunal Procedure (First-tier Tribunal) (General Regulatory Chamber) Rules 2009
HC	House of Commons
HL	House of Lords
IC	Information Commissioner
IT	Information Tribunal
IT(EA)Rules	Information Tribunal (Enforcement Appeals) Rules 2005
IT (NSA) Rules	Information Tribunal (National Security Appeals) Rules 2005
MoJ	Ministry of Justice
UT Rules	Tribunal Procedure (Upper Tribunal) Rules 2008
s.45 Code of Practice	Secretary of State for Constitutional Affairs' Code of Practice On the Discharge of Public Authorities' Functions under Part I of the Freedom of Information Act 2000. Presented to Parliament by the Secretary of State for Constitutional Affairs pursuant to section 45(5) of the FOIA, 25 November 2004.
s.46 Code of Practice	Lord Chancellor's Code of Practice on the Management of Records issued under section 46 of the Freedom of Information Act 2000. Presented to Parliament by the Lord Chancellor pursuant to section 46(6) of the FOIA, 16 July 2009.

WEB SOURCES

Primary material

UK material

UK cases and legislation:
www.bailii.org/

UK Information Commissioner:
www.ico.gov.uk/

Scottish Information Commissioner:
www.itspublicknowledge.info/

UK Information Tribunal:
www.informationtribunal.gov.uk/

MoJ, FOI home page (includes guidance):
www.justice.gov.uk/guidance/freedom-of-information.htm

DEFRA, EIR home page:
www.defra.gov.uk/corporate/opengov/eir/index.htm

DEFRA, Code of Practice issued under EIR reg 16(1):
www.defra.gov.uk/corporate/opengov/eir/cop.htm

DEFRA, Guidance on EIR:
www.defra.gov.uk/corporate/opengov/eir/guidance/full-guidance/index.htm

UK National Archives:
www.nationalarchives.gov.uk/

UK National Archives, policy on retention:
www.nationalarchives.gov.uk/ policy/ default.htm

UK National Archives, Departmental Management of Records Statement:
www.pro.gov.uk/about/access/system

Non-UK material

Australian cases and legislation:
www.austlii.edu.au/

Canadian cases and legislation:
www.canlii.org/

Irish cases and legislation:
www.bailii.org/

New Zealand cases and legislation:
www.nzlii.org/

US cases and legislation:
www.law.cornell.edu/

US Court of Appeals for the 1st circuit:
www.ca1.uscourts.gov/
  Substitute ca2 for 2nd circuit etc.
  Substitute cadc for the District of Columbia circuit

US, Executive Order 12,958 (as amended, 25 March 2003):
www.whitehouse.gov/news/releases/2003/03/20030325-11.html

European material

European Court of Human Rights:
cmiskp.echr.coe.int/tkp197/

European Court:

curia.europa.eu/en/

International material

Aarhus Convention:
www.unece.org/env/pp/documents/cep43e.pdf

UN Convention of Biological Diversity, concluded at Rio de Janiero, 5 June 1992:
www.biodiv.org/doc/legal/cbd-un-en.pdf

UN Convention Concerning the Protection of the World Cultural and Natural Heritage, concluded at Paris, 16 November 1972:
www.whc.unesco.org/world_he.htm

Secondary material

UK material

Cabinet Office, Open Government Code of Practice on Access to Government Information, 2nd edn (1997):
www.archive.official-documents.co.uk/document/caboff/foi/foi.htm

Cabinet Office, *Your Right to Know. The Government's Proposals for a Freedom of Information Act. White Paper* (Cm 3818, 1997):
www.archive.official-documents.co.uk/document/caboff/foi/foi.htm

House of Commons, Public Administration—Third Report (Cm 4355, 1999):
www.publications.parliament.uk/pa/cm199899/cmselect/cmpubadm/570/57002.htm

Secretary of State for Constitutional Affairs' Code of Practice On the Discharge of Public Authorities' Functions under Part I of the Freedom of Information Act 2000 (25 November 2004):
www.justice.gov.uk/guidance/foi-guidance-codes-practice.htm

Lord Chancellor's Code of Practice on the Management of Records under section 46 of the Freedom of Information Act 2000 (16 July 2009). Presented to Parliament by the Lord Chancellor pursuant to section 46(6) of the FOIA:
www.justice.gov.uk/guidance/foi-guidance-codes-practice.htm

DCA, *Review of Statutory Prohibitions on Disclosure*:
www.dca.gov.uk/statbarsrep2005sm1.pdf)

National Archives, Guidance on the FOI Act:
www.nationalarchives.gov.uk/policy/foi

Information Commissioner, Guidance on the FOI Act:
www.ico.gov.uk/eventual.aspx?id=33

Scottish Information Commissioner, Guidance on the FOI(S) Act
www.itspublicknowledge.info/legislation/briefings/briefings.htm

Non-UK material

Australian Law Reform Commission and Administrative Review Council, *Open Government: A Review of the Federal Freedom of Information Act 1982*, ALRC 77, ARC 40 (Canberra, 1995):
www.austlii.edu.au/au/other/alrc/publications/reports/77/

European material

The European Data Protection Supervisor, 'Public Access to Information and Data Protection', Background Paper Series, July 2005, No 1:

www.edps.europa.eu/EDPSWEB/edps/lang/en/pid/21Background

International material

Economic Commission for Europe, The Aarhus Convention. An Implementation Guide
(New York, United Nations, 2000):
www.unece.org/env/pp/acig.pdf

CHAPTER 1

Eliciting Official Information

1.   OVERVIEW OF OFFICIAL INFORMATION ACCESS LEGISLATION

1– 001 **Introduction**

The four decades leading to 2000 saw within the United Kingdom a gradual increase in the rights of an individual to elicit information from public authorities. The Public Bodies (Admission to Meetings) Act 1960 marked the first step in that process.[1] The Act had been introduced into Parliament as a private Member's Bill. The Member sponsoring the Bill spoke of a 'right to know'[2] and set out the purpose of that right:

> The public has the right...to know what its elected representatives are doing.... Unless the Press, which is to report to the public, has some idea from the documents before it what is to be discussed, the business of allowing the Press in becomes wholly abortive...The Press must have some idea from the documents what is the true subject to be discussed at a meeting to which its representatives are entitled to be admitted...I hope that hon. Members will think fit to give this Bill a Second Reading, and to consider that the paramount function of this distinguished House is to safeguard civil liberties rather than to think that

---

[1]   The Act applies to local authorities, education committees, parish meetings of rural parishes, various NHS boards, bodies and executive councils, as well as their committees. It makes the meetings of all such bodies open to the public, except where publicity 'would be contrary to the public interest'. Section 1(4)(b) provides that where the meeting is required to be open to the public, a newspaper can request, and on payment of postage must be supplied with, the agenda of the meeting '...together with such further statements or particulars, if any, as are necessary to indicate the nature of the items included or, if thought fit in the case of any item, with copies of any reports or other documents supplied to members of the body in connection with the item'. The Act is considered further at §§5– 012 to 5– 017.

[2]   In a speech by Lord Falconer (Constitutional Affairs Secretary and Lord Chancellor) to the International Conference of Information Commissioners, Manchester, 22 May 2006, he stated: 'Freedom of Information demands extra of our public officials, it requires cultural change within Governments and among public officials – a shift in mindset from the "need to know" to the "right to know".'

administrative convenience should take first place in law.[3]

The novelty of the Act lay in the conferral of a right to obtain access to official documents.[4] Although the scope of the right was narrow, to some its mere existence made the Act 'a very controversial piece of legislation'.[5] Its potential for extension, in particular to the ministries of central government, was immediately recognised.[6] Indeed, apart from the right of access to documents, there was little in the Act that was new:

> As the Hon Member for Islington North said, unless the spirit of the Bill is observed, it will do little more than the existing legislation. It will, however, do one thing more, and that is the most important feature to have come out of the Bill. It is not so much the admission of the public, curiously enough, but the provisions relating to the distribution of documents, that may well turn out to be the most important part of the Bill.[7]

The rationale for this early legislation and its identification of the competing considerations for and against disclosure of official information were to anticipate the preoccupations of Parliament 40 years later.

2 The Freedom of Information Act 2000

The enactment of the Freedom of Information Act 2000 represented a significant step in the process that had begun with the Public Bodies (Admission to Meetings) Act 1960. For the first time in the United Kingdom, Parliament conferred a right of access to official information that was not confined either by its permissible subject matter or by reference to the persons who may exercise that right. Its starting point is a right, described without reference to a subject-matter, conferred upon every person to have disclosed all information answering the terms of a request held by the requested public authority. Up until the Freedom of Information Act 2000, every right to elicit official information had been limited. The limitation had been generally referable to information answering a particular description or emanating from a particular source. But it had also been limited by reference to the persons on whom the right was conferred. In some cases, it was limited in both such respects. The access right conferred by the 2000 Act has no such limitation: it is given to every person, irrespective of that person's interest in the information; and it applies to all information, irrespective of its subject-matter. The right is, however, shaped by a series of specific exemptions.[8] To the extent that the

---

[3] Hansard HC vol 616 cols 1350–1358 (5 February 1960) (Margaret Thatcher, Finchley, Second Reading Speech. This was her maiden speech).

[4] The provision of a right for the press to attend meetings of local authorities had been introduced by The Local Authorities (Admission of the Press to Meetings) Act 1908, passed in consequence of the judgment in *Tenby Corp v Mason* [1908] 1 Ch 457. Section 3 of the 1908 Act provided that it was not to extend to any meeting of a committee of a local authority, other than education committees. The efficacy of the Act was reduced by the Local Government Act 1933 s 85, which empowered local authorities to appoint any committees they chose. As a result of this, many authorities went into committee of the full council in order to be able to exclude the press. Its efficacy was further reduced by the Education Act 1944, which removed education committees from the operation of the Act.

[5] Hansard HC vol 616 col 1366 (5 February 1960) (Mr GW Reynolds, Islington North).

[6] 'How Parliament would get on in those circumstances I really dread to think.' — Hansard HC vol 616 col 1384 (5 February 1960) (Mr Arthur Skeffington, member for Hayes and Harlington, quoting from the Official Report of the Standing Committee D on the Local Government Bill in 1958).

[7] Hansard HC vol 617 col 830 (13 May 1960) (Mr Peter Kirk, Gravesend).

[8] See FOIA s 1(2); FOI(S)A s 1(6). These make the rights or right, respectively, subject to (most importantly) s 2, thereby bringing in the provisions of Pt II of the Act.

requested information does not fall within one or more of those exemptions, it must be disclosed. There are two types of exemption. If information falls within the terms of a provision conferring 'absolute exemption' the right to disclosure is thereby disapplied.[9] If information falls within the terms of a provision conferring exemption, but not 'absolute exemption', then only if the public interest in maintaining that exemption outweighs the public interest in disclosure of the information will the right to disclosure be disapplied. The breadth of the Freedom of Information Act 2000 gives it greater significance than the earlier legislation conferring subject-specific rights of access.

1– 003   Earlier official information access legislation

Although the earlier patchwork of rights initiated by one paragraph in the Public Bodies (Admission to Meetings) Act 1960 has been eclipsed by the Freedom of Information Act 2000, it remains largely intact.[10] From the perspective of an individual seeking to elicit official information, the paramount concern will be the existence of a right to obtain that information, rather than the statutory provenance of that right. From the perspective of a public authority responding to a request for information under the Freedom of Information Act 2000, the existence of an alternative statutory right of access to the information will result in the displacement of the right of access to that information under the 2000 Act.[11] The earlier legislation thus remains significant. In this work, subject-specific rights of access have been considered thematically in Chapters 5, 6 and 8.

1– 004   Relationship between the FOI Act, the Data Protection Act and the Environmental Information Regulations

On the same day that the Freedom of Information Act 2000 came fully into force (1 January 2005), the Environmental Information Regulations 2004 also came into force. The Regulations provide a right of access to 'environmental information' held by public authorities. The Freedom of Information Act 2000, whilst unrestricted in its breadth, expressly acknowledges the proscriptions and the disclosure regimes of both the Data Protection Act 1998 and the Regulations. Both of these implement European Directives that had to be accommodated by the draftsman of the Freedom of Information Act 2000. This requirement was secured by routeing the treatment of requested information through the 1998 Act or the Regulations according to whether that information related to the applicant or was 'environmental information' (respectively). So far as personal information is concerned, an applicant's right of access to information of which he is the data subject is governed by s 7 of the Data Protection Act 1998. Where an applicant seeks personal information of which he is not the data subject, then the applicant's right of access is governed by the Freedom of Information Act. In this case,

---

[9] The verb 'disapply' in relation to the rights is used throughout this work to signify that one or both of the rights do not apply. It is recognised that the creation of express relationships between ss 1(1), 1(2), 2 and Pt II of the FOIA is simply a legislative technique for delineating the bounds of those substantive rights. In other words, these provisions shape the scope of the rights, rather than remove or negate a right already given. For a similar technique used elsewhere, see *Matthews v Ministry of Defence* [2003] 1 AC 1163, esp at [20], in relation to the Crown Proceedings Act 1947.

[10] Some rights have been repealed by the DPA, namely: the Access to Personal Files Act 1987; parts of the Access to Health Records Act 1990.

[11] FOIA s 21; FOI(S)A s 25.

however, disclosure under the Act will constitute a processing of personal data, which is a matter governed by the Data Protection Act 1998. The legislative regime reconciles the competing interests of the applicant and the subject of the personal information by importing into the Freedom of Information Act 2000 the protection given by certain of the data protection principles. Disclosure of personal information is considered in detail in Chapter 5 (personal information the only subject of which is the applicant) and Chapter 24 (personal information the subject of which is or includes someone other than the applicant). Where a request is for, or includes, environmental information, the request (or that part of the request) is governed by the Environmental Information Regulations 2004. This routeing is necessary in order to implement the more generous disclosure regime applicable to environmental information under European Parliament's Directive 2003/4/EC. Disclosure of environmental information is considered in Chapter 6.

2. TERMINOLOGY

5 **The basic rights**
It is convenient at this point to set out the principal terms that will be used in this work.
(1)   When this work refers to the 'FOI Acts', it generally means both the Freedom of Information Act 2000 and the Freedom of Information (Scotland) Act 2002. Footnotes identify the different section numbers, as well as differences between the two Acts. Where those differences are more substantive than can properly be set out in a footnote, they are treated separately in the main text.
(2)   When this work refers to the 'DPA', it means the Data Protection Act 1998. The DPA applies equally to Scotland.
(3)   The Environmental Information Regulations 2004 apply to public authorities and the Environmental Information (Scotland) Regulations 2004 apply to Scottish public authorities. Footnotes identify the different regulation numbers as well as differences between the two regimes. Footnotes also indicate the provenance of the regulations, both from Directive 2003/4/EC and the Aarhus Convention from which it was derived.
(4)   The FOI Acts confer on every person two distinct but interrelated entitlements:
(a)   First, an entitlement to be informed in writing by a public authority whether it holds information of the description specified in a request.[12] The FOI Acts label the duty of a public authority to comply with this entitlement as the *duty to confirm or deny*.[13] In shorthand, this may be called the *divulgence duty*. From the perspective of the person who made the request for the information, this may be called the *existence right*.
(b)   Secondly, but more importantly, if the public authority does hold information of the description specified in a request, an entitlement to

---

[12] FOIA s 1(1)(a). This does not exist as a discrete entitlement under the FOI(S)A.
[13] FOIA s 1(6).

have that information communicated to him.[14] The FOI Acts[15] refer to this at various points as *disclosure*. In this work, this duty has been variously called the *disclosure duty* or the *duty to communicate*. From the perspective of the person requesting the information, this may be called the *access right*. Although the FOI Acts locate this right after the existence right, it is better considered first: the existence right is academic if a decision has been made to disclose the information.[16]

(5) The Environmental Information Regulations 2004 and the Environmental Information (Scotland) Regulations 2004 confer a similar access right, but confined to 'environmental information'. There are significant differences in the breadth of the rights conferred by the FOI Acts and the right conferred by the Regulations. Generally, but not always, the Regulations provide a more liberal disclosure regime than the FOI Acts.

(6) The DPA confers on every person a right to be informed whether personal data of which the applicant is the data subject is being held and a right to have communicated to him those data.[17] The DPA speaks of data rather than of 'information', but the definition of 'data' makes it clear that data are simply information that has certain routine characteristics.[18] 'Personal data' means data that relate to a living individual who can be identified from the data, including any expressions of opinion about the individual.[19]

1– 006   Exemptions and exceptions

Part II of the FOI Acts and Part IV of the DPA enumerate a series of provisions, which in this work are called *exemptions*.[20] Part 3 of the Environmental Information Regulations 2004 and of the Environmental Information (Scotland) Regulations 2004 employ the term *exceptions* rather than *exemptions*. Nothing turns on the different terminology. Each of the provisions of Part II of the FOI Acts, in describing one or more types of information, renders it *exempt information*.[21] This designation is significant for the disclosure duty: the designation is a requirement for disapplication of that duty and, in relation to some of the provisions, is sufficient for disapplication of that duty. In relation to the duty to confirm or deny, each of the provisions in Part II (with two exceptions),[22] after describing a type of exempt information, is followed by

---

[14]   FOIA s 1(1)(b); FOI(S)A s 1(1).

[15]   FOIA ss 9(5), 13(3), 17(4), 22, 23(5), 26(1), 27(1) and (4), 28(1), 29(1), 33(2), 35(4), 36(2) and (7), 38(1), 40(3), 41(1), 42(2), 43(1), 44(1), 45(2), 53(7), 77(1), and 81(2); FOI(S)A ss 9(7), 13(4), 16(2), 26, 27, 28, 29(3), 30, 31(4), 32(1), 33(1) and (2), 35(1), 36(2), 38(2), 39(1), 40, 45, 50(7), 52(3), 60(2), 62(4), 64(1), 65(1).

[16]   As is implicitly recognised by the FOIA s 1(5).

[17]   DPA s 7(1)(a) and (c).

[18]   DPA s 1(1).

[19]   DPA s 1(1).

[20]   It is only the DPA that expressly refers to them as being 'exemptions'.

[21]   A term recognised throughout the FOI Acts: see FOIA s 84; FOI(S)A s 73. There are some specific sections in Pt II that are simply supportive of other provisions in that Part, eg FOIA s 25.

[22]   FOIA ss 21 and 43(1).

a closely corresponding provision preventing that duty from arising. The FOI Acts sometimes speak of the latter as an *exclusion* of the duty to confirm or deny,[23] and that term is used in this work.

7   Absolute exemptions

Some provisions in Part II of the FOI Acts confer what that Act calls *absolute exemption*.[24] The remaining provisions[25] in Part II of the FOI Acts confer what this work terms *qualified exemption*. The Environmental Information Regulations 2004 do not employ these terms, although the exceptions may be similarly divided. Where information falls within the terms of a provision that confers absolute exemption, the disclosure right does not apply and the public authority is thereby relieved from the duty to communicate. Similarly, where confirmation or denial of a holding would fall within one of the provisions in Part II under which the duty to confirm or deny is said not to arise and that provision confers absolute exemption, the right does not apply and the public authority is thereby relieved from the duty to confirm or deny. The Act speaks of an 'exclusion' of the duty to confirm or deny and of an 'exemption' from the duty to communicate.[26] Those duties may be said to be *disapplied*.[27] For information that falls within the terms of a provision that confers qualified exemption, the public authority may or may not be relieved from the duty to confirm or deny and from the duty to communicate depending upon a consideration of the public interest.[28]

8   Procedural terms

The person who seeks the information under the FOI Acts or the Environmental Information Regulations 2004 is called the *applicant*.[29] The person who seeks the information under the DPA is called the *recipient*.[30] Under both Acts and the Regulations, information is sought by a *request*.[31] A request under the FOI Acts and the Regulations is addressed to a *public authority*, which may be a government department, one of the Houses of Parliament, any emanation of local government or the National Health Service, any number of specifically named public bodies or officers, or a publicly owned company.[32] A request under the DPA is addressed to a *data controller*, which includes each government department as if it were a separate individual.[33] Under both Acts and the Regulations, once the public authority receives a valid request, it may give the applicant a *fees notice*, in which it sets out the amount it will charge the applicant for

---

[23]   FOIA ss 2(1)(a), 15(2)(a) and 17(3)(a).

[24]   FOIA s 2(3); FOI(S)A s 2(2). These provisions are listed at §14– 016.

[25]   Excluding the provisions that are purely supportive, such as s 25. The remaining provisions are listed at §14– 017.

[26]   FOIA s 2(1), (2)(b).

[27]   FOIA s 2(1) and (2); FOI(S)A s 2(1). See n 9.

[28]   See §§15– 010 to 15– 019.

[29]   FOIA s 84; FOI(S)A s 1(2); EIR reg 2(1); EI(S)R reg 2(1).

[30]   DPA s 70(1).

[31]   In the FOIA, called a 'request for information': ss 8 and 84. In Scotland, see FOI(S)A s 8. DPA s 7(2).

[32]   Public authorities are considered in detail at §§9– 018 to 9– 033. The definition is wider in the case of the EIR: see §6– 015.

[33]   DPA s 63. The DPA also applies to non-governmental persons, but this is outside the scope of this work.

complying with the request.[34] Where a public authority decides that some or all of the information sought should not be disclosed to the applicant, it must give the applicant notice of this, which this work calls a *refusal notice*. A public authority may decide to mask parts of a document disclosed to an applicant on the basis that it is not obliged to disclose those blanked out parts of the document. That blanking out process is called *redaction* and the document is said to be *redacted*.[35]

1– 009   Review, etc

The FOI Acts provide for two codes of practice. The *section 45 Code of Practice* is issued by the Secretary of State and provides guidance on the handling of requests for information.[36] The *section 46 Code of Practice* is issued by the Lord Chancellor and relates to the keeping, management and destruction of records.[37] The Environmental Information Regulations 2004 provide for one code of practice, similar to that issued under s 45.[38] An applicant who is dissatisfied with the way in which a public authority has dealt with his request under the FOI Acts may complain to that authority and seek *internal review* under the *section 45 Code of Practice*. If the applicant remains dissatisfied with the response, he may pursue what in this work is called a *2nd stage appeal* by making an *application* to the *Information Commissioner*.[39] At this point the applicant becomes a *complainant*.[40] If the Information Commissioner needs more information in order to determine an application, he may serve on the public authority an *information notice*.[41] If the Information Commissioner decides that the public authority has not complied with its disclosure duty or the duty to confirm or deny, he must serve a *decision notice* on the public authority and on the complainant.[42] If the Information Commissioner decides that the public authority has not otherwise properly complied with its duties in relation to a request, he may serve an *enforcement notice* on the public authority and on the complainant.[43] Either the complainant or the public authority may appeal against the Information Commissioner's decision to the *Tribunal*.[44] In this work, such an appeal is called a *3rd stage appeal*. In most cases,

---

[34] FOIA s 9(1): FOI(S)A s 9(1); DPA s 7(2)(b) and DP (Fees) Regs.

[35] Although not strictly a correct use of the word, this is the meaning it has come to assume in this and related areas of the law.

[36] FOIA s 45; FOI(S)A s 60. The Code is reproduced in the Appendix to this work.

[37] FOIA s 46; FOI(S)A s 61. The Code is reproduced in the Appendix to this work.

[38] EIR reg 18; EI(S)R reg 16.

[39] Similarly, under the EIR reg 18(1), EI(S)R reg 17. The Information Commissioner is simply a new name for the Data Protection Commissioner: FOIA s 18(1). In Scotland, the application is made to the Scottish Information Commissioner, who is referred to in the FOI(S)A s 73 as 'the Commissioner'. Appeals under the DPA are provided for by s 7(9), with jurisdiction vested in the High Court or a county court: s 15.

[40] FOIA s 50(1); EIR reg 18(1); EI(S)R reg 17.

[41] FOIA s 50(1); FOI(S)A s 50(1); EIR reg 18; EI(S)R reg 17.

[42] FOIA s 50(3)–(4); EIR reg 18. In Scotland the function of decision notices is absorbed within enforcement notices: FOI(S)A s 51; EI(S)R reg 17.

[43] FOIA s 52; EIR reg 18. In Scotland, an enforcement notice is employed wherever the Information Commissioner decides that the public authority has not properly complied with its duties in relation to a request: FOI(S)A s 51; EI(S)R reg 17.

[44] FOIA s 57(1); EIR reg 18. There is no such right of appeal in Scotland.

the tribunal will be the First-tier Tribunal, but in more significant cases it may go directly to the Upper Tribunal. The tribunal re-determines the issues based on its own evaluation of the evidence (including the requested information) before it. If a party is not satisfied with the decision of the tribunal, that party needs permission to have the tribunal's decision reviewed, either by the Upper Tribunal or, if the third-stage appeal was heard by the Upper Tribunal, by the Court of Appeal.

0   Miscellaneous terms

The FOI Acts, the DPA and the Environmental Information Regulations 2004 enable a *conclusive certificate* to be issued in certain circumstances by a Minister of the Crown or like official.[45] There are two types of conclusive certificate. An *exemption conclusive certificate* certifies either that a particular exemption or that a particular harm required for exemption is applicable, and the certificate stands as conclusive evidence of that 'fact', irrespective of what the reality might be.[46] A *compliance conclusive certificate* certifies that the person signing it has on reasonable grounds formed the opinion that the public authority has not failed to comply with the duty to disclose or the duty to confirm or deny,[47] irrespective of what the reality might be. The effect of both types of certificate is to remove altogether or cut down substantially an applicant's rights of appeal, either by express provision[48] or because of the deeming effect of the certificate. Although the FOI Acts, the DPA and the Environmental Information Regulations 2004 may excuse a public authority from disclosing certain information, the public authority may nevertheless decide to voluntarily disclose that information. In this work such disclosure is called *discretionary disclosure*. Legislation providing for access to official information exists in many other jurisdictions. In this work, where it has been thought enlightening, reference has been made to the jurisprudence of those jurisdictions whose legal systems and official information access legislation bear the closest resemblance to that of the United Kingdom: the United States of America, the Commonwealth of Australia, New Zealand, Canada and the Republic of Ireland. In this work, these are called *the comparative jurisdictions*.

3.   THE RATIONALE FOR OFFICIAL INFORMATION ACCESS LEGISLATION

1   Introduction

The Freedom of Information Act 2000 confers a right to secure the disclosure of certain information and imposes a correlative duty to disclose it. The short title of each of the FOI Acts tends to mask its compulsive character. The benefits typically attributed to the dissemination

---

[45]   FOIA ss 23(2), 24(3)–(4), 25, 34(3), 36(7), 53(2)–(3) and (6); FOI(S)A ss 31(2)–(3) and 52(2); DPA s 28(2)–(3); EIR reg 15; EI(S)R reg 12.

[46]   FOIA ss 23(2), 24(3)–(4), 25, 34(3) and 36(7); FOI(S)A s 31(2)–(3); DPA s 28(2)–(3); EIR reg 15; EI(S)R reg 12.

[47]   FOIA s 53(2)–(3) and (6); FOI(S)A s 52(2); EIR reg 18(6); EI(S)R reg 17.

[48]   FOIA s 60; EIR reg 18(1) and 18(7).

of official information, namely:[49]

— increased information in relation to the making of official decisions; and

— an electorate informed as to what its Government is or has been doing,

do not, in theory, require compulsion for their efficacy. The Act is not one that merely enables a public authority to do what otherwise it could not lawfully do for lack of statutory authority. Other than in limited circumstances,[50] it is and always has been perfectly open for a public authority to volunteer any information that it holds to anyone who requests it.[51] Such voluntary disclosure would, moreover, have been consistent with the spirit and letter of the Code of Practice on Access to Government Information.[52] A public authority owes its life to the public: unlike a private company or an individual, it has no interests that do not ultimately derive from that public. The compulsion that is at the heart of the FOI Acts recognises that a public authority to which a request for information has been made may be disinclined to disclose it. There is no deference in the Act to that disinclination. Disapplication of the duties under the Act only results where one or more of the statutory exemptions apply and, in some cases, the balance of specific facets of the public interest requires it.

1–012 The mischief at which the FOI Acts is aimed

It is conventional to speak of Parliament intending that an enactment remedy a particular mischief or vice.[53] From that convention, it is presumed that Parliament intends that courts and those administering an enactment should do so in such a manner that promotes the remedy: a purposive construction.[54] The task is of particular significance for a statute such as the FOI

---

[49] Or, put another way, 'to reinforce "the three basic principles of democratic government, namely, openness, accountability and responsibility."': *Commissioner of Police v District Court of New South Wales* (1993) 31 NSWLR 606 at 612; *Osland v Secretary to the Department of Justice* [2008] HCA 37, (2008) 234 CLR 27 at [62].

[50] For example: confidential information received by a public authority from a third party; information subject to a statutory or contractual proscription on disclosure; or personal information relating to a third person. See §§9– 034 to 9– 038.

[51] In *Reynolds v Times Newspapers Ltd* [2001] 2 AC 127 at 200, a case concerning qualified privilege, Lord Nicholls of Birkenhead said that 'the high importance of freedom to impart and receive information and ideas has been stated so often and so eloquently that this point calls for no elaboration in this case.'

[52] The Code ceased to operate on 31 December 2004. The Code only applied to central government departments and agencies.

[53] *Heydon's case* (1584) 3 Co Rep 7a. And, more recently: *Malloch v Aberdeen Corp* [1971] 1 WLR 1578 at 1583–1584 (Lord Reid); *Black-Clawson International Ltd v Papierwerke Waldhof-Aschaffenburg AG* [1975] AC 591 at 614 (Lord Reid); *AG ex rel Yorkshire Derwent Trust Ltd v Brotherton* [1992] 1 AC 425 at 442 and 447; *Attorney General v Associated Newspapers Ltd* [1994] 2 AC 238 esp at 259 (Lord Lowry); *R v Secretary of State for the Environment, Transport and the Regions, ex p Spath Holme Ltd* [2001] 2 AC 349 at 362, 376, 391 and 397; *Wilson v First County Trust* [2004] 1 AC 816 at [56] '...no legislation is enacted in a vacuum...'

[54] *Pepper v Hart* [1993] AC 593 at 617, 'The days have long passed when the courts adopted a strict constructionist view of interpretation which required them to adopt the literal meaning of the language. The courts now adopt a purposive approach which seeks to give effect to the true purpose of legislation and are prepared to look at much extraneous material that bears upon the background against which the legislation was enacted' (Lord Griffiths) and 635 (Lord Browne-Wilkinson); *Inland Revenue Commissioners v McGuckian* [1997] 1 WLR 991 at 999 (Lord Steyn) 'During the last 30 years there has been a shift away from literalist to purposive methods of construction'; *Macniven (HM Inspector of Taxes) v Westmoreland Investments Ltd* [2001] UKHL6, [2003] 1 AC 311 at [6] (Lord Nicholls). In relation to those administering the Act: *Padfield v Minister of Agriculture, Fisheries & Food* [1968] AC 977 at 1039 'Where some legal right or entitlement is conferred or enjoyed, and for the purpose of effectuating such right or entitlement a power is conferred upon someone, then words which are permissible in character will sometimes be construed as involving a duty to exercise the power. The purpose and the language of any particular enactment must be considered' (Lord Morris); *Crédit Suisse v Allerdale Borough Council* [1995] 1 Lloyd's Rep 315 at 345; *R v Secretary of State*

Acts.[55] The existence of a public authority's obligation to disclose or not to disclose information, as well as its obligation to confirm or deny that the information requested is held, is in many instances made to depend upon a balancing of competing facets of the public interest.[56] Whilst it is not unusual for the operation of a statutory provision to be part dependent upon the public interest,[57] it is unusual to ascribe to it an overriding importance about which an interested party[58] is given the adjudicative role. Identification of the purposes of the Act moderates the ability of the decision-maker to assess the public interest by undue reference to the interests of the public authority or to the idiosyncratic views of the decision-maker. Equally, an identification of purpose guides the exercise of the discretions conferred by the Act,[59] including that of whether or not a public authority should rely on an exemption.[60] The method for discerning the purpose of an Act or group of provisions in a statute is well known enough:

> In the absence of [looking at the legislative history and preparatory works] the courts have five principal avenues of approach to the ascertainment of the legislative intention: (1) examination of the social background, as specifically proved if not within common knowledge, in order to identify the social or juristic defect which is the likely subject of remedy; (2) a conspectus of the entire relevant body of the law for the same purpose; (3) particular regard to the long title of the statute to be interpreted (and, where available, the preamble), in which the general legislative objectives will be stated; (4) scrutiny of the actual words to be interpreted in the light of the established canons of interpretation; (5) examination of the other provisions of the statute in question (or of other statutes in pari materia) for the light which they throw on the particular words which are the subject of interpretation.[61]

---

for the Environment, Transport and the Regions, ex p Spath Holme Ltd [2001] 2 AC 349 at 362, 376, 397 and 400.

[55] Lord Falconer (Constitutional Affairs Secretary and Lord Chancellor), in a formal address to the International Conference of Information Commissioners, Manchester, 22 May 2006, said: '...unless FOI is consciously and carefully maintained, and its purposes are understood by people making requests, and by public officials, FOI can be perceived as a bureaucratic hassle, without any short-term benefit. The public become cynical, and officials fail to see FOI as part of public service and public communication.' The significance was addressed by Kirby J in *Osland v Secretary to the Department of Justice* [2008] HCA 37, (2008) 234 CLR 27 at [66] where he said: 'In the present setting, that purpose is a radical one. It assigns very high importance to a public interest in greater openness and transparency in public administration. Given the historical background, the attitudinal shift that FOI legislation demanded of Ministers, departments, agencies and the public service is nothing short of revolutionary. The courts ought not to obstruct that shift. On the contrary, they should strive to interpret FOI legislation in a manner harmonious with its objectives, doing so to the fullest extent that the text allows.' Although *Osland* was concerned with the Freedom of Information Act 1982 (Vic), the reasoning is equally applicable to all such legislation, including the FOI Acts.

[56] FOIA s 2(1) and (2); FOI(S)A s 2(1).

[57] Even though enactments may be seen as an expression of the public interest: *Bombay Province v Bombay Municipal Corp* [1947] AC 58 at 62–63.

[58] Namely, the public authority to whom a request for information has been made.

[59] 'Hansard has frequently been referred to with a view to ascertaining whether a statutory power has been improperly exercised for an alien purpose or in a wholly unreasonable manner': *Pepper v Hart* [1993] AC 593 at 639; *R v Northumbrian Water Ltd , ex p Newcastle and North Tyneside Health Authority* [1999] Env LR 715 at 727 (Collins J).

[60] See FOIA s 17(1); FOI(S)A s 16(1).

[61] *Ealing London Borough Council v Race Relations Board* [1972] AC 342 at 361, [1972] 1 All ER 105 at 114 (Lord Simon of Glaisdale). Similarly: *Black Clawson International Ltd v Papierwerke Waldhof-Aschaffenburg AG* [1975] AC 591 at 647, [1975] 1 All ER 810 at 844 (Lord Simon of Glaisdale).

1– 013   The background to the introduction of the legislation

The White Paper[62] that anticipated introduction of an FOI Bill spelled out the purpose of the legislation. In the preface by the Prime Minister it was said:

> This White Paper explains our proposals for meeting another key pledge—to legislate for freedom of information, bringing about more open Government. The traditional culture of secrecy will only be broken down by giving people in the United Kingdom the legal right to know. This fundamental and vital change in the relationship between government and governed is at the heart of this White Paper.

The Minister in charge of the Bill declared in his foreword:

> Openness is fundamental to the political health of a modern state. This White Paper marks a watershed in the relationship between the government and people of the United Kingdom. At last there is a government ready to trust the people with a legal right to information. This right is central to a mature democracy.

The opening paragraphs gave a straightforward statement of purpose:

> 1.1   Unnecessary secrecy in government leads to arrogance in governance and defective decision-making. The perception of excessive secrecy has become a corrosive influence in the decline of public confidence in government. Moreover, the climate of public opinion has changed: people expect much greater openness and accountability from government than they used to.
>
> 1.2   ......The purpose of the Act will be to encourage more open and accountable government by establishing a general statutory right of access to official records and information.[63]

1– 014   The purpose of the Act

Official information access legislation has been variously considered to serve the following purposes:

> (1)   To enable members of the public to be more informed as to the way in which administrative decisions are made and the basis for such decisions. The House of Commons Select Committee considered that this would improve the quality of government decision-making.[64]

---

[62]   Cabinet Office, *Your Right to Know. The Government's Proposals for a Freedom of Information Act. White Paper* (Cm 3818, 1997):
www.archive.official-documents.co.uk/document/caboff/foi/foi.htm
As to the permissibility of considering a White Paper, etc for the purpose of ascertaining the mischief and for drawing inferences as to Parliamentary intention, see: *Pepper v Hart* [1993] AC 593 at 630 and 635 (Lord Browne-Wilkinson); *R v Northumbrian Water Ltd , ex p Newcastle and North Tyneside Health Authority* [1999] Env LR 715 at 727 (Collins J); *R (on the application of Heather) v Leonard Cheshire Foundation* [2002] EWCA Civ 366, [2002] 2 All ER 936 [2002] HRLR 30; *Wilson v First County Trust* [2004] 1 AC 816 at [56] and [64]; *R (G) v London Borough of Barnet* [2004] 2 AC 208 at [84]–[85].

[63]   See also para 2.5 of the White Paper.

[64]   House of Commons, *Public Administration—Third Report* (Cm 4355, 1999) para 12:
www.publications.parliament.uk/pa/cm199899/cmselect/cmpubadm/570/57007.htm
For judicial support, see *London Regional Transport v Mayor of London* [2001] EWCA Civ 1491 [2003] EMLR 4 at [40], quoting Sullivan J with approval. In *Kuijer v Council of the European Union* (No 2) [2002] 1 WLR 1941 at [52] the Court of First Instance, dealing with Council Directive 93/731/EC, said: 'It is first necessary to point out that the principle of transparency is intended to secure a more significant role for citizens in the decision-making process and to ensure that the administration acts with greater propriety, efficiency and responsibility *vis-à-vis* the citizens in a democratic system. It helps strengthen the principle of democracy and respect for fundamental rights.' See, further: Case C-64/05 *IFAW gGmbH v European Commission* [2008] QB 902 (Opinion of Advocate General Maduro, 18 July 2007) at

(2)   To enable the curious to find out what information the instruments of government hold about themselves and others.[65]

(3)   To hold government and other bodies to account by drawing out information revealing maladministration.[66] Put another way, to supplement the operation of responsible government.[67]

(4)   To impose the discipline of potential revelation upon public authorities in their recording of information.

(5)   To counteract undue secrecy in the making of decisions and the formulation of policy.[68]

(6)   For any number of commercial ends.

(7)   As a form of pre-action disclosure or disclosure in judicial review or in connection with tribunal proceedings and the like.

The 'mischief' or 'vice' giving rise to the need for the Freedom of Information Act 2000 was acknowledged as a matter of public record by the Minister in introducing the Bill that became the Act:

> Unnecessary secrecy in Government and our public services has long been held to undermine good governance and public administration, ...the Bill will not only provide legal rights for the public and place legal duties on Ministers and public authorities, but will help to transform the culture of Government from one of secrecy to one of openness. It will transform the default setting from "this should be kept quiet unless" to "this should be published unless." By doing so, it should raise public confidence in the processes of government, and enhance the quality of decision making by the Government.[69]

And, a little later:

> The Bill will lead to cultural change throughout the public sector. There will be more information about how health authorities, local councils and the police deliver services. It will give citizens a right to know and a right to appeal to the commissioner if they do not get the information that they have sought. That is a fundamental change in the relationship between the citizens and the state.[70]

---

[53].

[65]   House of Commons, *Public Administration—Third Report* (Cm 4355, 1999) para 12 (see n 64).

[66]   *United States Department of Justice v Reporters Committee for Freedom of the Press*, 489 US 749 at 773.

[67]   *Osland v Secretary to the Department of Justice* [2008] HCA 37, (2008) 234 CLR 27 at [62]; *Egan v Willis* [1998] HCA 71 at [42] (High Court of Australia).

[68]   House of Commons, *Public Administration—Third Report* (Cm 4355, 1999) para 12 (see n 64).

[69]   Hansard HC vol 340 col 714 (7 December 1999) (Mr Jack Straw). In the construction of a statute, reference may be made to Parliamentary materials 'where (a) legislation is ambiguous, obscure or leads to an absurdity; (b) the material relied upon consists of one or more statements by a minister or other promoter of the Bill together if necessary with such other Parliamentary material as is necessary to understand such statements and their effect; (c) the statements relied upon are clear...': *Pepper v Hart* [1993] AC 593 at 640 (Lord Browne-Wilkinson). Satisfaction of these three conditions is critical to the entitlement to refer to the material: *R v Secretary of State for the Environment, Transport and the Regions, ex p Spath Holme Ltd* [2001] 2 AC 349 at 391–392 (Lord Bingham) and at 398–399 (Lord Nicholls). It has been said that the true purpose in referring to Hansard is to 'preven[t] the executive from placing a different meaning on the words used in legislation from that which they attributed to those words when promoting the legislation in Parliament...': *R v A (No 2)* [2001] UKHL 25, [2002] 1 AC 45 at [81] (Lord Steyn). Similarly stated in Johan Steyn, '*Pepper v Hart*: A re-examination' (2001) 21 *Oxford Journal of Legal Studies*, 59.

[70]   Hansard HC vol 340 col 725 (7 December 1999) (Mr Jack Straw). Similarly, cols 728, 738-739; 744–745 ('the legislation transforming the relationship between citizen and state'); 754–755; 771–772; Hansard HL vol 612 cols 830, 831, 835, 837, 847, 849, 853, 858–859, 862 (20 April 2000); Hansard HL vol 618 col 440 (25 October 2000).

It is implicit in the above statements that the voluntary code to which the same public sector had been subject for the preceding eight years had not effected the 'cultural' or 'fundamental' change hoped for the FOI Acts.[71] The most significant dissimilarity between the Code and the FOI Acts is the replacement of voluntariness with compulsion.[72] This dependence upon compulsion to secure the cultural change from the regime which pervaded under the voluntary Code gives support to the proposition that notions of due deference to a public authority's claims of exemption should play little or no part in the determination of claims of exemption save to the extent that they are substantiated by objective evidence. Domestic jurisprudence since the Act has come into force has recognised its basic objectives and significance:

> FOIA introduced a radical change to our law, and the rights of the citizen to be informed about the acts and affairs of public authorities.[73]

1–015 The purpose of freedom of information legislation: comparative jurisprudence

The US Supreme Court summarised the object of such legislation:

> The basic purpose of [the Freedom of Information Act] is to ensure an informed citizenry, vital to the functioning of a democratic society, needed to check against corruption and to hold the governors accountable to the governed.[74]

The Supreme Court of Canada expressed it as follows:

> The [Access to Information] Act is concerned with securing values of participation and accountability in the democratic process. The overarching purpose of access to information legislation is to facilitate democracy by helping to ensure that citizens have the information required to participate meaningfully in the democratic process and that politicians and bureaucrats remain accountable to the citizenry…Rights to state-held information are designed to improve the workings of government; to make it more effective, responsive and accountable.[75]

Most recently, in the High Court of Australia, Kirby J, after a consideration of the evolution of such legislation in Australia, said:[76]

> The basic purpose of the introduction of freedom of information legislation is the same in all jurisdictions. It is to reinforce "the three basic principles of democratic government, namely, openness, accountability and responsibility". The central objective is to strengthen

---

[71] Thus, Lord Phillips in *The BSE Inquiry—The Report* (2000) found that there had been 'positive censorship' (vol 3, para 2.175) in relation to information relating to zoonotic qualities of bovine spongiform encephalopathy (BSE); that there was a 'clear policy of restricting the disclosure of information about BSE' (vol 3, para 2.189); and he spoke of a policy of secrecy rather than one of openness (vol 3, para 2.191). Similarly, Sir Richard Scott's *Report of the Inquiry into the Export of Defence Equipment and Dual-Use Goods and Related Prosecutions* (1996): 'in circumstances where disclosure might be politically or administratively inconvenient, the balance struck by the government came down, time and time again, against full disclosure' (para D1.165). The unlikelihood of cultural change and the importance of compulsion were adverted to by the House of Commons, Constitutional Affairs Committee, *Freedom of Information—One Year On*, Seventh Report of Session 2005-06, HC 991 at paras 112–113:
www.publications.parliament.uk/pa/cm200506/cmselect/cmconst/991/991.pdf

[72] At any rate, so far as concerns central government departments and agencies.

[73] *OGC v IC* [2008] EWHC 774 (Admin), [2010] QB 98, [2008] ACD 54 at [68].

[74] *National Labor Relations Board v Robbins Tire & Rubber Co* (1978) 437 US 214 at 242. Similarly: *Natoinal Archives and Record Administration v Favish*, 541 US 157 (2004) at 171-72.

[75] *Dagg v Canada (Minister of Finance)* [1997] 2 SCR 403 at 432–433 and 450. Similarly, *Canada Post Corp v Canada (Minister of Public Works)* [1995] 2 FC 110 (FCA) at 124.

[76] *Osland v Secretary to the Department of Justice* [2008] HCA 37 at [62].

constitutional principles of governance not always translated into reality because of a lack of material information available to electors. Fundamentally, the idea behind such legislation is to flesh out the constitutional provisions establishing the system of representative government; to increase citizen participation in government beyond a fleeting involvement on election days; and to reduce the degree of apathy and cynicism sometimes arising from a lack of real elector knowledge about, or influence upon, what is going on in government.

And in Ireland:[77]

> The passing of the Freedom of Information Act 1997 constituted a legislative development of major importance. By it, the Oireachtas took a considered and deliberate step which dramatically alters the administrative assumptions and culture of centuries. It replaces the presumption of secrecy with one of openness. It is designed to open up the workings of government and administration to scrutiny. It is not designed simply to satisfy the appetite of the media for stories. It is for the benefit of every citizen. It lets light in to the offices and filing cabinets of our rulers. The principle of free access to publicly held information is part of a world-wide trend. The general assumption is that it originates in the Scandinavian countries. The Treaty of Amsterdam adopted a new Article 255 of the EC Treaty providing that every citizen of the European Union should have access to the documents of the European Parliament, Council and Commission.

6 The long title and the absence of a purpose clause

It is unusual for an Act of Parliament to have a purpose clause.[78] To the extent permitted by a single sentence, the purpose of an Act is normally only expressly articulated within a statute by its long title. For the reasons noted above, ascertainment of the purpose of the Act is of particular importance in statutes such as the FOI Acts.[79] An amendment to the Bill that would have seen a purpose clause included in the Act was defeated.[80] Instead, it was considered that changing the preposition *about* in the long title of the Bill to *for* would adequately articulate the purpose of the Act.[81] Although not having the status of a purpose clause, the following formal statement by the then Constitutional Affairs Secretary and Lord Chancellor, Lord Falconer, describes the aim more clearly than would be possible in a statute:

> FOI regimes, wherever they may be, are usually established from common principles. Governments have been motivated by citizen empowerment; by the desire to drive more democratic engagement; by the need to fight corruption; and by the simple notion that openness is a public good. More recently, Freedom of Information has been introduced in

---

[77] *Sheedy v Information Commissioner* [2005] 2 IR 272 at 275

[78] But not unknown, see eg: Health and Safety at Work, etc Act 1974 s 1; Proceeds of Crime Act 2002 s 240; Education Act 2002 s 1; Pollution Prevention and Control Act 1999 s 1.

[79] The inclusion of a purpose clause was recommended by the House of Commons, *Public Administration–Third Report* (Cm 4355, 1999) para 59 (see n 64). A purpose clause is to be found in: Freedom of Information Act 1982 (Cth of Australia) s 3 (substituted by the Freedom of Information Amendment (Reform) Act 2010); Official Information Act 1982 (NZ) s 4; Access to Information Act (1982)(Canada) s 2. The Freedom of Information Act 1997 (Ireland), although not including a purpose clause, includes a comprehensive statement of purpose in its long title.

[80] Hansard HC vol 347 col 830 (4 April 2000) (Amendment No 100). For discussion on the proposed purpose clause, see: Hansard HC vol 347 cols 830–855 (4 April 2000); Hansard HL vol 617 cols 886–888 and 892–900 (17 October 2000). It was opposed on the basis that it was 'pointless' because it would add nothing to what was explained 'more comprehensively' in the long title and that it would cause confusion to those minded to compare the long title with the purpose clause: Hansard HC vol 347 col 844 (4 April 2000) (Mr Mike O'Brien); Hansard HL vol 617 col 894 (17 October 2000) (Lord Brennan).

[81] An amendment proposed by Lord Archer: Hansard HL vol 617 col 890 (17 October 2000)

many countries because it is seen as a standard part of a liberal democracy.[82]

4.   BACKGROUND TO THE FREEDOM OF INFORMATION ACT 2000

1– 017   **Access to official information in the United Kingdom**
As noted above,[83] rights of access to official information in the United Kingdom increased in a piecemeal fashion in the 40 years prior to the enactment of the FOI Acts. It may fairly be observed that in that period Parliament showed a greater disposition to impose duties of disclosure upon the emanations of local government than it did upon central government departments or agencies. Notable increases in the right of access came with:

— the Local Government Act 1972 Part VA (ss 100A–100K) s 228, Sch 12A,[84]
— the Data Protection Act 1984,[85]
— the Health Service Joint Consultative Committees (Access to Information) Act 1986,[86]
— the Access to Personal Files Act 1987,[87]
— the Community Health Councils (Access to Information) Act 1988 (which applied, with modifications, the provisions of Part VA of the Local Government Act 1972 to community health councils established under s 20 of the National Health Service Act 1977),[88] and
— the Access to Health Records Act 1990.[89]

Where central government departments or agencies found themselves having to disclose

---

[82]   Speech by Lord Falconer (Constitutional Affairs Secretary and Lord Chancellor) to the International Conference of Information Commissioners, Manchester, 22 May 2006.

[83]   See §1– 001.

[84]   These provisions were inserted by the Local Government (Access to Information) Act 1985. They are considered in greater detail at §§8– 005 to 8– 022.

[85]   Section 21 of the Data Protection Act 1984 introduced the concept of a 'subject-access request' in which a person could seek access to information held by an organisation (which included private organisations as well as governmental organisations) about himself. The right was re-enacted and broadened by s 7 of the DPA. The right is considered in greater detail in ch 5.

[86]   Repealed by the Health Act 1999 s 65, Sch 4 para 72 and Sch 5, with effect from 1 April 2000 (in England) and 1 January 2001 (in Wales).

[87]   Repealed by the DPA s 74(2) Sch 16 Pt I, as from 1 March 2000. Similarly the Access to Personal Files (Social Services) Regulations 1989 and the Access to Personal Files (Housing) Regulations 1989 made under it. The purpose of this Act was to catch personal information that was recorded in 'manual files' and which, accordingly, fell outside the ambit of the Data Protection Act 1984. The Act came into force on 15 May 1987 and provided a right of access to personal information (which was defined in the same way as in the Data Protection Act 1984) falling within defined categories and held by 'Housing Act local authorities' and by 'local social services authorities'.

[88]   The Act is considered in greater detail at §8– 038.

[89]   This establishes a right of access to health records held by, inter alia, 'health service bodies' (ie a health authority, a health board, a special health authority or a National Health Service trust) for the individuals to whom the record relates and certain other persons. The Act is considered in greater detail at §8– 039.

information, this was generally the result of outside obligations.[90]

8 Attempts at a comprehensive right of access

From 1974 onwards, the Labour Party would before each General Election state a commitment to 'freedom of information'. The first indication of any realisation of that commitment was a directive issued in 1977 by the head of the Civil Service.[91] This promised to release more of the background detail and information behind Ministerial decisions. In March 1979 the Labour Government published a Green Paper on Open Government, which proposed a non-statutory code for the release of official information.[92] At about the same time a private member's Bill that would have compelled disclosure of official documents was introduced by Sir Clement Freud MP.[93] Both the non-statutory code and private Member's Bill did not survive the General Election of May 1979. In 1981 another freedom of information Bill, also drafted by the Outer Circle Policy Unit, was introduced by Frank Hooley MP. The Bill was opposed by the Conservative Government and defeated at second reading.

9 The Data Protection Act 1984

In 1981 the Council of Europe opened for signature and ratification its Convention for the Protection of Individuals with regard to the Automatic Processing of Personal Data. This ultimately led to the Data Protection Act 1984. Although this gave an individual a right of access to information relating to himself provided that it was held as part of a data processing system, the focus of the Act was not the extraction of information from governmental bodies: the right given by the Act applied to personal information irrespective of the identity of the body that held it. In 1984 a freedom of information Bill drafted by the Campaign for Freedom of Information was introduced by David Steel MP. At the same time the Campaign for Freedom of Information also pressed for the introduction of subject-specific legislation establishing more limited rights of access to information. Legislation receiving its support included the Local Government (Access to Information) Act 1985,[94] the Access to Personal Files

---

[90] Such as the Environmental Information Regulations 1992, which implemented Council Directive 90/313/EEC on the freedom of access to information on the environment, and the DPA, which implemented Directive 95/46, adopted by the European Parliament and European Council on 24 October 1998. These are considered in detail in chs 6 and 5 respectively.

[91] The Directive was actually a confidential memorandum from the Head of the Civil Service, Sir Douglas Allen, who became Lord Croham. It was published officially after it was leaked to *The Times*. The directive became known as the 'Croham directive'.

[92] *Open Government* (Cmnd 7520).

[93] Then Mr Clement Freud MP, Isle of Ely.

[94] It was introduced as a private member's Bill promoted by the Community Rights Project and introduced by Robin Squire MP. It gave the public wider rights of access to council meetings, reports and papers. See §§8– 005 to 8– 022.

Act 1987,[95] and the Access to Medical Reprts Act 1988.[96] The Campaign for Freedom of Information made another attempt at a comprehensive information access Bill in January 1991, but it only lasted 45 minutes in Parliament and did not get a second reading.[97] In the following year the Environmental Information Regulations 1992 were adopted to implement the Access to Environmental Information Directive of the European Community. In that same year, Roy Hattersley MP, the then shadow Home Secretary, promised that a freedom of information act would be the first piece of Home Office legislation if Labour were to win the election. The Conservatives won the election and William Waldegrave was given responsibility for implementing an 'open government' policy. In early 1993 a private member's Bill entitled The Right to Know Bill was introduced[98] into Parliament. This Bill had its second reading in the House of Commons and completed its Committee stage, but it failed to receive the necessary support.

5.   THE OPEN GOVERNMENT CODE OF PRACTICE

1– 020   The Code of Practice

In July 1993 the Conservative Government issued a White Paper which proposed a Code of Practice on Access to Government Information. In 1994 that Government issued a Code of Practice on Access to Government Information.[99] This was the first true attempt at a comprehensive scheme for the release of official information. But it was voluntary in nature, conferring no enforceable right of access. In 1996 the Select Committee on the Parliamentary Commissioner for Administration published its report on the operation of the voluntary scheme. It recommended that a freedom of information act be introduced. The Government rejected the recommendation and instead issued a slightly revised version of the Code in February 1997.

1– 021   Application

The Code applied to bodies falling within the jurisdiction of the Parliamentary Commissioner for Administration, and it was the Commissioner who enforced the Code.[100] These bodies included almost all central government departments and their agencies, as well as many other

---

[95] This was also the result of a private member's Bill promoted by the Campaign for Freedom of Information and introduced by Archy Kirkwood MP. It gave people the right to see manually held social work and housing records about themselves. The Bill originally also included access to school records, but this was later brought in under existing legislation by agreement with the Government.

[96] This was another private member's Bill drafted by the Campaign for Freedom of Information and introduced by Archy Kirkwood MP. It gives people the right to see any report produced by their own doctor for an employer or insurance company. See §8– 039.

[97] This was introduced by Archy Kirkwood MP.

[98] This was introduced by Mark Fisher MP.

[99] The code was revised in 1997 and remained in effect until 1 January 2005:
       www.foi.gov.uk/ogcode981.htm
     The Cabinet Office also published *Open Government Code of Practice on Access to Government Information: Guidance on Interpretation*, 2nd edn (1997).

[100] *Code of Practice*, paras 3 and 6.

public bodies. The Code contained a non-statutory, discretionary regime. It did not confer rights of access to information of any kind upon any person or class of persons. Nor did it override any statutory prohibitions upon the release of information or documents. Where information that fell, in principle, within the scope of the Code was also available pursuant to a statutory right of access, that right took precedence and the release of the information in question was governed thereby.[101] In particular, the Code expressly stated that it was not intended to override statutory provisions on access to public records, whether over or under 30 years old. The reason for this lay in the fact that the Ombudsman was not required, under s 12(3) of the Parliamentary Commissioner Act 1967, to question the merits of a decision if it had been taken without maladministration by a government department or other body in the exercise of a discretion vested in it; and decisions made in England and Wales with respect to public records by the Lord Chancellor, or in Scotland and Northern Ireland by the corresponding Secretary of State were such discretionary decisions.[102]

22 **The Code's five main commitments**
The Code's five main commitments were to supply facts and analysis with major policy decisions; to open up internal guidelines about departments' dealings with the public; to supply reasons for administrative decisions; to provide information about public services, what they cost, targets, performance, complaints and redress; and to respond to requests for information.

23 **The purpose and aims of the Code**
The Code was intended to give effect to the Government's stated policy of extending access to official information. The approach to the release of information that it embodied rested on an explicit assumption that information should be disclosed, except where its release would not be in the public interest.[103] Cases where the release of information would not be in the public interest were described in Part II of the Code. Exemptions under the Code may therefore be seen as the articulation of those circumstances where it was considered to have been not in the public interest (at least in the view of the Cabinet Office) to disclose information. The Code had three aims, subsidiary to its overall purposes.[104] These were: to improve policy-making and the democratic process by extending access to the facts and analyses which provide the basis for the consideration of proposed policy; to protect the interests of individuals and companies by ensuring that reasons are given for administrative decisions, except where there is statutory authority or established convention to the contrary; and to support and extend the principles of public service established by the Citizen's Charter.

24 **Protection of privacy and confidentiality under the Code**
The Code recognised that these objectives had to be balanced against the need to keep information private or confidential in certain circumstances. In particular, it expressly recognised that the aims of the Code had to be balanced against two countervailing

---

[101] *Code of Practice*, para 8. The bodies in question are listed in Sch 2 to the Parliamentary Commissioner Act 1967.

[102] *Code of Practice*, para 9.

[103] *Code of Practice*, para 1.

[104] *Code of Practice*, para 2.

requirements: namely, the need to maintain high standards of care in ensuring the privacy of personal and commercially confidential information, and the need to preserve confidentiality where disclosure would not be in the public interest or would breach personal privacy or the confidences of a third party in accordance with statutory requirements and Part II of the Code.[105]

1– 025   Information released under the Code

Subject to the exemptions contained in Part II, the Code committed Government departments and applicable public bodies to publishing the facts and analyses that the Government considered relevant and important in framing major policy proposals and decisions, and, ordinarily, to making such information available once those policies and decisions had been announced. The second Code commitment was to publish, or otherwise make available, explanatory material on departments' dealings with the public (including such rules, procedures, internal guidance to officials, and similar administrative manuals as would assist better understanding of departmental action in dealing with the public) except where publication could prejudice any matter which should properly be kept confidential under Part II of the Code. Thirdly, the Code enshrined a commitment on behalf of the bodies to which it applied to give reasons for administrative decisions to those affected, and to publish in accordance with the Citizen's Charter full information about how public services were run, how much they cost, who was in charge, and what complaints and redress procedures were available; and full and (where possible) comparable sets of information about what services were being provided, what targets were set, what standards of service were expected and the results that had been achieved. The final Code commitment was to release, in response to specific requests, information relating to the policies of the bodies covered, as well as information relating to their actions and decisions and other matters related to their areas of responsibility.[106] The Code did not require the release of information that the relevant public bodies did not themselves possess, or to provide information that had already been published, or to provide information which was provided as part of an existing service other than through that service.[107]

1– 026   Bodies specifically exempted from the Code

The Security and Intelligence Services were not within the scope of the Code, and information obtained from or relating to them was not covered by it.[108] The Code did not apply to or affect information held by courts or tribunals or inquiries, or information contained in the documents of such bodies.[109]

1– 027   Information excluded by Part II of the Code

Part II of the Code excluded fifteen categories of information from the commitment of disclosure set out in Part I. These categories of information were variously subject to two kinds

---

[105] *Code of Practice*, para 2.

[106] *Code of Practice*, para 3.

[107] *Code of Practice*, para 4.

[108] *Code of Practice*, para 6.

[109] *Code of Practice*, para 10.

of exemption from the assumption that information was to be disclosed, namely an exemption which applied in cases where a 'harm' or 'prejudice' test was satisfied, and an exemption that was absolute in the sense that no harm or prejudice test applied. 'Harm' and 'prejudice', for the purposes of Part II of the Code, included actual harm and prejudice and a risk or reasonable expectation of harm or prejudice. The Code explained that in such cases, consideration should be given to whether any harm or prejudice arising from disclosure was outweighed by the public interest in making the information available.[110] The Ombudsman interpreted the 'harm' test under the Code as allowing for a balancing of public interests, such that information should be disclosed when the public interest was best served thereby.[111] The categories of exempt information that were subject to a 'harm' test under Part II of the Code included information relating to defence,[112] security[113] and international relations;[114] and information whose disclosure would harm the frankness and candour of internal discussion.[115] The Code gave as examples of the latter kind of information: the proceedings of Cabinet and Cabinet committees; internal opinion, advice, recommendations, consultation and deliberation; projections and assumptions relating to internal policy and analysis, analysis of alternative policy options and information relating to rejected policy options; and confidential communications between departments, public bodies and regulatory bodies. The categories of information that were subject to an absolute exemption included information relating to confidential communications with the Royal Household;[116] and information relating to public employment and public appointments and honours.[117] Most of the fifteen categories of excluded information were, however, subject to a 'harm' or 'prejudice' test of some form or other.

8   Procedure for obtaining information covered by the Code

Information that was made available by the Code could be obtained simply by writing to the relevant department, agency or body and explaining what information was required. It was not necessary to specify particular files or documents. The Code specified that departments should reply to most requests within 20 working days, and should inform the maker of the request that they need longer to reply, if that was the case. Most information had to be provided free of charge, especially where it was needed to explain such matters as benefits, grants and entitlements; the standards and performances of services; the reasons for administrative decisions made with respect to the person requesting information; the way in which the person requesting information might exercise rights to appeal or complain about a decision; or regulatory requirements bearing upon the business of the person making the request. If the request did not fall within any one or more of the above categories, however, then a charge

---

[110] *Code of Practice*, Pt II.

[111] Case A8/00 HC 494 (1999–00), Case A31/99 HC 21 (1999–00).

[112] See now FOIA s 26, FOI(S)A s 31.

[113] See now FOIA ss 23, 24, FOI(S)A s 31.

[114] See now FOIA s 27, FOI(S)A s 32.

[115] See now FOIA ss 35, 36, FOI(S)A ss 29, 30.

[116] See now FOIA s 37, FOI(S)A s 41.

[117] See now FOIA s 37, FOI(S)A s 41.

could be imposed for supplying it.

1– 029 Enforcement of the Code

As noted above, the Code did not confer rights of access to information upon anyone. If a department did not comply with a request for information the matter might be taken up by the Ombudsman, who could, however, only instigate an investigation upon the referral of a complaint from an MP. The Ombudsman could then recommend disclosure or uphold the department's decision not to disclose. The Ombudsman's recommendations were not legally binding, although in practice most departments complied with them.

1– 030 Relationship between the Code and the Freedom of Information Act 2000

It will be noted from the above outline that the Code bore some resemblance to the Freedom of Information Act 2000 in its structure. Once the Act came fully into force (1 January 2005), the Code ceased to operate. Despite the absence of an enforceable right, the Code was an important step in the evolution of information rights in the United Kingdom. Given the continued official acknowledgment of a 'culture of secrecy' after its implementation, the attributes distinguishing the Freedom of Information Act 2000 from it may be seen as critical to countering that culture.[118] Most notable is the conferral of an enforceable right of access and the imposition of a correlative duty to disclose. The Code also provides valuable insight into the public interest in disclosure of information held by a public authority and in the public authority maintaining the various exemptions under the Freedom of Information Act 2000. It is to be noted that the Act provides a qualified exemption in respect of information that the Code did not exempt, so that the Code's treatment of that information could be of some relevance to the consideration of the public interest under s 2 of the Freedom of Information Act 2000.

1– 031 The Data Protection Act 1998

The Data Protection Act 1998 implemented an EC Directive on the protection of individuals with regard to the processing of personal data and on the free movement of such data.[119] It replaced the Data Protection Act 1984. The 1998 Act, and subordinate legislation made under it, effected major changes to the data protection regime, including access to personal data. The new Act removed the limitation on subject-access rights to computerised records, extending it to most manual records. It widened the definition of 'processing' so that it included obtaining, storing and disclosing of data.

---

[118] The difficulty of effecting a cultural change and the importance of the enforceable right was acknowledged by the House of Commons, Constitutional Affairs Committee, *Freedom of Information — One Year On*, Seventh Report of Session 2005–06, HC 991 at paras 112–113 (see n 71).

[119] Directive of the European Parliament and of the Council of 24 October 1995 on the Protection of Individuals with Regard to the Processing of Personal Data and on the Free Movement of Such Data 95/46/EC [1995] OJ L281/31.

6. ENACTMENT OF THE FREEDOM OF INFORMATION ACT 2000

Parliamentary history of the Freedom of Information Act 2000

Before the May 1997 General Election, both the Labour Party and Liberal Democrat party had promised to introduce freedom of information legislation if elected. The former secured election in May 1997, and in December 1997 a White Paper[120] was published, setting out its proposals for legislation. On 19 May 1998 the House of Commons Select Committee reported on the proposals,[121] stating in its Introduction:

> Freedom of Information Act is a major plank in the Government's proposals for constitutional reform, and a radical advance in open and accountable government. It will help to begin to change for good the secretive culture of the public service.
>
> Lack of openness and transparency in British government have featured in tribunals and inquiries as a contributory factor in many cases where things have gone seriously wrong ... [M]aking government more open is something which should have a serious impact on the daily lives of ordinary people. In other countries with Freedom of Information laws, most requests for information are for "my own file." Public authorities keep a vast amount of information about individuals. Some of this they can now get access to, under a patchwork of statutes and codes of practice. Some of it they still cannot get. Many people may want access to their files in order to pursue a dispute with a government department or other public authority. Individuals who are unhappy with the way they have been dealt with by, for example, the Child Support Agency or the Benefits Agency, or local Housing Authorities and Social Services Departments have a strong need to see how the authority concerned has handled their case...
>
> Freedom of Information should change the culture within the public sector so that the sort of obstruction that members of the public experienced in these cases no longer happens. We believe that the proposals, if implemented as presented in the White Paper, will have three purposes and effects. Increased access to information will:
>
> — Make it easier for members of the public to find out what information government holds about themselves.
>
> — Make it easier for politicians, journalists and members of the public to hold the government to account by making government cover-ups more difficult.
>
> — Make it easier for members of the public to participate in an informed way in the discussion of policy issues, and improve the quality of government decision-making because those drafting policy advice know that they must be able, ultimately, to defend their reasoning before public opinion. We believe that Dr Clark's proposals will begin to bring about a significant change in the culture of the UK Government.

The Report made a total of 44 recommendations and observations. In July 1998 responsibility for the Bill was transferred from the Cabinet Office to the Home Office. The Government

---

[120] *Your Right to Know—The Government's Proposals for a Freedom of Information Act* (Cm 3818, 1997): see n 62. The document was prepared by the Chancellor of the Duchy of Lancaster, Dr David Clark.

[121] *Third Report of the Select Committee on Public Administration: Your Right to Know—The Government's Proposals for a Freedom of Information Act*, HC (1997–1998) 398–I.

officially responded to the Report.[122] The Minister then responsible, Dr David Clark, said:

The Government's commitment to a radical Freedom of Information Act is clear, and has already been set out in Your Right to Know…FOI is a key part—and in my view a central part—of the Government's programme to modernise British politics through radical constitutional change. The Prime Minister has said that freedom of information is not some isolated constitutional reform, but a change that is absolutely fundamental to how we see politics developing in this country…

1– 033   The consultation paper and draft Bill

On 24 May 1999 the Government published a consultation paper with its proposals for freedom of information legislation, including a draft Bill.[123] The consultation paper was followed by a process of pre-legislative scrutiny by committees in both Houses of Parliament and a period of further public consultation. The House of Commons Select Committee on Public Administration reported on 29 July 1999,[124] summarising its conclusions and recommendations:

1. We welcome the fact that the Government has published a draft Freedom of Information Bill. Legislation on the information rights of citizens is a historic moment for our democracy. However, we believe that the present form of the Bill has significant deficiencies which, if not remedied, will undermine its potential. In particular we recommend that:

— There should be a purpose clause stating a clear presumption in favour of disclosure as a right of citizenship;

— The public interest in disclosing particular information in each case should be balanced against the prospect of harm in so doing; the information should be released if the public interest is greater; and decisions about where the balance lies in particular cases should be transparent, and reviewable by an Information Commissioner, whose decisions are enforceable;

— The right of access to information should apply as broadly as possible, and exemptions to it should be drawn as narrowly and precisely as possible with a more demanding harm test;

— A statutory freedom of information regime should contain, as much as possible, enforceable rights of access to information; not undertakings to consider the discretionary release of information,…

We believe that this will make the draft Bill better, our democracy stronger, and the information rights of citizens more effective.

The House of Lords appointed its own select committee on 17 June 1999, which reported on 27 July 1999.[125] Its recommendations included:

63.   The draft Bill should provide a framework for transforming the "culture of secrecy" in British government….

64.   If the draft Bill is to conform to true Freedom of Information principles, the most

---

[122] The Government's reply to the Report was the *Fourth Special Report of the Select Committee on Public Administration: Government Response to the Third Report from the Select Committee on Public Administration (Session 1997–1998) on Your Right to Know—The Government's Proposals for a Freedom of Information Act*, HC (1997–1998) 1020: www.parliament.the-stationery.co.uk/pa/cm199798/cmselect/cmpubadm/1020/102002.htm

[123] Home Office, *Freedom of Information: Consultation on draft legislation* (Cm 4355, May 1999): www.nationalarchives.gov.uk/ERORecords/HO/421/2/foi/dfoibill.htm

[124] *House of Commons, Public Administration—Third Report* (Cm 4355, 1999) (see n 64).

[125] *Draft Freedom of Information Bill—First Report* (Select Committee Report HL 97), Session 1998–1999, 27 July 1999: www.parliament.the-stationery-office.co.uk/pa/ld199899/ldselect/ldfoinfo/97/9701.htm

important single amendment needed is to give the Information Commissioner a public interest override power in clause 44 to overrule a ministerial decision under clause 14, and to order disclosure.

....

82.   The draft Bill does not need a purpose clause but the Long Title should be amended by leaving out the words "make provision about the disclosure of information" and substituting "facilitate the disclosure of information." This would clarify the draft Bill's purpose of providing a framework for transforming the "culture of secrecy" in British government.

The Government's response to the Report of the House of Commons Select Committee was published on 27 October 1999.[126] The document said that it agreed with the bulk of the Select Committee's recommendations. The Government's response to the Report of the House of Lords Select Committee was published on 17 January 2000.[127] That document, too, said that it agreed with the bulk of the Select Committee's recommendations.

4   The Freedom of Information Bill

The Freedom of Information Bill was introduced into the House of Commons on 18 November 1999, and received its second reading on 7 December 1999. It enjoyed a close Parliamentary scrutiny before receiving Royal Assent on 30 November 2000.[128]

5   Implementation of the Freedom of Information Act 2000

The Act was brought into force incrementally over the next four years. The initial implementation of the Act was concerned with publication schemes, the establishment of the Information Commissioner and the introduction of concepts basic to the operation of the Act.[129] A few further such provisions came into force on 1 February 2001.[130] The renaming of the Data Protection Tribunal took effect from 14 May 2001.[131] On 13 November 2001, the Lord Chancellor announced in Parliament an implementation plan for the Act:

---

[126] www.publications.parliament.uk/pa/cm199899/cmselect/cmpubadm/831/83102.htm

[127] www.nationalarchives.gov.uk/ERORecords/HO/421/2/foi/dfoilsc.htm

[128] The stages and dates of the Act's progress are as follows:
In the House of Commons: (1) Introduction, 18 November 1999, Hansard vol 339 col 124; (2) Second Reading, 7 December 1999, Hansard vol 340 cols 714–798; Committee, 1st Sitting, 21 December 1999; 2nd Sitting, 11 January 2000; 3rd Sitting, 11 January 2000; 4th Sitting, 18 January 2000; 5th Sitting, 18 January 2000; 6th Sitting, 20 January 2000 [Pt I]; 6th Sitting 20 January 2000 [Pt II]; 7th Sitting, 25 January 2000; 8th Sitting, 25 January 2000; 9th Sitting, 27 January 2000; 10th Sitting, 1 February 2000; 11th Sitting, 1 February 2000; 12th Sitting, 8 February 2000; 13th Sitting, 8 February 2000; 14th Sitting, 10 February 2000; (4) Report and Third Reading, 4 April 2000, Hansard vol 1857 cols 830–935; 5 April 2000, Hansard vol 1857 cols 981–1123; (5) Royal Assent, 30 November 2000 vol 1877 col 1231.
In the House of Lords: (1) Introduction, 6 April 2000, vol 1802, col 1490; (2) Second Reading, 20 April 2000, Hansard vol 612 cols 823–893; (3) Committee, 17 October 2000, Hansard vol 617 cols 883–954 and 971–1020; 19 October 2000, Hansard vol 617 cols 1208–1300; 24 October 2000, Hansard vol 618 cols 273–314; 25 October 2000, Hansard vol 618 cols 407–476; (4) Report, 14 November 2000, Hansard vol 1824 cols 134–158 and 173–266; (5) Third Reading, 22 November 2000, Hansard vol 1825 cols 817–852; (6) Royal Assent, 30 November 2000, Hansard vol 1826 col 1492.

[129] These provisions came into force on 30 November 2000: FOIA s 87(1).

[130] FOIA s 87(2).

[131] FOIA (Commencement No 1) Order 2001 SI 2001/1637. The Order also brought into force provisions relating to the appointment of members to the Tribunal and certain provisions relating to the Information Commissioner.

> The Act will be fully implemented by January 2005, 11 months before the timetable set out in the Act itself. The publication scheme provisions will be implemented first, on a rolling programme, starting with central government in November 2002. I am today placing a full schedule of organisations and dates of implementation in the Libraries of both Houses. This roll-out [ie of publication scheme provisions] will be completed in June 2004, and the individual right of access to information held by all public authorities, including government departments, will be implemented in January 2005.

The requirement on each public authority to produce a publication scheme began with named public authorities on 30 November 2002, widening over the course of 2003.[132] The requirement for the Lord Chancellor to issue a Code of Practice and for the Information Commissioner to issue practice recommendations and to promote good practice also took effect on that date. The publication scheme requirements were extended to smaller public authorities over the course of the first half of 2004.[133] The remainder of the Act, including the enforceable right of access to information held by public authorities, came into force on 1 January 2005.[134] On that same day, the Environmental Information Regulations 2004 came into force.

1–036 Developments since 1 January 2005

The principal changes to the freedom of information regime since 1 January 2005 have been:

    (1)   Numerous additional public authorities have been made subject to the Act.[135]

    (2)   On 18 December 2006 David Maclean MP introduced a Private Members Bill to amend the Freedom of Information Act 2000 so as to remove the House of Commons and the House of Lords as public authorities and to declare as exempt information correspondence between a Member of Parliament and a public authority.[136] On 19 January 2007 the Bill received an unopposed second reading in the House of Commons and on 7 February 2007 passed its Public Bill Committee stage. The Bill received backing from the Parliamentary Labour Party's committee, which urged Labour backbenchers to support it.[137] On 18 May 2007 the Bill was passed with a large majority by the House of Commons. However, the

---

[132] FOIA (Commencement No 2) Order 2002 SI 2002/2812.

[133] FOIA (Commencement No 3) Order 2003 SI 2003/2603.

[134] FOIA (Commencement No 4) Order 2004 SI 2004/1909, dealing with environmental information. FOIA (Commencement No 5) Order 2004 SI 2004/3122, dealing with everything else.

[135] Most notably, through:
> Freedom of Information (Additional Public Authorities) Order 2002 SI 2002/2623;
> Freedom of Information (Additional Public Authorities) Order 2003 SI 2003/1882;
> Freedom of Information (Additional Public Authorities) Order 2004 SI 2004/938;
> Freedom of Information (Additional Public Authorities) Order 2005 SI 2005/3593;
> Freedom of Information (Additional Public Authorities) Order 2008 SI 2008/1271;
> Freedom of Information (Additional Public Authorities) Order 2010 SI 2010/937.

Some public authorities have since been removed from the scope of the Act. See:
> Freedom of Information (Removal of References to Public Authorities) Order 2003 SI 2003/1883;
> Freedom of Information (Removal of References to Public Authorities) Order 2004 SI 2004/1641;
> Freedom of Information (Removal of References to Public Authorities) Order 2005 SI 2005/3594;
> Freedom of Information (Removal of References to Public Authorities) Order 2010 SI 2010/939.

[136] The Freedom of Information (Amendment) Bill 2006-07. A copy of the Bill is at:
> www.publications.parliament.uk/pa/cm200607/cmbills/039/2007039.pdf

[137] See: www.cfoi.org.uk/pdf/PLP.pdf

Bill did not survive in the House of Lords, with its Select Committee on the Constitution reporting that ' the Bill does not meet the requirements of caution and proportionality in enacting legislation of constitutional importance.'[138]

(3) With effect from 18 January 2010, the Information Tribunal ceased to exist and its functions were assumed by the First-tier Tribunal and the Upper Tribunal.[139]

(4) On 25 February 2010 amendments to the Constitutional Reform and Governance Bill 2009 were tabled in the House of Commons. The amendments to the Bill were in response to a report published in January 2009 recommending reduction to 20 years of the 30-year rule in relation to public records.[140] The Bill also expanded the exemption in s 37 for communications with the Royal Family and Royal Household and effected other minor changes in relation to historical records.

7. SCOTLAND, WALES AND NORTHERN IRELAND

7 Scotland: the demarcation

The applicability of the Freedom of Information Act 2000 and of the Data Protection Act 1998 to Scotland, as well as the scope of the Freedom of Information (Scotland) Act 2002, reflect the settlement of legislative powers effected by the Scottish devolution in 1998. Section 1(1) of the Scotland Act 1998 established a Scottish Parliament, which has a limited, devolved power to make laws with respect to certain matters in Scotland.[141] It does not have the power to make laws with respect to 'reserved matters', which remain within the exclusive competence of Westminster.[142] Moreover, Westminster retains its plenary power to make laws with respect to Scotland,[143] although the understanding is that it will not generally exercise that power in relation to devolved matters.[144] In relation to the right of access to official information, the legislative competence of the Scottish Parliament is limited to public authorities that operate purely in or as regards Scotland.[145]

---

[138] See: www.publications.parliament.uk/pa/ld200607/ldselect/ldconst/127/127.pdf

[139] The changes are considered further at §§27– 013 to 27– 021.

[140] Public Records Act 1958 s 3(4). See: www2.nationalarchives.gov.uk/30yrr/30-year-rule-report.pdf

[141] Scotland Act 1998 ss 28–29. Its statutes are known as Acts of the Scottish Parliament: s 28(1).

[142] Scotland Act 1998 ss 29(2)(b) and 30(1). Reserved matters are listed in Sch 5. Specifically reserved at Pt II s.B13 is 'public access to information held by public bodies or holders of public offices (including Government departments and persons acting on behalf of the Crown).' An exception to this reservation is made in relation to information held by the Scottish Parliament, any part of the Scottish Administration, the Scottish Parliamentary corporation and any Scottish public authority with mixed functions or no reserved functions, unless supplied by a Minister of the Crown or Government department and held in confidence. For an instance of a reserved matter relating to Scotland being covered by FOIA, rather than FOI(S)A, see *Scotland Office v IC*, IT, 8 August 2008.

[143] Scotland Act 1998 s 28(7).

[144] *Memorandum of Understanding and Supplementary Agreements between the United Kingdom Government, the Scottish Ministers, the Cabinet of the National Assembly of Wales and the Northern Ireland Executive Committee* (Cm 5240, 2001)(UK); SE/2002/54 (Scotland): www.justice.gov.uk/about/docs/odpm-dev-600629.pdf

[145] Scotland Act 1998 s 29(2)(a).

1– 038   Background

In July 1999 the Scottish Executive published a Code of Practice on Access to Scottish Executive Information.[146] The Code stated its aims and purpose as being:

1.   This Code of Practice supports Scottish Ministers' policy of extending access to official information, and responding to reasonable requests for information. The approach to release of information should in all cases be based on the assumption that information should be released except where disclosure would not be in the public interest, as specified in Part II of this Code.

2.   The aims of the Code are:

—   to facilitate policy-making and the democratic process by providing access to the facts and analyses which form the basis for the consideration of proposed policy;

—   to protect the interests of individuals and companies by ensuring that reasons are given for administrative decisions, except where there is statutory authority or established convention to the contrary; and

…

These aims are balanced by the need:

—   to maintain high standards of care in ensuring the privacy of personal and commercially confidential information; and

—   to preserve confidentiality where disclosure would not be in the public interest or would breach personal privacy or the confidences of a third party, in accordance with statutory requirements and Part II of the Code.

Like the Code for England and Wales issued in 1994 and revised in 1997,[147] it conferred no enforceable rights.

1– 039   Freedom of Information (Scotland) Act 2002

On 24 April 2002 the Freedom of Information (Scotland) Act 2002 was passed by the Scottish Parliament.[148] As noted above, the Act only applies to public authorities that operate purely in or as regards Scotland.[149] Westminster-established bodies, government departments, offices and office-holders when operating in Scotland, including what are termed cross-border public authorities,[150] are in any event not susceptible to coverage by the Freedom of Information (Scotland) Act 2002.[151] Difficult issues arise as to whether some of the exemptions in the Freedom of Information (Scotland) Act 2002 are outside the legislative competence of the

---

[146] A separate Code of Practice on Openness existed in relation to information held by the NHS in Scotland (covering Health Boards, NHS Trusts and other NHS organisations).

[147] See §1– 020.

[148] It received Royal Assent on 28 May 2002.

[149] These are listed in Sch 1 to the FOI(S)A.

[150] Cross-border authorities are listed in the Scotland Act 1998 (Cross-Border Public Authorities) (Specification) Order 1999 SI 1999/1319. These include the British Waterways Board, the Criminal Injuries Compensation Board and the Meat and Livestock Commission.

[151] See §1– 037. When operating in Scotland, these public authorities will be governed by the FOIA.

Scottish Parliament on the basis that they represent provisions that relate to reserved matters.[152]

40 Implementation of the Freedom of Information (Scotland) Act 2002
The Act was brought into force incrementally over the course of three years. The initial implementation of the Act brought into force those provisions that specified which bodies were to be subject to the Act, that provided for publication schemes and for the establishment of the Scottish Information Commissioner, and that effected certain amendments to public records legislation.[153] The remaining provisions for publication schemes, the Scottish Information Commissioner and immunity from suit were brought into force on 31 October 2003.[154] The remaining administrative provisions took effect from 30 April 2004.[155] Finally, the enforceable right of access was brought into force with effect from 1 January 2005.[156] On that same day, the Environmental Information (Scotland) Regulations 2004 came into force. Since that day, various additional Scottish public authorities have been made subject to the Act[157] and those that no longer exist have been taken out of the Act.

41 Differences between the two Acts
Although closely modelled on the Freedom of Information Act 2000, the Scottish Act treats a number of matters differently:

(1) The scheme for responses that neither confirm nor deny that the public authority holds information answering the terms of the request. The Freedom of Information Act 2000 spells out a separate duty on a public authority to inform an applicant whether it holds information of the description specified in the request.[158] In relation to all but one of the heads of exemption, that duty is disapplied where, or to the extent that, confirming or denying that the public authority holds the requested information would, or would be likely to, prejudice the matter protected by the head of exemption and, if the exemption is a qualified one, to do so would be contrary to the public interest.[159] The Freedom of Information (Scotland) Act 2002 creates no separate duty to confirm or deny that the information requested is

---

[152] An Act of the Scottish Parliament is not law in so far as any provision of it is outside the legislative competence of the Scottish Parliament: Scotland Act 1998 s 29(1). A provision will be outside the legislative competence of the Scottish Parliament if it relates to 'reserved matters': Scotland Act 1998 s 29(2)(b). Reserved matters are defined in Sch 5 to the Scotland Act 1998. Significantly, in light of the exemptions in the FOI(S)A, these include: international relations, including relations with territories outside the United Kingdom, the European Communities (and their institutions) and other international organisations; the defence of the realm and the naval, military or air forces of the Crown; data protection; national security, etc; social security; health and safety.

[153] FOI(S)A (Commencement No 1) Order 2002 SSI 2002/437.

[154] FOI(S)A (Commencement No 2) Order 2003 SSI 2003/477.

[155] FOI(S)A (Commencement No 3) Order 2004 SSI 2004/203.

[156] FOI(S)A (Commencement No 3) Order 2004 SSI 2004/203.

[157] For example: The Scottish Further and Higher Education Funding Council; Bòrd na Gàidhlig; and community justice authorities.

[158] FOIA s 1(1)(a). This is termed 'the duty to confirm or deny': s 1(6).

[159] FOIA ss 2(1), 22(2), 23(5), 24(2), 26(3), 27(4), 28(3), 29(2), 30(3), 31(3), 32(3), 33(3), 34(2), 35(3), 36(3), 37(2), 38(2), 39(3), 40(5), 41(2), 42(2), 43(3) and 44(2). The sole head of exemption that does not have a disapplication of the duty to confirm or deny is s 21.

held by the public authority. Instead, more elegantly, it provides that a refusal notice must, amongst other things, disclose that the public authority holds the information sought;[160] this requirement in relation to a refusal notice is then disapplied where information answering the terms of the request would be exempt under certain exemptions[161] and the public authority considers that it would be contrary to the public interest to reveal whether such information exists or is so held.[162]

(2) To the extent that there is an onus in engaging the public interest override in relation to the qualified exemptions, it is reversed. Under the Freedom of Information Act 2000, the duty to disclose exempt information is disapplied where, in all the circumstances of the case, the public interest in maintaining the exemption outweighs the public interest in disclosing the information.[163] Under the Freedom of Information (Scotland) Act 2002, the duty to disclose non-absolute exempt information only applies to the extent that, in all the circumstances of the case, the public interest in disclosing the information is not outweighed by the public interest in maintaining the exemption.[164]

(3) The harm level required to engage the prejudice-based exemptions is higher under the Freedom of Information (Scotland) Act 2002 ('would or might substantially prejudice')[165] than it is under the Freedom of Information Act 2000 ('would or might prejudice').[166] In light of the assurances given during the introduction into Parliament of the Freedom of Information Act 2000[167] the differences in practice ought to be less significant than the language might suggest.

(4) Under the Freedom of Information Act 2000, information held by a public authority is absolutely exempt if it was directly or indirectly supplied to the public authority by one of the security bodies or if it relates to one of the security bodies.[168] Moreover, a Minister of the Crown can sign a conclusive certificate certifying that the information to which the certificate applies was directly or indirectly supplied by, or relates to, any of the security bodies.[169] In Scotland, there is no such exemption.[170]

---

[160] FOI(S)A s 16(1)(a).

[161] The exemptions to which the duty to confirm or deny is disapplied are more limited than those under the FOIA: namely, ss 28–35, 39 and 41. The Scottish equivalents to the FOIA ss 22, 32, 33, 40, 41, 42 and 44 do not ground a refusal to confirm or deny under the FOI(S)A.

[162] FOI(S)A s 18.

[163] Section 2(2)(b). The effect of this provision is considered further in ch 15.

[164] Section 2(1)(b).

[165] FOI(S)A ss 27(2), 28(1), 30, 31(4), 32(1), 33(1), 33(2), 35(1) and 40.

[166] FOIA ss 26(1), 27(1), 28(1), 29(1), 31(1), 33(2), 36(2), 38(1) and 43(2).

[167] See §15– 021.

[168] FOIA s 23(1). The security bodies are those listed in s 23(3).

[169] FOIA s 23(2). The effect of a conclusive certificate is considered in §14– 039(1).

[170] This raises a serious issue in relation to the FOI(S)A. The exemption in the FOIA s 23 does not, of course, operate to render exempt information requested under the FOI(S)A.

(5) In England, Wales and Northern Ireland, information the disclosure of which would be a breach of parliamentary privilege enjoys an absolute exemption.[171] There is no such exemption under the Scottish Act.

(6) There are fewer grounds for issuing an exemption conclusive certificate under the Freedom of Information (Scotland) Act 2002[172] than there are under the Freedom of Information Act 2000.[173]

(7) The preconditions for the issue of a compliance conclusive certificate are more onerous under the Freedom of Information (Scotland) Act 2002 than they are under the Freedom of Information Act 2000. In both jurisdictions, where the Information Commissioner is satisfied that a public authority has failed to comply with any of the requirements of Part I of the Act, he may serve on that public authority an enforcement notice specifying the steps that the public authority must take.[174] In both jurisdictions, limited provision[175] is made for a high-ranking official to give the Information Commissioner, within a certain time, a certificate that causes the enforcement notice to cease to have effect.[176] Under the Freedom of Information Act 2000, the precondition for the high-ranking official issuing the certificate is that on reasonable grounds he has formed the opinion that, in respect of the request or requests concerned, there was no relevant[177] failure to comply with the Act.[178] In Scotland, the high-ranking official must also form the opinion that the information requested is of exceptional sensitivity.[179]

(8) The Freedom of Information (Scotland) Act 2002 gives no express right of review in relation to the decision to issue a conclusive certificate.[180]

(9) The Freedom of Information (Scotland) Act 2002 has no equivalent to s 81(1) of the Freedom of Information Act 2000, which treats each government department as a person separate from any other government department.

The Freedom of Information (Scotland) Act 2002 establishes the office of the Scottish

---

[171] FOIA s 34(1).

[172] The only ground is national security: s 31(2).

[173] The grounds are: security body information, s 23(2); national security, s 24(3); parliamentary privilege, s 34(3); and deliberative or cabinet information held by either House of Parliament, s 36(7).

[174] FOIA s 52(1); FOI(S)A s 51(1).

[175] Under the FOIA, the power to issue a certificate is confined to where the enforcement notice relates to: (a) a failure to inform an applicant that it holds information of the description specified in the request in circumstances where s 2(1) does not operate to disapply the duty to confirm or deny; (b) a failure to communicate information to an applicant in circumstances where s 2(2) does not operate to disapply the duty to disclose: FOIA s 53(1)(b). In Scotland, the power to issue a certificate is confined to where the enforcement notice relates to a failure to give information to an applicant in circumstances where s 2(1) does not operate to disapply the duty to disclose and the information is exempt information by virtue of s 29, 31(1), 32(1)(b), 34, 36(1) or 41(b): FOI(S)A s 52(1)(b).

[176] Under the FOIA, that high-ranking official is the 'accountable person' (itself defined in s 53(8)) and the time allowed is 20 working days: s 53(2). In Scotland that high-ranking official is the First Minister of the Scottish Executive and the time allowed is 30 working days: FOI(S)A s 52(2).

[177] In other words, a failure of the sort set out in n.175.

[178] FOIA s 53(2).

[179] FOI(S)A s 52(2).

[180] Either on national security or exceptional sensitivity grounds: FOI(S)A ss 31(2) and 52(2).

Information Commissioner.[181] This is independent of the office of the Information Commissioner, who is responsible for policing the Freedom of Information Act 2000. The Scottish Information Commissioner does not have responsibility for the enforcement of the Data Protection Act 1998 in Scotland.

1– 042   Environmental information: Scotland

In relation to 'environmental information', Scottish public authorities are subject to the Environmental Information (Scotland) Regulations 2004. Apart from their applying to Scottish public authorities, these Regulations are very similar to the Environmental Information Regulations 2004 which apply to Westminster public authorities. Both regimes are considered in Chapter 6 of this work.

1– 043   Subject-access requests: Scotland

Data protection is a reserved matter and responsibility for enforcement of the Data Protection Act 1998 lies with the Information Commissioner: the Scottish Information Commissioner does not have responsibility for enforcing the Data Protection Act 1998. Thus a request by an individual for information about himself will be exempt under the Freedom of Information (Scotland) Act 2002 and is instead to be treated as a subject access request under the Data Protection Act 1998, save to the extent that it also involves the disclosure of personal information about a third party.[182]

1– 044   Wales

Although the Government of Wales Act 1998 created a National Assembly for Wales, it was an administrative body rather than a legislative body. It had no power to make laws with respect to the granting of access to official information. The Government of Wales Act 2006 replaced the National Assembly with the Welsh Assembly Government, but did not alter the position in relation to the making of laws with respect to access rights to official information.[183] Accordingly, the Freedom of Information Act 2000 applies equally to public authorities in Wales as it does to public authorities in England.[184] Schedule 1 to the Act, which lists public authorities for the purposes of the Act, includes the National Assembly for Wales, Welsh county councils, borough councils and community councils, health authorities, maintained schools and other educational institutions, police authorities, and various other bodies ranging from the Ancient Monuments Board for Wales to the Welsh Optometric Committee. The National Assembly for Wales has its own Code of Practice on Public Access to Information,[185] which, like

---

[181] FOI(S)A s 42(1).

[182] See ch 5.

[183] As is evident from The Freedom of Information (Parliament and National Assembly for Wales) Order 2008 SI 2008 1967. Certain amendments to the Freedom of Information Act 2000 consequential upon the creation of the Welsh Assembly were effected by the Government of Wales Act 2006 (Consequential Modifications and Transitional Provisions) Order 2007 SI 2007/1388 Sch 1 para 80.

[184] The only difference is that where the Secretary of State for Justice proposes to add a body or office-holder to the list of public authorities in the Act and that body or office-holder is one whose functions are exercisable only or mainly in or as regards Wales, he must consult the National Assembly before doing so: FOIA s 4(7). The Secretary of State for Justice is not required to consult where he intends to add a police authority to the list.

[185] www.assemblywales.org/abthome/abt-nafw/abt-foi/abt-foi-cop-pub.htm

all such codes,[186] does not confer rights but merely states intent. It contemplates a more generous provision of information than the minimum that may be provided under the Freedom of Information Act 2000 and Environmental Information Regulations 2004. Since the initial coming into force of the Act, certain public authorities have been removed from its operation.[187]

45 Northern Ireland

The Freedom of Information Act 2000 extends to Northern Ireland[188] and specifically captures public authorities whose functions are exercisable only or mainly in or as regards Northern Ireland and relate only or mainly to transferred matters.[189] Schedule 1 to the Act includes the Northern Ireland Assembly, district councils, health and social services boards, schools and universities, the police authority, and various other bodies ranging from the Advisory Committee on Pesticides for Northern Ireland to the Northern Ireland Pig Production Development Committee.

---

[186] See §10– 008.

[187] Freedom of Information (Excluded Welsh Authorities) Order 2002 SI 2002/2832.

[188] FOIA s 88(2). The specific reference to Northern Ireland is, strictly speaking, superfluous, but simply accords with a drafting convention.

[189] FOIA s 84. 'Transferred matters' are defined in the Northern Ireland Act 1998 s 4(1).

CHAPTER 2

The Comparative Jurisdictions

1. INFORMATION RIGHTS LEGISLATION ELSEWHERE

01 Introduction

The enactment of the Freedom of Information Act 2000 was preceded by extensive consideration of analogous legislation in Australia, New Zealand, Canada and Ireland:[1] comparative tables of exemption were prepared; the different types of harm that could engage an exemption were considered; the various approaches to the public interest were analysed; and so forth.[2] This is reflected in the final product, whose structure and occasionally language resemble those employed in the legislation of the comparative jurisdictions.[3] The divergences are also pointed, with certain features of the comparative regimes having been considered but not adopted. An overview of each of the comparative regimes is given below. After a short history, the principal features of each regime are identified: the scope of the right; the approach to requests and permissible responses; the general treatment of exemptions, including classification by harm and by class; the role of the public interest; the specific heads of exemption; and the system of appeals and enforcement. These reveal certain universal issues, most notably the identification of those legitimate interests of an open, accountable and representative government that have paramountcy over the general right of access to government-held information. Elsewhere in this work, reference is made to authorities in these comparative jurisdictions where it is considered that it sheds light on the Freedom of Information Act 2000, the Environmental Information Regulations 2004 or the Data Protection Act 1998.

---

[1] Freedom of Information Act 1982 (Cth of Australia); Official Information Act 1982 (NZ); Access to Information Act (1982) (Canada); Freedom of Information Act 1997 (Ireland). Although it has the most developed body of jurisprudence on the topic, reference to the Freedom of Information Act (1966) 5 USC 552 (USA) was more limited.

[2] See: Cabinet Office, *Your Right to Know—The Government's Proposals for a Freedom of Information Act. White Paper* (Cm 3818, 1997) paras 3–12, Annexes A and B (see ch 1, n 62); *Background Material*, paras 33, 56–65, 70–71, 78, 108, 116–117, 125–129, 219. Hansard HC vol 340 cols 722, 728, 741, 746–749, 754, 759–761, 789 (7 December 1999); Hansard HC vol 347 cols 832, 837–839, 848–849, 922–926, 934 (4 April 2000); Hansard HC vol 347 cols 996, 1009, 1028, 1041, 1097, 1103 (5 April 2000); Hansard H vol 612 cols 830, 834, 838–839, 851, 867–868 (20 April 2000); Hansard HL vol 617 cols 888, 893, 939, 941, 946, 1010 (17 October 2000); Hansard HL vol 617 cols 1215, 1256, 1279 (19 October 2000); Hansard HL vol 618 cols 438, 441–442 (25 October 2000); Hansard HL vol 619 col 619 (14 November 2000).

[3] Most notably New Zealand and, to a slightly lesser extent, Australia.

2. UNITED STATES OF AMERICA

2–002 **Introduction**

In 1966 the United States Congress passed the Freedom of Information Act.[4] It had evolved after a decade of debate among agency officials, legislators and public interest group representatives.[5] The Act was not, however, entirely novel. The Administrative Procedure Act of 1964[6] had included a public disclosure section, although this was thought to have fallen short of its goals. In 1974 significant amendments to the Freedom of Information Act were made[7] and the Privacy Act was passed.[8] The latter granted individuals enhanced rights of access to agency records maintained about themselves;[9] it restricted the rights of agencies to disclose personally identifiable records maintained by an agency; and it granted a right to individuals to seek amendment of agency records maintained on themselves. Further amendments to the Freedom of Information Act were made in 1976, 1986, 1996 and 2007.[10] On 21 January 2009, President Obama signed the 'Presidential Memorandum for the Heads of Executive Departments and Agencies on the Freedom of Information Act,'[11] which directed all agencies

---

[4] 5 USC 1002 (1964) (amended in 1966 and now codified at 5 USC 552). The Act took effect on 4 July 1967.

[5] The main proponent of the legislation was a Californian Democrat Congressman, John Moss. A Republican Congressman, Donald Rumsfeld, signed as a co-sponsor. He explained the need for the Act: 'The unanimous action after years of delay results from the growing size and complexity of the federal government, of its increased role in our lives, and from the increasing awareness by Americans of the threat involved in Government secrecy in vital records affecting their fate…With the continuing tendency toward managed news and suppression of public information that the people are entitled to have, the issues have at last been brought home to the public…' (quoted in *The Arizona Republic*, 27 June 1966).

[6] 5 USC 1002. The Freedom of Information Act was in fact a revision of the public disclosure section of this Act.

[7] The 1974 amendments considerably narrowed the overall scope of the Act's law enforcement and national security exemptions. It also broadened many of the Act's procedural provisions, including fees, time limits, segregability, and *in camera* inspection by the courts. President Ford vetoed the bill effecting the changes, calling it 'unconstitutional and unworkable', but both Houses overrode his veto.

[8] 5 USC 552a. The Act took effect on 27 September 1975.

[9] 5 USC 552a(d)(1). There is an overlap between the right of access bestowed by the Freedom of Information Act and that which is granted by the Privacy Act. The latter only applies to requests for personal information relating to the person making the request. Such a request need not state under which statute it is made. The technique is first to consider whether any exemption under the Privacy Act applies: if it does not, then the information must be released irrespective of the applicability of an exemption under the Freedom of Information Act. If an exemption under the Privacy Act does apply, then exemptions under the Freedom of Information Act must be considered: if none applies, the requested information must be released notwithstanding the applicability of an exemption under the Privacy Act: 5 USC 552a(t)(1); *Martin v Office of Special Counsel*, 819 F 2d 1181 (DC Cir 1987); *Savada v Department of Defense*, 755 F Supp 6 (DDC 1991); *Viotti v United States Air Force*, 902 F Supp 1131 (D Colo 1995).

[10] The 1976 amendment narrowed the Act's incorporation of the non-disclosure provisions of other statutes. The Freedom of Information Reform Act (1986) provided broader exemption protection for law enforcement information, special law enforcement record exclusions, and created a new fee and fee waiver structure. The Electronic Freedom of Information Act Amendments (1996) dealt with electronic records, electronic reading rooms, agency backlogs of requests, and other procedural provisions. The OPEN Government Act of 2007 effected amendments including the definition of news media requesters, the recovery of attorney fees and litigation costs, computing and tolling (or stopping) the time limits for responding to requests and treatment of agency records maintained by government contractors. Smaller changes were also made in 1978 and 1984.

[11] www.whitehouse.gov/the_press_office/FreedomofInformationAct/

to administer the FOIA with a clear presumption in favour of disclosure, to resolve doubts in favor of openness, and to not withhold information based on 'speculative or abstract fears.' In addition, the President called on agencies to ensure that requests are responded to with 'a spirit of cooperation.'[12]

3 Scope of the right

Under the Freedom of Information Act, each federal 'agency'[13] is required to make its[14] 'records'[15] promptly available to any person[16] who makes a proper request for them[17]. The

---

[12] To similar effect, see Attorney General Holder's *Memorandum for Heads of Executive Departments and Agencies Concerning the Freedom of Information Act* (19 March 2009), available at: `www.usdoj.gov/ag/foia-memo-march2009.pdf`

[13] This extends to agencies within the executive branch of the federal Government, including the Executive Office of the President and independent regulatory agencies: 5 USC 552(f)(1). However, the Act does not apply to entities that are not controlled by the federal Government. Thus, organisations which, although having a relationship with the federal government, are autonomous, are outside the ambit of the Act: *Public Citizen Health Research Group v Department of Health, Education & Welfare*, 668 F 2d 537 (DC Cir 1981); *Irwin Memorial Blood Bank v American National Red Cross*, 640 F 2d 1051 (9th Cir 1981); *Gilmore v Department of Energy*, 4 F Supp 2d 912 (ND Cal 1998). Similarly, state Governments, municipal corporations, the courts, Congress and private citizens are not subject to the Act. Offices within the Executive Office of the President whose functions are limited to advising and assisting the President do not fall within the definition of 'agency': *Armstrong v Executive Office of the President*, 90 F 3d 553 (DC Cir 1996) (National Security Council not an agency); *Judicial Watch, Inc v Department of Energy*, 412 F 3d 125 (DC Cir 2005) (concluding that the National Energy Policy Development Group was not an agency subject to the Act, because 'its sole function [was] to advise and assist the President'). The Act does not cover Congressional documents: *United We Stand Am v Inland Revenue Service*, 359 F 3d 595 (DC Cir 2004); *Dow Jones & Co v Department of Justice*, 917 F 2d 571 (DC Cir 1990).

[14] 'Agency records' are records that are (1) either created or obtained by an agency, and (2) under agency control at the time of the request: *Department of Justice v Tax Analysts*, 492 US 136 (1989). The OPEN Government Act 2007 made it clear that agency records do not lose their status as such when physically maintained by a government contractor for the purposes of record management. In determining whether an agency has sufficient control over a record in order for it to be an 'agency record', there are four factors to be taken into account: (1) the intent of the record's creator to retain or relinquish control over the record; (2) the ability of the agency to use and dispose of the record as it sees fit; (3) the extent to which agency personnel have read or relied upon the record; and (4) the degree to which the record was integrated into the agency's record-keeping system or files: *Lindsey v Bureau of Prisons*, 736 F 2d 1462 (11th Cir 1984); *Tax Analysts v Department of Justice*, 845 F 2d 1060 (DC Cir 1988), affirmed, 492 US 136 (1989). Personal records which are maintained by agency employees are not considered to be agency records: *Bureau of National Affairs Inc v Department of Justice*, 742 F 2d 1484 (DC Cir 1984); *Spannaus v Department of Justice*, 942 F Supp 656 (DDC 1996); *Fortson v Harvey*, 407 F Supp 2d 13 (DDC 2005).

[15] The definition of 'record' was widened in 1996: see now 5 USC 552(f)(2). Before the inclusion of that definition, it had been held that 'records' did not include tangible, evidentiary objects: *Nichols v United States*, 325 F Supp 130 (D Kan 1971) (holding that archival exhibits consisting of guns, bullets, and clothing relating to the assassination of President Kennedy were not 'records'). However, 'record' had otherwise been given an expansive meaning to include: 'machine readable materials...regardless of physical form or characteristics' (*Forsham v Harris* 445 US 169 (1980)); an audiotape of Challenger astronauts on the basis that the Act 'makes no distinction between information in lexical and...non-lexical form' (*NY Times Co v NASA*, 920 F 2d 1002 (DC Cir 1990)); and a motion picture film (*Save the Dolphins v Department of Commerce*, 404 F Supp 407 (ND Cal 1975)).

[16] 'Any person' includes foreign citizens, partnerships, corporations, associations, states and state agencies, and foreign or domestic governments: 5 USC 552(2). Requests may also be made through an attorney or other representative on behalf of any person: *Constangy, Brooks & Smith v National Labor Relations Board*, 851 F 2d 839 (6th Cir 1988). However, fugitives may be denied access: *Doyle v Department of Justice*, 668 F 2d 1365 (DC Cir 1981); *Maydak v US Department of Education*, 150 F Appendix 136 (3d Cir 2005).

[17] 5 USC 552(a)(3)(A). *Stone v Export-Import Bank of US*, 552 F 2d 132 (5th Cir 1977). In 2002 Congress amended the Act to prohibit requests to intelligence agencies from or on behalf of foreign intelligence services, whether friendly or hostile: 5 USC 552(3)(E). 'Person' is defined at 5 USC 551(2).

37

reason for the making of a request has no bearing on the merits of that request.[18] Nor does the initial right of access depend upon the existence or extent of public interest in the records sought.[19] The scope of the right was curtailed by an amendment to the Act in 1986 which introduced the concept of 'exclusions'.[20] Three provisions create record 'exclusions', the effect of which is to expressly authorise federal law enforcement agencies, in relation to especially sensitive records under certain specified circumstances, to treat the records as not subject to the requirements of the Freedom of Information Act 1966.[21] The application of one of the three record exclusions results in a response stating that no records responsive to the request exist, even though they may exist. These exclusions do not provide additional bases for an agency to withhold documents from the public: the exclusions only apply to records that are already exempt from disclosure.

2– 004   Other rights

The Act does not speak of publication schemes, but contains two analogous provisions giving rise to automatic disclosure of certain agency information. Under the first, each agency is required to publish in the Federal Register certain information relating to itself for 'the guidance of the public'. This includes a description of the agency's organisation, functions and procedures; its substantive rules; and statements of general policy.[22] This requirement provides the public with automatic access to basic information regarding the transaction of agency business. Under the second, certain types of internal records, such as final agency opinions and orders rendered in the adjudication of cases, specific policy statements, certain administrative staff manuals, and some records previously processed for disclosure under the Act, must be routinely made 'available for public inspection and copying'.[23] This is generally referred to as

---

[18] *Environmental Protection Agency v Mink*, 410 US 73 (1973); *Department of Justice v Reporters Committee for Freedom of the Press*, 489 US 749 (1989).

[19] *Jordan v Department of Justice*, 591 F 2d 753 (DC Cir 1978). It may, of course, impinge upon the applicability of an exemption.

[20] 5 USC 552(c)(1), (c)(2), (c)(3).

[21] The first exclusion may be used when a request seeks information that is exempt because disclosure could reasonably be expected to interfere with a current law enforcement investigation (ie exemption (7)(A)). There are three specific prerequisites for the application of this exclusion. First, the investigation in question must involve a possible violation of criminal law. Second, there must be reason to believe that the subject of the investigation is not already aware that the investigation is underway. Third, disclosure of the existence of the records, as distinguished from the contents of the records, could reasonably be expected to interfere with enforcement proceedings. When all these conditions are satisfied, an agency may respond to a request as if the records were not subject to the requirements of the Act. The second exclusion applies to informant records maintained by a criminal law enforcement agency under the informant's name or personal identifier. The agency is not required to confirm the existence of these records unless the informant's status has been officially confirmed. This exclusion helps agencies to protect the identity of confidential informants. The third exclusion only applies to records maintained by the Federal Bureau of Investigation that relate to foreign intelligence, counter-intelligence, or international terrorism. When the *existence* of these types of records is classified, the FBI may treat the records as not subject to the requirements of the Act. This exclusion does not apply to all classified records on the specific subjects. It only applies when the records are classified and when the *existence* of the records is also classified.

[22] 5 USC 552(a)(1).

[23] 5 USC 552(a)(2). The importance of pro-active disclosure was underscored in President Obama's 21 January 2009 FOIA Memorandum. The reading rooms must also include information requested under the Act but which the agency considers is likely to be requested by others as well: 5 USC 552(a)(2)(D). The rationale for this is to prevent the development of agency 'secret law', known to agency personnel but not to members of the public who deal with agencies. It is for this reason that records that have no precedent value and which do not constitute the working

the 'reading room' provision of the Act.[24] A failure to comply with these requirements may provide a ground of challenge to an administrative decision that is related to information that ought to have been disclosed.[25] The effect of information falling within either provision is that it cannot be made the proper subject of a request under the Freedom of Information Act.[26] If an agency does not hold any record that answers the terms of a request, that agency is under no obligation to refer that request to any other agency where such records might be located. The Act contains no procedure entitling or enabling a third party to make representations before information relating to that third party is released to an applicant: this is dealt with, in part, by Executive Order.[27]

5   The request

A request must reasonably describe the records sought and it must be made in accordance with the agency's published regulations.[28] An agency is not required to create a record in order to respond to a request.[29] Nor is an agency required to answer a request for future information when it comes into existence.[30] However, an agency must undertake a search that is 'reasonably calculated to uncover all relevant documents'.[31] The Act provides for three levels of fees that may be assessed in response to a request according to categories of applicants.[32]

6   The response

Each agency is required to determine within 20 working days after the receipt of a proper request whether to comply with the request.[33] In 'unusual circumstances' an agency may have

---

   law of an agency are not required to be made available under this part of the Act: *National Labor Relations Board v Sears, Roebuck & Co*, 421 US 132 at 153–154 (1975); *Skelton v United States Postal Service*, 678 F 2d 35 at 41 (5th Cir 1982).

[24] Some of these records must be made available by agencies in 'electronic reading rooms'.

[25] *Checkosky v US Securities and Exchange Commission*, 23 F 3d 452 (DC Cir 1994); *Kennecott Utah Copper Corp v Department of the Interior*, 88 F 3d 1191 (DC Cir 1996).

[26] 5 USC 552(a)(3)(A).

[27] A more detailed comparative treatment of third party rights of consultation and of 'reverse FOI' is given at §11–043.

[28] 5 USC 552(a)(3)(A). The request will 'reasonably describe' the records sought if it enables a professional agency employee familiar with the subject area to locate the record with a reasonable amount of effort. Each agency must publish in the *Federal Register* its procedural regulations governing access to its records under the Act. These regulations must inform the public of where and how to address requests; its schedule of fees for search, review, and duplication; its fee waiver criteria; and its administrative appeal procedures.

[29] *National Labor Relations Board v Sears, Roebuck & Co*, 421 US 132 (1975).

[30] *Mandel Grunfeld & Herrick v United States Customs Service*, 709 F 2d 41 (11th Cir 1983).

[31] *Weisberg v Department of Justice*, 705 F 2d 1344 at 1351 (DC Cir 1983). The adequacy of the search will depend upon the specificity of the request. The courts may review the adequacy of the search, see: *Krikorian v Department of State*, 984 F 2d 461 (DC Cir 1993).

[32] 5 USC 552(a)(4)(A)(ii)(I), (II), (III).

[33] 5 USC 552(a)(6)(A)(i).

up to 10 days extra to answer.[34] The actual disclosure of records answering the terms of the request must follow promptly.[35] The agency can refuse to disclose if the applicant refuses to pay any fees.[36] An agency may charge an applicant three types of fee: the direct cost to the agency of searching for documents that answer the terms of the request; the direct cost to the agency in reviewing those documents to see what must be released; and duplication costs.[37] In permitting an agency to charge fees, the Act distinguishes records 'requested for commercial uses', requests made by 'an educational or non-commercial scientific institution whose purpose is scholarly or scientific research', requests from the media and requests from others. Provision is made for fee waiver or reductions where disclosure is in the public interest 'because it is likely to contribute significantly to public understanding of the operations or activities of government and is not primarily in the commercial interest of the requester'.[38] Disclosure must be in the form requested by the applicant.[39] If a request is refused in whole or in part, the agency must tell the applicant the reasons for the refusal.[40] The agency must also tell the applicant that there is a right to appeal.[41] If an agency fails to make a determination within the time limits, that may be treated as a constructive exhaustion of administrative remedies, entitling the applicant immediately thereafter to seek judicial review.[42] Where a record is not wholly comprised of exempt material the agency must, if it is reasonably practicable to do so, release any reasonably segregable portion that is not subject to an exemption.[43] The fact that supplying the records in answer to a properly described request would be burdensome does not of itself provide a

---

[34] Defined to mean circumstances in which the agency: (1) needs to search for and collect records from separate offices; (2) needs to examine a voluminous amount of records required by the request; or (3) needs to consult with another agency or agency component: 5 USC 552(a)(6)(B)(ii). The agency is required to notify the applicant whenever an extension is invoked.

[35] 5 USC 552(a)(6)(C)(i).

[36] *Trueblood v Department of the Treasury*, 943 F Supp 64 (DDC 1996).

[37] 5 USC(a)(4)(A).

[38] 5 USC 552(a)(4)(A)(ii)(II). Agencies can provide for the recovery of only the direct costs of search, duplication and review of records answering a request: 5 USC 552(a)(4)(A)(iv). Agencies are required to provide free of charge the first two hours of search time and the first 100 pages of duplication to all non-commercial requesters.

[39] Unless it is not readily reproducible in that form or format: 5 USC 552(a)(3)(B).

[40] 5 USC 552(a)(6)(F).

[41] 5 USC 552(a)(6)(A)(i), (a)(6)(C)(i).

[42] 5 USC 552(a)(6)(c)).

[43] 5 USC 552(b). The courts will scrutinise decisions to ensure that this obligation has been properly performed: *Trans-Pac Policing Agreement v United States Customs Service*, 177 F 3d 1022 at 1028 (DC Cir 1999). District courts have broad discretion to determine whether *in camera* inspection is necessary to evaluate the Government's claim that non-exempt material cannot be segregated from exempt material. There are limits to the obligation: see, generally: *Petroleum Information Corp v Department of the Interior*, 976 F 2d 1429 (DC Cir 1992); *Krikorian v Department of State*, 984 F 2d 461 (DC Cir 1993); *Solar Sources Inc v United States*, 142 F 3d 1033 (7th Cir 1998); *PHE Inc v Department of Justice*, 983 F 2d 249 (DC Cir 1993). Thus in *Students Against Genocide v Department of State*, 257 F 3d 828 at 837 (DC Cir 2001) the Court held that an agency is not obliged to segregate and release images from classified photographs by produc[ing] new photographs at a different resolution in order to mask the [classified] capabilities of the reconnaissance systems that took them. If, however, an agency determines that non-exempt material is so 'inextricably intertwined' that disclosure of it would leave only essentially meaningless words and phrases, the entire record may be withheld: *Neufeld v Inland Revenue Service*, 646 F 2d 661 at 663 (DC Cir 1981). In *Sherman v Department of the Army*, 244 F 3d 357 (5th Cir 2001) the court upheld the agency's decisions to require the requester to pay an estimated $350,000 to $1 million in costs for redacting social security numbers from a database of Vietnam medal awardees.

basis for non-compliance.[44]

07 Exemptions generally

An agency may refuse to disclose an agency record that falls within any of the nine statutory exemptions in the Freedom of Information Act. Generally speaking, the exemptions are discretionary in nature, so that it is open to an agency to grant disclosure to a record for which exemption could be claimed.[45] Access to a document that does not qualify as an 'agency record' may be refused on the basis that only agency records are available under the Act. Personal notes of agency employees may be refused on this basis. However, most records in the possession of an agency are 'agency records' within the meaning of the 1966 Act.

08 Specific exemptions

The right of access is disapplied to nine classes of matter:

(1) National security information concerning national defence or foreign policy, provided that that information has been classified in accordance with the procedural and substantive requirements of an executive order.[46] The information categories identified as proper bases for classification are:

(a) foreign government information;[47]

(b) vulnerabilities or capabilities of systems, installations, projects or plans

---

[44] *Yeager v Drug Enforcement Administration*, 678 F 2d 315 (DC Cir 1982); *Ruotolo v Department of Justice*, 53 F 3d 4 (2d Cir 1995); *Nation Magazine v United States Customs Service*, 71 F 3d 885 at 892 (DC Cir 1995).

[45] *Chrysler Corp v Brown*, 441 US 281 (1979); *Mobil Oil Corp v Environmental Protection Agency*, 879 F 2d 698 (9th Cir 1989); *Public Citizen v Department of State*, 11 F 3d 198 (DC Cir 1993); *Bartholdi Cable Co v Federal Communication Commission*, 114 F 3d 274 (DC Cir 1997); *Sherman v Department of the Army*, 244 F 3d 357 (5th Cir 2001). This was underscored in President Obama's 21 January 2009 FOIA Memorandum, which called on agencies to ensure that requests are responded to with 'a spirit of cooperation.'

[46] 5 USC 552(b)(1). Executive Order 12,958, made 14 October 1995, was amended by Executive Order 13,292, with effect from 25 March 2003. The Executive Order states that information may not be considered for classification unless it concerns one of the following categories: military plans, weapons systems, or operations; foreign government information; intelligence activities, sources or methods; foreign relations or foreign activities of the United States, including confidential sources; scientific, technological or economic matters relating to the national security; programmes for safeguarding nuclear materials or facilities; vulnerabilities or capabilities of systems, installations, projects or plans relating to the national security; or weapons of mass destruction. The Executive Order recognises three basic classifications according to the damage to the national security that might reasonably be expected to result from disclosure of the information to which the classification relates: top secret; secret; and confidential. The classification generally lasts for 10 years. In relation to foreign government information, see *Peltier v FBI*, 218 F App 30, 31 (2d Cir 2007), in which it was held that disclosure of foreign government information would 'breach express promises of confidentiality made to a foreign government, on which the provision of the information was expressly contingent';

[47] *Peltier v FBI*, 218 F App 30, 31 (2d Cir 2007) (where it was held that disclosure of foreign government information 'would breach express promises of confidentiality made to a foreign government, on which the provision of the information was expressly contingent';*Miller v Dept of Justice*, 562 F Supp. 2d 82, 102 (DDC 2008) (where it was held that disclosure of foreign government information would show that government's cooperation, capabilities and vulnerabilities, and would lead to negative diplomatic consequences and diminished intelligence capabilities); *Army v Dept of Defense*, 562 F Supp 2d 590, 600 (SDNY 2008) (where it was held that disclosure could be expected to 'impair the Department's ability to obtain information from foreign governments in the future, who will be less likely to cooperate with the United States if they cannot be confident that the information they provide will remain confidential').

relating to national security;[48] and

(c)   intelligence activities, sources or materials.

This exemption can be used to give a response that neither confirms nor denies the holding of records answering the terms of the request.[49]

(2)   Records that are 'related solely to the internal personnel rules and practices of an agency'.[50] This covers: (a) internal matters of a relatively trivial nature;[51] and (b) more substantial internal matters, the disclosure of which would risk circumvention of a statute or regulation.[52]

(3)   Information prohibited from disclosure by another statute, provided that that statute either requires that the information be withheld from the public in such a manner as to leave no discretion on the issue or that that statute establishes particular criteria for withholding or refers to particular types of information to be

---

[48]   The courts have consistently declined to reject agency assessments of a threat to national security on the basis that they are not equipped to second-guess such assessments: *Ray v Turner*, 587 F 2d 1187 (DC Cir 1978); *Halperin v CIA*, 629 F 2d 144 (DC Cir 1980); *Goldberg v Department of State*, 818 F 2d 71 (DC Cir 1987); *Bowers v Department of Justice*, 930 F 2d 350 (4th Cir 1991); *Young v CIA*, 972 F 2d 536 (4th Cir 1992); *Students Against Genocide v Department of State*, 257 F 3d 828 (DC Cir 2001); *American Civil Liberties Union v Department of Justice*, 265 F Supp 2d 20 (DDC 2003); *National Security Archive Fund, Inc v CIA*, 402 F Supp 2d 211 (DDC 2005); *Edmonds v US Department of Justice*, 405 F Supp 2d 23 (DDC 2005); *American Civil Liberties Union v FBI*, 429 F Supp 2d 179 (DDC 2006). Agencies, it is thought, have unique insights into such matters: *Miller v Department of State*, 779 F 2d 1378 (8th Cir 1985); *Cozen O'Connor v US Dept of Treasury*, 570 F Supp 2d 749, 773 (ED Pa 2008); *Makky v Chertoff*, 489 F Supp 2d 421, 441 (DNJ 2007); *Army v Dept of Defense*, 562 F Supp 2d 590, 597 (SDNY 2008). Judicial deference to agencies' say-so on matters of national security has increased: *Morley v CIA*, 508 F3d 1108, 1124 (DC Cir 2007); *Larson v Department of State*, 565 F3d857, 862 (DC Cir 2009) (noting that court need only examine whether agency's classification decision 'appears "logical" or "plausible"'; *Wolf v CIA*, 473 F3d 370, 374-75 (DC Cir 2007); *James Madison Project v CIA*, 605 F Supp 2d 99, 109 (DDC 2009); *Schoenman v FBI*, 575 F Supp 2d 136, 153 (DDC 2008). The Executive Order expressly acknowledges the 'mosaic' basis for refusal to disclose a record: Executive Order No 12,958 (as amended), para 1.7(e). This has also been recognised in the Courts: *Halperin v CIA*, 629 F 2d 144 (DC Cir 1980); *Edmonds v US Department of Justice*, 405 F Supp 2d 23 (DDC 2005); *American Civil Liberties Union v FBI*, 429 F Supp 2d 179 (DDC 2006) and authorities cited at §17– 029(1).

[49]   Executive Order No 12,958 (as amended), para 3.6(a). This, in the United States, is called a 'Glomar response', based on the judgment in *Phillippi v CIA*, 546 F 2d 1009 (DC Cir 1976). It is frequently used in conjunction with exemption (1).

[50]   5 USC 552(b)(2). As interpreted by the courts, there are two separate classes of documents that are generally held to fall within the second exemption. First, information relating to personnel rules or internal agency practices is exempt if it is a trivial administrative matter of no genuine public interest. Secondly, an internal administrative manual can be exempt if disclosure would risk circumvention of law or agency regulations. In order to fall into this category, the material will normally have to regulate internal agency conduct rather than public behaviour.

[51]   Often referred to as 'low 2' information. This covers routine internal personnel matters, such as performance standards and leave practices. The rationale for this part of the exemption is that the very task of processing and releasing these sorts of record would place an administrative burden on the agency that would not be justified by any genuine public benefit. The exemption does not apply where there is a genuine and significant public interest in disclosure of the records requested. In relation to the application of this provision: *Department of the Air Force v Rose*, 425 US 352 (1976); *Crooker v Bureau of Alcohol, Tobacco, Firearms and Explosives*, 670 F 2d 1051 (DC Cir 1981); *Dirksen v Department of Health and Human Services*, 803 F 2d 1456 (9th Cir 1986); *Maricopa Audubon Society v United States Forest Service*, 108 F 3d 1082 (9th Cir 1997).

[52]   Often referred to as 'high 2' information. This will extend to guidelines for conducting investigations, information that would reveal the identities of informants or undercover agents, information referring to the security techniques used in prisons, agency testing material, and so forth.

withheld.[53]

(4) Trade secrets[54] and commercial or financial information[55] obtained from a person that is privileged or confidential.[56] Information may also be withheld if disclosure would be likely to impair the Government's ability to obtain similar information in the future.[57] Only information obtained from a person other than a government agency qualifies under this exemption: information that an agency created on its own cannot normally be withheld under this exemption.[58] The provision protects the interests of both the Government and those who submit information to it.[59]

(5) Inter-agency or intra-agency[60] memoranda or letters 'which would not be available by law to a party other than an agency in litigation with the agency'.[61] This has been interpreted to mean records that would normally be privileged in civil proceedings.[62] These privileges are broader than those that are enjoyed by a public authority in the United Kingdom, and include: (a) deliberative process privilege,

---

[53] 5 USC 552(b)(3). In relation to this provision, see: *American Jewish Congress v Kreps*, 574 F 2d 624 (DC Cir 1978); *Hayden v National Security Agency*, 608 F 2d 1381 (DC Cir 1979); *Foundling Church of Scientology of Washington v National Security Agency*, 610 F 2d 824 (DC Cir 1979); *Halperin v CIA*, 629 F 2d 144 (DC Cir 1980); *Gardels v CIA*, 689 F 2d 1100 (DC Cir 1982); *CIA v Sims*, 471 US 159 (1985).

[54] 'Trade secrets' has been given a narrower definition than given to it in tort law, so as to be confined to 'a secret, commercially valuable plan, formula, process, or device that is used for the making, preparing, compounding, or processing of trade commodities and that can be said to be the end product of either innovation or substantial effort.' *Public Citizen Health Research Group v Food and Drugs Administration* 704 F 2d 1280 (DC Cir 1983). It requires that there be a direct relationship between the trade secret and the production process.

[55] Provided that the information relates to business or trade, the courts have generally accepted that it is commercial or financial information: *Public Citizen Health Research Group v Food and Drugs Administration*, 704 F 2d 1280 (DC Cir 1983); *Merit Energy Co v Department of the Interior*, 180 F Supp 2d 1184 (D Colo 2001). Detailed information on a company's marketing plans, profits, or costs can qualify as confidential business information.

[56] 5 USC 552(b)(4). In relation to confidentiality, a distinction is made between information submitted pursuant to obligation and information voluntarily submitted. In the former case, information is confidential for purposes of the exemption if disclosure of the information is likely to have either of the following effects: (1) to impair the Government's ability to obtain necessary information in the future; or (2) to cause substantial harm to the competitive position of the person from whom the information was obtained: *National Parks & Conservation Association v Morton*, 498 F 2d 765 (DC Cir 1974). In the case of voluntarily submitted information, it is protected from disclosure provided it is not customarily disclosed to the public by the third party: *Critical Mass Energy Project v Nuclear Regulatory Commission*, 975 F 2d 871 (DC Cir 1992).

[57] The Courts have drawn a sharp distinction between instances where a person has submitted information to an agency under compulsion and those cases where it has been volunteered to the agency: *Critical Mass Energy Project v Nuclear Regulatory Commission*, 975 F 2d 871 (DC Cir 1992); *Center for Auto Safety v National Highway Traffic Safety Administration*, 244 F 3d 144 (DC Cir 2001). The impairment must be significant: *Washington Post v Department of Health and Human Services*, 690 F 2d 252 (DC Cir 1982).

[58] *Grumman Aircraft Engineering Corp v Renegotiation Board*, 425 F 2d 578 (DC Cir, 1970).

[59] Although there is no formal requirement under the Act to do so, agencies will generally notify the person who submitted the business information that disclosure of the information is being considered.

[60] These terms are not rigidly exclusive and can include some records generated outside an agency: *Department of the Interior v Klamath Water Users Protective Association*, 532 US 1 (2001); *Center for International Environmental Law v Office of US Trade Representative*, 237 F Supp 2d 17 (DDC 2002).

[61] 5 USC 552(b)(5).

[62] *National Labor Relations Board v Sears, Roebuck & Co*, 421 US 132 (1975); *Federal Trade Commission v Grolier Inc*, 462 US 19 (1983).

also known as 'executive privilege';[63] (b) attorney work-product privilege;[64] and (c) attorney-client privilege.[65] The exemption will be unavailable where the privilege has been waived by disclosure to third parties or non-federal agencies.[66]

(6) Information about individuals[67] in 'personnel and medical files and similar files',[68] provided that the disclosure of that information 'would constitute a clearly unwarranted invasion of personal privacy'.[69]

---

[63] The protection of records revealing the deliberative policymaking process of government is said to be founded upon three policy considerations: (1) the encouragement of open, frank discussions on matters of policy between subordinates and superiors; (2) the protection against premature disclosure of proposed policies before they are finally adopted; and (3) the protection against public confusion that might result from disclosure of reasons and rationales that were not in fact ultimately the grounds for an agency's action: *Jordan v Department of Justice*, 591 F 2d 753 (DC Cir 1978); *Coastal States Gas Corp v Department of Energy*, 617 F 2d 854 (DC Cir 1980); *Russell v Department of the Air Force*, 682 F 2d 1045 (DC Cir 1982); *Heggestad v Department of Justice*, 182 F Supp 2d 1 (DDC 2000); *Kidd v Dept of Justice*, 362 F Supp 2d 291, 296 (DDC 2005) (protecting documents on basis that disclosure would 'inhibit drafters from freely exchanging ideas, language choice, and comments in drafting documents'). In order to rely on the exemption, there are two requirements. First, the record must predate the decision to which it relates: *National Labor Relations Board v Sears, Roebuck & Co*, 421 US 132 (1975); *Access Reports v Department of Justice*, 926 F 2d 1192 (DC Cir 1991). Determining this is not always an easy task and there is much authority on the point. Secondly, the record must be a direct part of the deliberative process, in that it makes recommendations and expresses opinions on legal or policy matters: *Vaughn v Rosen*, 523 F 2d 1136 (DC Cir 1975). This second requirement excludes factual material: *Coastal States Gas Corp v Department of Energy*, 617 F 2d 854 (DC Cir 1980). The provision has been generously interpreted: *Coastal States Gas Corp v Department of the Environment*, 617 F 2d 854 (DC Cir 1980); *Skelton v United States Postal Service*, 678 F 2d 35 (5th Cir 1982); *Afshar v Department of State*, 702 F 2d 1125 (DC Cir 1983); *Formaldehyde Institute v Department of Health and Human Services*, 889 F 2d 1118 (DC Cir 1989); *Access Reports v Department of Justice*, 926 F 2d 1192 (DC Cir 1991); *Wolfe v Department of Health and Human Services*, 839 F 3d 768 (DC Cir 1998); *Mapother v Dept of Justice*, 3 F3d 1533 (DC Cir 1993). The courts have recognised that there is no straightforward dichotomy between deliberative material and factual material.

[64] In other words, material prepared by a lawyer in contemplation of litigation. The privilege arises if litigation is probable: *Schiller v National Labor Relations Board*, 964 F 2d 1205 (DC Cir 1992). Privilege attaches provided that litigation was the primary factor in the decision to create the document: *Maine v Department of the Interior*, 285 F 3d 126 (1st Cir 2002).

[65] In other words, confidential communications between a lawyer and his client relating to a legal matter for which the client has sought professional advice: *Mead Data Center Inc v Department of the Air Force*, 566 F 2d 242 (DC Cir 1977).

[66] *Chilivis v Security & Exchange Commission*, 673 F 2d 12045 (11th Cir 1982); *Rockwell International v Department of Justice*, 235 F 3d 598 (DC Cir 2001).

[67] The exemption requires that the record relate to an identifiable specific individual, and not merely a large class of unidentified individuals: *Arieff v Department of the Navy*, 712 F 2d 1462 (DC Cir 1983). Corporations cannot fall within this exemption unless they are so small that there is no practicable difference between the individual and the corporation run by the individual: *Providence Journal Co v FBI*, 460 F Supp 778, 785 (DRI 1978); *Sims v CIA*, 642 F 2d 562 (DC Cir 1980). It would seem that deceased individuals do not have privacy interests: *Hale v Department of Justice*, 973 F 2d 894, 902 (10th Cir 1992); *Na Iwi O Na Kupuna v Dalton*, 894 F Supp 1397 (D Haw 1995).

[68] The words 'similar files' have been construed to mean all information that 'applies to a particular individual': *Department of State v Washington Post Co*, 456 US 595 (1982); *Sherman v Department of the Army*, 244 F 3d 357 (5th Cir 2001).

[69] 5 USC 552(b)(6). The last words import into the exemption a requirement to balance the public's right to disclosure against the individual's right to privacy: *Department of the Air Force v Rose*, 425 US 352 (1976). The words 'clearly warranted' have been interpreted to mean that information falling within the opening words of the exemption will nevertheless not enjoy exemption under it except where there is a clearly demonstrable unwarranted invasion of privacy: *Getman v National Labor Relations Board*, 450 F 2d 670 (DC Cir 1971); *Avondale Industries Inc v National Labor Relations Board*, 90 F 3d 955 (5th Cir 1996). If it is shown that a protectable privacy interest would be threatened by disclosure of the record, the public interest in disclosure must be weighed against the privacy interest in non-disclosure. As to the manner in which this task is to be carried out, see: *Department of Justice v Reporters Committee for Freedom of the Press*, 489 US 749 (1989); *Department of State v Ray*, 502 US 164 (1991); *Department of Defense v FLRA*, 510 US 487 (1994). As to what are protectable privacy interests, see: *Core v United States Postal Service*, 730 F 3d 946 (4th Cir 1984); *Nation Magazine v United States Customs Service*, 71 F 3d 885 (DC Cir 1995). The right to privacy of a public

(7) Records or information compiled for law enforcement purposes.[70] In order to engage the exemption it must also be shown that one or more of six types of harm would flow from the disclosure of such records or information:

(A) The production of such records or information could reasonably be expected[71] to interfere with enforcement proceedings.[72]

(B) The production of such records or information would deprive a person of a right to a fair trial or an impartial adjudication.[73]

(C) The production of such records or information could reasonably be expected to constitute an unwarranted invasion of personal privacy.[74]

(D) The production of such records or information could reasonably be expected

---

figure is a diluted one: *Fund for Constitutional Government v National Archives & Records Service*, 656 F 2d 856 (DC Cir 1981). The privacy interests of a public official are not as strong as those of a private citizen: *Lissner v Customs Service*, 241 F 3d 1220 (9th Cir 2001). While personal privacy normally concluded upon the death of the person to whom the information relates, relatives of the deceased may continue to have a privacy interest in the non-disclosure of information relating to the deceased: *National Archives & Records Administration v Favish*, 541 US 157 (2004). The onus is on the applicant to show that disclosure would be in the public interest of shedding light on an agency's performance of its statutory duties.

[70] The exemption has, by amendments in 1974 and 1986, been broadened in its scope. The phrase 'law enforcement purposes' has been given a broad interpretation, to include the enforcement of state laws and of foreign laws: *Bevis v Department of State*, 801 F 2d 1386 (DC Cir 1986); *Hopkinson v Shillinger*, 866 F 2d 1185 (10th Cir 1989). Information not initially obtained or generated for law enforcement purposes may still qualify under this exemption if it is subsequently compiled for a valid law enforcement purpose at any time prior to invocation of the exemption: *John Doe Agency v John Doe Corp*, 493 US 146 (1989). A particularly generous application of the provision is allowed for criminal law enforcement agencies, although this tends to vary with circuit. The exemption does not apply to information compiled in an agency's general internal monitoring of its own employees to ensure compliance with its own procedures.

[71] The 1986 amendment changed the required likelihood of harm from 'would interfere with' to 'could reasonably be expected to interfere with', thereby widening the scope of the exemption.

[72] The courts have held that the agency must be able to show some distinct harm could reasonably be expected to result if there were disclosure: *City of Chicago v Department of Treasury*, 287 F 3d 628 (7th Cir 2002) (holding that hypothetical scenarios are not enough). The protection afforded by the exemption only endures for so long as proceedings are pending or prospective: *National Labor Relations Board v Robbins Tire & Rubber Co*, 437 US 214 (1978). The types of harm which the courts have found might result from disclosure sufficient to engage the exemption include witness intimidation, fabrication of evidence, evasion of detection, premature revelation of evidence and revelation of strategies. A 'chilling' of witnesses will suffice: *Solar Inc v United States*, 142 F 3d 1033 (7th Cir 1998). Recently the Courts have carried over into exemption (7)(A) the notions of deference conventionally reserved for assessments of national security: 'just as we have deferred to the executive when it invokes Exemption 1 and 3, we owe the same deference under Exemption 7(A) in appropriate cases, such as this one' *Center for National Security Studies v Department of Justice*, 331 F 3d 918 (DC Cir 2003).

[73] This exemption is rarely used, with agencies generally relying on (7)(A) instead. The only authority on it is *Washington Post v Department of Justice*, 863 F 2d 96 (DC Cir 1988).

[74] Although there is an overlap between this exemption and exemption (6), the standard for engagement is different. Exemption (7)(C) protects against an unwarranted invasion of personal privacy, whereas exemption (6) protects against a clearly unwarranted invasion; exemption 7(C) allows the withholding of information that 'could reasonably be expected to' invade someone's privacy, whereas under exemption 6 information can be withheld only if disclosure 'would' invade someone's privacy. The exemption is given a generous interpretation: *Department of Justice v Reporters Committee for Freedom of the Press*, 489 US 749 (1989); *SafeCard Services v US Securities and Exchange Commission*, 926 F 2d 1197 (DC Cir 1991). It can also be relied upon to protect relatives of the person to whom the information relates: *National Archives & Records Administration v Favish*, 541 US 15 (2004).

to reveal the identity of a confidential source.[75]

(E) The production of such records or information would reveal techniques and procedures for law enforcement investigations or prosecutions, or would disclose guidelines for law enforcement investigations or prosecutions, provided that disclosure of the information could reasonably be expected to risk circumvention of the law.[76]

(F) The production of such records or information could reasonably be expected to endanger the life or physical safety of any individual.[77]

(8) Matters that are contained in or related to examination, operating, or condition reports prepared by, on behalf of, or for the use of an agency responsible for the regulation or supervision of financial institutions.[78]

(9) Geological and geophysical information and data, including maps, concerning wells.[79]

2– 009 Appeals and enforcement

An applicant has the right to an internal appeal on a merit basis against any adverse determination made by an agency.[80] If the agency upholds the decision, it must inform the applicant of its reasons and of the applicant's right of review in the federal courts.[81] Exclusive jurisdiction in relation to decisions under the Freedom of Information Act is vested in the United States district courts.[82] Before a district court will interfere with an agency's decision,

---

[75] A confidential source can include a state, local, or foreign agency or authority, or a private institution that furnished information on a confidential basis. In addition, the exemption protects information furnished by a confidential source if the data was compiled by a criminal law enforcement authority during a criminal investigation or by an agency conducting a lawful national security intelligence investigation. The courts have stated that the exemption must be given a 'robust' application in order to protect such sources of information: *Brant Construction Co v Environmental Protection Agency*, 778 F 2d 1258 (7th Cir 1985). The passage of time has no bearing on whether information should remain confidential: *Schmerler v FBI*, 900 F 2d 333 (DC Cir 1990). Thus, what matters is not the nature of the information itself but the source of that information: *Department of Justice v Landano*, 508 US 165 (1993).

[76] This only applies to techniques generally unknown to the public, and will not cover matters such as wire-tapping, eavesdropping, covert photography and so forth: *Albuquerque Publishing Co v Department of Justice*, 726 F Supp 851 (DDC 1989); *Jaffe v CIA*, 573 F Supp 377 (DDC 1983).

[77] This has been interpreted as giving a very wide protection from disclosure of those involved in law enforcement: *Spirko v United States Postal Service*, 147 F 3d 992 (DC Cir 1998); *Rugiero v Department of Justice*, 257 F 3d 534 (6th Cir 2001).

[78] 5 USC 552(b)(8). This has been given a generous interpretation: *Gregory v Federal Deposit Insurance Commission*, 631 F 2d 986 (DC Cir 1980); *Public Citizen v Farm Credit Administration*, 938 F 2d 290 (DC Cir 1991). The provision has been said to have two purposes underlying it: (1) to protect the security of financial institutions by withholding from the public reports that contain frank evaluations of a bank's stability; and (2) to promote co-operation and communication between employees and examiners: *Berliner, Zisser, Walter & Gallegos v US Securities and Exchange Commission*, 962 F Supp 1348 (D Colo 1997).

[79] 5 USC 552(b)(9). This exemption is rarely used.

[80] 5 USC 552(a)(6)(A). The request must be answered within 20 working days: 5 USC 552(a)(6)(A)(i).

[81] 5 USC 552(a)(6)(A). Unless there has been no response within the 20 working day limit to a properly made request, the internal review (known as the 'administrative remedy') must be exhausted before applying to the Court: *Taylor v Appleton*, 30 F 3d 1365 at 1367 (11th Cir 1994); *Pollack v Department of Justice*, 49 F 3d 115 at 118 (4th Cir 1995). If, after the 20 working days but before a District Court suit is filed, the agency responds to the request, then the administrative remedy must be exhausted before applying to the court: *Oglesby v Department of the Army*, 920 F 2d 57 at 61 (DC Cir 1990).

[82] 5 USC 552(a)(4)(B).

the applicant must show that the agency has improperly withheld agency records.[83] In effect this means judges determine the propriety of agency withholdings *de novo*, with agencies bearing the burden of proof in defending the non-disclosure of records.[84] Agencies are required to prepare an index supported by an affidavit that itemises each withheld document (whether in whole or in part), identifying on a document-by-document basis the specific exemption relied upon and the facts and matters relied upon by the agency to justify non-disclosure.[85] Although the index will often comprise the only evidence produced by the agency, it may be supplemented or displaced by the court's *in camera* inspection of the requested documents.[86] If the court finds that an exemption does apply, it has no inherent or equitable power to order disclosure.[87] The court is empowered to consider the adequacy of the search made by an agency.[88] Appeals from the district courts are heard in the Court of Appeals. Third parties may bring proceedings to prevent an agency from disclosing records under the Act.[89]

---

[83] *Kissinger v Reporters Committee for Freedom of the Press*, 445 US 136 at 150 (1980).

[84] 5 USC 552(a)(4)(B); *Natural Resources Defense Council v Nuclear Regulatory Commission*, 216 F 3d 1180 (DC Cir 2000). Although normally appeals are determined on a document-by-document basis, under certain circumstances courts have approved withholdings of entire, but discrete, categories of records which encompass all documents having similar contents: *National Labor Relations Board v Robbins Tire & Rubber Co*, 437 US 214 (1978). Before the court, the agency is not precluded from seeking to rely on an exemption that it did not rely upon at the administrative stage: *Young v CIA*, 972 F 2d 536 (4th Cir 1992). As to waiver of exemptions, see: *North Dakota ex rel Olson v Department of the Interior*, 581 F 2d 177 (8th Cir 1978); *Ryan v Department of Justice*, 617 F 2d 781 (DC Cir 1980); *Mobil Oil Corp v Environmental Protection Agency*, 879 F 2d 698 (9th Cir 1989); *Public Citizen v Department of State*, 11 F 3d 198 (DC Cir 1993); *Maydak v Department of Justice*, 218 F 3d 760 (DC Cir 2000).

[85] This document is generally called the 'Vaughn Index' after the judgment of the Court of Appeals for the District of Columbia Circuit in *Vaughn v Rosen* 484 F 2d 820 (1973). The index is required to be sufficiently detailed to enable the court to make a reasoned independent assessment of the claim of exemption. It must also be sufficiently specific to justify non-disclosure of the whole document, as opposed to just part of it: *Judicial Watch v Department of Health and Human Services*, 27 F Supp 2d 240 (DDC 1998); *Animal Legal Defense Fund Inc v Department of the Air Force*, 44 F Supp 2d 295 (DDC 1999). Where the documents are voluminous, a Vaughn Index may be prepared on the basis of representative samples: *Fensterwald v CIA*, 443 F Supp 667 (DDC 1977); *Weisberg v Department of Justice*, 745 F 2d 1476 (DC Cir 1984); *Bonner v Department of State*, 928 F 2d 1148 at 1151 (DC Cir 1991); *Campaign for Responsible Transplantation v FDA*, 180 F Supp 2d 29, 34 (DDC 2001).

[86] Sometimes the Vaughn Index (because it is available to the applicant) will include less detail than is necessary to make good the claim for exemption, with the agency relying instead on an *in camera* inspection of the records sought: *Ingle v Department of Justice*, 698 F 2d 259 (6th Cir 1983); *Simon v Department of Justice*, 980 F 2d 782 (DC Cir 1992); *Department of Justice v Landano*, 508 US 165 (1993); *Maynard v CIA*, 986 F 2d 547 (1st Cir 1993); *Quiñon v FBI*, 86 F 3d 198 (DC Cir 1993); *Fiduccia v Department of Justice*, 185 F 3d 1035 (9th Cir 1999).

[87] *Spurlock v FBI*, 69 F 3d 1010, 1016–1018 (9th Cir 1995).

[88] The agency must show that it made 'a good-faith effort to conduct a search for the requested records, using methods which can be reasonably expected to produce the information requested': *Weisberg v Department of Justice*, 745 F 2d 1476 at 1485 (DC Cir 1984); *Truitt v Department of State*, 897 F 2d 540 at 542 (DC Cir 1990); *Oglesby v Department of the Army*, 920 F 2d 57 at 61 (DC Cir 1990); *Campbell v Department of Justice*, 164 F 3d 20 at 28 (DC Cir 1998); *Rugiero v Department of Justice*, 257 F 3d 534 at 547 (6th Cir 2001). The court may use its powers to order discovery as part of the process: *Weisberg v Department of Justice*, 627 F 2d 365 (DC Cir 1980).

[89] These proceedings themselves are not based upon The Freedom of Information Act but upon the *Administrative Procedures Act* (5 USC 701–706): *Chrysler Corp v Brown* 441 US 281 (1979). As to reverse FOI generally, see: *CNA Finance Corp v Donovan*, 830 F 2d 1132 (DC Cir 1987); *McDonnell Douglas Corp v NASA*, 180 F 3d 303 (DC Cir 1999); *Campaign for Family Farms v Glickman*, 200 F 3d 1180 (8th Cir 2000); *McDonnell Douglas Corp v Department of the Air Force*, 375 F 3d 1182 (DC Cir 2004).

3.   COMMONWEALTH OF AUSTRALIA

2– 010   Introduction

In 1982 the Federal Parliament of Australia passed the Freedom of Information Act 1982.[90] It was the first such piece of legislation in a Westminster system of government. The origin of the Act lay in a report of an inter-departmental committee tabled in the Federal Parliament in November 1976. The first Bill was introduced into the Senate by the Attorney-General in June 1978. That was referred to various committees and inquiries before taking its final form. Since its enactment, the Act has been significantly amended on five occasions,[91] most substantially in 2010, with numerous smaller amendments.

2– 011   Scope of the right

Section 11 of the Freedom of Information Act 1982 gives every person[92] a legally enforceable[93] right to obtain access in accordance with the Act to a 'document'[94] of an 'agency'[95] and to an

---

[90] Since then each of the six states and one of the two internal territories has passed similar legislation: Freedom of Information Act 1982 (Vic); Freedom of Information Act 1989 (ACT); Freedom of Information Act 1989 (NSW); Freedom of Information Act 1991 (SA); Freedom of Information Act 1991 (Tas); Freedom of Information Act 1992 (Qld); Freedom of Information Act 1992 (WA).

[91] By the Freedom of Information Amendment Act 1983, the Freedom of Information Laws Amendment Act 1986, the Freedom of Information Amendment Act 1991, the Freedom of Information (Removal of Conclusive Certificates and Other Measures) Act 2009, and the Freedom of Information Amendment (Reform) Act 2010. The last is complemented by the Australian Information Commissioner Act 2010.

[92] This has been held to extend to a foreign corporation: *Re Lordsvale Finance Ltd and Department of the Treasury* (1985) 3 AAR 301, AAT. And to convicted felons: *Re Ward and Secretary, Department of Industry and Commerce* (1983) 8 ALD 324. But in Victoria, not to a severely mentally retarded person: *Wallace v Health Commission of Victoria* [1985] VR 403.

[93] Freedom of Information Act 1982 s 18. It has been suggested that this does not enable an 'unconscientious' use of the statute, eg to ask an agency for documents that would help the applicant in proceedings in an action against the agency: *Johnson Tiles Pty Ltd v Esso Australia Ltd* [2000] FCA 495.

[94] Document is defined broadly to include not only paper records but any other information which is capable of being reduced to written or visual form and which is capable of reproduction in that form: Freedom of Information Act 1982 s 4(1). There is a specific provision in relation to computer-based information: Freedom of Information Act 1982 s 17. Apart from this, however, the Act does not require the generation of documents in order to answer a request: *Re Redfern and the University of Canberra* (1995) 38 ALD 457. Documents created more than five years before the commencement of the Act are excluded from its operation: Freedom of Information Act 1982 s 12(2). It has been held that the Act does not extend to permit requests for documents that are received or created by the agency after the date of the request: *Re Edelsten and Australian Federal Police* (1985) 4 AAR 220 at 225, 9 ALN N65. But the reviewing Tribunal can make a decision with respect to documents that have come into existence after the date of the request for access in certain circumstances: *Murtagh v Federal Commissioner of Taxation* (1984) 54 ALR 313.

[95] 'Agency' is defined to mean principally a Department of State of the Commonwealth and a prescribed authority (itself defined to mean a body corporate or unincorporated established by statute for a public purpose, a statutory office-holder and other bodies declared to be agencies): Freedom of Information Act 1982 s 4(1). A court is not an agency, except for documents that relate to matters of an administrative nature: *Bienstein v Family Court of Australia* [2008] FCA 1138. 'Document of an agency' is itself defined to mean a document in the possession of the agency, whether created in the agency or received in the agency: Freedom of Information Act 1982 s 4(1) and see: *Loughnan (Principal Registrar, Family Court of Australia) v Altman* (1992) 111 ALR 445; *Re Sullivan and Department of Industry, Science and Technology* (1996) 23 AAR 59 (in relation to custody of a document); *Beesley v Australian Federal Police* [2001] FCA 836 (importing notions of constructive possession). Personal documents can become documents of an agency: *Re Barkhordar and Australian Capital Territory Schools Authority* (1987) 12 ALD 332.

'official document'[96] of a Minister, other than an 'exempt document'. The phrase 'exempt document' is defined[97] to mean:

(1)   A document that falls within one of the specific exemptions in Part IV of the Act;[98]

(2)   A document that is held by or received from one of the bodies that is exempted from the operation of the Act;[99] and

(3)   An official document of a Minister that contains some matter that does not relate to the affairs of an agency.

The right of access does not extend to documents that are publicly available independently of the Act[100] or to certain library, archive or museum collections.[101] An applicant is not required to demonstrate a need to know in order to exercise the general right of access.[102] The Act provides for publication schemes[103] and requires agencies to advise and assist those seeking to use its provisions.[104]

2   The request

A request must be in writing and must be sufficiently specific that the agency can identify the documents answering its terms.[105] If the request is made to the wrong agency, the recipient agency must direct the applicant to the correct agency.[106] Where an agency receives a request but does not hold the documents sought but either knows that another agency does or that the subject matter of the request is more closely connected with another agency, then the former

---

[96] Defined to mean a document that is in the possession of a Minister in his capacity as a Minister, being a document that relates to the affairs of an agency or of a Department of State: Freedom of Information Act 1982 s 4(1). The effect of the definition is to exclude from the Act those documents which the Minister holds in a political, party or personal capacity. A document held by a Member of Parliament in his representative capacity does not become an official document of a Minister because the Member is, incidentally, a Minister. In relation to the Victorian equivalent, see *Birrell v Department of Premier and Cabinet* [1988] VR 73. The definition expressly excludes library material maintained for reference purposes and Cabinet notebooks.

[97] Freedom of Information Act 1982 s 4(1).

[98] As to which, see §2–015.

[99] Freedom of Information Act 1982 s 7. The bodies listed in Sch 2 to the Act are exempted from the operation of the Act. Documents emanating from security bodies, being the bodies listed in s 7(2A), render the agency holding the documents exempt from the Act so far as those documents are concerned: Freedom of Information Act 1982 s 7(2A). A minister is similarly exempt from the operation of the Act in relation to a document that has originated with or has been received from any of the security bodies: s 7(2B).

[100] Freedom of Information Act 1982 s 12(1), but the Act expressly encourages alternative access: s 3A.

[101] Freedom of Information Act 1982 s 13. The right of access to information officially held in the archives collection is dealt with under the Archives Act 1983.

[102] Freedom of Information Act 1982 s 11(2). The Act can thus be used to achieve the same results as a *subpoena duces tecum* or discovery: *Johnson Tiles Pty Ltd v Esso Australia Ltd* (2000) 98 FCR 311.

[103] Freedom of Information Act 1982 ss 8 to 9. These were significantly enhanced by the FOI Am (Reform) Act 2010.

[104] Freedom of Information Act 1982 s 15(3)–(4).

[105] Freedom of Information Act 1982 s 15(2). The Tribunal has been reluctant to find that anything purporting to be a request is not a request: *Re Russell Island Development Association Inc and Department of Primary Industries and Energy* (1994) 33 ALD 683 at 692; *Re Redfern and University of Canberra* (1995) 38 ALD 457; *Re Collie and Deputy Commissioner of Taxation* (1997) 45 ALD 556 at 561.

[106] Freedom of Information Act 1982 s 15(4).

agency may transfer the request to the latter agency.[107]

2–013 The response

The agency can refuse a request if there is a 'practical refusal reason', such as that dealing with it would involve an unreasonable diversion of the agency's resources.[108] The request must be answered within 30 days, but there is power to extend that by a further 30 days.[109] Provided that it is reasonably practicable, access must be given in the form sought by the applicant.[110] The agency may charge fees for dealing with the request, which must be paid in order to give rise to the obligation to disclose.[111] In the event of the agency refusing to disclose, whether in whole or in part, it must give reasons for the refusal.[112] In certain cases, the Act permits an agency neither to confirm nor deny the existence of a document.[113] The Act specifically provides for discretionary disclosure[114] and, in relation to certain exemptions, for third parties to be invited to make representations before a decision is made to release documents.[115]

2–014 Exemptions generally

Once a valid request has been made and appropriate charges are paid, a document that is subject to the Act must be disclosed: the only legal reason for not complying with this obligation

---

[107] Freedom of Information Act 1982 s 16(1). The Administrative Appeals Tribunal does not have a general power to look behind a decision to transfer a request: *Re Reith and Minister of State for Aboriginal Affairs* (1988) 14 ALD 430.

[108] Freedom of Information Act 1982 ss 24, 24AA, 24AB. In relation to the use of multiple requests to evade the Victorian version of this provision, see: *Secretary, Department of Treasury and Finance v Kelly* [2001] VSCA 246.

[109] Freedom of Information Act 1982 s 15(5)–(6). If not made within this time, it is deemed to constitute a refusal: *Bienstein v Attorney General* [2009] FCA 1501 and now s 15AC. Extra time is allowed for voluminous requests: s 15AB.

[110] Freedom of Information Act 1982 s 20.

[111] Freedom of Information Act 1982 ss 18(1)(b) and 29. The charges regime is set out in the Freedom of Information (Fees and Charges) Regulations 1982. Charges may be remitted, but there is no right of review of a decision not to remit charges: *Re Waterford and Attorney-General's Department* (1985) 4 AAR 159.

[112] Freedom of Information Act 1982 s 26. Global responses can be given: *Day v Collector of Customs* (1995) 130 ALR 106.

[113] Freedom of Information Act 1982 s 25. The Act uses the device of a notional document containing information as to the existence of documents answering the terms of the request. If that notional document would itself be an exempt document under s 33 (national security, defence and international relations), s 33A (Commonwealth/State relations) or s 37 (law enforcement), then the agency is not required to confirm or deny the existence of the actual documents. The Tribunal and Courts have not readily accepted agency claims based on this section: *Department of Community Services v Jephcott* (1987) 15 FCR 122.

[114] Freedom of Information Act 1982 ss 14 and 18(2). This does not enable the Administrative Appeals Tribunal to grant discretionary disclosure: *Re Waterford and Department of Health* (1983) 5 ALN N139; *Re Waterford and Department of Treasury* (1983) 5 ALD 193. It has been held that a discretionary disclosure cannot give rise to an estoppel in relation to the subsequent invocation of an exemption in relation to like documents: *Re Lordsvale Finance Ltd and Department of Treasury* (1985) 3 AAR 301.

[115] Freedom of Information Act 1982 ss 26A (documents containing information that originated from a state), 27 (documents containing business information) and 27A (documents containing personal information). These provisions enable the third party to rely upon an exemption that is not sought to be engaged by the agency: *Re Parisi and Australian Federal Police* (1987) 14 ALD 11 at 15. However, the process need not be gone through if the agency is proposing to refuse access: *Motor Trades Association of Australia v Trade Practices Commission* (1993) ATPR 41–201 at 40–821. The pre-2010 amendment procedure was considered in *Mitsubishi Motors Australia Ltd v Department of Transport* (1986) 12 FCR 156, 68 ALR 626, where it was held that the reviewing Tribunal could, at the request of a third party, determine that a document treated by the agency as not exempt was exempt under s 43. A more detailed comparative treatment of third party rights of consultation and of 'reverse FOI' is given at §11–043.

is that the document is exempt.[116] The onus of proving that a document is exempt lies with the agency.[117] Resulting from its amendment in 2010, the Act divides exemptions into those that render a document unconditional exempt and those that render a document conditionally exempt. Access need not be given to a document that is unconditionally exempt. Access must be given to a conditionally exempt document unless that would be contrary to the public interest.[118] The Act spells out the public interest factors, including matters that are not relevant.[119] Although the Act always had a purpose clause, it was significantly strengthened by the Freedom of Information Amendment (Reform) Act 2010.[120] Exemptions in Part IV of the 1982 Act are either class-based or require that a particular harm would or would be likely to result from disclosure of the document. The measure of likelihood employed for the harm-based exemptions is that disclosure 'would, or could reasonably be expected', to cause the identified harm.[121] The level or type of harm required in order to engage the harm-based exemptions varies: 'caus[ing] damage'; having 'a substantial adverse effect'; 'caus[ing] prejudice'; being 'unreasonable.' Until removed in 2009, in relation to certain exemptions, a conclusive certificate could be issued where the relevant Minister had been satisfied that a document should not be disclosed.[122] The Act provides for severance of exempt material from a document that generally answers the terms of a request.[123] In certain circumstances, third parties are given rights to be informed that a request for access to documents has been made

---

[116] Freedom of Information Act 1982 s 18.

[117] Freedom of Information Act 1982 ss 55D and 61(1).

[118] Freedom of Information Act 1982 s 11A.

[119] Freedom of Information Act 1982 s 11B.

[120] Freedom of Information Act 1982 s 3. Under the earlier purpose clause, the courts had declined to interpret the exemptions by subject to any special restrictive presumptions: *News Corp Ltd v National Companies and Securities Commission* (1984) 1 FCR 64, 52 ALR 27; *Arnold v Queensland* (1987) 73 ALR 607; *Searle Australia Pty Ltd v Public Interest Advocacy Centre* (1992) 36 FCR 111, 108 ALR 163. In relation to the Victorian legislation, a contrary view had been taken by the High Court: *Public Service Board v Wright* (1986) 160 CLR 145 at 153–154.

[121] Employed in Freedom of Information Act 1982 ss 33(1), 33A(1), 37(1), 37(2), 40(1), 43(1) and 44(1). The Tribunal and Courts have interpreted this as being something more than fanciful but which need not be more likely than not: *News Corp Ltd v National Companies and Securities Commission* (1984) 57 ALR 550; *Attorney-General's Department v Cockroft* (1986) 10 FCR 180 at 190, 64 ALR 97; *Arnold (on behalf of Australians for Animals) v Australian National Parks and Wildlife Service* (1987) 73 ALR 607; *Re Environment Centre NT and Department of the Environment, Sport & Territories* (1994) 35 ALD 765 at 778. The Tribunal and Courts have generally been prepared to accept at face-value agency claims of likely harm: *Arnold (on behalf of Australians for Animals) v Australian National Parks and Wildlife Service* (1987) 73 ALR 607.

[122] Removed by the Freedom of Information (Removal of Conclusive Certificates and Other Measures) Act 2009. The provisions were: s 33 (national security, defence and international relations), s 33A (Commonwealth/State relations), s 34 (Cabinet documents), s 35 (Executive Council documents) and s 36 (deliberative process documents). The role of the Administrative Appeals Tribunal in reviewing such a certificate had been limited to asking whether or not reasonable grounds existed at the time of the hearing for the claims made in the certificate. This prevented the Tribunal from weighing public interest factors in favour of disclosure against public interest factors favouring non-disclosure: *McKinnon v Secretary, Department of Treasury* [2006] HCA 45, (2006) 229 ALR 187.

[123] Freedom of Information Act 1982 s 22(1). An agency is under a duty to consider whether some form of redacted document can be provided: *Day v Collector of Customs* (1995) 57 FCR 176 at 180, 130 ALR 106. The redacted document must not be misleading: *Re Carver and Department of the Prime Minister and Cabinet* (1987) 6 AAR 317 at 328, 12 ALD 447.

and to make submissions that access ought to be refused.[124] If, despite the representations of the third party, the agency decides that it will release the documents, the third party may apply to the Administrative Appeals Tribunal for a review of the agency's decision.[125]

2– 015   Specific exemptions

The exemptions may be grouped into 20 heads. The class-based exemptions are:

(1)   Cabinet documents and records.[126]

(2)   Executive Council documents.[127]

(3)   Documents and information the disclosure of which is proscribed by other statutes.[128]

(4)   Documents subject to legal professional privilege.[129]

(5)   Trade secrets.[130]

---

[124] Thus, where a request is received by an agency for documents that contain information concerning a person's or organisation's commercial affairs, and it appears that the person or organisation might wish to contest the disclosure of the documents, then that person or organisation must be given notice of the request: Freedom of Information Act 1982 s 27. Similar third party provision is made in relation to documents containing personal information relating to a third party (Freedom of Information Act 1982 s 27A) and in relation to documents containing information that originated from a State (Freedom of Information Act 1982 s 26A).

[125] Freedom of Information Act 1982 s 60AA. Section 53C defines who is 'an affected third party.' That person is given a right to apply for internal review of an access grant decision (s 54(2)), to be notified of a review application to the Information Commissioner (s 54P), to participate in that review (s 55A(1)(c)), to be given a copy of the Commissioner's decision (s 55K(6)), to appeal on a point of law to the Federal Court against the Commissioner's decision (s 56(1)), to apply to the Administrative Appeals Tribunal for merit review of the Commissioner's decision (s 57A) and to be notified of another person's appeal to the Tribunal (s 60AA(2)). A more detailed comparative treatment of third party rights of consultation and of 'reverse FOI' is given at §11– 043.

[126] Freedom of Information Act 1982 s 34, considered in *Re Telstra Corp Ltd and Department of Broadband, Communications and the Digital Economy* [2010] AATA 118. Purely factual material is generally exempted. The exemption applies to documents prepared for submission to Cabinet, even if not actually submitted to Cabinet: *Re Rae and Department of Prime Minister and Cabinet* (1986) 12 ALD 589; *Re Porter and Department of Community Services and Health* (1988) 14 ALD 403; *Re Reith and Minister for Aboriginal Affairs* (1988) 16 ALD 709. In relation to analogous legislation: *Department of Premier and Cabinet v Birrell (No 2)* [1990] VR 51.

[127] Freedom of Information Act 1982 s 35. Purely factual material is generally exempted.

[128] Freedom of Information Act 1982 s 38. This provision gave rise to considerable litigation prior to its amendment in 1991. The principles were summarised in *Harrigan v Department of Health* (1986) 72 ALR 293 at 294–295. See also: *Kavvadias v Commonwealth Ombudsman* (1984) 52 ALR 728; *News Corp Ltd v National Companies and Securities Commission* (1984) 57 ALR 550; *Federal Commissioner of Taxation v Swiss Aluminium Australia Ltd* (1986) 66 ALR 159. In relation to analogous legislation: *Secretary to the Department of Premier and Cabinet v Hulls* [1999] 3 VR 331.

[129] Freedom of Information Act 1982 s 42. It has been held that for the purposes of the Act, legal professional privilege attaches to confidential professional communications between a Government agency and its salaried legal officers provided that it is undertaken for the sole purpose of seeking or giving legal advice or in connection with anticipated or pending litigation: *Waterford v Commonwealth* (1987) 163 CLR 54; see also *Austin v Deputy Secretary, Attorney-General's Department* (1986) 67 ALR 585; *Secretary, Department of Health v Proudfoot* (1993) 114 FLR 384; *Commonwealth of Australia v Dutton* (2000) 102 FCR 168; *Comcare v Foster* [2006] FCA 6. In relation to analogous legislation: *Director of Public Prosecutions v Smith* [1991] VR 63 (documents relating to the sufficiency of evidence). The sole purpose test has since been reduced to a dominant purpose test: *Esso Australia Resources Ltd v Federal Commissioner of Taxation* (1999) 168 ALR 123. It has been held that, for the purposes of the Act, privilege can be waived: *Bennett v Chief Executive Officer of the Australian Customs Service* [2003] FCA 53.

[130] Freedom of Information Act 1982 s 43(1)(a). This whole section is designed to protect the interests of third parties: *Harris v Australian Broadcasting Corp* (1983) 78 FLR 236, 50 ALR 551. As to the meaning of this provision, see: *Searle Australia Pty Ltd v Public Interest Advocacy Centre* (1992) 108 ALR 163, 36 FCR 111; *Secretary, Department of Workplace Relations & Small Business v The Staff Development & Training Centre Pty Ltd* [2001] FCA 382, upheld at [2001] FCA 1375.

(6) Documents the disclosure of which would be a contempt of Court or of the Commonwealth or a State Parliament.[131]

(7) Certain documents arising out of companies and securities legislation.[132]

(8) Electoral rolls.[133]

The harm-based exemptions apply to a document whose disclosure would have one or more of the following effects:

(9) It would, or could be reasonably be expected to, cause damage to the national security, defence or international relations of Australia.[134]

(10) It would, or could be reasonably be expected to, cause damage to relations between the Commonwealth and a state.[135]

(11) It records the deliberative process of the federal Government[136] and its disclosure

---

[131] Freedom of Information Act 1982 s 46.

[132] Freedom of Information Act 1982 s 47.

[133] Freedom of Information Act 1982 s 47A.

[134] Freedom of Information Act 1982 s 33. This refers to Australia's ability to maintain good working relations with overseas governments and to protect the flow of confidential information between it and other governments: *Re Bui and Department of Foreign Affairs and Trade* (2005) 85 ALD 793. This head of exemption also exempts a document the disclosure of which would divulge any information communicated in confidence to the Australian Government by or on behalf of a foreign government, an authority of a foreign government or an international organisation. The information does not have to be confidential in nature: *Re Haneef and Australian Federal Police* [2009] AATA 51; *Gersten v Minister for Immigration and Multicultural Affairs* (2000) 61 ALD 445. Section 33 does not involve a consideration of whether disclosure would be contrary to the public interest: *Commonwealth of Australia v Hittich* (1994) 53 FCR 152 at 154. The section expresses an aspect of the public interest: *Re Mann and Australian Taxation Office* (1985) 3 AAR 261; *Re O'Donovan and Attorney-General's Department* (1985) 4 AAR 151, 8 ALD 528; *Re Edelsten and Australian Federal Police* (1985) 4 AAR 220. The Courts and Tribunal have been generally ready to accept agency assertions that this sort of harm would be caused: *Re Maher and Attorney-General's Department* (1985) 3 AAR 396; *Re Stolpe and Department of Foreign Affairs* (1985) 9 ALD 104; *Re Fewster and Department of Prime Minister and Cabinet (No 2)* (1987) 13 ALD 139; *Re Wang and Department of Employment, Education and Training* (1988) 15 ALD 497; *Re Bayliss and Department of Health and Family Services* (1997) 48 ALD 443; *Gersten v Minister for Immigration & Multicultural Affairs* [2000] FCA 1221, [2001] FCA 159. In this context, the Courts and Tribunal have been prepared to accept the 'mosaic theory' (see §§15– 024 to 15– 025): *Re McKnight and Australian Archives* (1992) 28 ALD 95. A document already in the public domain can still enjoy exemption under this section: *Commonwealth of Australia v Hittich* (1994) 53 FCR 152.

[135] Freedom of Information Act 1982 s 47B. The exemption is conditional. This head of exemption also exempts a document the disclosure of which would divulge information communicated in confidence by or on behalf of the Government of an Australian state to the federal Government. The earlier version of this exemption (s 33A) had been given a broad interpretation: *Re Mickelberg and Australian Federal Police* (1984) 6 ALN N176; *Re Anderson and Department of Special Minister of State* (1984) 7 ALN N155; *Re Angel and Department of Art, Heritage and Environment* (1985) 9 ALD 113; *Arnold (on behalf of Australians for Animals) v Australian National Parks and Wildlife Service* (1987) 73 ALR 607; *Re Guy and Department of Transport* (1987) 12 ALD 358; *Re Birch and Attorney-General's Department* (1994) 33 ALD 675; *Re Environment Centre NT Inc and Department of the Environment, Sport and Territories* (1994) 35 ALD 765.

[136] Freedom of Information Act 1982 s 47C. The exemption is conditional. The Courts and Tribunal had given the first paragraph of the earlier version of this exemption (s 36(1)) a broad interpretation, capable of encompassing most documents held by an agency recording any form of consideration of a decision: *Harris v Australian Broadcasting Corp* (1983) 78 FLR 236, 50 ALR 551 (interim reports should not be released because they could mislead); *Re James and Australian National University* (1984) 2 AAR 327; *Murtagh v Federal Commissioner of Taxation* (1984) 54 ALR 313 (documents showing process of making an assessment of taxation); *Re Waterford and Department of the Treasury (No 2)* (1984) 1 AAR 1, 5 ALD 588; *Re Toohey and Department of the Prime Minister and Cabinet* (1985) 9 ALN 94; *Re Howard and the Treasurer (Cth)* (1985) 3 AAR 169 at 172–175; *Re Chapman and Minister for Aboriginal and Torres Strait Islander Affairs* (1996) 23 AAR 142, 43 ALD 139; *Re Subramanian and Refugee Review Tribunal* (1997) 44 ALD 435; *Re The Staff Development and Training Centre and Secretary, Department of Employment, Workplace Relations and Small Business* (2000) 30 AAR 330 at 354. In relation to analogous legislation: *Director of Public Prosecutions v Smith* [1991] VR 63 (documents considering whether to prosecute). Operational information (defined in s 8A, and which must be published in any event (s 8)), purely factual material, reports, etc are excluded from the exemption. The meaning of the earlier

would be contrary to the public interest.[137]

(12) It would, or could be reasonably be expected to, cause damage to law enforcement, confidential sources of information relating to law enforcement, fair trials, or methods of criminal investigation.[138]

(13) It would have a substantial adverse effect on the financial or property interests of the Commonwealth of Australia or an agency.[139]

(14) It would, or could be reasonably be expected to, prejudice the effectiveness of audits or tests or to have a substantial adverse effect upon the running of an agency.[140]

(15) It would involve the unreasonable disclosure of personal information about any person (including a deceased person) other than the applicant.[141]

---

version (s 36) was considered in *Harris v Australian Broadcasting Corp (No 2)* (1984) 51 ALR 581.

[137] In order for the exemption to engage, the agency must demonstrate that disclosure would be contrary to the public interest. As to the matters which the Courts and Tribunal have taken into account under the rubric of the 'public interest', see: *Murtagh v Federal Commissioner of Taxation* (1984) 54 ALR 313; *Burns v Australian National University (No 1)* (1984) 1 AAR 456 at 458; *Re Howard and Treasurer, Commonwealth* (1985) 3 AAR 169; *Re Swiss Aluminium and Department of Trade* (1985) 9 ALD 243; *Ryder v Booth* [1985] VR 869 (inability to get further similar information); *Re Reith and the Attorney-General's Department* (1987) 11 ALD 345; *Re Fewster and Department of Prime Minister and Cabinet (No 2)* (1987) 13 ALD 139; *Re Reith and Minister of State for Aboriginal Affairs* (1988) 16 ALD 709; *Re Kamenka and Australian National University* (1992) 15 AAR 297; *Re Chapman and Minister for Aboriginal and Torres Strait Islander Affairs* (1996) 23 AAR 142 at 155–159; *Re Bartle and Secretary, Department of Employment, Education, Training and Youth Affairs* (1998) 28 AAR 140. If this exemption is relied upon, the ground of public interest must be specified.

[138] Freedom of Information Act 1982 s 37. This has been given a broad interpretation, covering: confidential sources of information (*McKenzie v Secretary to the Department of Social Security* (1986) 65 ALR 645); even if the information provided by the source is not in itself confidential (*Re Dale and Australian Federal Police* (1997) 47 ALD 417); policy documents setting out in what circumstances an agency would prosecute for a breach of statute (*Re Murphy and Australian Electoral Commission* (1994) 33 ALD 718); investigation manuals, even where large parts have been previously disclosed (*Re Arnold Bloch Leibler & Co and Australian Taxation Office (No 2)* (1985) 4 AAR 178, 9 ALD 7); any documents relating to public safety in a broad sense of the phrase (*Re Parisi and Australian Federal Police* (1987) 14 ALD 11); documents being used in an investigation (*News Corp Ltd v National Companies and Securities Commission* (1984) 57 ALR 550). But work accident investigation reports have been held not exempt under analogous Victorian legislation: *Accident Compensation Commission v Croom* [1991] 2 VR 322; nor is a police brief necessarily exempt: *Sobh v Police Force of Victoria* [1994] 1 VR 41.

[139] Freedom of Information Act 1982 s 47D. The exemption is conditional.

[140] Freedom of Information Act 1982 s 47E. The exemption is conditional. In relation to the earlier version of this exemption (s 40), the Courts and Tribunal had required a substantial degree of gravity before finding a 'substantial adverse effect': *Harris v Australian Broadcasting Corp* (1983) 78 FLR 236, 50 ALR 551; *Re Dyki and Commissioner of Taxation* (1990) 12 AAR 544, 22 ALD 124 (completed job applications not exempt); *Searle Australia Pty Ltd v Public Interest Advocacy Centre* (1992) 36 FCR 111, 108 ALR 163; *Re Kamenka and Australian National University* (1992) 15 AAR 297, 26 ALD 585; *Re Murphy and Australian Electoral Commission* (1994) 33 ALD 718.

[141] Freedom of Information Act 1982 s 47F. The exemption is conditional. Section 47F(2) prescribes matters that must be taken into account. Where the agency concludes that disclosure of the information would be detrimental to the health of the applicant, it may supply it instead to a medical practitioner, counsellor or social worker. It has been held that a company does not have 'personal affairs' within the meaning of the Act: *News Corp Ltd v National Companies and Securities Commission* (1984) 1 FCR 64, 52 ALR 277; *The University of Melbourne v Robinson* [1993] 2 VR 177. In New South Wales it has been held that the release of the name of a person is not necessarily information concerning the personal affairs of a person: *Commissioner of Police v District Court of NSW* (1993) 31 NSWLR 606. In Victoria, detailed references to the business affairs of victims of crime are not exempt where the victims had earlier disclosed them to the public: *Director of Public Prosecutions v Smith* [1991] VR 63. The words 'relating to' have been given a very wide interpretation: *Colakovski v Australian Telecommunications Corp* (1991) 29 FCR 429, 100 ALR 111; *Re Callejo and Department of Immigration and Citizenship* [2010] AATA 244. 'Personal affairs' itself has also been given a wide meaning: *Re Williams and Registrar, Federal Court of Australia* (1985) 8 ALD 219, 3 AAR 529; *Young v Wicks* (1986) 13 FCR 85; *Department of Social Security v Dyrenfurth* (1988) 80 ALR 533; *Bleicher v Australian Capital Territory Health Authority* (1990) 12 AAR 246; *Colakovski v Australian Telecommunications Corp* (1991) 29 FCR 429, 100 ALR 111.

(16) It could reasonably be expected to destroy or diminish the commercial value of any information.[142]

(17) It is information concerning the business, commercial or financial affairs of a person or organisation, the disclosure of which could reasonably be expected to have an unreasonably adverse effect upon that person or organisation or to prejudice the future supply of information to the Commonwealth of Australia.[143]

(18) It would be likely to result in an unreasonable exposure to disadvantage to specified agencies carrying out research that is incomplete.[144]

(19) It would, or could be reasonably be expected to, have a substantial adverse effect on the ability of the Commonwealth to manage the economy.[145]

(20) It would represent a breach of confidence other than that of the Commonwealth.[146]

6 Appeals and enforcement

Where an agency refuses access to documents, the first right of appeal is one of internal review by the principal officer of the agency.[147] Generally, the applicant is required to lodge a request for an internal review within 30 days of receiving notification of the original decision. The principal officer must review the decision within 30 days of receiving the request. If the applicant either does not receive a response within that time or receives an unfavourable decision, he is entitled to apply to the Information Commissioner for a further review of the decision. An application for review must generally be made within 60 days after the notice of the decision refusing access to a document was given to the applicant. The power given to the Information Commissioner is to review any decision that has been made by an agency or minister with respect to a request for access to a document and to decide the matter on the same basis as the agency or minister could have decided it. [148] A person may appeal against the Commissioner's decision, either to the Federal Court on a point of law or the Tribunal for merit review[149] The Tribunal may compel the production to it of the documents covered by the

---

[142] Freedom of Information Act 1982 s 43(1)(b). The section is designed to protect third party interests: *Harris v Australian Broadcasting Corp* (1983) 78 FLR 236, 50 ALR 551. As to the meaning of information having a commercial value, see: *Gill v Department of Industry Technology and Resources* [1987] VR 681; *Secretary, Dept of Workplace Relations & Small Business v The Staff Development & Training Centre Pty Ltd* [2001] FCA 382, upheld at [2001] FCA 1375.

[143] Freedom of Information Act 1982 s 47G. The exemption is conditional.

[144] Freedom of Information Act 1982 s 47H. The exemption is conditional.

[145] Freedom of Information Act 1982 s 47J. The exemption is conditional.

[146] Freedom of Information Act 1982 s 45. This had been interpreted to capture information for which a common law breach of confidence would not succeed: *Baueris v Commonwealth of Australia* (1987) 75 ALR 327; *Corrs Pavey Whiting & Byrne v Collector of Customs* (1987) 14 FCR 434. Section 45 was subsequently amended to remove this possibility.

[147] Freedom of Information Act 1982 ss 54 to 54D.

[148] Freedom of Information Act 1982 ss 54F to 54S. The Commissioner's power on review are set out in ss 54Z to 55Q.

[149] The Tribunal is not restricted to the grounds of exemption relied upon by the agency: *Searle Australia Pty Ltd v Public Interest Advocacy Centre* (1992) 108 ALR 163; *Victorian Casino and Gambling Authority v Hulls* [1998] 4 VR 718 (relating to the analogous Victorian scheme). The Appellant's representative may be given access to documents upon appropriate undertakings: *Day v Collector of Customs* (1995) 130 ALR 106; *cf News Corporation Ltd v National Companies and Securities Commission* (1984) 57 ALR 550; *Department of Industrial Relations v Forrest* (1990) 21 FCR 93, 91 ALR 417 (a certificate case).

request in order to make its decision.[150]   An appeal on a question of law lies from the Administrative Appeals Tribunal to the Federal Court.

4. NEW ZEALAND

2–017   **Introduction**

In New Zealand, the power to elicit official information originated in a 1962 statute establishing an ombudsman.[151]   In May 1978 a Committee on Official Information was established to consider the extent to which official information could be made more readily available to the public. Following the Committee's reports,[152] the Official Information Act 1982 came into force on 1 July 1983. The State-owned Enterprises Act 1986 brought state-owned enterprises within the Official Information Act 1982. In 1987, the Act was amended by replacing the original ministerial veto of the Ombudsman's recommendations with a collective veto by Order in Council; by expanding the protection for information about competitive commercial activities; by imposing time limits; and by extending coverage to additional organisations. In that same year, a separate Act was passed providing analogous rights of access to information held by local authorities.[153]   In 1993, the right of access to information where it related to a non-corporate applicant was transferred to the Privacy Act 1993. Thus, rights of access to official information are now split between three statutes:

(1)   In relation to information relating to the individual requesting it, under the Privacy Act 1993;[154]

(2)   In relation to other information held by local authorities, under the Local Government Official Information and Meetings Act 1987; and

(3)   In relation to all other information, under the Official Information Act 1982.[155]

2–018   **Scope of the right**

Section 12(1) of the Official Information Act 1982 enables citizens, residents and persons in New Zealand, as well as companies incorporated in New Zealand, to request a 'department or

---

[150] Freedom of Information Act 1982 s 58E.

[151] The Parliamentary Commissioner (Ombudsman) Act 1962. That statute empowered the Ombudsman to obtain information from governmental agencies and to disclose in any report such matters as in the Ombudsman's opinion needed to be disclosed in order to establish grounds for any conclusions and recommendations made in the report.

[152] Committee on Official Information, *Towards Open Government: General Report* (vol 1, 1980); *Towards Open Government: Supplementary Report* (vol 2, 1981). The Committee is commonly referred to as the Danks Committee and the reports as the Danks Report. The Supplementary Report contained a draft Bill that was to become the Official Information Act 1982.

[153] The Local Government Official Information and Meetings Act 1987.

[154] As to the division between the Official Information Act 1982 and the Privacy Act 1993, see *Director of Human Rights Proceedings v Commissioner of Police* [2008] NZHC 1286.

[155] There is a limited inter-relationship between the statutes, so that where the applicant seeks information under the Official Information Act 1982 or under the Local Government Official Information and Meetings Act 1987 for information relating to a third party, the provisions of the Privacy Act 1993 are relevant: Official Information Act 1982 s 9(2)(a); Local Government Official Information and Meetings Act 1987 s 7(2)(a). A more detailed comparative treatment of third party rights of consultation and of 'reverse FOI' is given at §11–043.

Minister of the Crown' to make available to the applicant any specified 'official information'.[156] The term 'official information' is defined to mean 'information'[157] that is 'held'[158] by a department,[159] Minister of the Crown or organisation.[160] The right of access to personal information[161] (whether of an individual or a company) is provided separately from the general right to information.[162] The access statutes require departments etc to give reasonable assistance to anyone using the Act.[163] The two main Acts also provide for publication schemes.[164]

19   The request

A request may be made orally or in writing, but it must have due particularity.[165]   The

---

[156] In relation to information held by a local authority, the provision is the Local Government Official Information and Meetings Act 1987 s 10(1).

[157] There is no definition of 'information'. As to the meaning given by the courts to 'information', see: *Commissioner of Police v Ombudsman* [1985] 1 NZLR 578 at 586, [1988] 1 NZLR 385 at 402 (CA) ('information' is 'that which informs, instructs, tells or makes aware'); *Ross v Tarnaki City Council* [1990] DCR 11 (information under the Local Government Official Information and Meetings Act 1987 must be tangible or retrievable); *Aldous v Auckland City Council* [1990] DCR 385; *R v Harvey* [1991] 1 NZLR 242 at 246; *Herewini v Ministry of Transport* [1992] 3 NZLR 482 at 498; *Leach v Ministry of Transport* [1993] 1 NZLR 106 at 108. Excluded from 'official information' is certain information held by universities and information contained in library or museum material made or acquired and preserved solely for reference or exhibition purposes and certain other information: see Official Information Act 1982 s 2(2).

[158] The Act does not define when information is 'held' by a department. See *R v Harvey* [1991] 1 NZLR 242 at 246.

[159] Departments are those listed in Pt I of the First Schedule to the Ombudsmen Act 1975.

[160] Official Information Act 1982 s 4; Local Government Official Information and Meetings Act 1987 s 2(1). 'Organisations' are those named in Part II of the First Schedule to the Ombudsmen Act 1975 and those named in the First Schedule to the Official Information Act 1982. Certain organisations are excluded: see Official Information Act 1982 s 2(6).

[161] That is, information that is about the person requesting the information. The distinction between 'personal' and 'non-personal' information has been described as 'both artificial and arbitrary': *Cornelius v Commissioner for Police* [1998] 3 NZLR 373 at 379; *cf Police v Keogh* [2000] 1 NZLR 736 at 742.

[162] Requests for personal information by individuals about themselves are governed by the Privacy Act 1993. That Act provides that where an agency holds personal information in such a way that it can be readily retrieved, the individual about whom the information relates has a legal right, enforceable in a Court of law, to obtain confirmation from the agency of whether or not it holds such information and to have access to that information: s 6, principle 6(1) and s 11(i). This right applies to any individual who is a New Zealand citizen, or a permanent resident of New Zealand, or a person in New Zealand: Privacy Act 1993 ss 33 and 34. Part IV of the Official Information Act 1982 (ss 24–27) is devoted to access to personal information by a body corporate. Section 24(1) bestows the right upon a body corporate to be given access to any personal information that is about that body corporate, subject to the exemptions in Pt I of the Act. In relation to local authorities, the right of access by a company to information relating to itself is bestowed by the Local Government and Official Information Act 1987 s 23.

[163] Official Information Act 1982 ss 13 and 24(3); Local Government Official Information and Meetings Act 1987 ss 11 and 23(2); Privacy Act 1993 s 38.

[164] Official Information Act 1982 s 20; Local Government Official Information and Meetings Act 1987 s 19. This requires the publication and updating of a document that describes the structure, functions, and responsibilities of all government departments and organisations subject to each of the Acts, as well as a description of the categories of documents held by each body and certain other details. Every person has a right of access to these last details: Official Information Act 1982 s 21; Local Government Official Information and Meetings Act 1987 s 20.

[165] Official Information Act 1982 s 12(2); Local Government Official Information and Meetings Act 1987 s 10(2). The request may be made by an agent: Official Information Act 1982 s 25(c); Local Government Official Information and Meetings Act 1987 s 24(c); Privacy Act 1993 s 45(c).

department may refuse to answer a request that is frivolous or vexatious;[166] where the information requested is trivial;[167] where making the information available would involve substantial collation or research;[168] or where the information is or will shortly be publicly available.[169] Where a department receives a request but either does not hold the information sought and believes that another department does, or if it considers that the information requested is more closely connected with another department, then the former department may transfer the request to the latter department.[170]

2– 020   The response

Within 20 working days of receiving a request, the department must inform the applicant whether access to the requested information is to be given and, if not, of the reasons for the decision.[171] The 20-working-day period may be extended for a reasonable period of time where the request is for a large quantity of information, requires searching through a large quantity of information, or requires consultations that cannot be completed within the original time limit.[172] If the requested information is not provided within the 20 working days or the extended period, the request is deemed to have been refused.[173] If the decision is to give access, that may take any of a number of forms: giving the applicant an opportunity to examine the document containing the information; providing a copy of it; providing information about a document's contents, etc.[174] If the decision is to refuse access, the department, etc must give reasons for the refusal and, if requested, the statutory grounds for that refusal.[175] A department, etc may only refuse to disclose information answering the terms of a proper request if it falls within one of the grounds of exemption.[176] In refusing a request, the department is not required to confirm or deny whether any information answering the terms of the request actually exists

---

[166] Official Information Act 1982 s 18(h); Local Government Official Information and Meetings Act 1987 s 17(h); Privacy Act 1993 s 29(1)(j).

[167] Official Information Act 1982 s 18(h); Local Government Official Information and Meetings Act 1987 s 17(h); Privacy Act 1993 s 29(1)(j).

[168] Official Information Act 1982 s 18(f); Local Government Official Information and Meetings Act 1987 s 17(f); Privacy Act 1993 s 29(2)(a).

[169] Official Information Act 1982 s 18(d); Local Government Official Information and Meetings Act 1987 s 17(d).

[170] Official Information Act 1982 s 14; Local Government Official Information and Meetings Act 1987 s 12(b)(i); Privacy Act 1993 s 39.

[171] Official Information Act 1982 ss 15(1) and 24(3); Local Government Official Information and Meetings Act 1987 ss 13 and 23(2); Privacy Act 1993 s 40(1)(a).

[172] Official Information Act 1982 ss 15A(1)(a) and 24(3); Local Government Official Information and Meetings Act 1987 ss 14(1)(a) and 23(2); Privacy Act 1993 s 41(1)(a).

[173] Official Information Act 1982 s 28(4).

[174] Official Information Act 1982 ss 16(1)(a)–(f) and 24(3); Local Government Official Information and Meetings Act 1987 ss 15(1)(a)–(f) and 23(2); Privacy Act 1993 s 42(2). The form of access must be that preferred by the applicant unless to do so would impair efficient administration and so forth: Official Information Act 1982 s 16(2); Local Government Official Information and Meetings Act 1987 s 15(2); Privacy Act 1993 s 42(2). This includes a requirement to make the information readable where it is stored in a way that is not visible to the applicant: *Commissioner of Police v District Court at Manukau* [2007] NZHC 101.

[175] Official Information Act 1982 s 19; Local Government Official Information and Meetings Act 1987 s 18.

[176] Official Information Act 1982 ss 18 and 27(1); Local Government Official Information and Meetings Act 1987 ss 17 and 26; Privacy Act 1993 s 30.

if to do so would be likely to damage security, defence, international relations, represent a breach of confidence, endanger individuals, reveal a trade secret or damage the economy.[177] A charge may be imposed for the disclosure of information, depending upon: the statute under which access is sought; whether the information sought is personal information; and whether the body to which the request is made is a public sector agency or a private sector agency.[178] Specific provision is made for excision of exempt information contained in a document.[179] Although there is no express power enabling a conditional release of information, there would appear to be an implicit power to do so, as the ombudsman is given power to investigate such conditions.[180] There is nothing proscribing the discretionary release of information that is exempt under the Act.[181]

1 Exemptions generally

Exemptions under the New Zealand legislation divide into two broad classes: those that are engaged upon their terms being satisfied;[182] and those that will be disengaged if, in the circumstances, the withholding of particular information is outweighed by other considerations which render it desirable in the public interest to make that information available.[183] The exemptions may also be categorised into prejudice-based exemptions, which require that disclosure 'be likely to prejudice' an identified interest,[184] and pure class-based exemptions, which do not require that prejudice flow from disclosure of the requested information. The applicability of exemptions varies according to whether the information sought is personal information and, if so, whether the person is a corporate person. In considering exemptions, the overarching principle is that information is to be made available unless there is good reason

---

[177] Official Information Act 1982 s 10; Local Government Official Information and Meetings Act 1987 s 8; Privacy Act 1993 s 32.

[178] Official Information Act 1982 ss 15(2) and 24(3); Local Government Official Information and Meetings Act 1987 s 13(1A); Privacy Act 1993 ss 35, 36 and 59.

[179] Official Information Act 1982 ss 17(1) and 24(3); Local Government Official Information and Meetings Act 1987 ss 16(1) and 23(2); Privacy Act 1993 s 43(1).

[180] Official Information Act 1982 s 28(1)(c); Local Government Official Information and Meetings Act 1987 s 27(1)(c); Privacy Act 1993 s 66(2)(a)(iii), where the power is vested in the Privacy Commissioner. Examples of conditions imposed are: (1) where information was released on the condition that the information could only be published together with a statement or explanation from the holder of the information; (2) where information was to be used for Court proceedings on the basis of undertakings by the parties that the information would not be made available to the media.

[181] Although where its disclosure breaches the privacy principles set out in the Privacy Act 1993 this may give rise to a complaint either under that Act or to the Ombudsman. Discretionary disclosure does not attract the protection given by the Official Information Act 1982 s 48.

[182] Official Information Act 1982 ss 18(c)(i) and 52(3); Local Government Official Information and Meetings Act 1987 ss 17(c)(i) and 44(2); Privacy Act 1993 s 7.

[183] Official Information Act 1982 ss 18(c)(ii) and 52(1); Local Government Official Information and Meetings Act 1987 ss 17(c)(ii) and 44(1); Privacy Act 1993 s 29(1)(i).

[184] The High Court has held that the test to be applied in determining whether withholding the information is necessary to protect one of the specified interests is one of 'reasonable' necessity, rather than 'strict' necessity: *Television New Zealand Ltd v Ombudsman* [1992] 1 NZLR 106 at 118. The 'would be likely' test has been held not to mean 'more likely than not', but to involve a lesser threshold, namely: 'a serious or real and substantial risk to a protected interest, a risk that might well eventuate': *Commissioner of Police v Ombudsman* [1988] 1 NZLR 385 (CA).

for withholding it.[185] Certificates may be issued by the Prime Minister or the Attorney-General on the grounds that disclosure of the requested information would be likely to prejudice: the defence or security of New Zealand or one of its dependencies; international relations; or the investigation, etc of offences.[186] The effect of a certificate is that the Ombudsman may not recommend the disclosure of the information to which the certificate relates.

2– 022   The absolute exemptions

Information may be withheld without a consideration of the public interest where:

(1)   Disclosure would be likely to prejudice the security or defence of New Zealand or certain external dependencies or the international relations of the New Zealand Government.[187]

(2)   Disclosure would be likely to prejudice the entrusting of information to the Government of New Zealand on a basis of confidence by the Government of any other country or any agency of such a government, or by any international organisation.[188]

(3)   Disclosure would be likely to prejudice the maintenance of the law, including the prevention, investigation, and detection of offences, and the right to a fair trial.[189]

(4)   Disclosure would be likely to endanger the safety of any person.[190]

(5)   Disclosure would be likely to damage seriously the New Zealand economy by disclosing prematurely decisions to change or continue government economic or financial policies relating to: exchange rates or the control of overseas exchange transactions; the regulation of banking or credit; taxation; the stability, control, and adjustment of prices of goods and services, rents, and other costs, and rates of wages, salaries, and other incomes; the borrowing of money by the New Zealand government; and the entering into of overseas trade agreements.[191]

(6)   Disclosure would be contrary to the provisions of another enactment.[192]

(7)   Disclosure would be a contempt of court or of the House of Representatives.[193]

2– 023   The qualified exemptions

The remaining exemptions involve a two-stage process. First, a consideration of whether

---

[185] Official Information Act 1982 s 5. The Courts have rejected the notion that there is a general presumption that exemptions are to be narrowly construed: *Commissioner of Police v Ombudsman* [1988] 1 NZLR 385 (CA).

[186] Official Information Act 1982 s 31.

[187] Official Information Act 1982 ss 6(a), 7 and 27(1)(a); Privacy Act 1993 ss 27(1)(a) and 27(2)(a)–(c).

[188] Official Information Act 1982 ss 6(b) and 27(1)(a); Privacy Act 1993 s 27(1)(b).

[189] Official Information Act 1982 ss 6(c) and 27(1)(a); Local Government Official Information and Meetings Act 1987 ss 6(a) and 26(1)(a); Privacy Act 1993 s 27(1)(c).

[190] Official Information Act 1982 ss 6(d) and 27(1)(a); Local Government Official Information and Meetings Act 1987 ss 6(b) and 26(1)(a); Privacy Act 1993 s 27(1)(d).

[191] Official Information Act 1982 ss 6(e) and 27(1)(a).

[192] Official Information Act 1982 ss 18(c)(i), 27(1)(a) and 52(3)(b); Local Government Official Information and Meetings Act 1987 ss 17(c)(i), 26(1)(a) and 44(2)(b); Privacy Act 1993 s 7(2)–(3).

[193] Official Information Act 1982 ss 18(c)(ii), 27(1)(a) and 52(1); Local Government Official Information and Meetings Act 1987 ss 17(c)(ii), 26(1)(a) and 44(1); Privacy Act 1993 s 29(1)(h).

withholding the requested information is necessary in order to protect particular interests or to avoid particular prejudice. Secondly, if it is so necessary, to consider whether the withholding of the information is outweighed by other considerations that nevertheless render it desirable in the public interest to make that information available. So far as the first stage is concerned, this will be satisfied where the withholding of the information is necessary:

(1) To protect the privacy of natural persons, including that of deceased natural persons.[194]

(2) To protect information where the making available of that information would disclose a trade secret, or would be likely to unreasonably prejudice the commercial position of the person who supplied or who is the subject of the information.[195]

(3) To protect information which is subject to an obligation of confidence or which any person has been or could be compelled to provide under the authority of any enactment.[196]

(4) To avoid prejudice to measures protecting the health or safety of members of the public.[197]

(5) To avoid prejudice to the substantial economic interests of New Zealand.[198]

(6) To avoid prejudice to measures that prevent or mitigate material loss to members of the public.[199]

(7) To maintain the constitutional conventions for the time being which protect: the confidentiality of communications by or with the Sovereign or her representative; collective and individual ministerial responsibility; the political neutrality of officials; and the confidentiality of advice tendered by ministers of the Crown and officials (these reasons are not applicable in the case of local authorities).[200]

(8) To maintain the effective conduct of public affairs, through the free and frank expression of opinions by or between or to ministers or members of a specified organisation or officers and employees of any department, organisation, or local authority in the course of their duty; or through the protection of such ministers, members, officers, and employees from improper pressure or harassment.[201]

---

[194] Official Information Act 1982 ss 9(2)(a) and 27(1)(b); Local Government Official Information and Meetings Act 1987 ss 7(2)(a) and 26(1)(b); Privacy Act 1993 s 29(1)(a). Although not involving a request under the Act, *Mafart and anor v Television New Zealand* [2006] NZCA 183 is illustrative of privacy interests being subordinated to the public interest by making important Court proceedings accessible to the public (video-tape of the committal proceedings of the Rainbow Warrior bombers).

[195] Official Information Act 1982 ss 9(2)(b)(i) and 27(1)(a); Local Government Official Information and Meetings Act 1987 ss 7(2)(b)(i) and 26(1)(a); Privacy Act 1993 s 28(1)(a)–(b).

[196] Official Information Act 1982 ss 9(2)(b)(ii) and 27(1)(c); Local Government Official Information and Meetings Act 1987 ss 7(2)(b)(ii) and 26(1)(c); Privacy Act 1993 s 29(1)(b)b. The courts have rejected the notion that the contractual provisions requiring confidentiality to be kept necessarily protected the information from being disclosed under the Act: *Wyatt Co (NZ) Ltd v Queenstown-Lakes District Council* [1991] 2 NZLR 180.

[197] Official Information Act 1982 s 9(2)(c); Local Government Official Information and Meetings Act 1987 s 7(2)(d); Privacy Act 1993 s 29(1)(c).

[198] Official Information Act 1982 s 9(2)(d).

[199] Official Information Act 1982 s 9(2)(e); Local Government Official Information and Meetings Act 1987 s 7(2)(e).

[200] Official Information Act 1982 s 9(2)(f).

[201] Official Information Act 1982 s 9(2)(g); Local Government Official Information and Meetings Act 1987 s 7(2)(f).

(9)   To maintain legal professional privilege.[202]

(10) To enable a minister, department, specified organisation, or local authority holding the information to carry out, without prejudice or disadvantage, commercial activities.[203]

(11) To enable a minister, department, specified organisation, or local authority holding the information to carry on negotiations without prejudice or disadvantage, including commercial or industrial negotiations.[204]

(12) To prevent the disclosure or use of official information for improper gain or improper advantage.[205]

2– 024   Appeals and enforcement

The first stage of the appeal system lies with the Ombudsman, who, upon a complaint, may investigate and review any decision to refuse access or to refuse to confirm or deny the existence of requested information.[206]   The Ombudsman has all the normal powers under the Ombudsmen Act 1975, including compelling the production of information.   After investigation, the Ombudsman must make a report with recommendations, setting out whether it is considered that the original decision was wrong or unreasonable.[207]   The department is obliged to observe a recommendation of the Ombudsman unless the Governor-General, by Order in Council, otherwise directs.[208]   Where no Order in Council is made, a person dissatisfied with the Ombudsman's recommendation may have it and the original decision judicially reviewed.   Where an Order in Council is made, an appeal may be made to the High Court on grounds that it was wrong in law[209] and, from there, to the Court of Appeal.[210]   There is statutory protection for those who in good faith release official information under the access acts.[211]

---

[202] Official Information Act 1982 ss 9(2)(h) and 27(1)(h); Local Government Official Information and Meetings Act 1987 ss 7(2)(g) and 26(1)(h); Privacy Act 1993 s 29(1)(f).

[203] Official Information Act 1982 s 9(2)(i); Local Government Official Information and Meetings Act 1987 s 7(2)(h).

[204] Official Information Act 1982 s 9(2)(j); Local Government Official Information and Meetings Act 1987 s 7(2)(i).

[205] Official Information Act 1982 s 9(2)(k); Local Government Official Information and Meetings Act 1987 s 7(2)(j).

[206] Official Information Act 1982 s 28(1); Local Government Official Information and Meetings Act 1987 s 27(1).

[207] Official Information Act 1982 s 30(1); Local Government Official Information and Meetings Act 1987 s 29(1).

[208] Official Information Act 1982 s 32(1); Local Government Official Information and Meetings Act 1987 s 31(1).

[209] Official Information Act 1982 s 32B; Local Government Official Information and Meetings Act 1987 s 34.

[210] Official Information Act 1982 s 32C; Local Government Official Information and Meetings Act 1987 s 35.

[211] Official Information Act 1982 s 48(1); Local Government Official Information and Meetings Act 1987 s 41(1); Privacy Act 1993 s 115(1). If the original supplier to the department did so in breach of confidence, that person will not enjoy the statutory protection where that information is disclosed under an access Act: *Attorney-General v Davidson* [1994] 3 NZLR 143 (CA).

5. CANADA

25 ### Introduction

In Canada, legislation giving a general right of access to government-held information originated in the provinces. In 1977 Nova Scotia became the first Canadian jurisdiction to pass such legislation, followed by New Brunswick in 1978, Newfoundland in 1981 and Quebec in 1982.[212] Federal legislation giving a general right of access to government-held information was passed in June 1982. Called the Access to Information Act, it was enacted at the same time as the Privacy Act,[213] and they came into force on 1 July 1983. All of the remaining provincial and territorial jurisdictions subsequently introduced similar legislation.[214] Since its enactment, the Access to Information Act has been amended on three occasions, all of which have been of relatively minor significance.[215]

26 ### Scope of the right

Section 4 of the Act gives Canadian citizens and permanent residents a right of access to records under the control of a government institution, subject only to specific exclusions[216] and exemptions.[217] The Act gives the Governor in Council power to extend this right to others, and in 1989 the access right was extended to include all individuals and incorporated entities present in the country.[218] The unit of disclosure under the Access to Information Act is a

---

[212] The original Nova Scotia Act was replaced in 1993 by the Freedom of Information and Protection of Privacy Act 1993 (Nova Scotia); Right to Information Act 1978 (New Brunswick); Freedom of Information Act 1990 (Newfoundland); An Act respecting Access to documents held by public bodies and the Protection of personal information 1982 (Quebec).

[213] The purpose of the Privacy Act is, broadly speaking, to protect the privacy of individuals with respect to personal information about themselves held by a government institution and to provide individuals with a right of access to that information: *Dagg v Canada (Minister of Finance)* [1997] SCJ 63 at [61]; *Attorney-General of Canada and Hartley v Information Commissioner of Canada* [2002] FCT 128.

[214] Freedom of Information Act 1998 (Manitoba); Freedom of Information and Protection of Privacy Act 1992 (Saskatchewan); Freedom of Information and Protection of Privacy Act 1988 (Ontario); Freedom of Information and Protection of Privacy Act 1996 (British Columbia); Freedom of Information and Protection of Privacy Act 1994 (Alberta); Freedom of Information and Protection of Privacy Act 2001 (Prince Edward Island); Access to Information and Protection of Privacy Act 1994 (Northwest Territories); Access to Information and Protection of Privacy Act 1996 (Yukon Territory).

[215] In 1992, the Act was amended to deal with the provision of records in alternative formats to individuals with sensory disabilities. In 1999, it was amended to make it a criminal offence to intentionally obstruct the right of access by destroying, altering, hiding or falsifying a record, or directing anyone else to do so. In 2001, it was amended by the Anti-terrorism Act which provides that a certificate by the Attorney-General prohibiting the disclosure of information for the purpose of protecting national defence or national security will override the provisions of the Access to Information Act.

[216] Published, library and museum material are generally excluded from the operation of the Act: Access to Information Act s 68. So, too, confidences of the Queen's Privy Council for Canada (ie cabinet material): Access to Information Act s 69. In relation to cabinet material generally, see: *Canada (Minister of Environment) v Canada (Information Commissioner)* [2003] FCA 68.

[217] Exemptions, which are provided for by Access to Information Act ss 13–26, are considered at §§2– 029 to 2– 032.

[218] Access to Information Act Extension Order No 1 (SOR/89–207).

'record',[219] as opposed to a 'document' or 'information'. In order for the right to arise, a record must be 'under the control'[220] of a 'government institution'.[221] Decisions granting or refusing access must be made by the 'head' of each government institution, with the head of each institution being designated by regulation.[222]

2– 027 The request

A request must be made in writing.[223] There is no power to refuse to answer a request that is frivolous, vexatious or abusive. The only control over burdensome requests lies in the fees regime.[224] Where a government institution receives a request but considers that another government institution has a greater interest in the record, the former institution may transfer the request to the latter institution.[225] The Act provides for a publication scheme.[226] The head of a government institution must give every reasonable assistance to a person making a request and to respond promptly.[227]

2– 028 The response

Within 30 days of receiving a request, a government institution must inform the applicant

---

[219] Access to Information Act s 3 defines 'record' to mean any documentary material, regardless of medium or form. It has been held that 'software' does not constitute a record: *Yeager v Canada (Correctional Service)* [2003] FCA 30. A 'record' can include something not yet in existence but that can be assembled from data already held, see: *Yeager v Canada (Correctional Service)* [2003] FCA 30.

[220] The Act does not define when a record is 'under the control' of an institution. The authorities indicate that any document that happens to be in the custody or in the hands of a government institution, regardless of how or upon what conditions, will be under its control: *Montana Band of Indians v Canada (Minister of Indian and Northern Affairs)* [1989] 1 FC 143 (TD), 51 DLR (4th) 306; *Ottawa Football Club v Canada (Minister of Fitness and Amateur Sports)* [1989] 2 FC 480 (TD); *Canada Post Corp v Canada (Minister of Public Works)* [1995] 2 FC 110, 30 Admin LR (2d) 242, affirming [1993] 3 FC 320, 19 Admin LR (2d) 230; *Rubin v Canada (Minister of Foreign Affairs and International Trade)* [2001] FCT 440 (a returned document is not 'under the control' of an institution); *Federation des Producteurs v Canadian Food Inspection Agency* [2007] FC 704. In relation to documents obtained by the institution from a third party through court disclosure or discovery, see *Andersen Consulting v Canada* [2001] 2 FC 324.

[221] Access to Information Act s 3 simply defines a 'government institution' as any department or ministry, body or office listed in Sch I of the Act. Schedule I lists 19 departments and ministries and a number of other bodies and offices. It also applies to Crown corporations and wholly-owned subsidiaries. But the Canadian Broadcasting Corporation enjoys similar exemption to that enjoyed by the BBC in the United Kingdom: Access to Information Act s 68.1. As to ministerial offices, see: *Canada (Attorney-General) v Canada (Information Commissioner)* [2000] FCA 26. As to the meaning of the phrase 'government institution,' see *Information Commissioner v Minister for National Defence* [2009] FCA 175, upholding [2009] 2 FCR 86 (considering the circumstances in which a record physically located in a Minister's office is nevertheless under the control of the government institution over which he presides).

[222] Access to Information Act Heads of Government Institutions Designation Order SI 1983/113.

[223] Access to Information Regulations (SOR/83–507) reg 4.

[224] Access to Information Act s 11 and Access to Information Regulations (SOR/83–507) reg 7 provide for an applicant to be charged an application fee, not exceeding $25, and also to be charged for: reasonable search and preparation time in excess of five hours; the costs of producing a record in an alternative format; the production of a machine-readable record; and reproduction costs. In all cases, specific amounts are set by regulation. Heads of institutions can require applicants to pay deposits, or to waive or repay a fee. The ability to use the fees regime to control what are considered to be frivolous or vexatious requests would appear to be limited: *Rubin v Canada (Minister of Finance)* (1987) 9 FTR 317, 35 DLR (4th) 517.

[225] Access to Information Act s 8; Access to Information Regulations (SOR/83–507) reg 6.

[226] Access to Information Act s 5.

[227] Access to Information Act s 4(2.1).

whether access to the requested record is to be given and, if so, to provide it.[228] The 30-day period may be extended 'for a reasonable period of time' where the request is for a large number of records, requires a search through a large number of records, requires consultations that cannot be completed within the original time limit, or where notice has to be given to third parties.[229] If a record is not provided within the original 30 days or the extended period, the request is deemed to have been refused.[230] If, after processing a request, it is decided to give access, that access takes the form of an opportunity to examine the record or the provision of a copy of the record.[231] If the institution decides to refuse access, it must cite the statutory ground for refusing access or what it would be if the record existed.[232] In refusing a request, the institution is not required to confirm whether any record answering the terms of the request actually exists.[233] An institution must so far as practicable excise exempted portions of records and provide access to the rest.[234] An institution must make reasonable efforts to give a third party that supplied information to it notice of its intention to disclose that information.[235]

9 Exemptions generally

The Access to Information Act divides exemptions into mandatory and discretionary exemptions.[236] Mandatory exemptions must be invoked; discretionary exemptions allow the head of a government institution to decide whether the exemption needs to be invoked. Each exemption is based on either an 'injury test' or 'class test'. Exemptions which incorporate an 'injury test' take into consideration whether the disclosure of certain information could 'reasonably be expected' to be injurious to a specified interest.[237] 'Class test' exemptions are those applying to a record that matches the description given in the statutory provision; in order to engage the exemption there is no need to demonstrate any likelihood of injury resulting from disclosure of the record. Two of the mandatory exemptions include public interest overrides. These allow the head of a government institution to disclose information where this would be

---

[228] Access to Information Act s 7.

[229] Access to Information Act s 9.

[230] As to the review by the courts of decisions to extend the time within which to respond to a request, see: *Canada (Information Commissioner) v Canada (Minister of External Affairs)* [1989] 1 FC 3, 32 Admin LR 265; *Canada (Information Commissioner) v Canada (Minister of External Affairs)* [1990] 3 FC 514; *X v Canada (Minister of National Defence)* [1991] 1 FC 670.

[231] Access to Information Act s 12(1); Access to Information Regulations (SOR/83–507) regs 5 and 8.

[232] Access to Information Act s 10(1).

[233] Access to Information Act s 10(2).

[234] Access to Information Act s 25. See *Sheldon Blank & Gateway Industries v Canada (Minister of Environment)* [2001] FCA 374.

[235] Access to Information Act s 27(1). The party can make representations in relation to the proposed disclosure: s 28. Similarly, if the Information Commissioner proposes to recommend disclosure, notice must be given to the third party: s 35(2)(c). As to the nature of the obligation to give a third party notice, see *Minister of Health v Merck Frosst Canada Ltd* [2009] FCA 166.

[236] There are no mandatory exemptions in the FOIA.

[237] The courts have interpreted this to mean that there must be a reasonable expectation of probable harm: *Canada Packers Inc v Canada (Minister of Agriculture)* [1989] 1 FC 47. Mere assertions will not suffice: *Jacques Whitford Environment Ltd v Canada (Minister of National Defence)* [2001] FCT 556; *Wyeth-ayerst Canada Inc v Canada (Attorney-General)* [2002] FCT 133; *Geophysical Service Inc v Canada-Newfoundland Offshore Petroleum Board* [2003] FCT 507.

in the public interest as defined in the provision.[238]

2–030 Onus, purpose clause and conclusive certificates

Although there is no specific provision in the Act specifying whether it is the institution or the applicant who must demonstrate the applicability or inapplicability of a ground of exemption, the courts have held that where there is a contest between disclosure and non-disclosure of a record, the burden rests upon the party resisting disclosure.[239] This approach is consistent with the Act's purpose clause, which includes a statement of principle that government information should be available to the public and that necessary exceptions to the right of access should be limited and specific.[240] Until late 2001, the Access to Information Act did not include any mechanism for taking particular documents outside of its operation or for reducing the ability to review a non-disclosure decision. The Anti-terrorism Act (2001) amended the Access to Information Act by adding a provision[241] which provides that a certificate by the Attorney-General prohibiting the disclosure of information for the purpose of protecting national defence or national security will override the provisions of the Access to Information Act. The certificates are subject to review by the Federal Court of Appeal.

2–031 Mandatory exemptions

There are seven class-based mandatory exemptions:

(1) Information received in confidence from other governments.[242]

(2) Information obtained or prepared by the Royal Canadian Mounted Police on provincial or municipal policing services.[243]

(3) Personal information.[244]

---

[238] Access to Information Act s 20(6) permits the head of an institution to disclose commercial information from a third party if this would be in the public interest as it relates to health, safety or protection of the environment, and the public interest in disclosure clearly outweighs any injury to the third party. Section 19 of the Access to Information Act provides a similar public interest override in relation to the exemption for personal information. The consideration of the public interest only as it concerns the specific exemption, rather than in general, is the model adopted in the FOIA.

[239] *Maislin Industries Ltd v Minister for Industry, Trade & Commerce* [1984] 1 FC 939; *Rubin v Canada (Canada Mortgage and Housing Corp)* [1989] 1 FC 265; *Canada (Information Commissioner) v Canada (Minister of External Affairs)* [1990] 3 FC 665. This also applies where a third party resists disclosure: *Wyeth-ayerst Canada Inc v Canada (Attorney-General)* [2002] FCT 133; *Cistel Technology Inc v Canada (Correctional Service)* [2002] FCT 253. Where proceedings are on foot, the position is governed by Access to Information Act s 48.

[240] Access to Information Act s 2.

[241] Access to Information Act s 69(1).

[242] Access to Information Act s 13(1). The exemption becomes discretionary if the body from whom the information was obtained either consents to its disclosure or makes it public itself: s 13(1). See *Sherman v Minister of National Revenue* [2003] FCA 202 (tax information exchanged under convention).

[243] Access to Information Act s 16(3).

[244] Access to Information Act s 19. As to the division between the Access to Information Act and the Privacy Act and the meaning of 'personal information', see: *Information Commissioner v Minister of Industry* [2002] FCA 212, (2002) 284 DLR (4th) 293; *Information Commissioner v Royal Canadian Mounted Police* [2003] 1 SCR 66; *Yaeger v National Parole Board* [2008] FCA 13. The Act adopts the definition of 'personal information' given in the Privacy Act s 3, which is that it is 'information about an identifiable individual that is recorded in any form' and then proceeds to give a series of specific inclusions. Personal information has been held to extend to qualitative evaluations of an employee's performance (*Canada (Information Commissioner) v Canada (Solicitor General)* [1988] 3 FC 557 and to the remuneration levels of various chairmen, heads, and presiding officials of an agency (*Rubin v Canada (Clerk of the Privy Council)* (1993)

(4)   Trade secrets of a third party.[245]

(5)   Financial, commercial, scientific or technical information received in confidence from a third party.[246]

(6)   Information the disclosure of which is restricted by or pursuant to any provision set out in Sch II to the Act.[247]

(6A) Information held by the Information Commissioner, the Privacy Commissioner, the Auditor-General, the Chief Electoral Officer and certain other office-holders, created or obtained by them in the course of an investigation, examination or audit conducted by them.[248]

There are two injury-based mandatory exemptions:

(7)   Records the disclosure of which could reasonably be expected to cause loss or gain

62 FTR 287). See also: *Canada (Information Commissioner) v Canada (Cultural Property Export Review Board)* [2001] FCT 1054; *Canada (Information Commissioner) v Canada (Royal Canadian Mounted Police)* [2001] 3 FC 70, [2001] FCA 56; *Canada (Information Commissioner) v Canada (Minister of Citizenship and Immigration)* [2002] FCA 270; *Canada (Information Commissioner) v Transportation Accident Investigation and Safety Board* [2006] FCA 157 [2007] 1 FCR 203 (holding that recordings of air traffic controllers did not constitute 'personal information'). An 'identifiable individual' does not include a corporation: *Geophysical Service Inc v Canada-Newfoundland Offshore Petroleum Board* [2003] FCT 507. As to the level of detail that makes information 'personal information', see *Gordon v Minister of Health* [2008] FC 258. The exemption is subject to a public interest override: s 19(6).

[245] Access to Information Act s 20(1)(a). The Courts have given this exemption a narrow interpretation: *Merck Frosst Canada Inc v Canada (Minister of Health and Welfare)* (1988) 20 FTR 73; *Canada Post Corp v Canada (Minister of Public Works)* [1993] 3 FC 320, affirmed (1993), 64 FTR 62; *Matol Botanical International Inc v Canada (Minister of National Health & Welfare)* (1994) 84 FTR 168; *Société Gamma Inc v Canada (Secretary of State)* (1994) 79 FTR 42; *PricewaterhouseCoopers, LLP v Canada (Minister of Canadian Heritage)* [2001] FCT 1040; *Wyeth-ayerst Canada Inc v Canada (Attorney-General)* [2002] FCT 133; *Cistel Technology Inc v Canada (Correctional Service)* [2002] FCT 253; *St Joseph Corp v Canada (Public Works and Government Services)* [2002] FCT 274; *Minister of Health v Merck Frosst Canada Ltd* [2009] FCA 166.

[246] Access to Information Act s 20(1)(b). The courts have held that the information must still have its confidentiality at the time of the request in order for the exemption to operate: *Maislin Industries Ltd v Minister for Industry, Trade & Commerce* [1984] 1 FC 939. The general approach of the courts has been to scrutinise carefully claims of confidentiality, whether these claims are made by the government institution or by the third party that supplied the information: *Noël v Great Lakes Pilotage Authority Ltd* [1988] 2 FC 77; *Intercontinental Packers Ltd v Canada (Minister of Agriculture)* (1987) 14 FTR 142; *Ottawa Football Club v Canada (Minister of Fitness and Amateur Sports)* [1989] 2 FC 480; *Canada Packers Inc v Canada (Minister of Agriculture)* [1989] 1 FC 47; *PricewaterhouseCoopers, LLP v Canada (Minister of Canadian Heritage)* [2001] FCT 1040; *Jacques Whitford Environment Ltd v Canada (Minister of National Defence)* [2001] FCT 556; *Canada (Minister of Health & Welfare) v Merck Frosst Canada & Co* [2005] FCA 215 (even if the format is different, once the information is in the public domain it can no longer be confidential); *Minister of Public Works and Government Services v The Hi-Rise Group Inc* [2004] FCA 99, (2004) 238 DLR (4th) 44 (the rent paid by a government agency for premises held not to be confidential: 'when a would-be contractor sets out to win a government contract through a confidential bidding process, he or she cannot expect that the monetary terms, in the event that the bid succeeds, will remain confidential'), and similarly *131 Queen Street Limited v Attorney-General* [2007] FC 347; *Heinz Company of Canada Ltd v Attorney-General of Canada* [2006] FCA 378 (rejecting a claim by Heinz that information supplied by it to government inspectors was confidential). The supply of information to a government institution on a confidential basis, while a relevant factor, will not be determinative, as a third party cannot trump the rights conferred by the Act: *Canadian Tobacco Manufacturers' Council v Minister of National Revenue* [2003] FC 1037.

[247] Access to Information Act s 24. The courts have said that it was intended that the invocation of provisions in other statutes to limit disclosure was intended to be as restrictive as possible: *Canada (Information Commissioner) v Canada (Immigration Appeal Board)* [1988] 3 FC 477.

[248] Access to Information Act ss 16.1 - 16.5.

to a third party or prejudice to competitive position.[249]

(8)   Records the disclosure of which could reasonably be expected to cause interference with contractual or other negotiations of a third party.[250]

2– 032   **Discretionary exemptions**

There are ten class-based discretionary exemptions. These grant exemption from disclosure for records that contain:

(1)   Information obtained or prepared by listed investigative bodies.[251]

(2)   Information on techniques or plans for investigations.[252]

(3)   Trade secrets or valuable financial, commercial, scientific or technical information belonging to the Government of Canada[253] or to various government-related agencies.[254]

(4)   Advice or recommendations developed by or for a government institution or a minister of the Crown.[255]

(5)   Any account of governmental consultations or deliberations in which government employees or a minister participates.[256]

(6)   Government negotiation plans.[257]

---

[249] Access to Information Act s 20(1)(c). The courts have treated claims for this exemption with circumspection, requiring real evidence to support the reasonable expectation and not just surmise: *Burns Meats Ltd v Canada (Minister of Agriculture)* (1987) 14 FTR 137; *Glaxo Canada Inc v Canada (Minister of National Health & Welfare)* (1992) 41 CPR (3d) 176; *Cyanamid Canada Inc v Canada (Minister of National Health and Welfare)* (1992) 45 CPR (3d) 390; *Prud'homme v Canada (Canadian International Development Agency)* (1994) 85 FTR 302; *Matol Botanical International Inc v Canada (Minister of National Health & Welfare)* (1994) 84 FTR 168; *Jacques Whitford Environment Ltd v Canada (Minister of National Defence)* [2001] FCT 556; *Brookfield Lepage Johnson Controls Facility Management Services v Minister of Public Works and Government Services* [2004] FCA 214.

[250] Access to Information Act s 20(1)(d). The courts have required the negotiations to be on foot and for the interference to amount to actual obstruction: *Société Gamma Inc v Canada (Secretary of State)* (1994) 79 FTR 42; *Saint John Shipbuilding Ltd v Canada (Minister of Supply and Services)* (1990) 67 DLR (4th) 315.

[251] Access to Information Act s 16(1)(a).

[252] Access to Information Act s 16(1)(b). For an example of its application, see *Rubin v Canada (Solicitor General)* (1986) 1 FTR 157.

[253] Access to Information Act s 18(a).

[254] Access to Information Act s 18.1.

[255] Access to Information Act s 21(1)(a). As to the meaning of 'advice or recommendations', see: *Canada Inc v Canada (Minister of Industry)* [2002] 1 FC 421. There is an exception where the record relates to a decision that is made in the exercise of a discretionary power or an adjudicative function and that affects the rights of a person: Access to Information Act s 21(2). Factual information falls outside the exemption: *Canadian Council of Christian Charities v Canada (Minister of Finance)* [1999] 4 FC 245; *Information Commissioner v Minister of the Environment* [2007] 3 FCR 125.

[256] Access to Information Act s 21(1)(b). There is an exception where the account relates to a decision that is made in the exercise of a discretionary power or an adjudicative function and that affects the rights of a person: Access to Information Act s 21(2). The courts have not inquired into the reasons for invoking this exemption: provided that the record answers the description, that will suffice: *Canada (Information Commissioner) v Canadian Radio-television and Telecommunications Commission* [1986] 3 FC 413; *Re Rubin and President of CMHC* (1987) 36 DLR (4th) 22. Factual information falls outside the exemption: *Canadian Council of Christian Charities v Canada (Minister of Finance)* [1999] 4 FC 245; *Information Commissioner v Minister of the Environment* [2007] 3 FCR 125.

[257] Access to Information Act s 21(1)(c). There is an exception where the record relates to a decision that is made in the exercise of a discretionary power or an adjudicative function and that affects the rights of a person: Access to Information Act s 21(2).

(7)　　Government personnel or organisational plans.[258]

(8)　　Solicitor-client privileged information.[259]

(9)　　Information that is likely to be published within 90 days.

(9A)　Draft internal audit reports of a government institution.[260]

There are nine injury-based discretionary exemptions. These apply to records the disclosure of which could 'reasonably be expected' to cause:[261]

(10)　Injury to the conduct of federal-provincial affairs.[262]

(11)　Injury to the conduct of international affairs, or to the defence of Canada or allied states.[263]

(12)　Injury to law enforcement or conduct of lawful investigations.[264]

(13)　Harm in facilitating the commission of a criminal offence.[265]

(14)　Threat to an individual's safety.[266]

(15)　Prejudice to the competitive position of government or to interfere with contractual or other negotiations of a government institution.[267]

(16)　Harm in depriving a government researcher of priority of publication.[268]

(17)　Injury to the financial or economic interests of Canada or of a government

---

[258] Access to Information Act s 21(1)(d). There is an exception where the record relates to a decision that is made in the exercise of a discretionary power or an adjudicative function and that affects the rights of a person: Access to Information Act s 21(2).

[259] Access to Information Act s 23. The common law test of privilege is applied, including concepts of waiver: *Weiler v Canada (Minister of Justice)* [1991] 3 FC 617; *Wells v Canada (Minister of Transport)* (1995) 63 CPR (3d) 201; *Professional Institute of the Public Service of Canada v Canadian Museum of Nature* (1995) 63 CPR (3d) 449; *Canadian Jewish Congress v Canada (Minister of Employment and Immigration)* [1996] 1 FC 268; *Stevens v Canada (Prime Minister)* [1998] 4 FC 89; *Sheldon Blank & Gateway Industries v Canada (Minister for Environment)* [2001] FCA 374 (whether privilege applies to documents incorporated by reference); *St Joseph Corp v Canada (Public Works and Government Services)* [2002] FCT 274. Litigation privilege is treated as coming to an end at the conclusion of proceedings: *Minister of Justice v Blank* [2006] SCC 39, [2006] 2 SCR 319, (2006) 270 DLR (4th) 257. The Supreme Court held that even if the documents were covered by litigation privilege, that would not prevent disclosure of a party's abuse of process or similar blameworthy conduct.

[260] Access to Information Act s 22.1. But only for 15 years after its creation and not once the final report has been published.

[261] Access to Information Act s 26.

[262] Access to Information Act s 14.

[263] Access to Information Act s 15. The courts have shown themselves comparatively deferential to respondent claims of exemption under defence grounds: *Canada (Information Commissioner) v Canada (Minister of National Defence)* [1990] 3 FC 22; *X v Canada (Minister of National Defence)* (1992) 58 FTR 93; *X v Canada (Minister of National Defence)* [1992] 1 FC 77.

[264] Access to Information Act s 16(1)(c). The courts have required that the respondent identify a particular investigation that would be prejudiced, and declined to uphold a refusal to disclose upon an assertion that investigations generally would be prejudiced: *Rubin v Canada (Clerk of the Privy Council)* [1993] 2 FC 391 [1994] 2 FC 707 (1996) 179 NR 320, SCC; *Information Commissioner v Minister of Citizenship and Immigration* [2002] FCA 270 ('chilling effect' argument rejected).

[265] Access to Information Act s 16(2).

[266] Access to Information Act s 17.

[267] Access to Information Act s 18(b).

[268] Access to Information Act s 18(c).

institution.[269]

(18) Prejudice to the use of audits or tests.[270]

2– 033   **Appeals and enforcement**

There is a two-tiered review process. Applicants have the right to complain to the Information Commissioner about an institution's handling of their request.[271] Following an investigation and report by the Commissioner to the head of the institution, both applicant and Information Commissioner have a right to seek a review of a denial of access in the Federal Court of Canada.[272] Third parties may also apply to the Federal Court in order to prevent disclosure of a record.[273] The appeal to the Federal Court is an appeal on judicial review grounds.[274] The Court is entitled to examine any record in dispute[275] and it is normally accepted practice to allow counsel for an applicant to see the disputed documents to enable the case to be properly heard, but on an undertaking not to disclose them to the client.[276]

---

[269] Access to Information Act s 18(d). This does not extend to information that would result in an increase in legitimate claims for deductions under tax legislation: *Canadian Council of Christian Charities v Canada (Minister of Finance)* [1999] 4 FC 245.

[270] Access to Information Act s 22. For an example, see *Bombardier v Canada (Public Service Commission)* (1990) 44 FTR 39.

[271] Access to Information Act s 30. There is a 60 day time limit: s 31.

[272] Access to Information Act ss 41 and 42. There must be a denial of access, so that if the institution claims that it has no documents, the applicant has no right of appeal; a court will not intervene where there is mere assertion that documents are held: *Creighton v Canada (Superintendent of Financial Institutions)* [1990] FCJ No 353, QL (FCTD); *Sheldon Blank & Gateway Industries Ltd v Canada (Minister of Environment)* [2001] FCA 374. The appeal is against the refusal to grant access, not the Information Commissioner's review: *Bellemare v Canada (Attorney-General)* [2000] FCT 429. However, the Court may properly take into account the Commissioner's views: *Canadian Council of Christian Charities v Canada (Minister of Finance)* [1999] 4 FC 245. As to an institution's ability to invoke for the first time an exemption during the appeal process, see: *Canada (Information Commissioner) v Canada (Minister of National Defence)* [1999] FCJ No 522, QL FCA.

[273] Access to Information Act s 44. A third party can invoke s 19 on a s 44 review: *Heinz Co of Canada Ltd v Attorney-General* [2006] 1 SCR 441, 2006 SCC 13.

[274] *Canadian Jewish Congress v Canada (Minister of Employment and Immigration)* [1996] 1 FC 268. The role of the Court is more limited where the exemption relied on turns on the head of a governmental institution reasonably believing that disclosure will result in an identified harm: *X v Canada (Minister of National Defence)* (1992) 58 FTR 93.

[275] Access to Information Act s 46. The purpose of this provision is to enable the Court to have the information and material necessary to ensure that the discretion given to the administrative head has been exercised within proper limits and on proper principles: *Rubin v Canada (Canada Mortgage and Housing Corp)* [1989] 1 FC 265. See also: *Canada (Minister of Environment) v Canada (Information Commissioner)* [2000] FCJ No 480, QL FCA. Protection against disclosure by the Court is given in s 47.

[276] *Maislin Industries Ltd v Minister for Industry, Trade & Commerce* [1984] 1 FC 939 (TD); *Robertson v Canada (Minister of Employment and Immigration)* (1987) 13 FTR 120 (FCTD); *Hunter v Canada (Consumer and Corporate Affairs)* [1991] 3 FC 186 (CA); *Bland v Canada (National Capital Commission)* [1991] 3 FC 325 (TD); *Sheldon Blank & Gateway Industries Ltd v Canada (Minister of the Environment)* [1999] FCJ No 571, QL (FCTD). Cross-examination of deponents of affidavits in support of exemptions is not normally allowed: *X v Canada (Minister of National Defence)* (1992) 58 FTR 93 (FCTD).

6. REPUBLIC OF IRELAND

4   Introduction

In Ireland, the first proposal to provide a right for access to official information came from a private member's Bill in 1985. It received little support and matters remained there until late 1994 when the Fine Gael/Labour Party made a commitment to introduce access legislation as part of their programme for government. The Freedom of Information Act 1997 was passed on 21 April 1997 and came into operation on 21 April 1998.[277] Significant amendments were effected in 2003, which generally increased the ability of public bodies to claim exemption both from disclosing records and from having to confirm or deny the holding of records.[278]

5   Scope of the right

Section 6(1) of the Act gives every person[279] a right of access to any 'record'[280] 'held'[281] by a 'public body'.[282] Certain records are, however, taken entirely outside the operation of the Act.

---

[277] Freedom of Information Act 1997 s 1(2). In relation to local authorities and health boards, the Act came into force on 21 October 1998. Its significance was described by the Supreme Court in *Sheedy v Information Commissioner* [2005] IESC 35 in these terms: 'The passing of the Freedom of Information Act constituted a legislative development of major importance. By it, the Oireachtas took a considered and deliberate step which dramatically alters the administrative assumptions and culture of centuries. It replaces the presumption of secrecy with one of openness. It is designed to open up the workings of government and administration to scrutiny. It is not designed simply to satisfy the appetite of the media for stories. It is for the benefit of every citizen. It lets light in to the offices and filing cabinets of our rulers.'

[278] Freedom of Information (Amendment) Act 2003. This Act effected amendments to the definition of 'record'; allowed access to personal information that predated the commencement of the Freedom of Information Act 1997; strengthened the provisions relating to the refusal to confirm or deny the existence of a record answering the terms of a request; converted the protection of records relating to meetings of Government from discretionary to mandatory; extended the non-disclosure period of records relating to meetings of Government from 5 to 10 years; generally widened the scope of the exemptions. The net effect of the amendments is to make the Freedom of Information Act 1997 the most restrictive of the comparative jurisdictions so far as a person's right of access to official information is concerned, notwithstanding the words in the long title of the Act. The High Court in *Deely v Information Commissioner* [2001] IEHC 91 and prior to the amendments, had described the Act as being 'on any view, a piece of legislation independent in existence, forceful in its aim and liberal in outlook and philosophy.'

[279] 'Person' is defined in the Interpretation Act 1937 to include a body corporate. The long title of the Freedom of Information Act 1997 suggests that the Act is principally intended to be for 'members of the public' rather than companies.

[280] 'Record' is defined to include any memorandum, book, plan, map, drawing, diagram, pictorial or graphic work or other document, any photograph, film or recording (whether of sound or images or both), any form in which data is held, any other form (including machine-readable form) or thing in which information is held or stored manually, mechanically or electronically: Freedom of Information Act 1997 s 2(1).

[281] The phrase 'held by a public body' is defined to include a record under the control of a public body: Freedom of Information Act 1997 s 2(5)(a). It also extends to records in the possession of a person who is providing a service for a public body under a contract for services, provided that the records relate to the service: Freedom of Information Act 1997 s 6(9). 'Control' suggests 'a degree of authority/dominion/management of the records rather than mere access to the records': *Minister for Enterprise Trade and Employment v Information Commissioner* [2006] IEHC 39.

[282] Public bodies are listed in the First Schedule and include local authorities, health boards, governmental departments, various bodies and organisations. The Act does not cover the police force, schools, universities, voluntary hospitals, nor various government agencies such as the Health and Safety Executive nor commercial state-sponsored bodies such as Aer Lingus. It only applies to a limited extent to the state broadcaster: *RTE v Information*

These are termed[283] 'exempt records' and include:

— most records held by a court or tribunal other than those of an administrative nature;[284]
— records held or created by the Attorney-General or the Director of Public Prosecutions, or their offices, other than those of a general administrative character;[285]
— records of the Ombudsman, and records relating to audits, to the President, or to any private papers of a member of either House of the Oireachtas;[286]
— records revealing the source of information relating to criminal law enforcement;[287] and
— records otherwise available to members of the public.[288]

With two exceptions, the right of access applies only to records created after the commencement of the Act.[289] The Act makes limited provision for the giving of assistance to people who seek access to information.[290] Under the Act, each public body must publish a 'reference book' setting out its functions and duties, the classes of records held by it, together with certain information in relation to the making of a request for access to records.[291] In addition to these rights, the Act grants individuals the right to require amendment of incorrect government records containing personal information concerning them.[292]

2– 036 **The request**

A request is normally to be made in writing and must be adequately particularised.[293] The

---

Commissioner [2004] IEHC 113.

[283] Freedom of Information Act 1997 s 2(1).

[284] Freedom of Information Act 1997 s 46(1)(a).

[285] Freedom of Information Act 1997 s 46(1)(b).

[286] Freedom of Information Act 1997 s 46(1)(c)–(e). These are also picked up by the second limb of the definition of 'exempt record' in s 2(1).

[287] Freedom of Information Act 1997 s 46(1)(f).

[288] Freedom of Information Act 1997 s 46(2). This does not extend to information available under the Data Protection Act 1988: Freedom of Information Act 1997 s 46(3).

[289] Freedom of Information Act 1997. The first exception is where earlier records are needed in order to understand post-commencement records: Freedom of Information Act 1997 s 6(5)(a). See further n 278. The second exception is in relation to records containing personal information relating to the person making the request: Freedom of Information Act 1997 s 6(5)(b). As to the meaning of the latter, see *EH v Information Commissioner* [2001] IEHC 182, where it was held that the record could constitute personal information about the requester even though the requester is not named in the record.

[290] Freedom of Information Act 1997 ss 7(7) and 10(2).

[291] Freedom of Information Act 1997 s 15. In addition, internal guidelines on the making of any decisions by a public body must be published: Freedom of Information Act 1997 s 16. Apart from s 16(3) no express provision is made for any sanction for non-compliance with s 15 or 16. The Information Commissioner is, however, given the power to examine practices and procedures adopted by public bodies for the purposes of compliance with the Act: Freedom of Information Act 1997 s 36(1).

[292] Freedom of Information Act 1997 s 17. Personal information can include records relating to a subject matter in which the applicant has a real and substantial interest, such as proceedings before a committee of the medical council: *EH v Information Commissioner* [2001] IEHC 182.

[293] Freedom of Information Act 1997 s 7(1). The request must specify the form of access sought.

reason for the request is irrelevant to the entitlement to obtain access.[294] A request that is frivolous or vexatious or which would cause a substantial and unreasonable interference with or disruption of the other work of the public body concerned need not be answered.[295] A request need not be answered if the required fee has not been paid.[296]

37   The response

The public body is required to take reasonable steps to ascertain the location of records answering the terms of the request.[297] If the public body does not hold records answering the terms of the request but actually or constructively knows that another public body does, the request must be transferred to that latter public body within two weeks of the receipt of the request.[298] Within four weeks of receipt of the request, the public body must notify the applicant of the decision on the application, together with the fees that must be paid in order to obtain access.[299] Failure to notify within the prescribed period is deemed to constitute a refusal.[300] If the decision involves a refusal, reasons must be given together with a statement of appeal rights.[301] If the public body decides to give access to a record, it can do so in any number of ways.[302] Where part of a record contains exempt material but the remainder does not, the public authority must give disclosure to as much of the non-exempt material as is practicable.[303] The public body can, in a wide range of circumstances, refuse to confirm or deny that it holds records answering the terms of a request.[304] The Act specifically provides for

---

[294] Freedom of Information Act 1997 s 8(4). Accordingly, the public body cannot impose restrictions on the purpose for which released records may be used or persons to whom they may be shown: *EH v Information Commissioner* [2001] IEHC 58, [2001] 2 IR 463.

[295] Freedom of Information Act 1997 s 10(1).

[296] Freedom of Information Act 1997 s 10(1)(f). The amount of the fee is set by Freedom of Information Act 1997 s 47. Fees can be waived: Freedom of Information Act 1997 s 47(5) and (6).

[297] Freedom of Information Act 1997 s 10(1). Where it is estimated that the cost of search and retrieval is likely to exceed £50.80, the public body is entitled to seek a deposit and need not commence the search until such time as the deposit is paid: Freedom of Information Act 1997 s 47(7).

[298] Freedom of Information Act 1997 s 7(3) and (6). Where the requested body holds some, but not all, of the records answering the terms of the request and the public body actually or constructively knows that another public body holds other records, the first public body must so notify the applicant: Freedom of Information Act 1997 s 7(4) and (6).

[299] Freedom of Information Act 1997 s 8(1). The period can be extended where the records involved are voluminous or where there have been other requests for the same records: Freedom of Information Act 1997 s 9(1).

[300] Freedom of Information Act 1997 s 41.

[301] Freedom of Information Act 1997 s 8(2).

[302] Freedom of Information Act 1997 s 12(1). Generally speaking, the public body must give access in the form sought by the applicant: Freedom of Information Act 1997 s 12(2). The public body cannot impose restrictions on the purpose for which released records may be used or the persons to whom they may be shown: *EH v Information Commissioner* [2001] IEHC 58, [2001] 2 IR 463.

[303] Freedom of Information Act 1997 s 13(1). The resultant redacted record must not be misleading: Freedom of Information Act 1997 s 13(2).

[304] Where to do so would be prejudicial to government business, s 19(5); where to do so would be prejudicial to parliamentary or court business, s 22(2); where to do so would be prejudicial to law enforcement, s 23(2); where to do so would be prejudicial to security, defence or international relations, s 24(3); where to do so would reveal confidential information, s 26(4); where to do so would reveal commercially sensitive information, s 27(4); and where to do so would reveal personal information about someone other than the applicant, s 28(5A).

discretionary disclosure.[305]

2–038   Exemptions generally

Certain exemptions are mandatory, the remainder are discretionary. Some of the exemptions are prejudice-based exemptions, others are purely class based. The likelihood of harm needed to engage the prejudice-based exemptions varies from 'could reasonably be expected' to occasion the identified harm,[306] to 'would be likely' to occasion the identified harm,[307] to 'could' occasion the identified harm.[308] Approximately half of the exemptions include a provision that disapplies the exemption where, in the opinion of the head of the public body, the public interest would on balance be better served by granting rather than by refusing the request for access.[309] The Act provides for conclusive certificates in relation to: records recording the deliberations of a public body; records whose access could be expected to prejudice law enforcement, investigations, public safety, domestic or national security, defence and international relations; and records containing certain confidential information or that might reveal the identity of certain informants.[310] The effect of a conclusive certificate is to remove the right of merit review in relation to the decision to treat the record as exempt.[311] Where the information included in a record to which access has been sought includes information obtained in confidence, commercially sensitive information or personal information, a third party to whom the information relates is given the opportunity to make submissions on the disclosure of it.[312] In such cases the onus is upon the public body to justify non-disclosure.[313] The courts construe the exemptions restrictively.[314]

2–039   Specific exemptions

There are 16 heads of exemption, half of which are mandatory and half of which are discretionary. The public body must refuse access where:

(1)   the record has been or is proposed to be submitted to the Government for

---

[305] Freedom of Information Act 1997 s 6(8). It is not clear whether a mandatory exemption represents a prohibition of access by law.

[306] Freedom of Information Act 1997 ss 21(1), 23(1), 24(1), 27(1)(b), 30(1)(b), 31(1) and 31(2)(n).

[307] Freedom of Information Act 1997 ss 26(1)(a) and 30(1)(a).

[308] Freedom of Information Act 1997 s 27(1)(b)–c).

[309] Freedom of Information Act 1997 ss 20(3), 21(2), 23(3)(b), 26(3), 27(3), 28(5) and 31(3). The language of these exemptions suggests that in so far as there may be an onus in relation to the balancing exercise, it may be said nominally to lie on the applicant: if the head of the public body has no particular view whether the public interest would be better served by granting or refusing the request, the exemption remains engaged.

[310] Freedom of Information Act 1997 ss 20(1A) and 25.

[311] There remains the more limited right to challenge the issue of the certificate on a point of law: Freedom of Information Act 1997 s 42(2). See also the limited right of review under Freedom of Information Act 1997 s 25(7) and (8).

[312] Freedom of Information Act 1997 s 29. A more detailed comparative treatment of third party rights of consultation and of 'reverse FOI' is given at §11–043.

[313] Freedom of Information Act 1997 s 34(12)(b).

[314] *Minister for Agriculture and Food v Information Commissioner* [2000] 1 IR 309 at 319; *Sheedy v Information Commissioner* [2005] 2 IR 272 at 275; *Health Service Executive v Information Commissioner* [2008] IEHC 298; *Rotunda Hospital v Information Commissioner* [2009] IEHC 315; *P v Information Commissioner* [2009] IEHC 574.

consideration by a Minister and was created for that purpose, or the record contains information for use at a meeting of the Government or consists of a communication between two or more members of the Government relating to the same;[315]

(2)   the record contains or reveals a statement made at a meeting of the Government;[316]

(3)   the record would be exempt from production in a court on the grounds of legal professional privilege; disclosure of the record would constitute a contempt of court; the record consists of the private papers of a member of the European Parliament, a member of a local authority or of a health board; or the record consists of the opinions, advice, recommendations or results of consultations considered by either House of the Oireachtas or its committees;[317]

(4)   the record contains information: obtained for intelligence purposes; relating to the security forces; revealing diplomatic communications; or revealing confidential communications from foreign state organisations;[318]

(5)   the record contains information given to the public body in confidence or the disclosure of which would constitute a breach of confidence;[319]

(6)   the record contains trade secrets, financial, etc information or contractual negotiations;[320]

(7)   disclosure would be of personal information not relating to the applicant;[321] and

---

[315] Freedom of Information Act 1997 s 19(1). Factual material is excluded and the exemption becomes inapplicable 10 years after the decision is made to which the record relates. The public body can refuse to confirm or deny the existence of any record falling within the terms of the exemption if it thinks that to do either would be contrary to the public interest: Freedom of Information Act 1997 s 19(5). The exemption will apply even if the record was not actually submitted to the Cabinet, provided that it was created for that purpose: *Minister for Education & Science v Information Commissioner* [2008] IEHC 279.

[316] Freedom of Information Act 1997 s 19(2).

[317] Freedom of Information Act 1997 s 22(1). The public body can refuse to confirm or deny the existence of any record falling within the terms of the exemption if it thinks that to do either would be contrary to the public interest: Freedom of Information Act 1997 s 22(2). For the purposes of the contempt provision, any disclosure will suffice: *EH v Information Commissioner* [2001] IEHC 58, [2001] 2 IR 463.

[318] Freedom of Information Act 1997 s 24(2). The relevant minister may issue a conclusive certificate if he takes the view that the exemption applies. The public body can refuse to confirm or deny the existence of any record falling within the terms of the exemption if it thinks that to do either would be contrary to the public interest: Freedom of Information Act 1997 s 24(3).

[319] Freedom of Information Act 1997 s 26(1). This exemption is disapplied where the public interest is better served by disclosure than by non-disclosure. The public body can refuse to confirm or deny the existence of any record falling within the terms of the exemption if it thinks that to do either would be contrary to the public interest: Freedom of Information Act 1997 s 26(4). This will be satisfied where the provider and the recipient regarded it as being confidential at the time of receipt: *Gannon v Information Commissioner* [2007] IEHC 17; *National Maternity Hospital v Information Commissioner* [2007] 3 IR 643; *Rotunda Hospital v Information Commissioner* [2009] IEHC 315.

[320] Freedom of Information Act 1997 s 27(1). This exemption is disapplied where the public interest is better served by disclosure than by non-disclosure. The public body can refuse to confirm or deny the existence of any record falling within the terms of the exemption if it thinks that to do either would be contrary to the public interest: Freedom of Information Act 1997 s 27(4).

[321] Freedom of Information Act 1997 s 28(1). This exemption is disapplied where the public interest is better served by disclosure than by non-disclosure. The public body can refuse to confirm or deny the existence of any record falling within the terms of the exemption if it thinks that to do either would be contrary to the public interest: Freedom of Information Act 1997 s 28(5A). The exemption was considered in: *Health Service Executive v Information Commissioner* [2008] IEHC 298; *Rotunda Hospital v Information Commissioner* [2009] IEHC 315; *P v Information Commissioner* [2009] IEHC 574.

(8)   disclosure of the information is prohibited by another statute.[322]

The public body may refuse access where:

(9)   the record contains matter relating to the deliberative process of the public body;[323]

(10)   disclosure of the record could reasonably be expected to prejudice the effectiveness of tests, inquiries, audits, etc carried out by a public body or have a significant adverse effect on staff management or disclose a negotiating position;[324]

(11)   the record relates to the appointment or business or proceedings of a tribunal or an inquiry;[325]

(12)   disclosure of the record could reasonably be expected to prejudice law enforcement and investigations or matters of internal security, or to reveal the name of a police informer;[326]

(13)   disclosure of the record could reasonably be expected to adversely affect the security or defence of the Republic of Ireland or its international relations;[327]

(14)   disclosure might be prejudicial to the health of the applicant;[328]

(15)   disclosure would reveal information about research in progress;[329] or

(16)   disclosure would have a serious adverse effect upon the financial interests of the state, on the ability to manage the economy, or might disturb business or could result in an unwarranted benefit or loss to a person or to a class of persons.[330]

2– 040   Appeals and enforcement

The first stage of appeal is a merit review by the 'branch head' of the public body to whom the request is made.[331]   The second stage of appeal is a merit review by the Information

---

[322] Freedom of Information Act 1997 s 32.

[323] Freedom of Information Act 1997 s 20(1). Factual and statistical material is excluded from the scope of the exemption. The exemption is disapplied where the public interest is better served by disclosure than by non-disclosure: Freedom of Information Act 1997 s 20(3). The relevant minister may issue a conclusive certificate if he takes the view that the exemption applies.

[324] Freedom of Information Act 1997 s 21(1). This exemption is disapplied where the public interest is better served by disclosure than by non-disclosure. This was considered in *Minister for Education and Science v Information Commissioner* [2001] IEHC 116 in relation to a request for education league tables.

[325] Freedom of Information Act 1997 s 22(1A).

[326] Freedom of Information Act 1997 s 23(1). The public body can refuse to confirm or deny the existence of any record falling within the terms of the exemption if it thinks that to do either would be contrary to the public interest: Freedom of Information Act 1997 s 23(2). A conclusive certificate may be issued in respect of this head of exemption: Freedom of Information Act 1997 s 25. This exemption is disapplied where the public interest is better served by disclosure than by non-disclosure.

[327] Freedom of Information Act 1997 s 24(1). The public body can refuse to confirm or deny the existence of any record falling within the terms of the exemption if it thinks that to do either would be contrary to the public interest: Freedom of Information Act 1997 s 24(3). A conclusive certificate may be issued in respect of this head of exemption: Freedom of Information Act 1997 s 25.

[328] Freedom of Information Act 1997 s 28(3).

[329] Freedom of Information Act 1997 s 30.

[330] Freedom of Information Act 1997 s 31. This exemption is disapplied where the public interest is better served by disclosure than by non-disclosure.

[331] Freedom of Information Act 1997 s 14(1). The review decision must be made within three weeks of the application for review having been received: Freedom of Information Act 1997 s 14(4). Failure to respond in that time is deemed to constitute a refusal: Freedom of Information Act 1997 s 41.

Commissioner.[332] The onus of proof lies upon the public body to justify the decision not to grant access.[333] A third party who would be affected by a disclosure will normally be entitled to have his views taken into account.[334] An appeal to the High Court on a point of law lies from a decision of the Information Commissioner[335] or from the decision to issue a conclusive certificate.[336] The Act provides for various enforcement provisions,[337] as well as granting immunity from legal proceedings for the disclosure of information pursuant to the Act.[338]

---

[332] Freedom of Information Act 1997 s 34. The Information Commissioner can rely on exemptions not invoked by the public body: *Minister for Education and Science v Information Commissioner* [2001] IEHC 116; cf *Minister for Agriculture and Food v Information Commissioner* [1999] IEHC 66, [2000] 1 IR 309, [2001] 1 ILRM 40. The Information Commissioner also has power to review a decision to defer access; a decision to grant access in the face of opposition from a third party under s 29; a decision to give access in one particular form, rather than another. The Information Commissioner has inquisitorial powers: Freedom of Information Act 1997 ss 35 and 37. He can refer questions of law to the High Court: Freedom of Information Act 1997 s 42(5).

[333] Freedom of Information Act 1997 s 34(12).

[334] *South Western Area Health Board v Information Commissioner* [2005] IEHC 177, [2005] 2 IR 547.

[335] Freedom of Information Act 1997 s 42(1). The limited nature of such an appeal was considered by the High Court in *Deely v Information Commissioner* [2001] IEHC 91, [2001] 3 IR 349; *Sheedy v Information Commissioner* [2005] 2 IR 272; *Rotunda Hospital v Information Commissioner* [2009] IEHC 315.

[336] Freedom of Information Act 1997 s 42(2).

[337] Freedom of Information Act 1997 s 37.

[338] Freedom of Information Act 1997 s 45.

CHAPTER 3

The Influence of the European Convention on Human Rights etc

1. THE INFLUENCE OF THE HUMAN RIGHTS ACT 1998 ON INFORMATION RIGHTS

3–001 Introduction

The principal human rights instruments do not directly address the right of access to officially-held information. Attempts to ground such a right in the right to freedom of expression as protected by article 10 of the European Convention on Human Rights[1] or article 19 of the International Covenant of Human Rights[2] have, by and large, failed. Article 10 of the ECHR is framed in narrower terms than article 19 of the ICCPR. The former right is limited to receiving and imparting information whilst the latter right includes the 'freedom to seek, receive and impart information'. But in relation to the ICCPR, the limited nature of enforcement mechanisms has curtailed significant development.[3] In the late 1970s a draft additional protocol to the ECHR was discussed which expressly extended the right to freedom of expression protected under article 10 of the ECHR to include the freedom to seek information. This draft protocol failed to secure widespread support and was abandoned.[4] This can be contrasted with the approach of the Inter-American Court of Human Rights, which has interpreted the right to freedom of thought and expression protected by article 13 of the American Convention on Human Rights[5] to include a general right to information held by

---

[1]   Article 10 of the ECHR provides:
1.   Everyone has the right to freedom of expression. This right shall include freedom to hold opinions and to receive and impart information and ideas without interference by public authority and regardless of frontiers. This article shall not prevent States from requiring the licensing of broadcasting, television or cinema enterprises.
2.   The exercise of these freedoms, since it carries with it duties and responsibilities, may be subject to such formalities, conditions, restrictions or penalties as are prescribed by law and are necessary in a democratic society, in the interests of national security, territorial integrity or public safety, for the prevention of disorder or crime, for the protection of health or morals, for the protection of the reputation or rights of others, for preventing the disclosure of information received in confidence, or for maintaining the authority or impartiality of the judiciary.

[2]   Article 19 of the ICCRP, para 2 provides that: 'Everyone shall have the right to freedom of expression: this right shall include freedom to seek, receive and impart information and ideas of all kinds, regardless of frontiers, either orally, in writing or in print, in the form of art or through any other media of his choice.'

[3]   Similar weaknesses in enforcement have inhibited development of protection under Article 19 of the UN Universal Declaration of Human Rights, 1948 which provides:
Everyone has the right to freedom of opinion and expression; this right includes freedom to hold opinions without interference and to seek, receive, and impart information and ideas through any media and regardless of frontiers.

[4]   See Malinverni, 'Freedom of Information in the European Convention on Human Rights and the International Covenant on Civil and Political Rights' (1983) 4 *Human Rights Law Journal* 443.

[5]   Article 13 of the American Convention on Human Rights, entitled 'Freedom of Thought and Expression', provides:
1.   Everyone has the right to freedom of thought and expression. This right includes freedom to seek, receive, and impart information and ideas of all kinds, regardless of frontiers, either orally, in writing, in print, in the form of art, or through any other medium of one's choice.
2.   The exercise of the right provided for in the foregoing paragraph shall not be subject to prior censorship but shall be subject to subsequent imposition of liability, which shall be expressly established by law to the extent necessary to ensure:
1.   respect for the rights or reputations of others; or
2.   the protection of national security, public order, or public health or morals.
3.   The right of expression may not be restricted by indirect methods or means, such as the abuse of government or private controls over newsprint, radio, broadcasting frequencies, or equipment used in the dissemination of information, or by any other means tending to impede the communication and circulation of ideas and opinions.
4.   Notwithstanding the provisions of paragraph 2 above, public entertainments may be subject by law to prior censorship for the sole purpose of regulating access to them for the moral protection of childhood and adolescence.
5.   Any propaganda for war and any advocacy of national, racial, or religious hatred that constitutes incitements to lawless violence or to any other similar action against any person or group of persons on any grounds including those of race, color, religion, language, or national origin shall be considered as offenses punishable by law.
The Convention was adopted by the nations of the Americas in 1969 and came into operation on 18 July 1978.

governments.[6] However, a right of access to official information has, in certain contexts, been recognised under the rubric of other human rights: in particular, the right to respect for private life protected by article 8 of the ECHR, the right to a fair trial protected by article 6 of the ECHR and the right to life protected by article 2 of the ECHR.

2. ARTICLE 8 OF THE ECHR

3– 002 **Strasbourg jurisprudence: introduction**

Whilst article 8 of the ECHR[7] does not provide for a generalised right of access to official information, in certain circumstances article 8 of the ECHR imposes on the State authorities a positive obligation to supply information of particular significance to an individual or group of individuals. Early case law focused on the right of access to personal data. In *Gaskin v United Kingdom*,[8] the Applicant successfully relied upon article 8 of the ECHR in challenging a local authority's refusal to supply personal data. The applicant had been fostered as a child. He sought access to his own records, which included contributions from a number of professionals, some of whom objected to disclosure. The European Court of Human Rights concluded that the right to access his file fell within the ambit of article 8 of the ECHR and that the local authority's blanket refusal to disclose the applicant's records unjustifiably interfered with his right.[9] In response to the judgment in *Gaskin*, the United Kingdom Government enacted legislation providing access to one's own 'personal data' which is now embodied within the Data

---

As at the date of writing, 24 of the 35 members of the Organization of American States are parties to the Convention.

[6] See §3– 013.

[7] Article 8 of the ECHR provides:
1.   Everyone has the right to respect for his private and family life, his home and his correspondence.
2.   There shall be no interference by a public authority with the exercise of this right except such as is in accordance with the law and is necessary in a democratic society in the interests of national security, public safety or the economic well-being of the country, for the prevention of disorder or crime, for the protection of health or morals, or for the protection of the rights and freedoms of others.

[8] (App no 10454/83) (1989) 12 EHRR 36, [1990] 1 FLR 167. Similarly *R (Rose) v Secretary of State for Health* [2002] EWHC 1593, [2002] 2 FLR 962, [2002] 3 FCR 731, [2002] UKHRR 1329, where the Claimant, who had been born by artificial insemination, sought judicial review of decisions of the Secretary of State and the Human Fertilisation and Embryology Authority which refused her requests for access to non identifying information and, where possible, identifying information in respect of anonymous sperm donors and for the establishment of a voluntary contact register. In partly granting the application, the Court held that respect for private and family life under art 8 required that persons should be able to establish details of their identity as human beings. This included establishing their origins and the opportunity to understand them. It also embraced their physical and social identity. The Court held that this included the right to obtain information concerning a biological parent who inevitably had contributed to the identity of the child.

[9] Contrast *Odièvre v France* (App no 42326/98) (2004) 38 EHRR 43, where the Grand Chamber concluded ten votes to seven that there was no positive obligation under art 8 to disclose to an applicant the identity of his or her mother who had, under domestic law, been permitted to give birth anonymously. The majority of the Grand Chamber held that, unlike in *Gaskin*, there were competing art 8 rights in issue: the child had a right to know where she came from, but the mother also had a right under art 8 to remain 'anonymous in order to protect her health by giving birth in appropriate medical conditions' (at [44]). The majority concluded that the balance struck between those competing interests by France was within the state's margin of appreciation.

Protection Act 1998. The existence of a right to appeal to an independent authority against the non-disclosure of certain records under the Data Protection Act 1998 has been held to be sufficient to discharge the State's positive obligation to supply personal information under article 8 of the ECHR.[10]

3 Strasbourg jurisprudence: medical records

The European Court takes a particular approach in relation to access to an individual's own medical records. In *KH v Slovakia*[11] the Court held that the right of effective access to information concerning a person's own health and reproductive status was a positive right protected by article 8. The positive obligation in such cases extended to making available to the data subjects physical copies of their data files.[12]

4 Strasbourg jurisprudence: police etc records

The ECHR has also considered a number of cases concerning the individual's right to access the information about him held secretly by police or security services. In *Leander v Sweden*,[13] the Court held that the interference with article 8 caused by the storing and releasing of information on a secret register was justified under article 8(2). The fact that information about the applicant on the register was released to military authorities but kept secret from the applicant could not by itself warrant the conclusion that the interference with not in accordance with article 8(2).[14] In *Rotaru v Romania*, however, the Grand Chamber held that the storing of information about the appellant by the Romanian secret police, and their use of it, coupled with a refusal to allow the applicant an opportunity to refute it, breached article 8, as the system employed by the Romanian secret police was not in accordance with law, nor did it have proper safeguards or supervision procedures.[15] The Grand Chamber held that public information (such as publication of political pamphlets or a criminal conviction) can fall within the scope of private life where it is systematically collected and stored in files held by authorities,

---

[10] See *MG v United Kingdom* (App no 39393/98) [2002] 3 FCR 289, (2003) 36 EHRR 3, (2003) 13 BHRC 179 (however, the European Court found a violation of art 8 of the ECHR from 1995 to 1 March 2000 prior to the coming into force of the DPA); *cf Martin v United Kingdom* (App no 27533/95) (1996) 21 EHRR CD112, where the European Commission of Human Rights declared inadmissible an application under art 8 of the ECHR for records relating to an intermittent period of mental health treatment for four years. The Court in *MG* distinguished *Martin* on the basis that, in *MG* the requested social service records contained the principal source of information for a significant part of the applicant's formative years, whereas the records in *Martin* were for a limited and intermittent period.

[11] (App no 32881/04) (2009) 49 EHRR 34. This concerned a group of women who, through their lawyers, tried to obtain copies of their medical files concerning their childbirths.

[12] At [47]-[56].

[13] (App no 9248/81) (1987) 9 EHRR 433.

[14] See also *Segerstedt-Wiberg v Sweden* (App no 62332/00) (2007) 44 EHRR 2 at [69]-[104], where the Court concluded that the state's refusal of full access to a national security police register when the state legitimately feared that the provision of such information might jeopardise the efficacy of a secret surveillance system designed to protect national security and combat terrorism was permissible under art 8; *Brinks v Netherlands* (App no 9940/04) (2005) 41 EHRR SE5, where the Court declared inadmissible a complaint by an academic for access to all information possibly held on him by the Dutch Secret Service.

[15] *Rotaru v Romania* (28341/95) (2000) 8 BHRC 449 at [45]-[46] and [59]-[62]. A concurring judgment, criticising the 'national security' justification for indiscriminate storing of information relating to individuals' private lives, was given by the President of the Grand Chamber and concurred in by six further judges.

particularly where the information concerns a person's distant past.[16]

3–005 Strasbourg jurisprudence: third-party information

The European Court has relied on article 8 to support access to information concerning a third party provided that there is a close relationship between the third party and the person requesting the information. In *TP and KM v United Kingdom*,[17] which concerned information relied upon by a local authority in taking the appellant's child into protective care, the Grand Chamber held that it was essential that such information be made available to the parent, even where it had not been directly requested. However, that right to information had to be curtailed where required by the interests of the child, and the decision as to what information should be released should be made by a court.

3–006 Strasbourg jurisprudence: public information

Whilst initially it was thought that article 8 of the ECHR was limited to granting a right to 'personal data', the European Court has adopted a broader interpretation and extended the right to access to include environmental information that has an impact on an individual's private life or home life. In *Guerra v Italy*,[18] the Court concluded that the state authorities were under a positive obligation to supply information about the dangers of a local chemical factory to local residents so that they could assess the extent of the risk and take steps to reduce that risk.[19] In *Roche v United Kingdom*[20] the Grand Chamber unanimously found a violation of article 8 arising from the Government's failure to provide an effective and accessible procedure enabling the applicant to have access to all relevant and appropriate information which would allow him to assess any risk to which he may have been exposed during his participation in tests at Porton Down.[21]

---

[16] At [43]. See also: *Copland v United Kingdom* (App no 62617/00) (2007) 45 EHRR 37 at [43]-[44]; *S v United Kingdom* (App nos 30562/04 and 30566/04) [2008] ECHR 1581; but compare *Chief Constable of Humberside Police & ors v IC and SSHD* [2009] EWCA 1079, where the Court of Appeal was equivocal about whether art 8 was applicable to the retention on the Police National Computer of old criminal convictions (at [50] and [78]-[81]). The Information Tribunal had explicitly held that processing included retention of information and that retention would breach art 8(1) unless it could be justified: *Chief Constable of Humberside and ors v IC*, IT, 21 July 2008 at [173]-[180].

[17] *TP and KM v United Kingdom* (App no 28945/95) (2001) 34 EHRR 42 at [80]-[82].

[18] *Guerra v Italy* (App no 14967/89) (1998) 26 EHRR 357, 4 BHRC 63 at [56]-[60].

[19] See also: *Lopez Ostra v Spain* (App no 16798/90) (1995) 20 EHRR 277; *McGinley and Egan v United Kingdom* (App nos 21825/93 and 23414/94) (1999) 27 EHRR 1, (1999) 4 BHRC 421, (1998) 42 BMLR 123, where the court concluded, by a majority of five to four that although there was a positive obligation pursuant to art 8 of the ECHR to supply information about nuclear tests at Christmas Island to individuals present in the area, this obligation was discharged in relation to the applicants by r 6 of the Pensions Appeals Tribunals (Scotland) Rules); *Taskin v Turkey* (App no 46117/99) (2006) 42 EHRR 50, where the court held that there was a violation of art 8 in relation to lack of information relating to operation of a goldmine using cyanide extraction methods that allegedly threatened the health of local residents.

[20] *Roche v United Kingdom* (App no 32555/96) (2006) 42 EHRR 30.

[21] At [164], the Grand Chamber distinguished the earlier decision in *McGinley and Egan v United Kingdom* on the basis that Mr McGinley and Mr Egan's search for documents was 'inextricably bound up with their domestic applications for pensions', whereas Mr Roche had made numerous attempts to obtain the relevant records independently of any litigation.

7   Domestic jurisprudence: personal information

Article 8 of the ECHR has been relied upon in a number of cases relating to private information although, so far, its impact has been limited. In *Linda Gunn-Russo v Nugent Care Society and The Secretary of State for Health*[22] the Claimant sought disclosure of her adoption records held by a voluntary adoption agency. The High Court concluded that in that context article 8 of the ECHR added nothing to the common law. The Court rejected the claimant's argument, based on *Gaskin*, that the voluntary adoption agency could not have the last word and there must be some form of appeal to an independent authority: unlike *Gaskin* the information sought included private information relating to others, namely the adoptive family rather than just the claimant. However, the courts have permitted access to third party information in the context of guardianship proceedings and care proceedings.[23]

8   Domestic jurisprudence: public information

Article 8 was deployed to support a right to public information in *R (Furness) v Environment Agency*,[24] where the claimants cited *Guerra* in relation to an alleged failure to protect their right to information affecting their homes. The claimants had been challenging the grant of an authorisation for incineration of municipal waste to take place at an industrial estate near their homes. Although the challenge failed,[25] the court appeared to accept that article 8 could require the provision of information if there were a substantial threat to health or property. The *Guerra/Roche* line of cases is yet to be properly considered by the Tribunal.[26]

9   Domestic jurisprudence: police etc information

Article 8 has also been relied on in relation to access to information held by the Security Service. In *Baker v SSHD*,[27] the appellant challenged the Security Service's refusal to confirm or deny (NCND) that it kept records about him, and the SSHD's certificate purporting to exempt the Security Service from the provisions of the Part II DPA 1998. The Information Tribunal held that article 8 was engaged, as NCND removed one of the preconditions of action by the data subject: knowledge as to whether his data was held.[28] However, NCND was justifiable in appropriate cases. The Tribunal went on to quash the certificate as it was found to be wider than necessary to protect national security.

---

[22]   [2001] EWHC (Admin) 56, [2002] 1 FLR 1, [2001] UKHRR 1320.

[23]   See also *R (Ann S) v Plymouth City Council and C* [2002] EWCA Civ 388, [2002] 1 WLR 2583, [2002] 1 FLR 1177, which concerned the disclosure to the appellant's mother and nearest relative of certain information contained in social service files concerning her adult but mentally incapacitated son, C. The Court of Appeal concluded, relying in part on art 8 that disclosure was appropriate. And similarly *Re B (Disclosure to other Parties)* [2001] 2 FLR 1017, [2002] 2 FCR 32 and *Re R (a child) (disclosure)* [2004] EWHC 2085, which concerned disclosure of documents in care proceedings.

[24]   *R (Furness) v Environment Agency* [2001] EWHC (Admin) 1058, [2002] Env LR 26.

[25]   At [25]-[27].

[26]   See *Civil Aviation Authority v Information Commissioner and Kirkaldie*, IT, 22 January 2010. Although art 10 was cited in *Hoyte v IC and CAA*, IT, 5 March 2008 at [90]-[95], the *Guerra* line of cases was not relied upon.

[27]   *Baker v SSHD* [2001] UKHRR 1275.

[28]   At [67]. See also *Gosling v SSHD*, Data Protection Tribunal, 1 August 2003 and *Hitchens v SSHD*, Data Protection Tribunal, 4 August 2003, which challenged the use of NCND permitted by the revised certificate.

3.   ARTICLE 10 OF THE ECHR

3– 010   Early Strasbourg jurisprudence

Article 10 of the ECHR expressly includes the right to receive information. Initially, it appeared that the right would be interpreted broadly to include some form of right of access to information held by States. In *X v Federal Republic Germany*[29] the European Commission on Human Rights stated:

> it follows from the context in which the right to receive information is mentioned…that it envisages first of all access to general sources of information…the right to receive information may under certain circumstances include a right of access by the interested person to documents which although not generally accessible are of particular importance.[30]

Subsequent case law from the European Court on Human Rights indicated that article 10 of the ECHR did not form the basis of a generalised right of access to information in circumstances where there was no 'willing speaker'. In *Leander v Sweden*[31] the European Court of Human Rights held, in relation to the State's refusal to reveal secret information:

> [T]he right to freedom to receive information basically prohibits a Government from restricting a person from receiving information that others wish or may be willing to impart to him. Article 10 does not, in circumstances such as the present case, confer on the individual a right of access to a register containing information on his personal position, nor does it embody an obligation on the Government to impart such information to the individual.[32]

A similar approach was adopted in *Gaskin v United Kingdom*[33] where the applicant complained that he had been refused access to a case record relating to him created when he was a minor and held by a local authority. The Court found that there was no violation of article 10 of the ECHR.[34] In both *Leander* and *Gaskin*, the information sought related to a specific individual and its disclosure could not be said to be in the public interest.

3– 011   Later Strasbourg jurisprudence

The disclosure of information that was in the public interest was considered in *Guerra v Italy*,[35] which concerned disclosure of information relating to the dangers of a chemical factory. The residents contended that the authorities were obliged under inter alia article 10 of the ECHR

---

[29]   *X v Federal Republic Germany* (App no 8383/78) (1979) 17 DR 227.

[30]   At 228–229.

[31]   (App no 9248/81) (1987) 9 EHRR 433.

[32]   At [74]. Cited with approval in *Brown v Executors of HM Queen Elizabeth* [2007] EWHC 1607 (Fam) at [68].

[33]   (1989) 12 EHRR 36, [1990] 1 FLR 167.

[34]   However, the European Court concluded that the applicant was entitled to the information sought under art 8 of the ECHR: see §3– 002.

[35]   (App no 14967/89) (1998) 26 EHRR 357, 4 BHRC 63. Similarly: *Oneryildiz v Turkey* (App no 48939/99) (2004) 39 EHRR 12 at [108]. Contrast *R (Furness) v Environment Agency* [2001] EWHC (Admin) 1058, [2002] Env LR 26, [2002] EHLR 8.

to inform them about the hazards of the activity undertaken at the factories and about major accident procedures. The European Commission of Human Rights held that article 10 of the ECHR not only placed states under an obligation to make environmental information accessible to the public, but also under a positive obligation to collect, process and disseminate information which, by its very nature, is not directly accessible and which cannot be known to the public unless the authorities act accordingly. However, the European Court refused to adopt the same approach and, reiterating its position previously expressed in *Leander*, ruled that article 10 of the ECHR was not applicable.[36] The Court categorically stated that the right to receive information referred to in article 10 of the ECHR 'cannot be construed as imposing on a State, in circumstances such as those of the present case, positive obligations to collect and disseminate information of its own motion'.[37] The Court distinguished the situation in *Guerra* from cases concerning the right to receive information as a corollary of the function of the press to impart information and ideas on matters of public interest.[38]

2 The emerging Strasbourg jurisprudence

There are indications of a broadening of the European Court's approach to the right to receive information. In *Sdruženi Jihočeské Matky v Czech Republic*,[39] the Court recognised that the refusal by the Czech authorities to provide the applicant ecological NGO with access to documents regarding a nuclear power station amounted to an interference with the right to receive information under art 10. After referring to its traditional case law, including *Leander*, *Guerra* and *Roche* and commenting that it was 'difficult to derive from [art 10] a general right to access to data and documents of an administrative character,' the Court went on to recognise that the particular refusal in issue an interference with the applicant's right to receive information and that it was one that had to be justified under article 10(2).[40] The significance of *Matky* was recognised in *Társasága Szabadságjogokért (Hungarian Civil Liberties Union) v Hungary*,[41] where it cited the *Matky* decision as indicative of a recent advance towards 'a broader interpretation of the notion of "freedom to receive information" … and thereby towards the recognition of a right

---

[36] However, again, the European Court found a violation under art 8 ECHR, see §3– 006.

[37] At [53]. Although the concurring opinion of the Judge, joined by five others, indicated that in certain circumstances there may be a positive obligation to make available to the public information which by its nature could not otherwise come to the attention of the public. See also the Grand Chamber decision in *Roche v United Kingdom* (App no 32555/96) (2006) 42 EHRR 30, 20 BHRC 99 where the Grand Chamber, although finding a violation of art 8 ECHR, unanimously concluded (at [172]) that there was no violation of art 10.

[38] At [53], citing *Observer and Guardian v United Kingdom* (App no 13585/88) (1992) 14 EHRR 153 (the 'Spycatcher' case) and *Thorgeirson v Iceland* (App no 13778/88) (1992) ECHR 51. See also *Romanenko v Russia*, ECHR, 8 October 2009 at [42] and *Eerikäinen v Finland*, ECHR, 10 February 2009 at [68].

[39] *Sdruženi Jihočeské Matky v Czech Republic* (App no 19101/03) ECHR 10 July 2006 (only available in French).

[40] The Court held the refusal was justified in the interests of protecting the rights of others (industrial secrets), national security (risk of terrorist attacks) and public health. The Court also held that the request for technical information about the nuclear power station did not reflect a matter of public interest. The application was therefore declared inadmissible. The Court's reasoning is not easy to discern. Two elements appear to have been important: the appellant NGO needed the information in order to disseminate it as part of its public role in debating the desirability of the nuclear power station; and the information was of the type that could usually be accessed through the Czech law on freedom of information (although the request for access had failed).

[41] *Társasága Szabadságjogokért (Hungarian Civil Liberties Union) v Hungary* (App no 37374/05) ECHR 14 April 2009.

of access to information.'[42] *Társasága* concerned the refusal to allow the applicant NGO access to the text of a constitutional complaint challenging amendments to drug-related offences in the Criminal Code. The applicant was active in the field of drug policy. The Court held that, in seeking to publicise the information gathered from the constitutional complaint, the applicant's activities amounted to an essential element of informed public debate on a matter of public importance. The applicant could therefore be characterised, like the press, as a social 'watchdog', and the Constitutional Court's refusal to provide information in which it had a monopoly amounted to a form of censorship which interfered with article 10(1).[43] The Court went on to find that the interference was not justified under article 10(2).[44] The above authorities appear to indicate a move by the ECHR towards recognising that art 10 confers a right of access to information which, in the public interest, should be disseminated. This is particularly significant for civil society organisations and the media, whose 'social watchdog' role has been endorsed by the Court. This is particularly significant for requests made under FOIA where the public authority invokes non-absolute exemptions, as it may colour the determination of the public interest in disclosure.

3–013 **American Convention on Human Rights**
The Strasbourg jurisprudence can be contrasted with that of the Inter-American Court of Human Rights which has recently concluded that article 13 of the Convention[45] includes a right of access to information. The Inter-American Commission in *Claude Reyes v Chile*[46] was of the view that the free expression rights guaranteed by Article 13 included a general right to access state-held information and a corresponding obligation for states to ensure that the information is available. The information sought in *Claude Reyes* concerned a major logging project. The Commission's view was affirmed by the American Court of Human Rights on 11 October 2006. The Court stated:

> With respect to the facts of the present case, the Court concludes that article 13 of the Convention, which specifically establishes the rights to "seek" and "receive" information protects the right of all persons to request access to information held by the State, with the exceptions permitted by the restrictions regime of the Convention. As a result, this article supports the right of persons to receive such information and the positive obligation on the State to supply it, so that the person may have access to the information or receive a reasoned response when, on grounds permitted by the Convention, the State may limit access to it in the specific case. The said information should be provided without a need to demonstrate a direct interest in obtaining it, or a personal interest, except in cases where a legitimate restriction applies. Disclosure to one person in turn permits it [the information] to circulate in society in such a way that it can be known, obtained and evaluated. In this way, the right to freedom of thought and of expression contemplates protection of the right of access to information under State control.[47]

---

[42] At [35].

[43] At [26]-[28].

[44] At [36]. In so doing the Court noted that the information sought by the applicant was 'ready and available' and did not require the collection of any data by the government, unlike the situation in *Guerra*.

[45] The provisions of art 13 of the American Convention on Human Rights are set out at n 5.

[46] Inter-American Commission on Human Rights, Report 31/05, Case 12.108.

[47] At [77].

The Court ordered Chile to provide the information requested about the logging project or adopt a reasoned decision as to why it was not providing it.[48] The Court further required the State to train public officials on the right of access to information.[49] It remains to be seen whether *Claude Reyes v Chile* has any influence on the European Court of Human Rights' thinking on the issue.[50] It is possible that the Strasbourg Court may seek to distinguish such case law on the basis that article 13 of the Inter-American Convention on Human Rights, unlike article 10 of the ECHR, includes the right to 'seek information' rather than merely receive and impart information.

4   Earlier domestic jurisprudence

There has been little domestic case law successfully relying on article 10 of the ECHR to found an entitlement to information held by a public authority. The early cases considered by the English Courts related to government inquiries. In *R (Wagstaff) v Secretary of State for Health*[51] the claimant successfully relied upon article 10 to require that the inquiry into Dr Shipman's activities be held in public. The *Wagstaff* decision was a high watermark, not least because it pre-dated the coming into force of the Human Rights Act 1998. Later cases concerning inquiries have been more reluctant to apply article 10. In *Persey v Secretary of State for Environment, Food and Rural Affairs*,[52] which concerned the inquiry into the outbreak of foot and mouth disease, the High Court held that article 10 was not engaged by a decision to hold a closed public inquiry.[53] The Court stated that article 10 does not impose a positive obligation on government to provide, in addition to existing means of communication, 'an open forum to achieve the yet wider dissemination of views.'[54] The Court was critical of the analysis of article 10 in *Wagstaff*, noting that the decision was not supported by the Strasbourg authorities.[55]

---

[48]   At [157]–[158].

[49]   At [164].

[50]   Reyes has been cited once by the Court, in *Stoll v Switzerland* (App no 69698/01) ECHR 10 December 2007 (Grand Chamber), but not in the context of the right to receive information. The case concerned the criminal prosecution of a journalist who published a leaked confidential memo sent from the Swiss Ambassador to the US head of a team conducting highly sensitive negotiations about repatriation of unclaimed assets held in Swiss banks by those presumed killed during the Holocaust. The Grand Chamber relied on *Reyes* in finding that press freedom assumes even greater importance in circumstances in which state activities and decisions escape democratic or judicial scrutiny on account of their confidential or secret nature (at [111]). However, the Court held that the prosecution was justified because the sensationalist and truncated nature of the news report was likely to mislead the public.

[51]   [2001] 1 WLR 292, [2000] HRLR 646, [2000] UKHRR 875.

[52]   [2002] EWHC 371, [2003] QB 794.

[53]   See also *R (Howard) v Secretary of State for Health* [2002] EWHC 396, [2003] QB 803, which held that art 10 was not engaged in a decision not to hold a public inquiry into circumstances surrounding the serious misbehaviour of a doctor.

[54]   At [53]. Similarly, in *R (Pelling) v Bow County Court (No 2)* [2001] UKHRR 165, [2001] ACD 1 (at [36]), the Divisional Court, after quoting from *Guerra v Italy* said: 'The point does not arise in this case, but it seems to me very pertinent that the Strasbourg court does not recognise an absolute right to receive information in the absence of willingness on the part of those holding that information to give it to him. …If the state makes arrangements to prevent that information flowing it does not, in my judgment, by that step alone, involve itself in any breach of Article 10.'

[55]   At [48]-[54].

Similar criticism was voiced in *R (Howard) v Secretary of State for Health*,[56] with Scott Baker J noting that article 10 'does not confer a right on individuals to receive information that others are not willing to impart.'[57] This line of authority may need to be adapted in light of the *Hungarian Civil Liberties Union* case[58] which found that article 10 does provide a limited right of access to information, provided that its dissemination is required by an established public interest.

3–015   Later domestic jurisprudence

Strasbourg jurisprudence on article 10 has so far not featured much in support of the right of access conferred by s 1(1) of the Freedom of Information Act 2000. In *BBC v Sugar*,[59] the first appeal to the High Court directly concerning the Act, the Court said:

> The FOIA is, in its way, an Act of an entirely new kind. However, it does have at least some kinship with aspects of the special purposes and exceptions contained in the Data Protection Act 1998; and clearly it must have major underpinning by reference to the concepts enshrined in Article 10 of the European Convention on Human Rights with regard to the freedom to receive and impart information: although it was rightly acknowledged before me that the FOIA goes very much further than Article 10 would of itself require.

The desirability for the press and other media to have access to information in order to foster legitimate and informed public debate was recognised by the High Court in *Stone v South East Coast Strategic Health Authority*.[60] However, the weight that should be given to this principle in the context of FOIA requests is yet to be properly considered. In *Guardian Newspapers Limited v IC and Chief Constable of Avon and Somerset Police*,[61] which concerned the refusal of a request for copies of police investigation files from 1978-79 relating to the criminal trial of the former leader of the Liberal Party, the appellant submitted that the balance of public interest favoured disclosure, relying on Article 10 as showing that there was a particular interest in disclosure and publication where political issues, the administration of justice or public figures are involved. That argument does not appear to have found favour with the Tribunal, as it was not included in the list of findings which bore on the weighing of competing interests.

4.   OTHER ARTICLES OF THE ECHR

3–016   Other articles of the ECHR

Article 6 of ECHR, which concerns the right to a fair trial, has been relied upon to require

---

[56]   [2002] EWHC 396, [2003] QB 803 at [99]-[112].

[57]   In *Higher Education Funding Council for England v Information Commissioner & anor*, IT, 13 January 2010 at [28], the Information Tribunal considered itself bound by *Howard*.

[58]   See §§3– 012 above.

[59]   *BBC v Sugar* [2007] EWHC 905 (Admin), [2007] 1 WLR 2583 at [15].

[60]   *Stone v South East Coast Strategic Health Authority* [2006] EWHC 1668 (Admin) at [51].

[61]   *Guardian Newspapers Limited v IC and Chief Constable of Avon and Somerset Police*, IT, 5 April 2007 at [22].

disclosure of documents that may be relevant to litigation.[62] Article 5(4) of the ECHR which concerns the right of access to a court to test the lawfulness of detention includes the right to access documents and information.[63] Article 2 of the ECHR, which protects the right to life may in certain circumstances require provision of information relating to matters concerning health and safety.[64] Article 2 of the ECHR also imposes positive obligations on states to establish effective mechanisms to investigate deaths in certain situations.[65]

5. IMPACT OF THE HUMAN RIGHTS ACT 1998

.7 Introduction

In introducing the second reading of the Freedom of Information Bill in the House of Commons, Jack Straw (the then Home Secretary), acknowledged that the Bill and the Human Rights Act 1998 were interrelated. He stated:

> The 1998 Act sets out the European Convention's statement of basic rights. Some of those rights are absolute, such as that provided in Article 3, guaranteeing freedom from torture or degrading treatment. The rights which we have had to wrestle in the Freedom of Information Bill are not absolutes, but have to be balanced one with another. Article 10 gives a right to freedom of expression, but that has to be set against Article 8 on the right to respect for a private life. We have therefore sought in the Bill to secure a balance between the right to information needed for the proper exercise of freedom of expression and the directly conflicting right of individuals to protection of information about themselves; the rights that institutions, including commercial companies should have to proper confidentiality; and the need for any organisation, including the Government, to be able to formulate its collective policies in private.[66]

All the bodies that are subject to the duties imposed by s 1 of the Freedom of Information Act

---

[62] See *KH v Slovakia* (2009) 49 EHRR 34, 27 BHRC 373 at [59]-[69] (disclosure of medical records prior to institution of civil proceedings); *McGinley and Egan v United Kingdom* (App nos 21825/93 and 23414/94) (1999) 27 EHRR 1, (1999) 4 BHRC 421, (1998) 42 BMLR 123 (disclosure of documents relating to nuclear tests for the purposes of litigation before the Pensions Appeals Tribunal. art 6(1) of the ECHR claim rejected as no documents detailing the fact that they had been exposed to dangerous levels of radiation existed). Article 6 of the ECHR was also invoked before the (App no 14967/89) European Court of Human Rights in *Lopez Ostra v Spain* (App no 16798/90) (1995) 20 EHRR 277 and *Guerra v Italy* (1998) 26 EHRR 357, 4 BHRC 63, [1998] HRCD 277. See also *Edwards v United Kingdom* (App no 13071/87) (1992) 15 EHRR 417 (defendants in criminal cases have the right to disclosure of information relevant to their trial). Cf Case C-450/06 *Varec v Belgium* [2008] 2 CMLR 24 at [43]-[55] in the context of access to documents under EU law in litigation to review the award of contracts. For consideration by domestic courts see: *Re B (Disclosure to other Parties)* [2001] 2 FLR 1017, [2002] 2 FCR 32, [2001] Fam Law 798; *R (Ann S) v Plymouth City Council and C* [2002] EWCA Civ 388, [2002] 1 WLR 2583, [2002] 1 FLR 1177; *Roberts v Nottingham Healthcare NHS Trust*, IT, 1 August 2008 at [19]-[25].

[63] See *Weeks v United Kingdom* (App no 9787/82) (1987) 10 EHRR 293; *Roberts v Nottingham Healthcare NHS Trust*, IT, 1 August 2008 at [19].

[64] See *Osman v United Kingdom* (2000) 29 EHRR 245, [1999] 1 FLR 193, (1999) 11 Admin LR 200. See also *Oneryildiz v Turkey* (App no 48939/99) [2004] 39 EHRR 12 where the Court found that the Government had violated art 2 of the Convention because it did not provide inhabitants living near an unsafe rubbish tip with information 'enabling them to assess the risks they might run as a result of the choices they had made'. In this context there is likely to be an overlap with art 8 of the ECHR.

[65] See *R v SSHD, ex p Amin* [2003] UKHL 5, [2004] 1 AC 653, [2003] 4 All ER 1264, [2004] HRLR 3, [2004] UKHRR 75.

[66] Hansard HC cols 719–720 (7 December 1999).

2000 are likely to be public authorities within the meaning of s 6 of the Human Rights Act 1998. Equally, the bodies that are responsible for enforcing the Freedom of Information Act 2000, including the Information Commissioner, the First-Tier Tribunal, the Upper Tribunal and the Courts, are also public authorities within the meaning of s 6 of the Human Rights Act 1998. All such bodies are required to act compatibly with the provisions of the European Convention of Human Rights. In most cases under the Freedom of Information Act 2000, no issues will arise under the European Convention of Human Rights. However, in certain cases the European Convention of Human Rights may have an impact. Such an impact is likely to occur in two areas: (a) the information sought engages a substantive provision of the Convention; (b) Article 6 of the ECHR may be relevant to the fairness of a hearing before the Information Commissioner, the First-Tier Tribunal, the Upper Tribunal or the Courts.

3–018   The Human Rights Act 1998: substantive impact

Public authorities holding information and equally the Information Commissioner and the Tribunals have a duty, pursuant to s 3 of the Human Rights Act 1998, to interpret the Freedom of Information Act 2000 so far as possible in a way that is compatible with the provisions of the European Convention on Human Rights incorporated into domestic law by the Human Rights Act 1998. In cases concerning personal information, and environmental information that may have an impact on an individual's private or home life, article 8 of the ECHR may well be of some relevance to the interpretation of the provisions of the Freedom of Information Act 2000. Article 2 will be relevant to investigations of deaths in custody. If a right under the European Convention of human rights is engaged this may require the public authority, the Commissioner or Tribunal to adopt a restrictive approach to the exemptions permitting the withholding of the information sought or the public interest balancing exercise (in relation to qualified exemptions). For example, where the information sought relates to environmental issues that could have an impact on the applicant's health or well being, the public authority holding the information is likely to be required to consider the impact of article 8 of the ECHR when deciding whether a particular exception applies and, if it is a qualified exemption, whether the public interest favours disclosure. Equally, if the public authority refuses disclosure and the applicant appeals to the Information Commissioner or the Tribunals, these bodies will also have to have regard to the right of the applicant under article 8 of the ECHR to such information when interpreting the scope of exceptions and whether the public interest is in favour of disclosure. The European Convention may also be invoked in support of any argument that the public interest favours withholding the information sought. Indeed, it is in this context that the European Convention on Human Rights has been invoked most often before the Tribunals. Respondents seeking to resist disclosure of information that is protected by legal professional privilege[67] and confidentiality[68] have invoked the European Convention is support of their arguments that the material sought should not be disclosed.

---

[67]   See, eg *Bellamy v Information Commissioner and DTI*, IT, 4 April 2006 at [11]; *Kitchener v Information Commissioner*, IT, 20 December 2006 at [16]–[17].

[68]   See, eg *Bustin v Information Commissioner*, IT, 16 December 2005 at [35].

9 The Human Rights Act 1998 and procedural fairness before the First-Tier Tribunal and other bodies

Article 6(1) of the ECHR[69] which protects the right to a fair trial applies to the determination of an individual's civil rights and obligations. The concept of 'civil rights and obligations' has been given an autonomous meaning under the Convention. It is likely that in the majority of cases, the right to access information will not give rise to a 'civil right or obligation' so as to engage article 6 of the ECHR. The European Commission of Human Rights in *Barry v France*[70] rejected an argument that article 6 of the ECHR applied to a rejection of an application for access to information relating to steps being taken by the French Foreign Ministry to inquire about and support political prisoners. Equally, the Commission dismissed a similar application in relation to a rejection of a request by an individual who was seeking access to redacted parts of his police file which disclosed the identity of members of the security services.[71] In both cases, the Commission dismissed the applications because the information sought could not be considered personal to the applicant. Clearly applications under the Data Protection Act 1998 are likely to engage article 6 of the ECHR because the information sought is, by definition, of a personal nature.[72] Of course, hearings before the First-Tier and Upper Tribunals will be subject to the domestic law requirements of natural justice which is concerned with similar issues to article 6 of the ECHR.[73]

---

[69] Article 6(1) of the ECHR provides:

> In the determination of his civil rights and obligations or of any criminal charge against him, everyone is entitled to a fair and public hearing within a reasonable time by an independent and impartial tribunal established by law. Judgment shall be pronounced publicly but the press and public may be excluded from all or part of the trial in the interests of morals, public order or national security in a democratic society, where the interests of juveniles or the protection of the private life of the parties so require, or to the extent strictly necessary in the opinion of the court in special circumstances where publicity would prejudice the interests of justice.

[70] *Barry v France* (App no 14497/89) 14 October 1991. But see now: *Syndicat CFDT des Etablissements et Arsenaux du Val-de-Marne and Vesque v France* (App no 11678/85) 7 December 1987; *Loiseau v France* (App No 46809/99) ECHR 18 November 2003; *Micallef v Malta* (App no 17056/06) ECHR 15 January 2008 at [39].

[71] See *Schaller Volpi v Switzerland* (App no 25147/94) 84 DR 106.

[72] See ch 5 on access to personal information.

[73] In *BBC v Sugar* [2007] EWHC 905 (Admin), [2007] 1 WLR 2583 at [45] the Court rejected an argument that art 6 was offended by the appeal system under the FOIA. This was upheld by the Court of Appeal ([2008] EWCA Civ 191, [2008] 1 WLR 2289 at [38]-[47]. The point was not appealed to the House of Lords: [2009] UKHL 9. [2009] 1 WLR 430.

CHAPTER 4
Rights of Access under European Union Law

1. BACKGROUND

)1   Introduction

The institutions of the European Union have neither a strong nor a lengthy tradition of providing access to documents or information held by them. They are thus closer to the British model of government, with a predisposition towards secrecy and non-disclosure,[1] than to the openness long practised by the Scandinavian members of the EU. In the last 10 years, however, there has been a considerable opening up by the EU institutions. This chapter focuses on the measures concerning access to documents held by and relating to the operation of EU institutions. This will include a discussion of the Code of Practice, Decisions 93/731 and 94/90 and the case law interpreting these decisions. Whilst the Code of Practice and decisions have now been repealed and replaced by Regulation 1049/2001, the case law under the earlier regime gives some indication as to how the European Court of First Instance and the Court of Justice will interpret Regulation 1049/2001.

02   The Maastricht Treaty

The first express recognition of the importance of transparency and openness appeared in Declaration No 17 annexed to the Final Act of the Treaty of the European Union (the Maastricht Treaty), which stated:

> The Conference considers that transparency of the decision-making process strengthens the democratic nature of the institutions and the public's confidence in the administration. The Conference accordingly recommends that the Commission submit to the Council no later than 1993, a report on measures to improve the public access to the information available to the institutions.[2]

This stated commitment to openness was reiterated by the European Council in their declaration issued at the conclusion of the Birmingham meeting on 16 October 1992 and reaffirmed by the European Council at Edinburgh in December 1992.

03   Article 255 of the Treaty of Amsterdam

The right of access to documents has now been recognised in the Treaty of Amsterdam. Article 255 (formerly article 191a) provides:[3]

1.   Any citizen of the Union, and any natural or legal person residing or having its registered office in a Member State, shall have a right of access to European Parliament, Council and Commission documents subject to the principles and conditions to be defined in accordance with paragraphs 2 and 3.

2.   General principles and limits on grounds of public or private interest governing this right of access to documents shall be determined by the Council, acting in accordance

---

[1]   See generally, V Deckmyn and I Thompson (eds), *Openness and Transparency in the European Union* (Maastricht, European Institute of Public Administration, 1998).

[2]   Declaration No 17 annexed to the Final Act of the Treaty of the European Union signed at Maastricht on 7 February 1992.

with the procedure referred to in Article 251 within two years of the entry into force of the Treaty of Amsterdam.

3. Each institution referred to above shall elaborate in its own Rules of Procedure specific provisions regarding access to its documents.[4]

4– 004   The European Charter of Fundamental Rights of The European Union

Article 42 of the Charter of Fundamental Rights replicates the first sentence of article 255 of the Treaty of Amsterdam and provides:

> Any citizen of the Union, and any natural or legal person residing or having its registered office in a Member State, has a right of access to European Parliament, Council and Commission documents.

The Lisbon Treaty, which came into effect on 1 December 2009, gives legal force to the Charter of Fundamental Rights,[5] but Article 42 merely rehearses rights already in existence.

4– 005   Environmental Information

On 25 June 1998, the UN Economic Commission for Europe (UNECE), at its Fourth Ministerial Conference in the 'Environment for Europe' process, adopted a Convention on Access to Information, Public Participation in Decision-Making and Access to Justice on Environmental Matters. This has become known as the 'Aarhus Convention'. The Convention entered into force on 30 October 2001. The European Community (as well as the UK) is a signatory to the Aarhus Convention. The Aarhus Convention established a number of rights of the public (citizens and their associations) with respect to the environment. It contains three broad themes or 'pillars': access to information, public participation, and access to justice.[6] On 28 January 2003 the European Parliament and the Council of the European Union adopted Directive 2003/4/EC 'on public access to environmental information'.[7] This required Member States to enact national legislation giving effect to the Directive, and thereby implement the first pillar of the Aarhus Convention. In the United Kingdom, this was done through the Environmental Information Regulations 2004 and the Environmental Information (Scotland) Regulations 2004. These regulations are considered in detail in Chapter 6. The European Community itself ratified the Aarhus Convention on 17 February 2005. On 26 September 2006 the European Parliament and Council adopted Regulation 1367/2006: this is known as the 'Aarhus Regulation'. The regulation came into effect on 28 June 2007. In effect, the Aarhus Regulation applies Directive 2003/4/EC to all institutions, bodies, offices and

---

[4] The Treaty of Amsterdam came into force on 21 May 1999, so that the regulation had to be adopted by 1 May 2001.

[5] Note the Protocol to the Lisbon Treaty on the application of the Charter of Fundamental Rights of the European Union to Poland and to the United Kingdom, which states that the Charter does not extend the ability of the Court of Justice of the EU, or any court or tribunal of Poland or the United Kingdom, to find that laws, regulations or administrative provisions, practices or actions of Poland or the United Kingdom are inconsistent with the fundamental rights, freedoms and principles that it reaffirms.

[6] Thus art 1 of the Aarhus Convention provides 'In order to contribute to the protection of the right of every person of present and future generations to live in an environment adequate to his or her health and well-being, each Party shall guarantee the rights of access to information, public participation in decision-making, and access to justice in environmental matters in accordance with the provisions of this Convention.'

[7] The Directive entered into force on 14 February 2003. Article 10 of the Directive obliges the Member States of the European Union to have their legislation in place at the latest by 14 February 2004.

agencies established by, or on the basis of, the EC Treaty.[8] Thus, in relation to 'environmental information' held by institutions, bodies, offices and agencies established by, or on the basis of, the EC Treaty, a person has a free-standing right of access to this information under the Aarhus Regulation. The discussion in Chapter 6, although directed to public authorities in the United Kingdom, can accordingly be applied to environmental information held by such institutions, bodies, offices and agencies.

2. THE CODE OF PRACTICE AND DECISIONS 93/731 AND 94/90

6 General principles

The commitment to openness and transparency expressed in Declaration No 17 annexed to the Maastricht Treaty was realised on 6 December 1993 when, with the approval of both the Commission and the Council, a Code of Conduct concerning public access to Council and Commission documents was published.[9] The Council and Commission subsequently adopted this Code of Conduct by decision.[10] The Code of Conduct followed the conventional template for access legislation: a universal right of access, immediately qualified by exceptions, enforceable with a right of review. 'Document' was defined widely as including 'any written text, whatever its medium, which contains existing data and is held by the Council or the Commission.'[11] However:

> [w]here the requested document was written by a natural or legal person, a Member State, another Community institution or body, or any other national or international body, the application must not be sent to the Council [or Commission][12] but direct to the author.[13]

Thus, the right of access to documents was limited to documents produced by the Council or Commission. The Commission and Council were obliged to inform applicants within one month whether the application was approved or rejected. The Code of Practice provided that a failure to reply within the period amounted to a refusal.[14] There was an obligation, if the request was refused, to give reasons for the refusal and set out further avenues of redress available, namely a complaint to the ombudsman under article 195 and judicial proceedings under article 230.[15]

---

[8]   The coverage of the Aarhus Regulation is thus broader than Regulation 1049/2001. That regulation applies only to the European Parliament, the Council and the Commission and, by extension, to the Community Agencies.

[9]   93/730/EC [1993] OJ L340/41.

[10] The Council adopted the Code of Conduct by Decision 93/731 on 20 December 1993 (93/731/EC, [1993] OJ L340/43). The Decision came into force on 1 January 1994. The Commission, on 8 February 1994, adopted Decision 94/90 which under art 1 formally adopted the Code of Conduct. Decisions 93/731 and 94/90 have now been repealed and replaced by Regulation No 1049/2001 discussed at §§4–010 to 4–028.

[11] See Code of Conduct, General Principles 93/730 Council Decision 93/731/EC art 1(2).

[12] See Code of Conduct.

[13] Decision 93/731/EC art 2(2).

[14] Decision 93/731/EC art 7(1).

[15] Decision 93/731/EC art 7(3).

4–007 **Exceptions**

There were two types of exception to the general right of access. First, mandatory exceptions which provided that access to the document should not be granted where its disclosure could undermine:

    (1)   the protection of the public interest (public security, international relations, monetary stability, court proceedings, inspections and investigations);

    (2)   the protection of the individual and privacy;

    (3)   the protection of commercial and industrial secrecy;

    (4)   the protection of the Community's financial interests;

    (5)   the protection of confidentiality as requested by the natural or legal person who supplied any of the information contained in the document or as required by the legislation of the Member State which supplied any of that information.[16]

Secondly, a discretionary exception that provided that access to a Council or Commission document might be refused 'in order to protect the confidentiality of the Council's proceedings.'[17]

4–008 **Legal basis, ambit and extension of the right to access to other European bodies**

The Netherlands challenged the legal basis of the Decision permitting access to documents held by the Council.[18] The legal bases for the decision were founded in the rule of procedure and in article 207(3) of the Treaty (vesting in the Council the power to adopt its own rules of procedure). The Netherlands Government argued that access to documents was a citizen's fundamental right and should therefore have a different legal basis. Advocate General Tesauro had some sympathy with the Dutch Government's arguments. The European Court of Justice was less convinced. The court appeared to refuse to hold that access to information was a general principle of Community law, although it did indicate that the public's right of access to documents could not be deduced from the Council's rules of procedure. But the court did not indicate what the legal basis was.[19] Whilst the Netherlands Government's arguments were rejected, the Court has since consistently emphasised the importance of openness on the basis that it strengthens the public's confidence in the administration as well as enabling citizens to carry out genuine and efficient monitoring of the exercise of the powers.[20] The European Court of Justice subsequently held that the right of access extended to documents in the

---

[16] Decision 93/731 art 4(1) and Code of Conduct exceptions (Commission).

[17] Decision 93/731 art 4(2) and Code of Conduct exceptions (Commission).

[18] *Netherlands v Council of the European Union* [1996] ECR I–2169, [1996] 2 CMLR 996.

[19] Numerous commentators have expressed the view that the only other legal basis for the decision is in a general principle of law, see: M Broberg, 'Access to documents: a general principle of Community law?' (2002) 27 *European Law Review* 194; U Öberg, 'EU Citizen's Right to Know: The Improbable Adoption of a European Freedom of Information Act' in A Dashwood and A Ward (eds), *Cambridge Yearbook of European Legal Studies*, vol 2 (Oxford, Hart Publishing, 2000) at p 315.

[20] See, eg, *Interporc Im und Export GmbH v Commission of the European Communities* [1998] ECR II–231, [1998] 2 CMLR 82.

possession of the Council or Commission that related to both second pillar[21] (common foreign and security policy) and third pillar[22] documents (justice and home affairs). The Court of First Instance[23] also concluded that the right of access extended to confidential documents.[24] As a result of an inquiry by the European Ombudsman into access of documents held by institutions and bodies other than the Council and the Commission, the Ombudsman concluded that:

> failure to adopt and make easily available to the public rules governing public access to documents constitutes an issue of maladministration.[25]

As a result of this ruling all of the bodies to which it was addressed, with the exception of the European Court of Justice, adopted rules governing public access to documents.[26]

09 Interpretation

Both the Commission and Council initially adopted a narrow approach to disclosing documents under Decisions 93/731 and 94/90. In *Carvel and Guardian Newspapers Ltd v Council of the European Union*[27] a newspaper sought access to preparatory reports, minutes and attendance and voting records of the Council of Ministers' meetings relating to social affairs, justice and agriculture. The Council refused disclosure of the documents relating to justice and agriculture on the grounds of confidentiality. This refusal was challenged by the newspaper with the support of the Danish and Dutch Governments and the European Parliament on the grounds that the decision amounted to a blanket refusal to release information. The newspaper contended that the Council had failed to exercise its discretion and balance the interests of the citizen in gaining

---

[21] *Heidi Hautala v Council of the European Union* [2002] 1 WLR 1930, [2002] 1 CMLR 15, [2002] CEC 127, on appeal from [2001] ECR I–9565, [1999] 3 CMLR 528.

[22] *Svenska Journalistforbundet v Council of the European Union* [1998] All ER (EC) 545, [1998] ECR II–2289, [1998] 3 CMLR 645 (refusal of various documents relating to the setting up of Europol. An application was made by Svenska to various Swedish bodies under Swedish legislation for twenty documents. The newspaper received 18 of the 20 documents. An identical application was made to the Council but only 4 out of the 20 were disclosed. The remaining 16 documents were refused on grounds of public interest (public security) and confidentiality because they disclosed positions taken by various member states. The Court of First Instance annulled the decision because the Council had failed to give adequate reasons. It was unclear which exception applied to which document. The Court further doubted that the disclosure would prejudice public security as the documents concerned negotiations on the adoption of the Europol Convention. In relation to the confidentiality exception there was no evidence that the Council had engaged in a balancing exercise).

[23] The differing roles of the Court of First Instance and the European Court of Justice are considered in §4– 028.

[24] *Rothmans International BV v Commissioner of the European Communities* [1998] ECR II–2463, [1999] 3 CMLR 66, where the Court of First Instance rejected an argument that a 'comitology committee', composed of Member State representatives and chaired by a Commission representative, was not distinct from and independent of the Commission. The Court held that the comitology committee, and others like it, were established to assist the Commission perform its functions and that since they had no individual resources they could not be viewed as 'another Community institution' nor as any other third party. The Court held that exceptions to the right of access were to be narrowly construed so as to not to frustrate the proper operation of the right.

[25] Decision of the European Ombudsman in his own initiative inquiry into public access to documents (616/PUBAC/F/IJH), p 7.

[26] Namely, the European Parliament, the Court of Auditors, The European Investment Bank, The Economic and Social Committee, The Committee of the Regions, The European Monetary Institute, The Office for Harmonisation of the Internal Market, The European Training Foundation, The European Foundation for the Improvement of Living and Working Conditions, The European Environment Agency, The Translation Centre for Bodies of the European Union, The European Monitoring Centre for Drugs and Drug Addiction, and the European Agency for the Evaluation of Medicinal Products.

[27] [1996] All ER (EC) 53, [1995] ECR II–2765, [1995] 3 CMLR 359, [1996] CEC 282.

access to its documents against any interests of its own in maintaining the confidentiality of its deliberations when making its judgment. The Court of First Instance annulled the decision on the grounds that the Council was obliged to balance relevant considerations and had failed to do so. *The Guardian* obtained the documents. The Court of First Instance indicated that the Commission was obliged to give reasons why it considered that the documents detailed in the request were within one of the exceptions.[28] The Court indicated that Decision 94/90 was designed to provide 'for the widest public access possible' and as such any exception was to be interpreted strictly.[29] In *Hautala v European Union Council*[30] the appellant, a Finnish Member of the European Parliament, sought disclosure of a report on criteria for conventional arms exports. Disclosure was refused on the grounds that it was necessary for the protection of the public interest (international relations) as disclosure would harm EU relations with third countries. The decision was annulled because the Court of First Instance concluded that the Council was under a duty to consider partial access to the document excluding the parts of the report that risked damaging the EU's relations with third countries. The Council appealed unsuccessfully to the European Court of Justice which reiterated its view that the exceptions were to be interpreted narrowly and laid down the following general principles:

(1)   the Code of Practice related not only to access to documents but also to information contained in such documents;

(2)   natural and legal persons had a right of access to information contained in a document not covered by one of the exceptions; and

(3)   the general principle of proportionality required the Council to consider partial disclosure of a document when disclosure of the whole document would fall within one of the exceptions.[31]

3.   REGULATION 1049/2001

4–010   **Introduction**

Regulation 1049/2001 marked a substantial enhancement of the right of access to documents held by the EU Institutions. The Regulation was adopted under the co-decision procedure and approved by the European Parliament on 3 May 2001 pursuant to article 255 EC. It came into force on 3 June 2001 and was applicable from 3 December 2001.[32] Its ambit is considerably

---

[28]   See also *World Wildlife Fund UK v Commission of the European Union* [1997] ECR II–313, CFI (refusal to disclose documents relating to EU funded visitors' centre to be located in Ireland on grounds of the protection of the public interest as the documents related to possible infringement proceedings and as such were related to inspections and investigations). Decision of Commission annulled because it had failed to give adequate reasons for refusal. CFI also found that the Commission had failed to balance interests adequately in relation to the confidentiality exception.

[29]   See also: *Van Der Wal v Commission of the European Communities* [2000] ECR I–1, [2002] 1 CMLR 16; *Bavarian Lager Company Ltd* [1999] ECR II–3217, [1999] 3 CMLR 544, [1999] CEC 543.

[30]   [2002] 1 WLR 1930, [2001] ECR I–9565, [2002] 1 CMLR 15, [2002] CEC 127.

[31]   [2002] 1 WLR 1930, [2002] 1 CMLR 15, [2002] CEC 127 at [23]–[27] and [31]–[32]. See also *Kuijer v Council of the European Union* [2002] 1 WLR 1941, [2003] All ER (EC) 276, [2002] 1 CMLR 42, [2002] CEC 238.

[32]   See art 19 of the Regulation 1049/2001.

wider than that of earlier EU schemes.[33] On 5 December 2001 the Commission of the European Communities amended its rules of procedure for the application of Regulation 1049/2001 to the European Commission.[34] As noted above,[35] there is a free-standing right of access to 'environmental information' held by EU institutions, conferred by the separate and more liberal regime implemented by Regulation 1367/2006.[36]

11 Further changes

On 9 November 2005 the Commission launched a 'European Transparency Initiative'. This included a proposal that there be a review of Regulation 1049/2001. On 4 April 2006 the European Parliament called on the Commission to come forward with proposals for amending the Regulation. On 18 April 2007 the Commission of the European Commission issued a green paper reviewing the Regulation.[37] The outcome of consultations on the green paper was summarised in a report published in January 2008. On 30 April 2008 the Commissioner proposed an updated regulations regarding public access to European Parliament, Council and Commission documents.[38] The Commission's proposed regulation has received a mixed response.[39] The regulation is to be adopted under the 'co-decision' mechanism whereby the Council of the European Union (the 27 governments) and the European Parliament have to agree on any changes. There has been some controversy over the proposed regulation with the Council and the Parliament disagreeing on the Parliament's authority to make amendments to the proposed regulation. The Parliament has sought to make changes increasing rights of access and the Council blocked the changes. This has led to an impasse and the proposed regulation has not moved any closer to adoption. The last action was the proposed amendments which were tabled by the Parliament on 11 March 2009.

12 Object of Regulation 1049/2001

Article 1 states that the purpose of the Regulation is:

    (1)   to define the principles, conditions and limits on grounds of public or private

---

[33] Recital (17) notes that 'Council Decision 93/731/EC of 20 December 1993 on public access to Council documents, Commission Decision 94/90/ECSC, EC, Euratom of 8 February 1994 on public access to Commission documents, European Parliament Decision 97/632/EC, ECSC, Euratom of 10 July 1997 on public access to European Parliament documents…should therefore, if necessary, be modified or be repealed.'

[34] The rules of procedure spell out the manner in which a request must be made, the manner in which the request is to be handled and the persons to be consulted before responding to the request.

[35] §4– 005.

[36] Unlike the environmental information regime in its application to public authorities in the United Kingdom, the right conferred by Regulation 1049/2001 applies equally in relation to environmental information held by EU bodies: Regulation 1049/2001 art 2(6). Thus, a person seeking access to environmental information held by a EU body has rights under both Regulation 1049/2001 and under Regulation 1367/2006. In practice, because the latter is more liberal than the former, where there is no right to information falling within the terms of a request (or some of the information falling within the terms of a request) because of the applicability of an exception under Regulation 1367/2006 and/or upon an application of the public interest test in that regulation, it is unlikely that the applicant will have a right to have that information disclosed under Regulation 1049/2001.

[37] At: www.ec.europa.eu/transparency/revision/docs/gp_en.pdf

[38] www.ec.europa.eu/transparency/access_documents/docs/229_en.pdf

[39] See, eg, the comments of Miamh Grogan and Gordon Christian in their article 'United Kingdom: Proposed Revisions of Regulation — A Step too Far' *Freedom of Information Journal*, July 2008 at:
    www.sjberwin.com/publicationdetails.aspx?mid=14&rid=14&lid=3&cid=1960

interest governing the right of access to institution documents provided for in artcile 255 of the EC Treaty in such a way as to ensure the widest possible access to documents;

(2)   to establish rules ensuring the easiest possible exercise of this right; and

(3)   to promote good administrative practice on access to documents.[40]

The introduction of the regulation was greeted with considerable optimism, with the Commission suggesting that the new rules represented 'major progress'.[41] The Council stated that the new regulation was 'an important step towards more openness of the institutions and better accessibility of their documents'.[42] The Court of First Instance has described the object of the Regulation as being:

> ...to secure a more significant role for citizens in the decision-making process, to ensure that the administration acts with greater propriety, efficiency and responsibility vis-à-vis the citizens in a democratic system and to help to strengthen the principles of democracy and respect for fundamental rights.[43]

Regulation 1049/2001 has had a considerable impact on institutional practice encouraging greater openness. Just under 80 per cent of requests for Council documents in 2007 were successful.[44] The figure for the Commission was slightly lower in 2007 at 72%, but rose to 82% in 2008.[45]

4–013   The register and publication

To make the citizen's right of access to documents as effective as possible, the institutions are obliged to provide public access in electronic form to a register of documents.[46] The institutions were obliged to have this register operational from 3 June 2002.[47] Each document must have a reference number, details of the subject matter and/or a short description of the content together with the date on which it was received or drawn up and recorded.[48] The institutions are under an obligation to make, as far as possible, documents publicly accessible in electronic form or through the register.[49] There is an obligation to make all legislative documents[50] directly accessible subject to arts 4 (exemptions) and 9 (sensitive information).[51] In addition to the Register, a number of documents must, subject to arts 4 and 9, be published in the official

---

[40]   Regulation 1049/2001 art 1.

[41]   European Commission, *European Governance. A White Paper*, Brussels, 25 July 2001 COM (2001) 428 at 11.

[42]   See 2346th Council meeting General Affairs, Brussels, 14–15 May, 2001, 8441/01 (presse 169).

[43]   Case T-84/03 *Turco v Council of the European Union* [2004] ECR II–4061 at [53].

[44]   See Council Annual Report on Access to Documents adopted in April 2008.

[45]   See Report from the Commission on the application in 2008 of the Regulation.

[46]   Regulation 1049/2001 art 10(2). The register is similar to publication schemes required of public authorities under the FIOA and FOI(S)A: see §§10– 013 to 10– 018.

[47]   Regulation 1049/2001 art 11(3).

[48]   Regulation 1049/2001 art 10(2).

[49]   Regulation 1049/2001 art 12(2).

[50]   'Legislative documents' are defined in art 12(2) as documents drawn up or received in the course of procedures for the adoption of acts which are legally binding in or for the Member States.

[51]   Regulation 1049/2001 art 12(2).

journal. Documents that must be so published include:

(1) Commission proposals;

(2) common positions adopted by the Council in accordance with the procedures referred to in arts 251 and 252 of the EC Treaty and the reasons underlying those common positions, as well as the European Parliament's positions in these procedures;

(3) framework decisions and decisions referred to in article 34(2) of the EU Treaty;

(4) conventions established by the Council in accordance with article 34(2) of the EU Treaty;

(5) conventions signed between Member States on the basis of article 293 of the EC Treaty;

(6) international agreements concluded by the Community or in accordance with article 24 of the EU Treaty.[52]

In addition, the following documents must be published so far as possible:

(7) initiatives presented to the Council by a Member State pursuant to article 67(1) of the EC Treaty or pursuant to article 34(2) of the EU Treaty;

(8) common positions referred to in article 34(2) of the EU Treaty;

(9) directives other than those referred to in article 254(1) and (2) of the EC Treaty, decisions other than those referred to in article 254(1) of the EC Treaty, recommendations and opinions.[53]

4 Information, administrative practice, copyright and reports

Although Regulation 1049/2001 does not expressly impose a duty on the institutions to advise and assist a person making a request for information,[54] a similar result is achieved through various provisions in the regulation. Article 14 places a duty on each of the institutions to take measures to inform the public of rights under the Regulation. Member States are obliged to co-operate with the institutions in providing this information. Article 15 provides that the institutions must develop good administrative practices. Article 16 provides that the Regulation is without prejudice to any existing rules on copyright which may limit a third party's right to reproduce or exploit released documents. Each institution is obliged to publish an annual report which must include the number of cases in which the institution refused to grant access to documents, the reasons for such refusals and the number of sensitive documents not recorded in the register.[55]

5 Persons entitled to exercise the right

By article 2(1) every citizen of the European Union and every natural or legal person residing or having its registered office in a Member State is given 'a right of access to documents of the institutions, subject to the principles, conditions and limits set out elsewhere in [the] Regulation'. There is no need to justify the request or explain why the request has been

---

[52] Regulation 1049/2001 art 13(1).

[53] Regulation 1049/2001 art 13(2).

[54] Compare the obligations imposed on public authorities in the United Kingdom: see §§10–001 to 10–006.

[55] Regulation 1049/2001 art 17(1).

made.[56] As with all comparative freedom of information regimes, the motive of an applicant in seeking a document is largely irrelevant to the efficacy of the request.[57] The institutions have a discretion to grant access to documents, subject to the same principles, conditions and limits, to any natural or legal person not residing in or not having a registered office in a Member State.[58]

4– 016   **Bodies against which the right may be exercised**
The Regulation applies to 'documents of the institutions'.[59] This is defined to mean the European Parliament, Council and Commission.[60] Unlike the earlier Code of Practice and Decisions 93/731 and 94/90, Regulation 1049/2001 applies not only to documents created by EU institutions but also to other documents held by the institutions, including documents drawn up or received by it and in its possession, in all areas of activity of the European Union.[61]

4– 017   **The information to which the Regulation applies**
The unit of disclosure in the regulation is a 'document' rather than 'information'. However, the Court of First Instance has held that the Regulation 'applies to information generally and not simply to documents.'[62] A part disclosure provision renders the difference largely insignificant.[63] 'Document' is defined widely to mean 'any content whatever its medium (written on paper or stored in electronic form or as a sound, visual or audiovisual recording) concerning a matter relating to the policies, activities and decisions falling within the institution's sphere of responsibility'.[64] The regime is not limited to documents created by the institutions, but includes all documents held by the institutions whether drawn up by one of the institutions or received by and in the possession of one of the institutions.[65] The Regulation would appear to be fully retrospective: that is to say, it covers documents created before its coming into force.[66] As with all comparative access regimes, the right is a right to information that is recorded in some form: it does not impose upon an institution an obligation to record

---

[56] Regulation 1049/2001 art 6(1). *Petrie v Commission of the European Communities* [2002] 1 CMLR 18, [2002] CEC 57 at [26], a decision under Decisions 93/731 and 94/90; *Verein fur Konsumenteninformation v Commission of the European Communities* [2005] 1 WLR 3302, [2005] All ER (EC) 813, [2005] ECR II–1121, [2006] 2 CMLR 60, [2005] 4 CMLR 21 at [109]; *Sison v Council of European Union* [2005] ECR II–1429, [2005] 2 CMLR 29 at [50], [52]; *Franchet v Commission of the European Communities* [2006] 3 CMLR 37 at [81]–[82].

[57] See §§9– 017 and 15– 015.

[58] Regulation 1049/2001 art 2(2).

[59] Regulation 1049/2001 art 2(1).

[60] Regulation 1049/2001 art 1(a).

[61] Regulation 1049/2001 art 2(3). And see Case T-380/04 *Terezakis v European Commission* (CFI 30 January 2008) at [38].

[62] Case T-264/04 *World Wildlife Fund EPP v EU Council* [2007] ECR II-911 at [67]. It is unclear what the Court meant by this statement, as it made clear that the duty on the institution was not to provide information contained in documents in its possession.

[63] Regulation 1049/2001 art 4(6).

[64] Regulation 1049/2001 art 3(a). The provision does not confer a right to interrogate the institution: Case T–264/04 *WWF European Policy Programme v European Union Council* (ECJ 25 April 2007) at [75]–[76].

[65] Regulation 1049/2001 art 2(3). As to the meaning of the term 'held' see §9– 009.

[66] See further §9– 011.

information.[67]

8   The request

Applications for access to a document must be made in written form, including electronic form, in one of the languages referred to in article 314 of the EC Treaty and in a sufficiently precise manner to enable the institution to identify the document.[68]   If a Member State receives a request for a document in its possession that originates from an institution, the Member State must consult with the institution concerned prior to disclosure unless it is clear to the Member State whether or not the document should be disclosed.[69] Alternatively, the Member State may refer the request to the institution concerned.[70]   An institution has 15 working days after registration of the application to either grant access to a document or provide reasons why access has been refused.[71]   This period can be extended by another 15 working days if the request is for a very long document or a large number of documents, although the institution must give reasons in advance for this delay.

9   The response

There has been considerable discussion in the case law as to the extent to which the institution has to undertake a concrete, individual examination of the documents before responding to a request. The Court of First Instance has concluded that there is, as a general rule, an obligation to examine each document referred to in the request to ascertain whether it should be disclosed or withheld.[72]   However, the Court has found this obligation discharged on the basis of very limited evidence.[73]   Further, it may, in exceptional circumstances, be possible to give a total refusal without individual examination of the documents if the administrative burden entailed by a concrete, individual examination is too heavy.[74]   The reasons for refusal can be brief.[75]   The institution must also consider whether a document caught by a request can be disclosed without harm to protected interests by redacting parts of the document.[76]   If the institution

---

[67] Case T–264/04 *World Wildlife Foundation v Council of the European Union*, (ECJ 25 April 2007) at [76].

[68] Regulation 1049/2001 art 6.

[69] Regulation 1049/2001 art 5; see also Recital 15.

[70] Regulation 1049/2001 art 5.

[71] Regulation 1049/2001 art 7(1). From the reasons it must be possible to understand and ascertain, first, whether the document requested did in fact fall within the sphere of the exception relied on by the institution and, secondly, whether the need for protection relating to that exception was genuine, see *Sison v Council of European Union* [2005] ECR II–1429, [2005] 2 CMLR 29 at [61].

[72] *Franchet v Commission of the European Communities* [2006] 3 CMLR 37 at [115]–[118].

[73] *Sison v Council of European Union* [2005] ECR II–1429, [2005] 2 CMLR 29 where the Court of First Instance concluded that a concrete assessment was demonstrated by the existence of a specific procedure for considering requests for sensitive documents together with the Council unanimously approving the refusal of access to such documents.

[74] *Verein für Konsumenteninformation v Commission of the European Communities* [2005] 1 WLR 3302, [2005] All ER (EC) 813, [2005] ECR II–1121, [2006] 2 CMLR 60, [2005] 4 CMLR 21 which concerned an application for an administrative file containing 47,000 pages.

[75] *Sison v Council of European Union* [2005] ECR II–1429, [2005] 2 CMLR 29 at [62]–[65].

[76] Regulation 1049/2001 art 4(6). Case T–264/04 *World Wildlife Foundation v Council of the European Union* (ECJ 25 April 2007) at [50].

makes a partial or total refusal of disclosure the applicant may, within 15 working days of receiving the institution's reply, make a confirmatory application asking the institution to reconsider its position.[77] If for whatever reason the institution fails to reply within the prescribed time limit an applicant is also entitled to make a confirmatory application.[78] The confirmatory application must also be decided within 15 working days from registration of the application, subject to the possibility of an extension of 15 working days if the request relates to a very long document or a large number of documents, although the institution must give reasons in advance for this delay.[79] In the event of a partial or total refusal, the institution must write to the applicant setting out the reasons for the refusal and informing him of the remedies open to him, namely instituting court proceedings and/or making a complaint to the ombudsman.[80] A failure to reply within the prescribed period will also entitle an applicant to initiate court proceedings and/or complain to the ombudsman.[81]

4– 020   Disclosure

If access to a document is granted, the applicant may either consult it at the institution in question or receive a copy, including, where available, an electronic copy according to his preference. Consultation on the spot, direct access in electronic form or through the register or copies of fewer than 20 A4 pages are free.[82] If the applicant is sent written documents exceeding 20 A4 pages the institution may charge the applicant although any charge must be limited to the real cost of producing and sending the copies.[83] To assist visually impaired individuals, documents must be supplied either in an existing version and format or in an alternative format such as Braille, large print or tape with full regard to the applicant's preference.[84] The Regulation does not expressly make provision for an institution to give a response that neither confirms nor denies that the requested document is held by it.[85]

4– 021   Exceptions – general principles

Article 4 sets out the various exceptions to the general right of access to documents. Uniquely amongst the comparative regimes, all the exceptions are mandatory: an institution must refuse access if a document falls within the terms of an exception.[86] The exceptions are divided into absolute exceptions (in relation to which the public interest need not be considered) and

---

[77] Regulation 1049/2001 art 7(3).

[78] Regulation 1049/2001 art 7(4).

[79] Regulation 1049/2001 art 8(2).

[80] Regulation 1049/2001 art 8(1). Article 230 EC lays down the conditions for instituting court proceedings, whilst art 95 EC lays down the conditions for making an application to the Ombudsman.

[81] Regulation 1049/2001 art 8(3).

[82] Regulation 1049/2001 art 10(1).

[83] Regulation 1049/2001 art 10(1).

[84] Regulation 1049/2001 art 10(3).

[85] However, arguably such a response can be given where (or to the extent that) a request for information captures or would capture sensitive documents: see §4– 026.

[86] *Sison v Council of European Union* [2005] ECR II–1429, [2005] 2 CMLR 29 at [51]; Case T–264/04 *World Wildlife Foundation v Council of the European Union* (ECJ 25 April 2007) at [44].

qualified exceptions (which have a public interest 'override'). In addition, certain sorts of documents are classed as 'sensitive documents'. Disclosure of sensitive documents is governed by a special regime.[87] The Regulation expressly recognises that the likelihood of harm from the disclosure of a document diminishes with time.[88] Furthermore, the majority of exceptions cannot be invoked in relation to documents more than 30 years old. In the case of documents that are not 'sensitive documents', only those exceptions relating to privacy or commercial interest can be invoked thereafter. In the case of 'sensitive documents' all exceptions can be invoked irrespective of the age of the documents. The EU Courts have frequently stated that the exceptions are to be interpreted and applied restrictively so as not to frustrate application of the general principle of giving the public the widest possible access to documents held by the Commission.[89] The onus is upon the institution to establish the applicability of an exception.[90]

22   Prejudice and the public interest

The measure of required harm to the interests protected by Arts 4(1) and 4(2) is that disclosure 'would undermine the protection' of either the public interest encapsulated in the interest (in the case of public security, defence and military matters, international relations and the financial, monetary or economic policy of the Community or a Member State) or the interest itself (in all other cases). The measure of required harm to the interests protected by article 4(3) is that disclosure 'would seriously undermine the institution's decision making process'. The Court of First Instance has made clear that it will be necessary for the institution to show 'concretely and effectively', and not generally or in an abstract fashion, that disclosure would undermine the decision-making process.[91] Thus, unlike the harm-based exemptions in the Freedom of Information Act 2000, for the engagement of any of the exemptions in arts 4(1)–(3), a mere likelihood of harm would appear to be insufficient.[92] It must be shown that the access in question was likely specifically and actually to undermine the interest protected by the exception.[93] Moreover, the phrases 'would undermine' and 'would seriously undermine' used in arts 4(1)–(3) arguably set a higher threshold of harm than the phrase 'would prejudice' as used in the Freedom of Information Act 2000.[94] In terms of the harm-based exceptions, the Court of First Instance has said that the:

> risk of a protected interest being undermined must be reasonably foreseeable and not purely

---

[87]   Regulation 1049/2001 arts 2(5) and 4(7); see §4– 026.

[88]   Regulation 1049/2001 art 4(7).

[89]   *Petrie v Commission of the European Communities* [2002] 1 CMLR 18, [2002] CEC 57 at [66], a decision under Decisions 93/731 and 94/90; *Turco v Council of the European Union* [2004] ECR II–4061 at [60], [71]; *Verein für Konsumenteninformation v Commission of the European Communities* [2005] 1 WLR 3302, [2005] All ER (EC) 813, [2005] ECR II–1121, [2006] 2 CMLR 60, [2005] 4 CMLR 21 at [106]; *Sison v Council of European Union* [2005] ECR II–1429, [2005] 2 CMLR 29 at [45]; *Franchet v Commission of the European Communities* [2006] 3 CMLR 37 at [84]; Case T-36/04 *Association de la presse internationale asbl v EC Commission* [2007] ECR II-3201, [2007] 3 CMLR 51 at [51]-[53]; Case T-194/04 *Bavarian Lager Co Ltd v EC Commission* [2007] ECR II-4523, [2008] 1 CMLR 35 at [94].

[90]   Case T-264/04 *WWF European Policy Programme v European Union Council* (ECJ 25 April 2007) at [39].

[91]   Case T-121/05 *Borax Europe Ltd v EC Commission* (CFI 11 March 2009) at [71].

[92]   For a further discussion of the likelihood requirement in the FOIA and FOI(S)A, see §§15– 022 to 15– 025.

[93]   Case T-144/05 *Muñiz v EC Commission* (CFI 18 December 2008) at [74].

[94]   For a further discussion of the level of harm required in the FOIA and the FOI(S)A, see §15– 021. And see Case T-144/05 *Muñiz v EC Commission* (CFI 18 December 2008) at [75].

hypothetical.[95]

The public interest override in arts 4(2) and 4(3) is expressed as an exception. In other words, a document captured by an exemption in those Articles is exempt from disclosure 'unless there is an overriding public interest in disclosure'. Again, this differs from the public interest balancing exercise employed in the Freedom of Information Act 2000.[96] In considering the overriding public interest, the Court of First Instance has said that there is no need to take into account a particular interest of the applicant in having access to the documents requested.[97] The Court's review of the public interest is limited to verifying whether the procedural rules and the duty to state reasons have been complied with, the facts have been accurately stated, and whether there has been a manifest error of assessment of the facts or a misuse of power.[98]

4–023 Absolute exceptions

The absolute exceptions are contained in article 4(1). This provides that institutions shall refuse access to a document where disclosure would undermine the protection of:

    (a)   the public interest as regards:
- public security;[99]
- defence and military matters;[100]
- international relations;[101] or
- the financial, monetary or economic policy of the Community or a Member State;[102] or

    (b)   privacy and the integrity of the individual, in particular in accordance with Community legislation regarding the protection of personal data.[103]

---

[95] *Franchet v Commission of the European Communities* [2006] 3 CMLR 37 at [115]. Similarly *Technische Glaswerke Ilmenau GmbH v Commission of the European Communities* [2007] 1 CMLR 39 at [77] where the Court said that the task for the institution was to determine 'whether access to the document would specifically and actually undermine the protected interest'.

[96] See further §§15–001 to 15–017.

[97] *Sison v Council of European Union* [2005] ECR II–1429, [2005] 2 CMLR 29 at [52], [54], [71]; *Franchet v Commission of the European Communities* [2006] 3 CMLR 37 at [137]. The Court's statement of principle is questionable, at least in relation to the administration of justice. An applicant may have a particular interest in having access to documents that might demonstrate or prevent a miscarriage of justice relating to himself. There is, however, a coincidental public interest, which is no less because of the applicant's self-interest.

[98] Case T-264/04 *WWF European Policy Programme v European Union Council* (ECJ 25 April 2007) at [40].

[99] Public security would appear to embrace both what, in domestic legislation, is termed national security and matters of law enforcement. See §§17–033 to 17–039 and 20–014 to 20–024.

[100] See §§17–063 to 17–072.

[101] See §§18–001 to 18–007 and 25–061 to 25–064.

[102] See §§19–001 to 19–009.

[103] As with all disclosure regimes, the rights of public access to information held by public bodies may collide with the right of an individual not to have personal data unnecessarily disclosed. In Case T-121/05 *Borax Europe Ltd v EC Commission* (CFI 11 March 2009) the Court of First Instance held that the Commission had unlawfully based a refusal to supply a recording of an experts meeting on the privacy and integrity exception. The Court emphasised the requirement for the institution to explain how access to the document would specifically and effectively undermine the interest protected (at [37]). In that case, the Commission had relied on the privacy and integrity exception but had not pleaded specific ground pertaining to the risk of undermining the protection of privacy. Further, in relation to the protection of integrity, the Court held that the Commission had made its decision 'on the basis of general grounds which are incapable of substantiating the existence' of a risk.

4   Qualified exceptions: article 4(2)

Article 4(2) provides that the institutions shall refuse access to a document where disclosure would undermine the protection of:

— commercial interests of a natural or legal person, including intellectual property;[104]
— court proceedings;[105]
— legal advice;[106] and
— the purpose of inspections, investigations and audits,[107]

unless there is an overriding public interest in disclosure.

5   Qualified exceptions: article 4(3)

Article 4(3) provides for a two-limbed qualified exception in relation to internal, deliberative documents:

(1)   Under the first limb, access to a document is to be refused where the decision to which the document relates has not been taken and disclosure of the document would seriously undermine the institution's decision-making process. All comparative regimes include such a provision, although article 4(3) would appear to impose a higher threshold of likely resultant harm than is required under the comparable provision in the Freedom of Information Act 2000.[108]

(2)   Under the second limb, even after the decision to which the document relates has

---

[104] In *Postbank NV v Commission of the European Communities* [1996] All ER (EC) 817, [1996] ECR II–921, [1997] 4 CMLR 33 at [87] the Court of First Instance stated that 'business secrets' concerns information of which not only disclosure to the public but also mere transmission to a person other than the one who provided the information may seriously harm the latter's interests. In relation to the corresponding exemption applicable in relation to a request for information held by a public authority in the United Kingdom, see §§25– 049 to 25– 060.

[105] In *Franchet v Commission of the European Communities* [2006] 3 CMLR 37 at [88]–[89] the Court of First Instance concluded that this exception precluded the disclosure of the content of documents drawn up solely for the purposes of specific court proceedings. The words 'documents drawn up solely for the purposes of specific court proceedings' should be understood to mean the pleadings or other documents lodged, internal documents concerning the investigation of the case, and correspondence concerning the case between the Directorate-General concerned and the Legal Service or a lawyers' office. The purpose of that definition of the scope of the exception was to ensure both the protection of work done within the Commission and confidentiality and the safeguarding of professional privilege for lawyers. In *Petrie v Commission of the European Communities* [2002] 1 CMLR 18, [2002] CEC 57 the Court of First Instance held that Member States are entitled to expect the Commission to guarantee confidentiality that might lead to infringement proceedings; this requirement of confidentiality remains even after the matter has been brought before the court. In relation to the corresponding exemption applicable in relation to a request for information held by a public authority in the United Kingdom, see ch 20.

[106] In *Turco v Council of the European Union* [2004] ECR II–4061 the Court of First Instance rejected an argument from the applicant that only documents capable of undermining the protection of legal advice drawn up in the context of court proceedings are covered by the exemption. The Court said (at [62]): 'the words "legal advice" must be understood as meaning that the protection of the public interest may preclude the disclosure of the contents of documents drawn up by the Council's legal service in the context of court proceedings but also for any other purpose.' The Court went on to observe (at [71]) that 'the fact that the document in question is a legal opinion cannot, of itself, justify application of the exception relied upon'. The Court placed the burden of proof regarding the 'public interest override' on applicants, ruling also that the override could not be invoked in the general interest of transparency. In relation to the corresponding exemption applicable in relation to a request for information held by a public authority in the United Kingdom, see ch 21.

[107] *Franchet v Commission of the European Communities* [2006] 3 CMLR 37 at [104]–[113]. In relation to the corresponding exemption applicable in relation to a request for information held by a public authority in the United Kingdom, see ch 20.

[108] See ch 22.

been taken, access to a document is to be refused where that document contains 'opinions for internal use as part of deliberations and preliminary consultations' *and* disclosure would seriously undermine the institution's decision-making process. Again, such an exemption is common to all the comparative regimes, but the language of this exception imposes a higher threshold of harm to the protected interest than that imposed by the comparable provision in the Freedom of Information Act 2000.[109]

4– 026   Sensitive documents

Sensitive documents are defined to be those documents originating from the institutions, the agencies establishing them, from Member States, third countries or International Organisations[110] that have been classified 'Très Secret/Top Secret', 'Secret' or 'Confidential' in accordance with the rules of the institution concerned. This system echoes that used in the United States pursuant to Executive Order.[111] The expectation is that such documents will be concerned with public security, defence and military matters. Applications for sensitive documents may be handled only by persons who have a right to acquaint themselves with those documents.[112] Sensitive documents shall be recorded in the register or released only with the consent of the originator.[113] Whilst an institution remains under a duty to give reasons if it refuses to disclose a sensitive document caught by the terms of the request, the reasons need only be provided in such a manner that does not harm the interests protected in article 4.[114] It is suggested that this might enable a neither confirm nor deny response, on the basis that in some circumstances any other response would indeed harm the interests protected in article 4.[115]

4– 027   Third parties and Member State veto

Where information in a document captured by a request originates from a 'third party' (in other words, from a legal person other than the institution to which the request is addressed), then, unless it is that the document does or does not fall within one of the exceptions in article 4(1) or (2), the institution receiving the request must consult that third party with a view to assessing whether any of the exceptions is applicable.[116] It is suggested that in this situation, the third

---

[109] See ch 22.

[110] As to the meaning of 'international organisations', see §18– 006.

[111] See §17– 010(1).

[112] Regulation 1049/2001 art 9(2). See *Sison v Council of European Union* [2005] ECR II–1429, [2005] 2 CMLR 29 which concerned sensitive documents.

[113] Regulation 1049/2001 art 9(3).

[114] Regulation 1049/2001 art 10(4).

[115] For a further discussion on the need in some circumstances for a neither confirm nor deny response, see §§17– 055 to 17– 058 and 17– 061.

[116] Regulation 1049/2001 art 4(4). In *IFAW Internationaler Tierschutz-Fonds GmbH v Commission of the European Communities* [2005] 1 WLR 1252, [2005] 2 CMLR 28 the Court of First Instance said: 'consultation of the third party is, as a general rule, a precondition for determining whether the exceptions to the right of access provided for in art 4(1) and (2) of the Regulation are applicable in the case of third-party documents' (at [55]). The consultation procedure is further spelled out in Commission Decision 2001/937/EC art 5. The involvement of third parties is considerably stronger than that provided for under the FOIA and FOI(S)A: see §§11– 041 to 11– 049. Case T–198/03 *Bank*

party could properly make submissions that an exception other than that proposed to be relied upon by the institution was applicable. It could also make submissions whether there was or was not an overriding public interest in disclosure. In addition to this provision, a Member State has a free-standing power to request that an institution shall not disclose a document originating from that Member State without its prior agreement.[117] In effect, this gives the Member State from which a document originates the power of veto over the disclosure of such documents.[118] The Member State does not have to provide any explanation for refusing its agreement.[119] Because of the expansive definition given to the word 'document', it is suggested that this will extend to a document (or that part of a document) generated within the institution but which reproduces information received from a Member State.

8 Appeals

The European Union has two courts:

— The Court of First Instance, which is the lower court. It deals with cases where individuals sue the EU institutions. Because most appeals against refusal of access to documents involve an institution denying an individual access to documents, the majority are heard before the Court of First Instance.

— The European Court of Justice. This court hears appeals against the judgments of the Court of First Instance (by individuals, by EU institutions or by Member States). It also hears cases where one EU institution sues another and cases between the EU institutions and the Member States. The European Court of Justices also answers questions about EU law referred from national courts. The European Court of Justice is assisted by Advocates General, who release a non-binding but influential Opinion about how to decide each case before the Court's judgment.

The courts cannot order the EU institutions to release documents. Instead, they have the more limited power to annul an institution's refusal to release them. This leaves the institution free to refuse access to the information requested on other grounds. The intensity of review of decisions by European Institutions refusing access was considered by the European Court of Justice in *Sison v Council*.[120] The European Court of Justice dismissed Mr Sison's appeal against the Court of First Instance's rejection of his challenge to the Council's refusal to disclose certain documents on the grounds that they fell within the ambit of article 4(1)(a). The Court stated:

> ...the Court of First Instance...correctly held...as regards the scope of the judicial review of the legality of a decision of the Council refusing public access to a document on the basis of

---

Austria Creditanstalt AG v Commission [2006] ECR II-1429, [2006] 5 CMLR 10 at [71].

[117] Regulation 1049/2001 art 4(5). The procedure is further spelled out in Commission Decision 2001/937/EC art 5. See, eg: Case T-187/03 *Scippacercola v Commission of the European Communities* [2005] 2 CMLR 54; *IFAW Internationaler Tierschutz-Fonds GmbH v Commission of the European Communities* [2005] 1 WLR 1252, [2005] 2 CMLR 28; Case T-380/04 *Terezakis v European Commission* (CFI 30 January 2008) at [39].

[118] *Mara Messina v Commission of the European Communities* [2003] ECR II-3203, [2005] 2 CMLR 21; *IFAW Internationaler Tierschutz-Fonds GmbH v Commission of the European Communities* [2005] 1 WLR 1252, [2005] 2 CMLR 28 (holding that where the originating Member State has requested that a document not be disclosed, the application for access to that document is governed by the relevant national provisions and not by the Regulation).

[119] *IFAW Internationaler Tierschutz-Fonds GmbH v Commission of the European Communities* [2005] 1 WLR 1252, [2005] 2 CMLR 28 at [59].

[120] [2005] ECR II–1429, [2005] 2 CMLR 29.

one of the exceptions relating to the public interest provided for in Article 4(1)(a) of Regulation No 1049/2001, that the Council must be recognised to have a wide discretion for the purpose of determining whether the disclosure of documents relating to the fields covered by those exceptions could undermine the public interest. The Court of First Instance also correctly held...that the Community Court's review of the legality of such a decision must therefore be limited to verifying whether the procedural rules and the duty to state reasons have been complied with, whether the facts have been accurately stated, and whether there has been a manifest error of assessment or a misuse of powers.[121]

---

[121] [2005] ECR II–1429, [2005] 2 CMLR 29 at [47].

CHAPTER 5

Access to Personal Information under the Data Protection Act 1998

111

1.   GENERAL PRINCIPLES

1   Introduction

Section 7 of the Data Protection Act 1998[1] confers upon an individual a right of access to personal data of which that individual is the subject, together with three associated rights.[2] These rights are collectively referred to as 'subject access rights'. They form one aspect of the Data Protection Act 1998. Broadly speaking, that Act:

—   controls the processing of personal data by prescribing certain data protection principles and imposing a duty on those who control personal data to comply with

---

[1]   The DPA applies equally to England, Northern Ireland, Scotland and Wales. Data protection is a reserved matter under the Scotland Act 1998 and, accordingly, is outside the legislative competence of the Scottish Parliament: see Scotland Act 1998 s 27(2)(b) and Sch 5, and §1– 037. As a matter of drafting convention rather than necessity, the DPA is expressly stated to apply to Northern Ireland: s 75(5) and (6).

[2]   The four rights are set out at §5– 030.

those principles;

— confers individual rights of access to and, to a limited extent, control over, personal information; and

— provides for the regulation and enforcement of those rights and duties.[3]

This chapter is concerned with subject access rights in relation to information held by public authorities.[4] The right of access within the subject access rights is qualified by a number of exemptions, as is the case with the right of access to information under the Freedom of Information Act 2000.

5– 002   Overview

The access regime created by the Data Protection Act 1998 co-exists with those created by the Freedom of Information Act 2000 and the Environmental Information Regulations 2004.[5] A single request for information made to a public authority may straddle any combination of these regimes. The statutory source of an applicant's right of access to information held by a public authority will define the scope of the right, the available exemptions and the applicant's right of appeal. For each unit of information captured by a request, that statutory source is determined by reference to the nature of the information (whether or not it is 'personal data') and by its relationship to the applicant (whether or not it is personal data 'relating to the applicant'). In summary:

(1)   In relation to personal data[6] that relate to the applicant himself and no one else, the right of access to that information falls to be determined by the Data Protection Act 1998.[7] Neither the Freedom of Information Act 2000 nor the Environmental Information Regulations 2004 will impinge upon the applicant's right of access to that information.[8]

(2)   In relation to personal data that relates both to the applicant and another individual, to the extent that the information can be disclosed without revealing the identity of that other individual or the individual has consented to disclosure or it would be reasonable not to secure that consent, the right of access to that

---

[3]   Other than those relating to the subject access rights, the provisions of the DPA are beyond the scope of this work. For a general treatment of the DPA, see: S Chalton, S Gaskill, D Walden and H Grant, *Encyclopaedia of Data Protection*, Sweet & Maxwell, looseleaf service; R Jay, *Data Protection Law and Practice*, 3rd edn (London, Sweet & Maxwell, 2007); P Carey, *Data Protection: A Practical Guide to UK and EU law*, 3rd edn (London, Oxford University Press, 2009).

[4]   The rights of access to personal information conferred by the DPA, unlike the rights of access to information conferred by the FOIA, are not confined to information held by a public authority. To the extent that the DPA confers rights of access to personal information held by a person or body other than a public authority, those rights are beyond the scope of this work, although the basic rights, exemptions and procedures are, with the exception of unstructured personal data, the same irrespective of the identity of the person or body holding the personal information.

[5]   And, in relation to Scottish public authorities, those created by the FOI(S)A and the EI(S)R.

[6]   As to the meaning of which, see §§5– 021 to 5– 026.

[7]   If a request were made for this sort of information under the FOIA, the public authority would be entitled to refuse the request without any consideration of the public interest: see s 40 of that Act; FOI(S)A s 38.

[8]   FOIA s 40(1); EIR reg 5(3). See *Wise v Information Commissioner*, First-Tier Tribunal, 3 February 2010. Nor, in relation to a request for information made of a Scottish public authority, will the FOI(S)A or the EI(S)R impinge upon the applicant's right of access: FOI(S)A s 38(1)(a); EI(S)R reg 11(1).

information falls to be determined by the Data Protection Act 1998.[9] To the extent that these conditions cannot be met, the Freedom of Information Act 2000, or in respect of 'environmental information', the Environmental Information Regulations 2004, will govern the applicant's right of access to that information.[10]

(3) In relation to personal data that relate to an individual (other than the applicant), the applicant's right of access to that information will fall to be determined by the Freedom of Information Act 2000 or, to the extent that that personal data is also 'environmental information',[11] by the Environmental Information Regulations 2004.[12] The Act and the Regulations each provide a specific exemption for certain sorts of personal data relating to an individual other than the applicant.[13] This exemption is considered in Chapter 24.

(4) In relation to information that is not personal data relating to an individual, the applicant's right of access will fall to be determined by the Freedom of Information Act 2000 or, to the extent that that information is 'environmental information',[14] by the Environmental Information Regulations 2004.[15]

(5) Where the request for information is made by a corporate entity, its right of access will fall to be determined by the Freedom of Information Act 2000 or, to the extent that 'environmental information'[16] is captured by the request, by the Environmental Information Regulations 2004.[17] A corporate entity has no right of access to information under the Data Protection Act 1998. To the extent that the request captures information relating to an individual, the Act and the Regulations each provide a specific exemption for certain sorts of personal data.[18] This exemption is considered in Chapter 24.

03 Comparative jurisdictions

This separate legislative treatment of the right of access to information relating to the applicant is common, but not universal, amongst the comparative jurisdictions. Thus:

(1) In the United States of America, the Privacy Act confers an additional, enhanced right of access to personal information, in addition to that enjoyed under the

---

[9] DPA ss 7(4)–(6) and 8(7). See further §5– 045.

[10] FOIA s 40(1); EIR reg 5(3). Nor, in relation to a request for information made of a Scottish public authority, will the FOI(S)A or the EI(S)R impinge upon the applicant's right of access: FOI(S)A s 38(1)(a); EI(S)R reg 11(1).

[11] As to the meaning of which, see §6– 010.

[12] Where the request for information is made to a Scottish public authority, it will fall to be determined by the FOI(S)A and the EI(S)R, respectively.

[13] FOIA s 40(2)–(4); FOI(S)A s 38(1)(b), (2), (3); EIR regs 12(3), 13; EI(S)R reg 10(3), 11(2)–(5).

[14] As to the meaning of which, see §6– 010.

[15] Where the request for information is made to a Scottish public authority, it will fall to be determined by the FOI(S)A and the EI(S)R, respectively.

[16] As to the meaning of which, see §6– 010.

[17] Where the request for information is made to a Scottish public authority, it will fall to be determined by the FOI(S)A and the EI(S)R, respectively.

[18] FOIA s 40(2)–(4); FOI(S)A s 38(1)(b), (2), (3); EIR regs 12(3), 13; EI(S)R reg 10(3), 11(2)–(5).

general right of access conferred by the Freedom of Information Act.[19]

(2)   In Australia, the right of access to personal information is that given by the Freedom of Information Act 1982, although the Privacy Act 1988 impinges upon the exercise of that right where personal information is sought.[20]

(3)   In New Zealand, the right of access to personal information was originally embodied within the general right of access to information in the Official Information Act 1982. In 1993 the right of access to personal information relating to the applicant was transferred to the Privacy Act 1993.[21]

(4)   In Canada, the right of access to personal information under the control of a government institution is governed by the Privacy Act, which came into force at the same time as the Access to Information Act.[22]

(5)   In the Republic of Ireland, the right of access to personal information is embodied in the general right of access to records held by a public body conferred by the Freedom of Information Act 1997.[23]

The United Kingdom is unusual in that the legislation protecting privacy[24] and, as part of that protection, giving a person a right of access to information relating to himself, long predated the legislation conferring a general right of access to information. Typically, statutory protection of an individual's privacy is exercisable against more than just public authorities. Thus, the focus of the Data Protection Act 1998 is the processing of personal data, irrespective of the identity of the body or person processing those data. Freedom of information legislation, on the other hand, is invariably concerned with information held by public authorities, and not with information held by private bodies. The Freedom of Information Act 2000 amended the Data Protection Act 1998 so as to expand the right of access given by the latter to cover all forms of recorded information held by a public authority relating to an individual.[25] The statutory division of the right of access to information held by a public authority according to whether the requested information is or is not the applicant's personal data is more readily understood when this legislative chronology and the provenance of the Data Protection Act 1998 are borne in mind.

5– 004   Origins of the access right

The predecessor to the Data Protection Act 1998 was the Data Protection Act 1984. It was more limited in scope than the Data Protection Act 1998, in particular being confined to 'automated data'.[26] However, it did grant an individual certain rights of access in respect of personal information:

---

[19] See §2– 002.

[20] See §2– 015(15).

[21] See §2– 017.

[22] See §2– 025. Personal information is a mandatory exemption under the Access to Information Act: see §2– 031(3).

[23] See §2– 034. There is an exemption from disclosure where the personal information is not related to the applicant: see §2– 039(7).

[24] Initially the Data Protection Act 1984 and, subsequently, the DPA.

[25] By the addition of para (e) of the definition of 'data' in DPA s 1(1). See also n 40.

[26] Effectively, information falling within either paragraph (a) or (b) of the definition of 'data' in DPA s 1(1).

—   a right to be informed whether personal data about him or her were being processed;

—   a right to be supplied with a copy of the information constituting any such personal data; and

—   an explanation, if one was necessary, to understand the information supplied.[27]

Those rights of access were subject to a number of exemptions. The Data Protection Act 1984 had its origins, in part, in the Convention for the Protection of Individuals with regard to Automatic Processing of Personal Data, adopted by the Council of Europe in 1981.[28] Specific rights of access to personal information were also provided subsequently by a number of individual statutes: for example, the Access to Personal Files Act 1987[29] and the Access to Health Records Act 1990.[30]

5   The Data Protection Directive

In 1995 the European Council issued what is generally termed the 'Data Protection Directive'.[31] This Directive applies not only to automated data[32] but also to certain types of manually stored data,[33] and it confers on the data subject a number of rights. These again include rights of access to personal data. Member States are required to guarantee data subjects the right to obtain from a data controller:

—   confirmation whether personal data about them are being processed;

—   information at least as to the purposes of such processing and the recipients or categories of recipients to whom the data are disclosed;

—   the data themselves in an intelligible form, together with any available information as to their source; and

—   knowledge of the logic involved in any automatic processing of data in the case of certain automated decisions.[34]

These rights are to be available to individuals without constraint at reasonable intervals and without excessive delay or expense.[35]

6   Implementation of the Directive

Member States were required to implement the Data Protection Directive by 24 October 1998. Implementation in the United Kingdom was by the enactment of the Data Protection Act 1998,

---

[27]   Data Protection Act 1984 s 21.

[28]   Convention for the Protection of Individuals with regard to Automatic Processing of Personal Data, 28 January 1981, ETS No 108.

[29]   The Act repealed by the DPA s 74(2), Sch 16, Pt I, as from 1 March 2000.

[30]   Except for the sections dealing with requests for access to records relating to deceased patients, this Act was repealed by DPA, s 74(2), Sch 16, Pt I, as from March 2000. See further §5– 059.

[31]   Council Directive 95/46/EC, [1995] OJ L281/31.

[32]   Effectively, information falling within either paragraph (a) or (b) of the definition of 'data' in DPA s 1(1). The Data Protection Act 1984 was only concerned with 'automated data'.

[33]   Council Directive 95/46/EC art 2(c) and 3(1).

[34]   Council Directive 95/46/EC art 12(a).

[35]   Council Directive 95/46/EC art 12(a)

which was brought fully into force on 1 March 2000. In the light of its origins in Directive 95/46/EC, much of the Data Protection Act 1998 must be construed in a purposive fashion, having regard to the aims of the Directive.[36] Nevertheless, both the Data Protection Directive and the Data Protection Act 1998 were principally directed at automated data[37] or organised data relating to an individual: neither applied to certain types of manually stored data. The right of access conferred by the Freedom of Information Act 2000 is indifferent to the distinctions between manually stored data and automated data. The unit of disclosure and of exemption is 'information',[38] with exemptions being based either upon the likelihood of an identified harm resulting from disclosure or on the basis of the information falling within a class description.[39] In order to maintain parity between the scope of the disclosure right conferred by each Act, it was necessary to amend the Data Protection Act 1998 in order to make it apply to all manually stored data held by a public authority.[40]

5–007 Personal information about third parties

As noted above, to the extent that a request for information captures personal information about a third party, the applicant's right of access to that information is governed by the Freedom of Information Act 2000 and not by the Data Protection Act 1998. The principles relating to the disclosure of such information are considered in Chapter 24. In broad terms, the provisions of the Freedom of Information Act 2000 are designed to ensure that such information is only provided under that Act if it could have been disclosed under the Data Protection Act 1998 both to the data subject and to the person making the request. Thus, information is exempt from disclosure under the Freedom of Information Act 2000 if:

(a) disclosure to a member of the public would breach any of the data protection principles;[41]

(b) in the case of most types of personal data[42] disclosure would contravene the individual's right under s 10 of the Data Protection Act 1998 to prevent processing likely to cause damage or distress;[43] or

(c) the information is exempt from the subject access rights of the Data Protection Act

---

[36] *Campbell v Mirror Group Newspapers Ltd* [2002] EWCA Civ 1373, [2003] QB 633 at [97] (the decision of the Court of Appeal was overturned on different grounds by the House of Lords: *Campbell v Mirror Group Newspapers* [2004] UKHL 22, [2004] 2 AC 457); *Durant v Financial Services Authority* [2003] EWCA 1746, [2004] FSR 28 at [3]; *R (Lord) v SSHD* [2003] EWHC 2073 (Admin) at [90]–[93]; *Johnson v Medical Defence Union* [2007] EWCA Civ 262, [2007] 3 CMLR 9, (2007) 96 BMLR 99 at [88]-[93].

[37] Effectively, information falling within either paragraph (a) or (b) of the definition of 'data' in DPA s 1(1).

[38] Defined to mean 'recorded information': FOIA s 84; FOI(S)A s 73.

[39] See §§14–015 to 14–023.

[40] Thus, the FOIA ss 68–73 effected the following amendments to the DPA: (1) the definition of 'data' was enlarged to include all recorded information held by a public authority; (2) 'held' was given the same meaning as in the FOIA; (3) 'public authority' was given the same meaning as in the FOIA; (4) a special provision, s 9A, was introduced to deal with unstructured personal data held by public authorities; (5) a limited ground of exemption, s 33A, was introduced to protect certain types of manual data held by a public authority; and (6) a further exemption, s 35A, was introduced to protect from disclosure where that was required to avoid an infringement of the privileges of either House of Parliament.

[41] FOIA s 40(2), (3)(a)(i), (3)(b); FOI(S)A s 38(1)(b), (2)(a)(i), (2)(b).

[42] As to which see §§5–021 to 5–024.

[43] FOIA s 40(3)(b); FOI(S)A s 38(2)(b).

1998.[44]

In Scotland, there are also exemptions under the Freedom of Information (Scotland) Act 2002 in respect of personal census information and a deceased person's health record.[45]

8   Overriding nature of the access rights

Subject access rights enjoy a general paramountcy over rules preventing disclosure of information. Section 27(5) of the Data Protection Act 1998 provides that, subject only to specific exemptions provided by that Act, the subject access rights[46] have effect notwithstanding any legislative provision or rule of law prohibiting or restricting the disclosure, or authorising the withholding, of information.[47] The Secretary of State does have a power to exempt from the subject access rights information the disclosure of which is subject to such a prohibition or restriction under other legislation, provided that he considers it necessary for safeguarding the interests of the data subject or the rights and freedoms of any other individual that the prohibition or restriction ought to prevail over the subject access provisions.[48] This paramountcy marks a fundamental difference between the right of access conferred by the Data Protection Act 1998 and the right of access conferred by the Freedom of Information Act 2000. The latter Act provides an absolute exemption for information the disclosure of which is prohibited by or under any enactment.[49]

9   Transitional provisions

Upon the coming into force of the Data Protection Act 1998 on 1 March 2000, its requirements applied in respect of all personal data being processed by a data controller, unless the data controller could take advantage of transitional exemptions. Certain transitional exemptions were available until 24 October 2001, and a further set was available until 24 October 2007. However, none of the remaining exemptions relates to the subject access rights.[50] There are also transitional provisions in respect of rights of data subjects under the Data Protection Act 1984 that were repealed by the Data Protection Act 1998. By virtue of these provisions, the repeals do not affect the application of the relevant provisions in respect of requests made pursuant to the right of access to personal data prior to the date of repeal;[51] compensation in respect of damage or distress suffered by reason of anything done or not done prior to the date of repeal;[52] and applications to the court for orders for rectification or erasure made before the date of repeal.[53]

---

[44] FOIA s 40(4); FOI(S)A s 38(3).

[45] FOI(S)A s 38(1)(c), (d).

[46] Together with the first data protection principle, referred to as the 'subject information provisions': DPA s 27(2), (5).

[47] DPA s 27(5).

[48] DPA s 38(1). See further at §5– 081.

[49] FOIA s 44(1)(a); FOI(S)A s 26(a). These provisions are considered in detail in §§26– 015 to 26– 024.

[50] DPA s 39, Sch 8.

[51] DPA Sch 14, para 3(1).

[52] DPA s 39, Sch 14, para 3(4).

[53] DPA Sch 14, para 3(5).

010 **Extra-territoriality**

The subject access rights are enjoyed by individuals regardless of their nationality or residence: the application of the Data Protection Act 1998 is determined by reference to the data controller and the data themselves.[54] The Act applies:

(1) To data controllers established in the United Kingdom[55] in respect of data processed in the context of that establishment.[56] Establishment in the United Kingdom covers:

— individuals ordinarily resident in the United Kingdom;

— bodies incorporated, and partnerships or unincorporated associations formed, under the law of any part of the United Kingdom; and

— persons who maintain offices, branches or agencies in the United Kingdom through which they carry on any activity, or who maintain a regular practice there.[57]

(2) To data controllers established neither in the United Kingdom nor elsewhere in the European Economic Area, but who use equipment in the United Kingdom for processing data, other than for the purposes of transit through the United Kingdom.[58] A transit exemption means that data merely passing through the United Kingdom, for instance emails routed through a United Kingdom server, are not caught by the Act. A data controller has to nominate a representative established in the United Kingdom for the purposes of the Data Protection Act 1998.[59]

Where a data subject with rights under the Data Protection Act 1998 is resident abroad in a country which is a party to the 1981 Convention for the Protection of Individuals with regard to Automatic Processing of Personal Data, the Information Commissioner is under certain obligations to assist that person in exercising his or her subject access rights; for instance, by notifying him or her of the data controller's address and of his or her rights in respect of subject access.[60]

2. THE SCOPE OF THE RIGHTS: PERSONAL DATA

5–011 **Types of information to which the access right applies**

The access related rights given to an individual by the Data Protection Act 1998 are confined

---

[54] DPA s 5. See also Information Commissioner, DPA: Legal Guidance, para 2.4.

[55] That is, England, Wales, Scotland and Northern Ireland: see Interpretation Act 1978, Sch 1.

[56] DPA s 5(1)(a).

[57] DPA s 5(3).

[58] DPA s 5(1)(b).

[59] DPA s 5(2).

[60] Data Protection (Functions of Designated Authority) Order 2000 SI 2000/186 art 4; Convention for the Protection of Individuals with regard to Automatic Processing of Personal Data, arts 8, 13 and 14. In relation to duties to give assistance, see ch 10.

to 'personal data' of which that individual is the 'data subject'.[61] The starting point in considering the access rights under the Data Protection Act 1998 is therefore the concepts of 'data', 'personal data' and 'data subject'.

12   Meaning of 'data'

Although it employs the term 'data', the manner in which that term is defined and employed in the Data Protection Act 1998 reveals that 'data' essentially means grouped information that is obtained, recorded, held or used in a particular way or by a particular body. Thus, the Act speaks of 'information contained in the data',[62] suggesting that data involves some grouping of information. The Act identifies five classes of information which will constitute 'data' for the purposes of the Act:[63]

(1)   information that is being processed by equipment operating automatically in response to instructions;

(2)   information that is recorded with the intention that it should be so processed;

(3)   information that is recorded as part of a 'relevant filing system' or with the intention that it should form part of such a system;

(4)   information that forms part of an 'accessible record'; and

(5)   any other recorded information that is held by a public authority.

These are considered separately below. The first three classes of data reflect the coverage of the Data Protection Directive.[64] The fifth class of data applies only to information held by a public authority. It was added by the Freedom of Information Act 2000 to ensure that an applicant's right of access to information relating to himself was not, on the ground of the manner of its holding, less than that given by the 2000 Act.[65] Whilst this fifth class will invariably mean that all recorded information held by a public authority will be 'data' for the purposes of the Data Protection Act 1998, whether the information falls into one of the first four data classes can nevertheless be important in terms of the format of the request,[66] the charging regime,[67] the exemptions available[68] and certain other matters.[69]

13   Data class 1: automatically processed data

The first class of information that constitutes 'data' for the purposes of the Data Protection Act 1998 is information that 'is being processed by means of equipment operating automatically

---

[61]   DPA s 7.

[62]   DPA s 1(2). See also, ss 14(2), 40(4) and Sch 1 Pt II paras 3(2)(b) and 7.

[63]   DPA s 1(1). The five classes are there labelled (a)–(e).

[64]   Council Directive 95/46/EC art 3(1).

[65]   This is underscored by DPA s 1(5).

[66]   DPA s 9A(2).

[67]   DPA s 9A(3)–(6).

[68]   DPA s 33A.

[69]   DPA Sch 8 para 14A, dealing with exemptions available during the period up to 24 October 2001 and up to 24 October 2007. Also, in relation to public authorities to which the FOIA has only limited application, by virtue of s 7 of that Act, an applicant will only have subject access rights in relation to information falling within the first four data classes: DPA s 1(6)

in response to instructions given for that purpose'. As noted below,[70] 'processing' is very broadly defined in the Act.[71] Most significantly for subject access rights, it includes 'holding' the information. Information held on computer-based storage (eg on hard disks, flash memory, tape drives, CD-ROMs) is information held by means of equipment operating automatically in response to instructions given for the purpose of processing that information.[72] Accordingly, any information being held by a public authority on computer-based storage will constitute 'data'. This class is sufficiently wide to include word-processed documents, electronically scanned documents and emails to the extent that they are being stored electronically, whether in live, archive or back-up systems. It will also include such information in a 'deleted' form where it can still technically be recovered.[73] The phrase is also wide enough to include information gathered and automatically processed by website operators. However, this class requires that the information is being processed by the automatically operating equipment. Information that is currently held on computer-based storage will satisfy the requirement; on the other hand, information that was once so held but is no longer so held will not satisfy the requirement. Thus, for example, where the electronic copy of a word-processed document has been irretrievably deleted but a paper copy has been retained, the paper copy will not be data within this class.[74]

5– 014   **Data class 2: information recorded with the intention that it be automatically processed**

The second class of information that constitutes 'data' for the purposes of the Data Protection Act 1998 is information that is recorded with the intention that it should be processed by means of equipment operating automatically in response to instructions given for that purpose. Unlike the first data class, the information need not be being 'processed' by automatically operating equipment: it is enough that it is recorded with that intention. For example, information recorded by hand on paper but with the intention that it be transferred to a computer based storage system (eg by being keyed in or by being scanned) will fall within the second data class but not the first.

5– 015   **Data class 3: information within a relevant filing system**

The third class of information that constitutes 'data' for the purposes of the Data Protection Act 1998 is information that is recorded as part of a 'relevant filing system' or with the intention that it should form part of such a system. A 'relevant filing system' is defined to mean:

---

[70]   §5– 029.

[71]   DPA s 1(1). But it does not include the manual selection of data the results of which are then, as part of the same operation, recorded or transmitted in electronic form. That decision-making process will precede the processing, which will ordinarily begin with the entry of the manually selected information onto a computer: *Johnson v Medical Defence Union* [2007] EWCA Civ 262 at [44]–[48].

[72]   Computer-based storage media are blank to begin with. Information is not stored on them without, ultimately, some instruction for that purpose.

[73]   Information Commissioner, Subject access to personal data contained in emails, DPA Compliance advice. See also *Harper v Information Commissioner*, IT, 15 November 2005 at [21] and §9– 008. In the case of a public authority, any paper copy will almost certainly fall within data class 5.

[74]   *Johnson v Medical Defence Union* [2004] EWHC 347 (Ch) at [34], not overruled in *Johnson v Medical Defence Union* [2007] EWCA Civ 262; *Smith v Lloyds TSB Bank plc* [2005] EWHC 246 (Ch) at [17]–[18].

any set of information relating to individuals to the extent that, although the information is not processed by means of equipment operating automatically in response to instructions given for that purpose, the set is structured, either by reference to individuals or by reference to criteria relating to individuals, in such a way that specific information relating to a particular individual is readily accessible.[75]

The starting-point for the third data class is that it comprises information that is not processed by automatically operating equipment. Most commonly, the third class will thus exclude information being held on computer-based storage. To fall in the third data class, this information must be structured, either by reference to individuals or by reference to criteria relating to individuals, in such a way that specific information relating to a particular individual is readily accessible.[76] Under the definition, in order to qualify as a relevant filing system, not only must the information be structured by reference to individuals or criteria relating to individuals, but it must be structured in such a way that specific information relating to a particular individual is readily accessible.

6 Data class 3: jurisprudence

In *Durant v Financial Services Authority* [77] the Court of Appeal held that it is only to the extent that manual filing systems are broadly equivalent to computerised systems in ready accessibility to relevant information capable of constituting personal data that they are within the system of data protection.[78] The Court held that 'relevant filing system' was to be restrictively interpreted, so as not to impose a disproportionate burden on a data controller, and that it is limited to a system:

(1)   in which the files forming part of it are structured or referenced in such a way as clearly to indicate at the outset of the search whether specific information capable of amounting to personal data about the individual requesting it is held within the system and, if so, in which files; and

(2)   which has as part of its own structure or referencing mechanism, a sufficiently sophisticated and detailed means of readily indicating whether and where in an individual file or files specific criteria or information about the applicant can be readily located.

Therefore it is not enough that a filing system leads a searcher to a file containing documents mentioning the data subject. The file must itself be so structured and/or indexed as to enable easy location within it, or any sub-files, of specific information about the data subject that he has requested. Thus a set of manual personnel files arranged alphabetically by employee name,

---

[75]   DPA s 1(1). The definition in Council Directive 95/46/EC art 2(c) states that the relevant filing system can be 'centralised, de-centralised or dispersed on a functional or geographical basis'. DPA s 1(1) does not reproduce this part of the Directive, but should nevertheless be purposively interpreted to accord with it, particularly when dealing with de-centralised or dispersed data sets.

[76]   DPA s 1(1).

[77]   [2003] EWCA Civ 1746, [2004] FSR 28 at [34], [45]–[50].

[78]   While the restrictive interpretation holds for other data protection purposes, the addition of the fifth class of 'data' in section 1(1) has largely undone this aspect of the Court of Appeal's judgment in relation to public authorities. At the time of *Durant v Financial Services Authority*, this fifth class of 'data' was not in force. However, *Smith v Lloyds TSB Bank plc* [2005] EWHC 246 (Ch) illustrates the effect of *Durant*, where a former client of Lloyds Bank was refused access to manual records in the form of unstructured bundles kept in boxes, which he maintained would evidence an oral agreement to provide him with substantial long-term finance.

each of which relates to a particular individual and contains, in no particular order, every document relating to that individual's employment, would not fall within the third data class. This interpretation is consistent with the Government's view, expressed by Lord Williams of Mostyn during the passage of the Data Protection Bill through Parliament.[79] It also appears to reflect the intentions of the Data Protection Directive itself. The Directive defines the equivalent concept — a 'personal data filing system' — as 'any structured set of personal data which are accessible according to specific criteria...'.[80] Recital 27 makes clear that the Directive is to apply only to filing systems, not to unstructured files, and that individual files, not simply the whole filing system, must be structured according to criteria relating to individuals.[81] In *Johnson v Medical Defence Union*,[82] the Court held that the definition of data refers to information which 'is' being processed or recorded, so the question as to whether information is data within the meaning of the 1998 Act is to be determined at the time when the data subject makes his data request.[83] The fact that data may at a prior stage have been held as part of an electronic filing system thus does not avail an applicant if, at the time of the request, the data is held only in an unstructured manual filing system.

5–017 **Data class 3: examples**

The requirement in the definition of 'relevant filing system' that the set of information is structured in such a way that specific information relating to a particular individual be 'readily' accessible reflects the reference to 'easy' access in recital 27. The Information Commissioner suggests as a rule of thumb for establishing whether a system is a relevant filing system the 'temp test': namely, whether a temporary administrative assistant would be able to extract specific information about an individual without any particular type of knowledge about the data controller's type of work or the documents it held.[84] Because the definition of 'data' includes information recorded with the intention that it should form part of a relevant filing system, it will include documents that will eventually form part of a structured set, but have not yet been filed: for example an employer's note of a conversation with an employee who phones in sick, intended, eventually, for his or her personnel file. The Data Protection Directive also makes clear that the structured set of personal data need not be held in one place: they may be centralised, decentralised or dispersed on a functional or geographical basis.[85] Thus, wage records held in one place and sickness records in another would still fall within the third data class.

5–018 **Data class 4: accessible records**

The fourth class of information that constitutes 'data' for the purposes of the Data Protection Act 1998 is information that does not fall within any of the preceding classes but is 'data' that

---

[79] Hansard HL vol 587 cols 467–468 (16 March 1998).

[80] Council Directive 95/46/EC art 2(c).

[81] Council Directive 95/46/EC recital 27.

[82] [2007] EWCA Civ 262, [2007] 3 CMLR 9, (2007) 96 BMLR 99.

[83] At [30]-[34]. See also *Smith v Lloyds TSB Bank plc* [2005] EWHC 246 (Ch) at [12]-[17].

[84] Information Commissioner, Frequently Asked Questions and Answers (Relevant Filing Systems).

[85] Council Directive 95/46/EC art 2(c).

form part of an 'accessible record'. There are three specific categories of accessible record:

— health records;

— educational records; and

— accessible public records.[86]

Each is defined in some detail in the Act.[87] Broadly speaking, a health record is a record of information relating to an individual's health made by a health professional, and an 'educational record' is a record of specified information relating to a present or former pupil at a maintained or special school. The term 'health professional' includes a wide range of professionals, from doctors, dentists and opticians to clinical psychologists and certain therapists.[88] Accessible public records are defined by reference to particular bodies or authorities. In England and Wales they are: a record of information held by a Housing Act local authority for the purpose of any of its tenancies and a record of information held by a local social services authority for any purpose of its social services functions.[89]

19   Data class 4: jurisprudence

The fourth class of data (and the associated exemption and access provisions dealt with below) has its origins in the decision of the European Court of Human Rights in *Gaskin v United Kingdom*.[90] There an individual had been denied access by a local authority in whose care he had been to certain records relating to him, in order to protect the confidence of individuals who had contributed to those records. The European Court upheld the domestic approach of striking a balance between an individual's right to respect for his private life (and access to the records in question) and the public interest in maintaining the confidence of those who contributed to such records, so as to ensure frankness in such contributions. The special regime in relation to 'accessible records' is secured through the inclusion of data class 4, together with special exemptions for each of the three categories.[91]

20   Data class 5: other recorded information held by a public authority

The final class of information, 'any other recorded information held by a public authority', was introduced into the Data Protection Act 1998 by the Freedom of Information Act 2000.[92] For a public authority, any recorded information held by it, but not falling within the preceding classes, will fall within this fifth data class. For the purposes of the Data Protection Act 1998,

---

[86] DPA s 1(1) s 68. See further IC Guidance Data Protection - Subject Access Request to Health Records (13 November 2001) Appendix 1 'Who is a "health professional"?'

[87] DPA ss 68(1)(a), (2), 69 (health record); DPA s 68(1)(b), Sch 11 (educational record); DPA s 68(1)(c), Sch 12 (accessible public record).

[88] DPA s 69.

[89] DPA s 68(1)(c) Sch 12 paras 1(a) and 2. In Scotland accessible public records are records of information held by a local authority for any purpose of its tenancies and records of information held by a social work authority for any purpose of specified social work functions: DPA s 68(1)(c) Sch 12 paras 1(b) and 4.

[90] (1989) 12 EHRR 36. Special transitional provisions applied (up until 24 October 2001) to 'accessible records': DPA Sch 8 para 3. See also DPA Sch 8 paras 14 and 14A for the period up to 24 October 2007.

[91] Data Protection (Subject Access Modification) (Health) Order 2000 SI 2000/413; Data Protection (Subject Access Modification) (Education) Order 2000 SI 2000/414; Data Protection (Subject Access Modification) (Social Work) Order 2000 SI 2000/415.

[92] DPA s 1(1); FOIA ss 68(1), (2), 86, Sch 8 Pt III. For the meaning of 'public authority' see §§9–018 to 9–026.

'public authority' has the same meaning as it has under the Freedom of Information Act 2000.[93] Likewise, the reference to information 'held' by a public authority is to be construed in accordance with s 3(2) of the Freedom of Information Act 2000.[94] The term 'recorded' is not defined.[95] In respect of some public authorities, the Freedom of Information Act 2000 has effect only in relation to specified information.[96] Where that is the case, other information held by the public authority is deemed not to fall within the final limb of the definition of data in the Data Protection Act 1998.[97] However, it seems that such information may still fall within the other limbs of the definition. As noted above, the addition of the fifth class of 'data' has, in practical terms, largely undone one aspect of the Court of Appeal's judgment in *Durant v Financial Services Authority*.[98] Thus, so far as a public authority is concerned, any recorded information held by it will constitute 'data' for the purposes of the Data Protection Act 1998.[99]

5– 021 **Meaning of 'personal data'**

The subject access rights are conferred only in relation to 'personal data'. Section 1(1) of the Data Protection Act 1998 provides:

> "personal data" means data which relate to a living individual who can be identified—
> - (a) from those data, or
> - (b) from those data and other information which is in the possession of, or is likely to come into the possession of, the data controller,
>
> and includes any expression of opinion about the individual and any indication of the intentions of the data controller or any other person in respect of the individual.

Under this definition, data will only be 'personal data' if they satisfy two requirements. First, the data must relate to a living individual. And, secondly, it must be possible to identify that individual either from the data themselves or from the data and any other information that is in the possession of the data controller or is likely to come into the controller's possession.[100] These requirements are considered separately below. In a change from the position under the Data Protection Act 1984, personal data now also includes any expression of opinion about the individual and any indication of the intentions of the data controller or any other person in respect of the individual.[101] This would cover, for example, employee appraisals and assessments of their promotion prospects (provided they fell within the definition of data).[102]

---

[93] DPA s 1(1). For detailed consideration of the meaning of 'public authority' see §§9– 018 to 9– 026.

[94] DPA s 1(5). For detailed consideration of the meaning of 'held' see §9– 009.

[95] The reference in the DPA to 'recorded information' mirrors the FOIA, which only applies to recorded information: see the definition of 'information' in the FOIA s 84 and in the FOI(S)A s 73. See further §§9– 001 to 9– 008.

[96] FOIA s 7, Sch 1. See further §§9– 022 and 9– 030.

[97] DPA s 1(6).

[98] [2003] EWCA Civ 1746, [2004] FSR 28 at [34], [45]–[50].

[99] But see the final sentence of §5– 013. As an example of its operation in relation to public authorities, see *A v Information Commissioner*, IT, 11 July 2006.

[100] DPA s 1(1). See also Information Commissioner, DPA: Legal Guidance, paras 2.2.1.– 2.2.4. For the meaning of 'data controller' see §5– 027.

[101] DPA s 1(1). For the meaning of 'data controller' see §5– 027.

[102] See also Information Commissioner, DPA: Legal Guidance, para 2.2.6.

22 **Requirement 1: the data must relate to a living individual**

The requirement that the data 'relate to' a living individual requires some sort of connection between the data and a living individual. As noted above,[103] data involve some grouping of information, so that in assessing whether the requirement is met it is the data (ie the grouped information), and not just the information on an item-by-item basis, that must be considered. The phrase 'relates to' is notoriously context-sensitive.[104] In *Durant v Financial Services Authority*[105] the Court of Appeal interpreted the phrase as used in s 1(1) to require a direct connection between the individual and the subject matter of the data:

> In conformity with the 1981 Convention and the Directive, the purpose of section 7, in entitling an individual to have access to information in the form of his "personal data" is to enable him to check whether the data controller's processing of it unlawfully infringes his privacy and, if so, to take such steps as the Act provides, for example in sections 10 to 14, to protect it. It is not an automatic key to any information, readily accessible or not, of matters in which he may be named or involved. Nor is it to assist him, for example, to obtain discovery of documents that may assist him in litigation or complaints against third parties. As a matter of practicality and given the focus of the Act on ready accessibility of the information – whether from a computerised or comparably sophisticated non-computerised system – it is likely in most cases that only information that names or directly refers to him will qualify. In this respect, a narrow interpretation of "personal data" goes hand in hand with a narrow meaning of "a relevant filing system".[106]

The Court of Appeal identified what would and would not suffice:

> It follows from what I have said that not all information retrieved from a computer search against an individual's name or unique identifier is personal data within the Act. Mere mention of the data subject in a document held by a data controller does not necessarily amount to his personal data. Whether it does so in any particular instance depends on where it falls in a continuum of relevance or proximity to the data subject as distinct, say, from transactions or matters in which he may have been involved to a greater or lesser degree. It seems to me that there are two notions that may be of assistance. The first is whether the information is biographical in a significant sense, that is, going beyond the recording of the putative data subject's involvement in a matter or an event that has no personal connotations, a life event in respect of which his privacy could not be said to be compromised. The second is one of focus. The information should have the putative data subject as its focus rather than some other person with whom he may have been involved or some transaction or event in which he may have figured or have had an interest, for example, as in this case, an investigation into some other person's or body's conduct that he

---

[103] §5– 012.

[104] See authorities cited at §22– 007. 'It may be accepted that there will always be a question of degree involved where the issue is the relationship between two subject matters. The words 'in relation to' are wide words which do no more, at least without reference to context, than signify the need for there to be some relationship or connection between two subject matters': *Smith v Federal Commissioner of Taxation* (1987) 164 CLR 513 at 533. Similarly: *PMT Partners Pty Ltd (in liquidation) v Australian National Parks and Wildlife Service* (1995) 184 CLR 328 and *Technical Products Pty Ltd v State Government Insurance Office (Qld)* (1989) 167 CLR 45 at 51.

[105] [2003] EWCA Civ 1746, [2004] FSR 28 at [27]–[28]. See also *Johnson v Medical Defence Union* [2004] EWHC 347 (Ch) at [37]–[49].

[106] At [27] (Auld LJ). See *Common Services Agency v Scottish Information Commissioner*, 2006 CSIH 58, 2007 SC 231 at [23], where the Scottish Court of Session held that statistical information that had been 'perturbed' by a recognised statistical method would not constitute personal data.

may have instigated. In short, it is information that affects his privacy, whether in his personal or family life, business or professional capacity.[107]

Given the impact of *Durant* on the scope of the DPA, the Information Commissioner issued guidance concerning the case.[108] The central role played by the concept of privacy in the definition of personal data is recognised by the Information Commissioner, who speculates that whether the information in question is capable of having an adverse impact on the individual should therefore form part of the determination of whether it amounts to personal data.[109] The Information Commissioner suggests that information about matters such as an individual's medical history, salary,[110] tax details[111] and spending preferences are likely to amount to personal data; by contrast with mere reference to his name,[112] his attendance at a business meeting[113] or his receipt of a document or email, which are unlikely to do so.[114] Reference to a person's name, when combined with another identifier such as an address or a telephone number, will generally amount to personal information.[115] On the other hand, it is not necessary that data identify the data subject by name in order to constitute personal data

---

[107] At [27] (Auld LJ). The Court of Appeal (Auld LJ) held (at [30]) that documents concerning Mr Durant's complaint to the FSA about Barclays Bank and concerning the FSA's own investigation of that complaint did not constitute 'personal data' relating to Mr Durant: 'Just because the FSA's investigation of the matter emanated from a complaint by him does not, it seems to me, render information obtained or generated by that investigation, without more, his personal data. For the same reason, either on the issue as to whether a document contains "personal data" or as to whether it is part of a "relevant filing system", the mere fact that a document is retrievable by reference to his name does not entitle him to a copy of it under the Act.' See also *Ezsias v Welsh Ministers* [2007] EWHC B15 (QB) at [65]-[66].

[108] Information Commissioner, The 'Durant' case and its impact on the interpretation of the DPA. In *Harcup v IC*, IT, 5 February 2008, the Tribunal commented at [23]: 'The Court of Appeal's approach in Durant was significantly to narrow the concept of personal data as it had been widely understood and applied. The attempt in the IC's Guidance to apply Durant in practice restores much of the previous width.'

[109] Information Commissioner, *The 'Durant' case and its impact on the interpretation of the DPA.* See also *England v IC*, IT, 10 May 2007 at [95]-[98]; *Kelway v IC and Northumbria Police*, IT, 14 April 2009 at [58]-[61]; *Guardian News & Media Ltd v IC and MoJ*, IT, 10 June 2009 at [83]-[85].

[110] In Case C-465/00 *Rechnungshof v Österreichischer Rundfunk* [2002] ECR I-4989 the ECJ confirmed that data concerning salaries and pensions of employees of the State, generated in the course of their employment and held by the State, were personal information (see [64]).

[111] The ECJ has accepted that information on income, wealth and taxes can amount to personal data: Case C-73/07 *Tietosuojavaltuutettu v Satakunnan* (ECJ 16 December 2008).

[112] In *Harcup v IC*, IT, 5 February 2008 at [18]-[27], the names of attendees of a public authority's hospitality events, listed without any reference to the organisations they worked for, were held not to be personal data. But cf *DBERR v IC and Friends of the Earth*, IT, 29 April 2008, which held at [91] that a list of names of individuals who attended meetings between ministers and/or senior civil servants (Grade 5 or above) and employees from the Confederation of British Industry (CBI) was personal data, as it would have 'biographical significance for the individual in that [the minutes of the meetings] record his/her employer's name, whereabouts at a particular time and that he/she took part in a meeting with a government department which would be of personal career or business significance.'

[113] *O'Connell v IC and CPS*, IT, 17 September 2009 at [9]; *Brett v IC and FCO*, IT, 21 August 2009 at [43].

[114] Information Commissioner, *The 'Durant' case and its impact on the interpretation of the DPA.* In *Corporate Officer of the House of Commons v Information Commissioner and Baker*, IT, 16 January 2007 at [38] the Information Tribunal held that a breakdown of MPs' travel expenses by name, mode of travel and amount, constituted 'personal data'.

[115] This was accepted by the ECJ in the first case on the Directive, *Re Lindqvist (Approximation of Laws)* [2004] QB 1014 at [24]. See also Case C-553/07 *College van burgemeester en wethouders van Rotterdam v Rijkeboer* [2009] 3 CMLR 28 at [42] and the references cited therein. In the domestic context, see *Benford v IC and DEFRA*, IT, 14 November 2007 at [48]-[51].

relating to that person.[116] Information about the business of a sole trader and about a specific individual in a partnership will be personal information, whereas information solely about a legal entity will not.[117]

23 Requirement 2A: the data subject must be identifiable from the data

The second requirement can be satisfied in either of two ways. First, it will be satisfied where it is possible to identify from the data the individual to whom the data relate. Once the first requirement is satisfied, the second requirement will often be satisfied at the same time: for example, where the data include the individual's name and address. But the reach of the Act is much broader. Article 2 of the Data Protection Directive defines personal data as information relating to an 'identified or identifiable' natural person, and provides that an identifiable person is:

> one who can be identified, directly or indirectly, in particular by reference to an identification number or to one or more factors specific to his physical, physiological, mental, economic, cultural or social identity.[118]

It is clear from recital 14 to the Data Protection Directive that this covers sound and image data relating to the individual. The Act does not specify by whom the individual must be identifiable. It is suggested that it will be sufficient if anyone, including the individual to whom the data relate, is able to identify the individual from the data. Thus, photographs and voice recordings, if sufficiently clear, may well suffice without any other identifier in the data. The Information Commissioner has expressed the view that an individual is capable of being identified if the data controller is able to process the data so as to distinguish the data subject from any other individual, and that this would be the case if the data subject could be treated differently from other individuals.[119] Thus, personal data would include, for example, closed-circuit television recordings of an individual from which he or she could be visually identified by reference to a photograph, physical description or physical features[120] and many email addresses, such as those including the individual's name and workplace.[121] In the context of the internet, personalised user profiles developed by website operators (eg through the use of 'cookies'), which are capable of being linked to an individual, through his or her name, postal address or email address for example, will also amount to personal data.[122] DNA, fingerprints or similar information have been recognised as personal data.[123]

---

[116] *A v Information Commissioner*, IT, 11 July 2006 at [11].

[117] See also Information Commissioner, *DPA: Legal Guidance*, para 2.2.1 and *Smith v Lloyds TSB Bank plc* [2005] EWHC 246 (Ch) at [31]-[33].

[118] Council Directive 95/46/EC art 2(a). In *Alcock v IC and Chief Constable of Staffordshire Police*, IT, 3 January 2007 at [25] the Information Tribunal held that information could identify an individual, even if not mentioning him by name.

[119] Information Commissioner, *DPA: Legal Guidance*, para 2.2.3. The approach in the Guidance has been criticised for being at odds with the broad approach to identifiability in the Directive: see R Jay, *Data Protection Law and Practice*, 5th ed (London, Sweet & Maxwell, 2007) at p 134-5, para 3-36.

[120] See also Council Directive 95/46/EC, recitals 14 and 26.

[121] Information Commissioner, *DPA: Legal Guidance*, para 2.2.3.

[122] Information Commissioner, *DPA: Legal Guidance*, para 2.2.3.

[123] *S and Marper v United Kingdom* [2008] ECHR 1581, (2009) 48 EHRR 50 at [63] and [68]. The ECHR held that the blanket and indiscriminate retention of fingerprint and DNA information breached the right to privacy.

5– 024   **Requirement 2B: the data subject must be otherwise identifiable**
The second way that the second requirement will be satisfied is where the individual to whom
the data relate can be identified from those data and other information in the possession of, or
likely to come into the possession of, the data controller. This limb of the definition will capture
data that relate to an individual but from which, without additional information, it is not
possible to identify that individual. For example, where the data only refer to an individual by
a number. If the data controller is able to tie that number to other information from which it
is possible to identify the individual, that will suffice to render the data 'personal data'.[124] The
identifying information need not be in the possession of the data controller: it is enough that
it is likely to come into the possession of the data controller. The Information Commissioner's
view is that information may be in the possession of a data controller not simply when it is in
his physical control but also, for example, when it is in the physical control of his contracted
data processor.[125] It is not clear what information may be said to be 'likely to come into the
possession of [a] data controller'. Recital 26 to the Data Protection Directive provides that in
order to determine whether a person is identifiable, account should be taken of 'all the means
likely reasonably to be used' either by the data controller or by any other person to identify the
individual.[126] This suggests that it is not simply identification by the data controller that is
important, but that identification by any other person would also count. On that basis it would
not matter whether the data controller took steps to avoid information coming into his
possession, if that information was reasonably likely to be used by a third party to identify the
individual. This appears to be beyond the scope of the definition in the Data Protection Act
1998, which is concerned only with identification by the data controller.[127]

5– 025   **Anonymised data**
The Data Protection Act 1998 and the Data Protection Directive do not apply to data
anonymised in such a way that the data subject is no longer identifiable.[128] However, care must
be taken in anonymising the data. If the data controller simply separates the personal
identifiers from the rest of the data, they will remain personal data, because the identifying
material will be information in the possession of the data controller.[129] The data controller must
get rid of the original data set and the separated identifying material, and in such a way that it

---

[124] Thus in *England and LB of Bexley v Information Commissioner*, IT, 10 May 2007 at [98] it was held that addresses of
empty residential properties constituted 'personal data' because that information was held together with ownership
details from the Council Tax register.

[125] Information Commissioner, *DPA: Legal Guidance*, para 2.2.4. See further §§9– 009 to 9– 010.

[126] Council Directive 95/46/EC, recital 26.

[127] Note that in *Collie and CSA* Scottish Information Commissioner decision 021/2005 at [63]–[65] it is suggested (based
on guidance from the OIC) that s 8(7) of the DPA applies in these circumstances. However, this seems on the face
of it to be inconsistent with the terms of the DPA. Section 8(7) is concerned with subject access requests under s 7
and not with the definition of personal data in s 1(1).

[128] *R v The Department of Health, ex p Source Informatics Ltd* [2000] 1 All ER 786 (CA); Directive 95/46/EC, recital 26.
Guidance on anonymised data is given in Information Commissioner, *DPA: Legal Guidance*, para 2.2.5.

[129] See *Dept of Health v IC and Pro-Life Alliance*, IT, 15 October 2009 at [31]-[45]; *Riniker v IC and MoJ*, IT, 22 September
2009 at [24].

is not likely to come into his possession.[130]

26   Meaning of 'data subject'

A data subject is an individual who is the subject of personal data.[131] It appears to follow from the definition of personal data that the data subject must be a living individual, and this has been confirmed by the Information Commissioner.[132] In the Data Protection Directive, reference is made to 'natural persons' rather than to living individuals.[133] There is no age restriction — children of any age enjoy the subject access rights conferred by the Data Protection Act 1998.

27   Meaning of 'data controller'

The access rights given to an individual by the Data Protection Act 1998 are rights as against the data controller.[134] A 'data controller' is a person who determines the purposes for which and the manner in which personal data are processed.[135] Where personal data are processed pursuant to an obligation imposed by or under an enactment, the person on whom the obligation to process the data is imposed is the data controller.[136] For example, where a local authority engages a contractor to acquire, hold or otherwise process personal data that it is under a statutory obligation to acquire, hold or otherwise process, the local authority will be the data controller of those data even though it is the contractor who carries out the processing. The definition of data controller follows fairly closely that in the Data Protection Directive.[137] The definition in the Data Protection Directive expressly includes public authorities, but covers all other natural or legal persons, agencies and other bodies.[138] This is in contrast to the Freedom of Information Act 2000, which applies only to public authorities. There may be more than one data controller in respect of the same personal data — the Act makes clear that a data controller may act alone, or jointly or in common with others.[139]

---

[130] In *Common Services Agency v IC* [2008] UKHL 47, [2008] 1 WLR 1550 the House of Lords considered the disclosure control method known as 'barnardisation' (named after Professor George Alfred Barnard (1915-2002), a professor of mathematical statistics at the University of Essex), which is used to render statistical information anonymous by randomly subtracting or adding 1 to some values in a table of statistics. It was considered that barnardisation might be able to render the data sufficiently anonymous that the data controller could no longer identify a living individual from that data, even though the data controller still held the original information on which the barnardised information was based (see [17]-[27] and [73]-[88]). Whether that was actually possible was left as a question of fact for the Scottish IC, which is yet to issue a further decision on the matter. The true utility of barnardisation is questionable where the data controller retains the original data set.

[131] DPA s 1(1). For the meaning of 'data controller' see §5– 027.

[132] Information Commissioner, *DPA: Legal Guidance*, para 2.2.6.

[133] Council Directive 95/46/EC art 2(a).

[134] DPA s 7.

[135] DPA s 1(1). For the meaning of processing see §5– 029.

[136] DPA s 1(4).

[137] Council Directive 95/46/EC art 2(d).

[138] Council Directive 95/46/EC art 2(d).

[139] DPA s 1(1).

131

5– 028 **Data controller: guidance**

The Information Commissioner has issued advice on the meaning of 'data controller'. The view expressed is that where one person determines the purposes for which personal data are processed, but that person delegates responsibility for determining the manner in which they are processed to someone else, it is the person who determines the purposes who is the data controller.[140] In the Commissioner's view, a decision as to the manner in which the data are to be processed is implicit in that determination, and thus determination of the purposes of processing takes precedence in identifying the data controller.[141]

5– 029 **Meaning of 'processing'**

'Processing' is an extremely broad concept under the Data Protection Act 1998. It covers simply obtaining, recording or holding information or data, as well as carrying out any operation or set of operations on it.[142] The carrying out of an operation receives a similarly broad (non-exhaustive) definition, including the organisation, adaptation or alteration of the information or data; their retrieval, consultation, use and disclosure; and their alignment, combination, blocking, erasure or destruction.[143] This reflects the definition of 'processing' in the Data Protection Directive.[144] Recital 14 to the Directive makes it clear that the capture, transmission, manipulation, recording, storage and communication of sound and image data are intended to be covered.[145] For the avoidance of doubt, in relation to personal data, obtaining or recording the data includes obtaining or recording the information to be contained in the data; and using or disclosing the data includes using or disclosing the information to be contained in the data.[146] Given the breadth of these definitions, it is difficult to conceive of an interaction with data that would not amount to processing.[147] That is also the view of the

---

[140] Information Commissioner, *DPA: Legal Guidance*, para 2.5.

[141] This appears to be at odds with the DPA and Council Directive 95/46/EC, neither of which indicate that one part of the definition should be given precedence over the other.

[142] DPA s 1(1). In *Campbell v Mirror Group Newspapers Ltd* [2002] EWCA Civ 1373, [2003] QB 633, the Court of Appeal held that the publication of material in hard copy, where it had previously been automatically processed, fell within the definition of 'processing'.

[143] DPA s 1(1).

[144] Council Directive 95/46/EC art 2(b).

[145] Council Directive 95/46/EC recital 14. In Case C-73/07 *Tietosuojavaltuutettu v Satakunnan* [2010] All ER (EC) 213, [2008] ECR I-9831at [35]-[49], the ECJ held that 'processing' includes collating information from publicly available documents held by a public authority; the provision of information on a CD-ROM and the provision of information via text message.

[146] DPA s 1(2). *A v Information Commissioner*, IT, 11 July 2006 at [14] and *R v Rooney* [2006] EWCA Crim 1841 at [12]-[13].

[147] In *Johnson v Medical Defence Union* [2007] EWCA Civ 262, [2007] 3 CMLR 9, (2007) 96 BMLR 99 an individual took the central role in processing, rather than it being automated. The processing revolved around a risk assessment of the claimant, performed by a risk manager creating a new data set by selecting information from computerised files (which fell within the DPA) and from various manual and microfiche files (which did not fall within the DPA), adding information to some of the computerised files and then adding new observations and allocating scores. The claimant alleged that the defendant had unfairly processed his personal data by 'selecting the information contained in the personal data and thereby presenting a false picture of the situation'. The Court of Appeal held by a majority that the operation did not fall within the s1(1) DPA. The majority of the court focussed on the fact that the relevant activities were conducted wholly by the human agent and involved an exercise of judgment (at [21]-[54] and [154]-

Information Commissioner.[148]

3. THE NATURE OF THE RIGHTS

0 **The four access-related rights granted by the Data Protection Act 1998**
Section 7 of the Data Protection Act 1998 gives an individual four access-related rights in respect of personal data of which that individual is the data subject. These are:

(1) to be informed by any data controller whether such data are being processed by or on behalf of the data controller;[149]

(2) if so, to be given by the data controller a description of the data, the purposes for which they are being or are to be processed, and the recipients or classes of recipients to whom they are or may be disclosed;[150]

(3) to have communicated in an intelligible form the information constituting the personal data and any information available to the data controller as to the source of those data;[151] and

(4) where such data are automatically processed in order to evaluate matters relating to the individual, such as the individual's work performance, creditworthiness, reliability or conduct, and such processing has constituted or is likely to constitute the sole basis for any decision significantly affecting the individual, to be informed by the data controller of the logic involved in that decision-taking.[152]

These rights reflect the rights conferred by article 12(a) of the Data Protection Directive.

1 **First right: to be informed whether data are being processed**
The first right is straightforward. If personal data about the data subject are not being processed, the data controller may simply inform the applicant of that fact, and the remaining rights are inapplicable. Typically, the first right will be satisfied by the data controller informing the data subject that the data controller holds personal data relating to the data subject. The first right is analogous to the 'existence right' in the Freedom of Information Act 2000.[153]

2 **Second right: description of data, purposes of processing and recipients**
The second right only arises where the data controller is processing personal data relating to the data subject. Where this is the case, the data subject has a right to be given by the data controller a description of the data, the purposes for which they are being or are to be

---

[156]). Arden LJ dissented, holding that the manual selection and presenting of information into automated form fell within s1(1) DPA (at [120]-[136]).

[148] Information Commissioner, *DPA: Legal Guidance*, para 2.3.

[149] DPA s 7(1)(a).

[150] DPA s 7(1)(b).

[151] DPA s 7(1)(c).

[152] DPA s 7(1)(d).

[153] FOIA s 1(1) (a), arising from the duty to confirm or deny.

processed, and the recipients or classes of recipients to whom they are or may be disclosed. As a necessary corollary to this right, information on the recipients or categories of recipient of data and on the content of data disclosed must be stored for an appropriate period of time, in order that it can be provided when requested.[154] The Act does not make clear the level of detail to which a data subject is entitled under the second right. So far as the description of the data is concerned, the data subject's entitlement under the Data Protection Directive is to information as to 'the categories of data concerned'.[155] This indicates that the description of the data may be confined to a statement of the categories of data being processed, rather than anything more detailed. The data controller does not have to name the recipients of the data; he may simply describe the categories into which they fall. A recipient is anyone to whom the data are disclosed, including employees or agents of the data controller to whom they are disclosed in the course of processing.[156] However, someone to whom the data are (or may be) disclosed as a result of, or with a view to, a particular inquiry made in the exercise of a legal power is not classed as a recipient.[157] So an employer would have to include, for example, the category of payroll employees to whom an individual's personal data were disclosed, but not the Inland Revenue, if those data were disclosed pursuant to a specific inquiry.

5–033 **Third right: information itself and information as to source**

The third right will almost always be the most important for a data subject. It is the right of the data subject to have communicated in an intelligible form the information constituting the personal data and any information available to the data controller as to the source of those data. The right to have the information relating to the data subject was also present in Data Protection Act 1984. It is the equivalent to the main right conferred by the Freedom of Information Act 2000.[158] The right of the data subject also to be provided with any available information as to the source of the data was new to the 1998 Act and has no equivalent in the Freedom of Information Act 2000. It is derived directly from the Data Protection Directive and adopts the same wording.[159] However, neither the Directive nor the Data Protection Act 1998 provides any indication as to the level of detail to be supplied, nor as to what information is to be classed as 'available'.[160] Presumably it includes any information in the possession of the data controller — there is no qualification that the information must be readily or reasonably available — but it is not clear whether it also covers information available to the data controller from third parties. Data controllers are not obliged to keep records of this type of information,

---

[154] C-553/07 *College van burgemeester en wethouders van Rotterdam v Rijkeboer* [2009] 3 CMLR 28, where the ECJ held that the appropriate period will depend on the period for which the 'basic data' (ie the personal information of or from which disclosure is made) is stored, tempered by the burden that storage places on the data controller (see [66]). The United Kingdom intervened in the *Rijkeboer* case, arguing that the right of access in art 12(a) exists only in the present and not the past (see [37]). The ECJ rejected that proposition (see [53]-[54]).

[155] Council Directive 95/46/EC art 12(a).

[156] DPA s 70(1).

[157] DPA s 70(1).

[158] FOIA s 1(1)(b).

[159] Council Directive 95/46/EC art 12(a).

[160] It is to be narrowly construed. It does not include 'every hand through which the data have passed', such as secretarial or administrative personnel: *Johnson v Medical Defence Union* [2004] EWHC 347 (Ch) at [55].

only to provide such information as is available at the time of the request. Requests for information as to the source of personal data may well involve information relating to other identifiable individuals, and as such will be subject to the third-party disclosure provisions.[161]

4   Fourth right: logic involved in automated decision-taking
The fourth right only arises in limited cases. Where personal data relating to the data subject are automatically processed in order to evaluate matters relating to the individual, such as the individual's work performance, creditworthiness, reliability or conduct, and such processing has constituted or is likely to constitute the sole basis for any decision significantly affecting the individual, the data subject has the right to be informed by the data controller of the logic involved in that decision-taking. This right, which is derived directly from the Data Protection Directive,[162] is linked to rights to object to such automated decisions being taken about oneself on important matters, and is presumably intended to enable the individual to inform himself in order properly to exercise those rights.[163] The Data Protection Act 1998 does not define the term 'logic'. This right only applies to data processed automatically in order to evaluate matters relating to the individual such as conduct, reliability and the like. So, for example, a system that rejected job applicants under the age of 18 would not be caught, whereas an automated psychometric testing system would. The decision-taker is not required to provide information as to the logic involved in any decision-taking if the information constitutes a trade secret.[164] Again, 'trade secret' is not defined.[165] It appears that it need not be a trade secret of the decision-taker, but may be a trade secret, for example, of the supplier of the automated system. This is the view of the Information Commissioner who has indicated, in relation to the employer/employee relationship, that the decision-taker is not required to disclose matters that either he or the system supplier would reasonably want to keep secret from a competitor on the basis that it provides a significant competitive advantage. That view is consistent with the broad and non-technical approach adopted by the courts in recent years.[166]

4.   THE REQUEST

5   Form of request
A data controller is not obliged to supply any of the information identified above unless he has received a written request.[167] A request sent by electronic means, which is received in legible form and is capable of being used for subsequent reference, satisfies the requirement that the

---

[161] DPA s 7(4), (5). See §5–045.

[162] Council Directive 95/46/EC art 12(a).

[163] DPA s 12; Council Directive 95/46/EC art 15.

[164] DPA s 8(5).

[165] As to its meaning under the FOIA, see §§25–049 to 25–054.

[166] See, eg *Lansing Linde Ltd v Kerr* [1991] 1 All ER 418 (CA) at 425 and 435.

[167] DPA s 7(2)(a). Query whether the obligation to submit a written request is a 'constraint' contrary to art 12(a) of the Data Protection Directive.

request be in writing.[168] This would appear potentially to cover text messages that can be printed or stored as well as emails.

5– 036 Requests made by an agent on behalf of adult

It appears that a subject access request may be made not only by a data subject but also by someone acting on the applicant's behalf, such as a solicitor or parent. The Information Commissioner advises data controllers that they should comply with subject access requests made by an agent on behalf of an intellectually capable adult individual if satisfied (eg by a written authority or power of attorney) that the individual has authorised the agent to make the request.[169]

5– 037 Requests by children and mentally incapacitated adults

So far as children are concerned, while the Data Protection Act 1998 does not place any age restriction on the right to exercise the subject access requests, the Information Commissioner's advice is that a data controller who receives a subject access request on behalf of a child will need to judge whether the child understands the nature of the request. If so, then the child is entitled to exercise the right and the data controller should reply to the child. If the child does not understand the nature of the request, someone with parental responsibility, or a guardian, is entitled to make the request on the child's behalf, and receive the response.[170] Similarly, where an adult is incapable of making decisions on his own behalf, an agent acting pursuant to an enduring power of attorney or appointed by the Court of Protection may exercise the subject access rights on his behalf.[171]

5– 038 Scope of request

The Data Protection Act 1998 expressly allows an individual in prescribed cases to limit his request to personal data of any prescribed description.[172] A request in relation to one of the first three rights is deemed to include a request in relation to the other two such rights.[173] However, the fourth right (information as to the logic involved in automated decision-taking) is treated separately. A general request is not deemed to include a request in respect of the fourth right unless it shows an express intention to that effect.[174] Similarly, a request in respect of the fourth right is not deemed to include a request in respect of the other rights unless it shows an express intention to that effect.[175] As noted above,[176] it is open to an individual to make a request of a public authority that straddles different information access regimes: for example, a request that

---

[168] DPA s 64. Unless the contrary intention appears, 'writing' includes other modes of representing or reproducing words in a visible form: see the Interpretation Act 1978 s 5.

[169] Information Commissioner, *DPA: Legal Guidance*, para 4.1.5.

[170] Information Commissioner, *DPA: Legal Guidance*, para 4.1.6.

[171] Information Commissioner, *DPA: Legal Guidance*, para 4.1.7.

[172] DPA s 7(7).

[173] DP (Fees) Regs reg 2(1).

[174] DP (Fees) Regs reg 2(2).

[175] DP (Fees) Regs reg 2(3).

[176] §5– 002.

seeks both personal information relating to the applicant himself (under the Data Protection Act 1998) as well as non-personal information or personal information relating to a third party (under both the Freedom of Information Act 2000 and the Environmental Information Regulations 2004).[177]

39   Particularising the request

A data controller may ask for further information from a person making a subject access request in certain circumstances, and is not obliged to comply with the request unless he is supplied with that further information.[178] The further information must be reasonably required by the data controller to enable him to satisfy himself as to the identity of the person making the request and to locate the information sought, and the data controller must inform the individual of this requirement.[179] The data controller may need to confirm the authenticity of the request, not by virtue of s 7 itself, but by virtue of other obligations imposed by the Data Protection Act 1998, in particular the obligation to comply with the data protection principles. The further information may again be provided by electronic means.[180]

40   Unstructured personal data

'Unstructured personal data' is defined to mean:

> any personal data falling within paragraph (e) of the definition of "data" in section 1(1), other than information which is recorded as part of, or with the intention that it should form part of, any set of information relating to individuals to the extent that the set is structured by reference to individuals or by reference to criteria relating to individuals.[181]

As noted above,[182] the fifth class of data was introduced into the Data Protection Act 1998 by the Freedom of Information Act 2000. It expands the subject access right conferred by the Data Protection Act to give it equivalence (in relation to information held by a public authority) with the right of access conferred by the Freedom of Information Act 2000. The amendment of the definition was principally a measure related to freedom of information, rather than to data protection. This is reflected in the expanded right under the Data Protection Act 1998 being given only in relation to data held by a public authority.[183] Information falling within the fifth data class is not conventionally within the grasp of data protection legislation. Because information in paragraph (e) falls outside the first four data classes, there is less scope for such information to impinge upon a data subject's privacy. Some information falling within paragraph (e) of the definition of 'data' will not constitute 'unstructured personal data', namely information that forms part of a set of information structured by reference to individuals or by reference to criteria relating to individuals. This brings in such information even though the set is structured in such a way that specific information relating to a particular individual is

---

[177] A specimen request is included in the Appendix to this work.

[178] DPA s 7(3).

[179] DPA s 7(3).

[180] DPA s 64.

[181] DPA s 9A(1). As to paragraph (e), see §5– 020.

[182] §§5– 012 and 5– 020.

[183] It is also reflected in DPA s 33A.

readily accessible.[184] This is illustrated by the examples given in the explanatory notes to the Freedom of Information Act 2000 (which implemented this provision).[185] While incidental personal information on a policy file or in loose papers would amount to unstructured personal data, a case file about an individual containing correspondence about a number of matters relating to that individual and indexed by reference only to correspondence dates would be structured personal data for these purposes.

5–041   Significance of unstructured personal data

To the extent that the subject access request relates to unstructured personal data, a public authority is not obliged to comply with the request unless it contains a description of the data.[186] The authority is therefore allowed to look to the data subject for help in identifying the data. Secondly, if the authority estimates that the cost of complying with the request so far as it relates to the unstructured personal data would exceed the relevant prescribed limit, it is not obliged to comply with it.[187] However, the public authority's obligation to comply with the first access related right, ie to inform the individual whether unstructured personal data in respect of which the applicant is the data subject are being processed by or on behalf of the data controller,[188] must also be considered separately. Only if the estimated cost of complying with that obligation alone would exceed the appropriate limit is the public authority relieved of the requirement of doing so.[189] When estimating the cost of compliance with the request, the public authority must comply with regulations made under the Freedom of Information Act 2000.[190] In making its estimate, the public authority may only take account of costs it reasonably expects to incur in determining whether it holds the information, locating the information (or a document that may contain it), or retrieving the information (or such a document and extracting the information from it).[191]

5–042   Fees

The general position is that a data controller is not obliged to comply with a subject access request unless he has received such fee as he may require, provided that the fee does not exceed the maximum prescribed by the Secretary of State for Justice.[192] The Secretary of State for Justice also has the power to prescribe cases in which no fee is payable.[193] In most cases the

---

[184] DPA s 9A(1).

[185] Explanatory Notes 215 and 216.

[186] DPA s 9A(2).

[187] DPA s 9A(3). The limit is prescribed by the Secretary of State for Justice by regulations and he may prescribe different amounts in relation to different cases: s 9A(5). The FOI & DP (Limit & Fees) Regs prescribe a limit of £600 for public authorities listed in Pt I of Sch 1 to the FOIA and a limit of £450 in the case of any other public authority. In relation to fees, see §§11– 014 to 11– 021.

[188] See §5– 031.

[189] DPA s 9A(4).

[190] DPA s 9A(6), FOIA s 12(5). The relevant regulations are the FOI & DP (Limit & Fees) Regs. See further §11– 018.

[191] FOI & DP (Limit & Fees) Regs reg 4.

[192] DPA s 7(2)(b), (10). The fee is set by the DP (Fees) Regs reg 3.

[193] DPA s 7(2)(b), (10).

normal maximum subject access fee prescribed is currently £10, except in the case of certain educational and health records.[194] In the case of educational records, no fee may be charged, unless a permanent copy of the information is to be provided, in which case the maximum fee varies from £1 to £50, according to the type and number of the copies in question.[195] In the case of health records, the maximum that may be charged for a copy of a non-automated record is £50. Where the request is restricted solely to data forming part of a health record that was created, at least in part, within the 40 days preceding the request, no fee may be charged, provided that no permanent copy of the information is to be supplied.[196] Requests may be specifically limited to conform to these circumstances.[197]

3 Vexatious requests

There is a tension between the need to deter vexatious requests and the fundamental right to obtain a copy of personal data. There is no specific power to refuse a request on the basis that it is vexatious.[198] The balance, instead, is struck in the Data Protection Directive by the requirement that individuals should be able to gain access to their data 'without excessive expense'.[199]

4 Limited request

Under the former Data Protection Act 1984 an individual was entitled to be supplied with a copy of the information constituting the personal data. Under that regime it had been held that once a subject access request had been received, all that a data controller could do was supply all the data held by it relating to the data subject.[200] The Data Protection Act 1998 provides that an individual making a subject access request may, in prescribed cases, specify that his request is limited to personal data of any prescribed description.[201] To date the only prescribed circumstance in which a limited request may be made relates to requests for access to health records, designed to enable individuals to confine their requests to those for which no fee may be charged.[202] Other than in this prescribed circumstance, it would seem that a data subject cannot confine his request to limited personal data relating to himself.

---

[194] For the definition of educational and health records, see §5–018.

[195] DP (Fees) Regs reg 5 and schedule.

[196] DP (Fees) Regs reg 6.

[197] DP (Fees) Regs reg 6.

[198] Contrast the position under the FOIA: see §§12–010 to 12–013.

[199] Directive 95/46/EC art 12.

[200] *R v Chief Constable of B County Constabulary, ex p Director of the National Identification Service, ex p R*, QBD, 24 November 1997 (Laws J).

[201] DPA s 7(7).

[202] DP (Fees) Regs reg 6.

5.   THE RESPONSE

5– 045   **Data that also relate to a third party**

The right conferred by s 7(1)(c) is a right to have communicated in an intelligible form the information constituting the personal data and any information available to the data controller as to the source of those data. As just noted, once a proper request is received, and if there is no applicable exemption, the data controller must ordinarily provide the data subject with all the data held by the data controller relating to the data subject. Where a data controller cannot comply with a subject access request without disclosing information relating to another individual[203] who can be identified from that information, the data controller is not obliged to comply with the request unless that other individual has consented to the disclosure or it is reasonable in all the circumstances for him to comply with the request without such consent.[204] Another individual can be identified from the information being disclosed if he can be identified merely from that information, or from that and any other information which, in the reasonable belief of the data controller, is likely to be in, or to come into, the possession of the data subject making the request.[205] Without more, s 7(4) would have the potential to defeat the subject access rights of many data subjects according to whether or not information relating to them also happened to relate to another person. To overcome this, s 7(5) provides that s 7(4):

> is not to be construed as excusing a data controller from communicating so much of the information sought by the request as can be communicated without disclosing the identity of the other individual concerned, whether by the omission of names or other identifying particulars or otherwise.

In relation to the data that discloses the identity of the other individual concerned, the Court of Appeal has emphasised that the data controller is only required to carry out that balancing act if the information about the third party is necessarily part of the data subject's personal data; otherwise the third-party information should simply be redacted.[206] The Data Protection Act 1998 specifies a number of factors to be taken into account in determining whether it is reasonable to comply with the request without such consent.[207] In addition, it has been suggested that the data controller should be able to ask himself what, if any, legitimate interest the data subject has in the disclosure of the identity of another individual.[208]

5– 046   **Time for compliance**

A data controller is required to comply with a subject access request promptly and in any event

---

[203] This includes information identifying an individual as the source of the information sought by the request: DPA s 7(5).

[204] DPA s 7(4).

[205] DPA s 8(7).

[206] *Durant v Financial Services Authority* [2003] EWCA Civ 1746, [2004] FSR 28 at [64]–[66].

[207] DPA s 7(6).

[208] *Durant v Financial Services Authority* [2003] EWCA Civ 1746, [2004] FSR 28 at [61]; *Johnson v Medical Defence Union* [2004] EWHC 347 (Ch) at [57]–[58].

within a prescribed period (40 days)[209] from the day on which he receives the request or, if later, the day on which he has both the required fee and any further information required by him pursuant to s 7(3).[210] The time for compliance is greater than that of the corresponding provision in the Freedom of Information Act 2000.[211]

7 Manner of compliance: data at time request received

The information supplied pursuant to a subject access request must be supplied by reference to the data in question at the time when the request was received, except that it may take account of any subsequent amendment or deletion provided that amendment or deletion would have been made regardless of the receipt of the request.[212] This means that data controllers can carry on with their routine processing despite the receipt of a subject access request. What they cannot do is make special deletions or amendments in response to the request.[213]

8 Manner of compliance: the right to a copy of the information

Specific requirements are imposed as to the manner of compliance for certain of the access-related rights. In particular, in order to comply with the obligation to communicate to the data subject in an intelligible form the information constituting any personal data of which he is the subject, the data controller must supply the data subject with a copy of the information in permanent form, unless that would be impossible or would involve disproportionate effort or the data subject agrees otherwise.[214] A copy of the information in permanent form would plainly embrace a photocopy, printout or video recording. If any of the information is expressed in terms that are not intelligible without explanation, the copy must be accompanied by an explanation of those terms.[215] The data controller is also under an obligation to disclose sources of information.[216] There is no obligation to maintain records of such sources, only to supply them if they are available in recorded form.[217]

9 Use by data subject of information supplied

The Data Protection Act 1998 imposes no restriction on the use that may be made of

---

[209] DPA s 7(10). In relation to subject access requests wholly or partly relating to personal data forming part of an accessible record which is an educational record within the meaning of Sch 11 to the Act, a period of 15 school days is allowed: DP (Fees) Regs reg 5(4).

[210] DPA s 7(8), (10). The Information Commissioner suggests that 'promptly' means 'as quickly as he can': see DPA: Legal Guidance, para 4.1.

[211] Note, however, that the DPA speaks of 'days' (ie including Saturdays and Sundays), whereas the FOIA speaks of 'working days'. See s 10(1) and FOI(S)A s 10(1). The statutory requirement is dealt with at §11–026.

[212] DPA s 8(6). In relation to the possibility of making a request for future information, see §9–011.

[213] See also Information Commissioner, DPA: Legal Guidance, para 4.1.

[214] DPA ss 7(1)(c)(i), 8(2). *Ezsias v Welsh Ministers* [2007] EWHC B15 (QB) at [95]-[97]. See further §§13–015 to 13–021.

[215] DPA s 8(2).

[216] DPA s 7(1)(c)(ii).

[217] *Ezsias v Welsh Ministers* [2007] EWHC B15 (QB) at [77]-[78]. See also Council Directive 95/46/EC art 12(a), which specifies that 'any available information' as to the source of the data has to be provided.

information supplied to a data subject pursuant to a subject access request.[218] There is nothing to stop the data subject from using the information supplied in support of proceedings, whether civil, criminal or administrative, against the organisation supplying the information or any other organisation. Nor does the Data Protection Act 1998 prevent a data subject from volunteering the information received under a subject access request to a third party. That being said, the underlying purpose of s 7 is not to assist a data subject, for example, to obtain discovery of documents that may assist him in litigation or complaints against third parties and this is reflected in a narrow interpretation of 'personal data'.[219]

5–050 **Proscription against compulsion to share information received**

The Data Protection Act 1998 provides safeguards to prevent individuals from being required to exercise their subject access rights in order to provide information to others, such as employers or prospective employers. These safeguards do not have their origin in the Data Protection Directive. The first set of safeguards relates, broadly speaking, to police, criminal and social security contribution records.[220] It is an offence for a person to require an individual or a third party to supply or produce a record obtained by virtue of a subject access request (a 'relevant record') in connection with the individual's recruitment, continued employment or engagement under a contract for the provision of services.[221] The protection is broad, applying not only to employees, but also to contractors and office holders.[222] Indeed, it is not confined to an employment situation. Suppliers of goods, facilities or services are similarly prohibited from requiring individuals or third parties to supply or produce a relevant record as a condition for the provision of such goods, facilities or services.[223] This would prevent, for example, an insurance company from requiring an individual to supply his or her criminal record as a condition for providing insurance cover. However, the prohibitions do not apply to a person who shows that the imposition of the requirement to supply or produce a relevant record was required or authorised by an enactment, a rule of law or a court order, or was, in the particular circumstances, justified as being in the public interest.[224]

5–051 **Certificates under the Police Act 1997**

These safeguards in the Data Protection Act 1998 go hand in hand with the regime under Part V of the Police Act 1997 for the provision of certificates as to criminal convictions and records by the Criminal Records Agency.[225] Under that Act, such certificates may only be obtained by the individuals to whom they relate and certain other registered persons.[226] In the absence of

---

[218] As to the ability of a data controller to impose such a condition, see §15–027.

[219] *Durant v Financial Services Authority* [2003] EWCA Civ 1746, [2004] FSR 28 at [27].

[220] DPA s 56(1), (2), (6). Social security contribution records are included because of the tendency of some employers to rely on a gap in contributions as evidence of time spent in prison.

[221] DPA s 56(1), (5).

[222] DPA s 56(1), (10).

[223] DPA s 56(2).

[224] DPA s 56(3). As to the meaning of the 'public interest', see §15–004.

[225] DPA s 75(4); Police Act 1997 Pt V.

[226] DPA s 75(4), Police Act 1997 Pt V.

s 56 of the Data Protection Act 1998, it would be open to employers to seek to circumvent that regime by requiring individuals to exercise their rights under the Data Protection Act 1998. The Secretary of State may by order add to the categories of information and suppliers thereof that constitute a relevant record.[227] This power addresses the concern that employers or others would find different ways of obtaining information as to individuals' criminal records via their subject access rights. In the light of the provision made by the Police Act 1997 for the supply of criminal record and conviction certificates, the Data Protection Act 1998 makes clear that the public interest defence will not be satisfied merely on the ground that the imposition of a requirement to supply a relevant record would assist in the prevention or detection of crime.[228]

2 Use of information required: health records
Safeguards also apply in the case of health records. Any contractual term or condition purporting to require an individual to supply or produce any health record obtained by virtue of a subject access request is deemed to be void.[229] This prevents employers from requiring their employees to obtain and disclose their medical records.

6. DISENTITLEMENT

3 Multiple and repeat requests
Where a data controller has previously complied with a subject access request, it is not obliged to comply with a subsequent identical or similar request made by the same individual unless a reasonable interval has elapsed between compliance with the previous request and the making of the current request.[230] This 'reasonable interval' limitation reflects the wording of the Data Protection Directive.[231] In determining whether a reasonable interval has elapsed, regard must be had to the nature of the data, the purpose for which they are processed and the frequency with which they are altered.[232]

4 Excessive cost of compliance
In so far as a subject access request relates to unstructured personal data,[233] the public authority is not obliged to comply with it if it estimates that the cost of doing so would exceed the relevant

---

[227] DPA s 56(8).

[228] DPA s 56(4).

[229] DPA s 57. As to the meaning of 'health record' see §5–018.

[230] DPA s 8(3).

[231] Directive 95/46/EC art 12(a). There is a corresponding provision in the FOIA s 14(2); FOI(S)A s 14(2). See further §§12–014 to 12–018.

[232] DPA s 8(4).

[233] As to the meaning of 'unstructured personal data', see §5–040.

prescribed limit.[234] In this context, the public authority's obligation to comply with the first access related right, ie to inform the individual whether unstructured personal data in respect of which he or she is the data subject are being processed by or on behalf of the data controller, must be considered separately. Only if the estimated cost of complying with that obligation alone would exceed the appropriate limit is the public authority relieved of the requirement of doing so.[235] When estimating the cost of compliance with the request, the public authority must comply with regulations made under the Freedom of Information Act 2000.[236] In making its estimate, the public authority may only take account of costs it reasonably expects to incur in: determining whether it holds the information, locating the information or a document that may contain it, retrieving the information or such a document and extracting the information from such a document.[237]

7.   EXEMPTIONS

5– 055   **Introduction**

Both the Data Protection Directive and the Data Protection Act 1998 set out a series of exemptions.[238] Where an exemption is engaged, the data controller is relieved of the obligation to meet the rights of access of the data subject.[239] The Act does not expressly make provision for part disclosure where only some of the information comprising the personal data falls within an exemption.[240] Engagement of an exemption turns on the character of the applicant's 'personal data' or the effect of disclosure of that data, rather than on the character of the actual information itself. This does not prevent the data controller from voluntarily supplying the data subject with the information sought.[241] The exemptions in the Data Protection Act 1998 are largely, but not entirely, mirrored in the Freedom of Information Act 2000. These are considered in detail in Chapters 14 to 26 of this work. What follows is a brief outline of each of the heads of exemption existing under the Data Protection Act 1998, cross-referenced to the detailed treatment of that exemption.

5– 056   **The Directive**

The Directive is deemed not to apply to personal data processed by a natural person in the

---

[234] DPA s 9A(3). The limit is prescribed by the Secretary of State for Justice by regulations and he may prescribe different amounts in relation to different cases: s 9A(5). The FOI & DP (Limit & Fees) Regs prescribe a limit of £600 for public authorities listed in Pt I of Sch 1 to the FOIA and a limit of £450 in the case of any other public authority. There is a parallel provision in the FOIA s 13(1); FOI(S)A s 12. In relation to fees, see §11– 018.

[235] DPA s 9A(4).

[236] DPA s 9A(6), FOIA s 12(5). See the FOI & DP (Limit & Fees) Regs.

[237] FOI & DP (Limit & Fees) Regs reg 4.

[238] DPA Pt IV ss 27–39.

[239] DPA s 27(1)–(2).

[240] Contrast FOIA s 17, FOI(S)A s 16, EIR reg 12(3)–(5), and EI(S)R reg 10(3)–(5). The definition of 'personal data' suggests all the information which, considered as a group, relate to the applicant: see §§5– 021 to 5– 022 and DPA s 7(1)(c)(i).

[241] See §§9– 034 to 9– 038 and 14– 007 to 14– 014.

course of a purely personal or household activity.[242] In addition, it provides for exemptions on a number of broad grounds:

— safeguarding of national security, defence and public security;
— the prevention and prosecution of crime and breaches of professional ethics;
— State economic and financial interests;
— certain regulatory functions;
— the protection of the data subject and the rights and freedoms of others.[243]

It provides for specific exemptions in relation to:

— scientific research and statistics;[244] and
— data processed for journalistic, artistic and literary purposes.[245]

These exemptions are on the whole reflected in the Data Protection Act 1998, although some of the exemptions under the Act appear only loosely related, at best, to the permissible exemptions under the Directive. The exemptions granted under Part IV of the Data Protection Act 1998 will now be considered in turn.

7 National security

Personal data are exempt from the subject access rights if exemption from those rights is required for the purpose of safeguarding national security.[246] As with the Freedom of Information Act 2000, a claim for exemption on the grounds of safeguarding national security may be the subject of a conclusive certificate signed by a Minister of the Crown.[247] A conclusive certificate stands as conclusive evidence of the 'fact' that exemption from the subject access rights is or at any time was required for the purpose of safeguarding national security.[248] The certificate may identify the personal data to which it applies by means of a general description; it may also be expressed to have prospective effect.[249] The principal effect of a conclusive certificate is to change the right of appeal against a decision to refuse access from one of independent merit review, in which the Upper Tribunal makes a fresh decision unconstrained by the original decision, to one in which the Upper Tribunal merely determines whether the

---

[242] Directive 95/46/EC art 3(2).

[243] Directive 95/46/EC arts 3(2), 13(1). Reference to 'the rights and freedoms of others' embraces those rights and freedoms conferred or recognised by the European Convention on Human Rights: see *R (Lord) v SSHD* [2003] EWHC 2073 (Admin) at [91]–[93].

[244] Directive 95/46/EC art 13(2).

[245] Directive 95/46/EC art 9.

[246] DPA s 28(1)(b). Detailed treatment of exemption on the grounds of national security is provided at §§17– 002 and 17– 040 to 17– 065. Equivalent provisions are found in the FOIA s 24, and in the FOI(S)A s 31(1). National security is a qualified exemption under the FOIA, so that it may be disengaged upon a consideration of the public interest. There is no such potential public interest override where the national security exemption is engaged under the DPA.

[247] DPA s 28(2). Detailed treatment of the effect of a conclusive certificate is provided at §§14– 032 et seq. The only Ministers that may issue a certificate are those who are members of the Cabinet or the Attorney-General or the Advocate General for Scotland: DPA s 28(10).

[248] A conclusive certificate may also be issued for purpose of defeating any of the other provisions of the DPA mentioned in s 28(1).

[249] DPA s 28(3).

Minister was reasonable in his decision to issue a certificate.[250] If a data controller claims that the terms of a conclusive certificate employing a general description applies to particular personal data, the certificate is presumed so to apply.[251] That presumption is itself capable of challenge by any party to proceedings before the Upper Tribunal, which may determine that the certificate does not apply to the personal data in question.[252] The Information Commissioner also has a role to play in relation to national security exemptions, as he must determine whether an exemption under section 28 of the Act has been properly claimed.[253] In any case where s 28 is relied upon (either through the issue of a certificate or otherwise), the Information Commissioner is entitled to satisfy himself that the requested material is indeed exempt, and in so doing he is entitled to request to see the material. If refused, the Commissioner can serve a notice under s 43 of the Act requiring the data controller to furnish him with the requested material.

5– 058 **Crime detection and tax collection**

Personal data are exempt from the subject access rights where they are held for the purpose of:
— crime prevention or detection;[254]
— the apprehension or prosecution of offenders; or
— the assessment or collection of any tax, duty or similar imposition,
but only in any case to the extent that such access would be likely to prejudice any such

---

[250] Appeals against non-certificated claims of exemption under the DPA are considered at §§28– 041 to 28– 045; appeals against certificated exemptions under the DPA are considered at §§5– 084 and 28– 046 to 28– 047. In *Norman Baker MP v SSHD* [2001] UKHRR 1275 the Data Protection Tribunal (as the Tribunal was then known) held that a national security exemption certificate applying effectively a blanket exemption to files held by MI5 was unreasonably wide. A revised form of the certificate was considered by the High Court in *Re Ewing* [2002] EWHC 3169 (QB), where it was held that the criticisms of the Information Tribunal had been addressed: '...a general [neither confirm nor deny] policy, in response to requests for personal data, including as to the existence (or non-existence) of personal data, is in principle justifiable and cannot be criticised as unreasonable or unnecessary' (at [60]). The Information Tribunal expressed the view in *Hitchens v SSHD*, IT, 4 August 2003 at [49] and *Gosling v SSHD*, IT, 1 August 2003 at [56] that the Investigatory Powers Tribunal established pursuant to the Regulation of Investigatory Powers Act 2000 had power to consider whether the Security Services were justified in claiming that a neither confirm nor deny policy was necessary in a particular case and, for this reason, found that the revised form of national security exemption certificate issued in those two cases had been issued on reasonable grounds. See also *Hilton v FCO*, IT, 28 June 2005, which applied the same reasoning in relation to GCHQ.

[251] DPA s 28(6).

[252] DPA s 28(6).

[253] DPA s 51, construed in light of Articles 13 and 28 of the Directive. See *R (SSHD) v Information Tribunal* [2006] EWHC 2958 (Admin), [2007] 2 All ER 703, where the Court upheld a decision by the Information Tribunal to quash a national security certificate which was made on the basis that the IC had no statutory role within the context of s 28 exemptions.

[254] In *Re Martin* [2002] NIQB 67 the High Court in Northern Ireland held that information held by the Health & Social Services Trust obtained by it when investigating allegations of sexual abuse by the applicant represented data processed for the purposes of the prevention or detection of crime. In *R (A) v Chief Constable of C* [2001] 1 WLR 461, [2001] 2 FCR 431 it was held that non-conviction information following a police vetting enquiry in respect of the applicant's application for the post of head-teacher represented data processed for the prevention and detection of crime. See also *Chief Constable of Humberside Police & ors v IC and SSHD* [2009] EWCA 1079 in relation to the retention of old criminal convictions on the police national computer.

purpose.[255] In order for the exemption to be engaged, a likelihood of prejudice to the exemption is required.[256] Similarly, personal data are exempt from the subject access rights where they are held for the purpose of discharging any statutory function, provided that those data were obtained for that purpose from a person who had them in his possession for any of the preceding purposes.[257] There is a further specific exemption in the case of personal data that consist of a classification applied to the data subject as part of a system of risk assessment operated for the purpose either of tax assessment or collection, or of the prevention or detection of crime involving unlawful claims for payment out of, or unlawful application of, public funds.[258] The exemption applies where the data controller operating the risk assessment system is a government department, a local authority or an authority administering housing benefit or council tax benefit.[259] The data are exempt to the extent to which exemption is required in the interests of the operation of that risk assessment system.[260]

9 Health information

The Data Protection Act 1998 does not by its own terms exempt from the subject access rights information relating to the health of a person.[261] Indeed, certain health records are specifically brought within the definition of an 'accessible record'.[262] Section 30 of the Act does, however, empower the Secretary of State to exempt or modify the subject access rights in relation to personal data consisting of information as to the physical or mental health of the data subject.[263] The Secretary of State has made an order[264] under this power. The order defines three circumstances in which information as to the physical or mental health of the data subject will be exempt from the subject access rights:

(1) Where the information is held by a court and it consists of information supplied to it in a report or other evidence given by certain bodies or individuals.[265]

---

[255] DPA s 29(1). Equivalent provisions are found in the FOIA s 31(1)(a), (b) and (d), and in the FOI(S)A s 35. These are considered in detail at §§20– 014 to 20– 019. Law enforcement is a qualified exemption under the FOIA, so that it may be disengaged upon a consideration of the public interest. There is no such potential public interest override where the law enforcement exemption is engaged under the DPA.

[256] As to the meaning of 'would be likely to prejudice', see §§15– 020 to 15– 028.

[257] DPA s 29(2). However, the exemption does not apply to personal data held by the Football Membership Authority for the purposes of the national football membership scheme: see the Football Spectators Act 1989 s 5(6).

[258] DPA s 29(4).

[259] DPA s 29(4), (5).

[260] DPA s 29(4).

[261] Limited exemptions for certain health information exist under the FOIA ss 31(2)(i), (j) and 38(1)(a) and the FOI(S)A ss 35(2)(i) and 39(1). Free-standing information access rights to certain medical information are given by other legislative provisions: see §§8– 036 to 8– 041.

[262] DPA s 68.

[263] DPA s 30(1). The Information Commissioner has issued detailed guidance in this area: Use and Disclosure of Health Data: Guidance on the Application of the DPA 1998 (May 2002).

[264] The Data Protection (Subject Access Modification) (Health) Order 2000 SI 2000/413.

[265] The Data Protection (Subject Access Modification) (Health) Order 2000 SI 2000/413 art 4. The bodies and persons are: a local authority; a Health and Social Services Board; a Health and Social Services Trust; a probation officer; and other persons who give evidence in the course of any proceedings to which the Family Proceedings Courts (Children Act 1989) Rules 1991, the Magistrates' Courts (Children and Young Persons) Rules 1992, the Magistrates'

(2)   Where application of the rights would be likely[266] to cause serious harm to the physical or mental health or condition of the data subject or any other person.[267] Where the data controller is not a health professional, the controller must consult (or have consulted) the appropriate health professional before withholding information on this ground.[268] However, the obligation to consult does not arise where the data controller is satisfied that the information requested has previously been seen by the data subject or is known to the data subject.[269]

(3)   Where a request is made on behalf of the data subject by the person with parental responsibility for the data subject (if the data subject is a child) or by the person appointed by the court to manage his affairs (if the data subject is incapable of doing so) and granting access would disclose information:

(i)   that the data subject had provided in the expectation that it would not be disclosed to the applicant;

(ii)   that was obtained as a result of an examination or investigation to which the data subject consented in the expectation that the information would not be so disclosed; or

(iii)   that the data subject had expressly indicated should not be so disclosed.[270]

5–060   Educational records

The Data Protection Act 1998 does not by its own terms exempt educational records from the subject access rights. Educational records[271] are specifically brought within the definition of an 'accessible record'.[272] But again, s 30 of the Act empowers the Secretary of State to exempt or modify the subject access rights in relation to certain sorts of educational information.[273] The Secretary of State has made an order under this power.[274] The order defines three circumstances in which personal data consisting of information constituting an 'educational record'[275] are exempt from the subject access provisions:

Courts (Criminal Justice (Children)) Rules (Northern Ireland) 1999, the Act of Sederunt (Child Care and Maintenance Rules) 1997 or the Children's Hearings (Scotland) Rules 1996 apply provided that under those rules the information may be withheld by the court in whole or in part from the data subject.

[266] In *Roberts v Nottingham Healthcare NHS Trust* [2008] EWHC 1934 (QB), [2009] FSR 4, [2008] MHLR 294, Cranston J adopted the meaning of 'likely' expounded in *R (Lord) v SSHD* [2003] EWHC 2073: the question is whether there may very well be a risk of harm to health even if the risk falls short of being more probable than not (at [7]-[9]).

[267] The Data Protection (Subject Access Modification) (Health) Order 2000 SI 2000/413 art 5. This is similar to the exemption granted by the FOIA s 38(1)(a) and the FOI(S)A s 39(1). These are considered at §§23–001 to 23–010.

[268] The Data Protection (Subject Access Modification) (Health) Order 2000 SI 2000/413 arts 5(2) and 7. As to the meaning of 'health professional' see the DPA s 69.

[269] The Data Protection (Subject Access Modification) (Health) Order 2000 SI 2000/413 art 6(2).

[270] The Data Protection (Subject Access Modification) (Health) Order 2000 SI 2000/413 art 5(3)–(4).

[271] Defined in the DPA Sch 11.

[272] DPA s 68(1).

[273] DPA s 30(2)(a). The exemption is restricted to data in respect of which the data controller is the proprietor of, or a teacher at, a school, and which consist of information relating to persons who are or have been pupils at the school. The proprietor of a school is the person or body responsible for its management, generally the governing body: DPA s 30(5) and Education Act 1996 s 579.

[274] The Data Protection (Subject Access Modification) (Education) Order 2000 SI 2000/414.

[275] As defined in the DPA Sch 11, para 1.

(1) where the data have been provided to a court in specified proceedings, and is information that the court may withhold from the data subject;[276]

(2) where the disclosure of the data would be likely to cause serious harm to the physical or mental health or condition of the data subject or any other person;[277]

(3) where the request is made on behalf of the data subject by a person with parental responsibility for the data subject (in the case of a child) or by a person appointed by the court to manage the data subject's affairs (in the case of a person incapable of doing so) and the request relates to information as to whether the data subject has been the subject of or may be at risk of child abuse. In such circumstances, the subject access rights do not apply in any case to the extent to which their application would not be in the best interests of the data subject.[278]

These exemptions do not apply to data to which the health exemption applies.[279]

5‑1 Health records of a deceased

Access to the health records of a patient who has died is provided by the Access to Health Records Act 1990. The right of access is given to the personal representative of the patient and to any person who may have a claim arising out of the patient's death. The right is also to be extended to a medical examiner stating or investigating the cause of the patient's death under section 20 of the Coroners and Justice Act 2009. The right of access is subject to several exemptions.[280]

5‑2 Social work records: the power to exempt

The Secretary of State has power to exempt or modify the subject access rights in relation to social work records.[281] The power to exempt applies to a much broader category of personal data than that to which the relevant accessible public record provisions apply (ie information held by a local social services authority for any purpose of its social services functions).[282] It

---

[276] The Data Protection (Subject Access Modification) (Education) Order 2000 SI 2000/414 art 4. The proceedings to which it applies are those under the Family Proceedings Courts (Children Act 1989) Rules 1991, the Magistrates' Courts (Children and Young Persons) Rules 1992, the Magistrates' Courts (Criminal Justice (Children)) Rules (Northern Ireland) 1999, the Act of Sederunt (Child Care and Maintenance Rules) 1997 or the Children's Hearings (Scotland) Rules 1996, provided that under those rules the information may be withheld by the court in whole or in part from the data subject.

[277] The Data Protection (Subject Access Modification) (Education) Order 2000 SI 2000/414 art 5(1). For an example of where it did not apply, see: In *A v Information Commissioner*, IT, 11 July 2006 at [17b]. In Scotland, where an education authority receives a request relating to relevant education information it believes to have originated from the Principal Reporter, it must notify the Principal Reporter of that request and may not communicate the information to the data subject unless the Principal Reporter has given his opinion that this ground of exemption (serious harm to the physical or mental health or condition of the data subject or any person) does not apply: art 6. This is similar to the exemption granted by the FOIA s 38(1)(a) and the FOI(S)A s 39(1). These are considered at §§23– 001 to 23– 010.

[278] The Data Protection (Subject Access Modification) (Education) Order 2000 SI 2000/414 art 5(2)–(5). This exemption does not apply in Scotland.

[279] The Data Protection (Subject Access Modification) (Education) Order 2000 SI 2000/414 art 3(2)(a). As to the health exemption, see §5– 059.

[280] See further §8– 037.

[281] DPA s 30(3).

[282] DPA s 68(1)(c) Sch 12.

applies to personal data consisting of information processed by government departments, local authorities, voluntary organisations or other bodies designated by the Secretary of State, where that information appears to him to be processed in the course of, or for the purposes of carrying out, social work in relation to the data subject or other individuals.[283] Social work is not defined. The power to exempt is therefore apt to attach to a broader category of records held by public authorities than simply the relevant accessible public records. The power to exempt or modify the subject access provisions is only exercisable where the Secretary of State considers that the application of those provisions would be likely to prejudice the carrying out of social work.[284]

5– 063 ## Social work records: the exemption order

The Secretary of State has exercised his power of exemption by the making of an order.[285] The order applies (1) to personal data processed by a diverse range of authorities and bodies pursuant to a variety of social services and other functions specified in the order, including information processed by local authorities in connection with their social services functions, and also, for example, data processed by probation committees, special health authorities, any court-appointed children's guardian and the National Society for the Prevention of Cruelty to Children in connection with specified functions;[286] and (2) to personal data processed by a court in specified proceedings.[287] The data will be exempt:

(1)   In the case of the former, where disclosure of the information would be likely to prejudice the carrying out of social work by reason of the fact that serious harm to the physical or mental health or condition of the data subject or any other person would be likely to be caused.[288] Note that two elements must be satisfied before the second exemption may be relied upon: not only must application of the relevant access rights be likely to cause serious harm to physical or mental health, but this must, in turn, be likely to prejudice the carrying out of social work.[289]

(2)   Again in the case of the former, where a request is made on behalf of the data subject and the information was provided by the data subject in the expectation that

---

[283] DPA s 30(3).

[284] DPA s 30(3).

[285] The Data Protection (Subject Access Modification) (Social Work) Order 2000 SI 2000/415 as amended.

[286] The Data Protection (Subject Access Modification) (Social Work) Order 2000 art 3(1) and sch para 1.

[287] The Data Protection (Subject Access Modification) (Social Work) Order 2000 art 3(1) and sch para 2.

[288] The Data Protection (Subject Access Modification) (Social Work) Order 2000 arts 3(1), 5(1)–(2) and Sch para 1. This exemption applies only to the second, third and fourth subject access rights: the data subject remains entitled to be informed whether personal data of which he or she is the subject are being processed by the data controller: The Data Protection (Subject Access Modification) (Social Work) Order 2000 SI 2000/415 art 5(1); DPA s 7(1).

[289] The Data Protection (Subject Access Modification) (Social Work) Order 2000 SI 2000/415 art 5(1). This reflects the qualification to the Secretary of State's exemption power. In Scotland, where a social work authority receives a request relating to relevant social work information it believes to have originated from the Principal Reporter, it must notify the Principal Reporter of that request and may not communicate the information to the data subject unless the Principal Reporter has given his opinion that this ground of exemption (prejudice to social work because of serious harm to the physical or mental health or condition of the data subject or any other person) does not apply: art 6.

it would not be disclosed to the person making the request.[290]

(3) In the case of the latter, where the information has been provided to a court in specified proceedings, and is information that the court may withhold from the data subject.[291] The social work exemptions do not apply to data to which the health or education exemptions apply.[292]

54 Prejudice to regulatory activity

Personal data that are held (or otherwise processed) for certain regulatory functions are exempt from the subject access rights to the extent that application of those subject access rights to the data would be likely to prejudice[293] the proper discharge of the regulatory functions.[294] Broadly, the regulatory functions covered by this exemption are:

(1) statutory, governmental or public functions designed to protect the public against financial loss at the hands of financial services professionals or corporate management,[295] bankrupts[296] and persons authorised to carry on professions or activities;[297]

(2) statutory, governmental or public functions designed for protecting charities or community interest companies against misconduct or mismanagement,[298] or for protecting or recovering their property;[299]

(3) statutory, governmental or public functions designed for securing the health, safety and welfare of persons at work[300] or for protecting other persons from risks to their health, safety and welfare arising out of the actions of persons at work;[301]

---

[290] The Data Protection (Subject Access Modification) (Social Work) Order 2000 SI 2000/415 arts 3(1), 5(3)–(4) and Sch para 1.

[291] DPA ss 3(1), 4 and Data Protection (Subject Access Modification) (Social Work) Order 2000 Sch para 2. The proceedings to which it applies are those to which the Family Proceedings Courts (Children Act 1989) Rules 1991, the Magistrates' Courts (Children and Young Persons) Rules 1992, the Magistrates' Courts (Criminal Justice (Children)) Rules (Northern Ireland) 1999, the Act of Sederunt (Child Care and Maintenance Rules) 1997, the Children's Hearings (Scotland) Rules 1996 or the Family Proceedings Rules 1991 apply provided that under those rules the information may be withheld by the court in whole or in part from the data subject.

[292] The Data Protection (Subject Access Modification) (Social Work) Order 2000 SI 2000/415 art 3(2)(a). As to the health exemption, see §5– 059. As to educational records, see §5– 060.

[293] As to the meaning of the word 'prejudice' and the phrase 'would be likely to prejudice' see §§15– 020 to 15– 028.

[294] DPA s 31.

[295] DPA s 31(1), (2)(a)(i), (3). Analogous provisions are contained in the FOIA s 31(2)(d) and the FOI(S)A s 35(2)(d). These are considered in §20– 032.

[296] DPA s 31(1), (2)(a)(ii), (3).

[297] DPA s 31(1), (2)(a)(iii), (3). Analogous provisions are contained in the FOIA s 31(2)(d) and the FOI(S)A s 35(2)(d). These are considered in §20– 032.

[298] DPA s 31(1), (2)(b), (3). Analogous provisions are contained in the FOIA s 31(2)(f)–(h) and the FOI(S)A s 35(2)(f)–(h). These are considered in §20– 032.

[299] DPA s 31(1), (2)(c), (2)(d), (3).

[300] DPA s 31(1), (2)(e), (3). As to the meaning of prejudice to health and safety see further §§23– 002 to 23– 003. Analogous provision are contained in the FOIA s 31(2)(i)–(j) and the FOI(S)A s 35(2)(i)–(j). These are considered in §20– 032.

[301] DPA s 31(1), (2)(f), (3).

(4)   the statutory functions of the various ombudsmen[302] designed for protecting members of the public against maladministration by public bodies and failures in services provided by public bodies;[303]

(5)   the statutory functions of the Financial Ombudsman Service established pursuant to Part XVI of the Financial Services and Markets Act 2000;[304]

(6)   the statutory functions of the Legal Services Board, where provision of the data would be likely to prejudice the proper discharge of those functions;

(7)   the function of considering a complaint under the scheme established under Part 6 of the Legal Services Act 2007 (legal complaints), where provision of the data would be likely to prejudice the proper discharge of that function;

(8)   the statutory functions of the Office of Fair Trading designed for protecting members of the public against conduct that may adversely affect their interests by persons carrying on a business, for regulating anti-competitive agreements and for regulating market abuses;[305] and

(9)   statutory functions relating to the handling and consideration of complaints relating to NHS redress, health care, social services and children looked after by local authorities.[306]

These heads of exemption are considered more extensively elsewhere in this work.[307]

5–065   **Journalism, literature and art**

Personal data held (or otherwise processed) only for journalistic, artistic or literary purposes ('the special purposes') are exempt from the subject access rights if:

—   they are held (or otherwise processed) with a view to the publication of journalistic, literary or artistic material; and

—   the data controller reasonably believes both that publication would be in the public interest and that compliance with the subject access rights would be incompatible with the special purposes.[308]

This exemption, which has its origins in article 9 of the Data Protection Directive, is concerned with the balance between the protection of individual privacy and the right to freedom of expression. Thus, in considering whether publication would be in the public interest, the data controller is required to have particular regard to the special importance of the public interest

---

[302] The Parliamentary Commissioner for Administration, the Commission for Local Administration in England, the Health Service Commissioner for England, the Public Services Ombudsman for Wales, the Assembly Ombudsman for Northern Ireland, the Northern Ireland Commissioner for Complaints and the Scottish Public Services Ombudsman: DPA s 31(4)(a).

[303] DPA s 31(4)(b).

[304] DPA s 31(4A).

[305] DPA s 31(5).

[306] DPA s 31(6).

[307] See §20– 032.

[308] DPA ss 32(1) and (2). There is no matching general exemption in the FOIA or in the FOI(S)A. However, Part VI of Schedule I to the FOIA establishes that the BBC, Channel 4 Television, The Gaelic Media Service and Sianel Pedwar Cymru are only subject to the Act 'in respect of information held for purposes other than those of journalism, art or literature'.

in freedom of expression.[309]   This exemption is unlikely to have much application to information held by public authorities.

66   Information held only for research purposes

Personal data held (or otherwise processed) only for 'research purposes' are exempt from the subject access rights provided that:

— the data are not held (or otherwise processed) in order to support measures or decisions with respect to particular individuals;

— they are not processed in such a way that substantial damage or distress is, or is likely to be, caused to any data subject; and

— the results of the research or any resulting statistics are not made available in a form which identifies any data subject.[310]

'Research purposes' includes statistical and historical purposes.[311]   Personal data are not treated as held otherwise than for research purposes simply because they are disclosed to a person for research purposes, or are disclosed to the data subject or a person acting on his behalf, or are disclosed at the request or with the consent of the data subject or a person acting on his behalf.[312]   Further, they are not treated as being so processed where the person making the disclosure has reasonable grounds for believing that one of those circumstances applies.[313]

67   Manual data relating to Crown employment

Personal data falling within the final limb of the definition of 'data', ie manual data recorded by a public authority,[314] and which relate to personnel matters concerning Crown employment are exempt from the subject access rights.[315]   The types of personnel matters concerned include appointments and removals, pay, discipline and superannuation.[316]   The exemption covers service in the armed forces, service in any office or employment under the Crown or a public authority, and service in any other office or employment or under any contract for services where the power to take action in respect of such personnel matters rests with Her Majesty, a Minister of the Crown, the National Assembly for Wales, a Northern Ireland Minister or any public authority.[317]   This exemption is designed to achieve parity between those who work for public authorities and those who work in the private sector.   The view is taken that the former should not have additional rights of access in the employment context merely because of the

---

[309] DPA s 32(1)(b).   The public interest is treated in greater detail at §§15–001 to 15–019.

[310] DPA s 33(1) and (4).   There is no matching exemption in the FOIA or in the FOI(S)A.   Indeed, under those Acts, statistical and 'factual' information is expressly taken out of certain of the exemptions: FOIA ss 35(2), 35(4) and 36(4); FOI(S)A ss 29(2) and 29(3).   Many research bodies are included in the list of public bodies to which FOIA applies.

[311] DPA s 33(1).

[312] DPA s 33(5)(a)–(c).

[313] DPA s 33(5)(d).

[314] As to which, see §5–020.

[315] DPA s 33A(2).   An applicant cannot circumvent the exemption by arranging for another person to request the information under the FOIA: see ss 40(2) and (4) of that Act and FOI(S)A ss 38(1)(b) and 38(3).   Both are absolute exemptions under those Acts.

[316] DPA s 33A(2).

[317] DPA s 33A(2).

identity of their employer.

5– 068 Information otherwise available

Where personal data are available to the public independently of the subject access rights, those data are exempt from the subject access rights.[318] This exemption applies to any personal data comprising information which the data controller is statutorily obliged to make available to the public, whether by publishing it or making it available for inspection or by making it available in some other way, and whether on payment of a fee or otherwise, apart from information the data controller is obliged to make available under the Freedom of Information Act 2000.

5– 069 Parliamentary privilege

Personal data are exempt from the subject access rights if the exemption is required for the purpose of avoiding an infringement of the privileges of either House of Parliament, ie parliamentary privilege.[319]

5– 070 Legal professional privilege

Personal data are exempt from the subject access rights if the data comprise information in respect of which a claim to legal professional privilege, or, in Scotland, confidentiality of communications, could be maintained in legal proceedings.[320]

5– 071 Domestic purposes

Personal data processed by an individual only for the purposes of the individual's personal, family or household affairs, including recreational purposes, are exempt from the subject access rights.[321] This exemption is, or at least should be, unlikely to have much application to information held by public authorities.

5– 072 Confidential references

Personal data are exempt from the subject access rights if they consist of a reference given (or to be given) in confidence[322] by the data controller for the purposes of the education, training or employment of the data subject; his or her appointment to any office; or the provision by him or her of any service.[323] It is notable that this exemption applies only to references given or to be given by the data controller. If the data controller has on file references provided by a previous employer, they do not fall within the scope of the exemption. However, the data

---

[318] DPA s 34. The analogous provisions are the FOIA s 21(1) and the FOI(S)A s 25(1). These exemptions are considered further in §§16– 001 to 16– 006.

[319] DPA s 35A. The analogous provision is the FOIA s 34. There is no analogous provision in the FOI(S)A. These exemptions are considered further in §§21– 001 to 21– 012.

[320] DPA s 37, Sch 7 para 10. The analogous provisions are the FOIA s 42(1) and FOI(S)A s 36(1). These exemptions are considered further in §§21– 013 to 21– 022.

[321] DPA s 36.

[322] As to the meaning of information given 'in confidence', see §§25– 001 to 25– 028. The FOIA s 41(1) and the FOI(S)A s 36, provide a general exemption for information acquired in confidence. The FOIA s 27(3) and the FOI(S)A s 32(1)(b) also deal with certain other information acquired by a public authority in confidence: see §§18– 016 to 18– 017.

[323] DPA s 37, Sch 7 para 1.

controller may, for example, decline to reveal the identity of the author of the reference, pursuant to s 7(4) and (5).

3 Judicial appointments and honours

Personal data are exempt from the subject access rights where they are held (or otherwise processed) for the purposes of assessing a person's suitability for judicial office or the office of Queen's Counsel, or for the purposes of the conferring by the Crown of any honour or dignity.[324]

4 Crown employment and Crown or Ministerial appointments

The Data Protection Act 1998 confers a power on the Secretary of State to exempt from the subject access rights personal data processed for the purposes of assessing a person's suitability for Crown employment or appointment to any office by Her Majesty, a Minister of the Crown or a Northern Ireland department.[325] This power has been exercised in relation to a variety of Crown appointments, including archbishops, bishops and certain other clergy; Lord-Lieutenants; Masters of certain Cambridge colleges; the Provost of Eton; the Poet Laureate and the Astronomer Royal.[326]

5 Armed forces

Personal data are exempt from the subject access rights in any case to the extent to which the application of those provisions would be likely to prejudice the combat effectiveness of any of the armed forces of the Crown.[327]

6 Management forecasts

Personal data processed for the purposes of management forecasting or management planning to assist the data controller in the conduct of any business or other activity are exempt from the subject access rights in any case to the extent to which the application of those provisions would be likely to prejudice the conduct of that business or activity.[328]

7 Corporate finance

There is an exemption in relation to personal data processed for the purposes of, or in connection with, a corporate finance service.[329] The concept of a 'corporate finance service'

---

[324] DPA s 37, Sch 7 para 3. An applicant cannot circumvent the exemption by arranging for another person to request the information under the FOIA: see ss 40(2) and (4) of that Act and FOI(S)A ss 38(1)(b) and 38(3). Both are absolute exemptions under those Acts.

[325] DPA s 37, Sch 7 para 4.

[326] The Data Protection (Crown Appointments) Order 2000 SI 2000/416.

[327] DPA s 37, Sch 7 para 2. The analogous provisions are the FOIA s 26(1), and the FOI(S)A s 31(4). These are qualified exemptions under the FOI Acts. These exemptions are considered in §§17–040 to 17–049, 17–052 to 17–055, 17–058 to 17–062 and 17–065. As to the meaning of the word 'prejudice' and the phrase 'would be likely to prejudice' see §§15–020 to 15–028.

[328] DPA s 37, Sch 7 para 5. There is no analogous provision under either the FOIA or the FOI(S)A. As to the meaning of the word 'prejudice' and the phrase 'would be likely to prejudice' see §§15–020 to 15–028. A public authority may be a 'business': *Friends of the Earth v Information Commissioner and DTI*, IT, 4 April 2007.

[329] DPA s 37, Sch 7 para 6.

is derived from the EC Directive on investment services in the securities field.[330] It covers certain activities relating to issues of specified instruments, as well as the provision of advice to undertakings on matters such as capital structure, industrial strategy and mergers.[331] Where personal data are processed for the purposes of, or in connection with, a corporate finance service provided by a relevant person,[332] the data are exempt from the subject access rights to the extent to which the application of those provisions could affect the price of any specified instrument (whether it already exists, or is to be or may be created).[333] This limb of exemption also extends to circumstances in which the data controller reasonably believes that the price of such an instrument could be so affected.[334] Such data are also exempt if exemption is required to safeguard an important economic or financial interest of the United Kingdom.[335] The Secretary of State has a power to specify matters to be taken into account in determining whether exemption on the latter ground is required, or circumstances in which exemption is (or is not) to be taken to be required.[336] This power has been exercised in relation to personal data to which the application of the subject information provisions could affect decisions whether to deal in, subscribe for or issue instruments or decisions which are likely to affect any business activity.[337] In such cases, the matter to be taken into account is the inevitable prejudicial effect on the orderly functioning of financial markets or the efficient allocation of capital within the economy resulting from the application of the subject access rights.[338]

5– 078 Negotiations

Personal data comprising records of the data controller's intentions in relation to any negotiations with the data subject are exempt from the subject access rights in any case to the extent to which the application of those provisions would be likely to prejudice those negotiations.[339]

5– 079 Examination marks and scripts

A group of exemptions and modifications relates to examination marks and scripts. Examination scripts, that is to say personal data consisting of information recorded by candidates during an academic, professional or other examination,[340] are exempt from the

---

[330] Council Directive 93/22/EEC. See DPA Sch 7 para 6(3).

[331] DPA Sch 7 para 6(3).

[332] Defined in DPA Sch 7 para 6(3).

[333] DPA Sch 7 para 6(1)(a)(i).

[334] DPA Sch 7 para 6(1)(a)(ii).

[335] DPA Sch 7 para 6(1)(b).

[336] DPA Sch 7 para 6(2).

[337] Data Protection (Corporate Finance Exemption) Order 2000 SI 2000/184 art 2(3).

[338] Data Protection (Corporate Finance Exemption) Order 2000 SI 2000/184 art 2(2).

[339] DPA s 37, Sch 7 para 7. As to the meaning of the word 'prejudice' and the phrase 'would be likely to prejudice' see §§15– 020 to 15– 028.

[340] DPA Sch 7 para 9(1).

subject access rights.[341] Those rights are modified in relation to examination marks or other information processed for the purpose of determining examination results, or of enabling those results to be determined, or in consequence of their determination.[342] The modifications prevent a data subject from using his or her subject access rights to obtain examination results before they are announced. They achieve this by extending the period for compliance with a subject access request.[343]

0   Self-incrimination

The privilege against self-incrimination is preserved by the Data Protection Act 1998. A person is not required to comply with a subject access request (or order under s 7) to the extent that to do so would, by revealing evidence of the commission of any offence (other than an offence under the Data Protection Act 1998) expose him to proceedings for that offence.[344] Furthermore, information disclosed by a person in compliance with such a request or order is not admissible against him in proceedings for an offence under the Data Protection Act 1998.[345]

1   Disclosure prohibited by other legislation

In addition to the exemptions conferred by the Data Protection Act 1998 itself, there are additional exemptions from the subject access rights made pursuant to a further general power of exemption conferred on the Secretary of State by the Act in respect of information the disclosure of which is already prohibited or restricted by other legislation. The Secretary of State may exempt personal data consisting of such information, where he considers it necessary for safeguarding the interests of the data subject or the rights and freedoms of any other individual that the prohibition or restriction should prevail over the subject access rights.[346] Pursuant to this power, there are exemptions in respect of certain information relating to human fertilisation and embryology,[347] adoption records and reports,[348] statements of special educational needs[349] and parental order records and reports.[350]

---

[341] DPA s 37, Sch 7 para 9.

[342] DPA Sch 7 para 8(1), (5).

[343] DPA Sch 7 para 8.

[344] DPA s 37 and Sch 7 para 11(1).

[345] DPA Sch 7 para 11(2).

[346] DPA s 38(1).

[347] The Data Protection (Miscellaneous Subject Access Exemptions) Order 2000 SI 2000/419 art 2 and sch Pt I.

[348] The Data Protection (Miscellaneous Subject Access Exemptions) Order 2000 SI 2000/419 art 2 and sch Pt II(a), III(a), IV(a) as amended by the Data Protection (Miscellaneous Subject Access Exemptions) (Amendment) Order 2000 SI 2000/1865. In Scotland information provided by a Principal Reporter for a children's hearing is also exempted: The Data Protection (Miscellaneous Subject Access Exemptions) Order 2000 SI 2000/419 art 2 and sch Pt III(b).

[349] The Data Protection (Miscellaneous Subject Access Exemptions) Order 2000 SI 2000/419 art 2 and Sch Pt II(b), III(c) (record of special educational needs in Scotland), Pt IV(b).

[350] The Data Protection (Miscellaneous Subject Access Exemptions) Order 2000 SI 2000/419 art 2 and Sch Pt II(c), III(d), IV(c).

8. APPEALS

5– 082 **Two routes of appeal**

There are two methods by which a person who is dissatisfied with the response by a data controller to a subject access request may seek to have that response reviewed. First, the person may appeal directly against that decision. That method is considered in this section and, in greater detail, in Chapter 28.[351] The nature of that appeal and the body to whom it is made will depend on whether or not there is a national security certificate in place. Secondly, the person may request an assessment by the Information Commissioner of the performance of the data controller. That is considered in section 9 below.[352] In this second method, once the Information Commissioner takes the view that there has been a breach of the data protection principles, it is the Commissioner who maintains the momentum against the data controller. The two methods are not mutually exclusive. In particular, the second method may, in some circumstances, provide a data subject with a more effective appeal right than the first method.

5– 083 **Ordinary appeals**

Where no national security certificate has been issued in respect of the data sought, the dissatisfied applicant may appeal to the High Court or a county court or, in Scotland, to the Court of Session or the sheriff against any failure to comply with a subject access request.[353] There is no provision or requirement for the dissatisfied applicant first to seek a reconsideration by the data controller of the decision. The question for the court on such an appeal is whether the data controller has failed to comply with the request in contravention of the provisions of s 7 of the Data Protection Act 1998.[354] In other words, the right of appeal involves the court considering afresh the applicability of any exemption, unfettered by the decision of the data controller: it is not a review of the reasonableness of the data controller's decision or of the methodology applied by the data controller in reaching the appealed decision. However, where the data controller itself is required to make an assessment of reasonableness — eg the reasonableness of complying with a subject access request without the consent of a third party about whom information will necessarily be disclosed — the court's role is not routinely to 'second-guess' the merits of the data controller's decision, rather, ordinarily, to carry out a review of its reasonableness based on anxious scrutiny.[355] To this end, the court is entitled to

---

[351] See §§28– 041 to 28– 050. Under the Data Protection Directive, Member States are required to provide individuals with a right to a 'judicial remedy' for any breach of the rights guaranteed to them: Directive 95/46/EC art 22. The rights of appeal are compliant with the Human Rights Act 1998: *MG v United Kingdom* [2002] 3 FCR 289, (2003) 36 EHRR 3, (2003) 13 BHRC 179. (However, the European Court found a violation of art 8 of the ECHR from 1995 to 1 March 2000 prior to the coming into force of the DPA). See further §§3– 002 to 3– 007.

[352] §§5– 086 to 5– 090.

[353] DPA s 15(1).

[354] DPA s 7(9). As the applicant's entitlement under s 7(1) is 'subject to the following provisions of [ss 7,] 8, 9 and 9A' of the Act, the court will have jurisdiction to consider whether the procedural requirements set out in those sections have been met in order to determine whether the failure to comply with the applicant's request is, in fact, in contravention of the applicant's entitlement.

[355] *Durant v Financial Services Authority* [2003] EWCA Civ 1746, [2004] FSR 28 at [58]–[61].

require the data controller to make available to the court any information held (or otherwise processed) by or on behalf of the data controller.[356]   Where the court does require the data controller to make available to it any such information, the court is not permitted to disclose to the applicant or his representative the information made available pending the determination of the appeal in the applicant's favour.[357]   The court has a 'general and untrammelled' discretion whether to order compliance with the request.[358]   It has been emphasised that this regime is quite separate from the disclosure regime under the Civil Procedure Rules.[359]   There is no reason in principle why the mere fact that data have been found to fall outside the scope of a subject access request should mean that they are not disclosable in accordance with the Civil Procedure Rules in an action, for example, under section 13 or 14 of the Data Protection Act 1998.[360]

4 National security certificate appeals

Where a certificate has been issued certifying in respect of some or all of the data sought that exemption from the subject access rights[361] is, or at any time was, required for the purpose of safeguarding national security (ie a national security certificate), then the certificate will be conclusive evidence of that 'fact'.[362]   A national security certificate effectively removes the right of a merit review to the extent that it relates to the data sought.   In its place, there are two rights of appeal to the Upper Tribunal:

(1)   A person directly affected by the issuing of a conclusive certificate may appeal against the reasonableness of the decision to issue the conclusive certificate.

(2)   There is a right of appeal as to the applicability of a national security certificate to particular data.

5 Procedure on appeals

The procedure on appeals is considered in detail in Chapter 28 below.[363]   In brief terms, ordinary appeals are governed by the rules of the court in which the appeal is heard.[364]   Both sorts of national security appeals are governed by a special regime, which is shared with

---

[356] The information that may be sought is not expressly limited to that answering the terms of the request.

[357] DPA s 15(2).

[358] *Durant v Financial Services Authority* [2003] EWCA Civ 1746, [2004] FSR 28 at [74]; *R (Lord) v SSHD* [2003] EWHC 2073 (Admin) at [160]; *Ezsias v Welsh Ministers* [2007] EWHC B15 (QB) at [102].

[359] *Ezsias v Welsh Ministers* [2007] EWHC B15 (QB) at [102]/

[360] *Johnson v Medical Defence Union* [2004] EWHC 2509 (Ch) at [28].

[361] Whether specifically or as part of any of the provisions mentioned in s 28(1) of the DPA.

[362] DPA s 28(2). A certificate may identify the personal data to which it applies by means of a general description; and it may be expressed to have prospective effect: DPA s 28(3). Conclusive certificates are considered further in §§14–032 et seq.

[363] See §§28– 041 to 28– 047.

[364] The court has special powers to call for the information that is the subject of the request and certain other information: see §5– 083.

national security appeals under the Freedom of Information Act 2000.[365]

9. ENFORCEMENT[366]

5–086 **Request for an assessment**
In addition to appealing to a court against any failure to comply with a subject access request,[367] a data subject (or a person on his behalf) may request the Information Commissioner for an assessment as to whether it is likely that the processing has been or is being carried out in compliance with the provisions of the Data Protection Act 1998.[368] Such a request may include seeking an assessment by the Information Commissioner whether the data controller has disclosed under s 7 and in accordance with the Act information held by the data controller relating to the data subject.[369] Where such a request is made, the Information Commissioner is obliged to make an assessment in such manner as appears to him to be appropriate.[370] The advantage for a data subject in making a request for an assessment by the Information Commissioner is that, if an exemption on any of the specified grounds is relied upon by the data controller, the Information Commissioner will be able to call for the data relating to the data subject (as well as other information)[371] and, having examined those data (and other information), consider whether the exemption has been properly relied upon.[372] This can assume importance, as the data controller, in answering a subject access request, may have not informed the data subject that data relating to him had been withheld, the basis upon which

---

[365] DPA s 28(12) and Sch 6. In relation to the FOIA s 60(1) and (4). The FOI(S)A gives no express right of review in relation to the decision to issue a conclusive certificate, whether issued on national security grounds (s 31(2)) or on exceptional sensitivity grounds (s 52(2)).

[366] See further ch 29.

[367] See §5–083.

[368] DPA s 42(1).

[369] DPA s 1(1), definition of 'processing', in particular para (c).

[370] DPA s 42(2). In determining what manner is appropriate, the Information Commissioner may have regard to the extent to which the request appears to him to raise a matter of substance, whether there has been undue delay in making the request and whether the person is entitled to make an application under DPA s 7 in relation to the request: DPA s 42(3).

[371] By the service of an 'information notice' under DPA s 43(1). A person served with an information notice may appeal to the First-Tier Tribunal against that notice: DPA s 48(1). Ordinarily, the information notice must not require compliance at a time sooner than the expiry of the time for an appeal: DPA s 43(4). However, if the Information Commissioner requires the information sought in the information notice as a matter of urgency, he may include in the information notice a statement to that effect: DPA s 43(5). In this case, the notice can require the information to be supplied 8 or more days after service of the information notice: DPA s 43(5). The data controller can include in an appeal against the information notice an appeal against the inclusion of such a statement: s 48(3). Appeals are governed by DPA Sch 6. The appeal is a merit-based appeal: DPA s 49.

[372] The power of the IC to require the data holder to provide him with information extends to situations where the information is held by the Security Services: *R (SSHD) v Information Tribunal* [2006] EWHC 2958 (Admin), [2007] 2 All ER 703.

it had been withheld or whether a national security certificate[373] is operating.[374] The minimum requirements of an assessment are that the Information Commissioner notify the person making the request whether he has made an assessment and, to the extent he considers appropriate, of the view he has formed or the action taken as a response to the request.[375] The action taken may include the service of an enforcement notice.

37   Enforcement notice

Where the Information Commissioner is satisfied that a data controller has contravened any of the data protection principles, the Commissioner may issue an 'enforcement notice'.[376] The sixth data protection principle requires personal data to be processed in accordance with the rights of data subjects under the Data Protection Act 1998, and it is a breach of that principle to fail to supply information in accordance with section 7.[377] Thus, where the Information Commissioner is satisfied that a data controller has failed to comply with a subject access request, the Commissioner may issue a notice requiring the data controller to comply with the request.[378] Although in practice a request for an assessment will ordinarily be the catalyst for such an enforcement notice, the Information Commissioner can issue an enforcement notice whenever he is satisfied that a data controller has contravened or is contravening any of the data protection principles.[379] In deciding whether or not to issue an enforcement notice (and whether or not an information notice was served in considering the request for assessment), the Information Commissioner will be able to call for the data relating to the data subject (as well as other information)[380] and, having examined those data (and other information), consider whether the exemption has been properly relied upon. An enforcement notice must contain a statement of the data protection principle that the Information Commissioner is satisfied has been or is being contravened and the Commissioner's reasons for reaching that conclusion.[381]

38   Cancellation or variation of an enforcement notice

The Information Commissioner may, after serving an enforcement notice, cancel or vary it.[382] At any time after the time for appeal against an enforcement notice has expired, the person on whom the notice has been served may apply to the Information Commissioner for a

---

[373] Under DPA s 28(2).

[374] Thus, in *R (SSHD) v Information Commissioner* [2006] EWHC 2958 (Admin), [2007] 2 All ER 703 (DC), the Home Department responded to the data subject's request by stating 'We have processed your request and enclose copies of all the information which [the Immigration and Nationality Directorate] is required to supply under the Data Protection Act 1998.' The Home Department's response did not indicate whether there was any further information that it held relating to the applicant and, if so, upon what basis it declined to disclose it to him, including the existence of a national security certificate.

[375] DPA s 42(4).

[376] DPA s 40(1).

[377] DPA Sch 1, Pt I and Pt II para 8(e).

[378] DPA s 40(1). See, eg: *DCLG v IC*, IT, 23 April 2009.

[379] DPA s 40(1).

[380] By the service of an 'information notice' under DPA s 43(1). See further n 371.

[381] DPA s 40(6)(a).

[382] DPA s 41(1).

cancellation or variation of the enforcement notice on the ground that, by reason of a change of circumstances, the notice need not be complied with in order to ensure compliance with the data protection principles.[383]

5– 089 Appeal against an enforcement notice

A data controller served with an enforcement notice may appeal to the First-Tier Tribunal against that notice.[384] A data controller may also appeal against the refusal of the Information Commissioner to cancel or vary an enforcement notice.[385] Appeals to the First-Tier Tribunal are merit-based and are considered in Chapter 28.[386]

5– 090 Non-compliance with an enforcement notice

Failure to comply with an enforcement notice is an offence, subject to a defence of due diligence.[387]

5– 091 Compensation

Where a data controller contravenes any of the requirements of the Data Protection Act 1998, an individual who suffers damage[388] or distress as a result is entitled to be compensated by the data controller.[389] The right to compensation for distress only arises if the individual also suffers damage by reason of the contravention, or if the contravention relates to the processing of personal data for journalistic, artistic or literary purposes.[390] It is a defence to a claim for damages for the data controller to prove that he took such care to comply with the requirement concerned as was reasonably required in all of the circumstances.[391] This appears to be somewhat more generous than the defence for which the Data Protection Directive provides, namely that the data controller was not responsible for the event giving rise to the damage.[392] The right to compensation is conferred only on individuals.[393] Compensation is awarded by the courts.

5– 092 Rectification and destruction

The court's powers to order the rectification, blocking, erasure or destruction of inaccurate

---

[383] DPA s 41(2).

[384] DPA s 48(1). Case C-353/01 *Mattila v EC Commission* [2004] ECR II-1073, [2004] 1 CMLR 32.

[385] DPA s 48(2).

[386] Appeals are governed by DPA Sch 6 and the Tribunal Procedure (First-tier Tribunal) (General Regulatory Chamber) Rules 2009 and, where there is a national security certificate, the Tribunal Procedure (Upper Tribunal) Rules 2008.

[387] DPA s 47.

[388] In *Sofola v Lloyds TSB Bank plc* [2005] EWHC 1335 (QB), [2005] All ER (D) 299 (Jun), Tugendhat J commented at [43] that the refusal of banking facilities would arguably fall within the meaning of the word 'damage' in s 13.

[389] DPA s 13. See also Directive 95/46/EC art 23.

[390] DPA ss 3 and 13(2). As to heads of compensation under s 13 see *Johnson v Medical Defence Union (No 2)* [2006] EWHC (Ch) 321, (2006) 89 BMLR 43 at [217]–[218].

[391] DPA s 13(3).

[392] Directive 95/46/EC art 23(2).

[393] DPA s 13(1) and (2).

personal data generally are outside the scope of this work. However, the court has a specific power to order such rectification, blocking, erasure or destruction following a contravention of any of the requirements of the Data Protection Act 1998, including the subject access rights, in respect of any personal data.[394] It may, on an application by the data subject, order the data controller to rectify, block, erase or destroy the personal data in question if it is satisfied both that the data subject has suffered damage by reason of the contravention, in circumstances entitling him to compensation under s 13, and that there is a substantial risk of further contravention in respect of those data in such circumstances.[395] Moreover, the court may additionally, if it considers it reasonably practicable, order the data controller to notify third parties to whom the data have been disclosed of their rectification, blocking, erasure or destruction.[396] The question of reasonable practicability is to be assessed, in particular, having regard to the number of persons who would have to be notified.[397]

93   Failure to comply with enforcement or information notice

It is not in itself an offence for a data controller to fail to comply with a subject access request. However, as noted above, it is an offence for him to fail to comply with an enforcement notice that orders him to comply with such a request[398] or to fail to comply with an information notice issued by the Commissioner in relation to such a request.[399]

94   Unlawful obtaining of personal data

It is an offence knowingly or recklessly to obtain or disclose personal data, or to procure their disclosure, without the consent of the data controller.[400] It appears that this applies as much to the data subject as to any other person: the data subject must obtain access to his personal data by exercising his rights under s 7. It is not an offence if the obtaining or disclosure was necessary for the prevention or detection of crime; was required or authorised by law or was reasonably believed to be; if the person obtaining or disclosing the data reasonably believed that the data controller would, in the circumstances, have consented; or if the obtaining or disclosure was justified as being in the public interest.[401]

95   Disclosure by Commissioner or Commissioner's staff

It is an offence for the Information Commissioner, or anyone who has worked for him or on

---

[394] DPA s 14(4). This remedy is independent of any claim for compensation. See *Sofola v Lloyds TSB Bank plc* [2005] EWHC 1335 (QB), [2005] All ER (D) 299 (Jun) at [47].

[395] DPA s 14(4).

[396] DPA s 14(5).

[397] DPA s 14(6).

[398] DPA ss 40(1), 47.

[399] DPA s 47.

[400] DPA s 55(1). *R v Rooney* [2006] EWCA Crim 1841.

[401] DPA s 55(2).

his behalf, knowingly or recklessly[402] to disclose any information obtained for the purposes of the Data Protection Act 1998 which relates to an identifiable individual or business and which is not already within the public domain, unless he or she has lawful authority to make such a disclosure.[403] A disclosure is made with lawful authority if the data subject or person carrying on the business consents; if it was made pursuant to or for the purposes of certain statutory functions[404] or obligations, or of criminal or civil proceedings; or if it was necessary in the public interest, having regard to the rights, freedoms and legitimate interests of others.[405] The prohibition on disclosure targets unauthorised or reckless breaches of confidentiality: it does not preclude the Information Commissioner from the due performance of his functions where that requires the disclosure of information supplied to him.[406]

5–096 Enforced subject access

As noted above, it is an offence for a person to require someone to supply him with certain records such as police and criminal records in connection with his recruitment, employment or retention under a contract of services.[407] This prevents individuals from being forced to exercise their subject access rights in such circumstances.

5–097 Prosecutions and penalties

Criminal proceedings for an offence under the Data Protection Act 1998 may only be brought by the Information Commissioner or with the consent of the Director of Public Prosecutions.[408] For all offences under the Data Protection Act 1998 the prescribed punishment, whether on summary conviction or on conviction on indictment, is a fine.[409] There are powers of entry and inspection under the Data Protection Act 1998.[410]

---

[402] As to a body vicariously acting 'knowingly and recklessly', see *Information Commissioner v London Borough of Islington* [2002] EWHC 1036, [2003] BLGR 38, where it was held that the London Borough of Islington could properly be convicted of having knowingly and recklessly contravened the proscription against holding personal data without a current registration: it was not necessary to show that the individual officer who accessed and used the data had acted recklessly. See also *Data Protection Registrar v Amnesty International* [1995] Crim LR 633.

[403] DPA s 59(1), (3). 'Business' is to be given a broad interpretation, covering any identifiable organisation, government department, local authority, charity, other organisation or association, whether or not the body has a commercial or profit-making purpose or function: *Friends of the Earth v Information Commissioner and DTI*, IT, 4 April 2007 at [15], [22] and [40].

[404] See *Roberts v IC and DBIS*, IT, 20 August 2009.

[405] DPA s 59(2).

[406] *Friends of the Earth v Information Commissioner and DTI*, IT, 4 April 2007 at [42].

[407] DPA s 56. See §5–050.

[408] DPA s 60(1).

[409] DPA s 60(2), (3).

[410] DPA s 50, Sch 9.

CHAPTER 6

Access under the Environmental Information Regulations

1. PROVENANCE OF THE ENVIRONMENTAL INFORMATION REGULATIONS

01   The Aarhus Convention

On 25 June 1998, the UN Economic Commission for Europe (UNECE), at its Fourth Ministerial Conference in the 'Environment for Europe' process, adopted a Convention on Access to Information, Public Participation in Decision-Making and Access to Justice on Environmental Matters.   This has become known as the 'Aarhus Convention'.   The Convention entered into force on 30 October 2001. The UK and the European Community is each a signatory to the Aarhus Convention. The Aarhus Convention establishes a number of rights of the public (citizens and their associations) with respect to the environment. It contains three broad themes or 'pillars': access to information, public participation, and access to justice.[1] The Convention recites as one of its goals the protection of the right of every person of present and future generations to live in an environment which is adequate to health and well-being.   The UNECE has described the Aarhus Convention as 'a new kind of environmental agreement', which links environmental rights and human rights, and government accountability and environmental protection.   Thus, it is not only an environmental agreement, but also an agreement about government accountability, transparency and responsiveness.[2] The then Secretary of State for the Environment stated that the UK government strongly supported the objectives of the Aarhus Convention, adding that the three areas in which it provides additional rights (namely, under the three 'pillars' referred to above) would allow the public[3] to be better informed and more involved in decision-making, and that 'more broadly based discussion can lead to better decisions and so make an important

---

[1]   Thus art 1 of the Aarhus Convention provides: 'In order to contribute to the protection of the right of every person of present and future generations to live in an environment adequate to his or her health and well-being, each Party shall guarantee the rights of access to information, public participation in decision-making, and access to justice in environmental matters in accordance with the provisions of this Convention.'

[2]   The Preamble to the Aarhus Convention states, inter alia, that the parties thereto agreed to its terms 'Affirming the need to protect, preserve and improve the state of the environment and to ensure sustainable and environmentally sound development; Recognising that adequate protection of the environment is essential to human well-being and the enjoyment of basic human rights, including the right to life itself; Recognising also that every person has the right to live in an environment adequate to his or her health and well-being, and the duty, both individually and in association with others, to protect and improve the environment for the benefit of present and future generations; Considering that, to be able to assert this right and observe this duty, citizens must have access to information, be entitled to participate in decision-making and have access to justice in environmental matters, and acknowledging in this regard that citizens may need assistance in order to exercise their rights; Recognising that, in the field of the environment, improved access to information and public participation in decision-making enhance the quality and the implementation of decisions, contribute to public awareness of environmental issues, give the public the opportunity to express its concerns and enable public authorities to take due account of such concerns; Aiming thereby to further the accountability and transparency in decision-making and to strengthen public support for decisions on the environment; Recognising the desirability of transparency in all branches of government and inviting legislative bodies to implement the principles of the Convention in their proceedings, [and] Recognising also that the public needs to be aware of the procedures for participation in environmental decision-making, have free access to them and know how to use them.'

[3]   'The public' is defined in art 2(4) of the Aarhus Convention to mean 'one or more natural or legal persons, and, in accordance with national legislation or practice, their associations, organisations or groups'.

contribution to achieving sustainable development'.[4] The European Community ratified the Aarhus Convention on 17 February 2005. The United Kingdom ratified it on 24 February 2005, becoming a full party to the Convention 90 days thereafter. In 2000, the United Nations published an 'Implementation Guide' to the Aarhus Convention.[5]

6– 002 **The first 'pillar' of the Aarhus Convention – access to information**

The Aarhus Convention provides for the right of everyone to receive environmental information that is held by public authorities. Within the United Kingdom, this pillar is implemented through Directive 2003/4/EC and the Environmental Information Regulations 2004.[6] The Convention provides an elaborate definition of 'environmental information'.[7] Having defined 'public authorities',[8] the Convention requires each Contracting Party to ensure that each public authority makes available, in response to a request and within the framework of national legislation, a copy of 'the actual documentation' containing or comprising the requested environmental information. The Convention expressly provides that the person making the request need not state an interest in the information sought.[9] The Convention requires a public authority to make the information available 'as soon as possible' and at the latest within one month after the request has been submitted.[10] The Convention permits a Contracting Party to make a charge 'for supplying information' according to a pre-published schedule of charges.[11] Charges must be reasonable.[12] A request for environmental information may be refused in the circumstances set out in Arts 4(3)–(4) of the Convention. Article 4.3 sets out procedural grounds for refusal: the information is not held by the recipient public authority, the request is manifestly unreasonable, or the information is deliberative material whose disclosure is customarily or expressly provided for. Article 4.4 sets out seven classes of protected

---

[4] Michael Meacher, Minister for the Environment, 6 October 2000 Explanatory Memorandum, Report from the Commission to the Council and the European Parliament on the experience gained in the application of Directive 90/313/EEC of 7 June 1990, on freedom of access to information on the environment and Proposal for a Directive of the European Parliament and of the Council on public access to environmental information, para 15.

[5] Available at:
> www.unece.org/env/pp/acig.pdf

For an annotated guide to case-law on the Convention, see: A Andrusevych, T Alge, C Clemens (eds), *Case Law of the Aarhus Convention Compliance Committee (2004-2008)* (RACSE, Lviv 2008), available at:
> www.rac.org.ua/fileadmin/user_upload/publications/CL3_en_web.pdf

[6] In relation to Scottish public authorities, it is implemented through the EI(S)R.

[7] Article 2.3, considered in §§6– 008 to 6– 012.

[8] 'Public authority' is defined in art 2.2 of the Aarhus Convention as meaning '(a) Government at national, regional and other level; (b) Natural or legal persons performing public administrative functions under national law, including specific duties, activities or services in relation to the environment; (c) Any other natural or legal persons having public responsibilities or functions, or providing public services, in relation to the environment, under the control of a person falling within subparagraphs (a) or (b) above; (d) the institutions of any regional economic integration organisation referred to in art 17 which is a party to this Convention.' Article 2 further states that the above definition of 'public authority' does not include bodies or institutions acting in a judicial or legislative capacity.

[9] Aarhus Convention art 4.1.

[10] Aarhus Convention art 4.2. This requirement is subject to the proviso that this period may be extended, if the volume and complexity of the information justifies the extension, to up to two months after the request. The applicant for information must be informed of any extension and the reasons for it.

[11] Aarhus Convention art 4.8.

[12] Aarhus Convention art 4.8.

interest. Under that Article, a public authority may refuse to disclose requested information to the extent that its disclosure would adversely affect:

— the confidentiality of the proceedings of public authorities, provided that such confidentiality is provided for under national law;[13]
— international relations, national defence or public security;[14]
— the course of justice, the ability of a person to receive a fair trial or the ability of a public authority to conduct an enquiry of a criminal or disciplinary nature;[15]
— the confidentiality of commercial and industrial information, where such confidentiality is protected by law in order to protect a legitimate economic interest;[16]
— intellectual property rights;[17]
— the confidentiality of personal data and/or files relating to a natural person, where that person has not consented to the disclosure of the information to the public and where such confidentiality is provided for in national law;[18]
— the interests of a third party which has supplied the information requested without that party being under or capable of being put under a legal obligation to do so, and where that party does not consent to the release of the material;[19] or
— the environment to which the information relates, such as the breeding sites of rare species.[20]

These grounds for refusal are not made subject to a public interest balancing test. Rather, the Convention provides that the grounds for refusal are to be interpreted in a restrictive way, taking into account the public interest served by the disclosure and taking into account whether the information requested relates to emissions into the environment.[21] The Convention imposes an obligation on a public authority that does not hold requested information to transfer the request to a public authority that it believes holds the requested information.[22] Alternatively, the public authority may inform the applicant that it believes that the other public authority holds the requested information. The Convention provides for redaction of exempt material.[23] Refusals must be in writing, must set out the reasons for refusal and must advise of the applicant's right of review.[24] The right of review must be determined by a court or an

---

[13] Aarhus Convention art 4.4(a). See §6– 046.

[14] Aarhus Convention art 4.4(b). See §6– 042.

[15] Aarhus Convention art 4.4(c). See §6– 044.

[16] Aarhus Convention art 4.4(d). This Article specifically provides that 'Within this framework, information on emissions which is relevant for the protection of the environment shall be disclosed.' See §6– 054.

[17] Aarhus Convention art 4.4(e). See §6– 056.

[18] Aarhus Convention art 4.4(f). See §6– 051.

[19] Aarhus Convention art 4.4(g). See §6– 052.

[20] Aarhus Convention art 4.4(h). See §6– 058.

[21] Aarhus Convention art 4.4.

[22] Aarhus Convention art 4.5.

[23] Aarhus Convention art 4.6.

[24] Aarhus Convention art 4.7.

independent body established by law.[25] The procedure must be free of charge or 'inexpensive'.[26] Under the Convention, public authorities also have a separate obligation to actively disseminate environmental information in their possession.[27] The first pillar, as it has been implemented in the United Kingdom, is considered in this chapter.

6–003 **The second 'pillar' of the Aarhus Convention — public participation**
Article 6 of the Aarhus Convention guarantees the right to participate from an early stage in environmental decision-making with respect to certain specified activities,[28] and with respect to activities that are not specified in the Aarhus Convention itself, but which may have a significant effect on the environment. Where the provisions of article 6 are applicable, the public concerned[29] must be informed, either by public notice or individually as appropriate, early in the environmental decision-making procedure, and in an adequate, timely and effective manner, inter alia, of the proposed activity and the application on which a decision will be taken; the nature of the possible decisions or draft decision; the public authority responsible for making the decision, the envisaged decision-making procedure; and the fact that the activity is subject to a national or trans-boundary environmental impact assessment procedure.[30] Each party to the Convention must require the competent public authorities to give the public concerned access for examination, upon request where so required under national law, free of charge and as soon as it becomes available, all information relevant to the decision-making referred to in article 6 that is available at the time of the public participation procedure, including at least a description of the site and the physical and technical characteristics of the proposed activity; a description of the significant effects of the proposed activity on the environment; a description of the measures envisaged to prevent and/or reduce the effects, including emissions; a non-technical summary of the above; an outline of the main alternatives studied by the applicant; and, in accordance with national legislation, the main reports and advice issued to the public authority at the time when the public concerned shall be informed in accordance with article 2.[31] The procedure for public participation must then allow for the public to submit, in writing or, as appropriate, at a public hearing or inquiry with the applicant, any comments, information, analyses, or opinions that it considers relevant to the proposed

---

[25] Aarhus Convention art 9.1.

[26] Aarhus Convention art 9.1. The Convention implies that if the procedure would not be 'inexpensive' for the appellant, legal aid or some other form of assistance must be made available.

[27] Aarhus Convention art 5.

[28] Namely, those listed in Annex I to the Aarhus Convention. These include activities carried out in the energy sector; in the course of the production and processing of materials; in the mineral and chemical industries; in waste management; by water treatment plants with a capacity exceeding 150,000 population equivalent; by industrial plants; in the construction of transport infrastructure such as railways, airports and roads; and other activities; as well as any activities not specifically mentioned where public participation is provided for under an environmental impact assessment procedure in accordance with national legislation.

[29] Namely by art 2.5, the public affected or likely to be affected by, or having an interest in, the environmental decision-making. Article 2.5 further provides that, for the purpose of the latter definition, non-governmental organisations promoting environmental protection and meeting any requirements under national law shall be deemed to have an interest.

[30] Aarhus Convention art 6.2.

[31] Aarhus Convention art 6.6. These provisions are without prejudice to the provisions of art 4 of the Aarhus Convention: Aarhus Convention art 6.6.

activity;[32] and the parties to the Convention must ensure that in the decision due account is taken of the outcome of the public participation.[33]

4 The third 'pillar' of the Aarhus Convention — access to justice

This pillar of the Aarhus Convention, which is set out in article 9, aims to provide access to justice in three contexts, namely, review procedures with respect to information requests; review procedures with respect to specific decisions that are subject to the public participation requirements, and challenges to breaches of environmental law in general. So far as access to information appeals are concerned, the Convention provides that a person who considers that his Convention request for information has been ignored, wrongfully refused, inadequately answered, or otherwise not dealt with in accordance with the provisions of that Article, must be provided with access to a review procedure by a court or another independent and impartial body established by law.[34] The Convention further provides that, in the circumstances where a party provides for such a review by a court of law, it must ensure that a complainant also has access to an expeditious procedure established by law, that is free of charge or inexpensive, for reconsideration by a public authority or review by an independent and impartial body other than a court of law. Secondly, article 9.2 provides that each party must, within the framework of its national legislation, ensure that members of the public concerned having a sufficient interest, or, alternatively, maintaining impairment of a right, where the administrative procedural law of a party requires this as a precondition, have access to a review procedure before a court of law and/or another independent and impartial body established by law to challenge the substantive and procedural legality of any decision, act or omission subject to the provisions of article 6 and, where so provided for under national law, of other relevant provisions of the Aarhus Convention.[35] Article 9.2 further provides that what constitutes a sufficient interest or impairment of a right shall be determined in accordance with the requirements of national law and consistently with the objective of giving the public concerned

---

[32] Aarhus Convention art 6.7.

[33] Further steps in the public participation procedure are provided for in arts 6.8–6.11. In addition, requirements for public participation concerning plans, programmes and policies relating to the environment are set out in art 7; while art 8 provides for public participation during the preparation of executive regulations and/or generally applicable legally binding normative instruments. The above-mentioned provisions are already largely reflected in the Environmental Impact Assessment procedure that is provided for in UK law under the Town and Country Planning (Environmental Impact Assessment) (England and Wales) Regulations 1999, which were drafted with the Aarhus Convention in mind. Similarly: Electricity Works (Environmental Impact Assessment) (England and Wales) Regulations 2000; Water Resources (Environmental Impact Assessment) (England and Wales) Regulations 2003; Gas Transporter Pipe-line Works (Environmental Impact Assessment) Regulations 1999; Harbour Works (Environmental Impact Assessment) Regulations 1999; Environmental Impact Assessment (Land Drainage Improvement Works) Regulations 1999; Environmental Impact Assessment (Fish Farming in Marine Waters) Regulations 1999; Highways (Environmental Impact Assessment) Regulations 2007; Infrastructure Planning (Environmental Impact Assessment) Regulations 2009; Nuclear Reactors (Environmental Impact Assessment for Decommissioning) Regulations 1999; Pipe-line Works (Environmental Impact Assessment) Regulations 2000; Public Gas Transporter Pipe-line Works (Environmental Impact Assessment) Regulations 1999;

[34] Aarhus Convention art 9.1.

[35] This provision is subject to art 9.3, which provides that in addition and without prejudice to the review procedures referred to in arts 9.1 and 9.2, each Party shall ensure that, where they meet the criteria, if any, laid down in its national law, members of the public have access to administrative or judicial procedures to challenge acts and omissions by private persons and public authorities which contravene provisions of its national law relating to the environment.

wide access to justice within the scope of the Convention. To this end, article 9.2 states, the interest of any non-governmental organisation meeting the requirements referred to in article 2.5 (namely non-governmental organisations which promote environmental protection and meeting any requirements under national law) shall be deemed sufficient; and that such organisations shall also be deemed to have rights capable of being impaired for the purposes of article 9.2.

6–005   Directive 2003/4/EC

On 28 January 2003 the European Parliament and the Council of the European Union adopted Directive 2003/4/EC on public access to environmental information ('the Directive').[36] The Directive repeals Council Directive 90/313/EEC,[37] which in Great Britain had been implemented through the Environmental Information Regulations 1992.[38] The recitals to the 2003 Directive record a general favouring of the disclosure of official information 'to the widest extent possible',[39] crediting increased public access to environmental information with:

> contribut[ing] to a greater awareness of environmental matters, a free exchange of views, more effective participation by the public in environmental decision-making and, eventually, to a better environment.[40]

The Directive records that its disclosure obligations are not intended to dissuade Member States from providing more extensive disclosure regimes than that which is required by the Directive.[41] The Directive imposes, in other words, the minimum acceptable level of disclosure of environmental information: it does not set the bounds of permissible disclosure.[42]

6–006   The Environmental Information Regulations 2004

Both the Parliament at Westminster and the Scottish Parliament have made regulations implementing the Directive. The Environmental Information Regulations 2004 implement the Directive in relation to public authorities that owe their existence to the Parliament at Westminster,[43] including those operating or holding information in Scotland. The Environmental Information (Scotland) Regulations 2004 implement the Directive in relation to public authorities that owe their existence to the Scottish Parliament, ie Scottish public

---

[36]   The Directive entered into force on 14 February 2003. Article 10 of the Directive obliges the Member States of the European Union to have their legislation in place at the latest by 14 February 2004.

[37]   With effect from 14 February 2005: art 11. Recital (6) of the 2003 Directive records that 'it is appropriate in the interest of increased transparency to replace Directive 90/313/EEC rather than to amend it, so as to provide interested parties with a single, clear and coherent legislative text.'

[38]   SI 1992/3240. These were amended by the Environmental Information (Amendment) Regulations 1998 SI 1998/1447, which reduced the exceptions from disclosure so as to make the 1992 regulations properly align with Council Directive 90/313/EEC.

[39]   Directive 2003/4/EC Recital (9).

[40]   Directive 2003/4/EC Recital (1).

[41]   Directive 2003/4/EC Recital (24).

[42]   This is acknowledged in the Code of Practice, February 2005, issued under reg 16, para 7.

[43]   These are the public authorities that are listed in Sch 1 of the FOIA or that are designated by order under s 5(1) of that Act.

authorities.[44] The two sets of Regulations are very similar. The Environmental Information Regulations 2004 may be invoked by a person in Scotland to seek information from a non-Scottish public authority. The Environmental Information (Scotland) Regulations 2004 may be invoked by a person in England, Wales or Northern Ireland to request information from a Scottish public authority. There is an obligation to interpret each set of Regulations 'as far as possible, in the light of the wording and the purpose of the Directive in order to achieve the result pursued by the latter'.[45] Although the Directive left it open for Member States to implement a more generous disclosure regime than the minimum prescribed by the Directive, there is nothing to indicate that the Environmental Information Regulations 2004 intended to do more than introduce into domestic law exceptions matching in their terms and their extent those permitted by the Directive.[46]

7 **Overview**

Information to which a person has a right of access under the Environmental Information Regulations 2004 is exempt information under the Freedom of Information Act 2000.[47] In this way, the Act attempts to funnel requests for 'environmental information' through the Regulations. The attempt is not entirely successful, as the exemption under the Freedom of Information Act 2000 is not absolute.[48] Accordingly, the right under the Act to environmental information is only disapplied to the extent that, in all the circumstances of the case, the public interest in maintaining the exemption outweighs the public interest in disclosing the information.[49] There is nothing to preclude an applicant making a composite request for specified information under both the Freedom of Information Act 2000 and the Environmental Information Regulations 2004. A public authority faced with such a request will need: (1) to determine which of the information captured by the request falls within the access right given by the Regulations (ie to determine which of that information falls within the definition of 'environmental information')[50]; (2) then, in relation to that 'environmental information', determine whether any of the exceptions in the Regulations applies, including a consideration of the public interest;[51] (3) in relation to the requested information that is 'environmental

---

44 These are the public authorities that are listed in Sch 1 of the FOI(S)A or that is designated by order under s 5(1) of that Act.

45 *ECGD v Friends of the Earth* [2008] EWHC 638 (Admin), [2008] Env LR 40, [2008] JPL 1813 at [20]; Case C–106/89 *Marleasing SA v La Comercial Internacional de Alimentación SA* [1992] 1 CMLR 305 at [8]; Case C–365/98 *Brinkmann Tabakfabriken GmbH v Hauptzollamt Bielefeld* [2002] 2 CMLR 36; *Perceval-Price v Department of Economic Development* [2000] IRLR 380, [2000] NI 141.

46 *Office of Communication v Information Commissioner* [2010] UKSC 3 at [3].

47 FOIA s 39(1)(a). And, similarly, information to which a person has a right of access under the EI(S)R is exempt information under the FOI(S)A s 39(2)(a). See further §§16– 010 to 16– 013.

48 FOIA s 2(3); FOI(S)A s 2(2).

49 FOIA s 2(2); FOI(S)A s 2(1)(b).

50 A single document or electronic file, all of which falls within the terms of a request, may be made up partly of environmental information (access to which falls to be decided under the EIR) and the remainder of information that is not environmental information (access to which falls to be decided under FOIA). The practical difficulties which this presents for any public authority was acknowledged by the Tribunal in *DBERR v IC and Friends of the Earth*, IT, 29 April 2008 at [29].

51 Under EIR reg 12(1)(b), or EI(S)R reg 10(1)(b).

information' but which, under (2), need not be disclosed, consider whether in all the circumstances the public interest in maintaining the s 39 exemption outweighs the public interest in disclosing that information; and (4) in relation to the requested information that is not 'environmental information', determine whether any of the other exemptions in the Act applies (including, where necessary, a consideration of the public interest). The definition of 'public authority' in the Regulations is different from that in the Act. Where environmental information is sought of a body that is a public authority under the Act, but not under the Regulations, the request will fall to be determined solely by reference to the Act.[52]

2. ENVIRONMENTAL INFORMATION

6– 008 **Introduction**

The Environmental Information Regulations 2004 establish a regime that overall confers a greater right of access than that conferred by the Freedom of Information Act 2000. The special treatment afforded to environmental information gives effect to the recited objectives of the Aarhus Convention and Directive 2003/4/EC. At their core is the belief that protection of the environment is a matter of legitimate individual concern and involvement. Each of the three pillars of the Convention require the Contracting Parties to bestow an individual right that enables that individual involvement. Each right partly depends on the two others for its efficacy. Informed public participation in the making of decisions relating to the environment requires access to information on the environment held by public authorities. Central to the regime established by the Directive, and faithfully reproduced in the Regulations, is the definition of 'environmental information'.[53] Although there are similarities with the definition given to the term by the 1992 Regulations,[54] the new definition has an increased number of paragraphs.[55] However, the required nexus has changed from information that 'relates to' any

---

[52] See further §6– 049.

[53] EIR reg 2(1), reproducing art 2.1 of the Directive. Similarly, EI(S)R reg 2(1). Their provenance is in art 2.3 of the Aarhus Convention, although there are slight variations: see §6– 010. The meaning given to the phrase 'environmental information' is significantly wider than that given to it in the Town and Country Planning (Environmental Impact Assessment) (England and Wales) Regulations 1999, as to which see *R (Richardson) v North Yorkshire County Council* [2003] EWHC 764 (Admin).

[54] The ECJ in *Mecklenburg v Kreis Pinneberg der Landrat* [1999] All ER (EC) 166, [1999] 2 CMLR 418 considered the concept of environmental information under Directive 90/313/EEC, upon which the 1992 Regulations were based, to be 'a broad one'. It was held that a statement of views given by a countryside protection authority in development consent proceedings would, if capable of influencing the outcome of those proceedings, constitute 'environmental information'. Subsequently, in Case C–316/01 *Glawischnig v Bundesminister für soziale Sicherheit und Generationen* [2003] ECR I-5995 the Court held that that Directive was not intended to give a general and unlimited right of access to all information held by public authorities that has a connection, however minimal, with one of the environmental factors mentioned in art 2(a): in order to be covered, the information had to fall within one or more of the categories set out in art 2(a). In that case the Court upheld the public authority's refusal to answer a request to the extent that it sought the names and producers of genetically-modified products in respect of which the authority had received complaints or had imposed penalties for non-compliance with product labelling laws. In *R v Secretary of State for the Environment, Transport and the Regions, ex p Alliance against Birmingham Northern Relief Road (No 1)* [1999] Env LR 447, [1999] JPL 231, Sullivan J found that a concession agreement did constitute 'environmental information' within the meaning of the 1992 Regulations, holding that the definition in the Regulations was deliberately 'very broad' (JPL at 249–250).

[55] See recital (10) in Directive 2003/4/EC.

of the paragraphs to information 'on' any of the paragraphs.[56] The changed nexus arguably requires a closer connection than was required under the 1992 Regulations. It is possible for information to 'relate to' a subject without being information 'on' that subject. The requirement for a closer connection may serve to explain the absence of some conventional exemptions from the right of access to information held by public authorities.[57] If any of the information sought by an applicant is outside the definition of 'environmental information', the right of access will fall to be decided principally by the Freedom of Information Act 2000.

9 The elements of the environment

The definition of 'environmental information' is expressly the same as that given in article 2(1) of the Directive.[58] Central to the definition of 'environmental information' are the 'elements of the environment'. The definition opens by providing that 'environmental information shall mean any information…on the state of the elements of the environment, such as air and atmosphere, water, soil, land, landscape and natural sites including wetlands, coastal and marine areas, biological diversity and its components, including genetically modified organisms and the interaction between these elements.' In relation to these 'elements of the environment', guidance issued by DEFRA suggests[59] that:

— 'air' should be taken to include the air within buildings and other natural and manmade structures above or below ground, ie not only ambient air, but indoor and workplace air as well.[60]

— 'water' should be taken to include underground and surface waters (both natural and in man-made structures) sewage and foul water, inland waters (ie rivers, canals, lakes), estuaries, seas, water tables and aquifers.

— 'soil' should be taken to include the in situ upper layer of the mantle rock in which plants grow.

— 'land' and 'landscape' should be taken to include all land surfaces, caves and underground strata.[61] Land covered by water is also included.

— 'natural sites' should be taken to include areas identified by reason of their flora, fauna, geological or physiographical features (eg Sites of Special Scientific Interest) or general environmental quality (eg Areas of Outstanding Natural Beauty). This could also include for example a tree or park of local significance.

— 'biological diversity' should be taken to include species of flora and fauna. The United Nation's Implementation Guide cross-refers to the definition given to the phrase in article 2 of the Convention on Biological Diversity:[62] namely, 'the

---

[56] See §22– 007 for a discussion of the meaning of 'relates to'.

[57] For example, information that is covered by legal professional privilege: see §6– 033.

[58] EIR reg 2(1); EI(S)R reg 2(1). Recital (10) of Directive 2003/4/EC recites the desirability of a clarified definition of 'environmental information'.

[59] DEFRA, *Guidance*, ch 3 'What is covered by the Regulations?', December 2006, para 3.5.

[60] The same view is taken in S Stec, S Casey-Lefkowitz & J Jendroska, *The Aarhus Convention: an Implementation Guide* (New York, United Nations, 2000) p 36.

[61] Similarly provided in the Interpretation Act 1978 Sch 1.

[62] Concluded at Rio de Janeiro on 5 June 1992. S Stec, S Casey-Lefkowitz & J Jendroska, *The Aarhus Convention: an Implementation Guide* (New York, United Nations, 2000) p 36.

variability among living organisms from all sources including, inter alia, terrestrial, marine and other aquatic ecosystems and the ecological complexes of which they are part; this includes diversity within species, between species and of ecosystems.' The Implementation Guide continues by stating that biodiversity 'includes, but is not limited to, ecosystem diversity, species diversity and genetic diversity. In addition, tangible entities identifiable as a specific ecosystem (a dynamic complex of plant, animal and micro-organism communities and their non-living environment interacting as a functional unit), are considered components of biodiversity.'

The statutory list of 'elements of the environment' is non-exhaustive. Both DEFRA Guidance and the United Nations Implementation Guide consider that radiation, in addition to being a factor, is an element of the environment.[63]

6– 010   The meaning of 'environmental information'

Having identified the 'elements of the environment', the Regulations define 'environmental information' to mean information[64] on:

(a)   The 'state' of the elements of the environment and the interaction amongst those elements.[65] The requirement on signatories to the Aarhus Convention to report regularly on 'the state of the environment' might suggest that information on the state of the elements of the environment is not concerned with the detail of information relating to each of these elements but with higher level analysis of them.[66]

(b)   'Factors' affecting or likely to affect the elements of the environment.[67] Examples given of these factors are 'substances, energy, noise, radiation or waste'.[68] This limb

---

[63]   DEFRA, *Guidance*, ch 3 'What is covered by the Regulations?', December 2006 para 3.5. S Stec, S Casey-Lefkowitz & J Jendroska, *The Aarhus Convention: an Implementation Guide* (New York, United Nations, 2000) p 37.

[64]   As to the meaning of 'information', see §§6– 012 and 9– 001 to 9– 008. In *Maile v Wigan MBC* [2001] Env LR 11, [2001] JPL 193 Eady J seemed to doubt whether a database that the Council had not finished compiling constituted 'information'. In the course of his judgment he said: 'The regulations are concerned with the availability of information (and I emphasise that word) and not speculation or preliminary thoughts based on limited research.' It may be observed that preliminary thoughts are just as much 'information' as concluded thoughts. The extent of research merely goes to the quality or character of the information, eg information as to the tentative views of the Council. Moreover, incomplete information is now specifically dealt with in EIR reg 12(4)(d) and EI(S)R reg 10(4)(d).

[65]   Derived from Aarhus Convention art 2.3(a) and Directive 2003/4/EC art 2.1(a). In *R v British Coal Corporation, ex p Ibstock Building Products Ltd* [1995] Env LR 277, a case under the 1992 Regulations, Harrison J held that the name of an informant who had advised a local authority that naval munitions had been dumped down a mineshaft in 1947 (a matter which impinged upon the grant of planning permission) was information that was capable of relating to the state of the land.

[66]   See Aarhus Convention art 5.4, and Directive 2003/4/EC art 7.3. In *Archer v IC and Salisbury DC*, IT, 9 May 2007 (at [32]) it was held that para (a) covered a joint report to a committee of a local council from the head of development services and the head of legal and democratic services which identified breaches of planning control and recommended certain legal action.

[67]   Derived from Aarhus Convention art 2.3(b), and Directive 2003/4/EC art 2.1(b).

[68]   In *OFCOM v IC and T-Mobile (UK) Ltd*, IT, 4 September 2007 the Tribunal rejected an argument that emission bore the narrow meaning given to it in Council Directive 96/6/EC and concluded that radiation emanating from mobile phone base stations are a type of 'emission' (at [25]). The Tribunal also concluded that the radio emissions were a form of energy or radiation that affected the elements of the environment (at [27]). The definition was found to be wide enough to cover the names of mobile network operators that owned the different base stations (at [31]).

is of uncertain width. On one reading it is confined to information that itself makes the link between the 'factors' and their affecting or likelihood of affecting the elements of the environment. An alternative reading is that it is sufficient that the information is on a 'factor' and that it can be shown that the elements of the environment etc are or are likely to be affected by them. The UN Implementation Guide favours the latter. The Guide considers that the level of likelihood required is a low one, and that this is reflected in the Russian and French texts of the Convention.[69] The example given in the Implementation Guide is information related to planning in transport or tourism, which 'would in most cases be covered by this definition'.

(c)   'Measures' and 'activities' affecting or likely to affect the elements of the environment or the 'factors', including those designed to protect the elements of the environment.[70] 'Measures' are stated to include administrative measures. The given examples of measures are policies, legislation, plans, programmes and environmental agreements. This limb would seem not to be concerned with routine information, but instead with information having sufficient formality for it to constitute a 'measure'.[71] It may be that documents recording the decision-making process leading to the passing of a measure are therefore outside the grasp of the paragraph. This would tend to explain the need for paragraph (e) of the definition, which might otherwise be superfluous. It is capable of covering officer reports to the committee of a local council.[72] The UN Implementation Guide considers that 'environmental agreements' applies to 'voluntary agreements such as those negotiated between government and industry, and may also apply to bilateral or multilateral environmental agreements among States... These agreements are sometimes published, and sometimes not published, and may be negotiated by committees dominated by either representatives of the regulated industry or by the officials who will be responsible for enforcing the regulations.'[73] As with paragraph (b) of the definition, this paragraph requires a nexus between the measure or activity and the elements in paragraph (a) or the factors in paragraph (b). The example given in the UN Implementation Guide is:

> if decisions about what land to conserve and what land to develop affect social conditions as described above in a particular area by changing the quality of air or water: [then]
> - Information relating to the decision-making would be environmental information under subparagraph (b);

---

[69] S Stec, S Casey-Lefkowitz & J Jendroska, *The Aarhus Convention: an Implementation Guide* (New York, United Nations, 2000) p 37.

[70] Derived from Aarhus Convention art 2.3(b), and Directive 2003/4/EC art 2.1(c).

[71] That appears to be how the word is used elsewhere in the Aarhus Convention (arts 3.1, 3.5, 5.5 and 5.6) and in Directive 2003/4/EC (recitals (2), (23) and (24) and arts 7.3 and 10). Hence, building regulation documents and planning agreements under the Town and Country Planning Act 1990 s 10 are not within the scope of 'measures': *Spurgeon v IC and Horsham DC*, IT, 29 June 2007 at [21].

[72] *Archer v IC and Salisbury DC*, IT, 9 May 2007 at [32].

[73] S Stec, S Casey-Lefkowitz & J Jendroska, *The Aarhus Convention: an Implementation Guide* (New York, United Nations, 2000) p 38.

- Information relating to the quality of air or water would be environmental information under subparagraph (a); and
- Information about the affected social conditions would be environmental information under subparagraph (c).[74]

(d) Reports on the implementation of environmental legislation.[75] This limb of the definition would appear to be directed to the report required to be produced at regular intervals under the Aarhus Convention and the Directive.[76]

(e) Cost-benefit and other economic analyses and assumptions used within the framework of the measures and activities referred to in (c). It is conventional in freedom of information regimes that exempt policy formulation or 'deliberative' documents, nevertheless to make available the background statistical information or purely factual material that informed the policy decision taken.[77]

(f) The state of human health and safety, conditions of human life, cultural sites and built structures, 'inasmuch as they are or may be affected by the state of the elements of the environment referred to in (a) or, through those elements, by any of the matters referred to in (b) and (c)'.[78] The quoted words materially reduce the scope of this paragraph. It is not clear whether the limb is confined to information that itself links the state of human health and safety, etc to the state of the elements of the environment, etc; or whether it is sufficient that the information is on the state of human health and safety, etc and that it can be shown that the state of the elements of the environment, etc are or may be affecting them. In *OFCOM v IC and T-Mobile (UK) Ltd*,[79] the Tribunal expressed the view that (f) was intended to apply to information on the state of human health (and not just information on factors that are suspected of possibly creating a risk to it) and that the information must be *on* the result of those factors affecting human health and not the factors themselves.[80] The UN Implementation Guide expresses the view:

> The Convention clearly requires a link between information on human health and safety, conditions of human life, etc and the elements, factors, activities or measures described in subparagraphs (a) and (b), in order to impose a reasonable limit on the vast kinds of human health and safety information potentially covered. The negotiating parties were faced with a situation in

---

[74] S Stec, S Casey-Lefkowitz & J Jendroska, *The Aarhus Convention: an Implementation Guide* (New York, United Nations, 2000) p 39.

[75] This limb is not in the definition of 'environmental information' in the Aarhus Convention.

[76] See Aarhus Convention arts 5.3(a) and 5.4, and Directive 2003/4/EC arts 7.2(d) and 7.3.

[77] See, eg: FOIA s 35(2) and (4); FOI(S)A s 29(3); Freedom of Information Act 1982 (Commonwealth of Australia) s 36; Official Information Act 1982 (New Zealand) s 9(2)(g); Access to Information Act 1985 (Canada) s 21; Freedom of Information Act 1997 (Republic of Ireland) s 20. The Aarhus Convention art 2.3(b), speaks of 'cost benefit and other economic analyses and assumptions used in environmental decision-making'. The words used in the Regulations derive from Directive 2003/4/EC art 2.1(f).

[78] Derived from Aarhus Convention art 2.3(c), and Directive 2003/4/EC art 2.1(f).

[79] IT, 4 September 2007 at [29].

[80] Thus, the Tribunal, following the findings of the Independent Expert Group on Mobile Phones ('the Stewart Report'), 28 April 2000, concluded that technical attributes of mobile phone cellular base stations did not fall within (f). A copy of the Stewart Report is available at:
www.iegmp.org.uk/report/text.htm

which looser language would have brought a whole range of human health and safety information unrelated to the environment under the definition, such as information relating to specific medical procedures or safety rules for the operation of specific tools.

Article 1 of the Convention Concerning the Protection of the World Cultural and Natural Heritage[81] gives the following definition of cultural sites:

works of man or the combined works of nature and man, and areas including archaeological sites which are of outstanding universal value from the historical, aesthetic, ethnological or anthropological point of view.

Overall, DEFRA Guidance suggests:

Experience from the implementation of the environmental information regime has established that "environmental information" is interpreted very broadly. The Government has treated information relating to GM crop trials, to pesticide testing, to diseased cattle and to land-use planning (including the reasons for decisions to approve as well as to refuse planning permission) as environmental information. The definition could also include reports on the implementation of environmental legislation and analysis resulting from an appraisal of policy, including any Regulatory Impact Assessment.'[82]

1 Environmental information – examples

The Tribunal has concluded that the following all constitute 'environmental information':

— an application for planning permission;[83]

— legal advice which included the enforceability of an agreement under section 106 of the Town and Country Planning Act 1990;[84]

— legal advice on a planning inspector's decision and on the meaning of certain provisions of planning legislation;[85]

— an enforcement file in connection with a breach of planning control;[86]

— an appraisal prepared in connection with negotiations for an agreement under s 106 of the Town and Country Planning Act 1990;[87]

— submissions to a Minister on a 'called-in' planning inquiry;[88]

— a river works licence;[89]

— information relating to land holdings of a public authority;[90]

---

[81] 16 November 1972, Paris.

[82] DEFRA, *Guidance*, ch 3 'What is covered by the Regulations?', December 2006, para 3.1.

[83] *Markinson v IC*, IT, 28 March 2006; *Robinson v IC and East Ridings of Yorkshire Council*, IT, 9 October 2007; cf *Spurgeon v IC and Horsham DC*, IT, 29 June 2007.

[84] *Kirkaldie v IC and Thanet DC*, IT, 4 July 2006. The actual request was for the legal advice that Thanet District Council had sought regarding the night-flying policy at Kent International Airport.

[85] *Burgess v IC and Stafford BC*, IT, 7 June 2007.

[86] *Young v IC and Dept for Environment for Northern Ireland*, IT, 12 December 2007.

[87] *South Gloucestershire Council v IC and Bovis Homes Ltd*, IT, 20 October 2009.

[88] *Lord Baker of Dorking v IC and DCLG*, IT, 1 June 2007, although all parties agreed that the information sought was environmental information.

[89] *Port of London Authority v IC and Hibbert*, IT, 31 May 2007, although not disputed by any of the parties in that appeal.

[90] *Perrins v IC and Wolverhampton City Council*, IT , 9 January 2007.

— information about a local authority's liability to construct a sea defence;[91]
— information about the location, ownership and technical attributes of mobile phone cellular base stations;[92]
— statements in support of an application to modify a right of way shown on the definitive map under the Wildlife and Countryside Act 1981;[93]
— information on 'energy policy' in respect of 'supply, demand and pricing';[94]
— records of a meeting held to consider perceived 'climate change';[95]
— records of the quantity, origin and prices of mussels imported and exported from certain fishery areas;[96]
— a draft report jointly commissioned by the Chancellor of the Exchequer and the Secretary of State for Transport to examine the long-term links between transport, economic productivity and competitiveness;[97]
— information relating to the building of a bridge and its tolling;[98] and
— certain information relating to an oil pipeline.[99]

The Tribunal has concluded that the following does not constitute 'environmental information':
— communications between UK and US authorities relating to decommissioned US warships containing toxic waste and to be dismantled in the United Kingdom.[100]

6–012   The format of the information

The right given by the Regulations is to 'information in written, visual, aural, electronic or any other material form'.[101] The medium on which the information is recorded does not affect the existence of the right. Unlike the Freedom of Information Act 2000, which defines 'information' as 'information recorded in any form',[102] there is no such requirement in the Environmental Information Regulations 2004 or in Directive 2003/4/EC. Arguably, 'information' in the Environmental Information Regulations 2004 extends to samples or specimens held by a public authority.[103] The form and format provision of the Environmental

---

[91] *McGlade v IC and Redcar and Cleveland BC*, IT, 23 November 2009.

[92] *OFCOM v IC and T-Mobile (UK) Ltd*, IT, 4 September 2007, on appeal *R (Office of Communications) v IC*, [2008] EWHC 1445 (Admin), [2008] ACD 65, [2009] Env LR 1, then *R (Office of Communications) v IC* [2009] EWCA Civ 90, [2009] ACD 48, and then *Office of Communication v IC* [2010] UKSC 3.

[93] *Dainton v IC and Lincolnshire CC*, IT, 10 September 2007.

[94] *DBERR v IC and Friends of the Earth*, IT, 29 April 2008 at [27].

[95] *DBERR v IC and Friends of the Earth*, IT, 29 April 2008 at [27].

[96] *North Western and North Wales Sea Fisheries Committee v IC*, IT, 8 July 2008.

[97] *SS for Transport v IC*, IT, 5 May 2009.

[98] *Mersey Tunnel Users Association v IC and Halton BC*, IT, 24 June 2009 at [54]-[70].

[99] *ECGD v IC and Corner House*, IT, 11 August 2009.

[100] *FCO v IC and Friends of the Earth*, IT, 29 June 2007.

[101] EIR reg 2(1); EI(S)R reg 2(1). Derived from Directive 2003/4/EC art 2.1.

[102] FOIA s 84; FOI(S)A s 73.

[103] See Directive 2003/4/EC art 8.2.

Information Regulations 2004[104] gives a public authority more flexibility in the method by which it meets a request than does the corresponding provision in the Freedom of Information Act 2000.[105] The former provision would enable a public authority to meet a request by making samples or specimens available for inspection.[106] Environmental information accordingly includes information contained in documents, pictures and records, where records are taken to include registers, reports, returns, computer records and other non-documentary records. DEFRA Guidance states:

> Maps will often contain environmental information. No types of information are excluded from the potential ambit of environmental information. It includes, for example, information contained in all types of documents such as decision letters, applications, inspection reports, concession agreements, contracts, tables, databases, spreadsheets, emails, photographs, sketches and handwritten notes or drawings and covers opinions and advice as well as facts. Information in raw and unprocessed form is capable of being environmental information as well as documents.[107]

3. THE RIGHT TO ENVIRONMENTAL INFORMATION

13 Scope of the right

The Regulations are retrospective in that they apply to 'environmental information' irrespective of whether it was created or received before the Regulations came into effect.[108] The Regulations do not specifically include a provision to 'freeze' the information captured by a request to that information which is held at the time when the request is received. Nevertheless, there are indications in the Regulations that point to this being the intention.[109] The 'snapshot' approach is consistent with what is expressly provided for in the Freedom of Information Act 2000.[110]

14 Persons enjoying the right

Save to the extent that it may be relevant to a consideration of the public interest, the motives

---

[104] R 6(1); EI(S)R reg 6(1).

[105] FOIA s 11(1); FOI(S)A s 11(2).

[106] Compare the FOIA and FOI(S)A ss 1 and 11, which provide for the communication of the requested information.

[107] DEFRA, *Guidance*, ch 3 'What is covered by the Regulations?', December 2006, para 3.6.

[108] The position is the same under the FOIA and under the FOI(S)A. This retrospectivity was confirmed by the Home Secretary during the passage of the Bill through the House of Commons: Hansard HC vol 340 col 728 (7 December 1999). See further §9– 011.

[109] See, eg regs 10(2)–(3), 12(4)(a) and 19(1); but cf reg 5(4). In Scotland, EI(S)R regs 12(4)(a), 14(2) and 19(1).

[110] Compare FOIA s 1(4) and FOI(S)A s 1(4). See further §9– 011. In *Kirkaldie v IC and Thanet DC*, IT, 4 July 2006, the Tribunal said (at [17]) that the position was not clear, but that 'it would not make much sense for a public authority to respond that it did not hold the information when it had just received it before sending the response. Also the public authority would no doubt be under a duty to advise and assist the applicant under Regulation 9 EIR that the information was not in its possession at the time the request was received although knowing that it was about to be received so that the applicant could then make a new request, if necessary, when the information was then held by the public authority. Alternatively the public authority could take the sensible and pragmatic approach and accept the request under the EIR and deal with it accordingly.'

of the person for making a request are irrelevant to the decision to disclose.[111] The Regulations speak of an applicant being a 'person'.[112] Consistently with the general position at law and with the Directive, this will extend to companies and other legal persons, corporate or unincorporate.[113] The Aarhus Convention states that the right should be exercisable by any person, irrespective of citizenship, nationality or domicile.[114] Although this did not find its way into either the Directive or the Regulations, it is questionable whether the right could be denied on the basis of any of these.[115] In particular, it is questionable whether a Scottish public authority could refuse a request made by a UK citizen resident in England.

6– 015   Bodies subject to the obligation

Under the Environmental Information Regulations 2004, the right of access is only exercisable against a 'public authority'.[116] Under the Environmental Information (Scotland) Regulations 2004, the right of access is only exercisable against a 'Scottish public authority'.[117] Each of the terms is given a similar, but not identical, definition to that which it bears under the corresponding Act.[118] The Environmental Information Regulations 2004 expand the definition given to 'public authority' in the Freedom of Information Act 2000 by adding to it two additional limbs. First, by para (c) of the definition, 'public authority' also embraces 'any other body or other person that carries out functions of public administration'. Most bodies and persons that carry out functions of public administration are already captured under paras (a) and (b) through the incorporation of the Act's definition. Paragraph (c) may serve to cover public authorities that have been excluded from s 3(1) by an order under s 4(5) or by statute.[119]

---

[111] See recital (8) to and art 3.1 of the Directive and Aarhus Convention art 4.1. S Stec, S Casey-Lefkowitz & J Jendroska, *The Aarhus Convention: an Implementation Guide* (New York, United Nations, 2000) p 54. See further §9– 017.

[112] Regulation 2(1).

[113] Recital (8) to and art 2.6 of the Directive. Similarly, Aarhus Convention art 2.4. Interpretation Act 1978 s 5 and Sch 1. See further §9– 013.

[114] Aarhus Convention art 3.9. See S Stec, S Casey-Lefkowitz & J Jendroska, *The Aarhus Convention: an Implementation Guide* (New York, United Nations, 2000) pp 39–40, 48.

[115] Article 3.1 of the Directive requires Member States to ensure that public authorities make available environmental information 'to any applicant' on request. See further §9– 014.

[116] EIR reg 5(1).

[117] EI(S)R reg 5(1).

[118] EIR reg 2(2); EI(S)R reg 2(1). This is so that the definition of 'public authority' accords with art 2.2 of the Directive. See also recital (11) of the Directive and art 2.2 of the Aarhus Convention.

[119] Bodies that the Commissioner has determined are public authorities within the meaning of the Regulations include: the Port of London Authority, Decision Notice FER0086096 (2 October 2006); Environment Resources Management Ltd, Decision Notice FER0090259 (7 June 2006). 'Functions of public administration' is vaguely similar to, but narrower than, the limb of the definition of a 'public authority' in s 6(3)(b) of the Human Rights Act 1998. In relation to which, see: *Cameron v Network Rail Infrastructure Ltd* [2006] EWHC 1133, [2007] 1 WLR 163, [2006] HRLR 31 (holding Network Rail not to be a public authority on the basis that the running of a railway was not intrinsically an activity of government); *Aston Cantlow and Wilmcote with Billesley Parochial Church Council v Wallbank* [2003] 3 All ER 1213 (parochial church council, a body corporate which formed part of the Church of England and whose functions included co-operating with the minister in promoting the Church's mission within the parish, not a public authority); *R (Johnson) v Havering London BC* [2006] EWHC 1714 (Admin) (a private body, in providing accommodation to persons in need of care and assistance, pursuant to arrangements made with a local authority in the exercise of that authority's functions under ss 21 and 26 of the National Assistance Act 1948 held not to be a public authority); *R (Heather) v Leonard Cheshire Foundation* [2002] 2 All ER 936 (charitable organisation providing accommodation pursuant to arrangements with a local authority in the discharge of its statutory duties under the

A body does not fall within paragraph (c) merely because it carries out functions of a public nature: they must be administrative functions.[120] It would seem most naturally to embrace persons or bodies discharging administrative powers and duties either conferred by statute or arising under prerogative. Thus, in *Port of London Authority v Information Commissioner and Hibbert*[121] the Tribunal, in deciding that the Port of London Authority was a public authority by virtue of para (c), examined the statute by which the Authority was created, noting that it imposed duties and conferred powers on the Authority, that it was subject to a degree of government control and regulation, that it was to a degree accountable to Parliament, that some of its board members were appointed by the Secretary of State, that it had compulsory purchase powers and that there was a right of appeal against certain of its decisions. Secondly, paragraph (d) of the definition in both Regulations adds any other body or person 'that is under the control of' a public authority (as defined in paras (a)–(c)) and that:

— has public responsibilities relating to the environment;

— exercises functions of a public nature relating to the environment; or

— provides public services relating to the environment.[122]

By contrast, in *Network Rail Ltd v Information Commissioner*[123] the Tribunal, noting that Network Rail operated like a listed public company in many respects, that the Government exercised no influence or control over its board and that it was not created by statute, held that it was not a body that carried out functions of public administration. Its receipt of large amounts of public funding, the fact that it served a public interest and that the State took responsibility for rail services, did not render its functions ones of 'public administration'.

Although the requirement that the body or person be 'under the control' of a public authority (as defined in paras (a)–(c)) might be thought to exclude utility companies in United Kingdom, DEFRA guidance suggests that governmental regulation might suffice:

> Examples of bodies that may be covered by EIR limb (d) are private companies or Public Private Partnerships with obvious environmental functions such as waste disposal, water, energy, transport regulators. Public utilities, for example, are involved in the supply of essential public services such as water, sewerage, electricity and gas and may fall within the scope of the EIRs.[124]

National Assistance Act 1948, held not to be a public authority); *Poplar Housing and Regeneration Community Association Ltd v Donoghue* [2001] 4 All ER 604.

[120] *Network Rail Ltd v IC and Network Rail Infrastructure Ltd*, IT, 17 July 2007 at [24].

[121] IT, 31 May 2007.

[122] This limb of the definition has no counterpart in the FOIA or in the FOI(S)A. This paragraph is derived from Directive 2003/4/EC, recital (11) and art 2.2(c).

[123] *Network Rail Ltd v IC and Network Rail Infrastructure Ltd*, IT, 17 July 2007.

[124] DEFRA, *EIR Guidance*, ch 2, July 2007, para 2.22. The same view is taken in S Stec, S Casey-Lefkowitz & J Jendroska, *The Aarhus Convention: an Implementation Guide* (New York, United Nations, 2000) pp 32–33 (specifically referring to providers of natural gas, electricity, water and sewage services). The notion that the Regulations apply to environmental information held by private companies is not easily reconciled with the purpose of the Regulations or with the other 'pillars' of the Aarhus Convention. The public does not normally participate in decisions made by private companies and are not normally thought to have a legitimate interest in doing so. It may be that where a non-public authority company carries out 'obvious environmental functions', this will constitute a powerful facet of the public interest in favour of the disclosure of information addressed to or received from that company but held by those public authorities regulating or otherwise communicating with that company. In this way, eg, confidential information relating to these functions and emanating from such a company but held by a public authority, may more readily be disclosed when carrying out the exercise required by regulation 12(1)(b) than like information

The guidance suggests that the degree of control is the determinant:

> It is important to note that the level of control needs to be sufficient to exert a decisive influence on the body – the simple existence of a contract with a public authority does not necessarily provide this control. The existence of one contract between, for example, a government body and a private company or other organisation will not necessarily bring that company or organisation within the scope of the regime, although it may do so. Each case will need to be considered on its merits and a range of factors would need to be taken into account.[125]

The Regulations do not apply to any public authority when it is acting in a judicial or legislative capacity.[126] It would seem that a body falling within para (c) or (d) can be a public authority in respect of some information that it holds but not other information.[127] However, it would further seem that provided that the information relates to a function of the body that is not purely 'private', then that information will be subject to the Regulations.[128]

6– 016   **The holding requirement**

A public authority is only obliged to disclose environmental information that it 'holds'.[129] The corollary of this is that the right of access is conferred only in relation to environmental information that is 'held' by a public authority. Information 'held by a public authority' is defined to extend to information held by third parties on behalf of that public authority.[130] Thus, the Regulations extend to information held on behalf of a public authority by consultants or archival companies. The term 'hold' itself suggests that information that neither is nor has been created, sought, used or consciously retained by a public authority will not be information 'held' by it.[131] Thus, the private papers of a member of staff of a public authority that that staff member brings into work will not be information 'held' by the public authority. The word 'held' also indicates that a public authority is not obliged to assemble and record what it knows nor to ascertain matters so as to produce information that answers a request. The Tribunal may, on an appeal, review the adequacy of a public authority's search for information

---

emanating from a company not engaged in such 'obvious environmental functions'.

[125] DEFRA, *EIR Guidance*, ch 2, July 2007, para 2.20.

[126] EIR reg 3(3); EI(S)R reg 3(2). See further §6– 049. In *R v Secretary of State for the Environment, Transport and Regions, ex p Marson*, 23 March 1998, Jowitt J rejected an argument made in relation to the analogous reg 2(1)(b) of the 1992 Regulations that this disapplied the Regulations where the information related to any function carried out in pursuance of a power conferred by primary or secondary legislation. The disapplication, he held, referred to those things done in the preparation and enactment of legislation. This part of his ruling did not form part of a subsequent challenge to the Court of Appeal [1998] 3 PLR 90, (1999) 77 P&CR 202, [1998] JPL 869.

[127] In *Port of London Authority v IC and Hibbert*, IT, 31 May 2007 it is recorded at [42] that both the Authority and the Information Commissioner submitted that it was possible that an organisation might be a public authority in respect of some of the information that they hold but not others, with the Tribunal stating that it did not dissent from this proposition. This view is not easy to reconcile with FOIA s 7, which, by virtue of EIR reg 2(2)(b)(i), also applies to the environmental information regime.

[128] *Port of London Authority v IC and Hibbert*, IT, 31 May 2007 at [44].

[129] EIR regs 4(1) and 5(1); EI(S)R regs 4(1) and 5(1). This is also the requirement in the Directive: see arts 1(a) and 3.1.

[130] EIR reg 3(2); EI(S)R reg 2(2). This is consistent with the requirements of the recital (12) and arts 1(a), 2.3, 2.4 and 3.1 of the Directive. This is acknowledged in DEFRA, *Code of Practice – Environmental Information Regulations*, February 2005, Foreword, para 14(iii).

[131] 'Hold' is similarly, but not identically, defined in s 3(2) of the Act. See further §9– 009.

answering the terms of a request.[132]

7 Historical records

Emulating the Freedom of Information Act 2000 rather than the Directive, the Regulations make special provision for 'historical records'.[133] A record becomes a historical record at the end of 30 years beginning with the year following that in which it was created.[134] The Regulations import various terms from the regime created by Part VI (ss 62–67) of the Freedom of Information Act 2000.[135] The Regulation's treatment of historical records is simpler and less generous than that of the Act. Whereas the Act provides for certain exemptions to fall away according to the age of the record,[136] the Regulations maintain all the exceptions[137] whatever the antiquity of the information. Instead, the Regulations require the public authority holding the information to consult certain bodies before deciding whether it is in the public interest to maintain the exception.[138]

8 Electronic reading rooms

The Directive exhorts public authorities to disseminate environmental information without specific request and to do so electronically.[139] While the Freedom of Information Act 2000 provides for publication schemes,[140] which serve a similar purpose, the Directive's emphasis on the use of electronic communications to achieve this takes its inspiration from the US Electronic Freedom of Information Act of 1996.[141] The Directive's exhortations find their way into the 2004 Regulations,[142] albeit they are not so emphatic. Although the availability of information through general dissemination does not remove the obligation to answer a request,[143] it does enable the public authority to decline to provide the applicant with the information in the particular form or format requested.[144] It would seem that the public authority may respond

---

[132] *Mersey Tunnel Users Association v IC and Halton BC*, IT, 24 June 2009 at [71]-[87].

[133] EIR reg 17. 'Historical record' is given the same meaning as it has in section 62 of the 2000 Act: reg 2(1). In Scotland, EI(S)R reg 15, and FOI(S)A s 57. See further §7– 036.

[134] See §7– 036.

[135] Thus: 'transferred public records' and 'open information'. In Scotland, FOI(S)A, Pt V (ss 57–59). As to the meaning of these, see §§7– 043 and 7– 045.

[136] FOIA s 63. See further §§7– 037 to 7– 039.

[137] What are termed 'exemptions' in the FOIA are termed 'exceptions' in the EIR. See further §6– 031.

[138] See further ch 7.

[139] See recitals (9), (14), (15) and (21) and Arts 1(b) and 7. The Aarhus Convention similarly encourages public authorities: see arts 5.3, 5.5 and 5.7.

[140] FOI ss 19 and 20; FOI(S)A ss 23–24. See further §§10– 013 to 10– 018.

[141] These amended the Freedom of Information Act 1966 by establishing a requirement for the electronic availability of 'reading room' records in what are referred to as 'electronic reading rooms': see 5 USC 552(a)(2) (D). Under these amendments, all federal agencies have FOI Act sites on the World Wide Web to serve this 'electronic reading room' function.

[142] EIR reg 4; EI(S)R reg 4. This regulation is not made under the power conferred by the FOIA s 74, but under the European Communities Act 1972 s 2(2).

[143] Cash flow. FOIA s 21(1) and FOI(S)A s 25, which are absolute exemptions.

[144] EIR reg 6(1); EI(S)R reg 6(1).

to the request by simply directing the applicant to its 'reading room' facility.

6– 019   Registers of environmental information

Article 3(5)(c) of the Directive requires each Member State to ensure that practical arrangements are defined for ensuring that the right of access to environmental information can be exercised, including (by way of example) through the maintenance of registers or lists of the environmental information held by public authorities. The Environmental Information Unit of DEFRA has created a central register, setting out where these registers can be found, generally by internet link.[145] Register information is also available from the Environment Agency.[146]

6– 020   Codes of Practice, Guidance and Practice Recommendations

The Secretary of State may issue and revise a code of practice providing guidance to public authorities as to desirable practice in carrying out the Regulations.[147] Before issuing the code of practice, the Secretary of State is required to consult the Information Commissioner. The code of practice must be laid before each House of Parliament. The Secretary of State issued a Code of Practice in February 2005. It 'outlines to public authorities the practice that it would, in the opinion of the Secretary of State, be desirable for them to follow in connection with the discharge of their duties under' the Regulations.[148] The Department for Environment, Food and Rural Affairs has also issued 'guidance' on the operation of the Regulations. The guidance is non-statutory, with neither the Regulations nor the Directive making provision for it.[149] As under the Freedom of Information Act 2000, the Information Commissioner may give practice recommendations.[150]

6– 021   Advice and assistance

Each public authority must provide applicants and prospective applicants with so much advice and assistance as would be reasonable.[151] The provision emulates the Freedom of Information Act 2000[152] but has its provenance in the Aarhus Convention[153] and Directive 2003/4/EC.[154] Compliance with the guidance given in the Code of Practice in relation to advice and assistance

---

[145] See: www.defra.gov.uk/corporate/opengov/eir/register.htm.

[146] See: www2.environment-agency.gov.uk/epr/.

[147] EIR r16(1). The Directive does not provide for a code of practice for public authorities. The only form of guidance it contemplates is for those seeking information: art 3.5.

[148] Foreword, para 9.

[149] The effect of such guidance is considered further at §10– 020.

[150] EIR reg 16; EI(S)R reg 18.

[151] EIR reg 9(1); EI(S)R reg 9(1). *Boddy v IC and North Norfolk DC*, IT, 23 June 2008 at [25].

[152] FOI s 16, considered further at §§10– 001 to 10– 006. The provision derives from art 3 of the Aarhus Convention. See further S Stec, S Casey-Lefkowitz & J Jendroska, *The Aarhus Convention: an Implementation Guide* (New York, United Nations, 2000) p 43.

[153] Article 3.2 requires each Contracting Party to endeavour to ensure that officials and authorities 'assist and provide guidance to the public in seeking access to information'.

[154] Article 3.5 provides that Member States are to ensure that 'officials are required to support the public in seeking access to information' and spells out certain specific requirements.

is deemed to constitute due compliance with the duty to advise and assist.[155] Examples given in the Code of assistance that 'might be appropriate' includes 'providing access to detailed catalogues and indexes, where these are available, to help the applicant ascertain the nature and extent of the information held by the authority'.[156] The Code requires public authorities to publish their procedures for dealing with requests for environmental information.[157] Where a request is inadequately particularised, the public authority is required to assist the applicant in providing the required detail.[158] Where a public authority proposes to charge for supplying an applicant with a copy of the information answering the terms of a request, the duty to advise and assist may require that public authority to offer the applicant an opportunity to inspect that information (without charge) in order to decide which of it he would like copied.[159] If a public authority fails to provide advice and assistance, it would appear that the public authority will not be able subsequently to refuse the request on the basis of that request being manifestly unreasonable.[160]

22 The request

For a person to exercise his right of access to environmental information held by a public authority, that person must make a request.[161] The Regulations do not prescribe any formalities for the request.[162] There is nothing to preclude an applicant making a request orally.[163] Although there is no obligation for an applicant to state his name or address, a failure to do so may make it impossible for the public authority to comply properly with its obligations where the response would include personal data. Where a request does not describe the information sought with sufficient particularity, the recipient public authority must ask the applicant as soon as possible (and in any event not more than 20 working days after receipt of the request) to provide more particulars in relation to the request and it must help the applicant to do so.[164] The particularity of a request will impinge upon its reasonableness and upon the

---

[155] EIR reg 9(3); EI(S)R reg 9(3).

[156] Code of Practice, February 2005, para 10.

[157] Article 3.3 of the Aarhus Convention requires each Contracting Party to 'promote environmental education and environmental awareness among the public, especially on how to obtain access to information.' The requirements of the Code give effect to art 3.5 of Directive 2003/4/EC.

[158] Code of Practice, February 2005, paras 15–16. See further §6– 022.

[159] *Keston Ramblers Association v IC and LB of Bromley*, IT, 26 October 2007 at [56]-[59].

[160] *Mersey Tunnel Users Association v IC and Halton BC*, IT, 24 June 2009 at [95].

[161] FEIR reg 5(1); EI(S)R reg 5(1). See further §§11– 001 to 11– 010.

[162] Cash flow. FOIA s 8(1); FOI(S)A s 8(1).

[163] As is acknowledged in the Code of Practice, February 2005, Foreword, para 14(iii) and main text paras 1–2, 8 and 15. This is the approach taken in the Aarhus Convention: S Stec, S Casey-Lefkowitz & J Jendroska, *The Aarhus Convention: an Implementation Guide* (New York, United Nations, 2000) p 54.

[164] EIR reg 9(2); EI(S)R, 9(2). Derived from Directive 2003/4/EC art 3.3. See further §11– 010. See Code of Practice, February 2005, paras 15–18. If a public authority maintains that a request lacks sufficient particularity, it is prudent for that public authority to seek further details from the applicant. On an appeal, the Tribunal may not share the public authority's difficulty: *Mersey Tunnel Users Association v IC and Halton BC*, IT, 24 June 2009 at [36]-[53]. Similarly, the Tribunal many not share a public authority's narrow construction of a request, resulting in a finding by the Tribunal that the public authority has not identified all the information held by it answering the terms of that request: *Mersey Tunnel Users Association v IC and Halton BC*, IT, 24 June 2009 at [73], [81]-[83].

cost of compliance. What may be 'manifestly unreasonable' in a single compendious request (whether itemised or not), may be split between two or more requests, each of which is reasonable. Splitting a request may make it more difficult for a public authority to award itself an extra 20 working days within which to answer the request.[165]

6– 023 Fees

The Regulations make provision for a public authority to charge an applicant 'for making the information available.'[166] It is not clear whether the charge can extend to the cost of searching for the information or to considering which exceptions might apply.[167] On one reading, the Directive appears to prevent a public authority from charging an applicant for examining *in situ* the requested information and to permit fees to be imposed only for 'supplying' the information (in the sense of making a copy of some sort).[168] The Regulations are to similar effect.[169] There is no obligation on a public authority to charge any fee.[170] A public authority may in any event not charge more than what it is satisfied is a reasonable amount.[171] On one reading of the Regulations, a public authority may not charge an applicant for the cost to it of refusing access to information held by it.[172] Such a reading is consistent with the ECJ's view under Directive 90/313/EEC. It held[173] that the term 'reasonable cost' precludes a Member State from passing on to an applicant 'the entire amount of the costs, in particular indirect ones, actually incurred for the State budget in conducting an information search' and that it also prevents a charge being imposed where a request is refused. A public authority, although not able (or limited in its ability) to charge for a time-consuming request may nevertheless consider the cost to itself in determining whether the request is 'manifestly unreasonable'[174] or formulated in too general

---

[165] Under EIR reg 7(1) and EI(S)R reg 7(1), it is the impracticality of answering a particular request that enables a public authority to award itself an extension of time: it is not the volume of requests received. Contrast the FOIA s 14(2), and FOI(S)A s 14(7), which entitle a public authority to refuse to comply with a request on the ground of a 'substantially similar' request from the applicant within a reasonable interval before. There is nothing to stop an applicant side-stepping this by asking another person to put in later requests on his behalf.

[166] EIR reg 8(1), EI(S)R reg 8(1). This is consistent with recital (18) and art 5.2 of the Directive and art 4.8 of the Aarhus Convention. Article 4.8 of the Convention and art 5.3 of Directive 2003/4/EC require public authorities to provide a schedule of the charges that may be levied and to set out the circumstances in which charges are to be levied or may be waived. See S Stec, S Casey-Lefkowitz & J Jendroska, *The Aarhus Convention: an Implementation Guide* (New York, United Nations, 2000) p 65.

[167] Article 5 of the Directive also makes it appear that the charge is for 'the supply' rather than for the cost of retrieval of information and of consideration of exemptions. This is to be contrasted with the FOIA ss 12 and 13, which treat separately the 'cost of compliance' with a request for information and the 'cost of communication'.

[168] Articles 5.1 and 5.2. See the *Code of Practice — EIR*, February 2005, para 28.

[169] EIR reg 8(2)(b); EI(S)R reg 8(2)(b). This view appears to receive some support from *Keston Ramblers Association v IC and LB of Bromley*, IT, 26 October 2007 at [56]-[59].

[170] Acknowledged in the *Code of Practice — EIR*, February 2005, para 28.

[171] EIR reg 8(3). The EI(S)R reg 8(3), use a more precise formula.

[172] The *Code of Practice — EIR*, February 2005 appears to favour this reading: see para 29. Similarly, DEFRA, *EIR Guidance*, ch 6, December 2006 is to like effect: 'A public authority may make a reasonable charge for the supply of environmental information. These [*sic*] should not exceed the cost of providing the information, eg, the cost of photocopies' (para.6.26).

[173] *Commission v Germany* [1999] 3 CMLR 277 at 300. This is also consistent with reg 8(1), which ties the ability to charge to 'making information available' and not to making it unavailable.

[174] EIR reg 12(4)(b); EI(S)R reg 10(4)(b). See the *Code of Practice — EIR*, February 2005, paras 20–21.

a manner.[175] Where a public authority requires advance payment of a charge, this has the effect of freezing the time for compliance with the request.[176] If the amount requested is not received within 60 working days of a notification of advance payment, the request effectively lapses.[177] An applicant may appeal to the Information Commissioner against the amount of any fees sought to be imposed.[178] In contrast to the Freedom of Information Act 2000, a public authority is not excused from processing a request for environmental information on the basis that it will involve costs in excess of a specified limit.[179]

4.   THE RESPONSE

11–024   Time for compliance

A public authority must make the requested information available 'as soon as possible and no later than 20 working days after the date of the receipt of the request.'[180] If further particulars of the request have been sought or if the public authority has notified the applicant that it requires advance payment of a charge, this has the effect of stopping the clock until these are received.[181] Where a public authority reasonably believes that the complexity or volume of information requested makes it impracticable to deal with a request, it may award itself a further 20 working days within which to deal with the request.[182] The Guidance suggests that in the latter case the public authority is expected to inform the applicant of this 'as soon as possible' and within 20 working days and that the public authority should also be as specific as possible in relation to the length of and reason for the delay.[183] In contrast to the Freedom of Information Act 2000, the time limit is not extended where the public authority is required to carry out a public interest balancing exercise.[184]

---

[175] EIR reg 12(4)(c); EI(S)R reg 10(4)(c).

[176] EIR reg 8(5)–(7); EI(S)R reg 8(5)–(6). There is no comparable provision in the Directive.

[177] EIR reg 8(5); EI(S)R reg 8(6).

[178] EIR reg 18(1)–(7) and FOIA s 50(1).; EI(S)R reg 17. The Tribunal has held that the proper role of the Commissioner is not to substitute his view of what a reasonable fee would be, but to assess whether the fee imposed by the public authority was within the range that a public authority could reasonably impose: *Markinson v IC*, IT, 28 March 2006.

[179] As is acknowledged in the *Code of Practice — EIR*, February 2005, paras 8 and 20, and in the Foreword, para 14(vi).

[180] EIR reg 5(2); EI(S)R reg 5(2). This roughly accords with the Directive, recital (13) and art 3.2 (which allows normally one month), and the Aarhus Convention art 4.2. 'Working day' is defined in FOIA, imported by reg 2(2). See further §11– 026. The *Code of Practice — EIR*, February 2005, para 25 expressly reminds public authorities that 'they must not delay responding until the end of the 20 working day period…if the information could reasonably have been provided earlier.' This accords with the UN view: S Stec, S Casey-Lefkowitz & J Jendroska, *The Aarhus Convention: an Implementation Guide* (New York, United Nations, 2000) pp 55–56.

[181] FEIR regs 9(4) and 8(5)–(6) respectively; EI(S)R regs 9(4) and 8(6)–(7). See the *Code of Practice — EIR*, February 2005, Foreword, para 14(iv).

[182] Regulation 7(1). This accords with art 4.2 of the Aarhus Convention and with art 3.2(b) of the Directive. See further §11– 030.

[183] *Code of Practice — EIR*, February 2005, para 26.

[184] As is acknowledged in the *Code of Practice — EIR*, February 2005, paras 8 and 26, and in the Foreword, para 14(v).

6– 025   **Transferring the request**

The Regulations provide for the transfer of a request for environmental information where the recipient public authority believes that another public authority holds the information requested.[185] The drafting of the provision seemingly only contemplates the situation where the recipient public authority holds no information answering the terms of the request, rather than where it holds some information but is aware that another public authority holds further information. The Guidance nevertheless contemplates that in this latter situation one of the options for the public authority is to transfer that part of the request that relates to information which is not held by it.[186] Given this arrangement, it is sensible for any applicant who considers that there is a prospect that information may also be held by other public authorities (bearing in mind that each government department is treated as a separate public authority)[187] to include in the request an express requirement that the public authority provide assistance by advising the applicant of any other public authorities it believes may also hold information of the kind requested.[188] The Code of Practice indicates that where such a transfer requirement is not included within the request, the public authority should first contact the applicant.[189] The Code also provides that all transfers of requests should take place 'as soon as possible'.[190] Where a request has been transferred to another public authority it becomes a new request received by that public authority, with time running afresh for answering the request.[191]

6– 026   **Communicating the information**

Once a public authority decides that it will disclose information it must normally do so in the form or format requested by the applicant.[192] If it decides not to use the applicant's preferred format, it must explain its decision to the applicant. This decision gives rise to a right to appeal

---

[185] EIR reg 10(1); EI(S)R reg 14(1). This is broadly consistent with art 4.1(a) of the Directive and art 4.5 of the Aarhus Convention. See S Stec, S Casey-Lefkowitz & J Jendroska, *The Aarhus Convention: an Implementation Guide* (New York, United Nations, 2000) pp 57, 63. The FOIA has no such provision. However, the Act's Code of Practice, paragraph 25, requires a similar exercise. See further §11– 038.

[186] EIR reg 9(1); EI(S)R reg 9(1). See the *Code of Practice — EIR*, February 2005, paras 31, 34–35.

[187] EIR reg 3(5). There is no comparable provision in the EI(S)R.

[188] EIR reg 9(1); EI(S)R reg 9(1).

[189] The *Code of Practice — EIR*, February 2005, para 36. DEFRA, *EIR Guidance*, ch 6, December 2006, para 6.18.

[190] The *Code of Practice — EIR*, February 2005, para 38.

[191] EIR reg 10(2); EI(S)R reg 14(2).

[192] EIR reg 6(1); EI(S)R reg 6(1). These provisions are derived from: Directive, recital (14) and arts 3.4 and 8.2, and Aarhus Convention art 4.1. This is also the view expressed in S Stec, S Casey-Lefkowitz & J Jendroska, *The Aarhus Convention: an Implementation Guide* (New York, United Nations, 2000) pp 54–55. In *Rhondda Cynon Taff CBC v IC*, IT, 5 December 2007 at [26]-[27] the Tribunal expressed the view that there was no obligation under the EIR 'to communicate' (by which it meant supply a copy of) information answering the terms of a request: the public authority could simply make the information available for inspection by the applicant. The Tribunal considered that it was at that point that an applicant could specify the mode of access and, if that mode was refused, could appeal that decision. Further, in that situation, the public authority would need to consider whether the information was required to be disclosed under FOIA, as that Act does give a right to have information communicated. The decision is questionable. By allowing a person to inspect documents, the information in those documents is being communicated. That is recognised in FOIA s 11(1)(b). Moreover, a well drawn request for information will specify the preferred mode of communication for information captured by its terms. See further §13– 017.

to the Information Commissioner. Unlike the Freedom of Information Act 2000,[193] the Regulations do not provide for communication of the requested information by means of the provision of a summary of that information. It is doubtful whether the provision of merely a summary of the information held would meet the obligation imposed by the Regulations.[194] The Code of Practice suggests that where the applicant requests that the information be provided by means of a summary, the public authority should generally comply with that request.[195]

27 Refusal notices

To the extent that a public authority refuses a request for information, whether because an exception applies to any of the information and the public interest weighs in favour of maintaining that exception,[196] because the request is procedurally flawed, because the request involves personal data or because the public authority did not hold the information when the request was received, the public authority must serve a 'refusal notice' that complies with the requirements of the Regulations.[197] The Regulations spell out the detail of reasons that are required in a refusal notice.[198] The refusal notice should not merely paraphrase the terms of an exception, but should state clearly the reasons why the public authority has decided to apply each particular exception to the information requested.[199] Where the exception is qualified, the refusal notice should specify the public interest factors for upholding the exception, and those for disclosure, that have been taken into account before reaching the decision (unless to do so would involve the disclosure of the excepted information).[200] A refusal notice should notify the applicant of the complaints (ie review) procedure.[201] A refusal notice must be served within 20 working days of the receipt of the request.[202] If neither a refusal notice nor the requested information is received within 20 working days (unless extended for one of the reasons described above), then:

(1)   the applicant has 40 days within which to make representations to the public

---

[193] Section 11(1)(c); FOI(S)A s 11(2)(b).

[194]   Article 4.1 of the Aarhus Convention requires Contracting States to pass legislation conferring a right to 'copies of the actual documentation containing or comprising [the requested] information.' See also Directive 2003/4/EC arts 3.1 and 3.4.

[195] The *Code of Practice — EIR*, February 2005, para 23. Under the terms of the Aarhus Convention, it is the information that must be provided, rather than just a summary of it: S Stec, S Casey-Lefkowitz & J Jendroska, *The Aarhus Convention: an Implementation Guide* (New York, United Nations, 2000) p 54. The UN authors consider that the applicant should be provided with 'the context' of the information.

[196] What are termed 'exemptions' in the FOIA are termed 'exceptions' in the EIR. See further §6– 031.

[197] EIR reg 14(1); EI(S)R reg 13(a). For the provenance of this provision, see: Directive, arts 3.3 and 4.5; Aarhus Convention, arts 4.3(b), 4.5–4.7, S Stec, S Casey-Lefkowitz & J Jendroska, *The Aarhus Convention: an Implementation Guide* (New York, United Nations, 2000) p 64. See further §§13– 009 to 13– 012.

[198] EIR reg 14(3); EI(S)R reg 13(c). The notice must also set out an applicant's right of representations and appeal: EIR reg 14(5); EI(S)R reg 13(e).

[199] The *Code of Practice — EIR*, February 2005, para 56.

[200] The *Code of Practice — EIR*, February 2005, para 56.

[201] The *Code of Practice — EIR*, February 2005, para 56. Directive 2003/4/EC art 4.5.

[202] EIR reg 13(2); EI(S)R, 13(a). This is slightly less generous to the public authority than is contemplated under the Directive art 4.5, and the Aarhus Convention art 4.7.

authority in relation to its failure to comply with its obligations;[203] and

(2) if, within 40 working days of receipt of the representations, the public authority either gives no response or gives a response with which the applicant is not satisfied, this will constitute non-compliance with Pt 2 of the Regulations, enabling the applicant to make a complaint to the Information Commissioner, who will look at the matter afresh.[204]

6– 028   Neither confirming nor denying

The Regulations enable a public authority to respond to a request by 'neither confirming or denying' that the information requested exists.[205] The Directive does not provide for such a response.[206] Such a notice can only be given under the Regulations where confirmation or denial that the public authority holds the requested information:

(1) would involve the disclosure of information that would adversely affect international relations, defence, national security or public safety; and

(2) in all the circumstances of the case, the public interest in not disclosing that information outweighs the public interest in disclosing the information.[207]

6– 029   Partial disclosure and redaction

The Regulations specifically require a public authority to treat discretely information that answers the terms of a request. Thus, the fact that a public authority is entitled to refuse to disclose a particular document relying on reg 12 does not detract from the obligation of the public authority to disclose all other information that it holds that answers the terms of the request, save to the extent that some exception applies to any of that remainder. Similarly, within any particular document, a public authority must consider whether it is possible to release part of the document, redacting, if necessary, parts that are excepted from disclosure.[208]

6– 030   Consultation with third parties

Information answering the terms of a request may have originated from a third party. Such information may have been volunteered to the public authority by the third party, it may have been supplied under compulsion or it may have been supplied in support of an application of

---

[203] EIR reg 11(1)–(2); EI(S)R reg 16(1)–(2).

[204] EIR regs 11(4) and 18(1), and FOIA s 50; EI(S)R regs 16(4) and 17 (the time limit in Scotland is 20 days). See further §11– 022. Appeal rights are considered further below.

[205] EIR reg 12(6); EI(S)R reg 10(8). In relation to 'neither confirm nor deny' responses under the FOIA, see §13– 011.

[206] The Regulations seek to address this anomaly through a quasi-deeming provision: EIR reg 12(7); EI(S)R reg 10(9). Presumably the FOIA s 74(3)(b), and FOI(S)A s 62(3)(b), are relied upon in this regard. Paragraph 4(ix) of the *Explanatory Memorandum* to the Regulations recognises that the basis for a 'neither confirm nor deny' response is not to be explicitly found in the Directive, but states that 'it is believed to be implicit'.

[207] EIR reg 12(6)–(7); EI(S)R reg 10(8)–(9). The scope for issuing a neither confirm nor deny response is thus considerably narrower than it is under the FOIA.

[208] EIR reg 12(11); EI(S)R reg 10(7). Derived from Directive 2003/4/EC, recital (17) and art 4.4, and Aarhus Convention art 4.6. This is required by the Aarhus Convention: S Stec, S Casey-Lefkowitz & J Jendroska, *The Aarhus Convention: an Implementation Guide* (New York, United Nations, 2000) p 63. See further §13– 014. Thus in *Archer v IC and Salisbury DC*, IT, 9 May 2007, the Tribunal ordered the disclosure of part of a joint report by officers of a local authority into planning control enforcement options whilst upholding a claim for exception in relation to other parts of that report.

some sort. A public authority is not obliged by the Regulations to consult the third party who supplied this information to it before communicating it to an applicant. The Code of Practice does not impose a requirement to consult the third party.[209] A public authority cannot contractually agree with a third party that it will not disclose information supplied by that third party to the public authority that subsequently falls within the terms of a request made under the Regulations. The Code of Practice exhorts public authorities against making agreements with such provisions.[210]

5. EXCEPTIONS – GENERAL PRINCIPLES

31 Introduction

The Regulations set out the circumstances in which a public authority may or must refuse to disclose requested information.[211] These are called 'exceptions'. The exceptions may be divided into three categories:

(1) Refusals on procedural grounds: namely, where the request is vague, the request is manifestly unreasonable,[212] or the public authority does not hold the requested information;[213]

(2) Where the information falls within one of the three purely class-based exceptions, namely:

— information that includes personal data of which the applicant is not the data subject;[214]

— where the request relates to incomplete material;[215] or

— where the request involves the disclosure of internal communications;[216]

(3) Where disclosure of the information would adversely affect one of a number of matters specifically protected.[217]

---

[209] The *Code of Practice — EIR*, February 2005, paras 40–45.

[210] The *Code of Practice — EIR*, February 2005, paras 46–55.

[211] EIR reg 12(3)–(5); EI(S)R reg 10(3)–(5).

[212] For example, by making overlapping requests or by making further requests before awaiting the outcome of earlier requests: *Latimer v IC and Environment Agency*, IT, 3 August 2009; *Carpenter v IC and Stevenage BC*, IT, 17 November 2008

[213] EIR reg 12(4)(a)–(c); EI(S)R reg 10(4)(a)-(c). Derived from art 4.1(a)-(c) of the Directive and art 4.3(a)–(b) of the Aarhus Convention. See further §6– 032. DEFRA, *EIR Guidance*, ch 7, July 2007, paras 7.4.2–7.4.3. the Tribunal has jurisdiction to consider whether a public authority holds more information answering the terms of a request than it claims: *McGlade v IC and Redcar and Cleveland BC*, IT, 23 November 2009; *Latimer v IC and Environment Agency*, IT, 3 August 2009.

[214] EIR reg 12(3); EI(S)R regs 10(3) and 11(1). Derived from art 4.2(f) of the Directive and art 4.4(f) of the Aarhus Convention. See further §6– 051.

[215] EIR reg 12(4)(d); EI(S)R regs 10(4)(d). Derived from art 4.1(d) of the Directive and art 4.3(c) of the Aarhus Convention. See further §6– 040.

[216] EIR reg 12(4)(e); EI(S)R reg 10(4)(e). Derived from art 4.1(e) of the Directive and art 4.3(c) of the Aarhus Convention. See further §6– 047.

[217] EIR reg 12(5); EI(S)R reg 10(5). Derived from art 4.2 of the Directive and art 4.4 of the Aarhus Convention. See further §§6– 042 to 6– 046 and 6– 052 to 6– 059.

Apart from information that includes personal data of which the applicant is not the data subject, the applicability of any of the above exceptions is not by itself enough to enable a public authority to refuse to disclose the requested information. It must also be shown that in all the circumstances of the case the public interest in maintaining the exception outweighs the public interest in disclosing the information.[218]

6–032   **Vague or unreasonable requests**

A public authority may refuse to disclose environmental information to the extent that the request for information is manifestly unreasonable.[219] Departmental guidance suggests that this might arise where the request would place 'a substantial and unreasonable burden on the resources of a public authority' because of the time it would take to search for the information or to redact excepted information.[220] The environmental information regime does not set a financial limit to the cost of compliance with a request, beyond which a public authority is not obliged to deal with it.[221] Whilst the cost of compliance may be taken into account in concluding that the request is manifestly unreasonable, the particular financial limits set by regulations under the Freedom of Information Act 2000 do not represent an expression of the dividing line between requests that, on the basis of the cost of compliance, are and are not manifestly unreasonable.[222] A public authority will not be able to claim that a request has been manifestly unreasonable if the public authority itself has acted unreasonably in dealing with a request: for example, by failing to comply with its duty to provide advice and assistance.[223] A public authority may also refuse to disclose environmental information to the extent that the request is formulated in too general a manner and the public authority has complied with its obligation to provide reasonable advice and assistance to the applicant.[224] In both cases, before refusing to disclose the information, the public authority will have to satisfy itself that in all the circumstances of the case, the public interest in maintaining the particular exception outweighs the public interest in disclosure.[225]

---

[218] EIR reg 12(1)(b); EI(S)R reg 10(1)(b). Loosely derived from arts 4.1(e) and 4.2 (antepenultimate sentence) of the Directive and art 4.4 (final sentence) of the Aarhus Convention. The Regulations differ from the Act in that refusal on procedural grounds under the Act does not involve any consideration of the public interest: FOIA ss 1(2)–(4) and 14; FOI(S)A ss 1 and 14.

[219] EIR reg 12(4)(b); EI(S)R, 10(4)(b). Derived from art 4.1(b) of the Directive and art 4.3(b) of the Aarhus Convention.

[220] DEFRA, *EIR Guidance*, ch 7, July 2007, para 7.4.2. This would appear to be focussing on what the request involves, rather than on the nature of the request: cf EIR reg 12(4)(e).

[221] Compare FOIA s 12. See §12–002 and *Mersey Tunnel Users Association v IC and Halton BC*, IT, 24 June 2009 at [90].

[222] *Mersey Tunnel Users Association v IC and Halton BC*, IT, 24 June 2009 at [92]-[98] (by inference).

[223] under EIR reg 9 and EI(S)R reg 9: *Mersey Tunnel Users Association v IC and Halton BC*, IT, 24 June 2009 at [95].

[224] EIR reg 12(4)(c); EI(S)R reg 10(4)(c). Derived from art 3.3 and 4.1 (c) of the Directive and art 4.3(b) of the Aarhus Convention. As to the duty to give advice and assistance when a request is too vague, see §§6–021 to 6–022. Suggested meanings of the provision in the Aarhus Convention are given in S Stec, S Casey-Lefkowitz & J Jendroska, *The Aarhus Convention: an Implementation Guide* (New York, United Nations, 2000) p 57. The public authority must comply with its duty to provide reasonable advice and assistance before invoking this as a basis for refusing to disclose: *Mersey Tunnel Users Association v IC and Halton BC*, IT, 24 June 2009 at [100].

[225] EIR reg 12(1)(b); EI(S)R reg 10(1)(b).

33 Comparison with the Freedom of Information Act exemptions

Apart from where the request would involve disclosure of 'internal communications',[226] the Regulations are more liberal in the disclosure of information than is the Freedom of Information Act 2000. First, there are fewer exceptions under the Regulations than there are exemptions under the Act. The Regulations do not provide an exception for:

— information available under an alternative access regime;[227]
— policy information;[228]
— information in respect of which a claim to legal professional privilege could be maintained;[229]
— information the disclosure of which would or would be likely to prejudice relations between any administrations within the United Kingdom;[230]
— information the disclosure of which would be or would be likely to be prejudicial to the economic or financial interests of the United Kingdom;[231] and
— information the disclosure of which is prohibited by or under any enactment or by rule of law (such as contempt of court).[232]

Secondly, a number of the exceptions in the Regulations are more narrowly drafted than are the equivalent exemptions in the Act:

— confidential or commercial information;[233] and
— information relating to the detection of crime or to the conduct of criminal proceedings.[234]

Thirdly, many of the exceptions in the Regulations that approximate class-based exemptions under the Act differ in their additional requirement that disclosure 'adversely affect' the interest

---

[226] EIR regs 12(4)(e) and 12(8); EI(S)R reg 10(4)(e). The Explanatory Memorandum to the EIR describes this exception as not being made under s 74 of the FOIA, but under s 2(2) of the European Communities Act 1972.

[227] Compare FOIA s 21; FOI(S)A s 25. However, under the EIR regime a public authority is not required to make information available if it is already publicly available and easily accessible to the applicant: EIR reg 6(1)(b); EI(S)R reg 6(1)(b). This means publicly available in the format sought by the applicant in the request for information: *OFCOM v IC and T-Mobile (UK) Ltd*, IT, 4 September 2007 at [69].

[228] Compare FOIA s 35(1); FOI(S)A s 29(1). Some policy information may be captured by EIR reg 12(4)(e) and the EI(S)R reg 10(4)(e). See further §6– 047 for the closest comparable provision.

[229] Compare FOIA s 42(1); FOI(S)A s 36. Although some protection may be afforded by EIR reg 12(5)(b) and (d), and EI(S)R reg 10(5)(b) and (d). The Tribunal in *Kirkaldie v IC and Thanet DC*, IT, 4 July 2006, considered (at [21]) that reg 12(5) 'exists in part to ensure that there should be no disruption to the administration of justice, including the operation of the courts and no prejudice to the right of individuals or organisations to a fair trial. In order to achieve this it covers legal professional privilege, particularly where a public authority is or is likely to be involved in litigation.' The conclusion is questionable, not least because legal professional privilege does not depend upon consequential adverse effects whereas reg 12(5)(b) requires it. A claim for exemption in respect of legal advice was similarly upheld in *Burgess v IC and Stafford BC*, IT, 7 June 2007.

[230] Compare FOIA s 28(1); FOI(S)A s 32.

[231] Compare FOIA s 29(1); FOI(S)A s 33.

[232] Compare FOIA s 44(1); FOI(S)A s 26. The EIR reg 5(6), and the EI(S)R reg 5(3), specifically disapply any enactment or rule of law that would prevent the disclosure of information in accordance with the Regulations. Contrast the 1992 Regulations reg 4(3)(a).

[233] Compare FOIA ss 41(1) and 43 with EIR reg 12(5)(e) and (f) and FOI(S)A ss 36 and 33, EI(S)R reg 10(5)(e) and (f).

[234] Compare FOIA ss 30(1) and 31(1) with EIR reg 12(5)(b), and FOI(S)A ss 34 and 35, EI(S)R reg 10(5)(b).

protected by the exception.[235]   And fourthly, all exceptions, save one, in the Regulations involve a consideration of the public interest before the public authority can refuse to communicate the requested information.[236]

6– 034   **Onus**

The more restrictive treatment of exceptions is further marked by a specific onus provision in the Regulations.[237]   The presumption in favour of disclosure informs both the specific exceptions and the public interest weighing exercise.[238]   The progenitors of the Regulations also include an interpretive provision that requires exceptions to be read restrictively:[239] no such provision is to be found in the Regulations, although it is stated in the departmental guidance.[240]

6– 035   **Discretionary disclosure**

The applicability of an exception merely means that an applicant has no entitlement under the Regulations to the disclosure of the information to which the exception applies.   Other than in relation to personal data of which the applicant is not the data subject,[241] it does not mean that the public authority is unable to disclose the information.[242]   In practice, there is a risk that voluntary disclosure of environmental information (other than of 'internal communications') will expose the public authority to a claim for breach of copyright, breach of confidentiality or breach of the data protection principles.[243]

---

[235] In other words, what in the FOIA is a purely class-based exemption becomes a prejudice-based exception in the EIR: see ss 27(2), 30(1), 32(1), 34(1), 35(1), 41(1), 42(1), 43(1) and 44(1).   And similarly as between the FOI(S)A ss 25(1), 26, 27(1), 29(1), 31(1), 32(1)(b), 33(1)(a), 34, 36, 37(1), 38(1), 39(2) and 41, and the EI(S)R.

[236] Namely, those exemptions not listed in the FOIA s 2(3), ie ss 21(1), 23(1), 32(1), 32(2), 34(1), 36(2), 40(1), 40(3)(a)(i,) 40(3)(b), 41(1) and 44(1).   In Scotland, FOI(S)A ss 27, 28, 29, 30, 31, 32, 33, 34, 35, 36(1), 39, 40 and 41.

[237] EIR reg 12(2), to which a public authority's power to refuse to disclose environmental information is made subject: reg 12(1).   In *Burgess v IC and Stafford BC*, IT, 7 June 2007 at [43] the Tribunal regarded this as a significant difference from the FOIA.   See further DEFRA, *EIR Guidance*, ch 7, July 2007, paras 7.1, 7.3.4–7.3.5.   EI(S)R reg 10(2), is to similar effect.   Directive 2003/4/EC, recital (16) states 'disclosure of information should be the general rule and…public authorities should be permitted to refuse a request for environmental information in specific and clearly defined cases.'

[238] There is, at most, only an implication of onus in the FOIA: see further §14– 025.

[239] EI(S)R do include a requirement that exceptions be interpreted in a restrictive way.   This derives from recital (16) to and art 4.2 (penultimate sentence) of the Directive and the concluding words of art 4.4 of the Aarhus Convention. This is consistent with the approach that the European Court of Justice has taken in relation to other freedom of information instruments: see *Hautala v Council of the European Union* [2002] 1 WLR 1930 at [25].   See further S Stec, S Casey-Lefkowitz & J Jendroska, *The Aarhus Convention: an Implementation Guide* (New York, United Nations, 2000) p 45 (the Aarhus Convention sets 'a floor, not a ceiling').   The Tribunal has recognised that recital (16) 'suggests that the grounds for refusal to disclose should be interpreted in a restrictive way' and that it followed that any rider to an exception (such as EIR reg 12(9)) should be given a broad interpretation: *OFCOM v IC and T-Mobile (UK) Ltd*, IT, 4 September 2007 at [25].   As to reading the exemptions in the Act restrictively, see §14– 030.

[240] DEFRA, *EIR Guidance*, ch 7, July 2007, paras 7.1 and 7.2.2.

[241] EIR reg 12(3); EI(S)R regs 10(3) and 11(1).   The matter here being protected is the privacy of a third person.

[242] EIR reg 12(1); EI(S)R reg 10(1).   In relation to discretionary disclosure, Directive 2003/4/EC, recital (24) and art 4.1, are to the same effect.   The Aarhus Convention is yet more emphatic in its support of discretionary disclosure: arts 3.5–3.6.   The FOIA s 78, affirms the position under the Act.   See further §§9– 036 to 9– 038.

[243] See further §9– 034.

36 Ministerial certificates

The Regulations make provision for a ministerial conclusive certificate.[244] The only circumstance in which a conclusive certificate may be issued is where the Minister states that disclosure of information under the regulations would adversely affect national security and would not be in the public interest applying the balancing test.[245] The effect of a conclusive certificate is evidential: the certificate stands as conclusive evidence of the 'fact' certified in it, irrespective of the reality. Once a conclusive certificate is issued, the ordinary appeal provisions are displaced and review is confined to the reasonableness of the certificate.[246] The Directive makes no provision for a conclusive certificate or any other such deeming device.[247] The Aarhus Convention does not provide any such exception to its specific requirement for independent review or reconsideration of refusals.[248]

37 The public interest

All the exceptions other than the personal data exception[249] are made subject to a weighing of the public interest.[250] Apart from where the personal data exception applies, the fact that particular environmental information falls within one of the exceptions in the regulations will not be enough to enable a public authority to refuse to disclose that information. What is also required is that in all the circumstances of the case the public interest in maintaining the exception must outweigh the public interest in disclosing the information.[251] In order for the public interest balancing exercise to have some independent function, it is implicit that there will be circumstances in which although it can be shown that disclosure would adversely affect one of the matters in the exceptions, there should nevertheless be disclosure of that information. The mere identification of the adverse effect that engages the exception cannot always be sufficient to outweigh the public interest in disclosure. As with the Freedom of Information Act

---

[244] EIR reg 15; EI(S)R reg 12. The FOIA allows for conclusive certificates to protect national security (s 24(3)), as well as in relation to information from or relating to nominated security bodies (s 23(2)), information the disclosure of which would infringe a privilege of a House of Parliament (s 34(2)) and certain information held by either House of Parliament (s 36(7)). In Scotland, FOI(S)A s 31(2) (national security). For the effect of a conclusive certificate, see further §14– 033.

[245] Although the wording might suggest that a generalised appraisal of the public interest is all that is required, the reference to reg 12(1)(b) (reg 10(1)(b) in Scotland) indicates that it is the outcome of that balancing exercise which the Minister must certify.

[246] EIR reg 18(3) and (7). As with the FOI(S)A, the EI(S)R do not make provision for an appeal against a conclusive certificate. For a more detailed treatment of the appeal provisions where a certificate has been issued, see §28– 027.

[247] Bearing in mind the effect of a conclusive certificate, there may be difficulty in reconciling reg 15 with art 6 of the Directive.

[248] Article 9.1. Article 6(1)(c) of the Aarhus Convention permits the Contracting Parties to deem public participation in environmental decision-making to be contrary to 'national defence purposes' but does not make analogous provision in relation to withholding the disclosure of environmental information.

[249] EIR reg 12(3); EI(S)R regs 10(3) and 11(1). The personal data exception involves a different and less focussed consideration of the public interest: see §6– 051.

[250] EIR reg 12(1); EI(S)R reg 10(1). The provision is derived from Directive 2003/4/EC art 4.2 (penultimate paragraph). The 'public interest' is a composite phrase and it is unlikely that its meaning is modified by the definition of 'public' in the Directive art 2.6, notwithstanding EIR reg 2(5), and EI(S)R reg 2(4).

[251] See further §15– 001.

2000, the public interest weighing exercise involves a focussed consideration of the public interest:

— On one side is the public interest in *maintaining* the exception. This involves an identification of the public interest that is embodied in the exception.[252] In earlier editions of this work, the view had been expressed that it is that public interest, rather than some general public interest thought to be served by the non-disclosure of the information, that is to be weighed in all the circumstances of the case.[253] This view has been partly rejected by the Court of Appeal in *R (Office of Communications) v Information Commissioner*.[254] It held that in carrying out the balancing exercise, the public interest in all exceptions applicable to a particular item of information must be aggregated and that aggregated public interest must be weighed against the public interest in disclosing that information. Public interest considerations against disclosure but not relevant to maintaining the applicable exceptions remain outside the balancing exercise.[255] Thus it remains important to identify the public interest in maintaining each particular exception. Where there is a variety of information captured by a request with different combinations of exceptions applicable to different items of information, the aggregated public interest in maintaining those exceptions will vary according to the combination of applicable exceptions.[256]

— On the other side is the public interest 'in disclosing the information'. This imports the basic purpose of the Regulations,[257] together with any particular benefit in disclosure of the subject information that may be thought to arise in all the circumstances of the case. Departmental guidance identifies this public interest:

> The Government is committed to freedom of information and to greater openness and transparency. Openness is central to a modern, mature and democratic society. It strengthens government and empowers people. It can improve policy-making and the democratic process by extending access to the facts and analysis that provide the basis for the consideration of policy.
>
> Access to environmental information has long been seen as particularly important. It is essential for achieving sustainable development. An informed

---

[252] *Archer v IC and Salisbury DC*, IT, 9 May 2007 at [59]. The focussed approach to the public interest balancing exercise is also employed in the FOIA s 2(2), and in the FOI(S)A s 2(1)(b): see further §15– 001 and 15– 010.

[253] Compare DEFRA, *EIR Guidance*, ch 7, July 2007, paras 7.3.1–7.3.3, which suggest that what is involved is a generalised appraisal of the pros and cons of disclosure.

[254] [2009] EWCA Civ 90, [2009] ACD 48. On further appeal (*Office of Communication v Information Commissioner* [2010] UKSC 3), the Supreme Court referred the question to the European Court of Justice, pursuant to Art 267 of the Treaty on the Functions of the European Union (formerly art 234 (EC)), with a 3-2 majority indicating a preference for the view expressed by the Court of Appeal.

[255] *R (Office of Communications) v IC* [2009] EWCA Civ 90, [2009] ACD 48 at [35].

[256] The practical difficulties that this interpretation presents to those charged with carrying out the exercise has been touched upon in a number of Tribunal decisions: *South Gloucestershire Council v IC and Bovis Homes Ltd*, IT, 20 October 2009 at [49]-[52]; *SS for Transport v IC*, IT, 5 May 2009 at [103].

[257] Elements of which are articulated in recitals (1), (8), (9) and (16) to and art 1(b) of the Directive and the recitals to and art 5.1(c) of the Aarhus Convention. DEFRA, *EIR Guidance*, ch 7, July 2007, para 7.3.6, states that 'if the public have information on environmental information they can hope to influence decisions from a position of knowledge rather than mere speculation. There may be instances where disclosure of information contributes towards scientific advancements, or assists in access to justice and other fundamental rights. Access to environmental information is particularly important as environmental issues affect the whole population.'

public can support effective decision-making by bringing a wide range of views into the discussion. This helps us to take account of the many potential impacts from the immediate and obvious implications, through those which may become apparent in the long term to global impacts that might easily go unrecognised.[258]

Facets of the public interest in disclosing information recognised by the Tribunal include: greater transparency and, through that, greater public confidence in official decision-making; greater accountability in official decision-making; better informed public debate; better public understanding of official decisions and the decision-making process (including the role played by lobbyists); more informed and meaningful public participation in the decision-making process; increased opportunity to challenge decisions; improved future decision-making; and satisfying those having a local or special interest in a particular decision.[259] In assessing this side of the public interest it is permissible to take into account a use that would be made of the information even though that use would involve an unlawful act.[260]

The various facets of the public interest are assessed at the moment at which the public authority received the request for information, even where this years earlier.[261] Given the stated objective of the Aarhus Convention to facilitate public participation in decisions whether to permit activities specified in Annex I to that Convention,[262] there may be a particularly compelling public interest in making available[263] environmental information conducive to that public participation. Depending on the information being considered and the exception being invoked, the result of the public interest balancing exercise may be time-sensitive. In carrying out the balancing exercise, it will also be necessary to consider the ECHR.[264] In particular, it has been held that article 8 will, in certain circumstances, impose a positive obligation to disclose 'essential information' relating to environmental matters.[265] Thus, in *McGinley v United Kingdom*[266] the Court, dealing with information relating to the exposure of individuals to radiation, said:

---

[258] DEFRA, *EIR Guidance*, ch 1, 23 March 2005, paras 1.1–1.2.

[259] *FCO v IC and Friends of the Earth*, IT, 29 June 2007 at [41]; *DBERR v IC and Friends of the Earth*, IT, 29 April 2008 at [132]-[133]; *Maiden v IC and King's Lynn and West Norfolk BC*, IT, 15 December 2008 at [42][-44]; *SS for Transport v IC*, IT, 5 May 2009 at [137]-254]; *Creekside Forum v IC and Dept for Culture Media and Sport*, IT, 28 May 2009 at [38]-[40]; *Mersey Tunnel Users Association v IC and Halton BC*, IT, 11 January 2010 at [49]; *Office of Communication v Information Commissioner* [2010] UKSC 3 at [6].

[260] For example, breach of a third party's copyright: *R (Office of Communications) v IC* [2009] EWCA Civ 90, [2009] ACD 48 at [54]-[59].

[261] As may be the case where the issue is reconsidered by the Tribunal: *Creekside Forum v IC and Dept for Culture Media and Sport*, IT, 28 May 2009 at [36]; *SS for Transport v IC*, IT, 5 May 2009 at [102]; *ECGD v IC and Corner House*, IT, 11 August 2009 at [16]; *DBERR v IC and Friends of the Earth*, IT, 29 April 2008 at [104]-[111].

[262] The list includes oil and gas refineries, power stations, various facilities for the production and processing of metals, various installations in the mineral and chemical industries, various facilities for waste management, most large transport facilities, pipelines, dams, large mines, and large pig or poultry farms.

[263] See art 6.6 of the Aarhus Convention.

[264] Human Rights Act 1998 ss 3 and 6.

[265] *Guerra v Italy* (1998) 26 EHRR 357, 4 BHRC 63, [1998] HRCD 277; *Roche v United Kingdom* (2006) 42 EHRR 30, 20 BHRC 99.

[266] (1999) 27 EHRR 1, 4 BHRC 421, (1998) 42 BMLR 123.

> Where a government engages in hazardous activities, such as those at issue in the present case, which might have hidden adverse consequences on the health of those involved in such activities, respect for private and family life under Article 8 requires that an effective and assessable procedure be established which enables such persons to seek all relevant and appropriate information.

And in *Taskin v Turkey*[267] the European Court of Human Rights summarised its views in this area:

> Where a State must determine complex issues of environmental and economic policy, the decision-making process must firstly involve appropriate investigations and studies in order to allow them to predict and evaluate in advance the effects of those activities which might damage the environment and infringe individuals' rights and to enable them to strike a fair balance between the various conflicting interests at stake. The importance of public access to the conclusions of such studies and to information which would enable members of the public to assess the danger to which they are exposed is beyond question.

6– 038   Ascertaining and weighing prejudice

The degree of prejudice required by the prejudice-based exceptions is that 'disclosure would adversely affect' the matters protected by those exceptions.[268]   This is in contrast to the prejudice-based exemptions in the Freedom of Information Act 2000, which employ the formula 'disclosure would, or would be likely to, prejudice' any of the protected matters.[269] Given that consideration of a request necessarily involves speculation as to the effects that disclosing the sought information will have, a requirement of apparent certainty rather than likelihood constitutes a significant divergence from the regime established by the Act.[270]

6.   SPECIFIC EXCEPTIONS

6– 039   Information accessible by other means

The Aarhus Convention does not expressly provide an exception for information that is otherwise accessible to an applicant.   However, excluded from the requirement for each Contracting Party to ensure that public authorities make available requested information to members of the public in the form requested is information that is already available in another

---

[267] (2006) 42 EHRR 50 at [119]. And similarly *Giacomelli v Italy* (2007) 45 EHRR 38 at [83].

[268] Prejudice-based exceptions are those listed in the EIR reg 12(5), and in the EI(S)R reg 10(5). These are derived from art 4.2 of the Directive and art 4.4 of the Aarhus Convention.

[269] Sections 26(1), 27(1), 29(1), 31(1), 33(2), 36(2), 38(1), 43(1) and (2). In Scotland, the FOI(S)A requires the same degree of likelihood but a higher degree of prejudice, employing the phrase 'would, or would be likely to, prejudice substantially' any of the protected interests: ss 27(2)(b), 28(1), 30, 31(4), 32(1)(a), 33(1)(b), 33(2), 35(1) and 40. See further §15– 022. Given that elsewhere in the Regulations (reg 2(1), paragraphs (b) and (c) of the definition of 'environmental information') the formula 'affect or likely to affect' is used, the exclusion of the latter limb is unlikely to have been an oversight. The deliberateness of the omission is supported by the terms of recital (10) and arts 2.1(b), (c), 7.2(e) and 7.4 of the Directive. See also S Stec, S Casey-Lefkowitz & J Jendroska, *The Aarhus Convention: an Implementation Guide* (New York, United Nations, 2000) p 58.

[270] *Archer v IC and Salisbury DC*, IT, 9 May 2007 at [51], after noting this and other differences from the FOIA, concluded: 'The result, in short, is that the threshold to justify non-disclosure is a high one.'

form.[271] Under the Regulations, a public authority may decline to provide an applicant with requested information where the information is already publicly available and easily accessible to the applicant in another form or format.[272] The implication is that if the information is available to the applicant in the *same* form or format, for example through some other access regime, that will not provide the public authority with a basis for refusing to provide it under the Regulations.[273]

10 Unfinished material

Subject to the public interest test, a public authority may refuse to disclose information to the extent that 'the request relates to material which is still in the course of completion, to unfinished documents or to incomplete data.'[274] The exception is purely class-based. The public authority may thus rely on the exception without having to show any harm or likelihood of harm which would result from disclosure. The comparable exemption in the Freedom of Information Act 2000 imposes a reasonableness requirement.[275] The focus of the exception does not appear to be the state of completion of the function, project or matter to which the information relates: rather, it is the state of completion of the material, documents or data with which it is concerned.[276] The exception will thus capture an incomplete draft of a document but not a finalised preliminary document.[277] As with the internal communications exception, whereas the unit of exception is usually 'information' to the extent that its disclosure would adversely affect any of the identified matters, the unit of exception in relation to this exception appears to be all information covered by the terms of the request.[278]

---

[271] Aarhus Convention art 4.1. This is reproduced in Directive 2003/4/EC, recital (14) and art 3.4(a).

[272] EIR reg 6(1)(b); EI(S)R reg 6(1)(b).

[273] *OFCOM v IC and T-Mobile (UK) Ltd*, IT, 4 September 2007 at [69].

[274] EIR reg 12(4)(d); EI(S)R reg 10(4)(d). Derived from art 4.1(d) of the Directive and art 4.3(c) of the Aarhus Convention. Regulation 4(2)(d) of the 1992 Regulations provided for a similar exception but without the public interest balancing test.

[275] FOI s 22(1)(c); FOI(S)A s 27(1)(c). See further §16– 009.

[276] Thus a request for a draft version of a document that has been subsequently finalised will fall within the exception: *SS for Transport v IC*, IT, 5 May 2009 at [66]-[83].

[277] In *Maile v Wigan MBC* [2001] Env LR 11, [2001] JPL 193 the applicant made a request to Wigan MBC for access to a database held by the Council comprising raw data relating to potentially contaminated sites. The database was being prepared in advance of the implementation of forthcoming remediation obligations imposed upon the Council by the Environment Act 1995 s 57. At the time of the request and before completing it, the Council had put this exercise 'on hold'. The Council refused access, relying on both reg 4(2)(c) and (d) of the Environmental Information Regulations 1992, stating that the data was incomplete and had inaccuracies. On a challenge to the lawfulness of that decision, Eady J upheld the Council's decision on both grounds. He said that 'to reveal these purely speculative thoughts could cause unnecessary alarm and despondency among the local citizens or landowners.' In relation to reg 4(2)(c) Eady J said that 'any deliberations as to how the Council and its officers should prepare for fulfilling the anticipated obligations of "remediation" need to be conducted in confidence.' In relation to reg 4(2)(d), Eady J said that it 'would be highly unsatisfactory to reveal to the public material which has variously been described as inchoate, embryonic and hypothetical....The fact that an operation may have been put, as it were, "on ice" at a preliminary stage does not mean that it should therefore be regarded as having been completed.'

[278] It is not clear whether the words 'to the extent that' and EIR reg 12(9) will be sufficient to displace this interpretation. The UN Implementation Guide takes a narrower view in relation to the source provision in the Aarhus Convention: S Stec, S Casey-Lefkowitz & J Jendroska, *The Aarhus Convention: an Implementation Guide* (New York, United Nations, 2000) pp 57–58.

6– 041   **Unfinished material: the public interest**

Even where the terms of this exception are met, the public authority may only not disclose that part of the information in respect of which it is satisfied that in all the circumstances the public interest in maintaining this and other exceptions applicable to it outweighs the public interest in the information's disclosure.[279]   Where there is no finished material on an environmental matter upon which a decision is to be made by the public authority, the stated public interest in disclosure of environmental information, namely public participation in that decision-making process, may in some circumstances compel the disclosure of unfinished material if that is required for effective public participation.   Where a final version of a draft document has been published at the time that the request for the draft is made, the public interest in maintaining the exception may be heightened (on account of disclosure of a draft serving to confuse matters)[280] and the public interest in disclosure reduced (on account of the public interest in disclosure having been served by disclosure of the finalised document)[281]   Where this exception is invoked as the basis for the refusal to disclose information, the public authority is required to specify, if known to the public authority, the name of any other public authority preparing the information and the estimated time within which the information will be finished or completed.[282]

6– 042   **International relations, defence, national security and public safety**

Subject to the public interest test, a public authority may refuse to disclose information to the extent that its disclosure would adversely affect 'international relations, defence, national security or public safety'.[283]   The Regulations give no guidance as to the meaning of any of these terms.[284]   There are analogues for each of the four in the Freedom of Information Act 2000, which are slightly more informative as to their scope.[285]   The operation of this exception is considered under the analogous provision of the Act.[286]   Examples of where the Tribunal has

---

[279] As to the public interest exercise in relation to 'unfinished material', see further §16– 009.

[280] It may legitimately be asked why in these circumstances the public authority retains the draft in its records, rather than destroying it.

[281] See, eg: *SS for Transport v IC*, IT, 5 May 2009 at [127]-[160]; *Mersey Tunnel Users Association v Information Commissioner and Halton BC*, IT, 11 January 2010 at [27]. Note, however, that this reasoning will weaken with time, normally being strongest immediately after publication of the final report: *SS for Transport v IC*, IT, 5 May 2009 at [166]. The continued retention of the draft will serve to indicate that it has some enduring significance.

[282] EIR reg 14(4); EI(S)R reg 13(d). Derived from Directive 2003/4/EC art 4.1 (final sentence).

[283] EIR reg 12(5)(a); EI(S)R, 10(5)(a). Derived from art 4.2(b) of the Directive and art 4.4(b) of the Aarhus Convention. The term 'public security' in the Directive and Convention is converted by the Regulations into 'national security' and 'public safety'. Regulation 4(2)(a) of the 1992 Regulations provided for a similar exception but without the public interest balancing test.

[284] The respondent in *R v British Coal Corporation, ex p Ibstock Building Products Ltd* [1995] Env LR 277 (considered in §6–010) sought unsuccessfully to rely on the analogous exception in the 1992 Regulations.

[285] FOI ss 27(1) (international relations), 26(1) (defence), 24(1) (national security) and 38(1)(b) (public safety), none of which is an absolute exemption. In Scotland, FOI(S)A ss 32(1), 31(4), 31(1) and 39(1), respectively.

[286] For the international relations exemption, see §§18– 001 to 18– 016. For the defence exemption, see §§17– 063 to 17– 072. For the national security exemption, see §§17– 040 to 17– 062. For the health and safety exemption, see §§23– 001 to 23– 009. For an instance in which the exception has been applied: *FCO v IC and Friends of the Earth*, IT, 29 June 2007.

held that this exception applies include:

— Information setting out the details of mobile phone base stations, including their grid references. The Tribunal held that disclosure of the information would provide some assistance to criminals.[287]

— Information about an oil pipeline in Turkey. The Tribunal held that the disclosure of the information would harm international relations.[288]

13 International relations, defence, national security and public safety: the public interest

Even where the terms of this exception are met, the public authority may only not disclose that part of the information in respect of which it is satisfied that in all the circumstances the public interest in maintaining this and other exceptions applicable to it outweighs the public interest in the information's disclosure.[289]

14 Interference with the course of justice

Subject to the public interest test, a public authority may refuse to disclose information to the extent that its disclosure would adversely affect 'the course of justice, the ability of a person to receive a fair trial or the ability of a public authority to conduct an inquiry of a criminal or disciplinary nature.'[290] It is questionable whether the exemption applies where justice has run its course and the proceedings or investigation is concluded.[291] Nevertheless, in the absence of any explicit exception for information in respect of which a claim to legal professional privilege could be maintained,[292] the Tribunal has upheld claims to protect such material on the basis

---

[287] *OFCOM v IC and T-Mobile (UK) Ltd*, IT, 4 September 2007 at [36]-[40]. Appeals at *R (Office of Communications) v IC*, [2008] EWHC 1445 (Admin), [2008] ACD 65, [2009] Env LR 1; *R (Office of Communications) v IC* [2009] EWCA Civ 90, [2009] ACD 48; *Office of Communication v Information Commissioner* [2010] UKSC 3.

[288] *ECGD v IC and Corner House*, IT, 11 August 2009.

[289] See §6– 037. For examples of the public interest balancing exercise being carried out with this exception, see: *OFCOM v IC and T-Mobile (UK) Ltd*, IT, 4 September 2007 at [41]-[42]; *FCO v IC and Friends of the Earth*, IT, 29 June 2007 at [37]-[45].

[290] EIR reg 12(5)(b); EI(S)R reg 10(5)(b). Derived from art 4.2(c) of the Directive and art 4.f(c) of the Aarhus Convention. Contrast the significantly narrower reg 4(2)(b) of the 1992 Regulations. In *R v British Coal Corporation, ex p Ibstock Building Products Ltd* [1995] Env LR 277 (considered further at §6– 010) Harrison J held that exception under the 1992 Regulations did not apply where a person had sought planning permission but had not appealed to an inquiry: 'the mere existence of a planning application does not mean that there is a prospective appeal' (at 283).

[291] This is the view taken in relation to the Aarhus Convention provision itself: S Stec, S Casey-Lefkowitz & J Jendroska, *The Aarhus Convention: an Implementation Guide* (New York, United Nations, 2000) p 59. The Tribunal in *Archer v IC and Salisbury DC*, IT, 9 May 2007, while prepared to uphold the exception in relation to an officer report to a local council committee suggesting options for enforcement of planning control, inferred that the position might be otherwise where the possibility of enforcement had passed (at [57]). Although it was not necessary for the Tribunal to decide, it also noted (at [65]) that the currency of the advice might have impinged upon the public interest balancing exercise. In *Burgess v IC and Stafford BC*, IT, 7 June 2007 at [28] and [38] the Tribunal concluded that reg 12(5)(b) could apply to counsel's advice on a planning inspector's decision letter on an enforcement appeal notwithstanding that enforcement was no longer in contemplation by the local authority to which the advice was provided.

[292] Cf FOIA s 42(1); FOI(S)A s 36. And see §§21– 013 to 21– 020.

that the disclosure of privileged material would interfere with the course of justice.[293] Information relating to civil investigations, other than those of a disciplinary nature, would appear to be outside the grasp of the exception.[294] Information that is revelatory of a public authority's strategy for dealing with regulatory breaches, including an assessment by the public authority of the strengths and weaknesses of its position, may have the adverse effect upon the protected interest.[295] Official documents, which may not be held by the prosecution or by the public authority responsible for the prosecution, can be of considerable importance in an environmental prosecution. The Regulations provide an accused person with scope for securing information from both the prosecuting authority and other public authorities more quickly and extensively than under criminal disclosure rules. It is not readily obvious that earlier, rather than later disclosure, of such information can properly be characterised as 'adversely affecting' the course of justice. The exception differs from its equivalent in the Freedom of Information Act 2000, the focus of which is prejudice to investigations and prosecutions.[296] It would seem that the exception has potentially wider operation than its equivalent under the Act in cases where a request for the information emanates from someone other than the person being investigated or prosecuted. In this situation, even if there is no prejudice to the investigation or prosecution from the disclosure, the Regulations provide a basis for non-disclosure where it would prejudice the rights of the accused to receive a fair trial or otherwise interfere with the course of justice.[297]

6–045 **Interference with the course of justice: the public interest**

Even where the terms of this exception are met, the public authority may only not disclose that part of the information in respect of which it is satisfied that in all the circumstances the public interest in maintaining this and other exceptions applicable to it outweighs the public interest in the information's disclosure.[298] Where this exception is relied upon on the basis that the information is subject to legal professional privilege, the Tribunal has tracked the approach which it has used when considering the express exemption in the Freedom of Information Act

---

[293] *Burgess v IC and Stafford BC*, IT, 7 June 2007 at [44]-[49]; *Boddy v IC and North Norfolk DC*, IT, 23 June 2008 at [33]-[37]; *Rudd v IC and Verderers of the New Forest*, IT, 29 September 2008 at [25]-[32]; *Maiden v IC and King's Lynn and West Norfolk BC*, IT, 15 December 2008 at [32]-[37]; *Creekside Forum v IC and Dept for Culture Media and Sport*, IT, 28 May 2009 at [29]-[34]; *Mersey Tunnel Users Association v Information Commissioner and Halton BC*, IT, 11 January 2010 at [38]-[44].

[294] Again, this is the view taken in relation to the Aarhus Convention provision itself: S Stec, S Casey-Lefkowitz & J Jendroska, *The Aarhus Convention: an Implementation Guide* (New York, United Nations, 2000) p 59.

[295] *Archer v IC and Salisbury DC*, IT, 9 May 2007 at [56].

[296] FOIA s 31(1); FOI(S)A s 35(1). This exception is considered further at §§20– 014 to 20– 018.

[297] See §20– 018. The Tribunal in *Kirkaldie v IC and Thanet DC*, IT, 4 July 2006, considered (at [21]) that reg 12(5) 'exists in part to ensure that there should be no disruption to the administration of justice, including the operation of the courts and no prejudice to the right of individuals or organisations to a fair trial. In order to achieve this it covers legal professional privilege, particularly where a public authority is or is likely to be involved in litigation.' Similarly: *Archer v IC and Salisbury DC*, IT, 9 May 2007 at [61]; *Burgess v IC and Stafford BC*, IT, 7 June 2007 at [33]; *Young v IC and Dept for Environment for Northern Ireland*, IT, 12 December 2007; but cf *Watts v IC*, IT, 20 November 2007. See §6–033.

[298] See §6– 037.

2000 for information subject to legal professional privilege.[299] The qualified nature of the exception acknowledges that there will be circumstances in which material subject to legal professional privilege must be disclosed. In particular, if the information evidences malfeasance, fraud or corruption, the public interest in disclosure will be heightened.[300] In considering where the balance of the public interest lies, the age of the information and the existence of current legal proceedings that relates to the information will both be relevant.[301]

6 Confidential public proceedings

Subject to the public interest test,[302] a public authority may refuse to disclose information to the extent that its disclosure would adversely affect 'the confidentiality of the proceedings of that or any other public authority where such confidentiality is provided by law'.[303] This would appear to be directed to *in camera* proceedings of one sort or another.[304] It is capable of applying to meetings of a local authority.[305] Provided that such proceedings enjoy legal protection of their confidentiality and that maintenance of it outweighs the public interest in disclosure, that protection is not disturbed by the Regulations. There is no direct equivalent in the Freedom of Information Act 2000. This exception does not apply to information on emissions.[306]

7 Communications within a public authority

Subject to the public interest test, a public authority may refuse to disclose information to the extent that 'the request involves the disclosure of internal communications'.[307] 'Internal communications' can include communications with an external advisor working under contract to a public authority. Whether communications by such an advisor are 'internal communications' will depend upon the facts in each case, in particular whether the advisor was physically located within the premises of the public authority, the extent to which the advisor

---

[299] See §§21– 019 to 21– 020: *Creekside Forum v IC and Dept for Culture Media and Sport*, IT, 28 May 2009 at [36]-[46]; *Mersey Tunnel Users Association v Information Commissioner and Halton BC*, IT, 11 January 2010 at [46]-[53]; *Boddy v IC and North Norfolk DC*, IT, 23 June 2008 at [38]-[47]; *Salmon v IC and King's College Cambridge*, IT, 17 July 2008 at [55]; *Rudd v IC and Verderers of the New Forest*, IT, 29 September 2008 at [35]-[42].

[300] *Creekside Forum v IC and Dept for Culture Media and Sport*, IT, 28 May 2009 at [40].

[301] *Creekside Forum v IC and Dept for Culture Media and Sport*, IT, 28 May 2009 at [45]; *Maiden v IC and King's Lynn and West Norfolk BC*, IT, 15 December 2008 at [38]-[47].

[302] See §6– 037.

[303] EIR reg 12(5)(d); EI(S)R reg 10(5)(d). Derived from art 4.2(a) of the Directive and art 4.4(a) of the Aarhus Convention. Contrast reg 4(2)(b) of the 1992 Regulations. The exception does not apply to information on (or, possibly, relating to) emissions: EIR reg 12(9); EI(S)R reg 10(6).

[304] For other suggestions, see S Stec, S Casey-Lefkowitz & J Jendroska, *The Aarhus Convention: an Implementation Guide* (New York, United Nations, 2000) p 59.

[305] *Archer v IC and Salisbury DC*, IT, 9 May 2007 at [68]. A document referred to at such a meeting will only fall within the exception, it would seem, if it was prepared exclusively for the discussions at that meeting (at [70]).

[306] EIR reg 12(9); EI(S)R reg 10(6). Derived from Directive 2003/4/EC art 4.2 (penultimate paragraph) and, more loosely, from the Aarhus Convention art 4.4(d) (last sentence) and the last sentence of art 4.4 itself.

[307] EIR reg 12(4)(e); EI(S)R reg 10(4)(e). Derived from art 4.1(e) of the Directive and art 4.3(e) of the Aarhus Convention. Regulation 4(2)(e) of the 1992 Regulations provided for a similar exception but without the public interest balancing test. The Explanatory Memorandum describes this exception as not being made under s 74 of the FOIA but under s 2(2) of the European Communities Act 1972. Whether particular information falls within this description is a question of fact and law: *SS for Transport v IC*, IT, 5 May 2009 at [84].

received support from the staff of the public authority and the extent to which the advisor had the final word on any document he was commissioned to produce.[308] Under the Westminster regulations, the operation of the exception is enlarged by providing that internal communications include communications between government departments.[309] The exception potentially applies to much environmental information that answers the terms of a request.[310] The exception is purely class based. The public authority may thus rely on either exception without having to show any harm or likelihood of harm which would result from disclosure. The comparable exemption in the Freedom of Information Act 2000 imposes a likelihood of an identified prejudice.[311] The Act also requires that invocation of the exemption be founded upon the reasonable opinion of a 'qualified person', being a high-level official in the public authority: there is no comparable requirement in the Regulations. Moreover, whereas the unit of exception under the Regulations is usually 'information' to the extent that its disclosure would adversely affect any of the identified matters, the unit of exception under the internal communications exception appears to be all information covered by the terms of the request.[312] Other than what has been sent to it by, or sent by it to, third parties, most of the information held by a public authority will be an 'internal communication'.[313]

6– 048   **Communications within a public authority: the public interest**

Even where the terms of this exception are met, the public authority may only not disclose that

---

[308] *SS for Transport v IC*, IT, 5 May 2009 at [84]-[98]; *South Gloucestershire Council v IC and Bovis Homes Ltd*, IT, 20 October 2009 at [24]-[33].

[309] EIR reg 12(8): cf reg 3(5). There is no equivalent provision in the EI(S)R. 'Government department' is not defined, although it may be inferred from reg 2(2) that it bears the same meaning as in the FOIA s 84. DEFRA, *EIR Guidance*, ch 7, July 2007, para 7.4.5 contends that 'the meaning of "Government Department" under the EIR can be a difficult question in law. In the UK context, it clearly includes all ministerial and non-ministerial departments of State. Executive agencies are part of their parent department, so can use this exception for communications both internal to the Executive Agency and between the Executive Agency and the parent department.'

[310] As is recognised in DEFRA, *EIR Guidance*, ch 7, July 2007, para 7.4.5: 'This exception could include, eg, correspondence between local authority council members or board members of a government agency, information passed between officials in the course of their duties, internal minutes, briefs and submissions to ministers in government departments. It could also include reports by inspectors or consultants (depending on the contractual relationship), instructed by or reporting to the authority or local authority committee, as part of the internal process for considering the report, where it is necessary to withhold the information pending a decision.' The UN Implementation Guide seems to suggest that the provision should have a narrower operation, excluding factual material or any material once it has been passed to a third party: S Stec, S Casey-Lefkowitz & J Jendroska, *The Aarhus Convention: an Implementation Guide* (New York, United Nations, 2000) p 58.

[311] FOI s 36(2). See further §§22– 020 to 22– 026.

[312] It is not clear whether the words 'to the extent that' and EIR reg 12(10), will be sufficient to displace this interpretation.

[313] In *R v Secretary of State for the Environment, Transport and Regions, ex p Marson*, 23 March 1998, Jowitt J considered (in a judicial review permission application) a challenge to the Secretary of State's refusal to produce under the 1992 Regulations a copy of a 'specific estimate' of the effects of a project on the environment as well as briefing documents, notes and appraisals. He upheld the Secretary of State's contention that the information was excepted under reg 4(1)(a) and 4(2)(c) ('confidential deliberation'): 'the Secretary of State is not required by the regulations to open up his files so as to make available the advice he has received from his officers and documents which record his own thinking about the matter leading up to his actual decision.' The Court of Appeal [1998] 3 PLR 90 at 98, (1999) 77 P&CR 202, [1998] JPL 869 merely accepted this part of the judgment. The Tribunal in *Archer v IC and Salisbury DC*, IT, 9 May 2007 at [72] had no difficulty in finding that an officer report to a local authority committee fell within the exception. The Tribunal's transposition to this exception of the public interest factors in maintaining the exception under reg 12(5)(b) is difficult to reconcile with its observations at [59].

part of the information in respect of which it is satisfied that in all the circumstances the public interest in maintaining this and other exceptions applicable to it outweighs the public interest in the information's disclosure.[314] Because disclosure of such information may well serve the interests described in the recitals to the Directive, the public interest balancing exercise will often prove determinative of disclosure.[315] There is no immediately obvious, universal public interest in maintaining an exception that entitles refusal on the basis that 'the request involves the disclosure of internal communications' without unpicking the objective of the Regulations.[316] The stated rationale for the exception is 'that it is often in the public interest that public authorities have a space within which to think in private as recognised in the Aarhus Convention.'[317] The rationale is not uniformly applicable and the metaphor has its limitations. Mere thoughts are not manifested and leave no record; they have no external consequences. The recording of thoughts, however tentative, reflects a process of selection and an intention that the thoughts either be communicated to others or serve as a reminder. Where the record is intended only to remind the writer of a thought, the rationale is well founded. Where, however, the record is intended to be communicated to others or to rest on the file, able to be consulted by others, the rationale is weaker and the metaphor inapt. Moreover, internal communications may represent the only indication of an intention to make a decision on a matter affecting the environment before a public authority formally takes that decision. Where there is no publicly-available means, or only limited means, of discovering an intention to make a decision on a matter affecting the environment, the stated public interest in disclosure of environmental information (namely, public participation in that decision-making process) may in some circumstances compel the disclosure of internal communications that would reveal that intention and the bases for it. The Tribunal, while recognising the differences between the public interest in maintaining the exception in reg 12(4)(e) and the public interest in maintaining the exemption in s 36 of the Freedom of Information Act 2000,[318] has adopted a

---

[314] As to the public interest exercise in relation to 'unfinished material', see further §16– 009.

[315] The Tribunal in *Friends of the Earth v IC and ECGD*, IT, 20 August 2007 at [76] considered that disclosure of the requested information before the public authority made the decision to which it related would, 'if anything, [be] likely to improve the quality of the deliberative process.'

[316] Namely, participation in the decision-making process: Principle 10 of the Rio Declaration on Environment and Development (1992). See S Stec, S Casey-Lefkowitz & J Jendroska, *The Aarhus Convention: an Implementation Guide* (New York, United Nations, 2000) pp 42, 49. See further §22– 002. In other administrative law spheres, it is recognised that where consultation is required, it must be at a formative stage and it must be adequate: *R v North & East Devon Health Authority, ex p Pow* (1997–98) 1 CCL Rep 280, (1998) 39 BMLR 77; *R (Essex CC) v Secretary of State for Transport, Local Government and the Regions* [2002] EWHC 2516, [2003] JPL 583, [2002] 49 EGCS 123; *R (Montpeliers and Trevors Association) v Westminster City Council* [2005] EWHC 16, [2006] BLGR 304; *R (Capenhurst) v Leicester City Council* [2004] EWHC 2124; *R (Newsum) v Welsh Assembly (No 2)* [2005] EWHC 538, [2006] Env LR 1, [2005] 2 P & CR 32, [2005] JPL 1486; *R (Madden) v Bury MBC* [2002] EWHC 1882.

[317] DEFRA, *EIR Guidance*, ch 7, July 2007, para 7.4.5.1. To similar effect, para 7.4.5.8: 'The rationale behind this exception is ensuring that the formulation and development of government policy and government decision making can proceed in the self-contained space needed to ensure that it is done well. The fact that this exception is subject to the public interest test ensures that the right balance is struck between disclosing information to enable proper public participation in policy debates and providing public authorities with the space they need in which to do their work best.' In fact, the Aarhus Convention, recital (17), acknowledges that 'public authorities hold environmental information in the public interest.'

[318] *Lord Baker of Dorking v IC and DCLG*, IT, 1 June 2007 at [18].

broadly similar approach in both cases.[319] In *Lord Baker of Dorking v Information Commissioner and Department for Communities and Local Government*[320] both the public authority and the Information Commissioner argued that any disclosure of advice given by civil servants would present a risk that they would be less frank and impartial in their advice and less punctilious in recording it. The Tribunal rejected the argument, deciding the public interest issue upon the facts of the case.[321] Of significance to the Tribunal's conclusion were:

— that the decision, namely whether to grant or to refuse planning permission, based upon the advice sought had been taken;[322]

— that the advice related to an administrative decision, rather than general policy;[323] and

— that the requested information would provide 'the whole picture' for a controversial decision:

> It seems to us, however, that one reason for having a freedom of information regime is to protect Ministers and their advisers from suspicion or innuendo to the effect that the public is not given a complete and accurate explanation of decisions; that the outcome is in some way "spun" (to adopt the term whose very invention illustrates this tendency towards cynicism and mistrust). Disclosure of internal communications is not therefore predicated by a need to bring to light any wrongdoing of this kind. Rather, by making the whole picture available, it should enable the public to satisfy itself that it need have no concerns on the point.
>
> ...We repeat that we believe that the strength of the argument in favour of disclosure and against maintaining the exemption is that disclosure will enable the public to form a view on what actually happened and not on what it can only guess at.[324]

The Tribunal has been similarly reluctant to find that the public interest in maintaining the exception is enhanced by related arguments that policy-making requires 'private space' and that that 'space' would be destroyed or polluted by disclosure, or that disclosure would send 'secondary signals.'[325]

6–049   **Information held by judicial or legislative bodies**

Both the Aarhus Convention and the Directive exclude from the definition of a public authority

---

[319] See §§22–013 and 22–025 to 22–026. *Friends of the Earth v IC and ECGD*, IT, 20 August 2007, on app *ECGD v Friends of the Earth* [2008] EWHC 638 (Admin), [2008] Env LR 40, [2008] JPL 1813; *SS for Transport v IC*, IT, 5 May 2009 at [105].

[320] *Lord Baker of Dorking v IC and DCLG*, IT, 1 June 2007 at [12].

[321] Similarly: *Friends of the Earth v IC and ECGD*, IT, 20 August 2007 at [49]-[76]; *SS for Transport v IC*, IT, 5 May 2009 at [108]-[126].

[322] *Lord Baker of Dorking v IC and DCLG*, IT, 1 June 2007 at [16], [22] and [29].

[323] *Lord Baker of Dorking v IC and DCLG*, IT, 1 June 2007 at [17]. The Tribunal considered that in some cases the public interest in maintaining the exception in relation advice on an administrative decision would be greater than where the information sought related to general policy.

[324] *Lord Baker of Dorking v IC and DCLG*, IT, 1 June 2007 at [24] and [28].

[325] *DBERR v IC and Friends of the Earth*, IT, 29 April 2008 at [113]-[131].

'bodies acting in a judicial or legislative capacity'.[326] This is carried through to the regulations.[327] This is not an 'exception' within the meaning of the Regulations. Rather, these are bodies that are outside the regime established by the Regulations such that, whether or not one of the exceptions applies, there is no right of access under the Regulations to information held by them. Accordingly, an applicant seeking environmental information held by such bodies or institutions will need to rely on the right of access given by the Freedom of Information Act 2000. Because these bodies and institutions are neither obliged by the Regulations to disclose, nor would be so obliged but for any exception contained in the Regulations, section 39 of the Freedom of Information Act 2000[328] is inapplicable: disclosure under the Act will fall to be determined by other exemptions in Part II of the Act.

50   Personal data — introduction

To the extent that information requested includes 'personal data' then:

— If the applicant is the data subject of that personal data, the applicant has no right under the Regulations to that information.[329] No consideration of the public interest is involved.

— If the applicant is not the data subject of that personal data, then in certain circumstances the public authority must not disclose under the Regulations that data.[330]

The terms 'data', 'personal data' and 'data subject' all have the meanings that are given to them in the Data Protection Act 1998.[331] These definitions are considered in Chapter 5 of this work. Although the Directive provides that this exception does not apply to information on emissions, the Regulations do not so provide.[332]

51   Personal data of which the applicant is not the data subject

Disclosure of environmental information that constitutes 'personal data' of which the applicant

---

[326] Aarhus Convention art 2.2; Directive 2003/4/EC art 2.2.

[327] EIR reg 3(3); EI(S)R reg 3(2).

[328] In relation to Scottish public authorities, FOI(S)A s 39.

[329] EIR reg 5(3); EI(S)R reg 11(1). The applicant will, however, have a right of access to that information under s 7 of the DPA, subject to the exemptions in that Act. The DPA does not have an equivalent of s 39 of the FOIA. DEFRA, *EIR Guidance*, ch 7, July 2007, para 7.6.3 suggests that where the request captures both environmental information and information that is personal data of which the applicant is the data subject, the public authority should treat the latter part separately as a subject access request, ie without requiring a separate request under the 1998 Act or, it seems, the usual fee required under that Act. This exception is not found in Directive 2003/4/EC: see art 4.2(d).

[330] EIR reg 12(3); EI(S)R reg 10(3). Derived from arts 4.2(f) and 4.4 (final sentence) of the Directive and art 4.4(f) of the Aarhus Convention. Regulation 4(3)(b) of the 1992 Regulations provided for a similar exception. The Regulations do not proscribe its disclosure should there be another right of access to some or all of the information.

[331] EIR reg 2(4); EI(S)R reg 2(3). Each of these terms is defined in s 1(1) of that Act.

[332] EIR reg 12(9); EI(S)R reg 10(6). Derived from Directive 2003/4/EC art 4.2 (penultimate paragraph) and, more loosely, from the Aarhus Convention art 4.4(d) (last sentence) and the last sentence of art 4.4 itself.

is not the data subject is governed by reg 13.[333] This exception is unique in that non-disclosure where the exception applies is mandatory.[334] The exception mimics s 40(2)–(4) of the Freedom of Information Act 2000, but adds onto it a consideration of the public interest in limited circumstances.[335] In summary, personal data of which the applicant is not the data subject must not be disclosed by a public authority under the Regulations if:

(1)   (in the case of non-manual data[336]), their disclosure would contravene any of the data protection principles;[337]

(2)   (in the case of manual data[338]), their disclosure would contravene any of the data protection principles disregarding the exemptions in s 33A(1) of the Data Protection Act 1998;[339]

(3)   (in the case of non-manual data where the data subject has previously given an effective written notice to the public authority under s 10 of the Data Protection Act 1998), their disclosure would contravene s 10 of the Data Protection Act 1998;[340] or

(4)   (in all cases), if the information had been requested under s 7(1) of the Data Protection Act 1998 (the subject-access provision) it would have been exempted from disclosure under that Act by virtue of one of the exemptions in Part IV of that Act *and* the public interest in not disclosing the information outweighs the public

---

[333] The Explanatory Memorandum notes: 'The handling of personal data is not covered explicitly under the Directive although art 4(2) refers to compliance with Directive 95/46/EC on the protection of individuals with regard to the processing of personal data and on the free movement of such data (the Data Protection Directive). Regulations 5(3), 12(3) and 13 relating to personal data contain similar provisions to those in section 40 of the FOIA and are believed to be compatible with the Data Protection Directive.' For an instance in which the exception has been applied: *Creekside Forum v IC and Dept for Culture Media and Sport*, IT, 28 May 2009 at [47]-[82].

[334] EIR regs 12(4) and 13(1); EI(S)R regs 10(4) and 11(2). Although art 4.2(f) of the Directive does not make non-disclosure mandatory art 4.4 (last sentence), in requiring compliance with Directive 95/46/EC, effectively makes mandatory non-disclosure of this class of information (on the basis of it not being a 'fair processing').

[335] The principles relating to this exception are considered in detail in ch 24.

[336] That is, information that is held or is intended to be held as part of a 'relevant filing system' (for the meaning of which, see §5– 015), or that is held as part of an 'accessible record' (for the meaning of which, see §5– 018), or that is processed or intended to be processed automatically (for the meaning of which, see §5– 014).

[337] EIR reg 13(2)(a)(i); EI(S)R reg 11(3)(a)(i). This exception is in the same terms as the FOIA s 40(3)(a)(i). For more detail as to its operation, see §24– 009.

[338] That is, information that is not held nor intended to be held as part of a 'relevant filing system' (for the meaning of which, see §5– 015), nor is held as part of an 'accessible record' (for the meaning of which, see §5– 018), nor is processed or intended to be processed automatically (for the meaning of which, see §5– 014).

[339] EIR reg 13(2)(b); EI(S)R reg 11(3)(b). This exception is in the same terms as the FOIA s 40(3)(b). For more detail as to its operation, see §24– 009.

[340] EIR reg 13(2)(a)(ii); EI(S)R reg 11(3)(a)(ii). This exception only applies where the information is held or is intended to be held as part of a 'relevant filing system' (for the meaning of which, see §5– 015), or is held as part of an 'accessible record' (for the meaning of which, see §5– 018), or is processed or intended to be processed automatically (for the meaning of which, see §5– 014). The exception is in the same terms as the FOIA s 40(3)(a)(ii), FOI(S)A s 38(2)(a)(ii). Disclosure under it may, however, differ in that section 40(3)(a)(ii) is not an absolute exemption and, accordingly, the public authority may only not disclose the information to the extent that, in all the circumstances, the public interest in maintaining the exemption outweighs the public interest in disclosing it: s 2(3)(f)(ii). For more detail as to its operation, see §24– 019.

interest in disclosing it.[341]

The first three circumstances protect the interests or privacy of the data subject. The fourth circumstance ensures that an applicant under the Regulations has, subject to the public interest, no greater right of access than a data subject making a request under s 7 of the Data Protection Act 1998 for information of which he is the data subject. The public interest balancing exercise, which is different from that which applies to the other exceptions,[342] may serve to enlarge the right of an applicant under the Regulations over that of an applicant under the 1998 Act. The exception is considered in greater detail in Chapter 24.

2 Non-consensual disclosure of information supplied by a third party

Subject to the public interest test,[343] a public authority may refuse to disclose information to the extent that its disclosure would adversely affect:

the interests of the person who provided the information where that person:

(i) was not under, and could not have been put under, any legal obligation to supply it to that or any other public authority,

(ii) did not supply it in circumstances such that that or any other public authority is entitled apart from these Regulations to disclose it, and

(iii) has not consented to its disclosure.[344]

The exception attempts to provide some protection for information held by a public authority that has been supplied to it by a third party. The list of conditions required for the exception to engage gives it a limited operation. First, the disclosure must adversely affect the interests of the person who provided the information. A mere likelihood of harm is not sufficient. Secondly, it must be information that was not supplied under compulsion, nor could have been legally required to be supplied. This is particularly limiting. There is little information that at least one public authority, if it so wishes, cannot compel an individual to supply to it. Moreover, information supplied under compulsion (or that could be legally required to be supplied) is often that which is most sensitive to the person supplying it: for example, tax and business information. It is not clear whether information required to be supplied to a public authority in order to secure a licence, permission, consent and so forth, would be treated as

---

[341] This exception is in the same terms as the FOIA s 40(4) and FOI(S)A s 38(3). The public interest test differs in that under the Act the contest is between the public interest in maintaining the exemption (rather than the public interest in not disclosing the information) and the public interest in disclosure For more detail as to the operation of FOIA s 40(4), and FOI(S)A s 38(3), see §24– 021. The Directive does not differentiate between the exceptions in its treatment of the public interest: see art 4.2 (penultimate paragraph).

[342] The public interest balancing exercise here involves balancing, on the one hand, the public interest in not disclosing the information (as opposed to the public interest in maintaining the exception) against the public interest, on the other hand, in disclosing the information: EIR reg 13(3); EI(S)R reg 11(4). The wording suggests that it is for the public authority to show that the public interest in non-disclosure outweighs the public interest in disclosure, rather than vice versa.

[343] See §6– 037.

[344] EIR reg 12(5)(f); EI(S)R reg 10(5)(f). Derived from art 4.2(g) of the Directive and art 4.4(g) of the Aarhus Convention. Regulation 4(3)(c) of the 1992 Regulations provided for a similar exception but without the public interest balancing test. In *R v Secretary of State for the Environment, Transport and the Regions, ex p Alliance against Birmingham Northern Relief Road (No 1)* [1999] Env LR 447, [1999] JPL 231, (summarised in §6– 008) Sullivan J held that parts of the concession agreement fell within reg 4(3)(c). The exception does not apply to information on (or, possibly, relating to) emissions: EIR reg 12(9); EI(S)R reg 10(6).

having been supplied under an obligation. Departmental guidance suggests that it would not.[345] Thirdly, few are the circumstances in which information, other than personal information, held by a public authority may not be disclosed by it or any other public authority: subject to proscriptions arising by statute or common law, a person (including a public authority) holding information may generally disclose it as it likes.[346]

6– 053 ## Non-consensual disclosure of third-party information: the public interest

Even where the terms of this exception are met, the public authority may only not disclose that part of the information in respect of which it is satisfied that in all the circumstances the public interest in maintaining this and other exceptions applicable to it outweighs the public interest in the information's disclosure.[347] Instances in which the Tribunal has held that the public interest in maintaining the exception outweighs the public interest in the disclosure include:

— Where disclosure of the information would weaken a public authority's ability to negotiate with a developer and so increase the cost to the public purse.[348]

— Where disclosure of a forensic accountant's report would damage the public authority's economic interests.[349]

This exception does not apply to information on emissions.[350]

6– 054 ## Adverse effect upon confidential commercial or industrial information

Subject to the public interest test,[351] a public authority may refuse to disclose information to the extent that its disclosure would adversely affect 'the confidentiality of commercial or industrial information where such confidentiality is provided by law to protect a legitimate economic interest.'[352] The exception imposes two requirements. First, the information must enjoy the

---

[345] DEFRA, *EIR Guidance*, ch 7, July 2007, para 7.5.7.4: 'The exception is not likely to apply to members of the public when applying for grants, permits and licences where the information is specifically required as part of the application process, even though the decision to apply for the grant etc may have been a voluntary action.' Similarly, S Stec, S Casey-Lefkowitz & J Jendroska, *The Aarhus Convention: an Implementation Guide* (New York, United Nations, 2000) p 61.

[346] DEFRA, *EIR Guidance*, ch 7, July 2007, para 7.5.7.5 suggests that 'this limb will be met wherever there is no specific statutory power to disclose the information because some public authorities with narrow powers to disclose information will, we can reasonably assume, be unable to disclose this information without such an explicit statutory power.' In fact, unless proscribed from doing so, a public authority needs no explicit statutory power to disclose information. See §9– 036.

[347] EIR reg 12(1)(b); EI(S)R reg 10(1)(b). See §6– 037.

[348] *South Gloucestershire Council v IC and Bovis Homes Ltd*, IT, 20 October 2009 at [46].

[349] *Salmon v IC and King's College Cambridge*, IT, 17 July 2008 at [57]-[58].

[350] EIR reg 12(9); EI(S)R reg 10(6). Derived from Directive 2003/4/EC art 4.2 (penultimate paragraph) and, more loosely, from the Aarhus Convention art 4.4(d) (last sentence) and the last sentence of art 4.4 itself.

[351] See §6– 037.

[352] EIR reg 12(5)(e); EI(S)R reg 10(5)(e). Derived from art 4.2(d) of the Directive and art 4.4(d) of the Aarhus Convention. The exception does not apply to information on (or, possibly, relating to) emissions: EIR reg 12(9); EI(S)R reg 10(6). Regulation 4(2)(e) of the 1992 Regulations provided for a similar exception but without the public interest balancing test. In *R v Secretary of State for the Environment, Transport and the Regions, ex p Alliance against Birmingham Northern Relief Road (No 1)* [1999] Env LR 447, [1999] JPL 231, the applicant sought access under the 1992 Regulations to a concession agreement, made under s 1 of the *New Roads and Street Works Act 1991* between Midland Express Motorway Ltd and the Secretary of State, by which Midland Express was to design, build, finance and operate a motorway. After the agreement had been made, the required public inquiry concluded with the Secretary of State deciding to make the necessary orders. The applicant was concerned that the Secretary of State, in deciding

quality of confidentiality.[353]   Secondly, the information must be 'commercial or industrial information'.   The exception straddles three separate exemptions in the Freedom of Information Act 2000.[354]   While all trade secrets will be covered, non-confidential commercial information will not be covered.   Nor will non-commercial or non-industrial confidential information be covered.   The Directive provision from which it derived confirms its more limited scope, providing for refusal of a request for environmental information where disclosure would adversely affect 'the confidentiality of commercial or industrial information where such confidentiality is provided for by national or Community law to protect a legitimate economic interest, including the public interest in maintaining statistical confidentiality and tax secrecy.'[355]

55   Adverse effect upon confidential commercial or industrial information: the public interest

Even where the terms of this exception are met, the public authority may only not disclose that part of the information in respect of which it is satisfied that in all the circumstances the public interest in maintaining this and other exceptions applicable to it outweighs the public interest in the information's disclosure.[356]   This exception does not apply to information on emissions.[357]

56   Adverse effect upon intellectual property rights

Subject to the public interest test, a public authority may refuse to disclose information to the extent that its disclosure would adversely affect 'intellectual property rights'.[358]   Conventionally, 'intellectual property rights' comprise rights for the protection of patents, secret processes, copyright, registered designs, plant breeders' rights, trade marks and any related or similar kinds of rights.   The Copyright, Designs and Patents Act 1988 provides that a disclosure

---

to make the orders, might have been influenced by the prospect of having to pay compensation to Motorway Express if he decided otherwise.   The Secretary of State refused to disclose the agreement, citing commercial confidentiality and reg 4(1)(a) and 4(2)(e) and the applicant challenged that refusal by way of judicial review. Sullivan J held that the issues of whether information was 'environmental information' and whether it was 'confidential' were objective issues to be determined in an objective manner (JPL at 247).   He found that the concession agreement was not intrinsically confidential (JPL at 253) and rejected a submission that because it was a commercial document having financial implications all of it was confidential (JPL at 254).   He accepted that information in the agreement relating to prices, costs, payment, compensation events and trade secrets should attract confidentiality (JPL at 255).

[353] As to which, see §§25– 015 to 25– 020.   The mere stamping of a document with the words 'confidential' (or the like) does not transform its contents into confidential information.   The duty of confidence may be owed to the body that supplied the information or to a third party: *South Gloucestershire Council v IC and Bovis Homes Ltd*, IT, 20 October 2009 at [39]-[42].   Or it may arise through a contractual provision: *Mersey Tunnel Users Association v Information Commissioner and Halton BC*, IT, 11 January 2010 at [58]-[61].

[354] ROI ss 41(1), 43(1) and 43(2); FOI(S)A ss 36 and 33(1).

[355] Directive art 4.2(d).

[356] EIR reg 12(1)(b); EI(S)R reg 10(1)(b).   See §6– 037.

[357] EIR reg 12(9); EI(S)R reg 10(6).   Derived from Directive 2003/4/EC art 4.2 (penultimate paragraph) and, more loosely, from the Aarhus Convention art 4.4(d) (last sentence) and the last sentence of art 4.4 itself.

[358] EIR reg 12(5)(c); EI(S)R reg 10(5)(c).   Derived from art 4.2(e) of the Directive and art 4.4(e) of the Aarhus Convention.   None of the instruments defines what is meant by 'intellectual property rights'.   Regulation 4(2)(e) of the 1992 Regulations provided for a similar exception but without the public interest balancing test.

'specifically authorised by an Act of Parliament' does not infringe copyright.[359] The fact that a disclosure under the Regulations would otherwise be a breach of copyright will thus not of itself be sufficient to engage the exception.[360]

6– 057   Adverse effect upon intellectual property rights: the public interest

Even where the terms of this exception are met, the public authority may only not disclose that part of the information in respect of which it is satisfied that in all the circumstances the public interest in maintaining this and other exceptions applicable to it outweighs the public interest in the information's disclosure.[361]

6– 058   Adverse effect upon environmental protection

Subject to the public interest test, a public authority may refuse to disclose information to the extent that its disclosure would adversely affect the protection of the environment to which the information relates.[362] There is no equivalent exemption in the Freedom of Information Act 2000. The scope for the operation of this exception is unclear.[363] The Regulations, the Directive and the Convention all expressly presuppose that disclosure of environmental information should work to assist protecting the environment.[364]

6– 059   Adverse effect upon environmental protection: the public interest

Even where the terms of this exception are met, the public authority may only not disclose that part of the information in respect of which it is satisfied that in all the circumstances the public interest in maintaining this and other exceptions applicable to it outweighs the public interest in the information's disclosure.[365] This exception does not apply to information on emissions.[366]

---

[359] Section 50(1). As the FOIA s 74(3), empowers the Secretary of State to make regulations 'for the purpose of implementing the information provisions of the Aarhus Convention' and as the Regulations constitute that implementation, it is suggested that a disclosure under the Regulations constitutes a disclosure 'specifically authorised by an Act of Parliament'. This is reinforced by EIR reg 5(6) and EI(S)R reg 5(3).

[360] The Tribunal has held that this exception will exempt the complete data set of mobile phone base stations, which the public authority had compiled from data supplied to it by the mobile phone operators: *OFCOM v IC and T-Mobile (UK) Ltd*, IT, 4 September 2007 at [43]-[58].

[361] EIR reg 12(1)(b); EI(S)R reg 10(1)(b). See §6– 037. By way of example, see: *OFCOM v IC and T-Mobile (UK) Ltd*, IT, 4 September 2007 at [59]-[62].

[362] EIR reg 12(5)(g); EI(S)R reg 10(5)(g). Derived from art 4.2(h) of the Directive and art 4.4(h) of the Aarhus Convention. Regulation 4(3)(d) of the 1992 Regulations provided for a similar exception but without the public interest balancing test.

[363] DEFRA, *EIR Guidance*, ch 7, July 2007, para 7.5.8.1 suggests, by way of example, that 'information about possible Sites of Special Scientific Interest should not normally be made available until a formal notice is served: especially if there is any risk that making information available prematurely could result in pre-emptive damage being caused before it was protected.'

[364] See the recitals to the Aarhus Convention and the recitals to the Directive.

[365] EIR reg 12(1)(b); EI(S)R reg 10(1)(b). See §6– 037.

[366] EIR reg 12(9); EI(S)R reg 10(6). Derived from Directive 2003/4/EC art 4.2 (penultimate paragraph) and, more loosely, from the Aarhus Convention art 4.4(d)(last sentence) and the last sentence of art 4.4 itself.

7.   APPEALS AND ENFORCEMENT

50   Appeals

The Regulations include a four-tiered review structure which imports most of the review provisions of the Freedom of Information Act 2000:

(1)   The first stage is an internal, merit-based reconsideration of the decision.[367]   In contrast to the Freedom of Information Act 2000, it is mandatory for a public authority to have a complaints and reconsideration procedure to deal with representations complaining of a failure to comply with the Regulations. A public authority is obliged to notify an applicant of his right of complaint.[368]   The Code provides that this notification should set out details of the public authority's complaints procedure, how it may be invoked and the right to complain to the Information Commissioner under section 50 of the Freedom of Information Act 2000 if the applicant is still dissatisfied after the public authority's review.[369]   The Code also provides that the complainant should be informed of the public authority's target date for determining the complaint.[370]   Complaints must, in any event, be responded to within 40 working days from the time when the complaint was received.[371]

(2)   If, after that, the applicant (who becomes a 'complainant'[372]) remains dissatisfied, an application can be made to the Information Commissioner.[373]   The Commissioner is given a wide remit to deal with refusals, the level of fee charged, the time taken and so forth.[374]   Unless a conclusive certificate has been issued, the Commissioner will undertake a merit review of the public authority's decision.[375]   The Commissioner's review results in what is termed a 'decision notice'. For the purpose of carrying out his review, the Information Commissioner can issue an 'information notice' which requires a public authority to furnish the Commissioner with relevant information within such time as the Commissioner specifies.[376]

---

[367]   EIR reg 11; EI(S)R reg 16. This meets the requirement of art 6.1 of the Directive, which permits reconsideration by the same body.

[368]   EIR reg 14(5). EI(S)R reg 16(5), is in different terms.

[369]   *Code of Practice — EIR*, February 2005, para 59.

[370]   *Code of Practice — EIR*, February 2005, para 62.

[371]   *Code of Practice — EIR*, February 2005, para 63.

[372]   FOIA s 50(1); FOI(S)A s 49(1).

[373]   EIR reg 18(1) and FOIA s 50(1), imported by reg 18(3) and (4). In Scotland, EI(S)R reg 17.

[374]   See §§28–006 to 28–014. In relation to fees, the Tribunal has held that the proper role of the Commissioner is not to substitute his view of what a reasonable fee would be, but to assess whether the fee imposed by the public authority was within the range that a public authority could reasonably impose: *Markinson v IC*, IT, 28 March 2006.

[375]   Directive 2003/4/EC art 6.2, and Aarhus Convention art 9.1, require a second-stage review process 'in which the acts or omissions of the public authority concerned can be reviewed and whose decisions may become final.'

[376]   FOIA s 51(1) and (7); FOI(S)A s 50(1).

Through this notice, the Commissioner is able to see the information that is being sought by the applicant in order to form a judgment as to whether it ought to be disclosed under the Regulations.

(3) The third stage of the appeal process is an appeal to the First-tier or Upper Tribunal under section 57 of the Freedom of Information Act 2000.[377] The appeal is normally to the First-tier Tribunal but the appeal can, in suitable cases (eg where the appeal is of considerable public importance or involves complex or unusual issues), be transferred to the Upper Tribunal.[378] The grounds of appeal are the same as under the Freedom of Information Act 2000.[379] It is not just the complainant who may appeal to the Tribunal: if a public authority does not care for the decision of the Information Commissioner, it too may appeal to the Tribunal.[380] The Tribunal must allow the appeal if the notice is 'not in accordance with the law'. If the Information Commissioner's decision involved the exercise of discretion, the Tribunal can interfere if it takes the view that the Commissioner should have exercised his discretion differently.[381]

(4) Under section 11 of Tribunals, Courts and Enforcement Act 2007 any party to a case has a right of appeal to the Upper Tribunal on any point of law arising from a decision made by the First-tier Tribunal.[382]

(5) Section 13 of Tribunals, Courts and Enforcement Act 2007 provides for an appeal from the decision of the Upper Tribunal to the Court of Appeal (or, in Scotland, to the Court of Session). Again, decisions in relation to national security certificates are excluded.[383]

A committee of experts has been appointed under article 15 of the Aarhus Convention to consider representations from the public concerning matters of implementation relating to the Convention. It is possible for cases to be brought to their attention. The committee would not normally expect to investigate a case unless all domestic routes for complaint and appeal have been exhausted.[384] The Regulations do not make specific provision for a third party who may be affected by a proposed disclosure of information to be invited to participate in the appeal process.[385]

6– 061   Practice recommendations

The general functions of the Information Commissioner under sections 47 to 49 of the Freedom

---

[377] There is no appeal to a Tribunal against a decision made in respect of a request for information made to a Scottish public authority, whether under the FOI(S)A or the EI(S)R.

[378] FTT Rules r 19(2)-(3). See further §27– 021.

[379] See further §28– 018.

[380] See further §28– 019.

[381] FOIA s 58(1). See further §§28– 020 to 28– 026.

[382] See further §28– 030. In Scotland, the Court of Sessions: FOI(S)A s 56. Arhus Convention art 3.8, implies that this is the first point at which costs may be awarded against an applicant.

[383] Tribunals, Courts and Enforcement Act 2007 s 13(8). See further §28– 032.

[384] See further: www.unece.org/env/pp/compliance/Pubcom0205.doc.

[385] Directive 2003/4/EC art 6.2, enables, but does not require, Member States to so provide. See further §6– 030.

of Information Act 2000 apply under the Environmental Information Regulations.[386] Under s 47 of the Act, the Information Commissioner has a duty to promote the observance by public authorities of the reg 16 Code of Practice. If it appears to the Commissioner that the practice of a public authority in the exercise of its functions under the Regulations does not conform with that proposed in the Code of Practice, he may give the public authority a practice recommendation under s 48, specifying the steps which should, in his opinion, be taken to promote such conformity. Unless the public authority appeals against the decision of the Commissioner, the public authority must comply with the practice recommendation of the Commissioner. A practice recommendation must be given in writing and must refer to the particular provisions of the Code of Practice with which, in the Commissioner's opinion, the public authority's practice does not conform. A practice recommendation is simply a recommendation and cannot be directly enforced by the Commissioner. However, a failure to comply with a practice recommendation may lead to a failure to comply with the Regulations. Further, a failure to take account of a practice recommendation may lead to an adverse comment in a report to Parliament by the Commissioner.

62 Information notices

The enforcement and appeal provisions of Freedom of Information Act 2000 apply to environmental information.[387] The Information Commissioner determines whether the practice of a public authority conforms to the reg 16 Code of Practice. Where an application has been received under s 50, the Information Commissioner may serve an information notice on the authority requiring it to provide information relating to its conformity with the Code.[388] If a public authority fails to comply with an information notice the Commissioner may certify in writing to the court that the public authority has failed to comply with that notice. The court may then inquire into the matter and, after hearing any witnesses who may be produced against or on behalf of the public authority and after hearing any statement that may be offered in defence, deal with the authority as if it had committed a contempt of court.[389]

63 Enforcement and offences

The Regulations similarly import the enforcement provisions of the Freedom of Information Act 2000.[390] By Sch 3 to the Act, the Information Commissioner may apply for a warrant to enter, search and seize material if it appears that a public authority is not complying with any of the requirements under the Act. Where a request for environmental information has been received by a public authority and the applicant would have been entitled to the information, it is an offence for a person to alter, deface, block, destroy or conceal any record held by the recipient public authority with the intention of preventing the applicant from obtaining disclosure of some of or all the information requested.[391]

---

[386] EIR reg 16(5); EI(S)R reg 18(5), applying FOI(S)A s 43.

[387] EIR reg 18; EI(S)R reg 17.

[388] FOIA s 51; FOI(S)A s 50.

[389] FOIA s 54.; FOI(S)A s 53.

[390] EIR reg 18; EI(S)R reg 17(1).

[391] EIR reg 19; EI(S)R reg 19. Section 77 is the comparable provision in the FOIA. See further §§29– 001 to 29– 007.

CHAPTER 7
Public Records

1. BACKGROUND

1   Introduction

A 'public record' may be described as a document created by a government or a department of government in the course of the business of government.[1] Such a description in a historical context necessarily begs a number of questions. The business of government varies over time: at some moments it may be thought to show an undue interest in men's souls; at other moments an indifference bordering on callousness. The historian AJP Taylor reckoned that until August 1914 a sensible, law-abiding Englishman could pass through life and hardly notice the existence of the State, beyond the post office and the policeman.[2] Since 1914 the position has changed dramatically. The extent of government business and the quantity of records generated by it have hugely increased. Furthermore, the means by which records can be maintained have also changed dramatically in the last 25 years. Nonetheless, what constitutes 'government' varies in context; for the mass of the population, until comparatively recently, what mattered in government was what occurred locally.

2   Medieval records

After the Norman Conquest there was, just as before 1066, no separation of records into those which might (according to later lights) have been classified as 'personal' to the King and those classified as 'public'.[3] All records were simply the King's personal records created in the course

---

[1]   A specific definition of 'public record' is given in the FOIA s 84, which picks up the definition in the Public Records Act 1958 s 10 and Sch 1: see §7– 017.

[2]   The opening line in AJP Taylor, *English History, 1914–1945*, Oxford History of England, vol 15, rev edn (Oxford, Oxford University Press, 1976) p 1.

[3]   For a more comprehensive treatment of the history of public records in Great Britain, reference should be made to: CP Cooper, *An Account of the Most Important Public Records of Great Britain, and the Publications of the Record Commissioners: Together With Other Miscellaneous, Historical, and Antiquarian Information. Compiled From Various Printed Books and Manuscripts*, (London, Baldwin & Cradock, 1872); JD Cantwell, *The Public Record Office 1838–1958* (London, The Stationery Office, 1991); JD Cantwell, *The Public Record Office 1959–1969* (Richmond, The Public Record Office, 2000).

of the business of governing his kingdom. Likewise, such records as were kept by feudal lords derived from their position in feudal society or the maintenance of their estates and were their personal records which simply happened to have been created in the course of governing a feudal society. The King carried on his business in a peripatetic manner, taking with him his exchequer, personal belongings and records. Documents were conveyed in large chests.[4] The Domesday Book[5] (1086) was one such record of the King and is now regarded as the best-known public record in England. It was, in effect, a government survey of William's realm of England.[6] The Domesday Book, as a record of public inquisition or survey, remains admissible as evidence of boundaries.[7] It was compiled by royal commissioners and contains a general survey of most of the counties of England. It specifies the name and local position of every place, its possessor both in the reign of King Edward the Confessor and at the time of the survey with particulars,[8] quantities and descriptions of the land. It is, principally, manors which are described in the Domesday Book, England being at the time of the survey (and for some time thereafter) largely divided into manors.[9] Some northern counties and the cities of London and Winchester, which were not within manors, are not within the Domesday Book.

7– 003 The development of state records

Royal administration, which was inseparable from the governance of the State, came to develop and grow in complexity. It also became more centralised, with others (notably the King's justices) travelling on the King's business. Records, by way of copies, came to be necessary so that instructions (for example, by a writ) could be conveyed, but knowledge maintained centrally. In addition, records of the royal income and expenditure were maintained. In this regard it can be observed that the essential purpose of the Domesday Book was the establishment of the terms of a new rating system to protect and enlarge the King's Revenue:[10] information is seldom obtained simply for the sake of obtaining information, no more than books are written simply for the sake of writing. Copies were made on parchment, that is to say on cleaned, dried and smoothed sheepskin. Copies were enrolled, ie sheets of parchment were sewn together to create rolls,[11] for easy carriage and storage. Departments of State

---

[4] Some of which are preserved in The National Archives in Kew, near Richmond, Surrey TW9 4DU.

[5] The document references for Domesday in The National Archives are E31/1 and E31/2. It consists of one folio volume of 382 pages and one quarto volume of 450 pages. The name 'Domesday' is from Old English 'Dom', meaning judgment.

[6] However, it is not the oldest document held at The National Archives; that is an Anglo-Saxon land deed dated 974. However, if this and other such deeds are regarded as private records, then the Domesday Book is the oldest public record held by The National Archives.

[7] *Iveagh v Martin* [1961] 1 QB 232 at 238; *Brackenborough v Spalding UDC* [1942] AC 310 at 313; *Nicholls v Ely Beet Sugar Factory* [1931] 2 Ch 84 at 89; *Harris v Earl of Chichester* [1911] AC 623 at 629, 632; *AG v Simpson* [1901] 2 Ch 671 at 688, 700; *Merttns v Hill* [1901] 1 Ch 842 at 850, 854; *Duke of Beaufort v John Aire & Co* (1904) 20 TLR 602; *Alcock v Cooke* (1829) 5 Bing 340.

[8] The Anglo-Saxon Chronicle for 1085 records that no pig was left out.

[9] C Jessel, *Law of the Manor* (Chichester, Barry Rose Law Publishers, 1998).

[10] See C Platt, *Medieval England: A Social History and Archaeology from the Conquest to AD 1600* (London, Routledge and Kegan Paul, 1978). The 'Domesday Book' was for some time used as a term to denote any book containing a list of the rateable value of land: see *Lumsden v Inland Revenue Commissioners* [1914] AC 877 at 897, 900; *Commissioners of Inland Revenue v Herbert* [1913] AC 326 at 348, 351, 356.

[11] Hence, the office of 'Master of the Rolls'.

gradually developed. The Exchequer was concerned with the financial side of medieval government and the Chancery was concerned with the administrative side. There was no systematic archiving of these records once their immediate use had passed. In the Tudor period the various secretaries of state retained many important state papers when they left office. In order to prevent this leakage and to make some permanent provision for the custody and arrangement of these papers, in 1578 the State Paper office was established. In the early eighteenth century the House of Lords established an inquiry into domestic records. As was the way, the inquiry proceeded through the reigns of Anne and George I. Before its conclusion, the House of Commons commenced its own inquiry, producing, some 30 years later, a report which observed that there were no indexes to the records and that such catalogues that did exist were incomplete. Another committee was appointed; but little was done over the following 40 years.

4   The establishment of a public record office

In all this time, no measures had been taken for the housing of the increasing mass of records. The casual or adventitious nature of storage created difficulties as to both access and maintenance. The usual places in which these records were stored,[12] such as the Chapter House at Westminster, the Tower of London and the stables in Holborn, were too small to contain the increasing mass of records, as well as being ill-suited to the purpose. That said, the purpose was not as it is today. From time to time, records might be consulted to resolve some legal controversy, but:

> ..except for these practical purposes they had hardly ever been consulted. Occasionally, indeed, historians had arisen who refused to base their story upon any but the best evidence. For the majority the study of the records under the then existing conditions was, to use Prynne's expression, too "heroic".[13]

The House of Commons committee, which had been appointed some 40 years earlier, produced a report; and the report prompted the appointment of a Record Commission in 1800 to investigate the state of the public records. Its minute book for June 28, 1809 has the following entry:

> On Wednesday the 28th of June, 1809, and the three following days, Mr Meaking of the Chirographer's Office brought and delivered into the Record Office at the Chapter House ten large cartloads of the transcript of Fines, each load being about one ton weight, and the number of bundles being about fourteen hundred.... Some of these bundles were brought from the Temple Church, where, from the dampness of the place, and a constant accumulation of filth and dirt, many of them are rendered almost completely useless, and many half-destroyed through lying in the wet, whereby they are become so fixed together as not to be separated without breaking them in pieces. The smell arising from the sad condition they were in rendered the arrangement of them etc very disagreeable and unhealthy.[14]

---

[12]   There were over 60 such places by the beginning of the nineteenth century.

[13]   W Holdsworth, *A History of English Law in Sixteen Volumes*, vol 5, 4th edn (London, Methuen, 1936) p 601.

[14]   W Holdsworth, *A History of English Law in Sixteen Volumes*, vol 5, 4th edn (London, Methuen, 1936) p 600.

The Commissioners reported in 1819,[15] as did a Select Committee in 1822,[16] and their work led to the passage of the Public Record Office Act 1838. This was the first legislation to protect public records by the creation of an official archive.

7–005 The Public Record Office

Section 8 of the Public Record Office Act 1838 established the Public Record Office under the direction of the Master of the Rolls. The principal concern of the Public Record Office Act 1838 was to make provision for the records of the Exchequer, Chancery and other ancient courts of law. The Record Office when first constituted was supposed to exist for the sake of litigants who wanted copies of documents, rather than for historians.[17] The records were brought together in a single repository, administered by professional staff in a new government department. The site chosen was a place where records had since the thirteenth century been stored and was the redundant chapel of a hostel called Domus Conversarium. Situated in Chancery Lane, it had been a lodging house for Jews who had converted to Christianity. However, all Jews had been expelled from England in 1290 and the chapel, thereby superfluous, was then converted and used for storage of the rolls of Chancery. The Master of the Rolls came to live on the site, which became known as the Rolls Estate. The Public Record Office Act 1838 created no compulsion for the transfer of records to the Public Record Office. Many records were given to the Public Record Office, but no selection occurred and some material was worthless. The Public Record Office Act 1877 authorised the destruction of such documents, provided that they did not predate 1715.

7–006 The Public Records Act 1958

As the business of government developed over the next hundred years or so, there was a corresponding growth in the quantity of records. This necessitated a reconsideration of the regime which had been established in 1838. A parliamentary committee was established under Sir James Grigg.[18] The recommendations of that committee in 1954 led to the Public Records Act 1958, which remains the principal piece of legislation governing the operations of The National Archives. As its long title records, it was an Act to make new provision with respect to public records and the Public Record Office and for connected purposes. Accordingly, the 1958 Act repealed the Public Record Office Acts 1838 to 1898.[19]

7–007 The Freedom of Information Act 2000

One of the matters dealt with in the Public Records Act 1958 was public access to public records. In general terms, the approach taken under the 1958 Act was to refuse access to records that were less than 50 years old (reduced in 1967 to 30 years old) held by the Public

---

[15] Reports from the Commissioners Appointed to Execute the Measures Recommended by the Committee of the House of Commons, Respecting the Public Records of the Kingdom with an Account of their Proceedings.

[16] Report from the Select Committee on Public Records of the Kingdom.

[17] W Holdsworth, *A History of English Law in Sixteen Volumes*, vol 5, 4th edn (London, Methuen, 1936) pp 601–602.

[18] Later, Lord Altrincham.

[19] That being the collective title for the Public Record Office Act 1838, the Public Record Office Act 1877 and the Public Record Office Act 1898. The 1898 Act enabled worthless documents created between 1660 and 1715 to be destroyed.

Record Office (ie The National Archives), but to extend the refusal period where disclosure 'could or might constitute a breach of good faith on the part of the Government.'[20] Whilst having a certain simplicity about it, the vagueness of such a determinant of access does not sit comfortably with a prescriptive scheme of disclosure such as is created by the Freedom of Information Act 2000. For this reason, the rudimentary access regime originally conferred by s 5 of the Public Records Act 1958 has been replaced by the regime created by s 1 of the Freedom of Information Act 2000 and, in relation to 'environmental information',[21] the Environmental Information Regulations 2004. The special characteristics of information held by the Public Record Office (ie The National Archives), the fact that public records are held by bodies other than the Public Record Office, and the fact that the interest of the Public Record Office in the contents of a record is different from that of the public authority which created that record, have all necessitated important modifications to the regime which ordinarily applies to information held by a public authority under the 2000 Act. These modifications are considered in detail below. What must be also kept in mind is that there is an important legislative distinction between the obligations in relation to the preservation of public records and those in relation to the access to such records. Generally, the framework given by the public records legislation[22] has been retained for the preservation of records, whilst the Freedom of Information Act 2000 controls the ability to access such records. It should also be added that the Public Record Office is itself a 'public authority' subject to the Freedom of Information Act 2000 and the Environmental Information Regulations 2004.

2. PUBLIC RECORD BODIES

The Public Record Office
The historical background to the Public Record Office (ie The National Archives) has already been outlined. The Public Record Office Act 1958 sets out the powers and duties of the Keeper of Public Records. These seemingly simple provisions belie the complexity of his functions. The National Archives[23] produces a manual, entitled Access to Public Records, which is intended to be a tool for use by those who need to understand the legal basis for the working of the public records system. As is there stated, from the moment of a record's creation to its final archiving in The National Archives, a complex web of legislative provisions, government policy instructions and departmental practices govern how it may be treated. It is the stated principal aim of The National Archives to assist and promote the study of the past in order to inform the present and the future. Whilst this work is not concerned with the preservation obligations as such, their inter-relationship with the rights of access necessitates some understanding of them. Before doing so, however, it is convenient to introduce the protagonists in the archiving of records.

---

[20] Public Records Act 1958 s 5.

[21] As to the meaning of which, see §6–010.

[22] Now the Public Records Act 1958.

[23] On 2 April 2003 the Public Record Office and the Historical Manuscripts Commission joined together to form a new organisation called 'The National Archives'.

7– 009 **The Keeper of Public Records**

Section 1 of the Public Records Act 1958 provided for the transfer of the direction of the Public Record Office from the Master of the Rolls to the Lord Chancellor. He was made generally responsible for the execution of the Public Records Act 1958 and required to supervise the care and preservation of public records. There was established by s 1(2) an Advisory Council on Public Records to advise the Lord Chancellor on matters concerning public records in general and, in particular, on those aspects of the work of the Public Record Office affecting members of the public who make use of the facilities provided by the Public Record Office (ie The National Archives). The Advisory Council on Public Records now operates within the Advisory Council on National Records and Archives. The Master of the Rolls is chairman of the Advisory Council on Public Records. The other members of the Council are appointed by the Lord Chancellor on such terms as he specifies. By s 1(2A), introduced by the Freedom of Information Act 2000, the matters on which the Advisory Council on Public Records may advise the Lord Chancellor include matters relating to the application of the Freedom of Information Act 2000 to information contained in public records which are historical records within the meaning of Part VI of the 2000 Act. Every year the Lord Chancellor must lay before Parliament a report of the work of the Public Record Office. The report has to include any report made to him by the Advisory Council on Public Records. Section 2 of the Public Records Act 1958 empowers the Lord Chancellor to appoint a Keeper of Public Records. The Keeper of Public Records takes charge, under the direction of the Lord Chancellor, of the Public Record Office (ie The National Archives) and of the records in it. Further, the Lord Chancellor may with the concurrence of the Treasury as to numbers and conditions of service appoint such other persons to serve in the Public Record Office as he thinks fit. The Keeper of Public Records has, by s 2 of the 1958 Act, power to do all such things as appear to him necessary or expedient for maintaining the utility of the Public Record Office. In particular, he may:

(a) compile and make available indexes and guides to, and calendars and texts of, the records in the Public Record Office;

(b) prepare publications concerning the activities of and facilities provided by the Public Record Office;

(c) regulate the conditions under which members of the public may inspect public and other records or use the other facilities of the Public Record Office;

(d) provide for the making and authentication of copies of and extracts from records required as evidence in legal proceedings or for other purposes;

(e) accept responsibility for the safe keeping of records other than public records;

(f) make arrangements for the separate housing of films and other records which have to be kept under special conditions;

(g) where the Lord Chancellor gives his approval, lend records for display at commemorative exhibitions or for other special purposes; and

(h) acquire records and accept gifts and loans.

The Public Record Office (Fees) (No 2) Regulations 2001[24] prescribe the fees which may be charged for inspection, authentication of records in the charge of the Keeper of Public Records

---

[24] SI 2001/3462 made under s 2(5) by the Lord Chancellor with the concurrence of the Treasury.

and other services given by officers of the Public Record Office.

10 The Historical Manuscripts Commission

The Historical Manuscripts Commission[25] was appointed by Royal Warrant dated April 2, 1869. The Commission's terms of reference were revised and extended by a further Royal Warrant given on 5 December 1959. Since then they have been:

— to make enquiry as to the existence and location of manuscripts, including records or archives of all kinds, of value for the study of history, other than records which are for the time being public records by virtue of the Public Records Act 1958;

— with the consent of the owners or custodians to inspect and report upon these;

— to record the particulars of such manuscripts and records in a National Register;

— to promote and assist the proper preservation and storage of such manuscripts and records;

— to assist those wishing to use such manuscripts or records for study or research;

— to consider and advise upon general questions relating to the location, preservation and use of such manuscripts and records;

— to promote the co-ordinated action of all professional and other bodies concerned with the preservation and use of such manuscripts and records; and

— to carry out in place of the Public Record Office the statutory duties of the Master of the Rolls in respect of manorial and tithe documents.

Since its inception, the Commission has, in summary, created and maintained:

— The National Register of Archives: a resource for those seeking information on the nature and location of records relating to British history. The National Register of Archives holds over 43,000 unpublished catalogues and listed manuscript collections and has been indexed. The indexes contain 150,000 references, with a further 300,000 connected records and these are available on the Historical Manuscripts Commission website.

— ARCHON: an up to date electronic directory of repositories in the United Kingdom and abroad and a portal to archival resources. ARCHON provides the framework for a virtual UK archival network.

— The Manorial Documents Register: an index to surviving manorial records in England and Wales. The Manorial Documents Register is administered by the Historical Manuscripts Commission on behalf of the Master of the Rolls. Some sections of the Manorial Documents Register have been stored on computer and are available on the Historical Manuscripts Commission website. The Manorial Documents Register records information on the whereabouts of manorial records excluding title deeds. Manorial records survive today in many national and local record offices and in some cases in private hands. The Historical Manuscripts Commission itself holds no manorial records. The Manorial Documents Register is not a register of title to manorial lordships and the Historical Manuscripts Commission does not collect or record information of this nature.

— Archives in Focus: an introduction to archives. It includes information on online

---

[25] The Historical Manuscripts Commission has offices in Quality House, Quality Court, Chancery Lane, London WC2A 1HP. It there provides access to the National Register of Archives and to the Manorial Documents Register.

archival resources designed for teachers, practical advice on what can be expected and what can be found when visiting a record office and guidance on how archives can be used for family, local and house history.

7– 011   The National Archives

On 2 April 2003 the Historical Manuscripts Commission informally merged with the Public Record Office to form The National Archives. The National Archives is, in fact, an umbrella term, with the two bodies remaining distinct for legislative purposes. In October 2006 the Office of Public Sector Information, previously attached to the Cabinet Office, merged with the National Archives. The Office of Public Sector Information, which is responsible for Her Majesty's Stationery Office, performs its role from within the structure of the National Archives. The National Archives is a non-ministerial government department and an executive agency of the Ministry of Justice. Although the legal entity to which the various legal provisions applies remains the Public Record Office, since April 2003 the Public Record Office has functioned as part of The National Archives and has been known by that name.[26]   For that reason, normally this work uses The National Archives to mean the Public Record Office.

7– 012   The Lord Chancellor

The Lord Chancellor is the government minister responsible for the National Archives. On normal policy matters concerning the National Archives, public and other records and the work of the Public Record Office and the Historical Manuscripts Commission he relies on advice from the Keeper of Public Records[27] and from his officials in the Lord Chancellor's Department. Since 1958, as minister responsible for the Public Record Office, he has had the benefit of independent advice on matters relating to public records from his Advisory Council on Public Records. For the moment he remains responsible for these, despite the transfer of certain functions formerly performed by him to the Secretary of State for Justice.[28]

7– 013   The Advisory Council on National Records and Archives

The Advisory Council[29] on National Records and Archives was established by the Lord Chancellor on 2 April 2003. It has advisory functions of its own in relation to strategic and policy matters relating to the National Archives and archival policy. The Advisory Council on National Records and Archives embraces two further bodies, which advise on specific areas: the Advisory Council on Public Records (created by s 1(2) of the Public Records Act 1958) to advise on public records issues; and the Advisory Council on Historical Manuscripts to advise on matters relating to non-public records and manuscripts. All three bodies are chaired by the Master of the Rolls who sits with unpaid members, appointed by the Lord Chancellor, who represent a wide range of different interests, including Parliament, regular users of historical

---

[26]   This is reflected in the s 46 Code of Practice.

[27]   Appointed under s 2 of the Public Records Act 1958.

[28]   See The Secretary of State for Justice Order 2007 SI 2007/2128. Up until 9 May 2007, the Secretary of State for Constitutional Affairs: see The Secretary of State for Constitutional Affairs Order 2003 SI 2003/1887.

[29]   The legal entity is the Advisory Council on Public Records, Since 2003 the Council has functioned as The Advisory Council on National Records and Archives, and that term is used in the s 46 Code of Practice. The Advisory Council's address is: The Advisory Council on National Records and Archives, The National Archives, Kew, near Richmond, Surrey TW9 4DU.

records and owners of private papers. The Council is independent of the Keeper of Public Records. The three Advisory Councils are all advisory Non-Departmental Public Bodies within the remits of the Parliamentary Commissioner for Administration (the Ombudsman), the Commissioner for Public Appointments and the Information Commissioner. None has any executive functions or powers.

14 The role of the Advisory Council

The Advisory Council's task is to advise the Lord Chancellor on any subject concerning archives and manuscripts, on issues relating to public access to the public records, and on the preservation of records, archives and manuscripts. It has no role in the day-to-day running of the National Archives, and no authority over the Keeper. The Council will normally meet four times a year, in February, June, October and December. Its most important task is to consider applications from departments for the extended closure of public records beyond the normal 30 years, or for the retention of public records by departments. The Lord Chancellor's practice is never to sign an instrument approving extended closures or retentions until he has received advice on it from the Advisory Council. The reasons for applications are scrutinised closely, and departments may be asked for further justification. This reconsideration can lead to a document being made available after all. The Advisory Council also considers subjects such as the corporate plan of the National Archives and its performance against its objectives and targets; the acceptance by the nation of papers in lieu of tax; the sale and export of historical manuscripts; public services provided by the National Archives and other UK archives; preservation policy for records and manuscripts of all sorts; and the level and fairness of fees. The Advisory Council reports to the Lord Chancellor every year in an annual report by the Master of the Rolls, which is published with the Keeper's Report. On matters of urgency or of particular importance it asks the Master of the Rolls to write to the Lord Chancellor directly.

15 The Master of the Rolls

Apart from his continuing responsibility in respect of the Chancery of England, the Master of the Rolls does not have charge and superintendence over, or custody of, any public records. Those public records which prior to the commencement of the 1958 Act were in the custody of the Master of the Rolls were thereafter (save for records of the Chancery of England) in the custody of the Keeper of Public Records or such other officer as the Lord Chancellor might from time to time appoint.

3. THE PRESERVATION OF RECORDS

16 Introduction

The utility of much information, whether official or otherwise, is ephemeral. A public authority will wish to hold information for as long as it appears to have some relevance, or at least potential relevance, to the performance of that public authority's functions. The significance to a public authority of any information held by it will with time generally diminish. If for no other reasons than those of space and management, a public authority will ordinarily wish to cull the 'non-current' information held by it, either by destroying it or by archiving it. As will be seen in this section, the public record regime provides an orderly and defined methodology for doing so which recognises that information that has lost its contemporaneity to a public authority may nevertheless hold a different, residual interest for others. As will be seen in the next section, as particular information 'ages', the grounds for exempting the information from disclosure, which remain founded in the Freedom of Information Act 2000, are reduced to a series of key exemptions.

7–017 **The meaning of 'public records'**

The Public Records Act 1958 distinguishes between public and other records. Section 10 provides that the phrase 'public records' has the meaning given by the first schedule to the Act and that the word 'records' includes not merely written records but records conveying information by any other means whatsoever.[30] When records for administrative purposes are kept together in one file they are, in consequence of s 10(2), treated for the purposes of the Act as having been created on the date of the last record. The provisions of Sch 1 of the Public Records Act 1958 have effect for determining what constitute public records. A comprehensive list is set out in the Schedule:

(1) The first category is administrative and departmental records belonging to Her Majesty, whether in the United Kingdom or overseas, in right of Her Majesty's Government in the United Kingdom.[31] This expressly embraces records of, or held in, any department of Her Majesty's Government in the United Kingdom or records of any office, commission or other body whatsoever under Her Majesty's Government in the United Kingdom. This first broad category is subject to a number of exemptions. These cover:

(a) the records of any government department or body which is wholly or mainly concerned with Scottish affairs, or which carries on its activities wholly or mainly in Scotland;

(b) registers, or certified copies of entries in registers, being registers or certified copies kept or deposited in the General Register Office under or in pursuance of any enactment, whether past or future, which provides for the registration of births, deaths, marriages or adoptions;

(c) except as provided by para 4 of the Schedule (which deals with records of court proceedings) records of the Duchy of Lancaster;

(d) records of the office of Public Trustee relating to individual trusts; and

(e) Welsh public records as defined in s 148 of the Government of Wales Act 2006.[32]

---

[30] See s 46 Code of Practice, para 3, which uses the definition in BS ISO 15489-1:2001 Information and documentation – Records management – Part 1: General.

[31] Public Records Act 1958 Sch 1 para 2.

[32] The following are defined by s 148(1) as 'Welsh public records':
(a) administrative and departmental records belonging to Her Majesty which are records of the Welsh Assembly Government,
(b) administrative and departmental records of the Auditor General,
(c) administrative and departmental records belonging to Her Majesty which are records of or held in any government department which is wholly or mainly concerned with Welsh affairs,
(d) administrative and departmental records belonging to Her Majesty which are records of any office, commission or other body or establishment under Her Majesty's Government which is wholly or mainly

        This first category will cover much of what is 'information held by a public authority' within the meaning of the Freedom of Information Act 2000.

(2)   The second category of public records is given by way of a table set out at the end of para 3 of the Schedule to the Act. This category is without prejudice to the generality of the first category and embraces the administrative and departmental records of the bodies and establishments set out in the table whether or not they are records belonging to Her Majesty. However, the provisions of para 3 of the Schedule are not taken as applying to records in any museum or gallery listed in the table which are part of its records acquired otherwise than by transfer from or under arrangements with a government department. The table (identifying public records), mentioned above, is divided into two parts. The first is a list of bodies and establishments under government departments and the second is a list of other establishments and organisations. Part I of the table, which has been substantially amended since 1958, includes such bodies as the Agricultural Wages Board and the Legal Services Commission. Part II, likewise much amended since 1958, includes such bodies as the Adult Learning Inspectorate and the War Works Commission. The table in the Act should be consulted as necessary, having in mind that by para 3A of the Schedule the table may, by Her Majesty in Council, be amended by adding to either part of the table an entry relating to any body or establishment which is specified in Sch 2 to the Parliamentary Commissioner Act 1967 (ie departments or other bodies subject to investigation) or a body or establishment which could be added to Sch 2 to the Act of 1967.

(3)   Records of courts and tribunals constitute the third category of public records.[33] Excluded from the scope of this category are records of any court or tribunal whose jurisdiction is restricted to Scotland or Northern Ireland. Records for the purposes of this category include records of any proceedings in the court or tribunal in question and includes rolls, writs, books, decrees, bills, warrants and accounts of, or in the custody of, the court or tribunal in question. Paragraph 4 of the Schedule gives a list of courts and tribunals, which has also been amended since 1958.

---

concerned with Welsh affairs in a field or fields in which the Welsh Ministers have functions, or the First Minister or the Counsel General has functions,

(e)   administrative and departmental records of the bodies and establishments specified in subsection (2) (but not records of health service hospitals in Wales which are of the descriptions excepted from being public records for the purposes of the Public Records Act 1958 (c 51) in the case of health service hospitals in England), and

(f)   any other description of records (other than records of the Assembly or the Assembly Commission or records of any court or tribunal or held in any department of the Supreme Court) which is specified by order made by the Lord Chancellor.

The bodies and establishments specified in s 148(2) are: (a) the Care Council for Wales, (b) the Countryside Council for Wales, (c) the Curriculum and Assessment Authority for Wales, (d) Family Practitioner Committees for localities in Wales, (e) the Further Education Funding Council for Wales, (f) the General Teaching Council for Wales, (g) health service hospitals, within the meaning of the National Health Service (Wales) Act 2006, in Wales, (h) the Higher Education Funding Council for Wales, (i) the Local Government Boundary Commission for Wales, (j) the National Council for Education and Training for Wales, (k) National Health Service Authorities for districts or localities in Wales, or for areas in or comprising Wales, including National Health Service trusts all of whose hospitals, establishments and facilities are situated in Wales, (l) the Qualifications, Curriculum and Assessment Authority for Wales, (m) the Wales Centre for Health, and (n) the Welsh Board of Health.

[33] Public Records Act 1958 Sch 1 para 4.

Further, the Lord Chancellor is given power to designate as public records those records of such other courts and tribunals as he specifies.[34] The list given by para 4 of Sch 1 to the 1958 Act includes records of, or held in, any department of the Supreme Court (including any court held under a commission of assize); records of county courts; quarter sessions; magistrates' courts; coroners' courts; courts-martial, whether held by any of Her Majesty's Forces in or outside the United Kingdom; naval courts in or outside the United Kingdom under enactments relating to merchant shipping; any court exercising jurisdiction held by Her Majesty within a country outside Her dominions; records of any tribunal having jurisdiction connected with any functions of a department of Her Majesty's Government in the United Kingdom or having jurisdiction in proceedings to which such a Government department is a party; records of the Lands Tribunal or of any Rent Tribunal or Local Valuation Court; of any Conveyancing Appeal Tribunal; of the Industrial Court; of umpires and deputy umpires appointed under the National Service Act 1948 or the Resumption in Civil Employment Act 1944; records of ecclesiastical courts when exercising certain testamentary and matrimonial jurisdictions; and of the Information Tribunal. The Lord Chancellor is, by s 8 of the 1958 Act, responsible for the public records of every court of record or magistrates' court which are not in the Public Record Office or a place of deposit appointed by him under the Act. The Lord Chancellor is given power to determine in the case of any such records the officer in whose custody they are for the time being to be placed. Section 124 of the Supreme Court Act 1981 requires all original wills and other documents which are under the control of the High Court in the Principal Registry or in any district probate registry to be deposited and preserved in such places as the Lord Chancellor may direct and, subject to the control of the High Court and probate rules, to be open to inspection. There is a particular saving (by s 8(5)) from the selection and transfer provisions of s 3 of the Act in respect of certain records of ecclesiastical courts but the Lord Chancellor is able, after consulting the President of the Family Division, to direct their transfer to a place of deposit which he appoints.[35]

(4)   Records of the Chancery of England are, other than any which are Welsh public records (as defined in s 148 of the Government of Wales Act 2006[36]), public records for the purposes of the Public Records Act 1958. Subject to the terms of s 7 of the Act, the Master of the Rolls continues to be responsible for, and to have custody of, the records of the Chancery of England and has power to determine where they

---

[34]   Public Records Act 1958 Sch 1 para 4(1)(o). The power is exercised by order in a statutory instrument.

[35]   There are certain public records, in the custody of the University of Oxford, included in an index a copy of which was transmitted to the principal probate registrar under s 2 of the Oxford University Act 1860 which are not required to be transferred. However, the Lord Chancellor has to make arrangements with the University of Oxford as to the conditions under which those records may be inspected by the public.

[36]   See n 32 above.

should be deposited.[37]   Section 3 of the Act, which deals with selection and preservation of public records, does not apply to the records of the Chancery of England; nor does s 6(4), which deals with consultation by the Lord Chancellor before appointing a place of deposit, apply. However, if records of the Chancery of England are deposited in the Public Record Office then they are in the custody of the Keeper of Public Records and subject to the directions of the Lord Chancellor, as in the case of any other records in The National Archives.

18   Extension of the meaning of 'public records'

Paragraphs 6, 7 and 8 of the First Schedule to the 1958 Act extend what is embraced by the definition of public records. Thus, public records include, other than any which are Welsh public records (as defined in s 148 of the Government of Wales Act 2006[38]):

— all records within the meaning of the Public Record Office Act 1838 or to which that Act was applied, which, at the commencement of the Public Records Act 1958,[39] were in the custody of the Master of the Rolls in pursuance of that Act;

— all records within the meaning of the Public Record Office Act 1838 or to which that Act was applied which at the commencement of the Public Records Act 1958 were in the Public Record Office and under the charge and superintendence of the Master of the Rolls; and

— all records forming part of the same series of documents as any series of documents falling under the previous heads. Paragraph 7 of the Schedule enables Her Majesty by order in Council to direct that any class of records (not being Welsh public records within the meaning of s 148 of the Government of Wales Act 2006[40]) not falling within the Schedule shall be treated as public records. No recommendation is to be made to Her Majesty for such an order unless a draft has been laid before Parliament and approved by each House.

Paragraph 7(2) provides that a question whether any records or class of records are public records for the purposes of the Act shall be referred to and determined by the Lord Chancellor who has to include his decisions on such questions in his annual report to Parliament. Furthermore, the Lord Chancellor has from time to time to compile and publish lists of the departments, bodies, establishments, courts and tribunals comprised in paras 2, 3 and 4 of the Schedule and lists describing more particularly the categories of records which are, or are not, public records as defined in the Schedule. Paragraph 8 of the Schedule declares that any class of government department, court, tribunal or other body or establishment in the Schedule by reference to which a class of public records is framed extends to a government department, court, tribunal or other body or establishment which has ceased to exist whether before or after the passing of the Public Records Act 1958. Further, by virtue of s 8(4) of the Public Records

---

[37] By s 73(1) of the Courts and Legal Services Act 1990 where the Master of the Rolls expects to be absent at a time when it may be appropriate for any relevant functions of his to be exercised he may appoint a judge of the Supreme Court to exercise those functions on his behalf. Relevant functions include functions under s 144A of the Law of Property Act 1922 (functions relating to manorial documents) and functions under s 7(1) of the Public Records Act 1958 (power to determine where records of the Chancery of England are to be deposited).

[38] See n 32 above.

[39] 1 January 1959: Public Records Act 1958 s 13(3).

[40] See n 32 above.

Act 1958 where private documents have remained in the custody of a court in England and Wales for more than 50 years without being claimed, the Keeper of Public Records may, with the approval of the Master of the Rolls, require their transfer to The National Archives, whereupon they become public records. Scotland and Northern Ireland have their own record offices and the National Assembly for Wales has the power to establish one for Wales. If one is established, the Lord Chancellor has power to impose (by statutory instrument) arrangements analogous to those in the Public Records Act 1958. The access regimes in Scotland and Northern Ireland mirror the access arrangements in England.

7– 019 Welsh public records

By s 146(1) of the Government of Wales Act 2006, Welsh public records are not public records for the purposes of the Public Records Act 1958. However, by subs.(2), the Public Records Act 1958 has effect in relation to Welsh public records until an order under s 147 imposes a duty on the National Assembly for Wales to preserve them. No such order has yet been made. Welsh public records are defined in s 148 of the Government of Wales Act 2006.[41]

7– 020 Preservation of records that are not public records

The Keeper of Public Records is empowered to accept records which are not public records. This is done where the Keeper is of the view that the records merit permanent preservation, and the body generating the records agrees to deposit them.[42] An agreement is entered into between the body and The National Archives. In relation to access and copying, the agreement renders the deposit similar to that by public record bodies. The organisation making the deposit must carry out the necessary selection and indexing work under the supervision of staff from The National Archives. The ownership of the records and their copyright status remain unaffected by the deposit. The Lord Chancellor is also able (in consequence of s 3(5)), if it appears to him in the interests of the proper administration of the Public Record Office, to direct that the transfer of any class of records shall be suspended until arrangements for their reception have been completed. As will be seen, although such records do not metamorphose into public records, they are 'historical records' with accompanying rights of access.

7– 021 The management of public records

The wide definition given to 'public records' covers the prosaic as well as the principal; and it will do so before any formal decision as to retention has been made by the public authority that brought the record into being. Inevitably, there must be some reduction in this mountain of material. The reduction process is spelled out in Part 1 of the s 46 Code of Practice and in the Public Records Act 1958 (in conjunction with Part 2 of the s 46 Code of Practice). The first secures the 'disposal' of material (including the destruction of day-to-day material that has no enduring significance). The second deals with material that has not been disposed of.

---

[41] See n 32 above.

[42] Other records can be deposited with The National Archives, eg: records relating to a dissolved company under the Companies Act 1985 s 707A(3); manorial documents, under the Law of Property Act 1922 s 144A; instruments of apportionment, under the Tithes Act 1936 s 36(3); and orders of exchange by the Inclosure Commissioners, under the Inclosure Act 1857 s 5.

22   Disposal of public records under the s 46 Code of Practice

Paragraph 8 of the s 46 Code of Practice provides that public authorities must keep the records they will need for business, regulatory, legal and accountability purposes. In deciding what they keep, paragraph 8 requires a public authority to take into account:

— The legislative and regulatory environment within which it operates;

— The need to refer to authoritative information about past actions and decisions for current business purposes;

— The need to protect legal and other rights of the authority, its staff and its stakeholders;

— The need to explain, and if necessary justify, past actions in the event of an audit, public inquiry or other investigation.

Paragraph 12 of the Code provides that each public authority should define how long it needs to keep particular records, that it should dispose of them when they are no longer needed and that it should be able to explain why records are no longer held. 'Dispose' here means destroyed or transferred to an archives service for permanent preservation or presented under s 3(6) of the Public Records Act 1958.[43] The Code provides that a public authority should not keep records (ie the records should be destroyed) after they have ceased to be of use to the authority unless:

(a)   The records are known to be the subject of litigation or a request for information. In this case, the public authority should delay destruction until the litigation is complete or, in the case of a request for information, all relevant complaint and appeal provisions have been exhausted.

(b)   The records have long-term value for historical or other research and have been or should be selected for permanent preservation.

(c)   The records contain or relate to information recently released in response to a request under the Act. This may indicate historical value and a public authority should delay destruction pending a re-assessment of that value.[44]

The Code suggests that disposal of records must adhere to the public authority's policies and disposal schedules.

23   Selection of public records for preservation

Section 3 of the Public Records Act 1958 imposes a duty on every person responsible for public records of any description which are not in the Public Record Office or a place of deposit appointed by the Lord Chancellor under the 1958 Act to make arrangements for the selection of those records which ought to be permanently preserved and for their safekeeping. These duties are to be performed under the guidance of the Keeper of Public Records, who is responsible for the co-ordination and supervision of all action taken under s 3. The obligation imposed by the Public Records Act 1958 is in respect of those which ought to be permanently

---

[43]   Presentation transfers ownership of the records to the receiving body and is undertaken by The National Archives in consultation with the public authority.

[44]   Section 46 Code of Practice para 12.3.

preserved.[45] Current practice has a two-stage selection process. Each government department has a Departmental Record Officer who is responsible for the management of its records.[46] He carries out the selection process under the guidance of The National Archives through the Central Records Management Department. The first review takes place, generally, five years[47] after a departmental file is closed. A public authority should have clearly established policies to assist in this task.[48] Records considered to be valueless are destroyed.[49] Those thought possibly necessary in the future for administrative or research purposes are kept for another 15 to 25 years. They are then assessed for permanent preservation on second review. Once selected for permanent preservation public records are, subject to a proviso, required to be transferred not later than 30 years after their creation either to The National Archives or to such other place of deposit appointed by the Lord Chancellor under the 1958 Act as the Lord Chancellor may direct.[50] Section 4 of the Act gives the Lord Chancellor power to appoint places of deposit. The proviso given by s 3(4) enables any records to be retained after 30 years if, in the opinion of the person responsible for them, they are required for administrative purposes or ought to be retained for any other special reason. If the person responsible is not the Lord Chancellor, then the Lord Chancellor must be informed of the facts and give his approval. The quantity annually transferred to The National Archives is about 1,830 metres.

7–024 Destruction of public records under the Public Records Act 1958

Those public records which have been rejected as not required for permanent preservation are destroyed or, in the case of records for which some person other than the Lord Chancellor is responsible, subject to the approval of the Lord Chancellor, are disposed of in any other way. Any question arising under s 3 as to the person whose duty it is to make arrangements under the section with respect to any class of public records is required to be referred to the Lord Chancellor for his decision. If it appears to the Keeper of Public Records that as respects any public records in the Public Record Office (ie The National Archives) or any place of deposit appointed under the Act that they are duplicated by other public records which have been selected for permanent preservation or that there is some other special reason why they should not permanently be preserved, he may, with the approval of the Lord Chancellor and of the minister or other person, appearing to the Lord Chancellor as primarily concerned with public records of the class in question, authorise the destruction of those records or, with the same approval, their disposal in any other way.[51] Section 3 of the 1958 Act, which deals with selection and presentation of public records, does not render it unlawful for the person responsible for any public record to transmit it to the Keeper of the Records of Scotland or to

---

[45] Section 3(3) of the Act requires that all public records created before 1660, ie the year of the restoration of the monarchy, be amongst those selected for permanent preservation.

[46] As explained by the National Archives System at: www.nationalarchives.gov.uk/policy/act/system.htm.

[47] This period of time is consistent with the policy of opening new files after five years of inactivity rather than adding to an existing file. If one merely added to the existing file, Public Records Act 1958 s 10(2) would, for the purposes of the Act, treat the record as having been created on the last date.

[48] Section 46 Code of Practice, paras 12.4 and 16.1.

[49] Section 46 Code of Practice, paras 12.3 and 16.1.

[50] Public Records Act 1958 s 3(4).

[51] Public Records Act 1958 s 6.

the Public Record Office of Northern Ireland.

25 Access to public records: regime to 1 January 2005

Section 5 of the Public Records Act 1958, as originally enacted, kept public records closed to public inspection for 50 years. This was reduced, subject to exceptions, to 30 years by the Public Records Act 1967 which amended s 5 with effect from 1 January 1968. The regime as given by s 5 of the 1958 Act was repealed by the Freedom of Information Act 2000[52] from 1 January 2005. Up until then, access by the public to public records in The National Archives (other than those to which the public had access before their transfer to The National Archives) was not permitted for a period of 30 years beginning with the first day of January in the year next after that in which they had been created.[53] However,[54] if it appeared to the person responsible[55] for any public records which had been selected by him for permanent preservation that they contained information which had been obtained from members of the public under such conditions that the opening of the records to the public after the 30-year period[56] might constitute a breach of good faith on the part of the Government or on the part of the persons who obtained the information, that person had to inform the Lord Chancellor accordingly so that those records were not available for public inspection after the expiration of 30 years or such other period as was determined except in circumstances as the person responsible for selection and the Lord Chancellor approved or after such further period of time as they approved. The 30-year closure period did not apply to records which had been open to the public prior to their transfer; they remained open. Further, s 5(1) gave the Lord Chancellor a discretion to open records, with the concurrence of the Minister concerned, earlier than the specified period. This was known as accelerated opening. Where a variation of the normal 30-year period occurred it was effected by a document signed by the Lord Chancellor and known as a Lord Chancellor's Instrument. The duty imposed on the Keeper of Public Records[57] was to arrange that reasonable facilities were available to the public for inspecting and obtaining copies of public records in the Public Record Office (ie The National Archives), subject to the time rule (ie the 30-year rule) and the good faith restraint, if applicable. It has been seen that the period of 30 years was capable of extension. This is illustrated by the records relating to the abdication in 1936 of King Edward VIII (later HRH the Duke of Windsor). Certain records were closed until after the death in 2002 of Her Majesty Queen Elizabeth, the Queen Mother.

26 Additional proscriptions against disclosure before 1 January 2005

The access rights was, in addition, subject to those enactments set out in the Second Schedule to the 1958 Act which prohibited the disclosure of certain information obtained from the public

---

[52] ss 67 and 86 and Sch 5 Pt I and Sch 8 Pt II.

[53] Or such other period as the Lord Chancellor may, with the approval, or at the request, of the Minister or other person, who appears to him to be principally concerned, prescribe as respects any particular class of public records.

[54] In consequence of the Public Records Act 1958 s 5(2).

[55] Under the Public Records Act 1958 s 3.

[56] Or other period determined under s 5(1).

[57] By the Public Records Act 1958 s 5(3).

except for certain limited purposes.[58] The Second Schedule listed a variety of enactments having this prohibitory effect, including the Coal Industry Nationalisation Act 1946 (s 56), the Statistics of Trade Act 1947 (s 9), the Industrial Organisation and Development Act 1947 (s 5), the Agricultural Statistics Act 1979 and the Film Levy Finance Act 1981 (s 8). Schedule 2 to the Act was repealed by the Freedom of Information Act 2000, with effect from 1 January 2005.

7– 027   **Disposition of public records to other places of deposit**
The National Archives has published a disposition policy providing a principled framework for the making of decisions to offer public records to archival institutions other than The National Archives. The power to appoint places of deposit was delegated by the Lord Chancellor to the Keeper of Public Records when, in 1992, the Public Record Office became an executive agency. There are about 235 archives, libraries, museums, galleries and government agencies which have been inspected by The National Archives and appointed to hold specified classes of public record. Throughout England and Wales local authority archive services have been appointed as places of deposit for public records of strong local interest. Many of the major national museums and galleries are appointed to hold their own administrative records or specialist material which falls within their collecting policies. Places of deposit are periodically inspected by a member of staff from The National Archives. It is usual for a major place of deposit, such as a county record office, to be visited once every five years. All inspections are carried out by professionally qualified archivists with experience of working in a record office. The purpose of these inspections is to determine whether places of deposit offer conditions for the storage of records and facilities for public access which meet The National Archives' standards. These standards are largely based on BS 5454 relating to Records in Places of Deposit. From the year 2000 onwards, a checklist based on the Standard for Access to Archives, which has been developed by the Public Services Quality Group, will also inform The National Archives' inspections of places of deposit, so that access to records by users has the same weight as preservation.

7– 028   **Other places of deposit**
The preceding paragraphs have been substantially concerned with access to material in The National Archives. The Lord Chancellor is required, for all public records in places of deposit appointed by him outside The National Archives, to arrange that facilities are available for their inspection by the public comparable to those for public records in The National Archives.

7– 029   **Transfer of public records instead of destruction**
In addition to transfers of public records to places of deposit, s 3(6) of the Public Records Act 1958 allows the Public Record Office (ie The National Archives), under powers delegated by the Lord Chancellor to the Keeper of Public Records, to present government records which have not been selected for permanent preservation to places of deposit and other bona fide institutions. In this way such records are preserved and made publicly available as an alternative to their destruction. Presented records become the property of the recipient and

---

[58] The duty is also subject to any other Act or instrument whether passed or made before or after the Public Records Act 1958 containing a similar prohibition.

cease to have public record status.[59]   These records are transferred subject to conditions stipulated by The National Archives. Normal conditions will be a restriction on the disposal of the records without advance consultation with The National Archives and a 30-year closure period.

4.   ACCESS TO PUBLIC RECORDS: THE NEW REGIME

Introduction

From 1 January 2005 the basic principles relating to access to public records became founded upon the rights to information held by a public authority. It is thus essential to a proper understanding of the new regime to be familiar with the two basic rights conferred by s 1 of the Freedom of Information Act 2000, together with the distinction between those provisions in Part II of the Act conferring absolute exemption and those provisions in Part II of the Act conferring a qualified exemption. These are dealt with elsewhere in this work.[60] But, in brief, by s 1(1) of the Freedom of Information Act 2000, any person making a request for information to a public authority is entitled to be informed in writing by the public authority whether it holds information of the description specified in the request and if that is the case to have that information communicated to him. Those rights are made subject to a number of other provisions in the Act,[61] most notably s 2, which brings in the provisions of Part II. Thus, the s 1 rights are shaped by the provisions of Part II. Where the information is 'environmental information'[62] the right of access will fall to be decided by the Environmental Information Regulations 2004, and not by the Freedom of Information Act 2000. The Environmental Information Regulations 2004 essentially incorporate a part, but not all, of the regime in the Freedom of Information Act 2000 relating to historical records. As noted earlier, the special characteristics of information held by The National Archives, the fact that public records are held by bodies other than The National Archives, and the fact that the interest of The National Archives in the contents of a record is different from that of the public authority which created that record, have all necessitated important modifications to the regime which ordinarily applies to information held by a public authority under the 2000 Act. As will be seen, these modifications are secured by s 15 of the Freedom of Information Act 2000, which makes special provision relating to public records transferred to The National Archives, and by Part VI of the Act (ss 62–67), which deals with historical records and records in The National Archives or the Public Record Office of Northern Ireland.

Administrative arrangements from 1 January 2005

Since 1 January 2005, the duty of the Keeper of Public Records[63] has been one of arranging that reasonable facilities are available to the public for inspecting and obtaining copies of those

---

[59] Accordingly, they are not 'transferred public records' within the meaning of s 15(4) of the FOIA.

[60] See, in particular, chs 1, 14 and 15. There is no distinct existence right under the FOI(S)A.

[61] FOIA s 1(2); FOI(S)A s 1(6).

[62] As to the meaning of which, see §6– 010.

[63] By virtue of a new s 5(3), inserted into the Public Records Act 1958 by the FOIA.

public records in The National Archives which fall to be disclosed in accordance with the Freedom of Information Act 2000 and the Environmental Information Regulations 2004.[64] Section 5(3) of the Public Records Act 1958 means that from 1 January 2005 the regime, so far as public records are concerned, is that their selection, deposit and destruction are governed by the 1958 Act, whilst their accessibility is controlled by the Freedom of Information Act 2000 or the Environmental Information Regulations 2004, as the case may be. Hence, the mechanics of maintenance of public records is given by the earlier Act whilst, consistent with the theme that access to information is substantially administered by one Act, securing access to information is given by the Freedom of Information Act 2000 and the Environmental Information Regulations 2004. It is to be kept in mind that, since the Public Record Office (ie The National Archives) is a government department, it constitutes a 'public authority' within the meaning of that Act and those Regulations. In this way, the manifold obligations imposed upon a public authority by the Freedom of Information Act 2000 attach to The National Archives.

7– 032   Summary of changes to the 1958 regime

The broad nature of the new regime, looking exclusively for the moment at The National Archives, is as follows.

(1)   First, the Public Record Office (ie The National Archives) is a public authority and subject to the obligations of the Freedom of Information Act 2000 and the Environmental Information Regulations 2004.

(2)   Secondly, in any event, the Public Records Act 1958, as amended, obliges access to public records held by The National Archives to be provided in accordance with the Freedom of Information Act 2000.

(3)   Thirdly, the access right is that given by s 1 of the Freedom of Information Act 2000, as shaped by the provisions in Part II of that Act or, in relation to environmental information, that give by reg 5(1) of the Environmental Information Regulations 2004 as shaped by the provisions in Part 3 of those Regulations.

(4)   Fourthly, some of those provisions confer absolute exemptions; the remainder confer a qualified exemption, which involves considering whether in all the circumstances the public interest in maintaining the exemption outweighs the public interest in disclosing the information.

(5)   Fifthly, the range of exemptions available under the Freedom of Information Act 2000 is reduced where the public record is a 'historical record'.

(6)   Sixthly, where information contained in a record that has been transferred to The National Archives falls within a provision of the Freedom of Information Act 2000 that confers a qualified exemption,[65] then, unless the information has been designated 'open information', the weighing of the public interest described in (4) above is determined by the 'responsible authority'[66] and not by The National Archives.

---

[64]   The Lord Chancellor is likewise obliged in respect of records held in places of deposit other than at The National Archives: Public Records Act 1958 s 5(5).

[65]   Or a qualified exclusion of the duty to confirm or deny.

[66]   As to the meaning of which, see §7– 044.

(7) Finally, the Act and the Regulations enable responsible authorities to designate information as 'open'.[67] This designation, putting the matter broadly, leaves the decision-making principally with The National Archives, but with some involvement by the Lord Chancellor where it is proposed to refuse access on the basis of a qualified exemption.

The regime operates in a similar way for places of deposit other than The National Archives.[68]

3 Designation of information as 'open'

Where a public authority transfers a record to The National Archives or another place of deposit, that public authority must consider whether that record should be released to the public: in other words, transferred as 'open'.[69] In reviewing a record for public release, a public authority must ensure that records become available to the public at the earliest possible time.[70] The public authority must consider which exemptions are applicable to the information in the record and whether the public interest supports the release of the information notwithstanding the applicability of an exemption.[71] If the outcome of the review is that records are to be transferred as open, the public authority should designate the records as 'open'. There is no formal review of this designation by The National Archives.[72] Where the public authority identifies specific information in the record which it considers ought not to be released under the terms of the Freedom of Information Act 2000, it should prepare a schedule identifying this information precisely, citing the relevant exemption(s), explaining why the information may not be released and identifying a date at which either release would be appropriate or a date at which the case for release should be reconsidered.[73] A public authority must consider whether the exempt information could be redacted from the record and the remainder made open.[74] The public authority must then send its schedule to The National Archives for review and advice.[75] The Advisory Council then considers the case in favour of withholding the records for a period longer than 30 years. The Advisory Council may respond: (a) by accepting that the information may be withheld for longer than 30 years and earmarking the records for release or rereview at the date identified by the authority; (b) by accepting that the information may be withheld for longer than 30 years but asking the authority to reconsider the later date designated for release or rereview; (c) by questioning the basis on which it is deemed that the information may be withheld for longer than 30 years and asking the authority to reconsider

---

[67] Curiously, no definition is given in the Act of open information; nor does the Act govern how information receives such a designation. The only process by which information is designated 'open' is that touched upon in the s 46 Code of Practice. The designation then assumes importance under FOIA s 66(1).

[68] FOIA s 15(5).

[69] Section 46 Code of Practice, paras 18.1 and 18.3.

[70] Section 46 Code of Practice, para 15.2.

[71] Section 46 Code of Practice, para 18.1(a)-(b).

[72] Section 46 Code of Practice, para 18.3.

[73] Section 46 Code of Practice, para 18.4. And similarly in relation to 'environmental information' with the applicable exceptions in the EIR being identified.

[74] Section 46 Code of Practice, para 18.5.

[75] Section 46 Code of Practice, para 18.6.

the case; (d) by advising the Lord Chancellor if it is not satisfied with the responses it receives from authorities in particular cases; e) by taking such other action as it deems appropriate within its role as defined in the Public Records Act.[76]

7– 034   Exemptions: introduction

The operation of the Public Records Act 1958, the Freedom of Information Act 2000 and the Environmental Information Regulations 2004 contemplate the Keeper of Public Records arranging reasonable facilities for the inspection and copying of those public records in The National Archives which fall to be disclosed in accordance with the Freedom of Information Act 2000 and the Environmental Information Regulations 2004.[77] That obligation to disclose is framed by the applicability of the exemptions in Part II of that Act. So far as public records are concerned, the way those exemptions and exceptions operate is affected by a variety of factors, but principally by the age of the record. It should be observed, parenthetically, that The National Archives will hold, just as other public authorities hold, information, for example about its current operating programme, for which access can be sought in the usual way under the Act. However, in this chapter we are concerned principally with the regime as it applies to public records.

7– 035   The reduction of exemptions and exclusions

The starting point is that the access right and the existence right apply equally to information held by The National Archives as they do to ordinary information held by a public authority: in other words, a person has the rights given by s 1(1) of the Freedom of Information Act 2000 in relation to all information held by The National Archives, those rights being shaped by the exemptions and exclusions in Part II of the Freedom of Information Act 2000. In the case of 'environmental information', a person has the rights given by reg 5 of the Environmental Information Regulations 2004, those rights being shaped by the exceptions in Part 3 of those Regulations. The fact that the information is contained in what the Public Records Act 1958 terms a 'public record' of itself effects no change to the ambit of the right to obtain access to that information under the Freedom of Information Act 2000, the Environmental Information Regulations 2004 or to the ambit of the existence right. Modification to the ambit of those rights occurs if and only if the information is contained in a 'historical record'. There is no modification to 'environmental information' contained in a historical record. Under the Freedom of Information Act 2000 the modifications then vary according to the age of the historical record in which the information is contained. In very general terms, what Part VI of the Freedom of Information Act 2000 does is to remove in respect of information contained in a historical record some of the exemptions in Part II of the Act, thereby extending the scope of the right of access.[78] The exemptions that are removed are those relating to:

— relations within the United Kingdom (s 28);
— criminal investigations and proceedings (s 30(1));
— court records, etc (s 32);
— audit functions (s 33);

---

[76] Section 46 Code of Practice, para 18.6.

[77] See §7– 031.

[78] FOIA s 63(1); FOI(S)A s 58(1).

- formulation of government policy, etc (s 35);
- prejudice to effective conduct of public affairs (s 36);
- communications with Her Majesty, etc (s 37(1)(a));
- legal professional privilege (s 42); and
- commercial interests (s 43).

A similar modification is made to the existence right given by s 1(1)(a) of the 2000 Act.[79] In the following paragraphs of this chapter, the term 'The National Archives' has for ease of understanding been used in place of 'the appropriate records authority'; however, it should be remembered that the points made equally apply to the other approved places of deposit and to the Public Record Office of Northern Ireland.

36 'Historical record'

Section 62 of the Freedom of Information Act 2000 introduces the concept of 'historical record'. A record, for the purposes of Part VI of the Act, becomes a historical record at the end of 30 years beginning with the year[80] following that in which it was created.[81] The period of 30 years appears to have been selected in the light of the period presently given by the Public Records Act 1958 for the commencement of access. A historical record is not necessarily a public record.[82] Thus, a record that is not a public record but which has been accepted by The National Archives for preservation[83] will constitute a 'historical record' provided that the age requirements of s 62 are met. Where records are created at different dates but are kept together in one file or other assembly, all the records are to be treated as having been created when the latest of those records was created.[84] Although the Environmental Information Regulations 2004 imports from the Freedom of Information Act 2000 its definition of historical record, it only uses the concept of a historical record to impose consultative obligations on the public authority holding the information at the time of the request.[85] There is no falling away of exceptions.

37 Historical records at most 60 years old

Having defined a 'historical record', the Freedom of Information Act 2000 removes an increasing number of the provisions in Part II of the Act according to the age of the record. Where up to 60 years has elapsed since the start of the year following that in which the record was created, information contained in it can only be exempt information under:

---

[79] FOIA s 63(2). Note, however, that the exclusions of the duty to confirm or deny that information is held granted by ss 30(3), 32(3), 35(3) and 37(2) are not removed in relation to historical records. There is no separate duty to confirm or deny under the FOI(S)A.

[80] A year is a calendar year: FOIA s 62(3).

[81] On 25 February 2010 amendments to the Constitutional Reform and Governance Bill 2009 were tabled in the House of Commons. The amendments to the Bill were in response to a report published in January 2009 recommending reduction to 20 years of the 30-year rule in relation to public records. See: www2.nationalarchives.gov.uk/30yrr/30-year-rule-report.pdf

[82] As is recognised by FOIA s 65.

[83] See §7–020.

[84] FOIA s 62(2); FOI(S)A s 57(2).

[85] EIR reg 17; EI(S)R reg 15.

— s 21, ie the information is accessible to the applicant by other means.[86] However, this exemption cannot operate if the historical record is in either The National Archives or the Public Record Office of Northern Ireland.[87]

— s 22, ie the information is intended for future publication.[88] However, this exemption cannot operate if the historical record is in either The National Archives or the Public Record Office of Northern Ireland.[89]

— s 23, ie the information is supplied by or relating to bodies dealing with security matters.[90]

— s 24, ie the information is required for the purpose of national security.[91]

— s 26, ie the information is such that its disclosure would prejudice or be likely to prejudice defence.[92]

— s 27, ie the information is such that its disclosure would or would be likely to prejudice international relations.[93]

— s 29, ie the information is such that its disclosure would or would be likely to prejudice the economic interests of the United Kingdom or the financial interests of any administration in the United Kingdom.[94]

— s 30(2), ie the information was obtained or recorded for the purposes of a public authority's functions relating to criminal investigations or proceedings as to impropriety (listed in s 31(2)) or civil proceedings, and it relates to obtaining information from confidential sources.[95]

— s 31, ie the information relates to law enforcement.[96]

— s 34, ie the information is required for the purpose of avoiding an infringement of the privileges of either House of Parliament.[97]

— s 37(1)(b), ie the information relates to the conferring by the Crown of any honour or dignity.[98]

— s 38, ie the information is such that its disclosure would or would be likely to endanger health or safety.[99]

— s 39, ie the information is environmental information which the holding public

---

[86] Similarly, FOI(S)A s 25. As to which exemption, see §§16–001 to 16–005.

[87] FOIA s 64(1).

[88] Similarly, FOI(S)A s 27. As to which exemption, see §§16–007 to 16–009.

[89] FOIA s 64(1).

[90] As to which exemption, see §§17–033 to 17–038. There is no analogous exemption under the FOI(S)A.

[91] Similarly, FOI(S)A s 31. As to which exemption, see §§17–040 to 17–049.

[92] Similarly, FOI(S)A s 31. As to which exemption, see §§17–063 to 17–072.

[93] Similarly, FOI(S)A s 32. As to which exemption, see §§18–001 to 18–016.

[94] Similarly, FOI(S)A s 33(2). As to which exemption, see §§19–001 to 19–009.

[95] Similarly, FOI(S)A s 34. As to which exemption, see §§20–004 to 20–013.

[96] Similarly, FOI(S)A s 35. As to which exemption, see §§20–014 to 20–026.

[97] As to which exemption, see §§21–001 to 21–011.

[98] Similarly, FOI(S)A s 41(b). As to which exemption, see §§26–008 to 26–014.

[99] Similarly, FOI(S)A s 39. As to which exemption, see §§23–001 to 23–008.

authority is obliged by regulations under s 74 to make available or would be obliged to but for an exemption under the regulations.[100]

— s 40, ie the information constitutes personal data of which the applicant is the data subject.[101]

— s 41, ie the disclosure of the information would constitute an actionable breach of confidence.[102]

— s 44, ie the disclosure of the information is prohibited by or under another enactment, is incompatible with any European Community obligation or would constitute or be punishable as a contempt of court.[103]

38 Historical records more than 60 years old

Where more than 60 years has elapsed since the start of the year following that in which the record containing the information was created, the potential grounds of exemption in respect of information in that record are further reduced by the removal of s 37(1)(b), ie the information cannot be exempt information by virtue of it relating to the conferring by the Crown of any honour or dignity.[104]

39 Historical records more than 100 years old

Where a historical record is more than 100 years old, then the potential grounds of exemption are further reduced by the removal of s 31, ie the information cannot be exempt information by virtue of it relating to law enforcement.[105]

40 The duty to confirm or deny

As has been noted elsewhere in this work, although the Freedom of Information Act 2000 places the duty to confirm or deny before the disclosure duty, the latter is more sensibly considered first. If a decision is made to disclose information then a public authority will not need to exercise itself with the duty to confirm or deny.[106] If, however, a decision is made to refuse disclosure of certain information, then a public authority will need to go on to consider separately the duty to confirm or deny.[107] As with the disclosure duty, the technique employed by the Act is to remove certain of the exclusions from the duty to confirm or deny in relation to a historical record, thereby widening the range of historical records in relation to which The

---

[100] Similarly, FOI(S)A s 39. As to which exemption, see §§16–010 to 16–013.

[101] Similarly, FOI(S)A s 38. As to which exemption, see §24–005.

[102] As to which exemption, see §§25–001 to 25–029. The position under the FOI(S)A is different.

[103] Similarly, FOI(S)A s 26. As to which exemption, see §§26–015 to 26–032.

[104] FOIA s 63(3); FOI(S)A s 58(2)(a).

[105] FOIA s 63(4); FOI(S)A s 58(2)(b), with additional exemptions falling away.

[106] FOIA s 1(5).

[107] Note also that if the decision on disclosure is made in two stages because the weighing of the public interest has not been completed within the 20 working day time limit (see FOIA s 17(2) and §11–028), then it is quite possible that the decision on the duty to confirm or deny will have to be concluded before the second stage of the decision on disclosure. This is both because the exclusions of the duty to confirm or deny given by various provisions in Pt II are not coincidental with the exemptions from disclosure given by that Part (see §§14–005 to 14–016 and 14–017) and because, in relation to historical records, the exclusions removed by s 63(2) are not as extensive as the exemptions removed by s 63(1) and (3).

National Archives (as a public authority) must discharge the duty to confirm or deny.[108] The result is as follows:

(1)   To the extent that the information held by The National Archives that answers, or that would answer, the terms of the request is not in a historical record, the scope of the duty to confirm or deny is the same as it is in relation to information held by any other public authority which is subject to the Freedom of Information Act 2000.[109]

(2)   To the extent that the information held by The National Archives that answers, or that would answer, the terms of the request is in a historical record that is less than 61 years old, the scope of the duty to confirm or deny is enlarged by the removal of the exclusions relating to:

— relations within the United Kingdom (s 28(3));
— audit functions (s 33(3));
— prejudice to effective conduct of public affairs (s 36(3));
— legal professional privilege (s 42(2)); and
— commercial interests (s 43(3)).[110]

(3)   To the extent that the information held by The National Archives that answers, or that would answer, the terms of the request is in a historical record that is more than 100 years old, the scope of the duty to confirm or deny is further enlarged by the removal of the exclusions relating to law enforcement (s 31(1)).[111]

7– 041   Practical considerations

The preceding paragraphs have shown that any information contained in a historical record may fall outside the disclosure obligation and the duty to confirm or deny. Theoretically this means that if access were sought to what is already reasonably accessible, say, the Domesday Book, the Duke of Marlborough's despatches or records relating to Lord Nelson, it would be possible to refuse access on the basis of the residual exemptions that apply to historical records more than 100 years old. From the perspective of The National Archives, the removal of s 21 as a ground of exemption[112] may seem odd, as it removes the opportunity for it to refuse requests for such information on the straightforward basis that that information is already reasonably accessible by the general access arrangements provided by The National Archives. Nevertheless, it is suggested that a request for information made to The National Archives for information which is contained in a historical record that is freely accessible in The National Archives will, in some circumstances, be a vexatious request, so that it will not have to be

---

[108] The reference in FOIA s 63(2) to 'a historical record' should probably be read as a reference to 'information contained in a historical record" as information is the unit of the obligation in s 1(1)(a): see §§9– 001 and 14– 001.

[109] This is because the reduction in exclusions only applies to historical records: FOIA s 63.

[110] FOIA s 63(2).

[111] FOIA s 63(5).

[112] FOIA s 64(1). This is not so in Scotland with the equivalent FOI(S)A s 25 remaining in place.

complied with.[113]

5. DECISION-MAKING RESPONSIBILITY IN RELATION TO PUBLIC RECORDS

42 Introduction

As noted earlier, whenever a request for information is made of a public authority, it is ordinarily that public authority which makes the disclosure decision in relation to all information answering the terms of the request which is held by it, irrespective of whether the information originated from another public authority. A request may be transferred by one public authority to another public authority: where this occurs, the receiving public authority will determine the request solely according to the information that it holds.[114] But for s 15 of the Freedom of Information Act 2000, the ordinary position would have had the result that if a request for information were made of The National Archives,[115] it would have been The National Archives that would have determined the request in relation to all information held by it, including records previously transferred by a public authority to The National Archives under the Public Records Act 1958. As will be seen, the Freedom of Information Act 2000, displaces the usual decision-maker only for the purposes of weighing the public interest and allocates decision-making responsibility on that point to the 'responsible authority'. There is thus a division of decision-making responsibility between The National Archives and the 'responsible authority'. It is first necessary to consider the four terms used by the Freedom of Information Act 2000 to secure this division of responsibility:

— 'transferred public record';
— 'responsible authority';
— 'appropriate records authority'; and
— 'open information'.

The Environmental Information Regulations 2004 secures the same objective in relation to 'environmental information' contained in a historical record.[116]

43 'Transferred public record'

Section 15(4) of the Freedom of Information Act 2000 introduces the concept of a 'transferred public record'. The term is imported into the Environmental Information Regulations 2004 for the purposes of 'environmental information'.[117] A 'transferred public record' is a public

---

[113] FOIA s 14(1); FOI(S)A s 14(1). In relation to vexatious requests, see §§12– 010 to 12– 013. If the person requesting the information expresses a preference for communication by means of a copy and, particularly if the person lives some distance from The National Archives, it may be more difficult to characterise the request as 'vexatious' unless the information is otherwise freely available.

[114] In relation to transfers, see §§11– 037 to 11– 038.

[115] Or another place of deposit appointed by the Lord Chancellor under the Public Records Act 1958 or the Public Records Office of Northern Ireland.

[116] EIR reg 17; EI(S)R reg 15.

[117] EIR reg 2(1); but not EI(S)R.

record[118] that has been transferred to The National Archives, to another place of deposit appointed by the Lord Chancellor under the Public Records Act 1958 or to the Public Record Office of Northern Ireland. Thus, when a public record is transferred from a public authority to The National Archives (or to another place of deposit, etc) it remains a 'public record' for the purposes of the Public Records Act 1958, but is labelled a 'transferred public record' for the purposes of the Freedom of Information Act 2000. As noted earlier, not all information held by The National Archives is a public record: the Office can accept and hold material that is not a public record;[119] by definition such material will not be a 'transferred public record'.[120] In relation to this non-public record material held by The National Archives (or other place of deposit, etc), all decision-making for the purposes of the Freedom of Information Act 2000 remains with The National Archives (or other place of deposit, etc).[121] It should also be noted that the division of responsibility is not confined to 'historical records': it applies equally to public records that are not historical records but that have been transferred to The National Archives (or other place of deposit, etc).

7–044 **'Responsible authority' and 'appropriate records authority'**
Section 15(5) of the Freedom of Information Act 2000 defines 'responsible authority' by reference both to the party transferring the public record and to the destination of the transferred public record. The term is imported into the Environmental Information Regulations 2004 for the purposes of 'environmental information'.[122]

(1)   In the case of a public record transferred from a government department either to The National Archives or to a place of deposit appointed by the Lord Chancellor, the 'responsible authority' is the Minister of the Crown who appears to the Lord Chancellor to be primarily concerned.

(2)   In the case of a public record transferred from any person other than a government department either to The National Archives or to a place of deposit appointed by the Lord Chancellor, the 'responsible authority' is the person who appears to the Lord Chancellor to be primarily concerned. Bearing in mind the wide definition given to 'public record',[123] it is readily apparent that that person may not be a public authority within the meaning of the Freedom of Information Act 2000.[124] In this situation, that person is deemed to be a public authority, with certain consequential obligations which are discussed below.[125]

(3)   In the case of a record transferred to the Public Record Office of Northern Ireland

---

[118] 'Public record' means public record as defined by the Public Records Act 1958: see §§7–017 to 7–018.

[119] See §7–020.

[120] FOIA s 15(4). There is a broadly similar regime in FOI(S)A s 22.

[121] On the basis that it will be treated as 'information held by a public authority' (ie The National Archives), but without the modifications effected by the FOIA in relation to transferred public records.

[122] EIR reg 2(1); but not EI(S)R.

[123] See §§7–017 to 7–018.

[124] See FOIA ss 3–7.

[125] FOIA s 66(6). As to those obligations, see §§7–046 to 7–047. The obligations can be lightened by simply designating all the information 'open information'.

from a government department in the charge of a Minister of the Crown, the responsible authority is that minister of the Crown who appears to the appropriate Northern Ireland Minister[126] to be primarily concerned. If the transfer is from a Northern Ireland department then the responsible authority is the Northern Ireland Minister who appears to the appropriate Northern Ireland Minister to be primarily concerned. If the record was transferred from any other person then the responsible authority is the person who appears to the appropriate Northern Ireland Minister to be primarily concerned.[127]

Section 15(5) of the Freedom of Information Act 2000 identifies the Public Record Office (ie The National Archives) as 'the appropriate records authority' in relation to public records transferred to The National Archives. The term is imported into the Environmental Information Regulations 2004 for the purposes of 'environmental information'.[128] In relation to a transferred public record transferred to a place of deposit appointed by the Lord Chancellor, the 'appropriate records authority' is the Lord Chancellor; if the record is in the Public Record Office of Northern Ireland, then 'the appropriate records authority' is the Public Record Office of Northern Ireland.

45 'Open information'

Section 66 of the Freedom of Information Act 2000 contains the only reference in the Act to 'open information'.[129] The term is not defined,[130] but the operation of ss 15, 65 and 66 allows its meaning to be discerned. 'Open information' is information contained in a transferred public record that the responsible authority has, at some stage prior to the receipt by The National Archives of a request relating to that information, designated as 'open information'. The process by which this is done has already been described.[131] The designation of such information as 'open information' has the result[132] that The National Archives, when it receives a request for information contained in a transferred public record:

(a)   need not consult the responsible authority in relation to a determination of whether that information is 'exempt information' (in other words, a determination whether the information falls within one or more of the provisions of Part II of the Act);

(b)   need not consult the responsible authority in relation to a determination of whether the duty to confirm or deny that the information requested is held (or would be held) has been excluded by one or more of the provisions of Part II of the Act;

(c)   retains for itself the task of balancing the public interest where the information is subject to a qualified exemption; and

---

[126] ie the Northern Ireland Minister in charge of the Department of Culture, Arts and Leisure in Northern Ireland@ FOIA s 84.

[127] The same remarks as in (2) apply in relation to a person that is not a 'public authority' within the meaning of the FOIA.

[128] EIR reg 2(1); but not EI(S)R.

[129] Similarly, EIR reg 17(2).

[130] Though it is in EI(S)R reg 15(8).

[131] §7– 033.

[132] Because the obligations in FOIA s 66(2)–(4) do not arise in relation to information contained in a transferred public record that the responsible authority has designated as open information: FOIA s 66(1). Similarly, EIR reg 17(2).

(d)   retains for itself the task of balancing the public interest where the exclusion of the duty to confirm or deny is a qualified exclusion.

It should be borne in mind that the designation of information as 'open information' by the responsible authority does not dictate the determination by The National Archives of matters (a)–(d). However, where the information has been designated as 'open information', then, if the information is contained in a historical record that is a public record, The National Archives must first consult the Lord Chancellor before refusing to disclose the information solely on the basis of a qualified exemption.[133]

7– 046   The first stage of a request

Where The National Archives receives a request under the Freedom of Information Act 2000 that relates to information that is contained in a 'transferred public record', then, after satisfying itself as to the usual formalities for a proper request,[134] The National Archives must, within the usual time allowed for a public authority to answer a request:[135]

(1)   identify the information held by it that answers the terms of the request;

(2)   in relation to that information, having consulted the responsible authority,[136] determine whether it is 'exempt information' within the meaning of the Freedom of Information Act 2000 (in other words, determine whether it falls within one or more of the provisions of Part II of the Act, bearing in mind the age of the record in which the information is contained and the removal of certain of those provisions in relation to a public record that is a historical record[137]);

(3)   if any of the information that is determined to be exempt information is only so by virtue of a 'qualified exemption', send a copy of the request to the responsible authority;[138]

(4)   where the information is 'exempt information',[139] and again having consulted the responsible authority,[140] further determine whether the duty to confirm or deny that information answering the terms of the request is held by The National Archives has been excluded by one or more of the provisions of Part II of the Freedom of Information Act 2000, again bearing in mind the age of the record in which the information sought is contained and the removal of certain of those provisions in

---

[133] FOIA s 65(1); EIR reg 17(1). Reading ss 65(2) and 66(1) together, it is apparent that s 65 applies to, inter alia, information that the responsible authority has not designated as open information.

[134] See §§11– 001 to 11– 012.

[135] See §§11– 022 to 11– 030.

[136] FOIA s 66(2)(b); EIR reg 17(2). The obligation to consult the responsible authority does not, however, arise if the responsible authority has previously designated the information as 'open information'.

[137] See §§7– 036 to 7– 041.

[138] FOIA s 15(1)–(2). In the case of 'environmental information', the responsible authority decides where the public interest lies, having consulted the Lord Chancellor: EIR reg 17(3)–(4).

[139] If it is determined not to be exempt information, it will have to be disclosed and the duty to confirm or deny will be taken to be complied with: FOIA s 1(5).

[140] FOIA s 66(2)(a). The obligation to consult the responsible authority does not, however, arise if the responsible authority has previously designated the information as 'open information'.

relation to a public record that is (or would be) a historical record;[141]

(5) if the duty to confirm or deny is only excluded by virtue of a 'qualified exclusion' and the request has not been sent under (3), send a copy of the request to the 'responsible authority';[142]

(6) communicate to the applicant any information that is not 'exempt information';[143] and

(7) in relation to any information that is 'exempt information':
   (i) give the applicant a notice under s 17(1); and
   (ii) in relation to any such information in respect of which it is necessary to weigh the public interest, give the applicant a notice as required under s 17(2).[144]

47   The second stage of a request

By the end of the first stage, The National Archives will have dealt with all information answering the terms of the request, except information that is exempt information only by virtue of a provision conferring a qualified exemption. The second stage of a request received by The National Archives that relates to information contained in a 'transferred public record' is thus concerned with the weighing of the public interest. The way in which this task must be carried out varies according to whether the responsible authority has designated information in question as 'open information' and to whether the duty to confirm or deny has prima facie been excluded:

(1) If the information has been designated as 'open information' and it has been determined in the first stage that the information is exempt information (but only by virtue of a 'qualified exemption'), then The National Archives must determine whether in all the circumstances of the case, the public interest in maintaining the exemption outweighs the public interest in disclosing the information.[145] In so far as the outcome of this exercise is that the public interest weighs in favour of disclosure, then that information must be communicated to the applicant.[146] In so far as the outcome of this exercise is that the public interest weighs in favour of maintaining the exemption, then The National Archives must first consult the Lord Chancellor[147] and, if that consultation does not cause it to change its mind, give a notice to the applicant stating the reasons for that decision.[148]

(2) If the information has not been disclosed to the applicant under (1) above, then, if it has been designated as 'open information' and it has been determined in the first

---

[141] See §§7–036 to 7–041.

[142] FOIA s 15(1)–(2).

[143] FOIA s 10(1); EIR reg 17(3)(c).

[144] See §§13–011 to 13–012.

[145] As to the general approach to this task, see §§15–010 to 15–017.

[146] FOIA s 11.; EIR reg 5(1).

[147] FOIA s 65(1)(a); EIR reg 17(1)(a).

[148] FOIA s 17(3): unless, or to the extent that, the statement would involve the disclosure of information which would itself be exempt information (s 17(4)). Plainly, it would be sensible for the notice to record that the Lord Chancellor had been consulted.

stage that the duty to confirm or deny does not arise in relation to it (but only by virtue of a 'qualified exclusion'), The National Archives must determine whether in all the circumstances of the case, the public interest in maintaining the exclusion of the duty to confirm or deny outweighs the public interest in disclosing whether The National Archives holds the information.[149] In so far as the outcome of this exercise is that the public interest weighs in favour of disclosing that The National Archives holds the information, then The National Archives must so inform the applicant. In so far as the outcome of this exercise is that the public interest weighs in favour of maintaining the exclusion, then The National Archives must give a notice to the applicant stating the reasons for that decision.[150]

(3) If the information has not been designated as 'open information' and it has been determined in the first stage that the information is exempt information (but only by virtue of a 'qualified exemption'), then the responsible authority[151] must determine whether in all the circumstances of the case, the public interest in maintaining the exemption outweighs the public interest in disclosing the information.[152] In so far as the outcome of this exercise is that the public interest weighs in favour of disclosure, then that information must be communicated to the applicant.[153] In so far as the outcome of this exercise is that the public interest weighs in favour of maintaining the exemption, then the responsible authority must first consult the Lord Chancellor[154] and, if that consultation does not cause it to change its mind, give a notice to the applicant stating the reasons for that decision.[155]

(4) On the footing that the information has not been disclosed to the applicant under (3) above, then, if the information has not been designated as 'open information' and it has been determined in the first stage that the duty to confirm or deny does not arise in relation to it (but only by virtue of a 'qualified exclusion'), the

---

[149] As to the general approach to this task, see §§15– 018 to 15– 019.

[150] FOIA s 17(3): unless, or to the extent that, the statement would involve the disclosure of information which would itself be exempt information (s 17(4)).

[151] By virtue of FOIA s 66(4).

[152] As to the general approach to this task, see §§15– 010 to 15– 017. In the case of 'environmental information' this determination is made by the responsible authority: EIR R17(3)(a).

[153] FOIA s 11. It is not entirely clear whether it is the responsible authority, rather than The National Archives, that is responsible for informing the applicant of the decision and of communicating the information. Section 66(6) of the FOIA tends to suggest that it is the responsible authority who must do so: if this be correct, presumably it would simply pass over the copy which it had received from The National Archives under s 15(1) or a copy of that copy. On the other hand, s 15(3) tends to suggest that the responsible authority simply makes the determination, leaving execution of that determination to The National Archives. Either way, the responsible authority must inform The National Archives of the determination reached by it in relation to the weighing of the public interest. It is clear that in relation to 'environmental information' the appropriate authority must inform the applicant: EIR reg 17(3)(c).

[154] FOIA s 66(5)(a); EIR reg 17(4)(a).

[155] FOIA s 17(3): unless, or to the extent that, the statement would involve the disclosure of information which would itself be exempt information (s 17(4)). Plainly, it would be sensible for the notice to record that the Lord Chancellor had been consulted. As to whether it is the responsible authority or The National Archives that must carry into effect the determination, see §7– 042.

responsible authority[156] must determine whether in all the circumstances of the case, the public interest in maintaining the exclusion of the duty to confirm or deny outweighs the public interest in disclosing whether The National Archives holds the information.[157] In so far as the outcome of this exercise is that the public interest weighs in favour of disclosing that The National Archives holds the information, then the responsible authority must so inform the applicant.[158] In so far as the outcome of this exercise is that the public interest weighs in favour of maintaining the exclusion, then the responsible authority must first consult the Lord Chancellor[159] and, if that consultation does not cause it to change its mind, give a notice to the applicant stating the reasons for that decision.[160]

In all cases, the task must be carried out within a reasonable time[161] and, in any event, within the time specified in the notice given in the first stage.[162]

---

[156] By virtue of FOIA s 66(3).

[157] As to the general approach to this task, see §§15– 018 to 15– 019.

[158] As to whether it is the responsible authority or The National Archives that must so inform the applicant, see §7– 047(3) fn 153.

[159] FOIA s 66(5)(a). The astute reader will have noticed that the obligation to consult the Lord Chancellor in relation to a determination neither to confirm nor deny that the information is held does not apply where the information is open information: see s 65(1).

[160] FOIA s 17(3): unless, or to the extent that, the statement would involve the disclosure of information which would itself be exempt information (s 17(4)). Plainly, it would be sensible for the notice to record that the Lord Chancellor had been consulted. As to whether it is the responsible authority or The National Archives that must carry into effect the determination, see §7– 042.

[161] FOIA s 10(3).

[162] FOIA s 17(2). It would seem that if there were good, objective reasons why the decision-making body could not determine the matter within the time specified in the earlier notice, then, provided that the decision were nevertheless made within a reasonable time, this would be satisfactory.

CHAPTER 8

Other Domestic Rights of Access

1. LOCAL GOVERNMENT

)01 **Introduction**

At common law an individual has no general right of access to information held by a public authority. However, the common law does recognise a limited right for a member of a local authority to see such documents as are reasonably necessary to enable him to carry out his duties.[1] Onto this very limited common law right are grafted a series of statutory rights specifically relating to information held by local authorities and cognate bodies. These rights of access are additional to those conferred by the Freedom of Information Act 2000, the Environmental Information Regulations 2004 and the Data Protection Act 1998. In each case, the scope of the right is dependent upon:

— the identity of the applicant;

— the nature of the information sought;

— the body by whom the information is held; and

— the applicability of an exemption to that right.

In very broad terms the principal provisions are:

(1) The Public Bodies (Admission to Meetings) Act 1960 gives a member of the press an entitlement to be supplied with a copy of the agenda and limited additional information relating to meetings of certain local government bodies that are required to be open to the public.[2]

(2) The Local Government (Records) Act 1962 confers on members of the public

---

[1] *R v Southwold Corporation, ex p Wrightson* (1907) 5 LGR 888; *R v Barnes BC, ex p Conlan* [1938] 3 All ER 226; *R v Lancashire County Council Police Authority, ex p Hook* [1980] QB 603; *R v Birmingham City Council, ex p O* [1983] 1 AC 578, [1983] 1 All ER 497, 81 LGR 259 (where the House of Lords held that a councillor has the right to have access to all written material in the possession of the local authority of which the councillor is a member provided that the councillor has a good reason for having access. That good reason will exist in relation to all documents held by a committee of which the councillor is a member; but otherwise some need to know will have to be demonstrated); *R v Hackney London Borough Council, ex p Gamper* [1985] 1 WLR 1229, [1985] 3 All ER 275. This right does not extend to documents that the member is merely curious to see: the member has to be actuated solely by the desire to discharge his public functions: *R v Hampstead Borough Council, ex p Woodward* (1917) 15 LGR 309.

[2] §§8– 002 to 8– 003.

limited rights of access to records held by a local authority.[3]

(3) Part VA of the Local Government Act 1972 gives members of the public a right of access to the agenda, reports and certain background papers used at meetings of a wide range of local government bodies.[4]

(4) Section 30 of the Local Government Act 1974 gives a right of public access to reports produced by the Local Commissioner into complaints of maladministration.[5]

(5) Section 96 of the Local Government, Planning and Land Act 1980 gives members of the public access to a register of certain land holdings of local authority bodies.[6]

(6) Section 13 of the Audit Commission Act 1998 gives members of the public access to reports produced by an auditor which have been transmitted to a public body or its chairman.[7]

(7) Paragraph 8 of Sch 9 to the Local Government Finance Act 1988 gives members of the public a right of access to certain information in local non-domestic rating lists.[8]

(8) The Local Government Finance Act 1992 gives members of the public certain rights to access information relating to local domestic rating lists.[9]

(9) Section 22 of the Local Government Act 2000 and the regulations made under it provide similar rights of access as Part VA of the Local Government Act 1972, but in relation to information put to meetings of local authority executives.[10]

(10) Paragraph 57 of Sch 1 to the Representation of the People Act 1983, and like rules in relation to European and local elections, provides a time-limited right of access to certain documents used or received in connection with Parliamentary, European and local elections.[11]

8– 002   Public Bodies (Admission to Meetings) Act 1960

The Public Bodies (Admission to Meetings) Act 1960 was passed at the instigation of Margaret Thatcher MP in 1960.[12] This Act opened up 'the meetings of certain bodies exercising public functions' to the press and other members of the public. The Act applies to the bodies listed in Sch 1 to the Act, including parish and community councils, the Welsh Development Agency,

---

[3] §8– 004.

[4] §§8– 005 to 8– 022.

[5] §8– 023.

[6] §8– 024.

[7] §8– 025.

[8] §8– 026.

[9] §8– 026.

[10] See further §§8– 027 to 8– 034.

[11] §8– 035.

[12] See further §1– 001.

the Commission for Health Improvement, Strategic Health Authorities, Primary Care Trusts,[13] regional and local flood defence committees, advisory committees established and maintained under s 12 of the Environment Act 1995, National Health Service Trusts established under s 5(1) of the National Health Service and Community Care Act 1990;[14] and, in Scotland, Health Boards constituted under the National Health Service (Scotland) Act 1978 (but only so far as regards the exercise of their executive functions), and National Health Service Trusts established under s 12A of the National Health Service (Scotland) Act 1978.[15] Section 1(1) of the Act provides that any meeting of a body exercising public functions to which the Act applies shall be open to the public.[16] Section 1(1) is, however, subject to a proviso contained in s 1(2), by virtue of which a public body may, by resolution, exclude the public from a meeting (whether during the whole or a part of the proceedings) whenever publicity would be prejudicial to the public interest by reason of the confidential nature of the business to be transacted or for other special reasons stated in the resolution and arising from the nature of the business or of the proceedings. Where such a resolution is passed, the Act does not require the meeting to be open to the public during the proceedings to which the resolution applies. Section 1(3) of the Public Bodies (Admission to Meetings) Act 1960 further provides that a body may, under s 1(2), treat the need to receive or consider recommendations or advice from sources other than members, committees or sub-committees of the body as a special reason why publicity would be prejudicial to the public interest, without regard to the subject or purport of the recommendations or advice, but that the making by s 1(3) of express provision for that case shall not be taken to restrict the generality of s 1(2) in relation to other cases (including, in particular, cases where the report of a committee or sub-committee of the body is of a confidential nature. This provision covers advice from officers.

03   The right to certain information under the Public Bodies (Admission to Meetings) Act 1960

Section 1(4) of the Public Bodies (Admission to Meetings) Act 1960 provides that where a body is required by the Act to be open to the public during the proceedings or any part of them, then, on request and payment of postage, a copy of the agenda for the meeting as supplied to the members of the body must be supplied for the benefit of any newspaper. The agenda so supplied may, if thought fit, exclude any item during which the meeting is likely not to be open to the public. That person must also be supplied with a copy of such further statements or particulars, if any, as are necessary to indicate the nature of the items included, or, if thought fit in the case of any item, with copies of any reports or other documents supplied to the members of the body in connection with the item. This provision thus provides a limited class of person with a limited right to information in limited circumstances. To the extent that the Public Bodies (Admission to Meetings) Act 1960 confers a right to information, that information

---

[13]   Except as regards the exercise of their functions under the National Health Service (Service Committees and Tribunal) Regulations 1992 or any regulations amending or replacing those Regulations: para 1(gg) of Sch 1 to the Public Bodies (Admission to Meetings) Act 1960.

[14]   Added by art 2 of the Public Bodies (Admission to Meetings) (National Health Service Trusts) Order 1997.

[15]   Added by art 2 of the Public Bodies (Admission to Meetings) (National Health Service Trusts) Order 1997.

[16]   This does not preclude the body from excluding a member of the public whose rowdiness is impeding business: *R v Brent Health Authority, ex p Francis* [1985] QB 869, [1985] 1 All ER 74; *R v Bude-Stratton Town Council, ex p Bennett* [2005] EWHC 2341; *R v London Borough of Brent, ex p Assegai* (1987) 151 LG Rev 891.

will be exempt information under the Freedom of Information Act 2000.[17] Section 1(4)(c) of the Public Bodies (Admission to Meetings) Act 1960 provides that, while the meeting is open to the public, the body lacks the power to exclude members of the public from the meeting. Duly accredited representatives of newspapers attending for the purpose of reporting the proceedings for those newspapers must, so far as practicable, be afforded reasonable facilities for making their report and, unless the meeting is held in premises not belonging to the body or on the telephone, for telephoning the report at their own expense.

8– 004   Local Government (Records) Act 1962

Section 1(1) of the Local Government (Records) Act 1962 confers on local authorities a broad discretion do all such things as appear to them necessary or expedient for enabling adequate use to be made of records under their control. In relation to such records, a local authority may in particular make provision for enabling persons, with or without charge and subject to such conditions as the authority may determine, to inspect records and to make or obtain copies thereof.[18]

8– 005   Local Government Act 1972 – Pt VA

The public have a right under Part VA of the Local Government Act 1972[19] to attend meetings of principal councils and their committees, as well as to be given access to certain documents connected with the proceedings of the latter bodies.[20] With modification, this right also extends to representation hearings conducted by the Mayor of London under section 2F of the Town and Country Planning Act 1990[21] and meetings of a standards committee, or a sub-committee of a standards committee of an authority[22] and to meetings of the Central Lincolnshire Joint Strategic Planning Committee.[23] Section 100A(1) of the Local Government Act 1972 provides that meetings of principal councils shall be open to the public, except to the extent that they are excluded under s 100A(2) or by resolution under s 100A(4). Public notice of the time and place of the meeting must be given by posting it at the offices of the council at least five clear days before the meeting, or if the meeting is convened at shorter notice, then at the time it is

---

[17] FOIA s 21(1). See §§16– 001 to 16– 005.

[18] Local Government (Records) Acts 1972 s 1(1)(a).

[19] Pt VA of the Local Government Act 1972 comprises ss 100A to 100K and Sch 12. Pt VA was inserted by the Local Government (Access to Information) Act 1985.

[20] But not 'working parties': *R v Warwickshire DC, ex p Bailey* [1991] COD 284. Nor a 'homelessness board': *R v London Borough of Tower Hamlets, ex p Khalique* [1995] 2 FCR 1074

[21] The Town and Country Planning (Mayor of London) Order 2008, SI 2008/580, art 9(1).

[22] Standards Committee (England) Regulations 2008, SI 2008/1085, reg 8(1). Part VA of the Local Government Act 1972 will not apply if the meeting is convened to consider an allegation received under section 57A(1) of the Local Government Act 2000 or to review a decision under s 57B of the Local Government Act 2000: Standards Committee (England) Regulations 2008, SI 2008/1085, reg 8 (5). Reference should also be made to reg 8(6), which sets out how Part VA of the Local Government Act 1972 applies to specific meetings of a standards committee, or a sub-committee of a standards committee.

[23] Central Lincolnshire Joint Strategic Planning Committee Order 2009, SI 2009/2467, art 9(1), Schedule, para 7.

convened.[24] While the meeting is open to the public, the council cannot exclude members of the public from the meeting.[25] While the meeting is open to the public, accredited newspaper representatives attending the meeting for the purpose of reporting the proceedings shall, so far as practicable, be afforded reasonable facilities for taking their report.[26] By s 100A(2), the public must be excluded from a meeting of a principal council during an item of business whenever it is likely, in view of the nature of the business to be transacted or the nature of the proceedings, that, if members of the public were to be present during that item, confidential information[27] would be disclosed to them in breach of the obligation of confidence. Section 100A(2) further provides that nothing in Part VA can be taken to authorise or require the disclosure of confidential information in breach of the obligation of confidence.

06 Meaning of 'principal council'
The primary meaning of a 'principal council' as the term is used in the Local Government Act 1972 is a council elected for a non-metropolitan county, for a district or for a London Borough and, in relation to Wales, for a county or for a county borough.[28] For the purposes of Part VA of the Act, the term also includes a joint authority,[29] the London Fire and Emergency Planning Authority,[30] the Common Council of the City of London,[31] the Broads Authority,[32] a National Park Authority,[33] a joint board or joint committee constituted under any enactment as a body corporate and discharging the functions of two or more principal councils,[34] a police authority established under s 3 of the Police Act 1996, the Metropolitan Police Authority, and a combined fire authority constituted by a scheme under section 2 of the Fire and Rescue Service Act 2004.[35]

---

[24] Local Government Act 1972, s100A (6) (a). As regards representation hearings conducted by the Mayor of London, seven clear days are required: the Town and Country Planning (Mayor of London) Order 2008, art 9(3)(c). In relation to meetings of a standards committee, the authority must give notice of the meeting to the parish council, in accordance with s100A(6)(a): Standards Committee (England) Regulations 2008, SI 2008/1085 reg 8(3)(a).

[25] Local Government Act 1972 s 100A(6)(b). This does not preclude the body from excluding a member of the public for misbehaviour at a meeting: s 100A(8).

[26] Local Government Act 1972 s 100A(6)(c).

[27] The term 'information', as it appears in Pt VA of the Local Government Act 1972, includes an expression of opinion, any recommendations and any decision taken: Local Government Act 1972 s 100K(1). The definition of 'confidential information' in the Local Government Act 1972 is materially different from its common law meaning: see §§25– 010 to 25– 029.

[28] Local Government Act 1972 s 270(1). These are listed in Sch 1 to the Act.

[29] That is, an authority established by Pt IV of the Local Government Act 1985: Local Government Act 1972 s 270(1).

[30] Established under the Local Government Act 1985, s 27 (now repealed) but reconstituted by the Greater London Authority Act 1999, Pt III.

[31] In other words, the mayor, aldermen and commons of the City of London in common council assembled: see City of London (Various Powers) Act 1958 s 5.

[32] As established by the Norfolk and Suffolk Broads Act 1988 s 1.

[33] These are established under the Environment Act 1995 ss 63 and 64 and Sch 7.

[34] Local Government Act 1972 s 100J(2).

[35] Local Government Act 1972 s 100J(1)(f).

8– 007   Meaning of 'confidential information'

For the purposes of Part VA of the Local Government Act 1972, 'confidential information' is defined to mean:

— information furnished to a principal council by a government department upon terms (however expressed) that forbid the disclosure of the information to the public; and

— information the disclosure of which to the public is prohibited by or under any enactment or by the order of a court.[36]

As noted above, the definition given to 'confidential information' is materially different from its common law meaning.[37]

8– 008   Power to exclude the public by resolution

Principal councils may resolve to exclude the public from a meeting during an item of business whenever it is likely, in view of the nature of the business to be transacted or the nature of the proceedings, that if members of the public were to remain during the item there would be disclosure to them of 'exempt information'.[38] The resolution must identify the proceedings, or the part of the proceedings, to which it applies[39] and it must state the description, in terms of Sch 12A to the Local Government Act 1972, of the exempt information giving rise to the exclusion of the public.[40] Where such a resolution is made, the meeting need not be open to the public during the proceedings to which the resolution relates.

8– 009   Exempt information under the Local Government Act 1972

Section 100I(1) defines 'exempt information' as information described in Part I of Sch 12A to the Local Government Act 1972, subject to any qualifications contained in Part II,[41] and as interpreted in the light of Part III.[42] The items of information specified in Part I of Sch 12A to the Local Government Act 1972 are:[43]

---

[36] Local Government Act 1972 s 100A(3)(a).

[37] As to which see §§25– 010 to 25– 029.

[38] Local Government Act 1972 s 100A(4). For examples of the exercise of this power see *R v Kensington and Chelsea LBC, ex p Stoop* [1992] 1 PLR 58 (public excluded during a consideration of an application for the grant of planning permission); and *R v Wandsworth LBC, ex p Darker Enterprises Ltd* (1999) 1 LGLR 601 (public excluded during consideration of an application for a renewal of a licence for a sex establishment). This power does not extend to the Mayor of London when conducting representation hearings : Town and Country Planning (Mayor of London) Order 2008 art 9(3)(a).

[39] Local Government Act 1972 s 100A(5)(a).

[40] Local Government Act 1972 s 100A(5)(b).

[41] By para 7 of Pt II of Sch 12A to the Local Government Act 1972, information falling within any paragraph of Pt I is not exempt information by virtue of that paragraph if it relates to proposed development for which the local planning authority can grant itself planning permission pursuant to Town and County Planning General Regulations 1992 SI 1992/1492 reg 3.

[42] In relation to Wales, exempt information is that described in Part 4 of Sch 12A, subject to any qualifications in Part 5 and as interpreted in light of Part 6: Local Government Act 1972 s 100I(1A).

[43] Information is not exempt information if it relates to proposed development for which the local planning authority may grant itself planning permission pursuant to reg 3 of the Town and Country Planning General Regulations 1992: Local Government Act 1972, Sch 12A, Part 2, para 9.

(1)   Information relating to any individual.[44]

(2)   Information which is likely to reveal the identity of an individual.[45]

(3)   Information relating to the financial or business affairs of any particular person (including the authority[46] holding that information).[47]

(4)   Information relating to any consultations or negotiations, or contemplated consultations or negotiations, in connection with any labour relations matter arising between the authority or a Minister of the Crown and employees of, or office holders under, the authority.[48]

(5)   Information in respect of which a claim to legal professional privilege could be maintained in legal proceedings.[49]

(6)   Information which reveals that the authority proposes (a) to give under any enactment a notice under or by virtue of which requirements are imposed on a person; or (b) to make an order or direction under any enactment.[50]

(7)   Information relating to any action taken or to be taken in connection with the prevention, investigation or prosecution of crime.[51]

10 Access to documents: agendas and reports

Section 100B of the Local Government Act 1972 confers a right of access upon members of the public to:

—   copies of the agenda for a meeting of a principal council; and

---

[44] Local Government Act 1972, Sch 12A, Part 1, para 1.

[45] Local Government Act 1972, Sch 12A, Part 1, para 2.

[46] Local Government Act 1972 Sch.12A Pt 3, para 1(2) provides that any reference in that Schedule to 'the authority' is a reference to the principal council, or, as the case may be, the committee or sub-committee in relation to whose proceedings or documents the question whether information is exempt or not falls to be determined; and includes a reference, in the case of a principal council, to any committee or sub-committee of the council, and, in the case of a committee, to any constituent principal council, any other principal council by which appointments are made to the committee or whose functions that committee discharges, and any other committee or sub-committee of a principal council of the above mentioned kinds. In the case of a subcommittee, references to 'the authority' include the committee or any committees of which it is a sub-committee and any principal council which falls within the above-mentioned kinds in relation to that committee. References in Sch 12A to 'the authority' include references to the Mayor of London: Town and Country Planning (Mayor of London) Order 2008 art 9(8).

[47] Local Government Act 1972, Sch 12A, Part 1, para 3. This is not exempt information by virtue of that paragraph if it is required to be registered under: (a) the Companies Acts (as defined in s 2 of the Companies Act 2006); (b) the Friendly Societies Act 1974; (c) the Friendly Societies Act 1992; (d) the Industrial and Provident Societies Acts 1965 to 1978; (e) the Building Societies Act 1986; or (f) the Charities Act 1993: Local Government Act 1972, Sch 12A, Part 2, para 8.

[48] Local Government Act 1972, Sch 12A, Part 1, para 4.

[49] Local Government Act 1972, Sch 12A, Part 1, para 5.

[50] Local Government Act 1972, Sch 12A, Part 1, para 6.

[51] Local Government Act 1972, Sch 12A, Part 1, para 7. Information which (a) falls within any of paragraphs 1 to 7 of the Local Government Act 1972, Sch 12A, Part 1 and (b) is not prevented from being exempt by virtue of para 8 or 9 Local Government Act 1972, Sch 12A, Part 2, is exempt information if and so long, as in all the circumstances of the case, the public interest in maintaining the exemption outweighs the public interest in disclosing the information: Local Government Act 1972, Sch 12A, Part 2, para 10.

    —   copies of any report for the meeting.[52]

These documents are required to be open to inspection by members of the public at least five clear days before the meeting in question, except that, where the meeting is convened at shorter notice, the copies of the agenda and reports must be open to inspection from the time the meeting is convened.[53] Where an item is added to an agenda, copies of which are open to inspection by the public, copies of the item (or of a revised agenda) and the copies of any report for the meeting relating to the item, must be open to inspection from the time the item is added to the agenda.[54] Copies of any agenda or report that is open to inspection by the public need not be made available to the public until copies have been made available to members of the council.[55] The right of access to copies of reports is subject to the power conferred upon the proper officer by s 100B(2), if he thinks fit, to exclude from such copies the whole or any part of a report which relates only to items during which, in his opinion, the meeting is likely not to be open to the public. Where the officer in question does take the view that the whole or part of any report should be excluded for this reason, every copy of the report, or part of the report, so excluded must be marked 'Not for publication',[56] and every copy of the whole or of the part of the report so excluded must state the description, in terms of Sch 12A to the Local Government Act 1972, of the exempt information by virtue of which the council are likely to exclude the public during the item to which the report relates.[57] An item of business may not be considered at a meeting of a principal council unless a copy of the agenda including the item (or a copy of the item) is open to inspection by members of the public for at least five clear days before the meeting or, where the meeting is convened at shorter notice, from the time the

---

[52] Local Government Act 1972 s 100B(1). In relation to the meetings of a standards committee, the authority must provide copies of the documents referred to in s 100B(1) to the parish council at least five clear days before the meeting: Standards Committee (England) Regulations 2008, SI 2008/1085 reg 8(3)(b). By s 100B(6), where a meeting of a principal council is required by s 100A to be open to the public during the proceedings or any part of them, a reasonable number of copies of the agenda, and subject to s 100B(8), of the reports for the meeting, must be made available for the use by members of the public present at the meeting. Section 100B(8) provides that s 100B(2) applies in relation to copies of reports provided in pursuance of s 100B(6)or 100B(7) as it applies in relation to copies of reports provided in pursuance of s 100B(1). In order to benefit from the rights of access to information under the Local Government Act 1972, it is sufficient that one is a local government elector, but it is not necessary that one should seek to obtain access to the information in question in that capacity. In *Stirrat v Edinburgh City Council* [1999] SLT 274 [1998] SCLR 971 the claimant, who was a partner in a firm providing a property enquiry service and also a council taxpayer in the City of Edinburgh, attended the Council's office in order to inspect documents in the exercise of his right to do so under s 101(1) of the Local Government (Scotland) Act 1973. Some documents were not available, and the Council refused the claimant access to them on the grounds of confidentiality and expense. The claimant presented a petition seeking a declaration that he was entitled to inspect the documents. The Council opposed the petition on the ground that the right to inspect the documents was linked to the right of the council taxpayer to object to the accounts, and did not apply where the inspection was for professional purposes. The Scottish Outer House granted the declaration, holding that the claimant had right and title to inspect the documents as a council taxpayer under s 101(1), and that the motive with which he sought to exercise that right was irrelevant.

[53] Local Government Act 1972 s 100B(3)(a). The reference to 'five clear days' means five working days: *R v Swansea City Council, ex p Elitestone* [1993] 46 EG 181. As regards representation hearings conducted by the Mayor of London, seven clear days are required: Town and Country Planning (Mayor of London) order 2008 art 9(4).

[54] Local Government Act 1972 s 100B(3)(b).

[55] Local Government Act 1972 s 100B(3).

[56] Local Government Act 1972. s 100B(5)(a).

[57] Local Government Act 1972 s 100B(5)(b).

meeting is convened;[58] or unless, by reason of special circumstances, which must be specified in the minutes, the chairman of the meeting is of the opinion that the item should be considered at the meeting as a matter or urgency.[59]

11 Access to documents: inspection of minutes and other documents after meetings

Once a meeting of a principal council has been held, members of the public are entitled to inspect at the offices of the council until the expiration of the period of six years beginning with the date of the meeting:

— the minutes of the meeting, or a copy of the minutes, excluding that part of the minutes of proceedings during which the meeting was not open to the public as disclosures of exempt information;[60]

— where applicable, a summary of the meeting;[61]

— a copy of the agenda for the meeting; and

— a copy of so much of any report for the meeting as relates to any item during which the meeting was open to the public.[62]

Where, as result of the exclusion of parts of the minutes that would disclose exempt information, the minutes of the meeting that are made open to inspection do not provide members of the public with a reasonably fair and coherent record of the whole or part of the proceedings, the proper officer must make a written summary of those (or that part of the) proceedings.[63]

12 Access to documents: inspection of background papers

If and so long as copies of the whole or part of a report for a meeting of a principal council are required by s 100B(1) or 100C(1) to be open to inspection by members of the public, then:

— those copies must include a copy of a list, compiled by the proper officer, of the background papers for the report or the part of the report,[64] and

— at least one copy of each of the documents included in that list must also be open to inspection at the offices of the council.[65]

Section 100D(1) does not require a copy of any document included in the list, to be open to

---

[58] Local Government Act 1972 s 100B(4)(a). As regards representation hearings conducted by the Mayor of London, seven clear days are required: Town and Country Planning (Mayor of London) Order 2008 art 9(4).

[59] Local Government Act 1972 s 100B(4)(b).

[60] Local Government Act 1972 s 100C(1)(a). See the Standards Committee (England) Regulations 2008 reg 8(3)(c) for its application to meetings of a standards committee.

[61] Local Government Act 1972 s 100C(1)(b).

[62] Local Government Act 1972 s 100C(1)(c).

[63] Local Government Act 1972 s 100C(2).

[64] Local Government Act 1972 s 100D(1)(a).

[65] Local Government Act 1972 s 100D(1)(b). Section 100D(3) further provides that where a copy of any background papers for a report is required by s 100D(1) to be open to inspection by members of the public, the copy shall be taken for the purposes of Pt VA of the Local Government Act 1972 to be so open if arrangements exist for its production to members of the public as soon as is reasonably practicable after the making of a request to inspect the copy.

inspection after the expiration of a period of four years beginning with the date of the meeting.[66] The background papers for a report are those documents relating to the subject-matter of the report that disclose any facts or matters on which, in the opinion of the proper officer, the report or an important part of the report is based, and that have, in that officer's opinion, been relied on to a material extent in preparing the report.[67] The material to be disclosed need not include any confidential information the disclosure of which would be in breach of the obligation of confidence.[68]

8–013   **Application to committees and sub-committees**

The above disclosure provisions apply to committees and sub-committees of principal councils as they apply in relation to principal councils.[69]

8–014   **Inspection of records relating to functions exercisable by members**

Where a member of a local authority discharges any function of the authority under section 236 of the Local Government and Public Involvement in Health Act 2007 (exercise of functions by local councillors in England), that member must—

(a)   ensure that a record is made in writing of any decision made or action taken in connection with the discharge of that function; and

(b)   within one month of the date on which the decision is made, or action taken, provide the record to the authority.[70]

Any written record provided to the authority under the Exercise of Functions by Local Councillors (Written Records) Regulations 2009, must be open to members of the public at the offices of the authority for a period of six years beginning with the date on which the decision was made or action taken.[71]

8–015   **Additional rights of access by members of principal councils**

Members of principal councils also have a right to inspect any document that is in the possession or under the control of a principal council and contains material relating to any business to be transacted at a meeting of the council or a committee or sub-committee of the

---

[66]   Local Government Act 1972 s 100D(2).   In *Maile v Wigan MBC* [2001] Env LR 11, [2001] JPL 193 Eady J held that a database dealing with potentially contaminated sites in the Council's area did not form part of the committee report for the purposes of s 100C of the Local Government Act 1972, and was not a 'background paper' for the purposes of s 100D of that Act, because the Council's environmental health officer had not relied upon the database when drafting his report to committee.   Consequently the claimant was not entitled to inspect the database under the provisions of the Local Government Act 1972.

[67]   Local Government Act 1972 s 100D(5).   The background papers for a report do not, however, include any published works.

[68]   Local Government Act 1972 s 100D(4).

[69]   Local Government Act 1972 s 100E(1).   As to the publication of notices of meetings of committees and sub-committees of principal councils, see s 100E(2) of the Local Government Act 1972.

[70]   Exercise of Functions by Local Councillors (Written Records) Regulations 2009, SI 2009/352, reg 2.   The regulations were made pursuant to section 100EA (1) of the Local Government Act 2000.

[71]   Section 100EA (2) of the Local Government Act 2000.

council.[72] In relation to a principal council in England, this provision does not, however, apply in respect of documents which appear to the proper officer to disclose exempt information,[73] unless the information is information of a description falling within any of paras 1 to 6, 9, 11, 12 and 14 of Part I of Sch 12A to the Local Government Act 1972.[74] In relation to a principal council in Wales, s 100F(1) does not require the document to be open to inspection if it appears to the proper officer that it discloses exempt information[75] unless the information is of a description falling within paragraph 14 or 17 of Sch12A of the Local Government Act 1972.[76]

16   Additional information

Principal councils are required to maintain a register stating:

— the name and address of every current member of the council and the ward or division which that member represents;[77]

— the name and address of every current member of each committee or sub-committee of the council.[78]

Principal councils must also maintain a list specifying those powers of the council which, for the time being, are exercisable from time to time by officers of the council in pursuance of arrangements made under the Local Government Act 1972 or any other enactment for their discharge by those officers and stating the title of the officer by whom each of the powers so specified is for the time being so exercisable.[79] Finally, principal councils are required to keep at their offices a written summary of the rights to attend the meetings of a principal council and of committees and sub-committees of a principal council, and of the rights to inspect and copy documents and to be furnished with documents which are conferred by Part VA of the Local Government Act 1972.[80] The above-mentioned register, list and summary must be kept open

---

[72]   This right is in addition to any other rights that members of principal councils may have apart from s 100F: Local Government Act 1972 s 100F(5). At common law, a member is entitled to see any document which is in the possession of an authority of which he is a member if sight of the document is reasonably necessary to enable him to discharge his functions as a member of that authority: see *R v Barnes Borough Council, ex p Conlan* [1938] 3 All ER 226, 36 LGR 524, DC; *R v Lancashire County Council Police Authority, ex p Hook* [1980] QB 603; *Birmingham City District Council v O* [1983] 1 AC 578, [1983] 1 All ER 497, HL.

[73]   Local Government Act 1972 s 100F(2). Section 100I(1) provides that in relation to principal councils in England, the descriptions of information which are exempt information are those specified in Part I of Sch 12A to the Local Government Act 1972, but subject to any qualifications contained in Part II of that Schedule. In respect of Wales, exempt information is that specified in Part IV of Sch 12 A, but subject to any qualifications in Part V of the Schedule. These classes of exempt information are listed at §8–009.

[74]   Local Government Act 1972 s 100F(2A).

[75]   Local Government Act 1972 s 100F(2C).

[76]   Local Government Act 1972 s 100F(2D).

[77]   Local Government Act 1972 s 100G(1)(a).

[78]   Local Government Act 1972 s 100G(1)(b). A substituted version of this paragraph (effected by the Local Government and Housing Act 1989 s 194, Sch 11 para 24), which would require additional information in relation to speaking rights at such committee and sub-committee meetings, has yet to be put in force.

[79]   Local Government Act 1972 s 100G(2). This section does not, however, require a power to be specified in the list if the arrangements for its discharge by the officer are made for a specified period not exceeding six months.

[80]   Local Government Act 1972 s 100G(3). The same written summary must also set out the rights to attend meetings and inspect, copy and be furnished with documents conferred by Pt XI of the Local Government Act 1972 and such other enactments as the Secretary of State by order specifies: Local Government Act 1972 s 100G(3). For the purposes of this subsection, references to the offices of every principal council have effect as if they were references

to inspection by the public at the offices of the council.[81]

8– 017 Times for inspection, payment and copying of documents

A document that, under the above provisions, is to be open to inspection must be so open at all reasonable hours[82] and without payment, except in the case of background papers for reports, where payment of a reasonable fee for inspection may be demanded.[83] Where a document is open to inspection by a person under the above provisions, the person may make copies of or extracts from the document,[84] or require the person having custody of the document to supply him with a photographic copy of the document or of extracts from it.[85] The rights so conferred are in addition, and without prejudice, to any such rights conferred by or under any other enactment.[86]

8– 018 Offences

It is a summary offence for a person having custody of a document which is required by s 100B(1), 100C(1) of 100EA(2) to be open to inspection under the above provisions to obstruct any person from exercising that right[87] or to refuse to furnish copies to any person entitled to obtain them.[88]

8– 019 Publication of defamatory material

Where, in pursuance of s 100B(7), any accessible document for a meeting to which that section applies is supplied to, or open to inspection by, a member of the public, or is supplied for the benefit of any newspaper, the publication thereby of any defamatory matter contained in the document is privileged, unless the publication is proved to be made with malice.[89] This applies[90] to any meeting of a principal council and any meeting of a committee or sub-committee of a principal council. The 'accessible documents' for a meeting are:

---

to the principal office of the Mayor of London: Town and Country Planning (Mayor of London) Order 2008 art 9(5)(a).

[81] Local Government Act 1972 s 100G(4). This applies with modification to the Mayor of London: Town and Country Planning (Mayor of London) Order 208 art 9(5)(b).

[82] Local Government Act 1972 s 100H(1).

[83] Local Government Act 1972 s 100H(1).

[84] Local Government Act 1972 s 100H(2)(a).

[85] Local Government Act 1972 s 100H(2)(b). Section 100H(2) does not require or authorise the doing of any act which infringes the copyright in any work, except that, where the owner of the copyright is a principal council, nothing done in pursuance of s 100H(2) constitutes an infringement of that copyright: Local Government Act 1972 s 100H(3). section 100H(3) has effect as if the Mayor of London were a principal council: Town and Country Planning (Mayor of London) Order 2008 art 9(6).

[86] Local Government Act 1972 s 100H(7).

[87] Local Government Act 1972 s 100H(4)(a). The offence is punishable on conviction by the imposition of a fine not exceeding level 1 on the standard scale.

[88] Local Government Act 1972 s 100H(4)(b).

[89] Local Government Act 1972 s 100H(5).

[90] By virtue of Local Government Act 1972 s 100H(6).

- — any copy of the agenda or of any item included in the agenda for the meeting;[91]
- — any such further statements or particulars for the purpose of indicating the nature of any item included in the agenda;[92]
- — any copy of a document relating to such an item which is supplied for the benefit of a newspaper in pursuance of s 100B(7)(c);[93]
- — any copy of the whole or part of a report for a meeting;[94] and
- — any copy of the whole or part of any background papers to a report for the meeting.[95]

20 Parish and community councils, joint authorities, police authorities and Broads authorities

The Local Government Act 1972 provides for the inspection by local government electors for the area of parish and community councils of the minutes of their proceedings, and such local government electors have the right, in addition, to make a copy of those minutes or an extract from them.[96] Orders for payments of money made by local authorities are also open to inspection by local electors,[97] while the accounts of local authorities, as well as those of any proper officer of a local authority, are open to inspection by the members of that authority, who may make a copy of those minutes or an extract from them.[98] These provisions apply to the minutes of proceedings and accounts of a joint authority, an economic prosperity board, a combined authority and police authorities established under s 3 of the Police Act 1996, as well as to the Metropolitan Police Authority, as if those authorities were local authorities and as if references to a local government elector for the area of the authority were references to a local government elector for any local government area in the area for which the authority is established.[99]

---

[91] Local Government Act 1972 s 100H(6)(a).

[92] Local Government Act 1972 s 100H(6)(b).

[93] Local Government Act 1972 s 100H(6)(c).

[94] Local Government Act 1972. s 100H(6)(d).

[95] Local Government Act 1972 s 100H(6)(e).

[96] Local Government Act 1972 s 228(1). Section 228 also applies to the minutes of proceedings and accounts of a parish meeting as if that meeting were a parish council: Local Government Act 1972 s 228(8).

[97] Local Government Act 1972 s 228(2).

[98] Local Government Act 1972 s 228(3). Documents directed by s 228 to be open to inspection must be so open at all reasonable hours and, except where otherwise provided, without payment: Local Government Act 1972 s 228(6). It is an offence punishable upon summary conviction by a fine not exceeding level 1 on the standard scale for a person having custody of a document required by s 228 to be open to the public to obstruct any person entitled to inspect the document or to make a copy or extract, or to refuse to give copies or extracts to any person entitled to obtain copies or extracts: Local Government Act 1972 s 228(7).

[99] Local Government Act 1972 s 228(7A). In its application to the Broads Authority, those references in that section to a local government elector are to be construed as references to an elector for the area of any of the local authorities mentioned in s 1(3)(a) of the Norfolk and Suffolk Broads Act 1988. The authorities in question are Norfolk County Council, Suffolk County Council, Broadland District Council, Great Yarmouth Borough Council, North Norfolk District Council, Norwich City Council, South Norfolk District Council and Waveney District Council.

8– 021 **Application to the Greater London Authority**

Part VA of the Local Government Act 1972 has effect as if the London Assembly were a principal council and any committee or sub-committee of the Assembly were a committee or sub-committee of a principal council, within the meaning of Part VA, with certain modifications.[100] The Assembly has an express power to require certain individuals to attend proceedings of the Assembly[101] for the purpose of giving evidence,[102] or to produce to the

---

[100] Greater London Authority Act 1999 s 58(1). By s 58(2) of the Greater London Authority Act 1999, in the application of Pt VA of the Local Government Act 1972 by s 58(1), any information furnished to the Greater London Authority and available to the Assembly must be treated as information furnished to the Assembly; any offices of or belonging to the Authority must be treated as also being offices of or belonging to the Assembly; and the proper officer of the Authority must be taken to be the proper officer in relation to the Assembly. By s 58(3), in the following provisions of the Local Government Act 1972, namely s 100A(2) and 100D(4), any reference to the disclosure (or likelihood of disclosure) of confidential information in breach of the obligation of confidence includes a reference to the disclosure of information of any of the descriptions specified in s 58(4) without the consent of the relevant body concerned. The descriptions in s 58(4) are: any information relating to the financial or business affairs of any particular person which was acquired in consequence of a relationship between that person and a relevant body; the amount of any expenditure proposed to be incurred by a relevant body under any particular contract, if and so long as disclosure would be likely to give an advantage to a person entering into, or seeking to enter into, a contract with the relevant body, whether the advantage would arise against the relevant body or another such person; any terms proposed or to be proposed by or to a relevant body in the course of negotiations for any particular contract, if and so long as disclosure would prejudice the relevant body in those or any other negotiations concerning the subject matter of the contract; and the identity of any person as the person offering any particular tender for a contract for the supply of goods or services to a relevant body. In s 58(4), the phrase 'relevant body' means Transport for London or the London Development Agency. By s 58(5) of the Greater London Authority Act 1999, any reference to the minutes of a meeting in s 100C of the Local Government Act 1972 shall, in the case of a meeting of the Assembly under s 52(3) of the Greater London Authority Act 1999, be taken to include a reference to the text of any question put pursuant to s 52(3) at the meeting and the text of any answer given to any such question, whether the question was put orally or in writing. By s 58(6), nothing in s 100D of the Local Government Act 1972 requires or authorises the inclusion of any such list as is referred to in s 100D(1) of any document which discloses anything which, by virtue of s 45(6) of the Greater London Authority Act 1999, is not required to be disclosed under s 45(3) or s 45(4) of the Greater London Authority Act 1999. By s 58(7) of the Greater London Authority Act 1999, in s 100E of the Local Government Act 1972 s 100E(3)(a) shall have effect as if s 55 of the Greater London Authority Act 1999 were included among the enactments specified in s 101(9) of the Local Government Act 1972. By s 58(8) of the Greater London Authority Act 1999, for the purposes of s 100F of the Local Government Act 1972, any document which is in the possession or under the control of the Authority and is available to the Assembly shall be treated as a document which is in the possession or under the control of the Assembly. By s 58(9) of the Greater London Authority Act 1999, in the case of the Assembly, the register of members required to be maintained under s 100G(1) of the Local Government Act 1972 shall, instead of stating the ward or division which a member represents, state whether the member is a London member or a constituency member, and if he is a constituency member, the Assembly constituency for which he is a member. By s 58(10) of the Greater London Authority Act 1999, for the purposes of s 100H(3) of the Local Government Act 1972, the Authority shall be treated as a principal council. Finally, by s 58(11) of the Greater London Authority Act 1999, in the application in relation to the Assembly of Sch 12A to the Local Government Act 1972, any reference to 'the authority' includes a reference to the Assembly.

[101] Greater London Authority Act 1999 s 61(1). Relevant indiviudals are defined within sub ss 61(2), (3), (4) and (5) of the Greater London Authority Act 1999. By virtue of s 61(2) individuals who could be required to give evidence include (a) any person who is a member of staff of the Authority, or of any functional body, to whom ss 1 to 3 of the Local Government and Housing Act 1989 apply, (b) any person who is the chairman of, or a member of, any functional body (defined in s 424(1) as being Transport for London, the London Development Agency, the Metropolitan Police Authority and the London Fire and Emergency Planning Authority), and (c) any person who has within the three years prior to the date of the requirement to be imposed under s 61(1) been the chairman of, or a member of, any functional body. Section 61(3) applies to (a) any person who has within the three years prior to the date of the requirement to be imposed under s 61(1) had a contractual relationship with the Authority, and (b) any person who is a member of, or a member of staff of, a body which has within the three years prior to the date of the requirement to be imposed under s 61(1) had such a relationship. Section 61(4) applies to (a) any person who has within the three years prior to the date of the requirement to be imposed under s 61(1) received a grant from

Assembly documents in their possession or under their control.[103] In respect of such proceedings, Part VA of the Local Government Act 1972 has effect with certain modifications.[104]

2   Relationship between Part VA of the Local Government Act 1972 and the Freedom of Information Act 2000

To the extent that one or other of the provisions of Part VA of the Local Government Act 1972 confers a right to information (whether directly or as extended to another body by a further statutory provision) that information will be exempt information under the Freedom of Information Act 2000.[105] Although not entirely clear, it would seem that s 100H(7) will not operate to preserve the rights of access conferred by the Freedom of Information Act 2000. This is because once a public authority is obliged by Part VA of the Local Government Act 1972 to communicate information to members of the public on request, that information becomes exempt information and the duty to communicate under the Freedom of Information Act 2000 does not apply.[106] There is, accordingly, no right remaining for s 100H(7) to add to. It should be noted, however, that the Freedom of Information Act 2000 draws a distinction for the purposes of this exemption between information that is required to be made available for inspection (to which the exemption will not apply) and information that is required to be communicated upon request (to which the exemption will apply).

---

the Authority, and (b) any person who is a member of, or a member of staff of, a body which has within the three years prior to the date of the requirement to be imposed under s 61(1) received such a grant. Section 61(5) applies to (a) any person who is an Assembly member, (b) any person who has within the three years prior to the date of the requirement to be imposed under s 61(1) been an Assembly member, and (c) any person who has within the three years prior to the date of the requirement to be imposed under s 61(1) been the Mayor.

[102] Greater London Authority Act 1999 s 61(1)(a).

[103] Greater London Authority Act 1999 s 61(1)(b).

[104] Greater London Authority Act 1999 s 65(1). By s 65(2), in the following provisions of the Local Government Act 1972, for the purpose of s 100B (access to agenda and connected reports) any reference to a report for a meeting includes a reference to any document (other than the agenda) supplied before, and for the purposes of, the evidentiary proceedings (a 'relevant document'). Section 65(3) provides that if a report or relevant document is supplied less than three clear days before the evidentiary proceedings, copies of the report or document shall be open to inspection by the public under sub s 100B(1) from the time such copies are available to Assembly members, notwithstanding anything in sub s.(3) of s 100B. By s 65(4), in s 100C (inspection of minutes and other documents after meetings) (a) any reference to the minutes of a meeting shall be taken to include a reference to a transcript or other record of evidence given in the course of the evidentiary proceedings; and (b) any reference to a report for the meeting includes a reference to a relevant document. Under s 65(5), in s 100D (inspection of background papers) any reference in sub ss.(1) to (4) of that section to background papers for a report (or part of a report) shall be taken as a reference to any additional documents supplied by a witness. 'Additional documents supplied by a witness' is defined in s 65(6) as meaning documents supplied, whether before, during or after the evidentiary proceedings, (a) by a person attending to give evidence at the proceedings, and (b) for the use of Assembly members in connection with the proceedings, but does not include any document which is a relevant document. Section 65(7) provides that for the purposes of s 100F (additional rights of access for members) sub ss.(2) to (4) shall not have effect in relation to documents which contain material relating to any business to be transacted at the evidentiary proceedings. Section 65(8) states that in s 100H (supplemental provisions and offences) in sub s.(6), in the definition of 'accessible documents' (a) the reference in paragraph (d) to a report for the meeting includes a reference to a relevant document; and (b) the reference in paragraph (e) to background papers for a report for a meeting shall be taken as a reference to any additional documents supplied by a witness.

[105] FOIA s 21(1). See §§16– 001 to 16– 005.

[106] By combination of FOIA ss 21(2)(b), 2(2)–(3) and 1(1)–(2), in that order.

8– 023 Local Government Act 1974 – right of access to the Reports of the Local Commissioner

Where a Local Commissioner conducts an investigation, or decides not to conduct an investigation, into a complaint of maladministration, the Local Government Act 1974 requires him to send a report of the results of the investigation, or a statement of his reasons for not conducting an investigation to – amongst others – the authority concerned.[107] Subject to s 30(7) the authority must for a period of three weeks make copies of the report available for inspection by the public without charge at all reasonable hours at one or more of its offices; and any person shall be entitled to take copies of, or extracts from, the report.[108] The authority must supply a copy of the report to any person on request if he pays such charge as the authority may reasonably require.[109] Not later than two weeks after the report is received by the authority, the proper officer of the authority must give public notice, by advertisement in newspapers and other ways as he considers appropriate, that copies of the report will be available and shall specify the date, being a date not more than one week after public notice is first given, from which the period of three weeks will begin.[110] Section 30(7) limits the operation of the section, by providing that the Local Commissioner may, if he thinks fit after taking into account the public interest as well as the interests of the complainant and of persons other than the complainant, direct that a report shall not be made available for inspection or for copying.

8– 024 Local Government, Planning and Land Act 1980

Under s 95 of the Local Government, Planning and Land Act 1980, the Secretary of State may maintain a register of land owned by the public bodies listed in Sch 16 to the Act. The Secretary of State must send to a Council in respect of whose area a register is maintained a copy of that register;[111] and such amendments as may be made to it.[112] A copy of a register sent to a council must be made available at the council's principal office for inspection by any member of the public at all reasonable hours.[113] If any member of the public requires a council to supply him with a copy of any information contained in such a copy of a register, the council must supply him with a copy of that information on payment of such reasonable charge for making it as the council may determine.[114] In addition, Part II of the Act imposes a general duty on local authorities to publish information relating to the discharge of their functions.

---

[107] Local Government Act 1974 s 30(1)(c).

[108] Local Government Act 1974 s 30(4). It is a summary offence for a person having custody of a report made available for inspection to obstruct any person seeking to inspect, or make a copy of, the report: Local Government Act 1974 s 30(6). The offence is punishable on conviction by the imposition of a fine not exceeding level 3 on the standard scale.

[109] Local Government Act 1974 s 30(4A).

[110] Local Government Act 1974 s 30(5).

[111] Local Government, Planning and Land Act 1980 s 96(1)(a).

[112] Local Government, Planning and Land Act 1980 s 96(1)(b).

[113] Local Government, Planning and Land Act 1980 s 96(3).

[114] Local Government, Planning and Land Act 1980 s 96(4).

5 Audit Commission Act 1998

Where an auditor has sent an immediate report[115] to a body (not including a health service body[116]) or its chairman, from the time when the report is received,[117] any member of the public may:

— inspect the report at all reasonable times without payment,[118]

— make a copy of it, or of any part of it,[119] and

— require the body or chairman to supply him with a copy of it, or of any part of it, on payment of a reasonable sum.[120]

In respect of non-immediate reports, the auditor may:

— notify any person he thinks fit of the fact that he has made the report,[121]

— publish the report in any way he thinks fit,[122] and

— supply a copy of the report, or of any part of it, to any person he thinks fit.[123]

When the report is sent by the auditor to the body, the auditor must ensure that any member of the public may inspect the report at all reasonable times without payment,[124] and make a copy of the report or of any part of it.[125] Any member of the public may require the auditor to supply him with a copy of the report, or of any part of it, on payment of a reasonable sum.[126] From the end of the period of one year beginning with the day when the report is sent, the obligations under s 13(3) cease to be the auditor's obligations,[127] but become obligations of the Commission instead.[128] A local government elector for the area of a body subject to audit other than a health service body, may inspect and make copies of any statement of accounts prepared by the body pursuant to regulations under section 27, inspect and make copies of any report, other than an immediate report, made to the body by an auditor; and require copies of any

---

[115] Audit Commission Act 1998, this is defined in s 8 as: 'In auditing accounts required to be audited in accordance with this Act, the auditor shall consider: (a) whether, in the public interest, he should make a report on any matter coming to his notice in the course of the audit, in order for it to be considered by the body concerned or brought to the attention of the public, and (b) whether the public interest requires any such matter to be made the subject of an immediate report rather than of a report to be made at the conclusion of the audit.'

[116] Audit Commission Act 1998 s 13(1).

[117] Audit Commission Act 1998 s 10(1) deals with the transmission and receipt of reports.

[118] Audit Commission Act 1998 s 13(2)(a)

[119] Audit Commission Act 1998 s 13(2)(b). Under s 13(5) a person who has the custody of an immediate report and obstructs a person in the exercise of a right conferred by s 13(2)(a) or (b), or refuses to supply a copy of the report is guilty of an offence and liable on summary conviction to a fine not exceeding level 3 on the standard scale.

[120] Audit Commission Act 1998 s 13(2)(c).

[121] Audit Commission Act 1998 s 13A(2)(a).

[122] Audit Commission Act 1998 s 13A(2)(b).

[123] Audit Commission Act 1998 s 13A(2)(c).

[124] Audit Commission Act 1998 s 13A(3)(a)(i), subject to s 13A(4).

[125] Audit Commission Act 1998 s 13A(3)(a)(ii).

[126] Audit Commission Act 1998 s 13A(3)(b).

[127] Audit Commission Act 1998 s 13A(4)(a).

[128] Audit Commission Act 1998 s 13A(4)(b).

such statement or report to be delivered to him on payment of a reasonable sum for each copy.[129] A local government elector is entitled to inspect a document under the section at all reasonable times and without payment.[130] At each audit under the Act, other than an audit of accounts of a health service body, any persons interested[131] may (a) inspect the accounts to be audited and all books, deeds, contracts, bills, vouchers and receipts relating to them, and (b) make copies of all or any part of the accounts and those other documents.[132]

8–026 **Local Government Finance Acts**

The rating of real property in the United Kingdom is divided between non-domestic rating and domestic rating. Although a local authority is made responsible for the collection of both, in the former case all sums received are paid over to Central Government. In both cases, the regime involves rating lists containing all of the hereditaments (non-domestic or domestic, as the case may be) in the area of the local authority. The lists are amended from time to time to take account of changes in the nature and value of a hereditament. Schedule 9 to the Local Government Finance Act 1988 deals with various aspects relating to the administration of the non-domestic rating system. The non-domestic system provides for three types of lists: non-domestic rating lists; central non-domestic rating lists; and rural settlement lists. Paragraph 8 of Sch 9 confers a right on every person to request a valuation officer[133] or a billing authority[134] to provide him with such information as will enable him to establish the state of the non-domestic rating list. Access to the information must be provided free of charge, but a charge may be imposed for any copying requested. Information as to proposals and amendments to the list may be similarly accessed.[135] The Local Government Finance Act 1992 confers a corresponding right of access to local domestic rating lists. A person may require a listing officer to give him access to such information as will enable him to establish what is the state of a list, or has been its state at any time since it came into force, if the officer is maintaining the list;[136] and the list is in force or has been in force at any time in the preceding five years.[137]

---

[129] Audit Commission Act 1998 s 14(1).

[130] Audit Commission Act 1998 s 14(2).

[131] See *R v Bedwellty UDC, ex p Price* [1934] 1 KB 333 and *R (HTV Ltd) v Bristol City Council* [2004] 1 WLR 2717 which consider the meaning of the phrase 'person interested'.

[132] Audit Commission Act 1998 s 15(1). See *R (Veolia ES Nottinghamshire Ltd) v Nottinghamshire County Council* [2009] EWHC 2382 (Admin), [2010] Env LR 12 which considers the ambit of section 15(1). Section 15(1) does not entitle a person to inspect any accounts or other document which contain personal information as defined by ss 15(3A) or (4). However, apart from this, the right of access conferred by s.15(1) does not provide for any exemptions, eg for confidential information held by the authority.

[133] A valuation officer is a person appointed by the Commissioners of Inland Revenue: Local Government Finance Act 1988 s 61.

[134] Billing authorities are district councils, London borough councils, the Common Council of the City of London and the Council of the Isles of Scilly (in relation to England), and county councils and county borough councils (in relation to Wales): Local Government Finance Act 1992 s 1(2), applied by Local Government Finance Act 1988 s 144(2).

[135] Local Government Finance Act 1988 Sch 9, para 9.

[136] Local Government Finance Act 1992 s 28(1)(a). Section 91, which is materially identical to s 28, applies solely in relation to Scotland.

[137] Local Government Finance Act 1992 s 28(1)(b).

7   The Local Government Act 2000

The Local Government Act 2000 makes provision for access to information held by local authority executives. Section 22(1) of the Local Government Act 2000 provides that meetings of a local authority executive, or a committee of such an executive, are to be open to the public or held in private. It is for a local authority executive to decide which of its meetings, and which of the meetings of any committee of the executive, are to be open to the public and which of those meetings are to be held in private. Written records must be kept of prescribed[138] decisions made at meetings of local authority executives or committees of such executives which are held in private,[139] and of prescribed decisions made by individual members of local authority executives.[140] These written records must include the reasons for the decisions to which they relate.[141] Further, the written records, together with such reports, background papers or other documents as may be prescribed, must be made available to members of the public in accordance with regulations made by the Secretary of State.[142] The regulations made by the Secretary of State are the Local Authorities (Executive Arrangements) (Access to Information) (England) Regulations 2000. These apply to county and district councils in England, and to London borough councils that operate executive arrangements under Part II of the Local Government Act 2000.[143]

8   Executive decisions made at meetings

Under the Local Authorities (Executive Arrangements) (Access to Information) (England) Regulations 2000, as soon as reasonably practicable after a private meeting or a public meeting of a decision-making body at which an executive decision[144] has been made, the proper officer,

---

[138] That is, prescribed by regulations made by the Secretary of State: Local Government Act 2000 s 22(13).

[139] Local Government Act 2000 s 22(3). Executive decisions made by decision-making bodies are prescribed decisions for the purpose of s 22(3) of the Local Government Act 2000: Local Authorities (Executive Arrangements) (Access to Information) (England) Regulations 2000 reg 3(4). A 'decision-making body', in relation to an executive decision, means the executive of a local authority; the committee of a local authority executive; a joint committee, where all members of the joint committee are members of the local authority executive; or a sub-committee of a joint committee where all the members of the joint committee are members of a local authority executive, and which is authorised to discharge the function to which the executive decision relates in accordance with the Local Authorities (Arrangements for the Discharge of Functions) (England) Regulations 2000: Local Authorities (Executive Arrangements) (Access to Information) (England) Regulations 2000 reg 2.

[140] Local Government Act 2000 s 22(4). Executive decisions made by individual members of local authority executives are prescribed decisions for the purposes of s 22(4) of the Local Government Act 2000: Local Authorities (Executive Arrangements) (Access to Information) (England) Regulations 2000 reg 4(3).

[141] Local Government Act 2000 s 22(5).

[142] The Local Government Act 2000 s 22(7) provides that regulations made under s 22(6) may make provision for or in connection with preventing the whole or part of any record or document containing prescribed information from being made available to members of the public. Further powers to make regulations in connection with local authority executive meetings are conferred on the Secretary of State by s 22(8), (9), (1), (11) and (12) of the Local Government Act 2000.

[143] For Wales, see Local Authorities (Executive Arrangements) (Decisions, Documents and Meetings) (Wales) Regulations 2001.

[144] Namely, a decision made or to be made, by a decision-maker, in connection with the discharge of a function which is the responsibility of the executive of a local authority: Local Authorities (Executive Arrangements) (Access to Information) (England) Regulations 2000 reg 2.

or in the event that the proper officer is not present at the meeting, the person presiding,[145] must ensure that a written statement is produced in respect of every executive decision made at that meeting.[146] This written statement must include the following information:

— a record of the decision;
— a record of the reasons for the decision;
— details of any alternative options considered and rejected by the decision-making body at the meeting at which the decision was made;
— a record of any conflict of interest in relation to the matter decided which is declared by any member of the decision-making body which made the decision; and
— in respect of any declared conflict of interest, a note of any dispensation granted by the local authority's standards committee.[147]

8– 029   Executive decisions made by individuals

Similar provisions apply in respect of executive decisions made by individual members of local authority executives,[148] as well as in respect of 'key decisions' made by officers.[149] A key decision is an executive decision which is likely to result in the local authority incurring expenditure which is, or the making of savings which are, significant having regard to the local authority's budget for the service or function to which the decision relates, or to be significant in terms of its effects on communities living or working in an area comprising two or more wards or electoral divisions in the area of the local authority.[150]

8– 030   Inspection of documents following executive decisions

After a private meeting or a public meeting of a decision-making body at which an executive decision has been made, after an individual member has made an executive decision, or after an officer has made a key decision, the proper officer is required to ensure that a copy of any records prepared in accordance with regs 3 or 4, or of any report considered at the meeting or, as the case may be, considered by the individual member or officer and relevant to a decision recorded in accordance with reg 3 or 4, or of that part, where only a part of the report is relevant to such a decision, shall be available for inspection by members of the public, as soon as is reasonably practicable, at the offices of the relevant local authority.[151] Where a request on behalf of a newspaper is made for a copy of any of the documents available for public inspection under reg 5(1), those documents must be supplied for the benefit of the newspaper by the local authority on payment by the newspaper to the local authority of postage, copying or other

---

[145] Namely, the person actually presiding, or the person nominated to preside at the meeting: Local Authorities (Executive Arrangements) (Access to Information) (England) Regulations 2000 reg 3(3).

[146] Local Authorities (Executive Arrangements) (Access to Information) (England) Regulations 2000 reg 3(1).

[147] Local Authorities (Executive Arrangements) (Access to Information) (England) Regulations 2000 reg 3(2).

[148] Local Authorities (Executive Arrangements) (Access to Information) (England) Regulations 2000 reg 4.

[149] Local Authorities (Executive Arrangements) (Access to Information) (England) Regulations 2000 reg 4(4).

[150] Local Authorities (Executive Arrangements) (Access to Information) (England) Regulations 2000, regs 2 and 8(1). Regulation 8(2) further provides that, in accordance with s 38 of the Local Government Act 2000, in determining the meaning of 'significant' for the purposes of reg 8(1), regard shall be had to any guidance issued for the time being by the Secretary of State.

[151] Local Authorities (Executive Arrangements) (Access to Information) (England) Regulations 2000 reg 5(1).

necessary charge for transmission.[152] When a copy of the whole or part of a report for a private or a public meeting is made available for inspection by members of the public in accordance with reg 5, at the same time a copy of the list compiled by the proper officer of the background papers to the report or part of the report must be included in the report or part of the report, and at least one copy of each of the documents included in that list must be made available for inspection by the public at the offices of the relevant local authority.[153] The above requirements are subject to certain provisions concerning confidential information, exempt information and advice given by political advisers or assistants.[154]

31 **Meetings to be held in public**
Where the executive leader, a s 11(2) mayor,[155] a council manager, or any other person likely to preside at a meeting[156] of a decision-making body, reasonably believes:

— that a decision to be made at that meeting will be a key decision;[157] or

— that a matter that is included in the forward plan[158] or is the subject of a notice given under reg 15 is likely to be discussed at the meeting, and the decision on that matter is likely to be made within 28 days, and an officer who is not a political adviser, assistant or council manager will be present at the discussion,[159]

the meeting (or that part of it) must be held in public.[160] This requirement is also subject to certain provisions concerning confidential information, exempt information and advice given by political advisers or assistants.[161]

---

[152] Local Authorities (Executive Arrangements) (Access to Information) (England) Regulations 2000 reg 5(2).

[153] Local Authorities (Executive Arrangements) (Access to Information) (England) Regulations 2000 reg 6.

[154] Local Authorities (Executive Arrangements) (Access to Information) (England) Regulations 2000 reg 21. See §8–032.

[155] Namely an elected mayor who is a member of a mayor-and-cabinet executive: Local Authorities (Executive Arrangements) (Access to Information) (England) Regulations 2000 reg 2.

[156] For the purposes of reg 7(1), 'meeting' does not include a meeting to which the circumstances specified in reg 7(2)(b) apply and the principal purpose of which is for an officer of the local authority to brief a decision-maker on matters connected with the making of an executive decision: Local Authorities (Executive Arrangements) (Access to Information) (England) Regulations 2000 reg 7(2A).

[157] Local Authorities (Executive Arrangements) (Access to Information) (England) Regulations 2000 reg 7(2)(a). A 'key decision' is defined by reg 8(1) of the Local Authorities (Executive Arrangements) (Access to Information) (England) Regulations 2000 as an executive decision which, is likely (a) to result in the local authority incurring expenditure which is, or the making of savings which are, significant having regard to the local authority's budget for the service or function to which the decision relates; or (b) to be significant in terms of its effects on communities living or working in an area comprising two or more wards or electoral divisions in the area of the local authority. The steps that must be taken to publicise key decisions are set out in reg 12. The steps that must be taken in relation to key decisions taken by individual executive members or officers are set out in reg 9. The procedure to be followed prior to public meetings generally is set out in reg 10.

[158] Forward plans are required to contain details of all the matters likely to be the subject of key decisions, and must be prepared in accordance with regs 13 and 14 of the Local Authorities (Executive Arrangements) (Access to Information) (England) Regulations 2000: Local Authorities (Executive Arrangements) (Access to Information) (England) Regulations 2000 reg 13(1).

[159] Local Authorities (Executive Arrangements) (Access to Information) (England) Regulations 2000 reg 7(2)(b).

[160] Local Authorities (Executive Arrangements) (Access to Information) (England) Regulations 2000 reg 7(1)).

[161] Local Authorities (Executive Arrangements) (Access to Information) (England) Regulations 2000 reg 21. See §8–032.

8–032   Confidential information, exempt information, and advice

The public may be excluded from a meeting of a decision-making body that is exercising an executive function where it is likely, in view of the nature of the business to be transacted or of the nature of the proceedings, that if members of the public were present during the transaction of an item of business:

— confidential information would be disclosed to them in breach of the obligation of confidence;[162]

— a resolution has been passed by the decision-making body concerned excluding the public during the transaction of an item of business where it is likely, in view of the nature of the item of business, that if members of the public were present during the transaction of that item, exempt information would be disclosed to them;[163]

— a resolution has been passed by the decision-making body concerned excluding the public during the transaction of an item of business where it is likely, in view of the nature of the item, that if members of the public were present during the transaction of that item, the advice of a political adviser or assistant would be disclosed to them;[164] or

— a lawful power is used to exclude a member or members of the public in order to maintain orderly conduct or to prevent misbehaviour at a meeting.[165]

An exclusion of the public on any of the first three of the above-mentioned bases may apply only to the part or parts of the meeting during which it is likely that confidential information, exempt information, or the advice of a political adviser or political assistant would be disclosed.[166] A local authority is not authorised by the Regulations to disclose to the public or make available for public inspection any document or part of a document if, in the opinion of the proper officer, that document or part of a document:

— contains or may contain confidential information;

— contains or is likely to contain exempt information or the advice of a political adviser or assistant.[167]

8–033   Access to agenda and connected reports

Copies of the agenda and every report for a public meeting must be available for inspection by the public at the offices of the local authority when they are made available to the members of the executive or decision-making body responsible for making the decision to which they

---

[162] Local Authorities (Executive Arrangements) (Access to Information) (England) Regulations 2000 reg 21(1)(a).

[163] Local Authorities (Executive Arrangements) (Access to Information) (England) Regulations 2000 reg 21(1)(b). A resolution under reg 21(1)(b) must identify the proceedings or part of the proceedings to which it applies, and state by reference to the descriptions in Sch 12A to the Local Government Act 1972 the description of exempt information giving rise to the exclusion of the public: Local Authorities (Executive Arrangements) (Access to Information) (England) Regulations 2000 reg 21(2).

[164] Local Authorities (Executive Arrangements) (Access to Information) (England) Regulations 2000 reg 21(1)(c).

[165] Local Authorities (Executive Arrangements) (Access to Information) (England) Regulations 2000 reg 21(1)(d).

[166] Local Authorities (Executive Arrangements) (Access to Information) (England) Regulations 2000 reg 21(3).

[167] Local Authorities (Executive Arrangements) (Access to Information) (England) Regulations 2000 reg 21(5) makes similar provision in respect of documents relating to executive decisions made in accordance with executive arrangements made by members of local authority executives and officers.

relate.[168] The proper officer is empowered to have excluded from the copy of any report the whole, or any part, of the report which relates only to the transaction of any item of business during which, in his opinion, the meeting is not likely to be open to the public.[169] Any document which is required to be available for inspection by the public must be available for inspection for at least five clear days before the meeting, except that, when the meeting is convened at shorter notice,[170] a copy of the agenda and associated reports must be available for inspection at the time when the meeting is convened; and, where an item which would be available for inspection by the public is added to the agenda, a copy of the revised agenda, and of any report relating to the item for consideration at the meeting, must be available for inspection by the public when the item is added to the agenda.[171] The local authority must, except during any part of a public meeting from which the public are excluded, make available for the use of members of the public present at the meeting a reasonable number of copies of the agenda and reports for the meeting.[172] In addition, local authorities must, following any request on behalf of a newspaper and on payment being made of postage charges or other necessary charge for transmission, supply to the newspaper a copy of the agenda for the public meeting and a copy of each of the reports for consideration at the meeting; such further statements or particulars, if any, as are necessary to indicate the nature of the items contained in the agenda; and, if the proper officer thinks fit in the case of any item, a copy of any other document supplied to members of the executive in connection with the item.[173]

34 **Additional rights of members of the local authority and of members of overview and scrutiny committees**

Under reg 17 of the Local Authorities (Executive Arrangements) (Access to Information) (England) Regulations 2000, any document which is in the possession, or under the control, of

---

[168] Local Authorities (Executive Arrangements) (Access to Information) (England) Regulations 2000 reg 11(1).

[169] Local Authorities (Executive Arrangements) (Access to Information) (England) Regulations 2000 reg 11(2). Where, by virtue of reg 11(2), the whole or any part of a report for a public meeting is not available for inspection by the public, every copy of the whole report, or the part of the report, as the case may be, must be marked 'not for publication'. Moreover, there must be stated on every copy of the whole or part of the report either that it contains confidential information; or exempt information and, by reference to the descriptions in Sch 12A to the Local Government Act 1972, the description of the exempt information by virtue of which the decision-making body discharging the executive function is likely to exclude the public during the item to which the report relates; or that the report, or a part of the report, contains the advice of a political adviser or assistant as the case may be: Local Authorities (Executive Arrangements) (Access to Information) (England) Regulations 2000 reg 11(5).

[170] In accordance with reg 15 or 16 of the Local Authorities (Executive Arrangements) (Access to Information) (England) Regulations 2000: Local Authorities (Executive Arrangements) (Access to Information) (England) Regulations 2000 regs 10 and 11(3)(a).

[171] Local Authorities (Executive Arrangements) (Access to Information) (England) Regulations 2000 reg 11(3). Regulation 11(3) is subject to reg 11(4), which provides that nothing in reg 11(3) shall require a copy of the agenda, item or report to be available for inspection by the public until a copy is available to members of the decision-making body concerned.

[172] Local Authorities (Executive Arrangements) (Access to Information) (England) Regulations 2000 reg 11(6).

[173] Subject to Local Authorities (Executive Arrangements) (Access to Information) (England) Regulations 2000 reg 21, as to which see §8– 032. The Local Authorities (Executive Arrangements) (Access to Information) (England) Regulations 2000 also contain provisions concerning times for inspection, payment and copying of documents, and provisions concerning offences involving the withholding of information, similar to those that are to be found in the Local Government Act 1972, see reg 22. Regulation 23 provides that it is a summary offence to obstruct any rights of access within the regulations, punishable by a level 1 fine.

the executive of a local authority, and contains material relating to any business to be transacted at a public meeting, must be available for inspection by any member of the local authority.[174] That member also has limited rights to information relating to any business transacted at a private meeting, any decision made by an individual member in accordance with executive arrangements and any key decision made by an officer in accordance with executive arrangements. These requirements do not apply where it appears to the proper officer that the document would disclose exempt information of a description falling within Part 1 of Sch 12A to the 1972 Act.[175]

8–035 Representation of the People Act 1983

Under the Representation of the People Act 1983 a person can, for a limited time after an election, request to be supplied with certain electoral documents, including a copy of the marked copies of the register, the postal voters list, the list of proxies and the proxy postal voters list. In the case of a parliamentary election, the Clerk of the Crown must retain for a year all documents relating to a parliamentary election that have been forwarded to him by a returning officer.[176] These documents, with the exception of ballot papers, counterfoils and certificates as to employment on duty on the day of the poll, are open to inspection by a member of the public, and a copy must be provided on request and payment of a prescribed fee.[177] Similar provisions exist in relation to papers produced in connection with European parliament elections,[178] local government elections,[179] Greater London Authority elections,[180] regional assembly elections and referenda.[181]

2. HEALTH, MEDICAL AND CARE RECORDS

8–036 Introduction

Rights of access to medical information are to be found in various legislative provisions. The nature of the information is such that ordinarily the person seeking the information will be the subject of that information. To the extent that medical information held by a public authority relating to the applicant is 'data' that are 'processed' (which includes information that is held)

---

[174] Local Authorities (Executive Arrangements) (Access to Information) (England) Regulations 2000 reg 17(1).

[175] Local Authorities (Executive Arrangements) (Access to Information) (England) Regulations 2000 reg 17(3).

[176] Representation of the People Act 1983 Sch 1 para 57(1). A returning officer is required to forward all such papers to the Clerk of the Crown upon completion of the counting. The papers that he is required to send are listed in para 55(1).

[177] Representation of the People Act 1983 Sch 1 para 57.

[178] European Parliamentary Elections Rules 2004 Sch 1 para 61.

[179] Local Elections (Principal Areas) (England and Wales) Rules 2006 Sch 2, para 53 and Sch 3 para 53; Local Elections (Parishes and Communities) Rules 2006 Sch 2 para 53 and Sch 3 para 53. An order must be obtained in relation to local government election documents.

[180] Greater London Authority Elections Rules 2004 Sch 1 para 50; Sch 2 para 53; Sch 3 para 55.

[181] Regional Assembly and Local Government Referendums Order 2004, Sch 1 para 65.

the usual avenue of disclosure will be by request made under the Data Protection Act 1998.[182]

37 Access to Health Records Act 1990

The Access to Health Records Act 1990 provided a right of access to 'manual health records'. This was largely repealed by the Data Protection Act 1998, the scope of which extended to information caught by the 1990 Act.[183] The 1990 Act now applies only to applications for access to records by the personal representative of a patient who has died or by a person who might have a claim arising out of the patient's death.[184] Such a person is not a data subject, and so falls outside the Data Protection Act 1998. Access to the health records of a patient who has died is provided by the Access to Health Records Act 1990.[185] The right of access is given to the personal representative of the patient and to any person who may have a claim arising out of the patient's death.[186] The right is also to be extended to a medical examiner stating or investigating the cause of the patient's death under section 20 of the Coroners and Justice Act 2009.[187] The right of access is subject to several exemptions:

(1)   Where the health record was made before 1 November 1991;[188]

(2)   Where disclosure would, in the opinion of the holder of the record, be likely to cause serious harm to the physical or mental health of any individual;[189]

(3)   Where the record contains information relating to or provided by an individual, other than the patient, who could be identified from the information;[190]

(4)   Where, in the opinion of the holder of the record, the patient expected that the information would not be disclosed to the applicant.[191]

Where the health record is to be disclosed, but information therein is expressed in terms which are unintelligible without explanation, an explanation of terms must be supplied.[192] Refusal to provide the health record is subject to appeal to the High Court or a county court.[193]

---

[182] See ch 5.

[183] See ch 5.

[184] Access to Health Records Act 1990 s 3(1)(f).

[185] See further IC Guidance Data Protection - Subject Access Request to Health Records (13 November 2001).

[186] Access to Health Records Act 1990 s 3(1)(f). Access is restricted to information which, in the opinion of the holder of the record, is relevant to any claim which may arise out of the patient's death: s 5(4).

[187] Inserted by the Coroners and Justice Act 2009 s 177(1) Sch 21 Pt 1 para 29(1). The date on which this is to come into force is yet to be appointed: see the Coroners and Justice Act 2009 s 182(4)(e).

[188] Except insofar as the information therein is required to make sense of a later disclosed record, Access to Health Records Act 1990 s 5(1)(b).

[189] Access to Health Records Act 1990 s 5(1)(a)(i).

[190] Access to Health Records Act 1990 s 5(1)(a)(ii). This provision does not apply where the individual concerned has consented to the application, or where that individual is a health professional who has been involved in the care of the patient: s 5(2)(a)-(b).

[191] Access to Health Records Act 1990 s 5(3)(a)-(b).

[192] Access to Health Records Act 1990 s 3(3).

[193] Access to Health Records Act 1990 s 8.

8– 038 **Rights of access to information concerning Community Health Councils**
Subject to certain modifications, ss 100A to 100D of the Local Government Act 1972 also apply to Community Health Councils as they apply to principal councils.[194] There are further provisions for access to information relating to members of Community Health Councils and to the right of members of the public to attend meetings of Community Health Councils and community health committees, and to inspect and copy and be furnished with documents relating to such Councils and committees.[195]

8– 039 **Rights of access to medical reports under the Access to Medical Reports Act 1988**
An individual has a right of access to any medical report relating to him which is to be or has been supplied by a medical practitioner for employment or insurance purposes.[196] In addition, medical practitioners have a duty to retain a copy of any medical report which they have supplied for employment or insurance purposes for at least six months from the date when it was supplied.[197] A medical practitioner, if so requested, must give an individual access to any medical report relating to him which the practitioner has supplied for employment or insurance purposes in the previous six months.[198]

8– 040 **Access to the register of NHS Foundation Trusts**
The Independent Regulator of NHS Foundation Trusts must maintain a register of NHS foundation trusts.[199] The register must contain in relation to each NHS foundation trust:
  (1)   a copy of the current constitution,
  (2)   a copy of the current authorisation,[200]
  (3)   a copy of the latest annual accounts and of any report of the auditor on them,
  (4)   a copy of the latest annual report,
  (5)   a copy of the latest document sent to the regulator under para 27 of Sch 7 to the National Health Act 2006 (forward planning), and
  (6)   a copy of any notice given under s 52 of the 2006 Act (failing NHS foundation trusts).[201]
Members of the public may inspect the register at any reasonable time.[202] Any person who requests it must be provided with a copy of, or extract from, any document contained in the

---

[194] §§8– 005 to 8– 019.

[195] Community Health Councils (Access to Information Act) 1988 s 2.

[196] Access to Medical Reports Act 1988 s 1.

[197] Access to Medical Reports Act 1988 s 6(1).

[198] Access to Medical Reports Act 1988 s 6(2). By s 6(3), the reference in s 6(2) to giving an individual access to a medical report is a reference to making a copy of the report available for his inspection, or supplying him with a copy of it.

[199] National Health Service Act 2006 s 39(1).

[200] As defined in National Health Service Act 2006 s 65.

[201] National Health Act 2006 s 39(2).

[202] National Health Act 2006 s 39(4).

register on payment of a reasonable charge.[203]

41   Access to information pertaining to the Children and Family Court Advisory and Support Service

Minutes of the meetings of the Children and Family Court Advisory and Support Service are to be taken of the proceedings of each meeting of the Service.[204] The minutes are to be open to public inspection in such manner as the Service shall decide, save where the minutes relate to:

(a)   officers or employees of the Service;

(b)   the remuneration of officers or employees of the Service;

(c)   individual cases;

(d)   matters which the Service considers to be commercially confidential or sensitive; or

(e)   legal advice obtained by the Service.[205]

3.   PLANNING, ENVIRONMENTAL, PUBLIC HEALTH AND SAFETY INFORMATION

42   Introduction

Although the Environmental Information Regulations 2004 are the main instrument for obtaining access to 'environmental information',[206] there remain in place a series of provisions giving access to specific sorts of similar information. While the Environmental Information Regulations 2004 will often provide the readiest means of obtaining access to all such information, these more specific regimes generally have fewer exemptions and more limited scope for charging for provision of the information. In summary, the regimes are those provided by:

(1)   s 86 of the National Parks and Access to the Countryside Act 1949;

(2)   the Control of Pollution Act 1974;

(3)   the Food and Environmental Protection Act 1985;

(4)   the Environment and Safety Information Act 1988;

(5)   the Environmental Protection Act 1990;

(6)   the Town and Country Planning Act 1990;

(7)   the Planning (Hazardous Substances) Act 1990; and

(8)   Sch 11 to the Environment Act 1995.

In addition to these, there are other provisions that provide for a right of access to specific planning information.

---

[203] National Health Service Act 2006 s 39(5).

[204] Children and Family Court Advisory and Support Service (Membership, Committee and Procedure) Regulations 2005 reg 21(1).

[205] Children and Family Court Advisory and Support Service (Membership, Committee and Procedure) Regulations 2005 reg 21(2).

[206] As to the meaning of which, see §6–010.

8– 043   **The Control of Pollution Act 1974**

Every local authority which has designated its area or any part of its area a noise abatement zone has to measure the level of noise emanating from premises within the zone which are of any class to which the relevant noise abatement order relates.[207] The measurements must be recorded in a 'noise level register', which is to be kept by the local authority for the purpose in accordance with regulations.[208] The register is open to public inspection at the principal office of the local authority free of charge at all reasonable hours, and the local authority must afford members of the public reasonable facilities for obtaining from the authority, on payment of reasonable charges, copies of entries in the register.[209]

8– 044   **The Food and Environment Protection Act 1985**

In order to ensure that food is not rendered unfit for human consumption by virtue of deposits into the sea, before any such deposit can be made, a licence is required. It is the duty of each licensing authority to maintain a register containing prescribed[210] particulars of or relating to:

   (a)   applications for licences made to that authority;

   (b)   the licences issued by that authority;

   (c)   variations of licences effected by that authority;

   (d)   revocations of licences effected by that authority;

   (e)   convictions for any offences under s 9;

   (f)   information obtained or furnished in pursuance of s 8(3), (4) or (5) of the Food and Environment Protection Act 1985;

   (g)   the occasions on which either of the responsible Ministers has carried out any operation under s 10 of the Food and Environment Protection Act 1985; and

   (h)   such other matters relating to operations for which licences are needed under Part II of the Act as may be prescribed.[211]

No information shall be included in any register which, in the opinion of either of the Ministers, is such that its disclosure on the register would be contrary to the interests of national security,[212] or would prejudice to an unreasonable degree some person's commercial interests.[213] A licensing authority is under a duty to secure that the register maintained by the authority is available, at all reasonable times, for inspection by the public free of charge;[214] and to afford to members of the public facilities for obtaining copies of entries, on payment of reasonable

---

[207] Control of Pollution Act 1974 s 64(1).

[208] Control of Pollution Act 1974 s 64(2).

[209] Control of Pollution Act 1974 s 64(7).

[210] 'Prescribed' means prescribed in regulations: Food and Environment Protection Act 1985 s 14(7). See, eg, Deposits in the Sea (Public Registers of Information) Regulations 1996.

[211] Food and Environment Protection Act 1985 s 14(1).

[212] Food and Environment Protection Act 1985 s 14(2)(a).

[213] Food and Environment Protection Act 1985 s 14(2)(b).

[214] Food and Environment Protection Act 1985 s 14(5)(a).

charges.[215] Registers may be kept in any form.[216]

45   The Environment and Safety Information Act 1988

The right of access to information conferred by this Act is limited. It requires certain authorities to keep a register of certain notices served by the authority, to ensure that the register is indexed and to ensure that the register and the index are open to inspection by the public free of charge at all reasonable hours.[217] On request, and upon payment of any reasonable fee as the authority may require, a person inspecting the register can require the authority to provide him with a copy of the entry in the register.[218] The only authorities to which the Act applies and the only notices to which the Act applies are:

(1)   notices issued by a fire authority[219] under arts 29-31 of the Regulatory Reform (Fire Safety) Order 2005;

(2)   notices issued by an enforcing authority[220] under ss 21 and 22 of the Health and Safety at Work etc Act 1974;

(3)   notices issued by a local authority[221] under s 10 of the Safety of Sports Grounds Act 1975; and

(4)   notices issued by the responsible authority[222] under ss 19(5) and 19(6) of the Food and Environment Protection Act 1985.

An exemption is provided where an entry would disclose a trade secret, but the provision requires the person upon whom the notice has been served to claim this exemption within 14 days of service.[223]

46   The Town and Country Planning Act 1990

Every local planning authority is required to keep a register containing prescribed information with respect to applications for planning permission.[224] The register must contain information

---

[215] Food and Environment Protection Act 1985 s 14(5)(b).

[216] Food and Environment Protection Act 1985 s 14(6).

[217] Environment and Safety Information Act 1988 s 1(1). The register can be kept on a computer: s 1(4).

[218] Environment and Safety Information Act 1988 s 1(1)(d). The authority can require the payment of a reasonable fee: presumably the cost of photocopying the page in the register.

[219] As defined in the Regulatory Reform (Fire Safety) Order 2005 art 25.

[220] As defined in the Health and Safety at Work etc Act 1974 s 18(7)(a).

[221] As defined in the Safety of Sports Grounds Act 1975 s 17(1).

[222] As defined in the Food and Environment Protection Act 1985 s 2(2).

[223] Environment and Safety Information Act 1988 s 4(1). As to trade secrets, see §§25– 049 to 25– 056.

[224] The Town and Country Planning Act 1990 s 69(1). This section has been substituted by the Planning and Compulsory Purchase Act 2004 s 118(1), Sch 6, paras 1, 3, for the purpose of making, or making provision by means of, subordinate legislation, and amended by the Planning Act 2008 s 190(4), for the purposes of applications for non-material changes to planning permission under s 96A of the 1990 Act. However, this latter amendment only comes into force on 6 April 2010 – see Planning Act 2008 (Commencement No 5 and Saving) Order 2010 art 3(b). Hence, as amended s 69(1) provides that the local planning authority must keep a register containing such information as is prescribed as to (a) applications for planning permission; (aa) applications for non-material changes to planning permission under s 96A; (b) requests for statements of development principles (within the meaning of s 61E); (c) local development orders; (d) simplified planning zone schemes. Under s 69(2) as amended the register must contain (a) information as to the manner in which applications mentioned in subs (1)(a) and (aa) and requests mentioned in subs.(1)(b) have been dealt with; (b) such information as is prescribed with respect to any local development order

as to the manner in which planning applications have been dealt with,[225] together with the type of information prescribed by a development order.[226] The register must be available for inspection by the public at all reasonable hours.[227] Each local planning register authority[228] is also required to keep, in two parts, a register of every application for planning permission relating to its area.[229] A third part is also required to deal with local development orders.[230] The register must contain information in respect of every application for a certificate of lawfulness of existing or proposed use or development made under s 191 or 192 of the Town and Country Planning Act 1990.[231] The register also has to record information about simplified planning zone schemes.[232] To enable any person to trace any entry in the register, every register includes an index together with a separate index of applications for development involving mining operations or the creation of mineral working deposits.[233] The local planning register authority is also required to keep a register under s 188 of the 1990 Act containing information with respect to enforcement notices and stop notices,[234] and breach of condition notices.[235] The register must include an index for enabling a person to trace any entry in the register by reference to the address of the land to which the notice relates.[236]

8–047   Planning (Hazardous Substances) Act 1990

Every hazardous substances authority must keep a register containing such information as may

---

or simplified planning zone scheme in relation to the authority's area. Section 69(4) states that each part of the development order must contain such information as is prescribed relating to the matters mentioned in subs (1)(a), (aa) and (b). Section 69(8) provides that the register must be kept available for inspection by the public at all reasonable hours.

[225] Town and Country Planning Act 1990 s 69(2)(a).

[226] Town and Country Planning Act 1990 s 69(2)(b).

[227] Town and Country Planning Act 1990 s 69(8).

[228] Town and Country Planning (General Development Procedure) Order 1995 art 25(1) provides that for the purposes of arts 25, 25A and 26 'the local planning register authority' means (a) in Greater London or a metropolitan county [or in Wales], the local planning authority (and references to the area of the local planning register authority are, in this case, to the area of the local planning authority); (b) in relation to land in a National Park (except in a metropolitan county [or in Wales]), the county planning authority (and references to the area of the local planning register authority are, in this case, to the area of the county planning authority within a National Park); (c) in relation to any other land, the district planning authority (and references to the area of the local planning register authority are, in this case, to the area of the district planning authority, other than any part of its area falling within a National Park).

[229] Town and Country Planning (General Development Procedure) Order 1995 art 25(2). Article 25(3) sets out in detail the contents of Pt I of the register, and art 25(4) deals with Pt II.

[230] Town and Country Planning (General Development Procedure) Order 1995 art 25A(1). Article 25A(2) sets out the contents of that Part.

[231] Town and Country Planning (General Development Procedure) Order 1995 art 25(6), specifies the required information.

[232] Town and Country Planning (General Development Procedure) Order 1995 art 25(7), sets out the required information.

[233] Town and Country Planning (General Development Procedure) Order 1995 art 25(8).

[234] Town and Country Planning (General Development Procedure) Order 1995 art 26(1).

[235] Town and Country Planning (General Development Procedure) Order 1995 art 26(1).

[236] Town and Country Planning (General Development Procedure) Order 1995 art 26(4).

be prescribed with respect to applications for hazardous substances consent made to that authority;[237] to applications under s 17(1) of the Act made to that authority;[238] to hazardous substances consent having effect by virtue of ss 11 or 12 with respect to land for which that authority is the hazardous substances authority;[239] to revocations or modifications of hazardous substances consent granted with respect to such land;[240] and to directions under s 27 sent to the authority by the Secretary of State.[241] Every such register is available for inspection by the public at all reasonable hours.[242]

8.48 Environmental Protection Act 1990

The Environmental Protection Act 1990 makes detailed provision for public registers containing a variety of information. The information required to be recorded is information relating to:

— contaminated land;[243]
— litter;[244]
— genetically modified organisms;[245]
— stray dogs.[246]

In respect of all registers:

— Information is excluded from being in the register if in the opinion of the Secretary of State it would be contrary to the interests of national security.[247]
— No information relating to the affairs of any individual or business shall be included in a register maintained under the Environmental Protection Act 1990, without the consent of that individual or the person for the time being carrying on that business, if and so long as the information is, in relation to him, commercially confidential.[248]
— It is the duty of each enforcing authority to secure that the registers maintained by them under the section are available, at all reasonable times, for inspection by the public free of charge;[249] and to afford to members of the public facilities for obtaining copies of entries, on payment of reasonable charges[250] and places may be prescribed by the Secretary of State at which any such registers or facilities are to

---

[237] Planning (Hazardous Substances) Act 1990 s 28(1)(a).

[238] Planning (Hazardous Substances) Act 1990 s 28(1)(aa).

[239] Planning (Hazardous Substances) Act 1990 s 28(1)(b).

[240] Planning (Hazardous Substances) Act 1990 s 28(1)(c).

[241] Planning (Hazardous Substances) Act 1990 s 28(1)(d).

[242] Planning (Hazardous Substances) Act 1990 s 28(3).

[243] Environmental Protection Act 1990 s 78R.

[244] Environmental Protection Act 1990 s 95.

[245] Environmental Protection Act 1990 s 122.

[246] Environmental Protection Act 1990 s 149(8).

[247] Environmental Protection Act 1990 ss 21(1), 78S and 123(1).

[248] Environmental Protection Act 1990 ss 22(1)(a), 78T(1)(a) and 123(3)(a).

[249] Environmental Protection Act 1990 ss 20(7)(a), 78R(8)(a), 95(4)(a), 122(2)(a), and 149(8).

[250] Environmental Protection Act 1990 ss 20(7)(b), 78R(8)(b), 95(4)(b) and 122(2)(b).

be available or afforded to the public in pursuance of the paragraph in question. Registers under the section may be kept in any form.[251]

8–049 Water Industry Act 1991

Various registers under Part II of the Water Industry Act 1991 must be maintained. The contents of the register must be available for inspection by the public at such times, and subject to the payment of such charges, as may be specified in an order made by the Secretary of State.[252] Any person may, on the payment of such fee as may be specified in an order so made, require the Authority to supply him with a copy of, or extract from, the contents of any part of the register, being a copy or extract which is certified by the Authority to be a true copy or extract.[253] Public registers must also be maintained by sewage undertakers and water undertakers. Registers must also be kept under the Water Resources Act 1991.[254]

8–050 Coal Mining Subsidence Act 1991

Where it is proposed to carry on any underground coal-mining operations, notice must be given of the operations to any local authority whose area includes land which may be affected by subsidence as a result of the operations.[255] Each local authority must ensure that copies of all notices and other information received by them under this section are made available, at all reasonable times, for inspection by the public free of charge;[256] and provide facilities for obtaining copies of such documents on payment of a reasonable fee.[257]

8–051 Waste and Emissions Trading Act 2003

Where the waste authorities for a two-tier area prepare a statement setting out their strategy for dealing with household waste, and waste similar to household waste, each of the authorities must keep a copy of the statement available at all reasonable times at one of its offices for inspection by the public free of charge;[258] and each of the authorities must supply a copy of the statement to any person who requests one, on payment by the person of such reasonable charge as the authority requires.[259]

---

[251] Environmental Protection Act 1990 ss 20(8), 78R(9), 95(5) and s 122(3).

[252] Water Industry Act 1991 s 195(4).

[253] Water Industry Act 1991 s 195(5).

[254] Water Resources Act 1991 s 189.

[255] Coal Mining Subsidence Act 1991 s 47(1).

[256] Coal Mining Subsidence Act 1991 s 47(5)(a).

[257] Coal Mining Subsidence Act 1991 s 47(5)(b).

[258] Waste and Emissions Trading Act 2003 s 32(7)(c).

[259] Waste and Emissions Trading Act 2003 s 32(7)(d).

4. LAND INFORMATION

52 Caravan Sites and Control of Development Act 1960

Every local authority must keep a register of site licences[260] issued in respect of land situated in their area. This register must be kept open for inspection at all reasonable times.[261]

53 Commons Registration Act 1965

Every registration authority[262] must keep a register of common land and a register of town or village greens.[263] The register must be kept open for inspection by the public at all reasonable times.[264]

54 Local Government, Planning and Land Act 1980

Section 96 of the Local Government, Planning and Land Act 1980 provides for registers of land holdings compiled and maintained under s 95 of that Act to be accessible by the public. In very general terms, the aim of the register is to list land holdings of local government bodies which, in the opinion of the Secretary of State, are being underutilised and to make that list open to the public. Under s 95(1), the Secretary of State is empowered to compile and maintain a register of land which satisfies certain conditions.[265] These conditions are:

— that a freehold or leasehold interest in the land is owned by a body to which Part X of the Act applies or a subsidiary of that body;[266]

— that it is situated in an area in relation to which Part X of the Act is in operation,[267]

---

[260] A 'site licence' is a licence issued under Pt I of the 1960 Act authorising the use of land as a caravan site for the time being in force as respects the land so used, Caravan Sites and Control of Development Act 1960 s 1(1). A 'caravan site' is defined as land on which a caravan is stationed for the purposes of human habitation and land which is used in conjunction with land on which a caravan is so stationed: Caravan Sites and Control of Development Act 1960 s 1(4).

[261] Caravan Sites and Control of Development Act 1960 s 25(1).

[262] The registration authority for the purposes of this Act is, in relation to any land situated in any county, the council of that county, and in relation to any land situated in Greater London, the council of the London borough in which the land is situated: Commons Registration Act 1965 s 2.

[263] Commons Registration Act 1965 s 3(1). The definitions of common land, and town and village greens are given in s 22(1) of 1965 Act.

[264] Commons Registration Act 1965 s 3(2). These provisions will be repealed on the appointment of the Commons Act 2006 s 53 and Sch 6 Pt I. The Commons Act 2006 places a duty on a commons registration authority to keep a register known as a register of common land, and a register known as a register of town or village greens: Commons Act 2006 s 1.

[265] These conditions are spelled out in s 95(2).

[266] Local Government, Planning and Land Act 1980 s 95(2)(a).

[267] The areas in relation to which Pt X of the Local Government, Planning and Land Act 1980 is in operation are determined by order made by statutory instrument by the Secretary of State in relation to the area of any district council or London borough council specified in the order: Local Government, Planning and Land Act 1980 s 94(2). See SIs 1980/1871 (in relation to certain specified areas of district and London borough councils); 1981/194 (in relation to certain specified areas of district and London borough councils); 1981/1251 (in relation to certain specified areas of district councils); 1981/1618 (in relation to all other areas of district councils in England, all other London Boroughs and the City of London); 1983/94 (in relation to certain specified areas of district councils); and

or is not so situated, but adjoins other land which is so situated and in which a freehold or leasehold interest is owned by a body to which Part X of the Act applies or a subsidiary of that body;[268] and

— that in the opinion of the Secretary of State the land is not being used or not being sufficiently used for the purposes of the body's functions.[269]

The Secretary of State has the power to enter on the register any such land satisfying the above conditions as he thinks fit.[270] He may also enter on the register any Crown land situated in an area in relation to which Part X of the Act is in operation or not so situated but adjoining other Crown land which is so situated.[271]

8– 055   Bodies to whom Part X applies

Part X of the Local Government, Planning and Land Act 1980 applies to any body for the time being specified in Sch 16 to the Act.[272] The bodies specified in Sch 16 are:

— a county council, a county borough council, a district council, a London borough council, and the Common Council of the City of London;
— a joint authority established by Part IV of the Local Government Act 1985;
— the London Fire and Emergency Planning Authority;
— a police authority established under s 3 of the Police Act 1996 and the Metropolitan Police Authority;
— an economic prosperity board established under section 88 of the Local Democracy, Economic Development and Construction Act 2009, or a combined authority under section 103;
— an authority established for an area in England under section 207 of the Local Government and Public Involvement in Health Act 2007;
— a development corporation established under the New Towns Act 1981 and an Urban Development Corporation established under the Local Government, Planning and Land Act 1980;
— a housing action trust established under Part III of the Housing Act 1988;
— the Regulator of Social Housing;
— the Civil Aviation Authority;
— British Shipbuilders, the Coal Authority, the British Broadcasting Association and the Environment Agency; and
— statutory undertakers, defined to mean persons authorised by any enactment to

1984/1493 (in relation to all other areas of district councils in Wales).

[268] Local Government, Planning and Land Act 1980 s 95(2)(b).

[269] Local Government, Planning and Land Act 1980 s 95(2)(c).

[270] Local Government, Planning and Land Act 1980 s 95(3).

[271] Local Government, Planning and Land Act 1980 s 95(4). Section 95(5) further provides that the information to be included in the register in relation to any land entered on it shall be such as the Secretary of State thinks fit.

[272] Local Government, Planning and Land Act 1980 s 93(1). The Secretary of State has the power to amend Sch 16 by order made by statutory instrument by adding an entry naming a public body not for the time being specified in that Sch or by amending or deleting any entry for the time being contained in the Schedule: Local Government, Planning and Land Act 1980 s 93(2). A statutory instrument containing an order under s 93(2) is subject to annulment in pursuance of a resolution of either House of Parliament: Local Government, Planning and Land Act 1980 s 93(3).

carry on any railway, light railway, road transport, water transport, canal, inland navigation, dock or harbour undertaking, or undertaking for the supply of hydraulic power; provided that where any persons carry on a business to the main purpose of which any such undertaking is merely ancillary, those persons shall not be treated as statutory undertakers.

956   Public access to the register

The Secretary of State must send to a council in respect of whose area a register is maintained a copy of that register and such amendments to it as he may from time to time consider appropriate.[273] That council has a duty to incorporate those amendments.[274] A copy of the register must be available at the council's principal office for inspection by any member of the public at all reasonable hours.[275] If any member of the public requires a council to supply him with a copy of any information contained in such a copy of the register, the council must supply him with a copy of that information on payment of such reasonable charge for making it as the council may determine.[276]

957   Land Registration Act 2002

The register of title maintained under the Land Registration Act 2002 is open to inspection by any person. Any person may make copies of, or of any part of, the register of title; any document kept by the registrar which is referred to in the register of title; any other document kept by the registrar which relates to an application by him; or the register of cautions against title.[277] This right is subject to rules which may provide for exceptions to the right and impose conditions on its exercise, including conditions requiring the payment of fees.[278] The registrar has a duty to keep an index for the purpose of enabling the following matters to be ascertained in relation to any parcel of land: whether any registered estate relates to the land; how any registered estate which relates to the land is identified for the purposes of the register; whether the land is affected by any, and if so, what, caution against first registration; and such other matters as rules may provide.[279] Rules may also make provision about how the index is to be kept, and may, in particular, make provision about the information to be contained in the index; the form in which information contained in the index is to be kept; and the arrangement of that information. Rules may make provision about official searches of the index.[280] Under s 69 of the Land Registration Act 2002, the registrar has a power to provide, on application,

---

[273] Local Government, Planning and Land Act 1980 s 96(1).

[274] Local Government, Planning and Land Act 1980 s 96(2).

[275] Local Government, Planning and Land Act 1980 s 96(3).

[276] Local Government, Planning and Land Act 1980 s 96(4).

[277] Land Registration Act 2002 s 66(1).

[278] Land Registration Act 2002 s 66(2). The relevant rules are contained in the Land Registration Rules 2003 SI 2003/1417, Part 13. In particular, rule 136(1) provides that a person may apply for the registrar to designate a document as an exempt document if it contains prejudicial information.

[279] Land Registration Act 2002 s 68(1). The relevant rules are contained in the Land Registration Rules 2003 SI 2003/1417.

[280] Land Registration Act 2002 s 68(2). The relevant rules are contained in the Land Registration Rules 2003 SI 2003/1417.

information about the history of a registered title;[281] and may arrange for the provision of information about the history of registered titles and may authorise anyone who has the function of providing information of the latter sort to have access on such terms as he thinks fit to any relevant information kept by him.[282]

8– 058 **Local Government Act 1972 – incidental power**

Although much of the material held by a local authority relating to land is required to be made available under the above provisions, not all land information held by it falls within these provisions. Generally local authorities have considered that the provision of information about a property to prospective purchasers of that property was incidental to their statutory function of collecting and holding that information.[283] While a local authority may charge for the provision of this information,[284] it is not under a duty to provide that information. However, to the extent that such information is necessary for a property transaction, a refusal by a local authority to provide that information would almost certainly be an unlawful decision, capable of challenge by way of judicial review.[285]

5. PERSONAL INFORMATION

8– 059 **Introduction**

In addition to the right of access to personal information relating to the applicant conferred by s 7 of the Data Protection Act 1998 and to the restricted right of access to third-party personal information under the Freedom of Information Act 2000,[286] a number of limited access rights to what might broadly be called personal information exist in other statutory provisions. These are, in summary:

(1)   a right of access to the register of disclaimers of peerage contained in the Peerage Act 1963;

(2)   a right of access to certain information relating to marriage and civil partnership;

(3)   a right of access to certain information relating to adoption;

(4)   a right of access to certain human donor information; and

(5)   a right of access to information as to licence conditions and supervision requirements of an offender exercisable by a victim of crime.

8– 060 **Register of disclaimers of hereditary peerages**

A person who succeeds to a peerage in England, Scotland, Great Britain or the United Kingdom may, by an instrument of disclaimer delivered to the Lord Chancellor within the

---

[281] Land Registration Act 2002 s 69(1). Section 69(2) provides that rules may make provision about applications for the exercise of the power conferred on the registrar by s 69(1): see the Land Registration Rules 2003 SI 2003/1417.

[282] Land Registration Act 2002 s 69(3).

[283] For which they were empowered under Local Government Act 1972 s 111 or Local Government Act 2000 s 2.

[284] The Local Authorities (England) (Charges for Property Searches) Regulations 2008 (SI 2008 No 3248)

[285] *Onesearch Direct Holdings Ltd (t/a Onesearch Direct) v City of York Council* [2010] EWHC 590 (Admin) at [83].

[286] Restricted principally by FOIA s 40.

prescribed period,[287] disclaim that peerage for life.[288] Where the Lord Chancellor is satisfied that an instrument of disclaimer in respect of a peerage has been delivered within the prescribed time, he shall furnish to the person disclaiming a peerage a certificate to that effect, and shall cause particulars of the instrument and of his certificate to be entered into a register kept by him for the purpose, which shall be open to inspection by the public at all reasonable times.[289]

61 Information relating to marriage and civil partnership

The Marriage Act 1949, the Births and Death Acts Registration Act 1953 and the Registration Service Act 1953, collectively govern the compulsory registration of births, deaths, marriages and civil partnerships. The Registration of Births and Deaths Regulations 1987[290] and the Registration of Marriage Regulations 1986[291] prescribe the information that must be recorded in the respective registers. Upon payment of the prescribed fee, a person may search the index of the register.

62 Information relating to adopted persons

The Adoption and Children Act 2002 provides adopted persons and others with certain rights of access to information where that adoption took place after 30 December 2005. The 2002 Act provides that there are two types of information: 'protected information'[292] and information which is not protected.[293] Section 57 of the 2000 Act provides that 'protected information' may only be disclosed to an adopted person in pursuance of sections 56 to 65.[294] Protected information is:

(1) Any 'section 56 information' kept by an adoption agency which is about an adopted person or any other person which is or includes identifying information[295] about the person in question.[296]

(2) Any information[297] kept by an adoption agency[298] which the agency has obtained from the Registrar General[299] and any other information which would enable the

---

[287] That being the period set out in the Peerage Act 1963 s 1(3).

[288] Peerage Act 1963 s 1(1).

[289] Peerage Act 1963 Sch 1 para 3.

[290] SI 1987/2088.

[291] SI 1986/1442.

[292] As defined in Adoption and Children Act 2002 s 57.

[293] See Adoption and Children Act 2002 s 58.

[294] Adoption and Children Act 2002 s 57(1) and (2). A registered adoption society which discloses any information in contravention of s 57 is guilty of an offence and is liable on summary conviction to a fine not exceeding level 5 on the standard scale: Disclosure of Adoption Information (Post-Commencement Adoptions) Regulations 2005 reg 21.

[295] 'Identifying information' about a person means information which, whether taken on its own or together with other information disclosed by an adoption agency, identifies the person or enables the person to be identified: Adoption and Children Act 2002 s 57(4).

[296] Adoption and Children Act 2002 s 57(1).

[297] 'Information' means 'information recorded in any form': Adoption and Children Act 2002 s 144(1).

[298] 'Adoption agency' is defined in Adoption and Children Act 2002 s 2(1).

[299] On an application pursuant to Adoption and Children Act 2002 s 79(5).

adopted person to obtain a certified copy of the record of his birth or which is information about an entry relating to the adopted person in the Adoption Contact Register.[300]

8– 063 The Registrar General

Where an adopted person who has attained the age of 18 years requests information from an adoption agency under s 60(2)(a) of the Adoption and Children Act 2002 that would entitle him to obtain a certified copy of the record of his birth and the agency does not have that information, the agency must seek that information from the Registrar General.[301] The Registrar General must disclose to any person (including an adopted person) at his request any information that the person requires to assist him to make contact with the appropriate adoption agency and disclose to the appropriate adoption agency any information that the agency requires, in relation to an application under s 60, 61 or 62 of the 2002 Act about any entry relating to an adopted person on the Adoption Contact Register.[302]

8– 064 Access to donor information

The Human Fertilisation and Embryology Authority is required to keep a register containing all information obtained by the Authority[303] that relates to the provision of treatment services for any identifiable individual, or the keeping or use of the gametes of any identifiable individual or an embryo taken from any identifiable woman, or if it shows that any identifiable individual was, or may have been, born in consequence of treatment services.[304] A person who has attained the age of 16 ('the applicant') may request the Authority to give the applicant notice stating whether or not the information contained in the register shows that a person other than a parent of the applicant would or might be a parent of the applicant and, if it does show that, giving the applicant so much of that information as relates to the person concerned as the Authority is required by regulations to give (but no other information) or stating whether or not that information shows that there are other persons of whom the donor is not the parent but would or might, but for the relevant statutory provisions, be the parent and if so the number of those other persons, the sex of each of them, and the year of birth of each of them.[305] There is a corresponding right conferred on an applicant to request the Authority to give the applicant information as to a person whom the applicant proposes to marry or enter into a civil partnership, or with whom the applicant is in (or proposes to enter in) an intimate physical

---

[300] Adoption and Children Act 2002 s 57(2). The 'Adoption Contact Register' is defined in s 80(1) as a register maintained by the Registrar General at the General Register Office.

[301] Disclosure of Adoption Information (Post-Commencement Adoptions) Regulations 2005 reg 19(1). Where the adoption agency seeks such information from the Registrar General, the agency must provide him in writing with the following information, so far as it is known, the name, date of birth and country of birth of the parents of the adopted person, the names of that person's adoptive father and mother, and the date of the adoption order. Disclosure of Adoption Information (Post-Commencement Adoptions) Regulations 2005 reg 19(2).

[302] Disclosure of Adoption Information (Post-Commencement Adoptions) Regulations 2005 reg 20(1).

[303] Human Fertilisation and Embryology Act 1990 s 31(1).

[304] Human Fertilisation and Embryology Act 1990 s 31(2). Information does not fall within s 31(2) if it is provided to the Authority for the purposes of any voluntary contact register as defined in s 31F(1): Human Fertilisation and Embryology Act 1990 s 31(3).

[305] Human Fertilisation and Embryology Act 1990 s 31ZA.

relationship.[306] The Authority must comply with that request if the information contained in the register shows that the applicant was, or may have been, born in consequence of treatment services and the applicant is a relevant individual,[307] the Authority receives notice in writing from the specified person consenting to the request being made and that notice has not been withdrawn, and the applicant and the specified person have each been given a suitable opportunity to receive proper counselling about the implications of compliance with the request.[308] The information that the Authority is required by regulations to give is set out in the Human Fertilisation and Embryology Authority (Disclosure of Donor Information) Regulations 2004.

65 Disclosure of information to victims of crime

If a court convicts a person ('the offender') of a sexual or violent offence and a relevant sentence[309] is imposed upon him in respect of the offence, the local probation board[310] for the area in which the sentence is imposed must take all reasonable steps to ascertain whether a person who appears to the board to be the victim[311] of the offence (or to act for the victim of the offence) wishes to receive information about any licence conditions or supervision requirements to which the offender is to be subject in the event of his release.[312] If a local probation board has ascertained that a person wishes to receive such information, the relevant local probation board must take all reasonable steps:

(1) to inform the person whether or not the offender is to be subject to any licence conditions or supervision requirements in the event of his release;

(2) if he is, to provide the person with details of any licence conditions or supervision requirements which relate to contact with the victim or his family, and

(3) to provide the person with such other information as the relevant local probation board considers appropriate in all the circumstances of the case.[313]

The Domestic Violence, Crime and Victims Act 2004 makes comparable provision for local probation boards to provide similar information (obtained from the Secretary of State and Mental Health Review Tribunal) to victims of persons subject to the Mental Health Act 1973. In general terms, the provisions require a local probation board to take reasonable steps to ascertain whether the victim wishes to receive information about any conditions to which the

---

[306] Human Fertilisation and Embryology Act 1990 s.31ZA.

[307] Defined in section 31(4) of the Human Fertilisation and Embryology Act 1990 as '…an individual who was or may have been born in consequence of (a) treatment services, other than basic partner treatment services, or (b) the procurement or distribution of any sperm (other than partner-donated sperm which has not been stored) in the course of providing non-medical fertility services.'

[308] Human Fertilisation and Embryology Act 1990 s 31ZB (3).

[309] As defined in the Domestic Violence, Crime and Victims Act 2004 s 45(1).

[310] Where the offender is to be supervised on release by an officer of a local probation board, that local probation board is the relevant probation board. In any other case, the relevant probation board is the local probation board for the area in which the prison or other place in which the offender is detained: Domestic Violence, Crime and Victims Act 2004 s 35(8).

[311] As defined in Domestic Violence, Crime and Victims Act 2004 s 52(2).

[312] Domestic Violence, Crime and Victims Act 2004 s 35(1), (3)(b) and (5).

[313] Domestic Violence, Crime and Victims Act 2004 s 35(7).

patient is to be subject in the event of his discharge from hospital. If so, the board is required to inform the victim of any such conditions, and with details of any conditions which relate to contact with the victim or his family.[314]

6. ECONOMIC AND BUSINESS INFORMATION

8– 066 Introduction

Although the Freedom of Information Act 2000 and the Environmental Information Regulations 2004 are the main instruments for obtaining any information held by a public authority, including economic and business information, there remain in place a series of provisions giving access to specific sorts of economic and business information. While the Freedom of Information Act 2000 and, to a lesser extent, the Environmental Information Regulations 2004 will often provide the readiest means of obtaining access to all such information, these more specific regimes generally have fewer exemptions and more limited scope for charging fees for provision of the information. In summary, these more limited regimes are:

(1) Under s 6 of the Nuclear Installations Act 1965, there is a right of public inspection of the list of sites in respect of which a nuclear site licence has been granted.

(2) Under s 27 of the Industry Act 1975, there is a right of access to certain economic planning information held by the Treasury.

(3) Under s 42 of the Harbours Act 1964 and s 14 of the Pilotage Act 1987, there is a right of public inspection of the annual accounts prepared by a statutory harbour undertaker which relate to the harbour activities and to revenue derived from the provision of or the expenditure on pilotage services.

(4) Under s 49 of the Electricity Act 1989, there is a right of public inspection of the register maintained by the Gas and Electricity Markets Authority relating to licences granted for the generation, transmission, distribution and supply of electricity.

(5) Under s 39 of the Radioactive Substances Act 1993, there is a limited right of access to information relating to radioactive substances, held by the chief inspector but generally supplied to him by those involved in that industry.

(6) Under the Railways Act 1993, there is a right of access to the Regulator's Register and the Franchising Director's Register.

(7) Under s 57 of the Coal Industry Act 1994, there is a right to a limited amount of information relating to the coal industry, held by the Coal Authority but generally

---

[314] Each provision should be examined for its precise terms. In relation to the case where the court convicts a person for a sexual or violent offence or makes a finding of insanity or unfitness to plead and then makes a hospital order with restrictions in respect of that patient: see Domestic Violence, Crime and Victims Act 2004 ss 36 and 38. In the case that the sentencing court makes a hospital direction and limitation direction in respect of an offender in addition to giving him a relevant prison sentence: see the Domestic Violence, Crime and Victims Act 2004 ss 39 and 41. Where an offender is transferred by the Home Secretary to hospital and restrictions are imposed under the powers in the Mental Health Act 1973: see Domestic Violence, Crime and Victims Act 2004 ss 42 and 44. In Northern Ireland: see Domestic Violence, Crime and Victims Act 2004 s 46 (amending the Justice (Northern Ireland) Act 2002).

supplied to it by those involved in that industry.

(8)   Under s 38 of the Postal Services Act 2000, there is a right of inspection of the register maintained by the Postal Services Commission recording matters relating to the provision of licences to convey a letter from one place to another.

(9)   Under s 35 of the Transport Act 2000, there is a right to inspect the register maintained by the Civil Aviation Authority relating to licences granted companies to provide air traffic services.

(10) Various rights of access under the Communications Act 2003.

(11) Various rights of access under the Gambling Act 2005.

67   The Nuclear Installations Act 1965

Under section 6 of the Nuclear Installations Act 1965, the Minister must maintain a list showing every site in respect of which a nuclear site licence has been granted. This must include a map or maps showing the position and limits of each such site. The Minister must make arrangements for the list or a copy thereof to be available for inspection by the public and he shall cause notice of these arrangements to be made public in such a manner as may appear to him to be appropriate.

68   Industry Act 1975

Section 27 of the Industry Act 1975 provides for the disclosure of information by Ministers of the Crown and the Treasury. The information in question is described in Sch 5 to the Industry Act 1975, and consists of a macro-economic model, to be kept by the Treasury, which is suitable for demonstrating the likely effects on economic events in the United Kingdom of different assumptions about the following matters, namely government economic policies; economic events outside the UK; and such (if any) other matters as appear to the Treasury from time to time likely to have a substantial effect on economic events in the UK.[315] The model must enable forecasts to be made of any of the following: the level of gross domestic product; unemployment; the balance of payments on current account; the general index of retail prices; and average earnings.[316] The model must also enable forecasts to be made of such (if any) other economic variables as are appropriate in the opinion of the Treasury from time to time.[317] The model must be maintained on a computer,[318] and be available to members of the public to make forecasts based on their own assumptions, using the computer during office hours upon payment of such reasonable fee as the Treasury may determine.[319] The Treasury also has a duty, under para 6 of Sch 5 to the Industry Act 1975, not less than twice in each year commencing with a date not later than one year from the coming into force of that Act,[320] to publish forecasts with the aid of the model as to such matters and based on such alternative

---

[315] Industry Act 1975 Sch 5 para 1.

[316] Industry Act 1975 Sch 5 para 2(a).

[317] Industry Act 1975 Sch 5 para 2(b). The references to forecasts in para 2 are references to forecasts relating to successive periods of three months, and not to shorter periods: Industry Act 1975 Sch 5 para 3.

[318] Industry Act 1975 Sch 5 para 4.

[319] Industry Act 1975 Sch 5 para 5.

[320] Namely November 20, 1975.

assumptions as appear to them to be appropriate;[321] and, under para 8, from time to time to publish an analysis of errors in such forecasts that would have remained even if the assumptions set out in the forecasts and on which they were based had been correct.

8– 069   **Harbours Act 1964 and Pilotage Act 1987**

Every statutory harbour undertaker must prepare an annual statement of accounts relating to the harbour activities[322] and to any associated activities carried on by him.[323] Copies of any statement of accounts identifying these matters shall be available for inspection by the public at all reasonable hours at the registered office of the competent harbour authority, and the competent harbour authority shall make copies available for purchase by members of the public at a reasonable charge.[324]

8– 070   **Electricity Act 1989**

The Gas and Electricity Markets Authority may grant a number of different licences relating to the generation, transmission, distribution and supply of electricity.[325] The Authority must maintain a register containing the provisions of every licence and every exemption[326] granted to a particular person, every modification or revocation of a licence, every direction or consent given or determination made under a licence and every final or provisional order,[327] every revocation of such an order and every notice under s 25(6) of the Electricity Act 1989,[328] and every penalty imposed under s 27A(1) and every notice under s 27A(5).[329] The contents of the register are available for inspection by the public during such hours and subject to the payment of such fee as may be specified in an order made by the Secretary of State.[330] Any person may, on the payment of such fee, require the Authority to supply him with a copy of, or an extract from, any part of the register, being a copy or extract which is certified by the Authority to be a true copy.[331] The provisions above also apply to licences granted under the Energy Act 2004.[332]

8– 071   **Radioactive Substances Act 1993**

Provision is made under the Radioactive Substances Act 1993 for the public to obtain access

---

[321] Any forecast under Sch 5 must indicate, where possible, the margin of error attaching to it: Industry Act 1975 Sch 5 para 7.

[322] 'Harbour activities' means activities involved in carrying on a statutory harbour undertaking or in carrying out harbour operations: Harbours Act 1964 s 42(9).

[323] Harbours Act 1964 s 42(1).

[324] Statutory Harbour Undertakings (Pilotage Accounts) Regulations 1988 reg 5, and the Pilotage Act 1987 s 14.

[325] Electricity Act 1989 s 6(1).

[326] As defined in Electricity Act 1989 ss 3A and 64(1).

[327] See Electricity Act 1989 ss 25(8) and 64(1).

[328] Being an order to secure compliance with a condition or requirement of a licence.

[329] Electricity Act 1989 s 49(2).

[330] Electrify Act 1989 s 49(5). See the Electricity (Register) Order 1990 arts 3 and 4.

[331] Electricity Act 1989 s 49(6).

[332] Energy Act 2004 ss 184(12) and 185(13).

to certain information concerning radioactive substances. Thus, under s 39 of the Act, the chief inspector[333] must keep copies of all applications made to him under any provision of the Radioactive Substances Act 1993;[334] of all documents issued by him under any provision of that Act;[335] of all other documents sent by him to any local authority pursuant to directions of the Secretary of State;[336] and of such records of convictions as may be prescribed in regulations.[337] The chief inspector must make copies of those documents available to the public,[338] except to the extent that this would involve the disclosure of information relating to any relevant process[339] or trade secret,[340] or would involve the disclosure of applications or certificates with respect to which the Secretary of State has directed[341] that knowledge should be restricted on grounds of national security. Every local authority must keep and make available to the public copies of all documents sent to the authority under any provision of that Act, unless directed by the chief inspector, or, as the case may be, the appropriate minister and the chief inspector, that all or any part of such document is not to be available for inspection.[342] It is not necessary for copies made available to the public by the chief inspector or a local authority to be kept in documentary form,[343] but the public nevertheless has the right to inspect such documents at all reasonable times and, on payment of a reasonable fee, to be provided with copies of such documents.[344] Because the right conferred is one of inspection, the existence of this right does not of itself cause the information to be exempt information under the Freedom of Information Act 2000.

72 Railways Act 1993

The Office of Rail Regulation is required to maintain a register ('the Regulator's Register')[345] containing matters relating to the provision of licences (being licences authorising a person to be an operator of railway assets),[346] matters relating to access agreements, access contracts and

---

[333] Namely the chief inspector appointed under s 4 of the Radioactive Substances Act 1993.

[334] Radioactive Substances Act 1993 s 39(1)(a).

[335] Radioactive Substances Act 1993 s 39(1)(b).

[336] Radioactive Substances Act 1993 s 39(1)(c).

[337] Radioactive Substances Act 1993 s 39(1)(d).

[338] Radioactive Substances Act 1993 s 39(1).

[339] 'Relevant process' means any process applied for the purposes of, or in connection with, the production or use of radioactive material: Radioactive Substances Act 1993 s 34(3).

[340] See §§25– 049 to 25– 056 for a consideration of the analogous exemption in the FOIA.

[341] Under Radioactive Substances Act 1993 s 25. In relation to what constitutes 'national security', see §§17– 040 to 17– 048, where it is considered in the context of the FOIA.

[342] Radioactive Substances Act 1993 s 39.

[343] Radioactive Substances Act 1993 s 39(4).

[344] Radioactive Substances Act 1993 s 39(5).

[345] Railways Act 1993 s 72(1).

[346] Railways Act 1993 s 72(2)(a).

installation access contracts,[347] matters relating to experimental passenger services,[348] closures[349] and the provisions of every railway administration order and of the discharge of such an order.[350] Similarly, the Secretary of State is required to maintain a register containing the provisions of every franchise exemption,[351] every franchise agreement,[352] every amendment of a franchise agreement[353] and other related matters ('the Franchise Director's Register').[354] The contents of the Regulator's register and the contents of the Franchise Director's register are available for inspection by the public, without payment of any fee, between 10.00am and 4.00pm on each working day.[355] Any person may, on the payment of such fee as may be specified in an order, require the Office of Rail Regulation to supply him with a copy of, or an extract from, any part of the Regulator's Register, being a copy or extract which is certified by the Office of Rail Regulation to be a true copy or extract.[356]

8–073   Coal Industry Act 1994

Provision for public access to information in respect of the coal industry is made under the Coal Industry Act 1994. Thus the Coal Authority is required to establish and maintain arrangements under which every person is entitled, on payment to the Authority of such fee and subject to such other conditions as the Authority may consider appropriate, to be furnished with certain information[357] and to have so much of the records maintained by the Authority as contain any such information, to be made available to him for inspection at such office of the Authority as it may determine and at such times as may be reasonable;[358] and also to make or be supplied with copies of or extracts from so much of the records maintained by the Authority as contain any such information.[359] For these purposes, 'records' includes registers, maps, plans and accounts, as well as computer records and other records kept otherwise than in documentary form.[360] The information that must be made available in this way is that

---

[347] Railways Act 1993 s 72(2)(b).

[348] Railways Act 1993 s 72(2)(d), 'experimental passenger services' being defined in Pt 4 of the Railways Act 2005.

[349] Railways Act 1993 s 72(2)(da); see Pt 4 of the Railways Act 2005.

[350] Railways Act 1993 s 72(2)(e).

[351] Railways Act 1993 s 73(2)(a).

[352] Railways Act 1993 s 73(2)(b).

[353] Railways Act 1993 s 73(2)(c).

[354] As contained in the Railways Act 1993 s 73(2)(d)–(ga). Section 73A imposes a similar obligation on the Scottish Ministers.

[355] Railways (Register) Order 1994 art 2; Railways Act 1993 s 72(7).

[356] Railways Act 1993 s 72(8); Railways (Register) Order 1994 art 3.

[357] Coal Industry Act 1994 s 57(2)(a).

[358] Coal Industry Act 1994 s 57(2)(b).

[359] Coal Industry Act 1994 s 57(2)(c).

[360] Coal Industry Act 1994 s 57(8). Records of the Coal Authority are public records for the purposes of the Public Records Act 1958: Coal Industry Act 1994 s 10.

contained in the register of licences and orders;[361] that contained in the register of rights;[362] and any of the following which is for the time being in the possession of the Authority: information about the geological or physiological features or characteristics of any land in which any unworked coal or any coal mine is situated or of any other land;[363] information about the identity of persons in whom interests and rights in any unworked coal or coal mine have been vested;[364] the contents of any plans of any coal mines or coal workings;[365] any other information about proposals for the carrying on by any person of any coal mining operations;[366] information about any subsidence or subsidence damage or about claims made under the Coal Mining Subsidence Act 1991;[367] and information about such other matters as the Secretary of State may prescribe by regulations.[368] In so far as the right of access conferred is one of inspection (and does not extend to being able to require the supply of a copy of the information), the existence of this right does not of itself cause the information to be exempt information under the Freedom of Information Act 2000.[369]

74 Postal Services Act 2000

The Postal Services Commission must maintain a register in which is recorded: the provisions of every licence,[370] being a licence to convey a letter from one place to another;[371] every modification, revocation or surrender of a licence[372] and various other matters relating to the licences issued under the Postal Services Act 2000.[373] The Commission must ensure that the contents of the register are available for inspection by the public during such hours as may be specified in an order by the Secretary of State and subject to such reasonable fees (if any) as the Commission may determine.[374] If requested by any person to do so and subject to such reasonable fees (if any) as the Commission may determine, the Commission shall supply the person concerned with a copy (certified to be true) of the register or of an extract from it.[375]

---

[361] That is, under Coal Industry Act 1994 s 35.

[362] That is, under Coal Industry Act 1994 s 56.

[363] Coal Industry Act 1994 s 57(1)(a).

[364] Coal Industry Act 1994 s 57(1)(b).

[365] Coal Industry Act 1994 s 57(1)(c). The Authority must maintain such records of information which comes into its possession and which falls into any of the preceding three heads as it considers appropriate: Coal Industry Act 1994 s 57(6).

[366] Coal Industry Act 1994 s 57(1)(d).

[367] Coal Industry Act 1994 s 57(1)(e).

[368] Coal Industry Act 1994 s 57(1)(f).

[369] See §16–001.

[370] Postal Services Act 2000 s 38(3)(a).

[371] Postal Services Act 2000 s 6(1).

[372] Postal Services Act 2000 s 38(3)(b).

[373] Postal Services Act 2000 ss 38(3)(c)–(e). The duty on the Commission to cause matters relating to licences to be entered into the register does not extend to anything of which the Commission is unaware: Postal Services Act 2000 s 38(4).

[374] Postal Services Act 2000 s 38(8); Postal Services Commission (Register) Order 2001.

[375] Postal Services Act 2000 s 38(9).

8–075   Transport Act 2000

The Civil Aviation Authority must maintain a register[376] containing details of licences[377] granted to a company authorising it to provide air traffic services in respect of an authorised area.[378] The CAA must ensure that the contents of the register are available for inspection by the public during such hours as may be specified in an order made by the Secretary of State.[379] If requested by any person to do so the CAA must supply him with a copy (certified to be true) of the register or of an extract from it.[380]

8–076   Communications Act 2003

The Office of Communication must maintain a register for the purposes of s 33 of the Communications Act 2003[381] recording every designation by them, every withdrawal by them of a designation, every notification received by them under s 33 and any deemed notification received under s 33.[382] Information recorded in the register must be recorded in such manner as OFCOM consider appropriate.[383] The register is available for public inspection, subject to the payment of a fee.[384] OFCOM must also maintain a public register of information[385] relating to the issue, renewal or variation of wireless telegraphy licences or grants or recognised spectrum access.[386] Subject to such conditions (including conditions as to payment) as may be prescribed by regulations, the register is open to inspection by the public.

8–077   Gambling Act 2005

The Gambling Commission must maintain a register of operating licences[387] containing such details of and relating to each licence as the Commission thinks appropriate.[388] The Commission shall make the register available for inspection by the public at all reasonable

---

[376] Transport Act 2000 s 35(1).

[377] Namely those matters set out in the Transport Act 2000 s 35(3). This duty does not extend to anything of which the CAA is unaware: Transport Act 2000 s 35(4).

[378] Transport Act 2000 s 5(1).

[379] Transport Act 2000 s 35(7). No such order has been made.

[380] Transport Act 2000 s 35(8). This provision does not apply if a charge required by a scheme or regulations made under s 11 of the Civil Aviation Act 1982, being a payment to be made to the CAA for the exercise of its functions, is not paid: Transport Act 2000 s 35(9).

[381] Communications Act 2003 s 44(1).

[382] Communications Act 2003 s 44(2).

[383] Communications Act 2003 s 44(3).

[384] Communications Act 2003 s 44(6).

[385] Wireless Telegraphy Act 2006 s 31(1); Wireless Telegraphy (Register) Regulations 2004 reg 3.

[386] Wireless Telegraphy (Register) Regulations 2004 reg 4(1).

[387] The Commission may issue an operating licence, which is a licence which states that it authorises the user to operate a casino, to provide facilities for playing bingo, to provide facilities for betting, to act as a betting intermediary, to make gaming machines available for use, to manufacture, supply, install, adapt, maintain or repair a gaming machine, to manufacture, etc gambling software or to promote a lottery: Gambling Act 2005 ss 65(1) and (2).

[388] Gambling Act 2005 s 106(1)(a).

times,[389] and shall make arrangements for the provision of a copy of an entry in the register to the public on request.[390] A licensing authority[391] shall maintain a separate register of each of the following:

    (1)   premises licences;[392]
    (2)   temporary use notices;[393]
    (3)   family entertainment centre gambling machine permits;[394]
    (4)   club gaming permits and club machine permits;[395]
    (5)   licensed premises gaming machine permits;[396]
    (6)   prize gaming permits.[397]

In relation to each of these registers, the authority shall make the register and the information contained in it available for inspection by members of the public at all reasonable times[398] and shall make arrangements for the provision of a copy of an entry in the register, or of information, to a member of the public on request.[399]

7.   EDUCATIONAL RECORDS

78   **Introduction**

The specific right to educational information differs somewhat from the other rights to official information in that it is in most part concerned with providing members of the public with general information relating to educational bodies, rather than information that is specifically

---

[389] Gambling Act 2005 s 106(1)(b).

[390] Gambling Act 2005 s 106(1)(c).

[391] As defined in s 2 of the Gambling Act 2005.

[392] Gambling Act 2005 s 156(1). A premises licence is a licence which states that it authorises premises to be used for the operation of a casino, the provision of facilities for the playing of bingo, making gaming machines available for use, or the provision of facilities for betting: Gambling Act 2005 s 150(1).

[393] Gambling Act 2005 s 234(1)(a). A temporary use notice is a notice provided by the holder of an operating licence which states his intention to carry on a prescribed activity for a period of less than 21 days in a period of 12 months: Gambling Act 2005 ss 214–218.

[394] Schedule 10 to the Gambling Act 2005 para 23(1)(a).

[395] Schedule 12 to the Gaming Act 2005 para 26(1)(a).

[396] Schedule 13 to the Gaming Act 2005 para 22(1)(a).

[397] Schedule 14 to the Gaming Act 2005 para 23(1)(a).

[398] In relation to the register for premises licences: see Gambling Act 2005 s 156(1)(b). In relation to the register for temporary use notices: see Gambling Act 2005 s 234(1)(b). In relation to the register for family entertainment centre gambling machine permits: see Sch 10 to the Gambling Act 2005 para 23(1)(b). In relation to the register for club gaming permits and club machine permits: see Sch 12 to the Gaming Act 2005 para 26(1)(b). In relation to the register for licensed premises gaming machine permits: see Sch 13 to the Gaming Act 2005 para 22(1)(b). In relation to the register for prize gaming permits: see Sch 14 to the Gaming Act 2005 para 23(1)(b).

[399] In relation to the register for premises licences: see Gambling Act 2005 s 156(1)(c). In relation to the register for temporary use notices: see Gambling Act 2005 s 234(1)(c). In relation to the register for family entertainment centre gambling machine permits: see Sch 10 of the Gambling Act 2005 para 23(1)(c). In relation to the register for club gaming permits and club machine permits: see Sch 12 to the Gaming Act 2005 para 26(1)(c). In relation to the register for licensed premises gaming machine permits: see Sch 13 to the Gaming Act 2005 para 22(1)(c). In relation to the register for prize gaming permits: see Sch 14 to the Gaming Act 2005 para 23(1)(c).

addressed to answering the terms of a request. In brief terms, legislation places a duty to provide certain information on the governing body of each school, the head teacher of a school and each local education authority. Specific rights are, however, conferred on parents to access their child's educational record. Similarly, there are various rights of access in relation to reports of inspections of schools.

8– 079   Education Act 1996

The Secretary of State is empowered to make regulations requiring the governing body of any institution that is maintained by a local education authority or a special school which is not maintained as such by such an authority, and the proprietor of every independent school to provide such information about the school as may be prescribed.[400] The regulations currently in force for England are the Education (School Information) (England) Regulations 2008.[401]

8– 080   Governing bodies

The governing body of a maintained school must publish the report containing special needs information referred to in s 317(5) of the Ehducation Act 1996 and any other general information relating to that school which they may decide to publish as a single document identified as the school prospectus.[402] Copies of the school prospectus must be made available at the school for distribution without charge to parents on request and for reference by parents and other persons.[403] The school prospectus must be published during the offer year and, except in the case of a special school, not later than six weeks before the date up to which parents may express a preference for a school in respect of the admission year.[404] In the case of a special school such information must also be published by copies being made available at the offices of the relevant authority for distribution without charge to parents on request and reference by parents and other persons.[405] In the case of any maintained secondary school, a copy of the school prospectus shall be provided without charge to the offices in the area served by the school of persons providing career services in accordance with arrangements made, or directions given, under section 10 of the Employment and Training Act 1973.[406]

8– 081   Head teachers

The head teacher of every maintained school must make available to parents of pupils at the school and other persons the following information:
— the times at which each school session begins and ends on a school day;
— particulars of the charging and remissions policies determined by the governing body of the school under s 457 of the Education Act 1996.
Copies of such information must be provided at the school for inspection by parents and other

---

[400] Education Act 1996 s 537(1).

[401] SI 2008/3093.

[402] School Information (England) Regulations 2008 (SI 2008/3093), reg 10(1).

[403] School Information (England) Regulations 2008 (SI 2008/3093), reg 10(2).

[404] School Information (England) Regulations 2008 (SI 2008/3093), reg 10(3).

[405] School Information (England) Regulations 2008 (SI 2008/3093), reg 10(4).

[406] School Information (England) Regulations 2008 (SI 2008/3093), reg 10(5).

persons at all reasonable times on a school day and for distribution without charge to parents on request.[407] The head teacher of any school maintained by a local education authority must, prior to the end of the summer term of every school year, prepare a head teacher's report in respect of every registered pupil at the school containing the information referred to in Sch 1 of the Education (Pupil Information) (England) Regulations 2005 and provide a copy of each such report to the following persons free of charge:

— in the case of any pupil who is aged 18 or over at the time the head teacher's report is due to be provided and who is not proposing to leave school by the end of the school year to which the report relates, the pupil himself and, if the head teacher considers there to be special circumstances which make it appropriate, the parents of that pupil;

— in any other case, the parents of the pupil to whom the report relates.[408]

The head teacher of every maintained school must prepare a school leaver's report in respect of any pupil who has ceased to be of compulsory school age and is proposing to leave or has left the school, containing brief particulars of the pupil's progress and achievements in subjects and activities forming part of the school curriculum (other than in relation to any public examination or vocational qualification) in the school year during or at the end of which the pupil proposes to leave or has left school. The head teacher must provide a copy of the school leaver's report to the pupil concerned by no later than September 30 following the end of the school year during or at the end of which the pupil left the school.[409]

2   Local education authorities

Local education authorities are also required to publish detailed information concerning schools in their area.[410] This information includes:

— the addresses and telephone numbers of the offices of the authority to which enquiries in respect of primary and secondary education in their area should be addressed;[411]

— the arrangements for parents to obtain the information specified in Sch 2 in the case of individual schools other than special schools;[412]

— as respects each school mentioned in the prospectus, other than a special school, the name, address and telephone number of the school and the name of a person to whom enquiries should be addressed, as well as the expected number of pupils at the school and their age range.[413]

Local education authorities must also publish the classification of each school maintained by

---

[407] Education (School Sessions and Charges and Remissions Policies) (Information) (England) Regulations 1999 reg 3.

[408] Education (Pupil Information) (England) Regulations 2005 reg 6(7).

[409] Education (Pupil Information) (England) Regulations 2005 reg 8.

[410] School Information (England) Regulations 2008 Pt 3 and Sch 3.

[411] School Information (England) Regulations 2008 Sch 2, para 1.

[412] As defined in s 337(1) of the Education Act 1996: School Information (England) Regulations 2008 Sch 3 Pt 1 para 2.

[413] School Information (England) Regulations 2008 Sch 2 Pt 2.

them;[414] the authority's general arrangements and policies in respect of transport for pupils of compulsory school age and below to and from schools and institutions within the further education sector, including in particular the provision of free transport, the carriage on school buses of pupils for whom free transport is not provided, and the payment in whole or in part of reasonable travel expenses.[415] Local education authorities must publish their general arrangements and policies in respect of the provision of milk, meals and other refreshments including, in particular, the remission in whole or in part of charges. Such authorities must also publish details of their general arrangements and policies in respect of the provision of school clothing (including uniform and physical training clothes), and the making of grants to defray expenses in respect of such clothing and, in particular, the address from which parents may obtain detailed information about the assistance which is available and eligibility for it.[416] Local education authorities must also publish further details of their general arrangements and policies, in the case of pupils attending any school maintained by them, in respect of the making of grants to defray other expenses and the granting of allowances in the case of pupils of compulsory school age, including, in particular, the address from which parents may obtain detailed information about the assistance which is available and eligibility for it. Finally, local education authorities must publish: their general policy in respect of the entering of pupils for public examination; their general arrangements and policies in respect of special educational provision[417] for pupils with special educational needs[418] including, in particular, the arrangements for parents to obtain information about the matters referred to in Part 2 of Sch 3; and the arrangements for parents and others to obtain copies of and to refer to particulars of the charging and remissions policies determined by the authority under s 457 of the Education Act 1996.[419]

8–083 **Information concerning special educational provision**

Local education authorities have a further duty to publish the information specified in Part II of Sch 3 to the School Information (England) Regulations 2008 concerning special educational provision.[420] This information includes the authority's detailed arrangements and policies in respect of the identification and assessment of children with special educational needs and the involvement of parents in that process; the provision made in community, voluntary and special schools maintained by them for pupils with special educational needs and the use made by them of such special schools maintained by other authorities; and special educational provision

---

[414] That is, as a community, foundation, voluntary controlled or voluntary aided school or a community special or foundation school; a primary, middle or secondary school; a comprehensive, secondary modern or grammar school; a co-educational or single sex school; and as a day or boarding school or (as the case may be) a school taking both day and boarding pupils; in the case of a school with selection arrangements, a partially selective school or a grammar school; in the case of a school designated as having a religious character by an order under section 69(3) SSFA, the religious denomination, or denominations, of the school; in the case of a school with specialist status, its specialism: School Information (England) Regulations 2008 Sch 2 Pt 2 para 11.

[415] School Information (England) Regulations 2008 Sch 3 Pt 1 para 11.

[416] School Information (England) Regulations 2008 Sch 3 Pt 2 paras 3 and 4.

[417] As defined in Education Act 1996 s 312: School Information (England) Regulations 2008 Sch 3 Pt 1 para 12.

[418] As defined in Education Act 1996 s 312: School Information (England) Regulations 2008 Sch 3 Pt 1 para 12.

[419] See also the School Information (England) Regulations 2008 Sch 3 Pt 1 para 8.

[420] As defined in s 312 of the Education Act 1996.

supplied otherwise than at school.[421] In addition, local education authorities must publish:

—   their arrangements and policies in respect of the use of non-maintained special and independent schools;[422]

—   the arrangements for parents who consider that their child may have special educational needs to obtain advice and further information;[423]

—   the authority's arrangements and policies in respect of transport for pupils of compulsory school age and below to and from maintained and non-maintained special schools and independent schools;[424] and

—   the arrangements for parents to obtain the information particularised in Sch 2 in the case of the special schools used by the authority which are maintained by them or other authorities.[425]

84   Further provisions concerning the publication of information by local education authorities

The information described in Sch 3 to the School Information (England) Regulations 2008 must be published by copies being made available for distribution without charge to parents on request, and for reference by parents and other persons at the office of the relevant authority and at every school maintained by the authority (other than nursery schools and special schools or a pupil referral unit).[426] Copies of the above-mentioned information must also be distributed without charge to parents of pupils at schools maintained by the relevant authority (other than nursery schools or special schools or a pupil referral unit) who, in the publication school year, are in the final year at such schools and who might transfer to other schools so maintained;[427] and by copies being made available for reference by parents and other persons at the public libraries in the area of the relevant authority.[428] Local authorities also have a duty, with respect to maintained schools,[429] to publish a composite prospectus containing the information specified in Sch 2 to the School Information (England) Regulations 2008 concerning those schools.[430]

85   Advice and information about provision for special educational needs

A local education authority must arrange for the parent of any child in the area with special educational needs to be provided with advice and information about matters relating to those needs.[431] In making the arrangements, the authority must have regard to any guidance given

---

[421] School Information (England) Regulations 2008 Sch 3 para 12.

[422] School Information (England) Regulations 2008 Sch 3 para 13.

[423] School Information (England) Regulations 2008 Sch 3 para 14.

[424] School Information (England) Regulations 2008 Sch 3 para 15.

[425] School Information (England) Regulations 2008 Sch 3 para 16.

[426] School Information (England) Regulations 2008 reg 9(1)(b).

[427] School Information (England) Regulations 2008 reg 9(1)(c).

[428] School Information (England) Regulations 2008 reg 9(1)(d).

[429] As defined by s 84(6) of the School Standards and Framework Act 1998.

[430] School Information (England) Regulations 2008 reg 5(1).

[431] Education Act 1996 s 332A(1).

in England by the Secretary of State, and in Wales, by the National Assembly for Wales.[432] The authority must take such steps as they consider appropriate for making the services provided known to the parents of children in the area, the head teachers and proprietors of schools in their area and such other persons as they consider appropriate.[433] A local authority must publish specific information in relation to special educational needs provision.[434] The local education authority must publish this information by providing a written copy of the information to any Primary Care Trust or social services authority which in the opinion of the local education authority has an interest in that information, making the information available on the internet and providing a written copy of the information to any person on request.[435] Any revisions to the information must be published by the local education authority as soon as reasonably practicable after a revision has been made by providing the revised information to a Primary Care Trust or social services authority previously provided with information by the local education authority, updating the website maintained by the authority on the internet to display the revised information and notifying the maintained schools in the authority's area of the revisions by post or by electronic communication.[436] The information must be published free of charge.[437]

8–086 **Access to child's educational record**

The governing body of any school maintained by a local education authority (other than a nursery school) and any special school not so maintained must make a pupil's educational record[438] available for inspection by the parent, free of charge, within 15 days of the parent's written request for access to that record.[439] The governing body must provide a copy of the pupil's educational record to the parent, on payment of such fee (not exceeding the cost of supply), if any, as the governing body may prescribe within 15 school days of receipt of the parent's written request for a copy of that record.[440] When complying with either request a governing body must not make available for inspection or provide a copy of any information which they could not lawfully disclose to the pupil himself under the Data Protection Act 1998 or in relation to which the pupil himself would have no right of access under that Act.[441]

---

[432] Education Act 1996 s 332A(2).

[433] Education Act 1996 s 332A(3).

[434] Special Educational Needs (Provision of Information by Local Education Authorities) (England) Regulations 2001 reg 2 Sch 1.

[435] Special Educational Needs (Provision of Information by Local Education Authorities) (England) Regulations 2001 reg 3(1).

[436] Special Educational Needs (Provision of Information by Local Education Authorities) (England) Regulations 2001 reg 3(4).

[437] Special Educational Needs (Provision of Information by Local Education Authorities) (England) Regulations 2001 reg 3(5).

[438] 'Educational record' is defined in Education (Pupil Information) (England) Regulations 2005 reg 3.

[439] Education (Pupil Information) (England) Regulations 2005 reg 5(2).

[440] Education (Pupil Information) (England) Regulations 2005 reg 5(3).

[441] Education (Pupil Information) (England) Regulations 2005 reg 5(4)

87 Access to reports by Her Majesty's Chief Inspector of Schools in England of school inspections

A copy of a report sent to an appropriate authority[442] by Her Majesty's Chief Inspector of Schools in England concerning an inspection of a school[443] must be made available by it for inspection by members of the public at such times and at such places as may be reasonable. The appropriate authority must also provide a copy of the report free of charge (or in prescribed cases on payment of such fee as they think fit which does not exceed the cost of supply) to any person who asks for one and must take such steps as are reasonably practicable to secure that every registered parent of a registered pupil at the school receives a copy of the report within such period following receipt of the report by the authority as may be prescribed.[444] There are corresponding provisions for interim statements.[445]

88 Access to reports by registered inspectors and members of the inspectorate of school inspections

A copy of any report and summary sent to an appropriate authority[446] by a registered inspector or member of the inspectorate concerning an inspection of a school[447] must be made available for inspection by members of the public at such times and at such place as may be reasonable. The appropriate authority must also provide a copy of the report and summary free of charge (or in prescribed cases on payment of such fee as they think fit which does not exceed the cost of supply) to any person who asks for one and must take such steps as are reasonably practicable to secure that every parent of a registered pupil at the school receives a copy of the summary within such period following receipt of the report by the authority as may be prescribed.[448] On receipt of such a report and summary, an appropriate authority must prepare a written statement of the action which it proposes to take in light of the report and the period within which it proposes to take it.[449] The appropriate authority must make any statement prepared by it under this section available for inspection by members of the public at such times and at such place as may be reasonable. The appropriate authority must provide a copy of the statement, free of charge (or in prescribed cases on payment of such fee as it sees fit which does not exceed the cost of supply) to any person who asks for one and must take such steps as are reasonably practicable to secure that every parent of a registered pupil at the school receives

---

[442] As defined in Education Act 2005 s 18.

[443] Namely a report issued pursuant to Education Act 2005 s 5.

[444] Education Act 2005 s 14. Where the school is a school other than a maintained school, the same duty falls on the proprietor of the school: Education Act 2005 s 16.

[445] Education Act 2005 ss 14A and 16A. Interim statements are defined in s 10A.

[446] As defined in Education Act 1996 s 43.

[447] Namely a report issued pursuant to Education Act 2005 s 28.

[448] Education Act 2005 s 38(4). Where the school is a school other than a maintained school, the same duty falls on the proprietor of the school: Education Act 2005 s 41(4).

[449] Education Act 2005 s 39(1). Where the school is a school other than a maintained school, the same duty falls on the proprietor of the school: Education Act 2005 s 42(1).

a copy of the statement as soon as reasonably practicable.[450] The latter requirement is taken to have been satisfied by the appropriate authority if it:

    (a)   takes such steps as are reasonably practicable to secure that every parent of a pupil at the school receives, as soon as is reasonably practicable, a copy of a document prepared by it which summarises the statement and contains a statement of the right to request a copy of it; and

    (b)   provides a copy of the statement to every parent of a registered pupil at the school who asks for one.[451]

8–089   **Access to reports as to the inspection of religious education in schools**
It is the duty of a governing body of any voluntary or foundation school in England which has been designated under s 69(3) of the School Standards and Framework Act 1998 by the Secretary of State as having a religious character to secure that any denominational education given to pupils and the contents of the school's collective worship are inspected.[452] A person conducting such an inspection must report on these matters to the governing body.[453] The governing body must make any such report available for inspection by members of the public, at such times and at such a place as may be reasonable.[454] The governing body must take such steps as are reasonably practicable to secure that every parent of a registered pupil at the school for whom the school provides denominational education or who takes part in collective worship receives a copy of the report as soon as is reasonably practicable.[455] The governing body must provide a copy of the report free of charge (or in prescribed cases on payment of such fee as they see fit which does not exceed the cost of supply) to any other person who asks for one.[456]

8.   INFORMATION RIGHTS IN CONNECTION WITH CIVIL LITIGATION

8–090   **Introduction**
Civil litigation generally brings with it an obligation upon the parties, and occasionally non-parties, to disclose information in the form of documents.[457] This obligation is called 'disclosure': it was formerly called 'discovery'. The obligation is not unique to public authorities and a public authority may enjoy a public interest immunity exemption not available to ordinary litigants. While a full treatment of the law of disclosure is beyond the scope of this

---

[450] Education Act 2005 s 39(7). Where the school is a school other than a maintained school, the same duty falls on the proprietor of the school: Education Act 2005 s 42(5).

[451] Education Act 2005 s 39(8).

[452] Education Act 2005 s 48(1).

[453] Education Act 2005 ss 48(4), 49(2) and 49(3).

[454] Education Act 2005 s 49(4)(a).

[455] Education Act 2005 s 49(4)(b).

[456] Education Act 2005 s 49(4)(c).

[457] 'Document' is defined in CPR 31.4 to mean anything in which information of any description is recorded.

book,[458] the disclosure obligation may impinge upon a person's rights under the Freedom of Information Act 2000 as well as represent a means of eliciting information from a public authority.

91 The concept of disclosure

Court rules[459] provide for a formal procedure, termed 'disclosure', by which one party to a civil case obtains the documents and other information relevant to those proceedings in advance of the trial from another party, or less usually from a non-party. It is a means of compelling the production of evidence and therefore applies in relation to all material that may constitute evidence, except that for which there is a lawful ground on which to resist compulsion. The obligation of disclosure extends to both documents and real evidence. 'Disclosure' is defined as 'stating that a document exists or has existed'.[460] Section 28 of the Crown Proceedings Act 1947 expressly provides that the general rules relating to (what were previously termed) discovery and interrogatories apply to the Crown. The rule of public interest immunity is preserved.[461] The disclosure obligations in the CPR apply in relation to 'documents'. A 'document' is 'anything in which information of any description is recorded'. This will be interpreted extremely broadly, and will certainly cover media such as photographs, films, microfilms, video tapes, audio tapes and computer discs. In order to be a document information must be included. Documents will be disclosable even though they may not be admissible in evidence, as long as they fall within the standard disclosure categories.

92 Court-ordered pre-action disclosure

The Practice Direction — Protocols provides that the court will expect parties, in accordance with the overriding objective, to act reasonably in exchanging information and documents relevant to the claim to avoid the necessity for the start of proceedings.[462] Applications for pre-action disclosure are permitted under s 33 of the Supreme Court Act 1981/Senior Courts Act 1981[463] and s 52 of the County Court Act 1984. These provisions empower the court in preliminary proceedings to order a potential defendant to subsequent proceedings to disclose documents in or likely to be in his possession, custody or power and which are relevant to an issue arising or likely to be so relevant.[464] The court may order disclosure before proceedings have commenced where:

— both the applicant and respondent are likely to be parties to proceedings if proceedings were commenced;[465]

---

[458] For a more comprehensive treatment, see P Matthews and H Malek, *Disclosure*, 3rd edn (Sweet & Maxwell, London, 2007).

[459] CPR 31.

[460] CPR 31.2.

[461] Also see RSC Ord 77 rr 12 and 14. Ord 77 still operates under the CPR.

[462] Practice Direction – Protocols, para 4.1.

[463] The Supreme Court Act 1981 is to be renamed the 'Senior Courts Act 1981' on the coming into force of the Constitutional Reform Act 2005 Sch 11 Pt 1 para 1(2).

[464] *Burns v Shuttlehurst Ltd* [1999] 1 WLR 1449 (CA); *Howe v David Brown Tractors (Retail) Ltd* [1991] 4 All ER 30.

[465] CPR 31.16(3)(a), (b).

— the respondent's duty by way of standard disclosure would extend to the documents or classes of documents sought;[466] and

— pre-action disclosure is desirable in order to dispose fairly of the anticipated proceedings, to assist in the resolution of the dispute without proceedings, or to save costs.[467]

An order for pre-action disclosure must specify the documents or class of documents to be disclosed.[468] The order may require the respondent to indicate what has happened to any documents which are no longer in his control.[469] The person much show that if proceedings were brought, the documents or classes of documents would fall within the respondent's duty by way of standard disclosure. This has been interpreted to mean that all the documents within a category or class must be subject to standard disclosure and the applicant must show that it is more probable than not that the documents are within the scope of standard disclosure with regard to the issues that are likely to arise.[470] The person applying for an order must 'be likely to be a party to subsequent proceedings' and the person against whom the order is sought must appear 'likely to be a party to the proceedings and to be likely to have or to have had in his possession, custody or power any documents which are relevant to an issue arising or likely to arise out of that claim.' 'Likely' means only 'may well', not 'more probable than not'.[471] If the applicant is bound to fail in the substantive case, or that substantive case does not amount to a prima facie case, then the requirement for pre-action disclosure is not met.[472] If the person seeking such disclosure does not yet have a cause of action then the claim is not 'likely' within the first requirement, and so the application would fail.[473] The fact that the prospective claimant is not yet able to plead a claim (ie without the disclosure) is not a bar to such early disclosure.[474] The court must consider whether the third criterion above, that disclosure be desirable for the fair disposal of the proceedings, is satisfied. Although no standard is expressed in the Civil Procedure Rules, it has been held that the standard is that of a real prospect in principle.[475] This is not a steep hurdle requiring anything like the showing of a probability that

---

[466] CPR 31.16(3)(c). *Mitsui & Co Ltd v Nexen Petroleum UK Ltd* [2005] EWHC 625 (Ch), [2005] 3 All ER 511 at [32]. This is a strict test but it may usually be surmounted by appropriate drafting. Also see *Hands v Morrison Construction Services Ltd* [2006] EWHC 2018 (Ch) at [26].

[467] CPR 31.16(3)(d). See *Bermuda International Securities Ltd v KPMG* [2001] EWCA Civ 269, [2001] Lloyd's Rep PN392; *Black v Sumitomo Corp* [2001] EWCA Civ 1819, [2002] 1 WLR 1562; *Central Exchange Ltd v Anaconda Nickel Ltd* [2001] WASC 128, Sup Ct of WA; *Arsenal Football Club v Elite Sports Distribution* [2002] EWHC 3057, [2003] FSR 26, (2003) 26(3) IPD 26017 (Ch); *Snowstar Shipping Co Ltd v Graig Shipping plc* [2003] EWHC 1367 (Comm); *Moresfield v Banners* [2003] EWHC 1602 (Ch).

[468] CPR 31.16(4).

[469] CPR 31.16(5).

[470] *Hutchinson 3G UK Ltd v O2 (UK) Ltd* [2008] EWHC 50 (Comm) at [28], [44]; *Hays Specialist Recruitment (Holdings) Ltd v Ions* [2008] EWHC 745 (Ch), [2008] IRLR 904 at [33].

[471] *Black v Sumitomo Corp* [2001] EWCA Civ 1819, [2002] 1 WLR 1562 at [70]–[73]; also *Moresfield v Banners* [2003] EWHC 1602 (Ch) at [32].

[472] *Mars UK Ltd v Waitrose* [2004] EWHC 2264 (Ch).

[473] *Burns Ltd v Shuttlehurst Ltd* [1999] 1 WLR 1449 (CA); *Gwelhayl Ltd v Midas Construction Ltd* [2008] EWHC 2316 (TCC), 123 Con LR 91.

[474] For example, *XL London Market v Zenith Syndicate Management* [2004] EWHC 1182 (Comm).

[475] *Black v Sumitomo Corp* [2001] EWCA Civ 1819, [2002] 1 WLR 1562 at [81].

a desirable objective of the rule will be achieved.[476] The requirement that this be desirable gives a wide discretion to the court.[477] Relevant facts include the nature of the loss; the clarity of issues identified; the nature of the documents requested; any pre-action inquiries; and the ability of the party to make his case without the material sought.[478] In almost every dispute, a case can be made out that pre-action would be useful in achieving a settlement or otherwise saving costs.[479] However, in order to obtain pre-action disclosure, the circumstances must be outside the 'usual run' to allow the hurdle to be surmounted.[480] The court must consider the discretionary question in detail and that is likely to call for an examination of each of the categories of documents requested in any multiple requests, rather than just an all or nothing approach. The court will also look at the matter in the round, considering whether the request generally furthers the overriding objective.[481]

93 Pre-action disclosure in personal injury and clinical negligence actions

There are specific protocols regulating pre-action disclosure in these types of claims. In respect of personal injury claims the protocol recommends that the claimant's solicitor identify in a letter of claim the particular categories of documents which he considers relevant.[482] If the defendant denies liability, he should enclose with the letter of reply documents in his possession which are material to the issues between the parties and which would be likely to be ordered to be disclosed by the court.[483] Annex B of the pre-action protocol for personal injury claims contains lists of the types of disclosure which should be given for different types of personal injury claims. The pre-action protocol for the resolution of clinical disputes contains detailed guidance on the obtaining of health records.[484] The protocol sets out those matters which the defendant should provide in response to a letter of claim.[485] Sanctions for non-compliance include costs and interest.[486] However one sanction not available to the court is to override a party's privilege in a report obtained following non-compliance with the protocol.[487] While the

---

[476] *Hands v Morrison Construction Services Ltd* [2006] EWHC 2018 (Ch) at [27].

[477] This requirement is described as having two stages or tests, a jurisdictional stage and a discretionary stage. However in practice it is difficult to disentangle the two: see the comments by Clarke J in *First Gulf Bank v Wachovia Bank* [2005] EWHC 2827.

[478] *Black v Sumitomo Corp* [2001] EWCA Civ 1819, [2002] 1 WLR 1562 at [88]. The nature of this discretion is explained at [81]–[83]. If the applicant can make his case without the disclosure then that is a good reason not to order it: *XL London Market Ltd v Zenith Syndicate Management Ltd* [2004] EWHC 1182 at [24]. If the documents are peripheral, a court is likely to refuse the application: *Northumbrian Water Ltd v British Telecommunications plc* [2005] EWHC 2408, [2006] BLR 38 at [32].

[479] *Hutchinson 3G UK Ltd v O2 (UK) Ltd* [2008] EWHC 50 (Comm) at [55].

[480] *Trouw UK Ltd v Mitsui & Co plc* [2007] EWHC 863 (Comm), [2007] UKCLR 921 at [43]. See also *Anglo Irish Bank Corporation v West LB AG* [2009] EWHC 207 (Comm).

[481] *Hands v Morrison Construction Services Ltd* [2006] EWHC 2018 ChDat [29]–[30].

[482] Pre-action Protocols for Personal Injury Claims, Notes of Guidance ('the Protocol') para 2.10.

[483] Protocol para 3.10.

[484] See paras 3.7 to 3.13 of that Protocol.

[485] See paras 3.23 to 3.27 and Annex C2 of the Protocol.

[486] Practice Direction on Protocols, paras 2.1 and 2.3.

[487] *Carlson v Townsend* [2001] EWCA Civ 511, [2001] 1 WLR 2415.

protocol encourages and promotes voluntary disclosure of medical reports, it does not specifically require this, and the withholding of a medical report does not constitute non-compliance with the protocol.[488] The pre-action protocol for personal injury claims should be followed in all cases. In certain types of cases of injury following road traffic accidents,[489] when intimating a claim the claimant's advisers should offer access to their client's vehicle to the defendant's insurers for the purpose of early examination if the defendant's insurers so wish, and give early disclosure, with irrelevant passages redacted if necessary, of any contemporaneous general practitioner's notes or other relevant medical notes.[490]

8– 094   **Pre-action disclosure in judicial review claims**

Like the other protocols, the pre-action protocol for judicial review claims contains detailed guidance on the matters to be set out in a letter of claim and a response to a letter before claim.[491] The introduction to the protocol states that the protocol does not impose a greater obligation on a public body to disclose documents or give reasons for its decision than that already provided for in statute and common law. However, where the court considers that a public body should have provided other documents or information, particularly where this failure is a breach of a statutory or common law requirement, then it may impose sanctions.[492] Lateness of instruction is unlikely to be a good reason for failure to comply with the protocol.[493]

8– 095   **Actions for disclosure — Norwich Pharmacal orders**

At common law[494] courts have power to order that persons caught up in the wrongful[495] acts of others disclose the identity and address[496] of the wrongdoers and the person into whose hands the subject property has passed, as well as other information.[497] These are often described as 'Norwich Pharmacal' orders.[498] Although such orders against a public authority are rarely

---

[488] *Carlson v Townsend* [2001] EWCA Civ 511, [2001] 1 WLR 2415.

[489] This guidance from the Court of Appeal was given in the context of a claim for personal injury arising out of a low velocity impact between two motor vehicles where the claimant claimed damages for a soft tissue injury to part of the spine, and the insurers of the other vehicle asserted that the impact had been so insignificant that the claimant could not have suffered the injury of which they had made complaint.

[490] *Kearsley v Klarfeld* [2005] EWCA Civ 1510, [2006] 2 All ER 303 at [50].

[491] See Pre-Action Protocol for Judicial Review, paras 8 to 12 (letter before claim) and 13 to 17 (letter of response).

[492] See para 6 of the introduction to the protocol.

[493] *R (Kemp) v Denbighshire Local Health Board* [2006] EWHC 181 (Admin), [2006] 3 All ER 141 at [63].

[494] The CPR do not limit the common law powers that courts possess to order disclosure before proceedings have started, or to order disclosure against third parties: CPR 31.18.

[495] The rule is no longer restricted to torts: *Ashworth Hospital Authority v MGN Ltd* [2002] UKHL 29, [2002] 1 WLR 2033, [2002] 4 All ER 193.

[496] *Coca-Cola Company v British Telecommunications plc* [1999] FSR 518.

[497] In theory the action can be used to obtain disclosure of documents from potential defendants, but in practice CPR 31.16 will often provide an adequate alternative to the common law action in such cases. See *Taylor v Anderton*, *The Times*, 21 October 1986.

[498] After the leading case, *Norwich Pharmacal Co v Commissioners of Customs & Excise* [1974] AC 133, where a person innocently caught up in a wrongdoing was required to disclose the wrongdoer's identity.

made,[499] there is no principle precluding their application to such a body. The requirements for the grant of such an order are as follows:

(1) A wrong has been carried out or at least arguably carried out.[500] The subject of inquiry may be any wrongdoing, whether criminal or civil.[501] The victim of a crime may seek the identity of the wrongdoer. In *Norwich Pharmacal* the wrong was a tort. However the principle covers all civil wrongs, eg breach of contract or confidence,[502] or a breach of trust or other equitable wrong.[503]

(2) The claimant intends to assert legal rights against the wrongdoer.

(3) There is a need for the court's intervention to enable action to be brought against the wrongdoer. The need usually consists of the need to identify the wrongdoer. It could be to discover whether a wrong has been committed at all.[504] Discovery must either be necessary to enable the claimant to take action, or at least that it should be just and convenient in the interests of justice to make the order sought.[505] This can be broken down into three elements: (a) whether the information sought can be shown to be necessary; (b) the extent of information which may be ordered to be disclosed; and (c) whether there is an alternative and more appropriate method to obtain the information sought. Note that relief may be refused where there is an alternative method of obtaining the information.[506]

(4) The defendant or respondent is a person who was caught up in or facilitated the wrongdoing or has some relationship with the wrongdoer sought to be identified.[507] It is not necessary to show that the respondent's actions were causative of the

---

[499] For an example, see *R (Mohamed) v Secretary of State for Foreign and Commonwealth Affairs* [2008] EWHC 2048 (Admin), [2009] 1 WLR 2579 (disclosure of sensitive material held by government which might assist in defence of terrorist charges before a US military commission.

[500] In *President of the State of Equatorial Guinea v Royal Bank of Scotland International* [2006] UKPC 7 [2006] 3 LRC 676 the Privy Council upheld the granting of a *Norwich Pharmacal* order for the purpose of pursuing those engaged in an as yet unrecognised tort arising out of a foreign coup, but the Privy Council suspended the order pending a determination by the English courts whether the *Norwich Pharmacal* applicants had a cause of action enforceable in English law. In the substantive proceedings that followed the defendant alleged that those substantive proceedings were merely a cynical attempt to satisfy an undertaking given to the foreign court hearing the *Norwich Pharmacal* application that the applicant would pursue substantive civil proceedings.

[501] *Ashworth Hospital Authority v MGN Ltd* [2002] UKHL 29, [2002] 1 WLR 2033, [2002] 4 All ER 193, disapproving *Interbrew SA v Financial Times* [2002] EWCA Civ 274, [2002] 1 Lloyd's Rep 542 (CA) on this aspect. Also see *Mersey Care NHS Trust v Ackroyd* [2003] EWCA Civ 663, *The Times*, 21 May 2003.

[502] *British Steel Corporation v Granada Television Ltd* [1981] AC 1096; *Hughes v Carratu International plc* [2006] EWHC 1791, [2006] All ER (D) 250 (Jul).

[503] *Bankers Trust v Shapira* [1980] 1 WLR 1274 (CA).

[504] *Carlton Film Distributors Ltd v VCI* [2003] FSR 47; *Mitsui v Nexen Petroleum* [2005] 2 All ER 511.

[505] As to the meaning of this test in this context see *President of the State of Equatorial Guinea v Royal Bank of Scotland International* [2006] UKPC 7 at [16]; *R (Mohamed) v Secretary of State for Foreign and Commonwealth Affairs* [2008] EWHC 2048 (Admin), [2009] 1 WLR 2579 at [94].

[506] In *Mitsui v Nexen Petroleum* [2005] 2 All ER 511 the order was refused as the information could be obtained from a prospective party, so there was no need to make an order against an innocent third party.

[507] For example, an internet search engine advertising the services of a party allegedly responsible for a copyright infringement is so mixed up in the infringement: *Grant v Google* [2005] EWHC 3444 (Ch). In a number of cases the Courts have ordered disclosure of information intended to identify so far as possible the sender of an e-mail: *Campaign Against Arms Trade v BAE Systems plc* [2007] EWHC 330; *Applause Store Productions Ltd v Raphael* [2008] EWHC 1781 (QB).

occurrence of the wrongdoing or that the respondent had knowledge of the wrongdoing.[508] A person is not required to so disclose the identity of another person if that first person is a 'mere witness' and is not caught up in the wrongdoing.[509] There is also a residual discretion as to whether it is right that an order should be made. The court will balance the interest in disclosure against the public and/or private interests asserted. Orders can also be granted for the disclosure of the holding of disputed property and the identity of trustees or the identity of further innocent parties caught up in the wrongdoing,[510] for example as recipients of property.[511] The information required to be disclosed is not just the identity of a person, but such full information as to enable a practical commercial judgment to be made as to enforcement of remedies against the wrongdoer.[512] The claimant need not show he intends to take legal proceedings against the wrongdoer.[513] An order can be obtained to require the employees or agents of a public authority to give the necessary information.[514] Orders are not made as of right; the court retains a discretion whether to make the order. There are four defences available: (1) disclosure will not be ordered if that would complete a cause of action; (2) the privilege against self-incrimination operates as a defence;[515] (3) s 10 of the Contempt of Court Act 1981 provides another defence for sources of information contained in publications in that a person responsible for a publication will not be required to give discovery of the source of information contained in that publication unless it is necessary in the interests of national security, the interests of justice, or for the prevention of disorder or crime;[516] and (4) an order will not be made if it would infringe the sovereignty of another country.[517] In addition, a public interest defence may be available to the source, and if there is an arguable public interest defence there may be no wrongdoer for the purpose of a *Norwich Pharmacal* Order.[518] Proceedings may be brought under either CPR 7 or CPR 8. The order may be the sole relief sought or ancillary relief.[519] The order is usually granted following a trial of the action, but can be granted on an interlocutory application, normally with notice but exceptionally without.[520] The claimant must identify the wrongdoing in general terms and

---

[508] *R (Mohamed) v Secretary of State for Foreign and Commonwealth Affairs* [2008] EWHC 2048 (Admin), [2009] 1 WLR 2579 at [69]-[71].

[509] *Ricci v Chow* [1987] 1 WLR 1658.

[510] *Re Murphy's Settlements* [1998] 3 All ER 1.

[511] *Bankers Trust v Shapira* [1980] 1 WLR 1274.

[512] *Norwich Pharmacal Co v Commissioners of Customs & Excise* [1974] AC 133 at 175; *Banker's Trust v Shapira* [1980] 1 WLR 1274 at 1281; *AXA Equity and Law Life Assurance Society plc v National Westminster Bank plc* [1998] PNLR 433.

[513] *Ashworth Hospital Authority v MGN Ltd* [2002] UKHL 29, [2002] 1 WLR 2033, where the claimant intended to dismiss the relevant employee.

[514] *Harrington v North London Polytechnic* [1984] 1 WLR 1293.

[515] *Re Westinghouse Electric Corp* [1978] AC 547.

[516] See, eg, *X Ltd v Morgan-Grampian (Publishers) Ltd* [1991] 1 AC 1; *Secretary of State for Defence v Guardian Newspapers Ltd* [1985] AC 339; *Ashworth Hospital Authority v MGN Ltd* [2002] UKHL 29, [2002] 1 WLR 2033.

[517] See, eg, *McKinnon v Donaldson Lufkin and Jenrette Securities Corp* [1986] Ch 482.

[518] *Mersey Care NHS Trust v Ackroyd* [2003] EWCA Civ 663, *The Times*, 21 May 2003.

[519] *Microsoft Corporation v Plato Technology Ltd* [1999] FSR 834.

[520] *Banker's Trust v Shapira* [1980] 1 WLR 1274.

identify the purposes for which disclosure will be used when made.[521]

96 Disclosure after commencement of litigation

Once civil proceedings have commenced all parties are subject to compulsory requirements of disclosure, as provided for in court rules. There are broadly two types of disclosure: standard and specific disclosure. Disclosure during the course of civil litigation will normally be limited to 'standard disclosure'.

97 Standard disclosure

Standard disclosure requires a party to disclose only documents on which he relies, documents adversely affecting one party's case or supporting another party's case, and documents required to be disclosed by reference to a practice direction.[522] This formulation significantly reduces the obligation to disclose from the *Peruvian Guano* test of relevance, which applied in relation to discovery prior to the introduction of the Civil Procedure Rules in 1999.[523] On the Fast Track the court is likely to direct less than standard disclosure.[524] A party must disclose documents on which it relies.[525] The Civil Procedure Rules contain no definition of 'reliance'. It probably means 'use in court', including use for cross-examination. It probably does not extend to all documents which a party may use in or out of court to advance the case. Documents which may cast doubt on the credibility of a party whose evidence is important are likely to 'adversely affect' that party's case. The concept of documents adversely affecting a party's case is not defined in the CPR. A document is not covered if it merely indicates a line of inquiry which may lead to other information having an adverse effect.[526] Parties need only disclose:

— documents which are or have been in their control, including those documents in their physical possession;

— documents over which they have the right to possession; and

— documents over which they have a right to inspect or take copies.[527]

In determining the issues in a party's case the pleadings are an essential reference point.[528] In judicial review claims disclosure is generally not required unless the Court orders it.[529] The Court will look to whether it is necessary to order disclosure in order to deal with a case fairly and justly, and the court has discretion to order disclosure of specific documents if necessary.[530]

---

[521] *Ashworth Hospital Authority v MGN Ltd* [2002] UKHL 29 at [60], [2002] 1 WLR 2033; *Mersey Care NHS Trust v Ackroyd* [2007] EWCA Civ 101, (2007) HRLR 19, [2008] EMLR 1, (2007) 94 BMLR 84.

[522] CPR r 31.6. Part 31 does not apply in relation to cases on the Small Claims Track. The court can give directions as to disclosure in such cases: CPR rr 27.2(2)(b), 27.4(1).

[523] *Compagnie Financière du Pacifique v Peruvian Guano Co* (1882) 11 QBD 55 at 63.

[524] CPR Pt 28 PD para 3.6(1)(c), (4).

[525] CPR r31.6(a).

[526] P Matthews and H Malek, *Disclosure*, 3rd edn (London, Sweet & Maxwell, 2007).

[527] CPR 31.8.

[528] *Harrods Ltd v Times Newspaper Ltd* [2006] EWCA Civ 294 at [12]; *EAA Securities Ltd v Chan Lin Mui* [2008] HKDC 205 at [26].

[529] CPR PD 54 para 12.1; *Save Guana Cay Reef Association Ltd v The Queen & Ors (Bahamas)* [2009] UKPC 44.

[530] *Tweed v Parades Commission for Northern Ireland* [2006] UKHL 53, [2007] 1 AC 650 at [2]–[3].

8–098   Electronic data

The civil disclosure obligation extends to 'documents', defined in CPR 31.4 to mean 'anything in which information of any description is recorded'. This extends to electronic documents, including email[531] and other electronic communications, word processed documents[532] and databases,[533] and includes both documents readily accessible from computer systems and other electronic devices and media, as well as material stored on servers and back-up systems as well as electronic documents which have been apparently deleted, but a record of which will often remain on the computer system.[534] The CPR[535] and the Admiralty & Commercial Courts Guide[536] both state that parties should discuss issues that arise regarding searches for and preservation of electronic documents.[537] Factors that may be relevant in deciding the reasonableness of a search for electronic documents include the number of documents involved; the nature and complexity of the proceedings; the ease and expense of retrieval of any particular document (the CPR and the Admiralty & Commercial Courts Guide set out detailed guidance as to the assessment of this); and the significance of any document which is likely to be located during the search.[538] It may be reasonable to search some or all of the parties' electronic storage systems. The very great volume of electronic documents means that issues of the scope and reasonableness of the search need careful consideration. Disclosure of electronic documents may be circumscribed to ensure the disclosure obligation is not too burdensome.[539] In some circumstances, it may be reasonable to search for electronic documents by means of keyword searches (agreed as far as possible between the parties) even where a full review of each and every document would be unreasonable.[540]

8–099   Specific disclosure

The court may make an order for specific disclosure, being an order that a party:

— disclose documents or classes of documents as specified;

— carry out a search to the extent stated in the order; and/or

— disclose any documents located as a result of the search.[541]

While the timing of such an application depends on the circumstances, often it will be appropriate to apply when directions are given, namely on allocation to a track and on filing

---

[531] For example: *Vellacott v The Convergence Group plc*, unreported, 3 February 2006 (Ch).

[532] For example: *Alliance & Leicester v Ghahremani* [1992] RVR 198.

[533] See CPR PD 31 para 2A.1. As to databases see *Derby & Co Ltd v Weldon (No 9)* [1992] 2 All ER 901; *Marlton v Tectronix UK Holdings plc* [2003] EWHC 383 (Ch).

[534] CPR PD 31 para 2A.1; Admiralty & Commercial Courts Guide, 8th edn (2009) para E2.5(a).

[535] Practice Direction to Pt 31, para 2A.2.

[536] Admiralty & Commercial Courts Guide, 8th ed (2009) para E2.5(b).

[537] CPR PD 31 para 2A.3; Admiralty & Commercial Courts Guide, 8th edn (2009) para E2.5(b).

[538] CPR PD 31 para 2A.4; Admiralty & Commercial Courts Guide, 8th edn (2006) para E2.5(d).

[539] For example: *Hands v Morrison Construction Services Ltd* [2006] EWHC 2018 (Ch).

[540] CPR PD 31 para 2A.5; Admiralty & Commercial Courts Guide, 8th edn (2009) para E2.5(e); *Digicel (St Lucia) Ltd v Cable & Wireless plc* [2008] EWHC 2522 (Ch), [2009] 2 All ER 1094.

[541] CPR 31.12.

of the listing questionnaire,[542] or at a case-management conference.[543] The party seeking the order must normally file an application notice, supported by evidence, specifying the order sought. The application should specify the document or classes of documents sought, using a schedule if appropriate. It is important to keep the materials sought within proper limits, and the application may be refused or amended if cast too broadly.[544] The same applies in relation to a search requested to be ordered. The grounds for seeking the order may be in the application notice or in the accompanying evidence.[545] The usual grounds for seeking the order are that it is alleged that the search carried out was unreasonably limited, and/or that the party believes that there are relevant documents which ought to be disclosed and it is appropriate to require their disclosure. The evidence should describe the material sought and/or extent of search sought, and explain why it is reasonable and proportionate that each aspect of the order be made. This should be done by reference to the issues in the action. If appropriate, the sources and grounds for believing that particular materials exist should be stated. For cases allocated to the Small Claims Track, Part 31 does not apply, so a party seeking specific disclosure must apply for special directions, and the court may hold a preliminary hearing to determine such an application.[546] Specific disclosure will only be granted if there is at least a prima facie basis for believing that the materials are in the control of the party and are relevant.[547] The court retains a discretion whether to make the order.[548] The court will consider all surrounding circumstances, the importance of the material sought, the nature of the issues, the cost and burden to the disclosing party of compliance and general proportionality.[549] A party opposing such an order should normally file evidence in opposition. The response to an order may be that the respondent party has no materials as sought by the order. Alternatively he may assert that the materials he holds are irrelevant, but only if the court has not already ruled that the particular materials are relevant. The CPR provide that where a party has access to information which is not reasonably available to the other party, the court may direct the party who has access to the information to prepare and file a document recording the information; and to serve a copy of that document on the other party.[550]

100   **Disclosure of copies**

A party need not disclose more than one copy of a document.[551] A copy of a document that

---

[542] As to the Fast Track see CPR PD 28 (The Fast Track) para 2.

[543] Although the Queen's Bench Guide para 7.85 discourages this practice for cases to which it relates. On the timing of specific disclosure applications, see P Matthews and H Malek, *Disclosure*, 3rd edn (London, Sweet & Maxwell, 2007) paras 5.42, 5.43, 5.47.

[544] *David Kahn Inc v Conway Stewart & Co* [1972] FSR 169, [1972] RPC 572; *Gotha City v Sotheby's* [1998] 1 WLR 114 at 123.

[545] CPR PD 31 paras 5.2 and 5.3.

[546] CPR 27.6; also see CPR 27.4(1)(a).

[547] *Portman Building Society v Royal Insurance plc* [1998] PNLR 672.

[548] *Berkeley Administration Inc v MacClelland* [1990] FSR 381.

[549] CPR PD 31 para 5.4.

[550] CPR 35.9.

[551] CPR 31.9(1).

contains the modification, obliteration or other marking feature on which the party intends to rely or which adversely effects his own case or another party's case or supports another party's case, is treated as a separate document.[552]

8–101   Lists of documents

The procedure for standard disclosure is by list. Each party must make and serve on the other party or parties a list of documents in the required form identifying the documents in a convenient order and manner and as concisely as possible.[553] The list must indicate those documents in respect of which the party claims a right or duty to withhold inspection and those documents that are no longer in their control and, in relation to them, what has happened to those documents.[554] The standard disclosure list must also include a disclosure statement setting out the extent of the search that has been made to locate disclosable documents; certifying the understanding of the party making disclosure of the duty to disclose documents; and certifying that to the best of their knowledge they have carried out that duty.[555]

8–102   Documents referred to in statements of case and experts' reports

A party also has the right to inspect documents mentioned in a statement of case, witness statement, witness summary, affidavit or expert's report.[556] Documents are probably only 'mentioned' for this purpose if the reference to them is specific and direct. Mere reference to a transaction which must have been carried out by a particular written document is probably insufficient.[557]

8–103   Non-party disclosure

The court has power to order a person who is not a party to the proceedings to disclose whether documents relevant to an issue in the claim are in that person's possession, custody or power, and to produce those documents.[558] Such an order shall not be made if compliance would be likely to be injurious to the public interest.[559] The court may only make such an order where the documents are likely to support the applicant's case or adversely affect another party's case, or if disclosure is necessary to dispose of the claim fairly or save costs.[560] This power applies to

---

[552] CPR 31.9(2).

[553] CPR 31.10(1)–(3).

[554] CPR 31.10(4).

[555] CPR 31.10(5), (6).

[556] CPR 31.14; *Expandable Ltd v Rubin* [2008] EWCA Civ 59, [2008] 1 WLR 1099.

[557] P Matthews and H Malek, *Disclosure*, 3rd edn (London, Sweet & Maxwell, 2007) ch 9.

[558] CPR 31.17. Supreme Court Act 1981/Senior Courts Act 1981 s 34 (The Supreme Court Act 1981 is to be renamed the 'Senior Courts Act 1981' on the coming into force of the Constitutional Reform Act 2005 Sch 11 Pt 1 para 1(2)); County Courts Act 1984 s 53. *Burrells Wharf Freeholds Ltd v Galliard Homes Ltd* [1999] 2 EGLR 81; *Hipwood v Gloucester Health Authority* [1995] ICR 999; *Re Howglen* [2001] 1 All ER 376; *Three Rivers District Council v Bank of England (Disclosure) (No 4)* [2002] EWCA Civ 1182, [2002] 4 All ER 881; *Rowe v Fryers* [2003] EWCA Civ 655; *Franlison v Home Office* [2003] EWCA Civ 665, [2003] 1 WLR 1952.

[559] Supreme Court Act 1981/Senior Courts Act 1981 s 35(1).

[560] CPR 31.17(3). *Re Howglen Ltd* [2001] 1 All ER 376; *Three Rivers District Council v Bank of England (No 4)* [2002] EWCA Civ 1182, [2003] 1 WLR 210; *Frankson v Home Office* [2003] EWCA Civ 655, [2003] 1 WLR 1952; *A v X and B (Non-party)* [2004] EWHC 447; *Flood v Times Newspapers Ltd* [2009] EWHC 411 (QB), [2009] EMLR 18.

all legal proceedings, not just those relating to personal injury or death (as was formerly the case). Disclosure can be ordered to be made to medical or legal advisers only,[561] or on the giving of certain undertakings.[562] Applications for disclosure by persons not a party to the proceedings are made, as with interlocutory applications generally, under Part 23. The application must be supported by evidence.[563] This can be achieved by simply verifying the application with a statement of truth, if the application covers the requisite matters.[564] The order must specify the documents or class of documents to be disclosed and require the respondent, when making disclosure, to specify which documents are no longer in his control or those in relation to which he claims a right or duty to withhold inspection.[565]

04 Access to documents used in other litigation

Where civil proceedings are held in open court, the public may attend, take notes and publish or otherwise use information heard during those proceedings.[566] The same generally applies to criminal cases,[567] though there are a number of important statutory exceptions.[568] The public normally are allowed access to witness statements and written submissions used in civil litigation.[569] Until such time as documents are read to or by the court, or referred to, at a hearing held in public, it is impermissible for a party to the proceedings to use disclosed documents for a collateral or ulterior purpose, without the leave of the court or the consent of the party providing the documents.[570] This principle is now articulated in the Civil Procedure Rules.[571] The principle applies equally to documents produced under a witness summons or under the '*Norwich Pharmacal*' procedure.[572]

05 Court records

Courts keep an accessible register of claims which have been issued out of that court. Members of the public may inspect that register, and any person who pays the prescribed fee may search

---

[561] Supreme Court Act 1981 s 34(2)(b).

[562] See, eg, *Church of Scientology v DHSS* [1979] 1 WLR 723.

[563] CPR 31.17(2).

[564] CPR PD 31 para 9.7.

[565] CPR 31.17(4).

[566] *Forbes v Smith* [1998] 1 All ER 973; *Hodgson v Imperial Tobacco* [1998] 2 All ER 673; cf *Clibbery v Allen* [2002] EWCA Civ 45, [2002] Fam 261, [2002] 1 All ER 865. In relation to proceedings held in private see s 12 of the Administration of Justice Act 1960.

[567] For example, under the Criminal Appeal Rules 1968, r 19 (transcripts).

[568] For example, under the Children and Young Persons Act 1933 s 37; Official Secrets Act 1920 s 8.

[569] *GIO Personal Investment Services Ltd v Liverpool and London Steamship, etc Ltd* [1999] 1 WLR 984.

[570] *Alterskye v Scott* [1948] 1 All ER 469; *Crest Homes plc v Marks* [1987] 1 AC 829; *Taylor v Serious Fraud Office* [1999] 2 AC 177. By 'collateral or ulterior' is meant any use not reasonably necessary for the proper conduct of the action in which they were disclosed: *Home Office v Harman* [1983] AC 280 at 302, 312 and 319. See also: *Woolgar v Chief Constable of Sussex* [2000] 1 WLR 25, [1999] 3 All ER 604; *Preston Borough Council v McGrath*, The Times, 19 May 2000 (CA); *McBride v The Body Shop International plc* [2007] EWHC 1658 (QB).

[571] CPR 31.22.

[572] *Sybron Corp v Barclays Bank plc* [1985] Ch 299 at 318–320.

the register of claims.[573] A party to proceedings may obtain from the records of the court a copy of any of the various types of documents listed in para 4.2A of the Practice Direction to Pt 5 of the CPR; and obtain from the records of the court a copy of any other document filed by a party or communication between the court and a party or another person.[574] In general a person who is not a party to proceedings may obtain from the court records copies of the following documents:

— a statement of case, but not any documents filed with or attached to the statement of case, or intended by the party whose statement it is to be served with it;

— a judgment or order given or made in public (whether made at a hearing or without a hearing); and

— if the court gives permission, a copy of any other document filed by a party, or a copy of any communication between the court and a party or another person.

8– 106 **Summonses to produce documents**

Prior to the Civil Procedure Rules, a person (including a public authority) could be subpoenaed to attend court to produce documents.[575] The procedure is now called a 'witness summons', which can be used to require a witness to attend court and produce documents.[576] Permission of the court is not generally required for the issue of a witness summons.[577] Both the recipient of the witness summons and a party with an interest in the document may apply to set it aside.[578]

9. INFORMATION RIGHTS IN CONNECTION WITH CRIMINAL PROCEEDINGS

8– 107 **Introduction**

Although in strict legal theory the prosecution of offences is commenced by private individuals, in practice the prosecutor in the vast majority of cases is a police officer acting in the course of his duties[579] or some other governmental or quasi-governmental body which is likely to be a public authority for the purposes of the Freedom of Information Act 2000 or the

---

[573] CPR 5.4.

[574] CPR 5.4B.

[575] A *subpoena duces tecum* under RSC O 38 r 14.

[576] CPR 34.2(1).

[577] Unless the summons is issued less than seven days before the date of the trial or is returnable other than at trial: CPR 34.3. The power to obtain disclosure against non-parties makes the early return date procedure less important than it was previously.

[578] See the discussion in Malek (ed), *Phipson on Evidence*, 17th ed (London, Sweet & Maxwell, 2010) ch 8.

[579] Which leads automatically to the prosecution being taken over by the Director of Public Prosecutions and the Crown Prosecution Service: Prosecution of Offences Act 1985 s 3(2)(a).

Environmental Information Regulations 2004.[580] In the course of criminal proceedings the prosecutor comes under various obligations to disclose information to the defendant. Such information obviously includes the evidence on which the prosecutor proposes to rely to prove his case; but it also includes material the prosecutor has which will not be relied on but which weakens the prosecution case or strengthens that of the defendant, which is traditionally referred to as 'unused material'. Fairness ordinarily requires that such material is disclosed and 'the golden rule is that full disclosure...should be made'.[581] The only derogation from that 'golden rule' is known as 'public interest immunity': in certain circumstances such material is withheld on the ground that its disclosure would risk serious prejudice to an important public interest.[582] The exact scope, timing and nature of the prosecution obligations of disclosure depend on the nature of the offence[583] and whether it is tried summarily in the magistrates' court or on indictment in the Crown Court. This section will deal first with the procedural framework, then with public interest immunity, then with the question of obtaining disclosure from third parties in the course of criminal proceedings and finally with the relationship between the rights of defendants given by the criminal process and statutory rights under the legislation with which this work is primarily concerned, namely the Freedom of Information Act, the Environmental Information Regulations, and the Data Protection Act 1998.

08 Evidence to be relied on — Crown Court

Although there is often some disclosure at an earlier stage,[584] the legal obligation on the prosecutor to disclose the evidence to be relied on generally arises after the case has been transferred to the Crown Court. Where a case is 'sent' to the Crown Court by the magistrates under s 51 of the Crime and Disorder Act 1998 (which will be the most common procedure

---

[580] For example: local authorities, which have numerous prosecutorial functions, the Health and Safety Executive (or inspectors appointed under s 19 of the Health and Safety at Work, etc Act 1974), the Environment Agency, HM Revenue & Customs, the DTI, DEFRA, the Food Standards Agency, Financial Services Authority, Office of Fair Trading or the General Medical Council.

[581] *R v H* [2004] UKHL 3 [2004] 2 AC 134, [2004] 1 All ER 1269, [2004] 2 Cr App R 10, [2004] HRLR 20 at [14] (Lord Bingham).

[582] *R v H* [2004] UKHL 3 [2004] 2 AC 134, [2004] 1 All ER 1269, [2004] 2 Cr App R 10, [2004] HRLR 20 at [18].

[583] In summary, triable only on indictment or triable 'either way'; readers will need to refer to standard books on criminal procedure for a full account of these terms and the procedure by which cases are assigned to the Crown Court or the magistrates' court, in particular *Archbold Criminal Pleading Evidence and Practice* and *Blackstone's Criminal Practice*.

[584] For example: (1) the police may decide to make disclosure of evidence to the defendant and/or his lawyer at the interview stage (note that the defendant must be informed at that stage of 'the nature of the offence' he is being interviewed about and of any significant statement or silence of his which might be evidence of guilt: see Police and Criminal Evidence Act 1984 Code C paras 11.1A and 11.4); (2) the prosecutor may be obliged if the defendant so requests to disclose 'advance information' in the form of witness statements or a summary in relation to an either-way offence before the magistrates consider mode of trial (see Criminal Procedure Rules Pt 21); (3) the CPS recommends that a standard package of advance information is served on the defendant for cases falling within the s 51 of the Crime and Disorder Act 1998 even though there is no mode of trial decision to be made; this will include the charge sheet, any summary of the prosecution case, key witness statements and a print-out of previous convictions (see: Sprack, *A Practical Approach to Criminal Procedure*, 11th edn para 13.14).

under which criminal cases come before the Crown Court)[585] the prosecutor must serve on the defendant copies of the documents containing the evidence 'on which any charge is based' within 70 days (or, if the defendant is in custody, 50 days).[586] At this stage the prosecutor is effectively bound to serve all the evidence needed to support a proper conviction since, if the evidence is insufficient, the judge must dismiss the charge and thereafter no further proceedings can be brought.[587] It still remains open to the prosecutor to use additional evidence at trial and in theory there is no obligation to give advance disclosure of it but the invariable modern practice is that notice of that intention is given to the defendant with a copy of a statement of the additional evidence at the earliest opportunity.[588]

8–109   Magistrates' Court

In cases which are to be tried in a magistrates' court, the Criminal Procedure Rules 2010 provide that the prosecutor must at or before the beginning of the day of the first hearing serve 'initial details' of the prosecution case, unless the court otherwise directs.[589] 'Initial details' consist of a summary of the evidence or any statement or other document setting out the facts and the Defendant's previous convictions.[590] Further, the courts have expressed the view that the Crown Prosecution Service should in all but exceptional cases supply the defendant with copies of prosecution witness statements[591] and the Attorney-General's Guidelines on Disclosure of Information in Criminal Proceedings also state that the prosecutor should provide the defendant with all evidence to be relied on in sufficient time for him to consider it.[592] A failure to give sufficient notice of the prosecution case might very well involve a breach of article 6 of the European Convention on Human Rights, in particular article 6(3)(b) (which requires that a criminal defendant be given adequate time and resources to prepare his defence), and form the basis for (at least) a successful application for an adjournment.

---

[585] At the time of writing committal proceedings still exist in relation to 'either-way' offences but the intention is that the procedure under s 51 of the Crime and Disorder Act 1998 of 'sending' cases to the Crown Court should entirely replace committal proceedings when Sch 3 to the Criminal Justice Act 2003 comes into force and when that happens all cases which would have been subject of committal proceedings and are tried in the Crown Court will either have been 'sent' or be the subject of a voluntary bill of indictment. While committal proceedings do still exist the prosecution obligation to disclose its evidence necessarily comes at an earlier stage (see Magistrates Court Act 1980 ss 4–6). Somewhat different rules apply in relation to child witness and serious fraud cases; in the latter the defendant must be given a statement of the evidence relied on at the same time as he is given a copy of the 'notice of transfer' to the Crown Court: see Criminal Justice Act 1987 (Notice of Transfer) Regulations 1988 SI 1988/1691.

[586] See Crime and Disorder Act 1998 (Service of Prosecution Evidence) Regulations 2005 SI 2005/902 reg 2; the court can extend time under reg 3.

[587] Save by preferment of a voluntary bill of indictment (which requires the consent of a High Court judge): see Crime and Disorder Act 1998 Sch 3 para 2(6)(a).

[588] It appears that failure to follow this practice would not make the evidence inadmissible but that if there was insufficient notice the court would grant a suitable adjournment or could exclude the evidence on the ground of unfairness under Police and Criminal Evidence Act 1984 s 78: see *R v Wright* (1934) 25 Cr App R 35 (Avory J) at 40.

[589] Criminal Procedure Rules 2010 rr 21.1 and 21.2.

[590] Civil Procedure Rules 2010, r.21.3.

[591] See *R v Stratford Justices, ex p Imbert* [1999] All ER (D) 115, [1999] 2 Cr App R 276 (Buxton LJ and Collins J).

[592] See para 57 of the Guidelines which can be accessed at:
www.cps.gov.uk/legal/a_to_c/attorney_generals_guidelines_on_disclosure/.

10 'Unused material' — Crown Court

The obligation on the prosecutor to disclose 'unused material' is now exclusively governed by the statutory rules found in Part I of the Criminal Procedure and Investigations Act 1996.[593] The prosecutor must disclose any material (the expression includes information)[594] which is in his possession or which he has inspected under the Code of Practice issued under Part II of the Act[595] and 'which might reasonably be considered capable of undermining the case for the prosecution against the accused or of assisting the case for the accused',[596] unless he successfully applies to the court for an order that it is not in the public interest that the material be disclosed[597] or its disclosure is prohibited by s 17 of the Regulation of Investigatory Powers Act 2000.[598] The prosecutor must comply with this duty as soon as reasonably practicable after the service of evidence when the case is sent to the Crown Court or after the preferring of a bill of indictment.[599] The legislation refers to that duty as 'the initial…duty to disclose' but the duty to disclose is a continuing one and the prosecutor must keep the existence of material that ought to be disclosed under review and disclose it to the defendant as soon as is reasonably practicable.[600] After the initial disclosure there is an obligation on the defendant to give a defence statement setting out the nature of his defence and indicating any matters of fact on which he takes issue with the prosecutor.[601] The service of a defence statement, which is designed to clarify the issues between prosecution and defence, typically results in further disclosure by virtue of the obligation on the prosecutor to keep the matter under review. It is

---

[593] See Criminal Procedure and Investigations Act 1996 s 21 (which excludes the earlier common law rules save in relation to whether public interest immunity applies).

[594] Criminal Procedure and Investigations Act 1996 s 2(4).

[595] The Code (which is set out in full in Blackstone's Criminal Practice) sets out the manner in which police officers (and other investigating officers: see para 1.1) are to record, retain and reveal to the prosecutor relevant material obtained in a criminal investigation. Importantly para 3.5 imposes an obligation on the investigator to pursue all reasonable lines of enquiry (and thereby obtain material) whether these 'point towards or away from the suspect'.

[596] Criminal Procedure and Investigations Act 1996 s 3(1) and (2); the Attorney-General's Guidelines on disclosure of information in criminal proceedings at para 10 point out that such material will include material which can be used in cross-examination, which may support submissions in support of the exclusion of evidence or a stay of proceedings as well as material which might suggest an explanation for a defendant's conduct. It will also include material helpful to a bail application or to sentence mitigation. Under para 2.4 of Code C of the codes of practice issued under the Police and Criminal Evidence Act 1984 the police are obliged to disclose a copy of the custody record which the custody officer is obliged to keep in respect of a defendant's detention at a police station to a solicitor or other adult as soon as practicable after their arrival at the station.

[597] Criminal Procedure and Investigations Act 1996 s 3(6); see also ss 7A(8) and 8(5); see §8– 112 under discussion of public interest immunity.

[598] Criminal Procedure and Investigations Act 1996 s 3(7); see also ss 7A(9) and 8(6).

[599] Criminal Procedure and Investigations Act 1996 s 13; but note that a failure to observe time limits does not on its own constitute grounds for staying proceedings unless it results in the defendant being denied a fair trial: s 10. para 55 of the Attorney-General's Guidelines on disclosure of information in criminal proceedings reminds prosecutors of the need to make disclosure before the duty arises under the Act where justice and fairness so requires where, eg, such disclosure would be relevant to a bail application.

[600] Criminal Procedure and Investigations Act 1996 s 7A(2) and (3).

[601] Criminal Procedure and Investigations Act 1996 ss 5 and 6A. The defence statement must be served within 14 days of the prosecutor complying (or purporting to comply) with his initial duty to disclose; the time limit can be extended but the application must be made before the time limit expires: see Criminal Procedure and Investigations Act 1996 (Defence Disclosure Time Limits) Regulations 1997 SI 1997/684 regs 2 and 3, and Criminal Procedure Rules r 25.7.

also a precondition to an application by the defendant for an order requiring disclosure by the prosecutor.[602] On such an application the court will have to decide whether the relevant material exists,[603] whether it might reasonably be considered capable of undermining the case for the prosecution or of assisting the case for the defence,[604] and, if the prosecutor makes an application at that stage, whether it is not in the public interest that the material be disclosed.[605]

8–111 Summary cases

In a criminal trial proceeding in the magistrates' court the initial duty to make disclosure and the duty to keep the matter under review apply to the prosecutor in the same way as in the Crown Court. However, the defendant does not have to serve a defence statement unless he chooses to do so,[606] but, if he does, it must comply with the same requirements and be served in the same time as a defence statement in the Crown Court. If the defendant does not serve a defence statement the prosecutor will obviously not be able to review disclosure in the light of it and the defendant cannot make an application for disclosure under s 8 of the Criminal Procedure and Investigations Act 1996, disadvantages which have to be taken into account when deciding whether or not to disclose his case to the prosecutor. Regardless of a defence statement being served the defendant retains the right to invite the court to review the question whether it is in, or not in, the public interest to disclose material but the court is not under a duty to keep the question under review as it is in the Crown Court.[607]

8–112 Public interest immunity — General

In certain circumstances material which may undermine the prosecution or assist the defence and which is held by the prosecutor nevertheless cannot be disclosed because to do so may risk serious prejudice to an important public interest. The most common relevant public interest is the effective investigation and prosecution of crime, which may involve informers or undercover agents or the use of surveillance or other techniques which cannot be disclosed without exposing individuals to risk or jeopardising other investigations;[608] other public interests include safeguarding national security and protecting children from the disclosure of sensitive information held by local authority social services departments. The Code of Practice made under Part II of the Criminal Procedure and Investigations Act 1996 contains a list of examples of so-called 'sensitive material' (the disclosure of which would give rise to a real risk of serious prejudice to an important public interest) which the police must list separately for the prosecutor: this list contains many common heads of public interest immunity, although not

---

[602] Criminal Procedure and Investigations Act 1996 s 8(1) and (2).

[603] Such an application can cover material in the prosecutor's possession, material which he has inspected under the Pt II Code and material which the prosecutor can require to have disclosed to him under that Code: s 8(3) and (4).

[604] Criminal Procedure and Investigations Act 1996 s 8(2) and 7A(2) and (3).

[605] Criminal Procedure and Investigations Act 1996 s 8(5): see §8–112 under discussion of public interest immunity.

[606] Criminal Procedure and Investigations Act 1996 s 6.

[607] cf Criminal Procedure and Investigations Act 1996 ss 13 and 14.

[608] See *R v H* [2004] UKHL 3, [2004] 2 AC 134, [2004] 1 All ER 1269, [2004] 2 Cr App R 10, [2004] HRLR 20 at [18].

necessarily all, and some are clearly stated too widely.[609] If it is concluded that the disclosure of certain material would prejudice the relevant public interest that is not the end of the matter: the court (not the prosecution) must carry out a balancing exercise and decide whether the public interest in non-disclosure outweighs the interests of justice in there being full disclosure in the case. If the court concludes that the material may prove a defendant's innocence or avoid a miscarriage of justice or (to put it another way) that any failure to disclose may have the effect of rendering '...the trial process, viewed as a whole, unfair to the defendant', the balance will come down resoundingly in favour of disclosure and the material must either be disclosed to the defence or the prosecution abandoned.[610] In carrying out the balancing exercise the court will seek to find a solution by adopting measures which give the maximum disclosure possible in order to achieve a fair trial while withholding only the information which the public interest in question requires it to withhold.[611]

3 Procedure

The court's role as the exclusive arbiter of whether disclosure is or is not required is now put on a firm statutory basis by the Criminal Procedure and Investigations Act 1996: if the prosecutor has possession of or has inspected material which might undermine his case or assist the defence he must either disclose it or apply for an order from the court that it is not in the public interest that he disclose it and if on such an application the court requires disclosure but the prosecutor still wants to withhold it the prosecution must be abandoned.[612] The procedure for such applications is laid down in Part 22 of the Criminal Procedure Rules 2010. Notice of the application, describing the material to which it relates, must be served on the defendant but only to the extent that serving it on the defendant would not disclose what the prosecutor thinks ought not to be disclosed and on any person who the prosecutor thinks would be directly affected by disclosure of the material.[613] The application is determined at a hearing normally held in private and, if the court so directs, it can take place wholly or partly in the defendant's absence,[614] but the judge should always involve the defence to the maximum extent possible without undermining the public interest to be protected and in really exceptional cases it may be appropriate for the court to appoint special counsel to protect the defendant's interests in a

---

[609] See para 6.12 of the Code for the list; 'material given in confidence' is clearly formulated too widely.

[610] See: *R v Keane* [1994] 2 All ER 478 at 483g to 484e; *R v H* [2004] UKHL 3, [2004] 2 AC 134, [2004] 1 All ER 1269, [2004] 2 Cr App R 10, [2004] HRLR 20 at [36(6)].

[611] For examples of how the court might seek to achieve this end see *R v H* [2004] UKHL 3, [2004] 2 AC 134, [2004] 1 All ER 1269, [2004] 2 Cr App R 10, [2004] HRLR 20 at [36] and the Code of Practice under Pt II of the Criminal Procedure and Investigations Act 1996 at para 10.5.

[612] See ss 3(6), 7A(8) and 8(5). Before the decision in *R v Ward* [1993] 1 WLR 619 the decision on public interest immunity was normally taken internally by the prosecution; in that case the Court of Appeal stated that the decision was one for the court and that the prosecution must always give notice to the defence that they proposed to withhold material on grounds of public interest immunity, but that rule was modified shortly thereafter so as to allow for ex parte applications to the court in limited circumstances, a position now reflected in the Criminal Procedure Rules Pt 25: see *R v Davis* [1993] 1 WLR 613. Note that unless the material is reasonably considered capable of weakening the prosecution or assisting the defence there is no question of the public interest being considered and the prosecution does not need to apply at all if it is clear that the material is not so capable: see *R v H* [2004] UKHL 3, [2004] 2 AC 134, [2004] 1 All ER 1269, [2004] 2 Cr App R 10, [2004] HRLR 20 at [35].

[613] Criminal Procedure Rules 2010 r 22.3(2)(b)(ii) and (iii).

[614] Criminal Procedure Rules 2010 r 22.3(6) and (7).

case where he and his lawyers cannot be heard.[615] Any third party who was involved in drawing the attention of the prosecutor to material and who claims to have an interest in it should be notified of an application and is entitled to make representations to the court on the application.[616] The court can only determine the application if satisfied that it has been able to take account of any rights of confidentiality in the material and the defendant's right to a fair trial.[617] Although this is not stated in the rules, it is submitted that it is always open to the court to inspect the material itself if it is necessary to do so in the course of an application, but in a national security case, once there is an actual or potential risk demonstrated by an appropriate ministerial certificate, the court will be reluctant to do so.[618] The court should state its reasons for making an order that it is not in the public interest for material to be disclosed and a record kept of such reasons, but only the prosecutor will be notified of the decision and reasons unless the court otherwise directs.[619] Once a decision has been made that material should not be disclosed that decision must be kept under review by the court throughout the trial process; in the Crown Court the court is obliged to keep the matter under review of its own motion whereas in the magistrates' court a review will only take place on an application by the defendant.[620]

8–114   Disclosure from third parties

The disclosure obligations discussed above lie on the prosecutor in a criminal case but it may be that a third party is in possession of material which may weaken the prosecution or strengthen the defence case. The Code of Practice issued under Part II of the Criminal Procedure and Investigations Act 1996 and the Attorney-General's Guidelines on disclosure of information in criminal proceedings referred to above contain provisions relevant to material held by third parties. Under the Code, investigators[621] are obliged to pursue all reasonable lines of inquiry (whether pointing towards or away from the suspect) and to seek relevant material[622] from any third parties who may be in possession of it[623] and retain it if obtained and make it available for the prosecutor to disclose if appropriate. The Guidelines also impose on prosecutors the obligation to seek relevant material from government departments or other Crown bodies and from other agencies (for example local authorities, social services

---

[615] *R v H* [2004] UKHL 3, [2004] 2 AC 134, [2004] 1 All ER 1269, [2004] 2 Cr App R 10, [2004] HRLR 20 at [22] and [36].

[616] See Criminal Procedure and Investigations Act 1996 s 16, and Criminal Procedure Rules 2010 r 22.3(2)(b)(ii) and 22.3(5)(b).

[617] Criminal Procedure Rules 2010 r 22.3(8).

[618] See comments of Roch LJ at p 8 of All England official transcript of *Powell v Chief Constable of North Wales Constabulary* (16 December 1999) and, in relation to ministerial certificates relating to national security, *Balfour v Foreign and Commonwealth Office* [1994] 2 All ER 588 at 596e; note that case was an unfair dismissal claim and in a criminal case the court is likely to be more ready to inspect a document to establish its materiality and how much assistance it would be likely to give to the defence before deciding the public interest immunity issue.

[619] Criminal Procedure Rules 2010 r 22.3(9).

[620] Criminal Procedure and Investigations Act 1996, ss 14 and 15; the procedure is in Criminal Procedure Rules 2010 r 22.6.

[621] That is, police officers and those charged with the duty of conducting investigations (see Code para 1.1).

[622] The test of relevance in the Code is wider than the test for disclosure: see definitions at para 2.1.

[623] Code paras 3.5 and 3.6.

departments, hospitals, doctors, schools) and, where they cannot obtain access to the material, to consider what further steps to take including notifying the defence and applying for a witness summons under the procedure discussed below.[624] If a third party is in possession of material which may be relevant to a criminal trial and will not voluntarily disclose it to the prosecutor or direct to the defence the only means within the criminal proceedings by which such disclosure can be enforced is an application under s 2 of the Criminal Procedure (Attendance of Witnesses) Act 1965 (in the Crown Court) or s 97 of the Magistrates' Courts Act 1980 (in the magistrates' court). These sections enable the court to issue a summons requiring a person to attend to give evidence or produce a 'document or thing' if he is likely to be able to give evidence or produce something which is likely to be 'material evidence'. However, the requirements for making an order under these sections are much stricter than those which impose a disclosure obligation on the prosecutor; in particular the authorities establish that: (1) in order to be material evidence for the purposes of the sections any documents must be admissible as such in evidence; (2) documents desired only for the purposes of possible cross-examination are not so admissible; (3) the applicant must show a 'real possibility' that the person has the document or can give the evidence and that it is 'material' and (4) it is not sufficient that the applicant merely wants to find out whether the person has the information or document: the procedure must not be used as a disguised attempt to obtain discovery.[625] The procedure relating to orders under these sections is set out in the Criminal Procedure Rules 2010 at Part 28. The Rules make clear that, even if the evidence sought is 'material', it must be in the interests of justice for an order to be made[626] and that rights of confidentiality are properly balanced against the reasons for making an order.[627] Further, it is of course open to an agency in possession of material evidence to object to an order on the basis that it is covered by public interest immunity, though this argument will frequently be coupled with the question whether the evidence is 'material' for the purposes of the sections at all. Notwithstanding the strict requirements referred to above, it is likely that in practice in serious criminal cases the judge will strain to adopt a 'pretty liberal regime' in order to enforce disclosure of documents by third party agencies which would assist the defence.[628] Further, it seems clear that in extreme cases the court can stay a prosecution where there is material which may undermine the prosecution or assist the defence which the third party refuses to disclose voluntarily notwithstanding that the prosecutor has conscientiously complied with all his disclosure obligations.[629]

---

[624] Guidelines paras 47 to 54.

[625] See *R v Reading Justices, ex p Berkshire County Council* [1996] FCR 535 at 542–3.

[626] Criminal Procedure Rules 2010 r 28.3(2)(b)(ii).

[627] See: Criminal Procedure Rules 2010 rr 28.5(4)(b), 28.6(1)(b), 28.7(1)(b)(iii), 28.7(1)(c)(iii).

[628] See *R v Brushett* [2000] All ER (D) 2432, a case in which the Court of Appeal approved of the judge's approach in a case where a defendant accused of abuse of children under his care sought access to social services files some of which were not strictly disclosable by the prosecutor. The judge said that if the files indicated victims making false allegations in the past or abuse by another adult he would order disclosure in any event, adopting a 'pretty liberal regime'.

[629] See *R v Alibhai* [2004] EWCA Crim 681 at [63]–[64].

8– 115 **Relationship between criminal disclosure rights and those under Freedom of Information Act 2000, Environmental Information Regulations 2004 and Data Protection Act 1998**

Apart from the criminal disclosure rules discussed above, the Freedom of Information Act 2000, the Environmental Information Regulations 2004 and the Data Protection Act 1998 contain rights of access to information which may in some circumstances be available and advantageous to a criminal defendant. The main distinctions between a defendant's rights under that legislation and those under the criminal disclosure rules are:

(1) Under the Freedom of Information Act and the Environmental Information Regulations the information must be held by a 'public authority' and (in the case of the regulations) amount to 'environmental information' and under the Data Protection Act 1998 it must amount to 'personal data' about the defendant held by a 'controller'; but if a defendant is entitled to information under the legislation he can seek it at any time, whereas any right to disclosure in a criminal case follows the timetable outlined above.

(2) There is no test of relevance or materiality to be satisfied under the legislation: provided the information comes within the terms of the relevant legislation and no exemption applies the defendant will be able to obtain disclosure without showing that it is relevant or material to the criminal case and without serving a defence statement.

(3) The prosecutor is under an obligation to obtain and disclose information of his own motion and to keep under review what further information ought to be disclosed: under the legislation it is up to the defendant to request specific information and he will need to be able to identify it in some way.

(4) Under the legislation disclosure can be obtained from any third party provided they are a 'public authority' or a 'data controller' as the case may be: there is no need to satisfy any higher test if disclosure is required from someone other than the prosecutor in the case.

(5) The decision as to whether the information must be disclosed under the criminal disclosure rules lies with the prosecutor and then with the court seized of the criminal proceedings; under the legislation the decision lies with the body from whom a request for information is made and then the county court under s 9 of the Data Protection Act 1998 or, as the case may be, the Information Commissioner and the First-tier or Upper Tribunal under the Freedom of Information Act 2000 or the Environmental Information Regulations 2004: it is likely that the decision of the criminal court in an individual case would be much quicker to obtain whenever there is a dispute as to entitlement.

(6) Under the criminal disclosure rules information satisfying the relevant test of materiality must (subject to public interest immunity) be disclosed; under the Acts there are various exemptions which may apply to requests by a defendant for such information, for example:

(a) any information held by a prosecutor or investigator for the purposes of the criminal proceedings themselves will very likely come within s 30(1) or (2) of the Freedom of Information Act 2000 (or subject to adverse effects within reg 12(5)(b) of the Environmental Information Regulations 2004) and thus be exempt from disclosure under the relevant legislation, subject to the normal public interest test; it is not clear whether in the application of that test the fact that disclosure under the criminal disclosure rules is to take place in any event at a later stage would point towards or away from disclosure under the legislation;

(b)   personal data about the defendant held by a prosecutor or investigator are likely to be exempt from the disclosure provisions in Data Protection Act 1998 by virtue of s 29 on the basis that their disclosure would be likely to prejudice the prosecution of crime; but in this case it may be that no relevant prejudice could be shown as resulting from the early disclosure of personal data which would later be disclosable in any event so that the exemption may not apply.

(7)   The sort of disclosure often sought from third parties by a defendant in the context of criminal proceedings may be exempted by s 38 (health and safety) or s 41 (information provided in confidence) of Freedom of Information Act 2000 or statutory instruments made under s 30 of Data Protection Act 1998 (health, education and social work); exemptions of this nature would be unlikely to be relevant to a request under the Freedom of Information Act 2000 or Environmental Information Regulations 2004 for environmental or other technical information in connection with regulatory criminal proceedings;

(8)   Section 21 of the Freedom of Information Act 2000[630] which exempts information which is 'reasonably accessible to the applicant otherwise than under' the Act, would arguably prevent a request under the Act by a defendant in criminal proceedings addressed to the police or the prosecutor. Section 21 is dealt with elsewhere in this work but it may be arguable that it should not apply to such a request on the grounds that (1) the request was made at a time when the disclosure rules had not made the information disclosable (and the precise issues in the criminal case may not be clear) or (2) if s 21(2)(b) is a definition rather than a deeming provision s 21 would not exempt information disclosable under the criminal disclosure rules since those rules clearly do not make information accessible to 'members of the public' as opposed to the defendant himself.[631]

(9)   The heads of public interest immunity applied under the criminal disclosure rules are broadly analogous to various exemptions on the basis of which disclosure under the Acts can be resisted[632] and there is a balancing exercise to be performed under the Freedom of Information Acts in relation to some of them; however, to the defendant's disadvantage there is no balancing exercise called for under the Data Protection Act 1998 and the balancing exercise under the Freedom of Information

---

[630] FOI(S)A s 25 is the corresponding section in relation to information held by Scottish public authorities; the exemption is absolute.

[631] cf DPA s 34, which makes it clear that for the exemption to apply the information must be otherwise accessible to the public as opposed to a particular individual.

[632] For example, prejudice to national security: cf FOIA ss 23 and 24 and DPA s 28(2) prejudice to criminal investigations; cf FOIA ss 30 and 31 and DPA s 29(3) maintenance of certain confidences: FOIA s 41.

Act 2000 or Environmental Information Regulations (where it applies)[633] is not strictly the same as under the criminal disclosure rules: under the Freedom of Information Act the question is whether the public interest in maintaining the exemption outweighs the public interest in disclosing the information generally;[634] under the criminal disclosure rules the balance is between the public interest in withholding disclosure and the interests of justice in having full disclosure in the particular case before the court (which balance, as mentioned above, is likely to come down resoundingly in favour of disclosure if the court, which will keep the matter under constant review, concludes there is a danger of a miscarriage of justice in the case).

(10) Information disclosed under the Acts can be used in any way the defendant wishes; disclosure under the Criminal Procedure and Investigations Act 1996 can be used only for the purposes of the criminal case in question unless it has already been revealed in open court or the court gives permission.[635]

---

[633] Which it does not, eg, if the information was supplied to the public authority by, or relates to, a security body (see FOIA s 23) or if it was supplied to the public authority by another person in circumstances where its disclosure would amount to a breach of confidence (see FOIA s 41)

[634] It is a moot point to what extent the interests of the particular defendant in respect of his criminal case are relevant to this general interest: see §§15– 015 to 15– 016.

[635] Criminal Procedure and Investigations Act 1996 ss 17 and 18(1). The procedure for applying for such provision is laid down in the Criminal Procedure Rules 2010 r 22.7.

CHAPTER 9
The Right to Information

1.   THE NATURE OF INFORMATION

9– 001   Introduction

The rights of access conferred by the Freedom of Information Act 2000 and the Environmental Information Regulations 2004 are rights conferred in relation to 'information'.[1] Similarly, engagement of any of the provisions of Part II of the Act,[2] which render information exempt information, turns upon the attributes of the information in question or upon the likely effects of its disclosure: it does not turn upon the attributes of the document or record containing the information sought nor upon the likely effects of disclosure of such a document or record. If a provision in Part II of the Act does apply, the information that caused it to apply will become exempt information. Only if the document or record is coincident with that information will it thereby be rendered exempt.[3] The unit of disclosure and of exemption may therefore be said to be 'information'.[4] Although information is at the heart of the Freedom of Information Act 2000 and of the Environmental Information Regulations 2004, in relation to the great majority of requests for information it is to be expected that there will be no real question whether that which falls within the terms of a request represents information. The mere ability to consider that a certain matter answers the terms of the request will normally be sufficient indication that that matter constitutes information. Thus, in most cases, the words appearing on the face of a document will represent recorded information capable of being the subject matter of a request. The simplicity of this part of the exercise in the vast majority of cases is deceptive. The word 'information' does not enjoy a clearly delineated, universal meaning, but varies

---

[1]   FOIA s 1; FOI(S)A s 1; EIR reg 5(1); EI(S)R reg 5(1). The DPA employs the term 'data', which is defined to mean 'information' having certain attributes: see further at §5– 012. It is suggested that the analysis below holds true for 'data' under that Act: *Durant v Financial Services Authority* [2003] EWCA Civ 1746, [2004] FSR 28 at [65]. Of the comparative jurisdictions, only New Zealand employs 'information' as the unit of disclosure: see §2– 018. In the United States, a person is entitled to access to 'records' of an agency: see §2– 003. In Australia, the right of access is to 'documents' of an agency: see §2– 011. In Canada, a person is given a right of access to 'records' under the control of a government institution: see §2– 026. And in the Republic of Ireland, a person is given a right of access to any 'record' held by a public institution: see §2– 035.

[2]   Similarly EIR Pt 3 and EI(S)R Pt 3.

[3]   Subject to FOIA s 2; FOI(S)A s 2(1); EIR reg 12(1); EI(S)R reg 10(1). See §14– 001.

[4]   That the distinction in the Act between 'information' and 'record' is both real and intentional is apparent from FOIA s 77 and FOI(S)A s 65. The significance of the distinction is discussed in: *DBERR v IC and Friends of the Earth*, IT, 29 April 2008 at [29]; *Glasgow City Council & anor v Scottish IC* [2009] CSIH 73 at [43]. Similarly in relation to 'data' under the DPA: *Durant v Financial Services Authority* [2003] EWCA Civ 1746, [2004] FSR 28 at [65].

according to the context in which it is used.[5] Subject to the qualification introduced by the limited definition of information in the Act,[6] it is suggested that so far as the Freedom of Information Act 2000 and the Environmental Information Regulations 2004 are concerned, 'information' is any matter that is capable of being recorded and of being communicated from one person to another. This definition, which is consistent with the ordinary meaning of the word, avoids the intractable difficulties which attach to any narrower definition of the word.

2   The meaning of 'information'

The term 'information' is defined in the Act to mean information recorded in any form,[7] implicitly recognising that information may also be unrecorded. The *New Shorter Oxford Dictionary* (1993) defines 'information' as:

    1.[....]

    2. Communication of the knowledge of some fact or occurrence.

    3.   a.   Knowledge or facts communicated about a particular subject, event, etc; intelligence, news.

            b.   [....]

            c.   Without necessary relation to a recipient: that which inheres in or is represented by a particular arrangement, sequence, or set, that may be stored in, transferred by, and responded to by inanimate things; Math. a statistically defined quantity representing the probability of occurrence of a symbol, sequence, message, etc as against a number of possible alternatives.

The dictionary definition does not turn upon the recipient's state of knowledge. While the extent, if any, to which material is informative will depend upon the knowledge of the recipient, even with the narrowest dictionary definition material will be 'information' if it is *capable* of being informative, irrespective of whether it is to the recipient. This accords with the nature of disclosure under the Freedom of Information Act 2000 and the Environmental Information Regulations 2004. As it is effectively disclosure to the world, the fact that certain material is wholly uninformative to the applicant does not cause that material to cease to be information.[8] Whether material constitutes information for the purposes of the Act should not, therefore, depend upon the state of knowledge of the applicant.[9] While the same issue may arise in

---

[5] Other fields of human endeavour have struggled to find a satisfactory definition of 'information', with the impetus largely originating with telecommunications and its need to identify the limits of message degradation before that which is received ceases to be information to the recipient. The starting point is generally considered to be found in CE Shannon, 'A mathematical theory of communication' (1948) 27 *Bell System Technical Journal* 379 and 623. There are many treatments of the subject: see, eg R Losee, 'A Discipline Independent Definition of Information' (1997) 48 *Journal of the American Society for Information Science* 254–269.

[6] FOIA s 84; FOI(S)A s 73. Under the environmental information regime, 'information' is not defined, but 'environmental information' is defined: EIR reg 2(1); EI(S)R reg 2(1).

[7] FOIA s 84; FOI(S)A s 73; cf EIR reg 2(1); EI(S)R reg 2(1). An exception is made for FOIA s 51(8), empowering the Information Commissioner to require a public authority to furnish him with information, whether recorded or not recorded, for the purpose of determining whether a public authority has complied or is complying with its duties under Part I of the Act, and for FOIA s 75(2), enabling the Secretary of State for Justice to override a statutory proscription on the disclosure of information, whether recorded or unrecorded, in order to give full effect to FOIA s 1. The equivalent provisions in FOI(S)A, are ss 50(9) and 64(2), respectively.

[8] Most people would, for example, recognise that the Rosetta Stone contains information, even if they were unable to read hieroglyphics, demotic or Greek.

[9] *FCO v IC and Friends of the Earth*, IT, 29 June 2007 at [36(5)].

relation to the state of knowledge of the public authority holding the information,[10] as a matter of practice it is difficult to imagine how a public authority could identify material as being information answering the terms of a request unless the nature of that material were understood by someone within the public authority.

9–003 **The medium on which information is recorded**

The medium on which matter is recorded should not, in principle, impinge upon its characterisation as information.[11] Material stored on the hard disk of a computer or on a video tape is just as much capable of being information as words appearing on a document. So, too, the fact that a machine or an instrument may be required to render the matter intelligible or readable is of no greater significance to its being information than are the spectacles of a long-sighted applicant. This is confirmed by the White Paper that anticipated the introduction of the Act, which indicated that information should extend to computer data, drawings, maps,[12] plans, photographs,[13] images, video and sound recordings.[14]

9–004 **Incorrect or worthless information**

On one view, information that is incorrect may be said not to be information at all. The Government appears to have taken the view during the passage of the Freedom of Information Bill through Parliament that issues about the accuracy of information are separate from the rights of access to information under the Act.[15] In terms of sheer practicality, there is much sense in ignoring inaccuracies in material in deciding whether that material constitutes information. This approach has been taken elsewhere when considering whether material represents information. Thus, in *Win v Minister for Immigration and Multicultural Affairs* the Federal Court of Australia considered that the term was sufficiently wide to cover material that was

---

[10] So that the inscriptions on the Rosetta Stone would represent information even if there were no-one in the British Museum who could read hieroglyphics, demotic or Greek. And, it may be added, the hieroglyphs were information even before Champollion completed his work.

[11] *Glasgow City Council & anor v Scottish IC* [2009] CSIH 73 at [43], [47]; *DBERR v IC and Peninsula Business Services*, IT, 28 April 2009 at [50].

[12] For an instance in which maps were requested: *OFCOM v IC and T-Mobile (UK) Ltd*, IT, 4 September 2007.

[13] For instances in which photographs were requested: *Francis v IC and GMC*, IT, 15 January 2009; *Freebury v IC and Chief Constable of Devon and Cornwall Constabulary*, IT, 5 October 2009.

[14] See, eg Home Office, *Your Right to Know* (1997), para 85,. These are no more than different means for the *storage* or *conveyance* of information. Information stored on a computer is no more than an array of binary digits, wholly unintelligible to an average person. Also included would be undeleted voice-box messages. The EIR specifically provide that 'environmental information' means information in written, visual, aural, electronic or any other material form: EIR reg 2(1) and EI(S)R reg 2(1).

[15] During the Bill's passage through Parliament, Mr David Lock, The Parliamentary Secretary, Lord Chancellor Department, rejected a proposed amendment that would have required a public authority to make a judgment on whether the information is accurate, saying: 'The authority may not know whether the information is accurate, and the cost ceiling for charges made under the freedom of information regime is designed only to cover finding and retrieving the information. The public authority should not have to go to further unlimited lengths in verifying the accuracy of information. If information is disclosed by a public authority under the duty and is subsequently found to be inaccurate, the manufacturer could subject the decision to legal proceedings, thereby placing severe burdens on a range of public authorities on whom the duty was placed. I remind hon. Members that the provisions of clause 13 apply, and that those are the better route' — Hansard HC vol 347 col 909 (4 April 2000).

completely worthless or that was bare assertion.[16]

5 The meaning given to 'information' in other contexts

Of the comparative jurisdictions, only New Zealand employs 'information' as the unit of disclosure. The jurisprudence of that country gives some indication of the scope that has been given to that word and of a general disinclination to refuse a request on the basis that what is sought does not constitute information. In *Commissioner of Police v Ombudsman*,[17] the applicant had been charged with various offences. His solicitors made a request under the Official Information Act 1982 for copies of the briefs of evidence of the witnesses that the police intended to call. This was refused. On appeal to the Ombudsman, he recommended that the information be made available. The police sought judicial review of the Ombudsman's decision. Although the police accepted that the briefs contained 'personal information', the High Court,[18] in a general overview of the Act, considered the meaning of the word 'information':

> Perhaps the most outstanding feature of the definition is that the word "information" is used which dramatically broadens the scope of the whole Act. The stuff of what is held by Departments, Ministers, or organisations is not confined to the written word but embraces any knowledge, however gained or held, by the named bodies in their official capacities. The omission, undoubtedly deliberate, not to define the word "information" serves to emphasise the intention of the Legislature to place few limits on relevant knowledge.[19]

On appeal, the Court of Appeal[20] said:

> Information is not defined in the Act. From this it may be inferred that the draftsman was prepared to adopt the ordinary dictionary meaning of that word. Information in its ordinary dictionary meaning is that which informs, instructs, tells or makes aware. It is reasonable to suppose that, by their very nature, the police briefs contain information pointing to the commission of offences of the kind charged against the appellant and to the involvement of

---

[16] [2001] FCA 56 at [17]–[21], (2001) 105 FCR 212 at 217–218. The case concerned the Migration Act 1958 s 503A, which provides that information communicated in confidence to a migration officer by particular agencies is to be protected from disclosure, including disclosure under the Freedom of Information Act 1982. On the other hand, in *WAGP of 2002 v Minister for Immigration & Multicultural & Indigenous Affairs* (2002) 124 FCR 276 at [26]–[29] the Full Court of the Federal Court held that mere 'observations' did not constitute information. The court there was considering the Migration Act 1958 s 424A, which provides that the Refugee Review Tribunal must give an applicant to that tribunal particulars of any information that it considers would be a reason for affirming a decision, in this case refusing to grant the applicant a protection visa. The Court held that neither of two observations by the Tribunal: (a) that the applicant did not refer to a particular matter in his evidence; and (b) that there was inconsistency between two pieces of information, constituted information. Similarly: *Paul v Minister for Immigration and Multicultural Affairs* (2001) 113 FCR 396 at [99]–[100], [107]–[108] and [116]; *NAIH of 2002 v Minister for Immigration & Multicultural & Indigenous Affairs* (2002) 124 FCR 223; *VAF v Minister for Immigration and Multicultural and Indigenous Affairs* (2004) 206 ALR 471; *SZECF v Minister for Immigration and Multicultural and Indigenous Affairs* [2005] FCA 1200.

[17] [1985] 1 NZLR 578.

[18] Which held that the information was exempt on the grounds that substantial disclosure before trial would be likely to prejudice the maintenance of the law.

[19] [1985] 1 NZLR 578 at 586. See also *Mecklenburg v Kreis Pinneberg der Landrat* [1999] 2 CMLR 418, [1999] Env LR D6, [1999] All ER (EC) 166, where the European Court of Justice had to interpret Council Directive (EEC) 1990/313 on the freedom of access to information on the environment. Article 2(a) of the Directive provides a more detailed definition of information than in the FOIA, but the ECJ showed a willingness to find that the Community legislature intended to make the concept of information a broad one: see para 19.

[20] Which allowed the appellant's appeal and found that the disclosure would not be likely to prejudice the maintenance of the law, including the prevention, investigation and detection of offences, and the right to a fair trial.

the appellant in them.[21]

In other legislative contexts, a similarly broad meaning has been given to the word. Thus, in relation to a trade descriptions offence, the mileage shown on the odometer of a car has been treated as information.[22] In relation to a defence of relying upon information supplied by another to a prosecution under the Consumer Credit Advertisements Regulations 1989, the Divisional Court has held that 'information' extended to advice as well as factual information.[23] And, in relation to the expenses to be borne by the purchaser of land where he requires verification of information not in the possession of the vendor[24] the Court of Appeal has said: '[t]he word "information" is as large as can be.'[25] The suggested definition[26] is sufficiently wide to avoid the need to inquire as to the intelligibility of what is sought to the applicant, or to any other person, or to ascertain its worth or reliability, whilst according with the dictionary meaning.[27]

9– 006   The information must be recorded

As noted above, the access right and the existence right only apply to information that is 'recorded in any form'.[28] In practical effect, the requirement that information be recorded places the Freedom of Information Act 2000 regime closer to the comparative regimes that confer rights to 'documents' and 'records'[29] than to that in New Zealand, which requires only that the information be held, not that it be recorded.[30] The Act and the Regulations specifically do not limit or prescribe the medium on which the information must be recorded. It will cover handwritten or typed information, information stored in any computer storage device, maps, plans, models, any film and any form of magnetic storage such as tapes and videos.[31]

9– 007   No obligation to record what is known

The purpose of the requirement that the information be recorded 'in any form' removes the

---

[21] [1988] 1 NZLR 385 at 402. Considered further in *R v Harvey* [1991] 1 NZLR 242. Not followed in *Vice-Chancellor Macquarie University v FM* [2005] NSWCA 192 dealing with a request under the Privacy and Personal Information Act 1998 (NSW).

[22] For the purposes of the Trade Descriptions Act 1968 s 24(1)(a): *Simmons v Potter* [1975] RTR 347, [1975] Crim LR 354.

[23] *Coventry City Council v Lazarus* (1996) 160 JP 188, [1996] C CLR 5.

[24] Now under the Law of Property Act 1925 s 45(4).

[25] *Re Stuart and Seadon* [1896] 2 Ch 328 at 334.

[26] See §9– 001.

[27] See definition 3c. at §9– 002. That the FOIA recognises that something may be information even though not recorded suggests that, for the purposes of the Act, matter takes on the quality of information before its articulation in one form or another.

[28] FOIA s 84; FOI(S)A s 73. Similarly EIR reg 2(1); EI(S)R reg 2(1).

[29] These terms are given an expanded definition in each of the Acts to cover non-written material and so forth: see §§2– 003, 2– 011, 2– 026 and 2– 035. Similarly, UK legislation regularly gives the term 'document' an expanded definition in order to capture the different media upon which information may be recorded, eg: CPR 31.4; Civil Evidence Act 1995 s 13; Criminal Justice Act 2003 s 134(1); Value Added Tax Act 1994 s 96(1); Charities Act s 97(2).

[30] See §9– 001.

[31] See §9– 003.

need for a public authority to identify and record information held by it but unrecorded.[32] Matters known to an officer or employee of a public authority but not recorded will thus be outside the scope of the Act.[33] Similarly, information that can be assembled from material held by a public authority but which has not been recorded at the time of the receipt of a request will not be information recorded in any form:[34]

> The only obligation under the Act is for the public authority to provide the information it holds of the description specified in the request.[35]

However, a request for information that would be answered by a public authority changing the form in which it holds that information will not involve the creation of new information.[36] The requirement to change the form may involve a considerable imposition on the public authority,[37] including the interrogation of computer database using software to yield a bespoke output directed to answering the request.[38]

8   Information stored in a computer

Computers, which are increasingly used to store the bulk of information held by a public authority, present three particular difficulties so far as the recording of information is concerned. First, any computer will typically store information in a variety of ways, principally

---

[32] Compare House of Commons, *Public Administration Third Report* (Cm 4355, 1999) Annex 6, para 3 (see ch 1 n 64) where the Freedom of Information Unit, Home Office stated, 'we think that it would be unworkable to include information which had not been recorded in any form whatsoever within the scope of the statutory right because of the difficulty of establishing whether such information actually exists. There is a need for absolute clarity when creating statutory rights and obligations.'

[33] Except for the purposes of FOIA ss 51(8) and 75(2). Even if officials of a public authority know more about the matter in respect of which an applicant has made a request for information, the public authority is not obliged to reduce what it knows into writing: *Reed v IC and Astley Abbotts Parish Council*, IT, 29 December 2008 at [12]; *Ingle v IC*, IT, 29 June 2007 at [8]. Nor is the Tribunal concerned with whether a public authority should have recorded or held particular information: *Brigden v IC and North Lincolnshire and Goole Hospitals NHS Trust*, IT, 5 April 2007. The position is the same under Council Regulation (EC) 1049/2001, with the entitlement being to recorded information and not to interrogate the organisation: Case T–264/04 *WWF European Policy Programme v European Union Council* (ECJ 25 April 2007) at [75]–[76].

[34] Thus, the fact that the information held by a public authority is inadequate for the purpose of its functions does not give rise to a right under the FOIA to more adequate information: *Simmons v IC*, IT, 16 December 2005.

[35] *Prior v IC*, IT, 27 April 2006 at [22]. In *Johnson v IC and Ministry of Justice*, IT, 13 July 2007 at [47] the Tribunal held that if answering a request for information merely requires 'simple collation of the raw data [already held] to arrive at the total figures that the Applicant has sought' this does not mean that the requested information is not 'held' by the public authority. In that case the applicant requested statistics on an annual basis of claims allocated to and struck out by individual masters of the High Court. Similarly in *Benford v IC and DEFRA*, IT, 14 November 2007 at [57] the Tribunal held that the production of a redacted list from a computer database did not represent the production of new information.

[36] *Common Services Agency v IC* [2008] UKHL 47, [2008] 1 WLR 1550, where the public authority was required to 'barnardise' the requested information (that is, add -1, 0 or 1 to very low values so as to make more difficult identification of the individuals reflected in those values) held by it. The House of Lords held that the process of barnardisation did not involve the creation of new information, but rather that it represented a change in the form in which the information might be provided.

[37] In *Common Services Agency v IC* [2008] UKHL 47, [2008] 1 WLR 1550 at [15] it was held that this part of the statutory regime should be construed in as liberal a manner as possible.

[38] *SSHD v IC*, IT, 15 August 2008 at [12]. The Tribunal held that there is no difference between 'information' held by a public authority and 'raw data' held on a database held by a public authority. The fact that the public authority had to run an existing computer programme (which it routinely used for other reporting purposes) in order to interrogate the database and yield the output so as to answer the request did not represent creating new information held by the authority.

according to the manner in which the computer needs to access the information at any given time. Its storage systems are conventionally divided into volatile and non-volatile.[39] Volatile memory may properly be said to lack the requisite degree of permanence to be described as having been 'recorded'. The position in relation to non-volatile memory is less straightforward, and this leads to the second difficulty. A computer ordinarily generates numerous temporary or working files during any session, without any specific intervention by the user. Some of these temporary files are stored in the volatile memory, but some are also written to the hard disk of the computer. The computer may automatically delete these files at the end of a session, after a set time, by overwriting them, or they may be left on the hard disk indefinitely. Information so stored can include accessed web pages, back-up files, unsaved documents, overflow files and so forth. These files are generally capable of being retrieved. The unifying feature of these files is that although they contain information, the information has been created and is stored within the computer without specific user intervention. It is arguable, but perhaps no more, that such information is not 'recorded' on the basis that that verb requires an animate subject or at least some conscious decision connected to the process.[40] Thirdly, most computer files, whether word processing and the like or the automatically generated variety, remain accessible for some time after 'deletion', whether deleted automatically or by human intervention.[41] On the footing that the file before its 'deletion' was recorded information, if such a file is deleted but remains accessible, it will continue to be subject to the Act and the Regulations.[42]

---

[39] Volatile memory is 'held' by an electrical charge which requires regular 'refreshing' if it is not to be lost. Unless there is some other source of power, shutting down a computer will result in the loss of this memory. Non-volatile memory does not require such refreshing, and will be stored on devices such as the computer's hard disk. Once 'written' to the disk, it will remain accessible, unless deleted or overwritten.

[40] The *New Shorter Oxford English Dictionary* (1993), gives as the meaning of the verb 'record': '4.a. Relate, tell, or narrate in writing; set down in writing or other permanent form; make a written record of. 4.b. Make an official record of (an action, decision, etc); set down officially or permanently.' In relation to information under the EIR and the EI(S)R, the argument is stronger as those regulations provide that information is held by a public authority 'if the information is in the authority's possession and has been produced or received by the authority': EIR reg 3(2); EI(S)R reg 3(2).

[41] Deletion normally only removes the leading character of the filename, so that that file no longer appears in the list of files which is accessible to most programs. Provided that the file has not been overwritten, it is normally a comparatively simple task to restore the totality, or the better part, of the file by assigning a character to replace the missing one.

[42] It may be that the restoration of the file will cause the cost of compliance to exceed the appropriate limit and enable the public authority to avoid answering the request. See FOIA s 13, FOI(S)A s 12 and §§12– 002 to 12– 007. There is no equivalent let-out in the EIR or the EI(S)R. In MoJ, *FOIA – Procedural Guidance*, undated, it is suggested that 'where it is intended that data should be permanently deleted, and this is not achieved only because the technology will not permit it, authorities may regard such data as having been permanently deleted. This information is no longer considered to be "held" by the authority and does not have to be retrieved or provided in response to a request. This approach is not justified where the information has only been temporarily deleted and is stored in such a way that it could easily be recovered, for example from the Deleted Items folder in Outlook. This information is still considered to be "held" by the Department and may have to be provided if a request is received.' The Tribunal has taken a more rigorous line: *Harper v IC and Royal Mail Group plc*, IT, 15 November 2005 at [17]–[27]. It is notable that certain public authorities, relying on their powers to have access to documents and other recorded information of, eg, taxpayers, will in the exercise of that power restore deleted files from a computer hard disk: see, generally, *R (Paul da Costa & Co (a firm)) v Thames Magistrates' Court* [2002] EWHC 40, [2002] STC 267, [2002] Crim LR 504. Parties to litigation are also required to give access to 'deleted' information on a computer: CPR PD 31 para 2A.

2. THE HOLDING REQUIREMENT

09 **When information is 'held' by a public authority**

For the purposes of the Freedom of Information Act 2000, information is 'held' by a public authority if it is held by the authority otherwise than on behalf of another person, or if it is held by another person on behalf of the authority.[43] The Act has avoided the technicalities associated with the law of disclosure, which has conventionally drawn a distinction between a document in the power, custody or possession of a person.[44] The Act imposes a duty on a public authority to search for information answering the terms of a request.[45] Putting to one side the effects of s 3(2) (see §9–010 below), the word 'held' suggests a relationship between a public authority and the information akin to that of ownership or bailment of goods. Information:

— that is, without request or arrangement, sent to or deposited with a public authority which does not hold itself out as willing to receive it and which does not subsequently use it;[46]

— that is accidentally left with a public authority;[47]

— that just passes through a public authority;[48] or

— that 'belongs' to an employee or officer of a public authority but which is brought[49]

---

[43] FOIA s 3(2). The position is the same under the FOI(S)A s 3(2), except for three differences: information is not held by an authority if it is held by the authority in confidence, having been supplied by a Minister of the Crown or by a department of the Government of the United Kingdom (s 3(2)(a)(ii)); the definition is subject to any qualification set out in Sch 1 (s 3(3)); and there is a particular exception relating to the Keeper of the Records of Scotland (s 3(4)). Differing approaches are taken in the comparative regimes. In the United States, the right attaches to 'agency records:' see §2–003. In Australia, the right attaches to 'documents of an agency:' see §2–011. In New Zealand, the right attaches to information 'held' by a department, etc: see §2–018. In Canada, the right attaches to a record 'under the control' of a government institution: see §2–026. This phrase, too, is vague and the Federal Court in *Canada Post Corp v Canada (Minister of Public Works)* [1995] 2 FC 110, 30 Admin CR (2d) 242 (affirming [1993] 3 FC 320, 19 Admin CR (2d) 230) held that the notion of control was not limited to the power to dispose of a record, that there was nothing in the Act that indicated that the word 'control should not be given a broad interpretation, and that a narrow interpretation would deprive citizens of a meaningful right of access under the Act. In the Republic of Ireland, the right attaches to any record 'held' by a public body: see §2–035.

[44] See P Matthews and H Malek, *Disclosure*, 3rd edn (London, Sweet & Maxwell, 2007) pp 107–114.

[45] See further §13–001.

[46] By analogy with a gratuitous bailment by deposit: *Howard v Harris* (1884) 1 Cab & El 253. In the law of bailment, a slight assumption of control of the chattel so deposited will render the recipient a depositary: *Newman v Bourne and Hollingworth* (1915) 31 TLR 309. For further examples, see N Palmer, *Bailment*, 3rd edn (London, Sweet & Maxwell, 2009) pp 39–44, 619–621 and 712–4.

[47] Also by analogy with a gratuitous bailment by deposit: *Mills v Brooker* [1919] 1 KB 555.

[48] In *Information Commissioner for Western Australia v Ministry of Justice* [2001] WASC 3 at [20] it was held that 'It may be that mere transient physical custody will not suffice. There may arise sometimes questions of knowledge or of intention. For example, there may be inadvertent delivery of documents to an agency, or documents may be presented to an agency for the purpose of inspection (eg when a person presents their birth certificate for the purpose of identification) in circumstances where it is plainly not intended that the document form any part of the records of the agency.'

[49] *Quaere* would this be the case if the employee or officer were to place the information on a computer of the public authority?

by that employee or officer onto the public authority's premises,[50] will, it is suggested, lack the requisite assumption by the public authority of responsibility for or dominion over the information that is necessary before it can be said that the public authority can be said to 'hold' the information. The position under the Environmental Information Regulations 2004 is clearer, those regulations expressly providing that environmental information must have been produced or received by the public authority if it is to be information 'held' by that public authority.[51] Under both regimes, information sent to a public authority without invitation and knowingly kept for any material length of time can probably be said to be held by the public authority. In short, information will not be 'held' by a public authority, it is suggested, where that information neither is nor has been created, sought, used or consciously retained by it. Thus, in the example given by the explanatory notes to the legislation,[52] a Minister's constituency papers would not be held by the department just because the Minister happens to keep them there.[53] It is quite possible for the same information to be held by more than one public authority. For example, if a document is sent by one public authority to another, but the first keeps a copy for itself, both public authorities will be holding the information comprised in the document. There is nothing to stop an applicant making a request to either or both public authorities for the same information.

9–010   Information held by or on behalf of others

Section 3(2) of the Act has two effects. First, to take out of the scope of 'documents held by a public authority' those documents which are held by it on behalf[54] of another person.[55] Secondly, to bring within the scope of 'documents held by a public authority' information held by another person on behalf of that public authority. Thus, where an authority uses a private data storage company to maintain its records,[56] or where information is processed by another on behalf of the authority,[57] that information will be treated as being held by the authority. The

---

[50]   This is the approach that has been taken in the comparative jurisdictions: *Re Horesh and Ministry of Education* [1986] 1 VAR 143 (departmental inquiry concerning the professional relationship between the applicant and the principal of the school at which he had taught, notes taken by a friend of the principal who was also the secretary of the relevant teachers association and not used by the authority were personal to the principal and not disclosable under Australian legislation); *Re Mann and Capital Territory Health Commission* (1983) 5 ALN N368; *Re O'Sullivan and Family Court of Australia* (1997) 47 ALD 765 (dealing with the meaning of the 'documents of a court'); *Loughman v Altman* (1992) 39 FCR 90, 111 ALR 445 (document held to be 'of a court' even though possessed by another agency); *Re Barkhordar and Australian Capital Territory Schools Authority* (1987) 12 ALD 332 (personal documents can become documents of an agency); *Bureau of National Affairs, Inc v US Department of Justice* 742 F (2d) 1484 (DC Cir 1984); *Canada (Privacy Commissioner) v Canada (Labour Relations Board)* [1996] 3 FC 609, (1996) 118 FTR 1, approved on appeal (1996) 180 FTR 313, 25 Admin LR (3d) 305 (notes taken by members of the Canada Labour Relations Board in the course of quasi-judicial proceedings are not under the control of the Board itself).

[51]   EIR reg 3(2); EI(S)R reg 2(2).

[52]   Stationery Office, *Explanatory Notes, Freedom of Information Act 2000*, para 31.

[53]   This has been held to be the case in Australia: *Re Said and Dawkins* (1993) 30 ALD 242.

[54]   The phrase 'on behalf of' suggests an agency relationship between the public authority and the person for whom the information is held.

[55]   Each government department is treated as a separate person: FOIA s 81(1); EIR reg 3(5).

[56]   See Stationery Office, Explanatory Notes, Freedom of Information Act 2000, para 31. See, for example: *Francis v IC and South Essex Partnership Foundation NHS Trust*, IT, 21 July 2008 at [21]-[38]; *Tuckley v IC and Birmingham City Council*, IT, 28 February 2008 at [24]-[32].

[57]   House of Commons, *Public Administration—Third Report* (Cm 4355, 1999) Annex 6, para 6 (see ch 1 n 64).

comparable provision in the Environmental Information Regulations 2004 has the second effect, but not the first effect.[58] A third-party database capable of being accessed by a public authority, as well as by others, is not information held by the public authority.[59] The Act does not expressly deal with the situation of a public authority that has contracted with a person who is not a public authority for the provision of goods or services to that public authority. Such a contract may include the provision of services that would otherwise be carried out by the public authority itself: for example, occupational health services in connection with the public authority's employees. It is not a normal incident of the performance of such a contract that each party to the contract is obliged to share with the other party the information generated by that party in the performance of its contractual obligations. It is suggested that in this case, information acquired or generated by a person with whom a public authority contracts will not, in the absence of some special contractual provision, be held 'on behalf of' the public authority.

11   Information previously or subsequently held

The information which is to be communicated, or to have its existence disclosed, is the information held at the time when the request is received, irrespective of the date at which the information was recorded or came to be held by the public authority.[60] The Freedom of Information Act 2000 and the Environmental Information Regulations 2004 are to this extent retrospective.[61] The public authority is not obliged when answering a request to consider information that is first held or recorded after the receipt of the request, even though this information answers the terms of the request.[62] It follows that a request which is specifically expressed to apply to information of a particular description that may, after receipt of the request, come to be held or recorded by the public authority, is ineffective.[63] Where an appeal is lodged against a decision of a public authority, the appeal body will be concerned with the information held by the public authority at the time of the request, and not at the time of the appeal. The receipt of a request does not, however, require the public authority to take a 'snapshot' of the information held by it at the time of the receipt of the request. The Act

---

[58]   EIR reg 3(2); EI(S)R reg 2(2).

[59]   *Marlow v IC*, IT, 1 June 2006 (Lexis Nexis Butterworths legal information database not information held by a public authority that had access to it).

[60]   FOIA s 1(4); FOI(S)A s 1(4); EIR reg 12(4)(a); EI(S)R reg 10(4)(a). The Tribunal has no power on an appeal to require a public authority to disclose information first held by that public authority after its receipt of the request: *OGC v IC* [2008] EWHC 774 (Admin), [2010] QB 98, [2008] ACD 54 at [105]-[109]. Also, if a public authority has shredded the requested information before a request for that information is received, the request may be refused on that basis: *Mitchell v IC*, IT, 10 October 2005. Similarly, *Harper v IC and Royal Mail Group plc*, IT, 15 November 2005 at [17].

[61]   In relation to the FOIA, this was confirmed by the Home Secretary during the passage of the Bill through the House of Commons: Hansard HC vol 340 col 728 (7 December 1999). Beyond this, the Act is not retrospective: *Mitchell v IC*, IT, 10 October 2005 at [14]. The position is the same in Canada and New Zealand. Only limited retrospectivity is granted by the Freedom of Information Act 1982 (Cth of Aust) s 12(2) and the Freedom of Information Act 1997 (Ireland) s 6(4).

[62]   FOIA s 1(4); EIR reg 12(4)(a); EI(S)R reg 10(4)(a). The wording in the FOI(S)A s 1(4) is slightly different, stating that any such amendment or deletion may be made before the information is given. In addition, the Scottish Act provides that the requested information is not, by virtue of s 1(4), to be destroyed before it can be given unless the circumstances are such that it is not reasonably practicable to prevent such destruction from occurring: s 1(5).

[63]   As has been generally held under the Australian Act: *Murtagh v Federal Commissioner of Taxation* (1984) 1 AAR 419, 54 ALR 313; *Re Edelsten and Australian Federal Police* (1985) 4 AAR 220.

specifically contemplates that a public authority might, in the time between receipt of a request and determination of that request, legitimately have sought to amend or delete information answering the terms of the request. Where such amendment or deletion has taken place, the public authority is not obliged to answer, but may answer, the request so far as the deleted or pre-amendment information is concerned.[64] Nevertheless, a public authority must be careful in amending or deleting information caught by the terms of a request. If a public authority deletes information as the result of its routine application of a pre-existing practice (eg the 6-monthly bulk deletion of email of more than a certain age), then, if that deletion occurs after receipt of a request but before the last date for compliance, that is a matter that may be taken into account under s 1(4) in deciding what information is held by the public authority.[65] If, on the other hand, a public authority, after receiving a request for information but before the date for compliance, decides to cull some of the information that it holds (which includes information covered by the terms of the request), the information deleted almost certainly cannot be taken into account under s 1(4) in deciding what information is held by the public authority.[66] Even in the former case, the deletion of information after receipt of the request may result in the public authority being required to make a greater effort to try to recover the 'deleted' information.[67]

9–012   Alteration, destruction, etc of records

The Freedom of Information Act 2000 does not impose an obligation on a public authority to keep information.[68] However, it is a criminal offence to alter, deface, block, erase, destroy or conceal any record[69] held by a public authority with the intention of preventing the disclosure by that authority of all or any part of the information, to the communication of which the applicant would have been entitled.[70] This applies to the public authority itself (but not a government department)[71] as well as to any person who is employed by, is an officer of, or is subject to the direction of that authority.[72] A prosecution for this offence, which is triable summarily only, can only be brought by the Information Commissioner or with the consent of

---

[64] There is no such let-out in the EIR.

[65] *Harper v IC and Royal Mail Group plc*, IT, 15 November 2005 at [17].

[66] *Harper v IC and Royal Mail Group plc*, IT, 15 November 2005 at [17].

[67] *Harper v IC and Royal Mail Group plc*, IT, 15 November 2005 at [18], [27].

[68] *Babar v IC and British Council*, IT, 14 November 2007 at [33]. However, a public authority is under a duty to comply with the Code of Practice issued under FOIA s 46, Part 1 of which deals with records management.

[69] Note the reference is to a 'record' rather than 'information'.

[70] FOIA s 77; FOI(S)A s 65; EIR reg 19(1); EI(S)R reg 19(1). Destruction of material before the FOIA came into force will not offend this provision: *Mitchell v IC*, IT, 10 October 2005.

[71] FOIA s 81(3). However, this only applies to the Government department itself. Section 77 applies to a person in the public service of the Crown as it does to any other person: s 81(3). In Scotland, the exemption is for the Scottish Parliament, the Parliamentary Corporation and the Scottish Administration, although again this immunity does not extend to members of staff of these entities or persons acting on their behalf: FOI(S)A s 68. In relation to environmental information, EIR reg 19(2), (5); EI(S)R reg 19(2), (4).

[72] FOIA s 77(2); FOI(S) s 65(2); EIR reg 19(2); EI(S)R reg 19(2).

the Director of Public Prosecutions.[73] The maximum fine is level five on the standard scale.[74]

3. PERSONS ENTITLED TO EXERCISE THE RIGHTS

13 Individuals, companies, unincorporated associations, etc
The rights conferred by s 1 of the Freedom of Information Act 2000 are rights conferred upon any 'person'.[75] The term 'person' extends to any body of persons corporate or incorporate,[76] so that companies, clubs and associations are able to rely on the Acts.

14 Territoriality of the rights
It is a principle of statutory interpretation that Parliament does not assert or assume jurisdiction that goes beyond the limits established by the common consent of nations. Provided that its language admits, an Act of Parliament is to be applied so as not to be inconsistent with the comity of nations or with the established principles of public international law.[77] The principle of comity between nations requires that each sovereign state should be left to govern its own territory.[78] Thus, while words in a statute may be expressed in universally applicable language, the rebuttable presumption is that Parliament is concerned with the conduct of persons taking place within the territories to which the Act extends, and with no other conduct.[79] In relation to rights conferred and obligations imposed by a statute, the presumption operates to limit these rights and obligations to those persons within the country at the time at which the right is sought to be exercised.[80] There is little within the Freedom of Information Act 2000 to suggest that the presumption against extra-territoriality was intended to be rebutted.[81] While the extra-

---

[73] FOIA s 77(4); EIR reg 19(4). In Northern Ireland, it is the consent of the Director of Public Prosecutions for Northern Ireland which is necessary. The FOI(S)A and the EI(S)R contain no limitation.

[74] FOIA s 77(3); FOI(S)A s 65(3); EIR reg 19(3); EI(S)R reg 19(3).

[75] The position is the same under the FOI(S)A, the EIR and the EI(S)R.

[76] 'Person' includes a body of persons corporate or unincorporated: Interpretation Act 1978 s 5 and Sch 1. It can include a committee: *Davey v Shawcroft* [1948] 1 All ER 827.

[77] See *Halsbury's Laws of England*, 4th edn, 1995 re-issue, vol 44(1), para 1317.

[78] *AG v Prince Ernest Augustus of Hanover* [1957] AC 436 at 462; *Gaudiya Mission v Brahmachary* [1998] Ch 341.

[79] F Bennion, *Statutory Interpretation*, 5th edn (London, LexisNexis, 2008) pp 327-9, 335-338, 360-384; *Halsbury's Laws of England*, 4th edn, 1995 re-issue, vol 44(1), para 1319; *Lawson v Serco* [2006] UKHL 3, [2006] 1 All ER 823, [2006] ICR 250; *Clark (Inspector of Taxes) v Oceanic Contractors Inc* [1983] 2 AC 130 at 144–145; *Al Sabah v Grupo Torras SA* [2005] UKPC 1, [2005] 2 AC 333 at [13]; *Agassi v Robinson (Inspector of Taxes)* [2006] UKHL 23, [2006] 1 WLR 1380 at [16] and [20]; *Al-Skeini & ors v Secretary of State for Defence* [2007] UKHL 26 at [11] and [44]–[55].

[80] *Jefferys v Boosey* (1854) 4 HL Cas 815 (copyright given by the Copyright Act 1709 to 'the author of any book' included only authors who were British subjects or were aliens resident in the country); *Tomalin v Pearson & Son Ltd* [1909] 2 KB 61 (where it was held that the Workmen's Compensation Act 1906, which provided for compensation to be paid 'if in any employment personal injury by accident arising out of and in the course of the employment is caused to any workman', did not apply to an English workman employed by an English company sent to carry out work in Malta); cf *Howgate v Bagnall* [1951] 1 KB 265, dealing with the Personal Injuries (Emergency Provisions) Act 1939.

[81] In the United States, foreign citizens, partnerships, corporations, associations, states and state agencies, and foreign or domestic governments could until very recently apply: 5 USC 551(2): see §2– 003. In Australia, the Freedom of Information Act 1982 is expressed to give every person a right of access. This has been held to extend to a foreign corporation: *Re Lordsvale Finance Ltd and Department of the Treasury* (1985) 3 AAR 301, AAT: see §2– 011. Section 12(1)

territorial application of the Act would not encroach upon the sovereignty of another state, it would confer rights on people all over the world who have little or no connection with the United Kingdom. Although the Freedom of Information Act 2000 will certainly extend to confer rights on a person in Scotland, it is doubtful whether the Freedom of Information (Scotland) Act 2002 extends to confer rights on a person in England, Wales or Northern Ireland, as the territorial limits of the Acts of the Scottish Parliament are the boundaries of Scotland. Nevertheless, the presumption against extra-territoriality is unlikely to make much practical difference, as a foreign applicant can always engage an undisclosed local agent to make the request. As well, in the case of a natural person, there is nothing to stop such a person coming into the jurisdiction for the purpose of making a request. It follows that a non-resident present in the United Kingdom, however fleetingly, is entitled to make a request under the Freedom of Information Act 2000.[82]

9–015 Convicted criminals

On the face of the Act, a convicted criminal and a law-abiding citizen are equally entitled to rely on the rights conferred by the Freedom of Information Act 2000. Depending upon the terms of the request, however, it may be that a request from the former will be more readily characterised as vexatious. The position in the comparative jurisdictions, none of which excepts convicted criminals, varies. In the USA, exceptions to the right of access have sometimes,[83] but not always,[84] been made in the case of criminals. In Australia, it has been held that the fact that a person had convictions for rape and armed robbery did not prevent him from applying for access to documents under the legislation.[85]

9–016 Children

The Freedom of Information (Scotland) Act 2002 provides that where a question falls to be determined as to the legal capacity of a person who has not attained the age of sixteen years to exercise any right conferred by any provision of this Act, any such person is to be taken to have

---

of the Official Information Act 1982 (New Zealand) enables citizens, residents and persons in New Zealand and companies incorporated in New Zealand to make a request for official information: see §2– 018. Section 4 of the Access to Information Act (Canada) gives Canadian citizens and permanent residents a right of access to records under the control of a government institution: see §2– 026. The review of the Act recommended that the Act be amended to provide that any person has a right of access: Government of Canada, *Report of the Access to Information Review Task Force* (June 2002), p 19. The Freedom of Information Act 1997 (Ireland) gives every person a right of access to records held by a public body: see §2– 035.

[82] Examples of recently-arrived persons enjoying statutory rights include: *R v Inhabitants of Eastbourne* (1803) 4 East 103; *R v Hillingdon London Borough Council, ex p Streeting* [1980] 1 WLR 1425; *Re Islam* [1983] 1 AC 688. In a speech by Lord Falconer (Constitutional Affairs Secretary and Lord Chancellor) to the International Conference of Information Commissioners, Manchester, 22 May 2006, he stated: 'From its introduction on 1 January 2005 any individual, from anywhere in the world, can submit requests to public bodies in the UK.' He did not state whether those individuals had to be within the UK at the time of making the request.

[83] *Doyle v US Department of Justice*, 668 F 2d 1365 (DC Cir 1981) (fugitive not entitled to enforcement of the Freedom of Information Act access provisions because he could not expect judicial aid in obtaining government records related to the sentence he was evading).

[84] *O'Rourke v US Department of Justice*, 684 F Supp 716 (DDC 1988) and *Doherty v US Department of Justice*, 596 F Supp 423 (SDNY 1984) (convicted criminal and fugitive from his own country and undergoing US deportation proceedings qualified as 'any person').

[85] *Re Ward and Secretary, Department of Industry and Commerce* (1983) 8 ALD 324.

that capacity who has a general understanding of what it means to exercise the right.[86] A child over 12 is presumed to have this understanding.[87] The Freedom of Information Act 2000[88] does not make any mention of applications by children and the Interpretation Act 1978 is silent on the question whether a reference to a 'person' is confined to persons of full age and capacity.[89] In both cases, any limitation can readily be circumvented by the application being made by someone on the minor's behalf.

17   Applicant's motives

An applicant's motives in making a request are irrelevant and so cannot be demanded by a public authority.[90] Nor does the absence of any actual or apparent motive for the request provide any basis for refusing it.[91] The Government considered an amendment to the Bill making this clear, but concluded that it was unnecessary:[92]

> It is perfectly legitimate for an official to have a discussion with the applicant with a view to helping the applicant to refine the request he or she is making so as to use better the provisions of the Bill. That is only for the purpose of assistance, not for examining motive with a view to determining whether to proceed with the request because that is quite irrelevant in the context of the Bill as drafted.[93]

---

[86]   FOI(S)A s 69(1). There is no equivalent in the EI(S)R.

[87]   FOI(S)A s 69(1).

[88]   And the EIR and the EI(S)R.

[89]   In *Wallace v Health Commission of Victoria* [1985] VR 403 the Supreme Court of Victoria held, in relation to a request made under the Freedom of Information Act 1982 (Vic) by a person lacking mental capacity, that it was a prerequisite to enforcement of the right of access that an application is made which is the conscious voluntary act of the person making it so that the person making it fully understood the nature and significance of the act and wished it to be done in order to obtain access to documents. Similarly, in a different context, *R v Oldham Metropolitan Borough Council, ex p Garlick* [1993] AC 509 at 520, although this may be explained on the basis that the wider interpretation of 'person' would have enabled a circumvention of restricted rights in the Housing Act 1985.

[90]   *Common Services Agency v IC* [2008] UKHL 47, [2008] 1 WLR 1550 at [29], [43]; *S v IC and The General Register Office*, IT, 9 May 2007 at [80]; *Berend v Information Commission and LB of Richmond upon Thames*, IT, 12 July 2007 at [46]. This is conventional in freedom of information legislation. Thus, in the USA, see *United States Department of Justice v Reporters Committee for Freedom of the Press*, 489 US 749 (1989); *Durns v Bureau of Prisons*, 804 F 2d 701 (DC Cir 1986) ('Congress granted the scholar and the scoundrel equal rights of access to agency records'); *Forsham v Califano*, 587 F 2d 1128 (DC Cir 1978); *O'Rourke v Department of Justice*, 684 F Supp 716 (DDC 1988). In Australia, see *Re Green and Australian and Overseas Telecommunications Corp* (1992) 28 ALD 655; *Re Russell Island Development Association Inc and Department of Primary Industry and Energy* (1994) 33 ALD 683; *Re Collie and Deputy Commissioner of Taxation* (1997) 45 ALD 556. And in Canada, see *Canada (Information Commissioner) v Canada (Commissioner of the Royal Canadian Mounted Police)*, [2003] 1 SCR 66 at [33]; *Intercontinental Packers Ltd v Canada (Minister of Agriculture)* (1987) 14 FTR 142; *Prud'homme v Canada (Canadian International Development Agency)* (1994) 85 FTR 302.

[91]   A lack of motive does not make a request 'vexatious'. However, a reasonable motive may prevent a request that would otherwise be vexatious from being so: *Adair v IC*, IT, 14 January 2010 at [40]-[42]; *Gowers v IC and LB of Camden*, IT, 13 May 2008; *Craven v IC*, IT, 13 May 2008.

[92]   Hansard HL vol 617 col 921 (17 October 2000) (Minister of State, Cabinet Office, Lord Falconer).

[93]   Hansard HL vol 617 col 921 (17 October 2000) (Minister of State, Cabinet Office, Lord Falconer). See also the Code of Practice on the Discharge of the Functions of Public Authorities under Pt I of the Freedom of Information Act (November 2002) (issued under s 45 of the Act), para 9 of which states:"where the applicant does not describe the information sought in a way which would enable the public authority to identify or locate it, or the request is ambiguous, the authority should, as far as practicable, provide assistance to the applicant to enable him or her to describe more clearly the information requested. Authorities should be aware that the aim of providing assistance is to clarify the nature of the information sought, not to determine the aims or motivation of the applicant. Care should be taken not to give the applicant the impression that he or she is obliged to disclose the nature of his or her interest or that he or she will be treated differently if he or she does".

Having said this, the absence of any apparent motive for a request may be relevant in considering whether a request is vexatious or in determining whether the public authority's response has been reasonable.[94] Where it is apparent that the applicant has a legitimate motive for making the request, that may be relevant in balancing the public interest for the purpose of qualified exemptions.[95]

4. BODIES AGAINST WHICH THE RIGHTS MAY BE EXERCISED

9–018 **Exhaustive definition**

The rights conferred by the Freedom of Information Act 2000 are only exercisable against 'public authorities'.[96] These are defined to mean:

(1)   any body,[97] person or office holder which or who is listed in Sch 1 of the Act;[98]

(2)   any body, person or office holder designated by order of the Secretary of State;[99] or

(3)   a publicly owned company.[100]

These categories are exhaustive[101] and are estimated to cover in excess of 50,000 bodies.[102]

9–019 **Schedule 1: public authorities under the Freedom of Information Act 2000**

Schedule 1 to the Freedom of Information Act 2000[103] provides the core list of those bodies, persons and office-holders who are deemed to be public authorities and against whom the s 1 rights may be exercised. These bodies are also subject to the Environmental Information Regulations 2004.[104] The Schedule is divided into seven numbered parts:

---

[94] For example, under the FOIA ss 17(3) and 22(1)(c); EIR reg 12(4)(b); EI(S)R reg 10(4)(b).

[95] *DTI v IC*, IT, 10 November 2006 at [53].

[96] Similarly the EIR, although the definition extends further: see §9– 026. Those conferred by the FOI(S)A and the EI(S)R are only exercisable against Scottish public authorities. In the case of the EI(S)R, the definition of Scottish public authorities extends further: see §9– 033.

[97] Body includes an unincorporated association: FOIA s 84; FOI(S)A s 73.

[98] FOIA s 3(1)(a)(i); FOI(S)A s 3(1)(a)(i). These are considered at §§9– 019 and 9– 027.

[99] FOIA s 3(1)(a)(ii); FOI(S)A s 3(1)(a)(ii); EIR reg 2(2). These are considered at §§9– 023 and 9– 031.

[100] FOIA s 3(1)(b); FOI(S)A s 3(1)(b). These are considered at §§9– 024 and 9– 032.

[101] The Home Office Freedom of Information Unit stated during the passage of the Bill: 'Because FOI applications are made direct by a person to an organisation, there needs to be absolute clarity as to whether any particular organisation is covered by the legislation. It is therefore necessary to spell out either in the Bill itself, or in an order, those organisations which are public authorities for the purpose of the legislation.' — House of Commons, *Public Administration—Third Report* (Cm 4355, 1999) Annex 6, para 1 (see ch 1 n 64). The importance of and rationale for this were acknowledged in *Sugar v BBC* [2009] UKHL 9, [2009] 1 WLR 430, [2009] 4 All ER 111 at [56].

[102] Government estimates have ranged from 50,000 (Hansard HC vol 347 col 883 (4 April 2000), Parliamentary Under-Secretary of State for the Home Department, Mr Mike O'Brien) to 88,000 (the Lord Chancellor's Advisory Group on implementation of the Freedom of Information Act).

[103] Which now includes those authorities added by various statutory instruments: see §9– 020.

[104] EIR reg 2(2)(a)-(b).

(I)   GENERAL: This includes all government departments,[105] both Houses of Parliament,[106] the Northern Ireland Assembly and the National Assembly for Wales, and most of the armed forces.[107] A Member of Parliament is not a public authority. Accordingly, information held by an individual Member of Parliament does not come within the scope of the Act (eg a Member's casework file). However, information held by departments within the House's administration service, by Select Committees, by the Parliamentary Archive or by the private office of Mr Speaker will be information held by the House of Commons.[108] A government department is defined to include any body or authority exercising statutory functions on behalf of the Crown,[109] so that information held by government agencies (eg the Child Protection Agency, Benefits Agency, etc) will be subject to the Act.[110] However, the Security Service, the Secret Intelligence Service and the Government Communications Headquarters are not included in the definition[111] and are therefore exempt from the operation of the Act.[112] The Tribunal has held that courts are not public authorities within the meaning of the Act:[113] this is a questionable conclusion.[114]

---

[105] Each government department is to be treated as a person separate from any other government department: FOIA s 81; EIR reg 3(5). However, a government department cannot rely upon this to claim a duty of confidence arising with respect to another government department so as to rely upon the exemption in s 41 (information provided in confidence): FOIA s 81(2). There is no equivalent provision under the FOI(S)A, the EIR or the EI(S)R. For information provided in confidence, see ch 25.

[106] The Houses of Parliament are not bodies corporate or any other kind of legal person. When dissolved by Her Majesty (for example, before a general election), they cease to exist. Nevertheless, the Houses of Parliament do not suspend rights of access when Parliament has been dissolved: *House of Commons v IC*, IT, 9 August 2007 at [34], [38]. Proceedings under the Act are brought against The Corporate Officer of the House of Commons by virtue of The Parliamentary Corporate Bodies Act 1992 s 2: *House of Commons v IC*, IT, 9 August 2007 at [42].

[107] The only exceptions are the special forces (meaning those units of the armed forces of the Crown the maintenance of whose capabilities is the responsibility of the Director of Special Forces or which are for the time being subject to the operational command of that Director: FOIA s 84) and any unit or part of a unit which is for the time being required by the Secretary of State to assist the Government Communications Headquarters in the exercise of its functions: FOIA Sch 1 Pt I para 6. As to the special exemption granted in relation to information supplied by these, and other, security bodies, to a public authority, see ch 17.

[108] *House of Commons v IC*, IT, 9 August 2007 at [38], [42]-[44]. The House of Commons, as a body of Members of Parliament, is distinct from The Corporate Officer of the House of Commons (established by The Parliamentary Corporate Bodies Act 1992 s 2) and from the Commission of the House of Commons (established by the House of Commons (Administration) Act 1978), although information held by them may, by virtue of s 3(2)(b), be treated as being held by the House of Commons.

[109] FOIA s 84.

[110] This was confirmed by the Government during the Bill's passage by the Parliamentary Under-Secretary of State: Hansard HL vol 619 col 231 (14 November 2000) (Lord Bassam).

[111] FOIA s 84.

[112] The Scottish Parliament, any part of the Scottish Administration, the Scottish Parliamentary Corporate Body, any Scottish public authority with mixed functions or no reserved functions (within the meaning of the Scotland Act 1998) and the National Assembly for Wales are also excluded from the definition of 'government department': FOIA s 84. All but the last are, of course, subject instead to the FOI(S)A.

[113] *Mitchell v IC*, IT, 10 October 2005 at [31].

[114] It is suggested that courts, or at the very least the Court Service, fall within the definition of 'government department' in FOIA s 84 (by virtue of being bodies that exercise statutory functions on behalf of the Crown–see, eg, Courts Act 1971 s 27, and Supreme Court Act 1981 s 1) and that, by virtue of Sch 1, Pt I, each is thereby a 'public authority'. Certainly, the Northern Ireland Court Service is a public authority: FOIA s 84, definition of

(II)   LOCAL GOVERNMENT: This Part contains a list of 29 types of local government bodies in England and Wales, including the Greater London Authority, county councils, London borough councils, district councils, parish councils, county borough councils, community councils, fire authorities, National Parks authorities, Transport for London, magistrates court committees, as well as all Northern Ireland district councils.

(III) THE NATIONAL HEALTH SERVICE: This covers core NHS bodies in England, Wales and Northern Ireland, such as health authorities, special health authorities, NHS and primary care trusts, community health councils and so forth. It also extends to individual GPs, dentists, opticians and pharmacists, but only in respect of information relating to the provision of medical services under the NHS.

(IV)   MAINTAINED SCHOOLS AND OTHER EDUCATIONAL INSTITUTIONS: Governing bodies of all maintained schools,[115] as well as further and higher education institutions, are all included in this Part. It was suggested by the Government in Parliament that information about institutions which do not have governing bodies, such as pupil referral units, will be accessible through the local education authority directly responsible for such institutions.[116] (The Teacher Training Agency, the Higher Education Funding Council in England and Wales and the Northern Ireland Higher Education Council, Her Majesty's Chief Inspector of Schools in Wales and the School Teachers Review Body are all listed in Part VI).

(V)   POLICE: This Part covers all police authorities in England, Wales and Northern Ireland, the chief officer of police forces (including the Chief Constable of the Royal Ulster Constabulary), the British Transport Police, the Ministry of Defence Police and any person (not otherwise covered by Sch 1) who has the statutory power to nominate individuals for appointment as special constables by magistrates (but only in respect of information relating to this function). (The National Crime Squad and the Police Complaints Authority are listed in Part VI, although the National Criminal Intelligence Service is not).

(VI)   OTHER PUBLIC BODIES AND OFFICES: GENERAL: This Part enumerates over 350 miscellaneous public bodies and offices, ranging from the Advisory Committee on Conscientious Objectors and the British Potato Council to the OSO Board and the Zoos Forum. Some are well known, such as the Health and Safety Executive, the Arts Council and the Post Office, whereas others such as the Unlinked Anonymous Serosurveys Steering Group, the Marshall Aid Commemoration Commission and the Place Names Advisory Committee are less so. The BBC, Channel 4 and Sianel Pedwar Cymru (S4C) are included (but only in respect of information held for purposes other than those of journalism art or literature),[117] as well as the Broadcasting Standards Commission, the Independent Television Commission, the Theatres Trust and most of the country's main museums and galleries. The Bank of England is included, but information relating to its functions with respect to monetary policy, financial operations intended to support

---

'government department'.

[115] Within the meaning of the School Standards and Framework Act 1998: FOIA Sch 1 Pt I para 52.

[116] Hansard HL vol 617 col 946 (17 October 2000) (Lord Falconer, Minister of State, Cabinet Office).

[117] In relation to determining whether a request for information falls within or outside the limits of operation, see §9–022.

financial institutions for the purposes of maintaining stability, and the provision of private banking and related services is all excluded. Bodies omitted include the British Board of Film Classification, those running prisons under contract, the Press Complaints Commission, and those assigned responsibility for running the railways.

(VII) OTHER PUBLIC BODIES AND OFFICES: NORTHERN IRELAND: This is a very similar list to that in Part (VI) above, containing over 80 bodies and offices which relate to Northern Ireland.

20 Adding public authorities to Schedule 1

The Secretary of State for Justice[118] has the power[119] to add to Sch 1 any body or holder of any office which satisfies two specified conditions.[120] The first specified condition is that the body or office is either (a) established by virtue of royal prerogative, an enactment or subordinate legislation,[121] or (b) is established in any other way by a Minister of the Crown (in his capacity as such), a government department or the Welsh Assembly.[122] The second condition is (in the case of a body) that the body is wholly or partly constituted by appointment made by the Crown, a Minister of the Crown, a government department or the Welsh Assembly,[123] or (in the case of an office) that appointments to the office are made by one of the same.[124] However, this power may not be exercised to add the Scottish Parliament, any part of the Scottish administration, the Scottish Parliamentary Corporate Body, or any Scottish public authority with mixed functions or no reserved functions (within the meaning of the Scotland Act 1998).[125] An order adding a public authority to Sch 1 in this way may relate to a specified person or

---

[118] The FOIA originally referred to the 'Secretary of State' but all his functions under the Act were first transferred to the Lord Chancellor by the Transfer of Functions (Miscellaneous) Order 2001 SI 2001/3500 and then to the Secretary of State for Constitutional Affairs by the Secretary of State for Constitutional Affairs Order 2003 SI 2003/1887 and on 9 May 2007 to the Secretary of State for Justice under The Secretary of State for Justice Order 2007 SI 2007/2128.

[119] FOIA s 4(1). Where such an order relates to a body or office-holder whose functions are exercisable only or mainly in or as regards Wales, or to a Northern Ireland public authority, the Secretary of State must consult either the National Assembly for Wales or the First Minister and deputy First Minister in Northern Ireland respectively: FOIA s 4(7). 'Northern Ireland public authority' means any public authority, other than the Northern Ireland Assembly or a Northern Ireland department, whose functions are exercisable only or mainly in or as regards Northern Ireland and relate only or mainly to transferred matters: FOIA s 84. 'Transferred matter' has the meaning given by s 4(1) of the Northern Ireland Act 1998: FOIA s 84. Such an order is subject to annulment in pursuance of a resolution of either House of Parliament: FOIA s 82(3).

[120] Five dedicated orders have been made: Freedom of Information (Additional Public Authorities) Order 2002 SI 2002/2623 Freedom of Information (Additional Public Authorities) Order 2003 SI 2003/1882; (Additional Public Authorities) Order 2004 SI 2004/938; Freedom of Information (Additional Public Authorities) Order 2005 SI 2005/3593; Freedom of Information (Additional Public Authorities) Order 2008 SI 2008/1271. In addition, other bodies have been added to Sch 1. These are brought within the EIR by the limb of the definition of 'public authority' in reg 2(2)(b)(ii).

[121] FOIA s 4(2)(a).

[122] FOIA s 4(2)(b).

[123] FOIA s 4(3)(a).

[124] FOIA s 4(3)(b).

[125] FOIA s 80.

office or to persons or offices falling within a specified description[126] and may list the new entry only in relation to information of a specified description.[127]

9–021 Removing or amending entries in Schedule 1

The Secretary of State for Justice has the power to limit any entry on Sch 1 to information of a specified description, as well as to remove any such limitation.[128] Whilst the removal of a limitation is unlikely to be controversial (at least outside the body in question), the power to introduce limits would allow the Government to cut down the Act's scope so far as rights of access to particular information are concerned. Concern about this was expressed during the Bill's passage through Parliament and in response to a proposed amendment removing this power, and a direct question asking what the Government's intention was in conferring this, Lord Bassam, the Parliamentary Under-Secretary of State, Home Office, replied as follows:

> The power to amend the entries in Schedule 1 so as to limit them to specific types of information is necessary in order to ensure that the bodies listed at Schedule 1 are covered by the Freedom of Information Act only in respect of those activities which should properly be the subject of the obligations in the Bill. It is not the Government's [intention] to apply the Bill to information held for purposes in respect of which it would be inappropriate and damaging to apply freedom of information principles. Journalistic information held by public sector broadcasters or private banking information held by the Bank of England are two current examples of such information.
>
> Where we have identified information which needs to be protected in this way, we have amended the entry in Schedule 1 accordingly. However, we cannot be certain that any of the bodies listed may not change their functions in the future. For that reason, we need to make provision for a power to amend the entry if this should be deemed necessary. To that extent, clause 7(3) is a just-in-case provision.
>
> The noble Lord asked for an example, hypothetical or otherwise, and I am happy to try to provide one. The entry in Schedule 1 relating to the Bank of England is already limited to certain information. Should the Bank decide to add, say, an insurance provision to the services it provides to its private customers, that private activity which would relate to private customers would be brought within the scope of the Freedom of Information Act, unless an order was made to limit the entry in Schedule 1 specifically to exclude it.
>
> That is why the power in clause 7(3) is necessary. I hope that the noble Lord will accept the example I have given and feel able to withdraw his amendment.[129]

The Act provides that all such orders must be approved by a resolution of each House of

---

[126] FOIA s 4(6). An example of this is found in Sch 1, Pt VI, 'any housing action trust established under Pt III of the Housing Act 1988.'

[127] FOIA s 7(2). For such partly-affected public authorities, see §9– 022.

[128] FOIA s 7(3). In other words, a public authority can be turned into a 'partly affected' public authority and vice versa: see §9– 022.

[129] Hansard HL vol 619 cols 182–183 (14 November 2000). Lord Mackay, who had tabled the amendment and asked the question, replied as follows: 'I am reasonably grateful for the answer. [Lord Bassam] set out a clear scenario and I hope that if the Secretary of State decides to go a good deal further a clever lawyer will be able to prevent him by using the courts and quoting what the noble Lord said and the example he gave. I am pleased to beg leave to withdraw my amendment.' — Hansard HL vol 619 col 183 (14 November 2000). See also the debate in the House of Commons, with Government pronouncements on very similar lines: Hansard HC vol 347 cols 871–890 (4 April 2000) (Mr Mike O'Brien, Parliamentary Under-Secretary of State for the Home Department).

Parliament.[130] A body or office-holder listed in Pts VI and VII of Sch 1 automatically ceases to be a public authority by virtue of its entry in the Schedule if it ceases to satisfy either of the two conditions specified above.[131] Where this happens, or where the body or office ceases to exist, the Secretary of State for Justice has the power to amend Sch 1 to reflect this change,[132] described in Parliament as a 'form of housekeeping... necessary so that the lists may be routinely updated to remove dead wood.'[133] So long as a body or office continues to fulfil the two specified conditions,[134] however, it can only be removed from Sch 1 by means of further primary legislation.

22 Partly-affected Schedule 1 public authorities

Some public authorities are listed in Sch 1 only in relation to information of a specified description.[135] In these cases, the rights conferred by the Freedom of Information Act 2000 do not apply to any other information held by that authority.[136] A partly-affected public authority is a public authority within the meaning of the Freedom of Information Act 2000 whatever the nature of the information held by it.[137] Once a request for information is made under the Act to a partly-affected public authority, the fact that it claims that the information is excluded under Schedule 1 does not mean that it thereby ceases to be a public authority under the Act.[138] The obligation of a partly-affected public authority under section 1 is to ascertain the extent to

---

[130] FOIA s 82(2).

[131] FOIA s 4(4). The two conditions are those in s 4(2)–(3), as to which see §9– 020.

[132] FOIA s 4(5). But this is not necessary as the removal occurs automatically under s 4(4).

[133] Hansard HL vol 617 col 952 (17 October 2000) (Lord Falconer, Minister of State, Cabinet Office). In contrast to other powers to add to or amend Sch 1 (see §§9– 020, 9– 021 and 9– 023), the FOIA requires only that such an order be laid before Parliament after being made: s 82(4). Orders removing public authorities are: Freedom of Information (Removal of References to Public Authorities) Order 2003 SI 2003/1883; Freedom of Information (Removal of References to Public Authorities) Order 2004 SI 2004/1641; Freedom of Information (Removal of References to Public Authorities) Order 2005 SI 2005/3594.

[134] That is, those in FOIA s 4(2)–(3): see §9– 020.

[135] For example: the Common Council of the City of London, in respect of information held in its capacity as a local authority, police authority or port health authority (Sch 1 Pt II para 9); the Sub-Treasurer of the Inner Temple or the Under-Treasurer of the Middle Temple, in respect of information held in his capacity as a local authority (Sch 1 Pt II para 9); any person providing primary medical services, primary dental services, general medical services, general dental services, general ophthalmic services or pharmaceutical services, etc under the NHS Act 1977, in respect of information relating to the provision of those services (Sch 1 Pt III paras 43A–45A, 51); the Bank of England, in respect of information held for purposes other than those of its functions with respect to: (a) monetary policy, (b) financial operations intended to support financial institutions for the purposes of maintaining stability, and (c) the provision of private banking services and related services (Sch 1 Pt VI); and the Traffic Commissioners, in respect of information held by them otherwise than as a tribunal (Sch 1 Pt VI).

[136] FOIA s 7(1). The Secretary of State for Justice has the power, in relation to any entry in Sch 1, to introduce, remove or amend any such limitation. FOIA s 7(3). If such an order relates to the National Assembly for Wales or a Welsh public authority, the Northern Ireland Assembly, or a Northern Ireland department or a Northern Ireland public authority, the Secretary of State for Justice must consult the National Assembly for Wales, the Presiding Officer of the relevant Northern Ireland Assembly, or the First Minister and deputy First Minister in Northern Ireland respectively before making such an order: FOIA s 7(4). As to the meaning of a 'Welsh public authority', see FOIA s 83. In any event, a draft of such an order must be laid before and approved by a resolution of each House of Parliament before it is made: FOIA s 82(2).

[137] *Sugar v BBC* [2009] UKHL 9, [2009] 1 WLR 430, [2009] 4 All ER 111.

[138] *Sugar v BBC* [2009] UKHL 9, [2009] 1 WLR 430, [2009] 4 All ER 111 at [90].

which the requested information that it holds is excluded in Schedule 1. If it is excluded, the public authority is entitled to reply that that part of the requested information does not form part of the information it holds, followed by the description of excluded information specified in Schedule 1.[139] Whether requested information is or is not within the exclusion is a question of law, for which there is only one correct answer.[140] The specified descriptions in Sch 1 vary in nature: in some cases the limiting characteristic is the capacity in which the public authority holds the information; in other cases it is the subject matter to which the information relates; and in others it is the purpose for which the information is held. Information falling within the excepted aspect of a public authority is treated as enjoying disapplication of the s 1(1) duties. One public authority in respect of which the Act has a limited operation is the BBC. It is listed in Part VI of Sch 1 to the Act as follows:

> The British Broadcasting Corporation, in respect of information held for purposes other than those of journalism art or literature.

The same limitation applies to other public broadcasters.[141] Where information is held for mixed purposes, some of which are for excepted aspects of a partly-affected public authority and some of which are not, if to any significant extent the authority holds the information for excepted aspects then it is not required to disclose that information.[142] Thus:

> the BBC has no obligation to disclose information which they hold to any significant extent for the purposes of journalism, art or literature, whether or not the information is also held for other purposes. The words do not mean that the information is disclosable if it is held for purposes distinct from journalism, art or literature, whilst it is also held to any significant extent for those listed purposes. If the information is held for mixed purposes, including to any significant extent the purposes listed in the Schedule or one of them, then the information is not disclosable.[143]

In establishing the purpose for which information is held, regard must be had to the reason that the information was created or acquired, the content of the information and the range of applications or purposes to which it is to be put in relation to the period in which the request was made and in relation to the public authority as a whole.[144] The term 'journalism' has been interpreted generously, embracing a public authority obligations of impartiality:

> Ensuring impartiality, whilst creating conditions in which challenging and penetrating journalistic coverage is possible, may well be described as strategic thinking and decision-making, but such a task is surely intrinsically concerned with journalistic output, even if the immediate activity of reviewing adherence to the Charter obligations may not be "journalism" in the sense of the activity of journalism.[145]

Similarly, financial information held for 'operational purposes' of a broadcaster is, it seems, not

---

[139] *Sugar v BBC* [2009] UKHL 9, [2009] 1 WLR 430, [2009] 4 All ER 111 at [33].

[140] *Sugar v BBC* [2009] UKHL 9, [2009] 1 WLR 430, [2009] 4 All ER 111 at [53].

[141] That is, Channel Four Television Corporation and Sianel Pedwar Cymru.

[142] Put another way, the phrase 'held for purposes other than' means 'held for purposes apart from or in addition to': *BBC v IC* [2009] EWHC 2348 (Admin), [2010] EMLR 6 at [62]. The question is not resolved by a consideration of the predominant purpose for which the information is held: *BBC v IC* [2009] EWHC 2348 (Admin), [2010] EMLR 6 at [63].

[143] *BBC v Sugar* [2009] EWHC 2349 (Admin), [2010] 1 All ER 782, [2010] ACD 3 at [65].

[144] *BBC v Sugar* [2009] EWHC 2349 (Admin), [2010] 1 All ER 782, [2010] ACD 3 at [84].

[145] *BBC v Sugar* [2009] EWHC 2349 (Admin), [2010] 1 All ER 782, [2010] ACD 3 at [76].

subject to the obligation to disclose.[146] Regardless of whether the requested information is outside the description in Schedule 1, the Information Commissioner has power to review the question whether the information is within the excepted aspect of a public authority and may issue a decision notice under s 50.[147]

23 Designated public authorities

An entity not listed in Sch 1 nor capable of being added to that list by an order under s 4(1) may be designated by order as a public authority for the purposes of the Act if it appears to the Secretary of State for Justice to exercise functions of a public nature or is providing under a contract made with a public authority any service whose provision is a function of that authority.[148] It is not necessary in this latter case that the contractor itself should be performing functions of a public nature.[149] The determination of what is and is not a 'function of a public nature' is a familiar one for the courts, being central to both judicial review and the Human Rights Act 1998.[150] When exercising this power, the Secretary of State for Justice may designate a specified person or office falling within a specified description.[151] Before making such an order the Secretary of State for Justice must consult every person to whom the order relates, or persons appearing to represent them.[152] An order of this type made in relation to a person who appears to exercise functions of a public nature[153] must specify the functions of the designated public authority with respect to which the order is to have effect. The general right of access under the Act to information held by the public authority does not apply to information held by the authority which does not relate to the exercise of those functions.[154] Similarly, where an order is made in relation to a person who is providing under a contract made with a public authority any service whose provision is a function of that authority,[155] it must specify the services provided under contract with respect to which the order is to have

---

[146] *BBC v IC* [2009] EWHC 2348 (Admin), [2010] EMLR 6 at [86]-[87]. An outcome for a publicly-funded body which is surprising given the objects of the FOIA.

[147] *Sugar v BBC* [2009] UKHL 9, [2009] 1 WLR 430, [2009] 4 All ER 111 at [23], [36]-[37], [73], [91].

[148] FOIA s 5(1). A draft of such an order must be laid before and approved by a resolution of each House of Parliament before it is made: FOIA s 82(2). Such a draft is not to be treated for the purposes of the Standing Orders of either House of Parliament as a hybrid instrument: s 82(5). As with orders under s 4(1) (as to which see §9– 020) this power cannot be exercised in relation to the Scottish Parliament, any part of the Scottish administration, the Scottish Parliamentary Corporate Body, or any Scottish public authority with mixed functions or no reserved functions (within the meaning of the Scotland Act 1998): ss 5(4) and 80.

[149] House of Commons, *Public Administration—Third Report* (Cm 4355, 1999) Annex 6, para 9 (Notes by the Freedom of Information Unit, Home Office) (see ch 1 n 64).

[150] Human Rights Act 1998 s 6 makes it unlawful for public authorities to act incompatibly with rights under the European Convention on Human Rights and provides that 'public authority' includes (a) a court or tribunal and (b) any person certain of whose functions are 'functions of a public nature'.

[151] FOIA s 5(2).

[152] FOIA s 5(3). It was also said by the Home Office that, 'as a matter of good administrative practice it is expected that the Secretary of State will consult other persons whom he believes have a legitimate and direct interest in the order.' — House of Commons, *Public Administration—Third Report* (Cm 4355, 1999) Annex 6, para 10 (Notes by the Freedom of Information Unit, Home Office) (see ch 1 n 64).

[153] That is, under FOIA s 5(1)(a).

[154] FOIA s 7(5).

[155] That is, under FOIA s 5(1)(b).

effect. The general right of access under the Act to information held by the public authority does not apply to information held by the authority which does not relate to the provision of those services.[156]

9– 024 Publicly owned companies

A company is a publicly owned company[157] and therefore a public authority under the Freedom of Information Act 2000 if it is wholly owned by either (1) the Crown; or (2) any public authority listed in Sch 1 to the Act, other than a government department or any authority listed only in relation to particular information.[158] For these purposes, a company is considered to be wholly-owned by the Crown if it has no members other than Ministers of the Crown,[159] government departments or companies wholly owned by the Crown, or persons acting on behalf of any of these.[160] A company is considered to be wholly owned by a public authority listed in Sch 1 other than a government department if it has no members except that public authority or companies wholly owned by that public authority, or persons acting on behalf of either of these.[161] However, the general right of access to information under the Act does not apply to any information held by a publicly owned company which is defined by order of the Secretary of State for Justice as 'excluded information' in relation to that company.[162]

9– 025 Welsh public authorities

Welsh public authorities are defined to mean any public authority listed in Pt II, III, IV or VI of Sch 1 whose functions are exercisable only or mainly in or as regards Wales, other than an 'excluded authority'.[163] These bodies will also fall within the scope of the Environmental Information Regulations 2004.[164] Welsh public authorities are also defined to include any public authority which is:

— a subsidiary of the Welsh Ministers (as defined by section 134(4) of the Government of Wales Act 2006);[165] or

— a subsidiary of the Assembly Commission (as defined by section 139(4) of the

---

[156] FOIA s 7(6).

[157] 'Company' includes any body corporate: FOIA s 6(3).

[158] FOIA s 6(1). For public authorities listed in Sch 1 only in relation to particular information see §9– 022.

[159] Including a Northern Ireland Minister: FOIA s 6(3).

[160] FOIA s 6(2)(a).

[161] FOIA s 6(2)(b).

[162] FOIA s 7(8).

[163] FOIA s 83(1)(a). An excluded authority is a public authority which is designated by the Secretary of State by order as an excluded authority for the purposes of FIOA s 83(1)(a): FOIA s 83(2). By Freedom of Information (Excluded Welsh Authorities) Order 2002 SI 2002/2832, the Lord Chancellor excluded four magistrates' court committees, the Advisory Committee on General Commissioners of Income Tax for certain areas, the Parliamentary Boundary Commission for Wales, and Sianel Pedwar Cymru, in respect of information held for purposes other than those of journalism art or literature, and certain other bodies.

[164] EIR reg 2(2)(b).

[165] FOIA s 83(1). It is defined by s 134(4) to mean: (a) any body corporate or other undertaking in relation to which, if the Welsh Ministers were an undertaking, the Welsh Ministers would be a parent undertaking, (b) any trust of which the Welsh Ministers are settlors, or (c) any charitable institution of which the Welsh Ministers are founders but which is neither a body corporate nor a trust.

Government of Wales Act).[166]

26   Other bodies holding environmental information

Under the Environmental Information Regulations 2004, the right of access is similarly exercisable against a 'public authority'.[167] However, the term is given a different definition from that which it bears under the Freedom of Information Act 2000.[168] The Environmental Information Regulations 2004 expand the definition given to 'public authority' in the Freedom of Information Act 2000 by adding to it two additional limbs. First, by para (c) of the definition, 'public authority' also embraces 'any other body or other person that carries out functions of public administration'. Most bodies and persons that carry out functions of public administration are already captured under paras (a) and (b) through the incorporation of the Act's definition. Paragraph (c) may serve to cover public authorities that have been excluded from s 3(1) by an order under section 4(5) or by statute. It would seem most naturally to bring into the Regulations persons or bodies discharging powers and duties either conferred by statute or arising under prerogative. Secondly, para (d) of the definition adds any other body or person 'that is under the control of' a public authority (as defined in paras (a)–(c)) and that:

— has public responsibilities relating to the environment;
— exercises functions of a public nature relating to the environment; or
— provides public services relating to the environment.

This has been held to cover the Port of London Authority,[169] but not to cover Network Rail.[170]

5.   SCOTTISH BODIES AGAINST WHICH THE RIGHT MAY BE EXERCISED

27   Schedule 1: public authorities under the Freedom of Information (Scotland) Act 2002

Schedule 1 to the Freedom of Information (Scotland) Act 2002 provides a similar list to that in Sch 1 to the Westminster Act. These bodies are also subject to the Environmental Information (Scotland) Regulations 2004.[171] It is estimated to cover some 9,000 authorities in total.[172]

(I)   MINISTERS, THE PARLIAMENT: This comprises the Scottish Ministers, the Scottish Parliament and the Scottish Parliamentary Corporate Body.

---

[166] FOIA s 83(1). It is defined by s 139(4) to mean: (a) any body corporate or other undertaking in relation to which the Assembly Commission is a parent undertaking, (b) any trust of which the Assembly Commission is settlor, or (c) any charitable institution of which the Assembly Commission is founder but which is neither a body corporate nor a trust.

[167] EIR reg 5(1).

[168] EIR reg 2(2). This is so that the definition of 'public authority' accords with art 2.2 of the Directive. See also recital (11) of the Directive and art 2.2 of the Aarhus Convention.

[169] *Port of London Authority v IC and Hibbert*, IT, 31 May 2007.

[170] *Network Rail Ltd v IC and Network Rail Infrastructure Ltd*, IT, 17 July 2007.

[171] EI(S)R reg 2(2)(a)–(b).

[172] According to the Scottish Information Commissioner at: www.itspublicknowledge.info.

(II)   NON-MINISTERIAL OFFICER HOLDERS IN THE SCOTTISH ADMINISTRATION: This includes such persons as the Chief Dental Officer and Chief Medical Officer of the Scottish Administration, Her Majesty's various Chief Inspectors of Constabulary and of Prisons, Her Inspector of Anatomy, of Fire Services and inspectors of schools for Scotland, the Keepers of the Records and Registers of Scotland, procurators fiscal, the Queen's and Lord Treasurer's Remembrancer, the Queen's Printer for Scotland, the Registrars of Births, Deaths and Marriages and of Independent Schools, rent officers[173] and social work inspectors.[174]

(III) LOCAL GOVERNMENT: This comprises Councils constituted, and assessors appointed, under the Local Government, etc (Scotland) Act 1994, joint boards within the meaning of s 235(1) of the Local Government (Scotland) Act 1973, licensing boards constituted in accordance with the provisions of s 1 of the Licensing (Scotland) Act 1976 and the Strathclyde Passenger Transport Authority.

(IV)   THE NATIONAL HEALTH SERVICE: This Part covers most NHS institutions in Scotland and, as with the Freedom of Information Act 2000, includes individual GPs, dentists, opticians and pharmacists, but only in respect of information relating to their provision of services under the NHS.

(V)   EDUCATIONAL INSTITUTIONS: This lists the board of management of colleges of further education, central institutions within the meaning of the Education (Scotland) Act 1980, and institutions in receipt of funding from the Scottish Higher Education Funding Council other than any institution whose activities are principally carried on outside Scotland.

(VI)   POLICE: Listed here are the chief constables of police forces in Scotland, joint police boards and the Police Advisory Board for Scotland.

(VII) OTHERS: This is a general list of 53 other public bodies and offices, similar to that contained in Part VI of Sch 1 to the Freedom of Information Act 2000.

9– 028 **Adding Scottish public authorities to Schedule 1**

The Scottish Ministers have the power[175] to add to Sch 1 any body or holder of any office which is either a part of the Scottish Administration or a Scottish public authority with mixed functions or no reserved functions.[176] The Act imposes no duty to consult before making such an order.[177] An order adding a Scottish public authority to Sch 1 in this way may relate to a specified person or office or to persons or offices falling within a specified description.[178] In

---

[173] Appointed under Rent (Scotland) Act 1984 s 43(3): FOI(S)A Sch 1 Pt 2 para 18.

[174] FOI(S)A Sch 1 Pt 2 para 19.

[175] FOI(S)A s 4(1). Such an order is subject to annulment in pursuance of a resolution of the Scottish Parliament: FOI(S)A s 72(2)(a). If the order is adding an authority only in relation to information of a specified description then a draft order must be laid before and approved by a resolution of that body before being made: FOI(S)A s 72(2)(b).

[176] 'Scottish public authority' has the meaning it has in the rest of the Act, as defined in FOI(S)A s 3(1), ie either a body or office which is listed in Sch 1 (although obviously that could not apply here, since this concerns adding a body or office to Sch 1), designated by the Scottish Ministers or a publicly-owned company. However, this reference to an authority with mixed functions or no reserved functions is to be construed in accordance with paras 1(4) and 2 of Pt III of Sch 5 to the Scotland Act 1998: FOI(S)A s 4(2).

[177] Contrast the position under the FOIA s 4(7): see §9– 020 fn 119.

[178] FOI(S)A s 4(3).

addition, the order may list the new entry only in relation to information of a specified description, in which case nothing in the Act applies to any other information held by the authority.[179]

29   Removing Scottish public authorities from Schedule 1

The Scottish Ministers have the power to remove from Sch 1 any entry listed there.[180]   There is no requirement for approval of such an order by the Scottish Parliament.[181]

30   Partly-affected Scottish public authorities

The Freedom of Information (Scotland) Act 2002 provides that any body listed in Sch 1 is considered a Scottish public authority for the purposes of that Act,[182] subject to any qualification in that Schedule.[183]   Therefore, as with the Freedom of Information Act 2000, there is no right of access to information held by such an authority if the information falls outside the description in the Schedule.   The difference is really only conceptual: the effect of the Scottish approach is that such a body is not considered by the Act to be a Scottish public authority in such circumstances, whereas under the Freedom of Information Act 2000 such a body remains at all times a public authority under the statute, although not always subject to the Act's main provisions.[184]   The Scottish Ministers have the power, in relation to any entry in Sch 1, to introduce, amend or remove any such limitation.[185]

31   Designated Scottish public authorities

A person who is not listed in Sch 1 nor capable of being added to that list by an order under s 4(1)[186] may be designated by order as a Scottish public authority for the purposes of the Act if he: (a) appears to the Scottish Ministers to exercise functions of a public nature, or (b) is providing under a contract made with a Scottish public authority any service whose provision is a function of that authority.[187]   In such cases, the order must specify the functions of a public nature which appear to be exercised or the service being provided.[188]   As with orders made under s 4(1) of the Freedom of Information Act 2000,[189] such an order may designate a specified

---

[179] FOI(S)A, s 7(1).

[180] FOI(S)A s 4(1)(b).

[181] As there is when adding bodies in relation to specified information, or introducing such a limitation to a body on Sch 1: see §9– 031.

[182] FOI(S)A s 3(1)(a)(i).

[183] FOI(S)A s 3(3). For example, Pt 4 (the National Health Service) has the entry, 'A person providing general medical services, general ophthalmic services or pharmaceutical services under Pt II of the National Health Service (Scotland) Act 1978, but only in respect of information relating to the provision of those services.'

[184] That is, those in Pts I to V of the FOI(S)A. See §9– 022.

[185] FOI(S)A s 7(2). Such an order must be laid before and approved by a resolution of the Scottish Parliament before being made: FOI(S)A s 72(2)(b).

[186] See §9– 028.

[187] FOI(S)A s 5(1)–(2). Such an order must be laid before and approved by a resolution of the Scottish Parliament before being made: FOI(S)A s 72(2)(b).

[188] FOI(S)A s 5(4).

[189] See §9– 023.

person or office or persons or offices falling within a specified description.[190] In contrast to the position under s 4(1),[191] however, before making this type of order the Scottish Ministers must consult every person to whom the order relates, or persons appearing to represent them.[192]

9–032 Publicly owned companies

A company is a publicly owned company[193] and therefore a Scottish public authority under the Freedom of Information (Scotland) Act 2002 if it is wholly owned by either (1) the Scottish Ministers; or (2) any other Scottish public authority listed in Sch 1 to the Act other than an authority listed only in relation to particular information.[194] For these purposes, a company is considered to be wholly owned by the Scottish Ministers if it has no members other than the Scottish Ministers or companies wholly owned by the Scottish Ministers, or persons acting on behalf of either of these.[195] A company is considered to be wholly owned by any other Scottish public authority if it has no members except that authority or companies wholly owned by that authority, or persons acting on behalf of either of these.[196] However, nothing in the Act applies to any information held by a publicly owned company which is of a description specified in relation to that company in an order made by the Scottish Ministers.[197]

9–033 Other bodies holding environmental information

Under the Environmental Information (Scotland) Regulations 2004, the right of access is similarly exercisable against a 'Scottish public authority'.[198] However, the term is given a different definition from that which it bears under the Freedom of Information (Scotland) Act 2002.[199] The Environmental Information Regulations (Scotland) 2004 expand the definition given to 'public authority' in the Freedom of Information (Scotland) Act 2000 by adding to it two additional limbs. First, by para (c) of the definition, 'public authority' also embraces 'any other Scottish public authority with mixed functions or no reserved function (within the meaning of the Scotland Act 1998).' Secondly, para (d) of the definition adds any other body or person 'that is under the control of' a public authority (as defined in paras (a)–(c)) and that:
— has public responsibilities relating to the environment;
— exercises functions of a public nature relating to the environment; or
— provides public services relating to the environment.
Paragraph (d) may be apt to cover private companies operating in certain regulated industries,

---

[190] FOI(S)A s 5(3).

[191] See §9–028.

[192] FOI(S)A s 5(3).

[193] 'Company' includes any body corporate: FOI(S)A s 6(3).

[194] FOI(S)A s 6(1). For Scottish public authorities listed in Sch 1 only in relation to particular information see §9–030.

[195] FOI(S)A s 6(2)(a).

[196] FOI(S)A s 6(2)(b).

[197] FOI(S)A s 7(4). This is the equivalent of the 'excluded information' provision in s 7(7)–(8) of the FOIA.

[198] EI(S)R reg 5(1).

[199] EI(S)R reg 2(2). This is so that the definition of 'public authority' accords with art 2.2 of the Directive. See also recital (11) of the Directive and art 2.2 of the Aarhus Convention.

such as water and public transport.[200]

6. THE OBLIGATION TO DISCLOSE AND CONSTRAINTS ON DISCLOSURE

34 **Data protection, confidentiality, copyright and other constraints**

A disclosure that for one person may represent 'freedom of information', may for another constitute an undue processing of personal data, a breach of confidence, a breach of copyright or a defamatory publication.[201] The Freedom of Information Act 2000 accommodates the first two of these competing interests by rendering information exempt information where it would offend either interest.[202] In these two cases, the right of access yields to another interest: to a person's right not to have personal data relating to himself unduly disclosed; and to a person's right not to have confidential information disclosed. Furthermore, the proscription against disclosure is left intact, such that the public authority must not disclose the information.[203] In the case of copyright and defamation, however, these interests generally yield to the right of access conferred by the Freedom of Information Act 2000. Section 50(1) of the Copyright, Designs and Patents Act 1988 provides:

> Where the doing of a particular act is specifically authorised by an Act of Parliament, whenever passed, then, unless the Act provides otherwise, the doing of that act does not infringe copyright.

Disclosure of information where there is a duty to do so under the Freedom of Information Act 2000 or the Environmental Information Regulations 2004 (because there is no exemption disapplying that duty) will be specifically authorised and so not constitute a breach of copyright.

35 **Defamatory material**

Neither the Freedom of Information Act 2000 nor the Environmental Information Regulations 2004 confers absolute privilege for the disclosure of information pursuant to the duty to disclose.[204] Generally, where a public authority is under a duty to disclose information to an applicant by reason of the Act or the Environmental Information Regulations 2004, that communication will attract qualified privilege.[205] Such a disclosure may be said to be a paradigm instance satisfying the duty-interest test. Information held by a public authority that is disclosed by it to a person where there is no obligation to do so (eg because an exemption

---

[200] See further §6–015.

[201] For the ability of an affected third party to participate in any decision to disclose information, see §§11–041 to 11–049.

[202] Thus: processing of personal data is protected by FOIA s 40; FOI(S)A s 38; EIR reg 13; EI(S)R reg 12; confidentiality is protected by FOIA ss 41 and 43; FOI(S)A ss 33 and 36; EIR reg 12(5)(d)–(f); EI(S)R reg 10(5)(d)–(f).

[203] See further §§9–037 and 11–041 to 11–049.

[204] Compare Parliamentary Commissioner Act 1967 s 10(5); Care Standards Act 2000 s 76(7); Competition Act 1998 s 57, and various other statutes.

[205] *Adam v Ward* [1917] AC 309 at 334; *Moore v Canadian Pacific SS Co* [1945] 1 All ER 128.

359

applies), will, if it is defamatory, not automatically enjoy qualified privilege.[206] In relation to information that a public authority is required to disclose under s 1 of the Freedom of Information Act 2000 but which was supplied to the public authority by a third person, the Act specifically provides that the publication to an applicant of any defamatory material contained in that information will be privileged unless the publication is shown to have been made with malice.[207] While qualified privilege will, as just discussed, invariably protect the public authority in such circumstances, the statutory provision is required to protect the third party. But for the provision, if a public authority, in answer to a request for information under the Act, supplied a defamatory statement made to the public authority by a third party, that supply would constitute a further publication for which the third party could be liable:[208]

> The law would part company with the realities of life if it were held that the damage caused by the publication of a libel began and ended with publication to the original publishee. Defamatory statements are objectionable not least because of their propensity to percolate through underground channels and contaminate hidden springs.[209]

Because the Freedom of Information Act 2000 imposes a duty on a public authority to disclose requested information, the foreseeability of the republication will be higher than if it were a matter of pure discretion:

> Where an actual duty is cast upon the person to whom the slander is uttered to communicate what he has heard to some third person, as when a communication is made to a husband, such as, if true, would render the subject of it unfit to associate with his wife and daughters, the slander cannot excuse himself by saying: "True, I told the husband, but I never intended that he should carry the matter to his wife." In such a case... the originator of the slander, and not the hearer of it, is responsible for the consequences.[210]

Provided that the republication is without malice, it will be privileged, protecting both the public authority and the third party. The third party will, of course, remain potentially liable for the original publication to the public authority.

7. DISCRETIONARY DISCLOSURE OF INFORMATION[211]

9–036 **Discretionary disclosure**

The Freedom of Information Act 2000 and the Environmental Information Regulations 2004

---

[206] *Wood v Chief Constable of the West Midlands* [2003] EWHC 2971, [2004] EMLR 17. But in *S v Newham LBC* [1998] 1 FLR 1061, [1999] EMLR 583 (CA) the defence was available to a local authority which, in accordance with ministerial guidelines, sent details concerning one of its social workers to the Department of Health for inclusion in an index of persons unsuitable for child care work.

[207] FOIA s 79; FOI(S)A s 67. There is no equivalent provision in the EIR or the EI(S)R.

[208] The republication may be treated either as a separate cause of action or (provided that it was not too remote) as part of the foreseeable damage resulting from the original publication to the public authority: *Toomey v Mirror Newspapers* (1985) 1 NSWLR 173 at 182–183; *Sims v Wran* [1984] 1 NSWLR 317.

[209] *Slipper v BBC* [1991] 1 QB 283 at 300 (Bingham LJ). See further *McManus v Beckham* [2002] EWCA Civ 939, [2002] 1 WLR 2982, [2002] 4 All ER 497; *Collins Stewart Ltd v Financial Times Ltd (No 2)* [2005] EWHC 262, [2006] EMLR 5.

[210] *Derry v Handley* (1867) 16 LT 263 at 264 (Cockburn CJ).

[211] See further §§14–007 to 14–014 in relation to the discretion to maintain a particular exemption.

do not set the limits of the information that a public authority may lawfully disclose.[212] Disclosure of information by a public authority where it is not under a duty to do so may be called *discretionary disclosure*. The Open Government Code of Practice, published in 1993 and applying to almost all central government bodies and their agencies, was a non-statutory, discretionary regime.[213] Implicit in the Code was an acknowledgment that the public authorities to which it applied could lawfully disclose information held by them despite the absence of a specific statutory provision empowering them to do so.

37   Duties, powers and unlawful disclosure

In any consideration of discretionary disclosure by a public authority, three concepts should be kept distinct:

(1)   Whether there is a *duty* on the public authority to disclose the particular information.

(2)   Whether the public authority has *power* to disclose the particular information; and

(3)   Whether it is *unlawful* for the public authority to disclose the particular information.

The Freedom of Information Act 2000 imposes a *duty* on public authorities to communicate information of the description specified in a request.[214] The exemptions in Part II of the Act do not make *unlawful* the disclosure of particular information: rather, they shape the *duty* imposed by s 1(1) of the Act.[215] Disclosure of information requested under the Freedom of Information Act that is not required to be disclosed is effectively a discretionary disclosure. Other legislation similarly imposes a duty on certain public authorities to disclose certain information to certain people at certain times.[216] The limit of each of those duties does not of itself make *unlawful* the disclosure of information beyond that limit. In certain circumstances, however, disclosure of information in the absence of a statutory obligation to do so (whether from the Freedom of Information Act 2000 or otherwise) will be *unlawful*. Thus:

(a)   Some legislative provisions *prohibit* the disclosure of certain information to certain people at certain times.[217] An exception to such a prohibition does not of itself give rise to a duty to disclose that information: it simply sets the limit of the prohibition. Similarly, disclosure may be prohibited by Community obligations.[218]

---

[212] FOIA s 78; FOI(S)A s 66.

[213] See §§1– 020 to 1– 030.

[214] FOIA,s 1(1)(b).

[215] FOIA s 1(2) in conjunction with s 2(2).

[216] See chs 5, 6 and 8.

[217] For examples of statutory prohibitions, see § 26– 018. A statutory prohibition on the disclosure of information renders that information exempt information under the FOIA, but not under the EIR: FOIA s 44(1)(a); FOI(S)A s 26(a); EIR reg 5(6); EI(S)R reg 5(3).

[218] See further §§26– 025 to 26– 026. Article 6 of Directive 2004/18/EC (dealing with the coordination of procedures for the award of public works contracts, public supply contracts and public service contracts) provides:
Confidentiality
Without prejudice to the provisions of this Directive, in particular those concerning the obligations relating to the advertising of awarded contracts and to the information to candidates and tenderers set out in Articles 35(4) and 41, and in accordance with the national law to which the contracting authority is subject, the contracting authority shall not disclose information forwarded to it by economic operators which they have designated as confidential; such information includes, in particular, technical or trade secrets and the confidential aspects of tenders.

(b)   Some statutory regimes provide that a disclosure is *unlawful* outside the circumstances mandated by the legislation. The most significant such regime is that imposed by the Data Protection Act 1998.[219]

(c)   Disclosure may interfere with a person's private life and, if not justified, may contravene Article 8 of the ECHR.[220] The more systematic the collection of the information, the longer that the information is held, the more it relates to things that are out of the public domain, the more likely that its disclosure will interfere with the subject's private life.[221]

(d)   Disclosure may be unlawful because it would breach some common law or equitable duty, such as respecting confidentiality, whether arising under contract or otherwise. Public authorities hold large quantities of commercially sensitive information provided to them by third parties, whether under compulsion or in order for those third parties to carry out an activity regulated or supervised by public authorities.

In all cases where a request under the Freedom of Information Act 2000 captures information that *may* be subject to such constraints but which the public authority is minded to disclose (because it considers the constraint inapplicable), it is prudent for the public authority to take all reasonable steps to invite the views of the bodies whose interests are protected by the constraint before disclosing the information.[222] Where a public authority discloses information that it is not required to disclose and whose disclosure is constrained in any of the above ways, the public authority will have acted unlawfully.[223] The public authority will not necessarily be excused from civil liability by its genuine belief that it was obliged to disclose the information under the Freedom of Information Act 2000.

9– 038   **The power to disclose information**

While a statute occasionally confers power on a public authority to disclose particular information, discretionary or voluntarily disclosure is not ordinarily specifically provided for. Nevertheless, it is an ordinary incident of a person (whether a natural person or a body corporate or public authority) holding information that that person may deal with that information (including disclosing it) as that person sees fit, subject to any prohibition, constraint

---

This now finds domestic expression in the Public Contracts Regulations 2006 reg 43. European jurisprudence founded upon Art 6 (and its predecessor, Directive 93/36/EEC Art 15(2)) acknowledge that the protection of confidential business information is a general principle against which rights of access must be balanced: *AKZO Chemie BV v EC Commission* (C-53/85) [1986] ECR 1965, [1987] 1 CMLR 231, [1987] FSR 203 at [28]; *Samenwerkende Elektriciteits-Produktiebedrijven NV v EC Commission* (C-36/92 P) [1994] ECR I-1911 at [37]; *Varec SA v Belgium* (C-450/06) [2009] All ER (EC) 772, [2008] ECR I-581, [2008] 2 CMLR 24 at [49]; *Productores de Musica de Espana (Promusicae) v Telefonica de Espana SAU* (C-275/06) [2008] All ER (EC) 809, [2008] ECR I-271, [2008] 2 CMLR 17 at [43], [57], [61]-[63], [68]-[70].

[219] See, generally, ch 24.

[220] *R (L) v Metropolitan Police Commissioner* [2009] UKSC 3, [2010] 1 All ER 113; *R v Chief Constable of North Wales Police, ex p Thorpe* [1999] QB 396 at 414, 416, 429.

[221] *R (L) v Metropolitan Police Commissioner* [2009] UKSC 3, [2010] 1 All ER 113 at [27], [71].

[222] Applying the reasoning in *R (L) v Metropolitan Police Commissioner* [2009] UKSC 3, [2010] 1 All ER 113 at [46]. See further §§11– 041 to 11– 049.

[223] And, in certain circumstances, potentially criminally.

or implied limitation.[224] The power of a public authority to voluntarily disclose information that it holds will be shaped by its functions. If there is no specific statutory power[225] to disclose particular information, a public authority will be acting lawfully in disclosing information that it holds provided that that voluntary disclosure is reasonably required to enable that public authority to properly carry out its functions, subject to any prohibition, limitation or constraint on that disclosure.[226] A power to disclose information may be impliedly limited where the disclosure of certain information would undermine a regulated statutory regime for the disclosure of that information.[227] It may also be limited where the disclosure would involve an interference with a person's private and family life, home or correspondence.[228] Defamation

---

[224] This may in part no more than reflect the fact that without more there is no property in information as such. In *Boardman v Phipps* [1967] AC 46 at 127–128 Lord Upjohn said: 'In general, information is not property at all. It is normally open to all who have eyes to read and ears to hear. The true test is to determine in what circumstances the information has been acquired. If it has been acquired in such circumstances that it would be a breach of confidence to disclose it to another then courts of equity will restrain the recipient from communicating it to another. In such cases such confidential information is often and for many years has been described as the property of the donor, the books of authority are full of such references; knowledge of secret processes, "know-how," confidential information as to the prospects of a company or of someone's intention or the expected results of some horse race based on stable or other confidential information. But in the end the real truth is that it is not property in any normal sense but equity will restrain its transmission to another if in breach of some confidential relationship.' Similarly, *Federal Commissioner of Taxation v United Aircraft Corp* (1944) 68 CLR 525 at 534–6 and *Moorgate Tobacco Co Ltd v Philip Morris Ltd (No 2)* (1984) 156 CLR 414 at 438. And, more recently, see *Douglas v Hello! (No 3)* [2006] QB 125 at [127]; *OBG Ltd v Allan* [2007] UKHL 21, [2007] 2 WLR 920 at [275]–[277], [282], [286].

[225] In the case of a local authority it may derive that power from the Local Government Act 1972 ss 142 and 111, or the Local Government Act 2000 s 2. As to the first provision, see: *Meek v Lothian Regional Council* [1983] SLT 494; *R v Inner London Education Authority, ex p Westminster City Council* [1986] 1 WLR 28, [1986] 1 All ER 19.

[226] *R v Chief Constable of North Wales Police, ex p Thorpe* [1999] QB 396 at 410–411, 415 and 429; *R v Local Authority in the Midlands* [2000] 1 FCR 736; *R (X) v Chief Constable of the West Midlands Police* [2005] 1 All ER 610 at [36]; *Green v Police Complaints Authority* [2004] 1 WLR 725 (HL).

[227] In *R v Liverpool City Council, ex p Baby Products Association* [1999] LGLR 689 the court considered that a local authority did not have power to issue a press release identifying models of babywalkers that did not comply with safety standards. This conclusion was reached on the basis that the issue of consumer warnings was governed by section 13 of the Consumer Protection Act 1987, which granted the Secretary of State the power to require companies to issue warnings only where he considered the goods unsafe and statutory safeguards were complied with. The Court held: 'It is apparent that these provisions comprise a detailed and carefully-crafted code designed, on the one hand, to promote the very important objective of protecting the public against unsafe consumer products and, on the other, to give fair protection to the business interests of manufacturers and suppliers... Mr Fordham [appearing for the Baby Products Association] accepted that, generally speaking, it was open to local authorities to publish information relating to their activities, at any rate within their areas. Had the Council issued suspension notices in accordance with section 14 of the Act, that fact could (he accepted) have been announced to the public. Had the Council initiated any criminal proceedings that fact, and the outcome of such proceedings, could similarly have been announced to the public. Sections 142(2) and 111(1) gave authority to make such announcements if statutory authority was needed. What, however, was impermissible was to make a public announcement having an intention and effect which could only be achieved by implementation of clear and particular procedures prescribed in an Act of Parliament when the effect of the announcement was to deny the companies the rights and protections which Parliament had enacted they should enjoy. So to act was to circumvent the provisions of the legislation and to act unlawfully.'

[228] *R (L) v Metropolitan Police Commissioner* [2009] UKSC 3, [2010] 1 All ER 113; *R v Chief Constable of North Wales Police, ex p Thorpe* [1999] QB 396 at 410–411, 415 and 429 (held lawful for Chief Constable to disclose information from the local press about T's convictions to a proprietor of a caravan site at which T (a married couple who had been released from prison after serving lengthy sentences for serious sexual offences against children) were staying); *R v Local Authority in the Midlands, ex p LM* [2000] 1 FCR 736, [2000] UKHRR 143, (2000) 2 LGLR 1043 (held unlawful for a local authority and local police authority to disclose to a county council, with whom the claimant had contracted to supply school transport, allegations made 10 years earlier that the claimant had sexually abused his daughter and a child in his care). Although the two earlier decisions were questioned in *R (X) v Chief Constable of the West Midlands* [2004] EWCA Civ 1068, [2005] 1 WLR 65, in *R (L) v Metropolitan Police Commissioner* [2009] UKSC

363

and data protection may constrain a public authority volunteering to a person information held by the public authority, whether that information was generated by it or was supplied by a third party. Where the information was supplied to the public authority by a third party, there may also be issues of breach of confidence and copyright that further constrain a voluntary disclosure. If the public authority obtained the information from a third party under some form of compulsion, fairness may require the public authority to notify that third party before voluntarily disclosing it.[229]

3, [2010] 1 All ER 113 at [44], [63] it was held that the latter decision had tilted the balance too far against the person to whom the information relates. See also: *R (A) v Chief Constable of C* [2001] 1 WLR 461, [2001] 2 FCR 43 (held lawful for a Chief Constable to disclose sensitive non-conviction information to a local education authority on the basis that the LEA had a lawful interest in the information and a pressing need to receive it); *Re C (Sexual Abuse: Disclosure to Landlords)* [2002] EWHC 234, [2002] 2 FLR 375, [2002] 2 FCR 385 (Court granting permission to Chief Constable and Director of Social Services to disclose to a local housing association with whom C housed findings of child sexual abuse made against C in care proceedings, but refusing permission to disclose to housing authorities that might house C in the future); *R (X) v Chief Constable of the West Midlands* [2004] EWCA Civ 1068, [2005] 1 WLR 65, [2005] 1 All ER 610 (held that Police Act 1997 s 115 put a Chief Constable under a duty to provide a potential employer with information on X, a social worker with no criminal convictions who was looking for work with children and vulnerable adults, contained in the 'Other Relevant Information' section of an enhanced criminal record certificate); *R (L) v Metropolitan Police Commissioner* [2006] EWHC 482 (held lawful for the Commissioner to disclose information not amounting to criminal conduct or potentially criminal conduct as part of an enhanced criminal record certificate); *R (D) v Secretary of State for Health* [2006] EWCA Civ 989 [2006] Lloyd's Rep Med 457 (held lawful for the Secretary of State to issue an alert letter advising NHS bodies of allegations of indecent assault made against claimant doctor).

[229] See *R (Kent Pharmaceuticals Limited) v SFO* [2004] EWCA Civ 1494, [2005] 1 All ER 449 (where the SFO did have an express statutory power to disclose to a government department information obtained from the claimant).

CHAPTER 10

The Duty to Advise and Assist, Codes of Practice and Publication Schemes

1. THE DUTY TO ADVISE AND ASSIST

001 Introduction

Section 16(1) of the Freedom of Information Act 2000 imposes a duty upon a public authority to provide advice and assistance to any person who proposes to make, or who has made, a request for information to it.[1] The scope of the duty is not open-ended, but is stated to be a duty to provide advice and assistance 'so far as would be reasonable to expect the authority to do'.[2] The duty was introduced on the basis that it represented an important step in achieving the cultural change stated to be sought by the legislation.[3] There had been an initial reluctance on the part of the government to impose such a duty, said to be because of difficulties in adequately describing the limits of the duty.[4] The expedient adopted was to leave the detail to one of the codes of practice.[5] A main object of providing such advice and assistance is to clarify the nature of the information required. Effective exercise of the rights conferred by the Act requires the person seeking information to know how to most appropriately describe what it is they are seeking. The Tribunal has emphasised the importance of providing as much practical assistance as possible to those making information requests.[6]

10– 002   Scope of the duty

Section 16(2) provides that a public authority that conforms with the Code of Practice issued under s 45 is to be taken to comply with the duty to advise and assist. That, however, does not mean that nothing less will suffice. To ascertain the minimum requirements of the duty it is necessary to consider the terms of the section before considering the effect of the Code of Practice. The duty is necessarily shaped by the underlying purpose of the Act, as manifested by its other provisions and its long title. There are a number of notable features about the duty to advise and assist. First, there is no identification of the matters with respect to which the public authority is obliged to provide advice and assistance: it is to a class of persons to which

---

[1]   Similarly: FOI(S)A s 15(1); EIR reg 9(1); EI(S)R reg 9(1). There is no duty to advise and assist in relation to a subject-access request made under s 7 of the DPA except in the very narrow circumstances contemplated by s 53 (where data is being processed for any of the special purposes and the matter is one of substantial public importance).

[2]   There are similar duties in three of the comparative jurisdictions: Freedom of Information Act 1982 (Cth of Aust) s 15(3); Official Information Act 1982 (NZ) s 13; Freedom of Information Act 1997 (Ireland), long title and ss 6(2), 7(7) and 10(2). There is no provision in either the US or the Canadian Act requiring an agency to give assistance. In the recent review of the Canadian Act, it was recommended that that Act be amended to require that the institution make a reasonable effort to assist an applicant upon request, and offer to help the requester reformulate the request in a way that will avoid negative outcomes: Government of Canada, *Report of the Access to Information Review Task Force* (June 2002) p 86. In its review of the Freedom of Information Act 1982, the Australian Law Reform Commission noted that many agencies did not seem to have an adequate commitment to the obligation to give assistance. The Review declined to prescribe further what assistance had to be given, instead considering that the FOI Commissioner should encourage agencies to do more than the bare statutory minimum. The Commission concluded: 'if agencies take care to find out exactly what information an applicant requires they may ultimately save resources and avoid disputes': Australian Law Reform Commission and Administrative Review Council, *Open Government: a review of the Federal Freedom of Information Act 1982*, ALRC 77, ARC 40 (Canberra, 1995) para 7.5. See also paras 7.14, 8.14 and 10.9.

[3]   See Hansard HL vol 617 cols 940 and 942 (17 October 2000).

[4]   See House of Commons, *Public Administration—Third Report* (Cm 4355, 1999) Annex 6, para 24(see ch 1 n 64); House of Commons, *Select Committee on Public Administration, 5th Special Report*, Appendix, 27 October 1999, p 11; Hansard HC vol 347 cols 856–870 (4 April 2000); Hansard HL vol 617 cols 938–945 (17 October 2000). For the final acceptance by the Government of this, see Hansard HL vol 619 cols 194–197 (14 November 2000).

[5]   During the passage of the Bill, it had been suggested that rather more detail should be spelt out in the Act itself: House of Commons, *Public Administration–Third Report* (Cm 4355, 1999) para 52 (see ch 1 n 64); House of Commons, *Select Committee on Public Administration 5th Special Report*, Appendix, 27 October 1999, p 5; Hansard HC vol 347 cols 868–870 (4 April 2000); Hansard HL vol 619 cols 250–252 (14 November 2000).

[6]   *Bellamy v IC and DTI*, IT, 4 April 2006 at [40]. Similarly, in relation to Scottish public authorities, *Common Services Agency v Scottish IC*, 2006 CSIH 58, 2007 SLT 7 at [16].

the duty is confined.[7] Secondly, the duty is not only engaged where the applicant seeks advice or assistance: the public authority may be required to volunteer advice and assistance.[8] Thirdly, the duty relates to both an unformed request and to one already made.[9] The former implies that the duty includes advising and assisting in the formulation of a request that meets the formal requirements of the Act.[10] Fourthly, the fact that the duty is not tied to advice and assistance in relation to the Freedom of Information Act 2000 suggests that a public authority may also be required to advise and assist where the request for information would be better made under other legislation, such as the Data Protection Act 1998 in relation to a request for personal information.[11] Fifthly, it is apparent from the wording of the section that the duty to advise and assist does not end with the receipt by the public authority of a properly formulated request. Thus the duty may require the giving of advice and assistance:

— where a public authority apprehends that the request is more likely to retrieve the information requested if directed to another public authority;

— where a public authority estimates that the cost of compliance with the request will exceed the appropriate limit, thereby removing the obligation upon the public authority to comply with the request[12] or, if it chooses to do so, to charge for meeting the request;[13]

— where a public authority considers that it requires further information in order to identify and locate the information requested by the applicant;[14]

— where a public authority considers that the request would be more successful if the applicant were to obtain the consent of a third party to disclosure and that could properly be suggested to the applicant without the disclosure of exempt information; and

— in relation to the applicant's appeal and enforcement rights.

And sixthly, the duty is one to give advice and assistance to the extent that it is reasonable to expect of the public authority. This suggests that the size and resources of the public authority will in part determine how much advice and assistance a public authority must give an applicant in the proper discharge of its duty. The Information Commissioner advises[15] that the authority should adopt a flexible approach; the duty to advise and assist will often be fulfilled

---

[7] Namely, 'persons who propose to make, or have made, requests for information': FOIA s 16(1).

[8] *Barber v IC*, IT, 20 February 2006 at [17]-[19].

[9] See, eg, *Hogan v IC and Oxford City Council*, IT, 17 October 2006, where Oxford City Council were held to have breached the duty to advise and assist in relation to what was held to be a modified request for information.

[10] That is, the requirements set out in the FOIA s 8(1), and the FOI(S)A s 8(1). See *Lamb v IC*, IT, 16 November 2006 at [2]. In relation to requests for environmental information, see §6– 021.

[11] A request for such information made under the FOIA could properly be refused by virtue of FOIA s 21, or FOI(S)A s 25.

[12] FOIA s 12(1); FOI(S)A s 12(1).

[13] FOIA s 13(1); FOI(S)A s 13(1). If a request is refused on grounds of excessive cost of compliance, it may then be appropriate for the authority to provide advice and assistance to help the person who made the request to focus their request: see the Information Commissioner's Awareness Guidance No 23 (1 July 2009). But see *Roberts v IC*, IT, 4 December 2008 where it was held that a failure to advise and assist did not render a costs estimate invalid.

[14] FOIA s 1(3); FOI(S)A s 1(3).

[15] Awareness Guidance No 23 (1 July 2009).

by the provision of standard information.

10–003 No duty to record information

The Tribunal has made it clear that the duty does not extend to creating intelligible information from raw data held by the public authority. The Freedom of Information Act 2000 does not have an equivalent to the requirement in the Data Protection Act 1998 that the holding body communicate information in an 'intelligible form.'[16] Furthermore, where a public authority comes to the objectively reasonable conclusion that a request is vexatious, it will not be held to have breached the duty to provide advice and assistance by not engaging in further communications with the applicant.[17]

10–004 The role of the Code of Practice

Section 45(1) of the Freedom of Information Act 2000 obliges the Secretary of State for Justice to issue a Code of Practice providing guidance to public authorities as to the practice which it would be desirable for public authorities to follow in connection with the discharge of their functions under Part I of the Act.[18] The section specifically requires the Code of Practice to cover the provision of advice and assistance by public authorities to persons who propose to make, or have made, requests for information.[19] The present Code of Practice under s 45 was laid before Parliament on 25 November 2004.[20] As noted above, the Act provides that conformity with the Code will constitute compliance with the duty to advise and assist, so that so far as this duty is concerned it may go beyond the minimum that is required of a public authority. Other Acts of Parliament may also be relevant to the way in which authorities provide advice and assistance to applicants or potential applicants, such as the Disability Discrimination Act 1995.[21] The Code's requirements do not, of course, prevent an authority from offering additional assistance if it wishes.[22]

10–005 The requirements of the Code of Practice

Although paras 3 to 15 of the Code of Practice are specifically directed to the duty to advise and assist, the full extent to which the code describes the duty requires a consideration of all its provisions. In summary, the requirements of the Code so far as the duty is concerned are:

(1)   For each public authority to publish its procedures for dealing with a request for information, which may, but need not, include a standard procedure for a transfer of the request from one public authority to another where the public authority does

---

[16]   *Evans v IC and MoD*, IT, 26 October 2007 at [48]-[50].

[17]   *Billings v IC*, IT, 6 February 2008 at [13]-[14]. This is also the view of the Information Commissioner: Awareness Guidance No 23 (1 July 2007).

[18]   Similarly: FOI(S)A s 60; EIR reg 16; EI(S)R reg 18.

[19]   FOIA s 45(2)(a); FOI(S)A s 60(2)(a).

[20]   It is reproduced in the Appendix. In relation to the Code of Practice under the EIR and the EI(S)R, see §6–020.

[21]   See the Foreword to the s 45 Code of Practice, para 14, and the Scottish Ministers Code of Practice on the Discharge of Functions by Public Authorities under the FOI(S)A, Introduction.

[22]   See Hansard HL vol 619 col 196 (14 November 2000) (Lord Falconer, Minister of State, Cabinet Office).

not hold the information requested.[23]

(2) For a public authority to alert a potential applicant that it may need to consult other public authorities or third persons before determining the application.[24]

(3) The procedures should include the following contact details to which requests for information and assistance should be directed: mailing address, email address, telephone number and name of a specific individual to contact.[25]

(4) For a public authority to volunteer the existence of the Act to those who are unaware of it.[26]

(5) For a public authority to assist an applicant in formulating a request that is both proper and that enables it to locate the requested information.[27]

(6) For a public authority to indicate to an applicant which information of the kind sought is available free of charge.[28]

(7) For a public authority to advise an applicant that it does not hold all or part of the requested information.[29] Where the public authority to which the request has been made believes that some or all of that information is held by another public authority, the public authority that has received the request is expected to consider the most helpful way of assisting the applicant, which will normally include advising the applicant of the identity of that other public authority and suggesting that application is made to it.[30] If the public authority does not know the identity of another public authority that might hold the requested information, the first-mentioned public authority must at least consider what advice it can give the applicant to assist him with his request.[31]

It is suggested that the line between the minimum duty such as can be discerned from the words of s 45(1) and the duty as described in the Code of Practice is a fine one.

006 Enforcement of the duty to advise and assist

There are two principal mechanisms contemplated in the Act for enforcement of the duty to advise and assist. First, a duty is imposed upon the Information Commissioner to promote the following of 'good practice', which is defined to include compliance with the requirements of the Act and the provisions of the Code of Practice.[32] Where it appears to the Information Commissioner that the practice of a particular public authority does not conform with the

---

[23] See para 4 of the s 45 Code of Practice. Transfers of requests for information are treated in §§11– 037 to 11– 038.

[24] Section 45 Code of Practice, para 4.

[25] Section 45 Code of Practice, para 5. But see *Berend v IC and LB of Richmond*, IT, 12 July 2007 at [49] where the Tribunal pointed out that a named individual need only be identified 'where possible.'

[26] Section 45 Code of Practice, para 6.

[27] Section 45 Code of Practice, paras 7–11.

[28] Section 45 Code of Practice, paras 13–14. And see §10– 013 as to the lawfulness of charges for information supplied pursuant to a publication scheme.

[29] Section 45 Code of Practice, para 17.

[30] Section 45 Code of Practice, paras 17-23.

[31] Section 45 Code of Practice, para 24.

[32] FOIA s 47(1); FOI(S)A s 43(1); EIR reg 16(5); EI(S)R reg 18(5).

requirements laid out in the Code of Practice, the Information Commissioner can issue a 'practice recommendation' that specifies the steps which, in the opinion of the Information Commissioner, ought to be taken in order to promote conformity.[33] The first mechanism, then, does not depend upon the applicant in order for it to be instigated. The second mechanism is applicant-driven. In addition to being able to apply to the Information Commissioner on the basis of non-disclosure of requested information, a person may apply to the Information Commissioner on the grounds that the advice and assistance that he was entitled to receive from the public authority after having made a request was not provided to him.[34] In order to be able to make the application, the person must have made a request for information that meets all the formal requirements.[35] The latter is probably more hypothetical than real, in that once an applicant makes complaint to the Information Commissioner the applicant will normally be seeking the Commissioner's decision upon a refusal to disclose, irrespective of the level of help that might have been given. A complainant in person should not be expected to be familiar with s 16 of the Act, and even if such a complainant does not specify a breach of the duty to advise and assist in his complaint, the Commissioner may still be obliged to consider whether s 16 has been complied with.[36] The Commissioner may issue a decision notice that specifies whether the public authority has or has not breached its duty under s 16.[37] A party dissatisfied with that decision notice may appeal to the First-Tier Tribunal in relation to the finding as to the provision of advice and assistance.[38] The Tribunal has stated that non-compliance with s 16 'may go to the very nature of the request and that any exercise of discretion by the Commissioner which does not take this into account may be flawed'; and that failure to consider compliance with s 16 may mean that the Commissioner has not complied with s 47 of the Act, which is the general duty to promote good practices.[39]

2. THE CODES OF PRACTICE

10–007 Introduction

The Freedom of Information Act 2000 requires two Codes of Practice to be issued: the first, to

---

[33] FOIA s 48(1); FOI(S)A s 44(1); EIR reg 16(5); EI(S)R reg 18(5).

[34] FOIA s 50(1); EIR reg 18. The position would appear to be otherwise in Scotland: see FOI(S)A s 47.

[35] FOIA ss 8(1) and 50(1).

[36] *Barber v IC*, IT, 11 November 2005 at [17]–[18]; cf *Johnson v IC*, IT, 28 April 2006 at [2].

[37] See §28–011.

[38] See further §§28–026 to 28–026. For example: *Hogan and Oxford City Council v IC*, IT, 17 October 2006 at [17]–[21]; *Campsie v IC*, IT, 5 April 2007; *Lamb v IC*, IT, 16 November 2006 at [2]–[4] and [19]–[20], where the Information Tribunal found that a public authority should have asked the applicant to specify more precisely the information that was being requested. In *Urmenyi v IC and LB of Sutton*, IT, 13 July 2007, the Tribunal held that the public authority had failed in its duty to advise and assist where the cost of complying with the applicant's request for information would have exceeded the appropriate limit and the public authority did not suggest ways in which the applicant could reduce the scope of his request so as not to exceed that limit.

[39] *Barber v IC*, IT, 20 February 2006 at [17]–[18].

be issued by the Secretary of State for Justice,[40] providing guidance to public authorities on good practice in dealing with requests for information;[41] the second, to be issued by the Lord Chancellor, providing guidance to relevant authorities[42] on good practice in keeping, managing and destroying records.[43] The Secretary of State for Justice and the Lord Chancellor may amend the respective codes from time to time.[44] The Information Commissioner is under a duty to promote observance of the codes by public authorities.[45] The Data Protection Act 1998 also provides for codes of practice.[46] As at 1 June 2010 the versions of the Codes are:

— Section 45 Code of Practice on the Discharge of the Functions of Public Authorities under Part I of the Freedom of Information Act, the second edition of which was published and laid before Parliament in November 2004.

— Lord Chancellor's Code of Practice on the Management of Records under section 46, which was revised and re-issued on 16 July 2009.

There is also a Code of Practice relating to the Environmental Information Regulations.

008   Status of the codes

The Codes of Practice issued under the Freedom of Information Act 2000 do not have any

---

[40]   The Act originally assigned the function to the Secretary of State, but that function was first transferred to the Lord Chancellor by the Transfer of Functions (Miscellaneous) Order 2001 SI 2001/3500 and then to the Secretary of State for Constitutional Affairs by the Secretary of State for Constitutional Affairs Order 2003 SI 2003/1887 and, from 9 May 2007, to the Secretary of State for Justice under The Secretary of State for Justice Order 2007 SI 2007/2128.

[41]   FOIA s 45; FOI(S)A s 60. In Scotland, the duty is cast upon the Scottish Ministers. These provisions set out what must be included in the code, and allow for different provisions to be made for different public authorities. The former also provides that before issuing or revising any code under this section, the Secretary of State for Justice must consult the Information Commissioner and then must subsequently lay any code or revised code before each House of Parliament. In relation to the EIR, see §6– 020.

[42]   'Relevant authority' means: (a) any public authority, and (b) any office or body which is not a public authority but whose administrative and departmental records are public records for the purposes of the Public Records Act 1958 or the Public Records Act (Northern Ireland) 1923: FOIA s 46(7).

[43]   FOIA s 46; FOI(S)A s 61. In exercising his functions under this section the Secretary of State for Justice is required to have regard to the public interest in allowing public access to information held by relevant authorities. The code may make different provisions for different relevant authorities. Before issuing or revising any code under this section the Secretary of State for Justice must consult the Secretary of State, the Information Commissioner and (in relation to Northern Ireland), the appropriate Northern Ireland Minister, and then must subsequently lay any code or revised code before both Houses of Parliament.

[44]   The Secretary of State for Justice and the Lord Chancellor must consult the Information Commissioner before revising a Code of Practice: FOIA ss 45(4) and 46(5). In Scotland, the Scottish Ministers must consult the Information Commissioner before revising a Code of Practice: FOI(S)A ss 60(4) and 61(5). Any revision to a Code of Practice must be laid before both Houses of Parliament: FOIA ss 45(5) and 46(6). In Scotland, revisions must be laid before the Parliament: FOI(S)A ss 60(5) and 61(6).

[45]   FOIA s 47(1); FOI(S)A s 43(1). The s 45 Code of Practice, para 3, provides that authorities are expected to abide by the Code unless there are good reasons, capable of being justified to the Information Commissioner, why it would be inappropriate to do so.

[46]   DPA s 51(3). The codes of practice are issued by the Information Commissioner upon direction by the Secretary of State for Justice or where the Commissioner considers it appropriate to do so. There is a consultation process that reflects all the preoccupations of the DPA, rather than merely the right of access to personal data. Although no specific code of practice relating to subject-access requests has been issued, the Information Commissioner has issued certain documents providing 'compliance advice'.

statutory force.[47] The Act imposes no direct duty on public authorities to follow or even to have regard to them. Instead, where it appears to the Information Commissioner that the practice of a public authority in relation to the exercise of its functions under the Freedom of Information Act 2000 does not conform with that proposed in the codes of practice, the Information Commissioner can give the public authority a written 'practice recommendation' specifying the steps which in the opinion of the Information Commissioner ought to be taken for promoting such conformity.[48] In contrast to non-compliance with a decision notice, information notice or enforcement notice issued by the Information Commissioner (which can amount to contempt of court), the Act does not specify the consequences of a failure to comply with a practice recommendation. The Government referred to this during the Bill's passage through Parliament, and commented as follows:

> [C]ompliance with the published codes of practice would not be enforceable in the courts in the same way that a statutory duty might be. We believe it would be an exceptional authority which ignored a [practice] recommendation, particularly given the commissioner's powers to name and shame in any report that she might make to Parliament. An additional point is that the code of practice could be referred to in any test case which was the subject of judicial review. The power of naming and shaming should not be underestimated in regard to public sector bodies keen to keep the confidence of the public they serve.[49]

10–009 Other methods of compelling compliance

Although it would be open to the Information Commissioner to seek judicial review of a public authority's refusal to follow a practice recommendation, the non-statutory nature of the codes of practice, the fact that the refusal relates to a recommendation rather than a direction, and the absence of any statutory duty to follow or have regard to a Practice Direction, would materially weaken such a claim.[50] It is suggested that unless non-compliance with a practice recommendation also represents a breach of the Act, a court would rule that the appropriate forum for securing compliance is a political one and not the courts. Similarly, judicial review by any other person based solely on a breach of a code of practice is unlikely to succeed.[51] However, non-compliance with the codes could form part of a wider challenge to the discharge by a public authority of its duties under the Act, such as a failure in relation to the duty to

---

[47] See s 45 Code of Practice, para 3; Scottish Ministers Code of Practice on the Discharge of Functions by Public Authorities under the FOI(S)A, Introduction, issued pursuant to FOI(S)A s 60.

[48] FOIA s 48(1); FOI(S)A s 44(1); EIR reg 16(5); EISR reg 18(5). The Information Commissioner is required to consult the Keeper of the Public Records (or the Deputy Keeper of the Records of Northern Ireland) before giving a practice recommendation relating to conformity with the Lord Chancellor's Code of Practice on record-keeping: FOIA s 48(3) and (4).

[49] Hansard HL vol 617 col 944 (17 October 2000) (Lord Bassam of Brighton, Parliamentary Under-Secretary of State, Home Office). See also the s 45 Code of Practice, Foreword, para 7, which states: 'practice recommendation is simply a recommendation and cannot be directly enforced by the Information Commissioner. However, a failure to comply with a practice recommendation may lead to a failure to comply with the Act. Further a failure to take account of a practice recommendation may lead to an adverse comment in a report to Parliament by the Commissioner.'

[50] See §10–020.

[51] Compare *R (Munjaz) v Mersey Care NHS* [2003] EWCA Civ 1036 at [77] where the Court of Appeal treated a hospital's breach of code as enabling the affected individual to seek a declaration of illegality, possible damages for tort (unlawful detention) and damages under the Human Rights Act 1998.

advise and assist.[52] In these circumstances, the Information Commissioner could serve an enforcement notice. By itself, however, the failure of a public authority to comply with either of the codes of practice does not provide a basis for a disgruntled applicant to make an application to the Information Commissioner under s 50.[53]

010 The aims of the section 45 code

The s 45 code of practice provides guidance to public authorities as to the practice which it would, in the opinion of the Secretary of State, be desirable for them to follow in connection with the discharge of their functions under Part I of the Act.[54] The Code sets out its aims as follows:[55]

(1) to facilitate the disclosure of information under the Act by setting out good administrative practice that it is desirable for public authorities to follow when handling requests for information, including, where appropriate, the transfer of a request to a different authority;

(2) to protect the interests of applicants by setting out standards for the provision of advice which it would be good practice to make available to them and to encourage the development of effective means of complaining about decisions taken under the Act;

(3) to ensure that the interests of third parties who may be affected by any decision to disclose information are considered by the authority by setting standards for consultation; and

(4) to ensure that authorities consider the implications for Freedom of Information before agreeing to confidentiality provisions in contracts and accepting information in confidence from a third party more generally.

011 The contents of the section 45 code

The code is divided into 12 overlapping topics:

(1) An introduction. Notably, this recites the code's lack of statutory force.

(2) The provision of advice and assistance to persons making requests for information. As noted before, the code goes little beyond what is required by the terms of the Act.[56]

(3) The handling of requests for information that appear to be part of an organised campaign. Section 12(4) of the Freedom of Information Act 2000 and the fees regulations[57] enable aggregation in certain circumstances of the cost of compliance of multiple requests. The code suggests that in these circumstances disclosure by publication on the public authority's website may be appropriate, but otherwise

---

[52] This is suggested by the Foreword to the s 45 Code of Practice.

[53] This is because compliance with the codes of practice is not a requirement of Pt I of the Act: see FOIA s 50(1). This is confirmed by FOIA s 51(1)(b), which contradistinguishes the requirements of Pt I of the Act from the codes of practice.

[54] FOIA s 45.

[55] Section 45 Code of Practice, para 4.

[56] §10–004.

[57] FOI & DP (Limit & Fees)R.

adds little to the scheme established by the Act.

(4)   Timeliness in dealing with requests for information. Section 10(1) of the Act provides a basic 20 working day limit for compliance with a request that does not involve a qualified exemption.[58] The code exhorts earlier compliance if possible. In relation to a request involving a qualified exemption, for which the Act provides no time limit for responding to the request, the code encourages a response within the basic 20 working-day time limit.

(5)   Charging fees. The code does little more than recite the position under the Freedom of Information Act 2000 and the charging regulations made under it.[59]

(6)   Transferring requests for information. The code sets out what a public authority should do where it either holds none or just some of the requested information, with the balance being held by some other public authority. The code encourages such transfers to take place as quickly as possible.[60] The code states that in most cases the authority receiving the request will contact the person who made it, explain that there is another public authority which holds the information, provide the contact details of that authority, and advise the person to make a request to that authority. The code also states that in some cases it may be more appropriate to transfer the original request directly to that other authority.

(7)   Consultation with third parties. Given that the Freedom of Information Act 2000 makes no express provision for third-party involvement in the determination of a request for information, this part of the code is of particular importance.[61] Where the absence of consent from a third party would necessarily defeat a request for information (eg because the requested information was supplied in confidence to the public authority by the third party), the Code of Practice exhorts the public authority to seek the consent of the third party unless that third party cannot be located or the cost of doing so is disproportionate. Consultation with a third party is also commended where disclosure would impinge upon the interests of that third party, where it might assist in the determination of the applicability of an exemption, or where it might assist the public authority in determining where the public interest lies. If, however, the information sought will be rendered exempt by another provision of the Act, the code dispenses with the need to consult an interested third party.

(8)   Freedom of information and public sector contracts. The code advises public authorities to refuse to enter into private sector contracts that include a term that purports to restrict or oust the operation of the Act in relation to the contract and to ensure that only truly confidential information is received on an in-confidence basis from private sector contractors.

(9)   Accepting information in confidence from third parties. The code cautions against public authorities receiving information from third parties on an in-confidence basis

---

[58]   See further §§11–022 to 11–030.

[59]   See further §§11–014 to 11–021.

[60]   See further §§11–037 to 11–038.

[61]   See §25–009. The Information Commissioner has issued guidance in relation to requests for data under the DPA that contain third-party information.

unless:(a) it is necessary to obtain that information in connection with the exercise of any of the authority's functions;(b) the information would not otherwise be provided to the public authority by the third party; and(c) the information is confidential in nature.

(10) Consultation with devolved administrations. The code builds on s 28 of the Act by suggesting that public authorities should consult with a devolved administration directly concerned with the information proposed to be disclosed irrespective of whether any prejudice to relations with the devolved administration would be caused by a disclosure.

(11) Refusal of request. The code requires public authorities, when refusing a request, to do more than incant the words of the provision relied upon to found the exemption and, where a qualified exemption is relied upon, to enumerate the public interest factors relied upon in the weighing exercise.[62]

(12) Complaints procedure. The code encourages public authorities to have a complaints procedure, which should provide an effective right of internal appeal, and to advise applicants of their statutory rights of appeal.

012 The section 46 code
This Code of Practice was revised and re-issued on 16 July 2009.[63] Its aims are:
(1) To set out practices which public authorities, and bodies subject to the Public Records Act 1958 and the Public Records Act (NI) 1923, should follow in relation to the creation, keeping, management and destruction of their records (including specific provision for management of electronic records) (Part I of the Code); and
(2) To describe the arrangements which public record bodies should follow in reviewing public records and transferring them to The National Archives or to a place of deposit for public records or to the Public Record Office of Northern Ireland (Part II of the Code).

3. PUBLICATION SCHEMES

013 Introduction
Public authorities should not be solely reactive to specific requests for information, but also take steps to ensure that some of their information is publicly available. The Freedom of Information Act 2000 does not limit the pre-existing powers of public authorities to disclose their information.[64] Every public authority must adopt and maintain a scheme, called a

---

[62] See §§13– 008 to 13– 014.

[63] The code is reproduced in the Appendix. The original code was issued in November 2002.

[64] FOIA s 78.

'publication scheme'.[65] A publication scheme sets out the classes of information which the public authority intends to make available to the public as a matter of course.[66] In that publication scheme, the public authority must specify the classes of information that it publishes or intends to publish, the manner in which it publishes each class of information, and state whether the material is available to the public free-of-charge or on payment.[67] The publication scheme is not intended to be a list of information held by the authority.[68] The rationale for the scheme is two-fold: to spare a public authority from having to deal with standard requests under the Act which it may be anticipated will be sought; and to encourage a culture of openness within public authorities:[69]

> The Freedom of Information Act must be a catalyst for changes in the way that public authorities approach openness. Experience overseas consistently shows the importance of changing the culture through requiring active disclosure, so that public authorities get used to making information publicly available in the course of their activities. This helps ensure that FOI does not simply become a potentially confrontational arrangement under which nothing is released unless someone has specifically asked for it. We believe it is important that further impetus is given to the pro-active release of information. So, the Act will impose duties upon public authorities to make certain information publicly available, as a matter of

---

[65] FOIA s 19(1); FOI(S)A s 23(1). In relation to environmental information, see §6– 018. The freedom of information legislation in each of the comparative jurisdictions includes the equivalent of a publication scheme. Most of the comparative regimes also require their statutory equivalent of a public authority to prepare and make available a statement that sets out the organisation, functions and adopted policies of the public authority. So far as equivalents of the publication scheme are concerned, in the United States, the Freedom of Information Act 1966 s 552(a)(2) requires that certain sorts of records, such as policy statements and certain administrative staff manuals, be routinely made available for public inspection and copying. This is often referred to as the 'reading room' provision of the Act, and certain records must also be made available in 'electronic reading rooms'. In Australia, the Freedom of Information Act 1982 ss 8 - 8D include a comprehensive regime obliging agencies to publish a wide range of accurate, up-to-date information about themselves and their functions. The Information Commissioner may review information publications schemes: s 8F. In Canada, the Access to Information Act 1982 s 5(1) requires the designated Minister to publish at least once a year 'a description of all classes of records under the control of each government institution in sufficient detail to facilitate the exercise of the right of access under [the] Act.' The Minister must also prepare a bulletin at least twice a year, and both documents must be 'made available throughout Canada in conformity with the principle that every person is entitled to reasonable access thereto.' In New Zealand, the Official Information Act 1982 s 20 requires the Ministry of Justice to publish for each Department and organisation subject to the Act a general description of the categories of documents held by it, a description of the manuals containing policies by which decisions are made, as well as the officer to whom requests for information should be sent. Under s 21, a person is entitled to access to the latest edition of the publication, and there are various provisions giving a person an absolute right to particular documents. In Ireland, the Freedom of Information Act 1997 ss 15 and 16 require each public body to prepare and publish a 'reference book' containing, amongst other things, a general description of the classes of records held by it, giving such particulars as are reasonably necessary to facilitate the exercise of the right of access as well as the rules, procedures, etc used by the body for the purposes of any enactment or scheme administered by it.

[66] MoJ, *Freedom of Information Act–Procedural Guidance*, undated, Annex A.

[67] FOIA s 19(2); FOI(S)A s 23(2). Note that local authorities are only empowered to impose charges for such services where authorised by Parliament to do so (*McCarthy & Stone plc v London Borough of Richmond* [1992] 2 AC 48; *R (Stennett) v Manchester CC* [2002] UKHL 34, [2002] 4 All ER 124) and the provisions of the Freedom of Information legislation do not authorise such charging where the information is supplied to a publication scheme, particularly where the statutory scheme makes detailed provision for charges levied on information provided pursuant to specific requests.

[68] House of Commons, *Public Administration—Third Report* (Cm 4355, 1999) Annex 6, para 18 (see ch 1 n 64).

[69] Hansard HL vol 612 col 826 (20 April 2000) (Minister of State, Cabinet Office, Lord Falconer).

course.[70]

There is a particular incentive for authorities to publish information under a publication scheme, as it grounds an absolute exemption under Part II of the Act[71] or, in the case of information intended to be published, a qualified exemption, as the information is already reasonably accessible to the applicant.[72] Under the Environmental Information Regulations, there is no requirement for publication schemes as such, but there is provision for dissemination of environmental information electronically.[73]

014 Duties on public authorities

The publication scheme requirement comprehends three discrete duties upon a public authority:

    (1)   to adopt and maintain a publication scheme that is approved by the Information Commissioner;

    (2)   to publish information in accordance with its publication scheme; and

    (3)   from time to time to review that publication scheme.[74]

015 Model publication schemes: England, Wales and Northern Ireland

As from 1 January 2009 there has in England, Wales and Northern Ireland been one approved model scheme which must be adopted by all public authorities. The approval for all previous schemes expired on 31 December 2008. The new model scheme lists information under seven broad classes:

    (1)   Who we are and what we do;

    (2)   What we spend and how we spend it;

    (3)   What our priorities are and how we are doing;

    (4)   How we make decisions;

    (5)   Our policies and procedures;

    (6)   Lists and registers; and

    (7)   The services we offer.

Each public authority must prepare a guide to information for the public, which gives details of what the authority will provide under the scheme. Authorities established after 1 November 2008 have 60 days to comply from the date they were created. Information published by the Information Commissioner on the Model Publication Scheme states that it is the only scheme approved by the Information Commissioner and should be adopted by all public authorities. It also states that the model scheme should not be altered or amended and removes the requirement for public authorities to inform the Information Commissioner that they have adopted the scheme. The Information Commissioner has published 'Definition Documents' setting out the information that he would expect to be made available in the model publication scheme in relation to certain sectors. The sectors for which Definition Documents are currently

---

[70] Cabinet Office, *Your Right to Know—The Government's Proposals for a FOI Act. White Paper* (Cm 3818, 1997) paras 2.17–2.18.

[71] FOIA s 21(1); FOI(S)A s 25(1). also see MoJ, *Freedom of Information Act – Procedural Guidance*, undated, Annex A.

[72] FOIA s 22(1); FOI(S)A s 27(1).

[73] §6– 018.

[74] FOIA s 19(1); FOI(S)A s 23(1).

available are:

— authorities established to manage museums, libraries, and archives (including art galleries and historical collections);
— charter trustees;
— colleges of further education;
— community health councils;
— education and library boards, Northern Ireland;
— Government departments;
— health and social services councils;
— health bodies in England;
— health bodies in Northern Ireland;
— health bodies in Wales;
— health regulators;
— joint authorities and boards;
— non-departmental public bodies
— Northern Ireland district councils;
— Northern Ireland government departments;
— police authorities;
— police forces;
— principal local authorities;
— the House of Commons;
— the House of Lords;
— Welsh Assembly Government sponsored bodies;
— local fisheries;
— national parks and broads;
— Northern Ireland non-departmental public bodies;
— schools in England;
— schools in Northern Ireland;
— schools in Wales;
— armed forces of the Crown;
— the National Assembly for Wales;
— the Northern Ireland Assembly;
— the Welsh Assembly Government;
— universities; and
— wholly-owned companies.

10–016 Model publication schemes: Scotland

The position in Scotland is different. In 2004 all Scottish public authorities produced publication schemes which were approved by the Commissioner. The approval for these schemes will expire between 2008 and 2012, starting with central government schemes in 2008. On expiry, each public authority will be required to submit a new publication scheme to the Commissioner for approval prior to the expiry of their existing scheme. The Scottish Commissioner has produced new guidance to assist authorities in fulfilling the duty to adopt and maintain a publication scheme. The Scottish Commissioner has published a Publication Scheme template but there is not a single approved scheme in Scotland. Authorities are able to submit publication schemes for approval as was the case previously in England, Wales and Northern Ireland.

017 Scotland: bespoke publication schemes

If a Scottish public authority does not wish to adopt a model scheme, it must develop its own bespoke scheme and submit that scheme to the Information Commissioner for approval. The requirements of a publication scheme are that it must:

    (1)   specify classes of information which the public authority publishes or intends to publish;

    (2)   specify the manner in which information of each class is, or is intended to be, published; and

    (3)   specify whether the material is, or is intended to be, available to the public free of charge or on payment.[75]

In adopting or reviewing a publication scheme, a public authority must have regard to the public interest in allowing public access to information held by the authority and in the publication of reasons for decisions made by the authority.[76] If the Commissioner refuses to approve a proposed model publication scheme he must give reasons for the refusal.[77] If the Commissioner gives approval to a publication scheme, he can provide that the approval is to expire at the end of a specified period.[78] Once it is approved, the public authority must publish its publication scheme, but can do so in whatever manner it thinks fit.[79] Approval for a publication scheme can be revoked by the Commissioner at any time, but he must give six months' notice[80] and must also give reasons for the revocation.[81] The Commissioner has published advice for public authorities on how to develop their own publication schemes.[82]

018 Enforcing the publication scheme regime

Each public authority is required to adopt a publication scheme that has been approved by the Information Commissioner. Where a public authority breaches its statutory duty to do so, the Commissioner can serve an enforcement notice on the authority requiring it to remedy this.[83] Similarly, where a public authority has adopted a model publication scheme and the Commissioner considers that the authority does not fall within the class to which that model

---

[75] FOI(S)A s 23(2). As to the legality of charges for information supplied pursuant to a publication scheme, see §10–013.

[76] In adopting or reviewing its publication scheme a Scottish public authority must have regard to the public interest in: (a) allowing public access to information held by it and in particular to information which relates to the provision of services by it, the cost to it of providing them or the standards attained by services so provided or which consists of facts, or analyses, on the basis of which decisions of importance to the public have been made by it; and (b) the publication of reasons for decisions made by it: FOI(S)A s 23(3).

[77] FOI(S)A s 23(6)(a).

[78] FOI(S)A s 23(5)(a).

[79] FOI(S)A s 23(4).

[80] FOI(S)A s 23(5)(b).

[81] FOI(S)A s 23(6)(b).

[82] Available on the Commissioner's website at: www.dataprotection.gov.uk.

[83] Under FOIA s 52(1), or FOI(S)A s 51(1). See FOIA s 52, and FOI(S)A s 52, discussed in §§28– 013 and 28– 016.

379

scheme relates, he can serve an enforcement notice.[84] The expectation is that the Information Commissioner should exercise an active supervisory role in relation to the adequacy and suitability of each public authority's publication scheme:

> Authorities will not be able to get away with weak or self-serving publication schemes. They will all have to be approved by the Commissioner and she will ensure they are strong and meaningful.[85]

Accordingly, if the Information Commissioner conclude that a public authority's publication scheme falls short of the statutory requirements, the Commissioner is not obliged to be deferential to the views of the public authority before exercising his powers of enforcement. Although the Commissioner can ensure that model codes he prepares are strong and meaningful, he has much less control over publication schemes prepared by others since he cannot rewrite them, only withhold approval.[86] In England, Wales and Northern Ireland, this lack of control has been addressed by the publication of a single approved model scheme which all public authorities are obliged to adopt. Authorities have no statutory right of appeal against the refusal of the Commissioner to approve a publication scheme or a decision to revoke approval for a scheme. A public authority could seek judicial review against a decision of the Information Commissioner to refuse such approval. Once a scheme is approved, the authority is required to publish it in such manner as it thinks fit.[87] The government rejected proposed amendments that would have required authorities to publish their publication schemes in certain forms and free-of-charge, stating as follows:

> The Government are confident that public authorities will not wish to embarrass themselves by making people pay unreasonably for copies of their publication schemes. We have made it clear all along that we expect public authorities to bear most of the additional cost of freedom of information....All publication schemes will have to have the approval of the information commissioner. She is bound to question any unreasonable proposals with regard to charging. She will also be best placed to judge what is the most appropriate form for the publication of these schemes in individual cases....The Bill offers the best way of ensuring that public authorities will publish their schemes in the manner most appropriate in the circumstances and that they will make them available either free or at minimal cost....The commissioner will not have the power to approve the manner of the publication of the scheme, but she can issue guidance as to how it is done. In any event, we believe that it is in the interests of the authority for the public body to make its scheme known widely, as the aim of such schemes is to minimise the burden on an authority from individual requests for information that it makes available generally.[88]

Applying ordinary principles of public law, a public authority may charge a person for access to information held by it where there is a statutory mandate to do so.[89] There is no provision in the Freedom of Information Act 2000 authorising a public authority to charge for making its publication scheme available. Moreover, restricting access to a publication scheme to those

---

[84] On the basis that the authority has not adopted a publication scheme in accordance with the statutory provisions and has therefore failed to comply with one of the requirements of Pt I of the Act.

[85] Hansard HL vol 612 col 826 (20 April 2000) (Minister of State, Cabinet Office, Lord Falconer).

[86] House of Commons, *Public Administration—Third Report* (Cm 4355, 1999) Annex 6, para 21 (see ch 1 n 64).

[87] FOIA s 19(4); FOI(S)A s 23(4).

[88] Hansard HL vol 619 cols 199–200 (14 November 2000) (Lord Bach).

[89] See §10– 013.

who had paid to see it would be difficult to reconcile with a public authority having actually published that scheme. Furthermore, authorities are under a statutory duty to publish information in accordance with their publication scheme.[90] If an authority fails or refuses to do this, the Commissioner can issue an enforcement notice.[91] In these circumstances it would be open to make an application for a standard request under the Act and the exemptions otherwise open to the public authority on the basis of the information being otherwise available will not be open to the public authority.[92]

4. DEPARTMENTAL GUIDANCE

019 Sources of guidance

The Ministry of Justice has issued guidance on the operation of the Freedom of Information Act 2000. The Information Commissioner has also issued guidance on the operation of the Act. The Information Commissioner also has issued guidance concerning the duty to advice and assist.[93] This guidance advises public authorities to keep a record of the advice and assistance that has been given. If the authority has responded that it needs more information to identify the information sought, then it is not required to comply with the request, but it should provide advice and assistance to clarify the request.[94] If a request is refused on grounds of excessive cost of compliance, it may then be appropriate for the authority to provide advice and assistance to help the person who made the request to focus their request.[95] There is separate guidance relating to the Environmental Information Regulations.[96]

020 Status of departmental guidance

The guidance documents issued by the Ministry of Justice and the Information Commissioner do not have any statutory force. The Freedom of Information Act 2000 neither provides for nor requires such guidance to be given.[97] Nor is there any statutory requirement upon a public authority either to follow or even to have regard to such guidance.[98] The guidance documents

---

[90] FOIA s 19(1)(b); FOI(S)A s 23(1)(b).

[91] On the basis that a request for information has not been dealt with in accordance with Pt I of the Act. For enforcement notices, see FOIA s 52 and FOI(S)A s 52 discussed in §§28–013 and 28–016.

[92] FOIA ss 21 and 22; FOI(S)A ss 25 and 27.

[93] *Awareness Guidance No 23* (16 July 2009).

[94] Information Commissioner, *Awareness Guidance No 23* (16 July 2009).

[95] Information Commissioner, *Awareness Guidance No 23* (16 July 2009). See also *Urmenyi v IC and LB of Sutton*, IT, 13 July 2007 at [49].

[96] See §6–020.

[97] Indeed, FOIA s 45-46 and 60-61 contemplate that any guidance that is to be given will find expression in the s 45 Code of Practice or the s 46 Code of Practice. The position is the same with FOI(S), the EIR and the EI(S)R.

[98] Even where there is a duty to have regard to a code of practice, it has been held that this does not mean it has to be applied: *R (Wirral MBC) v Chief Schools Adjudicator* [2001] ELR 574; *R (Munjaz) v Mersey Care NHS* [2003] EWCA Civ 1036, [2003] 3 WLR 1505 at [71]–[74], concerning a code of practice prepared under s 118(2) of the Mental Health Act 1983, where the Court of Appeal considered that since the code related to matters where a person's human rights were or might be engaged, 'the arguments for according the code the greater status [ie the status of

issued by the Ministry of Justice and the Information Commissioner are no more authoritative than any other statement of opinion by a public official. However they are relevant considerations to be taken into account in decision-making by public bodies.[99] If any parts of such guidance are not consistent with an Act then the guidance may be unlawful to the extent of the inconsistency. Assuming the relevant part of the guidance is lawful, then regard should be had to it; in this situation, if the public body is to depart from it, it must only do so for good reasons and should state such reasons clearly; and if the public body fails to understand the relevant part of the guidance or Code properly, then any decision may be quashed for that reason.[100]

10– 021 **Practice recommendations**

Where the Information Commissioner considers that the practice of a public authority in relation to the exercise of its functions under the Act does not conform with that proposed in the Codes of Practice, the Commissioner can give the public authority a written 'practice recommendation' specifying the steps which in the opinion of the Commissioner ought to be taken for promoting such conformity.[101] Non-compliance with a Code of Practice could form part of a wider challenge to the discharge by a public authority of its duties under the Act.[102]

---

being required to be followed unless there is some good reason to the contrary, as opposed to a code which a public authority is free not to follow unless to do so would be Wednesbury unreasonable] are compelling.'

[99] For example, *R v Islington LBC, ex p Rixon* [1997] ELR 66.

[100] As to these principles, see *Gransden v Secretary of State for the Environment* (1985) P & CR 86 at 93–94; also see M Fordham, *Judicial Review Handbook*, 5th edn (Oxford, Hart Publishing, 2005) paras 6.2.8 to 6.2.11 and cases cited therein.

[101] FOIA s 48(1); FOI(S)A s 44(1); EIR reg 16(5); EI(S)R reg 18(5). See §10– 008.

[102] See the discussion in §10– 009.

CHAPTER 11

The Request

1. THE REQUEST FOR INFORMATION

11– 001 Introduction

Under the Freedom of Information Act 2000, for a person to exercise his right to information held by a public authority, he must first make a 'request for information'.[1] A 'request for information' is one that:[2]

— is made in writing;
— states the name of the applicant;
— states an address for correspondence; and
— describes the information requested.

For an individual to exercise his corresponding right under the Data Protection Act 1998, all that is required is that he make a request in writing.[3] A request for 'environmental information' may be made orally.[4] Quite apart from meeting the formal requirements of each statutory

---

[1] FOIA s 1(1). The FOI(S)A does not invoke the concept of a defined 'request for information' but gives an entitlement to 'a person who requests information': FOI(S)A s 1(1). Section 8(1) of the FOI(S)A provides that a reference in that Act to 'requesting' information is a reference to a request which, save for the requirement that it be in writing, has the same characteristics as a 'request for information' under the FOIA.

[2] FOIA s 8(1).

[3] DPA s 7(2)(a). However, in certain circumstances a data controller need not comply with a request unless the individual provides certain information: see §11– 005.

[4] EIR reg 5(1); EI(S)R reg 5(1).

regime, the terms of a request are fundamentally important to the whole disclosure exercise. An applicant's description of the information sought will impinge upon the efficacy of the request; upon the cost of compliance; upon the public authority's obligation to comply with the request on the grounds of particularity, repetitiveness, etc; upon the information yielded; and, thereafter, the applicable exemptions. It is suggested that, save for routine requests, it will generally be in the interests of both the applicant and the public authority for a request to describe the information sought by reference to one or more of the following attributes:

a)   the date or period over which the information was created or first held by the public authority;

(b)   the subject matter of the information, with as much precision as possible;

(c)   the types of information sought (eg correspondence, reports, internal documents and so forth);

(d)   the authorship or provenance of the information, if needs be by class;

(e)   the original intended recipient of the information; and

(f)   the manner in which the information is recorded (eg written or stored on a computer, etc).

This is not to say that an applicant should strive to guess precisely what information is held by a public authority: it is simply a matter of reflecting upon the attributes of the information that is being sought and attempting, so far as is reasonably practicable, to articulate those attributes. Whilst an applicant's motives for requesting information are irrelevant to a request,[5] where an applicant anticipates that some or all of the information may fall within a qualified exemption, it may be in the applicant's interests to set out in the request any facts and matters which may relate to the public interest in disclosing the information.[6] Finally, there will be circumstances in which it will be mutually advantageous for an applicant to take a staged approach to requesting information from a public authority. For example, a properly-drawn first request may be designed to elicit information that will assist in the subsequent identification of the information sought to be disclosed.[7]

-002   Request must be in writing

A request made under the Freedom of Information Act 2000 (or of a data controller under the Data Protection Act 1998) must be made in writing.[8] 'Writing' means the representation or reproduction of words in a visible form.[9] A request is deemed to have been made in writing where it has been transmitted by electronic means, it has been received in legible form and it

---

[5]   See §§9– 017, 12– 011 and 15– 015.

[6]   See §§15– 011, 15– 012 and 15– 018.

[7]   For example, a request for a list of files relating to a particular topic may, when answered, help the applicant to identify from which of those files a second request for information should be answered. If the second request does not yield the information expected, the applicant can make a third request identifying other files from the list, and so on. Although this may provoke a claim of 'fishing', this is to be preferred to 'trawling'. The s 45 Code of Practice, para 10, appears to support this sort of approach.

[8]   FOIA s 8(1)(a); DPA s 7(2)(a); cf EIR reg 5; EI(S)R reg 5; and see further §6– 022. The FOI(S)A provides that although such a request may be made in writing, it may also be made in another form which has some permanency: see §11– 004.

[9]   Interpretation Act 1978 s 5 and Sch 1.

is capable of being used for subsequent reference.[10] Accordingly, a request made by way of a facsimile transmission or email should qualify as a request made in writing.

11– 003 Request made orally

The requirement under the Acts that a request be made in writing means that an oral request will not be sufficient to give rise to an obligation on a public authority or a data controller to communicate information.[11] However, on the basis that an individual who makes a request orally should be regarded as someone who is proposing to make a request for information and that it would normally be reasonable to expect a public authority to inform such an individual of the formal requirements of a request for information, in most such cases a public authority's duty to provide advice and assistance[12] will require it to advise the individual that his request should be made in writing. The *Code of Practice* suggests that where a person is unable to put his request in writing, the public authority should provide appropriate assistance to enable that person to make a request for information, such as pointing him or her towards another person who could assist him (such as a Citizen's Advice Bureau) or, in exceptional circumstances, by taking a note of the person's request and then sending it to him for confirmation (in which case receipt of the confirmed note would constitute a written request).[13]

11– 004 Request in other permanent form in Scotland

In Scotland, a request need not be made in writing but may be made in another form which, by reason of it having some permanency, is capable of being used for subsequent reference.[14] The Freedom of Information (Scotland) Act 2002 cites recordings made on audio or video tape as specific examples of such a form,[15] and presumably a request by email would also suffice.

11– 005 Request must state name of the applicant

A request made under the Freedom of Information Act 2000 or the Freedom of Information (Scotland) Act 2002 must state the name of the applicant.[16] In this context, 'the applicant' is the person who is making the request.[17] As noted elsewhere,[18] the identity of the applicant will only be relevant to a public authority's obligation to communicate information in limited

---

[10]   FOIA s 8(2); FOI(S)A s 8(2); DPA s 64(2).

[11]   In Scotland, an oral request recorded onto audio or video tape would be sufficient: see §11– 004.

[12]   As to the duty to provide advice and assistance, see ch 10.

[13]   Section 45 Code of Practice, para 7. This was anticipated by the House of Commons' *Public Administration Committee's Third Report* (Cm 4355, 1999) Annex 6, para 13 (see ch 1 n 64). The Scottish Ministers' Code of Practice goes further and suggests that in such a case a public authority should even provide the applicant with a stamped addressed envelope in which he or she can return the duly confirmed request (Scottish Ministers' Code of Practice, para 19).

[14]   FOI(S)A s 8(1)(a).

[15]   FOI(S)A s 8(1)(a). Quite why anyone would wish to make a request by video tape is not obvious.

[16]   FOIA s 8(1)(b); FOI(S)A s 8(1)(b). There is no such requirement in relation to a request for 'environmental information': EIR reg 5(1); EI(S)R reg 5(1); and see §6– 022.

[17]   FOIA s 84; FOI(S)A s 1(2); EIR reg 2(1); EI(S)R reg 2(1). In the House of Lords debate on this provision, it was suggested by the Parliamentary Under-Secretary of State for the Home Office that s 8(1)(b) of the FOIA did not require an applicant to give his real name: Hansard HL vol 619 col 184 (14 November 2000). However, the requirement in s 8(1)(b) to give '*the* name *of*' the applicant rather than '*a* name *for*' the applicant suggests the contrary.

[18]   See §§12– 011 and 15– 015.

circumstances.[19] The fact that 'any person' may make a request for information means that there is no reason why one individual cannot apply on behalf of another,[20] there is no need for an applicant to have any particular standing to seek information and an applicant need not be a United Kingdom national or resident.[21] Although there is no express requirement for a person making a request under the Data Protection Act 1998 to provide his name, a data controller is not obliged to comply with a request unless he is supplied with such information as he reasonably requires in order to satisfy himself as to the identity of the person making the request.[22] Given that the right conferred by that Act is to information constituting personal data of which the applicant is the data subject and given the proscriptions against unauthorised processing of data,[23] it would be reasonable for a data controller to require confirmation of the name of the person making the request before satisfying himself as to that person's identity.

06 Request must state address for correspondence
A request made under the Freedom of Information Act 2000 or the Freedom of Information (Scotland) Act 2002 must state an address for correspondence.[24] There is no such requirement under the Data Protection Act 1998 or the Environmental Information Regulations 2004. Neither the Freedom of Information Act 2000 nor the Freedom of Information (Scotland) Act 2002 specifies what is meant by 'an address for correspondence'. In particular, it is not specified whether, in the light of the fact that a request may be made by electronic means,[25] the provision of an electronic address (such as an email address or a fax number) would be sufficient to meet the requirements of the Acts. During debate on the Bill the view expressed was that the provision of an electronic address would not be sufficient.[26] The stated fear was that practical difficulties might ensue if a public authority were obliged to communicate a large volume of information which was recorded in documentary form where the public authority had only been provided with an electronic address.[27] In any event, an individual who makes a request which includes only an electronic address should at the very least be regarded as someone who is proposing to make a request for information and, as it would normally be reasonable to expect a public authority to inform such an individual of the formal requirements

---

[19] For example, in the case of vexatious or repeated requests (see §§12– 010 to 12– 017) or if a request relates to information which is personal data (see §12– 018).

[20] As was recognised in the House of Commons' Public Administration Committee's *Third Report* (Cm 4355, 1999) Annex 6, para 14 (see ch 1 n 64).

[21] As is recognised in the *Explanatory Notes to the Freedom of Information Act 2000*, para 49. As to applications made by persons outside the United Kingdom, see §9– 014.

[22] DPA s 7(3). As to the proper construction of DPA s 7(3), see §11– 013.

[23] DPA s 7(1) and Pt V. 'Processing' includes disclosure: DPA s 1(1): see §5– 029.

[24] FOIA s 8(1)(b); FOI(S)A s 8(1)(b).

[25] See §11– 002.

[26] Hansard HL vol 619 col 184 (14 November 2000).

[27] As to the means by which information should be communicated, see §§13– 015 to 13– 019. In fact there may be instances in which electronic communication is easier. In the USA, agencies establish 'electronic reading rooms' to deal with disclosure of policy statements, staff manuals, records previously processed for disclosure and other documents routinely sought: see §2– 004.

of a request for information, a public authority's duty to provide advice and assistance[28] will generally require it to advise the individual that his request should include a postal address. In practice, requests are frequently made and responded to by email.

11– 007 Request must describe information requested

A request for information must describe the information requested.[29] There is no formal obligation on an applicant to describe the information sought in a particular way and, in particular, an applicant is not required to describe a particular record.[30] It is questionable whether it would be sufficient for an applicant to request a random sample of information, as this does not identify the information requested but requires the intercession of an act of selection by the public authority.[31] Where a request does not describe the information requested with sufficient particularity, the recipient public authority ought to consider whether it should advise or assist the applicant in relation to the proper particularisation of his request, whether it should inform the applicant that it requires further particulars,[32] or both. The emphasis in the *Code of Practice* is on the provision of assistance and it suggests possible examples of such assistance as being the provision of an outline of the different types of information which might meet the terms of the request as made, the provision of detailed catalogues or indexes to help the applicant ascertain the nature of the information held by the public authority, or the provision of a general response setting out options for further information which could be provided.[33] Although there is no requirement that a person making a request under the Data Protection Act 1998 describe the information requested, in certain circumstances a data controller is not obliged to comply with a request if he reasonably requires further information in order to locate the information sought by the person making the request.[34] Public authorities should take care to look beyond the language or tone of a request for information and should focus on the substance of what is being requested.[35] The mere fact that a public authority does not approve of the language used, or allegations made, in a request does not prevent such a request being a request for the purposes of the legislation.[36] The Tribunal takes a fairly liberal, rather than literal, approach to requests.[37]

---

[28] As to the duty to provide advice and assistance, see §§10– 001 to 10– 006.

[29] FOIA s 8(1)(c); FOI(S)A s 8(1)(c).

[30] As is recognised in the *Explanatory Notes to the Freedom of Information Act 2000*, para 23. But see §11– 001.

[31] See *Redfern v University of Canberra* (1995) 38 ALD 457 in relation to the comparable s 15(2)(b) of the Freedom of Information Act 1982 (Cth of Australia).

[32] As to requiring particulars in order to identify and locate requested information, see §§11– 011 to 11– 012. In relation to a request for, or to the extent that a request includes, 'environmental information', this is required by EIR reg 9(2); EI(S)R reg 9(2); see further §6– 022.

[33] Section 45 Code of Practice, para 10.

[34] DPA s 7(3). As to requesting particulars under the DPA, see §11– 013.

[35] *Barber v IC*, IT, 20 February 2006 at [9] and [12]. The fact that the request is in accusatorial terms should not generally be used as a basis for refusing to treat the request as valid.

[36] Subject, of course, to the provisions on vexatious requests: see §§12– 010 to 12– 013.

[37] See, eg, *Alcock v IC and Chief Constable of Staffordshire Police*, IT, 3 January 2007 at [25].

)08 Matters not required

There is no requirement in the Freedom of Information Act 2000[38] for a request for information to make reference to the fact that it is being made under the Act. Nevertheless, as a public authority has a duty to provide advice and assistance to those who make requests under the Act, it is desirable that a request for information states that it is being made under the Freedom of Information Act 2000. Further, as there is no requirement in the Act that a request for information be sent to a particular individual or department within a public authority, it will be necessary for public authorities to ensure that all staff who might receive such requests are aware of the appropriate procedures for dealing with them.[39]

)09 Treatment of a request for information under the Data Protection Act 1998

Where a request for information is made under any of paras (a), (b) or (c) of s 7(1) of the Data Protection Act 1998, it is to be treated as also extending to the other two paragraphs of those three.[40] Any such request will only be treated as extending to information under para (d) of s 7(1) where the request shows an express intention that it should do so.[41] Conversely, unless a request for information made under s 7(1)(d) of the Data Protection Act 1998 shows an express intention that it should extend to information under any of the other three paragraphs in s 7(1), then it is not to be treated as extending to information under any of those other paragraphs.[42]

010 Duty to provide advice and assistance

A public authority has a duty to provide advice and assistance, so far as it is reasonable to expect it to do so, to persons who have made or who propose to make requests for information to it pursuant to the Freedom of Information Acts.[43] Compliance with the relevant provisions of the *Code of Practice*[44] is deemed to be compliance with the duty to provide advice and assistance.[45] The terms of the Code of Practice indicate that there is a strong emphasis on public authorities providing advice and assistance to applicants and potential applicants and that public authorities will be discouraged from relying upon formal or procedural defects in would-be requests for information to avoid having to comply with requests which would otherwise have been valid.

---

[38]   Or the FOI(S)A, DPA, EIR, or EI(S)R.

[39]   This is recommended by para 15 of the foreword to the s 45 Code of Practice.

[40]   DP (Fees) Regs reg 2(1). As to the difference, see §§5– 030 to 5– 034.

[41]   DP (Fees) Regs reg 2(2).

[42]   DP (Fees) Regs reg 2(3).

[43]   FOIA s 16(1); FOI(S)A s 15(1); EIR reg 9(1); EI(S)R reg 9(1). See §§10– 001 to 10– 006 and, in relation to 'environmental information', see §6– 021.

[44]   As to the s 45 Code of Practice, see §§10– 007 to 10– 011.

[45]   FOIA s 16(2); FOI(S)A s 15(2).

2. PARTICULARISING THE REQUEST

11–011 Introduction

Although a request for information under the Freedom of Information Act 2000 or the Freedom of Information (Scotland) Act 2002 must describe the information requested,[46] provision is made under these Acts, and also under the Data Protection Act 1998, for the situation where an applicant does not provide sufficient particulars of the information sought to enable the public authority to identify and locate that information.[47]

11–012 Insufficient particularity under the Freedom of Information Acts

Under the Freedom of Information Act 2000, where a public authority reasonably requires further particulars in order to identify and locate the information requested, then, as long as it has informed the applicant of that requirement,[48] the public authority is not obliged to provide the information requested unless it is furnished with the further particulars that it requires to identify and locate that information.[49] In such a case, the time allowed for the public authority to comply with the request for information only starts to run from the date on which it receives the further particulars.[50] A public authority may only seek further particulars which are relevant to identifying the information sought by the applicant and not, for example, to seek information which is relevant to the applicant or his motives.[51] Further, a public authority may not seek further particulars which an applicant could not reasonably be expected to have, such as a file number or the exact location of the information sought.[52] The *Code of Practice* recommends that, where a request for information is insufficiently particularised, the public authority should assist the applicant to enable him or her to describe more clearly the information sought.[53] A failure to seek to elicit greater particularity may constitute a failure of

---

[46] As to the requirement that a request for information must describe the information requested, see §11–007.

[47] In relation to a request for, or to the extent that a request includes, 'environmental information', see EIR reg 9(2); EI(S)R reg 9(2). As to the treatment of inadequately particularised requests under the EIR, see §6–021.

[48] The original version of s 1(3) of the FOIA did not feature the requirement that a public authority must inform an applicant that it requires further particulars before it is absolved of its obligations under s 1(1): Freedom of Information Bill 1999, cl 8(3).

[49] FOIA s 1(3); FOI(S)A s 1(3).

[50] As to the time for compliance generally, see §11–022. To the extent that a request for information captures 'environmental information', see §6–024.

[51] Section 45 Code of Practice, para 9. See also the House of Commons' *Public Administration –Committee's Third Report* (Cm 4355, 1999) Annex 6, para 25 (see ch 1 n 64). As to the irrelevancy of motives, see §9–017.

[52] Section 45 Code of Practice, para 11. See also the House of Commons' *Public Administration Committee's Third Report* (Cm 4355, 1999) Annex 6, para 25.

[53] Section 45 Code of Practice, para 8.

the duty to advise and assist.[54]

013 **Insufficient particularity under the Data Protection Act 1998**
Where a data controller reasonably requires further particulars in order to satisfy himself as to the identity of the person making a request and to locate the information which that person seeks and has informed that person of that requirement, the data controller is not obliged to comply with the request unless it is supplied with those further particulars.[55] It is suggested that the two reasons for requiring further information set out in s 7(3)(a) of the Data Protection Act 1998 need to be read disjunctively in order to give proper effect to that section. Thus a data controller may avail himself of the provisions of s 7(3) if either he requires further particulars in order to satisfy himself as to the identity of the person making the request or he requires further particulars in order to locate the information which that person seeks.

3. FEES

014 **Introduction**
Both the Freedom of Information Act 2000 and the Freedom of Information (Scotland) Act 2002 establish a framework for the charging of fees by any public authority that receives a request for information.[56] Neither Act obliges a public authority to charge fees. In some cases, a public authority will have had the practice of voluntarily providing information pursuant to informal requests: there is nothing in the Freedom of Information Act 2000 to prevent such a practice continuing.[57] Nevertheless, a public authority exercising its discretion to charge a fee must do so in accordance with normal public law principles. Thus, improper discrimination between different types of requests or a lack of consistency in approach in relation to the imposition of fees may be unlawful. The level of fee is to be determined in accordance with regulations.[58] The relevant regulations are the Freedom of Information and Data Protection (Appropriate Limit and Fees) Regulations 2004 SI 2004/3244.[59] The Ministry of Justice has

---

[54] See §§10–001 to 10–006. This may be the subject of complaint to the Information Commissioner and of appeal to the First-Tier Tribunal: see, eg, *Lamb v IC*, IT, 16 November 2006 at [2]–[4] and [19]–[20], where the Information Tribunal found that a public authority should have asked the applicant to specify more precisely the information that was being requested.

[55] DPA s 7(3).

[56] FOIA s 9; FOI(S)A s 9. The EIR also provide for the charging of fees: EIR reg 8; EI(S)R reg 8. As to the charging of fees under the EIR, see further §6–023. It is suggested that where a request for information captures information some of which falls to be disclosed under the FOI/FOI(S)A regime and some of which falls to be disclosed under the EIR/EI(S)R regime, it is impermissible for a public authority to aggregate the two or deal with them other than under their respective regimes. This is because the right to each of the two classes of information has a distinct statutory provenance.

[57] See §11–015. Arguably, the disclosure remains one under FOIA, rather than a true discretionary disclosure: see §§9–036 to 9–038.

[58] FOIA s 9(3); FOI(S)A s 9(4). This restriction does not apply where provision is made by or under another enactment for the charging of a fee by a public authority for the disclosure of the information (FOIA s 9(5); FOI(S)A s 9(7)).

[59] In Scotland, the Freedom of Information (Fees for Required Disclosure) (Scotland) Regulations 2004 SSI 2004/467.

issued non-statutory guidance on these regulations.[60] Under the Data Protection Act 1998, except in prescribed cases, a data controller is not required to supply any information unless he has received such fee as he may require (subject to a prescribed maximum).[61]

11–015 Fees notice

Where a public authority receives a request for information, it may, within the period of time allowed for it to comply with its duties under s 1(1) of the Freedom of Information Act 2000, give the applicant a fees notice. A fees notice is a notice in writing which states that a fee of the amount stated in the notice is to be charged by the public authority for complying with its duties under s 1(1).[62] Section 9 gives a public authority a 'time window' within which to give an applicant a fees notice.

11–016 Fees notice in Scotland

In Scotland, a fees notice must set out the manner in which the fee has been calculated.[63] A fees notice in Scotland must also comply with the formal requirements prescribed by s 19 of the Freedom of Information (Scotland) Act 2002.[64] A fees notice in Scotland must therefore also contain particulars of the procedure provided by the public authority for dealing with complaints about the handling by it of requests for information[65] and about the rights of the applicant to apply for a review of the public authority's actions and to apply to the Commissioner for a decision as to whether the public authority has acted in accordance with Part I of the Act.[66]

11–017 Determination of fees

Unless provision is made by or under some other enactment for the charging of fees by a public authority for the disclosure of information,[67] then any fee must be determined in accordance with the relevant regulations.[68] Accordingly, although the fees regime gives a public authority a discretion as to whether to give an applicant a fees notice, if it decides to give a fees notice, it has no discretion as to whether it applies the fees regulations. However, as will be seen, those regulations prescribe the maximum fee that may be charged but, subject to that upper limit, a public authority has a discretion as to the amount of fee that it charges.

---

[60] See 'Fees and Aggregation' in: www.justice.gov.uk/guidance/foi-procedural-fees.htm. In Scotland, the relevant guidance is to be found in the (statutory) Scottish Ministers' Code of Practice, paras 59 to 61 and Annex 3.

[61] DPA s 7(2)(b). Fees under the DPA are considered at §5–042.

[62] FOIA s 9(1); FOI(S)A s 9(1).

[63] Freedom of Information (Fees for Required Disclosure) (Scotland) Regulations 2004 SSI 2004/467 reg 4(4).

[64] FOI(S)A s 9(2).

[65] FOI(S)A s 19(a).

[66] FOI(S)A s 19(b).

[67] FOIA s 9(3) and (5); FOI(S)A s 9(4) and (7).

[68] FOIA s 9(3); FOI(S)A s 9(4). The relevant regulations are the FOI & DP (Limit & Fees) Regs (in relation to the FOIA) and the Freedom of Information (Fees for Required Disclosure) (Scotland) Regulations 2004 SSI 2004/467 (in relation to the FOI(S)A).

18 Amount of fees

The Freedom of Information and Data Protection (Appropriate Limit and Fees) Regulations 2004 provide that the fee is not to exceed a maximum equivalent to the total costs that the public authority reasonably expects to incur in informing the person making the request whether it holds the information and in communicating the information.[69] The costs that the public authority may take into account when calculating the total costs that it expects to incur include the costs of complying with any obligation under s 11(1) as to the means or form of communicating the information, the costs of reproducing any document containing the information and the costs of postage and any other forms of transmitting the information.[70] However a public authority may not take into account any costs which are attributable to the time which persons undertaking the activities of informing the applicant whether the public authority holds the information or of communicating the information are expected to spend on those activities.[71] Nor may a public authority take into account what may prove to be the most time-consuming part of the exercise, ie ascertaining whether the information is exempt information and, if so, the public interest balancing exercise. It is to be noted that the regulations prescribe a maximum fee but do not prescribe a minimum fee. Nor do the regulations prescribe a particular method for calculating the amount of any fee that is to be charged. Accordingly, where a public authority exercises its discretion to charge a fee, it has a further discretion as to the amount of the fee that it charges (provided always that it does not exceed the prescribed maximum). Nevertheless, a public authority exercising its discretion as to the amount of the fee to be charged must do so in accordance with normal public law principles.[72] Thus, improper discrimination between different types of requests or a lack of consistency in approach in relation to the amount of fees may be unlawful.

19 Amount of fees in Scotland

The Freedom of Information (Fees for Required Disclosure) (Scotland) Regulations 2004 invoke the concept of 'projected costs' in the context of the amount of fees that may be charged.[73] In relation to a request for information, the 'projected costs' are the total costs, whether direct or indirect, which a public authority reasonably estimates that it is likely to incur in locating, retrieving and providing such information.[74] However, in estimating projected costs, no account may be taken of costs incurred in determining whether the public authority holds the information specified in the request or whether the person seeking the requested information is entitled to receive it (or, if not so entitled, whether he should nevertheless be provided with it or refused it).[75] Further, any estimate of the cost of staff time shall not exceed £15 per hour

---

[69] FOI & DP (Limit & Fees) Regs reg 6(1) and (2). In relation to fees for environmental information, see §6– 023.

[70] FOI & DP (Limit & Fees) Regs reg 6(3).

[71] FOI & DP (Limit & Fees) Regs reg 6(4).

[72] For an example of a case where the Tribunal held that the fees charged by a public authority were unreasonable (in the context of the EIR), see *Markinson v IC*, IT, 28 March 2006.

[73] Freedom of Information (Fees for Required Disclosure) (Scotland) Regulations 2004 SSI 2004/467 reg 4.

[74] Freedom of Information (Fees for Required Disclosure) (Scotland) Regulations 2004 SSI 2004/467 reg 3(1).

[75] Freedom of Information (Fees for Required Disclosure) (Scotland) Regulations 2004 SSI 2004/467 reg 3(2)(a).

per member of staff.[76] Where the projected costs do not exceed £100, no fee shall be payable[77] and where the projected costs exceed £100 but do not exceed £600,[78] the fee shall not exceed ten per cent of the difference between the projected costs and £100.[79]

11– 020   Effect of fees notice

Where a public authority gives a fees notice to an applicant, it is not required to comply with s 1(1) of the relevant Act unless the applicant pays the fee within the period of three months beginning with the day on which the fees notice is given to the applicant.[80] However, if an applicant indicates that he is not prepared to pay the fee, the public authority should consider whether it can provide any of the information free of charge.[81] Where a fees notice has been given to an applicant and he has paid the fee within the requisite period, the time taken for the applicant to pay the fee is to be discounted when calculating the date on which the public authority is required to comply with s 1(1).[82] The combined effect of the provisions makes it prudent for a public authority to serve a fees notice as soon as possible after receipt of a request. In this way a public authority may lessen the possibility of abortive costs where an applicant subsequently indicates that he is not prepared to pay. The fact that a public authority gives a fee notice in which the fee is calculated on the basis of a prospective estimate of costs means that, should the actual cost of complying with the request for information be higher than the fee stated in the fees notice, the public authority cannot then claim that additional sum from the applicant: the public authority must bear the burden of any additional cost.[83]

11– 021   Fees in cases where cost of compliance is excessive

In cases where a public authority is not obliged to comply with a request for information because the cost of complying with it is deemed to be excessive,[84] where the communication of the information is not otherwise required by law, and where no provision is made by or under another enactment for the charging of fees, if the public authority nevertheless decides to

---

[76]   Freedom of Information (Fees for Required Disclosure) (Scotland) Regulations 2004 SSI 2004/467 reg 3(2)(b).

[77]   Freedom of Information (Fees for Required Disclosure) (Scotland) Regulations 2004 SSI 2004/467 reg 4(2).

[78]   That is, the amount prescribed under reg 5 of the Freedom of Information (Fees for Required Disclosure) (Scotland) Regulations 2004 SSI 2004/467.

[79]   Freedom of Information (Fees for Required Disclosure) (Scotland) Regulations 2004 SSI 2004/467 reg 4(3). The intention may have been that, when projected costs exceed £600, the excessive cost provisions come into play. However, this is not necessarily the case: see §12– 004.

[80]   FOIA s 9(2); FOI(S)A s 9(3). This is a similar formulation to that used in other comparable legislation, such as s 111(2)(a) of the Employment Rights Act 1996. It is suggested that a similar approach to the calculation of the relevant period should be adopted as is adopted under that Act. This would mean that the correct method for determining the final day of the period is to take the day and the date immediately before the date on which the fees notice was given to the applicant and then go forward three months: *Pruden v Cunard Ellerman Ltd* [1993] IRLR 317, EAT.

[81]   Section 45 Code of Practice, para 13.

[82]   FOIA s 10(2); FOI(S)A s 10(3).

[83]   See 'Fees and Aggregation' in: www.justice.gov.uk/guidance/foi-procedural-fees.htm. The same guidance suggests that, should it transpire that the actual cost of complying with a request for information is less than the fee stated in a fees notice, the public authority should consider refunding the excess to the applicant.

[84]   As to the situation where the cost of complying with a request for information would be excessive, see §§12– 001 to 12– 009.

communicate the information it may charge a fee for doing so.[85] In such a case, it will be good practice for the public authority to provide an indication of what information could be provided within the costs ceiling or to advise the applicant that a reformulated request for information may result in information being supplied for a lower, or no, fee.[86] The fee is to be determined by the public authority in accordance with regulations.[87]

4. TIME FOR COMPLIANCE

22 Introduction

A public authority is required to comply with a request for information promptly and in any event not later than the twentieth working day following the 'date of receipt'.[88] Although the date of receipt is generally the date on which the public authority receives the request,[89] it is effectively postponed in cases where a public authority has sought further particulars of a request.[90] Further, the period for compliance is in effect extended where a public authority has given a fees notice to an applicant.[91] Where a request is made under the Data Protection Act 1998, a data controller is required to comply with a request promptly and in any event before the end of the period which has been prescribed by the relevant regulations.[92]

023 Legislative history

The provisions of the Freedom of Information Act 2000 relating to time for compliance[93] are largely the same as those proposed in the Freedom of Information Bill 1999,[94] save in two important respects. First, the original outer time-limit was 40 days rather than 20 working days.[95] The 20-working-day time limit was introduced in response to suggestions at the Committee stages that as the 40-day time limit had originated in the Data Protection Act 1984, when information processing technology was less advanced that it is today and as the Code of Practice on Access to Government Information had suggested a time limit of 20 days, a time

---

[85] FOIA s 13(1) and (3); FOI(S)A s 13(1) and (4).

[86] Section 45 Code of Practice, para 14.

[87] FOIA s 13(1); FOI(S)A s 13(1). The relevant regulations are the FOI & DP (Limit & Fees) Regs and the Freedom of Information (Fees for Disclosure under section 13) (Scotland) Regulations 2004.

[88] FOIA s 10(1). The FOI(S)A s 10(1) does not invoke a defined concept of 'date of receipt', but its effect is the same. The EIR require information to be made available 'as soon as possible and no later than 20 days after the date of receipt of the request': EIR reg 5(2). As to the time for compliance with requests for information under the EIR, see §6– 024.

[89] FOIA s 10(6); FOI(S)A s 10(1)(a).

[90] FOIA ss 1(3) and 10(6); FOI(S)A ss 1(3) and 10(1)(b).

[91] FOIA s 10(2); FOI(S)A s 10(3).

[92] DPA s 7(8). See §5– 046.

[93] FOIA s 10.

[94] Freedom of Information Bill 1999, cl 10.

[95] Freedom of Information Bill 1999, cl 10(1).

limit of 40 days was overly generous.[96] Secondly, the Freedom of Information Bill did not provide for public authorities to have an additional amount of time to conduct the public interest balancing exercise which is now allowed where information falls within the terms of a qualified exemption. The introduction of the provision was the cause of some controversy, as it was feared that the absence of a finite time limit would result in procrastination on the part of public authorities.[97]

11–024 Promptness

The primary obligation on a public authority is that it must promptly comply with s 1(1) of the Act.[98] Accordingly, the requirement that a public authority comply in any event not later than the 20th working day following the date of receipt is simply an outer, or 'long-stop', time-limit:[99] the fact that a public authority complies within 20 working days will not necessarily mean that it has complied promptly.[100] It is implicit[101] in the dual requirement that there will be instances in which compliance in 20 or fewer working days will not constitute prompt compliance. There is no provision in the Freedom of Information Act 2000 to deal with the situation where a request for information is particularly urgent.[102] However, the urgency or otherwise of a request is likely to be one of the factors relevant to an assessment of whether a public authority has promptly complied with its obligations under s 1(1).

11–025 Date of receipt

Ordinarily, the period for compliance with a request for information is calculated from the date of actual receipt, namely the day on which the public authority receives the request for information.[103] However, in a case where a public authority has sought further particulars about a request,[104] then the date of receipt is deemed to be the day on which the public authority receives the further particulars sought by it.[105]

---

[96] See the House of Commons' Select Committee on Public Administration, *Fifth Special Report*, 27 October 1999, Appendix. A shortening of the time-limit was also recommended by the House of Lords Select Committee on the Draft Freedom of Information Bill: House of Lords' Select Committee on the Draft Freedom of Information Bill, *First Report*, 29 July 1999, para 56.

[97] Hansard HL vol 617 cols 1000–1006 (17 October 2000); vol 619 cols 187–190 (14 November 2000); Hansard HC vol 357 cols 727–729 (27 November 2000).

[98] FOIA s 10(1); FOI(S)A s 10(1).

[99] This was the intention: see Hansard HC vol 347 col 858 (4 April 2000).

[100] This accords with the approach adopted to similar provisions in the former RSC Ord 53 r 3(4) (see now CPR 54.5(1)): *R v Independent Television Commission, ex p TV NI Ltd*, *The Times*, 30 December 1991 (CA).

[101] On the basis that there is a strong presumption that every word in a statute must be given some effective meaning: *McMonagle v Westminster City Council* [1990] 2 AC 716 at 727; *Gubay v Kingston* [1984] 1 WLR 163 (HL) at 172.

[102] Compare the Official Information Act 1982 (New Zealand) s 12(3), which provides that an applicant may inform the body of which he makes his request that the request is urgent and the reasons why it is urgent.

[103] FOIA s 10(6)(a); FOI(S)A s 10(1)(a).

[104] As to requiring particulars in order to identify and locate requested information, see §§11–011 to 11–013.

[105] FOIA s 10(6)(b); FOI(S)A s 10(1)(b).

26 Meaning of a 'working day'

A 'working day' is any day other than a Saturday, a Sunday, Christmas Day, Good Friday or a bank holiday 'in any part of the United Kingdom'.[106]

27 Cases where public authority has given a fees notice to the applicant

Where a public authority has given a fees notice to an applicant and the fee is paid within the specified period,[107] the working days in the period beginning with the day on which the fees notice is given to the applicant and ending on the day on which the fee is received by the public authority are to be discounted when calculating the 20th working day following the date of receipt.[108]

28 Requests involving information subject to a qualified exemption

To the extent that the requested information is exempt information by virtue of one of the qualified exemptions[109] in Part II of the Freedom of Information Act 2000, then the ordinary 20-working-day time limit for compliance is extended, but only for the purpose of conducting the public interest balancing exercise.[110] For this exercise, the public authority is allowed 'such time as is reasonable in the circumstances'.[111] Some idea of what is meant by 'reasonable in the circumstances' can be deduced from the fact that where s 10(3) applies, the only addition to the public authority's burden in dealing with the request is the balancing exercise set out in s 2(1) and (2) of the Act. On the assumption that Parliament, in specifying the ordinary time limit in s 10(1), was not setting a time limit that it thought was or might be unreasonable in any circumstance, it is to be inferred that the 'reasonable time' permitted by s 10(3) can only exceed the time limit set by s 10(1) to the extent, if any, that is reasonably required to carry out the public interest balancing exercise. This reading is confirmed by the requirements of s 17, relating to the giving of a refusal notice. Section 10(3) expressly retains the obligation to give

---

[106] FOIA s 10(6); FOI(S)A s 73. The FOI(S)A only excludes bank holidays 'in Scotland' from the definition of a 'working day' and Good Friday is a working day for the purposes of the FOI(S)A. Because bank holidays under the Banking and Financial Dealings Act 1971 differ in the various parts of the United Kingdom, the effect of the FOIA referring to a bank holiday under the Banking and Financial Dealings Act 1971 'in any part' of the United Kingdom is to exclude each of the following days: New Year's Day (or, if New Year's Day be a Sunday, 3 January), 2 January (or, if 2 January be a Sunday, 3 January), 17 March (or if 17 March be a Sunday, 18 March), Easter Monday, the first Monday in May, the last Monday in May, the first Monday in August, the last Monday in August, 25 December, 26 December (if it not be a Sunday) and 27 December (in a year in which 25 or 26 December is a Sunday): see Banking and Financial Dealings Act 1971 Sch 1.

[107] As to the period within which fees must be paid, see §11– 020.

[108] FOIA s 10(2); FOI(S)A s 10(3). Where a request is for, or to the extent that a request includes, 'environmental information', see EIR reg 8(5)–(6); EI(S)R reg 8(6)–(7); and see further §6– 023.

[109] The qualified exemptions are listed at §14– 017.

[110] *Prior v IC*, IT, 27 April 2006 at [24]. There is no such extension of time to the extent that a request is for or extends to 'environmental information'.

[111] FOIA s 10(3). There is no comparable provision in the FOI(S)A. It is difficult to see what practical difference s 10(3)(a) makes to the operation of s 10(3). The public authority's consideration of whether it is obliged to communicate information logically precedes a discrete consideration of the obligation to confirm or deny: see §1– 005(4)(b) and FOIA s 1(5). Exclusion of the duty to confirm or deny will at most be co-extensive with exemption from the duty to disclose. Accordingly, other than where information is exempt information by virtue of a qualified exemption in Pt II of the FOIA, there are no circumstances in which the duty to confirm or deny does not arise or apply, and extension of the ordinary time limit will already have been secured by s 10(3)(b).

a refusal notice within the ordinary 20-working-day time limit, even where a qualified exemption is involved. Where s 10(3) applies, however, if the public interest balancing exercise has not been determined within that ordinary time limit, the refusal notice must state that an exemption applies and that no decision has been taken on the balancing exercise required by the Act, and must give an estimate of the date on which the public authority expects that such a decision will be taken.[112] Where a request for information relates to information, some of which is exempt information by virtue of one of the qualified exemptions and the rest of which is either not exempt or is exempt information by virtue of one of the absolute exemptions, the public authority must both disclose the non-exempt information and give a refusal notice (dealing with everything save for the public interest balancing exercise) within the ordinary time limit.

11– 029   Time limits for refusal notices

If a public authority is required to give a refusal notice to an applicant,[113] then it must do so within the time allowed for compliance with s 1(1) of the Freedom of Information Act 2000.[114] In other words, the back-stop time for compliance (save for the public interest balancing exercise) is the same whether a public authority is communicating the information to the applicant or whether it is giving the applicant a refusal notice, or a combination of the two. The special provisions that relate to cases where a public authority has sought further particulars of a request for information[115] or where a public authority has given a fees notice to an applicant[116] equally apply to extend the time given to a public authority for giving a refusal notice.

11– 030   Extended periods of time for compliance

There is power to modify by regulations references to the 20th working day to another working day not more than the 60th working day after the date of receipt.[117] To date, the only such regulations are the Freedom of Information (Time for Compliance with Request) Regulations 2004 SI 2004/3364.[118] No such regulations have been made in Scotland.

---

[112] FOIA s 17(2) and see ch 13. The s 45 Code of Practice, para 18, states that these estimates should be realistic and reasonable and that in the majority of cases public authorities will be expected to comply with their estimates. It also states that if an estimate is exceeded, the public authority should apologise and provide reasons for the delay. In *Berend v IC and LB of Richmond upon Thames*, IT, 12 July 2007 at [61] the Tribunal criticised the use of a s 17 notice lacking identification of the invoked exemptions but claiming consideration of the public interest as a means of 'buying time'.

[113] The requirements of a refusal notice are considered at §§13– 008 to 13– 012.

[114] FOIA s 17(1); FOI(S)A s 16(1). In relation to 'environmental information', see: EIR reg 13(2); EI(S)R reg 13(a).

[115] As to seeking further particulars of a request for information, see §§11– 011 to 11– 013.

[116] As to fees notices, see §11– 015.

[117] FOIA s 10(4); FOI(S)A s 10(4).

[118] As to which, see §§11– 031 to 11– 034. The Parliamentary Secretary for the Lord Chancellor's Department told Parliament that such regulations would only be made in 'exceptional circumstances' — Hansard HC vol 347 col 858 (4 April 2000). However, it is difficult to envisage what new 'exceptional circumstances' might have been thought to have arisen since the enactment of the FOIA to necessitate the FOI (Time) Regs.

31 Maintained schools

Time for compliance with a request for information may be extended where the request is received by the governing body of a maintained school or a maintained nursery school or it relates to information which is held by the recipient public authority only by virtue of the information being situated in a school which is maintained by the Secretary of State for Defence (and which provides primary or secondary education or both).[119] In such a case, any references in s 10(1) and (2) of the Freedom of Information Act 2000 to the 20th working day following receipt of the request are to be read as either a reference to the 20th working day following receipt disregarding any working day which is not a school day[120] or a reference to the 60th working day following the date of receipt, whichever occurs first.[121]

32 Archives

Time for compliance with a request for information is extended where a request for information is received by an appropriate records authority[122] or by a person at an appointed place of deposit[123] and the request relates wholly or partly to information that may be contained in a transferred public record[124] and that has not been designated as open information.[125] In such a case, any references in s 10(1) and (2) of the Freedom of Information Act 2000 to the 20th working day following the date of receipt are to be read as references to the 30th working day following the date of receipt.[126]

33 Armed forces operations

Time for compliance with a request for information may be extended where the public authority cannot comply with s 1(1) of the Freedom of Information Act 2000 without obtaining information (whether or not that information is recorded) from any individual who is actively involved in an operation of the armed forces of the Crown or in the preparations for such an operation, whether or not that individual is himself a member of the armed forces.[127] In such a case, the public authority may apply to the Information Commissioner for, in effect, an

---

[119] FOI (Time) Regs reg 3(1).

[120] In this context, a 'school day' means any day on which at the relevant school there is a session: FOI (Time) Regs reg 3(3).

[121] FOI (Time) Regs reg 3(2).

[122] That is, the Public Records Office, the Lord Chancellor or the Public Records Office of Northern Ireland: FOIA s 15(5). As to appropriate records authorities, see §7– 044.

[123] That is, a place of deposit appointed under s 4(1) of the Public Records Act 1958: FOI (Time) Regs reg 4(1)(b). As to appointed places of deposit, see §7– 027.

[124] That is, a public record which has been transferred to the Public Records Office, an appointed place of deposit, or the Public Records Office of Northern Ireland: FOIA s 15(4). As to transferred public records, see §7– 043.

[125] That is, designated as open information for the purposes of s 66(1) of the FOIA. As to open information, see §7– 045.

[126] FOI (Time) Regs reg 4(2). To the extent that the request is for 'environmental information', the time limit remains that provided by the EIR.

[127] FOI (Time) Regs reg 5(1).

extension of time for complying with the request for information.[128] Such an application is to be made within 20 working days following receipt of the request for information by the public authority.[129] If such an application is duly made, the Information Commissioner shall specify such a day as he considers reasonable in all the circumstances,[130] not later than the 60th working day following the date of receipt of the request for information.[131] Any reference in s 10(1) and (2) of the Freedom of Information Act 2000 is then to have effect as if any reference to the 20th working day following the date of receipt of the request for information were a reference to the day specified by the Information Commissioner.[132] Neither the Freedom of Information (Time for Compliance with Request) Regulations 2004 nor the Freedom of Information Act 2000 provide any definition of what is meant by an 'operation' in this context. However, assuming the word is to be given its ordinary dictionary meaning, it refers to 'a strategic movement of troops, ships, etc for military action'.[133]

11–034 Information held outside the United Kingdom

Time for compliance with a request for information may be extended where the request may relate to information not held in the United Kingdom[134] or may require information[135] that is not held in the United Kingdom to be obtained in order to comply with it[136] and, for that reason, the public authority would not be able to obtain the information within such time as to comply with the request for information within the 20-working-day period.[137] In such a case, the public authority may apply to the Information Commissioner for, in effect, an extension of time for complying with the request for information.[138] Such an application is to be made within 20 working days following receipt of the request for information by the public authority.[139] If such an application is duly made, the Information Commissioner shall specify such a day as he considers reasonable in all the circumstances,[140] not later than the 60th working day following the date of receipt of the request for information.[141] Any reference in s 10(1) and (2) of the Freedom of Information Act 2000 then has effect as if any reference to the

---

[128] FOI (Time) Regs reg 5(2) and (3). To the extent that the request is for 'environmental information', the time limit remains that provided by the EIR.

[129] FOI (Time) Regs reg 5(3)(b).

[130] FOI (Time) Regs, reg 5(3).

[131] FOI (Time) Regs reg 5(2).

[132] FOI (Time) Regs reg 5(2).

[133] *New Shorter Oxford English Dictionary* (1993).

[134] FOI (Time) Regs reg 6(1)(a)(i).

[135] Whether or not that other information is held by a public authority: FOI (Time) Regs reg 6(1)(a)(ii).

[136] FOI (Time) Regs reg 6(1)(a)(ii).

[137] FOI (Time) Regs reg 6(1) (b). To the extent that the request is for 'environmental information', the time limit remains that provided by the EIR.

[138] FOI (Time) Regs reg 6(2) and (3).

[139] FOI (Time) Regs reg 6(3)(b).

[140] FOI (Time) Regs, reg 6(3).

[141] FOI (Time) Regs reg 6(2).

20th working day following the date of receipt of the request for information were a reference to the day specified by the Information Commissioner.[142] The provisions relating to information held outside the United Kingdom proceed on the basis of an unusual dichotomy. In effect, for them to apply, it need only be possible that the information is not held in the United Kingdom, or may require such information,[143] but it must be certain that that possibility would prevent compliance with the normal time limit.[144] It is difficult to see how a possibility could give rise to a certainty in such a way. Accordingly, the circumstances in which a public authority will actually be able to avail itself of the provisions relating to information held outside the United Kingdom may be limited to those where it can be certain that the information is not held in the United Kingdom.

35 Keeper of the Records of Scotland

Under the Freedom of Information (Scotland) Act 2002, where the public authority of whom the request is made is the Keeper of the Records of Scotland and the request is one that relates to information which is contained in a record transferred to him by a public authority and which has not been designated by the public authority as open information,[145] then references to the 20th working day are to be read as references to the 30th working day.[146]

36 Time limits under the Data Protection Act 1998

The primary obligation on a data controller is also to comply promptly with a request.[147] This primary obligation is supplemented by a further obligation to comply with the request within a period which has been prescribed by regulations.[148] The relevant day on which the prescribed period begins is the day on which the data controller receives the request or, where later, the first day on which the data controller receives both the required fee[149] and any further particulars[150] requested by him.[151] In this respect, the Data Protection Act 1998 is similar to the Freedom of Information Act 2000.[152] In a case where the request relates wholly or partly to personal data forming part of an accessible record[153] that is part of an educational record,[154] and where the address of the data controller is in England or Wales, then the prescribed period is

---

[142] FOI (Time) Regs reg 6(2).

[143] By virtue of the word 'may' in reg 6(1)(a) of the FOI (Time) Regs.

[144] By virtue of the word 'would' in reg 6(1)(b) of the FOI (Time) Regs.

[145] FOI(S)A s 22(1). As to 'open information', see §7– 045.

[146] FOI(S)A s 10(2). To the extent that the request is for 'environmental information', the time limit remains that provided by the EIR.

[147] DPA s 7(8).

[148] DPA s 7(8). As to the interrelationship between the duty to act promptly and the duty in any event to comply with a request within a specified period, see §11– 024.

[149] As to fees under the DPA, see §5– 042.

[150] As to requiring further particulars under the DPA, see §11– 013.

[151] DPA s 7(8) and (10).

[152] As to the equivalent position under the FOIA, see §§11– 022, 11– 024, 11– 027 and 11– 029.

[153] As defined in the DPA s 68(1). As to accessible records, see §§5– 018 to 5– 019.

[154] As defined in Sch 11 to the DPA. As to educational records, see §5– 060.

15 school days.[155] These obligations are subject to the provisions relating to the disclosure of information relating to third parties.[156] For example, if a data controller were to take reasonable steps to seek the consent of a third party to the disclosure of the information (and it was not reasonable to comply with the request without obtaining that consent), then any delay in complying with the request occasioned by the taking of those steps would not amount to a lack of promptness contrary to s 7(8) of the Data Protection Act 1998.

5.   TRANSFERRING REQUESTS FOR INFORMATION

11– 037   Introduction

The Freedom of Information Act 2000 does not expressly deal with the situation where a public authority receives a request for information which it itself does not hold, but which it believes is held by a different public authority.[157] This is relegated to the Code of Practice issued under s 45 of the Act.[158]

11– 038   Provisions of Code of Practice on transferring requests for information

The Code of Practice states that where a public authority receives a request for information that it does not hold, but which it believes is held by another public authority, then it should consider whether to transfer the request to that other public authority.[159] The Code of Practice states that before transferring a request, the public authority should ascertain whether the other public authority holds the information, consider whether a transfer is appropriate and whether the applicant would have any grounds to object to a transfer.[160] If a public authority reasonably considers that an applicant would not have any grounds to object, then it may transfer a request without further reference to him, but if it reasonably considers that an applicant would object, then it should only transfer with his consent.[161] Furthermore, the public authority's duty to provide advice and assistance may require it to inform the applicant that it believes that the information requested is held by a different public authority.[162] The process of transfer should

---

[155] DP (Fees) R reg 5(4). For these purposes, a 'school day' means any day on which at the relevant school there is a school session: Education Act 1996 s 579(1).

[156] See the DPA s 7(4)

[157] This is in contrast to the EIR, which do make provision for such situations: EIR reg 10. As to the transfer of requests under the EIR, see §6– 025. This is also in contrast to freedom of information legislation in other jurisdictions. See, eg Freedom of Information Act 1982 s 16 (Commonwealth of Australia); Official Information Act 1982 s 14 (New Zealand); Freedom of Information Act 1997 s 7(3) (Republic of Ireland).

[158] In Scotland, under FOI(S)A s 60. For a general treatment of the s 45 Code of Practice, see ch 10.

[159] Section 45 Code of Practice, para 19. However, it should be noted that the s 45 Code of Practice envisages that, in most cases, assisting the applicant with his request will only involve contacting him and informing him that the information requested may be held by another public authority, suggesting that the applicant reapplies to that other public authority, and providing him with the contact details of that other public authority.

[160] Section 45 Code of Practice, para 20. In Scotland, in contrast, the Scottish Ministers' Code of Practice states that transferring requests 'will not generally be appropriate' unless an applicant has made it clear that his application should be transferred (Scottish Ministers' Code of Practice, paras 30 and 32).

[161] Section 45 Code of Practice, paras 20 to 21.

[162] Section 45 Code of Practice, paras 17 to 18. As to the duty to provide advice and assistance, see ch 10.

be conducted as soon as is practicable[163] and it does not relieve the public authority of its normal obligations, which continue to apply whether the public authority holds some or none of the information requested. Where a public authority receives a transferred request for information, it should treat it in the same way as if it had been received directly from the applicant.[164]

6. FAILURE TO LOCATE INFORMATION

039 Failure to locate any information

The Freedom of Information Act 2000 does not deal expressly with what is required of a public authority before it may respond to a request by stating that it does not hold any information of the type requested by an applicant.[165] A failure to locate any information answering the terms of the request does not constitute a 'refusal' of that request and, accordingly, none of the notice requirements of s 17 is applicable.[166] The Code of Practice gives no guidance as to the thoroughness of the search that is required before a public authority may properly conclude that it holds no information answering the terms of the request[167] nor of the form of response that must be given to an applicant in those circumstances.[168] Since the duty to confirm or deny applies (subject to Part II and s 2(1)) irrespective of whether a public authority holds the information requested, it is to be deduced that any search must be completed within 20 working days[169] and that the minimum entitlement of the applicant is to be informed in writing that the public authority does not hold information of the description specified in the request.[170] In contrast, the Freedom of Information (Scotland) Act 2002 does expressly provide for the giving

---

[163] Section 45 Code of Practice, paras 23 and 29.

[164] Section 45 Code of Practice, para 22.

[165] In the USA, the yardstick used is that an agency must undertake a search that is 'reasonably calculated to uncover all relevant documents' — *Weisberg v United States Department of Justice*, 705 F 2d 1344 (DC Cir 1983). This involves a consideration of: (a) how the agency conducted its search in light of the scope of the request; (b) the applicant's description of the records sought; (c) the standards the agency used in determining where the records were likely to be found; and (d) whether the agency believes the records sought may exist.

[166] Compare the Freedom of Information Act 1982 (Commonwealth of Australia) s 24A, which expressly provides for the refusal of a request for access to a document if all reasonable steps have been taken to find the document and the relevant public authority is satisfied that it cannot be found. The Information Commissioner can require further searches: s 55V. See also the similar provision in the Freedom of Information Act 1997 (Republic of Ireland) s 10(1)(a). In Canada, the Federal Court has suggested that a total failure to make a search or an adequate search might, if proven, be tantamount to a refusal to disclose: *X v Canada (Minister of National Defence)* (1992) 58 FTR 93.

[167] For a discussion of the duties on public authorities to search for 'deleted' information on computer systems, see *Harper v IC*, IT, 15 November 2005 at [20] to [27] (cf the MOJ *Procedural Guidance*, Information Covered by the Act). Elsewhere the view taken is that the public authority must carry out a search that is reasonable in the circumstances: *Re Anti-Fluoridation Association of Victoria v Secretary to the Department of Health* (1985) 8 ALD 163.

[168] Elsewhere, the view taken is that where documents answering the terms of the request cannot be located, it is not sufficient to state merely that no such documents exist, on the basis that this is a bare statement of ultimate fact: *Re Luton and Commissioner of Taxation* (1996) 22 AAR 492 at 496.

[169] FOIA s 10(1). See §§11–022 to 11–030.

[170] FOIA s 1(1)(a).

of written notice that information is not held.[171] Where no information is found, the public authority is entitled to give an applicant a fees notice under s 9(1), but the amount required by that notice is, strictly speaking, confined to the costs of complying with s 1(1)(a): in other words, the cost of informing the applicant, and not the cost of the search.

11– 040 Partial location of information

The Code of Practice states that where a public authority has been able to identify and locate some information, but not other information, then it should provide the information that it has located and explain to the applicant why it has not been able to identify or locate the remainder.[172] Given that the unit of disclosure is 'information', this does not take matters much beyond what is required by the terms of the Act: the public authority is required to communicate all the information that it holds answering the terms of the request.

7.   CONSULTATION WITH THIRD PARTIES

11– 041 Introduction

In addition to generating information themselves, public authorities are repositories of large amounts of third-party information, either collected by those public authorities or, more commonly, provided to them by members of the public, businesses, foreign governments and international organisations.[173] In some cases, the information will have been truly volunteered to a public authority. But in most cases, the information will have been provided either under compulsion (such as an income tax return) or by practical necessity in order to secure a licence, grant, permit, authorisation, dispensation or some other such advantage. The information may have been supplied with no thought or warning as to public rights of access to information held by the recipient public authority. Indeed, the information may have been supplied before such rights were put on the statute books. The person who supplied the information may have done so expecting that it, or at least some of it, should not be used by the recipient public authority other than for the purpose for which it was supplied. While sometimes the expectations and wishes of that person, and the reasons for them, will be self-evident to the recipient public authority, in other cases these will either not be obvious or not fully appreciated. Those expectations and wishes may moreover reflect a wider public interest in non-disclosure. Neither the Freedom of Information Act 2000 nor the Environmental Information Regulations 2004[174] makes express provision for third-party involvement in the determination of a request for information. There is no legal obligation to notify or consult a third party whose interests would be affected by the disclosure of information. Nor do third parties have a statutory right to challenge or seek a review of decisions to disclose information. Thus, although many of the

---

[171] FOI(S)A s 17.

[172] Section 45 Code of Practice, para 12. For implicit criticism by the Tribunal of a failure to adopt this approach, see *Johnson v IC*, IT, 28 April 2006 at [2].

[173] In addition, a person may have supplied information to one public authority and that public authority may, without reference to the person supplying the information, have supplied it to one or more other public authorities.

[174] Similarly the FOI(S)A and the EI(S)R.

exemptions under the Acts are designed to protect third parties' interests, the Acts themselves do not provide procedural mechanisms for protecting those interests.

042 Comparative jurisdictions

The differing approaches taken in the comparative jurisdictions are illuminating, showing the importance that has been attached to the rights of third parties.[175] Thus:

(1) In the USA, the Freedom of Information Act 1966 makes no provision for a third party to attempt to stop disclosure of information. In *Chrysler Corp v Brown*[176] the Supreme Court held that jurisdiction for a reverse FOI action cannot be based on the Freedom of Information Act itself 'because Congress did not design the FOIA exemptions to be mandatory bars to disclosure.' Instead, the Court found that review of an agency's decision to disclose requested records can be brought under the Administrative Procedure Act.[177] As a result, a third party will ordinarily argue that an agency's contemplated release would violate the Trade Secrets Act and thus would 'not be in accordance with law' or would be 'arbitrary and capricious' within the meaning of the Administrative Procedure Act. The third party's right of challenge is thus on judicial review grounds, and not one of merit review. On top of this, Executive Order 12,600 requires that notice be given to submitters of confidential commercial information whenever an agency 'determines that it may be required to disclose' the requested information. When a third party is given notice, it must be given a reasonable period of time within which to object to disclosure of any of the requested material. If the third party's objection is not upheld by the agency, the third party must be notified in writing and given a brief explanation of the agency's decision. The notification must be provided a reasonable number of days before the disclosure date, so as to give the third party an opportunity to seek judicial relief.

(2) In Australia, the Freedom of Information Act 1982 provides that before an agency discloses documents containing information that originated from a state, that contain business information or contain personal information (each of which is an exemption), the agency holding the documents is required to give the potentially affected third party an opportunity to make representations as to whether the relevant exemption applies.[178] If, despite the representations, the agency intends to disclose the documents, the third party may request the Information Commissioner to review the decision and thereafter appeal to the Tribunal.[179] The third party is entitled to put forward any of the grounds of exemption, including those not relied

---

[175] Given that the FOIA was the last of its comparators and that those comparators were the subject of close scrutiny (see §2– 001), it is a little surprising that its treatment of third parties' interests is the most primitive.

[176] (1979) 441 US 281.

[177] 5 USC 701–706 (2000).

[178] Sections 26A, 27 and 27A (substituted by the Freedom of Information (Amendment) Reform Act 2010). The third party can request internal review: ss. 53C and 54A(2).

[179] Commissioner: ss 54M(3)(a), 54P, 54Q, 54S(2), 55A(1)(c) and 55D(2). Tribunal: ss 60AA, 60AB(2) and 61(2).

upon by the agency holding the documents.[180] The Act is silent as to whether the third party should be advised of the identity of the applicant.[181]

(3) In New Zealand, the Official Information Act 1982 imposes no binding obligation upon an agency to consult with a third party before releasing information relating to that party. Instead, s 30(3) of the Official Information Act 1982 and s 18(3) of the Ombudsmen Act 1975 require an Ombudsman, before making any report or recommendation that may adversely affect any person, to give that person an opportunity to be heard.[182] Limited provision is also made by the Privacy Act 1993 in relation to personal information.

(4) In Canada, the Access to Information Act, deals methodically with the rights of third parties.[183] Section 20 provides a number of exemptions for records specifically relating to third parties: trade secrets; financial, commercial, scientific or technical information supplied by third parties in confidence; information disclosure of which might cause material financial loss or gain to, or prejudice the competitive position of, a third party; information disclosure of which might prejudice negotiations of a third party. Under s 27, where the institution intends to disclose a record that contains, or that the head of the institution has reason to believe might contain, matter specifically exempted by s 20, notice must be given to the third party giving him 20 days within which to make representations as to whether the record should be disclosed.[184] Section 28 deals with the manner in which a third party is required to make representations. Section 33 provides that a third party is to be given notice of a complaint against a non-disclosure decision, provided that notification under s 27 would have been required had it been intended to disclose. Section 35 gives a third party a right, where necessary, to make representations to the Information Commissioner and the third party will, in those circumstances, receive a copy of his report (s 37(2)). An affected, or potentially affected, third party is given a right to participate in a review application and is notified of the same (s 43). A third party may also itself apply for a review order to prevent disclosure of a record (s 44). The statutory scheme is said to give a third party a vested right to have its information withheld from unqualified requesters.[185] The courts have taken the view that a third

---

[180] The third party may be made a party to the proceedings by the Administrative Appeals Tribunal Act 1975, ss 27(1) and 30(1A). But see *Mitsubishi Motors Australia Ltd v Department of Transport* (1986) 12 FCR 156, 68 ALR 626, where the Federal Court held that a third party could only apply to the Tribunal for review in respect of a decision that a document was not exempt under s 43: the Tribunal did not have jurisdiction to deal with the whole question of access to that document, including other grounds of exemption. The Federal Court expressly recognised that, where s 43 was not being relied upon, the third party could seek judicial review of the agency's decision to disclose a document. The decision must now be read in light of the Freedom of Information Reform (Amendment) Act 2010.

[181] In its review of the Freedom of Information Act 1982, the Australian Law Reform Commission said that revealing the identity of the applicant to the third party was best left to the discretion of the agency, although it was sensible to consult the applicant before doing so: Australian Law Reform Commission and Administrative Review Council, *Open Government: a Review of the Federal Freedom of Information Act 1982*, ALRC 77, ARC 40 (Canberra, 1995) para 10.17.

[182] See *Wyatt Co (NZ) Ltd v Queenstown-Lakes District Council* [1991] 2 NZLR 180.

[183] Access to Information Act ss 20, 27, 28, 33, 37, 43 and 44.

[184] Outside the grounds specified in s 27, a third party has no right to be notified of a disclosure and, accordingly, no right of review under s 44: *Twinn v Canada (Minister of Indian Affairs and Northern Development)* [1987] 3 FC 368.

[185] *Glaxo Canada Inc v Canada (Minister of National Health and Welfare)* [1990] 1 FC 652.

party is not able to invoke exemptions with which it has no connections, such as injury to international relations, if the government institution has chosen not to invoke it.[186]

(5) In Ireland, there are two separate procedures in the Freedom of Information Act 1997 obliging a public body to consult with a third party before deciding to disclose records answering the terms of the request. The first applies where the records stand to fall within the scope of one of three particular exemptions: records obtained in confidence, commercially sensitive information and personal information about third parties.[187] Where a record answering the terms of a request falls within the scope of one or more of these exemptions but the head of the public body is nevertheless of the opinion that the public interest lies in favour of disclosure, that public body is required to inform a third party to whom the record relates of this fact.[188] The third party has a right to make written representations in relation to the access request.[189] The second procedure applies to certain categories of record relating to matters before government: the head of a public body may not release the record until he has consulted with the leader of each political party to which a member of the Government belonged that made any decision to which the record relates.[190] A person notified under the first procedure must be advised in writing of the decision and of his right of appeal.[191] The Act is silent as to whether the third party should be advised of the identity of the applicant.

043 Protection of third-party interests under the Freedom of Information Act 2000
The only recognition of the interests of a third party affected by disclosure under the Freedom of Information Act 2000 is a non-statutory statement of expectation that such a third party should in some circumstances be consulted before any such disclosure.[192] The absence of any statutory protection in the draft freedom of information legislation drew considerable criticism during its passage through Parliament.[193] Businesses concerned about their commercial interests, as well as others concerned at the possible implications of the release of information

---

[186] *Saint John Shipbuilding Ltd v Canada (Minister of Supply and Services)* (1988) 24 FTR 32; on appeal, (1990) 67 DLR (4th) 315.

[187] Freedom of Information Act 1997 ss 26, 27 and 28, respectively.

[188] Freedom of Information Act 1997 s 29.

[189] Freedom of Information Act 1997 s 29(3). The third party has three weeks in which to do so. The head is obliged to take the submissions into account before making his decision.

[190] Freedom of Information Act 1997 s 19.

[191] Freedom of Information Act 1997 s 29(3). If the public body accedes to the third party's representations, the applicant may also appeal: Freedom of Information Act 1997 ss 34(1) and 34(15). There is no internal review in relation to the third-party consultation procedure.

[192] Section 45 Code of Practice paras 34-38. There are similar provisions in the codes applying to FOI(S)A, EIR and EI(S)R. The Information Commissioner has issued guidance in relation to requests for data under the DPA that contain third-party information.

[193] Hansard, HL, vol 617, 17 October 2000, cols 983-990. An amendment was moved to impose a notification upon a public authority: col 983. Similarly, Hansard, vol 347, 4 April 2000, col 890. While the original White Paper (*Cabinet Office, Your Right to Know: The Government's Proposals for a Freedom of Information Act* (Cm 3818, 1997) invited views on whether a mechanism for protecting third parties was needed (at para 5.19), the draft bill contained no such mechanism.

about them (a striking example being the Research Defence Society, which expressed concerns about the implications for holders of licences for scientific research involving animals) argued that the protection afforded to third parties by a code of practice was inadequate, and there were recommendations that third parties should be given a legal right to be consulted and to challenge decisions to disclose information about them. However, professed concerns about the administrative burden and lack of flexibility to which such an approach would give rise, its cost to the public purse by comparison with reliance on third parties' existing legal rights (eg by way of action for breach of confidence) and its putative potential to undermine the very principle of access to information, were seized upon to defeat the concerns of third parties.[194]

11– 044 The requirements of the Code of Practice

Apart from any free-standing bases for controlling disclosure[195] all that remains for an affected third party is the s 45 Code of Practice.[196] Whereas the first version of the Code of Practice provided some concrete guidelines for the consultation of third parties before disclosure of information,[197] the current version is more plastic, to the disadvantage of those third parties.[198] So far as third party consultation is concerned, the Code of Practice advises that:

(1) There will be some cases where it will be necessary to consult directly and individually with a third party: but the Code gives no clue to their nature.[199]

(2) But 'in a range of other circumstances it will be good practice to do so; for example where a public authority proposes to disclose information relating to third parties, or information which is likely to affect their interests, reasonable steps should, where appropriate, be taken to give them advance notice, or failing that, to draw it to their attention afterwards.'[200]

(3) Where the information affects a number of third parties, a public authority may consult representative organisations, or even representative samples of numbers of individuals.[201]

11– 045 Other third-party rights

Given the absence of any statutory provision or substantive provision in the Code of Practice requiring an invitation to or the participation of an affected third party, other means of influencing a public authority's decision to disclose come to assume greater importance. Those

---

[194] See, eg *House of Commons Select Committee on Public Administration—Third Report* (Cm 355, 1999) paras 107–110; *Report from the House of Lords Select Committee appointed to consider the draft Freedom of Information Bill*, 27 July 1999, paras 40–47, 76; House of Commons, *Select Committee on Public Administration—Fifth Special Report*, Appendix, p 10, 27 October 1999; Hansard HC vol 347 cols 890–915 (4 April 2000); Hansard HL vol 617 cols 983–991 (17 October 2000).

[195] See §11– 045.

[196] In relation to the force of which, see §10– 008.

[197] Paragraphs 34–38.

[198] In relation to consultation with an affected third party, the s 45 Code of Practice probably falls short of providing any promise or requirement to adopt a practice such that adherence could be secured through judicial review proceedings: see *R (Nadarajah and Abdi) v SSHD* [2005] EWCA Civ 1363 at [68].

[199] Section 45 Code of Practice, para 27.

[200] Section 45 Code of Practice, para 27.

[201] Section 45 Code of Practice, para 30.

other means will almost certainly require an underlying and recognisable right, such as:

— a third party's rights under art 8 of the ECHR;

— a third party's intellectual property in the information proposed to be disclosed;

— a right of confidentiality (including one arising out of a contract);

— a right arising out of the Data Protection Act 1998;

— rights arising out of the law of defamation; or

— parliamentary privilege.

A threatened breach of such a right may provide a direct basis upon which to seek injunctive relief. Alternatively, it may provide a basis for challenging by way of judicial review the decision or the proposed decision of a public authority. The facts and circumstances giving rise to the underlying right will often also result in the information falling within one of the exemptions in Part II of the Act.[202] Depending on whether the exemption is absolute (and, if not, where the public interest balance lies), that will have the effect of making any such disclosure not one required by the Act,[203] ie a voluntary disclosure.[204] Various statutory protections provided to a public authority where a disclosure is required by statute[205] will be thereby removed. In both cases, the real issue for most third parties will be knowing of the decision to disclose before the disclosure has been made. In all cases, a third party can improve its prospects of being invited for its views and in subsequent coercive proceedings by formally advising a public authority that it expects to be consulted should that public authority propose to disclose particular information to any other person, including another public authority. Such notification can accompany the provision of the information or can be given subsequently. In relation to personal data, a data subject may serve a notice under s 10 of the Data Protection Act 1998. A notification that supplies grounds of justification and contact details will further enhance those prospects. Where a public authority has disclosed information in circumstances where an exemption could have been invoked and in breach of one of the above rights, an affected third party may be able to bring an action in damages.[206]

046 Requests involving personal information about third parties

Where compliance with a request for information may entail disclosure of personal information about a third party there are specific provisions to protect the interests of that individual. A distinction is drawn between:

(1) requests for access to personal information about the person making the request (ie

---

[202] For example, s 34, 40, 41 or 43.

[203] FOIA s 2(1)–(2).

[204] As to which, see §§9– 036 to 9– 038.

[205] For example: FOIA s 79; Copyright, Designs and Patents Act 1988 s 50; DPA Sch 2. And see further §§9– 034 to 9– 035.

[206] The action would most likely be founded upon a breach of the underlying right. Damages for a breach of an underlying private law right could be sought as part of judicial review proceedings: Supreme Court Act 1981 s 31(7); CPR 54.3(2). A court may also order a public authority to pay damages under the Human Rights Act 1998 s 8, where that public authority has acted in a way that is incompatible with a right derived from the European Convention on Human Rights. In this case, the court will have to be satisfied that an award of damages is necessary to ensure just satisfaction for the person concerned, having regard to the other remedies granted and the consequences of the unlawful act: *R (Anufrijeva) v London Borough Southwark* [2003] EWCA Civ 1406, [2004] QB 1124; *R (N) v SSHD* [2003] EWHC 207, [2003] HRLR 20, [2003] UKHRR 546. In an egregious case it might be possible to mount a claim on the basis of misfeasance in public office.

subject access requests) which also entail the disclosure of personal information about a third party; and

(2)   requests for the disclosure of personal information about a third party.

The latter are dealt with under the Freedom of Information Act 2000 and are considered in detail in Chapter 24. As already noted, the issue of consultation is addressed through the Code of Practice.[207] The former, as with all subject access requests, are channelled through the Data Protection Act 1998.

11– 047   Data Protection Act 1998

Since the Code of Practice is directed at public authorities exercising their functions under Part I of the Freedom of Information Act 2000, it has no application in the case of requests for access to personal information under the Data Protection Act 1998. Where a data controller cannot comply with a subject access request without disclosing information relating to another individual[208] who can be identified from that information,[209] he is not obliged to comply with the request unless:

(1)   the other individual has consented to the disclosure; or

(2)   it is reasonable in all the circumstances to comply with the request without such consent.[210]

The balancing process this calls for mirrors that required under article 8 of the European Convention on Human Rights[211] and it has been suggested that in this context data controllers should have in mind the principles of necessity and proportionality.[212] In determining whether it is reasonable to comply with the request without the third party's consent, particular regard must be paid to any duty of confidentiality owed to the third party, any steps the data controller has taken with a view to seeking the third party's consent, the capacity of the third party to consent and any express refusal of consent by the third party.[213] The requirement, in particular, to have regard to the steps taken with a view to seeking the third party's consent may be thought to give rise, at the least, to a pragmatic need to consult the third party or to attempt to do so. This is recognised in guidance issued by the Information Commissioner on this specific

---

[207] Section 45 Code of Practice, para 33.

[208] This includes information identifying an individual as the source of the information sought by the request: DPA s 7(5). However, the information must necessarily form part of the personal data requested by the data subject, otherwise no question of balancing under s 7(4) arises at all: see *Durant v Financial Services Authority* [2003] EWCA Civ 1746, [2004] FSR 28 at [65].

[209] Another individual can be identified from the information being disclosed if he can be identified from that information, or from that and any other information which, in the reasonable belief of the data controller, is likely to be in, or to come into, the possession of the data subject making the request: DPA s 8(7).

[210] DPA s 7(4). See further §24– 007.

[211] As to which, see *R (L) v Metropolitan Police Commissioner* [2009] UKSC 3, [2010] 1 All ER 113.

[212] *Durant v Financial Services Authority* [2003] EWCA Civ 1746, [2004] FSR 28 at [54], [60].

[213] DPA s 7(6). Recent jurisprudence points to a growing expectation that a public authority take all reasonable steps to consult a third party whose personal interests would stand to be affected by that public authority disclosing personal information relating to him: *R (L) v Metropolitan Police Commissioner* [2009] UKSC 3, [2010] 1 All ER 113 at [46].

aspect of the Data Protection Act 1998.[214] The Commissioner advises that data controllers may at the very least need to take steps to seek consent in order to demonstrate that it was reasonable in the circumstances to make the disclosure without consent.[215] As the Commissioner notes, these provisions may give rise to complex judgments for data controllers, weighing on the one hand the data subject's right of access (and the potential breach of the sixth data protection principle to which non-disclosure might give rise) and on the other hand the third party's right to respect for his private life.[216] While the right to privacy and other legitimate interests of third parties identified in or identifiable from the data subject's personal data will be highly relevant, so too will the question of what, if any, legitimate interest the data subject has in the disclosure of that third party's identity.[217] In an application under s 7(9) of the Act concerning this balance, the role of the court is, ordinarily, confined to a review of the reasonableness of the data controller's judgment — albeit on an anxious scrutiny basis — and does not entail a review of the merits.[218] The Court of Appeal has suggested that the starting-point for the data controller is a 'presumption' against disclosure of third-party information without that third party's consent, but beyond this has expressed reluctance to attempt to devise any generally applicable principles.[219]

048 Disclosure without revealing the identity of a third party
Where the data controller can communicate part of the information sought by the data subject without disclosing the third party's identity, for example by omitting the third party's name or other identifying particulars, then he must do so. The prohibition on disclosure applies only to the information from which the third party can be identified.[220]

049 Requests involving confidential information of a third party
Where the disclosure of information to the public (otherwise than under the Freedom of Information Act 2000) by the public authority holding it would constitute a breach of confidence actionable by a third party, that information will be rendered exempt information if it was that third party which supplied the information to the public authority.[221] It would seem that the exemption does not extend to information held by a public authority which it did not obtain directly from that third party. Nevertheless, even in this situation other proscriptions against disclosure may apply, thereby rendering it exempt information.[222] Whilst in some

[214] *Data Protection Act 1998: Subject Access Rights and Third Party Information*, 2 March 2000. However, in *Durant v Financial Services Authority* [2003] EWCA Civ 1746, [2004] FSR 28 at [56] the Court of Appeal emphasised that s 7(4) leaves the data controllers with a choice whether to do so: it does not oblige them to do so. This must be read in the light of *R (L) v Metropolitan Police Commissioner* [2009] UKSC 3, [2010] 1 All ER 113 at [46].

[215] *Data Protection Act 1998: Subject Access Rights and Third Party Information*, 2 March 2000, para 7.5.

[216] *Data Protection Act 1998: Subject Access Rights and Third Party Information*, 2 March 2000, paras 2–4.

[217] *Durant v Financial Services Authority* [2003] EWCA Civ 1746, [2004] FSR 28 at [61].

[218] *Durant v Financial Services Authority* [2003] EWCA Civ 1746, [2004] FSR 28 at [59]–[60].

[219] *Durant v Financial Services Authority* [2003] EWCA Civ 1746, [2004] FSR 28 at [55], [66].

[220] DPA s 7(5).

[221] FOIA s 41; FOI(S)A s 36.

[222] FOIA s 44(1); FOI(S)A s 26. See further §§26– 015 to 26– 026.

situations it will be clear whether or not disclosure of the information to the public will constitute an actionable breach of confidence, where it is not a person by whom such a breach would be actionable may be well placed to contribute to the public authority's understanding of the qualities of the information. A public authority's failure to seek those views before releasing such information will expose the public authority to a claim for damages.

CHAPTER 12
Disentitlement

1. EXCESSIVE COST OF COMPLIANCE

001 Introduction

One of the risks of a freedom of information regime is that an applicant may make applications for information which would result in a public authority incurring disproportionate cost or in an unreasonable diversion of a public authority's resources.[1] The Freedom of Information Act 2000 does not require a public authority to comply with a request for information where the

---

[1] This was a potential problem identified in the White Paper: Cabinet Office, *Your Right to Know: The Government's Proposals for a Freedom of Information Act. White Paper* (Cm 3818, 1997) para 2.26. The concept of a 'substantial and unreasonable diversion of resources' is deployed expressly in the Australian legislation (Freedom of Information Act 1982 (Commonwealth of Australia) ss 24AA(1)(a).

cost of complying with the request would exceed a specified limit.[2] However, where the cost of compliance does exceed the specified limit and the duty to disclose does not arise, a public authority nevertheless has a power to provide the information and may charge for the same.[3] As will be seen, the combined operation of the provisions has the result that:

— when a public authority is determining whether there is no duty to comply with a request for information because the cost of compliance would be excessive, it takes into account the cost of determining whether or not it holds the information, the cost of locating the information and the cost of retrieving it;

— however, once a public authority has properly determined that there is no duty to comply with a request for information because the cost of compliance would be excessive, but it nevertheless decides to exercise its power to do so, it may charge not just for the cost of determining whether or not it holds the information, the cost of locating the information and the cost of retrieving it, but also for the cost of informing the applicant whether it holds the information and the cost of communicating the information to the applicant.

There is no provision for a public authority, in estimating the costs at either stage, to take into account matters such as the cost of considering whether the information is exempt information or the cost of considering public interest issues.

12–002 No obligation to comply with request where cost of compliance is excessive

Where a public authority estimates that the cost of complying with a request for information would exceed the appropriate limit,[4] then it is relieved of its two obligations under s 1(1) of the Freedom of Information Act 2000.[5] This has been described as 'a guillotine which prevents the burden on the public authority from becoming too onerous under the Act.'[6] However, a public authority is only relieved of its duty to confirm or deny if the estimated cost of complying with that duty alone would exceed the appropriate limit.[7] It is notable that the Acts use the word 'would' rather than 'might'. This is likely to be of particular relevance where a public authority is unable to estimate the costs of compliance with any certainty. In such a case, if the public authority were to estimate that the cost of compliance would fall somewhere between a lower and an upper figure, it is unlikely that it would be able to take advantage of the provisions on excessive cost of compliance where the lower figure was below the appropriate limit. In such

---

[2] FOIA s 12(1); FOI(S)A s 12(1). There is no equivalent provision in the environmental information regime: see §6–023 and see *Mersey Tunnel Users Association v IC and Halton BC*, IT, 24 June 2009 at [90]. Nor is there an equivalent in the DPA, save to the extent that the request is for unstructured personal data: see §§5–040 and 5–041.

[3] FOIA s 13(1); FOI(S)A s 13(1).

[4] FOIA s 12(1). Although the FOI(S)A does not invoke the concept of an 'appropriate limit', the effect of the relevant provisions is broadly the same (see the FOI(S)A s 12(1)). As to the 'appropriate limit', see §12–005.

[5] Or its obligation under s 1(1) of the FOI(S)A, as the case may be: *Quinn v IC and Home Office*, IT, 15 November 2006 at [50]; *Johnson v IC and MoJ*, IT, 13 July 2007 at [52]. As to a public authority's obligations under s 1(1) of the FOIA or s 1(1) of the FOI(S)A, see §1–005(4). The position under the DPA is considered at §5–042.

[6] *Quinn v IC and SSHD*, IT, 15 November 2006 at [50].

[7] FOIA s 12(2). A precise calculation is not required but the estimate must be 'sensible, realistic and supported by cogent evidence': *Randall v IC and Medicines and Healthcare Products Regulatory Agency*, IT, 30 October 2007 at [12]. For what is required when arriving at a reasonable estimate, see: *James v IC and DTI*, IT, 25 September 2007 at [45]-[49]; *Roberts v IC*, IT, 4 December 2008 at [12]. There is no equivalent provision in the FOI(S)A.

a case, it could not be said that the estimated costs 'would' exceed the appropriate limit. Where a request for information captures information some of which falls to be disclosed under the freedom of information regime and some of which falls to be disclosed under the environmental information regime, it is suggested that it is impermissible for a public authority to take into account the cost of complying with the latter. This is because the latter is not a request for information to which s 1(1) of the Freedom of Information Act 2000 would to any extent apply.[8]

003 Estimating the cost of compliance

The Freedom of Information Act 2000 does not itself prescribe the type of costs which a public authority is entitled to take into account, or the manner of estimating those costs, when assessing whether the cost of complying with a request for information would exceed the appropriate limit. The Act makes provision for such matters to be prescribed by regulations.[9] Those regulations are the Freedom of Information and Data Protection (Appropriate Limit and Fees) Regulations 2004.[10] The Ministry of Justice has published non-statutory guidance on the application of these regulations.[11] The Regulations provide that a public authority may, for the purpose of estimating whether the cost of complying with a request for information[12] would exceed the appropriate limit, take account only of the costs it reasonably expects to incur in determining whether it holds the information,[13] locating the information (or a document which may contain the information),[14] retrieving the information (or a document which may contain the information),[15] and extracting the information from a document containing it.[16] Further, where any of those costs are attributable to the time which persons undertaking any of those activities[17] on behalf of the public authority are expected to spend on those activities, those costs are to be estimated at the rate of £25 per person per hour.[18] Accordingly, the costs that may be taken into account at the stage when a public authority is determining whether or not the cost of compliance would exceed the appropriate limit do not include the costs of considering

---

[8] Being the opening requirement in FOI & DP (Limit & Fees) Regs reg 5(1). Section 1(1) does not apply to environmental information because of FOIA ss 1(2), 2(1), 2(2) and 39. This will be the case regardless of whether the request for environmental information is contained within the same document as the request for information under the FOIA.

[9] FOIA s 12(5); FOI(S)A s 12(4).

[10] As to the position in Scotland, see §12–004.

[11] MoJ, Freedom of Information Act–Procedural Guidance, undated, 'Fees and Aggregation' section. In Scotland, guidance on the regulations is set out in the (statutory) Scottish Ministers' Code of Practice, paras 59 to 61 and Annex 3.

[12] That is, a request for information to which s 1(1) of the FOIA would, apart from the appropriate limit, to any extent apply: FOI & DP (Limit & Fees) Regs reg 4(1) and (2)(b). The same regulation applies to a request for unstructured personal data within the meaning of s 9A(1) of the DPA and to which s 7(1) of the DPA would, apart from the appropriate limit, to any extent apply: FOI & DP (Limit & Fees) Regs reg 4(2)(a): see §5–041.

[13] FOI & DP (Limit & Fees) Regs reg 4(3)(a).

[14] FOI & DP (Limit & Fees) Regs reg 4(3)(b).

[15] FOI & DP (Limit & Fees) Regs reg 4(3)(c).

[16] FOI & DP (Limit & Fees) Regs reg 4(3)(d). This does not include the cost of redaction: *Jenkins v IC and DEFRA*, IT, 2 November 2007.

[17] That is, the activities referred to in FOI & DP (Limit & Fees) Regs reg 4(3).

[18] FOI & DP (Limit & Fees) Regs reg 4(4). It should be noted that this is a fixed, not a maximum, figure.

whether the information is exempt information, the costs of considering public interest issues, the costs of informing the applicant whether it holds the information, or the costs of communicating the information to the applicant.[19]

12–004 Estimating the cost of compliance, Scottish public authorities

Section 12(4) of the Freedom of Information (Scotland) Act 2002 enables regulations to be made which make provision for the costs to be estimated and the manner in which those costs are to be estimated. The Regulations make provision for the estimation of the 'projected costs' in relation to a request for information.[20] The projected costs are stated to be the total costs, whether direct or indirect, which the public authority reasonably estimates it is likely to incur in locating, retrieving and providing such information. The Regulations state that in estimating projected costs no account may be taken of costs in determining:

(a) whether the authority holds the information specified in the request;[21] and

(b) whether the person seeking the information is entitled to receive the requested information or, if not so entitled, should nevertheless be provided with it or should be refused it.[22]

The Scottish regime differs from that of the FOIA in that the public authority is not allowed to include the cost of determining whether it holds the information. Under both FOIA and FOI(S)A, public authorities are not allowed to take into account the cost of considering whether the information is exempt information. Under FOI(S)A the public authority is at liberty to take into account the costs of informing the applicant that it holds the information and the cost of communicating that information to the applicant.

12–005 The 'appropriate limit'

The Freedom of Information Act 2000 provides that the 'appropriate limit' is to be prescribed by regulations, which may provide that different limits apply in different cases.[23] Those regulations are, again, the Freedom of Information and Data Protection (Appropriate Limit and Fees) Regulations 2004. These provide that in the case of a public authority which is listed in Part I of Sch 1 to the Freedom of Information Act 2000 or in the case of a public authority in Scotland, the appropriate limit is £600.[24] In the case of any other public authority, the appropriate limit is £450.[25]

---

[19] Further examples of matters that may not be taken into account are given in the *Guidance on the application of the Freedom of Information and Data Protection (Appropriate Limit and Fees) Regulations 2004*, para 2.3.5.

[20] Freedom of Information (Fees for Required Disclosure) (Scotland) Regulations 2004 SSI 2004/467 reg 3 (see further §11–019) and Freedom of Information (Fees for Disclosure under Section 13) (Scotland) Regulations SSI 2004/376 reg 3 (see further §12–009).

[21] Regulation 3(2)(a)(i).

[22] Regulation 3(2)(a)(ii).

[23] FOIA s 12(3). Although the FOI(S)A does not invoke the concept of an 'appropriate limit', the FOI(S)A s 12(1) provides that the relevant amount should be prescribed by regulations.

[24] FOI & DP (Limit & Fees) Regs reg 3(2) and Freedom of Information (Fees for Required Disclosure) (Scotland) Regulations 2004 SSI 2004/467 reg 5. Although the FOI(S)A does not invoke the concept of an 'appropriate limit', the effect of the relevant provisions is the same.

[25] FOI & DP (Limit & Fees) Regs reg 3(3).

006 Cumulative cost of complying with separate requests

The Freedom of Information Act 2000 anticipates the possibility that the provisions protecting public authorities from incurring excessive costs in complying with requests could be emasculated in a situation where several separate requests are submitted.[26] Accordingly, the Act makes provision for regulations to prescribe that in certain circumstances, where two or more requests for information are made to a public authority by one person, or by different persons who appear to the public authority to be acting in concert[27] or in pursuance of a campaign,[28] the public authority may treat the estimated cost of compliance as being the estimated cost of complying with all of the requests.[29] Pursuant to the regulations, where two or more such requests relate, to any extent, to the same or similar information and they are received by the public authority within any period of 60 consecutive working days,[30] then the estimated cost of complying with any of the requests is to be taken to be the total costs which may be taken into account by the public authority of complying with all of them.[31] The guidance exhorts public authorities to be cautious about treating separate requests in this way, particularly where the cumulative cost of complying exceeds the appropriate limit by only a small amount.[32] It is suggested that in a case where the cumulative cost of complying with related requests is excessive, the public authority may wish to consider whether the information could be communicated in a more cost-effective manner, such as by publication on its website.

007 Cumulative cost of complying with separate requests in Scotland

The power of a Scottish public authority to refuse to comply with separate requests on grounds of excessive cumulative cost is much more limited than that of public authorities covered by the Freedom of Information Act 2000. Where two or more requests are made to a Scottish public

---

[26] This was a potential problem identified in the white paper (Cabinet Office, *Your Right to Know: The Government's Proposals for a Freedom of Information Act. White Paper* (Cm 3818, 1997) para 2.26.

[27] A phrase normally associated with a criminal enterprise (see *DPP v Merriman* [1973] AC 584). It generally connotes a joining together of two or more persons to do what is sought to be done.

[28] FOIA s 12(4); FOI(S)A s 12(2). The FOI(S)A differs slightly from the FOIA in this respect, in that it does not refer to different persons who appear to be acting in pursuance of a campaign, but refers to different persons whose requests appear to have been instigated wholly or mainly for a purpose other than the obtaining of the information itself: FOI(S)A s 12(2)(b). As to the position in Scotland, see §12–007.

[29] FOIA s 12(4); FOI(S)A s 12(2). The relevant regulations are the FOI & DP (Limit & Fees) Regs and the Freedom of Information (Fees for Required Disclosure) (Scotland) Regulations 2004 SSI 2004/467.

[30] In this context, a working day means any day other than a Saturday, a Sunday, Christmas Day, Good Friday or a day which is a bank holiday under the Banking and Financial Dealings Act 1971 in any part of the United Kingdom: FOI & DP (Limit & Fees) Regs reg 5(3). Because bank holidays under the Banking and Financial Dealings Act 1971 differ in the various parts of the United Kingdom, the effect of the regulations referring to a bank holiday under the Banking and Financial Dealings Act 1971 'in any part' of the United Kingdom is to exclude each of the following days: New Year's Day (or, if New Year's Day be a Sunday, January 3), January 2 (or if January 2 be a Sunday, January 3), March 17 (or if March 17 be a Sunday, March 18), Easter Monday, the first Monday in May, the last Monday in May, the first Monday in August, the last Monday in August, December 25, December 26 (if it not be a Sunday) and December 27 (in a year in which December 25 or 26 is a Sunday): see Banking and Financial Dealings Act 1971, Sch 1.

[31] FOI & DP (Limit & Fees) Regs reg 5(1) and (2).

[32] DCA, Freedom of Information Act–Procedural Guidance, undated, 'Fees and Aggregation' section.

authority by different persons,[33] the public authority is only relieved of the duty to comply with either or any of those requests where the information sought in the requests covers the same subject or overlaps to a significant extent,[34] the authority estimates that the total cost of complying with both or all of the requests would exceed £600,[35] and, on the basis that it considers it reasonable to do so,[36] the public authority makes the information available to the public at large within the period of 20 working days of receipt by it of the first of the requests.[37] In addition to the significantly more restrictive criteria that must be met in the case of a Scottish public authority (as compared to public authorities governed by the Freedom of Information Act 2000) which are expressly imposed by the relevant provisions, there is also a restrictive criterion which is implicit in them. Before a Scottish public authority may take advantage of the excessive cumulative cost of compliance provisions, it must have sent to each applicant the requisite notice within 20 working days of receipt by it of the first of the requests.[38] Accordingly, it may only take advantage of those provisions in relation to requests which are made within 20 working days of each other. This is a significantly shorter period than the period of 60 consecutive working days applicable to public authorities covered by the Freedom of Information Act 2000.[39]

12– 008 Notices in cases where cost of compliance is excessive

Where a public authority claims that it is not obliged to comply with its duties under s 1(1) of the Freedom of Information Act 2000 because the cost of complying with it would be excessive, it must within the time for compliance with that section give the applicant a notice stating that fact.[40]

12– 009 Fees in cases where cost of compliance is excessive

The Freedom of Information Act 2000 makes provision for public authorities to charge for the provision of information which might not otherwise be provided because of cost considerations.[41] In cases where a public authority is not obliged to comply with a request for information because the cost of complying with it is deemed to be excessive,[42] where the communication of the information is not otherwise required by law, and where no provision is made by or under another enactment for the charging of fees, then the public authority may

---

[33] Freedom of Information (Fees for Required Disclosure) (Scotland) Regulations 2004 SSI 2004/467 reg 6.

[34] Freedom of Information (Fees for Required Disclosure) (Scotland) Regulations 2004 SSI 2004/467 reg 6(a).

[35] That is, the amount prescribed under the Freedom of Information (Fees for Required Disclosure) (Scotland) Regulations 2004 SSI 2004/467 reg 5 — see reg 6(b).

[36] Freedom of Information (Fees for Required Disclosure) (Scotland) Regulations 2004 SSI 2004/467 reg 6(c).

[37] That is, the period specified in reg 6(d) of the Freedom of Information (Fees for Required Disclosure) (Scotland) Regulations 2004 SSI 2004/467 — see reg 6(e). The public authority must, within the same period, notify each requester of this decision.

[38] Freedom of Information (Fees for Required Disclosure) (Scotland) Regulations 2004 SSI 2004/467 reg 6(d).

[39] FOI & DP (Limit & Fees) Regs reg 5(2)(b).

[40] FOIA s 17(5); FOI(S)A s 16(4). As to notices in cases where the cost of compliance with a request for information would be excessive, see further §13– 010.

[41] Explanatory Notes to the FOIA, para 58.

[42] As to cases where the cost of compliance with a request for information would be excessive, see §12– 008.

charge a fee for the communication of that information.[43] In such a case, however, the Code of Practice suggests that the public authority may wish to consider providing an indication of what information could be provided within the costs ceiling.[44] If a fee is to be charged, it is to be determined by the public authority in accordance with regulations, which prescribe a maximum fee.[45] The maximum fee which may be charged is a sum equivalent to the total of two categories of costs. First, the costs that the public authority is entitled to take into account when estimating the cost of complying with a request.[46] However, costs in this first category must not include any costs which the public authority is entitled to take into account solely by virtue of the provisions relating to the cumulative cost of complying with separate requests.[47] Secondly, the costs that the public authority reasonably expects to incur in informing the applicant whether it holds the information and in communicating the information to the applicant.[48] Costs in the second category which may be taken into account include the costs of giving effect to any preference expressed by the applicant as to the means or form of communicating the information,[49] the costs of reproducing any document containing the information,[50] and the costs of postage and other forms of transmitting the information.[51] Where any of the costs which relate to informing the applicant whether the public authority holds the information and communicating the information to the applicant are attributable to the time which persons undertaking any of those activities[52] on behalf of the public authority are expected to spend on those activities, those costs are to be estimated at the rate of £25 per person per hour.[53] Where a Scottish public authority proposes to communicate information in a case where the cost of compliance with a request for information is excessive, it is subject to two restrictions. First, it must notify the fee to, and agree it with, the applicant before the information is communicated.[54] Secondly, the fee shall not in any case exceed the sum of £50 plus the amount by which the 'projected costs' exceed £600.[55] In this context, the 'projected costs' are the total costs, whether direct or indirect, which a public authority reasonably

---

[43] FOIA s 13(1) and (3); FOI(S)A s 13(1) and (4).

[44] Section 45 Code of Practice, para 14.

[45] FOIA s 13(1); FOI(S)A s 13(1). The relevant regulations are the FOI & DP (Limit & Fees) Regs and the Freedom of Information (Fees for Disclosure under Section 13) (Scotland) Regulations 2004 SSI 2004/376.

[46] That is, the costs which the public authority may take into account under reg 4 of the FOI & DP (Limit & Fees) Regs: FOI & DP (Limit & Fees) Regs reg 7(2)(a). As to such costs, see §§12–003 to 12–004.

[47] FOI & DP (Limit & Fees) Regs reg 7(3). As to the provisions on the cumulative costs of complying with separate requests, see §§12–006 to 12–007.

[48] FOI & DP (Limit & Fees) Regs reg 7(2)(b).

[49] FOI & DP (Limit & Fees) Regs reg 7(4)(a).

[50] FOI & DP (Limit & Fees) Regs reg 7(4)(b).

[51] FOI & DP (Limit & Fees) Regs reg 7(4)(c).

[52] That is, the activities referred to in FOI & DP (Limit & Fees) Regs reg 7(2)(b).

[53] FOI & DP (Limit & Fees) Regs regs 4(4) and 7(5). It should be noted that this is a fixed, and not a maximum, figure.

[54] Freedom of Information (Fees for Disclosure under Section 13) (Scotland) Regulations 2004 SSI 2004/376 reg 4.

[55] Freedom of Information (Fees for Disclosure under Section 13) (Scotland) Regulations 2004 SSI 2004/376 reg 4. This provides some continuity with the fees which may be charged in a case which does not involve excessive cost of compliance: see §12–005.

estimates that it is likely to incur in locating, retrieving and providing the information.[56] However, in estimating projected costs, no account may be taken of costs incurred in determining whether the public authority holds the information specified in the request or whether the applicant is entitled to receive it (or, if not so entitled, whether he should nevertheless be provided with it or refused it).[57] Further, any estimate of the cost of staff time shall not exceed £15 per hour per member of staff.[58] It is to be noted that both sets of provisions impose a maximum fee but make no other provision for the calculation of fees. Nevertheless, a public authority in exercising its discretion to charge a particular level of fee must do so in accordance with normal public law principles.[59] Accordingly, improper discrimination between different types of requests or a lack of consistency in approach in relation to the level of fees may be unlawful.

2. VEXATIOUS REQUESTS

12– 010 Introduction

A public authority is not obliged to comply with a request for information[60] under the Freedom of Information Act 2000 if the request is vexatious.[61] There is no equivalent provision in the Data Protection Act 1998.[62]

12– 011 Meaning of 'vexatious'

The Freedom of Information Act 2000 does not provide any assistance as to what is meant by 'vexatious'.[63] It has been suggested that an analogy may be drawn with the concept of vexatious litigants,[64] but such an analogy may mislead. The Freedom of Information Acts adopt what has been termed an 'applicant-blind' approach.[65] Accordingly, it matters not whether an applicant

---

[56]   Freedom of Information (Fees for Disclosure under Section 13) (Scotland) Regulations 2004 SSI 2004/376 reg 3(1).

[57]   Freedom of Information (Fees for Disclosure under Section 13) (Scotland) Regulations 2004 SSI 2004/376 reg 3(2)(a).

[58]   Freedom of Information (Fees for Disclosure under Section 13) (Scotland) Regulations 2004 SSI 2004/376 reg 3(2)(b).

[59]   For an example of a case where the Tribunal held that the fees charged by a public authority were unreasonable (in the context of the EIR), see *Markinson v IC*, IT, 28 March 2006.

[60]   That is, the public authority is not obliged to comply with its duties under s 1(1) of the FOIA (or of the FOI(S)A, as the case may be).

[61]   FOIA s 14(1); FOI(S)A s 14(1). The EIR provide for a similar exception in the case of requests which are 'manifestly unreasonable': EIR reg 12(4); EI(S)R reg 10(4). As to manifestly unreasonable requests under the EIR, see §6– 032.

[62]   See §5– 043.

[63]   The Australian Law Reform Commission rejected an amendment to the Australian Freedom of Information Act 1982 which would have allowed requests to be rejected on the basis that they were vexatious, arguing that vexatiousness is a vague concept likely to result in unpredictable implementation (Australian Law Reform Commission and Administrative Review Council, *Open Government: a Review of the Federal Freedom of Information Act* (Canberra, Australian Law Reform Commission,1982) para 7.18).

[64]   This analogy was drawn in the white paper (Cabinet Office, *Your Right to Know: the Government's Proposals for a Freedom of Information Act. White Paper* (Cm 3818, 1997) para 2.25).

[65]   Hansard HL vol 617 col 1015 (17 October 2000).

is vexatious: the proper question is whether a particular request is vexatious.[66] The motive of an applicant for making a request cannot transform an otherwise proper request into a vexatious request,[67] unless perhaps it is apparent that the applicant has no interest in receiving the information requested but is bent on creating administrative difficulty for the public authority.[68] Similarly, it is questionable whether the manner in which a request is made will be sufficient to render an otherwise proper request vexatious,[69] although an abusive or offensively-worded request might be considered vexatious. What will amount to a vexatious request will depend on all the circumstances.[70] Examples of requests which are likely to be vexatious[71] are those which go beyond the point at which no further information can be provided,[72] those that seek to reopen issues that have already been considered by the public authority before[73] and those which amount to an attempt to interfere with or undermine the integrity of court processes.[74] The Information Commissioner has indicated that he will be sympathetic towards public authorities where a request would impose a significant burden and it clearly does not have any serious purpose or value, is designed to cause disruption or annoyance, has the effect of harassing the public authority, or can otherwise fairly be characterised as obsessive or manifestly unreasonable.[75]

012 Vexatious requests — examples

The Tribunal has found the following requests to be vexatious:

— Where the tone of the correspondence indicated that the request was obsessive, the requests affected the health and well-being of officers in the public authority and the volume, length and repetitive nature of the requests was a distraction from the public authority's key functions.[76]

---

[66] MoJ, Freedom of Information Act–Procedural Guidance, undated, 'Vexatious and Repeated Requests' section. Accordingly, a better analogy may be with vexatious claims. See, eg, the Employment Tribunals (Constitution and Rules of Procedure) Regulations 2001, Sch 1, para 15(2)(c) and the old RSC Ord 18 r 19(1)(b). Because a large measure of protection is already given to a public authority from such requests through the 'excessive cost of compliance' and 'repeat request' mechanisms, it is difficult to see the particular need for this provision. Other comparable jurisdictions, such as Canada, have managed without it, although it is fair to observe that the Report of the Access to Information Review Task Force, June 2002, recommended that such a provision be inserted in the Canadian Act (p 73).

[67] There is nothing in the Freedom of Information Acts which require or preclude anything in terms of motive: see §§9– 017 and 15– 015.

[68] MoJ, Freedom of Information Act–Procedural Guidance, undated, 'Vexatious and Repeated Requests' section. See, by way of analogy, *AG v Barker* [2000] 2 FCR 1 at 6d-f (Lord Bingham).

[69] Explanatory Notes to the FOIA, para 59: the fact that an applicant 'vents his frustration' in a request will not be sufficient to render that request vexatious. See, eg, *Barber v IC*, IT, 11 November 2005.

[70] *Ashmore v British Coal Corporation* [1990] 2 QB 338 at 348A-C (Stuart-Smith LJ), dealing with abuse of process as an aspect of frivolous or vexatious claims in the Employment Tribunal.

[71] Further examples are set out in the Information Commissioner's *Detailed Specialist Guide*, 'Vexatious and Repeated Requests' (3 December 2008) and in the Scottish Ministers' Code of Practice, para 23.

[72] Hansard HL vol 617 col 1014 (17 October 2000).

[73] *Ahilathirunayagam v IC*, IT, 20 June 2007.

[74] *Johnson Tiles Pty v Esso Australia Ltd* [2000] FCA 495 at [48]–[54], [56] (Merkel J).

[75] Information Commissioner's *Awareness Guidance No 22*.

[76] *Coggins v IC*, IT, 13 May 2008.

— Where, given the content and history of the case, the request was harassing, likely to impose a significant burden and obsessive.[77]

— Where the request was an attempt to re-open issues which had already been disputed several times.[78]

The principles that have emerged from the authorities were summarised in *Carpenter v Information Commissioner and Stevenage Borough Council*:[79]

(1) It is important to ensure that the standard for establishing that a request is vexatious is not too high.

(2) The various considerations identified in AG22 (summarised at Paragraph 31 of the Decision Notice) are a useful interpretive guide to help public authorities to navigate the concept of a "vexatious request." There should not however be an overly-structured approach to the application of those considerations and every case should be viewed on its own particular facts.

(3) When deciding whether a request is vexatious a public authority is not obliged to look at the request in isolation. It could consider both the history of the matter and what lay behind the request. A request could appear, in isolation, to be entirely reasonable yet could assume quality of being vexatious when it is construed in context.

(4) Every case turns on its own facts. Considerations which may be relevant to the overall analysis include:

(a) the request forming part of an extended campaign to expose alleged improper or illegal behaviour in the context of evidence tending to indicate that the campaign is not well founded;

(b) the request involving information which had already been provided to the applicant;

(c) the nature and extent of the applicant's correspondence with the authority whether this suggests an obsessive approach to disclosure;

(d) the tone adopted in the correspondence being tendentious and/or haranguing;

(e) whether the correspondence could reasonably be expected to have a negative effect on the health and well-being of officers; and

(f) whether responding to the request would be likely to entail substantial and disproportionate financial and administrative burdens.

12–013 Notices in cases of vexatious requests

If a public authority is relying on a claim that it is not obliged to comply with a request for information because the request is vexatious, then it must (subject to one exception)[80] give a notice to that effect to the applicant within the time for compliance with s 1(1) of the Freedom of Information Act 2000.[81]

---

[77] *Betts v IC*, IT, 19 May 2008.

[78] *Fortune v IC and National Patient Safety Agency*, IT, 16 April 2008; *Betts v IC*, IT, 19 May 2008; *Adair v IC*, IT, 14 January 2010.

[79] IT, 17 November 2008 at [51]. Similarly: *Gowers v IC and LB of Camden*, IT, 13 May 2008 at [27]-[29].

[80] As to the exception to the duty to give a notice to the applicant in cases where the request for information is vexatious, see §13–009.

[81] FOIA s 17(5); FOI(S)A s 16(5). As to the time for compliance, see §§11–022 to 11–030. As to the requirement to give a notice in cases where a request for information is vexatious, see §13–009.

3. REPEAT REQUESTS

014 Introduction

A public authority is not obliged to comply with a request for information where it is a request for information[82] which is identical or substantially similar to a previous request made by the same applicant, where the public authority has already complied with that previous request and where a reasonable interval has yet to elapse between compliance with the previous request and the making of the current request.[83] Similar provisions apply under the Data Protection Act 1998.[84]

015 Identical or substantially similar request

The Freedom of Information Act 2000 does not give any guidance as to what is meant by 'identical' or 'substantially similar'. Whilst the former concept should not prove problematic for most public authorities, it is likely that the concept of 'substantially similar' will provoke differences of opinion between public authorities and applicants. The provision is unfortunately worded, in that by altering a mere word or two used in a first request it is possible to change completely the information sought in a second request. In particular, an applicant may very properly restrict a request for information by reference to a period within which the information was created or first held by the public authority. Such a temporal restriction will generally be mutually advantageous, limiting the scope of the task for the public authority and helping to ensure that the cost of compliance does not exceed the applicable limit. It may be that this temporally-limited request does not yield the information anticipated or that it yields information that points to further information outside the original limit. Accordingly, a staged approach to the request process is generally to be commended rather than condemned. This reasoning, together with the concatenation of the phrase 'substantially similar' with the word 'identical', suggests that the mischief to which the provision is directed is the wasting of a public authority's resources through the provision of information to an applicant who has already been provided with that information. It is not intended to preclude a request the words of which may be substantially similar to a previous request but where the information that answers its terms is materially different.[85] It is notable that the provisions on repeat requests only apply where the requests are made by the same person, so its effect may be side-stepped by the

---

[82] In other words, the public authority is not obliged to comply with its duties under s 1(1) of the FOIA or under s 1 of the FOI(S)A.

[83] FOIA s 14(2); FOI(S)A s 14(2). The EIR regime has no specific provision to this effect. However, the same objective is arguably secured by it excluding manifestly unreasonable requests: EIR reg 12(4)(b); EI(S)R reg 10(4)(b); see §6–032.

[84] See §5–053.

[85] The Home Office Freedom of Information Unit suggested that one of the factors which could be taken into account when assessing whether a request was 'substantially similar' to an earlier one was whether it was reasonable to expect that fresh information would be disclosed on the new request: House of Commons, *Public Administration Committee—Third Report* (Cm 4355, 1999) Annex 6, para 31 (see ch 1 n 64). However, it would seem that this is a matter which goes to the reasonableness of the interval between the requests (as to which, see §12–016) rather than to the similarity of the requests.

expedient of placing a request through another person. Where identical or substantially similar requests are made by different persons, it may be appropriate to consider whether the later request is vexatious.[86]

12–016 A reasonable interval between requests

Unlike the Data Protection Act 1998,[87] the Freedom of Information Act 2000 does not give any guidance as to what should be taken into account when determining whether a reasonable interval has elapsed. However, it is likely that similar considerations will apply, such as the nature of the information, the purpose for which the information is held and the frequency with which the information is altered.[88]

12–017 Notices in cases of repeat requests

If a public authority is relying on a claim that it is not obliged to comply with a request for information because the request is a repeat request, then (subject to one exception)[89] it must give a notice to that effect to the applicant within the time for compliance with s 1(1) of the Freedom of Information Act 2000.[90]

12–018 Position under the Data Protection Act 1998

Where a data controller has previously complied with a request made under s 7 of the Data Protection Act 1998, he is not obliged to comply with a subsequent identical or similar request made by the same individual unless a reasonable interval has elapsed between compliance with the previous request and the making of the current request.[91] When deciding what constitutes a reasonable interval for these purposes, regard is to be had to the nature of the data, the purpose for which the data are processed and the frequency with which the data are altered.[92]

---

[86] As to vexatious requests, see §§12–010 to 12–013.

[87] As to the assessment of a 'reasonable interval' under the DPA, see §5–053.

[88] See the DPA s 8(4). During the debate in the House of Lords, the frequency with which the information is altered was put forward by the government spokesman as one of the factors which would affect the reasonableness of an interval: Hansard HL vol 617 col 1014 (17 October 2000).

[89] As to the exception to the duty to give a notice to the applicant in cases where the request for information is a repeat request, see §13–009.

[90] FOIA s 17(5); FOI(S)A s 16(5). As to the requirement to give a notice to the applicant in cases where the request for information is a repeat request, see also §13–009.

[91] DPA s 8(3).

[92] DPA s 8(4).

CHAPTER 13
The Response

1. THE DUTY TO SEARCH

001 The nature of the duty

The basic duties imposed by s 1 of the Freedom of Information Act 2000 apply to information held by the public body at the time that the request is received.[1] That information to which the duties apply includes information held by another person on behalf of the public authority.[2] Invariably a public authority will have to search through the information that it holds in order to respond to a request for information, whether in order to identify the information that it holds which answers the terms of that request or to establish that it does not hold any information answering the terms of that request. A public authority may require an applicant to provide further particulars in order to identify and locate the information requested.[3] The s 46 Code of Practice encourages public authorities to have record systems that include the capacity to search for information requested under the Freedom of Information Act 2000.[4]

13– 002 The extent of the duty

The Act does not stipulate the extent to which a public authority must search for information answering the terms of a request. However, the time which a public authority spends, or would need to spend, locating and retrieving the information answering the terms of a request is relevant to whether the cost of compliance would be excessive.[5] On a complaint by an applicant, the Information Commissioner will investigate the adequacy of the search made by the public authority. The Commissioner should not accept the public authority's bare assertion that it has carried out an adequate search.[6] An applicant who is unsatisfied with the conclusion reached by the Information Commissioner may appeal to the Tribunal. The Tribunal will review the Commissioner's conclusion, if necessary hearing evidence on the issue. Provided that a statement from the public authority is thorough, not contradicted by other material and seemingly accurate, the Tribunal will not necessarily permit an oral hearing to have the adequacy of the search explored in cross-examination.[7] The Tribunal will decide the issue on the balance of probabilities.[8] The Tribunal does not demand certainty.[9] A public authority must carry out a reasonable search.[10] In deciding whether the search has been a reasonable one, the Tribunal will consider all relevant factors, including the public authority's analysis of the request, the scope of its search, and the rigour and efficiency with which it conducted the search.[11] The measure of what is reasonable is coloured by the cost limit set by the

---

[1] FOIA s 1(1), (4); FOI(S)A s 1(1), (4); EIR reg 5(1); EI(S)R reg 5(1).

[2] FOIA s 3(2)(b); FOI(S)A s 3(2)(b); EIR reg 3(2); EI(S)R reg 3(3). See further §9– 010.

[3] FOIA s 1(3); FOI(S)A s 1(3). See further §11– 012

[4] Section 46 Code of Practice para 9.3.

[5] FOI & DP (Limit & Fees) Regs reg 4(3). See §§12– 001 to 12– 009. There is no equivalent provision in the environmental information regime.

[6] *Berend v IC and LB of Richmond*, IT, 12 July 2007 at [84].

[7] *Ames v IC and Cabinet Office*, IT, 24 April 2008 at [14].

[8] *Bromley v IC and Environment Agency*, IT, 31 August 2007 at [13]; *Fortune v IC and National Patient Safety Agency*, IT, 16 April 2008 at [6]; *Ames v IC and Cabinet Office*, IT, 24 April 2008 at [10]; *Reed v IC*, IT, 3 July 2009 at [32]-[38].

[9] *Bromley v IC and Environment Agency*, IT, 31 August 2007 at [13]; *Dudley v IC*, IT, 20 April 2009 at [31]; *Innes v IC*, IT, 27 October 2009.

[10] *Reed v IC*, IT, 3 July 2009 at [42].

[11] *Bromley v IC and Environment Agency*, IT, 31 August 2007 at [12]-[13]; *Ames v IC and Cabinet Office*, IT, 24 April 2008 at [107]; *Malcolm v IC*, IT, 19 December 2008; *Dudley v IC*, IT, 20 April 2009 at [24]-[47]; *Reed v IC*, IT, 3 July 2009 at [39][-56].

Regulations.[12] It would seem that in reviewing the reasonableness of a public authority's search, the Tribunal will do so on the basis of the filing systems available to the public authority notwithstanding shortcomings in those systems.[13]

2. NON-SUBSTANTIVE RESPONSES

003 Introduction

A person's entitlement to receive information requested and to be informed whether the information requested is held by the public authority[14] is made subject to certain other provisions of the Freedom of Information Act 2000.[15] The bases upon which a public authority may refuse to comply with a request may conveniently be grouped into two broad classes:

    (1)   Procedural bases, where the form of the request is defective in a manner that entitles the public authority to treat it as not representing a proper request.

    (2)   Substantive bases, where the information is exempt information, either by virtue of a provision conferring absolute exemption or where the information is exempt information by virtue of a qualified exemption and the public interest is on balance against disclosure.

The basis for refusal influences the form of the refusal notice that must be given to the applicant.

004 Requests defective in form

There are four types of formal defect that entitle a public authority to refuse or to place in abeyance a request for information:

    (1)   Inadequately particularised request: where a public authority reasonably requires further particulars in order to identify and locate the information requested, then, provided that it has informed the applicant of that requirement, it is not obliged to provide the information requested until it is provided with the further particulars that it requires to identify and locate that information.[16]

    (2)   Vexatious or repeat request: a public authority is not obliged to comply with a request for information if that request is vexatious.[17] Nor is a public authority obliged to comply with a request for information if it is a request which is identical or substantially similar to a previous request made by the same applicant, the public

---

[12] The FOI & DP (Limits & Fees) Regs: see *Francis v IC and South Essex Partnership Foundation NHS Trust*, IT, 21 July 2008. In other words, 18 hours or 24 hours (at £25 per hour), depending on the type of public authority.

[13] *Francis v IC and South Essex Partnership Foundation NHS Trust*, IT, 21 July 2008 at [18]-[19]; *Dudley v IC*, IT, 20 April 2009 at [24]-[47].

[14] Termed, in this work, 'the access right' and 'the existence right', respectively: see §1– 005(4).

[15] FOIA s 1(2); FOI(S)A s 1(6).

[16] FOIA s 1(3); FOI(S)A s 1(3). As to requiring further particulars of a request for information, see §11– 011 to 11– 013. An analogous exemptions applies in relation to environmental information: EIR reg 12(4)(c); EI(S)R reg 10(4)(c); and see §§6– 022 and 6– 032. Similarly in relation to the DPA: s 7(3); and see §5– 039.

[17] FOIA s 14(1); FOI(S)A s 14(1). In relation to environmental information: EIR reg 12(4)(b); EI(S)R reg 10(4)(b). In relation to the DPA, there is no such let out: see §5– 043. As to vexatious requests, see §§12– 010 to 12– 013.

authority has already complied with the previous request, and a reasonable interval has yet to elapse between compliance with the previous request and the making of the current request.[18]

(3)   Failure to pay required fee: where a public authority has given a fees notice to an applicant, it is not obliged to comply with the request for information unless the applicant pays the fee within the period of three months beginning with the day on which the fees notice was given to the applicant.[19]

(4)   Excessive cost of compliance: where a public authority estimates that the cost of complying with a request for information would exceed the appropriate limit, it is not obliged to comply with that request.[20]

13–005 Substantive refusals

Where a request is made in respect of information which is exempt information by virtue of a provision conferring absolute exemption, a public authority is not obliged to communicate the information to the applicant.[21] Similarly, where a request is made in respect of information which is exempt information (but not by virtue of a provision conferring absolute exemption), a public authority is not obliged to communicate that information to the applicant where the public interest in maintaining the exemption outweighs the public interest in disclosing the information.[22] In either such case, however, the public authority is not automatically relieved of its duty to confirm or deny that it holds the information.

13–006 Information excluded from the duty to confirm or deny

Where a request is made in respect of information in relation to which an absolute exclusion from the duty to confirm or deny applies, a public authority is not obliged to comply with the request.[23] Where a request is made in respect of information in relation to which there is an exclusion (but not an absolute exclusion) of the duty to confirm or deny, a public authority is not obliged to comply with the request where the public interest in maintaining the exclusion of the duty to confirm or deny outweighs the public interest in disclosing whether the public authority holds the information.[24]

13–007 Deferred decision

Where a request is made in respect of information in relation to which there is an exclusion (but not an absolute exclusion) of the duty to confirm or deny or in respect of information which is exempt information (but not by virtue of a provision conferring absolute exemption), a public

---

[18] FOIA s 14(2); FOI(S)A s 14(2); DPA s 8(3). The EIR and the EI(S)R have no specific provision on repeat requests. As to repeat requests, see §§12–014 to 12–018.

[19] FOIA s 9(2); FOI(S)A s 9(3); DPA s 7(2)(b). As to fees notices, see §§11–014 to 11–021. As to the position under the EIR and the EI(S)R, see §6–023.

[20] FOIA s 12(1); FOI(S)A s 12(1). As to the situations where the cost of complying with a request for information would be excessive, see §§12–001 to 12–009.

[21] FOIA s 2(2)(a); FOI(S)A s 2(1)(a); EIR regs 5(1) and 12(3); EI(S)R reg 5(1) and 10(3); DPA s 7(1).

[22] FOIA s 2(2)(b); FOI(S)A s 2(1)(b); EIR regs 5(1) and 12(3); EI(S)R reg 5(1) and 10(3).

[23] FOIA s 2(1)(a); DPA s 7(1)(a).

[24] FOIA s 2(1)(b); EIR reg 12(6); EI(S)R reg 10(8).

authority may defer compliance with the request for such time as is reasonable in the circumstances pending a decision on where the public interest lies.[25]

3. REFUSAL TO COMMUNICATE

008 Introduction

Where a public authority relies on a claim that it is not obliged to comply with a request for information, it is required to give the applicant a notice to that effect.[26] The purpose of a refusal notice is not just to ensure that an applicant is informed of the outcome of a request for information, but also to ensure that an unsuccessful applicant is aware of the reasons why his request has been refused and to enable him to decide on an informed basis whether to take the matter further.[27] The expectation is that the requirement to give such a notice will make it less likely that a public authority will make an unjustified claim that it is not obliged to comply with a request for information, as it will be required to apply its mind to the justification at the time.[28] The nature of a refusal notice and the time within which it is to be provided to an applicant depend upon the basis for refusal, as well as upon what it is that is being refused. These may be divided into the following categories:

(1) refusal notices where a request is vexatious or is a repeat request;

(2) refusal notices where the cost of compliance is excessive;

(3) refusal notices where the information falls within Part II of the Act but no public interest balancing exercise is involved; and

(4) refusal notices where information falls within Part II of the Act and a public interest balancing exercise is involved.

An applicant may apply to the Information Commissioner under s 50 complaining that a refusal notice does not comply with the requirements of Part I of the Act.[29] The Commissioner may issue a decision notice that specifies whether the public authority has or has not complied with the requirements of s 17. A party dissatisfied with that decision notice may appeal to the Tribunal in relation to the finding as to the adequacy of the refusal notice.[30]

009 Refusal notice where request is vexatious or is a repeat request

Where a public authority is relying on a claim that it is not obliged to comply with a request for

---

[25] FOIA s 10(3). There is no equivalent provision in FOI(S)A, EIR, EI(S)R or DPA.

[26] FOIA s 17; FOI(S)A s 16; EIR reg 14; EI(S)R reg 13. As to refusal notices under the EIR, see §6– 027.

[27] In some jurisdictions, public authorities are subject to more onerous duties in relation to explaining their decisions. See, eg, the Freedom of Information Act 1997 (Republic of Ireland) s 10(2), the Freedom of Information Act 1982 (Cth of Australia) s 26(1) and *Re Luton and Commissioner of Taxation* (1996) AAR 492.

[28] See, eg, Australian Law Reform Commission and Administrative Review Council, *Open Government: A Review of the Federal Freedom of Information Act 1982*, ALRC 77, ARC 40 (Canberra, 1995) para 7.19.

[29] See §28– 007.

[30] See further §§28– 017 to 28– 029. For example: *Hogan and Oxford CC v IC*, IT, 17 October 2006 at [22]–[24].

information because it is a vexatious or repeat request,[31] then (subject to one exception) it must give the applicant a notice stating that fact.[32] The exception is that the public authority need not give such a notice where it has previously given the applicant a notice in relation to a previous request for information stating that it is relying on such a claim[33] and, in all the circumstances, it would be unreasonable to expect the public authority to serve a further notice in relation to the current request.[34] The Freedom of Information Act 2000 does not impose upon a public authority a duty to state why it considers a request to be a vexatious or repeat request and it must be questionable whether it would be reasonable to expect a public authority which is faced with a vexatious or repeat request to provide advice and assistance in this respect to the applicant.[35] As is the case with other refusal notices, any such notice must contain particulars of the public authority's procedures for dealing with complaints about requests for information (or state that the authority does not have such a procedure)[36] and it must provide details of the right to apply for a decision by the Information Commissioner as to whether the request has been properly dealt with.[37] Any notice must be served within the time for compliance with s 1(1) of the Freedom of Information Act 2000.[38]

13–010 Refusal notice where cost of compliance is excessive

Where a public authority is relying on a claim that it is not obliged to comply with a request for information because the cost of compliance would be excessive,[39] then it must give the applicant a notice stating that fact.[40] The Freedom of Information Act 2000 does not impose upon a public authority an express duty to state why it considers that the cost of complying with a request would be excessive, but it may be reasonable to expect a public authority which is faced

---

[31] Under FOIA s 14, or FOI(S)A s 14. As to vexatious requests, see §§12–010 to 12–013. As to repeat requests, see §§12–014 to 12–018.

[32] FOIA s 17(5); FOI(S)A s 16(5).

[33] The FOIA s 17(6)(b) refers to a previous notice that the public authority is relying on a claim that s 14 applies and not just a previous notice that the public authority is relying on a claim that a request was vexatious. Accordingly, it would seem that a public authority is entitled to rely upon the provisions of s 17(6) where it has previously served either a notice that a request is vexatious or a notice that a request is a repeat request. The Scottish provisions are slightly more restrictive, in that a public authority is only excused from giving a notice if it has previously given a notice in respect of an identical or substantially similar request: FOI(S)A s 16(5)(a).

[34] FOIA s 17(6); FOI(S)A s 16(5). In relation to information held by Scottish public authorities, there is an additional requirement that the previous request was identical or substantially similar to the current request: FOI(S)A s 16(5)(a).

[35] That is, pursuant to the duty imposed by s 16(1) of the FOIA or s 15(1) of the FOI(S)A. Paragraph 15 of the s 45 Code of Practice suggests that a public authority is not expected to provide assistance to applicants whose requests are vexatious.

[36] FOIA s 17(7)(a); FOI(S)A s 19(a).

[37] That is, the right conferred by the FOIA s 50 or the FOI(S)A s 47: FOIA s 17(1)(b); FOI(S)A s 19(b). In relation to information held by Scottish public authorities, the notice must also contain particulars of the right to apply to the public authority for a review of its decision under s 20(1): FOI(S)A s 19(b).

[38] FOIA s 17(5). In relation to information held by Scottish public authorities, the notice must be given within the time for compliance laid down by s 10 of the FOI(S)A: FOI(S)A s 16(5). As to the time for compliance, see §§11–022 to 11–030.

[39] Under the FOIA s 12 or the FOI(S)A s 12. As to the situation where the cost of complying with a request for information would be excessive, see §§12–001 to 12–009.

[40] FOIA s 17(5); FOI(S)A s 16(4).

with such a request to provide advice and assistance in this respect to the applicant.[41] As is the case with other refusal notices, such a notice must contain particulars of the public authority's procedures for dealing with complaints about requests for information (or state that the authority does not have such a procedure)[42] and it must provide details of the right to apply for a decision by the Information Commissioner as to whether the request has been properly dealt with.[43] The notice must be given within the time for compliance with s 1(1) of the Freedom of Information Act 2000.[44]

11 Refusal notice where information is excluded from the duty to confirm or deny or where information is exempt information

Where a public authority is to any extent relying on a claim that any of the information requested is excluded from the duty to confirm or deny (whether an absolute exclusion or otherwise) or a claim that information is exempt information, it must give the applicant a notice to that effect.[45] Such a notice must state that the public authority is relying on the relevant claim,[46] it must specify the exclusion or exemption in question[47] and it must state (if it would not otherwise be apparent) why the exclusion or exemption applies.[48] Given that: (a) a public authority is in an advantaged position to determine whether information held by it falling within the terms of a request for information is or is not exempt information and, where it is exempt information by virtue of a qualified exemption, to determine the outcome of the public interest test in s 2(2) of the Act; (b) the subject of that determination is a matter in which the recipient public authority will often have an interest; and (c) the duty under s 16(1) to provide

---

[41] Pursuant to the duty imposed by the FOIA s 16(1) or the FOI(S)A s 15(1). para 14 of the s 45 Code of Practice suggests that in such a case a public authority should give an indication of what information could be provided within the cost ceiling and should consider advising the applicant that by reforming or refocusing the request, it may be possible to supply information for a lower, or no, fee.

[42] FOIA s 17(7)(a); FOI(S)A s 19(a).

[43] In other words, the right conferred by s 50 in the FOIA and s 47 in the FOI(S)A: FOIA s 17(1)(b); FOI(S)A s 19(b). In relation to information held by Scottish public authorities, the notice must also contain particulars of the right to apply to the public authority for a review of its decision under s 20(1): FOI(S)A s 19(b). The applicant can further appeal to the Tribunal, and the Tribunal can inquire into the matters that have and have not been taken into account by the public authority in carrying out the estimate and make an overall judgment as to its reasonableness: *Urmenyi v IC and LB of Sutton*, IT, 13 July 2007 at [16].

[44] FOIA s 17(5). In relation to information held by Scottish public authorities, the notice must be given within the time for compliance laid down by s 10: FOI(S)A s 16(4). As to the time for compliance, see §§11–022 to 11–030.

[45] FOIA s 17(1); FOI(S)A s 16(1).

[46] FOIA s 17(1)(a); FOI(S)A s 16(1)(b). In relation to information held by Scottish public authorities, subject to s 18 of the FOI(S)A, the notice must also state that the public authority holds the information: FOI(S)A s 16(1)(a). The difference in treatment presumably arises from the fact that s 16(1) of the FOI(S)A applies only to requests for information which the public authority holds, whereas s 17(1) of the FOIA applies to any request for information. Section 18 of the FOI(S)A disapplies s 16(1)(a) and (2) in a case where the public authority considers that to reveal whether the information exists or is held would be contrary to the public interest.

[47] FOIA s 17(1)(b); FOI(S)A s 16(1)(c).

[48] FOIA s 17(1)(c); FOI(S)A s 16(1)(d). In this context it is unlikely that it will be sufficient for the public authority merely to paraphrase the wording of the exemption. The addition of this requirement was a departure from the position in the Freedom of Information Bill 1999, cl 15. See also House of Commons, *Public Administration—Third Report* (Cm 4355, 1999) Annex 6, para 39B (see ch 1 n 64) and House of Lords, *Draft Freedom of Information Bill—First Report* (Select Committee Report HL 97), Session 1998–1999, 27 July 1999, paras 51 to 54 (see ch 1 n 125). This is the line that has been taken by the Tribunal: *Hogan and Oxford CC v IC*, IT, 17 October 2006 at [22].

431

assistance to a person who has made a request for information, it is suggested that a public authority in discharging its duty under s 17(1) must be astute to describe and characterise accurately the information that answers the request for information. While the statement provided under s 17(1) ought not itself disclose exempt information, that statement must describe the information sufficiently in order to state why an exemption applies. A misdescription or mischaracterisation of that information, particularly if it facilitates reliance upon an exemption, will not constitute a notice which 'states' why the exemption applies. The experience of the comparative jurisdictions is that where there are a significant number of 'pieces' of information to which different exemptions apply, a statement is often most conveniently done in tabular form, with a row for each discrete piece of information and a column for each exemption and explanations for the same. However, the public authority is not required to state why an exemption applies if, and to the extent that, that statement would involve the disclosure of information which would itself be exempt information.[49] As is the case with other refusal notices, such a notice must contain particulars of the public authority's procedures for dealing with complaints about requests for information (or state that the authority does not have such a procedure)[50] and it must provide details of the right to apply for a decision by the Information Commissioner as to whether the request has been properly dealt with.[51] The notice must be served within the time for compliance with s 1(1) of the Freedom of Information Act 2000.[52]

13–012 Refusal notice where disclosure would be contrary to the public interest

Where a public authority is to any extent relying on a claim that any information is exempt information (but not by virtue of a provision conferring absolute exemption) and that the public interest in maintaining the exemption outweighs the public interest in disclosing the information, then it must (subject to one exception)[53] state the reasons why it has so decided.[54] Similarly, where a public authority is to any extent relying on a claim that any information is subject to an exclusion (but not an absolute exclusion) from the duty to confirm or deny (but not by virtue of a provision conferring absolute exclusion) and that the public interest in maintaining the exclusion of the duty to confirm or deny outweighs the public interest in disclosing whether the public authority holds the information, then it must (subject to one

---

[49] FOIA s 17(4); FOI(S)A s 16(3).

[50] FOIA s 17(7)(a); FOI(S)A s 19(a).

[51] In other words, the right conferred by s 50 of the FOIA and s 47 of the FOI(S)A: FOIA s 17(1)(b); FOI(S)A s 19(b). In relation to information held by Scottish public authorities, the notice must also contain particulars of the right to apply to the public authority for a review of its decision under s 20(1): FOI(S)A s 19(b).

[52] FOIA s 17(1). In relation to information held by Scottish public authorities, the notice must be served in accordance with the time allowed for compliance with the request by s 10: FOI(S)A s 16(1).

[53] In relation to information held by Scottish public authorities, a second exception applies: see n 57.

[54] FOIA s 17(3); FOI(S)A s 16(2). In this context it would be prudent for the public authority to specify the public interest factors, both for and against disclosure, that it has taken into account. Failure to do so may result in a finding by the Tribunal that the public authority has failed to provide a valid refusal notice: see, eg, *Hogan and Oxford CC v IC*, IT, 17 October 2006 at [22]–[24].

exception)[55] state the reasons why it has so decided.[56] The exception in each case is that the public authority need not make such a statement if, and to the extent that, the statement would involve the disclosure of information which would itself be exempt information.[57] The reasons must be stated in the refusal notice or in a separate notice given within such time as is reasonable in the circumstances.[58] The provision for separate notice to be given is to allow for the situation where the public authority has deferred its decision on where the public interest lies.[59] Where a public authority has deferred its decision on where the public interest lies, then the notice given to the applicant[60] must:

(a) state that the public authority has not yet reached a decision as to where the balance of the public interest lies;

(b) contain an estimate of the date by which the public authority expects that it will have reached that decision;[61] and

(c) contain all the usual matters that must be included in a refusal notice where the information is exempt.[62]

013 Partial refusal

It may be the case that a request for information will seek both information which a public authority is required to communicate to the applicant and information which it is not required to communicate, for example, because it is exempt information. In such a case, a public authority must communicate the information which it is required to communicate in the normal way and follow the normal procedures in relation to that information which it refuses to communicate.

014 Redaction

The Freedom of Information Act 2000 provides for the communication of information to

---

[55] In relation to information held by Scottish public authorities, a second exception applies: see n 57.

[56] FOIA s 17(3); FOI(S)A s 16(2). In this context it would be prudent for the public authority to specify the public interest factors, both for and against disclosure, that it has taken into account.

[57] FOIA s 17(4); FOI(S)A s 16(3). In relation to information held by Scottish public authorities, FOI(S)A s 18, provides for a further exception in a case where the public authority considers that to reveal whether the information exists or is held would be contrary to the public interest.

[58] FOIA s 17(3). As the FOI(S)A does not provide for a public authority to defer a decision on where the public interest lies in such a case, that Act contains no provision for a separate notice to be served at a time after the service of the refusal notice.

[59] See the FOIA s 10(3) and §11–028. As to the position in relation to information held by Scottish public authorities, see §11–028 fn 111.

[60] That is, the notice given in accordance with s 17(1) of the FOIA.

[61] These estimates should be realistic and reasonable, particularly as it is likely that public authorities will be expected to comply with their estimates. If an estimate is exceeded, the public authority should apologise and provide reasons for the delay.

[62] FOIA s 17(2). As to requirement (c), see §13–011. As the FOI(S)A does not provide for a public authority to defer such a decision, that Act contains no similar provisions as to notices.

applicants and not for the provision of documents.[63] Accordingly, where an applicant requests information which forms part of a document and that document also contains other information which the applicant is not entitled to receive (for example, because the information is exempt information or because it is outside the terms of the request), the public authority must decide whether it will:

— provide the applicant with the entire document, thereby effectively waiving the exemption in relation to any exempt information[64] or providing the applicant with information that has not been requested;[65]

— redact the document so that the applicant only receives what he is entitled to and what has been asked for; or

— provide the information by a means other than the provision of a copy of the document (eg by the provision of a newly created document containing only those parts of the original document containing information to which the applicant is entitled or by the provision of a summary of the document).

Whichever option is adopted, the public authority is not entitled to avoid its obligations in relation to the requested information that is either not exempt information or is exempt information solely by virtue of a qualified exemption for which the public interest weighs in favour of disclosure.[66] Where the second or third option is chosen, a public authority should be careful to ensure that any new or redacted document does not create a misleading impression of the information which is held by the public authority. If there is a risk of such a misleading impression being created, then it might be more appropriate to consider providing the information in an alternative manner, such as by way of a summary.[67] In relation to statistical information, the House of Lords has held that perturbation of the information by a process of 'barnardisation'[68] is a matter of presentation of information, rather than altering the

---

[63] Similarly, EIR, EI(S)R and DPA (with the last speaking of 'data'). This is in contrast to freedom of information legislation in all but one of the comparable jurisdictions. Where provision is made for access to documents, provision is also made for the redaction of those documents. See, eg, the Freedom of Information Act 1982 (Commonwealth of Australia) s 22(1) (substituted in 2010); Access to Information Act 1982 (Canada) s 25; Freedom of Information Act 1997 (Republic of Ireland) s 13.

[64] In other words, a discretionary disclosure: see §§9– 036 to 9– 038 and 14– 007 to 14– 014.

[65] In Australia (where the unit of disclosure and exemption is a 'document'), the approach taken where disclosure of a single document would disclose information that would reasonably be regarded as irrelevant to a request, is to ask whether such disclosure would reasonably, as opposed to irrationally or absurdly, be considered or looked on as irrelevant and, if so, not include it in the response: *Re Russell Island Development Association Inc and Department of Primary Industries and Energy* (1994) 33 ALD 683.

[66] This is spelled out in the environmental information and data protection regimes: EIR reg 12(11); EI(S)R reg 10(7); DPA s7(5). This accords with the view expressed by the government spokesman in the House of Lords: Hansard HL vol 617 cols 930–931 (17 October 2000). The House of Commons Public Administration Committee had recommended that an express provision to this effect be included in the Act: House of Commons, *Public Administration—Third Report* (Cm 4355, 1999) para 120 (see ch 1 n 64). This is the approach adopted in the Official Information Act 1982 (New Zealand) s 17.

[67] It is likely that the difficulty of redacting information which an applicant is not entitled to see is one of the circumstances which a public authority would be entitled to take into account when deciding whether it is reasonably practicable to give effect to an applicant's preference as to the means of communication of the information: FOIA s 11; FOI(S)A s 11. As to the applicant's preference as to the means of communication of the information, see §13– 017. See also *Craven v IC*, IT, 13 May 2008 at [29].

[68] That is, by expressly adding -1, 0 or 1 to very low values so as to make more difficult identification of the individuals reflected in those values.

information.[69]

4. COMMUNICATION OF INFORMATION

015 Introduction

The primary obligation on a public authority which communicates information pursuant to the Freedom of Information Act 2000 is to communicate that information by any means which are reasonable in the circumstances.[70] It is implicit in the Freedom of Information Act 2000 that the communication of information does not necessarily involve the provision of a copy of that information to an applicant, and that in certain circumstances the provision of a summary or of an opportunity to inspect a record of it will be sufficient.[71] More onerous obligations apply under the Data Protection Act 1998 (as will be seen in §13– 021).

016 Obligation to provide information by reasonable means

Without the expression of a preference by an applicant for a particular means of communication, a public authority may comply with a request for information by communicating that information by any means which are reasonable in the circumstances.[72] The notion of 'reasonableness' of communication must be informed by the purpose of the Act, which is to facilitate rather than hinder the disclosure of information held by public authorities.[73] The circumstances which will be relevant for these purposes would normally include the form in which the relevant information is held by a public authority, the volume of the information to be communicated, the cost of different means of communication and the applicant's ability to receive or read different means of communication. There seems no sensible reason why different 'pieces' of information answering the terms of a request should not be communicated by different means, if that is what is reasonable in the circumstances. The House of Lords has held that, provided that it notifies the applicant that it has done so, a public authority can 'perturb' requested statistical information by a process of 'barnardisation'[74] and that this perturbation will simply be a matter of presentation of requested information, rather than constituting an alteration of the information held by the public authority.[75]

017 Preferences expressed by the applicant

The entitlement of a public authority to communicate the information requested by any means

---

[69] *Common Services Agency v IC* [2008] UKHL 47, [2008] 1 WLR 1550 at [15].

[70] FOIA s 11(4); FOI(S)A s 11(4). The environmental information regime leans more towards compliance with the applicant's wishes: EIR reg 6(1); EI(S)R reg 6(1); and see §6– 026. The data protection regime similarly leans in favour of an applicant's wishes: DPA s 7(1)(c) and 8(2); and see §5– 048.

[71] See, eg, the FOIA s 11(1)(b) and the FOI(S)A s 11(2)(c).

[72] FOIA s 11(4); FOI(S)A s 11(4).

[73] See §§1– 012, 1– 014 and 1– 032 to 1– 034.

[74] That is, by expressly adding -1, 0 or 1 to very low values so as to make more difficult identification of the individuals reflected in those values.

[75] *Common Services Agency v IC* [2008] UKHL 47, [2008] 1 WLR 1550 at [15].

435

that are reasonable in the circumstances is subject to the authority's obligation to communicate in accordance with an applicant's expressed preference, provided that that preference is one of the three enumerated in s 11(1) and to the extent that giving effect to the preference is reasonably practicable.[76] It should be noted, however, that the obligation to give effect to a preference expressed by an applicant only arises where he expresses it 'on making his request for information'.[77] Accordingly, it would seem that the obligation only arises if the applicant expresses his preference at the time when he makes his request for information and it does not arise if the preference is only expressed subsequently. In subordinating subs.(4) to subs.(1), it is implicit that the expressed preference may be for a means that is not reasonable in the circumstances. However, in so far as it is reasonably practicable to comply with an expressed preference, then the public authority must comply with it.[78] The specified means are the provision to the applicant of a copy of the information in a permanent form (or another form acceptable to the applicant),[79] the provision to the applicant of a reasonable opportunity to inspect a record containing the information,[80] and the provision to the applicant of a digest or summary of the information in a permanent form (or another form acceptable to the applicant).[81] The use of the phrase 'one or more' indicates that the applicant is not limited to expressing a preference for only one of the specified means. Again, there seems no sensible reason why an applicant should not be able to specify a particular means of communication for certain information and another means for the remainder. Alternatively, an applicant may express a preference for a particular means if the information answering the terms of the request is less than a particular quantity and for a different means if it is more. Such a course may be sensible having regard to fees, the cost of compliance and copyright issues.

13– 018   Reasonable practicability

The obligation to give effect to a preference expressed by an applicant for communication by way of one or more specified means only extends as far as it is reasonably practicable for the public authority to give effect to it.[82] In other contexts, the phrase 'reasonably practicable' has been equated to 'reasonable feasibility'.[83] Although this is a somewhat circular explanation, it is clear that the test of reasonable practicability falls somewhere between the two extremes of

---

[76] In relation to the environmental information regimes: EIR reg 6(1); EI(S)R reg 6(1); and see §6– 026.

[77] FOIA s 11(1). The FOI(S)A refers to an applicant expressing a preference 'in requesting information': FOI(S)A s 11(1). And see *Glasgow City Council & anor v Scottish IC* [2009] CSIH 73 at [53]-[57].

[78] FOIA s 11(1); FOI(S)A s 11(1).

[79] FOIA s 11(1)(a); FOI(S)A s 11(2)(a).

[80] FOIA s 11(1)(b); FOI(S)A s 11(2)(c).

[81] FOIA s 11(1)(c); FOI(S)A s 11(2)(b). The latter provision does not require that the digest or summary be in any particular form.

[82] FOIA s 11(1); FOI(S)A s 11(1). Section 11(5) of the FOI(S)A expressly provides that a public authority cannot rely upon the 'reasonable practicability' test to side-step any duty to make reasonable adjustments imposed upon it by the Disability Discrimination Act 1995 s 21.

[83] *Palmer and Saunders v Southend-on-Sea Borough Council* [1984] 1 WLR 1129, [1984] 1 All ER 945 (CA).

mere reasonableness and physical possibility.[84] A public authority may have regard to all the circumstances when deciding whether it is reasonably practicable to give effect to an applicant's preference, including the cost of doing so.[85] In addition to cost, such circumstances would normally include the form in which the relevant information is held by a public authority, the ease with which it can be converted from its existing form to the preferred form, the volume of the information to be communicated or summarised, and, where copies have been requested, any relevant copyright restrictions. It is suggested that where it is difficult to provide the applicant with information in a particular form without also providing him with information to which he is not entitled (for example, exempt information or information outside the scope of the request), this will be a relevant circumstance for the public authority to take into account.[86] Where a public authority determines that it is not reasonably practicable to comply with an applicant's preference, it must notify the applicant of its reasons for that determination.[87]

019   Other matters to be taken into account

When considering how to communicate information, a public authority will need to take into account any duties that it has under other legislation, where relevant.[88] The view has been taken by the Information Commissioner that, without some other statutory duty, there is no obligation on a public authority to translate information from one language to another for the purposes of responding to a request for information, apparently on the basis that if no information is held in that other language, then no such information exists.[89] Whilst this analysis might give rise to some interesting semiotic arguments, it would nevertheless be prudent for a public authority to consider whether its duty to provide advice and assistance requires it to translate information for the benefit of an applicant.[90] Further, a public authority may wish to consider whether its duty to provide advice and assistance requires it to provide some warning to an applicant in an appropriate case that the information being provided to him or her is subject to copyright and that this may restrict his or her future dealing with it.[91]

020   Effect of communication of information on the duty to confirm or deny

Where a public authority has complied with any obligation to communicate information to an

---

[84]   *Edwards v National Coal Board* [1949] 1 KB 704 at 712 (a health and safety case); *Marshall v Gotham Co Ltd* [1954] AC 360 at 370 (a health and safety case); *Palmer and Saunders v Southend-on-Sea Borough Council* [1984] 1 WLR 1129, [1984] 1 All ER 945 (CA); *London Underground Ltd v Noel* [2000] ICR 109 (CA).

[85]   FOIA s 11(2); FOI(S)A s 11(3).

[86]   As to redaction of documents, see §13– 014.

[87]   FOIA s 11(3); FOI(S)A s 11(3).

[88]   For example, duties under the Disability Discrimination Act 1995 or the Welsh Language Act 1993. A discussion of these duties is outside the scope of this work, but for examples of the guidance on this point, see the Scottish Ministers' Code of Practice, paras 7 to 8 and MoJ, *Fees and Aggregation Procedural Guidance*.

[89]   Information Commissioner's *Awareness Guidance No 29*.

[90]   As to the duty to provide advice and assistance, see §§10– 001 to 10– 006.

[91]   See, further: the Scottish Ministers' Code of Practice, paras 13 to 14; *Guidance on the Application of the Freedom of Information and Data Protection (Appropriate Limit and Fees) Regulations 2004*, para 9.2; MoJ, *Fees and Aggregation Procedural Guidance*; and Section 45 Code of Practice para 28.

applicant, then it is deemed to have complied with its duty to confirm or deny under the Freedom of Information Act 2000.[92]

13–021 Communication of information pursuant to the Data Protection Act 1998

The obligations relating to the manner in which information is communicated pursuant to the Data Protection Act 1998 are more onerous than the corresponding duties under the Freedom of Information Act 2000. In particular, the obligation to communicate to an individual information constituting personal data and information as to the source of those data[93] must be complied with by providing the individual with a copy of the information in permanent form.[94] A data controller is only absolved from this obligation if the supply of such a copy is not possible or would involve disproportionate effort[95] or if the individual agrees otherwise.[96] Further, where any of the information is expressed in terms which are not intelligible without explanation, the copy must be accompanied by such an explanation.[97] The Data Protection Act 1998 also prevents a data controller from deliberately modifying information in response to a request. The information communicated must be supplied by reference to the data in question as they stood at the time when the relevant request was made, and it may only take account of any amendments or deletions made since the time of the request if those amendments or deletions would have been made regardless of the receipt of the request.[98] Where a data controller is obliged to inform an individual of the logic involved in any decision-making process,[99] then that obligation does not extend to informing the individual of any information as to the decision-taking process which is a trade secret.[100]

---

[92] FOIA s 1(5).

[93] DPA s 7(1)(c).

[94] DPA s 8(2).

[95] DPA s 8(2)(a).

[96] DPA s 8(2)(b).

[97] DPA s 8(2).

[98] DPA s 8(6). See further §5–047.

[99] DPA s 7(1)(d).

[100] DPA s 8(5). As to the meaning of trade secrets, see §§25–049 to 25–056.

CHAPTER 14

Exemptions: General Principles

1.   THE UNIT OF EXEMPTION

14–001 Information, not documents

As noted earlier,[1] under the freedom of information regimes[2] both the existence and the access rights attach to 'information' rather than to documents or records.[3] Although the distinction is narrowed by 'information' being defined to mean 'recorded information',[4] the terms are not synonymous: a document or record may contain any number of discrete pieces of information. Similarly, engagement of each of the exemptions and consideration of the public interest both turn upon the quality or characteristics of the particular 'information', rather than of the document or record containing that information. It is information that has that quality or characteristic, rather than the document or record containing it, which becomes exempt from the duty to confirm or deny and from the duty to disclose.[5]

---

[1]   See §9–001.

[2]   That is, the FOIA, the FOI(S)A, the EIR, the EI(S)R and the DPA s 7.

[3]   FOIA s 1(1); FOI(S)A s 1(1); EIR regs 6(1), 12(6); EI(S)R regs 6(1), 10(8). The DPA s 7(1), gives a right to 'personal data' and s 1(1) defines 'data' to mean 'information' possessing certain characteristics.

[4]   FOIA s 84; FOI(S)A s 73. In the environmental information regime, information means 'information in written, visual, aural, electronic or any other material form': EIR reg 2(1); EI(S)R reg 2(1). Note that for the Commissioner's purposes in serving an information notice under s 51, information extends to unrecorded information: FOIA s 51(8); FOI(S)A s 50(9); EIR reg 18; EI(S)R reg 17. Although 'information' is not defined in the DPA, paras (b) and (c) of the s 1(1) definition require it to be recorded.

[5]   FOIA s 2(1) and (2); FOI(S)A ss 2(1) and 18(1); EIR regs 5(1) and 12(1); EI(S)R regs 5(1) and 10(1). *DBERR v IC and Friends of the Earth*, IT, 29 April 2008 at [28]-[30].

002 Exempt information

Information that falls within one or other of the exemptions in Part II of the Freedom of Information Act 2000 is termed 'exempt information'.[6] Only 'exempt information' is capable of being excused from the duty to disclose. If information falls within one of the 'absolute exemptions'[7] within Part II, then that will be sufficient to disapply the duty to communicate that information. If it does not fall within one of the absolute exemptions, disapplication of the duty to communicate will depend upon a consideration of the public interest. Similarly, under the environmental information regime, only 'environmental information' that falls within one of the exceptions in Part 3 (regs 12–15) is excused from the duty to disclose.[8] Apart from environmental information that includes personal data, disapplication of the duty to make such information available will depend upon a consideration of the public interest.[9]

003 Partial disclosure

A single document or record may contain some information that (or the existence of which) need not be disclosed and other information that (or the existence of which) must be disclosed. Where the information in a document is segregable then, provided that the information in the remainder of the document or record falls within the terms of a request, a public authority remains under its two duties in relation to that information. The use of 'information' as the unit of disclosure and of exemption makes it unnecessary for there to be a specific provision requiring a public authority to redact and disclose a document of which only a part contains information that is excused from disclosure.[10] An amendment to the Freedom of Information Bill that would have compelled a public authority to consider partial disclosure[11] was withdrawn following this explanation:

> We have been discussing whether the Bill in effect permits partial disclosure. It will in fact require that when some of the information that is requested is exempt but other information is not. The right of access in Clause 1 involves information that is recorded in any form. That means that the right of access attaches to the content of documents or records rather than to the documents or records themselves. When a document contains a mixture of disclosable and non-disclosable information, the disclosable information must be communicated to the applicant.[12]

---

[6] FOIA s 84, referring to ss 21(1), 22(1), 23(1), 24(1), 26(1), 27(1), 28(1), 29(1), 30(1) and (2), 31(1), 32(1) and (2), 33(2), 34(1), 35(1), 36(2), 37(1), 38(1), 39(1), 40(1) and (2), 41(1), 42(1), 43(1) and (2), and 44(1). FOI(S)A s 73, referring to ss 25(1), 26, 27(1) and (2), 28(1), 29(1), 30, 31(1) and (4), 32(1), 33(1) and (2), 34(1)–(4), 35(1), 36(1) and (2), 37(1), 38(1), 39(1) and (2), 40 and 41.

[7] FOIA s 2(2); FOI(S)A s 2(1). Absolute exemptions are considered at §14– 016.

[8] EIR reg 5(1); EI(S)R reg 5(1). But see EIR reg 3(4).

[9] EIR reg 12(1); EI(S)R reg 10(1).

[10] This is made explicit in the environmental information regime: EIR reg 12(11); EI(S)R reg 10(7). This is the approach taken in most of the comparative regimes: Freedom of Information Act 1982 (Cth of Aust) s 22(1) (substituted in 2010); The Official Information Act 1982 (NZ) s 17; Access to Information Act, (1982) (Canada) s 25; Freedom of Information Act 1997 (Ireland) s 13.

[11] Amendment no 25, moved by Lord Lucas: Hansard HL vol 617 col 930 (17 October 2000); withdrawn, col 932.

[12] Hansard HL vol 617 col 931 (17 October 2000) (Lord Falconer of Thoroton).

14–004 The moment at which exemption is determined

In many cases it will make no difference whether determination of the applicability of an exemption and the public interest balancing test are carried out at the moment of receipt of the request or at the time that the request is decided. However, in some circumstances even a small amount of time may effect a significant difference: for example, where in the intervening period information on the same topic as the requested information is formally released. The Tribunal's approach has generally been that the applicability of an exemption and the public interest balancing exercise should be determined by reference to the facts and circumstances as they stood at the time that the request should have been answered.[13] The approach is questionable.[14] However, a public authority may properly take into account circumstances or matters that come to light after the date of the request where those subsequent circumstances or matters shed light on the public interest at the time that it falls to be decided.[15] If an applicant is disadvantaged by this approach, the disadvantage can be circumvented by lodging a fresh request in identical terms.[16]

---

[13] In ordinary circumstances, the 20-day working limit is merely the endstop date, so that normally responses should be given before then. The date for consideration can normally be approximated as being within a short period after receipt of the request for information. See: *Bellamy v IC and DTI*, IT, 4 April 2006 at [6]; *DTI v IC*, IT, 10 November 2006 at [44], [46]; *DWP v IC*, IT, 5 March 2007 at [30]; *Campaign against the Arms Trade v IC and MoJ*, IT, 26 August 2008 at [43]-[53] (where it was held that the public authority had to consider matters as at the date at which it was obliged to respond to the request); *DCLG v IC*, IT, 22 July 2008; *Dept of Culture, Media and Sport v IC*, IT, 29 July 2008 at [4].

[14] While the Tribunal is correct in relation to the identification of the information that answers the terms of the request (FOIA s 1(4)); FOI(S)A s 1(4), and see §9– 011), it is difficult to understand the Tribunal's reason for extending this to the determination of whether the information is exempt information and, in the case of an applicable qualified exemption, to whether the public interest in maintaining the exemption outweighs the public interest in disclosing the information (eg: *DfES v IC and The Evening Standard*, IT, 19 February 2007 at [20(iv)]; *Baker v IC and Cabinet Office*, IT, 28 February 2007 at [25]; *Evans v IC and MoD*, IT, 26 October 2007 at [23]; *DBERR v IC and Friends of the Earth*, IT, 29 April 2008 at [104]; *Campaign against the Arms Trade v IC and MoJ*, IT, 26 August 2008 at [43]-[53]; *DBERR v IC and Friends of the Earth*, IT, 29 April 2008 at [104]-[111]; *Bellamy v IC and DBIS*, FTT, 23 February 2010 at [38(iii)]). Section 1(4) limits the extent of the public authority's duties under s 1(1) by reference to the information – not the exempt information – that the public authority holds at the time at which it receives the request. As with any administrative decision, unless statute otherwise provides, satisfaction of statutory requirements is decided on the basis of the facts known to the decision-maker at the time that the decision is made. On an appeal to a merit-review tribunal, that tribunal should, unless statute otherwise provides, determine an appeal based on the facts known to it at the time that it makes its decision: *Saber v SSHD* [UKHL 97, [2008] 3 All ER 97 at [2] ('common sense indicates that the final decision, whenever it is made, should be based on the most up to date evidence that is available,' dealing with an asylum-seeker was in need of international protection, although the common sense is not unique to that jurisdiction). This is the position that has been taken in other jurisdictions when dealing with requests under freedom of information legislation and having a provision similar to FOIA s 1(4): *Re Radar Investments and Health Insurance Commission* (2004) 80 ALD 733 at [30]-[42]. The Tribunal's power under FOIA s 58(2) is ample for this purpose. The FOIA does not confer an accrued right to information; nor does it impose an accrued liability to communicate information. In these circumstances, the taking of evidence in order to make findings so as to confirm or overturn an evaluative conclusion on a state of facts as they existed long before is not a fruitful exercise. In *OGC v IC* [2008] EWHC 774 (Admin), [2010] QB 98, [2008] ACD 54 at [98], the High Court doubted whether the Tribunal's approach was correct.

[15] *DTI v IC*, IT, 10 November 2006 at [46]–[47].

[16] If the facts and circumstances have truly changed, this should render the interval between the requests a 'reasonable' one, so that the applicant should not fall foul of the proscription against repeat requests: see §§12– 014 to 12– 016.

2. THE DUTY TO CONFIRM OR DENY

005 Exemption from the duty to confirm or deny: England, Wales & Northern Ireland

Under the Freedom of Information Act 2000, dispensation from the duty to confirm or deny turns upon the purpose for which the information is held, the nature of the information sought or, most commonly, the effect that confirmation or denial of holding the sought information would have. In the last case, the effect required in order to trigger dispensation varies according to the ground of exemption. In summary:

(1) Where the information sought:

    (a) has at any time been held for the purposes of a criminal investigation or is confidential information obtained for the purposes of the authority's functions relating to such an investigation;

    (b) has at any time been held as part of court or arbitral proceedings;

    (c) is held by a government department and relates to the formulation of policy or to Ministerial communications;

    (d) relates to communications with the Royal Family or the conferring of honours or dignities;

    (e) is required to be made available under the access to environmental information provisions; or

    (f) constitutes personal data of which the requester is the data subject,

then the public authority is excused from the duty to confirm or deny that such information is held.[17]

(2) Where, or to the extent that, exemption from confirmation or denial of a holding of the information sought is required:

    (a) to safeguard national security;

    (b) to avoid an infringement of the privileges of either House of Parliament;

    (c) to avoid an actionable breach of confidence;

    (d) to maintain the possibility of a claim of legal professional privilege; or

    (e) to avoid contravention of an enactment or of a community obligation, or to avoid a contempt of court,

then the public authority is excused from the duty to confirm or deny that any information answering the request is held.[18]

(3) Where the information sought:

    (a) is intended for future publication;

    (b) is supplied by, or relates to, bodies dealing with security matters; or

    (c) is confidential information obtained from the Government of any state other than the United Kingdom or from an international organisation or court,

then the duty to confirm or deny does not arise if, or to the extent that,

---

[17] FOIA ss 30(3), 32(2), 35(3), 37(2), 39(2) and 40(5)(a), respectively.

[18] FOIA ss 24(2), 34(2), 41(2), 42(2) and 44(2), respectively.

confirmation or denial that the requested public authority holds the information sought would itself involve the disclosure of any information so exempted from disclosure.[19]

(4) Where confirmation or denial that the public authority holds the information sought would, or would be likely to, prejudice:

    (a)   the defence of the nation or the effectiveness of the armed forces;

    (b)   relations between the United Kingdom and another state or an international organisation or the interests of the United Kingdom abroad;

    (c)   governmental relations within the United Kingdom;

    (d)   the economic interests of the United Kingdom or the financial interests of any administration within the United Kingdom;

    (e)   the efficacy of law enforcement;

    (f)   the exercise of an auditing body's functions;

    (g)   cabinet confidentiality, the frank provision of advice or the effective conduct of public affairs;

    (h)   the physical or mental health or safety of an individual; or

    (i)   the commercial interests of a person,

then the duty to confirm or deny is, to that extent, disapplied.[20]

(5) Where the information sought constitutes personal data of which the requester is not the data subject and where confirmation or denial that the public authority holds the information requested would contravene one of the data protection principles or s 10 of the Data Protection Act 1998 or the information is exempt from s 7(1)(a) of that Act, then the duty to confirm or deny is, to that extent, disapplied.[21]

(6) In relation to:

    (a)   information accessible to a requester by other means; or

    (b)   information that constitutes a trade secret,

there is no disapplication of the duty to confirm or deny the existence of such information.[22]

The existential regime in relation to 'environmental information'[23] is simpler and more limited. To the extent that confirmation or denial that the public authority holds the requested information would involve the disclosure of information that would adversely affect international relations, defence, national security or public safety, and that disclosure would not satisfy the public interest balancing test, then the public authority may issue a notice neither confirming nor denying that it holds the requested information.[24] Under the data protection regime, exemption from the duty to advise that personal data answering the terms of the

---

[19] FOIA ss 22(2), 23(5) and 27(4)(b), respectively.

[20] FOIA ss 26(3), 27(4)(a), 28(3), 29(2), 31(1), 33(3), 36(3), 38(2) and 43(3)), respectively.

[21] FOIA s 40(4)(b).

[22] FOIA ss 21 and 43(1), respectively.

[23] As to the meaning of which, see §6–010.

[24] EIR reg 12(6).

request are being processed by the public authority[25] turns on whether compliance with that duty would prejudice one of the protected interests in Part IV (ss 27–39).

006 **Exemption from the duty to confirm or deny: Scottish public authorities**

There is no discrete duty in the Freedom of Information (Scotland) Act 2002 to confirm or deny the existence of information answering the terms of a request. A Scottish public authority nevertheless can, in certain circumstances, reply to a request for information by neither confirming or denying the existence of the information, or some of the information, sought.[26] The ability to do so does not, of course, depend upon the existence of the information sought: to so confine it would rob the provision of its efficacy. The exercise involves assuming that the sought information exists (irrespective of whether or not it does). If, on that assumed basis, the public authority could give a refusal notice on the basis that that information would be exempt by virtue of:

— its disclosure substantially prejudicing relations between United Kingdom administrations;

— it relating to the formulation of Scottish Administration policy;

— its disclosure substantially prejudicing the effective conduct of public affairs;

— its exemption being required to safeguard national security;

— its disclosure being substantially prejudicial to the defence of the country;

— its disclosure being substantially prejudicial to international relations;

— it constituting a trade secret;

— its disclosure being substantially prejudicial to commercial interests or the economic or financial interest of the country;

— it having been held for the purposes of a criminal investigation;

— its disclosure being substantially prejudicial to a criminal investigation, prosecution, the administration of justice, tax collection, immigration controls and so forth;

— its disclosure endangering the health or safety of an individual; or

— it relating to communications with Her Majesty or other members of the Royal Family,[27]

then the public authority may proceed to consider whether confirming or denying the existence of the information would be contrary to the public interest.[28] If confirmation or denial would be so contrary to the public interest, the public authority is permitted to give the applicant a refusal notice that neither discloses that it holds the sought information nor sets out its reasoning in relation to the public interest.[29] Under the Environmental Information (Scotland) Regulations 2004, to the extent that a confirmation or denial that the public authority holds the requested information would involve the disclosure of information that would adversely affect international relations, defence, national security or public safety, and that disclosure would not satisfy the public interest balancing test, then the public authority may issue a notice neither

---

[25] That is, DPA s 7(1)(a).

[26] FOI(S)A s 18(1); EI(S)R reg 10(8).

[27] FOI(S)A ss 28, 29, 30, 31(1), 31(4), 32, 33(1)(a), 33(1)(b) and 33(2), 34, 35, 39(1) and 41 respectively.

[28] FOI(S)A s 18(1).

[29] FOI(S)A s 18(2).

confirming nor denying that it holds the requested information.[30]

3. THE DISCRETION TO MAINTAIN AN EXEMPTION[31]

14–007 Introduction

The Freedom of Information Act 2000 opens by describing an unrestricted entitlement to be informed as to the existence of, and to have communicated, information held by a public authority.[32] These broadly-described entitlements are shaped by a series of exemptions, some of which involve a consideration of the public interest. The applicability of an exemption, whether an absolute one or a qualified one, does not preclude the public authority from otherwise disclosing the information: a 'discretionary disclosure'. It simply means that the applicant has no entitlement under the Freedom of Information Act 2000 to the disclosure of that information. The Act expressly affirms this position.[33] In relation to central government departments it has occasionally been suggested that they may disclose and disseminate information under a prerogative power of the Crown.[34] Alternatively, the power to disclose and disseminate information may be seen as a common law power possessed by the Crown by virtue of its legal personality as a corporation sole.[35] Regardless of Crown status, all public authorities will also have power to disclose information where this is expressly provided for by statute or is necessarily incidental or conducive to the exercise of another statutory, prerogative or common law function: subject, of course, to any countervailing restrictions on disclosure:

(a) Some legislative provisions *prohibit* the disclosure of certain information to certain people at certain times.[36]

(b) Some statutory regimes provide that a disclosure is *unlawful* outside the circumstances mandated by the legislation. The most significant such regime is that imposed by the Data Protection Act 1998.[37]

---

[30] EI(S)R reg 10(8).

[31] See further §§9– 036 to 9– 038.

[32] FOIA s 1(1). And similarly: FOI(S)A s 1(1), in relation to information held by Scottish public authorities; EIR reg 5(1), in relation to environmental information; EI(S)R reg 5(1), in relation to environmental information held by Scottish public authorities. Under the DPA s 7(1)(c), the entitlement is to personal data of which the applicant is the data subject.

[33] FOIA s 78; FOI(S)A s 65. See also FOIA s 17, and FOI(S)A s 16(1), which speak of 'relying' on a 'claim' that information is exempt information, that the duty to confirm or deny does not arise and that the public interest is against disclosure. This is acknowledged in MoJ, *Exemptions Guidance — Introduction*, undated, para 3.4. The EIR, the EI(S)R and the DPA contain no equivalent, FOIA s 78. The FOIA resembles, in this respect, the Freedom of Information Act 1982 (Cth of Aust) and Official Information Act 1982 (New Zealand), but differs from those in the Access to Information Act, (1982) (Canada) and the Freedom of Information Act 1997 (Ireland) which spell out circumstances in which a request may be refused and circumstances in which a request must be refused.

[34] *Jenkins v AG* (1971) *The Times*, August 14 (issue of a pamphlet on the common market); *R v Secretary of State for the Environment, ex p Greenwich London Borough Council* [1989] COD 530 (DC) (publication of a leaflet about the 'poll tax').

[35] *Malone v Metropolitan Police Commissioner* [1979] Ch 344, sub nom. *Malone v Metropolitan Police Commissioner (No 2)* [1979] 2 All ER 620; *R v Secretary of State for Health, ex p C* [2000] 1 FLR 627 (CA).

[36] See further §9– 037.

[37] See, generally, ch 24.

(c)   Disclosure may interfere with a person's private life and, if not justified, may contravene Article 8 of the ECHR.[38]

(d)   Disclosure may be unlawful because it would breach some common law or equitable duty, such as respecting confidentiality, whether arising under contract or otherwise.

The power to make a voluntary disclosure may be precluded by a statutory bar or by a comprehensive statutory regime which provides for similar disclosures subject to specific requirements and which must be read as displacing any more general power to act outside that regime.[39]

008   The nature of the discretion

Other than perhaps through its long title, the Act does not expressly encourage the discretionary disclosure of information.[40] Some encouragement can be found in the statutory recognition of a public interest in disclosing exempt information, at least in relation to qualified exemptions.[41] The decision to provide discretionary disclosure of information is distinct from the conclusion that results from weighing the public interest in maintaining a qualified exemption against the public interest in disclosing the information.[42] Other than in relation to information the disclosure of which is unlawful,[43] a public authority does not require a statutory mandate to disclose information held by it.[44] It is an ordinary incident of holding information that the person holding it may choose to disclose it to others. A public authority may, however, be constrained by other considerations, most notably the effect of any disclosure upon either the public generally or specific individuals.[45]

---

[38]   See further §9– 037.

[39]   *R v Liverpool City Council, ex p Baby Products Association* [2000] BLGR 171, 2 LGR 689; *AG v De Keyser's Royal Hotel Ltd* [1920] AC 508; *R v SSHD, ex p Fire Brigades Union* [1995] 2 AC 513.

[40]   Compare EIR reg 12(2); EI(S)R reg 10(2). Compare also Freedom of Information Act 1982 s 3A (Cth of Aust), which expressly records that the Act is not intended to discourage the disclosure of information otherwise than under the Act, including information that is exempt under the Act.

[41]   FOIA s 2(2); FOI(S)A s 2(1). Amendments to the Bill that would have recorded that the purpose of the Act was to encourage the provision of information by public authorities to the public were unsuccessful: Hansard HL vol 617 cols 886–888 (17 October 2000). Lord Falconer of Thoroton (the Minister of State, Cabinet Office) said that a purpose clause was not 'appropriate': Hansard HL vol 617 col 898 (17 October 2000). He later said: 'We make it clear, and made it clear in Committee, that what we are interested in seeking to achieve is a change of culture in relation to freedom of information... [the Government's amendments] put beyond doubt the Government's resolve that information must be disclosed except where there is an overriding public interest in keeping specific information confidential. Perhaps I may repeat that: information must be disclosed except where there is an overriding public interest in keeping specific information confidential.' — Hansard HL vol 619 col 143 (14 November 2000). See §1–013.

[42]   See FOIA ss 17 and 18; FOI(S)A s 16(1). It is tolerably clear from s 17 (in Scotland, s 16(1)) that a public authority makes a decision whether to rely both on the applicability of a provision in Pt II and on the result of the public interest weighing exercise.

[43]   Whether because it is defamatory, a breach of copyright, a breach of confidentiality, a breach of privacy rights, a breach of the DPA or contravenes a statutory proscription against disclosure.

[44]   *AG v Guardian Newspapers Ltd (No 2)* [1990] 1 AC 109 at 256: 'The general rule is that anyone is entitled to communicate anything he pleases to anyone else, by speech or in writing or in any other way.'

[45]   See further §§9– 036 to 9– 038.

14– 009 Scope for discretionary disclosure

It is nevertheless difficult to see much scope for discretionary disclosure under the Freedom of Information Act 2000, certainly in relation to information that is not required to be disclosed on the basis of a qualified exemption: the public authority will necessarily already have concluded that the public interest in maintaining the exemption outweighs the public interest in disclosing the information.[46] In relation to environmental information, although the regime provides express encouragement to make it available to the public by electronic means which are easily accessible and for public authorities to 'take reasonable steps to organise the information relevant to [their] functions with a view to the active dissemination to the public of the information', that general duty only applies to information that would be required to be disclosed if a request were made.[47]

14– 010 Waiver by discretionary disclosure

A discretionary disclosure of information may impinge upon the subsequent ability of a public authority to rely on a claim[48] of exemption or exclusion in relation to similar requests for information. Elsewhere it has been held that a decision not to maintain any of the available grounds of exemption and to release information that could properly be withheld does not prevent the subsequent maintenance of grounds of exemption.[49] In the United States, the starting-point is that an agency may make a discretionary disclosure of material that is exempt under the Freedom of Information Act 2000 without undue concern that it will be impairing its ability subsequently to invoke applicable exemptions in relation to like information. Notions of waiver have usually been resisted on the basis that they would tend to thwart the purpose of the Act:

> Implying such a waiver could tend to inhibit agencies from making any disclosures other than those explicitly required by law because voluntary release of documents exempt from disclosure requirements would expose other documents [of a related nature] to risk of disclosure. An agency would have an incentive to refuse to release all exempt documents if it wished to retain an exemption for any documents...[R]eadily finding waiver of confidentiality for exempt documents would tend to thwart the [FOI Act's] underlying statutory purpose, which is to implement a policy of broad disclosure of government records.[50]

---

[46] The House of Commons Select Committee appeared to consider that there was scope for discretionary disclosure in relation to purely class-based exemptions: House of Commons, *Public Administration — Third Report* (Cm 4355, 1999) para 60 (see ch 1 n 64).

[47] EIR reg 4; cf EI(S)R reg 3(3).

[48] See FOIA s 17 and FOI(S)A s 16(1). See *Mitchell v IC*, IT, 10 October 2005 at [22].

[49] *Re Lordsvale Finance Ltd v Department of Treasury* (1985) 9 ALD 16, 3 AAR 301 (Australia).

[50] *Mobil Oil Corp v Environmental Protection Agency*, 879 F 2d 698 (9th Cir 1989), where the applicant argued that by making a discretionary disclosure of certain records that could have been withheld under the FOI Act, the agency had waived its right to invoke that exemption for a group of related records. The Court did hold that the release of the documents amounted to a waiver of the exemptions for those documents so released. Similarly: *Nationwide Building Maintenance Inc v Sampson*, 559 F 2d 704 at 712 (DC Cir 1977) ('The FOI Act should not be construed so as to put the federal bureaucracy in a defensive or hostile position with respect to the Act's spirit of open government and liberal disclosure of information.'); *Mehl v Environmental Protection Agency*, 797 F Supp 43 at 47 (DDC 1992) ('A contrary rule would create an incentive against voluntary disclosure of information.'); *Greenberg v United States Department of Treasury*, 10 F Supp (2d) at 23–24 (DDC 1998).

Although it is possible for a claim of waiver to meet with success, such claims have been met with a preliminary requirement that the applicant establish that the exempt information sought duplicates or sufficiently matches the information that previously has been voluntarily disclosed.[51] Moreover, in order to found a waiver, the previous disclosure must have been an authorised one[52] and it must have been made voluntarily.[53]

011 Effect of discretionary disclosure upon prejudiced-based exemptions
There is a distinction between the effect of discretionary disclosure upon the subsequent invocation of a purely class-based exemption and the subsequent invocation of a prejudice-based exemption. In the former case, previous disclosure of like information does not impede subsequent information from falling within the terms of the exemption. In the latter case, the exemption requires that disclosure 'would or would be likely to' cause some prejudice. The requirement that it 'cause' or 'be likely to cause' prejudice may be lost by the earlier disclosure of like information.[54] Similarly, discretionary disclosure may impinge upon a subsequent weighing of the public interest in maintaining an exemption in respect of like information.

012 Other consequences of discretionary disclosure
In granting discretionary disclosure, a public authority will not enjoy any protection should that disclosure represent a publication of defamatory matter. That protection only applies to publication effected by a communication of information under the Freedom of Information Act 2000.[55] Other statutory protections may also only be engaged where disclosure is pursuant to the statutory duty imposed by s 1.[56] Where a public authority decides to give discretionary disclosure it may charge for the cost of the communication of that information.[57]

013 Review of discretionary disclosure
A decision not to effect a voluntary disclosure will not engage the appeal structure set out in the

---

[51] *Public Citizen v Department of State*, 276 F 3d 634 at 645 (DC Cir 2002); *Afshar v Department of State*, 702 F 2d 1125 at 1132 (DC Cir 1983).

[52] *Public Citizen Health Research Group v FDA*, 953 F Supp 400 (DDC 1996) (no waiver where material accidentally released); *Simmons v United States Department of Justice*, 796 F 2d 709 (4th Cir 1986) (unauthorised disclosure does not constitute waiver); similarly *Medina-Hincapie v Department of State*, 700 F 2d 73 (DC Cir 1983).

[53] *Lead Industry Association v OSHA*, 610 F 2d 70 (2d Cir 1979).

[54] As, eg, in *John Connor Press Associates v IC*, IT, 25 January 2006, where the disclosure of certain commercial information relating to a particular transaction precluded exemption under FOIA s 43(2), for the remaining commercial information relating to that transaction.

[55] FOIA s 79; FOI(S)A s 67.

[56] See further §§9–034 to 9–035.

[57] FOIA s 13(1)(b); FOI(S)A s 13(1)(b). The provisions do not enable the public authority to charge for the cost of locating the information, determining whether the information is exempt information or considering the public interest: see §§11–017 to 11–019. A voluntary disclosure of environmental information is not a disclosure under the EIR (because of regs 4(3) and 5(1)), but constitutes the disclosure of exempt information under the FOIA (because of s 39). In relation to environmental information held by Scottish public authorities, a voluntary disclosure will be under the EI(S)R reg 3(3). There is no power to charge for the provision of such information.

Freedom of Information Act 2000.[58] Such a decision is theoretically justiciable by judicial review, but other than in relation to an unjustifiably selective discretionary disclosure of exempt information, it is questionable whether there is much scope for judicial review of a refusal to provide discretionary disclosure.

14–014 Non-reliance upon an exemption

Where there is more than one ground upon which a public authority can rely for the disapplication of its duty to confirm or deny or of its duty to disclose information, it may when giving a refusal notice choose not to rely on one or more of those grounds of exemption.[59] The distinction between this and discretionary disclosure is that here the public authority maintains that confirmation or denial, or that disclosure, of the information should be resisted. The public authority, in choosing not to rely on a particular exemption, makes no concession other than as to its assessment of the most convenient or apposite exemption. Moreover, by having not disclosed the information, it will remain open for the disclosure of the information to have, or to be likely to have, a prescribed prejudicial effect. Accordingly, the decision of a public authority not to invoke a potential ground of exemption does not preclude a subsequent invocation of that ground of exemption, either in relation to a subsequent like request or in the enforcement or appeal procedure.[60]

4. CLASSIFICATION OF EXEMPTIONS

14–015 Introduction

Part II of the Freedom of Information Act 2000 enumerates discrete grounds upon which a public authority is excused both from its duty to confirm or deny that it holds the information sought and from its duty to disclose that information.[61] A classification of the different grounds for dispensation from the duty to confirm or deny has been considered above.[62] More generally and in relation to both duties, the Freedom of Information Act 2000 divides each of the exemptions into absolute exemptions and qualified exemptions. Each exemption can also be characterised either as being a purely class-based exemption or as being a prejudice-based exemption. Depending on the circumstances, the applicability of an exemption will be either

---

[58] And similarly: FOI(S)A; EIR; EI(S)R. So held in Australia in relation to the analogous s 14 Freedom of Information Act 1982: *Re Waterford and Department of Treasury* (1983) 5 ALD 193; *Re Waterford and Department of Health* (1983) 5 ALN N139. Section 14 has since been repealed, but see now s 3A.

[59] FOIA s 17(1); FOI(S)A s 16(1).

[60] In relation to a public authority relying in a Tribunal appeal upon an exemption not previously relied upon, see §28–022.

[61] FOIA ss 21–44; FOI(S)A ss 25–41. Pt 2 of the latter Act relates only to exemption from the duty to disclose information. In relation to the circumstances in which a Scottish public authority is excused from revealing in a refusal notice whether the information sought exists, see §1–041(1). In relation to the classification of exceptions under the environmental information regime, see §6–031. In relation to the classification of exemptions under the data protection regime, see §5–056.

[62] See §14–005.

a question of law or a question of mixed fact and law.[63]

016 Absolute exemptions

Absolute exemptions are defined in the Freedom of Information Act 2000[64] to be those conferred in respect of:

— information that is reasonably accessible to the applicant otherwise than under the Freedom of Information Act 2000;[65]

— information held by the requested public authority that was directly or indirectly supplied to it by, or that relates to, any of the defined security bodies;[66]

— information held by the requested public authority only by virtue of that information being contained in a formal document filed with a court or tribunal, in a formal document served for the purposes of court or tribunal proceedings, or in a formal document created by a court or by staff of a court;[67]

— information held by the requested public authority only by virtue of it being contained in a document placed in the custody of a person conducting an inquiry or arbitration, or in a document created by a person conducting an inquiry or arbitration, for the purposes of the inquiry or arbitration;[68]

— information for which exemption is required for the purpose of avoiding an infringement of the privileges of either House of Parliament;[69]

— information held by the House of Commons or the House of Lords that, in the reasonable opinion of the Speaker of the House of Commons or the Clerk of the Parliaments respectively, if disclosed under the Freedom of Information Act 2000, would or would be likely to:

— prejudice the convention of the collective responsibility of Ministers of the Crown, etc;

— inhibit the free and frank provision of advice or exchange of views for the purposes of deliberation; or

— otherwise prejudice the effective conduct of public affairs;[70]

— information that constitutes personal data of which the applicant is the data subject;[71]

— information that is not unstructured manual data but which constitutes personal

---

[63] *DWP v IC*, IT, 5 March 2007 at [16].

[64] FOIA s 2(3); FOI(S)A s 2(2).

[65] FOIA s 21(1); FOI(S)A s 25(1).

[66] FOIA s 23(1). This does not constitute an absolute exemption in relation to information held by a Scottish public authority.

[67] FOIA s 32(1); FOI(S)A s 37(1)(a).

[68] FOIA s 32(2); FOI(S)A s 37(1)(b).

[69] FOIA s 34(1). This does not constitute an absolute exemption in relation to information held by a Scottish public authority.

[70] FOIA s 36(2). This does not constitute an absolute exemption in relation to information held by a Scottish public authority.

[71] FOIA s 40(1); FOI(S)A s 38(1)(a). In relation to information held by a Scottish public authority, personal census information and a deceased person's health record are also absolute exemptions: s 38(1)(c) and (d).

        data of which the applicant is not the data subject, the disclosure of which would contravene a data protection principle;[72]

—   information that is unstructured manual data and constitutes personal data of which the applicant is not the data subject, the disclosure of which would contravene one of the data protection principles disregarding the exemptions from the data protection principles granted by s 33A of the Data Protection Act 1998;[73]

—   information obtained by the public authority from any other person (including another public authority) the disclosure of which would constitute an actionable breach of confidence by the public authority;[74] and

—   information the disclosure of which is prohibited by or under an enactment, is incompatible with any Community obligation or would constitute a contempt of court.[75]

Under the environmental information regime, there is only an absolute exception to the extent that the requested information includes personal data or where disclosure would involve an infringement of the privileges of a House of Parliament.[76] None of the exemptions under the data protection regime involves an express consideration of the public interest. Where information satisfies a provision conferring absolute exemption, that will be sufficient to disapply both the duty to confirm or deny the existence of that information and the duty to disclose that information.[77] Subject to any proscription against disclosure, a public authority may, in its discretion, nevertheless decide to disclose the information.[78]

14–017 Qualified exemptions

The remaining exemptions, which may for convenience be termed 'qualified exemptions', are those conferred in respect of:

—   information intended for future publication;[79]

—   information for which exemption from the duties is required for the purpose of safeguarding national security;[80]

—   information whose disclosure would or would be likely to prejudice the defence of the British Isles;[81]

—   information whose disclosure would or would be likely to prejudice relations between the United Kingdom and any other state or international organisation or

---

[72] FOIA s 40(3)(a)(i); FOI(S)A s 38(1)(a).

[73] FOIA s 40(3)(b); FOI(S)A s 38(1)(b).

[74] FOIA s 41(1); FOI(S)A s 36(2).

[75] FOIA s 44(1); FOI(S)A s 26.

[76] EIR regs 3(4), 5(3), 12(1) and 12(3); EI(S)R regs 10(1), 10(3) and 11(1).

[77] FOIA ss 2(1)(a) and 2(1)(b); FOI(S)A s 2(1)(a); EIR reg 12(6)–(7); EI(S)R reg 10(7)–(8). In relation to information held by a Scottish public authority it will not automatically lead to that public authority being excused from revealing in a refusal notice whether the information sought exists: see §14– 006.

[78] See §§9– 034 to 9– 035 and 14– 007 to 14– 009.

[79] FOIA s 22(1); FOI(S)A s 27(1).

[80] FOIA s 24(1); FOI(S)A s 31(1).

[81] FOIA s 26(1); FOI(S)A s 31(4).

to prejudice the interests of the United Kingdom abroad;[82]

— confidential information obtained from a foreign state or from an international organisation or court;[83]

— information whose disclosure would or would be likely to prejudice relations between administrations within the United Kingdom;[84]

— information the disclosure of which would or would be likely to prejudice the economic or financial interests of the United Kingdom or any part of it;[85]

— information held by a public authority for the purposes of a criminal investigation or proceedings;[86]

— information the disclosure of which would or would be likely to prejudice the prevention or detection of crime, etc;[87]

— information that would or would be likely to prejudice an auditing body's audit functions;[88]

— information relating to government policy;[89]

— information, other than that held by the House of Commons or the House of Lords that, in the reasonable opinion of a qualified person, if disclosed under the Freedom of Information Act 2000, would or would be likely to:

  — prejudice the convention of the collective responsibility of Ministers of the Crown, etc;

  — inhibit the free and frank provision of advice or exchange of views for the purposes of deliberation; or

  — otherwise prejudice the effective conduct of public affairs;[90]

— communications with Her Majesty or the Royal Household;[91]

— information the disclosure of which would or would be likely to endanger the physical or mental health of an individual or endanger an individual's safety;[92]

— environmental information;[93]

— information in respect of which a claim to legal professional privilege could be maintained;[94]

— information that constitutes a trade secret or the disclosure of which would or would

---

[82] FOIA s 27(1); FOI(S)A s 32(1)(a).

[83] FOIA s 27(2); FOI(S)A s 32(1)(b).

[84] FOIA s 28(1); FOI(S)A s 28(1).

[85] FOIA s 29(1); FOI(S)A s 33(2).

[86] FOIA s 30(1); FOI(S)A s 34(1).

[87] FOIA s 31(1); FOI(S)A s 35(1).

[88] FOIA s 33(2); FOI(S)A s 40.

[89] FOIA s 35(1); FOI(S)A s 29(1).

[90] FOIA s 36(2). FOI(S)A s 30.

[91] FOIA s 37(1); FOI(S)A s 41.

[92] FOIA s 38(1); FOI(S)A s 39(1).

[93] FOIA s 39(1); FOI(S)A s 39(2).

[94] FOIA s 42(1); FOI(S)A s 36(1).

be likely to prejudice the commercial interests of any person.[95]

In relation to environmental information held by a public authority, each of the exceptions set out in reg 12(4)–(5) is qualified.[96]

14–018 Principal significance of the division between absolute and qualified exemptions

As noted above, where information satisfies a provision conferring absolute exemption, that will be sufficient to disapply the duty to disclose that information.[97] And similarly a provision conferring absolute exclusion from the duty to confirm or deny the existence of information. Where information satisfies a provision conferring qualified exemption then:

(a) the duty to confirm or deny will be disapplied where, in all the circumstances of the case, the public interest in maintaining the exclusion of the duty to confirm or deny outweighs the public interest in disclosing whether the public authority holds the information; and

(b) the duty to disclose will be disapplied where, in all the circumstances of the case, the public interest in maintaining the exemption outweighs the public interest in disclosing the information.[98]

That which is being balanced thus differs according to the duty being disapplied. Although the public interest in 'maintaining the exclusion of the duty to confirm or deny' may be thought to be less pressing than the public interest in 'maintaining the exemption', the counterbalancing public interest in 'disclosing whether the public authority holds the information' may be thought to be correspondingly less compelling than the public interest in 'disclosing the information'. The public interest in maintaining the exclusion of the duty to confirm or deny will involve a consideration of the terms of the request. A highly specific request is more likely than a general request to result in the public interest in maintaining the exclusion of the duty to confirm or deny outweighing the public interest in disclosing whether the public authority holds the information: answering a highly specific request can effectively amount to a disclosure of the information sought. The public interest in maintaining the exemption from disclosure will, on the other hand, involve a greater emphasis on the information itself, rather than on the terms of the request.

14–019 Significance of distinction for time-limits

The distinction between the two categories of exemption has significance for the time within which a public authority must reply to a request. The time-limit for complete compliance with a request under the Freedom of Information Act 2000 varies according to whether there are any qualified grounds of exemption applicable to the information sought. To the extent that a public authority, in claiming a disapplication of the duty to confirm or deny or to

---

[95] FOIA s 43(1) and (2); FOI(S)A s 33(1).

[96] EIR reg 12(1). In relation to environmental information held by a Scottish public authority, similarly under EI(S)R regs 10(1), (4) and (5).

[97] FOIA ss 2(1) and (2); FOI(S)A s 2(1); EIR reg 12(1); EI(S)R reg 10(1): Scottish public authorities are not under a separate duty to confirm or deny the existence of information sought under FOI(S)A.

[98] As to what exactly this entails and the significance of the phrase 'the public interest in maintaining the exemption', see Philip Coppel, 'The public interest and the Freedom of Information Act 2000' *Judicial Review*, vol 10, issue 4, December 2005.

communicate particular information, relies exclusively upon one or more absolute exemptions, the public authority must give notice of its refusal within 20 working days.[99] To the extent that a public authority, in claiming a disapplication of the duty to confirm or deny or to communicate particular information, relies upon one or more qualified exemptions, the public authority must first, within 20 working days, give notice specifying the exemption relied upon and the reason it applies, but advising the applicant that no decision in relation to the weighing of the public interest has yet been reached and giving an estimate of when it expects that exercise to be completed.[100] The public authority then has a reasonable time within which to carry out the exercise of weighing the public interest[101] and a further reasonable time to give the applicant notice of that decision.[102] In relation to environmental information held by a public authority, the time limit is set at 20 working days regardless of whether a consideration of the public interest is involved.[103]

)20 Significance of distinction for enforcement

The distinction between the two categories of exemption also has significance for the ability of certain public authorities to shield themselves from decision notices and enforcement notices. Certain core, central government public authorities, when served with a decision notice or an enforcement notice, may give the Information Commissioner a certificate under s 53(2).[104] In general terms, the effect of the certificate is to shield that public authority from its duty to comply with a decision notice or an enforcement notice.[105] In relation to the communication obligation, the ability to serve such a notice is confined to where there has been a failure to comply with the duty to communicate in respect of exempt information. In relation to the duty to confirm or deny, the ability to serve such a notice is confined to where there has been a failure to comply with the duty to confirm or deny in respect of information falling within any provision of Part II stating that that duty does not arise. In those circumstances, the 'accountable person' of the public authority can give the Information Commissioner a certificate stating that he has on reasonable grounds formed the opinion that, in respect of the request, there has been no failure to comply with the s 1 duty. Because certification can only apply to a decision notice or an enforcement notice that relates to a failure to comply with the s 1 duty, the issue of whether the information falls within any provision of Part II is outside the certification process under s 53. The s 53(2) certificate is directed to the accountable person's opinion in relation to the weighing of the public interest: it is only that weighing which can reasonably induce an accountable person to form the opinion that there has been no failure to comply with the s 1(1) duties where the information is exempt information. In short, the effect

---

[99] FOIA ss 17(1) and 10(1)); FOI(S)A ss 17(1) and 10(1). See §11– 029.

[100] FOIA ss 17 and 10(1). No additional time for responding is provided under the FOI(S)A. See further §§11– 022 to 11– 030.

[101] FOIA s 10(3); FOI(S)A s 33(1).

[102] FOIA s 17(3); FOI(S)A s 33(1).

[103] EIR reg 5(2); EI(S)R reg 5(2). The environmental information regime does, however, provide for an extension of time from 20 to 40 working days, but availability of this extension depends upon the complexity of the request and the amount of environmental information requested: EIR reg 7(1); EI(S)R reg 7(1).

[104] FOI(S)A s 52(2); EIR regs 15(1), 18(2)–(3); EI(S)R regs 12(1), 17(2).

[105] See §14– 032.

of a s 53(2) certificate is confined to shielding certain central government public authorities from the Information Commissioner's determination that information falling within a qualified exemption ought to be disclosed in the public interest.[106]

14– 021 Implicit significance of the statutory distinction

Underlying each of the exemptions in Part II of the Freedom of Information Act 2000 is a public interest against the disclosure of information falling within the terms of the exemption. It is implicit in the creation of the qualified exemptions that the public interest in a public authority confirming or denying that it holds certain information and in it communicating that information are each capable of outweighing the underlying public interest in maintaining each of the exemptions. Approximately half of the qualified exemptions, in order to be engaged, expressly require that disclosure of the information under the Act would cause, or would be likely to cause, some form of prejudice.[107] The existence of that prejudice or of the likelihood of that prejudice will not automatically represent an adequate counterbalancing public interest against disclosure, as that would effectively elevate the exemption into an absolute exemption.[108] The Freedom of Information Act 2000 recognises that where a qualified exemption is engaged, the public interest in the maintenance of that exemption is not of fixed weight, but that it will vary according to 'all the circumstances of the case'. Similarly, the Freedom of Information Act 2000 recognises that whilst there always exists a public interest in disclosing whether a public authority holds information and in disclosing that information, the weight to be afforded to this interest will vary according to 'all the circumstances of the case'.[109]

---

[106] As is confirmed in *Explanatory Notes to the FOIA*, para 180. This was also confirmed to Parliament by Lord Falconer of Thoroton (the Minister of State, Cabinet Office) who said: 'Contrary to what my noble friend Lord Brennan said, it is worth noting that the effect of this provision is not that any decision of the information commissioner can be overridden: the only decision of the information commissioner that can be overridden is one on the balance of the public interest under cl13. If, for example, the information commissioner determined that something was not covered by an exemption, then the ministerial override would never apply. Once it is not exempt, disclosure is automatic. The ministerial override under Clause 13 applies only where something is exempt and the Minister or the public authority concerned has refused to override the exemption in the public interest." — Hansard HL vol 618 cols 445–446 (25 October 2000). See also: Hansard HL vol 619 col 258 (14 November 2000) (Lord Falconer of Thoroton).

[107] FOIA ss 26(1), 27(1), 28(1), 29(1), 31(1), 33(2) and (3), 36(2), 38(1) and 43(2); FOI(S)A ss 28(1), 30, 31(4), 32(1)(a), 33(1)(b), 33(2), 35(1), 39(1) and 40; EIR reg 12(5); EI(S)R reg 10(5). The requirement in relation to information held by a Scottish public authority is that the prejudice be a 'substantial' one before the exemption is engaged and before considering whether nevertheless the public interest in disclosing the information is not outweighed by the public interest in maintaining the exemption.

[108] See generally: Hansard HL vol 617 cols 901–905, 912–913, and 923–924 (17 October 2000) (Lord Falconer of Thoroton, the Minister of State at the Cabinet Office, during Committee Stage of the FOI Bill in the House of Lords and introducing the amendment that resulted in s 2). Questioned as to what a public official was to do when required to weigh the competing public interests, he said (col 921): 'As far as public interest between disclosure on the one hand and the maintenance of exemption on the other is concerned, it has to be looked at objectively. One looks at the impact of disclosure, that is, making it public. What is the impact of the exemption being maintained? That should be looked at objectively rather than in terms of whatever the motive may be of the person applying. That does not mean that the motive of the person applying may not coincide with factors that could be relevant to what damage may be done and what assistance could be served by making the matter public. But individual motives will not be relevant to that.. The FOI Bill as originally introduced (cl14, later cl 13) required a public authority to consider 'discretionary disclosure' of exempt information: see House of Commons, *Public Administration — Third Report*, (Cm 4355, 1999) para 60 (see ch 1 n 64).

[109] The necessity of carrying out this exercise on a case-by-case basis was acknowledged by Lord Falconer of Thoroton: Hansard HL vol 619 col 831 (22 November 2000).

022 Purely class-based exemptions

Independently of the statutory distinction between absolute and qualified exemptions, it is possible to characterise some of the exemptions as purely class based,[110] whereas others require some form of prejudice before the exemption is engaged. Purely class-based exemptions are those conferred in respect of:

— information that is reasonably accessible to the applicant otherwise than under the Freedom of Information Act 2000;[111]

— information intended for future publication;[112]

— information held by the requested public authority that was directly or indirectly supplied to it by, or that relates to, any of the defined security bodies;[113]

— confidential information obtained from a foreign state or from an international organisation or court;[114]

— information held by a public authority for the purposes of a criminal investigation or proceedings;[115]

— information held by the requested public authority only by virtue of that information being contained in a formal document filed with a court or tribunal, in a formal document served for the purposes of court or tribunal proceedings, or in a formal document created by a court or by staff of a court;[116]

— information held by the requested public authority only by virtue of it being contained in a document placed in the custody of a person conducting an inquiry or arbitration, or in a document created by a person conducting an inquiry or arbitration, for the purposes of the inquiry or arbitration;[117]

— information for which exemption is required for the purpose of avoiding an infringement of the privileges of either House of Parliament;[118]

— information relating to government policy;[119]

— communications with Her Majesty or the Royal Household;[120]

---

[110] Although the term 'class-based exemption' is not used in the Act, they were so described in the *Explanatory Notes, FOI Act 2000* (see paras 12 and 85) and in House of Commons, *Public Administration — Third Report*, (Cm 4355, 1999) para 60. The following categorisation is consistent with that given in the *Explanatory Notes, FOI Act 2000* and in the *Public Administration — Third Report*.

[111] FOIA s 21(1); FOI(S)A s 25(1).

[112] FOIA s 22(1); FOI(S)A s 27(1).

[113] FOIA s 23(1). This does not constitute an absolute exemption in relation to information held by a Scottish public authority.

[114] FOIA s 27(2); FOI(S)A s 32(1)(b).

[115] FOIA s 30(1); FOI(S)A s 34(1).

[116] FOIA s 32(1); FOI(S)A s 37(1)(a).

[117] FOIA s 32(2); FOI(S)A s 37(1)(b).

[118] FOIA s 34(1). This does not constitute an absolute exemption in relation to information held by a Scottish public authority.

[119] FOIA s 35(1); FOI(S)A s 29(1).

[120] FOIA s 37(1); FOI(S)A s 41.

— environmental information;[121]

— information that constitutes personal data;[122]

— information obtained by the public authority from any other person (including another public authority) the disclosure of which would constitute an actionable breach of confidence by the public authority;[123]

— information in respect of which a claim to legal professional privilege could be maintained;[124]

— information that constitutes a trade secret;[125] and

— information the disclosure of which is prohibited by or under an enactment, is incompatible with any Community obligation or would constitute a contempt of court.[126]

A small number of exceptions in the environmental information regime are class-based.[127] In relation to each of these exemptions and exceptions, the fact that the disclosure of the information would be demonstrably harmless will not detract from it being 'exempt information'. Where the exemption is a qualified exemption, that harmlessness may, however, impinge upon the public interest in maintaining the exemption.

14– 023 Prejudice-based exemptions

The remaining exemptions all require 'prejudice' in order for the exemption to be engaged; or, in the case of Scotland, 'substantial prejudice'. Prejudice-based exemptions are those conferred in respect of:

— information for which exemption from the duties is required for the purpose of safeguarding national security;[128]

— information whose disclosure would or would be likely to prejudice the defence of the British Isles;[129]

— information whose disclosure would or would be likely to prejudice relations between the United Kingdom and any other state or international organisation or to prejudice the interests of the United Kingdom abroad;[130]

— information whose disclosure would or would be likely to prejudice relations between administrations within the United Kingdom;[131]

— information the disclosure of which would or would be likely to prejudice the

---

[121] FOIA s 39(1); FOI(S)A s 39(2).

[122] FOIA s 40(1); FOI(S)A s 38(1)(a). In relation to information held by a Scottish public authority, personal census information and a deceased person's health record are also absolute exemptions: s 38(1)(c) and (d).

[123] FOIA s 41(1); FOI(S)A s 36(2).

[124] FOIA s 42(1); FOI(S)A s 36(1).

[125] FOIA s 43(1); FOI(S)A s 33(1).

[126] FOIA s 44(1); FOI(S)A s 26.

[127] EIR regs 3(4), 5(3), 12(3), 12(4)(d) and 12(4)(e); EI(S)R regs 10(3), 10(4)(d), 10(4)(e) and 11(1).

[128] FOIA s 24(1); FOI(S)A s 31(1).

[129] FOIA s 26(1); FOI(S)A s 31(4).

[130] FOIA s 27(1); FOI(S)A s 32(1)(a).

[131] FOIA s 28(1); FOI(S)A s 28(1).

economic or financial interests of the United Kingdom or any part of it;[132]

— information the disclosure of which would or would be likely to prejudice the prevention or detection of crime, etc;[133]

— information that would or would be likely to prejudice an auditing body's audit functions;[134]

— information held by the House of Commons or the House of Lords that, in the reasonable opinion of the Speaker of the House of Commons or the Clerk of the Parliaments respectively, if disclosed under the Freedom of Information Act 2000, would or would be likely to:

    — prejudice the convention of the collective responsibility of Ministers of the Crown, etc;

    — inhibit the free and frank provision of advice or exchange of views for the purposes of deliberation; or

    — otherwise prejudice the effective conduct of public affairs;[135]

— information the disclosure of which would or would be likely to endanger the physical or mental health of an individual or endanger an individual's safety;[136] and

— information the disclosure of which would or would be likely to prejudice the commercial interests of any person.[137]

The majority of exceptions in the environmental information regime are prejudice-based.[138]

5. INTERPRETATION OF EXEMPTIONS AND ONUS

024 Introduction

The Freedom of Information Act 2000 does not explicitly specify whether it is for the applicant to show that he has a right to the information requested or for the public authority to show that it is excused from disclosing the information requested; or whether there is a shifting 'onus' of some sort.[139] In this, the Act is no different from most statutes that confer upon an individual a right against a public authority.[140] The environmental information regime does specifically

---

[132] FOIA s 29(1); FOI(S)A s 33(2).

[133] FOIA s 31(1); FOI(S)A s 35(1).

[134] FOIA s 33(2); FOI(S)A s 40.

[135] FOIA s 36(2); FOI(S)A s 30. This does not constitute an absolute exemption in Scotland.

[136] FOIA s 38(1); FOI(S)A s 39(1).

[137] FOIA s 43(1) and (2); FOI(S)A s 33(1).

[138] EIR reg 12(5); EI(S)R reg 10(5).

[139] However, FOIA s 10(3), in speaking of 'if the condition in section 2(1)(b) were satisfied' implies some sort of a burden on the authority. Similarly, FOIA s 17 and FOI(S)A s 16(1), in referring to 'relying on a claim' that any of the provisions in Pt II applies.

[140] The freedom of information legislation of most comparative jurisdictions does specifically state that the onus of establishing an exemption lies upon the recipient public authority or agency: Freedom of Information Act 1982 ss 3, 59D and 61 (Cth of Australia); Access to Information Act, (1982) (Canada) s 48; Freedom of Information Act 1997 (Ireland) s 34(12). In New Zealand there is a general statement of principle: Official Information Act 1982 (NZ) s 5. This has been held not to create an onus upon the agency seeking to rely upon an exemption: *Commissioner of Police*

provide that a public authority is to apply a presumption in favour of disclosure.[141] It is unlikely that the difference will make any operative difference.[142] It has been held in the context of a confidentiality claim:

> it is incumbent upon the Crown, in order to restrain disclosure of Government secrets, not only to show that the information is confidential, but also to show that it is in the public interest that it should not be published .... The reason for this additional requirement in cases concerned with Government secrets appears to be that, although in the case of private citizens there is a public interest that confidential information should as such be protected, in the case of Government secrets the mere fact of confidentiality does not alone support such a conclusion, because in a free society there is a continuing public interest that the workings of government should be open to scrutiny and criticism. From this it follows that, in such cases, there must be demonstrated some other public interest which requires that publication should be restrained.[143]

And, in relation to adoption information held by a local authority:

> the bias, if any, should be in favour of allowing access to information rather than concealing information.[144]

These statements predate the Freedom of Information Act 2000. It may be thought that their sentiments are sufficiently embodied within the Act as not to require the application of any gloss to its provisions.

14–025   Onus or burden of proof: exempt information

The scope of the rights given by s 1(1) of the Freedom of Information Act 2000 is shaped by whether the information to which a request relates is or is not 'exempt information'. To be exempt information, the information must fit within one or more of the descriptions of exempt information given by the provisions of Part II of the Act. Some of these descriptions involve an identification of some specific sort of prejudice or likely prejudice: matters on which there will often be legitimate differences of view. It is generally considered inappropriate to speak of a formal 'onus of proof' in the exercise of an administrative duty or discretion.[145] The convention is that a public authority is presumed to have properly and duly performed its

---

v Ombudsman [1988] 1 NZLR 385 (CA), on appeal from [1985] 1 NZLR 578. In debate on the FOI Bill, it was thought to be 'seriously defective' in not having a clear presumption in favour of disclosure, with most debate as to presumption concerned with the presumption in relation to the weighing of the aspects of the public interest, rather than the presumption in relation to whether information falls within one or other of the provisions of Pt II of the Freedom of Information Act 2000: Hansard HL vol 619 col 136 (14 November 2000) (Lord Lester of Herne Hill).

[141] EIR reg 12(2); EI(S)R reg 10(2).

[142] *Guardian Newspapers Ltd and Heather Brooke v IC and BBC*, IT, 8 January 2007 at [82], where the Information Tribunal spoke of a default setting of disclosure. However, there is no such presumption in favour of the release of personal information (*Common Services Agency v IC* [2008] UKHL 47, [2008] 1 WLR 1550 at [7], [68]) and, by parity of reasoning, in any other circumstance where disclosure might impinge upon the rights of a third party.

[143] *AG v Guardian Newspapers (No 2)* [1990] 1 AC 109 at 283 (Lord Goff). See also the quotation at §25–028 from *A-G (UK) v Heinemann Publishers Pty Ltd* (1987) 10 NSWLR 86 at 191, 75 ALR 353 at 454.

[144] *Birmingham City District Council v O* [1983] 1 AC 578 at 596.

[145] *Pye (Oxford) Estates Ltd v Secretary of State for the Environment* [1982] JPL 575 (in relation to a planning appeal). The point has been considered elsewhere at length: *McDonald v Director General of Social Security* (1986) 6 ALD 6; *Lodkowski v Comcare* (1998) 53 ALD 371 at 386; *Re VBN and Prudential Regulatory Authority (No 5)* (2006) 92 ALD 259 at 328-31.

statutory duties:[146]

> The legal, as contrasted with the evidential, burden being on the applicant to establish his entitlement to relief, [the courts] are entitled and are very willing to assume that the authority has acted in accordance with law, until the contrary is shown. But authorities assist neither themselves nor the courts, if their response is a blanket assertion of having acted in accordance with law or one which begs the question. If the issue is whether an authority took a particular factor into account, it will be a sufficient response to show that it did. But if the allegation is that a decision is prima facie irrational and that there are grounds for inquiring whether something immaterial may have been considered or something material omitted from consideration, it really does not help to assert baldly that all relevant matters and no irrelevant matters were taken into consideration without condescending to mention some at least of the principal factors on which the decision was based.[147]

Where a public authority is required to be satisfied of something or to form some opinion, then, absent evidence to the contrary, in public law its say-so that it was satisfied or formed that opinion will generally suffice.[148] The transposition of this principle to the prejudice-based exemptions in the freedom of information regime requires a public authority to make a disinterested assessment of those wider interests, uncoloured by its disinclination to disclose. Although official material leading to the passage of the Act spoke of 'a presumption of openness', there is no such presumption expressed in the Act itself.[149] The short title of the Freedom of Information Act 2000 might suggest some sort of presumption of openness, although as an interpretative tool it is of limited use.[150] Nevertheless, the basic scheme of the Act and the language employed suggest that it is for a public authority to demonstrate the applicability of a provision in Part II of the Act before it may rely on that provision.[151] The Tribunal has noted:

> The FOIA, in s 1, conferred an important new fundamental right to information held by public bodies. It is a right subject to exceptions, or conditions as they were termed by Lord Turnbull. Where such an exception is relied on by a public authority, it is for that authority to justify such reliance. If it says there is an absolute exemption, it must demonstrate it. If prejudice is a requisite factor, it must prove it.[152]

---

[146] *Point of Ayr Collieries Ltd v Lloyd-George* [1943] 2 All ER 546; *Wilover Nominees Ltd v Inland Revenue Commissioners* [1973] 1 WLR 1393 at 1389; *R v Inland Revenue Commissioners, ex p Rossminster* [1980] AC 952 at 1009, 1013; *R v Inland Revenue Commissioners, ex p TC Coombs & Co* [1991] 2 AC 283 at 300.

[147] *R v Lancashire County Council, ex p Huddleston* [1986] 2 All ER 941 at 945–946 (Donaldson MR).

[148] *Wilover Nominees Ltd v Inland Revenue Commissioners* [1973] 1 WLR 1393 at 1389; *Stoke-on-Trent City Council v B&Q (Retail) Ltd* [1984] Ch 1; *R v Inland Revenue Commissioners, ex p TC Coombs & Co* [1991] 2 AC 283 at 299–302.

[149] Cabinet Office, *Your Right to Know. The Government's Proposals for a FOI Act. White Paper* (Cm 3818, 1997) para 3.1. In *R (Rose) v Secretary of State for Health* [2002] 2 FLR 962, [2002] UKHRR 13 at [47] Scott Baker J (in the context of an application by an individual conceived through artificial insemination for information about the donor) said: 'We live in a much more open society than even 20 years ago. Secrecy nowadays has to be justified where previously it did not.'

[150] *Re Vexatious Actions Act 1886, Re Boaler* [1915] 1 KB 21 at 40; *R v Wheatley* [1979] 1 WLR 144 at 147; *Lonrho Ltd v Shell Petroleum Co Ltd (No 2)* [1982] AC 173 at 187.

[151] As noted above, this is expressly required by the environmental information regime: EIR reg 12(2); EI(S)R reg 10(2).

[152] *DfES v IC and The Evening Standard*, IT, 19 February 2007 at [61]. In *Toms v IC*, IT, 19 June 2006 at [2] the Information Tribunal stated that 'the 2000 Act contains a presumption in favour of disclosure.' Similarly: *DTI v IC*, IT, 10 November 2006 at [54]; *Guardian Newspapers Ltd and Heather Brooke v IC and BBC*, IT, 8 January 2007 at [82]–[83]; *DWP v IC*, IT, 5 March 2007 at [25]; *Reith v IC and LB Hammersmith & Fulham*, IT, 1 June 2007 at [41]. Similarly, the President of the Scottish Court of Session has held that 'as each [provision in Part II] is an exemption

The specifying of 'exemptions' from 'a general right of access' implies a requirement that the operative words of any of those exemptions must be satisfied in order for it to be triggered[153] on the basis of:

> the orthodox principle (common to both the criminal and the civil law) that exceptions, etc are to be set up by those who rely on them.[154]

The exemptions do not, however, set up a threshold of the harm that must be caused.[155]

14–026 Onus of proof elsewhere

In the analogous regime in New Zealand, the courts have held[156] that the ombudsman, to whom an appeal against an agency's decision lies, has no pre-determined starting point and that the agency withholding the information is under no obligation to establish affirmatively each element of the exemption. Nevertheless, despite avoiding use of terms such as 'onus', the courts there have held that the withholding agency bears an obligation:

> to justify its refusal to disclose ... with sufficient particularity for the ombudsman to make his or her decision and recommendation.[157]

14–027 Onus of proof: public interest

Having established that information answering the terms of the request falls within one of the provisions of Part II, if those provisions do not confer absolute exemption it will be necessary to weigh the competing aspects of the public interest to determine if the duty to acknowledge and the duty to communicate are disapplied.[158] When the public interest override was first introduced in the FOI Bill, it provided that, if information fell within one of the qualified exemptions, then it would only be required to be communicated to the applicant if:

---

to a general entitlement it is for the public authority relying on it to demonstrate that the exemption is engaged.' — *Scottish Ministers v Scottish IC* [2007] CSIH 8, 2007 SCLR 253 at [12]. In relation to exceptions in the environmental information regime, see: *Friends of the Earth v IC and ECGD*, IT, 20 August 2007 at [53]. In *Burgess v IC and Stafford Borough Council*, IT, 7 June 2007 at [43] the Tribunal considered that the express presumption in favour of disclosure in the EIR made them 'significantly different' from the FOIA: see further §6– 034.

[153] Similarly, when refusing a request, it is for the public authority to rely upon a claim that one of the provisions of Pt II applies: FOIA s 17(2); FOI(S)A s 16(2). In Canada, the view taken is that since the basic principle of the statute is to codify the right of public access to government information two things follow: first, that such public access ought not to be frustrated by the Courts except upon the clearest grounds so that doubt ought to be resolved in favour of disclosure; secondly, the burden of persuasion must rest upon the party resisting disclosure whether it be a private corporation, citizen or the Government: *Maislin Industries Limited v Minister for Industry, Trade & Commerce* [1984] 1 FC 939; *Rubin v Canada (Canada Mortgage and Housing Corp)* [1989] 1 FC 265 (CA) ('the general rule is disclosure, the exception is exemption and the onus of proving the entitlement to the benefit of the exception rests upon those who claim it.'); *Canada (Information Commissioner) v Canada (Minister of External Affairs)* [1990] 3 FC 665; *Rubin v Canada (Solicitor General)* (2000) 187 DLR (4th) 675. Note, however, that the Access to Information Act, (1982) (Canada) has both a purpose clause (s 2) and an onus provision in relation to appeals (s 48).

[154] *Nimmo v Alexander Cowan & Sons Ltd* [1968] AC 107 at 130 (Lord Wilberforce). Similarly: *R v Hunt* [1987] AC 352 at 373–375 (Lord Griffiths).

[155] *ECGD v Friends of the Earth* [2008] EWHC 638 (Admin), [2008] Env LR 40, [2008] JPL 1813 at [31]-[37], criticising the Tribunal for requiring a public authority to specify clearly and precisely the harm or harms that would be caused were disclosure to be ordered.

[156] *Commissioner of Police v Ombudsman* [1988] 1 NZLR 385 (CA), on appeal from [1985] 1 NZLR 578.

[157] *Commissioner of Police v Ombudsman* [1988] 1 NZLR 385 at 406.

[158] FOIA s 2(1)(b) and 2(2)(b); FOI(S)A s 2(1)(b). In Canada the two-stage burden, ie that the information falls within the exemption and that the public interest is against disclosure, is recognised: *Rubin v Canada (Solicitor General)* (2000) 187 DLR (4th) 675.

in all the circumstances of the case, the public interest in disclosing the information outweighs the public interest in maintaining the exemption.[159] In the face of criticism,[160] the section was modified to its present form, which reversed the order. In moving the amendments, it was specifically stated:

> the starting point is the public right of access and the public interest in disclosure, and it is for the public authority to justify non-disclosure on the basis that public disclosure is outweighed in the circumstances of the case by the public interest in non-disclosure .... The burden of proof, as lawyers would say, is placed upon the public authority to show that there is some pressing need for non-disclosure and that the restriction on the public right of access is necessary in the sense of being a proportionate way of meeting that need.[161]

The suggested amendments were accepted by the Minister in charge of the Bill in the House of Lords, saying they:

> will result in an important and significant shift towards greater openness. They will put beyond doubt the Government's resolve that information must be disclosed except where there is an overriding public interest in keeping specific information confidential. Perhaps I may repeat that: information must be disclosed except where there is an overriding public interest in keeping specific information confidential .... They significantly contribute to the change in culture. They contribute significantly to ensuring that the public authority must make out the case for non-disclosure before there is non-disclosure. That is why we have agreed to accept them.[162]

Section 2, in speaking of the acknowledgement and communication duties being disapplied where 'the public interest in maintaining the exemption outweighs the public interest in disclosing the information', posits a starting position of disclosure.[163] This is acknowledged in guidance both from the Ministry of Justice and the Information Commissioner:

> The starting point in considering the balance of the public interest is that there is a general public interest in disclosure. The existence of the Freedom of Information Act, and other access regimes, is testimony to that. In contrast, there is no general public interest in non-disclosure.[164]

In *Hogan v Oxford City Council and Information Commissioner* the Tribunal took the same line:

---

[159] Under this, it was recognised that if evenly-balanced, there should be no disclosure: Hansard HL vol 617 col 914 (17 October 2000) (Lord Falconer of Thoroton).

[160] It was described as turning the burden the wrong way round: Hansard HL vol 617 col 907 (17 October 2000) (Lord Goodhart). And, later on, as making the balance to be in favour of concealment: Hansard HL vol 619 col 134 (14 November 2000) (Lord Archer).

[161] Hansard HL vol 619 col 137 (14 November 2000) (Lord Lester of Herne Hill).

[162] Hansard HL vol 619 cols 143–144 (14 November 2000) (Minister of State, Cabinet Office, Lord Falconer of Thoroton). See also: Hansard HC vol 357 cols 719, 721–72 (27 November 2000), where, in introducing the amendment that led to s 2, the Parliamentary Under-Secretary of State for the Home Department (Mr O'Brien), said: 'the amendment also reverses the way in which the test works, so that the public interest in disclosing the information must be outweighed by the public interest in maintaining an exemption before any information can be withheld.'

[163] Similarly, EIR reg 12(1)(b); EI(S)R reg 10(1)(b). The position under the FOI(S)A is slightly different. The duty to disclose non-absolute exempt information only applies to the extent that, in all the circumstances of the case, the public interest in disclosing the information is not outweighed by the public interest in maintaining the exemption: s 2(1)(b). The provision is couched as part of the circumscription of the parameters of the right of access, rather than as an exception to be invoked in order to disapply the right of access.

[164] MoJ, *Exemptions Guidance — The public interest*, undated. Similarly, Information Commissioner, *Freedom of Information Act Awareness Guidance No 3*, undated, p 4 ('there is a presumptions running through the Act that openness is, in itself, to be regarded as something which is in the public interest.').

> [The Act] does not include any general provision that there is a presumption in favour of the disclosure of information held by public authorities. However in one important respect FOIA does contain a presumption in favour of disclosure. The duty to communicate under s 1(1)(a) [*sic*] is displaced by a qualified exemption under s 2(2)(b) only if the public interest in maintaining the exemptions *outweighs* the public interest in disclosure of the information sought. So if the interests are equally balanced, then the public authority, in our view, must communicate the information sought.[165]

Similarly, in *Dept for Education and Skills v Information Commissioner and The Evening Standard* the Tribunal held:

> Section 2(2)(b) is clear: the authority must disclose unless the public interest in withholding the information outweighs the public interest in disclosure. If the scales are level, it must disclose. Such an equilibrium may not be a purely theoretical result: there may be many cases where the apparent interests in disclosure and in maintaining the exemption are equally slight. The weighing exercise begins with both pans empty and therefore level. Disclosure follows if that remains the position.[166]

These views have been endorsed by the High Court:

> In my judgment, it is both implicit and explicit in FOIA that, in the absence of a public interest in preserving confidentiality, there is a public interest in the disclosure of information held by public authorities. That public interest is implicitly recognised in section 1, which confers, subject to specified exceptions, a general right of access to information held by public authorities...
>
> The public interest in disclosure is explicitly recognised and affirmed in section 19(3). Section 19(1) imposes on every public authority a duty to adopt and to maintain a scheme for the publication of information by it....[167]

These views have been endorsed by the High Court.[168] Put another way, the mere fact that information falls within a qualified exemption does not necessarily mean that disclosure would damage the interest protected by that exemption.[169] Accordingly, it is for a public authority that does not wish to communicate or acknowledge the existence of information falling within one of the provisions of Part II, other than one conferring absolute exemption, to demonstrate that in all the circumstances that stance is supported by a weighing of the relevant aspects of the public interest.[170] The Tribunal has rejected the notion that certain qualified exemptions

---

[165] IT, 17 October 2006 at [56]. Similarly, *Kitchener v IC and Derby City Council*, IT, 20 December 2006 at [13]; *Dept of Culture, Media and Sport v IC*, IT, 29 July 2008 at [22]; *DBERR v IC and Friends of the Earth*, IT, 29 April 2008 at [112(a)]; *Scotland Office v IC*, IT, 8 August 2008 at [77]; *Galloway v IC and NHS*, IT, 20 March 2009 at [69]; *ECGD v IC and Campaign Against Arms Trade*, IT, 21 October 2009 at [50(i)].

[166] *DfES v IC and The Evening Standard*, IT, 19 February 2007 at [64]–[65]. Similarly: *DTI v IC*, IT, 10 November 2006 at [54].

[167] *OGC v IC* [2008] EWHC 774 (Admin), [2010] QB 98, [2008] ACD 54 at [69]-[70]. See also [78], [82].

[168] *OGC v IC* [2008] EWHC 774 (Admin), [2010] QB 98, [2008] ACD 54 at [79]; *Home Office and MoJ v IC* [2009] EWHC 1611 (Admin) at [35].

[169] *DfES v IC and The Evening Standard*, IT, 19 February 2007 at [60], [62]; approved in *OGC v IC* [2008] EWHC 774 (Admin), [2010] QB 98, [2008] ACD 54 at [79].

[170] *DfES v IC and The Evening Standard*, IT, 19 February 2007 at [64]–[67]; *DWP v IC*, IT, 5 March 2007 at [27]–[29].

have an inherently greater public interest against disclosure than others.[171]

028 Standard of proof

In administrative matters, to the extent that there is any standard of proof, the civil standard of proof applies.[172] In other spheres where the courts have had to consider the public interest in disclosing and in not disclosing information, a mere say-so of harm, other than in cases involving national security, has not sufficed.[173]

029 Principles of interpretation: special characteristics

Applying the ordinary principles of administrative law, a public authority must exercise its discretion so as to promote the policy and objects of the Freedom of Information Act 2000, and not so as to frustrate that policy and those objects.[174] In the comparative jurisdictions, it has sometimes been argued that the nature of freedom of information legislation calls for any ambiguity to be decided in favour of wider disclosure. Underlying this argument is the notion that legislation providing for access to official information is akin to a constitutional instrument and that special principles of interpretation apply.[175] Whilst support can be found in judgments from comparative jurisdictions for the idea that official information access legislation may rank as a constitutional measure, those same judgments have not taken the additional step of giving the legislation a benevolent interpretation as a result of it.[176]

030 Principles of interpretation: general

Putting to one side characterisation of 'freedom of information' legislation as a constitutional measure, an issue that has arisen elsewhere is whether ambiguities in freedom of information legislation should as a rule be resolved so as to favour disclosure. In relation to the Freedom of Information (Scotland) Act 2002, Lord Marnoch in the Court of Session expressed the view:

---

[171] The argument has been run repeatedly before the Tribunal despite judicially approved decisions of the Tribunal: *DfES v IC and The Evening Standard*, IT, 19 February 2007 at [60]-[63]; *OGC v IC* [2008] EWHC 774 (Admin), [2010] QB 98, [2008] ACD 54 at [79]; *DBERR v IC and Friends of the Earth*, IT, 29 April 2008 at [103]. On the other hand, the Tribunal itself appears to countenance the suggestion: *Bellamy v IC and DBIS*, FTT, 23 February 2010

[172] *R v SSHD, ex p Khawaja* [1984] AC 74.

[173] *AG v Guardian Newspapers (No 2)* [1990] 1 AC 109 at 263 and 283. Although the standard remains the civil one, if the predicted consequence is inherently unlikely that will affect the cogency of the evidence required to satisfy the civil standard: *Re D* [2008] UKHL 33, [2008] 1 WLR 1499; *Re H (minors) (sexual abuse: standard of proof)* [1996] AC 563 at 586, [1996] 1 All ER 1 at 16 (Lord Nicholls); *SSHD v Rehman* [2001] UKHL 47, [2003] 1 AC 153 at [55] (Lord Hoffmann); *R (AN) v Mental Health Review Tribunal (Northern Region)* [2005] EWCA Civ 1605, [2006] QB 468 at [60], [62]–[71] (where it is said that the more serious the allegation or the more serious the consequences if the allegation is proved, the stronger must be the evidence before a court will find the allegation proved on the balance of probabilities).

[174] *Padfield v Minister of Agriculture, Fisheries and Food* [1968] AC 997 at 1030; *London Boroughs Transport Committee v Freight Transport Assocn Ltd* [1991] 1 WLR 828 at 836. As to the purpose of the FOIA, see §§1– 011 to 1– 016.

[175] In relation to the principles of construction of a true constitutional instrument, see *Minister of Home Affairs v Fisher* [1980] AC 319 at 329; *Riley v AG of Jamaica* [1983] 1 AC 719. In *Thoburn v Sunderland City Council* [2002] EWHC 195 Admin, [2003] QB 151 at [62] Laws LJ spoke of a hierarchy of 'ordinary' and 'constitutional' statutes, with the former being amenable to implied repeal and the latter not: 'In my opinion a constitutional statute is one which (a) conditions the legal relationship between citizen and State in some general, overarching manner, or (b) enlarges or diminishes the scope of what we would now regard as fundamental constitutional rights.'

[176] *Commissioner of Police v Ombudsman* [1988] 1 NZLR 385 (CA) at 391, 402 and 411; *Wyatt Co Ltd v Queenstown Lakes District Council* [1991] 2 NZLR 180.

...that the statute, whose whole purpose is to secure the release of information, should be construed in as liberal a manner as possible and, as long as individual and other rights are respected, and the cost limits are not exceeded, I do not myself see any reason why the Commissioner should not be accorded the widest discretion in deciding the form and type of information which should be released in furtherance of its objectives.[177]

This was not endorsed by the House of Lords on appeal:[178]

[7] In my opinion there is no presumption in favour of the release of personal data under the general obligation that the 2002 Act lays down. The references which that Act makes to provisions of the 1998 Act must be understood in the light of the legislative purpose of that Act, which was to implement Council Directive 95/46/EC.

[68] Where the legislature has thus worked out the way that the requirements of data protection and freedom of information are to be reconciled, the role of the courts is just to apply the compromise to be found in the legislation. The 2002 Act gives people, other than the data subject, a right to information in certain circumstances and subject to certain exemptions. Discretion does not enter into it. There is, however, no reason why courts should favour the right to freedom of information over the rights of data subjects. If Lord Marnoch's observations [32], were intended to suggest otherwise, I would respectfully disagree.

Nevertheless the principle may survive where there is no countervailing third party interest against disclosure.[179]

14–031 Principles of interpretation: comparative jurisprudence

In Australia, the High Court has said:

In the light of [s 3 and s 16] it is proper to give to the relevant provisions of the Act a construction which would further, rather than hinder, free access to information.[180]

More recently, Kirby J, in considering the Victorian Freedom of Information Act, stated:[181]

The starting point for resolving the issues presented by the present appeal is an appreciation of the duty of this Court, in this context, to do what we are constantly instructing other courts to do in giving effect to legislation. This is to read the legislative text in its context (including against the background of the significant change that the legislation introduces) and, so far as the text and context permit, to give effect to the legislative purpose.

In the present setting, that purpose is a radical one. It assigns very high importance to a public interest in greater openness and transparency in public administration. Given the historical background, the attitudinal shift that FOI legislation demanded of Ministers,

---

[177] *Common Services Agency v Scottish IC*, 2006 CSIH 58, 2007 SLT 7 at [32].

[178] *Common Services Agency v IC* [2008] UKHL 47, [2008] 1 WLR 1550, per Lord Hope and Lord Rodger respectively.

[179] On the basis that since any such third party interest weighs against disclosure (resulting in an even opening public interest balance), where there is no such countervailing interest against disclosure, the opening public interest balance should be in favour of disclosure.

[180] *Victorian Public Service Board v Wright* (1986) 160 CLR 145 at 153, considering the FOI Act of the State of Victoria. Similarly: *Accident Compensation Commission v Croom* [1991] 2 VR 322; *Sobh v Police Force of Victoria* [1994] 1 VR 41, although these decisions are in part based on an objects section in the legislation. See also: *Commissioner of Police v District Court of NSW and Perrin* (1993) 31 NSWLR 606; *Re Eccleston and Dept of Family Services and Aboriginal and Islander Affairs* (1993) 1 QAR 60. Contrast decisions of the Federal Court, considering the Commonwealth Act: *Kavvaadias v Commonwealth Ombudsman* (1984) 1 FCR 80 at 85; *News Corporation Ltd v National Companies & Securities Commission* (1984) 1 FCR 64; *Attorney-General's Department v Cockcroft* (1986) 10 FCR 180 at 195; *Commissioner of Taxation v Swiss Aluminium Australia Ltd* (1986) 10 FCR 321 at 327; *Searle Australia Pty Ltd v Public Interest Advocacy Centre* (1992) 36 FCR 111 at 114–115; cf *Arnold v Queensland* (1987) 13 ALD 195 at 205.

[181] *Osland v Secretary to the Department of Justice* [2008] HCA 37 at [65]-[66].

departments, agencies and the public service is nothing short of revolutionary. The courts ought not to obstruct that shift. On the contrary, they should strive to interpret FOI legislation in a manner harmonious with its objectives, doing so to the fullest extent that the text allows.

In Canada, the view taken is that public access ought not to be frustrated by the Courts except upon the clearest grounds, so that doubt ought to be resolved in favour of disclosure.[182] European case law in relation to Decision 93/731, article 4, has consistently stated that exceptions must be construed and applied restrictively so as not to defeat the general principle enshrined in that decision.[183] The European Court of Justice has consistently said:

> The aim pursued by Decision 93/731, as well as being to ensure the internal operation of the Council in conformity with the interests of good administration . . . is to provide the public with the widest possible access to documents held by the Council, so that any exception to that right of...access must be interpreted and applied strictly.[184]

In Ireland a similar view has been expressed:

> (In) the light of the preamble, it seems to me that there can be no doubt but that it was the intention of the legislature when enacting the provisions of the Freedom of Information Act 1997, that it was only in exceptional cases that members of the public at large should be deprived of access to information in the possession of public bodies and this intention is exemplified by the provision of s 34(12)(b) of the Act which provides that a decision to refuse to grant access to information sought shall be presumed not to have been justified until the contrary is shown.[185]

And later:

> ... given the policy and object of the Act to give wide and generous access to the documents held by public bodies, any exemptions or restrictions, such as those contained in Part III of the Act (ss. 19 to 32) ought to be given a narrow restrictive interpretation so as to derogate as little as possible from the main purpose of the Act[186]

---

[182] *Maislin Industries Limited v Minister for Industry, Trade & Commerce* [1984] 1 FC 939.

[183] *World Wide Fund for Nature v Commission of the European Communities* [1997] ECR II–313, [1997] All ER (EC) 300 [1997] Env LR 242 at [5]; *Svenska Journalistförbundet v Council of the European Union* [1998] ECR II–2289, [1998] All ER (EC) 545 at [110]; *Hautala v Council of the European Union* [1999] 3 CMLR 528 at [84]; *Denkavit Nederland BV v Commission of the European Communities* [2000] 3 CMLR 1014 at [45]; *Kuijer v Council of the European Union* [2002] 1 WLR 1941 at [55] and [57] ('Decision 93/731 must be interpreted in the light of the principle of the right to information and the principle of proportionality.'); *Franchet v Commission of European Communities* [2006] 3 CMLR 37 at [84], [105]. In relation to Decision 93/731 [1993] OJ L340/43 generally, see ch 6.

[184] *Hautala v Council of the European Union* [2002] 1 WLR 1930 at [25]. Similarly: *Verein für Konsumenteninformation v Commission* [2005] 1 WLR 3302, [2005] All ER (EC) 813, [2005] ECR II–1121, [2006] 2 CMLR 60, [2005] 4 CMLR 21 at [69] and [72]; *Franchet v Commission of European Communities* [2006] 3 CMLR 37 at [115]; Case T-121/05 *Borax Europe Ltd v EC Commission* (CFI 11 March 2009) at [31]-[35].

[185] *Minister for Agriculture and Food v Information Commissioner* [2000] 1 IR 309 at 319.

[186] *Health Service Executive v Information Commissioner and Another* [2008] IEHC 298.

6.   CONCLUSIVE CERTIFICATES*

14–032 Introduction

The Freedom of Information Act 2000, the Data Protection Act 1998 and the Environmental Information Regulations 2004 all provide for the signing and issuing of 'conclusive certificates'. The effect of a conclusive certificate is evidential: the certificate stands as conclusive evidence of the 'facts' certified in it, irrespective of the reality. The 'facts' that may be so certified are:

(1)   that particular information was directly or indirectly supplied by, or relates to, any of the security bodies specified in s 23(3) of the Freedom of Information Act 2000;[187]

(2)   that exemption from s 1(1)(b) (the disclosure duty) or s 1(1)(a) and (b) (the existence duty and the disclosure duty) of the Freedom of Information Act 2000, is, or at any time was, required for the purpose of safeguarding national security;[188]

(3)   that exemption from the disclosure duty, or from the existence duty and the disclosure duty, under the FOI Act 2000 is required for the purpose of avoiding an infringement of the privileges of either House of Parliament;[189]

(4)   that disclosure of information held by either House of Parliament would, or would be likely to, have any of the effects mentioned in s 36(2) of the Freedom of Information Act 2000 (in other words, it would be prejudicial to the maintenance of the convention of the collective responsibility of the Ministers of the Crown; it would inhibit the free and frank provision of advice or the free and frank exchange of views for the purposes of deliberation; or it would otherwise prejudice the effective conduct of public affairs);[190]

(5)   that the exemption of personal data from all or any of the provisions of the data protection principles or Pts II–III or V or ss 54A or 55 of the Data Protection Act 1998 is, or at any time was, required for the purpose of safeguarding national security;[191]

(6)   that a refusal to disclose information under reg 12(1) of the Environmental Information Regulations 2004 is because the disclosure would adversely affect national security and would not be in the public interest under reg 12(1)(b).[192]

Section 53 of the Freedom of Information Act 2000[193] also sets out circumstances in which the duty to comply with a decision notice or enforcement notice may be excepted through the issue

---

*   By Oliver Sanders, 1 Crown Office Row.

[187] FOIA s 23(2). Neither the certificate provision nor the underlying exemption exists in FOI(S)A.

[188] FOIA s 24(3); FOI(S)A s 31(2).

[189] FOIA s 34(2). Neither the certificate provision nor the underlying exemption exists in FOI(S)A.

[190] FOIA s 36(7). Although the underlying exemption is provided for by FOI(S)A s 30, it does not provide for conclusive certificates to facilitate its engagement.

[191] DPA s 28(2).

[192] EIR reg 15(1); EI(S)R reg 12.

[193] FOI(S)A s 52(2).

of a certificate. A certificate under s 53 has a prescribed statutory effect: it is not a conclusive evidential certificate as such. Certificates under s 53 are considered elsewhere in this work.[194]

033 General effect of a conclusive certificate

Each of the six types of conclusive certificate effectively deems that a prerequisite to the application of a particular exemption is satisfied, thereby facilitating the application of that exemption for the purposes of the relevant enactment.[195] These conclusive certificates fall into two categories: appealable ministerial 'national security certificates' under ss 23(2) and 24(3) of the Freedom of Information Act 2000, s 28(2) of the Data Protection Act 1998 and reg 15(1) of the Environmental Information Regulations 2004; and non-appealable 'Parliamentary certificates' under ss 34(3) and 36(7) of the Freedom of Information Act 2000. The former may be signed by certain Ministers of the Crown[196] and the latter may be signed by the Speaker of the House of Commons or the Clerk of the Parliaments ('the House Authorities').[197] Each of the underlying exemptions can nevertheless operate independently of conclusive certificates: the issue of an appropriate certificate is a sufficient but not a necessary condition for the engagement of each one.[198]

034 Types of ouster clause

Statutory provisions which seek to confer finality on determinations of the executive by excluding judicial review of those determinations are often referred to as 'preclusive clauses' or 'ouster clauses' because they seek to preclude or oust the supervisory jurisdiction of the courts over the executive.[199] Such clauses can take the form of 'finality' clauses, 'no certiorari' clauses, 'as if enacted' clauses, 'shall not be questioned' clauses and 'conclusive evidence' clauses.[200] An ouster clause which seeks to preclude judicial review other than by way of an exclusive statutory appeal or a review mechanism is known as a 'partial' ouster clause and, where the prescribed mechanism must be invoked within a particular limitation period, as a 'time-limited' clause.[201]

---

[194] See §28– 014.

[195] Both Acts confer power to 'sign' such certificates but talk in terms of their being 'issued' in relation to appeals. See also FOI(S)A s 31(2)–(3).

[196] FOIA s 25(3); DPA s 28(10); EIR reg 15(6). EIR reg 15(2) further provides that a Minister of the Crown may designate a person to certify the matters in reg 15(1) on his behalf.

[197] FOIA ss 34(4) and 36(5)(d)–(e) and (7).

[198] *Beam v IC and FCO*, IT, 12 May 2009, where the Tribunal upheld reliance upon FOIA s 23(1), (3)(b) without the need for a ministerial certificate under FOIA s 23(2). The FCO had stated in its evidence that 'we did not feel it necessary or helpful to the parties concerned to take up ministerial time by going down that line in this case' (at [11]) and the Tribunal made it clear that production of a ministerial certificate is not always necessary and may be disproportionate (at [15]).

[199] H Woolf, J Jowell and A Le Sueur, *De Smith's Judicial Review*, 6th edn (London, Sweet & Maxwell, 2007) paras 4–014 to 4–055; W Wade and C Forsyth, *Administrative Law*, 10th edn (Oxford, Oxford University Press, 2009) pp 610–631.

[200] H Woolf, J Jowell and A Le Sueur, *De Smith's Judicial Review*, 6th edn (London, Sweet & Maxwell, 2007) paras 4–019 to 4–022; W Wade and C Forsyth, *Administrative Law*, 10th edn, (Oxford, Oxford University Press, 2009) pp 610–615; M Fordham, *Judicial Review Handbook*, 5th edn (Oxford, Hart Publishing, 2008) ch P28.

[201] H Woolf, J Jowell and A Le Sueur, *De Smith's Judicial Review*, 6th edn (London, Sweet & Maxwell, 2007) paras 4–023 to 4–025, 4–038 and 4–055; W Wade and C Forsyth, *Administrative Law*, 10th edn (Oxford, Oxford University Press, 2009) pp 607–609 and 621–626; M Fordham, *Judicial Review Handbook*, 5th edn (Oxford, Hart Publishing, 2005), ch P36.

The provisions in the Freedom of Information Act 2000, the Data Protection Act 1998 and the Environmental Information Regulations 2004 allowing for the issue of conclusive certificates thus contain a species of conclusive evidence clause:[202] in relation to ss 23(2) and 24(3) of the Freedom of Information Act 2000, s 28(2) of the Data Protection Act 1998 and reg 15(1) of the Environmental Information Regulations 2004 these are partial ouster clauses because national security certificates signed thereunder are appealable. In relation to ss 34(3) and 36(7) of the Freedom of Information Act 2000, they are absolute as there is no scope for challenging parliamentary certificates.

14–035 Judicial approach to ouster clauses

In very general terms, the courts have been prepared to enforce partial and time-limited ouster clauses on the basis that they do not altogether preclude judicial oversight.[203] By contrast, the courts have had a long-standing reluctance to give full literal effect to absolute ouster clauses, eventually leading to a complete unwillingness to read 'shall-not-be-questioned' clauses as ousting their supervisory jurisdiction over subordinate authorities in particular.[204] In modern times, the domestic courts have upheld conclusive evidence clauses[205] and accepted that they cannot go behind or scrutinise non-appealable national security certificates unless and in so far

---

[202] For examples of traditional certificate-based conclusive evidence clauses see: the Race Relations Act 1976, ss 42 and 69 as originally enacted (subsequently amended by the Employment Rights Act 1996 and the Race Relations (Amendment) Act 2000); and the Fair Employment (Northern Ireland) Act 1976 s 42 (subsequently repealed and replaced by the Fair Employment and Treatment (Northern Ireland) Order 1998 SI 1998/3162 (NI 21)). Both sets of provisions were amended or replaced so as to allow, inter alia, for appeals to be brought against the relevant type of ministerial national security certificate following the decision of the European Court of Human Rights in *Tinnelly and Sons Ltd v United Kingdom* (1999) 27 EHRR 249 (ECtHR). For further examples see: Parliamentary Commissioner Act 1967 s 8(4) allowing the Secretary to the Cabinet to issue a certificate with the approval of the Prime Minister certifying conclusively that any information, question, document or part of a document relates to proceedings of the Cabinet or any committee of the Cabinet and is thus immune from compulsory disclosure or production under that Act (such a certificate was issued in the *Court Line* case: HC 498, 1974–1975, para 9: W Wade and C Forsyth, *Administrative Law*, 10th edn (Oxford, Oxford University Press, 2009) p 87); Trade Union and Labour Relations (Consolidation) Act 1992 s 183; Disability Discrimination Act 1995, Sch 3, Pt II, para 8; Protection from Harassment Act 1997 s 12; Northern Ireland Act 1998, ss 90–91; International Criminal Court Act 2001 s 39; Privacy and Electronic Communications (EC Directive) Regulations 2003 SI 2003/2426 reg 28; Civil Contingencies Act 2004 s 46.

[203] *Smith v East Elloe RDC* [1956] AC 736 (HL); *R v Secretary of State for the Environment, ex p Ostler* [1977] QB 122 (CA); *R v Cornwall CC, ex p Huntington* [1992] 3 All ER 566; *R v Dacorum DC, ex p Cannon* [1996] 2 PLR 45 (DC); cf *Anisminic Ltd v Foreign Compensation Commission* [1969] 2 AC 147 (HL) at 171 (Lord Reid), 200 (Lord Pearce), 210 (Lord Wilberforce).

[204] *Anisminic Ltd v Foreign Compensation Commission* [1969] 2 AC 147; *R v Hull University Visitor, ex p Page* [1993] AC 682; *Boddington v British Transport Police* [1999] 2 AC 143; *R v SSHD, ex p Fayed* [1998] 1 WLR 763 (CA). See also the debate on the abandoned ouster clause originally included in Asylum and Immigration (Treatment of Claimants, etc) Bill 2003, cl 11: H Wade and C Forsyth, *Administrative Law*, 10th edn (Oxford, Oxford University Press, 2009) pp 617–618, n 279; Jowell, 'Heading for Constitutional Crisis?' (2004) 154 *New Law Journal* 401; Le Sueur, 'Three Strikes and It's Out? The UK Government's Strategy to Oust Judicial Review from Immigration and Asylum Decision Making' [2004] *Public Law* 225; Rawlings, 'Review, Revenge and Retreat' (2005) 68 *Modern Law Review* 378; Thomas, 'After the Ouster: Review and Reconsideration in a Single Tier Tribunal' [2006] *Public Law* 674.

[205] *R v Registrar of Companies, ex p Central Bank of India* [1986] QB 1114 (CA); cf *R v Preston Supplementary Benefits Appeal Tribunal, ex p Moore* [1975] 1 WLR 624 (CA). See also the Tribunals and Inquiries Act 1958 s 11, Tribunals and Inquiries Act 1971 s 14 and Tribunals and Inquiries Act 1992 s 12.

as obtained or issued in bad faith.[206]   However, recent decisions of the European Court of Justice and the European Court of Human Rights founded on human rights principles have, in effect, declared certain conclusive evidence clauses precluding any judicial oversight to be incompatible with fundamental rights.[207]

036   Human rights

Human rights issues[208] are therefore potentially important to the application and effectiveness of the conclusive evidence clauses in the Freedom of Information Act 2000, the Data Protection Act 1998 and the Environmental Information Regulations 2004.   If it can be shown that a conclusive certificate issued under one of these Acts has interfered with the enjoyment or exercise of a 'Convention right' within the meaning of the Human Rights Act 1998[209] or a right under European Community law that can be relied upon before the domestic courts,[210] this will

---

[206] See the references to the various unreported judicial review proceedings in the Northern Ireland High Court before Nicholson and McCollum JJ which preceded *Tinnelly and Sons Ltd v United Kingdom* (1999) 27 EHRR 249 (ECtHR) at [18]–[32], [64], [66]–[67] and [74]–[75] and before Kerr J which preceded *Devlin v United Kingdom* (2002) 34 EHRR 43 (ECtHR) at [12]–[14].   See also: *R v Secretary of State for Foreign and Commonwealth Affairs, ex p Vidler* [1993] COD 305 (national security certificate under the Employment Protection (Consolidation) Act 1978, Sch 9, para 2); *R v Secretary of State for Transport, ex p Evans and Commission for Racial Equality* [1992] COD 196 (national security certificate under the Race Relations Act 1976, ss 42 and 69); and *R v Secretary of State for Northern Ireland, ex p Gilmore* (unreported, 10 April 1987) referred to in White, 'Security Vetting, discrimination and the right to a fair trial' [1999] *Public Law* 406.

[207] Case 222/84 *Johnston v Chief Constable of the Royal Ulster Constabulary* [1987] QB 129 (ECJ); *Tinnelly and Sons Ltd v United Kingdom* (1999) 27 EHRR 249 (ECtHR); *Devlin v United Kingdom* (2002) 34 EHRR 43 (ECtHR); *Devenney v United Kingdom* (2002) 35 EHRR 24 (ECtHR).   See further §14– 036.

[208] For the role of the ECHR in relation to FOIA generally, see ch 3.

[209] Human Rights Act 1998 s 1(1)–(3), Sch 1 define 'the Convention rights' for the purposes of that Act as the rights and fundamental freedoms set out in arts 2–12 and 14 of the Convention for the Protection of Human Rights and Fundamental Freedoms (Cmd 8969, 1953), arts 1–3 of the First Protocol and arts 1–2 of the Sixth Protocol. The ECHR, arts 1 and 13 are notable omissions from 'the Convention rights'. Primary and subordinate legislation must, so far as possible, be read and given effect in a way which is compatible with the Convention rights (s 3) and it is unlawful for public authorities (including courts) to act in a way which is incompatible with them unless left with no alternative by primary legislation (s 6).

[210] In this regard, reliance can be placed on Community law in accordance with the doctrine of direct effect including the subsidiary or related doctrines of vertical, indirect and incidental direct effect: P Craig and G De Búrca, *EU Law: Text, Cases and Materials*, 4th edn (Oxford, Oxford University Press, 2007) chs 8–9; D Wyatt and A Dashwood, *European Union Law*, 5th edn (London, Sweet & Maxwell, 2004) ch 5.   In particular, the doctrine of incidental direct effect requires that national law implementing Directives is interpreted and applied in accordance with Community law and norms and is therefore relevant to DPA (implementing European Community Data Protection Directive 95/46/EC) and EIR (implementing European Community Public Access to Environmental Information Directive 2003/4/EC): Case 14/83 *Von Colson v Land Nordrhein-Westfalen* [1984] ECR 1891 (ECJ); Case C–106/89 *Marleasing SA v La Comercial Internacional de Alimentacion SA* [1990] ECR I–4135 (ECJ); Cases C–240–244/98 *Océano Grupo Editorial v Rocio Murciano Quintero* [2000] ECR I–449 (ECJ); P Craig, 'Directives: Direct Effect, Indirect Effect and the Construction of National Legislation' (1997) 22 EL Rev 519.   In relation to the interpretation of DPA see in particular: *Campbell v MGN Ltd* [2002] EWCA Civ 1373, [2003] QB 633 (CA) at [96] (Phillips MR); *Durant v Financial Services Authority* [2003] EWCA Civ 1746, [2004] FSR 28 (CA) at [3]–[4] (Auld LJ); *R (Lord) v SSHD* [2003] EWHC 2073 (Admin) at [83] (Munby J); *R (SSHD) v Information Tribunal* [2006] EWHC 2958 (Admin), [2007] 2 All ER 703 (DC) at [15] (Latham LJ).   Where Community law can be relied upon, the legality of acts done by European Community member states in the exercise of powers conferred or reserved by Community law falls to be determined by reference to the 'general principles of Community law' which include principles of administrative or procedural fairness: J Usher, *General Principles of EC Law*, (London, Longmans, 1998); T Tridimas, *The General Principles of EU Law*, 2nd edn (Oxford, Oxford University Press, 2006); P Craig and G De Búrca, *EU Law: Text, Cases and Materials*, 4th edn (Oxford, Oxford University Press, 2007), ch 11.   In relation to procedural fairness, these principles can confer a right to a fair hearing (Case 17/74 *Transocean Marine Paint Association v EC Commission* [1974] ECR 1063 (ECJ) at 1080) and to judicial oversight and control (Case 222/84 *Johnston v Chief Constable of the Royal Ulster Constabulary*

have two important consequences. First, the Tribunal and the courts will need to be persuaded that there is sufficient judicial control over the operation of the relevant provisions when reading and giving effect to them generally and when considering whether it is possible and appropriate to intervene in relation to decisions taken thereunder.[211] Secondly, the Tribunal and the courts will apply a more intensive proportionality-based standard of scrutiny if and when called upon to review any such decisions.[212] Whether any relevant Convention or Community rights will be engaged by the issue of conclusive certificates for these purposes is

---

[1987] QB 129 (ECJ) at 147 (although note that the decision itself rested on 'the principle of effective judicial control laid down in article 6 of Council Directive (76/207/EEC) of 9 February 1976': see 155)).

[211] The scope for appealing national security certificates issued under FOIA ss 23(2) and 24(3), DPA s 28(2) and EIR reg 15(1) should suffice for these purposes but questions may nevertheless arise as to the grounds and intensity of the review thereby allowed and as to the absence of any provision allowing for a further appeal to the High Court on a point of law (cf the non-appealability of parliamentary certificates issued under FOIA ss 34(3) and 36(7) and the scope for further appeals under FOIA s 59 and DPA s 49(6)). In *Tinnelly and Sons Ltd v United Kingdom* (1999) 27 EHRR 249 (ECtHR) two non-appealable certificates had been signed by the Secretary of State under the Fair Employment (Northern Ireland) Act 1976 s 42 certifying conclusively that certain decisions were acts done for the purpose of safeguarding national security, etc. The European Court of Human Rights held that: civil rights under the ECHR art 6(1) were engaged (at [61]–[63]); the scope for judicial review of the certificates was limited to a review of whether they had been obtained or issued in bad faith and could not entail 'full scrutiny' of their factual basis (at [74]–[75]); and the exclusion of a judicial determination of the merits of the complaints constituted a disproportionate interference with the applicants' rights under the ECHR, Article 6(1) (at [77] and [79]). In Case 222/84 *Johnston v Chief Constable of the Royal Ulster Constabulary* [1987] QB 129 (ECJ) a non-appealable certificate had been signed by the Secretary of State under the Sex Discrimination (Northern Ireland) Order 1976 SI 1976/1042 (NI 15) art 53(2) certifying conclusively that Mrs Johnston had been refused employment on the grounds of national security, etc. The ECJ held that the exclusion of judicial review was contrary to Community law: 'The requirement of judicial control stipulated by [Article 6 of the Equal Treatment Directive] reflects a general principle of law which underlies the constitutional traditions common to the member states. That principle is also laid down in articles 6 and 13 of the [ECHR]' (at 147); and 'The principle of effective judicial control laid down in article 6 of Council Directive (76/207/EEC) of 9 February 1976 does not allow a [national security certificate]…to exclude the exercise of any power of review by the courts' (at 155).

[212] The traditional standard of review for reasonableness is that enunciated in *Associated Provincial Picture Houses Ltd v Wednesbury Corp* [1948] 1 KB 223 (CA) and *Council of Civil Service Unions v Minister for the Civil Service* [1985] AC 374 at 410 (Lord Diplock). As a matter of common law principle, a heightened standard of review will be applied where 'fundamental rights' are engaged (*R v Ministry of Defence, ex p Smith* [1996] QB 517 (CA) at 554 (Bingham MR)) and where 'Convention rights' are engaged for the purposes of the Human Rights Act 1998 a yet more intensive proportionality-based standard of review is appropriate (*R (Daly) v SSHD* [2001] UKHL 26, [2001] 2 AC 532 at [26]–[27] (Lord Steyn)). In the light of these principles, the Information Tribunal adopted a proportionality-based standard of review in *Baker v SSHD* [2001] UKHRR 1275 in an appeal under DPA s 28(4) against a certificate issued by the Home Secretary which effectively conferred a blanket exemption allowing the Security Service to respond with a 'neither confirm nor deny' reply to every request made to it under DPA s 7(1)(a) without considering each request on its individual merits (at [83]). Having referred in general terms to the Council of Europe Convention for the Protection of Individuals with Regard to Automatic Processing of Personal Data dated 28 January 1981, the European Community Data Protection Directive 95/46/EC dated 24 October 1995 and the Human Rights Act 1998 ss 1, 3 and 6, the Tribunal asked itself whether the issue of the certificate was 'reasonable in the extended sense of proportionate by reference to the precepts of the ECHR' (at [63]) and concluded that the certificate had an 'unnecessarily wide effect' and should be quashed accordingly (summary, [14]). See also *Gosling v SSHD*, IT, 1 August 2003; *Hitchens v SSHD*, IT, 4 August 2003; *Hilton v FCO*, IT, 28 June 2005; *Stevenson v SSHD*, IT, 30 April 2009. Whether or not human rights are engaged for these purposes, it remains the case that the courts will show 'considerable deference' to the executive's assessment of national security matters whilst bearing in mind that they must do so 'in a manner appropriate to the national security context': *Baker v SSHD* [2001] UKHRR 1275 at [76]; *Gosling v SSHD*, IT, 1 August 2003 at [44] and [48]; *SSHD v Rehman* [2001] UKHL 47, [2003] 1 AC 153 at [50] and [62] (Lord Hoffmann) and at [16] (Lord Slynn); *A v SSHD* [2004] UKHL 56, [2005] 2 AC 68, 'Safeguarding national security is (with the possible exception of some questions of macro-economic policy and allocation of resources) the area of policy in which the courts are most reluctant to question or interfere with the judgment of the executive or (a fortiori) the enacted will of the legislature' at [192] (Lord Walker dissenting).

another matter[213] but the rights which are most likely to be relied upon in this regard are: rights to procedural fairness and judicial oversight under article 6 of the ECHR and the general principles of Community law;[214] rights to privacy and data protection rights under article 8 of the ECHR and the European Community Data Protection Directive 95/46/EC;[215] and rights to freedom of expression under article 10 of the ECHR.[216]

037 Legislative history

The policy and consultation documents which preceded and underlay the Freedom of Information Act 2000 contain very little discussion of its conclusive evidence clauses.[217] Section 28 of the Data Protection Act 1998 was plainly the model for s 24 of the Freedom of Information Act 2000[218] and thus provided a template for adopting a certification procedure in relation to the national security exemption.[219] So far as parliamentary debate is concerned, Mr O'Brien, the Home Office Minister, made the following points during the Report and Third Reading debate in the House of Commons in relation to the clauses which became ss 23–24 of the Freedom of Information Act 2000:

— information covered by certificates signed under these provisions will be 'extremely sensitive' and should not therefore be seen by the Information Commissioner or his staff;

— such certificates can only be signed 'at the highest level'; and

— they will not operate as 'ministerial vetoes' because they are 'nothing more than

---

[213] See §§14–042 to 14–045.

[214] See §14–043. See, generally, §3–016.

[215] See §14–044. See, generally, §§3–002 to 3–007.

[216] See §14–045. See, generally, §§3–010 to 3–015.

[217] As already mentioned, the use of conclusive certificate provisions is by no means unprecedented, particularly in the national security context, and once an exemption has been settled on as a matter of principle, the technicalities of its application are much less likely to generate political or public interest or debate.

[218] 'The clause [which became FOIA s 24] is drafted in similar terms to section 28 of the Data Protection Act 1998. The two provisions have the same purpose. It is therefore sensible for them to be drafted in similar language. Any difference of approach between the provisions could lead to them being interpreted differently. Clearly, that is not the intention' (Mr O'Brien, the Home Office Minister, Report and Third Reading debate on the Freedom of Information Bill in the House of Commons: Hansard HC vol 347 col 1060 (5 April 2000).

[219] DPA s 28 was itself preceded by the national security exemption in the Data Protection Act 1984 s 27 which provided that, 'Any question whether the exemption mentioned in subsection (1) above is or at any time was required for the purpose there mentioned [ie the purpose of safeguarding national security] in respect of any personal data shall be determined by a Minister of the Crown; and a certificate signed by a Minister of the Crown certifying that the exemption is or at any time was so required shall be conclusive evidence of that fact.' — Data Protection Act 1984 s 27(2), see also s 27(3). The 'required for the purpose of safeguarding national security' test was therefore the same under both Acts, the key difference being the addition of an appeal mechanism in DPA s 28. This was explained during the parliamentary passage of the 1998 Data Protection Bill as follows: 'This is broadly familiar from the 1984 provision, but it contains two important changes. First, it allows a certificate confirming the need for the exemption to be expressed in general terms and to be prospective, and, secondly, it allows a limited right of appeal to the Data Protection Tribunal for individuals who are affected by such a certificate.' — Hansard HL vol 585 col 441 (2 February 1998) (Home Office Minister, Lord Williams, Second Reading). Similarly: 'The right of appeal against a national security certificate is an important new safeguard. It represents an advance on the 1984 Act, which offered no appeal rights.' — Hansard HC vol 315 col 586 (2 July 1998) (Home Office Minister, Mr Howarth, Report and Third Reading).

evidential certificates' subject to challenge before the Tribunal.[220]

During Committee Stage in the House of Lords, Lord Falconer of Thoroton, the Cabinet Office Minister, said he could not conceive that a conclusive certificate issued under the clause which became s 23 of the Freedom of Information Act 2000 could ever be subject to an exemption itself or be anything other than a public document.[221]

14– 038 The comparative jurisdictions

At the time that the Freedom of Information Act 2000 was enacted, the Freedom of Information Act 1982 (Cth of Aust) and the Freedom of Information Act 1997 (Ireland) both[222] provided for the issue of conclusive certificates as a means of activating certain exemptions:[223]

(1)   Under the Freedom of Information Act 1982 (Cth of Aust), conclusive certificates could be issued by ministers under s 33(2) and (4) (documents affecting national security, defence or international relations), s 33A(2) and (4) (documents affecting relations with States) and s 36(3) (internal working documents),[224] by the Secretary to the Department of the Prime Minister and Cabinet under s 34(2) and (4) (Cabinet documents) and by the Secretary to the Executive Council (or a person performing his or her duties) under s 35(2) and (4) (Executive Council documents). Such certificates were required, where appropriate, to identify the part or parts of the document covered by the relevant exemption[225] and they had to make clear the particular kind of document in respect of which the exemption had been claimed.[226] While they remained in force,[227] such certificates were conclusive in their effect subject to the relevant review procedures in Part VI of the Freedom of Information Act 1982 (Cth of Aust). In this latter regard, the Administrative Appeals Tribunal, on an application under s 55, could not review the decision to give the certificate but could review 'whether there existed reasonable grounds' for claiming that

---

[220] Hansard HC vol 347 col 1060 (5 April 2000).

[221] Hansard HL vol 617 col 1259 (19 October 2000). See also J Wadham and J Griffiths, *Blackstone's Guide to the Freedom of Information Act 2000*, 3rd edn (Oxford, Oxford University Press, 2007) para 7.3.2 contending that the minister's assertion is 'open to question.'

[222] As to the position under the Access to Information Act (1982) (Canada) see §§2– 025 to 2– 030.

[223] Official Information Act 1982 s 31 (NZ) allows for certificates to be issued preventing an Ombudsman from recommending the disclosure of information where this would be likely to prejudice: (a) security, defence or international relations (power conferred on Prime Minister); or (b) the prevention, investigation or detection of offences (power conferred on Attorney-General). These are not 'conclusive certificates' as such but they operate in a similar way and demonstrate a common approach in relation to the provision of executive override mechanisms in areas generally regarded as being particularly sensitive. See §2– 021.

[224] Ministerial certificates were required to specify the relevant ground of exemption: Freedom of Information Act 1982, ss 33(2) and (4), 33A(2) and (4) and 36(3) (Cth of Aust). In relation to certificates under Freedom of Information Act 1982 s 36(3) (Cth of Aust), see *McKinnon v Secretary, Department of Treasury* [2006] HCA 45, (2006) 229 ALR 187. These were abolished by the Freedom of Information (Removal of Conclusive Certificates and Other Measures) Act 2009.

[225] Freedom of Information Act 1982 ss 33(3), 33A(3), 34(3), 35(3), 36(4) (Cth of Aust).

[226] *Department of Industrial Relations v Forrest* (1990) 21 FCR 93, 11 AAR 256, 91 ALR 417 (certificate under Freedom of Information Act 1982 s 34 (Cth of Aust) invalid for uncertainty).

[227] Freedom of Information Act 1982 s 36A (Cth of Aust).

the relevant exemption applies.[228]   It had been held 'that it is a heavy thing for the Tribunal to reject a certified claim.'[229]   However, the above-mentioned provisions were all repealed with effect from 7 October 2009 by the Freedom of Information (Removal of Conclusive Certificates and other Measures) Act 2009 (Cth of Aust),[230] thereby removing conclusive certificates entirely from the scheme of the Freedom of Information Act 1982 (Cth of Aust).

(2)   In relation to the Freedom of Information Act 1997 (Ireland), conclusive certificates can be issued by ministers under s 25 in order to declare that a record is exempt by virtue of s 23 (law enforcement and public safety) or s 24 (security, defence and international relations).[231]   Such certificates can only be issued where access to a record has been refused in reliance on one of these exemptions and the minister is satisfied that the record is of 'sufficient sensitivity or seriousness' to 'justify' the issue of a certificate.[232]   While they remain in force,[233] such certificates are conclusive in their effect[234] subject to appeal to the High Court on a point of law under s 42(2) of the Freedom of Information Act 1997 (Ireland).   The Act also establishes various mechanisms for monitoring, controlling and publicising the use of such certificates.[235]

039 National security certificates

Appealable ministerial national security certificates may be issued under the Freedom of Information Act 2000, the Data Protection Act 1998 and the Environmental Information

---

[228]   Freedom of Information Act 1982 s 58(3), (4), (5) and (5A) (Cth of Aust). The issue for the Tribunal under s 58(4), (5) and (5A) had been whether the view expressed in the certificate was reasonably open to the Minister and not whether it was reasonable to release the document: *Re Bracken and Minister of State for Education and Youth Affairs* (1984) 2 AAR 406, (1985) 7 ALD 243; *Re Waterford and the Treasurer of the Commonwealth (No 2)* (1985) 8 ALN N37; *Re Porter and Department of Community Services* (1988) 8 AAR 335, 14 ALD 403; *Department of Industrial Relations v Burchill* (1991) 33 FCR 122, 14 AAR 408, 105 ALR 327; *Re Cleary and Department of the Treasury* (1993) 18 AAR 83; *Australian Doctors Fund Ltd v Commonwealth* (1994) 49 FCR 478, 34 ALD 451; *McKinnon v Secretary, Department of Treasury* [2006] HCA 45, (2006) 229 ALR 187. Specific provision is made regarding the constitution of the Tribunal and its hearings in cases where a conclusive certificate has been issued: Freedom of Information Act 1982, ss 58B, 58C and 58E (Cth of Aust). Where the Tribunal determines that there do not exist reasonable grounds for claiming that an exemption applies, the appropriate minister has 28 days either to revoke the certificate or follow the special procedure for deciding not to do so: Freedom of Information Act 1982 s 58A (Cth of Aust). The existence of these review procedures does not oust the scope for judicial review of the issue of conclusive certificates: *Shergold v Tanner* [2002] HCA 19, (2002) 188 ALR 302.

[229]   *Re Porter and Department of Community Services and Health* (1988) 14 ALD 403 at 405–406.

[230]   Section 1, Sch 3.

[231]   M McDonagh, *Freedom of Information Law in Ireland* , 2nd edn (Dublin, Thomson Round Hall, 2006), pp 154–158.

[232]   Freedom of Information Act 1997 s 25(1)(a) (Ireland).

[233]   Freedom of Information Act 1997 s 25(9), (10) and (13) (Ireland).

[234]   Freedom of Information Act 1997 s 25(3) (Ireland). The issue of a certificate cannot therefore be subject to internal review or review by the Information Commissioner: Freedom of Information Act 1997 s 25(3)(b) (Ireland).

[235]   Under the Freedom of Information Act 1997 s 25(6)(b) (Ireland) the Taoiseach (and prescribed ministers) must be provided with a copy of every certificate and a statement explaining why it was issued and, under s 25(7), they must in turn carry out periodic reviews of the operation of s 25(1). The Taoiseach also has power under s 25(8) to conduct specific reviews of the operation of s 25(1) in relation to particular ministers or certificates. In accordance with s 25(9), both periodic and specific reviews can result in requests that a certificate be revoked which must be complied with. Each minister must also provide the Information Commissioner with a written annual return detailing the number of conclusive certificates issued by him or her in the preceding year and these are then appended to the Commissioner's annual report to the Houses of the Oireachtas: ss 25(11) and 40(1)(b).

Regulations 2004 as follows:

(1)   Under s 23(2) of the Freedom of Information Act 2000 a Minister of the Crown may sign a certificate certifying that the information to which it applies was directly or indirectly supplied by, or relates to, any of the 'security bodies' specified in s 23(3). Such a certificate will then stand as conclusive evidence of that fact, thus confirming the engagement of the s 23 exemption, unless and until withdrawn or revoked[236] or quashed on an appeal under s 60(1) of the Freedom of Information Act 2000. The coincidence between what is certified by a s 23(2) certificate and what is required to engage the s 23(1) exemption is not perfect. The certificate will not certify whether the information was directly or indirectly supplied *to* the public authority *by* any of the s 23(3) bodies. It is possible that a public authority's holding of information to which a certificate applies may not result, directly or indirectly, from a supply by any of the bodies specified in s 23(3). For example, where a public authority has acquired the information independently or where it has acquired it from a third party that has itself acquired it independently.[237] There is no provision allowing such a certificate to identify the information to which it applies by means of a general description or to be expressed to have prospective effect.[238] Such a certificate may only be signed by a Minister who is a member of the Cabinet or by the Attorney-General, the Advocate General for Scotland or the Attorney-General for Northern Ireland.[239] While a s 23(2) certificate facilitates the rendering of information as exempt information and the disapplication of the disclosure duty, it is not determinative of the separate question whether the duty to confirm or deny arises, although it will undoubtedly bear on this issue.

(2)   Under s 24(3) of the Freedom of Information Act 2000 a Minister of the Crown may sign a certificate certifying that exemption from the disclosure duty in s 1(1)(b), or from the divulgence and disclosure duties in s 1(1)(a) and (b), is, or at any time was, required for the purpose of safeguarding national security.[240] Such a certificate will then stand as conclusive evidence of that fact, thus confirming the engagement of the s 24 exemption, unless and until withdrawn or revoked or quashed on an appeal under s 60(1) or (4) of the Freedom of Information Act 2000. If a s 24(3) certificate is confined to exemption from s 1(1)(b), determination of the existence duty will be decided on the ordinary basis, unaffected by the certificate. A s 24(3)

---

[236] There is no obvious reason for construing FOIA ss 23(2), 24(3), 34(3) or 36(7), DPA s 28(2) or EIR reg 15(1) as preventing the withdrawal or revocation of certificates or rendering their signatories *functus officio*. Changes in circumstances may very well make the withdrawal or revocation of a certificate appropriate without the need (where this route is open) for an appeal to the Upper Tribunal. See: *Al Fayed v SSHD*, IT, 28 February 2002 at [9] and [15]–[16]; W Wade and C Forsyth, *Administrative Law*, 10th edn (Oxford, Oxford University Press, 2009) pp 193–196; and the Interpretation Act 1978 s 12.

[237] Always assuming, of course, that it does not relate to any of the s 23(3) bodies.

[238] Compare FOIA s 24(4) and DPA s 28(3).

[239] FOIA s 25(3).

[240] FOI(S)A s 31(2)–(3). Under FOI(S)A s 31(2) a certificate may be signed by a member of the Scottish Executive and will stand as being conclusive of the fact certified (ie exemption from s 1(1) is required for the purpose of safeguarding national security): FOI(S)A does not expressly provide or allow for any appeal or review. Under FOI(S)A s 31(3), such a certificate may identify the information to which it applies by means of a general description and may be expressed to have prospective effect.

certificate may not deem that the public interest in maintaining the exemption outweighs the public interest in divulgence or disclosure but may identify the information to which it applies by means of a general description and may be expressed to have prospective effect.[241] Such a certificate may only be signed by a Minister who is a member of the Cabinet or by the Attorney-General, the Advocate General for Scotland or the Attorney-General for Northern Ireland.[242]

(3) Under s 28(2) of the Data Protection Act 1998 a Minister of the Crown may sign a national security certificate certifying that exemption from all or any of the provisions of the data protection principles or Pts II, III or V or ss 54A or 55 of the Data Protection Act 1998 (which includes the subject access rights given by s 7) is, or at any time was, required for the purpose of safeguarding national security in respect of any personal data. Such a certificate will then stand as conclusive evidence of that fact, thus confirming the engagement of the s 28 exemption, unless and until withdrawn or revoked or quashed on an appeal under s 28(4) or (6) of the Data Protection Act 1998. Such a certificate may identify the personal data to which it applies by means of a general description and may be expressed to have prospective effect.[243] Such a certificate may only be signed by a Minister who is a member of the Cabinet or by the Attorney-General, the Advocate General for Scotland or the Attorney-General for Northern Ireland.[244]

(4) Under reg 15(1) of the Environmental Information Regulations 2004 a Minister of the Crown may certify that a refusal to disclose information under reg 12(1) is required because the disclosure would adversely affect national security and would not be in the public interest under reg 12(1)(b).[245] For these purposes, Ministers of the Crown may designate persons to certify these matters on their behalf and a refusal to disclose information under reg 12(1) includes a neither confirm nor deny response under reg 12(6).[246] A certificate issued in accordance with reg 15(1) will then stand as conclusive evidence of the fact that disclosure would adversely affect national security and would not be in the public interest, unless and until withdrawn or revoked or quashed on an appeal under s 60 of the Freedom of Information Act 2000.[247] A national security certificate under reg 15(1) of the Environmental Information Regulations 2004 may identify the information to which it relates in

---

[241] FOIA s 24(4). Pursuant to FOIA s 60(4) a public authority may claim in proceedings under or by virtue of that Act that a certificate issued under s 24(3) which identifies the information to which it applies by means of a general description applies to particular information and, subject to any contrary determination by the Upper Tribunal on appeal, the certificate will be conclusively presumed so to apply.

[242] FOIA s 25(3).

[243] DPA s 28(3). Pursuant to DPA s 28(6) a data controller may claim in proceedings under or by virtue of that Act that a certificate issued under s 28(2) which identifies the personal data to which it applies by means of a general description applies to any personal data and, subject to any contrary determination by the Upper Tribunal on appeal, the certificate will be conclusively presumed so to apply.

[244] DPA s 28(10).

[245] See also EI(S)R reg 12.

[246] EIR reg 15(2).

[247] FOIA s 60 is applied for the purposes of the EIR with modifications by EIR reg 18(1), (3)–(4), (7). As to appeals, see §28– 027.

general terms but there is no express provision allowing for such certificates to be expressed to have prospective effect.[248] The power to sign such a certificate or to designate another person to certify the relevant matters is only exercisable by a Minister who is a member of the Cabinet or by the Attorney-General, the Advocate General for Scotland or the Attorney-General for Northern Ireland.[249]

14– 040 Appeals against national security certificates

The appeals procedure is considered in detail later in this work.[250] In summary, certificates issued under ss 23(2) and 24(3) of the Freedom of Information Act 2000, s 28(2) of the Data Protection Act 1998 and reg 15(1) of the Environmental Information Regulations 2004 may be appealed to the Upper Tribunal under a common appeal mechanism provided for by ss 60–61 of the Freedom of Information Act 2000, s 28 of, and Sch 6 to, the Data Protection Act 1998 and reg 18 of the Environmental Information Regulations 2004.

(1) In relation to certificates issued under ss 23(2) and 24(3) of the Freedom of Information Act 2000 and reg 15(1) of the Environmental Information Regulations 2004, such an appeal may be brought by the Information Commissioner or any applicant whose request for information is affected and, in relation to certificates issued under s 28(2) of the Data Protection Act 1998, such an appeal may be brought by any person directly affected.[251] The Tribunal may allow the appeal and quash the certificate if it finds: in relation to a certificate under s 23(2) of the Freedom of Information Act 2000, that the information referred to in the certificate was not exempt information by virtue of s 23(1);[252] or, in relation to a certificate under s 24(3) of the Freedom of Information Act 2000, s 28(2) of the Data Protection Act 1998 or reg 15(1) of the Environmental Information Regulations 2004, that, applying the principles applied by the court on an application for judicial review, the Minister or the person designated by him did not have reasonable grounds for issuing the certificate.[253]

---

[248] Compare FOIA s 24(4) and DPA s 28(3).

[249] EIR reg 15(6) giving the term 'Minister of the Crown' in reg 15(1)–(2) and (5) the same meaning as in FOIA s 25(3).

[250] See §§28– 027 to 28– 030 and 28– 046 to 28– 047.

[251] FOIA s 60(1) and EIR reg 18(7)(a); DPA s 28(4). FOIA s 60 is applied for the purposes of the EIR with modifications by EIR reg 18(1), (3)–(4), (7). Appeals under FOIA s 60, DPA s 28 and EIR reg 18(7) are governed by UT Rules. Where a national security certificate is issued under DPA s 28(2) in response to an assessment by the Information Commissioner under DPA s 42 and/or the issue by the Information Commissioner of an information notice under DPA s 43, the Information Commissioner will be a 'person directly affected' by the issuing of that certificate for the purposes of DPA s 28(4) who will therefore be able to appeal to the Upper Tribunal against the certificate (see *R (SSHD) v Information Tribunal* [2006] EWHC 2958 (Admin), [2007] 2 All ER 703 (DC) at [41] (Latham LJ)).

[252] FOIA s 60(2). The Tribunal is thus given full appellate jurisdiction to review the matter, unconstrained by any caveat that it 'apply the principles applied by the court on an application for judicial review' and assess only whether the minister had 'reasonable grounds for issuing the certificate' (cf FOIA s 60(3), DPA s 28(5) and EIR reg 18(7)).

[253] FOIA s 60(3); DPA s 28(5); EIR reg 18(7). In determining whether the minister did or did not have reasonable grounds for issuing the certificate, the Tribunal will inevitably have to assess whether the minister did or did not have reasonable grounds for concluding, in relation to FOIA s 24(3) and DPA s 28(2), that exemption from the relevant provision is, or at any time was, required for the purpose of safeguarding national security or, in relation to EIR reg 15(1), that disclosure would adversely affect national security and would not be in the public interest. It would appear that the Tribunal is thus confined to applying only one of the three heads of judicial review

(2)   A second type of appeal may be brought under s 60(4) of the Freedom of Information Act 2000 or s 28(6) of the Data Protection Act 1998 by a party to any proceedings under or by virtue of the relevant Act if it is claimed by a public authority or a data controller that a certificate issued under s 24(3) of the Freedom of Information Act 2000 or s 28(2) of the Data Protection Act 1998 which identifies the information or the personal data to which it applies by means of a general description applies to particular information or personal data. It is arguable that such an appeal may also be brought under s 60(4) of the Freedom of Information Act 2000 by a party to any proceedings under the Environmental Information Regulations 2004 where similar claims are made by a public authority in relation to a certificate issued under reg 15(1) of the Regulations.[254] Appeals of this type are also dealt with elsewhere in this work,[255] but it should be noted here that the Tribunal has power to determine that the certificate in question does not apply to the information or personal data referred to by the public authority or data controller.[256]

---

identified in *Council of Civil Service Unions v Minister for the Civil Service* [1985] AC 374 at 410 (Lord Diplock) (ie irrationality but not illegality or procedural impropriety): if the minister took into account an irrelevant consideration or failed to take into account a relevant consideration, made an error of law or failed to act fairly in a procedural sense this will only be relevant if and in so far as it led or contributed to him not having reasonable grounds for issuing the certificate. So far as concerns 'the principles applied by the court on an application for judicial review' in relation to 'reasonable grounds', the Tribunal will review whether the minister's decision was reasonable or so unreasonable that no reasonable minister could have taken it (*Associated Provincial Picture Houses Ltd v Wednesbury Corp* [1948] 1 KB 223 (CA)) and the intensity of its scrutiny will increase if it can be shown that 'fundamental rights' are engaged (*R v Ministry of Defence, ex p Smith* [1996] QB 517 (CA) at 554 (Bingham MR). If satisfied that a 'Convention right' as defined by the Human Rights Act 1998 has also been affected by the minister's decision and the appellant may have been the 'victim' of this for the purposes of that Act, the Tribunal will also need to go further and determine whether the decision to issue a certificate was compatible with that Convention right and would thus have to apply a more intensive proportionality-based standard of review: *R (Daly) v SSHD* [2001] UKHL 26, [2001] 2 AC 532 at [26]–[27] (Lord Steyn); *Baker v SSHD* [2001] UKHRR 1275, at [63]; *Gosling v SSHD*, IT, 1 August 2003 at [48]. The language used in FOIA s 60(3) and DPA s 28(5) might also be thought to suggest that the Tribunal must focus solely on the grounds which the minister had in his mind at the time he issued the certificate (to the exclusion of other grounds which he might now wish to rely upon). However, this will not affect the eventual outcome because there is nothing to prevent a minister from issuing a fresh certificate on new grounds to replace one that has been quashed.

[254] EIR reg 18(1), (3), (4)(a)–(b) and (7)(a). This assumes that EIR reg 18(7)(a) operates to apply FOIA s 60(4) as if the reference therein to a certificate under FOIA s 24(3) were substituted by a reference to a certificate issued in accordance with EIR reg 15(1). The interaction between these provisions is not perfect, however, as EIR reg 18(7)(a) refers to 'the reference' in FOIA s 60 to a certificate under FOIA s 24(3) when there are three such references. Moreover, EIR reg 15(3)(b) allows for a certificate to 'identify the information to which it relates in general terms' while FOIA s 60(4) applies to a certificate 'which identifies the information to which it relates by means of a general description.'

[255] See §28– 027.

[256] The Tribunal is thus given full appellate jurisdiction to review such matters unconstrained by any caveat that it 'apply the principles applied by the court on an application for judicial review' and assess only whether the minister had 'reasonable grounds for issuing the certificate' (cf FOIA s 60(3), DPA s 28(5) and EIR reg 18(7)). The explanation for this is no doubt that the minister can issue a new certificate with a much clearer application if dissatisfied with a determination made by the Tribunal under FOIA s 60(5) or DPA s 28(7). FOIA s 60(4) or DPA s 28(6) only provide for the resolution by way of appeal of a dispute over a certificate's applicability where it arises, in relation to FOIA, 'in any proceedings under this Act', in relation to DPA, 'in any proceeding under or by virtue of this Act' and, in relation to EIR, 'in any proceedings under these Regulations.' — see EIR, reg 18(4)(a)(i). The reason for the different formulations is unclear and their effect depends on whether the need for 'proceedings' is given a strict or generous construction; the latter would expand the scope for having disputes over a certificate's applicability resolved by the Tribunal without the procedural need for separate 'proceedings'.

14–041 Parliamentary certificates

Non-appealable parliamentary certificates may be issued under the Freedom of Information Act 2000 as follows:

(1) Under s 34(3) of the Freedom of Information Act 2000, the 'appropriate authority' may sign a certificate certifying that exemption from the disclosure duty in s 1(1)(b), or from the divulgence and disclosure duties in s 1(1)(a) and (b), is, or at any time was, required for the purpose of avoiding an infringement of the privileges of either House of Parliament.[257] Such a certificate will then stand as conclusive evidence of that fact, thus confirming the engagement of the s 34 exemption, unless and until withdrawn or revoked or (in so far as this is possible given that parliamentary privilege should be in play and there is no scope for an appeal under the Freedom of Information Act 2000) quashed on an application for judicial review.[258] The 'appropriate authority' for these purposes is, in relation to the House of Commons, the Speaker of that House, and in relation to the House of Lords, the Clerk of the Parliaments.[259] If a s 34(3) certificate is confined to exemption from s 1(1)(b), determination of the existence duty will be decided on the ordinary basis, unaffected by the certificate.

(2) Under s 36(7) of the Freedom of Information Act 2000, a 'qualified person' may sign a certificate certifying that, in his reasonable opinion, disclosure of information held by either House of Parliament or compliance with the divulgence duty in s 1(1)(a) by either House would, or would be likely to, have any of the effects mentioned in s 36(2) of the Freedom of Information Act 2000 (in other words, it would be prejudicial to the maintenance of the convention of the collective responsibility of the Ministers of the Crown; it would inhibit the free and frank provision of advice or the free and frank exchange of views for the purposes of deliberation; or it would otherwise prejudice the effective conduct of public affairs). Such a certificate will then stand as conclusive evidence of the 'fact' that disclosure or divulgence would, or would be likely to, produce any of those effects, thus facilitating application of the s 36 exemption. The certificate is not determinative of the application of the exemption, as it will also be necessary to demonstrate that the information satisfies the description in s 36(1). The certificate stands unless and until withdrawn or revoked or (in so far as this is possible given that parliamentary privilege may be in play and there is no scope for an appeal under the Freedom of Information Act 2000) quashed on an application for judicial review.[260] The 'qualified person' for these purposes is, in relation to information held by the House of Commons, the Speaker of that House, and in relation to information held by the

---

[257] A certificate under FOIA s 34(3) was not signed in *House of Commons v IC and Brooke, Leapman, Ungoed-Thomas* [2008] EWHC 1084 (Admin), [2009] 3 All ER 403 at [2]. See also DPA s 35A exempting personal data from certain data protection principles and provisions of that Act if required for the purpose of avoiding an infringement of the privileges of either House of Parliament. Provision inserted by FOIA s 73, Sch 6, para 2.

[258] FOIA ss 2(3) and 34 confer an 'absolute exemption'.

[259] FOIA s 34(4).

[260] FOIA ss 2(3) and 36 (so far as relates to information held by the House of Commons or the House of Lords) confer an 'absolute exemption'.

House of Lords, the Clerk of the Parliaments.[261] If a s 36(7) certificate is confined to exemption from s 1(1)(b), determination of the existence duty will be decided on the ordinary basis, unaffected by the certificate.

- 042 Challenges to parliamentary certificates

As mentioned above, certificates issued by the House Authorities under ss 34(3) and 36(7) of the Freedom of Information Act 2000 are not subject to any express appeal procedure. The following factors tend to suggest that the courts would probably be disinclined to intervene if an attempt were made to challenge such a certificate by way of judicial review: the wording of the relevant conclusive evidence clauses follows a format which has previously been given full effect as a matter of statutory construction without any consideration of human rights;[262] the clear intention not to provide for any oversight by way of an appeal to the Upper Tribunal;[263] and the fact that considerations of parliamentary privilege will inevitably be engaged in circumstances where the courts will not as a matter of principle interfere with the affairs of Parliament.[264] As already explained, were it possible to establish that a parliamentary certificate had interfered with the enjoyment or exercise of a Convention or Community right, the courts might be more inclined to intervene.[265] The scope for relying on such arguments is limited in this context, however, and the very strong constitutional and policy reasons which inhibit the courts from interfering with the affairs of Parliament would probably be enough to establish that any infringement of rights was necessary and proportionate in any event.

- 043 Rights to procedural fairness and judicial supervision of conclusive certificates

Article 6(1) of the ECHR confers a right of access to a fair and effective hearing before an independent and impartial tribunal in relation to 'the determination of civil rights and obligations' and Community law can also require a similar level of judicial oversight and effective judicial protection in relation to the exercise, enjoyment and implementation of Community rights. Such rights only guarantee a certain level of procedural protection,

---

[261] FOIA s 36(5)(d)–(e) and (7).

[262] See: §14– 035; *Tinnelly and Sons Ltd v United Kingdom* (1999) 27 EHRR 249 (ECtHR) at [18]–[32], [64], [66]–[67] and [74]–[75]; *Devlin v United Kingdom* (2002) 34 EHRR 43 (ECtHR) at [12]–[14]; *R v Secretary of State for Foreign and Commonwealth Affairs, ex p Vidler* [1993] COD 305; *R v Secretary of State for Transport, ex p Evans and Commission for Racial Equality* [1992] COD 196.

[263] Compare FOIA ss 23(2), 24(3) and 60(1) and (4), DPA s 28(4) and (6) and EIR reg 18.

[264] *Prebble v Television New Zealand Ltd* [1995] 1 AC 321 (PC) at 332: 'wider principle... that the courts and Parliament are both astute to recognise their respective constitutional roles. So far as the courts are concerned they will not allow any challenge to be made to what is said or done within the walls of Parliament in performance of its legislative functions and protection of its established privileges.' (Lord Browne-Wilkinson). See also: *Bradlaugh v Gossett* (1884) 12 QBD 271 (DC); *Pickin v British Railways Board* [1974] AC 765; *Hamilton v Al Fayed* [2001] 1 AC 395; *R v Parliamentary Commissioner for Standards, ex p Al Fayed* [1998] 1 WLR 669 (CA); *OGC v IC* [2008] EWHC 774 (Admin), [2010] QB 98. Support for this can also be found in H Woolf, J Jowell and A Le Sueur, *De Smith's Judicial Review*, 6th edn (London, Sweet & Maxwell, 2007) para 4–027 where it is suggested, in relation to statutory formulae purporting to exclude judicial review by general but comprehensive language, that in the context of the working of the parliamentary system there is a much stronger probability that the courts will give the words prohibiting judicial review a literal interpretation (referring to the Parliament Act 1911 s 3). See also the Ministerial and other Salaries Act 1975 s 2(2).

[265] See §14– 036.

however, and they cannot confer, or alter the substantive extent of, any freestanding rights of access to information or personal data.[266] Having said this, the relevance of such rights to procedural fairness and judicial oversight in relation to conclusive certificates issued under the Freedom of Information Act 2000, the Data Protection Act 1998 or the Environmental Information Regulations 2004 is not without question. There is an argument that article 6 of the ECHR cannot be relied upon in this context in relation to any of these enactments, although the argument is more tenuous in relation to the Data Protection Act 1998 and the Environmental Information Regulations 2004:

(1) So far as concerns article 6 of the ECHR, a question may arise whether the rights of access to information and personal data conferred by the Freedom of Information Act 2000, the Data Protection Act 1998 or the Environmental Information Regulations 2004 have the requisite 'private law' character to count as 'civil rights' for the purposes of article 6(1). In this regard: 'article 6(1) is engaged where the decision which is to be given is of an administrative character, that is to say one given in an exercise of a discretionary power, as well as a dispute in a court of law regarding the private rights of the citizen, provided that it directly affects civil rights and obligations and is of a genuine and serious nature.'[267] If it were possible to show that article 6(1) is prima facie engaged through the presence of a relevant 'civil right', it would next be necessary to show that the issue of a conclusive certificate or the operation of the relevant exemption has interfered with the exercise or enjoyment of that right.[268] In other words, it would have to be shown that the certificate or the exemption has operated to 'defeat' or 'cut off' an otherwise enforceable entitlement to the information or personal data in question rather than having acted simply to define and confirm the substantive bounds of a right which never extended

---

[266] ECHR art 6 can itself confer a subsidiary right of access to information but only where it has already been established that art 6 is engaged and it is then shown that access to the information in question is essential to the exercise of the right to a fair trial: *McGinley and Egan v United Kingdom* (1998) 27 EHRR 1 (ECtHR); *R (S) v Plymouth City Council* [2002] EWCA Civ 388, [2002] 1 WLR 2583; *Roche v United Kingdom* (2006) 42 EHRR 30 (ECtHR). In general terms, the rules and procedures on disclosure and witness summonses in domestic civil and criminal proceedings (eg CPR 31 and CPR 34, Employment Tribunals Rules of Procedure, r. 10(2) at Employment Tribunals (Constitution and Rules of Procedure) Regulations 2004 SI 2004/1861 Sch 1 and Criminal Procedure Rules 2010 SI 2010/60 Pts 22, 28) can be seen as satisfying art 6 for these purposes and FOIA need not be seen as contributing to this: *McGinley and Egan v United Kingdom* (1998) 27 EHRR 1, 4 EHRC 421 (ECtHR) at [86] and [90].

[267] *R (Alconbury Developments Ltd) v Secretary of State for the Environment, Transport and the Regions* [2001] UKHL 23, [2003] 2 AC 295, [2001] 2 All ER 929 at [150] (Lord Clyde) and [79]–[80] (Lord Hoffmann); *Ringeisen v Austria (No 1)* (1979–80) 1 EHRR 455 (ECtHR) at [94]; *König v Germany* (1978) 2 EHRR 170 (ECtHR); *Le Compte, Van Leuwen and De Meyere v Belgium* (1981) 4 EHRR 1 (ECtHR) at [46] and [49]; *H v France* (1990) 12 EHRR 74 (ECtHR) at [47]. The right must be a private law right or it must be 'decisive for private rights and obligations'. In *Tinnelly and Sons Ltd v United Kingdom* (1999) 27 EHRR 249 (ECtHR) it was held that the right not to be discriminated against conferred by the Fair Employment (Northern Ireland) Act 1976 was a 'civil right' for the purposes of the ECHR art 6(1) 'having regard to the context in which it applied and to its pecuniary nature' and that s 42 of that Act did not define the scope of that substantive right *in limine* but provided a respondent with a defence to a complaint of unlawful discrimination (at [61]–[63]). The same reasoning was applied and the same conclusion reached in the employment context in *Devlin v United Kingdom* (2002) 34 EHRR 43 (ECtHR) at [26] and *Devenney v United Kingdom* (2002) 35 EHRR 24 (ECtHR).

[268] *Matthews v Ministry of Defence* [2003] UKHL 4, [2003] 1 AC 1163 at [3] (Lord Bingham); *Wilson v First County Trust Ltd (No 2)* [2003] UKHL 40, [2004] 1 AC 816 at [32]–[35] (Lord Nicholls), [103]–[105] (Lord Hope), [132] (Lord Hobhouse) and [165] (Lord Scott); *Golder v United Kingdom* (1979–80) 1 EHRR 524 (ECtHR); *König v Germany* (1978) 2 EHRR 170 (ECtHR); *Fayed v United Kingdom* (1994) 18 EHRR 393 (ECtHR) at [65]–[67]; *Tinnelly and Sons Ltd v United Kingdom* (1999) 27 EHRR 249 (ECtHR) at [72]–[79]; *Z v United Kingdom* [2001] 2 FLR 612 (ECtHR) at [87].

further.[269] If these hurdles can be overcome, non-appealable national security certificates have been found to operate as procedural bars to the judicial resolution of disputes in contravention of article 6(1), unless justified by reference to principles of proportionality.[270] However, the context and structure of the Freedom of Information Act 2000, the Data Protection Act 1998 and the Environmental Information Regulations 2004 are very different and there is an argument that the relevant exemptions (whether or not engaged via the issue of a conclusive certificate) do not infringe rights to information or personal data whose non-disclosure is required for the purpose of safeguarding national security but rather confirm the total absence of any such right.[271]

(2) Community law has no bearing on the application or enforcement of the Freedom of Information Act 2000 but it is relevant to the Data Protection Act 1998, which implements the European Community Data Protection Directive 95/46/EC, and the Environmental Information Regulations 2004, which implement European Community Public Access to Environmental Information Directive 2003/4/EC. The Data Protection Act 1998 and the Environmental Information Regulations 2004 must therefore be construed and given effect in accordance with the terms of their parental Directives and the general principles of Community law.[272] As a consequence, there may be greater scope for relying on Community rights to effective judicial protection by this route in relation to s 28 of the Data Protection Act 1998 and regs 15 and 18 of the Environmental Information Regulations 2004. In any event, limited practical consequences would flow from being able to show that rights to procedural fairness and judicial oversight are engaged and arguably infringed in relation to the issue of conclusive certificates under the Freedom of Information Act 2000, the Data Protection Act 1998 or the Environmental Information Regulations 2004. In this regard, the scope for appealing national security certificates issued under ss 23(2) and 24(3) of the Freedom of Information Act 2000, s 28(2) of the Data Protection Act 1998 and reg 18 of the Environmental Information Regulations 2004 arguably provides a respectable measure of judicial oversight[273] that should justify the restrictions entailed, bearing in mind the importance of national security matters and the fact that the executive is generally considered better qualified and

---

[269] *Matthews v Ministry of Defence* [2003] UKHL 4, [2003] 1 AC 1163 at [141] (Lord Walker).

[270] *Tinnelly and Sons Ltd v United Kingdom* (1999) 27 EHRR 249 (ECtHR); *Devlin v United Kingdom* (2002) 34 EHRR 43 (ECtHR); *Devenney v United Kingdom* (2002) 35 EHRR 24 (ECtHR). However, note the emphasis on the context and the pecuniary nature of the right not to be discriminated against.

[271] While FOIA s 1(1) does enact what is described in the side-note as a 'general right of access to information held by public authorities' this is immediately qualified by s 1(2) which brings in the remainder of s 1, ss 2, 9, 12 and 14 and, in turn, Pt II. It is made clear in s 1(2) that s 1(1) 'has effect' throughout and is at all times 'subject to' these provisions (see also the language of 'section 1(1)(a) does not apply' and 'section 1(1)(b) does not apply' (in s 2) and 'the duty to confirm or deny does not arise' (throughout)). See especially the ultimate conclusion reached by the House of Lords on whether ECHR, art 6(1) was engaged in *Matthews v Ministry of Defence* [2003] UKHL 4, [2003] 1 AC 1163.

[272] See §14– 036.

[273] Questions may nevertheless arise as to the grounds and intensity of the review thereby allowed and as to the absence of any provision allowing for a further appeal to the High Court on a point of law (cf the non-appealability of Parliamentary certificates issued under FOIA ss 34(3) and 36(7)).

equipped to judge related issues.[274] As a consequence, the successful invocation of Community rights is unlikely to go further than encouraging the Upper Tribunal to apply a more intensive proportionality-based standard of scrutiny when considering this type of appeal.

14– 044 Rights to privacy and data protection rights

The right to respect for private and family life contained in article 8 of the ECHR can confer a right of access to personal information where this is essential to the exercise and enjoyment of that right.[275] Although it is not inconceivable that information falling within this category might be sought under the Freedom of Information Act 2000 or the Environmental Information Regulations 2004, it is much more likely that requests under the Data Protection Act 1998 will seek such information. So far as concerns conclusive certificates issued under s 28 of the Data Protection Act 1998, Convention rights under article 8 may therefore be engaged in a very direct way and Community rights may also come into play by virtue of the fact that the Data Protection Act 1998 implements the European Community Data Protection Directive 95/46.[276] Of course, article 8 of the ECHR, the Data Protection Directive and the Data Protection Act 1998 do not confer absolute rights and all three expressly allow, where necessary and proportionate, for the curtailment and denial of these rights in the interests of national security.[277] The rights of appeal under ss 28(4) and (6) of the Data Protection Act 1998 and the adequacy of the judicial oversight they provide will therefore be crucial if it is to be demonstrated that the use of national security certificates thereunder, and the application of the exemption therein, is compatible with Convention rights and Community law. In this regard, it is notable that in relation to the first substantive decision taken by the Information Tribunal under s 28(4) of the Data Protection Act 1998, a more intensive proportionality-based standard of review was applied and the certificate in question was quashed for having an 'unnecessarily

---

[274] It is important to note that the right of access to the courts secured by the ECHR art 6(1) is not absolute and may be subject to limitations provided they do not restrict or reduce the access left to the individual in such a way or to such an extent that the very essence of the right is impaired, provided that they pursue a legitimate aim and provided that there is a reasonable relationship of proportionality between the means employed and the aim sought to be achieved: *Fayed v United Kingdom* (1994) 18 EHRR 393 (ECtHR) at [65]–[67]; *Tinnelly and Sons Ltd v United Kingdom* (1999) 27 EHRR 249 (ECtHR) at [74]; *Lithgow v United Kingdom* (1986) 8 EHRR 329 (ECtHR) at [194].

[275] *Gaskin v United Kingdom* (1989) 12 EHRR 36 (EctHR) at [60]; *Botta v Italy* (1998) 26 EHRR 241 (ECtHR); *Guerra v Italy* (1998) 26 EHRR 357 (EctHR) at [60]; *McGinley and Egan v United Kingdom* (1998) 27 EHRR 1 (ECtHR) at [101] and [103]; *R (S) v Plymouth City Council* [2002] EWCA Civ 388, [2002] 1 WLR 2583; *MG v United Kingdom* (2003) 36 EHRR 3, [2002] 3 FCR 289 (ECtHR); *Craxi v Italy (No1)* (2004) 28 EHRR 47 (ECtHR); *Roche v United Kingdom* (2006) 42 EHRR 30, (2006) BHRC99. Note that in *MG v United Kingdom* it was held that ECHR art 8 required only the establishment of a procedure facilitating access to local authority care records relating to significant periods of the applicant's formative years and that the violation of art 8 therefore ceased on entry into force of the DPA. See further ch 3.

[276] Indeed, the connection between rights to privacy (including under the ECHR art 8) and data protection is strongly emphasised throughout the recitals to the European Community Data Protection Directive 95/46/EC (see especially recitals (1)–(3), (7) and (9)–(11)) and in art 1. See §§14– 036 to 14– 044 and especially 14– 043 on the way in which the Community law connection can engage rights to effective judicial oversight.

[277] ECHR art 8(2); European Community Data Protection Directive 95/46/EC, recital (16) and art 13(1); DPA s 28.

wide effect'.[278]

)45 Rights to freedom of expression

Although expressed to include 'the right to receive and impart information and ideas without interference' the right to freedom of expression guaranteed by article 10 to the ECHR has been consistently held not to confer or entail a general right of access to information.[279] For this reason, and in the absence of some development in the jurisprudence on this,[280] it will not be possible to invoke article 10 rights in order to bring or enhance a challenge to the issue of a conclusive certificate under ss 23–24, 34 or 36 of the Freedom of Information Act 2000, s 28 of the Data Protection Act 1998 or reg 15 of the Environmental Information Regulations 2004 or to the application of one of the exemptions whose engagement may be certified thereunder. The practical significance of this should not be overstated, however, particularly in the national security context, as article 10(2) of the ECHR expressly recognises that the right to freedom of expression may be restricted, where necessary and proportionate, in the interests of national security.

---

[278] *Baker v SSHD* [2001] UKHRR 1275. Note the emphasis on Convention and Community rights at [50]–[64] and, more generally, see §14– 036. In *Gosling v SSHD*, IT, 1 August 2003 a replacement certificate whose application depended upon a consideration of the requirements of national security in relation to the need for particular exemptions in each individual case was subsequently upheld by the Information Tribunal albeit upon limited grounds (at [28]) and the Tribunal again emphasised the relevance of Convention and Community rights when considering the appropriate intensity of its review (at [48]). This decision was followed in *Hitchens v SSHD*, IT, 4 August 2003, *Hilton v FCO*, IT, 28 June 2005 and *Stevenson v SSHD*, IT, 30 April 2009.

[279] *R (Persey) v Secretary of State for the Environment, Food and Rural Affairs* [2002] EWHC 371 (Admin), [2003] QB 794 (DC) at [52]–[53] (Simon Brown LJ); *R (Howard) v Secretary of State for Health (Note)* [2002] EWHC 396 (Admin) at [103] (Scott Baker J); *Leander v Sweden* (1987) 9 EHRR 433 (ECtHR); *Gaskin v United Kingdom* (1989) 12 EHRR 36 (ECtHR); *Guerra v Italy* (1998) 26 EHRR 357 (ECtHR); *BBC, Petitioners (No 2)* 2000 JC 521; *cf R (Wagstaff) v Secretary of State for Health* [2001] 1 WLR 292 (DC). See further ch 3.

[280] See, eg Sir Stephen Sedley, 'Information as a Human Right' in J Beatson and Y Cripps (eds), *Freedom of Expression and Freedom of Information: Essays in Honour of Sir David Williams* (Oxford, Oxford University Press, 2000).

CHAPTER 15
Prejudice and the Public Interest

1. THE PUBLIC INTEREST

001 Introduction

The Freedom of Information Act 2000 implicitly recognises a public interest underlying each of the grounds of exemption, as well as a public interest in divulging whether information is held and in disclosing that information.[1] Indeed, most of the exemptions simply articulate a public interest in non-disclosure that has been well recognised in other contexts, most notably public interest immunity, confidentiality and the protection of privacy and personal data.[2] Where information falls within one of the qualified exemptions within Part II of the Act, the competition between the relevant aspects of the public interest is determinative of whether the duty to confirm or deny and the duty to communicate are disapplied or not. In requiring such a balancing exercise, the FOI Acts also recognise that the force of an aspect of the public interest will vary according to the information sought and 'all the circumstances of the case'. This latter phrase requires that for each request a public authority should take account of all the circumstances that bear upon the public interest in maintaining the applicable exemptions and upon the public interest in disclosing the information sought.[3] A blanket approach by a public authority to requests of a particular sort will not take into account all the circumstances of the case.[4]

002 Aggregating relevant aspects of the public interest

In relation to the disclosure of exempt information under a qualified exemption, the task under s 2 is not to 'weigh'[5] the public interest in non-disclosure against the public interest in disclosure: the task is to weigh the public interest 'in maintaining the exemption'[6] that renders it exempt information against the public interest in disclosing that information.[7] Only if the weighing

---

[1] FOIA s 2(1) and (2). Similarly: FOI(S)A s 2(1); EIR reg 12(1)(b); EI(S)R s 10(1)(b).

[2] The public interest in disclosing official information has itself been long recognised: *British Steel Corporation v Granada Television Ltd* [1981] AC 1096 at 1129, (Lord Denning). Similarly: *X v Morgan-Grampian (Publishers) Ltd* [1991] 1 AC 1 at 40 ('The courts have always recognised an important public interest in the free flow of information'); *Camelot Group plc v Centaur Communications Ltd* [1999] QB 124 at 139 (the 'general public interest in access to information'); *Hyde Park Residence Ltd v Yelland* [2001] Ch 143 at 170 ('the public interest in knowing the truth' (Mance LJ)).

[3] *OGC v IC* [2008] EWHC 774 (Admin), [2010] QB 98, [2008] ACD 54 at [87].

[4] *Galloway v IC and NHS*, IT, 20 March 2009 at [70(c)]; *ECGD v IC and Campaign Against Arms Trade*, IT, 21 October 2009 at [50(iv)].

[5] The FOI Acts employ the term 'outweigh', although as has been observed in relation to public interest immunity it is 'a rough metaphor' and 'a more complex process than merely using the scales': *Science Research Council v Nassé* [1980] AC 1028 at 1067 (Lord Wilberforce).

[6] 'Exemption' here cannot mean exemption from the duty to communicate, as that only arises after the weighing process: it cannot, at this stage, be said to be being 'maintained'. The same phraseology is used in the environmental information regime: EIR reg 12(1)(b); EI(S)R reg 10(1)(b). See, also, Pt IV of the DPA, which terms the provisions analogous to those in Pt II of the FOI Acts as 'exemptions'.

[7] MoJ Guidance still states otherwise:
   The public interest test need not focus solely on the particular considerations relevant to the specific exemption(s) engaged. Section 2(2) requires that 'all the circumstances of the case' should be taken in to account when determining whether to maintain a qualified exemption. Therefore, in considering a

process favours maintenance of the applicable exemptions is the duty to communicate disapplied. Accordingly, the balancing exercise does not involve a consideration of all aspects of the public interest that weigh against disclosure.[8] The consideration of the public interest, so far as it weighs against disclosure, is focussed upon the public interest embodied in the exemptions by which the information sought is rendered exempt information. Previously, the Tribunal, and earlier editions of this work, had interpreted s 2(2) as requiring the public interest in maintaining each exemption applicable to an item of information to be weighed singly against the public interest in disclosing that information: only if there was a qualified exemption in the maintenance of which the public interest outweighed the public interest in disclosure would s 2(2)(b) disapply the s 1(1)(b) duty to communicate that information.[9] That approach was rejected by the Court of Appeal in *R (Office of Communications) v Information Commissioner*.[10] The Court of Appeal held that in carrying out the balancing exercise, the public interest in all exceptions applicable to a particular item of information must be aggregated and that it is that aggregated public interest which must be weighed against the public interest in disclosing that information.[11] Public interest considerations against disclosure but not relevant to maintaining the applicable exemptions remain outside the balancing exercise.[12] Similarly, public interest considerations relating to exemptions that have not been invoked are not included in the aggregated public interest.[13] Thus it remains important to identify the public interest in maintaining each particular exemption.[14] Where there is a variety of information captured by a request with different combinations of exemptions applicable to different items of information, the aggregated public interest in maintaining those exemptions may vary according to the

---

request for information that engages section 29 (the economy), any damage to the UK's economic interests resulting from disclosure would be considered, but wider considerations, such as any potential prejudice to the free and frank exchange of views, should also be taken into account.
www.justice.gov.uk/guidance/foi-exemptions-public-interest.htm
This neither mirrors the language of the Act nor is faithful to *R (Office of Communications) v IC* [2009] EWCA Civ 90, [2009] ACD 48 at [35]. The slant given to s 2(2) in the MoJ Guidance increases the ability of a public authority to refuse disclosure by introducing its own assessment of the desirability of disclosure, unconstrained by any reference to the applicable exemptions. Given the history of the Act, the statutory duty that animates it, and the conspicuous failure of the voluntary code to persuade public authorities to embrace a culture of openness, an intention to reserve such a power to those same public authorities is thought unlikely. On the other hand, the Information Commissioner's *Guidance No 3* (3 July 2009) accurately sets out the position:
www.ico.gov.uk/upload/documents/library/freedom_of_information/detailed_speci
alist_guides/fep038_public_interest_test_v3.pdf
The Information Commissioner suggests that the aggregated approach required by the Court of Appeal in *R (Office of Communications) v IC* applies only to exceptions under the EIR, and not to exemptions under FOIA. In relation to applicable exemptions under FOIA, he considers that the approach previously taken by the Tribunal and in earlier editions of this book should be adhered to.

[8]   *R (Office of Communications) v IC* [2009] EWCA Civ 90, [2009] ACD 48 at [35].

[9]   *Bellamy v IC and DTI*, IT, 4 April 2006 at [5]; *Toms v IC*, IT, 19 June 2006 at [5]–[7]; *Hogan and Oxford City Council v IC*, IT, 17 October 2006 at [59]–[60].

[10] *R (Office of Communications) v IC* [2009] EWCA Civ 90, [2009] ACD 48. An appeal to the House of Lords saw the matter being referred to the European Court of Justice, but with an indication that the majority favoured the view expressed in the Court of Appeal: *Office of Communication v Information Commissioner* [2010] UKSC 3.

[11] See further n 44.

[12] *R (Office of Communications) v IC* [2009] EWCA Civ 90, [2009] ACD 48 at [35].

[13] *ECGD v IC and Campaign Against Arms Trade*, IT, 21 October 2009 at [52]-[53].

[14] *ECGD v IC and Campaign Against Arms Trade*, IT, 21 October 2009 at [50(v)].

different combinations of applicable exemptions.[15]

003 The nature of the balancing exercise

The public interest balancing exercise does not involve the exercise of discretion.[16] It is an issue of mixed law and fact,[17] and the Tribunal may substitute its judgment for that of the Commissioner.[18]

004 The nature of the public interest

The 'public interest', whether unlimited in its scope or focussed upon a particular matter, is not a reference to something that is of interest to the public.[19] It signifies something that is in the interests of the public; that is, for the common welfare.[20] Thus:

> The public are interested in many private matters which are no real concern of theirs and which the public have no pressing need to know.[21]

And:

> There is a wide difference between what is interesting to the public and what it is in the public interest to make known.[22]

---

[15] The practical difficulties that this interpretation presents to those charged with carrying out the exercise has been touched upon in a number of Tribunal decisions: *South Gloucestershire Council v IC and Bovis Homes Ltd*, IT, 20 October 2009 at [49]-[52]; *SS for Transport v IC*, IT, 5 May 2009 at [103].

[16] *Common Services Agency v IC* [2008] UKHL 47, [2008] 1 WLR 1550 at [68].

[17] In *Currie v Commissioners of Inland Revenue* [1921] 2 KB 332 at 339, Scrutton LJ, in considering the question whether a particular person carried on a 'profession' within the meaning of a Finance Act, said:
> I rather agree with what Lord Parker said in *Farmer v Cotton's Trustees* [1915] AC 922 at 932 "It may not always be easy to distinguish between questions of fact and questions of law for the purpose of the Taxes Management Act, 1880, or similar provisions in other Acts of Parliament. The views from time to time expressed in this House have been far from unanimous." I think the reason is, as has been suggested by the Master of the Rolls, that there has been a very strong tendency, arising from the infirmities of human nature, in a judge to say, if he agrees with the decision of the Commissioners, that the question is one of fact, and if he disagrees with them that it is one of law, in order that he may express his own opinion the opposite way.

Where there is a question of mixed law and fact, whether the facts in issue are *capable* of falling within the statutory condition is the question of law (since it requires a determination of the bounds of the condition), and whether the facts *actually* fall within those bounds is a question of fact.

[18] See: *Bellamy v IC and DTI*, IT, 4 April 2006 at [34]; *Hogan and Oxford CC v IC*, IT, 17 October 2006 at [55]; *Hemsley v IC and Chief Constable of Northamptonshire*, IT, 10 April 2006 at [18]; *Toms v IC*, IT, 19 June 2006; *DWP v IC*, IT, 5 March 2007 at [22]; *CPS v IC*, FTT, 25 March 2010 at [14].

[19] *DTI v IC*, IT, 10 November 2006 at [50]; *Mersey Tunnel Users Association v Information Commissioner and Halton BC*, IT, 11 January 2010 at [48(vii)]; *Bellamy v IC and DBIS*, FTT, 23 February 2010 at [38(viii)]. Some Tribunal decisions have appeared to suggest otherwise: *Cabinet Office v IC*, IT, 27 January 2009 at [14]; *Pugh v IC and MoD*, IT, 17 December 2007 at [48]; *Barrett v IC and Office for National Statistics*, IT, 23 April 2008 at [26]; *ECGD v IC and Campaign Against Arms Trade*, IT, 21 October 2009 at [50(xi)]. The first three may be thought the product of loose language rather than of loose thought.

[20] The definition given to it in the *Shorter Oxford English Dictionary*, 2nd edn, (Oxford, Oxford University Press, 1993).

[21] *Lion Laboratories Ltd v Evans* [1985] QB 526 at 537, [1984] 2 All ER 417 (CA). In *Francome v Mirror Group Newspapers Ltd* [1984] 1 WLR 892 (at 898) the Court of Appeal spoke of the newspapers as being 'peculiarly vulnerable to the error of confusing the public interest with their own interest.'

[22] *Hyde Park Residences Ltd v Yelland* [2001] Ch 143 at 164; *Reynolds v Times Newspapers Ltd* [2001] 2 AC 127 at 202; *Douglas v Hello!* [2001] QB 967 at 997–998; *British Steel Corporation v Granada Television Ltd* [1981] AC 1096 at 1168 (Lord Wilberforce). Similarly: *R v Inhabitants of the County of Bedfordshire* (1855) 24 LJQB 81 at 84; *Sinclair v Mining Warden at Maryborough* (1975) 132 CLR 473 at 480; *Director of Public Prosecutions v Smith* [1991] 1 VR 63 at 75. Similarly in *AG for the United Kingdom v Wellington Newspapers Limited* [1988] 1 NZLR 129 at 178–179, McMullin J said:

Thus, there may be a public interest in obtaining access to information on an issue even though the number of individuals affected by that issue is numerically low.[23] Where a statute speaks of a decision-maker being able to do something when that is in the public interest, that operates as a device by which the discretion vested in the decision-maker is directed away from matters of narrower or immediate concern to the decision-maker and to matters which are not necessarily of direct interest to the decision-maker:

> [T]he expression "in the public interest", when used in a statute, classically imports a discretionary value judgment to be made by reference to undefined factual matters, confined only "in so far as the subject matter and the scope and purpose of the statutory enactments may enable...given reasons to be [pronounced] definitely extraneous to any objects the legislature could have had in view".[24]

15–005 The time at which the public interest is considered

The public interest is not immutable.[25] In some circumstances even a small amount of time may effect a significant difference: for example, where in the intervening period information on the same topic as the requested information is formally released. As already noted,[26] the Tribunal's approach has been to determine the public interest balancing exercise by reference to the facts and circumstances as they stood at or about the moment that the request was received.[27] The approach is questionable.[28] However, a public authority may properly take into account circumstances or matters that come to light after the date of the request where

---

'By public interest is meant something more than that which catches one's curiosity or merely raises the interest of the gossip. It is something which may be of real concern to the public.' Similarly: *Guardian Newspapers Ltd and Brooke v IC and BBC*, IT, 8 January 2007 at [34].

[23] *Bellamy v IC and DTI*, IT, 4 April 2006 at [35]; *DTI v IC*, IT, 10 November 2006 at [50].

[24] *O'Sullivan v Farrer* (1989) 168 CLR 210 at 216, cited with approval in *McKinnon v Secretary, Department of Treasury* [2006] HCA 45, (2006) 229 ALR 187 at [55].

[25] *AG v Times Newspapers Ltd* [1974] AC 273 at 320.

[26] §14–004.

[27] *Bellamy v IC and DTI*, IT, 4 April 2006 at [6]; *DTI v IC*, IT, 10 November 2006 at [44], [46]; *DWP v IC*, IT, 5 March 2007 at [30]; *DfES v IC and The Evening Standard*, IT, 19 February 2007 at [20]; *Baker v IC & ors*, IT, 28 February 2007 at [25]; *Campaign against the Arms Trade v IC and MoJ*, IT, 26 August 2008 at [43]-[53] (where it was held that the public authority had to consider matters as at the date at which it was obliged to respond to the request); *DCLG v IC*, IT, 22 July 2008; *Dept of Culture, Media and Sport v IC*, IT, 29 July 2008 at [4]; *DBERR v IC and Friends of the Earth*, IT, 29 April 2008 at [104]-[111]; *Home Office and MoJ v IC* [2009] EWHC 1611 (Admin) at [34]; *ECGD v IC and Campaign Against Arms Trade*, IT, 21 October 2009 at [50(vi)]; *Bellamy v IC and DBIS*, FTT, 23 February 2010 at [38(iii)]).

[28] As with any administrative decision, unless statute otherwise provides, satisfaction of statutory requirements is decided on the basis of the facts known to the decision-maker at the time that the decision is made. On an appeal to a merit-review tribunal, that tribunal should, unless statute otherwise provides, determine an appeal based on the facts known to it at the time that it makes its decision: *Saber v SSHD* [2008] UKHL 97, [2008] 3 All ER 97 at [2] ('common sense indicates that the final decision, whenever it is made, should be based on the most up to date evidence that is available,' dealing with an asylum-seeker in need of international protection, although the sense is not unique to that jurisdiction). This is the position that has been taken in other jurisdictions when dealing with requests under freedom of information legislation and having a provision similar to FOIA s 1(4): *Re Radar Investments and Health Insurance Commission* (2004) 80 ALD 733 at [30]-[42]. The Tribunal's power under FOIA s 58(2) is ample for this purpose. The FOIA does not confer an accrued right to information; nor does it impose an accrued liability to communicate information. In these circumstances, the taking of evidence in order to make findings so as to confirm or overturn an evaluative conclusion on a state of facts as they existed long before is not a fruitful exercise. In *OGC v IC* [2008] EWHC 774 (Admin), [2010] QB 98, [2008] ACD 54 at [98], the High Court doubted whether the Tribunal's approach was correct.

those subsequent circumstances or matters shed light on the public interest at the time that it falls to be decided.[29] If an applicant is disadvantaged by this approach, the disadvantage can be circumvented by lodging a fresh request in identical terms.[30] Any change in those circumstances may influence the outcome of the balancing exercise. Accordingly, while a public authority may properly refuse to disclose information subject to a qualified exemption, where a subsequent request is made for the same information a change in the surrounding circumstances may result in the public authority being obliged to disclose that information.

006 **Evidence as to the public interest**

Both the identification of relevant aspects of the public interest and the balancing of those aspects are evaluative matters exclusively for the public authority in the first instance, the Information Commissioner on a complaint, and the Tribunal on an appeal.[31] The Tribunal should, of course, receive evidence of anticipated consequences of disclosure or non-disclosure of the requested information so far as it is relevant to the claimed exemptions.[32] That evidence should include bringing forward facts that validate any expression of opinion by a public authority as to type and likelihood of harm that would result from disclosure of the requested information. The evidence given to the Tribunal will inform its conclusions whether the predicted adverse effects to protected interests are likely to result from disclosure of the requested information (in the case of harm-based exemptions) and the strength of the evidential underpinning for the relevant public interest considerations (particularly in the case of public interest considerations that express a predicted harm resulting from disclosure). The Tribunal should not defer to the views of a public authority or those employed by it, either as to the likely effects of disclosure of information (whether upon an interest protected by an exemption or upon a matter that a recognised public interest is designed to protect) or as to what the outcome of the public interest balancing exercise should be.[33] It is the Tribunal which is charged with the task of evaluating the evidence.[34] Relevant evidence from a public authority will, however, be useful to identify and explain matters of recognised public interest, including putting before the Tribunal facts that support any predictions of the effect of disclosing the requested information.

007 **Weight of the public interest**

A decision-maker must take into account all considerations that are relevant to the public interest balancing exercise and not take into account any that are irrelevant to that exercise. On an appeal to the Tribunal, it is required to take the same approach. It is well established that while a decision-maker may be required to take certain matters into account in making a decision in exercise of a function, unless otherwise required the weight to be given to such

---

[29] *DTI v IC*, IT, 10 November 2006 at [46]–[47].

[30] If the facts and circumstances have truly changed, this should render the interval between the requests a 'reasonable' one, so that the applicant should not fall foul of the proscription against repeat requests: see §§12–014 to 12–016.

[31] *HM Treasury v IC* [2009] EWHC 1811 (Admin) at [39], [62].

[32] *Guardian Newspapers Ltd v IC and BBC*, IT, 8 January 2007 at [92]; *HM Treasury v IC* [2009] EWHC 1811 (Admin) at [41].

[33] *Home Office and MoJ v IC* [2009] EWHC 1611 (Admin) at [29].

[34] Moreover, the appeal will generally be against the decision of the public authority.

material considerations is quintessentially one for the decision-maker.[35] This has been acknowledged in relation to the s 2(2) exercise.[36] There is nothing in the Freedom of Information Act 2000 stipulating the particular weight to be given to the applicable aspects of the public interest in maintaining the qualified exemptions. The statutory bifurcation of exemptions into those that are absolute and those that are not, together with the requirement that in the latter case regard is to be had to 'all the circumstances', is not without significance to the character of the public interest balancing exercise that is to be carried out. Nevertheless, the High Court has on occasions maintained that it is 'incumbent' on the Tribunal to give 'significant weight' to the public interest built in to certain exemptions.[37]

15– 008   The two balancing exercises

The FOI Acts distinguish the public interest in disclosing whether a public authority holds certain information from the public interest in disclosing that information. Although the FOI Acts place the balancing exercise for the purpose of disclosure after the balancing exercise for the purpose of the duty to confirm or deny,[38] the former is better considered before the latter. If it is in the public interest for a public authority to disclose certain information, it follows that it will be in the public interest for that public authority to disclose that it holds that information. Logically, then, the need to carry out the weighing exercise set out in s 2(1) of the FOI Acts will only arise if the result of carrying out the separate weighing exercise in s 2(2) is a decision not to disclose the information.

15– 009   The public interest in comparative official information access legislation

This focussed approach to the public interest in the FOI Acts distinguish them from the freedom of information legislation of comparative jurisdictions. The FOI Acts of Australia, New Zealand and Ireland all require the decision-maker, if he is to rely on certain exemptions, to be satisfied that the disclosure of the document would be contrary to 'the public interest'.[39]

---

[35] *Tesco Stores v SSE* [1995] 1 WLR 759 (HL) at 764, 770 and 780; *R (von Brandenburg) v East London and The City Mental Health NHS Trust* [2001] EWCA Civ 239, [2002] QB 235 at [41] ('The principle that the weight to be given to such facts is a matter for the decision-maker, moreover, does not mean that the latter is free to dismiss or marginalise things to which the structure and policy of the Act attach obvious importance'). The nature of the right that stands to be affected by the decision will colour a court's preparedness to interfere on the basis of the weight given by a decision-maker: *R (Samaroo) v SSHD* [2001] EWCA Civ 1139, [2001] UKHRR 1150 at [39].

[36] *ECGD v Friends of the Earth* [2008] EWHC 638 (Admin), [2008] Env LR 40, [2008] JPL 1813 at [38]; *Home Office and MoJ v IC* [2009] EWHC 1611 (Admin).

[37] *DBERR v O'Brien and IC* [2009] EWHC 164 (QB) at [41], [51], [53], [54]; *HM Treasury v IC* [2009] EWHC 1811 (Admin) at [42]-[43], [51].

[38] That is, FOIA ss 2(2) and 2(1), respectively. In relation to information held by a Scottish public authority, FOI(S)A ss 18(1) and 2(1) respectively. In relation to a request made under the environmental information regime, there is no discrete duty on a public authority to disclose whether or not it holds the requested information.

[39] Freedom of Information Act 1982 (Cth of Australia), ss 47B, 47C, 47E, 47F, 47G, 47H and 47J, which require considering whether disclosing the documents would be contrary to the public interest, but do not require a general or focused weighing of it; Official Information Act 1982 (NZ) s 9(1); Freedom of Information Act 1997 (Ireland), ss 20(1), 21(2), 22(3), 23(3), 26(3), 27(3), 30(3) and 31(3), cf 28(5)(a). The Access to Information Act (1982) (Canada) does not involve consideration of the public interest, except where the request relates to 'third party information', in which case the decision-making involves a focussed treatment of the public interest: s 20(6). Within the terms of the Freedom of Information Act 1966 (USA) itself, the role of the public interest is confined to considering whether the information requested should be provided free of charge: 5 USC 552(a)(4)(A)(i). In relation to declassification decisions, Executive Order 12,958 3.2(b) authorises agencies to apply a balancing test: namely, to determine

This generalised reference to the public interest enables a broad range of matters to be taken into account as part of the balancing exercise.[40] But it also means that despite a superficial similarity with the regime in the United Kingdom,[41] their jurisprudence on this issue is limited in its comparative value.

2. WEIGHING THE PUBLIC INTEREST: DISCLOSURE

010 The public interest in maintaining the exemption

As noted above,[42] where information is covered by a qualified exemption, displacement of the duty to communicate that information involves weighing the public interest in maintaining the applicable exemptions, rather than all aspects of the public interest that are against disclosure of that information:

> The public authority's assessment of the public interest in maintaining the exemption should focus on the public interest factors specifically associated with that particular exemption, rather than on a more general consideration of the public interest in withholding the information: see the decision the Tribunal in *Hogan and Oxford City Council v Information Commissioner* at [59]. This exercise requires the public authority to stand back and abnegate its own interests except and in so far as those interests are properly viewed as part of the public interest.[43]

The public interest in all exceptions applicable to a particular item of information must be aggregated and it is that aggregated public interest which must be weighed against the public interest in disclosing that information.[44] It will never be enough for a public authority simply

---

'whether the public interest in disclosure outweighs the damage to national security that might reasonably be expected from disclosure.'

[40] See, eg: *Re Howard and the Treasurer* (1985) 7 ALD 626, 3 AAR 169; *Director of Public Prosecutions v Smith* [1991] 1 VR 63. The absence of any such focus led the Australian Law Reform Commission and the Administrative Review Council in their joint review of the operation of the Freedom of Information Act 1982 to recommend that the FOI Commissioner issue guidelines listing the factors that are relevant and that are irrelevant when weighing the public interest: Australian Law Reform Commission and Administrative Review Council, *Open Government: a review of the Federal Freedom of Information Act 1982* (Canberra, 1995) para 8.14, recommendation 37.

[41] That is, the FOIA, FOI(S)A, EIR and EI(S)R.

[42] §§15–001 to 15– 002.

[43] *DWP v IC*, IT, 5 March 2007 at [24]. Similarly: *Bellamy v IC and DTI*, IT, 4 April 2006 at [5]; *Hogan and Oxford City Council v IC*, IT, 17 October 2006 at [55]; *Office of Commerce v IC*, IT, 2 May 2007 at [51]; *Student Loans Company Ltd v IC*, IT, 17 July 2009 at [53].

[44] Although the Court of Appeal was concerned with the public interest weighing exercised expressed in the EIR, its reasoning is equally applicable to the FOIA: the phraseology used in the EIR mimics that used in the FOIA, and not vice versa. This appears to be confirmed by *Home Office and MoJ v IC* [2009] EWHC 1611 (Admin) at [25] and the Court's analysis. It is also the view taken by the Tribunal: *ECGD v IC and Campaign Against Arms Trade*, IT, 21 October 2009 at [51]. The Information Commissioner considers otherwise: see n 7. The treatment of the public interest in FOIA differs markedly from that which had originally been proposed in cl 14(3) of the original FOI Bill. Some indication of this change appears from Hansard HL vol 617 cols 901–902 (17 October 2000) (Minister of State, Cabinet Office, Lord Falconer of Thoroton), when introducing the amendment that led to s 2, and in Hansard HL vol 617 col 1265 (19 October 2000), where Lord Falconer of Thoroton gave an example of how it should work in practice. For a fuller consideration of the genesis of the public interest balancing exercise, see Philip Coppel, 'The public interest and the Freedom of Information Act 2000' *Judicial Review*, vol 10, issue 4, December 2005.

to rely upon the public interest against disclosure that is inherent in the particular qualified exemption that applies to the information sought without a consideration of the particular circumstances relating to the information.[45] To allow this would effectively be to elevate a qualified exemption into an absolute exemption. Nevertheless, it is legitimate to take into account the public interest in avoiding the harm sought to be protected by the exemption and the likelihood of that harm eventuating from disclosure of the requested information.[46] Section 2(2) contemplates instances in which information rendered exempt information by a qualified exemption will be required to be disclosed. The specific aspect of the public interest that underlies each of the qualified exemptions is considered in more detail in the chapters that deal with particular exemptions. The only 'internal' indication of the public interest in maintaining the exemptions comes from the provisions reducing the exemptions in relation to historical records.[47] Implicit in the removal of those exemptions is that if the information is without contemporaneity there is no significant public interest served by the exemption. With all qualified exemptions, the public interest balancing exercise will often be time sensitive.[48]

15–011 The public interest in disclosure

The FOI Acts describe at various points a public interest in disclosing information.[49] In introducing the Bill and in commending its provisions, the objectives and aspirations for it were said to be:

> ... the Bill will not only provide legal rights for the public and place legal duties on Ministers and public authorities, but will help to transform the culture of Government from one of secrecy to one of openness. It will transform the default setting from "this should be kept quiet unless" to "this should be published unless." By doing so, it should raise public confidence in the processes of government, and enhance the quality of decision making by the Government'[50]

It may be thought that the public interest in disclosure lies partly in the attainment of those stated objectives. The significance of the public interest was described by those supporting the Bill in these terms:

> The duty to disclose information in the public interest is one of the most important aspects of the Bill. It is the key to creating the new culture of openness in the public sector with which the Government intend to replace the secrecy that, as everyone accepts, permeates Whitehall and too much of the public sector. We are introducing the Bill because we want to change that. The question is how to achieve the necessary balance between opening up the public sector and recognising that openness does not always have a monopoly on righteousness. It needs to be balanced against the need for personal privacy, commercial

---

[45] MoJ, *Exemptions Guidance—Introduction*, undated, para 3.6; *Bellamy v IC and DBIS*, FTT, 23 February 2010 at [38(iv)].

[46] *DTI v IC*, IT, 10 November 2006 at [48]–[49].

[47] FOIA s 63; FOI(S)A s 58. See §§7– 036 to 7– 039. Under the environmental information regime, the exceptions are the same for information contained in historical records as it is for information not so contained: EIR reg 17; EI(S)R reg 15.

[48] *Hogan and Oxford City Council v IC*, IT, 17 October 2006 at [58] and [71].

[49] FOIA ss 2(2)(b), 17(3)(b), 19(3), 35(4) and 46(3); FOI(S)A ss 2(1)(b), 16(2), 23(3), 29(3) and 61(3). See also §14–024 in relation to the presumption of openness in the FOI Acts.

[50] Hansard HC vol 340 (7 December 1999) (Mr Jack Straw, second reading speech).

confidentiality and effective government.[51]

A consideration of the provisions and structure of the Act reveals that it is the disclosure of information that animates it.[52] The purposes of the FOI Acts, although not recited within their provisions, guide the public interest in disclosure.[53] To the extent that discernment of the public interest in disclosure is left in the hands of the courts, it may be thought that some guidance may be found in this underlying philosophy of the Act:

> Where over a period of years there can be discerned a steady trend in legislation which reflects the view of successive Parliaments as to what the public interest demands in a particular field of law, development of the common law in that part of the same field which has been left to it ought to proceed upon a parallel rather than a diverging course.[54]

012 Tribunal cases

The approach taken by the Tribunal has been to start from a position that assumes a public interest in disclosure of requested information.[55] Absent any public interest against maintaining an applicable qualified exemption, the public interest in disclosure will prevail, requiring the information to be disclosed. In assessing the harm that might result from disclosure (and, connected to that, the public interest in maintaining an exemption), the Tribunal is not bound to follow the views expressed by public officials:

> Mr Crow argued, in effect, that the Tribunal had no real alternative to accepting the evidence of the eminent witnesses that he called on these matters, in the absence of any evidence to refute them. We accept without question their assertions as to the vital importance of the principles listed in the last paragraph and others which they cited. Indeed, as we have already said, nobody cast doubt upon them. When it comes to the effects of disclosure, however, we have listened with care and respect to their warnings but remain entitled, indeed under a duty, to reach our own conclusions, applying our commonsense and, as to the lay members, our experience to our decision.[56]

The appeals decided by the Tribunal have recognised a particular public interest in disclosure in various circumstances:

> — There is a public interest in the accountability and transparency of the decision-making process of a public authority, including the provision of reasons for those decisions.[57]
>
> — There is a public interest in the proper conduct of investigative processes and

---

[51] Hansard HC vol 357 col 719 (27 November 2000) (Parliamentary Under-Secretary of State for the Home Department, Mr O'Brien, introducing amendments to the public interest provisions of the Bill).

[52] See: *Common Services Agency v Scottish IC*, 2006 CSIH 58, 2007 SLT 7 at [32].

[53] The purposes of the FOI Acts are considered in ch 1.

[54] *Erven Warnink Besloten Vennootschap v J Townend & Sons (Hull) Ltd* [1979] AC 731 at 743 (Lord Diplock). See also the quotation at §25– 028 from *A-G (UK) v Heinemann Publishers Pty Ltd* (1987) 10 NSWLR 86 at 191, 75 ALR 353 at 454.

[55] *Hogan and Oxford City Council v IC*, IT, 17 October 2006 at [56]; *DTI v IC*, IT, 10 November 2006 at [42]–[43], [45] and [54]; *Reith v IC and LB Hammersmith & Fulham*, IT, 1 June 2007 at [41]; *Bellamy v IC and DBIS*, FTT, 23 February 2010 at [38(i)]. Similarly the Scottish Court of Session: *Scottish Ministers v Scottish IC* [2007] CSIH 8, 2007 SCLR 253 at [11]. See further §14– 027.

[56] *DfES v IC and The Evening Standard*, IT, 19 February 2007 at [72].

[57] *Burgess v IC and Stafford Borough Council*, IT, 7 June 2007 at [45]; *Ministry of Defence v IC and Evans*, IT, 20 July 2007 at [14]–[68]; *OGC v IC*, IT, 19 February 2009 at [146]-[147], [149], [162]; *Galloway v IC and NHS*, IT, 20 March 2009 at [70(d)].

procedures carried out by public authorities, particularly those which might lead to criminal proceedings.[58]

— There is a public interest in ensuring the accountability of a public authority, including its decision to launch care proceedings[59] and to take enforcement action in support of planning control.[60] However, there must be some link between the attainment of this objective and the disclosure of the information sought.[61]

— There is a public interest in divulging a current policy that is used by a public authority to make decisions.[62]

— There is a public interest in the disclosure of information if it would disclose a cause of action legitimately open to the applicant.[63]

— There is a public interest in disclosing the workings of a public body, particularly one that is in receipt of public funds[64] or one in relation to a matter where government does not have a good track record.[65]

— There is a public interest in a disclosure that would promote public debate and meaningful participation in any aspect of the democratic process,[66] including upon important government decisions (eg introduction of an ID card).[67]

— There is a public interest in being able to test whether the assessments of a minister are robust or where disclosure of information will allow the public to better judge the Government's performance in a particular sphere.[68]

— There is a public interest in disclosing information that reveals corruption, illegality

---

[58] *DTI v IC*, IT, 10 November 2006 at [57]. However, it is necessary to bear in mind whether existing systems and procedures provide sufficient means of ensuring the proper conduct of such processes and procedures (at [62]); *McTeggart v IC*, IT, 4 June 2007 at [44].

[59] *Kitchener v IC and Derby City Council*, IT, 20 December 2006 at [13]–[14].

[60] *Archer v IC and Salisbury District Council*, IT, 9 May 2007 at [60].

[61] *ECGD v IC and Campaign Against Arms Trade*, IT, 21 October 2009 at [50(ix)]; *Dept of Culture, Media and Sport v IC*, IT, 29 July 2008 at [28].

[62] *Kitchener v IC and Derby City Council*, IT, 20 December 2006 at [15]. In *Department of Economic Policy and Development of the City of Moscow and another v Bankers Trust Co and another* [2004] EWCA Civ 314, [2005] QB 207 at [39] Mance LJ spoke of 'the public interest in ensuring appropriate standards of fairness in the conduct of arbitrations militates in favour of a public judgment in respect of judgments given on applications under section 68 [of the Arbitration Act 1996]. The desirability of public scrutiny as a means by which confidence in the courts can be maintained and the administration of justice made transparent applies here as in other areas of court activity under the principles of *Scott v Scott* [1913] AC 417 and article 6.'

[63] *Alcock v IC and Chief Constable of Staffordshire Police*, IT, 3 January 2007 at [41]. In *AG's Reference No 5* [2004] UKHL 40, [2005] 1 AC 167 at [20] Lord Bingham spoke of the 'obvious public interest' in the disclosure of information that would reveal that a telephone intercept was unlawful.

[64] *Guardian Newspapers Ltd and Heather Brooke v IC and BBC*, IT, 8 January 2007 at [120]–[121]. In *Archer v IC and Salisbury District Council*, IT, 9 May 2007 at [60] the IT identified a public interest in knowing why public money has been used abortively. This public interest is conventionally recognised in freedom of information regimes: *Harris v Australian Broadcasting Corporation* (1983) 78 FLR 236, 50 ALR 551.

[65] *OGC v IC*, IT, 19 February 2009 at [152] (the procurement of large information technology projects, such as the ID card system).

[66] *Dept of Culture, Media and Sport v IC*, IT, 29 July 2008 at [28]; *Galloway v IC and NHS*, IT, 20 March 2009 at [70(d)].

[67] *DWP v IC*, IT, 5 March 2007 at [97]; *OGC v IC*, IT, 19 February 2009 at [152]-[162].

[68] *DWP v IC*, IT, 5 March 2007 at [99]–[101].

or mismanagement on the part of public officials.[69]

— There is a legitimate public interest in ensuring the security of the postal system.[70]

— There is a public interest that all persons or parties subject to a Companies Act investigation be acquainted with the reasons for the investigation.[71]

013 Public interest in disclosing information already in the public domain

If the Tribunal, having examined the requested information, is of the view that it will add little to what is already in the public domain, the public interest in the disclosure of that information may be diminished.[72] On the other hand, to the extent that relevant aspects of the public interests are directed to protecting an interest from harm arising from disclosure, the fact that the requested information is already in the public domain will generally mean that no harm will be caused by the release of the requested information. It will matter not that the original release did cause harm, as what is required is that the disclosure in answer to the request be causative of harm. On the other hand, the relevant aspects of the public interest in maintaining an exemption or in disclosing the requested information (or both) may be substantially restored if the same information, although in the public domain, has not been officially released and the official releasing of the information would have significance.

014 Relevance of use to the public interest exercise

In assessing the public interest in disclosing the requested information, it is permissible to take into account a use that would be made of that information, even though that use would involve an unlawful act.[73] If the cumulative effect of similar requests gives rise to a well-founded fear of misuse of the information, that may be a legitimate factor to be taken into account in

---

[69] *Mitchell v IC*, IT, 10 October 2005 at [6]. This reflects the stance taken in other areas of the law: *Beloff v Pressdram Ltd* [1973] 1 All ER 241 at 260 ('disclosure justified in the public interest, of matters carried out or contemplated, in breach of the country's security, or in breach of law, including statutory duty, fraud, or otherwise destructive of the country or its people, including matters medically dangerous to the public; and doubtless other misdeeds of similar gravity.'); *AG v Guardian Newspapers (No 2)* [1990] 1 AC 109 ('possibly the public interest in the exposure of iniquity in the Security Service' at 212 (Dillon LJ); also, 268–269 (Lord Griffiths) and at 282–283 (Lord Goff); Lord Salmon in *British Steel Corporation v Granada Television Ltd* [1981] AC 1096 at 1185; *Sankey v Whitlam* (1978) 142 CLR 1; *Director of Public Prosecutions v Smith* [1991] 1 VR 63; *Cochran v United States*, 770 F 2d 949 (11th Cir 1985); *Columbia Packing Co v USDA*, 563 F 2d 495. See also the Public Interest Disclosure Act 1998, which inserted Pt IVA (ss 43A–43L) into the Employment Rights Act 1996. One of the classes of 'qualifying disclosure' which are said to be in the public interest is a disclosure tending to show 'that a criminal offence has been committed, is being committed or is likely to be committed.' – s 43B(1)(a).

[70] *Toms v IC*, IT, 19 June 2006 at [18] and [22].

[71] *DTI v IC*, IT, 10 November 2006 at [51]; *FCO v IC*, IT, 22 January 2008 at [27]-[28].

[72] See eg: *FCO v IC and Friends of the Earth*, IT, 29 June 2007. It will be necessary to consider the similarity between the information that falls within the terms of the request and that which is in the public domain. If it is identical, a public authority should generally be relying upon FOIA s 21(1) if it does not wish to release the requested information. A public authority must be careful not to deploy the principle that effectively requires an applicant to have a legitimate motive for making the request for information.

[73] *R (Office of Communications) v IC* [2009] EWCA Civ 90, [2009] ACD 48 at [54]-[59] (breach of a third party's copyright).

maintaining an exemption.[74]

15– 015 The significance of the identity and motive of the applicant

Although the identity of and motive for the applicant seeking access to information provide no separate grounds for declining to answer a request,[75] these can impinge upon the public interest in disclosing the information[76] (as well as whether the request for information is vexatious). Case law in most comparative jurisdictions recognises that the public interest in disclosure embraces the right of an individual to have disclosed documents that relate to him or that may affect his interests.[77] Under the FOI Acts, where what is requested amounts to personal information relating to the applicant, the information enjoys absolute exemption under the FOI Acts,[78] so that the public interest in its disclosure need not be considered. The issue may, nevertheless, arise in other circumstances. Information, although not personal information, may be of especial interest to, or significance for, the applicant: for example, where it does touch upon the applicant, albeit falling short of having the biographical requirement of personal information;[79] or information relating to an institution with which the applicant is associated.[80]

15– 016 External indications of the public interest in disclosure

The precursor to the Freedom of Information Act 2000, the *Code of Practice on Access to Government*

---

[74] *Hemsley v IC and Chief Constable of Northamptonshire*, IT, 10 April 2006 at [23]. The appellant had sought detailed information relating to speed offences recorded by a particular speed camera. The Tribunal found that the information fell within FOIA s 31(1). In considering the public interest balancing exercise, it held (at [23]): '...we are impressed by the argument as to setting a precedent. Whilst every request must be dealt with on its merits, if this request were granted, it is not hard to envisage the difficulties faced by police authorities in dealing with future requests for such information, justified more or less plausibly, as designed to test the efficacy of signs, the hazards posed by weather conditions or the vigilance of drivers at particular times of day. It might be difficult to distinguish between the public spirited motivation of such as the appellant and others whose purpose was less admirable, eg the creation of a commercial website selling forecasts on the operation of safety cameras.'

[75] As was stated in *Burns v Bureau of Prisons*, 804 F 2d 701 at 706 (DC Cir 1986), 'Congress granted the scholar and the scoundrel equal rights of access to agency records.' More prosaically: *Dept of Culture, Media and Sport v IC*, IT, 29 July 2008 at [4]; *Armstrong v IC and HMRC*, IT, 14 October 2008 at [75], [96]; *MoD v IC and Evans*, IT, 20 July 2007 at [50]-[51]; *S v IC and General Register Office*, IT, 9 May 2007 at [19], [80]; *O'Brien v IC and DBERR*, IT, 20 July 2009 at [38]; *East Riding of Yorkshire Council v IC and Stanley Davis Group Ltd*, FTT, 15 March 2010 at [28].

[76] In *Hogan and Oxford City Council v IC*, IT, 17 October 2006 at [32], the IT considered that the motive of an applicant could be relevant for the purposes of determining the degree of prejudice likely to result from disclosure.

[77] *Burns v Australian National University (No 1)* (1984) 6 ALD 193, 1 AAR 456; *Burns v Australian National University (No 2)* (1985) 7 ALD 425. The courts in the US have been generally less receptive to this notion, taking the view that although the public interest may affect the priority of processing requests, it has no bearing on an individual's rights of access under the FOI Act: *EPA v Mink*, 410 US 73 (1973) (the FOI Act 'is largely indifferent to the intensity of a particular requester's need'); *United States Department of Justice v Reporters Committee for Freedom of the Press*, 489 US 749 (1989); *Forsham v Califano*, 587 F 2d 1128 (DC Cir 1978). Thus, it has been held that a convicted criminal's wish to establish his own innocence through the requested documents does not create a FOI Act-recognised public interest: *Landano v United States Department of Justice*, 956 F 2d 422 (3d Cir 1991); *Hale v United States Department of Justice*, 973 F 2d 894 (10th Cir 1992); *Neely v FBI*, 208 F 3d 461 (4th Cir 2000).

[78] FOIA s 40(1); FOI(S)A s 38(1); EIR regs 5(3) and 12(3); EI(S)R regs 10(3) and 11(1). It is instead normally accessible under the DPA s 7. The ability of the data subject to rectify, etc such information under s 14 would serve to enhance the public interest in that individual being granted access to it.

[79] See §§5– 021 to 5– 024.

[80] As in *Burns v Australian National University (No1)* (1984) 6 ALD 193, 1 AAR 456.

Information,[81] stated that its aims were:

— to improve policy-making and the democratic process by extending access to the facts and analyses which provide the basis for the consideration of proposed policy;

— to protect the interests of individuals and companies by ensuring that reasons are given for administrative decisions, except where there is statutory authority or established convention to the contrary; and

— to support and extend the principles of public service established under the Citizen's Charter.[82]

The 2000 Act was intended to represent a development from the Code of Practice, but there is nothing to suggest that its core purpose was materially different from that of the Code.[83]

017 The public interest: confusion, partial accounts and misinformation

The Tribunal has rejected as a relevant consideration the possibility that members of the public might be confused by the information disclosed: if a public authority entertains that fear, it can always volunteer information that will redress any imbalance.[84] There is a public interest in the disclosure of information that is needed to disclose the full picture: in other words, where there has been a partial disclosure of information upon a particular matter the selection of which is unrepresentative of the whole.[85] Similarly, there is a public interest in the disclosure of information where that would correct misinformation that is in the public domain, particularly where the origin of the misinformation is the public authority to whom the request has been made.[86]

---

[81] In relation to information held by Scottish public authorities, see §§1– 039 to 1– 041.

[82] 2nd edn 1997, para 2.

[83] The most significant distinction between the Act and the Code is that the former imposes an enforceable duty to disclose in certain circumstances, whereas the latter merely exhorted disclosure in certain circumstances.

[84] *Kitchener v IC and Derby City Council*, IT, 20 December 2006 at [19]; *Hogan and Oxford City Council v IC*, IT, 17 October 2006; *DWP v IC*, IT, 5 March 2007, argument at [92] not accepted; *OGC v IC*, IT, 2 May 2007 at [75]; *House of Commons v IC and Brooke, Leapman, Ungoed-Thomas* [2008] EWHC 1084 (Admin), [2009] 3 All ER 403 at [79(e)]; *OGC v IC*, IT, 19 February 2009 at [161], [182].

[85] *Woodward v Hutchins* [1977] 1 WLR 760 at 764 ('If the image which they fostered was not a true image, it is in the public interest that it should be corrected. In these cases of confidential information it is a question of balancing the public interest in knowing the truth.' (Lord Denning)). Significant doubts have been expressed about this authority: it was said to be 'framed in astonishingly wide terms' in *Douglas v Hello! Ltd* [2001] QB 967 at [96]; and it was doubted by Lightman J at first instance in *Campbell v Frisbee* [2002] EWHC 328 (Ch), [2002] EMLR 656 at [40]–[41] and the Court of Appeal (reversing his decision) said his doubts 'may well be right', [2002] EWCA Civ 1374, [2003] ICR 141 at [34]. Moreover, Australian courts have expressly departed from it in favour of a narrower approach: *Castrol Australia Pty Ltd v Emtech Associates Pty Ltd* (1980) 33 ALR 31 at 56 (Rath J). Less controversially, in *AG v Guardian Newspapers (No 2)* [1990] 1 AC 109 at 196 Lord Donaldson MR spoke of 'the legitimate public interest in being fully informed.'

[86] *Hyde Park Residence Ltd v Yelland* [2001] Ch 143 at 170 ('the public interest in knowing the truth' (Mance LJ)).

3.   WEIGHING THE PUBLIC INTEREST: CONFIRMATION AND DENIAL

15– 018   **The public interest in maintaining the exclusion of the duty to confirm or deny**

As noted above,[87] the need to undertake the weighing exercise set out in subs 2(1)[88] will only arise if the result of carrying out the separate weighing exercise in subs 2(2) is a decision not to disclose the information.[89] Unlike the weighing exercise in relation to the duty to communicate, under subs 2(1) there is no focussing of the public interest upon the particular provision of Part II by which the duty to confirm or deny does not arise. The identified public interest is the maintenance of 'the exclusion of the duty to confirm or deny'. The public interest in maintaining the exclusion of the duty to confirm or deny will vary with the specificity of the request: the more specifically the request identifies the information sought, the more readily may it be determined that the public interest in maintaining the exclusion of the duty to confirm or deny outweighs the public interest in disclosing whether the public authority holds the information. Authorities from the USA illustrate the types of request that have there been held entitle a public authority in the name of the public interest neither to confirm nor deny holding any documents of the sort requested.[90]

15– 019   **The public interest in disclosing whether the public authority holds the information**

This public interest is analogous to the public interest in disclosing the information. However, as the applicant is not receiving the information requested but only an acknowledgment that it is or is not held by a particular public authority, it may be thought that the public interest in it is generally less compelling than the public interest in communicating the information requested. The analogy, moreover, has its limitations. In order to be effective, disapplication of the duty to confirm or deny must be invoked consistently to requests of a particular type, whether or not the public authority holds information of the precise sort requested. Unless this is done, a response neither confirming or denying that the sought information is held by the

---

[87]   See §15– 008.

[88]   In relation to information held by Scottish public authorities, see s 18(1).

[89]   In relation to information held by Scottish public authorities, see s 2(1). The exemptions to which the duty to confirm or deny is disapplied are more limited than those under the FOIA: namely, ss 28–35, 39 and 41. The Scottish equivalents to the FOIA ss 22, 32, 33, 40, 41, 42 and 44 do not ground a refusal to confirm or deny under the FOI(S)A. In relation to the differences between the approach taken to the duty to confirm or deny in the FOIA and that which is taken in the FOI(S)A, see §1– 041(1). Where the request is made under the environmental information regime, there is no discrete obligation on a public authority to disclose whether or not it holds the requested information.

[90]   *Frugone v CIA*, 169 F 3d 772 (DC Cir 1999) (where it was upheld that the CIA's refusal to confirm or deny whether plaintiff was ever employed by CIA on the basis that disclosure could cause 'diplomatic tension between Chile and the United States' or could 'lessen the burden facing a foreign intelligence agency attempting to track the CIA's covert activities abroad'); *Miller v Casey*, 730 F 2d 773 (DC Cir 1984) (upholding a refusal to confirm or deny holding any record reflecting any attempt by western countries to overthrow the Albanian government); *Gardels v CIA*, 689 F 2d 1100 (DC Cir 1982) (upholding a refusal to confirm or deny holding any record revealing any covert CIA connection with the University of California). In the United States, this is often called a 'Glomar response'.

public authority will be understood to represent an acknowledgment that that information is in fact held. The public interest in disclosing whether an authority holds the information sought thus involves a consideration of the public interest in generally disclosing whether that authority holds information of the type requested. For example:[91] an applicant may request all information received by a public authority from X that contributed to the public authority's decision to discontinue benefits to the applicant; the public authority holds no such information received from X; the public authority nevertheless declines to disclose whether it holds the information sought on the basis that unless it uniformly so declines all requests for information on informants, irrespective of the identity or existence of the informant, its ability to conceal the identity of its informants will be prejudiced. The public interest here is that of protecting the anonymity of informants.

4. ASCERTAINING AND WEIGHING PREJUDICE

020 **Introduction**

With the exception of the national security and health and safety exemptions, under each of the prejudice-based exemptions[92] information only becomes exempt information if its disclosure under the FOI Acts 'would, or would be likely to, prejudice' that which the particular exemption seeks to protect.[93] If a public authority is to refuse a request for information, it must specify the exemption relied on and the reason it applies.[94] Where a prejudice-based exemption is specified in the refusal notice, that will involve, if it is not otherwise apparent, stating the basis upon which disclosure 'would, or would be likely to, prejudice' that which the particular exemption seeks to protect.

021 **The meaning of 'prejudice'**

Some indication of what was said to be intended by the word 'prejudice' appears from the Second Reading speech in the House of Lords:

> I want to emphasise the strength of the prejudice test. Prejudice is a term used in other legislation relating to the disclosure of information. It is a term well understood by the courts and the public. It is not a weak test. The commissioner will have the power to overrule an authority if she feels that any prejudice caused by a disclosure would be trivial or insignificant. She will ensure that an authority must point to prejudice which is "real, actual or of substance." We do not think that reliance on undefined terms such as "substantial" or "significant" is a sensible way forward. We do not know how they will be interpreted by the commissioner or the courts. We can never deliver absolute certainty, but we can avoid

---

[91] The example is loosely based on the Australian case of *Department of Community Services v Jephcott* (1987) 15 FCR 122, 73 ALR 493 (Federal Court on appeal from the Administrative Appeals Tribunal to which the matter had previously been remitted by the Federal Court – see (1985) 8 FCR 85, 62 ALR 421).

[92] FOIA ss 26(1), 27(1), 28(1), 29(1), 31(1), 33(2), 36(2), 38(1) and 43(2); FOI(S)A ss 27(2), 28(1), 30, 31(4), 32(1), 33(1), 33(2), 35(1) and 40.

[93] In Scotland the requirement is to show 'serious prejudice'.

[94] FOIA s 17(1); FOI(S)A s 16(1).

making uncertainty worse by adding ill-defined terminology into the Bill.[95]

In rejecting a proposed amendment that would have required the prejudice to be 'substantial' or 'probable', it was said:

> .. qualification of the term is unnecessary. The Government have consistently stated their views that prejudice means prejudice that is actual, real or of substance.[96]

And similarly in the House of Lords:

> There were also complaints about the "harm" test. A number of noble Lords said that the reference should be to "substantial harm". That was the kind of test they were looking for. The word that was chosen where we are dealing with a harm test is "prejudice". To all lawyers present—there are depressingly few—"prejudice" will mean some real harm to government, or whatever the reference is in a particular part of the Bill. It is something real, and it is harm. Should it be "substantial harm", or should it be "prejudice"? That sounds like the kind of discussion that a lawyer would like to enter into, but it does not cut to the heart of the debate. It sounds much more theological, if I may use that word in this context, rather than cutting to the fundament of the Bill.[97]

This has been endorsed by the Tribunal:

> An evidential burden rests with the decision maker to be able to show that some causal relationship exists between the potential disclosure and the prejudice and that the prejudice is, as Lord Falconer of Thoroton has stated, "real, actual or of substance" (Hansard HL vol 162 col 827 (20 April 2000)). If the public authority is unable to discharge this burden satisfactorily, reliance on "prejudice" should be rejected. There is therefore effectively a *de minimis* threshold which must be met.[98]

The statutory formulation 'would be likely to prejudice...' embodies protection against 'risks,' spelling out the precise probability and consequence that will engage the exemption.[99] In this way, it can properly be said that the identified risks constitute a prejudice that is 'real, actual and of substance.'

---

[95] Hansard HL vol 162 col 827 (20 April 2000) (Minister of State, Cabinet Office, Lord Falconer of Thoroton). When the Lord Chancellor (Lord Irvine) announced in the House of Lords the publication of the *White Paper, Your Right to Know* (Cm 3818, 1997) Hansard HL vol 584 col 245 (11 December 1997), he identified as one of the key features of the proposed FOI regime: 'Thirdly, fewer exemptions. ...Significantly, in most cases information could only be withheld if its disclosure would cause "substantial" harm – a further important advance on the Code.' The House of Lords, *Draft FOI Bill – First Report*, (Select Committee Report HL 97), Session 1998–99, 29 July 1999, had recommended that prejudice be qualified by 'substantial.' — para 32 (see ch 1 n 125).

[96] Hansard HC vol 347 col 1067 (5 April 2000) (Mr Mike O'Brien). The Government advised the House of Commons Select Committee that the formula required 'probable prejudice, not just possible prejudice': House of Commons, *Public Administration — Third Report* (Cm 4355, 1999) para 65–71 (see ch 1 n 64); Annex 6, para 47–48. The Home Secretary specifically invited reliance upon his explanation in Parliament as a tool of interpretation in the Courts: para 68.

[97] Hansard HL vol 612 col 889 (20 April 2000) (Minister of State, Cabinet Office, Lord Falconer of Thoroton). See also: Hansard HL vol 617 col 1267 (19 October 2000) – the harm must be 'real'. The House of Commons, *Public Administration — Third Report* (Cm 4355, 1999) para 65, although considering them to be synonymous, preferred the word 'prejudice' to 'harm' on the basis that it was 'more common in other legislation', citing the Local Government Act 1972 Sch 12A, para 4, Taxes Management Act 1970 s 20(8H), Drug Trafficking Act 1994 s 53(2)(b), and DPA ss 29, 30 and 31.

[98] *Hogan and Oxford City Council v IC*, IT, 17 October 2006 at [30]. Similarly: *Hemsley v IC and Chief Constable of Northamptonshire*, IT, 10 April 2006 at [17] ('some prejudice' is sufficient); *Ministry of Defence v IC and Evans*, IT, 20 July 2007 at [73].

[99] It is suggested that to the extent that *Campaign against the Arms Trade v IC and MoJ*, IT, 26 August 2008, at [81], and *Gilby v IC and FCO*, IT, 22 October 2008, at [23], consider that a 'risk of harm' to a protected interest is synonymous with harm to that protected interest, they are wrong.

022 The required degree of likelihood

With the exception of the national security exemption, each of the prejudice-based exemptions employs the formula 'would, or would be likely to prejudice' (or 'endanger', in the case of the health and safety exemption). The range of meaning that might be given to the phrase was noted by the House of Commons Select Committee, which quoted one witness before it:

> I think the words "likely to prejudice" are ones which are not the most desirable to have in this field because there is a very considerable risk of conflict as to what the word "likely" means. Does it mean "likely to rain," as in the possibility that it is going to rain, or does it mean "it is more likely than that," in other words that it is more probable than that. ...If "prejudice" is the appropriate word, surely the issue is whether some interest would be prejudiced, and the word "likely" can be somewhat weasel.[100]

In *R (Lord) v Secretary of State for the Home Department*[101] Munby J had cause to consider the meaning of the phrase 'would be likely to prejudice' for the purpose of considering certain exemptions under the Data Protection Act 1998. In the course of judgment, he said:

> I accept that "likely" in section 29(1) [of the Data Protection Act 1998] does not mean more probable than not. But on the other hand, it must connote a significantly greater degree of probability than merely "more than fanciful". A "real risk" is not enough. I cannot accept that the important rights intended to be conferred by section 7 are intended to be set at nought by something which measures up only to the minimal requirement of being real, tangible or identifiable rather than merely fanciful. Something much more significant and weighty than that is required....In my judgment "likely" in section 29(1) connotes a degree of probability where there is a very significant and weighty chance of prejudice to the identified public interests. The degree of risk must be such that there "may very well" be prejudice to those interests, even if the risk falls short of being more probable than not.

This passage has been quoted with approval by the Tribunal when considering the phrase as used in the Freedom of Information Act 2000:

> We interpret the expression "likely to prejudice" as meaning that the chance of prejudice being suffered should be more than a hypothetical or remote possibility; there must have been a real and significant risk.[102]

And similarly:

> It means that inhibition would probably occur (ie, on the balance of probabilities, the chance being greater than 50%) or that there would be a "very significant and weighty chance" that it would occur. A "real risk" is not enough; the degree of risk must be such that there "may very well be" such inhibition, even if the risk falls short of being more probable than not.[103]

---

[100] Lord Woolf, quoted in House of Commons, *Public Administration — Third Report* (Cm 4355, 1999) para 66 (see ch 1 n 64). The Government had argued before the Committee that the phrase required the prejudice to be at least 'likely' or 'probable', rather than merely 'possible': *Public Administration — Third Report* (Cm 4355, 1999) para 68.

[101] [2003] EWHC 2073 (Admin) at [106].

[102] *John Connor Press Associates v IC*, IT, 25 January 2006 at [15]. Similarly: *Hogan and Oxford City Council v IC*, IT, 17 October 2006 at [34]; *McIntyre v IC and MoD*, IT, 4 February 2008 at [40]; *Craven v IC*, IT, 13 May 2008 at [14], [19], [24]; *Keene v IC and Central Office of Information*, IT, 14 September 2009 at [36]; *Bangar v IC and Transport for London*, IT, 23 November 2009 at [5]. An attack on the applicability of *R (Lord) v SSHD* to the FOIA was rejected by the Tribunal in *Office of Commerce v IC*, IT, 2 May 2007 at [48].

[103] *Guardian Newspapers Ltd v IC and BBC*, IT, 8 January 2007 at [53]. Similarly: *Evans v IC and MoD*, IT, 26 October 2007 at [21]; *Galloway v IC and NHS*, IT, 20 March 2009 at [93]. For the interpretation given to the word 'likely' in s 12(3) of the Human Rights Act 1998, see *Cream Holdings Ltd v Banerjee* [2003] EWCA Civ 103, [2003] 2 All ER 318 at [12(i)] and [83].

The mere assertion of inhibition resulting from disclosure, while not necessarily fatal to a claim for exemption, will be an important consideration.[104] The Tribunal has indicated that it expects to receive evidence of the likelihood, severity, extent or frequency of the claimed inhibition.[105]

15– 023 Approach elsewhere

Similar formulae of likelihood of harm are used in the prejudice-based exemptions of other FOI Acts. In Australia, the phrase 'would or could reasonably be expected to' has been consistently been held to mean that the decision-maker must have real and substantial grounds for the expectation that harm will occur: it requires more than a possibility, risk or chance of the event occurring.[106] In New Zealand, the phrase 'likely to prejudice' has been held to mean no more than a distinct or significant possibility, and that it is enough if there is a serious or real and substantial risk to a protected interest or that a risk might well eventuate.[107] In Canada, in order to rely on a prejudice-based exemption,[108] it has been held that the agency need not prove direct causation between disclosure and harm: indirect causality will suffice.[109] However, in order to uphold non-disclosure on an appeal, the Courts have required evidence to justify the apprehension of prejudice: evidence that describes in a most general way certain consequences that could ensue from disclosure has been held to fall short of meeting the burden of proving the harm that disclosure would cause.[110] Similarly, mere affirmations that the disclosure would cause the harm required by the section will not suffice where the expectation of the harm is not self-evident.[111] European case law in relation to Decision 93/731 art 4, requires that 'the risk of the public interest being undermined must ... be reasonably foreseeable and not purely

---

[104] *Guardian Newspapers Ltd and Heather Brooke v IC and BBC*, IT, 8 January 2007 at [78].

[105] *Guardian Newspapers Ltd and Heather Brooke v IC and BBC*, IT, 8 January 2007 at [99]–[102].

[106] *News Corporation v National Companies and Securities Commission* (1984) 5 FCR 88, 57 ALR 550, where (at ALR 561) a distinction was drawn between the two phrases 'would or could reasonably be expected to prejudice' and 'would or might prejudice', with the former requiring more than the latter; *Attorney-General's Department v Cockcroft* (1986) 10 FCR 180, 64 ALR 97; *Arnold v Queensland* (1987) 13 ALD 195 at 215; *Re Binnie and Department of Agriculture and Rural Affairs* [1989] VR 836; *Searle Australia Pty Ltd v Public Interest Advocacy Centre and Department of Community Services and Health* (1992) 108 ALR 163; *George v Rocket* (1990) 170 CLR 104. See Freedom of Information Act 1982 (Cth of Australia), ss 33, 33A, 37, 43A, 47E, 47G and 47J.

[107] *Commissioner of Police v Ombudsman* [1988] 1 NZLR 385 at 391, 404 and 411, which considered the various possible shades of meaning that could be given to the word 'likely'. The Official Information Act 1982, ss 6 and 7 render information exempt from disclosure where that disclosure 'would be likely to prejudice/endanger/damage seriously' one of the protected interests. Exemption is also granted where that 'is necessary to protect/avoid prejudice/ maintain the constitutional conventions which would protect/maintain the effective conduct of public affairs/enable a Minister to carry out/prevent the disclosure of use of official information for improper gain' (s 9).

[108] Section 20(1)(c) of the Access to Information Act creates a mandatory exemption for 'information the disclosure of which could reasonably be expected to result in material financial loss or gain to, or could reasonably be expected to prejudice the competitive position of, a third party.' See also: ss 14, 15 and 16, which use 'could reasonably be expected to be injurious' (s 16), 'could reasonably be expected to facilitate the commission of an offence' (s 17), 'could reasonably be expected to threaten' (s 18), 'could reasonably be expected to prejudice' (s 18) and 'could reasonably be expected to result in an undue benefit'.

[109] *Canada Packers Inc v Canada (Minister of Agriculture)* [1989] 1 FC 47.

[110] *Ottawa Football Club v Canada (Minister of Fitness and Amateur Sports)* [1989] 2 FC 480; *Merck Frosst Canada Inc v Canada (Minister of Health and Welfare)* (1988), 20 FTR 73 30 CPR (3d) 473; *Canada Post Corp v Canada (Minister of Public Works)* [1993] 3 FC 320, affirmed (1993) 64 FTR 62.

[111] *Canadian Broadcasting Commission v National Capital Commission* (1998) 147 FTR 264.

hypothetical.'[112]

024 'Mosaic' or cumulative prejudice

Although disclosure of particular information, when considered in isolation, may fail to satisfy the prejudice requirement, consideration of the prejudice caused by the disclosure of that information together with that caused by the disclosure of other similarly non-prejudicial information may yield a different result. This is variously termed 'jigsaw', 'mosaic' or 'cumulative' prejudice. There is nothing in the FOI Acts requiring such an exercise to be carried out. A provision in the FOI Bill specifically enabling such an exercise was criticised by both the House of Commons Select Committee and the House of Lords Select Committee, and did not find its way into the statute.[113]

025 'Mosaic' or cumulative prejudice elsewhere

Freedom of information legislation in comparative jurisdictions invariably prescribes certain exemptions on the basis of anticipated prejudice or harm resulting from disclosure. The concept of 'mosaic' or cumulative prejudice has been accepted as capable of constituting that prejudice or harm, albeit only in particular spheres of governmental activity. In the United States, mosaic prejudice is well-recognised in relation to intelligence gathering activities,[114] and is now explicitly recognised by Executive Order.[115] In Australia, security and criminal investigation agencies have usually been able to sustain claims of exemption founded upon prejudice to the integrity of their intelligence from incremental disclosure.[116] In Canada, there is less authority on the point: it has on one occasion received passing acceptance in relation to police information.[117]

026 Information already in the public domain

Each of the prejudice-based exemptions requires that disclosure 'would, or would be likely to, prejudice' a particular protected interest. If that anticipated prejudice has already resulted from

---

[112] *Kuijer v Council of the European Union* [2002] 1 WLR 1941 at [56]; *Verein für Konsumenteninformation v Commission* [2005] 1 WLR 3302, [2005] All ER (EC) 813, [2005] ECR II–1121, [2006] 2 CMLR 60, [2005] 4 CMLR 21 at [69] and [72]; *Franchet v Commission of European Communities* [2006] 3 CMLR 37 at [115].

[113] House of Commons, *Public Administration—Third Report* (Cm 4355, 1999) paras 113–116; Annex 6, paras 70–72; House of Lords, *Draft FOI Bill—First Report*, (Select Committee Report HL 97), Session 1998–99, 29 July 1999, paras 36–37, referring to cl 37 (see ch 1 n 125). In relation to mosaic prejudice and intelligence and national security matters, see §17– 029(1).

[114] *Halperin v CIA*, 629 F 2d 144 (DC Cir 1980), 'each individual piece of intelligence information, much like a piece of a jigsaw puzzle, may aid in piecing together other bits of information even when the individual piece is not of obvious importance in itself'; *Salisbury v United States*, 690 F 2d 966; *Taylor v Department of the Army*, 684 F 2d 99.

[115] Executive Order 12,958, 1.8(e).

[116] *Re Low and Department of Defence* (1984) 2 AAR 142 at 149; *Re Actors' Equity Association of Australia and Australian Broadcasting Tribunal (No 2)* (1985) 7 ALD 584 (information sought relating to commercial television licensees); *Re Robinson and Department of Foreign Affairs* (1986) 11 ALN N48; *Re Throssell and Australian Archives* (1986) 10 ALD 403 at 406 and 407; *Re Throssell and Department of Foreign Affairs* (1987) 14 ALD 296; *Re Slater and Cox (Director General, Australian Archives)* (1988) 15 ALD 20 at 27; *Re McKnight v Australian Archives* (1992) 28 ALD 95 at 112; *Re Ewer and Australian Archives* (1995) 38 ALD 789.

[117] *Ruby v Canada (Royal Canadian Mounted Police)* [1998] 2 FC 351 (TD). The Court of Appeal appeared less enthusiastic about it: *Ruby v Canada (Solicitor General)* [2000] 3 FC 589 (CA) at [89] *et seq.*

an earlier disclosure, it will be difficult to attribute any material prejudice[118] to a later disclosure of the same or like information. The fact that there has been an earlier disclosure of the same or like information does not, however, necessarily mean that the anticipated prejudice has already occurred. The manner in which information is disclosed can impinge upon the prejudice resulting from that disclosure. In particular, the prejudice resulting from an unintentional or unauthorised disclosure of information may, in some circumstances, be different from that resulting from an official disclosure of the same information.[119] Official confirmation carries with it secondary information as to the accuracy of the earlier disclosure: this secondary information can turn theory into fact and render others more likely to act upon it. In the United States the courts have held that, in asserting a claim of prior public disclosure, the applicant bears the initial burden of pointing to specific information in the public domain that appears to duplicate that being withheld.[120] If the public authority itself has made the information available to certain quarters of the public, it will be difficult to sustain a prejudice-based exemption.[121]

15–027 The nature of disclosure under statute

Once the access right is engaged, it not having been disapplied by any provision in the Act, the duty on a public authority is to communicate the requested information in one of the ways specified in the Act. There is nothing in the FOI Acts enabling a public authority when communicating information to place restrictions on the use of that information.[122] The unqualified nature of any disclosure required under the Act is shared by the FOI legislation in comparative jurisdictions. Attempts in the USA and Australia to impose restrictions on the use

---

[118] See §15– 021 for the meaning of 'prejudice'.

[119] *S v IC and The General Register Office*, IT, 9 May 2007 at [80]; *Ministry of Defence v IC and Evans*, IT, 20 July 2007 at [57]; *Gilby v IC and FCO*, IT, 22 October 2008 at [42]-[44]. In Australia, in *Ascic v Australian Federal Police* (1986) 11 ALN N184, it was held that the mere fact that information in respect of which an agency claimed exemption may have been 'leaked' did not necessarily prejudice the merits of the exemption claimed: disclosure by order under the Act being considered a very different thing with very different consequences to unauthorised access. In Canada the jurisprudence indicates that once information is public from another source the release of the same information by the Government will be less likely to cause harm; the courts have required the Government to show specific reasons why its release of the same information would cause harm: *Canada (IC) v Canada (Prime Minister)* [1993] 1 FC 427 (TD); *Cyanamid Canada Inc v Canada (Minister of Health and Welfare)* (1992) 45 CPR (3d) 390 (FCA).

[120] *Afshar v Department of State*, 702 F 2d 1125 (DC Cir 1983); *Assassination Archives & Research Centre v CIA*, 177 F Supp 2d 1 (DDC 2001) (holding that CIA's prior disclosure of some intelligence methods employed in Cuba does not oblige it to disclose all forms of intelligence gathering in Cuba); *Billington v Department of Justice*, 11 F Supp 2d 45 (DDC 1998) (holding that because the release of similar types of information by the FBI in one case did not warrant disclosure in the instant case); *Hunt v CIA*, 981 F 2d 1116 (9th Cir 1992) (held that although some information about subject of request may have been made public by other governmental agencies, CIA's 'neither confirm nor deny' response was warranted).

[121] *Kuijer v Council of the European Union (No 2)* [2002] 1 WLR 1941 at paras 73–74 (Court of First Instance of the European Communities). For an example of how disclosure by a public authority of some of the requested information can make a claim for a prejudice-based exemption unsustainable, see *John Connor Press Associates v IC*, IT, 25 January 2006, where the disclosure of certain commercial information relating to a particular transaction precluded exemption under FOIA s 43(2), for the remaining commercial information relating to that transaction. See also *Hogan and Oxford City Council v IC*, IT, 17 October 2006 at [42]–[50] and [71].

[122] *Hogan and Oxford City Council v IC*, IT, 17 October 2006 at [31]; *S v IC and The General Register Office*, IT, 9 May 2007 at [80].

of disclosed information have been held unlawful.[123]

028 Significance of the nature of disclosure

The inability of a public authority to restrict the use made of information disclosed under the Act is of particular significance in the determination of the prejudice-based exemptions. The prejudice that is to be measured is that resulting from an unrestricted disclosure, and not just a disclosure to the applicant.[124] There is nothing in the FOI Acts to prevent a person when requesting information and who anticipates that the public authority may claim that disclosure would prejudice a protected interest, to reduce the scope for prejudice by offering to limit use of the information so disclosed. Such undertakings have, however, been rejected in the US.[125]

---

[123] *Schiffer v FBI* 78 F 3d 1405 (9th Cir 1996). The FOI Act (US) does not provide for limited disclosure; rather, it 'speaks in terms of disclosure and nondisclosure [and] ordinarily does not recognize degrees of disclosure, such as permitting viewing, but not copying, of documents' — *Julian v United States Department of Justice*, 806 F 2d 1411 at 1419 n.7 (9th Cir 1986). In Australia, *Re Dwyer and Department of Finance* (1985) 8 ALD 474.

[124] *Hogan and Oxford City Council v IC*, IT, 17 October 2006 at [31]; *Guardian Newspapers Ltd and Brooke v IC and BBC*, IT, 8 January 2007 at [52].

[125] *Maricopa Audobon Society v United States Forest Service*, 108 F 3d 1082 at 1088–89 (9th Cir 1997) on the basis that the 'FOI Act does not permit selective disclosure of information to only certain parties, and that once the information is disclosed to [the plaintiff], it must be made available to all members of the public who request it.'

CHAPTER 16

Information Otherwise Accessible

1. INFORMATION OTHERWISE ACCESSIBLE

16– 001 Introduction

Information that is reasonably accessible to the applicant otherwise than under the Freedom of Information Act 2000 is exempt information.[1] The exemption is absolute, so that if information falls within s 21(1) it is not necessary to consider the public interest. The underlying rationale for the exemption would appear to be two-fold. First, where an applicant has a right under a specific legislative regime to obtain access to particular information, then that specific legislative regime should normally be used rather than the Freedom of Information Act 2000. By this mechanism, the exemption ensures that an applicant does not circumvent the fees regime or other constraints of a specific legislative regime by using the Freedom of Information Act 2000. Where there is no such fees regime, the exemption is not so rigid in its application. Secondly, where information is made available by a public authority under a publication scheme, then a public authority cannot be required to communicate that information to a person making a request under the Act. A broadly equivalent exemption is

---

[1] FOIA s 21(1); FOI(S)A s 25(1).

508

to be found in the freedom of information legislation of most of the comparative jurisdictions.[2] There is no equivalent exception in the Environmental Information Regulations 2004.[3] Accordingly, where (or to the extent that) information that answers the terms of a request for information is 'environmental information',[4] the fact that that information is otherwise available to the applicant will not excuse the public authority from complying with the request.[5] The exemption had a relatively uneventful passage through Parliament.[6] Both the Ministry of Justice and the Information Commissioner have issued non-statutory guidance on the exemption.[7]

002   Scope of the exemption

The sole criterion for exemption is that the information be 'reasonably accessible to the applicant' otherwise than under the Freedom of Information Act 2000. The provision[8] deems certain duties to communicate as providing reasonable accessibility and deems certain other access to information as not providing reasonable accessibility. Where no deeming applies, in

---

2 There is no directly comparable exemption in the Freedom of Information Act, 1966 (USA). Although the Federal Court had suggested that an agency was not required to make requested records available by giving copies of them to a requester if the agency preferred to make the records available in one central location for examination (ie the reading room system) (*Oglesby v United States Department of the Army*, 920 F 2d 57, 70 (DC Cir 1990)), the Department of Justice recommends that such documents be copied to the requester: Freedom of Information Act Update, vol vol XII, No 2, at p 5. The Freedom of Information Act 1982 (Cth of Australia) s 12(1) removes the right of access to certain documents: '(a) a document, or a copy of a document, which is, under the Archives Act 1983, within the open access period within the meaning of that Act unless the document contains personal information (including personal information about a deceased person); or (b) a document that is open to public access, as part of a public register or otherwise, in accordance with another enactment, where that access is subject to a fee or other charge; or (ba) a document that is open to public access, as part of a land title register, in accordance with a law of a State or Territory where that access is subject to a fee or other charge; or (c) a document that is available for purchase by the public in accordance with arrangements made by an agency' — see §2–011. The Official Information Act 1982 (New Zealand) s 18(d), provides a discretionary exemption for information that 'is or will soon be publicly available' — see § 2–019. The Access to Information Act (Canada) s 68, provides that the Act does not apply to published material or material available for purchase by the public nor to library material: see §2–026(9). However, ss 2(2) and 19(2)(b) appear to specifically enable the Act to be used notwithstanding that the same material is available under other legislation or another source: see *Cyanamid Canada Inc v Canada (Minister of Health and Welfare)* (1992) 41 CPR (3d) 512 (FCTD). The Freedom of Information Act 1997 (Ireland) s 46(2), provides that the Act does not apply to a record that is available for inspection by members of the public, whether upon payment or free of charge, nor to a record where a copy is available for purchase or removal free of charge by members of the public, whether under an enactment or otherwise: see §2–035.

3 *Friends of the Earth v IC and ECGD*, IT, 20 August 2007 at [77].

4 As to the meaning of which, see §6–010.

5 However, a public authority is not obliged to comply with a request to the extent that the information sought is already publicly available and easily accessible to the applicant: EIR reg 6(1)(b); EI(S)R reg 6(1)(b). Alternative availability may also make the request for information 'manifestly unreasonable': eg, if the environmental information is readily available from public sources accessible to the applicant. In these circumstances the public authority may refuse to disclose: EIR reg 12(4)(b); EI(S)R reg 10(4)(b).

6 The provision (cl 19) originally referred to information that was reasonably accessible to members of the public, but this was amended early on in its passage: see Hansard HC vol 347 col 1053 (5 April 2000). Another amendment that would have taken information reasonably accessible in one format (eg paper) but not in another format (eg electronic) out of the exemption was withdrawn: Hansard HL vol 617 cols 1011–1012 (17 October 2000).

7 MoJ, *Exemptions guidance – Section 21: information available by other means* (14 May 2008); Information Commissioner, *Freedom of Information Act Awareness Guidance No 6*, ver 2 (updated January 2006).

8 In *Glasgow City Council & anor v Scottish IC* [2009] CSIH 73 the Court of Session described the Scottish provision (which is modelled on FOIA s 21) as 'not a model of clarity' (at [59]).

deciding whether information is reasonably accessible otherwise than under the Freedom of Information Act 2000, consideration must be given to whether:

(a)   the information sought[9] is accessible pursuant to an enforceable right or is accessible without any statutory or pre-existing contractual entitlement;

(b)   whether the information is accessible with or without charge;

(c)   whether the access obligation is merely to make the information available for inspection or whether an applicant is entitled to obtain a copy of the information;

(d)   whether the information is accessible on request or without the need for a request; and

(e)   whether the information is the subject of the publication scheme of the public authority.

An applicant's preferred mode of access is irrelevant in determining reasonable accessibility.[10] Similarly, information in a document comprising or reproducing what is contained in another document (the latter document being reasonably accessible) will itself thereby be reasonably accessible.[11]

16– 003   Information deemed reasonably available or deemed not reasonably available
Information is deemed to be reasonably accessible to the applicant if it is information which the public authority or any other person is obliged by or under any enactment[12] to communicate to members of the *public* on request, whether free of charge or on payment.[13] An obligation to communicate in this context does not include an obligation to make information available for inspection.[14] Where neither the public authority nor any other person is obliged by or under any enactment to copy the information to members of the public on request, then the position is more complicated.

(1)   If the public authority or another person is obliged by or under any enactment to

---

[9]   The provision looks to the reasonable accessibility of the information sought. It is not concerned with whether a reasonable amount of the information requested is otherwise available: *England and LB of Bexley v IC*, IT, 10 May 2007 at [113]; *Ames v IC and Cabinet Office*, IT, 24 April 2008 at [18].

[10]   *Glasgow City Council & anor v Scottish IC* [2009] CSIH 73 at [56].

[11]   *Glasgow City Council & anor v Scottish IC* [2009] CSIH 73 at [52].

[12]   As to the meaning of 'enactment', see §26– 017. The exemption thus cannot be invoked where the only right of access is a common law right, eg a common law right enjoyed by a member of a council: see §8– 001.

[13]   FOIA s 21(2)(b); FOI(S)A s 25(2)(b). Examples would include: documents available under the Radioactive Substances Act 1993 s 39; the register kept under the Local Government, Planning and Land Act 1980 s 95. If the obligation to communicate is limited to particular individuals (eg the applicant, because of certain attributes he holds), FOIA s 21(2)(b) will not apply as the obligation is not to *members of the public*.

[14]   FOIA s 21(2)(b); FOI(S)A s 25(2)(b). By way of example, the following rights to consult will not render the information 'reasonably accessible' for the purposes of s 21: the building notice register kept by each local authority under the Building Act 1984 s 56; the minutes of a magistrates' court committee kept under the Justices of the Peace Act 1997 s 30; the register kept by the General Chiropractic Council under the Chiropractors Act 1994 s 9; the register of persons to whom the electronic communications code applies, which is kept by OFCOM under the Communications Act 2003 s 108; the registers kept by waste regulation authorities and waste collection authorities under the Control of Pollution Act 1974 s 64; a local authority's summary of its housing allocation rules, kept under the Housing Act 1985 s 106 (but cf the Housing Act 1996 s 168, which gives an entitlement to receive a copy of the rules); the register of hazardous substances, kept under the Planning (Hazardous Substances) Act 1990 s 28; the registers of planning applications and of enforcement and stop notices kept by every local planning authority under the Town and Country Planning Act 1990, ss 69 and 188; sewer maps and so forth prepared by sewerage undertakers and provided to each local authority under the Water Industry Act 1991, ss 199 and 200.

give access to the information but that public authority or person is not obliged to copy the information (eg where it is obliged to allow members of the public to inspect documents in which the information is recorded), then if the applicant is permitted to take a copy of the information (whether on payment of a fee or free of charge) that may constitute reasonable accessibility, rendering the information exempt information.[15] If the applicant must request the public authority or other person in order to obtain a copy of the information (whether or not a payment of a fee is also required), it is arguable that that also constitutes reasonable accessibility, rendering the information exempt information.[16] If the applicant is not permitted to take a copy of the information to which he is entitled to have access, then unless (3) applies, the information is not to be regarded as reasonably accessible.[17]

(2)   If the public authority is not obliged by or under any enactment to give access to the information, but nevertheless the public authority does make it available on request to the applicant (whether on payment of a fee or free of charge) but not under its publication scheme, then the information is not to be regarded as reasonably accessible.[18] Any regime to which a public authority may be subject that merely encourages or recommends disclosure of particular information, or indicates that disclosure of particular information should be forthcoming, will not result in that information being captured by s 21. If the public authority is not obliged by or under any enactment to give access to the information, but nevertheless the information is accessible to the applicant from a source other than the public authority (whether on payment of a fee or free of charge), then provided that source is reasonably accessible to the applicant, the information will be exempt information in the hands of that public authority.[19]

(3)   If the public authority is not obliged by or under any enactment to give access to the information, but nevertheless the public authority does make it available to members of the public in accordance with its publication scheme (including such charges as are prescribed in that scheme), then the information is to be regarded as reasonably accessible.[20] It is to be noted that for these purposes the information

---

[15] FOIA s 21(2)(a); FOI(S)A s 25(2)(a). The disapplication effected by s 21(3) would not apply as the information is not merely 'available...on request' but is being permitted to be copied without the need for a request. If the copying charge is beyond that allowed under the freedom of information regime (see ch 11) or under the public authority's publication scheme, then that may result in the information not being reasonably accessible to the applicant.

[16] FOIA s 21(2)(a); FOI(S)A s 25(2)(a). Although not without doubt, it is arguable that the disapplication effected by s 21(3) would not apply as the information is not merely being 'made available' (in the sense of being inspected) but that the public authority has gone further and copied the information. Again, if the copying charge is beyond that allowed under the freedom of information regime (see ch 11) or under the public authority's publication scheme, then that may result in the information not being reasonably accessible to the applicant.

[17] FOIA s 21(3); FOI(S)A s 25(3).

[18] FOIA s 21(3); FOI(S)A s 25(3). In relation to publication schemes, see ch 10.

[19] FOIA s 21(2)(a); FOI(S)A s 25(2)(a). The disapplication effected by s 21(3) would not apply as the information is not 'available from the public authority itself on request' but is available from another person (including another public authority). Whether the other source provides reasonable accessibility will depend upon: whether that source only permits inspection of the information or whether it allows a copy to be taken; whether a charge is made and the level of that charge; the ease with which the applicant can get to that source.

[20] FOIA s 21(3); FOI(S)A s 25(3). *Glasgow City Council & anor v Scottish IC* [2009] CSIH 73 at [51].

must be made available by the public authority to which the applicant has made his request: for the purposes of s 21(3) it is not enough that another public authority has made the information requested available through its publication scheme.[21] However, provided that this is the case, then availability under a publication scheme will represent reasonable accessibility, even though it does not provide a practical means of access for a particular applicant.[22]

16–004   The information must be reasonably accessible to the applicant

If the information is neither deemed reasonably accessible nor deemed not reasonably accessible, the exemption applies where the information is reasonably accessible to the applicant.   The fact that information may be reasonably accessible to another person is insufficient to render it exempt information under s 21.   There are two aspects to this requirement:

(1)   Some legislation gives a right of access to certain information only to a particular class of person.[23] In order for information under such an alternative right to fall within s 21, the applicant must belong to the class of person who is entitled to exercise that right.[24]

(2)   Where the information is available (but not as of right) to the applicant, the public authority must consider the personal circumstances of the applicant in determining whether that information is reasonably accessible.[25] Factors affecting an individual applicant's ability to access information include the form in which the information is accessible (for example, digitally or otherwise), geographical restrictions or financial means. Thus, if the applicant's means are particularly limited or the fee payable for access to the information is excessively high, the information may not be reasonably accessible. Conversely, information may be significantly more accessible to a well-resourced applicant with access to all forms of information dissemination so that reliance on the exemption is justified. A public authority seeking to rely on the exemption will be required to address the applicant's individual circumstances in its response to the request.[26]

More generally, reasonable accessibility may depend upon the comparative ease with which an applicant may secure access to the information. For example, where an applicant seeks very specific information, which is available on a website but only by much searching of it, the website access may fall short of representing reasonable accessibility.[27]

---

[21]   Assuming, of course, that the requested information is held by both public authorities.

[22]   *Glasgow City Council & anor v Scottish IC* [2009] CSIH 73 at [60]. This may, however, indicate that the publication scheme is not a reasonable one.

[23]   See ch 8.

[24]   *Glasgow City Council & anor v Scottish IC* [2009] CSIH 73 at [67].

[25]   *MOJ v IC*, IT, 29 July 2008 at [34]. That is so even if the publication scheme allows a public authority to charge for the provision of information under it.

[26]   FOIA s 17(1)(c); FOI(S)A s 16(1)(d).

[27]   *Ames v IC and Cabinet Office*, IT, 24 April 2008 at [19]; *Glasgow City Council & anor v Scottish IC* [2009] CSIH 73 at [59].

005 Information available from a source other than the requested public authority

In order for s 21 to apply it is not necessary that the information be reasonably accessible to the applicant from the public authority to which the request under the Freedom of Information Act 2000 has been made. Section 21 is capable of applying irrespective of the identity of the alternative source of the information. Thus, information available from a public library or from a readily-available newspaper will generally fall within the terms of the exemption. Similarly, transcript of legal proceedings available on request from a court may be exempt information under the Act.[28] It should be noted that information contained in a historical record in the Public Record Office (ie The National Archives) or the Public Record Office of Northern Ireland cannot be exempt information by virtue of s 21.[29]

006 The Data Protection Act 1998

Section 34 of the Data Protection Act 1998 deals with information available to the public by or under an enactment. It provides that personal data[30] are exempt from, inter alia, the access rights[31] in s 7 of the Data Protection Act 1998 if the data consist of information which the data controller[32] is obliged by or under any enactment[33] to make available to the public, whether by publishing it,[34] making it available for inspection or otherwise and whether gratuitously or on payment of a fee. Three differences between this exemption and the corresponding exemption in the Freedom of Information Act 2000 are evident. First, under the Data Protection Act 1998 the exemption applies only where the data are in the hands of a given data controller and does not extend to information in the hands of third parties. Secondly, under the 1998 Act data are exempted when they are made available for inspection by or under any enactment. Thus, for example, information contained in the Register of Births, Marriages and Deaths is available within the meaning of the 1998 Act and will fall within the exemption: under the Freedom of Information Act 2000 such information is not deemed to be reasonably accessible. Thirdly, the data controller under the 1998 Act is not required to consider whether the information is reasonably accessible to the public, merely whether it is available. Thus, the personal circumstances of the applicant and the form in which the data are available are not relevant considerations.

---

[28] *Armstrong v IC and HMRC*, IT, 14 October 2008 at [37]-[57].

[29] FOIA s 64. There is no comparable provision in the FOI(S)A. In relation to historical records, see ch 7.

[30] As to the meaning of which, see §§5–021 to 5–024.

[31] As to the meaning of which, see §§5–030 to 5–034. Section 7 is one of 'the subject information provisions' — see DPA s 27(2).

[32] As to the meaning of which, see §5–027.

[33] Including one passed after the DPA: see s 70(1).

[34] In relation to journalistic, literary or artistic material, 'publish' means make available to the public or any section of the public: DPA s 32(6).

2. INFORMATION INTENDED FOR FUTURE PUBLICATION

16– 007 Introduction

Under s 22(1) of the Freedom of Information Act 2000[35] information held by a public authority is exempt information if:

(a) the information is held by it with a view to its future publication (whether by the public authority to which the request is made or any other person), whether or not the date for publication has been determined;

(b) at the time of the request, the information was already being held with a view to such publication; and

(c) it is reasonable in all the circumstances that the information should not be disclosed until the future date.[36]

Section 22(2) provides that the duty to confirm or deny does not arise if, or to the extent that, compliance with that duty would involve the disclosure of any information (whether or not already recorded) that falls within s 22(1).[37] Both exemption from the disclosure duty and exclusion from the duty to divulge are non-absolute. Thus, the duty to communicate information that falls within s 22(1) does not apply only if, or to the extent that, in all the circumstances of the case, the public interest in maintaining the exemption outweighs the public interest in disclosing the information.[38] Similarly, the duty to confirm or deny that such information is held remains excluded only if, in all the circumstances of the case, the public interest in maintaining the exclusion of that duty outweighs the public interest in divulging whether the public authority holds the information.[39] An equivalent exemption is to be found in the freedom of information legislation of two of the comparative jurisdictions.[40] The Environmental Information Regulations 2004 provide an exception to broadly similar effect.

---

[35] FOI(S)A s 27(1).

[36] Both the Ministry of Justice and the Information Commissioner have issued non-statutory guidance on this exemption: MoJ, *Exemptions guidance – Section 22: information intended for future publication* (14 May 2008); Information Commissioner, *Freedom of Information Act Awareness Guidance No 7, Information for Future Publication*, ver 2 (updated June 2006). The exemption has not been considered by the Tribunal, with only a passing reference in *Lawton v IC and NHS Direct*, IT, 5 March 2008 at [11].

[37] There is no corresponding provision in the FOI(S)A.

[38] FOIA s 2(2)(b).

[39] FOIA s 2(1)(b).

[40] There is no directly comparable exemption in the Freedom of Information Act, 1966 (USA), the Freedom of Information Act 1982 (Cth of Australia) or the Freedom of Information Act 1997 (Ireland). Both the Freedom of Information Act 1982 (Cth of Australia) s 47H, and the Freedom of Information Act 1997 (Ireland) s 30(1)(a), contain a very narrow exemption for documents or records (respectively) containing information in relation to research being carried out that has not been completed the disclosure of which would expose the person carrying out the research or the subject matter of the research to serious disadvantage. The Official Information Act 1982 (New Zealand) s 18(d), provides a discretionary exemption for information that 'is or will soon be publicly available' — see §2– 019. The Access to Information Act (Canada) s 26, provides a discretionary exemption for a record where the head of the institution believes on reasonable grounds that the material in the record or part thereof will be published by a government institution, agent of the Government of Canada or minister of the Crown within 90 days after the request is made: see §2– 032(9).

Regulation 12(4)(d) provides that where or to the extent that a request relates to matter which is still in the course of completion, to unfinished documents or to incomplete data, the public authority may refuse to disclose the information.[41] The exception is a qualified exception. There is no corresponding exemption in the Data Protection Act 1998.

008 Scope of the exemption

The principal purpose of the exemption is to spare a public authority that is, at the time of a request for information, engaged in the collation of information intended for future publication from being disrupted in that task by having to retrieve, edit and copy parts or all of that information in order to answer the request. The exemption is not concerned to protect a public authority from harm resulting from the premature release of information. In relation to this sort of harm, the information will be exempt under one or more of the other provisions of Part II of the Freedom of Information Act 2000: it will be a matter for an applicant to re-submit his request for information at a later time when the harm resulting from disclosure will have diminished or disappeared. In order to rely on the exemption, the public authority must show that the three conditions set out in paras (a)-(c) are met. The information must be held by the public authority with a 'view' to its publication at a future date. This connotes more than a mere hope or aspiration that the information will be published and suggests rather a concluded intention that the information will be published. The point at which the public authority must assess whether it holds the information with a view to future publication is the moment at which the request is received. The public authority is not entitled to decide on receipt of a request that it will avoid disclosure by publishing the information. The intention must predate the request for the exemption to be relied on. The information may be published by the public authority or a third party such as a commercial publisher or an internet service provider. Section 22(1)(a) does not require that a date is fixed for publication in order to allow reliance on the exemption, although the more uncertain the timetable for future publication, the less likely it is that the information is held with a view to its eventual publication and the less likely it is that it would be reasonable to withhold the information. The exemption applies to *information* held with a view to final publication. It will be a question of fact and degree whether the information contained in a draft *document*, which the public authority holds with a view to its publication once finalised, can properly be said to be held with a view to its future publication. In these circumstances, the degree to which the public authority anticipates the final version will include information not in the draft and vice versa is likely to be decisive. Finally, it must be reasonable in 'all the circumstances' for the information to be withheld until the proposed future publication. The test of reasonableness must be applied to the withholding of the information, not, for example, to some aspect of a public authority's policy on the early release of information. Whether or not it is reasonable to withhold the information must be assessed objectively, having regard to a wide range of factors. These will include the extent of the information requested, the imminence or otherwise of the future publication date, the significance of the information to the applicant, whether undue disturbance would be caused to any person or persons by the early release of information, and the time and resources which must be devoted to answering the request. If a commercial price is to be obtained for the

---

[41] In relation to a request for environmental information made of a Scottish public authority, EI(S)R reg 10(4)(d), provides a like exception. The exception is considered more fully at §6– 040.

published information, it is thought that loss of revenue could affect whether or not it is reasonable in all the circumstances for the information to be withheld although this will also depend on other factors. It is difficult to see why a single limited piece of information should be withheld, merely because it will at some point in the future form a small part of an expensive book.

16– 009   The public interest

Even if information is exempt because it falls within the scope of s 22(1), an applicant will still be entitled to have the information communicated to him unless, in all the circumstances of the case, the public interest in maintaining the exemption outweighs the public interest in disclosing the information.[42] Similarly, even if the duty to confirm or deny does not arise as a result of the operation of s 22(2), an applicant will still be entitled to be informed that the public authority holds the information requested unless, in all the circumstances of the case, the public interest in maintaining the exclusion outweighs the public interest in divulging its existence.[43] The decision of the legislature not to make exemption under s 22 absolute contemplates some situations in which information falling within s 22(1) will have to be disclosed. This decision cannot properly be undone by giving the public interest in maintaining the exemption such weight as to make the public interest in disclosure unable to outweigh it. The interplay between para 22(1)(c) and the public interest may be problematic. On the one hand it is difficult to see how it is possible for the public authority to determine that it is not reasonable in all the circumstances for the information to be withheld, but to determine that nonetheless it is in the public interest not to disclose the information. Nonetheless the Freedom of Information Act 2000 appears to contemplate this possibility. On the other hand, it is possible to envisage situations where it is thought reasonable to withhold information because of time and resources considerations but those considerations are outweighed by the public interest in a significant piece of information being aired in public as soon as possible.

3.   ENVIRONMENTAL INFORMATION

16– 010   Introduction

The right of access to 'environmental information'[44] held by a public authority is now governed by the Environmental Information Regulations 2004 and not, with one largely theoretical possibility, the Freedom of Information Act 2000.[45] The right of access to environmental information held by public authorities is considered in detail in Chapter 6. In very general terms, the Freedom of Information Act 2000 removes the s 1 rights[46] in relation to any

---

[42]   FOIA s 2(2)(b).

[43]   FOIA s 2(1)(b).

[44]   As to the meaning of which, see §6– 010.

[45]   Similarly in relation to environmental information held by Scottish public authorities, it is governed by the EI(S)R and not the FOI(S)A.

[46]   In other words, the right to have the requested information communicated and the right to know whether the requested information is held by the public authority.

information for which there is a right of access under the Environmental Information Regulations 2004. The practical difficulties in divining what is and what is not 'environmental information' are magnified by the unit of exemption (information) not being necessarily coincident with the unit in which information is normally recorded (a document or an electronic file). Within a single document or electronic file there may be both information that is 'environmental information' and other information that is not 'environmental information.' The public authority must identify which is which and, according to the applicable regime, decide whether particular material must be disclosed.[47]

011 The exemption

Under s 39(1) of the Freedom of Information Act 2000 information is exempt information if the public authority holding it:

(a)   is obliged by the Environmental Information Regulations 2004 to make the information available to the public in accordance with the regulations;[48] or

(b)   would be so obliged but for any exemption contained in the regulations.[49]

Section 39(2) provides that the duty to confirm or deny does not arise if, or to the extent that, compliance with that duty would involve the disclosure of any information (whether or not already recorded) that falls within s 39(1).[50] Both exemption from the disclosure duty and exclusion from the duty to divulge are non-absolute. Thus, the duty to communicate information that falls within s 39(1) does not apply only if, or to the extent that, in all the circumstances of the case, the public interest in maintaining the exemption outweighs the public interest in disclosing the information.[51] Similarly, the duty to confirm or deny that such information is held remains excluded only if, in all the circumstances of the case, the public interest in maintaining the exclusion of that duty outweighs the public interest in divulging whether the public authority holds the information.[52] There is no corresponding exemption in the Data Protection Act 1998.

012 Scope of the exemption

The purpose of the exemption is not to prevent or impede access to environmental information. Rather, its purpose is to give exclusivity to the Environmental Information Regulations 2004 in so far as the information answering the terms of the request is 'environmental information'.[53] Unlike the system of precedence established by s 21 of the Freedom of Information Act 2000 (which does not disapply an applicant's s 1 rights where the information is exempted under the other access regime), s 39(1) also gives the Environmental Information Regulations 2004 paramountcy in relation to its exceptions. Thus, if information falls within the scope of the

---

[47] *DBERR v IC and Friends of the Earth*, IT, 29 April 2008 at [29].

[48] FOIA s 39(1)(a); FOI(S)A s 39(2)(a).

[49] FOIA s 39(1)(b); FOI(S)A s 39(2)(b).

[50] There is no corresponding provision in the FOI(S)A.

[51] FOIA s 2(2)(b).

[52] FOIA s 2(1)(b).

[53] In *Rhondda Cynon Taff CBC v IC*, IT, 5 December 2007 at [24] the Tribunal said that it was 'not quite correct to consider EIR and FOIA as mutually exclusive regimes.' It saw the two as running 'in parallel'. The decision is considered further in ch 6 at n 192.

Environmental Information Regulations 2004 but is rendered exempt by those regulations, that information will be also exempt information for the purposes of the Freedom of Information Act 2000.[54] Information is exempt under s 39 only if there is an obligation on the public authority holding it to make the information available to the public in accordance with the Environmental Information Regulations 2004. Thus information available at discretion is not rendered exempt information by s 39.

16–013 The public interest

Even if information is exempt because it falls within the scope of s 39(1), an applicant will still be entitled to have the information communicated to him unless, in all the circumstances of the case, the public interest in maintaining the exemption outweighs the public interest in disclosing the information.[55] Similarly, even if the duty to confirm or deny does not arise as a result of the operation of s 39(2), an applicant will still be entitled to be informed that the public authority holds the information requested unless, in all the circumstances of the case, the public interest in maintaining the exclusion outweighs the public interest in divulging its existence.[56] As with all other qualified exemptions, the decision of the legislature not to make exemption under s 39 absolute contemplates some situations in which information falling within s 39(1) will have to be disclosed. Given that: (a) the only public interest in maintaining the exemption created by s 39(1) is the upholding of an exclusive, as opposed to a parallel, regime of access to environmental information; (b) that the Freedom of Information Act 2000 is itself an articulation of the public interest in the disclosure of information that is not exempt information under its own terms; and (c) that there is a particular public interest in the disclosure of environmental information, it is theoretically possible that information exempted under the Environmental Information Regulations 2004 will be accessible under the Freedom of Information Act 2000, provided of course that none of the other exemptions in the Act applies.

---

[54] FOIA s 39(1)(b); FOI(S)A s 39(2)(b).

[55] FOIA s 2(2)(b).

[56] FOIA s 2(1)(b).

CHAPTER 17
Security Bodies, National Security and Defence

1. INTRODUCTION

001 Overview of the security and defence provisions in the Freedom of Information Act 2000

Sections 23 to 26 of the Freedom of Information Act 2000 provide a series of exemptions and exclusions for information that, broadly speaking, relates to national security or defence matters.[1] Collectively, these provisions operate to exclude certain security bodies from the Freedom of Information Act 2000 regime and to prescribe three overlapping classes of exempt information.[2] Thus:

---

*   By Oliver Sanders, 1 Crown Office Row.

[1]   See §17– 008 in relation to FOI(S)A s 31.

[2]   The government document *Factual and Background Material* published under *Your Right to Know: The Government's Proposals for a Freedom of Information Act* (Cm 3818, 1997) para 3.13 drew a distinction between 'two basic ways' of protecting specific bodies and types of information from the disclosure requirements of Freedom of Information legislation, namely, 'exclusions' (for bodies) and 'exemptions' (for types of information) (paras 24–30). Later parts

(1)   Certain bodies dealing with security matters ('security bodies') are excluded from the definition of a 'public authority' in s 3 of, and Sch 1 to, the Freedom of Information Act 2000 and are thus institutionally excluded from the regime of the Act altogether. As a result, an effective request for information cannot be made to these bodies and they are not subject to any of the provisions or duties which otherwise apply to those listed or designated as public authorities by or under the Freedom of Information Act 2000.[3]

(2)   Information held by a public authority which was directly or indirectly supplied to it by, or which relates to, a security body is subject to an absolute exemption under s 23 of the Freedom of Information Act 2000. In respect of such information, the duty to confirm or deny and the duty to communicate do not arise.[4]

(3)   Information held by a public authority which was not directly or indirectly supplied to it by, and which does not relate to, any of the security bodies is subject to a qualified exemption under s 24 of the Freedom of Information Act 2000 if this is required for the purpose of safeguarding national security. In respect of such information, the duty to communicate does not arise if the public interest in maintaining the exemption outweighs the public interest in disclosing the information. Similarly, the duty to confirm or deny is excluded where or to the extent that the public interest in maintaining the exclusion outweighs the public interest in divulging whether the public authority holds the information.[5]

(4)   Information whose disclosure under the Freedom of Information Act 2000 would, or would be likely to, prejudice the defence of the British Islands or of any colony or the capability, effectiveness or security of the armed forces of the Crown or of any forces co-operating with those forces is also subject to a qualified exemption under s 26 of the Freedom of Information Act 2000. The duty to communicate does not arise in relation to such information if or to the extent that the public interest in maintaining the exemption outweighs the public interest in its disclosure. Similarly, the duty to confirm or deny does not arise in relation to such information if divulging whether the public authority holds it would, or would be likely to, prejudice the same defence interests and if the public interest in maintaining the exclusion of that duty outweighs the public interest in disclosure.[6]

The institutional exclusion of the security bodies outlined at (1) above and the exemptions outlined at (2)–(4) above potentially provide four layers of protection for sensitive security and defence information. The institutional exclusion of the security bodies is insurmountable and will conceal information regardless of its sensitivity. But other public authorities also hold security and defence information. This will be accessible unless one or more of the three exemptions is applicable and, in relation to the latter two exemptions, the public interest in

---

of the document blurred the clarity of this distinction somewhat by referring to the 'exclusion' as well as the 'exemption' of types of information (paras 93–99).

[3] See §§17–011 to 17–032.

[4] See §§17–033 to 17–039, 17–051, 17–054 to 17–057 and 17–062.

[5] See §§17–051, 17–054 to 17–057, and 17–062 to 17–064.

[6] See §§17–063 to 17–064 and 17–067 to 17–072.

maintaining the exemption is shown to outweigh the public interest in disclosure.

002 Overview of the security and defence provisions in the Data Protection Act 1998

Unlike the Freedom of Information Act 2000, the Data Protection Act 1998 does not contain any institutional exclusions or exceptions for security bodies.[7] Bodies such as the intelligence services all count as 'data controllers' for the purposes of the Act and they must therefore comply with its requirements. However, s 28 of the Data Protection Act 1998 does exempt personal data from the provisions of the data protection principles and Pts II-III and V and ss 54A and 55 of the Act if exemption from the relevant provision is required for the purpose of safeguarding national security.[8] Personal data may therefore be exempt from the right of access under s 7 of the Data Protection Act 1998, other related rights and the regulatory requirements of the regime of that Act if this is required for the purpose of safeguarding national security. Schedule 7 to the Data Protection Act 1998 further exempts personal data from the subject information provisions to the extent that the application of those provisions would be likely to prejudice the combat effectiveness of any of the armed forces of the Crown.[9]

003 Overview of the security and defence provisions in the Environmental Information Regulations 2004

Where (or to the extent that) a request for information relates to 'environmental information'[10] that request (or that part of that request) will fall to be determined by the Environmental Information Regulations 2004 and not by the Freedom of Information Act 2000.[11] The Regulations give the term 'public authority' a broader meaning than in the Freedom of Information Act 2000. In particular, there are no institutional exclusions or exceptions for security bodies. Regulation 12 of the Environmental Information Regulations 2004 provides an exception allowing for the non-disclosure of environmental information whose dissemination or disclosure would adversely affect international relations, defence, national security or public safety.[12] Disclosure may only be refused on this basis if, in all the circumstances of the case, the public interest in maintaining the exception outweighs the public interest in disclosing the information.[13] If doing so would involve the disclosure of information which would adversely affect international relations, defence, national security or public safety and would not be in the public interest, the relevant public authority may also refuse to confirm or deny whether the

---

[7] There was, of course, no scope for such an approach to be followed in DPA given that it was enacted to implement the European Community Data Protection Directive 95/46/EC which neither contains nor allows for institutional exclusions or exemptions.

[8] See §§17– 042 to 17– 049, 17– 052 to 17– 055, 17– 058 to 17– 062 and 17– 065.

[9] DPA s 37, Sch 7, para 2.

[10] For the meaning of 'environmental information', see §§6– 008 to 6– 010.

[11] FOIA s 39. Similarly, in relation to Scottish public authorities, it will fall to be determined by the EI(S)R and not the FOI(S)A; FOI(S)A s 39.

[12] As with DPA, the more inclusive approach was dictated by the European Community Environmental Information Directive 2003/4/EC, which EIR were intended to implement. The exception from the obligation to disclose arises through: EIR regs 4(3), 5(1), 12(1)–(2) and (5)(a). See further §§6– 042, 17– 042 and 17– 061. Important differences between the environmental information regime and the regime under the FOIA are set out in ch 6.

[13] EIR reg 12(1)(b); EI(S)R reg 10(1)(b).

requested information exists and is held 'whether or not it holds such information'.[14] The reg 12 exception is itself made subject to a requirement that public authorities apply a presumption in favour of disclosure.[15]

17– 004   Policy background

The Code of Practice on Access to Government Information contained an exemption for 'information whose disclosure would harm national security or defence'.[16] The accompanying Guidance on Interpretation stated that the purpose of this exemption encompassed, so far as national security was concerned, the protection of 'information which could be of assistance to those engaged in espionage, sabotage, subversion or terrorism', 'individuals and sites which may be at risk' and 'the operations, sources and methods of the security and intelligence services' and, so far as defence was concerned, the protection of 'the operational effectiveness of the armed forces and their capacity to protect the country from external aggression' and 'servicemen and their civilian support staff, including those of friendly forces, and those under their protection'.[17] The White Paper, *Your Right to Know: The Government's Proposals for a Freedom of Information Act*, described 'national security, defence and international relations' as one of seven key 'specified interests' which could require non-disclosure if liable to be harmed by disclosure.[18] Both the White Paper[19] and the accompanying *Factual and Background Material*[20] went on to propose that a number of security bodies be excluded from the scope of any Act in order to preserve their effectiveness. When reporting on these proposals the House of Commons Public Administration Select Committee recommended against the institutional exclusion of the security bodies after noting that the comparable statutes in the USA, New Zealand and Canada contained exemptions for security and defence information but did not altogether exclude security bodies from the scope of their access regimes.[21]

17– 005   The Freedom of Information Bill: drafting

The provisions containing the security and defence exemptions in the draft Freedom of

---

[14]   EIR reg 12(6)–(7); EI(S)R reg 10(6)–(7).

[15]   EIR reg 12(2); EI(S)R reg 10(2). See further §6– 034.

[16]   *Open Government Code of Practice on Access to Government Information* (2nd edn, 1997), Pt II, para 1(a). Although the exemption referred to 'harm' there was nevertheless a presumption that such information should be disclosed unless the harm likely to arise from disclosure would outweigh the public interest in making the information available. See also: *White Paper on Open Government* (Cm 2290, 1993) paras 3.5–3.7 and Annex A, Pt II, para i; Scottish Executive's *Code of Practice on Access to Scottish Executive Information*, 2nd edn (2003) Pt II, para 1(a); and National Assembly for Wales *Code of Practice on Public Access to Information*, 3rd edn (2004), Annex B.

[17]   *Open Government Code of Practice on Access to Government Information: Guidance on Interpretation*, 2nd edn (1997) Pt II, para 1.3.

[18]   (Cm 3818, 1997) paras 3.8–3.11.

[19]   (Cm 3818, 1997) para 2.3.

[20]   Published under (Cm 3818, 1997) para 3.13. See para 96.

[21]   House of Commons Public Administration Select Committee Third Report Session 1997–1998 *Your Right to Know: the Government's Proposals for a Freedom of Information Act*, (HC 398–I), 1998, paras 38–39. See also House of Lords Draft Freedom of Information Bill Select Committee First Report Session 1998–1999 *Report from the Select Committee Appointed to Consider the Draft Freedom of Information Bill* (HL 97) 1999, para 39 (see ch 1 n 125).

Information Bill published on 24 May 1999[22] underwent only minor revision before being included in the Freedom of Information Bill introduced in the House of Commons on 18 November 1999.[23]   When reporting on the draft Bill, the House of Commons Public Administration Select Committee referred to arguments opposing the blanket exclusion of the security bodies put forward by a former Legal Adviser to the security and intelligence services[24] but ultimately accepted that the approach adopted was reasonable.[25] In relation to the security and defence exemptions, the introduction print of the Bill only differed from the draft version in two respects: cls 21(5), 22(2) and 24(3) of the introduction print took a textually different approach to the engagement of the relevant exemptions and the non-application of the duty to confirm or deny;[26] and cl 22 on national security did not feature a 'jigsaw puzzle' exemption expressly ensuring the non-disclosure of apparently harmless information which might be harmful when looked at in conjunction with other pieces of a wider jigsaw puzzle.[27] Section 28 of the Data Protection Act 1998 was plainly the model for the clauses which became s 24 of the Freedom of Information Act 2000.[28]

006 The Freedom of Information Bill: passage

The relevant clauses in the introduction print of the Freedom of Information Bill did not

---

[22] *Freedom of Information: Consultation on Draft Legislation* (Cm 4355, 1999) Pt II, cls 18 (information supplied by, or relating to, bodies dealing with security matters), 19 (national security), 20 (certificates under ss 18 and 19: supplementary provisions) and 21 (defence) (see ch 1 n 64).

[23] Clauses 21 (information supplied by, or relating to, bodies dealing with security matters), 22 (national security), 23 (certificates under ss 21 and 22: supplementary provisions) and 24 (defence).

[24] That is, Mr David Bickford. See M Urban, *UK Eyes Alpha: The Inside Story of British Intelligence* (London, Faber & Faber, 1996), pp 85–86.

[25] House of Commons Public Administration Select Committee Third Report Session 1998–1999 *Freedom of Information Draft Bill* (HC 570–I) 1999, paras 74–77 and Annex 6, paras 43–48.

[26] Compare draft Freedom of Information Bill published on 24 May 1999, cls 18(5), 19(2), 21(3).

[27] Compare draft Freedom of Information Bill published on 24 May 1999, cl 19(3) which provided as follows 'Where, in relation to any information ("the information requested"), exemption from section 8(1)(b)–(a) is not required for the purpose of safeguarding national security, but (b) would be required for that purpose if any other information (whether or not held by the public authority and whether or not accessible, or likely to become accessible, to members of the public) became available at the same time or subsequently, the exemption shall be taken for the purposes of this section to be required for that purpose in relation to the information requested.' See House of Lords Draft Freedom of Information Bill Select Committee First Report Session 1998–1999 *Report from the Select Committee Appointed to Consider the Draft Freedom of Information Bill* (HL 97) 1999, paras 36–37 (see ch 1 n 125). See also §17–029(1).

[28] Thus: 'The clause [which became FOIA s 24] is drafted in similar terms to s 28 of DPA. The two provisions have the same purpose. It is therefore sensible for them to be drafted in similar language. Any difference of approach between the provisions could lead to them being interpreted differently. Clearly, that is not the intention.' — Hansard HC vol 347 col 1060 (5 April 2000) (Home Office Minister, Mr O'Brien, Report and Third Reading debate on the Freedom of Information Bill). Section 28 of DPA replaced the national security exemption in the Data Protection Act 1984 s 27 which provided that, '[A]ny question whether the exemption mentioned in subsection (1) above is or at any time was required for the purpose there mentioned [ie the purpose of safeguarding national security] in respect of any personal data shall be determined by a Minister of the Crown; and a certificate signed by a Minister of the Crown certifying that the exemption is or at any time was so required shall be conclusive evidence of that fact' (Data Protection Act 1984 s 27(2), see also s 27(3)). The 'required for the purpose of safeguarding national security' test was therefore the same under both Acts, the key difference being the addition of an appeal mechanism in DPA s 28: 'The right of appeal against a national security certificate is an important new safeguard. It represents an advance on the 1984 Act, which offered no appeal rights' — Hansard HC vol 315 col 586 (2 July 1998) (Home Office Minister, Mr Howarth, Report and Third Reading debate on the Data Protection Bill).

thereafter change on their way to enactment as ss 23–26 of the Freedom of Information Act 2000, save for the inclusion in the list of security bodies of the Tribunal newly established under s 65 of the Regulation of Investigatory Powers Act 2000.[29] Indeed the security and defence exemptions in the Freedom of Information Act 2000 passed through Parliament with very little controversy. Amendments were put forward, but later withdrawn, which would have omitted the (s 23) exemption for information supplied by, or relating to, the security bodies altogether and made the operation of both that exemption and the (s 24) national security exemption dependent on the satisfaction of a prejudice or harm test.[30] These proposals were all partly justified by reference to the broader crime-related functions of some of the security bodies such as the Security Service[31] and the National Criminal Intelligence Service.[32] Amendments were also put forward which would have made the operation of the defence exemption dependent on the satisfaction of a 'substantial' prejudice requirement but these were defeated on a vote.[33]

17– 007 Scottish public authorities

Under the Scotland Act 1998, the Scottish Parliament cannot make legislation which relates to or modifies the law on 'reserved matters'.[34] Corresponding restrictions apply in relation to the exercise of certain functions by the Scottish Ministers.[35] The following are in turn defined as 'reserved matters' for the purposes of the Scotland Act 1998: the functions of the Security Service, the Secret Intelligence Service and the Government Communications Headquarters;[36] the defence of the realm, the naval, military or air forces of the Crown (including reserve forces), visiting forces, international headquarters and defence organisations;[37] national security, the interception of communications, official secrets and terrorism;[38] and public access to information held by public bodies or holders of public offices other than certain Scottish public authorities.[39] In terms of the Scottish devolution settlement, it therefore follows that the Scottish Parliament had limited scope for creating access rights in relation to security and

---

[29] FOIA s 23(3)(e) (inserted pursuant to a government amendment): Hansard HL vol 619 cols 205–207 (14 November 2000).

[30] In relation to the proposed omission of cl 21 (information supplied by, or relating to, bodies dealing with security matters) and the amendment of cl 22 (national security) see: Hansard HC vol 347 cols 1054–1062 (5 April 2000) (House of Commons Report and Third Reading). In relation to the proposed amendment of cl 21 (information supplied by, or relating to, bodies dealing with security matters) see: Hansard HL vol 617 cols 1256–1259 (19 October 2000) (House of Lords Committee Stage).

[31] Including under the Security Service Act 1996 and the Security Service's 'management consultancy' type work advising other public bodies on matters such as security systems and controls.

[32] Including, eg in relation to football hooliganism.

[33] Hansard HC vol 347 cols 1062–1071 (5 April 2000) (House of Commons Report and Third Reading).

[34] Scotland Act 1998 ss 28–30, Sch 4, Pt I, paras 2, 3, Sch 5 (on 'legislative competence').

[35] Scotland Act 1998 ss 53–54 (on 'devolved competence').

[36] Scotland Act 1998 s 30, Sch 5, Pt I, paras 1, 2(4).

[37] Scotland Act 1998 s 30, Sch 5, Pt I, para 9(1)(a)–(d).

[38] Scotland Act 1998 s 30, Sch 5, Pt II, s.B8.

[39] Scotland Act 1998 s 30, Sch 5, Pt II, s.B13. The subject matter of DPA and the European Community Data Protection Directive 95/46/EC ([1995] OJ L281/31) is also a 'reserved matter' under Scotland Act 1998 s 30, Sch 5, Pt II, s.B2.

defence information in the Freedom of Information (Scotland) Act 2002.[40] More generally, the reservation of these matters in the Scottish devolution settlement (and their similar treatment in the Northern Ireland[41] and Wales[42] devolution settlements) derives from and reflects their national importance and may thus help to explain the cautious approach taken to them in the Freedom of Information Act 2000.

008 Overview of the security and defence provisions in the Freedom of Information (Scotland) Act 2002

The Freedom of Information (Scotland) Act 2002 follows the Freedom of Information Act 2000 fairly closely in its approach to security and defence matters. Given the limitations on the legislative competence of the Scottish Parliament referred to above, the security bodies are inevitably excluded from the definition of a 'Scottish public authority' in s 3 of, and Sch 1 to, the Freedom of Information (Scotland) Act 2002.[43] Information held by a Scottish public authority is subject to a qualified exemption under s 31 of the Freedom of Information (Scotland) Act 2002 if this is required for the purpose of safeguarding national security or if its disclosure under that Act would, or would be likely to, prejudice substantially the defence of the British Islands or of any colony or the capability, effectiveness or security of the armed forces of the Crown or of any forces co-operating with those forces. These exemptions closely follow those in ss 24 and 26 of the Freedom of Information Act 2000 and both exclude the operation of the general entitlement to information in s 1 of the Freedom of Information (Scotland) Act 2002 if or to the extent that the public interest in disclosing the information is outweighed by the public interest in maintaining the exemption.[44] The Freedom of Information (Scotland) Act 2002 departs from the Freedom of Information Act 2000 model in relation to security and defence matters in two main respects: first, there is no express exemption for information held by a Scottish public authority which was directly or indirectly supplied to it by, or which relates to, a security body;[45] and, secondly, the exemption for defence information operates by

---

[40] This is not to say that FOI(S)A as enacted is necessarily outside the legislative competence of the Scottish Parliament: it does not obviously contain any provisions which 'relate to' any 'reserved' security or defence 'matters' when the expression 'relates to' is read in accordance with the Scotland Act 1998 s 29(3); and the proviso to the Scotland Act 1998 Sch 5, Pt II, s.B13 would also appear to envisage legislation along the lines of FOI(S)A. See §1–039.

[41] Northern Ireland Act 1998 ss 4(1), 6(2), 14(5), Sch 2, paras 1, 4, 17. Devolution in Northern Ireland was suspended for the time being on 15 October 2002 pursuant to the Northern Ireland Act 2000, ss 1, 4, Sch 1 and the Northern Ireland Act 2000 (Suspension of Devolved Government) Order 2002 SI 2002/2574 art 2. Devolution was restored with effect from 8 May 2007 pursuant to the Northern Ireland (St Andrews Agreement) Act 2006 s 2, Sch 2 (as modified by the Northern Ireland (St Andrews Agreement) Act 2007 s 1) and a restoration order made under the Northern Ireland Act 2000 s 2(2). See Burns, 'Devolution... At Last?' (2007) 157 *New Law Journal* 248.

[42] Government of Wales Act 1998 s 22, Sch 2 and the Transfer of Functions Orders made thereunder, ie SI 1999/672 SI 2000/253, SI 2000/1829, SI 2000/1830, SI 2001/3679, SI 2004/3044, SI 2005/1958, SI 2006/1458, SI 2006/3334. The Government of Wales Act 2006 contains a saving for these Orders (s 162, Sch 11) and the reformed devolution settlement provided for thereunder takes an identical approach to the non-devolution of security and defence matters (ss 58, 94, 108, Schs 3, 5, 7).

[43] See also Scotland Act 1998, ss 29–30, Sch 5, Pt II, s.B13.

[44] FOI(S)A s 2(1)(b).

[45] Compare FOIA ss 2, 23. Given the limitations on the legislative competence of the Scottish Parliament referred to above, it may have been felt unnecessary or even inappropriate to include an equivalent exemption in FOI(S)A and/or the omission may simply reflect the narrower responsibilities and competences of the Scottish public authorities and the limited extent to which they are likely to hold information supplied by or relating to the security

reference to the 'substantial prejudice' test adopted elsewhere in the Freedom of Information (Scotland) Act 2002.[46]

17–009 Overview of the security and defence provisions in the Environmental Information (Scotland) Regulations 2004

The Environmental Information (Scotland) Regulations 2004 apply to the same group of 'Scottish public authorities' as the Freedom of Information (Scotland) Act 2002 together with a relatively small group of additional authorities and other persons with environmental functions of a public nature.[47] As with the Freedom of Information (Scotland) Act 2002, the security bodies fall outside this group and are not therefore subject to the requirements of the Environmental Information (Scotland) Regulations 2004.[48] Regulation 10 of the Environmental Information (Scotland) Regulations 2004 provides an exception allowing for the non-disclosure of environmental information whose disclosure would prejudice substantially international relations, defence, national security or public safety.[49] A Scottish public authority may refuse to disclose such information if, in all the circumstances, the public interest in making the information available is outweighed by that in maintaining the exception.[50] In considering the application of this exception, Scottish public authorities are moreover required to interpret it 'in a restrictive way' and 'apply a presumption in favour of disclosure'.[51] In this regard, the Environmental Information (Scotland) Regulations 2004 closely mirror the Environmental Information Regulations 2004 save that the exemption for security and defence information operates by reference to the 'substantial prejudice' test found in the Freedom of Information (Scotland) Act 2002 rather than the 'adverse affect' test applied in the Environmental Information Regulations 2004.[52] If doing so would involve making information available which would, or would be likely to, prejudice substantially international relations, defence, national security or public safety and would not be in the public interest, the relevant Scottish public authority may also respond to a request by not revealing whether the requested information exists or is held 'whether or not it holds such information'.[53]

17–010 The comparative jurisdictions

National security exemptions are common to the freedom of information legislation of each of

---

bodies in practice. Having said this, a number of the Scottish public authorities (eg the Scottish Ministers and other authorities with criminal justice functions in relation to policing, prisons and parole) presumably hold some information within the terms of FOIA s 23(1). See further §1–039.

[46] FOI(S)A s 31(4); cf FOIA s 26(1). See further §1–041(3).

[47] EI(S)R reg 2(1).

[48] See §17–008.

[49] EI(S)R regs 5(2)(b), 10(1)–(2), (5)(a).

[50] EI(S)R reg 10(1).

[51] EI(S)R reg 10(2).

[52] EI(S)R reg 10(5)(a); cf EIR reg 12(5)(a).

[53] EI(S)R reg 10(8)–(9).

the comparative jurisdictions:[54]

(1) *United States of America.* 'Exemption 1' of the federal Freedom of Information Act 1966 (USA) exempts matters that are specifically authorised to be kept secret in the interest of national defence or foreign policy under criteria established by a Presidential Executive Order and are in fact properly classified pursuant to such an Order.[55] The Presidential Order for these purposes is currently Executive Order 12,958 which was issued by President Clinton in 1995 and amended by President Bush on 25 March 2003.[56] This Order provides that information may not be classified unless 'its disclosure reasonably could be expected to cause damage to the national security'.[57] The Order further provides that documents may only be classified by persons at certain designated levels[58] and that information may not be considered for classification unless it concerns at least one of the following matters: (a) military plans, weapons systems or operations; (b) foreign government information; (c) intelligence activities (including special activities), intelligence sources or methods or cryptology; (d) foreign relations or foreign activities of the United States, including confidential sources; (e) scientific, technological or economic matters relating to the national security including defence against transnational terrorism; (f) United States Government programmes for safeguarding nuclear materials or facilities; (g) vulnerabilities or capabilities of systems, installations, infrastructures, projects, plans or protection services relating to the national security including defence against transnational terrorism; or (h) weapons of mass destruction.[59] Classification generally lasts for 10 years but is subject to various provisions regarding review and declassification.[60] There is no institutional exclusion for security, intelligence or defence bodies.

(2) *Commonwealth of Australia.* Section 33 of the Freedom of Information Act 1982 (Cth of Aust) exempts documents if their disclosure under the Act would, or could reasonably be expected to, cause damage to the security or defence of the

---

[54] Freedom of Information Act 1966 5 USC 552 (2000 & Supp III 2003) (USA); Freedom of Information Act 1982 s 33(1)(a)(i) (Cth of Aust); Official Information Act 1982 ss 6(a), 31 (NZ); Access to Information Act (1982), ss 15(1), 16 (Canada); Freedom of Information Act 1997 s 24(1) (Ireland).

[55] Freedom of Information Act 1966 5 USC 552(b)(1) s 6F(b) (USA). See also 5 USC 552(a)(3)(E), (b)(7)(D), (c)(3). See further §2– 008(1). See also: S Dyeus, A Berney, W Banks and P Raven-Hansen, *National Security Laws*, 4th edn (New York, Aspen Publishers, 2007) pp 979-1019 (also covering the Presidential Records Act 1978 44 USC 2201-2207 (2000) USE, Privacy Act 1974 5 USC 552a (2000) (USA), Government in the Sunshine Act 5 USC 552b (2000) (USA) and Federal Advisory Committee Act 5 USC App (2000) (USA)).

[56] Executive Order 12,958 replaced Executive Order 12,356, which was issued by President Reagan in 1982. According to its preamble, Executive Order 12,958 (as amended) 'prescribes a uniform system for classifying, safeguarding, and declassifying national security information'.

[57] Under Executive Order 12,958 (as amended): 'damage to the national security' means 'harm to the national defense or foreign relations of the United States from the unauthorized disclosure of information, taking into consideration such aspects of the information as the sensitivity, value, utility, and provenance of that information' (Pt 6 s 6.1(j)); there are three basic classifications, ie Top Secret, Secret and Confidential (Pt 1 s 1.2(a)); and these are applied according to the damage to national security that might reasonably be expected to result from disclosure, ie exceptionally grave damage (Top Secret), serious damage (Secret) and damage (Confidential).

[58] Executive Order 12,958 (as amended), Pt 1, s 1.3.

[59] Executive Order 12,958 (as amended), Pt 1, s 1.4.

[60] Executive Order 12,958 (as amended), Pt 1, s 1.5, Pt 3.

Commonwealth.[61] The expression 'security of the Commonwealth' is in turn defined to extend to: (a) matters relating to the detection, prevention or suppression of activities, whether within or outside Australia, subversive of, or hostile to, the interests of the Commonwealth or of any country allied or associated with the Commonwealth; and (b) the security of any communications system or cryptographic system of the Commonwealth or of another country used for the defence of the Commonwealth or of any country allied or associated with the Commonwealth or the conduct of the international relations of the Commonwealth.[62] The Freedom of Information Act 1982 (Cth of Aust) also contains provisions which produce a similar effect to s 23 of the Freedom of Information Act 2000 and the institutional exclusion of the security bodies under that Act: the Australian Secret Intelligence Service, Australian Security Intelligence Organisation and Inspector-General of Intelligence and Security are exempt agencies which are deemed not to be 'prescribed authorities' for the purposes of the Freedom of Information Act 1982 (Cth of Aust);[63] the Defence Imagery and Geospatial Organisation, Defence Intelligence Organisation and Defence Signals Directorate are deemed not to be included in the Department of Defence or to be agencies in their own right for those purposes;[64] and all agencies and ministers are exempt from the operation of the Freedom of Information Act 1982 (Cth of Aust) in relation to documents that have originated with, or have been received from, any of the Australian security or defence bodies already mentioned or the Office of National Assessments.[65]

(3)   *New Zealand.* Sections 6 and 31 of the Official Information Act 1982 (NZ) provide that information may be withheld from disclosure under the Act if making it available would be likely to prejudice the security or defence of New Zealand.[66] There is no institutional exclusion for security, intelligence or defence bodies: the

---

[61] Freedom of Information Act 1982 s 33(1)(a)(i)–(ii) (Cth of Aust). See further §2– 015(9). The section does not involve a consideration of whether disclosure would be contrary to the public interest: *Commonwealth of Australia v Hittich* (1994) 53 FCR 152 at 154. Rather, the section is an expression of the content of the public interest: *Re Mann and Australian Taxation Office* (1985) 3 AAR 261; *Re O'Donovan and Attorney-General's Department* (1985) 4 AAR 151 8 ALD 528; *Re Edelsten and Australian Federal Police* (1985) 4 AAR 220. See also the Archives Act 1983 s 33(1)(a) (Cth of Aust). Ministers previously had power to issue conclusive certificates specifying the relevant ground of exemption, the part or parts of the document covered and the particular kind of document in respect of which the exemption has been claimed under Freedom of Information Act 1982 s 33(2)–(4) (Cth of Aust), but these provisions were repealed with effect from 7 October 2009 by the Freedom of Information (Removal of Conclusive Certificates and Other Measures) Act 2009 s 3 and Sch 1 (Cth of Aust). See §14– 038(1).

[62] Freedom of Information Act 1982 s 4(5) (Cth of Aust). In *Re Slater and Cox* (1988) 15 ALD 20 it was held that damage to the security of the country would be found where disclosure would enable those engaged in espionage, sabotage, subversion, terrorism or similar activities to resist attempts by official security organisations to obtain information about their activities. In *Re Aarons and Australian Archives* (1986) 12 ALD 155 disclosure of symbols and expressions used by the security service ASIO was held to be contrary to national security.

[63] Freedom of Information Act 1982 s 7(1), Sch 2, Pt I, Div.1 (Cth of Aust).

[64] Freedom of Information Act 1982 s 7(1A), Sch 2, Pt I, Div.2 (Cth of Aust). The three Defence Organisations are all parts of the Department of Defence (s 4(1)).

[65] Freedom of Information Act 1982 s 7(2A)-(2B) (Cth of Aust).

[66] Official Information Act 1982 ss 6(a), 31 (NZ). See §2– 022(1). The Prime Minister may certify that disclosure would be likely to have this effect. Requests for personal information under Official Information Act 1982 s 24 (NZ) may also be refused if disclosure would be likely to prejudice the security or defence of New Zealand: s 27(1)(a).

New Zealand Security Intelligence Service is expressly subject to the provisions of the Official Information Act 1982 (NZ).[67]

(4) *Canada.* Sections 15–16 of the federal Access to Information Act (1982) (Canada) contain exemptions for information relating to international relations and defence (s 15) and law enforcement and investigations (s 16).[68] Under s 15 of the Access to Information Act (1982) (Canada) the head of a government institution has a discretion to refuse to disclose any record requested under the Act that contains information the disclosure of which could reasonably be expected to be injurious to the conduct of international affairs, the defence of Canada or any state allied or associated with Canada or the detection, prevention or suppression of subversive or hostile activities (including information relating to various specific defence and intelligence matters).[69] Section 16 of the Access to Information Act (1982) (Canada) confers a similar discretion to withhold information obtained or prepared by certain investigative bodies in the course of lawful investigations pertaining to criminal and law enforcement matters and activities suspected of constituting threats to the security of Canada. There is no institutional exclusion for security, intelligence or defence bodies: the Canadian Security Intelligence Service, the Office of the Inspector General of the Canadian Security Intelligence Service, the Security Intelligence Review Committee and the Department of National Defence are all listed in Sch 1 to the Access to Information Act (1982) (Canada) as 'government institutions' subject to the requirements of the Act.

(5) *Republic of Ireland.* Section 24 of the Freedom of Information Act 1997 (Ireland) provides that the head of a public body may refuse to grant a request under s 7 in relation to a record if, in the opinion of the head, access to it could reasonably be expected to affect adversely the security, defence or international relations of the State or matters relating to Northern Ireland.[70] Such a refusal must be issued in relation to records which contain information that was obtained or prepared for the

---

[67] Official Information Act 1982 s 2, Sch 1 (NZ).

[68] Access to Information Act 1982, ss 15(1) and 16 (Canada). See §2– 032(1) and (11).

[69] On appeal, the court must form its own opinion in determining whether the explanations provided by the head of the government institution for refusing to disclose the requested records are reasonable but it is not entitled to order disclosure simply because it would have reached a different conclusion: *X v Canada (Minister of National Defence)* [1992] 1 FC 77 (TD); *X v Canada (Minister of National Defence)* (1992) 58 FTR 93 (FCTD). In this regard, the Canadian courts have shown themselves moderately deferential to respondent claims of exemption based on defence grounds: *Canada (IC) v Canada (Minister of National Defence)* [1990] 3 FC 22 (TD); *X v Canada (Minister of National Defence)* (1992) 58 FTR 93 (FCTD); *X v Canada (Minister of National Defence)* [1992] 1 FC 77 (TD); *Do-ky v Canada (Minister of Foreign Affairs and International Trade)* [1999] FCJ No 673, QL (FCA); *Dzevad Cemerlic MD v Canada (Solicitor General)* [2003] FCT 133, (2003) 228 FTR 1: 'In order to claim the exemption under section 21, the head of a government institution must demonstrate there is a reasonable expectation of injury' (at [24]). The Courts have accepted the 'mosaic' principle: *Ternette v Canada (Solicitor General)* [1992] 2 FC 75 at [35].

[70] Freedom of Information Act 1997 s 24(1) (Ireland); as amended by Freedom of Information (Amendment) Act 2003 s 19 (Ireland). See §2– 039(4) and (13). Ministers can issue conclusive certificates in order to declare that a record is exempt by virtue of Freedom of Information Act 1997 s 24 (Ireland) provided that access to a record has been refused in reliance on this exemption and the minister is satisfied that the record is of 'sufficient sensitivity or seriousness' to 'justify' the issue of a certificate. While they remain in force, such certificates are conclusive in their effect subject to appeal to the High Court on a point of law under the Freedom of Information Act 1997 s 42(2) (Ireland). See: Freedom of Information Act 1997 s 25 (Ireland); M McDonagh, *Freedom of Information Law in Ireland*, 2nd edn (Dublin, Thomson Round Hall, 2006) pp 154–159; and see further §14– 038(2).

purpose of intelligence in respect of the security or defence of the State or relate to specified security or defence interests.[71] The head of the public body must also refuse to confirm or deny the existence of any such records if satisfied that this would prejudice any of these matters.[72] While the main departments of state and the defence forces are listed as 'public bodies' for the purposes of the Freedom of Information Act 1997 (Ireland),[73] no security or intelligence bodies are listed as such.

2. THE SECURITY BODIES

17– 011 The specified security bodies

As mentioned above, certain security bodies are excluded from the Freedom of Information Act 2000 regime altogether and information held by other public authorities is subject to an absolute exemption if it was directly or indirectly supplied to them by, or relates to, any of those bodies. The excluded security bodies are specified in s 23(3) of the Freedom of Information Act 2000[74] as:

(a)   the Security Service;

(b)   the Secret Intelligence Service ('SIS');

(c)   the Government Communications Headquarters ('GCHQ');

(d)   the special forces;

(e)   the Regulation of Investigatory Powers Act 2000 Tribunal ('the RIPA Tribunal');[75]

(f)   the Interception of Communications Act 1985 Tribunal ('the IOCA Tribunal');[76]

(g)   the Security Service Act 1989 Tribunal ('the SSA Tribunal');[77]

(h)   the Intelligence Services Act 1994 Tribunal ('the ISA Tribunal');[78]

(i)   the Security Vetting Appeals Panel;

(j)   the Security Commission;

(k)   the National Criminal Intelligence Service ('NCIS');

(l)   the Service Authority for NCIS; and

(m)   the Serious Organised Crime Agency ('SOCA').

The following paragraphs of this section deal with the institutional exclusion of the security bodies from the Freedom of Information Act 2000 regime, describe the identity and functions of each body and provide contextual information on the legal and constitutional framework

---

[71] Freedom of Information Act 1997 s 24(1)–(2) (Ireland).

[72] Freedom of Information Act 1997 s 24(3) (Ireland).

[73] Freedom of Information Act 1997 s 2, Sch 1 (Ireland).

[74] There were originally twelve security bodies in FOIA as enacted. FOIA s 23(3)(m) and the thirteenth security body, the Serious Organised Crime Agency, were added by the Serious Organised Crime and Police Act 2005 s 59, Sch 4, paras 158–159 with effect from 1 April 2006.

[75] Established under the Regulation of Investigatory Powers Act 2000 s 65.

[76] Established under the Interception of Communications Act 1985 s 7.

[77] Established under the Security Service Act 1989 s 5.

[78] Established under the Intelligence Services Act 1994 s 9.

within which they operate and the extent to which this achieves secrecy and accountability.[79]

012 The security bodies: exclusion

The 13 security bodies are not expressly excluded from the Freedom of Information Act 2000 regime by reference to the list in s 23(3) of the Freedom of Information Act 2000 or any other list. Their exclusion is instead achieved through their omission from the list of 'public authorities' in Sch 1 to the Freedom of Information Act 2000.[80] In this regard, s 1(1) only confers a general right of access to information held by a 'public authority' and in relation to requests for information made to a 'public authority'. The expression 'public authority' is in turn defined for present purposes by s 3(1)(a)(i) as 'any body which, any other person who, or the holder of any office which is listed in Sch 1'.[81] None of the security bodies specified in s 23(3) is 'listed in Schedule 1' and it follows that none of them is a 'public authority' for the purposes of the Act.[82] It is not clear whether any is exempt from the Environmental Information Regulations 2004. Arguably each of them 'carries out functions of public administration' and, on that basis, would be subject to the Regulations. What is clear is that none of the security bodies is excluded or exempted from the provisions of the Data Protection Act 1998: in so far as each security body is a data controller for the purposes of the Data Protection Act 1998,[83] it is obliged to comply with its provisions and the obligations conferred thereunder subject, of course, to any relevant exemptions in Part IV.[84]

---

[79] The Intelligence Services Commissioner, Interception of Communications Commissioner and Intelligence and Security Committee (which have close links with the security bodies) are also institutionally excluded from FOIA in the sense that they are not listed as 'public authorities' in Sch 1 but they are not then specified as security bodies in s 23(3) and are therefore treated as distinct from the security bodies in this chapter: see §17– 030(2), (3) and (6).

[80] Furthermore, FOIA does not expressly bind the Crown and therefore only binds the Crown to the extent required by necessary implication: *Province of Bombay v Municipal Corporation of Bombay* [1947] AC 58 (PC); *AG of Ceylon v A D Silva* [1953] AC 461 (PC); *Madras Electric Supply Corp Ltd v Boarland* [1955] AC 667; *Ministry of Agriculture v Jenkins* [1963] 2 QB 317 (CA); *Wood v Leeds Area Health Authority* [1974] ICR 535; and *Lord Advocate v Strathclyde Regional Council* [1990] 2 AC 580. This 'doctrine of Crown immunity' is expressly saved and recognised by the Crown Proceedings Act 1947 ss 31(1), 40(2)(f). Following *BBC v Johns (Inspector of Taxes)* [1965] Ch 32 (CA) at 81 (Diplock LJ) the Crown's 'immunity' from the FOIA regime will also be enjoyed by the Crown's servants and agents to the extent that they are not brought under that regime by express provision or necessary implication (see also F Bennion, *Statutory Interpretation*, 5th edn (London, LexisNexis, 2008) p 207; W Wade and C Forsyth, *Administrative Law*, 10th edn (Oxford, Oxford University Press, 2009) pp 712–713). As FOIA does not expressly bind the Crown it therefore follows that the Crown's servants and agents are only bound to the extent that they are expressly listed as 'public authorities' in FOIA Sch 1 or to the extent that their being bound is required by necessary implication. See also s 81(3) and, in relation to the intelligence services, see the definition of 'government department' in s 84 at sub-para.(b). The exclusion of those security bodies which are servants or agents of the Crown is thus doubly ensured through the operation of the presumption that statutes do not bind the Crown. The criminal offence provisions in FOIA s 77 and Sch 3, para 12 are nevertheless applied to all persons in the public service of the Crown as they apply to any other person: FOIA s 81(3).

[81] For these purposes, 'body' includes an unincorporated association (FOIA s 84; FOI(S)A s 73) and 'person' includes a body of persons corporate or unincorporate (Interpretation Act 1978 s 5, Sch 1).

[82] None of the security bodies is a 'Scottish public authority' for the purposes of FOI(S)A s 3, Sch 1. See also the Scotland Act 1998 ss 29–30, Sch 5, Pt II, s.B13.

[83] DPA ss 1(1) and (4), 5. Each of the intelligence services is a data controller for these purposes: *Baker v SSHD* [2001] UKHRR 1275 at [4] and [9]; *Al Fayed v SSHD*, IT, 28 February 2002 at [3]; *Gosling v SSHD*, IT, 1 August 2003 at [2]; *Hitchens v SSHD*, IT, 4 Augusut 2003 at [2]; *Hilton v FCO*, IT, 28 June 2005 at [2]; *Stevenson v SSHD*, IT, 30 April 2009 at [3].

[84] For example DPA s 28 (on national security).

17– 013 **The security bodies: order**

The order in which the security bodies are listed in s 23(3) of the Freedom of Information Act 2000 would appear to be intentional. The security bodies are not listed in alphabetical order and they have not been ordered simply according to their size or practical importance, otherwise NCIS and SOCA would appear higher up the list.[85] Rather, the appearance of the Security Service, SIS, GCHQ and the special forces at the head of the list appears to reflect a certain primacy in terms of the nature and quality of the type of information which these bodies may supply to public authorities or which may relate to them: these four would appear to be the most important of the security bodies. Whether or not the final order was intended to convey a particular message or came about simply because the later entries were, in policy or drafting terms, just that,[86] the final order can be said to reflect a division between principal and ancillary security bodies as follows:

    (1)   The principal security bodies:

        (a)   the three 'intelligence services', that is to say, the Security Service, SIS and GCHQ,[87] come first as the key operational bodies whose exclusion from the Freedom of Information Act 2000 regime is most important and most easily explained in policy terms;[88]

        (b)   the special forces come next as an operational body, akin to a fourth intelligence service, whose exclusion from the Freedom of Information Act 2000 regime is seen as being equally important.[89]

    (2)   The ancillary security bodies:

        (a)   the RIPA, IOCA, SSA and ISA Tribunals, the Security Vetting Appeals Panel and the Security Commission come next as a collection of non-operational oversight bodies whose exemption is, presumably, required by reason of their close connections with the principal security bodies or security

---

[85] FOIA adopts an alphabetical approach to the straightforward lists of 'other public bodies and offices' in Sch 1, Pts VI–VII but a more hierarchical approach in other areas where bodies are ordered according to their relative size or importance, with national bodies coming before devolved or regional bodies and with bodies from Scotland, Northern Ireland and Wales appearing in that order (eg FOIA ss 28(2), 59, 76, Sch 1 Pts I–III).

[86] See §17– 014.

[87] The compendious expression 'the intelligence services' is used in this chapter to refer to the Security Service, SIS and GCHQ in the same way as in the Regulation of Investigatory Powers Act 2000 s 81(1). The alternative expression 'the security and intelligence services' appears in the Official Secrets Act 1989 s 1 without further definition but there is no reason to think it goes any further than the three intelligence services. At the time the Official Secrets Act 1989 was enacted the Security Service Act 1989 (which would place the Security Service on a statutory basis upon coming into force) had only just been enacted and SIS and GCHQ still had no legal status: the Official Secrets Act 1989 received Royal Assent on 11 May 1989 and came into force on 1 March 1990 (see Official Secrets Act 1989 s 16(6) and Official Secrets Act 1989 (Commencement) Order 1990 SI 1990/199) while the Security Service Act 1989 received Royal Assent a fortnight before on 27 April 1989 and came into force on 18 December 1989 (see Security Service Act 1989 s 7(2) and Security Service Act 1989 (Commencement) Order 1989 SI 1989/2093). Although the Intelligence Services Act 1994 treated SIS as 'the Intelligence Service' (s 1(1)) its short title, coupled with its provisions relating to the Security Service, could be read as suggesting that it regarded all three services as 'intelligence services' (cf ss 8 and 10 in relation to the Intelligence Services Commissioner (originally distinct from the Security Service Commissioner) and the naming of the Intelligence and Security Committee with 'intelligence and security' in alphabetical order).

[88] FOIA s 23(3)(a)–(c).

[89] FOIA s 23(3)(d).

and intelligence matters generally;[90]

(b)   SOCA (the successor to, among others, NCIS and its Service Authority) has an operational role but would appear to be the most borderline of the security bodies and its exemption presumably came about by reason of the close connections with the Security Service which NCIS had and SOCA assumed.[91]

014   The security bodies: selection

The criteria by which the security bodies were selected for designation as such were never fully articulated prior to the enactment of the Freedom of Information Act 2000. The exclusion of the principal security bodies, the intelligence services and the special forces, was proposed at the outset but the selection of the ancillary security bodies and the non-selection of other apparently similar bodies were not the subject of much scrutiny or debate. The White Paper, *Your Right to Know: The Government's Proposals for a Freedom of Information Act*, stated that the four principal security bodies would be excluded because they 'could not carry out their duties effectively in the interests of the nation if their operations and activities were subject to freedom of information legislation'.[92] Continuing this theme, the accompanying *Factual and Background Material*[93] referred again to the principal security bodies as candidates for exclusion 'requiring careful consideration' together with 'support provided to them by other bodies and information originating from them but held by other bodies'.[94] The government consultation paper *Freedom of Information: Consultation on Draft Legislation* first mentioned NCIS as a likely candidate for exclusion on the basis that its work is 'closely analogous' to that of the intelligence services.[95] The proposed exclusion of the IOCA, SSA and ISA Tribunals[96] was similarly explained on the grounds that 'their work is wholly concerned with security and intelligence matters' and 'they would not be able to carry out their work effectively if their activities, or even their administrative functions, were subject to freedom of information legislation'.[97] The designation of the Security Vetting Appeals Panel and the Security Commission as security bodies was not discussed at all in the policy and consultation documents which preceded and underlay the Freedom of Information Act 2000.

---

[90]   FOIA s 23(3)(e)–(j).

[91]   FOIA s 23(3)(k)–(m).

[92]   Cm 3818, 1997 para 2.3. This passage goes on to state, 'These organisations, and the information they provide, will be excluded from the Act, as will information about these organisations held by other public authorities.'

[93]   Published under Cm 3818, 1997 para 3.13.

[94]   Paragraph 96. This passage goes on to state, 'It is argued that reliance solely on a harm tested exemption would lead to the cumulative disclosure of a significant quantity of the agencies' records or of operational information. This would undermine confidence among those individuals and bodies on whose co-operation the effective functioning of the agencies relies, and would have a deleterious impact on the effectiveness of the Special Forces'.

[95]   Cm 4355, 1999 para 26.

[96]   The explanation is to be found in notes produced by the Home Office Freedom of Information Unit for the House of Commons Public Administration Select Committee on the clause in the draft Freedom of Information Bill published on 24 May 1999 which eventually formed the basis for FOIA s 23 (see *Freedom of Information: Consultation on Draft Legislation* (Cm 4355, 1999) Pt II, cl 18).

[97]   House of Commons Public Administration Select Committee Third Report Session 1998–1999 *Freedom of Information Draft Bill* (HC 570–I) 1999, Annex 6, para 43.

17– 015 **The intelligence services**

The Security Service, SIS and GCHQ are specifically excluded from the Freedom of Information Act 2000 regime by s 84 which provides that they are not 'government departments' for the purposes of the Act.[98] Their identities and functions are prescribed and regulated primarily by the Security Service Act 1989, the Intelligence Services Act 1994 and the Regulation of Investigatory Powers Act 2000.[99] Taking each service in turn:

    (1)   *The Security Service.* The Security Service (more commonly known as 'MI5') was 'placed on a statutory basis' by the Security Service Act 1989 which provides that 'there shall continue to be a Security Service'.[100] The Security Service is under the authority of the Home Secretary who appoints a Director General to control its operations and be responsible for its efficiency.[101] The Director General in turn makes an annual report on the work of the Security Service to the Prime Minister and Home Secretary and may at any time report to either of them on any matter

---

[98]   The intelligence services are not otherwise listed as 'public authorities' in FOIA Sch 1. Each one on the face of it satisfies the test of being a 'body or authority exercising statutory functions on behalf of the Crown', which would make it a 'government department' for the purposes of FOIA s 84, Sch 1, Pt I, para 1 but for the fact that each one is expressly excluded from the definition of 'government department' in s 84.

[99]   See generally: *Halsbury's Laws of England*, 4th edn, 1996 re-issue, vol 8(2), title 'Constitutional Law and Human Rights', paras 471–476; I Leigh and L Lustgarten, 'The Security Service Act 1989' (1989) 52 *Modern Law Review* 801; L Lustgarten and I Leigh, *In From the Cold: National Security and Parliamentary Democracy* (Oxford, Oxford University Press, 1994); J Wadham, 'The Intelligence Services Act 1994' (1994) 57 *Modern Law Review* 916; M Urban, *UK Eyes Alpha: The Inside Story of British Intelligence* (London, Faber & Faber, 1996); A Bradley and K Ewing, *Constitutional and Administrative Law*, 14th edn (London, Pearson Longman, 2007) pp 599–609; O Hood Phillips and P Jackson, *Constitutional and Administrative Law*, 8th edn (London, Sweet & Maxwell, 2001) paras 19–038 to 19–040; S Twigge, E Hampshire and G Macklin, *British Intelligence: Secrets, Spies and Services*, (Kew, The National Archives, 2008); C Andrews, *The Defence of the Realm: The Authorised History of MI5*, (London, Allen Lane, 2009). See also the official government publications: Cabinet Office, *National Intelligence Machinery*, 4th edn (London, TSO, 2006); Intelligence and Security Committee, *Intelligence Oversight* (London, 2002); Home Office, *MI5: The Security Service*, 4th edn (2002); Cabinet Office, *Improving the Central Intelligence Machinery* 2009. Further information can also be found via the following websites: www.cabinetoffice.gov.uk/security-and-intelligence.aspx (Cabinet Office website for 'Security, Intelligence and Resilience'); www.mi5.gov.uk (Security Service); www.mi6.gov.uk (Secret Intelligence Service); www.gchq.gov.uk (GCHQ).

[100]   Security Service Act 1989 s 1(1). This Act was passed against a background which had seen Lord Donaldson MR call for the Security Service to be placed on a statutory basis (comments made in the Court of Appeal on 10 February 1988 during the course of *AG v Guardian Newspapers Ltd (No 2)* [1990] 1 AC 109) and the commencement of *Hewitt and Harman v United Kingdom* (1992) 14 EHRR 657 (ECtHR). In ECHR terms, it had already been held in *Leander v Sweden* (1987) 9 EHRR 433 (ECtHR) that it is legitimate for member states to establish security or secret services to gather and disclose information about their citizens provided that such services are placed on a clear legal basis and made subject to adequate and effective safeguards against abuse (see also *Klass v Germany* (1979–80) 2 EHRR 214 (ECtHR)). The Security Service Act 1989 was itself modelled on the Interception of Communications Act 1985 which had been passed following *Malone v United Kingdom* (1985) 7 EHRR 14 (ECtHR). Prior to this the operation of the Security Service was governed by a directive issued by the Home Secretary, Sir David Maxwell Fyffe, to the Director General in 1952 as publicised by Lord Denning MR in his *Report on the Profumo Affair* (Cmnd 2152, 1963) and in his judgment in *R v SSHD, ex p Hosenball* [1977] 3 All ER 452 (CA). A great deal of the Maxwell Fyffe Directive found expression in the Security Service Act 1989 (Cabinet Office, *National Intelligence Machinery*, 2nd edn (London, HMSO, 2001) p 9). See also the House of Commons Home Affairs Select Committee Third Report Session 1998–1999 *Accountability of the Security Service* (HC 291) 1999.

[101]   Security Service Act 1989 ss 1(1), 2(1).

relating to this work.[102] The Security Service has the following functions:[103] the protection of national security and, in particular, its protection against threats from espionage, terrorism[104] and sabotage, from the activities of agents of foreign powers and from actions intended to overthrow or undermine parliamentary democracy by political, industrial or violent means;[105] to safeguard the economic well-being of the United Kingdom against threats posed by the actions or intentions of persons outside the British Islands;[106] and to act in support of the activities of police forces, SOCA and other law enforcement agencies in the prevention and detection of serious crime.[107]

---

[102] Security Service Act 1989 s 2(4).

[103] According to Home Office, *MI5: The Security Service*, 4th edn (2002), the Security Service fulfils its functions by: 'collecting and disseminating intelligence, investigating and assessing threats and working with others to counter them, advising on protection and providing effective support for those tasks' (p 5); working 'closely' with SIS, GCHQ, the Home Office, the Foreign and Commonwealth Office, the Cabinet Office, the Northern Ireland Office, the Department of Trade and Industry, the Ministry of Defence and its Defence Intelligence Staff, law enforcement agencies (ie the United Kingdom's 56 police forces, the National Crime Squad, NCIS and HM Customs and Excise), the armed forces and various foreign security and intelligence services (pp 20 and 25–26); and by gathering intelligence through covert human intelligence sources, the interception of communications and directed and intrusive surveillance (p 22). See also Cabinet Office, *National Intelligence Machinery*, 4th edn (London, TSO, 2006) pp 11–13. The Security Service has very close working relationships with the 53 police Special Branches in the United Kingdom, so much so that the Special Branches have been described as an executive partner of the Security Service and a major extension to its intelligence collection capability (*Intelligence and Security Committee Annual Report 2002–2003* (Cm 5837, 2003) paras 68–71). Note that with effect from 2 October 2006 the Metropolitan Police Special Branch merged with the former Anti-Terrorist Branch to form a new Counter-Terrorism Command (also known as 'SO 15'). The Special Branch had itself been established in March 1883 as the Special Irish Branch, tasked with countering Irish 'Fenian' terrorism on mainland Great Britain

[104] In May 1992, following the end of the Cold War, the Security Service acquired from the police responsibility for the collection of intelligence regarding Irish Republican terrorism in Great Britain: Hansard HC vol 207 cols 297–306 (8 May 1992); *Intelligence and Security Committee Report on Security Service Work Against Organised Crime* (Cm 3065, 1995); M Urban, *UK Eyes Alpha: The Inside Story of British Intelligence* (London, Faber & Faber, 1996), chs 15 and 21; A Bradley and K Ewing, *Constitutional and Administrative Law*, 14th edn (London, Pearson Longman, 2007) pp 601–603. In October 2007 the Security Service acquired the same responsibility in relation to Northern Ireland: Hansard HC vol 431 col 62WS (24 February 2005). The Security Service is largely responsible for two inter-departmental bodies, the Centre for the Protection of National Infrastructure ('CPNI') (www.cpni.gov.uk) and the Joint Terrorism Analysis Centre ('JTAC') whose Heads are both accountable to the Director General of the Security Service. CPNI was established in February 2007 through the abolition and merger of the former National Security Advice Centre and the National Infrastructure Security Co-ordination Centre. JTAC was established in June 2003 through the expansion of the Counter-Terrorist Analysis Centre itself established in October 2001: *Government Response to the Intelligence and Security Committee Inquiry into Intelligence, Assessments and Advice Prior to the Terrorist Bombings on Bali 12 October 2002* (Cm 5765, 2003) para 11; *Intelligence and Security Committee Annual Report 2002–2003* (Cm 5837, 2003) para 62; *Government Response to the Intelligence and Security Committee's Annual Report 2002–2003* (Cm 5838, 2003) para 13; Cabinet Office, *National Intelligence Machinery*, 4th edn (London, TSO, 2006) p 16 where JTAC is listed as a separate 'intelligence and security agency' and a part of 'the United Kingdom's intelligence machinery'; Home Office, *Threat Levels: The System to Assess the Threat from International Terrorism* (London, TSO, 2006) pp 3, 5; HM Government, *Countering International Terrorism: The United Kingdom's Strategy* (Cm 6888, 2006) p 16; HM Government, *Pursue, Prevent, Protect, Prepare: The United Kingdom's Strategy for Countering International Terrorism* (Cm 7547, 2009) p 39.

[105] Security Service Act 1989 s 1(2).

[106] Security Service Act 1989 s 1(3). See §17– 067.

[107] Security Service Act 1989 s 1(4) as inserted by the Security Service Act 1996 s 1(1) and amended by the Police Act 1997 s 134(1), Sch 9, para 60 and then the Serious Organised Crime and Police Act 2005 s 59, Sch 4, paras 55–56. The Director General must also ensure that there are arrangements, agreed with the Director General of SOCA, for co-ordinating the activities of the Security Service in pursuance of the Security Service Act 1989 s 1(4) with the activities of police forces, SOCA and other law enforcement agencies: Security Service Act 1989 s 2(2)(c) as inserted by the Security Service Act 1996 s 1(1) and (3) and amended by the Police Act 1997 ss 12 and 134(1), Sch 9, para

(2)   *The Secret Intelligence Service.* SIS (more commonly known as 'MI6') was placed on a statutory basis by the Intelligence Services Act 1994 which provided that 'there shall continue to be a Secret Intelligence Service'.[108] SIS is under the authority of the Foreign Secretary who appoints a Chief of the Intelligence Service to control its operations.[109] The Chief makes an annual report on the work of SIS to the Prime Minister and Foreign Secretary and may at any time report to either of them on any matter relating to this work.[110] The functions of SIS are to obtain and provide information relating to the actions or intentions of persons outside the British Islands and to perform other tasks relating to the actions or intentions of such persons.[111] These functions are exercisable only in the interests of national security, with particular reference to the defence and foreign policies of Her Majesty's Government in the United Kingdom, in the interests of the economic well-being of the United Kingdom or in support of the prevention or detection of serious crime.[112]

(3)   *GCHQ.* GCHQ was also placed on a statutory basis by the Intelligence Services Act 1994 which provided that 'there shall continue to be a Government Communications Headquarters'.[113] GCHQ is under the authority of the Foreign Secretary who appoints a Director of GCHQ to control its operations.[114] The Director makes an annual report on the work of GCHQ to the Prime Minister and Foreign Secretary and may at any time report to either of them on any matter relating to this work.[115] GCHQ has two main functions under the Intelligence Services Act 1994: first, to monitor or interfere with electromagnetic, acoustic and other emissions and any equipment producing such emissions and to obtain and provide information derived from or related to such emissions or equipment and from encrypted material;[116] and, secondly, to provide advice and assistance about languages (including terminology used for technical matters) and cryptography and other matters relating to the protection of information and other material to the

---

61 and then the Serious Organised Crime and Police Act 2005 s 59, Sch 4, paras 55, 57. Note also Cabinet Office, *National Intelligence Machinery*, 4th edn (London, TSO, 2006) p 12 — 'Since the establishment of [SOCA] the [Security] Service has suspended work on serious crime in order to concentrate more resources on counter-terrorism.'

[108] Intelligence Services Act 1994 s 1(1). The Intelligence Services Act 1994 was modelled on the Security Service Act 1989 and the Interception of Communications Act 1985. (Indeed, the Security Service Act 1989 was itself modelled on the Interception of Communications Act 1985).

[109] Intelligence Services Act 1994 ss 1(1) and 2(1).

[110] Intelligence Services Act 1994 s 2(4).

[111] Intelligence Services Act 1994 s 1(1). According to Cabinet Office, *National Intelligence Machinery*, 4th edn (London, TSO, 2006), SIS 'uses human and technical sources' and 'liaison with a wide range of foreign intelligence and security services' to fulfil its functions (p 7).

[112] Intelligence Services Act 1994 s 1(2).

[113] Intelligence Services Act 1994 s 3(1).

[114] Intelligence Services Act 1994 ss 3(1), 4(1).

[115] Intelligence Services Act 1994 s 4(4).

[116] Intelligence Services Act 1994 s 3(1)(a).

armed forces of the Crown, Her Majesty's Government in the United Kingdom, Northern Ireland departments and any other organisation determined in such manner as may be specified by the Prime Minister.[117]   The first (monitoring) function is exercisable only in the interests of national security, with particular reference to the defence and foreign policies of Her Majesty's Government in the United Kingdom, in the interests of the economic well-being of the United Kingdom in relation to the actions or intentions of persons outside the British Islands or in support of the prevention or detection of serious crime.[118] The second (advisory) function is not subject to a specific purpose condition.[119]

016   The special forces: identity
The special forces are not themselves a 'public authority' for the purposes of the Freedom of Information Act 2000 and they are not a part of the wider 'public authority' comprising the armed forces of the Crown.[120] Section 84 of the Freedom of Information Act 2000 defines 'the special forces' to mean 'those units of the armed forces of the Crown the maintenance of whose capabilities is the responsibility of the Director of Special Forces or which are for the time being subject to the operational command of that Director'. The identities of the Director of Special Forces and of the units under his responsibility or command are not clarified further in the Freedom of Information Act 2000. The only official statements made by the government on this topic in connection with the Freedom of Information Bill linked the special forces to the Special Air Service and the Special Boat Service.[121] More generally, the Government has elsewhere confirmed that the 'United Kingdom Special Forces Group' includes three Special Air Service Regiments (the Regular 22 SAS Regiment and the Territorial Army Reserve 21 and 23 SAS Regiments), a number of Special Boat Service Squadrons (Regular and Reserve), a Special Reconnaissance Regiment and a Special Forces Support Group.[122]

---

[117] Intelligence Services Act 1994 s 3(1)(b).

[118] Intelligence Services Act 1994 s 3(2).

[119] GCHQ's advisory function is in part fulfilled through its 'Information Assurance' arm, Communications Electronics Security Group ('CESG') (www.cesg.gov.uk).

[120] The 'armed forces of the Crown' are listed as a 'public authority' in FOIA Sch 1 Pt I para 6 but the special forces and units of the armed forces which are for the time being required by the Secretary of State to assist GCHQ in the exercise of its functions are expressly excepted from this provision by Sch 1 Pt I para 6(a)–(b).

[121] *Your Right to Know: The Government's Proposals for a Freedom of Information Act* (Cm 3818, 1997) para 2.3 and the Factual and Background Material (1997), para 96 (published under Your Right to Know, para 3.13), both contain explanatory references to the 'SAS' and 'SBS', after references to the special forces and a written answer to a Parliamentary Question about the clause in the Freedom of Information Bill which became the FOIA s 4 confirmed that these initials stand for 'Special Air Service' and 'Special Boat Service': Hansard HL vol 612 col 124 (20 April 2000).

[122] This information can be gleaned from: *Ministry of Defence Performance Report* 2001/2002 (Cm 5661, 2002) Annex E, table3; *'R' v AG for England and Wales* [2003] UKPC 22, [2003] EMLR 499 at [36] (Lord Hoffmann); www.army.mod.uk/uksf; www.army.mod.uk/para; and www.royalnavy.mod.uk. It is apparent that the Special Air Service and Special Reconnaissance Regiments are parts of the Army and the Special Boat Service Squadrons are parts of the Royal Marines. So far as concerns the establishment of the Special Reconnaissance Regiment (with effect from 6 April 2005) and the Special Forces Support Group (with effect from 3 April 2006), see the government announcements at: Hansard HC vol 428 col 1796 (16 December 2004); Hansard HC vol 432 col 130WS (5 April 2005); and Hansard HC vol 445 col 25WS (20 April 2006).

17– 017 The special forces: functions

There is very little publicly available official information about the special forces to explain their exclusion from the Freedom of Information Act 2000 regime.[123] This is largely attributable to the long-standing government policy of not commenting publicly on special forces matters.[124] However, a small number of public statements have been made. In 1996 the Government stated that the special forces have four primary roles, namely, reconnaissance, offensive action, the provision of support to indigenous forces and counter-terrorism.[125] During the course of the Strategic Defence Review begun in 1997, the government further stated that the special forces are involved in war-fighting operations and counter-terrorism work[126] and that they are a 'Spearhead' component of the 'First Echelon' of the United Kingdom's 'Joint Rapid Reaction Forces'.[127] In 2002, the Government also confirmed that it was planning to enhance the capabilities of the special forces and their 'enablers' in order to maximise their utility and flexibility.[128] And, in 2010, the Government confirmed its view that special forces 'have demonstrated their value across a broad spectrum of activity, from operating alongside our conventional forces in Iraq and Afghanistan to capacity building with our partners or hostage rescue.'[129] Further information about the role of the special forces can be derived from: the introduction in 1996 of a Defence Council Instruction making the signing of a confidentiality

---

[123] Indeed, the exclusion of the special forces from the FOIA regime can itself be seen as a public pronouncement on the nature of their functions: '*R' v AG for England and Wales* [2003] UKPC 22, [2003] EMLR 499 at [36] (Lord Hoffmann).

[124] *The Threat from Terrorism: Government Response*, para 39 at House of Commons Defence Select Committee, *Fourth Special Report of 2001–02* (HC 667), Appendix: 'The Government has in the past made it known that the UK has Special Forces which, as well as their war-fighting roles, are used in support of its counter-terrorist policy, and to provide assistance in this area to the law enforcement agencies. However, successive governments have adopted a policy of not commenting, save in exceptional circumstances, on Special Forces matters. The effectiveness of the Special Forces in the counter-terrorist role depends on maintaining secrecy about their operations, methods, capabilities (including numbers) and equipment. Moreover, we need to protect their identities because they and their families are at risk from terrorist groups. This therefore constrains what we can say in public about our plans for Special Forces.' See also *Statement on the Defence Estimates 1996* (Cm 3223, 1996) para 731, 'as a general rule, the government will not comment on matters which are judged to have an unacceptable impact on the successful conduct of operations or on the best interests of special forces personnel.' Cf the Prime Minister's announcement regarding the deployment of Special Forces in Afghanistan in 2009: Hansard HC vol 501 cols 835-836 (30 November 2009).

[125] *Statement on the Defence Estimates 1996* (Cm 3223, 1996) para 727. See also the remainder of the section headed 'disclosure of information on the special forces' at paras 727–731.

[126] *Strategic Defence Review* (Cm 3999, 1998). The conclusions of the *Strategic Defence Review* were approved by the House of Commons: Hansard HC vol 317 cols 1097–1177 (20 October 1998).

[127] *Strategic Defence Review* (Cm 3999, 1998).

[128] *Strategic Defence Review: A New Chapter* (Cm 5566, 2002), para 45.

[129] Ministry of Defence, *Adaptability and Partnership: Issues for the Strategic Defence Review* (Cm 7794, 2010) p 19, para 2.1. It can also be noted that the draft House of Commons resolution proposed by the Government in March 2008 for the establishment of a new process for the Parliamentary approval of commitments of HM Armed Forces into armed conflict contained an exception for 'conflict decisions' involving the special forces deployed only for the purpose of assisting the Special Forces: MoJ White Paper, *The Governance of Britain – Constitutional Renewal* (Cm 7342, 2008) pt I para 217, Annex A 'Draft Detailed War Powers Resolution' para 4.

contract a prerequisite to all service with the special forces;[130] and the issue in 2000 of an amended 'DA-Notice' reiterating the counter-terrorist role of the special forces and suggesting that they are 'involved with' covert operations, sources and methods of the intelligence services.[131]

018 The RIPA, IOCA, SSA and ISA Tribunals: identities

In general terms, the RIPA Tribunal established under s 65 of the Regulation of Investigatory Powers Act 2000 deals with proceedings and complaints relating to the intelligence services and the use by those services and other public authorities of investigatory powers under the Intelligence Services Act 1994 and the Regulation of Investigatory Powers Act 2000.[132] The RIPA Tribunal has effectively replaced the IOCA, SSA, and ISA Tribunals which are now defunct except in relation to complaints made before 2 October 2000.[133] None of these Tribunals is listed as a 'public authority' in Sch 1 to the Freedom of Information Act 2000.

019 The RIPA Tribunal: functions

So far as concerns the jurisdiction of the RIPA Tribunal: the Intelligence Services Act 1994 makes provision for warrants to be issued by a relevant Secretary of State authorising the intelligence services to enter on or interfere with property or wireless telegraphy or to do certain acts outside the British Islands;[134] the Regulation of Investigatory Powers Act 2000 makes

---

[130] *AG for England and Wales v Television New Zealand Ltd* (1999) 44 IPR 123 (CA) (NZ) at 124–126 (Henry J); '*R' v AG for England and Wales* [2003] UKPC 22, [2003] EMLR 499 at [2]–[10] (Lord Hoffmann) on appeal from *AG for England and Wales v 'R'* [2002] 2 NZLR 91 (CA) (NZ) (see at [16]–[19] and [24] (Tipping J)); *MoD v Griffin* [2008] EWHC 1542 (QB). The Defence Council Instruction ('DCI') was issued on 4 October 1996 and provided, 'From the date of this DCI all Armed Forces personnel serving currently or in future on the establishment of units under the operational or administrative command of the Director of Special Forces will be required to sign a contract binding the signatory to a lifelong commitment not to disclose, without prior permission of the [Ministry of Defence], any information gained during service with Special Forces' (*AG for England and Wales v 'R'* [2002] 2 NZLR 91 (CA) (NZ) (see at [19] (Tipping J)).

[131] Standing Defence Advisory Notice 5, 'United Kingdom Security and Intelligence Services and Special Forces' (DA-Notice 5) issued by the Defence, Press and Broadcasting Advisory Committee ('DPBAC') on 24 May 2000. This was retitled 'United Kingdom Security and Intelligence Services and Special Services' on 20 April 2005 but the substance relating to special forces remains the same. The DPBAC is a non-statutory advisory body which provides 'advice and guidance to the media about defence and counter-terrorist information the publication of which would be damaging to national security' on a voluntary and confidential basis (www.dnotice.org.uk). The DPBAC itself comprises senior civil servants and editors from national and regional newspapers, periodicals, news agencies, television and radio and is chaired by the Permanent Under Secretary of State for Defence. The DA-Notices cannot therefore be regarded as government statements as such but they are drafted within government and reviewed by the Secretary to the DPBAC before being agreed and issued by the DPBAC as a whole. See: Jaconelli, 'The D Notice System' [1982] *Public Law* 37; HC 773 (1979–1980); *The Protection of Military Information* (Cmnd 9112, 1983); Fairley, 'D Notices, Official Secrets and the Law' (1990) 10 OJLS 430; A Bradley and K Ewing, *Constitutional and Administrative Law*, 14th edn (London, Pearson Longman, 2007) pp 620–621; O Hood Phillips and P Jackson, *Constitutional and Administrative Law*, 8th edn (London, Sweet & Maxwell, 2001) para 26-011.

[132] Regulation of Investigatory Powers Act 2000 ss 65–69, Sch 3; Investigatory Powers Tribunal Rules 2000 SI 2000/2665; *Interception of Communications in the United Kingdom: A Consultation Paper* (Cm 4368, 1999).

[133] Interception of Communications Act 1985 s 7 and Sch 1 (establishing the IOCA Tribunal), Security Service Act 1989 s 5 and Schs 1–2 (establishing the SSA Tribunal) and Intelligence Services Act 1994 s 9 and Schs 1–2 (establishing the ISA Tribunal) were repealed except in relation to complaints made to those Tribunals before 2 October 2000 by the Regulation of Investigatory Powers Act 2000 ss 70, 82(2), Sch 5 and the Regulation of Investigatory Powers Act 2000 (Commencement No 1 and Transitional Provisions) Order 2000 SI 2000/2543.

[134] Intelligence Services Act 1994 ss 5–7 (ss 5–6 replacing Security Service Act 1989 s 3). See also Regulation of Investigatory Powers Act 2000 ss 42, 44, 74.

similar provision for interception warrants to be issued by a relevant Secretary of State authorising, amongst others, the intelligence services and SOCA, to intercept communications;[135] and the Regulation of Investigatory Powers Act 2000 also makes provision in relation to the authorisation of the acquisition and disclosure of communications data[136] and the authorisation of directed surveillance (eg the covert monitoring of a target's activities, conversations and movements), intrusive surveillance (eg sound or video eavesdropping in a target's residential premises or private vehicle) and the conduct and use of covert human intelligence sources (ie under-cover officers and agents).[137] Any member of the public who is aggrieved by any conduct which they believe to have been carried out in relation to them by or on behalf of the intelligence services or who wishes to bring proceedings against them under s 7 of the Human Rights Act 1998 may make a complaint to or bring such proceedings before the RIPA Tribunal.[138] So far as concerns the RIPA Tribunal's handling of sensitive information, its Rules oblige it to carry out its functions 'in such a way as to secure that information is not disclosed to an extent, or in a manner, that is contrary to the public interest or prejudicial to national security, the prevention or detection of serious crime, the economic well-being of the United Kingdom or the continued discharge of the functions of any of the intelligence services.'[139]

17–020 The Security Vetting Appeals Panel

The creation of the Security Vetting Appeals Panel was formally announced in both Houses of Parliament on 19 June 1997 in written answers to two Parliamentary Questions asking 'what are the arrangements for hearing appeals from those who need to have access to protectively marked Government assets and have been refused security clearance or have had that clearance

---

[135] Regulation of Investigatory Powers Act 2000 Pt I, c I (see esp ss 5–11). Interception warrants under s 5 may be issued to, inter alia, the Director General of the Security Service, Chief of the Secret Intelligence Service, Director of GCHQ, Director General of SOCA and Chief of Defence Intelligence (ss 6(2)(a)–(d) and (i) and 7(3)(a)).

[136] Regulation of Investigatory Powers Act 2000 Pt I, c II (acquisition and disclosure of communications data). The intelligence services and SOCA are 'relevant public authorities' for the purposes of these provisions and certain of their members can therefore grant authorisations and engage in certain conduct in relation to communications data (s 25(1)).

[137] Regulation of Investigatory Powers Act 2000 Pt II (surveillance and covert human intelligence sources). The intelligence services, SOCA and any of Her Majesty's forces are 'relevant public authorities' for the purposes of ss 28–29 and certain of their members can therefore authorise directed surveillance and the conduct and use of covert human intelligence sources: s 30, Sch 1, paras 2 and 5–6 and Regulation of Investigatory Powers (Directed Surveillance and Cover Human Intelligence Sources) Order 2003 SI 2003/3171. A relevant Secretary of State and the Director General of SOCA are among those who can authorise intrusive surveillance on the application of the intelligence services, the Ministry of Defence and the armed forces (in the case of a Secretary of State) and SOCA (in the case of the Director General of SOCA) under the Regulation of Investigatory Powers Act 2000 s 32. See also: ss 33–40 (which are modelled on the Police Act 1997, Pt III) in relation to police authorisations granted and applied for by members of SOCA and the additional requirements regarding Surveillance Commissioner approval, etc that apply in relation to intrusive surveillance authorisations granted and applied for by members of SOCA; s 41 in relation to Secretary of State intrusive surveillance authorisations; and ss 42 and 44 in relation to the grant by the Secretary of State of authorisations to the intelligence services.

[138] See *R (A) v Director of Establishments of the Security Service* [2009] UKSC 12, [2010] 2 WLR 1. The Regulation of Investigator Powers Act 2000 s 62(2)(a) confers exclusive jurisdiction on the RIPA Tribunal to hear claims under the Human Rights Act 2000 s 7(1)(a) against any of the intelligence services.

[139] Investigatory Powers Tribunal Rules 2000 SI 2000/2665 r 6. See also Regulation of Investigatory Powers Act 2000 s 69(6)(b).

withdrawn?' These written answers read as follows:[140]

> An independent Security Vetting Appeals Panel, chaired by Sir Anthony May, will be established on July 1 to hear appeals against the refusal or withdrawal of clearance at Security Check (SC) or Developed Vetting (DV) levels and to advise the head of the organisation concerned. The Panel will be available to all those, other than recruits, in the public and private sectors and in the Armed Forces who are subject to security vetting at these levels, have exhausted existing appeals mechanisms within their own organisations and remain dissatisfied with the result. Separate arrangements are available to staff of the security and intelligence agencies. The establishment of the Panel therefore brings to an end the role of the Three Advisers who, since 1948, have been available to consider cases where security clearance was refused or withdrawn on the grounds of subversion.

The Security Vetting Appeals Panel is not listed as a 'public authority' in Sch 1 to the Freedom of Information Act 2000 and is not a 'government department' for the purposes of para 1 of that Schedule.[141] In formal terms, the Panel is an advisory non-departmental public body sponsored by the Cabinet Office.[142]

021 The Security Commission

The creation of the Security Commission was formally announced by the Prime Minister, Sir Alec Douglas-Home, on 23 January 1964 after fears of possible security lapses that came to light after the resignation of Mr John Profumo MP.[143] The Commission's original terms of reference, which have since been slightly modified, were:[144]

> If so requested by the Prime Minister, to investigate and report upon the circumstances in

---

[140] Hansard HC vol 296 cols 245–246 (19 June 1997) (question by Mr Rooney MP, answer by the Prime Minister, Mr Blair); Hansard HL vol 580 col 123 (19 June 1997) (question by Lord Graham of Edmonton, answer by the Lord Privy Seal, Lord Richards). In March 1948 the Prime Minister, Mr Attlee, announced that all Communists and Fascists would be excluded from work 'vital to the security of the state' via a vetting system: Hansard HC vol 44 cols 3417–3426 (25 March 1948). This system evolved into the current Security Vetting Scheme which was last re-announced in a statement made by the Prime Minister, Mr Major Hansard HC vol 25 cols 764–766 (15 December 1994) and which operates in conjunction with the Government's Protective Marking Scheme whereby documents and other 'assets' are classified 'RESTRICTED', 'CONFIDENTIAL', 'SECRET', 'TOP SECRET', etc. See: Hennessy and Brownfield 'Britain's Coldwar Security Purge: the Origins of Positive Vetting' (1982) 25 *The Historical Journal* 4, pp 965–973; Joelson, 'The Dismissal of Civil Servants in the Interests of National Security' [1963] *Public Law* 51; A Bradley and K Ewing, *Constitutional and Administrative Law*, 14th edn (London, Pearson Longman, 2007) pp 610–612; White, 'Security vetting, discrimination and the right to a fair trial' [1999] *Public Law* 406.

[141] FOIA s 84.

[142] See the Cabinet Office publications *Public Bodies 2009* (2009), p 17, annex A and *Cabinet Office Annual Report and Accounts 2008-2009* (HC 442, 2009) pp 105, 206. On non-departmental public bodies generally see also *Halsbury's Laws of England*, 4th edn, 1996 re-issue, vol 8(2), title 'Constitutional Law and Human Rights', paras 951–954.

[143] The actual basis for Mr Profumo's resignation was his having denied in Parliament that there had been 'impropriety' in his relationship with a Miss Keeler when, in fact, 2 years earlier for a period of weeks he had had a sexual relationship with her. The relationship was known to the security services and ended upon the advice of the head of MI5. See further: I Leigh and L Lustgarten, 'The Security Commission: Constitutional Achievement or Curiosity' [1991] *Public Law* 215; L Lustgarten and I Leigh, *In From the Cold: National Security and Parliamentary Democracy* (Oxford, Oxford University Press, 1994), pp 476–492; A Bradley and K Ewing, *Constitutional and Administrative Law*, 14th edn (London, Pearson Longman, 2007) pp 621–622.

[144] Hansard HC vol 687 cols 1271–1275 (23 January 1964). The Security Commission has been unflatteringly described as a 'lightning conductor' for security crises (*The Times*, 24 January 1964 cited in D Williams, *Not in the Public Interest: the Problem of Security in Democracy* (London, Hutchinson, 1965), pp 167–169) and a 'stable door operation' Hansard HC vol 145 cols 64–65 (16 January 1989). The terms of reference were twice expanded by the Prime Minister, Mr Wilson: Hansard HC vol 712 col 34 (10 May 1965) and Hansard HC vol 780 col 311 (26 March 1969).

which a breach of security is known to have occurred in the public service, and upon any related failure in departmental security arrangements or neglect of duty; and, in the light of any such investigations, to advise whether any change in security arrangements is desirable. The Security Commission is not listed as a 'public authority' in Sch 1 to the Freedom of Information Act 2000 and is not a 'government department' for the purposes of para 1 of that Schedule.[145] In formal terms, the Commission is an advisory non-departmental public body sponsored by the Cabinet Office.[146] There is some overlap between the respective remits of the Security Commission and the Intelligence and Security Committee established under the Intelligence Services Act 1994.[147] It remains to be seen whether this will eventually result in the decline or even demise of the Security Commission, but early statements made by the Intelligence and Security Committee appeared to suggest its desire to take primacy in cases of overlap.[148] As mentioned above, the basis for the Security Commission's specification as a security body was not explained prior to the passage of the Freedom of Information Act 2000, but it can be observed that some of its reports have never been published, or at least not wholly.[149]

17– 022 NCIS and its Service Authority: abolition

NCIS and its Service Authority, together with the National Crime Squad and its Service Authority, were abolished and subsumed within SOCA with effect from 1 April 2006.[150] Both NCIS and its Service Authority nevertheless remain specified as 'security bodies' in s 23(3) of the Freedom of Information Act 2000. As with the defunct IOCA, SSA, and ISA Tribunals, the logic of this is that other public authorities may still hold information which was supplied to them by, or relates to, NCIS or its Service Authority.

17– 023 NCIS and its Service Authority: identities

NCIS was established in 1992 on a non-statutory basis as a common police service under the aegis of the Home Office before being placed on a statutory footing by the Police Act 1997 and becoming an executive non-departmental public body sponsored by the Home Office under

---

[145] FOIA s 84.

[146] See the Cabinet Office publications *Public Bodies 2009* (2009), p 17, annex A and *Cabinet Office Annual Report and Accounts 2008-2009*(HC 442, 2009) pp 105, 206. On non-departmental public bodies generally see also *Halsbury's Laws of England*, 4th edn, 1996 re-issue, vol 8(2), title 'Constitutional Law and Human Rights', paras 951–954. Since its creation in 1964, the Security Commission has conducted 18 separate inquiries to date including: Cmnd 2722, 1965 on Bossard and Allen; Cmnd 3151, 1966 on Squadron Leader Reen; Cmnd 3365, 1967 on Helen Keenan; Cmnd 3856, 1968 on Chief Technician Britten; Cmnd 3892, 1969 on Clive Bland; Cmnd 5367, 1973 on Earl Jellicoe and Lord Lambton; Cmnd 8235, 1981 on John Wagstaff; Cmnd 8540, 1982 on civil service security procedures; Cmnd 8876, 1983 on Geoffrey Prime; Cmnd 9212, 1984 on Lance Corporal Aldridge; Cmnd 9514, 1985 on Michael Bettaney; Cmnd 9923, 1986 on security in Static Signals Units; Cm 2930, 1995 on Michael Smith; Cm 4578, 2000 on Steven Hayden; Cm 6177, 2004 on Ryan Parry and the security of the Royal Household.

[147] See §17– 030(6).

[148] Intelligence and Security Committee Annual Report 1997–1998 (Cm 4073, 1998) para 59; Intelligence and Security Committee Annual Report 1998–1999 (Cm 4532, 1999) para 75.

[149] For example the report on Sir Roger Hollis: see Hansard HC vol 1 cols 1079–1085 (26 March 1981). In lieu of the report's publication, Cmnd 8540, 1982 was issued containing a summary of certain action taken in response to some of the recommendations contained in the report. A large part of the report on Michael Bettaney also remains unpublished (see Cmnd 9514, 1985).

[150] Serious Organised Crime and Police Act 2005 Pt 1.

the Criminal Justice and Police Act 2001.[151] The Police Act 1997 provided for the establishment of NCIS and its Service Authority (neither of which was listed as a 'public authority' in Sch 1 to the Freedom of Information Act 2000)[152] as well as the National Crime Squad and its Service Authority (which were both listed as 'public authorities' for these purposes).[153] The NCIS Service Authority had legal personality as a body corporate consisting of 11 members,[154] whilst NCIS itself was a body consisting of its Director General together with police and civilian members.[155]

024 NCIS and its Service Authority: functions

The NCIS Service Authority operated under a Chairman and was charged with maintaining NCIS which in turn had the following functions: (1) to gather, store and analyse information in order to provide criminal intelligence; (2) to provide criminal intelligence to police forces in Great Britain, the Police Service for Northern Ireland, the National Crime Squad and other law enforcement agencies; and (3) to act in support of those bodies carrying out their criminal intelligence activities.[156] In discharging its functions, the NCIS Service Authority was obliged to have regard to various objectives, targets, service plans, codes of practice and directions, ensure that NCIS was efficient and effective and to produce service plans and reports on an annual basis.[157] NCIS was itself under the direction and control of a Director General with the rank of chief constable who was appointed by the Home Secretary and who was obliged to have regard to the Service Authority's service plan in discharging his functions and to produce an annual report.[158]

---

[151] See Cabinet Office *Public Bodies 2006* (2006), p 242. In relation to NCIS and its Service Authority see: Police Act 1997, Pt I; Criminal Justice and Police Act 2001 Pt V. Relevant provisions repealed with effect from 1 April 2006 by the Serious Organised Crime and Police Act 2005 ss 59, 174(2), Sch 4, paras 94–95, 162, 166, Sch 17, Pt 2.

[152] It is plain that neither NCIS nor its Service Authority were meant to be 'public authorities' for the purposes of FOIA; contrast the approach taken to the similarly constituted National Crime Squad and its Service Authority which were both listed in FOIA Sch 1, Pt VI.

[153] In relation to the National Crime Squad and its Service Authority see: Police Act 1997 Pt II; Criminal Justice and Police Act 2001 Pt V; FOIA Sch 1, Pt VI. Relevant provisions repealed with effect from 1 April 2006 by the Serious Organised Crime and Police Act 2005 ss 59, 174(2), Sch 4, paras 94–96, 162, 166, Sch 17, Pt 2. The original proposal that a National Crime Squad be established in place of the previous Regional Crime Squads was made in House of Commons Home Affairs Select Committee Third Report Session 1994–1995 *Organised Crime* (HC 18–11) 1995. The National Crime Squad thereafter came into being under the Police Act 1997 on 1 April 1998, its principal function being to prevent and detect serious crime which was of relevance to more than one police area. Like NCIS, the National Crime Squad was also an executive non-departmental public body sponsored by the Home Office: see the Cabinet Office publication *Public Bodies 2006* (2006), p 241.

[154] Police Act 1997 ss 1, 46 and 90. Repealed by the Serious Organised Crime and Police Act 2005 ss 59, 174(2) Sch 4 paras 94–96, Sch 17 Pt 2.

[155] Police Act 1997 ss 2, 9, 46, 90. Repealed by the Serious Organised Crime and Police Act 2005 ss 59, 174(2) Sch 4 paras 94–96, Sch 17 Pt 2.

[156] Police Act 1997 ss 1, 2, 46 and 90. Repealed by the Serious Organised Crime and Police Act 2005 ss 59, 174(2) Sch 4, paras 94–96, Sch 17 Pt 2.

[157] Police Act 1997 ss 2–5. Repealed by the Serious Organised Crime and Police Act 2005 ss 59, 174(2) Sch 4 paras 94–95, Sch 17 Pt 2.

[158] Police Act 1997 ss 6 and 10–11. Repealed by the Serious Organised Crime and Police Act 2005 ss 59 174(2) Sch 4 paras 94–95, Sch 17 Pt 2.

17– 025 SOCA: identity

SOCA was established as a body corporate with effect from 1 April 2006.[159] It consists of a Board comprising a Chairman, a Director General and other members, who are all appointed by the Home Secretary, together with a capped number of internal *ex officio* members, themselves appointed by the Director General after consultation with the Chairman.[160] Although the Director General is appointed by the Home Secretary (following consultation with the Scottish Ministers and, in practice, the Northern Ireland Secretary) he maintains general operational control of SOCA on an independent basis.[161] SOCA has a nation wide remit operating across the United Kingdom as an executive non-departmental public body sponsored and funded by the Home Office.[162] SOCA is a civilian body, not a police force, and it does not act on behalf of the Crown.[163] Police officers, Revenue and Customs officers and immigration officers seconded to work at SOCA automatically lose any special powers they had in their previous capacities as such and the Director General then has power to confer such powers on individual members of staff (whether permanent or seconded) by designation according to the business needs of the Agency.[164] SOCA is not listed as a 'public authority' in Sch 1 to the Freedom of Information Act 2000.[165]

17– 026 SOCA: functions

SOCA not only replaced and assumed the functions of NCIS and the National Crime Squad, it also acquired certain functions of the Home Office and HM Revenue and Customs relating respectively to organised immigration crime and serious drug trafficking. SOCA's principal statutory functions are preventing and detecting serious organised crime and contributing to the reduction of such crime in other ways and to the mitigation of its consequences.[166] SOCA also acquired certain functions of the former Assets Recovery Agency in relation to the recovery of the proceeds of crime, with effect from 1 April 2008, and it absorbed the UK Human

---

[159] Serious Organised Crime and Police Act 2005 s 1 Sch 1. For the policy background, see: the Home Secretary's announcement at Hansard HC vol 417 cols 58–60WS (9 February 2004); the Home Office White Paper *One Step Ahead: A 21st Century Strategy to Defeat Organised Crime* (Cm 6167, 2004).

[160] Serious Organised Crime and Police Act 2005 Sch 1 paras 1, 8–9.

[161] Serious Organised Crime and Police Act 2005 s 21, Sch 1 para 9. The Security Service Act 1989 s 2(2)(c) (as amended) places a duty on the Director General of the Security Service to ensure that there are arrangements, agreed with the Director General of SOCA, for co-ordinating the activities of the Security Service in pursuance of the Security Service Act 1989 s 1(4) with the activities of police forces, SOCA and other law enforcement agencies. Prior to the amendment of this provision by the Serious Organised Crime and Police Act 2005 s 59 Sch 4 paras 55, 57, arrangements of this kind had to be agreed with the Director General of NCIS.

[162] SOCA, *SOCA Annual Plan 2010/11* (2010), pp 5, 7-8.

[163] Serious Organised Crime and Police Act 2005 s 179 Sch 1 para 20.

[164] Serious Organised Crime and Police Act 2005 ss 43–50.

[165] By confirming SOCA's status as a non-Crown body, Serious Organised Crime and Police Act 2005 s 179 Sch 1 para 20 precludes any argument to the effect that SOCA is a 'public authority' for the purposes of FOIA by virtue of its being a 'body or authority exercising statutory functions on behalf of the Crown' and therefore a 'government department' within the meaning of FOIA s 84, Sch 1, Pt I, para 1.

[166] Serious Organised Crime and Police Act 2005 s 2(1). There are limits on SOCA's power to act against revenue fraud or serious or complex fraud without the agreement of either HM Revenue and Customs or the Serious Fraud Office (s 2(3)–(4)).

Trafficking Centre, with effect from 1 April 2010.[167] It also has ancillary functions as to the gathering, storing, analysis, disclosure and dissemination of information relevant to the prevention, detection, investigation, prosecution and reduction of all crime (not just serious organised crime) and 'general powers' to institute criminal proceedings and act in support of other police forces and law enforcement agencies.[168] In exercising its functions SOCA is obliged to have regard to its own annual plan, priorities and targets together with strategic priorities and codes of practice issued by the Home Secretary and it must also publish an annual report.[169] In practical terms, SOCA is at least partially reliant on other police forces and law enforcement agencies for assistance and for the use and loan of staff, facilities, equipment, premises and services albeit that the provision of assistance may be mutual.[170] Given its remit, the inclusion of SOCA within s 23(3) of the Freedom of Information Act 2000 confers absolute exemption on types of information which were previously accessible under the Act through requests made to the National Crime Squad, Home Office and HM Revenue and Customs.

027 The security bodies: importance of secrecy

In *Attorney-General v Guardian Newspapers Ltd (No 2)* Lord Griffiths advanced the following basic proposition: 'The security and intelligence services are necessary for our national security. They are, and must remain, secret services if they are to operate efficiently.'[171] This proposition has three limbs: first, the implicit point that national security is itself an important public interest objective;[172] secondly, the recognition that operationally effective intelligence services (and other security bodies) are essential to the achievement and maintenance of this objective; and, thirdly, the more practical point that their effectiveness is in turn dependent upon secrecy.[173] This secrecy is said to be necessary because of the 'special nature'[174] of the functions of the principal security bodies outlined above. In this regard, the principal security bodies deal in intelligence and surveillance and counter-intelligence and counter-surveillance and they undertake covert and clandestine operations: their activities, capabilities, equipment, methods, operations, organisation, personnel, plans, procedures, sources, systems and techniques must

---

[167] Serious Organised Crime and Police Act 2005 s 2A and Proceeds of Crime Act 2002 ss 2A-2B. Relevant amendments and transfers of functions were made by and under the Serious Crime Act 2007. The UK Human Trafficking Centre is a non-statutory 'multi-agency centre' which was formerly sponsored by the Association of Chief Police Officers as part of the South Yorkshire Police.

[168] Serious Organised Crime and Police Act 2005 ss 3, 5, 32–36, 38.

[169] Serious Organised Crime and Police Act 2005 ss 4, 6–7, 9–10.

[170] Serious Organised Crime and Police Act 2005 ss 23–28.

[171] [1990] 1 AC 109 at 269, endorsed in *R v Shayler (David)* [2002] UKHL 11, [2003] 1 AC 247 at [25] (Lord Bingham). See also the reference to the Security Service needing to 'operate under and be protected by a cloak of secrecy' in *R v Shayler (David)* [2002] UKHL 11, [2003] 1 AC 247 at [98] (Lord Hutton).

[172] This is because national security, properly performed, provides part of the foundation for a stable and democratic society in which human rights are protected and may be enjoyed. It is a matter of historic record that some of what has been done in the name of national security, even by democratic nations, has been done to destabilise governments, including those democratically elected.

[173] It is important not to lose sight of the first of these limbs because the effectiveness and secrecy of the intelligence services are not simply ends in themselves, they are also means to the greater (but not ultimate) end of national security.

[174] *R v Shayler (David)* [2002] UKHL 11, [2003] 1 AC 247 at [36] (Lord Bingham).

therefore remain secret, otherwise their targets will be able to adopt evasive or counteractive measures.[175] The indisputable importance of secrecy is, however, tempered by the recognition that the security bodies are not immune from making mistakes, that such mistakes can have a profound and damaging impact on individuals, and that unrestricted secrecy is less likely to reveal such mistakes than some form of external disclosure.[176]

17– 028   The security bodies: maintenance of secrecy

For information to remain secret it must be accessible to only a limited number of people. Once information becomes 'generally accessible'[177] it loses the quality of confidence and ceases to be secret. At a very basic level, information supplied by, or relating to, the security bodies only needs to be kept secret to prevent its being exploited to the disadvantage of national security. However, despite the fact that the vast majority of the general public would have neither the desire nor the ability to exploit information of this kind in such a way, it will normally need to be kept secret from them in order to prevent it becoming accessible to those who might. Apart from the Freedom of Information Act 2000, the Data Protection Act 1998 and the Environmental Information Regulations 2004, various other statutory and non-statutory legal rules regulate the accessibility and disclosure of information supplied by, or relating to, the security bodies. These reflect a consistent approach by the courts, Parliament and the government to such issues and form the legal and policy background into which the relevant exemptions in the aforementioned enactments fit and must be understood. The most significant of these rules are mentioned in outline below:

 (1) *Criminal law.* In criminal terms, the Official Secrets Act 1989 makes it an offence for serving or former members of the security and intelligence services, other Crown servants,[178] and government contractors to disclose certain types of information,

---

[175] *R v Shayler (David)* [2002] UKHL 11, [2003] 1 AC 247 at [25], 'There is much domestic authority pointing to the need for a security or intelligence service to be secure. The commodity in which such a service deals is secret and confidential information. If the service is not secure those working against the interests of the state, whether terrorists, other criminals or foreign agents, will be alerted, and able to take evasive action; its own agents may be unmasked; members of the service will feel unable to rely on each other; those upon whom the service relies as sources of information will feel unable to rely on their identity remaining secret; and foreign countries will decline to entrust their own secrets to an insecure recipient' (Lord Bingham). See also the references in the same speech at [25]–[26] to: *AG v Guardian Newspapers Ltd (No 2)* [1990] 1 AC 109 at 118, 213–214, 259, 265 and 269; *AG v Blake* [2001] 1 AC 268 at 287; *Engel v The Netherlands (No 1)* (1979–80) 1 EHRR 647 (ECtHR) at [100]–[103]; *Klass v Federal Republic of Germany* (1979–80) 2 EHRR 214 (ECtHR) at [48]; *Leander v Sweden* (1987) 9 EHRR 433 (ECtHR) at [59]; *Hadjianastassiou v Greece* (1993) 16 EHRR 219 (ECtHR) at [45]–[47]; *Esbester v United Kingdom* (1994) 18 EHRR CD 72 (ECommHR) at [74]; *Brind v United Kingdom* (1994) 18 EHRR CD 76 (ECommHR) at [83]–[84]; *Murray v United Kingdom* (1995) 19 EHRR 193 (ECtHR) at [58]; *Vereniging Weekblad Bluf! v The Netherlands* (1995) 20 EHRR 189 (ECtHR) at [35], [40].

[176] The point need not be laboured with illustrations, but some of the resultant tensions between interests are explored by the High Court of Australia in *A v Hayden* [1984] HCA 67, (1984) 156 CLR 532.

[177] *AG v Guardian Newspapers Ltd (No 2)* [1990] 1 AC 109 at 282 (Lord Goff); *Barclays Bank plc v Guardian News & Media Ltd* [2009] EWHC 591 (QB).

[178] As discussed above, it is not thought that 'the security and intelligence services' means anything other than the three intelligence services: §17– 013. The expression 'Crown Servant' includes Ministers of the Crown, civil servants, members of the naval, military or air forces of the Crown and any constable and any other person employed or appointed in or for the purposes of SOCA (Official Secrets Act 1989 s 12(1)(a) and (c)–(e)). It also includes the Comptroller and Auditor General, the staff of the National Audit Office and the Parliamentary Commissioner for Administration (Official Secrets Act 1989 s 12(1)(g); Official Secrets Act 1989 (Prescription) Order 1990 SI 1990/200 sch 2.

documents or other articles without lawful authority.[179] Members of the security and intelligence services are thus prohibited from making any unauthorised disclosures of information, etc relating to security or intelligence.[180] Furthermore, all Crown servants and government contractors are prohibited from making 'damaging' unauthorised disclosures of information, etc relating to security or intelligence,[181] defence[182] or international relations.[183] There are also offences

[179] See generally: *Departmental Committee on Section 2 of the Official Secrets Act 1911, vols 1–4* (Cmd 5104, 1972) (The Franks Report); the Home Office White Paper *Reform of Section 2 of the Official Secrets Act 1911* (Cm 408, 1988); R Thomas, *Espionage and Secrecy: the Official Secrets Acts 1911–1989 of the United Kingdom* (London, Routledge, 1991); Palmer, 'The Government Proposals for Reforming Section 2 of the Official Secrets Act 1911' [1988] *Public Law* 523; Palmer, 'Tightening Secrecy Law: the Official Secrets Act 1989' [1990] *Public Law* 243; Bailin, 'The last Cold War Statute' (2008) 8 Crim LR 625. The ancillary offences provided for by the Official Secrets Act 1989 ss 5–6 and 8 and the other offences provided by the Official Secrets Act 1911 and 1920 are not dealt with further in this chapter, but see further *R v James (Daniel)* [2009] EWCA Crim 1261, [2010] 1 Cr App R (S) 57. The RIPA Tribunal can give 'official authorisations' and impose 'official restrictions' for the purposes of the Official Secrets Act 1989 (s 7(5)); Official Secrets Act 1989 (Prescription) Order 1990 SI 1990/200 sch 3. The IOCA, SSA and ISA Tribunals were formerly prescribed for the same purposes but replaced by the RIPA Tribunal under the Official Secrets Act 1989 (Prescription) (Amendment) Order 2003 SI 2003/1918 art 2(3), sch 2.

[180] Official Secrets Act 1989 s 1(1)–(2), (5) and (9). The information, document or article must be or have been in the person's possession by virtue of their position as a member of any of the security or intelligence services (s 1(1)). 'Security or intelligence' is defined to mean the work of, or in support of, the security and intelligence services or any part of them and references to information relating to security or intelligence are defined to include references to information held or transmitted by those services or by persons in support of them, or any part of them (s 1(9)). See *R v Shayler (David)* [2002] UKHL 11, [2003] 1 AC 247, confirming that Official Secrets Act 1989 s 1 is not incompatible with Convention rights.

[181] Official Secrets Act 1989 s 1(3)–(5), (9). The information, document or article must be or have been in the person's possession by virtue of their position as a Crown servant or government contractor (s 1(3)). 'Security or intelligence' and references to information relating to security or intelligence have the same meaning as in s 1(1)–(2) (s 1(9)). For the purposes of s 1(3) a disclosure is damaging if it causes damage to the work of, or any part of, the security and intelligence services or would be likely to cause such damage (s 1(4)).

[182] Official Secrets Act 1989 s 2. The information, document or article must be or have been in the person's possession by virtue of their position as a Crown servant or government contractor (s 2(1)). 'Defence' is defined to mean (a) the size, shape, organisation, logistics, order of battle, deployment, operations, state of readiness and training of the armed forces of the Crown, (b) the weapons, stores or other equipment of those forces and the invention, development, production and operation of such equipment and research relating to it, (c) defence policy and strategy and military planning and intelligence and (d) plans and measures for the maintenance of essential supplies and services that are or would be needed in time of war (s 2(4)). For the purposes of s 2(1) a disclosure is damaging if it (a) damages the capability of, or any part of, the armed forces of the Crown to carry out their tasks or leads to loss of life or injury to members of those forces or serious damage to the equipment or installations of those forces, (b) endangers the interests of the United Kingdom abroad, seriously obstructs the promotion or protection by the United Kingdom of those interests or endangers the safety of British citizens abroad or (c) would be likely to have any of those effects (s 2(2), see also s 3(2)). Serving members of the armed forces of the Crown are also subject to service discipline under the Naval Discipline Act 1957, Army Act 1955 and Air Force Act 1955 ('the Service Discipline Acts'), the Armed Forces Act 2006, the Queen's Regulations for the Royal Navy, Army and Royal Air Force and the Manuals of Naval, Military and Air Force Law which themselves restrict unauthorised disclosures of information.

[183] Official Secrets Act 1989 s 3. See *In re Times Newspapers Ltd* [2007] EWCA Crim 1926, [2008] 1 WLR 234; *R v Keogh (David)* [2007] EWCA Crim 528, [2007] 1 WLR 1500. The offence covers information, etc relating to international relations (s 3(1)(a)) and confidential information, etc obtained from a state other than the United Kingdom or an international organisation (s 3(1)(b)). The information, document or article must be or have been in the person's possession by virtue of his or her position as a Crown servant or government contractor (s 3(1)). 'International relations' are defined to mean the relations between states, between international organisations or between one or more states and one or more such organisations and includes any matter relating to a state other than the United Kingdom or to an international organisation which is capable of affecting the relations of the United Kingdom with another state or with an international organisation (s 3(5)). For the purposes of s 3(1) a disclosure is damaging if it (a) endangers the interests of the United Kingdom abroad, seriously obstructs the promotion or protection by the

prohibiting all Crown servants and government contractors from making unauthorised disclosures of information, etc which have or would be likely to have certain effects in relation to the commission, prevention or detection of offences or the apprehension, prosecution or detention of offenders[184] or which are connected with interceptions of communications under, or other actions authorised by, warrants under various statutes.[185]

(2)   *Civil law.* In civil law terms, actionable private law obligations not to disclose, without authority, information which is confidential to the Crown or which was acquired during the course of Crown service can arise at equity or common law under the general law of confidence,[186] contract[187] or fiduciary duties.[188] The Government can and does seek to enforce or vindicate such obligations through the pursuit of civil proceedings seeking any combination of injunctive relief, a declaration of right, an account of profits, damages, the delivery up or destruction of material and costs. Proceedings with similar objectives may also be brought to prevent or remedy infringements of intellectual property rights[189] or tortious

---

United Kingdom of those interests or endangers the safety of British citizens abroad or (b) would be likely to have any of those effects (s 3(2), see also s 2(2)(b)–(c)). In relation to the exemption under FOIA for international relations, see §§18– 001 to 18– 016.

[184] Official Secrets Act 1989 s 4(1)–(2) and (4)–(6).

[185] Official Secrets Act 1989 s 4(1) and (3)–(6). The statutes in question are the Interception of Communications Act 1985, the Security Service Act 1989, the Intelligence Services Act 1994 and the Regulation of Investigatory Powers Act 2000. See especially the Regulation of Investigatory Powers Act 2000 s 19 which makes it an offence for the heads of the intelligence services and SOCA, every person holding office under the Crown and every member of the staff of SOCA to disclose certain information about the interception of communications.

[186] For example, *AG v Guardian Newspapers Ltd (No 2)* [1990] 1 AC 109; *Lord Advocate v The Scotsman Publications Ltd* [1990] 1 AC 812; *The Observer & The Guardian v United Kingdom* (1991) 14 EHRR 153; *The Sunday Times v United Kingdom (No 2)* (1991) 14 EHRR 229; *AG v Shayler* [2006] EWHC 2285. It is also notable that the conventions governing the publication by former ministers of memoirs and other works relating to their experience as ministers (known as the 'Radcliffe Rules') provide that the consent of the Cabinet Secretary (with a right of appeal to the Prime Minister) is always required in relation to the publication of two categories of information, namely, information whose revelation would contravene the requirements of national security and information whose disclosure would be injurious to the United Kingdom's relations with other nations. See: the statement made to the House of Commons on behalf of the Prime Minister, Mr Attlee, by the Lord President of the Council, Mr Morrison, at Hansard HC vol 426 cols 1207–1208 (1 August 1946); the *Report of the Committee of Privy Counsellors [chaired by Lord Radcliffe] on Ministerial Memoirs* (Cmnd 6386, 1976) paras 79 and 91–92 produced following the 'Crossman Affair' and *AG v Jonathan Cape Ltd* [1976] QB 752; A Bradley and K Ewing, *Constitutional and Administrative Law*, 14th edn (London, Pearson Longman, 2007) pp 569–571; the reference to the Radcliffe Report in *Open Government Code of Practice on Access to Government Information: Guidance on Interpretation*, 2nd edn (1997) Pt II, para 2.3 in relation to the 'internal discussion and advice' exemption under that Code. The same restrictions apply, in relation to these two categories of information, to similar publications by former members of the Civil Service and Diplomatic Service under their respective Management Codes. See House of Commons, Public Administration Select Committee Tenth Report of Session 2008-09, *Leaks and Whistleblowing in Whitehall* (HC 83, 2009).

[187] For example '*R' v AG for England and Wales* [2003] UKPC 22, [2003] EMLR 499; *MoD v Griffin* [2008] EWHC 1542 (QB).

[188] For example *IDC Ltd v Cooley* [1972] 1 WLR 443; *Island Export Finance Ltd v Umunna* [1986] BCLC 460; *AG v Shayler* [2006] EWHC 2285; cf *AG v Blake* [1998] Ch 439 (CA) at 453–455 (Lord Woolf MR) (in relation to existence of fiduciary duties after service; a point not considered on appeal in *AG v Blake* [2001] 1 AC 268.

[189] For example under Copyright, Designs and Patents Act 1988 s 163; or on the grounds suggested in *AG v Guardian Newspapers Ltd (No 2)* [1990] 1 AC 109, Ch at 139–140 (Scott J) and HL at 263 (Lord Keith), 266 (Lord Brightman) and 275–276 (Lord Griffiths) and *Paragon Finance plc v Thakerar & Co* [1999] 1 All ER 400 (CA) at 409 (Millett LJ).

interferences with other civil law rights and obligations.[190] Lastly, the Government can and does bring ancillary proceedings for contempt of court against those who have breached or undermined the purpose of related court orders.[191]

(3) *Public law.* In public law terms, the Security Service Act 1989 and Intelligence Services Act 1994 put the head of each intelligence service under a duty to ensure that there are arrangements for securing that no information is obtained by his service except so far as necessary for the proper discharge of its functions or disclosed by it except so far as necessary for that purpose, in the interests of national security, for the prevention or detection of serious crime or for the purpose of any criminal proceedings.[192] The relevant provisions thus establish a statutory bar to the onward disclosure of security and defence information held by the intelligence services.[193] If and in so far as these provisions or the arrangements arrived at thereunder 'prohibit' other public authorities from disclosing the same information, s 44(1)(a) of the Freedom of Information Act 2000 confers a further absolute exemption on such information.[194]

(4) *Employment law.* In employment law terms, the 'whistle-blower' provisions inserted into the Employment Rights Act 1996[195] by the Public Interest Disclosure Act 1998 do not apply to employment for the purposes of the intelligence services or operate to protect disclosures which entail the commission of an offence under the Official

---

[190] For example A Dugdale and M Jones (eds), *Clerk and Lindsell On Torts*, 19th edn (London, Sweet & Maxwell, 2006) ch 25; Sales and Stilitz, 'Intentional Infliction of Harm by Unlawful Means' (1999) 115 *Law Quarterly Review* 411.

[191] *AG v Newspaper Publishing plc* [1988] Ch 333 (CA); *AG v Times Newspapers Ltd* [1992] 1 AC 191; *AG v Punch Ltd* [2002] UKHL 50, [2003] 1 AC 1046.

[192] Security Service Act 1989 s 2(2)(a) (in relation to the Security Service); Intelligence Services Act 1994 ss 2(2)(a) and 4(2)(a) (in relation to SIS and GCHQ respectively). See the *Second Report to Parliament on the Review of Legislation Governing the Disclosure of Information* (November 2002) referring to the Security Service Act 1989 s 2(2)(a) and the Intelligence Services Act 1994 ss 2(2)(a), 4(2)(a), 5(2)(c), 7(3)(c), 10(7). In relation to the latter set of provisions the report records that, '[T]he Foreign and Commonwealth Office, in consultation with the Home Office, considers that these provisions form an essential and integral part of the statutory governance of the Agencies and it is right that the provisions are retained within the primary legislation for that purpose. The Agencies are not covered by FOIA and therefore these items will be retained'. This report is in turn referred to in the report published under FOIA s 87(5) by the Lord Chancellor, *Freedom of Information Annual Report* (HC 6) 2002 s 5. See also Department for Constitutional Affairs *Review of Statutory Provisions on Disclosure* (2005), p 50 referred to in Department for Constitutional Affairs *Freedom of Information Annual Report 2005: Operation of the FOI Act in Central Government* (2006), p 13.

[193] The Interception of Communications Act 1985 s 6 provided, in similar terms, that the Secretary of State should make arrangements minimising the disclosure and use of intercepted material. In *R v Preston* [1994] 2 AC 130 it was held that the Interception of Communications Act 1985 ss 2 and 6 entirely prevented the disclosure of such material in criminal proceedings despite the fact that they did not impose prohibitions or criminal sanctions in connection with the making or observance of the relevant arrangements. See at 143 (Lord Jauncey) and 166, 168–169, 172 (Lord Mustill).

[194] FOIA ss 2(3)(h), 44(1)(a). The wording of the absolute exemption in FOIA s 23 means that this point is unlikely to have any practical significance in relation to that Act. However, it could have a potentially greater significance in relation to FOI(S)A which does not contain an exemption for information supplied by, or relating to, the security bodies equivalent to FOIA s 23 but which does confer an absolute exemption on information whose disclosure by a Scottish public authority is prohibited by or under an enactment (FOI(S)A ss 2(2)(b) and 26(a)). See further §17–008. EIR reg 5(6) provides that 'any enactment or rule of law which would prevent the disclosure of information in accordance with these Regulations shall not apply' and EI(S)R reg 5(3) is in similar terms.

[195] Employment Rights Act 1996, Pt IVA, ss 47B, 103A, 105(6A) and other provisions added by the Public Interest Disclosure Act 1998. These provisions protect workers from victimisation, dismissal and redundancy in the event that they make specified types of 'protected disclosures' relating to specified types of misconduct and malpractice.

Secrets Act 1989.[196] Section 202 of the Employment Rights Act 1996 also imposes more general restrictions on certain disclosures of information in the employment rights context which 'in the opinion of any Minister of the Crown' would be 'contrary to the interests of national security'.

(5) *Evidence, procedure and public interest immunity.* In evidential and procedural terms, it has long been recognised that public interest immunity[197] may be claimed to prevent the disclosure and inspection of documents, the asking of written and oral questions and the admission of evidence in criminal and civil proceedings and inquests and inquiries before courts and tribunals[198] where this would cause harm or damage to, inter alia, national security and defence interests.[199] The European Court of Human Rights has held that the exclusion of similar material from public law proceedings regarding the validity of certain decisions taken on national security grounds can constitute an unjustifiable interference with Convention rights

---

[196] Employment Rights Act 1996 ss 43B(3), 193. Those in Crown employment (including members of the intelligence services and the armed forces) are otherwise able to rely on the bulk of the employment rights conferred under that Act: see Employment Rights Act 1996 ss 191–193.

[197] See generally: *Conway v Rimmer* [1968] AC 910; *Balfour v Foreign Office* [1994] 1 WLR 681 (CA); *R v Chief Constable of the West Midlands Police, ex p Wiley* [1995] 1 AC 274; *R v H* [2004] UKHL 3, [2004] 2 AC 134; *R v McDonald* [2004] EWCA Crim 2614; *R (Mohamed) v Secretary of State for Foreign & Commonwealth Affairs (No. 1)* [2008] EWHC 2048 (Admin), [2009] 1 WLR 2579 (DC); *R (Al-Sweady) v Secretary of State for Defence* [2009] EWHC 1687 (Admin) (DC); *R(Mohamed) v Secretary of State for Foreign & Commonwealth Affairs* [2010] EWCA Civ 65. Crown Proceedings Act 1947 s 28; Criminal Procedure and Investigations Act 1996, ss 3(6), 14–16, 21(2); Criminal Procedure Rules 2010 SI 2010/60 Pt 22; CPR 31.19; H Woolf, J Jowell and A Le Suer, *De Smith's Judicial Review*, 6th edn, (London, Sweet & Maxwell, 2007) paras 8–006 to 8–014; W Wade and C Forsyth, *Administrative Law*, 10th edn (Oxford, Oxford University Press, 2009) pp 717–727; O Hood Phillips and P Jackson, *Constitutional and Administrative Law*, 8th edn (London, Sweet & Maxwell, 2001) paras 33–022 to 33–028; *Halsbury's Laws of England*, 4th edn, 2002 re-issue, vol 17(1), title 'Evidence', paras 436–440. Central government's current approach to public interest immunity issues is set out in identical statements made in both Houses of Parliament by the Lord Chancellor, Lord Mackay, and the Attorney-General, Sir Nicholas Lyell, on 18 December 1996: Hansard HC vol 287 cols 949–950 (18 December 1996) and Hansard HL vol 576 cols 1507–1508 (18 December 1996). These statements were made following a wide-ranging consultation exercise which itself followed the publication of the Scott Report (*Inquiry into the Export of Defence Equipment and Dual Use Goods to Iraq and Related Prosecutions* (HC 115) 1995–1996 and *R v Chief Constable of the West Midlands Police, ex p Wiley* [1995] 1 AC 274. The statements were accompanied by a detailed paper which was placed in the libraries of both Houses of Parliament and were endorsed by the incoming Labour administration in a written answer dated 11 July 1997: Hansard HC vol 297 cols 616–617 (11 July 1997). See M Supperstone and J Coppel, 'A New Approach to Public Interest Immunity' [1997] *Public Law* 211.

[198] The doctrine of public interest immunity applies to both criminal and civil proceedings but its application may differ according to the nature of the proceedings and the differing considerations involved (eg if the liberty of the subject is at stake): *R v Governor of Brixton Prison, ex p Osman* [1991] 1 WLR 281 (DC) at 287 (Mann LJ). Public interest immunity rulings in civil cases are therefore not necessarily of direct relevance in criminal cases where the public interest in disclosure may be stronger and where the abandonment of the prosecution always remains a fall-back option in circumstances where both disclosure and non-disclosure are deemed unacceptable. In relation to public inquiries, see now the Inquiries Act 2005 ss 19–21, 25(4)–(7).

[199] In terms of domestic law see: *Duncan v Cammell Laird & Co Ltd* [1942] AC 624; *Asiatic Petroleum Co Ltd v Anglo-Persian Oil Co Ltd* [1916] 1 KB 822 (CA); *Balfour v Foreign Office* [1994] 1 WLR 681 (CA); *R v H* [2004] UKHL 3, [2004] 2 AC 134. The European Court of Human Rights has endorsed public interest immunity claims upheld on such grounds in criminal proceedings provided the domestic courts exercise effective control and oversight: *Rowe and Davis v United Kingdom* (2000) 30 EHRR 1, 8 BHRC 325, [2000] Crim LR 584; *Jasper v United Kingdom* (2000) 30 EHRR 441, [2000] Crim LR 586; *Fitt v United Kingdom* (2000) 30 EHRR 480; *Edwards and Lewis v United Kingdom*, [2003] Crim LR 891, (2005) 40 EHRR 24, (2003) 15 BHRC 189. See also the Regulation of Investigatory Powers Act 2000 s 17 which prohibits the disclosure in legal proceedings of certain information about interceptions of communications.

including the right of effective access to justice under article 6 of the ECHR.[200] For this reason, a number of instruments now provide that documents and hearings dealing with sensitive material which must remain closed to parties in such proceedings should instead be handled by 'special advocates' who will act in the interests of those parties but who will not disclose that material to them.[201] It has further been suggested that the courts have an inherent discretionary power to request the appointment by the Attorney-General of, and to hear, special advocates on an extra-statutory basis in other proceedings.[202] Sensitive identities and information can also be protected in legal proceedings through mechanisms which do not involve complete non-disclosure such as: private hearings;[203] orders and directions prohibiting the collateral and onward use of disclosed materials;[204] orders or directions requiring witnesses to give evidence anonymously or screened from

---

[200] *Chahal v United Kingdom* (1997) 23 EHRR 413, 1 BHRC 40 (ECtHR); *Tinnelly and Sons Ltd v United Kingdom* (1999) 27 EHRR 249, 4 BHRC 393 (ECtHR); *Al-Nashif v Bulgaria* (2003) 36 EHRR 655 (ECtHR).

[201] An adjudicative process involving the use of closed material and special advocates is capable of being compatible with Convention rights under ECHR, arts 5(4), 6 and 13: *A v SSHD (No.1)* [2002] EWCA Civ 1502, [2004] 1 QB 335 (CA) at [57] (Lord Woolf CJ) (decision reversed by House of Lords but not on this point, see [2004] UKHL 56, [2005] 2 AC 68; *A v SSHD (No 2)* [2004] EWCA Civ 1123, [2005] 1 WLR 414 at [51]–[52] (Pill LJ) and [235] (Laws LJ) (detention certificate proceedings under the Anti-terrorism, Crime and Security Act 2001) (decision reversed by House of Lords but not on this point, see [2005] UKHL 71, [2006] 2 AC 221); *SSHD v MB* [2007] UKHL 46, [2008] 1 AC 440; *RB (Algeria) v SSHD* [2009] UKHL 10, [2009] 2 WLR 512; *A v United Kingdom* (2009) 49 EHRR 29 (EctHR); *SSHD v F* [2009] UKHL 28, [2009] 3 WLR 74. Provision is made for the appointment and appearance of special advocates in proceedings under: Special Immigration Appeals Commission Act 1997 and Special Immigration Appeals Commission (Procedure) Rules 2003 SI 2003/1034; Northern Ireland Act 1998 and Northern Ireland Act Tribunal (Procedure) Rules 1999 SI 1999/2131; Terrorism Act 2000 and Proscribed Organisations Appeal Commission (Procedure) Rules 2007 SI 2007/1286; Anti-terrorism, Crime and Security Act 2001 and Pathogens Access Appeal Commission (Procedure) Rules 2002 SI 2002/1845; Life Sentences (Northern Ireland) Order 2001 SI 2001/2564 (NI 2)) and Life Sentence Review Commissioners' Rules 2001 SRNI 2001/317; Employment Tribunals (Constitution and Rules of Procedure) Regulations 2004 SI 2004/1861 Schs 1–2 (see *Tariq v Home Office* [2010] ICR 223 (EAT)); Employment Appeal Tribunal Rules 1993 SI 1993/2854 as amended by Employment Appeal Tribunal (Amendment) Rules 2001 and 2004 SI 2001/1128 and SI 2004/2526; Prevention of Terrorism Act 2005 and CPR 76; Town and Country Planning Act 1990 s 321; Planning (Listed Buildings and Conservation Areas) Act 1990 Sch 3; Planning (Hazardous Substances) Act 1990 Sch 1; Counter-Terrorism Act 2008 and CPR 79; Constitutional Reform Act 2005 and Supreme Court Rules 2009 SI 2009/1603.

[202] *R v Shayler (David)* [2002] UKHL 11, [2003] 1 AC 247 at [34] (Lord Bingham) and [113] (Lord Hutton); *SSHD v Rehman* [2000] 3 WLR 1240 (CA) at [31]–[32] (Lord Woolf MR); *R v H* [2004] UKHL 3, [2004] 2 AC 134; *R (Roberts) v Parole Board* [2005] UKHL 45, [2005] 2 AC 738; *R (Malik) v Manchester Crown Court* [2008] EWHC 1362 (Admin), [2008] 4 All ER 403 (DC); *Campaign against the Arms Trade v IC and MoJ*, IT, 26 August 2008; *MH v SSHD* [2009] EWCA Civ 287, [2009] 1 WLR 2049; *Al Rawi v Security Service* [2009] EWHC 2959 (QB); Ip, 'The Rise and Spread of the Special Advocate, [2008] *Public Law* 717 .

[203] For example Administration of Justice Act 1960 s 12(1)(c); Official Secrets Act 1920 s 8(4); Criminal Justice Act 1988 s 159(1); Official Secrets Act 1989 s 11(4); Criminal Procedure Rules 2010 SI 2010/60 Pts 16.10 and 69; Coroners Rules 1984 SI 1984/552 r 17; CPR 39.2(3), CPR PD 39.1 see esp CPR 39.2(3)(b) 'a hearing, or any part of it, may be in private if it involves matters relating to national security'. See *R v Shayler (David)* [2003] EWCA Crim 2218, [2003] ACD 327 (CA) at [18]–[22] (Kennedy LJ); *In re A* [2006] EWCA Crim 4, [2006] 1 WLR 1361 (CA); *R (Malik) v Central Criminal Court* [2006] EWHC 1539 (Admin), [2006] 4 All ER 1141 (DC).

[204] Criminal Procedure and Investigations Act 1996, ss 17–18; Criminal Procedure Rules 2010 SI 2010/60 Pt 22; CPR 18.2, 31.22, 32.12; *Davies (Joy Rosalie) v Eli Lilly & Co (No 1)* [1987] 1 WLR 428 (CA) at 431–432 (Lord Donaldson MR).

public view;[205] and reporting restrictions.[206]

17– 029   The security bodies: the rationale for institutional exclusion

So far as concerns the treatment of the security bodies in the Freedom of Information Act 2000, the key issue is whether and why the legitimate preservation of their secrecy should be pursued by absolute rather than qualified means: that is to say, does the need for secrecy require or justify the institutional exclusion of the security bodies from the regime of the Act and the absolute exemption of all information supplied by, or relating to, them irrespective of whether its disclosure might harm those bodies or national security?   Many of the judicial pronouncements regarding the intelligence services and the importance of, and relationship between, their effectiveness and secrecy have been made in connection with decisions reviewing and affirming the need for a 'brightline rule' prohibiting all unauthorised disclosures by their members and former members.[207]   Certain aspects of the rationale for this rule are not relevant in the freedom of information context, however, as disclosures under access to information legislation are not unauthorised and, provided they are controlled by reference to an adequate harm or prejudice test, they should not run the risk of damaging the trust of others in, or the morale of, the intelligence services.[208]   Moreover, it is well established that there are occasions when government can and should consider and authorise the disclosure of information supplied by, or relating to, security bodies.   Such occasions may arise in relation to: the disclosure and inspection of documents in legal proceedings and the application of the doctrine of public interest immunity;[209] requests for authorisation to publish memoirs and books relating to service with the principal security bodies;[210] and the disclosure of information to, and the inclusion of

---

[205] For example CPR 39.2(4), PD 39.1; *R v Lord Saville of Newdigate, ex p A* [2000] 1 WLR 1855, [1999] 4 All ER 860, [1999] COD 436 (CA); *R v Shayler (David)* [2003] EWCA Crim 2218, [2003] ACD 79 (CA) (permission to appeal) at [10]–[17] (Kennedy LJ); *R v Davis* [2006] EWCA Crim 1155, [2006] 1 WLR 3130,; *R (Bennett) v HM Coroner for Inner South London* [2004] EWCA Civ 1439, [2005] UKHRR 44 (CA); *R v HM Coroner for Newcastle Upon Tyne, ex p A* (1998) *The Times*, 19 January 1998; *Re Ministry of Defence's Application* [1994] NI 279 (CA) (NI); *Doorson v The Netherlands* (1996) 22 EHRR 330 (ECtHR); *X v United Kingdom* (1993) 15 EHRR CD 113 (EcommHR); *In re Officer* [2007] UKHL 36, [2007] 1 WLR 2125; *In re Times Newspapers Ltd* [2008] EWCA Crim 2396, [2009] 1 WLR 1015.

[206] For example Administration of Justice Act 1960 s 12; Contempt of Court Act 1981, ss 4 and 11.

[207] *AG v Guardian Newspapers Ltd* [1990] 1 AC 109 at 269 (Lord Griffiths). Cited with approval in: *Lord Advocate v The Scotsman Publications Ltd* [1990] 1 AC 812 at 828 (Lord Jauncey); *AG v Blake* [2001] 1 AC 268 (Lord Nicholls); *R v Shayler (David)* [2002] UKHL 11, [2003] 1 AC 247 at [25] and [36] (Lord Bingham). See also: *The Observer & The Guardian v United Kingdom* (1991) 14 EHRR 153; *The Sunday Times v United Kingdom (No 2)* (1991) 14 EHRR 229; *AG v Shayler* [2006] EWHC 2285. A categorical or 'brightline' rule against unauthorised disclosures is imposed by the Official Secrets Act 1989 s 1 (on members of the intelligence services) and the general law of confidence (on members of the intelligence services and, arguably, others in a similar position). Membership of 'the intelligence services' is not necessarily an essential or exclusive pre-condition in this regard: note the reference to 'members or former members of those services who have had access to information relating to national security' in *R v Shayler (David)* [2002] UKHL 11, [2003] 1 AC 247 at [68] (Lord Hope).

[208] *AG v Blake* [2001] 1 AC 268 at 287 (Lord Nicholls); *R v Shayler (David)* [2002] UKHL 11, [2003] 1 AC 247 at [100] (Lord Hutton); *AG v Shayler* [2006] EWHC 2285.

[209] See §17– 028(5).

[210] For example S Rimington, *Open Secret: The Autobiography of the Former Director General of MI5* (Hutchinson, London, 2001). Refusals of authorisation to publish are judicially reviewable see: *AG v Guardian Newspapers Ltd (No 2)* [1990] 1 AC 109 at 163 (Scott J, Ch); *R v Shayler (David)* [2002] UKHL 11, [2003] 1 AC 247 at [31]–[35] (Lord Bingham) at [72]–[85] (Lord Hope) and at [107]–[116] (Lord Hutton); *'R' v AG for England and Wales* [2003] UKPC 22, [2003] EMLR 499 at [36] (Lord Hoffmann); *AG v Shayler* [2006] EWHC 2285; *R (A) v Director of Establishments of the Security Service* [2009] UKSC 12, [2010] 2 WLR 1.

material in the published versions of reports produced by, oversight bodies.[211] There would appear to be two main justifications for taking an absolutist approach to secrecy in the freedom of information context:

(1) *Mosaic prejudice.* First is the contention that any disclosure of information supplied by, or relating to, security bodies is necessarily harmful because it will contribute pieces to a public domain 'mosaic' or 'jigsaw' of information about those bodies. This argument gives rise to the theory that such disclosures cause 'mosaic prejudice' because apparently innocuous information connected with security and intelligence matters can prove to be acutely revealing when read in conjunction with other pieces of the mosaic or when used as the basis for deductions and inferences about gaps in the picture.[212] Most of the domestic judicial dicta dealing with the dangers of mosaic prejudice have arisen in relation to the need for the brightline rule mentioned above and have stressed the particular risks run by individuals who attempt to assess for themselves how an intended disclosure will add to the public mosaic.[213] It could therefore be argued that the force of these dicta diminishes in the freedom of information context, where decisions to disclose can be taken by or in consultation with the security bodies.[214] Against this, a pre-

---

[211] See §17– 030(2), (3) and (6).

[212] See §§15– 024 to 15– 025 for a general discussion of 'mosaic prejudice'. The Government certainly regarded mosaic prejudice as a live issue when it published the consultation paper *Freedom of Information: Consultation on Draft Legislation* (Cm 4355, 1999). As mentioned above, cl 19(3) of the draft Bill annexed to this paper contained an express 'jigsaw puzzle' exemption which would have ensured the non-disclosure of apparently harmless information which might be harmful when looked at in conjunction with other pieces of the wider puzzle: 'Where, in relation to any information ("the information requested"), exemption from section 8(1)(b)–(a) is not required for the purpose of safeguarding national security, but (b) would be required for that purpose if any other information (whether or not held by the public authority and whether or not accessible, or likely to become accessible, to members of the public) became available at the same time or subsequently, the exemption shall be taken for the purposes of this section to be required for that purpose in relation to the information requested'. This draft provision was criticised for being too broad (eg House of Lords Draft Freedom of Information Bill Select Committee First Report Session 1998–1999, *Report from the Select Committee Appointed to Consider the Draft Freedom of Information Bill* (HL 97) 1999, paras 36–37: see ch 1 n 125) and was not repeated in the Freedom of Information Bill introduced in the House of Commons on 18 November 1999.

[213] In relation to unauthorised disclosures see: *AG v Guardian Newspapers Ltd (No 2)* [1990] 1 AC 109 at 269, 'What may appear to the writer to be trivial may in fact be the one missing piece in the jigsaw sought by some hostile intelligence agency' (Lord Griffiths); *R v Shayler (David)* [2002] UKHL 11, [2003] 1 AC 247 at [101], 'such a decision [ie whether a disclosure would or would not be damaging] could not safely be left to that individual because he may not have a full appreciation of how that piece of information fits into a wider picture and of what effect the disclosure might have on other aspects of the work of the service of which he is unaware or of which he lacks a full appreciation' (Lord Hutton).

[214] The courts in the US and Australia have usually endorsed the mosaic approach to prejudice in relation to national security exemption claims in the freedom of information context. Because the security bodies in the US (eg the CIA) do not enjoy the institutional exclusion enjoyed by their UK counterparts under the FOIA, 'mosaic prejudice' has been accepted by the courts in a way that secures a similar result to institutional exclusion. Because the absolute exclusion of security bodies has been otherwise secured in the UK, it is suggested that caution must be exercised before transposing the principles and reasoning of US decisions on 'mosaic prejudice' to information held by public authorities in the UK. The standard authorities on 'mosaic prejudice' in the US are: *Halperin v CIA*, 629 F 2d 144, 150 (DC Cir 1980) ('each individual piece of intelligence information, much like a piece of a jigsaw puzzle, may aid in piecing together other bits of information even when the individual piece is not of obvious importance in itself'); *Salisbury v United States*, 690 F 2d 966, 971 (DC Cir 1982) (referring to the 'mosaic-like nature of intelligence gathering'); *American Friends Services Committee v Department of Defense*, 831 F 2d 441, 444–45 (3d Cir 1987) ('compilation' theory); *Taylor v Department of the Army*, 684 F 2d 99, 105 (DC Cir 1982); *National Security Archive v FBI*, 759 F Supp 872, 877 (DDC 1991) (held that disclosure of code names and designator phrases could provide a hostile intelligence analyst with a 'common denominator' permitting the analyst to piece together seemingly unrelated data into a snapshot of specific FBI counter-intelligence activity); *Jan-Xin Zang v FBI*, 756 F Supp 705, 709–10 (WDNY 1991)

disclosure assessment and authorisation process might not entail a particularly effective use of time and resources within the security bodies and it would not provide total immunity from mosaic prejudice in any event. While the security bodies can evaluate the pieces of the mosaic they know to be in the public domain and the extent to which a particular disclosure would add to the overall publicly accessible picture, they cannot know every piece of information held by hostile forces and individuals (which may not be in the public domain but may make the proposed disclosure more damaging) and they cannot predict the subsequent emergence of further pieces of information which will elucidate the picture even further.

(2)   *Countervailing human rights.* A more defensive argument in support of the absolutist approach takes the need for secrecy and the risk of mosaic prejudice as its starting point before asserting that there is no human rights based reason for taking a more qualified approach. The need to act compatibly with 'Convention rights' within the meaning of the Human Rights Act 1998[215] or rights under European Community law that can be relied upon before the domestic courts,[216] may require that disclosures of information are

---

(upholding classification of any source-identifying word or phrase, which could by itself or in aggregate lead to disclosure of an intelligence source); *Berman v CIA*, 378 F Supp 2d 1209 at 1215–1217 and 1222 (ED Cal 2005); *Edmonds v US Department of Justice*, 405 F Supp 2d 23, 33 (DDC 2005), holding that the mosaic theory 'comports with the legal framework'; *American Civil Liberties Union v Department of Justice*, 321 F Supp 2d 24, 37 (DDC 2004) where, in holding that the Department of Justice could withhold statistical intelligence-collection data, the court commented that 'even aggregate data is revealing', and concluded that disclosure 'could permit hostile governments to accurately evaluate the FBI's counterintelligence capabilities'; *Bassiouni v CIA*, 392 F 3d 244, 246 (7th Cir 2004) ('when a pattern of responses itself reveals classified information, the only way to keep secrets is to maintain silence uniformly'); *Centrer for National Security Studies v US Department of Justice*, 331 F 3d 918, 928 (DC cir 2003) ('[a] complete list of names informing terrorists of every suspect detained by the government at any point during the September 11 investigation' could 'allow terrorists to better evade the ongoing investigation and more easily formulate or revise counter-efforts.' Mosaic prejudice is also now recognised in the USA by Executive Order 12,958 (as amended), para 1.7(e). In relation to Australia see: *Re Low and Department of Defence* (1984) 2 AAR 142 at 149; *Re Actors' Equity Association of Australia and Australian Broadcasting Tribunal (No 2)* (1985) 7 ALD 584; *Re Robinson and Department of Foreign Affairs* (1986) 11 ALN N48; *Re Throssell and Australian Archives* (1986) 10 ALD 403 at 406–407; *Re Throssell and Department of Foreign Affairs* (1987) 14 ALD 296; *Re Slater and Cox (Director General, Australian Archives)* (1988) 15 ALD 20 at 27; *Re McKnight v Australian Archives* (1992) 28 ALD 95 at 112; *Re Ewer and Australian Archives* (1995) 38 ALD 789; *Re Dunn and Department of Defence* [2004] AATA 1040. A mechanical application or an unquestioning acceptance of all claims of mosaic prejudice will, of course, emasculate the rights given by FOIA. See Pozen, 'The Mosaic Theory, National Security and the Freedom of Information Act' (2005) 115 *Yale LJ* 628.

[215] Human Rights Act 1998 s 1(1)–(3), Sch 1 define 'the Convention rights' for the purposes of that Act as the rights and fundamental freedoms set out in arts 2–12 and 14 of the Convention for the Protection of Human Rights and Fundamental Freedoms (Cmd 8969, 1953) ('ECHR') and arts 1–3 of the First Protocol and arts 1–2 of the Sixth Protocol thereto. The ECHR, arts 1 and 13 are notable omissions from 'the Convention rights'. Primary and subordinate legislation must, so far as possible, be read and given effect in a way which is compatible with the Convention rights (s 3) and it is unlawful for public authorities (including courts and tribunals) to act in a way which is incompatible with them unless left with no alternative by primary legislation (s 6).

[216] In this regard, reliance can be placed on Community law in accordance with the doctrine of direct effect including the subsidiary or related doctrines of vertical, indirect and incidental direct effect: P Craig and G De Búrca, *EU Law: Text, Cases and Materials*, 4th edn (London, Oxford University Press, 2007) chs 8–9; D Wyatt and A Dashwood, *European Union Law*, 5th edn (London, Sweet & Maxwell, 2002) ch 5. In particular, the doctrine of incidental direct effect requires that national law implementing Directives is interpreted and applied in accordance with Community law and norms and is therefore relevant to DPA (implementing European Community Data Protection Directive 95/46/EC) and EIR (implementing European Community Public Access to Environmental Information Directive 2003/4/EC): Case 14/83 *Von Colson v Land Nordrhein-Westfalen* [1984] ECR 1891; Case C–106/89 *Marleasing SA v La Comercial Internacional de Alimentacion SA* [1990] ECR I–4135; Cases C–240–244/98 *Océano Grupo Editorial v Rocio Murciano Quintero* [2000] ECR I–4491; Craig 'Directives: Direct Effect, Indirect Effect and the Construction of National Legislation' (1997) 22 EL Rev 519. In relation to the interpretation of DPA see in particular: *Campbell v MGN Ltd* [2002] EWCA Civ 1373, [2003] QB 633 at [96] (Phillips MR); *Durant v Financial Services Authority* [2003]

considered by reference to a harm or prejudice test where such rights are in play. In this way, the following are capable of requiring a public authority to allow or authorise the disclosure of information: the right to life under article 2 of the ECHR;[217] the right to a fair trial under article 6 of the ECHR;[218] the right to respect for private and family life under article 8 of the ECHR;[219] Community rights under the European Community Data Protection Directive 95/46/EC;[220] and the right to freedom of expression under article 10 of the ECHR.[221] Although none of these rights is absolute and each of them may have to give way to the requirements of national security,[222] their engagement effectively requires that the competing interests involved be weighed against each other before a final decision is taken on disclosure. The engagement of these rights thus precludes the adoption of an absolutist approach to secrecy and requires that non-disclosure be supported by some evidence of the harm that disclosure would cause.[223] When it comes to general requests for information under the Freedom of Information Act 2000, however, there are unlikely to be any countervailing rights in play as neither the ECHR nor Community law confers a general right of access to information; an absolutist approach may therefore be seen as less objectionable.[224] It should also be remembered that in

---

EWCA Civ 1746, [2004] FSR 28 at [3]–[4] (Auld LJ); *R (Lord) v SSHD* [2003] EWHC 2073 (Admin) at [83] (Munby J); *R (SSHD) v IT* [2006] EWHC 2958 (Admin), [2007] 2 All ER 703 (DC) at [15] (Latham LJ).

[217] *Öneryildiz v Turkey* (2004) 39 EHRR 12 (ECtHR) at [84]; affirmed at (2005) 41 EHRR 20 (ECtHR) (GC) at [62], [90].

[218] *R (S) v Plymouth City Council* [2002] EWCA Civ 388, [2002] 1 WLR 2583; *McGinley and Egan v United Kingdom* (1998) 27 EHRR 1 (ECtHR).

[219] *Gaskin v United Kingdom* (1989) 12 EHRR 36 (ECtHR) at [60]; Botta*Botta v Italy* (1998) 26 EHRR 241 (ECtHR); *Guerra v Italy* (1998) 26 EHRR 357 (ECtHR) at [60]; *McGinley and Egan v United Kingdom* (1998) 27 EHRR 1, 4 BHRC 421, (1998) 42 BMLR 123 (ECtHR) at [101] and [103]; *R (S) v Plymouth City Council* [2002] EWCA Civ 388, [2002] 1 WLR 2583, [2002] 1 FLR 1177, [2002] BLGR 565; *MG v United Kingdom* [2002] 3 FCR 289, (2003) 36 EHRR 3 (ECtHR); *Craxi v Italy (No1)* (2004) 28 EHRR 47 (ECtHR); *Roche v United Kingdom* (2006) 42 EHRR 30 (ECtHR).

[220] [1995] OJ L281/31. Indeed, the connection between rights to privacy (including under the ECHR art 8) and data protection is strongly emphasised throughout the recitals to the European Community Data Protection Directive 95/46/EC (see esp recitals (1)–(3), (7) and (9)–(11)) and in art 1. The importance of countervailing rights favouring disclosure in the DPA context has been emphasised by the Information Tribunal in *Baker v SSHD* [2001] UKHRR 1275 at [50]–[64] and *Gosling v SSHD*, IT, 1 August 2003 at [48]. The engagement of countervailing rights and the limited scope for security and defence exemptions under the Data Protection Directive no doubt explain the absence of any institutional exclusion for the security bodies in DPA. See further §§5– 004 to 5– 008 and 5– 057.

[221] See n 210 in connection with requests for authority to publish service memoirs by former members of the security bodies.

[222] In relation to ECHR art 6 see: *Fayed v United Kingdom* (1994) 18 EHRR 393 (ECtHR) at [65]–[67]; *Tinnelly and Sons Ltd v United Kingdom* (1999) 27 EHRR 249, 4 BHRC 393 (ECtHR) at [74]; *Lithgow v United Kingdom* (1986) 8 EHRR 329 (ECtHR) at [194]. In relation to ECHR, arts 8 and 10 see: ECHR, arts 8(2) and 10(2). In relation to personal data rights see: European Community Data Protection Directive 95/46/EC ([1995] OJ L281/31), recital (16) and art 13(1)(a)–(c); DPA s 28. See further ch 3.

[223] Establishing a real risk of mosaic prejudice may or may not suffice in this regard, but there is no automatic presumption that it will and each case must be dealt with on its merits.

[224] Although the right to freedom of expression under ECHR art 10 includes 'the right to receive and impart information and ideas without interference', it has been consistently held not to confer or entail a general right of access to information: *R (Persey) v Secretary of State for the Environment, Food and Rural Affairs* [2002] EWHC 371 (Admin), [2003] QB 794 (DC) at [52]–[53] (Simon Brown LJ); *R (Howard) v Secretary of State for Health (Note)* [2002] EWHC 396 (Admin), [2003] QB 830 at [103] (Scott Baker J); *Leander v Sweden* (1987) 9 EHRR 433 (ECtHR); *Gaskin v United Kingdom* (1989) 12 EHRR 36, [1990] 1 FLR 167 (ECtHR); *Guerra v Italy* (1998) 26 EHRR 357 (ECtHR); *BBC, Petitioners (No 2)* 2000 JC 521; *cf R (Wagstaff) v Secretary of State for Health* [2001] 1 WLR 292 (DC). Compare Sir

circumstances where countervailing rights operate in other contexts to require the disclosure of information supplied by, or relating to, the security bodies, it may nevertheless be possible to restrict the number of people to whom that information is disclosed, thus minimising the risk of mosaic prejudice;[225] such measures cannot be taken under the Freedom of Information Act 2000.[226]

17– 030 **The security bodies: accountability and supervision**

Having set out the high level of secrecy conferred on the security bodies, the wider institutional and constitutional context in which they operate needs to be understood. This context will help determine the practical consequences of the security bodies' exclusion from the Freedom of Information Act 2000 regime in terms of the effect it has on other public authorities and the accessibility of information more generally. The extent to which the security bodies are subject to authorities and mechanisms allowing for the oversight and regulation of their work is also critical to an evaluation of two interdependent issues: first, the effectiveness and transparency of their public accountability and, secondly, the justifiability of their institutional exclusion from the Freedom of Information Act 2000 regime. In terms of the ancillary security bodies, the RIPA, IOCA, SSA and ISA Tribunals, the Security Vetting Appeals Panel and the Security Commission are themselves oversight bodies, whilst SOCA is subject to the complaints and misconduct regime operated by the Independent Police Complaints Commission.[227] In terms of the principal security bodies, an amount of accountability and supervision is provided by some of the ancillary security bodies, as has already been mentioned, together with (1) the Comptroller and Auditor General and National Audit Office, (2) the Intelligence Services Commissioner, (3) the Interception of Communications Commissioner, (4) the Parliamentary Commissioner for Administration and, in more limited circumstances, (5) the Privy Council. In addition to this, (6) the Intelligence and Security Committee and (7) the various Cabinet Office Committees have an oversight role in relation to the intelligence services.[228] A brief outline of the functions of the seven additional oversight bodies follows:

(1) *The Comptroller and Auditor General.* The National Audit Office is listed as a 'public authority' in Part VI of Sch 1 to the Freedom of Information Act 2000 and it supervises, and therefore holds information about, the security bodies and their

---

Stephen Sedley, 'Information as a Human Right' in J Beatson and Y Cripps (eds), *Freedom of Expression and Freedom of Information: Essays in Honour of Sir David Williams* (Oxford, Oxford University Press, 2000). See ch 3.

[225] Even where the disclosure of confidential information is required on public interest grounds, the courts recognise that this does not necessarily extend to publication to the world at large and may be limited to the police or appropriate regulators: *AG v Guardian Newspapers Ltd (No 2)* [1990] 1 AC 109 at 269 (Lord Griffiths) and 283 (Lord Goff); *Francome v MGN Ltd* [1984] 1 WLR 892; *Re a Company's Application* [1989] Ch 477. *cf Initial Services Ltd v Putterill* [1968] 1 QB 396 at 405–406; *Lion Laboratories Ltd v Evans* [1985] QB 526; *Barrymore v News Group Newspapers Ltd* [1997] FSR 600 at 603; *London Regional Transport v Mayor of London* [2001] EWCA Civ 1491, [2003] EMLR 4. See also §17– 028(5) on the restrictions that may be placed on the collateral and onward use of materials disclosed in legal proceedings.

[226] See §§15– 027 to 15– 028.

[227] Police Reform Act 2002 Pt 2.

[228] The special forces are not subject to any equivalent Committees or Commissions, although the House of Commons Defence Select Committee examines the expenditure, administration and policy of the Ministry of Defence: HC Standing Order, No 152 *Departmental Evidence and Response to Select Committees* (1999); A Bradley and K Ewing, *Constitutional and Administrative Law*, 14th edn (London, Pearson Longman, 2007) pp 218–221; O Hood Phillips and P Jackson, *Constitutional and Administrative Law*, 8th edn (London, Sweet & Maxwell, 2001) paras 12–029 to 12–033.

sponsoring departments.[229] Since 1994 the government has brought forward in a single published vote, known as the Single Intelligence Account, the aggregate expenditure and budget provision for the intelligence services in a form that is 'fully open to scrutiny by the Comptroller and Auditor General, apart from limited restrictions to protect the identities of certain sources of information and the details of particularly sensitive operations'.[230] The Single Intelligence Account is decided by Ministers through the biennial Spending Review mechanism and has the Cabinet Secretary as its Accounting Officer.[231] The total allocation for the intelligence services is made known to Parliament and the public, but the details (including the apportionment to each service) are only revealed to the Comptroller and Auditor General, the Intelligence and Security Committee and the Chairman of the House of Commons Public Account Committee.[232]

(2) *The Intelligence Services Commissioner.* The Regulation of Investigatory Powers Act 2000 established a new combined Intelligence Services Commissioner in place of the former Security Service Commissioner and Intelligence Services Commissioner created under the Security Service Act 1989 and Intelligence Services Act 1994 respectively.[233] The Intelligence Services Commissioner is not listed as a 'public authority' in Sch 1 to the Freedom of Information Act 2000. The Intelligence Services Commissioner is appointed by the Prime Minister to keep under review, so far as they are not required to be kept under review by the Interception of Communications Commissioner, the exercise and performance by the relevant Secretaries of State, the intelligence services, the Ministry of Defence and the armed

[229] National Audit Act 1983; *Halsbury's Laws of England*, 4th edn, 1996 re-issue, vol 8(2), title 'Constitutional Law and Human Rights', paras 716–717, 720 and 724–726; A Bradley and K Ewing, *Constitutional and Administrative Law*, 14th edn (London, Pearson Longman, 2007) pp 374–376; O Hood Phillips and P Jackson, *Constitutional and Administrative Law*, 8th edn (London, Sweet & Maxwell, 2001) paras 12–018 to 12–019.

[230] Hansard HC vol 233 col 52 (24 November 1993) (written answer by the Prime Minister, Mr Major, to a Parliamentary Question tabled by Mr Robinson). See: A Bradley and K Ewing, *Constitutional and Administrative Law*, 14th edn (London, Pearson Longman, 2007) pp 375–376 and 600; Cabinet Office, *National Intelligence Machinery*, 4th edn (London, TSO, 2006) p 5.

[231] The Cabinet Secretary acted as Accounting Officer until 1 August 2002 when the role was transferred to the newly created Cabinet Office Security and Intelligence Co-ordinator. This post was renamed 'Permanent Secretary, Intelligence, Security and Resilience', and merged with the Chairmanship of the Joint Intelligence Committee with effect from the appointment to both positions of Sir Richard Mottram on 14 November 2005 (Cabinet Office, *National Intelligence Machinery*, 4th edn (London, TSO, 2006) p 22; *Intelligence and Security Committee Annual Report 2005–2006* (Cm 6864, 2006) paras 7–12). However, the Cabinet Secretary resumed responsibility for the Single Intelligence Account in 2007 when the functions of the Permanent Secretary, Intelligence, Security and Resilience were split between a separate Chairman of the Joint Intelligence Committee and Head of Intelligence Assessment, on the one hand, and a Security Adviser to the Prime Minister and Cabinet Secretary known as the Head of Intelligence, Security and Resilience, on the other; Intelligence and Security Committee Annual Report 2006-2007 (Cm 7299, 2008) paras 73-74; Intelligence and Security Committee Annual Report 2007-2009 (Cm 7542, 2009) paras 129-133.

[232] Intelligence and Security Committee, *Intelligence Oversight* (London, 2002), p 8; Cabinet Office, *National Intelligence Machinery*, 4th edn (London, TSO, 2006) pp 5–6. Security Service Act 1989 s 2(3A)(b) permits the disclosure of information by the Security Service to the Comptroller and Auditor General. Intelligence Services Act 1994 ss 2(3)(b) and 4(3)(b) permit the disclosure of information by SIS and GCHQ respectively to the Comptroller and Auditor General.

[233] Regulation of Investigatory Powers Act 2000 ss 59–60. Security Service Act 1989 s 4 (establishing the Security Service Commissioner) and Intelligence Services Act 1994 s 8 (establishing the Intelligence Services Commissioner) were repealed by the Regulation of Investigatory Powers Act 2000 ss 59(8) and 82(2), Sch 5.

forces of various functions relating to the issue of warrants authorising directed and intrusive surveillance, interferences with property and the use of covert human intelligence sources.[234] Those involved are obliged to provide the Intelligence Services Commissioner with all the information he needs and the Commissioner is in turn required to assist the RIPA Tribunal and report to the Prime Minister on particular subjects from time to time and provide him with annual reports which are presented to Parliament and published.[235]

(3) *The Interception of Communications Commissioner.* The Regulation of Investigatory Powers Act 2000 established a new Interception of Communications Commissioner in place of the identically named Commissioner established under the Interception of Communications Act 1985.[236] The Interception of Communications Commissioner is not listed as a 'public authority' in Sch 1 to the Freedom of Information Act 2000. The Commissioner is appointed by the Prime Minister and his functions are to review the Secretary of State's role in authorising interception warrants, the operation of the regime for acquiring communications data, any notices requiring the decryption of data authorised by the Secretary of State and the adequacy of the arrangements made by the Secretary of State for the protection of intercepted material.[237] All persons involved in requesting, authorising or carrying out interception are required to co-operate with the Interception of Communications Commissioner and provide him with any information he needs.[238] The Commissioner in turn reports to the Prime Minister on particular subjects from time to time and provides him with annual reports which are presented to Parliament and published.[239]

(4) *The Parliamentary Commissioner for Administration.* The Parliamentary Commissioner for Administration[240] has a limited role to play in relation to the oversight of the security bodies: none of the security bodies is directly subject to his investigative remit (save for SOCA which may only be investigated in respect of the exercise of

---

[234] Regulation of Investigatory Powers Act 2000 s 59; Cabinet Office, *National Intelligence Machinery*, 4th edn (London, TSO, 2006) p 32.

[235] Regulation of Investigatory Powers Act 2000 ss 59(3) and 60. The published reports omit any matter whose publication would be contrary to the public interest or prejudicial to national security and other related interests.

[236] Regulation of Investigating Powers Act 2000 ss 57–58 (replacing the Interception of Communications Commissioner established under the Interception of Communications Act 1985 s 8; see the Regulation of Investigatory Powers Act 2000 s 57(8)). See also Regulation of Investigatory Powers Act 2000 s 61 in relation to the Investigatory Powers Commissioner for Northern Ireland.

[237] Regulation of Investigatory Powers Act 2000 s 57; Cabinet Office, *National Intelligence Machinery*, 4th edn (London, TSO, 2006) p 32.

[238] Regulation of Investigatory Powers Act 2000 s 58.

[239] Regulation of Investigation Powers Act 2000 s 58(4)–(7). The published reports omit any matter whose publication would be contrary to the public interest or prejudicial to national security and other related interests.

[240] Parliamentary Commissioner Act 1967; A Bradley and K Ewing, *Constitutional and Administrative Law*, 14th edn (London, Pearson Longman, 2007) pp 715–724; O Hood Phillips and P Jackson, *Constitutional and Administrative Law*, 8th edn (London, Sweet & Maxwell, 2001) paras 34–005 to 34–014.

certain asset recovery functions);[241] and, although their sponsoring departments are subject to such investigation,[242] various security and defence related matters are nevertheless excluded.[243] As a 'public authority' listed in Part VI of Sch 1 to the Freedom of Information Act 2000, the Parliamentary Commissioner for Administration may be asked to disclose information, but his ability to do so will be subject to the exemptions in Part II of that Act and the provisions on onward disclosure in s 11 of the Parliamentary Commissioner Act 1967.[244] The Parliamentary Commissioner for Administration may also exchange certain types of information with the Information Commissioner[245] and provide him with information which relates to certain matters within the Information Commissioner's remit or the commission of certain offences under the Freedom of Information Act 2000 or the Data Protection Act 1998.[246]

---

[241] Save for SOCA, none of the security bodies is listed as a government department, corporation or unincorporated body subject to investigation by the Commissioner in the Parliamentary Commissioner Act 1967, Sch 2 and it follows that action taken by or on behalf of the security bodies in the exercise of their administrative functions cannot be investigated under the Parliamentary Commissioner Act 1967 s 5. In relation to the limited coverage of SOCA, see Parliamentary Commissioner Act 1967 Sch 2 n 12.

[242] Parliamentary Commissioner Act 1967 Sch 2. The list includes the Cabinet Office (not including any of the Secretariats (including intelligence and security functions carried out by the Chairman of the Joint Intelligence Committee and the Prime Minister's Security Adviser respectively) or the office of the Secretary of the Cabinet and Head of the Home Civil Service: Parliamentary Commissioner Act 1967, Sch 2, n 3), Foreign and Commonwealth Office, Home Office and Ministry of Defence (including the Defence Council, Admiralty Board, Army Board and Air Force Board: Parliamentary Commissioner Act 1967 Sch 2, n 14).

[243] Parliamentary Commissioner Act 1967 s 5, Sch 4, paras 1–5. The Parliamentary Commissioner Act 1967 s 11(3) does envisage the Commissioner having access to documents or information whose disclosure might be prejudicial to the safety of the State or otherwise contrary to the public interest and if he did investigate or obtain security or defence information he could, in theory, disclose it to others but only for certain specified purposes (including the purposes of the investigation in question and of any report to be made thereon) and subject also to any notices in writing given by a Minister of the Crown specifying documents or information or classes of documents or information whose disclosure would, in the opinion of the Minister, be prejudicial to the safety of the State or otherwise contrary to the public interest (s 11(2)–(3)).

[244] These provisions effectively prevent the disclosure under FOIA of any information obtained by the Parliamentary Commissioner for Administration in the course of or for the purposes of an investigation under the Parliamentary Commissioner Act 1967. See also FOIA s 44. The provisions on ministerial notices in Parliamentary Commissioner Act 1967 s 11(3) do not apply in relation to disclosures made by the Parliamentary Commissioner for Administration under FOIA, as they only operate to prevent the Parliamentary Commissioner Act 1967 from being construed as authorising or requiring the disclosure of any document or information specified in a relevant notice. This is unlikely to be significant, however, as FOIA, Pt II and Parliamentary Commissioner Act 1967 s 11(2) will almost inevitably prevent the disclosure of any information that might have been covered by a ministerial notice under Parliamentary Commissioner Act 1967 s 11(3).

[245] FOIA s 76(1) (disclosure by the Information Commissioner) and Parliamentary Commissioner Act 1967 s 11AA (disclosure by the Parliamentary Commissioner for Administration) (inserted by FOIA Sch 7 para 2). The Information Commissioner may disclose to the Parliamentary Commissioner for Administration information obtained by, or furnished to, him under or for the purposes of FOIA or DPA if it appears to him to relate to a matter which could be the subject of an investigation by the Parliamentary Commissioner for Administration (FOIA s 76(1)). Information obtained by the Parliamentary Commissioner for Administration by virtue of this provision is nevertheless subject to Parliamentary Commissioner Act 1967 s 11(2)–(3) on onward disclosure and ministerial notices: Parliamentary Commissioner Act 1967 s 11(5), inserted by FOIA Sch 7 para 1.

[246] Parliamentary Commissioner Act 1967 s 11AA (inserted by FOIA Sch 7 para 2). The disclosure of information by the Parliamentary Commissioner for Administration under this provision is nevertheless subject to Parliamentary Commissioner Act 1967 s 11(3) on ministerial notices (Parliamentary Commissioner Act 1967 s 11AA(2)). While such disclosure need not be made for a purpose specified in Parliamentary Commissioner Act 1967 s 11(2), a Minister of the Crown may prevent it by giving the Parliamentary Commissioner for Administration notice in

(5)   *The Privy Council.* Issues of constitutional importance, including issues connected with security and defence matters, are sometimes referred to ad hoc committees of the Privy Council for advice. In this way, public service security arrangements,[247] the legal basis for and practice relating to telephone tapping,[248] government policy towards the Falkland Islands prior to Argentina's invasion in 1982[249] and intelligence on weapons of mass destruction[250] have been reviewed by such committees. One reason for referring such matters to the Privy Council is that Privy Counsellors take an oath on appointment binding them not to disclose anything said or done 'in Council' without the consent of the Sovereign and sensitive information can therefore be disclosed to them on 'Privy Counsellor terms'.[251] A further reason is that committees of the Privy Council can be political and yet non-partisan and can also examine the work of past administrations.[252] It would appear that the Privy Council is not a 'public authority' for the purposes of the Freedom of Information Act 2000.[253]

(6)   *The Intelligence and Security Committee.* The Intelligence and Security Committee was established under the Intelligence Services Act 1994 to examine the expenditure, administration and policy of the intelligence services.[254] In practice, the Committee

---

writing under Parliamentary Commissioner Act 1967 s 11(3) that disclosure would, in his or her opinion, be prejudicial to the safety of the State or otherwise contrary to the public interest (see also FOIA s 44).

[247] A committee, convened in the aftermath of the Burgess and Maclean defections, was in fact referred to as a conference of Privy Counsellors. For the background see Hansard HC vol 545 col 1609 (7 November 1955) and Hansard HC vol 546 col 1462 (23 November1955). Its report was not published, but a summary was made public (Cmnd 9715, 1956).

[248] *Report of the Privy Councillors appointed to inquire into the interception of communications* (Cmnd 283, 1957) (Birkett Report).

[249] *Falkland Islands Review: Report of a Committee of Privy Counsellors* (Cmnd 8787, 1983). The Prime Minister, Mrs Thatcher, consulted five former Prime Ministers to secure their consent to the committee on Falkland Islands policy having access to the papers of previous governments and secret intelligence assessments. See: A Bradley and K Ewing, *Constitutional and Administrative Law*, 14th edn (London, Pearson Longman, 2007) p 254; Lord Hunt, 'Access to a Previous Government's Papers' [1982] *Public Law* 514; Hansard HC vol 26 col 1039 (1 July 1982); Hansard HC vol 27 col 469 (8 July 1982).

[250] *Review of Intelligence on Weapons of Mass Destruction* (HC 898) 2004 (Butler Report).

[251] *Halsbury's Laws of England*, 4th edn, 1996 re-issue, vol 8(2), title 'Constitutional Law and Human Rights', para 523; A Bradley and K Ewing, *Constitutional and Administrative Law*, 14th edn (London, Pearson Longman, 2007) pp 253–254; O Hood Phillips and P Jackson, *Constitutional and Administrative Law*, 8th edn (London, Sweet & Maxwell, 2001) para 16-003.

[252] I Leigh and L Lustgarten, 'The Security Commission: Constitutional Achievement or Curiosity' [1991] *Public Law* 215 at 216.

[253] The Privy Council is not listed in FOIA Sch 1 and it cannot easily be described as a 'body or authority exercising statutory functions on behalf of the Crown' and thus a 'government department' for the purposes of s 84, Sch 1, Pt I, para 1. However, the Privy Council Office which, under the Lord President of the Council, is responsible for preparing business for the Privy Council and its committees has been described as, to a certain extent, 'a real administrative department': *Halsbury's Laws of England*, 4th edn, 1996 re-issue, vol 8(2), title 'Constitutional Law and Human Rights', para 526. See also §17– 012, n 80 on the 'immunity' of certain Crown bodies from the provisions of FOIA.

[254] Intelligence Services Act 1994 s 10(1), Sch 3. The Intelligence and Security Committee published a guide to its work: *Intelligence Oversight* (London, 2002), and it has a website: www.cabinet-office.gov.uk/intelligence. See also: *Halsbury's Laws of England*, 4th edn, 1996 re-issue, vol 8(2), title 'Constitutional Law and Human Rights', para 475; A Bradley and K Ewing, *Constitutional and Administrative Law*, 14th edn (London, Pearson Longman, 2007) pp 624–625; Cabinet Office, *National Intelligence Machinery*, 4th edn (London, TSO, 2006) pp 30–31.

has also 'developed its oversight remit' to take in the work of the Joint Intelligence Committee and the Cabinet Office Joint Intelligence and Security Secretariat and to allow it to consider evidence provided by the Defence Intelligence Staff.[255] The Committee operates within the so-called 'ring of secrecy', which means that the members of the Committee and its Secretariat are formally notified that they are subject to the provisions of s 1 of the Official Secrets Act 1989.[256] The Committee makes an annual report on the discharge of the functions of the intelligence services to the Prime Minister and may at any time report to him on any matter relating to the discharge of those functions.[257] The Prime Minister then publishes the annual reports by laying a copy before each House of Parliament,[258] although he may exclude from the published report any matter whose publication would be prejudicial to the continued discharge of the functions of the intelligence services.[259] The Committee is given access to information unless it is 'sensitive' or the Secretary of State has determined that it appears to him to be of such a nature that it would not be disclosed to a Departmental Select Committee.[260] The Committee is not a Parliamentary Select Committee as such, but it consists of nine members of Parliament drawn from both Houses of Parliament who are not Ministers of the Crown and who are appointed by the Prime Minister, after consultation with the Leader of the Opposition, on a cross-party basis.[261] Since June 1999, the Committee have also had their own Investigator whom they can deploy to pursue

---

[255] *Intelligence and Security Committee Annual Report 2005–2006* (Cm 6864, 2006) preface, para 1.

[256] Official Secrets Act 1989 s 1(1)(b) and (6)–(8). This was confirmed by the Foreign Secretary, Mr Hurd, at the press conference on publication of the Intelligence Services Bill on 23 November 1993 and the Chancellor of the Duchy of Lancaster, Mr Waldegrave, subsequently told the House of Commons 'The Committee will be fully trusted, and fully inside the secret wall' Hansard HC vol 238 col 240 (22 February 1994). See: Wadham, 'The Intelligence Services Act 1994' (1994) 57 *Modern Law Review* 916, pp 926–927; *Intelligence and Security Committee Interim Report 1994–1995* (Cm 2873, 1995); A Bradley and K Ewing, *Constitutional and Administrative Law*, 14th edn (London, Pearson Longman, 2007) p 624; Cabinet Office, *National Intelligence Machinery*, 4th edn (London, TSO, 2006) p 30; *Intelligence and Security Committee Annual Report 2005–2006* (Cm 6864, 2006) preface, para 3.

[257] Intelligence Services Act 1994 s 10(5).

[258] Intelligence Services Act 1994 s 10(6). In practice, at least some of the non-annual reports on specific subjects are also published in the same way.

[259] Intelligence Services Act 1994 s 10(6)–(7).

[260] Intelligence Services Act 1994 Sch 3, para 3. 'Sensitive information' is defined by Sch 3 para 4 as (a) information which might lead to the identification of, or provide details of, sources of information, other assistance or operational methods available to the intelligence services, (b) information about particular operations which have been, are being or are being proposed to be undertaken in pursuance of any of the functions of those bodies and (c) information provided by, or by an agency of, the Government of a territory outside the United Kingdom where that Government does not consent to the disclosure of the information. Such information may still be disclosed to the Committee if the head of the relevant intelligence service considers it safe to do so or the Secretary of State considers it desirable in the public interest (Sch 3 para 3(2)–(3)). The bases on which information may be withheld from Select Committees are set out in the Cabinet Office Memorandum expressing the 'Osmotherly Rules' in *Departmental Evidence and Response to Select Committees* (1999); see esp paras 80–87 which allow for the provision to Select Committees of 'sensitive information, including that carrying a protective security marking', on the basis that it will not be published and will be treated in confidence.

[261] Intelligence Services Act 1994 s 10(2)–(3). The Committee has been described as 'a committee of Parliamentarians, but emphatically not a committee of Parliament' in Liaison Committee (ie the Committee of Parliamentary Select Committee Chairmen) *Shifting the Balance: Select Committees and the Executive* (HC 300) 1999–2000, para 90.

specific matters in greater detail.[262] The Committee was given 'an enhanced scrutiny and public role' and its appointments process was made more akin to that of a Select Committee pursuant to the non-statutory reforms implemented in 2009.[263] The Foreign and Home Secretaries have both signed a certificate under s 28 of the Data Protection Act 1998 in relation to personal data processed by the Intelligence and Security Committee and its Secretariat.[264] The Committee is not listed as a 'public authority' in Sch 1 to the Freedom of Information Act 2000.

(7)   *Cabinet Office Committees.* Previous editions of this work referred at this point to a Ministerial Committee on the Intelligence Services chaired by the Prime Minister, which comprised the Deputy Prime Minister, the Defence, Foreign and Home Secretaries and the Chancellor of the Exchequer and had the following terms of reference: 'to keep under review policy on the security and intelligence services'.[265] This Ministerial Committee was itself assisted by a Permanent Secretaries' Committee on the Intelligence Services, which was chaired by the Cabinet Office Permanent Secretary, Intelligence, Security and Resilience, and which provided advice periodically on intelligence collection requirements, the intelligence services' programmes and expenditure and other issues related to intelligence.[266] The non-statutory management and supervision by central government, particularly the Cabinet Office, of the intelligence services and matters of 'intelligence policy' has since undergone significant administrative reform. There is now a Ministerial Committee on National Security, International Relations and Development with an Intelligence Sub-Committee (comprising the Prime Minister, Chancellor of the Exchequer and Foreign, Home and Defence Secretaries) and a corresponding Permanent Secretaries' Committee and Sub-Committee at official level. These are in turn supported by a National Security Secretariat and a Security and Intelligence Directorate within the Cabinet (itself established in 2007).[267] None of these

---

[262] The introduction of an Investigator was proposed by the Intelligence and Security Committee (see *Intelligence and Security Committee Annual Report 1997–1998* (Cm 4073, 1998) para 69 and *Intelligence and Security Committee Annual Report 1998–1999* (Cm 4532, 1999) paras 84–86) and accepted by the government subject to arrangements set out by the Prime Minister in *Government Response to the Intelligence and Security Committee's Annual Report 1998–1999* (Cm 4569, 2000) para 34. See also Intelligence and Security Committee, *Intelligence Oversight* (London, 2002) p 9.

[263] HM Government Green Paper, *The Governance of Britain* (CM 7170, 2007) para 93; MoJ, White Paper, *The Governance of Britain – Constitutional Renewal* (Cm 7342, 2008) Pt I, paras 235-244; *Intelligence and Security Committee Annual Report 2007-2008* (Cm 7542, 2009) paras 9-15; Resolution of the House of Commons and New Standing Order, Hansard HC vol 479 cols 501-502 (17 July 2008).

[264] *Intelligence and Security Committee Annual Report 2001–2002* (Cm 5542, 2002) paras 49–50 and Appendix 2.

[265] Cabinet Office, *National Intelligence Machinery*, 4th edn (London, TSO, 2006) p 17.

[266] Cabinet Office, *National Intelligence Machinery*, 4th edn (London, TSO, 2006) p 18. The Cabinet Secretary acted as Chairman of the Committee until 1 August 2002, when the duty was transferred to the newly created Cabinet Office Security and Intelligence Co-ordinator. This post was renamed Permanent Secretary, Intelligence, Security and Resilience and merged with the Chairmanship of the Joint Intelligence Committee with effect from the appointment to both positions of Sir Richard Mottram on 14 November 2005 (Cabinet Office, *National Intelligence Machinery*, 4th edn (London, TSO, 2006) p 22; *Intelligence and Security Committee Annual Report 2005–2006* (Cm 6864, 2006) paras 7–12).

[267] Cabinet Office, *The National Security Strategy of the United Kingdom: Security in an Interdependent World* (CM 7291, 2008); Cabinet Office, *The National Security Strategy of the United Kingdom: Update 2009: Security for the Next Generation* (CM 7590, 2009), Cabinet Office, *Improving the Central Intelligence Machinery* (2009) paras 35-36, Annex 1.

Committees is excluded from the Freedom of Information Act 2000 regime (they would appear to be parts of the Cabinet Office, which is a public authority for the purposes of Sch 1 to that Act)[268] and their practical importance is difficult to judge.

031 Other parts of the national intelligence machinery

One notable feature of the approach taken to the security bodies is the omission from the list specified in s 23(3) of the Freedom of Information Act 2000 of two other bodies which undoubtedly deal with security matters and which complete the government's 'national intelligence machinery',[269] namely, the Defence Intelligence Staff ('DIS') and the Joint Intelligence Committee ('JIC'):[270]

(1) *The Defence Intelligence Staff.* In the official government publication *National Intelligence Machinery* the DIS is dealt with under the heading, 'the intelligence and security agencies', but treated not as an additional intelligence service as such, but as 'an essential element' of the national intelligence machinery.[271] The DIS is a part of the Ministry of Defence funded out of the Defence Votes that was created in 1964 by the amalgamation of the Navy, Army and Air Force intelligence staffs and the civilian Joint Intelligence Bureau.[272] The DIS does not have any statutory basis or identity but its tasks are to analyse information, from both overt and covert sources, and to provide intelligence assessments, advice and strategic warning to the JIC, the Ministry of Defence, military commands and deployed forces.[273] The DIS also has responsibility for two separate organisations, Defence Geospatial Intelligence and the Defence Intelligence and Security Centre, which are responsible for providing imagery, geographic products and intelligence training.[274] The Defence Secretary is responsible for the DIS and its operations are controlled by the Chief of Defence Intelligence who reports to the Chief of the Defence Staff and the Permanent Secretary of the Ministry of Defence and who is also a Deputy Chairman of the

---

[268] FOIA s 84, Sch 1, Pt 1, para 1. See also FOIA s 35(4) on 'committees of the Cabinet'.

[269] *Intelligence and Security Committee Annual Report 1999–2000* (Cm 4897, 2000) paras 17–23; *Government Response to the Intelligence and Security Committee's Annual Report 1999–2000* (Cm 5013, 2000) paras 5–9; Cabinet Office, *National Intelligence Machinery* (4th edn, TSO, London, 2006); *Intelligence and Security Committee Annual Report 2001–2002* (Cm 5542, 2002) paras 8–12.

[270] For these purposes, references to the JIC should be read as a compendious short-hand for the entirety of the central intelligence machinery within the Cabinet Office which comprises the JIC itself, the Chairman of the JIC and Head of Intelligence Assessment, and their supporting staff.

[271] Cabinet Office, *National Intelligence Machinery*, 4th edn (London, TSO, 2006) pp 14–15. See: Ministry of Defence, *The Defence Intelligence Staff* (2005); *Inquiry into the Export of Defence Equipment and Dual Use Goods to Iraq and Related Prosecutions* (HC 115) 1995–1996, para C2.26 (Scott Report); A Bradley and K Ewing, *Constitutional and Administrative Law*, 14th edn (London, Pearson Longman, 2007) pp 603–604. See also the information on the Ministry of Defence website: www.mod.uk/DefenceInternet/AboutDefence/WhatWeDo/SecurityandIntelligence/DIS.

[272] Cabinet Office, *National Intelligence Machinery*, 4th edn (London, TSO, 2006) p 14. This followed the enactment of the Defence (Transfer of Functions) Act 1964 and the creation of a unified Secretary of State for Defence and Ministry of Defence: *Halsbury's Laws of England*, 4th edn, 1996 re-issue, vol 8(2), title 'Constitutional Law and Human Rights', paras 439–447.

[273] Cabinet Office, *National Intelligence Machinery*, 4th edn, (London, TSO, 2006) p 14.

[274] Cabinet Office, *National Intelligence Machinery*, 4th edn, (London, TSO, 2006) p 14; Ministry of Defence, *The Defence Intelligence Staff* (2005), p 6.

JIC.[275]

(2)   *The Joint Intelligence Committee.* The JIC is a part of the Cabinet Office which also has no statutory basis or identity.[276] The JIC is chaired by a Chairman who is also the Head of Intelligence Assessment and it comprises: senior officials in the Foreign and Commonwealth Office, Home Office, Ministry of Defence, Department of Business, Innovation & Skills, and HM Treasury; the heads of the intelligence services; and its Deputy Chairman, the Chief of Defence Intelligence.[277] The JIC is designed to bring an overall coherence to the tasking of the intelligence services, the assessment of their product and the determination of their resource needs and performance.[278] To this end, the JIC has two main functions, first, it produces assessments using secret intelligence and open-source material for ministers and officials and, secondly, it establishes the Government's requirements and priorities for secret intelligence. The JIC thus advises on priorities for intelligence gathering and provides ministers and senior officials with assessments of the resulting intelligence in the fields of security, defence and foreign affairs and is supported by the Assessments Staff.[279]

Neither the DIS nor the JIC is listed as a 'public authority' in Sch 1 to the Freedom of Information Act 2000 but, as already mentioned, they are parts of the Ministry of Defence and Cabinet Office respectively which are both 'public authorities' for these purposes.[280] It follows that neither the DIS nor the JIC is institutionally excluded from the Freedom of Information

---

[275] Cabinet Office, *National Intelligence Machinery*, 2nd edn (London, HMSO, 2001) pp 11–12.

[276] Parliamentary Commissioner Act 1967 Sch 2 n 2 formally acknowledges the existence of the Joint Intelligence Committee in providing that the Cabinet Office does not include, for the purposes of its being a department subject to investigation by the Parliamentary Commissioner for Administration, 'any of the Secretariats (including the intelligence and security functions carried out by the Chairman of the Joint Intelligence Committee and the Prime Minister's Security Adviser, respectively) or the office of the Secretary of the Cabinet and Head of the Home Civil Service': revised wording substituted by Parliamentary Commissioner Order 2008 SI 2008/3115 Sch 2 with effect from 12 November 2009.

[277] Cabinet Office, *National Intelligence Machinery*, 4th edn, (London, TSO, 2006) p 23.

[278] Cabinet Office, *National Intelligence Machinery*, 4th edn, (London, TSO, 2006) pp 23–27 and 37–39; *Review of Intelligence on Weapons of Mass Destruction* (HC 898) 2004 (Butler Report); *Review of Intelligence on Weapons of Mass Destruction: Implementation of its Conclusions* (Cm 6492, 2005); Hansard HC vol 432 col 432 (23 March 2005).

[279] The JIC's full terms of reference were revised in October 2009 in light of Cabinet Office, *Improving the Central Intelligence Machinery* (2009) (and related reforms) and now reads as follows: 'The role of the Joint Intelligence Committee is: To assess events and situations relating to external affairs, defence, terrorism, major international criminal activity, scientific, technical and international economic matters and other transnational issues, drawing on secret intelligence, diplomatic reporting and open source material; To monitor and give early warning of the development of direct and indirect threats and opportunities in those fields to British interests or policies and to the international community as a whole; To keep under review threats to security at home and overseas and to deal with such security problems as may be referred to it; To contribute to the formulation of statements of the requirements and priorities for intelligence gathering and other tasks to be conducted by the Intelligence Agencies; To maintain oversight of the intelligence community's analytical capability through the Professional Head of Intelligence Analysis; To maintain liaison with Commonwealth and foreign intelligence organisations as appropriate, and to consider the extent to which its product can be made available to them. Members of the Committee are to bring to the attention of their Ministers and Departments, as appropriate, assessments that appear to require operational, planning or policy action. The Chairman is specifically charged with ensuring that the Committee's monitoring and warning role is discharged effectively. The Committee may constitute such permanent and temporary sub-committees and working parties as may be required to fulfil its responsibilities.'

[280] They are both 'government departments' within FOIA s 84 and Sch 1 Pt I para 1.

Act 2000 regime.

032 The SCOPE information technology programme

According to the Intelligence and Security Committee's annual report for 2005–2006:

> SCOPE is a major IT programme designed to enable organisations across the intelligence community to improve fundamentally the way they work together, by transferring data electronically in a secure and timely manner. SCOPE has ten departmental and agency partners who contribute to its costs and share oversight of its development. The programme is directed and managed by the Cabinet Office, while support services will be provided from two locations outside London.[281]

The 'partners' referred to are the three intelligence services, SOCA and six government departments which are listed as 'public authorities' in Sch 1 to the Freedom of Information Act 2000, namely, the Cabinet Office, the Department of Trade and Industry, the Foreign and Commonwealth Office, the Home Office, HM Revenue and Customs and the Ministry of Defence.[282] Before becoming operational, the SCOPE system was hailed as marking 'the beginning of the end of hard copy intelligence distribution.'[283] However, its future is now in question: 'Phase 1' of its delivery was implemented in late 2007 but 'Phase 2' was then abandoned in April 2008 and the Intelligence and Security Committee has since refrained from reporting further on its fate due to a 'contractual dispute process.'[284] If 'Phase 1' of SCOPE achieved any lasting practical effects or if 'Phase 2' is ever implemented, questions may therefore arise whether a departmental partner 'holds' information on the system for the purposes of s 1 of the Freedom of Information Act 2000 and, if so, whether this was supplied by, or relates to, any of the security bodies for the purposes of s 23.

3. INFORMATION SUPPLIED BY, OR RELATING TO, THE SECURITY BODIES

033 Terms of the exemption in section 23 of the Freedom of Information Act 2000

As already indicated, information held by a public authority which was directly or indirectly supplied to it by, or which relates to, a security body is subject to an absolute exemption under

---

[281] *Intelligence and Security Committee Annual Report 2005–2006* (Cm 6864, 2006) para 82. The Committee has also said the following about SCOPE: 'This ambitious programme, which is aimed at fundamentally changing the way the UK Intelligence Community interacts through the introduction of a secure web-based information system, links the 10 main producers and consumers of intelligence' (*Intelligence and Security Committee Annual Report 2004–2005* (Cm 6510, 2005) para 70); 'The SCOPE programme will build on the current messaging system, the UK Intelligence Messaging Network (UKIMN), as well as delivering additional functionality, such as shared databases and the ability of the intelligence community to work across organisational boundaries' (*Intelligence and Security Committee Annual Report 2003–2004* (Cm 6240, 2004) para 116). See also *Intelligence and Security Committee Annual Report 2002–2003* (Cm 5837, 2003) paras 63–65.

[282] *Intelligence and Security Committee Annual Report 2005–2006* (Cm 6864, 2006) para 82.

[283] *Intelligence and Security Committee Annual Report 2005–2006* (Cm 6864, 2006) para 88.

[284] *Intelligence and Security Committee Annual Report 2007-2008* (Cm 7542, 2009) paras 147-150; *Intelligence and Security Committee Annual Report 2008-2009* (Cm 7807, 2010) paras 123-124; *Intelligence and Security Committee Annual Report 2009-2010* (CM 7844, 2010) pars 61-63.

s 23 of the Freedom of Information Act 2000.[285] Section 1 of the Freedom of Information Act 2000 does not apply in respect of such information so that the duty to communicate does not arise.[286] So far as concerns the duty to confirm or deny, public authorities need not inform applicants whether they hold information covered by the s 23 exemption if, or to the extent that, this would itself involve the disclosure of information which was directly or indirectly supplied by, or which relates to, a security body, whether or not that information is already recorded.[287] In this regard, the expression 'whether or not already recorded' is significant because the term 'information' would otherwise be confined to information recorded in any form.[288] Having said this, a public authority must specify the exemption relied upon when refusing to divulge or communicate information in reliance on s 23.[289] The exemption in s 23 of the Freedom of Information Act 2000 applies irrespective of whether the information in question is confidential, known to the applicant or wholly non-confidential.[290]

17– 034 The direct or indirect supply of information by the security bodies

For information supplied to a public authority by a security body to be caught by the exemption in s 23 of the Freedom of Information Act 2000 it need not have been obtained by the security body in the exercise of any particular function or supplied by it in writing or in confidence. The public authority holding the information need not have received it directly from the security body: it may have passed through a number of hands before indirectly reaching that authority. There is also no requirement that the information should have originated with the security body: it may simply have been supplied by that body to a third party on its way to the recipient public authority. One result of this is that where the same piece of information reaches authority 'A' via a security body and authority 'B' by some other non-security body route, it will be exempt from disclosure by authority 'A' under s 23 but available from authority 'B' as of right unless it relates to a security body or is subject to some other exemption in Part II of the

---

[285] Once a record containing particular information directly or indirectly supplied by, or relating to, a security body has been transferred to The National Archives or the Public Record Office of Northern Ireland in accordance with the Public Records Act 1958 or the Public Records Act (Northern Ireland) 1923, the exemption conferred on that information by FOIA s 23 ceases to be absolute. As a result, FOIA s 1 will not apply in respect of such information, and the duty to confirm or deny and the duty to communicate will not arise, only if the public interest in maintaining the exclusion of the relevant duty outweighs the public interest in divulging whether the public authority holds the information or in disclosing the information itself: s 64(2). The latter provision achieves this outcome by providing that, in relation to any information falling within s 23(1) which is contained in a historical record in The National Archives or the PRO of Northern Ireland s 2(3) shall have effect with the omission of the reference to s 23. It is also important to bear in mind here that information contained in a historical record in the PRO or the PRO of Northern Ireland cannot be exempt information by virtue of ss 21–22: s 64(1). In relation to historical records, see §§?, 7– 030 to 7– 041.

[286] FOIA s 23(1) engages s 2(2)(a) and (3)(b) so as to prevent the duty to communicate from arising in respect of the exempt information. FOIA s 23(5) engages s 2(1)(a) and (3)(b) so as to prevent the duty to confirm or deny from arising in relation to the exempt information.

[287] FOIA s 23(5).

[288] FOIA s 84.

[289] FOIA s 17(1)(b) and (5). See further §§17– 051 to 17– 056.

[290] See §17– 047 in relation to the relevance of confidentiality to the application of FOIA s 24. In *McCarthy v IC*, IT, 27 April 2007 at [11] the Tribunal rejected an argument that art 2 of the ECHR (right to life) impinged upon the operation of s 23: 'Whether or not he saw the [requested information] could not affect the risk of the United Kingdom becoming involved in a conflict which might endanger his life, even if such a risk engaged his art 2 rights, which it does not.'

Act. This is merely a concomitant of the institutional exemption afforded to information held by, emanating from or passing through the security bodies rather than a lapse in the protection provided by the Act. Another result is that a public authority which has received the same piece of information independently from security body and non-security body sources may nevertheless treat it as exempt under s 23. Lastly, there may be circumstances where a security body forwards information without assessing its contents or considering its dissemination in an active way or where the security body has no intention or desire that it should end up in the hands of the public authority in question: issues could then arise whether this has involved a meaningful act of 'supply to' that public authority 'by' the security body for the purposes of s 23.

035 Meaning of 'relates to'

Whether information 'relates to' a security body will be a question of both fact and law. The expression is conventionally used to require a link between subject and object.[291] The phrase 'relates to' (and cognate forms) was often used to link the power of devolved or colonial legislatures to make laws to particular subject matters. In this regard s 4(1) of the Government of Ireland Act 1920 (now repealed) prevented the old Parliament of Northern Ireland from making laws 'in respect of' certain excepted matters. Phrases such as 'in respect of', 'in relation to' and 'dealing with' describe the nature and extent of the connection between a law and particular permitted or, more usually, prohibited subject matters. As a matter of ordinary construction, laws can 'relate to' more than one matter.[292] Applying these principles, one would say that information does not 'relate to' a security body if it merely 'touches on' the body in question. However, the information need not be 'solely or mainly' concerned with or focused on that body or have that body as its 'pith and substance'. In this regard, information which relates to a security body's sources, methods, activities, plans or members, will generally relate to that body.

036 Where the absence of information relating to the security bodies is itself information which relates to those bodies

In certain circumstances, the fact that a public authority does not hold information which was supplied to it by, or which relates to, a security body could itself reveal the lack of any security body involvement in the subject matter of the relevant information request. The question may therefore arise whether the disclosure of requested information (without reference to or reliance on s 23) will thus involve the disclosure of exempt information falling within s 23 of the

---

[291] See further the discussion and authorities at §22– 007.

[292] See *R (Hume) v Londonderry Justices* [1972] NI 91(DC) at 110–113 (Lord Lowry CJ) (in relation to the Government of Ireland Act 1920 s 4) approving the analysis put forward in H Calvert, *Constitutional Law in Northern Ireland: a study in regional government* (London, Stevens, 1968) pp 187–196 and rejecting the approach taken in *Gallagher v Lynn* [1937] AC 863 where the 'doctrine of pith and substance' (applied in *Russell v The Queen* (1882) 7 App Cas 829 (PC) in relation to the Constitution Act 1867, formerly the British North America Act 1867) was applied at p 870 (Lord Atkin). The doctrine of pith and substance evolved in relation to the Constitution Act 1867 because that Act required that a law had to 'relate to' a particular matter within the exclusive area of either dominion or provincial legislative competence. A strained construction and search for each law's single pith and substance was thus required but in the absence of exceptional circumstances requiring such an approach, the doctrine of dual respection will ordinarily apply. Note the gloss on 'relates to' in the Scotland Act 1998 s 29(3) and the Government of Wales Act 2006, ss 94(7) and 108(7), the general clarification of 'deals with' in the Northern Ireland Act 1998 s 98(2) and the specific qualification of 'deals with' in the Northern Ireland Act 1998, Sch 2, para 22 and Sch 3, para 42. See the discussion in §22– 008, dealing with the same phrase in FOIA s 35.

Freedom of Information Act 2000. The answer to this may lie in the approach taken to the meaning of 'information' in s 23(1)–(2) and the effect of the reference to 'information (whether or not already recorded)' in s 23(5).[293] This can be demonstrated by reference to two hypothetical requests for information made to a government department or police authority regarding the involvement of the security bodies in a particular operation: request A asks for a list of every agency that was involved and request B asks for a list of every security body that was involved. If a security body was involved in the operation, the department or authority can respond to both requests with a partial list and a partial refusal notice which states that the authority is not obliged to confirm or deny whether it holds information relating to the involvement of the security bodies or to disclose any such information by virtue of s 23. If no security bodies were involved in the operation, however, the department or authority could only respond in the same fashion if: it holds information 'recorded in any form' which confirms the non-involvement of the security bodies;[294] or it does not hold any such information but the fact of security body non-involvement is nevertheless 'information (whether or not already recorded)' within s 23(5) and this would be disclosed if the applicant were informed that the requested information is not held. The Government takes the view that 'information (whether or not already recorded)' in s 23(5) is synonymous with 'unrecorded information' and extends to the absence of recorded information and the fact of security body non-involvement more generally.[295] It also considers that s 23(5) may therefore allow a neither confirm nor deny refusal to divulge, irrespective of whether the requested information is held and s 23(1) is engaged.

17– 037   Information which relates to GCHQ and the special forces: identities over time

The terms of the Freedom of Information Act 2000 allow scope for the composition of both GCHQ and the special forces to change over time as different units of the armed forces are

---

[293] FOIA s 84 gives 'information' the default meaning of 'information recorded in any form'. As to the meaning of 'information' as it is otherwise used in the Act, see §§9– 001 to 9– 008. FOIA ss 22(2), 23(5), 27(4)(b) and 42(2) all include references to 'any information (whether or not already recorded)' while FOIA ss 51(8) and 75(2) both refer to 'unrecorded information'. Although the two expressions would appear synonymous, it may be possible to discern some significance in the use of the different formulations, eg it could be argued that the use of 'already' confines 'any information (whether or not already recorded)' to information which is not yet recorded but which will or would be recorded at some point in the future or in the ordinary course of events.

[294] FOIA s 1(4) would prevent the department or authority from generating a record of security body non-involvement (following receipt of the information request) simply to enable it to say that it therefore holds recorded information relating to the security bodies.

[295] See MoJ, *Exemptions Guidance — Section 23: information supplied by, or related to, bodies dealing with security matters*, 14 May 2008: 'The fact that a public authority does not hold information supplied by one of the security bodies can itself be information relating to those bodies' (p 2); 'confirming that information is not held and thus that there is, or has been, no [security body] involvement in an issue can be as sensitive as confirming that there is or has been such involvement. Such information is itself information about a [security body] and is exempt under section 23' (p 3); 'The use of neither confirm nor deny...may be undermined not only by confirming that there is information held (ie implying that the [security bodies] have an interest in the subject) but also by confirming that no information is held (ie implying that the [security bodies] do not have an interest. Thus, to protect from disclosure the fact that no information is held the use of section 23(5) alone or section 23(5) and section 24(2) together may be justified' (p 5). See also *Baker v IC & ors*, IT, 28 February 2007 at [34].

transferred to or from duties assisting GCHQ or the remit of the Director of Special Forces.[296] Whether or not such transfers take place at all, questions could arise whether a unit of the armed forces was a part of GCHQ or the special forces at the time it supplied certain information or whether information relating to that unit relates to, or has ceased to relate to, GCHQ or the special forces for the purposes of s 23 of the Freedom of Information Act 2000. The relevant references to units of the armed forces being part of GCHQ or the special forces 'for the time being' tend to suggest that what matters is their status as such when the information request is made. So far as concerns the supply of information, what matters for the purposes of s 23 is that the unit of the armed forces which directly or indirectly supplied the information to the public authority was a part of GCHQ or the special forces at the time it did so. The question which s 23 appears to pose, namely whether information currently relates to any of the security bodies, is capable of raising more complicated issues. On a straightforward reading, information relating to sensitive work done by a unit of the armed forces at a time when it was a part of GCHQ or the special forces will cease to be exempt under s 23 once that unit ceases to be a part of GCHQ or the special forces. By the same token, information relating to non-sensitive work done by a unit of the armed forces at a time when it was not a part of GCHQ or the special forces will be exempt under s 23 once it becomes a part of GCHQ or the special forces. These outcomes may seem counter-intuitive at first blush because the sensitive information is left unprotected and the non-sensitive information is exempt. However, past membership of GCHQ or the special forces, possibly for a very short period, cannot confer permanent 'security body' status under s 23 and the past modus operandi of a unit which has since assumed more sensitive duties may well require protection. In practice, of course, the type of information likely to be affected by such questions will very often 'relate to' the unchanging core of GCHQ or the special forces in any event and, if not exempted by s 23, there may yet be a role for ss 24 and 26 of the Freedom of Information Act 2000.

038 Public authorities likely to hold information supplied by, or relating to, the security bodies

Bearing in mind the functions of the security bodies set out above, it is to be expected that numerous public authorities listed in Sch 1 to the Freedom of Information Act 2000 will hold information which was supplied to them by, or which relates to, those bodies. Candidates

---

[296] In relation to GCHQ, see FOIA ss 23(4) and 84 (definition of 'government department') and Sch 1, Pt I, para 6(b) and note that by virtue of s 23(4) GCHQ in s 23(3)(c) includes units or parts of units of the armed forces which are 'for the time being' required to assist GCHQ. Although there is no obvious reason why FOIA s 23(4) (and the Intelligence Services Act 1994 s 3(3)) refer to units of the armed forces assisting GCHQ 'in carrying out its functions' while FOIA Sch 1, Pt I, para 6(b) refers to them assisting GCHQ 'in the exercise of its functions', it is submitted that the different formulations are intended to have the same meaning and effect. In relation to the special forces, see FOIA s 84 (definition of 'the special forces') and Sch 1, Pt I, para 6(a) and note that the special forces are those units of the armed forces (no allowance is made for parts of units) the maintenance of whose capabilities is the responsibility of the Director of Special Forces (the words 'for the time being' are not included) or which are 'for the time being' subject to the operational command of that Director. So far as concerns the words 'for the time being' being applied in relation to those units subject to the operational command of the Director of Special Forces but not in relation to those units the maintenance of whose capabilities is the responsibility of that Director, for the latter type of unit to be a part of the special forces it must nevertheless be true to say that the maintenance of its capabilities '*is* the responsibility of the Director of Special Forces'. It would therefore appear that the use or non-use of 'for the time being' is not of great significance and may simply reflect the fact that periods of 'operational command' can be of varying length whilst the maintenance of a unit's capabilities will tend to be a more long-term responsibility.

include: major ministerial departments of state such as the Attorney-General's Office, Cabinet Office, Department for Communities and Local Government, Department for International Development, Department of Business, Innovation & Skills, Foreign and Commonwealth Office, Home Office, Ministry of Defence, Ministry of Justice, Northern Ireland Office and HM Treasury; the armed forces of the Crown; non-ministerial departments and agencies such as HM Revenue and Customs, the Treasury Solicitor's Department and the Defence Vetting Agency; law enforcement agencies and prosecuting authorities such as the police, Crown Prosecution Service and Serious Fraud Office; regulatory and financial bodies such as the Bank of England and the Financial Services Authority; oversight bodies such as the National Audit Office and the Parliamentary Commissioner for Administration; and a number of other public authorities such as the Armed Forces Pay Review Body, the Civil Service Appeal Board, the Defence Nuclear Safety Committee, the Diplomatic Service Appeal Board, the Imperial War Museum, the National Army Museum, the National Maritime Museum, the Royal Air Force Museum and the United Kingdom Atomic Energy Authority.

17– 039   Selection of the security bodies and treatment of other associated bodies

The selection of the security bodies specified in s 23(3) of the Freedom of Information Act 2000 and the omission of other similar bodies raises some questions about the purpose and effect of s 23. In relation to the principal security bodies, the question arises as to why the DIS and JIC are not also institutionally excluded from the Freedom of Information Act 2000 regime. In relation to the RIPA, IOCA, SSA and ISA Tribunals, the Security Vetting Appeals Panel and the Security Commission, the question arises as to why information supplied by, or relating to, the Interception of Communications Commissioner, the Intelligence and Security Committee and the Intelligence Services Commissioner, (which have similar oversight functions and are also not 'public authorities' for the purposes of the Freedom of Information Act 2000), is not also subject to the s 23 exemption. In relation to NCIS and its Service Authority, the question originally arose as to why the National Crime Squad and its Service Authority and the various police Special Branches were not also excluded from the Freedom of Information Act 2000 regime.[297] In constitutional terms, the answer must be that the selection of the security bodies and the treatment of other associated bodies in the Freedom of Information Act 2000 reflects an overall policy judgement as to the competing public interests involved. The difference of approach between, on the one hand, the ancillary security bodies, and, on the other hand, the DIS, JIC, Interception of Communications Commissioner, Intelligence and Security Committee and Intelligence Services Commissioner, is nevertheless difficult to explain: although it is easy to imagine in relation to the latter group that their designation as security bodies for the purposes of s 23 of the Freedom of Information Act 2000 would not have added much to its impact, it is more difficult to imagine that the non-designation of the former group would have diluted that impact to a significant degree.

---

[297] Albeit that the more recent inclusion in FOIA s 23 of the new SOCA has excluded the interests of the former, and now abolished, National Crime Squad from the FOIA regime, thereby expanding the scope of the institutional exclusion provided for by s 23. See §§17– 025 to 17– 026.

4. INFORMATION WHOSE EXEMPTION IS REQUIRED FOR NATIONAL SECURITY PURPOSES

040 Terms of the exemption in section 24 of the Freedom of Information Act 2000
As already indicated, information held by a public authority which was not directly or indirectly supplied to it by, and which does not relate to, any of the security bodies is subject to a qualified exemption under s 24 of the Freedom of Information Act 2000 if this is required for the purpose of safeguarding national security. However, the detailed terms of the exemption require closer examination:[298]

   (1)   Section 24(1) renders information that does not fall within s 23(1) (ie information which was not directly or indirectly supplied by, and does not relate to, any of the security bodies) exempt information if or to the extent that exemption from the duty to communicate is required for the purpose of safeguarding national security. The exemption is a qualified exemption, so that even if information falls within the description of the exemption (and is thus exempt information) it is then necessary to consider whether in all the circumstances the public interest favours disclosure of the information or maintenance of the exemption.[299] The fact that the exemption is qualified implies that there may be instances in which it will be in the public interest to disclose information, notwithstanding that exemption is required for the purpose of safeguarding national security.[300]

   (2)   Section 24(2) provides that 'the duty to confirm or deny does not arise if, or to the extent that, exemption from s 1(1)(a) is required for the purpose of safeguarding national security'. Unlike s 24(1), this limb of the national security exemption is not expressed to apply only to 'information which does not fall within s 23(1)'. Indeed s 24(2) is not expressed to relate to any particular category of information and it does not itself stand as a 'provision' which 'states that the duty to confirm or deny does not arise in relation to any information' for the purposes of s 2(1). As it was plainly not the intention that s 24(2) should operate independently of s 2(1),[301] s 24(2) must nevertheless be made to interact with s 2(1). This can be achieved by reading s 24 as a whole for the purposes of s 2(1), so that s 24 is itself a 'provision' which 'states that the duty to confirm or deny does not arise in relation to any

---

[298] This analysis appeared in the first edition of this work and was set out in full and endorsed by the Tribunal in *Baker v IC & ors*, IT, 28 February 2007 at [30]–[33].

[299] FOIA s 2(2)(b).

[300] Otherwise the exemption will be effectively metamorphosed into an absolute exemption.

[301] The same can be said of all the other provisions in Pt II which state that the duty to confirm or deny does not arise without stating that this is the case 'in relation to any information', ie FOIA ss 22(2), 26(3), 27(4)(a), 28(3), 29(3), 31(3), 33(3), 34(2), 38(2), 41(2), 43(3) and 44(2); cf ss 23(5), 27(4)(b), 30(3), 32(3), 35(3), 36(3), 37(2), 39(2) and 42(2).

information'.[302] On this basis, s 24 provides that the duty to confirm or deny does not arise in relation to information which does not fall within s 23(1) (ie information which was not directly or indirectly supplied by, and does not relate to, any of the security bodies) if, or to the extent that, exemption from s 1(1)(a) is required for the purpose of safeguarding national security. Again, the exclusion is a qualified one, so that even if the terms of s 24(2) are satisfied (and thus the duty to confirm or deny does not arise) it is then necessary to consider whether in all the circumstances the public interest favours confirmation or denial or maintenance of the exclusion.[303] The fact that the exclusion is qualified implies that there may be instances in which it will be in the public interest to divulge the existence of information, notwithstanding that exclusion of that duty is required for the purpose of safeguarding national security.

17– 041 Terms of the exemption in section 28 of the Data Protection Act 1998

As also indicated above, s 28 of the Data Protection Act 1998 exempts personal data from the provisions of the data protection principles and Pts II-III and V and ss 54A and 55 of the Data Protection Act 1998 (which include the subject-access right) if exemption from the relevant provision is required for the purpose of safeguarding national security. Personal data may therefore be exempt from the right of access under s 7 of the Data Protection Act 1998, other related rights and the regulatory requirements of the regime of that Act if this is required for the purpose of safeguarding national security. The national security exemption in s 28 of the Data Protection Act 1998 does not operate, and cannot be overridden, by reference to any public interest balancing test.

17– 042 Terms of the exception in regulation 12 of the Environmental Information Regulations 2004

As already indicated, reg 12 of the Environmental Information Regulations 2004 provides a qualified exception to the duty to disclose environmental information which allows public authorities to refuse to disclose information to the extent that its disclosure would adversely

---

[302] Reading FOIA ss 2(1) and 24(1)–(2) together in this way is consistent with s 2(3) in two respects: first, s 2(3) treats whole sections as 'provisions in Part II' for the purposes of s 2(1)–(2); and, secondly, s 2(3) does not designate s 24 as conferring absolute exemption and it is therefore clear that s 24 was intended to confer a qualified exemption subject to a public interest balancing test, which in turn requires that s 24(2) should engage s 2(1). It is further clear from FOIA s 24(3) that s 24(2) was not meant to operate independently of s 24(1): national security certificates under s 24(3) may certify that exemption from s 1(1)(b) is or was required for national security reasons (ie a duty to communicate certificate under s 24(1)) or that exemption from both s 1(1)(a) and (b) is or was required for national security reasons (ie a duty to confirm or deny and duty to communicate certificate under s 24(1) and (2)). The equivalent provision in the draft Freedom of Information Bill at *Freedom of Information: Consultation on Draft Legislation* (Cm 4355, 1999) Pt II (ie cl 19(2)) was more explicit in this regard: 'In relation to information which is exempt information by virtue of subsection (1), the duty to confirm or deny does not arise if, or to the extent that, exemption from section 8(1)(a) is required for the purpose of safeguarding national security.' The opening words '[I]n relation to information which is exempt information by virtue of subsection (1)' were not included in the equivalent provision in the Freedom of Information Bill introduced in the House of Commons on 18 November 1999 (ie cl 22(2)), but this change appears to have been a stylistic one made to all the exemptions based on the same template rather than a deliberate attempt to disengage s 2(1).

[303] FOIA s 2(2)(b).

affect international relations, defence, national security or public safety.[304] Disclosure may only be refused on this basis if, in all the circumstances of the case, the public interest in maintaining the exception outweighs the public interest in disclosing the information.[305] If doing so would involve the disclosure of information which would adversely affect international relations, defence, national security or public safety and would not be in the public interest, the relevant public authority may also refuse to confirm or deny whether the requested information exists and is held 'whether or not it holds such information'.[306] The reg 12 exception is also made subject to a requirement that public authorities apply a presumption in favour of disclosure and this should arguably govern their assessment of whether, first, disclosure would adversely affect one of the prescribed interests for the purposes of reg 12(1)(a) and, secondly, the public interest in maintaining the exception outweighs the public interest in disclosure for the purposes of reg 12(1)(b).[307] Regulation 4(3) of the Environmental Information Regulations 2004 moreover provides that the general duty to disseminate environmental information does not extend to information which a public authority would be entitled to refuse to disclose under reg 12.

043 Meaning of 'national security'
The expression 'national security' is not defined in the Freedom of Information Act 2000, the Data Protection Act 1998 or the Environmental Information Regulations 2004 and it has not been the subject of exhaustive definition in any other statutes or judicial decisions.[308] A number of general themes can, however, be extracted from a variety of sources:

(1)   In 1985 the Home Office White Paper, *Interception of Communications in the United Kingdom*, stated that the interests of national security encompass 'terrorist, espionage or major subversive activity, or [the] support of the Government's defence and foreign policies.'[309]

(2)   In 1988 the Prime Minister, Mrs Thatcher, stated in answer to a Parliamentary Question,

> National security is generally understood to refer to the safeguarding of the State and the community against threats to their survival or well-being. I am not aware that any previous administration has thought it appropriate to adopt

---

[304] EIR reg 12(1)(a) and (5)(a). See also EI(S)R reg 10(1)–(2) and (5)(a) applying the 'would, or would be likely to, prejudice substantially' test and an additional requirement that reg 10(4)–(5) are interpreted 'in a restrictive way' to an otherwise similarly worded national security 'exception'.

[305] EIR reg 12(1)(b). See also EI(S)R reg 10.

[306] EIR reg 12(6). See also EIR reg 12(7), 'For the purposes of a response under paragraph (6), whether information exists and is held by the public authority is itself the disclosure of information.' See also EI(S)R reg 10(8)–(9).

[307] EIR reg 12(2). By contrast, the 'presumption in favour of disclosure' in EI(S)R reg 10(2)(b) is to be applied by Scottish public authorities 'in considering the application of the exceptions referred to in paragraphs (4) and (5)', ie in considering whether disclosure would, or would be likely to, prejudice substantially national security for the purposes of reg 10(1)(a) but, arguably, not in considering whether the public interest in making the information available is outweighed by that in maintaining the exception for the purposes of reg 10(1)(b).

[308] *Esbester v United Kingdom* (1993) 18 EHRR CD 72 (ECommHR); *Hitchens v SSHD*, IT, 4 August 2003 at [47]. See generally: L Lustgarten and I Leigh, *In From the Cold: National Security and Parliamentary Democracy* (Oxford, Oxford University Press, 1994), pp 3–35; I Cameron, *National Security and the European Convention on Human Rights* (The Hague, Kluwer Law International, 2000) pp 39–58; MoJ, *Exemptions Guidance—Section 24: National security*, 14 May 2008, pp 3-4.

[309] Cmnd 9438, 1985 para 21.

a specific definition of the term.[310]

(3)   The Security Service Act 1989 envisages that the protection of national security requires that it be protected against threats from espionage, terrorism and sabotage, from the activities of agents of foreign powers and from actions intended to overthrow or undermine Parliamentary democracy by political, industrial or violent means,[311] but that it does not itself extend to safeguarding the economic well-being of the United Kingdom against threats posed by the actions or intentions of persons outside the British Islands or preventing or detecting serious crime.[312]

(4)   In 1991 the Report of the Security Service Commissioner for 1990 stated,

> The concept of national security however is wider than this and is not easily defined; indeed it is probably undesirable that I attempt an all-embracing definition. In my opinion it includes the defence of the realm and the government's defence and foreign policies involving the protection of vital national interests in this country and abroad. In this regard I would draw a distinction between national interest and the interests, which are not necessarily the same, of the government of the day. What is a vital national interest is a question of fact and degree, more easily recognised when being considered than defined in advance.[313]

(5)   The European Commission of Human Rights and the European Court of Human Rights[314] have held that the following may pose a threat to national security and may therefore be countered in the interests of national security: disloyalty in the public services (in relation to security vetting procedures);[315] espionage;[316] inciting disaffection of military personnel;[317] indiscipline in the armed forces and the

---

[310] Hansard HC vol 126 col 7 (25 January 1988).

[311] Security Service Act 1989 s 1(2).

[312] Security Service Act 1989 s 1(3)–(4). The same distinction between the interests of national security, on the one hand, and the interests of the economic well-being of the United Kingdom and the prevention or detection of serious crime, on the other, is drawn in the Security Service Act 1989 s 2(2)(a) and the Intelligence Services Act 1994 ss 1(2), 2(2)(a), 3(2) and throughout the Regulation of Investigatory Powers Act 2000 (see eg s 5(3)). This is also reflected in the separate provision made for the economic interests of the United Kingdom and law enforcement in FOIA ss 29–31. See further chs 19 and 20.

[313] Cm1480, 1991 para 10.

[314] In *Hewitt and Harman v United Kingdom* (1 September 1993) No 20317/92 (ECommHR) an application based on the ECHR art 8 brought following the implementation of the Security Service Act 1989 was ruled inadmissible by the European Commission of Human Rights. In relation to the Security Service Act 1989 the Commission said 'the principles referred to above do not necessarily require a comprehensive definition of "the interests of national security"' and 'the Commission considers that in the present case the law is formulated with sufficient precision to enable the applicants to anticipate the role of the Security Service' (p 13).

[315] *Glasenapp v Federal Republic of Germany* (1987) 9 EHRR 25 (ECtHR) at [86]–[87]; *Kosiek v Federal Republic of Germany* (1987) 9 EHRR 328 (ECtHR) at [79]–[80]; *Vogt v Federal Republic of Germany* (1996) 21 EHRR 205 (ECtHR) at [49]–[51].

[316] *Klass v Federal Republic of Germany* (1978) 2 EHRR 214 (ECtHR) at [48]; *Hadjianastassiou v Greece* (1992) 16 EHRR 219 (ECtHR) at [43].

[317] *Arrowsmith v United Kingdom* (1979) 19 DR 5 (ECommHR) at [24].

police;[318] separatist organisations;[319] subversion;[320] and terrorism.[321]

(6)   *National Security and the European Convention on Human Rights* by Iain Cameron states:

It would also seem clear that, in an era of global interdependence, the ordinary meaning of "national security" cannot be limited to the simple preservation of territorial integrity and political independence from external armed attack, or dictatorial interference by foreign powers. National security must also logically encompass espionage, economic or political, and covert (destabilising) action by foreign powers. Moreover, notwithstanding a lack of foreign involvement, purely internal threats to change the existing political order of the state by force (ie revolutionary subversion and terrorism) must also be covered. Certainly these are regarded by most if not all governments as legitimate national security concerns.[322]

(7)   In *Secretary of State for the Home Department v Rehman*,[323] the House of Lords made following points: 'national security' means 'the security of the United Kingdom and its people';[324] the interests of national security are not limited to action by an individual which can be said to be 'targeted at' the United Kingdom, its system of government or its people;[325] the protection of democracy and the legal and constitutional systems of the state is a part of national security as well as military defence;[326] 'action against a foreign state may be capable indirectly of affecting the security of the United Kingdom';[327] and 'reciprocal co-operation between the United Kingdom and other states in combating international terrorism is capable

---

[318]   *VDSÖ and Gubi v Austria* (1995) 20 EHRR 56 (ECtHR); *Grigoriades v Greece* (1999) 27 EHRR 464 (ECtHR) at [41]; *Rekvényi v Hungary* (2000) 30 EHRR 519 (ECtHR) at [39]; *Smith and Grady v United Kingdom* (1999) 29 EHRR 493 (ECtHR); *Lustig-Prean and Beckett v United Kingdom* (2000) 29 EHRR 548 (ECtHR).

[319]   *United Communist Party of Turkey v Turkey* (1998) 26 EHRR 121 (ECtHR) at [39]–[41]; *Socialist Party v Turkey* (1999) 27 EHRR 51 (ECtHR) at [33]–[36].

[320]   *Leander v Sweden* (1987) 9 EHRR 433 (ECtHR) at [59].

[321]   *Klass v Federal Republic of Germany* (1978) 2 EHRR 214 (ECtHR) at [48]; *Zana v Turkey* (1999) 27 EHRR 667 (ECtHR) at [48]–[50].

[322]   I Cameron, *National Security and the European Convention on Human Rights* (The Hague, Kluwer Law International, 2000) p 43.

[323]   [2001] UKHL 47, [2003] 1 AC 153. The House of Lords approved the Court of Appeal's rejection of the narrower definition of 'national security' adopted by the Special Immigration Appeals Commission, namely, 'a person may be said to offend against national security if he engages in, promotes, or encourages violent activity which is targeted at the United Kingdom, its system of government or its people. This includes activities directed against the overthrow or destabilisation of a foreign government if that foreign government is likely to take reprisals against the United Kingdom which affect the security of the United Kingdom or of its nationals. National security extends also to situations where United Kingdom citizens are targeted, wherever they may be' (see the speeches of Lord Slynn at [2] and Lord Hoffmann at [43]). *SSHD v Rehman* [2001] UKHL 47, [2003] 1 AC 153 at [15]–[17] and [50] are referred to by the Information Tribunal under the heading 'definition of national security' in *Baker v IC & ors*, IT, 28 February 2007 at [26]. See also Tomkins, 'Defining and delimiting national security' (2002) 118 *Law Quarterly Review* 200.

[324]   *SSHD v Rehman* [2001] UKHL 47, [2003] 1 AC 153 at [50] (Lord Hoffmann) and [64] (Lord Hutton).

[325]   *SSHD v Rehman* [2001] UKHL 47, [2003] 1 AC 153 at [15] (Lord Slynn).

[326]   *SSHD v Rehman* [2001] UKHL 47, [2003] 1 AC 153 at [16] (Lord Slynn).

[327]   *SSHD v Rehman* [2001] UKHL 47, [2003] 1 AC 153 at [16]–[17] (Lord Slynn). See also at [53] and [62] (Lord Hoffmann) and [64] (Lord Hutton).

of promoting the United Kingdom's national security'.[328]

(8) By way of contrast with the foregoing, the second of the 'Johannesburg Principles on National Security, Freedom of Expression and Access to Information' proposes a much narrower formulation:

> A restriction [on expression or information] sought to be justified on the ground of national security is not legitimate unless its genuine purpose and demonstrable effect is to protect a country's existence or its territorial integrity against the use or threat of force, or its capacity to respond to the use or threat of force, whether from an external source, such as a military threat, or an internal source, such as incitement to violent overthrow of the government.[329]

17– 044 Judicial approach to national security: traditional common law approach

Throughout the twentieth century the domestic courts consistently held that national security is the primary responsibility of the executive, that the executive has the particular experience and expertise necessary to make assessments and decisions relating to national security, together with democratic responsibility for doing so, and that the courts are not in a position to question the executive in this regard once it has been shown, on credible evidence, that national security considerations are in play.[330] The degree to which these authorities suggested that national

---

[328] *SSHD v Rehman* [2001] UKHL 47, [2003] 1 AC 153 at [17] (Lord Slynn).

[329] Adopted on 1 October 1995 by a group of experts on international law, national security and human rights convened by Article 19, the International Centre Against Censorship, in collaboration with the Centre for Applied Legal Studies of the University of the Witwatersrand, Johannesburg: Article 19 and Liberty, *Secrets, Spies and Whistleblowers: Freedom of Expression and National Security in the United Kingdom* (London, Liberty, 2000), Appendix 1 and recommendation 4; S Coliver, 'Commentary on the Johannesburg Principles' in S Coliver (ed), *Secrecy and Liberty: National Security, Freedom of Expression and Access to Information* (Cambridge Mass, Martinus Nijdhoff, 1999). See also *SSHD v Rehman* [2001] UKHL 47, [2003] 1 AC 153 at [14] (Lord Slynn).

[330] *The Zamora* [1916] 2 AC 77 (PC) at 107 'Those who are responsible for national security must be the sole judge of what the national security requires. It would obviously be undesirable that such matters should be made the subject of evidence in a court of law or otherwise discussed in public' (Lord Parker); *Chandler v DPP* [1964] AC 763 at 798 (Viscount Radcliffe) and 811 (Lord Devlin) (in relation to the defence of the realm); *R v SSHD, ex p Hosenball* [1977] 1 WLR 766 (CA) at 778 and 783 (Lord Denning MR) and 783–784 (Lane LJ); *Council of Civil Service Unions v Minister for the Civil Service* [1985] AC 374 at 402–403 (Lord Fraser), 404 and 406–407 (Lord Scarman), 410 and 412 (Lord Diplock), 420–421 (Lord Roskill) and 423 (Lord Brightman); *R v SSHD, ex p Ruddock* [1987] 1 WLR 1482, at 1490–1492 (Taylor J); *NHS v SSHD* [1988] Imm AR 389 (CA) at 395 (Dillon LJ); *R v Director of GCHQ, ex p Hodges* [1988] COD 123; *R v Secretary of State for Foreign and Commonwealth Affairs, ex p Everett* [1989] QB 811 (CA); *R v SSHD, ex p B, The Times*, 29 January 1991; *R v SSHD, ex p Cheblak* [1991] 1 WLR 890 (CA) at 902 and 906–907 (Lord Donaldson MR), 912 (Beldam LJ) and 916 (Nolan LJ); *R v SSHD, ex p Chahal* [1995] 1 WLR 526 (CA) at 531 and 535 (Staughton LJ); *R v SSHD, ex p McQuillan* [1995] 4 All ER 400 at 424 (Sedley J); *Jahromi v SSHD* [1996] Imm AR 20 (CA) at 26 (Roch LJ). See also: Lee, 'GCHQ: Prerogative and Public Law Principles' [1985] *Public Law* 186; Morris, 'The Ban on Trade Unions at Government Communications Headquarters' [1985] *Public Law* 177; Sir Simon Brown, 'Public Interest Immunity' [1994] *Public Law* 579, 589–590; Dickson, 'Judicial Review and National Security' in B Hadfield (ed), *Judicial Review: A Thematic Approach* (Dublin, Gill & Macmillan, 1995). The same approach is taken in the USA: *Center for National Security Studies v Department of Justice* 331 F 3d 918 (DC Cir 2003) '...the courts must defer to the executive on decisions of national security...' (at 932); *LA Times Communications v Department of the Army*, 442 F Supp 880 at 899 (CD Cal 2006), stating that 'the Court defers' to army officers' evaluation of how release of information could benefit insurgents in Iraq; *Department of the Navy v Egan*, 484 US 518 at 530 (1988); cf Brandeis J (diss) in *Olmstead v United States*, 277 US 438 at 479 'Experience should teach us to be most on our guard to protect liberty when the Government's purposes are beneficent. Men born to freedom are naturally alert to repel invasion of their liberty by evil-minded rulers. The greatest dangers to liberty lurk in insidious encroachment by men of zeal, well-meaning but without understanding.' The Supreme Court of Canada has adopted a similar line to that taken in the United Kingdom: *Suresh v Canada (Minister of Citizenship and Immigration)* [2002] 1 SCR 3, 208 DLR (4th) 1, 37 Admin LR (3d) 159. The Australian courts, whilst acknowledging the special position of the executive in assessing matters of national security, reserve for themselves a supervisory role and have

security was non-justiciable or that evidence of national security concerns could be demanded and reviewed to establish their bona fides and credibility varied a little from case to case, but the basic message remained the same: the courts would not interfere in the executive's assessment of national security matters.

· 045 **Judicial approach to national security: human rights and proportionality**
The judicial organs of the ECHR[331] and the European Community[332] have taken a broadly similar approach, but, whilst they have expressly recognised and emphasised the wide margin of appreciation enjoyed by the executive in this area, they have also stressed the need for effective judicial control by means of judicial review on proportionality-based grounds. In the light of this jurisprudence, the domestic courts have recently restated and recast their approach in cases where human rights are engaged, whilst retaining the same basic respect and deference for the conclusions of the executive when it comes to national security matters.[333] In a different but related context, national authorities have been given a wide, although not unfettered, margin of appreciation in determining whether there exists a 'public emergency threatening the

---

avoided express reference to their being 'deferential': *A v Hayden* [1984] HCA 67, (1984) 156 CLR 532; *Australian Communist Party v Commonwealth* [1951] HCA 5, (1951) 83 CLR 1, where Dixon J said at 188 'History and not only ancient history, shows that in countries where democratic institutions have been unconstitutionally superseded, it has been done not seldom by those holding the executive power. Forms of government may need protection from dangers likely to arise from within the institutions to be protected. In point of constitutional theory the power to legislate for the protection of an existing form of government ought not to be based on a conception, if otherwise adequate, adequate only to assist those holding power to resist or suppress obstruction or opposition or attempts to displace them or the form of government they defend.' Similar legislation was, on the other hand, upheld by a majority of the US Supreme Court in *American Communications Association v Dodds* (1950) 339 US 382.

[331] *Ireland v United Kingdom* (1979–80) 2 EHRR 25 (ECtHR) at [206]; *Chahal v United Kingdom* (1997) 23 EHRR 413 (ECtHR) at [131] and [138]; *Tinnelly and Sons Ltd v United Kingdom* (1999) 27 EHRR 249 (ECtHR) at [78]; *R v Ministry of Defence, ex p Smith* [1996] QB 517 (CA) and *Smith and Grady v United Kingdom* (1999) 29 EHRR 493 (ECtHR).

[332] Case 222/84 *Johnston v Chief Constable of the Royal Ulster Constabulary* [1987] QB 129 (ECJ); Case 175/94 *R v SSHD, ex p Gallagher* [1995] ECR I–4253, [1996] 1 CMLR 557 (ECJ); Case 273/97 *Sirdar v Secretary of State for Defence* [1999] ECR I–7403 (ECJ).

[333] *SSHD v Rehman* [2001] UKHL 47, [2003] 1 AC 153 at [16] and [26] (Lord Slynn) and [49]–[50], [53]–[54] and [62] (Lord Hoffmann). See esp at [31], while 'issues of national security do not fall beyond the competence of the courts' it is 'self-evidently right that national courts must give great weight to the views of the executive on matters of national security' (Lord Steyn); at [50] 'the question of whether something is "in the interests" of national security is not a question of law. It is a matter of judgment and policy. Under the constitution of the United Kingdom and most other countries, decisions as to whether something is or is not in the interests of national security are not a matter for judicial decision. They are entrusted to the executive' (Lord Hoffmann); and at [62] 'It is not only that the executive has access to special information and expertise in these matters. It is also that such decisions, with serious potential results for the community, require a legitimacy which can be conferred only by entrusting them to persons responsible to the community through the democratic process. If the people are to accept the consequences of such decisions, they must be made by persons whom the people have elected and whom they can remove' (Lord Hoffmann). See also: *R v DPP, ex p Kebilene* [2000] 2 AC 326 at 380–381 (Lord Hope); *Brown v Stott* [2003] 1 AC 681 (PC) at 834–835 (Lord Bingham); *A v SSHD (No 1)* [2004] UKHL 56, [2005] 2 AC 68 at [107]–[108] (Lord Hope), [154] (Lord Scott), [175]-[178] (Lord Rodger), [192]–[193] and [196]-[209] (Lord Walker diss); *International Transport Roth GmbH v SSHD* [2002] EWCA Civ 158, [2003] QB 728 (CA) at [77] and [80]–[87] (Laws LJ); *R v SSHD, ex p Farrakhan* [2002] EWCA Civ 606, [2002] QB 1391; *R (Mohamed) v Secretary of State for Foreign & Commonwealth Affairs* [2010] EWCA Civ 65 at [44]-[51] (Lord Judge CJ), [131]-[132], [137] (Lord Neuberger MR), [233] (Sir Anthony May); *A v SSHD (No 1)* [2002] EWCA Civ 1502, [2004] QB 335 at [40] (Lord Woolf CJ) and at [66] and [81] (Brooke LJ); *SSHD v MB* [2006] EWCA Civ 1140, [2007] QB 415; *R(Al Rawi) v Secretary of State for Foreign & Commonwealth Affairs* [2006] EWCA Civ 1279, [2008] QB 289 at [144]-[148] (Laws LJ); *Re Freddie Scappaticci's Application* [2003] NIQB 56 at [17]–[19] (Carswell CJ) (NI); *Baker v SSHD* [2001] UKHRR 1275 at [76]; *Gosling v SSHD*, IT, 1 August 2003 at [44] and [48]. In relation to the language of 'deference' see now *R (Pro-Life Alliance) v BBC* [2003] UKHL 23, [2004] 1 AC 185 at [74]–[77] (Lord Hoffmann) and [144] (Lord Walker).

life of the nation' so as to enable them to exercise their right to derogate from certain articles of the ECHR under article 15(1) thereof.[334] In this context, it was recently stated that, 'Safeguarding national security is (with the possible exception of some questions of macro-economic policy and allocation of resources) the area of policy in which the courts are most reluctant to question or interfere with the judgment of the executive or (a fortiori) the enacted will of the legislature.'[335]

17–046 Information whose exemption is required for the purpose of safeguarding, or whose disclosure would adversely affect, national security

Based on the authorities mentioned in the two foregoing paragraphs, the executive's assessment of whether exemption from the relevant provisions of the Freedom of Information Act 2000 and Data Protection Act 1998 is required for the purpose of safeguarding national security will not generally be gainsaid.[336] The same goes for its assessment of whether disclosure would adversely affect national security so as to engage the relevant exception in Part 3 of the Environmental Information Regulations 2004, albeit that this must be undertaken subject to a presumption in favour of disclosure.[337] In this regard, the executive may legitimately adopt a preventative or precautionary approach to the protection of national security and may consider not only direct or immediate threats but also the 'real possibility' of adverse affects on, and subsequent risks to, national security whether direct or indirect.[338] So far as concerns the communication of information or personal data under s 1(1)(b) of the Freedom of Information Act 2000 or s 7(1)(b)-(d) of the Data Protection Act 1998, the assessment to be made is simply whether non-disclosure is required for the purpose of safeguarding national security on the basis that disclosure would give rise to the real possibility of direct or indirect damage being done to national security. In relation to the dissemination or disclosure of information under regs 4(1)(a) or 5(1) of the Environmental Information Regulations 2004, a similar assessment is also

---

[334] See *Lawless v Ireland (No 3)* (1961) 1 EHRR 15 (ECtHR) at para 28; *The Greek Case* (1969) 12 YB 1 (ECommHR) at [153]; *Ireland v United Kingdom* (1978) 2 EHRR 25 (ECtHR) at [207]; *Brannigan and McBride v United Kingdom* (1993) 17 EHRR 539 (ECtHR) at [43]; *A v SSHD (No 2)* [2004] UKHL 56, [2005] 2 AC 68 at [27]–[29] (Lord Bingham), [79]–[81] (Lord Nicholls), [107]–[108], [112], [115]–[119] (Lord Hope), [154] (Lord Scott), [165]–[166], [175]–[177] (Lord Rodger), [192], [196], [208] (Lord Walker) and [226] (Baroness Hale).

[335] *A v SSHD (No 2)* [2004] UKHL 56, [2005] 2 AC 68 (Lord Walker, diss).

[336] Despite this, the Information Tribunal had little difficulty in dismissing the Ministry of Defence's reliance upon s 24 in relation to an application for the directory (listing names, posts, work addresses, telephone numbers and email addresses) of the Defence Expert Services Organisation: *Ministry of Defence v Information Commission and Evans*, IT, 20 July 2007 at [807]. *American Civil Liberties Union v Department of Defense*, 389 F Supp 2d 547 (SDNY 2005) offers a reminder of the limits to this, notwithstanding highly developed notions of deference in jurisprudence under the US Act: see §2–008(1).

[337] EIR, reg 12(1). See §17–042.

[338] *SSHD v Rehman* [2001] UKHL 47, [2003] 1 AC 153 at [16]–[17] and [22] (Lord Slynn) and [29] (Lord Steyn) (both approving *SSHD v Rehman* [2000] 3 WLR 1240 (CA) at [44] (Lord Woolf MR)); *Secretary of State for Defence v Guardian Newspapers Ltd* [1985] AC 339 at 355 (Lord Diplock), 371 (Lord Roskill) and 373 (Lord Bridge). MoJ, *Exemptions Guidance—Section 24: National security*, 14 May 2008, p 2 refers to the need to 'identify an undesirable effect on national security, or the risk of such an undesirable effect, that would occur if the information were released.' ICO, *Section 24: The National Security Exemption* (2009) p 2 says of the FOIA s 24 exemption: 'It does not apply simply because the information relates to national security. The word "required" means "reasonably necessary." It may not be vital to apply the exemption but it must certainly be more than just useful or convenient. The exemption should not be applied in a blanket fashion. There must be evidence that disclosure would pose a real and specific threat to national security.'

required subject again to the presumption in favour of disclosure. However, a wider variety of factors may have to be taken into account in relation to confirmation or denial decisions under s 1(1)(a) of the Freedom of Information Act 2000, s 7(1)(a) of the Data Protection Act 1998 or reg 12(6) of the Environmental Information Regulations 2004, as confirmation that a public authority holds or does not hold information or personal data of a particular description might be harmless in one case and yet give rise to damaging deductions and inferences if similar confirmation has to be withheld in another case. This may be accommodated on the basis that the public interest in disclosing whether the public authority holds information is, by itself, less compelling than the public interest in disclosing information.[339] Reference has already been made to the risk of mosaic prejudice being caused by the disclosure of information in the security and intelligence context and this will often be a factor in relation to national security assessments under s 24 of the Freedom of Information Act 2000, s 28 of the Data Protection Act 1998 and reg 12 of the Environmental Information Regulations 2004.[340]

047 Non-confidential information

Section 24 of the Freedom of Information Act 2000, s 28 of the Data Protection Act 1998 and reg 12 of the Environmental Information Regulations 2004 are all capable of conferring exemption on information or personal data that is known to the applicant or wholly non-confidential, just as much as on confidential information.[341] The question nevertheless arises whether the exemption of information which is already known to the applicant or in the public domain can realistically be required for the purpose of safeguarding national security or the disclosure of such information can be said to be capable of having an adverse affect on national security.[342] The first point to note here is that where information enters the public domain[343] without there being any official confirmation of its accuracy, it may nevertheless remain inherently unreliable.[344] Formal disclosure by a public authority will authenticate the information and thus entail the disclosure of an extra piece of information, namely, the fact that the information is true. It is therefore entirely possible for non-confidential information to attract the protection of s 24 of the Freedom of Information Act 2000, s 28 of the Data

---

[339] See generally §15– 019.

[340] See §17– 029(1) and references therein.

[341] Neither provision is expressly or implicitly confined to confidential information. See generally §15– 026.

[342] DPA s 28 could require the exemption of such information, but it may be more difficult to justify this, particularly in relation to a data subject who, eg, is a former servant or agent of the intelligence services or has been subject to a prosecution involving evidence supplied by the intelligence services and who therefore knows that they hold personal data about him. The Information Tribunal has recognised that establishing the need for a neither confirm nor deny response in such cases is not a foregone conclusion: *Baker v SSHD* [2001] UKHRR 1275 at [4] and [9]; *Gosling v SSHD*, IT, 1 August 2003; *Hitchens v SSHD*, IT, 4 August 2003; *Hilton v FCO*, IT, 28 June 2005.

[343] In this regard, it has been said that for information to enter the public domain means 'no more than that the information in question is so generally accessible that, in all the circumstances, it cannot be regarded as confidential': *AG v Guardian Newspapers Ltd (No 2)* [1990] 1 AC 109 at 282 (Lord Goff). See also *Barclays Bank plc v Guardian News & Media Ltd* [2009] EWHC 591 (QB).

[344] At least while some doubt remains whether or not it is true, false or the product of speculation and that doubt is greater than that which ordinarily attaches to official information of the same kind. See the first instance judgment of Scott J in *AG v Observer Ltd* [1990] 1 AC 109 at 165: 'It is of importance to note that, save in the case of the Granada TV broadcast, none of the allegations that had previously been publicly made had been publicly made by an "insider". Mr Alexander is, in my view, entitled to say that allegations acquire, when made by an insider, a ring of authenticity that they did not previously possess.'

Protection Act 1998 or reg 12 of the Environmental Information Regulations 2004. This is largely borne out by reference to the experience in the USA under the federal Freedom of Information Act 1966 (USA)[345] where the approach taken is that national security exemption claims are not undermined by a generalised allegation that classified information has been leaked to the press or otherwise made available to members of the public. Information is not considered to be in the public domain unless it has been the subject of an official disclosure.[346] Where a person seeks to defeat a national security claim for exemption on the ground that the information is in the public domain, the burden rests upon that applicant to point to specific information officially placed in the public domain that appears to duplicate[347] the withheld information.[348] Reports in the media, even if widespread, about the general subject matter of the information requested will not defeat a claim for national security exemption for that type of information.[349] Public statements by former government officials do not constitute such an official disclosure[350] and it would appear that even Congressional publications may not constitute an official disclosure.[351] Much the same conclusion has been arrived at in Australia in relation to information known to the applicant.[352]

17–048 Will the public interest in protecting national security always outweigh the public interest in disclosure?

---

[345] Freedom of Information Act 1966 5 USC 552(b)(1) (2000 & Supp III 2003) (USA).

[346] For example, *Simmons v Department of Justice*, 796 F 2d 709, 712 (4th Cir 1986); *Abbotts v Nuclear Regulatory Commission*, 766 F 2d 604, 607–08 (DC Cir 1985); *AFSHAR v Department of State*, 702 F 2d 1125 (DC Cir 1983) (foreign government can ignore 'unofficial leaks and public surmise... but official acknowledgement may force a government to retaliate'); *Steinberg v Department of Justice*, 801 F Supp 800, 802 (DDC 1992) ('passage of time, media reports and informed or uninformed speculation based on statements by participants cannot be used... to undermine [government's] legitimate interest in protecting international security [information]'), affirmed at 23 F 3d 548, 553 (DC Cir 1994). cf *Lawyers Comm for Human Rights v INS*, 721 F Supp 552, 569 (SDNY 1989) (national security exemption is not available when the same documents were disclosed by foreign government or when the same information was disclosed to press in 'off-the-record exchanges').

[347] It would appear that any material difference between that being requested and that which is in the public domain will allow the national security exemption to be maintained: *Public Citizen v Department of State* 11 F 3d at 199 (DC Cir 1993); *Public Citizen v Department of State*, 787 F Supp 12, 13, 15 (DDC 1992) (public Congressional testimony of the US Ambassador to Iraq did not constitute such a waiver so as to prevent the agency from invoking the national security exemption to withhold related records; his public testimony had not 'waived' Exemption 1 protection because the context of the information in the documents was sufficiently different so as to not negate their confidentiality).

[348] *Fitzgibbon v CIA*, 911 F 2d 755, 765 (DC Cir 1990); *Afshar v Department of State*, 702 F 2d 1125, 1130 (DC Cir 1983); *Billington v Department of Justice*, 11 F Supp 2d 45, 54–56 (DDC 1998); *Steinberg v Department of Justice*, 179 FRD 357, 361 (DDC 1998); *Pfeiffer v CIA*, 721 F Supp 337, 342 (DDC 1989).

[349] *Schlesinger v CIA*, 591 F Supp 60, 66 (DDC 1984) (CIA records relating to Guatemala were properly classified despite the fact that the public domain contained significant information and speculation about CIA involvement in the 1954 coup in Guatemala: 'CIA clearance of books and articles, books written by former CIA officials, and general discussions in Congressional publications do not constitute official disclosures').

[350] *Hudson River Sloop Clearwater, Inc v Department of the Navy*, 891 F 2d 414, 421–22 (2d Cir 1989).

[351] For example, *Salisbury v United States*, 690 F 2d 966, 971 (DC Cir 1982) (holding that inclusion of information in Senate report 'cannot be equated with disclosure by the agency itself'); *Military Audit Project v Casey*, 656 F 2d 724, 744 (DC Cir 1981) (publication of Senate report does not constitute official release of agency information).

[352] *Re Reithmuller and Australian Federal Police* (1985) 8 ALN N92; *Re Robinson and Department of Foreign Affairs* (1986) 11 ALN N48 (inadvertent earlier disclosure by the agency); *Commonwealth of Australia v Hittich* (1994) 53 FCR 152; *Gersten v Minister for Immigration and Multicultural Affairs* [2000] FCA 1221, on app [2001] FCA 159.

Even if information is rendered prima facie exempt or excepted (or if the duty to confirm or deny does not arise) for the purpose of safeguarding national security under s 24 of the Freedom of Information Act 2000 or because disclosure would adversely affect national security under reg 12 of the Environmental Information Regulations 2004, disclosure or divulgence will still have to take place under s 1 of the Act or regs 4–5 of the Regulations if, in all the circumstances of the case, the public interest in disclosure or divulgence outweighs, or is equal to, the public interest in maintaining the exemption or exception.[353] The legislative decision not to make exemption under these provisions absolute cannot properly be undone by giving the public interest in maintaining the exemption such weight as to make it automatically or intrinsically heavier than the public interest in disclosure.[354] The public interest balancing exercise must therefore be carried out in such a manner as to recognise that in some circumstances the public interest in disclosure will be sufficiently powerful to displace, or equal, an inherently compelling national security interest.[355] Were it assessed that the public interest in maintaining the relevant exemption and the public interest in disclosure were evenly balanced and in exact equipoise, the former could not be said to outweigh the latter and so disclosure would have to be the result: hence the above statement that disclosure must take place where the public interest in disclosure is equal to the public interest in maintaining the exemption.[356] The scales could also be made to tip in favour of disclosure or divulgence, for example, in relation to widely known non-confidential information whose exemption is nevertheless necessary for the purpose of safeguarding national security:[357] in such a case, the public interest in maintaining the exemption may have to be ascribed a more limited weight in accordance with the more limited effect it will have.

049 Approach to national security issues in the United States of America

In the US, once a document has engaged the national security exemption by being classified under the federal Freedom of Information Act 1966 (USA)[358] and the relevant Presidential

---

[353] FOIA s 2(1)(b) and (2)(b) and EIR reg 12(1)(b) and (6). DPA s 28 is not subject to an express public interest override provision but an assessment of the proportionality of any claim that its application is required for the purpose of safeguarding national security will nevertheless involve a similar balancing of national security interests, on the one hand, against the data subject's rights under DPA and the European Community Data Protection Directive 95/46/EC, on the other hand: *Baker v SSHD* [2001] UKHRR 1275 at [63] and [83]; *Gosling v SSHD*, IT, 1 August 2003; *Hitchens v SSHD*, IT, 4 August 2003; *Hilton v FCO*, IT, 28 June 2005.

[354] MoJ, *Exemptions Guidance—Section 24: National security*, 14 May 2008, p 5 states, 'There is obviously a very strong public interest in safeguarding national security. If non-disclosure is required to safeguard national security it is likely to be only in exceptional circumstances that consideration of other public interest factors will result in disclosure.'

[355] A crucial factor here will be the engagement of legally recognised countervailing human rights (as against a more generalised public interest) favouring disclosure over non-disclosure. Such rights will not be absolute, and they are unlikely to be determinative in any event, but they will at least provide something extra of substance to go into the balance..

[356] The presumption in favour of disclosure in EIR reg 12(2) could also have an effect in tipping finely balanced scales towards disclosure.

[357] See §17–047.

[358] 5 USC para 552(b)(1) s 6F(b) (USA).

Order thereunder,[359] the focus of challenge becomes the propriety of this classification.[360] While the courts have over the years increased their preparedness to scrutinise claims for exemption on this ground, it remains an exemption in respect of which the courts are loath to substitute their judgment for that of the executive. In 1973 the Supreme Court[361] held that records classified under proper procedures were necessarily exempt from disclosure, without any possibility of judicial scrutiny.[362] Following this decision, Congress amended the Freedom of Information Act in 1974 to provide expressly for de novo review by the courts and for the in camera review of classified documents.[363] Despite these amendments, the courts, in the absence of evidence of bad faith on the part of an agency, routinely upheld agency classification decisions.[364] Although the courts subsequently increased their use of the in camera review procedures in order to facilitate full de novo reviews of national security claims even where bad faith was not an issue,[365] it was recognised that they should first 'accord substantial weight to an agency's affidavit concerning the details of the classified status of the disputed record.'[366] Provided an agency's affidavit evidence discloses no bad faith and the requisite degree of particularity, examination of the documents by the court will either not be required or will be limited to sample documents.[367] Claims for exemption can be supported by in camera affidavits[368] which the legal representatives of the person seeking access will not be allowed to

---

[359] Executive Order 12,958 as amended by Executive Order 13,292. The latter order was issued by President Bush on 25 March 2003. The former Executive Order was issued by President Clinton on 17 April 1995. See further §2– 008(1) and the footnotes therein. 'National security' means the national defence or foreign relations of the United States: Executive Order 12,958, para 6.1(y).

[360] Thus the issue on review is whether the classification was justified at the time that it was made and an agency may, as a matter of discretion, re-examine its classification decisions under a newly issued Executive Order in order to take into account changed international and domestic circumstances: *King v Department of Justice*, 830 F 2d 210 at 217 (DC Cir 1987).

[361] *EPA v Mink* 410 US 73 (1973).

[362] *EPA v Mink*, 410 US 73 (1973) at 84.

[363] USC § 552(a)(4)(B).

[364] For example, *Weissman v CIA*, 565 F 2d 692 (DC Cir 1977) at 698.

[365] Starting with *Ray v Turner*, 587 F 2d 1187 (DC Cir 1978) at 1194–95.

[366] *Ray v Turner*, 587 F 2d 1187 (DC Cir 1978) at 1194–95.

[367] For example, *Doherty v Department of Justice*, 775 F 2d 49, 53 (2nd Cir 1985) ('the court should restrain its discretion to order in camera review'); *Hayden v National Security Agency*, 608 F 2d 1381, 1387 (DC Cir 1979) ('[w]hen the agency meets its burden by means of affidavits, in camera review is neither necessary nor appropriate'); *Public Education Center Inc v Department of Defense*, 905 F Supp 19, 22 (DDC 1995) (declining in camera review of withheld videotapes after according substantial weight to agency's affidavit that public disclosure would harm national security); *King v Department of Justice*, 586 F Supp 286, 290 (DDC 1983) (characterising in camera review as a last resort); *American Civil Liberties Union v Department of Justice*, 265 F Supp 2d 20 (DDC 2003), where the court held that the test for determining whether a document was properly classified 'is not whether the court personally agrees in full with the [agency's] evaluation of the danger – rather, the issue is whether on the whole record the Agency's judgment objectively survives the test of reasonableness, good faith, specificity, and plausibility in this field of foreign intelligence in which the [agency] is expert and given by Congress a special role.'

[368] For example, *Patterson v FBI*, 893 F 2d 595, 599–600 (3d Cir 1990); *Simmons v Department. of Justice*, 796 F 2d 709, 711 (4th Cir 1986); *Ingle v Department of Justice*, 698 F 2d 259, 264 (6th Cir 1983) (ruling that in camera review should be secondary to testimony or affidavits). The approach taken is that in such cases the agency is under a duty to 'create as complete a public record as is possible' before resorting to an in camera affidavit: *Phillippi v CIA*, 546 F 2d 1009, 1013 (DC Cir 1976). See also *Armstrong*, 97 F 3d at 580 (holding that when district court uses an in camera affidavit, even in national security cases, 'it must both make its reasons for doing so clear and make as much as possible of the in camera submission available to the opposing party' (citing *Lykins v Department of Justice*, 725 F 2d 1455, 1465

see.[369] The courts will give substantial deference to agency expertise in national security matters[370] and have expressed a reluctance to substitute their judgment for that of the agency's 'unique insights' in the areas of national defence and foreign relations.[371] Even where the person requesting access has adduced expert evidence as to the security implications, this has not usually caused the courts to upset the agency's assessment of the national security implications of disclosure.[372] Thus, claims for exemption are generally upheld if the agency's affidavits are reasonably specific and there is no evidence of bad faith.[373] A similar degree of

---

(DC Cir 1984)); *Patterson v FBI*, 893 F 2d 595 at 600 (3d Cir 1990); *Simmons v Department of Justice*, 796 F 2d at 710 (4th Cir 1986); *Scott v CIA*, 916 F Supp 42, 48–49 (DDC 1996) (denying request for in camera review until agency 'creates as full a public record as possible'); *Public Education Centre, Inc v Department of Defense*, 905 F Supp 19, 22 (DDC 1995) (ordering in camera review only after agency created 'as full a public record as possible').

[369] *Phillippi v CIA*, 546 F 2d 1009, 1013 (DC Cir 1976).

[370] For example, *Young v CIA*, 972 F 2d 536, 538–39 (4th Cir 1993) (finding district court properly deferred to agency because no evidence of bad faith); *Bowers v Department of Justice*, 930 F 2d 350, 357 (4th Cir 1991) (observing that '[w]hat fact... may compromise national security is best left to the intelligence experts'); *Doherty v Department of Justice*, 775 F 2d 49, 52 (2d Cir 1985) (according 'substantial weight' to agency declaration); *Miller v Casey*, 730 F 2d 773, 776 (DC Cir 1984) (same); *Taylor v Department of the Army*, 684 F 2d 99, 109 (DC Cir 1982) (holding that classification affidavits are entitled to 'the utmost deference') (reversing district court disclosure order); *Badalementi v Department of State*, 899 F Supp 542, 546 (D Kan 1995) (according substantial weight to agency's affidavit and granting motion for summary judgment in light of agency's expertise in national security matters); *Canning v Department of Justice*, 848 F Supp 1037, 1042 (DDC 1994) (describing how in according such deference, courts 'credit agency expertise in evaluating matters of national security by focusing attention primarily on whether affidavits are sufficiently specific and by ensuring that they are not controverted by contradictory evidence or evidence of bad faith'); *Abbotts v Nuclear Regulatory Commission*, 766 F 2d 604 (DC Cir 1985) overturning the district court's disclosure because it 'did not give the required "substantial weight" to the [agency's] uncontradicted affidavits.'

[371] For example, *Miller v Department of State*, 779 F 2d 1378, 1387 (8th Cir 1985); *Maynard v CIA*, 986 F 2d 547, 556 n 9 (1st Cir 1993) (a court is 'not in a position to "second-guess"' agency's determination regarding need for continued classification of material); *Krikorian v Department of State*, 984 F 2d 461, 464–65 (DC Cir 1993) (where it was held that an agency has 'unique insights' in areas of national defence and foreign relations); *Willens v NSC*, 726 F Supp 325, 326–27 (DDC 1989) (where it was held that a court cannot second-guess agency's national security determinations when they are 'credible and have a rational basis'). But see *King v Department of Justice*, 830 F 2d 210, 226 (DC Cir 1987) (holding that trial court erred in deferring to agency's judgment that information more than 35 years old remained classified when Executive Order presumed declassification of information over 20 years old and agency merely indicated procedural compliance with Order); *Lawyers Comm for Human Rights v INS*, 721 F Supp 552, 561 (SDNY 1989) (reminding that such deference does not give agency *carte blanche* to withhold responsive documents without 'valid and thorough affidavit'). *Wolf v CIA*, 473 F 3d 370, 379 (DC Cir 2007), where the Court, in refusing to compel the CIA to confirm or deny whether it held information relating to Jorge Eliecer Gaitan (a Columbian presidential candidate who had been assassinated on 9 April 1948), said: 'it is logical to conclude that the need to assure confidentiality to a foreign source includes neither confirming nor denying the existence of records even decades after the death of the foreign national.' Similarly: *National Security Archive Fund, Inc v CIA*, 402 F Supp 2d 211, 216 (DDC 2005); *American Civil Liberties Union v US Department of Justice*, 429 F Supp 2d 179, 188 (DDC 2006), holding that 'the court must recognize that the executive branch departments responsible for national security and national defense have unique insights and special expertise concerning the kind of disclosures that may be harmful.'

[372] For example, *Hudson River Sloop Clearwater, Inc v Department of the Navy*, 891 F 2d 414, 421–22 (2d Cir 1989) (retired admiral's opinion); *Gardels v CIA*, 689 F 2d 1100, 1106 n 5 (DC Cir 1982) (former agent of the CIA); *Pfeiffer v CIA*, 721 F Supp 337, 340–41 (DDC 1989) (retired CIA historian). Prior to 1986, no appellate court had ever upheld, on the substantive merits of the case, a decision to reject an agency's classification claim.

[373] *Halperin v CIA*, 629 F 2d 144, 148 (DC Cir 1980); *Goldberg v Department of State*, 818 F 2d 71 (DC Cir 1987); *Schrecker v Department of Justice*, 74 F Supp 2d 26, 30 (DDC 1999); *Voinche v FBI*, 46 F Supp 2d 26, 29 (DDC 1999); *Billington v Department of Justice*, 11 F Supp 2d 45, 54, 58 (DDC 1998); *Canning v Department of Justice*, 848 F Supp 1037, 1 042–43 (DDC 1994); *Students Against Genocide v Department of State*, 257 F 3d 828 (DC Cir 2001). Thus, in *Rosenfeld v Department of Justice*, 57 F 3d 803, 807 (9th Cir 1995) the Court affirmed a district court disclosure order, finding the Government had failed to show with 'any particularity' why classified portions of several documents should be withheld. Similarly, *Wiener v FBI*, 943 F 2d 972, 978–79 (9th Cir 1991), where the applicant sought the FBI's files on John Lennon; these documented the FBI's role in the Nixon Administration's attempt to deport John Lennon

judicial deference to the assessments of the executive has also been shown by the Australian courts in the freedom of information context.[374]

5. NATIONAL SECURITY CERTIFICATES AND THE OPERATION OF THE RELATED EXEMPTIONS

17– 050 National security exemptions and the use of conclusive certificates
As is covered in more detail in the following paragraphs, the Freedom of Information Act 2000, the Data Protection Act 1998 and the Environmental Information Regulations 2004 all contain special provisions governing ministerial national security certificates which may be issued to certify conclusively that a national security exemption or exception applies to specified information or personal data. It is nevertheless important to recognise that the exemptions in ss 23 and 24 of the Freedom of Information Act 2000 and s 28 of the Data Protection Act 1998 and the exception in reg 15 of the Environmental Information Regulations 2004 are all free-standing and may all be relied upon to justify the refusal of a request for information or personal data without recourse to a ministerial certificate.[375] The following paragraphs therefore contain general points of principle which are applicable to the operation of these provisions irrespective of whether they are engaged by way of a national security certificate.

17– 051 National security certificates under sections 23 and 24 of the Freedom of Information Act 2000
National security certificates may be issued under ss 23 and 24 of the Freedom of Information Act 2000 as follows:

(1) Under s 23(2) of the Freedom of Information Act 2000 a Minister of the Crown may sign a certificate certifying that the information to which it applies was directly or indirectly supplied by, or relates to, any of the security bodies specified in s 23(3). Such a certificate will then stand as conclusive evidence of that fact (irrespective of whether it is a fact), thus confirming the engagement of the s 23 exemption, unless

---

in 1972; the FBI refused to disclose the information on national security grounds: Wiener, *Gimme Some Truth: The John Lennon FBI Files* (Berkeley, Univ of California Press, 2000). Also: *Oglesby v Department of the Army*, 920 F 2d 57, 66 n 12 (DC Cir 1990); *Scott v CIA*, 916 F Supp 42, 44–49 (DDC 1996).

[374] *Re Maher and Attorney-General's Department* (1985) 3 AAR 396; *Re Stolpe and Department of Foreign Affairs* (1985) 9 ALD 104; *Re Fewster and Department of Prime Minister and Cabinet (No 2)* (1987) 13 ALD 139; *Re Wang and Department of Employment, Education and Training* (1988) 15 ALD 497; *Re Bayliss and Department of Health and Family Services* (1997) 48 ALD 443; *Gersten v Minister for Immigration & Multicultural Affairs* [2000] FCA 1221, [2001] FCA 159. See further §2– 015(9).

[375] *Baker v IC & ors*, IT, 28 February 2007 at [5]: 'It should be noted that the Commissioner has reached an agreement with the Secretary of State for Constitutional Affairs acting on behalf of central government departments that a Ministerial Certificate under sections 23(2) and 24(3) would only be obtained in the event of a complaint to the Commissioner. In this case no such certificate was issued. In the Decision Notice the Commissioner welcomed the fact that the Cabinet Office had not made use of a Ministerial Certificate but, rather, had chosen to explain the reasons for its refusal in a letter to Mr Baker of 5th May 2006.' And see *Beam v IC and FCO*, IT, 12 May 2009 at [11] and [15]. See also MoJ, *Exemptions Guidance—Section 23: Information supplied by, or related to, bodies dealing with security matters*, 14 May 2008, pp 6-7 and MoJ, *Exemptions Guidance—Section 24: National security*, 14 May 2008, pp 7-8, Annex A on the consequence of reliance or non-reliance on a certificate in terms of the consequences this will have for the applicable enforcement and appeals procedures.

and until withdrawn or revoked[376] or quashed on an appeal under s 60(1) of the Freedom of Information Act 2000. There is no provision allowing such a certificate to identify the information to which it applies by means of a general description or to be expressed to have prospective effect.[377] Such a certificate may only be signed by a Minister who is a member of the Cabinet or by the Attorney-General, the Advocate General for Scotland or the Attorney-General for Northern Ireland.[378]

(2) Under s 24(3) of the Freedom of Information Act 2000 a Minister of the Crown may sign a certificate certifying that exemption from the disclosure duty in s 1(1)(b) or from the divulgence and disclosure duties in s 1(1)(a) and (b) is, or at any time was, required for the purpose of safeguarding national security.[379] Such a certificate will then stand as conclusive evidence of that fact (irrespective of whether it is a fact), thus confirming the engagement of the s 24 exemption subject to the application of the public interest balancing tests,[380] unless and until withdrawn or revoked or quashed on an appeal under s 60(1) or (4) of the Freedom of Information Act 2000.[381] It is important to note here that such a certificate cannot certify for the purposes of s 2(1)(a) and (2)(a) of the Freedom of Information Act 2000 that, in all the circumstances of the case, the public interest in maintaining the exemption outweighs the public interest in divulging whether the public authority holds the information or in disclosing the information itself. The assessment and balancing of these competing facets of the public interest will therefore be subject to review by the Information Commissioner in the normal way. A national security certificate under s 24(3) may identify the information to which it applies by means of a general description and may be expressed to have prospective effect.[382] Such a certificate may only be signed by a Minister who is a member of the Cabinet or by the Attorney-General, the Advocate General for Scotland or the Attorney-General for Northern Ireland.[383]

---

[376] There is no obvious reason for construing FOIA ss 23(2), 24(3), 34(3) and 36(7), FOI(S)A s 31(2), DPA s 28(2) or EIR reg 15(1) as preventing the withdrawal or revocation of certificates or rendering the signatories *functus officio*. Changes in circumstances may very well make the withdrawal or revocation of a certificate appropriate without the need (where this route is open) for an appeal to the Upper Tribunal. See: *Al Fayed v SSHD*, Information Tribunal, 28 February 2002 at [9] and [15]–[16]; W Wade and C Forsyth, *Administrative Law*, 10th edn (Oxford, Oxford University Press, 2009) pp 193-196; Interpretation Act 1978 s 12.

[377] Compare FOIA s 24(4) and DPA s 28(3).

[378] FOIA s 25(3).

[379] FOI(S)A s 31(2)–(3). Under FOI(S)A s 31(2) a certificate may be signed by a member of the Scottish Executive and will stand as being conclusive of the fact certified (ie exemption from s 1(1) is required for the purpose of safeguarding national security): FOI(S)A does not expressly provide or allow for any appeal or review. Under FOI(S)A s 31(3), such a certificate may identify the information to which it applies by means of a general description and may be expressed to have prospective effect.

[380] FOIA s 2(1)(b) and (2)(b).

[381] As to appeals, see §28–027.

[382] FOIA s 24(4). Pursuant to FOIA s 60(4) a public authority may claim in proceedings under or by virtue of that Act that a certificate issued under s 24(3) which identifies the information to which it applies by means of a general description applies to particular information and, subject to any contrary determination by the Tribunal on appeal, the certificate will be conclusively presumed so to apply.

[383] FOIA s 25(3).

17–052 **National security certificates under section 28 of the Data Protection Act 1998**

Under s 28(2) of the Data Protection Act 1998 a Minister of the Crown may sign a national security certificate certifying that exemption from all or any of the provisions of the data protection principles or Pts II, III or V or ss 54A or 55 of the Data Protection Act 1998 (which includes the subject access rights given by s 7) is, or at any time was, required for the purpose of safeguarding national security in respect of any personal data. In this regard, it should be noted that national security requirements may vary depending upon whether the concern is disclosure to a data subject under s 7 of the Data Protection Act 1998 or disclosure to the Information Commissioner in the context of an assessment or information notice under s 42 or 43 respectively of the Act.[384] Such a certificate will then stand as conclusive evidence of that fact (irrespective of whether it is a fact), thus confirming the engagement of the s 28 exemption, unless and until withdrawn or revoked or quashed on an appeal under s 28(4) or (6) of and Sch 6 to the Data Protection Act 1998.[385] Such a certificate may identify the personal data to which it applies by means of a general description and may be expressed to have prospective effect.[386] Such a certificate may only be signed by a Minister who is a member of the Cabinet or by the Attorney-General, the Advocate General for Scotland or the Attorney-General for Northern Ireland.[387]

17–053 **National security certificates under regulation 15 of the Environmental Information Regulations 2004**

Under reg 15(1) of the Environmental Information Regulations 2004 a Minister of the Crown may certify that a refusal to disclose information under reg 12(1) is because the disclosure would adversely affect national security and would not be in the public interest.[388] For these purposes, Ministers of the Crown may designate persons to certify these matters on their behalf and a refusal to disclose information under reg 12(1) includes a neither confirm nor deny response under reg 12(6).[389] A certificate issued in accordance with reg 15(1) will then stand as conclusive evidence of the fact that disclosure would adversely affect national security and would not be in the public interest (irrespective of whether it would), unless and until withdrawn or revoked or quashed on an appeal under s 60 of the Freedom of Information Act 2000.[390] A national security certificate under reg 15(1) of the Environmental Information Regulations 2004 may identify the information to which it relates in general terms but there is no express provision

---

[384] *R (SSHD) v Information Tribunal* [2006] EWHC 2958 (Admin), [2007] 2 All ER 703 (DC) at [39]–[41] (Latham LJ).

[385] As to which, see §§28–046 to 28–047.

[386] DPA s 28(3). Pursuant to DPA s 28(6) a data controller may claim in proceedings under or by virtue of that Act that a certificate issued under s 28(2) which identifies the personal data to which it applies by means of a general description applies to any personal data and, subject to any contrary determination by the Tribunal on appeal, the certificate will be conclusively presumed so to apply.

[387] DPA s 28(10).

[388] See also EI(S)R reg 12.

[389] EIR reg 15(2).

[390] FOIA s 60 is applied for the purposes of the EIR with modifications by EIR reg 18(1), (3)–(4) and (7). As to appeals, see §28–027.

allowing for such certificates to be expressed to have prospective effect.[391] The power to sign such a certificate or to designate another person to certify the relevant matters is only exercisable by a Minister who is a member of the Cabinet or by the Attorney -General, the Advocate General for Scotland or the Attorney-General for Northern Ireland.[392]

054 National security certificates: appeals

The circumstances in, grounds on and procedures by which national security certificates issued under ss 23(2) and 24(3) of the Freedom of Information Act 2000, s 28(2) of the Data Protection Act 1998 and reg 15(1) of the Environmental Information Regulations 2004 may be appealed to the Upper Tribunal under s 60(1) of the Freedom of Information Act 2000 or s 28(4) of the Data Protection Act 1998 are dealt with elsewhere in this work.[393] For present purposes, however, the following points should be noted.

(1) The Tribunal may allow such an appeal and quash the relevant certificate if it finds: in relation to a certificate under s 23(2) of the Freedom of Information Act 2000, that the information referred to in the certificate was not exempt information by virtue of s 23(1);[394] or, in relation to a certificate under s 24(3) of the Freedom of Information Act 2000, s 28(2) of the Data Protection Act 1998 or reg 15(1) of the Environmental Information Regulations 2004, that, applying the principles applied by the court on an application for judicial review, the Minister or the person designated by him did not have reasonable grounds for issuing the certificate.[395]

(2) A second type of appeal may be brought under s 60(4) of the Freedom of Information Act 2000 or s 28(6) of the Data Protection Act 1998 by a party to any proceedings under or by virtue of the relevant Act if it is claimed by a public authority or a data controller that a certificate issued under s 24(3) of the Freedom of Information Act 2000 or s 28(2) of the Data Protection Act 1998 which identifies the information or the personal data to which it applies by means of a general description applies to particular information or personal data. It is arguable that such an appeal may also be brought under s 60(4) of the Freedom of Information Act 2000 by a party to any proceedings under the Environmental Information Regulations 2004 where similar claims are made by a public authority in relation to a certificate issued under reg 15(1) of the Regulations.[396] Appeals of this type are

---

[391] Compare FOIA s 24(4) and DPA s 28(3).

[392] EIR reg 15(6) giving the term 'Minister of the Crown' in reg 15(1)–(2) and (5) the same meaning as in FOIA s 25(3).

[393] See §§14– 032 to 14– 045, 28– 028 and 28– 046 to 28– 047. FOIA s 60 is applied for the purposes of the EIR with modifications by EIR reg 18(1), (3)–(4) and (7). Appeals under FOIA s 60, DPA s 28 and EIR reg 18(7) are governed by UT Rules.

[394] FOIA s 60(2). The Tribunal is thus given full appellate jurisdiction to review the matter, unconstrained by any caveat that it 'apply the principles applied by the court on an application for judicial review' and assess only whether the minister had 'reasonable grounds for issuing the certificate' (cf FOIA s 60(3), DPA s 28(5) and EIR reg 18(7)).

[395] FOIA s 60(3); DPA s 28(5); EIR reg 18(7). See further at §14– 040.

[396] EIR reg 18(1), (3), (4)(a)–(b) and (7)(a). This assumes that EIR reg 18(7)(a) operates to apply FOIA s 60(4) as if the reference therein to a certificate under FOIA s 24(3) were substituted by a reference to a certificate issued in accordance with EIR reg 15(1). The interaction between these provisions is not perfect, however, as EIR reg 18(7)(a) refers to 'the reference' in FOIA s 60 to a certificate under FOIA s 24(3) when there are three such references. Moreover, EIR reg 15(3)(b) allows for a certificate to 'identify the information to which it relates in general terms' while FOIA s 60(4) applies to a certificate 'which identifies the information to which it relates by means of a general

also dealt with in Chapter 28, but it should be noted here that the Tribunal has power to determine that the certificate in question does not apply to the information or personal data referred to by the public authority or data controller.[397]

17– 055 The principle of neither confirming nor denying

Whether described as keeping a secret or concealing the truth, the exercise of withholding information is in substance the same. So long as questions are not asked about the information or its existence, the secret can be kept and the truth concealed, often without significant misinformation or evasion.[398] Once such questions are asked, however, the picture changes because truthful answers may betray the underlying secret. The only way to continue withholding the information is then by way of a misleading or evasive response. Where the reply must come from a public authority, a misleading response is rarely acceptable and an evasive response is therefore the only option consistent with continuing to keep the secret; this will inevitably take the form of a non-committal 'neither confirm nor deny' or 'no comment' response.[399] The picture becomes even more complicated once multiple questions may be asked, because it will then be possible to compare evasive and non-evasive responses and the questions which elicited them in order to deduce or infer the underlying existence or nature of withheld information. These complications in part stem from, and are intimately bound up with, the nature of mosaic prejudice.[400] Accommodating these considerations will tend to require that the neither confirm nor deny blanket be extended to cover all requests on a particular topic which are sufficiently specific that any variation in the use of evasive or non-evasive responses to them could give something away. Courts in the comparative jurisdictions have, in general terms, approved the adoption of a neither confirm nor deny response to statutory information requests where this is necessary to preserve the secrecy of information

---

description.'

[397] The Tribunal is thus given full appellate jurisdiction to review such matters unconstrained by any caveat that it 'apply the principles applied by the court on an application for judicial review' and assess only whether the Minister had 'reasonable grounds for issuing the certificate' (cf FOIA s 60(3), DPA s 28(5) and EIR reg 18(7)). The explanation for this is no doubt that the Minister can issue a new certificate with a much clearer application if dissatisfied with a determination made by the Tribunal under FOIA s 60(5) and DPA s 28(7). FOIA s 60(4) or DPA s 28(6) only provide for the resolution by way of appeal of a dispute over a certificate's applicability where it arises, in relation to FOIA, 'in any proceedings under this Act', in relation to DPA, 'in any proceeding under or by virtue of this Act' and, in relation to EIR, 'in any proceedings under these Regulations' (see EIR reg 18(4)(a)(i)). The reason for the different formulations is unclear and their effect depends on whether the need for 'proceedings' is given a strict or generous construction; the latter would expand the scope for having disputes over a certificate's applicability resolved by the Tribunal without the procedural need for separate 'proceedings'.

[398] The position may be different where there has been official disclosure of other information relating to the same subject and what is not released impinges upon the former's worth or reliability.

[399] The alternative is not to answer at all, but it would then be uncertain whether the question or the answer has reached its intended recipient.

[400] See §§15– 024 to 15– 025, and 17– 029(1). See also MoJ, *Exemptions Guidance—Section 24: National Security*, 14 May 2008, Annex C and ICO, *Freedom of Information Act Awareness Guidance 21 – the duty to confirm or deny*, (2008), pp 4-5. For a recent exposition and consideration of the reasons for adopting and adhering to a 'neither confirm nor deny' policy in the security and intelligence context see: *Re Freddie Scappaticci's Application* [2003] NIQB 56 at [6] and [15] (Carswell CJ) (NI).

whose sensitivity is recognised and protected by the legislation in question.[401] The application of these principles to ss 23 and 24 of the Freedom of Information Act 2000, s 28 of the Data Protection Act 1998 and reg 12 of the Environmental Information Regulations 2004 is dealt with below.[402]

056 The relationship between sections 23 and 24 of the Freedom of Information Act 2000 and the problem of giveaway refusals

Before turning to this, it is important to note four points regarding ss 23 and 24 of the Freedom of Information Act 2000:

(1) Sections 23 and 24 confer very different types of exemption. Section 23 is absolute and applies in a mechanical way according to the satisfaction of factual criteria regarding the historical supply and current content of the requested information. Section 23 thus leaves little scope for considering the desirability of a neither confirm nor deny approach in the particular circumstances of each case or as a matter of general policy for cases of the same type. By contrast, s 24 is qualified and applies in a purposive way where exemption is required for live and ongoing national security reasons. Section 24 therefore allows regard to be had not only to the content and sensitivity of the requested information, but also to the particular and general consequences of disclosure and, following on from this, the desirability of a neither confirm nor deny approach.

(2) Sections 23 and 24 are also mutually exclusive and do not overlap: s 24(1) only applies to information which does not fall within s 23(1); s 24(2) must be read as being subject to the same limitation in order to engage s 2(1); and s 24(3)–(4) must necessarily share the same limitation as well.[403] Moreover, s 23 takes precedence over s 24: it is not possible to rely on ss 23 and 24 in relation to the same information; and s 24 may only be relied upon if and to the extent that s 23 is not in play. One consequence of this is that reliance on s 23, which must be revealed under s 17(1)(b) of the Freedom of Information Act 2000, will inevitably inform the applicant that his request has engaged information of the kind described in s 23 while reliance on s 24 instead, which must also be revealed under s 17(1)(b), will inevitably inform the applicant that his request has not had this effect: refusals based

---

[401] In the US such a response is known as a 'Glomar' response after the 'Glomar Explorer', a vessel involved in the leading case *Phillippi v CIA* 546 F 2d 1009 (DC Cir 1976). See also: Presidential Executive Order No 12,958 (as amended), para 3.6(a) 'An agency may refuse to confirm or deny the existence or non-existence of requested records whenever the fact of their existence or non-existence is itself classified under this order or its predecessors'; *Gardels v CIA* (1982) 689 Fed Rep (2d) Ser 1100. The security bodies in the USA are generally successful in defending their 'Glomar' responses: eg *Frugone v CIA*, 169 F 3d 772 (DC Cir 1999); *Wheeler v CIA*, 271 F Supp 2d 132 (DDC 2003); *Miller v Casey*, 730 F 2d 773 (DC Cir 1984); *Minier v CIA*, 88 F 3d 796 (9th Cir 1996). Somewhat atypically, in *American Civil Liberties Union v Department of Defense*, 389 F Supp 2d 547 at 561 (SDNY 2005) the Court observed that the 'danger of Glomar responses is that they encourage an unfortunate tendency of government officials to over-classify information, frequently keeping secret that which the public already knows, or that which is more embarrassing than revelatory of intelligence sources or methods.' See further §2– 013 (Australia); §2– 020 (New Zealand); §2– 028 (Canada); and §2– 037 (Ireland).

[402] See §§17– 057 to 17– 061.

[403] The foundation of this analysis is set out at §17– 040. Substantially the same text appeared in the first edition of this work and was repeated and endorsed by the Information Tribunal in *Baker v IC & ors*, IT, 28 February 2007 at [30]–[33].

on ss 23 and 24 may therefore have a 'tell-tale' or 'giveaway' effect. A further consequence is that the effectiveness of s 24 and its ability to have regard to the desirability of the neither confirm nor deny approach are hampered by its confinement to information which does not fall within s 23(1).

(3) Having said this, it should be borne in mind that the amount of information revealed by the giveaway effect will always be limited. First, bare reference to s 23 under s 17(1)(b) will not identify the particular security body or bodies in question or reveal anything specific about their involvement, although this may be apparent from the context. Secondly, the institutional exclusion of the security bodies from the Freedom of Information Act 2000 regime means there is less scope for strategic sequential requests liable to yield variable responses and designed to flush out information through the giveaway effect. Thirdly, simultaneous joint reliance on ss 23 and 24 may be possible in relation to a single information request where different pieces of the information requested are subject to those provisions, and it may also be possible to rely on different exemptions in the alternative.[404] Fourthly, and as already discussed,[405] s 23(5) of the Freedom of Information Act 2000 allows a neither confirm nor deny response where divulgence would disclose unrecorded as well as recorded security body information and, because the fact that no such information is held is itself capable of being unrecorded information and may suggest that the security bodies did not and do not have any involvement in the subject matter of the request, there is considerable scope for reliance on FOIA, s 23 even in cases where the security bodies are not involved. This will also limit the giveaway effect because it may not be clear whether s 23(5) has been invoked by reason of security body involvement or the total absence thereof.

(4) Following the publication of the first edition of this work, the then-Department of Constitutional Affairs published non-statutory guidance notes on the various exemptions in Part II of the Freedom of Information Act 2000 which adopted a different interpretation of the relationship between ss 23 and 24 from that outlined above[406] and, following the publication of the second edition of this work, the Ministry of Justice has done likewise.[407] In short, the Department asserted that the 'use of section 23(5) and section 24(2) together is possible under the Act (in contrast to section 23(1) and section 24(1) which are expressly mutually exclusive)'[408] and the Ministry likewise claims:

By using both exemptions it obscures the fact that a section 23 body may or

---

[404] In this latter regard, FOIA ss 23 and 24 may be exclusive but each is capable of overlapping with, eg ss 26 and 27. So, while there is no room for choosing between reliance on ss 23 or 24 (if s 23 is in play, s 24 is not), it is perfectly possible to rely on ss 26 or 27 in addition or in preference to either ss 23 or 24.

[405] See §§17–033 and 17–040.

[406] DCA, *Exemptions Guidance—Section 23*, undated, and DCA, *Exemptions Guidance—Section 24*, undated.

[407] MoJ, *Exemptions Guidance—Section 23: information supplied by, or related to, bodies dealing with security matters*, 14 May 2008 and MoJ, *Exemptions Guidance—Section 24: National security*, 14 May 2008.

[408] DCA, *Exemptions Guidance—Section 23*, undated, para 4.2. See also DCA, *Exemptions Guidance—Section 24*, undated, para 4.4 and the Cabinet Office evidence set out in *Baker v IC & ors*, IT, 28 February 2007 at [34]. Neither document explains why FOIA ss 23(1) and 24(1) are admittedly exclusive while FOIA ss 23(5) and 24(2) are said to be capable of co-operation and no rationale for the difference of approach is advanced.

may not have been involved. This is permissible in contrast to the application of section 23(1) and 24(1)...where exemptions are mutually exclusive....The ability to use section 23(5) and 24(2) together in respect of the same information is important in order to maintain the principle that information about section 23 bodies is exempt.[409]

Although the current Ministry of Justice guidance claims that the Information Tribunal 'agreed with' the Government's approach in *Baker v Information Commissioner & ors*,[410] the reality is that the point has not yet been tested.[411] Furthermore, the Government's approach, while understandable, involves stretching the language of the provisions. It is submitted that the most straightforward construction of the relevant provisions gives rise to the conclusion that ss 23(5) and 24(2) are (like ss 23(1) and 24(1)) mutually exclusive and may not be the subject of simultaneous joint reliance. Although this allows for the occurrence of the giveaway effect, the practical, as opposed to the purely imagined, implications of that effect are likely to be very modest, if discernible at all. Indeed, it might be said that the actual language used reflects Parliament's assessment that the effect was not attended by a sufficient likelihood of harm to the protected interests.

057 Sections 23 and 24 of the Freedom of Information Act 2000: the scope for neither confirming nor denying

Under the Freedom of Information Act 2000 a neither confirm nor deny response may be given where the duty to confirm or deny does not arise by virtue of a Part II exemption which prevents the application of s 1(1)(a).[412] As indicated above, the mutually exclusive operation of

---

[409] MoJ, *Exemptions Guidance—Section 23: information supplied by, or related to, bodies dealing with security matters*, 14 May 2008 p 4; MoJ, *Exemptions Guidance—Section 24: National security*, 14 May 2008 pp 5-6. Again, the mutual exclusivity of FOIA ss 23(1) and 24(1) and the contrasting co-operation between 23(5) and 24(2) are not explained.

[410] IT, 28 February 2007. MoJ, *Exemptions Guidance—Section 23: information supplied by, or related to, bodies dealing with security matters*, 14 May 2008 p 4; MoJ, *Exemptions Guidance—Section 24: National security*, 14 May 2008 p 6.

[411] *Baker v IC & ors*, IT, 28 February 2007, the Tribunal upheld a decision of the Information Commissioner (Decision Notice, No FS50086063, dated 11 July 2006) which in turn approved a Cabinet Office refusal to confirm or deny whether requested information was held (Tribunal decision, [43]–[45]; Commissioner decision, para 2.3). The refusal was overtly based on FOIA ss 23(5) and 24(2) in conjunction but the lawfulness of this simultaneous joint reliance and the general co-operation or mutual exclusivity of these provisions were apparently not argued, considered or determined as live issues. The appeal was, moreover, determined on the papers and without an oral hearing. Interestingly, the Tribunal did endorse the logic of the position upon which the above conclusion as to mutual exclusivity is based (see §17– 040 and *Baker v IC & ors*, IT, 28 February 2007 at [30]–[33]). Having said this, it would appear that the Information Commissioner does not accept the Government's approach and its reading of *Baker v IC*: ICO, *Exemptions Guidance – Section 23: Information supplied by or relating to security bodies* (2009) p 4; ICO, *Exemptions Guidance – Section 24: The National Security Exemption* (2009) pp 3-4.

[412] During the passage of the Freedom of Information Bill, the Cabinet Officer Minister, Lord Falconer of Thoroton, gave the following example of a situation in which it might be necessary to give a neither confirm nor deny response to an information request: 'The clearest and easiest example is endangering the defence of the realm. You do not have to communicate information which endangers the defence of the realm. Nor do you have to confirm or deny whether such information exists when, if you did confirm or deny its existence, that in itself would endanger the defence of the realm. I give the obvious example. "Do you have detailed information concerning the chemical warfare capacities of the following countries?"; and then a list of countries is given. It could well damage the defence of the realm if one indicated the extent to which one had that information.' — Hansard HL vol 617 col 1252 (19 October 2000) (House of Lords Committee Stage). See also MoJ, *Exemptions Guidance—Section 23: information supplied by, or related to, bodies dealing with security matters*, 14 May 2008 pp 3-5; MoJ, *Exemptions Guidance—Section 24: National*

ss 23 and 24 of the Freedom of Information Act 2000 means that reliance on one exemption and not the other may itself be thought to reveal something. The extent to which this is thought to be the case will depend on the practical operation of s 23 in general and s 23(5) in particular[413] and the scope allowed thereunder for the use of neither confirm nor deny responses.[414] In this regard, further reference can be made to two hypothetical requests for information made to a government department or police authority regarding the involvement of the security bodies in a particular operation, namely, request A asking for a list of every agency that was involved and request B asking for a list of every security body that was involved.[415] As set out above, if a security body was involved in the operation the department can refuse to comment on this in reliance on s 23 and if no security bodies were involved it can adopt the same approach, provided the fact of this non-involvement is information held by it in recorded form or amounts to unrecorded information which relates to the security bodies for the purposes of s 23(5).[416] In relation to such a request, the use or non-use of s 23 will only prove revealing if it cannot be relied upon in cases of security body non-involvement. However, if it can be used in such circumstances, so as to obscure the significance of the application of s 23, it might in practice need to be relied upon in analogous situations.[417]

17– 058 Section 24 of the Freedom of Information Act 2000 and section 28 of the Data Protection Act 1998: the scope for neither confirming nor denying

Leaving to one side the effect which the exclusive precedence of s 23 of the Freedom of Information Act 2000 has on the application of the exemption in s 24 of that Act, the basic

---

security, 14 May 2008 p 4, Annex C.

[413] FOIA s 23(5) prevents the duty to confirm or deny the existence or non-existence of recorded information from arising if, or to the extent that, compliance would involve the disclosure of any information, whether or not already recorded, which was supplied by, or relates to, a security body; see also s 17(4). Because s 23(1)–(2) does not include the formulation 'whether or not already recorded', national security certificates issued thereunder may apply only to recorded information unless it can be argued (by reference to the default definition of 'information' in s 84) that 'the context otherwise requires' a different construction of 'information' in s 23(2) (ie one that imports 'whether or not already recorded' because these words appear in s 23(5)). Not adopting such a construction would lead to the result that a national security certificate under s 23(1)–(2) could not be issued to support a refusal to confirm or deny the existence of recorded information to the extent that this refusal is based on a need to prevent the disclosure of unrecorded information which was supplied by, or relates to, a security body: the absence of a national security certificate in a s 23 case would then point to reliance on s 23(5) unrecorded information and this could itself be revealing. Nor does the additional category of unrecorded information which falls within s 23(5) present an area of possible overlap with s 24 even though it is not information falling within s 23(1): this is because s 24 itself only applies to 'information which does not fall within s 23(1)' in the default sense of 'information recorded in any form which does not fall within s 23(1)'.

[414] The extent to which reliance on FOIA s 23 and not s 24 (or vice versa) will in practice be capable of revealing significant information will, in any event, be somewhat limited for the reasons given at §17– 056(3).

[415] See §17– 036.

[416] See §§17– 033 and 17– 036.

[417] This is because the fact of security body non-involvement will arise as an implicit issue or piece of information in many situations. Returning to hypothetical requests A and B, the possibility that the only agencies involved in the operation might have been security bodies complicates the picture even further: if the fact of the operation is a matter of public record and no agencies are referred to in response to either request A or request B, it could be readily inferred that they must all have been security bodies. Avoiding this through adherence to the principle of neither confirming nor denying would, however, require a blanket refusal to comment on the involvement of state agencies in almost any security or defence type operation. MoJ, *Exemptions Guidance—Section 24: National security*, 14 May 2008 p 6 may anticipate this difficulty when it talks in terms of information which 'could reasonably have been' supplied by or related to a security body.

purposive formulation of that exemption, and the equivalent exemption in s 28 of the Data Protection Act 1998, leaves scope for both provisions to be applied in a way that has regard to the desirability of a neither confirm nor deny approach in comparable situations and the general risks of mosaic prejudice.[418] This is probably of more immediate significance in relation to s 28 of the Data Protection Act 1998, because s 7 of that Act allows individuals to request that the security bodies themselves confirm whether they are processing personal data of which they are the data subject and disclose the source of any such data and information. The intelligence services in particular have sought to pursue a neither confirm nor deny policy when responding to such requests and various national security certificates have been issued and relied upon under s 28 of the Data Protection Act 1998 in order to allow them to do so. The history and success for them of this policy to date is outlined in the following two paragraphs.

059 National security certificates under the Data Protection Act 1998: original intelligence service certificates

Three national security certificates under s 28(2) of the Data Protection Act 1998 were originally issued by the Home Secretary (in relation to the Security Service) and the Foreign Secretary (in relation to SIS and GCHQ) in July 2000.[419] These certificates purported to confer a blanket exemption, allowing each intelligence service to respond with a vague and non-committal neither confirm nor deny reply to every request made to it under s 7(1)(a) of the Data Protection Act 1998 without considering whether a different response might be acceptable in the particular circumstances of the case in question. On an appeal brought under s 28(4) of the Data Protection Act 1998 the Information Tribunal quashed the Home Secretary's original certificate on the basis that its effect was 'unnecessarily wide'[420] and the Foreign Secretary's original certificates were subsequently withdrawn.[421]

060 National security certificates under the Data Protection Act 1998: replacement intelligence service certificates

Three replacement certificates under s 28(2) of the Data Protection Act 1998 were then issued by the Home Secretary (in relation to the Security Service) and the Foreign Secretary (in relation to SIS and GCHQ) in December 2001, together with documents giving explanatory reasons.[422] The replacement certificates are expressed in broadly similar general and

---

[418] See §17–029(1).

[419] The Home Secretary's certificate was dated 22 July 2000 and the Foreign Secretary's certificates were dated 30 July 2000.

[420] *Baker v SSHD* [2001] UKHRR 1275, an appeal under DPA s 28(4). Having referred in general terms to the Council of Europe Convention for the Protection of Individuals with Regard to Automatic Processing of Personal Data dated 28 January 1981, the European Community Data Protection Directive 95/46/EC dated 24 October 1995 and the Human Rights Act 1998 ss 1, 3 and 6, the Tribunal asked itself whether the issue of the certificate was 'reasonable in the extended sense of proportionate by reference to the precepts of the ECHR' (at [63]) and concluded that the certificate had an 'unnecessarily wide effect' and should be quashed accordingly (summary, [14]).

[421] *Al Fayed v SSHD*, IT, 28 February 2002 at [9] and [15]–[16].

[422] The Home Secretary's certificate was dated 10 December 2001 and the Foreign Secretary's certificates were dated 8 December 2001. Copies of the certificate and reasons document relating to the Security Service are annexed to the decisions of the Information Tribunal in *Gosling v SSHD*, IT, 1 August 2003 and *Hitchens v SSHD*, IT, 4 August 2003. The certificate and reasons document relating to GCHQ were also accompanied by a document headed 'GCHQ Arrangements' setting out the Foreign Secretary's policy in relation to requests made under DPA s 7 and

prospective terms and confer exemption from different provisions of the Data Protection Act 1998 on personal data processed by the intelligence services depending on the purposes and types of data involved. The replacement certificates provide: first, that no data shall be exempt from s 7(1)(a) of the Data Protection Act 1998 if the intelligence service in question determines that adherence to the principle of neither confirming nor denying whether it holds data about an individual is not required for the purpose of safeguarding national security; and, secondly, that no data shall be exempt from s 7(1)(b)-(d) of the Data Protection Act 1998 if the intelligence service in question determines that the non-communication of such data or any description of such data is not required for the purpose of safeguarding national security. On appeals brought under s 28(4) of the Data Protection Act 1998 the Information Tribunal has effectively upheld the format of all three certificates,[423] although it should be noted that it has only done so in response to appeals founded on somewhat limited grounds.[424] In this regard, the Information Tribunal held that there were reasonable grounds for, in effect, delegating to the Security Service the power to determine the requirements of national security in relation to each request, bearing in mind the scope for challenging such determinations before the RIPA Tribunal under s 65 of the Regulation of Investigatory Powers Act 2000 or, possibly, by way of judicial review.[425]

17– 061 Regulation 12 of the Environmental Information Regulations 2004: the scope for neither confirming nor denying

Regulation 12(6) of the Environmental Information Regulations 2004 allows for a 'neither confirm nor deny' response to a request for environmental information, whether or not the public authority holds such information, if confirmation or denial would involve the disclosure of information which would adversely affect international relations, defence, national security or public safety.[426] As with s 24 of the Freedom of Information Act 2000 and s 28 of the Data Protection Act 1998, this provision allows the public authority to consider the desirability of a neither confirm nor deny approach in comparable situations and the general risks of mosaic prejudice when determining the risk of an adverse affect on any of those interests.[427] Having said this, the public authority must also apply the presumption in favour of disclosure imposed by reg 12(2) of the Environmental Information Regulations 2004 and this could conceivably cause it to decide against adopting a neither confirm nor deny stance in circumstances where

---

the procedure to be followed by GCHQ when responding to them (*Hitchens v SSHD*, IT, 4 August 2003 at [48]). Copies of the certificates and reasons documents for all three intelligence services were also placed in the Libraries of both Houses of Parliament (*Intelligence and Security Committee Annual Report 2001–2002* (Cm 5542, 2002) para 50). The Foreign and Home Secretaries both signed a similar certificate under s 28(2) of DPA in relation to personal data processed by the Intelligence and Security Committee established under s 10 of the Intelligence Services Act 1994 or by its Secretariat, and the Committee in turn issued its own explanatory reasons document (*Intelligence and Security Committee Annual Report 2001–2002* (Cm 5542, 2002) paras 49–50 and Appendix 2).

[423] *Gosling v SSHD*, IT, 1 August 2003 followed in *Hitchens v SSHD*, IT, 4 August 2003 and *Hilton v FCO*, IT, 28 June 2005; *Stevenson v SSHD*, IT, 30 April 2009.

[424] *Gosling v SSHD*, IT, 1 August 2003 at [28]; *Hitchens v SSHD*, IT, 4 August 2003 at [42].

[425] *Gosling v SSHD*, IT, 1 August 2003 at [56]; *Hitchens v SSHD*, IT, 4 August 2003 at [49]; *Hilton v FCO*, IT, 28 June 2005. As to the scope for judicial review, see now *R (A) v Director of Establishments of the Security Service* [2009] UKSC 12, [2010] 2 WLR 1.

[426] See EIR reg 12(7). See also EI(S)R reg 10(8)–(9).

[427] See §17– 029(1).

it might have done so under equivalent provisions in the Freedom of Information Act 2000 or the Data Protection Act 1998. It is clear from the inclusion of 'whether or not it holds such information' in reg 12(6) of the Environmental Information Regulations 2004 and from reg 12(7), which provides that whether information exists and is held by a public authority is itself the disclosure of information, that neither confirm nor deny responses may be made thereunder irrespective of whether the public authority holds any sensitive information. If knowledge of the fact that the authority does not hold any such information could itself imperil one of the specified interests, a neither confirm nor deny response will be legitimate.

062 The date to which a certificate relates

National security certificates under s 23(2) of the Freedom of Information Act 2000 may certify that information was directly or indirectly supplied by any of the security bodies as a matter of historical fact or that it relates to any of those bodies as a matter of current fact.[428] National security certificates under reg 15(1) of the Environmental Information Regulations 2004 may certify that the disclosure of information 'would' adversely affect national security and thus must mean if disclosure were to take place now or at any time in the future while the certificate remains in force.[429] However, national security certificates under s 24(3) of the Freedom of Information Act 2000 and s 28(2) of the Data Protection Act 1998 may certify that the exemption of the information or personal data to which it applies 'is or at any time was required' for the purpose of safeguarding national security. The past tense formulation 'or at any time was' is included to allow for national security certificates which are issued after the relevant exemption has been relied upon by the public authority in question.[430] It does not enable a Minister to claim exemption where this is no longer required for the purpose of safeguarding national security, because the operative exemption provisions only apply in circumstances where exemption 'is required' for that purpose.[431]

6. INFORMATION PREJUDICIAL TO DEFENCE OR THE ARMED FORCES

063 Introduction

As already indicated, information whose disclosure under the Freedom of Information Act 2000 would, or would be likely to, prejudice the defence of the British Islands or of any colony or the capability, effectiveness or security of the armed forces of the Crown or of any forces co-operating with those forces ('the s 26 defence interests') is also subject to a qualified exemption under s 26 of that Act. A similar exemption is to be found in the freedom of information

---

[428] See §17– 051.

[429] See §17– 053.

[430] In relation to FOIA s 24, this was confirmed in House of Commons Public Administration Select Committee Third Report Session 1998–1999 *Freedom of Information Draft Bill* (HC 570–I), 1999, paras 74–77 and Annex 6, para 44.

[431] FOIA s 24(1)–(2); DPA s 28(1).

legislation of each of the comparative jurisdictions.[432] The phrase 'would or would be likely to prejudice' is common to most of the prejudice-based exemptions in the Act. The nature of prejudice and the degree of likelihood which the phrase requires are considered elsewhere in this work.[433]

17– 064 **Terms of the exemption in section 26 of the Freedom of Information Act 2000**

Section 26(1) of the Freedom of Information Act 2000[434] provides that information is exempt information if its disclosure under the Act would, or would be likely to, prejudice any of the s 26 defence interests. Having reached that threshold, the duty to communicate will not apply where, in all the circumstances of the case, the public interest in maintaining the exemption outweighs the public interest in disclosing the information.[435] Section 26(3) provides a corresponding exclusion of the duty to confirm or deny where, or to the extent that, compliance with the duty to divulge the existence of information would, or would be likely to, prejudice any of the s 26 defence interests. Section 26(3) is not expressed to relate to any particular category of information and does not itself stand as a 'provision' which 'states that the duty to confirm or deny does not arise in relation to any information' for the purposes of s 2(1). However, for the reasons set out above in relation to s 24(2),[436] the whole of s 26 needs to be read as the 'provision' which 'states that the duty to confirm or deny does not arise in relation to any information' and which therefore engages s 2(1). On this basis, if the s 26(3) description is met, the duty to confirm or deny does not apply only where, in all the circumstances of the case, the public interest in maintaining the exclusion of the divulgence duty outweighs the public interest

---

[432] In the United States, the Freedom of Information Act, 1966, 5 USC 552(b)(1) s 6F(b) (USA), exempts from disclosure national security information concerning national defence or foreign policy, provided that that information has been classified in accordance with the requirements of a Presidential Executive Order: see §2– 008(1). The Freedom of Information Act 1982 s 33(1)(a) (Cth of Aust), provides an exemption where the disclosure of the requested document would, or could be reasonably be expected to, cause damage to (i) the security of the Commonwealth of Australia; or (ii) the defence of the Commonwealth of Australia: see §2– 015(9). The Act makes provision for neither confirming nor denying the existence of the requested documents where to do so would or could reasonably be expected to cause damage to these interests (see §2– 013). The Official Information Act 1982 ss 6(a), 7 and 27(1)(a) (NZ) and the Privacy Act 1993 ss 27(1)(a) and 27(2)(a)–(c) provide absolute exemptions where the disclosure of the information would be likely to prejudice the security or defence of New Zealand or certain external dependencies: see §2– 022(1). The Official Information Act 1982 (NZ) provides for a conclusive certificate to be issued in relation to this exemption in connection with investigations by the Ombudsman (see §2– 021) and makes provision for neither confirming nor denying the existence of the requested documents where to do so would or could reasonably be expected to cause damage to these interests (see §2– 020). The Access to Information Act (1982) s 15 (Canada), provides a discretionary exemption for records the disclosure of which could reasonably be expected to cause injury to the defence of Canada or allied states: see §2– 032(11). 'Defence of Canada', etc is defined to include the efforts of Canada and of foreign states toward the detection, prevention and suppression of activities of any foreign state directed toward actual or potential attack or other acts of aggression against Canada or any state allied or associated with Canada: s 15(2). The Freedom of Information Act 1997 s 24(1) (Ireland), provides a discretionary exemption for records the disclosure of which could reasonably be expected to adversely affect the security or defence of the Republic of Ireland: see §2– 039(13). The public body can refuse to confirm or deny the existence of any record falling within the terms of the exemption if it thinks that to do either would be contrary to the public interest: Freedom of Information Act 1997 s 24(3) (Ireland): see §2– 037. A conclusive certificate may be issued in respect of this head of exemption: Freedom of Information Act 1997 s 25 (Ireland): see §2– 038.

[433] See §§15– 020 to 15– 028.

[434] FOI(S)A s 31(4).

[435] FOIA s 2(2)(b).

[436] See §17– 040(1).

in disclosing whether the public authority holds the information requested.[437]

065   Terms of the exemption in Schedule 7 to the Data Protection Act 1998

As already indicated, Sch 7 to the Data Protection Act 1998 further exempts personal data from the subject access provisions in that Act[438] in any case to the extent to which the application of those provisions would be likely to prejudice the combat effectiveness of any of the armed forces of the Crown.[439] This is a much narrower exemption than s 26 of the Freedom of Information Act 2000 for the following reasons: it does not wholly exempt the type of information in question from the entirety of the Data Protection Act 1998 regime; it is confined to the combat effectiveness of the armed forces of the Crown and does not extend to their general effectiveness; it does not protect the defence of the British Islands or of any colony or the capability or security of the armed forces of the Crown; and it does not protect forces co-operating with them. The adoption of this narrower formulation was not expressly required by the European Community Data Protection Directive 95/46/EC, which allowed for restrictions and exemptions where necessary to safeguard defence.[440] The armed forces exemption in Sch 7 to the Data Protection Act 1998 does not operate, and cannot be overridden, by reference to any public interest balancing test, but its application is subject to the full range of enforcement mechanisms in Part V of that Act. The remainder of this section concentrates on the exemption in s 26 of the Freedom of Information Act 2000, but the same definition of the armed forces of the Crown and the same considerations as to the executive's assessment of likely prejudice to their combat effectiveness are nevertheless relevant to the armed forces exemption in Sch 7 to the Data Protection Act 1998.

066   Terms of the exception in regulation 12 of the Environmental Information Regulations 2004

As already indicated, reg 12 of the Environmental Information Regulations 2004 provides a qualified exception to the duty to disclose environmental information which allows public authorities to refuse to disclose information to the extent that its disclosure would adversely affect international relations, defence, national security or public safety.[441] This exception operates in exactly the same way in relation to defence interests as it does in relation to national security interests and its terms do not require further description here.[442]

067   The British Islands and the colonies

While s 24 of the Freedom of Information Act 2000 is concerned with safeguarding national

---

[437] FOIA s 26(3) (read with s 26(1)) thus engages s 2(1)(b) so as to prevent s 1(1)(a) from applying and the duty to confirm or deny from arising in relation to the exempt information if the public interest balance favours non-divulgence.

[438] The subject information provisions include the subject access rights under s 7: DPA ss 27(2) and 71.

[439] DPA s 37 Sch 7 para 2. cf FOIA s 26(1) which uses the more exhaustive formulation 'would, or would be likely to, prejudice'.

[440] [1995] OJ L281/31 art 13(1)(b).

[441] EIR reg 12(1)(a) and (5)(a). See also EI(S)R reg 10(1)–(2) and (5)(a) applying the 'would, or would be likely to, prejudice substantially' test and an additional requirement that reg 10(4)–(5) are interpreted 'in a restrictive way' to an otherwise similarly worded 'exception'.

[442] See §17–042.

security, meaning 'the security of the United Kingdom and its people',[443] s 26 of the Act might be thought to have a geographically wider purview in that it is overtly concerned with the defence of the British Islands and of any colony.[444] The significance of this should not be overstated, however, as it has been recognised that action overseas may be capable of indirectly affecting the security of the United Kingdom even if directed towards a foreign State.[445] For the purposes of s 26 of the Freedom of Information Act 2000, the British Islands means the United Kingdom, the Channel Islands and the Isle of Man (but not the Republic of Ireland which could be said to fall within the British Isles).[446] The United Kingdom in turn means Great Britain (ie England, Scotland and Wales)[447] and Northern Ireland, while the Channel Islands means the Bailiwick of Jersey and the Bailiwick of Guernsey, Alderney and Sark and their respective dependencies.[448] Colony means any part of Her Majesty's dominions outside the British Islands,[449] except countries having fully responsible status within the Commonwealth[450] and their respective dependencies.[451]

17– 068   The armed forces of the Crown

The expression 'the armed forces of the Crown' is not defined in the Freedom of Information Act 2000 or the Data Protection Act 1998 but must include the regular, reserve and auxiliary naval, military and air forces of the Crown and the women's services of those forces.[452]

---

[443] *SSHD v Rehman* [2001] UKHL 47, [2003] 1 AC 153, at [50] (Lord Hoffmann) and [64] (Lord Hutton).

[444] FOIA s 26(1); FOI(S)A s 31(4).

[445] *SSHD v Rehman* [2001] UKHL 47, [2003] 1 AC 153 at [16]–[17] (Lord Slynn). See also at [53] and [62] (Lord Hoffmann) and [64] (Lord Hutton). It is at least conceivable that some colonies may be of little or no significance to the national security of the United Kingdom so that considerations relating to their defence could engage FOIA s 26 but not s 24.

[446] Interpretation Act 1978 ss 5 22(1) Sch 1 Sch 2 para 4(2); F Bennion, *Statutory Interpretation*, 5th edn (London, LexisNexis, 2008), p 343.

[447] Interpretation Act 1978 ss 5 22(1) Sch 1 Sch 2 para 5(a); Union with Scotland Act 1706 preamble art 1.

[448] F Bennion, *Statutory Interpretation*, 5th edn (London, LexisNexis, 2008), pp 343-344.

[449] Interpretation Act 1978 s 5 Sch 1; F Bennion, *Statutory Interpretation*, 5th edn (London, LexisNexis, 2008), p345. MoJ, *Exemptions Guidance—Section 26: Defence* (14 May 2008), Annex A, lists the colonies as Anguilla, Bermuda, British Antarctic Territories, British Indian Ocean Territories, British Virgin Islands, Cayman Islands, Falkland Islands, Gibraltar, Montserrat, Pitcairn Island, South Georgia and South Sandwich Islands, Sovereign Base Area of Cyprus, St Helena and dependencies (Ascension Island and Tristan da Cunha), and Turks and Caicos Islands.

[450] That is, countries other than the United Kingdom which are part of Her Majesty's independent dominions.

[451] The statutory expression is 'territories for whose external relations a country other than the United Kingdom is responsible'. Associated states are also excluded from the definition of a colony, but this is now a defunct category as there are no longer any territories maintaining a status of association with the United Kingdom in accordance with the West Indies Act 1967.

[452] This is supported by the definition of 'the armed forces of the Crown raised in the United Kingdom at the present day' at *Halsbury's Laws of England*, 4th edn, 2003 re-issue, vol 2(2), title 'Armed Forces', para 1. The Armed Forces Act 1981 s 20(1) Sch 3 Pts I–II further provide that 'the armed forces of the Crown' (raised in the United Kingdom and excluding the Royal Navy) includes the women's services of those forces administered by the Defence Council: see also *Halsbury's Laws of England*, 4th edn, 2003 re-issue, vol 2(2), title 'Armed Forces', para 18. On this basis, the armed forces of the Crown comprise: the regular forces (ie the Royal Navy, Army, Royal Air Force and Royal Marines); the reserve and auxiliary forces (including the Territorial Army); and the women's services and their reserves. The alternative expression 'Her Majesty's forces' is also used in some legislation, eg Regulation of Investigatory Powers Act 2000 s 81(1) and Armed Forces Act 2006, Pts 1, 3, 6, 14, 16–18. As to the armed forces more generally see: A Bradley and K Ewing, *Constitutional and Administrative Law*, 14th edn (Pearson Longman,

Authority for the existence and maintenance of the naval forces derives from the royal prerogative, while authority for the existence and maintenance of the military and air forces derives from statute.[453] In terms of the principal and most important statutes, regard should be had to the Armed Forces Act 2006, as well the Naval Discipline Act 1957 (dealing with discipline in the naval forces), the Army Act 1955 (dealing with the raising and maintenance of, and the keeping of discipline within, the military forces) and the Air Force (Constitution) Act 1917 and the Air Force Act 1955 (dealing with the raising and maintenance of, and the keeping of discipline within, the air forces).[454] Similarly, the territorial forces, the naval, military and air force reserves and the women's services are raised and maintained primarily under the Reserve Forces Act 1996, the Armed Forces Act 2006 and the prerogative.[455] The supreme government, command and disposition of all the armed forces by sea, land and air, and of all defence establishments, is ultimately vested in the Crown by prerogative right at common law and by statute.[456] However, these powers are now exercised on the advice of ministers and most matters relating to the armed forces are regulated by statute and administered by and through ministers, the Ministry of Defence, the Defence Council and the Admiralty, Army and Air Force Boards.[457]

069   Other relevant forces

Although certain forces raised under the law of a colony, protectorate or trust territory and

---

London, 2007) pp 343–358; O Hood Phillips and P Jackson, *Constitutional and Administrative Law*, 8th edn (Sweet & Maxwell, London, 2001) paras 19–002 to 19–018; FW Maitland, *The Constitutional History of England* (Cambridge, Cambridge University Press, 1919) pp 275–280, 324–329 and 447–462; W Anson, *Law and Custom of the Constitution*, 4th edn (Oxford, Oxford University Press, 1907) vol II(ii), pp 199–222; Rowe 'The Crown and Accountability for the Armed Forces' in M Sunkin and S Payne (eds), *The Nature of the Crown: a Legal and Political Analysis* (Oxford, Oxford University Press, 1999). The special forces and any unit or part of a unit which is for the time being required by the Secretary of State to assist GCHQ in the exercise of its functions are not excluded from the definition of the armed forces of the Crown for the purposes of FOIA s 26, cf Sch 1, Pt I, para 6. See also MoJ, *Exemptions Guidance — Section 26: Defence* (18 May 2008) Annex A.

[453] Bill of Rights Act (1688 or 1689) art 1 prevents the Crown from raising or keeping a standing army within the United Kingdom in times of peace without the consent of Parliament; *Halsbury's Laws of England*, 4th edn, 1996 re-issue, vol 8(2), title 'Constitutional Law and Human Rights', paras 883 and 886–887; *Halsbury's Laws of England*, 4th edn, 2003 re-issue, vol 2(2), title 'Armed Forces', paras 1–9.

[454] The Army Act 1955, Air Force Act 1955 and Naval Discipline Act 1957 ('the Service Discipline Acts') are each continued in force for one year at a time by Army, Air Force and Naval Discipline (Continuation) Orders made annually during the course of five-year periods, in turn instituted by quinquennial Armed Forces Acts. *Halsbury's Laws of England*, 4th edn, 1996 re-issue, vol 8(2), title 'Constitutional Law and Human Rights', para 887; *Halsbury's Laws of England*, 4th edn, 2003 re-issue, vol 2(2), title 'Armed Forces', para 3. The Service Discipline Acts were repealed and replaced by the Armed Forces Act 2006 and will ultimately constitute the relevant provisions as to discipline in the armed forces in a harmonised and consolidated 'tri-service' format. Much of the Air Force (Constitution) Act 1917 will remain in force.

[455] Much of the Reserve Forces Act 1996 and the whole of the Army and Air Force (Women's Service) Act 1948 have been repealed and replaced by the Armed Forces Act 2006: see ss 378(2), 383(2), Sch 17. See generally: *Halsbury's Laws of England*, 4th edn, 1996 re-issue, vol 8(2), title 'Constitutional Law and Human Rights', paras 888–889.

[456] *Halsbury's Laws of England*, 4th edn, 1996 re-issue, vol 8(2), title 'Constitutional Law and Human Rights', para 884.

[457] Defence (Transfer of Functions) Act 1964; *Halsbury's Laws of England*, 4th edn, 1996 re-issue, vol 8(2), title 'Constitutional Law and Human Rights', paras 439–447 and 885–886; *Halsbury's Laws of England*, 4th edn, 2003 re-issue, vol 2(2), title 'Armed Forces', paras 1–2.

certain visiting forces can become subject to United Kingdom service law and discipline,[458] they are not 'armed forces of the Crown' for the purposes of the Freedom of Information Act 2000.[459] Any forces co-operating with the armed forces of the Crown or any part of those forces are, however, relevant forces for the purposes of s 26 of the Freedom of Information Act 2000.[460] Colonial, Commonwealth and other allied armed forces could fall into this category when co-operating with the armed forces of the Crown on operations or exercises on any kind of bilateral or multilateral basis or under the auspices of, for example, the North Atlantic Treaty Organisation or the United Nations.[461] There is also no express requirement that these co-operating forces be either armed or foreign and so it might be argued that domestic or foreign police or security forces are included. One question arising in relation to other relevant forces is whether general prejudice to their capability, effectiveness or security is enough to engage s 26 or whether what matters is their capability, effectiveness or security whilst they are 'co-operating with' the armed forces of the Crown: the latter interpretation seems preferable, since otherwise account could be taken of prejudice to the capability, effectiveness or security of forces which co-operate only occasionally with the armed forces of the Crown.

17–070 Prejudice to the defence of the British Islands or of any colony

Whether disclosure of particular information under the Freedom of Information Act 2000 would prejudice, or would be likely to prejudice, the defence of the British Islands or of any colony cannot properly be determined without some consideration of what the defence of the nation may reasonably require in the prevailing circumstances. Distinctions may be drawn between what is legitimately required for the defence of a nation in peacetime, during a time of preparation for war, during actual hostilities, upon the cessation of hostilities and in the transition to peace.[462] Prejudice to the defence of the nation will reflect those distinctions. The defence of the nation is not confined to the resistance of external threats to the nation, but extends to matters whose purpose is the protection of the nation.[463] Accordingly, there is bound

---

[458] Armed Forces Act 2006 ss 367–369; Visiting Forces (British Commonwealth) Act 1933 ss 4–6; Visiting Forces Act 1952; International Headquarters and Defence Organisations Act 1964; *Halsbury's Laws of England*, 4th edn, 2003 re-issue, vol 2(2), title 'Armed Forces', paras 10–11, 20, 22 and 135–150.

[459] Note the exclusion of Commonwealth forces from the definitions of 'Her Majesty's air forces', 'Her Majesty's forces' and 'Her Majesty's military forces' in Armed Forces Act 2006 s 374.

[460] FOIA s 26(2)(b); FOI(S)A s 31(5)(b)(ii).

[461] The involvement of foreign States or international organisations might also engage the international relations exemption in FOIA s 27, FOI(S)A s 32(1).

[462] For a discussion of the fluctuating nature of what may legitimately be done under the aegis of the defence of the nation, see: *Stenhouse v Coleman* (1944) 69 CLR 457 at 471–472. The Constitution of Australia gives the Federal legislature the power to make laws with respect to the 'defence of the Commonwealth'. In general terms, the view taken is that in a period of stable and amicable international relations the extent of what may be done in the name of the defence of the Commonwealth is small: there can be no reasonable justification for interference with most ordinary civil activities. But at a period of international discord, the danger to the nation of becoming involved in war may be great and what may legitimately be done in the name of the defence of the nation is broader: *Farey v Burvett* (1916) 21 CLR 433 at 453; *Victorian Chamber of Manufacturers v The Commonwealth of Australia* (1943) 67 CLR 335 at 339; *Adelaide Company of Jehovah's Witnesses Incorporated v Commonwealth of Australia* (1943) 67 CLR 116.

[463] MoJ, *Exemptions Guidance—Section 26: Defence* (18 May 2008) Annex A states that defence, 'is achieved by maintaining the ability to use military force in support of legitimate political objectives, in particular the protection of the UK, overseas territories and national interests. Defence can therefore include self-defence, as well as measures taken in conjunction with other countries or under the auspices of an international organisation. Such measures may include steps for the detection, prevention and suppression of aggressive activities of any foreign state or party against the

to be some overlap between information whose disclosure would, or would be likely to, prejudice, on the one hand, the defence of the British Islands or of any colony and, on the other hand, the capability, effectiveness or security of any relevant forces, as well as a substantial overlap with information whose non-disclosure is required for the purpose of safeguarding national security. The s 26 defence interests are akin to the national security interests covered by s 24 of the Freedom of Information Act 2000. The courts may therefore be expected to adopt an analogous approach to the executive's assessment of their protection and the type of disclosure which would be likely to cause them prejudice: the executive will thus be entitled to take a preventative or precautionary approach to the protection of the s 26 defence interests, taking into account the risks of mosaic prejudice,[464] and the courts can be expected to show a certain deference to its conclusions.[465] Section 2 of the Official Secrets Act 1989[466] provides some guidance as to the type of matters that may be relevant to 'defence'[467] and the type of effects which are 'damaging' to defence interests.[468]

UK, overseas territories and national interests, and may include counter terrorist and resilience measures'. For the government line on prejudice to defence interests generally, see MoJ, *Exemptions Guidance — Section 26: Defence* (18 May 2008) pp 3-4.

[464] See §17– 029(1). This has been the approach taken by the High Court of Australia in determining whether a law is one with respect to the defence of the Commonwealth: 'It is not the duty or the function of the court to consider whether in its opinion such regulations are 'necessary' for defence purposes. Questions of legislative policy are determined by the legislature, not by the courts. If it can reasonably be considered that there is a real connection between the subject matter of the legislation and defence, the court should hold that the legislation is authorised by the power to make laws with respect to defence' (*Dawson v The Commonwealth* (1946) 73 CLR 157 at 173). However, the High Court has rejected the notion that the Parliament's or the executive's determination of the needs of defence can be conclusive: *Australian Communist Party v The Commonwealth of Australia* (1951) 83 CLR 1, where the Court held that a law *inter alia* dissolving the Australian Communist Party which, in its recital, was declared to be detrimental to the defence of the nation could not, in fact, be said to be related to the defence of the nation.

[465] See §§17– 040 to 17– 049. See also: *R v Jones (Margaret)* [2006] UKHL 16, [2007] 1 AC 136 at [30], 'there are well-established rules that the courts will be very slow to review the exercise of prerogative powers in relation to the conduct of foreign affairs and the deployment of the armed services' (Lord Bingham citing: *Chandler v DPP* [1964] AC 763; *Council of Civil Service Unions v Minister for the Civil Service* [1985] AC 374; *Lord Advocate's Reference (No1 of 2000)* 2001 JC 143; *R (Marchiori) v Environment Agency* [2002] EWCA Civ 3, [2002] Eu LR 225 (CA)) and at [65]–[67] (Lord Hoffmann). For analogous wartime cases see: *Lipton Ltd v Ford* [1917] 2 KB 647; *Hudson's Bay Co v Maclay* (1920) 36 TLR 469; *John Robinson & Co Ltd v The King* [1921] 3 KB 183 at 197; *Fort Frances Pulp and Paper Co v Manitoba Free Press Co* [1923] AC 695 at 705–705; *Victorian Chamber of Manufactures v Commonwealth of Australia* (1943) 67 CLR 347 ('when a nation is in peril, applying the maxim *salus populi suprema lex*, the courts must concede to the Parliament and to the Executive which it controls a wide latitude to determine what legislation is required to protect the safety of the realm' at 400); *Hamilton v Kentucky Distilleries & Warehouse Co* (1919) 251 US 146 ('to the Congress, in the exercise of its powers, not least the war upon which the very life of the nation depends, a wide latitude of discretion must be accorded' at 163).

[466] See §17– 028(1).

[467] Official Secrets Act 1989 s 2(4) defines 'defence' to mean (a) the size, shape, organisation, logistics, order of battle, deployment, operations, state of readiness and training of the armed forces of the Crown, (b) the weapons, stores or other equipment of those forces and the invention, development, production and operation of such equipment and research relating to it, (c) defence policy and strategy and military planning and intelligence and (d) plans and measures for the maintenance of essential supplies and services that are or would be needed in time of war. See also MoJ, *Exemptions Guidance — Section 26: Defence* (18 May 2008) pp 3-4.

[468] For the purposes of Official Secrets Act 1989 s 2(1) a disclosure is damaging if it (a) damages the capability of, or any part of, the armed forces of the Crown to carry out their tasks or leads to loss of life or injury to members of those forces or serious damage to the equipment or installations of those forces, (b) endangers the interests of the United Kingdom abroad, seriously obstructs the promotion or protection by the United Kingdom of those interests or endangers the safety of British citizens abroad or (c) would be likely to have any of those effects (s 2(2)).

17– 071 **Prejudice to the capability, effectiveness or security of the armed forces**

So far as concerns the capability, effectiveness and security of any relevant forces, the Ministry of Justice has published its own guidance on the meaning of these terms:[469]

Capability: Capability involves having the necessary skills to operate in a particular situation. In relation to defence it is derived from having trained manpower, serviceable equipment, the supporting systems and information needed to deploy to and conduct operations that meet the policy objectives set by government.

Effectiveness: Effectiveness relates to the successful use of defence capability. This requires a readiness to undertake operations in a structured way that is appropriate to the situation, in conjunction with government departments and, where appropriate, other states and international organisations

Security: Security is achieved through the protection of personnel from attack, both at a collective and at an individual level, and from the threat of compromise to the confidentiality, integrity and/or availability of defence assets.

The Information Commissioner has also issued guidance on this topic suggesting that information about the reliability of military equipment 'might' be exempt under s 26 of the Freedom of Information Act 2000 'if it would enable an enemy to sabotage that equipment but not if the weakness was impossible to exploit or if it were one that was impossible to conceal.'[470] Finally, the Ministry of Defence publication *The Green Book: MoD Working Arrangements with the Media* provides guidance on procedures that the Ministry will adopt 'in working with the media throughout the full spectrum of military operations.'[471] Under the heading 'Restrictions on Reporting' there is a list of 'Subjects that correspondents may not be allowed to include in copy, or radio or television reports without specific approval.'[472] These categories give a further indication of the types of information whose disclosure may be capable of prejudicing the capability, effectiveness or security of the armed forces.[473] The s 26 defence interests, of course, go much wider than this and are not confined to periods of operational activity.

---

[469] MoJ, *Exemptions Guidance — Section 26: Defence* (18 May 2008) Annex A.

[470] Information Commissioner, *Freedom of Information Act Awareness Guidance No 10: The Defence Exemption*, (2006), Pt C. The remainder of this passage reads as follows: 'The timing of a disclosure is likely to be crucial. Information which might prejudice the effectiveness of a military operation that was either planned or underway might cause no harm once the operation had been concluded. This is not an absolute rule, and there will certainly be many cases where the disclosure of information about the tactics or weaponry involved in a successful operation might prejudice the chances of success in a similar operation in the future. When assessing whether disclosure would prejudice the purpose of defence, consideration should also be given to what information is already in the public domain. Where the same information is available from other, reliable sources, it will rarely be possible to argue that repeated disclosure would cause prejudice. By contrast, where the information available from elsewhere is of a more speculative nature (even though, in fact, true), then it will be easier to argue prejudice. Similarly, a public authority may legitimately decide to withhold information which is in itself relatively innocuous if that information would cause prejudice in combination with another piece of information which has already been put in the public domain.'

[471] The Green Book can be found at: www.mod.uk/DefenceInternet/AboutDefence via the links for 'Corporate Publications' and 'Doctrine Operations and Diplomacy Publications'.

[472] Ministry of Defence, *The Green Book: MoD Working Arrangements with the Media* (2008) para 43.

[473] The categories are: (a) composition of the force and the locations of ships, units and aircraft; (b) details of military movements; (c) operational orders; (d) plans or intentions; (e) casualties; (f) organisations; (g) place names; (h) tactics, details of defensive positions, camouflage methods, weapon capabilities or deployments, force protection measures; (i) names or numbers of ships, units or aircraft; (j) names of individual servicemen; (k) prisoners of war. See also MoJ *Exemptions Guidance — Section 26: Defence* (18 May 2008) pp 3-4.

072 Will the public interest in protecting defence interests always outweigh the public interest in disclosure?

Even if non-compliance with the duty to confirm or deny or the duty to communicate is required because divulgence or disclosure would, or would be likely to, prejudice any of the s 26 defence interests, divulgence or disclosure will still have to take place under s 1 of the Freedom of Information Act 2000 if, in all the circumstances of the case, the public interest in divulgence or disclosure is not outweighed by the public interest in preventing, or avoiding the risk of, such prejudice.[474] As with the safeguarding of national security interests under s 24 of the Freedom of Information Act 2000, the decision of Parliament not to make exemption under s 26 absolute cannot properly be undone by giving the public interest in maintaining the exemption such weight as to guarantee that the public interest in disclosure will necessarily be lighter.[475] The exercise must be carried out in such a manner as to recognise that in some circumstances the public interest in disclosure will be sufficiently powerful to match an inherently compelling public interest in maintaining the exemption.[476] For example, the public interest in complying with s 1 of the Freedom of Information Act 2000 may prevail where the degree of likelihood attaching to the apprehended prejudice is low. The United Kingdom public interest in defending a colony or protecting the capability, effectiveness or security of foreign forces may also deserve a lower weighting, particularly if the national security and international relations exemptions in ss 24 and 27 of the Freedom of Information Act 2000 are not engaged.[477] Moreover, it is generally recognised that the public interest in information about defence matters can be very great. The *Guidance on Interpretation* accompanying the *Code of Practice on Access to Government Information* stated in relation to the exemption for 'information whose disclosure would harm defence'[478] that this was not intended to prevent the disclosure of 'factual information relating to legitimate concerns on such matters as loss of life, or hazards and

---

[474] FOIA s 2(1)(b) and (2)(b). Similarly, if the disclosure of environmental information or the confirmation or denial of whether or not such information is held would adversely affect defence, an exception to the duty to disclose will arise under EIR reg 12 but only if, in all the circumstances of the case, the public interest in disclosure outweighs, or is equal to, the public interest in maintaining the exception (EIR reg 12(1)(b) and (6)).

[475] MoJ, *Exemptions Guidance — Section 26: Defence* (18 May 2008) p 7 states, 'The public interest in avoiding prejudice to defence and the Armed Forces is strong and in most cases, will tend to outweigh the public interest in disclosing such information. However, where the risk of prejudice has been assessed as being minimal, or where the harm that is likely to result is of a trivial nature, or where the public interest in disclosure is itself particularly strong, this may tip the public interest balance in favour of disclosure.'

[476] See §17–048.

[477] By way of a parallel, public interest immunity cannot be claimed by a foreign state or on the ground that disclosure would infringe the public interest of a foreign state: *Buttes Gas & Oil Co v Hammer (No 3)* [1981] QB 223 (CA) at 247, 251 and 262. However, it has been recognised that because the public interest of the United Kingdom requires continued co-operation, and recognises a convergence of interests, with foreign sovereign states, public interest immunity can nevertheless apply to various communications between British and foreign government departments or prosecuting authorities on international relations grounds: *Buttes Gas & Oil Co v Hammer (No 3)* [1981] QB 223 (CA) at 256; *R v Governor of Brixton Prison, ex p Osman* [1991] 1 WLR 281 (DC) at 285–286; *R v Horseferry Road Magistrates' Court, ex p Bennett (No 2)* (1995) 99 Cr App R 123 (DC) at 126; *R (Mohamed) v Secretary of State for Foreign & Commonwealth Affairs* [2010] EWCA Civ 65. Mention has already been made of the fact that action overseas may be capable of indirectly affecting the security of the United Kingdom, even if directed towards a foreign State: *SSHD v Rehman* [2001] UKHL 47, [2003] 1 AC 153 at [16]–[17] (Lord Slynn), [53] and [62] (Lord Hoffmann) and [64] (Lord Hutton).

[478] *Open Government Code of Practice on Access to Government Information*, 2nd edn (1997) Pt II, para 1(a).

environmental intrusion arising from military operations or use of land.'[479]   The guidance published by the Ministry of Justice states:[480]

> There is widespread interest in defence policy and the activities of the armed forces, and it is appropriate for the public to understand how and why key decisions are taken in these areas. The public interest will therefore be strong in relation to the disclosure of information that will inform debate and improve public understanding. Examples might include the disclosure of information relating to concerns on matters such as: national security; the safety of military personnel or loss of life; risks to the safety of civilians; the use of land or environmental impact of military activity (section 39 may also be relevant here); the factual and analytical basis used to develop defence policies; procurement; the use of public funds. On the other hand, the public interest is likely to weigh against the disclosure of information which could undermine the conduct of a specific military operation or have an adverse impact on security or safety. In addition, the disclosure of information in the face of an objection from an allied country, or in breach of a clear undertaking to preserve confidentiality, may well prejudice the UK's defence relations by restricting exchanges of information or by jeopardizing military co-operation.

---

[479] *Government Code of Practice on Access to Government Information: Guidance on Interpretation*, 2nd edn (1997) Pt II, para 1.1.

[480] MoJ, *Exemptions Guidance — Section 26: Defence* (18 May 2008) pp 7-8.

CHAPTER 18

International and Internal Relations

1. INTERNATIONAL RELATIONS

001 Overview

Section 27(1) of the Freedom of Information Act 2000[1] provides a four-limbed exemption in

---

[1] The FOI(S)A s 32(1)(a) is in similar terms, save that 'substantial prejudice' to the protected matters is required, rather than prejudice simpliciter. There is an argument that the Scottish provision relates to a matter outside the legislative competence of the Scottish Parliament. Under the Scotland Act 1998, the Scottish Parliament cannot make legislation which relates to or modifies the law on 'reserved matters' and corresponding restrictions apply in relation to the exercise of certain functions by the Scottish Ministers: Scotland Act 1998, ss 28–30, Sch 4, Pt I, paras 2, 3, Sch 5 (on 'legislative competence'), and Scotland Act 1998, ss 53–54 (on 'devolved competence'). The following are

respect of information the disclosure of which, broadly speaking, would be likely to be prejudicial to relations between the government of the United Kingdom and a foreign state or which otherwise would be likely to be prejudicial to the interests of the United Kingdom abroad.[2] Section 27(2) of the Act provides a separate exemption for confidential information obtained from a foreign state or from an international organisation or international court.[3] The latter exemption is purely class based, with no requirement of harm or likelihood of harm resulting from disclosure. Both exemptions are qualified exemptions, so that whether or not there is a duty to disclose such exempt information will turn upon whether in all the circumstances of the case the public interest in maintaining the exemption outweighs the public interest in disclosing the information.[4] Section 27 also includes a corresponding exclusion of the duty to confirm or deny. Although a particular piece of information may readily fall within both sub-sections, the focus of each of the two provisions is basically different. Section 27(1) is concerned to protect the interests of the United Kingdom in its dealings with and in other states. Section 27(2) is concerned to protect a facet of international comity. Whilst it can be said that any conduct that is potentially harmful to international comity is indirectly harmful to the interests of the United Kingdom, that harm may often be difficult to identify or measure at the time of proposed disclosure and it may have to compete with immediate interests that are clearly served by disclosure. Thus s 27(2) is capable of applying to information not captured by s 27(1). Moreover, determination of the applicability of s 27(2) is more straightforward, looking to the character of the information (ie whether it is confidential) and to the source of the information (ie whether it was obtained from a state other than the United Kingdom or from an international organisation or international court), rather than conjecturing about the effect of disclosure upon 'the interests of the United Kingdom abroad' and upon international relations. The issue of confidentiality and the scope of the s 27(2) exemption are considered in the main chapter on confidentiality.[5] The s 27(1) exemption, as well as the required sources of information for the s 27(2) exemption to operate, are considered in this chapter. With the exception of the US, similar exemptions of varying scope exist in each of the comparative jurisdictions.[6]

---

in turn defined as 'reserved matters' for the purposes of the Scotland Act 1998: (1) international relations, including relations with territories outside the United Kingdom, the European Communities (and their institutions) and other international organisations (under the heading 'foreign affairs etc'.): Scotland Act 1998 s 30, Sch 5, Pt I, para 7; and (2) public access to information held by public bodies or holders of public offices other than certain Scottish public authorities: Scotland Act 1998 s 30, Sch 5, Pt II, s.B13.

[2]   The provision echoes the language used in ss 3 and 6 of the Official Secrets Act 1989.

[3]   The FOI(S)A s 32(1)(b) is identical.

[4]   FOIA s 2(2); FOI(S)A s 2(1).

[5]   See in particular §§25– 061 to 25– 064.

[6]   In the United States, the Freedom of Information Act 1966 contains no specific exemption for information that might damage international relations or for information that was obtained from a foreign government in confidence. In practice, such information may be found to be exempt under Exemption 1 (national security information) provided that it has been earlier classified: see §2– 008(1) and Executive Order No 12,958 (as amended by Executive Order No 13,392), s 1.1(d). The amendment to the Executive Order instructed agencies to presume harm to the national security in releasing foreign government information. In order to be exempted, 'foreign government information' must be shown to have been provided to the US Government with an expectation of confidentiality and classified at the time as such: see *Weatherhead v United States*, 157 F 3d 735 (9th Cir 1998) and, on appeal, *Weatherhead v United States*, 527 US 1063 (1999), where a letter sent by the British Home Office to the Department of Justice was ordered to be disclosed because it had not been so classified. In *Weatherhead*, the British Government,

002 Environmental information

Where (or to the extent that) the information answering the terms of a request for information is environmental information,[7] the request (or that part of the request) falls to be determined by the Environmental Information Regulations 2004 and not by the Freedom of Information Act 2000.[8] Subject to a public interest test, a public authority may refuse to disclose information to the extent that its disclosure would adversely affect 'international relations'.[9] Unless another exception applies, even where the terms of this exception are met the public authority may only not disclose that part of the information in respect of which it is satisfied that in all the circumstances the public interest in maintaining this exception outweighs the public interest in the information's disclosure.[10] It is suggested that the phrase 'international relations' encapsulates the four matters described in section 27(1) of the Freedom of Information Act 2000. The requirement in regulation 12(5)(a) that disclosure would 'adversely affect'

---

upon being asked by the State Department whether it consented to release, stated that it was unable to agree because 'the normal line in cases like this is that all correspondence between Governments is confidential unless papers have been formally requisitioned'. If it has been classified, then exemption will generally be upheld. Thus, in *Krikorian v Department of State*, 984 F 2d 461 (DC Cir 1993) the court found that a telegram reporting discussion between an agency official and a high-ranking foreign diplomat regarding terrorism was properly withheld as foreign government information; release would jeopardise reciprocal confidentiality between governments. Differing views have been taken on whether the agency must demonstrate that the foreign state provided the information in confidence or whether that is to be presumed: *Steinberg v United States Department of Justice*, 179 FRD 357 (DDC 1998) and *Billington v Department of Justice*, 11 F Supp 2d 45 (DDC 1998) and 69 F Supp 2d 128 (DDC 1999). Exemption can also be secured under Exemption 7: §2– 008(7). The Freedom of Information Act 1982 (Cth of Australia) s 33, provides two exemptions that broadly correlate to the two provisions in FOIA s 27(1) and (2). Under Freedom of Information Act 1982 s 33(1)(a)(iii), a document is exempt where its disclosure would, or could be reasonably be expected to, cause damage to the international relations of Australia; under s 33(1)(b) a document is exempt if its disclosure would divulge any information communicated in confidence by or on behalf of a foreign government, etc: see §2– 015(9). The provision does not involve a consideration of the public interest. The Official Information Act 1982 (New Zealand), provides two separate absolute exemptions to cover analogous information. First, information may be withheld without a consideration of the public interest where disclosure would be likely to prejudice the international relations of the New Zealand Government: Official Information Act 1982 ss 6(b) and 27(1)(a); Privacy Act 1993 s 27(1)(b); and see §2– 022(1). Secondly, information may also be withheld without a consideration of the public interest where disclosure would be likely to prejudice the entrusting of information to the Government of New Zealand on a basis of confidence by the Government of any other country or any agency of such a government, or by any international organisation: Official Information Act 1982 ss 6(b) and 27(1)(a); Privacy Act 1993 s 27(1)(b); and see §2– 022(1). The Act provides for the Prime Minister to issue a conclusive certificate in support of the first: s 31. The Access to Information Act (Canada) s 15 provides a discretionary exemption for records the disclosure of which could 'reasonably be expected' to cause injury to the conduct of international affairs: see §2– 032(11). The Canada Evidence Act allows the Attorney-General to issue a certificate prohibiting the disclosure of information in connection with a legal proceeding for the purpose of inter alia protecting information obtained in confidence from foreign entities. The Freedom of Information Act 1997 (Ireland), ss 24(1)(c) provides a discretionary exemption for records the disclosure of which could reasonably be expected to affect adversely the international relations of the State of Ireland: see §2– 039(13). The Act provides for a conclusive certificate in support of the exemption: s 25.

[7] As to the meaning of which, see §6– 010.

[8] In the case of a request for information made of a Scottish public authority, it will fall to be determined by the EI(S)R and not by the FOI(S)A.

[9] EIR reg 12(5)(a); EI(S)R, 10(5)(a). Derived from art 4.2(b) of the Directive and art 4.4(b) of the Aarhus Convention. The term 'public security' in the Directive and Convention are converted by the Regulations into 'national security' and 'public safety'. Regulation 4(2)(a) of the 1992 Regulations provided for a similar exception but without the public interest balancing test.

[10] See §6– 037.

international relations presents a higher threshold for successful invocation than the corresponding requirement in section 27(1) that disclosure 'would, or would be likely to, prejudice' any of the matters in paras (a)–(d). Although the Environmental Information Regulations 2004 do not include an equivalent exception to the exemption in s 27(2) of the Freedom of Information Act 2000, there will be instances where the disclosure of confidential information obtained from a foreign state or, less likely, from an international organisation or international court will adversely affect international relations.[11] The inclusion of a separate exemption in s 27(2) acknowledges that harm to international relations will not necessarily result from the disclosure of confidential information obtained from a foreign state or from an international organisation or international court. The exception in reg 12(5)(a), unlike the exemption in s 27(1), is not confined to prejudice to relations between the United Kingdom and another country. Thus, resultant prejudice to international relations between two foreign states will suffice.

18– 003 Scope of the section 27(1) exemption

Section 27(1) of the Freedom of Information Act 2000[12] provides that where the disclosure of information under the Act would or would be likely to prejudice:

    (a)   relations between the United Kingdom[13] and any other state,

    (b)   relations between the United Kingdom and any international organisation or international court,

    (c)   the interests of the United Kingdom abroad, or

    (d)   the promotion or protection by the United Kingdom of its interests abroad,

then the information is exempt information. It is the relations and interests of the United Kingdom with which s 27(1) is concerned: it is not directly concerned with the interests of individual companies or enterprises as such.[14]

18– 004 Prejudice and likelihood of prejudice

The phrase 'would or would be likely to prejudice' is common to most of the prejudice-based exemptions in the Act. The nature of prejudice and the degree of likelihood which the phrase requires are considered elsewhere in this work.[15] The required probability of prejudice to the protected interests is that disclosure of the requested information be 'likely' to prejudice one or more of those protected interests. In considering s 27(1), the Tribunal has said that it:

> require[s] consideration of what is probable as opposed to possible or speculative. Prejudice is not defined, but we accept that it imports something of detriment in the sense of impairing relations or interests or their promotion or protection and further we accept that the

---

[11] See §§18– 008 to 18– 011.

[12] And similarly the FOI(S)A s 32(1)(a), but with a requirement of substantial prejudice.

[13] 'United Kingdom' bears its ordinary meaning under the Interpretation Act 1978: in other words, Great Britain and Northern Ireland: s 5 and Sch 1. Great Britain consists of England, Scotland and Wales.

[14] *Campaign against the Arms Trade v IC and MoJ*, IT, 26 August 2008, at [81].

[15] See §§15– 020 to 15– 028. The Information Tribunal in *FCO v IC and Friends of the Earth*, IT, 29 June 2007 at [34] confirmed that the Tribunal's approach to prejudice in other exemptions was equally applicable to s 27.

prejudice must be real, actual or of substance.[16]

The Tribunal went on to effectively reduce the required level of probability by including 'risk of harm' as a species of 'prejudice'.[17] It is suggested that the only point at which the probability of prejudice to a protected interest enters s 27(1) is through the words 'would be likely', and that a risk of prejudice and actual prejudice are not synonymous.[18]

005 The State and its organs

The Freedom of Information Act 2000 defines the word 'State' to include the 'government of any State and any organ of its government',[19] thereby alluding to its meaning in international law. There is no means of determining objectively the existence of a state: it is a matter of recognition by one state of another state, with recognition being largely presumed.[20] The stated view of the United Kingdom is:

> The normal criteria which the government apply for recognition as a state are that it should have, and seem likely to continue to have, a clearly defined territory with a population, a government who are able of themselves to exercise effective control of that territory, and independence in their external relations. Other factors, including some United Nations resolutions, may also be relevant.[21]

An entity unrecognised by the Foreign Office as a state will generally be treated by the courts as if it did not exist.[22] The constituent parts of a federated state, although often termed 'states' in their domestic law, are not states in the international law sense.[23] Whilst identification of a state itself will generally be straightforward, identification of the 'organs of its government' involves a consideration of the degree to which an entity is distinct from the executive elements

---

[16] *Campaign against the Arms Trade v IC and MoJ*, IT, 26 August 2008, at [80]. And similarly *Gilby v IC and FCO*, IT, 22 October 2008, at [23].

[17] *Campaign against the Arms Trade v IC and MoJ*, IT, 26 August 2008, at [81]. And similarly *Gilby v IC and FCO*, IT, 22 October 2008, at [23].

[18] Since 'risk' means the possibility of an adverse circumstance, by employing the formula 'would be likely to prejudice' a protected interest, s 27(1) already spells out the precise 'risk' that will engage the exemption. This is consistent with the manner in which the other exemptions employing the same prejudice formula have been applied by the Tribunal.

[19] FOIA s 27(5); FOI(S)A s 32(3).

[20] See generally RY Jennings and AD Watts (eds), *Oppenheim's International Law*, 9th edn (London, Longman, 1992) pp 120–123.

[21] Hansard HC vol 102 col 977 (23 October 1986) (written answer). See also Hansard HC vol 169 cols 449–450 (19 March 1990) (written answer). This accords with the view taken in RY Jennings and AD Watts (eds), *Oppenheim's International Law*, 9th edn (London, Longman, 1992), pp 120–123, where four conditions are identified as being necessary for the existence of a state: (1) a people, being an aggregate of individuals who live together as a community; (2) a territory in which the people are settled, even if its frontiers be disputed; (3) a government, meaning that there must be one or more persons who act for the people and govern according to the law of the land; and (4) a sovereign government, meaning that its domestic authority must not be dependent upon any other earthly authority.

[22] *The Annette* [1919] P 105; *Luther v Sagor* [1921] 1 KB 456, [1921] 3 KB 532.

[23] Such as the 50 states of the United States or the six states of Australia. Thus in *R (Alamieyeseigha) v Crown Prosecution Service* [2005] EWHC 2704, [2006] Crim LR 669 the Divisional Court held that Bayelsa State, a constituent part of the Federal Republic of Nigeria, did not conduct international relations.

of the government of the State.[24] The above starting-point has, in part, been displaced by the definition of 'state' given in s 27(5). Certainly so far as s 27(2) is concerned and seemingly so far as s 27(1) is concerned, the phrase 'State other than the United Kingdom' is defined to include references to any territory outside the United Kingdom. This is considerably wider than a state in its international law sense, and is sufficiently broad to include British territories.[25]

18– 006 International organisations

Section 27(5) of the Freedom of Information Act 2000 defines 'international organisation' to mean 'any international organisation whose members include any two or more states, or any organ of such an organisation',[26] thereby alluding to its meaning in international law. There is no fixed meaning in international law of the phrase 'international organisation'. However, the universal core attributes of an international organisation are:

— that it is created by a treaty between two or more states;[27]
— possession of what might be called a constitution;
— that it is a legal entity in international law, in the sense of being a juridical person or having legal personality; and
— generally, but not always, having an exclusive membership of states or governments, or at any rate membership that is predominantly composed of states or governments.[28]

International organisations of which the United Kingdom is a member are readily identifiable as they are declared to be such by Order in Council[29] or, in a limited number of cases, by statute.[30] Some international organisations of which the United Kingdom is not a member are also readily identifiable by virtue of their having certain privileges and immunities conferred

---

[24] *FCO v IC and Friends of the Earth*, IT, 29 June 2007 at [36(1)]. In *Coreck Maritime v Sevrybokholodflot*, 1994 SLT 893 (a state-owned shipping company held not to be an organ of the state on the basis that it was a commercial company, it had its own legal personality, it was substantially free of government control and it exercised no governmental functions).

[25] That is: Anguilla, Ascension Island, Bermuda, British Antarctic Territory, British Indian Ocean Territory, British Virgin Islands, Cayman Islands, Falkland Islands, Gibraltar, Monserrat, Pitcairn Islands, St Helena, South Georgia and South Sandwich Islands, Tristan da Cunha, and Turks & Caicos Islands.

[26] Similarly FOI(S)A s 32(3).

[27] *JH Rayner (Mincing Lane) Ltd v DTI* [1989] Ch 72 at 143 (Kerr LJ) where he also observed that most such treaties will be called a 'convention' or 'agreement'. Thus in *Westland Helicopters Ltd v Arab Organisation for Industrialisation* [1995] QB 282, [1995] 2 All ER 387, [1994] 2 Lloyd's Rep 608 the Arab Organisation for Industrialisation, which was created by treaty, whose members were states and which was given legal personality in each of its four member states, was recognised to be an 'international organisation'.

[28] See CF Amerasinghe, *Principles of the Institutional Law of International Organizations*, 2nd edn (Cambridge, Cambridge University Press, 2005) ch 1; G Schwarzenberger, *International Law as applied by International Courts and Tribunals* (London, Stevens & Sons, 1976) vol III, pp 5–8.

[29] See the International Organisations Act 1968 s 1, replacing the International Organisations (Immunities and Privileges) Act 1950. Any such Order in Council must be laid in draft before Parliament and approved by a resolution of each House: s 10(1).

[30] Such as the Bretton Woods Agreements Act 1945 and the International Sugar Organisation Act 1973.

on them by Order in Council.[31]   The list of international organisations that the United Kingdom has either recognised or upon which it has conferred privileges and immunities is extensive,[32] but more notable inclusions are: the Asian Development Bank;[33] the Council of Europe;[34] the European Court of Human Rights;[35] the European Bank for Reconstruction and Development;[36] the European Space Agency;[37] the European Union and its organs;[38] the International Atomic Energy Agency; the International Bank for Reconstruction and Development;[39] the International Court of Justice;[40] the International Monetary Fund;[41] the International Finance Corporation;[42] the North Atlantic Treaty Organisation;[43] the Organisation for Economic Co-operation and Development;[44] the United Nations (including various specialised agencies of the United Nations, such as the Food and Agriculture Organisation, the International Labour Organisation, the International Telecommunications Union, the United Nations Educational, Scientific and Cultural Organisation, the Universal Postal Union, the World Health Organisation, the World Meteorological Organisation, and

---

[31]   For example, because the United Kingdom has entered into 'headquarters agreement' with an international organisation which has its headquarters in the United Kingdom. This includes: the International Cocoa Organisation; the International Coffee Organisation; the International Whaling Commission; the International Maritime Organisation; INTELSAT.

[32]   See the list in *Halsbury's Laws of England*, 5th edn , vol 61 (London, LexisNexis, 2010), paras 459-461, 533-534.

[33]   Asian Development Bank (Immunities and Privileges) Order 1974 SI 1974/1251.

[34]   General Agreement on Privileges and Immunities of the Council of Europe, Paris, 2 September 1949 (Cmd 8852, 1949).

[35]   Second Protocol to the General Agreement on Privileges and Immunities of the Council of Europe, Paris, 15 December 1956 (Cmnd 579, 1957) (Commission of Human Rights); Fourth Protocol to the General Agreement on Privileges and Immunities of the Council of Europe, Paris, 16 December 1961 (Cmnd 4739, 1961).

[36]   European Bank for Reconstruction and Development (Immunities and Privileges) Order 1991 SI 1991/757.

[37]   European Space Agency (Immunities and Privileges) Order 1978 SI 1978/1105.

[38]   Protocol on the Privileges and Immunities of the European Communities, Brussels, 8 April 1965 (Cmnd 5179, 1965) (as amended).

[39]   Articles of Agreement of the International Bank for Reconstruction and Development (Washington, 27 December 1945 (Cmd 6885, 1946) art I. The International Bank for Reconstruction and Development was established by an agreement drawn up at the United Nations Monetary and Financial Conference held at Bretton Woods, New Hampshire, USA in July 1944: see the Bretton Woods Agreement Act 1945 preamble (repealed). See also International Bank for Reconstruction and Development (1988 General Capital Increase) Order 1988 SI 1988/1486.

[40]   United Nations and International Court of Justice (Immunities and Privileges) Order 1974 SI 1974/1261.

[41]   The International Monetary Fund was created at the Bretton Woods Conference in 1944. The constitution of the International Monetary Fund can be found in the Articles of Agreement of the International Monetary Fund (Washington, 27 December 1945 (Cmd 6885, 1946) (amended by TS 44 (Cmnd 7205, 1978); TS 83 (Cmnd 7331, 1978)). See also International Monetary Fund Act 1979 s 5.

[42]   The International Finance Corporation is an affiliate of the International Bank for Reconstruction and Development: Articles of Agreement of the International Finance Corporation (Washington, 25 May 1955, TS 37 (Cmnd 1377, 1961) art I. See also International Finance Corporation (1991 General Capital Increase) Order 1993 SI 1993/1059.

[43]   Agreement on the Status of the North Atlantic Treaty Organisation, National Representatives and International Staff, Ottawa, 20 September 1951 (Cmnd 9383, 1951).

[44]   Organisation for Economic Co-operation and Development (Immunities and Privileges) Order 1974SI 1974/1258.

the World Intellectual Property Organisation);[45] and the World Trade Organisation.[46] In addition to these readily recognisable international organisations, there exist many other international organisations (in the international law sense) including the Arab League, The Organisation of American States, The Organisation of African Unity, and The Association of South-East Asian Nations. So, too, the Commonwealth Secretariat.[47] These, too, will fall within the definition given by s 27(5), notwithstanding that these organisations do not enjoy any privileges and immunities in the United Kingdom.[48]

18– 007 International courts

Section 27(5) of the Freedom of Information Act 2000 defines 'international court' to mean
> any international court which is not an international organisation and which is established:
> (a) by a resolution of an international organisation of which the United Kingdom is a member, or (b) by an international agreement to which the United Kingdom is a party.

A number of notable international courts are international organisations,[49] but the operation of s 27 is the same whether the body falls within the definition of 'international organisation' or within the definition of 'international court'. The phrase 'international court' has no fixed meaning in international law, but the essential attributes would appear to be that:

— it is created by a treaty between two or more states;
— it has a legal personality derived from international law;
— it enjoys the usual immunities enjoyed by an international organisation; and
— it has had conferred on it powers and duties that are essentially judicial, even if it also performs administrative acts.[50]

International courts vary in nature, but may be divided into:

(1) Courts of universal scope, which includes the International Court of Justice, the International Tribunal for the Law of the Sea, the Dispute Settlement System of the World Trade Organisation, and the International Criminal Court.

(2) Ad hoc criminal tribunals, which includes the International Criminal Tribunal for the former Yugoslavia and the International Tribunal for Rwanda.

(3) Regional Human Rights Courts, which includes the European Court of Human Rights, the Inter-American Court of Human Rights, and the African Court of Human and Peoples Rights.

(4) Judicial bodies of regional economic integration and the like, including the Court of Justice of the European Communities (comprising the European Court of Justice and the European Court of First Instance), the Court of Justice of the European

---

[45] Specialised Agencies of the United Nations (Immunities and Privileges) Order 1974 SI 1974/1260.

[46] World Trade Organisation (Immunities and Privileges) Order 1995 SI 1995/266.

[47] *Sukuman Ltd v Commonwealth Secretariat* [2006] EWHC 304 (Comm), [2006] 1 All ER (Comm) 621, [2006] 2 Lloyd's Rep 53.

[48] See *Arab Monetary Fund v Hashim (No 3)* [1991] 1 AC 114 at 167, which suggests that in such cases, in order to be recognised as an international organisation, the entity must be created not by treaty but by one or more of the member states.

[49] The European Court of Human Rights, see n 35; the International Court of Justice, see n 40; and the International Criminal Court.

[50] See P Sands *et al, Manual on International Courts and Tribunals* (London, Butterworths, 1999); CF Amersainghe, *Jurisdiction of International Tribunals* (The Hague, Kluwer Law International, 2003) pp 42–43.

Free Trade Agreement, the Court of Justice of the Benelux Economic Union, the Central American Court of Justice, the Court of Justice of the Andean Community, the Court of Justice of the Common Market for Eastern and Southern Africa, the Common Court of Justice and Arbitration of the Organisation for the Harmonisation of Corporate Law in Africa, the Judicial Tribunal of the Organisation of Arab Petroleum Exporting Countries, and the Court of Justice of the Arab Maghrev Union.

008 Prejudice to international relations

There are basically two broad classes of information the disclosure of which may cause any of the types of prejudice identified in s 27(1)(a)–(b). The first class is information that has been supplied by a foreign State on the understanding or in the expectation that it will not be further disseminated without the approval of the foreign State. Whilst information in this class may, of course, be rendered exempt information by s 27(2), it is also potentially exempt under s 27(1). The second class embraces information the disclosure of which, on the basis of what would actually be disclosed, could be expected to cause prejudice to relations between the United Kingdom and another state or an international organisation or court. Here, the potential prejudice does not arise from the mere fact of disclosure of information that has been provided by a foreign state upon a particular understanding: it arises from a likely effect of the disclosure of particular information upon the international relations of the United Kingdom having regard to the information itself.

009 Prejudice by breaking an understanding

The Tribunal has rejected an argument that it should necessarily follow the assessment of the Foreign and Commonwealth Office of the likely prejudice to result from a disclosure of communications between officials of the United Kingdom and those of a foreign state:

> the Tribunal does not accept that this was or is for the FCO's judgment either in the sense contended for or at all and rejects any contention as submitted by the FCO that the judgement of a public authority in such a case must be accepted unless otherwise perverse or in some other way as to be so unreasonable that no tribunal could accept it.[51]

That judgment is, nevertheless, a valid consideration that the Tribunal should take into account.[52] In *Campaign against the Arms Trade v IC and MoJ*,[53] the Tribunal placed similar reliance upon evidence from diplomats of the anticipated reaction from the foreign government. In

---

[51] *FCO v IC and Friends of the Earth*, IT, 29 June 2007 at [39(1)].

[52] *FCO v IC and Friends of the Earth*, IT, 29 June 2007 at [36(3)] and [47]. MoJ, *Exemptions Guidance—Section 27: International relations*, 14 May 2008, p 11. The weight to be given to the different facets of the public interest, whilst it will take into account evidence of harm that will or would be likely to result from disclosure of the requested information (which may include valuable evidence from FCO officials), is exclusively a matter for the Tribunal. The *Guidance* cites *R v Secretary of State for the Home Department ex parte Launder* [1997] 1 WLR 839 per Lord Hope at 857 in support of the proposition that the courts have consistently acknowledged the special expertise of the Executive in assessing what actions would protect or promote international relations. In fact, in that case the courts only had a supervisory jurisdiction in respect of the impugned decision (whereas, in appeals under FOIA, the Tribunal effectively stands in the shoes of the decision-maker) and, moreover, that decision was one which had had to be taken 'amidst an atmosphere of mistrust and suspicion which a court is in no position to penetrate.'

[53] IT, 26 August 2008, at [86]-[89].

Gilby v IC and FCO,[54] the Tribunal readily concluded that disclosure of information concerning arms contracts with the Kingdom of Saudi Arabia would result in or would be likely to result in prejudice to relations between the United Kingdom and that State, as well as to the interests of the United Kingdom. In reaching this conclusion the Tribunal found that it was highly likely that any disclosure under the Freedom of Information Act 2000 would come to the attention of officials within the Kingdom of Saudi Arabia and that the damage would be distinct and greater than that caused by earlier unofficial ad hoc disclosures to similar effect.[55]

18–010 Breaking an understanding – comparative jurisdictions

The jurisprudence of the comparative jurisdictions reveals that public authorities often maintain that disclosure of information in the first class would damage international relations. These claims have enjoyed a measure of success, although such claims have been approached with a degree of circumspection in order not to convert what is a prejudice-based exemption into a purely class-based exemption. In Australia, the Administrative Appeals Tribunal has been generally receptive to such claims. In *Re Maher and Attorney-General's Department*[56] the President of the Tribunal upheld exemption on this basis for documents revealing negotiations that led to a treaty between Australia and United States on limiting the extra-territorial effect of anti-trust litigation in the United States:

> The phrase "damage to international relations of the Commonwealth" [of Australia] comprehends intangible damage to Australia's reputation though such damage may be difficult to assess. International relations have never been matters easy to define or to quantify. Regard must be had, inter alia, to the relationships between particular persons in one government and persons in another. Damage to personal relationships may cause considerable harm for a time at least.
>
> I accept that it must be shown that the publication of a document claimed to be exempt could reasonably be expected to cause damage to the international relations of the Commonwealth. A mere allegation to that effect is not enough. There must be cause and effect which can reasonably be anticipated. But if it can reasonably be anticipated that disclosure of the document would lessen the confidence which another country would place on the Government of Australia, that is a sufficient ground for a finding that the disclosure of the document could reasonably be expected to damage international relations. Trust and confidence are intangible aspects of international relations.

In *Re Slater and Cox (Director-General of Australian Archives)*[57] the Tribunal was concerned with documents relating to the establishment of the Australian Secret Service and the Australian Secret Intelligence Service some 30 or so years before the making of the request. In its necessarily sparse reasons[58] the Tribunal said:

---

[54] IT, 22 October 2008 at [42]-[44].

[55] See further §15– 026.

[56] (1985) 7 ALD 731, 3 AAR 396 at [40]–[41]. Referred to in *Campaign against the Arms Trade v IC and MoJ*, IT, 26 August 2008, at [81], with seeming support.

[57] (1988) 15 ALD 20. Later authorities have followed this reasoning: *Secretary, Department of Foreign Affairs & Trade v Whittaker* [2005] FCAFC 15; *Bui v Dept of Foreign Affairs and Trade* [2005] AATA 97; *Re O'Donovan & Attorney-General's Department* (1985) 8 ALD 528; *Commonwealth of Australia v Hittich* (1994) 53 FCR 152; *Wang v Department of Employment, Education and Training* (1988) 15 ALD 497.

[58] As the Tribunal explained: 'The Scylla of disclosure of confidential material (or worse, of the contents of a document in issue), and the Charybdis of inadequate explanation must each be avoided.'

It is necessary to have some regard to differences in attitude, and to reflect the views, of foreign governments which provide information, etc to the Australian Government or its agencies. Failure to respect such views could lead to a diminution in co-operation and consequently damage relations. Considerable weight should be given by the Tribunal to the views of objecting foreign governments since they are usually in the best position to assess the local, regional or international consequences of disclosure...If it can be anticipated that disclosure of the document would lessen the confidence which another country would place in the Government of Australia, that is sufficient ground for a finding that the disclosure of the document could reasonably be expected to damage international relations (though a mere allegation of damage or an expression of concern may not be sufficient).[59]

It is, of course, important to distinguish contrived prejudice (which may or may not be supported by the foreign Government that supplied the information) or mere diplomatic irritation from true prejudice to relations between the United Kingdom and another state. In this regard, it is worth remembering that information supplied by the United Kingdom to the United States was from time to time disclosed under the Freedom of Information Act (USA) without any apparent prejudice to the publicly declared special relationship between the two countries.

011 Inherent prejudice

Quite apart from breaking any understanding with a foreign state, disclosure of certain information may risk souring relations between the United Kingdom and another state because of the very contents of that information. The Tribunal has held that in assessing the effect on relations, it is relevant to take into account that the precepts of openness and transparency that underpin the Freedom of Information Act 2000 are alien to the foreign state.[60]

012 Inherent prejudice – comparative jurisprudence

In *Kuijer v EU Council (No 2)*[61] the applicant had made a request to the Secretary General of the European Council for access to certain reports that had been prepared by or with the Centre for Information, Discussion and Exchange on Asylum. The request was refused on the ground that:

> This report contains very sensitive information about the political, economical and social situation in [the country concerned], which was provided by the heads of the European Union member state missions in that country. The Council is of the opinion that disclosure

---

[59] At [35]–[36] and [50]. The Tribunal quoted with approval from the decision of Neaves J in *Re Throssell and Department of Foreign Affairs (No 2)* (1987) 14 ALD 296 at [16]: 'The material before the Tribunal tends to support the conclusion that the disclosure to the public of the records identified in the certificate could have the result of impairing the degree of trust and confidence which foreign governments place in the Government of the Commonwealth and, in consequence, of inhibiting the flow of information relating to security which might otherwise come to Australia from the overseas governmental agencies concerned and, possibly, similar agencies in other overseas countries. If such a result ensued, damage would be caused to the security and international relations of the Commonwealth. Whether such action on the part of the foreign governments and agencies would be a rational or otherwise proper reaction to the disclosure of these particular records is not to the point. The question is whether such action could reasonably be expected in the event of access being granted.'

[60] *Campaign against the Arms Trade v IC and MoJ*, IT, 26 August 2008, at [91]; *Gilby v IC and FCO*, IT, 22 October 2008, at [43]-[44].

[61] [2002] 1 WLR 1941, Court of First Instance of the European Communities. This was a request for information under the access regime then applicable to institutions of the European Union: see further ch 3. See also: *Sison v Council of the European Union* [2005] ECR II–1429, [2005] 2 CMLR 29.

of this information might damage the relations between the European Union and [country]. The Council has therefore decided that access to this document has to be denied on the basis of article 4(1) of [Decision 93/731] (international relations).

The Council explained that the Report contained very detailed information on the general political situation and the protection of human rights in third countries, which could be construed as criticism of those countries. The Court upheld the applicant's application for annulment of the decision to refuse access to the reports. While the Court accepted the principle that the contents of a document could be of such a nature as to make its disclosure harmful to international relations,[62] it did not accept that that could be said of the documents in question:

> Although it is the case that some documents, such as reports containing sensitive military information, may have sufficient features in common for their disclosure to be refused, that is not the case of the documents at issue. In such circumstances, the mere fact that certain documents contain information or negative statements about the political situation, or the protection of human rights, in a third country does not necessarily mean that access to them may be denied on the basis that there is a risk that the public interest may be undermined. That fact, in itself and in the abstract, is not a sufficient basis for refusing a request for access. Rather, refusal of access to the reports in question must be founded on an analysis of factors specific to the contents or the context of each report, from which it can be concluded that, because of certain specific circumstances, disclosure of such a document would pose a danger to a particular public interest. As regards their contents, the reports at issue do not concern directly or primarily the relations of the European Union with the countries concerned. They contain an analysis of the political situation and of the position as regards the protection of human rights in general in each of those countries and also refer to the ratification of international treaties concerning human rights. They also contain more specific information on the protection of human rights, the possibility of internal migration to escape persecution, the return of nationals to their country of origin and the economic and social situation.[63]

It was relevant that much of the information related to facts that had already been made public or that were common knowledge.[64] The risk of the claimed harm was reduced:

— by the significant political changes that had occurred since the analysis recorded in the report;

— by the fact that the situation in the country concerned had already been criticised by institutions of the European Union;

— by the fact that relations with the country concerned might be such that they could not be damaged by disclosure of criticism; and

---

[62] Although, had the request for information been one under the FOIA, various examples given by the Court would have engaged other exemptions.

[63] At [60]–[62].

[64] At [63]. This is one of the factors identified in MoJ, *Exemptions Guidance—Section 27: International relations*, 14 May 2008, pp 6-7. The Guidance makes the legitimate point that the applicability of the exemption may be affected by whether the earlier disclosure was from the other State or was unauthorised. The suggestion that disclosure under the FOIA of information already disclosed 'could give rise to prejudice that would not otherwise have existed...for example where reading the disclosed information alongside information already in the public domain allows deductions to be made that could themselves be prejudicial' is questionable: proof of the causative element of disclosure, would be, it is suggested, almost impossible in such circumstances.

—   by the fact that some of the observations in the report were positive.[65]
The only parts of the requested documents that the court was prepared to withhold from disclosure were those that would reveal the names of persons who had provided the information in question. Whilst the above authority exemplifies an attempt to employ the spectre of harm to international relations so as to secure exemption for commonplace material, it is suggested that prejudice to international relations can properly be said to be likely where, for example, the requested information comprises current appraisals of foreign political leaders or assessments of the relations between two foreign nations and so forth (at least to the extent that these views have not been previously made officially known).[66]

013   Prejudice to the interests of the United Kingdom

Paragraphs(c)–(d) of s 27(1) protect from disclosure information that would or would be likely to prejudice 'the interests of the United Kingdom abroad'. The phrase is sufficiently elastic to potentially embrace any financial, economic or proprietary interest abroad with which the United Kingdom (as a state) has some interest.[67] On the other hand, it is also susceptible to a narrower interpretation that confines it to matters of sovereign interest abroad.

014   The public interest

As noted above, the exemption is qualified: it only applies if the public interest in maintaining the exemption outweighs the public interest in disclosing the information.[68] Depending on the information that stands to be disclosed, the following may be relevant to a consideration of the public interest:

(1)   The recognised public interest in maintaining the confidentiality of diplomatic communications, in particular where the disclosure would interfere with the State's ability to negotiate delicate situations by stating different or even contradictory things to other states without the contradictions being too apparent.[69] The public interest will be particularly pressing if disclosure were to weaken the Government's bargaining position in negotiations with another state. Although the weight of this facet of the public interest will be time-sensitive, where the fragility of the negotiations is such there is a real risk that harm to future negotiations would result from merely revealing communications of the sort involved, the public interest in

---

[65]   At [66].

[66]   The MoJ, *Exemptions Guidance—Section 27: International relations*, 14 May 2008, p 7, notes that 'potentially prejudicial comments about the policies of a foreign government may diminish in sensitivity after a change of government'.

[67]   For examples of its application: *Campaign against the Arms Trade v IC and MoJ*, IT, 26 August 2008; *Gilby v IC and FCO*, IT, 22 October 2008. MoJ, *Exemptions Guidance—Section 27: International relations*, 14 May 2008, rightly states: 'The United Kingdom's interests abroad, and the subject matter of its international relations, cover a wide and changing range of matters, including for example trade, defence, environment, human rights and the fight against terrorism and international crime.'

[68]   See: FOIA ss 2(1)(b) and 2(2)(b) and FOI(S)A s 2(1)(b). For a general discussion of this topic, see §§15– 001 to 15–019.

[69]   *Gilby v IC and FCO*, IT, 22 October 2008, at [49]-[52]. See the *White Paper on Open Government* (Cm 2290, 1993) paras 3.8–3.9 and Annex A, Pt II, para i; the Scottish Executive's *Code of Practice on Access to Scottish Executive Information*, 2nd edn (2003), Pt II; and the National Assembly for Wales's *Code of Practice on Public Access to Information*, 2nd edn (2001) Annex B. According to Harold Nicolson, *Diplomacy, a Basic Guide to the Conduct of Contemporary Foreign Affairs* (London, Thornton Butterworth, 1939) diplomats are 'sent abroad to lie for their country'.

maintaining the exemption will subsist for a longer period.[70]

(2)　The public interest in avoiding other forms of prejudice to relations between the United Kingdom and other states or international organisations or courts, such as might result from revealing previously undisclosed critical appraisals of foreign states or their institutions.

(3)　There is a public interest in avoiding a disclosure that would impede international negotiations, for example, by revealing a negotiating or fall-back position, or weakening the Government's bargaining position.[71]

(4)　Whether the disclosure would have an adverse impact upon the relationship between the Governments of the United Kingdom and of another State.[72]

(5)　Whether the disclosure would have an adverse impact upon the protection and promotion of UK interests abroad.[73]

In weighing the public interest in maintaining the exemption, it may be relevant to take into account the general attitude taken by the foreign state to the disclosure of official information.[74] For example, the public interest in maintaining exemption under s 27(1) in relation to a communication from the European Commission (which is an international organisation) where that exemption is founded upon likely prejudice to relations arising from the mere fact of disclosure is arguably diminished by the encouragement which various European Union instruments give to disclosure of official documents.[75] Although what is in the public interest of a foreign State is not directly relevant to an assessment of the public interest under the Freedom of Information Act 2000, it may indirectly impinge upon that assessment.[76] On the other side of the balance, and underpinned by the rules of comity and international law, lies the principle that foreign states and organisations dealing with the public authorities in the United Kingdom must take the country as it is, including its laws relating to the disclosure of

---

[70] This is the line that was taken by the Federal Court of Canada in *Do-Ky v Canada (Minister of Foreign Affairs & International Trade)* [1997] 2 FC 907. The difference with the 'candour' argument in relation to the development of government policy by officials (see §22– 011) is that the relationship is not one of master and servant, with the foreign State being under no obligation to convey information to the United Kingdom and potentially having an agenda of its own that may be compromised by the disclosure.

[71] *Open Government Code of Practice on Access to Government Information: Guidance on Interpretation*, 2nd edn (1997) Pt II, para 1.5.

[72] *Campaign against the Arms Trade v IC and MoJ*, IT, 26 August 2008 at [96]; *Gilby v IC and FCO*, IT, 22 October 2008 at [51].

[73] *Campaign against the Arms Trade v IC and MoJ*, IT, 26 August 2008 at [96]; *Gilby v IC and FCO*, IT, 22 October 2008 at [51].

[74] *Campaign against the Arms Trade v IC and MoJ*, IT, 26 August 2008, at [91], [96]; *Gilby v IC and FCO*, IT, 22 October 2008, at [43]-[44], [51].

[75] Most notably art 255 of the Treaty of Amsterdam and art 42 of the Charter of Fundamental Rights of the European Union: see §§4– 003 to 4– 004. It will, in each case, be necessary to consider the general thrust of the legislative regime.

[76] By way of a parallel, public interest immunity cannot be claimed by a foreign state or on the ground that disclosure would infringe the public interest of a foreign state: *Buttes Gas & Oil Co v Hammer (No 3)* [1981] QB 223 (CA) at 247, 251 and 262. However, it has been recognised that because the public interest of the United Kingdom requires continued co-operation, and recognises a convergence of interests, with foreign sovereign states, public interest immunity can nevertheless apply to various communications between British and foreign government departments or prosecuting authorities on international relations grounds: *Buttes Gas & Oil Co v Hammer (No 3)* [1981] QB 223 (CA) at 256; *R v Governor of Brixton Prison, ex p Osman* [1991] 1 WLR 281 (DC) at 285–286; *R v Horseferry Road Magistrates' Court, ex p Bennett (No 2)* (1994) 99 Cr App R 123 (DC) at 126.

information.[77] Accordingly, the usual public interest in securing openness and transparency will weigh in favour of disclosure, with the particular weight depending on what will be disclosed. Thus, for example, the public interest in disclosing information that might reveal official corruption or that would enhance transparency in government transactions, especially where the subject matter is one of legitimate public concern (such as arms contracts), is particularly weighty.[78]

015   The duty to confirm or deny

Where, if a public authority were to inform an applicant that it holds or does not hold information of the description specified in the applicant's request, that revelation:

(a)   would or would be likely to prejudice any of the matters set out in s 27(1); or

(b)   would involve the disclosure of information (whether or not already recorded) which is confidential information obtained from a state other than the United Kingdom or from an international organisation or an international court,

then, to that extent, the duty to confirm or deny does not arise.[79] The precise terms of the request are critical to determining what would be revealed by confirming or denying that such information is held. A request that more specifically identifies the information sought will be more likely to fall within the exclusion than a request in general terms. The exclusion of the duty to confirm or deny is qualified. Accordingly, even if the request satisfies the terms of s 27(4) it will be necessary to consider whether, in all the circumstances, the maintenance of the exclusion of this duty is outweighed by the public interest in disclosing whether the public authority holds the information. This public interest balancing exercise is materially different from that employed for the purpose of determining whether the duty to communicate does not apply.[80]

016   Scope of the confidential information exemption

Section 27(2) of the Freedom of Information Act 2000[81] provides that 'confidential information' obtained by a state other than the United Kingdom[82] or from an international organisation[83] or international court[84] is exempt information. Section 27(3) defines what is meant by confidential information:

> For the purposes of this section, any information obtained from a State, organisation or court is confidential at any time while the terms on which it was obtained require it to be held in

---

[77] Just as the foreign entity would have to accept that if the information it conveyed to the public authority was personal information relating to the applicant, then that information would, notwithstanding that it had been conveyed to the public authority in confidence, have to be conveyed to the applicant if an application were made under s 7 of the DPA, subject to any applicable exemptions under that Act.

[78] *Campaign against the Arms Trade v IC and MoJ*, IT, 26 August 2008 at [97]-[98]; *Gilby v IC and FCO*, IT, 22 October 2008 at [51], [55]-[57].

[79] FOIA s 27(4). Similarly: EIR reg 12(6); EI(S)R reg 10(8). There is no equivalent provision under the FOI(S)A.

[80] See §§15– 018 to 15– 019 as to what it involves.

[81] And FOI(S)A s 32(1)(b).

[82] As to the meaning of 'a state other than the United Kingdom', see §18– 005.

[83] As to the meaning of 'international organisation', see §18– 006.

[84] As to the meaning of 'international court', see §18– 007.

confidence or while the circumstances in which it was obtained make it reasonable for the State, organisation or court to expect that it will be so held.

The special provision of an exemption for confidential information emanating from foreign state bodies and the like (in addition to the general exemption for confidential information provided by s 41), reflects the particular sensitivities arising from the disclosure of such material.[85] The scope of the exemption is considered in the chapter dealing with confidential information.[86]

18–017 The Data Protection Act 1998

There is no analogous exemption under the Data Protection Act 1998 or any statutory instrument made under it.

2. INTERNAL RELATIONS*

18–018 Scope of the section 28(1) exemption

Section 28(1) of the Freedom of Information Act 2000 provides that information is exempt information if its disclosure under the Act would, or would be likely to, prejudice relations between any administration in the United Kingdom[87] and any other such administration ('internal relations').[88] The phrase 'would or would be likely to prejudice' is common to most of the prejudice-based exemptions in the Act. The nature of the prejudice and the degree of likelihood which that phrase requires are considered elsewhere in this work.[89] Section 28(2) defines 'administration in the United Kingdom' for the purposes of the section to mean:

(a)   the government of the United Kingdom ('the Westminster Government');

(b)   the Scottish Administration;

(c)   the Executive Committee of the Northern Ireland Assembly; or

(d)   the Welsh Assembly Government.[90]

Section 28(3) provides that the duty to confirm or deny does not arise if, or to the extent that, compliance with s 1(1)(a) of the Freedom of Information Act 2000 would, or would be likely to,

---

[85]   See §18–008.

[86]   See §§25–061 to 25–064.

*   By Oliver Sanders, 1 Crown Office Row.

[87]   United Kingdom means Great Britain (ie England, Scotland and Wales) and Northern Ireland: Interpretation Act 1978 ss 5 22(1) Sch 1 Sch 2 para 5(a); Union with Scotland Act 1706 preamble art 1.

[88]   FOI(S)A s 28 is identically worded save that it follows the slightly different drafting format and 'substantial prejudice' test adopted elsewhere in that Act. See *Scottish Ministers v Scottish IC* [2007] CSIH 8, 2007 SLT 274, 2007 SCLR 253 at [21]-[22]. Information contained in a 'historical record' (as to the meaning of which, see §7–036) for the purposes of FOIA s 62 cannot be exempt information by virtue of s 28 and compliance with the duty to confirm or deny under s 1(1)(a) in relation to such a record is not to be taken to be capable of having any of the effects referred to in s 28(3): FOIA s 63(1)–(2).

[89]   See §§15–020 to 15–028.

[90]   As originally enacted, FOIA s 28(2)(d) referred to the (former) National Assembly for Wales. The reference to the (new) Welsh Assembly Government was substituted with effect from 25 May 2007 by way of an amendment made by the Government of Wales Act 2006 (Consequential Modifications and Transitional Provisions) Order 2007 SI 2007/1388 Sch 1 para 80.

prejudice internal relations. The exclusion and the exemption in s 28 of the Freedom of Information Act 2000 are non-absolute: the duty to confirm or deny does not arise in relation to information prejudicial to internal relations only if, in all the circumstances of the case, the public interest in maintaining the exclusion of that duty outweighs the public interest in divulging whether the public authority holds the information;[91] and the duty to communicate in relation to such information does not arise only if, or to the extent that, in all the circumstances of the case, the public interest in maintaining the exemption outweighs the public interest in disclosing the information.[92] There is no equivalent exception in the Environmental Information Regulations 2004. Where (or to the extent that) the information answering the terms of a request for information is environmental information,[93] the request (or that part of the request) falls to be determined by the Environmental Information Regulations 2004 and not by the Freedom of Information Act 2000.[94] Accordingly, the fact that disclosure of environmental information would, or would be likely to, prejudice relations between any administration in the United Kingdom and any other such administration will not of itself remove the duty to disclose that information under the Regulations.

019 The administrations in the United Kingdom

As already indicated, the administrations covered by s 28 of the Freedom of Information Act 2000 are the Westminster Government, together with the 'devolved administrations', namely, the Scottish Administration, Executive Committee of the Northern Ireland Assembly and the Welsh Assembly Government. A brief outline of each devolved administration follows:[95]

    (1)   The Scottish Administration. The Scottish Administration was established under Part II of the Scotland Act 1998[96] and the reference in s 28(2)(b) of the Freedom of Information Act 2000 to the Scottish Administration must be construed as a reference to both its office-holders and their staff.[97]

    (2)   The Executive Committee of the Northern Ireland Assembly. The Executive

---

[91] FOIA s 28(3) (read with s 28(1)) engages s 2(1)(b) so as to prevent s 1(1)(a) from applying and the duty to confirm or deny from arising in relation to the exempt information if the public interest balance favours non-divulgence.

[92] FOIA s 28(1) thus engages s 2(2)(b) so as to prevent s 1(1)(b) from applying and the duty to communicate from arising in relation to the exempt information if the public interest balance favours non-disclosure.

[93] As to the meaning of which, see §6–010.

[94] In the case of a request for information made of a Scottish public authority, it will fall to be determined by the EI(S)R and not by the FOI(S)A.

[95] As to devolution generally see: O Hood Phillips and P Jackson, *Constitutional and Administrative Law*, 8th edn (London, Sweet & Maxwell, 2001) ch 5; Mitchell, 'The Creation of the Scottish Parliament: Journey without End' (1999) 52 Parl Affairs 651; McAllister, 'The Road to Cardiff Bay: The Process of Establishing the National Assembly for Wales' (1999) 52 Parl Affairs 635; MoJ, *Exemptions Guidance—Section 28: Relations within the United Kingdom*, 14 May 2008, Annex A.

[96] The Scotland Act 1998 was passed to implement policy proposals set out in the government White Paper *Scotland's Parliament* (Cm 3658, 1997) and followed a referendum held in Scotland in September 1997 under the Referendums (Scotland and Wales) Act 1997.

[97] Scotland Act 1998 s 126(6)–(7). The office-holders are the members of the Scottish Executive (ie the Scottish Ministers including the First Minister and the Lord Advocate and Solicitor General for Scotland), junior Scottish Ministers and the holders of offices in the Scottish Administration which are not ministerial offices (ie the Registrar General of Births, Deaths and Marriages for Scotland, the Keeper of the Registers of Scotland, the Keeper of the Records of Scotland and certain other specified officers): Scotland Act 1998 ss 44–49, 126(7)(a), (8); Scottish Administration (Offices) Order 1999 SI 1999/1127.

Committee of the Northern Ireland Assembly was established under Part III of the Northern Ireland Act 1998.[98] The Committee consists of the First Minister and deputy First Minister and the Northern Ireland Ministers appointed under that Act.[99] Devolution in Northern Ireland was suspended with effect from 15 October 2002 before being restored on 8 May 2007.[100]

(3) As originally enacted, s 28(2)(d) of the Freedom of Information Act 2000 referred to the National Assembly for Wales which was established under Part I of the Government of Wales Act 1998[101] as a body corporate consisting of elected members.[102] The terms of the Welsh devolution settlement were then reformed with effect from 3 May 2007 by the Government of Wales Act 2006.[103] The National Assembly for Wales thereafter continued in being as a purely legislative elected body and devolved Welsh executive functions were assumed by the Welsh Assembly Government established under Part 2 of the Government of Wales Act 2006. The Welsh Assembly Government consists of the First Minister, Welsh Ministers, Counsel General and Deputy Welsh Ministers. It was substituted for the National Assembly of Wales in s 28(2)(d) of the Freedom of Information Act 2000 with effect from 25 May 2007.[104]

It can therefore be noted that, for the purposes of s 28 of the Freedom of Information Act 2000, the Scottish Administration includes staff as well as office-holders, whilst the Northern Ireland and Wales devolved administrations include only their elected ministers and not their staff.

18–020 Background

No exemption equivalent to s 28 of the Freedom of Information Act 2000 was included in the *Code of Practice on Access to Government Information*[105] or proposed in the White Paper *Your Right to*

---

[98]   The Northern Ireland Act 1998 was passed (together with the Northern Ireland (Sentences) Act 1998) to implement the Belfast Agreement (also known as the Good Friday Agreement) set out in the *Agreement Reached at Multi-Party Talks on Northern Ireland* (Cm 3883, 1998) and followed referendums held in Northern Ireland and the Republic of Ireland in May 1998. See also the related agreements between the United Kingdom and Republic of Ireland Governments: *Agreement Establishing Implementing Bodies* (Cm 4293, 1998); *Agreement Establishing a North-South Ministerial Council* (Cm 4294, 1998); *Agreement Establishing a British-Irish Council* (Cm 4296, 1998).

[99]   Northern Ireland Act 1998 s 20.

[100] Pursuant to the Northern Ireland (St Andrews Agreement) Act 2006 s 2 Sch 2 (as modified by the Northern Ireland (St Andrews Agreement) Act 2007 s 1). As a result of that, the Northern Ireland (St Andrews Agreement) Act 2006 s 2 Sch 4 repealed the Northern Ireland Act 2000 with effect from 10 May 2007. See Burns, 'Devolution ... At Last?' (2007) 157 *New Law Journal* 248.

[101] The Government of Wales Act 1998 was passed to implement policy proposals set out in the government White Paper *A Voice for Wales* (Cm 3718, 1997) and followed a referendum held in Wales in September 1997 under the Referendums (Scotland and Wales) Act 1997. See also the Transfer of Functions Orders made under the Government of Wales Act 1998 s 22, Sch 2, ie SI 1999/672, SI 2000/253, SI 2000/1829, SI 2000/1830, SI 2001/3679, SI 2004/3044, SI 2005/1958, SI 2006/1458, SI 2006/3334.

[102] Government of Wales Act 1998 ss 1(2), 2.

[103] For the background to this reform, see the government White Papers *Better Governance for Wales* (Cm 6582, 2005): www.official-documents.gov.uk/document/cm65/6582/6582.pdf

[104] Government of Wales Act 2006 (Consequential Modifications and Transitional Provisions) Order 2007 SI 2007/1388 Sch 1 para 80.

[105] *Open Government Code of Practice on Access to Government Information*, 2nd edn (1997).

Know: The Government's Proposals for a Freedom of Information Act.[106] This is not surprising as both documents preceded the establishment of the devolved administrations.[107] The draft Freedom of Information Bill published on 24 May 1999[108] and the Freedom of Information Bill introduced in the House of Commons on 18 November 1999 post-dated the 1998 devolution statutes and both contained clauses equivalent to s 28 of the Freedom of Information Act 2000.[109] During the passage of the Freedom of Information Bill two examples were given by the government of information held by a Westminster Government department which might be covered by the exemption, namely, 'a thumbnail sketch of the strengths and weaknesses of the individual members of an executive' and 'comments on a devolved administration's policy proposals or Acts'.[110]

021 The comparative jurisdictions

Exemptions similar to s 28 of the Freedom of Information Act 2000 are provided for in the comparable legislation of Australia, New Zealand and Canada. Sections 26A and 33A of the Freedom of Information Act 1982 (Cth of Aust) contain a discretionary exemption for information whose disclosure would, or could reasonably be expected to, cause damage to relations between the Commonwealth and a State or divulge certain confidential Commonwealth-State communications.[111] As with s 28 of the Freedom of Information Act 2000, the Australian equivalent is subject to a public interest override for information whose disclosure would, on balance, be in the public interest.[112] Section 7(a) of the Official Information Act 1982 (NZ) provides that information may be withheld if its disclosure would be likely to prejudice relations between any of the Governments of New Zealand, the self-governing state of the Cook Islands or the self-governing state of Niue. Section 14 of the federal Access to Information Act (1982) (Canada) contains a discretionary exemption for information which could reasonably be expected to be injurious to the conduct by the Government of Canada of federal-provincial affairs including information on federal-provincial consultations or deliberations and the strategy or tactics adopted or to be adopted by the Government of Canada relating to the conduct of federal-provincial affairs.

022 Prejudice to internal relations

All the administrations have agreed a Memorandum of Understanding and a series of Supplementary Agreements 'setting out the principles which underlie the relations between them' and a series of bilateral agreements have also been agreed between various Westminster

---

[106] (Cm 3818, 1997).

[107] Note, however, the reference to devolution in the White Paper (Cm 3818, 1997) para 2.1.

[108] *Freedom of Information: Consultation on Draft Legislation* (Cm 4355, 1999) Pt II.

[109] Draft Bill, cl 23; Introduction Print of Bill, cl 26.

[110] Cabinet Office Minister, Lord Falconer of Thoroton, Hansard HL vol 617 col 1280 (19 October 2000) (House of Lords Committee Stage).

[111] The words 'relations between the Commonwealth and a State' refer to the totality of their relationships at every level: *Arnold v Queensland* (1987) 6 AAR 463 at 472 (Wilcox J).

[112] Freedom of Information Act 1982 s 47B (Cth of Aust).

Government departments and their devolved counterparts.[113] Although these agreements are expressed to be non-binding statements of political intent, they reflect the way in which the administrations intend and would wish to relate to each other and may therefore provide a useful guide for what would and would not be liable to prejudice internal relations.[114] Although in legal terms each of the devolved administrations exercises its functions on behalf of the same Crown, their members may have very different political views and there is a constitutional distinction between the Crown in right of Her Majesty's Government in the United Kingdom, the Crown in right of the Scottish Administration, the Crown in right of Her Majesty's Government in Northern Ireland, and the Crown in right of the Welsh Assembly Government.[115] The logic of s 28 of the Freedom of Information Act 2000 is as follows: given that the Westminster Government and the devolved administrations do need to co-operate closely in a variety of areas, particularly in relation to the implementation of and compliance with the United Kingdom's obligations under European Community law, good internal relations are plainly a matter of great practical importance and they should not therefore be needlessly prejudiced or put at risk unless this is necessary on overriding public interest grounds. Whether the remaining exemptions in Part II of the Freedom of Information Act 2000 ought to suffice for these purposes is another matter, but the comparative jurisdictions at least show some consistency of approach to such issues and provide a precedent for s 28.

18–023 The Data Protection Act 1998

There is no analogous exemption under the Data Protection Act 1998 or any statutory instrument made under it.

---

[113] See the Memorandum of Understanding and Supplementary Agreements Between the United Kingdom Government, Scottish Ministers, the Cabinet of the National Assembly for Wales and the Northern Ireland Executive Committee (Cm 5240, 2001) and the Memorandum of Understanding and Supplementary Agreements between the United Kingdom Government, the Scottish Ministers, the Welsh Ministers and the Northern Ireland Executive Committee (2010), respectively:
    www.foi.fco.gov.uk/content/en/foi-releases/2009/293-concordat
    www.justice.gov.uk/guidance/docs/devolution-mou-mar-10.pdf
The principal agreement is the Memorandum of Understanding and there are five supplementary agreements: an Agreement on the Joint Ministerial Committee; and three Concordats on Co-ordination of European Union Policy Issues, Financial Assistance to Industry and International Relations. In very general terms, the importance of communicating and exchanging information between the administrations is stressed throughout, but there is also a recognition that some of this may need to take place on a confidential basis: see the Memorandum, paras 5–6, 12. See also MoJ, *Exemptions Guidance—Section 28: Relations within the United Kingdom*, 14 May 2008, pp 4-5, Annexes A–C; Information Commissioner, *Freedom of Information Act Awareness Guidance No 13: Relations within the UK* (2008) Pt B; and Welsh Assembly Government, *Code of Practice on Access to Information* (2007) Pts 1, 3, Annex B.

[114] The Westminster government department with overall responsibility for devolution (currently the Ministry of Justice, formerly the Department for Constitutional Affairs, the Office of the Deputy Prime Minister and the Cabinet Office) also publishes Devolution Guidance Notes on various topics and these may be capable of providing some illumination in relation to the same issues: eg *Devolution Guidance Note No 6: Circulation of Inter-Ministerial And Inter-Departmental Correspondence*, 2005. In *Scotland Office (Stage 2) v IC*, IT, 10 March 2009, the Tribunal's approach to FOIA s 28 was 'informed by' its approach to FOIA s 27 (international relations) in *Campaign against the Arms Trade v IC and MoJ*, IT, 26 August 2008 (at [80], [81]). In other words, the Tribunal considered whether prejudice was probable as opposed to possible or speculative, and it looked for something of detriment in the sense of impairing relations or interests or their promotion or protection (at [52]-[53]).

[115] See: Scotland Act 1998 s 99; Northern Ireland Act 1998 Sch 13 para 9(3); Government of Wales Act 1998 s 1(3); Government of Wales Act 1998 s 89.

CHAPTER 19
Economic and Financial Interests

001 Introduction

By s 29(1) of the Freedom of Information Act 2000 information is rendered exempt information where its disclosure would prejudice, or would be likely to prejudice:

(a) the economic interests of the United Kingdom[1] or of any part of the United Kingdom; or

(b) the financial interests of any administration in the United Kingdom.[2]

An 'administration in the United Kingdom' is defined to mean the Government of the United Kingdom, the Scottish Administration, the Executive Committee of the Northern Ireland Assembly and the National Assembly for Wales.[3] The phrase 'would or would be likely to prejudice' is common to most of the prejudice-based exemptions in the Act. The nature of prejudice and the degree of likelihood which the phrase generally requires are considered elsewhere in this work.[4] Section 29(2) provides that the duty to confirm or deny does not arise if, or to the extent that, compliance with that duty would prejudice, or would be likely to prejudice, the interests protected by s 29(1). Both exemption from the disclosure duty and exclusion from the duty to divulge are non-absolute. Thus, the duty to communicate information whose disclosure would be prejudicial (or would be likely to be prejudicial) to the interests protected by s 29 does not arise only if, or to the extent that, in all the circumstances of the case, the public interest in maintaining the exemption outweighs the public interest in disclosing the information.[5] Similarly, the duty to confirm or deny that such information is held

---

[1]   The United Kingdom means Great Britain (ie England, Scotland and Wales) and Northern Ireland: Interpretation Act 1978 ss 5 and 22(1) Sch 1 Sch 2 para 5(a); Union with Scotland Act 1706 preamble art 1.

[2]   FOI(S)A s 33(2) is in similar terms, save that the prejudice must be substantial.

[3]   FOIA s 28(2); FOI(S)A s 28(2).

[4]   See §§15– 020 to 15– 028.

[5]   FOIA s 2(2)(b).

remains excluded only if, in all the circumstances of the case, the public interest in maintaining the exclusion of that duty outweighs the public interest in divulging whether the public authority holds the information.[6] A broadly equivalent exemption is to be found in the freedom of information legislation of most of the comparative jurisdictions.[7] Where (or to the extent that) the information answering the terms of a request for information is 'environmental information'[8] that request (or that part of that request) falls to be determined by the Environmental Information Regulations 2004 and not by the Freedom of Information Act 2000.[9] The Environmental Information Regulations 2004 do not provide for an analogous exception. Accordingly, unless another exception applies to the information and the public interest balance favours maintenance of that exception, such environmental information must be released notwithstanding prejudice or likely prejudice to the economic interests of the United Kingdom or to the financial interests of any administration in the United Kingdom.

19– 002 Provenance of the exemption

Although the terms of the exemption are imprecise, the provenance of the exemption gives some clue as to its intended breadth. The exclusion of information whose disclosure could be harmful to the economy was in the Code of Practice. The amended version of the Code included an exemption for:

> information whose disclosure would harm the ability of the Government to manage the

---

[6] FOIA s 2(1)(b).

[7] There is no directly comparable exemption in the Freedom of Information Act, 1966 (USA). The Freedom of Information Act 1982 (Cth of Australia) s 47H, provides an exemption where the disclosure of the requested document would, or could be reasonably be expected to, have a substantial adverse effect on the ability of the Commonwealth to manage the economy: see §2– 015(19). The exemption does not involve a consideration of the public interest. The AAT in *Re Waterford and Treasurer of Commonwealth of Australia (No 2)* (1985) 8 ALN N37 stated that if the document entitled Forward Estimates of Budget Receipts had the potential to have a significant impact on the government's ability to control the economy, then its disclosure would be contrary to the public interest and it would be exempt. The Administrative Review Council in its review of the Australian Act considered the exemption superfluous (because information could be exempted under other provisions) and recommended that it be repealed: Australian Law Reform Commission and the Administrative Review Council, *Open Government: a review of the Federal Freedom of Information Act 1982*, ALRC 77, ARC 40 (Canberra, 1995) para 9.28. The Official Information Act 1982 (New Zealand), ss 6(e) and 27(1)(a) provide absolute exemptions where the disclosure of the information would be likely to damage seriously the New Zealand economy by disclosing prematurely decisions to change or continue government economic or financial policies relating to: exchange rates or the control of overseas exchange transactions; the regulation of banking or credit; taxation; the stability, control, and adjustment of prices of goods and services, rents, and other costs, and rates of wages, salaries, and other incomes; the borrowing of money by the New Zealand government; and the entering into of overseas trade agreements: see §2– 022(5). The Official Information Act 1982 makes provision for neither confirming nor denying the existence of the requested documents where to do so would or could reasonably be expected to cause damage to the economy (see §2– 020). The Access to Information Act (Canada) s 18, provides a discretionary exemption for records the disclosure of which could reasonably be expected to cause injury to the financial or economic interests of Canada: see §2– 032(17). The Canadian Courts have required clear proof of a reasonable belief on the part of the Minister that there was a reasonable expectation of probable harm of the prescribed kinds: see *Canadian Council of Christian Charities v Canada (Minister of Finance)* [1999] 4 FC 245. In that case, the Federal Court held that the phrase 'injurious to the financial interests of the Government of Canada' in s 18(d) should not be interpreted as including revenue loss resulting from an increase in legitimate claims to deduction under the Income Tax Act. The Freedom of Information Act 1997 (Ireland) s 24(1), provides a discretionary exemption for records the disclosure of which could reasonably be expected to have a serious adverse effect upon the financial interests of the state or on the ability to manage the economy: see §2– 039(16).

[8] As to the meaning of which, see §6– 010.

[9] And, in relation to a request for information made of a Scottish public authority, by the EI(S)R and not the FOI(S)A.

economy, prejudice the conduct of official market operations, or could lead to improper gain or advantage.[10]

The Explanatory Guidance on the Code gave a non-exhaustive list of examples of information that it considered fell within the exemption, as well as the underlying rationale for the exemption:

> Information about some types of proposals, or even the admission that certain possibilities are being considered, can lead to speculation, disturbance of the markets and even improper gain. It will therefore be necessary to consider the harm test set out in the exemption before releasing information regarding such matters as:
>
> — the currency, coinage or legal tender of the United Kingdom;
> — proposals for expenditure;
> — a contemplated change in the rate of bank interest or in Government borrowing;
> — a contemplated change in tariff rates, taxes, duties or any other revenue services;
> — a contemplated change in the conditions of operation of financial institutions;
> — a contemplated sale or acquisition of land or property; or
> — a contemplated sale or purchase of securities or of foreign or United Kingdom currency.[11]

The fact that information relates to one of these matters was not enough in itself: the exemption in the Code, as in the Freedom of Information Act 2000 now, was harm-based. The Explanatory Guidance simply sets out those classes of information that might, if disclosed, result in harm to the economy.

003 Legislative history

The Bill leading to the Freedom of Information Act 2000 included an exemption[12] in substantially the same terms as s 29. An attempt was made to amend the Bill so that its terms would more closely resemble the exemption in the Code. Lord Mackay of Ardbrecknish argued:

> I can be brief on this, because it is a straightforward argument between the terms of the Bill and the code of practice. The Government thought the code of practice inadequate, but it is stronger than the Bill. The amendment would replace the provisions for a contents exemption in the Bill with the wording used in the code of practice. It would tighten up the Bill, ensuring that only information that would genuinely harm a specific economic interest would be exempt. At the moment, the clause would catch all information relating to the economy. The Government must not be allowed to include such catch-all exemptions, especially as they have drawn up the Bill in such a way that, if information is covered by an exemption, the public authority, rather than the information commissioner, decides whether it should be released. For those reasons, the exemptions should be worded as tightly as possible. The wording in the code is far superior in this regard to that in the Bill. The Government's supporters, who have just come so willingly to their aid in the Division, should ask themselves whether they believed that they fought the election for a Bill that is weaker than the code introduced by the previous Government.[13]

---

[10] *Open Government Code of Practice on Access to Government Information,* 2nd edn (1997) Pt II, para 6(a).

[11] Cabinet Office, *Open Government: Code of Practice on Access to Government Information Guidance on Interpretation* 2nd edn (1997) para 6.1.

[12] Clause 24.

[13] Hansard HL vol 617 col 1286 (1 October 2000).

The response of Lord Bach was:

> I do not dispute that the interests identified in the amendment are important, but the Government do not believe that they are the only important economic or financial considerations in relation to which the inappropriate disclosure of information could lead to real harm being done to the economy.[14]

Lord Bach gave an example of information that would be captured by the proposed exemption but which would not be captured by the exemption in the code:

> Public authorities such as the DTI may hold documents which set out the advantages and disadvantages of investing in different regions. If that type of information were disclosed to an overseas business organisation which was contemplating setting up a factory in the UK, the organisation may be put off its proposed investment. However, if this amendment were carried, that would not exempt such information from disclosure.[15]

Other examples of information thought to be captured by s 29 but not by the Code were given by Lord Bassam of Brighton:

> I should like to assist Members of the Committee by providing some examples. First, the Treasury holds information about the performance of different sectors of the economy and information about whether it intends to raise or lower taxes—important information. Such information has an effect on the United Kingdom economy and its release needs to be carefully managed. Secondly, there exist research projects, the findings of which it would be unreasonable, impractical and inappropriate to publish before the project has been completed. Some research projects could easily run for longer than three months, but under this exemption they would have to supply information on request before the project was completed, with the possible effect of nullifying the results of that project.[16]

19– 004 Scope of the exemption

The terms 'economic interests' and 'financial interests' are capable of a considerable degree of overlap. However, the scope for overlap, as well as the ambit of the exemption itself, is reduced by these two interests being tied to different entities. In each case it is that entity whose interests are required to be prejudiced by disclosure. In order to be captured by s 29(1)(a), the economic interests required to be prejudiced by the disclosure are those of the United Kingdom or any part of the United Kingdom. It would seem that a city council is a 'part of the United Kingdom'.[17] In order to be captured by s 29(1)(b), the financial interests required to be prejudiced by the disclosure are those of any administration in the United Kingdom.[18] A further insight into the scope of the exemption comes from Part VI of the Act dealing with historical records.[19] It is not easy to conceive of information 30, 60 or 100 years old the disclosure of which would prejudice, or would be likely to prejudice, the economic interests of the United Kingdom or the financial interests of any administration of the United Kingdom.

---

[14] Hansard HL vol 617 col 1288 (1 October 2000).

[15] Hansard HL vol 617 col 1288 (19 October 2000).

[16] Hansard HL vol 617 col 1244 (19 October 2000).

[17] *Derry City Council v IC*, IT, 11 December 2006 at [29]. It is suggested that any unit significantly smaller than a local authority area cannot properly be characterised as a 'part of the United Kingdom': the word 'part' is here being used in its sense as a region, rather than as any portion of the whole.

[18] As to the meaning of 'any administration in the United Kingdom' see §19– 001.

[19] See, more generally, ch 6.

Nevertheless, the s 29 exemption is not removed where the information is contained in a historical record,[20] nor where it is contained in a record created 60 or 100 years earlier.[21] The decision to exclude s 29 from the exemptions that fall away with time can best be explained by the importance of the interest that is protected by the exemption, rather than by the nature of the information itself. While the quantity and type of information the disclosure of which would prejudice the economic interests of the United Kingdom, etc may be very greatly diminished when the information is, say, 60 years old, if that in fact is what the effect of its disclosure would be, then the desirability of avoiding the adverse effect is not lessened by the age of the information.

005 Economic interests

Not all information relating to the economy of the United Kingdom (or a part of the United Kingdom) will be exempted from disclosure by s 29. It is information prejudicing economic interests, rather than economic affairs, which is exempted by the section. Beyond the obvious instances of economic interests affecting the United Kingdom generally at a national level, such as forthcoming budgetary or fiscal policy decisions, the exemption would appear to cover information relating to a whole sector of the national economy.[22] As well as making strategic decisions, the State also acts as economic participant (buyer, seller, investor and lender) and as regulator and enforcer. It is arguable that, bearing in mind the scope of its activities in the economy and its corresponding interests, disclosure of information prejudicing or likely to prejudice these interests is also captured by the exemption.

006 Financial interests

So far as financial interests are concerned, the exemption would appear to have a narrower application than in relation to economic interests. As noted above, the financial interests exemption may only be invoked if it relates to the financial interests of an administration as defined. A substantial part of the finances of such administrations are a matter of public record, as in the case of the public sector pay review, for example.

007 The Bank of England

It is to be noted that, while 'any government department' is deemed to be a public authority[23] (and therefore the Treasury is a potential recipient of a request), the Bank of England is a public authority for the purposes of the Act only in respect of information held for purposes other than those of its functions with respect to:
— monetary policy,
— financial operations intended to support financial institutions for the purposes of maintaining stability, and
— the provision of private banking services and related services.[24]

---

[20] FOIA s 63(1).

[21] FOIA s 63(3) and (4).

[22] See *Norway v EFTA Surveillance Authority* [1999] 1 CMLR 851.

[23] FOIA s 3(1)(a)(i) and Sch 1, para 1.

[24] FOIA Sch 1, Pt VI.

Thus information relating to future or past interest rate changes or interventions to support a market sector is inaccessible as the Bank of England is not a public authority for the purposes of a request for such information.

19–008 Actual or likely prejudice

Demonstrating the likely prejudice from a disclosure of information under the Act presents particular problems so far as this exemption is concerned:

(1) Non-statutory guidance from the Ministry of Justice gives some straightforward examples of information, the disclosure of which, at a particular time, would be likely to prejudice the economic interests of the United Kingdom. The examples given include: information relating to the Budget, prior to its being delivered by the Chancellor; information relating to proposed interest rate changes, prior to the proposed change taking effect; proposed tax changes, prior to their being formally announced; premature disclosure of the government's cash flows or borrowing requirements.[25]

(2) As the above examples illustrate, where the disclosure of information would reveal a forthcoming government decision or announcement intended to benefit or protect the economy of the United Kingdom and that disclosure would be likely to result in pre-emptive behaviour that will reduce or negate the efficacy of the decision or announcement, it is suggested that the exemption will be satisfied. It is not in the economic interests of the United Kingdom that the government's power to regulate the economy be rendered ineffective or materially less effective. Beyond the more obvious examples, such as where premature disclosure could reasonably be expected to result in pre-emptive behaviour that makes it more difficult or expensive for the government to implement the decision or where premature disclosure will otherwise render the decision once made or announced less effective, engagement of the exemption is not straightforward. It is easy to assert the prejudice; but proof, even to a level sufficient for an administrative decision, will often be rather more difficult. Expert evidence may be required to demonstrate the likelihood of such prejudice. The currency of the information will often be critical to the application of the exemption. The economic interests of the United Kingdom are shaped by its adherence to a free-market system. The response of that market, and the freedom of that market to respond, to government decisions, whilst it may have adverse consequences for the Government, is not readily to be characterised as being prejudicial to 'the economic interests of the United Kingdom'.

(3) Since 1997, the Government has continued to publish the minutes of monthly meetings between the Chancellor of the Exchequer and the Bank of England. These minutes disclose sensitive economic and financial information. That this information is regularly dispersed to the public without apparent damage makes it more difficult to contend that disclosure of other economic information has, or would be likely to have, the prejudicial effect required by s 29.

(4) Some consideration must also be given to official information relating to the economy that is otherwise liable to be disclosed. Section 27 of the Industry Act

---

[25] MoJ, *Exemption Guidance — section 29*, undated.

1975 provides that Ministers of the Crown and the Treasury must publish, make available and provide access to information and analysis as set out in Sch 5 to that Act. That Schedule provides:

1. For the purposes of this Schedule the Treasury shall keep a macro-economic model suitable for demonstrating the likely effects on economic events in the United Kingdom of different assumptions about the following matters, namely:
   (a) government economic policies;
   (b) economic events outside the United Kingdom; and
   (c) such (if any) other matters as appear to the Treasury from time to time likely to have a substantial effect on economic events in the United Kingdom.

2. The model shall enable forecasts to be made:
   (a) of any of the following, namely:
      (i) the level of gross domestic product;
      (ii) unemployment;
      (iii) the balance of payments on current account;
      (iv) the general index of retail prices; and
      (v) average earnings; and
   (b) of such (if any) other economic variables as are appropriate in the opinion of the Treasury from time to time.

   ...

6. Not less than twice in each year commencing with a date not later than one year from the coming into force of this Act, the Treasury shall publish forecasts produced with the aid of the model as to such matters and based on such alternative assumptions as appear to them to be appropriate.

7. Any forecast under this Schedule shall indicate, where possible, the margin of error attaching to it.

8. The Treasury shall from time to time publish an analysis of errors in such forecasts that would have remained even if the assumptions set out in the forecasts and on which they were based had been correct.

It is difficult to contend that disclosure of analogous information (for example, a micro-economic model) under the Freedom of Information Act 2000 would or would be likely to prejudice the economic interests of the United Kingdom if that class of information is liable to be disclosed under another Act of Parliament. The existence of this free-standing right to certain information that may impinge upon the economic interests of the United Kingdom is also relevant to the weighing exercise required by s 2 of the Act: it is difficult to see that the public interest in maintaining the exemption has particular force if another Act of Parliament gives a statutory entitlement to the disclosure of information of the same class.

009 The public interest

Even if information is exempt because it answers the terms of s 29(1), an applicant will still be entitled to have the information communicated to him unless, in all the circumstances of the case, the public interest in maintaining the exemption outweighs the public interest in disclosing the information.[26] Similarly, even if the duty to confirm or deny does not arise as a result of the operation of s 29(2), an applicant will still be entitled to be informed that the public authority holds the information requested unless, in all the circumstances of the case, the public interest in maintaining the exclusion outweighs the public interest in divulging its existence.[27] The decision of the legislature not to make exemption under s 29 absolute cannot properly be undone by giving the public interest in maintaining the exemption such weight as to make the public interest in disclosure unable to outweigh it. The exercise must be carried out in such a manner as to recognise that in some circumstances the public interest in disclosure will be sufficiently powerful to displace an inherently compelling public interest in maintaining the exemption. In practice, the balancing exercise will comprise mainly weighing up the public interest in disclosure against the public interest in protecting the economic and financial welfare of the nation, the constituent parts of the nation, and the various national administrations. For information relating to past decisions involving the matters protected by s 29, it may be more difficult to find that the public interest in maintaining the exemption outweighs the public interest in disclosure.[28] So far as information relating to future decisions involving the protected matters, for example the imposition of exchange rate controls, the public interest in maintaining the exemption will, as a general rule, more readily outweigh the public interest in disclosure. The years since Black Wednesday have provided ample illustration of how entire markets and economic sectors can be destabilised by the acts of a very few speculators. Access to information which enables or informs such speculation cannot readily be characterised as being in the public interest. On the other hand, a potential investor seeking information about the future of a regional development will not necessarily be acting contrary to the public interest. Such an investor may well argue that a whole region will benefit from enhanced infrastructure and the creation of jobs by investment and that it is in the public interest that access to such information be provided.

19–010   The Data Protection Act 1998

There is no directly comparable exemption in the Data Protection Act 1998. However, para 6(1) of Sch 7[29] provides that where personal data are processed for the purposes of, or in connection with, a 'corporate finance service'[30] provided by a 'relevant person'[31] they may be exempt from the 'subject information provisions' (which includes the s 7 access rights) if the 'exemption is required for the purpose of safeguarding an important economic or financial interest of the United Kingdom'. Paragraph 6(2) of Sch 7 enables the Secretary of State to

---

[26]   FOIA s 2(2)(b).

[27]   FOIA s 2(1)(b).

[28]   Thus, in *Derry City Council v IC*, IT, 11 December 2006 at [29], although the information was held to fall within s 29, the passage of 6 years enabled the Information Tribunal to conclude that the public interest in maintaining the exemption was outweighed by the public interest in disclosure. Contrast the position taken by the European Court of Justice when considering the analogous exemption under Regulation 1049/2001: Case T-3/00 *Pitsiorlas v EU Council* [2007] ECR II-4779, [2008] 1 CMLR 47 at [231]-[288].

[29]   Schedule 7 provides miscellaneous exemptions for the purposes of the 'subject information provisions', which are defined in s 27(2) to include the access right provided by s 7 of the DPA.

[30]   Defined in §6(3) of Sch 7.

[31]   Also defined in §6(3) of Sch 7: in very general terms, a person who is authorised under Ch III of Pt I of the Financial Services Act 1986 or who is an exempted person under Ch IV of Pt I of that Act.

specify by order 'matters to be taken into account in determining whether exemption from the subject information provisions is required for the purposes of safeguarding an important economic or financial interest of the United Kingdom'. The Secretary of State has exercised this power,[32] with the matters to be taken into account spelt out as:

> ...the inevitable prejudicial effect on:
> (a)   the orderly functioning of financial markets, or
> (b)   the efficient allocation of capital within the economy,
> which will result from the application (whether on an occasional or regular basis) of the
> subject information provisions to data to which paragraph (3) applies.

The data referred to are personal data to which application of the relevant provisions of the Data Protection Act 1998 could reasonably be believed to affect: (a) any decision of any person whether or not to deal in, subscribe to or issue any instrument which is already in existence or is to be or may be created; or (b) any decision of any person to act or not to act in a way that is likely to have an effect on any business activity.

---

[32] Data Protection (Corporate Finance Exemption) Order 2000 SI 2000/184.

CHAPTER 20

Investigation, Audit, Law Enforcement and the Courts

1.   INTRODUCTION

001 Overview

This chapter is principally concerned with a group of provisions that exempt information from the disclosure obligations so as not to undermine the enforcement of the law (principally, but not exclusively, the criminal law) and the administration of justice. The exemptions take many different forms and often overlap in a haphazard way. Some depend on the purposes for which the information is held, some on whether disclosure will cause prejudice (and some on a combination of the two);[1] some require the information still to be held for the relevant purpose, some that it was once so held; in some cases the current holder of the information must have had the relevant purpose, in others this is not required; in some the original source of the information or the purposes for which it was communicated to the public authority is relevant, in others not. In this chapter, this group of exemptions has been divided into seven sections. In each section, separate consideration is given to the scope of the exemption from the duty to communicate under the Freedom of Information Acts, to the role of the public interest, to the duty to confirm or deny, and to any equivalent exemption under the two sets of Environmental Information Regulations[2] and the Data Protection Act 1998. It is worth emphasising at the outset that neither the courts nor the courts service is a public authority, so that information held by them is not required to be disclosed under either the Freedom of Information Act 2000

---

[1]   See in particular DPA s 29(1). In relation to the FOIA, see §§14– 022 to 14– 023.

[2]   The EIR and the EI(S)R.

or the Environmental Information Regulations 2004.[3]

20– 002 The public interest generally

The general purpose of these exemptions is set out in the White Paper which led to the introduction of the Freedom of Information Act 2000:

> [freedom of information] should not undermine the investigation, prosecution or prevention of crime, or the bringing of civil or criminal proceedings by public bodies. The investigation and prosecution of crime involve a number of essential requirements. These include the need to avoid prejudicing effective law enforcement, the need to protect witnesses and informers, the need to maintain the independence of the judicial and prosecution processes, and the need to preserve the criminal court as the sole forum for determining guilt. Because of this, the Act will exclude information relating to the investigation and prosecution functions of the police, prosecutors, and other bodies carrying out law enforcement work such as the Department of Social Security or the Immigration Service. The Act will also exclude information relating to the commencement or conduct of civil proceedings.[4]

With the exception of provisions relating to court records,[5] none of the Freedom of Information Act exemptions in this group is absolute: they only apply if the public interest in maintaining the exemption outweighs the public interest in disclosing the information.[6] This public interest requirement must be satisfied even in cases where the test for exemption is whether prejudice will or is likely to be caused. Thus it is possible that although a particular disclosure would cause prejudice to the enforcement of the law or the administration of justice, nevertheless the information must be disclosed because the public interest in disclosure outweighs the prejudice. Nevertheless, there is a recognised public interest in maintaining these exemptions where disclosure would provide undesirable forewarning to the subjects of investigation or would prejudice confidential sources of information needed for such purposes.[7] As with the other qualified exemptions, in weighing the competing public interests, the relevant decision maker[8] will have to take into account all the circumstances of the case[9] and any relevant provisions of the European Convention for the Protection of Human Rights and Fundamental Freedoms.[10] There is no express public interest requirement to be satisfied in relation to this group of exemptions as they appear in the Data Protection Act 1998.

---

[3] There is a free-standing right under the CPR to access certain documents held by the courts: see §8– 105.

[4] *Your Right to Know. The Government's Proposals for a FOI Act* (Cm 3818, 1997) §2.21. Although the form of the Act as enacted was quite different from that intended in 1997, the basic intention behind the provisions dealt with in this chapter is that revealed in the quotation.

[5] FOIA s 32; FOI(S)A s 37.

[6] FOIA ss 2(1)(b) and 2(2)(b); FOI(S)A s 2(1)(b); EIR reg 12(1)(b); EI(S)R reg 10(1)(b). The exemptions in Pt IV of the DPA have no specific requirement to consider the public interest. For a general discussion of this topic, see §§15– 001 to 15– 019.

[7] *DTI v IC*, IT, 10 November 2006 at [57], [60]–[61].

[8] That is, the public authority from which information is sought, the Information Commissioner, the Tribunal or the courts.

[9] FOIA ss 2(1)(b) and 2(2)(b); FOI(S)A s 2(1)(b); EIR reg 12(1)(b); EI(S)R reg 10(1)(b).

[10] As to which, see ch 3.

003 Limits on exemptions

As with all exemptions under Part II of the Freedom of Information Act 2000, Part 3 of the Environmental Information Regulations 2004 and Part IV of the Data Protection Act 1998, they only operate in relation to the obligations of disclosure provided by the relevant Act: they do not exempt a public authority from making disclosures required by other legislation or rules of law. Thus, they do not exempt a public authority from its obligations to disclose material to the accused in criminal proceedings[11] or to the other party in civil proceedings[12] and they do not affect its power to do so.[13]

2. INFORMATION HELD FOR PURPOSES OF CRIMINAL INVESTIGATIONS OR PROCEEDINGS

004 Introduction

This and the following two sections involve three separate, but in practice largely overlapping, heads of exemption:

(1) information held for the purposes of a criminal investigation or criminal proceedings;

(2) information relating to the obtaining of information from confidential sources; and

(3) information whose disclosure might prejudice the enforcement of criminal law.

It will be noted that only the third involves a consideration of resultant prejudice. Similar exemptions are to be found in each of the comparative jurisdictions.[14]

005 The exemption

Section 30(1) of the Freedom of Information Act 2000 exempts information held by a public authority if it has been held by it at any time for the purposes of any investigation which it has a duty to carry out with a view to it being ascertained whether to charge someone with an offence or whether a person charged is guilty,[15] or, if the authority itself has power to conduct

---

[11] See §§8– 107 to 8– 115.

[12] See §§8– 090 to 8– 106.

[13] See, eg FOIA s 78; FOI(S)A s 66; DPA s 35.

[14] In the United States, the Freedom of Information Act, 1966, 5 USC § 552(b)(7), exempts from disclosure records or information compiled for law enforcement purposes: see §2– 008(7). The Freedom of Information Act 1982 (Cth of Australia) s 37, provides an exemption where the disclosure of the requested document would, or could be reasonably be expected to, cause damage to law enforcement, confidential sources of information relating to law enforcement, fair trials, or methods of criminal investigation: see §2– 015(12). The Official Information Act 1982 (New Zealand), ss 6(c) and 27(1)(a), provides an exemption where the disclosure of the information would be likely to prejudice the maintenance of the law, including the prevention, investigation, and detection of offences, and the right to a fair trial: see §2– 022(3). The Access to Information Act (Canada) s 16(1)(c), provides a discretionary exemption for records the disclosure of which could reasonably be expected to cause injury to law enforcement or conduct of lawful investigations: see §2– 032(12). The Freedom of Information Act 1997 (Ireland), provides a discretionary exemption for records the disclosure of which could reasonably be expected to prejudice law enforcement and investigations or matters of internal security, or to reveal the name of a police informer: see §2– 039(12).

[15] See FOIA s 30(1)(a).

criminal proceedings, for the purposes of an investigation carried out by it which may lead to criminal proceedings[16] or for the purposes of such criminal proceedings.[17] This is a class-based exemption: in spite of considerable parliamentary pressure,[18] and in contrast to the position in much of the comparative legislation,[19] there is no requirement for any prejudice to any investigation or proceedings to be shown for the exemption to apply. The exemption appears to be designed to relate to information held for the purposes of specific investigations or criminal proceedings, rather than to investigations or proceedings generally,[20] although the wording of the provision is possibly ambiguous.[21] It applies most obviously to information coming to the police,[22] the National Crime Squad, the Serious Fraud Office, the Crown Prosecution Service or the Director of Public Prosecutions in the course of specific investigations; but it may also apply to information held by many other bodies which have the power to conduct criminal proceedings of all sorts, including proceedings relating to quite minor offences.[23] For the exemption to apply the authority holding the information must be the same as the one which held it for the relevant purpose,[24] but it can have held it for that purpose at any time in the past,[25] it need not have obtained it for that purpose originally and the information does not have to be required any longer for that purpose.[26] Thus, information once coming within the exemption is always potentially exempt and the potential exemption applies even if a decision was made not to prosecute or if a prosecution has been completed, however long ago the investigation or prosecution was completed.[27]

---

[16] FOIA s 30(1)(b).

[17] FOIA s 30(1)(c).

[18] For example: Hansard HL vol 617 col 1291 (19 October 2000).

[19] See, eg Freedom of Information Act 1982 (Cth of Aust) s 37(1)(a); Freedom of Information Act 1997 (Ireland) s 23(1)(a).

[20] As, eg, internal documents of the police showing investigation methods or procedures which are likely to be covered by FOIA s 31(1)(a) and (b).

[21] See the view of the Minister, Lord Falconer of Thoroton, in Hansard HL vol 612 col 827 (20 April 2000).

[22] See, eg: *Digby-Cameron v IC and Bedfordshire Police*, IT, 26 January 2009; *Kelway v IC and Northumbria Police*, IT, 14 April 2009.

[23] For example, local authorities which have numerous prosecutorial functions, the Health and Safety Executive (or inspectors appointed under s 19 of the Health and Safety at Work etc Act 1974), the Environment Agency, HM Revenue & Customs (see: *Armstrong v IC and HMRC*, IT, 14 October 2008 at [60]), the DTI (see: *DTI v IC*, IT, 10 November 2006, involving an investigation under Companies Act 1985 s 447), DEFRA, the Food Standards Agency, Financial Services Authority, Office of Fair Trading, General Medical Council, but not, generally, the Independent Police Complaints Commission whose main function is to supervise the investigation by the police of alleged misconduct on the part of officers (rather than to conduct the investigation themselves). Note that FOIA s 30(5) expressly includes proceedings before courts-martial and other military courts within the concept of criminal proceedings.

[24] The exemption is designed for prosecuting authorities as such.

[25] *Creekside Forum v IC and Dept for Culture Media and Sport*, IT, 28 May 2009 at [13].

[26] But the Tribunal has drawn a distinction between information 'used' for the purpose of an investigation and information 'held' for that purpose: *Digby-Cameron v IC and Bedfordshire Police*, IT, 26 January 2009 at [14].

[27] This appears to go further than was necessary to carry out the Government's expressed purpose for the provision, Lord Falconer of Thoroton stating that it was necessary 'to ensure that criminal proceedings are not jeopardised by the premature disclosure of information and to preserve the criminal courts as the sole forum for determining guilt': Hansard HL vol 612 col 827 (20 April 2000). But these issues may be relevant in assessing where the 'public interest' lies: see §20– 006.

006 The public interest

If the information in question comes within the section, the duty to disclose does not apply if and to the extent that the public interest in maintaining the exemption outweighs the public interest in disclosing the information.[28] The weighing exercise necessitates an identification of the public interest in the maintenance of the exemption, always recognising that that public interest must be delineated in such a fashion that it is capable in practice of being outweighed.[29] Superficially, the public interest protected by this exemption might seem to be confined to protecting the successful investigation and prosecution of specific criminal offences.[30] However, this objective has numerous strands, a view supported by the Ministry of Justice[31] and the Tribunal.[32] A more restrictive view would produce unfortunate consequences.[33] On this basis, it is thought that the public interest in maintaining the exemption will be taken to include the factors identified by the Ministry of Justice, namely the promotion of the chances of a successful prosecution or bringing future charges or making arrests, the promotion of the chances of a fair trial taking place, fairness to those not prosecuted, assistance with gathering intelligence information from confidential sources, protecting all who participate in the investigations or criminal proceedings,[34] assisting ongoing or further proceedings and the prevention of crime.[35] The force of the public interest in maintaining this exemption will in material part depend on the importance of the information to the investigation or proceedings,[36] the currency of the

---

[28] FOIA ss 30(1) and 2(2)(b). That there is a particular public interest in the disclosure of information relating to the commission of a criminal offence is reflected in Pt IVA of the Employment Rights Act 1996 as inserted by the Public Interest Disclosure Act 1998, which sanctions as being in the public interest a disclosure by an employee tending to show 'that a criminal offence has been committed, is being committed or is likely to be committed': s 43B(1)(a).

[29] To avoid metamorphosing it into an absolute exemption.

[30] The advantage of non-disclosure in support of this public interest is obvious: to avoid warning those who are being investigated that this is the case and to avoid contamination of evidence, as to which see *R v Police Complaints Authority, ex p Green* [2004] UKHL 6, [2004] 1 WLR 725, [2004] 2 All ER 209, [2004] HRLR 19, [2004] UKHRR 939 at [71] (Lord Rodger). Once a prosecution is started the prosecutor will be obliged to disclose any relevant material to the accused (unless the court concludes that to do so is not in the public interest) under ss 3 and 7A of the Criminal Procedure and Investigations Act 1996; but the accused can only use or disclose such material for the purposes of the case or if disclosed in open court or with the court's permission (s 17 of the 1996 Act): see ?(10).

[31] See MoJ, *Exemptions Guidance – Section 30* (14 May 2008) pp 12-13, which lists preventing the commission of crime and assisting future proceedings as relevant factors along with, eg, the promotion of the chances of a successful prosecution or a fair trial.

[32] See *Toms v IC*, IT, 19 June 2006, where the Information Tribunal upheld reliance on s 30(1) by the Royal Mail on the basis that the disclosure of the information requested would 'facilitate the commission of similar crimes [to those being investigated]' (at [9] and [23]). See also: *Digby-Cameron v IC and Bedfordshire Police*, IT, 26 January 2009 at [14].

[33] If s 30 applies to make information 'exempt' s 31 (information whose disclosure would prejudice the prevention of crime) cannot apply: see s 31(1). Thus, if prejudice to the prevention of future crime was not relevant to the weighing of the public interest under s 30(1), it could result in information having to be disclosed once a particular investigation or prosecution was complete notwithstanding that its disclosure might prejudice the prevention of future crime.

[34] This applies in particular to witnesses, though different considerations may apply in the case of police witnesses: see *McCluskey v IC and Public Prosecution Service for Northern Ireland*, IT, 21 December 2007 at [26]; *Armstrong v IC and HMRC*, IT, 14 October 2008 at [78].

[35] See MoJ, *Exemptions Guidance – Section 30* (14 May 2008) pp 12-13.

[36] *Freebury v IC and Chief Constable of Devon and Cornwall Constabulary*, IT, 5 October 2009 at [40].

investigation or proceedings,[37] whether the information, or like information, has been earlier released and, if so, to whom, on what basis and for what purpose. The passage of time, the completion of a prosecution, the release of similar information into a public forum[38] and the inconsequentiality of the information can all be expected to weaken the public interest in the maintenance of the exemption.[39] There is likely to be a public interest in the disclosure of information about the commission of a criminal offence and the public interest in disclosure may, for example, be heightened:

— where disclosure would allay legitimate public concerns about an investigation or prosecution;[40]

— where it can be inferred from the documents that there has been a lack of vigour or proper vigilance in an investigation, irrespective of the vintage of that investigation;[41]

— where the information already officially released relating to an investigation or prosecution is unrepresentative of all such information held by the public authority;[42] or

— where some decision affecting the applicant has been made that is based, whether in whole or in part, on the information.[43]

20– 007 The duty to confirm or deny

Where the requested information is, or if it were held would be, exempt information under s 30(1), then the discrete duty to confirm or deny that that information is held by the public authority does not arise but, again, this is a qualified exclusion of duty.[44] It will therefore be necessary to consider whether, in all the circumstances, the maintenance of the exclusion of this duty outweighs the public interest in disclosing whether the public authority holds the information. Despite its superficial similarity, this public interest balancing exercise is materially different from that employed for the purpose of determining whether the duty to

---

[37] *Kelway v IC and Northumbria Police*, IT, 14 April 2009 at [69]-[70].

[38] *Freebury v IC and Chief Constable of Devon and Cornwall Constabulary*, IT, 5 October 2009 at [37].

[39] See Hansard HL vol 618 col 274 (24 October 2000) and vol 619 cols 223–4 (14 November 2000). Note also the Access to Information Act 1982 (Canada) which provides at s 16(1)(a) that the corresponding exemption only applies to information less than 20 years old. In *Guardian Newspapers Ltd v IC and Chief Constable of Avon & Somerset Police*, IT, 5 April 2007 at [37] the Information Tribunal regarded the passage of 30 or so years from the creation of the documents sought (the complete files of a police force relating to the prosecution of Jeremy Thorpe for conspiracy to murder and for incitement to murder) and the date of the request as a 'double-edged sword'. Whilst it reduced the risk of prejudice to future investigations, it similarly weakened the legitimate public interest in knowing more of the background facts to the investigation.

[40] Including a decision not to prosecute: see *McCluskey v IC and Public Prosecution Service for Northern Ireland*, IT, 21 December 2007 at [27].

[41] *Guardian Newspapers Ltd v IC and Chief Constable of Avon & Somerset Police*, IT, 5 April 2007 at [35].

[42] See §§15– 012 and 15– 017.

[43] The public interest is capable of recognising the peculiar interest of an applicant in having access to information that touches upon or relates to that individual's rights or to matters of particular and legitimate concern to that individual: see §15– 015.

[44] FOIA s 2(1)(b).

communicate does not apply.[45] As a general rule, the broader the terms of the request, the more difficult it will become for the public authority to contend that the public interest in excluding the duty to confirm or deny that such information is held by it outweighs the public interest in compliance with that duty, if only because it will be self-evident that the public authority does hold information of that description. But public authorities are likely to refuse to confirm or deny the holding of information relating to a particular investigation since even that limited disclosure might assist those who are under investigation.

008 Scottish Act

The Scottish counterpart to s 30(1) is s 34(1) of the Freedom of Information (Scotland) Act 2002. The Scottish provision does not explicitly require the information to be held by the Scottish public authority which previously held it for the purposes of the investigation. Also, it does not cover the possibility of the authority which held the information itself having power to institute criminal proceedings; rather, it refers to an investigation which may lead to a report to the Procurator Fiscal.[46] There is also a special provision in s 34(2) of the Scottish Act making information exempt if it is held by a Scottish public authority for the purposes of an inquiry under the Fatal Accidents and Sudden Deaths Inquiry (Scotland) Act 1976[47] or if it has been held by such an authority for the purposes of any other investigation into the cause of death of any person. Apart from these differences, as well as the different manner in which the Scottish Act generally deals with the duty to confirm or deny,[48] the Scottish provision is materially the same as s 30(1) of the Freedom of Information 2000.

3. INFORMATION RELATING TO THE OBTAINING OF INFORMATION FROM CONFIDENTIAL SOURCES

009 First requirement of the exemption

Section 30(2) of the Freedom of Information Act 2000 contains specific provisions exempting information held by a public authority which was obtained or recorded for the purposes of the public authority's functions relating to criminal investigations or proceedings, as well as certain civil investigations or proceedings (relating, for example, to the disqualification of company directors). In each such case, however, there is an additional requirement that the information 'relates to the obtaining of information from confidential sources'.[49] In so far as this exemption relates to information obtained or recorded for the purpose of criminal investigation or proceedings, such information will very likely also be rendered exempt information by s 30(1). However, s 30(2), unlike s 30(1), would seem not to require that the information has been held for the purpose of any particular investigation: it would seem to be enough that the information

---

[45] See §§15– 018 to 15– 019 as to what it involves.

[46] There are similar provisions in the FOIA in the application of s 30 to Scottish public authorities: see s 30(6).

[47] But if the inquiry is still continuing, see FOI(S)A s 34(2)(a).

[48] See §1– 041.

[49] FOIA s 30(2)(a)(i) and (ii) and (b).

was obtained for the purposes of the public authority's functions relating to criminal investigations and proceedings generally. In so far as this exemption relates to particular civil investigations and proceedings, it does not overlap with s 30(1).

20– 010 Second requirement of the exemption

The second requirement in s 30(2) is that the information 'relates to the obtaining of information from confidential sources'. This was said to be intended to protect the identity of particular sources of information,[50] but it is arguable that it is more limited. A neutral reading of the exemption results in it only comprehending general information relating to the obtaining of information from confidential sources, and not a particular piece of information obtained from such a source in the course of a specific investigation or the identity of the particular source.[51] Whatever is precisely covered by the section, it is clear that it is not a requirement that the information itself is 'confidential' and it does not exempt any information simply on the grounds of confidentiality. Rather, it seeks to exempt information about the obtaining of information from confidential sources.[52] The phrase 'confidential sources' is likely to be construed as referring to sources who supply information 'on the understanding, whether express or implied, that his or her identity will remain confidential'.[53]

20– 011 The public interest

Exemption under s 30(2) is qualified.[54] An assessment of the public interest in maintaining this exemption should involve a consideration of both paragraphs of the exemption. So far as paragraph (a) is concerned, where the information relates to a criminal investigation or criminal proceedings, the relevant factors will be similar to those which arise upon an assessment of the public interest under s 30(1).[55] So far as paragraph (b) is concerned, the public interest in the maintenance of confidential sources of information will be of particular significance,[56] as will

---

[50] See Lord Falconer of Thoroton in Hansard HL vol 619 col 220 (14 November 2000).

[51] Compare the clearer and more explicit foreign legislation: Freedom of Information Act 1982 (Cth of Aust) s 37(1)(b); Official Information Act 1982 (New Zealand) s 9(2)(ba)(i); Access to Information Act 1982 (Canada) s 16(1)(c)(ii); Freedom of Information Act 1997 (Ireland) s 23(1)(a)(i) and (b); exemption 7(D) in the Freedom of Information Act 1966 (USA) referred to in *Pope v USA* (1979) 599 F 2d 1383 and note not only the wording of FOIA s 30(2)(b) but also the use of the phrase 'for the purposes of its functions relating to….investigations [and]…proceedings' in s 30(2)(a). It is likely that the identity of confidential sources would be protected in any event by the very general prejudice based exemption in s 31(1)(a) and (b) or by s 30(1). The Tribunal has found that the identity of a particular source comes within the exemption: *Alcock v IC and Chief Constable of Staffordshire Police*, IT, 3 January 2007 at [35].

[52] Note not just the identity of such sources: it might include, eg, details of an investigation or surveillance operation associated with the management of external confidential sources.

[53] See *Dept of Health v Jephcott* (1985) 62 ALR 421 at 426. See also *Luzaich v United States* (1977) 435 F Supp 31 at 35, which talks of a 'pledge of confidentiality'. Note the source does not have to be 'covert'; and the fact that a source is 'covert' does not necessarily make it 'confidential': eg, undercover police officers or concealed cameras are covert sources but they are not confidential sources.

[54] FOIA s 2(3).

[55] As to which, see §20– 006.

[56] *DTI v IC*, IT, 10 November 2006 at [57], [60], [61]. See for a discussion of the public interest in preserving confidential sources in this and analogous contexts: *D v NSPCC* [1978] AC 171 (in particular 218C–F, 230A–B, 232F–G, 241C–D); *R v Police Complaints Authority, ex p Green* [2004] UKHL 6, [2004] 1 WLR 725, [2004] 2 All ER 209, [2004] HRLR 19, [2004] UKHRR 939 at [73] (Lord Rodger); *R v H* [2004] UKHL 3, [2004] 2 AC 134, [2004] 1 All ER 1269, [2004] 2 Cr App R 10, [2004] HRLR 20 at [18]: 'Circumstances may arise in which material

the ability of a person adversely affected by a decision based on the information to controvert it. Where disclosure would assist the subject of an investigation or the public in understanding an investigative decision taken by police, where disclosure would help in holding the police accountable for their actions and use of public funds, or where disclosure would assist the applicant or any member of the public in righting an injustice to a person investigated, the public interest in disclosure could be weightier.[57] If the public authority has a structured system for assessing the validity of information provided to them by informants, then these public interest factors will be reduced in weight as the public interest in disclosure will to some extent already have been served by that system.[58] There may be circumstances where the public interest in maintaining the exemption can be satisfied by the redacting of names, addresses and other details of confidential sources from information supplied by them but obviously this will not always be sufficient, since the very existence of that information may disclose too much about the identity or methods or mere fact of information being obtained from confidential sources.

012 The duty to confirm or deny

Where the requested information is, or if it were held would be, exempt information under s 30(2), then the discrete duty to confirm or deny that that information is held by the public authority does not arise. The exclusion of this duty is a qualified one. It will be necessary to consider whether, in all the circumstances, the maintenance of the exclusion of this duty is outweighed by the public interest in disclosing whether the public authority holds the information. As noted above,[59] this public interest balancing exercise is materially different from that employed for the purpose of determining whether the duty to communicate does not apply.[60]

013 Scottish provisions

Analogous provisions exist in the Freedom of Information (Scotland) Act 2002,[61] albeit slightly narrower in scope than under the Westminster Act.[62]

---

held by the prosecution and tending to undermine the prosecution or assist the defence cannot be disclosed to the defence, fully or even at all, without the risk of serious prejudice to an important public interest. The public interest most regularly engaged is that in the effective investigation and prosecution of serious crime, which may involve resort to informers and undercover agents, or the use of scientific or operational techniques (such as surveillance) which cannot be disclosed without exposing individuals to the risk of personal injury or jeopardising the success of future operations.' See also *Pope v USA* (1979) 599 F 2d 1383 and *Jarvie v Magistrates' Court of Victoria at Brunswick* [1995] 1 VR 84 at 88: 'There is a public interest in preserving the anonymity of informers, since otherwise these wells of information will dry up and the police will be hindered in preventing and detecting crime; moreover, the public interest on which the need to protect informers rests is based in part on a regard for their personal safety, considered, not as a matter of expediency, but as an object in itself' (Brooking J).

[57] *Alcock v IC and Chief Constable of Staffordshire Police*, IT, 3 January 2007 at [38].

[58] *Alcock v IC and Chief Constable of Staffordshire Police*, IT, 3 January 2007 at [40].

[59] See §20– 007, where this duty is considered further.

[60] See §§15– 018 to 15– 019 as to what it involves.

[61] FOI(S)A s 34(3).

[62] The FOI(S)A does not include an equivalent of the FOIA s 30(2)(a)(i) or (ii). The FOIA s 30(2)(a)(iii) is equivalent to the FOI(S)A s 34(3); s 30(2)(a)(iv) is equivalent to 34(4), save that the second requirement is absent in relation to information held by Scottish public authorities.

4. INFORMATION WHOSE DISCLOSURE MIGHT PREJUDICE THE ENFORCEMENT OF CRIMINAL LAW

20– 014 The exemption

By s.31(1)(a) and (b) of the Freedom of Information Act 2000 information which is not exempt under s.30[63] is nevertheless exempt if its disclosure under the Act would, or would be likely to, prejudice the prevention or detection of crime or the apprehension or prosecution of offenders.[64] The basic distinction between ss.30 and 31 is that:

— the former is concerned with information held by the public authority for the purpose of a specific investigation or criminal proceedings conducted by it, and with investigative material that relates to the obtaining of information from confidential sources;

— the latter is concerned with information, which although not held by the public authority for the purpose of a specific investigation or criminal proceedings conducted by it (nor relating to the obtaining of information from confidential sources), nevertheless would, if disclosed, prejudice or be likely to prejudice the enforcement of the law.

The latter is, therefore, more concerned with adverse revelations of methodology.[65] Similar exemptions as to law enforcement procedures are to be found in the comparative jurisdictions.[66] The phrase 'would be likely to prejudice' in the context of this provision will be taken to mean that the prejudice must be a real possibility, or something which 'may well' result, as opposed

---

[63] See §§20– 004 to 20– 008.

[64] FOIA s 31(1)(a) and (b).

[65] It is questionable whether s 31 can be used to prevent the disclosure of confidential source information to any useful extent. First, the information will be exempt information by virtue of s 30 and therefore outside s 31. Secondly, a general assertion that the disclosure of such material will, or would be likely to, prejudice enforcement of the law is apt to metamporphose s 31 into a pure class-based exemption. This approach has been rejected elsewhere. In Canada, the Courts have required the public authority to identify a particular investigation that would be prejudiced, and have declined to uphold a refusal to disclose upon an assertion that investigative processes would generally be prejudiced: *Rubin v Canada (Clerk of the Privy Council)* [1993] 2 FC 391, TD, [1994] 2 FC 707, CA; (1996), 179 NR 320, SCC; *Lavigne v Canada (Commissioner of Official Languages)* [2000] FCJ 1412, QL FCA; *Information Commissioner v Minister of Citizenship and Immigration* [2002] FCA 270 ('chilling effect' argument rejected).

[66] In the United States, the Freedom of Information Act, 1966, 5 USC § 552(b)(7)(E), exempts from disclosure records or information that would reveal techniques and procedures for law enforcement investigations or prosecutions or that would disclose guidelines for law enforcement investigations or prosecutions, provided that disclosure of the information could reasonably be expected to risk circumvention of the law: see §2– 008(7)(E). The Freedom of Information Act 1982 (Cth of Australia), s 37, provides an exemption where the disclosure of the requested document would, or could be reasonably be expected to, prejudice an investigation or enforcement of the law or to disclose confidential sources of information in relation to the enforcement or administration of the law: see §2– 015(12). The Official Information Act 1982 (New Zealand), ss 6(c) and 27(1)(a), provides an exemption where the disclosure of the information would be likely to prejudice the maintenance of the law, including the prevention, investigation, and detection of offences, and the right to a fair trial: see §2– 022(3). The Access to Information Act (Canada), s 16(1)(c), provides a discretionary exemption for records the disclosure of which could reasonably be expected to cause injury to law enforcement or conduct of lawful investigations: see §2– 032(12). The Freedom of Information Act 1997 (Ireland), provides a discretionary exemption for records the disclosure of which could reasonably be expected to prejudice law enforcement and investigations or matters of internal security, or to reveal the name of a police informer: see §2– 039(12).

to being 'more probable than not.'[67] Thus, not only insignificant harm but also fanciful or improbable risks of harm to the relevant interest are to be disregarded. Provided the relevant likelihood of prejudice is established, it does not matter which public authority holds the information[68] and it need not relate to a specific investigation or prosecution. Thus, the exemption might apply not only to information held for the purposes of a current investigation (assuming for some reason it was not in any event covered by s 30(1) of the Freedom of Information Act 2000) but also to information disclosing methods and procedures for investigating or preventing crime.[69] Examples of information which might come within this exemption are as follows:

— policy documents setting out in what circumstances a public authority would prosecute for a breach of statute;[70]

— investigation manuals;[71]

— information about planned police operations or tactics;

— intelligence about anticipated criminal activities;

— witness statements held by another public authority in relation to an anticipated prosecution by the police or CPS;[72]

— information about the criteria the police apply when considering the possible installation of secret surveillance equipment;

— information as to the registration numbers of unmarked police cars;

— information whose disclosure may facilitate the commission of an offence;[73]

— information as to the physical security of buildings or IT and telephone systems;[74]

— information as to numbers of police officers deployed in a particular area.

It should also be noted that the particular information in itself may appear innocuous but nevertheless come within the exemption because, when combined with other information which

---

[67] See the Information Tribunal decisions in *Hogan and Oxford City Council v IC*, IT, 17 October 2006 at [34]-[36] and *John Connor Press Associates Ltd v IC*, IT, 25 January 2006 at [15], following the approach of Munby J in *R v Secretary of State for the Home Office ex parte Lord* [2003] EWHC 2073 (Admin). Generally, see §§ 15– 020 to 15– 028.

[68] See, eg, *Hargrave v IC and National Archives*, IT, 3 December 2007, which related to the police file on a murder which took place in 1954 which had been passed to the National Archives but where the Tribunal found on the basis of closed evidence that there was still some prospect of the murderer being detected and prosecuted [34]-[37].

[69] See the corresponding provision in the Freedom of Information Act 1982 (Cth of Aust), s 37(2)(b).

[70] For a similar example in Australia, see: *Re Murphy and Australian Electoral Commission* (1994) 33 ALD 718.

[71] For a similar example in Australia, see:*Re Arnold Bloch Leibler & Co and Australian Taxation Office (No 2)* (1985) 4 AAR 178, 9 ALD 7.

[72] See, eg, *R v Police Complaints Authority, ex p Green* [2004] UKHL 6, [2004] 1 WLR 725 at [71] Lord Rodger sets out the prejudice that can result from the disclosure of such witness statements and the public interest in their non-disclosure. In general criminal proceedings themselves should of course be open to public scrutiny: see art 6 of the European Convention.

[73] For example: *Hogan and Oxford City Council v IC*, IT, 17 October 2006 (in which it was successfully argued that the disclosure of the vehicle information numbers (VINs) for vehicles kept by the Council would be likely to increase the risk of 'vehicle cloning'); *Hemsley v IC and Chief Constable of Northamptonshire*, IT, 10 April 2006 (in which it was successfully argued that disclosing details of all speeding offences recorded by a particular speed camera may encourage drivers to speculate as to when the camera was active and to speed when they thought it was not); *England and LB of Bexley v IC*, IT, 10 May 2007 (in which it was successfully argued that the addresses of vacant residential properties fell within s 31(1)(a)).

[74] See *King v IC and DWP*, IT, 20 March 2008, which concerned a risk assessment carried out for the Department of Work and Pensions when setting up a new system for claiming benefits by telephone.

may be in the public domain or be otherwise accessible, its disclosure will or may result in the relevant prejudice.[75] There is an analogous exception in the Environmental Information Regulations 2004 at regulation 12(5)(b), which covers 'information to the extent that its disclosure would adversely affect ... the ability of a public authority to conduct an inquiry of a criminal ... nature.' It is probably more limited than the FOIA exemption which includes information which is likely to prejudice '... the prevention ... of crime' as well as its investigation.

20– 015 The public interest

If the information in question comes within the section, the duty to disclose the information does not apply if the public interest in maintaining the exemption outweighs the public interest in disclosing the information. The general principles relating to the public interest weighing exercise are as for other exemptions:[76] the nature, degree and likelihood of the prejudice (to the prevention or detection of crime or the apprehension or prosecution of offenders) will need to be balanced against and to outweigh the public interest in disclosure of the interest in question.[77] As a general rule, the less significant the prejudice to the protected interest is shown to be, the greater the chance that the public interest balancing exercise will tilt in favour of disclosure.[78] The balancing exercise will be different according to which limb of the exemption is relied upon. The public interest in maintaining the exemption will be stronger where disclosure would prejudice the prevention or detection of crime than where it is merely likely to have that effect.[79]

20– 016 The duty to confirm or deny

Where the requested information is, or if it were held would be, exempt information under s 31(1)(a) or (b), then the discrete duty to confirm or deny that that information is held by the public authority does not arise. The exclusion of this duty is a qualified one, and the principles relating to the public interest weighing exercise are likely to be similar to those in relation to s 30(1).[80]

20– 017 Scottish provisions

The Freedom of Information (Scotland) Act 2002 contains provisions that are identical to those

---

[75] The so-called 'mosaic' or 'jigsaw' principle. See §§15– 024 to 15– 025. This was effectively adopted by the IT in *Hemsley v IC and Chief Constable of Northamptonshire*, IT, 10 April 2006 at [23].

[76] See §§15– 010 to 15– 017.

[77] If disclosure would reveal a miscarriage of justice, then this will almost certainly trump the harm that might be caused to enforcement of the criminal law. That there is a particular public interest in the disclosure of information relating to the miscarriage of justice is reflected in Pt IVA of the Employment Rights Act 1996, as inserted by the Public Interest Disclosure Act 1998, which sanctions as being in the public interest a disclosure by an employee tending to show 'that a miscarriage of justice has occurred, is occurring or is likely to occur' – s 43B(1)(c). Promoting public confidence in the security of a system and enabling the public to encourage public authorities to make them more robust are factors which can increase the weight of the public interest in disclosure: see *England and LB of Bexley v IC*, IT, 10 May 2007 at [62].

[78] *Hogan and Oxford City Council v IC*, IT, 17 October 2006 at [54]; *England and LB of Bexley v IC*, IT, 10 May 2007 at [29].

[79] *Hogan and Oxford City Council v IC*, IT, 17 October 2006 at [54]; *England and LB of Bexley v IC*, IT, 10 May 2007 at [78].

[80] See §20– 007.

in the Freedom of Information Act 2000, save that the relevant prejudice must be 'substantial'.[81]

018 Environmental Information Regulations

Regulation 12(5)(b) of the Environmental Information Regulations 2004 states that (subject to the public interest test in reg 12(1)(b)) a public authority may refuse to disclose environmental information to the extent that its disclosure 'would adversely affect...the course of justice...or the ability of a public authority to conduct an inquiry of a criminal...nature'.[82] These provisions are considered in more detail above[83] but are analogous to those in the Freedom of Information Acts considered in this section. One obvious difference is that the Environmental Information Regulations require that disclosure 'would' cause the relevant adverse effect while the analogous provisions in the Freedom of Information Acts include cases where there is only a likelihood of prejudice.[84]

019 Data Protection Act 1998

Section 29(1) of the Data Protection Act 1998 also provides an analogous exemption in relation to a request for personal data. Under that section, personal data processed (which includes information 'held') for the purposes of the prevention or detection of crime or the apprehension or prosecution of offenders is exempt from the subject access rights in any case where disclosure would be likely to prejudice those purposes. Section 29(2) of the Act also provides an exemption for information being processed for the purpose of discharging statutory functions which has been obtained for that purpose from a person who had it in his possession for the purpose of preventing or detecting crime or apprehending or prosecuting offenders, provided that disclosure would be likely to prejudice the latter purposes.

5. OTHER LAW ENFORCEMENT

020 Introduction

All three Acts exempt information from disclosure if its disclosure is likely to prejudice[85] any of a large number of other law enforcement activities not directly concerned with crime in the narrow sense and the two Freedom of Information Acts also expressly exempt information whose disclosure is likely to prejudice 'the administration of justice' in general. All three Acts are cast in slightly different terms, but their scope is broadly the same. The most obvious difference of substance, apart from the different structure and terminology used in the Data Protection Act 1998, is that the Freedom of Information (Scotland) Act 2002 requires substantial prejudice to be shown, as opposed to prejudice *simpliciter*.[86] The Environmental

---

[81] FOI(S)A s 35(1)(a) and (b).

[82] The equivalent Scottish public authority provisions are EI(S)R reg 10(1)(b) and 10(5)(b).

[83] §§6– 044 to 6– 044.

[84] See §20– 014.

[85] For the meaning of 'prejudice' and the degree of likelihood required, see §§15– 020 to 15– 028 and 20– 014.

[86] As to the practical difference that the adjective 'substantial' makes, see §15– 021.

Information Regulations 2004 similarly expressly allow public authorities to refuse to disclose environmental information to the extent that (subject to the public interest test) its disclosure would 'adversely affect the course of justice [or] the ability of a person to receive a fair trial' or the ability of a public authority to conduct an inquiry of a criminal or disciplinary nature.[87]

20–021 Administration of justice

There is no definition of 'administration of justice' in the Freedom of Information Acts but presumably the phrase must be given a wide interpretation and the public interest in the administration of justice will be accorded considerable weight.[88] Justice must include not only justice as administered in the traditional courts but also justice administered in tribunals and by lay magistrates and even by arbitrators. It would also include non-contentious matters like inquiries and the business of coroners' courts. Prejudice in this context would include prejudice to a particular case and to the system of justice as a whole. Thus, a disclosure which might prejudice a fair trial or prevent a judge or jury doing their job properly in a particular criminal case or which might discourage witnesses from coming forward to give evidence or from giving their evidence openly or frankly[89] would come within the exemption as would a disclosure which might undermine the ability of litigants to bring their cases to court generally or undermine the legal aid system or the judicial appointments system or the authority of individual judges.[90] There is considerable potential overlap between this exemption and others within ss 30 or 31 of the Freedom of Information Act 2000 and those provided by s 32 (court records), s 42 (legal professional privilege) and s 44 (contempt of court).

20–022 Tax and similar impositions

The two Freedom of Information Acts exempt information if its disclosure will or is likely to prejudice 'the assessment or collection of any tax or duty or of any imposition of a similar nature'.[91] This would cover not only information which might prejudice a particular investigation of a taxpayer's affairs but also internal HM Revenue & Customs information which showed, say, minimum financial limits below which they do not, as a matter of policy, investigate a self-assessment or details of plans to close tax 'loopholes'. The Data Protection Act 1998 contains more elaborate provisions relating to tax assessment and collection. Under it, personal data processed for the purposes of tax assessment or collection are exempt if disclosure would be likely to prejudice such assessment or collection.[92] And personal data held by government departments, local authorities and authorities administering council tax and housing benefit are exempt from the subject access rights to the extent that the exemption is

---

[87] See further §§6–044 to 6–044. The relevant provisions are EIR reg 12(1)(b) and 12(5)(b) and, in relation to Scottish public authorities, EI(S)R reg 10(1)(b) and 10(5)(b).

[88] That was the view of the Department of Constitutional Affairs anyway: see DCA, *Exemptions Guidance – Section 31*, undated, §3.1 (currently undergoing revision).

[89] See in relation to witnesses generally *British Broadcasting Corporation, Petitioners (No 1)* 2000 SLT 845 at [25]–[27] and *R v Police Complaints Authority, ex p Green* [2004] UKHL 6, [2004] 1 WLR 725, [2004] 2 All ER 209, [2004] HRLR 19, [2004] UKHRR 939 at [71]–[73]. The trial itself will of course generally be held in the open: see art 6 of the European Convention.

[90] See *Guardian News & Media Ltd v IC and MoJ*, IT, 10 June 2009 at [104]-[107].

[91] See FOIA s 31(1)(d); FOI(S)A s 35(1)(d).

[92] DPA s 29(1)(c); see also DPA s 29(2) referred to in §20–019.

necessary for the operation of a system of risk assessment for the purpose of collecting and assessing tax or similar impositions or of preventing, detecting or prosecuting offenders for making unlawful claims to, or applications of, public funds.[93]

023 Immigration

The two Freedom of Information Acts exempt information if its disclosure will or is likely to prejudice the operation of immigration controls.[94] This might cover, for example, instructions to immigration officers as to how to conduct inquiries of those seeking entry to the country or information as to proposed changes to visa regimes (which usually take place with little or no notice).

024 Prisons

The two Freedom of Information Acts exempt information if its disclosure will or is likely to prejudice the maintenance of security and good order in prisons and other lawful detention centres.[95] This would cover, for example, plans of the layout of prisons.

025 The public interest

If the information in question comes within the section, the duty to disclose it does not apply if the public interest in maintaining the exemption outweighs the public interest in disclosing the information.[96] The principles relating to the public interest weighing exercise are the same as those in relation to s 31(1)(a) and (b).[97] The particular public interest in maintaining these various exemptions and the countervailing public interest in disclosure which must be outweighed will be largely self-evident.[98]

026 The duty to confirm or deny

Where the requested information is, or if it were held would be, exempt information under s 31(1), then the discrete duty to confirm or deny that that information is held by the public authority does not arise. The exclusion of this duty is a qualified one, and the principles relating to the public interest weighing exercise are likely to be similar to those in relation to s 30(1).[99]

---

[93] DPA ss 29(4) and (5).

[94] FOIA s 31(1)(e); FOI(S)A s 35(1)(e).

[95] FOIA s 31(1)(f); FOI(S)A s 35(1)(f). The exemption would cover young offender institutions, secure hospitals, secure training centres, local authority secure accommodation and immigration detention and removal centres.

[96] FOIA ss 31(1) and 2(2)(b).

[97] See §20– 015.

[98] See, eg, in relation to prisons, the examples set out in MoJ, *Exemptions Guidance – Section 31*, undated, §6.2 (currently undergoing revision). See also *In re L (sexual abuse: disclosure)* [1999] 1 WLR 299 for an example of a balancing exercise carried out by a court analogous to the balancing exercise required in relation to the exemption based on likely prejudice to the 'administration of justice': the administration of justice in proceedings concerning the care of children requires non-disclosure of information arising in the proceedings in order to engender maximum frankness against which had to be weighed the public interest in the disclosure of child abuse in order to bring offenders to justice and protect other children.

[99] See §20– 007.

6. OTHER INVESTIGATORY AND REGULATORY FUNCTIONS

20– 027 **Regulatory functions**

All three Acts exempt the disclosure of information if that is likely to prejudice the discharge of a wide range of investigatory and regulatory functions of public authorities.[100] The relevant functions are defined in the Data Protection Act 1998 as meaning functions conferred on any person by or under an enactment, any function of the Crown or a Minister or government department and any other function of a public nature exercised in the public interest.[101] The exemption in each of the Acts applies to the exercise of the relevant functions for specified purposes. These purposes include:

— ascertaining whether any person has failed to comply with the law;[102]

— ascertaining whether any person is responsible for improper conduct;[103]

— ascertaining whether circumstances exist which would justify regulatory action under an enactment;[104]

— ascertaining a person's fitness or competence in relation to management of companies or in any professional activity;[105]

— ascertaining the cause of an accident;[106]

— protecting charities against misconduct and mismanagement and the loss of their property and recovering property which has been lost;[107] and

---

[100] DPA s 31(1)–(3); FOIA s 31(1)(g) and (2); FOI(S)A s 35(1)(g) and (2).

[101] DPA s 31(3).

[102] FOIA s 31(1)(g) and (2)(a); FOI(S)A s 35(1)(g) and (2)(a).

[103] FOIA s 31(1)(g) and (2)(b); FOI(S)A s 35(1)(g) and (2)(b). See also DPA s 31(1) and (2)(a)(i)–(iii): the DPA refers to functions designed to protect the public against financial loss caused by improper conduct of those carrying on financial services or managing companies or those who are bankrupts or improper conduct of persons authorised to carry on professions or other activities, but it is thought that the same type of information is likely to be exempted under these differently worded provisions. For an example, see HMRC v IC, IT, 10 March 2009 at [55].

[104] FOIA ss 31(1)(g) and 31(2)(c); FOI(S)A s 35(2)(c). In *Reith v IC and LB Hammersmith & Fulham*, IT, 1 June 2007, the Tribunal rejected an argument that disclosure of the local authority's policy on the towing away of vehicles under parking regulations would result in an increase in illegal parking. However, the paucity of the evidence should be noted: 'The Tribunal has not seen any evidence to suggest that this risk [ie a claimed significant risk that the overall deterrent effect in relation to illegal parking would be lost] has been demonstrated or is even likely. [The local authority] rely upon their parking enforcement expertise, however their evidence is not independent, and being unsupported amounts to bare assertion. Such examples as given by [the local authority] do not demonstrate anything more than an unsupported fear that disclosure might increase illegal parking' (at [32]). The Information Tribunal has decided that the enforcement of the penalty charge regime in connection with the congestion charge by Transport for London is clearly within s. 31(2)(c): see *Bangar v IC and Transport for London*, IT, 23 November 2009 at [7].

[105] FOIA s 31(2)(d); FOI(S)A s 35(2)(d). This would cover investigations by DfES into fitness of teachers under sections 141 and 142 of the Education Act 2002 and by DBIS in relation to orders under the Company Directors Disqualification Act 1986.

[106] FOIA s 31(2)(e); FOI(S)A s 35(2)(e). This would cover investigations by the Health and Safety Commission into accidents at work, the Air Accident Branch of the Department for Transport in relation to air accidents and the police in relation to road traffic accidents.

[107] FOIA s 31(2)(f)–(h); FOI(S)A s 35(2)(f)–(h); DPA s 31(2)(b)–(d).

— securing the health safety and welfare of people at work[108] and protecting the public against risks to their health and safety from people at work.[109]

028 Information covered by regulatory functions exemption

It is clear that this group of exemptions will cover information whose disclosure might prejudice inquiries into the causes of all kinds of matters which come within the purview of particular public authorities (eg local authorities, the Civil Aviation Authority, the Health and Safety Executive, the Official Receiver and NHS Trusts[110]). What is not so clear is whether, and if so the extent to which, the prejudice need not relate to the specific inquiry for which the information has been obtained. The Canadian case *Rubin v Canada (Minister of Transport)*[111] neatly illustrates the issue. The applicant sought from Transport Canada a post-accident safety review report undertaken as a result of a Nationair aircraft crash in Jeddah, Saudi Arabia on 11 July 1991, in which 249 Nigerian passengers and 14 Canadian crew members were killed. It had been the worst airline disaster in Canadian history. Transport Canada refused the request. The trial judge ordered that Transport Canada should disclose only those parts of the report which could have been obtained through regulatory means or otherwise, without relying on confidential sources, but refused access to the remainder. He found a reasonable expectation of probable harm to the conduct of *future* accident safety reviews were the report to be disclosed, and that the public interest in maintaining confidential reviews outweighed the public right to access contemplated in the Canadian Act. Mr Rubin appealed and the Court of Appeal allowed his appeal, rejecting the trial judge's reasoning:

> to allow his judgment to stand, would protect from public review most non-regulatory investigations "past, present and future" on the nebulous ground that to disclose this information might have a chilling effect on future investigations. Given that the purpose of the Act is to broaden the public's access to government information, this cannot have been Parliament's intent.

The Court of Appeal was also influenced by the fact that such a broad interpretation of the exemption would render other exemptions in the Act practically superfluous. The Court of Appeal concluded that the exemption only referred to a specific, ongoing investigation or one that was about to be undertaken: it did not apply to the general investigative process. This line does not appear to have been followed in full by the Tribunal, which has accepted that possible apprehension by witnesses in future investigations of a similar type to the one in question may be relevant prejudice when the contents of an investigatory report are sought[112] and found similar prejudice where 'raw statements' themselves were sought.[113] The Tribunal has also found that disclosure of material about a particular matter which was likely to affect the voluntary flow of information in future to a financial regulator could in principle amount to

---

[108] FOIA s 31(2)(i); FOI(S)A s 35(2)(i); DPA s 31(2)(e).

[109] FOIA s 31(2)(j); FOI(S)A s 35(2)(j); DPA s 31(2)(f).

[110] See *Galloway v IC and NHS*, IT, 20 March 2009, where the Tribunal found that an inquiry into a 'serious untoward incident' came within s 31(2)(b), (e) and (j).

[111] [1998] 2 FC 430, (1997) 154 DLR (4th) 414, Court of Appeal. The analogous provision is the Access to Information Act s 16(1)(c).

[112] See *HMRC v IC*, IT, 10 March 2009 at [55]-[60]

[113] See case *Galloway v IC and NHS*, IT, 20 March 2009 at [57]-[68]

prejudice to its investigatory function, although in that case the Tribunal was not persuaded on the facts that such was the likely effect given the incentives on financial institutions to make voluntary disclosure.[114]

20– 029   The public interest

If the information in question comes within the section, the duty to disclose the information does not apply if the public interest in maintaining the exemption outweighs the public interest in disclosing the information.[115]   The broad principles relating to the public interest weighing exercise have been considered above.[116]   However, the nature of the investigations and regulatory activities with which the exemptions at hand are concerned will often be of wider public concern than the run-of-the-mill prosecution: accidents, particularly those involving trains or aircraft, invariably provoke public concern; so, too, maladministration that has been the subject of an official investigation of any sort.   This particular public interest must be reflected in the balancing exercises that must be carried out under s 2 of the Freedom of Information Act 2000.   The particular public interest was recognised by the Canadian Court of Appeal in *Rubin v Canada (Minister of Transport):*[117]

> Having stated the important role that post-accident safety reviews play in the overall safety of the aeronautics industry, I think it is also important not to underestimate the public's interest in disclosure and the positive impact disclosure may have on the regulation of the aeronautics industry.   It should not be forgotten that in passing this Act, Parliament has specified the important role public scrutiny of government information plays in a democratic system.   Indeed, as Justice La Forest recently affirmed in *Dagg,*[118] "The overarching purpose of access to information legislation... is to facilitate democracy.   It does so in two related ways.   It helps to ensure first, that citizens have the information required to participate meaningfully in the democratic process, and secondly, that politicians and bureaucrats remain accountable to the citizenry".

In a case where there has been an adequate report the public interest in disclosure of individual 'raw' witness statements may well be outweighed by the public interest in avoiding prejudice to future investigations, but the position may be different where an inadequate report has been prepared.[119]

20– 030   The duty to confirm or deny

Where the requested information is, or if it were held would be, exempt information under s 31(1), then the discrete duty to confirm or deny that that information is held by the public authority does not arise.   The exclusion of this duty is a qualified one, and the principles

---

[114]   See: *Craven v IC*, IT, 13 May 2008 at [18]-[25]; *Bangar v IC and Transport for London*, IT, 23 November 2009 at [9]-[12], where the relevant risk of prejudice was not established on the evidence.

[115]   FOIA ss 30(1) and 2(2)(b). It is important to bear in mind that the mere finding of a relevant risk of prejudice is not the end of the matter; the public interest in avoiding that prejudice must outweigh the public interest in disclosure: see *Bangar v IC and Transport for London*, IT, 23 November 2009 at [13].

[116]   See §20– 006.

[117]   [1998] 2 FC 430, (1997) 154 DLR (4th) 414 (CA).   The analogous provision is the Access to Information Act s 16(1)(c).

[118]   *Dagg v Canada (Minister of Finance)* [1997] 2 SCR 403 at 432–433.

[119]   *Galloway v IC and NHS*, IT, 20 March 2009 at [76].

relating to the public interest weighing exercise are the same as those in relation to s 30(2).[120]

031 Environmental Information Regulations
The two sets of Environmental Information Regulations provide that, subject to the public interest test, a public authority may refuse to disclose environmental information if its disclosure would adversely affect '...the ability of a public authority to conduct an inquiry of a...disciplinary nature'.[121] Again the public authority holding the information does not have to be the same as the public authority conducting the inquiry.

032 Data Protection Act 1998
Given that the Data Protection Act 1998 is concerned with 'personal data', the significance of this head of exemption is less immediate than it is under the Freedom of Information Act 2000. Nevertheless, the Data Protection Act 1998 provides a broadly analogous ground of exemption for information the disclosure of which would prejudice regulatory bodies.[122] Specific exemption is provided for personal data processed for the purpose of discharging any function conferred on various commissioners and ombudsmen, as well as the Director General of Fair Trading, provided that those functions are designed to protect members of the public against maladministration, failures and other forms of sub-standard conduct.[123]

7. CIVIL PROCEEDINGS

033 Investigations
There are specific provisions in the two Freedom of Information Acts relating to information obtained by public authorities for the purposes of civil proceedings arising out of investigations of various sorts, although the details of the provisions in the two Acts differ. Section 30(2)(a)(iv) of the Freedom of Information Act 2000 exempts information obtained for the purposes of civil proceedings brought by or on behalf of the authority arising out of investigations conducted by it for any of the purposes set out in s 31(2),[124] provided the information relates to the obtaining of information from confidential sources.[125] Section 34(4) of the Freedom of Information (Scotland) Act 2002 exempts information held by a Scottish public authority if it was obtained for the purposes of civil proceedings arising out of such investigations or out of criminal investigations, but there is no requirement about confidential sources. In neither case is it necessary for there to be any prejudice shown.

034 Prejudice to administration of justice
Both Freedom of Information Acts specifically exempt information held by a public authority

---

[120] See §20– 012.

[121] EIR reg 12(1)(b) and 12(5)(b) and EI(S)R reg 10(1)(b) and 10(5)(b). See further §§6– 044 to 6– 044.

[122] DPA s 31(1)–(2).

[123] DPA s 31(4)–(5).

[124] See §20– 027.

[125] FOIA s 30(2)(b).

the disclosure of which would or would be likely to prejudice 'the administration of justice':[126] this provision might include information held by the public authority in connection with civil proceedings being brought by or against it, although in general the paramount requirement for open justice would mean that no relevant prejudice would apply or the public interest in disclosure would prevail. Both Freedom of Information Acts also exempt information if its disclosure would or would be likely to prejudice any civil proceedings brought by any public authority and arising out of an investigation conducted for any of the purposes set out in s 31(2) of the Freedom of Information Act 2000[127] by virtue of the royal prerogative or under statutory powers.[128] Although the Environmental Information Regulations provide that a public authority may refuse to disclose environmental information to the extent that its disclosure 'would adversely affect...the course of justice'[129] that provision is likely to be interpreted as referring only to criminal justice.[130]

20– 035 Information in court documents

Section 32(1) of the Freedom of Information Act 2000[131] provides that information is exempt information under the Act if it is held by a public authority only by virtue of being contained in: (a) a document filed or lodged with a court for the purposes of particular proceedings; (b) a document served on or by a public authority for the purposes of particular proceedings; or (c) a document created by a court or its administrative staff for the purposes of particular proceedings.[132] The exemption is absolute.[133] The word 'court' is defined to include any tribunal or body exercising judicial power of the State.[134] As noted at the outset of this chapter, neither the courts nor the court service is 'public authority' for the purposes of the Act.[135] The

---

[126] FOIA s 31(1)(c); FOI(S)A s 35(1)(c). As to the phrase 'likely to prejudice', see §20– 014.

[127] Or the FOI(S)A s 35(2).

[128] See: FOIA s 31(1)(h); FOI(S)A s 35(1)(h). The FOIA s 31(1)(i) contains a similar exemption if disclosure may prejudice an inquiry held under the Fatal Accidents and Sudden Deaths Inquiries (Scotland) Act 1976.

[129] EIR reg 12(5)(b) and EI(S)R reg 10(5)(b).

[130] See §§6– 044 to 6– 044..

[131] FOI(S)A s 37(1)(a) provides a like exemption in relation to information held by Scottish public authorities. There is no equivalent under the environmental information regime. Similarly, there is no equivalent under the DPA.

[132] The words 'any document created by...a court' in s..32(1)(c)(i) were interpreted by the Tribunal as referring to documents created by a 'judge' as opposed to documents created by the court in the sense of an institution and therefore to include documents like draft directions and judgments produced by a judge personally but not to include a copy of a transcript of proceedings in a criminal trial in *Mitchell v IC*, IT, 10 October 2005 but the Tribunal has subsequently acknowledged that this decision was wrong: *MOJ v IC*, IT, 29 July 2008 at [32].

[133] FOIA s 2(3); FOI(S)A s 2(2).

[134] FOIA s 32(4)(a); FOI(S)A s 37(2). This would include, eg employment tribunals (see *DBERR v IC and Peninsula Business Services*, IT, 28 April 2009), the Employment Appeal Tribunal, mental health tribunals, Special Educational Needs Tribunals etc. It probably also encompasses the European Court of Justice and the European Court of Human Rights, which, though they do not exercise the judicial power of any state, are undoubtedly courts.

[135] *Mitchell v IC*, IT, 10 October 2005 at [31]. It is suggested that there is a respectable argument that the Court Service falls within the definition of 'government department' in FOIA s 84 (by virtue of being bodies that exercise statutory functions on behalf of the Crown – see, eg, Courts Act 1971 s 27, and Supreme Court Act 1981 s 1) and that, by virtue of Sch 1, Pt I, it is thereby a 'public authority'. Certainly, the Northern Ireland Court Service is a public authority: FOIA s 84, definition of 'government department'. The position in relation to tribunals may be the same, given that their existence and functions are entirely statute-based.

word 'document' has been held to include other recording media, such as a tape-recording.[136] The principal object of s 32(1) is to exempt information received or generated by a court in connection with proceedings in that court, but held by a public authority. Most commonly this will arise where the public authority is or has been a party to court proceedings. The exemption will also cover information contained in documents generated or received by a public authority in the course of legal proceedings. The thinking behind the exemption is that the disclosure of information contained in court documents (which may include confidential information and which may have special restrictions upon its re-use) should be regulated by the procedure applying in the court or tribunal in question, rather than by the general freedom of information regime.[137] The exemption will cover information contained in statements of case, application notices, witness statements, affidavits, skeleton arguments, and lists of documents and disclosed documents served in the course of proceedings,[138] provided always that the information is held by the public authority only by virtue of being contained in such a document.[139] It will also include a transcript of proceedings held by a public authority for other reasons.[140] Where information contained in one of the sorts of document described in (a)–(c) is also held by a public authority for other reasons, that information will not be exempt information by virtue of s 32(1): but the fact that information which is within s 32(1) is used or processed by a public authority in other ways does not prevent the exemption applying.[141] The exemption may also apply in the context of criminal proceedings.[142]

036 Information in inquiry and arbitration documents
Section 32(2) of the Freedom of Information Act 2000[143] provides that information is exempt information under the Act if it is held by a public authority only by virtue of being contained

---

[136] *Mitchell v IC*, IT, 10 October 2005 at [21]: 'we are in no doubt that the tapes are themselves a 'document' for the purpose of s 32(1), as the Respondent contends, since that term is broadly construed in an age offering so many recording media'. If it were otherwise then s 32(1) would not cover information recorded on the hard disk of a court service computer, even though strictly speaking a document is only created when the information is printed. This was followed in *Kennedy v IC and Charity Commission*, IT, 14 June 2009 at [58] and upheld in the High Court in *Kennedy v IC and Charity Commission*[2010] EWHC 475 (Admin) at [78]-[79]. On this basis, there would appear to be no distinction between the term 'information' as used in FOIA and the term 'document' as used in s 32.

[137] Thus, eg, in civil litigation in the High Court and county courts, CPR 5.4C now governs access by non-parties to documents coming into existence in the course of proceedings. In summary (a) there is a right to inspect served claim forms and judgments of the court; (b) other documents lodged with the court may be inspected with permission; (c) witness statements which have formed evidence in chief are open to inspection unless the court otherwise directs and in the circumstances set out in CPR 32.13(3); (d) access by third parties to transcripts of recordings of hearings before the High Court and county courts is governed by CPR PD39 paras 6.3 to 6.4. In criminal proceedings the dissemination of transcripts is governed by Crim PR 2010 rule 65.9. This is the explanation given by the Information Tribunal in *Mitchell v IC*, IT, 10 October 2005 at [33]–[34]. It mirrors the thinking of the Advocate-General as to what the position should be under European law (see Case C-515-07 *Sweden v Associated Press International* (Opinion of Advocate General Maduro, 1 October 2009).

[138] *Mitchell v IC*, IT, 10 October 2005 at [33].

[139] As to the effect of the provision, see §20– 036.

[140] *MOJ v IC*, IT, 29 July 2008.

[141] *DBERR v IC and Peninsula Business Services*, IT, 28 April 2009 at [52]-[53].

[142] 'Cause or matter' is not defined in the FOIA but the Supreme Court Act 1981 s 151(1) defines cause to mean 'any action or any criminal proceedings'.

[143] FOI(S)A s 37(1)(b) provides a like exemption in relation to information held by Scottish public authorities. There is no equivalent under the environmental information regime. There is no equivalent under the DPA.

in: (a) a document placed in the custody of a person conducting an inquiry or arbitration, for the purposes of the inquiry or arbitration; and (b) any document created by a person conducting an inquiry or arbitration, for the purposes of the inquiry or arbitration.[144] It is irrelevant that the inquiry or arbitration is complete, provided that the information is still held only by virtue of being contained in the relevant documents.[145] It can even extend to documents first acquired by a public authority before the initiation of an inquiry if the public authority subsequently passes those documents to the inquiry.[146] 'Inquiry' in the subsection means an inquiry held under a statutory provision and an arbitration means an arbitration to which the Arbitration Act 1996 applies.[147] Inquiries within the subsection include an inquiry by the Charity Commission instituted under section 8 of the Charities Act 1993[148] and an inquiry by the Comptroller of Patents under the Register of Patent Agent Rules into alleged misconduct by a patent agent.[149] Other examples would be the Bloody Sunday Inquiry under the Tribunals of Inquiry (Evidence) Act 1921, the Marchioness Inquiry under section 268 of the Merchant Shipping Act 1995 and a planning inquiry, but not Lord Butler's review of the intelligence on weapons of mass destruction or Lord Phillips' inquiry into BSE. Information held by a Scottish public authority for the purposes of an inquiry under the Fatal Accidents and Sudden Deaths Inquiry (Scotland) Act 1976 is not covered by this exemption.[150] The exemption is absolute.[151] Save that it applies to inquiries and arbitrations, rather than court proceedings, the exemption is similar to that provided by s 32(1).

20– 037 The duty to confirm or deny

Where the requested information is, or if it were held would be, exempt information under s 32(1) or (2), then the discrete duty to confirm or deny that that information is held by the public authority does not arise.[152] The exclusion of this duty is an absolute one.[153]

---

[144] For these purposes an inquiry means an inquiry held under a provision contained in an enactment (not eg the inquiry into inequalities in health requested by the Minister but not set up under a statute) and an arbitration means an arbitration under Pt I of the Arbitration Act 1996 (not, eg, under a consumer arbitration agreement under Pt II of that Act).

[145] *Kennedy v IC and Charity Commission*, IT, 14 June 2009 at [86]-[87], endorsed by the High Court in *Kennedy v IC and Charity Commission* [2010] EWHC 475.

[146] *Kennedy v IC and Charity Commission*, IT, 14 June 2009 at [86]-[87], endorsed by the High Court in *Kennedy v IC and Charity Commission* [2010] EWHC 475 (despite those documents having been held, presumably for a purpose, prior to the inquiry).

[147] FOIA s 32(4). Inquiries can be constituted: (1) under the Inquiries Act 2005; (2) under specific enactments (examples of which are given in the main text); or (3) by prerogative power of the Crown. Inquiries constituted under the Inquiries Act 2005 are provided with a complete procedural code. That code disapplies FOIA s 32(2) for those inquiries: see Inquiries Act 2005 ss 18(3) and 41. Where an inquiry is constituted under the Inquiries Act 2005, documents held by a public authority in connection or arising from that inquiry may nevertheless be exempt information under one or more other provisions in Pt II of FOIA.

[148] *Kennedy v IC and Charity Commission*, IT, 14 June 2009 endorsed by the High Court in *Kennedy v IC and Charity Commission* [2010] EWHC 475.

[149] *Szucs v IC and UK Intellectual Property Office*, IT, 26 February 2008.

[150] FOI(S)A s 37(3).

[151] FOIA s 2(3); FOI(S)A s 2(2).

[152] FOIA s 32(3).

[153] FOIA s 2(3).

8.   AUDIT

038   The exemption

There are provisions in both Freedom of Information Acts exempting information held by public authorities which have functions[154] in relation to auditing the accounts of other public authorities or examining the economy, efficiency and effectiveness with which they use their resources if its disclosure would or would be likely to prejudice (or, in the case of Scottish public authorities, prejudice substantially) the exercise of such audit functions.[155] The likelihood of harm to the protected interest and the level of harm are the same as are required for the other harm-based exemptions in the Act.[156]

039   The bodies covered

The exemption only applies to information held by public authorities which have the relevant audit functions: this will most obviously cover information held by the National Audit Office or the Audit Commission for Local Authorities and the National Health Service in England and Wales,[157] but is likely also to cover the Commission for Healthcare Audit and Inspection, HM Inspectorate of Court Administration, HM Inspectorate of Constabulary, HM Inspectorate of Prisons, Ofsted, the Office of Government Commerce[158] and Commission for Social Care Inspection. It does not relate to internal audits by public authorities. The Ministry of Justice has also expressed the view that it would include *ad hoc* non-statutory audit functions, a view which the Information Commissioner appears not to share.[159] Although private firms of accountants employed by public audit bodies are not themselves subject to the Freedom of Information Acts, the information generated by them in the course of carrying out work for a public authority may be information 'held' by the public authority even if it is in the physical possession of the private firm.[160]

---

[154] The word 'function' in such a context is usually a reference to a specific statutory function.

[155] FOIA s 33; FOI(S)A s 40. There are similar exemptions in three of the comparative regimes. The Freedom of Information Act 1982 (Cth of Australia) s 47E, provides an exemption where the disclosure of the requested document would, or could be reasonably be expected to, prejudice the effectiveness of audits or tests or to have a substantial adverse effect upon the running of an agency: see §2– 015(14). The Access to Information Act (Canada) s 22, provides a discretionary exemption for records the disclosure of which could reasonably be expected to prejudice the use of audits or tests: see §2– 032(18). The Freedom of Information Act 1997 (Ireland) s 46(1), treats records relating to audits as 'exempt records', thereby taking them outside the scope of the Act: see §2– 035.

[156] See §§15– 021 to 15– 022. In *Office of Government Commerce v IC*, IT, 2 May 2007 the IT specifically rejected an argument that a lesser likelihood of harm or a lesser degree of harm would suffice for the purposes of the exemption.

[157] Known as 'the Audit Commission.' See further below at §20– 044.

[158] This would appear to have been accepted by the Information Tribunal in *Office of Government Commerce v IC*, IT, 2 May 2007.

[159] See MoJ, *Exemptions Guidance section 33*, (14 May 2008) p 2; cf Information Commissioner's *Guidance* (May 2004) at p 2.

[160] See *Chantrey Martin v Martin* [1953] 2 QB 286 at 293; *Gibbon v Pease* [1905] 1 KB 810; *Leicestershire County Council v Michael Faraday & Partners* [1941] 2 All ER 483; *Formica Ltd v ECGD* [1995] 1 Lloyd's Rep 692 at 703.

20– 040 The information covered

The audit function of such bodies may be prejudiced by the disclosure of information in various ways. For example: relations with bodies being audited may be undermined by the disclosure of information supplied by them to auditors on a voluntary basis because such bodies may be less willing thereafter to supply information on that basis; audit methods may be disclosed in a way that undermines the effectiveness of the audit, either by revealing individual files to be audited beforehand or by disclosing methods to be used in future by auditors; or the disclosure of preliminary audit reports for discussion may create a misleading and unfair impression which is not borne out in the final report. The kind of information likely to be covered by the exemption would therefore comprise draft reports, audit methodology statements and correspondence between auditors and the bodies subject to audit. The applicability of the exemption is likely to be time-sensitive, with the risk of harm diminishing within even a fairly short span of time.[161] If information comes within the definition of 'environmental information' under the Environmental Information Regulations 2004 or Environmental Information (Scotland) Regulations 2004 those regulations will govern the matter and since there is no equivalent to the public audit exemption under the regulations such information will be subject to disclosure under the regulations unless some other exemption applies.

20– 041 The public interest

If the information in question comes within the section, the duty to disclose the information does not apply if the public interest in maintaining the exemption outweighs the public interest in disclosing the information.[162] The principles relating to the public interest weighing exercise are the same as those in relation to s 31.[163] Given that the exemption is prejudice based, the particular public interest in maintaining these exemptions may be self-evident, but should be identified and analysed carefully before the weighing exercise is carried out.[164] It is unlikely that the public interest in maintaining the exemption would outweigh the public interest in disclosure in the case of standard audit methodologies or information already in the public domain and, once an audit is complete, it is obviously less likely that the public interest in maintaining the exemption would outweigh the public interest in disclosure. A public authority with audit functions may be well advised to consult an audited body from which information had come before making disclosure in order to have a full appreciation of the public interest issues.

20– 042 The duty to confirm or deny

The discrete duty to confirm or deny the existence of information provided by s 1(1)(a) of the Freedom of Information Act 2000 does not apply if and to the extent that compliance would

---

[161] While the Tribunal in *Office of Government Commerce v IC*, IT, 2 May 2007 found that the 'gateway review' reports did fall within the exemption (ie the likely risk of prejudice was established) (at [52]), the age of the reports was also relevant to its consideration of the public interest in maintaining the exemption (at [85]). The decision was successfully appealed, although this point was not over-ruled: see *OGC v IC* [2008] EWHC 774 (Admin), [2008] ACD 54 at [84]-[91].

[162] FOIA ss 33(2) and 2(2)(b).

[163] See §20– 015.

[164] Case *OGC v IC* [2008] EWHC 774 (Admin), [2008] ACD 54 at [84]-[91].

or would be likely to prejudice the exercise by a public authority of its audit functions.[165] It is thought unlikely that there will often be such prejudice by the mere confirmation that such a public authority holds information but there may be cases where this would be so, for example if the authority was asked to confirm that information had been provided by a 'whistle-blower'.

043 Data Protection Act 1998
Analogous grounds of exemption are provided by s 35(2) of the Data Protection Act 1998.

044 The Audit Commission
There is special provision in the Audit Commission Act 1998 allowing interested persons to inspect accounts being audited by the Commission along with related documents and to obtain information from the auditor about the accounts.[166]

---

[165] FOIA ss 33(3) and 2(1)(b).

[166] Audit Commission Act 1988 s 15. This is considered further in §8– 025.

CHAPTER 21
Privilege

1. PARLIAMENTARY PRIVILEGE

21–001 Overview

Each House of Parliament is a 'public authority' within the meaning of the Freedom of

Information Act 2000.[1] Each House is accordingly subject to the information disclosure regime provided by that Act, as well as those of the Environmental Information Regulations 2004 and the Data Protection Act 1998. Although the Houses of Parliament have submitted to these three regimes, respect for the special status of business conducted within the Houses of Parliament is maintained through an exemption for Parliamentary privilege. Specifically, to the extent that information captured by a request would, if communicated to the applicant, result in an infringement of the privileges of either House of Parliament, that information is exempt information for the purposes of the Freedom of Information Act 2000.[2] There is a provision in the Environmental Information Regulations 2004 that produces the same result in relation to 'environmental information'.[3] There is a similar exemption from the subject access rights in the Data Protection Act 1998.[4] The operation of these exemptions accordingly turns upon the scope of the privileges of Parliament. While these exemptions will principally apply to information held by either House of Parliament, they are not so confined, and the exemptions will apply equally to information held by other public authorities to the extent that its disclosure would infringe the privilege.[5] In all cases the exemption is an absolute one, so that there is no need to consider whether the public interest in disclosing the information outweighs the public interest in maintaining the exemption.[6] Similarly, in all cases where the mere confirmation or denial by a public authority that it holds the information requested would constitute an infringement of the privileges of either House of Parliament, the duty to confirm or deny will not arise.[7] There is no equivalent in relation to Scottish public authorities.[8] The

---

[1] FOIA Sch 1 Pt I. They are thereby public authorities for the purposes of the EIR: EIR reg 2(2). The DPA applies to personal data processed (including held or stored) by or on behalf of the Houses of Parliament: DPA s 63A(1). The Corporate Officer of the House of Commons and the Corporate Officer of the House of Lords are the 'data controllers' in respect of those data: DPA s 63A(2)–(3). As at the date of writing, a private member's bill had been introduced into Parliament that would amend the FOIA: (a) by deleting the Houses of Parliament from FOIA Sch 1, Pt I; and (b) by adding a further exemption (s 34A) that would exempt any communication between a member of the House of Commons (acting in his capacity as such) and a public authority.

[2] FOIA s 34(1). With the result that the duty to communicate the information under FOIA s 1(1)(b), does not apply.

[3] EIR reg 3(4). As to the meaning of 'environmental information' see §6– 010.

[4] DPA s 35A. See further §21– 012.

[5] The Information Commissioner advises that as a matter of good practice, where a public authority other than one of the Houses of Parliament is considering relying on s 34 to withhold information, it should on all occasions contact the Freedom of Information Officer at the appropriate House of Parliament to discuss the details of the request: Information Commissioner, *Freedom of Information Awareness Guidance No 28*, December 2004 (updated January 2006) `www.ico.gov.uk/upload/documents/library/freedom_of_information/detailed_specialist_gui des/awareness_guidance_28_-_parliamentary_privilege.pdf`. Since disclosure of information in breach of parliamentary privilege is punishable by Parliament, where a public authority proposes to disclose information that might conceivably be covered by that privilege it is also good practice to contact the Freedom of Information Officer at the appropriate House of Parliament.

[6] FOIA s 2(3)(d). This does not, of itself, mean that there cannot be discretionary disclosure of the information: see §§9– 036 to 9– 038.

[7] FOIA s 34(2); EIR reg 3(4). The disapplication of this duty under FOIA is also absolute, so that it is not necessary to consider the public interest. Disapplication of the duty to confirm or deny is more likely to arise where the request is very specific, such that mere confirmation or denial is revelatory of the information sought. The EIR achieves the same result by disapplying the whole of the Regulations to the extent required for the purpose of avoiding an infringement of the privileges of either House of Parliament: EIR reg 3(4). The subject access rights include the right to be informed whether the data controller is processing (which includes holding or storing) personal data relating to the data subject (ie applicant): DPA s 7(1)(a). See further, §5– 031.

[8] That is, under FOI(S)A or EI(S)R.

privilege does not apply to proceedings in the National Assemblies of Northern Ireland or of Wales. Similar exemptions are to be found in each of the comparative jurisdictions except the United States and Canada.[9]

21– 002 **Documents in the custody of a House**

As with all other public authorities, it is only information that is 'held' by one of the Houses of Parliament that is within the scope of the rights conferred by the Freedom of Information Act 2000.[10] Members of Parliament and political parties are not 'public authorities' within the meaning of the Act. As such, papers held by them that are not 'in the custody of the House' are outside the right of access conferred by the Freedom of Information Act 2000.[11] Information that is in the 'custody of the House' includes documents in the possession of officers of Parliament and officers of its Committees, and Members of Parliament, held for some function of the work of Parliament and its committees. The term may, depending on the circumstances, extend to any of the following types of material:[12]

(a)   records of committee proceedings held in private, where that record is held by another public authority;

(b)   memoranda and draft memoranda submitted to committees;

(c)   reports or draft reports of a Parliamentary Committee held by another public authority prior to that report's disclosure by the Parliamentary Committee itself;

(d)   factual briefs or briefs of suggested questions prepared by the committee staff for the use of committee chairmen and members, and draft Reports which may be in the possession of a department as a result of a Minister being, or having been, a member of such a committee;

(e)   internal papers prepared by Officers of either House, including advice of all kinds to the Speaker, briefs for the chairmen and other members of committees, and informal notes of deliberative meetings of committees;

(f)   papers prepared by the libraries of either House, or by other House agencies such as the Parliamentary Office of Science and Technology;

(g)   papers relating to investigations by the Parliamentary Commissioner for Standards;

---

[9]   The Freedom of Information Act 1982 (Cth of Australia) s 46(b), provides an exemption where the disclosure of the requested document would infringe the privileges of the Commonwealth Parliament, State Parliaments and Territorial Assemblies: see §2– 015(6). The Official Information Act 1982 (New Zealand), ss 18(c)(ii) and 52(1), provides an absolute exemption where the disclosure of the information would constitute a contempt of the House: see §2– 022(7). This is a wider concept than Parliamentary privilege, and includes anything which has a tendency to obstruct or impede the House in its business, even something for which there is no precedent. The Freedom of Information Act 1997 (Ireland) s 22(1)(c), provides a mandatory exemption where the record consists of the private papers of a member of the European Parliament, a member of a local authority or of a health board, or where it consists of the opinions, advice, recommendations or the results of consultations considered by either House of the Oireachtas or its committees: see §2– 039(3).

[10] And similarly the Environmental Information Regulations 2004. See further §§6– 016 and 9– 009 to 9– 011.

[11] House of Commons, *Public Administration Committee, Third Report, Session 1997–98*, 19 May 1998, para 37. Such papers are similarly outside the scope of the regime in Australia (see §2– 011), New Zealand (see §2– 018), Canada (see §2– 026) and Ireland (see §2– 035).

[12] MoJ, *Exemptions Guidance Section 34 – Parliamentary privilege* (14 May 2008), pp 4-5 at:
       `www.justice.gov.uk/guidance/docs/foi-exemption-s34.pdf`

(h)   papers relating to the Registers of Members' Interests;[13]

(i)   bills, amendments and motions originating from Parliament or a Member rather than from parliamentary counsel or another government department;

(j)   confidential legal advice of Law Officers or by the legal branch of any other Department to the Speaker, a committee chairman or a committee;

(k)   any unpublished correspondence between Ministers and a member or official of either House, relating specifically to proceedings on any question, draft bill, motion or amendment, either in the relevant House, or in a committee;

(l)   any correspondence with or relating to the proceedings of the Parliamentary Commissioner for Standards or the Registrar of Members' Interests.

003   Meaning of the 'privileges of Parliament'

The House of Lords and the House of Commons claim for their members, both individually and collectively, certain rights and privileges which each House requires for the proper discharge of its functions and which exceed the rights possessed by other bodies and individuals. These are conventionally called the 'privileges of the Houses of Parliament'.[14] The privileges of the Houses of Parliament include the freedom of speech and debate in Parliament, the freedom from arrest (other than on a criminal charge or for contempt) and exemption from jury service. For present purposes, the privilege that is of greatest significance is the freedom of each House to control its own proceedings without external supervision, whether by the courts or otherwise. Each House is thus said to have 'exclusive cognisance' of its own 'proceedings'. That exclusive cognisance includes control over the disclosure of information within the custody of the House. The exemption in s 34 of the Freedom of Information Act 2000 operates to leave undisturbed the control by the Houses of Parliament over the disclosure of such information.

004   Provenance and rationale

Parliamentary privilege is protected by article 9 of the Bill of Rights 1689[15] and by common law authorities refusing to allow any challenge to what is said or done within the walls of Parliament

---

[13] This does not, of course, mean that it is subject to Parliamentary privilege: see *Rost v Edwards* [1990] 2 QB 460. In *Corporate Office of The House of Commons v IC & Norman Baker*, IT, 16 January 2007, the applicant made a request under FOIA to the House of Commons for a breakdown of the already published aggregate figure for travel claims by MPs, for the most recent year for which figures were available. He asked for the information 'in a format which would show for each MP the amount claimed by mode of travel, and therefore giving specific figures for rail, road, air and bicycle.' Notably, while the request was refused on the basis of s 40, the Parliamentary privilege exemption was not invoked. The Information Tribunal decided that the information should be released.

[14] Most of the privileges are common to both Houses, but some (not relevant for present purposes) are unique to each. For a fuller treatment of the privileges of the Houses of Parliament, see *Report from the Select Committee on Parliamentary Privilege* (HC Paper 34 (1967–68)); *Recommendations of the Select Committee on Parliamentary Privilege* (HC Paper 417 (1976–77)); and Joint Committee on Parliamentary Privilege, *Report*, April 1999, HL Paper 43, HC 214.

[15] 'That the freedom of speech and debates or proceedings in Parlyament ought not to be impeached or questioned in any court or place out of Parlyament.' Article 9 is not a comprehensive statement of the privilege, but is simply a manifestation of the principle that the courts and Parliament are both astute to recognise their respective constitutional roles: *Prebble v Television New Zealand* [1995] 1 AC 321 at 332D; *OGC v IC* [2008] EWHC 774 (Admin), [2010] QB 98 at [31].

in performance of its legislative function and established privileges.[16] The privilege is founded upon two principles:

— the need to avoid any risk of interference with free speech in Parliament; and

— the separation of powers, which requires the executive and the legislature to abstain from interference with the judicial function and requires the judiciary not to interfere with or to criticise the proceedings of the legislature.[17]

The courts determine the identity of the privileges of the Houses of Parliament but the manner of their exercise is within the exclusive domain of the Houses of Parliament.[18]

21– 005 The nature of the privilege

Parliamentary privilege prevents:

(1) the deployment in court or tribunal proceedings of statements made during proceedings in Parliament, but only where the object of the court or tribunal proceedings is to render the maker of the statement legally liable;[19]

(2) parties to litigation bringing into question anything said or done during proceedings in Parliament by suggesting (whether by direct evidence, cross-examination, inference or submission) that the actions or words were inspired by improper motives or were untrue or misleading;[20]

(3) a challenge to the veracity or accuracy of something said during proceedings in Parliament.[21]

Parliamentary privilege does not prevent reliance on evidence of what was said during

---

[16] *Prebble v Television New Zealand* [1995] 1 AC 321 at 332. In a defence to a defamation action, Television New Zealand asserted justification and relied inter alia on statements by ministers in the House which Television New Zealand alleged were calculated to mislead the House or were otherwise improperly motivated. Mr Prebble, a government minister and plaintiff in the defamation action, applied to strike out that part of the defence said to rely on privileged material. The Privy Council upheld the striking out of pleadings, ruling that the privilege applied to the material in question. It was an infringement of the privilege for any party to question in legal proceedings words spoken or actions done in Parliament by suggesting they were untrue, misleading or done for improper motives, even when done in defence of proceedings brought by a member of the legislature.

[17] *OGC v IC* [2008] EWHC 774 (Admin), [2010] QB 98 at [46].

[18] *Stockdale v Hansard* (1839) 9 Ad. & El. 1: '...the members of each House of Parliament are the sole judges whether their privileges have been violated, and whether thereby any person has been guilty of a contempt of their authority; and so they must necessarily adjudicate on the extent of their privileges...' (at 195). In *R v Richards, ex p Fitzpatrick and Browne* (1955) 92 CLR 157 at 162 Dixon CJ, speaking for the whole court of the High Court of Australia, said: '... it is for the courts to judge of the existence in either House of Parliament of a privilege, but, given an undoubted privilege, it is for the House to judge of the occasion and of the manner of its exercise.' Similarly, *New Brunswick Broadcasting Co v Nova Scotia* [1993] 1 SCR 319 at 384; *Egan v Willis* (1998) 195 CLR 424; *Halden v Marks* (1995) 17 WAR 447 at 462. In *Rost v Edwards* [1990] 2 QB 460 Popplewell J said (at 478): 'There are clearly cases where Parliament is to be the sole judge of its affairs. Equally there are clear cases where the courts are to have exclusive jurisdiction. In a case which may be described as a grey area a court, while giving full attention to the necessity for comity between the courts and Parliament, should not be astute to find a reason for ousting the jurisdiction of the court and for limiting or even defeating a proper claim by a party to litigation before it. If Parliament wishes to cover a particular area with privilege it has the ability to do so by passing an Act of Parliament giving itself the right to exclusive jurisdiction. Ousting the jurisdiction of the court has always been regarded as requiring the clearest possible words.' To similar effect, see *AG of Ceylon v de Livera* [1963] AC 103 (PC) at 120.

[19] *OGC v IC* [2008] EWHC 774 (Admin), [2010] QB 98 at [32].

[20] *Prebble v Television New Zealand* [1995] 1 AC 321 at 337A

[21] *Hamilton v Al-Fayed (No 1)* [2001] 1 AC 395 at 403; *OGC v IC* [2008] EWHC 774 (Admin), [2010] QB 98 at [39]-[40].

proceedings in Parliament to show what was the motivation of the executive's action outside Parliament.[22]   However, the reliance must not be such as to put another party to the proceedings at a disadvantage by that party being unable to contradict what was said during proceedings in Parliament. In particular, reliance upon an opinion or evaluative conclusion expressed during proceedings in Parliament may effect an unfairness upon another party and may be impermissible on that basis.[23] It is thus always important to identify the purpose for which evidence of proceedings in Parliament is relied upon.[24]

006 Parliamentary privilege and the exemption

So far as section 34 of the Freedom of Information Act 2000 is concerned, in making each House of Parliament a 'public authority' for the purposes of the Act, Parliament elected to submit itself to the obligations imposed by that Act: most notably, the obligation to provide a person with requested information held by it save to the extent otherwise prescribed by the Act. As such, where no exemption (apart from s.34) is applicable, the obligation to disclose requested information held by a House of Parliament will not normally constitute an infringement of the privileges of that House unless publication of that information has previously been restricted by a House. Each House of Parliament, should it deem it expedient, may prohibit the publication of its proceedings. In relation to proceedings of the House of Lords, the printing or publishing of anything relating to its proceedings is subject to the privileges of the House.[25] In relation to proceedings of the House of Commons, it resolved in 1971 that:

> notwithstanding the resolution of the House of 3 March 1762 and other such resolutions, this House will not entertain any complaint of contempt of the House or breach of privilege in respect of the publication of the debates and proceedings of the House or of its committees except when any such debates or proceedings shall have been conducted with closed doors or in private, or when such publication shall have been expressly prohibited by the House.[26]

Parliamentary privilege may be invoked to prevent the publication of evidence taken by a select committee before it has been reported to the House, including the publication of draft reports, in cases where such publication has not been authorised by the select committee or, in the Commons, if the select committee is no longer in existence, has not been authorised by the Speaker.[27]

---

[22] *Toussaint v The Attorney General of Saint Vincent and the Grenadines* [2007] UKPC 48, [2007] 1 WLR 2825. In that case, the claimant had alleged that a compulsory purchase order constituted discriminatory or illegitimate expropriation. The claimant was entitled to rely on the Minister's statement to Parliament to show the true motivation for the compulsory purchase. The claimant did not allege that the Minister had misled Parliament; to the contrary, it was alleged that what he said to Parliament disclosed his true motivation. The allegedly wrongful act in that case was not the statement to Parliament, but the compulsory purchase to which it related.

[23] *OGC v IC* [2008] EWHC 774 (Admin), [2010] QB 98 at [58]-[59].

[24] *Toussaint v The Attorney General of Saint Vincent and the Grenadines* [2007] UKPC 48, [2007] 1 WLR 2825 at [120]; *OGC v IC* [2010] QB 98 at [49], [62].

[25] HL Standing Orders (Public Business) (2007) no 16.

[26] 226 Commons Journals 548–549.

[27] Select committees are themselves empowered to publish evidence given to them, as is the Speaker if a select committee is no longer in existence: see HC Standing Orders (Public Business) (2009) no 135. When evidence has been given before a select committee meeting in public, no complaint of privilege will be entertained on the ground that it has been published before having been reported to the House: HC Standing Orders (Public Business) (2009) no 136.

21– 007 Proceedings in Parliament

Although the phrase has never been precisely defined, 'proceedings in Parliament' have been said to comprise:

> The primary meaning of proceedings, as a technical parliamentary term, . . . is some formal action, usually a decision, taken by the House in its collective capacity. This is naturally extended to the forms of business in which the House takes action, and the whole process, the principal part of which is debate, by which it reaches a decision. An individual member takes part in a proceeding usually by speech, but also by various recognised forms of formal action, such as voting, giving notice of a motion, or presenting a petition or report from a committee, most of such actions being time-saving substitutes for speaking. Officers of the House take part in its proceedings principally by carrying out its orders, general or particular. Strangers also may take part in the proceedings of a House, for example by giving evidence before it or one of its committees, or by securing presentation of a petition.[28]

It most obviously covers the various forms of business in which either House takes action and the whole process by which either House reaches a decision. It also embraces things said or done by a Member of Parliament in the exercise of his functions as a member in a committee of either House and everything said or done in either House in the transaction of Parliamentary business, whether by a member of either House or by an officer of either House.[29] The phrase thus indisputably covers debates, motions, proceedings on bills, votes, parliamentary questions, proceedings within committees formally appointed by either House, proceedings within sub-committees of such committees, and public petitions, once presented. Similarly, statements made and documents produced in the course of these proceedings, notices of these proceedings, internal House or committee papers of an official nature directly related to the proceedings, and communications arising directly out of such proceedings (as where a member seeks further information in the course of proceedings and another member agrees to provide it), all constitute proceedings in Parliament.[30] So too are the steps taken in carrying out an order of either House. The workings of the Parliamentary Commissioner for Standards form part of the proceedings of Parliament.[31]

21– 008 Matters that are not proceedings in Parliament

Certain activities of members are not 'proceedings in Parliament', even though they may take place within the House or a committee. A casual conversation between members in either

---

[28] W McKay (ed), *Erskine May's treatise on the law, privileges, proceedings and usage of Parliament*, 23rd edn (London, Butterworths, 2004) p 111.

[29] *AG of Ceylon v de Livera* [1963] AC 103 (PC) at 120–121; *Rost v Edwards* [1990] 2 QB 460.

[30] Joint Committee on Parliamentary Privilege, *Report*, April 1999, HL Paper 43, HC 214, para 100. In *O'Chee v Rowley* [1997] QCA 401, (1997) 150 ALR 199 (dealing with the Parliamentary Privileges Act 1987 (Cth of Aust), which is said to be declaratory of some of the privileges of the Parliament of the Commonwealth of Australia) the Queensland Court of Appeal held that documents said by a Senator to have been created, prepared or brought into existence for purposes of or incidental to the transacting of Senate business were within the scope of Parliamentary privilege. In *Crane v Gething* [2000] FCA 45, (2000) 97 FCR 9 the Federal Court reiterated the proposition that courts of law were not the proper forum for determining whether the privilege applied to the documents in question.

[31] *Hamilton v Al-Fayed (No 1)* [2001] 1 AC 395.

House even during a debate is not a proceeding in Parliament.[32] Nor are the proceedings of committees not appointed or nominated by either House, such as backbench and party committees, or the Ecclesiastical Committee. Proceedings in Parliament do not extend to the volunteering of information by a member of either House in his personal capacity;[33] nor do they include the writing of a letter by a Member to a Minister.[34] But they may include the provision of information to a member of Parliament in connection with the exercise of the member's parliamentary duties.[35] The Ministry of Justice suggests that a Member's correspondence, including correspondence with Ministers or other Members of either House, or their officers, is not privileged, unless it relates to actual or potential proceedings of the relevant House or committee.[36] In most such cases, however, it is unlikely that the information will be in the custody of a House of Parliament: as such, the information will not be within the grasp of the Freedom of Information Act 2000.[37] Other examples of information within the custody of Parliament but that will not form part of the proceedings in Parliament (and so not be within s 34) are:[38]

— Papers prepared by the libraries of either House, or other House agencies, intended to provide general or specific background information on matters not currently under examination, or expected or planned to be considered, in formal proceedings of either House or their committees.

— Members' correspondence and other communications not specifically related to proceedings of either House or of one of its formally constituted committees. For example, correspondence between a Member and a Minister about a constituency issue that is not the subject of proceedings.

— The deliberations of parliamentary bodies established by statute (although if they are discussing matters relating to the preparation of formal proceedings in parliament, those deliberations may well be privileged).

— Many administrative functions of Parliament, such as personnel matters, catering

---

[32] Joint Committee on Parliamentary Privilege, *Report*, April 1999, HL Paper 43, HC 214, §101, citing *Coffin v Coffin* (1808) 4 Mass 1, HC (1938–39) 101.

[33] HC Paper 112 (1954–55). See *Halsbury's Laws of England*, 5th edn, vol 78, para 1082.

[34] In 1958 the House ruled that a letter sent by a Member of Parliament to a Minister was not covered by privilege as a proceeding of the House. An MP, Mr Strauss, wrote a letter to the Minister for Power complaining about various actions of the London Electricity Board. The Minister referred the letter to the Board, who took issue with the allegations in the letter and threatened to sue Mr Strauss unless he retracted the comments. The House Committee on Privileges determined that the letter was subject to privilege and the Board and its solicitors had acted in breach of the privilege. Following a lengthy debate the Commons voted 218 to 213 to hold that the letter was not a 'proceeding in Parliament' and therefore the Board and its solicitors had not breached the privileges of the Parliament. See Hansard HC vol 591 cols 208–346 (8 July 1958).

[35] *R v Rule* [1937] 2 KB 375; *Beach v Freeson* [1972] 1 QB 14; *Rivlin v Bilainkin* [1953] 1 QB 485.

[36] MoJ, *Exemptions Guidance Section 34 – Parliamentary privilege* (14 May 2008) p 6, at: www.justice.gov.uk/guidance/docs/foi-exemption-s34.pdf

[37] See §21–002.

[38] As suggested in MoJ, *Exemptions Guidance Section 34 – Parliamentary privilege* (14 May 2008) p 6, at: www.justice.gov.uk/guidance/docs/foi-exemption-s34.pdf

669

and other household activities.[39]

21–009 **The effect of the exemption**

As noted above, the exemption in s 34 of the Freedom of Information Act 2000 operates to leave undisturbed the control by the Houses of Parliament over the disclosure of documents produced in the course of proceedings in Parliament, notices of these proceedings, internal House or committee papers of an official nature directly related to the proceedings, and communications arising directly out of such proceedings. Most such documents will be in the custody of one of the Houses of Parliament. However, the privilege can extend to information held by other public authorities, most commonly central government departments. Examples of information not in the custody of Parliament but the disclosure of which might infringe one of the privileges of Parliament are:[40]

— Unpublished working papers of a select committee of either House, including factual briefs or briefs of suggested questions prepared by the committee staff for the use of committee chairmen and/or other members, and draft Reports. These are most likely to be in the possession of a central government department as a result of a Minister being, or having been, a member of such a committee.

— Legal advice submitted in confidence by the Law Officers or by the legal branch of any other Department to the Speaker, a committee chairman or a committee, or any official of either House.

— Drafts of motions, bills or amendments, which have not otherwise been published or laid on the Table of either House.

— Any unpublished correspondence between Ministers (or departmental officials) on the one hand, and, on the other hand, any member or official of either House, relating specifically to proceedings on any Question, draft bill, motion or amendment, either in the relevant House, or in a committee.

— Any correspondence with or relating to the proceedings of the Parliamentary Commissioner for Standards or the Registrar.

21–010 **Material published by Parliament**

Most debates are conducted in public and most Parliamentary reports are available to the public. However Parliament retains the right to prohibit publication of its proceedings as it considers appropriate. Since 1971 this has been restricted to proceedings conducted in private or when publication has been expressly prohibited by the House, and the House allows publication of its proceedings which do not fall into those categories.[41] In 1980 the Commons resolved to allow its Official Report, published reports and public evidence taken by committees

---

[39] For example, *R v Graham Campbell, ex p Herbert* [1935] 1 KB 594 (Court declining jurisdiction on a complaint that liquor was sold without a licence from the Parliamentary building). Also see the House of Commons, Research Paper 99/98, *The Freedom of Information Bill, 3 December 1999*, p 40. For the background on whether administrative functions were to be covered by the FOIA see pp 39–40. The House of Commons Select Committee on Public Administration stated that such information should not be protected from disclosure: see their *Third Report, Session 1997–98*, 19 May 1998, para 37.

[40] As suggested in MoJ, *Exemptions Guidance Section 34 – Parliamentary privilege* (14 May 2008) pp 5-6, at: `www.justice.gov.uk/guidance/docs/foi-exemption-s34.pdf`

[41] See 226 *Commons Journal*, 548–549.

to be referred to in court proceedings without the need formally to petition the House for such permission.[42] Parliament has the right to prevent publication of the evidence taken by a select committee before it has been reported to the House.[43] So, for example, an application for disclosure of a Parliamentary Select Committee report, or of workings of that Committee, could not be sustained if such documents have not been released by Parliament itself. The same would apply to an unpublished draft report. Parliament also routinely publishes internal administrative documents and individual members' allowances and expenditure. Such materials may remain privileged even following publication.[44] However disclosure of previously published information is unlikely to be an 'infringement' of the privilege. Further, such information is likely to be exempt information under s 21 of the Freedom of Information Act 2000 (information otherwise available).[45]

011 Conclusive certificates

The Speaker of the House of Commons or, in relation to the House of Lords, the Clerk of the Parliaments may issue a conclusive certificate for the purpose of exempting a public authority from its disclosure duty or both its disclosure duty and its duty to confirm or deny that it holds any of the information requested. Such a certificate is conclusive evidence of the 'fact' that exemption from the duty or duties is, or at any time was, required for the purpose of avoiding an infringement of the privileges of either House of Parliament.[46] The effect of such a certificate in relation to information to which it applies is to remove practically all, if not all, an applicant's rights to challenge a decision not to communicate the information covered by the certificate and a decision neither confirming nor denying that the information requested is held by the public authority.[47] The Act provides no right of appeal against the issue of a certificate. Any attempt to seek to judicially review the decision to issue such a certificate is likely to be dismissed as itself contrary to the privilege.[48]

012 The Data Protection Act 1998

To the extent that a person applies for information relating to himself, that application will fall to be decided by the Data Protection Act 1998 and not by the Freedom of Information Act

---

[42] 236 *Commons Journal* 823.

[43] This would certainly be the case where Parliament has actively proscribed publication. It could arguably be otherwise where Parliament has merely taken no steps to publish committee evidence. However it is likely that the privilege applies in this latter situation as well, unless and until Parliament has taken a positive step to waive the privilege that would otherwise attach.

[44] Publication by Parliament does not necessarily entail a waiver of privilege such as applies to the disclosure of material covered by legal professional privilege.

[45] See ch 16. There is no equivalent exemption or exception in the DPA. There is a narrowed exception in EIR reg 6(1)(b).

[46] FOIA s 34(3)–(4).

[47] Appeals are considered generally in ch 28. A potential avenue of challenge in relation to a s 34(2) certificate is considered at §28–037.

[48] However, query the situation if the Clerk of the Parliaments issued a certificate purporting to rely on a privilege of Parliament not previously recognised. Both Houses recognised in 1705 that they had no power to create new privileges (see 14 Commons Journal 555, 560, 17 Lords Journal 677). It may be that such a certificate would be ineffective as not being a claim to Parliamentary privilege.

2000.[49] Section 35A of the Data Protection Act 1998 provides an exemption from the subject access rights that is in materially identical terms to s 34(1) of the Freedom of Information Act 2000.[50] As with all exemptions under the Data Protection Act 1998, there is no public interest 'override'. However, there is no provision for a conclusive certificate such as exists under s 34 of the Freedom of Information Act 2000.

2. LEGAL PROFESSIONAL PRIVILEGE

21–013 Overview

Information in respect of which a claim to legal professional privilege could be maintained in legal proceedings is rendered exempt information under the Freedom of Information Act 2000.[51] A similar exemption is provided in the Data Protection Act 1998.[52] There is no express reference to legal professional privilege in the Environmental Information Regulations 2004,[53] but the Tribunal has held that a similar exemption applies under those Regulations by virtue of reg 12(5)(b).[54] The exemption under the Freedom of Information Act 2000 is not absolute, so that disapplication of the disclosure duty requires consideration of whether the public interest in the maintenance of the exemption outweighs the public interest in disclosure.[55] There is a correlative exemption from the duty to confirm or deny that information answering the terms of the request is held by the public authority.[56] Similar exemptions are to be found in each of the comparative jurisdictions.[57] Section 42 does not cover the privilege in aid of negotiations

---

[49] See §5– 002. So, too, if the information is 'environmental information': see §6– 050.

[50] See DPA s 35A, which came into force on 1 January 2005: SI 2004/1909 art 2(1), (2)(f), (3).

[51] FOIA s 42(1). The nearest Scottish provision covers 'Information in respect of which a claim to confidentiality of communications could be maintained in legal proceedings is exempt information' – FOI(S)A s 36(1).

[52] DPA s 35.

[53] See §§6– 046 and 6– 049. Regulation 12(5)(d), (f) covers disclosure which would adversely affect confidentiality of proceedings where such confidentiality is protected by law, and the interests of persons providing information where that person was not under any legal obligation to so supply the information. The Scottish provisions are to the same effect: see the EI(S)R reg 10(5)(d), (f).

[54] *Kirkaldie v IC and Thanet DC*, IT, 4 July 2006 at [18]–[23]. Regulation 12(5)(b) covers disclosure which would adversely affect 'the course of justice, the ability of a person to receive a fair trial or the ability of a public authority to conduct an inquiry of a criminal or disciplinary nature.' The Tribunal in *Kirkaldie* gave little explanation of why it considered that disclosure of legally privileged information would necessarily adversely affect the course of justice. It may be thought advantageous to the course of justice for a fact-finder to have access to all relevant information in order to best discover the truth. Similarly *Archer v IC and Salisbury District Council*, IT, 9 May 2007 at [62]–[64].

[55] FOIA s 2(3).

[56] FOIA s 42(2). See §21– 021.

[57] In the United States, the Freedom of Information Act, 1966, 5 USC 552(b)(5), exempts from disclosure inter-agency or intra-agency memoranda or letters 'which would not be available by law to a party other than an agency in litigation with the agency', which has been interpreted to include records or information covered by attorney work-product privilege and attorney-client privilege: see §2– 008(5). The Freedom of Information Act 1982 (Cth of Australia) s 42, provides an exemption where the requested documents are subject to legal professional privilege: see §2– 015(4). In New Zealand, the Official Information Act 1982 ss 9(2)(h) and 27(1)(h), the Local Government Official Information and Meetings Act 1987 ss 7(2)(g) and 26(1)(h), and the Privacy Act 1993 s 29(1)(f), all provide a qualified exemption where non-disclosure is required to maintain legal professional privilege: see §2– 023(9). In Canada, the Access to Information Act, 1982 s 23, provides a discretionary exemption for solicitor-client privileged

(commonly termed 'without prejudice privilege'), which is a separate and distinct rule. However such negotiations may be treated as confidential, and so be affected by the principles discussed in Chapter 25. Guidance on section 42 has been issued by the Ministry of Justice[58] and by the Information Commissioner.[59]

014 Scope and meaning

'Legal professional privilege' is a rule or a collection of rules which seek to protect the confidentiality of legal communications, specifically:

(1)   information imparted by a client to a lawyer for the purpose of seeking advice;

(2)   communications in which advice is given; and

(3)   certain communications between a lawyer and third parties for the purpose of preparing for litigation.[60]

In *Bellamy v Information Commissioner and DTI*[61] the Information Tribunal described the privilege as:

a set of rules or principles which are designed to protect the confidentiality of legal or legally related communications and exchanges between the client and his, her or its lawyers, as well as exchanges which contain or refer to legal advice which might be imparted to the client, and even exchanges between the clients and their parties if such communications or exchanges come into being for the purposes of preparing for litigation.

The privilege is a bar to the compulsion of evidence: it is not a rule of inadmissibility. The confidentiality of legal communications is recognised as a human right under both arts 6 and 8 of the European Convention on Human Rights.[62] It is a fundamental and substantive legal right.[63]

015 Legal advice privilege and litigation privilege

There are two distinct branches of legal professional privilege: legal advice privilege and

---

information: see §2– 032(8). The Freedom of Information Act 1997 (Ireland) s 22(1), provides a mandatory exemption where the record would be exempt from production in a court on the grounds of legal professional privilege: see §2– 039(3).

[58]   MoJ, *Exemptions Guidance – Section 42* (20 June 2008)
        www.justice.gov.uk/guidance/docs/foi-exemption-section42.pdf.

[59]   Information Commissioner, *The Exemption for Legal Professional Privilege* (11 November 2008).

[60]   See generally: P Matthews and H Malek, *Disclosure*, 3rd edn (London, Sweet & Maxwell, 2007) chs 9 and 10; J Auburn, *Legal Professional Privilege: Law and Theory* (Oxford, Hart Publishing, 2000); C Passmore, *Privilege*, 2nd ed (London, CLT Publishing, 2006); H Malek (ed), *Phipson on Evidence*, 17th edn (London, Sweet & Maxwell, 2009), ch 22.

[61]   *Bellamy v IC and DTI*, IT, 4 April 2006 at [9]. In that case privilege applied to advice given by Treasury Counsel, and the privilege was not outweighed by the Appellant's interests in disclosure.

[62]   For example, *Golder v United Kingdom* (1979–80) 1 EHRR 524 (art 6); *Niemietz v Germany* (1993) 16 EHRR 97 (art 8). See the pre-incorporation House of Lords' decision in *R v SSHD, ex p Simms* [2000] 2 AC 115. Also see *Tamosius v United Kingdom* (2002) 35 EHRR CD323; *Foxley v United Kingdom* (2001) 31 EHRR 25; *McE v Prison Service of Northern Ireland* [2009] UKHL 15, [2009] 1 AC 908.

[63]   *Three Rivers DC v Bank of England (no 6)* [2004] UKHL 48, [2005] 1 AC 610, [2005] 4 All ER 948 at [26]; *Canada (Privacy Commissioner) v Blood Trive Department of Health* [2008] 2 SCR 574 (Sup Ct of Canada)

litigation privilege.[64] Legal advice privilege covers confidential[65] communications between a lawyer[66] and client for the purpose[67] of giving or obtaining legal advice.[68] The scope of legal advice privilege in England was for a short time thrown into doubt by the Court of Appeal's decisions in the *Three Rivers DC v Bank of England* litigation,[69] but the orthodox understanding of the principle was restored by the House of Lords in *Three Rivers DC v Bank of England (No 6)*.[70] Litigation privilege covers confidential communication after litigation has commenced or once litigation is reasonably in prospect,[71] between a lawyer and his client, a lawyer and his non-professional agent or a lawyer and third party, for the sole or dominant[72] purpose of the litigation.[73] Communications between parties with a common interest in litigation for the dominant purpose of informing each other of the advice received or of obtaining legal advice are also protected.[74] In England it appears that a corporate entity may be divided into constituent parts and correspondence within the corporation but between those parts for the purpose of seeking legal advice may not benefit from legal advice privilege.[75]

---

[64] For the distinction between legal advice privilege and litigation privilege, see *Three Rivers District Council v Bank of England (No 5)* [2003] EWCA Civ 474, [2003] All ER (D) 59 (Apr). Also see *Winterthur Swiss Insurance Company v AG (Manchester) Ltd* [2006] EWHC 839 (Comm).

[65] Communications between a lawyer and client in circumstances where they could not reasonably have expected confidentiality to be maintained are not covered, eg where the lawyer and client speak in a room with a police officer present.

[66] This will include: solicitors in private practice, as well as their employees and trainees acting on their behalf (*Wheeler v Le Marchant* (1881) 17 ChD 675 at 682); barristers in private practice; in-house solicitors and barristers (*Geraaghty v Minister for Local Government* [1975] IR 300; *AG for the Northern Territory v Kearney* (1985) 158 CLR 500; *Waterford v Commonwealth of Australia* (1987) 163 CLR 54; *Commonwealth of Australia v Dutton* (2000) 102 FCR 168; *Three Rivers District Council v Bank of England (No 3)* [2003] EWCA Civ 474, [2003] QB 1556). See further: P Matthews and H Malek, *Disclosure*, 3rd edn (London, Sweet & Maxwell, 2007) ch 11.

[67] In other jurisdictions such as Australia a test of 'dominant purpose' is used in both limbs of the privilege (eg see *Esso Australia Ltd v Federal Commissioner of Taxation* [1999] HCA 67). However the House of Lords in *Three Rivers DC v Bank of England (No 6)* [2005] 1 AC 610 did not appear to adopt this formulation for the legal advice limb of the privilege.

[68] Where legal advice is sought for the purpose of resisting a letters rogatory it is legal advice not litigation privilege that is in issue: *USA v Philip Morris* [2004] EWCA Civ 330.

[69] *Three Rivers DC v Bank of England (No 3)* [2003] EWCA Civ 474, [2003] QB 1556; *Three Rivers DC v Bank of England (No 6)* [2004] QB 916, [2005] 1 AC 610. In the latter case the Court of Appeal had accepted an argument that communications between the Bank of England and its lawyers was only covered by legal advice privilege to the extent that it was given in the furtherance of advice as to the Bank's legal rights and obligations, and did not extend to legal assistance for the dominant purpose of putting relevant factual material before an inquiry in an orderly and attractive fashion rather than for the taking of advice on such material.

[70] [2005] 1 AC 610.

[71] *Re Highgrade Traders* [1984] BCLC 151 at 172; *Mitsubishi Electric Australia Pty Ltd v Victorian Work Cover Authority* [2002] VSCA 59 at [16]–[19]; *USA v Philip Morris* [2004] EWCA Civ 330.

[72] This test has been thought to be too broad to be the foundation for an FOI exemption: see Australian Law Reform Commission, *Open Government*, report No 77 (Canberra, 1995) §10.26. Its breadth under the FOIA is tempered by the public interest override: see below.

[73] *Anderson v Bank of British Columbia* (1876) 2 Ch D 644; *Wheeler v Le Marchant* (1881) 17 Ch D 675.

[74] *Buttes Gas and Oil Co v Hammer (No 3)* [1981] QB 223; *Dadourian Group International Inc v Simms* [2008] EWHC 1784 (Ch).

[75] This is a possible application of the Court of Appeal decision in *Three Rivers DC v Bank of England (No 3)* [2003] EWCA Civ 474, [2003] QB 1556, concerning communications between the Bank of England's 'Bingham Investigation Unit' and others parts of the Bank for the purpose of seeking legal advice did not benefit from the privilege. In the subsequent case of *Three Rivers DC v Bank of England (No 6)* [2005] 1 AC 610 the House of Lords

016 Exceptions to the privilege

Certain communications that would otherwise fall within the general scope of the rule[76] are excepted from the privilege:

(1) Communications in furtherance of a crime or fraud are not communications within the ordinary scope of the professional lawyer-client relationship and so not privileged.[77]

(2) The privilege in the totality of a document may be waived or lost where part of that document has been disclosed such that it would be unfair for the disclosing party to continue to assert privilege over the remainder.[78] If privilege is waived there is no need to apply the public interest test and the information must be disclosed.[79]

(3) Privilege will also be waived where reference to a document is made in court documents, such as statements of case and witness statements[80] or where there has been reference to the content of legal advice received.[81]

(4) Privilege in a document will be waived where reference is made to it during the course of a trial, including in the course of advocate's speeches to the court, or by calling evidence of a privileged conversation[82] or having taken counsel's advice.

(5) Privilege does not extend to a copy of a privileged document in the hands of

---

heard argument on this point but expressly declined to decide it: see Lord Scott at [47] and Lord Carswell at [118]. Doubts remain as to the correctness of *Three Rivers DC v Bank of England (No 3)* and it is unfortunate that the House of Lords did not take the opportunity to overturn it when the matter was squarely before them and had been fully argued.

[76] See §21–014.

[77] *R v Cox and Railton* (1884) 14 QBD 153; *R v Central Criminal Court, ex p Francis & Francis* [1989] 1 AC 346; *Derby & Co v Weldon (No 7)* [1990] 1 WLR 1156; *Kuwait Airways Corp v Iraqi Airways Company* [2005] EWCA Civ. 286; The Times, 25 April 2006; *R v Gibbins* [2004] EWCA Crim 311; *C v C* [2007] WTLR 753. This exception can also apply in relation to litigation privilege, eg *R (Hallinan Blackburn) v Middlesex Crown Court* [2004] EWHC 2726 (Admin), [2005] 1 WLR 766.

[78] *Great Atlantic Insurance Co v Home Insurance Co* [1981] 2 All ER 485; *Nea Karteria Maritime Co Ltd v Atlantic and Great Lakes Steamship Corp* [1981] Comm LR 138; *General Accident Corp v Tanter* [1984] 1 WLR 100; *Re Konigsberg (a bankrupt)* [1989] 3 All ER 289; *R v Secretary of State for Transport and Factortame Ltd* [1998] 1 All ER 736 (Note); *Somatra Ltd v Sinclair, Roche & Temperley* [2000] 1 WLR 2453. See also the MoJ, *Exemptions Guidance – Section 34* (20 June 2008) www.justice.gov.uk/guidance/docs/foi-exemption-section42.pdf. In *Kirkaldie v IC and Thanet DC*, IT, 4 July 2006 at [24]–[43] the Information Tribunal held that a Council had waived privilege over its legal advice by providing an oral summary of the principal conclusions of that advice during a public session of the Council.

[79] *Kirkaldie v IC and Thanet DC*, IT, 4 July 2006 at [43].

[80] *Great Atlantic Insurance Co v Home Insurance Co* [1981] 1 WLR 529 at 538; *Derby v Weldon (No 10)* [1991] 2 All ER 908. The rule is based on the need to ensure the disclosing party has not misled the court by disclosing a selection of the document out of context or in a manner that is not properly representative of the whole. The material must be 'deployed' in court. Mere reference is usually insufficient. See also: *Expandable Ltd v Rubin* [2008] EWCA Civ 59, [2008] 1 WLR 1099.

[81] Authorities on the issue are reviewed in *Dunlop Slazenger International Ltd v Joe Bloggs Sports Ltd* [2003] EWCA Civ. 901. Disclosure in a letter of the gist or conclusions of legal advice may waive privilege over all of that advice: *Bennett v Chief Executive Officer, Australian Customs Service* [2004] FCAFC 237, (2004) 210 ALR 220. Also see *Fulham Leisure Holdings Ltd v Nicolson Graham & Jones* [2006] EWHC 158 (Ch), [2006] 2 All ER 599, [2006] PNLR 23 (waiver of privilege over advice concerning one transaction did not necessarily lead to waiver over all advice relating to the dispute).

[82] *George Doland Ltd v Blackburn Robson Coates & Co* [1972] 1 WLR 1338.

another party.[83]

(6)   In some jurisdictions (though not in England[84] or Australia[85]) the privilege may be taken to be overridden where the evidence may prove an accused innocent of a serious criminal charge.[86]

(7)   There are various statutory exceptions to the privilege, such as s 39 of the Banking Act 1987, which allows the Bank of England to require a person to produce material, including privileged material in certain circumstances; and s 291 of the Insolvency Act 1986, by which a bankrupt cannot withhold privileged documents from the Official Receiver. To the opposite effect it has been held that there was no express reference in s 20(1) of the Taxes Management Act 1970 to legal professional privilege and that section could not be construed as necessarily implying that a tax inspector could, by the issue of a notice, require the disclosure of documents which were subject to legal professional privilege.[87]

21–017   The public interest—the conceptual issue

It may be thought odd that the exemption for legal professional privilege is a qualified one.[88] It has been a defining feature of legal professional privilege that it involves no such balancing exercise. Courts in the United Kingdom and in the rest of the Commonwealth have frequently stated that the concept of legal professional privilege is itself the result of a balancing process,[89] which was performed once and for all in the sixteenth century,[90] and that such arguments were either presumed[91] or considered and rejected[92] in the course of the development of the common law, and therefore once the rule applies no further balancing process should be carried out:[93]

courts have for very many years regarded legal professional privilege as the predominant

---

[83]   *Calcraft v Guest* [1898] 1 QB 759; though the privilege-holder may seek an injunction under the principles in *Ashburton v Pape* [1913] 2 Ch 469.

[84]   *R v Derby Magistrates' Court, ex p B* [1996] 1 AC 487. It may be doubted whether this decision will survive the incorporation into domestic English law of art 6 of the European Convention on Human Rights.

[85]   *Carter v The Managing Partner, Northmore Hale Davy & Leake* (1995) 183 CLR 121.

[86]   *R v Gray* (1992) 74 CCC (3d) 267) (British Columbia Supreme Court); *S v Safatsa* (1988) 1 SA 868 (Appellate Division, South Africa). Also see *R v Craig* [1975] 1 NZLR 597 and *R v Dunbar and Logan* (1982) 138 DLR (3d) 221; *R v McClure* (2001) 195 DLR (4th) 513; *R v Brown* (2000) 210 DLR (4th) 341; *Goodis v Ontario* 2006 SCC 31, [2006] 2 SCR 32, 271 DLR (4th) 407.

[87]   *Three Rivers DC v Bank of England (No 6)* [2005] 1 AC 610; *R (Morgan Grenfell & Co Ltd) v Special Commissioner of Income Tax* [2002] UKHL 21, [2003] 1 AC 563. See also: *B v Auckland District Law Society* [2003] UKPC 8, [2003] 2 AC 736; *Woolworths v Fels* [2002] HCA 50, (2002) 193 ALR 1; *Daniels Corp v Accc* [2002] HCA 49, (2002) 194 ALR 561. As to whether provisions of the CPR override the privilege see *Lucas v Barking Havering and Redbridge Hospitals NHS Trust* [2003] 4 All ER 720; *Vasiliou v Hajigeorgiou* [2005] 3 All ER 17.

[88]   As is the case in New Zealand: see §2–023(9).

[89]   For example, *Waterford v The Commonwealth* (1987) 163 CLR 54 at 64–65; *Australian Federal Police v Propend Finance* (1997) 141 ALR 545 at 592, 609.

[90]   *R v Derby Magistrates' Court, ex p B* [1996] 1 AC 487 at 508.

[91]   *R v Uljee* [1982] 1 NZLR 561 at 576–577.

[92]   *Carter v The Managing Partner, Northmore Hale Davy & Leake* (1995) 183 CLR 121 at 138.

[93]   *Waterford v The Commonwealth* (1987) 163 CLR at 64, 74, 98–99; *AG (NT) v Kearney* (1985) 158 CLR 500 at 532; *Carter v The Managing Partner, Northmore Hale Davy & Leake* (1995) 183 CLR 121 at 128, 134 and 137; *Australian Federal Police v Propend Finance* (1997) 141 ALR at 592, 609.

public interest. A balancing exercise is not required in individual cases, because the balance must always come down in favour of upholding the privilege.[94]

The use of a balancing test within the privilege would, it has been repeatedly said, fundamentally undermine the raison d'être of the privilege, namely a client's confidence in the sanctity of his legal communications:

> once any exception to the rule is allowed, the client's confidence is necessarily lost.[95]

Section 42 of the Freedom of Information Act 2000 cuts across these notions, but in a more measured fashion than a general consideration of the public interest would entail.

018 The public interest balancing exercise

The weighing exercise imposed by s 2 of the Freedom of Information Act 2000 necessitates an identification of the public interest in the maintenance of the exemption, always recognising that that public interest must be delineated in such a fashion that it is capable in practice of being outweighed.[96] Cases concerning privileged information have largely involved claims of a general instrumental consideration underlying lawyer-client relationships in the abstract.[97] For example, in *Bellamy v Information Commissioner* the public interest asserted was that in being able 'to receive disinterested and frank legal advice in order to assist [public bodies] in making appropriate decisions and there is less likelihood that they would receive such advice if those giving it knew it was to be made public…in order to allow legal advice to be provided unfettered by concerns about disclosure'[98] and the Tribunal applied this general instrumental public interest, stating that 'there is a strong element of public interest inbuilt into the privilege itself.'[99] That there is a strong public interest in non-disclosure in-built into legal professional privilege has been accepted by the Tribunal in a long line of decisions, and this has been accepted as being the correct approach.[100] A proper weighing of the public interest in maintaining the exemption will involve both general and specific considerations.

---

[94] Lord Lloyd in *R v Derby Magistrates' Court, ex p B* [1996] 1 AC 487 at 509. Also see *Carter v The Managing Partner, Northmore Hale Davy & Leake* (1995) 183 CLR at 128–9, where Brennan J held that 'there is no occasion for the courts to undertake a balancing of public interests: the balance is already struck by the allowing of the privilege…if there can be no public interest which defeats the privilege, there can be no individual interest which does so.'

[95] *R v Derby Magistrates' Court, ex p B* [1996] 1 AC 487 at 508. In *Carter v The Managing Partner, Northmore Hale Davy & Leake* (1995) 183 CLR 121 at 139 the view expressed was that departure from this principle would mean that lawyers would become duty bound to recite the court's powers as to disclosure and this would intensify the chilling effect.

[96] To avoid metamorphosing it into an absolute exemption: *Kitchener v IC and Derby City Council*, IT, 20 December 2006 at [17]. The exercise is antithetical to orthodox privilege theory that 'once privileged, always privileged'. Thus, in *Calcraft v Guest* [1898] 1 QB 759 the privilege was asserted 110 years after the relevant communication. The House of Commons Select Committee favoured widespread disclosure of old opinions. Thus the House of Commons Public Administration Committee in its *Third Report, Session 1997–98*, 19 May 1998, stated at para 31: 'In the spirit of openness, the Government's vast storehouse of legal opinions on every conceivable subject should be made available to interested members of the public.'

[97] This is the main way the public interest is put in the MoJ, *Exemptions Guidance – Section 34* (20 June 2008) www.justice.gov.uk/guidance/docs/foi-exemption-section42.pdf.

[98] *Bellamy v IC and DTI*, IT, 4 April 2006 at [24].

[99] *Bellamy v IC and DTI*, IT, 4 April 2006 at [35]; *Archer v IC and Salisbury DC*, IT, 9 May 2007 at [62]-[63]; *Rosenbaum v IC and House of Lords Appointments Commission*, IT, 4 November 2008 at [32]-[37].

[100] *DBERR v O'Brien and IC* [2009] EWHC 164 (QB) at [53].

21–019 Public interest—general considerations

In relation to the general considerations, the general maintenance of the confidentiality of communications between any lawyer and his client is a matter which is in the public interest.[101] It is recognised that care should be taken to ensure that freedom of information principles do not undermine the well established common law right to legal professional privilege, which enables a public authority to put all relevant facts before its legal advisers, and to receive advice based on them, without fear that either the facts or the advice will be disclosed to others without its consent.[102] Here, the issue is not the effect that disclosure might have on particular information or in a particular solicitor-client relationship: it is the effect that disclosure might have on future legal communications in general.[103] There has been relatively little analysis of whether these concerns should apply in precisely the same manner in the public sector as they do in the private sector. There does appear to be some concern among the public that they be told the basis of legal advice given to their government on matters of important public concern.[104] The assertion of this general type of concern for the detrimental effect of recognising an exception to the privilege is a highly speculative exercise at best. There are widely differing views on the effect of individual disclosures on the continued confidence of clients in the sanctity of their legal communications. On the one hand, it is often claimed that it is essential to the maintenance of continued candid lawyer-client relations that there are no new exceptions to the privilege.[105] An alternative view is that these concerns have been overplayed, and that the privilege could survive the recognition of exceptions without the collapse of lawyer-client relations.[106] There will, of course, be occasions when the public interest in disclosure will outweigh the public interest in maintaining privilege, such as where the harm likely to be suffered by the party entitled to privilege is slight or the requirement for disclosure is overwhelming.[107] However, the general trend has been to refuse disclosure, informed by the general interest in maintaining legal professional privilege.[108]

21–020 Public interest – specific considerations

The second aspect involves a consideration of the specific information captured by the request

---

[101] For a more detailed analysis of the public interests advanced by the maintenance of the privilege, see J Auburn, *Legal Professional Privilege: Law and Theory* (Oxford, Hart Publishing, 2000) ch 4. In the European Union context, see: Case T-84/03 *Turco v EU Council* [2004] ECR II-4061; Case T-36/04 *Association de la presse internationale asbl v EC Commission* [2007] ECR II-3201

[102] *Shipton v IC and National Assembly of Wales*, IT, 11 January 2007; *Gillingham v IC*, IT, 26 September 2007 at [16] and [36]; *Pugh v IC and MoD*, IT, 17 December 2007 at [28]-[33]; *Mersey Tunnel Users Association v IC and Merseytravel*, IT, 15 February 2008 at [26]-[34]; *Francis v IC and South Essex Partnership Foundation NHS Trust*, IT, 21 July 2008 at [45].

[103] See §21–017.

[104] For example, the furore over the Government's refusal to disclose the legal advice given to it by the Attorney-General concerning the legality of Britain's involvement in military action against Iraq in 2003.

[105] For example, Lord Taylor CJ in *R v Derby Magistrates' Court, ex p B* [1996] 1 AC 487 at 508 'once any exception to the rule is allowed, the client's confidence is necessarily lost.'

[106] For example, *Saunders v Punch* [1998] 1 WLR 986 at 996.

[107] *Shipton v IC and National Assembly of Wales*, IT, 11 January 2007 at [14(b)]; *Kessler v IC and HMRC*, IT, 29 November 2007 at [53] and [55].

[108] See, eg: *Burgess v IC and Stafford BC*, IT, 7 June 2007.

and that stands to be disclosed. One set of relevant factors may relate to the age of the relevant information:[109] when it was created; whether the purpose for which it was created is 'spent' in the sense that the information may no longer be relevant to present or future proceedings;[110] whether all limitation periods for an action based on the information have expired. Another relevant factor may be the official release by the requested or another public authority of other information on the same subject matter as the information which enjoys legal professional privilege: if the information officially released, particularly if released as a discretionary disclosure, is unrepresentative of the entirety of the information held, the public interest in maintaining the exemption may be weakened where disclosure would redress the situation. The public interest in disclosure[111] will vary according to the information sought. Some clear, compelling and specific justification for disclosure must be shown so as to override the obvious interest in legal professional privilege.[112] Circumstances where specific considerations may be in favour of disclosure despite legal professional privilege include:

— where the harm likely to be suffered by the party entitled to the privilege is likely to be slight;[113]

— where there is reason to believe that the authority is misrepresenting the advice that it has received;[114]

— where the public authority is pursuing a policy which appears to be unlawful or where there are clear indications that it has ignored advice that it has received;[115]

— where there is an overriding interest in openness and transparency on the facts or where advice on the topic has already been disclosed;[116]

— where the information protected by legal professional privilege shows evidence of malfeasance, fraud or corruption.[117]

The Tribunal has readily found that the public interest tilts in favour of maintaining the exemption where there is any degree of currency to a legal advice.[118] However, in one case where the general public interest in accountability and transparency had been poorly served, disclosure was ordered to provide fuller reasoning as to how a particular conclusion had been

---

[109] *Kessler v IC and HMRC*, IT, 29 November 2007 at [57(8)]. As a general rule, the public interest in maintaining an exemption diminishes over time: *Mersey Tunnel Users Association v IC and Halton BC*, IT, 11 January 2010 at [48(x)].

[110] Compare *Bellamy v IC and DTI*, IT, 4 April 2006 at [24]: The Commissioner also noted that the particular issue raised by the legal advice and exchanges sought remained 'live' which rendered it 'particularly sensitive'. The importance of currency was emphasised by the Information Tribunal in *Kitchener v IC and Derby City Council*, IT, 20 December 2006 at [18].

[111] See §15–011.

[112] *Mersey Tunnel Users Association v IC and Halton BC*, IT, 24 June 2009 at [48(ix)].

[113] *Shipton v IC and National Assembly of Wales*, IT, 11 January 2007 at [14(b)].

[114] *Osland v Secretary to the Department of Justice* [2008] HCA 37, (2008) 234 CLR 27 (High Court of Australia).

[115] *FCO v IC*, IT, 29 April 2008 at [29].

[116] *Maiden v IC and King's Lynn and West Norfolk BC*, IT, 15 December 2008 at [43]-[44].

[117] *Mersey Tunnel Users Association v IC and Halton BC*, IT, 11 January 2010 at [50].

[118] *Kitchener v IC and Derby City Council*, IT, 20 December 2006. But the fact that disclosure of legal advice may give rise to legal proceedings against the public authority is not a public interest factor in maintaining the exemption: *Kitchener* at [19].

reached.[119] A number of Commonwealth courts have developed a principle that the privilege may give way to a far weightier public interest where the privilege-holders no longer have a recognised interest to protect.[120] It may be that this principle, previously disfavoured in England (as well as Australia),[121] will now be relevant in weakening the case for continued confidentiality.

21–021 Duty to confirm or deny

Where or to the extent that a public authority, by confirming or denying that it holds the requested information, would thereby disclose exempt information under s 42(1), then the discrete duty to confirm or deny that that information is held by the public authority does not arise.[122] Confirmation or denial that information answering the terms of a request is held will only be likely to involve the disclosure of information in respect of which a claim to legal professional privilege could be maintained where the request is couched in very specific terms: for example, a request for advice to a particular effect. Again, this is a qualified exclusion of duty. It will be necessary to consider whether, in all the circumstances, the maintenance of the exclusion of this duty is outweighed by the public interest in disclosing whether the public authority holds the information. Despite its superficial similarity, this public interest balancing exercise is materially different from that employed for the purpose of determining whether the duty to communicate does not apply.[123] As a general rule, the broader the terms of the request, the more difficult it will become for the public authority to contend that the public interest in excluding the duty to confirm or deny that such information is held by it outweighs the public interest in compliance with that duty; if only because it will be self-evident that the public authority does hold information of that description.

21–022 Scotland

The Scottish exemption is much wider, covering any information for which a claim to 'confidentiality of communications' could be maintained in legal proceedings.[124] In Scotland priests may have a form of privilege not recognised in England and Wales.[125] There already existed in Scottish law a general judicial discretion not to require answers that may betray

---

[119] *Kessler v IC and HMRC*, IT, 29 November 2007 at [70].

[120] *R v Craig* [1975] 1 NZLR 597 (NZ); *R v Dunbar and Logan* (1982) 138 DLR (3d) 221 at 252; *R v McClure* (2001) 195 DLR (4th) 513, [2001] 1 SCR 45; *R v Brown* [2002] 210 DLR (4th) 341 (Canada); *R v Ataou* [1988] QB 798, but over-ruled in *R v Derby Magistrates' Court, ex p B* [1996] 1 AC 487; *Carter v The Managing Partner, Northmore Hale Davy & Leake*, (unreported) 15 July 1993, Supreme Court of Western Australia (Full Court) at 30–31 (Rowland J).

[121] *Carter v The Managing Partner, Northmore Hale Davy & Leake* (1995) 183 CLR 121.

[122] FOIA s 42(2).

[123] See §§15–018 to 15–019 as to what it involves.

[124] FOIA s 42(2); FOI(S)A s 36(1).

[125] ID Macphail, *Research paper on the Law of Evidence of Scotland* (Edinburgh, Scottish Law Commission, 1979) paras 18.38–18.40; D Field, *The Law of Evidence in Scotland* (Edinburgh, W Green, 1988) p 265. Compare the position in England: *R v Hay* (1860) 2 F & F 4; *Pais v Pais* [1971] P 119, though the waiver analysis in this case is questionable if there is no privilege recognised.

confidences, even though the evidence is otherwise relevant and admissible.[126]

023 Related FOI exemptions

There is a separate exemption for communications relating to advice given by Law Officers.[127] Law Officers include the Attorney-General, Solicitor General, Advocate General for Scotland, Lord Advocate, Solicitor-General for Scotland and the Attorney-General for Northern Ireland.[128]

024 The Data Protection Act 1998

To the extent that a person applies for information relating to himself, that application will fall to be decided by the Data Protection Act 1998 and not by the Freedom of Information Act 2000.[129] The Data Protection Act 1998 exempts privileged documents from the non-disclosure provisions.[130] As with all exemptions under the Data Protection Act 1998, there is no public interest 'override', but otherwise the principles are the same as under s 34 of the Freedom of Information Act 2000.

---

[126] *HM Advocate v Airs* 1975 JC 64 at 70, SLT 177 at 180. However this is unlikely to be a sufficient explanation for the very different Scottish FOI exemption, as a similar discretion operated in England: *AG v Clough* [1963] 1 QB 773 at 792; *AG v Mulholland* [1963] 2 QB 477 at 489–490, 492.

[127] FOIA s 35(1)(c).

[128] FOIA s 35(5).

[129] See §5–002. So, too, if the information is 'environmental information': see §6–050.

[130] DPA s 35; also see Sch 7 para 10.

CHAPTER 22
Policy Formulation and Public Affairs

1. INTRODUCTION

001 Overview

This chapter is concerned with two connected provisions of the Freedom of Information Act 2000 which exempt:

—   information relating to government policy and ministerial communications;[1] and

—   information the disclosure of which would be prejudicial to the conduct of public affairs.[2]

The first of these exemptions applies only to information held by government departments or by the National Assembly for Wales: it does not apply to information held by any other public authority.[3] This exemption is a purely class-based exemption, such that it does not matter that harm will not result from disclosure of the information concerned.[4] The exemption is a qualified exemption, so that even if information falls within the description of the exemption, it is then necessary to consider whether the public interest favours disclosure or the maintenance of the exemption. The second exemption can apply to information held by any type of public authority, but so far as information held by a government department or the National Assembly of Wales is concerned, those bodies may only rely on it if the first exemption is inapplicable. The second exemption is a prejudice-based exemption. It is only applicable if disclosure would, or would be likely to, prejudice the effective conduct of public affairs in any one or more of the ways specified in s 36(2). This exemption is an absolute exemption in the case where the information is held by the House of Commons or the House of Lords; but otherwise it is a qualified exemption.[5] Where (or to the extent that) a request for information is for 'environmental information'[6] the obligation to disclose that information will fall to be determined by the Environmental Information Regulations 2004 and not by the Freedom of Information Act 2000.[7] The Environmental Information Regulations 2004 provide no exception that is directly comparable to either of these two exemptions. The Environmental Information Regulations 2004 do, however, provide a qualified exception for 'internal

---

[1]   FOIA s 35; FOI(S)A s 29.

[2]   FOIA s 36. The comparable provision in the FOI(S)A s 30, is in materially different terms: see §22– 021.

[3]   In relation to information held by Scottish public authorities, the comparable exemption is only applicable to information held by the Scottish Administration.

[4]   Though it may be relevant to a consideration of the public interest. In *DWP v IC*, IT, 5 March 2007, the Tribunal observed that 'the exemption in s 35(1)(a)... is a "class" exemption... in order for the exemption to be engaged the public authority does not need to demonstrate that any specific prejudice or harm would flow from the disclosure of the information in question... [in considering whether the public interest in maintaining the exemption outweighs the public interest in disclosure of the information sought] it is relevant to consider what specific harm would flow from the disclosure of the particular information in question' at [23]-[24]. This statement was approved by Mitting J in *ECGD v Friends of the Earth* [2008] EWHC 638 (Admin) at [28].

[5]   FOIA s 2(3)(e); FOI(S)A s 2(2).

[6]   As to the meaning of which, see §§6– 008 to 6– 011.

[7]   Where the request is made for information held by a Scottish public authority, it will fall to be determined by the EI(S)R and not by the FOI(S)A.

communications'.[8] The exception is neither content-related (cf s 35) nor prejudice based (cf s 36), with the result that the principles relating to ss 35 and 36 cannot be readily transposed to the exception under the Regulations.[9] The internal communications exception is separately considered in Chapter 6.[10]

22– 002   Application of the 'public interest' test

Apart from information held by the House of Commons or the House of Lords,[11] the exemptions considered in this chapter are all qualified. Accordingly, even if information falls within any of the descriptions in s 35 or s 36, the duty to disclose (and the duty to confirm or deny) will still apply unless the public interest in maintaining the exemption outweighs the public interest in disclosure (or the public interest in maintaining the exclusion of the duty to confirm or deny outweighs the public interest in disclosing whether the public authority holds the information). Thus, s 36 of the Freedom of Information Act 2000 allows for the possibility that the disclosure of information relating to public affairs being prejudicial to the interests described in s 35, but nonetheless being in the public interest. By contrast, policy information falling under s 35 of the Act is exempt from the duty of disclosure irrespective of whether or not its disclosure would be 'prejudicial'. However, the fact that no prejudice would be caused to anyone by the disclosure of such information in any given case may well count as a significant consideration in favour of it being in the public interest that the exemption should not be maintained and that the information should be disclosed. As with the other qualified exemptions, the relevant decision-maker will have to take into account all of the circumstances of the case and any relevant provisions of the European Convention for the Protection of Human Rights and Fundamental Freedoms.[12] The weighing of the competing public interests poses particular problems in relation to information that falls within s 35(1). As noted previously,[13] on one side of the 'balance' introduced by s 2 is the public interest in *maintaining the exemption*: it is not the public interest in non-disclosure. A public authority must therefore identify the public interest that is expressed in the particular exemption and adjudge the extent to which disclosure of each item of information falling within the terms of the request would offend that public interest. The exercise requires the public authority to stand back and abnegate its own interests except and in so far as those interests are properly viewed as part of the public interest. Where what is at stake is national security, the defence of the realm, international relations, criminal investigations and so forth, that task is difficult, but may be achieved through a disciplined thought process. The public interest in maintaining an exemption for information held by a government department relating to 'the formulation or development of public policy' (to use the first of the limbs of exemption in s 35(1))[14] presents two

---

[8]   EIR reg 12(4)(e); EI(S)R reg 10(4)(e).

[9]   Although the public interest in maintaining the exception bears a similarity with the public interest in maintaining the exemptions.

[10]   §6– 047.

[11]   But only in so far as the exemption provided by s 36 is concerned.

[12]   See ch 3.

[13]   §§15– 001 and 15– 010.

[14]   The point applies equally to the other three limbs of exemption in s 35(1).

additional challenges. First, there is nothing in the description itself that urges non-disclosure; or at least not without some rejection of the underlying premise of all freedom of information legislation.[15] This is further evidenced by the limited range of public authorities to which the exemption applies: if there is a public interest served by exempting information relating to the formulation or development of policy, it is not immediately obvious why that public interest stops with government departments and does not include the formulation or development of policy of, say, a local authority. Secondly and largely because of the first, a public authority's self-interest in non-disclosure of this class of information is apt to be presented or even perceived as the public interest in maintaining the exemption, with the public authority effectively determining its own cause. The exemptions therefore require government departments to steel themselves, and where required find that the public interest in maintaining these exemptions is outweighed by the public interest in disclosure.[16]

003 Inter-relationship between the two provisions

Apart from the restriction of s 35 to 'information held by a government department or by the National Assembly for Wales', the two provisions have a fair measure of overlap. In particular, the proceedings of the Cabinet, of the Executive Committee of the Northern Ireland Assembly and of the executive committee of the National Assembly for Wales are apt to be caught by both provisions. Similarly, it is to be anticipated that it will often be claimed that the disclosure of information relating to the formulation or development of government policy would, or would be likely to, inhibit the free and frank exchange of views for the purpose of deliberation. The inapplicability of s 36 to information held by a government department or by the National Assembly for Wales that is not exempt information by virtue of s 35[17] has wide-reaching consequences. Because s 35 is purely class based and because it is cast in such wide terms, there will be much that will be 'exempt information by virtue of s 35'. As noted above, the commonplace attributes required to render information exempt under s 35 may often result in a public authority struggling to conclude that the public interest in maintaining that exemption outweighs the public interest in disclosure, with the result that that provision may well not operate to disapply the disclosure or existence duty. However, the result of the public interest weighing exercise does not affect the inapplicability of s 36 to such information. The criterion in s 36(1)(a) is that it not be 'exempt information by virtue of section 35'. Where the public interest in maintaining the exemption does not outweigh the public interest in disclosing the information, s 2(2) does not metamorphose that exempt information into non-exempt information: it merely disapplies the rights conferred by s 1(1) of the Act in relation to that exempt information. Thus, it is to be anticipated that there will be circumstances where a government department holding information relating to, say, the formulation of government policy finds that the public interest in maintaining the s 35 exemption does not outweigh the

---

[15] In *OGC v IC* [2008] EWHC 774 (Admin), [2008] ACD 54 Stanley Burnton J confirmed that s 35 does not create a presumption of a public interest in non-disclosure [75-79]. This was applied in *DBERR v IC and Friends of the Earth*, IT, 29 April 2008 at [103].

[16] To do otherwise will effectively promote the exemptions into absolute exemptions. These propositions (as set out identically in the 1st edition of this text) were approved expressly by the Information Tribunal in *DWP v IC*, IT, 5 March 2007 at [31]–[32].

[17] See FOIA s 36(1)(a). This does not apply under the FOI(S)A: information can be rendered exempt information upon both ss 29 and 30 of the Act.

public interest in disclosure, but is unable to look to s 36 as an alternative means of refusing disclosure of the information. Because the public interest exercise is concerned with the *maintenance* of the exemption conferred by the particular provision it will not be permissible to sweep in under the rubric of 'the public interest' the attributes which, in s 36(2), are used to render information exempt information. To do that would make s 36(1)(a) pointless.

22–004 Legislative history

The two kinds of information that are now dealt with separately in ss 35 and 36 of the Freedom of Information Act 2000 were not distinguished in the 1997 White Paper. Instead, they were both considered under the single heading of information relating to government decision-making and policy advice.[18] In the White Paper, the Government proposed that the question of whether or not such information would be disclosed should be determined by a test of 'harm', whereas the test to be applied in the great majority of cases would be one of 'substantial harm'.[19] The draft Bill published in May 1999 substituted the term 'prejudice' for that of 'harm' as the key term in the applicable test,[20] and made information now falling within the scope of s 35 of the Freedom of Information Act 2000 subject to a purely class-based exemption.[21] The 'prejudice' test and the introduction of a class-based exemption in respect of policy information held by government departments were also retained in the Bill published in November 1999,[22] which later became the Freedom of Information Act 2000.

22–005 Controversies surrounding the form of the exemptions

The provisions of the Freedom of Information Bills concerning government information were recognised to be 'one of the especially difficult areas for freedom of information legislation'.[23] Both the introduction of a class-based exemption in relation to policy information held by government departments and the imposition of a test of 'prejudice' rather than 'substantial prejudice' in respect of information relating to public affairs were controversial. They were roundly criticised both at the Committee stage and in Parliament.[24] In particular, the

---

[18] Cabinet Officer, *Your Right to Know: The Government's Proposals for a Freedom of Information Act* (Cm 3818, 1997) para 3.12.

[19] Cabinet Officer, *Your Right to Know: The Government's Proposals for a Freedom of Information Act* (Cm 3818, 1997) paras 3.7, 3.12. The decision to impose a simple 'harm' test on such information rather than a test of 'substantial harm' was explained on the basis that 'now, more than ever, government needs space and time in which to assess arguments and conduct its own debates with a degree of privacy. Experience from overseas suggests that the essential governmental functions of planning ahead, delivering solutions to issues of national importance and determining options on which to base policy decisions while still maintaining collective responsibility, can be damaged by random and premature disclosure of its deliberations under Freedom of Information legislation ...': para 3.12.

[20] This was done in order to make the Bill consistent in its terminology with other legislation including, notably, the DPA and the Local Government Act 1972: see House of Commons Select Committee on Public Administration, *Third Report* (Cm 4355, 1999) para 65.

[21] Clause 28.

[22] Clauses 33 and 34.

[23] House of Commons Select Committee on Public Administration, *Third Report* (Cm 4355, 1999) para 83.

[24] For criticism of the former class-based exemption, see, eg, House of Commons Select Committee on Public Administration, *Third Report* (Cm 4355, 1999) para 89; Mr Robert McLennan MP, Hansard HC vol 340 col 748 (7 December 1999); Lord Mackay of Ardbrecht, Hansard HL vol 618 col 275–276 (24 October 2000). For criticisms of the imposition of a test of 'prejudice' as opposed to 'substantial prejudice', see, eg, House of Lords, *Draft Freedom of Information Bill: First Report*, 27 July 1999, paras 32, 34–35.

introduction of a class-based exemption in respect of policy information held by government departments was objected to on the basis that the exemption was more restrictive than the provisions of the Code that applied in respect of this kind of information, according to which such information should only be withheld if its disclosure would harm the frankness and candour of internal discussion, and if that harm outweighed the public interest in openness.[25]

006 Justification for the current form of the exemptions

The Government nevertheless insisted that the exemptions in respect of policy information and of information relating to public affairs were both justified. The imposition of a class-based exemption in respect of policy information was said to be necessary on the basis that, while the purpose of the Freedom of Information Bill was to increase openness in government, it was 'appropriate that policy-making should not take place in a goldfish bowl' and that there should be a process which allowed Ministers, public authorities and civil servants 'to exchange views in a way that they feel will be private to give them space to think and make decisions'.[26] The preference for a test of 'prejudice' as opposed to 'substantial prejudice' was explained on the basis that a public authority who sought to justify a decision to apply the exemption from the duty of disclosure to information relating to public policy on the basis that its disclosure would cause 'prejudice' of the relevant kind would in any event be required to show that the prejudice in question, or the risk of prejudice, was 'real, actual or of substance'. Consequently, there was nothing to be gained by including an additional requirement in the Bill that any 'prejudice' should also be 'substantial'.[27] The fact that 'prejudice', when viewed properly, entails real, actual or substantial prejudice provides a further indication of the Government's rationale in subjecting policy-information to a class-based exemption, rather than a 'simple prejudice' exemption.[28]

---

[25] See eg, Lord Mackay of Ardbrecht, Hansard HL vol 618 col 275–276 (24 October 2000). It is to be noted that in the 1997 White Paper, the Government itself criticised the Code of Practice on the basis that the tests for harm contained therein were 'insufficient'. In particular, the exemptions contained in the Code of Practice, for the most part, gave 'no indication of the extent of harm against which the disclosure or withholding of the information should be judged'. In the Government's view, as expressed in the White Paper, 'the test to determine whether disclosure is to be refused should normally be set in specific and demanding terms. We therefore propose to move in most areas from a simple harm test to a substantial harm test, namely will the disclosure of this information cause substantial harm?' — *Your Right to Know: The Government's Proposals for a Freedom of Information Act*, paras 3.6–3.7. Note also that, whereas the White Paper proposed (in para 3.12) that a simple harm test should nevertheless be retained in respect of information relating to government decision-making and policy advice, the Government's final position, as explained by Lord Falconer of Thoroton, appears to be that the test of 'prejudice' applicable in respect of information relating to public affairs in fact requires a demonstration of 'substantial prejudice' before the exemption can be said to apply.

[26] Hansard HL vol 612 col 827 (20 April 2000) (Lord Falconer). The explanation of the rationale for the exemption illuminates the public interest weighing exercise: if the policy decision has been made by the time that the request is received there will be little public interest in maintaining the exemption; they will have had their space to think and make decisions. Moreover, so far as the existence duty is concerned, it is difficult to see how confirming or denying that information is held should stop anyone of normal sensitivity from having 'space to think and make decisions'.

[27] Lord Falconer of Thoroton, Hansard HL vol 612 col 827 (20 April 2000).

[28] That is, in accordance with the approach taken in the White Paper (*Your Right to Know: The Government's Proposals for a Freedom of Information Act*, paras 3.6 to 3.7 and 3.12).

2. INFORMATION RELATING TO THE FORMULATION OF GOVERNMENT POLICY, ETC

22– 007 Introduction

Information held by a government department or by the National Assembly for Wales is exempt information if it relates to:

    (a)   the formulation or development of government policy;[29]

    (b)   Ministerial communications;[30]

    (c)   the provision of advice by any of the Law Officers or any request for the provision of such advice;[31] or

    (d)   the operation of any Ministerial private office.[32]

As noted at the outset of this Chapter, the exemption applies only to information held by government departments or by the National Assembly for Wales: it does not apply to information held by any other public authority.[33] The exemption has four discrete limbs, which need to be considered separately. So far as the first and second limbs of the exemption are concerned, special provision is made in relation to background statistical information.[34] So far as the first limb is concerned, special provision is also made in relation to background factual information.[35] The exemption is a qualified exemption,[36] and there is a corresponding exclusion of the duty to confirm or deny.[37] In relation to each of the limbs, the required connection is that the information 'relate to' what is described by the limb. The phrase 'relate to' and cognate expressions are notoriously vague.[38]

---

[29]   FOIA s 35(1)(a); FOI(S)A s 29(1)(a). 'Government policy' is defined in FOIA s 35(5), and in FOI(S)A s 29(4).

[30]   FOIA s 35(1)(b); FOI(S)A s 29(1)(b). 'Ministerial communications' is defined in FOIA s 35(5), and in FOI(S)A s 29(4).

[31]   FOIA s 35(1)(c); FOI(S)A s 29(1)(c). 'The Law Officers' is defined in FOIA s 35(5), and in FOI(S)A s 29(4).

[32]   FOIA s 35(1)(d); FOI(S)A s 29(1)(d). 'Ministerial private office' is defined in FOIA s 35(5), and in FOI(S)A s 29(4).

[33]   In relation to information held by Scottish public authorities, the comparable exemption is only applicable to information held by the Scottish Administration.

[34]   FOIA s 35(2); FOI(S)A s 29(2). See §22– 016.

[35]   FOIA s 35(4); FOI(S)A s 29(3). See §22– 017.

[36]   See §§22– 001 to 22– 002.

[37]   FOIA s 35(3). There is no separate duty to confirm or deny under the FOI(S)A. See §22– 019.

[38]   See, eg: *R v Smith* [1975] QB 531 at 542B ('the words "relating to" are very wide. They are equivalent to "connected with" or "arising out of"') (Lord Denning). The active voice suggests that the required link to the protected interest may need to be apparent from the information itself. Thus, in *Tooheys Limited v Commissioner of Stamp Duties* (1961) 105 CLR 602 at 622 Taylor J said that 'the vital question is whether the instrument "relates" and not whether it may be "related" by an examination of extraneous circumstances.' Authorities considering the phrase in other contexts are illustrative of the interpretive technique used to resolve the flexibility inherent in the phrase: *Rein v Lane* (1867) LR 2 QB 144; *R v Sheffield Crown Court ex p Brownlow* [1980] QB 530 at 538G-539D; *re Smalley* [1985] AC 622 at 643D-644F; *R v Central Criminal Court ex p Randle* [1991] 1 WLR 1087; *Tooheys Limited v. Commissioner of Stamp Duties* (1961) 105 CLR 602 at 613-614, 617, 619 and 620-622; *PMT Partners P/L v. Aust National Parks and Wildlife Services* (1995) 184 CLR 301 at 313 and 330-331, where there is a survey of various other authorities; *EH v Information Commissioner* [2002] 3 IR 600; *Rotunda Hospital v Information Commissioner* [2009] IEHC 315; *Durant v FSA* [2003] EWCA Civ 1746. The last three are concerned with the meaning of the phrase in the context of a right to personal

008 Formulation or development of government policy: scope

The first limb of s 35(1) renders material exempt information if it relates to the formulation or development of government policy. A broadly similar class of exemption is found in most of the comparable jurisdictions, with differences partly reflecting the differences in the systems of governance.[39] 'Government policy' is defined to include the policy of the Executive Committee of the Northern Ireland Assembly and the policy of the National Assembly for Wales.[40] The 1997 White Paper considered that there was a readily-identifiable core class of documents and materials that contain information falling within the exemption, including 'high-level' government records such as Cabinet and Committee papers,[41] as well as draft consultation papers and advice on policy prepared by civil servants for the benefit of Ministers. The House of Commons Select Committee on Public Administration, on the other hand, doubted that 'information relating to the formulation or development of policy' was a sufficiently well-defined class of information. It also took the view that such information should be included within the scope of the prejudice-based exemption contained in what is now s 36 of the Freedom of Information Act 2000.[42] In *Department for Education and Skills v Information Commissioner and Evening Standard*, the Tribunal concluded that, while the presence of s 36 might be some indication that s 35 should not be too liberally construed, the phrases 'relates to' and 'formulation and development of policy' should be given a reasonably broad interpretation.[43] By way of example, the Tribunal noted that if a meeting or a discussion of a particular topic within it was as a whole caught by s 35(1)(a) activities, then everything that was said and done is covered by s 35.[44] Further, the immediate factual background to policy discussions is itself caught by s 35(1)(a).[45] There are two grey areas in relation to the limb, at least at its extremities:

(1) in determining what is and what is not 'policy'; and

---

information. Generally, the authorities illustrate that resolution of any uncertainty is guided by an interpretation that will secure the object of the legislation without creating results that unnecessarily cut across existing legal rights or otherwise creating harsh results. See also: §§5– 022 and 17– 035.

[39] In the United States, the Freedom of Information Act, 1966, 5 USC 552(b)(5), exempts from disclosure records that enjoy 'deliberative process privilege': see §2– 008(5). The Freedom of Information Act 1982 (Cth of Australia) s 47C, provides an exemption in relation to 'matter in the nature of, or relating to, opinion, advice or recommendation …in the course of the deliberative processes involved in the functions of an agency or Minister …and [the disclosure of which] would be contrary to the public interest': see §2– 015(11). The Official Information Act 1982 (New Zealand), ss 6(e) and 27(1)(a), provides a comparatively narrow, but absolute, exemption for information relating to decisions to change or continue government economic or financial policies: see §2– 022(5). The Access to Information Act 1985 (Canada) s 21(1), provides a discretionary exemption for records that contain advice or recommendations developed by or for a government institution or a minister of the Crown and for any account of governmental consultations or deliberations: see §2– 032(4) and (5). The Freedom of Information Act 1997 (Ireland) s 20(1), provides a discretionary exemption where the record contains matter relating to the deliberative process of the public body: see §2– 039(9).

[40] FOIA s 35(5).

[41] Cabinet Office, *Your Right to Know: The Government's Proposals for a Freedom of Information Act* (Cm 3813, 1997) para 3.12.

[42] House of Commons Select Committee on Public Administration, *Third Report* (Cm 4355, 1999) para 89.

[43] *DfES v IC and The Evening Standard*, IT, 19 February 2007 at [52]–[53]. In *O'Brien v IC and DBERR*, IT, 7 October 2008, the Tribunal held (at [20]) that information does not have to come into existence before the policy is formed for s 35(1)(a) to apply.

[44] *DfES v IC and The Evening Standard*, IT, 19 February 2007 at [58].

[45] A conclusion said to be supported by s 35(4): *DfES v IC and The Evening Standard*, IT, 19 February 2007 at [55].

(2)   in determining when the 'formulation or development' of policy starts and ends. In relation to the first area, the wording of the limb appears to contemplate a dichotomy between 'policy' decisions and operational decisions made by government departments, with information relating to the latter falling outside of the scope of the exemption. As was recognised at the time of the Bill, however, the distinction will not always be clear,[46] and this is borne out by those occasions on which the word has been subject to judicial consideration.[47] In *Department for Education and Skills v Information Commissioner and Evening Standard*, the Tribunal recognised that s 35(2) appeared to envisage policy being formulated as a series of decisions rather than a continuing process of evolution.[48] This was confirmed in *Secretary of State for Work and Pensions v Information Commissioner* which found that on the facts of that case the two stage decision and policy formulation process could be considered separately at each stage rather than as a continuum.[49]   In relation to the second area, s 35(2) recognises that at some identifiable point a decision will be taken as to government policy such that it can no longer be said to be being formulated or developed. In *Department for Education and Skills v Information Commissioner and Evening Standard*, the Tribunal stated that when the formulation or development of a particular policy is complete is a question of fact.[50] The Tribunal concluded that:

> ... a parliamentary statement announcing the policy... will normally mark the end of the process of formulation. There may be some interval before development. We do not imply by that that any public interest in maintaining the exemption disappears the moment that a minister rises to his or her feet in the House... each case must be decided in the light of the circumstances. As is plain however, we do not regard a "seamless web" approach to policy as a helpful guide to the question whether discussions on formulation are over.[51]

It is not clear whether information relating to a review of the practical efficacy of a policy

---

[46]   The breadth of the exemption under s 35(1)(a) was objected to in Parliament: see, eg, Hansard HL vol 618 col 276 (24 October 2000). The Campaign for Freedom of Information described the exemption under s 35(1)(a) of the Freedom of Information Act 2000 as a 'gigantic' class exemption: see col 278.

[47]   In *Bushell v Secretary of State for the Environment* [1981] AC 75, which involved consideration of the refusal by an Inspector at a public inquiry into the construction of certain motorways to permit certain questions by way of cross-examination, Lord Diplock (at 98B) said: '"Policy" as descriptive of departmental decisions to pursue a particular course of conduct is a protean word and much confusion in the instant case has, in my view, been caused by the failure to define the sense in which it can properly be used to describe a topic which is unsuitable to be the subject of an investigation as to the merits at an inquiry at which only persons with local interests affected by the scheme are entitled to be represented. A decision to construct a nationwide network of motorways is clearly one of government policy in the widest sense of the word.' Lord Edmund Davies said (at 115D)'...matters of policy are matters which involve the exercise of political judgment, and matters of fact and expertise do not become "policy" merely because a department of government relies on them.' In *Auckland Regional Council v North Shore City Council* [1995] 3 NZLR 18 at 23 the New Zealand Court of Appeal expressed similar sentiments in attempting to ascertain the meaning of the word 'policy' in the Resources Management Act 1991: 'It is obvious that in ordinary present-day speech a policy may be either flexible or inflexible, either broad or narrow. Honesty is said to be the best policy. Most people would prefer to take some discretion in implementing it, but if applied remorselessly it would not cease to be a policy. Counsel for the defendants are on unsound ground in suggesting that in everyday speech or in parliamentary drafting or in etymology, policy cannot include something highly specific.'

[48]   *DfES v IC and The Evening Standard*, IT, 19 February 2007 at [57]. Similarly: *DWP v IC*, IT, 5 March 2007 at [56], [100]; *Office of Commerce v IC*, IT, 2 May 2007 at [56] (where the Tribunal drew a distinction between information relating to policy formulation or review and information concerned with implementation and delivery of those policies).

[49]   *DWP v IC*, IT, 5 March 2007 at [56].

[50]   *DfES v IC and The Evening Standard*, IT, 19 February 2007 at [75(v)].

[51]   *DfES v IC and The Evening Standard*, IT, 19 February 2007 at [75(v)].

already in place is properly to be characterised as representing information relating to the development of that policy.

009 Formulation or development of government policy: comparative jurisdictions
In each of the comparative jurisdictions there exists a similar exemption.

(1) In the USA, the Freedom of Information Act 1966 provides an exemption for inter-agency or intra-agency memoranda or letters 'which would not be available by law to a party other than an agency in litigation with the agency'.[52] This has been interpreted to mean records that would normally be privileged in civil proceedings. These privileges are broader than those that are enjoyed by a public authority in the United Kingdom and include deliberative process privilege, also known as 'executive privilege'. This protects records revealing the deliberative policymaking process of government. The Supreme Court has held that 'deliberative process privilege' exists to 'prevent injury to the quality of agency decisions'.[53] The injuries are thought to be occasioned by:

(i) an impairment of open, frank discussions on matters of policy between subordinates and superiors;

(ii) premature disclosure of proposed policies before they are finally adopted; and

(iii) public confusion that might result from disclosure of reasons and rationales that were not in fact ultimately the grounds for an agency's action.[54]

(2) In Canada, the Access to Information Act provides a discretionary exemption for advice or recommendations developed by or for a government institution or a minister of the Crown.[55] In relation to this exemption, the Federal Court has held that:

> despite the importance of governmental openness as a safeguard against the abuse of power, and as a necessary condition for democratic accountability, it is equally clear that governments must be allowed a measure of confidentiality in the policy-making process. To permit or to require the disclosure of advice given by officials, either to other officials or to ministers, and the disclosure of confidential deliberations within the public service on policy options, would erode government's ability to formulate and to justify its policies. It would be an intolerable burden to force ministers and their advisors to disclose to public scrutiny the internal evolution of the policies ultimately adopted. Disclosure of such material would often reveal that the policy-making process included false starts, blind alleys, wrong turns, changes of mind, the solicitation and rejection of advice, and the re-evaluation of priorities and the re-weighing of the relative importance of the relevant factors as a problem is studied more closely. In the hands of journalists or political opponents this is combustible material liable to fuel a fire that could quickly destroy governmental credibility and effectiveness. On the other hand, of course, democratic principles require that the public, and

---

[52] 5 USC 552(b)(5). Discussed further at §2–008(5).

[53] *National Labor Relations Board v Sears, Roebuck & Co* (1975) 421 US 132 at 151.

[54] *Russell v Department of the Air Force*, 682 F 2d 1045 (DC Cir 1982); *Coastal States Gas Corp v Department of Energy*, 617 F 2d 854 (DC Cir 1980); *Jordan v United States Department of Justice*, 591 F 2d 753 (DC Cir 1978).

[55] Section 21(1)(a). Considered further at §2–032(4).

this often means the representatives of sectional interests, are enabled to participate as widely as possible in influencing policy development. Without a degree of openness on the part of government about its thinking on public policy issues, and without access to relevant information in the possession of government, the effectiveness of public participation will inevitably be curbed.[56]

(3) In Australia, the Freedom of Information Act 1982 provides an exemption for documents that record the deliberative process of the federal government[57] the disclosure of which would be contrary to the public interest. In considering the public interest for the purposes of this provision, the Federal Court of Australia had held that disclosure of communications made in the course of the development and subsequent promulgation of policy tends not to be in the public interest and that the disclosure of such documents could inhibit frankness and candour in future pre-decisional communications as well as lead to confusion and 'unnecessary debate'. In particular, disclosure of documents that did not fairly disclose the reasons for a decision subsequently taken might be unfair to a decision-maker and may prejudice the integrity of the decision-making process.[58] This view, briefly held,[59] subsequently lost judicial favour,[60] although the argument continued to be run from time to time.[61] There remains a rift in judicial view, but with the majority taking the line that if the candour is to be successful, the public authority is obliged 'to demonstrate, as a factual rather than theoretical proposition, that disclosure would be contrary to the public interest.'[62]

---

[56] *Canadian Council of Christian Charities v Canada (Minister of Finance)* [1999] 4 FC 245 at [30]–[32].

[57] Freedom of Information Act 1982 s 47C. Considered further at §2– 015(11).

[58] *Re Howard and the Treasurer* (1985) 7 ALD 626, 3 AAR 169, in which the then Deputy Leader of the Opposition sought access to the documents provided by the Treasurer or his department to the Australian Council of Trade Unions during the government's bargaining session over the content and shape of the 1984/85 Budget. See also *Harris v Australian Broadcasting Corporation* (1983) 50 ALR 551, 78 FLR 236. These decisions were given early in the regime, with Davies J expressly acknowledging in *Re Howard* (at 635) that as time went on and with greater experience it might be necessary to revisit the principles he laid out. Later Australian decisions have been more circumspect in their acceptance of the candour argument: *Re Rae and Department of Prime Minister and Cabinet* (1986) 12 ALD 589; *Re Fewster and Department of Prime Minister and Cabinet (No 2)* (1987) 13 ALD 139; *Re Kamenka and the Australian National University* (1992) 26 ALD 585; *Re Cleary and Department of the Treasury* (1993) 31 ALD 214; *Re Eccleston and Department of Family Services and Aboriginal and Islander Affairs* (1993) 1 QAR 60. Even before *Re Howard* scepticism had been expressed, with a requirement that any such claim be supported by evidence: *Murtagh v Federal Commissioner of Taxation* (1984) 84 ATC 4516.

[59] See §22– 025 and §22– 026.

[60] In *General Manager, Workcover Authority of New South Wales v Law Society of New South Wales* [2006] NSWCA 84 at [154] the New South Wales Court of Appeal considered that the earlier decisions (such as *Re Howard*) were derived from Crown privilege authorities and that these 'were not an apt point of reference…Freedom of information legislation, as the earlier discussion reveals, was intended to cast aside the era of closed government and principles developed in that era may, with the benefit of twenty or more years of experience, be seen as anachronisms.'

[61] *Accredited (Wholesale Tobacco) Distributors Pty Ltd v Griffiths* [2003] VSC 20. It has now been statutorily removed.

[62] *General Manager, Workcover Authority of New South Wales v Law Society of New South Wales* [2006] NSWCA 84 at [158]. In *McKinnon v Secretary, Department of Treasury* [2006] HCA 45, (2006) 229 ALR 187 Callinan and Heydon JJ dismissed evidence from a former Secretary of the Attorney-General's Department (who had also served as President of the Australian Law Reform Commission and as a member of the Administrative Review Council) of his experience that disclosure of information, even very sensitive information, did not impede candid advice to a minister: 'One must question his, indeed anyone's, ability to express an opinion of that kind. We would, for ourselves, have given it little weight, as we would his rejection of other grounds relied upon by the respondent based upon his own personal experience' (at [116]). Nevertheless, they found no difficulty in accepting the Minister's assertion to the opposite

(4)　In New Zealand, the Official Information Act 1982 provides a discretionary exemption where the withholding of the requested information is necessary to maintain the effective conduct of public affairs, through the free and frank expression of opinions by or between or to ministers or members of a specified organisation or officers and employees of any department, organisation, or local authority in the course of their duty; or through the protection of such ministers, members, officers, and employees from improper pressure or harassment.[63]

(5)　In Ireland, the Freedom of Information Act 1997 provides a discretionary exemption where the record contains matter relating to the deliberative process of the public body.[64]

010　Formulation or development of government policy: background

Section 35(1)(a) of the Freedom of Information Act 2000 resembles one of the grounds of public interest immunity that the Crown used to rely upon to avoid what would otherwise have been its disclosure obligations in litigation.[65] That exemption enjoyed diminishing success in the Courts over the last half of the twentieth century, partly on the basis of the countervailing public interest in disclosure but also because the very notion that potential disclosure would inhibit candour was received with increasing scepticism.[66] It is fair to say that some judges were more receptive to the sentiment than others, but the preponderance of judicial view leaned increasingly against the notion that the potential of disclosure would adversely affect the

---

effect: 'The second ground, which speaks of jeopardy to candour, and the desirability of written communications, obviously cannot readily be dismissed, and it seems to us that this is a matter upon which a Minister's opinion and experience are likely to be as well informed and valuable as those of anyone else, including senior officials' (at [121]). The Court did not identify the Minister's experience in these matters. In *McKinnon* there was a conclusive certificate under s 36(3), which rendered the question for the Tribunal one of whether there existed reasonable grounds for the claim that the disclosure of the document would be contrary to the public interest: cf FOIA s 36(2). Such certificates are no longer possible: Freedom of Information (Removal of Conclusive Certificates and Other Measures) Act 2009.

[63]　Official Information Act 1982 s 9(2)(g); Local Government Official Information and Meetings Act 1987 s 7(2)(f). Considered further at §2– 023(8).

[64]　Freedom of Information Act 1997 s 20(1). Factual and statistical material is excluded from the scope of the exemption. The exemption is disapplied where the public interest is better served by disclosure than by non-disclosure: Freedom of Information Act 1997 s 20(3). The relevant minister may issue a conclusive certificate if he takes the view that the exemption applies. Considered further at §2– 039(9).

[65]　This class of exemption was referred to in *Smith v East India Co* (1841) 1 Ph 50 at 55 (Lord Lyndhurst): 'it is quite obvious that public policy requires…that the most unreserved communication should take place ….that it should be subject to no restraints or limitations; but it is also quite obvious, that if, at the suit of a particular individual, those communications should be subject to be produced in a court of justice, the effect of that would be to restrain the freedom of the communications, and to render them more cautious, guarded and reserved.'

[66]　Starting with *Duncan v Cammell, Laird & Co* [1942] AC 642. In *Conway v Rimmer* [1968] AC 910 the House of Lords, whilst recognising that candour could be impaired by disclosure, rejected this as a class-claim. Lord Upjohn was more sceptical of the claim: '...the executive have relied upon the *Cammell, Laird* case to claim privilege in class cases on the ground that the public interest requires that the writings of every member of the executive from the highest to the lowest ….must be protected from production for the reason that the writer of the document must have a full, free and uninhibited right to pen his views without fear that they will ever be subject to the public gaze; in other words, secure in such knowledge he can then, and apparently only then, write with the complete candour necessary for the discharge of his functions as a member of the public service' (at 992). And later: 'I cannot believe that any Minister or any high level military official or civil servant would feel in the least degree inhibited in expressing his honest views in the course of his duty on some subject, such as even the personal qualifications and delinquencies of some colleague, by the thought that his observations might one day see the light of day' (at 994).

candour of civil servants:

> The notion that any competent and conscientious public servant would be inhibited at all
> in the candour of his writings by consideration of the off-chance that they might have to be
> produced in a litigation is in my opinion grotesque. To represent that the possibility of it
> might significantly impair the public service is even more so. Nowadays the state in
> multifarious manifestations impinges closely upon the lives and activities of individual
> citizens. Where this has involved a citizen in litigation with the state or one of its agencies,
> the candour argument is an utterly insubstantial ground for denying him access to relevant
> documents.[67]

Even before its formal abandonment, the position had been reached where the notion that
those involved in the formulation or development of government policy would be legitimately
inhibited in expressing their views or giving advice were it apprehended that those views or that
advice might be disclosed enjoyed diminished respect in the higher courts.[68] The concept is no
longer employed by government departments in support of public interest immunity claims.[69]

---

[67] *Burmah Oil Company Limited v Bank of England* [1980] AC 1090 at 1133 (Lord Keith). See also: *Sankey v Whitlam* (1978) 148 CLR 1 at 40 (Gibbs ACJ), 63 (Stephen J) and 96 (Mason J); *Williams v Home Office* [1981] 1 All ER 1151. Contrast with Lord Wilberforce in *Burmah Oil Company Limited v Bank of England* [1980] AC 1090 at 1112; *Air Canada v Secretary of State for Trade* [1983] 2 AC 394 at 437. The Tribunal in *Guardian Newspapers Ltd and Heather Brooke v IC and BBC*, IT, 8 January 2007 at [115] although questioning whether this statement was of particular assistance or relevance in the context of s 36, added that the passages served as 'a reminder that assertions of inhibition should perhaps not be too readily accepted.' In *DfES v IC and The Evening Standard*, IT, 19 February 2007 at [74] the Tribunal, after acknowledging different passages in *Conway v Rimmer* and *Burmah Oil*, said: '...we do not entirely ignore the fact that similar claims to those made to us have met with a degree of scepticism in much less transparent times than ours.'

[68] Starting with Lord Radcliffe in the *Glasgow Corporation v Central Land Board* 1956 SC (HL) 1 at 20 who said that he would have supposed Crown servants to be 'made of sterner stuff', a view shared by Harman LJ in *Re Grosvenor Hotel, London (No 2)* [1965] Ch 1210 at 1255E. In *Rogers v Home Secretary* [1973] AC 388 at 413E-F Lord Salmon spoke of a 'candour argument' run by the Attorney-General as 'smack[ing] of the old fallacy that any official in the government service would be inhibited from writing frankly and possibly at all unless he could be sure that nothing he wrote could ever be exposed to the light of day.' See also *R v SSHD, ex p Duggan* [1994] 3 All ER 277 at 285e.

[69] In a statement to the House of Commons on the future of public interest immunity in relation to Government documents, the Attorney-General (Sir Nicholas Lyell) spelled out that the new approach was to focus directly on the damage that disclosure would cause, with the former division between class exemptions and contents exemptions no longer being maintained: Hansard HC vol 287 cols 949–950 (18 December 1996); see also Hansard HC vol 297 cols 616–617 (11 July 1997). The Government's new approach was set out in a document that was placed in the libraries of both Houses of Parliament. Entitled *Annex C: Paper which Accompanied 1996 HMG Hansard Statement on PII*, it reiterates the abandonment of purely class-based claims (para.2.3), describing the distinction between class claims and contents claims as 'unhelpful and obscure' (para.3.3) and noting the particular difficulty with 'the advice to ministers class' (para.3.4). The new approach heralded is 'therefore based on the principle that PII can only ever apply where disclosure of material could cause real damage to the public interest' (para.4.1). In the section on 'Examples of the Government's approach', under the heading 'Internal discussion and advice' the paper states: 'The class is widely represented as reinforcing the executive's tendency to secrecy and unaccountability. In practice this type of PII claim is only considered, let alone made, on comparatively rare occasions, since it is only rarely this kind of document is relevant to litigation. Government documents should not attract PII on the basis of any special privilege but merely on the basis, as for any other document, that in certain circumstances their disclosure would cause real harm. The Government accepts that an approach to PII which claimed a kind of blanket protection for pre-defined categories of documents would be wrong in principle...A claim will not be made simply because the document constitutes high level advice to ministers' (paras 5.5–5.6, 5.12). Wholly absent from the document was any suggestion that a claim might be made out on the basis that disclosure would inhibit the candour of civil servants or somehow prevent the free and frank exchange of ideas.

Candour has, however, been successfully deployed in other contexts.[70] In any event, the Tribunal has repeatedly stated that it derives little assistance from these statements, which were made in a different era and in the context of civil litigation.[71]

011 Formulation or development of government policy: the public interest

The public interest generally thought to be embraced by this head of exemption is that disclosure of the deliberative process whilst it is being undertaken will cramp the ability of those engaging in it to freely explore the full range of options, including toying with the presently unthinkable.[72] The Government has described the adverse effects said to flow from such disclosure as being the loss of frankness and candour, a danger of government by cabal, the damaging effect of disclosure on difficult policy decisions, an impact on record-keeping and damage to relations between civil servants and ministers and to the role of civil servants in the formation of policy.[73] In *Department for Education and Skills v Information Commissioner and Evening*

---

[70] In *Cleveland County Council v F* [1995] 1 WLR 785, [1995] 2 All ER 236, [1995] 1 FLR 797 Hale J held that candour was a relevant consideration in determining an application to disclose material relating to wardship proceedings; see also *Oxfordshire County Council v L and F* [1997] 1 FLR 235, 251 (Stuart-White J) In *R (Persey) v Secretary of State for the Environment, Food and Rural Affairs* [2002] EWHC 371, [2003] 1 QB 794 the likely lack of candour of witnesses at a public inquiry into the outbreak of foot and mouth disease was a relevant consideration for the Secretary of State in determining that the inquiry into the disease should sit in private. *Compare R (Wagstaff) v Secretary of State for Health* [2001] 1 WLR 292, [2000] HRLR 646, [2000] UKHRR 875 the Divisional Court described the candour argument, which was there being used in support of the decision to hold in private an inquiry into a series of deaths caused by a NHS medical practitioner, as 'plainly now what might be described as a diminishing minority point of view, incapable in the circumstances of this case, where no vulnerable witnesses are apparently involved, of standing up to the weight of the arguments in favour of an open inquiry.'

[71] *Lord Baker of Dorking v IC and DCLG*, IT, 1 June 2007 at [19]; *DfES v IC and The Evening Standard*, IT, 19 February 2007 at [74]; *Guardian Newspapers Ltd v IC and BBC*, IT, 8 January 2007 at [115].

[72] See the quotations at §22–006. The fact that the 'thinking' has been thought worthy of articulation and then of being recorded in some form distinguishes it from the thinking and general discussion which generally precede the preparation of drafts, option statements and the like. It may be thought that the fact of something having been thought worthy of recording and official retention indicates that it has taken more definite form than the mere thoughts and discussion leading to it.

[73] *DfES v IC and The Evening Standard*, IT, 19 February 2007 at [35] (by way of evidence given by the former Cabinet Secretary and head of the civil service, Lord Turnbull). In *Office of Commerce v IC*, IT, 2 May 2007 Counsel for the public authority enumerated 14 types of adverse effect which were said would be likely to result should 'gateway review' reports become routinely discloseable soon after publication. A 'gateway review' is a review of a public delivery programme or procurement project carried out at a key decision point by a team of people independent of the team running the project: the objective of the review process is to secure best value for money in government procurement by examination of projects at critical stages through their life-cycle. The Tribunal (at [81]) rejected these collectively as being tantamount to a claim for absolute class exemption. Reiterating its stance in the *DWP* and *DfES* decisions in recognising 'that Government needs to operate in a safe space to protect information in the early stages of policy formulation and development', the Tribunal found (at [85]) that the public interest was not in the maintenance of the exemption because the critical decision (namely, to introduce identity cards) had already been taken, a Bill had been presented to Parliament and was being debated publicly: 'We therefore find that in the circumstances of this case it was no longer so important to maintain the safe space at the time of the requests.' That part of the Tribunal's decision was upheld by Stanley Burnton J in *OGC v IC* [2008] EWHC 774 (Admin), [2010] QB 98, [2008] ACD 54 at [100]-[101]. The Tribunal has declared itself unimpressed by claims that the risk of disclosure would have a chilling effect on the ability of Ministers to consider the full range of policy options and on the ability of civil servants to provide full and frank advice to Ministers: *HM Treasury v IC*, IT, 7 November 2007 at [61]-[63] and *ECGD v IC and Campaign Against Arms Trade*, IT, 21 October 2009 at [79]-[80]. The Tribunal has taken a similarly sceptical approach to assertions that a risk of disclosure would have an inhibiting effect upon lobbyists: see *MOD v IC and Evans*, IT, 20 July 2007 at [31], [33]-[34] and *DBERR v IC and Friends of the Earth*, IT, 29 April 2008 [113]-[134], and on non-civil servant Ministerial advisers, see *Cabinet Office v IC*, IT, 21 October 2008 at [29]-[30], and (in the context of the EIR) *SS for Transport v IC*, IT, 5 May 2009 at [124]-[126]. On the other hand, Mitting J in *ECGD v Friends of the Earth* [2008] EWHC 638 (Admin), [2008] Env LR 40, [2008] JPL 1813 (at [38]) was readier

Standard,[74] the Tribunal set out the following principles to be applied to disclosure where information falls within s 35 and the public authority claims that the public interest in maintaining that exemption outweighs the public interest in disclosure:

(i) The central question in every case is the content of the particular information in question. Every decision is specific to the particular facts and circumstances under consideration. Whether there may be significant indirect and wider consequences from the particular disclosure must be considered case by case.[75]

(ii) No information within s 35(1) is exempt from the duty of disclosure simply on account of its status, of its classification as minutes or advice to a minister nor of the seniority of those whose actions are recorded.

(iii) … the purpose of confidentiality, where the exemption is to be maintained, is the protection from compromise or unjust public opprobrium of civil servants, not ministers … we were unable to discern the unfairness in exposing an elected politician, after the event, to challenge for having rejected a possible policy option in favour of a policy which is alleged to have failed.

(iv) The timing of a request is of particular importance to the decision. We fully accept the … argument … that disclosure of discussions of policy options, whilst policy is in the process of formulation, is highly unlikely to be in the public interest, unless, for example, it would expose wrongdoing within government. Ministers and officials are entitled to time and space, in some instances to considerable time and space, to hammer out policy by exploring safe and radical policies alike …

(v) If the information requested is not in the public domain, we do not regard publication of other information relating to the same topic for consultation, information or other purposes as a significant factor in a decision as to disclosure.

(vii) In judging the likely consequences of disclosure on officials' future conduct, we are entitled to expect of them the courage and independence that has been the hallmark of our civil servants … These are highly educated and sophisticated public servants who well understand the importance of their impartial role as counsellors to ministers of conflicting convictions …

(viii) … there may be good reason in some cases for withholding the names of… junior civil servants who would never expect their roles to be exposed to public gaze. These are questions to be decided on the particular facts, not by blanket policy…

(ix) ….

---

to accept departmental prognostications in support of their claims for exemption, stating that 'there is a legitimate public interest in maintaining the confidentiality of advice within and between government departments on matters that will ultimately result, or are expected ultimately to result, in a ministerial decision. The weight to be given to those considerations will vary from case to case… But I can state with confidence that the cases in which it will not be appropriate to give any weight to those considerations will, if they exist at all, be few and far between' [38]. The notion of 'confidentiality of advice' within a public authority or between public authorities such as to weaken the rights conferred by FOIA is not without difficulty.

[74] *DfES v IC and The Evening Standard*, IT, 19 February 2007 at [75]. The Tribunal (at [66]) expressly rejected a statement of Lord Falconer that 'information of this nature should be disclosed only where it is in the public interest to do so' on the basis that it inverted the public interest test in FOIA s 2(2)(b). The Tribunal has since applied the reasoning in the *DfES* decision: *HM Treasury v IC*, IT, 7 November 2007 at [58]-[64]; *Scotland Office v IC*, IT, 5 August 2008 [47]-[73]; *Cabinet Office v IC*, IT, 21 October 2008 at [35]-[38]; *Bowden Consulting Ltd v IC and Cabinet Office*, IT, 26 August 2009 at [46]-[54]. See also *O'Brien v IC and DBERR*, IT, 7 October 2008 [37]-[39], a decision upheld in part by Wyn Williams J (he rejected a challenge to the Tribunal's reasoning in relation to s 35) in *DBERR v O'Brien and IC* [2009] EWHC 164 (QB) at [21]-[33].

[75] A passage approved by Mitting J in *ECGD v Friends of the Earth* [2008] EWHC 638 (Admin), [2008] Env LR 40, [2008] JPL 1813 at [28].

(x)   ....

(xi)   A blanket policy of refusing to disclose the names of civil servants wherever they appear in departmental records cannot be justified because, in many cases disclosure will do no harm to anyone, even if it does little good... There must... be a specific reason for omitting the name of the official where the document is otherwise disclosable. That reason may not need to be utterly compelling where, as will often be the case, there is little or no public interest in learning the name.

The Tribunal expressly rejected the notion that disclosing the names of the civil servants involved in making policy recommendations would prejudice them or their future role in the civil service.[76] Similarly, the Tribunal rejected the notion that the 'level' of a policy document could by itself provide support for the maintenance of the exemption:

Is the very status of these minutes, the fact that they record meetings of the most senior officials discussing the funding issue, a factor which supports the maintenance of the exemption? In our view, it is not. It may, in some or many cases, increase the sensitivity of the matters minuted, disclosing, for example, whilst policy is being reviewed, that radical options are being discussed at a very high level. If it does, that will be a factor which can properly be taken into consideration when a government department is confronted with an FOIA request. To treat such status as automatically conferring exemption would be tantamount to inventing within s 35(1) a class of absolutely exempt information, for which the subsection gives no warrant and is a stance which the DFES quite rightly disclaimed. However, we do not consider that the matter ends there. We agree with the DFES submission that the weighing of the public interests involves in this case a consideration of any evidence of a wider impact on the conduct of government which might result from the Commissioner's decision – Lord Turnbull's "secondary signals". That conclusion seems to us to flow from the introductory words of s 2(2)(b) quoted above, "in all the circumstances of the case". They include indirect consequences.[77]

In *Secretary of State for Work and Pensions v Information Commissioner*[78] the Tribunal asked two questions in order to determine the public interest in the information being disclosed. First, what is the intrinsic value of the information? Where the intrinsic value of the information is

---

[76]   At [68]. See also, in the context of FOIA s 36, *MoD v IC and Evans*, IT, 20 July 2007, in which the Tribunal stated 'those persons who expend public money must in general terms be expected to stand up and account for the activities they carry out in so doing' [60], and see [61]-[62]. But that does not mean that in all instances their names should be disclosed: see, eg,*DWP v IC*, IT, 5 March 2007 at [94]. In *DBERR v IC and Friends of the Earth*, IT, 29 April 2008 the Tribunal stated (at [101]):

(a) Senior officials of both the government department and lobbyists attending meetings and communicating with each other can have no expectation of privacy.
(b) The officials to whom this principle applies should not be restricted to the senior spokesperson for the organisation. It should also relate to any spokesperson.
(c) Recorded comments attributed to such officials at meetings should similarly have no expectation of privacy or secrecy.
(d) In contrast, junior officials, who are not spokespersons for their organisations or merely attend meetings as observers or stand-ins for more senior officials should have an expectation of privacy. This means that there may be circumstances where junior officials who act as spokespersons for their organisations are unable to rely on an expectation of privacy.
(e) The question as to whether a person is acting in a senior or junior capacity or as a spokesperson is one to be determined on the facts of each case...

[77]   At [69]-[70]. In *DWP v IC*, IT, 5 March 2007 at [82] the Tribunal reiterated that there is no necessary harm in the disclosure of information falling within s 35(1). In *FCO v IC and Friends of the Earth*, IT, 29 June 2007 a differently constituted Tribunal said that it was 'loath to regard that [ie that information could be exempt merely because of the seniority of those whose actions are recorded] as a principle of general application' at [42].

[78]   *DWP v IC*, IT, 5 March 2007.

greater, then the weightier is the public interest in maintaining the exemption.[79] Secondly, how relevant is the information to assist the public in understanding Government thinking on the relevant issue?[80]

22– 012 Information relating to ministerial communications: scope

The second limb of s 35(1) renders material exempt information if it relates to 'ministerial communications'. That phrase is defined to mean any communications between Ministers of the Crown; or between Northern Ireland Ministers, including Northern Ireland junior Ministers; or between Assembly Secretaries, including the Assembly Secretary.[81] The term also includes, in particular, proceedings of the Cabinet or of any committee of the Cabinet, proceedings of the Executive Committee of the Northern Ireland Assembly, and proceedings of the Executive Committee of the National Assembly for Wales. 'Northern Ireland junior Minister' is itself defined to mean a member of the Northern Ireland Assembly appointed as a junior Minister under s 19 of the Northern Ireland Act 1998.[82] It is to be noted that the exemption is for information that 'relates to' ministerial communications, rather than being for ministerial communications themselves.[83] Thus, information that recounts or relays a ministerial communication will be captured by the exemption, but, possibly, not the communication itself. As the number of degrees of remove between the information in question and the original ministerial communication increases, it will become harder to maintain that the information 'relates to' the ministerial communication.[84]

22– 013 Information relating to ministerial communications: the public interest

This exemption has no analogous exemption in any of the comparative jurisdictions. The exemption presents peculiar difficulties so far as the public interest is concerned. Save for the effect of s 2, the exemption effectively takes out of the access regime all information relating to ministerial communications, irrespective of their content, irrespective of the harmlessness of their disclosure and irrespective of the origins of the information itself. This removal of a class of information that, on its face, has no characteristic requiring it to be cloaked in secrecy may be thought to be antithetical to the purpose of the Act.[85] The Secretary of State for the Home Department began the second reading speech for the Bill thus:

> Unnecessary secrecy in Government and our public services has long been held to undermine good governance and public administration, and my party has long been committed to change. At the last election, our manifesto stated: "We are pledged to a Freedom of Information Act, leading to more open government." The Bill will make that promise a reality. The Bill, by its first clause, lays down for the first time in our constitutional history that the public have a right to know about the work of Government and all other public authorities. Again for the first time, that right of access to information will be

---

[79] *DWP v IC*, IT, 5 March 2007 at [85] and [108].

[80] *DWP v IC*, IT, 5 March 2007 at [108].

[81] FOIA s 35(5).

[82] FOIA s 35(5).

[83] See *O'Brien v IC and DBERR*, IT, 7 October 2008 at [20].

[84] See §22– 007.

[85] See §§1– 011 to 1– 016 and §22– 011.

enforced by an independent Information Commissioner and an Information Tribunal with clear powers to override the decisions of Ministers or any other public authority as to whether information should be released. Moreover, the Bill will not only provide legal rights for the public and place legal duties on Ministers and public authorities, but will help to transform the culture of Government from one of secrecy to one of openness. It will transform the default setting from "this should be kept quiet unless" to "this should be published unless." By doing so, it should raise public confidence in the processes of government, and enhance the quality of decision making by the Government.[86]

A full reconciliation of this sentiment with the terms of s 35(1)(b) is only possible through the public interest balancing exercise prescribed in s 2 of the Act.[87] Against the backdrop of the Freedom of Information Act 2000 having set its face against non-disclosure of official information without objectively good reason and of s 35(1)(b) not having been made an absolute exemption, the decision-maker must identify the public interest which is served by maintaining an exemption for information whose only required attribute is that it relates to Ministerial communications. It will not be permissible to elevate the limb into a de facto absolute exemption by alighting on characteristics that invariably attend a Ministerial communication. In *Scotland Office v IC*, the Tribunal held that the principles established in *Department for Education and Skills v Information Commissioner and Evening Standard*[88] have 'considerable relevance' in the case of information falling within s 35(1)(b) as well as s 35(1)(a).[89] To the extent that such information would reveal the proceedings of the Cabinet, etc the public interest question may be fairly readily answered: the purpose served by the secrecy attaching to the records of Cabinet proceedings is well recognised.[90] This will be particularly compelling in relation to information that reveals the actual deliberations within Cabinet, but may be less compelling in relation to reports or submissions prepared for the assistance of Cabinet.[91] Otherwise, however, the public interest in maintaining the exemption is not readily divined.[92]

---

[86] Hansard HC vol 340 col 714 (7 December 1999).

[87] See the introductory remarks at §22– 002.

[88] IT, 19 February 2007 at [75].

[89] IT, 5 August 2008 at [79]. See further §21– 013 above. The principles have also been applied to the EIR reg 12(4)(d)-(e): *Secretary of State for Transport v IC*, IT, 5 May 2009 at [105].

[90] See *Conway v Rimmer* [1968] AC 910 at 952 and *AG v Jonathan Cape Ltd* [1976] QB 752. Similar statements are made in the comparative jurisdictions, apart from the USA: *AG v Hamilton* [1993] 2 IR 250 at 266; *Egan v Chadwick* [1999] NSWCA 176, (1999) 46 NSWLR 563 esp at 573–576 and at 589–592, which sets out a very useful history of the convention and its rationale.

[91] *Commonwealth v Northern Land Council* (1993) 176 CLR 604; *Commonwealth v Construction, Forestry, Mining and Energy Union* (2000) 98 FCR 31; *Egan v Chadwick* [1999] NSWCA 176, (1999) 46 NSWLR 563; *Northern Australian Aboriginal Legal Service v Bradley* [2001] FCA 1080; *National Tertiary Education Industry Union v Commonwealth of Australia* [2001] FCA 610, (2001) 111 FCR 583. This is on the basis that disclosure of the actual deliberations will almost inevitably be inconsistent with the doctrine of collective responsibility, whereas disclosure of reports or submissions may not.

[92] This passage was considered by the Tribunal in *Scotland Office v IC*, IT, 5 August 2008. The Tribunal stated (at [78]): 'we do see some force in the argument... that the factors in favour of maintaining the exemption for some types of information in this category will, almost always, be strong and that "very cogent and compelling" reasons for disclosure would be needed before the balance tips in favour of disclosure in those situations. This is not to turn the public interest test around, or to say that just because the exemption is engaged that is a factor weighing against disclosure, but recognisees the weight that should be given to the public interest factors for maintaining the exemption.'

22– 014 Information relating to advice from a Law Officer

The third limb of s 35(1) renders material exempt information if it relates to the provision of advice by any of the 'Law Officers' or any request for the provision of such advice. The phrase the 'Law Officers' is defined to mean the Attorney-General, the Solicitor-General, the Advocate General for Scotland, the Lord Advocate, the Solicitor-General for Scotland and the Attorney-General for Northern Ireland.[93] This exemption will inevitably overlap with the exemption for information in respect of which a claim to legal professional privilege could be maintained.[94] It extends the scope of protection by picking up information that might not be privileged itself: for example, because it merely recounts or relays legal advice received. The public interest in the maintenance of this exemption is akin to the public interest in maintaining the exemption for information in respect of which a claim to legal professional privilege could be maintained.[95] It has long been a convention within Government that neither the fact of having sought the opinion of the Law Officers of the Crown, nor the content of that advice, is disclosed without the Law Officers' consent. In relation to the former, in *HM Treasury v IC*[96] Blake J held that 'Parliament intended real weight should continue to be afforded to this aspect of the Law Officers' Convention', and that 'the general considerations of good government underlining the history and nature of the convention were capable of affording weight to the interest in maintaining an exemption even in the absence of particular damage.'[97] Blake J held that the FOIA had preserved the Convention, but rendered it amenable to being outweighed by greater considerations of the public interest requiring disclosure of information in either limb of the Convention.[98]

22– 015 Information relating to the operation of any ministerial private office

The final limb of s 35(1) renders material exempt information if it relates to the operation of any 'Ministerial private office'. This phrase is defined to mean any part of a government department which provides personal administrative support to a Minister of the Crown, to a Northern Ireland Minister or a Northern Ireland junior Minister, or any part of the administration of the National Assembly for Wales providing personal administrative support to the Assembly First Secretary or an Assembly Secretary.[99] Most of the comparative

---

[93] FOIA s 35(5).

[94] FOIA s 42; FOI(S)A s 36(1). See ch 21.

[95] See §§21– 017 to 21– 020.

[96] [2009] EWHC 1811 (Admin), [2010] 2 WLR 931. On appeal from the decision of the Tribunal in *HM Treasury v IC*, IT, 15 May 2008.

[97] At [54].

[98] At [54].

[99] FOIA s 5. The House of Commons Select Committee on Public Administration stated, in their *Third Report* (Cm 4355, 1999) para 89 that they did not believe that a class-based exemption for the operation of a private Ministerial office was appropriate. In their view, such information should be included within the scope of the prejudice-based exemption that is now to be found in s 36 of the FOIA.

jurisdictions remove such material from the operation of the legislation.[100]   The policy underpinning this exemption is that information relating to the operation of a Minister's private office does not serve any of the purposes of the Act.   On that basis, the public interest in disclosure of such information may be expected to be readily displaced by the public interest in maintaining the exemption.

016 Statistical information

Section 35(2) of the Freedom of Information Act 2000 provides that once a decision as to government policy has been taken, then any statistical information that has been used to provide 'an informed background' to that decision is to be taken out of the scope of the first two limbs of s 35(1).[101]   In *Secretary of State for Work and Pensions v Information Commissioner*[102] the Tribunal approved the definition of 'statistical information' suggested in the MoJ Guidance, namely that it requires 'mathematical operations performed on a sample of observations or some other factual information'.[103]   The fact that statistical information is at a certain point taken out of the scope of s 35 does not mean that that information must be disclosed.   Indeed, once exemption under s 35 drops away, the limitation imposed by the concluding words in s 36(1)(a) is disengaged, enabling the public authority to rely on this section to protect it from having to disclose to a member of the public any statistical information that it used to inform its policy decisions.[104]   The subsection implies that statistical information can represent information relating to the formulation or development of government policy.

017 Factual information: background

It is conventional for freedom of information legislation, when exempting policy deliberations from disclosure, to make some sort of exception for the factual material used in the course of those deliberations.[105]   In introducing freedom of information legislation into Westminster, the

---

[100] In Australia, such material is excluded as a result of the definition of 'official document' in s 4 of the Freedom of Information Act 1982: see §2– 011. The definition of 'official information' in s 2 of the Official Information Act 1982 (New Zealand) excludes some, but not all, such information. The Freedom of Information Act 1997 (Ireland) s 46(1), treats such material as 'exempt records' and therefore outside the main operation of the Act: see §2– 035.

[101] FOI(S)A s 29(2).

[102] *DWP v IC*, IT, 5 March 2007 at [75]–[77].

[103] MoJ, *Exemptions Guidance—Section 35*, 14 May 2008, p 9.

[104] See §22– 003. In relation to statistical information falling within the scope of s 36, the Commissioner has the power to review the decision not to disclose that information without being subject to the restriction that is applicable in respect of other kinds of information falling under s 36: namely, that that review must be limited to a consideration of whether the view of the relevant 'qualified person' that such information should not be disclosed was 'reasonable'. The Government conferred this broader power of review upon the Commissioner in respect of statistical information in order to underline its stated commitment to openness: Lord Falconer of Thoroton, Hansard HL vol 618 col 287 (24 October 2000).

[105] In the United States, under the Freedom of Information Act, 1966, 5 USC 552(b)(5), the 'deliberative process privilege' does not include the underlying factual material: see §2– 008(5). The Freedom of Information Act 1982 (Cth of Australia) s 47C takes out of the 'deliberative process' exemption 'purely factual material:' see §2– 015(11). However, purely factual material within Cabinet records or records of the Executive Council remain within these exemptions: see §2– 015(1)–(2). The Official Information Act 1982 (New Zealand), bucks convention so as to retain an exemption for factual and statistical information. The New Zealand Law Commission, in its Review of the Official Information Act 1982, October 1997, saw no reason to change this. In Canada, factual material falls outside of the exemption provided by the Access to Information Act s 21(1): see §2– 032(4)–(5). The exemption provided by the Freedom of Information Act 1997 (Ireland) s 19(1), does not extend to factual material and the

Government indicated that it intended that as much as possible factual and background information gathered by public authorities in the process of devising policy and making decisions should be made publicly available.[106] Thus, the 1997 White Paper recorded that the protection which the Government envisaged would be imposed with respect to the disclosure of information relating to policy and public affairs was intended 'primarily to protect opinion and analytical information, not the raw data and factual background material which have contributed to the policy-making process'.[107] The White Paper promised that public authorities would be encouraged to make such information available, even where opinion and advice based upon it needed to remain confidential. Nonetheless, neither the draft Bill published in May 1999 nor the second draft introduced into Parliament on 18 November 1999 distinguished between policy information and advice, on the one hand, and factual or statistical background material on the other. Both versions of the Bill were heavily criticised for this. In its first Report on the May 1999 draft Bill, the House of Commons Select Committee on Public Administration recommended that the exemption for decision-making and policy formulation should 'specifically not be taken to apply to purely factual information held by public authorities, not to analysis, if that information has been created in order to inform policy decisions, and this distinction should be drawn clearly in the Bill.'[108] This position was also endorsed by the House of Lords Select Committee that commented on the Bill. Parliament, likewise, pressed strongly for a distinction between factual and statistical information, on the one hand, and policy information, on the other, to be made in the Bill, and for factual and statistical information to be excluded from the scope of the policy exemption.[109] The Government resisted these criticisms on the basis that, while factual material used to provide an informed background to decision-taking should be made available wherever possible, it could not be made available as of right, because:

the dividing line between facts and opinions, or advice, is simply not that clear...There will

exemption provided by s 20 extends neither to factual information nor to statistical information: see §2– 039(1) and 2– 039(9).

[106] Cabinet Office, *Your Right to Know: The Government's Proposals for a Freedom of Information Act* (Cm 3813, 1997) para 3.13.

[107] Cabinet Office, *Your Right to Know: The Government's Proposals for a Freedom of Information Act* (Cm 3818, 1997) para 3.13.

[108] House of Commons Select Committee on Public Administration, Third Report (Cm4355, 1999) para 93. The House of Lords Select Committee, in its *First Report on the Draft Freedom of Information Bill* (27 July 1999) accepted the arguments justifying a class-based exemption for policy advice, but agreed with the House of Commons Select Committee that policy advice should be distinguished from 'separable factual background' to that advice; and that 'such factual background should be exempt only if its disclosure "would substantially or would be likely substantially to prejudice the interests set forth in clause 28(3)"' — House of Lords, *Draft Freedom of Information Bill: First Report* (27 July 1999), para 34.

[109] Dr Tony Wright MP (Cannock Chase), eg, said in the course of the second reading of the second draft Bill 'We had discussions on the [first draft Bill] and the Home Secretary told the Select Committee on Public Administration that the "issue of factual or background information is important...and I think on the whole ought to be disclosed". Unfortunately, the Bill does not convert that desire into legislative provision, but I am heartened by the fact that it might still do that. .... We have a cumulative body of evidence which says that it is both desirable and practical to have such distinctions. However, the distinction is not made in the Bill, contrary to the developing practice to which I have pointed, and contrary to freedom of information regimes elsewhere, notably in New Zealand and Ireland. Hon members should be clear about what that means. It means that all information relating in any way to the development of policy—including purely factual background information—stands exempt. I simply do not believe that the House will allow that to be sustained. Clauses 33 and 34 [the precursors to ss 35 and 36] represent the hole in the centre of the Bill. At the very least, we need the facts, and an analysis of them...' — Hansard HC vol 340 col 753 (7 December 1999).

be occasions where "facts" are part of the discussion or argumentation about options under consideration and where it will not be possible to disentangle facts from opinions or advice. On these occasions the disclosure of such information would, of itself, affect the decision-taking process. Thus there will be a need to withhold such information on a few occasions.[110]

The Government agreed, however, that greater openness could be achieved than the Bill allowed for[111] and amendments containing the provisions now to be found in ss 35(2)[112] and 35(4)[113] were introduced as a result.[114]

018 Factual information: approach

The approach taken by s 35(4) of the Freedom of Information Act 2000 is to exhort the decision-maker, when weighing the competing public interests in s 2, to have regard 'to the particular public interest in the disclosure of factual information which has been used, or is intended to be used, to provide an informed background to decision-making'.[115] This, of course, requires an identification of what is and what is not 'factual information'. As Wigmore observed at the outset of his treatise on evidence 'everything in the cosmos is a fact or a phenomenon'.[116] The phrase 'factual information' is innately vague: whether an opinion is held is a matter of fact even if the opinion itself is not.[117] On the other hand, the choice of factual material and its presentation may constitute a matter of opinion,[118] just as the reaching of a conclusion or a view upon factual material may itself be a fact.[119] These complexities and distinctions are borne out by the comparative jurisprudence. In the United States, the Courts will normally allow agencies to withhold factual material in an otherwise 'deliberative' document in two situations. First, if a document comprises or includes a conscious selection of factual information out of a larger group of factual information, the act of selection of those

---

[110] Lord Falconer of Thoroton, Hansard HL vol 612 col 827 (20 April 2000); Hansard HL vol 619 col 832 (22 November 2000). See also Jack Straw, Hansard HC vol 347 col 1027 (5 April 2000).

[111] Lord Falconer of Thoroton, Hansard HL vol 618 col 287 (24 October 2000).

[112] Lord Falconer of Thoroton, Hansard HL vol 618 col 287 (24 October 2000).

[113] Hansard HL vol 619 col 147 (14 November 2000). The formulation contained in s 35(4) was preferred to various alternatives that were proposed which would have had the effect of excluding factual information altogether from the scope of the exemption now contained in s 35(1): see eg Hansard HC vol 347 col 997 (5 April 2000).

[114] The amendment with respect to statistical information was welcomed in Parliament, but the majority of members of the House of Commons and House of Lords who spoke on the Bill continued to press for an exception from the exemption in respect of factual information, as well as statistical information: see, eg Hansard HL vol 618 cols 288–302.

[115] In relation to information held by Scottish public authorities, FOI(S)A s 29(3). As an example of the provision in operation, see *DWP v IC*, IT, 5 March 2007 at [71]–[74].

[116] JH Wigmore, *Treatise on the Anglo-American System of Evidence in Trials at Common Law*, 3rd edn (Boston, Little Brown, 1940), vol 1, p 1, para 1.

[117] That there is no logical dichotomy between fact and opinion is recognised in the FOIA itself: s 36(2) and (7) involve a statutory transposition of fact and opinion.

[118] The Federal Court of Australia in *Harris v Australian Broadcasting Corporation* (1984) 51 ALR 581 held that summaries of factual material could not be classified as 'purely factual material' for the purposes of s 47C (then, s 36) of the Freedom of Information Act 1982 if they were 'of such a character as to disclose a process of selection involving opinion, advice or recommendation for the purpose of the deliberative process'.

[119] In *Harris v Australian Broadcasting Corporation* (1984) 51 ALR 581 the Federal Court held that 'conclusions expressed as findings' could be a statement of 'purely factual material notwithstanding it involves a conclusion based upon primary facts'.

facts is treated as deliberative in nature, entitling the selected facts to enjoy the deliberative process privilege exemption.[120] Secondly, factual information may be withheld in circumstances where it is so inextricably connected to the deliberative material that its disclosure would expose or cause harm to the agency's deliberations.[121]

22– 019 The duty to confirm or deny

Section 35 also provides a corresponding qualified exclusion from the duty to confirm or deny.[122] The way in which the exclusion is worded is such that, if a given piece of information relating to the formulation of policy, etc is exempt information under s 35(1), then the corresponding duty to confirm or deny that the information is held does not arise. It should be noted that the public interest exercise differs for the two duties, so that even though the public interest may weigh in favour of maintaining the exemption from disclosure, it may nevertheless not weigh in favour of maintaining the exclusion of the duty to confirm or deny.

3.   INFORMATION THE DISCLOSURE OF WHICH WOULD BE PREJUDICIAL TO PUBLIC AFFAIRS

22– 020 Introduction

Section 36 of the Freedom of Information Act 2000 provides a further array of exemptions for what might loosely be described as information recording the deliberations of a public authority.[123] The scope and operation of the provision varies according to the identity of the public authority holding the information:

— If the information is held by a government department or by the National Assembly for Wales and the information is exempt information by virtue of s 35, then s 36 is inapplicable.[124]

— If the information is held by the House of Commons or the House of Lords, then

---

[120] *Montrose Chemical Corp v Train*, 491 F 2d 63, 66 (DC Cir 1974); *Mapother v Department of Justice*, 3 F(3d) 1533 (DC Cir 1993), where the Court held, in relation to a report which consisted of factual materials prepared for the Attorney-General's decision whether to allow former UN Secretary General Kurt Waldheim to enter the United States, that 'the majority of [the report's] factual material was assembled through an exercise of judgment in extracting pertinent material from a vast number of documents for the benefit of an official called upon to take discretionary action', and that it therefore fell within the deliberative process privilege. On the other hand, the Court held that a chronology of his military career was not deliberative, as it was 'neither more nor less than a comprehensive collection of the essential facts' and 'reflect[ed] no point of view'.

[121] *Wolfe v United States Department of Health and Human Services*, 839 F 2d 768 (DC Cir 1988).

[122] FOIA s 35(3).

[123] Similarly, in relation to information held by Scottish public authorities, FOI(S)A s 30. The exemption is highly time-sensitive, in that the greater the passage of time between the creation of the information and the information request, the less force there is likely to be in an argument that the public interest in maintaining the exemption outweighs the public interest in disclosure: *Scottish Ministers v Scottish IC* [2007] CSIH 8, 2007 SCLR 253 at [16].

[124] FOIA s 36(1)(a). As to the inter-relationship of the two provisions, see §22– 003. There is no equivalent restriction under the FOI(S)A.

the exemption is an absolute exemption for the purposes of s 2[125] and provision is made for a conclusive certificate.[126]

— If the information is held by any other public authority, then the exemption is a qualified exemption and there is no provision for a conclusive certificate.

The section provides three overlapping heads of exemption, each of which requires a reasonable expectation of prejudice, or the likelihood of prejudice, to the interest protected by the head.[127] A similar exemption exists in each of the comparative jurisdictions except the United States of America.[128] Since the exemption in the Freedom of Information Act 2000 is prejudice-based as well as subject to a public interest override, it is the narrowest exemption of its type amongst the comparative jurisdictions.[129] The meaning of 'prejudice' and the required

---

[125] FOIA s 2(3)(e). No analogous distinction is drawn in the FOI(S)A. The House of Commons Select Committee on Public Administration did not accept that the justification for the exclusion of Parliament from the right to official information had been made out. In their view, 'the exclusion of Parliament may well convey the wrong impression to the general public, given the purpose of this legislation' (*Third Report* (Cm 4355, 1999) para 37).

[126] FOIA s 36(7). No provision is made for a conclusive certificate under s 30 of the FOI(S)A.

[127] In *Guardian Newspapers Ltd and Heather Brooke v IC and BBC*, IT, 8 January 2007, the Tribunal interpreted the phrase 'would, or would be likely to' within s 36 (2)(b) as meaning 'inhibition would probably occur (ie on the balance of probabilities, the chance being greater than 50%) or that there would be a "very significant and weighty chance" that it would occur. A "real risk" is not enough; the degree of risk must be such that there "may very well be" such inhibition, even if the risk falls short of being more probable than not' (at [53]). See further §15– 022.

[128] The Freedom of Information Act 1982 (Cth of Australia) s 34(1) provides a very broad exemption that embraces any record of Cabinet, a document brought into existence for the purpose of submission to Cabinet and so submitted, extracts from such documents, and any document that would disclose the deliberations or decisions of Cabinet other than an official document. An exception is made for purely factual material: s 34(1A). There is no public interest requirement or override and there is no requirement that prejudice result from the disclosure. The Official Information Act 1982 (New Zealand) s 9(2) (f)(ii) is in substantially identical terms to s 36(2)(a) of the FOIA. The provision has the effect of affording a good reason for non-disclosure for the purposes of s 5 of the Act unless 'the withholding of that information is outweighed by other considerations which render it desirable, in the public interest, to make that information available.' The New Zealand Law Commission, in its Review of the Official Information Act 1982, October 1997, para 217, noted that this had been interpreted to mean that 'the protection afforded is not a categorical one. It is not enough, for instance, to show that the relevant information is set out in a Cabinet document. Rather a judgment, involving an element of damage, is required: the person wishing to withhold must show that the withholding is necessary to maintain the particular interest. That phrase has been interpreted by the Ombudsmen as requiring that release would go 'to the heart' of the relevant interest. Factors such as the age of the information, or the timing of the request, may be relevant.' In Canada, s 69 of the Access to Information Act provides that the Act does not apply to confidences of the Queen's Privy Council for Canada (which includes the Cabinet and committees of Cabinet), including memoranda the purpose of which is to present proposals or recommendations to Council; discussion papers the purpose of which is to present background explanations, analyses of problems or policy options to Council for consideration by Council in making decisions; agenda of Council or records recording deliberations or decisions of Council; records used for or reflecting communications or discussions between ministers of the Crown on matters relating to the making of government decisions or the formulation of government policy; records the purpose of which is to brief ministers of the Crown in relation to matters that are before, or are proposed to be brought before, Council; and records that contain information about the contents of any record within any of the preceding classes of records. Section 19(1) of the Freedom of Information Act 1997 (Ireland), provides a mandatory exemption (it was, until the amendments made in 2003, a discretionary exemption) for any record: submitted, or proposed to be submitted, to the Government for their consideration by a Minister; containing information (including advice) for a member of the Government, the Attorney-General, a Minister of State, the Secretary to the Government or the Assistant Secretary to the Government for use by him solely for the purpose of the transaction of any business of the Government at a meeting of the Government; that consists of a communication between two or more members of the Government relating to a matter that is under consideration by the Government or is proposed to be submitted to the Government. 'Government' is defined in s 19(6) to be broadly akin to the Cabinet.

[129] Although the information may independently be rendered exempt by s 35.

probability of prejudice are generally considered earlier in this work.[130] The Government's preference for a test of 'prejudice', rather than substantial prejudice, was the source of some controversy during the passage of the Bill through Parliament. The decision to retain a test of 'prejudice' was, however, justified on the ground that, according to the Government, the test of prejudice was not a weak test; and the commissioner, who would have the power to overrule an authority if it was thought that any prejudice caused by a disclosure would be trivial or insignificant, would ensure that the authority was able to point to prejudice that was 'real, actual, or of substance'.[131] An argument that, although this provision does not per se provide for a class exemption, its application might in some circumstances involve the identification of documents by class, has been rejected in Scotland.[132] Finally, it should be noted that the Freedom of Information (Scotland) Act 2002 requires 'substantial prejudice' for the purposes of this and other prejudice-based exemptions.

22– 021 **The reasonable opinion of a qualified person**

Section 36 is unique amongst the 23 sections of the Act conferring exemptions in its making the 'reasonable opinion' of a particular person determinative of its operation.[133] The 'reasonable opinion' criterion is not used in the regime applying to Scottish public authorities. Under that regime, the comparable exemption employs objective criteria, requiring substantial prejudice, or a likelihood of substantial prejudice, to the protected interest.[134] The reaching of a reasonable opinion is, in relation to each public authority, entrusted to a particular 'qualified person',[135] who is invariably at the highest level of accountability so far as that public authority

---

[130] See §§15– 020 to 15– 028.

[131] Lord Falconer of Thoroton, Hansard HL vol 612 col 827 (20 April 2000). Lord Falconer said 'I want to emphasise the strength of the prejudice test …. It is not a weak test. The commissioner will have the power to overrule an authority if she feels that any prejudice caused by a disclosure would be trivial or insignificant. She will ensure that an authority must point to prejudice which is "real, actual or of substance." We do not think that reliance on undefined words such as "substantial" or "significant" is a sensible way forward. We do not know how they will be interpreted by the commissioner or the courts. We can never deliver absolute certainty, but we can avoid making uncertainty worse by adding ill-defined terminology into the Bill.'

[132] *Scottish Ministers v Scottish IC* [2007] CSIH 8, 2007 SCLR 253 at [14]. The correct approach, the Court held, was for each case to be assessed on its own facts and circumstances and that this will 'necessarily begin with the scrutiny of relevant individual documents and the ascertainment whether they contain particular information which, read in the context of related information, has or is likely to have the specified prejudicial effect…it is only after such scrutiny that it will be possible to say whether such information will have or is likely to have such an effect. The circumstance that one ends up with a "class", namely, with pieces of information of that particular kind, does not mean that a class-based approach to the exercise is ever legitimate' (at [13]).

[133] Although, of course, there are provisions for conclusive certificates under ss 23, 24 and 34.

[134] FOI(S)A s 30. The difference is further marked by the requirement under the FOI(S)A for substantial prejudice, rather than just prejudice. The experience of Scottish public authorities may be relevant to the FOIA s 2 balancing exercise in adjudging claims of the public interest in maintaining the exemption. In *Salmon v IC and King's College Cambridge*, IT, 17 July 2008 the Tribunal concluded that the acting provost of King's College, Cambridge was not a 'qualified person' for the purposes of section 36(5)(o) as that fell outwith the Minister's authorisation at the material time (although see the subsequent designation of 27 July 2007 which authorises the head of college by whatever title used of colleges within collegiate universities) [35].

[135] In *Sugar v IC and BBC*, IT, 14 May 2009 the Tribunal concluded (at [10]) that the wording of s 36(2) did not require the opinion to be obtained at the time of the request. Rather, the section only requires that a reasonable opinion is obtained whether there would be, or would be likely to be, prejudice to the effective conduct of public affairs before the exemption is claimed.

is concerned.[136] This unique aspect of the exemption was controversial and was criticised, both at the Committee stage and as the Bill went through Parliament, on the basis that the question of whether or not such information should be disclosed was one that the Commissioner should be free to determine on the merits, without being limited to a review of the qualified person's opinion.[137] The role of the qualified person's opinion in determining whether a public authority is under a duty to disclose has two related limitations. First, the 'reasonable opinion' determinant is confined to deciding whether the disclosure of the information would have, or would be likely to have,[138] any of the effects set out in paras (a)-(c) of s 36(2). As noted above, except in relation to information held by the House of Commons or the House of Lords the exemption is a qualified exemption. Accordingly, the exercise prescribed by s 2(1) and (2) must then be carried out, not necessarily by the 'qualified person' who held the 'reasonable opinion', to determine whether the public interest in maintaining the exemption outweighs the public interest in disclosing the information.[139] The public interest in maintaining the exemption will, in part, be informed by the fact that the exemption is engaged by an opinion rather than an actuality. In this way, it may be that the extent to which the qualified person's opinion is borne out by the actuality will fall to be considered at this stage. Secondly, on its face, s 36 restricts the Commissioner's role in an appeal to assessing whether the qualified person's opinion was reasonable: in other words, a review of the qualified person's decision akin to the *Wednesbury* irrationality test.[140] Again, however, even if the Commissioner does find that the qualified

---

[136] The qualified person for each type of public authority is set out in FOIA s 36(5). For this reason, the s 36(2) opinion is not delegable: *Guardian Newspapers Ltd and Brooke v IC and BBC*, IT, 8 January 2007 at [26]. Qualified persons are listed at:

> www.foi.gov.uk/guidance/exguide/sec36/annex-d.htm

[137] See the House of Commons Select Committee on Public Administration, *Third Report* (Cm 4355, 1999) para 90; the House of Lords, *Draft Freedom of Information Bill: First Report*, 27 July 1999, para 35; Hansard HC vol 340 col 782 (7 December 1999); Hansard HC vol 347 cols 1079–1088 (5 April 2000); Hansard HL vol 618 cols 303–313 (24 October 2000); and Hansard HL vol 619 cols 833–842 (22 November 2000). The Government justified the retention of the clause on the basis that 'the issues involved in the decision-taking process of public authorities are so near the heart of government that ...only a qualified person, as defined by the Bill, can have a full understanding of them. Although the issues in [s 36] are less sensitive than those in [s 35] and a class exemption is not justified, the Government do not believe that it would be right for the commissioner to substitute her view for that of the authority on the question of prejudice; hence the test of the reasonable opinion of a qualified person.' — Hansard HC vol 347 col 1085 (5 April 2000). This is the view taken by the Tribunal of its own role when reviewing a claim for exemption under s 36: *Guardian Newspapers Ltd and Brooke v IC and BBC* , IT, 8 January 2007 at [54].

[138] As to the meaning of 'would, or would be likely to', see §15– 022. The same standard is required in s 36 as in other exemptions using this formula: *Guardian Newspapers Ltd and Heather Brooke v IC and BBC*, IT, 8 January 2007 at [53]. The Tribunal in *McIntyre v IC and MOD*, 4 February 2008, declined to find that the Information Commissioner could not find that the opinion of the qualified person was reasonable where the Minister failed to specify which limb of the prejudice test he relied upon [45]. The Tribunal concluded (at [45]) that 'where the qualified person does not designate the level of prejudice, that Parliament still intended that the reasonableness of the opinion should be assessed by the Commissioner, but in the absence of designation as to level of prejudice that the lower threshold of prejudice applies, unless there is other clear evidence that it should be at the higher level.'

[139] *Guardian Newspapers Ltd and Heather Brooke v IC and BBC*, IT, 8 January 2007 at [69].

[140] Thus Lord Falconer of Thoroton indicated that the Commissioner might overturn the qualified person's decision if she took the view that it was 'irrational' or 'perverse', or a view that 'no reasonable Minister or qualified person' would take; and he added that the Commissioner's review of the qualified person's decision would be conducted 'on a judicial review basis' — see Hansard HL vol 618 cols 305 and 306. See also Hansard HC vol 347 col 1085 (5 April 2000). This was the approach adopted by the Tribunal in *Guardian Newspapers Ltd and Heather Brooke v IC and BBC*, IT, 8 January 2007, although the Tribunal pointed out that as neither party sought to refer the Tribunal to *Hansard*, the Tribunal had not therefore taken into account Lord Falconer's statement (at [56]). The Tribunal was referred to the Information Commissioner's Awareness Guidance No 25, relating to s 36, and expressly stated that

person's opinion is reasonable, he must then decide whether or not the information should be disclosed in accordance with the provisions of s 2 of the Freedom of Information Act 2000.[141] In so doing, the Commissioner will have to determine how much weight should be given to the opinion of the qualified person that disclosing the information will have a prejudicial effect.[142] That task cannot properly be carried out without the Commissioner reaching his own view of whether the protected interests set out in paras (a)-(c) of s 36(2) would be, or would be likely to be, prejudiced by the disclosure of the information.[143] And, thirdly, a review before the

---

it did not endorse the view advanced in that Guidance that '...any opinion which is not outrageous, or manifestly absurd or made on the basis of irrelevant facts or without consideration of all relevant factors will satisfy the test [of reasonableness.].' The Tribunal considered that this was 'incorrect and should be disregarded' as an opinion could be objectively unreasonable without suffering from any of the defects cited in the Guidance. The Tribunal noted that it was not clear from the statutory wording the extent to which, if at all, in addition to being substantively reasonable, the opinion had to be reasonably arrived at; it concluded that in order to satisfy s 36(2) the opinion had to be both reasonable in substance and reasonably arrived at, stating that '...precisely because the opinion is essentially a judgment call on what might happen in the future, on which people may disagree, if the process were not taken into account, in many cases the reasonableness of the opinion would be effectively unchallengeable; we cannot think that was the Parliamentary intention' (at [64]). That the Tribunal may disagree with the qualified person's opinion does not mean that the qualified person's opinion was not a reasonable one for the purposes of s 36, see *MoD v IC and Evans*, IT, 20 July 2007 at [38]-[42]. See also *McKinnon v Secretary, Department of Treasury* [2006] HCA 45, (2006) 229 ALR 187 at [59], where the High Court of Australia, when considering whether there existed 'reasonable grounds for the claim that the disclosure of the document would be contrary to public interest' as required by s 58(5) of the Freedom of Information Act 1982 (Cth of Australia), stated that '...the expression "not irrational, absurd or ridiculous" is not synonymous with "reasonable grounds".'

[141] The Tribunal has applied the principles established in *DfES v IC and The Evening Standard*, IT, 19 February 2007 at [75] (see §25–011 above) to information falling within s 36: *Shipton v IC and National Assembly of Wales*, IT, 11 January 2007 at [16]-[17]; *MoD v IC and Evans*, IT, 20 July 2007 at [72]; *FCO v IC*, IT, 22 January 2008 at [24]-[28]; *SSHD v IC*, IT, 20 November 2008 at [41]-[67]; *Cabinet Office v IC*, IT, 27 January 2009 at [17]-[26]; *ECGD v IC and Campaign Against Arms Trade*, IT, 21 October 2009 at [62]-[115]; and *University of Central Lancashire v IC and Colquhoun*, IT, 8 December 2009 at [51]-[62].

[142] The Tribunal has considered the relevance of the opinion of the 'qualified person' for the test in s 2 on two occasions, with conflicting results. In *Guardian Newspapers Ltd v IC and BBC*, IT, 8 January 2007, the Tribunal stated that the Commissioner, having accepted the reasonableness of the qualified person's opinion that the disclosure of the information would, or would be likely to, inhibit the free and frank exchange of views for the purpose of deliberation, 'must give weight to that opinion as an important piece of evidence in his assessment of the balance of public interest' at [92]. In *Evans v IC and MoD*, IT, 26 October 2007 a differently constituted Tribunal disagreed, stating (at [36]) that 'we do not see the logic of then placing the Minister's opinion in the scales as a factor to be weighed in favour of maintaining an exemption whose engagement has been triggered by that very opinion. This seems to us like double counting the opinion which is a necessary safeguard to prevent inhibition being claimed without due cause ... we regard the opinion as a threshold condition, required to engage section 36, rather than a major piece of evidence in its own right.'

[143] See Hansard HL vol 619 col 836 (22 November 2000) (Lord Falconer). Again, this is supported by the view of the Tribunal in *Guardian Newspapers Ltd and Heather Brooke v IC and BBC*, IT, 8 January 2007, which stated that '...when it comes to weighing the balance of public interest under s 2(2)(b), it is impossible to make the required judgment without forming a view on the likelihood of inhibition or prejudice' [88]. The Tribunal (at [91] and [92]) then proceeded: '...the qualified person has made a judgment about the degree of likelihood that such inhibition will occur. It does not necessarily imply any particular view as to the severity or extent of such inhibition or the frequency with which it will or may occur, save that it will not be so trivial, minor or occasional, as to be insignificant...in order to perform the balancing judgment required by s 2(2)(b), the Commissioner is entitled, and will need, to form his own view on the severity, extent and frequency with which inhibition of the free and frank exchange of views for the purposes of deliberation will or may occur.' Indeed, in reaching its conclusion that the material in question was not covered by the exemption contained within s 36, the Tribunal referred to the lack of evidence before it on the severity, extent and frequency of any future inhibition.

Tribunal will also involve a consideration of the manner by which the opinion was reached.[144]

022 Statistical information

Section 36(4) of the Freedom of Information Act 2000 makes special provision in relation to the rendering of 'statistical information' into exempt information.[145] In relation to statistical information, the exemption created by s 36(2) operates like any of the other 22 provisions in the Act creating exemptions. In other words, the statistical information is exempt information if its disclosure would have, or would be likely to have, any of the consequences set out in paras (a)-(c): it is not exempt information merely because, in the reasonable opinion of the qualified person, its disclosure would have, or would be likely to have, any of the consequences set out in paras (a)-(c).[146] On any review by the Information Commissioner, the question for the Commissioner will be similarly modified where the information in question is statistical information.

023 The convention of the collective responsibility of Ministers of the Crown: scope

The first of the three limbs in s 36(2) describes information the disclosure of which would, or would be likely to, prejudice 'the maintenance of the convention of the collective responsibility of Ministers of the Crown'. In order to appreciate whether something would prejudice or would be likely to prejudice the convention, it is necessary to understand the exact nature of the convention and what end it is designed to serve. The matter was considered in *Attorney-General v Jonathan Cape Ltd*,[147] where the Attorney-General sought in 1975 to prevent the publication of a book, entitled *Diaries of a Cabinet Minister*, written by Richard Crossman, who had been a Cabinet Minister from 1964 to 1970, based upon a diary he had kept recording Cabinet discussions. The Attorney-General contended that publication of the book would undermine the doctrine of joint Cabinet responsibility, that it would represent a breach of the confidentiality and a breach of oath that every Cabinet Minister, as a Privy Councillor, is required to take, and that publication was therefore contrary to the public interest. Lord Widgery disagreed and the action was dismissed. The Court heard extensive evidence as to the nature of the convention, not all of it consistent, and concluded:

> It has always been assumed by lawyers and, I suspect, by politicians, and the Civil Service, that Cabinet proceedings and Cabinet papers are secret, and cannot be publicly disclosed until they have passed into history. It is quite clear that no court will compel the production

---

[144] *Guardian Newspapers Ltd and Heather Brooke v IC and BBC*, IT, 8 January 2007 at [64], [71]. The Tribunal in *MoD v IC and Evans*, IT, 20 July 2007 noted (at [14]) 'the question of whether the process of arriving at the opinion can be challenged is not without doubt.' The Tribunal in *McIntyre v IC and MoD*, IT, 4 February 2008 applied the approach in *Guardian and Brooke*, but with two caveats. First, where the opinion is overridingly reasonable in substance then, even though the method or process by which that opinion is arrived at is flawed in some way, this need not be fatal to a finding that it is a reasonable opinion. Second, the Tribunal should take a broad view of the way the opinion is arrived at, so that even if there are flaws in the process these can be subsequently corrected , provided that this is within a reasonable time period which would usually be no later than the internal review (at [31]). In *University of Central Lancashire v IC and Colquhoun*, IT, 8 December 2009 the Tribunal concluded (at [58]-[61]) that the 'perfunctory' process of forming the opinion supported a conclusion that it was not reasonably arrived at.

[145] See *Cabinet Office v IC*, IT, 21 October 2008 at [39]-[40].

[146] This special provision is, of course, not required for the regime applying to Scottish public authorities.

[147] [1976] QB 752.

of Cabinet papers in the course of discovery in an action, and the Attorney-General contends that not only will the court refuse to compel the production of such matters, but it will go further and positively forbid the disclosure of such papers and proceedings if publication will be contrary to the public interest.

The basis of this contention is the confidential character of these papers and proceedings, derived from the convention of joint Cabinet responsibility whereby any policy decision reached by the Cabinet has to be supported by all members of the Cabinet whether they approve of it or not, unless they feel compelled to resign. It is contended that Cabinet decisions and papers are confidential for a period to the extent at least that they must not be referred to outside the Cabinet in such a way as to disclose the attitude of individual Ministers in the argument which preceded the decision. Thus, there may be no objection to a Minister disclosing (or leaking, as it was called) the fact that a Cabinet meeting has taken place, or, indeed, the decision taken, so long as the individual views of Ministers are not identified.[148]

The Attorney-General had argued that all Cabinet papers and discussions were *prima facie* confidential and that publication of them ought to be restrained if the public interest in concealment outweighed the public interest in a right to free publication: the court could, it was argued, restrain disclosure of Cabinet documents or proceedings that would reveal the individual views or attitudes of a Minister and confidential advice from civil servants (whether contained in Cabinet papers or not).[149] Lord Widgery CJ concluded:

> ...it seems to me that the degree of protection afforded to Cabinet papers and discussion cannot be determined by a single rule of thumb. Some secrets require a high standard of protection for a short time. Others require protection until a new political generation has taken over....I find overwhelming evidence that the doctrine of joint responsibility is generally understood and practised and equally strong evidence that it is on occasion ignored
> ...To leak a Cabinet decision a day or so before it is officially announced is an accepted exercise in public relations, but to identify the Ministers who voted one way or another is objectionable because it undermines the doctrine of joint responsibility.[150]

Lord Widgery CJ concluded that publication of the Crossman diaries would, as a matter of fact, not prejudice the maintenance of the convention of the collective responsibility of Ministers of the Crown:

> ...I cannot believe that the publication at this interval [ie 1975 in a volume relating to 1964-1966] of anything in volume one would inhibit free discussion in the Cabinet of today, even though the individuals involved are the same, and the national problems have a distressing similarity with those of a decade ago. It is unnecessary to elaborate the evils which might flow if at the close of a Cabinet meeting a Minister proceeded to give the press an analysis of the voting, but we are dealing in this case with a disclosure of information nearly 10 years later. It may, of course, be intensely difficult in a particular case, to say at what point the material loses its confidential character, on the ground that publication will no longer undermine the doctrine of joint Cabinet responsibility. It is this difficulty which prompts some to argue that Cabinet discussions should retain their confidential character for a longer and arbitrary period such as 30 years, or even for all time, but this seems to me to be excessively restrictive. The court should intervene only in the clearest of cases where the continuing confidentiality of the material can be demonstrated. In less clear cases—and this,

---

[148] [1976] QB 752 at 764.

[149] [1976] QB 752 at 765.

[150] [1976] QB 752 at 767, 770.

in my view, is certainly one—reliance must be placed on the good sense and good taste of the Minister or ex-Minister concerned....The Attorney-General...has not satisfied me that publication would in any way inhibit free and open discussion in Cabinet hereafter.[151]

It is suggested that unless there is some measure of contemporaneity about the information or the subject matter of the information that falls to be released, it will be difficult to reasonably conclude that its disclosure would be likely to prejudice the maintenance of the convention of the collective responsibility of Ministers of the Crown.[152]

024 The convention of the collective responsibility of the Cabinet: the public interest

Lord Widgery's judgment in *Attorney-General v Jonathan Cape Ltd* also provides a useful insight into the public interest embodied in the exemption:

> I have already indicated some of the difficulties which face the Attorney-General when relied simply on the public interest as a ground for his actions. That such ground is enough in extreme cases is shown by the universal agreement that publication affecting national security can be restrained in this way. It may be that in the short run (for example, over a period of weeks or months) the public interest is equally compelling to maintain joint Cabinet responsibility and the protection of advice given by civil servants, but I would not accept without close investigation that such matters must, as a matter of course, retain protection after a period of years.[153]

Quite apart from its diminution in the likelihood of prejudice to the maintenance of the convention of the collective responsibility of Ministers of the Crown, the passage of time is likely also to diminish the public interest in the maintenance of the exemption.

025 Inhibiting the free and frank provision of advice or views

The second limb in s 36(2) describes information the disclosure of which would, or would be likely to, inhibit 'the free and frank provision of advice or the free and frank exchange of views for the purposes of deliberation'. The shortcomings in the 'candour argument' and its fate as a head of public interest immunity in this country have already been noted in relation to the

---

[151] [1976] QB 752 at 771. In *Cabinet Office v IC*, IT, 27 January 2009, the Tribunal noted (at [19]) that 'even assuming that there was a serious risk that the disclosure of [the information] would have led to the inference being drawn that there had been a disagreement between Ministers at the time it was prepared, we do not see how such an inference would have undermined the collective responsibility principle... The collective responsibility principle requires Ministers to support a decision once it has been reached, not to agree about everything before decisions have even been taken. The principle would only have been at risk of prejudice if specific views had been rehearsed in the paper which could then have been used to embarrass those holding them if a decision had gone against them.'

[152] Some further support for this proposition comes from the fact that such information in a 'historical record' cannot be exempt information: see FOIA s 63(1) and §7– 035. In *Cabinet Office v IC and Lamb*, IT, 27 January 2009, a majority of the Tribunal concluded (at [78]) that the importance of maintaining the Convention was diluted by the extent to which some of the information had already been disclosed, both formally and informally, and the trend of important matters being discussed in small groups outside Cabinet.

[153] [1976] QB 752 at 768. In *Sankey v Whitlam* (1978) 148 CLR 1, Mason J, in referring to Lord Widgery's judgment, said: 'I also agree with his Lordship that the efficiency of government would be seriously compromised if Cabinet decisions and papers were disclosed whilst they or the topics to which they relate are still current or controversial. But I base this view, not so much on the probability of ill-formed criticism with its inconvenient consequences, as upon the inherent difficulty of decision making if the decision-making processes of Cabinet and the materials on which they are based are at risk of premature publication. Cabinet proceedings have always been regarded as secret and confidential' (at 98).

parallel exemption in s 35.[154] On the basis of these, it is suggested that, whatever might have been the position in past decades, it can no longer seriously be maintained that officials, either by dint of advising on matters of policy or of their seniority, would be likely to neglect their duty to give frank advice if that advice were to be released pursuant to a legislative obligation to do so.[155]

22– 026 Otherwise prejudicing the effective conduct of public affairs
The last of the three limbs in s 36(2) describes information the disclosure of which would, or would be likely to, 'otherwise prejudice the effective conduct of public affairs'. The potential application of this provision is limited.[156] It is not easy to imagine what prejudice, apart from undermining Cabinet secrecy and the questionable impact upon public officials' ability to advise candidly, would be likely to be caused to the effective conduct of public affairs from the 'disclosure of...information under [the Freedom of Information Act]'.[157] If the information has a further attribute (eg it is confidential information or it comprises sensitive national security material) then it may be that disclosure will result in prejudice to the effective conduct of public affairs: however, that additional attribute will invariably render the information exempt information under another provision of the Act.[158] It is suggested that resultant criticism cannot properly be characterised as representing prejudice to the effective conduct of public affairs.[159]

---

[154] See §22– 011.

[155] See, eg, *Cabinet Office v IC and Lamb*, IT, 27 January 2009 at [77]-[82].

[156] In *McIntyre v IC and MoD*, IT, 4 February 2008, the Tribunal found (at [25]) that the s 36(2)(c) exemption is intended to apply to those cases 'where it would be necessary in the interests of good government to withhold information, but which are not covered by another specific exemption, and where the disclosure would prejudice the public authority's ability to offer an effective public service or to meet its wider objectives or purposes due to the disruption caused by the disclosure or the diversion of resources in managing the impact of disclosure.' In *McIntyre v IC and MoD*, IT, 4 February 2008, the request was for information relating to the process for promotion in the Ministry of Defence, disclosure of which the Ministry of Defence contended would adversely affect the integrity of the promotion scheme. See also *Galloway v IC and NHS*, IT, 20 March 2009, where the exemption was successfully invoked by an NHS Trust in relation to the requested disclosure of witness statements from staff provided in the course of an investigation of a 'serious untoward incident' – see [96], [99]-[112].

[157] In *Sankey v Whitlam* (1978) 148 CLR 1 a similar 'sweep-up' claim was made in support of a public interest immunity claim before the High Court of Australia. Mason J observed (at 97): 'They [the Executive] have sought refuge in the amorphous statement that non-disclosure is necessary for the proper functioning of the Executive Government and of the public service, without saying why disclosure would be detrimental to their functions, except for the reference to want of "candour." Perhaps affidavits in this form were acceptable in the days when it was thought that the court should uphold an objection once made by the Crown through its appropriate representative. But they are plainly unacceptable now that the court is to resolve the issue for itself, after an inspection of the documents when that is thought to be appropriate. An affidavit claiming Crown privilege should state with precision the grounds on which it is contended that documents or information should not be disclosed so as to enable the court to evaluate the competing interests.'

[158] In *MoD v IC and Evans*, IT, 20 July 2007, the Ministry of Defence sought to rely on the exemption contained in s 36(2)(c) in the alternative to its reliance upon s 36(2)(b), deploying identical arguments for the former exemption as for the latter. The Tribunal noted (at [53]) that 'if the same arguments are to be advanced, then the prejudice feared is not "otherwise". Some prejudice other than that to the free and frank expression of advice (or views, as far as section 36(2)(b)(ii) is concerned) has to be shown for section 36(2)(c) to be engaged.'

[159] In *Commonwealth of Australia v John Fairfax & Sons Ltd* (1980) 147 CLR 39 at 50–51 Mason J in granting an interlocutory injunction restraining the defendant on breach of copyright grounds from publishing but declining to grant an injunction on breach of duty-of-confidence grounds on the basis that disclosure was unlikely to injure the public interest said: 'The question then, when the executive government seeks the protection given by equity, is: What detriment does it need to show? The equitable principle has been fashioned to protect the personal, private and proprietary interests of the citizen, not to protect the very different interests of the executive government. It

The Tribunal has rejected a claim that disclosure might discourage proper minute-taking.[160]

027 **The duty to confirm or deny**

Section 36 also provides a corresponding exclusion from the duty to confirm or deny.[161] There is a subtle but important distinction in the operation of this exclusion from the exclusion given by s 35(3). Under s 35(3), if a given piece of information relating to the formulation of policy, etc is exempt information under s 35(1), then the corresponding duty to confirm or deny that the information is held does not arise. Under s 36(3), where information is exempt from the duty of disclosure under s 36(2), that is not determinative of whether the duty to confirm or deny arises under s 36(3).[162] Instead, the duty to confirm or deny does not arise where, in the reasonable opinion of a 'qualified person', informing the applicant that the public authority holds or does not hold the information requested would be, or would be likely to be, prejudicial to public affairs in one of the ways set out in s 36(2).[163] The exemption is qualified: the matters to be weighed, which are different from those weighed for the purposes of determining whether the duty to disclose applies, is treated elsewhere in this work.[164]

---

acts, or is supposed to act, not according to standards of private interest, but in the public interest. This is not to say that equity will not protect information in the hands of the government, but it is to say that when equity protects government information it will look at the matter through different spectacles. It may be a sufficient detriment to the citizen that disclosure of information relating to his affairs will expose his actions to public discussion and criticism. But it can scarcely be a relevant detriment to the government that publication of material concerning its actions will merely expose it to public discussion and criticism. It is unacceptable in our democratic society that there should be a restraint on the publication of information relating to government when the only vice of that information is that it enables the public to discuss, review and criticise government action...The court will not prevent the publication of information which merely throws light on the past workings of government, even if it be not public property, so long as it does not prejudice the community in other respects. Then disclosure will itself serve the public interest in keeping the community informed and in promoting discussion of public affairs. If, however, it appears that disclosure will be inimical to the public interest because national security, relations with foreign countries or the ordinary business of government will be prejudiced, disclosure will be restrained.' This authority was cited with approval in *AG v Observer Ltd* [1990] 1 AC 109 at 151–152 (Scott J), at 203 (Dillon LJ), at 218, 221 (Bingham LJ), at 258 (Lord Keith), at 270 (Lord Griffiths), at 283 'in a free society there is a continuing public interest that the workings of government should be open to scrutiny and criticism' (Lord Goff).

[160] *Guardian Newspapers Ltd and Heather Brooke v IC and BBC*, IT, 8 January 2007 at [107].

[161] FOIA s 36(3).

[162] FOIA s 2(1).

[163] The different ways in which the duty to confirm or deny has been disapplied under the FOIA is considered in §14–005.

[164] See §§15–018 to 15–019.

CHAPTER 23

Health and Safety

23–001 Introduction

Where the disclosure of information under the Freedom of Information Act 2000 would or would be likely: (a) to endanger the physical or mental health of any individual; or (b) to endanger the safety of any individual, then that information is exempt information by virtue of s 38(1).[1] The exemption is a qualified exemption, so that whether or not there is a duty to disclose such exempt information will turn upon whether in all the circumstances of the case the public interest in maintaining the exemption outweighs the public interest in disclosing the information. Similarly, to the extent that, if a public authority were to inform an applicant that it held information of the description specified in the applicant's request, that informing would or would be likely: (a) to endanger the physical or mental health of any individual; or (b) to endanger the safety of any individual, then the duty to confirm or deny does not arise.[2] The exclusion of this duty is also qualified, so that in such circumstances the public authority will be excused from informing the applicant that it holds the requested information only if the public interest in maintaining the exclusion outweighs the public interest in disclosing whether the public authority holds the information. Similar exemptions of varying scope exist in each of the comparative jurisdictions.[3] A substantial amount of information relating to health and

---

[1] FOI(S)A s 39(1), is effectively identical. EIR reg 12(5)(a) and EI(S)R reg 10(5)(a) provide for a qualified exception in respect of information the disclosure of which would adversely affect public safety.

[2] FOIA s 38(2). There is no separate duty to confirm or deny under the FOI(S)A.

[3] In the United States, the Freedom of Information Act, 1966, 5 USC 552(b)(7), exempts from disclosure records or information the production of which could reasonably be expected to endanger the life or physical safety of any individual: see §2–008(7)(F). The Freedom of Information Act 1982 (Cth of Australia) s 37(1)(c), provides an exemption where the disclosure of the requested document would, or could be reasonably be expected to, endanger the life or physical safety of any person. Section 37(2)(c) provides a separate exemption for a document the disclosure of which would, or could reasonably be expected to, prejudice the maintenance or enforcement of lawful methods for the protection of public safety. Section 41(3) provides a special method of disclosure where it appears

safety is likely to be 'environmental information'[4] and therefore exempt under s 39 of the Freedom of Information Act 2000. If this is the case, its disclosure falls to be considered under the Environmental Information Regulations 2004 and not under the Freedom of Information Act 2000.[5]

002 Scope of the exemption

The scope for the disclosure of information to directly endanger health or safety is limited. If the applicant, or a person to whom the information can reasonably be expected to be conveyed, has a vulnerability or sensitivity, then it is conceivable that receipt of the information, if touching upon that vulnerability or sensitivity, may directly endanger that individual's health. In those circumstances, the information will be exempt information. Such a determination by a public authority presupposes some knowledge on its part of the individual's vulnerabilities or sensitivities which the public authority may well not have. Apart from such direct endangering, information that is disclosed under the Freedom of Information Act 2000 may be *used* in such a way as to endanger an individual's health or safety. Whether in these circumstances it is apposite to describe *the disclosure* of the information as endangering health or safety, as opposed to *the likely use* that will be made of disclosed information endangering health or safety, is essentially a question of causation. On the usual principles of causation, if it is readily predictable that particular information, once disclosed, will be used in such a way as would risk harming the health or safety of an individual, then it may be said that the disclosure of the

---

to the agency that the disclosure of the information to the applicant might be detrimental to the applicant's physical or mental health, or well-being. The Official Information Act 1982 (New Zealand) s 9(2)(c) provides a qualified exemption where disclosure would cause prejudice to measures protecting the health or safety of members of the public: see §2– 023(4). Sections 6(d) and 27(1)(a) provide an absolute exemption where disclosure would be likely to endanger the safety of any person: see §2– 022(4). The Access to Information Act (Canada) s 17 provides a discretionary exemption for records the disclosure of which could 'reasonably be expected' to cause a threat to an individual's safety: see §2– 032(14). There is no analogous exemption in respect of information the disclosure of which could reasonably be expected to threaten an individual's physical or mental health. The *Report of the Access to Information Task Force* (June 2002, Ottawa), p 56, recommended that one be included. The Privacy Act (Canada) s 28, provides discretionary exemption for any personal information that relates to the physical or mental health of the individual who requested it where the examination of the information by the individual would be contrary to the best interests of the individual. Section 25 of that Act provides a discretionary exemption where disclosure could reasonably be expected to threaten the safety of individuals. Section 20(6) of the Access to Information Act also specifically provides that the head of a government institution (being the primary decision-maker for the purposes of the Act) may disclose third party confidential information (which would otherwise be exempt) where disclosure under the Act 'would be in the public interest as it relates to public health, public safety or protection of the environment and, if the public interest in disclosure clearly outweighs in importance any financial loss or gain to, prejudice to the competitive position of or interference with contractual or other negotiations of a third party.' The Freedom of Information Act 1997 (Ireland), ss 23(1)(aa) and 28(3), respectively provide a discretionary exemption for records the disclosure of which might endanger the life or safety of any person or that might be prejudicial to the health of the applicant: see §2– 039(14). A separate exemption is provided for disclosures that could reasonably be expected to prejudice or impair lawful methods, etc for ensuring the safety of the public and of persons. Sections 27(2)(e) and 28(2)(e) provide a similar override to the Canadian Act in relation to confidential third party information the disclosure of which is 'necessary in order to avoid a serious and imminent danger to the life or health of an individual.'

[4]   As to the meaning of which, see §6– 010.

[5]   And, in the case of information held by Scottish public authorities, under the EI(S)R and not the FOI(S)A. In relation to access to environmental information, see ch 6.

information will endanger the health or safety of that individual.[6] On the other hand, where there is a mere possibility that certain information may be misused in such a way as to endanger health or safety it becomes more difficult to say the disclosure of that information 'would or would be likely to endanger' health or safety.[7] This is particularly so if there is an obvious use that may be made of the information that would not be likely to endanger health or safety. The level of probability required by the exemption is the same as that used in other exemptions ('would or would be likely to'): this is considered elsewhere in this work.[8] The exemption is unique in its use of the word 'endanger' rather than the word 'prejudice'.[9] Arguably, it is easier for a disclosure to 'endanger' an interest than it is for a disclosure to prejudice that interest, as the word 'endanger' connotes a risk of harm rather than harm itself.[10]

23– 003 The distinction between health and safety

Although there is a considerable degree of potential overlap between the information caught by s 38(1)(a) (physical or mental health)[11] and the information caught by s 38(1)(b) (safety),[12] the

---

[6]   In other areas of the law it is conventional to seek to identify the 'effective' or 'dominant' cause of an outcome: *Galoo v Bright Grahame Murray* [1994] 1 WLR 1360 at 1374–1375. Ultimately it will depend upon a commonsense interpretation of the facts. Intervening acts by third persons have always presented particular problems in relation to causation, and the following authorities provide useful illustrations, albeit in different contexts: *Weld-Blundell v Stephens* [1920] AC 956 (where the defendant, in breach of his contract, negligently left a libellous letter written by the plaintiff, where it was read by a third party, who was likely to, and did, communicate its contents to the persons libelled: the latter recovered damages for libel from the plaintiff, who then turned around and sued the defendant. The House of Lords, by a majority, held that the act of the third party, although foreseeable, was a 'new and independent' cause).

[7]   The Tribunal has taken a less strict line. Thus, in *Hemsley v IC and Chief Constable of Northamptonshire*, IT, 10 April 2006 it was prepared to find that a request for information relating to a specific speed camera, including times of its operation, would satisfy s 38(1). Similarly in *Ministry of Defence v IC and Evans*, IT, 20 July 2007 at [76] the Tribunal was satisfied that there was 'a sufficiently serious suggestion' of the requisite likelihood of prejudice to health from the publication of a directory of staff, notwithstanding a certain amount of external circulation of the directory.

[8]   See §§15– 022 to 15– 027. In *MoD v IC and Evans*, IT, 20 July 2007 at [76], the Tribunal held that these principles applied to s 38. According to MoJ, *Exemptions Guidance—Section 38* (14 May 2008) in the context of FOIA s 38, it connotes risk of harm rather than harm itself; 'likely to' suggests a result which could reasonably be expected, but which does not have to be specifically foreseeable (p 3).

[9]   As to the meaning of 'likely to prejudice' see §15– 022.

[10]   In *Hemsley v IC and Chief Constable of Northamptonshire*, IT, 10 April 2006 at [14] the Tribunal held that no practical distinction arose between prejudicing and endangering, at least for the purposes of that appeal. In a very different context, see *R v Whitehouse* [2000] Crim LR 172 which concerned the issue of whether the use of a mobile phone on an aircraft was doing an act 'likely to endanger an aircraft' contrary to art 5 Air Navigation (No 2) Order 1995. The Court of Appeal concluded that 'likely to endanger' in this context would be satisfied if there was a real risk of endangerment. This case turned more on the meaning of 'likely' than of 'endanger'. In *R v Pearce* [1967] 1 QB 150 at 154–155 the Court of Appeal, again in a different context, spoke of endangering as being concerned with 'causing a source of danger'. See also MoJ, *Exemptions Guidance—Section 38* (14 May 2008) which suggests that 'likely to endanger' means 'likely to put someone's health or safety at risk, or at greater risk.' However, the Information Commissioner's Guidance No 19 suggests that there is no difference between the scope of 'endanger' and 'prejudice'.

[11]   MoJ, *Exemptions Guidance—Section 38* (14 May 2008) suggests that 'A broad approach should be taken when considering potential risks: mental health should include general emotional and psychological well-being, but should not necessarily include mere distress, while safety should be taken to mean general protection from harm.'

[12]   MoJ, *Exemptions Guidance—Section 38* (14 May 2008), suggests that 'safety' should again be given its ordinary meaning to include protection from harm. The OED defines safety as: 'the state of being protected from or guarded against any hurt or injury; freedom from danger.' According to the Guidance, as in the present context the term concerns the safety of individuals, a broad approach is likely to be right.

comparative jurisprudence illustrates that their coverage is by no means identical. In particular, whereas the former exemption has greater potential direct application, the latter is only readily engaged by some predicted use of the information.

— In the US, under the safety exemption, where the applicant had previously threatened federal employees and third persons connected with law enforcement matters, the courts have upheld non-disclosure of the names and identifying information of persons in that class, provided that withholding that information is necessary in order to protect them from possible harm.[13]

— In Australia, exemption on the analogous safety ground has been upheld for documents relating to a surveillance operation carried out by the police into members of a sect, the Tribunal considering that release would give rise to a reasonable expectation that the life or physical safety of a person might be in danger.[14] Similarly, exemption has been upheld where disclosure of information such as a person's identity, views or whereabouts would make that person a potential target of violence by another person or group of persons. However, the Tribunal and Courts have required objective evidence to support a reasonable apprehension of danger.[15] Thus, where an applicant, who had four convictions for assault and who had been a recipient of a disability support pension that had been cancelled and then reinstated, sought access to the underlying documents for the cancellation decision, it was held not to be enough to engage the safety exemption that (a) the psychologist who had examined the applicant had requested that his report not be provided to the applicant because of his potential to react violently; (b) the applicant had made statements suggesting that he would act violently; and (c) when interviewed, the applicant had had a threatening demeanour, and the officer concerned had felt threatened by him.[16]

— Also in Australia, disclosure has been refused on safety grounds in relation to a

---

[13] *Blanton v United States Department of Justice*, 182 F Supp 2d 81 (DDC 2002), where, on the grounds of safety, the Court refused to order disclosure so as to protect the identities of FBI Special Agents and non-law enforcement personnel assisting in an investigation, even though the requester was incarcerated, on the basis that his threats against persons responsible for his arrest and conviction made it possible that those individuals could be targets of physical harm.; *LA Times Communications, LLC v Department of the Army*, 442 F Supp 2d 880 (CD Cal 2006) where it was held that disclosure of private security contractor company names operating in concert with US military forces in Iraq could endanger the life or physical safety of many individuals; *Brady-Lunny v Massey*, 185 F Supp 2d 928 (CD Ill 2002) where the court held that disclosure of a list of the names of detainees in a prison would endanger life and physical safety given security risks that always are present in inmate populations.

[14] *Re Anderson and Australian Federal Police* (1987) 11 ALD 356. But the Administrative Appeals Tribunal will scrutinise agency claims that disclosure of information to the applicant will result in physical danger: *Scholes v Australian Federal Police* (1996) 44 ALD 299 at [121]–[128].

[15] *Re Boehm and Department of Industry Technology and Commerce* (1985) 7 ALN N186. On the other hand, the exemption has been held not to be satisfied where evidence was produced that one of several institutions where animal experiments were conducted had received a bomb threat. It was held that danger to lives or physical safety was only considered to be a possibility, not a real chance: *Re Binnie and Department of Agriculture and Rural Affairs* (1987) 1 VAR 361.

[16] *Centerlink v Dykstra* [2002] FCA 1442. The Tribunal had taken into account that the medical evidence was two years old and that the applicant had never actually attempted to harm any official. Although the Federal Court allowed an appeal, that was on the basis that the Tribunal had failed to take into account relevant material, and it otherwise upheld the decision-making methodology of the Tribunal: in particular, that the fear of the officers could not be determinative of the issue.

portion of an army manual relating to the tactical response to terrorism and to Army procedures to meet requests for assistance in dealing with terrorism on the basis that if the relevant section of the manual were made public, there would be a significant risk to security.[17]

— In New Zealand, the disclosure of possible examination questions for pilots has been refused on safety grounds.[18] Other safety examples can be expected to include: the disclosure of plans of a prison,[19] and the disclosure of the new identity, or the location of, a recently released convicted child killer.[20] In each of these two cases it is difficult to see a legitimate need for the information sought by any applicant under the Act.

23– 004 Examples where the exemption has applied

The following are examples where a public authority has successfully invoked s 38:

(1) *Hemsley v Information Commissioner and Chief Constable of Northamptonshire*,[21] where the applicant sought information relating to a specific speed camera, including its times of operation. In upholding the claim for exemption, it is unclear whether the Tribunal considered that the information was exempt under s 38 or s 31(1) (prejudice to the prevention or detection of crime).

(2) *Lawton v IC and NHS Direct*,[22] where the applicant sought the local telephone numbers of the 22 NHS Direct call centres, so that he did not have to use the national 0845 number which carried a time-based fee for its use. The Tribunal accepted evidence that disclosure of the numbers would side-step the automatic routeing system that minimised call-waiting times and would prejudice the operation of the system. The Tribunal held that although the probability of an adverse health consequence was low (delayed access to medical advice), the health consequence itself could be severe, so that s 38 was 'clearly engaged.'

23– 005 Examples where the exemption has not applied

The following are examples where a public authority has been unsuccessful in its attempt to invoke s 38:

(1) *MoD v IC and Evans*,[23] where the Tribunal rejected an argument that disclosure of a directory published by the Defence Export Services Organisation, listing names, job titles, work addresses, telephone numbers and e-mail addresses of its staff would

---

[17] *Re Hocking and Department of Defence* (1987) 12 ALD 554.

[18] 8 CCNO 78 and 9 CCNO 143.

[19] In Australia, the Administrative Appeals Tribunal upheld an exemption in relation to a request by an applicant who had been interned during the Second World War on the grounds that the information referred to methods for protecting public safety during wartime: *Re Parisi and Australian Federal Police* (1987) 14 ALD 11 at 17. It is not clear how the Tribunal considered this continued to remain a threat to safety some 40 years later.

[20] See *Venables v News Group Newspapers* [2001] Fam 430. In such circumstances art 2 ECHR protecting the right to life is likely to be relevant when carrying out the balancing test relating to the public interest.

[21] IT, 10 April 2006.

[22] IT, 5 March 2008.

[23] IT, 20 July 2007 at [76]-[77].

be harmful to their health and safety. It was claimed that this information, used in conjunction with other information, could be deployed to harm them. Although the Tribunal acknowledged that there was some risk, it considered that it was too low to engage s 38.

(2) In *Bucks Free Press v IC*,[24] the applicant sought the number of notices of intended prosecution arising from two particular speed cameras. The Tribunal held that since the information sought would not reveal enforcement patterns and so not affect driver behaviour, 'the connection between the incidence of speeding and the danger of accidents occurring is so obvious that it must follow that the section 38 exemption is ... not engaged.'

006 The public interest

As noted above, the health and safety exemption is qualified or non-absolute: it only applies if the public interest in maintaining the exemption outweighs the public interest in disclosing the information.[25] This public interest must be satisfied even in cases where the endangerment of physical or mental health or safety is likely to occur. As with the other qualified exemptions, in weighing the competing public interests, the relevant decision maker[26] will have to take into account all the circumstances of the case[27] and any relevant provisions of the European Convention for the Protection of Human Rights and Fundamental Freedoms. Articles 2, 3 and 8 ECHR are all potentially engaged in relation to this exemption.[28] Relevant factors that will need to be considered no doubt include the risk and severity of any adverse effects on someone's health and the strength of the public interest in disclosure. It is suggested that the public interest in maintaining an exemption where it is the anticipated *use* of information that renders it exempt information will be liable to be displaced by the public interest in disclosure if there are legitimate uses for the information. Thus, the public interest in maintaining an exemption for information revealing the risks, however slight, in treatments or medicines on the basis that a proportion of the population will turn away from them (despite their beneficial effects), can only readily predominate over the public interest in disclosure of such information by rejecting the fundamental precepts of freedom of information legislation. In the parliamentary debates there was considerable discussion about withholding information about the risks of eating beef

---

[24] IT, 18 January 2007 at [18].

[25] See: FOIA ss 2(1)(b) and 2(2)(b); FOI(S)A s 2(1)(b); EIR reg 12(1)(b); EI(S)R reg 10(1)(b). For a general discussion of this topic, see §§15– 001 to 15– 019. That there is particular public interest in the disclosure of information relating to health and safety of an individual is reflected in Pt IVA of the Employment Rights Act 1996, as inserted by the Public Interest Disclosure Act 1998, which sanctions on the basis of it being in the public interest of a disclosure by an employee tending to show 'that the health and safety of any individual has been, is being or is likely to be endangered' – s 43B(1)(d).

[26] That is: the public authority from which information is sought, the Information Commissioner, the Tribunal, or the courts.

[27] FOIA ss 2(1)(b) and 2(2)(b); FOI(S)A s 2(1)(b)); EIR reg 12(1)(b); EI(S)R reg 10(1)(b); DPA s 35. MoJ, *Exemptions Guidance—Section 38* (14 May 2008) suggests that details to be considered will include: the size of the risk involved, the likelihood of the outcome in question, and the extent to which steps might be taken to reduce or manage that risk; the nature and seriousness of the resulting outcome were that risk to come about; the possibility that disclosure would help to protect the health or safety of other individuals; the possibility that the anticipated danger could be prevented or managed by other, reasonable, precautions.

[28] See ch 3.

during the BSE controversy. Mr O'Brien, the Parliamentary Under-Secretary of State for the Home Department stated:

> Where public health is seriously at risk and information is held by the Government, it is difficult to see, on any reading of the Bill, how it could be justified for a Minister to take the view that the public interest was in favour of secrecy, unless a criminal investigation were about to be undertaken, in which case the public interest would have to be weighed very carefully. In circumstances where there is a clear view that public health would be at risk—particularly in the sort of situation in which BSE arose—under the Bill, it would always be in the public interest for that information to be in the public domain.[29]

23– 007 Examples where the public interest has favoured maintaining the exemption

The following are examples where a public authority has successfully invoked s 38:

(1) *Hemsley v Information Commissioner and Chief Constable of Northamptonshire*,[30] where the Tribunal found that the public interest in maintaining the exemption outweighed the public interest in disclosure having regard to: the considerable quantity of information already available to the public in relation to safety cameras; the lack of legitimate utility in the particular information sought; the fear of misuse by others of the particular information sought by the applicant; and the fact that if it were provided in answer to this request, all such information would have to be disclosed.

(2) *Lawton v IC and NHS Direct*,[31] where there was evidence that disclosure of the requested information would on occasions delay the public getting health advice, the Tribunal held that the public interest in maintaining the information outweighed the right of access to that information.

23– 008 Examples where the public interest has favoured disclosure

The following are examples where a public authority has been unsuccessful in its attempt to invoke s 38:

(1) *MoD v IC and Evans*,[32] in which the Tribunal found that even if s 38 had been engaged, the public interest in maintaining the exemption was 'easily outweighed' by the public interest in disclosure of the list.

(2) *Bucks Free Press v IC*,[33] where the Tribunal held that since the requested information would not reveal enforcement patterns, the connection between it and driver behaviour was 'tenuous' such that 'the public interest in the undoubtedly important issues of speeding offences and public safety is not sufficiently strong to outweigh the public interest in informing the public debate on the fairness and efficiency of the management of the speeding camera facilities in the area.'

23– 009 The duty to confirm or deny

Where the requested information is, or if it were held would be, exempt information under s 38

---

[29] Hansard HC vol 357 col 723 (27 November 2000).

[30] IT, 10 April 2006, outlined at §23– 004.

[31] IT, 5 March 2008, outlined at §23– 004.

[32] IT, 20 July 2007 at [76], outlined at §23– 005.

[33] IT, 18 January 2007 at [24], outlined at §23– 005.

(1), then the discrete duty to confirm or deny that the information is held by the public authority does not arise.[34] The exclusion of this duty is a qualified one. It will be necessary to consider whether, in all the circumstances, the maintenance of the exclusion of this duty is outweighed by the public interest in disclosing whether the public authority holds the information. This public interest balancing exercise is materially different from that employed for the purpose of determining whether the duty to communicate does not apply.[35] It will only be in limited circumstances that the decision maker will be exempted from confirming or denying that it holds such information. The need for an exemption to the duty to confirm or deny was debated by Parliament. Lord Goodhart, the Liberal Democrat peer, commented:

> There are certain possible circumstances in which the mere disclosure that information was held would be a potential danger, either to someone who would be seriously upset—mentally perhaps—by the realisation that such information was in the possession of a public authority, or to someone who had supplied the information. The fact that that was known might induce someone to take steps against him.[36]

Whilst, it is suggested, 'upset' — whether mental or otherwise — is not a sufficient reason for refusing to confirm or deny the existence of information, there may be certain circumstances where such disclosure could cause, or exacerbate, mental illness. Further, the disclosure of the existence of information, provided that the request is sufficiently narrowly formulated, might indicate the identity of an informer.

010   The Data Protection Act 1998

The Data Protection (Subject Access Modification) (Health) Order 2000[37] provides an analogous exemption in relation to a request for personal data. Under this Order, data is exempted from subject access requirements of s 7 of the Data Protection Act 1998 to the extent to which disclosure under the section would be likely to cause serious harm to the physical or mental health or condition of the data subject or any other person.[38] The qualification of harm as limited to 'serious' harm is likely to compensate for the absence of an express public interest requirement in the Data Protection Act 1998 and hence exemption from disclosure under both Acts is likely to be similar. It is suggested that the addition of the word 'condition' adds little; the phrase 'mental health' is sufficiently broad to include mental conditions.

---

[34] EIR reg 12(6); EI(S)R reg 10(8). Not applicable under the FOI(S)R.

[35] See §§15– 018 to 15– 019 as to what it involves.

[36] Hansard HL vol 617 col 1250 (19 October 2000).

[37] SI 2000/413.

[38] See §5– 059.

CHAPTER 24

Personal Information

1. INTRODUCTION

24–001 Overview

Section 40 of the Freedom of Information Act 2000[1] creates two exemptions in order to achieve two objectives:

(1) The objective of s 40(1) is that where (or to the extent that) an applicant's request for information captures personal data[2] relating to the applicant himself, that

---

[1] Similarly: FOI(S)A s 38; EIR regs 5(3), 12(3) and 13; EI(S)R regs 10(3) and 11.

[2] As to the meaning of 'personal data' see §§5–012 and 5–021 to 5–025. Broadly speaking, 'personal data' are data relating to living and identified or identifiable individuals.

request (or that part of the request) is to be exclusively determined in accordance with the access provisions of the Data Protection Act 1998. Section 40(1) achieves this objective by rendering those personal data exempt information for the purposes of the Freedom of Information Act 2000,[3] while leaving in place the applicant's free-standing right under the Data Protection Act 1998 to be given access to information relating to himself. This free-standing right, with its own set of exemptions, is considered in Chapter 5.

(2)   The objective of s 40(2) is that where (or to the extent that) an applicant's request for information captures personal information relating to a person other than the applicant, the applicant's right of access under the Freedom of Information Act 2000 is curtailed so as to respect the 'privacy' of that other person.[4] Section 40(2) achieves this objective by rendering such information exempt information for the purposes of the Freedom of Information Act 2000 where certain conditions are met.[5] Those conditions import into the Freedom of Information Act 2000 the data protection principles and use those principles as the governing measure of privacy.

To the extent that the information captured by a request for information is 'environmental information', the applicant's right of access will fall to be determined by the Environmental Information Regulations 2004 and not the Freedom of Information Act 2000.[6] However, the Environmental Information Regulations 2004 deal with personal data within 'environmental information' in the same way as the Freedom of Information Act 2000, creating exceptions in identical terms to the above-mentioned exemptions.[7] Central to both regimes is the concept of 'personal data'. This concept is considered in detail in Chapter 5.[8] In summary, the mere reference in a document to an individual will not normally render that document, or any part of it, 'personal data'. Rather, the information must be 'biographical in a significant sense...going beyond the recording of [the individual's] involvement in a matter or event that has no personal connotations....'[9] Section 40 also contains two correlative exclusions of the duty to confirm or deny.[10]

002   The approach adopted

When the Freedom of Information Act was first proposed, it was intended that the two access

---

[3] Similarly: FOI(S)A s 38(1)(a); EIR reg 5(3); EI(S)R reg 11(1). To the extent that the information captured by a request relates both to the applicant and another person, the applicant's right to that information similarly falls to be determined by the DPA: see §5– 045.

[4] Similarly: FOI(S)A s 38(1)(b); EIR regs 12(3) and 13; EI(S)R regs 10(3) and 11(2). The Data Protection Act 1998 gives an applicant no right of access to information of which he is not the data subject.

[5] FOIA s 40(3)–(4); FOI(S)A s 38(2)–(3); EIR reg 13(2)–(3); EI(S)R reg 11(3)–(4).

[6] FOIA s 39; FOI(S)A s 39. Rights of access under the EIR are dealt with in ch 6.

[7] EIR regs 5(3), 12(3) and 13; EI(S)R regs 10(3) and 11.

[8] Defined in DPA s 1(1). See §§5– 021 to 5– 025.

[9] *Durant v FSA* [2003] EWCA Civ 1746, [2004] FSR 28, more extensively quoted at §5– 022. However, it is not necessary for the data subject to be named in order for it to constitute personal data relating to him: *A v IC*, IT, 11 July 2006 at [11].

[10] FOIA s 40(5). Similarly: EIR reg 13(5) (but only in relation to information relating to a third party); EI(S)R reg 11(6). There is no separate duty to confirm or deny under the FOI(S)A.

schemes (ie under the Data Protection Act 1998 and the Freedom of Information Act) would run in parallel as a dual access regime, with their systems aligned as far as possible.[11] However, that proposal was abandoned when the Bill was drafted.[12] One alternative approach debated when the Bill received its third reading was to make the third party disclosure exemption under the Freedom of Information Act 2000 applicable when disclosure would be likely to result in a public authority breaching its obligation to respect the private life of individuals pursuant to article 8 of the European Convention on Human Rights; but this did not find favour.[13]

24– 003 The rationale for the first exemption

Access to personal information is a key element of any freedom of information regime. Individuals in the United Kingdom enjoyed rights of access to certain types of personal information about themselves well before the Freedom of Information Act 2000 came into force. Since 1998 the principal source of those rights has been the Data Protection Act 1998 (which implements the Data Protection Directive).[14] That Act, like the earlier Data Protection Act 1984, also provides safeguards in respect of the processing of personal data, most importantly by requiring data controllers to comply with eight data protection principles.[15] The advent of the Freedom of Information Act 2000, having at its core a general right of access to any information held by a public authority, gave rise to a potential overlap between the two Acts in relation to personal information held by public authorities. The solution arrived at was to channel a request by an applicant for information relating to himself through the Data Protection Act 1998 and to enhance the subject access right (but only in so far as it related to information held by a public authority) by enlarging the definition of 'data'.[16] The enlarged definition of 'data' now captures information relating to an individual that is not part of a structured file relating to that individual. In this way, the coverage of a subject access request, in so far as it relates to personal data held by a public authority, resembles the coverage given by the Freedom of Information Act 2000 in relation to non-personal data held by a public authority.

24– 004 The rationale for the second exemption

The second category of requests for personal information — requests for personal information about third parties — was placed within the province of the Freedom of Information Act 2000. There is an inherent tension between the objective of freedom of information and the objective of protecting personal privacy. These objectives will often conflict when an applicant seeks access to personal information about a third party. The conflict poses three related challenges

---

[11] Cabinet Office, *Your Right to Know. The Government's Proposals for a Freedom of Information Act. White Paper* (Cm 3818, 1997) paras 4.6–4.1; House of Commons Library, The Freedom of Information Bill: Data Protection Issues, Research Paper 99/99, 3 December 1999, p 7.

[12] For example, from the Data Protection Registrar in her evidence to the Public Administration Committee: *Third Report of 1998–1999, Freedom of Information Draft Bill*, Vol II: HC 570–II of 1998–99, 16 August 1999, memorandum 2, p 18 para 4; *Third Report of 1998–1999, Freedom of Information Draft Bill*, Vol II: HC 570–I of 1998–99, 29 July 1999, para 98.

[13] Hansard HC vol 347 col 982 (5 April 2000); Hansard HL vol 618 cols 409–412 (25 October 2000).

[14] See ch 5.

[15] As to which, see §24– 011.

[16] DPA s 1(1)(e), inserted by FOIA s 68(2)(a).

for governments: first, to determine where the balance should be struck between those aims; and, secondly, to determine the mechanisms for dealing with requests for such information.[17] The conflict between the right to personal privacy and the public interest in the disclosure of personal information was recognised by the Government when it first proposed freedom of information legislation[18] and there was continued recognition of that difficulty throughout the passage of the Bill.[19] As enacted, the balance is struck so as to give primacy to protection against intrusive disclosure of personal information by making personal information relating to another person exempt from disclosure under the Freedom of Information Act 2000 to the extent that that disclosure would offend the protection given by the Data Protection Act 1998.[20] The description adopted by the Tribunal is that s 40(2) of the Freedom of Information Act 2000

> seeks to ensure that the interests of those requesting information from a public authority do not undermine, unnecessarily, the interests of those individuals whose personal data might find its way into the public domain as a result of the public authority complying with such a request.[21]

The interests of the person to whom the information relates are left with the public authority to advocate. Thus, while aspects of the scheme appear to favour a third party's privacy,[22] the Freedom of Information Act 2000 is alone amongst comparable legislation in not making provision for consulting a third party where information relating to that third party is sought by an applicant.[23] Nor is a third party given any right to initiate or to participate in appeal proceedings.

---

[17] This is reflected in the approach taken by the majority of the comparative jurisdictions, where the right of access to personal information is found exclusively in a Privacy Act and not in the freedom of information legislation: see §5–003.

[18] Cabinet Office, *Your Right to Know. The Government's Proposals for a Freedom of Information Act. White Paper* (Cm 3818, 1997) para 3.11(3).

[19] See eg House of Commons, *Select Committee on Public Administration Third Report, Session 1997–1998*, 19 May 1998, paras 10–18.

[20] FOIA s 40; FOI(S)A s 38; EIR regs 5(3), 12(3) and 13; EI(S)R regs 10(3) and 11. See *LB of Camden v IC*, IT, 19 December 2007 at [22]. There is a further layer of complexity in Scotland, where the Information Commissioner, based in England, is responsible for the promotion and enforcement of the DPA, even if the request is made in Scotland. The Scottish Information Commissioner and the Information Commissioner have signed a memorandum of understanding setting out the relationship between them in relation to freedom of information legislation, the intention being that they will co-operate with and provide assistance to one another.

[21] *A v IC*, IT, 11 July 2006 at [11]; *Blake v IC and Wiltshire CC*, IT, 2 November 2009 at [24].

[22] For example, in relation to personal information about public officials, where the FOIA draws no distinction between personal information that might be termed 'public' and that which is 'private'. The Data Protection Registrar had suggested that public officials should be afforded the same level of protection for information relating to their private lives as that enjoyed by others, but that there should be provision for greater disclosure of information relating to their public activities: *Third Report of 1998–1999, Freedom of Information Draft Bill, vol II*: HC 570–II of 1998–99, 16 August 1999, memorandum 2, p 19 paras 4.4–4.5. The Access to Information Act (Canada), s 3, definition of 'personal information', draws this distinction.

[23] See further §§11–041 to 11–049.

2. PERSONAL DATA OF WHICH THE APPLICANT IS THE DATA SUBJECT

24– 005 Introduction

Under s 40(1) of the Freedom of Information Act 2000,[24] information that constitutes 'personal data'[25] of which the applicant is the 'data subject'[26] is rendered exempt information. The exemption is an absolute exemption.[27] The result is that an applicant seeking information about himself has no rights under s 1 of the Freedom of Information Act 2000 but, instead, must look to the Data Protection Act 1998 to obtain that information. Under the 1998 Act, such a request is termed a 'subject access request'. The data answering the terms of a subject access request may also reveal personal information relating to a third party. Such requests are also dealt with under the Data Protection Act 1998.[28] In broad terms, where a data controller cannot comply with a subject access request without disclosing information relating to another identifiable individual he is not obliged to do so unless that individual has consented to the disclosure or it is reasonable in all the circumstances to comply with the request without such consent.[29] This is different from the situation where only part of the information caught by a request represents personal data relating the requester (whether or not that part also contains personal data relating to others). In that situation, only those parts that constitute personal data relating to the requester will be exempt under s 40(1); the remainder will fall to be considered under any other applicable exemptions in the Freedom of Information Act 2000.[30]

24– 006 The duty to confirm or deny

Section 40(5)(a) grants a correlative exclusion of the duty to confirm or deny in relation to information which constitutes personal data of which the applicant is the data subject.[31] It is to be noted that the exclusion of the duty does not require that confirmation or denial would or might itself disclose the existence of the information or cause any particular prejudice.[32] The

---

[24] Similarly: FOI(S)A s 38(1)(a); EIR reg 5(3); EI(S)R reg 11(1).

[25] Defined in: FOIA s 40(7); FOI(S)A s 38(5); EIR reg 2(4); EI(S)R reg 2(3). See §§5– 012 and 5– 021 to 5– 025. Broadly speaking, 'personal data' are data relating to living and identified or identifiable individuals.

[26] Defined in: FOIA s 40(7); FOI(S)A s 38(5); EIR reg 2(4); EI(S)R reg 2(3). A data subject is an individual who is the subject of personal data: see §5– 026.

[27] FOIA s 2(3)(f); FOI(S)A s 2(2)(e); EIR reg 12(1) and (3); EI(S)R reg 10(3).

[28] In *Fenney v IC*, IT, 26 June 2008 at [10]-[14], the Tribunal rejected the argument that information containing both the requester's personal data and third party personal data fell outwith s40(1) because the requester's data was less extensive and less significant.

[29] DPA s 7(4). This provision is considered at §5– 045. The right of an applicant to personal data of which the applicant is the data subject is considered in ch 5.

[30] See *Freeborn v IC and Sussex Police*, IT, 5 August 2008 at [1]-[8] and [19]; *Stevenson v IC and Chief Constable of West Yorkshire Police*, IT, 14 October 2008 at [1]-[24]; *Kelway v IC and Northumbria Police*, IT, 14 April 2009 at [55]-[61].

[31] Similarly, EI(S)R reg 11(6), but not the EIR. There is no separate duty to confirm or deny under the FOI(S)A. For the meaning of a 'duty to confirm or deny', see §1– 005.

[32] See the distinctions drawn in §14– 005.

exclusion of the duty to confirm or deny is absolute.[33] Thus, where or to the extent that a public authority receives a request under the Freedom of Information Act 2000 for information that constitutes personal data of which the applicant is the data subject, the public authority need neither provide the information nor advise the applicant whether or not it holds the information. However, the public authority should, under s 16 of the Freedom of Information Act 2000, offer advice and assistance by referring the applicant to the subject access rights under the Data Protection Act 1998.

3. PERSONAL DATA OF WHICH THE APPLICANT IS NOT THE DATA SUBJECT

007 Introduction

The second exemption in s 40 deals with personal information that relates to one or more third parties.[34] This second exemption can only apply to information that constitutes personal data of which the applicant is not the data subject or one of the data subjects.[35] That is to say, the data must relate to a living individual whom it is possible to identify, either from those data alone or from those data and any other information that is in the possession of the data controller or is likely to come into his possession, and the request for information must be made by an individual who is not the subject of those personal data.[36] In relation to this third party personal information, the exemption in s 40(2) will apply to the extent that the information satisfies either of two conditions.

(1)   The objective of the first condition is the protection of the privacy of the person to whom the data relates. The first condition (considered below) can be met in a number of different ways, the availability of which partly depends upon whether the information in question falls within paras (a) to (d) of the definition of 'data' in s 1(1) of the Data Protection Act 1998[37] or whether, instead, it falls within para (e) of that definition.[38] Where the first condition is satisfied, the exemption is absolute other than in limited circumstances.[39]

(2)   The objective of the second condition is to ensure that an applicant does not have a greater right of access to information relating to a third party than that third party

---

[33]   FOIA s 2(3)(f) and similarly EI(S)R reg 11(6).

[34]   FOIA s 40(2)–(7); FOI(S)A s 38(1)(b) and (2)–(5); EIR reg 13(2)–(3); EI(S)R reg 11(3)–(4).

[35]   FOIA s 40(1), (2)(a) and (7); EIR reg 13(1); EI(S)R reg 11(2). The exemption in section 40(2) will not apply where the data relate both the to the applicant and to a third party. In this situation, the information will be rendered exempt information by FOIA s 40(1) and the applicant's right of access to this information will fall to be determined by the DPA. This is not a requirement under the FOI(S)A.

[36]   DPA s 1(1) definition of 'data subject', brought in by FOIA s 40(7), FOI(S)A s 38(5), EIR reg 2(4), EI(S)R reg 2(3). See §§5– 021 to 5– 026.

[37]   See §§5– 012 to 5– 019.

[38]   See §5– 020. Crudely summarised, it covers paper-based information that is not in a file arranged so that information relating to an individual is readily accessible.

[39]   Namely, where the condition is only satisfied because disclosure would contravene DPA s 10: FOIA s 2(3)(f)(ii); FOI(S)A s 2(2)(e)(ii); EIR reg 13(2)(a)(ii); EI(S)R reg 11(3)(a)(ii).

would himself have. The second condition (considered in §24– 021) imports the exemptions from disclosure in Part IV of the Data Protection Act 1998. These are the exemptions that would apply to that third party were he to make a request under s 7 of the Data Protection Act 1998 for data relating to himself. The second condition does not depend upon which paragraph of the definition of 'data' applies. Where information satisfies the second condition, the exemption is not absolute and the obligation to disclose will turn upon a consideration of the public interest.[40]

24– 008 The first condition

The operation of the first condition varies according to whether or not the requested information belongs to any of the first four classes of 'data' in s 1(1) of the Data Protection Act 1998. Those first four classes[41] capture information which:

(a) is being processed by means of equipment operating automatically in response to instructions given for that purpose,

(b) is recorded with the intention that it should be processed by means of such equipment,

(c) is recorded as part of a relevant filing system or with the intention that it should form part of a relevant filing system, or

(d) does not fall within paragraph (a), (b) or (c) but forms part of a health record,[42] an educational record[43] or an accessible public record.[44]

Information falling into any of these classes is rendered exempt information for the purposes of the Freedom of Information Act 2000 if its disclosure otherwise than under the 2000 Act[45] would:

(1) contravene any of the data protection principles;[46] or

(2) contravene s 10 of the Data Protection Act 1998 by causing substantial damage or distress to the data subject.[47]

In case (1), exemption is absolute; in case (2), exemption is qualified.[48] To the extent that the

---

[40] FOIA s 2(3)(f); FOI(S)A s 2(2)(e); EIR reg 13(3); EI(S)R reg 11(4).

[41] See further §§5– 012 to 5– 019.

[42] As defined by DPA s 68(2).

[43] As defined by DPA Sch 11.

[44] As defined by DPA Sch 12.

[45] The inclusion of the phrase 'otherwise than under this Act' in FOIA s 40(3) makes it clear that the proposed disclosure has to be evaluated only under the DPA, as though FOIA or EIR did not exist. The culture of openness fostered by FOIA is thus subordinated to the protection of privacy as it finds expression in the data protection principles. Nor can the existence of FOIA fulfil any requirement of lawfulness or constitute a legal obligation under DPA 1998. See *House of Commons v IC and Norman Baker*, IT, 16 January 2007 at [46]-[50] (this point was not appealed).

[46] See §§24– 009 to 24– 012.

[47] See §24– 019. DPA s 10 only comes into operation where the data subject has served on the data controller a written notice requiring the data controller to cease (or not to begin) processing personal data of which he is the data subject on the ground that the processing will cause (or will be likely to cause) him or another substantial damage or distress and that that damage or distress is unwarranted.

[48] FOIA s 2(3)(f)(ii); FOI(S)A s 2(2)(e)(ii); EIR reg 13(2)(a)(ii); EI(S)R reg 11(3)(a)(ii).

information falls within para (e) of the definition of 'data' in the Data Protection Act 1998[49] (ie it is unstructured manual data), it is rendered exempt information for the purposes of the Freedom of Information Act 2000 if its disclosure to a member of the public otherwise than under the Act would contravene any of the data protection principles.[50] In this case, exemption is absolute.[51]

009   Contravention of the data protection principles

The grasp of the data protection principles is reduced by the exemptions in Part IV (ss 27-39) of the Data Protection Act 1998. The exemptions operate by removing certain data and certain forms of processing from one or more of the data protection principles.[52] Accordingly, in considering whether there has been a contravention of any of the data protection principles, those principles are not simply to be read in their 'raw' form as they appear in Sch 1, but must be read in light of the exemptions in Part IV (ss 27-39). The exemptions in Part IV of the Data Protection Act 1998 are considered in Chapter 5.[53] For the purposes of exemption under s 40(2) of the Freedom of Information Act 2000, the effect is that where a provision in Part IV of the Data Protection Act 1998 exempts personal data from a data protection principle,[54] the first condition in s 40(3) will not be satisfied.[55] Instead, disclosure of that personal data will fall to be considered under the second condition in s 40(4).[56] Whereas information that satisfies the first condition enjoys absolute exemption, information that satisfies the second condition enjoys qualified exemption.

010   The duty to confirm or deny

In relation to the duty to confirm or deny, the position is similar to the disclosure duty: if the mere confirmation or denial of the holding of information answering the terms of the request would contravene any of the data protection principles, then the duty to confirm or deny will be excluded.[57] Exclusion of the duty is qualified, so that it is necessary for a public authority to consider whether the public interest in maintaining the exclusion of the duty to confirm or

---

[49]   See §5– 020. Crudely summarised, it covers paper-based information that is not in a file arranged so that information relating to an individual is readily accessible.

[50]   FOIA s 40(3)(b); FOI(S)A s 38(2)(b); EIR reg 13(2)(b); EI(S)R reg 11(3)(b).

[51]   FOIA s 2(3)(f)(ii); FOI(S)A s 2(2)(e)(ii); EIR reg 13(2)(a)(ii); EI(S)R reg 11(3)(a)(ii).

[52]   FOIA s 40(7) defines 'the data protection principles' to mean the principles set out in Part I of Sch 1 of the DPA, but read as subject to Part II of that Schedule and s 27(1) of that Act. Similarly: FOI(S)A s 38(5); cf EIR reg 2(4); EI(S)R reg 2(3). DPA s 27(1) provides that 'references in any of the data protection principles to "personal data" or to the "processing of personal data" do not include references to data or processing which, by virtue of [Part IV of the Data Protection Act 1998], are exempt from that principle.'

[53]   §§5– 055 to 5– 081.

[54]   Although the exemptions in DPA Part IV only apply to certain forms of processing, apart from DPA s 33, all those exemptions apply to disclosure of information. Accordingly, if information belongs to the class described by the exemption, that exemption will (apart from the case of s 33) apply to the disclosure of that information.

[55]   Unless either: (a) that disclosure would contravene DPA s 10 (because a notice had earlier been given); or (b) some other data protection principle remains contravened.

[56]   As to which, see §24– 021.

[57]   FOIA s 40(5)(b)(i); EIR reg 13(5)(a); EI(S)R reg 11(6). There is no separate duty to confirm or deny under FOI(S)A and s 18 is inapplicable to this exemption. For the meaning of a 'duty to confirm or deny', see §1– 005.

deny outweighs the public interest in disclosing the information.[58] There is no duty to confirm or deny where giving such confirmation or denial would contravene a s 10 DPA notice.

24– 011 **The data protection principles**
The eight data protection principles are enumerated in Part I of Sch 1 to the Data Protection Act 1998.[59] Part II of Sch 1 sets out a binding[60] statement of the manner in which those principles in Part I are to be interpreted. It must always be borne in mind that s 1(1) of the Data Protection Act 1998 defines 'processing' very widely, and that it expressly includes holding, disclosure or otherwise making available of information. In very general terms, the eight data protection principles are principles that must be followed by every data controller in his processing of personal data. Because the Data Protection Act 1998 relates to all aspects of the 'processing'[61] of data, the data protection principles reflect the breadth of that term and do not always have an immediate application to the disclosure of data such as would result from a public authority providing information in answer to a request under the Freedom of Information Act 2000. Nevertheless, as disclosure is one of the defined facets of 'processing', if disclosure of personal data of which the applicant is not the data subject contravenes any of the data protection principles and none of the exemptions in Part IV of the Data Protection Act 1998 applies, this will render those data 'exempt information' for the purposes of the Freedom of Information Act 2000. It is therefore necessary to consider each of the data protection principles, recognising that some are inapposite to the disclosure of information by a public authority to an applicant. For the reasons set out below, it is suggested that only contravention of the first and sixth principles will have any potential application to such a disclosure.

(1) *First Principle*: Personal data must be processed fairly and lawfully[62] and, in particular, must not be processed unless: (a) at least one of the conditions in Sch 2 of the Data Protection Act 1998 is also met;[63] and (b) in the case of sensitive personal data, at least one of the conditions in Sch 3 of the Data Protection Act 1998 is met.[64] Paras 1 to 4 of Part II of Sch 1 provide binding interpretive guidance as to the requirement to process fairly. Because of the intricacies of the first principle and given its potential to apply to a disclosure under the Freedom of Information Act 2000, it has been considered separately below.

(2) *Second Principle*: Personal data must be obtained only for some specified and lawful purpose or purposes, and must not be further processed in any manner that is

---

[58] FOIA ss 2(1), 2(3)(f) and 40(5)(b)(i). Exemption from the duty to confirm or deny is absolute under the EIR and EI(S)R. As to the application of the public interest test in this context see MoJ *Exemptions Guidance. Section 40 – Personal information* (14 May 2008) p 17.

[59] DPA s 4, Sch 1; see also Sch 2. These replaced the eight data protection principles that were in the Data Protection Act 1984.

[60] DPA s 4(2).

[61] Defined in the DPA s 1(1) to include obtaining, recording, holding, organising, retrieving, consulting, use, transmitting, etc of data.

[62] Helpful guidance on what is meant by lawful and fair processing is contained in Information Commissioner, Freedom of Information Awareness Guidance No 1 (undated).

[63] See §24– 016.

[64] See §24– 017.

incompatible with that purpose or those purposes.[65] The first part of the second principle relates to the *obtaining* of personal data: disclosure of personal information by a public authority is not going to result in a contravention of this part of the principle. The second part of the second principle is directed to all forms of processing, which will include disclosure. Paragraph 6 of Part II of Sch 1 explains that in determining whether any disclosure of personal data is compatible with the purpose or purposes for which the data were obtained, regard is to be had to the purpose or purposes for which the personal data are intended to be processed by any person to whom they are disclosed. It is questionable whether this has any application to a disclosure of personal data by a public authority. At any rate, the disclosure of more extensive information on the same subject matter as that already disclosed does not constitute an additional 'purpose' or further processing of that information.[66]

(3) *Third Principle*: Personal data must be adequate, relevant and not excessive in relation to the purposes for which they are processed. Part II of Sch 1 does not include interpretive provisions for this principle and there is no definition of or guidance as to what is 'adequate', 'relevant' or 'excessive'.[67] As this principle is principally directed to the obtaining of data, it is difficult to see how disclosure of information could by itself involve a contravention of the principle.[68]

(4) *Fourth Principle*: Personal data should be accurate and, where necessary, kept up-to-date. Paragraph 7 of Part II of Sch 1 explains that the fourth principle is not to be regarded as being contravened by reason of any inaccuracy in personal data which accurately record information obtained by the data controller from the data subject or a third party in a case where: (a) having regard to the purpose or purposes for which the data were obtained and further processed, the data controller has taken reasonable steps to ensure the accuracy of the data; and (b) if the data subject has notified the data controller of the data subject's view that the data are inaccurate, the data indicate that fact. As this principle is directed to the holding or keeping of data, it is difficult to see how disclosure of personal information could by itself involve a contravention of the principle.

(5) *Fifth Principle*: Personal data processed for any purpose or purposes must be kept no longer than is necessary for that purpose or those purposes. The Act gives no guidance as to what is meant by 'longer than is necessary' or the factors that are to

---

[65] The 'purpose' does not have to be a core or operational purpose of the data controller; a data controller can process data for any lawful purpose: *Chief Constable of Humberside Police & ors v IC and SSHD* [2009] EWCA 1079 at [31], [56], [66] and [104]. Purposes can be notified to the IC under broad heads: *House of Commons v IC and Norman Baker*, IT, 16 January 2007 at [98].

[66] *Corporate Officer of the House of Commons v IC and Baker*, IT, 16 January 2007 at [97].

[67] For an example of the application of this principle, see *Chief Constable of Humberside Police & ors v IC and SSHD* [2009] EWCA 1079.

[68] In *Chief Constable of Humberside Police & ors v IC and SSHD* [2009] EWCA 1079 at [44], [57] and [66], the Court of Appeal was critical of the Information Tribunal for taking account of possible disclosure in determining whether the obtaining of data concerning criminal conviction and its retention on the Police National Computer breached the Third Principle.

be taken into account.[69]   However, as this principle is directed to the keeping of data, it is difficult to see how disclosure of personal information could by itself involve a contravention of the principle.[70]

(6)   *Sixth Principle*: Personal data must be processed in accordance with a data subject's rights under the Data Protection Act 1998. Paragraph 8 of Part II of Sch 1 explains that this principle is only to be regarded as having been contravened by failing to supply information in accordance with s 7 or by failing to comply with a notice under s 10(1), 11(1) or 12(1). The only potential contravention of this principle by a disclosure by a public authority would be where a data subject has previously written to the public authority as data controller requiring it to cease, or not begin, processing personal information in respect of which he is the data subject on the ground that that processing would cause or would be likely to cause substantial damage or distress to him or another person which is unwarranted.

(7)   *Seventh Principle*: Appropriate technical and organisational measures must be taken against unauthorised or unlawful processing of personal data and against accidental loss or destruction of, or damage to, personal data. This is further explained in paras 9 to 12 of Part II of Sch 1. This underscores the focus of the seventh principle, which is the taking of technical and organisational measures to safeguard personal data. Again, it is difficult to see how disclosure by a public authority could by itself involve a contravention of the principle.

(8)   *Eighth Principle*: Personal data must not be transferred to a country or territory outside the European Economic Area[71] unless that country or territory ensures an adequate level of protection of the rights and freedoms of data subjects in relation to the processing of personal data. This principle is further explained in paras 13 to 15 of Part II of Sch 1. This, too, is unlikely to have any particular relevance to a disclosure by a public authority.

24–012 The first data protection principle

On the above analysis, a public authority's disclosure (otherwise than under the Freedom of Information Act 2000) of third party personal information will very rarely contravene any data protection principle other than the first data protection principle.[72] Accordingly, whether personal information relating to a third party is or is not exempt information will often turn on whether the disclosure of that information, otherwise than under the Freedom of Information Act 2000, would contravene the first data protection principle. The first data protection

---

[69]   For an example of the application of this principle, see *Chief Constable of Humberside Police & ors v IC and SSHD* [2009] EWCA 1079.

[70]   In *Chief Constable of Humberside Police & ors v IC and SSHD* [2009] EWCA 1079 [44], [57] and [66], the Court of Appeal was critical of the Information Tribunal for taking account of possible disclosure in determining whether the obtaining of data concerning criminal conviction and its retention on the Police National Computer breached the Third Principle.

[71]   Comprising the Member States of the European Union together with Norway, Iceland and Liechtenstein. Article 25(1) of the Directive imposes a stricter prohibition on any transfer outside the European Union.

[72]   Information Commissioner, Freedom of Information Awareness Guidance No 1 (undated), identifies compliance with the first principle as the key issue when considering an application for third party data.

principle involves three separate and cumulative requirements.[73] First, the personal data must be processed 'fairly'. In the present context, this means that the public authority's disclosure to an applicant of personal information relating to another person would be 'fair'. The 'fairness' is to be adjudged on the basis of a disclosure otherwise than in compliance with any duty imposed by the Freedom of Information Act 2000. Secondly, the personal data must be processed (ie disclosed) 'lawfully'. Again, the lawfulness is to be adjudged on the basis of a disclosure otherwise than in compliance with any duty imposed by the Freedom of Information Act 2000. Thirdly, the disclosure must satisfy at least one of the conditions in Sch 2 and, in the case of 'sensitive personal data', the disclosure must also satisfy at least one of the conditions in Schedule 3.

013 Disclosure would be fair: procedural fairness
The first data protection principle is largely concerned with what may be characterised as procedural process rights. Part II of Sch 1 to the Data Protection Act 1998 spells out the basis on which such fairness is to be judged.

— Paragraph 1 of Part II is concerned with the manner in which the information was obtained. It requires regard to be had to the method by which the data was obtained, including in particular whether any person from whom the information was obtained was deceived or misled as to the purpose for which the information would be processed.[74]

— Paragraphs 2 and 3 of Part II set out circumstances in which personal data are not to be treated as processed fairly. Crudely summarised, these paragraphs provide that personal data is not to be treated as processed fairly unless the data subject has been provided with, or had made readily available to him, the purposes for which the personal data are intended to be processed and the identity of the processor. Data protection notices can be given in reasonably generous terms.[75] However, if a public authority has stated that information provided to it will be used for a particular purpose, it will be more difficult to demonstrate that it would be fair to disclose that information in answer to a request for information.[76] This will be of particular importance where the person has volunteered the information, as opposed to supplying it under compulsion or in return for permission of some sort.[77]

It has become increasingly common for public authorities to forewarn people supplying information to them (whether in completing a form or however) that that information may be

---

[73] DPA s 4, Sch 1, Sch 2. *A v IC*, IT, 11 July 2006 at [17a].

[74] See, eg, *British Gas Trading Ltd v Data Protection Registrar*, Data Protection Tribunal, 24 March 1998, which concerned personal data held by British Gas Trading Ltd (BGTL) as a result of its former monopoly in supplying gas. Because of its monopoly status, those who used gas had little option but to provide their personal data. The Tribunal held that it would be fair for BGTL to process the data for gas-related marketing uses, and even for electricity-related marketing, but that processing for wider non-gas related marketing uses (such as banking services) would be unfair.

[75] See: *Grow with Us Ltd v Green Thumb (UK) Ltd* [2006] EWCA Civ1201; *House of Commons v IC and Norman Baker*, IT, 16 January 2007.

[76] See, eg, *England and LB of Bexley v IC*, IT, 10 May 2007 at [106].

[77] Although in *England and LB of Bexley v IC*, IT, 10 May 2007 certain information was required to be supplied by property owners in their Council Tax return, it was not mandatory to record that the property was empty and the evidence was that some owners did not include that information (at [103]).

disclosed under the Freedom of Information Act 2000. Where information has been supplied to a public authority that has given such a warning, the requirement of fairness is more likely to be satisfied, and conversely.[78] Nevertheless, it would appear that the fairness requirement does not necessarily require a statement of intent by the public authority that one of the purposes for which it processes the data is to supply it to a person who requests it regardless of whether the public authority is under a duty to do so.[79] Where no notice has been given of the possibility that data may be disclosed under FOIA, the data controller should consider the possibility of giving notice once a FOIA request has been made but before any disclosure is provided. The data controller should also consider the related question of whether the provision of the notice would 'involve a disproportionate effort'.[80]

24–014 Disclosure would be fair: substantive fairness

The use of the expression 'in particular' in paragraph 1(1) of the first principle has been held to mean that there is a general obligation to process data fairly, in addition to the requirement to comply with the detailed conditions listed in Schedule 2.[81] This entails an assessment of the nature of the data, the identity of the person to whom the information is to be disclosed and the possible implications for the data subject.[82] It does not, however, involve a consideration of the interests or motives of the person seeking the information. Where the data subject is an officer or an employee of a public authority, fairness may assume less importance:

> when assessing the fair processing requirements under the DPA...the consideration given to the interests of data subjects, who are public officials where data are processed for a public function, is no longer first or paramount. Their interests are still important, but where data subjects carry out public functions, hold elective office or spend public funds they must have the expectation that their public actions will be subject to greater scrutiny than would be the case in respect of their private lives. This principle still applies even where a few aspects of their private lives are intertwined with their public lives but where the vast majority of processing of personal data relates to the data subject's public life.[83]

There is a sliding scale of protection depending on where the data subject stands with regard to carrying out public functions and the public authority's duty to respect its employees'

---

[78] In *England and LB of Bexley v IC*, IT, 10 May 2007 the Information Tribunal found at [106] that it would be unfair to disclose personal data (namely, the ownership of vacant properties in the area of the local authority) without the consent of the owner. Whether that line could be maintained for information received after the FOIA came fully into force and its effect widely known is not clear.

[79] DPA Sch 1, Pt II, para 2(3)(c). The Information Tribunal has held that where the processing would involve the disclosure of the name of a police informant, it will be relevant that the informant had specifically requested that his name be kept confidential and that the informant believed that, if revealed, the applicant would take reprisals: *Alcock v IC and Chief Constable of Staffordshire Police*, IT, 3 January 2007. *Quaere* whether the mere mentioning of an informant's name renders information personal information in relation to the informant. This would also seem to follow from *Murray v Express Newspapers plc* [2007] EWHC 1908 at [73]–[74].

[80] DPA Sch 1 Part II para 3(2)(a).

[81] *Blake v IC and Wiltshire CC*, IT, 2 November 2009 at [28].

[82] The question of the likelihood of identifiability of individuals from statistics, and by whom such individuals could be identified, is integral to the question of the fairness of disclosure of such statistics: *Dept of Health v IC and Pro-Life Alliance*, IT, 15 October 2009 at [52].

[83] *House of Commons v IC and Norman Baker*, IT, 16 January 2007 at [78].

reasonable expectations of privacy.[84] There is a strong expectation of privacy where personal data was obtained for the purposes of an internal investigation during the course of a person's employment, even if the data subject is a senior member of staff.[85] Those who are paid from the public purse should expect some information about their salaries to be made public.[86] Disclosure of salary scales or bands is generally appropriate; disclosure of exact salaries will only be appropriate in exceptional circumstances.[87] The Information Commissioner has identified five non-exhaustive factors relevant to the determination of whether the disclosure of a public official's salary information would be fair:[88]

(a)   what the individual in question was told at the commencement of, or during the course of, employment;

(b)   the relevant contractual or non-contractual provisions and conditions surrounding the employment as well as the general surrounding circumstances;

(c)   the level of the individual's grade and position within the public authority;

(d)   the expectation and the degree to which other salary-related information was publicised and/or otherwise made available, eg salary/pay bands and other general information taking into account the contents of any published accounts;

(e)   the need to strike a balance between information relating to the public position of the individual and the individual's private life.[89]

015   Disclosure would be lawful

The Data Protection Act 1998 does not specify what is meant by lawful processing. Any disclosure of information proscribed by statute would certainly not be lawful processing.[90] Disclosure where data controllers know that the disclosed data would be used for direct marketing purposes would be unlawful if the data subject had made an objection under section 11 of the Data Protection Act 1998.[91] A disclosure of information that would give rise to a civil liability (eg because it is a breach of confidence) would probably not constitute lawful processing.[92] The question of whether disclosure is lawful also requires a consideration of

---

[84]   *Salmon v IC and King's College Cambridge*, IT, 17 July 2008 at [44].

[85]   *Salmon v IC and King's College Cambridge*, IT, 17 July 2008; *Waugh v IC and Doncaster College*, IT, 29 December 2008 at [40]; *Blake v IC and Wiltshire CC*, IT, 2 November 2009 at [34]; *Magherafelt District Council v IC*, First-Tier Tribunal, 3 February 2010 at [47]-[49].

[86]   See Information Commissioner's Guidance *When Should Salaries be Disclosed?* (23 February 2009).

[87]   Information Commissioner's Guidance *When Should Salaries be Disclosed?* (23 February 2009) p 4.

[88]   This approach was endorsed by the Tribunal in *Gibson v IC*, First-Tier Tribunal, 22 January 2010 at [16] and [36].

[89]   Citing *House of Commons v IC and Norman Baker*, IT, 16 January 2007, especially at [78].

[90]   The Tribunal has suggested that disclosure which would be contrary to government guidance would also be unlawful: *England v IC*, IT, 10 May 2007. This is questionable, given that guidance is not legally binding.

[91]   *Robertson v Wakefield DC and SSHD* [2001] EWHC Admin 915, [2002] QB 1052. This case concerned a challenge under DPA 1998 and HRA 1998 to the practice of making information on the electoral register available to organisations, some of which would use the names and addresses on the register for the purposes of direct marketing. The claimant succeeded on all his grounds, including breach of his Article 8 right to private life and the right to free elections under Article 3 of Protocol 1 ECHR.

[92]   *Blake v IC and Wiltshire CC*, IT, 2 November 2009 at [37].

whether disclosure would breach the Human Rights Act 1998.[93] Any disclosure that would amount to a breach of the data subject's Article 8 right to private life would not be lawful.[94] The ECJ has held that communication of personal data to third parties amounts to an interference with Article 8, and that the provisions of Council Directive 95/46/EC permitting such communication must be interpreted in accordance with Article 8.[95]

24–016 Schedule 2 of the Data Protection Act 1998

The third requirement of the first data protection principle is satisfaction of at least one of the conditions in Sch 2. So far as potentially applicable to a disclosure under the Freedom of Information Act 2000, the conditions in Sch 2 are that:

1. The data subject has given his consent to the processing.

2. ...

3. The processing is necessary for compliance with any legal obligation to which the data controller is subject, other than an obligation imposed by contract.

4. ...

5. The processing is necessary—
    (a) for the administration of justice;
    (aa) for the exercise of any functions of either House of Parliament;
    (b) for the exercise of any functions conferred on any person by or under any enactment;
    (c) for the exercise of any functions of the Crown, a Minister of the Crown or a government department; or
    (d) for the exercise of any other functions of a public nature exercised in the public interest by any person.

6.(1) The processing is necessary for the purposes of legitimate interests pursued by the data controller or by the third party or parties to whom the data are disclosed, except where the processing is unwarranted in any particular case by reason of prejudice to the rights and freedoms or legitimate interests of the data subject.

(2) ....

Because the focus of the first condition in s 40(3)(a) is contravention of the data protection principles by the disclosure of information *otherwise than under the Freedom of Information Act 2000*, that Act cannot supply the legal obligation for the purposes of condition 2 nor the necessity for the purposes of conditions 5 and 6.[96] In relation to condition 6(1), if it could be shown that the

---

[93] Because there is no clear positive right to information or right to publish information, the consideration of lawfulness under HRA will likely be restricted to art 8.

[94] See *Dept of Health v IC and Pro-Life Alliance*, IT, 15 October 2009 at [71]-[72].

[95] Case C-465/00 *Rechnungshof v Österreichischer Rundfunk* [2002] ECR I-4989, [2003] 3 CMLR 10 at [68] and [73]-[75].

[96] In *Corporate Officer of the House of Commons v IC and Baker*, IT, 16 January 2007 at [50] the Information Tribunal held 'once section 40(2) FOIA is engaged that Parliament intended that the request be considered under the DPA, without further consideration of FOIA. This means that information which is protected under the DPA may not be disclosed under FOIA.' The conclusion is questionable. It is suggested that another view might be that a person's right to have disclosed information that constitutes third party personal data is and always remains that conferred by the FOIA s 1. Section 40(2) and (3), in setting a particular bound to that right, do not change its statutory source. Certain of the data protection principles turn on whether the processing by the data controller is pursuant to an enactment. If disclosure under the FOIA (which is a form of processing) had not been excepted by the words 'otherwise than under this Act' the qualification of a data subject's rights by the existence of a statutory function would have been equally required where that function was the duty imposed by FOIA s 1. Accordingly, there is nothing absurd in the inclusion of the words.

disclosure of the information to the applicant was necessary[97] for the purposes of legitimate interests pursued by the applicant,[98] then subject to the balancing exercise required for that condition, the condition will be satisfied.[99] Public interest in the disclosure of official information can amount to a legitimate interest for the purposes of condition 6(1).[100] However, 'legitimate interest' is a wider concept than 'public interest'.[101] For example, the pursuit of a legitimate business has been held to be a legitimate interest.[102] In order for condition 6(1) to be satisfied, the legitimate interests of those to whom the data would be disclosed (ie members of the public) must outweigh the prejudice to the rights, freedoms and legitimate interests of the data subject.[103]

017 Schedule 3 of the Data Protection Act 1998

Where the data being processed are 'sensitive personal data',[104] the first data protection

---

[97] The word 'necessary' carried with it connotations from the ECHR; ie whether a pressing social need is involved and whether the disclosure is proportionate to the legitimate aim pursued: *House of Commons v IC and Brooke, Leapman, Ungoed-Thomas* [2008] EWHC 1084 (Admin), [2009] 3 All ER 403 at [43]. See also *R (Ellis) v Chief Constable of the Essex Police* [2003] EWHC 1321 (Admin) (DC), [2003] 2 FLR 566 at [29].

[98] In relation to this provision, it is the legitimate interests of the actual requester (who is the person who would have a right to receive the information under the Act) which must be considered; the fact that a disclosure under the Act is a disclosure 'to the world' is properly taken into account at the stage of considering the extent of the prejudice which would be caused to the data subject by the disclosure: *Digby-Cameron v IC and Bedfordshire Police*, IT, 26 January 2009 at [16].

[99] In *A v Information Commissioner*, IT, 11 July 2006 the Information Tribunal found that the legitimate interests of a local education authority in disclosing the identities of two teachers who had expressed concern about a particular pupil being returned to class without additional teaching support to the parent of that child was outweighed by the legitimate interests of those teachers. In *Alcock v IC and Chief Constable of Staffordshire Police*, IT, 3 January 2007 at [32] the Information Tribunal held that even if an applicant were pursuing a legitimate interest in finding the name of an informant whose information had resulted in a damaging police investigation of the applicant, disclosure was nevertheless unwarranted by reason of the prejudice to the legitimate interest of the data subject, who had specifically requested that his identity be kept confidential. In *Evans v IC and MoD*, IT, 23 June 2008 the Tribunal held that it was necessary for a journalist to have access to raw data in order to publish a story about lobbyists' access to ministers, but that the prejudice caused to the lobbyist in question by release of the information (concerning his business) outweighed the public interest in disclosure.

[100] This follows from Recital 72 of Directive 95/46/EC: see *House of Commons v IC and Leapman, Brooke and Thomas*, IT, 26 February 2008 at [53]-[55].

[101] See *Evans v IC and MoD*, IT, 23 June 2008 at [20]: 'We recognise that legitimate interest is not the same as public interest: legitimate interest goes wider than the narrower concept of public interest: someone may have a legitimate interest in pursuing particular information which is of very little public interest.'

[102] *Murray v Express Newspapers plc* [2007] EWHC 1908 at [76].

[103] *Corporate Officer of the House of Commons v IC and Baker*, IT, 16 January 2007 at [90]; *England and LB of Bexley v IC*, IT, 10 May 2007 at [108]; *McTaggart v IC*, IT, 4 June 2007. The Tribunal in *Ministry of Defence v IC*, IT, 20 July 2007 at [79] held that disclosure of a directory of certain Ministry staff satisfied the conditions of para 6(1). However, a request for a full copy of an enforcement file concerning a property did not satisfy para 6(2) and was refused under EIR regs 12(5)(b) and 13: *Young v IC and Dept for Environment for Northern Ireland*, IT, 12 December 2007.

[104] Which, under s 2 of the DPA, means personal data consisting of information as to: (a) the racial or ethnic origin of the data subject; (b) his political opinions; (c) his religious beliefs or other beliefs of a similar nature; (d) whether he is a member of a trade union (within the meaning of the Trade Union and Labour Relations (Consolidation) Act 1992); (e) his physical or mental health or condition; (f) his sexual life; (g) the commission or alleged commission by him of any offence; or (h) any proceedings for any offence committed or alleged to have been committed by him, the disposal of such proceedings or the sentence of any court in such proceedings. A photograph of a person showing him to be Caucasian will constitute sensitive personal data: *Murray v Express Newspapers plc* [2007] EWHC 1908 at [80].

principle imposes a fourth requirement, namely satisfaction of at least one of the conditions in Sch 3 of the Data Protection Act 1998. To the extent that information captured by a request is 'sensitive personal data' relating to a person other than the applicant, this will operate to widen the circumstances in which that information will be exempt information by operation of s 40(2).[105] So far as potentially relevant to a disclosure under the Freedom of Information Act 2000, the conditions in Sch 3 are that:

1. The data subject has given his explicit consent to the processing of the personal data.
2. ...
3. The processing is necessary[106]—
    (a) in order to protect the vital interests[107] of the data subject or another person, in a case where—
        (i) consent cannot be given by or on behalf of the data subject; or
        (ii) the data controller cannot reasonably be expected to obtain the consent of the data subject; or
    (b) in order to protect the vital interests of another person, in a case where consent by or on behalf of the data subject has been unreasonably withheld.
4. ...
5. The information contained in the personal data has been made public as a result of steps deliberately taken by the data subject.
6. The processing—
    (a) is necessary for the purpose of, or in connection with, any legal proceedings (including prospective legal proceedings);
    (b) is necessary for the purpose of obtaining legal advice; or
    (c) is otherwise necessary for the purposes of establishing, exercising or defending legal rights.
7(1). The processing is necessary—
    (a) ...
    (aa) for the exercise of any functions of either House of Parliament;
    (b) for the exercise of any functions conferred on any person by or under an enactment;[108] or
    (c) for the exercise of any functions of the Crown, a Minister of the Crown or a government department.
    (2) ....
8(1). The processing is necessary for medical purposes and is undertaken by—
    (a) a health professional, or
    (b) a person who in the circumstances owes a duty of confidentiality which is equivalent to that which would arise if that person were a health professional.
    (2) In this paragraph "medical purposes" includes the purposes of preventative medicine,

---

[105] Similarly: FOI(S)A s 38(1)(b); EIR reg 13(1); EI(S)R reg 11(2).

[106] 'Necessary' bears the same meaning in Sch 3 as it does in Sch 2: see n 97.

[107] A 'vital interest' is one that concerns a matter of life or death: *Heath v IC*, IT, 16 September 2009 at [15].

[108] See eg *Dept of Health v IC and Pro-Life Alliance*, IT, 15 October 2009 at [109]-[110]. In *Stone v South East Coast Strategic Health Authority* [2006] EWHC 1668 (Admin) at [64]-[65], the court rejected the contention that the qualification 'subject to the provision of suitable safeguards' should be read into paragraph 7 of Schedule 3, in order to construe it consistently with art 8(4) of the Directive.

medical diagnosis, medical research, the provision of care and treatment and the management of healthcare services.[109]

9. ...

10. The personal data are processed in circumstances specified in an order made by the Secretary of State for the purposes of this paragraph.

-018 Orders made in relation to sensitive personal data

Pursuant to paragraph 10 of Schedule 3, the Secretary of State has made a number of Orders setting out circumstances in which sensitive personal data may be processed. These broadly relate to processing that is necessary for:

— preventing or detecting any unlawful act;

— protecting the public against certain improper conduct or maladministration;

— providing confidential counselling, advice or support;

— carrying on insurance business or administering occupational pension schemes;

— monitoring equality of opportunity;

— carrying on political activities by registered political parties;

— research;

— certain types of publication for the purposes of journalism or artistic or literary purposes;[110]

— exercising functions conferred on constables by law;[111]

— dealing with requests made by individuals to elected representatives;[112] and

— administering accounts relating to payment cards used in the commission of offences relating to indecent photographs of children.[113]

To the extent that information captured by a request falls within one of the exemptions in one of these orders, paragraph 10 of Schedule 3 will apply. As such, one of the conditions in Schedule 3 will have been met and disclosure will not contravene the first data protection principle if the disclosure (otherwise than under the Freedom of Information Act 2000) also meets the requirements of fairness[114] and one of the conditions in Schedule 2[115] is satisfied.

-019 Disclosure would contravene section 10 of the Data Protection Act 1998

As noted above,[116] the first condition of s 40(2) of the Freedom of Information Act 2000 may

---

[109] In *Stone v South East Coast Strategic Health Authority* [2006] EWHC 1668 (Admin), the court held that the publication of a report produced by an Inquiry into the psychiatric and medical care, treatment and supervision of a man convicted of a notorious double murder fell within the ambit of 'medical purposes', as relating to 'the management of healthcare services'.

[110] Data Protection (Processing of Sensitive Personal Data) Order 2000 SI 2000/417 Sch para 3. See *Brett v IC and FCO*, IT, 21 August 2009.

[111] The Data Protection (Processing of Sensitive Personal Data) Order 2000 SI 2000/417 (the exemptions which introduce a requirement of 'the substantial public interest').

[112] The Data Protection (Processing of Sensitive Personal Data) (Elected Representatives) Order 2002 SI 2002/2905.

[113] The Data Protection (Processing of Sensitive Personal Data) Order 2006 SI 2006/2068.

[114] See §§ 24–013 to 24–014.

[115] See §24–016.

[116] See §24–008.

739

be satisfied in either of two ways. The second way only arises where the third party to whom the personal data relate has, under s 10 of the Data Protection Act 1998, notified the public authority that processing of personal data relating to himself is causing or would be likely to cause damage or distress. The second way only applies to information that falls within any of paragraphs (a) to (d) of the definition of 'data' in s 1(1) of the Data Protection Act 1998: it does not apply to information that is 'data' only by virtue of para (e) of the definition.[117] Section 10 of the Data Protection Act 1998 gives an individual a right, which may be exercised at any time by notice in writing to the data controller (ie here, the public authority holding the information), to require the data controller to cease or not begin processing (which will include holding or disclosing) any personal data in respect of which he is the data subject on the ground that the processing of those data is causing or is likely to cause substantial damage or distress to him or another person and that the damage is or would be unwarranted. A data subject does not have the right to give such a notice where any of the conditions in paras 1 to 4 of Sch 2 applies.[118] Where such a notice has been given, then, to the extent that disclosure of information (other than information that is within para (e) of the definition of 'data') captured by a request under the Freedom of Information Act 2000 would contravene s 10 of the Data Protection Act 1998, that information will be exempt information.[119] Such a disclosure will only contravene s 10 of the Data Protection Act 1998 if the notice is justified or justified to any extent.[120] The exemption is not absolute,[121] so that the public authority must weigh the public interest in upholding the exemption against the public interest in disclosing the information. There is a corresponding exemption from the duty to confirm or deny where giving to a member of the public a confirmation or denial that the requested information is held by the public authority would itself contravene s 10 of the Data Protection Act 1998.[122]

24–020 Unorganised, paper-based data held by public authorities

As previously indicated,[123] to the extent that the information captured by a request does not fall within any of paras (a)-(d) of the definition of 'data' in s 1(1) of the Data Protection Act 1998 but does fall within para (e) of that definition,[124] the first condition will only be met if its disclosure to a member of the public otherwise than under the Freedom of Information Act 2000 would contravene any of the data protection principles.[125] Accordingly, in relation to this sort of

---

[117] The limiting of this alternative to the first four categories of data reflects the position under s 33A of the DPA, by virtue of which s 10 does not apply to manual data held by public authorities.

[118] DPA s 10(2)(a). No orders have been made by the Secretary of State for the purposes of DPA s 10(2)(b). As to paras 1–4 of Sch 2, see §24–016.

[119] FOIA s 40(3)(b)(ii); FOI(S)A s 38(2)(a)(ii); EIR reg 13(2)(a)(ii); EI(S)R reg 11(3)(a)(ii).

[120] DPA s 10(3).

[121] FOIA s 2(3)(f)(ii); FOI(S)A s 2(2)(e)(ii); EIR reg 13(2)(b); EI(S)R reg 11(3)(a)(ii).

[122] FOIA s 40(5)(b)(i); EIR reg 13(5)(a); EI(S)R reg 11(6). Exemption from the duty to confirm or deny is absolute. There is no separate duty to confirm or deny under FOI(S)A and s 18 of that Act does not apply to exemption under s 38.

[123] See §24–008.

[124] See §5–020. Crudely summarised, it covers paper-based information that is not in a file arranged so that information relating to an individual is readily accessible.

[125] FOIA s 40(3)(b); FOI(S)A s 38(2)(b); EIR reg 13(2)(b); EI(S)R reg 11(3)(b).

information, the above discussion[126] of the data protection principles is applicable, but the discussion[127] of contravention of a s 10 notice is inapplicable. The particular treatment of data falling within para (e) of the definition of 'data' reflects the generally more restricted application of the Data Protection Act 1998 to this class of data.[128] Where the first condition is so met, exemption from the duty is absolute.[129] In relation to this class of data, there is a corresponding exemption from the duty to confirm or deny where giving to a member of the public a confirmation or denial that the requested information is held by the public authority would itself involve a contravention of the data protection principles.[130]

021 The second condition

As already noted,[131] to the extent that information captured by a request relates to a person other than the applicant, that information will be exempt information where either of two conditions is satisfied. The first condition ensures that there is no undue intrusion into the privacy of the person to whom the information relates. The second condition is concerned to ensure that an applicant does not have a greater right of access to information relating to a third party than that third party himself would have. The Freedom of Information Act 2000 achieves this objective by putting the person who made the request for information in the position that the person to whom the information relates would be in had the latter person made a subject access request under the Data Protection Act 1998. Thus, information falling within any of the paragraphs of the definition of 'data' is exempt information for the purposes of the Freedom of Information Act 2000 if that information, had it been sought under the Data Protection Act 1998 by the data subject, would be exempt from communication to the data subject.[132] In carrying out this process, if the person to whom the data relate would not have been entitled to that information because one of the exemptions in Part IV of the Data Protection Act 1998 applied, the information will be exempt information under the Freedom of Information Act 2000. Exemption under the second condition is a qualified exemption, so that the public authority will need to go on and consider whether the public interest in maintaining this exemption outweighs the public interest in disclosure.[133] Similarly, the duty to confirm or deny is disapplied, where, had the person to whom the information relates made a subject access request, the public authority holding the information would not be required to inform that person whether it was holding or otherwise processing the information.[134]

---

[126] See §§24–011 to 24–018.

[127] See §24–019.

[128] Thus, DPA s 33A exempts this class of data from certain of the data protection principles, section 10 and various other provisions of the Act.

[129] FOIA s 2(3)(f)(ii); FOI(S)A s 2(2)(e)(ii); EIR reg 13(2)(b); EI(S)R reg 11(3)(b).

[130] FOIA s 40(5)(b)(i); EIR reg 13(5)(a); EI(S)R reg 11(6). Exemption from the duty to confirm or deny is absolute. There is no separate duty to confirm or deny under FOI(S)A and its s 18 does not apply to exemption under s 38.

[131] See §24–007.

[132] FOIA s 40(4); FOI(S)A s 38(3); EIR reg 13(3); EI(S)R reg 11(4).

[133] FOIA s 2(3)(f); FOI(S)A s 2(2)(e); EIR reg 13(3); EI(S)R reg 11(4).

[134] This is a separate right given to a data subject under DPA s 7(1)(a). The disapplication of the duty under the FOIA is effected by FOIA s 40(5)(b)(ii). And similarly, EIR reg 13(5)(b); EI(S)R reg 11(6). The exemption from the duty to confirm or deny is, in the case of the FOIA, qualified.

CHAPTER 25

Confidential Information

1. BREACH OF CONFIDENCE: INTRODUCTION[1]

25– 001 The exemption

By s 41(1) of the Freedom of Information Act 2000, information is rendered exempt information where it was obtained by a public authority from any other person (including another public authority)[2] and the disclosure of the information to the public (otherwise than under the Act) by the public authority holding it would constitute a breach of confidence actionable by that or any other person.[3] Similarly, the duty to confirm or deny does not arise if, or to the extent that, a confirmation or denial that the public authority holds the information specified in the request would (apart from the Act) constitute an actionable breach of confidence.[4] The exemption and the exclusion of the duty to confirm or deny are absolute.[5] Accordingly, disapplication of the duty to disclose and of the duty to confirm or deny does not expressly depend upon a balancing of the public interest in maintaining the exemption (or in excluding the duty to confirm or deny), on the one hand, against the public interest in disclosure (or in disclosing whether the public authority holds the requested information), on the other hand.[6] However, a public interest defence is available to a claim for breach of confidence.[7] Therefore, a consideration of the public interest is required to determine whether disclosure would constitute an actionable breach of confidence. In addition, so far as government secrets are concerned, the Crown is not entitled to restrain disclosure or to obtain redress on confidentiality grounds unless it can establish that disclosure has damaged or would be likely to damage the public interest.[8] For these reasons, although the wording of the Act itself does not require any such evaluation to be made, the applicability of s 41 will involve in each instance some consideration of the public interest in disclosure and the public interest in maintaining the confidence. In balancing competing interests, the Tribunal has tended to take as a starting point 'the assumption that confidentiality should be preserved unless outweighed

---

[1] For a more general treatment of the law of confidentiality, see: RG Toulson and CM Phipps, *Confidentiality*, 2nd ed (Sweet & Maxwell, 2006); F Gurry, *Breach of Confidence* (Oxford, Oxford University Press, 1984); BC Reid, *Confidentiality and the Law* (London, Waterlow, 1986); L Clarke (ed), *Confidentiality and the Law* (London, Lloyd's of London, 1990); S Ricketson, *The Law of Intellectual Property: Copyright, Designs & Confidential Information*, 2nd edn (Sydney, Law Book Company, 1999); P Lavery, *Commercial Secrets: the Action for Breach of Confidence in Ireland* (Dublin, Round Hall, 1996).

[2] But see §25– 006.

[3] FOIA s 41(1); FOI(S)A s 36(2). For the position in relation to 'environmental information', see §25– 003. Under the DPA there is an exemption for confidential references, but otherwise no exemption for confidential information: DPA s 37, Sch 7, para 1, and see §5– 072.

[4] FOIA s 41(2). In relation to Scottish public authorities, see §1– 041(1).

[5] FOIA s 2(3)(g); FOI(S)A s 2(2)(c). Presumably because consideration of the public interest is inherent in determining whether there is an actionable breach of confidence.

[6] FOIA s 2(1)–(2); FOI(S)A s 2(1)–(2).

[7] *Derry City Council v IC*, IT, 11 December 2006 at [30]; *S v IC and General Register Office*, IT, 9 May 2007 at [26]-[28]; *McTeggart v IC and Dept for Culture*, Arts and Leisure, IT, 4 June 2007 at [28]-[29].

[8] *AG v Guardian Newspapers Ltd (No 2)* [1990] 1 AC 109, 256, 265, 270, 282 and 293. See further §25– 028.

by countervailing factors'.[9] This approach is unobjectionable so far as concerns the cause of action for breach of confidence in its traditional form. It can be reconciled with the taxonomy of that cause of action as extended to accommodate claims relating to private information,[10] although the Tribunal has been criticised for failing to take proper account of the way the law of confidence has developed in the latter regard.[11] A similar exemption for confidential information is to be found in each of the comparative jurisdictions.[12]

002 Private information

The cause of action for breach of confidence has been extended in recent years to cover misuse of private information. To accommodate this extension, the principles of confidentiality have been substantially adapted to the particular requirements of private information. As discussed in greater detail below,[13] the prevailing judicial analysis is that privacy claims have been accommodated by expanding (or, as some would say, distorting) the traditional cause of action for breach of confidence. Lord Nicholls has gone further, stating:

> As the law has developed, breach of confidence, or misuse of confidential information, now covers two distinct causes of action, protecting two different interests: privacy, and secret ("confidential") information.[14]

However, whether the better view is that misuse of private information has come to be protected by radically modifying the traditional cause of action or due to the creation of a new and distinct cause of action, there seems no doubt that the basis on which such protection is provided is by a claim for breach of confidence. At the same time, because the elements of an actionable breach of confidence and the limitations that apply to that cause of action have undergone radical transformation in this extended territory, it is more convenient to consider separately the principles of confidentiality in relation to private or personal information.[15]

---

[9] *Derry City Council v IC*, IT, 11 December 2006 at [35(m)], followed in *Anderson v IC and Parades Commission*, IT, 29 April 2008 at [31].

[10] See §25– 038.

[11] See *British Union for the Abolition of Vivisection v SSHD* [2008] EWHC 892 (QB), Eady J at [27]-[35], a criticism adopted by the Court of Appeal in *British Union for the Abolition of Vivisection v SSHD* [2008] EWCA Civ 870, [2009] 1 All ER 44, [2009] 1 WLR 636 at [23], and heeded by the Tribunal in *Higher Education Funding Council for England v IC & anor*, IT, 13 January 2010 at [42].

[12] In the United States, the Freedom of Information Act, 1966, 5 USC § 552(b)(4), exempts from disclosure records or information obtained from a person that is confidential: see §2– 008(7)(D). The Freedom of Information Act 1982 (Cth of Australia) s 45, provides an exemption where the disclosure of the requested document would represent a breach of confidence other than that of the Commonwealth: see §2– 015(20). In New Zealand, the Official Information Act 1982 ss 9(2)(b)(ii) and 27(1)(c), the Local Government Official Information and Meetings Act 1987 ss 7(2)(b)(ii) and 26(1)(c) and the Privacy Act 1993 s 29(1)(b) provide a qualified exemption where the non-disclosure is required to protect information which is subject to an obligation of confidence: see §2– 023(3). The Access to Information Act (Canada) s 16(1)(c), provides a mandatory exemption for financial, commercial, scientific or technical information received in confidence from a third party: see §2– 031(5). The Freedom of Information Act 1997 (Ireland), provides a mandatory exemption where the requested record contains information given to the public body in confidence or the disclosure of which would constitute a breach of confidence: see §2– 039(5).

[13] See §25– 031.

[14] *OBG Ltd v Allan* [2007] UKHL 21, [2008] 1 AC 1.

[15] At §§25– 030 to 25– 048.

25– 003 Environmental information

Information to which a person has a right of access under the Environmental Information Regulations 2004 is exempt information under s 39(1)(a) of the Freedom of Information Act 2000.[16] Those regulations give a right of access to 'environmental information'.[17] To the extent that a request for information captures 'environmental information', the Act effectively routes that part of the request through the Environmental Information Regulations 2004.[18] Although those regulations do provide some protection for certain sorts of confidential information, they take a significantly different approach from the Act in relation to confidentiality. The protection they give is accordingly considered separately in this Chapter.[19]

25– 004 Overview

A public authority faced with a request for information that includes confidential or commercial information or a trade secret will first need to identify which of that information captured by the request constitutes 'environmental information'.[20] In relation to requested information that is 'environmental information' the public authority will need to determine whether the special confidentiality exceptions that only apply to 'environmental information' are engaged.[21] In relation to the requested information that does not constitute 'environmental information', the public authority will need:

(1) To determine whether any of it constitutes a trade secret.[22]

(2) To determine whether the disclosure of any of it would, or would be likely to, prejudice the commercial interests of any person, including the public authority itself.[23]

(3) To determine whether any of the information was obtained from a State other than the United Kingdom or from an international organisation or international court.[24]

(4) To determine which of that information was 'obtained from any other person'[25] and, if so:

  (a) whether and to what extent that information falls within the ambit of the cause of action for breach of confidence in its traditional form;[26] and

  (b) whether and to what extent that information falls within the ambit of that

---

[16] In relation to Scottish public authorities, FOI(S)A s 39, similarly renders 'environmental information' exempt information for the purposes of that Act.

[17] In relation to Scottish public authorities, a like right is given by the EI(S)R.

[18] For a general treatment of the EIR and the EI(S)R, see ch 6.

[19] See §§25– 065 to 25– 067.

[20] See §6– 010.

[21] See §§25– 065 to 25– 067.

[22] See §§25– 049 to 25– 056.

[23] See §§25– 057 to 25– 060.

[24] See §§25– 061 to 25– 064.

[25] See §25– 005.

[26] See §§25– 010 to 25– 029.

cause of action as extended to private information.[27]

To the extent that the requested information falls within limb (b), that information will often also be rendered exempt information by s 40(2) of the Freedom of Information Act 2000.[28] In those circumstances, s 40(2) will generally provide a more straightforward means of rendering information exempt information than s 41(1) in its application to private information.[29] Section 40(2)–(4) ensures that disclosure of personal information under the Act accommodates the data protection principles and, through them, the protection of an individual's privacy.[30]

005 Information created by the requested public authority

The s 41 exemption only applies to information obtained by the public authority from another person.[31] The public authority therefore cannot rely upon the exemption as a basis for refusing to disclose information that it has itself created. Information that is obtained from an officer or employee of the public authority will not be obtained 'from any other person' if the officer or employee has disclosed the information in the course of his employment and acting solely in his capacity as an officer or employee. No doubt this will generally be the case. It is, however, possible that information may be disclosed to the public authority by an officer or employee in a private capacity and in the expectation that it will be kept confidential. In those circumstances, the exemption contained in s 41 would potentially apply to it.[32] Like considerations may apply where information is generated by contract workers who are engaged by a public authority and who may well carry out work within its buildings (eg doctors in an occupational health unit, supplied pursuant to a service agreement made between a public authority and a company which provides the public authority with occupational health services). The Tribunal has held that a concluded contract between a public authority and a third party does not constitute information obtained by that public authority from any other person for the purposes of s 41. The Tribunal went further and held on the facts that a document setting out the terms on which an airline company would use airport facilities provided by a public authority and by reference to which the parties had conducted themselves, even though not constituting a contract, was not information obtained by that public authority

---

[27]   See §§25– 030 to 25– 048.

[28]   Similarly: FOI(S)A s 38(1)(b); EIR regs 12(3) and 13; EI(S)R regs 10(3) and 11.

[29]   FOIA s 40(2)–(4); FOI(S)A; s 38, EIR regs 12(3) and 13; EI(S)R regs 10(3) and 11. These are considered in ch 24. Because of the narrow meaning given to 'personal data' by the Court of Appeal in *Durant v Financial Services Authority* [2003] EWCA Civ 1746, [2004] FSR 28, it is possible that certain information that constitutes private information for the purposes of limb (b), will not constitute 'personal data' for the purposes of s 40(2). In *Durant* Buxton LJ said (at [81]) that 'in future, those contemplating such proceedings [ie under DPA s 7] and those advising them must carefully scrutinise the guidance given by my Lord's [ie Auld LJ] judgment before going any further. That process should prevent the wholly unjustifiable burden and expense that has been imposed on the data controller in this case'. There is no good reason why the exhortation should not equally apply to public authorities invoking FOIA s 40(2). Although the FOIA was not fully in force at the time of *Durant*, important parts of it were and, given the FSA's representation, it is most unlikely that the Respondent was unaware of the FOIA and its inter-relationship with the DPA. It is suggested that where information relating to a person falls short of the requirements set by the Court of Appeal in *Durant*, a public authority will need to consider exemption under FOIA s 41(1), limb (b).

[30]   Similarly: FOI(S)A s 38(1)(b); EIR regs 12(3) and 13; EI(S)R regs 10(3) and 11.

[31]   Similarly: FOI(S)A s 36(2); EIR reg 12(5)(f); EI(S)R reg 10(5)(f).

[32]   MoJ, *Exemptions Guidance—Section 41* (14 May 2008) p 5.

from any other person:

> We are aware that the effect of our conclusion is that the whole of any contract with a public authority may be available to the public, no matter how confidential the content or how clearly expressed the confidentiality provisions incorporated in it, unless another exemption applies (most probably, that one or both parties to the contract could show that its disclosure would be likely to prejudice its commercial interests, so as to bring section 43 into play). We are also conscious of the fact that contracts will sometimes record more than just the mutual obligations of the contracting parties. They will also include technical information, either in the body of the contract or, more probably, in separate schedules. Depending, again, on the particular circumstances in which the point arises, it may be that material of that nature could still be characterised as confidential information "obtained" by the public authority from the other party to the contract, (or perhaps a "trade secret" under section 43(1) of the Act) in which event it may be redacted in any disclosed version.[33]

Information included in a document provided by a contractor to an authority but which originates from the authority rather than the contractor, is not obtained from another person for the purposes of s 41.[34]

25–006 Information received from another government department

The effect of s 81 of the Freedom of Information Act 2000[35] is that, in general, the disclosure by one government department of information originating from another government department is not to be regarded as giving rise to an actionable breach of confidence, and so will fall outside the scope of the exemption contained in s 41. The reason for this is that, although s 81(1) provides that for the purposes of the Act each government department is to be treated as a person separate from any other government department, s 81(2) goes on to provide that s 81(1) does not enable:

(a) a government department which is not a Northern Ireland department to claim for the purposes of s 41(1)(b) that the disclosure of any information by it would constitute a breach of confidence actionable by any other government department (not being a Northern Ireland department); or

(b) a Northern Ireland department to claim for those purposes that the disclosure of information by it would constitute a breach of confidence actionable by any other Northern Ireland department.

As s 81(2) does not apply to information provided by a Northern Ireland department to a government department, and vice versa, the disclosure of such information may constitute an actionable breach of confidence, and it may fall within the scope of the exemption. This appears to have been the intention of the legislature. If the information supplied by a government department originates from a third party (in other words, it does not originate from another government department), then, subject to any loss of confidentiality resulting from the transmission between departments, it will retain the confidentiality that it had when held by the transmitting department.

---

[33] *Derry City Council v Information Commissioner*, IT, 11 December 2006 at [32(e)].

[34] *Dept of Health v IC*, IT, 18 November 2008 at [33]-[37].

[35] Although EIR reg 3(5), provides that each government department is to be treated as a person separate from any other government department, that particular regulation does not apply to Part 3, being the Part containing reg 12. There is no equivalent to s 81 under the FOI(S)A or to reg 3(5) under the EI(S)R.

007 The meaning of 'actionable'

The exemption applies only to any disclosure by the public authority holding the information which would constitute a breach of confidence 'actionable' by the person who provided the information to that authority or by any other person.[36] One possible meaning of the word 'actionable' is that it will be satisfied whenever the circumstances afford 'grounds for an action at law'.[37] If that meaning applied here, the exemption would appear to be available wherever there is in existence a claim for breach of confidence which satisfies the test of 'real prospect of success' or arguability.[38] Another possible interpretation is that 'actionable' means a breach of confidence that satisfies the essential elements for a successful breach of confidence claim,[39] but without a consideration of whether any of the public interest defences to the claim would defeat it.[40] A third interpretation is that the claim is only actionable if the claim would be successful, taking into account any public interest defences. The Tribunal has suggested a fourth meaning:

> which arises when the word "actionable" is used, not to indicate the test to be applied in assessing whether a possible cause of action should be taken into consideration, but for the purpose of indicating who has the necessary status to assert it.[41]

During the introduction of the Act into Parliament, Lord Falconer of Thoroton, Minister of State at the Cabinet Office, advised Parliament that an 'actionable breach' meant one that affords grounds for a claim for breach of confidence that will succeed: in other words, one that 'would be upheld by the courts'.[42] That approach has since been endorsed by the Ministry of Justice:

> This exemption only applies if a breach of confidence would be "actionable". A breach of confidence will only be "actionable" if a person could bring a legal action and be successful. The courts have recognised that a person will not succeed in an action for breach of confidence if the public interest in disclosure outweighs the public interest in keeping the confidence. So although the Act requires no explicit public interest test, an assessment of the public interest must still be made. However, the factors the courts have considered to date

---

[36] One possible reason for the inclusion of the word 'actionable' was to avoid the uncertainties which the equivalent provision in the Freedom of Information Act 1982 (Cth of Aust) encountered before its amendment: see §25–015(20).

[37] *Oxford English Dictionary*. That is, eg, the sense in which the word is used in the headnote to *Stephens v Avery* [1988] Ch 449, [1988] 2 All ER 477, [1988] FSR 510, in which Browne-Wilkinson VC refused to strike out a statement of case complaining of the misuse of information relating to a lesbian sexual relationship between the claimant and another woman, on the basis that it was arguable that the claimant's confidant and the editor and publisher of a newspaper to whom the confidant had imparted the information were bound by a duty of confidence with regard to the information.

[38] Under CPR 3.4; or for resisting a claim for summary judgment under CPR 24. A claim satisfies that test if it is not merely fanciful: *Swain v Hillman* [2001] 1 All ER 91; *Krafft v London Borough of Camden* (2001) 3 LGR 37. In *Three Rivers District Council v Bank of England (No 3)* [2001] UKHL 16, [2001] 2 All ER 513 Lord Hope of Craighead observed that: 'The difference between a test which asks the question "is the claim bound to fail?" and one which asks the question "does the claim have a real prospect of success?" is not easy to determine.' For examples of claims and defences which were and which were not held to have 'a real prospect of success' under CPR 24 see *Celador Productions Ltd v Melville; Boone v ITV Network; Baccini v Celador Productions Ltd* [2004] EWHC 2362 (Ch), [2004] All ER (D) 298; and *Associated Newspapers Ltd v HRH the Prince of Wales* [2006] EWCA Civ 1776, [2007] 2 All ER 139.

[39] See §25–012.

[40] See §§25–024 to 25–029.

[41] *Higher Education Funding Council for England v IC & anor*, IT, 13 January 2010 at [25(c)].

[42] Hansard HL vol 618 col 416; (25 October 2000); vol 619 cols 175–176 (14 November 2000).

and the weight they give to them are not the same as the factors considered by the Tribunal under the public interest test in section 2 of the Act.[43]

The Information Commissioner has expressed the matter in more circumspect terms:

"Actionable" means that an aggrieved party would have the right to take the authority to court as a result of the disclosure. There are essentially two considerations…The authority must be satisfied the information in question is in fact confidential…The aggrieved party must have the legal standing to take action.[44]

The Tribunal has taken the view that Lord Falconer's statement in promoting the legislation put the issue 'beyond doubt.'[45] At all events, under each of these approaches, the wording of s 41 points to a consideration of:

(i)   the elements of a claim for breach of confidence; and

(ii)   the grounds on which such a claim may be defeated.

25– 008 The duty to confirm or deny

The duty to confirm or deny does not arise if, or to the extent that, a confirmation or denial that the public authority holds the information specified in the request would (apart from the Act) constitute an actionable breach of confidence.[46] This is an absolute exclusion of duty.[47] As a matter of practice, other than where the request is so specific that the mere confirmation that the information is held (without a disclosure of that information) would be to disclose the gist of the information, it is difficult to contemplate circumstances in which a public authority could properly refuse to confirm or deny that it held information under s 41(2).

25– 009 Consultation with other persons

There is no statutory obligation on the public authority to consult with persons to whom the information requested relates or whose interests are likely to be affected by the disclosure of information to the public pursuant to s 41 of the Freedom of Information Act 2000. In accordance with s 45(2)(c) of the Act, however, consultation with such third parties is covered by Part IV of the Code of Practice issued by the Lord Chancellor pursuant to s 45(1) 'providing guidance to public authorities as to the practice which he considers it desirable for them to follow in connection with the discharge of their functions under Part I of the Act.' The Code of Practice advises, among other things, that public authorities should ensure that third parties are aware of the public authority's duty to comply with the Act; that in some cases it will be necessary to consult with third parties in order to determine whether or not an exemption applies to the information requested, and that in a range of other circumstances it will be good practice to do so; and that it may also be appropriate to consult third parties about such matters as whether any further explanatory material or advice should be given to the applicant together with the information in question.[48] In practice, therefore, such persons are very likely to be

---

[43]   MoJ, *Exemptions Guidance – section.41* (14 May 2008) p 2.

[44]   Freedom of Information Act Awareness Guidance No 2, version 4, 12 September 2008, p 4. In relation to a similarly worded provision, see *Re B and Brisbane North Regional Health Authority* [1994] 1 QAR 279, 296.

[45]   *Higher Education Funding Council for England v IC & anor*, IT, 13 January 2010 at [26]-[27].

[46]   FOIA s 41(2). In relation to Scottish public authorities, see §1– 041(1).

[47]   FOIA s 2(3).

[48]   See s 45 Code of Practice, paras 25–30.

consulted by the public authority before any disclosure is made. If the persons consulted consent to disclosure, and no other person is entitled to maintain any claim to confidentiality with regard to the information in question, then the public authority will be released from any obligation of confidence that it would otherwise have had, and it will not be able to rely on the exemption to resist disclosure. If the persons consulted do not consent to disclosure, and the public authority considers that disclosure would constitute a breach of confidence actionable by them, it is likely that the terms of their objection will bolster the public authority's stance. If the persons consulted do not consent to disclosure and claim it would constitute a breach of confidence actionable by them and the public authority disagrees with that view, the matter may well end up being resolved by the court either in proceedings brought by such persons for injunctive relief, or, conceivably, in proceedings brought against them by the public authority for declaratory relief. If any dispute is not resolved by those means, and the public authority decides to make disclosure in spite of such claims, any person whose rights of confidentiality are breached by the disclosure will be entitled to claim pecuniary relief in respect of such disclosure, subject to any common law defences that may be available to the public authority: these rights are not conferred by the Act, but arise at common law.

2. CONVENTIONAL BREACH OF CONFIDENCE[49]

010 The sources of obligations of confidentiality

Obligations of confidentiality conventionally arise from contract, equity or statute.[50] The same facts may give rise to an obligation of confidentiality arising under more than one of these sources.[51] A contractual obligation of confidentiality may arise orally or in writing, and it may be express or implied. It is arguable that an express contractual duty of confidence carries more weight, at least when balanced against the restriction of the right of freedom of expression, than an implied duty of confidentiality.[52] Further, it is clear from the decisions of the Court of Appeal in *McKennitt v Ash*[53] and in *HRH the Prince of Wales v Associated Newspapers Ltd*[54] that a pre-existing confidential relationship is a matter of considerable importance when striking the

---

[49] In other words, breaches of confidence other than of private information, which are considered at §§25– 030 to 25– 048.

[50] Prior to *Prince Albert v Strange* (1849) 1 Mac & G 25, (1849) 1 De G & Sm. 652 where there was a misuse or a threatened misuse of confidential information, the courts would only intervene if it could be shown that that misuse constituted an infringement by the defendant of a right of property recognised at common law, a breach of contract by the defendant, a breach of trust by the defendant, or a use of information obtained by the defendant from a third party in the knowledge that that third party was in breach of contract or trust. See further: Lord Oliver, 'Spycatcher: Confidence, Copyright and Contempt', *Israel Law Review*, (1989) 23(4) 407.

[51] *Robb v Green* [1895] 2 QB 315 (CA); *Nichrotherm Electrical Co Ltd v Percy* [1957] RPC 207 (CA); *Ackroyds (London) Ltd v Islington Plastics Ltd* [1962] RPC 97.

[52] *HRH the Prince of Wales v Associated Newspapers Ltd* [2006] EWCA Civ 1776, [2008] Ch 57 at [69]; *Campbell v Frisbee* [2002] EWCA Civ 1374, [2003] EMLR 3 at [22], contrasting *London Regional Transport v Mayor of London* [2001] EWCA Civ 1491, [2003] EMLR 4 at [46] with *AG v Barker* [1990] 3 All ER 257 at 260.

[53] *McKennitt v Ash v* [2006] EWCA Civ 1714, [2008] QB 73 (see, eg, Buxton LJ at [8(v)] and [15]–[24]).

[54] *HRH the Prince of Wales v Associated Newspapers Ltd* [2006] EWCA Civ 1776, [2008] Ch 57 (see Lord Phillips CJ at, eg, [24] – [36], [48], [53], [65] – [68] and [74]).

balance between competing Conventions rights, such that:

> a significant element to be weighed in the balance is the importance in a democratic society of upholding duties of confidence that are created between individuals. It is not enough to justify publication that the information in question is a matter of public interest.... For these reasons, the test to be applied when considering whether it is necessary to restrict freedom of expression in order to prevent disclosure of information received in confidence is not simply whether the information is a matter of public interest but whether, in all the circumstances, it is in the public interest that the duty of confidence should be breached. The court will need to consider whether, having regard to the nature of the information and all the relevant circumstances, it is legitimate for the owner of the information to seek to keep it confidential or whether it is in the public interest that the information should be made public.[55]

In addition, the scope of express and implied obligations may be different. In *Balston Ltd v Headline Filters Ltd*,[56] for example, Scott J observed in the context of contracts of employment:

> the criteria that determine whether or not an express covenant in a contract of employment restricting the use or disclosure of particular information after the determination of the employment is enforceable are very different from the criteria that determine whether or not an obligation restricting the use or disclosure of that information can be implied into the contract. The implied obligation will always, I think be unlimited in time and probably in area as well...If the information sought to be protected is not fit for protection, unlimited by time or area, it is very difficult to see how protection can be supplied by an implied term. On the other hand, an express covenant against use or disclosure is very likely to be limited both as to time and as to area.

Independently of contract, it is well established that there is free-standing jurisdiction in equity to protect confidence.[57] The nature of the action was explained by Lord Oliver in a lecture given in 1989:[58]

> Now the action of confidence is entirely an equitable invention...The common law recognised the right of property of an author in his unpublished work, but what it protected was the mode of expression not the information expressed. The idea that information

---

[55] *HRH the Prince of Wales v Associated Newspapers Ltd* at [67]–[68]. As Bingham LJ observed in *AG v Guardian Newspapers (No 2)* [1990] 1 AC 109:

> In the ordinary case where an employer, principal or other confider sues to restrain the disclosure of confidential information confided in a commercial context, the role of the court is very limited. It will consider whether the information was and remains confidential, whether it was imparted or acquired in circumstances giving rise to a duty of confidence and whether there has been a breach or threatened breach of the duty. If those ingredients of the cause of action are established, and in the absence of an iniquity defence, a restraint on disclosure would ordinarily be imposed unless the confider would be adequately compensated by damages which the other party could pay. There would in such a case be no public interest in favour of disclosure which could outweigh or counter-balance the public interest in upholding the confider's right to preserve the confidentiality of his information. Indeed, such a case between two private citizens would not be seen as involving the public interest at all.

[56] *Balston Ltd v Headline Filters Ltd* [1987] FSR 330 at 348. For the outcome at trial see [1990] FSR 385. Among other things, this case concerned the extent to which preparations for the establishment of a competing business by a director become unlawful and place the director in breach of fiduciary duty, as to which see, also, *British Midland Tool Ltd v Midland International Trading Ltd* [2003] 2 BCLC 523 and *Shepherds Investments Ltd v Walters* [2006] EWHC 836 (Ch), [2007] IRLR 110, [2006] All ER (D) 213.

[57] The landmark authority is *Saltman Engineering Co Ltd v Campbell Engineering Co Ltd* (1948) 65 RPC 203, where, although there was a contract, the defendant's liability was found to rest on a breach of confidence.

[58] A lecture given to the Hebrew University of Jerusalem, reproduced as 'Spycatchter: Confidence, Copyright and Contempt', *Israel Law Review*, (1989) 23(4) 407 at 413.

imparted or acquired in confidence or as a result of a confidential relationship, such as a doctor and a patient, could be legally protected by the courts seems to have arisen only in the early nineteenth century.

As no contract or privity is required, the equitable jurisdiction is of potentially wider application than the contractual jurisdiction. Where confidentiality arises by statute, the information will almost certainly be independently rendered exempt information by s 44(1)(a).[59]

011   Breach of confidence for the purposes of the Act

It is not clear whether s 41(1), in referring to 'a breach of confidence actionable by [the person from whom the public authority obtained the information] or any other person', is referring solely to confidences that are or would be actionable under the courts' equitable jurisdiction or whether it also covers all information deemed confidential (irrespective of whether it is commonplace) provided under a contract. It is suggested that the reference to a 'breach of confidence' (rather than to a 'breach of contract') and to it being actionable 'by that or any other person' point to the former. Plainly, however, the presence of such a contractual provision will be relevant to a determination of whether disclosure of the information would be protected by equity. This is consistent with the approach taken by Scott J at first instance in *Attorney-General v Guardian Newspapers Ltd (No 2)*:

> The dicta in these two cases[60] places the origin of the duty of confidence not in contract, express or implied, but in equity. But the ambit of the duty of confidence imposed by equity will depend, in my view, on the same type of judicial approach to the surrounding circumstances of the case as that adopted where an implicit term is treated as the basis of the duty. As long ago as 1893 the Court of Appeal concluded that there was no distinction between the duty of confidence placed on an agent by implied contract and that imposed on him by equity; see *Lamb v Evans* [1893] 1 Ch 218.

If, contrary to this view, the phrase does extend to all information covered by a contractual prohibition on disclosure (including commonplace information), it will then be necessary to consider whether the contractual prohibition is actionable.[61]

012   The essential elements of an actionable breach of confidence

The conventional starting point for considering the nature and scope of the equitable duty of confidentiality remains[62] the three-fold test identified in the judgment of Megarry J in *Coco v A N Clark (Engineers) Ltd*:[63]

> In my judgment, three elements are normally required if, apart from contract, a case of

---

[59] Similarly, by FOI(S)A s 26(a). See further §§26– 015 to 26– 019.

[60] *Moorgate Tobacco Co Ltd v Philip Morris Ltd (No 2)* (1984) 156 CLR 414; *Commonwealth of Australia v John Fairfax & Sons Ltd* (1980) 147 CLR 39.

[61] It will be unenforceable where or to the extent that: (1) it would prevent an ex-employee from making proper use of his skills or otherwise constitutes an unreasonable restraint on trade; (2) it conflicts with competition law; (3) it would prevent publication that is in the public interest; or (4) it would otherwise be unlawful.

[62] See *R v Department of Health, ex p Source Informatics Ltd* [2001] QB 424, [2001] 1 All ER 786 at [14]; *Douglas v Hello! Ltd (No 3)* [2006] EWCA Civ 595, [2006] QB 125 at [55].

[63] *Coco v A N Clark (Engineers) Ltd* [1969] RPC 41 at 47. The information in that case was technical information which was of value for commercial purposes; it was held not to be of a confidential nature because it was already in the public domain. See more recently: *Murray v Yorkshire Fund Managers Ltd* [1998] 1 WLR 96 (CA); *A v B plc* [2001] 1 WLR 2341, [2002] 1 All ER 449.

breach of confidence is to succeed. First, the information itself, in the words of Lord Greene MR in *Saltman Engineering Co Ltd v Campbell Engineering Co Ltd*,[64] must "have the necessary quality of confidence about it". Secondly, that information must have been imparted in circumstances importing an obligation of confidence. Thirdly, there must be an unauthorised use of that information to the detriment of the party communicating it.

In *Attorney-General v Guardian Newspapers Ltd (No 2)*[65] Lord Goff of Chieveley stated the broad, general principle (non-definitively) as being:

> that a duty of confidence arises when confidential information comes to the knowledge of a person (the confidant) in circumstances where he has notice, or is held to have agreed, that the information is confidential, with the effect that it would be just in all the circumstances that he should be precluded from disclosing the information to others ... in the vast majority of cases ... the duty of confidence will arise from a transaction or relationship between the parties ... But it is well settled that a duty of confidence may arise in equity independently of such cases .

25–013 Underlying public policy considerations

The equitable jurisdiction is founded on obligations of conscience, and its essential basis is the duty to act in good faith.[66] It also rests on the notion that there is a public interest in the maintenance of confidences, and to this extent it is governed by public policy considerations. Such considerations mean that regard must be had to countervailing public interests. One such countervailing public interest is that of freedom of trade. Concern for this interest, coupled with the difficulties for employees of identifying what information of their employers is truly confidential, as opposed to forming part of the general stock of knowledge of those engaged in any particular line of business, has led the courts to observe that the proper way for employers to protect themselves:

> would be by exacting covenants from their employees restricting their field of activity after they have left their employment, not by asking the court to extend the general equitable doctrine to prevent breaking confidence beyond all reasonable bounds.[67]

Another countervailing public interest is that of freedom of expression. As Lord Keith of Kinkel said in *Attorney-General v Guardian Newspapers Ltd (No 2)*:[68]

> The general rule is that anyone is entitled to communicate anything he pleases to anyone else, by speech or in writing or in any other way. That rule is limited by the law of defamation and other restrictions similar to those mentioned in Article 10 of [the Convention]. All those restrictions are imposed in the light of considerations of public interest such as to countervail the public interest in freedom of expression.

There is also a public interest in promoting the accountability of government. It is this consideration that underpins the distinction made by Lord Scott of Foscote between the

---

[64] *Saltman Engineering Co Ltd v Campbell Engineering Co Ltd* [1948] 65 RPC 203 at 215, [1963] 3 All ER 413 (Note).

[65] *Attorney-General v Guardian Newspapers Ltd (No 2)* [1990] 1 AC 109 at 281.

[66] See the discussion of the relevant principles of law by Bingham LJ in *AG v Guardian Newspapers Ltd (No 2)* [1990] 1 AC 109 at 214–216.

[67] *Printers & Finishers Ltd v Holloway* [1965] 1 WLR 1 at 6, [1963] 3 All ER 731; see also, to similar effect, *AT Poeton (Gloucester Plating) Ltd v Horton* [2000] ICR 1208, [2001] FSR 14 (CA). However, the employer is not obliged to point out to the employee the precise limits of what is sought to be protected as confidential information: see *Lancashire Fires Ltd v Lyons & Co Ltd* [1996] FSR 629 at 673–674.

[68] *Attorney-General v Guardian Newspapers Ltd (No 2)* [1990] 1 AC 109 at 256.

principles that ought to represent the foundation of the law of confidence.[69] Lord Scott expressed the view that, on the one hand, there is a principle that private persons are entitled to protection against disclosure without their consent of confidential information about themselves and their activities in the absence of a sufficient public interest reason for disclosure of such information; but, on the other hand, there is a principle that the various manifestations of government are not entitled to protection against disclosure of information about themselves and their activities unless there is a sufficient public interest requiring such information to be protected from disclosure.[70]

014 The first element: the circumstances of acquisition

Where the person providing the information to the public authority expressly states that it is being provided in confidence, that will usually suffice to satisfy the first element.[71] Where a person is under a statutory duty to supply particular information to a public authority, that will often satisfy the first element, particularly if the public authority is under a statutory duty not to use the information other than in connection with its core functions. For example, a taxpayer who supplies to HM Revenue & Customs information relating to his income. Similarly, if a public authority received information in the exercise of its functions, although the provider is not obliged to supply it, that public authority will generally owe a duty to the provider not to use it for unrelated purposes.[72] The scope of the duty may vary from case to case according to the circumstances in which, and the purposes for which, the information was received.[73] Lord Goff's non-definitive formulation of the broad general principle makes clear that it is not essential that there should be a pre-existing relationship between the person seeking to enforce the duty and the person to whom the information was disclosed. The extent to which these principles will apply to information supplied to a public authority after the coming into force of the Freedom of Information Act is unclear and not without difficulty. First, although the cited decisions have relied on notions of confidentiality, often the outcome has turned on an analysis of the duties and powers of the public authority that acquired the information and whether the use to which the information has been put advances any of those functions. Those uses may be quite different from the purpose for which the person supplied the information to the public authority. Secondly, persons supplying information to a public authority after 2000 do so knowing that public authorities are subject to the disclosure obligations imposed by the Act and, more recently, the Environmental Information Regulations

---

[69] See Lord Scott's essay 'Confidentiality' in J Beatson and Y Cripps (eds), *Freedom of Information—Essays in Honour of Sir David Williams* (Oxford, Oxford University Press, 2000) pp 267–274.

[70] See §§15– 011 to 15– 016 for a treatment of the public interest considerations weighing in favour of disclosure.

[71] This will be most easily satisfied where a contract provides that all information received is received in confidence. As in *Dunford & Elliott v Johnson & Firth Brown* [1978] FSR 143.

[72] For example: *S v IC and The General Register Office*, IT, 9 May 2007, notes taken by the registrar of deaths during a question and answer session of a person registering a death held to be attended by an expectation of confidentiality.

[73] Thus in *Hellewell v Chief Constable of Derbyshire* [1995] 1 WLR 804 the court held that the police could make reasonable use of a 'mug shot' of an arrested person for the purposes of the prevention and detection of crime, investigation of alleged offences and apprehension of suspects. In *Marcel v Commissioner of Police* [1992] Ch 225 the court held that the police should not have allowed a party in civil proceedings to inspect documents seized by them in connection with a subsequently dropped criminal investigation. See also *Re Arrows Ltd (No 4)* [1995] 2 AC 75; *Taylor v Director of the Serious Fraud Office* [1999] AC 177.

2004. This should not affect the position of a person who is under a duty to supply information to a public authority (eg a tax return of a taxpayer). Where, however, a person volunteers information, the position may be different. A distinction may be drawn between the person who is required to provide information in order to secure a licence,[74] permission, grant, benefit, etc and the pure volunteer. In both cases, however, it is suggested that the stronger the potential requirement on the public authority, in the proper exercise of its functions, to share the information received (eg with a person who stands to be affected by it), the more difficult it will be to satisfy the first element. In those circumstances, the public authority receives the information knowing that the due performance of its functions may require the dissemination of the information that it receives. It is suggested that this is consistent with the general principle that a person to whom confidential information has been disclosed may disclose that information where legitimate interests in disclosure outweigh those of protecting the confidence.[75]

25–015 The second element: the confidential nature of the information

The requirement that the information be of a 'confidential nature' is linked to the first element. The circumstances in which information is received will shape whether the information itself is of a confidential nature. The necessary quality is that 'the information must not be something which is public property and public knowledge.'[76] In other words, in order to be confidential the information must have about it 'the basic attribute of inaccessibility'.[77] Self-classification of the information as 'confidential', whether or not acquiesced to by the recipient public authority, does not give it the necessary quality of confidence.[78] The information must

---

[74] Such as the plaintiffs in *R v Licensing Authority established under Medicines Act 1968, ex p Smith Kline & French Laboratories Ltd* [1990] 1 AC 64.

[75] See *Webster v James Chapman & Co* [1989] 3 All ER 939 at 945. See further §22–024.

[76] *Saltman Engineering Co Ltd v Campbell Engineering Co Ltd* [1948] 65 RPC 203 at 215. In *Douglas v Hello! Ltd (No 3)* [2006] EWCA Civ 595, [2006] QB 125, [2005] 4 All ER 128 at [55] the Court of Appeal said: 'This is not the clearest of definitions. It seems to us that information will be confidential if it is available to one person (or a group of persons) and not generally available to others, provided that the person (or group) who possesses the information does not intend that it should become available to others.' In some cases, however, the courts use the expression 'quality of confidentiality' to describe a threshold requirement which information needs to satisfy in order to be capable of being confidential, and treat this requirement as embracing considerations which are different from, or additional to, the requirement of inaccessibility. See, eg, *Tillery Valley Foods v Channel Four Television* [2004] EWHC 1075; Ch, [2004] 101 (22) LSG 31, in which, following *Australian Broadcasting Corp v Lenah Game Meats Pty Ltd* [2001] HCA 63, Mann J held that an employee's filming of his workplace, workmates and their working activities did not necessarily result in the information captured on film having the quality of confidentiality.

[77] *AG v Guardian Newspapers Ltd (No 2)* [1990] 1 AC 109 at 215.

[78] *Derry City Council v IC*, IT, 11 December 2006 at [34(a)], where the Information Tribunal held that the fact that some communication between the third party and the public authority was marked 'private and confidential' and that the agreement itself imposed an express obligation of confidence in relation to one piece of information, did not provide much assistance in determining whether the whole agreement was confidential. See also: *Worsley & Co v Cooper* [1939] 1 All ER 290; *Re Dalrymple* [1957] RPC 449; *Re Gallay Ltd's Application* [1959] RPC 141; *Drake Personnel Ltd v Beddison* [1979] VR 13; *Faccenda Chicken Ltd v Fowler* [1987] Ch 117 at 138; *Kone Elevators Pty Ltd v McNay* (1997) 19 ATPR 41–564; *cf Wright v Gasweld Pty Ltd* (1991) 22 NSWLR 317 at 333, where Kirby P said that courts should exercise a 'modest disinclination to hold that information is not confidential when parties have taken the trouble to say that it is.' In an employment context, the fact that the employer makes it clearly known to the employee that the employer considers certain information to be 'confidential' will be relevant: *Printers and Finishers Ltd v Holloway (Confidential Information)* [1965] RPC 239 at 256; *Lancashire Fires Ltd v SA Lyons & Co Ltd* [1997] IRLR 113(CA) at [18].

be such that a reasonable person would regard it as confidential.[79] Usages and practices of the industry or profession may be relevant.[80] So, too, may be the measures taken by the information provider to guard the information from wider dissemination.[81] In relation to certain classes of information the Courts have readily found that information has the requisite confidential nature:

— Correspondence between a person and his legal advisers.[82]

— Medical records relating to an individual, although readily characterised as part of a person's private life, have been held confidential on a conventional analysis of the cause of action.[83]

— Statements made to the police in the course of a criminal investigation.[84]

— Tender documents for a commercial contract[85] and other documents received by a public authority from a counterparty in the course of commercial negotiations.[86]

— Information supplied to a public authority by a person under legal compulsion, such as a tax return.[87]

— Information supplied to a public authority which, although provided under legal compulsion, is of a highly personal and sensitive nature.[88]

016 False information

A claim for breach of confidentiality, at least in a case involving personal information, may be successfully mounted even though the information is false.[89]

---

[79] *Lancashire Fires Ltd v SA Lyons & Co Ltd* [1996] FSR 629 at 646, 656; *Dunford & Elliott v Johnson & Firth Brown* [1978] FSR 143 at 148.

[80] *Thomas Marshall (Exports) Ltd v Guinle* [1979] Ch 227 at 248; *Weir Pumps Ltd v CML Pumps Ltd* [1984] FSR 33.

[81] *E Worsley & Co Ltd v Cooper* [1939] 1 All ER 290 at 307; *Ansell Rubber Co Pty Ltd v Allied Rubber Industries Pty Ltd* [1967] VR 37 at 50.

[82] *Watkins v SSHD* [2006] UKHL 17, [2006] 2 AC 395.

[83] *Ashworth Security Hospital v MGN Ltd* [2002] UKHL 29, [2002] 1 WLR 2033; *R (B) v Stafford Combined Court* [2006] EWHC 1645, [2007] All ER 102, [2006] 2 Cr App R 34; *R (Axon) v Secretary of State for Health* [2006] EWHC 37, [2006] QB 539; *LB of Brent v N* [2005] EWHC 1676, [2006] 1 FLR 310; *Mersey Care NHS Trust v Ackroyd (No1)* [2003] EWCA Civ 663, [2003] EMLR 36; *A Health Authority v X (No1)* [2001] EWCA Civ 2014, [2002] 2 All ER 780, [2002] 1 FLR 1045.

[84] *Taylor v Serious Fraud Office* [1999] 2 AC 177 at 211 (even though the material may be given in the knowledge that it will be made public in Court); *Frankson v SSHD* [2003] EWCA Civ 655, [2003] 1 WLR 1952; *Woolgar v Chief Constable of Sussex Police* [2000] 1 WLR 25; *Bunn v BBC* [1998] 3 All ER 552.

[85] *London Regional Transport v Mayor of London* [2001] EWCA Civ 1491, [2003] EMLR 4.

[86] *Derry City Council v IC*, IT, 11 December 2006 at [34], where the Information Tribunal readily accepted that commercial negotiations between a third party and a public authority be subject to an expectation of confidentiality. That obligation would remain in place until the information in question had either passed into the public domain or had ceased to have commercial significance.

[87] *Mount Murray Country Club Ltd & Ors v Commission of Inquiry into Mount Murray* [2003] UKPC 53, [2003] STC 1525, 75 TC 197, [2004] BTC 76.

[88] For example: *S v IC and The General Register Office*, IT, 9 May 2007, notes taken by the registrar of deaths during a question and answer session of a person registering a death held to be attended by an expectation of confidentiality.

[89] *McKennitt v Ash v* [2006] EWCA Civ 1714, [2008] QB 73.

25– 017 Information intended subsequently to be published

A claim for breach of confidentiality may be successfully mounted to restrain the disclosure of information in advance of the time that the confider proposes to make public the information.[90]

25– 018 The effect of the death of the confider on the existence of the duty

In *Bluck v Information Commissioner and Epsom & St Helier University NHS Trust*[91] the appellant's adult daughter had died at a hospital. Five years later the appellant learned that the hospital had admitted liability for her daughter's death and had reached a settlement with her widower on behalf of himself and the two children of their marriage under which substantial compensation had been paid. The appellant's attempts at obtaining information from the hospital concerning her daughter's death were unsuccessful, because it refused to share such information without the consent of the widower, as the deceased daughter's next of kin. The appellant sought to overcome that refusal by making a request for information under the Freedom of Information Act 2000. The Information Commissioner upheld the hospital's claim that the information was exempt under s 41, on the grounds that (1) the health records were subject to an obligation of confidence, (2) this obligation survived the death of the person to whom the records related, (3) the personal representatives could bring an action if the information were disclosed other than under the Act, and (4) as the s 41 exemption was absolute, there was no need to consider whether the public interest in maintaining that exemption was outweighed by the public interest in disclosure. The decision was upheld by the Information Tribunal. The Tribunal were right[92] (1) to agree with the authors of *Toulson & Phipps on Confidentiality*[93] that 'Equity may impose a duty of confidentiality towards another after the death of the original confider. The question is not one of property (whether a cause of action owned by the deceased has been assigned) but of conscience', (2) to agree also[94] with the authors' view that equity may in principle regard a doctor as owing a duty of conscience to a deceased's estate, in keeping with the maxim that equity will not suffer a wrong to be without a remedy[95] and (3) to cite *Z v Finland*[96] in support of the proposition that medical data is of fundamental importance not only to the Article 8 rights of the individual but also to both the private and public interests of maintaining confidence in health services.[97]

---

[90] *Khashoggi v Smith* (1980) 124 SJ 149; *Shelley Films Ltd v Rex Features Ltd* [1994] EMLR 134; *Creation Records Ltd v New Group Papers Ltd* [1997] EMLR 444.

[91] *Bluck v Information Commissioner and Epsom & St Helier University NHS Trust* IT, 17 September 2007.

[92] *Bluck v IC and Epsom & St Helier University NHS Trust*, IT, 17 September 2007 at [18]-[21].

[93] Second edition, at para 11–953.

[94] *Bluck v IC and Epsom & St Helier University NHS Trust*, IT, 17 September 2007 at [24].

[95] See also *Armioniene v Lithuania* [2009] EMLR 7, (2009) 48 EHRR 53, 27 BHRC 389.

[96] *Z v Finlandi* (1997) 25 EHRR 371 at [26].

[97] Nevertheless, it is suggested that these principles did not compel the answer that the exemption should be upheld. The appellant's interest in the cause(s) of her daughter's death would appear to have been both understandable and reasonable. Moreover, she was only seeking disclosure to herself, not to the world at large. It was far from clear, therefore, whether it ought to have troubled the conscience of the hospital to make the disclosure that was sought; or, in Article 8 terms, whether the deceased had a reasonable expectation of privacy that her medical records would not be disclosed to her own mother by the hospital where she died, or whether that expectation should prevail over her mother's Article 10 rights. These considerations were strengthened on the facts by the circumstances that: the

019 Confidential information that has entered the public domain

Confidential information will cease to be confidential once it has entered the public domain. This means:

> no more than that the information in question is so generally accessible that, in all the circumstances, it cannot be regarded as confidential.[98]

A clear example was given by Bingham LJ in *Attorney-General v Guardian Newspapers Ltd (No 2)*[99]

> Forty-four years ago there can have been few, if any, national secrets more confidential than the date of the planned invasion of France. Any Crown servant who divulged such information to an unauthorised recipient would plainly have been in flagrant breach of his duty. But it would be absurd to hold such a servant bound to treat the date of the invasion as confidential on or after (say) 9 June 1944 when the date had become known to the world. A purist might say that the Allies, as confiders and owners of the information, had by their own act destroyed its confidentiality and so disabled themselves from enforcing the duty, but the common sense view is that the date, being public knowledge, could no longer be regarded as the subject of confidence.

Whether information is so generally accessible that it is not confidential is a matter of fact and degree. Relevant considerations include the realities of accessibility, the nature of the information, and the lapse of time since dissemination took place.[100] For example, information in a library book filed under a specialised heading or on the website of a government department which would not be accessed without some degree of background knowledge may not be 'realistically accessible' or properly regarded as 'public knowledge'.[101] The disclosure of highly specific personal information (for example, carefully selected photographs of a wedding that had been sold on an exclusive basis) will not result in the loss of confidentiality for other information on the same subject matter (for example, other photographs of the same occasion taken surreptitiously and offered for sale without the consent of the subjects).[102]

020 The effect of a disclosure upon the duty of confidence

The basic principle is that the duty of confidence is imposed not only on the person to whom information is confided but also on any third party who acquires the information and who

---

deceased had died some five years previously; the hospital had admitted negligence; and that part of the medical records had already been released in correspondence, press statements and court records disclosed to the appellant without restriction. As was the case in *W v Egdell* [1990] Ch 359 (CA), the real question before the Tribunal was not as to the existence of the duty of confidentiality but as to its breadth, and that the correct answer to the issue that was raised on the facts involved striking a balance between competing interests. The Tribunal should, perhaps, have been more hesitant to arrive at a conclusion that was contrary to its clear sympathy for the appellant (at [13]). It is also suggested that, both as a matter of principle having regard to equitable concepts that inform the law of confidence and in light of the result arrived at by the Tribunal in this case, it is not necessarily right to regard all requests for information in a manner that is 'applicant blind' and/or 'motive blind'.

[98] See *AG v Guardian Newspapers (No 2) Ltd* [1990] 1 AC 109, Lord Goff at 282.

[99] *AG v Guardian Newspapers (No 2) Ltd* [1990] 1 AC 109 at 215.

[100] In *S v IC and The General Register Office*, IT, 9 May 2007 the Information Tribunal found that a limited disclosure of the requested information did not cause it to lose its confidential character (at [70]–[73]).

[101] *AG v Greater Manchester Newspapers Ltd* [2001] TLR 668, at [33]–[34]. Although it may be observed that in a modern society important information is often intelligible only to a limited number of people. On that basis, the issue is not that the information be generally accessible, but that it be readily accessible to a person interested in it.

[102] *OBG Ltd v Allan* [2007] UKHL 21, [2008] 1 AC 1 at [122], [302], [329].

knows that it is subject to an obligation of confidence. In this context, the question arises whether a recipient who is bound by an obligation of confidence can rely upon disclosure to the world at large, including as a matter of logic his own disclosure, to say that he is no longer bound by that obligation.[103] On one view, he can, because the consequence of any disclosure to the world at large, including a disclosure by the recipient, is that 'the secret, as a secret, has ceased to exist'.[104] The contrary view is that of the majority in *Schering Chemicals Ltd v Falkman Ltd*.[105] In that case Shaw LJ said:

> It is not the law that where confidentiality exists it is terminated or eroded by adventitious publicity. Nor is the correlative duty to preserve that confidentiality. The public interest may demand that the duty be gainsaid; but it cannot be arbitrarily cast aside. An order of a court of law may relieve the confidant of the burden of secrecy and may, after due inquiry, require him to reveal the subject matter of the confidence; but it is not to be sloughed at will for self-interest.[106]

The significance of this approach to the exemption contained in s 41 of the Freedom of Information Act 2000 is that it cannot be assumed that the fact that information in the possession of the public authority which is subject to an obligation of confidence has been placed in the public domain releases the public authority from that obligation — particularly in the event that the information has been placed in the public domain in breach of the public authority's own obligation. The disclosure, or further disclosure, by the public authority of the information which it holds may still be actionable, in spite of the fact that the information is already in the public domain.[107]

25–021 The third element: detriment

It is an open question whether detriment to the claimant is an essential ingredient of an action for breach of confidence.[108] If detriment does need to be established, however, it may well constitute sufficient detriment to the confider that information is to be disclosed to persons whom he would prefer not to know of it.[109]

25–022 Limiting principles

In *Attorney-General v Guardian Newspapers (No 2) Ltd*[110] Lord Goff identified three limiting concepts to the broad general principle that he had stated. The first, that the principle of confidentiality does not apply to information that is generally accessible, has already been considered above.[111]

---

[103] The House of Lords alluded to the point in their speeches in *AG v Guardian Newspapers Ltd (No 2)* [1990] 1 AC 109, but it did not require to be resolved in that case because no relief was sought against Peter Wright, the author of 'Spycatcher', and he neither appeared nor was represented at any level in that litigation.

[104] *O Mustad & Son v Dosen (Note)* [1964] 1 WLR 109, 111.

[105] *Schering Chemicals Ltd v Falkman Ltd* [1982] QB 1, [1981] 2 All ER 321.

[106] At 26–27, and see Templeman LJ at 37–38. See also *Exchange Telegraph Co Ltd v Central News Ltd* [1897] 2 Ch 48.

[107] Further, as to personal information and 'public domain' see §25–042.

[108] *AG v Guardian Newspapers Ltd (No 2)* [1990] 1 AC 109 at 281–282. Similarly, *AG (UK) v Heinemann Publishers Australia Pty Ltd* (1987) 10 NSWLR 86 at 90; *Carindale Country Club Estate Pty Ltd v Astill* (1993) 42 FCR 307, 115 ALR 112.

[109] *AG v Guardian Newspapers Ltd (No 2)* [1990] 1 AC 109 at 255–256.

[110] *AG v Guardian Newspapers Ltd (No 2)* [1990] 1 AC 109 at 282.

[111] See §§25–019 to 25–020.

The second is that the duty of confidence does not apply to information that is useless or trivial.[112] Although Lord Goff said that he did not need to develop this point, it has since assumed particular importance as a result of the extension of the law of confidence beyond its traditional boundaries and into the realms of intrusion into personal autonomy.[113] The third limiting concept identified by Lord Goff is that in certain circumstances the public interest in maintaining confidence may be outweighed by the public interest in disclosure.[114]

023 Useless or trivial information

Where the information for which a claim for confidence is made is of a commercial nature, the claim will be defeated if the information is, from an objective standpoint, trivial or useless.[115]

024 Public interest defence: the principle

Public interest is available as a defence[116] to claims for breach of confidence, and it is a general defence[117] not limited to the refusal of equitable relief.[118] The basic principles are that:

(1) the public interest in disclosure may outweigh both private and public interests in the protection of confidences;

(2) where the balancing exercise comes down in favour of disclosure, it may favour only limited disclosure—either in the form of disclosure to less than the world at large or in the form of partial disclosure; and

(3) in the era of the Human Rights Act 1998, the Court, as a public authority, has a duty to act compatibly with Convention rights (as defined by section 1 of that Act), including the right to respect for private and family life, home and correspondence that is guaranteed by Article 8 and the right to freedom of expression that is guaranteed by Article 10, and where there is a tension between competing rights (including, it is suggested, the 'societal interests' such as the protection of information received in confidence that is recognised by Article 10(2)) to carry out

---

[112] This is dealt with at §25– 023.

[113] See further §§25– 030 to 25– 048.

[114] This is dealt with at §§25– 024 to 25– 027.

[115] *AG v Guardian Newspapers Ltd (No 2)* [1990] 1 AC 109 at 282 (Lord Goff). At first instance, Scott J had given as an example *McNicol v Sportsman's Book Stores* (1930) McGCC 116, where the plaintiff was the originator of a betting system based on the age of the moon and had sought to restrain publication of his system.

[116] This is how the point is characterised in, eg, *London Regional Transport v Mayor of London* [2003] EWCA Civ 1491, [2003] EMLR 4, by Robert Walker LJ at [35]. There is a school of thought that the true analysis is not so much that the public interest affords a defence but rather that the public interest principle is of relatively narrow application and that, where it does apply, it has the effect that no obligation of confidence arises at all. This characterisation has usually been preferred by the Australian courts: *Corrs Pavey Whiting & Byrne v Collector of Customs (Vic)* (1987) 14 FCR 434 at 451, 74 ALR 428 at 445 *et seq.*; *Smith Kline & French Laboratories (Aust) Ltd v Secretary, Department of Community Services and Health* (1990) 22 FCR 87 at 110, 95 ALR 87 at 124.

[117] Although most of the reported cases have been concerned with the grant or refusal of an interlocutory injunction, it is submitted that the policy reasons given in the judgments apply with equal force to final injunctions and to pecuniary remedies.

[118] Indeed, it now seems clear that essentially the same defence is also available to a claim for infringement of copyright (which, unlike a claim for breach of confidence, is clearly a claim that is based on a property right), and that the existence and scope of the defence is informed and bolstered by free-speech considerations in view of the effective incorporation into English law of art 10 by the Human Rights Act 1998: see *Hyde Park Residence Ltd v Yelland* [2001] Ch 143; *Ashdown v Telegraph Ltd* [2002] Ch 149.

the parallel analysis mandated by the House of Lords in *Re S (Identification: Restrictions on Publication).*[119]

In *Attorney-General v Guardian Newspapers Ltd (No 2)*[120] Lord Goff of Chieveley summed the matter up as follows:

> The third limiting principle is of far greater importance. It is that, although the basis of the law's protection of confidence is that there is a public interest that confidences should be preserved and protected by the law, nevertheless that public interest may be outweighed by some other countervailing public interest which favours disclosure. This limitation may apply, as the learned judge pointed out, to all types of confidential information. It is this limiting principle which may require a court to carry out a balancing operation, weighing the public interest in maintaining confidence against a countervailing public interest favouring disclosure. Embraced within this limiting principle is, of course, the so called defence of iniquity. In origin, this principle was narrowly stated, on the basis that a man cannot be made "the confidant of a crime or a fraud": see *Gartside v Outram*[121] per Sir William Page Wood VC. But it is now clear that the principle extends to matters of which disclosure is required in the public interest: see *Beloff v Pressdram Ltd,*[122] per Ungoed-Thomas J, and *Lion Laboratories Ltd v Evans*[123] per Griffiths LJ. It does not however follow that the public interest will in such cases require disclosure to the media, or to the public by the media. There are cases in which a more limited disclosure is all that is required: see *Francome v Mirror Group Newspapers Ltd.*[124] A classic example of a case where limited disclosure is required is a case of alleged iniquity in the Security Service.

In the context of giving guidance as to the grant of interim injunctions, the Court of Appeal has said that in many situations the public have an understandable and so legitimate interest in being told the information, which can be taken into account by the court in deciding on what side of the line a case falls; and that the court must not ignore the fact that if newspapers do not publish information in which the public are interested, there will be fewer newspapers published which will not be in the public interest.[125] This is not to equate the public interest with what

---

[119] *Re S (Identification: Restrictions on Publication)* [2004] UKHL 47, [2005] 1 AC 593, Lord Steyn at [17].

[120] *Attorney-General v Guardian Newspapers Ltd (No 2)* [1990] 1 AC 109 at 282.

[121] *Gartside v Outram* (1857) 26 LJ Ch 113 at 114.

[122] *Beloff v Pressdram Ltd* [1973] 1 All ER 241 at 260.

[123] *Lion Laboratories Ltd v Evans* [1985] QB 526 at 550. In that case, claims for breach of confidence and infringement of copyright were made in respect of documents taken by former employees which cast doubt on the accuracy of electronic breath testing equipment supplied by the claimant company to the police for the purpose of measuring the level of intoxication of motorists. Public interest was the only defence argued in the Court of Appeal, which held that the public interest may afford just cause or excuse for breaking confidence or infringing copyright, and that there was on the facts sufficient just cause and excuse so that no interim injunction should be granted restraining use or disclosure. All three judges held that the defence was not limited to cases of wrongdoing on the part of the claimant, that the disclosure of iniquity was merely an instance of the essential just cause or excuse, and that the test is whether there is legitimate ground for supposing that it is in the public interest for disclosure to be made. See, in particular, Stephenson LJ at 538.

[124] *Francome v Mirror Group Newspapers Ltd* [1984] 1 WLR 892.

[125] See *A v B plc* [2003] QB 195 at [11](xii). The Court of Appeal in *Campbell v Mirror Group Newspapers Ltd* [2002] EWCA Civ 1373, [2003] QB 633 later explained (at [40]) that this was not intended to refer to private facts which a fair-minded person would consider it offensive to disclose and (at [41]) that the fact that an individual has achieved prominence on the public stage does not mean that his private life can be laid bare by the media.

is of interest to the public (or the media), which would be wrong.[126] However, it does underline that there is a public interest in freedom of expression itself;[127] and, although there is also a public as well as a private interest in the maintenance of confidences, this may provide scope for the public interest defence to the cause of action for breach of confidence to be interpreted more liberally and treated as having more strength and breadth in the post-Human Rights Act 1998 era than it did in the past. The Courts have had to grapple with this issue most acutely in cases concerning private information, where some uncertainty still prevails as to precisely where boundaries should properly be drawn. This is partly because each case falls to be decided on its own particular facts and partly because the importance of injunctions in this area of the law (where the interim result is often for all practical purposes dispositive of the dispute) means that fully reasoned post-trial decisions are a rarity. The circumstances in which a public interest defence to a claim for breach of confidence may enjoy success can conveniently be considered under three headings, which may, of course, overlap:

—   first, the public interest in the disclosure of iniquity;
—   secondly, the public interest in the public not being misled;
—   thirdly, the public interest in the disclosure of matters of public concern.

The extent to which it will be possible to make an assessment of these considerations for the purposes of s 41 of the Freedom of Information Act 2000 will vary from case to case. This may be especially difficult if, either by analogy with the position of the media, or (in a case involving a request under the Act from the media) in order to enable the free press to fulfil its proper role in a modern democracy, some latitude or margin of appreciation ought properly to be allowed as to how much information it is justifiable to disclose (or unjustifiable to withhold).[128] The public authority may be able to make such an assessment from the information itself, or by having regard to a combination of the information, the nature of the request, and consultation with other persons.

025   Public interest in the disclosure of iniquity
Although the defence of public interest is not confined to cases involving wrongdoing, that is the paradigm instance in which it operates. The courts have always refused to uphold the right to confidence when to do so would cover up wrongdoing: in the words of Wood VC in *Gartside v Outram*[129] there is 'no confidence as to the disclosure of iniquity'. In addition, in the era of the

---

[126] See, eg, *Francome v Mirror Group Newspapers Ltd* [1984] 1 WLR 892, Sir John Donaldson MR at 898: 'The "media", to use a term which comprises not only the newspapers, but also television and radio, are an essential foundation of any democracy. In exposing crime, anti-social behaviour and hypocrisy and in campaigning for reform and propagating the view of minorities, they perform an invaluable function. However, they are peculiarly vulnerable to the error of confusing the public interest with their own interest. Usually these interests march hand in hand, but not always. In the instant case, pending a trial, it is impossible to see what public interest would be served by publishing the contents of the tapes which would not equally be served by giving them to the police or to the Jockey Club. Any wider publication could only serve the interests of the "Daily Mirror".'

[127] Reflected in the provisions of s 12 of the Human Rights Act 1998, and in the provisions of, eg, the Press Complaints Commission Code of Conduct, which is a privacy code within the meaning of s 12(4) and the provisions of which accordingly have to be taken into account thereunder. Clause 3 of the PCC Code is asterisked to show that it is subject to the public interest exception contained in the Code, and that exception includes the statement that 'There is a public interest in freedom of expression itself'.

[128] See *Campbell v MGN Ltd* [2004] UKHL 22, [2004] 2 AC 457 at [28]-[29], [61]-[65], [108], [112], [143].

[129] *Gartside v Outram* (1857) 26 LJ Ch (NS) 113 at 114. The case is reported in differing terms in three other sets of reports: (1856) 3 Jur (NS) 39, 5 WR 35 and 28 LT(OS) 120.

Human Rights Act 1998, such a public interest consideration may be an exception under article 8(2) to the article 8(1) right to respect for private and family life. The reason that exposure of wrongdoing should not be prevented, even if it is in breach of confidence, is that 'no private obligations can dispense with that universal one which lies on every member of society to discover every design which may be formed contrary to the laws of the society to destroy the public welfare'.[130] An allegation of wrongdoing will justify exposure in the public interest if it is a credible allegation from an apparently reliable source.[131] An illustration of the operation of the principle at the interim stage is provided by *Cream Holdings Ltd v Banerjee*,[132] in which the principal events related to tax evasion. The House of Lords, reversing the majority decision of the Court of Appeal, agreed with the dissenting judgment of Sedley LJ that these events were clearly matters of serious public interest such that restraint by interim injunction was inappropriate. In that case, the source of the information was an employee, and one of the arguments upon which the claimant employer relied[133] was that the situation was governed by, or at least should be appraised by reference to, express statutory provisions which applied to disclosures by employees. In rejecting this argument, Lord Nicholls, giving the leading speech with which the other members of the House of Lords agreed, stated that:

> The graduated protection afforded to "whistleblowers" by sections 43A to 43L of the Employment Rights Act 1996, inserted by the Public Interest Disclosure Act 1998, section 1, does not militate against this appraisal. Authorities such as the Inland Revenue owe duties of confidentiality regarding the affairs of those with whom they are dealing. The "whistleblower" provisions were intended to give additional protection to employees, not to cut down the circumstances where the public interest may justify private information being published at large.

25– 026   Public interest in the public not being misled

There is also a public interest in the public not being misled. Typically, this principle comes into play if a public figure misleads the public, where the media may be entitled to put the record straight.[134] The application of this principle to the facts of any particular case, and especially one involving the media, is, also, informed by free speech considerations.

---

[130] *Annersley v Anglesea (Earl)* (1743) LR 5 QB 317n 17 State Tr 1139, cited by Lord Denning MR in *Initial Services v Putterill* [1968] 1 QB 396 at 405.

[131] *AG v Guardian Newspapers Ltd (No 2)* [1990] 1 AC 109 at 283. In *S v IC and The General Register Office*, IT, 9 May 2007 the Information Tribunal, whilst holding that in relation to information found to be confidential 'the public interest would likely be in favour of disclosure if the disputed information provided evidence of criminal conduct, having regard to the contents of the letter the Tribunal is satisfied that it does not' (at [62]).

[132] *Cream Holdings Ltd v Banerjee* [2004] UKHL 44, [2005] 1 AC 253, [2004] 4 All ER 617.

[133] In the course of dealing with this argument, the House of Lords accepted that the Inland Revenue owed a duty of confidentiality to the claimant. This is supported by, eg, *Mount Murray Country Club Ltd v Commission of Inquiry into Mount Murray & Anr* [2003] UKPC 53 Lord Walker of Gestingthorpe at [33]: 'A taxpayer's returns of income are not covered by legal professional privilege. In the hands of the Revenue they are entitled to be treated as confidential, and subject to public interest immunity, because they relate to the taxpayer's personal affairs and are obtained by the Revenue under statutory compulsion.' It did not follow, however, that the defendants in *Cream Holdings Ltd v Banerjee* [2004] UKHL 44, [2005] 1 AC 253 (an employee and a local newspaper to which she revealed information) should not be permitted to publish information about the claimant's income and tax affairs, including its dealings with the Inland Revenue, where that disclosure was otherwise justified in the public interest.

[134] See, eg, *Woodward v Hutchins* [1977] 1 WLR 760. See also *Theakston v MGN Ltd* [2002] EWHC 137, [2002] EMLR 22; *Campbell v MGN Ltd* [2004] UKHL 22, [2004] 2 AC 457.

027 Public interest in the disclosure of matters of public concern

In *Initial Services Ltd v Putterill*,[135] the Court of Appeal held, first, that the exception allowing disclosure of information and documents obtained by an employee in the course of his employment extended to any disclosure that was justified in the public interest and operated with regard to a claim in damages; and, second, that disclosure to the press can fall within the principle. In *Fraser v Evans*[136] Lord Denning MR said:

> There are some things which are of such public concern that the newspapers, the Press, and, indeed, everyone is entitled to make known the truth and to make fair comment on it. This is an integral part of the right of free speech and expression. It must not be whittled away.

In *London Regional Transport v Mayor of London*[137] the Court of Appeal held that there was a public interest in enabling the general public (and especially the travelling public in London) to be informed of serious criticism from a responsible source of the value for money evaluation of the proposed public-private partnership involvement in the London Underground; and that this outweighed the preservation of commercial confidentiality in an interim report prepared by a firm of accountants which was based on commercially sensitive and confidential information that had been disclosed by private-sector bidders subject to express confidentiality agreements. An injunction to restrain the publication of a redacted version of that report—which, although interim in form, would in practice have irreversible consequences—was, accordingly, refused. The Court accepted the concession that there is a need for proportionality in any restraint of freedom of expression if the restraint is to be justifiable under article 10(2) of the Convention.[138] Sedley LJ suggested that the concept of proportionality that formed the basis for deciding a variety of Convention issues in accordance with the jurisprudence of the European Court of Human Rights enabled the elastic concept of whether a reasonable recipient's conscience would be troubled to be replaced by a structured inquiry:

> Does the measure meet a recognised and pressing social need? Does it negate the primary right or restrict it more than is necessary? Are the reasons given for it logical? ...for my part, I find it more helpful today to postulate a recipient who, being reasonable, runs through the proportionality checklist in order to anticipate what a court is likely to decide, and who adjusts his or her conscience and conduct accordingly.[139]

In *Jockey Club v Buffham*,[140] Gray J held that questions of the integrity and fairness of bookmaking to the betting public; the relationship of bookmakers to trainers and racing stables; and the effectiveness of the Jockey Club's regulatory role over the sport and industry of horseracing, were questions of proper and serious interest and concern to the public and, in particular, to the very many hundreds of thousands of people interested in horseracing, very many of whom will place bets from time to time. Accordingly, he ruled that the BBC should be allowed to broadcast information relating to such matters notwithstanding that it had been obtained from

---

[135] *Initial Services Ltd v Putterill* [1968] 1 QB 396.

[136] *Fraser v Evans* [1969] 1 QB 349 at 363.

[137] *London Regional Transport v Mayor of London* [2003] EWCA Civ 1491, [2003] EMLR 4.

[138] *London Regional Transport v Mayor of London* [2003] EWCA Civ 1491, [2003] EMLR 4, Robert Walker LJ at [49].

[139] *London Regional Transport v Mayor of London* [2003] EWCA Civ 1491, [2003] EMLR 4, Sedley LJ at [57]–[58].

[140] *Jockey Club v Buffham* [2003] QB 462.

a 'whistleblower' who divulged it to the BBC in breach of express contractual obligations.[141] The Tribunal has applied the reasoning in *London Regional Transport v Mayor of London*[142] to s 41(1) of the Freedom of Information Act 2000. In *Derry City Council v Information Commissioner*[143] it found that there was a public interest in disclosing commercial information where it shed light on a debate of wider concern (funding of an airport by a public authority):

> ...we consider that the weight that it should be given in that exercise will depend on our perception of its nature and importance – it should be "proportional". Clearly, considerable weight should be attributed to an issue on which the public is justifiably exercised at the time, regardless of whether it falls within a category that has previously been approved by the courts. Conversely, less weight should be attributed if, for example, the public interest extends only as far as a half hearted wish to be more fully informed in the context of a desultory public debate on a matter of relatively low significance.

The Tribunal concluded that accountability of public funding for an airport used by private operators was sufficiently weighty to displace the confidentiality that attached to negotiations between the public authority and the airline operator.[144]

25– 028 Government secrets

Where confidential information is produced by the workings of government,[145] the question arises as to the extent to which it is open to the government to rely upon the law of confidence to restrain use and disclosure of such information (whether by its own servants or agents, or by third parties to whom such information has been communicated). The reasons why a different approach is appropriate in the case of government secrets[146] from that which applies to private

---

[141] In reaching this decision, Gray J had regard to what the Court of Appeal had said in *Grobbelaar v News Group Newspapers Ltd* [2001] 2 All ER 437 at [47], [201] about the public interest in whether there was corruption in football, to what Morland J had said in *Chandler v Buffham* [2002] EWHC 1426 on an earlier application for injunctive relief in relation to two of the documents with which the application before Gray J was concerned, and to what had been said by Sir Thomas Bingham MR in *R v Disciplinary Committee of the Jockey Club, ex p Aga Khan* [1993] 1 WLR 909 at 912, 914.

[142] *London Regional Transport v Mayor of London* [2003] EWCA Civ 1491, [2003] EMLR 4.

[143] *Derry City Council v Information Commissioner*, IT, 11 December 2006 at [35].

[144] On the other hand, in *S v IC and The General Register Office*, IT, 9 May 2007, the Information Tribunal (at [63]–[64]) rejected an argument by the Commissioner that disclosure of confidential information would be in the public interest on the basis that it would provide confidence in the public authority's decision-making process. The Tribunal considered that that public interest could be satisfied in other ways that did not involve the disclosure of confidential information and that there were compelling factors (identified at [67]) in maintaining the confidentiality of the information.

[145] Where government is not the source, but the recipient, of confidential information different considerations apply, for here the essential confidence is, or is likely to be, that of others, typically citizens. Broadly speaking, two different sets of circumstance are likely to arise. First, the information may have been imparted consensually, in which case it will be subject to ordinary principles, and confidence will not be lost unless, eg, the public interest in disclosure outweighs the public interest in maintaining the confidence: *London Regional Transport v Mayor of London* [2003] EWCA Civ 1491 provides an illustration of how this might work in practice. Secondly, the information may have been imparted pursuant to an obligation imposed on the citizen (typically by statute), in which case the material legislation may stamp the information with confidentiality, and, in some instances, may expressly prohibit disclosure or restrict the uses to which the information may be put: the census and fiscal legislation provide examples.

[146] In *British Steel Corp v Granada Television Ltd* [1981] AC 1096, the majority of the House of Lords held or assumed that the need for a different approach did not extend to statutory corporations, treated the claimant public authority as entitled to the same rights as a private organization, and regarded accountability to Parliament as a sufficient check. Contrast the approach taken in *Esso Australia Resources Ltd v Plowman* (1985) 183 CLR 10, 128 ALR 391 (HCA)

or commercial confidences were explained in *A-G (UK) v Heinemann Publishers Pty Ltd*[147] by McHugh JA in the following terms:

> ...the relationship between the modern State and its citizens is so different in kind from that which exists between private citizens that rules worked out to govern the contractual, property, commercial and private confidences of citizens are not fully applicable where the plaintiff is a government or one of its agencies. Private citizens are entitled to protect or further their own interests, no matter how selfish they are in doing so. Consequently, the publication of confidential information which is detrimental to the private interest of a citizen is a legitimate concern of a court of equity. But governments act, or at all events are constitutionally required to act, in the public interest. Information is held, received and imparted by governments, their departments and agencies to further the public interest. Public and not private interest, therefore, must be the criterion by which equity determines whether it will protect information which a government or governmental body claims is confidential.

029 **Role of the public interest in relation to government secrets**

In *Attorney-General v Jonathan Cape Ltd*[148] the Attorney-General sought an injunction to restrain publication of Richard Crossman's book *Diaries of a Cabinet Minister*. Having said that 'when a Cabinet Minister receives information in confidence the improper publication of such information can be restrained by the court', Lord Widgery CJ went on to hold that the claimant had to establish not only (a) that publication would be a breach of confidence but in addition (b) that the public interest required that the publication be restrained, and (c) that there were no other facets of the public interest contradictory of and more compelling than that relied upon (by the claimant). In fact, the events described in the diaries were 10 years old, and there had been three general elections in the intervening period. In the result, Lord Widgery CJ refused an injunction, because:

> I cannot believe that publication at this interval of anything in volume one would inhibit free discussion in the Cabinet of today, even though the individuals involved are the same, and the national problems have a distressing similarity with those of a decade ago.

In *Commonwealth v John Fairfax and Sons Ltd*[149] Mason J proceeded on the basis that detriment was a necessary element of a cause of action for breach of confidence, and continued:

> The question then, when the executive government seeks the protection given by equity, is: What detriment does it need to show?
> The equitable principle has been fashioned to protect the personal, private and proprietary interests of the executive government. It acts, or is supposed to act, not according to standards of private interest, but in the public interest. This is not to say that equity will not protect information in the hands of the government, but it is to say that when equity protects government information it will look at the matter through different spectacles. It may be a sufficient detriment to the citizen that disclosure of information relating to his affairs will expose his actions to public discussion and criticism. But it can scarcely be a relevant detriment to the government that publication of material concerning its actions will merely expose it to public discussion and criticism. It is unacceptable in our democratic society that

[147] *A-G (UK) v Heinemann Publishers Pty Ltd* (1987) 10 NSWLR 86 at 191, 75 ALR 353 at 454, and subsequently adopted in *Coulthard v South Australia* (1995) 63 SASR 531 and in *Smith, Kline & French Laboratories (Aust) Ltd v Secretary, Department of Community Services and Health* (1991) 99 ALR 679, 23 FCR 291.

[148] *Attorney-General v Jonathan Cape Ltd* [1976] QB 752 at 770–771.

[149] *Commonwealth v John Fairfax and Sons Ltd* (1980) 147 CLR 39 at 51.

there should be a restraint on the publication of information relating to government when the only vice of that information is that it enables the public to discuss, review and criticize government action.

Accordingly, the court will determine the government's claim to confidentiality by reference to the public interest. Unless disclosure is likely to injure the public interest, it will not be protected.

The court will not prevent the publication of information which merely throws light on the past workings of government, even if it be not public property, so long as it does not prejudice the community in other respects. Then disclosure will itself serve the public interest in keeping the community informed and in promoting discussion of public affairs. If, however, it appears that disclosure will be inimical to the public interest because national security, relations with foreign countries or the ordinary business of government will be prejudiced, disclosure will be restrained. There will be cases in which the conflicting considerations will be finely balanced, where it is difficult to decide whether the public's interest in knowing and expressing its opinion outweighs the need to protect confidentiality.

Mason J and Lord Widgery CJ accordingly adopted substantially the same approach. The passage from the judgment of Mason J set out above has been accepted as representing the law in England[150] and in Scotland.[151]

3.   PRIVACY AND BREACH OF CONFIDENCE

25–030   Introduction

By tying the exemption in s 41 to an actionable breach of confidence, the Freedom of Information Act 2000 imports the conceptual difficulties which surround the basis upon which the common law is prepared to offer protection against certain invasions of privacy. Because of these difficulties and the resultant uncertainties, it is convenient to give separate consideration to the concept of an actionable breach of confidence which concerns private information. Whatever the nomenclature used, information will only be exempt from the disclosure duty if that disclosure may properly be characterised as an actionable breach of confidence.[152]   It is worth repeating the point made earlier: where or to the extent that personal information relating to a third person is captured by a request for information, s 40(2) will generally provide a more straightforward means of rendering information exempt information than will s 41(1).[153]

25–031   English law of privacy before the Human Rights Act 1998

The view that English law does not recognise invasion of privacy as an independent cause of

---

[150] See *AG v Guardian Newspapers Ltd* [1987] 1 WLR 1248 at 1261–1262, [1987] 3 All ER 316 at 325–6; *AG v Guardian Newspapers Ltd (No 2)* [1990] 1 AC 109 at 150–2, 203, 218, 221–2, 257–8, 270, 283; *AG v Punch Ltd* [2001] QB 1028 at [40]; *R v Department of Health, ex p Source Informatics Ltd* [2001] QB 424 at [25]; *R v Shayler* [2001] 1 WLR 2206 at [71]–[72]. See also (in related litigation) the position in New Zealand *A-G for UK v Wellington Newspapers Ltd* [1988] 1 NZLR 129 at 176.

[151] *Lord Advocate v Scotsman Publications Ltd* [1990] 1 AC 812 at 828, [1989] 2 All ER 852 at 862.

[152] FOIA s 41(1); FOI(S)A s 36(2).

[153] Unless the third person is deceased, in which case the data protection principles are inapplicable: DPA s 1(1), definition of 'personal data', and FOIA s 40(7). By way of example, see *Bluck v IC and Epsom & St Helier University NHS Trust*, IT, 17 September 2007.

action was clearly articulated by the Court of Appeal in *Kaye v Robertson*.[154] Even at that time, however, that starting point was subject to two significant qualifications. First, the facts of cases in which privacy issues arise often constitute another cause of action that is recognised by English law, most notably for a breach of confidence. Lord Hoffmann in his 1996 Goodman Lecture[155] expressed the view that breach of confidence – which was not even argued – might have afforded a basis for relief in *Kaye v Robertson*.[156] In *Attorney-General v Guardian Newspapers Ltd (No 2)*,[157] Lord Keith referred to cases 'where the breach of confidence involves no more than an invasion of personal privacy', specifically mentioned *Argyll v Argyll*[158] and marital confidences, and concluded that 'the right to personal privacy is clearly one which the law should in this field seek to protect'. Secondly, even before the Human Rights Act 1988 came into force on 2 October 2000 it appeared that the law might be moving toward recognition of a discrete right of privacy of some description. In *Morris v Beardmore*[159] the question was whether a motorist who refused to take a breath test at the request of a policeman who was trespassing at the time was acting unlawfully. The House of Lords held that he was not. The common law rights in question were trespass to land and physical compulsion to blow into a breathalyser. Lord Edmund Davies, Lord Keith, Lord Scarman and Lord Roskill nevertheless alluded to the exercise of the relevant police powers in terms of invasion of privacy. Lord Scarman referred to the 'invasion of fundamental private rights and liberties' and said that 'the adjective "fundamental" ... is apt to describe the importance attached by the common law to the privacy of the home.' Lord Roskill referred to 'the right of the ordinary citizen not to have his property, and thus his privacy, invaded against his will, save where such invasion is directly authorised by law.' In *R v Khan*,[160] Lord Nolan said that there was no right of privacy in English law in terms similar to article 8 of the Convention, and Lord Keith agreed with him. However, Lord Browne-Wilkinson, Lord Slynn and Lord Nicholls left open the question whether English law recognised a right of privacy, and, if so, what were the limitations of that right. Lord Nicholls referred to 'the important question whether the present, piecemeal protection of privacy has now developed to the extent that a more comprehensive principle can be seen to exist.'

032 The relevant Convention rights

In accordance with s 1 of the Human Rights Act 1998, the Convention rights to which the Act applies include the rights and fundamental freedoms set out in Articles 8 and 10 of the

---

[154] [1991] FSR 62: 'It is well-known that in English law there is no right to privacy, and accordingly there is no right of action for breach of a person's privacy. The facts of the present case are a graphic illustration of the desirability of Parliament considering whether and in what circumstances statutory provision can be made to protect the privacy of individuals' at [66] (Glidewell LJ); 'This case nonetheless highlights, yet again, the failure of both the common law of England and statute to protect in an effective way the personal privacy of individual citizens' at [70] (Bingham LJ); 'This right has so long been disregarded here that it can be recognised now only by the legislature' at [71] (Leggatt LJ).

[155] Lord Bingham, on the other hand, saw a need for development: see 'Should There be a Law to Protect Rights of Personal Privacy?' [1996] EHLR 45.

[156] *Kaye v Robertson* [1991] FSR 62.

[157] *Attorney-General v Guardian Newspapers Ltd (No 2)* [1990] 1 AC 109 at 255.

[158] *Argyll v Argyll* [1967] Ch 302.

[159] *Morris v Beardmore* [1981] AC 446, [1980] 2 All ER 753.

[160] *R v Khan* [1997] AC 558.

Convention.[161] The rights set out in both Articles are qualified. In the case of article 8, the qualifications include the article 10 right to freedom of expression. In the case of article 10, the qualifications include both the article 8 right to respect for private and family life and the protection of information received in confidence. Although the latter is not, itself, a Convention right it is unclear whether this makes any, or any significant, difference in practice when the Courts are required to carry out a balancing exercise between competing rights. In *Cream Holdings Ltd v Banerjee*,[162] for example, the confidential information was of a commercial nature, but there is no suggestion in the speeches of their Lordships that, on this ground, and as a matter of principle, less weight should be attached to the protection to which it might be entitled. So far as protection of reputation is concerned, the distinction between Convention rights, on the one hand, and societal interests, on the other hand, has been reduced or eliminated, at least in the case of claims by individuals, by the recognition that the right to protection of reputation is part of the right to respect for private and family life that is guaranteed by article 8.[163]

25–033 The Human Rights Act 1998

Section 6(1) of the Human Rights Act 1998 provides that it is unlawful for a public authority to act in a way which is incompatible with a Convention right. Obviously, this has the effect that a public authority which wrongly applies s 41(1) of the Freedom of Information Act 2000 may be in breach of this duty: the public authority may act incompatibly with article 10 rights if it asserts that information is exempt when it is not; and, conversely, it may act incompatibly with article 8 rights if it discloses information which is in truth exempt information. In order to understand the process by which the Human Rights Act 1998 has had the effect of extending the boundaries of what constitutes an actionable breach of confidence, however, it is necessary to have regard to further provisions of that Act. First, s 2 requires any court or tribunal determining a question which has arisen in connection with a Convention right to take into account any relevant Strasbourg jurisprudence. Secondly, by virtue of s 6(3), a 'public authority' includes a court or tribunal. The effect of these provisions is that it is ordinarily the duty of the English courts, save where and so far as constrained by primary domestic legislation, to give practical recognition to the principles laid down by the Strasbourg institutions as governing the Convention rights specified in section 1(1) of the Human Rights Act 1998.[164] It

---

[161] These are set out at §§3–002 to 3–015.

[162] *Cream Holdings Ltd v Banerjee* [2004] UKHL 44, [2005] 1 AC 253.

[163] See *Greene v Associated Newspapers Ltd* [2004] EWCA Civ 1462, [2005] QB 972 at [68], citing *Affaire Radio France v France* (2005) 40 EHRR 706 at [31]. It is now well established that protection of reputation is a right that is covered by the right to respect for private life under Article 8: *Lindon v France* (2008) 46 EHRR 35 at O-I18, p799; *Chauvy v France* (2005) 41 EHRR 29.

[164] *Kay v Lambeth London Borough Council* [2006] UKHL 10, [2006] 2 AC 465, Lord Bingham at [28]. See, further, *R (Alconbury Developments Ltd) v Secretary of State for the Environment, Transport and the Regions* [2001] UKHL 23, [2003] 2 AC 295, Lord Slynn at [26]: 'In the absence of some special circumstances it seems to me the court should follow any clear and constant jurisprudence of the European Court of Human Rights'; *R (Anderson) v Secretary of State for the Home Department* [2002] UKHL 46, [2003] 1 AC 837, Lord Bingham at [18]: 'While the duty of the House under section 2(1)(a) of the Human Rights Act 1998 is to take into account any judgment of the European Court, whose judgments are not strictly binding, the House will not without good reason depart from the principles laid down in a carefully considered judgment of the court sitting as a Grand Chamber'; *R (Ullah) v Special Adjudicator* [2004] UKHL 26, [2004] 2 AC 323, Lord Bingham at [20] 'It is of course open to member states to provide for rights more generous than those guaranteed by the Convention, but such provision should not be the product of interpretation of the

may be open to an English court to hold that it is not bound by previous decisions of English courts which are incompatible with Convention rights, on the grounds that those previous decisions have not had regard to and given effect to relevant Convention rights and relevant Strasbourg case law.[165] However, a court which would ordinarily be bound to follow the decision of another court higher in the domestic curial hierarchy remains bound to follow that decision even if it appears to be inconsistent with a later ruling of the court in Strasbourg:

> Certainty is best achieved by adhering, even in the Convention context, to our rules of precedent. It will of course be the duty of judges to review Convention arguments addressed to them, and if they consider a binding precedent to be, or possibly to be, inconsistent with Strasbourg authority, they may express their views and give leave to appeal, as the Court of Appeal did here. Leap-frog appeals may be appropriate. In this way, in my opinion, they discharge their duty under the 1998 Act. But they should follow the binding precedent, as again the Court of Appeal did here.[166]

034 Current analysis of the application of the Human Rights Act 1988

Numerous commentators — both academics and judges speaking or writing in an extra-judicial capacity — have expressed varying degrees of criticism and concern about the efficacy of judicial attempts to expand and distort the cause of action for breach of confidence in order to provide a basis for privacy claims. In part, these views focus on the inadequacy of the incremental (case by case) evolution of an existing cause of action to cater for what would otherwise be the failure of the law to provide protection against invasions of privacy in a host of different factual situations; and in part on the suggested desirability of maintaining a distinction between breach of confidence on the one hand and privacy on the other. It is suggested that the incremental approach results in uncertainty, delay and costs. As Buxton LJ observed when comparing *Campbell v MGN Ltd*[167] and *Von Hannover v Germany*:[168]

> Had the House had the benefit of *Von Hannover's* case a shorter course might have been taken.[169]

This is particularly so because (as discussed above):[170]

Convention by national courts, since the meaning of the Convention should be uniform throughout the states party to it. The duty of national courts is to keep pace with the Strasbourg jurisprudence as it evolves over time: no more, but certainly no less'; *R (S) v Chief Constable of South Yorkshire Police* [2004] UKHL 39, [2004] 1 WLR 2196, Lord Steyn at [27]: 'I do accept that when one moves on to consider the question of objective justification under Article 8(2) the cultural traditions in the United Kingdom are material. With great respect to Lord Woolf CJ the same is not true under article 8(1). The question whether the retention of fingerprints and samples engages Article 8(1) should receive a uniform interpretation throughout member states, unaffected by different cultural traditions. And the current Strasbourg view, as reflected in decisions of the Commission, ought to be taken into account'.

[165] See, eg, *D v East Berkshire Community NHS Trust* [2003] EWCA Civ 1151, [2004] QB 558 in which the Court of Appeal held that the decision of the House of Lords in *X (Minors) v Bedfordshire County Council* [1995] 2 AC 633 could not survive the introduction of the Human Rights Act 1998; and *McKennitt v Ash v* [2006] EWCA Civ 1714, [2008] QB 73, especially per Buxton LJ at [62-64], in which the Court of Appeal held that the earlier decision of the Court of Appeal in *A v B plc* [2002] EWCA Civ 337, [2003] QB 195 'cannot be read as any sort of binding authority on the content of Articles 8 and 10'.

[166] *Kay v Lambeth London Borough Council* [2006] UKHL 10, [2006] 2 AC 465, Lord Bingham at [43].

[167] *Campbell v MGN Ltd* [2004] UKHL 22, [2004] 2 AC 457.

[168] *Von Hannover v Germany* (2005) 40 EHRR 1.

[169] *McKennitt v Ash v* [2006] EWCA Civ 1714, [2008] QB 73 at [39].

[170] See §25– 033.

Put shortly, the precedential rules of English domestic law apply to interpretations of Convention jurisprudence.[171]

Accordingly, when, in *Murray v Express Newspapers plc*,[172] the Court of Appeal was asked to rule on whether there was a tension between the decision of the House of Lords in *Campbell v MGN Ltd*[173] and that of the European Court of Human Rights in *Von Hannover v Germany*,[174] the Court focussed on providing an exegesis of the decision of the House of Lords,[175] which it then applied to the presumed facts of the case before it. The Court did not consider it necessary to analyse *Von Hannover v Germany* in any detail:

> Suffice it to say that, in our opinion, the view we have expressed is consistent with that in *Von Hannover* … we have little doubt that, if the assumed facts of this case were to be considered by the ECtHR, the court would hold that David had a reasonable expectation of privacy and it seems to us to be more likely than not that, on the assumed facts, it would hold that the article 8/10 balance would come down in favour of David.

25–035 Applicability of Convention rights to the law of confidence

At the same time, the Convention rights in accordance with the Human Rights Act 1998 do not include article 1, which forms the foundation of the positive duty of a State when it is brought before the international court which has the duty of enforcing the duties of Member States under the Convention. At one time it was thought that this raised a potential difficulty for a court called upon to determine a question which has arisen in connection with a Convention right within the meaning of the Act and which is required to take into account a relevant Strasbourg judgment which has made it clear that the law-making body of the Member States has a positive duty.[176] However, guidance as to the correct approach was given in *Venables v News Group Newspapers Ltd*,[177] where Dame Elizabeth Butler-Sloss P stated:

> The decisions of the European Court of Human Rights in Glaser's case[178] and *X and Y v The Netherlands*,[179] seem to dispose of any argument that a court is not to have regard to the Convention in private law cases.......That obligation on the court does not seem to me to encompass the creation of a free-standing cause of action based directly upon the articles of the Convention....The duty on the court, in my view, is to act compatibly with Convention rights in adjudicating upon existing common law causes of action, and that includes a

---

[171] *McKennitt v Ash v* [2006] EWCA Civ 1714, [2008] QB 73.

[172] *Murray v Express Newspapers plc* [2008] EWCA Civ 446, [2009] Ch 481.

[173] *Campbell v MGN Ltd* [2004] UKHL 22, [2004] 2 AC 457.

[174] *Von Hannover v Germany* (2005) 40 EHRR 1.

[175] *Murray v Express Newspapers plc* [2008] EWCA Civ 446, [2009] Ch 481 at [21]-[35].

[176] *Douglas v Hello! Ltd* [2001] QB 967 at [91] (Brooke LJ).

[177] *Venables v News Group Newspapers Ltd* [2001] Fam 430, [2001] 1 All ER 908 at [25]–[27]. And in *Douglas v Hello! Ltd* [2001] QB 967 Brooke LJ observed at [91]: 'Where Parliament in this country has been so obviously content to leave the development of the law to the judges, it might seem strange if the absence of art 1 from our national statute relieved the judges from taking into account the positive duties identified by the court at Strasbourg when they develop the common law.'

[178] *Glaser v United Kingdom* [2000] 3 FCR 193 at 208–209, [2001] 1 FLR 153, (2001) 33 EHRR 1, where the European Court of Human Rights, sitting as a Chamber, declared admissible an application by a father seeking the enforcement of contact orders made in private law proceedings between him and the mother of his children.

[179] *X and Y v The Netherlands* (1985) 8 EHRR 235.

positive as well as a negative obligation.[180]

Subsequently, in *A v B plc*, Lord Woolf CJ explained that the court, as a public authority, was able to fulfil its duty under section 6 of the Human Rights Act 1998 Act 'by absorbing the rights which articles 8 and 10 protect into the long-established action for breach of confidence.'[181] He went on to say:

> There is a tension between the two articles which requires the court to hold the balance between the conflicting interests they are designed to protect. This is not an easy task but it can be achieved by the courts if, when holding the balance, they attach proper weight to the important rights both articles are designed to protect. Each article is qualified expressly in a way which allows the interests under the other article to be taken into account.[182]

This approach was endorsed by the House of Lords in *Campbell v MGN Ltd*,[183] where Lord Nicholls said:

> The time has come to recognise that the values enshrined in articles 8 and 10 are now part of the cause of action for breach of confidence. As Lord Woolf CJ has said, the courts have been able to achieve this result by absorbing the rights protected by articles 8 and 10 into this cause of action: *A v B plc* [2003] QB 195, 202, para 4. Further, it should now be recognised that for this purpose these values are of general application. The values embodied in articles 8 and 10 are as much applicable in disputes between individuals or between an individual and a non-governmental body such as a newspaper as they are in disputes between individuals and a public authority.
>
> In reaching this conclusion it is not necessary to pursue the controversial question whether the European Convention itself has this wider effect. Nor is it necessary to decide whether the duty imposed on courts by section 6 of the Human Rights Act 1998 extends to questions of substantive law as distinct from questions of practice and procedure. It is sufficient to recognise that the values underlying articles 8 and 10 are not confined to disputes between individuals and public authorities.[184]

In *Douglas v Hello! Ltd (No 3)*[185] the Court of Appeal carried out an extensive review of the case law, and concluded that:

> in so far as private information is concerned, we are required to adopt, as the vehicle for performing such duty as falls on the courts in relation to Convention rights, the cause of action formerly described as breach of confidence. As to the nature of that duty, it seems to

---

[180] In addition to the cases cited in this passage, see *Stjerna v Finland* (1994) 24 EHRR 195 at [38] and *Verliere v Switzerland* Reports of Judgments and Decisions 2001–VII, p 413 and *Von Hannover v Germany* (2005) 40 EHRR 1, [2004] EMLR 21, 16 BHRC 545 at [57]: 'The court reiterates that although the object of article 8 is essentially that of protecting the individual against arbitrary interference by the public authorities, it does not merely compel the state to abstain from such interference: in addition to this primarily negative undertaking, there may be positive obligations inherent in an effective respect for private or family life. These obligations may involve the adoption of measures designed to secure respect for private life even in the sphere of the relations of individuals between themselves ... That also applies to the protection of a person's picture against abuse by others.'

[181] *A v B plc* [2003] QB 195 at [4].

[182] *A v B plc* [2003] QB 195 at [6].

[183] *Campbell v MGN Ltd* [2004] UKHL 22, [2004] 2 AC 457. See, also, Baroness Hale at [132]–[133]: 'The 1998 Act does not create any new cause of action between private persons. But if there is a relevant cause of action applicable, the court as a public authority must act compatibly with both parties' Convention rights ... our law cannot, even if it wanted to, develop a general tort of invasion of privacy. But where existing remedies are available, the court not only can but must balance the competing Convention rights of the parties.'

[184] *Campbell v MGN Ltd* [2004] UKHL 22, [2004] 2 AC 457 at [17]–[18].

[185] *Douglas v Hello! Ltd (No 3)* [2006] EWCA Civ 595, [2006] QB 125.

us that sections 2, 3, 6 and 12 of the Human Rights Act 1998 all point in the same direction. The court should, in so far as it can, develop the action for breach of confidence in such a manner as will give effect to both article 8 and article 10 rights. In considering the nature of those rights, account should be taken of the Strasbourg jurisprudence. In particular, when considering what information should be protected as private pursuant to article 8, it is right to have regard to the decisions of the European Court of Human Rights.[186]

Thus, Articles 8 and 10 are now 'the very content of the domestic tort that the English court has to enforce.'[187]

25–036 Privacy and confidence since the Human Rights Act 1998

Almost as soon as the Human Rights Act 1998 came into force,[188] the courts began grappling with the differences between the elements and parameters of the traditional claim for breach of confidence and the claim for protection of private information, and with whether this was any more than a labelling issue. In *Douglas v Hello! Limited*,[189] Sedley LJ said:

> What a concept of privacy does, however, is accord recognition to the fact that the law has to protect not only those people whose trust has been abused but those who simply find themselves subjected to an unwanted intrusion into their personal lives. The law no longer needs to construct an artificial relationship of confidentiality between intruder and victim: it can recognise privacy itself as a legal principle drawn from the fundamental value of personal autonomy.[190]

In the same case, Keene LJ said:

> The nature of the subject matter or the circumstances of the defendant's activities may suffice in some instances to give rise to liability for breach of confidence. That approach must now be informed by the jurisprudence of the Convention in respect of article 8. Whether the resulting liability is described as being for breach of confidence or for breach of a right of privacy may be little more that deciding what label is to be attached to the cause of action, but there would seem to be merit in recognising that the original concept of breach of confidence has in this particular category of cases now developed into something different from the commercial and employment relationships with which confidentiality is mainly concerned.[191]

Thereafter the courts began to give effect to privacy interests by expanding the boundaries of the law of confidence.

25–037 Confidentiality and the protection of private information

In *A v B plc*[192] the Court of Appeal set out guidelines to be followed by judges of first instance on applications for interim injunctions in cases involving personal information:

> (ix)...A duty of confidence will arise whenever the party subject to the duty is in a situation where he either knows or ought to know that the other person can reasonably expect his

---

[186] *Douglas v Hello! Ltd (No 3)* [2006] EWCA Civ 595, [2006] QB 125 at [53].

[187] *McKennitt v Ash v* [2006] EWCA Civ 1714, [2008] QB 73, Buxton LJ at [11].

[188] On 2 October 2000.

[189] *Douglas v Hello! Limited* [2001] QB 967.

[190] *Douglas v Hello! Limited* [2001] QB 967 at [126].

[191] *Douglas v Hello! Limited* [2001] QB 967 at [166].

[192] *A v B plc* [2002] EWCA Civ 337, [2003] QB 195.

privacy to be protected: see Lord Goff of Chieveley in *Attorney-General v Guardian Newspapers Ltd (No 2)*.[193] The range of situations in which protection can be provided is therefore extensive. Obviously, the necessary relationship can be expressly created. More often its existence will have to be inferred from the facts. Whether a duty of confidence does exist which courts can protect, if it is right to do so, will depend on all the circumstances of the relationship between the parties at the time of the threatened or actual breach of the alleged duty of confidence.

(x) If there is an intrusion in a situation where a person can reasonably expect his privacy to be respected then that intrusion will be capable of giving rise to liability in an action for breach of confidence unless the intrusion can be justified.[194]

In the first edition of this book it was stated that it seemed tolerably clear from this general statement of principle and these particular guidelines that where a person has a reasonable expectation of privacy he or she has a right to be protected against intrusion into that privacy, and that the law of confidence will provide protection for that right unless the intrusion in question can be justified. It was further stated that the fact that the Court of Appeal intended to make clear that the right of protection against intrusion on personal privacy falls within, and, in the era following the coming into force of the Human Rights Act 1988, can properly be assimilated into, the law of confidence seemed apparent from the reformulation of Lord Goff's words in *Attorney-General v Guardian Newspapers Ltd (No 2)*[195] that appear in guideline (ix).[196] These propositions have been borne out by cases decided after the first edition of this book was published.[197] However, the path which English law has chosen to follow has not made matters at all straightforward either for litigants or for the courts.[198] In this regard, the Court of Appeal in *Douglas v Hello! Ltd (No 3)*[199] remarked:

We cannot pretend that we find it satisfactory to be required to shoehorn within the cause of action of breach of confidence claims for publication of unauthorised photographs of a private occasion.

As time has gone on, the practical effect of this process has been to create a cause of action relating to the misuse of private information that, in all but name, is distinct from the traditional cause of action of breach of confidence.[200] As is apparent from the discussion below,[201] when transposed to cases involving the use or disclosure of private information, both the essential elements of an actionable breach of confidence and the limiting principles that apply to that cause of action have either effectively been dispensed with or have undergone substantial

---

[193] *Attorney-General v Guardian Newspapers Ltd (No 2)* [1990] 1 AC 109 at 281.

[194] *A v B plc* [2002] EWCA Civ 337, [2003] QB 195 at [11].

[195] *Attorney-General v Guardian Newspapers Ltd (No 2)* [1990] 1 AC 109 at 281.

[196] See, further, *Douglas v Hello! Ltd* [2003] EWHC 786, [2003] 3 All ER 996 (Ch, Lindsay J) at [186 (ix)–(x)].

[197] Considered in §25–035.

[198] Or, of course, for the reasons given in §25–030, for those concerned with interpreting and operating FOIA s 41.

[199] *Douglas v Hello! Ltd (No 3)* [2006] EWCA Civ 595, [2006] QB 125 at [53].

[200] In his Blackstone Lecture 'Sex, Libels and Video-surveillance' of 13 May 2006, Sedley LJ said that 'There are well-recognised constitutional objections to the creation by the courts of new torts. There are fewer such objections to the development, and even the renaming, of old causes of action to meet new conditions…Yet the situation we have now reached, where privacy is entitled to the protection of the law in everything but name, reduces the distinction between development and innovation to an abstraction.'

[201] §§25–038 to 25–048.

qualification or metamorphosis. It is suggested that the principal reasons for this are not difficult to identify: essentially, the underlying values and interests (that is to say, personal autonomy and protection from intrusion) that are jeopardised by the misuse of private information differ in significant respects from the underlying values and interests that are recognised and protected by more traditional claims for breach of confidence. And, where such differences exist, it is unsurprising that there should be differences as to the legal tests that are applicable, as to what is required before the law will grant protection, and as to the circumstances in which and the form in which the courts will be prepared to provide a remedy.

25– 038 The essential elements of an actionable breach of confidence in respect of private information

The unauthorised disclosure of information about a person's private life will be an a violation of article 8 of the ECHR where both:

(1) The disclosure relates to information in respect of which the person has a reasonable expectation of privacy, either because the information is obviously private or because its disclosure is one that would cause substantial offence to a reasonable person of ordinary sensibilities placed in the same position as that person.[202] This issue is determined objectively:

> The question is what a reasonable person of ordinary sensibilities would feel if she was placed in the same position as the claimant and faced with the same publicity.[203]

(2) Having weighed any legitimate interests in the disclosure, there remains on balance no good and sufficient reason justifying the interference. The issue here is:

> whether in all the circumstances the interest of the owner of the information must yield to the right of freedom of expression conferred on the publisher by article 10?[204]

Typically this requires separate consideration to be given to different items or classes of information.[205]

A disclosure that meets both requirements will constitute an actionable breach of confidence.

25– 039 Private life

The first question which falls to be considered is: what constitutes part of an individual's private life in the eyes of the law? The European Court of Human Rights has taken a broad, open-ended approach to the meaning of private life. In *Neimetz v Germany*[206] the Court said:

> The Court does not consider it possible or necessary to attempt an exhaustive definition of the notion of "private life." However, it would be too restrictive to limit the notion to an "inner circle" in which an individual may choose to live his personal life as he chooses and to exclude entirely the outside world not encompassed within that circle. Respect for private life must also comprise to a certain degree the right to establish and develop relationships

---

[202] *Campbell v MGN Ltd* [2004] UKHL 22, [2004] 2 AC 457.

[203] *Murray v Express Newspapers plc* [2008] EWCA Civ 446, [2009] Ch 481 at [35], quoting Lord Hope in *Campbell v MGN Ltd* [2004] UKHL 22, [2004] 2 AC 457 at [99].

[204] *Murray v Express Newspapers plc* [2008] EWCA Civ 446, [2009] Ch 481 at [27].

[205] See, eg, *Lord Browne of Madingley v Associated Newspapers Ltd* [2007] EWCA Civ 295, [2008] QB 103.

[206] *Neimetz v Germany* (1992) 16 EHRR 97 at [29].

with other human beings.

There appears, furthermore, to be no reason in principle why this understanding of the notion of "private life" should be taken to exclude the activities of a professional or business nature since it is, after all, in the course of their working lives that the majority of people have a significant, if not the greatest, opportunity of developing relationships with the outside world.[207]

In *Peck v United Kingdom*[208] the European Court of Human Rights held that 'private life' is a broad term not susceptible to exhaustive definition but includes the right to establish and develop relationships with other human beings, such that there is a zone of interaction of a person with others, even in a public context, which may fall within the scope of 'private life'.[209] Disclosure of material to the public in a manner which could never have been foreseen may give rise to such an interference.[210] Recognised facets of an individual's private life include:

— a person's health;[211]
— a person's ethnic identity;[212]
— a person's personal relationships;[213]
— a person's sexual conduct;[214]
— a person's religious or philosophical convictions;[215] and

---

[207] See also: *Bensaid v United Kingdom* (2001) 33 EHRR 208 at [47]: '"Private life" is a broad term not susceptible to exhaustive definition. The Court has already held that elements such as gender identification, name and sexual orientation and sexual life are important elements of the personal sphere protected by Article 8…Mental health must also be regarded as a crucial part of private life associated with the aspect of moral integrity. Article 8 protects a right to identity and personal development, and the right to establish and develop relationships with other human beings and the outside world.' Personal telephone calls from an employee's workplace will prima facie be covered by the notion of 'private life' and 'correspondence' for the purposes of art 8(1); personal emails sent from an employee's workplace and information derived from the monitoring of internet usage are similarly protected by art 8: *Copland v United Kingdom* (2007) 45 EHRR 37, [2007] ECHR 253.

[208] *Peck v United Kingdom (Application No 44647/98)* [2003] EMLR 15, (2003) 36 EHRR 41, 13 BHRC 669. Peck had been captured on closed circuit television when he had attempted suicide by cutting his wrists on a high street. Although the images used did not show the attempted suicide, they clearly identified Peck brandishing a kitchen knife in a public place. Although the police had attended the scene, Peck was not charged with any criminal offence. The images were used in a campaign to reflect the effectiveness of closed circuit television in combating crime. No attempt was made to mask Peck's identity. He subsequently appeared on a number of television broadcasts to discuss the publications of the footage and photographs, but nevertheless complained to the relevant media commissions about the disclosures. Peck tried unsuccessfully to obtain judicial review of the local authority's disclosure. Before the European Court, Peck complained: (1) that the disclosure by a local authority of closed circuit television footage and photographs which had resulted in images of himself being published and broadcast on a local and national level was a breach of his right to respect for family and private life under art 8; and (2) that it had been a breach of art 13 in that no effective domestic remedy existed in relation to the violation of his art 8 right.

[209] *Peck v United Kingdom (Application No 44647/98)* [2003] EMLR 15, (2003) 36 EHRR 41, 13 BHRC 669 at [57].

[210] *Peck v United Kingdom (Application No 44647/98)* [2003] EMLR 15, (2003) 36 EHRR 41, 13 BHRC 669 at [60].

[211] *Campbell v MGN Ltd* [2004] UKHL 22, [2004] 2 AC 457 (the position of the subject there was different on account of her having made public denials of the particular health aspect disclosed - see esp [56], [60]); *Z v Finland* (1997) 25 EHRR 371 at [71]; *S and Marper v UK* (2009) 48 EHRR 50 at [66]-[67].

[212] *S and Marper v UK* (2009) 48 EHRR 50 at [66]-[67].

[213] *Douglas v Hello! Ltd (No 3)* [2006] EWCA Civ 595, [2006] QB 125; *McKennitt v Ash v* [2006] EWCA Civ 1714, [2008] QB 73; *Standard Verlags GmbH v Austria (No 2)* [2009] ECHR 853.

[214] *Mosley v News Group Newspapers Ltd* [2008] EWHC 687 (QB), [2008] EMLR 679; *S and Marper v UK* (2008) 48 EHRR 50 at [66].

[215] *Folgero v Norway* [2007] ECHR 546 at [98]. But not a belief in fox-hunting: *Whaley & Anor v Lord Advocate* [2003] ScotCS 178.

— a person's image.[216]

It will be noticed that these facets resemble what is 'sensitive personal data' within the meaning of the Data Protection Act 1998.[217] A person's private life is not confined to what takes place in the home or out of the public eye.[218] The fact that the subject is a public or political figure does not take information relating to that person out of the realm of private life. Thus, in *Standard Verlags GmbH v Austria (No 2)*,[219] the Court observed that even in the case of a public political figure:

> idle gossip about the state of his or her marriage or alleged extra-marital relationships ... does not contribute to any public debate in respect of which the press has to fulfil its role of "public watchdog", but merely serves to satisfy the curiosity of a certain readership.... while reporting on true facts about a politician's or other public person's private life may be admissible in certain circumstances, even persons known to the public have a legitimate expectation of protection of and respect for their private life.

---

[216] *Sciacca v Italy* (2005) 43 EHRR 20 at [29]; *S and Marper v UK* (2009) 48 EHRR 50 at [66]. Where photographs are concerned, it is relevant to consider whether they relate to private or public matters and whether they were envisaged for limited use or likely to be made available to the general public: *Von Hannover v Germany* [2009] ECHR 853 at [61]. The Court held that disclosure to an extent which far exceeds the exposure to the public at the time may constitute a serious interference with the right to respect for private life (at [62]). In *Reklos & Davourlis v Greece* [2009] ECHR 200, [2009] EMLR 290, the European Court of Human Rights stated:
> A person's image constitutes one of the chief attributes of his or her personality, as it reveals the person's unique characteristics and distinguishes the person from his or her peers. The right to the protection of one's image is thus one of the essential components of personal development and presupposes the right to control use of that image. Whilst in most cases the right to control such use involves the possibility of an individual to refuse publication of his or her image, it also covers the individual's right to object to recording, conservation and reproduction of an image by another person. As a person's image is one of the characteristics attached to his or her personality, its effective protection presupposes, in principle and in circumstances such as those of the present case, obtaining the consent of the person concerned at the time the picture is taken and not simply if and when it is published. Otherwise an essential attribute of personality would be retained in the hands of a third party and the person concerned would have no control over any subsequent use of that image.

[217] Section 2, as well as the European Directive which it implements: see §24– 017. The DPA regulates the 'processing' of personal data. The term 'processing' covers holding, receiving, retrieval, dissemination and publication of personal data. The DPA restricts by reference to 'data protection principles' (set out in DPA Sch 1) the processing that the body may carry out: see ch 24 generally. Schedules 2 and 3 of the DPA are linked to the first data protection principle. These Schedules, by giving paramountcy to certain matters, embody a balance having similarities to that sought through the application of Articles 8 and 10 and the requirement of sufficient interference.

[218] *Von Hannover v Germany* (2005) 40 EHRR 1, [2004] EMLR 21, 16 BHRC 545, where the claimant had been photographed in her daily outdoor life: playing tennis, on horseback, cycling, visiting a horse show and so forth. The Court held that although these activities occurred in public places, they were of a purely private nature and, accordingly, were within the scope of the claimant's private life.

[219] *Standard Verlags GmbH v Austria (No 2)* [2009] ECHR 853 at [52]-[53]. Contrast: *Karhuvaara and Iltalehti v Finland* (2005) 41 EHRR 51, where the Court found that, even assuming the facts gave rise to an interference with the Article 8 rights of a politician, that interference was justified where a newspaper article printed a story concerning her husband's conviction for drunk and disorderly behaviour and affray; *Leempoel v Belgium* (No 64772/01, 9 November 2006), where the Court said:
> In matters relating to striking a balance between protecting private life and the freedom of expression that the Court had had to rule upon, it has always emphasised ... the requirement that the publication of information, documents or photographs in the press should serve the public interest and make a contribution to the debate of general interest ... Whilst the right for the public to be informed, a fundamental right in a democratic society that under particular circumstances may even relate to aspects of the private life of public persons, particularly where political personalities are involved ... publications whose sole aim is to satisfy the curiosity of a certain public as to the details of the private life of a person, whatever their fame, should not be regarded as contributing to any debate of general interest to society.

040 Sufficiency of interference

Not every disclosure relating to a person's private life will constitute an interference with that person's private life: it must be a 'sufficiently serious' disclosure. Strasbourg jurisprudence considers that the mere storing of data relating to the private life of an individual amounts to an interference within the meaning of Article 8 of the Convention. However, the Court will have regard to the manner of acquisition and retention, the nature of the records, the way in which it has been used and the results that may be obtained.[220] Examples provide the clearest guide to what will and will not suffice. In the following cases the Court held that the interference was sufficiently serious:

(1)   *Douglas v Hello! Ltd (No 3)*,[221] which, as noted above, concerned photographs which had been taken surreptitiously at the wedding of two film stars.

(2)   *Von Hannover v Germany*[222] which involved a complaint by Princess Caroline of Monaco that her article 8 rights had been infringed by the publication in German magazines of photographs showing her in the following places: with a boyfriend in the courtyard of a restaurant; horse riding; out in public places either alone or with people such as her boyfriend, children and bodyguard, including doing activities such as shopping, bicycling, and leaving her house in Paris; on a skiing holiday; with Prince Ernst August von Hannover at a horse show; at the Monte Carlo Beach Club.

(3)   *McKennitt v Ash*[223] which concerned the publication of a book about a celebrated composer and performer of folk music. The book was written by a close friend of the claimant. The court upheld claims of confidentiality in relation to disclosures of the claimant's house:

> To describe a person's home, the décor, the layout, the state of cleanliness, or how occupiers behave inside it, is generally regarded as unacceptable. To convey such details, without permission, to the general public is almost as objectionable as spying into the home with a long distance lens and publishing the resulting photographs.[224]

Descriptions of the claimant's health, her relationship with her fiancé, her reaction to his death, and disclosure of the claimant's acquisition of property were all protected. On the other hand, a description of a shopping trip was not protected.

(4)   *Mosley v News Group Newspapers Ltd*,[225] which concerned newspaper and online publication of a story and internet publication of video film relating to sex sessions which included sado-masochistic practices involving the head of Formula 1 and a number of women.

> Where the law is not breached, as I said earlier, the private conduct of adults is essentially no-one else's business. The fact that a particular relationship

---

[220] *S and Marper v UK* (2009) 48 EHRR 50 at [66]-[67].

[221] *Douglas v Hello! Ltd (No 3)* [2006] EWCA Civ 595, [2006] QB 125.

[222] *Von Hannover v Germany* (2005) 40 EHRR 1, [2004] EMLR 21, 16 BHRC 545.

[223] *McKennitt v Ash* [2005] EWHC 3003, [2006] EMLR 10.

[224] *McKennitt v Ash* [2005] EWHC 3003, [2006] EMLR 10 at [135].

[225] *Mosley v News Group Newspapers Ltd* [2008] EWHC 687 (QB), [2008] EMLR 679.

happens to be adulterous, or that someone's tastes are unconventional or "perverted", does not give the media *carte blanche*.

25–041 Examples of insufficiently serious interferences

In the following cases the Court held that the interference was not sufficiently serious:

(1) In *Mahmood v Galloway*[226] the court refused to restrain by interim injunction the publication on a website of two photographs of a journalist on the grounds (among others) that one of the photographs did not show him engaged in any activity which could be described as private but was 'simply a photograph of his face',[227] and that it could be assumed that he was aware that the other photograph was being taken when it was and that:

> As with anybody who consents to having his photograph taken [by a subject he was investigating or as part of a social occasion] he can be taken to have consented to its subsequent publication.[228]

(2) In *John v Associated Newspapers Ltd*[229] the court refused to restrain the publication in a newspaper of photographs that showed the claimant, Sir Elton John, standing in the street, outside his home in London, wearing a baseball cap and tracksuit, on the grounds (among others) that he had not established that he was more likely than not to obtain an injunction at trial, either on the basis that he had a reasonable expectation of privacy in the circumstances in which he found himself, or—if he did have such an expectation—on the basis that his article 8 rights would prevail over the article 10 rights of the newspaper. The Court said that a photograph of an individual leaving his car and going to his front gate was analogous to the activity of 'popping out for a pint of milk',[230] which Baroness Hale had said could be photographed without objection.[231] On this occasion, *Von Hannover v Germany*[232] was distinguished on the grounds that 'the element of harassment' was an important factor in that case.[233] Further, the court was not persuaded:

> that there is, as yet, any doctrine operative in English law whereby it is necessary to demonstrate that to publish a photograph one has to show that the subject of the photograph gave consent.[234]

25–042 Private information and the public domain

The question of whether the material is in the public domain involves careful analysis of:

(1) the information's accessibility, and how general it is;

---

[226] *Mahmood v Galloway* [2006] EWHC 1286, [2006] EMLR 26.

[227] *Mahmood v Galloway* [2006] EWHC 1286, [2006] EMLR 26 at [19].

[228] *Mahmood v Galloway* [2006] EWHC 1286, [2006] EMLR 26 at [20]. *Von Hannover v Germany* was said to be 'not in point' (at [19]).

[229] *John v Associated Newspapers Ltd* [2006] EWHC 1611, [2006] EMLR 27.

[230] *John v Associated Newspapers Ltd* [2006] EWHC 1611, [2006] EMLR 27 at [15].

[231] In *Campbell v MGN Ltd* [2004] UKHL 22, [2004] 2 AC 457 at [154].

[232] *Von Hannover v Germany* (2005) 40 EHRR 1, [2004] EMLR 21, 16 BHRC 545.

[233] *Von Hannover v Germany* (2005) 40 EHRR 1, [2004] EMLR 21, 16 BHRC 545 at [16].

[234] *Von Hannover v Germany* (2005) 40 EHRR 1, [2004] EMLR 21, 16 BHRC 545 at [21].

(2)   the extent to which the information has, or is likely to have been, or continues to be, accessed in consequence of that accessibility; and

(3)   the extent to which the information can be said to have lost the necessary quality of confidentiality in light of (1) and (2) taking account of, amongst other things, the extent of further harm that may be caused by continued or further publication.

The need to adopt a more purposive examination of public domain in order to give effective protection in cases of private information has repeatedly been recognised in the decided cases. So far as personal information is concerned:

> the fact that a matter has once been in the public domain cannot prevent its resurrection, possibly many years later, from being an invasion of privacy. Whether in such a case there is an unwarranted invasion of privacy is a matter of fact and degree.[235]

In short, while the general position remains that public accessibility will deprive information that is placed in the public domain of the protection of the law of confidence, it may well not do so if the information is of a private or personal nature. The touchstone will be whether such use or disclosure has an adverse impact on article 8 rights.[236] In *Douglas v Hello! Ltd (No 3)*[237] the Court of Appeal stated:

> In general, however, once information is in the public domain, it will no longer be confidential or entitled to the protection of the law of confidence, though this may not always be true: see *Gilbert v Star Newspaper Co Ltd* (1894) 11 TLR 4 and *Creation Records Ltd v News Group Newspapers Ltd* [1997] EMLR 444, 456. The same may generally be true of private information of a personal nature. Once intimate personal information about a celebrity's private life has been widely published it may serve no useful purpose to prohibit further publication. The same will not necessarily be true of photographs. In so far as a photograph does more than convey information and intrudes on privacy by enabling the viewer to focus on intimate personal detail, there will be a fresh intrusion of privacy when each additional viewer sees the photograph and even when one who has seen a previous publication of the photograph is confronted by a fresh publication of it…There is thus a further important potential distinction between the law relating to private information and that relating to other types of confidential information.[238]

The Court of Appeal rejected the argument that, as a result of their agreement to sell the story and photographs of the wedding to a magazine, the couple were precluded from contending that their wedding was a private occasion and, as such, protected by the law of confidence. Indeed, the Court of Appeal said[239] that, applying the reasoning of the decisions of the House

---

[235] *R v BCC, ex p Granada Television Ltd* [1995] EMLR 163 at 168.

[236] *A v M (Family Proceedings: Publicity)* [2001] 1 FLR 562 (children likely to suffer harm if allegations already made public were repeated); *R (Robertson) v Wakefield MDC* [2001] EWHC 915 (Admin), [2002] QB 1052 and *R(Robertson) v SSHD* [2003] EWHC 1760 (restraint on use of addresses on electoral register for direct marketing); *X and Y (Children), Re* [2004] EWHC 762, [2004] EMLR 29 (restraint on republication of information already in the public domain, where it would have a significant effect on the art 8 rights of children); *Green Corns Ltd v Claverley Group Ltd* [2005] EWHC 958, [2005] EMLR 31, [2005] 2 FCR 309 (restraint on newspaper publication of addresses of houses used to provide care for troubled children, including addresses which could be ascertained by a search of HM Land Registry). See also *Venables v News Group Newspapers Ltd* [2001] Fam 430, [2001] 1 All ER 908 and *AG v Greater Manchester Newspapers Ltd* [2001] TLR 668, (2001) 145 SJLB 279.

[237] *Douglas v Hello! Ltd (No 3)* [2006] EWCA Civ 595, [2006] QB 125, [2005] 4 All ER 128.

[238] *Douglas v Hello! Ltd (No 3)* [2006] EWCA Civ 595, [2006] QB 125, [2005] 4 All ER 128 at [105].

[239] *Douglas v Hello! Ltd (No 3)* [2006] EWCA Civ 595, [2006] QB 125, [2005] 4 All ER 128 at [251] – [259].

of Lords in *Campbell v MGN Ltd*[240] and the European Court of Human Rights in *Von Hannover v Germany*,[241] 'the Douglases appeared to have a virtually unanswerable case for contending that publication of the unauthorised photographs would infringe their privacy'; and that, as there was no good reason for refusing an interim injunction (for example, on the basis that publication would be in the public interest), and as damages were not an adequate remedy for the Douglases, an injunction ought to have been granted to restrain publication. The Court of Appeal said with regard to photographs:

> It is quite wrong to suppose that a person who authorises publication of selected personal photographs taken on a private occasion, will not reasonably feel distress at the publication of unauthorised photographs taken on the same occasion. There is a further point. The objection to the publication of unauthorised photographs taken on a private occasion is not simply that the images that they disclose convey secret information, or impressions that are unflattering. It is that they disclose information that is private. The offence is caused because what the claimant could reasonably expect would remain private has been made public. The intrusion into the private domain is, of itself, objectionable. To the extent that an individual authorises photographs taken on a private occasion to be made public, the potential for distress at the publication of other, unauthorised, photographs, taken on the same occasion, will be reduced. This will be very relevant when considering the amount of any damages. The agreement that authorised photographs can be published will not, however, provide a defence to a claim, brought under the law of confidence, for the publication of unauthorised photographs…the Douglases retained a residual right of privacy, or confidentiality, in those details of their wedding which were not portrayed by those of the official photographs which they released…[The unauthorised photographs] invaded the area of privacy which the Douglases had chosen to retain.[242]

As against that, some cases concerning personal information contain statements to the effect that a person who has placed or allowed to be placed in the public domain information concerning a certain aspect or 'zone' of his private life may not be entitled to complain about the publication of other information concerning the same area — or, possibly, in an extreme case, any area — of his private life.[243] However, there is a faint echo of this approach in the decided cases concerning commercial confidences,[244] where 'within the law of confidentiality in its normal reach' the exceptions to protection of (among other things) public domain are specific to the material in question.[245] In *Campbell v MGN Ltd*[246] the Court of Appeal sounded

---

[240] *Campbell v MGN Ltd* [2004] UKHL 22, [2004] 2 AC 457, .

[241] *Von Hannover v Germany* (2005) 40 EHRR 1, [2004] EMLR 21, 16 BHRC 545.

[242] *Douglas v Hello! Ltd (No 3)* [2006] EWCA Civ 595, [2006] QB 125, [2005] 4 All ER 128 at [106]–[107], [136]. This part of the judgment was not the subject of appeal to the House of Lords in *OBG Ltd v Allan* [2007] UKHL 21, [2008] 1 AC 1. That appeal was exclusively concerned with the claim by OK! for breach of a commercial confidence.

[243] *Theakston v MGN Ltd* [2002] EWHC 137, [2002] EMLR 398 at [68]; *A v B plc* [2002] EWCA Civ 337, [2003] QB 195 at [11(xii)]; *A v B, C and D* [2005] EWHC 1651, [2005] EMLR 851 at [16]–[23]; *Lennon v News Group Newspapers Ltd* [1978] FSR 573, 574–575.

[244] But see *Jockey Club v Buffham* [2002] EWHC 1866, [2003] QB 462 in which Gray J said at [57(v)] with regard to certain press releases issued by the claimant that 'The effect of placing such material in the public domain does in my view result in some loosening of the ties of confidence.'

[245] *Theakston v MGN Ltd* [2002] EWHC 137, [2002] EMLR 398 at [65]–[66].

[246] *Campbell v MGN Ltd* [2002] EWCA Civ 1373, [2003] QB 633.

a note of caution about the extent to which the courts will be prepared to adopt this approach to the ambit of the public domain exception in cases involving personal information:

> When Lord Woolf CJ spoke of the public having "an understandable and so a legitimate interest in being told" information, even including trivial facts, about a public figure, he was not speaking of private facts which a fair-minded person would consider it offensive to disclose. That is clear from his subsequent commendation of the guidance on striking a balance between Article 8 and Article 10 rights provided by the Council of Europe Resolution 1165 of 1998.
>
> For our part we would observe that the fact that an individual has achieved prominence on the public stage does not mean that his private life can be laid bare by the media. We do not see why it should necessarily be in the public interest that an individual who has been adopted as a role model, without seeking this distinction, should be demonstrated to have feet of clay.[247]

Further, in *McKennitt v Ash* the Court of Appeal held that:

> ...it seems clear that *A v B* [2003] QB 195 cannot be read as any sort of binding authority on the content of Articles 8 and 10. To find that content, therefore, we do have to look to *Von Hannover*. The terms of that judgment are very far away from the automatic limits placed on the privacy rights of public figures by *A v B*.[248]

The significance of these considerations to the exemption contained in s 41 of the Freedom of Information Act 2000 is that whether, and to what extent, the fact that information has come into the public domain has the effect that it ceases to be confidential because it no longer has 'the necessary quality of confidence' depends upon the nature of the information. It is clear from cases such as *Campbell v MGN Ltd* and *Peck v United Kingdom*[249] that whether information is private or public does not depend upon whether it is accessible to the public. In short:

> ...it is not possible in a case about personal information to apply Lord Goff's test of whether the information is generally accessible, and to conclude that, if it is, then that is an end of the matter.[250]

043 Information whose disclosure is offensive

Although certain information may not be obviously private – that is, not be information on one of the facets of an individual's private life[251] – nevertheless, if it is information the disclosure of which would cause substantial offence to a reasonable person of ordinary sensibilities placed in the same position as that person, that will constitute an actionable breach of confidence, subject to the weighing of legitimate interests in disclosure.[252] Again, examples provide the clearest guide to what will suffice:

---

[247] *Campbell v MGN Ltd* [2002] EWCA Civ 1373, [2003] QB 633 at [40]–[41]. Echoed in the House of Lords (where the decision of the Court of Appeal was reversed) by Baroness Hale of Richmond at [2004] UKHL 22, [2004] 2 AC 457 at [151]: 'It might be questioned why, if a role model has adopted a stance which all would agree is beneficial rather than detrimental to society, it is so important to reveal that she has feet of clay. But the possession and use of illegal drugs is a criminal offence and a matter of serious public concern. The press must be free to expose the truth and put the record straight.'

[248] *McKennitt v Ash* [2006] EWCA Civ 1714, [2008] QB 73 at [64] (Buxton LJ).

[249] *Peck v United Kingdom* (2003) 36 EHRR 719.

[250] *Green Corns Ltd v Claverley Group Ltd* [2005] EWHC 958, [2005] EMLR 31, [2005] 2 FCR 309 at [78] (Tugendhat J).

[251] See §25– 039.

[252] See §§25– 048 ff.

(1) *Campbell v MGN Ltd*[253] where a newspaper published reports and pictures of a well-known fashion model attending meetings of a self-help group for drug addiction. The claimant had previously made public statements that she did not have a drug problem. She accepted that in those circumstances the newspaper was entitled to publish the fact that she was receiving treatment for her addiction, but successfully claimed that publication of the details of the meetings and of covert photographs of her attendance constituted a breach of confidentiality. Lord Hope said:

> Miss Campbell could not have complained if the photographs had been taken to show the scene in the street by a passer-by and later published as street scenes. But these were not just pictures of a street scene where she happened to be when the photographs were taken. They were taken deliberately, in secret and with a view to publication with the article. The zoom lens was directed at the doorway of the place where the meeting had been taking place. The faces of others in the doorway were pixilated so as not to reveal their identity. Hers was not, the photographs were published and her privacy was invaded.[254]

(2) *Murray v Express Newspapers plc*[255] which concerned a photograph of the infant son of a well known author taken without consent when his mother and father were pushing him in a buggy in a public street. The photograph was taken covertly with a long lens. It later appeared in a magazine. By his litigation friend the child sought an injunction to prevent further publication of the photograph, notwithstanding that the photograph showed nothing embarrassing or untoward. At first instance, Patten J found that the photographs were of innocuous conduct in a public place such as were not to give rise to a reasonable expectation of privacy, and he struck out the action. That decision was reversed in the Court of Appeal, where it was held:

> We do not share the predisposition identified by the judge ... that routine acts such as a visit to a shop or a ride on a bus should not attract any reasonable expectation of privacy. All depends upon the circumstances.

Instances of what will not suffice have already been given.[256] In this context, the court is particularly sensitive to the potential offence caused by photographs:

> Special considerations attach to photographs in the field of privacy. They are not merely a method of conveying information that is an alternative to verbal description. They enable the person viewing the photograph to act as a spectator, in some circumstances voyeur would be the more appropriate noun, of whatever it is that the photograph depicts. As a means of invading privacy, a photograph is particularly intrusive. This is quite apart from the fact that the camera, and the telephoto lens, can give access to the viewer of the photograph to scenes where those photographed could reasonably expect that their appearances or actions would not be brought to the notice of the public.[257]

The courts are also astute to protect against disclosures involving children.[258]

---

[253] *Campbell v MGN Ltd* [2004] UKHL 22, [2004] 2 AC 457.

[254] *Campbell v MGN Ltd* [2004] UKHL 22, [2004] 2 AC 457 at [123].

[255] *Murray v Express Newspapers plc* [2008] EWCA Civ 446, [2009] Ch 481.

[256] See §25–041.

[257] *Douglas v Hello! Ltd (No 3)* [2006] EWCA Civ 595, [2006] QB 125 at [84], [104]-[107].

[258] *Murray v Express Newspapers plc* [2008] EWCA Civ 446, [2009] Ch 481 at [45].

044 The nature of the balancing exercise

As indicated above, the second requirement for an actionable breach of confidence in respect of private information is that, having weighed any legitimate interests in disclosure, there remains on balance no good and sufficient reason justifying the interference. The interest of an individual not to have details of his private life disclosed will not translate into a right where there is a more compelling interest justifying disclosure. Where the interference is a publication by the media, the Courts have balanced the Convention right to freedom of expression against the interference.[259] When balancing Articles 8 and 10, the Court carries out a parallel analysis:

> First, neither article has *as such* precedence over the other. Secondly, where the values under the two articles are in conflict, an intense focus on the comparative importance of the specific rights being claimed in the individual case is necessary. Thirdly, the justifications for interfering with or restricting each right must be taken into account. Finally, the proportionality test must be applied to each.[260]

As the structure of Articles 8 and 10 of the Convention are the same, the like considerations apply to Article 8(2) as apply to Article 10(2):

> It is plain from the language of article 10 (2), and the European Court has repeatedly held, that any national restriction on freedom of expression can be consistent with article 10(2) only if it is prescribed by law, is directed at one or more of the objectives specified in the article and is shown by the state concerned to be necessary in a democratic society. 'Necessary' has been strongly interpreted: it is not synonymous with 'indispensable', neither has it the flexibility of such expressions as 'admissible', 'ordinary', 'useful', 'reasonable' or 'desirable': *Handyside v United Kingdom*.[261] One must consider whether the interference complained of corresponded to a pressing social need, whether it is proportionate to the legitimate aim pursued and whether the reasons given by the national authority to justify it are relevant and sufficient under article 10(2).[262]

An interference with the right to respect for private life cannot be said to be 'necessary in a democratic society' unless:

(a)   relevant and sufficient reasons are given by the national authority to justify the restriction;

(b)   the restriction on protection corresponds to a 'pressing social need'; and

(c)   it is proportionate to the legitimate aim pursued.[263]

045 Factors relevant to the balancing exercise between Articles 8 and 10

On the Article 8 side of the equation, 'the more intimate the aspect of private life that is being

---

[259] See the cases considered at §§25– 039 to 25– 042.

[260] *Re S (Identification: Restrictions on Publication)* [2004] UKHL 47, [2005] 1 AC 593 at [17].

[261] *Handyside v United Kingdom* (1976) 1 EHRR 734, 754 at [48].

[262] *R v Shayler (David)* [2002] UKHL 11, [2003] 1 AC 247 at [23]. See also Lord Hope at [36].

[263] See the decisions of the European Court of Human Rights cited and applied by Lord Bingham in *R v Shayler* in the passage cited above. In a concurring speech in *R v Shayler*, Lord Hope (at [61]) elaborated on the meaning of proportionality in this context and concluded that the following three stage test should be applied: (a) whether the objective to be achieved - the pressing social need - is sufficiently important to justify limiting the fundamental right; (b) whether the means chosen to limit that right are rational, fair and not arbitrary; and (c) whether the means used impair the right as minimally as possible. The same approach can be applied to conflicts involving other Convention rights, such as Article 6, or involving 'societal' interests, such as the duty of confidence.

interfered with, the more serious must be the reasons for interference before the latter can be legitimate.'[264] Further, when striking a balance between competing rights, the Court is not restricted to considering the Article 8 rights of the immediate parties alone, but, where appropriate, can and should take account of the extent to which the threatened publication would adversely affect the Article 8 rights of others, such as close family members.[265] On the Article 10 side of the equation:

> There are undoubtedly different types of speech, just as there are different types of private information, some of which are more deserving of protection in a democratic society than others. Top of the list is political speech. The free exchange of information and ideas on matters relevant to the organisation of the economic, social and political life of the country is crucial to any democracy. Without this, it can scarcely be called a democracy at all. This includes revealing information about public figures, especially those in elective office, which would otherwise be private but is relevant to their participation in public life. Intellectual and educational speech and expression are also important in a democracy, not least because they enable the development of individuals' potential to play a full part in society and in our democratic life. Artistic speech and expression is important for similar reasons, in fostering both individual originality and creativity and the free-thinking and dynamic society we so much value. No doubt there are other kinds of speech and expression for which similar claims can be made. But it is difficult to make such claims on behalf of the publication with which we are concerned here. The political and social life of the community, and the intellectual, artistic or personal development of individuals, are not obviously assisted by pouring over the intimate details of a fashion model's private life.[266]

25– 046 Application to disclosure under the Freedom of Information Act 2000

Disclosure under the Freedom of Information Act 2000 will not necessarily engage the Convention right or any corresponding public interest. Disclosure under the Act is to the person who made the request. An applicant's motive in making a request for information is generally irrelevant to the processing of that request.[267] It is therefore suggested that where a request for information under the Act captures private information (ie either of the first two conditions is made out in respect of that information) that will ordinarily suffice to render that information exempt under s 41. However, it may be possible for an applicant to advance particular reasons why disclosure would be in the public interest or would otherwise justify the interference with a person's private life.

25– 047 Private or personal life – summary

It follows from these formulations that what is capable of being protected as part of an individual's private life may vary from case to case. In particular, whether or not use or disclosure of particular information infringes a person's privacy cannot be tested by asking whether, considered in isolation, the information is trivial or useless. On the contrary, that will depend upon all the circumstances, including, for example, where the information which is said to be private falls to be considered together with other material that would otherwise be of a

---

[264] *Douglas v Hello! Ltd (No 3)* [2006] EWCA Civ 595, [2006] QB 125, Keene LJ at [168].

[265] See, eg, *CC v AB* [2006] EWHC 3083 (QB), [2007] EMLR 312, Eady J at [42].

[266] *Campbell v MGN Ltd* [2004] UKHL 22, [2004] 2 AC 457, Baroness Hale at [158]-[159].

[267] See §9– 017.

private character, whether such material has already entered the public domain, when that other material entered the public domain, the extent to which that other material has been publicised, and whether that other material has been publicised with the consent or involvement of the claimant; and, with regard to the information which is said to be private, the manner in which and the purposes for which it was obtained, how it was stored or processed, the purposes for which it was or is intended to be published, and the consequences of publication. It is suggested that this appears from the cases considered above,[268] and may be especially true of photographs.[269]

048 Infringement of privacy and false information

Traditionally, the law has drawn a clear distinction between the use or disclosure of true information on the one hand and the publication of false information on the other hand. The former can be the subject of a claim for breach of confidence, whereas (assuming it is injurious to the claimant's reputation) the latter is properly the subject of a claim for defamation. In *Campbell v MGN Ltd*,[270] Lord Hope said that 'there is a vital difference between inaccuracies that deprive the information of its intrusive qualities and inaccuracies that do not.'[271] In *McKennitt v Ash*,[272] Eady J described as 'somewhat simplistic' the proposition that 'a reasonable expectation of protection, or a duty of confidence, *cannot* arise in relation to false allegations', and continued as follows:[273]

> As I observed in the case of *Beckham v Gibson*, 29 April 2005 (unreported), the protection of the law would be illusory if a claimant, in relation to a long and garbled story, was obliged to spell out which of the revelations are accepted as true, and which are said to be false or distorted: see also *W v Westminster City Council* [2005] EWHC 102, Tugendhat J.

In *W v Westminster City Council*[274] it was said that, in the event that the Council had received the false information that the claimant was the person of the same name who was a convicted paedophile and (acting entirely in good faith) had then kept that information on the family file, the claimant would have been able to rely on article 8 to bring a claim under s 7 of the Human Rights Act 1998 against the local authority in order to establish that he was not the person of the same name who had been convicted of sex offending, without having to wait for publication of that information to occur, such as to found a claim in libel. The Court of Appeal in

---

[268] At §§25– 039 to 25– 042.

[269] For the particular significance which may be attached to photographs taken without consent see (in addition to the cases cited in the main body of the text): *R v Broadcasting Standards Commission, ex p BBC (Liberty intervening)* [2001] QB 885, [2000] 3 All ER 989; *R v Loveridge* [2001] EWCA Crim 973; *Theakston v MGN Ltd* [2002] EWHC 137, [2002] EMLR 398 at [40]–[41]; *D v L* [2003] EWCA Civ 1169, [2004] EMLR 1 at [23] (Waller LJ): 'A court may restrain the publication of an improperly obtained photograph even if the taker is free to describe the information which the photograph provides or even if the information revealed by the photograph is in the public domain. It is no answer to the claim to restrain the publication of an improperly obtained photograph that the information portrayed by the photograph is already in the public domain.'

[270] *Campbell v MGN Ltd* [2004] UKHL 22, [2004] 2 AC 457.

[271] *Campbell v MGN Ltd* [2004] UKHL 22, [2004] 2 AC 457 at [102].

[272] *McKennitt v Ash* [2006] EMLR 10 at [178].

[273] *McKennitt v Ash* [2006] EMLR 10 at [78].

[274] *W v Westminster City Council* [2005] EWHC 102 at [288].

McKennitt v Ash[275] has now made clear that provided the matter in question is of a kind to which the law of private or confidential information applies, then it does not matter whether it is true or false – although falsity may be highly relevant to whether there is any or any arguable defence that it would be in the public interest for the matter to be published. So far as concerns the applicability of s 41(1) of the Freedom of Information Act 2000, therefore, disclosure of information of a private nature may be actionable as a breach of confidence even if that information contains inaccuracies, or even if it is entirely false.

4.   TRADE SECRETS

25–049 Introduction

Information that constitutes a trade secret[276] is rendered exempt information by s 43(1) of the Freedom of Information Act 2000.[277] Where the information is 'environmental information', exemption from disclosure falls to be determined under the Environmental Information Regulations 2004 and not the Freedom of Information Act 2000.[278] Although those regulations do not provide an exception for 'trade secrets', some trade secrets may be excepted from disclosure under an analogous exception.[279] The trade secret exemption in the Freedom of Information Act 2000 is a class exemption, in that it applies to any information that amounts to a trade secret, irrespective of the consequences of disclosure. The exemption is not absolute, so that disapplication of the duty to disclose requires a weighing of the public interest in maintaining the exemption against the public interest in disclosure of the information.[280] There is no correlative disapplication of the duty to confirm or deny. A similar exemption is to be found in each of the comparative jurisdictions.[281]

---

[275] *McKennitt v Ash* [2006] EWCA Civ 1714, [2008] QB 73 at [78]–[80] (Buxton LJ), [82] (Latham LJ) and [85]–[87] (Longmore LJ).

[276] For a more general treatment of the law of trade secrets, see: S Mehigan and A Kamerling, *Restraint of Trade and Business Secrets*, 4th edn (London, Sweet & Maxwell, 2004); AE Turner, *The Law of Trade Secrets* (London, Sweet & Maxwell, 1962); R Dean, *The Law of Trade Secrets and Personal Secrets* (Sydney, Law Book Company, 2002); A Coleman, *The Legal Protection of Trade Secrets* (London, Sweet & Maxwell, 1992); The Institute of Law Research and Reform, *Trade Secrets* (Edmonton, The Institute of Law Research, 1986); P Lavery, *Commercial Secrets* (Dublin, Round Hall, 1996).

[277] In relation to Scottish public authorities, it is rendered exempt information by FOI(S)A s 33(1) (a). There is a limited exemption for trade secrets under DPA s 8(5): see §5– 034.

[278] The disclosure regime under the EIR is considered in ch 6. In relation to Scottish public authorities, disclosure of environmental information falls to be determined under the EI(S)R.

[279] See §25– 067.

[280] FOIA s 2(2)(b); FOI(S)A s 2.

[281] In the United States, the Freedom of Information Act, 1966, 5 USC § 552(b)(4), exempts from disclosure trade secrets: see §2– 008(4). The Freedom of Information Act 1982 (Cth of Australia) s 47, provides an exemption for trade secrets: see §2– 015(5). The Official Information Act 1982 (New Zealand) ss 9(2)(b)(i) and 27(1)(a), provide a qualified exemption where the disclosure would disclose a trade secret: see §2– 023(2). The Access to Information Act (Canada) s 20(1)(a), provides a mandatory exemption for trade secrets: see §2– 031(4); s 18(a) provides a discretionary exemption for trade secrets belonging to the Government of Canada: see §2– 032(3). The Federal Court has held that given the existence of other, restricted exemptions for confidential information, the term 'trade secrets' had to be given a reasonably narrow interpretation. It considered that a trade secret must be something probably of a technical nature which is guarded very closely and is of such peculiar value to the owner of the trade

050 The nature of a trade secret

The ambit of this exemption depends upon the scope of the concept of a trade secret in English law.[282] As there is no statutory definition of what constitutes a trade secret, guidance on the point needs to be sought in the case law.[283] Although the case law yields no exact definition of a trade secret, it does provide useful guidelines. In *Ansell Rubber Co Pty Ltd v Allied Rubber Industries Pty Ltd*,[284] Gowans J suggested the following guidelines:

> An exact definition of a trade secret is not possible. Some factors to be considered in determining whether given information is one's trade secret are: the extent to which information is known outside of his business; the extent to which it is known by employees and others involved in his business; the extent of measures taken by him to guard the secrecy of the information; the value of the information to him and his contemporaries; the amount of effort or money expended by him in developing the information; the ease or difficulty with which the information could be properly acquired or duplicated by others.

Similar guidelines are found in the judgment of Sir Robert Megarry VC in *Thomas Marshall (Exports) Ltd v Guinle*.[285] Although in the following passage he did not attempt to distinguish between trade secrets and other confidential commercial information, his criteria are of assistance in establishing the minimum requirements that must be met before information could properly be said to amount to a trade secret:

> If one turns from the authorities and looks at the matter as a question of principle, I think (and I say this very tentatively, because the principle has not been argued out) that four elements may be discerned which may be of some assistance in identifying confidential information or trade secrets which the court will protect. I speak of such information or secrets only in an industrial or trade setting. First, I think that the information must be information the release of which the owner believes would be injurious to him or of advantage to his rivals or others. Second, I think the owner must believe that the information is confidential or secret, ie, that it is not already in the public domain.[286] It may be that some or all of his rivals already have the information: but as long as the owner

---

secret that harm to him would be presumed by its mere disclosure: *Société Gamma Inc v Canada (Secretary of State)* (1994) 56 CPR (3d) 58, 79 FTR 42. The Freedom of Information Act 1997 (Ireland) s 27(1) provides a mandatory exemption for any record that contains a trade secret: see §2– 039(6).

[282] As to the meaning given to 'trade secret' in the context of freedom of information legislation in Australia, see: *Searle Australia Pty Ltd v Public Interest Advocacy Centre* (1992) 108 ALR 163, 36 FCR 111, where it was held by the full court of the Federal Court that the essential attributes of a trade secret were: (a) that it must be used in or usable in trade; in other words, an asset of the trade; (b) it must be used for the benefit of the owner's business; (c) it must not be in the public domain; (d) technicality is not required, but the more technical the information is, the more likely it is to be characterised as a trade secret. The Federal Court accepted that, in 'an appropriate case', the names of customers and the goods that they buy would be a trade secret, provided that these would be to the advantage of rivals to obtain.

[283] The term has been used for over a century: in *Allsopp v Wheatcroft* (1872) Law Rep 15 Eq 59 at 64–65 Sir John Wickens referred to a 'clearly lawful restriction against divulging a trade secret'. See also: *Davies v Davies* (1887) 36 Ch D 359 at 385.

[284] *Ansell Rubber Co Pty Ltd v Allied Rubber Industries Pty Ltd* [1967] VR 373.

[285] *Thomas Marshall (Exports) Ltd v Guinle* [1979] Ch 227, [1978] 3 All ER 193, [1979] FSR 208.

[286] Thus, under the equivalent provision under the Canadian Access to Information Act 1982, the Federal Court held that dosage information for a drug which was disclosed in a monograph available to health professionals was in the public domain: *Merck Frosst Canada Inc v Canada (Minister of Health and Welfare)* (1988) 20 FTR 73, 30 CPR (3d) 473; *Canada Post Corp v Canada (Minister of Public Works)* [1993] 3 FC 320, affirmed (1993) 64 FTR 62 (Fed. Court of Appeal); *Matol Botanical International Inc v Canada (Minister of National Health & Welfare)* (1994) 84 FTR 168.

believes it to be confidential I think he is entitled to try and protect it. Third, I think that the owner's belief under the two previous heads must be reasonable. Fourth, I think that the information must be judged in the light of the usage and practices of the particular industry or trade concerned. It may be that information which does not satisfy all these requirements may be entitled to protection as confidential information or trade secrets: but I think that any information which does satisfy them must be of a type which is entitled to protection.

25–051 **Distinction between trade secrets and ordinarily acquired work knowledge**
In *Faccenda Chicken Ltd v Fowler*[287] the Court of Appeal distinguished between trade secrets (which at common law may not be disclosed, quite apart from any contractual proscription against disclosure) and the information which an employee will inevitably acquire whilst employed (which is not subject to an implied obligation not to disclose). The correct characterisation of any particular item of information does not depend purely upon the attributes of the information, but will also depend upon the nature of the employment, the degree to which the employer impressed on the employee the confidentiality of the information, and whether the relevant information can be easily isolated from other information which the employee is free to use or disclose. When discussing those matters, the Court of Appeal said:

> In our judgment the information will only be protected if it can properly be classed as a trade secret or as material which, while not properly to be described as a trade secret, is in all the circumstances of such a highly confidential nature as to require the same protection as a trade secret *eo nomine* … It is clearly impossible to provide a list of matters which will qualify as trade secrets or their equivalent. Secret processes of manufacture provide obvious examples, but innumerable other pieces of information are capable of being trade secrets, though the secrecy of some information may be only short-lived. In addition, the fact that the circulation of certain information is restricted to a limited number of individuals may throw light on the status of the information and its degree of confidentiality…though an employer cannot prevent the use or disclosure merely by telling the employee that certain information is confidential, the attitude of the employer towards the information provides evidence which may assist in determining whether or not the information can properly be regarded as a trade secret … For our part we would not regard the separability of the information in question as being conclusive, but the fact that the alleged "confidential" information is part of a package and that the remainder of the package is not confidential is likely to throw light on whether the information in question is really a trade secret.

The distinction made by the Court of Appeal in *Faccenda Chicken Ltd v Fowler*[288] was considered by Hoffmann J in *Lock International plc v Beswick*:[289]

> There will be a good deal of … information which an employee could not without breach of duty disclose while he was employed but which he is free to use as part of his own skill and knowledge after his employment has ceased…It would not, for example, be sufficient to say in general terms that they were extremely familiar with the way Metalcheck detectors worked with, as the plaintiff's witnesses repeatedly say, their "strengths and weaknesses." There may have been some particular strength or weakness which was indeed a trade secret, but general familiarity is pre-eminently the kind of skill and knowledge which the honest employee cannot help taking away with him…In the Technical Appendix I have considered all the

---

[287] *Faccenda Chicken Ltd v Fowler* [1987] Ch 117, [1986] 1 All ER 617, [1986] FSR 291.

[288] *Faccenda Chicken Ltd v Fowler* [1987] Ch 117, [1986] 1 All ER 617, [1986] FSR 291.

[289] *Lock International plc v Beswick* [1989] 1 WLR 1268 at 1274–1275, 1281, [1989] 3 All ER 373.

alleged secrets and it seems to me that the only one in respect of which the plaintiff has even an arguable case is that relating to a particular weakness in the tuner diodes used in one circuit. Some of the claims to trade secrets, such as the use of marine ply or a common microprocessor, I regard as frankly absurd…Many [employers] have great difficulty in understanding the distinction between genuine trade secrets and skill and knowledge which the employee may take away with him. In cases in which the plaintiff alleges misuse of trade secrets or confidential information concerning a manufacturing process, a lack of particularity about the precise nature of the trade secrets is usually a symptom of an attempt to prevent the employee from making legitimate use of the knowledge and skills gained in the plaintiff's service…Judges dealing with ex parte applications are usually also at a disadvantage in dealing with alleged confidential knowledge of technical processes described in technical language, such as the electric circuitry in this case. It may look like magic but turn out merely to embody a principle discovered by Faraday or Ampere.[290]

FSS Travel and Leisure Systems Ltd v Johnson[291] affords one example of a case in which a claim by an employer failed, essentially for the reasons discussed in the above passage. The Court of Appeal, agreeing with the decision of the deputy judge at first instance, held that the employer had not established an entitlement to any identifiable trade secrets, but, rather, was seeking to rely upon a restrictive covenant to lay claim, in effect, to the employee's skill, experience, know-how and general knowledge gained during the course of his employment.

052   Trade secrets—examples

The case law needs to be considered with care, as the distinction between confidential information and trade secrets is often unarticulated, if appreciated at all. Nevertheless, the following appear to have been characterised as trade secrets in the properly-understood sense:

— special methods of design and construction;[292]
— technical knowledge and experience connected with the manufacture of particular goods;[293]
— trade practices and processes which would be harmful if it fell into the hands of competitors;[294] and

---

[290] See also: *Lansing Linde v Kerr* [1991] 1 WLR 251, where Staughton LJ referred to *Herbert Morris Ltd v Saxelby* [1916] 1 AC 688, *Faccenda Chicken Ltd v Fowler* [1987] Ch 117, *Balston Ltd v Headline Filters Ltd* [1987] FSR 330 and *Lock International plc v Beswick* [1989] 1 WLR 1268, and went on to say (at 259–260): 'It appears to me that the problem is one of definition: what are trade secrets, and how do they differ (if at all) from confidential information?' Staughton LJ considered a definition suggested by Counsel that 'a trade secret is information which, if disclosed to a competitor, would be liable to cause real (or significant) harm to the owner of the secret', and continued: 'I would add first, that it must be information used in a trade or business, and secondly that the owner must limit the dissemination of it or at least not encourage or permit widespread publication. That is my preferred view of the meaning of trade secret in this context. It can thus include not only secret formulae for the manufacture of products but also, in an appropriate case, the names of customers and the goods which they buy. But some may say that not all such information is a trade secret in ordinary parlance. If that view be adopted, the class of information which can justify a restriction is wider, and extends to some confidential information which would not ordinarily be called a trade secret.'

[291] *FSS Travel and Leisure Systems Ltd v Johnson* [1999] FSR 505, [1998] IRLR 382, [1999] ITCLR 218.

[292] *Reid & Sigrist Ltd v Moss and Mechanism Ltd* (1932) 49 RPC 461 (manufacture of aircraft turn indicators); *Standex International Ltd v CB Blades Ltd* [1976] FSR 114 (a unique mould engraving process).

[293] *Cranleigh Precision Engineering v Bryant* [1964] 3 All ER 289 (a swimming pool); *Balston Ltd v Headline Filters* [1987] FSR 330; *Nordenfelt v Maxim Nordenfelt Guns and Ammunition Company* [1894] AC 535 (know-how in relation to machine guns); *Amber Size and Chemical Company, Limited v Menzel* [1913] 2 Ch 239.

[294] *Malden Timber v McLeish* [1992] SLT 727; *Littlewoods Organisation v Harris* [1977] 1 WLR 1472.

— information relating to sales, prices and customers which would be of advantage to a competing company.[295]

It should be noted that the information that was held not to be capable of protection as a trade secret in *Faccenda Chicken Ltd v Fowler*[296] comprised the following sales information: the names and addresses of customers; the most convenient routes to be taken to reach individual customers; the usual requirements of individual customers; the days of the week and times of day when deliveries were made to individual customers; and the prices charged to individual customers. There is not necessarily any tension between this result and the approach suggested by Staughton LJ in *Lansing Linde v Kerr*,[297] who qualified his statement that the names of customers and the goods which they buy may amount to a trade secret by the words 'in an appropriate case'. The conclusion of the Court of Appeal in *Faccenda Chicken Ltd v Fowler*[298] that the sales information did not constitute a trade secret was reached by reference to the various matters (discussed above) that the court had held needed to be considered in order to determine whether any particular item of information fell within the implied term that was the subject of the decision of the court in that case.

25–053 Technical information

It is clear from the cases discussed above that it is neither a necessary nor a sufficient requirement for information to constitute a trade secret that it should be technical in nature, although technical information may — subject always to Hoffmann J's warnings about the danger of lawyers being blinded with science — more readily be held to amount to a trade secret. These conclusions are in line with the Australian cases. In *Searle Australia Pty Ltd v Public Interest Advocacy Centre*[299] the court observed that: 'It may be that the more technical the information is, the more likely it is that, as a matter of fact, the information will be classed as a trade secret. But technicality is not required.'[300]

25–054 Trade secrets — unifying principles

In summary, therefore, in order for information to amount to a trade secret more is required than that it should be (a) trade information having a commercial value and (b) confidential to the person(s) claiming that it constitutes a trade secret.[301] What is required is a sufficiently high degree of confidentiality. Whether or not information is of such a high degree of confidentiality as to constitute a trade secret will depend on all the circumstances. Relevant considerations include: the value of the information, the investment made in developing the information, the extent to which it truly is secret, the extent to which access to it has been restricted or its secrecy

---

[295] *Sir WC Leng & Co Ltd v Andrews* [1909] 1 Ch 763; *Harben Pumps (Scotland) v Lafferty* [1989] SLT 752; *Lansing Linde Ltd v Kerr* [1991] 1 All ER 418; *cf Faccenda Chicken Ltd v Fowler* [1987] Ch 117, [1986] 1 All ER 617, [1986] FSR 291.

[296] *Faccenda Chicken Ltd v Fowler* [1987] Ch 117, [1986] 1 All ER 617, [1986] FSR 291.

[297] *Lansing Linde v Kerr* [1991] 1 WLR 251.

[298] *Faccenda Chicken Ltd v Fowler* [1987] Ch 117, [1986] 1 All ER 617, [1986] FSR 291.

[299] *Searle Australia Pty Ltd v Public Interest Advocacy Centre* (1992) 108 ALR 163, 36 FCR 111.

[300] *Searle Australia Pty Ltd v Public Interest Advocacy Centre* (1992) 108 ALR 163 at 174.

[301] Contrast the suggestion made by the House of Lords Select Committee which considered the draft Freedom of Information Bill that a trade secret is 'information of commercial value which is protected by the law of confidence' — *Report of the Select Committee*, 27 July 1998, para 45.

and importance have been emphasised, and the extent to which it is separate and distinct from other information which cannot properly be regarded as a trade secret. Technicality is not required, although secret processes of manufacture, formulae and designs and so forth may more readily be regarded as trade secrets than information about costs, prices, sales and customers.[302] Technical information may have the appearance of distinctiveness and sophistication, but in truth be trite or inseparable from a general stock of skill and knowledge which an employee may take away with him; in which case, it will not constitute a trade secret. Conversely, although it often may not do so, in an appropriate case financial and customer information may constitute a trade secret (eg where one or more of the following apply: dissemination of such information has been restricted; it is of great value; release of it would cause serious harm to the person from whom the information originates).

055 The public interest

If the information in question constitutes a trade secret, the duty to disclose the information does not apply if the public interest in maintaining the exemption outweighs the public interest in disclosing the information.[303] The weighing exercise necessitates an identification of the public interest in the maintenance of the exemption, always recognising that that public interest must be delineated in such a fashion that it is capable in practice of being outweighed.[304] The public interest in the maintenance of this exemption should, it is suggested, involve an appreciation of:

— the maintenance of rights of intellectual property; and

— the potential of a chilling effect upon the provision to public authorities of information constituting trade secrets if such secrets are routinely disclosed upon a request being made under the Freedom of Information Act 2000.

056 The duty to confirm or deny

The discrete duty to confirm or deny upon a public authority that it holds information of the description specified in a request[305] is not displaced on the ground that to comply with that duty would disclose a trade secret.

5. PREJUDICE TO COMMERCIAL INTERESTS

057 Introduction

By s 43(2) of the Freedom of Information Act 2000 information is rendered exempt if its disclosure would, or would be likely to, prejudice the commercial interests of any person,

---

[302] In Canada, in the equivalent provision of the Access to Information Act 1982, the Federal Court held that the term 'trade secret' should be reserved for more technical production information: *Merck Frosst Canada Inc v Canada (Minister of Health and Welfare)* (1988) 20 FTR 73, 30 CPR (3d) 473.

[303] FOIA s 2(2)(b); FOI(S)A s 2.

[304] To avoid metamorphosing it into an absolute exemption.

[305] FOIA s 1(1)(a). There is no separate duty to confirm or deny under the FOI(S)A.

including the public authority holding it.[306] Where the information is 'environmental information', exemption from disclosure falls to be determined under the Environmental Information Regulations 2004 and not the Freedom of Information Act 2000.[307] Those regulations provide an analogous exception (considered separately below)[308] for confidential commercial or industrial information the non-disclosure of which is provided by law to protect a legitimate economic interest. The exemption under the Freedom of Information Act 2000 is not absolute, so that disapplication of the duty to disclose requires a weighing of the public interest in maintaining the exemption against the public interest in disclosure of the information.[309] The duty to confirm or deny is similarly excluded where, or to the extent that, informing the applicant that the information specified in the request is or is not held would, or would be likely to, prejudice the commercial interests of any person.[310] The exclusion of the duty to confirm or deny is also not absolute.[311] Of the comparative jurisdictions, a similar exemption is to be found only in the Australian and New Zealand regimes.[312]

25–058 The scope of the exemption
The exemption involves a consideration of:
— the notion of 'prejudice';
— the requisite degree of likelihood of prejudice; and
— the matter that is the proper subject of protection from that prejudice or likely prejudice.

The concept of 'prejudice' and the requisite degree of likelihood of prejudice are the same as those which are used for most of the other harm-based exemptions. These have been considered elsewhere in this work.[313] The object of the harm that forms the subject of the provision is the commercial interests of any person (including the public authority holding the information in question). This wording is of wide scope. In particular, there is no limitation on the nature or extent of the commercial interests that are material to the operation of the exemption. For example, there is no requirement that such interests should be serious or

---

[306] In relation to Scottish public authorities, there is a similar exemption under FOI(S)A s 33(1)(b).

[307] The disclosure regime under the EIR is considered in ch 6. In relation to Scottish public authorities, disclosure of environmental information falls to be determined under the EI(S)R.

[308] EIR reg 12(5)(e); EI(S)R reg 10(5)(e). See §25–067.

[309] FOIA s 2(2)(b); FOI(S)A s 2.

[310] FOIA s 43(3). There is no separate duty to confirm or deny under the FOI(S)A.

[311] FOIA s 2(1)(b).

[312] The Freedom of Information Act 1982 (Cth of Australia) s 47G provides an exemption in respect of information concerning a person in respect of his or her business or professional affairs or concerning the business, commercial or financial affairs of an organisation or undertaking, being information the disclosure of which would, or could reasonably be expected to, unreasonably affect that person adversely in respect of his or her lawful business or professional affairs or that organisation or undertaking in respect of its lawful business, commercial or financial affairs: see §2–015(17). The Official Information Act 1982 (New Zealand), ss 9(2)(b)(i) and 27(1)(a), provides a qualified exemption where the making available of that information would be likely to unreasonably prejudice the commercial position of the person who supplied or who is the subject of the information: see §2–023(2). In the other jurisdictions, protection from disclosure is provided through the confidentiality and trade secrets exemptions.

[313] In relation to 'prejudice' generally, see §§15–020 to 15–028. In relation to the required degree of likelihood, see specifically §15–022. In *John Connor Press Associates v IC*, IT, 25 January 2006, the Tribunal found that, because of earlier disclosures of similar information, there was no likelihood of harm.

substantial;[314] nor is there any requirement that the protection of such interests should have any public interest element or justification. The phrase 'commercial interests' is apt to cover:

— the existing business of a person or organisation, including its know-how;[315]

— a proposed venture; and

— the assets of a commercial enterprise, including its contracts.

The Tribunal has observed that the meaning of the word 'commercial' depends upon the context in which it is used, and in the present context it should not be tied to 'competitive participation in buying and selling goods and services'.[316] By way of example, the Tribunal has accepted as prejudicial to commercial interest a disclosure of the detail of an agreement made six years earlier between a council operating an airport with an airline operator (which provided 60 per cent of the airport's business) on the basis that it would give a counterparty in ongoing negotiations with that council an indication of the council's negotiating position.[317]

059   The public interest

If the information in question comes within the section, the duty to disclose the information does not apply if the public interest in maintaining the exemption outweighs the public interest in disclosing the information.[318] The weighing exercise necessitates an identification of the public interest in the maintenance of the exemption, always recognising that that public interest must be delineated in such a fashion that it is capable in practice of being outweighed.[319] Given the quintessentially private nature of the interest being protected by the exemption (the commercial interests of a person), it is difficult to see immediately what particular public interest there is in maintaining the exemption without importing interests that already stand to be protected by other provisions in Part II of the Act. It is suggested that it would be impermissible to use the public interest weighing exercise for the purposes of s 43(2) effectively to reshape and enlarge the discrete exemptions provided elsewhere in the Act: most notably, the exemptions for confidential information and trade secrets. The public interest balancing exercise may be

---

[314] This is, it seems, the deliberate intention of the legislature. The Select Committee had recommended that the phrase 'substantial prejudice' be used, but this recommendation was rejected: *Report from the Select Committee Appointed to Consider the Draft Freedom of Information Bill 1998–9,* July 1999, HL, para 32; *Select Committee on Public Administration, Third Report,* Sessions 1998–9, July 1999, HC 570–1, para 71. Contrast, also, the test of 'substantial harm' which had been proposed in *Your Right to Know. The Government's Proposals for a Freedom of Information Act. White Paper* (Cm 3818, 1997) para 3.7.

[315] In Australia, under the equivalent provision in the Freedom of Information Act 1982, this exemption has been successfully invoked to exempt documents with information as to the nature of, techniques used in, and results of tests carried out into a pharmaceutical product *(Re Pfizer Pty Ltd and the Department of Health, Housing and Community Services* (1993) 30 ALD 647). See also: *Re Organon (Australia) Pty Ltd and Department of Community Services and Health* (1987) 13 ALD 588 at 595 (the fact that considerable time and money had been expended upon the compilation of statistical information supplied to the department and that the publication of the statistics would reduce the value of that investment was sufficient to meet the requirements of the exemption); *Gill v Department of Industry, Technology and Resources* [1987] VR 681 at 687; *Re The Staff Development and Training Centre and Secretary, Department of Employment, Workplace Relations and Small Business* (2000) 30 AAR 330 at 365–368; *Searle Australia v Public Interest Advocacy Centre* (1992) 36 FCR 111, 108 ALR 163 (the exemption does not apply to the compilation of material otherwise publicly available).

[316] *Student Loans Company Ltd v IC,* IT, 17 July 2009 at [42], endorsed in *University of Central Lancashire v IC and Colquhoun,* IT, 8 December 2009 at [31].

[317] *Derry City Council v IC,* IT, 11 December 2006 at [25].

[318] FOIA s 2(2)(b); FOI(S)A s 2.

[319] To avoid metamorphosing it into an absolute exemption.

time-sensitive.[320]

25–060 Duty to confirm or deny

Where compliance with the duty to confirm or deny would, or would be likely to, prejudice the commercial interests of any person (including the public authority holding the information), then the discrete duty to confirm or deny that that information is held by the public authority does not arise.[321] This is a qualified exclusion of duty.[322] It will therefore be necessary to consider whether, in all the circumstances, the maintenance of the exclusion of this duty is outweighed by the public interest in disclosing whether the public authority holds the information. As noted previously, despite its superficial similarity, this public interest balancing exercise is materially different from that employed for the purpose of determining whether the duty to communicate does not apply.[323] Short of a purely confirmatory request that, in its terms, sets out the information or the gist of the information sought, it is difficult to imagine any particular public interest in maintaining an exemption from the duty to confirm or deny that information is held. On the other hand, other than the public interest articulated through the Freedom of Information Act 2000 itself, it is also difficult to identify any particular public interest in confirming or denying the holding.

6. INTERNATIONAL CONFIDENCES

25–061 Introduction

Section 27(2) of the Freedom of Information Act 2000 exempts information if it is confidential information obtained from a state other than the United Kingdom or from an international organisation or international court.[324] Where the information is 'environmental information',

---

[320] As in *Derry City Council v IC*, IT, 11 December 2006 where the Information Tribunal held that although the requested information was covered by s 43 'the risk of prejudice to the Council's commercial interests by the time the Complainant made his request was not sufficient to outweigh the public interest in having the Ryanair Financial Information disclosed' (at [28(b)]).

[321] FOIA s 43(3). In relation to Scottish public authorities, there is no separate duty to confirm or deny under the FOI(S)A.

[322] FOIA s 2(1).

[323] See §§15–018 to 15–019 as to what it involves.

[324] In relation to information held by a Scottish public authority, exemption is provided by FOI(S)A s 32(2). There is no comparable exemption under the DPA. In the United States, exemption for information communicated by foreign governments in confidence is generally secured through Executive Order 12,958 and exemption 1: see §2–008(1) and *Krikorian v Department of State* 984 F 2d 461 (DC Cir 1993). There must be a contemporaneous expectation of confidentiality: *Weatherhead v United States*, 157 F(3d) 735 (9th Cir 1998), concerning information from the British Government. The Freedom of Information Act 1982 (Cth of Australia) s 33(1), exempts a document the disclosure of which would divulge any information communicated in confidence by or on behalf of a foreign government, an authority of a foreign government or an international organisation to the Australian Government: see §2–015(9). The Official Information Act 1982 (New Zealand), ss 6(b) and 27(1)(a), provides an absolute exemption where the disclosure of the information would be likely to prejudice the entrusting of information to the government of New Zealand on a basis of confidence by the government of any other country or any agency of such a government, or by any international organisation: see §2–022(2). The Access to Information Act (Canada) s 13(1), provides a mandatory exemption for records containing information received in confidence from other governments: see §2–031(1). The Freedom of Information Act 1997 (Ireland) s 24(2) provides a mandatory exemption for records containing information revealing diplomatic communications; or revealing confidential communications from

exemption from disclosure falls to be determined under the Environmental Information Regulations 2004 and not the Freedom of Information Act 2000.[325] Those regulations do not provide a separate exception in relation to confidential information obtained from another State or from an international organisation or international court. However, the exception provided in those regulations for certain confidential information (considered separately below)[326] may except the information from disclosure. The exemption in the Freedom of Information Act 2000 is a qualified exemption. What is confidential for the purposes of s 27(2) is statutorily defined by the Act as any information obtained from a State, organisation or court where (a) the terms on which it was obtained require it to be held in confidence or (b) the circumstances in which it was obtained make it reasonable for the State, organisation or court to expect that it will be held in confidence.[327] 'State', 'international organisation' and 'international court' are each statutorily defined by the Act.[328] The definitions are cast in wide terms.[329]

062 Scope of the exemption

This is a class exemption, so that it applies to any information that falls within this definition without regard to the consequences of disclosure. It is therefore potentially of wide scope. The exemption is capable of exempting information the disclosure of which would not 'constitute a breach of confidence actionable' by the supplier of the information or another person.[330] However, its practical operation is materially reduced by two considerations. First, although the focus of the definition is on the terms on which or the circumstances in which the information was obtained, and whether those terms or circumstances require it to be held or give rise to a reasonable expectation that it will be held in confidence, the definition also

---

foreign state organisations: see §2– 039(4).

[325] The disclosure regime under the EIR is considered in ch 6. In relation to Scottish public authorities, disclosure of environmental information falls to be determined under the EI(S)R.

[326] EIR reg 12(5)(e); EI(S)R reg 10(5)(e). See §25– 066.

[327] FOIA s 27(2); FOI(S)A s 32(2).

[328] See FOIA s 27(5); FOI(S)A s 32(3).

[329] See §§18– 003 to 18– 008 for a consideration of the exemption under FOIA s 27(1). The exemption may, in some circumstances, be able to be relied upon to exempt foreign confidential information on the basis that to disclose such information would be prejudicial to international relations.

[330] Being the words used in FOIA s 41(1)(b) and FOI(S)A s 36(2)(b): *Campaign against the Arms Trade v IC and MoJ*, IT, 26 August 2008, at [57]. In Australia, where the Freedom of Information Act 1982 s 33(1)(b) provides an exemption where disclosure 'would divulge any information or matter communicated in confidence by or on behalf of a foreign government, an authority of a foreign government or an international organization to the Government of the Commonwealth, to an authority of the Commonwealth ...' It has been held that that exemption is not confined to communications which if disclosed would give rise to an action in breach of confidence. It extends to information which was communicated and received under an express or inferred understanding that it would be kept confidential: *Re Maher and Attorney-General's Department* (1985) 7 ALD 731 (it was enough that the information was supplied pursuant to a general understanding that communications of a particular nature would be treated in confidence); *Re Throssell and Australian Archives (No 2)* (1987) 14 ALD 296. Nor is it necessary that the agency make inquiries as to the motives of the person who supplied the information or whether it is based on false information: *Gersten v Minister for Immigration & Multicultural Affairs* [2000] FCA 1221. Nor, apparently, does it make any difference that the information is in the public domain: *Commonwealth of Australia v Hittich* (1994) 53 FCR 152, 35 ALD 717. The view taken in the comparative jurisdictions is that the evidence of the views of foreign governments should be afforded considerable weight, but is not determinative: *Re Slater and Cox*, (1988) 15 ALD 20; *O'Donovan and Attorney-General's Dept* (1985) 8 ALD 528 at 534; *Do-Ky v Minister for Foreign Affairs* [1997] 2 FC 907.

contains a temporal limitation. Information is only confidential within the meaning of the statutory definition for so long as that requirement or that expectation continues in effect.[331] For example, the terms on which the information was obtained may have the effect that if and in so far as it enters the public domain it is no longer required to be held in confidence by the public authority.[332] Similarly, the circumstances in which the information was obtained may mean that if and in so far as it enters the public domain there ceases to be a reasonable expectation that it will be held in confidence. Second, the section only applies to information that has itself been obtained from a foreign state or international organisation. Where the information sought originates from a public authority in the United Kingdom, but has been prepared using information from a foreign state or an international organisation, unless and to the extent that the former will reveal the latter, the domestic information will not be exempt information under this provision.[333] However, the Tribunal has held that a memorandum of understanding could fall within the provision where a foreign State had provided the information for the purposes of that memorandum.[334] In *Campaign against the Arms Trade v IC and MoJ*,[335] the Tribunal upheld a claim for exemption under s 27(3) in relation to various memoranda of understanding between the Governments of the United Kingdom and of Saudi Arabia relating to the supply of defence equipment. The Tribunal, relying on s 27(3) and having regard to the subject-matter of the information and the consistent basis upon which the Saudi Arabian Government had supplied the source information to the United Kingdom Government, held that it was reasonable for the former to expect that the information would be held in confidence:

> the correct approach to that question is to consider what it would have been reasonable for the [Kingdom of Saudi Arabia] to have expected in all the circumstances. That does not justify imposing on the KSA our particular customs and principles as to transparency or democratic accountability. It should be judged against what would have been reasonable for the KSA to have expected....The concept of freedom of information and transparency is generally alien to their culture...To this extent the senior rulers and in particular the King could not be expected easily to accept or respond to the principles of disclosure and transparency to which we have referred in the context of the FOIA. We are satisfied on the evidence that these MoU were entered into on a basis on which the KSA would have expected that each government would respect the confidentiality of those agreements at least in the absence of the other consenting to disclosure. The MoU were marked secret and regarded as confidential.[336]

---

[331] FOIA s 27(3); FOI(S)A s 32(2).

[332] In the United States, a distinction is drawn between information that has unofficially 'leaked' into the public domain and that which has officially come into the public domain. Thus, in *Afshar v Department of State* 702 F 2d 1125 (DC Cir 1983) it was observed that a foreign government can ignore 'unofficial leaks and public surmise ... but official acknowledgment may force a government to retaliate.'

[333] This is the approach which was taken by the Federal Court of Appeal in Canada in *Sherman v Canada (Minister of National Revenue)* [2003] FCA 202, where the applicant sought records containing statistics generated by the Canadian Revenue but derived from information obtained in confidence from the United States pursuant to a bilateral convention with respect to taxes on income and capital.

[334] *Campaign against the Arms Trade v IC and MoJ*, IT, 26 August 2008 at [64].

[335] *Campaign against the Arms Trade v IC and MoJ* IT, 26 August 2008.

[336] *Campaign against the Arms Trade v IC and MoJ*, IT, 26 August 2008 at [75]-[77].

A similar conclusion was reached in *Gilby v IC and FCO*.[337]

063 The public interest

As noted above, the exemption is a qualified exemption. In other words, in each instance the exemption is subject to whether the public interest in maintaining it outweighs the public interest in disclosure.[338] Where no specific harm would result from the disclosure of the information, the public interest requirement may have the effect that the exemption does not apply. As against that, however, it may be argued that harm generally results from the disclosure of information in circumstances where that contradicts either the terms on which it was obtained or the reasonable expectation of the entity from which it was obtained, and that there is a public interest in upholding compliance with such terms or expectations and avoiding the harm in the shape of lack of trust (and, in all probability, a reduced flow of information) that results from not upholding compliance with the same:

> Parliament recognised and we accept that there is an inherent disservice to the public interest in flouting international confidence.[339]

Against that and underpinned by the rules of comity and international law, lies the principle that foreign states and organisations dealing with the public authorities in the United Kingdom must take the country as it is, including its laws relating to the disclosure of information. By conveying or transmitting information to a public authority in this country, the foreign entity must accept that that will be attended by certain loss of control over the further dissemination of the information.[340] Accordingly, a consideration of the public interest in maintaining the exemption will need to take into account:

— whether the particular information or information of that class has been identified by the source as being confidential;[341]

— whether, quite apart from any formal identification, the information is of a sort conventionally considered to be confidential;

— whether, if the source of the information has designated it as confidential, that was done as a matter of course or perfunctorily;

— whether the other State understood that information of the class sought to be disclosed would be kept confidential;[342]

— whether the disclosure would have an adverse impact upon the relationship between the Governments of the United Kingdom and of another State;[343]

---

[337] *Gilby v IC and FCO* IT, 22 October 2008, at [46], most of the reasons for which are apparently recorded in the closed part of its decision.

[338] FOIA s 2(2)(b); FOI(S)A s 2(1)(b).

[339] *Campaign against the Arms Trade v IC and MoJ*, IT, 26 August 2008 at [95].

[340] Just as the foreign entity would have to accept that if the information it conveyed to the public authority was personal information relating to the applicant, then that information would, notwithstanding that it had been conveyed to the public authority in confidence, have to be conveyed to the applicant if an application were made under s 7 of the DPA, subject to any applicable exemptions under that Act.

[341] In *Campaign against the Arms Trade v IC and MoJ*, IT, 26 August 2008 at [96], this was considered to be of paramount importance.

[342] *Gilby v IC and FCO*, IT, 22 October 2008 at [54].

[343] *Campaign against the Arms Trade v IC and MoJ*, IT, 26 August 2008 at [96]; *Gilby v IC and FCO*, IT, 22 October 2008 at [51].

— whether the disclosure would have an adverse impact upon the protection and promotion of UK interests abroad;[344] and

— where the information emanates from the European Union, article 255 of the Amsterdam Treaty;

On the other side of the balance, it is in the public interest to disclose information that might reveal corruption and that would enhance transparency in government transactions, especially where the subject matter is one of legitimate public concern (such as arms contracts).[345]

25–064 Duty to confirm or deny

The duty to confirm or deny does not arise if, or to the extent that, the confirmation or denial that would have to be given to comply with the duty would, or would be likely to, involve the disclosure of any confidential information (whether or not already recorded) which is obtained from a State other than the United Kingdom or from an international organisation or international court.[346] This disapplication of the duty to confirm or deny is only operative if, in all the circumstances of the case, the public interest in maintaining the exclusion of the duty outweighs the public interest in disclosing whether the public authority holds the information.[347]

7. ENVIRONMENTAL INFORMATION AND CONFIDENTIALITY

25–065 Introduction

Information to which a person has a right of access under the Environmental Information Regulations 2004 is exempt information under s 39(1)(a) of the Freedom of Information Act 2000.[348] In this way, whether or to the extent that a request for information captures 'environmental information', disclosure must be determined in accordance with the Environmental Information Regulations 2004 and not the Freedom of Information Act 2000.[349] The disclosure regime under the Environmental Information Regulations 2004 is considered in detail in Chapter 6. In summary, to the extent that a request for information captures information 'obtained from any other person' which is properly regarded as a request for 'environmental information', issues of confidentiality will be governed by the Environmental Information Regulations 2004.[350] The Regulations provide two exceptions from disclosure on confidentiality-related grounds. While the principles relating to confidentiality under the

---

[344] *Campaign against the Arms Trade v IC and MoJ*, IT, 26 August 2008 at [96]; *Gilby v IC and FCO*, IT, 22 October 2008 at [51].

[345] *Campaign against the Arms Trade v IC and MoJ*, IT, 26 August 2008 at [97]-[98]; *Gilby v IC and FCO*, IT, 22 October 2008 at [51], [55]-[57].

[346] FOIA s 27(4)(b). In relation to Scottish public authorities, there is no free-standing duty to confirm or deny.

[347] FOIA s 2(1)(b).

[348] Similarly, in relation to Scottish public authorities, FOI(S)A s 39.

[349] And, in relation to Scottish public authorities, the request must be determined in accordance with the EI(S)R and not the FOI(S)A.

[350] In the case of a request made to a Scottish public authority, issues of confidentiality will be governed by the EI(S)R.

Freedom of Information Act 2000[351] are also basic to the confidentiality-related exceptions in the Environmental Information Regulations 2004, the exceptions are materially narrower than their counterparts in the Act. It follows that where a request for information raises issues of confidentiality, it will be important to determine which (if any) of the information captured by the request is 'environmental information'.[352] Further, both exceptions are qualified by a public interest balancing test.[353]

- 066 Non-consensual disclosure of information supplied by a third party

Subject to the public interest test,[354] a public authority may refuse to disclose environmental information to the extent that its disclosure would adversely affect:

the interests of the person who provided the information where that person:

(i)   was not under, and could not have been put under, any legal obligation to supply it to that or any other public authority,

(ii)   did not supply it in circumstances such that that or any other public authority is entitled apart from these Regulations to disclose it, and

(iii)   has not consented to its disclosure.[355]

The exception attempts to provide some protection for information held by a public authority that has been supplied to it by a third party. The list of conditions required for the exception to engage gives it a limited operation. First, the disclosure must adversely affect the interests of the person who provided the information. A mere likelihood of harm is not sufficient. The regulations do not identify what sort of interests must be adversely affected, but it is suggested that any financial interest will qualify. Secondly, it must be information that was neither supplied under compulsion nor could have been obtained as a result of enforcement of any legal obligation. This is particularly limiting.[356] Thirdly, there are few circumstances in which information, other than personal information, held by a public authority may not lawfully be disclosed by it or any other public authority.[357] Unless another exception applies, even where the terms of this exception are met the public authority may only not disclose that part of the information in respect of which it is satisfied that in all the circumstances the public interest in maintaining this exception outweighs the public interest in the information's disclosure.[358] This

---

[351] See §§25– 010 to 25– 029.

[352] See §6– 010.

[353] EIR reg 12(1); EI(S)R reg 10(1). The provision is derived from Directive 2003/4/EC art 4.2 (penultimate paragraph). See further §6– 037.

[354] See §6– 037.

[355] EIR reg 12(5)(f); EI(S)R reg 10(5)(f). Derived from art 4.2(g) of the Directive and art 4.4(g) of the Aarhus Convention. Regulation 4(3)(c) of the 1992 Regulations provided for a similar exception but without the public interest balancing test. In *R v Secretary of State for the Environment, Transport and the Regions, ex p Alliance against Birmingham Northern Relief Road (No 1)* [1999] Env LR 447, [1999] JPL 231, Sullivan J held that parts of the concession agreement fell within reg 4(3)(c). The exception does not apply to information on (or, possibly, relating to) emissions: EIR reg 12(9); EI(S)R reg 10(6).

[356] See the discussion in §6– 052.

[357] Again, see the discussion in §§6– 052 and 9– 034 to 9– 035.

[358] EIR reg 12(1)(b); EI(S)R reg 10(1)(b). See §§6– 037 and 9– 036.

exception does not apply to information on emissions.[359] What would seem to be left so as to engage the exception is information volunteered by a third person to a public authority, disclosure of which would constitute a breach of confidence[360] enforceable by the third party, provided always that the public interest in maintaining the particular exception outweighs the public interest in disclosure.

25– 067 Adverse effect upon confidential commercial or industrial information

Subject to the public interest test,[361] a public authority may also refuse to disclose environmental information to the extent that its disclosure would adversely affect 'the confidentiality of commercial or industrial information where such confidentiality is provided by law to protect a legitimate economic interest'.[362] The exception imposes two requirements. First, the information must enjoy the quality of confidentiality. It is suggested that this substantially imports the requirements of s 41(1) of the Freedom of Information Act 2000.[363] Secondly, the information must be 'commercial or industrial information'. This takes out of the scope of the exception the private information limb of confidentiality.[364] The exception straddles three separate exemptions in the Freedom of Information Act 2000.[365] While all trade secrets will be covered, non-confidential commercial information will not be covered. Nor will non-commercial or non-industrial confidential information be covered. The Directive provision from which it derived confirms its more limited scope, providing for refusal of a request for environmental information where disclosure would adversely affect 'the confidentiality of commercial or industrial information where such confidentiality is provided for by national or Community law to protect a legitimate economic interest, including the public interest in

---

[359] EIR reg 12(9); EI(S)R reg 10(6). Derived from Directive 2003/4/EC art 4.2 (penultimate paragraph) and, more loosely, from the Aarhus Convention art 4.4(d) (last sentence) and the last sentence of art 4.4 itself.

[360] As to which, see §§25– 010 to 25– 048.

[361] See §6– 037.

[362] EIR reg 12(5)(e); EI(S)R reg 10(5)(e). Derived from art 4.2(d) of the Directive and art 4.4(d) of the Aarhus Convention. The exception does not apply to information on (or, possibly, relating to) emissions: EIR reg 12(9); EI(S)R reg 10(6). Regulation 4(2)(e) of the 1992 Regulations provided for a similar exception but without the public interest balancing test. In *R v Secretary of State for the Environment, Transport and the Regions, ex p Alliance against Birmingham Northern Relief Road (No 1)* [1999] Env LR 447, [1999] JPL 231, the applicant sought access under the 1992 Regulations to a concession agreement, made under s 1 of the New Roads and Street Works Act 1991 between Midland Express Motorway Ltd and the Secretary of State, by which Midland Express was to design, build, finance and operate a motorway. After the agreement had been made, the required public inquiry concluded with the Secretary of State deciding to make the necessary orders. The applicant was concerned that the Secretary of State, in deciding to make the orders, might have been influenced by the prospect of having to pay compensation to Motorway Express if he decided otherwise. The Secretary of State refused to disclose the agreement, citing commercial confidentiality and reg 4(1)(a) and 4(2)(e) and the applicant challenged that refusal by way of judicial review. Sullivan J held that the issues of whether information was 'environmental information' and whether it was 'confidential' were objective issues to be determined in an objective manner (JPL at 247). He found that the concession agreement was not intrinsically confidential (JPL at 253) and rejected a submission that because it was a commercial document having financial implications all of it was confidential (JPL at 254). He accepted that information in the agreement relating to prices, costs, payment, compensation events and trade secrets should attract confidentiality (JPL at 255).

[363] As to which, see §§25– 010 to 25– 015.

[364] As set out in §§25– 030 to 25– 048.

[365] Sections 41(1), 43(1) and 43(2); FOI(S)A ss 36 and 33(1).

maintaining statistical confidentiality and tax secrecy'.[366] Unless another exception applies, even where the terms of this exception are met the public authority may only not disclose that part of the information in respect of which it is satisfied that in all the circumstances the public interest in maintaining this exception outweighs the public interest in the information's disclosure.[367] This exception does not apply to information on emissions.[368]

---

[366] Directive art 4.2(d).

[367] EIR reg 12(1)(b); EI(S)R reg 10(1)(b). See §6– 037.

[368] EIR reg 12(9); EI(S)R reg 10(6). Derived from Directive 2003/4/EC art 4.2 (penultimate paragraph) and, more loosely, from the Aarhus Convention art 4.4(d)(last sentence) and the last sentence of art 4.4 itself.

CHAPTER 26
Miscellaneous Exemptions

1. COMMUNICATIONS WITH HER MAJESTY, ETC*

001 Introduction

By virtue of s 37(1)(a) of the Freedom of Information Act 2000, information that relates to communications with Her Majesty,[1] other members of the Royal Family or the Royal Household is exempt information.[2] Similarly, the duty to confirm or deny does not arise in relation to such information.[3] Both the exemption and the exclusion are qualified.[4] Accordingly, even if information is exempt information under this provision, the public authority holding that information must disclose it unless the public interest in maintaining the

---

* By Oliver Sanders, 1 Crown Office Row.

[1] The reference to Her Majesty is to be construed as a reference to the Sovereign for the time being: Interpretation Act 1978 s 10.

[2] Similarly, FOI(S)A s 41. See §26– 013.

[3] FOIA s 37(2). There is no discrete duty to confirm or deny under FOI(S)A.

[4] FOIA s 2(3); FOI(S)A s 2(2). At the time of writing, the Government's Constitutional Reform and Governance Bill was before Parliament. If enacted as drafted as at 3 March 2010, cl 86 and Sch 15 to this Bill would amend FOIA ss 2(3) and 37(1) so as to make the exemption in s 37 absolute in its application to information that relates to communications with the Sovereign, the heir to the Throne, the second in line to the Throne or a person who (after the communication but before the request is made) becomes the Sovereign, heir or second in line. Information relating to communications with other members of the Royal Family or with the Royal Household (other than communications made or received on behalf of the Sovereign, heir or second in line) would remain subject to the existing qualified exemption. Schedule 15 para 6 to the Bill would further insert a new s 80A into FOIA providing for the continued application of s 37 in its current form to information held by Northern Ireland public bodies.

exemption outweighs the public interest in disclosing the information.[5] There is no equivalent exception in the Environmental Information Regulations 2004. Accordingly, where (or to the extent that) information that answers the terms of a request for information is 'environmental information',[6] the fact that that information also relates to communications with Her Majesty, other members of the Royal Family or the Royal Household will not excuse the public authority from complying with the request.[7]

26–002 Background

The *Code of Practice on Access to Government Information* contained a similar, but narrower, exemption for 'information relating to confidential communications between Ministers and Her Majesty the Queen or other Members of the Royal Household, or relating to confidential proceedings of the Privy Council'.[8] The accompanying *Guidance on Interpretation* stated that that exemption was designed to protect confidences.[9] More long-standing restrictions have prevented parliamentary questions being asked of ministers regarding certain matters connected with the monarch, the Royal Family and the Royal Household.[10] The relevant exemptions in the draft Freedom of Information Bill published on 24 May 1999[11] and the Freedom of Information Bill introduced in the House of Commons on 18 November 1999[12] were identically worded.

26–003 The comparative jurisdictions

Section 9(2)(f)(i) of the Official Information Act 1982 (NZ) provides for the withholding of information where necessary to maintain the constitutional conventions that protect the confidentiality of communications by or with the Sovereign or her representative unless it is

---

[5] Similarly, the duty to confirm or deny. FOIA s 37(1) and (2) engage s 2(2)(b) and (1)(b) respectively so as to prevent from arising, first, the duty to confirm or deny and, secondly, the duty to communicate, if the public interest in divulgence or disclosure (respectively) is outweighed.

[6] As to the meaning of which, see §6–010.

[7] FOIA s 39; FOI(S)A s 39.

[8] *Open Government Code of Practice on Access to Government Information*, 2nd edn (1997) Pt II, para 3. The exemption did not refer to harm or prejudice and it was not therefore subject to any balancing exercise weighing the public interest in disclosure against the public interest in non-disclosure. See also: the Scottish Executive's *Code of Practice on Access to Scottish Executive Information*, 2nd edn (2003) Pt II, para 3; and the National Assembly for Wales's *Code of Practice on Public Access to Information*, 3rd edn (2004) Annex B.

[9] *Open Government Code of Practice on Access to Government Information: Guidance on Interpretation*, 2nd edn (1997) Pt II, paras 3.1 to 3.2.

[10] W McKay (ed), *Erskine May's treatise on the law, privileges, proceedings and usage of Parliament*, 23rd edn (London, Butterworths, 2004) p 298. Although the *White Paper on Open Government* (Cm 2290, 1993) did not offer any additional commentary upon the exemption which eventually found expression in the *Open Government Code of Practice on Access to Government Information*, 2nd edn (1997) Pt II, para 3, it did propose a further exemption which was not taken further for 'information which could not be sought in a parliamentary question' (see Annex A, Pt II, para xv). Information Commissioner, *Freedom of Information Act Awareness Guidance No 26: Communications with Her Majesty and the Awarding of Honours*, (2006), Pt B(a) states, 'It has been suggested by those with experience of royal matters that in practice very little additional information will become available under FOI – it will be a case of codifying and establishing more formal guidelines for the existing arrangements public authorities already have in place for dealing with information relating to royal communications.'

[11] *Freedom of Information: Consultation on Draft Legislation* (Cm 4355, 1999) Pt II, cl 29(1).

[12] Clause 35(1).

more desirable in the public interest that the information be made available.[13] Section 46(1)(d) of the Freedom of Information Act 1997 (Ireland) also excludes records relating to the President from the provisions of that Act. None of the other comparative jurisdictions has any exemptions in their access to information regimes equivalent to s 37(1) of the Freedom of Information Act 2000.

004 The Royal Family

Her Majesty and the other members of the Royal Family are not 'public authorities' for the purposes of the Freedom of Information Act 2000[14] and are thus not subject to the regime established by the Act.[15] The expression 'the Royal Family' is not defined in the Freedom of Information Act 2000 and does not have any specific legal definition elsewhere. The monarch, his or her parents and grandparents, his or her spouse and their children, children-in-law and grandchildren are plainly members of the Royal Family.[16] How much further the Royal Family extends to others who are related to the monarch by blood or marriage falls to be answered by reference to convention, their styles, titles, forms of precedence and special privileges, their subjection to the monarch's general authority in relation to the supervision of minors and royal marriages, their inclusion in the Civil List and the applicability of special common law and statutory provisions.[17] While it will often be clear in practice whether a particular

---

[13] See I Eagles, M Taggart & G Liddell, *Freedom of Information in New Zealand* (Auckland, Oxford University Press, 1992), pp 364–367.

[14] Her Majesty and the other members of the Royal Family are also not 'Scottish public authorities' for the purposes of FOI(S)A s 3, Sch 1: see also the Scotland Act 1998 ss 29–30, Sch 5, Pt II, s.B13.

[15] Furthermore, FOIA does not expressly bind the Crown and therefore only binds the Crown to the extent required by necessary implication: *Province of Bombay v Municipal Corporation of Bombay* [1947] AC 58 (PC); *AG of Ceylon v A D Silva* [1953] AC 461 (PC); *Madras Electric Supply Corp Ltd v Boarland* [1955] AC 667; *Ministry of Agriculture v Jenkins* [1963] 2 QB 317 (CA); *Wood v Leeds Area Health Authority* [1974] ICR 535; and *Lord Advocate v Strathclyde Regional Council* [1990] 2 AC 580. This 'doctrine of Crown immunity' is expressly saved and recognised by the Crown Proceedings Act 1947 ss 31(1), 40(2)(f). Following *BBC v Johns (Inspector of Taxes)* [1965] Ch 32 (CA) at 81 (Diplock LJ) the Crown's 'immunity' from the FOIA regime will also be enjoyed by the Crown's servants and agents to the extent that they are not brought under that regime by express provision or necessary implication (see also F Bennion, *Statutory Interpretation*, 5th edn (London, LexisNexis, 2008) p 207, and W Wade and C Forsyth, *Administrative Law*, 10th edn (Oxford, Oxford University Press, 2009) pp 712–713). In practice, a great number of servants and agents of the Crown and other Crown bodies are brought under the FOIA regime by being expressly listed as 'public authorities' in FOIA Sch 1. The criminal offence provisions in FOIA s 77 and Sch 3, para 12 are also applied to persons in the public service of the Crown as they apply to any other person: FOIA s 81(3).

[16] MoJ, *Exemptions Guidance—Section 37*, undated, Annex A sets out a list of 'Members of the Royal Family since 1 January 1975 (as at June 2004)' which comprises 'Those entitled to use the title Majesty or Royal Highness and their spouses'. MoJ, *Exemptions Guidance—Section 37*, undated, Pt 1, para 1.2 states, 'The list will change over time, especially through marriage or birth. If an authority is in doubt as to whether someone should be included in the list (for example, not all those entitled to the title of Royal Highness may choose to use it) the Private Secretary to the Queen should be consulted.' Information Commissioner, *Freedom of Information Act Awareness Guidance No 26: Communications with Her Majesty and the Awarding of Honours*, (2006), Pt B states, 'As a general rule the Royal Family will include all those individuals who hold or are entitled to hold the title of Majesty or Royal Highness and their spouses.'

[17] *Halsbury's Laws of England*, 4th edn, 1998 re-issue, vol 12(1), title 'Crown and Royal Family', paras 27, 35–36. The Royal Family would certainly appear to extend beyond those entitled to the style of 'Royal Highness:' *Halsbury's Laws of England*, 4th edn, 1998 re-issue, vol 12(1), title 'Crown and Royal Family', para 34. Complications may arise in relation to current members of the Royal Family who did not have their status as such when a particular communication took place and, conversely, in relation to former members of the Royal Family who have lost that status since a particular communication took place. It is notable that a less comprehensive protection from the regime is afforded to information that relates to communications with the Royal Family and Household than is

communication has passed from or to someone who is a member of the Royal Family for the purposes of s 37(1)(a) of the Freedom of Information Act 2000, formal membership for these purposes may depend upon questions of fact in the circumstances of each case. Once membership has been established, however, it is notable that s 37(1)(a) of the Freedom of Information Act 2000 exempts all information regardless of whether the Family member in question was acting in a public or private capacity in relation to the relevant communication.

26–005   The Royal Household

The Royal Household is also not a 'public authority' for the purposes of the Freedom of Information Act 2000[18] and is not subject to the Freedom of Information Act 2000 regime.[19] The expression 'the Royal Household' is not defined in the Freedom of Information Act 2000 and does not have any specific legal definition elsewhere.[20] The Royal Household assists the monarch in carrying out official duties and it includes the monarch's Household together with the Households of other members of the Royal Family who undertake public engagements. The Royal Household is under the overall authority of the Lord Chamberlain who is the senior member of the monarch's household and it is divided into five departments: the Private Secretary's Office; the Privy Purse and Treasurer's Office; the Master of the Household's Department; the Lord Chamberlain's Office; and the Royal Collection Department.[21] While it will often be clear in practice whether a particular communication has passed from or to someone who is a member of the Royal Household for the purposes of s 37(1)(a) of the Freedom

---

afforded by s 23(1) to information supplied by or relating to the security bodies. Basic precepts of statutory interpretation suggest that some effect must be given to the use of different formulae. It is also significant that information contained in a 'historical record' (as to the meaning of which, see §7– 036) cannot be exempt information by virtue of s 37(1)(a), suggesting that the contemporaneity of the information is central to the rationale for the exemption.

[18]   The Royal Household is also not a 'Scottish public authority' for the purposes of FOI(S)A s 3, Sch 1: see also the Scotland Act 1998, ss 29–30, Sch 5, Pt II, s.B13.

[19]   See also n 14.

[20]   MoJ, *Exemptions Guidance—Section 37*, undated, Pt 1, para 1.3 states that the Royal Household 'should generally be taken to include those individuals who are authorised to act on behalf of a member of the Royal Family (eg their employees, servants or agents) in fulfilling of [sic] public, official and constitutional roles'. The same passage continues: 'It will clearly include members of the Private Offices of members of the Royal Family. Contractors who supply goods and services to the Royal Household (such as holders of royal warrants) do not form part of the Royal Household. In cases of doubt, Departments should consult the private office of the member of the Royal Family to determine the precise role performed by the individual concerned when he or she was in communication with the Department.' Information Commissioner, *Freedom of Information Act Awareness Guidance No 26: Communications with Her Majesty and the Awarding of Honours*, (2006), Pt B states, 'The Royal Household comprises all the Households of members of the Royal Family. Each Household comprises the permanent members of the relevant private office and those who from time to time assist members of the Royal Family with their private and public duties. Contractors supplying goods and services to the Royal Household, including by royal warrant are not included.'

[21]   The respective heads of these five departments are: the Private Secretary (constitutional, official and political matters and media relations); the Keeper of the Privy Purse (financial, personnel, property and revenue matters and the management of the Civil List); the Master of the Household (domestic, hospitality and staff matters); the Comptroller (ceremonial and formal matters); and the Director of the Royal Collection (co-ordinating the work of the Surveyor of the Queen's Pictures, the Surveyor of the Queen's Works of Art and the Royal Librarian). The five heads of department meet under the chairmanship of the Lord Chamberlain as the Lord Chamberlain's Committee. The Private Secretary is also a Privy Counsellor: O Hood Phillips and P Jackson, *Constitutional and Administrative Law*, 8th edn (London, Sweet & Maxwell, 2001) para 14–011. The Royal Household also includes the Great Officers of State (eg the Earl Marshal and the Lord Great Chamberlain), other ancient officers together with numerous other domestic servants and staff who work for or on behalf of the Royal Family (eg ladies-in-waiting and footmen).

of Information Act 2000, the precise boundaries of that organisation may depend upon questions of fact in the circumstances of each case.[22] Furthermore, s 37(1)(a) of the Freedom of Information Act 2000 only exempts information relating to communications 'with the Royal Household' (and not communications with its members) so that the exemption only applies to communications with Household members if and in so far as they were acting in their official capacity in relation to the relevant communication.[23] A possible complication could arise in this regard out of the fact that certain officers of the Household are *ex-officio* government whips who continue to be appointed on a political basis at the nomination of the Prime Minister.[24]

006 Communications with the Royal Family and Household

The reference in s 37(1)(a) of the Freedom of Information Act 2000 to 'communications with' a member of the Royal Family or the Royal Household is broad enough to encompass all manner of written and oral transmissions and exchanges of information whether conducted directly or indirectly and whether passing from or to the Royal side.[25] The exemption in s 37(1)(a) of the Freedom of Information Act 2000 also applies irrespective of whether the public authority which holds the requested information, or indeed any public authority, is or was involved in or party to the communication in question. Information regarding the fact of such communications, details of the 'when, where, how, why, by whom, to whom' kind and the content of the information communicated can all 'relate to' those communications and so the

---

[22] For example, Royal Collection Enterprises Limited is a trading subsidiary of the Royal Collection Trust which in turn funds the activities of the Royal Collection Department within the Royal Household. To this end, Royal Collection Enterprises Limited manages public access to certain castles and palaces, connected shops and certain image and intellectual property rights. The Keeper of the Privy Purse is Chairman of Royal Collection Enterprises Limited. The Director of the Royal Collection is responsible for its day-to-day operation but the company has its own Managing Director. It will be a question of fact in each case whether a particular communication with someone working for or on behalf of Royal Collection Enterprises Limited constitutes a communication with the Royal Household for the purposes of FOIA s 37(1)(a). Although each Royal Household is formally dissolved upon the death of its monarch (signified by the symbolic breaking of the Lord Chamberlain's staff over the grave of the deceased monarch), information relating to prior communications with that Household may nevertheless benefit from the exemption in FOIA s 37(1)(a). See also n 14.

[23] Any information relating to a letter sent by Her Majesty is exempt under FOIA s 37(1)(a), but information relating to a private letter sent by someone who happens to be a member of Her Household is not, unless sent on behalf of the Royal Household and in the course of their official duties.

[24] These are the Treasurer, Comptroller and Vice-Chamberlain of Her Majesty's Household in the House of Commons and the Captain of the Honourable Corps of the Gentlemen-at-Arms, the Captain of the Queen's Bodyguard of the Yeomen of the Guard and up to five Lords and/or Baronesses in Waiting in the House of Lords: *Halsbury's Laws of England*, 4th edn, 1996 re-issue, vol 8(2), title 'Constitutional Law and Human Rights', para 546; O Hood Phillips and P Jackson, *Constitutional and Administrative Law*, 8th edn (London, Sweet & Maxwell, 2001) para 10–024. Strictly speaking, these whips are members of the Royal Household and it could be argued that information relating to communications with them is subject to FOIA s 37(1)(a). However, they are paid their salaries out of money provided by Parliament as part of the expenses of the Treasury and the argument that communications with them should be regarded as 'communications with the Royal Household' for the purposes of FOIA s 37(1)(a) is therefore weak: Ministerial and other Salaries Act 1975 s 3(1)(a) and (b), Sch 1 Pts IV and V para 2(f). MoJ, *Exemptions Guidance—Section 37*, undated, Pt 1 para 1.4 acknowledges that there is an issue here and states in relation to the relevant offices, 'Their activities as government whips are not covered by this exemption.'

[25] Such information could take the form of answers, assertions, claims, demands, ideas, messages, offers, opinions, propositions, questions, requests, responses or warnings and could be exchanged or transmitted by way of conversation, correspondence or discussion and on any basis ranging from one-off unilateral notification to fully inter-active dialogue. The choice of 'communications with' over 'communications between' leaves more room for the inclusion of one-sided or passive transmissions and exchanges. In this regard, the use of 'communications' in the plural should not be seen as requiring a sequence or series of communications — Interpretation Act 1978 s 6(c): 'words in the plural include the singular.'

exemption is of potentially broad application. However, it is also important to recognise its limitations: the exemption does not extend as far as all information directly or indirectly supplied by or relating to the Royal Family or the Royal Household;[26] it does not exempt information about the Royal Family or the Royal Household per se; and the precise meaning and limits of the expression 'communications with' will need to be established on a case-by-case basis. So far as the last point is concerned, it might be said that communicating 'with' someone requires that they be engaged to some degree so that unsuccessful or incomplete transmissions of information (eg a letter that is sent but recalled or not understood) do not count. Questions may also arise as to whether the copying or side-copying of documents to members of the Royal Family or the Royal Household necessarily entails any 'communication with' the relevant copy recipients.

26–007 Communications with the Royal Family and Household: the public interest

As the exemption conferred by s 37(1)(a) of the Freedom of Information Act 2000 is a qualified exemption, it is implicit that some information relating to communications with Her Majesty or with other members of the Royal Family or with the Royal Household is to be disclosed under the Freedom of Information Act 2000.[27] The task of weighing the public interest in maintaining an exemption that is purely class based (in other words, that does not have some type of prejudice as one of its composite elements) is always difficult. The task is particularly difficult where, as in s 37(1), the exemption does not reflect a well-understood proscription against disclosure: for example, safeguarding national security, legal professional privilege, trade secrets and so forth. Whereas in the latter cases it is always possible to assess the extent to which exemption is required in order to protect against that well-recognised harm, there is no such familiar protection to be secured by s 37(1), leaving the weighing exercise particularly prone to idiosyncratic views of the underlying public interest perceived to be protected by the exemption. With this caveat, it is suggested that the strength of the public interest in maintaining the exclusion of the duty to confirm or deny the existence of, or the duty to communicate, information relating to communications with members of the Royal Family or with the Royal Household will depend on the nature and public importance of that information. The monarch performs a number of important constitutional, legal and political functions and maintains open lines of communication with Parliament and the government at the highest level at all times. Members of the Royal Family more generally fulfil other public and official functions and are the recipients of public funds in return. The nature and content of their interactions with the outside world when they are acting in a public capacity and at public expense may therefore be of considerable public interest and the countervailing factors favouring non-disclosure will turn largely on the extent to which exposure to public scrutiny would prejudice the effective working of the Royal Family and the Royal Household given their status and importance.[28] Where communications have taken place with members of the Royal

---

[26] Compare FOIA s 23 on information directly or indirectly supplied by or relating to any of the security bodies: see n 14 and §§17–033 to 17–038.

[27] See §15–011.

[28] MoJ, *Exemptions Guidance—Section 37*, undated, Pt 1, paras 3.3-3.8 place particular emphasis on the confidentiality of communications with the Sovereign and the heir to the throne. See para 3.3: 'It is a fundamental constitutional principle that communications between the Queen and her Ministers and other public bodies are essentially confidential in nature and there is therefore a fundamental public interest in withholding information relating to

Family acting in their private capacities, however, the public interest in disclosure may be less strong and the legitimate interest in ensuring their privacy and dignity will acquire more force.

2. HONOURS AND DIGNITIES*

008 Introduction

By virtue of s 37(1)(b) of the Freedom of Information Act 2000, information that relates to the conferring by the Crown of any honour or dignity is exempt information.[29] Similarly, the duty to confirm or deny does not arise in relation to such information.[30] Both the exemption and the exclusion are qualified.[31] Accordingly, even if information is exempt under this provision, the public authority holding that information must disclose it unless the public interest in maintaining the exemption outweighs the public interest in disclosing the information.[32] There is no equivalent exception in the Environmental Information Regulations 2004. Accordingly, where (or to the extent that) information that answers the terms of a request for information is 'environmental information',[33] the fact that that information also relates to the conferring by the Crown of any honour or dignity will not excuse the public authority from complying with the request.[34]

009 Background

The *Code of Practice on Access to Government Information* contained a similar, but narrower, exemption for 'information, opinions and assessments given in relation to recommendations for honours'.[35] The accompanying *Guidance on Interpretation* stated that the exemption was aimed

---

such communications. That is so because the Sovereign has the right and the duty to counsel, encourage and warn her government. She is thus entitled to have opinions on government policy and to express them to her ministers. She is, however, constitutionally bound to accept and act on the advice of her ministers. Any communications which have preceded the giving of that advice remain confidential, because of the need to maintain the political neutrality of the Queen in public affairs (its reality and appearance); this itself is fundamental to the UK system of constitutional monarchy.' See also Information Commissioner, *Freedom of Information Act Awareness Guidance No 26: Communications with Her Majesty and the Awarding of Honours*, (2006), Pt B(b).

* By Oliver Sanders, 1 Crown Office Row.

[29] FOI(S)A s 41 is identically worded save that reference is made to 'the exercise by Her Majesty of Her prerogative of honour' (FOI(S)A s 41(a)) instead of 'the conferring by the Crown of any honour or dignity' (FOIA s 37(1)(b)): see §26– 013.

[30] FOIA s 37(2). There is no discrete duty to confirm or deny under FOI(S)A.

[31] FOIA s 2(3); FOI(S)A s 2(2).

[32] Similarly, the duty to confirm or deny. FOIA s 37(1) and (2) engage s 2(2)(b) and (1)(b) respectively so as to prevent from arising, first, the duty to confirm or deny and, secondly, the duty to communicate, if the public interest in divulgence or disclosure (respectively) is outweighed. Information cannot be exempt information by virtue of s 37(1)(b) after the end of the period of 60 years beginning with the year following that in which the record containing the information was created: FOIA s 63(3).

[33] As to the meaning of which, see §6– 010.

[34] FOIA s 39; FOI(S)A s 39.

[35] *Open Government Code of Practice on Access to Government Information*, 2nd edn (1997) Pt II, para 8c. The exemption did not refer to harm or prejudice and it was not therefore subject to any balancing exercise weighing the public interest in disclosure against the public interest in non-disclosure: see Pt II.

at ensuring frankness, candour and honesty in the honours recommendation and selection process.[36] More long-standing restrictions have prevented parliamentary questions being asked of ministers regarding the granting of honours.[37] The relevant exemptions in the draft Freedom of Information Bill published on 24 May 1999[38] and the Freedom of Information Bill introduced in the House of Commons on 18 November 1999[39] were identically worded. The only difference between these provisions and s 37(1) of the Freedom of Information Act 2000 is the additional inclusion in the latter of a reference to the conferring by the Crown of dignities as well as honours.[40]

26–010 Honours and dignities

There is an important distinction between honours and dignities which is maintained in numerous statutes.[41] Reference has already been made to the inclusion in s 37(1)(b) of the Freedom of Information Act 2000 of the reference to dignities (as well as honours) which was specifically achieved by way of amendment to the Freedom of Information Bill.[42] Awards, decorations and medals for bravery, gallantry, heroism and public service in the civilian and military spheres, the civic styles 'lord mayor', 'deputy lord mayor' and 'right honourable' and

---

[36] *Open Government Code of Practice on Access to Government Information: Guidance on Interpretation*, 2nd edn (1997) Pt II, paras 8.9–8.12. Paragraph 8.12 states that the exemption for information, opinions and assessments given in relation to recommendations for honours 'links in with' the restriction on the matters subject to investigation by the Parliamentary Commissioner for Administration in the Parliamentary Commissioner for Administration Act 1967 s 5 Sch 4 para 11: 'the grant of honours, awards or privileges within the gift of the Crown, including the grant of Royal Charters.'

[37] W McKay (ed), *Erskine May's treatise on the law, privileges, proceedings and usage of Parliament*, 23rd edn (London, Butterworths, 2004) p 298. The *White Paper on Open Government* (Cm 2290, 1993) did not offer any additional commentary upon the exemptions which eventually found expression in the *Open Government Code of Practice on Access to Government Information*, 2nd edn (1997) Pt II, para 8c.

[38] *Freedom of Information: Consultation on Draft Legislation* (Cm 4355, 1999) Pt II, cl 29(1).

[39] Clause 35(1).

[40] FOIA s 37(1)(b). The words 'or dignity' were inserted pursuant to a government amendment moved by Lord Falconer of Thoroton at Committee Stage in the House of Lords: Hansard HL vol 618 col 315 (24 October 2000). The amendment was described as 'merely clarificatory' and explained as follows: 'The term "dignity" refers to peerages, and the amendment ensures that the exemption applies to the granting of peerages as well as meritorious awards' — Hansard HL vol 618 col 315 (24 October 2000). Compare FOI(S)A s 41(a).

[41] For example, Honours (Prevention of Abuses) Act 1925 s 1; Legitimation (Scotland) Act 1968 s 8; Adoption Act 1976 s 44; Legitimacy Act 1976 Sch 1, paras 3–4; Race Relations Act 1976 s 76; Law Reform (Parent And Child) (Scotland) Act 1986 s 9; Family Law Reform Act 1987 ss 19 and 27; Human Fertilisation And Embryology Act 1990 s 29; Private International Law (Miscellaneous Provisions) Act 1995 s 6; Scotland Act 1998 s 30, Sch 5, para 2(3); Northern Ireland Act 1998 s 4, Sch 2, para 6; Adoption and Children Act 2002 s 71. It is notable that FOI(S)A s 41 refers to 'the exercise by Her Majesty of Her prerogative of honour' without mentioning the conferring of dignities.

[42] See §26–009. FOIA also amended DPA so as to exempt personal data processed for the purposes of the conferring of any dignity (as well as any honour) from the subject information provisions in that Act: DPA Sch7, para 3 as amended by FOIA s 73, Sch 6, para 6 (this amendment having come into force on 14 May 2001 under FOIA s 87(3) and the Freedom of Information Act 2000 (Commencement No 1) Order 2001 SI 2001/1637 art 2(d)). FOIA s 73, Sch 6, para 6 was itself inserted into the Freedom of Information Bill by way of amendment at the same time as the words 'or dignity' were added to what became s 31(1)(b) in order to ensure 'that the corresponding provision in the Data Protection Act is similarly amended.' — Hansard HL vol 618 col 315 (24 October 2000).

civic status as a city or royal borough are all conferred under the prerogative of honour.[43] Peerages, baronetcies, knighthoods, arms and precedence are conferred as dignities.[44] Appointment by the Crown as a Privy Counsellor or Queen's Counsel also carries with it certain consequences in terms of precedence and the right to use (as appropriate) the style 'right honourable' or the post-nominal initials 'QC'.[45] While the office of Queen's Counsel would not appear to constitute an honour or dignity as such, it has been suggested that the office of Privy Counsellor does constitute an honour.[46] That peerages are a type of dignity is probably the most important point to note here because, at least for the time being, the conferral of a life peerage carries with it the right to sit and vote in the House of Lords.[47] Whether the link

---

[43] *Prince's Case* (1606) 8 Co Rep 1a at 18b, 4 Co Inst 361 at 363, 1 Bl Com (14th edn) 271; *Halsbury's Laws of England*, 4th edn, 1996 re-issue, vol 8(2), title 'Constitutional Law and Human Rights', paras 831, 834; *Halsbury's Laws of England*, 4th edn, 1994 re-issue, vol 35, title 'Peerages and Dignities', para 969. Examples are the Victoria Cross, the Order of Victoria and Albert, the Albert Medal, the George Cross, the Imperial Order of the Crown of India, the Royal Red Cross, the Distinguished Service Order, the Order of Merit, the Imperial Service Order, the Edward Medal, the Territorial Decoration, the Order of the Companions of Honour and the Order of the British Empire. It is arguable whether the grant of borough status by royal charter under the Local Government Act 1972 ss 245–245A amounts to the conferring by the Crown of an honour for the purposes of FOIA s 37(1)(b).

[44] *Halsbury's Laws of England*, 5th edn, 2008, vol 79, title 'Peerages and Dignities', para 801. The right to bear arms is a dignity but the Crown's power to grant armorial bearings to individuals is delegated to the Kings of Arms: *Manchester Corporation v Manchester Palace of Varieties Ltd* [1955] P 133 at 147 (Lord Goddard) (Court of Chivalry); *Halsbury's Laws of England*, 5th edn, 2008, vol 79, title 'Peerages and Dignities', paras 801, 870-875. Arms are therefore not conferred on individuals 'by the Crown' for the purposes of FOIA s 37(1)(b). The position in relation to the conferring of arms on local authorities is more complicated: the power of grant was historically exercised by the Royal College of Arms (*Halsbury's Laws of England*, 5th edn, 2009, vol 69, title 'Local Government', para 112); but Her Majesty may by Order in Council authorise a new local authority to bear and use specified armorial bearings in certain circumstances under the Local Government Act 1972 s 247 and such grants arguably amount to the conferring 'by the Crown' of a dignity for the purposes of FOIA s 37(1)(b) (eg the Local Authorities (Armorial Bearings) Order 2006 SI 2006/3330). MoJ, *Exemptions Guidance—Section 37*, undated, Pt 2, para 2.2 states that 'some Crown appointments (both secular and ecclesiastical) will come within the category of 'honour or dignity' and so will come within this section. For example, some senior Church appointments (the appointment of archbishops, diocesan bishops, suffragan bishops, deans of cathedrals, deans and canons of the two Royal Peculiars and the First and Second Church Estates Commissioners) are dignities and so will fall within this section' (see also para 3.6).

[45] *Halsbury's Laws of England*, 4th edn, 1996 re-issue, vol 8(2), title 'Constitutional Law and Human Rights', paras 521–522 and 524; *Halsbury's Laws of England*, 5th edn, 2009, title 'Legal Professions', para 1124.

[46] See, eg A Bradley and K Ewing, *Constitutional and Administrative Law*, 14th edn (London, Pearson Longman, 2007) p 253 where membership of the Privy Council is described as a 'titular honour' and it is recorded that,'[T]he office is a recognised reward for public and political service, and appointments to it figure in the honours lists.' As to Queen's Counsel, see DPA s 37, Sch 7, para 3(a) and note the inclusion of honours and dignities in DPA s 37, Sch 7, para 3(b). MoJ, *Exemptions Guidance—Section 37*, undated, Pt 2, paras 2.1 and 2.3–2.4 exclude appointment to Queen's Counsel but include information relating to 'appointments to the Privy Council' (but not the Judicial Committee to the Privy Council) as covered by FOIA s 37(1)(b). See also Information Commissioner, *Freedom of Information Act Awareness Guidance No 26: Communications with Her Majesty and the Awarding of Honours*, (2006), Pt C.

[47] *Norfolk Earldom Case* [1907] AC 10 HL (Committee for Privileges); *Wensleydale Peerage Case* (1856) 5 HLC 958 HL (Committee for Privileges); LJ 38; Life Peerages Act 1958 s 1(2)(b); *Halsbury's Laws of England*, 5th edn, 2008, vol 79, title 'Peerages and Dignities', para 824; House of Lords Act 1999. The House of Lords currently comprises the Lords Spiritual and the Lords Temporal. All of the Lords Temporal are entitled to sit and vote in the House of Lords by virtue of the conferring by the Crown of a dignity (ie their peerage) while the Lords Spiritual are not because, while they are Lords of Parliament, they are not peers as such: *Halsbury's Laws of England*, 5th edn, 2010, vol 78, title 'Parliament', para 832; W McKay (ed), *Erskine May's treatise on the law, privileges, proceedings and usage of Parliament*, 23rd edn (London, Butterworths, 2004) p 12; O Hood Phillips and P Jackson, *Constitutional and Administrative Law*, 8th edn (London, Sweet & Maxwell, 2001) p 176, n 19; and *Standing Orders of the House of Lords Relating to Public Business* (HL 147) 2007, No 6. For these purposes, the Lords Spiritual are the archbishops and certain bishops of the Church of England and the Lords Temporal are life peers created under the Life Peerages Act 1958, Lords of Appeal in Ordinary created peers for life under the Appellate Jurisdiction Act 1876 and 92 hereditary peers given continued membership of the House of Lords under the House of Lords Act 1999 and

between peerages and membership of the House of Lords will survive further reform remains open to question.[48]

26– 011 The conferring by the Crown of any honour or dignity

The monarch is the fountain of all honour and dignity and enjoys the sole right of conferring all titles of honour and dignities.[49] By convention the monarch's powers in relation to titles of honour and dignities are exercised on the advice of the Prime Minister.[50] In relation to honours conferred on individuals for non-political reasons, a body known as the Main Honours Advisory Committee makes recommendations to the monarch via the Prime Minister.[51] In

---

relevant standing orders: *Halsbury's Laws of England*, 5th edn, 2010, vol 78, title 'Parliament', paras 834-843; *Halsbury's Laws of England*, 4th edn, 2002 re-issue, vol 10, title 'Courts', para 352. Since the implementation of the House of Lords Act 1999, only the following 92 members of the House of Lords have been hereditary peers: 75 elected under that Act either by their own political party's hereditary peers or cross-bench grouping in proportion to that party or grouping's share of the hereditary peers, 15 elected under that Act by the House as a whole to act as Deputy Speakers or Committee Chairmen plus the hereditary Royal appointments of Earl Marshal and the Lord Great Chamberlain.

[48] See: Report of the Royal Commission on the Reform of the House of Lords, *A House for the Future* (Cm 4534, 2000); Lord Chancellor's Department, *The House of Lords: Completing the Reform* (Cm 5291, 2001) paras 78–79 proposing to break the link; Department for Constitutional Affairs, *Constitutional Reform: Next Steps for the House of Lords* (CP 14/03), 2003, paras 21 and 24–28 abandoning the plan to break the link; and HM Government, *The House of Lords: Reform* (Cm 7027, 2007) paras 1.12, 1.15 and 9.36 reinstating the plan to break the link. However, note that the House of Commons and House of Lords came to different conclusions as to the appropriate composition of a reformed second chamber of Parliament in free votes on 7 March 2007 and 14 March 2007 respectively (see Hansard HC vol 457 col 1390 *et seq* (6 March 2007) and col 1524 *et seq* (7 March 2007) and Hansard HL vol 690 col 451 *et seq* (12 March 2007), col 571 *et seq* (13 March 2007) and col 741 *et seq* (14 March 2007). These votes were followed by a further White Paper (MoJ, *An Elected Second Chamber: Further Reform of the House of Lords* (Cm 7438, 2008)) and a response from the House of Commons Public Administration Select Committee (Fifth Report of Session 2008-09, *Response to White Paper: 'An Elected Second Chamber'* (HC 137)), but a clear consensus has yet to emerge.

[49] *Prince's Case* (1606) 8 Co Rep 1a at 18b, 4 Co Inst 361, 363, 1 Bl Com (14th edn) 271; *Halsbury's Laws of England*, 4th edn, 1996 re-issue, vol 8(2), title 'Constitutional Law and Human Rights', para 831; *Halsbury's Laws of England*, 5th edn, 2009, vol 69, title 'Local Government', para 107; *Halsbury's Laws of England*, 5th edn, 2008, vol 79, title 'Peerages and Dignities', paras 801; O Hood Phillips and P Jackson, *Constitutional and Administrative Law*, 8th edn (London, Sweet & Maxwell, 2001) para 15–015(f).

[50] However, the monarch reserves absolute discretion in conferring the Order of Merit, the Order of the Garter, the Order of the Thistle and the Royal Victorian Order: *Halsbury's Laws of England*, 4th edn, 1996 re-issue, vol 8(2), title 'Constitutional Law and Human Rights', paras 831–832. Thus Elizabeth II made the Governor of Southern Rhodesia a KCVO at the time of the Unilateral Declaration of Independence in November 1965: O Hood Phillips and P Jackson, *Constitutional and Administrative Law*, 8th edn (London, Sweet & Maxwell, 2001) p 316, n 4.

[51] The Main Honours Advisory Committee was established in its current form as a non-departmental public body in October 2005 as part of the programme of reform set out in Cabinet Office, *Reform of the Honours System* (Cm 6479, 2005). See also: Public Administration Select Committee, Fifth Report of Session 2003–04, *A Matter of Honour: Reforming the Honours System* (HC 212–I) 2004; Sir Hayden Phillips, *Review of the Honours System* (2004); Public Administration Select Committee, Second Report of Session 2007-08, *Propriety and Peerages* (HC 153); and Cabinet Office, *Three Years of Operation of the Reformed Honours System* (2008). The Main Committee reviews the work of eight specialist Sub-Committees covering the subject areas: Arts and Media; Sport; Health; Education; Science and Technology; the Economy; Community, Voluntary and Local Services; and State. The former Honours Scrutiny Committee, established in 1923, was wound up with effect from 31 March 2005 (Cabinet Office, *Public Bodies 2006* (2006), p 330). See: *Report of the Royal Commission on Honours* (Cmd 1789, 1922) paras 24–28; 57 HL Official Report (5th series) 26 June 1924, col 1068; *Halsbury's Laws of England*, 4th edn, 1996 re-issue, vol 8(2), title 'Constitutional Law and Human Rights', paras 526, 832; O Hood Phillips and P Jackson, *Constitutional and Administrative Law*, 8th edn (London, Sweet & Maxwell, 2001) para 15–015(f). The Honours Scrutiny Committee was originally named the Political Honours Scrutiny Committee before being renamed in 2002 pursuant to a recommendation made in Committee on Standards in Public Life, Fifth Report *Standards in Public Life* (Cm 4057, 1998) pp 14 and 193, R100. Despite its abolition, the Political Honours Scrutiny Committee remains listed as a public authority in FOIA Sch 1.

relation to peerages and party-political honours, an independent House of Lords Appointments Commission recommends non-party-political persons for cross-bench life peerages and scrutinises the propriety and suitability of all nominations, first, to life peerages including those put forward by the political parties (excluding peers appointed to take on ministerial responsibility) and, secondly, for party-political and other honours proposed independently of the Main Honours Advisory Committee system.[52] Both the Political Honours Scrutiny Committee (now abolished) and the House of Lords Appointments Commission are listed as 'public authorities' in Sch 1 to the Freedom of Information Act 2000.[53] Titles of honour are conferred by express grant in the form of letters patent and dignities are conferred by writ of summons in the case of peerages, by letters patent in the case of baronetcies and some knighthoods, by direct corporeal investiture in the case of most knighthoods or by warrants of precedence.[54] The expression 'the conferring by the Crown' in s 37(1)(b) of the Freedom of Information Act 2000 raises questions as to how far the exemption captures information relating to the earlier selection and recommendation process which precedes formal conferral by the Crown itself as well as information relating to non-conferral where a candidate is rejected, for whatever reasons, by the Crown or by those involved lower down. A Forfeiture Committee, comprising the Cabinet Secretary, Treasury Solicitor and the Permanent Secretaries to the Home Office and the Scottish Executive, makes recommendations on the cancellation of honours in the case of recipients convicted of criminal offences and it is likewise open to question whether related information is exempt under s 37(1)(b) the Freedom of Information Act 2000.[55]

012 The conferring by the Crown of any honour or dignity: the public interest
The particular difficulties affecting the public interest so far as s 37(1) of the Freedom of Information Act 2000 is concerned have already been considered in relation to s 37(1)(a), and

---

[52] The House of Lords Appointments Commission is an advisory non-departmental public body established by the Prime Minister on 4 May 2000 on a non-statutory basis pursuant to proposals set out in the government White Paper *Modernising Parliament: Reforming the House of Lords* (Cm 4183, 1999) ch 6, paras 9–14. According to Cabinet Office, *Public Bodies 2006* (2006), p 4, the Commission's terms of reference are, 'To make recommendations on the appointment of non-party-political peers. The Commission also vets for propriety all nominations for life peerages, including those made by the political parties, and all individuals added to honours lists by the Prime Minister'. In relation to cross-bench life peerages, the Prime Minister invites a fixed number of recommendations from the Commission and passes these on to Her Majesty for approval 'except in the most exceptional of circumstances'. The Commission acquired its functions relating to honours in April 2005 pursuant to the reforms set out in Cabinet Office, *Reform of the Honours System* (Cm 6479, 2005). The significance of this is likely to diminish following the Prime Minister's announcement in March 2006 that he will no longer add his own names to the twice yearly honours lists (Public Administration Select Committee, Fourth Report of Session 2005–06, *Propriety and Honours: Interim Findings* (HC 1119) 2006, paras 12–14). See also: O Hood Phillips and P Jackson, *Constitutional and Administrative Law*, 8th edn (London, Sweet & Maxwell, 2001) para 9–011; Report of the Royal Commission on the Reform of the House of Lords, *A House for the Future* (Cm 4534, 2000); Lord Chancellor's Department, *The House of Lords: Completing the Reform* (Cm 5291, 2001) paras 65–68; Department for Constitutional Affairs, *Constitutional Reform: Next Steps for the House of Lords* (CP 14/03), 2003, paras 29–43 and 53–60; Public Administration Select Committee, Fourth Report of Session 2005–06, *Propriety and Honours: Interim Findings* (HC 1119) 2006, paras 50–53; and HM Government, *The House of Lords: Reform* (Cm 7027, 2007) paras 8.11–8.20.

[53] FOIA s 3 Sch 1 Pt VI.

[54] Bl Com (14th edn) 272; *Halsbury's Laws of England*, 4th edn, 1996 re-issue, vol 8(2), title 'Constitutional Law and Human Rights', para 831; *Halsbury's Laws of England*, 5th edn, 2008, vol 79, title 'Peerages and Dignities', paras 814–815, 821–822, 829, 861 and 865; the Life Peerages Act 1958 s 1.

[55] FOIA s 37(1)(a) may still be relevant in any event.

these are equally applicable to s 37(1)(b).[56] While the conferring of honours and dignities is undoubtedly a matter of public interest,[57] it does not often carry any great practical consequences in legal, political or constitutional terms and the selection process often involves an evaluative assessment of personal information and the exercise of a very broad discretion. A public interest in maintaining the exclusion of the duty to communicate related information may therefore arise out of the need to protect confidences and to ensure frankness, candour and honesty in the recommendation and selection process[58] and the need to protect the feelings and privacy of those considered and their families particularly where it has been decided not to confer an honour.[59] A public interest in maintaining the exclusion of the duty to confirm or deny may also arise out of the same considerations, although this is less likely to be the case in circumstances where an honour or dignity *has* been conferred. So far as concerns information relating to the conferring of honours and most dignities (other than life peerages) on individuals, the public interest balance may therefore be thought normally to weigh in favour of non-disclosure rather than disclosure. The public interest balance may, however, be more likely to shift in favour of disclosure in relation to the conferring of honours on corporations or groups of people (where questions of privacy and personal distress are less likely to arise)[60] and in relation to the conferring of life peerages (where receipt of the dignity carries with it important consequences in terms of the right to sit and vote in Parliament and eligibility for ministerial office).[61]

26–013 Communications with Her Majesty, etc and honours: the Freedom of Information (Scotland) Act 2002

Section 41 of the Freedom of Information (Scotland) Act 2002 is the Scottish equivalent of s 37

---

[56] See §26–007.

[57] The public interest in the fairness and transparency of the honours system has long been recognised: *Report of the Royal Commission on Honours* (Cmd 1789, 1922) paras 24–28; 57 HL Official Report (5th series) June 26, 1924, col 1068; the Honours (Prevention of Abuses) Act 1925. The public interest in the conferring of both honours and dignities more generally is also implicitly recognised by the inclusion of the Political Honours Scrutiny Committee (now abolished) and the House of Lords Appointments Commission in FOIA Sch 1, Pt VI as 'public authorities'.

[58] See §26–009 and *Open Government Code of Practice on Access to Government Information: Guidance on Interpretation*, 2nd edn (1997) Pt II, paras 8.9–8.12 on the equivalent exemption in the Open Government Code of Practice on Access to Government Information, 2nd edn (1997) Pt II, para 8c. The exemptions for personal and confidential information in FOIA ss 40–41 would protect a certain amount of personal information in any event.

[59] See the remarks made by Lord Falconer of Thoroton at Committee Stage in the House of Lords in connection with a proposed government amendment to the relevant clause in the Freedom of Information Bill: 'The conferring of honours raises questions of personal confidentiality and the government believes that it should receive substantial protection under the Bill. The conferring of honours raises such questions not just in relation to the candidates for honours themselves and members of their families, but also in relation to those who contribute to the process of selection. Questions of confidentiality can arise just as easily in regard to posthumous awards. It will be obviously embarrassing, and potentially distressing, for surviving relatives to discover that the deceased was considered but rejected for an honour' — Hansard HL vol 618 col 315 (24 October 2000).

[60] For example, the conferring of city or royal borough status on a local authority, the award of the George Cross to 'the Island Fortress of Malta' by George VI on 15 April 1942 and the award of the George Cross to the Royal Ulster Constabulary by Elizabeth II on 23 November 1999. Where a local authority has applied for and been refused city status it may well want to disclose information relating to its application in order to show it put forward the best case possible and in such cases it may make voluntary disclosure regardless of FOIA s 37(1)(b).

[61] The greater 'constitutional significance' of peerages (which ought to represent appointments for future service) when compared with honours (which reflect past achievement) was emphasised throughout Public Administration Select Committee, Second Report of Session 2007-08, *Propriety and Peerages* (HC 153) (see paras 19, 35 and 39).

of the Freedom of Information Act 2000 and, as mentioned above, it follows the wording of its Westminster counterpart save that reference is made to 'the exercise by Her Majesty of Her prerogative of honour' instead of 'the conferring by the Crown of any honour or dignity'.[62] Information held by Scottish public authorities which relates to the conferring by the Crown of any dignity will not therefore be exempt under the terms of s 41(b) of the Freedom of Information (Scotland) Act 2002. The only way of avoiding this conclusion is to argue that the conferring of dignities is an 'exercise by Her Majesty of Her prerogative of honour' but this is not a particularly persuasive proposition given the distinction drawn between honours and dignities elsewhere. The different approach in s 41(b) of the Freedom of Information (Scotland) Act 2002 also raises two other questions which may lead to different results under the two regimes: first, whether there are any honours which may be conferred by the Crown other than in the exercise of Her prerogative of honour; and, secondly, whether there is any difference between the amount and type of honours-related information capable of 'relating to' the conferring by the Crown of any honour or dignity, on the one hand, and the exercise by Her Majesty of Her prerogative of honour, on the other.

014 Communications with Her Majesty, etc and honours: the Data Protection Act 1998

The Data Protection Act 1998 binds the Crown and contains special provision for its application to the Royal Household, the Duchy of Lancaster and the Duchy of Cornwall.[63] Personal data processed for the purposes of the conferring by the Crown of any honour or dignity are also exempt from the subject information provisions in the Data Protection Act 1998.[64]

3. PROHIBITIONS ON DISCLOSURE

015 Introduction

By s 44(1) of the Freedom of Information Act 2000 information is exempt from the disclosure

---

[62] It might be argued that FOI(S)A is outside the legislative competence of the Scottish Parliament to the extent that it confers a qualified entitlement (subject to a public interest override) to information about honours and a general entitlement to information about dignities because the Scottish Parliament cannot enact provisions which 'relate to' 'reserved matters' (Scotland Act 1998 ss 28–30; 'honours and dignities' are defined as 'reserved matters' by the Scotland Act 1998 s 30, Sch 5, paras 1, 2(3)). This is not a strong argument for a number of reasons. First, FOI(S)A does not obviously contain any provisions which 'relate to' the conferring of honours or dignities when the expression 'relates to' is read in accordance with the Scotland Act 1998 s 29(3). Secondly, if and in so far as Scottish public authorities hold information about honours and dignities, it would be odd if the Scottish Parliament were unable to regulate public access to it particularly when FOIA regulates public access to such information when held by other (non-Scottish) public authorities. Thirdly, the proviso to the Scotland Act 1998 Sch 5 Pt II, s.B13 would appear to envisage legislation along the lines of FOI(S)A.

[63] DPA s 63(3) provides: where the purposes for which and the manner in which any personal data are, or are to be, processed are determined by, inter alia, any person acting on behalf of the Royal Household, the data controller in respect of those data for the purposes of that Act shall be the Keeper of the Privy Purse. The Keeper of the Privy Purse is not liable to prosecution under DPA but the criminal offence and liability provisions in s 55 and Sch 9, para 12 do apply to persons in the service of the Crown as they apply to any other person (DPA s 63(5)).

[64] DPA s 37 Sch 7 para 3(b) as amended by FOIA s 73 Sch 6, para 6 (this amendment having come into force on 14 May 2001 under FOIA s 87(3) and the FOIA (Commencement No 1) Order 2001SI 2001/1637 art 2(d)).

obligation in s 1(1)(b) 'if its disclosure (otherwise than under [the Act itself]) by the public authority holding it (a) is prohibited by or under any enactment, (b) is incompatible with any Community obligation or (c) would constitute or be punishable as a contempt of court.' The exemption is an absolute one, so that no question of weighing competing public interests arises.[65] The duty to confirm or deny whether the public authority holds information requested provided by s 1(1)(a) of the Act does not arise if compliance with that duty would fall within any of paras (a), (b) or (c) above.[66] Section 26 of the Freedom of Information (Scotland) Act 2002 contains a provision in almost identical terms to s 44(1) of the 2000 Act.[67] The basic position under the two Freedom of Information Acts is therefore that existing legal prohibitions on disclosure by the public authority 'trump' any rights given by the Acts and, where such prohibitions apply, not only is there no obligation to disclose under the Acts but there is no discretion to do so either. This is in contrast to the position under the Environmental Information Regulations 2004 which oblige public authorities to disclose 'environmental information' regardless of any enactment or rule of law which would prevent such disclosure[68] and the Data Protection Act 1998, which provides that the 'subject information provisions' have effect notwithstanding any enactment or rule of law prohibiting or restricting the disclosure.[69]

26–016 General difficulties

Before considering separately these three categories of prohibition, it should be noted that although s 44 is on its face fairly straightforward practical difficulties can arise in applying it.[70] In particular, although the section is likely to raise questions of law and issues particularly appropriate for decision by a court, the question whether the requested disclosure would be prohibited by any enactment or would be incompatible with a Community obligation or would constitute a contempt of court falls to be decided in the first instance by the public authority itself; and subsequently, if the applicant pursues the matter further, by the Information Commissioner.[71] It is only at the stage of the Tribunal[72] (or, in Scotland, the Court of Session)[73] that the decision-maker will necessarily be legally-qualified and sitting in a judicial capacity. There is also a potential problem in that the decision whether the section applies involves (particularly in relation to contempt of court) a prediction of whether or not something which

---

[65] FOIA s 2(2)(a), 2(3)(h).

[66] FOIA s 2(2)(a), 2(3)(h).

[67] See also FOI(S)A s 2(2)(b); the duty to confirm or deny whether the public authority holds requested information does not arise under the Scottish legislation.

[68] EIR reg 5(6); EI(S)R reg 5(3).

[69] DPA s 27(5). This provision is of benefit only to an applicant if he is the data subject of the information requested since s 7 of the DPA only gives rights to data subjects.

[70] As it appears there were under the original s 38 of the Freedom of Information Act 1982 (Cth of Australia) which contained the corresponding provisions in relation to statutory prohibitions: *News Corp Ltd v National Companies and Securities Commission* (1984) 52 ALR 277; *Kavvadias v Ombudsman (Cth)* (1984) 1 FCR 80, 52 ALR 728; *Federal Commissioner of Taxation v Swiss Aluminium Ltd* (1986) 10 FCR 321.

[71] See §28–006.

[72] See §28–017.

[73] See §28–029.

has not happened would infringe the law. Moreover, the assumed facts on which the prediction must be based are not made entirely clear by the section: thus, it is not made clear to whom, for what purpose and in what circumstances the disclosure whose legality is to be judged would be made (other than that it is otherwise than under the Act). This is in contrast to the position in the corresponding provision dealing with contempt of court under the Australian legislation which refers to 'public disclosure' of the relevant document.[74]

4. PROHIBITIONS BY OR UNDER ENACTMENT

017 Definition of 'enactment'

In its ordinary sense, an 'enactment' is a legal proposition laid down in an Act or other legislative text with the effect that, when facts fall within an indicated area, specified legal consequences follow.[75] It seems clear that the word 'enactment' in section 44 is intended to include any enactment made by subordinate legislation,[76] although the word is not expressly defined in these terms for the purposes of s 44.[77] The relevant enactment can have been passed at any time as long as it prohibits the disclosure of the information at the time the question falls to be considered. It is thus possible in principle for rights under the Freedom of Information Acts to be removed by subordinate legislation made under different primary legislation without the Acts themselves being amended. However, the provision clearly does not cover departmental circulars or codes of practice even if issued under statutory authority; nor does it cover any prohibition on disclosure provided by the common law, whether constituting a crime, tort or breach of contract.[78] However, the exemption applies not only to disclosures which would amount to criminal offences but also to those which are subject to regulatory or civil law enforcement, so long as the prohibition in question arises by virtue of an enactment.

018 Form and content of enactments prohibiting disclosure

There is a vast amount of legislation which potentially prohibits disclosure of information by public authorities.[79] Such legislation covers the whole range of government activities. There

---

[74] Freedom of Information Act 1982 (Cth of Australia) s 46.

[75] This definition is taken from F Bennion, *Statutory Interpretation*, 5th edn (London, LexisNexis, 2008) p 396. As the author notes, the proposition containing the enactment may, as is most usual, be embodied in a single sentence of an Act or other instrument; or it may fall to be collected from two or more sentences, whether consecutive or not. The Interpretation Act 1889 s 35(1) appeared to take the view that an enactment was to be found within a single section or subsection. The provision is not repeated in the Interpretation Act 1978.

[76] This was assumed by the Information Tribunal in *Meunier v Information Commissioner and National Savings & Investments*, IT, 5 June 2007 at [64]–[78].

[77] See: FOIA ss 75(2)(b) and 84; FOI(S)A ss 46(2) and 73.

[78] Such disclosures may well be covered by another exemption (for example, breach of confidence which is dealt with at s 41 FOIA and s 36 FOI(S)A. Note also there is specific provision in s 79 FOIA (and s 67 FOI(S)A) giving immunity to public authorities from a defamation action arising from disclosure of information under the Acts unless the publication is made with malice.

[79] The Department of Constitutional Affairs mentioned a total of 448 statutory provisions in its *Review of Statutory Prohibitions on Disclosure* (which can be accessed at: www.dca.gov.uk/statbarsrep2005sm1.pdf) although it also says that on investigation 122 of these do not operate as bars to disclosure under FOIA and that 116 had already been repealed or amended in the course of the review. Lists of statutory prohibitions on disclosure can also be found

are numerous rationales for such prohibitions, although most commonly it is to preserve the confidentiality of information provided under compulsion by the citizen to public authorities. The following statutory provisions have been relied on in cases coming before the Tribunal:

— Abortion Regulations 1991 reg 5;[80]
— Animals (Scientific Procedures) Act 1986 s 24;[81]
— Census Act 1982 s 8;[82]
— Civil Aviation Act 1982 s 23;[83]
— Commissioners for Revenue and Customs Act 2005 ss 18 and 23;[84]
— Communications Act 2003 s 393;[85]
— Data Protection Act 1998 s 59;[86]
— Enterprise Act 2002 s 237;[87]
— Financial Services and Markets Act 2000 s 348;[88]
— Health Service Commissioners Act 1993 s 15;[89]
— Legal Aid Act 1988 s 38;[90]
— Local Government Act 1974 s 32;[91]
— Parliamentary Commissioner Act 1967 s 11;[92]
— Premium Savings Bond Regulations 1972 reg 30;[93]
— Police Act 1996 s 80;[94] and
— Public Service Contracts Regulations 1993 reg 30 and Public Contracts Regulations 2006 reg 43.[95]

Other examples of relevant statutory provisions would be:

---

at: www.dca.gov/foi/statbars.htm and www.dca.gov.uk/foi/statbarssi.htm.

[80] *Dept of Health v IC and Pro-Life Alliance*, IT, 15 October 2009.

[81] *SSHD v British Union for the Abolition of Vivisection* [2008] EWCA Civ 870, [2009] 1 All ER 44, [2009] 1 WLR 636, on appeal from [2008] EWHC 892 (QB), itself on appeal from Information Tribunal, 30 January 2008.

[82] *Barrett v IC and Office for National Statistics*, IT, 23 April 2008.

[83] *Hoyte v IC and CAA*, IT, 5 March 2008; *CAA v IC and Kirkaldie*, IT, 22 January 2010; *Phillips v IC*, IT, 10 February 2010.

[84] *Allison v IC and HMRC*, IT, 22 April 2008; *HMRC v IC*, IT, 10 March 2009; *Waugh v IC and HMRC*, IT, 27 March 2009.

[85] *Morrissey v IC and Office of Communications*, IT, 11 January 2010.

[86] *Friends of the Earth v IC and DTI*, 4 April 2007.

[87] *Dey v IC and OFT*, IT, 16 April 2007; *Dumfries and Galloway Council v Scottish IC* [2008] CSIH 12, 2008 SC 327.

[88] *Slann v IC and FSA*, IT, 11 July 2006; *Craven v IC*, IT, 13 May 2008; *FSA v IC*, IT, 13 October 2008; *Calland v IC and FSA*, IT, 8 August 2008; *Rowland and FSA v IC*, IT, 3 April 2009; *FSA v IC* [2009] EWHC 1548 (Admin).

[89] *Parker v IC and Parliamentary and Health Service Ombudsman*, IT, 15 October 2007.

[90] *Stephen v IC and Legal Services Commission*, IT, 25 February 2009.

[91] *Commission for Local Administration in England v IC*, IT, 11 March 2008; *Edmunds v IC*, IT, 20 May 2008.

[92] *Bluck v IC*, IT, 7 October 2009.

[93] *Meunier v IC and National Savings and Investments*, IT, 5 June 2007.

[94] *Higginson v IC*, IT, 2 May 2006.

[95] *Dept of Health v IC*, IT, 18 November 2008.

- Police and Criminal Evidence Act 1984 s 64A(4) (which prevents the disclosure of a photograph taken by the police of someone in custody);
- Representation of the People Act 1983 s 66(3) (which prohibits disclosure of information as to voting) ;
- Civil Procedure Rules 1998 rule 31.22 (which controls the subsequent use of documents disclosed in civil litigation).

The precise wording of all these statutory provisions varies substantially from enactment to enactment and it is essential that consideration is given to the precise terms of the prohibition in order to see whether it applies.[96] Often, legislation creates offences if certain categories of information are disclosed by members or employees of a public authority without lawful authority or excuse and/or otherwise than in the course of their duties and/or otherwise than for specified purposes and/or without the consent of specified persons and/or for prohibited purposes and such legislation often contains defences which apply if the defendant can show a subjective belief that he had lawful authority or that he did not know that the information came within the relevant category.[97] In many such cases it might be argued that the prohibition does not apply to a disclosure by the public authority at all or that if the public authority as a body was able to decide, in response to a specific request, that information should be disclosed notwithstanding the other exemptions in Part II, there would also be lawful authority for disclosure by an individual civil servant or officer on behalf of the public authority.[98] In some cases Ministers are given express powers effectively to prohibit the disclosure of information on the grounds of national security, or commercial confidentiality or simply the 'public interest'.[99]

019 Jurisprudence

Where a statutory provision, in proscribing the disclosure of particular information, provides a saving for any power or duty to disclose that information, the information will nevertheless fall within s 44(1): the right conferred by s 1 is not shaped[100] to survive the proscription.[101] Equally, where a provision allows disclosure for the purpose of enabling a public authority to

---

[96] A point made in MoJ, *Exemptions guidance Section 44 – Prohibitions on disclosure*, (14 May 2008) p 3. For example, the definition of 'confidential information' must be considered by reference to the statute in question and cannot be equated with that in FOIA s 41: *British Union for the Abolition of Vivisection v SSHD* [2008] EWHC 892 (QB); *British Union for the Abolition of Vivisection v SSHD* [2008] EWCA Civ 870, [2009] 1 All ER 44, [2009] 1 WLR 636; *Rowland and FSA v IC*, IT, 3 April 2009 at [15].

[97] See, eg, Army Act 1955 s 60; Census Act 1920 s 8; Finance Act 1989 s 182; Official Secrets Act 1911 s 1; Human Fertilisation and Embryology Act 1990 s 33..

[98] The DCA appears not to have appreciated this point when drafting the Freedom of Information (Removal and Relaxation of Statutory Prohibitions on Disclosure of Information) Order 2004 (SI 2004/3363): see eg s 59 of the Shops and Railway Premises Act 1963 and s 154 of the Factories Act 1961 which clearly only apply to the actual individuals who have obtained information in the course of inspections and allow such an individual to disclose such information 'in the performance of his duty' but which were nevertheless the subject of amendment by SI 2004/3363 by the introduction of ss 59A and 154A respectively which disapply ss 59 and 154A where the disclosure is made by or on behalf of a public authority for the purposes of the FOIA. In *Meunier v Information Commissioner and National Savings & Investments*, IT, 5 June 2007, the Information Tribunal assumed there was no difference between a disclosure by the public authority and disclosure by a person employed by that public authority. In practice, the answer will often be that the public authority cannot have a disclosure save through an act of a member of its staff.

[99] See, eg: Parliamentary Commissioner Act 1967 s 11(3); Environment Act 1995 s 113(3)(b); Airports Act 1986 s 30(7).

[100] See §1– 002.

[101] *Dey v Information Commissioner and Office of Fair Trading*, IT, 16 April 2007.

discharge its statutory functions, such functions will not be taken to include those under FOIA itself.[102] In the case of information which may only be disclosed with the consent of specified persons, the Tribunal has decided that, although public authorities may be expected to take steps to obtain such consent,[103] if consent is required for disclosure and it has not been obtained the disclosure remains prohibited and s 44(1)(a) of the Freedom of Information Act 2000 applies to exempt the information from disclosure.[104] Where the statutory prohibition is subject to a discretion on the part of the public authority to disclose, a decision by the public authority not to do so can only be challenged on the basis that the discretion had been exercised unlawfully under public law principles, ie in a way that was Wednesbury unreasonable, irrational or perverse.[105]

26– 020 Human Rights Act 1998

It has been argued that the Human Rights Act may itself, through a combination of section 6 and Articles 6 or 8 of the European Convention, prohibit disclosure of certain information by public authorities.[106] This argument was considered by the Information Tribunal in *Bluck v Information Commissioner*.[107] Although not necessary for its decision (because it found that the information was exempt under section 41 of FOIA), the Tribunal expressed the view that the general principles laid down by Article 8 of the Convention could not be elevated to the status of a specific legal prohibition of the type which section 44 was designed to uphold, and that the principles in Article 8 had already been taken account of in considering whether the information was confidential so that section 41 would apply to make it exempt.

26– 021 Comparative legislation

In contrast to the position in other jurisdictions, the section applies to 'any enactment' rather than to enactments that are expressly listed in the Act concerned.[108] There is no provision, as in Ireland, for particular enactments to be listed as not applying.[109] Nor, unlike the position in New Zealand, is there an express requirement that the decision-maker who relies on the section to specify the enactment relied on.[110] On the other hand, in some ways this exemption in the Freedom of Information Acts is narrower in scope than in some of the comparable legislation. Thus, the enactment must 'prohibit' the disclosure rather than 'restrict' it, as is the case in

---

[102] *Slann v IC and FSA*, IT, 11 July 2006 at [37]-[38]; *Dumfries and Galloway C v Scottish IC* [2008] CSIH 12, 2008 SC 327.

[103] This is also the line taken by the Scottish Information Commissioner: see his Briefing on section 26 of the FOI(S)A at p 3.

[104] See *Slann v Information Commissioner and Financial Services Authority*, IT, 11 July 2006, which dealt with a prohibition in s 348 of the Financial Services and Markets Act 2000.

[105] *Hoyte v IC and CAA*, IT, 5 March 2008 at [53].

[106] This appears to be the view of MoJ, *Exemptions guidance Section 44 – Prohibitions on disclosure*, (14 May 2008), p 4.

[107] *Bluck v IC and Epsom & St Helier University NHS Trust*, IT, 17 September 2007 at [31]-[32].

[108] Compare Access to Information Act (Canada) s 24(1) and Sch II and Freedom of Information Act 1982 (Cth of Australia) s 38(1)(b).

[109] See Freedom of Information Act 1997 (Ireland) s 32(1).

[110] See Official Information Act 1982 (New Zealand) s 18(c)(i). In practice this is very likely to happen in any event in the United Kingdom by reason of FOIA s 17(1)(c) and FOI(S)A s 16(1)(d).

Canada and New Zealand;[111] and there is no scope for continued reliance on statutory provisions which give the public authority a discretion whether to disclose information or not, as is the case in the United States and Ireland.[112]

022 Review and repeal or amendment

The Government stated during the passage of the Freedom of Information Bill that it would review all existing statutory prohibitions to disclosure and would repeal or amend any which on consideration could no longer be justified.[113] This intention found expression in s 75 of the Freedom of Information Act 2000, which enables the Secretary of State to repeal or amend any enactment by order[114] if it appears that by virtue of s 44(1) the enactment is capable of preventing the disclosure of information under the Act and in the review carried out by the then Department for Constitutional Affairs, published in June 2005.

023 Secretary of State's power to remove statutory prohibitions

Section 75 of the Freedom of Information Act 2000 empowers the Secretary of State for Justice to repeal or amend the enactment 'for the purpose of removing or relaxing the prohibition'. Section 75(2) expressly defines 'enactment' for the purposes of the section as any enactment contained in an Act passed before or in the same Session as the Freedom of Information Act 2000 and any enactment contained in Northern Ireland legislation or subordinate legislation passed or made before the passing of the Act. It is therefore clear that the power does not relate to legislation passed after the Freedom of Information Act 2000; this is presumably on the basis that Parliament and other legislators will be expected to take account of the principles enshrined in the Freedom of Information Act 2000 when passing new legislation. There is an ambiguity in s 75(2)(b) as to whether the subordinate legislation there referred to is only Northern Ireland subordinate legislation; it may be that the draftsman did intend this result on the basis that there would automatically be power to amend or repeal United Kingdom secondary legislation without the need for the express power[115] but this is unlikely to arise as an issue in practice. There is a similar power in the Freedom of Information (Scotland) Act 2002,[116] which allows Scottish Ministers to repeal or amend an enactment for the same purposes 'in so far as it relates to any Scottish public authority'. Subject to that limitation it is clear that the Scottish Ministers have power under the section to amend by order provisions in a United Kingdom Act of Parliament.[117] At the time of writing the power to repeal or amend

---

[111] See Access to Information Act (Canada) s 24(1); Official Information Act 1982 (New Zealand) s 52(3)(b)(i).

[112] See: Freedom of Information Act, 5 USC 552(b)(3)(B); Freedom of Information Act 1997 (Ireland) s 32(1)(b). The Lord Chancellor's Department's second report to Parliament on its review of legislation governing the disclosure of information (November 2002: `www.dca.gov.uk/foi/foidoirpt2.htm`) states that the FOIA will 'overlay...existing discretionary powers with an access right ...' (para.7).

[113] See Hansard, Standing Committee B, Freedom of Information Bill, 1 February 2000, col 385 per David Lock (Parliamentary Secretary, Lord Chancellor's Dept) and Hansard HL vol 617 col 905 (17 October 2000) (Lord Falconer).

[114] Subject to approval by a resolution of each House of Parliament (FOIA s 82(2)(b)) or the Scottish Parliament (FOI(S)A s 72(2)(b)).

[115] See Interpretation Act 1978 s 14.

[116] See FOI(S)A s 64.

[117] See definition of 'enactment' in FOI(S)A s 64(2).

enactments under these provisions has only been exercised twice, by the Freedom of Information (Removal and Relaxation of Statutory Prohibitions on Disclosure of Information) Order 2004,[118] which deals with eight Acts of Parliament, and by the Freedom of Information (Relaxation of Statutory Prohibitions on Disclosure of Information) (Scotland) Order 2008[119] in relation to Scottish public authorities.

26– 024 Government review

The last word in relation to the Government's review at the time of writing was a report entitled 'Review of Statutory Prohibitions on Disclosure' which was published by the Department of Constitutional Affairs in June 2005.[120] The report stated that there were 238 statutory provisions which had been identified as potentially operating as bars to disclosure but which on further consideration had been found not to operate in this way (in the case of 116 of them this was because they had been repealed or amended by other legislation in the course of the review).[121] 210 statutory provisions were identified as prohibiting disclosure under the Freedom of Information Act 2000. Of these, 20 implement international confidentiality obligations and cannot therefore be removed; 7 were passed after the Freedom of Information Act 2000 and could not therefore come within s 75; 13 were amended or repealed by the Freedom of Information (Removal and Relaxation of Statutory Prohibitions on Disclosure of Information) Order 2004; 40 were to be amended or repealed and 19 time limited by further orders under s 75; the balance of 111 would be retained for reasons set out in the report or were still under review. The main expressed reasons for retaining prohibitions were as follows: the provision protects information obtained under compulsion (this is not a ground of exemption under the Freedom of Information Acts); the provision applies to organisations which are not subject to the Freedom of Information Act 2000 and it would not be practical to have different regimes in force; the provision implements an international obligation; the provision is limited and there is a partial access regime provided in the relevant legislation. Notwithstanding the expressed intention to amend, repeal or time limit a number of provisions, only the two orders mentioned in the preceding paragraph have been passed.

5.   INCOMPATIBILITY WITH COMMUNITY OBLIGATIONS

26– 025 Introduction

Section 44(1)(b) of the Freedom of Information Act 2000 confers an absolute exemption on information the disclosure of which (but for any obligation under the Act itself) is incompatible

---

[118] SI 2004/3363.

[119] SI 2008/339.

[120] The web address from which it can be downloaded is:
    www.dca.gov.uk/StatutoryBarsReport2005.pdf

[121] Most notably by the Enterprise Act 2002 which according to the MoJ report at page 3 repealed or amended a large number of statutory prohibitions on disclosure and replaced them with a single coherent access regime for consumer information.

with any Community obligation.[122] 'Community obligation' is defined as any obligation created by or arising under the Treaties (as defined in the European Communities Act 1972), whether an enforceable Community obligation or not:[123] such obligations comprise any legal obligation in the Treaties or emanating from any of the European institutions whether or not they are directly enforceable without further enactment in the United Kingdom.[124] An example of such a provision is art 19 of the European Council Directive of 23 April 1990 on the deliberate release into the environment of genetically modified organisms.[125] This Article provides that the competent authorities in the Member States (which would be 'public authorities' under the Freedom of Information Acts) shall not divulge to third parties any confidential information notified to them under the Directive[126] and that, if a notification under the Directive is withdrawn, the competent authorities must respect the confidentiality of information supplied.[127] If the relevant information comes within the terms of the prohibition in the Directive there is no question of applying the public interest test as there would be if the public authority were applying, say, the exemption in s 43 of Freedom of Information Act 2000 ('commercial interests'), though of course it must be recognised that the concept of 'confidentiality' itself is somewhat elastic and the decision whether information is confidential may itself involve public interest considerations.[128]

026 **European Regulation 1049/2001**

The House of Commons Public Administration Committee expressed concern about s 44(1)(b): the Committee said that they considered the European rules on disclosure of information to be too restrictive.[129] After the publication of the Committee's Report, the European Parliament and Council have adopted Regulation 1049/2001 of 30 May 2001 regarding access to European Parliament, Council and Commission documents.[130] This is considered in more detail elsewhere in this work,[131] but in brief the Regulation provides a right of access to documents of the institutions subject to exceptions set out in article 4. Article 5 of the Regulation provides a special regime for documents held by Member States which originate from a European institution. In view of the supremacy of European law, this special regime

---

[122] See the remarks made at §§ 26– 015 to 26– 016.

[123] See: Interpretation Act 1978 s 5 and Sch 1 and European Communities Act 1972 s 1 and Sch 1 Pt II.

[124] See European Communities Act 1972 s 2(1) for definition of 'enforceable Community obligation'. Article 10 of the EC treaty requires Member States to abstain from any measure which jeopardises the attainment of the Treaty's objectives. Note that once the provisions of a directive have been enacted into UK law (eg the Financial Services and Markets Act 2000 (Disclosure of Confidential Information) Regulations 2001 SI 2001/2188 implementing provisions of the Investment Services Directive (93/22/EEC)) any prohibition on disclosure will come within s 44(1)(a) as well as s 44(1)(b).

[125] Council Directive 90/220.

[126] Article 19(1).

[127] Article 19(5).

[128] See §§25– 024 to 25– 027.

[129] See House of Commons *Public Administration Committee Third Report 1998–9 Session* (Cm 4355, 1999) para 111.

[130] The Regulation entered into force on 3 December 2001 and is binding in its entirety and directly applicable in all Member States.

[131] See §§4– 010 to 4– 028.

would apply in place of the provisions of the Freedom of Information Acts in relation to requests for access to such documents or information contained therein. Unless it is clear under the terms of the Regulation that a particular document or information should or should not be disclosed, the Member State must consult the institution concerned in order to take a decision on the matter or may simply refer the matter to the institution concerned. Articles 4(1), (2) and (3) provide that access to a document must be refused in the circumstances there set out. That proscription would therefore engage s 44(1)(b) of the Freedom of Information Act 2000 so as to defeat the domestic rights conferred by s 1. Although the exceptions in the Regulation are broadly similar to the exemptions provided in the Freedom of Information Acts, they are not identical.[132] Accordingly, the information that must be disclosed under the Regulation will not be exactly the same as the information that must be disclosed under the Freedom of Information Act 2000. In particular, the question of where the public interest lies in a particular case will be a matter not for the public authority in the United Kingdom but for the Community institution and, ultimately, the European Court of Justice. It should also be noted that if disclosure is required under the Regulation it must be given even if under the Freedom of Information Acts it could have been refused.

6. CONTEMPT OF COURT

26–027 Introduction

Information whose disclosure by the public authority holding it would constitute or be punishable as a contempt of court is exempt from disclosure under the Freedom of Information Acts.[133] This exemption appears to give precedence to the policy of preventing interference with the administration of justice (which is the underlying policy of the law of contempt of court) over the policy of free disclosure of information held by public authorities (which is the policy underlying the Freedom of Information Acts).[134] It should be noted that in many cases, the exemption provided by s 44(1)(c) of the Freedom of Information Act 2000 will also be provided by another provision in Part II, though generally the other provision will be subject to the public interest test in s 2.[135] There is no directly equivalent exception in the Environmental Information Regulations 2004. Accordingly, where (or to the extent that) information that answers the terms of a request for information is 'environmental information',[136] the fact that disclosure of that information would constitute or be punishable as a contempt of court will not excuse the public authority from complying with the request.[137] However, in such circumstances it may, depending on the facts. be arguable that disclosure

---

[132] See §4–012.

[133] FOIA s 44(1)(c); FOI(S)A s 26(c). See the introductory comments made at §§26–015 to 26–016.

[134] See *AG v Times Newspapers Ltd* [1974] AC 273 at 294E (Lord Reid) for a discussion of the public policy underlying the law of contempt and its interaction with the public interest in freedom of speech.

[135] This applies in particular to the exemptions provided by ss 30(1)(c), 31(1)(c), 32, 40, 41, 42 and 43; the same comment applies mutatis mutandis in relation to FOI(S)A.

[136] As to the meaning of which, see §6–010.

[137] FOIA s 39; FOI(S)A s 39.

would adversely affect 'the course of justice'.[138] In that case, subject to a consideration of the public interest balancing exercise, the public authority would be excused from its duty to disclose the information. There are provisions similar to s 44(1)(c) in the freedom of information statutes in Australia,[139] New Zealand[140] and Ireland.[141] Although this exemption has not so far featured in the jurisprudence arising out of the Freedom of Information Act 2000, a brief introduction of the relevant law and how in practice it might apply to the Act follow.

028   The law of contempt

The law of contempt can be highly technical and uncertain and is largely governed by common law rules.[142] The European Convention for the Protection of Human Rights and Fundamental Freedoms often plays an important role.[143] A person's guilt or innocence of contempt can depend on subjective knowledge and intent and on the practical effect of the act concerned and may be dependent on such questions as whether the legal proceedings concerned are civil or criminal, what stage they have reached, whether there is a jury, and the extent to which any information is already in the public domain. Proceedings are generally taken at the behest of the Attorney-General who has to make a fine judgment in the public interest as to whether they are appropriate.

029   Classification of contempts of court

Contempt of court can arise in a myriad of ways. The traditional classification into 'civil' and 'criminal' contempts is no longer helpful. Of greater assistance is a re-classification into (a) conduct which involves a breach, or which assists in a breach, of a court order and (b) any other conduct which involves an interference with the due administration of justice, either in a particular case or, more generally, as a continuing process, the first category being a special form of the latter, with such interference being a characteristic common to all contempts. In general, breach of a court order is treated as a matter for the parties to raise by way of complaint to the court, whereas other forms of contempt are considered to be a matter for the Attorney-General to raise as guardian of the public interest in the administration of justice.[144] The Phillimore Report on the law of contempt[145] divided contempts between:

(a)   'contempt in the face of the court', for example, throwing missiles at the judge,

---

[138] EIR reg 12(5)(b); EI(S)R reg 10(5)(b).

[139] Freedom of Information Act 1982 (Cth of Australia), s 46(a).

[140] Official Information Act 1982 (New Zealand) ss 18(c)(ii) and 52(1).

[141] Freedom of Information Act 1997 (Ireland) s 22(1)(b).

[142] Notwithstanding the Contempt of Court Act 1981. For a more detailed account of the law of contempt, reference should be made to the authoritative texts: D Eady and A Smith, *Aldridge, Eady & Smith on Contempt*, 3rd edn (London, Sweet & Maxwell, 2005); Borrie and Lowe, *The Law of Contempt*, 4th edn (London, LexisNexis, 2010); CJ Miller, *Contempt of Court*, 3rd edn (Oxford, Oxford University Press, 2000). For a general account see *Halsbury's Laws of England*, 4th edn, 1998 re-issue, vol 9(1), para 401 *et seq*.

[143] In particular, arts 6 (fair trial), 8 (private life) and 10 (freedom of expression): see *Sunday Times v UK* (1979–80) 2 EHRR 245; *Goodwin v United Kingdom* (1996) 22 EHRR 123; *Omar v France* (2000) 29 EHRR 210; *Daltel Europe Ltd (In Liquidation) v Makki (Committal for Contempt)* [2006] EWCA Civ 94, [2006] 1 WLR 2704.

[144] See *AG v Newspaper Publishing Ltd* [1988] Ch 333 at 362 (Donaldson MR).

[145] Report of the Committee on Contempt of Court (Cmnd.5794, 1974).

insulting persons in court, demonstrating in court; and

(b)   'contempt out of court', subdivided into:

(i)   reprisals against witnesses after the conclusion of proceedings;

(ii)   'scandalising the court', for example, abusing a judge *qua* judge or attacking his impartiality or integrity;

(iii) disobedience to court orders;

(iv)   conduct, whether intentional or not, liable to interfere with the course of justice in particular proceedings.[146]

Disclosure of information by a public authority is only ever likely to constitute a contempt under (b)(iii) or (iv) in this classification, by being contrary to a court order or undertaking or by tending to prejudice proceedings or to undermine the administration of justice.

26– 030   Decisions on the application of section 44(1)(c)

As has been pointed out,[147] the application of this difficult area of law will have to be carried out in the first instance by the decision-maker in the relevant public authority or the Information Commissioner.   This task is not made easier by the fact that the precise circumstances of the assumed disclosure by the public authority are not made clear by the section.   What is clear, however, is that it is the act of disclosure by the public authority itself which must constitute the act of contempt (rather than possible acts by the recipient of the information,[148] although knowledge of the intentions of the recipient may be relevant).   It is also clear that in order for the exemption to apply there must be almost certainty that a contempt will be committed.[149]

26– 031   Practical examples

Cases where the exemption may apply are as follows:

(1)   The most obvious and straightforward example would be a case where there is an order addressed directly to, or an undertaking[150] given expressly by, the public authority in question forbidding it from disclosing the relevant information:[151] in these circumstances there would clearly be no obligation to disclose it pursuant to a request made under Freedom of Information Act 2000 as to do so would almost certainly constitute a contempt of court.[152]

(2)   If a public authority is a party to litigation it will be subject to the implied undertakings as to the use of disclosed documents which are now codified in

---

[146] See *The Sunday Times v UK* (1979) 2 EHRR 245 at 257.

[147] See §§26– 015 to 26– 016.

[148] See *Altman v Family Court of Australia* (1992) 15 AAR 236 (Administrative Appeals Tribunal) at [38].

[149] The section requires that disclosure would constitute or be punishable as a contempt: see the discussion in relation to the New Zealand legislation in I Eagles, M Taggart & G Liddell, *Freedom of Information in New Zealand* (Auckland, Oxford University Press, 1992), at p 456.

[150] As to undertakings, see *Halsbury's Laws of England*, 4th edn, 1998 re-issue, vol 9(1), para 482.

[151] Such information is also likely to come within one or more other exemptions: eg under FOIA s 40 (personal information), s 41 (information provided in confidence), or s 43 (commercially sensitive information).

[152] Assuming, of course, that the public authority was aware of the order and its terms: see *Halsbury's Laws of England*, 4th edn, 1998 re-issue, vol 9(1), para 458, note 3.

CPR 31.22: to disclose a document or the information contained therein in breach of the terms of that rule would almost certainly constitute a contempt of court.[153]

(3) A public authority with the requisite knowledge and intent could also be in contempt of court if it disclosed information whose disclosure by another party was in breach of an injunction or undertaking, on the basis either that it was aiding and abetting the third party's breach of the order or undertaking[154] or, in the case of an interlocutory order or undertaking preventing the disclosure of information which may be confidential, on the basis that the disclosure destroyed the confidentiality which it was the purpose of the order or undertaking to preserve and that there had therefore been an interference with the administration of justice.[155]

(4) It is a contempt of court under the 'strict liability rule' to publish information which creates a substantial risk that the course of justice in particular proceedings will be seriously impeded or prejudiced[156] if the proceedings are 'active' (regardless of intent):[157] however, it seems unlikely that a public authority complying with a request for information under the Freedom of Information Acts would be committing such a contempt since the disclosure of any such information would be unlikely to constitute a 'publication' for the purposes of the 'strict liability rule'.[158] It may be that if the public authority knew that a journalist or news organisation seeking formation intended to publish it in breach of the 'strict liability rule', disclosure by the public authority would amount to a contempt by aiding and abetting, which would allow the public authority to refuse disclosure under s 44(1)(c).[159]

(5) It is also a contempt of court to create a real risk of prejudice to the administration of justice (regardless of whether the proceedings are active) with the intention of doing so.[160] Since this form of contempt normally takes the form of a publication

---

[153] See, eg: *Home Office v Harman* [1983] AC 280; *Alterskye v Scott* [1948] 1 All ER 469. The information may well also be exempt information under FOIA s 41 and such disclosure would probably also be exempt under s 44(1)(a) as being prohibited by CPR 31.22.

[154] On aiding and abetting, see *Halsbury's Laws of England*, 4th edn, 1998 re-issue, vol 9(1), para 490.

[155] See, on this form of contempt: *AG v Times Newspapers Ltd* [1992] 1 AC 191; *Jockey Club v Buffham* [2003] QB 462; *AG v Punch Ltd* [2002] UKHL 50, [2003] 1 AC 1046, [2003] 1 All ER 289. Note that information in this category is likely to be exempt under FOIA s 31(1)(c).

[156] The forms of information which might have this effect are numerous, including: information inducing bias in the court (eg information on the personal character or antecedents of an accused which would tend to influence a jury, information as to alleged confessions, comments on the merits of litigation or the court by the Government); information prejudicing the court's ability to determine the true facts (eg comments tending to discourage witnesses or to affect the content of their evidence, information as to without-prejudice offers in civil litigation, reports of private investigations or interviews with witnesses); information tending to discourage or deter a litigant from pursuing litigation.

[157] Contempt of Court Act 1981 ss 1–5.

[158] A publication must be 'addressed to the public at large or any section of the public': see Contempt of Court Act 1981 s 2(1).

[159] The factual hypothesis is perhaps unlikely; if these circumstances applied, the public authority would probably be able to rely on FOIA s 31(1)(b) or (c) and/or s 30(1)(c).

[160] See Contempt of Court Act 1981 s 6(c) and *AG v News Group plc* [1989] QB 110; *AG v Hislop* [1991] 1 QB 514; *AG v Sport Newspapers Ltd* [1991] 1 WLR 1194: the precise scope of this form of contempt is not at all clear.

to the public and since it is hard to see how the public authority, if it had the relevant intent, would seek to rely on it in order to avoid the very disclosure which it intended to make, it seems most unlikely that this form of contempt would ever be relevant for the purposes of the Freedom of Information Acts.

(6)   It is a contempt of court to disclose particulars of anything said in the jury room.[161] Thus, if for some reason (which it is hard to imagine in practice) a public authority had such information it would be committing a contempt in disclosing it and it would therefore be exempt information for the purposes of Freedom of Information Acts.

(7)   There are numerous specific statutory restrictions on the reporting of criminal and civil proceedings whose breach may also amount to a contempt of court.[162] Again, there will be a question whether disclosure of the information by the public authority itself pursuant to a request under the Freedom of Information Acts would involve publishing it sufficiently widely so as to breach such a restriction, but knowledge of an intention to do so by a journalist or news organisation seeking the information is likely to mean that the public authority could rely on s 44(1)(c) on the basis that such disclosure would amount to aiding and abetting such a breach.[163] In this context it should also be noted that the court itself has various powers to make orders binding on the world which restrict the publication of information concerning criminal or civil proceedings[164] and that a breach of such orders would also constitute a contempt of court. The same comments apply in relation to such orders as to the statutory provisions mentioned above.

(8)   There is a class of contempt referred to as 'scandalising the court' which arises when a court or judicial officer is grossly insulted or has its integrity impugned.[165] It is just conceivable that there exist in the Lord Chancellor's Department (or the Ministry of Justice) comments about individual judges which if disclosed would involve such a contempt.

26–032 Disclosure punishable as a contempt

Section 44(1)(c) of Freedom of Information Act 2000 also exempts information whose disclosure by the public authority would 'be punishable as a contempt of court'. Various statutes provide

---

[161] Contempt of Court Act 1981 s 8.

[162] See *Halsbury's Laws of England*, 4th edn, 1998 re-issue, vol 9(1), paras 430 and 431; Magistrates' Court Act 1980 s 8; Criminal Justice Act 1987 s 11; Sexual Offences (Amendment) Act 1976 Children and Young Persons Act 1933 s 39; Youth Justice and Criminal Evidence Act 1999 ss 44 and 45, Administration of Justice Act 1960 s 12. In theory, these statutory provisions might give rise to a prohibition on disclosure by or under an enactment for the purposes of s 44(1)(a) of FOIA, but the act of disclosure itself is unlikely to amount to publication (though if the journalist was known to have the relevant intention it might amount to aiding and abetting the relevant offence).

[163] And no doubt it could also rely on FOIA ss 30 and/or 31.

[164] Note in particular Contempt of Court Act 1981 ss 4(2) and 11 (examples of information which the court has power to withhold from the public apart from those provided by statute are secret processes and the name of complainants in blackmail cases (*R v Socialist Worker* [1975] QB 637)), Children and Young Persons Act 1933 s 39 and the inherent power of the Family Division of the High Court in certain circumstances to make orders which protect children from publicity (see: *Re S* [2004] UKHL 47, [2005] 1 AC 593, [2004] 4 All ER 683).

[165] See *Halsbury's Laws of England*, 4th edn, 1998 re-issue, vol 9(1), para 433 and *Altman v Australian Family Court* (1992) 15 AAR 236 at [37] (Administrative Appeals Tribunal).

that where a person does anything in relation to a particular tribunal which, if it were a court, would amount to a contempt of court, the tribunal can certify that fact to a court and the court can investigate the matter and punish the person as if they had committed a contempt of court.[166] It is thought that the words 'punishable as a contempt of court' are designed to deal with actions which would be caught by this kind of provision. Given that the tribunals in question may have limited powers to grant injunctions and given that they are unlikely to be easily influenced by publications in the way that a jury would, it seems unlikely that this provision would arise for consideration very often.

7. MISCELLANEOUS EXEMPTIONS UNDER THE DATA PROTECTION ACT 1998

033 Information held only for research purposes

Personal data processed only for research purposes are exempt from the subject access rights under the Data Protection Act 1998 provided:

— that the data are not processed in order to support measures or decisions with respect to particular individuals;

— that they are not processed in such a way that substantial damage or distress is, or is likely to be, caused to any data subject; and

— that the results of the research or any resulting statistics are not made available in a form which identifies any data subject.[167]

Research purposes includes statistical and historical purposes.[168] Personal data are not treated as processed otherwise than for research purposes simply because they are disclosed to a person for research purposes, or are disclosed to the data subject or a person acting on his behalf, or are disclosed at the request or with the consent of the data subject or a person acting on his behalf.[169] Further, they are not treated as being so processed where the person making the disclosure has reasonable grounds for believing that one of those circumstances applies.[170] The Information Commissioner advises that, as a matter of good practice, when processing for research, historical or statistical purposes, data controllers should always consider whether it is necessary to process personal data in order to achieve this purpose, and that wherever possible they should only process data that have been stripped of all identifying features.[171]

034 Manual data relating to Crown employment

Personal data falling within the final limb of the definition of data, ie manual data recorded by

---

[166] See, eg: Army Act 1955 s 101; Air Force Act 1955 s 101; Naval Discipline Act 1957 s 65; Tribunals of Inquiry (Evidence) Act 1921 s 1(2); Parliamentary Commissioner Act 1967 s 9.

[167] DPA s 33(1), (4).

[168] DPA s 33(1).

[169] DPA s 33(5)(a)–(c).

[170] DPA s 33(5)(d).

[171] The Information Commissioner, *DPA: Legal Guidance* para 5.7.

a public authority, and that relate to personnel matters concerning Crown employment are exempt from the subject access rights (and other provisions) of the Data Protection Act 1998.[172] The types of personnel matters concerned include appointments and removals, pay, discipline and superannuation.[173] The exemption covers service in the armed forces, service in any office or employment under the Crown or a public authority, and service in any other office or employment or under any contract for services where the power to take action in respect of such personnel matters rests with Her Majesty, a Minister of the Crown, the National Assembly for Wales, a Northern Ireland Minister or any public authority.[174] This exemption is designed to achieve parity between those who work for public authorities and those who work in the private sector. The view is taken that the former should not have additional rights of access in the employment context merely because of the identity of their employer.

26–035 Journalistic, literary and artistic material held with a view to publication

Personal data processed only for journalistic, artistic or literary purposes ('the special purposes')[175] are exempt from the subject access rights (and certain other provisions) of the Data Protection Act 1998 if they are processed with a view to the publication of journalistic, literary or artistic material and the data controller reasonably believes both that publication would be in the public interest and that compliance with the subject access rights would be incompatible with the special purposes.[176] As the Information Commissioner has noted in his published Legal Guidance on the Data Protection Act 1998, the data controller must be satisfied that each of the four conditions (processing solely for the special purposes, processing with a view to publication of journalistic, literary or artistic material, belief that publication would be in the public interest, belief that compliance with the Data Protection Act 1998 would be incompatible with the special purposes) is satisfied in respect of the specific provision of the Data Protection Act 1998 from which exemption is claimed.[177] This exemption, which has its origins in article 9 of the Data Protection Directive, is concerned with the balance between the protection of individual privacy and the right to freedom of expression.[178] Thus, in considering whether publication would be in the public interest, the data controller is required to have particular regard to the special importance of the public interest in freedom of expression.[179] The ECJ has held in relation to Article 9 that the publication of data within the public domain, which publication was done for profit-making purposes, fell within the definition of activity

---

[172] DPA s 33A(2).

[173] DPA s 33A(2).

[174] DPA s 33A(2).

[175] Data processing by journalists or the media that is not related to the special purposes (such as processing subscriber data for billing or direct marketing) is not covered by the exemption).

[176] DPA s 32(1), (2). In *Campbell v Mirror Group Newspapers Ltd* [2002] EWCA Civ 1373, [2003] QB 633 the exemption was successfully relied on by a newspaper in relation to the publication of information about the drug addiction and treatment of a model, along with a photograph of the model leaving a drug rehabilitation clinic.

[177] The Information Commissioner, *DPA: Legal Guidance* para 5.6.

[178] See Case C-73/07 *Tietosuojavaltuutettu v Satakunnan* [2010] All ER (EC) 213, [2008] ECR I-9831 at [54]-[56].

[179] DPA s 32(1)(b). The ECJ held in Case C-73/07 *Tietosuojavaltuutettu v Satakunnan* [2010] All ER (EC) 213, [2008] ECR I-9831 at [56] that in order to take account of the importance of the right to freedom of expression in a democracy, it is necessary to give a broad interpretation to notions relating to that freedom, such as 'journalism'.

undertaken 'solely for journalistic purposes'.[180]

-036 Confidential references

A number of exemptions relate broadly to information provided or processed in relation to the employment, engagement or appointment of individuals to posts, offices and the like. The first relates to confidential references. Personal data are exempt from the subject access rights if they consist of a reference given (or to be given) in confidence by the data controller for the purposes of the education, training or employment of the data subject; his or her appointment to any office; or the provision by him or her of any service.[181] It is notable that this exemption applies only to references given or to be given by the data controller. If the data controller has on file references provided by a previous employer, they do not fall within the scope of the exemption.[182] However, the data controller may, for example, decline to reveal the identity of the author of the reference, pursuant to s 7(4) and (5).

-037 Judicial appointments and honours

The next related exemption concerns judicial appointments and honours. It covers a broader category of information than confidential references: all personal data processed for the purposes of assessing a person's suitability for judicial office[183] or the office of Queen's Counsel, or for the purposes of the conferring by the Crown of any honour or dignity,[184] are exempt from the subject access rights (and other provisions).[185]

-038 Crown employment and Crown or ministerial appointments

The final related exemption concerns other Crown and Ministerial appointments or employment. Again, it covers a broader category of information than confidential references. Rather than providing a blanket exemption, the Data Protection Act 1998 confers a power on the Secretary of State to exempt from the subject access rights personal data processed for the purposes of assessing a person's suitability for Crown employment or appointment to any office by Her Majesty, a Minister of the Crown or a Northern Ireland department.[186] This power has been exercised in relation to a variety of Crown appointments, including archbishops, bishops and certain other clergy; Lord Lieutenants; Masters of certain Cambridge colleges; the Provost of Eton; the Poet Laureate and the Astronomer Royal.[187]

-039 Armed forces

Personal data are exempt from the subject access rights (and other provisions) in any case to the

---

[180] Case C-73/07 *Tietosuojavaltuutettu v Satakunnan* [2010] All ER (EC) 213, [2008] ECR I-9831 at [59].

[181] DPA s 37 Sch 7 para 1.

[182] See also: The Information Commissioner, *DPA: Legal Guidance*, para 5.13.

[183] In *Guardian News & Media Ltd v IC and MoJ*, IT, 10 June 2009 at [91] the Tribunal held that this encompasses a review of the person's performance whilst in office, thereby exempting disciplinary actions taken against judges.

[184] As to the meaning of which, see generally §§26– 008 to 26– 014.

[185] DPA s 37 Sch 7 para 3.

[186] DPA s 37 Sch 7 para 4.

[187] The Data Protection (Crown Appointments) Order 2000 SI 2000/416.

extent to which the application of those provisions would be likely to prejudice the combat effectiveness of any of the armed forces of the Crown.[188]

26– 040 Management forecasts

Personal data processed for the purposes of management forecasting or management planning to assist the data controller in the conduct of any business or other activity are exempt from the subject access rights (and other provisions) in any case to the extent to which the application of those provisions would be likely to prejudice the conduct of that business or activity.[189]

26– 041 Corporate finance

There is an exemption in relation to personal data processed for the purposes of, or in connection with, a corporate finance service.[190] The concept of a 'corporate finance service' is derived from the EC Directive on investment services in the securities field.[191] It covers certain activities relating to issues of specified instruments, as well as the provision of advice to undertakings on matters such as capital structure, industrial strategy and mergers.[192] Where personal data are processed for the purposes of, or in connection with, a corporate finance service provided by a relevant person,[193] the data are exempt from the subject access rights (and other provisions) to the extent to which the application of those provisions could affect the price of any specified instrument (whether it already exists, or is to be or may be created).[194] This limb of exemption also extends to circumstances in which the data controller reasonably believes that the price of such an instrument could be so affected.[195] Such data are also exempt if exemption is required to safeguard an important economic or financial interest of the United Kingdom.[196] The Secretary of State has a power to specify matters to be taken into account in determining whether exemption on the latter ground is required, or circumstances in which exemption is or is not to be taken to be required.[197] This power has been exercised in relation to personal data to which the application of the subject information provisions could affect decisions whether to deal in, subscribe for or issue instruments or decisions which are likely to affect any business activity.[198] In such cases, the matter to be taken into account is the inevitable prejudicial effect on the orderly functioning of financial markets or the efficient allocation of capital within the economy resulting from the application of the subject access

---

[188] DPA s 37 Sch 7 para 2. See generally §§17– 063 to 17– 072.

[189] DPA s 37 Sch 7 para 5.

[190] DPA s 37 Sch 7 para 6.

[191] Council Directive 93/22. See DPA Sch7 para 6(3).

[192] DPA Sch 7 para 6(3).

[193] Defined in DPA Sch 7 para 6(3).

[194] DPA Sch 7 para 6(1)(a)(i).

[195] DPA s 37 Sch 7 para 6(1)(a)(ii).

[196] DPA s 37 Sch 7 para 6(1)(b).

[197] Data Protection 1998 Act Sch 7 para 6(2).

[198] Data Protection (Corporate Finance Exemption) Order 2000 SI 2000/184 art 2(3).

rights.[199]

042 Negotiations

Personal data comprising records of the data controller's intentions in relation to any negotiations with the data subject are exempt from the subject access rights (and other provisions) in any case to the extent to which the application of those provisions would be likely to prejudice those negotiations.[200] One example of the application of this exemption is the situation in which an organisation is in dispute with a former employee and records a potential settlement figure for its own budget forecasting. Disclosure of the figure to the ex-employee might prejudice the negotiations between those parties.[201]

043 Examination marks and scripts

A group of exemptions and modifications relates to examination marks and scripts. Examination scripts, that is to say personal data consisting of information recorded by candidates during an academic, professional or other examination,[202] are exempt from the subject access rights.[203] Those rights are modified in relation to examination marks or other information processed for the purpose of determining examination results, or of enabling those results to be determined, or in consequence of their determination.[204] The modifications prevent a data subject from using his or her subject access rights to obtain examination results before they are announced. They achieve this by extending the period for compliance with a subject access request.[205]

044 Self-incrimination

The privilege against self-incrimination is preserved by the Data Protection Act 1998. A person is not required to comply with a subject access request (or order under s 7) to the extent that to do so would, by revealing evidence of the commission of any offence (other than an offence under the Data Protection Act 1998) expose him to proceedings for that offence.[206] Furthermore, information disclosed by a person in compliance with such a request or order is not admissible against him in proceedings for an offence under the Data Protection Act 1998.[207]

045 Disclosure prohibited by other legislation

In addition to the exemptions conferred by the Data Protection Act 1998 itself, there are additional exemptions from the subject access rights made pursuant to a further general power of exemption conferred on the Secretary of State by the Act in respect of information the

---

[199] Data Protection (Corporate Finance Exemption) Order 2000 SI 2000/184 art 2.

[200] DPA s 37 Sch 7 para 7.

[201] The Information Commissioner, *DPA: Legal Guidance*, para 5.18.

[202] DPA Sch 7 para 9(1).

[203] DPA s 37 Sch 7 para 9.

[204] DPA s 37 Sch 7 para 8(1), (5).

[205] DPA Sch 7 para 8.

[206] DPA s 37 Sch 7 para 11(1).

[207] DPA s 37 Sch 7 para 11(2).

disclosure of which is already prohibited or restricted by other legislation.[208] The Secretary of State may exempt personal data consisting of such information, where he considers it necessary for safeguarding the interests of the data subject or the rights and freedoms of any other individual that the prohibition or restriction should prevail over the subject access rights.[209] Pursuant to this power, there are exemptions in respect of certain information relating to human fertilisation and embryology,[210] adoption records and reports,[211] statements of special educational needs[212] and parental order records and reports.[213]

---

[208] As to the potential scope of the provision, see §§26– 015 to 26– 024.

[209] DPA s 38(1).

[210] The Data Protection (Miscellaneous Subject Access Exemptions) Order 2000 SI 2000/419 art 2 and sch Pt I.

[211] The Data Protection (Miscellaneous Subject Access Exemptions) Order 2000 SI 2000/419 sch Pts II(a), III(a), IV(a) as amended by the Data Protection (Miscellaneous Subject Access Exemptions) (Amendment) Order 2000 SI 2000/1865. In Scotland information provided by a principal reporter for a children's hearing is also exempted: The Data Protection (Miscellaneous Subject Access Exemptions) Order 2000 SI 2000/419 art 2 and sch Pt III(b).

[212] The Data Protection (Miscellaneous Subject Access Exemptions) Order 2000 SI 2000/419 art 2 and sch Pts II(b), III(c) (record of special educational needs in Scotland), IV(b).

[213] The Data Protection (Miscellaneous Subject Access Exemptions) Order 2000 SI 2000/419 schedule Pts II(c), III(d), IV(c).

CHAPTER 27

The Information Commissioners and the First-tier and Upper Tribunals

1. THE FUNCTIONS AND DUTIES OF THE INFORMATION COMMISSIONERS

27–001 The Information Commissioner

The main responsibility for enforcing the Data Protection Act 1998, the Freedom of Information Act 2000 and the Environmental Information Regulations 2004 lies with the Information Commissioner.[1] The office was originally established as that of the Data Protection Registrar.[2] It was renamed the Data Protection Commissioner by the Data Protection Act 1998[3] and later the Information Commissioner by the Freedom of Information Act 2000.[4] The last name change coincided with the office being given responsibilities under that Act in addition to its responsibilities under the Data Protection Act 1998.[5] The Information Commissioner is also responsible for the enforcement of the Environmental Information Regulations 2004 and the Privacy and Electronic Communications (EC Directive) Regulations 2003.[6] The Information Commissioner is also the 'supervisory authority' in the United Kingdom for the purposes of the Data Protection Directive and the 'designated authority' in the United Kingdom for the purpose of art 13 of the 1981 Convention for the Protection of Individuals with regard to the Automatic Processing of Personal Data.[7] The Information Commissioner is subject to the supervision of the Tribunals and Inquiries Act 1992.[8] In addition to his specific statutory duties, the Commissioner sets himself the aims of providing a general inquiry service for individuals and organizations and influencing thinking on privacy and access issues. He currently employs more than 200 staff and handles more than 2,600 freedom of information complaints a year, along with 24,000 data protection complaints and 182,000 telephone calls. A serious backlog of freedom of information cases built up which it is hoped will be addressed by the new Commissioner.[9]

---

[1] Since June 2009 the Commissioner has been Christopher Graham, formerly Director General of the Advertising Standards Agency. The website (www.ico.gov.uk) describes his Office as 'the UK's independent authority set up to uphold information rights in the public interest, promoting openness by public bodies and data processing for individuals. The Ministry of Justice is [the] sponsoring department within the Government.'

[2] Under the Data Protection Act 1984 s 3(1)(a).

[3] DPA s 5(1).

[4] FOIA s 18(1), with effect from 30 January 2001.

[5] The combination of the two roles into one post was the source of some controversy in Parliament. The Government's justifications for combining the two roles were given in Hansard HC vol 347 cols 1040–1042 (5 April 2000) as: (1) the two roles were said by the then Commissioner to be complementary and she supported the idea; (2) consistent decisions would be made as to what should be disclosed; (3) the public would have a single point of contact when they sought information; (4) this was said to be the course adopted in Australia, New Zealand and Ireland. See also Hansard HL vol 617 col 1214 (15 October 2000).

[6] SI 2004/3391 and SI 2003/2426 respectively.

[7] DPA s 54(1).

[8] Tribunals and Inquiries Act 1992 s 1 and Sch I Pt I para 14(a).

[9] See further §28-006 below.

-002 Terms of appointment

The Information Commissioner is appointed by the Crown by Letters Patent.[10] Part I of Sch 5 to the Data Protection Act 1998 lays down the detailed terms of his appointment and powers. The Commissioner is a corporation sole and neither he nor his officers and staff are servants or agents of the Crown.[11] His tenure is normally for five years (renewable twice) and he can be removed from office only in pursuance of an address by both Houses of Parliament.[12] Provision is made for his salary and pension and for the appointment by him of one or two deputy commissioners and other officers and staff.[13] The funds required by the Commissioner are to be paid to him by the Secretary of State for Justice out of money provided by Parliament.[14] He must keep proper accounts and records.[15] Each year he must lay a general report before Parliament on the exercise of his functions under the Data Protection Act 1998 and the Freedom of Information Act 2000.[16]

-003 Functions under the Data Protection Act 1998

The main functions of the Information Commissioner under the Data Protection Act 1998 are:

— maintaining the register of notifications by 'data controllers'[17] under Pt III of the Data Protection Act 1998;

— enforcing compliance with the 'data protection principles'[18] by data controllers by issuing 'enforcement notices'[19] and investigating compliance with the Act and those principles in respect of the processing of 'personal data'[20] by data controllers;[21]

— promoting good practice and the observance of the requirements of the Act by data controllers;[22]

— disseminating information and advice about the Act to the public[23] and preparing and disseminating codes of practice if he considers it appropriate

---

[10] DPA s 5(2).

[11] DPA Sch5 Pt I para 1.

[12] DPA Sch5 Pt I para 2.

[13] DPA Sch5 Pt I paras 5 and 6.

[14] DPA Sch5 Pt I para 8.

[15] DPA Sch5 Pt I para 10.

[16] DPA s 52(1); FOIA s 49(1). The reports are prepared for the year ending March 31 and can be accessed on the Information Commissioner's website.

[17] As to the meaning of 'data controller,' see §5– 027.

[18] These principles are set out in DPA, Sch 1, Pt I, and elucidated in Sch 1, Pt II and Schs 2–4.

[19] DPA ss 40 and 41. As to enforcement notices, see §§5– 086 to 5– 090.

[20] As to the meaning of 'personal data,' see §§5– 021 to 5– 024.

[21] DPA ss 42–46. 'Processing' is defined by s 1(1) of the Act to include obtaining, recording, holding or carrying out defined operations on the data.

[22] DPA s51(1).

[23] DPA s 51(2).

or the Secretary of State so directs by order;[24]

— encouraging trade associations to prepare and disseminate and approve codes of practice;[25]

— disseminating information about European decisions and the protection of data subjects' rights in the rest of the world;[26]

— providing assistance to individuals who are parties to proceedings under Pt II of the Act[27] which relate to personal data processed for the 'special purposes' if he considers the case to involve a matter of substantial public importance;[28]

— instituting proceedings for offences under the Act;[29]

— making annual reports to Parliament about the exercise of his functions under the Act;[30] and

— being the 'designated authority' and the 'supervisory authority' for the purposes of the Convention for the Protection of Individuals with regard to Automatic Processing of Personal Data and the Data Protection Directive respectively and carrying out various functions under the Directive and the Convention and other international obligations of the United Kingdom as provided by the Secretary of State.[31]

The Information Commissioner and the Director of Public Prosecutions have sole authority for bringing prosecutions under the Act.[32] The Information Commissioner is also responsible for enforcing the Privacy and Electronic Communications (EC Directive) Regulations 2003,[33] which implement a large part of Directive 2002/58/EC of the European Parliament and Council concerning the processing of personal data and the protection of privacy in the electronic communications sector. From October 2005 a new form of regulatory action became available to the Commissioner under Part 8 of the Enterprise Act 2002 which enables him to apply to the courts for an enforcement order in cases where breaches of the 2003 Regulations are considered harmful to individual consumers.[34]

---

[24] DPA s 51(3).

[25] DPA s 51(4).

[26] DPA 51(6).

[27] These include proceedings under DPA s7(9) to enforce the right of access to personal data by individuals who are the subject of it.

[28] DPA s 53. 'Special purposes' are defined by s 3 as the purposes of journalism, artistic purposes and literary purposes.

[29] DPA s 60. Offences under the Act are considered at §§5– 086 to 5– 097.

[30] DPA s 52.

[31] DPA s 54. Note that the Data Protection Directive (Directive 95/46/EC) expressly provides by art 28 that the supervisory authority shall act with 'complete independence'. The following orders have been made under the section: Data Protection (Functions of Designated Authority) Order 2000 SI 2000/186 and the Data Protection (International Co-operation) Order 2000 SI 2000/190.

[32] DPA s 60(1).

[33] SI 2003/2426. Regulation 31 extends the provisions of Pt V of DPA relating to enforcement for the purposes of the regulations and reg 32 entitles OFCOM or any aggrieved person to request the Commissioner to exercise his enforcement functions and provides that those functions can also be exercised without any such request.

[34] See Commissioner's Annual Report 2005–2006 p 24 and Enterprise Act 2002 s 213(2) and SI 2003/1399.

004 Functions under the Freedom of Information Act 2000

The main functions of the Information Commissioner under the Freedom of Information Act 2000 are investigating and determining whether public authorities have dealt with requests for information in accordance with Part I of the Act, or are otherwise complying with Part I of the Act and the codes of practice issued by the Lord Chancellor and the Secretary of State under it, and enforcing such compliance.[35] He also has the general functions of:

— approving 'publication schemes' by public authorities;[36]
— preparing and/or approving 'model publication schemes';[37]
— promoting good practice by public authorities in following the provisions of the Act and the codes of practice;[38]
— disseminating information about the Act and about good practice;[39]
— assessing (with consent) whether public authorities are following good practice;[40]
— consulting the Keeper of Public Records about the promotion of the observance by local authorities of codes of practice issued by the Lord Chancellor under s 46;[41]
— giving recommendations to public authorities if it appears that their practice does not comply with such codes of practice;[42]
— reporting to Parliament at least annually on the exercise of his functions;[43]
— disclosing information to the appropriate ombudsman if it appears to him that it could be relevant to an investigation by that ombudsman.[44]

The Lord Chancellor or must consult the Information Commissioner before issuing or revising a code of practice under s 45(1) of the Act providing guidance to public authorities in connection with the discharge of their functions under Part I or under s 46(1) in connection with the keeping, management and destruction of public records.[45] The Information Commissioner also has responsibility for bringing criminal proceedings against a public authority, or its officers and employees, which alters records to prevent disclosure pursuant to the Act or the Data Protection Act 1998.[46] The Information Commissioner is also responsible for the enforcement of the Environmental Information Regulations 2004 and has other functions under the regulations analogous to those under the Freedom of Information Act

---

[35] FOIA Pt IV (ss 50–56).

[36] FOIA s 19(1)(a). As to publication schemes, see ch 10.

[37] FOIA s 20(1).

[38] FOIA s 47(1). As to codes of practice, see ch 10. The Information Commissioner has himself issued numerous guides to the working of the FOIA in particular relating to the exemptions; they are available on his website.

[39] FOIA s 47(2).

[40] FOIA s 47(3).

[41] FOIA s 47(5). As to codes of practice under s 46, see §10– 012.

[42] FOIA s 48.

[43] FOIA s 49.

[44] FOIA s 76.

[45] FOIA s 45(4) and 46(5)(b). See further §10– 007.

[46] FOIA s 77(4). See also §29– 007.

2000.[47]

27–005 The Scottish Information Commissioner

The Freedom of Information (Scotland) Act 2002 and Environmental Information (Scotland) Regulations 2004 are enforced by the Scottish Information Commissioner. He is appointed by Her Majesty on the nomination of the Scottish Parliament.[48] He holds office for an initial term not exceeding five years on the terms and conditions determined by the Scottish Parliamentary corporation.[49] Schedule 2 to the Freedom of Information (Scotland) Act 2002 lays down similar terms in relation to the Scottish Information Commissioner as Sch 5 to the Data Protection Act 1998. The Scottish Information Commissioner must also lay a report each year before the Scottish Parliament on the exercise of his functions under the Act, which must include a record of the number of occasions on which he failed to reach a decision on a s 47(1) application within the four months specified by s 47(3)(b).[50] The Scottish Information Commissioner has a staff of 24 and has taken approximately 800 decisions since 2005.[51]

27–006 Functions of Scottish Information Commissioner

The main function of the Scottish Information Commissioner is enforcing the Freedom of Information (Scotland) Act 2002 by investigating and deciding whether Scottish public authorities have dealt with requests for information in accordance with Pt 1 of the Act or are otherwise complying with Pt 1.[52] He also has the general functions of:

— promoting the following of good practice by Scottish public authorities in relation to the Act and the codes of practice issued under it and assessing whether they are following such good practice;[53]

— disseminating information to and advising the public about the operation of the Act;[54]

— making proposals to the Scottish Ministers about their power under ss.4 and 5 of the Act to designate Scottish public authorities for the purpose thereof;[55] and

— issuing practice recommendations to Scottish public authorities if he considers they are not following the codes of practice issued by the Scottish Ministers as to their functions under the Act and as to keeping, management and destruction of records issued under ss 60 and 61 thereof.[56]

The Scottish Information Commissioner also has responsibility for enforcing the Environmental

---

[47] See EIR regs 16(5) and 18.

[48] FOI(S)A s 42(1). The current appointee is Kevin Dunion.

[49] FOI(S)A s 42(2)–(5).

[50] FOI(S)A s 46(1) and (2).

[51] See his website at: www.itspublicknowledge.info/home/ScottishInformationCommissioner.asp

[52] FOI(S)A s 43(1) and (3). As to codes of practice, see ch 9.

[53] POI(S)A Pt 4 (ss 50–56), which is in similar terms to FOIA Pt IV (ss 47–56).

[54] POI(S)A s 43(2).

[55] POI(S)A s 43(4).

[56] FOI(S)A s 44. As to public records, see ch 7.

Information (Scotland) Regulations 2004 and other functions under those regulations analogous to his functions under the Freedom of Information (Scotland) Act 2002.[57]

007   Information Commissioners' duties of confidentiality

The Information Commissioners have extensive powers and opportunities to obtain information in the course of enforcing compliance with the Data Protection Act 1998, the two Freedom of Information Acts and the two Environmental Information Regulations, including information held by public authorities.[58] Further, no enactment or rule of law prohibiting or restricting the disclosure of information precludes any person from furnishing the Commissioners with any information necessary for the discharge of their functions under the Data Protection Act 1998 or Freedom of Information Acts.[59] The Commissioners and their staff are therefore potentially privy to much sensitive information, which may not in the event be made public. They commit an offence if they disclose, without lawful authority, any information which has been furnished to the Commissioner under the Data Protection Act 1998 or the Freedom of Information Act 2000 which relates to an identified or identifiable individual or business and which is not available to the public from other sources.[60] There appears to be a lacuna in the English legislation, however, in that there is no provision making it an offence for the Commissioner or his staff to disclose information which comes to them under the Freedom of Information Act 2000 unless it relates to an identified or identifiable individual or business; there is no such lacuna in the Freedom of Information (Scotland) Act 2002, which provides that the Scottish Commissioner or his staff or agents commit an offence (punishable on summary conviction by the maximum fine and on indictment by an unlimited fine) if they disclose without lawful authority any information which is received by them under the Act and which is not in the public domain.[61]

008   Disclosure with lawful authority

Disclosure with lawful authority is defined for the purposes of the Data Protection Act 1998 and the Freedom of Information Act 2000 as being only where:

   (1)   the disclosure is with consent of the individual or person carrying on the business concerned;

   (2)   the information was provided for the purpose of being made available to the public under any provision of the Acts;

   (3)   the disclosure is made for the purposes of and is necessary for the discharge of functions under the Acts or any Community obligation;

   (4)   the disclosure is made for the purposes of any proceedings, whether criminal or civil; or

   (5)   the disclosure is necessary in the public interest having regard to the rights and

---

[57] EI(S)R regs 17 and 18(5).

[58] In particular by virtue of: FOIA s 51; FOI(S)A s 50; DPA s 43; EIR reg 18(2); EI(S)R reg 17(1).

[59] DPA s 58 (which applies to the discharge of functions under the FOIA as well); FOI(S)A s 50(7).

[60] DPA s 59.

[61] FOI(S)A s 45(1), (3), (4).

freedoms or legitimate interests of any person.[62]

Under the Freedom of Information (Scotland) Act 2002 the definition of disclosure with lawful authority is similar save that:

(1)   the relevant consent is of the person from whom the information was obtained; and

(2)   there is also provision that in a case where the Commissioner himself or the public authority which provided the information would have been obliged to disclose the information under the Freedom of Information (Scotland) Act 2002 a disclosure is lawful if made by the Commissioner.[63]

Both the Freedom of Information Act 2000 and the Freedom of Information (Scotland) Act 2002 contain specific provisions authorising the Commissioners to disclose information coming to them under the Data Protection Act 1998 and the Freedom of Information Act 2000 or the Freedom of Information (Scotland) Act 2002 respectively to various ombudsmen where the Commissioner believes the information would be relevant to these ombudsmen's investigations.[64]

27–009   Human Rights Act 1998

The Information Commissioners are themselves subject to the Human Rights Act 1998.[65] Articles 6, 8 and 10 of the European Convention on Human Rights are potentially relevant to the exercise of their functions.[66] Article 6 of the Convention has very limited application to the work of the Commissioners in deciding whether applicants are entitled to information under the Acts since the rights granted are not 'civil rights'[67] within the meaning of the Convention (although the civil rights of third parties may be affected), and, in any event, the various rights of appeal against their decisions probably mean that article 6 will be satisfied. The European Court has decided[68] that article 10 (which includes the right 'to receive information') only prohibits a government from restricting a person from receiving information from others who want to provide it and does not cast any obligation to provide information to an applicant against its will; but in the same case the Court decided that the failure by a public authority to disclose certain personal data might involve a breach of the right to respect for private and family life provided by article 8. It seems likely that this decision would only impinge on

---

[62]   DPA s 59(2).

[63]   FOI(S)A s 45(2), in particular paras (a) and (e).

[64]   FOIA s 76 and FOI(S)A s 63. Similarly, EIR reg 18(10) and EI(S)R reg 17(5).

[65]   See, in relation to England and Wales, Human Rights Act 1998 s 6(1) and (3).

[66]   See ch 3.

[67]   See the admissibility decision of the European Human Rights Commission in *Barry v France* (App No 14497/89) 14 October 1991 and *McGinley v United Kingdom* (1998) 27 EHRR 1 at paras 85–6. See, also, ; *Syndicat CFDT des Etablissements et Arsenaux du Val-de-Marne and Vesque v France* (App 11678/85) 7 December 1987; *Loiseau v France* (App No 46809/99) ECHR 18 November 2003; *Micallef v Malta* (App no 17056/06) ECHR 15 January 2008 at [39]. See further ch 3.

[68]   *Gaskin v United Kingdom* (1990) 12 EHRR 36. The actual decision in *Gaskin* was that the failure to provide medical records relating to the applicant at his request was an interference with his art 8 right to respect for his private and family life; this decision led to the enactment of DPA ss 68 and 69 which *inter alia* make health records, in whatever form they are kept, subject to the DPA and in particular the access rights provided by s 7, thereby potentially allowing individuals a right to obtain access to their own health records. See, further, ch 3. See also in the English courts *R (Persey) v Environment Secretary* [2003] QB 794 at [51]–[52].

applications for information under the Data Protection Act 1998. The Commissioners are also themselves public authorities for the purposes of the Freedom of Information Acts[69] and potentially 'data controllers' subject to the Data Protection Act 1998, and they must accordingly comply with the provisions of these Acts and the Environmental Information Regulations.

2. MONITORING COMPLIANCE WITH THE ACTS

010 Monitoring the right of access to personal data
The right of access to 'personal data'[70] held by a 'data controller' provided by Part II of the Data Protection Act 1998 is mainly enforced by means of an application to court by the individual who is the subject of such personal data.[71] The Information Commissioner's monitoring and enforcement functions relate to data controllers' 'processing' of personal data and their compliance with 'the data protection principles',[72] rather than directly to their compliance with their obligations to give access to personal data.

011 Monitoring the right of access to information held by public authorities
There is no express provision of the Freedom of Information Act 2000 requiring the Information Commissioner to monitor compliance by public authorities with their duty to give access to information pursuant to Part I of the Act. The normal mechanism for enforcement of that duty is for a complainant to apply to the Commissioner seeking from him a decision notice requiring steps to be taken by a public authority pursuant to s 50 of the Act.[73] However, there are a number of provisions of the Act from which such a free-standing obligation on the part of the Commissioner can be implied:

(1) The Commissioner has power, with the consent of the public authority, to assess whether it is following 'good practice' in the discharge of its functions under Part I of the Act;[74]

(2) The Commissioner can make recommendations as to good practice in any case where it appears to him that the practice of a public authority does not comply with a code of practice issued under s 45 of the Act in connection with the discharge of public authorities' functions under Part I thereof;[75]

(3) The Commissioner has power to require a public authority to furnish him with information for the purpose of determining whether it has complied with Part I of

---

[69] FOIA Sch 1 Pt VI, FOI(S)A, Sch 1 Pt 7.

[70] As to the meaning of 'personal data', see §§5– 021 to 5– 025.

[71] DPA s 7(9). See §5– 083. Note that in *R (SSHD) v IT (IC interested party)* [2006] EWHC 2958 (Admin), [2007] 2 All ER 703 (DC) the Information Commissioner treated a complaint arising from a request under s 7 of the DPA as a request for an assessment under s 42 of the Act and proceeded to deal with the matter.

[72] See in particular DPA ss 40(1), 42(1) and 43(1).

[73] See §28– 006.

[74] See FOIA ss 47(3) and (6).

[75] FOIA s 48.

the Act or a code of practice issued under s 45[76] and power to seek a warrant allowing entry, search and seizure of documents and other evidence if there is reason for suspecting a breach of Part I of the Act,[77] whether or not there has been a complaint and, if he is satisfied that the public authority has failed to comply with any requirement of Part I of the Act, he has power to serve an 'enforcement notice' on the public authority under s 52(1) of the Act, again whether or not there has been a complaint.

The functions and powers of the Information Commissioner under ss 47 and 48 and Part IV (ss 50-56) of the Freedom of Information Act 2000 apply also for the purposes of monitoring and enforcing compliance with the Environmental Information Regulations 2004.[78]

27–012 Monitoring the right of access to information held by Scottish public authorities

The position under the Freedom of Information (Scotland) Act in relation to the Scottish Information Commissioner is very similar,[79] save that the Scottish Information Commissioner does not require the consent of the public authority before undertaking an assessment as to whether the authority is following good practice and in particular complying with the requirements of the Act.[80] The Scottish Information Commissioner has the same functions and powers in relation to monitoring and enforcing compliance with the Environmental Information (Scotland) Regulations 2004 as he has under the Act.[81]

3. THE FIRST-TIER AND UPPER TRIBUNALS

27–013 The Information Tribunal

Under the original scheme of the legislation, judicial supervision of information rights was primarily provided by the Information Tribunal[82] (although it had no jurisdiction in relation to the Freedom of Information (Scotland) Act 2002 and no equivalent for it is provided under that Act).[83] The Information Tribunal was originally constituted as a statutory tribunal under the Data Protection Act 1984[84] as the Data Protection Tribunal. It was continued in existence

---

[76] FOIA s 51(1)(b).

[77] FOIA s 55, Sch 3 paras 1 and 2.

[78] EIR regs 16(5) and 18.

[79] See FOI(S)A ss 43(3), 44(1), 50(1)(b) and 51, and Sch 3.

[80] FOI(S)A s 43(1), (3) and (8).

[81] EI(S)R regs 17 and 18(5).

[82] FOIA ss 57 and 60 and EIR reg 18. In relation to the DPA, where no national security certificate has been issued under the DPA, judicial supervision is provided by the County Courts and the High Court (see §§5– 083 and 28– 042); where a national security certificate has been issued, judicial supervision is provided by the Tribunal (see §§5– 084 and 28– 046).

[83] Appeals from decisions of the Scottish Information Commissioner are heard by the Court of Session: FOI(S)A s 56.

[84] DPA s 3(1)(b).

by the Data Protection Act 1998[85] and its name was changed to the Information Tribunal by s 18(2) of the Freedom of Information Act 2000,[86] which Act also extended its functions substantially. The jurisdiction of the Tribunal was purely statutory. However, by virtue of Art 2(3)(a) of the Transfer of Tribunal Functions Order 2010,[87] with effect from 18 January 2010 all the functions of the Information Tribunal were transferred to the First-tier Tribunal (and, to a limited extent, the Upper Tribunal)[88] established under the Tribunals, Courts and Enforcement Act 2007.[89] Cases formerly heard by the Information Tribunal ('information rights cases')[90] have been assigned to the General Regulatory Chamber of the First-tier Tribunal and the Administrative Appeals Chamber of the Upper Tribunal.[91]

014 Membership of the Tribunals

Pursuant to section 6(4) of the Data Protection Act 1998, the Lord Chancellor had appointed members of the Information Tribunal. Prior to 18 January 2010, there were a chairman,[92] 11 deputy chairmen and 34 other members.[93] On that date, the chairman and deputy chairmen and the other members of the Information Tribunal became judges and other members of the First-tier and Upper Tribunals.[94] They were assigned to the General Regulatory Chamber and

---

[85] DPA s 6(3).

[86] With effect from 30 January 2001.

[87] SI 2010/22.

[88] Tribunal Procedure Rules are to determine which cases are assigned to the Upper Tribunal: the relevant rule is r 19 of the FTT Rules: this provides that national security cases must be transferred to the Upper Tribunal (r 19(1A)) and that other cases may be referred to the President of the General Regulatory Chamber and then transferred to the Upper Tribunal on his direction with the concurrence of the President of the Administrative Appeals Chamber of the Upper Tribunal (see rr 19(2) and (3)). It is envisaged that cases will only be suitable for transfer where some special feature merits this course; examples may be where the case is of considerable public importance or involves complex or unusual issues.

[89] Part 1 of this Act was designed to provide a new unified tribunals service by setting up the First-tier and Upper Tribunals under a new judicial office holder, the Senior President of Tribunals (currently Sir Robert Carnwath); it enabled the Lord Chancellor by order to transfer the jurisdiction of existing tribunals to the new tribunals; for the background see Sir Andrew Leggatt's report *Review of Tribunals* published in August 2001 and the Government's *White Paper Transforming Public Services: Complaints, Redress and Tribunals* published by the DCA in July 2004; the Upper Tribunal is to be a 'superior court of record': s 3(5). The Lord Chancellor is under a statutory duty to ensure that there is an efficient and effective system to support the carrying on of business by the Tribunals: see s 39 of the 2007 Act.

[90] That is, appeals under the DPA, FOIA, the Privacy and Electronic Communications (EC Directive) Regulations 2003 and the EIR: see definition in the Practice Statement on composition of Tribunals issued by the Senior President of Tribunals dated 21 August 2009.

[91] The First-tier Tribunal and Upper Tribunal (Chambers) Order 2008 (SI 2008/2684) (as amended by SI 2009/1590) arts 2(e), 5B(a), 6, 7(a)(vii).

[92] Professor John Angel. He became President of the General Regulatory Chamber and Principal Judge of the Information Rights jurisdiction under the new structure.

[93] Pen portraits of all the members are available at: www.informationtribunal.gov.uk

[94] See art 4 and Schedule 1 to the 2010 Order. Note that the chairman and deputy chairmen designated to hear national security appeals under para 2 of Schedule 6 to the Data Protection Act 1998 became deputy judges of the Upper Tribunal and transferred-in judges of the First-tier Tribunal and other deputy chairmen became transferred-in judges of the First-tier Tribunal (Parts 3 and 4 of Schedule 1); all the other ('lay') members of the Information Tribunal are transferred-in other members of the Upper Tribunal and, as such, are automatically other members of the First-tier Tribunal (see: s4(3)(c) of Tribunals, Courts and Enforcement Act 2007).

Administrative Appeals Chamber[95] with the intention that they should continue to hear information rights cases as before. The former chairman of the Information Tribunal was appointed the Chamber President of the General Regulatory Chamber and the Principal Judge of the information rights jurisdiction. New judges and other members of the First-tier and Upper Tribunals will be appointed and assigned to those Chambers and to the information rights jurisdiction in accordance with the relevant provisions of the Tribunals, Courts and Enforcement Act 2007 and secondary legislation and directions made thereunder.[96]

27– 015 Constitution of Tribunals in particular cases

The First-tier and Upper Tribunal's functions of deciding information rights cases is to be exercised by a member or members of the General Regulatory or Administrative Appeals Chamber (as the case may be) chosen by the Senior President of Tribunals,[97] who can delegate that (and any other function) to any other judge,[98] in particular the relevant Chamber President or Principal Judge of the information rights jurisdiction. In practice, the judges chosen to hear information rights cases will be those with experience of such cases (initially those transferred-in from the Information Tribunal). The composition of Tribunals in the General Regulatory Chamber is regulated by the Senior President's Practice Statement dated 21 August 2009,[99] which provides that a decision that disposes of proceedings[100] or determines a preliminary issue must be made by a judge (who must preside) and two other members '… where each other member has substantial experience of data protection or of freedom of information (including environmental information) rights' but that any other decision (including striking out a case or giving directions) must be made by one judge.[101] In the Upper Tribunal, any decision is to be made by one judge unless the Senior President determines it should be decided by two or three members determined by the Senior President.[102]

27– 016 Data Protection Act 1998 appeals

The First-tier and Upper Tribunals have jurisdiction to determine the following appeals under the Data Protection Act 1998:

— an appeal under s 28(4) of the Act to quash a certificate relating to national security issued by a Minister under s 28(2) of the Act;[103]

— an appeal under s 28(6) of the Act for a determination under s 28(7) that such a

---

[95] Pursuant to paras 9 to 12 of Schedule 4 to the Tribunals, Courts and Enforcement Act 2007.

[96] See Schs 2 to 4 to the Tribunals, Courts and Enforcement Act 2007.

[97] Para 14 of Schedule 4 to the 2007 Act.

[98] Section 8(1)(a) of the 2007 Act

[99] Made under para 15 Schedule 4 to the 2007 Act and the First-tier and Upper Tribunal (Composition of Tribunal) Order 2008 (SI 2008/2835).

[100] This does not include a decision to strike out a party's case under rule 8 of the FTT Rules: para 1(d) of the Practice Statement.

[101] See paras 3, 10, 14 and 15 of the Practice Statement.

[102] First-tier and Upper Tribunal (Composition of Tribunal) Order 2008 (SI 2008/2835) paras 3, 4, and 6 to 8.

[103] A certificate signed by a Minister of the Crown is, by virtue of the DPA s 28(2), conclusive evidence that exemption from the provisions of all or any of the provisions mentioned in s 28(1) (which include Pt II, which itself includes s 7: the right of access to personal data) is required for the purposes of safeguarding national security.

certificate does not relate to particular personal data;[104]

— an appeal under s 48(1) of the Act against an 'enforcement notice',[105] an 'information notice'[106] or a 'special information notice'[107] served by the Information Commissioner;

— an appeal under s 48(2) of the Act against the refusal of the Information Commissioner to cancel or vary an enforcement notice after an application under s 41(2);

— an appeal under s 48(3) against a statement of urgency in relation to an enforcement notice, information notice or special information notice included by the Information Commissioner under ss 40(8), 43(5) or 44(6) of the Act respectively; and

— an appeal under s 48(4) of the Act by a data controller against a determination by the Information Commissioner under s 45(1) that particular data is not being processed only for 'special purposes'.[108]

017 Freedom of Information Act 2000 appeals

The First-tier and Upper Tribunals have jurisdiction to determine the following appeals under the Freedom of Information Act 2000:

— an appeal under s 57(1) by a complainant or a public authority[109] against a decision notice served by the Information Commissioner under s 50(3)(b) following a complaint under s 50(1) that the public authority had failed to deal with a request for information in accordance with Part I of the Act;[110]

— an appeal under s 57(2) by a public authority against an 'information notice'[111] or an 'enforcement notice'[112] served on it;[113]

— an appeal under s 60(1) by the Information Commissioner or any applicant whose request for information has been affected by a Minister's issue of a national security

---

[104] Appeals under s.28 must be transferred to the Upper Tribunal: see rule 19(1A) of the FTT Rules.

[105] DPA s 40. Enforcement notices under the DPA are considered at §5– 087.

[106] DPA s 43. Information notices under the DPA are considered at §5– 093.

[107] DPA s 44. As to the meaning of 'special purposes', see §5– 065.

[108] DPA ss 3 and 45(1)(b).

[109] Or, in the case of 'transferred public records' (FOIA s 15(4)) within s 66 of the Act, the 'responsible authority' as defined in s 15(5) thereof: s 57(3).

[110] This does not include determining whether a request for information made of a body to which the Act has limited operation falls or does not fall within the limited area of operation: *BBC v Sugar and IC* [2007] EWHC 905 (Admin), [2007] 1 WLR 2583. See further §9– 022.

[111] FOIA s 51(1). Information notices under the FOIA are dealt with at §28– 012.

[112] FOIA s 52(1). Enforcement notices under the FOIA are dealt with at §28– 013.

[113] Or, in the case of 'transferred public records' (FOIA s 15(4)) within s 66 of the Act, the 'responsible authority' as defined in s 15(5) thereof: s 57(3).

certificate under s 23(2)[114] or s 24(3);[115] and

— an appeal under s 60(4) by a party to proceedings under the Act on the grounds that a certificate issued under s 24(3) identifying the information to which it applies by means of a general description does not apply to the particular information in question as claimed by the public authority holding it.[116]

27– 018 Environmental Information Regulations 2004 appeals
By virtue of regulation 18 of the Environmental Information Regulations 2004, the First-tier and Upper Tribunals have jurisdiction to hear appeals against decision notices served by the Information Commissioner in relation to applications for environmental information under the Regulations and by a public authority against an information notice or an enforcement notice as under s 57(1) and 57(2) of the Freedom of Information Act 2000. By virtue of regulation 18(7) the Upper Tribunal also has jurisdiction to hear appeals relating to ministerial certificates made under regulation 15(1) equivalent to those provided by s 60(1) and 60(4) of the Freedom of Information Act 2000.

27– 019 Practice and procedure
Section 22 of the Tribunals, Courts and Enforcement Act 2007 makes provision for a Tribunal Procedure Committee to make rules governing the practice and procedure to be followed in the First-tier and Upper Tribunal. There are two relevant sets of rules in force:[117]

— The Tribunal Procedure (First-tier Tribunal) (General Regulatory Chamber) Rules 2009[118] which govern all information rights appeals to the First-tier Tribunal;

— The Tribunal Procedure (Upper Tribunal) Rules 2008[119] which govern appeals transferred to the Upper Tribunal under rule 19 of the The Tribunal Procedure (First-tier Tribunal) (General Regulatory Chamber) Rules 2009, in particular national security certificate appeals.[120]

Further, section 23 of Tribunals, Courts and Enforcement Act 2007 enables the Senior

---

[114] FOIA s 23(2) provides that a certificate signed by a Minister of the Crown certifying that information was supplied by or relates to any of the security bodies listed in s 23(3) is conclusive evidence of that 'fact' so as to make it 'exempt information' by virtue of s 23(1). Conclusive certificates on the grounds of national security are dealt with at §§17– 050 to 17– 062. Appeals where there has been such a certificate are dealt with at §§14– 039 to 14– 040, 28– 017, 28– 027 to 28– 028.

[115] FOIA s 24(3) provides that a certificate signed by a Minister of the Crown certifying that exemption from s 1(1)(b) or ss 1(1)(a) and (b) is required shall be conclusive evidence of that 'fact' for the purposes of s 24(1) and (2) which provide exemption in those circumstances from the duties to state whether information is held and to communicate it pursuant to s 1(1)(a) and (b) of the Act respectively. Conclusive certificates under s 24 are dealt with at §§17– 050 to 17– 062. Appeals where there has been such a certificate are dealt with at §§14– 039 to 14– 040, 28– 017, 28– 027 to 28– 028, and 28– 046 to 28– 047.

[116] Appeals under s 60 must be transferred to the Upper Tribunal under rule 19(1A) of the FTT Rules.

[117] These rules apply to appeals in information rights cases even if they were started before the Information Tribunal (ie before 18 January 2010) except that the new tribunal (First-tier or Upper as the case may be) can disapply them and apply the procedural rules in force before (as to which see the previous edition of this book) and that an order for costs can only be made in such cases if and to the extent it could have been made by the Information Tribunal: see Transfer of Tribunal Functions Order 2010 (SI 2010/22) Schedule 5 paras 2 and 3.

[118] SI 2009/1976 as amended by SI 2010/43.

[119] SI 2008/2698 as amended by SIs 2009/274, 2009/1975, 2010/43 and 2010/44.

[120] That is, appeals under DPA s 28 and FOIA s 60 (see definition in UT Rules rule 1).

President to give practice directions as to the practice and procedure in the two Tribunals with the approval of the Lord Chancellor, and the Chamber President to give practice directions as to the practice and procedure in the chamber with the approval of the Lord Chancellor and the Senior President.[121]

020 The Tribunal Procedure (First-tier Tribunal) (General Regulatory Chamber) Rules 2009

These rules are of general application and not specific to information rights appeals. In accordance with modern practice, they contain an 'overriding objective' provision.[122] An appeal to the First-tier Tribunal must be brought within 28 days of the relevant notice. An appeal is initiated by a notice of appeal compliant with rule 22 and sent to the Tribunal.[123] The Rules make generous provision for parties to be added to an appeal.[124] Unless striking out a case under rule 8, the Tribunal must hold a hearing before making a final decision unless each party agrees to it being determined without a hearing and the Tribunal is satisfied that it can properly determine the case in that way.[125] Rule 8 confers power on the Tribunal to strike out the whole or any part of proceedings or bar a respondent to an appeal from taking further part in the proceedings in any case if the Tribunal considers that there is no reasonable prospect of the relevant party's case (or part of it) succeeding. The Tribunal has wide powers to govern the extent and nature of any submissions and evidence it requires to receive; it can admit any evidence regardless of its strict admissibility at a civil trial and it can exclude otherwise admissible evidence where it would be unfair to admit it.[126] Rule 14 governs prevention of disclosure or publicity of documents and information. Rule 14(6) is of particular significance in information rights cases in that it enables the Tribunal to direct that documents and information are disclosed to it without being disclosed to a party. Rule 14(10) directs the Tribunal to conduct its proceedings and record its decision and reasons in such a way as not to undermine the effect of such a direction and rule 35(4) enables the Tribunal to exclude a party from any part of a hearing if necessary in order to give effect to rule 14(10). Part 4 of the Rules contains provisions which are new to this jurisdiction in that the Tribunal is given power on an application for permission to appeal under section 11 of the Tribunals, Courts and Enforcement Act 2007 (itself new) to review a decision if it is satisfied that there was an error of law in it.[127]

---

[121] The writer is not aware of any relevant practice directions although there is a Practice Note dated 1 February 2010 applying to appeals before the First-tier Tribunal in information rights cases which practitioners should be familiar with. Although it is headed 'Protection of Confidential Information' it covers a wide range of general topics in relation to such appeals, including joinder, witnesses, documents and decisions.

[122] Rule 2.

[123] There is a general jurisdiction to extend time: rule 5(3)(a).

[124] Rule 9.

[125] Rule 32: note 'hearing' is defined in rule 1.

[126] Rule 15.

[127] Rule 44(1).

27– 021 **The Tribunal Procedure (Upper Tribunal) Rules 2008**

National security certificate appeals[128] and other appeals on the direction of the President of the General Regulatory Chamber with the concurrence of the President of the Administrative Appeals Chamber of the Upper Tribunal are transferred and determined by the Upper Tribunal.[129] Such appeals are not appeals from the First-tier Tribunal but are direct appeals from the relevant decision of the Information Commissioner or Minister but they are governed by the same set of procedural rules as those which govern appeals from the First-tier Tribunal.[130] These Rules include an 'overriding objective' and case management powers similar to those in The Tribunal Procedure (First-tier Tribunal) (General Regulatory Chamber) Rules 2009. They contain at rule 14(10) specific provision that the Upper Tribunal must ensure that information is not disclosed contrary to the interests of national security and consequential provisions in relation to hearings and decisions.[131] In contrast to the position in the First-tier Tribunal, the Upper Tribunal can make any decision without a hearing.[132] Schedule 2 to the Rules makes special provision in relation to national security certificate cases.

27– 022 **Costs**

In the First-tier Tribunal the only costs orders that can be made are (a) wasted costs orders under section 29(4) of the Tribunals, Courts and Enforcement Act 2007[133] or (b) if the Tribunal considers that a party has acted unreasonably in bringing, defending or conducting the proceedings.[134] In relation to proceedings transferred or referred by, or on appeal from, the First-tier Tribunal (which would include not only appeals from decisions of the Information Commissioner transferred to the Upper Tribunal but also appeals from the First-tier Tribunal under section 11 of the Tribunals, Courts and Enforcement Act 2007) the Upper Tribunal can make the same costs orders as the First-tier Tribunal.[135] There are also special costs provisions in relation to national security certificate appeals under section 28 of the Data Protection Act 1998 or section 60 of the Freedom of Information Act 2000 (or regulation 18(7) of the Environmental Information Regulations 2004). The Tribunal can make:

---

[128] That is, under DPA s 28 or FOIA s 60 or under that section as applied and modified by EIR reg 18.

[129] Rule 19 of FTT Rules. Appeals other than national security appeals are likely to have some special feature, eg to be of considerable public importance or involve complex or unusual issues.

[130] Save that the rules in Part 3 (including rules 23 (Notice of Appeal), 24 (Response to Notice of Appeal) and 25 (Appellant's reply) only apply to the extent provided for by directions given by the Upper Tribunal: see rule 26A(2); it appears to be envisaged that the notice of appeal in all transferred cases must comply with rule 22 of the FTT Rules and that following transfer to the Upper Tribunal, that tribunal shall consider the case and give 'tailor-made' directions: see rule 26A(2)(a) of the UT Rules.

[131] Rules 14(11), 37 and 40.

[132] Rule 34.

[133] Orders in relation to costs wasted as a result of the improper, unreasonable or negligent act or omission of a legal or other representative of a party.

[134] See rule 10 of the FTT Rules which also lays down the procedure in relation to making costs orders. In relation to the similarly-worded provision in the IT(EA) Rules, see *HM Treasury v IC and Times Newspapers Ltd*, IT, 26 July 2007.

[135] Rule 10(1)(b) of UT Rules.

— a wasted costs orders under section 29(4);

— a costs order if it considers that a party or its representative has acted unreasonably in bringing, defending or conducting the proceedings;

— if a certificate is quashed, a costs order against the relevant Minister and in favour of the appellant; and

— if the appeal is against the application of a certificate, a costs order against the appellant if the appeal is dismissed, and in his favour if the appeal is allowed.[136]

The above costs rules only apply to appeals started before 18 January 2010 if and to the extent that an order for costs could have been made by the Information Tribunal under its rules of procedure.[137]

023 Contempt jurisdiction and enforcement powers of Tribunals

The Upper Tribunal is a 'superior court of record'[138] and (as well as being given the same powers as the High Court in relation to judicial review)[139] it is given the same powers, rights, privileges and authority as the High Court (and in Scotland, the Court of Session) in relation to the attendance of witnesses, the production of documents and all other matters incidental to its functions.[140] This presumably includes the power to imprison for contempt of court,[141] whether for failure to obey an order of the Upper Tribunal (by, for example, failing to answer a witness summons, citation or order)[142] or for interfering with its process (by, for example, committing a contempt in the face of the court or interfering with witnesses). However, there are no rules relating to this jurisdiction apart from rule 16 of the Tribunal Procedure (Upper Tribunal) Rules 2008 relating to the issue of witness summonses and related orders,[143] and presumably the Upper Tribunal would follow the practice and procedure of the High Court as closely as possible. The First-tier Tribunal has no similar powers but rule 7(3) of the Tribunal Procedure (First-tier Tribunal) (General Regulatory Chamber) Rules 2009 provides that the First-tier Tribunal can refer to the Upper Tribunal and ask it to exercise its powers under section 25 of the Tribunals, Courts and Enforcement Act 2007 to deal with any failure

---

[136] Rule 10(1A).

[137] Reference should be made to previous editions of this book and the relevant rules: IT(EA) Rules rr 20 and 29 and IT (NSA) Rules rr 23 and 29.

[138] Tribunals, Courts and Enforcement Act 2007 s 3(5). As to the meaning and significance of this, see *R (Cart) v Upper Tribunal* [2009] EWHC 3052 (Admin), [2010] 2 WLR 1012, where the Upper Tribunal was described as 'an alter ego of the High Court: it constitutes an authoritative, impartial and independent judicial source for the interpretation and application of the relevant statutory texts....It is a court possessing the final power to interpret for itself the law it must apply....[The Upper Tribunal's] role at the apex of a new and comprehensive judicial structure ought to be respected and given effect' (at [94]). The Divisional Court held that decisions of the Upper Tribunal were not generally amenable to judicial review (at [97]-[100]).

[139] Tribunals, Courts and Enforcement Act 2007 ss 15-21.

[140] Tribunals, Courts and Enforcement Act 2007 s 25(1) and (2).

[141] The power of the High Court is discussed in *Halsbury's Laws of England* 4th edn, Butterworths 1998 re-issue, vol 9(1) paras 506-509. By Contempt of Court Act 1981 s 14, the power is limited to one of committal for two years in the case of a superior court.

[142] As to which there is specific provision in UT Rules r 16.

[143] Cryptically, rule 16(6)(b) states that a summons issued under the rule must state the consequences of non-compliance without mentioning what those consequences might be; it is thought that they must be the possibility of contempt proceedings.

by a person to comply with any requirement to attend to give evidence or swear an oath or give evidence or produce a document. Presumably the First-tier Tribunal would be considered an 'inferior court' for the purposes of RSC Ord 52 r1(2)(a)(iii) so that a Divisional Court of the Queen's Bench Division would have jurisdiction to make an order for committal for a contempt committed in connection with its proceedings.[144] It also seems likely that the First-tier Tribunal would be considered a 'court' for the purposes of section 42 of the Senior Courts Act 1981 (which deals with vexatious litigants) in the same way as the Information Tribunal was.[145] It should be noted that the orders made by the First-tier Tribunal at the conclusion of information rights appeals will amount to the original or a substituted decision, information or enforcement notice of the Information Commissioner:[146] such notices are enforceable at the instance of the Commissioner himself by certification to the High Court or Court of Session.[147] As for enforcement of monetary awards, section 27 of the Tribunals, Courts and Enforcement Act 2007 provides that sums payable under a decision of the First-tier or Upper Tribunal are recoverable as if they were payable under an order of the county court or High Court, with analogous provisions in relation to Scotland and Northern Ireland.

27–024 **Human Rights Act 1998**

The Tribunals themselves are subject to the Human Rights Act 1998.[148] Although it seems unlikely that the rights given by the Freedom of Information Act 2000 give rise to 'civil rights and obligations' such as to require the Tribunals to comply with article 6 of the European Convention in deciding cases under that Act, there may be occasions (particularly in relation to the Data Protection Act 1998) where article 6 does apply: for example, where the civil rights of a third party are affected[149] or where the information is personal and relates particularly to the applicant. Furthermore, the Tribunals will obviously have regard to other provisions of the European Convention in exercising its jurisdiction (particularly in considering where the public interest lies when considering the applicability of any of the exemptions to disclosure in the Freedom of Information Act 2000). Although the Tribunals are probably not public authorities for the purposes of the Freedom of Information Act 2000, they may be 'data controllers' for the purposes of the Data Protection Act 1998.

---

[144] See, eg in relation to industrial tribunals, *Peach Grey & Co v Sommers* [1995] 1 All ER 100.

[145] See case *Re Ewing* [2002] EWHC 3169 at [40], but note that that case was, strictly speaking, only concerned with the Information Tribunal sitting on an appeal under DPA s 28(4).

[146] FOIA s 58.

[147] See discussion of this procedure below at §§29–002 to 29–004.

[148] Human Rights Act 1998 s 6(1) and (3). See the discussion on the impact of the Human Rights Act in ch 3.

[149] For example, a disclosure that will arguably breach contractual rights in relation to confidential information.

CHAPTER 28
Appeals

A. APPEALS UNDER THE FREEDOM OF INFORMATION ACTS

1. FIRST STAGE: INTERNAL RECONSIDERATION

28– 001 First stage

A person who is dissatisfied with the response of a public authority to his request for information under the Freedom of Information Act 2000 or Environmental Information Regulations 2004 will normally first seek internal reconsideration by the public authority before resorting to the Information Commissioner, the tribunal system or the courts.

28– 002 Complaints under the section 45 Code of Practice

The code of practice issued under s 45 of the Freedom of Information Act 2000 requires public authorities to provide internal procedures for dealing with complaints about the handling by them of requests for information.[1] Such complaints will include complaints by persons who have made requests for information about a failure to comply with s 1(1)(a) or (b) of the Act promptly[2] or objections to the contents of a notice of refusal by the public authority made under s 17(1), (3) or (5) relying on an exemption in Part II of the Act or stating that s 12 or s 14 apply to relieve it of the duty to comply with the request.[3] A notice under s 17 must, if appropriate, contain reasons for reliance on an exemption in Part II of the Act and reasons for claiming that the public interest in disclosure is outweighed by the public interest in maintaining the exemption[4] and must contain details of any complaints procedure and of the right to complain to the Information Commissioner under s 50.[5] The code provides that any written reply from an applicant expressing dissatisfaction with a public authority's response to a valid request for information should be treated as a complaint.[6] The complaints procedure should provide for a fair and thorough review of decisions under the Act; it should enable a fresh decision to be taken on reconsideration of all relevant factors; procedures should be as clear and simple as possible and encourage a prompt determination;[7] if possible, complaints should be handled by someone senior to the person who took the original decision;[8] complainants should be informed of the outcome of their complaint and complaints should be dealt with within target time periods;[9] the information requested should be provided as soon as practicable if that is the outcome of the procedure;[10] and a complainant should be informed of his right to apply to the Information Commissioner if still dissatisfied.[11]

003 Statutory encouragement for internal procedure

The policy of the Act is to encourage attempts at resolving disputes by means of the internal complaints procedure. Thus, any notice of refusal of a request under s 17 of the Act must include particulars of any complaints procedure maintained by the public authority or state that it does not have one[12] and the Information Commissioner should not deal with an application to him under s 50 of the Act if it appears to him that the complainant has not exhausted any

---

[1] See FOIA s 45(2)(e) and Pt VI of the Code. The current version of the Code was issued by the Secretary of State for Constitutional Affairs in November 2004. The Code is dealt with more specifically in ch 10.

[2] Sections 1(1)(a) and (b) give the basic rights to be informed whether the public authority holds the information and to have it communicated; s 10(1) generally requires compliance within 20 working days of a request, but permits extensions in certain circumstances: see §§11– 022 to 11– 030.

[3] Section 12 provides exemption where the cost of compliance would exceed an appropriate limit and s 14 provides exemption where the request is vexatious. See ch 12.

[4] FOIA s 17(1)(c) and 17(3) and §§13– 011 to 13– 012.

[5] FOIA s 17(7).

[6] FOIA s 45; Code of Practice, para 38. The Tribunal has taken a similarly generous line in relation to what will constitute a request for internal review: see *Hogan and Oxford City Council v IC*, IT, 17 October 2006 at [20].

[7] Code of Practice, para 39.

[8] Code of Practice, para 40.

[9] Code of Practice, paras 41 and 42.

[10] Code of Practice, para 44.

[11] Code of Practice, para 46.

[12] FOIA s 17(7)(a).

complaints procedure which complies with the Code of Practice.[13]

28–004 Internal review by Scottish public authorities

The Freedom of Information (Scotland) Act 2002 adopts a different approach from that in the Freedom of Information Act 2000. There is a statutory procedure for an internal review by the public authority which is a precondition of any application to the Scottish Information Commissioner[14] and any refusal notice must include details of the applicant's right to such a review.[15] The statutory procedure allows an applicant who is dissatisfied with the way that a Scottish public authority has dealt with a request for information under the Act to require the authority to review its actions and decisions in relation to the request.[16] The requirement for a review must be made not later than the fortieth working day after the time limit for dealing with a request or a purported compliance with a request or service of a notice refusing to supply the information if later,[17] but the public authority can, in effect, extend time.[18] Unless the requirement for a review or the original request for information was vexatious,[19] the public authority must comply with a requirement for a review promptly and in any event not later than the twentieth working day after receipt thereof.[20] On the review, the public authority can confirm, vary or substitute any decision or reach an original decision if the complaint is that no decision has been reached.[21] The public authority must give the applicant a notice in writing as to what it has done on the review or that it considers the requirement or request to have been vexatious.[22] Special provisions apply in relation to certain reviews when the relevant public authority is the Keeper of the Records of Scotland.[23] There is some further guidance on the requirements of a review in the Scottish Ministers' Code of Practice on the Discharge of Functions by Public Authorities Under the Freedom of Information (Scotland) Act 2002.[24]

28–005 Internal review — environmental information

To the extent that a request for information captures 'environmental information',[25] the applicant's right of internal review is conferred by the Environmental Information

---

[13] FOIA s 50(2)(a).

[14] FOI(S)A s 47(1) which provides for applications to the Commissioner only by a person dissatisfied with a decision given by the public authority on such review under ss 21(5) or (9) or with the failure of the public authority to deal with a requirement for a review.

[15] FOI(S)A s 19(b).

[16] FOI(S)A s 20(1).

[17] FOI(S)A s 20(5).

[18] FOI(S)A s 20(6).

[19] FOI(S)A s 21(8).

[20] FOI(S)A s 21(1).

[21] FOI(S)A s 21(4).

[22] FOI(S)A ss 21(5) and (9). It is against notices under these subsections or a failure to carry out a review that application is made to the Scottish Commissioner under s 47(1).

[23] FOI(S)A ss 21(2) and 22.

[24] See Code at paras 63 to 71.

[25] As to the meaning of which, see §6–010.

Regulations.[26] Where an applicant's request for information covers both 'environmental information' and other information, although the provenance of the applicant's right to internal consideration is different, the practical consequences are negligible. The internal review procedure under the Environmental Information Regulations 2004 is considered in Chapter 6.[27]

2.   SECOND STAGE: APPLICATION TO THE INFORMATION COMMISSIONER

006   Application to Information Commissioner
The second stage for a person who is dissatisfied with the response by a public authority to a request for information is an application to the Information Commissioner under s 50(1) of the Freedom of Information Act 2000 or that section as imported by the Environmental Information Regulations 2004.[28] The section is framed in such a way that it is only the person who made the original request for information who can apply. The application is for a decision whether, in any specified respect, the request for information has (or, by implication, has not) 'been dealt with in accordance with the requirements of Part I [of the Act]'.[29] There are no procedural requirements for making a complaint to the Information Commissioner although he has published on his website a standard complaint form for use in relation to the Freedom of Information Act 2000 and Environmental Information Regulations 2004. This indicates that complaints will be dealt with on a 'first-come, first-served' basis. There have been serious delays in the process of dealing with these applications over the last few years, such that the entire system is in danger of being undermined.[30] It is understood that the new Information Commissioner at the time of writing, Christopher Graham, firmly intends to address the backlog and the delay.

007   Grounds for complaint—procedural matters
The reference in s 50(1) to a request not having been dealt with in accordance with the requirements of Part I of the Act encompasses a wide range of potential complaints of a procedural nature. A complainant may apply to the Commissioner for a decision whether any of the following matters are in accordance with the Act:

(1)   Whether a request for information made of a body to which the Act has limited operation (eg the BBC) falls or does not fall within the limited area of operation;[31]

---

[26] EIR reg 11; EI(S)R reg 16. No doubt by an oversight there is no modification to s 50(2)(a) of the FOIA provided in EIR reg 18(4), although in the case of requests for environmental information the complaints procedure will be under reg 11 not the Code of Practice.

[27] See §6– 060.

[28] EIR reg 18. See further §6– 060.

[29] FOIA s 50(1).

[30] This has been referred to in many Tribunal decisions: see *Student Loans Company Ltd v IC*, IT, 17 July 2009 at [4]-[7] and *Cabinet Office v IC*, IT, 5 January 2009 at [18].

[31] *Sugar v BBC* [2009] UKHL 9, [2009] 1 WLR 430, [2009] 4 All ER 111 at [35]-[36].

(2)   The level of fee sought by the public authority for complying with its duty to inform the applicant whether it holds information of the description specified in the request and for communicating that information to him;[32]

(3)   The time taken by the public authority for complying with the request;[33]

(4)   The means by which the public authority communicated the information to the applicant;[34]

(5)   The refusal of a public authority to comply with a request on the basis of the cost of compliance being estimated to exceed the appropriate limit;[35]

(6)   The refusal of a public authority to deal with a request on the basis that it is vexatious or is identical or substantially identical to an earlier request from the applicant;[36]

(7)   The failure by an appropriate records authority upon receipt of a request to comply with its obligations under s 15 of the Act;

(8)   The failure by a public authority to provide advice and assistance;[37] and

(9)   The failure of a refusal notice to contain the information required under s 17 of the Act.

28–008   Grounds for complaint—refusals

Where none of the procedural matters are relevant and a public authority either:

—   does not inform an applicant whether or not it holds information of the description specified in his request; or

—   does not communicate to that applicant some or all of the requested information held by it,

the applicant's request will not have been dealt with in accordance with the requirements of Part I of the Act (unless one or more of the qualifications introduced by s 1(2) and s 2 of the Act apply). An applicant may complain that, notwithstanding a public authority's denial that it holds information coming within the terms of the request,[38] it does in fact do so and that section 1(1)(a) and (subject to the effect of any exemptions) section 1(1)(b) have not been complied with. This raises a straight issue of fact which has to be determined on the balance of probabilities.[39]

---

[32]   FOIA s 9.

[33]   FOIA s 10. Even if there has been a breach of s 10, the Information Commissioner will have no power to specify any steps that must be taken by the public authority: *Harper v IC and Royal Mail Group plc* [2005], IT, 15 November 2005. The Commissioner can, however: (1) make a good practice recommendation under FOIA s 48; (2) mention the matter in his annual report under FOIA s 49; or (3) issue an enforcement notice under FOIA s 52, requiring adherence to time-limits.

[34]   FOIA s 11.

[35]   FOIA ss 12 and 13.

[36]   FOIA s 14.

[37]   FOIA s 16.

[38]   The request must be read objectively in the light of the background circumstances: *Berend v IC and LB of Richmond*, IT, 12 July 2007 at [86]; *Dept for Culture, Media & Sport v IC*, IT, 22 February 2010 at [16].

[39]   When such an issue is raised it is open to the Commissioner (and in due course the relevant Tribunal) to review the adequacy of the public authority's search for the information having regard if appropriate to the Lord Chancellor's Code of Practice on the keeping, management and destruction of records issued under FOIA s 46: see *Bromley v IC and Environment Agency*, IT, 31 August 2007 at [13]; *Babar v IC and British Council*, IT, 14 November 2007 at [31]; *Ames*

If the public authority seeks to rely on any of the qualifications in s 2, the Commissioner must consider:

(1) whether the information held by the public authority answering the terms of the request is exempt information by virtue of any provision in Part II (ss 21-44);

(2) if a provision by which the information is rendered exempt information does not confer absolute exemption, whether the public interest in maintaining the exemption outweighs the public interest in disclosing that information;

(3) whether the duty to confirm or deny that the public authority holds information of the description specified in the request has been disapplied by any provision in Part II; and

(4) if the duty to confirm or deny has been disapplied by any provision in Part II, whether the public interest in maintaining the exclusion of that duty outweighs the public interest in disclosing whether the public authority holds that information.

Depending upon the exemption, (1) and (3) involve considering, in relation to each piece of information, whether the particular attributes identified in the exemption are present or the likely effects of its disclosure upon an identified interest. Where a conclusive certificate has been issued, (1) and (3) above will be answered to the extent that the information sought is covered by the certificate.

009 Approach on review

It is for the Information Commissioner himself to decide in any particular case whether any provision of Part II applies[40] and, in particular, where the 'public interest' lies in the case of a non-absolute exemption (as opposed to it being for him to review the decision of the public authority on the question).[41] Since on a complaint under section 50 of the Freedom of Information Act 2000 the Commissioner must consider whether the request for information has been dealt by the public authority in accordance with Part I of the Act, his decision must be based on the factual position as it existed at the date when the public authority made its decision (including any review decision).[42] It has been suggested that if circumstances have changed since the public authority's refusal to disclose information such that, notwithstanding a decision that the public authority ought to have disclosed the information at the time of the request, it is undesirable that it should do so at the time of the Commissioner's decision (because, eg, criminal proceedings have been started which may be prejudiced), the Commissioner may decide that the public authority need take no steps notwithstanding the breach of the Act.[43] Obviously the Commissioner (and the Tribunal) can only require

---

v IC and Cabinet Office, IT, 24 April 2008 at [10]; Weait v IC, IT, 17 July 2007; James v IC and DTI, IT, 25 September 2007. See further §13– 002. t has frequently happened that additional information has emerged in the course of proceedings before the Information Commissioner or Tribunal.

[40] Subject to the certification procedure under FOIA ss 23(2), 24(3) 34(3) or 36(7).

[41] This was the view before the Act was passed (see the debate in House of Lords, Hansard vol 619 col 218 (14 November 2000) (Lord Goodhart) and is the approach of the Tribunal (see Hogan and Oxford City Council v IC, IT, 17 October 2006 at [55]). The Commissioner's decision would also be subject to an appropriate certificate under FOIA s 53: see §28– 014.

[42] Campaign against the Arms Trade v IC and MoJ, IT, 26 August 2008 at [38]-[40]; Roberts v IC, IT, 4 December 2008 at [27].

[43] OGC v IC [2008] EWHC 774 (Admin), [2010] QB 98, [2008] ACD 54 at [98].

disclosure of information which comes within the terms of the relevant request.[44] There is no provision dealing with who bears the burden of persuading the Information Commissioner that the public authority has or has not acted in accordance with the Act.[45] The Tribunal has expressed the view that the Information Commissioner should normally communicate with the complainant and the public authority before reaching any decision rather than merely relying on the complaint notice and accompanying documentation; and that he should draw attention to any perceived breach of the duty to provide advice and assistance under s 16 of the Freedom of Information Act 2000 notwithstanding that the complainant has not expressly raised that matter.[46] In a case where the Commissioner agrees with a public authority that information need not be disclosed, it is of particular importance that the Commissioner himself sees the disputed information and makes a full investigation.[47] The Commissioner can encourage the parties to settle, but if the parties cannot agree he must reach a decision on the complaint and specify the steps that the public authority must take to comply with its obligations under the Act.[48]

28– 010   New grounds of exemption

Despite the procedure and time limits laid down by ss 10 and 17 of the Freedom of Information Act 2000,[49] on a complaint under s 50 the public authority may rely on exemptions not previously invoked by it. Similarly, the Information Commissioner is not limited to the exemptions invoked by the public authority.[50] However, the Tribunal has made it clear that the Commissioner should only allow exemptions to be relied on for the first time before him if there is a reasonable justification in the particular circumstances of the case: to permit otherwise would risk making the complaint and appeal system cumbersome and uncertain, as well as permitting public authorities to take a cavalier attitude to their obligations under sections 10 and 17.[51] The Tribunal has also expressed the view that the failure to claim an exemption in a refusal notice does not involve a breach of section 17 but means that the Information Commissioner must consider whether to allow a claim of reliance on such exemption at all.[52]

---

[44] *OGC v IC* [2008] EWHC 774 (Admin), [2010] QB 98, [2008] ACD 54 at [109]-[110].

[45] Compare the Australian Freedom of Information Act 1982 s 61 referred to in §28– 020. In relation to the burden of proof, see §§14– 024 to 14– 030.

[46] See *Barber v IC*, IT, 20 February 2006 at [16]–[19].

[47] See: *Beam v IC and FCO*, IT, 12 May 2009 at [14]-[15]; and *Health Professionals Council v IC*, IT, 14 March 2008 at [52].

[48] See FOIA s 50(4) and the discussion in *King v IC and DWP*, IT, 20 March 2008 at [73]-[89].

[49] And similarly under FOI(S)A, EIR and EI(S)R.

[50] In *England and LB of Bexley v IC*, IT, 10 May 2007 at [109] the Tribunal, without deciding, doubted whether the Information Commissioner could claim on behalf of the public authority an exemption which the public authority itself had not relied upon.

[51] See *DBERR v IC and Friends of the Earth*, IT, 29 April 2008 at [41]-[45]. See also §28– 022 below, which considers the claiming of late exemptions for the first time at the Tribunal stage for relevant considerations and specific examples: for obvious reasons, there is more likely to be a reasonable justification for considering an exemption first raised before the Commissioner than one first raised before the Tribunal.

[52] See *FSA v IC and Riverstone Managing Agency Ltd*, IT, 25 November 2008 at [20].

011 Formalities of Commissioner's decision

Unless the Information Commissioner forms the view that the complainant has not exhausted an internal complaints procedure, that there has been 'undue delay' in making the application, that it is frivolous or vexatious or that it has been withdrawn or abandoned,[53] he must make a decision on the application and serve a 'decision notice' on the complainant and the public authority in question.[54] There is no set form for a decision notice: it is just a 'letter setting out the Commissioner's decision.'[55] If the decision is that the public authority has failed to communicate information or to confirm or deny whether it holds the information as required by s 1(1) of the Act or that it has failed to comply with any of the requirements of s 11[56] or s 17,[57] the decision notice must specify the steps to be taken by the authority to comply with its obligations and the period within which they must be taken.[58] The decision notice must also contain details of the right of appeal to the Tribunal provided by s 57 of the Act.[59] There is no express provision requiring that reasons be given, and there are arguments both for and against,[60] but the better view is probably that the Commissioner is under a duty to provide such reasons as he can.[61] In practice the Commissioner does give reasons, sometimes quite substantial ones.[62]

012 Information notices

The Information Commissioner has power, in connection with an application by a complainant under s 50(1) (or if he reasonably requires information to determine whether a public authority is complying with Part I of the Act or any code of practice issued under s 45 or 46), to serve on

---

[53] In any of which cases he must notify the complainant accordingly and let him know the grounds for not making a decision: FOIA ss 50(2) and 50(3)(a).

[54] FOIA s 50(3)(b).

[55] *Sugar v BBC* [2009] UKHL 9, [2009] 1 WLR 430, [2009] 4 All ER 111 at [37].

[56] Obligations of public authority as to means by which information is communicated.

[57] Obligations of public authority in relation to notices of refusal of requests for information.

[58] FOIA s 50(4).

[59] FOIA s 50(5).

[60] For example: *against*: (1) the fact that there is an express requirement to give 'grounds' when refusing to make a decision in FOIA s 50(3)(a); (2) the fact that in many cases there may be difficulties in giving reasons which do not themselves reveal the information which is the subject-matter of a request and the lack of any statutory guidance as to how this problem should be dealt with (compare in relation to the First-tier Tribunal: FTT Rules r 28; *for*: (1) the need for a party considering an appeal under FOIA s 57 to have some basis for deciding whether or not to appeal (2) in particular the provision at s 58(2) that the Tribunal can review 'any finding of fact on which the notice in question was based' and (3) the fact that the public authority in question must give reasons for deciding that an exemption under Pt II of FOIA applies and for claiming that the public interest in disclosing the information in question is outweighed by the public interest in maintaining the exemption (see FOIA ss 17(1)(c) and 17(3)).

[61] *Scottish Ministers v Scottish Information Commissioner* [2007] CSIH 8, 2007 SCLR 253 at [17]. Whether or not a claim for exemption is upheld, the Commissioner's ability to give reasons will be constrained by the need to avoid disclosing the information for which exemption is claimed. See generally in relation to the duty to give reasons: *Halsbury's Laws of England*, 4th edn, Butterworths 2001, vol 1(1), 2001 re-issue, paras 112 and 113; *Halsbury's Laws of England*, 5th edn, vol 61 (London, LexisNexis, 2010) paras 646-647.

[62] See, eg, the Enforcement Notice dated 22 May 2006 addressed to the Law Officers concerning requests for information relating to advice given to the Prime Minister by the Attorney-General about the legality of the war against Iraq.

the public authority an 'information notice' requiring it to furnish him with relevant information (including unrecorded information)[63] within such time as may be specified.[64] The Commissioner does not have to serve such a notice and is at liberty to use informal methods of investigation.[65] The notice must contain details of the right of appeal to the Tribunal provided by s 57 of the Act and if an appeal is brought it need not be complied with pending appeal.[66] The public authority is not required to provide legally privileged information relating to the complainant's rights and obligations under the Act or made in connection with proceedings or contemplated proceedings under it,[67] but otherwise the public authority must comply with the notice.[68] The Tribunal has stated that a public authority appealing against an information notice would have a 'very high hurdle' to clear in convincing it that the Commissioner could and should carry out his functions under the Act without seeing the information in dispute.[69] Thus, the Information Commissioner is able to see the information which is being sought by the applicant in order to form a judgment as to whether it or its existence ought to be disclosed under the Freedom of Information Act 2000.[70]

28– 013 Enforcement notices

If the Information Commissioner is satisfied that a public authority has failed to comply with any of the requirements of Part I of the Act,[71] he may serve on it an 'enforcement notice' requiring it to take within a specified time such steps as may be specified to comply.[72] In general such a notice would be served following an independent investigation by the Information Commissioner rather than following a complaint under s 50(1), although there is nothing in Part IV of the Act to prevent an enforcement notice being served in respect of the same matter which is the subject of a decision notice.[73] An enforcement notice must give details of the failure to comply with Part I and of the right of appeal under s 57 of the Act.[74] The obligation to comply with the notice is suspended pending an appeal.[75]

---

[63] FOIA s 51(8): the effect of this provision is that the Information Commissioner is able to require a public authority to provide evidence of its staff's recollection of relevant events.

[64] FOIA ss 51(1), (7). For an example of the use of an information notice see *R (SSHD) v IT (IC)* [2006] EWHC 2958, [2007] 2 All ER 703 (DC).

[65] *King v IC and DWP*, IT, 20 March 2008 at [90].

[66] FOIA ss 51(3), (4).

[67] FOIA ss 51(5), (6). See *MoJ v IC*, IT, 6 August 2007.

[68] Note that there is no provision against self incrimination similar to that in DPA s 43(8). Note also that s 58 of that Act expressly states that no enactment or rule of law precludes anyone furnishing the Information Commissioner with any information necessary for the discharge of his functions under the FOIA or the DPA.

[69] *Health Professionals Council v IC*, IT, 14 March 2008 at [52].

[70] See, in relation to the Commissioner's duties of confidentiality, §27– 007.

[71] This would include in particular FOIA ss 1, 10, 11, 15, 16, 17 and 19.

[72] FOIA s 52(1).

[73] This was envisaged as a possibility in *Harper v IC and Royal Mail Group plc*, IT, 15 November 2005.

[74] FOIA s 52(2).

[75] FOIA s 52(3).

-014 Certificated exemption from compliance with certain decision or enforcement notices

There is a provision allowing a government department or the National Assembly for Wales (or any other public authority specified in an order made by the Secretary of State) to avoid the effect of a decision or enforcement notice served on it relating to a failure to comply with s 1(1) in respect of exempt information[76] where within 20 days of the notice there is a certificate signed by an 'accountable person' given to the Information Commissioner stating that he has on reasonable grounds formed the opinion that there was no failure.[77] The 'accountable person' must give reasons to the complainant for the opinion he has formed unless that would involve the disclosure of exempt information.[78] An 'accountable person' (apart from special provisions about the National Assembly of Wales and the Northern Ireland Assembly) is a member of the cabinet or the Attorney-General and a copy of the certificate must be laid before Parliament.[79] This provision in effect removes the supervision of the Tribunal as to where the public interest lies in relation to the disclosure of exempt information and represents a kind of 'trump card' in the hand of the higher executive.[80] The only way of challenging such a certificate would be by an application for judicial review.[81]

-015 Scottish provisions

Under the Freedom of Information (Scotland) Act 2002 a person dissatisfied with the decision (or failure to take a decision) of a Scottish public authority on a review under the statutory review procedure set out in ss 20–22 of that Act can apply to the Scottish Information Commissioner for a decision whether the request for information was dealt with in accordance with Part 1 of the Act.[82] This provision along with the remainder of Part 4 of the Freedom of

---

[76] In other words, information falling within one or more of the provisions in Pt II of the Act, irrespective of whether the public interest weighs in favour of disclosure: FOIA s 84.

[77] FOIA ss 53(1), (2). Such a certificate was issued by Jack Straw, the Secretary of State for Justice on 24 February 2009 in respect of *Cabinet Office v IC and Lamb*, IT, 27 January 2009, upholding a decision of the Commissioner dated 19 February 2008, requiring the disclosure of minutes of Cabinet meetings of 13 and 17 March 2003 relating to the invasion of Iraq.

[78] FOIA ss 53(6) and (7).

[79] FOIA s 53(8) and (3).

[80] It seems clear that a certificate can only relate to the public interest question and not to the prior question of whether information is exempt. The trumping effect of such certificates is a feature of freedom of information legislation in each of the Westminster-style comparative jurisdictions. See §§2–014 (Australia); 2–021 (New Zealand); 2–030 (Canada); and 2–038 (Ireland). In the USA, an equivalent is achieved with exclusions: see §2–003.

[81] See §28–037. There is a question whether s 53, by effectively removing the jurisdiction of the Tribunal, might involve a breach of art 6.1 of the European Convention on Human Rights. It is thought that this is unlikely for at least two reasons: (1) it seems unlikely that in many cases the right of access to information could properly be categorised as a 'civil right' within the meaning of art 6.1, since there is unlikely to be any direct financial or property right at stake (see: decision of the European Human Rights Commission on admissibility in *Barry v France*, (App No 14497/89) 14 October 1991; *Syndicat CFDT des Establissements et Arsenaux du Val-de-Marne and Vesque v France* (App 11678/85) 7 December 1987; *Loiseau v France* (App No 46809/99) ECHR 18 November 2003; *Micallef v Malta* (App no 17056/06) ECHR 15 January 2008 at [39]); and (2) the question of entitlement involves a weighing of the public interest and the decision of the minister on the matter will be open to judicial review, which is an appropriate way of testing such a decision in any event.

[82] FOI(S)A s 47(1). The language is materially the same as the FOIA s 50(1): see §28–006.

Information (Scotland) Act 2002 relating to enforcement is also applied for the purposes of the Environmental Information (Scotland) Regulations 2004.[83] Unlike the Freedom of Information Act 2000, the Scottish Act lays down detailed provisions as to the form and contents of the application and the time within which it is to be brought (basically, six months from the date of the review).[84] Once he has received an application the Scottish Information Commissioner must make a decision unless it is excluded[85] or he thinks it is frivolous or vexatious or it has been withdrawn or abandoned.[86] Again, unlike the Freedom of Information Act 2000, the Scottish Act provides a time limit of four months[87] for the Scottish Information Commissioner to make a decision and expressly provides that the Scottish Information Commissioner must invite the public authority's comments on the application and that he may endeavour to effect a settlement of the case.[88] Once he has made a decision the Scottish Information Commissioner must serve a 'decision notice' on the parties and must specify the steps which the Scottish public authority must take and the time within which it must do so in order to comply with Part 1 of the Scottish Act.[89] The decision notice must also contain particulars of the right of appeal against the notice provided by s 56 of the Scottish Act, which, unlike the position under the Freedom of Information Act 2000, is an appeal to the Court of Session on a point of law. As with decisions of the Information Commissioner,[90] there is no express requirement on the Scottish Information Commissioner to give reasons in a decision but there is a common law duty to do so.[91]

28–016   Scottish provisions as to information notices and enforcement notices

The provisions in the Freedom of Information (Scotland) Act 2002 in relation to information and enforcement notices are very similar to those in the Freedom of Information Act 2000.[92] The Scottish Act expressly provides that neither an obligation to maintain secrecy nor any other restriction on disclosure affects the public authority's duty to comply with an information notice[93] and the particulars of a right of appeal which are to be given are of an appeal under s 56 of the Scottish Act, namely to the Court of Session on a point of law. The exception from compliance with a decision or enforcement notice provided by s 53 of the Freedom of Information Act 2000[94] is mirrored in s 52 of the Scottish Act, but in more limited terms: the

---

[83]   EI(S)R reg 17.

[84]   FOI(S)A s 47(2)–(7).

[85]   By s 48 FOI(S)A, which excludes such applications in relation to the Commissioner himself, the Procurator Fiscal and the Lord Advocate in his prosecutorial role.

[86]   FOI(S)A s 49(1), (2).

[87]   A time-limit which would, apparently, have been impossible for the UK Information Commissioner to achieve.

[88]   FOI(S)A s 49(3), (4).

[89]   FOI(S)A s 49(5)–(7).

[90]   See §28–011.

[91]   *Scottish Ministers v Scottish IC* [2007] CSIH 8, 2007 SLT 274, 2007 SCLR 253.

[92]   FOI(S)A ss 50, 51: see §§28–012 and 28–013.

[93]   FOI(S)A s 50(7).

[94]   See §28–014.

decision or enforcement notice must have been given to the Scottish Administration,[95] the categories of exempt information on which a certificate can rely are expressly set out,[96] and the certificate can only be given by the First Minister, who must also certify his opinion that the information requested is 'of exceptional sensitivity'.[97]

3. THIRD STAGE: APPEAL TO THE TRIBUNALS

017 Appeal to the First-tier or Upper Tribunal
The third stage of the appeal process is an appeal to the First-tier or Upper Tribunal under section 57 of the Freedom of Information Act 2000.[98] The appeal is normally to the First-tier Tribunal but the appeal can, in suitable cases (eg where the appeal is of considerable public importance or involves complex or unusual issues), be transferred to the Upper Tribunal.[99]

018 Grounds for an appeal
The only basis for the appeal is that the relevant notice was not in accordance with the law or was based on an exercise of discretion by the Commissioner which the Tribunal would exercise differently.[100] In addition to these 'ordinary appeals', s 60 provides for a separate right of appeal where a national security certificate has been issued under s 23(2) or 24(3): this right of appeal is considered separately below.[101] The Information Tribunal had no power to dispose of an appeal by consent but the First-tier and Upper Tribunals do, provided they think it appropriate to do so.[102]

019 Parties to an appeal
An appeal to a Tribunal may be launched:
— by a person who requested information under the Freedom of Information Act 2000 or the Environmental Information Regulations 2004 and received a decision

---

[95] FOI(S)A s 52(1)(a).

[96] FOI(S)A s 52(1)(b).

[97] FOI(S)A s 52(2).

[98] There is no appeal to a Tribunal against a decision made in respect of a request for information made to a Scottish public authority, whether under the FOI(S)A or the EI(S)R.

[99] FTT Rules r 19(2)-(3). See further §27– 021.

[100] FOIA s 58(1).

[101] FOIA s 60(1). See also EIR reg 18(7) which applies the provisions of s 60 for the purposes of appeals against national security certificates relating to environmental information made under reg 15(1). There is no equivalent provision for an appeal against conclusive evidence certificates issued under s 34(3) ('parliamentary privilege') and s 36(7) ('prejudice to effective conduct of public affairs') or a certificate issued under s 53(2). For s 53(2) certificates see §28– 014. It may be possible to seek a judicial review of these three types of certificates: see §§28– 033 to 28– 037.

[102] See: FTT Rules r 37(1); UT Rules r 39(1). It is suggested that care would be required in a case where an appeal is brought by a public authority and the Commissioner decides to concede the appeal but the original requestor is not a party to the appeal: see, for an example of such a case, *FSA v IC and Riverstone Managing Agency Ltd*, IT, 25 November 2008 at [17].

notice under s 50,[103] but who remains dissatisfied with the information (if any) he has received in response to that request;[104]

— by a person who made a request for information under either regime, who received a 'nil information' response from the public authority and who has received a decision notice under s 50 confirming that response;[105]

— by a person who made a request for information, who was otherwise dissatisfied with the response, or the manner of response, of the public authority and who has received a decision notice under s 50 with which he is dissatisfied;[106]

— by a public authority that has been required by a decision notice issued by the Information Commissioner to communicate information that it considers is exempt or to disclose the existence of information where it considers that it should not be required to do so;[107]

— by a public authority against a decision notice finding that it failed to provide advice and assistance, or that it failed to provide a valid refusal notice;[108] and

— by a public authority against an information notice or an enforcement notice.[109]

There can be no appeal to the Tribunal where the Information Commissioner has decided not to issue one of the three sorts of notice: but that refusal may found a claim for judicial review.[110] The Information Commissioner will be the respondent to any appeal under s 57. Where the appellant is a public authority, the person who made the request for information may apply to be joined as an additional party to the appeal.[111] That person will often be able to make a valuable contribution to the appeal, particularly in adducing evidence of the public interest in disclosure and of the likelihood of harm to a protected interest that would result from a disclosure of the requested information. Where the appellant is the person who made the

---

[103] An appeal only lies to the Tribunal under FOIA s 57(1) where a s 50 decision notice has been served, but there is no requirement as to the form of such a notice: *Sugar v BBC* [2009] UKHL 9, [2009] 1 WLR 430, [2009] 4 All ER 111 at [37].

[104] FOIA s 57(1); EIR reg 18. This includes an appeal against a response that neither confirms nor denies the existence of the information requested: eg *Johnson v IC*, IT, 28 April 2006.

[105] See, eg: *Smith v IC*, IT, 20 March 2006; *Bustin v IC*, IT, 16 December 2005; *Johnson v IC*, IT, 28 April 2006; *Wales v IC and Newcastle NHS Trust*, IT, 31 May 2006; *Roberts v IC*, IT, 16 June 2006; *Harper v IC and Royal Mail Group plc*, IT, 15 November 2005. But the Tribunal does not have jurisdiction to consider whether a public authority should have recorded or held information that would have answered the terms of the request for information: *Brigden v IC Brigden v IC and North Lincolnshire and Goole Hospitals NHS Trust*, IT, 5 April 2007 at [27].

[106] Including considering whether a public authority has properly complied with its duty to advise and assist: see, eg, *Lamb v IC*, IT, 16 November 2006 at [2]–[4] and [19]–[20], where the Tribunal found that a public authority should have asked the applicant to specify more precisely the information that was being requested. Similarly: *Campsie v IC*, IT, 5 April 2007; *Spurgeon v IC and Horsham DC*, IT, 29 June 2007 at [20]; *Urmenyi v IC and LB of Sutton*, IT, 13 July 2007. It would seem that the Tribunal will also consider whether the Information Commissioner's investigation of a complaint was incomplete or otherwise unsatisfactory: *Meunier v IC and National Savings & Investments*, IT, 5 June 2007.

[107] FOIA s 57(1); EIR reg 18. This includes an appeal against a decision notice that requires the public authority to inform the applicant whether it holds information of the description specified in a request.

[108] See, eg: *Hogan and Oxford City Council v IC*, IT, 17 October 2006 at [17]–[24].

[109] FOIA s 57(2); EIR reg 18.

[110] See below at §28– 035.

[111] FTT Rules r 9(3); UT Rules r 9(3).

request, the public authority may apply to be joined as an additional party to the appeal. Again, the public authority will often be able to make a valuable contribution to the appeal, both in relation to the public interest and in adducing interest of likely resultant harm to one of the interests protected by Part II of the Act. The Tribunal has invariably acceded to both sorts of joinder applications. Whether the appellant is the person who made the request or the public authority that received the request, the Information Commissioner can make submissions in support of the decision notice. Where both the person who made the request and the public authority to whom it was addressed are dissatisfied with a decision notice, they may both appeal to the Tribunal.[112]

- 020   Nature of an ordinary appeal

As stated above, the only basis for an appeal is that the relevant notice is not in accordance with the law or that the Tribunal would exercise any discretion differently.[113] However, the Tribunal is entitled to review any finding of fact on which the notice was based[114] and for this purpose it can (and almost invariably does) receive evidence which was not before the Commissioner.[115] It thus undertakes a full review of the merits of the Commissioner's decision (and not a review like that undertaken by the High Court on a judicial review application) and substitutes its own view if it considers that the decision of the Commissioner was wrong.[116] The appeal is against the decision of the Commissioner[117] and not against the way he has expressed his reasons[118] or a means of raising complaints which were never before the Commissioner.[119]

- 021   The approach on appeal

In assessing where the 'public interest' lies when considering s 2(1)(b) or 2(2)(b) of the Freedom of Information Act 2000, the Tribunal exercises its own judgment. The public interest balancing exercise does not involve the exercise of discretion: it is an issue of mixed fact and law, and the Tribunal may substitute its judgment for that of the Commissioner.[120] The Tribunal will look at all the documents submitted with an appeal notice, at least in the case of an appellant acting in person, to ascertain what are the grounds of appeal.[121] Where the public authority has refused to comply with a request for information on the ground that it has

---

[112] See, eg: *Hogan and Oxford City Council v IC*, IT, 17 October 2006.

[113] FOIA s 58(1).

[114] FOIA s 58(2).

[115] *Stephen v IC and Legal Services Commission*, IT, 25 February 2009 at [26].

[116] For a concise summary of the nature of the appeal jurisdiction, see *Guardian Newspapers Ltd v IC and BBC*, IT, 8 January 2007 at [14].

[117] In other words, the outcome of the complaint to the Information Commissioner.

[118] *Billings v IC*, IT, 6 February 2008 at [5]-[9].

[119] *Randall v IC and Medicines and Healthcare Products Regulatory Agency*, IT, 30 October 2007 at [20]-[21]

[120] See: *Bellamy v IC and DTI*, IT, 4 April 2006 at [34]; *Hogan and Oxford CC v IC*, IT, 17 October 2006; *Hemsley v IC and Chief Constable of Northamptonshire*, IT, 10 April 2006 at [18]; *Toms v IC*, IT, 19 June 2006 at [21]; *DTI v IC*, IT, 10 November 2006 at [54]; *Guardian Newspapers Ltd and Brooke v IC and BBC*, IT, 8 January 2007 at [14(3), (5)] *Corporate Officer of the House of Commons v IC and Baker*, IT, 16 January 2007 at [34]; *DfES v IC and The Evening Standard*, IT, 19 February 2007 at [20].

[121] *Prior v IC*, IT, 27 April 2006 at [8].

estimated the cost of compliance would exceed the appropriate limit, the Tribunal can inquire into the matters that have and have not been taken into account in performing this exercise and make an overall judgment as to its reasonableness.[122]

28–022 New grounds of exemption

Under the Tribunal jurisprudence it has been decided that the Tribunal has a discretion whether or not to consider exemptions raised by a public authority for the first time at the appeal stage; the discretion will be exercised 'case by case' and the Tribunal will only consider a new exemption if there is 'reasonable justification' for doing so taking account of all relevant factors.[123] Such factors may include: the length of the delay in raising the point; the stage proceedings have reached; any explanation supplied for the late raising of the exemption; the nature of the exemption relied on; any prejudice that will be suffered by the parties or the original requester if not a party; the position of third parties; the stage at which the information was discovered; and the knowledge public authorities can be expected to have of the Freedom of Information Act 2000 and its workings. Public authorities, and in particular government departments, have argued strongly against this approach and sought to persuade the Tribunal that they are entitled to raise an exemption at any stage but the Tribunal has rejected their arguments[124] and the higher courts, although invited to rule on the point, have not yet done so.[125]

28–023 Onus

There is nothing in s 57 of the Act or the procedural rules to suggest that the onus of persuading the Tribunal to allow an appeal against a decision notice does not lie on the appellant in the normal way[126] and this is the approach that has been taken by the Tribunal.[127] Accordingly, while the Tribunal can make findings of fact different from those of the Information Commissioner, it will follow those of the Commissioner unless fresh evidence is adduced.[128]

28–024 Evidence

Although the Tribunal can take account of new evidence and of certain developments since the Commissioner's decision,[129] in relation to an appeal against a decision notice it, like the

---

[122] *Urmenyi v IC and LB of Sutton*, IT, 13 July 2007 at [16].

[123] See *DBERR v IC and Friends of the Earth*, IT, 29 April 2008 at [41]-[45]. For an example, see *Dept for Culture, Media & Sport v IC*, IT, 22 February 2010 at [19]-[20].

[124] See eg DCMS v IC EA2009/0038 22.2.10 [18]

[125] *Home Office and MoJ v IC* [2009] EWHC 1611 (Admin) at [41]-[46].

[126] This is in contrast to the position in Australia, where it is expressly provided that in an appeal to the Australian Administrative Appeals Tribunal the burden of establishing that a decision to withhold information was justified lies on the public authority: Freedom of Information Act 1982 (Cth of Aust) s 61. The position is otherwise in relation to appeals against information and enforcement notices by public authorities: see rule 26 of the IT (EA) Rules which casts the onus of proof onto the Commissioner but which expressly excludes appeals under s 57(1).

[127] *Roberts v IC*, IT, 16 June 2006 at [14]; *Quinn v IC and Home Office*, IT, 15 November 2006 at [32]; cf *DTI v IC*, IT, 10 November 2006 at [54].

[128] *Guardian Newspapers Ltd and Brooke v IC and BBC*, IT, 8 January 2007 at [14(4) and (6)].

[129] For example, changes in position of the parties or the discovery of information answering the request for information.

Commissioner,[130] must consider the factual position as it was at the date of the decision by the public authority.[131] The Tribunal will receive opinion evidence as to likelihood of harm to an interest protected by an exemption.[132]

– 025 The requested information

The Information Commissioner will normally be able to use as evidence the information that is caught by the request. In the case of an appeal by a public authority, this will enable the Information Commissioner to make valuable submissions supporting disclosure in a way that is not open to the person who made the request. In the case of an appeal by the person who made the request, the Information Commissioner's submissions may be expected to be less self-interested than those of the public authority. The Tribunal may at any stage call for and inspect the information that is captured by the terms of the request, even if the parties themselves do not make the suggestion.[133] This information will often constitute the best evidence for the purpose of determining an appeal.[134]

– 026 Relief on an ordinary appeal

On an appeal under s 57:

— if the Tribunal considers that the decision notice is 'not in accordance with the law' or,

— to the extent that the decision notice involved an exercise of discretion by the Information Commissioner, if the Tribunal considers that the Commissioner ought to have exercised his discretion differently,

the Tribunal must allow the appeal or substitute an alternative notice such as could have been served by the Commissioner; but otherwise it must dismiss the appeal.[135] The Tribunal is not restricted to dealing with matters that are the subject of the appeal notice:[136]

> …where the Tribunal serves a substitute decision notice, the substitute decision notice needs to set out the information to be disclosed within a time period. Alternatively, the substitute decision notice might acknowledge that all the relevant information has been communicated, but has been done so late, or that the public authority had failed to comply with other procedural requirements of FOIA.[137]

The Tribunal can also make a recommendation to the Information Commissioner that he use his powers under s 48 to make a practice recommendation to the public authority concerned.[138]

---

[130] See §28– 009 above.

[131] See: *Digby-Cameron v IC and Bedfordshire Police*, IT, 26 January 2009 at [12]; *Cabinet Office v IC*, IT, 27 January 2009 at [10].

[132] *Guardian Newspapers Ltd and Brooke v IC and BBC*, IT, 8 January 2007 at [41].

[133] See, eg: *Bellamy v IC and DTI*, IT, 4 April 2006 at [32].

[134] See further §27– 020.

[135] FOIA s 58(1). The use of the word 'or' between 'allowing the appeal' and 'substitute an alternative notice' is indeed 'odd' as the Tribunal put it in *Mitchell v IC*, IT, 10 October 2005 at [45]. The word must be read as 'and/or': *Guardian Newspapers Ltd and Brooke v IC and BBC*, IT, 8 January 2007 at [22]–[23].

[136] *Bowbrick v IC and Nottingham City Council*, IT, 28 September 2006 at [22]–[25].

[137] *Bowbrick v IC and Nottingham City Council*, IT, 28 September 2006 at [26].

[138] For an example, see *Bowbrick v IC and Nottingham City Council*, IT, 28 September 2006 at [70].

A costs order may be made.[139]

28–027 Nature of an appeal against a national security certificate

The certificate of a Minister of the Crown[140] under s 23(2) (to the effect that certain information was supplied by or relates to certain security bodies)[141] or s 24(3) (to the effect that exemption from the right of access to information is required for the purpose of safeguarding national security)[142] is conclusive evidence of the 'fact' certified and, accordingly, if the certificate applies to the information in question, provides exemption to the public authority under the Act. Further, if in any proceedings under the Act the public authority claims that a certificate under s 24(3) which identifies information in general terms covers the information in question, it shall be conclusively presumed that the certificate does cover that information.[143] Section 60 provides that the Information Commissioner and any applicant whose request for information is affected by a certificate under s 23(2) or 24(3) may appeal against that certificate.[144] These appeals are to the Upper Tribunal.[145] An appeal relating to a certificate under s 23(2) or relating to the presumption as to the applicability of a s 24(3) certificate is in the nature of a determination whether, as a matter of fact, the certificate is true or does apply to the information in question.[146] The appeal relating to a certificate under s 24(3) is quite different: the appeal can be allowed and the certificate quashed only if the Tribunal, applying judicial review principles, finds that the Minister did not have reasonable grounds for issuing the certificate.[147] Where in any proceedings under the Act the public authority claims that the

---

[139] See further §27–022. In relation to cases started before 18 January 2010, the rules as to costs to be applied are those supplied by IT(EA) Rules rr 20 and 29. In relation to cases started on or after 18 January 2010, the rules relating to costs are those in FTT Rules r 10 and UT Rules r 10: Transfer of Tribunal Functions Order 2010 Sch 5 paras 2 and 3(7).

[140] That is, a member of the Cabinet or the Attorney-General or in Scotland the Advocate General: FOIA s 25(3).

[141] Listed in the FOIA s 23(3).

[142] The relevant information for the purposes of such a certificate can be identified by means of a general description: FOIA s 24(4).

[143] FOIA s 60(4).

[144] FOIA s 60(1), (4).

[145] FTT Rules r 19(1A).

[146] FOIA ss 60(2) and 60(5).

[147] FOIA s 60(3); DPA s 28(5). In determining whether the Minister did or did not have reasonable grounds for issuing the certificate, the Tribunal will inevitably have to assess whether the Minister did or did not have reasonable grounds for concluding that exemption from the relevant provision is, or at any time was, required for the purpose of safeguarding national security. It would appear that the Tribunal is thus confined to applying only one of the three heads of judicial review identified in *Council of Civil Service Unions v Minister for the Civil Service* [1985] AC 374 at 410 (Lord Diplock) (ie irrationality but not illegality or procedural impropriety): if the Minister took into account an irrelevant consideration or failed to take into account a relevant consideration, made an error of law or failed to act fairly in a procedural sense this will only be relevant if and in so far as it led or contributed to him not having reasonable grounds for issuing the certificate. So far as concerns 'the principles applied by the court on an application for judicial review' in relation to 'reasonable grounds', the Tribunal will review whether the Minister's decision was reasonable or so unreasonable that no reasonable Minister could have taken it (*Associated Provincial Picture Houses Ltd v Wednesbury Corpn* [1948] 1 KB 223) and the intensity of its scrutiny will increase if it can be shown that 'fundamental rights' are engaged (*R v Ministry of Defence, ex p Smith* [1996] QB 517 at 554 (Bingham MR). If satisfied that a 'Convention right' as defined by the Human Rights Act 1998 has also been affected by the Minister's decision and the appellant may have been the 'victim' of this for the purposes of that Act, the Tribunal will also need to go further and determine whether the decision to issue a certificate was compatible with that Convention right

general description given in a s 24(3) certificate applies to particular information, any other party to these proceedings may appeal to the Upper Tribunal on the ground that the certificate does not so apply.[148] The Tribunal decides the issue on its merits.[149]

028 Practice and procedure

The general practice and procedure of the First-tier and Upper Tribunals has been considered above. The relevant rules of procedure in relation to information rights appeals are the Tribunal Procedure (First-tier Tribunal) (General Regulatory Chamber) Rules 2009[150] and the Tribunal Procedure (Upper Tribunal) Rules 2008.[151] Regard should also be had to the Practice Note dated 1 February 2010.[152] Although it does not have statutory authority, it provides useful guidance and parts of it will often be incorporated by reference in directions issued by the First-tier Tribunal. Although entitled 'Protection of Confidential Information in Information Appeals before the First-tier Tribunal', it covers more topics than confidentiality. So far as confidentiality is concerned, it explains the need for the Tribunal to maintain the confidentiality of information which a public authority maintains should not be disclosed and it deals with the ways in which this is ensured, in particular the holding of parts of hearings in the absence of the requestor under rule 35 of The Tribunal Procedure (First-tier Tribunal) (General Regulatory Chamber) Rules 2009 and the preparation of 'closed' parts of decisions and reasons. In very rare cases, which are likely to be both sensitive and of great public interest, it is open to the Tribunal to order that a party excluded from the closed hearing and unable to see withheld material be represented by a 'special advocate'.[153] There are also special rules in relation to national security certificate appeals to the Upper Tribunal under section 60 of the Freedom of Information Act 2000 which are considered further below in the context of such appeals under section 28 of the Data Protection Act 1998.[154]

029 Appeals under section 56 of the Freedom of Information (Scotland) Act 2002

Section 56 of the Freedom of Information (Scotland) Act 2002 gives a direct right of appeal on a point of law to the Court of Session against decisions of the Scottish Commissioner under ss 49, 50 and 51 of the Scottish Act in relation to decision notices, enforcement notices and

---

and would thus have to apply a more intensive proportionality-based standard of review: *R (Daly) v SSHD* [2001] UKHL 26, [2001] 2 AC 532 at [26]–[27] (Lord Steyn); *Baker v SSHD* [2001] UKHRR 1275 para 63. On the question whether Convention rights will be engaged, see §§14– 043 to 14– 045. The language used in the FOIA s 60(3) and DPA s 28(5) might also be thought to suggest that the Tribunal must focus solely on the grounds which the Minister had in his mind at the time he issued the certificate (to the exclusion of other grounds which he might now wish to rely upon). However, this will not affect the eventual outcome because there is nothing to prevent a Minister from issuing a fresh certificate on new grounds to replace one that has been quashed.

[148] FOIA s 60(4).

[149] FOIA s 60(5).

[150] Abbreviated in this work to 'FTT Rules'.

[151] Abbreviated in this work to 'UT Rules'.

[152] www.informationtribunal.gov.uk/Documents/PracticeNote_Confidential_Infor.pdf

[153] *Campaign against the Arms Trade v IC and MoJ*, IT, 26 August 2008 at [15] and [21]: this was a case concerning national security, although it was not a 'national security certificate appeal'.

[154] See §§28– 046 to 28– 047.

information notices.[155] Such an appeal may be expected to be analogous to that to the Upper Tribunal from the First-tier Tribunal under s 11 of the Tribunals, Courts and Enforcement Act 2007.[156] There is the same right of appeal in relation to decisions of the Scottish Commissioner under the Environmental Information (Scotland) Regulations 2004.[157]

4. FOURTH STAGE: APPEAL FROM FIRST-TIER TRIBUNAL TO UPPER TRIBUNAL

28–030 Appeal to the Upper Tribunal
Under section 11 of Tribunals, Courts and Enforcement Act 2007 any party to a case has a right of appeal to the Upper Tribunal on any point of law arising from a decision made by the First-tier Tribunal. Section 11(5)(b) and (c) exclude from this right decisions of the First-tier Tribunal on appeals concerning national security certificates but such appeals are in any event automatically referred to the Upper Tribunal under rule 19(1A) of the Tribunal Procedure (First-tier Tribunal) (General Regulatory Chamber) Rules 2009. An appeal on a 'point of law' would be on the grounds (a) that the Tribunal misdirected itself in law or misunderstood or misapplied the law; (b) that there was no evidence to support a particular conclusion or finding of fact made by the Tribunal; or (c) that the decision was perverse in that it was one which the Tribunal, directing itself properly on the law, could not have reached or one which was obviously wrong.[158] This right of appeal is similar to that formerly provided by section 59 of Freedom of Information Act 2000 for appeals from the Information Tribunal to the High Court, so that further guidance as to the nature of the appeal and what amounts to a 'point of law' can be sought in cases under that section.[159]

28–031 Practice and procedure
The right of appeal under section 11 of Tribunals, Courts and Enforcement Act 2007 may only be exercised with permission of the First-tier or Upper Tribunal.[160] The requirement for permission is not an additional requirement of the right to appeal: it is designed to filter out 'appeals' which do not in fact raise any point of law at all. On an application to the First-tier

---

[155] See §§28– 015 to 28– 016.

[156] See §28– 030.

[157] See EI(S)R reg 17.

[158] See, in relation to the analogous provisions about appeals from employment tribunals to the Employment Appeal Tribunal: *British Telecommunications plc v Sheridan* [1990] IRLR 27 at 30; *Melon v Hector Powe Ltd* [1981] ICR 43, [1980] IRLR 477; *Neale v Hereford and Worcester County Council* [1986] ICR 471, [1986] IRLR 168; *Watling v William Bird & Son (Contractors) Ltd* [1976] ITR 70.

[159] See, eg: *BBC v Sugar* [2008] EWCA Civ 191, [2008] 1 WLR 2289 at [15], [17] (jurisdiction); *BBC v IC* [2009] EWHC 2348 (Admin), [2010] EMLR 6 at [52] (point of law equivalent to judicial review), [83]-[85] (respect for decisions of specialist tribunal: this point may not apply in the context of an appeal from the First-tier to Upper Tribunal, which are both within the tribunal system and have access to specialisation); *HM Treasury v IC* [2009] EWHC 1811 (Admin), [2010] 2 WLR 931 at [54] (errors in tribunal's approach to public interest balance).

[160] There is a standard application form with guidance notes which can be obtained from the Tribunal website: www.informationtribunal.gov.uk/Documents/1_Noticeofappealform_Mar10.pdf

Tribunal for permission to appeal, it is open to the First-tier Tribunal to itself review and re-make the decision if it is satisfied that there has been an error of law in the decision,[161] which may obviate the need for an appeal. On an appeal, the Upper Tribunal can set aside the decision of the First-tier Tribunal and either re-make the decision itself or refer the matter back to the First-tier Tribunal.[162] The procedure on the appeal will be governed by the Tribunal Procedure (Upper Tribunal) Rules 2008.[163] Although the rules give the Upper Tribunal power to admit evidence whether or not it was available to the previous decision maker,[164] it is thought that the Upper Tribunal would be reluctant to admit new evidence given that the appeal is on a point of law and that the First-tier Tribunal will have undertaken a full merits review of the Commissioner's decision.

5. FIFTH STAGE: APPEAL FROM UPPER TRIBUNAL TO COURT OF APPEAL

032 Appeal to Court of Appeal

Section 13 of Tribunals, Courts and Enforcement Act 2007 provides for an appeal from the decision of the Upper Tribunal to the Court of Appeal (or, in Scotland, to the Court of Session). Again, decisions in relation to national security certificates are excluded.[165] The appeal is with permission of the Upper Tribunal or the Court of Appeal on the application of any party,[166] but such permission may only be granted if the court or tribunal considers that the proposed appeal would raise some important point of principle or practice or there is some other compelling reason for the appellate court to hear the appeal.[167] The Court of Appeal has power on the appeal to set aside the Upper Tribunal's decision and either re-make it or refer the matter back to the Upper Tribunal or the First-tier Tribunal.[168] The procedure in the Court of Appeal is governed by the Civil Procedure Rules Part 52. Appeals to the Supreme Court from the Court of Appeal will be governed by the normal rules governing such appeals.

---

[161] FTT Rules r 44 and section 9 of the Tribunals, Courts and Enforcement Act 2007 s 9.

[162] Tribunals, Courts and Enforcement Act 2007 s 12.

[163] See §§27–021 to 27–023.

[164] See UT Rules r 15(2). Note, there is no equivalent of rule 15(2A) which restricts new evidence in an asylum or immigration case.

[165] Tribunals, Courts and Enforcement Act 2007 s 13(8).

[166] Tribunals, Courts and Enforcement Act 2007 s 13(4).

[167] The Appeals from the Upper Tribunal to the Court of Appeal Order 2008 (SI 2008/2834).

[168] Tribunals, Courts and Enforcement Act 2007 s 14.

6. JUDICIAL REVIEW

28– 033 Limits to judicial review

The Freedom of Information Act 2000 and Environmental Information Regulations 2004 provide for numerous decisions and actions to be taken by 'public authorities', and by the Information Commissioner, the Secretary of State, and Ministers and others who are given power to sign certificates (in particular, the Speaker of the House of Commons and the Clerk of the Parliaments).[169] There is no provision in the Act expressly excluding the supervisory jurisdiction of the Administrative Court to grant judicial review under Part 54 of the Civil Procedure Rules 1998 in relation to such decisions and actions,[170] so that in principle they would be susceptible to judicial review. In most cases, however, the Act itself provides an appeal or other means of challenge[171] and the court would be unlikely to give permission for, or grant, judicial review in such cases unless there were exceptional circumstances.[172] There are, however, a few cases where judicial review by an applicant may be appropriate because of a gap in the appeal rights provided by the Act.

28– 034 Public authorities

It is thought unlikely that any judicial review would lie against the handling by a public authority of a request for information given the wide powers of the Information Commissioner under s 50 of the Act.

28– 035 Information Commissioner

As for the Commissioner, the exercise of more general powers such as issuing codes of practice might in principle be open to judicial review, but his decision notices, enforcement notices and information notices, which are subject to the extensive rights of appeal given by s 57, are unlikely to be open to such review. There is one decision of the Commissioner, namely a decision not to pursue a complaint under s 50(2), however, which is not subject to any right of appeal under the Act and which would therefore be susceptible to judicial review.[173] A failure by the Commissioner to take a decision at all might also be the subject of a judicial review

---

[169] See, eg: FOIA ss 23(2), 24(3), 34(3), 36(7) and 53(2).

[170] Section 56(1) states that the Act 'does not confer any right of action in civil proceedings in respect of any failure to comply with any duty imposed by or under [it]' but is unlikely to be construed as excluding judicial review: compare similar (but stronger) exclusionary wording considered in, *ex p Waldron* [1986] QB 824, [1985] 3 All ER 775 (CA).

[171] For example, the right to complain to the Information Commissioner under s 50(1) that a public authority has not complied with Pt I of the Act, the right to appeal against a decision of the Information Commissioner under s 57(1), the right to appeal against national security certificates under s 60, the right to appeal against the decisions of the Information Tribunal under s 59.

[172] See: *Halsbury's Laws of England*, 5th edn , vol 61 (London, LexisNexis, 2010) para 657.

[173] For example, in the *Sugar* litigation, Mr Sugar commenced judicial review proceedings in the face of the Information Commissioner's assertion (upheld by the High Court and Court of Appeal but not the House of Lords: see *Sugar v BBC* [2009] UKHL 9, [2009] 1 WLR 430, [2009] 4 All ER 111 at [36]) that there was no appeal against his finding that the information requested was not held by the BBC in its capacity as a public authority since it did not amount to a decision under section 50 of Freedom of Information Act 2000.

claim,[174] as might a failure to take one within a reasonable time even though, in contrast to the position in Scotland,[175] there is no express time limit on the taking of a decision.

036 The Tribunals

As for decisions of the Tribunals, those under s 57 are subject to an appeal to the Upper Tribunal or Court of Appeal,[176] but those relating to national security certificates are not the subject of any appeal procedure.[177] It is therefore possible that the Upper Tribunal would be susceptible to judicial review in respect of its decisions on appeals relating to national security certificates. However, it is a moot point whether decisions of the Upper Tribunal can be judicially reviewed[178] and, in practice, foreign experience suggests it will be difficult to challenge successfully any such certificate.[179]

037 Certificates

National security certificates are open to challenge under s 60 so there is unlikely to be any basis for a judicial review of the act of the relevant Minister in signing the certificate.[180] However, certificates signed under ss 34(3), 36(7) and 53(2) are not open to such challenge. Certificates signed by a Cabinet minister or the Attorney-General will be open to judicial review.[181] Those signed by the Speaker of the House of Commons or the Clerk of the Parliaments under ss 34(3) and 36(7) are probably not amenable to judicial review, on the basis of parliamentary privilege.[182] However the scope of Parliamentary privilege is ultimately for the courts and not Parliament itself to define. Parliament cannot create new forms of privilege. Therefore a certificate may only be conclusive as to whether disclosure would infringe an established privilege. It would still appear to be open to an individual or the Information Commissioner to challenge non-disclosure on the basis that disclosure would not infringe any established form

---

[174] *Tuckley v IC and Birmingham City Council*, IT, 28 February 2008 at [37].

[175] See FOI(S)A s 49(3)(b) and §28– 015.

[176] See §§28– 030 to 28– 032.

[177] See Tribunals, Courts and Enforcement Act 2007 s 13(8).

[178] The Upper Tribunal is a 'superior court of record' and itself has a judicial review jurisdiction, so there must be doubt whether its decisions can be reviewed.

[179] See §§2– 008(1), 2– 015(9) and 2– 032(11).

[180] There is a suggestion in *Norman Baker MP* [2001] UKHRR 1275 at [48] that there may be a distinction between the Minister not having reasonable grounds for issuing a national security certificate and it being unlawful for him to have done so; in the latter case there is no express provision for an appeal to the Tribunal in s 60(3) so that, the Tribunal thought, in such a case it would be necessary (and presumably possible) to apply to the Administrative Court for judicial review. It is thought unlikely that this would arise in practice.

[181] As the Minister, Lord Falconer of Thoroton, assured Parliament at the second reading of the Bill in dealing with what became s 53. He also stated that the Commissioner would have locus to apply for such a judicial review: Hansard HL vol 612 col 828 (20 April 2000). See also the Australian case *Shergold v Tanner* [2002] HCA 19, (2002) 188 ALR 302.

[182] See on parliamentary privilege *Halsbury's Laws of England*, 5th edn , vol 78 (London, LexisNexis, 2010) paras 1076-1093; *R v Parliamentary Commissioner for Standards, ex p Al Fayed* [1998] 1 WLR 669, [1998] 1 All ER 93 (CA). There may be a legitimate distinction to be drawn between s 34(3) certificates and s 36(7) certificates: s 34(3) certificates are to the effect that the relevant parliamentary officer certifies that exemption is necessary to avoid an infringement of parliamentary privilege (more likely to be privileged) whereas s 36(7) certificates relate to the opinion of such officer that disclosure of information by Parliament would prejudice the effective conduct of public affairs (an opinion which may be open to review without considering whether parliamentary privilege is properly claimed).

of privilege, and that the Speaker of the House of Commons or the Clerk of the Parliaments has misconstrued the ambit of Parliamentary privilege.[183] Under the Freedom of Information (Scotland) Act 2002 and the Environmental Information (Scotland) Regulations 2004 there is no provision for an appeal against ministerial certificates relating to national security issued under s 31(2) and reg 12(1) respectively; it seems likely that such certificates would however be open to judicial review.

7. THIRD PARTIES: INSTITUTION OF APPEALS AND PARTICIPATION IN APPEALS

28–038 Introduction

As noted earlier,[184] a person or body other than the public authority to which a Freedom of Information Act request for information is made may have a legitimate interest in seeing that some or all of the information answering the terms of a request is not communicated, either to that applicant or to anyone else.[185] That third party may be similarly concerned to see that any appeal against a refusal to communicate is adequately resisted and that the third party's interests in having the information not disclosed are properly articulated before the appellate body. As well as participating in any appeal, a third party may himself wish to initiate proceedings or an appeal where a decision has been or is proposed to be made by the public authority or by the appellate body to disclose information.

28–039 Participation in appeals

Notwithstanding these legitimate interests a third party is given no right to participate in any decisions or appeals arising out of a request for information under the Acts. Although a public authority, when making its original decision in relation to disclosure, may have informed the third party of the request and invited the third party's views on disclosure, there is nothing in either of the Acts or the Code issued under s 45 of the Freedom of Information Act 2000 requiring the public authority to inform the third party either of the outcome of the request or of whether an appeal has been instituted[186] and a third party is given no entitlement to seek internal reconsideration.[187] Likewise a third party has no entitlement to apply to the Commissioner for a decision whether a request has been dealt with in accordance with Part I of the Act,[188] and there is nothing obliging the Information Commissioner, when an application

---

[183] However for a more restrictive interpretation of the court's powers in determining the ambit of Parliamentary privilege see Eagles, Taggart and Liddell, *Freedom of Information in New Zealand*, (Auckland, Oxford University Press, 1992) pp 469–470. Also see Lock [1985] *Public Law* 64.

[184] See §§11–041 to 11–047.

[185] Disclosure under the Act is disclosure to the world: the public authority cannot itself restrict what the applicant does with the information once it is disclosed to him.

[186] Although the Code deals in Pt IV with consultation with third parties it does so in permissive terms.

[187] Part VI of the Code does not contemplate any participation by a third party. In Scotland, only an applicant is entitled to seek internal review: FOI(S)A s 20(1).

[188] Similarly, in Scotland: FOI(S)A s 47(1).

has been made to him, to inform a third party of that application, to invite representations from the third party or to advise the third party of the outcome of it. There is no entitlement to appeal to the Tribunals;[189] however, they have power to order any person to be joined as a party to an appeal under s 57 of the Freedom of Information Act 2000, which may give third parties an opportunity to be heard.[190] The position of third parties has been treated more generously in comparative jurisdictions.[191]

040 Institution of appeals and other proceedings
Although a third party's rights are therefore limited, a third party who has a recognised interest in seeing that information is not disclosed may well, on ordinary principles, be able to apply for a judicial review of a decision of a public authority, of the Information Commissioner or of the Tribunals that would result in the disclosure of that information.[192] Also, in certain circumstances a third party will be able to institute proceedings to restrain disclosure although there may be procedural difficulties if a court were to take a different view on an issue of confidentiality to that taken by the Information Commissioner or the Tribunals.[193]

B.   APPEALS UNDER THE DATA PROTECTION ACT 1998

8.   ORDINARY APPEALS

041 Subject access rights
The means by which the subject access rights under s 7 of the Data Protection Act 1998 are pursued are quite different from those by which the equivalent rights under the Freedom of Information Acts are pursued. First, in contrast to the position under the Freedom of Information Acts, there is no specific requirement for codes of practice issued or approved by the Commissioner under s 51(3) of the Data Protection Act 1998 to require authorities to institute internal complaints procedures. As at 1 June 2010 the Information Commissioner had not issued a code laying down such a requirement in relation to s 7 requests.[194]

---

[189] In Scotland, to the Court of Session: FOI(S)A s 56.

[190] FTT Rules r 9 and UT Rules r 9 and the First-Tier Tribunal Information Rights Practice Note (dated 1 February 2010) §§ 14-20. If the decision is likely to affect the 'civil rights' of the third party it might be argued that the Human Rights Act 1998 and art 6 of the European Convention would require the Tribunal to join him to the appeal so that such rights could be determined by an independent and impartial tribunal established by law: see *Zander v Sweden* (1993) 18 EHRR 175. Note in this context FTT Rules r 9(4) and UT Rules r 9(4).

[191] As to the role that it has been held third parties in appeals can play in the comparative jurisdictions, see: §§2– 013 and 2– 014 (Australia); §§2– 031 and 2– 033 (Canada); §2– 038 (Ireland).

[192] This is the route adopted in the USA: see §2– 009.

[193] See §25– 009.

[194] The Lord Chancellor issued non-statutory guidance dated April 2002 to government departments which makes no such requirement: see www.dca.gov.uk/foi/dpasaguide.htm.

28–042 Application to court under section7(9) of the Data Protection Act 1998

The main remedy for an individual dissatisfied with the response to a request under s 7(1) of the Data Protection Act 1998 in relation to data of which he is the 'data subject' is by way of an application to a court under s 7(9), rather than an application to the Information Commissioner. If the court on such an application is satisfied that the data controller in question has failed to comply with the request in contravention of any provision of s 7 it can order him to comply with the request.

28–043 Practice and procedure on an application under s 7(9)

Both the High Court and a county court (or in Scotland the Court of Session or the sheriff) have jurisdiction to hear such an application.[195] The question for the court on such an appeal is whether the data controller has failed to comply with the request in contravention of the provisions of s 7 of the Data Protection Act 1998.[196] In other words, the right of appeal involves the court considering afresh the applicability of any exemption, unfettered by the decision of the data controller: it is not a review of the reasonableness of the data controller's decision or of the methodology applied by the data controller in reaching the appealed decision. In determining whether an applicant is entitled to the information which he seeks (including any question whether it is exempt from s 7 by virtue of Part IV of the Act) the court has power to require the information in question[197] to be made available for its own inspection but must not, pending a decision in the applicant's favour, require it to be disclosed to him whether by way of discovery or otherwise.[198] Subject to the rights of appeal to the Upper Tribunal mentioned below,[199] if a national security certificate has been issued under s 28(1) of the Act in relation to any data which is relied on by the data controller in the proceedings, this will constitute conclusive evidence that the exemption of that data from the provisions of s 7 of the Act is required for the purpose of safeguarding national security.[200] If the data controller claims in the course of the proceedings that a national security certificate in general terms applies to the personal data in question, the certificate will be conclusively deemed so to apply.[201] Presumably, if an applicant faced with such a certificate indicated that he wished to appeal to the Upper Tribunal on either of those points, the court would grant an adjournment of the proceedings pending a decision of the Upper Tribunal. There are no specific rules of procedure relating to an application to the court under the Data Protection Act 1998 and the Civil Procedure Rules 1998 will therefore apply;[202] it is likely that most claims will be brought

---

[195] DPA s 15(1).

[196] DPA s 7(9). As the applicant's entitlement under s 7(1) is 'subject to the following provisions of ss 7, 8, 9 and 9A' of the Act, the court will have jurisdiction to consider whether the procedural requirements set out in those sections have been met in order to determine whether the failure to comply with the applicant's request is, in fact, in contravention of the applicant's entitlement.

[197] And information as to the logic involved in any decision-taking as mentioned in s 7(1)(d).

[198] DPA s 15(2).

[199] See §28–046 for rights of appeal which are provided by DPA ss 28(4) and (6).

[200] DPA s 28(2).

[201] DPA s 28(6).

[202] CPR 2.1.

under Part 8 of the Civil Procedure Rules 1998. An appeal from the decision of the court dealing with the application may with leave be made to either the High Court or the Court of Appeal under Part 52 of the Civil Procedure Rules 1998.[203]

044 The roles of the Information Commissioner and the Tribunals

In relation to the access rights as against public authorities granted by s 7 of the Data Protection Act 1998, the roles of the Information Commissioner and the Tribunals are likely to be limited. Contravention of s 7 by a public authority by failing to supply information in accordance with that section would constitute a breach of the 'sixth data protection principle'.[204] Such contravention could be the subject of an 'enforcement notice' by the Information Commissioner pursuant to s 40 of the Act requiring the public authority to take steps to comply with its obligations, and could also in principle be the subject of a request for an assessment by the Information Commissioner under s 42 of the Act[205] and of an 'information notice' served by the Information Commissioner on the public authority under s 43[206] of the Act in connection with such an assessment or for determining whether the data protection principles had been complied with.[207] An information notice under s 43 is very similar to one under s 51 of the Freedom of Information Act 2000 save that s 43 includes an express provision, not found in s 51, that a person does not have to comply with an information notice if to do so would expose him to proceedings for an offence save for an offence under the Data Protection Act 1998 itself.[208]

045 Appeal against enforcement or information notice

Under s 48 of the Data Protection Act 1998[209] a data controller may appeal to the First-tier Tribunal or Upper Tribunal against an enforcement or information notice. The Tribunal must allow such an appeal if it considers that the notice was not in accordance with the law or if any discretion of the Information Commissioner ought to have been exercised differently and it may review any determination of fact on which the notice was based.[210] These appeals will be dealt

---

[203] CPR 52.3; an appeal from the High Court is to the Court of Appeal; an appeal from the county court is normally to the High Court but is likely to be assigned to the Court of Appeal either on the basis that it has been allocated to the multi-track under rr 26.5 and 26.7(2) or if the court exercises its power under r 52.14 (see: CPR PD 52 paras 2A.1, 2A.2 and 2A.6).

[204] DPA s 4(4) Sch 1 Pt I para 6; Sch 1 Pt II, para 8(a).

[205] The complaint made by the applicant in *R (SSHD) v IT* [2006] EWHC 2958 (Admin), [2007] 2 All ER 703 (DC) was treated as a request under DPA s 42. Such a request must be complied with by the Information Commissioner unless he has not been supplied with sufficient information to identify the person requesting the assessment and the 'processing' in question: DPA s 42(2).

[206] Or, in theory, a 'special information notice' under s 44, though it is probably unlikely that a public authority will claim that 'personal data' were being processed by it for journalistic, artistic or literary purposes.

[207] But note in this context DPA s 42(3)(c), which would suggest that the Commissioner would generally expect a data subject to seek to exercise his rights to apply to court under s 7(9) before proceeding with any assessment or serving an enforcement notice; presumably the failure of the Commissioner to carry out an assessment or serve an enforcement notice could in principle be the subject of an application for judicial review, but since a direct application under s 7(9) could be made against the real wrong-doer this is unlikely to be granted in practice.

[208] DPA s 43(8).

[209] Read with Transfer of Tribunal Functions Order 2010 (SI 2010/22) art 2(3).

[210] DPA s 49(1), (2).

with under the Tribunal Procedure (First-tier Tribunal) (General Regulatory Chamber) Rules 2009 and the Tribunal Procedure (Upper Tribunal) Rules 2008 as appropriate.[211]

9.   NATIONAL SECURITY CERTIFICATE APPEALS

28- 046   National security certificate appeals

Where a national security certificate has been issued certifying in respect of some or all of any relevant data that exemption from the data protection principles or Parts II, III or V and/or s 55 of the Data Protection Act 1998[212] is, or at any time was, required for the purpose of safeguarding national security, then the certificate will be conclusive evidence of that 'fact'.[213] Although an applicant for data is not disentitled from appealing to a court where a conclusive certificate has been issued, the certificate will render the proceedings a foregone conclusion provided that it relates to the information sought. Instead, there are two discrete rights of appeal to the Upper Tribunal:[214]

(1)   A person directly affected by the issuing of a conclusive certificate may appeal to the Tribunal against the decision to issue the conclusive certificate.[215] The task for the Tribunal on such an appeal is to consider whether, applying the principles applied by a court on an application for judicial review, the Minister did not have reasonable grounds for issuing the certificate: the Tribunal does not consider afresh whether exemption is in fact required for the purpose of safeguarding national security. Unless the Tribunal finds that the Minister did not have reasonable grounds for issuing the certificate, it must dismiss the appeal; if it finds that the Minister did not have reasonable grounds for issuing the certificate, it may allow the appeal and quash the certificate.[216]

---

[211] See §§27– 020 to 27– 021.

[212] These include the right of access under DPA s 7 and the enforcement provisions available to the Information Commissioner in Part V of the Act.

[213] DPA s 28(2). A certificate may identify the personal data to which it applies by means of a general description; and it may be expressed to have prospective effect: DPA s 28(3). Conclusive certificates are considered further in §§14– 032 to 14– 045.

[214] Assuming that an applicant in a particular case has a 'civil right' to disclosure of the data sought it seems that the Human Rights Act 1998 and art 6 of the European Convention in particular would be satisfied by these arrangements (compare *Tinnelly & Sons Ltd v UK* (1998) 27 EHRR 249 where there was no independent or judicial scrutiny of the ministerial national security certificate). The Upper Tribunal has inherited this jurisdiction under the Transfer of Tribunal Functions Order 2010 SI 2010/22 art 2(3) and the FTT Rules r 19(1A).

[215] DPA s 28(4). A person directly affected can include not only the data subject but also the Information Commissioner: see *R (SSHD) v Information Tribunal* [2006] EWHC 2958 (Admin), [2007] 2 All ER 703 (DC) in which the Information Commissioner issued an information notice under s 43 of the Act in the course of an assessment under s 42 following a complaint by a data subject in response to which the Secretary of State issued a certificate to the effect that exemption from s 43 was required for the purposes of safeguarding national security and the Information Commissioner appealed to the Information Tribunal.

[216] DPA s 28(5). In *Norman Baker MP v SSHD* [2001] UKHRR 1275 the Data Protection Tribunal (as the Information Tribunal was then known) held that a national security exemption certificate applying effectively a blanket exemption to files held by MI5 was unreasonably wide. The difficulty with the exemption was that the security service did not have to consider in any individual case whether responding to the request (even with a 'neither confirm nor deny' response) would harm national security. A revised form of the certificate was considered by the

(2)   Where a dissatisfied applicant has made a 'merit review' application to the relevant court against a failure to comply with a subject access request[217] and the data controller has claimed in those proceedings that a national security certificate that identifies information by means of a general description[218] applies to the information sought, then any other party to those proceedings may appeal to the Upper Tribunal on the ground that the certificate does not apply to the personal data in question.[219] The task for the Upper Tribunal is to consider whether the generally-worded certificate is apt to apply to all the information sought.

047   Practice and procedure

Procedure in national security certificate appeals is governed by the Tribunal Procedure (Upper Tribunal) Rules 2008. The notice of appeal will be addressed to the First-tier Tribunal but, in accordance with rule 19(1A) of the Tribunal Procedure (First-tier Tribunal) (General Regulatory Chamber) Rules 2009, the appeal will automatically be transferred to the Upper Tribunal at which point the Upper Tribunal must give directions as to the consideration and disposal of the proceedings.[220] The Tribunal Procedure (Upper Tribunal) Rules 2008 are dealt with in general above[221] to which reference should be made but there are a number of special rules which should also be noted. First, schedule 2 to the Rules provides additional rules, relating to the notification and participation of the relevant Minister[222] and objections by the Minister to the publication of his response or any record of the Tribunal's decision. Rule 14(10) specifically enjoins the Upper Tribunal to ensure that information is not disclosed contrary to the interests of national security and the Tribunal must conduct proceedings and record its decision and reasons so as not to undermine the effect of that provision.[223] Rule 10(1A) makes special provision in relation to costs, in particular costs may be awarded against the relevant Minister if it allows an appeal against a certificate (without the usual requirement that he has acted unreasonably).[224] There is no provision for an appeal from a determination of the Upper Tribunal on an appeal relating to a national security certificate, so that judicial review of the

---

High Court in *Re Ewing* [2003] EWHC 3169 (QB), where it was held that the criticisms by the Information Tribunal had been addressed.: '... a general [neither confirm nor deny] policy, in response to requests for personal data, including as to the existence (or non-existence) of personal data, is in principle justifiable and cannot be criticised as unreasonable or unnecessary' (at [60]). In *R (SSHD) v IT* [2006] EWHC 2958 (Admin), [2007] 2 All ER 703 the Divisional Court upheld the decision of the Information Tribunal that the Secretary of State in issuing a certificate under s 28(2) of the Act was obliged to take account of the Information Commissioner's role under s 51(1) of 'checking' that an exemption had been properly claimed under s 28(1) as against the data subject and that, in failing to take account of the Information Commissioner's role, he did not have reasonable grounds for issuing the certificate as against the Information Commissioner.

[217] That is, under the DPA s 7(9).

[218] Relying on DPA s 28(3).

[219] DPA s 28(6).

[220] UT Rules r 26A(2).

[221] See §§27–021 to 27–023.

[222] Rule 35(2) gives him a specific entitlement to attend any hearing, though note that rule 34(1) enables the Upper Tribunal to make any decision without a hearing.

[223] See rule 14(11); see also rules 37(2A) and 37(4)(c) in relation to hearings and the exclusion of parties from them.

[224] See rule 10(3)(d).

Tribunal's decision might, in principle, be possible.[225]

10. JUDICIAL REVIEW

28– 048 Judicial review

The position in relation to judicial review of acts and decisions under the Data Protection Act 1998 is similar to that under the Freedom of Information Act 2000.[226] Again, there is no provision expressly excluding judicial review but, so far as an applicant is concerned, it will ordinarily be excluded by the principle that the court will not generally grant judicial review where there is some other remedy available. This exclusion would not apply to decisions of the Upper Tribunal on national security appeals under s 28 of the Data Protection Act 1998[227] or to a failure to act on the part of the Information Commissioner on a request for an assessment under s 42(2) of the Act.

11. THIRD PARTIES: INSTITUTION OF APPEALS AND PARTICIPATION IN APPEALS

28– 049 Introduction

The issues which arise under the Data Protection Act 1998 in respect of third party participation in appeals are very similar to those which arise under the Freedom of Information Act 2000.[228] However, the manner in which these issues have been addressed under the Data Protection Act 1998 is slightly different.

28– 050 Participation in and institution of appeals

A third party is not entitled to initiate an appeal under s 7 of the Act.[229] However, the Data Protection Act 1998 provides a free-standing right by any person who is, or believes himself to be, directly affected by any processing of personal data for an assessment by the Information Commissioner as to whether it is likely or unlikely that the processing has been or is being carried out in compliance with the provisions of the Act.[230] As 'processing' is defined to include the disclosure of information, this would appear to permit a third party who is, or would stand to be, directly affected by the disclosure of information to make application to the Information

---

[225] See above at §28– 036.

[226] See §§28– 033 to 28– 037.

[227] See, eg, *R (SSHD) v Information Tribunal* [2006] EWHC 2958 (Admin), [2007] 2 All ER 703 (DC) where the Secretary of State brought an unsuccessful judicial review of the Information Tribunal's decision under DPA s 28(5) quashing a national security certificate issued by him. But note the position of the Upper Tribunal may well be different: see §28– 036.

[228] See §§ 28– 038 to 28– 040.

[229] An appeal can only be made by the person who has made the request under s 7: DPA s 7(9).

[230] DPA s 42(1).

Commissioner for an assessment. The Commissioner is only required to provide the person making the request with details of any view formed or action taken to the extent that the Information Commissioner considers appropriate.[231] Upon such an application being made, the Information Commissioner can issue an information notice,[232] a special information notice[233] or an enforcement notice.[234] The statutory right of appeal to the Tribunals only extends to a public authority against whom one or more of the above three notices has been served.[235] Outside these statutory rights of appeal, the position of a dissatisfied third party is akin to that under the Freedom of Information Act 2000.[236]

---

[231] DPA s 42(2).

[232] DPA s 43.

[233] DPA s 44.

[234] DPA s 40.

[235] DPA s 48. These appeals are considered at §28– 045.

[236] See §§28– 038 to 28– 040.

CHAPTER 29
Enforcement

1. FREEDOM OF INFORMATION ACTS

29– 001 Immunities from private suit

Both the Freedom of Information Act 2000 and the Environmental Information Regulations 2004, as well as their Scottish counterparts, state that they do not confer any right of action in civil proceedings in respect of a failure to comply with a duty imposed by or under the Act.[1] There is also specific provision giving protection against proceedings for defamation brought in respect of information supplied to a public authority by a third party which is published to applicants under the Acts unless the publication is made with malice.[2] The protection is conferred in relation to information communicated pursuant to the duty imposed by statute on the public authority. Accordingly, the statutory protection will not apply where a public authority discloses information to an applicant in response to a request but without being

---

[1] FOIA s 56(1); FOI(S)A s 55(1); EIR reg 18 (applying FOIA Pt IV (ss 50–56), incl Sch 3); EI(S)R reg 17 (applying FOI(S)A, Pt IV (ss 47–56), incl Sch 3). These provisions are concerned with setting the limits of the rights conferred by these statutes. A breach of any of them will thus not give rise to a cause of action for the tort of breach of statutory duty. However, it is arguable that a breach could form *an element* of a cause of action for misfeasance in public office as that tort requires other elements before a right of civil action arises. It is doubtful that these provisions exclude judicial review proceedings: *Re Waldron (No1)* [1986] QB 824, [1985] 3 All ER 775 (CA).

[2] FOIA s 79; FOI(S)A s 67. There is no direct equivalent in the environmental information regime, although EIR reg 5(6) and EI(S)R reg 5(3) may serve the same purpose. In relation to internally generated material that is defamatory, see §9– 035.

obliged to do so (eg because the information is exempt from the duty to communicate).[3] Similarly, the protection will not apply where a public authority volunteers information to a person other than the person who has made a request for that information (eg by posting the requested information onto the internet).

002 Enforcement by Information Commissioners

Enforcement of the duties of public authorities under the Acts is primarily in the hands of the two Information Commissioners. They have power to issue decision notices,[4] enforcement notices,[5] and information notices[6] requiring public authorities to take steps to comply with their obligations under the Acts or to supply information in order to determine whether they have complied with such obligations. If a decision notice, enforcement notice or information notice issued by the Information Commissioner (and not successfully appealed against)[7] is not complied with, the Information Commissioner may certify that that is the case to the High Court or the Court of Session.[8] The court may then inquire into the matter and, after hearing evidence and any statement which may be offered in defence, it may deal with the public authority 'as if it had committed a contempt of court'.[9]

003 Means of dealing with a contempt of court

If it was ever required in practice,[10] there may be difficulties in applying the provision for contempt of court. The normal ways of dealing with a person who has committed a contempt of court are by way of an order of committal to prison, a sequestration order, a fine, an injunction, an order that the contemnor pay the costs of the hearing (often on an indemnity basis) and (possibly) a declaration.[11] It seems unlikely that committal, sequestration or a fine would ever be appropriate in relation to a public authority (even assuming the public authority in question was an individual and therefore amenable to an order of committal) and, at least in relation to government departments, the House of Lords has expressed the view that a *finding*

---

[3] See §§9– 034 to 9– 038.

[4] FOIA s 50; FOI(S)A s 49; FOIA s 56(1); EIR reg 18 (applying FOIA, Pt IV (ss 50–56), incl Sch 3); EI(S)R reg 17 (applying FOI(S)A, Pt IV (ss 47–56), incl Sch 3). These are discussed in §§28– 011 and 28– 015.

[5] FOIA s 52; FOI(S)A s 52; EIR reg 18 (applying FOIA, Pt IV (ss 50–56), incl Sch 3); EI(S)R reg 17 (applying FOI(S)A, Pt IV (ss 47–56), incl Sch 3). These are discussed in §§28– 013 and 28– 016.

[6] FOIA s 51; FOI(S)A s 50; EIR reg 18 (applying FOIA, Pt IV (ss 50–56), incl Sch 3); EI(S)R reg 17 (applying FOI(S)A, Pt IV (ss 47–56), incl Sch 3). These are discussed in §§28– 012 and 28– 016. Note that failure to comply with an information notice includes making a false statement in purported compliance with the information notice: FOIA s 54(2) and FOI(S)A s 53(2).

[7] FOIA s 57; FOI(S)A s 56; EIR reg 18 (applying FOIA, Pt V (ss 57–61)); EI(S)R reg 17 (applying FOI(S)A, Pt IV (ss 47–56), incl Sch 3). These appeals are dealt with in ch 28. An appeal can result in a substitute notice issued under FOIA s 58 which will operate and be enforceable as if it had been issued by the Information Commissioner.

[8] FOIA s 54(1); FOI(S)A s 53(1); EIR reg 18 (applying FOIA, Pt IV (ss 50–56), incl Sch 3); EI(S)R reg 17 (applying FOI(S)A, Pt IV (ss 47–56), incl Sch 3).

[9] FOIA s 54(3); FOI(S)A s 53(3); EIR reg 18 (applying FOIA, Pt IV (ss 50–56), incl Sch 3); EI(S)R reg 17 (applying FOI(S)A, Pt IV (ss 47–56), incl Sch 3).

[10] The Home Office's Freedom of Information Unit expressed the view that the provision was only there 'to give the Commissioner's notices the appropriate status': see Public Administration Committee, *Third Report*, 1998–99 Session, Annex 6, para 90.

[11] *Halsbury's Laws of England*, 4th edn, Butterworths 1998 re-issue, vol 9(1), paras 506–509.

of contempt should suffice in any case.[12] Because the provision refers to dealing with the authority it does not seem that the court could make an order of committal or sequestration against individual officers who were personally responsible (even in a contumacious way) for the failure of the authority to comply with a notice by the Commissioner, as the court can normally do in the case of a breach of one of its own orders,[13] although it would presumably be open to the court to grant an injunction which could itself thereafter be enforced if still not complied with in this way.

29–004 Procedure

The power of the High Court to punish for contempt under the Freedom of Information Act 2000 can be exercised by a single judge of the Queen's Bench Division.[14] There is no procedure expressly laid down but it is thought that the matter would be brought before the court by the Attorney-General issuing a claim form[15] and that it would be dealt with in accordance with CPR Sch 1 (RSC Ord 52) and the Practice Direction thereto. There is an automatic right of appeal to the Court of Appeal against the making of a committal order by a High Court judge if that were the outcome.[16]

29–005 Search and seizure

As well as the power to serve information notices against public authorities in order to collect evidence in relation to compliance with the Freedom of Information Acts, both Commissioners have power to seek a warrant from a circuit judge or a sheriff authorising them or their officers to enter and search premises, inspect and seize documents or other material which might be evidence of non-compliance with the Act, and to inspect, examine, operate and test equipment found there in which information may be recorded if there are reasonable grounds for suspecting such non-compliance and that evidence thereof is to be found on any premises.[17] Save in cases of urgency or where this would defeat the object of the exercise, the occupier of the premises must have been given seven days notice that access was required and have refused it and been warned of the application for a warrant and been heard on the matter.[18] This reflects a clear policy that agreement should be reached if possible, which no doubt also reflects the hope that public authorities will not normally destroy or hide evidence.

---

[12] See *M v Home Office* [1994] 1 AC 377, [1993] 3 All ER 537 (Lord Woolf).

[13] See RSC Ord 45 r 5(1)(b)(ii) and (iii).

[14] See RSC Ord 52 r 1(4).

[15] See, eg *AG v Clough* [1963] 1 QB 773 (showing practice under Tribunals of Enquiry (Evidence) Act 1921) and RSC Ord 52 r 4.

[16] CPR 52.3(1)(a)(i).

[17] FOIA s 55 and Sch 3, para 1; FOI(S)A s 54 and Sch 3, para 1; EIR reg 18 (applying FOIA, Pt IV (ss 50–56), incl Sch 3); EI(S)R reg 17 (applying FOI(S)A, Pt IV (ss 47–56), incl Sch 3). These powers are comparable to those given to the Inland Revenue Commissioners in relation to serious fraud by the Taxes Management Act 1970 s 20C and to constables by the Companies Act 1985 s 448, with the interesting result that, under the Freedom of Information Acts, it would be public authorities which are on the receiving end of the search and seizure order.

[18] FOIA Sch 3 para 2; FOI(S)A, Sch 3 para 2; EIR reg 18 (applying FOIA Pt IV (ss 50–56), incl Sch 3); EI(S)R reg 17 (applying FOI(S)A, Pt IV (ss 47–56), incl Sch 3).

006 Procedure on warrant

The warrant must be executed within seven days[19] and the person executing it can use reasonable force and must execute it at a reasonable time unless this would mean the evidence would not be found.[20] The powers of inspection and seizure are not exercisable in respect of information which is exempt on national security grounds or communications subject to legal professional privilege in relation to advice or proceedings about obligations, rights or liabilities arising under the Freedom of Information Acts themselves.[21]

007 Criminal offences

There are various criminal offences underpinning this system of enforcement. The Freedom of Information Acts both make it an offence to interfere with any records held by a public authority with the intention of preventing disclosure by the authority of information to which the applicant would have been entitled after having made a request for information.[22] The offence can be committed by a public authority or any of its officers or employees or anyone subject to its direction[23] but a government department[24] (or, in Scotland, the Parliament or the Parliamentary corporation or the Scottish Administration) is not liable to prosecution under the Acts, though servants of the Crown (and members of staff of the Scottish bodies mentioned) are.[25] It is a summary offence, punishable with a fine on level 5.[26] Under the Freedom of Information Act 2000 a prosecution can only be brought in England and Wales by the Information Commissioner or by or with the consent of the Director of Public Prosecutions.[27] It is also an offence to obstruct or to fail, without reasonable excuse, to give reasonably required assistance to a person executing a warrant under the procedure set out above.[28] The Scottish Act specifies that this is a summary offence punishable with a fine at level 5.[29]

---

[19] FOIA Sch 3 para 1(2); FOI(S)A, Sch 3 para 1(2); EIR reg 18 (applying FOIA Pt IV (ss 50–56), incl Sch 3); EI(S)R reg 17 (applying FOI(S)A, Pt IV (ss 47–56), incl Sch 3).

[20] FOIA Sch 3 paras 4 and 5; FOI(S)A, Sch 3 paras 3 and 4; EIR reg 18 (applying FOIA Pt IV (ss 50–56), incl Sch 3); EI(S)R reg 17 (applying FOI(S)A, Pt IV (ss 47–56), incl Sch 3).

[21] FOIA Sch 3 paras 8 and 9; FOI(S)A, Sch 3 paras 7 and 8; EIR reg 18 (applying FOIA Pt IV (ss 50–56), incl Sch 3); EI(S)R reg 17 (applying FOI(S)A, Pt IV (ss 47–56), incl Sch 3).

[22] FOIA s 77(1); FOI(S)A s 65(1); EIR reg 19(1); EI(S)R reg 19(1).

[23] FOIA s 77(2); FOI(S)A s 65(2); EIR reg 19(2); EI(S)R reg 19(2).

[24] As defined in FOIA s 84 (with certain exceptions, 'any body or authority exercising statutory functions on behalf of the Crown').

[25] FOIA s 81(3); FOI(S)A s 68; EIR reg 19(5); EI(S)R reg 19(4).

[26] FOIA s 77(3); FOI(S)A s 65(3); EIR reg 19(3); EI(S)R reg 19(3).

[27] FOIA s 77(4); EIR reg 19(4).

[28] FOIA, Sch 3, para 12; FOI(S)A, Sch 3, para 10; EIR reg 18 (applying FOIA, Pt IV (ss 50–56), incl Sch 3); EI(S)R reg 17 (applying FOI(S)A, Pt IV (ss 47–56), incl Sch 3). See §29– 006.

[29] FOI(S)A, Sch 3, para 10(2); EI(S)R reg 17 (applying FOI(S)A, Pt IV (ss 47–56), incl Sch 3).

2. DATA PROTECTION ACT 1998

29–008 Private action to enforce access rights

As discussed in Chapters 5 and 28,[30] the primary means by which the access rights under the Data Protection Act 1998 are pursued are by an application to the court under s 7(9), which provides that the court can, if satisfied that the data controller has failed to comply with a request in contravention of the Act, order it to do so. The jurisdiction is exercisable by both the High Court or the county court, or, in Scotland, by the Court of Session or the sheriff. If a public authority was ordered to comply with a request and failed to do so, it would be open to the applicant to seek enforcement of the order in the normal way pursuant to the relevant rules of court.[31] As discussed above, it is most unlikely that a public authority would ever be committed to prison (assuming, of course, that the authority in question was a natural person) or that an order for sequestration or a fine would be made, but it would be open, in principle, for the court to make an order for committal against an individual officer of the authority[32] in appropriate circumstances, no doubt involving actual fault on the part of the officer.

29–009 Compensation

Under the Data Protection Act 1998 it is also open to an individual who suffers damage by reason of a contravention of the Act by a data controller to obtain compensation for the damage, and such compensation can include compensation for distress provided there is other damage.[33] The jurisdiction is again in the High Court or a county court (or as appropriate in Scotland) and there is a defence that the data controller took reasonable care to comply with the requirements of the Act.[34]

29–010 Information Commissioner's role

As discussed earlier,[35] there is also a limited role for the Information Commissioner in enforcing the right of access to personal data provided by the Data Protection Act 1998. The Commissioner can serve enforcement notices on the data controller if satisfied that it has contravened any of the data protection principles[36] (including the sixth principle, which can come about by a contravention of s 7 of the Act)[37] and can serve information notices in connection with inquiries into such a contravention.[38] A failure to comply with any such notice

---

[30] See §§5–082 to 5–085 and 28–041 to 28–043.

[31] In the High Court RSC Ord 45 r 5 and Ord 52 and in a county court CCR Ord 29.

[32] See RSC Ord 45 r 5(1)(b)(iii) and CCR Ord 29 r 1(1).

[33] DPA s 13. See further §5–091.

[34] DPA s 13(3).

[35] §§5–086 to 5–090 and 28–044.

[36] DPA s 40(1).

[37] DPA Sch 1 Pt II para 8(a).

[38] DPA s 43(1).

(including, in the case of an information notice, deliberately or recklessly making a false statement in response thereto) is an offence.[39] It is a defence to the charge to show that all due diligence was exercised.[40] The offence is triable either summarily or on indictment and punishable with the maximum or an unlimited fine. Proceedings must be brought by the Information Commissioner or by or with the consent of the DPP.[41] No government department[42] is liable to prosecution under the Data Protection Act 1998[43] but individual servants of the Crown may be.[44]

– 011 Search and seizure

As with the Freedom of Information Acts, the Information Commissioner has power to seek a warrant authorising entry search and seizure if there are reasonable grounds for suspecting a contravention of the data protection principles or that an offence under the Data Protection Act 1998 is being or has been committed and that evidence of the contravention or the offence is to be found on any premises.[45] The detailed provisions in the Data Protection Act 1998 in relation to these powers are very similar to those in the Freedom of Information Acts.[46]

– 012 Criminal offences

As in relation to the Freedom of Information Acts, it is a criminal offence to interfere with records held by a public authority with the intention of preventing the disclosure of information to which a person who had made a request would have been entitled in accordance with s 7 of the Data Protection Act 1998.[47] It is also an offence under the Data Protection Act 1998 to obstruct a person in the execution of a warrant under the Act or to fail to give reasonable assistance in the same way as in relation to a warrant under the Freedom of Information Acts.[48] Proceedings for this offence must be brought by the Information Commissioner or by or with the consent of the DPP, it is triable summarily and the maximum penalty is a fine on level 5;[49] although a government department cannot be liable to prosecution for this offence Crown servants can be guilty of the offence.[50]

---

[39] DPA s 47(1) and (2).

[40] DPA s 47(3).

[41] DPA s 60(1) and (2).

[42] Defined by the Data Protection Act s 70(1) as including any 'body or authority exercising statutory functions on behalf of the Crown'.

[43] DPA s 63(5).

[44] The position is unclear: the Data Protection Act s 63(5) does not refer expressly to offences under s 47 of failing to comply with a notice and the effect of DPA s 61(1) is not clear where the body corporate (in this case the government department) is itself not 'liable to prosecution'.

[45] DPA s 50 and Sch 9, para 1.

[46] See §29– 005.

[47] FOIA ss 77 and 81(3).

[48] DPA Sch 9 para 12; see §29– 007.

[49] DPA s 60(1) and (3).

[50] DPA s 63(5).

MATERIALS

Tribunal Rules, Orders and Practice Notes

Statutory Codes of Practice

European Union Directives and Regulations

Conventions

Freedom of Information Act 2000

(as amended to 1 February 2010)

CHAPTER 36

An Act to make provision for the disclosure of information held by public authorities or by persons providing services for them and to amend the Data Protection Act 1998 and the Public Records Act 1958; and for connected purposes.

30 November 2000

BE IT ENACTED by the Queen's most Excellent Majesty, by and with the advice and consent of the Lords Spiritual and Temporal, and Commons, in this present Parliament assembled, and by the authority of the same, as follows:—

PART I

ACCESS TO INFORMATION HELD BY PUBLIC AUTHORITIES

PART II

EXEMPT INFORMATION

PART III

GENERAL FUNCTIONS OF LORD CHANCELLOR AND INFORMATION COMMISSIONER

PART IV

ENFORCEMENT

SCHEDULES

PART I

ACCESS TO INFORMATION HELD BY PUBLIC AUTHORITIES

Right to information

General right of access to information held by public authorities

1(1)   Any person making a request for information to a public authority is entitled--

(a) to be informed in writing by the public authority whether it holds information of the description specified in the request, and

(b) if that is the case, to have that information communicated to him.

(2)   Subsection (1) has effect subject to the following provisions of this section and to the provisions of sections 2, 9, 12 and 14.

(3)   Where a public authority--

(a) reasonably requires further information in order to identify and locate the information requested, and

(b) has informed the applicant of that requirement,

the authority is not obliged to comply with subsection (1) unless it is supplied with that further information.

(4)   The information—

(a) in respect of which the applicant is to be informed under subsection (1)(a), or

(b) which is to be communicated under subsection (1)(b),

is the information in question held at the time when the request is received, except that account may be taken of any amendment or deletion made between that time and the time when the information is to be communicated under subsection (1)(b), being an amendment or deletion that would have been made regardless of the receipt of the request.

(5)   A public authority is to be taken to have complied with subsection (1)(a) in relation to any information if it has communicated the information to the applicant in accordance with subsection (1)(b).

(6)   In this Act, the duty of a public authority to comply with subsection (1)(a) is referred to as "the duty to confirm or deny".

NOTES

Commencement
1 January 2005: SI 2004/3122 art 2.

Scottish public authority equivalent
FOI(S)A s 1

Defined terms
"applicant": s 84
"duty to confirm or deny": subs (6)
"information": s 84
"public authority": s 3(1)
"request for information": s 8

Effect of the exemptions in Part II

2(1)   Where any provision of Part II states that the duty to confirm or deny does not arise in relation to any information, the effect of the provision is that where either—

(a) the provision confers absolute exemption, or

(b) in all the circumstances of the case, the public interest in maintaining the exclusion of the duty to confirm or deny outweighs the public interest in disclosing whether the public authority holds the information,

section 1(1)(a) does not apply.

(2) In respect of any information which is exempt information by virtue of any provision of Part II, section 1(1)(b) does not apply if or to the extent that—

    (a) the information is exempt information by virtue of a provision conferring absolute exemption, or

    (b) in all the circumstances of the case, the public interest in maintaining the exemption outweighs the public interest in disclosing the information.

(3) For the purposes of this section, the following provisions of Part II (and no others) are to be regarded as conferring absolute exemption—

    (a) section 21,

    (b) section 23,

    (c) section 32,

    (d) section 34,

    (e) section 36 so far as relating to information held by the House of Commons or the House of Lords,

    (f) in section 40—

        (i) subsection (1), and

        (ii) subsection (2) so far as relating to cases where the first condition referred to in that subsection is satisfied by virtue of subsection (3)(a)(i) or (b) of that section,

    (g) section 41, and

    (h) section 44.

NOTES

Commencement
1 January 2005: SI 2004/3122 art 2.

Scottish public authority equivalent
FOI(S)A s 2

Defined terms
"duty to confirm or deny": s 1(6)
"exempt information": s 84 and Pt II

Public authorities

3(1) In this Act "public authority" means—

    (a) subject to section 4(4), any body which, any other person who, or the holder of any office which—

        (i) is listed in Schedule 1, or

        (ii) is designated by order under section 5, or

    (b) a publicly-owned company as defined by section 6.

(2) For the purposes of this Act, information is held by a public authority if—

    (a) it is held by the authority, otherwise than on behalf of another person, or

    (b) it is held by another person on behalf of the authority.

NOTES

Commencement
30 November 2000: s 87(1)(a).

Defined terms
"information": s 84
"public authority": subs (1)

Scottish public authority equivalent
FOI(S)A s 2

Amendment of Schedule 1

4(1)   The Secretary of State may by order amend Schedule 1 by adding to that Schedule a reference to any body or the holder of any office which (in either case) is not for the time being listed in that Schedule but as respects which both the first and the second conditions below are satisfied.

(2)   The first condition is that the body or office—

(a) is established by virtue of Her Majesty's prerogative or by an enactment or by subordinate legislation, or

(b) is established in any other way by a Minister of the Crown in his capacity as Minister, by a government department or by the Welsh Ministers, the First Minister for Wales or the Counsel General to the Welsh Assembly Government.

(3)   The second condition is—

(a) in the case of a body, that the body is wholly or partly constituted by appointment made by the Crown, by a Minister of the Crown, by a government department or by the Welsh Ministers, the First Minister for Wales or the Counsel General to the Welsh Assembly Government, or

(b) in the case of an office, that appointments to the office are made by the Crown, by a Minister of the Crown, by a government department or by the Welsh Ministers, the First Minister for Wales or the Counsel General to the Welsh Assembly Government.

(4)   If either the first or the second condition above ceases to be satisfied as respects any body or office which is listed in Part VI or VII of Schedule 1, that body or the holder of that office shall cease to be a public authority by virtue of the entry in question.

(5)   The Secretary of State may by order amend Schedule 1 by removing from Part VI or VII of that Schedule an entry relating to any body or office—

(a) which has ceased to exist, or

(b) as respects which either the first or the second condition above has ceased to be satisfied.

(6)   An order under subsection (1) may relate to a specified person or office or to persons or offices falling within a specified description.

(7)   Before making an order under subsection (1), the Secretary of State shall—

(a) if the order adds to Part II, III, IV or VI of Schedule 1 a reference to—

      (i) a body whose functions are exercisable only or mainly in or as regards Wales, or

     (ii) the holder of an office whose functions are exercisable only or mainly in or as regards Wales, consult the Welsh Ministers, and

  (b) if the order relates to a body which, or the holder of any office who, if the order were made, would be a Northern Ireland public authority, consult the First Minister and deputy First Minister in Northern Ireland.

(8)   This section has effect subject to section 80.

(9)   In this section "Minister of the Crown" includes a Northern Ireland Minister.

NOTES

Commencement
30 November 2000: s 87(1)(a).

Defined terms
"public authority": s 3(1)

Scottish public authority equivalent
FOI(S)A s 4

Further power to designate public authorities

5(1)   The Secretary of State may by order designate as a public authority for the purposes of this Act any person who is neither listed in Schedule 1 nor capable of being added to that Schedule by an order under section 4(1), but who—

  (a) appears to the Secretary of State to exercise functions of a public nature, or

  (b) is providing under a contract made with a public authority any service whose provision is a function of that authority.

(2)   An order under this section may designate a specified person or office or persons or offices falling within a specified description.

(3)   Before making an order under this section, the Secretary of State shall consult every person to whom the order relates, or persons appearing to him to represent such persons.

(4)   This section has effect subject to section 80.

NOTES

Commencement
30 November 2000: s 87(1)(a).

Defined terms
"public authority": s 3(1)

Scottish public authority equivalent
FOI(S)A s 5

Publicly-owned companies

6(1)   A company is a "publicly-owned company" for the purposes of section 3(1)(b) if—

  (a) it is wholly owned by the Crown, or

(b) it is wholly owned by any public authority listed in Schedule 1 other than—
    (i) a government department, or
    (ii) any authority which is listed only in relation to particular information.

(2) For the purposes of this section—
    (a) a company is wholly owned by the Crown if it has no members except—
        (i) Ministers of the Crown, government departments or companies wholly owned by the Crown, or
        (ii) persons acting on behalf of Ministers of the Crown, government departments or companies wholly owned by the Crown, and
    (b) a company is wholly owned by a public authority other than a government department if it has no members except—
        (i) that public authority or companies wholly owned by that public authority, or
        (ii) persons acting on behalf of that public authority or of companies wholly owned by that public authority.

(3) In this section—
"company" includes any body corporate;
"Minister of the Crown" includes a Northern Ireland Minister.

NOTES

Commencement
30 November 2000: s 87(1)(a).

Scottish public authority equivalent
FOI(S)A s 6

Defined terms
"company": subs (3)
"government department": s 84
"Minister of the Crown": subs.(3), s 84 of the Ministers of the Crown Act 1975 (c.26)
"Northern Ireland Minister": s 84
"public authority": s 3(1)

Public authorities to which Act has limited application

7(1) Where a public authority is listed in Schedule 1 only in relation to information of a specified description, nothing in Parts I to V of this Act applies to any other information held by the authority.

(2) An order under section 4(1) may, in adding an entry to Schedule 1, list the public authority only in relation to information of a specified description.

(3) The Secretary of State may by order amend Schedule 1—
    (a) by limiting to information of a specified description the entry relating to any public authority, or
    (b) by removing or amending any limitation to information of a specified description which is for the time being contained in any entry.

(4) Before making an order under subsection (3), the Secretary of State shall—
    (a) if the order relates to the National Assembly for Wales or a Welsh public authority referred to in section 83(1)(b)(ii) (subsidiary of the Assembly Commission), consult

the Presiding Officer of the National Assembly for Wales,

(aa) if the order relates to the Welsh Assembly Government or a Welsh public authority other than one referred to in section 83(1)(b)(ii), consult the First Minister for Wales,

(b) if the order relates to the Northern Ireland Assembly, consult the Presiding Officer of that Assembly, and

(c) if the order relates to a Northern Ireland department or a Northern Ireland public authority, consult the First Minister and deputy First Minister in Northern Ireland.

(5) An order under section 5(1)(a) must specify the functions of the public authority designated by the order with respect to which the designation is to have effect; and nothing in Parts I to V of this Act applies to information which is held by the authority but does not relate to the exercise of those functions.

(6) An order under section 5(1)(b) must specify the services provided under contract with respect to which the designation is to have effect; and nothing in Parts I to V of this Act applies to information which is held by the public authority designated by the order but does not relate to the provision of those services.

(7) Nothing in Parts I to V of this Act applies in relation to any information held by a publicly-owned company which is excluded information in relation to that company.

(8) In subsection (7) "excluded information", in relation to a publicly-owned company, means information which is of a description specified in relation to that company in an order made by the Secretary of State for the purposes of this subsection.

(9) In this section "publicly-owned company" has the meaning given by section 6.

NOTES

Commencement
30 November 2000: s 87(1)(a).

Scottish public authority equivalent
FOI(S)A s 7

Defined terms
"excluded information": subs (8)
"information": s 84
"publicly owned company": subs (9), s 6
"public authority": s 3(1)

Request for information

8(1) In this Act any reference to a "request for information" is a reference to such a request which—

(a) is in writing,

(b) states the name of the applicant and an address for correspondence, and

(c) describes the information requested.

(2) For the purposes of subsection (1)(a), a request is to be treated as made in writing where the text of the request—

(a) is transmitted by electronic means,

(b) is received in legible form, and

(c) is capable of being used for subsequent reference.

NOTES

Commencement

30 November 2000: s 87(1)(a)

Scottish public authority equivalent

FOI(S)A s 8

Defined terms

"applicant": s 84

"information": s 84

Fees

9(1)   A public authority to whom a request for information is made may, within the period for complying with section 1(1), give the applicant a notice in writing (in this Act referred to as a "fees notice") stating that a fee of an amount specified in the notice is to be charged by the authority for complying with section 1(1).

(2)   Where a fees notice has been given to the applicant, the public authority is not obliged to comply with section 1(1) unless the fee is paid within the period of three months beginning with the day on which the fees notice is given to the applicant.

(3)   Subject to subsection (5), any fee under this section must be determined by the public authority in accordance with regulations made by the Secretary of State.

(4)   Regulations under subsection (3) may, in particular, provide—

    (a) that no fee is to be payable in prescribed cases,

    (b) that any fee is not to exceed such maximum as may be specified in, or determined in accordance with, the regulations, and

    (c) that any fee is to be calculated in such manner as may be prescribed by the regulations.

(5)   Subsection (3) does not apply where provision is made by or under any enactment as to the fee that may be charged by the public authority for the disclosure of the information.

NOTES

Commencement

30 November 2000: s 87(1)(a) (in so far as this section confers powers to make any order, regulations or code of practice): see s 87(1)(m).

For remaining purposes, 1 January 2005: SI 2004/3122 art 2

Scottish public authority equivalent

FOI(S)A s 9

Defined terms

"applicant": s 84

"fees notice": subs (1)

"public authority": s 3(1)

"request for information": s 8

Subordinate legislation

Freedom of Information and Data Protection (Appropriate Limit and Fees) Regulations 2004, SI 2004/3244. Reproduced at p 1137 ff.

Time for compliance with request

10(1)   Subject to subsections (2) and (3), a public authority must comply with section 1(1) promptly and in any event not later than the twentieth working day following the date of receipt.

(2) Where the authority has given a fees notice to the applicant and the fee is paid in accordance with section 9(2), the working days in the period beginning with the day on which the fees notice is given to the applicant and ending with the day on which the fee is received by the authority are to be disregarded in calculating for the purposes of subsection (1) the twentieth working day following the date of receipt.

(3) If, and to the extent that—
    (a) section 1(1)(a) would not apply if the condition in section 2(1)(b) were satisfied, or
    (b) section 1(1)(b) would not apply if the condition in section 2(2)(b) were satisfied,
the public authority need not comply with section 1(1)(a) or (b) until such time as is reasonable in the circumstances; but this subsection does not affect the time by which any notice under section 17(1) must be given.

(4) The Secretary of State may by regulations provide that subsections (1) and (2) are to have effect as if any reference to the twentieth working day following the date of receipt were a reference to such other day, not later than the sixtieth working day following the date of receipt, as may be specified in, or determined in accordance with, the regulations.

(5) Regulations under subsection (4) may—
    (a) prescribe different days in relation to different cases, and
    (b) confer a discretion on the Commissioner.

(6) In this section—
    "the date of receipt" means—
    (a) the day on which the public authority receives the request for information, or
    (b) if later, the day on which it receives the information referred to in section 1(3);
    "working day" means any day other than a Saturday, a Sunday, Christmas Day, Good Friday or a day which is a bank holiday under the Banking and Financial Dealings Act 1971 in any part of the United Kingdom.

NOTES

Commencement

30 November 2000 (in so far as this section confers powers to make any order, regulations or code of practice): see s 87(1)(m).

1 January 2005 (for remaining purposes): SI 2004/3122 art 4.

Scottish public authority equivalent

FOI(S)A s 10

Defined terms

"applicant": s 84
"date of receipt": subs (6)
"fees notice": s 9(1)
"information": s 84
"public authority": s 3(1)
"request for information": s 8
"working day": subs (6)

Subordinate legislation

Freedom of Information (Time for Compliance with Request) Regulations 2004, SI 2004/3364. Reproduced at p 1137 ff.

Means by which communication to be made

11(1)   Where, on making his request for information, the applicant expresses a preference for communication by any one or more of the following means, namely—

   (a) the provision to the applicant of a copy of the information in permanent form or in another form acceptable to the applicant,

   (b) the provision to the applicant of a reasonable opportunity to inspect a record containing the information, and

   (c) the provision to the applicant of a digest or summary of the information in permanent form or in another form acceptable to the applicant,

the public authority shall so far as reasonably practicable give effect to that preference.

(2)   In determining for the purposes of this section whether it is reasonably practicable to communicate information by particular means, the public authority may have regard to all the circumstances, including the cost of doing so.

(3)   Where the public authority determines that it is not reasonably practicable to comply with any preference expressed by the applicant in making his request, the authority shall notify the applicant of the reasons for its determination.

(4)   Subject to subsection (1), a public authority may comply with a request by communicating information by any means which are reasonable in the circumstances.

NOTES

Commencement
1 January 2005: SI 2004/3122 art 2.

Scottish public authority equivalent
FOI(S)A s 11

Defined terms
"applicant": s 84
"information": s 84
"public authority": s 3(1)
"request for information": s 8

Exemption where cost of compliance exceeds appropriate limit

12(1)   Section 1(1) does not oblige a public authority to comply with a request for information if the authority estimates that the cost of complying with the request would exceed the appropriate limit.

(2)   Subsection (1) does not exempt the public authority from its obligation to comply with paragraph (a) of section 1(1) unless the estimated cost of complying with that paragraph alone would exceed the appropriate limit.

(3)   In subsections (1) and (2) "the appropriate limit" means such amount as may be prescribed, and different amounts may be prescribed in relation to different cases.

(4)   The Secretary of State may by regulations provide that, in such circumstances as may be prescribed, where two or more requests for information are made to a public authority—

   (a) by one person, or

   (b) by different persons who appear to the public authority to be acting in concert or in pursuance of a campaign, the estimated cost of complying with any of the requests is to be taken to be the estimated total cost of complying with all of them.

(5)   The Secretary of State may by regulations make provision for the purposes of this section as to the costs to be estimated and as to the manner in which they are to be estimated.

NOTES

Commencement
30 November 2000 in so far as this section confers powers to make any order, regulations or code of practice): see s87(1)(m).
1 January 2005 (for remaining purposes): SI 2004/3122 art 2.

Scottish public authority equivalent
FOI(S)A s 12

Defined terms
"appropriate limit": subs (3)
"public authority": s 3(1)
"request for information": s 8

Subordinate legislation
Freedom of Information and Data Protection (Appropriate Limit and Fees) Regulations 2004, SI 2004/3244. Reproduced at p 1134 ff.

Fees for disclosure where cost of compliance exceeds appropriate limit

13(1)   A public authority may charge for the communication of any information whose communication—

(a) is not required by section 1(1) because the cost of complying with the request for information exceeds the amount which is the appropriate limit for the purposes of section 12(1) and (2), and

(b) is not otherwise required by law,

such fee as may be determined by the public authority in accordance with regulations made by the Secretary of State.

(2)   Regulations under this section may, in particular, provide—

(a) that any fee is not to exceed such maximum as may be specified in, or determined in accordance with, the regulations, and

(b) that any fee is to be calculated in such manner as may be prescribed by the regulations.

(3)   Subsection (1) does not apply where provision is made by or under any enactment as to the fee that may be charged by the public authority for the disclosure of the information.

NOTES

Commencement
30 November 2000 (in so far as this section confers powers to make any order, regulations or code of practice): see s 87(1)(m).
1 January 2005 (for remaining purposes): SI 2004/3122 art 2.

Scottish public authority equivalent
FOI(S)A s 13

Defined terms
"appropriate limit": s12(3)
"information": s 84
"public authority": s 3(1)

Subordinate legislation
Freedom of Information and Data Protection (Appropriate Limit and Fees) Regulations 2004, SI 2004/3244. Reproduced at p 1137 ff.

Vexatious or repeated requests

14(1)   Section 1(1) does not oblige a public authority to comply with a request for information if the request is vexatious.

(2)   Where a public authority has previously complied with a request for information which was made by any person, it is not obliged to comply with a subsequent identical or substantially similar request from that person unless a reasonable interval has elapsed between compliance with the previous request and the making of the current request.

NOTES

Commencement

1 January 2005: SI 2004/3122 art 2.

Scottish public authority equivalent

FOI(S)A s 14

Defined terms

"public authority": s 3(1)

"request for information": s 8

Special provisions relating to public records transferred to Public Record Office, etc

15(1)   Where—

(a) the appropriate records authority receives a request for information which relates to information which is, or if it existed would be, contained in a transferred public record, and

(b) either of the conditions in subsection (2) is satisfied in relation to any of that information,

that authority shall, within the period for complying with section 1(1), send a copy of the request to the responsible authority.

(2)   The conditions referred to in subsection (1)(b) are—

(a) that the duty to confirm or deny is expressed to be excluded only by a provision of Part II not specified in subsection (3) of section 2, and

(b) that the information is exempt information only by virtue of a provision of Part II not specified in that subsection.

(3)   On receiving the copy, the responsible authority shall, within such time as is reasonable in all the circumstances, inform the appropriate records authority of the determination required by virtue of subsection (3) or (4) of section 66.

(4)   In this Act "transferred public record" means a public record which has been transferred—

(a) to the Public Record Office,

(b) to another place of deposit appointed by the Lord Chancellor under the Public Records Act 1958, or

(c) to the Public Record Office of Northern Ireland.

(5)   In this Act—

"appropriate records authority", in relation to a transferred public record, means—

(a) in a case falling within subsection (4)(a), the Public Record Office,

(b) in a case falling within subsection (4)(b), the Lord Chancellor, and

(c) in a case falling within subsection (4)(c), the Public Record Office of Northern Ireland;

"responsible authority", in relation to a transferred public record, means—

(a) in the case of a record transferred as mentioned in subsection (4)(a) or (b) from a government department in the charge of a Minister of the Crown, the Minister of the Crown who appears to the Lord Chancellor to be primarily concerned,

(b) in the case of a record transferred as mentioned in subsection (4)(a) or (b) from any other person, the person who appears to the Lord Chancellor to be primarily concerned,

(c) in the case of a record transferred to the Public Record Office of Northern Ireland from a government department in the charge of a Minister of the Crown, the Minister of the Crown who appears to the appropriate Northern Ireland Minister to be primarily concerned,

(d) in the case of a record transferred to the Public Record Office of Northern Ireland from a Northern Ireland department, the Northern Ireland Minister who appears to the appropriate Northern Ireland Minister to be primarily concerned, or

(e) in the case of a record transferred to the Public Record Office of Northern Ireland from any other person, the person who appears to the appropriate Northern Ireland Minister to be primarily concerned.

NOTES

Commencement
Subss (4), (5): 1 January 2005: SI 2004/1909 art 2(1)-(3)
Subss (1)-(3): 1 January 2005: SI 2004/3122 art 2.

Scottish public authority equivalent
FOI(S)A s 22

Defined terms
"appropriate records authority": subs (5)
"public record": s 84 of the Public Records Act 1958 (c 51), Public Records Act (Northern Ireland) 1923
"responsible authority": subs (5)
"request for information": s 8
"transferred public record": subs (5)

Duty to provide advice and assistance

16(1) It shall be the duty of a public authority to provide advice and assistance, so far as it would be reasonable to expect the authority to do so, to persons who propose to make, or have made, requests for information to it.

(2) Any public authority which, in relation to the provision of advice or assistance in any case, conforms with the code of practice under section 45 is to be taken to comply with the duty imposed by subsection (1) in relation to that case.

NOTES

Commencement
1 January 2005: SI 2004/3122 art 2.

Scottish public authority equivalent
FOI(S)A s 15

Defined terms
"public authority": s 3(1)
"request for information": s 8

Refusal of request

17(1) A public authority which, in relation to any request for information, is to any extent relying on a claim that any provision of Part II relating to the duty to confirm or deny is relevant to the request or on a claim that information is exempt information must, within the time for complying with section 1(1), give the applicant a notice which—

(a) states that fact,

(b) specifies the exemption in question, and

(c) states (if that would not otherwise be apparent) why the exemption applies.

(2) Where—

(a) in relation to any request for information, a public authority is, as respects any information, relying on a claim—

(i) that any provision of Part II which relates to the duty to confirm or deny and is not specified in section 2(3) is relevant to the request, or

(ii) that the information is exempt information only by virtue of a provision not specified in section 2(3), and

(b) at the time when the notice under subsection (1) is given to the applicant, the public authority (or, in a case falling within section 66(3) or (4), the responsible authority) has not yet reached a decision as to the application of subsection (1)(b) or (2)(b) of section 2,

the notice under subsection (1) must indicate that no decision as to the application of that provision has yet been reached and must contain an estimate of the date by which the authority expects that such a decision will have been reached.

(3) A public authority which, in relation to any request for information, is to any extent relying on a claim that subsection (1)(b) or (2)(b) of section 2 applies must, either in the notice under subsection (1) or in a separate notice given within such time as is reasonable in the circumstances, state the reasons for claiming—

(a) that, in all the circumstances of the case, the public interest in maintaining the exclusion of the duty to confirm or deny outweighs the public interest in disclosing whether the authority holds the information, or

(b) that, in all the circumstances of the case, the public interest in maintaining the exemption outweighs the public interest in disclosing the information.

(4) A public authority is not obliged to make a statement under subsection (1)(c) or (3) if, or to the extent that, the statement would involve the disclosure of information which would itself be exempt information.

(5) A public authority which, in relation to any request for information, is relying on a claim that section 12 or 14 applies must, within the time for complying with section 1(1), give the applicant a notice stating that fact.

(6) Subsection (5) does not apply where—

(a) the public authority is relying on a claim that section 14 applies,

(b) the authority has given the applicant a notice, in relation to a previous request for information, stating that it is relying on such a claim, and

    (c) it would in all the circumstances be unreasonable to expect the authority to serve a further notice under subsection (5) in relation to the current request.

(7)   A notice under subsection (1), (3) or (5) must—

    (a) contain particulars of any procedure provided by the public authority for dealing with complaints about the handling of requests for information or state that the authority does not provide such a procedure, and

    (b) contain particulars of the right conferred by section 50.

NOTES

Commencement

1 January 2005: SI 2004/3122 art 2.

Scottish public authority equivalent

FOI(S)A s 16

Defined terms

"duty to confirm or deny": s 1(6)

"exempt information": s 84 and Part II

"public authority": s 3(1)

"request for information": s 8

The Information Commissioner

18(1)   The Data Protection Commissioner shall be known instead as the Information Commissioner.

(3)   In this Act—

    (a) the Information Commissioner is referred to as "the Commissioner"

(4)   Schedule 2 (which makes provision consequential on subsections (1) and (2) and amendments of the Data Protection Act 1998 relating to the extension by this Act of the functions of the Commissioner and the Tribunal) has effect.

(5)   If the person who held office as Data Protection Commissioner immediately before the day on which this Act is passed remains in office as Information Commissioner at the end of the period of two years beginning with that day, he shall vacate his office at the end of that period.

(6)   Subsection (5) does not prevent the re-appointment of a person whose appointment is terminated by that subsection.

(7)   In the application of paragraph 2(4)(b) and (5) of Schedule 5 to the Data Protection Act 1998 (Commissioner not to serve for more than fifteen years and not to be appointed, except in special circumstances, for a third or subsequent term) to anything done after the passing of this Act, there shall be left out of account any term of office served by virtue of an appointment made before the passing of this Act.

NOTES

Commencement

Subs (1): 30 January 2001: s 87(2)(a).

Subs (2), (3), (5)-(7): 14 May 2001: SI 2001/1637 art 2(a)

Subs (4): 30 January 2001 (for certain
   purposes): s 87(2)(a); 14 May 2001 (for other purposes):
   SI 2001/1637 art 2(a); 30 November 2002 (for

Defined terms

"Commissioner": subs (3)

"Information Commissioner": subs (1)

remaining purposes): SI 2002/2812 art 2(h).

Scottish public authority equivalent
None

Publication schemes

19(1)   It shall be the duty of every public authority—

    (a) to adopt and maintain a scheme which relates to the publication of information by the authority and is approved by the Commissioner (in this Act referred to as a "publication scheme"),

    (b) to publish information in accordance with its publication scheme, and

    (c) from time to time to review its publication scheme.

(2)   A publication scheme must—

    (a) specify classes of information which the public authority publishes or intends to publish,

    (b) specify the manner in which information of each class is, or is intended to be, published, and

    (c) specify whether the material is, or is intended to be, available to the public free of charge or on payment.

(3)   In adopting or reviewing a publication scheme, a public authority shall have regard to the public interest—

    (a) in allowing public access to information held by the authority, and

    (b) in the publication of reasons for decisions made by the authority.

(4)   A public authority shall publish its publication scheme in such manner as it thinks fit.

(5)   The Commissioner may, when approving a scheme, provide that his approval is to expire at the end of a specified period.

(6)   Where the Commissioner has approved the publication scheme of any public authority, he may at any time give notice to the public authority revoking his approval of the scheme as from the end of the period of six months beginning with the day on which the notice is given.

(7)   Where the Commissioner—

    (a) refuses to approve a proposed publication scheme, or

    (b) revokes his approval of a publication scheme,

he must give the public authority a statement of his reasons for doing so.

NOTES

Commencement
30 November 2000 (in relation to publication schemes): s 87(1)(b).
Subs (1)-(4) (depending upon the public authority): 30 November 2002, 28 February 2003, 30 June 2003: SI 2002/2812; 31 October 2003: SI 2003/2603.

Defined terms
"Commissioner": s 18(3)
"information": s 84
"public authority": s 3(1)
"publication scheme": subs (1)

Scottish public authority equivalent
FOI(S)A s 23

Model publication schemes

20(1)   The Commissioner may from time to time approve, in relation to public authorities falling within particular classes, model publication schemes prepared by him or by other persons.

(2)   Where a public authority falling within the class to which an approved model scheme relates adopts such a scheme without modification, no further approval of the Commissioner is required so long as the model scheme remains approved; and where such an authority adopts such a scheme with modifications, the approval of the Commissioner is required only in relation to the modifications.

(3)   The Commissioner may, when approving a model publication scheme, provide that his approval is to expire at the end of a specified period.

(4)   Where the Commissioner has approved a model publication scheme, he may at any time publish, in such manner as he thinks fit, a notice revoking his approval of the scheme as from the end of the period of six months beginning with the day on which the notice is published.

(5)   Where the Commissioner refuses to approve a proposed model publication scheme on the application of any person, he must give the person who applied for approval of the scheme a statement of the reasons for his refusal.

(6)   Where the Commissioner refuses to approve any modifications under subsection (2), he must give the public authority a statement of the reasons for his refusal.

(7)   Where the Commissioner revokes his approval of a model publication scheme, he must include in the notice under subsection (4) a statement of his reasons for doing so.

NOTES

Commencement

30 November 2000 (so far as relating to the approval and preparation by the Commissioner of model publication schemes): s 87(1)(c)
30 November 2002 (for remaining purposes): SI 2002/2812 art 2(a)

Defined terms

"Commissioner": s 18(3)
"public authority": s 3(1)
"publication scheme": s 19(1)

Scottish public authority equivalent
FOI(S)A s 24

PART II

EXEMPT INFORMATION

Information accessible to applicant by other means

21(1)   Information which is reasonably accessible to the applicant otherwise than under section 1 is exempt information.

(2)   For the purposes of subsection (1)—
   (a) information may be reasonably accessible to the applicant even though it is accessible only on payment, and
   (b) information is to be taken to be reasonably accessible to the applicant if it is information which the public authority or any other person is obliged by or under any enactment to communicate (otherwise than by making the information available for inspection) to members of the public on request, whether free of charge or on payment.

(3)   For the purposes of subsection (1), information which is held by a public authority and does not fall within subsection (2)(b) is not to be regarded as reasonably accessible to the applicant merely because the information is available from the public authority itself on request, unless the information is made available in accordance with the authority's publication scheme and any payment required is specified in, or determined in accordance with, the scheme.

NOTES

Commencement
1 January 2005: SI 2004/3122 art 2.

Scottish public authority equivalent
FOI(S)A s 25

Exemption type
Absolute: s 2(3)(a)

Defined terms
"applicant": s 84
"exempt information": s 84
"information": s 84
"publication scheme": s 19(1)
"public authority": s 3(1)fs

Information intended for future publication

22(1)   Information is exempt information if—
   (a) the information is held by the public authority with a view to its publication, by the authority or any other person, at some future date (whether determined or not),
   (b) the information was already held with a view to such publication at the time when the request for information was made, and
   (c) it is reasonable in all the circumstances that the information should be withheld from disclosure until the date referred to in paragraph (a).

(2)   The duty to confirm or deny does not arise if, or to the extent that, compliance with section 1(1)(a) would involve the disclosure of any information (whether or not already recorded) which falls within subsection (1).

Commencement
1 January 2005: SI 2004/3122 art 2.

Scottish public authority equivalent
FOI(S)A s 27

Exemption type
Not absolute: s 2(3)

NOTES
Defined terms
"duty to confirm or deny": s 16
"exempt information": s 84
"information": s 84
"public authority": s 3(1)

Information supplied by, or relating to, bodies dealing with security matters

23(1)   Information held by a public authority is exempt information if it was directly or indirectly supplied to the public authority by, or relates to, any of the bodies specified in subsection (3).

(2)   A certificate signed by a Minister of the Crown certifying that the information to which it applies was directly or indirectly supplied by, or relates to, any of the bodies specified in subsection (3) shall, subject to section 60, be conclusive evidence of that fact.

(3)   The bodies referred to in subsections (1) and (2) are—
   (a) the Security Service,
   (b) the Secret Intelligence Service,
   (c) the Government Communications Headquarters,
   (d) the special forces,
   (e) the Tribunal established under section 65 of the Regulation of Investigatory Powers Act 2000,
   (f) the Tribunal established under section 7 of the Interception of Communications Act 1985,
   (g) the Tribunal established under section 5 of the Security Service Act 1989,
   (h) the Tribunal established under section 9 of the Intelligence Services Act 1994,
   (i) the Security Vetting Appeals Panel,
   (j) the Security Commission,
   (k) the National Criminal Intelligence Service,
   (l) the Service Authority for the National Criminal Intelligence Service,
   (m) the Serious Organised Crime Agency.

(4)   In subsection (3)(c) "the Government Communications Headquarters" includes any unit or part of a unit of the armed forces of the Crown which is for the time being required by the Secretary of State to assist the Government Communications Headquarters in carrying out its functions.

(5)   The duty to confirm or deny does not arise if, or to the extent that, compliance with section 1(1)(a) would involve the disclosure of any information (whether or not already recorded) which was directly or indirectly supplied to the public authority by, or relates to, any of the bodies specified in subsection (3).

NOTES

Commencement
1 January 2005: SI 2004/3122 art 2.

Scottish public authority equivalent
None

Exemption type
Absolute: s 2(3)(b)

Defined terms
"duty to confirm or deny": s 1(6)
"exempt information": s 84
"information": s 84
"Minister of the Crown": s 84 of the Ministers of the Crown Act 1975
"public authority": s 3(1)

National security

24(1)   Information which does not fall within section 23(1) is exempt information if exemption from section 1(1)(b) is required for the purpose of safeguarding national security.

(2)   The duty to confirm or deny does not arise if, or to the extent that, exemption from section 1(1)(a) is required for the purpose of safeguarding national security.

(3)   A certificate signed by a Minister of the Crown certifying that exemption from section 1(1)(b), or from section 1(1)(a) and (b), is, or at any time was, required for the purpose of safeguarding national security shall, subject to section 60, be conclusive evidence of that fact.

(4)   A certificate under subsection (3) may identify the information to which it applies by means of a general description and may be expressed to have prospective effect.

NOTES

Commencement
1 January 2005: SI 2004/3122 art 2.

Scottish public authority equivalent
FOI(S)A s 31

Exemption type
Not absolute: s 2(3)

Defined terms
"duty to confirm or deny": s 1(6)
"exempt information": s 84
"information": s 84
"Minister of the Crown": s 84, Ministers of the Crown Act 1975
"special forces": s 84

Certificates under ss 23 and 24: supplementary provisions

25(1)   A document purporting to be a certificate under section 23(2) or 24(3) shall be received in evidence and deemed to be such a certificate unless the contrary is proved.

(2)   A document which purports to be certified by or on behalf of a Minister of the Crown as a true copy of a certificate issued by that Minister under section 23(2) or 24(3) shall in any legal proceedings be evidence (or, in Scotland, sufficient evidence) of that certificate.

(3)   The power conferred by section 23(2) or 24(3) on a Minister of the Crown shall not be exercisable except by a Minister who is a member of the Cabinet or by the Attorney General, the Advocate General for Scotland or the Attorney General for Northern Ireland.

NOTES

Commencement
1 January 2005: SI 2004/3122 art 2.

Defined terms
"Minister of the Crown": s.84, Ministers of the Crown
Act 1975

Scottish public authority equivalent
None

Defence

26(1)   Information is exempt information if its disclosure under this Act would, or would be likely to, prejudice—

     (a) the defence of the British Islands or of any colony, or

     (b) the capability, effectiveness or security of any relevant forces.

(2)   In subsection (1)(b) "relevant forces" means—

     (a) the armed forces of the Crown, and

     (b) any forces co-operating with those forces,

or any part of any of those forces.

(3)   The duty to confirm or deny does not arise if, or to the extent that, compliance with section 1(1)(a) would, or would be likely to, prejudice any of the matters mentioned in subsection (1).

NOTES

Commencement
1 January 2005: SI 2004/3122 art 2.

Defined terms
"duty to confirm or deny": s 1(6)
"exempt information": s 84

Scottish public authority equivalent
FOI(S)A s 31

"information": s 84
"relevant forces": subs.(2)

Exemption type
Not absolute: s 2(3)

International relations

27(1)   Information is exempt information if its disclosure under this Act would, or would be likely to, prejudice—

     (a) relations between the United Kingdom and any other State,

     (b) relations between the United Kingdom and any international organisation or international court,

     (c) the interests of the United Kingdom abroad, or

     (d) the promotion or protection by the United Kingdom of its interests abroad.

(2)   Information is also exempt information if it is confidential information obtained from a State other than the United Kingdom or from an international organisation or international court.

(3) For the purposes of this section, any information obtained from a State, organisation or court is confidential at any time while the terms on which it was obtained require it to be held in confidence or while the circumstances in which it was obtained make it reasonable for the State, organisation or court to expect that it will be so held.

(4) The duty to confirm or deny does not arise if, or to the extent that, compliance with section 1(1)(a)—

(a) would, or would be likely to, prejudice any of the matters mentioned in subsection (1), or

(b) would involve the disclosure of any information (whether or not already recorded) which is confidential information obtained from a State other than the United Kingdom or from an international organisation or international court.

(5) In this section—

"international court" means any international court which is not an international organisation and which is established—

(a) by a resolution of an international organisation of which the United Kingdom is a member, or

(b) by an international agreement to which the United Kingdom is a party;

"international organisation" means any international organisation whose members include any two or more States, or any organ of such an organisation;

"State" includes the government of any State and any organ of its government, and references to a State other than the United Kingdom include references to any territory outside the United Kingdom.

NOTES

Commencement
1 January 2005: SI 2004/3122 art 2.

Scottish public authority equivalent
FOI(S)A s 32

Exemption type
Not absolute: s 2(3)

Defined terms
"duty to confirm or deny": s 196)
"exempt information": s 84
"information": s 84
"international court": subs.(5)
"international organisation": subs.(5)
"State": subs.5

Relations within the United Kingdom

28(1) Information is exempt information if its disclosure under this Act would, or would be likely to, prejudice relations between any administration in the United Kingdom and any other such administration.

(2) In subsection (1) "administration in the United Kingdom" means—

(a) the government of the United Kingdom,

(b) the Scottish Administration,

(c) the Executive Committee of the Northern Ireland Assembly, or

(d) the Welsh Assembly Government.

(3)   The duty to confirm or deny does not arise if, or to the extent that, compliance with section 1(1)(a) would, or would be likely to, prejudice any of the matters mentioned in subsection (1).

NOTES

Commencement
1 January 2005: SI 2004/3122 art 2.

Scottish public authority equivalent
FOI(S)A s 28

Exemption type
Not absolute: s 2(3)

Defined terms
"administration in the United Kingdom": subs.(2)
"duty to confirm or deny": s 1(6)
"exempt information": s 84
"information": s 84

The economy

29(1)   Information is exempt information if its disclosure under this Act would, or would be likely to, prejudice—

    (a) the economic interests of the United Kingdom or of any part of the United Kingdom, or

    (b) the financial interests of any administration in the United Kingdom, as defined by section 28(2).

(2)   The duty to confirm or deny does not arise if, or to the extent that, compliance with section 1(1)(a) would, or would be likely to, prejudice any of the matters mentioned in subsection (1).

NOTES

Commencement
1 January 2005: SI 2004/3122 art 2.

Scottish public authority equivalent
FOI(S)A s 33

Exemption type
Not absolute: s 2(3)

Defined terms
"duty to confirm or deny": s 1(6)
"exempt information": s 84
"information": s 84

Investigations and proceedings conducted by public authorities

30(1)   Information held by a public authority is exempt information if it has at any time been held by the authority for the purposes of—

    (a) any investigation which the public authority has a duty to conduct with a view to it being ascertained—

        (i) whether a person should be charged with an offence, or

        (ii) whether a person charged with an offence is guilty of it,

(b) any investigation which is conducted by the authority and in the circumstances may lead to a decision by the authority to institute criminal proceedings which the authority has power to conduct, or

(c) any criminal proceedings which the authority has power to conduct.

(2) Information held by a public authority is exempt information if—

    (a) it was obtained or recorded by the authority for the purposes of its functions relating to—

        (i) investigations falling within subsection (1)(a) or (b),

        (ii) criminal proceedings which the authority has power to conduct,

        (iii) investigations (other than investigations falling within subsection (1)(a) or (b)) which are conducted by the authority for any of the purposes specified in section 31(2) and either by virtue of Her Majesty's prerogative or by virtue of powers conferred by or under any enactment, or

        (iv) civil proceedings which are brought by or on behalf of the authority and arise out of such investigations, and

    (b) it relates to the obtaining of information from confidential sources.

(3) The duty to confirm or deny does not arise in relation to information which is (or if it were held by the public authority would be) exempt information by virtue of subsection (1) or (2).

(4) In relation to the institution or conduct of criminal proceedings or the power to conduct them, references in subsection (1)(b) or (c) and subsection (2)(a) to the public authority include references—

    (a) to any officer of the authority,

    (b) in the case of a government department other than a Northern Ireland department, to the Minister of the Crown in charge of the department, and

    (c) in the case of a Northern Ireland department, to the Northern Ireland Minister in charge of the department.

(5) In this section—

"criminal proceedings" includes service law proceedings (as defined by section 324(5) of the Armed Forces Act 2006);

"offence" includes a service offence (as defined by section 50 of that Act).

(6) In the application of this section to Scotland—

    (a) in subsection (1)(b), for the words from "a decision" to the end there is substituted "a decision by the authority to make a report to the procurator fiscal for the purpose of enabling him to determine whether criminal proceedings should be instituted",

    (b) in subsections (1)(c) and (2)(a)(ii) for "which the authority has power to conduct" there is substituted "which have been instituted in consequence of a report made by the authority to the procurator fiscal", and

    (c) for any reference to a person being charged with an offence there is substituted a reference to the person being prosecuted for the offence.

NOTES

Commencement	**Defined terms**
1 January 2005: SI 2004/3122 art 2.	"criminal proceedings": subs.(5)
	"duty to confirm or deny": s 1(6)
Scottish public authority equivalent	"enactment": s 84
FOI(S)A s 34	"exempt information": s 84
	"held": s 3(2)
Exemption type	"information": s 84
Not absolute: s 2(3)	"Northern Ireland Minister": s 84
	"public authority": s 3(1)

Law enforcement

31(1)   Information which is not exempt information by virtue of section 30 is exempt information if its disclosure under this Act would, or would be likely to, prejudice—

(a) the prevention or detection of crime,

(b) the apprehension or prosecution of offenders,

(c) the administration of justice,

(d) the assessment or collection of any tax or duty or of any imposition of a similar nature,

(e) the operation of the immigration controls,

(f) the maintenance of security and good order in prisons or in other institutions where persons are lawfully detained,

(g) the exercise by any public authority of its functions for any of the purposes specified in subsection (2),

(h) any civil proceedings which are brought by or on behalf of a public authority and arise out of an investigation conducted, for any of the purposes specified in subsection (2), by or on behalf of the authority by virtue of Her Majesty's prerogative or by virtue of powers conferred by or under an enactment, or

(i) any inquiry held under the Fatal Accidents and Sudden Deaths Inquiries (Scotland) Act 1976 to the extent that the inquiry arises out of an investigation conducted, for any of the purposes specified in subsection (2), by or on behalf of the authority by virtue of Her Majesty's prerogative or by virtue of powers conferred by or under an enactment.

(2)   The purposes referred to in subsection (1)(g) to (i) are—

(a) the purpose of ascertaining whether any person has failed to comply with the law,

(b) the purpose of ascertaining whether any person is responsible for any conduct which is improper,

(c) the purpose of ascertaining whether circumstances which would justify regulatory action in pursuance of any enactment exist or may arise,

(d) the purpose of ascertaining a person's fitness or competence in relation to the management of bodies corporate or in relation to any profession or other activity which he is, or seeks to become, authorised to carry on,

(e) the purpose of ascertaining the cause of an accident,

(f) the purpose of protecting charities against misconduct or mismanagement (whether by trustees or other persons) in their administration,

(g) the purpose of protecting the property of charities from loss or misapplication,

(h) the purpose of recovering the property of charities,

(i) the purpose of securing the health, safety and welfare of persons at work, and

(j) the purpose of protecting persons other than persons at work against risk to health or safety arising out of or in connection with the actions of persons at work.

(3) The duty to confirm or deny does not arise if, or to the extent that, compliance with section 1(1)(a) would, or would be likely to, prejudice any of the matters mentioned in subsection (1).

NOTES

Commencement
1 January 2005: SI 2004/3122 art 2.

Scottish public authority equivalent
FOI(S)A s 35

Exemption type
Not absolute: s 2(3)

Defined terms
"duty to confirm or deny": s 1(6)
"enactment": s 84
"exempt information": s 84
"information": s 84
"public authority": s 3(1)

Court records, etc

32(1) Information held by a public authority is exempt information if it is held only by virtue of being contained in—

(a) any document filed with, or otherwise placed in the custody of, a court for the purposes of proceedings in a particular cause or matter,

(b) any document served upon, or by, a public authority for the purposes of proceedings in a particular cause or matter, or

(c) any document created by—

(i) a court, or

(ii) a member of the administrative staff of a court,

for the purposes of proceedings in a particular cause or matter.

(2) Information held by a public authority is exempt information if it is held only by virtue of being contained in—

(a) any document placed in the custody of a person conducting an inquiry or arbitration, for the purposes of the inquiry or arbitration, or

(b) any document created by a person conducting an inquiry or arbitration, for the purposes of the inquiry or arbitration.

(3) The duty to confirm or deny does not arise in relation to information which is (or if it were held by the public authority would be) exempt information by virtue of this section.

(4) In this section—

(a) "court" includes any tribunal or body exercising the judicial power of the State,

(b) "proceedings in a particular cause or matter" includes any inquest or any investigation under Part 1 of the Coroners and Justice Act 2009, any inquest under the Coroners Act (Northern Ireland) 1959 and any post-mortem examination,

(c) "inquiry" means any inquiry or hearing held under any provision contained in, or made under, an enactment, and

(d) except in relation to Scotland, "arbitration" means any arbitration to which Part I of the Arbitration Act 1996 applies.

NOTES

Commencement
1 January 2005: SI 2004/3122 art 2.

Scottish public authority equivalent
FOI(S)A s 37

Exemption type
Absolute: s 2(3)(c)

Defined terms
"arbitration": subs.(4), Arbitration Act 1996
"court": subs.(4)
"duty to confirm or deny": s 116)
"exempt information": s 84
"held": s 3(2)
"information": s 84
"inquiry": subs.(4)
"proceedings in any cause or matter": subs.(4)
"public authority": s 84

Audit functions

33(1) This section applies to any public authority which has functions in relation to—

(a) the audit of the accounts of other public authorities, or

(b) the examination of the economy, efficiency and effectiveness with which other public authorities use their resources in discharging their functions.

(2) Information held by a public authority to which this section applies is exempt information if its disclosure would, or would be likely to, prejudice the exercise of any of the authority's functions in relation to any of the matters referred to in subsection (1).

(3) The duty to confirm or deny does not arise in relation to a public authority to which this section applies if, or to the extent that, compliance with section 1(1)(a) would, or would be likely to, prejudice the exercise of any of the authority's functions in relation to any of the matters referred to in subsection (1).

NOTES

Commencement
1 January 2005: SI 2004/3122 art 2.

Scottish public authority equivalent
FOI(S)A s 40

Exemption type
Not absolute: s 2(3)

Defined terms
"duty to confirm or deny": s 11(6)
"exempt information": s 84
"held": s 3(2)
"information": s 84
"public authority": s 84

Parliamentary privilege

34(1)   Information is exempt information if exemption from section 1(1)(b) is required for the purpose of avoiding an infringement of the privileges of either House of Parliament.

(2)   The duty to confirm or deny does not apply if, or to the extent that, exemption from section 1(1)(a) is required for the purpose of avoiding an infringement of the privileges of either House of Parliament.

(3)   A certificate signed by the appropriate authority certifying that exemption from section 1(1)(b), or from section 1(1)(a) and (b), is, or at any time was, required for the purpose of avoiding an infringement of the privileges of either House of Parliament shall be conclusive evidence of that fact.

(4)   In subsection (3) "the appropriate authority" means—
   (a) in relation to the House of Commons, the Speaker of that House, and
   (b) in relation to the House of Lords, the Clerk of the Parliaments.

NOTES

Commencement
1 January 2005: SI 2004/3122 art 2.

Scottish public authority equivalent
None

Exemption type
Absolute: s 2(3)(d)

Defined terms
"duty to confirm or deny": s 1(3)
"exempt information": s 84
"information": s 84

Formulation of government policy, etc

35(1)   Information held by a government department or by the Welsh Assembly Government is exempt information if it relates to—
   (a) the formulation or development of government policy,
   (b) Ministerial communications,
   (c) the provision of advice by any of the Law Officers or any request for the provision of such advice, or
   (d) the operation of any Ministerial private office.

(2)   Once a decision as to government policy has been taken, any statistical information used to provide an informed background to the taking of the decision is not to be regarded—
   (a) for the purposes of subsection (1)(a), as relating to the formulation or development of government policy, or
   (b) for the purposes of subsection (1)(b), as relating to Ministerial communications.

(3)   The duty to confirm or deny does not arise in relation to information which is (or if it were held by the public authority would be) exempt information by virtue of subsection (1).

(4)   In making any determination required by section 2(1)(b) or (2)(b) in relation to information which is exempt information by virtue of subsection (1)(a), regard shall be had to the

particular public interest in the disclosure of factual information which has been used, or is intended to be used, to provide an informed background to decision-taking.

(5) In this section—

"government policy" includes the policy of the Executive Committee of the Northern Ireland Assembly and the policy of the Welsh Assembly Government;

"the Law Officers" means the Attorney General, the Solicitor General, the Advocate General for Scotland, the Lord Advocate, the Solicitor General for Scotland, the Counsel General to the Welsh Assembly Government and the Attorney General for Northern Ireland;

"Ministerial communications" means any communications—

(a) between Ministers of the Crown,

(b) between Northern Ireland Ministers, including Northern Ireland junior Ministers, or

(c) between members of the Welsh Assembly Government,

and includes, in particular, proceedings of the Cabinet or of any committee of the Cabinet, proceedings of the Executive Committee of the Northern Ireland Assembly, and proceedings of the Cabinet or any committee of the Cabinet of the Welsh Assembly Government;

"Ministerial private office" means any part of a government department which provides personal administrative support to a Minister of the Crown, to a Northern Ireland Minister or a Northern Ireland junior Minister or any part of the administration of the Welsh Assembly Government providing personal administrative support to the members of the Welsh Assembly Government;

"Northern Ireland junior Minister" means a member of the Northern Ireland Assembly appointed as a junior Minister under section 19 of the Northern Ireland Act 1998.

NOTES

Commencement
1 January 2005: SI 2004/3122 art 2.

Scottish public authority equivalent
FOI(S)A s 29

Exemption type
Not absolute: s 2(3)

Defined terms
"duty to confirm or deny": s 116

"exempt information": s 84
"government department": s 84
"government policy": subs.(6)
"held": s 3(2)
"information": s 84
"Law Officer": subs.(6)
"Minister of the Crown": s 84, Ministers of the Crown Act 1975
"Ministerial communication": subs.(6)
"Ministerial private office": subs.(6)
"Northern Ireland junior Minister": subs.(6)
"Northern Ireland Minister": s 84

Prejudice to effective conduct of public affairs

36(1) This section applies to—

(a) information which is held by a government department or by the Welsh Assembly Government and is not exempt information by virtue of section 35, and

(b) information which is held by any other public authority.

(2)   Information to which this section applies is exempt information if, in the reasonable opinion of a qualified person, disclosure of the information under this Act—
    (a) would, or would be likely to, prejudice—
        (i) the maintenance of the convention of the collective responsibility of Ministers of the Crown, or
        (ii) the work of the Executive Committee of the Northern Ireland Assembly, or
        (iii) the work of the Cabinet of the Welsh Assembly Government,
    (b) would, or would be likely to, inhibit—
        (i) the free and frank provision of advice, or
        (ii) the free and frank exchange of views for the purposes of deliberation, or
    (c) would otherwise prejudice, or would be likely otherwise to prejudice, the effective conduct of public affairs.

(3)   The duty to confirm or deny does not arise in relation to information to which this section applies (or would apply if held by the public authority) if, or to the extent that, in the reasonable opinion of a qualified person, compliance with section 1(1)(a) would, or would be likely to, have any of the effects mentioned in subsection (2).

(4)   In relation to statistical information, subsections (2) and (3) shall have effect with the omission of the words "in the reasonable opinion of a qualified person".

(5)   In subsections (2) and (3) "qualified person"—
    (a) in relation to information held by a government department in the charge of a Minister of the Crown, means any Minister of the Crown,
    (b) in relation to information held by a Northern Ireland department, means the Northern Ireland Minister in charge of the department,
    (c) in relation to information held by any other government department, means the commissioners or other person in charge of that department,
    (d) in relation to information held by the House of Commons, means the Speaker of that House,
    (e) in relation to information held by the House of Lords, means the Clerk of the Parliaments,
    (f) in relation to information held by the Northern Ireland Assembly, means the Presiding Officer,
    (g) in relation to information held by the Welsh Assembly Government, means the Welsh Ministers or the Counsel General to the Welsh Assembly Government,
    (ga) in relation to information held by the National Assembly for Wales, means the Presiding Officer of the National Assembly for Wales,
    (gb) in relation to information held by any Welsh public authority (other than one referred to in section 83(1)(b)(ii) (subsidiary of the Assembly Commission), the Auditor General for Wales or the Public Services Ombudsman for Wales), means—
        (i) the public authority, or
        (ii) any officer or employee of the authority authorised by the Welsh Ministers or the Counsel General to the Welsh Assembly Government",

(gc) in relation to information held by a Welsh public authority referred to in section 83(1)(b)(ii), means—
  (i) the public authority, or
  (ii) any officer or employee of the authority authorised by the Presiding Officer of the National Assembly for Wales,

(i) in relation to information held by the National Audit Office, means the Comptroller and Auditor General,

(j) in relation to information held by the Northern Ireland Audit Office, means the Comptroller and Auditor General for Northern Ireland,

(k) in relation to information held by the Auditor General for Wales, means the Auditor General for Wales,

(ka) in relation to information held by the Public Services Ombudsman for Wales, means the Public Services Ombudsman for Wales,

(l) in relation to information held by any Northern Ireland public authority other than the Northern Ireland Audit Office, means—
  (i) the public authority, or
  (ii) any officer or employee of the authority authorised by the First Minister and deputy First Minister in Northern Ireland acting jointly,

(m) in relation to information held by the Greater London Authority, means the Mayor of London,

(n) in relation to information held by a functional body within the meaning of the Greater London Authority Act 1999, means the chairman of that functional body, and

(o) in relation to information held by any public authority not falling within any of paragraphs (a) to (n), means—
  (i) a Minister of the Crown,
  (ii) the public authority, if authorised for the purposes of this section by a Minister of the Crown, or
  (iii) any officer or employee of the public authority who is authorised for the purposes of this section by a Minister of the Crown.

(6) Any authorisation for the purposes of this section—
  (a) may relate to a specified person or to persons falling within a specified class,
  (b) may be general or limited to particular classes of case, and
  (c) may be granted subject to conditions.

(7) A certificate signed by the qualified person referred to in subsection (5)(d) or (e) above certifying that in his reasonable opinion—
  (a) disclosure of information held by either House of Parliament, or
  (b) compliance with section 1(1)(a) by either House,
would, or would be likely to, have any of the effects mentioned in subsection (2) shall be conclusive evidence of that fact.

NOTES

Commencement
1 January 2005: SI 2004/3122 art 2.

Scottish public authority equivalent
FOI(S)A s 30

Exemption type
Absolute, so far as relates to information held by the
  House of Commons or House of Lords, not absolute
  otherwise: s 2(3)(e)

Defined terms
"duty to confirm or deny": s 1(6)
 "exempt information": s 84
"government department": s 84
"held": s 3(2)
"information": s 84
"Minister of the Crown": s 84, Ministers of the Crown
  Act 1975
"Northern Ireland Minister": s 84
"public authority": s 3(1)
"qualified person": subs.(5)

Communications with Her Majesty, etc and honours

37(1)   Information is exempt information if it relates to—

        (a) communications with Her Majesty, with other members of the Royal Family or with the Royal Household, or

        (b) the conferring by the Crown of any honour or dignity.

(2)   The duty to confirm or deny does not arise in relation to information which is (or if it were held by the public authority would be) exempt information by virtue of subsection (1).

NOTES

Commencement
1 January 2005: SI 2004/3122 art 2.

Scottish public authority equivalent
FOI(S)A s 41

Exemption type
Not absolute: s 2(3)

Defined terms
"duty to confirm or deny": s 1(6)
"exempt information": s 84
"information": s 84

Health and safety

38(1)   Information is exempt information if its disclosure under this Act would, or would be likely to—

        (a) endanger the physical or mental health of any individual, or

        (b) endanger the safety of any individual.

(2)   The duty to confirm or deny does not arise if, or to the extent that, compliance with section 1(1)(a) would, or would be likely to, have either of the effects mentioned in subsection (1).

NOTES

Commencement
1 January 2005: SI 2004/3122 art 2.

Scottish public authority equivalent
FOI(S)A s 39

Defined terms
"duty to confirm or deny": s 1(6)
"exempt information": s 84
"information": s 84

Exemption type
Not absolute: s 2(3)

Environmental information

39(1)   Information is exempt information if the public authority holding it—

(a) is obliged by environmental information regulations to make the information available to the public in accordance with the regulations, or

(b) would be so obliged but for any exemption contained in the regulations.

(1A)   In subsection (1) "environmental information regulations" means—

(a) regulations made under section 74, or

(b) regulations made under section 2(2) of the European Communities Act 1972 for the purpose of implementing any Community obligation relating to public access to, and the dissemination of, information on the environment.

(2)   The duty to confirm or deny does not arise in relation to information which is (or if it were held by the public authority would be) exempt information by virtue of subsection (1).

(3)   Subsection (1)(a) does not limit the generality of section 21(1).

NOTES

Commencement
1 January 2005: SI 2004/3122 art 2.

Scottish public authority equivalent
FOI(S)A s s 39

Exemption type
Not absolute: s 2(3)

Defined terms
"duty to confirm or deny": s 1(6)
"exempt information": s 84
"held": s 3(2)
"information": s 84
"public authority": s 3(1)

Personal information

40(1)   Any information to which a request for information relates is exempt information if it constitutes personal data of which the applicant is the data subject.

(2)   Any information to which a request for information relates is also exempt information if—

(a) it constitutes personal data which do not fall within subsection (1), and

(b) either the first or the second condition below is satisfied.

(3)   The first condition is—

(a) in a case where the information falls within any of paragraphs (a) to (d) of the definition of "data" in section 1(1) of the Data Protection Act 1998, that the disclosure of the information to a member of the public otherwise than under this Act would contravene—

(i) any of the data protection principles, or

(ii) section 10 of that Act (right to prevent processing likely to cause damage or distress), and

(b) in any other case, that the disclosure of the information to a member of the public otherwise than under this Act would contravene any of the data protection principles if the exemptions in section 33A(1) of the Data Protection Act 1998 (which relate to manual data held by public authorities) were disregarded.

(4) The second condition is that by virtue of any provision of Part IV of the Data Protection Act 1998 the information is exempt from section 7(1)(c) of that Act (data subject's right of access to personal data).

(5) The duty to confirm or deny—

(a) does not arise in relation to information which is (or if it were held by the public authority would be) exempt information by virtue of subsection (1), and

(b) does not arise in relation to other information if or to the extent that either—

(i) the giving to a member of the public of the confirmation or denial that would have to be given to comply with section 1(1)(a) would (apart from this Act) contravene any of the data protection principles or section 10 of the Data Protection Act 1998 or would do so if the exemptions in section 33A(1) of that Act were disregarded, or

(ii) by virtue of any provision of Part IV of the Data Protection Act 1998 the information is exempt from section 7(1)(a) of that Act (data subject's right to be informed whether personal data being processed).

(6) In determining for the purposes of this section whether anything done before 24th October 2007 would contravene any of the data protection principles, the exemptions in Part III of Schedule 8 to the Data Protection Act 1998 shall be disregarded.

(7) In this section—

"the data protection principles" means the principles set out in Part I of Schedule 1 to the Data Protection Act 1998, as read subject to Part II of that Schedule and section 27(1) of that Act;

"data subject" has the same meaning as in section 1(1) of that Act;

"personal data" has the same meaning as in section 1(1) of that Act.

NOTES

Commencement
1 January 2005: SI 2004/3122 art 2.

Scottish public authority equivalent
FOI(S)A s 38

Exemption type
Absolute in relation to subsection (1); absolute in relation to subsection (2) so far as relating to cases where the first condition referred to in it is satisfied by virtue of subsection (3)(a)(I) or (b); not absolute otherwise: s 2(3)(f)

Defined terms
"applicant": s 84
"data protection principles": subs.(7)
"data subject": subs.(7), Data Protection Act 1998, s 1(1)
"duty to confirm or deny": s 1(6)
"exempt information": s 84
"information": s 84
"personal data": subs.(7), Data Protection Act 1998, s 1(1)
"request for information": s 8

Information provided in confidence

41(1) Information is exempt information if—

(a) it was obtained by the public authority from any other person (including another public authority), and

(b) the disclosure of the information to the public (otherwise than under this Act) by the public authority holding it would constitute a breach of confidence actionable by that or any other person.

(2) The duty to confirm or deny does not arise if, or to the extent that, the confirmation or denial that would have to be given to comply with section 1(1)(a) would (apart from this Act) constitute an actionable breach of confidence.

NOTES

Commencement
1 January 2005: SI 2004/3122 art 2.

Scottish public authority equivalent
FOI(S)A s 36

Exemption type
Absolute: s 2(3)(**g**)

Defined terms
"duty to confirm or deny": s 1(6)
"exempt information": s 84
"information": s 84
"public authority": s 3(1)

Legal professional privilege

42(1) Information in respect of which a claim to legal professional privilege or, in Scotland, to confidentiality of communications could be maintained in legal proceedings is exempt information.

(2) The duty to confirm or deny does not arise if, or to the extent that, compliance with section 1(1)(a) would involve the disclosure of any information (whether or not already recorded) in respect of which such a claim could be maintained in legal proceedings.

NOTES

Commencement
1 January 2005: SI 2004/3122 art 2.

Scottish public authority equivalent
FOI(S)A s 36

Exemption type
Not absolute: s 2(3)

Defined terms
"duty to confirm or deny": s 1(6)
"exempt information": s 84
"information": s 84

Commercial interests

43(1) Information is exempt information if it constitutes a trade secret.

(2) Information is exempt information if its disclosure under this Act would, or would be likely to, prejudice the commercial interests of any person (including the public authority holding it).

(3)   The duty to confirm or deny does not arise if, or to the extent that, compliance with section 1(1)(a) would, or would be likely to, prejudice the interests mentioned in subsection (2).

NOTES

Commencement
1 January 2005: SI 2004/3122 art 2.

Scottish public authority equivalent
FOI(S)A s 33

Exemption type
Not absolute: s 2(3)

Defined terms
"duty to confirm or deny": s 1(6)
"exempt information": s 84
"information": s 84
"public authority": s 3(1)

Prohibitions on disclosure

44(1)   Information is exempt information if its disclosure (otherwise than under this Act) by the public authority holding it—

(a) is prohibited by or under any enactment,

(b) is incompatible with any Community obligation, or

(c) would constitute or be punishable as a contempt of court.

(2)   The duty to confirm or deny does not arise if the confirmation or denial that would have to be given to comply with section 1(1)(a) would (apart from this Act) fall within any of paragraphs (a) to (c) of subsection (1).

NOTES

Commencement
1 January 2005: SI 2004/3122 art 2.

Scottish public authority equivalent
FOI(S)A s 26

Exemption type
Absolute: s 2(3)(h)

Defined terms
"duty to confirm or deny": s 1(6)
"enactment": s 84
"exempt information": s 84
"information": s 84
"public authority": s 3(1)

PART III

GENERAL FUNCTIONS OF LORD CHANCELLOR AND INFORMATION COMMISSIONER

Issue of code of practice

45(1)   The Secretary of State shall issue, and may from time to time revise, a code of practice providing guidance to public authorities as to the practice which it would, in his opinion, be desirable for them to follow in connection with the discharge of the authorities' functions under Part I.

(2)   The code of practice must, in particular, include provision relating to—
- (a) the provision of advice and assistance by public authorities to persons who propose to make, or have made, requests for information to them,
- (b) the transfer of requests by one public authority to another public authority by which the information requested is or may be held,
- (c) consultation with persons to whom the information requested relates or persons whose interests are likely to be affected by the disclosure of information,
- (d) the inclusion in contracts entered into by public authorities of terms relating to the disclosure of information, and
- (e) the provision by public authorities of procedures for dealing with complaints about the handling by them of requests for information.

(3)   The code may make different provision for different public authorities.

(4)   Before issuing or revising any code under this section, the Secretary of State shall consult the Commissioner.

(5)   The Secretary of State shall lay before each House of Parliament any code or revised code made under this section.

NOTES

Commencement

30 November 2000 (for the purpose of exercising the power to make codes of practice): s 87(1)(m)
For remaining purposes, 30 November 2002: SI 2002/2812

Scottish public authority equivalent
FOI(S)A s 60

Defined terms

"Commissioner": s 18(3)

The Code
The Code is reproduced at p 1264 ff.

Issue of code of practice by Lord Chancellor

46(1)   The Lord Chancellor shall issue, and may from time to time revise, a code of practice providing guidance to relevant authorities as to the practice which it would, in his opinion, be desirable for them to follow in connection with the keeping, management and destruction of their records.

(2)   For the purpose of facilitating the performance by the Public Record Office, the Public Record Office of Northern Ireland and other public authorities of their functions under this Act in relation to records which are public records for the purposes of the Public Records Act 1958 or the Public Records Act (Northern Ireland) 1923, the code may also include guidance as to—
- (a) the practice to be adopted in relation to the transfer of records under section 3(4) of the Public Records Act 1958 or section 3 of the Public Records Act (Northern Ireland) 1923, and
- (b) the practice of reviewing records before they are transferred under those provisions.

(3)   In exercising his functions under this section, the Lord Chancellor shall have regard to the public interest in allowing public access to information held by relevant authorities.

(4)   The code may make different provision for different relevant authorities.

(5)   Before issuing or revising any code under this section the Lord Chancellor shall consult—
          (a) the Secretary of State,
          (b) the Commissioner, and
          (c) in relation to Northern Ireland, the appropriate Northern Ireland Minister.

(6)   The Lord Chancellor shall lay before each House of Parliament any code or revised code made under this section.

(7)   In this section "relevant authority" means—
          (a) any public authority, and
          (b) any office or body which is not a public authority but whose administrative and departmental records are public records for the purposes of the Public Records Act 1958 or the Public Records Act (Northern Ireland) 1923.

NOTES

Commencement

30 November 2000 (for the purpose of exercising the power to make codes of practice): s 87(1)(m)
For remaining purposes, 30 November 2002: SI 2002/2812

Scottish public authority equivalent

FOI(S)A s 61

Defined terms

"Commissioner": s 18(3)
"Northern Ireland Minister": s 84
"public authority": s 3(1)
"relevant authority": subs.(7)

The code

The code is reproduced at p 1276 ff

General functions of Commissioner

47(1)   It shall be the duty of the Commissioner to promote the following of good practice by public authorities and, in particular, so to perform his functions under this Act as to promote the observance by public authorities of—
          (a) the requirements of this Act, and
          (b) the provisions of the codes of practice under sections 45 and 46.

(2)   The Commissioner shall arrange for the dissemination in such form and manner as he considers appropriate of such information as it may appear to him expedient to give to the public—
          (a) about the operation of this Act,
          (b) about good practice, and
          (c) about other matters within the scope of his functions under this Act,
and may give advice to any person as to any of those matters.

(3)   The Commissioner may, with the consent of any public authority, assess whether that authority is following good practice.

(4) The Commissioner may charge such sums as he may with the consent of the Secretary of State determine for any services provided by the Commissioner under this section.

(5) The Commissioner shall from time to time as he considers appropriate—

(a) consult the Keeper of Public Records about the promotion by the Commissioner of the observance by public authorities of the provisions of the code of practice under section 46 in relation to records which are public records for the purposes of the Public Records Act 1958, and

(b) consult the Deputy Keeper of the Records of Northern Ireland about the promotion by the Commissioner of the observance by public authorities of those provisions in relation to records which are public records for the purposes of the Public Records Act (Northern Ireland) 1923.

(6) In this section "good practice", in relation to a public authority, means such practice in the discharge of its functions under this Act as appears to the Commissioner to be desirable, and includes (but is not limited to) compliance with the requirements of this Act and the provisions of the codes of practice under sections 45 and 46.

NOTES

Commencement
30 November 2000 for subsections (2)-(6): s 87(1)(d)
30 November 2002 for subsection (1): SI 2002/2812

Scottish public authority equivalent
FOI(S)A s 43

Defined terms
"Commissioner": s 18(3)
"good practice": subs.(6)
"public authority": s 3(1)

Recommendations as to good practice

48(1) If it appears to the Commissioner that the practice of a public authority in relation to the exercise of its functions under this Act does not conform with that proposed in the codes of practice under sections 45 and 46, he may give to the authority a recommendation (in this section referred to as a "practice recommendation") specifying the steps which ought in his opinion to be taken for promoting such conformity.

(2) A practice recommendation must be given in writing and must refer to the particular provisions of the code of practice with which, in the Commissioner's opinion, the public authority's practice does not conform.

(3) Before giving to a public authority other than the Public Record Office a practice recommendation which relates to conformity with the code of practice under section 46 in respect of records which are public records for the purposes of the Public Records Act 1958, the Commissioner shall consult the Keeper of Public Records.

(4) Before giving to a public authority other than the Public Record Office of Northern Ireland a practice recommendation which relates to conformity with the code of practice under section 46 in respect of records which are public records for the purposes of the

Public Records Act (Northern Ireland) 1923, the Commissioner shall consult the Deputy Keeper of the Records of Northern Ireland.

NOTES

Commencement
Subsections (1), (2), 30 November 2002: SI 2002/2812
Subsections (3), (4), 1 January 2005: SI 2004/1909

Scottish public authority equivalent
FOI(S)A s 44

Defined terms
"Commissioner": s 18(3)
"code of practice": subs.(1), ss.45,46
"public authority": s 3(1)
"practice recommendation": subs.(1)

Reports to be laid before Parliament

49(1)   The Commissioner shall lay annually before each House of Parliament a general report on the exercise of his functions under this Act.

(2)   The Commissioner may from time to time lay before each House of Parliament such other reports with respect to those functions as he thinks fit.

NOTES

Commencement
30 November 2000: s 87(1)(e)

Scottish public authority equivalent
FOI(S)A s 46

Defined terms
"Commissioner": s 18(3)

PART IV

ENFORCEMENT

Application for decision by Commissioner

50(1)   Any person (in this section referred to as "the complainant") may apply to the Commissioner for a decision whether, in any specified respect, a request for information made by the complainant to a public authority has been dealt with in accordance with the requirements of Part I.

(2)   On receiving an application under this section, the Commissioner shall make a decision unless it appears to him—
(a)   that the complainant has not exhausted any complaints procedure which is provided by the public authority in conformity with the code of practice under section 45,
(b)   that there has been undue delay in making the application,
(c)   that the application is frivolous or vexatious, or
(d)   that the application has been withdrawn or abandoned.

(3)   Where the Commissioner has received an application under this section, he shall either—

(a) notify the complainant that he has not made any decision under this section as a result of the application and of his grounds for not doing so, or

(b) serve notice of his decision (in this Act referred to as a "decision notice") on the complainant and the public authority.

(4) Where the Commissioner decides that a public authority—

(a) has failed to communicate information, or to provide confirmation or denial, in a case where it is required to do so by section 1(1), or

(b) has failed to comply with any of the requirements of sections 11 and 17, the decision notice must specify the steps which must be taken by the authority for complying with that requirement and the period within which they must be taken.

(5) A decision notice must contain particulars of the right of appeal conferred by section 57.

(6) Where a decision notice requires steps to be taken by the public authority within a specified period, the time specified in the notice must not expire before the end of the period within which an appeal can be brought against the notice and, if such an appeal is brought, no step which is affected by the appeal need be taken pending the determination or withdrawal of the appeal.

(7) This section has effect subject to section 53.

NOTES

Commencement
1 January 2005: SI 2004/1909

Scottish public authority equivalent
FOI(S)A s 47

Defined terms
"Commissioner": s 18(3)
"complainant": subs.(1)
"decision notice": subs.(3)
"information": s 84
"public authority": s 3(1)
"request for information": s 8

Information notices

51(1) If the Commissioner—

(a) has received an application under section 50, or

(b) reasonably requires any information—

(i) for the purpose of determining whether a public authority has complied or is complying with any of the requirements of Part I, or

(ii) for the purpose of determining whether the practice of a public authority in relation to the exercise of its functions under this Act conforms with that proposed in the codes of practice under sections 45 and 46,

he may serve the authority with a notice (in this Act referred to as "an information notice") requiring it, within such time as is specified in the notice, to furnish the Commissioner, in such form as may be so specified, with such information relating to the application, to compliance with Part I or to conformity with the code of practice as is so specified.

(2) An information notice must contain—

(a) in a case falling within subsection (1)(a), a statement that the Commissioner has received an application under section 50, or

(b) in a case falling within subsection (1)(b), a statement—

    (i) that the Commissioner regards the specified information as relevant for either of the purposes referred to in subsection (1)(b), and

    (ii) of his reasons for regarding that information as relevant for that purpose.

(3) An information notice must also contain particulars of the right of appeal conferred by section 57.

(4) The time specified in an information notice must not expire before the end of the period within which an appeal can be brought against the notice and, if such an appeal is brought, the information need not be furnished pending the determination or withdrawal of the appeal.

(5) An authority shall not be required by virtue of this section to furnish the Commissioner with any information in respect of—

(a) any communication between a professional legal adviser and his client in connection with the giving of legal advice to the client with respect to his obligations, liabilities or rights under this Act, or

(b) any communication between a professional legal adviser and his client, or between such an adviser or his client and any other person, made in connection with or in contemplation of proceedings under or arising out of this Act (including proceedings before the Tribunal) and for the purposes of such proceedings.

(6) In subsection (5) references to the client of a professional legal adviser include references to any person representing such a client.

(7) The Commissioner may cancel an information notice by written notice to the authority on which it was served.

(8) In this section "information" includes unrecorded information.

NOTES

Commencement

In relation to the issue and enforcement of information notices relating to the conformity with the code of practice under s 45 hereof of the practice of public authorities in relation to the exercise of their functions under the publication scheme provisions): 30 November 2002: see SI 2002/2812, art 2(d), (e).

For remaining purposes: 1 January 2005: see SI 2004/1909, art 2(1), (2)(c), (3).

Defined terms

"Commissioner": s 18(3)

"information": s 84, subs.(8)

"information notice": subs.(2)

"public authority": s 3(1)

"Tribunal": s 18(3)

Scottish public authority equivalent

FOI(S)A s 50

Enforcement notices

52(1) If the Commissioner is satisfied that a public authority has failed to comply with any of the requirements of Part I, the Commissioner may serve the authority with a notice (in this Act referred to as "an enforcement notice") requiring the authority to take, within such time as may be specified in the notice, such steps as may be so specified for complying with those requirements.

(2) An enforcement notice must contain—
  (a) a statement of the requirement or requirements of Part I with which the Commissioner is satisfied that the public authority has failed to comply and his reasons for reaching that conclusion, and
  (b) particulars of the right of appeal conferred by section 57.

(3) An enforcement notice must not require any of the provisions of the notice to be complied with before the end of the period within which an appeal can be brought against the notice and, if such an appeal is brought, the notice need not be complied with pending the determination or withdrawal of the appeal.

(4) The Commissioner may cancel an enforcement notice by written notice to the authority on which it was served.

(5) This section has effect subject to section 53.

NOTES

Commencement

In relation to the enforcement of the requirements on public authorities under the publication scheme provisions): 30 November 2002: see SI 2002/2812, art 2(e).

For remaining purposes: 1 January 2005: see SI 2004/1909, art 2(1), (2)(c), (3).

Defined terms

"Commissioner": s 18(3)
"enforcement notice": subs.(1)
"public authority": s 3(1)

Scottish public authority equivalent

FOI(S)A s 51

Exception from duty to comply with decision notice or enforcement notice

53(1) This section applies to a decision notice or enforcement notice which—
  (a) is served on—
    (i) a government department,
    (ii) the Welsh Assembly Government, or
    (iii) any public authority designated for the purposes of this section by an order made by the Secretary of State, and
  (b) relates to a failure, in respect of one or more requests for information—
    (i) to comply with section 1(1)(a) in respect of information which falls within any provision of Part II stating that the duty to confirm or deny does not arise, or
    (ii) to comply with section 1(1)(b) in respect of exempt information.

(2)   A decision notice or enforcement notice to which this section applies shall cease to have effect if, not later than the twentieth working day following the effective date, the accountable person in relation to that authority gives the Commissioner a certificate signed by him stating that he has on reasonable grounds formed the opinion that, in respect of the request or requests concerned, there was no failure falling within subsection (1)(b).

(3)   Where the accountable person gives a certificate to the Commissioner under subsection (2) he shall as soon as practicable thereafter lay a copy of the certificate before—
    (a) each House of Parliament,
    (b) the Northern Ireland Assembly, in any case where the certificate relates to a decision notice or enforcement notice which has been served on a Northern Ireland department or any Northern Ireland public authority, or
    (c) the National Assembly for Wales, in any case where the certificate relates to a decision notice or enforcement notice which has been served on—
      (i)   the Welsh Assembly Government,
      (ii) the National Assembly for Wales, or
      (iii) any Welsh public authority.

(4)   In subsection (2) "the effective date", in relation to a decision notice or enforcement notice, means—
    (a) the day on which the notice was given to the public authority, or
    (b) where an appeal under section 57 is brought, the day on which that appeal (or any further appeal arising out of it) is determined or withdrawn.

(5)   Before making an order under subsection (1)(a)(iii), the Secretary of State shall—
    (a) if the order relates to a Welsh public authority, consult the Welsh Ministers,
    (aa)   if the order relates to the National Assembly for Wales, consult the Presiding Officer of that Assembly,
    (b) if the order relates to the Northern Ireland Assembly, consult the Presiding Officer of that Assembly, and
    (c) if the order relates to a Northern Ireland public authority, consult the First Minister and deputy First Minister in Northern Ireland.

(6)   Where the accountable person gives a certificate to the Commissioner under subsection (2) in relation to a decision notice, the accountable person shall, on doing so or as soon as reasonably practicable after doing so, inform the person who is the complainant for the purposes of section 50 of the reasons for his opinion.

(7)   The accountable person is not obliged to provide information under subsection (6) if, or to the extent that, compliance with that subsection would involve the disclosure of exempt information.

(8)   In this section "the accountable person"—

(a) in relation to a Northern Ireland department or any Northern Ireland public
  authority, means the First Minister and deputy First Minister in Northern Ireland
  acting jointly,

(b) in relation the Welsh Assembly Government, the National Assembly for Wales or
  any Welsh public authority, means the First Minister for Wales, and

(c) in relation to any other public authority, means—

    (i) a Minister of the Crown who is a member of the Cabinet, or

    (ii) the Attorney General, the Advocate General for Scotland or the Attorney
    General for Northern Ireland.

(9) In this section "working day" has the same meaning as in section 10.

NOTES

Commencement

30 November 2000 (in so far as this section confers
powers to make any order, regulations or code of
practice):: see s 87(1)(m).

For remaining purposes: 1 January 2005: see SI
2004/1909, art 2(1), (2)(c), (3).

Scottish public authority equivalent

FOI(S)A s 52

Defined terms

"accountable person": subs.(8)

"Commissioner": s 18(3)

"complainant": s 50(1)

"decision notice": s 50(3)

"duty to confirm or deny": s 1(6)

"enforcement notice": s 52(1)

"exempt information": s 84, Part II

"government department": s 84

"information": s 84

"Minister of the Crown": s 84, Ministers of the Crown
Act 1975

"Northern Ireland public authority": s 84

"public authority": s 3(1)

"request for information": s 8

"working day": s 10(6)

Failure to comply with notice

54(1) If a public authority has failed to comply with—

    (a) so much of a decision notice as requires steps to be taken,

    (b) an information notice, or

    (c) an enforcement notice,

the Commissioner may certify in writing to the court that the public authority has failed
to comply with that notice.

(2) For the purposes of this section, a public authority which, in purported compliance with
an information notice—

    (a) makes a statement which it knows to be false in a material respect, or

    (b) recklessly makes a statement which is false in a material respect,

is to be taken to have failed to comply with the notice.

(3) Where a failure to comply is certified under subsection (1), the court may inquire into the
matter and, after hearing any witness who may be produced against or on behalf of the

public authority, and after hearing any statement that may be offered in defence, deal with the authority as if it had committed a contempt of court.

(4)   In this section "the court" means the High Court or, in Scotland, the Court of Session.

NOTES

Commencement

In relation to the enforcement of information notices relating to the conformity with the code of practice under s 45 hereof of the practice of public authorities in relation to the exercise of their functions under the publication scheme provisions): 30 November 2002: see SI 2002/2812, art 2(d), (e).

For remaining purposes: 1 January 2005: see SI 2004/1909, art 2(1), (2)(c), (3).

Defined terms

"Commissioner": s 18(3)
"decision notice": s 50(3)
"enforcement notice": s 52(1)
"information notice": s 51(1)
"public authority": s 3(1)

Scottish public authority equivalent

FOI(S)A s 53

Powers of entry and inspection

55   Schedule 3 (powers of entry and inspection) has effect.

NOTES

Commencement

For certain purposes: 30 November 2002: see SI 2002/2812, art 2(d)-(f).

For remaining purposes: 1 January 2005: see SI 2004/1909, art 2(1), (2)(c), (3).

Scottish public authority equivalent

FOI(S)A s 54

No action against public authority

56(1)   This Act does not confer any right of action in civil proceedings in respect of any failure to comply with any duty imposed by or under this Act.

(2)   Subsection (1) does not affect the powers of the Commissioner under section 54.

NOTES

Commencement

30 November 2002: see SI 2002/2812, art 2(g)

Defined terms

"Commissioner": s 18(3)

Scottish public authority equivalent

FOI(S)A s 55

PART V

APPEALS

Appeal against notices served under Part IV

57(1) Where a decision notice has been served, the complainant or the public authority may appeal to the Tribunal against the notice.

(2) A public authority on which an information notice or an enforcement notice has been served by the Commissioner may appeal to the Tribunal against the notice.

(3) In relation to a decision notice or enforcement notice which relates—
   (a) to information to which section 66 applies, and
   (b) to a matter which by virtue of subsection (3) or (4) of that section falls to be determined by the responsible authority instead of the appropriate records authority,
   subsections (1) and (2) shall have effect as if the reference to the public authority were a reference to the public authority or the responsible authority.

NOTES

Commencement
Subss.(1), (3): 1 January 2005: see SI 2004/1909, art 2(1), (2)(d), (3).
Subs.(2): 30 November 2002: see SI 2002/2812, art 2(g).

Scottish public authority equivalent
FOI(S)A s 56

Defined terms
"appropriate records authority": s 15(5)
"Commissioner": s 18(3)
"complainant": s 50(1)
"decision notice": s 50(3)
"enforcement notice": s 52(1)
"information notice": s 51(1)
"public authority": s 3(1)
"responsible authority": s 15(5)
"Tribunal": s 18(3)

Determination of appeals

58(1) If on an appeal under section 57 the Tribunal considers—
   (a) that the notice against which the appeal is brought is not in accordance with the law, or
   (b) to the extent that the notice involved an exercise of discretion by the Commissioner, that he ought to have exercised his discretion differently,
   the Tribunal shall allow the appeal or substitute such other notice as could have been served by the Commissioner; and in any other case the Tribunal shall dismiss the appeal.

(2) On such an appeal, the Tribunal may review any finding of fact on which the notice in question was based.

NOTES

Commencement
30 November 2002: see SI 2002/2812, art 2(g).

Defined terms
"Commissioner": s 18(3)
"Tribunal": s 18(3)

Scottish public authority equivalent

59 *Repealed*

Appeals against national security certificate

60(1)   Where a certificate under section 23(2) or 24(3) has been issued—

(a) the Commissioner, or

(b) any applicant whose request for information is affected by the issue of the certificate,

may appeal to the Tribunal against the certificate.

(2)   If on an appeal under subsection (1) relating to a certificate under section 23(2), the Tribunal finds that the information referred to in the certificate was not exempt information by virtue of section 23(1), the Tribunal may allow the appeal and quash the certificate.

(3)   If on an appeal under subsection (1) relating to a certificate under section 24(3), the Tribunal finds that, applying the principles applied by the court on an application for judicial review, the Minister did not have reasonable grounds for issuing the certificate, the Tribunal may allow the appeal and quash the certificate.

(4)   Where in any proceedings under this Act it is claimed by a public authority that a certificate under section 24(3) which identifies the information to which it applies by means of a general description applies to particular information, any other party to the proceedings may appeal to the Tribunal on the ground that the certificate does not apply to the information in question and, subject to any determination under subsection (5), the certificate shall be conclusively presumed so to apply.

(5)   On any appeal under subsection (4), the Tribunal may determine that the certificate does not so apply.

NOTES

Commencement

1 January 2005: see SI 2004/1909, art 2(1), (2)(d),

Defined terms

"applicant": s 84

"Commissioner": s 18(3)

"exempt information": s 84 and Pt.II

"information": s 84

"Tribunal": s 18(3)

Appeal proceedings

61(1)   The provisions of Schedule 6 to the Data Protection Act 1998 have effect (so far as applicable) in relation to appeals under this Part.

NOTES

Commencement
Subs.(1): For certain purposes: 14 May 2001: see SI
  2001/1637, art 2(c).
Subs.(1): For certain purposes: 30 November 2002: see SI
  2002/2812, art 2(i).
Subs.(1): For remaining purposes: 1 January 2005: see SI
  2004/1909, art 2(1), (2)(d), (3).
Subs.(2):30 November 2002: see SI 2002/2812, art 2(g).

PART VI

HISTORICAL RECORDS AND RECORDS IN PUBLIC RECORD OFFICE OR PUBLIC RECORD OFFICE OF NORTHERN IRELAND

Interpretation of Part VI

62(1)   For the purposes of this Part, a record becomes a "historical record" at the end of the period of thirty years beginning with the year following that in which it was created.

(2)   Where records created at different dates are for administrative purposes kept together in one file or other assembly, all the records in that file or other assembly are to be treated for the purposes of this Part as having been created when the latest of those records was created.

(3)   In this Part "year" means a calendar year.

NOTES

Commencement   **Defined terms**
1 January 2005: see SI 2004/1909, art 2(1), (2)(e), (3).   "historical record": subs.(1)

Scottish public authority equivalent
FOI(S)A s 57

Removal of exemptions: historical records generally

63(1)   Information contained in a historical record cannot be exempt information by virtue of section 28, 30(1), 32, 33, 35, 36, 37(1)(a), 42 or 43.

(2)   Compliance with section 1(1)(a) in relation to a historical record is not to be taken to be capable of having any of the effects referred to in section 28(3), 33(3), 36(3), 42(2) or 43(3).

(3)   Information cannot be exempt information by virtue of section 37(1)(b) after the end of the period of sixty years beginning with the year following that in which the record containing the information was created.

(4) Information cannot be exempt information by virtue of section 31 after the end of the period of one hundred years beginning with the year following that in which the record containing the information was created.

(5) Compliance with section 1(1)(a) in relation to any record is not to be taken, at any time after the end of the period of one hundred years beginning with the year following that in which the record was created, to be capable of prejudicing any of the matters referred to in section 31(1).

NOTES

Commencement
1 January 2005: SI 2004/3122 art 2.

Scottish public authority equivalent
FOI(S)A s 58

Defined terms
"exempt information": s 84 and Pt.II
"historical information": s 62(1)
"information": s 84

Removal of exemptions: historical records in public record offices

64(1) Information contained in a historical record in the Public Record Office or the Public Record Office of Northern Ireland cannot be exempt information by virtue of section 21 or 22.

(2) In relation to any information falling within section 23(1) which is contained in a historical record in the Public Record Office or the Public Record Office of Northern Ireland, section 2(3) shall have effect with the omission of the reference to section 23.

NOTES

Commencement
1 January 2005: SI 2004/3122 art 2.

Defined terms
"exempt information": s 84
"historical record": s 62(1)
"information": s 84

Decisions as to refusal of discretionary disclosure of historical records

65(1) Before refusing a request for information relating to information which is contained in a historical record and is exempt information only by virtue of a provision not specified in section 2(3), a public authority shall—
   (a) if the historical record is a public record within the meaning of the Public Records Act 1958, consult the Lord Chancellor, or
   (b) if the historical record is a public record to which the Public Records Act (Northern Ireland) 1923 applies, consult the appropriate Northern Ireland Minister.

(2) This section does not apply to information to which section 66 applies.

NOTES

Commencement
1 January 2005: SI 2004/3122 art 2.

Defined terms
"appropriate Northern Ireland Minister": s 84
"exempt information": s 84 and Part II

"historical record": s 62(1)
"information": s 84
"public authority": s 3(1)
"request for information": s 8

Decisions relating to certain transferred public records

66(1) This section applies to any information which is (or, if it existed, would be) contained in a transferred public record, other than information which the responsible authority has designated as open information for the purposes of this section.

(2) Before determining whether—
(a) information to which this section applies falls within any provision of Part II relating to the duty to confirm or deny, or
(b) information to which this section applies is exempt information,
the appropriate records authority shall consult the responsible authority.

(3) Where information to which this section applies falls within a provision of Part II relating to the duty to confirm or deny but does not fall within any of the provisions of that Part relating to that duty which are specified in subsection (3) of section 2, any question as to the application of subsection (1)(b) of that section is to be determined by the responsible authority instead of the appropriate records authority.

(4) Where any information to which this section applies is exempt information only by virtue of any provision of Part II not specified in subsection (3) of section 2, any question as to the application of subsection (2)(b) of that section is to be determined by the responsible authority instead of the appropriate records authority.

(5) Before making by virtue of subsection (3) or (4) any determination that subsection (1)(b) or (2)(b) of section 2 applies, the responsible authority shall consult—
(a) where the transferred public record is a public record within the meaning of the Public Records Act 1958, the Lord Chancellor, and
(b) where the transferred public record is a public record to which the Public Records Act (Northern Ireland) 1923 applies, the appropriate Northern Ireland Minister.

(6) Where the responsible authority in relation to information to which this section applies is not (apart from this subsection) a public authority, it shall be treated as being a public authority for the purposes of Parts III, IV and V of this Act so far as relating to—
(a) the duty imposed by section 15(3), and
(b) the imposition of any requirement to furnish information relating to compliance with Part I in connection with the information to which this section applies.

NOTES

Commencement
1 January 2005: SI 2004/3122 art 2.

Defined terms
"appropriate Northern Ireland Minister": s 84
"appropriate records authority": s 15(5)
"duty to confirm or deny": s 1(6)
"exempt information": s 84
"information": s 84

"public authority": s 3(1)
"responsible authority": s 15(5)
"transferred public record": s 15(4)

Amendments of public records legislation

67   Schedule 5 (which amends the Public Records Act 1958 and the Public Records Act (Northern Ireland) 1923) has effect.

NOTES

Commencement

30 November 2000 (for certain purposes): see s 87(1)(j).
For certain purposes: 30 November 2002: see SI
  2002/2812, art 2(j).
For remaining purposes: 1 January 2005: see SI
  2004/3122, art 2.

Defined terms

Scottish public authority equivalent

FOI(S)A s 70

PART VII

AMENDMENTS OF DATA PROTECTION ACT 1998

Amendments relating to personal information held by public authorities

Extension of meaning of "data"

68(1)   Section 1 of the Data Protection Act 1998 (basic interpretative provisions) is amended in accordance with subsections (2) and (3).

(2)   In subsection (1)—
   (a) in the definition of "data", the word "or" at the end of paragraph (c) is omitted and after paragraph (d) there is inserted
       "or
       (e) is recorded information held by a public authority and does not fall within any of paragraphs (a) to (d);", and
   (b) after the definition of "processing" there is inserted—
       "'public authority' has the same meaning as in the Freedom of Information Act 2000;".

(3)   After subsection (4) there is inserted—
       "(5)   In paragraph (e) of the definition of "data" in subsection (1), the reference to information "held" by a public authority shall be construed in accordance with section 3(2) of the Freedom of Information Act 2000.
       (6) Where section 7 of the Freedom of Information Act 2000 prevents Parts I to V of that Act from applying to certain information held by a public authority, that

information is not to be treated for the purposes of paragraph (e) of the definition of "data" in subsection (1) as held by a public authority."

(4) In section 56 of that Act (prohibition of requirement as to production of certain records), after subsection (6) there is inserted—

"(6A) A record is not a relevant record to the extent that it relates, or is to relate, only to personal data falling within paragraph (e) of the definition of "data" in section 1(1)."

(5) In the Table in section 71 of that Act (index of defined expressions) after the entry relating to processing there is inserted—

"public authority   section 1(1)"."

NOTES

Commencement   **Defined terms**

1 January 2005: SI 2004/3122 art 2.

Right of access to unstructured personal data held by public authorities

69(1) In section 7(1) of the Data Protection Act 1998 (right of access to personal data), for "sections 8 and 9" there is substituted "sections 8, 9 and 9A".

(2) After section 9 of that Act there is inserted—

"9A Unstructured personal data held by public authorities

(1) In this section "unstructured personal data" means any personal data falling within paragraph (e) of the definition of "data" in section 1(1), other than information which is recorded as part of, or with the intention that it should form part of, any set of information relating to individuals to the extent that the set is structured by reference to individuals or by reference to criteria relating to individuals.

(2) A public authority is not obliged to comply with subsection (1) of section 7 in relation to any unstructured personal data unless the request under that section contains a description of the data.

(3) Even if the data are described by the data subject in his request, a public authority is not obliged to comply with subsection (1) of section 7 in relation to unstructured personal data if the authority estimates that the cost of complying with the request so far as relating to those data would exceed the appropriate limit.

(4) Subsection (3) does not exempt the public authority from its obligation to comply with paragraph (a) of section 7(1) in relation to the unstructured personal data unless the estimated cost of complying with that paragraph alone in relation to those data would exceed the appropriate limit.

(5) In subsections (3) and (4) "the appropriate limit" means such amount as may be prescribed by the Secretary of State by regulations, and different amounts may be prescribed in relation to different cases.

(6) Any estimate for the purposes of this section must be made in accordance with regulations under section 12(5) of the Freedom of Information Act 2000."."

(3)   In section 67(5) of that Act (statutory instruments subject to negative resolution procedure), in paragraph (c), for "or 9(3)" there is substituted ", 9(3) or 9A(5)".

NOTES

Commencement

Defined terms

30 November 2000 (in so far as this section confers
    powers to make any order, regulations or code of
    practice): see s 87(1)(m).
For remaining purposes): 1 January 2005: see SI
    2004/1909, art 2(1), (2)(f), (3).

Exemptions applicable to certain manual data held by public authorities

70(1)   After section 33 of the Data Protection Act 1998 there is inserted—

"**33A Manual data held by public authorities**

(1) Personal data falling within paragraph (e) of the definition of "data" in section 1(1) are exempt from—

   (a) the first, second, third, fifth, seventh and eighth data protection principles,

   (b) the sixth data protection principle except so far as it relates to the rights conferred on data subjects by sections 7 and 14,

   (c) sections 10 to 12,

   (d) section 13, except so far as it relates to damage caused by a contravention of section 7 or of the fourth data protection principle and to any distress which is also suffered by reason of that contravention,

   (e) Part III, and

   (f) section 55.

(2) Personal data which fall within paragraph (e) of the definition of "data" in section 1(1) and relate to appointments or removals, pay, discipline, superannuation or other personnel matters, in relation to—

   (a) service in any of the armed forces of the Crown,

   (b) service in any office or employment under the Crown or under any public authority, or

   (c) service in any office or employment, or under any contract for services, in respect of which power to take action, or to determine or approve the action taken, in such matters is vested in Her Majesty, any Minister of the Crown, the National Assembly for Wales, any Northern Ireland Minister (within the meaning of the Freedom of Information Act 2000) or any public authority, are also exempt from the remaining data protection principles and the remaining provisions of Part II."

(2)   In section 55 of that Act (unlawful obtaining etc of personal data) in subsection (8) after "section 28" there is inserted "or 33A".

(3)   In Part III of Schedule 8 to that Act (exemptions available after 23rd October 2001 but before 24th October 2007) after paragraph 14 there is inserted—

"14A

(1) This paragraph applies to personal data which fall within paragraph (e) of the definition of "data" in section 1(1) and do not fall within paragraph 14(1)(a), but does not apply to eligible manual data to which the exemption in paragraph 16 applies.

(2) During the second transitional period, data to which this paragraph applies are exempt from—

(a) the fourth data protection principle, and

(b) section 14(1) to (3)."

(4) In Schedule 13 to that Act (modifications of Act having effect before 24th October 2007) in subsection (4)(b) of section 12A to that Act as set out in paragraph 1, after "paragraph 14" there is inserted "or 14A".

NOTES

Commencement

1 January 2005: see SI 2004/1909, art 2(1), (2)(f), (3).

Defined terms

Particulars registrable under Part III of Data Protection Act 1998

71 In section 16(1) of the Data Protection Act 1998 (the registrable particulars), before the word "and" at the end of paragraph (f) there is inserted—

"(ff) where the data controller is a public authority, a statement of that fact,".

NOTES

Commencement

1 January 2005: see SI 2004/1909, art 2(1), (2)(f), (3).

Defined terms

Availability under Act disregarded for purpose of exemption

72 In section 34 of the Data Protection Act 1998 (information available to the public by or under enactment), after the word "enactment" there is inserted "other than an enactment contained in the Freedom of Information Act 2000".

NOTES

Commencement

30 November 2002: see SI 2002/2812, art 2(k).

Defined terms

Other amendments

Further amendments of Data Protection Act 1998

73 Schedule 6 (which contains further amendments of the Data Protection Act 1998) has effect.

NOTES

Commencement
30 November 2000: (for certain purposes): s87(1)(k).
14 May 2001 (for other purposes): SI 2001/1637, art 2(d).
1 January 2005 (for remaining purposes): SI 2004/1909,
  art 2(1), (2)(f), (3).

Defined terms

PART VIII

MISCELLANEOUS AND SUPPLEMENTAL

Power to make provision relating to environmental information

74(1)   In this section "the Aarhus Convention" means the Convention on Access to Information, Public Participation in Decision-making and Access to Justice in Environmental Matters signed at Aarhus on 25th June 1998.

(2)   For the purposes of this section "the information provisions" of the Aarhus Convention are Article 4, together with Articles 3 and 9 so far as relating to that Article.

(3)   The Secretary of State may by regulations make such provision as he considers appropriate—

(a) for the purpose of implementing the information provisions of the Aarhus Convention or any amendment of those provisions made in accordance with Article 14 of the Convention, and

(b) for the purpose of dealing with matters arising out of or related to the implementation of those provisions or of any such amendment.

(4)   Regulations under subsection (3) may in particular—

(a) enable charges to be made for making information available in accordance with the regulations,

(b) provide that any obligation imposed by the regulations in relation to the disclosure of information is to have effect notwithstanding any enactment or rule of law,

(c) make provision for the issue by the Secretary of State of a code of practice,

(d) provide for sections 47 and 48 to apply in relation to such a code with such modifications as may be specified,

(e) provide for any of the provisions of Parts IV and V to apply, with such modifications as may be specified in the regulations, in relation to compliance with any requirement of the regulations, and

(f) contain such transitional or consequential provision (including provision modifying any enactment) as the Secretary of State considers appropriate.

(5)   This section has effect subject to section 80.

NOTES

Commencement
30 November 2000: see s 87(1)(f).

Defined terms
"Aarhus Convention": subs.(1)
"information provisions": subs.(2)

Scottish public authority equivalent
FOI(S)A s 62

Power to amend or repeal enactments prohibiting disclosure of information

75(1) If, with respect to any enactment which prohibits the disclosure of information held by a public authority, it appears to the Secretary of State that by virtue of section 44(1)(a) the enactment is capable of preventing the disclosure of information under section 1, he may by order repeal or amend the enactment for the purpose of removing or relaxing the prohibition.

(2) In subsection (1)—
"enactment" means—
  (a) any enactment contained in an Act passed before or in the same Session as this Act, or
  (b) any enactment contained in Northern Ireland legislation or subordinate legislation passed or made before the passing of this Act;
"information" includes unrecorded information

(3) An order under this section may do all or any of the following—
  (a) make such modifications of enactments as, in the opinion of the Secretary of State, are consequential upon, or incidental to, the amendment or repeal of the enactment containing the prohibition;
  (b) contain such transitional provisions and savings as appear to the Secretary of State to be appropriate;
  (c) make different provision for different cases.

NOTES

Commencement
30 November 2000: see s 87(1)(g).

Scottish public authority equivalent
FOI(S)A s 64

Defined terms
"enactment": s 84 and subs.(2)
"information": s 84 and subs.(2)
"public authority": s 3(1)

Disclosure of information between Commissioner and ombudsmen

76(1) The Commissioner may disclose to a person specified in the first column of the Table below any information obtained by, or furnished to, the Commissioner under or for the purposes of this Act or the Data Protection Act 1998 if it appears to the Commissioner that the information relates to a matter which could be the subject of an investigation by that person under the enactment specified in relation to that person in the second column of that Table.

TABLE

Ombudsman	Enactment
The Parliamentary Commissioner for Administration.	The Parliamentary Commissioner Act 1967 (c 13).
The Health Service Commissioner for England.	The Health Service Commissioners Act 1993 (c 46).

A Local Commissioner as defined by section 23(3) of the Local Government Act 1974.	Part III or Part 3A of the Local Government Act 1974 (c 7).
The Scottish Public Services Ombudsman Act 2002 (asp 11)	The Public Services Ombudsman for Wales
Part 2 of the Public Services Ombudsman (Wales) Act 2005	The Northern Ireland Commissioner for Complaints.
The Commissioner for Complaints (Northern Ireland) Order 1996 (SI 1996/1297 (NI 7)).	The Assembly Ombudsman for Northern Ireland.
The Ombudsman (Northern Ireland) Order 1996 (SI 1996/1298 (NI 8)).	The Commissioner for Older People in Wales.
The Commissioner for Older People (Wales) Act 2006.	

(2)   Schedule 7 (which contains amendments relating to information disclosed to ombudsmen under subsection (1) and to the disclosure of information by ombudsmen to the Commissioner) has effect.

NOTES

Commencement
30 January 2001: see s 87(2)(b).

Defined terms
"Commissioner": s 18(3)
"information": s 84

Disclosure between Commissioner and Scottish Information Commissioner

76A   The Commissioner may disclose to the Scottish Information Commissioner any information obtained or furnished as mentioned in section 76(1) of this Act if it appears to the Commissioner that the information is of the same type that could be obtained by, or furnished to, the Scottish Information Commissioner under or for the purposes of the Freedom of Information (Scotland) Act.

NOTES

Commencement
1 January 2005: see SI 2004/3089, art 1.

Defined terms
"Commissioner": s 18(3)
"information": s 84

Offence of altering etc records with intent to prevent disclosure

77(1)   Where—
(a) a request for information has been made to a public authority, and
(b) under section 1 of this Act or section 7 of the Data Protection Act 1998, the applicant would have been entitled (subject to payment of any fee) to communication of any information in accordance with that section,
any person to whom this subsection applies is guilty of an offence if he alters, defaces, blocks, erases, destroys or conceals any record held by the public authority, with the intention of preventing the disclosure by that authority of all, or any part, of the information to the communication of which the applicant would have been entitled.

(2)   Subsection (1) applies to the public authority and to any person who is employed by, is an officer of, or is subject to the direction of, the public authority.

(3)   A person guilty of an offence under this section is liable on summary conviction to a fine not exceeding level 5 on the standard scale.

(4)   No proceedings for an offence under this section shall be instituted—
        (a) in England or Wales, except by the Commissioner or by or with the consent of the Director of Public Prosecutions;
        (b) in Northern Ireland, except by the Commissioner or by or with the consent of the Director of Public Prosecutions for Northern Ireland.

NOTES

Commencement
1 January 2005: see SI 2004/1909, art 2(1), (2)(g), (3).

Scottish public authority equivalent
FOI(S)A, ss 65 and 68

Defined terms
"applicant": s 84
"information": s 84
"public authority": s 3(1)
"request for information": s 8

Saving for existing powers

78   Nothing in this Act is to be taken to limit the powers of a public authority to disclose information held by it.

NOTES

Commencement
30 November 2000: see s 87(1)(h).

Scottish public authority equivalent
FOI(S)A s 66

Defined terms
"held": s 3(2)
"information": s 84
"public authority": s 3(1)

Defamation

79   Where any information communicated by a public authority to a person ("the applicant") under section 1 was supplied to the public authority by a third person, the publication to the applicant of any defamatory matter contained in the information shall be privileged unless the publication is shown to have been made with malice.

NOTES

Commencement
30 November 2000: see s 87(1)(h).

Scottish public authority equivalent
FOI(S)A s 67

Defined terms
"public authority": s 3(1)

Scotland

80(1)   No order may be made under section 4(1) or 5 in relation to any of the bodies specified in subsection (2); and the power conferred by section 74(3) does not include power to make provision in relation to information held by any of those bodies.

(2)   The bodies referred to in subsection (1) are—
   (a)   the Scottish Parliament,
   (b)   any part of the Scottish Administration,
   (c)   the Scottish Parliamentary Corporate Body, or
   (d)   any Scottish public authority with mixed functions or no reserved functions (within the meaning of the Scotland Act 1998).

(3)   Section 50 of the Copyright, Designs and Patents Act 1988 and paragraph 6 of Schedule 1 to the Copyright and Rights in Databases Regulations 1997 apply in relation to the Freedom of Information (Scotland) Act 2002 as they apply in relation to this Act.

NOTES

Commencement
30 November 2000: see s 87(1)(h).

Defined terms
"held": s 3(2)
"information": s 84
"body": s 84

Application to government departments, etc

81(1)   For the purposes of this Act each government department is to be treated as a person separate from any other government department.

(2)   Subsection (1) does not enable—
   (a)   a government department which is not a Northern Ireland department to claim for the purposes of section 41(1)(b) that the disclosure of any information by it would constitute a breach of confidence actionable by any other government department (not being a Northern Ireland department), or
   (b)   a Northern Ireland department to claim for those purposes that the disclosure of information by it would constitute a breach of confidence actionable by any other Northern Ireland department.

(3)   A government department or the Welsh Assembly Government is not liable to prosecution under this Act, but section 77 and paragraph 12 of Schedule 3 apply to a person in the public service of the Crown as they apply to any other person.

(4)   The provisions specified in subsection (3) also apply to a person acting on behalf of either House of Parliament or on behalf of the Northern Ireland Assembly or the National Assembly for Wales as they apply to any other person.

NOTES

Commencement
30 November 2000: see s 87(1)(h).

Defined terms
"government department": s 84
"information": s 84

Orders and regulations

82(1) Any power of the Secretary of State to make an order or regulations under this Act shall be exercisable by statutory instrument.

(2) A statutory instrument containing (whether alone or with other provisions)—
  (a) an order under section 5, 7(3) or (8), 53(1)(a)(iii) or 75, or
  (b) regulations under section 10(4) or 74(3),
shall not be made unless a draft of the instrument has been laid before, and approved by a resolution of, each House of Parliament.

(3) A statutory instrument which contains (whether alone or with other provisions)—
  (a) an order under section 4(1), or
  (b) regulations under any provision of this Act not specified in subsection (2)(b),
and which is not subject to the requirement in subsection (2) that a draft of the instrument be laid before and approved by a resolution of each House of Parliament, shall be subject to annulment in pursuance of a resolution of either House of Parliament.

(4) An order under section 4(5) shall be laid before Parliament after being made.

(5) If a draft of an order under section 5 or 7(8) would, apart from this subsection, be treated for the purposes of the Standing Orders of either House of Parliament as a hybrid instrument, it shall proceed in that House as if it were not such an instrument.

NOTES

Commencement **Defined terms**
30 November 2000: see s 87(1)(h).

Meaning of "Welsh public authority"

83(1) In this Act "Welsh public authority" means—
  (a) any public authority which is listed in Part II, III, IV or VI of Schedule 1 and whose functions are exercisable only or mainly in or as regards Wales, other than an excluded authority, or
  (b) any public authority which is—
    (i) a subsidiary of the Welsh Ministers (as defined by section 134(4) of the Government of Wales Act 2006), or
    (ii) a subsidiary of the Assembly Commission (as defined by section 139(4) of that Act).

(2) In paragraph (a) of subsection (1) "excluded authority" means a public authority which is designated by the Secretary of State by order as an excluded authority for the purposes of that paragraph.

(3) Before making an order under subsection (2), the Secretary of State shall consult the First Minister for Wales.

959

NOTES

Commencement
30 November 2000: see s 87(1)(h).

Defined terms
"excluded authority": subs.(2)
"public authority": s 3(1)
"Welsh public authority": subs.(1)

Interpretation

84   In this Act, unless the context otherwise requires—

"applicant", in relation to a request for information, means the person who made the request;

"appropriate Northern Ireland Minister" means the Northern Ireland Minister in charge of the Department of Culture, Arts and Leisure in Northern Ireland;

"appropriate records authority", in relation to a transferred public record, has the meaning given by section 15(5);

"body" includes an unincorporated association;

"the Commissioner" means the Information Commissioner;

"decision notice" has the meaning given by section 50;

"the duty to confirm or deny" has the meaning given by section 1(6);

"enactment" includes an enactment contained in Northern Ireland legislation;

"enforcement notice" has the meaning given by section 52;

"exempt information" means information which is exempt information by virtue of any provision of Part II;

"fees notice" has the meaning given by section 9(1);

"government department" includes a Northern Ireland department, the Northern Ireland Court Service and any other body or authority exercising statutory functions on behalf of the Crown, but does not include—

(a) any of the bodies specified in section 80(2),

(b) the Security Service, the Secret Intelligence Service or the Government Communications Headquarters, or

(c) the Welsh Assembly Government;

"information" (subject to sections 51(8) and 75(2)) means information recorded in any form;

"information notice" has the meaning given by section 51;

"Minister of the Crown" has the same meaning as in the Ministers of the Crown Act 1975;

"Northern Ireland Minister" includes the First Minister and deputy First Minister in Northern Ireland;

"Northern Ireland public authority" means any public authority, other than the Northern Ireland Assembly or a Northern Ireland department, whose functions are exercisable only or mainly in or as regards Northern Ireland and relate only or mainly to transferred matters;

"prescribed" means prescribed by regulations made by the Secretary of State;

"public authority" has the meaning given by section 3(1);

"public record" means a public record within the meaning of the Public Records Act 1958 or a public record to which the Public Records Act (Northern Ireland) 1923 applies;

"publication scheme" has the meaning given by section 19;

"request for information" has the meaning given by section 8;

"responsible authority", in relation to a transferred public record, has the meaning given by section 15(5);

"the special forces" means those units of the armed forces of the Crown the maintenance of whose capabilities is the responsibility of the Director of Special Forces or which are for the time being subject to the operational command of that Director;

"subordinate legislation" has the meaning given by subsection (1) of section 21 of the Interpretation Act 1978, except that the definition of that term in that subsection shall have effect as if "Act" included Northern Ireland legislation;

"transferred matter", in relation to Northern Ireland, has the meaning given by section 4(1) of the Northern Ireland Act 1998;

"transferred public record" has the meaning given by section 15(4);

"the Tribunal", in relation to any appeal under this Act, means—

    (a) the Upper Tribunal, in any case where it is determined by or under Tribunal Procedure Rules that the Upper Tribunal is to hear the appeal; or

    (b) the First-tier Tribunal, in any other case;

"Welsh public authority" has the meaning given by section 83.

NOTES

Commencement
30 November 2000: see s 87(1)(h).

Defined terms

Scottish public authority equivalent
FOI(S)A s 73

Expenses

85   There shall be paid out of money provided by Parliament—

    (a) any increase attributable to this Act in the expenses of the Secretary of State in respect of the Commissioner, the Tribunal or the members of the Tribunal,

    (b) any administrative expenses of the Secretary of State attributable to this Act,

    (c) any other expenses incurred in consequence of this Act by a Minister of the Crown or government department or by either House of Parliament, and

    (d) any increase attributable to this Act in the sums which under any other Act are payable out of money so provided.

NOTES

Commencement
30 November 2000: see s 87(1)(h).

Defined terms
"Commissioner": s 18(3)
"government department": s 84
"Minister of the Crown": s 84 of the Ministers of the
   Crown Act 1975
"Tribunal": s 18(3)

Repeals

86   Schedule 8 (repeals) has effect.

NOTES

Commencement   **Defined terms**
30 November 2000: see s 87(1)(h).

Commencement

87(1)   The following provisions of this Act shall come into force on the day on which this Act is passed—

(a) sections 3 to 8 and Schedule 1,

(b) section 19 so far as relating to the approval of publication schemes,

(c) section 20 so far as relating to the approval and preparation by the Commissioner of model publication schemes,

(d) section 47(2) to (6),

(e) section 49,

(f) section 74,

(g) section 75,

(h) sections 78 to 85 and this section,

(i) paragraphs 2 and 17 to 22 of Schedule 2 (and section 18(4) so far as relating to those paragraphs),

(j) paragraph 4 of Schedule 5 (and section 67 so far as relating to that paragraph),

(k) paragraph 8 of Schedule 6 (and section 73 so far as relating to that paragraph),

(l) Part I of Schedule 8 (and section 86 so far as relating to that Part), and

(m) so much of any other provision of this Act as confers power to make any order, regulations or code of practice.

(2)   The following provisions of this Act shall come into force at the end of the period of two months beginning with the day on which this Act is passed—

(a) section 18(1),

(b) section 76 and Schedule 7,

(c) paragraphs 1(1), 3(1), 4, 6, 7, 8(2), 9(2), 10(a), 13(1) and (2), 14(a) and 15(1) and (2) of Schedule 2 (and section 18(4) so far as relating to those provisions), and

(d) Part II of Schedule 8 (and section 86 so far as relating to that Part).

(3)   Except as provided by subsections (1) and (2), this Act shall come into force at the end of the period of five years beginning with the day on which this Act is passed or on such day before the end of that period as the Secretary of State may by order appoint; and different days may be appointed for different purposes.

(4)   An order under subsection (3) may contain such transitional provisions and savings (including provisions capable of having effect after the end of the period referred to in that subsection) as the Secretary of State considers appropriate.

(5)   During the twelve months beginning with the day on which this Act is passed, and during each subsequent complete period of twelve months in the period beginning with that day and ending with the first day on which all the provisions of this Act are fully in force, the Secretary of State shall—

(a) prepare a report on his proposals for bringing fully into force those provisions of this Act which are not yet fully in force, and

(b) lay a copy of the report before each House of Parliament.

NOTES

Commencement   **Defined terms**

30 November 2000: see s 87(1)(h).

Short title and extent

88(1)   This Act may be cited as the Freedom of Information Act 2000.

(2)   Subject to subsection (3), this Act extends to Northern Ireland.

(3)   The amendment or repeal of any enactment by this Act has the same extent as that enactment.

NOTES

Commencement   **Defined terms**

30 November 2002: SI 2002/2812

Scottish public authority equivalent

FOI(S)A s 76

SCHEDULE 1

PUBLIC AUTHORITIES

Section 3(1)(a)(i)

PART I

GENERAL

1   Any government department other than the Office for Standards in Education, Children's Services and Skills.

1A   The Office for Standards in Education, Children's Services and Skills, in respect of information held for purposes other than those of the functions exercisable by Her

Majesty's Chief Inspector of Education, Children's Services and Skills by virtue of section 5(1)(a)(iii) of the Care Standards Act 2000.

2   The House of Commons, in respect of information other than—

     (a) information relating to any residential address of a member of either House of Parliament,

     (b) information relating to travel arrangements of a member of either House of Parliament, where the arrangements relate to travel that has not yet been undertaken or is regular in nature,

     (c) information relating to the identity of any person who delivers or has delivered goods, or provides or has provided services, to a member of either House of Parliament at any residence of the member,

     (d) information relating to expenditure by a member of either House of Parliament on security arrangements.

     Paragraph (b) does not except information relating to the total amount of expenditure incurred on regular travel during any month.

3   The House of Lords, in respect of information other than—

     (a) information relating to any residential address of a member of either House of Parliament,

     (b) information relating to travel arrangements of a member of either House of Parliament, where the arrangements relate to travel that has not yet been undertaken or is regular in nature,

     (c) information relating to the identity of any person who delivers or has delivered goods, or provides or has provided services, to a member of either House of Parliament at any residence of the member,

     (d) information relating to expenditure by a member of either House of Parliament on security arrangements.

     Paragraph (b) does not except information relating to the total amount of expenditure incurred on regular travel during any month.

4   The Northern Ireland Assembly.

5   The National Assembly for Wales, in respect of information other than—

     (a) information relating to any residential address of a member of the Assembly,

     (b) information relating to travel arrangements of a member of the Assembly, where the arrangements relate to travel that has not yet been undertaken or is regular in nature,

     (c) information relating to the identity of any person who delivers or has delivered goods, or provides or has provided services, to a member of the Assembly at any residence of the member,

     (d) information relating to expenditure by a member of the Assembly on security arrangements.

     Paragraph (b) does not except information relating to the total amount of expenditure incurred on regular travel during any month.

5A   The Welsh Assembly Government.

6   The armed forces of the Crown, except—
     (a) the special forces, and
     (b) any unit or part of a unit which is for the time being required by the Secretary of State to assist the Government Communications Headquarters in the exercise of its functions.

PART II

LOCAL GOVERNMENT

England and Wales

7   A local authority within the meaning of the Local Government Act 1972, namely—
     (a) in England, a county council, a London borough council, a district council or a parish council,
     (b) in Wales, a county council, a county borough council or a community council.

8   The Greater London Authority.

9   The Common Council of the City of London, in respect of information held in its capacity as a local authority, police authority or port health authority.

10   The Sub-Treasurer of the Inner Temple or the Under-Treasurer of the Middle Temple, in respect of information held in his capacity as a local authority.

11   The Council of the Isles of Scilly.

12   A parish meeting constituted under section 13 of the Local Government Act 1972.

13   Any charter trustees constituted under section 246 of the Local Government Act 1972.

14   A fire and rescue authority constituted by a scheme under section 2 of the Fire and Rescue Services Act 2004 or a scheme to which section 4 of that Act applies.

15   A waste disposal authority established by virtue of an order under section 10(1) of the Local Government Act 1985.

15A An authority established for an area in England by an order under section 207 of the Local Government and Public Involvement in Health Act 2007 (joint waste authorities).

16   A port health authority constituted by an order under section 2 of the Public Health (Control of Disease) Act 1984.

18   An internal drainage board which is continued in being by virtue of section 1 of the Land Drainage Act 1991.

19   A joint authority established under Part IV of the Local Government Act 1985 (fire and rescue services and transport).

19A An economic prosperity board established under section 88 of the Local Democracy, Economic Development and Construction Act 2009.

19B A combined authority established under section 103 of that Act.

20 The London Fire and Emergency Planning Authority.

21 A joint fire authority established by virtue of an order under section 42(2) of the Local Government Act 1985 (reorganisation of functions).

22 A body corporate established pursuant to an order under section 67 of the Local Government Act 1985 (transfer of functions to successors of residuary bodies, etc).

23 A body corporate established pursuant to an order under section 17 of the Local Government and Public Involvement in Health Act 2007 (residuary bodies).

24 The Broads Authority established by section 1 of the Norfolk and Suffolk Broads Act 1988.

25 A joint committee constituted in accordance with section 102(1)(b) of the Local Government Act 1972.

26 A joint board which is continued in being by virtue of section 263(1) of the Local Government Act 1972.

27 A joint authority established under section 21 of the Local Government Act 1992.

28 A Passenger Transport Executive for an integrated transport area for the purposes of Part 2 of the Transport Act 1968.

29 Transport for London.

30 The London Transport Users Committee.

31 A joint board the constituent members of which consist of any of the public authorities described in paragraphs 8, 9, 10, 12, 15, 16, 20 to 31, 57 and 58.

32 A National Park authority established by an order under section 63 of the Environment Act 1995.

33 A joint planning board constituted for an area in Wales outside a National Park by an order under section 2(1B) of the Town and Country Planning Act 1990.

35 The London Development Agency.

35A A local fisheries committee for a sea fisheries district established under section 1 of the Sea Fisheries Regulation Act 1966.

35B An inshore fisheries and conservation authority for a district established under section 149 of the Marine and Coastal Access Act 2009.

Northern Ireland

36   A district council within the meaning of the Local Government Act (Northern Ireland) 1972.

PART III

THE NATIONAL HEALTH SERVICE

England and Wales

36A A Strategic Health Authority established under section 13 of the National Health Service Act 2006.

38   A special health authority established under section 28 of the National Health Service Act 2006 or section 22 of the National Health Service (Wales) Act 2006.

39   A primary care trust established under section 18 of the National Health Service Act 2006.

39A A Local Health Board established under section 11 of the National Health Service (Wales) Act 2006.

40   A National Health Service trust established under section 25 of the National Health Service Act 2006 or section 18 of the National Health Service (Wales) Act 2006.

40A An NHS foundation trust.

41   A Community Health Council established under section 182 of the National Health Service (Wales) Act 2006.

43A Any person providing primary medical services, primary dental services or primary ophthalmic services—
       (a) in accordance with arrangements made under section 92 or 107 of the National Health Service Act 2006, or section 50 or 64 of the National Health Service (Wales) Act 2006; or
       (b) under a contract under section 84, 100 or 117 of the National Health Service Act 2006 or section 42 or 57 of the National Health Service (Wales) Act 2006;
       in respect of information relating to the provision of those services.

44   Any person providing general medical services, general dental services, general ophthalmic services or pharmaceutical services under the National Health Service Act 2006 or the National Health Service (Wales) Act 2006, in respect of information relating to the provision of those services.

45   Any person providing personal medical services or personal dental services under arrangements made under section 28C of the National Health Service Act 1977, in respect of information relating to the provision of those services.

45A Any person providing local pharmaceutical services under—
       (a) a pilot scheme established under section 134 of the National Health Service Act 2006 or section 92 of the National Health Service (Wales) Act 2006; or

(b) an LPS scheme established under Schedule 12 to the National Health Service Act 2006 or Schedule 7 to the National Health Service (Wales) Act 2006,

in respect of information relating to the provision of those services.

Northern Ireland

48   A Health and Social Services Trust established under Article 10 of the Health and Personal Social Services (Northern Ireland) Order 1991.

49   A special agency established under Article 3 of the Health and Personal Social Services (Special Agencies) (Northern Ireland) Order 1990.

51   Any person providing primary medical services, general dental services, general ophthalmic services or pharmaceutical services under Part VI of the Health and Personal Social Services (Northern Ireland) Order 1972, in respect of information relating to the provision of those services.

51A The Regional Business Services Organisation established under section 14 of the Health and Social Services (Reform) Act (Northern Ireland) 2009.

51B The Patient and Client Council established under section 16 of the Health and Social Care (Reform) Act (Northern Ireland) 2009.

51C The Regional Health and Social Care Board established under section 7 of the Health and Social Care (Reform) Act (Northern Ireland) 2009.

51D The Regional Agency for Public Health and Social Well-being established under section 12 of the Health and Social Care (Reform) Act (Northern Ireland) 2009.

PART IV

MAINTAINED SCHOOLS AND OTHER EDUCATIONAL INSTITUTIONS

England and Wales

52   The governing body of—
(a) a maintained school, as defined by section 20(7) of the School Standards and Framework Act 1998, or
(b) a maintained nursery school, as defined by section 22(9) of that Act.

53(1)   The governing body of—
(a) an institution within the further education sector,
(b) a university receiving financial support under section 65 of the Further and Higher Education Act 1992,
(c) an institution conducted by a higher education corporation,

(d) a designated institution for the purposes of Part II of the Further and Higher Education Act 1992 as defined by section 72(3) of that Act, or

(e) any college, school, hall or other institution of a university which falls within paragraph (b).

53(2) In sub-paragraph (1)—

(a) "governing body" is to be interpreted in accordance with subsection (1) of section 90 of the Further and Higher Education Act 1992 but without regard to subsection (2) of that section,

(b) in paragraph (a), the reference to an institution within the further education sector is to be construed in accordance with section 91(3) of the Further and Higher Education Act 1992,

(c) in paragraph (c), "higher education corporation" has the meaning given by section 90(1) of that Act, and

(d) in paragraph (e) "college" includes any institution in the nature of a college.

Northern Ireland

54(1) The managers of—

(a) a controlled school, voluntary school or grant-maintained integrated school within the meaning of Article 2(2) of the Education and Libraries (Northern Ireland) Order 1986, or

(b) a pupil referral unit as defined by Article 87(1) of the Education (Northern Ireland) Order 1998.

54(2) In sub-paragraph (1) "managers" has the meaning given by Article 2(2) of the Education and Libraries (Northern Ireland) Order 1986.

55(1) The governing body of—

(a) a university receiving financial support under Article 30 of the Education and Libraries (Northern Ireland) Order 1993,

(b) a college of education in respect of which grants are paid under Article 66(2) or (3) of the Education and Libraries (Northern Ireland) Order 1986, or

(c) an institution of further education within the meaning of the Further Education (Northern Ireland) Order 1997.

55(2) In sub-paragraph (1) "governing body" has the meaning given by Article 30(3) of the Education and Libraries (Northern Ireland) Order 1993.

56 Any person providing further education to whom grants, loans or other payments are made under Article 5(1)(b) of the Further Education (Northern Ireland) Order 1997.

PART V

POLICE

England and Wales

969

57   A police authority established under section 3 of the Police Act 1996.

58   The Metropolitan Police Authority established under section 5B of the Police Act 1996.

59   A chief officer of police of a police force in England or Wales.

Northern Ireland.

60   The Northern Ireland Policing Board.

61   The Chief Constable of the Police Service of Northern Ireland.

Miscellaneous

62   The British Transport Police.

63   The Ministry of Defence Police established by section 1 of the Ministry of Defence Police Act 1987.

63A The Civil Nuclear Police Authority.

63B The chief constable of the Civil Nuclear Constabulary.

64   Any person who—
        (a) by virtue of any enactment has the function of nominating individuals who may be appointed as special constables by justices of the peace, and
        (b) is not a public authority by virtue of any other provision of this Act,
        in respect of information relating to the exercise by any person appointed on his nomination of the functions of a special constable.

PART VI

OTHER PUBLIC BODIES AND OFFICES: GENERAL

The Adjudication Panel for Wales.
The Adjudicator for the Inland Revenue and Customs and Excise.
The Administration of Radioactive Substances Advisory Committee.
The Administrative Justice and Tribunals Council.
The Advisory Board on Restricted Patients.
The Advisory Board on the Registration of Homoeopathic Products.
The Advisory Committee for Disabled People in Employment and Training.
The Advisory Committee for the Public Lending Right.
The Advisory Committee on Advertising.
The Advisory Committee on Animal Feedingstuffs.
The Advisory Committee on Borderline Substances.
The Advisory Committee on Business and the Environment.

The Advisory Committee on Business Appointments.
The Advisory Committee on Conscientious Objectors.
The Advisory Committee on Consumer Products and the Environment.
The Advisory Committee on Dangerous Pathogens.
The Advisory Committee on Distinction Awards.
The Advisory Committee on the Government Art Collection.
The Advisory Committee on Hazardous Substances.
The Advisory Committee on Historic Wreck Sites.
An Advisory Committee on Justices of the Peace in England and Wales.
The Advisory Committee on the Microbiological Safety of Food.
The Advisory Committee on Novel Foods and Processes.
The Advisory Committee on Organic Standards.
The Advisory Committee on Overseas Economic and Social Research.
The Advisory Committee on Packaging.
The Advisory Committee on Pesticides.
The Advisory Committee on Releases to the Environment.
The Advisory Committee on Statute Law.
The Advisory Committee on Telecommunications for the Disabled and Elderly.
The Advisory Council on Historical Manuscripts.
The Advisory Council on Libraries.
The Advisory Council on the Misuse of Drugs.
The Advisory Council on National Records and Archives.
The Advisory Council on Public Records.
The Advisory Group on Hepatitis.
The Advisory Group on Medical Countermeasures.
The Advisory Panel on Beacon Councils.
The Advisory Panel on Public Sector Information.
The Advisory Panel on Standards for the Planning Inspectorate.
The Aerospace Committee.
An Agricultural Dwelling House Advisory Committee.
An Agricultural Wages Board for England and Wales.
An Agricultural Wages Committee.
The Agriculture and Environment Biotechnology Commission.
The Agriculture and Horticulture Development Board.
The Air Quality Expert Group.
The Airborne Particles Expert Group.
The Alcohol Education and Research Council.
The All-Wales Medicines Strategy Group.
The Animal Procedures Committee.
The Animal Welfare Advisory Committee.
The Appointments Commission.
The Architects Registration Board.
The Armed Forces Pay Review Body.
The Arts and Humanities Research Council.

The Arts Council of England.

The Arts Council of Wales.

The Audit Commission for Local Authorities and the National Health Service in England.

The Auditor General for Wales.

The Bank of England, in respect of information held for purposes other than those of its functions with respect to—

      (a) monetary policy,

      (b) financial operations intended to support financial institutions for the purposes of maintaining stability, and

      (c) the provision of private banking services and related services.

The Better Regulation Task Force.

The Big Lottery Fund.

The Biotechnology and Biological Sciences Research Council.

The Board of the Pension Protection Fund.

The Britain-Russia Centre and East-West Centre.

The British Association for Central and Eastern Europe.

The British Broadcasting Corporation, in respect of information held for purposes other than those of journalism, art or literature.

The British Coal Corporation.

The British Council.

The British Educational Communications and Technology Agency.

The British Hallmarking Council.

The British Library.

The British Museum.

The British Pharmacopoeia Commission.

The British Railways Board.

British Shipbuilders.

The British Tourist Authority.

The British Transport Police Authority.

The British Waterways Board.

The British Wool Marketing Board.

The Broadcasting Standards Commission.

The Building Regulations Advisory Committee.

The Care Council for Wales.

The Care Quality Commission.

The Central Advisory Committee on War Pensions.

The Central Rail Users' Consultative Committee.

The Certification Officer.

The Channel Four Television Corporation, in respect of information held for purposes other than those of journalism, art or literature.

The Chemical Weapons Convention National Authority Advisory Committee.

The Child Maintenance and Enforcement Commission.

The Children and Family Court Advisory and Support Service.

The Children's Commissioner.

The Children's Commissioner for Wales.

The Civil Aviation Authority.

The Civil Justice Council.

The Civil Procedure Rule Committee.

The Civil Service Appeal Board.

The Civil Service Commissioners.

The Coal Authority.

The Commission for Architecture and the Built Environment.

The Commission for Equality and Human Rights.

The Commission for Integrated Transport.

The Commission for Local Administration in England.

Commission for Rural Communities.

The Commissioner for Older People in Wales.

Commissioner for Parliamentary Investigations.

The Commissioner for Public Appointments.

The Commissioners of Northern Lighthouses.

The Committee for Monitoring Agreements on Tobacco Advertising and Sponsorship.

The Committee on Agricultural Valuation.

The Committee on Carcinogenicity of Chemicals in Food, Consumer Products and the Environment.

The Committee on Chemicals and Materials of Construction For Use in Public Water Supply and Swimming Pools.

The Committee on Climate Change.

The Committee on Medical Aspects of Food and Nutrition Policy.

The Committee on Medical Aspects of Radiation in the Environment.

The Committee on Mutagenicity of Chemicals in Food, Consumer Products and the Environment.

The Committee on Radioactive Waste Management.

The Committee on Safety of Devices.

The Committee on Standards in Public Life.

The Committee on Toxicity of Chemicals in Food, Consumer Products and the Environment.

The Committee on the Medical Effects of Air Pollutants.

The Committee on the Safety of Medicines.

The Commonwealth Scholarship Commission in the United Kingdom.

Communications for Business.

The Community Development Foundation.

The Competition Commission, in relation to information held by it otherwise than as a tribunal.

The Competition Service.

A conservation board established under section 86 of the Countryside and Rights of Way Act 2000.

The Construction Industry Training Board.

Consumer Communications for England.

The Consumer Council for Water.

The Consumer Panel established under section 16 of the Communications Act 2003.

The Council for Healthcare Regulatory Excellence.

The Council for the Central Laboratory of the Research Councils.

The Council for Science and Technology.

The Countryside Council for Wales.

A courts board established under section 4 of the Courts Act 2003.

The Covent Garden Market Authority.

The Criminal Cases Review Commission.

The Criminal Injuries Compensation Authority.

The Criminal Justice Consultative Council.

The Criminal Procedure Rule Committee.

The Crown Court Rule Committee.

The Dartmoor Steering Group and Working Party.

The Darwin Advisory Committee.

The Defence Nuclear Safety Committee.

The Defence Scientific Advisory Council.

The Design Council.

The Diplomatic Service Appeal Board.

The Director of Fair Access to Higher Education.

The Disability Employment Advisory Committee.

The Disability Living Allowance Advisory Board.

The Disabled Persons Transport Advisory Committee.

The Distributed Generation Co-Ordinating Group.

The East of England Industrial Development Board.

The Economic and Social Research Council.

The Electoral Commission.

The Engineering Construction Industry Training Board.

The Engineering and Physical Sciences Research Council.

The English Sports Council.

The English Tourist Board.

The Environment Agency.

The Ethnic Minority Business Forum.

The Expert Advisory Group on AIDS.

The Expert Group on Cryptosporidium in Water Supplies.

An Expert Panel on Air Quality Standards.

The Export Guarantees Advisory Council.

The Family Justice Council.

The Family Procedure Rule Committee.

The Family Proceedings Rules Committee.

The Farm Animal Welfare Council.

The Financial Reporting Advisory Board.

The Financial Services Authority.

The Fire Services Examination Board.

The Firearms Consultative Committee.

The Food Advisory Committee.

Food from Britain.

The Football Licensing Authority.

The Fuel Cell Advisory Panel.

The Fuel Poverty Advisory Group.

The Gaelic Media Service, in respect of information held for purposes other than those of journalism, art or literature.

The Gambling Commission.

Gangmasters Licensing Authority.

The Gene Therapy Advisory Committee.

The General Chiropractic Council.

The General Dental Council.

The General Medical Council.

The General Optical Council.

The General Osteopathic Council.

The General Social Care Council.

The General Teaching Council for England.

The General Teaching Council for Wales.

The Genetic Testing and Insurance Committee.

The Government Hospitality Advisory Committee for the Purchase of Wine.

The Government-Industry Forum on Non-Food Use of Crops.

The Government Chemist.

The Great Britain-China Centre.

The Health Professions CouncilThe Health Protection Agency.

The Health and Safety Commission.

The Health and Safety Executive.

The Health Service Commissioner for England.

The Hearing Aid Council.

Her Majesty's Chief Inspector of Education and Training in Wales or Prif Arolygydd Ei Mawrhydi dros Addysg a Hyfforddiant yng Nghymru.

Her Majesty's Commissioners for Judicial Appointments.

The Higher Education Funding Council for England.

The Higher Education Funding Council for Wales.

The Historic Buildings and Monuments Commission for England.

The Historic Royal Palaces Trust.

The Homes and Communities Agency.

The Horserace Betting Levy Board.

The Horserace Totalisator Board.

Horticulture Research International.

The House of Lords Appointments Commission.

Any housing action trust established under Part III of the Housing Act 1988.

The Human Fertilisation and Embryology Authority.

The Human Tissue Authority.

The Human Genetics Commission.

The Immigration Services Commissioner.

The Imperial War Museum.

The Independent Advisory Group on Teenage Pregnancy.

The Independent Board of Visitors for Military Corrective Training Centres.

The Independent Case Examiner for the Child Support Agency.

The Independent Groundwater Complaints Administrator.

The Independent Living Funds.

Any Independent Monitoring Board established under section 6(2) of the Prison Act 1952.

The Independent Parliamentary Standards Authority.

The Independent Police Complaints Commission.

The Independent Regulator of NHS Foundation Trusts.

The Independent Review Panel for Advertising.

The Independent Review Panel for Borderline Products.

The Independent Scientific Group on Cattle Tuberculosis.

The Independent Television Commission.

The Industrial Development Advisory Board.

The Industrial Injuries Advisory Council.

The Information Commissioner.

The Infrastructure Planning Commission.

The Inland Waterways Advisory Council.

The Insolvency Rules Committee.

The Integrated Administration and Controls System Appeals Panel.

The Intellectual Property Advisory Committee.

Investors in People UK.

The Joint Committee on Vaccination and Immunisation.

The Joint Nature Conservation Committee.

The Joint Prison/Probation Accreditation Panel.

The Judicial Appointments Commission.

The Judicial Appointments and Conduct Ombudsman.

The Judicial Studies Board.

The Know-How Fund Advisory Board.

The Land Registration Rule Committee.

The Law Commission.

The Learning and Skills Council for England.

The Legal Deposit Advisory Panel.

The Legal Services Board.

The Legal Services Commission.

The Local Better Regulation Office.

The Local Government Boundary Commission for England.

The Local Government Boundary Commission for Wales.

The Local Government Commission for England.

A local probation board established under section 4 of the Criminal Justice and Court Services Act 2000.

The London and South East Industrial Development Board.

The London Pensions Fund Authority.

The Low Pay Commission.

The Magistrates' Courts Rules Committee.

The Marine Management Organisation.

The Marshall Aid Commemoration Commission.

The Measurement Advisory Committee.

The Medical Research Council.

The Medicines Commission.

The Museum of London.

The National Army Museum.

The National Audit Office.

The National Care Standards Commission.

The National Employers' Liaison Committee.

The National Employment Panel.

The National Endowment for Science, Technology and the Arts.

The National Forest Company.

The National Gallery.

The National Heritage Memorial Fund.

The National Identity Scheme Commissioner.

The National Information Governance Board for Health and Social Care.

The National Library of Wales.

The National Lottery Commission.

The National Maritime Museum.

The National Museum of Science and Industry.

The National Museums and Galleries of Wales.

The National Museums and Galleries on Merseyside.

The National Policing Improvement Agency.

The National Portrait Gallery.

Natural England.

The Natural Environment Research Council.

The Natural History Museum.

The New Deal Task Force.

The North East Industrial Development Board.

The North West Industrial Development Board.

The Northern Ireland Judicial Appointments Ombudsman.

The Nuclear Decommissioning Authority.

The Nuclear Research Advisory Council.

The Nursing and Midwifery Council.

The Office of Communications.

The Office of Government Commerce.

The Office of the Health Professions Adjudicator.

The Office for Legal Complaints.

The Office of Manpower Economics.

Office for Tenants and Social Landlords.

The Oil and Pipelines Agency.

The Olympic Delivery Authority.

The Olympic Lottery Distributor.

The Ombudsman for the Board of the Pension Protection Fund.

The OSO Board.

The Overseas Service Pensions Scheme Advisory Board.

The Panel on Standards for the Planning Inspectorate.

The Parliamentary Boundary Commission for England.

The Parliamentary Boundary Commission for Scotland.

The Parliamentary Boundary Commission for Wales.

The Parliamentary Commissioner for Administration.

The Parole Board.

The Particle Physics and Astronomy Research Council.

The Pensions Ombudsman.

The Pensions Regulator.

The Pesticide Residues Committee.

The Pesticides Forum.

The Poisons Board.

The Police Advisory Board for England and Wales.

The Police Negotiating Board.

The Political Honours Scrutiny Committee.

The Postgraduate Medical Education and Training Board.

The Post Office.

The Prison Service Pay Review Body.

A probation trust.

The Public Private Partnership Agreement Arbiter.

The Public Services Ombudsman for Wales

The Qualifications Curriculum Authority.

The Race Education and Employment Forum.

The Race Relations Forum.

The Radio Authority.

The Radioactive Waste Management Advisory Committee.

A Regional Cultural Consortium.

Any regional development agency established under the Regional Development Agencies Act 1998, other than the London Development Agency.

Any regional flood defence committee.

The Registrar General for England and Wales.

The Registrar of Public Lending Right.

Remploy Ltd.

The Renewable Energy Advisory Committee.

The Renewables Advisory Board.

Resource: The Council for Museums, Archives and Libraries.

The Review Board for Government Contracts.

The Review Body for Nursing Staff, Midwives, Health Visitors and Professions Allied to Medicine.

The Review Body on Doctors and Dentists Remuneration.

The Reviewing Committee on the Export of Works of Art.

The Royal Air Force Museum.

The Royal Armouries.

The Royal Botanic Gardens, Kew.

The Royal College of Veterinary Surgeons, in respect of information held by it otherwise than as a tribunal.

The Royal Commission on Ancient and Historical Monuments of Wales.

The Royal Commission on Environmental Pollution.

The Royal Commission on Historical Manuscripts.

The Royal Hospital at Chelsea.

The Royal Mint Advisory Committee on the Design of Coins, Medals, Seals and Decorations.

The Royal Pharmaceutical Society of Great Britain, in respect of information held by it otherwise than as a tribunal.

The School Teachers' Review Body.

The Scientific Advisory Committee on Nutrition.

The Scientific Committee on Tobacco and Health.

The Scottish Committee of the Administrative Justice and Tribunals Council.

The Sea Fish Industry Authority.

The Security Industry Authority.

The Senior Salaries Review Body.

The Sentencing Council for England and Wales.

The Sentencing Advisory Panel.

The Sentencing Guidelines Council.

Sianel Pedwar Cymru, in respect of information held for purposes other than those of journalism, art or literature.

Sir John Soane's Museum.

The Small Business Council.

The Small Business Investment Task Force.

The Social Care Institute for Excellence.

The social fund Commissioner appointed under section 65 of the Social Security Administration Act 1992.

The Social Security Advisory Committee.

The Social Services Inspectorate for Wales Advisory Group.

The South West Industrial Development Board.

The Specialist Advisory Committee on Antimicrobial Research.

The Spongiform Encephalopathy Advisory Committee.

The Sports Council for Wales.

The Standards Board for England.

The Standing Advisory Committee on Industrial Property.

The Standing Advisory Committee on Trunk Road Assessment.

The Standing Dental Advisory Committee.

The Steering Committee on Pharmacy Postgraduate Education.

The Strategic Investment Board.

Strategic Rail Authority.

The subsidence adviser appointed under section 46 of the Coal Industry Act 1994.

The Substance Misuse Advisory Panel.

The Sustainable Development Commission.

The Sustainable Energy Policy Advisory Board.

The TB Advisory Group.

The Tate Gallery.

The Teacher Training Agency.

The Technical Advisory Board.

The Theatres Trust.

The Traffic Commissioners, in respect of information held by them otherwise than as a tribunal.

The Training and Development Agency for Schools.

The Treasure Valuation Committee.

The trustee corporation established by section 75 of the Pensions Act 2008.

The UK Advisory Panel for Health Care Workers Infected with Bloodborne Viruses.

The UK Chemicals Stakeholder Forum.

The UK Commission for Employment and Skills.

The UK Sports Council.

The United Kingdom Atomic Energy Authority.

The United Kingdom Xenotransplantation Interim Regulatory Authority.

The University for Industry.

The Unlinked Anonymous Serosurveys Steering Group.

The Unrelated Live Transplant Regulatory Authority.

The Valuation Tribunal Service.

The verderers of the New Forest, in respect of information held by them otherwise than as a tribunal.

The Veterinary Products Committee.

The Veterinary Residues Committee.

The Victoria and Albert Museum.

The Wales Centre for Health.

The Wallace Collection.

The War Pensions Committees.

The Water Regulations Advisory Committee.

The Welsh Committee of the Administrative Justice and Tribunals Council.

The Welsh Committee for Professional Development of Pharmacy.

The Welsh Dental Committee.

The Welsh Industrial Development Advisory Board.

The Welsh Language Board.

The Welsh Medical Committee.

The Welsh Nursing and Midwifery Committee.

The Welsh Optometric Committee.

The Welsh Pharmaceutical Committee.
The Welsh Scientific Advisory Committee.
The Westminster Foundation for Democracy.
The West Midlands Industrial Development Board.
The Wilton Park Academic Council.
The Wine Standards Board of the Vintners' Company.
The Women's National Commission.
The Yorkshire and the Humber and the East Midlands Industrial Development Board.
The Youth Justice Board for England and Wales.
The Zoos Forum.

PART VII

OTHER PUBLIC BODIES AND OFFICES: NORTHERN IRELAND

An advisory committee established under paragraph 25 of the Health and Personal Social
    Services (Northern Ireland) Order 1972.
The Advisory Committee on Justices of the Peace in Northern Ireland.
The Advisory Committee on Pesticides for Northern Ireland.
The Agri-food and Biosciences Institute.
The Agricultural Wages Board for Northern Ireland.
The Arts Council of Northern Ireland.
The Assembly Ombudsman for Northern Ireland.
The Attorney General for Northern Ireland.
The Belfast Harbour Commissioners.
The Board of Trustees of National Museums and Galleries of Northern Ireland.
The Boundary Commission for Northern Ireland.
A central advisory committee established under paragraph 24 of the Health and Personal Social
    Services (Northern Ireland) Order 1972.
The Certification Officer for Northern Ireland.
The Charities Advisory Committee.
The Charity Commission for Northern Ireland
The Chief Electoral Officer for Northern Ireland.
The Chief Inspector of Criminal Justice in Northern Ireland.
The Civil Service Commissioners for Northern Ireland.
Comhairle na Gaelscolaíochta.
Commissioner for Children and Young People for Northern Ireland.
The Commissioner for Public Appointments for Northern Ireland.
The Commissioner for Victims and Survivors for Northern Ireland.
The Construction Industry Training Board.
The consultative Civic Forum referred to in section 56(4) of the Northern Ireland Act 1998.
The Council for Catholic Maintained Schools.
The Council for Nature Conservation and the Countryside.

The County Court Rules Committee (Northern Ireland).

The Criminal Injuries Compensation Appeals Panel for Northern Ireland, in relation to information held by it otherwise than as a tribunal.

A development corporation established under Part III of the Strategic Investment and Regeneration of Sites (Northern Ireland) Order 2003.

The Disability Living Allowance Advisory Board for Northern Ireland.

The Distinction and Meritorious Service Awards Committee.

A district policing partnership.

The Drainage Council for Northern Ireland.

An Education and Library Board established under Article 3 of the Education and Libraries (Northern Ireland) Order 1986.

Enterprise Ulster.

The Equality Commission for Northern Ireland.

The Family Proceedings Rules Committee (Northern Ireland).

The Fisheries Conservancy Board for Northern Ireland.

The General Consumer Council for Northern Ireland.

The General Teaching Council for Northern Ireland.

The Governors of the Armagh Observatory and Planetarium.

The Harbour of Donaghadee Commissioners.

The Health and Safety Agency for Northern Ireland.

The Historic Buildings Council.

The Historic Monuments Council.

The Independent Assessor of Military Complaints Procedures in Northern Ireland.

An independent monitoring board appointed under section 10 of the Prison Act (Northern Ireland) 1953.

The Independent Reviewer of the Northern Ireland (Emergency Provisions) Act.

The Independent Commissioner for Holding Centres.

Invest Northern Ireland.

The Labour Relations Agency.

The Laganside Corporation.

The Law Reform Advisory Committee for Northern Ireland.

The Lay Observer for Northern Ireland.

The Legal Aid Advisory Committee (Northern Ireland).

The Livestock & Meat Commission for Northern Ireland.

The Local Government Staff Commission.

The Londonderry Port and Harbour Commissioners.

The Magistrates' Courts Rules Committee (Northern Ireland).

The Mental Health Commission for Northern Ireland.

The Northern Ireland Audit Office.

The Northern Ireland Authority for Utility Regulation.

The Northern Ireland Building Regulations Advisory Committee.

The Northern Ireland Civil Service Appeal Board.

The Northern Ireland Commissioner for Complaints.

The Northern Ireland Community Relations Council.

The Northern Ireland Council for the Curriculum, Examinations and Assessment.
The Northern Ireland Court of Judicature Rules Committee.
The Northern Ireland Crown Court Rules Committee.
The Northern Ireland Events Company.
The Northern Ireland Fire and Rescue Service Board.
The Northern Ireland Fishery Harbour Authority.
The Northern Ireland Health and Personal Social Services Regulation and Improvement Authority.
The Northern Ireland Higher Education Council.
The Northern Ireland Housing Executive.
The Northern Ireland Human Rights Commission.
The Northern Ireland Insolvency Rules Committee.
The Northern Ireland Judicial Appointments Commission.
The Northern Ireland Law Commission.
The Northern Ireland Legal Services Commission.
The Northern Ireland Local Government Officers' Superannuation Committee.
The Northern Ireland Museums Council.
The Northern Ireland Pig Production Development Committee.
The Northern Ireland Practice and Education Council for Nursing and Midwifery.
The Northern Ireland Social Care Council.
The Northern Ireland Tourist Board.
The Northern Ireland Transport Holding Company.
The Parades Commission.
Parole Commissioners for Northern Ireland.
The Pharmaceutical Society of Northern Ireland, in respect of information held by it otherwise than as a tribunal.
The Poisons Board (Northern Ireland).
The Police Ombudsman for Northern Ireland.
The Probation Board for Northern Ireland.
The Rural Development Council for Northern Ireland.
The Sentence Review Commissioners appointed under section 1 of the Northern Ireland (Sentences) Act 1998.
The social fund Commissioner appointed under Article 37 of the Social Security (Northern Ireland) Order 1998.
The Sports Council for Northern Ireland.
The Staff Commission for Education and Library Boards.
The Statistics Advisory Committee.
The Statute Law Committee for Northern Ireland.
A sub-group established under section 21 of the Police (Northern Ireland) Act 2000.
Ulster Supported Employment Ltd.
The Warrenpoint Harbour Authority.
The Waste Management Advisory Board.
The Youth Council for Northern Ireland.

SCHEDULE 2

THE COMMISSIONER AND THE TRIBUNAL

Section 18(4)

PART I

PROVISION CONSEQUENTIAL ON S 18(1) AND (2)

General

1(1) Any reference in any enactment, instrument or document to the Data Protection Commissioner or the Data Protection Registrar shall be construed, in relation to any time after the commencement of section 18(1), as a reference to the Information Commissioner.

2(1) Any reference in this Act or in any instrument under this Act to the Commissioner shall be construed, in relation to any time before the commencement of section 18(1), as a reference to the Data Protection Commissioner.

Remainder not reproduced

PART II

AMENDMENTS RELATING TO EXTENSION OF FUNCTIONS OF COMMISSIONER AND TRIBUNAL

Information provided to Commissioner or Tribunal

18   In section 58 of that Act (disclosure of information to Commissioner or Tribunal), after "this Act" there is inserted "or the Freedom of Information Act 2000".

19(1)   Section 59 of that Act (confidentiality of information) is amended as follows.

(2)   In subsections (1) and (2), for "this Act", wherever occurring, there is substituted "the information Acts".

(3)   After subsection (3) there is inserted—
        "(4)   In this section "the information Acts" means this Act and the Freedom of Information Act 2000.".

Deputy commissioners

20(1)   Paragraph 4 of Schedule 5 to that Act (officers and staff) is amended as follows.

(2)   In sub-paragraph (1)(a), after "a deputy commissioner" there is inserted "or two deputy commissioners".

(3)   After sub-paragraph (1) there is inserted—

"(1A) The Commissioner shall, when appointing any second deputy commissioner, specify which of the Commissioner's functions are to be performed, in the circumstances referred to in paragraph 5(1), by each of the deputy commissioners.".

Exercise of Commissioner's functions by others

21(1) Paragraph 5 of Schedule 5 to that Act (exercise of functions of Commissioner during vacancy etc) is amended as follows.

(2) In sub-paragraph (1)—

(a) after "deputy commissioner" there is inserted "or deputy commissioners", and

(b) after "this Act" there is inserted "or the Freedom of Information Act 2000".

(3) In sub-paragraph (2) after "this Act" there is inserted "or the Freedom of Information Act 2000".

Money

22 In paragraph 9(1) of Schedule 5 to that Act (money) for "or section 159 of the Consumer Credit Act 1974" there is substituted ", under section 159 of the Consumer Credit Act 1974 or under the Freedom of Information Act 2000".

SCHEDULE 3

POWERS OF ENTRY AND INSPECTION

Section 55

Issue of warrants

1(1) If a circuit judge or a District Judge (Magistrates' Courts) is satisfied by information on oath supplied by the Commissioner that there are reasonable grounds for suspecting—

(a) that a public authority has failed or is failing to comply with—

(i) any of the requirements of Part I of this Act,

(ii) so much of a decision notice as requires steps to be taken, or

(iii) an information notice or an enforcement notice, or

(b) that an offence under section 77 has been or is being committed,

and that evidence of such a failure to comply or of the commission of the offence is to be found on any premises specified in the information, he may, subject to paragraph 2, grant a warrant to the Commissioner.

(2) A warrant issued under sub-paragraph (1) shall authorise the Commissioner or any of his officers or staff at any time within seven days of the date of the warrant—

(a) to enter and search the premises,

(b) to inspect and seize any documents or other material found there which may be such evidence as is mentioned in that sub-paragraph, and

      (c) to inspect, examine, operate and test any equipment found there in which information held by the public authority may be recorded.

2(1) A judge shall not issue a warrant under this Schedule unless he is satisfied—

      (a) that the Commissioner has given seven days' notice in writing to the occupier of the premises in question demanding access to the premises, and

      (b) that either—

          (i) access was demanded at a reasonable hour and was unreasonably refused, or

          (ii) although entry to the premises was granted, the occupier unreasonably refused to comply with a request by the Commissioner or any of the Commissioner's officers or staff to permit the Commissioner or the officer or member of staff to do any of the things referred to in paragraph 1(2), and

      (c) that the occupier, has, after the refusal, been notified by the Commissioner of the application for the warrant and has had an opportunity of being heard by the judge on the question whether or not it should be issued.

(2) Sub-paragraph (1) shall not apply if the judge is satisfied that the case is one of urgency or that compliance with those provisions would defeat the object of the entry.

3   A judge who issues a warrant under this Schedule shall also issue two copies of it and certify them clearly as copies.

Execution of warrants

4   A person executing a warrant issued under this Schedule may use such reasonable force as may be necessary.

5   A warrant issued under this Schedule shall be executed at a reasonable hour unless it appears to the person executing it that there are grounds for suspecting that the evidence in question would not be found if it were so executed.

6(1) If the premises in respect of which a warrant is issued under this Schedule are occupied by a public authority and any officer or employee of the authority is present when the warrant is executed, he shall be shown the warrant and supplied with a copy of it; and if no such officer or employee is present a copy of the warrant shall be left in a prominent place on the premises.

(2) If the premises in respect of which a warrant is issued under this Schedule are occupied by a person other than a public authority and he is present when the warrant is executed, he shall be shown the warrant and supplied with a copy of it; and if that person is not present a copy of the warrant shall be left in a prominent place on the premises.

7(1) A person seizing anything in pursuance of a warrant under this Schedule shall give a receipt for it if asked to do so.

(2) Anything so seized may be retained for so long as is necessary in all the circumstances but the person in occupation of the premises in question shall be given a copy of anything that

is seized if he so requests and the person executing the warrant considers that it can be done without undue delay.

Matters exempt from inspection and seizure

8   The powers of inspection and seizure conferred by a warrant issued under this Schedule shall not be exercisable in respect of information which is exempt information by virtue of section 23(1) or 24(1).

9(1) Subject to the provisions of this paragraph, the powers of inspection and seizure conferred by a warrant issued under this Schedule shall not be exercisable in respect of—

    (a) any communication between a professional legal adviser and his client in connection with the giving of legal advice to the client with respect to his obligations, liabilities or rights under this Act, or

    (b) any communication between a professional legal adviser and his client, or between such an adviser or his client and any other person, made in connection with or in contemplation of proceedings under or arising out of this Act (including proceedings before the Tribunal) and for the purposes of such proceedings.

(2) Sub-paragraph (1) applies also to—

    (a) any copy or other record of any such communication as is there mentioned, and

    (b) any document or article enclosed with or referred to in any such communication if made in connection with the giving of any advice or, as the case may be, in connection with or in contemplation of and for the purposes of such proceedings as are there mentioned.

(3) This paragraph does not apply to anything in the possession of any person other than the professional legal adviser or his client or to anything held with the intention of furthering a criminal purpose.

(4) In this paragraph references to the client of a professional legal adviser include references to any person representing such a client.

10   If the person in occupation of any premises in respect of which a warrant is issued under this Schedule objects to the inspection or seizure under the warrant of any material on the grounds that it consists partly of matters in respect of which those powers are not exercisable, he shall, if the person executing the warrant so requests, furnish that person with a copy of so much of the material in relation to which the powers are exercisable.

Return of warrants

11   A warrant issued under this Schedule shall be returned to the court from which it was issued—

    (a) after being executed, or

    (b) if not executed within the time authorised for its execution;

and the person by whom any such warrant is executed shall make an endorsement on it stating what powers have been exercised by him under the warrant.

Offences

12 Any person who—
    (a) intentionally obstructs a person in the execution of a warrant issued under this Schedule, or
    (b) fails without reasonable excuse to give any person executing such a warrant such assistance as he may reasonably require for the execution of the warrant,
is guilty of an offence.

Vessels, vehicles etc

13 In this Schedule "premises" includes any vessel, vehicle, aircraft or hovercraft, and references to the occupier of any premises include references to the person in charge of any vessel, vehicle, aircraft or hovercraft.

Scotland and Northern Ireland

14 In the application of this Schedule to Scotland—
    (a) for any reference to a circuit judge there is substituted a reference to the sheriff, and
    (b) for any reference to information on oath there is substituted a reference to evidence on oath.

15 In the application of this Schedule to Northern Ireland—
    (a) for any reference to a circuit judge there is substituted a reference to a county court judge, and
    (b) for any reference to information on oath there is substituted a reference to a complaint on oath.

SCHEDULE 4

APPEAL PROCEEDINGS: AMENDMENTS OF SCHEDULE 6

TO DATA PROTECTION ACT 1998

Section 61(1)

Not reproduced

SCHEDULE 5

AMENDMENTS OF PUBLIC RECORDS LEGISLATION

Section 67

Not reproduced

SCHEDULE 6

FURTHER AMENDMENTS OF DATA PROTECTION ACT 1998

Section 73

Not reproduced

SCHEDULE 7

DISCLOSURE OF INFORMATION BY OMBUDSMEN

Section 76(2)

Not reproduced

SCHEDULE 8

REPEALS

Section 86

Not reproduced

Data Protection Act 1998

(as amended to 1 February 2010)

CHAPTER 29

An Act to make new provision for the regulation of the processing of information relating to individuals, including the obtaining, holding, use or disclosure of such information.

16 July 1998

BE IT ENACTED by the Queen's most Excellent Majesty, by and with the advice and consent of the Lords Spiritual and Temporal, and Commons, in this present Parliament assembled, and by the authority of the same, as follows:–

PART I

PRELIMINARY

PART II

RIGHTS OF DATA SUBJECTS AND OTHERS

PART III

NOTIFICATION BY DATA CONTROLLERS

PART IV

EXEMPTIONS

PART V

ENFORCEMENT

PART VI

MISCELLANEOUS AND GENERAL

SCHEDULES

PART I

PRELIMINARY

Basic interpretative provisions

1(1)   In this Act, unless the context otherwise requires–
        "data" means information which–
        (a) is being processed by means of equipment operating automatically in response to instructions given for that purpose,
        (b) is recorded with the intention that it should be processed by means of such equipment,
        (c) is recorded as part of a relevant filing system or with the intention that it should form part of a relevant filing system,
        (d) does not fall within paragraph (a), (b) or (c) but forms part of an accessible record as defined by section 68; or

(e) is recorded information held by a public authority and does not fall within any of paragraphs (a) to (d);

"data controller" means, subject to subsection (4), a person who (either alone or jointly or in common with other persons) determines the purposes for which and the manner in which any personal data are, or are to be, processed;

"data processor", in relation to personal data, means any person (other than an employee of the data controller) who processes the data on behalf of the data controller;

"data subject" means an individual who is the subject of personal data;

"personal data" means data which relate to a living individual who can be identified–
  (a) from those data, or
  (b) from those data and other information which is in the possession of, or is likely to come into the possession of, the data controller,

and includes any expression of opinion about the individual and any indication of the intentions of the data controller or any other person in respect of the individual;

"processing", in relation to information or data, means obtaining, recording or holding the information or data or carrying out any operation or set of operations on the information or data, including–
  (a) organisation, adaptation or alteration of the information or data,
  (b) retrieval, consultation or use of the information or data,
  (c) disclosure of the information or data by transmission, dissemination or otherwise making available, or
  (d) alignment, combination, blocking, erasure or destruction of the information or data;

"public authority" means a public authority as defined by the Freedom of Information Act 2000 or a Scottish public authority as defined by the Freedom of Information (Scotland) Act 2002;

"relevant filing system" means any set of information relating to individuals to the extent that, although the information is not processed by means of equipment operating automatically in response to instructions given for that purpose, the set is structured, either by reference to individuals or by reference to criteria relating to individuals, in such a way that specific information relating to a particular individual is readily accessible.

(2) In this Act, unless the context otherwise requires–
  (a) "obtaining" or "recording", in relation to personal data, includes obtaining or recording the information to be contained in the data, and
  (b) "using" or "disclosing", in relation to personal data, includes using or disclosing the information contained in the data.

(3) In determining for the purposes of this Act whether any information is recorded with the intention–
  (a) that it should be processed by means of equipment operating automatically in response to instructions given for that purpose, or
  (b) that it should form part of a relevant filing system,

it is immaterial that it is intended to be so processed or to form part of such a system only after being transferred to a country or territory outside the European Economic Area.

(4)   Where personal data are processed only for purposes for which they are required by or under any enactment to be processed, the person on whom the obligation to process the data is imposed by or under that enactment is for the purposes of this Act the data controller.

(5)   In paragraph (e) of the definition of "data" in subsection (1), the reference to information "held" by a public authority shall be construed in accordance with section 3(2) of the Freedom of Information Act 2000 or section 3(2), (4) and (5) of the Freedom of Information (Scotland) Act 2002.

(6)   Where
  (a) section 7 of the Freedom of Information Act 2000 prevents Parts I to V of that Act or
  (b) section 7(1) of the Freedom of Information (Scotland) Act 2002 prevents that Act,
from applying to certain information held by a public authority, that information is not to be treated for the purposes of paragraph (e) of the definition of "data" in subsection (1) as held by a public authority.

NOTES

Defined terms

"accessible record": s 68 and Schs 11 and 12
"the Commissioner": s 70(1)
"data": s 1(1)
"data controller": ss1(1) and (4) and 63(3)
"data processor": s 1(1)
"data protection principles": s 4 and Sch1
"data subject": s 1(1)
"disclosing": s 1(2)(b)
"EEA State": s 70(1)
"enactment": s 70(1)
"held": s 1(6) and Freedom of Information Act 2000, s 3(2)

"obtaining": s 1(2)(a)
"personal data": s 1(1)
"processing": s 1(1)
"public authority": s 1(1) and Freedom of Information Act 2000, s 3(1)
"recording": s 1(2)(a)
"relevant filing system": s 1(1)
"sensitive personal data": s 2
"the special purposes": s 3
"the Tribunal": s 70(1)
"using": s 1(2)(b)

Sensitive personal data

2   In this Act "sensitive personal data" means personal data consisting of information as to—
  (a) the racial or ethnic origin of the data subject,
  (b) his political opinions,
  (c) his religious beliefs or other beliefs of a similar nature,
  (d) whether he is a member of a trade union (within the meaning of the Trade Union and Labour Relations (Consolidation) Act 1992,

(e) his physical or mental health or condition,

(f) his sexual life,

(g) the commission or alleged commission by him of any offence, or

(h) any proceedings for any offence committed or alleged to have been committed by him, the disposal of such proceedings or the sentence of any court in such proceedings.

NOTES

Defined terms
"data subject": s 1(1)

"sensitive personal data": s 2

The special purposes

3   In this Act "the special purposes" means any one or more of the following–

(a) the purposes of journalism,

(b) artistic purposes, and

(c) literary purposes.

The data protection principles

4(1)   References in this Act to the data protection principles are to the principles set out in Part I of Schedule 1.

(2)   Those principles are to be interpreted in accordance with Part II of Schedule 1.

(3)   Schedule 2 (which applies to all personal data) and Schedule 3 (which applies only to sensitive personal data) set out conditions applying for the purposes of the first principle; and Schedule 4 sets out cases in which the eighth principle does not apply.

(4)   Subject to section 27(1), it shall be the duty of a data controller to comply with the data protection principles in relation to all personal data with respect to which he is the data controller.

NOTES

Defined terms
"data controller": s 1(1)
"data protection principles": s 4 and Sch1

"personal data": s 1(1)
"sensitive personal data": s 2

Application of Act

5(1)   Except as otherwise provided by or under section 54, this Act applies to a data controller in respect of any data only if–

(a) the data controller is established in the United Kingdom and the data are processed in the context of that establishment, or

(b) the data controller is established neither in the United Kingdom nor in any other EEA State but uses equipment in the United Kingdom for processing the data otherwise than for the purposes of transit through the United Kingdom.

(2) A data controller falling within subsection (1)(b) must nominate for the purposes of this Act a representative established in the United Kingdom.

(3) For the purposes of subsections (1) and (2), each of the following is to be treated as established in the United Kingdom–

(a) an individual who is ordinarily resident in the United Kingdom,

(b) a body incorporated under the law of, or of any part of, the United Kingdom,

(c) a partnership or other unincorporated association formed under the law of any part of the United Kingdom, and

(d) any person who does not fall within paragraph (a), (b) or (c) but maintains in the United Kingdom–

(i) an office, branch or agency through which he carries on any activity, or

(ii) a regular practice;

and the reference to establishment in any other EEA State has a corresponding meaning.

NOTES

Defined terms

"data": s 1(1)

"data controller": s 1(1)

"EEA State": s 70(1)

"established": s 5(3)

"processing": s 1(1)

The Commissioner and the Tribunal

6(1) For the purposes of this Act and of the Freedom of Information Act 2000 there shall be an officer known as the Information Commissioner (in this Act referred to as "the Commissioner").

(2) The Commissioner shall be appointed by Her Majesty by Letters Patent.

(7) Schedule 5 has effect in relation to the Commissioner .

NOTES

Defined terms

"processing": s 1(1)

"Commissioner": s 6(1)

"data controller": s 1(1)

"data subject": s 1(1)

"Tribunal": s 6(3)

PART II

RIGHTS OF DATA SUBJECTS AND OTHERS

Right of access to personal data

7(1) Subject to the following provisions of this section and to sections 8, 9 and 9A, an individual is entitled–

(a) to be informed by any data controller whether personal data of which that individual is the data subject are being processed by or on behalf of that data controller,

(b) if that is the case, to be given by the data controller a description of–

(i) the personal data of which that individual is the data subject,

(ii) the purposes for which they are being or are to be processed, and

(iii) the recipients or classes of recipients to whom they are or may be disclosed,

(c) to have communicated to him in an intelligible form–

(i) the information constituting any personal data of which that individual is the data subject, and

(ii) any information available to the data controller as to the source of those data, and

(d) where the processing by automatic means of personal data of which that individual is the data subject for the purpose of evaluating matters relating to him such as, for example, his performance at work, his creditworthiness, his reliability or his conduct, has constituted or is likely to constitute the sole basis for any decision significantly affecting him, to be informed by the data controller of the logic involved in that decision-taking.

(2) A data controller is not obliged to supply any information under subsection (1) unless he has received–

(a) a request in writing, and

(b) except in prescribed cases, such fee (not exceeding the prescribed maximum) as he may require.

(3) Where a data controller–

(a) reasonably requires further information in order to satisfy himself as to the identity of the person making a request under this section and to locate the information which that person seeks, and

(b) has informed him of that requirement,

the data controller is not obliged to comply with the request unless he is supplied with that further information.

(4) Where a data controller cannot comply with the request without disclosing information relating to another individual who can be identified from that information, he is not obliged to comply with the request unless–

(a) the other individual has consented to the disclosure of the information to the person making the request, or

(b) it is reasonable in all the circumstances to comply with the request without the consent of the other individual.

(5)   In subsection (4) the reference to information relating to another individual includes a reference to information identifying that individual as the source of the information sought by the request; and that subsection is not to be construed as excusing a data controller from communicating so much of the information sought by the request as can be communicated without disclosing the identity of the other individual concerned, whether by the omission of names or other identifying particulars or otherwise.

(6)   In determining for the purposes of subsection (4)(b) whether it is reasonable in all the circumstances to comply with the request without the consent of the other individual concerned, regard shall be had, in particular, to–
        (a) any duty of confidentiality owed to the other individual,
        (b) any steps taken by the data controller with a view to seeking the consent of the other individual,
        (c) whether the other individual is capable of giving consent, and
        (d) any express refusal of consent by the other individual.

(7)   An individual making a request under this section may, in such cases as may be prescribed, specify that his request is limited to personal data of any prescribed description.

(8)   Subject to subsection (4), a data controller shall comply with a request under this section promptly and in any event before the end of the prescribed period beginning with the relevant day.

(9)   If a court is satisfied on the application of any person who has made a request under the foregoing provisions of this section that the data controller in question has failed to comply with the request in contravention of those provisions, the court may order him to comply with the request.

(10)   In this section–
        "prescribed" means prescribed by the Secretary of State by regulations;
        "the prescribed maximum" means such amount as may be prescribed;
        "the prescribed period" means forty days or such other period as may be prescribed;
        "the relevant day", in relation to a request under this section, means the day on which the data controller receives the request or, if later, the first day on which the data controller has both the required fee and the information referred to in subsection (3).

(11)   Different amounts or periods may be prescribed under this section in relation to different cases.

NOTES

Defined terms
"court" s 15(1)
"data controller": s 1(1)
"data subject": s 1(1)
"personal data": s 1(1)

"prescribed period": s 7(10)
"processing": s 1(1)
"recipients": s 70(1)
"relevant day": s 7(10)

"prescribed": s 7(10)
"prescribed maximum": s 7(10)

Subordinate legislation
Data Protection (Subject Access) (Fees and Miscellaneous
  Provisions) Regulations 2000, SI 2000/191.
  Reproduced at p 1148 ff.

Provisions supplementary to section 7

8(1)   The Secretary of State may by regulations provide that, in such cases as may be prescribed, a request for information under any provision of subsection (1) of section 7 is to be treated as extending also to information under other provisions of that subsection.

(2)   The obligation imposed by section 7(1)(c)(i) must be complied with by supplying the data subject with a copy of the information in permanent form unless–

(a) the supply of such a copy is not possible or would involve disproportionate effort, or

(b) the data subject agrees otherwise;

and where any of the information referred to in section 7(1)(c)(i) is expressed in terms which are not intelligible without explanation the copy must be accompanied by an explanation of those terms.

(3)   Where a data controller has previously complied with a request made under section 7 by an individual, the data controller is not obliged to comply with a subsequent identical or similar request under that section by that individual unless a reasonable interval has elapsed between compliance with the previous request and the making of the current request.

(4)   In determining for the purposes of subsection (3) whether requests under section 7 are made at reasonable intervals, regard shall be had to the nature of the data, the purpose for which the data are processed and the frequency with which the data are altered.

(5)   Section 7(1)(d) is not to be regarded as requiring the provision of information as to the logic involved in any decision-taking if, and to the extent that, the information constitutes a trade secret.

(6)   The information to be supplied pursuant to a request under section 7 must be supplied by reference to the data in question at the time when the request is received, except that it may take account of any amendment or deletion made between that time and the time when the information is supplied, being an amendment or deletion that would have been made regardless of the receipt of the request.

(7)   For the purposes of section 7(4) and (5) another individual can be identified from the information being disclosed if he can be identified from that information, or from that and any other information which, in the reasonable belief of the data controller, is likely to be in, or to come into, the possession of the data subject making the request.

NOTES

Defined terms
"data": s 1(1)
"data controller": s 1(1)
"data subject": s 1(1)
"processing": s 1(1)

Subordinate legislation
Data Protection (Subject Access) (Fees and Miscellaneous
   Provisions) Regulations 2000, SI 2000/191.
   Reproduced at p 1148 ff.

Application of section 7 where data controller is credit reference agency

9(1)   Where the data controller is a credit reference agency, section 7 has effect subject to the provisions of this section.

(2)   An individual making a request under section 7 may limit his request to personal data relevant to his financial standing, and shall be taken to have so limited his request unless the request shows a contrary intention.

(3)   Where the data controller receives a request under section 7 in a case where personal data of which the individual making the request is the data subject are being processed by or on behalf of the data controller, the obligation to supply information under that section includes an obligation to give the individual making the request a statement, in such form as may be prescribed by the Secretary of State by regulations, of the individual's rights–

    (a) under section 159 of the Consumer Credit Act 1974 , and

    (b) to the extent required by the prescribed form, under this Act.

NOTES

Defined terms
"credit reference agency": s 70(1)
"data controller": s 1(1)
 "data subject": s 1(1)
"personal data": s 1(1)

"prescribed": s 7(10)

Subordinate legislation
Data Protection (Subject Access) (Fees and Miscellaneous
   Provisions) Regulations 2000, SI 2000/191.
   Reproduced at p 1148 ff.

Unstructured personal data held by public authorities

9A(1)   In this section "unstructured personal data" means any personal data falling within paragraph (e) of the definition of "data" in section 1(1), other than information which is recorded as part of, or with the intention that it should form part of, any set of information relating to individuals to the extent that the set is structured by reference to individuals or by reference to criteria relating to individuals.

(2)   A public authority is not obliged to comply with subsection (1) of section 7 in relation to any unstructured personal data unless the request under that section contains a description of the data.

(3)   Even if the data are described by the data subject in his request, a public authority is not obliged to comply with subsection (1) of section 7 in relation to unstructured

personal data if the authority estimates that the cost of complying with the request so far as relating to those data would exceed the appropriate limit.

(4) Subsection (3) does not exempt the public authority from its obligation to comply with paragraph (a) of section 7(1) in relation to the unstructured personal data unless the estimated cost of complying with that paragraph alone in relation to those data would exceed the appropriate limit.

(5) In subsections (3) and (4) "the appropriate limit" means such amount as may be prescribed by the Secretary of State by regulations, and different amounts may be prescribed in relation to different cases.

(6) Any estimate for the purposes of this section must be made in accordance with regulations under section 12(5) of the Freedom of Information Act 2000.

NOTES

Defined terms
"data": s 1(1)
"data subject": s 1(1)

"personal data": s 1(1)
"public authority": FOIA s 3(1)

Right to prevent processing likely to cause damage or distress

10(1) Subject to subsection (2), an individual is entitled at any time by notice in writing to a data controller to require the data controller at the end of such period as is reasonable in the circumstances to cease, or not to begin, processing, or processing for a specified purpose or in a specified manner, any personal data in respect of which he is the data subject, on the ground that, for specified reasons–
    (a) the processing of those data or their processing for that purpose or in that manner is causing or is likely to cause substantial damage or substantial distress to him or to another, and
    (b) that damage or distress is or would be unwarranted.

(2) Subsection (1) does not apply–
    (a) in a case where any of the conditions in paragraphs 1 to 4 of Schedule 2 is met, or
    (b) in such other cases as may be prescribed by the Secretary of State by order.

(3) The data controller must within twenty-one days of receiving a notice under subsection (1) ("the data subject notice") give the individual who gave it a written notice–
    (a) stating that he has complied or intends to comply with the data subject notice, or
    (b) stating his reasons for regarding the data subject notice as to any extent unjustified and the extent (if any) to which he has complied or intends to comply with it.

(4) If a court is satisfied, on the application of any person who has given a notice under subsection (1) which appears to the court to be justified (or to be justified to any extent),

that the data controller in question has failed to comply with the notice, the court may order him to take such steps for complying with the notice (or for complying with it to that extent) as the court thinks fit.

(5)   The failure by a data subject to exercise the right conferred by subsection (1) or section 11(1) does not affect any other right conferred on him by this Part.

NOTES

Defined terms
"court": s 15(1)
"data": s 1(1)
"data controller": s 1(1)
"data subject": s 1(1)

"data subject notice": s 10(3)
"personal data": s 1(1)
"prescribed": s 7(10)
"processing": s 1(1)

Right to prevent processing for purposes of direct marketing

11(1)   An individual is entitled at any time by notice in writing to a data controller to require the data controller at the end of such period as is reasonable in the circumstances to cease, or not to begin, processing for the purposes of direct marketing personal data in respect of which he is the data subject.

(2)   If the court is satisfied, on the application of any person who has given a notice under subsection (1), that the data controller has failed to comply with the notice, the court may order him to take such steps for complying with the notice as the court thinks fit.

(2A)   This section shall not apply in relation to the processing of such data as are mentioned in paragraph (1) of regulation 8 of the Telecommunications (Data Protection and Privacy) Regulations 1999 (processing of telecommunications billing data for certain marketing purposes) for the purposes mentioned in paragraph (2) of that regulation.

(3)   In this section "direct marketing" means the communication (by whatever means) of any advertising or marketing material which is directed to particular individuals.

NOTES

Defined terms
"court": s 15(1)
"data controller": s 1(1)

"direct marketing": s 11(3)
"data subject": s 1(1)
"personal data": s 1(1)
"processing": s 1(1)

Rights in relation to automated decision-taking

12(1)   An individual is entitled at any time, by notice in writing to any data controller, to require the data controller to ensure that no decision taken by or on behalf of the data controller which significantly affects that individual is based solely on the processing by automatic means of personal data in respect of which that individual is the data subject for the purpose of evaluating matters relating to him such as, for example, his performance at work, his creditworthiness, his reliability or his conduct.

(2)   Where, in a case where no notice under subsection (1) has effect, a decision which significantly affects an individual is based solely on such processing as is mentioned in subsection (1)–

(a)   the data controller must as soon as reasonably practicable notify the individual that the decision was taken on that basis, and

(b)   the individual is entitled, within twenty-one days of receiving that notification from the data controller, by notice in writing to require the data controller to reconsider the decision or to take a new decision otherwise than on that basis.

(3)   The data controller must, within twenty-one days of receiving a notice under subsection (2)(b) ("the data subject notice") give the individual a written notice specifying the steps that he intends to take to comply with the data subject notice.

(4)   A notice under subsection (1) does not have effect in relation to an exempt decision; and nothing in subsection (2) applies to an exempt decision.

(5)   In subsection (4) "exempt decision" means any decision–

(a)   in respect of which the condition in subsection (6) and the condition in subsection (7) are met, or

(b)   which is made in such other circumstances as may be prescribed by the Secretary of State by order.

(6)   The condition in this subsection is that the decision–

(a)   is taken in the course of steps taken–

(i)   for the purpose of considering whether to enter into a contract with the data subject,

(ii) with a view to entering into such a contract, or

(iii) in the course of performing such a contract, or

(b)   is authorised or required by or under any enactment.

(7)   The condition in this subsection is that either–

(a)   the effect of the decision is to grant a request of the data subject, or

(b)   steps have been taken to safeguard the legitimate interests of the data subject (for example, by allowing him to make representations).

(8)   If a court is satisfied on the application of a data subject that a person taking a decision in respect of him ("the responsible person") has failed to comply with subsection (1) or (2)(b), the court may order the responsible person to reconsider the decision, or to take a new decision which is not based solely on such processing as is mentioned in subsection (1).

(9)   An order under subsection (8) shall not affect the rights of any person other than the data subject and the responsible person.

NOTES

Defined terms
"court": s 15(1)
"data controller": s 1(1)

"exempt decision": s 12(5)
"personal data": s 1(1)
"prescribed": s 7(10)

"data subject": s 1(1)
"data subject notice": s 12(3)
"enactment": s 70(1)

"processing": s 1(1)
"responsible person": s 12(8)

Compensation for failure to comply with certain requirements

13(1)   An individual who suffers damage by reason of any contravention by a data controller of any of the requirements of this Act is entitled to compensation from the data controller for that damage.

(2)   An individual who suffers distress by reason of any contravention by a data controller of any of the requirements of this Act is entitled to compensation from the data controller for that distress if–

(a) the individual also suffers damage by reason of the contravention, or

(b) the contravention relates to the processing of personal data for the special purposes.

(3)   In proceedings brought against a person by virtue of this section it is a defence to prove that he had taken such care as in all the circumstances was reasonably required to comply with the requirement concerned.

NOTES

Defined terms
"data controller": s 1(1)
"personal data": s 1(1)

"processing": s 1(1)
"special purposes": s 3

Rectification, blocking, erasure and destruction

14(1)   If a court is satisfied on the application of a data subject that personal data of which the applicant is the subject are inaccurate, the court may order the data controller to rectify, block, erase or destroy those data and any other personal data in respect of which he is the data controller and which contain an expression of opinion which appears to the court to be based on the inaccurate data.

(2)   Subsection (1) applies whether or not the data accurately record information received or obtained by the data controller from the data subject or a third party but where the data accurately record such information, then–

(a) if the requirements mentioned in paragraph 7 of Part II of Schedule 1 have been complied with, the court may, instead of making an order under subsection (1), make an order requiring the data to be supplemented by such statement of the true facts relating to the matters dealt with by the data as the court may approve, and

(b) if all or any of those requirements have not been complied with, the court may, instead of making an order under that subsection, make such order as it thinks fit for securing compliance with those requirements with or without a further order requiring the data to be supplemented by such a statement as is mentioned in paragraph (a).

(3) Where the court
   (a) makes an order under subsection (1), or
   (b) is satisfied on the application of a data subject that personal data of which he was the data subject and which have been rectified, blocked, erased or destroyed were inaccurate,

it may, where it considers it reasonably practicable, order the data controller to notify third parties to whom the data have been disclosed of the rectification, blocking, erasure or destruction.

(4) If a court is satisfied on the application of a data subject–
   (a) that he has suffered damage by reason of any contravention by a data controller of any of the requirements of this Act in respect of any personal data, in circumstances entitling him to compensation under section 13, and
   (b) that there is a substantial risk of further contravention in respect of those data in such circumstances,

the court may order the rectification, blocking, erasure or destruction of any of those data.

(5) Where the court makes an order under subsection (4) it may, where it considers it reasonably practicable, order the data controller to notify third parties to whom the data have been disclosed of the rectification, blocking, erasure or destruction.

(6) In determining whether it is reasonably practicable to require such notification as is mentioned in subsection (3) or (5) the court shall have regard, in particular, to the number of persons who would have to be notified.

NOTES

Defined terms
"court": s 15(1)
"data" s 1(1)
"data controller": s 1(1)

"data subject": s 1(1)
"inaccurate (in relation to data)": s 70(2)
"personal data": s 1(1)
"third party": s 70(1)

Jurisdiction and procedure

15(1) The jurisdiction conferred by sections 7 to 14 is exercisable by the High Court or a county court or, in Scotland, by the Court of Session or the sheriff.

(2) For the purpose of determining any question whether an applicant under subsection (9) of section 7 is entitled to the information which he seeks (including any question whether any relevant data are exempt from that section by virtue of Part IV) a court may require the information constituting any data processed by or on behalf of the data controller and any information as to the logic involved in any decision-taking as mentioned in section 7(1)(d) to be made available for its own inspection but shall not, pending the determination of that question in the applicant's favour, require the

information sought by the applicant to be disclosed to him or his representatives whether by discovery (or, in Scotland, recovery) or otherwise.

NOTES

Defined terms   "data controller": s 1(1)
"data": s 1(1)   "processing": s 1(1)

PART III

NOTIFICATION BY DATA CONTROLLERS

Preliminary

16(1)   In this Part "the registrable particulars", in relation to a data controller, means–

    (a) his name and address,

    (b) if he has nominated a representative for the purposes of this Act, the name and address of the representative,

    (c) a description of the personal data being or to be processed by or on behalf of the data controller and of the category or categories of data subject to which they relate,

    (d) a description of the purpose or purposes for which the data are being or are to be processed,

    (e) a description of any recipient or recipients to whom the data controller intends or may wish to disclose the data,

    (f) the names, or a description of, any countries or territories outside the European Economic Area to which the data controller directly or indirectly transfers, or intends or may wish directly or indirectly to transfer, the data,

    (ff) where the data controller is a public authority, a statement of that fact

    (g) in any case where–

        (i) personal data are being, or are intended to be, processed in circumstances in which the prohibition in subsection (1) of section 17 is excluded by subsection (2) or (3) of that section, and

        (ii) the notification does not extend to those data,

    a statement of that fact, and

    (h) such information about the data controller as may be prescribed under section 18(5A).

(2)   In this Part–

"fees regulations" means regulations made by the Secretary of State under section 18(5) or 19(4) or (7);

"notification regulations" means regulations made by the Secretary of State under the other provisions of this Part;

"prescribed", except where used in relation to fees regulations, means prescribed by notification regulations.

(3)   For the purposes of this Part, so far as it relates to the addresses of data controllers–

(a) the address of a registered company is that of its registered office, and

(b) the address of a person (other than a registered company) carrying on a business is that of his principal place of business in the United Kingdom.

NOTES

Defined terms
"address": s 16(3)
"business": s 70(1)
"data": s 1(1)
"data controller": s 1(1) and (4) and 63(3).
"data subject": s 1(1)
"disclosing": s 1(2)(b)
"EEA State": s 70(1)

"fees regulations": s 16(2)
"notification regulations": s 16(2)
"personal data": s 1(1)
"prescribed": s 16(2)
"processing": s 1(1)
"recipient": s 70(1)
"registered company": s 70(1)
"registrable particulars": s 16(1)

Prohibition on processing without registration

17(1)   Subject to the following provisions of this section, personal data must not be processed unless an entry in respect of the data controller is included in the register maintained by the Commissioner under section 19 (or is treated by notification regulations made by virtue of section 19(3) as being so included).

(2)   Except where the processing is assessable processing for the purposes of section 22, subsection (1) does not apply in relation to personal data consisting of information which falls neither within paragraph (a) of the definition of "data" in section 1(1) nor within paragraph (b) of that definition.

(3)   If it appears to the Secretary of State that processing of a particular description is unlikely to prejudice the rights and freedoms of data subjects, notification regulations may provide that, in such cases as may be prescribed, subsection (1) is not to apply in relation to processing of that description.

(4)   Subsection (1) does not apply in relation to any processing whose sole purpose is the maintenance of a public register.

NOTES

Defined terms
"accessible record": s 68
"assessable processing": s 22(1)
"the Commissioner": s 70(1)
"data": s 1(1)
"data controller": ss1(1) and (4) and 63(3)
"data subject": s 1(1)
"notification regulations": s 16(2)
"personal data": s 1(1)

"prescribed": s 16(2)
"processing": s 1(1)
"public register": s 70(1)

Subordinate legislation
Data Protection (Notification and Notification Fees)
    Regulations 2000, SI 2000/188.

Notification by data controllers

18(1)   Any data controller who wishes to be included in the register maintained under section 19 shall give a notification to the Commissioner under this section.

(2)   A notification under this section must specify in accordance with notification regulations–
   (a) the registrable particulars, and
   (b) a general description of measures to be taken for the purpose of complying with the seventh data protection principle.

(3)   Notification regulations made by virtue of subsection (2) may provide for the determination by the Commissioner, in accordance with any requirements of the regulations, of the form in which the registrable particulars and the description mentioned in subsection (2)(b) are to be specified, including in particular the detail required for the purposes of section 16(1)(c), (d), (e) and (f) and subsection (2)(b).

(4)   Notification regulations may make provision as to the giving of notification–
   (a) by partnerships, or
   (b) in other cases where two or more persons are the data controllers in respect of any personal data.

(5)   The notification must be accompanied by such fee as may be prescribed by fees regulations.

(5A)   Notification regulations may prescribe the information about the data controller which is required for the purpose of verifying the fee payable under subsection (5).

(6)   Notification regulations may provide for any fee paid under subsection (5) or section 19(4) to be refunded in prescribed circumstances.

NOTES

Defined terms
"the Commissioner": s 70(1)
"data controller": ss1(1) and (4) and 63(3)
"data protection principles": s 4 and Schedule 1
"fees regulations": s 16(2)
"notification regulations": s 16(2)
"personal data": s 1(1)

"prescribed": s 16(2)
"registrable particulars": s 16(1)

Subordinate legislation
Data Protection (Notification and Notification Fees)
   Regulations 2000, SI 2000/188.

Register of notifications

19(1)   The Commissioner shall–
   (a) maintain a register of persons who have given notification under section 18, and
   (b) make an entry in the register in pursuance of each notification received by him under that section from a person in respect of whom no entry as data controller was for the time being included in the register.

(2)   Each entry in the register shall consist of–
   (a) the registrable particulars notified under section 18 or, as the case requires, those particulars as amended in pursuance of section 20(4), and

(b) such other information as the Commissioner may be authorised or required by notification regulations to include in the register.

(3) Notification regulations may make provision as to the time as from which any entry in respect of a data controller is to be treated for the purposes of section 17 as having been made in the register.

(4) No entry shall be retained in the register for more than the relevant time except on payment of such fee as may be prescribed by fees regulations.

(5) In subsection (4) "the relevant time" means twelve months or such other period as may be prescribed by notification regulations; and different periods may be prescribed in relation to different cases.

(6) The Commissioner–
    (a) shall provide facilities for making the information contained in the entries in the register available for inspection (in visible and legible form) by members of the public at all reasonable hours and free of charge, and
    (b) may provide such other facilities for making the information contained in those entries available to the public free of charge as he considers appropriate.

(7) The Commissioner shall, on payment of such fee, if any, as may be prescribed by fees regulations, supply any member of the public with a duly certified copy in writing of the particulars contained in any entry made in the register.

(8) Nothing in subsection (6) or (7) applies to information which is included in an entry in the register only by reason of it falling within section 16(1)(h).

NOTES

Defined terms
"the Commissioner": s 70(1)
"data controller": ss1(1) and (4) and 63(3)
"fees regulations": s 16(2)
"notification regulations": s 16(2)
"prescribed": s 16(2)

Subordinate legislation
Data Protection (Fees under section 19(7)) Regulations 2000, SI 2000/187. Reproduced at p 1147 ff.
Data Protection (Notification and Notification Fees) Regulations 2000, SI 2000/188

Duty to notify changes

20(1) For the purpose specified in subsection (2), notification regulations shall include provision imposing on every person in respect of whom an entry as a data controller is for the time being included in the register maintained under section 19 a duty to notify to the Commissioner, in such circumstances and at such time or times and in such form as may be prescribed, such matters relating to the registrable particulars and measures taken as mentioned in section 18(2)(b) as may be prescribed.

(2) The purpose referred to in subsection (1) is that of ensuring, so far as practicable, that at any time–

(a) that at any time the entries in the register maintained under section 19 contain current names and addresses and describe the current practice or intentions of the data controller with respect to the processing of personal data,

(aa) that the correct fee is paid under section 19(4), and

(b) that at any time the Commissioner is provided with a general description of measures currently being taken as mentioned in section 18(2)(b).

(3) Subsection (3) of section 18 has effect in relation to notification regulations made by virtue of subsection (1) as it has effect in relation to notification regulations made by virtue of subsection (2) of that section.

(4) On receiving any notification under notification regulations made by virtue of subsection (1), the Commissioner shall make such amendments of the relevant entry in the register maintained under section 19 as are necessary to take account of the notification.

NOTES

Defined terms
"address": s 70(1)
"Commissioner": s 70(1)
"data controller": s 1(1)
"notification regulations": s 16(2)

"personal data": s 1(1)
"prescribed": s 16(2)
"processing": s 1(1)
"registrable particulars": s 16(1)

Offences

21(1) If section 17(1) is contravened, the data controller is guilty of an offence.

(2) Any person who fails to comply with the duty imposed by notification regulations made by virtue of section 20(1) is guilty of an offence.

(3) It shall be a defence for a person charged with an offence under subsection (2) to show that he exercised all due diligence to comply with the duty.

NOTES

Defined terms
"data controller": s 1(1)

"notification regulations": s 16(2)

Preliminary assessment by Commissioner

22(1) In this section "assessable processing" means processing which is of a description specified in an order made by the Secretary of State as appearing to him to be particularly likely–

(a) to cause substantial damage or substantial distress to data subjects, or

(b) otherwise significantly to prejudice the rights and freedoms of data subjects.

(2) On receiving notification from any data controller under section 18 or under notification regulations made by virtue of section 20 the Commissioner shall consider–

(a) whether any of the processing to which the notification relates is assessable processing, and

(b) if so, whether the assessable processing is likely to comply with the provisions of this Act.

(3) Subject to subsection (4), the Commissioner shall, within the period of twenty-eight days beginning with the day on which he receives a notification which relates to assessable processing, give a notice to the data controller stating the extent to which the Commissioner is of the opinion that the processing is likely or unlikely to comply with the provisions of this Act.

(4) Before the end of the period referred to in subsection (3) the Commissioner may, by reason of special circumstances, extend that period on one occasion only by notice to the data controller by such further period not exceeding fourteen days as the Commissioner may specify in the notice.

(5) No assessable processing in respect of which a notification has been given the Commissioner as mentioned in subsection (2) shall be carried on unless either–

(a) the period of twenty-eight days beginning with the day on which the notification is received by the Commissioner (or, in a case falling within subsection (4), that period as extended under that subsection) has elapsed, or

(b) before the end of that period (or that period as so extended) the data controller has received a notice from the Commissioner under subsection (3) in respect of the processing.

(6) Where subsection (5) is contravened, the data controller is guilty of an offence.

(7) The Secretary of State may by order amend subsections (3), (4) and (5) by substituting for the number of days for the time being specified there a different number specified in the order.

NOTES

Defined terms
"Commissioner": s 70(1)

"data subject": s 1(1)
"processing": s 1(1)

Power to make provision for appointment of data protection supervisors

23(1) The Secretary of State may by order–

(a) make provision under which a data controller may appoint a person to act as a data protection supervisor responsible in particular for monitoring in an independent manner the data controller's compliance with the provisions of this Act, and

(b) provide that, in relation to any data controller who has appointed a data protection supervisor in accordance with the provisions of the order and who complies with such conditions as may be specified in the order, the provisions of this Part are to have effect subject to such exemptions or other modifications as may be specified in the order.

(2)   An order under this section may–
    (a) impose duties on data protection supervisors in relation to the Commissioner, and
    (b) confer functions on the Commissioner in relation to data protection supervisors.

NOTES

Defined terms
"Commissioner": s 70(1)

"data controller": s 1(1)

Duty of certain data controllers to make certain information available

24(1)   Subject to subsection (3), where personal data are processed in a case where–
    (a) by virtue of subsection (2) or (3) of section 17, subsection (1) of that section does not apply to the processing, and
    (b) the data controller has not notified the relevant particulars in respect of that processing under section 18,
the data controller must, within twenty-one days of receiving a written request from any person, make the relevant particulars available to that person in writing free of charge.

(2)   In this section "the relevant particulars" means the particulars referred to in paragraphs (a) to (f) of section 16(1).

(3)   This section has effect subject to any exemption conferred for the purposes of this section by notification regulations.

(4)   Any data controller who fails to comply with the duty imposed by subsection (1) is guilty of an offence.

(5)   It shall be a defence for a person charged with an offence under subsection (4) to show that he exercised all due diligence to comply with the duty.

NOTES

Defined terms
"data controller": s 1(1)

"data subject": s 1(1)
"personal data" s 1(1)
"processing": s 1(1)

Functions of Commissioner in relation to making of notification regulations

25(1)   As soon as practicable after the passing of this Act, the Commissioner shall submit to the Secretary of State proposals as to the provisions to be included in the first notification regulations.

(2)   The Commissioner shall keep under review the working of notification regulations and may from time to time submit to the Secretary of State proposals as to amendments to be made to the regulations.

(3)   The Secretary of State may from time to time require the Commissioner to consider any matter relating to notification regulations and to submit to him proposals as to amendments to be made to the regulations in connection with that matter.

(4)   Before making any notification regulations, the Secretary of State shall–

(a)   consider any proposals made to him by the Commissioner under subsection (2) or (3), and

(b)   consult the Commissioner.

NOTES

Defined terms
"Commissioner": s 70(1)

"notification regulations": s 16(2)

Fees regulations

26(1)   Fees regulations prescribing fees for the purposes of any provision of this Part may provide for different fees to be payable in different cases.

(2)   In making any fees regulations, the Secretary of State shall have regard to the desirability of securing that the fees payable to the Commissioner are sufficient to offset–

(a)   the expenses incurred by the Commissioner in discharging his functions under this Act and any expenses of the Secretary of State in respect of the Commissioner so far as attributable to those functions; and

(b)   to the extent that the Secretary of State considers appropriate–

(i)   any deficit previously incurred (whether before or after the passing of this Act) in respect of the expenses mentioned in paragraph (a), and

(ii)   expenses incurred or to be incurred by the Secretary of State in respect of the inclusion of any officers or staff of the Commissioner in any scheme under section 1 of the Superannuation Act 1972.

NOTES

Defined terms
"Commissioner": s 70(1)
"fees regulations": s 16(2)
"Tribunal": s 70(1)

Subordinate legislation
Data Protection (Notification and Notification Fees)
Regulations 2000, SI 2000/188

PART IV

EXEMPTIONS

Preliminary

27(1)　References in any of the data protection principles or any provision of Parts II and III to personal data or to the processing of personal data do not include references to data or processing which by virtue of this Part are exempt from that principle or other provision.

(2)　In this Part "the subject information provisions" means–
(a) the first data protection principle to the extent to which it requires compliance with paragraph 2 of Part II of Schedule 1, and
(b) section 7.

(3)　In this Part "the non-disclosure provisions" means the provisions specified in subsection (4) to the extent to which they are inconsistent with the disclosure in question.

(4)　The provisions referred to in subsection (3) are–
(a) the first data protection principle, except to the extent to which it requires compliance with the conditions in Schedules 2 and 3,
(b) the second, third, fourth and fifth data protection principles, and
(c) sections 10 and 14(1) to (3).

(5)　Except as provided by this Part, the subject information provisions shall have effect notwithstanding any enactment or rule of law prohibiting or restricting the disclosure, or authorising the withholding, of information.

Defined terms
"data": s 1(1)
"data protection principles": s 4 and Sch1
"disclosing": s 1(2)(b)
"enactment": s 70(1)

NOTES
"the non-disclosure provisions": s 27(3)
"personal data": s 1(1)
"processing": s 1(1)
"the subject information provisions": s 27(2)

National security

28(1)　Personal data are exempt from any of the provisions of–
(a) the data protection principles,
(b) Parts II, III and V, and
(c) sections 54A and 55,
if the exemption from that provision is required for the purpose of safeguarding national security.

(2)　Subject to subsection (4), a certificate signed by a Minister of the Crown certifying that exemption from all or any of the provisions mentioned in subsection (1) is or at any time was required for the purpose there mentioned in respect of any personal data shall be conclusive evidence of that fact.

(3) A certificate under subsection (2) may identify the personal data to which it applies by means of a general description and may be expressed to have prospective effect.

(4) Any person directly affected by the issuing of a certificate under subsection (2) may appeal to the Tribunal against the certificate.

(5) If on an appeal under subsection (4), the Tribunal finds that, applying the principles applied by the court on an application for judicial review, the Minister did not have reasonable grounds for issuing the certificate, the Tribunal may allow the appeal and quash the certificate.

(6) Where in any proceedings under or by virtue of this Act it is claimed by a data controller that a certificate under subsection (2) which identifies the personal data to which it applies by means of a general description applies to any personal data, any other party to the proceedings may appeal to the Tribunal on the ground that the certificate does not apply to the personal data in question and, subject to any determination under subsection (7), the certificate shall be conclusively presumed so to apply.

(7) On any appeal under subsection (6), the Tribunal may determine that the certificate does not so apply.

(8) A document purporting to be a certificate under subsection (2) shall be received in evidence and deemed to be such a certificate unless the contrary is proved.

(9) A document which purports to be certified by or on behalf of a Minister of the Crown as a true copy of a certificate issued by that Minister under subsection (2) shall in any legal proceedings be evidence (or, in Scotland, sufficient evidence) of that certificate.

(10) The power conferred by subsection (2) on a Minister of the Crown shall not be exercisable except by a Minister who is a member of the Cabinet or by the Attorney General or the Advocate General for Scotland.

(11) No power conferred by any provision of Part V may be exercised in relation to personal data which by virtue of this section are exempt from that provision.

(12) Schedule 6 shall have effect in relation to appeals under subsection (4) or (6) and the proceedings of the Tribunal in respect of any such appeal.

NOTES

Defined terms

"data controller": s 1(1) and (4) and 63(3)
"data protection principles": s 4 and Schedule 1

"Minister of the Crown": s 70(1)
"personal data" : s 1(1)
"the Tribunal": s 70(1)

Crime and taxation

29(1) Personal data processed for any of the following purposes–

       (a) the prevention or detection of crime,

       (b) the apprehension or prosecution of offenders, or

       (c) the assessment or collection of any tax or duty or of any imposition of a similar nature,

are exempt from the first data protection principle (except to the extent to which it requires compliance with the conditions in Schedules 2 and 3) and section 7 in any case to the extent to which the application of those provisions to the data would be likely to prejudice any of the matters mentioned in this subsection.

(2)   Personal data which–

       (a) are processed for the purpose of discharging statutory functions, and

       (b) consist of information obtained for such a purpose from a person who had it in his possession for any of the purposes mentioned in subsection (1),

are exempt from the subject information provisions to the same extent as personal data processed for any of the purposes mentioned in that subsection.

(3)   Personal data are exempt from the non-disclosure provisions in any case in which–

       (a) the disclosure is for any of the purposes mentioned in subsection (1), and

       (b) the application of those provisions in relation to the disclosure would be likely to prejudice any of the matters mentioned in that subsection.

(4)   Personal data in respect of which the data controller is a relevant authority and which–

       (a) consist of a classification applied to the data subject as part of a system of risk assessment which is operated by that authority for either of the following purposes–

           (i) the assessment or collection of any tax or duty or any imposition of a similar nature, or

           (ii) the prevention or detection of crime, or apprehension or prosecution of offenders, where the offence concerned involves any unlawful claim for any payment out of, or any unlawful application of, public funds, and

       (b) are processed for either of those purposes,

are exempt from section 7 to the extent to which the exemption is required in the interests of the operation of the system.

(5)   In subsection (4)–

"public funds" includes funds provided by any Community institution;

"relevant authority" means–

       (a) a government department,

       (b) a local authority, or

       (c) any other authority administering housing benefit or council tax benefit.

NOTES

Defined terms

"data": s 1(1)

"data controller": ss1(1) and (4) and 63(3)

"data subject": s 1(1)

"data protection principles": s 4 and Sch1

"government department": s 70(1)

"the non-disclosure provisions": s 27(3)

"personal data" : s 1(1)

"processing": s 1(1) and para5 of Sch8

"public funds": s 29(5)

"disclosing": s 1(2)(b)

"relevant authority": s 29(5)
"the subject information provisions": s 27(2)

Health, education and social work

30(1)   The Secretary of State may by order exempt from the subject information provisions, or modify those provisions in relation to, personal data consisting of information as to the physical or mental health or condition of the data subject.

(2)   The Secretary of State may by order exempt from the subject information provisions, or modify those provisions in relation to–

(a) personal data in respect of which the data controller is the proprietor of, or a teacher at, a school, and which consist of information relating to persons who are or have been pupils at the school, or

(b) personal data in respect of which the data controller is an education authority in Scotland, and which consist of information relating to persons who are receiving, or have received, further education provided by the authority.

(3)   The Secretary of State may by order exempt from the subject information provisions, or modify those provisions in relation to, personal data of such other descriptions as may be specified in the order, being information–

(a) processed by government departments or local authorities or by voluntary organisations or other bodies designated by or under the order, and

(b) appearing to him to be processed in the course of, or for the purposes of, carrying out social work in relation to the data subject or other individuals;

but the Secretary of State shall not under this subsection confer any exemption or make any modification except so far as he considers that the application to the data of those provisions (or of those provisions without modification) would be likely to prejudice the carrying out of social work.

(4)   An order under this section may make different provision in relation to data consisting of information of different descriptions.

(5)   In this section–

"education authority" and "further education" have the same meaning as in the Education (Scotland) Act 1980 ("the 1980 Act"), and

"proprietor"–

(a) in relation to a school in England or Wales, has the same meaning as in the Education Act 1996,

(b) in relation to a school in Scotland, means–

(ii) in the case of an independent school, the proprietor within the meaning of the 1980 Act,

(iii) in the case of a grant-aided school, the managers within the meaning of the 1980 Act, and

(iv) in the case of a public school, the education authority within the meaning of the 1980 Act, and

(c) in relation to a school in Northern Ireland, has the same meaning as in the Education and Libraries (Northern Ireland) Order 1986 and includes, in the case of a controlled school, the Board of Governors of the school.

NOTES

Defined terms

"data": s 1(1)
"data controller": ss1(1) and (4) and 63(3)
"data subject": s 1(1)
"educational record": Schedule 11, paragraph 1
"government department": s 70(1)
"health professional": s 69(1)
"personal data": s 1(1)
"processing": s 1(1)
"proprietor": s 30(5)
"pupil": s 70(1)
"school": s 70(1)
"teacher": s 70(1)
"the subject information provisions": s 27(2)

Subordinate legislation

Data Protection (Subject Access Modification) (Health) Order 2000, SI 2000/413. Reproduced at p 1152 ff.
Data Protection (Subject Access Modification) (Education) Order 2000, SI 2000/414. Reproduced at p 1156 ff.
Data Protection (Subject Access Modification) (Social Work) Order 2000, SI 2000/415. Reproduced at p 1159 ff.

Regulatory activity

31(1)   Personal data processed for the purposes of discharging functions to which this subsection applies are exempt from the subject information provisions in any case to the extent to which the application of those provisions to the data would be likely to prejudice the proper discharge of those functions.

(2)   Subsection (1) applies to any relevant function which is designed–
    (a) for protecting members of the public against–
        (i) financial loss due to dishonesty, malpractice or other seriously improper conduct by, or the unfitness or incompetence of, persons concerned in the provision of banking, insurance, investment or other financial services or in the management of bodies corporate,
        (ii) financial loss due to the conduct of discharged or undischarged bankrupts, or
        (iii) dishonesty, malpractice or other seriously improper conduct by, or the unfitness or incompetence of, persons authorised to carry on any profession or other activity,
    (b) for protecting charities or community interest companies against misconduct or mismanagement (whether by trustees, directors or other persons) in their administration,
    (c) for protecting the property of charities or community interest companies from loss or misapplication,
    (d) for the recovery of the property of charities or community interest companies,
    (e) for securing the health, safety and welfare of persons at work, or
    (f) for protecting persons other than persons at work against risk to health or safety arising out of or in connection with the actions of persons at work.

(3) In subsection (2) "relevant function" means–
  (a) any function conferred on any person by or under any enactment,
  (b) any function of the Crown, a Minister of the Crown or a government department, or
  (c) any other function which is of a public nature and is exercised in the public interest.

(4) Personal data processed for the purpose of discharging any function which–
  (a) is conferred by or under any enactment on–
    (i) the Parliamentary Commissioner for Administration,
    (ii) the Commission for Local Administration in England,
    (iii) the Health Service Commissioner for England,
    (iv) the Public Services Ombudsman for Wales,
    (v) the Assembly Ombudsman for Northern Ireland.
    (vi) the Northern Ireland Commissioner for Complaints, or
    (vii) the Scottish Public Services Ombudsman, and
  (b) is designed for protecting members of the public against–
    (i) maladministration by public bodies,
    (ii) failures in services provided by public bodies, or
    (iii) a failure of a public body to provide a service which it was a function of the body to provide,
are exempt from the subject information provisions in any case to the extent to which the application of those provisions to the data would be likely to prejudice the proper discharge of that function.

(4A) Personal data processed for the purpose of discharging any function which is conferred by or under Part XVI of the Financial Services and Markets Act 2000 on the body established by the Financial Services Authority for the purposes of that Part are exempt from the subject information provisions in any case to the extent to which the application of those provisions to the data would be likely to prejudice the proper discharge of the function.

(4B) Personal data processed for the purposes of discharging any function of the Legal Services Board are exempt from the subject information provisions in any case to the extent to which the application of those provisions to the data would be likely to prejudice the proper discharge of the function.

(4C) Personal data processed for the purposes of the function of considering a complaint under the scheme established under Part 6 of the Legal Services Act 2007 (legal complaints) are exempt from the subject information provisions in any case to the extent to which the application of those provisions to the data would be likely to prejudice the proper discharge of the function.

(5) Personal data processed for the purpose of discharging any function which–
  (a) is conferred by or under any enactment on the Office of Fair Trading, and
  (b) is designed–

      (i) for protecting members of the public against conduct which may adversely affect their interests by persons carrying on a business,

      (ii) for regulating agreements or conduct which have as their object or effect the prevention, restriction or distortion of competition in connection with any commercial activity, or

      (iii) for regulating conduct on the part of one or more undertakings which amounts to the abuse of a dominant position in a market,

are exempt from the subject information provisions in any case to the extent to which the application of those provisions to the data would be likely to prejudice the proper discharge of that function.

(5A)   Personal data processed by a CPC enforcer for the purpose of discharging any function conferred on such a body by or under the CPC Regulation are exempt from the subject information provisions in any case to the extent to which the application of those provisions to the data would be likely to prejudice the proper discharge of that function.

(5B)   In subsection (5A)–

      (a) "CPC enforcer" has the meaning given to it in section 213(5A) of the Enterprise Act 2002 but does not include the Office of Fair Trading;

      (b) "CPC Regulation" has the meaning given to it in section 235A of that Act.

(6)   Personal data processed for the purpose of the function of considering a complaint under section 14 of the NHS Redress Act 2006, section 113(1) or (2) or 114(1) or (3) of the Health and Social Care (Community Health and Standards) Act 2003, or section 24D, 26 or 26ZB of the Children Act 1989, are exempt from the subject information provisions in any case to the extent to which the application of those provisions to the data would be likely to prejudice the proper discharge of that function.

(7)   Personal data processed for the purpose of discharging any function which is conferred by or under Part 3 of the Local Government Act 2000 on–

      (a) the monitoring officer of a relevant authority,

      (b) an ethical standards officer, or

      (c) the Public Services Ombudsman for Wales,

are exempt from the subject information provisions in any case to the extent to which the application of those provisions to the data would be likely to prejudice the proper discharge of that function.

(8)   In subsection (7)–

      (a) "relevant authority" has the meaning given by section 49(6) of the Local Government Act 2000, and

      (b) any reference to the monitoring officer of a relevant authority, or to an ethical standards officer, has the same meaning as in Part 3 of that Act.

NOTES

Defined terms
"business": s 70(1)
"data": s 1(1)
"enactment": s 70(1)
"government department": s 70(1)

"Minister of the Crown": s 70(1)
"personal data": s 1(1)
"processing": s 1(1)
"relevant function": s 31(3)
"the subject information provisions": s 27(2)

Journalism, literature and art

32(1) Personal data which are processed only for the special purposes are exempt from any provision to which this subsection relates if–

(a) the processing is undertaken with a view to the publication by any person of any journalistic, literary or artistic material,

(b) the data controller reasonably believes that, having regard in particular to the special importance of the public interest in freedom of expression, publication would be in the public interest, and

(c) the data controller reasonably believes that, in all the circumstances, compliance with that provision is incompatible with the special purposes.

(2) Subsection (1) relates to the provisions of–

(a) the data protection principles except the seventh data protection principle,

(b) section 7,

(c) section 10,

(d) section 12, and

(e) section 14(1) to (3).

(3) In considering for the purposes of subsection (1)(b) whether the belief of a data controller that publication would be in the public interest was or is a reasonable one, regard may be had to his compliance with any code of practice which–

(a) is relevant to the publication in question, and

(b) is designated by the Secretary of State by order for the purposes of this subsection.

(4) Where at any time ("the relevant time") in any proceedings against a data controller under section 7(9), 10(4), 12(8) or 14 or by virtue of section 13 the data controller claims, or it appears to the court, that any personal data to which the proceedings relate are being processed–

(a) only for the special purposes, and

(b) with a view to the publication by any person of any journalistic, literary or artistic material which, at the time twenty-four hours immediately before the relevant time, had not previously been published by the data controller,

the court shall stay the proceedings until either of the conditions in subsection (5) is met.

(5) Those conditions are–

(a) that a determination of the Commissioner under section 45 with respect to the data in question takes effect, or

(b) in a case where the proceedings were stayed on the making of a claim, that the claim is withdrawn.

(6) For the purposes of this Act "publish", in relation to journalistic, literary or artistic material, means make available to the public or any section of the public.

Defined terms
"the Commissioner": s 70(1)
"data": s 1(1)
 "data controller": ss1(1) and (4) and 63(3)
"data protection principles": s 4 and Sch1
"exempt manual data": Sch13, para1(4)
"personal data": s 1(1)

NOTES
"processing": s 1(1)
"publish": s 32(6)
"relevant time": s 32(4)
"the special purposes": s 3

Subordinate legislation
Data Protection (Designated Codes of Practice) (No 2) Order 2000

Research, history and statistics

33(1)   In this section–
"research purposes" includes statistical or historical purposes;
"the relevant conditions", in relation to any processing of personal data, means the conditions–
(a) that the data are not processed to support measures or decisions with respect to particular individuals, and
(b) that the data are not processed in such a way that substantial damage or substantial distress is, or is likely to be, caused to any data subject.

(2) For the purposes of the second data protection principle, the further processing of personal data only for research purposes in compliance with the relevant conditions is not to be regarded as incompatible with the purposes for which they were obtained.

(3) Personal data which are processed only for research purposes in compliance with the relevant conditions may, notwithstanding the fifth data protection principle, be kept indefinitely.

(4) Personal data which are processed only for research purposes are exempt from section 7 if–
(a) they are processed in compliance with the relevant conditions, and
(b) the results of the research or any resulting statistics are not made available in a form which identifies data subjects or any of them.

(5) For the purposes of subsections (2) to (4) personal data are not to be treated as processed otherwise than for research purposes merely because the data are disclosed–
(a) to any person, for research purposes only,
(b) to the data subject or a person acting on his behalf,
(c) at the request, or with the consent, of the data subject or a person acting on his behalf, or

(d) in circumstances in which the person making the disclosure has reasonable grounds for believing that the disclosure falls within paragraph (a), (b) or (c).

Manual data held by public authorities

33A(1)   Personal data falling within paragraph (e) of the definition of "data" in section 1(1) are exempt from–

    (a) the first, second, third, fifth, seventh and eighth data protection principles,

    (b) the sixth data protection principle except so far as it relates to the rights conferred on data subjects by sections 7 and 14,

    (c) sections 10 to 12,

    (d) section 13, except so far as it relates to damage caused by a contravention of section 7 or of the fourth data protection principle and to any distress which is also suffered by reason of that contravention,

    (e) Part III, and

    (f) section 55.

(2)   Personal data which fall within paragraph (e) of the definition of "data" in section 1(1) and relate to appointments or removals, pay, discipline, superannuation or other personnel matters, in relation to–

    (a) service in any of the armed forces of the Crown,

    (b) service in any office or employment under the Crown or under any public authority, or

    (c) service in any office or employment, or under any contract for services, in respect of which power to take action, or to determine or approve the action taken, in such matters is vested in Her Majesty, any Minister of the Crown, the National Assembly for Wales, any Northern Ireland Minister (within the meaning of the Freedom of Information Act 2000) or any public authority,

are also exempt from the remaining data protection principles and the remaining provisions of Part II.

Information available to the public by or under enactment

34   Personal data are exempt from–

(a) the subject information provisions,

(b) the fourth data protection principle and section 14(1) to (3), and

(c) the non-disclosure provisions,

if the data consist of information which the data controller is obliged by or under any enactment other than an enactment contained in the Freedom of Information Act 2000 to make available to the public, whether by publishing it, by making it available for inspection, or otherwise and whether gratuitously or on payment of a fee.

NOTES

Defined terms
"data": s 1(1)
"data controller": ss1(1) and (4) and 63(3)
"data protection principles": s 4 and Sch1

"enactment": s 70(1)
"the non-disclosure provisions": s 27(3)
"personal data": s 1(1)
"the subject information provisions": s 27(2)

Disclosures required by law or made in connection with legal proceedings etc

35(1)   Personal data are exempt from the non-disclosure provisions where the disclosure is required by or under any enactment, by any rule of law or by the order of a court.

(2)   Personal data are exempt from the non-disclosure provisions where the disclosure is necessary–

(a) for the purpose of, or in connection with, any legal proceedings (including prospective legal proceedings), or

(b) for the purpose of obtaining legal advice,

or is otherwise necessary for the purposes of establishing, exercising or defending legal rights.

NOTES

Defined terms
"disclosing": s 1(2)(b)
"enactment": s 70(1)

"the non-disclosure provisions": s 27(3)
"personal data": s 1(1)

Parliamentary privilege

35A   Personal data are exempt from–

(a) the first data protection principle, except to the extent to which it requires compliance with the conditions in Schedules 2 and 3,

(b) the second, third, fourth and fifth data protection principles,

(c) section 7, and

(d) sections 10 and 14(1) to (3),

if the exemption is required for the purpose of avoiding an infringement of the privileges of either House of Parliament.

NOTES

Defined terms
"data protection principles": s 4 and Sch1
"personal data": s 1(1)

Domestic purposes

36   Personal data processed by an individual only for the purposes of that individual's personal, family or household affairs (including recreational purposes) are exempt from the data protection principles and the provisions of Parts II and III.

NOTES

Defined terms
"data protection principles": s 4 and Sch 1

"personal data": s 1(1)
"processing": s 1(1) Sch 8, para 5

Miscellaneous exemptions

37   Schedule 7 (which confers further miscellaneous exemptions) has effect.

Powers to make further exemptions by order

38(1)   The Secretary of State may by order exempt from the subject information provisions personal data consisting of information the disclosure of which is prohibited or restricted by or under any enactment if and to the extent that he considers it necessary for the safeguarding of the interests of the data subject or the rights and freedoms of any other individual that the prohibition or restriction ought to prevail over those provisions.

(2)   The Secretary of State may by order exempt from the non-disclosure provisions any disclosures of personal data made in circumstances specified in the order, if he considers the exemption is necessary for the safeguarding of the interests of the data subject or the rights and freedoms of any other individual.

NOTES

Defined terms
"data subject": s 1(1)
"disclosing": s 1(2)(b)
"enactment": s 70(1)
"the non-disclosure provisions": s 27(3)
"personal data": s 1(1)
"the subject information provisions": s 27(2)

Subordinate legislation
Data Protection (Miscellaneous Subject Access Exemptions) Order 2000, SI 2000/419. Reproduced at p 1171 ff.

Transitional relief

39   Schedule 8 (which confers transitional exemptions) has effect.

PART V

ENFORCEMENT

Enforcement notices

40(1)   If the Commissioner is satisfied that a data controller has contravened or is contravening any of the data protection principles, the Commissioner may serve him with a notice (in this Act referred to as "an enforcement notice") requiring him, for complying with the principle or principles in question, to do either or both of the following–

(a) to take within such time as may be specified in the notice, or to refrain from taking after such time as may be so specified, such steps as are so specified, or

(b) to refrain from processing any personal data, or any personal data of a description specified in the notice, or to refrain from processing them for a purpose so specified or in a manner so specified, after such time as may be so specified.

(2)   In deciding whether to serve an enforcement notice, the Commissioner shall consider whether the contravention has caused or is likely to cause any person damage or distress.

(3)   An enforcement notice in respect of a contravention of the fourth data protection principle which requires the data controller to rectify, block, erase or destroy any inaccurate data may also require the data controller to rectify, block, erase or destroy any other data held by him and containing an expression of opinion which appears to the Commissioner to be based on the inaccurate data.

(4)   An enforcement notice in respect of a contravention of the fourth data protection principle, in the case of data which accurately record information received or obtained by the data controller from the data subject or a third party, may require the data controller either–

(a) to rectify, block, erase or destroy any inaccurate data and any other data held by him and containing an expression of opinion as mentioned in subsection (3), or

(b) to take such steps as are specified in the notice for securing compliance with the requirements specified in paragraph 7 of Part II of Schedule 1 and, if the Commissioner thinks fit, for supplementing the data with such statement of the true facts relating to the matters dealt with by the data as the Commissioner may approve.

(5)   Where–

(a) an enforcement notice requires the data controller to rectify, block, erase or destroy any personal data, or

(b) the Commissioner is satisfied that personal data which have been rectified, blocked, erased or destroyed had been processed in contravention of any of the data protection principles, an enforcement notice may, if reasonably practicable, require the data controller to notify third parties to whom the data have been disclosed of the rectification, blocking, erasure or destruction; and in determining whether it is reasonably practicable to require such notification regard shall be had, in particular, to the number of persons who would have to be notified.

(6) An enforcement notice must contain–

 (a) a statement of the data protection principle or principles which the Commissioner is satisfied have been or are being contravened and his reasons for reaching that conclusion, and

 (b) particulars of the rights of appeal conferred by section 48.

(7) Subject to subsection (8), an enforcement notice must not require any of the provisions of the notice to be complied with before the end of the period within which an appeal can be brought against the notice and, if such an appeal is brought, the notice need not be complied with pending the determination or withdrawal of the appeal.

(8) If by reason of special circumstances the Commissioner considers that an enforcement notice should be complied with as a matter of urgency he may include in the notice a statement to that effect and a statement of his reasons for reaching that conclusion; and in that event subsection (7) shall not apply but the notice must not require the provisions of the notice to be complied with before the end of the period of seven days beginning with the day on which the notice is served.

(9) Notification regulations (as defined by section 16(2)) may make provision as to the effect of the service of an enforcement notice on any entry in the register maintained under section 19 which relates to the person on whom the notice is served.

(10) This section has effect subject to section 46(1).

NOTES

Defined terms

"the Commissioner": s 70(1)
"data": ss1(1)
"data controller": ss1(1) and (4) and 63(3)
"data protection principles": s 4 and Sch1
"data subject": s 1(1)
"disclosing": s 1(2)(b)

"enforcement notice": s 40(1)
"inaccurate": s 70(2)
"notification regulations": s 16(2)
"personal data": s 1(1)
"processing": s 1(1)
"third party": s 70(1)

Cancellation of an enforcement notice

41(1) If the Commissioner considers that all or any of the provisions of an enforcement notice need not be complied with in order to ensure compliance with the data protection principle or principles to which it relates, he may cancel or vary the notice by written notice to the person on whom it was served.

(2) A person on whom an enforcement notice has been served may, at any time after the expiry of the period during which an appeal can be brought against that notice, apply

in writing to the Commissioner for the cancellation or variation of that notice on the ground that, by reason of a change of circumstances, all or any of the provisions of that notice need not be complied with in order to ensure compliance with the data protection principle or principles to which that notice relates.

NOTES

Defined terms
"the Commissioner": s 70(1)

"data protection principles": s 4 and Sch1
"enforcement notice": s 40(1)

Assessment notices

41A(1) The Commissioner may serve a data controller within subsection (2) with a notice (in this Act referred to as an "assessment notice") for the purpose of enabling the Commissioner to determine whether the data controller has complied or is complying with the data protection principles.

(2) A data controller is within this subsection if the data controller is–
  (a) a government department,
  (b) a public authority designated for the purposes of this section by an order made by the Secretary of State, or
  (c) a person of a description designated for the purposes of this section by such an order.

(3) An assessment notice is a notice which requires the data controller to do all or any of the following–
  (a) permit the Commissioner to enter any specified premises;
  (b) direct the Commissioner to any documents on the premises that are of a specified description;
  (c) assist the Commissioner to view any information of a specified description that is capable of being viewed using equipment on the premises;
  (d) comply with any request from the Commissioner for–
    (i) a copy of any of the documents to which the Commissioner is directed;
    (ii) a copy (in such form as may be requested) of any of the information which the Commissioner is assisted to view;
  (e) direct the Commissioner to any equipment or other material on the premises which is of a specified description;
  (f) permit the Commissioner to inspect or examine any of the documents, information, equipment or material to which the Commissioner is directed or which the Commissioner is assisted to view;
  (g) permit the Commissioner to observe the processing of any personal data that takes place on the premises;
  (h) make available for interview by the Commissioner a specified number of persons of a specified description who process personal data on behalf of the data controller (or such number as are willing to be interviewed).

(4)   In subsection (3) references to the Commissioner include references to the Commissioner's officers and staff.

(5)   An assessment notice must, in relation to each requirement imposed by the notice, specify–
      (a) the time at which the requirement is to be complied with, or
      (b) the period during which the requirement is to be complied with.

(6)   An assessment notice must also contain particulars of the rights of appeal conferred by section 48.

(7)   The Commissioner may cancel an assessment notice by written notice to the data controller on whom it was served.

(8)   Where a public authority has been designated by an order under subsection (2)(b) the Secretary of State must reconsider, at intervals of no greater than 5 years, whether it continues to be appropriate for the authority to be designated.

(9)   The Secretary of State may not make an order under subsection (2)(c) which designates a description of persons unless–
      (a) the Commissioner has made a recommendation that the description be designated, and
      (b) the Secretary of State has consulted–
            (i) such persons as appear to the Secretary of State to represent the interests of those that meet the description;
            (ii) such other persons as the Secretary of State considers appropriate.

(10) The Secretary of State may not make an order under subsection (2)(c), and the Commissioner may not make a recommendation under subsection (9)(a), unless the Secretary of State or (as the case may be) the Commissioner is satisfied that it is necessary for the description of persons in question to be designated having regard to–
      (a) the nature and quantity of data under the control of such persons, and
      (b) any damage or distress which may be caused by a contravention by such persons of the data protection principles.

(11) Where a description of persons has been designated by an order under subsection (2)(c) the Secretary of State must reconsider, at intervals of no greater than 5 years, whether it continues to be necessary for the description to be designated having regard to the matters mentioned in subsection (10).

(12) In this section–
      "public authority" includes any body, office-holder or other person in respect of which–
      (a) an order may be made under section 4 or 5 of the Freedom of Information Act 2000, or
      (b) an order may be made under section 4 or 5 of the Freedom of Information (Scotland) Act 2002;

"specified" means specified in an assessment notice.

NOTES

Defined terms
"business": s 70(1)
"the Commissioner": s 70(1)
"data": s 1(1)
"data controller": s 1(1)
"data protection principles": s 4 and Sch 1

"government department": s 70(1)
"personal data": s 1(1)
"processing": s 1(1)

Assessment notices: limitations

41B(1)   A time specified in an assessment notice under section 41A(5) in relation to a requirement must not fall, and a period so specified must not begin, before the end of the period within which an appeal can be brought against the notice, and if such an appeal is brought the requirement need not be complied with pending the determination or withdrawal of the appeal.

(2)   If by reason of special circumstances the Commissioner considers that it is necessary for the data controller to comply with a requirement in an assessment notice as a matter of urgency, the Commissioner may include in the notice a statement to that effect and a statement of the reasons for that conclusion; and in that event subsection (1) applies in relation to the requirement as if for the words from "within" to the end there were substituted "of 7 days beginning with the day on which the notice is served".

(3)   A requirement imposed by an assessment notice does not have effect in so far as compliance with it would result in the disclosure of–
    (a) any communication between a professional legal adviser and the adviser's client in connection with the giving of legal advice with respect to the client's obligations, liabilities or rights under this Act, or
    (b) any communication between a professional legal adviser and the adviser's client, or between such an adviser or the adviser's client and any other person, made in connection with or in contemplation of proceedings under or arising out of this Act (including proceedings before the Tribunal) and for the purposes of such proceedings.

(4)   In subsection (3) references to the client of a professional legal adviser include references to any person representing such a client.

(5)   Nothing in section 41A authorises the Commissioner to serve an assessment notice on–
    (a) a judge,
    (b) a body specified in section 23(3) of the Freedom of Information Act 2000 (bodies dealing with security matters), or
    (c) the Office for Standards in Education, Children's Services and Skills in so far as it is a data controller in respect of information processed for the purposes of

functions exercisable by Her Majesty's Chief Inspector of Eduction, Children's Services and Skills by virtue of section 5(1)(a) of the Care Standards Act 2000.

(6) In this section "judge" includes–
(a) a justice of the peace (or, in Northern Ireland, a lay magistrate),
(b) a member of a tribunal, and
(c) a clerk or other officer entitled to exercise the jurisdiction of a court or tribunal; and in this subsection "tribunal" means any tribunal in which legal proceedings may be brought.

NOTES

Defined terms
"assessment notice": s 40A(1)
"the Commissioner": s 70(1)
"data": s 1(1)
"data controller": s 1(1)

"government department": s 70(1)
"personal data": s 1(1)
"processing": s 1(1)

Code of practice about assessment notices

41C(1) The Commissioner must prepare and issue a code of practice as to the manner in which the Commissioner's functions under and in connection with section 41A are to be exercised.

(2) The code must in particular–
(a) specify factors to be considered in determining whether to serve an assessment notice on a data controller;
(b) specify descriptions of documents and information that–
(i) are not to be examined or inspected in pursuance of an assessment notice, or
(ii) are to be so examined or inspected only by persons of a description specified in the code;
(c) deal with the nature of inspections and examinations carried out in pursuance of an assessment notice;
(d) deal with the nature of interviews carried out in pursuance of an assessment notice;
(e) deal with the preparation, issuing and publication by the Commissioner of assessment reports in respect of data controllers that have been served with assessment notices.

(3) The provisions of the code made by virtue of subsection (2)(b) must, in particular, include provisions that relate to–
(a) documents and information concerning an individual's physical or mental health;
(b) documents and information concerning the provision of social care for an individual.

(4) An assessment report is a report which contains–

(a) a determination as to whether a data controller has complied or is complying with the data protection principles,

(b) recommendations as to any steps which the data controller ought to take, or refrain from taking, to ensure compliance with any of those principles, and

(c) such other matters as are specified in the code.

(5) The Commissioner may alter or replace the code.

(6) If the code is altered or replaced, the Commissioner must issue the altered or replacement code.

(7) The Commissioner may not issue the code (or an altered or replacement code) without the approval of the Secretary of State.

(8) The Commissioner must arrange for the publication of the code (and any altered or replacement code) issued under this section in such form and manner as the Commissioner considers appropriate.

(9) In this section "social care" has the same meaning as in Part 1 of the Health and Social Care Act 2008 (see section 9(3) of that Act).

NOTES

Defined terms
"assessment notice": s 40A(1)
"the Commissioner": s 70(1)

Request for assessment

42(1) A request may be made to the Commissioner by or on behalf of any person who is, or believes himself to be, directly affected by any processing of personal data for an assessment as to whether it is likely or unlikely that the processing has been or is being carried out in compliance with the provisions of this Act.

(2) On receiving a request under this section, the Commissioner shall make an assessment in such manner as appears to him to be appropriate, unless he has not been supplied with such information as he may reasonably require in order to–

(a) satisfy himself as to the identity of the person making the request, and

(b) enable him to identify the processing in question.

(3) The matters to which the Commissioner may have regard in determining in what manner it is appropriate to make an assessment include–

(a) the extent to which the request appears to him to raise a matter of substance,

(b) any undue delay in making the request, and

(c) whether or not the person making the request is entitled to make an application under section 7 in respect of the personal data in question.

(4) Where the Commissioner has received a request under this section he shall notify the person who made the request–

(a) whether he has made an assessment as a result of the request, and

(b) to the extent that he considers appropriate, having regard in particular to any exemption from section 7 applying in relation to the personal data concerned, of any view formed or action taken as a result of the request.

Information notices

43(1) If the Commissioner–

(a) has received a request under section 42 in respect of any processing of personal data, or

(b) reasonably requires any information for the purpose of determining whether the data controller has complied or is complying with the data protection principles,

he may serve the data controller with a notice (in this Act referred to as "an information notice") requiring the data controller, within such time as is specified in the notice, to furnish the Commissioner, in such form as may be so specified, with such information relating to the request or to compliance with the principles as is so specified to furnish the Commissioner with specified information relating to the request or to compliance with the principles.

(1A) In subsection (1) "specified information" means information–

(a) specified, or described, in the information notice, or

(b) falling within a category which is specified, or described, in the information notice.

(1B) The Commissioner may also specify in the information notice–

(a) the form in which the information must be furnished;

(b) the period within which, or the time and place at which, the information must be furnished.

(2) An information notice must contain–

(a) in a case falling within subsection (1)(a), a statement that the Commissioner has received a request under section 42 in relation to the specified processing, or

(b) in a case falling within subsection (1)(b), a statement that the Commissioner regards the specified information as relevant for the purpose of determining whether the data controller has complied, or is complying, with the data protection principles and his reasons for regarding it as relevant for that purpose.

(3) An information notice must also contain particulars of the rights of appeal conferred by section 48.

(4)   Subject to subsection (5), the time specified in an information notice shall not expire a period specified in an information notice under subsection (1B)(b) must not end, and a time so specified must not fall, before the end of the period within which an appeal can be brought against the notice and, if such an appeal is brought, the information need not be furnished pending the determination or withdrawal of the appeal.

(5)   If by reason of special circumstances the Commissioner considers that the information is required as a matter of urgency, he may include in the notice a statement to that effect and a statement of his reasons for reaching that conclusion; and in that event subsection (4) shall not apply, but the notice shall not require the information to be furnished before the end of the period of seven days beginning with the day on which the notice is served.

(6)   A person shall not be required by virtue of this section to furnish the Commissioner with any information in respect of–
    (a) any communication between a professional legal adviser and his client in connection with the giving of legal advice to the client with respect to his obligations, liabilities or rights under this Act, or
    (b) any communication between a professional legal adviser and his client, or between such an adviser or his client and any other person, made in connection with or in contemplation of proceedings under or arising out of this Act (including proceedings before the Tribunal) and for the purposes of such proceedings.

(7)   In subsection (6) references to the client of a professional legal adviser include references to any person representing such a client.

(8)   A person shall not be required by virtue of this section to furnish the Commissioner with any information if the furnishing of that information would, by revealing evidence of the commission of any offence other than an offence under this Act, , other than an offence under this Act or an offence within subsection (8A), expose him to proceedings for that offence.

(8A)   The offences mentioned in subsection (8) are–
    (a) an offence under section 5 of the Perjury Act 1911 (false statements made otherwise than on oath),
    (b) an offence under section 44(2) of the Criminal Law (Consolidation) (Scotland) Act 1995 (false statements made otherwise than on oath), or
    (c) an offence under Article 10 of the Perjury (Northern Ireland) Order 1979 (false statutory declarations and other false unsworn statements).

(8B)   Any relevant statement provided by a person in response to a requirement under this section may not be used in evidence against that person on a prosecution for any offence under this Act (other than an offence under section 47) unless in the proceedings–
    (a) in giving evidence the person provides information inconsistent with it, and

(b) evidence relating to it is adduced, or a question relating to it is asked, by that person or on that person's behalf.

(8C) In subsection (8B) "relevant statement", in relation to a requirement under this section, means–

(a) an oral statement, or

(b) a written statement made for the purposes of the requirement.

(9) The Commissioner may cancel an information notice by written notice to the person on whom it was served.

(10) This section has effect subject to section 46(3).

NOTES

Defined terms
"the Commissioner": s 70(1)
"data controller": ss1(1) and (4) and 63(3)
"data protection principles": s 4 and Sch1

"information notice": s 43(1)
"personal data": s 1(1)
"processing": s 1(1)
"the Tribunal": s 70(1)

Special information notices

44 If the Commissioner–

(a) has received a request under section 42 in respect of any processing of personal data, or

(b) has reasonable grounds for suspecting that, in a case in which proceedings have been stayed under section 32, the personal data to which the proceedings relate–

(i) are not being processed only for the special purposes, or

(ii) are not being processed with a view to the publication by any person of any journalistic, literary or artistic material which has not previously been published by the data controller,

he may serve the data controller with a notice (in this Act referred to as a "special information notice") requiring the data controller, within such time as is specified in the notice, to furnish the Commissioner, in such form as may be so specified, with such information as is so specified for the purpose specified in subsection (2) to furnish the Commissioner with specified information for the purpose specified in subsection (2).

(1A) In subsection (1) "specified information" means information–

(a) specified, or described, in the special information notice, or

(b) falling within a category which is specified, or described, in the special information notice.

(1B) The Commissioner may also specify in the special information notice–

(a) the form in which the information must be furnished;

(b) the period within which, or the time and place at which, the information must be furnished.

(2) That purpose is the purpose of ascertaining–

(a) whether the personal data are being processed only for the special purposes, or

(b) whether they are being processed with a view to the publication by any person of any journalistic, literary or artistic material which has not previously been published by the data controller.

(3) A special information notice must contain–

(a) in a case falling within paragraph (a) of subsection (1), a statement that the Commissioner has received a request under section 42 in relation to the specified processing, or

(b) in a case falling within paragraph (b) of that subsection, a statement of the Commissioner's grounds for suspecting that the personal data are not being processed as mentioned in that paragraph.

(4) A special information notice must also contain particulars of the rights of appeal conferred by section 48.

(5) Subject to subsection (6), the time specified in a special information notice shall not expire a period specified in a special information notice under subsection (1B)(b) must not end, and a time so specified must not fall, before the end of the period within which an appeal can be brought against the notice and, if such an appeal is brought, the information need not be furnished pending the determination or withdrawal of the appeal.

(6) If by reason of special circumstances the Commissioner considers that the information is required as a matter of urgency, he may include in the notice a statement to that effect and a statement of his reasons for reaching that conclusion; and in that event subsection (5) shall not apply, but the notice shall not require the information to be furnished before the end of the period of seven days beginning with the day on which the notice is served.

(7) A person shall not be required by virtue of this section to furnish the Commissioner with any information in respect of–

(a) any communication between a professional legal adviser and his client in connection with the giving of legal advice to the client with respect to his obligations, liabilities or rights under this Act, or

(b) any communication between a professional legal adviser and his client, or between such an adviser or his client and any other person, made in connection with or in contemplation of proceedings under or arising out of this Act (including proceedings before the Tribunal) and for the purposes of such proceedings.

(8) In subsection (7) references to the client of a professional legal adviser include references to any person representing such a client.

(9) A person shall not be required by virtue of this section to furnish the Commissioner with any information if the furnishing of that information would, by revealing evidence of the commission of any offence other than an offence under this Act, , other than an

offence under this Act or an offence within subsection (9A), expose him to proceedings for that offence.

(9A) The offences mentioned in subsection (9) are–

(a) an offence under section 5 of the Perjury Act 1911 (false statements made otherwise than on oath),

(b) an offence under section 44(2) of the Criminal Law (Consolidation) (Scotland) Act 1995 (false statements made otherwise than on oath), or

(c) an offence under Article 10 of the Perjury (Northern Ireland) Order 1979 (false statutory declarations and other false unsworn statements).

(9B) Any relevant statement provided by a person in response to a requirement under this section may not be used in evidence against that person on a prosecution for any offence under this Act (other than an offence under section 47) unless in the proceedings–

(a) in giving evidence the person provides information inconsistent with it, and

(b) evidence relating to it is adduced, or a question relating to it is asked, by that person or on that person's behalf.

(9C) In subsection (9B) "relevant statement", in relation to a requirement under this section, means–

(a) an oral statement, or

(b) a written statement made for the purposes of the requirement.

(10) The Commissioner may cancel a special information notice by written notice to the person on whom it was served.

NOTES

Defined terms
"the Commissioner": s 70(1)
"data controller": ss1(1) and (4) and 63(3)
"personal data": s 1(1)
"processing": s 1(1)
"publish": s 32(6)
"special information notice": s 44(1)
"the special purposes": s 3
"the Tribunal": s 70(1)

Determination by Commissioner as to the special purposes

45(1) Where at any time it appears to the Commissioner (whether as a result of the service of a special information notice or otherwise) that any personal data–

(a) are not being processed only for the special purposes, or

(b) are not being processed with a view to the publication by any person of any journalistic, literary or artistic material which has not previously been published by the data controller,

he may make a determination in writing to that effect.

(2) Notice of the determination shall be given to the data controller; and the notice must contain particulars of the right of appeal conferred by section 48.

(3)   A determination under subsection (1) shall not take effect until the end of the period within which an appeal can be brought and, where an appeal is brought, shall not take effect pending the determination or withdrawal of the appeal.

NOTES

Defined terms
"the Commissioner": s 70(1)
"data controller": ss1(1) and (4) and 63(3)
"personal data": s 1(1)

"processing": s 1(1)
"publish": s 32(6)
"special information notice": s 44(1)
"the special purposes": s 3

Restriction on enforcement in case of processing for the special purposes

46(1)   The Commissioner may not at any time serve an enforcement notice on a data controller with respect to the processing of personal data for the special purposes unless–

(a) a determination under section 45(1) with respect to those data has taken effect, and

(b) the court has granted leave for the notice to be served.

(2)   The court shall not grant leave for the purposes of subsection (1)(b) unless it is satisfied–

(a) that the Commissioner has reason to suspect a contravention of the data protection principles which is of substantial public importance, and

(b) except where the case is one of urgency, that the data controller has been given notice, in accordance with rules of court, of the application for leave.

(3)   The Commissioner may not serve an information notice on a data controller with respect to the processing of personal data for the special purposes unless a determination under section 45(1) with respect to those data has taken effect.

NOTES

Defined terms
"the Commissioner": s 70(1)
"data controller": ss1(1) and (4) and 63(3)
"data protection principles": s 4 and Sch1
"enforcement notice": s 40(1)

"information notice": s 43(1)
"personal data": s 1(1)
"processing": s 1(1)
"the special purposes": s 3

Failure to comply with notice

47(1)   A person who fails to comply with an enforcement notice, an information notice or a special information notice is guilty of an offence.

(2)   A person who, in purported compliance with an information notice or a special information notice–

(a) makes a statement which he knows to be false in a material respect, or

(b) recklessly makes a statement which is false in a material respect,

is guilty of an offence.

(3)   It is a defence for a person charged with an offence under subsection (1) to prove that he exercised all due diligence to comply with the notice in question.

Rights of appeal

48(1)   A person on whom an enforcement notice, an assessment notice, an information notice or a special information notice has been served may appeal to the Tribunal against the notice.

(2)   A person on whom an enforcement notice has been served may appeal to the Tribunal against the refusal of an application under section 41(2) for cancellation or variation of the notice.

(3)   Where an enforcement notice, an assessment notice, an information notice or a special information notice contains a statement by the Commissioner in accordance with section 40(8), 41B(2), 43(5) or 44(6) then, whether or not the person appeals against the notice, he may appeal against–
   (a) the Commissioner's decision to include the statement in the notice, or
   (b) the effect of the inclusion of the statement as respects any part of the notice.

(4)   A data controller in respect of whom a determination has been made under section 45 may appeal to the Tribunal against the determination.

(5)   Schedule 6 has effect in relation to appeals under this section and the proceedings of the Tribunal in respect of any such appeal.

Determination of appeals

49(1)   If on an appeal under section 48(1) the Tribunal considers–
   (a) that the notice against which the appeal is brought is not in accordance with the law, or
   (b) to the extent that the notice involved an exercise of discretion by the Commissioner, that he ought to have exercised his discretion differently,
   the Tribunal shall allow the appeal or substitute such other notice or decision as could have been served or made by the Commissioner; and in any other case the Tribunal shall dismiss the appeal.

(2)   On such an appeal, the Tribunal may review any determination of fact on which the notice in question was based.

(3)   If on an appeal under section 48(2) the Tribunal considers that the enforcement notice ought to be cancelled or varied by reason of a change in circumstances, the Tribunal shall cancel or vary the notice.

(4)   On an appeal under subsection (3) of section 48 the Tribunal may direct–
        (a) that the notice in question shall have effect as if it did not contain any such statement as is mentioned in that subsection, or
        (b) that the inclusion of the statement shall not have effect in relation to any part of the notice,
        and may make such modifications in the notice as may be required for giving effect to the direction.

(5)   On an appeal under section 48(4), the Tribunal may cancel the determination of the Commissioner.

NOTES

Defined terms
"address": s 49(7)
"the Commissioner": s 70(1)

"enforcement notice": s 40(1)
"the Tribunal": s 70(1)

Powers of entry and inspection

50   Schedule 9 (powers of entry and inspection) has effect.

PART VI

MISCELLANEOUS AND GENERAL

Functions of Commissioner

General duties of Commissioner

51(1)   It shall be the duty of the Commissioner to promote the following of good practice by data controllers and, in particular, so to perform his functions under this Act as to promote the observance of the requirements of this Act by data controllers.

(2)   The Commissioner shall arrange for the dissemination in such form and manner as he considers appropriate of such information as it may appear to him expedient to give to the public about the operation of this Act, about good practice, and about other matters within the scope of his functions under this Act, and may give advice to any person as to any of those matters.

(3)   Where–
        (a) the Secretary of State so directs by order, or

(b) the Commissioner considers it appropriate to do so,

the Commissioner shall, after such consultation with trade associations, data subjects or persons representing data subjects as appears to him to be appropriate, prepare and disseminate to such persons as he considers appropriate codes of practice for guidance as to good practice.

(4) The Commissioner shall also–

    (a) where he considers it appropriate to do so, encourage trade associations to prepare, and to disseminate to their members, such codes of practice, and

    (b) where any trade association submits a code of practice to him for his consideration, consider the code and, after such consultation with data subjects or persons representing data subjects as appears to him to be appropriate, notify the trade association whether in his opinion the code promotes the following of good practice.

(5) An order under subsection (3) shall describe the personal data or processing to which the code of practice is to relate, and may also describe the persons or classes of persons to whom it is to relate.

(5A) In determining the action required to discharge the duties imposed by subsections (1) to (4), the Commissioner may take account of any action taken to discharge the duty imposed by section 52A (data-sharing code).

(6) The Commissioner shall arrange for the dissemination in such form and manner as he considers appropriate of–

    (a) any Community finding as defined by paragraph 15(2) of Part II of Schedule 1,

    (b) any decision of the European Commission, under the procedure provided for in Article 31(2) of the Data Protection Directive, which is made for the purposes of Article 26(3) or (4) of the Directive, and

    (c) such other information as it may appear to him to be expedient to give to data controllers in relation to any personal data about the protection of the rights and freedoms of data subjects in relation to the processing of personal data in countries and territories outside the European Economic Area.

(7) The Commissioner may, with the consent of the data controller, assess any processing of personal data for the following of good practice and shall inform the data controller of the results of the assessment.

(8) The Commissioner may charge such sums as he may with the consent of the Secretary of State determine for any services provided by the Commissioner by virtue of this Part.

(9) In this section–

"good practice" means such practice in the processing of personal data as appears to the Commissioner to be desirable having regard to the interests of data subjects and others, and includes (but is not limited to) compliance with the requirements of this Act;

"trade association" includes any body representing data controllers.

NOTES

Defined terms
"Commissioner": s 70(1)
"data controller": ss1(1) and (4) and 63(3)
"Data Protection Directive": s 70(1)
"data subject": s 1(1)

"good practice": s 51(a)
"personal data": s 1(1)
"processing": s 1(1)
"trade association": s 51(a)

Reports and codes of practice to be laid before Parliament

52(1)   The Commissioner shall lay annually before each House of Parliament a general report on the exercise of his functions under this Act.

(2)   The Commissioner may from time to time lay before each House of Parliament such other reports with respect to those functions as he thinks fit.

(3)   The Commissioner shall lay before each House of Parliament any code of practice prepared under section 51(3) for complying with a direction of the Secretary of State, unless the code is included in any report laid under subsection (1) or (2).

NOTES

Defined terms
"Commissioner": s 70(1)

Data-sharing code

52A(1)   The Commissioner must prepare a code of practice which contains–
   (a) practical guidance in relation to the sharing of personal data in accordance with the requirements of this Act, and
   (b) such other guidance as the Commissioner considers appropriate to promote good practice in the sharing of personal data.

(2)   For this purpose "good practice" means such practice in the sharing of personal data as appears to the Commissioner to be desirable having regard to the interests of data subjects and others, and includes (but is not limited to) compliance with the requirements of this Act.

(3)   Before a code is prepared under this section, the Commissioner must consult such of the following as the Commissioner considers appropriate–
   (a) trade associations (within the meaning of section 51);
   (b) data subjects;
   (c) persons who appear to the Commissioner to represent the interests of data subjects.

(4)   In this section a reference to the sharing of personal data is to the disclosure of the data by transmission, dissemination or otherwise making it available.

NOTES

Defined terms
"Commissioner": s 70(1)
"data controller": ss1(1) and (4) and 63(3)
"Data Protection Directive": s 70(1)
"data subject": s 1(1)

"personal data": s 1(1)
"processing": s 1(1)
"trade association": s 51(a)

Data-sharing code: procedure

52B(1)   When a code is prepared under section 52A, it must be submitted to the Secretary of State for approval.

(2)   Approval may be withheld only if it appears to the Secretary of State that the terms of the code could result in the United Kingdom being in breach of any of its Community obligations or any other international obligation.

(3)   The Secretary of State must–
        (a) if approval is withheld, publish details of the reasons for withholding it;
        (b) if approval is granted, lay the code before Parliament.

(4)   If, within the 40-day period, either House of Parliament resolves not to approve the code, the code is not to be issued by the Commissioner.

(5)   If no such resolution is made within that period, the Commissioner must issue the code.

(6)   Where–
        (a) the Secretary of State withholds approval, or
        (b) such a resolution is passed,
        the Commissioner must prepare another code of practice under section 52A.

(7)   Subsection (4) does not prevent a new code being laid before Parliament.

(8)   A code comes into force at the end of the period of 21 days beginning with the day on which it is issued.

(9)   A code may include transitional provision or savings.

(10)   In this section "the 40-day period" means the period of 40 days beginning with the day on which the code is laid before Parliament (or, if it is not laid before each House of Parliament on the same day, the later of the 2 days on which it is laid).

(11)   In calculating the 40-day period, no account is to be taken of any period during which Parliament is dissolved or prorogued or during which both Houses are adjourned for more than 4 days.

NOTES

Alteration or replacement of data-sharing code

52C(1) The Commissioner–
>   (a) must keep the data-sharing code under review, and
>   (b) may prepare an alteration to that code or a replacement code.

(2) Where, by virtue of a review under subsection (1)(a) or otherwise, the Commissioner becomes aware that the terms of the code could result in the United Kingdom being in breach of any of its Community obligations or any other international obligation, the Commissioner must exercise the power under subsection (1)(b) with a view to remedying the situation.

(3) Before an alteration or replacement code is prepared under subsection (1), the Commissioner must consult such of the following as the Commissioner considers appropriate–
>   (a) trade associations (within the meaning of section 51);
>   (b) data subjects;
>   (c) persons who appear to the Commissioner to represent the interests of data subjects.

(4) Section 52B (other than subsection (6)) applies to an alteration or replacement code prepared under this section as it applies to the code as first prepared under section 52A.

(5) In this section "the data-sharing code" means the code issued under section 52B(5) (as altered or replaced from time to time).

Publication of data-sharing code

52D(1) The Commissioner must publish the code (and any replacement code) issued under section 52B(5).

(2) Where an alteration is so issued, the Commissioner must publish either–
>   (a) the alteration, or
>   (b) the code or replacement code as altered by it.

Effect of data-sharing code

52E(1)   A failure on the part of any person to act in accordance with any provision of the data-sharing code does not of itself render that person liable to any legal proceedings in any court or tribunal.

(2)   The data-sharing code is admissible in evidence in any legal proceedings.

(3)   If any provision of the data-sharing code appears to–
    (a) the Tribunal or a court conducting any proceedings under this Act,
    (b) a court or tribunal conducting any other legal proceedings, or
    (c) the Commissioner carrying out any function under this Act,
to be relevant to any question arising in the proceedings, or in connection with the exercise of that jurisdiction or the carrying out of those functions, in relation to any time when it was in force, that provision of the code must be taken into account in determining that question.

(4)   In this section "the data-sharing code" means the code issued under section 52B(5) (as altered or replaced from time to time).

Defined terms   "the Tribunal": s 70(1)
"Commissioner": s 70(1)

Assistance by Commissioner in cases involving processing for the special purposes

53(1)   An individual who is an actual or prospective party to any proceedings under section 7(9), 10(4), 12(8) or 14 or by virtue of section 13 which relate to personal data processed for the special purposes may apply to the Commissioner for assistance in relation to those proceedings.

(2)   The Commissioner shall, as soon as reasonably practicable after receiving an application under subsection (1), consider it and decide whether and to what extent to grant it, but he shall not grant the application unless, in his opinion, the case involves a matter of substantial public importance.

(3)   If the Commissioner decides to provide assistance, he shall, as soon as reasonably practicable after making the decision, notify the applicant, stating the extent of the assistance to be provided.

(4)   If the Commissioner decides not to provide assistance, he shall, as soon as reasonably practicable after making the decision, notify the applicant of his decision and, if he thinks fit, the reasons for it.

(5)   In this section–
    (a) references to "proceedings" include references to prospective proceedings, and

(b) "applicant", in relation to assistance under this section, means an individual who applies for assistance.

(6)   Schedule 10 has effect for supplementing this section.

NOTES

Defined terms
"applicant": s 53(5)(b)
"Commissioner": s 70(1)

"personal data": s 1(1)
"proceedings": s 53(5)
"special purposes": s 3

International co-operation

54(1)   The Commissioner–
        (a) shall continue to be the designated authority in the United Kingdom for the purposes of Article 13 of the Convention, and
        (b) shall be the supervisory authority in the United Kingdom for the purposes of the Data Protection Directive.

(2)   The Secretary of State may by order make provision as to the functions to be discharged by the Commissioner as the designated authority in the United Kingdom for the purposes of Article 13 of the Convention.

(3)   The Secretary of State may by order make provision as to co-operation by the Commissioner with the European Commission and with supervisory authorities in other EEA States in connection with the performance of their respective duties and, in particular, as to–
        (a) the exchange of information with supervisory authorities in other EEA States or with the European Commission, and
        (b) the exercise within the United Kingdom at the request of a supervisory authority in another EEA State, in cases excluded by section 5 from the application of the other provisions of this Act, of functions of the Commissioner specified in the order.

(4)   The Commissioner shall also carry out any data protection functions which the Secretary of State may by order direct him to carry out for the purpose of enabling Her Majesty's Government in the United Kingdom to give effect to any international obligations of the United Kingdom.

(5)   The Commissioner shall, if so directed by the Secretary of State, provide any authority exercising data protection functions under the law of a colony specified in the direction with such assistance in connection with the discharge of those functions as the Secretary of State may direct or approve, on such terms (including terms as to payment) as the Secretary of State may direct or approve.

(6)   Where the European Commission makes a decision for the purposes of Article 26(3) or (4) of the Data Protection Directive under the procedure provided for in Article 31(2) of the Directive, the Commissioner shall comply with that decision in exercising

his functions under paragraph 9 of Schedule 4 or, as the case may be, paragraph 8 of that Schedule.

(7) The Commissioner shall inform the European Commission and the supervisory authorities in other EEA States–

    (a) of any approvals granted for the purposes of paragraph 8 of Schedule 4, and

    (b) of any authorisations granted for the purposes of paragraph 9 of that Schedule.

(8) In this section–

"the Convention" means the Convention for the Protection of Individuals with regard to Automatic Processing of Personal Data which was opened for signature on 28th January 1981;

"data protection functions" means functions relating to the protection of individuals with respect to the processing of personal information.

NOTES

Defined terms

"the Commissioner": s 70(1)

"the Convention": s 54(8)

"the Data Protection Directive": s 70(1)

"data protection functions": s 54(8)

"EEA State": s 70(1)

Subordinate legislation

Data Protection (Functions of Designated Authority) Order 2000. Reproduced at p 1144 ff.

Data Protection (International Co-operation) Order 2000

Inspection of overseas information systems

54A(1) The Commissioner may inspect any personal data recorded in–

    (a) the Schengen information system,

    (b) the Europol information system,

    (c) the Customs information system.

(2) The power conferred by subsection (1) is exercisable only for the purpose of assessing whether or not any processing of the data has been or is being carried out in compliance with this Act.

(3) The power includes power to inspect, operate and test equipment which is used for the processing of personal data.

(4) Before exercising the power, the Commissioner must give notice in writing of his intention to do so to the data controller.

(5) But subsection (4) does not apply if the Commissioner considers that the case is one of urgency.

(6) Any person who–

    (a) intentionally obstructs a person exercising the power conferred by subsection (1), or

    (b) fails without reasonable excuse to give any person exercising the power any assistance he may reasonably require,

is guilty of an offence.

(7)   In this section—

"the Customs information system" means the information system established under Chapter II of the Convention on the Use of Information Technology for Customs Purposes,

"the Europol information system" means the information system established under Title II of the Convention on the Establishment of a European Police Office,

"the Schengen information system" means the information system established under Title IV of the Convention implementing the Schengen Agreement of 14th June 1985, or any system established in its place in pursuance of any Community obligation.

NOTES

Defined terms   "processing": s 1(1)
"Commissioner": s 70(1)
"data controller": ss1(1) and (4) and 63(3)
"data subject": s 1(1)

Unlawful obtaining etc of personal data

55(1)   A person must not knowingly or recklessly, without the consent of the data controller—

(a) obtain or disclose personal data or the information contained in personal data, or

(b) procure the disclosure to another person of the information contained in personal data.

(2)   Subsection (1) does not apply to a person who shows—

(a) that the obtaining, disclosing or procuring—

(i) was necessary for the purpose of preventing or detecting crime, or

(ii) was required or authorised by or under any enactment, by any rule of law or by the order of a court,

(b) that he acted in the reasonable belief that he had in law the right to obtain or disclose the data or information or, as the case may be, to procure the disclosure of the information to the other person,

(c) that he acted in the reasonable belief that he would have had the consent of the data controller if the data controller had known of the obtaining, disclosing or procuring and the circumstances of it,

(ca)that he acted—

(i) for the special purposes,

(ii) with a view to the publication by any person of any journalistic, literary or artistic material, and

(iii) in the reasonable belief that in the particular circumstances the obtaining, disclosing or procuring was justified as being in the public interest, or

(d) that in the particular circumstances the obtaining, disclosing or procuring was justified as being in the public interest.

(3)   A person who contravenes subsection (1) is guilty of an offence.

(4)   A person who sells personal data is guilty of an offence if he has obtained the data in contravention of subsection (1).

(5)   A person who offers to sell personal data is guilty of an offence if–
    (a) he has obtained the data in contravention of subsection (1), or
    (b) he subsequently obtains the data in contravention of that subsection.

(6)   For the purposes of subsection (5), an advertisement indicating that personal data are or may be for sale is an offer to sell the data.

(7)   Section 1(2) does not apply for the purposes of this section; and for the purposes of subsections (4) to (6), "personal data" includes information extracted from personal data.

(8)   References in this section to personal data do not include references to personal data which by virtue of section 28 or 33A are exempt from this section.

NOTES

Defined terms
"data controller": ss1(1) and (4) and 63(3)
"disclosing": s 1(2)(b)
"enactment": s 70(1)

"obtaining": s 1(2)(a)
"personal data : s 1(1)
"special purposes": s 3

Power of Commissioner to impose monetary penalty

55A(1) The Commissioner may serve a data controller with a monetary penalty notice if the Commissioner is satisfied that–
    (a) there has been a serious contravention of section 4(4) by the data controller,
    (b) the contravention was of a kind likely to cause substantial damage or substantial distress, and
    (c) subsection (2) or (3) applies.

(2)   This subsection applies if the contravention was deliberate.

(3)   This subsection applies if the data controller–
    (a) knew or ought to have known–
      (i)   that there was a risk that the contravention would occur, and
      (ii) that such a contravention would be of a kind likely to cause substantial damage or substantial distress, but
    (b) failed to take reasonable steps to prevent the contravention.

(3A)   The Commissioner may not be satisfied as mentioned in subsection (1) by virtue of any matter which comes to the Commissioner's attention as a result of anything done in pursuance of–
    (a) an assessment notice;
    (b) an assessment under section 51(7).

(4)   A monetary penalty notice is a notice requiring the data controller to pay to the Commissioner a monetary penalty of an amount determined by the Commissioner and specified in the notice.

(5)   The amount determined by the Commissioner must not exceed the prescribed amount.

(6)   The monetary penalty must be paid to the Commissioner within the period specified in the notice.

(7)   The notice must contain such information as may be prescribed.

(8)   Any sum received by the Commissioner by virtue of this section must be paid into the Consolidated Fund.

(9)   In this section–
       "data controller" does not include the Crown Estate Commissioners or a person who is a data controller by virtue of section 63(3);
       "prescribed" means prescribed by regulations made by the Secretary of State.

NOTES

Monetary penalty notices: procedural rights

55B(1)   Before serving a monetary penalty notice, the Commissioner must serve the data controller with a notice of intent.

(2)   A notice of intent is a notice that the Commissioner proposes to serve a monetary penalty notice.

(3)   A notice of intent must–
       (a) inform the data controller that he may make written representations in relation to the Commissioner's proposal within a period specified in the notice, and
       (b) contain such other information as may be prescribed.

(4)   The Commissioner may not serve a monetary penalty notice until the time within which the data controller may make representations has expired.

(5)   A person on whom a monetary penalty notice is served may appeal to the Tribunal against–
       (a) the issue of the monetary penalty notice;
       (b) the amount of the penalty specified in the notice.

(6)   In this section, "prescribed" means prescribed by regulations made by the Secretary of State.

NOTES

Defined terms
"the Commissioner": s 70(1)

"data controller": ss1(1) and (4) and 63(3)

Guidance about monetary penalty notices

55C(1)   The Commissioner must prepare and issue guidance on how he proposes to exercise his functions under sections 55A and 55B.

(2)   The guidance must, in particular, deal with–
  (a) the circumstances in which he would consider it appropriate to issue a monetary penalty notice, and
  (b) how he will determine the amount of the penalty.

(3)   The Commissioner may alter or replace the guidance.

(4)   If the guidance is altered or replaced, the Commissioner must issue the altered or replacement guidance.

(5)   The Commissioner may not issue guidance under this section without the approval of the Secretary of State.

(6)   The Commissioner must lay any guidance issued under this section before each House of Parliament.

(7)   The Commissioner must arrange for the publication of any guidance issued under this section in such form and manner as he considers appropriate.

(8)   In subsections (5) to (7), "guidance" includes altered or replacement guidance.

NOTES

Defined terms
"the Commissioner": s 70(1)

Monetary penalty notices: enforcement

55D(1)   This section applies in relation to any penalty payable to the Commissioner by virtue of section 55A.

(2)   In England and Wales, the penalty is recoverable–
  (a) if a county court so orders, as if it were payable under an order of that court;
  (b) if the High Court so orders, as if it were payable under an order of that court.

(3)   In Scotland, the penalty may be enforced in the same manner as an extract registered decree arbitral bearing a warrant for execution issued by the sheriff court of any sheriffdom in Scotland.

(4)   In Northern Ireland, the penalty is recoverable–
  (a) if a county court so orders, as if it were payable under an order of that court;
  (b) if the High Court so orders, as if it were payable under an order of that court.

NOTES

Notices under sections 55A and 55B: supplemental

55E(1) The Secretary of State may by order make further provision in connection with monetary penalty notices and notices of intent.

(2) An order under this section may in particular–

(a) provide that a monetary penalty notice may not be served on a data controller with respect to the processing of personal data for the special purposes except in circumstances specified in the order;

(b) make provision for the cancellation or variation of monetary penalty notices;

(c) confer rights of appeal to the Tribunal against decisions of the Commissioner in relation to the cancellation or variation of such notices;

(e) make provision for the determination of appeals made by virtue of paragraph (c);

(3) An order under this section may apply any provision of this Act with such modifications as may be specified in the order.

(4) An order under this section may amend this Act.

NOTES

Defined terms
"the Commissioner": s 70(1)

"special purposes": s 3
"the Tribunal": s 70(1)

Records obtained under data subject's right of access

Prohibition of requirement as to production of certain records

56(1) A person must not, in connection with–

(a) the recruitment of another person as an employee,

(b) the continued employment of another person, or

(c) any contract for the provision of services to him by another person,

require that other person or a third party to supply him with a relevant record or to produce a relevant record to him.

(2) A person concerned with the provision (for payment or not) of goods, facilities or services to the public or a section of the public must not, as a condition of providing or offering to provide any goods, facilities or services to another person, require that other person or a third party to supply him with a relevant record or to produce a relevant record to him.

(3) Subsections (1) and (2) do not apply to a person who shows–

(a) that the imposition of the requirement was required or authorised by or under any enactment, by any rule of law or by the order of a court, or

(b) that in the particular circumstances the imposition of the requirement was justified as being in the public interest.

(4) Having regard to the provisions of Part V of the Police Act 1997 (certificates of criminal records etc), the imposition of the requirement referred to in subsection (1) or (2) is not to be regarded as being justified as being in the public interest on the ground that it would assist in the prevention or detection of crime.

(5) A person who contravenes subsection (1) or (2) is guilty of an offence.

(6) In this section "a relevant record" means any record which–

(a) has been or is to be obtained by a data subject from any data controller specified in the first column of the Table below in the exercise of the right conferred by section 7, and

(b) contains information relating to any matter specified in relation to that data controller in the second column,

and includes a copy of such a record or a part of such a record.

Table

Data controller		Subject-matter	
1 Any of the following persons–		(a)	Convictions.
(a)	a chief officer of police of a police force in England and Wales.	(b)	Cautions
(b)	a chief constable of a police force in Scotland.		
(c)	the Chief Constable of the Police Service of Northern Ireland.		
(d)	the Director General of the Serious Organised Crime Agency.		
2 The Secretary of State.		(a)	Convictions.
		(b)	Cautions.
		(c)	His functions under section 92 of the Powers of Criminal Courts (Sentencing) Act 2000, section 205(2) or 208 of the Criminal Procedure (Scotland) Act 1995 or section 73 of the Children and Young Persons Act (Northern Ireland) 1968 in relation to any person sentenced to detention.
		(d)	His functions under the Prison Act 1952, the Prisons (Scotland) Act 1989 or the Prison Act (Northern Ireland) 1953 in relation to any person imprisoned or detained.
		(e)	His functions under the Social Security Contributions and Benefits Act 1992, the Social Security Administration Act 1992 or the Jobseekers Act 1995.
		(f)	His functions under Part V of the

		Police Act 1997.
	(g)	His functions under the Safeguarding Vulnerable Groups Act 2006 or the Safeguarding Vulnerable Groups (Northern Ireland) Order 2007.
3 The Department of Health and Social Services for Northern Ireland.		Its functions under the Social Security Contributions and Benefits (Northern Ireland) Act 1992, the Social Security Administration (Northern Ireland) Act 1992 or the Jobseekers (Northern Ireland) Order 1995.4 The Independent Barring Board.Its functions under the Safeguarding Vulnerable Groups Act 2006 or the Safeguarding Vulnerable Groups (Northern Ireland) Order 2007.

(6A) A record is not a relevant record to the extent that it relates, or is to relate, only to personal data falling within paragraph (e) of the definition of "data" in section 1(1).

(7) In the Table in subsection (6)–

"caution" means a caution given to any person in England and Wales or Northern Ireland in respect of an offence which, at the time when the caution is given, is admitted;

"conviction" has the same meaning as in the Rehabilitation of Offenders Act 1974 or the Rehabilitation of Offenders (Northern Ireland) Order 1978.

(8) The Secretary of State may by order amend–

(a) the Table in subsection (6), and

(b) subsection (7).

(9) For the purposes of this section a record which states that a data controller is not processing any personal data relating to a particular matter shall be taken to be a record containing information relating to that matter.

(10) In this section "employee" means an individual who–

(a) works under a contract of employment, as defined by section 230(2) of the Employment Rights Act 1996, or

(b) holds any office,

whether or not he is entitled to remuneration; and "employment" shall be construed accordingly.

NOTES

Defined terms
"data controller": ss1(1) and (4) and 63(3)
"enactment": s 70(1)

"personal data": s 1(1)
"third party": s 70(1)

Avoidance of certain contractual terms relating to health records

57(1) Any term or condition of a contract is void in so far as it purports to require an individual–

(a) to supply any other person with a record to which this section applies, or with a copy of such a record or a part of such a record, or

(b) to produce to any other person such a record, copy or part.

(2) This section applies to any record which–

(a) has been or is to be obtained by a data subject in the exercise of the right conferred by section 7, and

(b) consists of the information contained in any health record as defined by section 68(2).

NOTES

Defined terms   "health record": s 68(2)
"data subject": s 1(1)

Information provided to Commissioner or Tribunal

Disclosure of information

58 No enactment or rule of law prohibiting or restricting the disclosure of information shall preclude a person from furnishing the Commissioner or the Tribunal with any information necessary for the discharge of their functions under this Act or the Freedom of Information Act 2000.

NOTES

Defined terms   "enactment": s 70(1)
"Commissioner": s 70(1)   "Tribunal": s 70(1)

Confidentiality of information

59(1) No person who is or has been the Commissioner, a member of the Commissioner's staff or an agent of the Commissioner shall disclose any information which–

(a) has been obtained by, or furnished to, the Commissioner under or for the purposes of the information Acts,

(b) relates to an identified or identifiable individual or business, and

(c) is not at the time of the disclosure, and has not previously been, available to the public from other sources,

unless the disclosure is made with lawful authority.

(2) For the purposes of subsection (1) a disclosure of information is made with lawful authority only if, and to the extent that–

(a) the disclosure is made with the consent of the individual or of the person for the time being carrying on the business,

(b) the information was provided for the purpose of its being made available to the public (in whatever manner) under any provision of the information Acts,

(c) the disclosure is made for the purposes of, and is necessary for, the discharge of–

    (i) any functions under the information Acts, or

    (ii) any Community obligation,

(d) the disclosure is made for the purposes of any proceedings, whether criminal or civil and whether arising under, or by virtue of, the information Acts or otherwise, or

(e) having regard to the rights and freedoms or legitimate interests of any person, the disclosure is necessary in the public interest.

(3) Any person who knowingly or recklessly discloses information in contravention of subsection (1) is guilty of an offence.

(4) In this section "the information Acts" means this Act and the Freedom of Information Act 2000.

NOTES

Defined terms
"Commissioner": s 70(1)

General provisions relating to offences

Prosecutions and penalties

60(1) No proceedings for an offence under this Act shall be instituted–

    (a) in England or Wales, except by the Commissioner or by or with the consent of the Director of Public Prosecutions;

    (b) in Northern Ireland, except by the Commissioner or by or with the consent of the Director of Public Prosecutions for Northern Ireland.

(2) A person guilty of an offence under any provision of this Act other than section 54A and paragraph 12 of Schedule 9 is liable–

    (a) on summary conviction, to a fine not exceeding the statutory maximum, or

    (b) on conviction on indictment, to a fine.

(3) A person guilty of an offence under section 54A and paragraph 12 of Schedule 9 is liable on summary conviction to a fine not exceeding level 5 on the standard scale.

(4) Subject to subsection (5), the court by or before which a person is convicted of–

    (a) an offence under section 21(1), 22(6), 55 or 56,

    (b) an offence under section 21(2) relating to processing which is assessable processing for the purposes of section 22, or

    (c) an offence under section 47(1) relating to an enforcement notice,

may order any document or other material used in connection with the processing of personal data and appearing to the court to be connected with the commission of the offence to be forfeited, destroyed or erased.

(5)   The court shall not make an order under subsection (4) in relation to any material where a person (other than the offender) claiming to be the owner of or otherwise interested in the material applies to be heard by the court, unless an opportunity is given to him to show cause why the order should not be made.

NOTES

Defined terms   "personal data": s 1(1)
"Commissioner": s 70(1)   "processing": s 1(1)

Liability of directors etc

61(1)   Where an offence under this Act has been committed by a body corporate and is proved to have been committed with the consent or connivance of or to be attributable to any neglect on the part of any director, manager, secretary or similar officer of the body corporate or any person who was purporting to act in any such capacity, he as well as the body corporate shall be guilty of that offence and be liable to be proceeded against and punished accordingly.

(2)   Where the affairs of a body corporate are managed by its members subsection (1) shall apply in relation to the acts and defaults of a member in connection with his functions of management as if he were a director of the body corporate.

(3)   Where an offence under this Act has been committed by a Scottish partnership and the contravention in question is proved to have occurred with the consent or connivance of, or to be attributable to any neglect on the part of, a partner, he as well as the partnership shall be guilty of that offence and shall be liable to be proceeded against and punished accordingly.

Amendments of Consumer Credit Act 1974

Amendments of Consumer Credit Act 1974

62(1)   *Not reproduced*

General

Application to Crown

63(1)   This Act binds the Crown.

(2)   For the purposes of this Act each government department shall be treated as a person separate from any other government department.

(3)   Where the purposes for which and the manner in which any personal data are, or are to be, processed are determined by any person acting on behalf of the Royal Household, the Duchy of Lancaster or the Duchy of Cornwall, the data controller in respect of those data for the purposes of this Act shall be–
       (a) in relation to the Royal Household, the Keeper of the Privy Purse,

   (b) in relation to the Duchy of Lancaster, such person as the Chancellor of the Duchy appoints, and

   (c) in relation to the Duchy of Cornwall, such person as the Duke of Cornwall, or the possessor for the time being of the Duchy of Cornwall, appoints.

(4)   Different persons may be appointed under subsection (3)(b) or (c) for different purposes.

(5)   Neither a government department nor a person who is a data controller by virtue of subsection (3) shall be liable to prosecution under this Act, but sections 54A and 55 and paragraph 12 of Schedule 9 shall apply to a person in the service of the Crown as they apply to any other person.

NOTES

Defined terms
"data controller": ss1(1) and (4) and 63(3)

"government department": s 70(1)
"personal data": s 1(1)
"processing": s 1(1)

Application to Parliament

63A(1)   Subject to the following provisions of this section and to section 35A, this Act applies to the processing of personal data by or on behalf of either House of Parliament as it applies to the processing of personal data by other persons

(2)   Where the purposes for which and the manner in which any personal data are, or are to be, processed are determined by or on behalf of the House of Commons, the data controller in respect of those data for the purposes of this Act shall be the Corporate Officer of that House.

(3)   Where the purposes for which and the manner in which any personal data are, or are to be, processed are determined by or on behalf of the House of Lords, the data controller in respect of those data for the purposes of this Act shall be the Corporate Officer of that House.

(4)   Nothing in subsection (2) or (3) is to be taken to render the Corporate Officer of the House of Commons or the Corporate Officer of the House of Lords liable to prosecution under this Act, but section 55 and paragraph 12 of Schedule 9 shall apply to a person acting on behalf of either House as they apply to any other person.

NOTES

Defined terms
"data controller": ss1(1) and (4) and 63(3)
"data protection principles": s 4 and Sch 1

"personal data": s 1(1)
"processing": s 1(1)

Transmission of notices etc by electronic or other means

64(1)   This section applies to
       (a) a notice or request under any provision of Part II,

(b) a notice under subsection (1) of section 24 or particulars made available under that subsection, or

(c) an application under section 41(2),

but does not apply to anything which is required to be served in accordance with rules of court.

(2) The requirement that any notice, request, particulars or application to which this section applies should be in writing is satisfied where the text of the notice, request, particulars or application–

(a) is transmitted by electronic means,

(b) is received in legible form, and

(c) is capable of being used for subsequent reference.

(3) The Secretary of State may by regulations provide that any requirement that any notice, request, particulars or application to which this section applies should be in writing is not to apply in such circumstances as may be prescribed by the regulations.

Service of notices by Commissioner

65(1) Any notice authorised or required by this Act to be served on or given to any person by the Commissioner may–

(a) if that person is an individual, be served on him–

(i) by delivering it to him, or

(ii) by sending it to him by post addressed to him at his usual or last-known place of residence or business, or

(iii) by leaving it for him at that place;

(b) if that person is a body corporate or unincorporate, be served on that body–

(i) by sending it by post to the proper officer of the body at its principal office, or

(ii) by addressing it to the proper officer of the body and leaving it at that office;

(c) if that person is a partnership in Scotland, be served on that partnership–

(i) by sending it by post to the principal office of the partnership, or

(ii) by addressing it to that partnership and leaving it at that office.

(2) In subsection (1)(b) "principal office", in relation to a registered company, means its registered office and "proper officer", in relation to any body, means the secretary or other executive officer charged with the conduct of its general affairs.

(3) This section is without prejudice to any other lawful method of serving or giving a notice.

NOTES

Defined terms

"the Commissioner": s 70(1)

Exercise of rights in Scotland by children

66(1)   Where a question falls to be determined in Scotland as to the legal capacity of a person under the age of sixteen years to exercise any right conferred by any provision of this Act, that person shall be taken to have that capacity where he has a general understanding of what it means to exercise that right.

(2)   Without prejudice to the generality of subsection (1), a person of twelve years of age or more shall be presumed to be of sufficient age and maturity to have such understanding as is mentioned in that subsection.

Orders, regulations and rules

67(1)   Any power conferred by this Act on the Secretary of State to make an order, regulations or rules shall be exercisable by statutory instrument.

(2)   Any order, regulations or rules made by the Secretary of State under this Act may–
   (a) make different provision for different cases, and
   (b) make such supplemental, incidental, consequential or transitional provision or savings as the Secretary of State considers appropriate;
and nothing in section 7(11), 19(5), 26(1) or 30(4) limits the generality of paragraph (a).

(3)   Before making–
   (a) an order under any provision of this Act other than section 75(3),
   (b) any regulations under this Act other than notification regulations (as defined by section 16(2)),
the Secretary of State shall consult the Commissioner.

(4)   A statutory instrument containing (whether alone or with other provisions) an order under–
       section 10(2)(b),
       section 12(5)(b),
       section 22(1),
       section 30,
       section 32(3),
       section 38,
       section 41A(2)(c),
       section 55E(1),
       section 56(8),
       paragraph 10 of Schedule 3, or
       paragraph 4 of Schedule 7,
shall not be made unless a draft of the instrument has been laid before and approved by a resolution of each House of Parliament.

(5)   A statutory instrument which contains (whether alone or with other provisions)–
   (a) an order under–
           section 22(7),

section 23,

section 41A(2)(b),

section 51(3),

section 54(2), (3) or (4),

paragraph 3, 4 or 14 of Part II of Schedule 1,

paragraph 6 of Schedule 2,

paragraph 2, 7 or 9 of Schedule 3,

paragraph 4 of Schedule 4,

paragraph 6 of Schedule 7,

(b) regulations under section 7 which–

   (i) prescribe cases for the purposes of subsection (2)(b),

   (ii) are made by virtue of subsection (7), or

   (iii) relate to the definition of "the prescribed period",

(c) regulations under section 8(1) , 9(3) or 9A(5),

(ca) regulations under section 55A(5) or (7) or 55B(3)(b),

(d) regulations under section 64,

(e) notification regulations (as defined by section 16(2)), or

(f) rules under paragraph 7 of Schedule 6,

and which is not subject to the requirement in subsection (4) that a draft of the instrument be laid before and approved by a resolution of each House of Parliament, shall be subject to annulment in pursuance of a resolution of either House of Parliament.

(6)   A statutory instrument which contains only–

(a) regulations prescribing fees for the purposes of any provision of this Act, or

(b) regulations under section 7 prescribing fees for the purposes of any other enactment,

shall be laid before Parliament after being made.

NOTES

Defined terms

"the Commissioner": s.70(1)

Meaning of "accessible record"

68(1)   In this Act "accessible record" means–

(a) a health record as defined by subsection (2),

(b) an educational record as defined by Schedule 11, or

(c) an accessible public record as defined by Schedule 12.

(2)   In subsection (1)(a) "health record" means any record which–

(a) consists of information relating to the physical or mental health or condition of an individual, and

(b) has been made by or on behalf of a health professional in connection with the care of that individual.

Meaning of "health professional"

69(1)   In this Act "health professional" means any of the following–

    (a) a registered medical practitioner,

    (b) a registered dentist as defined by section 53(1) of the Dentists Act 1984,

    (c) a registered dispensing optician or a registered optometrist within the meaning of the Opticians Act 1989,

    (d) a registered pharmacist or registered pharmacy technician within the meaning of the Pharmacists and Pharmacy Technicians Order 2007 or a registered person as defined by Article 2(2) of the Pharmacy (Northern Ireland) Order 1976,

    (e) a registered nurse or midwife,

    (f) a registered osteopath as defined by section 41 of the Osteopaths Act 1993,

    (g) a registered chiropractor as defined by section 43 of the Chiropractors Act 1994,

    (h) any person who is registered as a member of a profession to which the Health Professions Order 2001 for the time being extends,

    (i) a child psychotherapist,

    (j) and

    (k) a scientist employed by such a body as head of a department.

(2)   In subsection (1)(a) "registered medical practitioner" includes any person who is provisionally registered under section 15 or 21 of the Medical Act 1983 and is engaged in such employment as is mentioned in subsection (3) of that section.

(3)   In subsection (1) "health service body" means–

    (a) a Strategic Health Authority established under section 13 of the National Health Service Act 2006,

    (b) a Special Health Authority established under section 28 of that Act, or section 22 of the National Health Service (Wales) Act 2006,

    (bb)   a Primary Care Trust established under section 18 of the National Health Service Act 2006,

    (bbb)   a Local Health Board established under section 11 of the National Health Service (Wales) Act 2006,

    (c) a Health Board within the meaning of the National Health Service (Scotland) Act 1978,

    (d) a Special Health Board within the meaning of that Act,

    (e) the managers of a State Hospital provided under section 102 of that Act,

    (f) a National Health Service trust first established under section 5 of the National Health Service and Community Care Act 1990, section 25 of the National Health Service Act 2006, section 18 of the National Health Service (Wales) Act 2006 or section 12A of the National Health Service (Scotland) Act 1978,

    (fa) an NHS foundation trust;

    (g) a Health and Social Services Board established under Article 16 of the Health and Personal Social Services (Northern Ireland) Order 1972,

(h) a special health and social services agency established under the Health and Personal Social Services (Special Agencies) (Northern Ireland) Order 1990, or

(i) a Health and Social Services trust established under Article 10 of the Health and Personal Social Services (Northern Ireland) Order 1991.

Supplementary definitions

70(1) In this Act, unless the context otherwise requires–

"business" includes any trade or profession;

"the Commissioner" means the Information Commissioner;

"credit reference agency" has the same meaning as in the Consumer Credit Act 1974;

"the Data Protection Directive" means Directive 95/46/EC on the protection of individuals with regard to the processing of personal data and on the free movement of such data;

"EEA State" means a State which is a contracting party to the Agreement on the European Economic Area signed at Oporto on 2nd May 1992 as adjusted by the Protocol signed at Brussels on 17th March 1993;

"enactment" includes an enactment passed after this Act and any enactment comprised in, or in any instrument made under, an Act of the Scottish Parliament;

"government department" includes a Northern Ireland department and any body or authority exercising statutory functions on behalf of the Crown;

"government department" includes–

(a) any part of the Scottish Administration;

(b) a Northern Ireland department;

(c) the Welsh Assembly Government;

(d) any body or authority exercising statutory functions on behalf of the Crown;

"Minister of the Crown" has the same meaning as in the Ministers of the Crown Act 1975;

"public register" means any register which pursuant to a requirement imposed–

(a) by or under any enactment, or

(b) in pursuance of any international agreement,

is open to public inspection or open to inspection by any person having a legitimate interest;

"pupil"–

(a) in relation to a school in England and Wales, means a registered pupil within the meaning of the Education Act 1996,

(b) in relation to a school in Scotland, means a pupil within the meaning of the Education (Scotland) Act 1980, and

(c) in relation to a school in Northern Ireland, means a registered pupil within the meaning of the Education and Libraries (Northern Ireland) Order 1986;

"recipient", in relation to any personal data, means any person to whom the data are disclosed, including any person (such as an employee or agent of the data controller, a data processor or an employee or agent of a data processor) to whom they are disclosed in the course of processing the data for the data controller, but does not include any person to whom disclosure is or may be made as a result of, or with a view to, a particular inquiry by or on behalf of that person made in the exercise of any power conferred by law;

"registered company" means a company registered under the enactments relating to companies for the time being in force in the United Kingdom;

"school"–

   (a) in relation to England and Wales, has the same meaning as in the Education Act 1996,

   (b) in relation to Scotland, has the same meaning as in the Education (Scotland) Act 1980, and

   (c) in relation to Northern Ireland, has the same meaning as in the Education and Libraries (Northern Ireland) Order 1986;

"teacher" includes–

   (a) in Great Britain, head teacher, and

   (b) in Northern Ireland, the principal of a school;

"third party", in relation to personal data, means any person other than–

   (a) the data subject,

   (b) the data controller, or

   (c) any data processor or other person authorised to process data for the data controller or processor;

"the Tribunal" means the Information Tribunal.

(2) For the purposes of this Act data are inaccurate if they are incorrect or misleading as to any matter of fact.

Index of defined expressions

71 The following Table shows provisions defining or otherwise explaining expressions used in this Act (other than provisions defining or explaining an expression only used in the same section or Schedule)–

   accessible record section 68

   address (in Part III) section 16(3)

   business section 70(1)

   the Commissioner section 70(1)

   credit reference agency section 70(1)

   data section 1(1)

   data controller sections 1(1) and (4) and 63(3)

   data processor section 1(1)

   the Data Protection Directive section 70(1)

   data protection principles section 4 and Schedule 1

   data subject section 1(1)

   disclosing (of personal data) section 1(2)(b)

   EEA State section 70(1)

enactment   section 70(1)

enforcement notice   section 40(1)

fees regulations (in Part III) section 16(2)

government department   section 70(1)

health professional   section 69

inaccurate (in relation to data) section 70(2)

information notice   section 43(1)

Minister of the Crown   section 70(1)

the non-disclosure provisions (in Part IV) section 27(3)

notification regulations (in Part III)   section 16(2)

obtaining (of personal data) section 1(2)(a)

personal data section 1(1)

prescribed (in Part III)   section 16(2)

processing (of information or data) section 1(1) and paragraph 5 of Schedule 8

public authority   section 1(1)

public register   section 70(1)

publish (in relation to journalistic, literary or artistic material) section 32(6)

pupil (in relation to a school)   section 70(1)

recipient (in relation to personal data) section 70(1)

recording (of personal data) section 1(2)(a)

registered company   section 70(1)

registrable particulars (in Part III)   section 16(1)

relevant filing system   section 1(1)

school section 70(1)

sensitive personal data   section 2

special information notice   section 44(1)

the special purposes section 3

the subject information provisions (in Part IV)   section 27(2)

teacher   section 70(1)

third party (in relation to processing of personal data)section 70(1)

the Tribunal section 70(1)

using (of personal data) section 1(2)(b).

Modifications of Act

72   During the period beginning with the commencement of this section and ending with 23rd October 2007, the provisions of this Act shall have effect subject to the modifications set out in Schedule 13.

Transitional provisions and savings

73   Schedule 14 (which contains transitional provisions and savings) has effect.

Minor and consequential amendments and repeals and revocations

74(1)   Schedule 15 (which contains minor and consequential amendments) has effect.

(2)   The enactments and instruments specified in Schedule 16 are repealed or revoked to the extent specified.

Short title, commencement and extent

75(1)   This Act may be cited as the Data Protection Act 1998.

(2)   The following provisions of this Act–
   (a) sections 1 to 3,
   (b) section 25(1) and (4),
   (c) section 26,
   (d) sections 67 to 71,
   (e) this section,
   (f) paragraph 17 of Schedule 5,
   (g) Schedule 11,
   (h) Schedule 12, and
   (i) so much of any other provision of this Act as confers any power to make subordinate legislation,

shall come into force on the day on which this Act is passed.

(3)   The remaining provisions of this Act shall come into force on such day as the Secretary of State may by order appoint; and different days may be appointed for different purposes.

(4)   The day appointed under subsection (3) for the coming into force of section 56 must not be earlier than the first day on which sections 112, 113 and 115 of the Police Act 1997 (which provide for the issue by the Secretary of State of criminal conviction certificates, criminal record certificates and enhanced criminal record certificates) are all in force.

(4A)   Subsection (4) does not apply to section 56 so far as that section relates to a record containing information relating to–
   (a) the Secretary of State's functions under the Safeguarding Vulnerable Groups Act 2006 or the Safeguarding Vulnerable Groups (Northern Ireland) Order 2007, or
   (b) the Independent Barring Board's functions under that Act or that Order.

(5)   Subject to subsection (6), this Act extends to Northern Ireland.

(6)   Any amendment, repeal or revocation made by Schedule 15 or 16 has the same extent as that of the enactment or instrument to which it relates.

SCHEDULE 1

THE DATA PROTECTION PRINCIPLES

Section 4(1) and (2)

PART I

THE PRINCIPLES

1. Personal data shall be processed fairly and lawfully and, in particular, shall not be processed unless–
    (a) at least one of the conditions in Schedule 2 is met, and
    (b) in the case of sensitive personal data, at least one of the conditions in Schedule 3 is also met.

2. Personal data shall be obtained only for one or more specified and lawful purposes, and shall not be further processed in any manner incompatible with that purpose or those purposes.

3. Personal data shall be adequate, relevant and not excessive in relation to the purpose or purposes for which they are processed.

4. Personal data shall be accurate and, where necessary, kept up to date.

5. Personal data processed for any purpose or purposes shall not be kept for longer than is necessary for that purpose or those purposes.

6. Personal data shall be processed in accordance with the rights of data subjects under this Act.

7. Appropriate technical and organisational measures shall be taken against unauthorised or unlawful processing of personal data and against accidental loss or destruction of, or damage to, personal data.

8. Personal data shall not be transferred to a country or territory outside the European Economic Area unless that country or territory ensures an adequate level of protection for the rights and freedoms of data subjects in relation to the processing of personal data.

PART II

INTERPRETATION OF THE PRINCIPLES IN PART I

The first principle

1(1) In determining for the purposes of the first principle whether personal data are processed fairly, regard is to be had to the method by which they are obtained, including in particular whether any person from whom they are obtained is deceived or misled as to the purpose or purposes for which they are to be processed.

(2)   Subject to paragraph 2, for the purposes of the first principle data are to be treated as obtained fairly if they consist of information obtained from a person who–
    (a) is authorised by or under any enactment to supply it, or
    (b) is required to supply it by or under any enactment or by any convention or other instrument imposing an international obligation on the United Kingdom.

2(1)   Subject to paragraph 3, for the purposes of the first principle personal data are not to be treated as processed fairly unless–
    (a) in the case of data obtained from the data subject, the data controller ensures so far as practicable that the data subject has, is provided with, or has made readily available to him, the information specified in sub-paragraph (3), and
    (b) in any other case, the data controller ensures so far as practicable that, before the relevant time or as soon as practicable after that time, the data subject has, is provided with, or has made readily available to him, the information specified in sub-paragraph (3).

(2)   In sub-paragraph (1)(b) "the relevant time" means–
    (a) the time when the data controller first processes the data, or
    (b) in a case where at that time disclosure to a third party within a reasonable period is envisaged–
        (i) if the data are in fact disclosed to such a person within that period, the time when the data are first disclosed,
        (ii) if within that period the data controller becomes, or ought to become, aware that the data are unlikely to be disclosed to such a person within that period, the time when the data controller does become, or ought to become, so aware, or
        (iii) in any other case, the end of that period.

(3)   The information referred to in sub-paragraph (1) is as follows, namely–
    (a) the identity of the data controller,
    (b) if he has nominated a representative for the purposes of this Act, the identity of that representative,
    (c) the purpose or purposes for which the data are intended to be processed, and
    (d) any further information which is necessary, having regard to the specific circumstances in which the data are or are to be processed, to enable processing in respect of the data subject to be fair.

3(1)   Paragraph 2(1)(b) does not apply where either of the primary conditions in sub-paragraph (2), together with such further conditions as may be prescribed by the Secretary of State by order, are met.

(2)   The primary conditions referred to in sub-paragraph (1) are–
    (a) that the provision of that information would involve a disproportionate effort, or

(b) that the recording of the information to be contained in the data by, or the disclosure of the data by, the data controller is necessary for compliance with any legal obligation to which the data controller is subject, other than an obligation imposed by contract.

4(1) Personal data which contain a general identifier falling within a description prescribed by the Secretary of State by order are not to be treated as processed fairly and lawfully unless they are processed in compliance with any conditions so prescribed in relation to general identifiers of that description.

(2) In sub-paragraph (1) "a general identifier" means any identifier (such as, for example, a number or code used for identification purposes) which–
 (a) relates to an individual, and
 (b) forms part of a set of similar identifiers which is of general application.

The second principle

5. The purpose or purposes for which personal data are obtained may in particular be specified–
 (a) in a notice given for the purposes of paragraph 2 by the data controller to the data subject, or
 (b) in a notification given to the Commissioner under Part III of this Act.

6. In determining whether any disclosure of personal data is compatible with the purpose or purposes for which the data were obtained, regard is to be had to the purpose or purposes for which the personal data are intended to be processed by any person to whom they are disclosed.

The fourth principle

7. The fourth principle is not to be regarded as being contravened by reason of any inaccuracy in personal data which accurately record information obtained by the data controller from the data subject or a third party in a case where–
 (a) having regard to the purpose or purposes for which the data were obtained and further processed, the data controller has taken reasonable steps to ensure the accuracy of the data, and
 (b) if the data subject has notified the data controller of the data subject's view that the data are inaccurate, the data indicate that fact.

The sixth principle

8. A person is to be regarded as contravening the sixth principle if, but only if–
 (a) he contravenes section 7 by failing to supply information in accordance with that section,
 (b) he contravenes section 10 by failing to comply with a notice given under subsection (1) of that section to the extent that the notice is justified or by failing to give a notice under subsection (3) of that section,

(c) he contravenes section 11 by failing to comply with a notice given under subsection (1) of that section, or

(d) he contravenes section 12 by failing to comply with a notice given under subsection (1) or (2)(b) of that section or by failing to give a notification under subsection (2)(a) of that section or a notice under subsection (3) of that section.

The seventh principle

9. Having regard to the state of technological development and the cost of implementing any measures, the measures must ensure a level of security appropriate to–

(a) the harm that might result from such unauthorised or unlawful processing or accidental loss, destruction or damage as are mentioned in the seventh principle, and

(b) the nature of the data to be protected.

10. The data controller must take reasonable steps to ensure the reliability of any employees of his who have access to the personal data.

11. Where processing of personal data is carried out by a data processor on behalf of a data controller, the data controller must in order to comply with the seventh principle–

(a) choose a data processor providing sufficient guarantees in respect of the technical and organisational security measures governing the processing to be carried out, and

(b) take reasonable steps to ensure compliance with those measures.

12. Where processing of personal data is carried out by a data processor on behalf of a data controller, the data controller is not to be regarded as complying with the seventh principle unless–

(a) the processing is carried out under a contract–

(i) which is made or evidenced in writing, and

(ii) under which the data processor is to act only on instructions from the data controller, and

(b) the contract requires the data processor to comply with obligations equivalent to those imposed on a data controller by the seventh principle.

The eighth principle

13. An adequate level of protection is one which is adequate in all the circumstances of the case, having regard in particular to–

(a) the nature of the personal data,

(b) the country or territory of origin of the information contained in the data,

(c) the country or territory of final destination of that information,

(d) the purposes for which and period during which the data are intended to be processed,

(e) the law in force in the country or territory in question,

(f) the international obligations of that country or territory,

(g) any relevant codes of conduct or other rules which are enforceable in that country or territory (whether generally or by arrangement in particular cases), and

(h) any security measures taken in respect of the data in that country or territory.

14. The eighth principle does not apply to a transfer falling within any paragraph of Schedule 4, except in such circumstances and to such extent as the Secretary of State may by order provide.

15(1) Where–

(a) in any proceedings under this Act any question arises as to whether the requirement of the eighth principle as to an adequate level of protection is met in relation to the transfer of any personal data to a country or territory outside the European Economic Area, and

(b) a Community finding has been made in relation to transfers of the kind in question,

that question is to be determined in accordance with that finding.

(2) In sub-paragraph (1) "Community finding" means a finding of the European Commission, under the procedure provided for in Article 31(2) of the Data Protection Directive, that a country or territory outside the European Economic Area does, or does not, ensure an adequate level of protection within the meaning of Article 25(2) of the Directive.

SCHEDULE 2

CONDITIONS RELEVANT FOR PURPOSES OF THE FIRST PRINCIPLE: PROCESSING OF ANY PERSONAL DATA

Section 4(3)

1. The data subject has given his consent to the processing.

2. The processing is necessary–
   (a) for the performance of a contract to which the data subject is a party, or
   (b) for the taking of steps at the request of the data subject with a view to entering into a contract.

3. The processing is necessary for compliance with any legal obligation to which the data controller is subject, other than an obligation imposed by contract.

4. The processing is necessary in order to protect the vital interests of the data subject.

5. The processing is necessary–
   (a) for the administration of justice,
   (aa) for the exercise of any functions of either House of Parliament,

(b) for the exercise of any functions conferred on any person by or under any enactment,

(c) for the exercise of any functions of the Crown, a Minister of the Crown or a government department, or

(d) for the exercise of any other functions of a public nature exercised in the public interest by any person.

6(1) The processing is necessary for the purposes of legitimate interests pursued by the data controller or by the third party or parties to whom the data are disclosed, except where the processing is unwarranted in any particular case by reason of prejudice to the rights and freedoms or legitimate interests of the data subject.

(2) The Secretary of State may by order specify particular circumstances in which this condition is, or is not, to be taken to be satisfied.

SCHEDULE 3

CONDITIONS RELEVANT FOR PURPOSES OF THE FIRST PRINCIPLE: PROCESSING OF SENSITIVE PERSONAL DATA

Section 4(3)

1. The data subject has given his explicit consent to the processing of the personal data.

2(1) The processing is necessary for the purposes of exercising or performing any right or obligation which is conferred or imposed by law on the data controller in connection with employment.

(2) The Secretary of State may by order–
    (a) exclude the application of sub-paragraph (1) in such cases as may be specified, or
    (b) provide that, in such cases as may be specified, the condition in subparagraph (1) is not to be regarded as satisfied unless such further conditions as may be specified in the order are also satisfied.

3. The processing is necessary–
    (a) in order to protect the vital interests of the data subject or another person, in a case where–
        (i) consent cannot be given by or on behalf of the data subject, or
        (ii) the data controller cannot reasonably be expected to obtain the consent of the data subject, or
    (b) in order to protect the vital interests of another person, in a case where consent by or on behalf of the data subject has been unreasonably withheld.

4. The processing–
    (a) is carried out in the course of its legitimate activities by any body or association which–
        (i) is not established or conducted for profit, and

(ii) exists for political, philosophical religious or trade-union purposes,

(b) is carried out with appropriate safeguards for the rights and freedoms of data subjects,

(c) relates only to individuals who either are members of the body or association or have regular contact with it in connection with its purposes, and

(d) does not involve disclosure of the personal data to a third party without the consent of the data subject.

5.   The information contained in the personal data has been made public as a result of steps deliberately taken by the data subject.

6.   The processing–

(a) is necessary for the purpose of, or in connection with, any legal proceedings (including prospective legal proceedings),

(b) is necessary for the purpose of obtaining legal advice, or

(c) is otherwise necessary for the purposes of establishing, exercising or defending legal rights.

7(1)   The processing is necessary–

(a) for the administration of justice,

(aa)   for the exercise of any functions of either House of Parliament,

(b) for the exercise of any functions conferred on any person by or under an enactment, or

(c) for the exercise of any functions of the Crown, a Minister of the Crown or a government department.

(2)   The Secretary of State may by order–

(a) exclude the application of sub-paragraph (1) in such cases as may be specified, or

(b) provide that, in such cases as may be specified, the condition in subparagraph (1) is not to be regarded as satisfied unless such further conditions as may be specified in the order are also satisfied.

7A(1)   The processing–

(a) is either–

(i) the disclosure of sensitive personal data by a person as a member of an anti-fraud organisation or otherwise in accordance with any arrangements made by such an organisation; or

(ii) any other processing by that person or another person of sensitive personal data so disclosed; and

(b) is necessary for the purposes of preventing fraud or a particular kind of fraud.

(2)   In this paragraph "an anti-fraud organisation" means any unincorporated association, body corporate or other person which enables or facilitates any sharing of information to prevent fraud or a particular kind of fraud or which has any of these functions as its purpose or one of its purposes.

8(1)   The processing is necessary for medical purposes and is undertaken by–
        (a) a health professional, or
        (b) a person who in the circumstances owes a duty of confidentiality which is equivalent to that which would arise if that person were a health professional.

(2)   In this paragraph "medical purposes" includes the purposes of preventative medicine, medical diagnosis, medical research, the provision of care and treatment and the management of healthcare services.

9(1)   The processing–
        (a) is of sensitive personal data consisting of information as to racial or ethnic origin,
        (b) is necessary for the purpose of identifying or keeping under review the existence or absence of equality of opportunity or treatment between persons of different racial or ethnic origins, with a view to enabling such equality to be promoted or maintained, and
        (c) is carried out with appropriate safeguards for the rights and freedoms of data subjects.

(2)   The Secretary of State may by order specify circumstances in which processing falling within sub-paragraph (1)(a) and (b) is, or is not, to be taken for the purposes of sub-paragraph (1)(c) to be carried out with appropriate safeguards for the rights and freedoms of data subjects.

10.   The personal data are processed in circumstances specified in an order made by the Secretary of State for the purposes of this paragraph.

SCHEDULE 4

CASES WHERE THE EIGHTH PRINCIPLE DOES NOT APPLY

Section 4(3)

1.   The data subject has given his consent to the transfer.

2.   The transfer is necessary–
        (a) for the performance of a contract between the data subject and the data controller, or
        (b) for the taking of steps at the request of the data subject with a view to his entering into a contract with the data controller.

3.   The transfer is necessary–
        (a) for the conclusion of a contract between the data controller and a person other than the data subject which–
            (i) is entered into at the request of the data subject, or
            (ii) is in the interests of the data subject, or
        (b) for the performance of such a contract.

4(1)   The transfer is necessary for reasons of substantial public interest.

(2)   The Secretary of State may by order specify–
    (a) circumstances in which a transfer is to be taken for the purposes of subparagraph (1) to be necessary for reasons of substantial public interest, and
    (b) circumstances in which a transfer which is not required by or under an enactment is not to be taken for the purpose of sub-paragraph (1) to be necessary for reasons of substantial public interest.

5.   The transfer–
    (a) is necessary for the purpose of, or in connection with, any legal proceedings (including prospective legal proceedings),
    (b) is necessary for the purpose of obtaining legal advice, or
    (c) is otherwise necessary for the purposes of establishing, exercising or defending legal rights.

6.   The transfer is necessary in order to protect the vital interests of the data subject.

7.   The transfer is of part of the personal data on a public register and any conditions subject to which the register is open to inspection are complied with by any person to whom the data are or may be disclosed after the transfer.

8.   The transfer is made on terms which are of a kind approved by the Commissioner as ensuring adequate safeguards for the rights and freedoms of data subjects.

9.   The transfer has been authorised by the Commissioner as being made in such a manner as to ensure adequate safeguards for the rights and freedoms of data subjects.

SCHEDULE 5

THE INFORMATION COMMISSIONER AND THE INFORMATION TRIBUNAL

Section 6(7)

PART I

THE COMMISSIONER

Status and capacity

1(1)   The corporation sole by the name of the Data Protection Registrar established by the Data Protection Act 1984 shall continue in existence by the name of the Information Commissioner.

(2)   The Commissioner and his officers and staff are not to be regarded as servants or agents of the Crown.

Tenure of office

2(1)   Subject to the provisions of this paragraph, the Commissioner shall hold office for such term not exceeding five years as may be determined at the time of his appointment.

(2)   The Commissioner may be relieved of his office by Her Majesty at his own request.

(3)   The Commissioner may be removed from office by Her Majesty in pursuance of an Address from both Houses of Parliament.

(4)   The Commissioner shall in any case vacate his office–
    (a) on completing the year of service in which he attains the age of sixty-five years, or
    (b) if earlier, on completing his fifteenth year of service.

(5)   Subject to sub-paragraph (4), a person who ceases to be Commissioner on the expiration of his term of office shall be eligible for re-appointment, but a person may not be re-appointed for a third or subsequent term as Commissioner unless, by reason of special circumstances, the person's re-appointment for such a term is desirable in the public interest.

Salary etc

3(1)   There shall be paid–
    (a) to the Commissioner such salary, and
    (b) to or in respect of the Commissioner such pension,
as may be specified by a resolution of the House of Commons.

(2)   A resolution for the purposes of this paragraph may–
    (a) specify the salary or pension,
    (b) provide that the salary or pension is to be the same as, or calculated on the same basis as, that payable to, or to or in respect of, a person employed in a specified office under, or in a specified capacity in the service of, the Crown, or
    (c) specify the salary or pension and provide for it to be increased by reference to such variables as may be specified in the resolution.

(3)   A resolution for the purposes of this paragraph may take effect from the date on which it is passed or from any earlier or later date specified in the resolution.

(4)   A resolution for the purposes of this paragraph may make different provision in relation to the pension payable to or in respect of different holders of the office of Commissioner.

(5)   Any salary or pension payable under this paragraph shall be charged on and issued out of the Consolidated Fund.

(6)   In this paragraph "pension" includes an allowance or gratuity and any reference to the payment of a pension includes a reference to the making of payments towards the provision of a pension.

Officers and staff

4(1)   The Commissioner–
(a) shall appoint a deputy commissioner or two deputy commissioners, and
(b) may appoint such number of other officers and staff as he may determine.

(1A)   The Commissioner shall, when appointing any second deputy commissioner, specify which of the Commissioner's functions are to be performed, in the circumstances referred to in paragraph 5(1), by each of the deputy commissioners.

(2)   The remuneration and other conditions of service of the persons appointed under this paragraph shall be determined by the Commissioner.

(3)   The Commissioner may pay such pensions, allowances or gratuities to or in respect of the persons appointed under this paragraph, or make such payments towards the provision of such pensions, allowances or gratuities, as he may determine.

(4)   The references in sub-paragraph (3) to pensions, allowances or gratuities to or in respect of the persons appointed under this paragraph include references to pensions, allowances or gratuities by way of compensation to or in respect of any of those persons who suffer loss of office or employment.

(5)   Any determination under sub-paragraph (1)(b), (2) or (3) shall require the approval of the Secretary of State.

(6)   The Employers' Liability (Compulsory Insurance) Act 1969 shall not require insurance to be effected by the Commissioner.

5(1)   The deputy commissioner or deputy commissioners shall perform the functions conferred by this Act or the Freedom of Information Act 2000 on the Commissioner during any vacancy in that office or at any time when the Commissioner is for any reason unable to act.

(2)   Without prejudice to sub-paragraph (1), any functions of the Commissioner under this Act or the Freedom of Information Act 2000 may, to the extent authorised by him, be performed by any of his officers or staff.

Authentication of seal of the Commissioner

6.   The application of the seal of the Commissioner shall be authenticated by his signature or by the signature of some other person authorised for the purpose.

Presumption of authenticity of documents issued by the Commissioner

7.   Any document purporting to be an instrument issued by the Commissioner and to be duly executed under the Commissioner's seal or to be signed by or on behalf of the Commissioner shall be received in evidence and shall be deemed to be such an instrument unless the contrary is shown.

Money

8. The Secretary of State may make payments to the Commissioner out of money provided by Parliament.

9(1) All fees and other sums received by the Commissioner in the exercise of his functions under this Act, under section 159 of the Consumer Credit Act 1974 or under the Freedom of Information Act 2000 shall be paid by him to the Secretary of State.

(2) Sub-paragraph (1) shall not apply where the Secretary of State, with the consent of the Treasury, otherwise directs.

(3) Any sums received by the Secretary of State under sub-paragraph (1) shall be paid into the Consolidated Fund.

Accounts

10(1) It shall be the duty of the Commissioner–
   (a) to keep proper accounts and other records in relation to the accounts,
   (b) to prepare in respect of each financial year a statement of account in such form as the Secretary of State may direct, and
   (c) to send copies of that statement to the Comptroller and Auditor General on or before 31st August next following the end of the year to which the statement relates or on or before such earlier date after the end of that year as the Treasury may direct.

(2) The Comptroller and Auditor General shall examine and certify any statement sent to him under this paragraph and lay copies of it together with his report thereon before each House of Parliament.

(3) In this paragraph "financial year" means a period of twelve months beginning with 1st April.

Application of Part I in Scotland

11. Paragraphs 1(1), 6 and 7 do not extend to Scotland.

PART II

THE TRIBUNAL

Tenure of office

12(1) Subject to the following provisions of this paragraph, a member of the Tribunal shall hold and vacate his office in accordance with the terms of his appointment and shall, on ceasing to hold office, be eligible for re-appointment.

(2) Any member of the Tribunal may at any time resign his office by notice in writing to the Lord Chancellor (in the case of the chairman or a deputy chairman) or to the Secretary of State (in the case of any other member).

(3)   A person who is the chairman or deputy chairman of the Tribunal shall vacate his office on the day on which he attains the age of seventy years; but this sub-paragraph is subject to section 26(4) to (6) of the Judicial Pensions and Retirement Act 1993 (power to authorise continuance in office up to the age of seventy-five years).

Salary etc

13.   The Secretary of State shall pay to the members of the Tribunal out of money provided by Parliament such remuneration and allowances as he may determine.

Officers and staff

14.   The Secretary of State may provide the Tribunal with such officers and staff as he thinks necessary for the proper discharge of its functions.

Expenses

15.   Such expenses of the Tribunal as the Secretary of State may determine shall be defrayed by the Secretary of State out of money provided by Parliament.

SCHEDULE 6

APPEAL PROCEEDINGS

Sections 28(12), 48(5)

Tribunal Procedure Rules

7(1)   Tribunal Procedure Rules may make provision for regulating the exercise of the rights of appeal conferred–
    (a) by sections 28(4) and (6) and 48 of this Act, and
    (b) by sections 47(1) and (2) and 60(1) and (4) of the Freedom of Information Act 2000.

(2)   In the case of appeals under this Act and the Freedom of Information Act 2000, Tribunal Procedure Rules may make provision–
    (a) for securing the production of material used for the processing of personal data;
    (b) for the inspection, examination, operation and testing of any equipment or material used in connection with the processing of personal data;
    (c) for hearing an appeal in the absence of the appellant or for determining an appeal without a hearing.

Obstruction etc

8(1)   If any person is guilty of any act or omission in relation to proceedings before the Tribunal which, if those proceedings were proceedings before a court having power to commit for contempt, would constitute contempt of court, the Tribunal may certify the offence to the High Court or, in Scotland, the Court of Session.

(2)   Where an offence is so certified, the court may inquire into the matter and, after hearing any witness who may be produced against or on behalf of the person charged with the offence, and after hearing any statement that may be offered in defence, deal with him in any manner in which it could deal with him if he had committed the like offence in relation to the court.

SCHEDULE 7

MISCELLANEOUS EXEMPTIONS

Section 37

Confidential references given by the data controller

1.   Personal data are exempt from section 7 if they consist of a reference given or to be given in confidence by the data controller for the purposes of–
     (a) the education, training or employment, or prospective education, training or employment, of the data subject,
     (b) the appointment, or prospective appointment, of the data subject to any office, or
     (c) the provision, or prospective provision, by the data subject of any service.

Armed forces

2.   Personal data are exempt from the subject information provisions in any case to the extent to which the application of those provisions would be likely to prejudice the combat effectiveness of any of the armed forces of the Crown.

Judicial appointments and honours

3.   Personal data processed for the purposes of–
     (a) assessing any person's suitability for judicial office or the office of Queen's Counsel, or
     (b) the conferring by the Crown of any honour or dignity,
     are exempt from the subject information provisions.

Crown employment and Crown or Ministerial appointments

4(1)   The Secretary of State may by order exempt from the subject information provisions personal data processed for the purposes of assessing any person's suitability for–
     (a) employment by or under the Crown, or
     (b) any office to which appointments are made by Her Majesty, by a Minister of the Crown or by a Northern Ireland authority.

(2)   In this paragraph "Northern Ireland authority" means the First Minister, the deputy First Minister, a Northern Ireland Minister or a Northern Ireland department.

Management forecasts etc

5. Personal data processed for the purposes of management forecasting or management planning to assist the data controller in the conduct of any business or other activity are exempt from the subject information provisions in any case to the extent to which the application of those provisions would be likely to prejudice the conduct of that business or other activity.

Corporate finance

6(1) Where personal data are processed for the purposes of, or in connection with, a corporate finance service provided by a relevant person—
  (a) the data are exempt from the subject information provisions in any case to the extent to which either—
    (i) the application of those provisions to the data could affect the price of any instrument which is already in existence or is to be or may be created, or
    (ii) the data controller reasonably believes that the application of those provisions to the data could affect the price of any such instrument, and
  (b) to the extent that the data are not exempt from the subject information provisions by virtue of paragraph (a), they are exempt from those provisions if the exemption is required for the purpose of safeguarding an important economic or financial interest of the United Kingdom.

(2) For the purposes of sub-paragraph (1)(b) the Secretary of State may by order specify—
  (a) matters to be taken into account in determining whether exemption from the subject information provisions is required for the purpose of safeguarding an important economic or financial interest of the United Kingdom, or
  (b) circumstances in which exemption from those provisions is, or is not, to be taken to be required for that purpose.

(3) In this paragraph—
  "corporate finance service" means a service consisting in—
  (a) underwriting in respect of issues of, or the placing of issues of, any instrument,
  (b) advice to undertakings on capital structure, industrial strategy and related matters and advice and service relating to mergers and the purchase of undertakings, or
  (c) services relating to such underwriting as is mentioned in paragraph (a);
  "instrument" means any instrument listed in section C of Annex I to Directive 2004/39/EC of the European Parliament and of the Council of 21 April 2004 on markets in financial instruments;
  "price" includes value;
  "relevant person" means—
  (a) any person who, by reason of any permission he has under Part IV of the Financial Services and Markets Act 2000, is able to carry on a corporate finance service without contravening the general prohibition, within the meaning of section 19 of that Act,

(b) an EEA firm of the kind mentioned in paragraph 5(a) or (b) of Schedule 3 to that Act which has qualified for authorisation under paragraph 12 of that Schedule, and may lawfully carry on a corporate finance service,

(c) any person who is exempt from the general prohibition in respect of any corporate finance service—

(i) as a result of an exemption order made under section 38(1) of that Act, or

(ii) by reason of section 39(1) of that Act (appointed representatives),

(cc) any person, not falling within paragraph (a), (b) or (c) who may lawfully carry on a corporate finance service without contravening the general prohibition,

(d) any person who, in the course of his employment, provides to his employer a service falling within paragraph (b) or (c) of the definition of "corporate finance service", or

(e) any partner who provides to other partners in the partnership a service falling within either of those paragraphs.

Negotiations

7. Personal data which consist of records of the intentions of the data controller in relation to any negotiations with the data subject are exempt from the subject information provisions in any case to the extent to which the application of those provisions would be likely to prejudice those negotiations.

Examination marks

8(1) Section 7 shall have effect subject to the provisions of sub-paragraphs (2) to (4) in the case of personal data consisting of marks or other information processed by a data controller—

(a) for the purpose of determining the results of an academic, professional or other examination or of enabling the results of any such examination to be determined, or

(b) in consequence of the determination of any such results.

(2) Where the relevant day falls before the day on which the results of the examination are announced, the period mentioned in section 7(8) shall be extended until—

(a) the end of five months beginning with the relevant day, or

(b) the end of forty days beginning with the date of the announcement,

whichever is the earlier.

(3) Where by virtue of sub-paragraph (2) a period longer than the prescribed period elapses after the relevant day before the request is complied with, the information to be supplied pursuant to the request shall be supplied both by reference to the data in question at the time when the request is received and (if different) by reference to the data as from time to time held in the period beginning when the request is received and ending when it is complied with.

(4)   For the purposes of this paragraph the results of an examination shall be treated as announced when they are first published or (if not published) when they are first made available or communicated to the candidate in question.

(5)   In this paragraph–
"examination" includes any process for determining the knowledge, intelligence, skill or ability of a candidate by reference to his performance in any test, work or other activity;
"the prescribed period" means forty days or such other period as is for the time being prescribed under section 7 in relation to the personal data in question;
"relevant day" has the same meaning as in section 7.

Examination scripts etc

9(1)   Personal data consisting of information recorded by candidates during an academic, professional or other examination are exempt from section 7.

(2)   In this paragraph "examination" has the same meaning as in paragraph 8.

Legal professional privilege

10   Personal data are exempt from the subject information provisions if the data consist of information in respect of which a claim to legal professional privilege or, in Scotland, to confidentiality of communications could be maintained in legal proceedings.

Self-incrimination

11(1)   A person need not comply with any request or order under section 7 to the extent that compliance would, by revealing evidence of the commission of any offence other than an offence under this Act, , other than an offence under this Act or an offence within sub-paragraph (1A), expose him to proceedings for that offence.

(1A)   The offences mentioned in sub-paragraph (1) are–
(a) an offence under section 5 of the Perjury Act 1911 (false statements made otherwise than on oath),
(b) an offence under section 44(2) of the Criminal Law (Consolidation) (Scotland) Act 1995 (false statements made otherwise than on oath), or
(c) an offence under Article 10 of the Perjury (Northern Ireland) Order 1979 (false statutory declarations and other false unsworn statements).

(2)   Information disclosed by any person in compliance with any request or order under section 7 shall not be admissible against him in proceedings for an offence under this Act.

SCHEDULE 8

TRANSITIONAL RELIEF

Section 39

PART I

INTERPRETATION OF SCHEDULE

1(1)   For the purposes of this Schedule, personal data are "eligible data" at any time if, and to the extent that, they are at that time subject to processing which was already under way immediately before 24th October 1998.

(2)   In this Schedule–
"eligible automated data" means eligible data which fall within paragraph (a) or (b) of the definition of "data" in section 1(1);
"eligible manual data" means eligible data which are not eligible automated data;
"the first transitional period" means the period beginning with the commencement of this Schedule and ending with 23rd October 2001;
"the second transitional period" means the period beginning with 24th October 2001 and ending with 23rd October 2007.

PART II

EXEMPTIONS AVAILABLE BEFORE 24TH OCTOBER 2001

Manual data

2(1)   Eligible manual data, other than data forming part of an accessible record, are exempt from the data protection principles and Parts II and III of this Act during the first transitional period.

(2)   This paragraph does not apply to eligible manual data to which paragraph 4 applies.

3(1)   This paragraph applies to–
(a) eligible manual data forming part of an accessible record, and
(b) personal data which fall within paragraph (d) of the definition of "data" in section 1(1) but which, because they are not subject to processing which was already under way immediately before 24th October 1998, are not eligible data for the purposes of this Schedule.

(2)   During the first transitional period, data to which this paragraph applies are exempt from–
(a) the data protection principles, except the sixth principle so far as relating to sections 7 and 12A,
(b) Part II of this Act, except–
(i) section 7 (as it has effect subject to section 8) and section 12A, and

(ii) section 15 so far as relating to those sections, and

(c) Part III of this Act.

4(1) This paragraph applies to eligible manual data which consist of information relevant to the financial standing of the data subject and in respect of which the data controller is a credit reference agency.

(2) During the first transitional period, data to which this paragraph applies are exempt from–

(a) the data protection principles, except the sixth principle so far as relating to sections 7 and 12A,

(b) Part II of this Act, except–

(i) section 7 (as it has effect subject to sections 8 and 9) and section 12A, and

(ii) section 15 so far as relating to those sections, and

(c) Part III of this Act.

Processing otherwise than by reference to the data subject

5. During the first transitional period, for the purposes of this Act (apart from paragraph 1), eligible automated data are not to be regarded as being "processed" unless the processing is by reference to the data subject.

Payrolls and accounts

6(1) Subject to sub-paragraph (2), eligible automated data processed by a data controller for one or more of the following purposes–

(a) calculating amounts payable by way of remuneration or pensions in respect of service in any employment or office or making payments of, or of sums deducted from, such remuneration or pensions, or

(b) keeping accounts relating to any business or other activity carried on by the data controller or keeping records of purchases, sales or other transactions for the purpose of ensuring that the requisite payments are made by or to him in respect of those transactions or for the purpose of making financial or management forecasts to assist him in the conduct of any such business or activity,

are exempt from the data protection principles and Parts II and III of this Act during the first transitional period.

(2) It shall be a condition of the exemption of any eligible automated data under this paragraph that the data are not processed for any other purpose, but the exemption is not lost by any processing of the eligible data for any other purpose if the data controller shows that he had taken such care to prevent it as in all the circumstances was reasonably required.

(3) Data processed only for one or more of the purposes mentioned in subparagraph (1)(a) may be disclosed–

(a) to any person, other than the data controller, by whom the remuneration or pensions in question are payable,

(b) for the purpose of obtaining actuarial advice,

(c) for the purpose of giving information as to the persons in any employment or office for use in medical research into the health of, or injuries suffered by, persons engaged in particular occupations or working in particular places or areas,

(d) if the data subject (or a person acting on his behalf) has requested or consented to the disclosure of the data either generally or in the circumstances in which the disclosure in question is made, or

(e) if the person making the disclosure has reasonable grounds for believing that the disclosure falls within paragraph (d).

(4) Data processed for any of the purposes mentioned in sub-paragraph (1) may be disclosed–

(a) for the purpose of audit or where the disclosure is for the purpose only of giving information about the data controller's financial affairs, or

(b) in any case in which disclosure would be permitted by any other provision of this Part of this Act if sub-paragraph (2) were included among the non-disclosure provisions.

(5) In this paragraph "remuneration" includes remuneration in kind and "pensions" includes gratuities or similar benefits.

Unincorporated members' clubs and mailing lists

7   Eligible automated data processed by an unincorporated members' club and relating only to the members of the club are exempt from the data protection principles and Parts II and III of this Act during the first transitional period.

8   Eligible automated data processed by a data controller only for the purposes of distributing, or recording the distribution of, articles or information to the data subjects and consisting only of their names, addresses or other particulars necessary for effecting the distribution, are exempt from the data protection principles and Parts II and III of this Act during the first transitional period.

9   Neither paragraph 7 nor paragraph 8 applies to personal data relating to any data subject unless he has been asked by the club or data controller whether he objects to the data relating to him being processed as mentioned in that paragraph and has not objected.

10   It shall be a condition of the exemption of any data under paragraph 7 that the data are not disclosed except as permitted by paragraph 11 and of the exemption under paragraph 8 that the data are not processed for any purpose other than that mentioned in that paragraph or as permitted by paragraph 11, but–

(a) the exemption under paragraph 7 shall not be lost by any disclosure in breach of that condition, and

(b) the exemption under paragraph 8 shall not be lost by any processing in breach of that condition,

if the data controller shows that he had taken such care to prevent it as in all the circumstances was reasonably required.

11   Data to which paragraph 10 applies may be disclosed–

(a) if the data subject (or a person acting on his behalf) has requested or consented to the disclosure of the data either generally or in the circumstances in which the disclosure in question is made,

(b) if the person making the disclosure has reasonable grounds for believing that the disclosure falls within paragraph (a), or

(c) in any case in which disclosure would be permitted by any other provision of this Part of this Act if paragraph 10 were included among the non-disclosure provisions.

Back-up data

12   Eligible automated data which are processed only for the purpose of replacing other data in the event of the latter being lost, destroyed or impaired are exempt from section 7 during the first transitional period.

Exemption of all eligible automated data from certain requirements

13(1)   During the first transitional period, eligible automated data are exempt from the following provisions–

(a) the first data protection principle to the extent to which it requires compliance with–
(i) paragraph 2 of Part II of Schedule 1,
(ii) the conditions in Schedule 2, and
(iii) the conditions in Schedule 3,

(b) the seventh data protection principle to the extent to which it requires compliance with paragraph 12 of Part II of Schedule 1;

(c) the eighth data protection principle,

(d) in section 7(1), paragraphs (b), (c)(ii) and (d),

(e) sections 10 and 11,

(f) section 12, and

(g) section 13, except so far as relating to–
(i) any contravention of the fourth data protection principle,
(ii) any disclosure without the consent of the data controller,
(iii) loss or destruction of data without the consent of the data controller, or
(iv) processing for the special purposes.

(2)   The specific exemptions conferred by sub-paragraph (1)(a), (c) and (e) do not limit the data controller's general duty under the first data protection principle to ensure that processing is fair.

PART III

EXEMPTIONS AVAILABLE AFTER 23RD OCTOBER 2001 BUT BEFORE 24TH OCTOBER 2007

Not reproduced

PART IV

EXEMPTIONS AFTER 23RD OCTOBER 2001 FOR HISTORICAL RESEARCH

15.   In this Part of this Schedule "the relevant conditions" has the same meaning as in section 33.

16(1)   Eligible manual data which are processed only for the purpose of historical research in compliance with the relevant conditions are exempt from the provisions specified in sub-paragraph (2) after 23rd October 2001.

(2)   The provisions referred to in sub-paragraph (1) are–
      (a) the first data protection principle except in so far as it requires compliance with paragraph 2 of Part II of Schedule 1,
      (b) the second, third, fourth and fifth data protection principles, and
      (c) section 14(1) to (3).

17(1)   After 23rd October 2001 eligible automated data which are processed only for the purpose of historical research in compliance with the relevant conditions are exempt from the first data protection principle to the extent to which it requires compliance with the conditions in Schedules 2 and 3.

(2)   Eligible automated data which are processed–
      (a) only for the purpose of historical research,
      (b) in compliance with the relevant conditions, and
      (c) otherwise than by reference to the data subject,
are also exempt from the provisions referred to in sub-paragraph (3) after 23rd October 2001.

(3)   The provisions referred to in sub-paragraph (2) are–
      (a) the first data protection principle except in so far as it requires compliance with paragraph 2 of Part II of Schedule 1,
      (b) the second, third, fourth and fifth data protection principles, and
      (c) section 14(1) to (3).

18   For the purposes of this Part of this Schedule personal data are not to be treated as processed otherwise than for the purpose of historical research merely because the data are disclosed–
      (a) to any person, for the purpose of historical research only,
      (b) to the data subject or a person acting on his behalf,

(c) at the request, or with the consent, of the data subject or a person acting on his behalf, or

(d) in circumstances in which the person making the disclosure has reasonable grounds for believing that the disclosure falls within paragraph (a), (b) or (c).

Part V

Exemption from Section 22

19 Processing which was already under way immediately before 24th October 1998 is not assessable processing for the purposes of section 22.

SCHEDULE 9

Powers of Entry and Inspection

Section 50

Issue of warrants

1(1) If a circuit judge or a District Judge (Magistrates' Courts) is satisfied by information on oath supplied by the Commissioner that there are reasonable grounds for suspecting–
(a) that a data controller has contravened or is contravening any of the data protection principles, or
(b) that an offence under this Act has been or is being committed,
and that evidence of the contravention or of the commission of the offence is to be found on any premises specified in the information, he may, subject to subparagraph (2) and paragraph 2, grant a warrant to the Commissioner.

(1A) Sub-paragraph (1B) applies if a circuit judge or a District Judge (Magistrates' Courts) is satisfied by information on oath supplied by the Commissioner that a data controller has failed to comply with a requirement imposed by an assessment notice.

(1B) The judge may, for the purpose of enabling the Commissioner to determine whether the data controller has complied or is complying with the data protection principles, grant a warrant to the Commissioner in relation to any premises that were specified in the assessment notice; but this is subject to sub-paragraph (2) and paragraph 2.

(2) A judge shall not issue a warrant under this Schedule in respect of any personal data processed for the special purposes unless a determination by the Commissioner under section 45 with respect to those data has taken effect.

(3) A warrant issued under sub-paragraph (1) this Schedule shall authorise the Commissioner or any of his officers or staff at any time within seven days of the date of the warrant to enter the premises, to search them, to inspect, examine, operate and test any equipment found there which is used or intended to be used for the processing

of personal data and to inspect and seize any documents or other material found there which may be such evidence as is mentioned in that sub-paragraph –

(a) to enter the premises;

(b) to search the premises;

(c) to inspect, examine, operate and test any equipment found on the premises which is used or intended to be used for the processing of personal data;

(d) to inspect and seize any documents or other material found on the premises which–

  (i) in the case of a warrant issued under sub-paragraph (1), may be such evidence as is mentioned in that paragraph;

  (ii) in the case of a warrant issued under sub-paragraph (1B), may enable the Commissioner to determine whether the data controller has complied or is complying with the data protection principles;

(e) to require any person on the premises to provide an explanation of any document or other material found on the premises;

(f) to require any person on the premises to provide such other information as may reasonably be required for the purpose of determining whether the data controller has contravened, or is contravening, the data protection principles.

2(1)   A judge shall not issue a warrant under this Schedule unless he is satisfied–

(a) that the Commissioner has given seven days' notice in writing to the occupier of the premises in question demanding access to the premises, and

(b) that either–

  (i) access was demanded at a reasonable hour and was unreasonably refused, or

  (ii) although entry to the premises was granted, the occupier unreasonably refused to comply with a request by the Commissioner or any of the Commissioner's officers or staff to permit the Commissioner or the officer or member of staff to do any of the things referred to in paragraph 1(3), and

(c) that the occupier, has, after the refusal, been notified by the Commissioner of the application for the warrant and has had an opportunity of being heard by the judge on the question whether or not it should be issued.

(1A)   In determining whether the Commissioner has given an occupier the seven days' notice referred to in sub-paragraph (1)(a) any assessment notice served on the occupier is to be disregarded.

(2)   Sub-paragraph (1) shall not apply if the judge is satisfied that the case is one of urgency or that compliance with those provisions would defeat the object of the entry.

3   A judge who issues a warrant under this Schedule shall also issue two copies of it and certify them clearly as copies.

Execution of warrants

4   A person executing a warrant issued under this Schedule may use such reasonable force as may be necessary.

5   A warrant issued under this Schedule shall be executed at a reasonable hour unless it appears to the person executing it that there are grounds for suspecting that the evidence in question would not be found object of the warrant would be defeated if it were so executed.

6   If the person who occupies the premises in respect of which a warrant is issued under this Schedule is present when the warrant is executed, he shall be shown the warrant and supplied with a copy of it; and if that person is not present a copy of the warrant shall be left in a prominent place on the premises.

7(1) A person seizing anything in pursuance of a warrant under this Schedule shall give a receipt for it if asked to do so.

(2)   Anything so seized may be retained for so long as is necessary in all the circumstances but the person in occupation of the premises in question shall be given a copy of anything that is seized if he so requests and the person executing the warrant considers that it can be done without undue delay.

Matters exempt from inspection and seizure

8   The powers of inspection and seizure conferred by a warrant issued under this Schedule shall not be exercisable in respect of personal data which by virtue of section 28 are exempt from any of the provisions of this Act.

9(1) Subject to the provisions of this paragraph, the powers of inspection and seizure conferred by a warrant issued under this Schedule shall not be exercisable in respect of–
      (a) any communication between a professional legal adviser and his client in connection with the giving of legal advice to the client with respect to his obligations, liabilities or rights under this Act, or
      (b) any communication between a professional legal adviser and his client, or between such an adviser or his client and any other person, made in connection with or in contemplation of proceedings under or arising out of this Act (including proceedings before the Tribunal) and for the purposes of such proceedings.

(2)   Sub-paragraph (1) applies also to–
      (a) any copy or other record of any such communication as is there mentioned, and
      (b) any document or article enclosed with or referred to in any such communication if made in connection with the giving of any advice or, as the case may be, in connection with or in contemplation of and for the purposes of such proceedings as are there mentioned.

(3)   This paragraph does not apply to anything in the possession of any person other than the professional legal adviser or his client or to anything held with the intention of furthering a criminal purpose.

(4)   In this paragraph references to the client of a professional legal adviser include references to any person representing such a client.

10   If the person in occupation of any premises in respect of which a warrant is issued under this Schedule objects to the inspection or seizure under the warrant of any material on the grounds that it consists partly of matters in respect of which those powers are not exercisable, he shall, if the person executing the warrant so requests, furnish that person with a copy of so much of the material as is not exempt from those powers.

Return of warrants

11   A warrant issued under this Schedule shall be returned to the court from which it was issued–
        (a) after being executed, or
        (b) if not executed within the time authorised for its execution;
and the person by whom any such warrant is executed shall make an endorsement on it stating what powers have been exercised by him under the warrant.

Offences

12   Any person who–
        (a) intentionally obstructs a person in the execution of a warrant issued under this Schedule, or
        (b) fails without reasonable excuse to give any person executing such a warrant such assistance as he may reasonably require for the execution of the warrant,
        (c) makes a statement in response to a requirement under paragraph (e) or (f) of paragraph 1(3) which that person knows to be false in a material respect, or
        (d) recklessly makes a statement in response to such a requirement which is false in a material respect,
    is guilty of an offence.

Vessels, vehicles etc

13   In this Schedule "premises" includes any vessel, vehicle, aircraft or hovercraft, and references to the occupier of any premises include references to the person in charge of any vessel, vehicle, aircraft or hovercraft.

Scotland and Northern Ireland

14   In the application of this Schedule to Scotland–
        (a) for any reference to a circuit judge there is substituted a reference to the sheriff,

(b) for any reference to information on oath there is substituted a reference to evidence on oath, and

(c) for the reference to the court from which the warrant was issued there is substituted a reference to the sheriff clerk.

15 In the application of this Schedule to Northern Ireland–

(a) for any reference to a circuit judge there is substituted a reference to a county court judge, and

(b) for any reference to information on oath there is substituted a reference to a complaint on oath.

Self-incrimination

16 An explanation given, or information provided, by a person in response to a requirement under paragraph (e) or (f) of paragraph 1(3) may only be used in evidence against that person–

(a) on a prosecution for an offence under–

(i) paragraph 12,

(ii) section 5 of the Perjury Act 1911 (false statements made otherwise than on oath),

(iii) section 44(2) of the Criminal Law (Consolidation) (Scotland) Act 1995 (false statements made otherwise than on oath), or

(iv) Article 10 of the Perjury (Northern Ireland) Order 1979 (false statutory declarations and other false unsworn statements), or

(b) on a prosecution for any other offence where–

(i) in giving evidence that person makes a statement inconsistent with that explanation or information, and

(ii) evidence relating to that explanation or information is adduced, or a question relating to it is asked, by that person or on that person's behalf.

SCHEDULE 10

FURTHER PROVISIONS RELATING TO ASSISTANCE UNDER SECTION 53

Section 53(6)

1 In this Schedule "applicant" and "proceedings" have the same meaning as in section 53.

2 The assistance provided under section 53 may include the making of arrangements for, or for the Commissioner to bear the costs of–

(a) the giving of advice or assistance by a solicitor or counsel, and

(b) the representation of the applicant, or the provision to him of such assistance as is usually given by a solicitor or counsel–

(i) in steps preliminary or incidental to the proceedings, or

(ii) in arriving at or giving effect to a compromise to avoid or bring an end to the proceedings.

3   Where assistance is provided with respect to the conduct of proceedings–

(a) it shall include an agreement by the Commissioner to indemnify the applicant (subject only to any exceptions specified in the notification) in respect of any liability to pay costs or expenses arising by virtue of any judgment or order of the court in the proceedings,

(b) it may include an agreement by the Commissioner to indemnify the applicant in respect of any liability to pay costs or expenses arising by virtue of any compromise or settlement arrived at in order to avoid the proceedings or bring the proceedings to an end, and

(c) it may include an agreement by the Commissioner to indemnify the applicant in respect of any liability to pay damages pursuant to an undertaking given on the grant of interlocutory relief (in Scotland, an interim order) to the applicant.

4   Where the Commissioner provides assistance in relation to any proceedings, he shall do so on such terms, or make such other arrangements, as will secure that a person against whom the proceedings have been or are commenced is informed that assistance has been or is being provided by the Commissioner in relation to them.

5   In England and Wales or Northern Ireland, the recovery of expenses incurred by the Commissioner in providing an applicant with assistance (as taxed or assessed in such manner as may be prescribed by rules of court) shall constitute a first charge for the benefit of the Commissioner–

(a) on any costs which, by virtue of any judgment or order of the court, are payable to the applicant by any other person in respect of the matter in connection with which the assistance is provided, and

(b) on any sum payable to the applicant under a compromise or settlement arrived at in connection with that matter to avoid or bring to an end any proceedings.

6   In Scotland, the recovery of such expenses (as taxed or assessed in such manner as may be prescribed by rules of court) shall be paid to the Commissioner, in priority to other debts–

(a) out of any expenses which, by virtue of any judgment or order of the court, are payable to the applicant by any other person in respect of the matter in connection with which the assistance is provided, and

(b) out of any sum payable to the applicant under a compromise or settlement arrived at in connection with that matter to avoid or bring to an end any proceedings.

SCHEDULE 11

EDUCATIONAL RECORDS

Section 68(1)(b)

Meaning of "educational record"

1   For the purposes of section 68 "educational record" means any record to which paragraph 2, 5 or 7 applies.

England and Wales

2   This paragraph applies to any record of information which–
    (a) is processed by or on behalf of the governing body of, or a teacher at, any school in England and Wales specified in paragraph 3,
    (b) relates to any person who is or has been a pupil at the school, and
    (c) originated from or was supplied by or on behalf of any of the persons specified in paragraph 4,
other than information which is processed by a teacher solely for the teacher's own use.

3   The schools referred to in paragraph 2(a) are–
    (a) a school maintained by a local education authority, and
    (b) a special school, as defined by section 6(2) of the Education Act 1996, which is not so maintained.

4   The persons referred to in paragraph 2(c) are–
    (a) an employee of the local education authority which maintains the school,
    (b) in the case of–
        (i) a voluntary aided, foundation or foundation special school (within the meaning of the School Standards and Framework Act 1998), or
        (ii) a special school which is not maintained by a local education authority,
a teacher or other employee at the school (including an educational psychologist engaged by the governing body under a contract for services),
    (c) the pupil to whom the record relates, and
    (d) a parent, as defined by section 576(1) of the Education Act 1996, of that pupil.

Scotland

Not reproduced

Northern Ireland

Not reproduced

England and Wales: transitory provisions

SCHEDULE 12

ACCESSIBLE PUBLIC RECORDS

Section 68(1)(c)

Meaning of "accessible public record"

1 For the purposes of section 68 "accessible public record" means any record which is kept by an authority specified–
    (a) as respects England and Wales, in the Table in paragraph 2,
    (b) as respects Scotland, in the Table in paragraph 4, or
    (c) as respects Northern Ireland, in the Table in paragraph 6,
and is a record of information of a description specified in that Table in relation to that authority.

Housing and social services records: England and Wales

2 The following is the Table referred to in paragraph 1(a).

Table of Authorities and Information

Housing Act local authority.	Information held for the purpose of any of the authority's tenancies.
Local social services authority.	Information held for any purpose of the authority's social services functions.

3(1) The following provisions apply for the interpretation of the Table in paragraph 2.

(2) Any authority which, by virtue of section 4(e) of the Housing Act 1985, is a local authority for the purpose of any provision of that Act is a "Housing Act local authority" for the purposes of this Schedule, and so is any housing action trust established under Part III of the Housing Act 1988.

(3) Information contained in records kept by a Housing Act local authority is "held for the purpose of any of the authority's tenancies" if it is held for any purpose of the relationship of landlord and tenant of a dwelling which subsists, has subsisted or may subsist between the authority and any individual who is, has been or, as the case may be, has applied to be, a tenant of the authority.

(4) Any authority which, by virtue of section 1 or 12 of the Local Authority Social Services Act 1970, is or is treated as a local authority for the purposes of that Act is a "local social services authority" for the purposes of this Schedule; and information contained in records kept by such an authority is "held for any purpose of the authority's social services functions" if it is held for the purpose of any past, current or proposed exercise of such a function in any case.

(5) Any expression used in paragraph 2 or this paragraph and in Part II of the Housing Act 1985 or the Local Authority Social Services Act 1970 has the same meaning as in that Act.

Housing and social services records: Scotland

Not reproduced

Housing and social services records: Northern Ireland

Not reproduced

SCHEDULE 13

MODIFICATIONS OF ACT HAVING EFFECT BEFORE 24TH OCTOBER 2007

Section 72

Not reproduced

SCHEDULE 14

TRANSITIONAL PROVISIONS AND SAVINGS

Section 73

Not reproduced

SCHEDULE 15

MINOR AND CONSEQUENTIAL AMENDMENTS

Section 74(1)

Not reproduced

SCHEDULE 16

REPEALS AND REVOCATIONS

Section 74(2)

Not reproduced

Environmental Information Regulations 2004 (SI 2004/3391)

Made 21st December 2004

Coming into force 1st January 2005

Whereas a draft of these Regulations has been approved by resolution of each House of Parliament in pursuance of paragraph 2(2) of Schedule 2 to the European Communities Act 1972;

Now, therefore, the Secretary of State, being a Minister designated for the purposes of section 2(2) of the European Communities Act 1972 in relation to freedom of access to, and dissemination of, information on the environment held by or for public authorities or other bodies, in exercise of the powers conferred on her by that section, makes the following Regulations:

PART 1

INTRODUCTORY

1   Citation and commencement

These Regulations may be cited as the Environmental Information Regulations 2004 and shall come into force on 1st January 2005.

NOTES

Scottish public authority equivalent
EI(S)R reg 1

2   Interpretation

(1)   In these Regulations--

"the Act" means the Freedom of Information Act 2000;

"applicant", in relation to a request for environmental information, means the person who made the request;

"appropriate records authority", in relation to a transferred public record, has the same meaning as in section 15(5) of the Act;

"the Commissioner" means the Information Commissioner;

"the Directive" means Council Directive 2003/4/EC on public access to environmental information and repealing Council Directive 90/313/EEC;

"environmental information" has the same meaning as in Article 2(1) of the Directive, namely any information in written, visual, aural, electronic or any other material form on--

(a) the state of the elements of the environment, such as air and atmosphere, water, soil, land, landscape and natural sites including wetlands, coastal and marine areas, biological diversity and its components, including genetically modified organisms, and the interaction among these elements;

(b) factors, such as substances, energy, noise, radiation or waste, including radioactive waste, emissions, discharges and other releases into the environment, affecting or likely to affect the elements of the environment referred to in (a);

(c) measures (including administrative measures), such as policies, legislation, plans, programmes, environmental agreements, and activities affecting or likely to affect the elements and factors referred to in (a) and (b) as well as measures or activities designed to protect those elements;

(d) reports on the implementation of environmental legislation;

(e) cost-benefit and other economic analyses and assumptions used within the framework of the measures and activities referred to in (c); and

(f) the state of human health and safety, including the contamination of the food chain, where relevant, conditions of human life, cultural sites and built structures inasmuch as they are or may be affected by the state of the elements of the environment referred to in (a) or, through those elements, by any of the matters referred to in (b) and (c);

"historical record" has the same meaning as in section 62(1) of the Act;

"public authority" has the meaning given by paragraph (2);

"public record" has the same meaning as in section 84 of the Act;

"responsible authority", in relation to a transferred public record, has the same meaning as in section 15(5) of the Act;

"Scottish public authority" means--

(a) a body referred to in section 80(2) of the Act; and

(b) insofar as not such a body, a Scottish public authority as defined in section 3 of the Freedom of Information (Scotland) Act 2002;

"transferred public record" has the same meaning as in section 15(4) of the Act; and

"working day" has the same meaning as in section 10(6) of the Act.

(2) Subject to paragraph (3), "public authority" means--

(a) government departments;

(b) any other public authority as defined in section 3(1) of the Act, disregarding for this purpose the exceptions in paragraph 6 of Schedule 1 to the Act, but excluding--

(i) any body or office-holder listed in Schedule 1 to the Act only in relation to information of a specified description; or

(ii) any person designated by Order under section 5 of the Act;

(c) any other body or other person, that carries out functions of public administration; or

(d) any other body or other person, that is under the control of a person falling within sub-paragraphs (a), (b) or (c) and--

(i) has public responsibilities relating to the environment;

(ii) exercises functions of a public nature relating to the environment; or

(iii) provides public services relating to the environment.

(3) Except as provided by regulation 12(10) a Scottish public authority is not a "public authority" for the purpose of these Regulations.

(4) The following expressions have the same meaning in these Regulations as they have in the Data Protection Act 1998, namely--

(a) "data" except that for the purposes of regulation 12(3) and regulation 13 a public authority referred to in the definition of data in paragraph (e) of section 1(1) of that Act means a public authority within the meaning of these Regulations;

(b) "the data protection principles";

(c) "data subject"; and

(d) "personal data".

(5) Except as provided by this regulation, expressions in these Regulations which appear in the Directive have the same meaning in these Regulations as they have in the Directive.

NOTES

Scottish public authority equivalent

EI(S)R reg 2(1) but excluding definitions of "appropriate records authority" , "historical record" , "public record" , "responsible authority" and "transferred public record."

Application

3(1) Subject to paragraphs (3) and (4), these Regulations apply to public authorities.

(2) For the purposes of these Regulations, environmental information is held by a public authority if the information--

(a) is in the authority's possession and has been produced or received by the authority; or(b) is held by another person on behalf of the authority.

(3) These Regulations shall not apply to any public authority to the extent that it is acting in a judicial or legislative capacity.

(4) These Regulations shall not apply to either House of Parliament to the extent required for the purpose of avoiding an infringement of the privileges of either House.

(5) Each government department is to be treated as a person separate from any other government department for the purposes of Parts 2, 4 and 5 of these Regulations.

NOTES

Scottish public authority equivalent

EI(S)R regs 2(2), 3

Defined terms

"environmental information": reg 2(1)

"public authority": regs 2(1)-(3) and 12(10); Freedom of Information Act 2000, s 3(1) and Sch 1

PART 2

ACCESS TO ENVIRONMENTAL INFORMATION HELD BY PUBLIC AUTHORITIES

Dissemination of environmental information

4(1)   Subject to paragraph (3), a public authority shall in respect of environmental information that it holds–

(a) progressively make the information available to the public by electronic means which are easily accessible; and

(b) take reasonable steps to organize the information relevant to its functions with a view to the active and systematic dissemination to the public of the information.

(2)   For the purposes of paragraph (1) the use of electronic means to make information available or to organize information shall not be required in relation to information collected before 1st January 2005 in non-electronic form.

(3)   Paragraph (1) shall not extend to making available or disseminating information which a public authority would be entitled to refuse to disclose under regulation 12.

(4)   The information under paragraph (1) shall include at least–

(a) the information referred to in Article 7(2) of the Directive; and

(b) facts and analyses of facts which the public authority considers relevant and important in framing major environmental policy proposals.

NOTES

Scottish public authority equivalent
EI(S)R reg 4

Defined terms
"the Act": reg 2(1)
"the Directive": reg 2(1)
"environmental information": reg 2(1)

"information held by a public authority": reg 2(5);
Council Directive 2003/4/EC, art 2(3)
"public": reg 2(5); Council Directive 2003/4/EC, art 2(6)
"public authority": reg 2(1)-(3) and 12(10); Freedom of
Information Act 2000, s.3(1) and Sch 1

Duty to make available environmental information on request

5(1)   Subject to paragraph (3) and in accordance with paragraphs (2), (4), (5) and (6) and the remaining provisions of this Part and Part 3 of these Regulations, a public authority that holds environmental information shall make it available on request.

(2)   Information shall be made available under paragraph (1) as soon as possible and no later than 20 working days after the date of receipt of the request.

(3)   To the extent that the information requested includes personal data of which the applicant is the data subject, paragraph (1) shall not apply to those personal data.

(4)   For the purposes of paragraph (1), where the information made available is compiled by or on behalf of the public authority it shall be up to date, accurate and comparable, so far as the public authority reasonably believes.

(5)   Where a public authority makes available information in paragraph (b) of the definition of environmental information, and the applicant so requests, the public authority shall, insofar as it is able to do so, either inform the applicant of the place where information, if available, can be found on the measurement procedures, including methods of analysis, sampling and pre-treatment of samples, used in compiling the information, or refer the applicant to a standardised procedure used.

(6)   Any enactment or rule of law that would prevent the disclosure of information in accordance with these Regulations shall not apply.

NOTES

Scottish public authority equivalent
EI(S)R regs 5, 11(1)

Defined terms
"applicant": reg 2(1)

"data": reg 2(4); Data Protection Act 1998, s 1(1)
"data subject": reg 2(4); Data Protection Act 1998, s 1(1)
"environmental information": reg 2(1)
"personal data": reg 2(4); Data Protection Act 1998, s 1(1)
"public authority": regs 2(1)-(3) and 12(10); Freedom of Information Act 2000, s 3(1) and Sch 1
"working day": reg 2(1); Freedom of Information Act 2000, s 10(6)

Form and format of information

6(1)   Where an applicant requests that the information be made available in a particular form or format, a public authority shall make it so available, unless–
        (a) it is reasonable for it to make the information available in another form or format; or
        (b) the information is already publicly available and easily accessible to the applicant in another form or format.

(2)   If the information is not made available in the form or format requested, the public authority shall–
        (a) explain the reason for its decision as soon as possible and no later than 20 working days after the date of receipt of the request for the information;
        (b) provide the explanation in writing if the applicant so requests; and
        (c) inform the applicant of the provisions of regulation 11 and of the enforcement and appeal provisions of the Act applied by regulation 18.

NOTES

Scottish public authority equivalent
EI(S)R reg 6

Defined terms

"information held by a public authority": reg 2(5); Council Directive 2003/4/EC, art 2(3)
"public": reg 2(5); Council Directive 2003/4/EC, art 2(6)
"public authority": regs 2(1)-(3) and 12(10); Freedom of

"the Act": reg 2(1)
"applicant": reg 2(1)

Information Act 2000, s 3(1) and Sch 1
"working day": reg 2(1); Freedom of Information Act
2000, s 10(6)

Extension of time

7(1) Where a request is made under regulation 5, the public authority may extend the period of 20 working days referred to in the provisions in paragraph (2) to 40 working days if it reasonably believes that the complexity and volume of the information requested means that it is impracticable either to comply with the request within the earlier period or to make a decision to refuse to do so.

(2) The provisions referred to in paragraph (1) are–
  (a) regulation 5(2);
  (b) regulation 6(2)(a); and
  (c) regulation 14(2).

(3) Where paragraph (1) applies the public authority shall notify the applicant accordingly as soon as possible and no later than 20 working days after the date of receipt of the request.

NOTES

Scottish public authority equivalent
EI(S)R reg 7

Defined terms
"applicant": reg 2(1)

"public authority": regs 2(1)-(3) and 12(10); Freedom of
  Information Act 2000, s 3(1) and Sch 1
"working day": reg 2(1); Freedom of Information Act
  2000, s 10(6)

Charging

8(1) Subject to paragraphs (2) to (8), where a public authority makes environmental information available in accordance with regulation 5(1) the authority may charge the applicant for making the information available.

(2) A public authority shall not make any charge for allowing an applicant–
  (a) to access any public registers or lists of environmental information held by the public authority; or
  (b) to examine the information requested at the place which the public authority makes available for that examination.

(3) A charge under paragraph (1) shall not exceed an amount which the public authority is satisfied is a reasonable amount.

(4) A public authority may require advance payment of a charge for making environmental information available and if it does it shall, no later than 20 working days after the date of receipt of the request for the information, notify the applicant of this requirement and of the amount of the advance payment.

(5)   Where a public authority has notified an applicant under paragraph (4) that advance payment is required, the public authority is not required–

      (a) to make available the information requested; or

      (b) to comply with regulations 6 or 14,unless the charge is paid no later than 60 working days after the date on which it gave the notification.

(6)   The period beginning with the day on which the notification of a requirement for an advance payment is made and ending on the day on which that payment is received by the public authority is to be disregarded for the purposes of determining the period of 20 working days referred to in the provisions in paragraph (7), including any extension to those periods under regulation 7(1).

(7)   The provisions referred to in paragraph (6) are–

      (a) regulation 5(2);

      (b) regulation 6(2)(a); and

      (c) regulation 14(2).

(8)   A public authority shall publish and make available to applicants–

      (a) a schedule of its charges; and

      (b) information on the circumstances in which a charge may be made or waived.

NOTES

Scottish public authority equivalent
EI(S)R reg 8

Defined terms
"applicant": reg 2(1)
"environmental information": reg 2(1)

"information held by a public authority": reg 2(5);
   Council Directive 2003/4/EC, art 2(3)
"public": reg 2(5); Council Directive 2003/4/EC, art 2(6)
"public authority": reg 2(1)-(3) and 12(10); Freedom of
   Information Act 2000, s 3(1) and Sch 1
"working day": reg 2(1); Freedom of Information Act
   2000, s 10(6)

Advice and assistance

9(1)   A public authority shall provide advice and assistance, so far as it would be reasonable to expect the authority to do so, to applicants and prospective applicants.

(2)   Where a public authority decides that an applicant has formulated a request in too general a manner, it shall–

      (a) ask the applicant as soon as possible and in any event no later than 20 working days after the date of receipt of the request, to provide more particulars in relation to the request; and

      (b) assist the applicant in providing those particulars.

(3)   Where a code of practice has been made under regulation 16, and to the extent that a public authority conforms to that code in relation to the provision of advice and assistance in a particular case, it shall be taken to have complied with paragraph (1) in relation to that case.

(4) Where paragraph (2) applies, in respect of the provisions in paragraph (5), the date on which the further particulars are received by the public authority shall be treated as the date after which the period of 20 working days referred to in those provisions shall be calculated.

(5) The provisions referred to in paragraph (4) are–
- (a) regulation 5(2);
- (b) regulation 6(2)(a); and
- (c) regulation 14(2).

NOTES

Scottish public authority equivalent
EI(S)R reg 9

Defined terms
"applicant": reg 2(1)

"public authority": regs 2(1)-(3) and 12(10); Freedom of Information Act 2000, s 3(1) and Sch 1
"working day": reg 2(1); Freedom of Information Act 2000, s 10(6)

Transfer of a request

10(1) Where a public authority that receives a request for environmental information does not hold the information requested but believes that another public authority or a Scottish public authority holds the information, the public authority shall either–
- (a) transfer the request to the other public authority or Scottish public authority; or
- (b) supply the applicant with the name and address of that authority, and inform the applicant accordingly with the refusal sent under regulation 14(1).

(2) Where a request is transferred to a public authority, for the purposes of the provisions referred to in paragraph (3) the request is received by that public authority on the date on which it receives the transferred request.

(3) The provisions referred to in paragraph (2) are–
- (a) regulation 5(2);
- (b) regulation 6(2)(a); and
- (c) regulation 14(2).

NOTES

Scottish public authority equivalent
EI(S)R reg 14

Defined terms
"applicant": reg 2(1)
"environmental information": reg 2(1)

"information held by a public authority": reg 2(5); Council Directive 2003/4/EC, art 2(3)
"public authority": regs 2(1)-(3) and 12(10); Freedom of Information Act 2000, s 3(1) and Sch 1
"Scottish public authority": reg 2(1); Freedom of Information Act 2000, s 80(2)

Representations and reconsideration

11(1)   Subject to paragraph (2), an applicant may make representations to a public authority in relation to the applicant's request for environmental information if it appears to the applicant that the authority has failed to comply with a requirement of these Regulations in relation to the request.

(2)   Representations under paragraph (1) shall be made in writing to the public authority no later than 40 working days after the date on which the applicant believes that the public authority has failed to comply with the requirement.

(3)   The public authority shall on receipt of the representations and free of charge–
(a) consider them and any supporting evidence produced by the applicant; and
(b) decide if it has complied with the requirement.

(4)   A public authority shall notify the applicant of its decision under paragraph (3) as soon as possible and no later than 40 working days after the date of receipt of the representations.

(5)   Where the public authority decides that it has failed to comply with these Regulations in relation to the request, the notification under paragraph (4) shall include a statement of–
(a) the failure to comply;
(b) the action the authority has decided to take to comply with the requirement; and
(c) the period within which that action is to be taken.

NOTES

Scottish public authority equivalent
EI(S)R reg 16

Defined terms
"the Act": reg 2(1)
"applicant": reg 2(1)

"environmental information": reg 2(1)
"public authority": regs 2(1)-(3) and 12(10); Freedom of Information Act 2000, s 3(1) and Sch 1
"working day": reg 2(1); Freedom of Information Act 2000, s 10(6)

PART 3

EXCEPTIONS TO THE DUTY TO DISCLOSE ENVIRONMENTAL INFORMATION

Exceptions to the duty to disclose environmental information

12(1)   Subject to paragraphs (2), (3) and (9), a public authority may refuse to disclose environmental information requested if–
(a) an exception to disclosure applies under paragraphs (4) or (5); and
(b) in all the circumstances of the case, the public interest in maintaining the exception outweighs the public interest in disclosing the information.

(2)   A public authority shall apply a presumption in favour of disclosure.

(3)   To the extent that the information requested includes personal data of which the applicant is not the data subject, the personal data shall not be disclosed otherwise than in accordance with regulation 13.

(4)   For the purposes of paragraph (1)(a), a public authority may refuse to disclose information to the extent that–
    (a) it does not hold that information when an applicant's request is received;
    (b) the request for information is manifestly unreasonable;
    (c) the request for information is formulated in too general a manner and the public authority has complied with regulation 9;
    (d) the request relates to material which is still in the course of completion, to unfinished documents or to incomplete data; or
    (e) the request involves the disclosure of internal communications.

(5)   For the purposes of paragraph (1)(a), a public authority may refuse to disclose information to the extent that its disclosure would adversely affect–
    (a) international relations, defence, national security or public safety;
    (b) the course of justice, the ability of a person to receive a fair trial or the ability of a public authority to conduct an inquiry of a criminal or disciplinary nature;
    (c) intellectual property rights;
    (d) the confidentiality of the proceedings of that or any other public authority where such confidentiality is provided by law;
    (e) the confidentiality of commercial or industrial information where such confidentiality is provided by law to protect a legitimate economic interest;
    (f)   the interests of the person who provided the information where that person–
        (i)   was not under, and could not have been put under, any legal obligation to supply it to that or any other public authority;
        (ii) did not supply it in circumstances such that that or any other public authority is entitled apart from these Regulations to disclose it; and
        (iii) has not consented to its disclosure; or
    (g) the protection of the environment to which the information relates.

(6)   For the purposes of paragraph (1), a public authority may respond to a request by neither confirming nor denying whether such information exists and is held by the public authority, whether or not it holds such information, if that confirmation or denial would involve the disclosure of information which would adversely affect any of the interests referred to in paragraph (5)(a) and would not be in the public interest under paragraph (1)(b).

(7)   For the purposes of a response under paragraph (6), whether information exists and is held by the public authority is itself the disclosure of information.

(8)   For the purposes of paragraph (4)(e), internal communications includes communications between government departments.

(9) To the extent that the environmental information to be disclosed relates to information on emissions, a public authority shall not be entitled to refuse to disclose that information under an exception referred to in paragraphs (5)(d) to (g).

(10) For the purposes of paragraphs (5)(b), (d) and (f), references to a public authority shall include references to a Scottish public authority.

(11) Nothing in these Regulations shall authorise a refusal to make available any environmental information contained in or otherwise held with other information which is withheld by virtue of these Regulations unless it is not reasonably capable of being separated from the other information for the purpose of making available that information.

NOTES

Scottish public authority equivalent
EI(S)R reg 10

Defined terms
"applicant": reg 2(1)
"data": reg 2(4); Data Protection Act 1998, s 1(1)
"data subject": reg 2(4); Data Protection Act 1998, s 1(1)
"environmental information": reg 2(1)

"information held by a public authority": reg 2(5); Council Directive 2003/4/EC, art 2(3)
"personal data": reg 2(4); Data Protection Act 1998, s 1(1)
"public": reg 2(5); Council Directive 2003/4/EC, art 2(6)
"public authority": rr2(1)-(3) and 12(10); Freedom of Information Act 2000, s 3(1) and Sch 1
"Scottish public authority": reg 2(1); Freedom of Information Act 2000, s 80(2)

Personal data

13(1) To the extent that the information requested includes personal data of which the applicant is not the data subject and as respects which either the first or second condition below is satisfied, a public authority shall not disclose the personal data.

(2) The first condition is–
    (a) in a case where the information falls within any of paragraphs (a) to (d) of the definition of "data" in section 1(1) of the Data Protection Act 1998, that the disclosure of the information to a member of the public otherwise than under these Regulations would contravene–
        (i) any of the data protection principles; or
        (ii) section 10 of that Act (right to prevent processing likely to cause damage or distress) and in all the circumstances of the case, the public interest in not disclosing the information outweighs the public interest in disclosing it; and
    (b) in any other case, that the disclosure of the information to a member of the public otherwise than under these Regulations would contravene any of the data protection principles if the exemptions in section 33A(1) of the Data Protection Act 1998 (which relate to manual data held by public authorities) were disregarded.

(3) The second condition is that by virtue of any provision of Part IV of the Data Protection Act 1998 the information is exempt from section 7(1) of that Act and, in all

the circumstances of the case, the public interest in not disclosing the information outweighs the public interest in disclosing it.

(4) In determining whether anything done before 24th October 2007 would contravene any of the data protection principles, the exemptions in Part III of Schedule 8 to the Data Protection Act 1998 shall be disregarded.

(5) For the purposes of this regulation a public authority may respond to a request by neither confirming nor denying whether such information exists and is held by the public authority, whether or not it holds such information, to the extent that–

(a) the giving to a member of the public of the confirmation or denial would contravene any of the data protection principles or section 10 of the Data Protection Act 1998 or would do so if the exemptions in section 33A(1) of that Act were disregarded; or

(b) by virtue of any provision of Part IV of the Data Protection Act 1998, the information is exempt from section 7(1)(a) of that Act.

NOTES

Scottish public authority equivalent
EI(S)R reg 11

Defined terms
"applicant": reg 2(1)
"data": reg 2(4); Data Protection Act 1998, s 1(1)

"data protection principles": reg 2(4); Data Protection Act 1998, s 4(1) and Sch 1
"information held by a public authority": reg 2(5); Council Directive 2003/4/EC, art 2(3)
"personal data": reg 2(4); Data Protection Act 1998, s 1(1)
"public": reg 2(5); Council Directive 2003/4/EC, art 2(6)
"public authority": regs 2(1)-(3) and 12(10); Freedom of Information Act 2000, s 3(1) and Sch 1

Refusal to disclose information

14(1) If a request for environmental information is refused by a public authority under regulations 12(1) or 13(1), the refusal shall be made in writing and comply with the following provisions of this regulation.

(2) The refusal shall be made as soon as possible and no later than 20 working days after the date of receipt of the request.

(3) The refusal shall specify the reasons not to disclose the information requested, including–

(a) any exception relied on under regulations 12(4), 12(5) or 13; and

(b) the matters the public authority considered in reaching its decision with respect to the public interest under regulation 12(1)(b) or, where these apply, regulations 13(2)(a)(ii) or 13(3).

(4) If the exception in regulation 12(4)(d) is specified in the refusal, the authority shall also specify, if known to the public authority, the name of any other public authority preparing the information and the estimated time in which the information will be finished or completed.

(5)   The refusal shall inform the applicant–
      (a) that he may make representations to the public authority under regulation 11; and
      (b) of the enforcement and appeal provisions of the Act applied by regulation 18.

NOTES

Scottish public authority equivalent
EI(S)R reg 13

Defined terms
"the Act": reg 2(1)
"applicant": reg 2(1)

"environmental information": reg 2(1)
"public authority": regs 2(1)-(3) and 12(10); Freedom of Information Act 2000, s 3(1) and Sch 1
"working day": reg 2(1); Freedom of Information Act 2000, s 10(6)

Ministerial certificates

15(1)   A Minister of the Crown may certify that a refusal to disclose information under regulation 12(1) is because the disclosure–
      (a) would adversely affect national security; and
      (b) would not be in the public interest under regulation 12(1)(b).

(2)   For the purposes of paragraph (1)--
      (a) a Minister of the Crown may designate a person to certify the matters in that paragraph on his behalf; and
      (b) a refusal to disclose information under regulation 12(1) includes a response under regulation 12(6).

(3)   A certificate issued in accordance with paragraph (1)--
      (a) shall be conclusive evidence of the matters in that paragraph; and
      (b) may identify the information to which it relates in general terms.

(4)   A document purporting to be a certificate under paragraph (1) shall be received in evidence and deemed to be such a certificate unless the contrary is proved.

(5)   A document which purports to be certified by or on behalf of a Minister of the Crown as a true copy of a certificate issued by that Minister under paragraph (1) shall in any legal proceedings be evidence (or, in Scotland, sufficient evidence) of that certificate.

(6)   In paragraphs (1), (2) and (5), a "Minister of the Crown" has the same meaning as in section 25(3) of the Act.

NOTES

Scottish public authority equivalent
EI(S)R reg 12

Defined terms
"the Act": reg 2(1)
"public": reg 2(5); Council Directive 2003/4/EC, art 2(6)

Issue of a code of practice and functions of the Commissioner

16(1)   The Secretary of State may issue, and may from time to time revise, a code of practice providing guidance to public authorities as to the practice which it would, in the Secretary of State's opinion, be desirable for them to follow in connection with the discharge of their functions under these Regulations.

(2)   The code may make different provision for different public authorities.

(3)   Before issuing or revising any code under this regulation, the Secretary of State shall consult the Commissioner.

(4)   The Secretary of State shall lay before each House of Parliament any code issued or revised under this regulation.

(5)   The general functions of the Commissioner under section 47 of the Act and the power of the Commissioner to give a practice recommendation under section 48 of the Act shall apply for the purposes of these Regulations as they apply for the purposes of the Act but with the modifications specified in paragraph (6).

(6)   For the purposes of the application of sections 47 and 48 of the Act to these Regulations, any reference to–
   (a) a public authority is a reference to a public authority within the meaning of these Regulations;
   (b) the requirements or operation of the Act, or functions under the Act, includes a reference to the requirements or operation of these Regulations, or functions under these Regulations; and
   (c) a code of practice made under section 45 of the Act includes a reference to a code of practice made under this regulation.

NOTES

Scottish public authority equivalent
EI(S)R reg 18

Defined terms
"the Act": reg 2(1)

"the Commissioner": reg 2(1)
"public authority": regs 2(1)-(3) and 12(10); Freedom of
   Information Act 2000, s 3(1) and Sch 1

The Code
The code is reproduced a p 1301ff

Historical and transferred public records

17(1)   Where a request relates to information contained in a historical record other than one to which paragraph (2) applies and the public authority considers that it may be in the public interest to refuse to disclose that information under regulation 12(1)(b), the public authority shall consult–
   (a) the Lord Chancellor, if it is a public record within the meaning of the Public Records Act 1958; or

(b) the appropriate Northern Ireland Minister, if it is a public record to which the Public Records Act (Northern Ireland) 1923 applies, before it decides whether the information may or may not be disclosed.

(2) Where a request relates to information contained in a transferred public record, other than information which the responsible authority has designated as open information for the purposes of this regulation, the appropriate records authority shall consult the responsible authority on whether there may be an exception to disclosure of that information under regulation 12(5).

(3) If the appropriate records authority decides that such an exception applies–

(a) subject to paragraph (4), a determination on whether it may be in the public interest to refuse to disclose that information under regulation 12(1)(b) shall be made by the responsible authority;

(b) the responsible authority shall communicate its determination to the appropriate records authority within such time as is reasonable in all the circumstances; and

(c) the appropriate records authority shall comply with regulation 5 in accordance with that determination.

(4) Where a responsible authority is required to make a determination under paragraph (3), it shall consult–

(a) the Lord Chancellor, if the transferred public record is a public record within the meaning of the Public Records Act 1958; or

(b) the appropriate Northern Ireland Minister, if the transferred public record is a public record to which the Public Records Act (Northern Ireland) 1923 applies,before it determines whether the information may or may not be disclosed.

(5) A responsible authority which is not a public authority under these Regulations shall be treated as a public authority for the purposes of–

(a) the obligations of a responsible authority under paragraphs (3)(a) and (b) and (4); and

(b) the imposition of any requirement to furnish information relating to compliance with regulation 5.

NOTES

Scottish public authority equivalent
EI(S)R reg 15

Defined terms
"appropriate records authority": reg 2(1)
"historical record": reg 2(1) and Freedom of Information Act 2000, s 62(1)

"public authority": regs 2(1)-(3) and 12(10); Freedom of Information Act 2000, s 3(1) and Sch 1
"public record": reg 2(1); Freedom of Information Act 2000, s 84
"responsible authority": reg 2(1); Freedom of Information Act 2000, s 15(5)
"transferred public record": reg 2(1); Freedom of Information Act 2000, s 15(4)

Enforcement and appeal provisions

18(1) The enforcement and appeals provisions of the Act shall apply for the purposes of these Regulations as they apply for the purposes of the Act but with the modifications specified in this regulation.

(2) In this regulation, "the enforcement and appeals provisions of the Act" means–
   (a) Part IV of the Act (enforcement), including Schedule 3 (powers of entry and inspection) which has effect by virtue of section 55 of the Act; and
   (b) Part V of the Act (appeals).

(3) Part IV of the Act shall not apply in any case where a certificate has been issued in accordance with regulation 15(1).

(4) For the purposes of the application of the enforcement and appeals provisions of the Act–
   (a) for any reference to–
      (i) "this Act" there shall be substituted a reference to "these Regulations"; and
      (ii) "Part I" there shall be substituted a reference to "Parts 2 and 3 of these Regulations";
   (b) any reference to a public authority is a reference to a public authority within the meaning of these Regulations;
   (c) for any reference to the code of practice under section 45 of the Act (issue of a code of practice by the Secretary of State) there shall be substituted a reference to any code of practice issued under regulation 16(1);
   (d) in section 50(4) of the Act (contents of decision notice)--
      (i) in paragraph (a) for the reference to "section 1(1)" there shall be substituted a reference to "regulation 5(1)"; and
      (ii) in paragraph (b) for the references to "sections 11 and 17" there shall be substituted references to "regulations 6, 11 or 14";
   (e) in section 56(1) of the Act (no action against public authority) for the words "This Act does not confer" there shall be substituted the words "These Regulations do not confer";
   (f) in section 57(3)(a) of the Act (appeal against notices served under Part IV) for the reference to "section 66" of the Act (decisions relating to certain transferred public records) there shall be substituted a reference to "regulations 17(2) to (5)";
   (g) in paragraph 1 of Schedule 3 to the Act (issue of warrants) for the reference to "section 77" (offence of altering etc records with intent to prevent disclosure) there shall be substituted a reference to "regulation 19"; and
   (h) in paragraph 8 of Schedule 3 to the Act (matters exempt from inspection and seizure) for the reference to "information which is exempt information by virtue of section 23(1) or 24(1)" (bodies and information relating to national security) there shall be substituted a reference to "information whose disclosure would adversely affect national security".

(5) In section 50(4)(a) of the Act (contents of decision notice) the reference to confirmation or denial applies to a response given by a public authority under regulation 12(6) or regulation 13(5).

(6) Section 53 of the Act (exception from duty to comply with decision notice or enforcement notice) applies to a decision notice or enforcement notice served under Part IV of the Act as applied to these Regulations on any of the public authorities referred to in section 53(1)(a); and in section 53(7) for the reference to "exempt information" there shall be substituted a reference to "information which may be refused under these Regulations".

(7) Section 60 of the Act (appeals against national security certificate) shall apply with the following modifications–
    (a) for the reference to a certificate under section 24(3) of the Act (national security) there shall be substituted a reference to a certificate issued in accordance with regulation 15(1);
    (b) subsection (2) shall be omitted; and
    (c) in subsection (3), for the words, "the Minister did not have reasonable grounds for issuing the certificate" there shall be substituted the words "the Minister or person designated by him did not have reasonable grounds for issuing the certificate under regulation 15(1)".

(8) A person found guilty of an offence under paragraph 12 of Schedule 3 to the Act (offences relating to obstruction of the execution of a warrant) is liable on summary conviction to a fine not exceeding level 5 on the standard scale.

(9) A government department is not liable to prosecution in relation to an offence under paragraph 12 of Schedule 3 to the Act but that offence shall apply to a person in the public service of the Crown and to a person acting on behalf of either House of Parliament or on behalf of the Northern Ireland Assembly as it applies to any other person.

(10) Section 76(1) of the Act (disclosure of information between Commissioner and ombudsmen) shall apply to any information obtained by, or furnished to, the Commissioner under or for the purposes of these Regulations.

NOTES

Scottish public authority equivalent
EI(S)R reg 17

Defined terms
"the Act": reg 2(1)

"the Commissioner": reg 2(1)
"public authority": regs 2(1)-(3) and 12(10); Freedom of Information Act 2000, s 3(1) and Sch 1

Offence of altering records with intent to prevent disclosure
19(1) Where–

(a) a request for environmental information has been made to a public authority under regulation 5; and

(b) the applicant would have been entitled (subject to payment of any charge) to that information in accordance with that regulation,

any person to whom this paragraph applies is guilty of an offence if he alters, defaces, blocks, erases, destroys or conceals any record held by the public authority, with the intention of preventing the disclosure by that authority of all, or any part, of the information to which the applicant would have been entitled.

(2) Subject to paragraph (5), paragraph (1) applies to the public authority and to any person who is employed by, is an officer of, or is subject to the direction of, the public authority.

(3) A person guilty of an offence under this regulation is liable on summary conviction to a fine not exceeding level 5 on the standard scale.

(4) No proceedings for an offence under this regulation shall be instituted–
    (a) in England and Wales, except by the Commissioner or by or with the consent of the Director of Public Prosecutions; or
    (b) in Northern Ireland, except by the Commissioner or by or with the consent of the Director of Public Prosecutions for Northern Ireland.

(5) A government department is not liable to prosecution in relation to an offence under paragraph (1) but that offence shall apply to a person in the public service of the Crown and to a person acting on behalf of either House of Parliament or on behalf of the Northern Ireland Assembly as it applies to any other person.

NOTES

Scottish public authority equivalent
EI(S)R reg 19

Defined terms
"applicant": reg 2(1)

"the Commissioner": reg 2(1)
"environmental information": reg 2(1)
"public authority": regs 2(1)-(3) and 12(10); Freedom of
    Information Act 2000, s 3(1) and Sch 1

Amendment

20(1) Section 39 of the Act is amended as follows.

(2) In subsection (1)(a), for "regulations under section 74" there is substituted "environmental information regulations".

(3) After subsection (1) there is inserted–
    "(1A) In subsection (1) "environmental information regulations" means–
        (a) regulations made under section 74, or
        (b) regulations made under section 2(2) of the European Communities Act 1972 for the purpose of implementing any Community obligation relating to public access to, and the dissemination of, information on the environment.".

NOTES

Defined terms
"the Act": reg 2(1)

Revocation

21   The following are revoked–

    (a) The Environmental Information Regulations 1992 and the Environmental Information (Amendment) Regulations 1998 except insofar as these apply to Scottish public authorities; and

    (b) The Environmental Information Regulations (Northern Ireland) 1993 and the Environmental Information (Amendment) Regulations (Northern Ireland) 1998.

NOTES

Scottish public authority equivalent
EI(S)R reg 21

Public Records Act 1958

CHAPTER 51

An Act to make new provision with respect to public records and the Public Record Office, and for connected purposes

23rd July 1958

BE IT ENACTED by the Queen's most Excellent Majesty, by and with the advice and consent of the Lords Spiritual and Temporal, and Commons, in this present Parliament assembled, and by the authority of the same, as follows:–

TABLE OF PROVISIONS

General responsibility of the Lord Chancellor for public records

1(1)   The direction of the Public Record Office shall be transferred from the Master of the Rolls to the Lord Chancellor, and the Lord Chancellor shall be generally responsible for the execution of this Act and shall supervise the care and preservation of public records.

(2)   There shall be an Advisory Council on Public Records to advise the Lord Chancellor on matters concerning public records in general and, in particular, on those aspects of the work of the Public Record Office which affect members of the public who make use of the facilities provided by the Public Record Office.
The Master of the Rolls shall be chairman of the said Council and the remaining members of the Council shall be appointed by the Lord Chancellor on such terms as he may specify.

(2A)   The matters on which the Advisory Council on Public Records may advise the Lord Chancellor include matters relating to the application of the Freedom of Information Act 2000 to information contained in public records which are historical records within the meaning of Part VI of that Act.

(3)   The Lord Chancellor shall in every year lay before both Houses of Parliament a report on the work of the Public Record Office, which shall include any report made to him by the Advisory Council on Public Records.

Commencement
1 January 1959

NOTES

Defined terms
"public records" s 10(1) and Sch 1;
"records" s 10(1)

The Public Record Office

2(1)   The Lord Chancellor may appoint a Keeper of Public Records to take charge under his direction of the Public Record Office and of the records therein and may, with the concurrence of the Treasury as to numbers and conditions of service, appoint such other persons to serve in the Public Record Office as he may think fit.

(2)   The Keeper of Public Records and other persons appointed under this Act shall receive such salaries and remuneration as the Treasury may from time to time direct.

(3)   It shall be the duty of the Keeper of Public Records to take all practicable steps for the preservation of records under his charge.

(4)   The Keeper of Public Records shall have power to do all such things as appear to him necessary or expedient for maintaining the utility of the Public Record Office and may in particular--

(a) compile and make available indexes and guides to, and calendars and texts of, the records in the Public Record Office;

(b) prepare publications concerning the activities of and facilities provided by the Public Record Office;

(c) regulate the conditions under which members of the public may inspect public and other records or use the other facilities of the Public Record Office;

(d) provide for the making and authentication of copies of and extracts from records required as evidence in legal proceedings or for other purposes;

(e) accept responsibility for the safe keeping of records other than public records;

(f) make arrangements for the separate housing of films and other records which have to be kept under special conditions;

(g) lend records, in a case where the Lord Chancellor gives his approval, for display at commemorative exhibitions or for other special purposes;

(h) acquire records and accept gifts and loans.

(5)   The Lord Chancellor may by regulations made with the concurrence of the Treasury and contained in a statutory instrument prescribe the fees which may be charged for the inspection of records under the charge of the Keeper of Public Records, for authenticated copies or extracts from such records and for other services afforded by officers of the Public Record Office and authorise the remission of the fees in prescribed cases.

(6) Fees received under the last foregoing subsection shall be paid into the Exchequer.

NOTES

Commencement
1 January 1959

Defined terms
"public records" s 10(1) and Sch 1;
"records" s 10(1)

Selection and preservation of public records

3(1) It shall be the duty of every person responsible for public records of any description which are not in the Public Record Office or a place of deposit appointed by the Lord Chancellor under this Act to make arrangements for the selection of those records which ought to be permanently preserved and for their safe-keeping.

(2) Every person shall perform his duties under this section under the guidance of the Keeper of Public Records and the said Keeper shall be responsible for co-ordinating and supervising all action taken under this section.

(3) All public records created before the year sixteen hundred and sixty shall be included among those selected for permanent preservation.

(4) Public records selected for permanent preservation under this section shall be transferred not later than thirty years after their creation either to the Public Record Office or to such other place of deposit appointed by the Lord Chancellor under this Act as the Lord Chancellor may direct:Provided that any records may be retained after the said period if, in the opinion of the person who is responsible for them, they are required for administrative purposes or ought to be retained for any other special reason and, where that person is not the Lord Chancellor, the Lord Chancellor has been informed of the facts and given his approval.

(5) The Lord Chancellor may, if it appears to him in the interests of the proper administration of the Public Record Office, direct that the transfer of any class of records under this section shall be suspended until arrangements for their reception have been completed.

(6) Public records which, following the arrangements made in pursuance of this section, have been rejected as not required for permanent preservation shall be destroyed or, subject, in the case of records for which some person other than the Lord Chancellor is responsible, to the approval of the Lord Chancellor, disposed of in any other way.

(7) Any question as to the person whose duty it is to make arrangements under this section with respect to any class of public records shall be referred to the Lord Chancellor for his decision.

(8) The provisions of this section shall not make it unlawful for the person responsible for any public record to transmit it to the Keeper of the Records of Scotland or to the Public Record Office of Northern Ireland.

NOTES

Commencement
1 January 1959

Defined terms
"public records" s 10(1) and Sch 1;
"records" s 10(1)

Place of deposit of public records

4(1)   If it appears to the Lord Chancellor that a place outside the Public Record Office affords suitable facilities for the safe-keeping and preservation of records and their inspection by the public he may, with the agreement of the authority who will be responsible for records deposited in that place, appoint it as a place of deposit as respects any class of public records selected for permanent preservation under this Act.

(2)   In choosing a place of deposit under this section for public records of--
  (a) courts of quarter sessions or magistrates' courts, or
  (b) courts of coroners of counties or boroughs,
the Lord Chancellor shall have regard to any arrangements made by the person for the time being responsible for the records with respect to the place where those records are to be kept and, where he does not follow any such arrangements, shall, so far as practicable, proceed on the principle that the records of any such court ought to be kept in the area of the administrative county or county borough comprising the area for which the court acts or where it sits, except in a case where the authorities or persons appearing to the Lord Chancellor to be mainly concerned consent to the choice of a place of deposit elsewhere.

(3)   The Lord Chancellor may at any time direct that public records shall be transferred from the Public Record Office to a place of deposit appointed under this section or from such a place of deposit to the Public Record Office or another place of deposit.

(4)   Before appointing a place of deposit under this section as respects public records of a class for which the Lord Chancellor is not himself responsible, he shall consult with the Minister or other person if any who appears to him to be primarily concerned and, where the records are records of a court of quarter sessions the records of which are, apart from the provisions of this Act, subject to the directions of a custos rotulorum, the Lord Chancellor shall consult him.

(5)   Public records in the Public Record Office shall be in the custody of the Keeper of Public Records and public records in a place of deposit appointed under this Act shall be in the custody of such officer as the Lord Chancellor may appoint.

(6)   Public records in the Public Record Office or other place of deposit appointed by the Lord Chancellor under this Act shall be temporarily returned at the request of the person by whom or department or office from which they were transferred.

NOTES

Commencement
1 January 1959

Defined terms
"public records" s 10(1) and Sch 1;
"records" s 10(1)

Access to public records

5(3)   It shall be the duty of the Keeper of Public Records to arrange that reasonable facilities are available to the public for inspecting and obtaining copies of those public records in the Public Record Office which fall to be disclosed in accordance with the Freedom of Information Act 2000.

(5)   The Lord Chancellor shall as respects all public records in places of deposit appointed by him under this Act outside the Public Record Office require arrangements to be made for their inspection by the public comparable to those made for public records in the Public Record Office.

NOTES

Commencement
1 January 1959

Defined terms
"public records" s 10(1) and Sch 1;
"records" s 10(1)

Office or other place of deposit

6   If as respects any public records in the Public Record Office or any place of deposit appointed under this Act it appears to the Keeper of Public Records that they are duplicated by other public records which have been selected for permanent preservation or that there is some other special reason why they should not be permanently preserved, he may, with the approval of the Lord Chancellor and of the Minister or other person, if any, who appears to the Lord Chancellor to be primarily concerned with public records of the class in question, authorise the destruction of those records or, with that approval, their disposal in any other way.

NOTES

Commencement
1 January 1959

Defined terms
"public records" s 10(1) and Sch 1;
"records" s 10(1)

Records for which Master of the Rolls remains responsible

7(1)   Subject to the provisions of this section, the Master of the Rolls shall continue to be responsible for, and to have custody of, the records of the Chancery of England, including those created after the commencement of this Act, and shall have power to determine where the said records or any of them are for the time being to be deposited.

(2)   Section three and subsection (6) of section four of this Act shall not apply to any of the said records but if and so long as any of them are deposited in the Public Record Office those records shall be in the custody of the Keeper of Public Records and subject to the directions of the Lord Chancellor as in the case of any other records in the Public Record Office.

(3)   Subject to the foregoing provisions of this section, the Master of the Rolls shall not have charge and superintendence over, or custody of, any public records and any

public records which at the commencement of this Act were in the custody of the Master of the Rolls (other than records of the Chancery of England) shall thereafter be in the custody of the Keeper of Public Records or such other officer as the Lord Chancellor may from time to time appoint.

NOTES

Commencement
1 January 1959

Defined terms
"public records" s 10(1) and Sch 1;
"records" s 10(1)

Court records

8(1)   The Lord Chancellor shall be responsible for the public records of every court of record or magistrates' court which are not in the Public Record Office or a place of deposit appointed by him under this Act and shall have power to determine in the case of any such records other than records of the Supreme Court, the officer in whose custody they are for the time being to be:

(1A)   Records of the Supreme Court for which the Lord Chancellor is responsible under subsection (1) shall be in the custody of the chief executive of that court.

(4)   Where any private documents have remained in the custody of a court in England or Wales for more than fifty years without being claimed, the Keeper of Public Records may, with the approval of the Master of the Rolls, require the documents to be transferred to the Public Record Office and thereupon the documents shall become public records for the purposes of this Act.

(5)   Section three of this Act shall not apply to such of the records of ecclesiastical courts described in paragraph (n) of sub-paragraph (1) of paragraph 4 of the First Schedule to this Act as are not held in any office of the Senior Courts or in the Public Record Office, but, if the Lord Chancellor after consulting the President of the Family Division so directs as respects any of those records, those records shall be transferred to such place of deposit as may be appointed by the Lord Chancellor and shall thereafter be in the custody of such officer as may be so appointed.

(6)   The public records which at the commencement of this Act are in the custody of the University of Oxford and which are included in the index a copy of which was transmitted to the principal probate registrar under section two of the Oxford University Act 1860 shall not be required to be transferred under the last foregoing subsection but the Lord Chancellor shall make arrangements with the University of Oxford as to the conditions under which those records may be inspected by the public.

NOTES

Commencement
1 January 1959

Defined terms
"public records" s 10(1) and Sch 1;
"records" s 10(1)

Legal validity of public records and authenticated copies

9(1) The legal validity of any record shall not be affected by its removal under the provisions of this Act, or of the Public Record Office Acts 1838 to 1898, or by any provisions in those Acts with respect to its legal custody.

(2) A copy of or extract from a public record in the Public Record Office purporting to be examined and certified as true and authentic by the proper officer and to be sealed or stamped with the seal of the Public Record Office shall be admissible as evidence in any proceedings without any further or other proof thereof if the original record would have been admissible as evidence in those proceedings.

(3) An electronic copy of or extract from a public record in the Public Record Office which--
   (a) purports to have been examined and certified as true and authentic by the proper officer; and
   (b) appears on a website purporting to be one maintained by or on behalf of the Public Record Office, shall, when viewed on that website, be admissible as evidence in any proceedings without further or other proof if the original record would have been admissible as evidence in those proceedings.

(4) In this section any reference to the proper officer is a reference to the Keeper of Public Records or any other officer of the Public Record Office authorised in that behalf by the Keeper of Public Records, and, in the case of copies and extracts made before the commencement of this Act, the deputy keeper of the records or any assistant record keeper appointed under the Public Record Office Act 1838.

NOTES

Commencement
1 January 1959

Defined terms
"public records" s 10(1) and Sch 1;
"records" s 10(1)

Interpretation

10(1) In this Act "public records" has the meaning assigned to it by the First Schedule to this Act and "records" includes not only written records but records conveying information by any other means whatsoever.

(2) Where records created at different dates are for administrative purposes kept together in one file or other assembly all the records in that file or other assembly shall be treated for the purposes of this Act as having been created when the latest of those records was created.

NOTES

Commencement
1 January 1959

Defined terms
"public records" s 10(1) and Sch 1;
"records" s 10(1)

Northern Ireland

12(1)   It shall be lawful for any government department or other body or person having the custody of any public records relating exclusively or mainly to Northern Ireland to transmit those records to the Public Record Office of Northern Ireland.

Short title, repeals and commencement

13(1)   This Act may be cited as the Public Records Act 1958.

(3)   This Act shall come into force on the first day of January, nineteen hundred and fifty-nine.

SCHEDULE 1

DEFINITION OF PUBLIC RECORDS

Section 10

1.   The provisions of this Schedule shall have effect for determining what are public records for the purposes of this Act.

Departmental records

2(1)   Subject to the provisions of this paragraph, administrative and departmental records belonging to Her Majesty, whether in the United Kingdom or elsewhere, in right of Her Majesty's Government in the United Kingdom and, in particular,--

   (a) records of, or held in, any department of Her Majesty's Government in the United Kingdom, or

   (b) records of any office, commission or other body or establishment whatsoever under Her Majesty's Government in the United Kingdom,

shall be public records.

(2)   Sub-paragraph (1) of this paragraph shall not apply--

   (a) to records of any government department or body which is wholly or mainly concerned with Scottish affairs, or which carries on its activities wholly or mainly in Scotland, or

   (b) to registers, or certified copies of entries in registers, being registers or certified copies kept or deposited in the General Register Office under or in pursuance of any enactment, whether past or future, which provides for the registration of births, deaths, marriages, civil partnerships or adoptions, or

   (c) except so far as provided by paragraph 4 of this Schedule, to records of the Duchy of Lancaster, or

   (d) to records of the office of the Public Trustee relating to individual trusts or

   (e) to Welsh public records (as defined in the Government of Wales Act 2006).

3(1)   Without prejudice to the generality of sub-paragraph (1) of the last foregoing paragraph, the administrative and departmental records of bodies and establishments set out in the Table at the end of this paragraph shall be public records, whether or not they are records belonging to Her Majesty.

(2)   The provisions of this paragraph shall not be taken as applying to records in any museum or gallery mentioned in the said Table which form part of its permanent collections (that is to say records which the museum or gallery has acquired otherwise than by transfer from or arrangements with a government department).

TABLE

PART I

BODIES AND ESTABLISHMENTS UNDER GOVERNMENT DEPARTMENTS

Responsible Government Department

Not reproduced

PART II

OTHER ESTABLISHMENTS AND ORGANISATIONS

Anglo-Egyptian Resettlement Board.
Armouries.
Arts and Humanities Research Council.
The Authorised Conveyancing Practitioners Board.
The Big Lottery Fund.
The Board of the Pension Protection Fund.
The Board of Trustees of the National Museums and Galleries on Merseyside.
British Coal Corporation.
British Council.
British Museum (including the Natural History Museum).
British Telecommunications.
Care Council for Wales.
the Care Quality Commission.
Catering Wages Commission.
Central Police Training and Development Authority.
Child Maintenance and Enforcement Commission.
Civil Nuclear Police Authority.
Coal Authority.
Coal Industry Social Welfare Organisation.
Commission for Architecture and the Built Environment.
The Commission for Equality and Human Rights.

Commission for Health Improvement.

Commission for Patient and Public Involvement in Health.

Commission for Rural Communities.

Commission on Industrial Relations.

Commissioner for Parliamentary Investigations.

The Committee on Climate Change.

Competition Commission.

Competition Service.

Consumer Council for Water.

The Conveyancing Ombudsman.

Criminal Cases Review Commission.

Crown Agents for Oversea Governments and Administrations (before and after their reconstitution as a body corporate) except when acting for governments or authorities outside Her Majesty's Dominions.

Crown Agents Holding and Realisation Board.

Council for Healthcare Regulatory Excellence.

A development agency established under section 1 of the Regional Development Agencies Act 1998.

Development Commission.

Director of Fair Access to Higher Education.

Economic and Social Research Council.

Electoral Commission.

Engineering and Physical Sciences Research Council.

The Environment Agency.

Funding Agency for Schools.

Further Education Funding Council for England.

Gangmasters Licensing Authority.

General Social Care Council.

General Teaching Council for England.

General Teaching Council for Wales.

Higher Education Funding Council for England.

Historic Buildings and Monuments Commission for England.

The Homes and Communities Agency.

Human Tissue Authority.

Imperial War Museum.

The Independent Parliamentary Standards Authority.

Information Commissioner.

Infrastructure Planning Commission.

Irish Sailors' and Soldiers' Land Trust.

Learning and Skills Council for England.

The Legal Services Board.

The Legal Services Consultative Panel.

The Legal Services Ombudsman.

Local Better Regulation Office.

Local Government Boundary Commission for England.
London Museum.
The Lord Chancellor's Advisory Committee on Legal Education and Conduct.
The Marine Management Organisation.
Medical Research Council.
National Audit Office.
National Gallery.
National Lottery Commission.
National Maritime Museum.
National Policing Improvement Agency.
National Portrait Gallery.
National Savings Committee.
Natural England.
Natural Environment Research Council.
Nuclear Decommissioning Authority.
Occupational Pensions Regulatory Authority.
Office of Communications.
Office of Fair Trading.
The Office of the Health Professions Adjudicator.
The Office for Legal Complaints.
Office for Tenants and Social Landlords.
Olympic Delivery Authority.
Olympic Lottery Distributor.
The Ombudsman for the Board of the Pension Protection Fund.
Pensions Compensation Board.
Pensions Ombudsman.
The Pensions Regulator.
Police Information Technology Organisation.
Post Office.
Post Office company (within the meaning of Part IV of the Postal Services Act
    2000).
Qualifications and Curriculum Authority.
Qualifications and Curriculum Development Agency.
Rail Passengers' Committees.
Rail Passengers' Council.
Remploy Limited.
Royal Botanic Gardens, Kew.
Royal Greenwich Observatory.
School Curriculum and Assessment Authority.
Science Museum.
Scottish Criminal Cases Review Commission.
Security Industry Authority.
Serious Organised Crime Agency.
The Simpler Trade Procedures Board.

Tate Gallery.

Training and Development Agency for Schools.

Teacher Training Agency.

Technology Strategy Board.

Traffic Director for London.

The trustee corporation established by section 75 of the Pensions Act 2008.

Trustee Savings Banks Inspection Committee.

United Kingdom Atomic Energy Authority.

University Grants Committee.

Valuation Tribunal Service.

Victoria and Albert Museum.

Wallace Collection.

War Works Commission.

Any body established for the purpose of determining the boundaries of constituencies of the Parliament of the United Kingdom, or of local authorities in England.

3A(1)   Her Majesty may by Order in Council amend the Table at the end of paragraph 3 of this Schedule by adding to either Part of the Table an entry relating to any body or establishment--

    (a) which, at the time when the Order is made, is specified in Schedule 2 to the Parliamentary Commissioner Act 1967 (departments, etc subject to investigation), or

    (b) in respect of which an entry could, at that time, be added to Schedule 2 to that Act by an Order in Council under section 4 of that Act (which confers power to amend that Schedule).

(2)   An Order in Council under this paragraph may relate to a specified body or establishment or to bodies or establishments falling within a specified description.

(3)   An Order in Council under this paragraph shall be subject to annulment in pursuance of a resolution of either House of Parliament.

Records of courts and tribunals.

4(1)   Subject to the provisions of this paragraph, records of the following descriptions shall be public records for the purposes of this Act:–

    (za) records of the Supreme Court;

    (a) records of, or held in any department of, the Senior Courts (including any court held under a commission of assize);

    (b) records of county courts and of any other superior or inferior court of record established since the passing of the County Courts Act 1846;

    (d) records of courts of quarter sessions;

    (e) records of magistrates' courts;

    (f) records of coroners' courts;

(fa) records of the Court Martial, the Summary Appeal Court or the Service Civilian Court;

(g) records of courts-martial held whether within or outside the United Kingdom by any of Her Majesty's forces raised in the United Kingdom;

(h) records of naval courts held whether within or outside the United Kingdom under the enactments relating to merchant shipping;

(i) records of any court exercising jurisdiction held by Her Majesty within a country outside Her dominions;

(j) records of any tribunal (by whatever name called)--

    (i) which has jurisdiction connected with any functions of a department of Her Majesty's Government in the United Kingdom; or

    (ii) which has jurisdiction in proceedings to which such a Government department is a party or to hear appeals from decisions of such a Government department;

(k) records of any Rent Tribunal or Local Valuation Court;

(kk) records of any Conveyancing Appeal Tribunal;

(l) records of the Industrial Court, of the Industrial Disputes Tribunal, and of the National Arbitration Tribunal (which was replaced by the Industrial Disputes Tribunal);

(m) records of umpires and deputy-umpires appointed under the National Service Act 1948 or the Reinstatement in Civil Employment Act 1944;

(n) records of ecclesiastical courts when exercising the testamentary and matrimonial jurisdiction removed from them by the Court of Probate Act 1857 and the Matrimonial Causes Act 1857 respectively;

(o) records of such other courts or tribunals (by whatever name called) as the Lord Chancellor may by order contained in a statutory instrument specify.

(1A) Records of, or held in any department of, the Senior Courts within sub-paragraph (1)(a) of this paragraph include the records of the Chancery Court of the county palatine of Lancaster and the Chancery Court of the county palatine of Durham (which were abolished by the Courts Act 1971).

(1B) Records of county courts within sub-paragraph (1)(b) of this paragraph include the records of the following courts (which were abolished by the Courts Act 1971)--

    (a) the Tolzey and Pie Poudre Courts of the City and County of Bristol;

    (b) the Liverpool Court of Passage;

    (c) the Norwich Guildhall Court; and

    (d) the Court of Record for the Hundred of Salford.

(2) This paragraph shall not apply to any court or tribunal whose jurisdiction extends only to Scotland or Northern Ireland.

(3) In this paragraph "records" includes records of any proceedings in the court or tribunal in question and includes rolls, writs, books, decrees, bills, warrants and accounts of, or in the custody of, the court or tribunal in question.

Records of the Chancery of England

5   The records of the Chancery of England, other than any which are Welsh public
records (as defined in the Government of Wales Act 2006), shall be public records for
the purposes of this Act.

Records in Public Record Office

6   Without prejudice to the foregoing provisions of this Schedule, public records for the
purposes of this Act shall include--
     (a) all records within the meaning of the Public Record Office Act 1838, or to
         which that Act was applied, which at the commencement of this Act are in the
         custody of the Master of the Rolls in pursuance of that Act, and
     (b) all records (within the meaning of the said Act or to which that Act was applied)
         which at the commencement of this Act are in the Public Record Office and,
         in pursuance of the said Act, under the charge and superintendence of the
         Master of the Rolls, and
     (c) all records forming part of the same series as any series of documents falling
         under sub-paragraph (a) or sub-paragraph (b) of this paragraph
other than any which are Welsh public records (as defined in the Government of Wales
Act 2006).

Power to add further categories of records and to determine cases of doubt

7(1) Without prejudice to the Lord Chancellor's power of making orders under paragraph
4 of this Schedule, Her Majesty may by Order in Council direct that any description
of records not falling within the foregoing provisions of this Schedule and not being
Welsh public records (as defined in the Government of Wales Act 2006) shall be
treated as public records for the purposes of this Act but no recommendation shall be
made to Her Majesty in Council to make an Order under this sub-paragraph unless
a draft of the Order has been laid before Parliament and approved by resolution of
each House of Parliament.

(2)   A question whether any records or description of records are public records for the
purposes of this Act shall be referred to and determined by the Lord Chancellor and
the Lord Chancellor shall include his decisions on such questions in his annual report
to Parliament and shall from time to time compile and publish lists of the departments,
bodies, establishments, courts and tribunals comprised in paragraphs 2, 3 and 4 of this
Schedule and lists describing more particularly the categories of records which are, or
are not, public records as defined in this Schedule.

Interpretation

8   It is hereby declared that any description of government department, court, tribunal
or other body or establishment in this Schedule by reference to which a class of public
records is framed extends to a government department, court, tribunal or other body

or establishment, as the case may be, which has ceased to exist, whether before or after the passing of this Act.

Freedom of Information and Data Protection (Appropriate Limit and Fees) Regulations 2004 (SI 2004/3244)

Made 7th December 2004
Laid before Parliament 9th December 2004
Coming into force 1st January 2005

The Secretary of State, in exercise of the powers conferred upon him by sections 9(3) and (4), 12(3), (4) and (5), and 13(1) and (2) of the Freedom of Information Act 2000, and by sections 9A(5) and 67(2) of the Data Protection Act 1998, and having consulted the Information Commissioner in accordance with section 67(3) of the Data Protection Act 1998, hereby makes the following Regulations:

Citation and commencement

1   These Regulations may be cited as the Freedom of Information and Data Protection (Appropriate Limit and Fees) Regulations 2004 and come into force on 1st January 2005.

Interpretation

2   In these Regulations–
"the 2000 Act" means the Freedom of Information Act 2000;
"the 1998 Act" means the Data Protection Act 1998; and
"the appropriate limit" is to be construed in accordance with the provision made in regulation 3.

The appropriate limit

3(1)   This regulation has effect to prescribe the appropriate limit referred to in section 9A(3) and (4) of the 1998 Act and the appropriate limit referred to in section 12(1) and (2) of the 2000 Act.

(2)   In the case of a public authority which is listed in Part I of Schedule 1 to the 2000 Act, the appropriate limit is £600.

(3)   In the case of any other public authority, the appropriate limit is £450.

Estimating the cost of complying with a request – general

4(1)   This regulation has effect in any case in which a public authority proposes to estimate whether the cost of complying with a relevant request would exceed the appropriate limit.

(2)   A relevant request is any request to the extent that it is a request–
(a) for unstructured personal data within the meaning of section 9A(1) of the 1998 Act, and to which section 7(1) of that Act would, apart from the appropriate limit, to any extent apply, or

(b) information to which section 1(1) of the 2000 Act would, apart from the appropriate limit, to any extent apply.

(3) In a case in which this regulation has effect, a public authority may, for the purpose of its estimate, take account only of the costs it reasonably expects to incur in relation to the request in–

(a) determining whether it holds the information,

(b) locating the information, or a document which may contain the information,

(c) retrieving the information, or a document which may contain the information, and

(d) extracting the information from a document containing it.

(4) To the extent to which any of the costs which a public authority takes into account are attributable to the time which persons undertaking any of the activities mentioned in paragraph (3) on behalf of the authority are expected to spend on those activities, those costs are to be estimated at a rate of £25 per person per hour.

Estimating the cost of complying with a request – aggregation of related requests

3(1) In circumstances in which this regulation applies, where two or more requests for information to which section 1(1) of the 2000 Act would, apart from the appropriate limit, to any extent apply, are made to a public authority–

(a) by one person, or

(b) by different persons who appear to the public authority to be acting in concert or in pursuance of a campaign,

the estimated cost of complying with any of the requests is to be taken to be the total costs which may be taken into account by the authority, under regulation 4, of complying with all of them.

(2) This regulation applies in circumstances in which–

(a) the two or more requests referred to in paragraph (1) relate, to any extent, to the same or similar information, and

(b) those requests are received by the public authority within any period of sixty consecutive working days.

(3) In this regulation, "working day" means any day other than a Saturday, a Sunday, Christmas Day, Good Friday or a day which is a bank holiday under the Banking and Financial Dealings Act 1971 in any part of the United Kingdom.

Maximum fee for complying with section 1(1) of the 2000 Act

6(1) Any fee to be charged under section 9 of the 2000 Act by a public authority to whom a request for information is made is not to exceed the maximum determined by the public authority in accordance with this regulation.

(2) Subject to paragraph (4), the maximum fee is a sum equivalent to the total costs the public authority reasonably expects to incur in relation to the request in–

    (a) informing the person making the request whether it holds the information, and

    (b) communicating the information to the person making the request.

(3)   Costs which may be taken into account by a public authority for the purposes of this regulation include, but are not limited to, the costs of–

    (a) complying with any obligation under section 11(1) of the 2000 Act as to the means or form of communicating the information,

    (b) reproducing any document containing the information, and

    (c) postage and other forms of transmitting the information.

(4)   But a public authority may not take into account for the purposes of this regulation any costs which are attributable to the time which persons undertaking activities mentioned in paragraph (2) on behalf of the authority are expected to spend on those activities.

Maximum fee for communication of information under section 13 of the 2000 Act

7(1)   Any fee to be charged under section 13 of the 2000 Act by a public authority to whom a request for information is made is not to exceed the maximum determined by a public authority in accordance with this regulation.

(2)   The maximum fee is a sum equivalent to the total of–

    (a) the costs which the public authority may take into account under regulation 4 in relation to that request, and

    (b) the costs it reasonably expects to incur in relation to the request in–

      (i) informing the person making the request whether it holds the information, and

      (ii) communicating the information to the person making the request.

(3)   But a public authority is to disregard, for the purposes of paragraph(2)(a), any costs which it may take into account under regulation 4 solely by virtue of the provision made by regulation 5.

(4)   Costs which may be taken into account by a public authority for the purposes of paragraph (2)(b) include, but are not limited to, the costs of–

    (a) giving effect to any preference expressed by the person making the request as to the means or form of communicating the information,

    (b) reproducing any document containing the information, and

    (c) postage and other forms of transmitting the information.

(5)   For the purposes of this regulation, the provision for the estimation of costs made by regulation 4(4) is to be taken to apply to the costs mentioned in paragraph (2)(b) as it does to the costs mentioned in regulation 4(3).

Freedom of Information (Time for Compliance with Request) Regulations 2004 (SI 2004/3364)

Made 16th December 2004
Coming into force 1st January 2005

Whereas a draft of these Regulations has been approved by resolution of both Houses of Parliament in pursuance of section 82(2) of the Freedom of Information Act 2000;

Now, therefore, the Secretary of State, in exercise of the powers conferred by section 10(4) and (5) of the Freedom of Information Act 2000, hereby makes the following Regulations:

Citation and commencement

1   These Regulations may be cited as the Freedom of Information (Time for Compliance with Request) Regulations 2004 and come into force on 1st January 2005.

Interpretation

2   In these Regulations, "the Act" means the Freedom of Information Act 2000.

Governing body of a maintained school or maintained nursery school and schools maintained by the Secretary of State for Defence

3(1)   This regulation applies–

(a) to a request for information that is received by the governing body of a maintained school or a maintained nursery school; and

(b) to a request for information which is held by the public authority only by virtue of the information being situated in a school which is maintained by the Secretary of State for Defence and which provides primary or secondary education, (or both primary and secondary education).

(2)   Where this regulation applies, subsections (1) and (2) of section 10 of the Act have effect as if any reference to the twentieth working day following the date of receipt were a reference to either–

(a) the twentieth working day following the date of receipt, disregarding any working day which, in relation to the school referred to in paragraph (1), is not a school day, or

(b) the sixtieth working day following the date of receipt, whichever occurs first.

(3)   "School day", for the purposes of this regulation, means any day on which, at the school referred to in paragraph (1) above, there is a session.

Archives

4(1)   This regulation applies where–

(a) a request for information is received by an appropriate records authority or by a person at a place of deposit appointed under section 4(1) of the Public Records Act 1958; and

(b) the request relates wholly or partly to information:

(i)   that may be contained in a transferred public record, and

(ii) that has not been designated as open information for the purposes of section 66 of the Act.

(2)   Where this regulation applies, subsections (1) and (2) of section 10 of the Act have effect as if any reference to the twentieth working day following the date of receipt were a reference to the thirtieth working day following the date of receipt.

Operations of armed forces of the Crown

5(1)   This regulation applies, in relation to a request for information, where–

(a) a public authority cannot comply with section 1(1) of the Act without obtaining information (whether or not recorded) from any individual (whether or not a member of the armed forces of the Crown) who is actively involved in an operation of the armed forces of the Crown, or in the preparations for such an operation, and

(b) for that reason, the public authority would not be able to obtain the information within such time as to enable it to comply with the request within the time referred to in subsections (1) and (2) of section 10 of the Act.

(2)   Where this regulation applies, subsections (1) and (2) of section 10 of the Act have effect as if any reference to the twentieth working day following the date of receipt were a reference to such other day, not being later than the sixtieth working day following the date of receipt, as the Information Commissioner may specify in accordance with paragraph (3).

(3)   Where–

(a) the public authority applies to the Information Commissioner for specification of a day in accordance with this regulation, and

(b) that application is made within twenty working days following the date of receipt of the request,

the Information Commissioner shall specify such day as he considers reasonable in all the circumstances.

Information held outside the United Kingdom

6(1)   This regulation applies to a request for information which–

(a) may

(i)   relate to information not held in the United Kingdom, or

      (ii) require information (including information held by a person who is not a public authority) that is not held in the United Kingdom to be obtained in order to comply with it, and

   (b) for that reason, the public authority would not be able to obtain the information within such time as to enable it to comply with the request within the time referred to in subsections (1) and (2) of section 10 of the Act.

(2)   Where this regulation applies, subsections (1) and (2) of section 10 of the Act have effect as is any reference to the twentieth working day following the date of receipt were a reference to such other day, not being later than the sixtieth working day following the date of receipt, as the Information Commissioner may specify in accordance with paragraph (3).

(3)   Where–

   (a) the public authority applies to the Information Commissioner for specification of a day in accordance with this regulation, and

   (b) that application is made within twenty working days following the date of receipt of the request,

the Information Commissioner shall specify such day as he considers reasonable in all the circumstances.

Freedom of Information
(Excluded Welsh Authorities) Order 2002
(SI 2002/2832)

Made 11th November 2002
Coming into force 30th November 2002

The Lord Chancellor, in exercise of the powers conferred upon him by section 83(2) of the Freedom of Information Act 2000, and after consultation with the National Assembly for Wales in accordance with section 83(3) of that Act, hereby makes the following Order:

1   This Order may be cited as the Freedom of Information (Excluded Welsh Authorities) Order 2002 and shall come into force on 30th November 2002.

2   The public authorities listed in the Schedule to this Order are designated as excluded authorities for the purposes of section 83(1)(a) of the Freedom of Information Act 2000.

SCHEDULE
EXCLUDED AUTHORITIES

Article 2

PART I

LOCAL GOVERNMENT

The magistrates' court committee established under section 27 of the Justices of the Peace Act 1997 for each of the following areas:
Dyfed Powys;
Gwent;
North Wales; and
South Wales.

PART II

OTHER BODIES AND OFFICES: GENERAL

The Advisory Committee on Justices of the Peace for each of the following areas:
Clwyd;
Dyfed-Carmarthen;
Dyfed-Ceredigion;
Dyfed-Pembroke;
Gwent;
Gwynedd;

Mid Glamorgan;
Powys;
South Glamorgan; and
West Glamorgan.
The Parliamentary Boundary Commission for Wales.
Sianel Pedwar Cymru, in respect of information held for purposes other than those of journalism, art or literature.
The Traffic Commissioner for the Welsh Traffic Area, in respect of information held otherwise than as a tribunal.

Data Protection (Conditions under Paragraph 3 of Part II of Schedule 1) Order 2000 (SI 2000/185)

Made 31st January 2000
Laid before Parliament 7th February 2000
Coming into force 1st March 2000

The Secretary of State, in exercise of the powers conferred upon him by section 67(2) of, and paragraph 3(1) of Part II of Schedule 1 to, the Data Protection Act 1998, and after consultation with the Data Protection Commissioner in accordance with section 67(3) of that Act, hereby makes the following Order:

Citation and commencement

1   This Order may be cited as the Data Protection (Conditions under Paragraph 3 of Part II of Schedule 1) Order 2000 and shall come into force on 1st March 2000.

Interpretation

2   In this Order, "Part II" means Part II of Schedule 1 to the Data Protection Act 1998.

General provisions

3(1)   In cases where the primary condition referred to in paragraph 3(2)(a) of Part II is met, the provisions of articles 4 and 5 apply.

(2)   In cases where the primary condition referred to in paragraph 3(2)(b) of that Part is met by virtue of the fact that the recording of the information to be contained in the data by, or the disclosure of the data by, the data controller is not a function conferred on him by or under any enactment or an obligation imposed on him by order of a court, but is necessary for compliance with any legal obligation to which the data controller is subject, other than an obligation imposed by contract, the provisions of article 4 apply.

Notices in writing

4(1)   One of the further conditions prescribed in paragraph (2) must be met if paragraph 2(1)(b) of Part II is to be disapplied in respect of any particular data subject.

(2)   The conditions referred to in paragraph (1) are that–
    (a) no notice in writing has been received at any time by the data controller from an individual, requiring that data controller to provide the information set out in paragraph 2(3) of that Part before the relevant time (as defined in paragraph 2(2) of that Part) or as soon as practicable after that time; or
    (b) where such notice in writing has been received but the data controller does not have sufficient information about the individual in order readily to determine whether he is processing personal data about that individual, the data controller shall send to the individual a written notice stating that he cannot provide the

information set out in paragraph 2(3) of that Part because of his inability to make that determination, and explaining the reasons for that inability.

(3)   The requirement in paragraph (2) that notice should be in writing is satisfied where the text of the notice–

(a) is transmitted by electronic means,

(b) is received in legible form, and

(c) is capable of being used for subsequent reference.

Further condition in cases of disproportionate effort

5(1)   The further condition prescribed in paragraph (2) must be met for paragraph 2(1)(b) of Part II to be disapplied in respect of any data.

(2)   The condition referred to in paragraph (1) is that the data controller shall record the reasons for his view that the primary condition referred to in article 3(1) is met in respect of the data.

Data Protection
(Functions of Designated Authority) Order 2000
(SI 2000/186)

Made 31st January 2000
Laid before Parliament 7th February 2000
Coming into force 1st March 2000

The Secretary of State, in exercise of the powers conferred upon him by sections 54(2) and 67(2) of the Data Protection Act 1998 and after consultation with the Data Protection Commissioner in accordance with section 67(3) of that Act, hereby makes the following Order:

Citation and commencement

1   This Order may be cited as the Data Protection (Functions of Designated Authority) Order 2000 and shall come into force on 1st March 2000.

Interpretation

2(1)   In this Order:"the Act" means the Data Protection Act 1998;"foreign designated authority" means an authority designated for the purposes of Article 13 of the Convention by a party (other than the United Kingdom) which is bound by that Convention;"register" means the register maintained under section 19(1) of the Act;"request", except in article 3, means a request for assistance under Article 14 of the Convention which states–
   (a) the name and address of the person making the request;
   (b) particulars which identify the personal data to which the request relates;
   (c) the rights under Article 8 of the Convention to which the request relates;
   (d) the reasons why the request has been made;
and "requesting person" means a person making such a request.

(2)   In this Order, references to the Commissioner are to the Commissioner as the designated authority in the United Kingdom for the purposes of Article 13 of the Convention.

Co-operation between the Commissioner and foreign designated authorities

3(1)   The Commissioner shall, at the request of a foreign designated authority, furnish to that foreign designated authority such information referred to in Article 13(3)(a) of the Convention, and in particular the data protection legislation in force in the United Kingdom at the time the request is made, as is the subject of the request.

(2)   The Commissioner shall, at the request of a foreign designated authority, take appropriate measures in accordance with Article 13(3)(b) of the Convention, for furnishing to that foreign designated authority information relating to the processing of personal data in the United Kingdom.

(3)   The Commissioner may request a foreign designated authority to furnish to him or, as the case may be, to take appropriate measures for furnishing to him, the information referred to in Article 13(3) of the Convention.

Persons resident outside the United Kingdom

4(1)   This article applies where a person resident outside the United Kingdom makes a request to the Commissioner under Article 14 of the Convention, including a request forwarded to the Commissioner through the Secretary of State or a foreign designated authority, seeking assistance in exercising any of the rights under Article 8 of the Convention.

(2)   If the request–
      (a) seeks assistance in exercising the rights under section 7 of the Act; and
      (b) does not indicate that the data controller has failed, contrary to section 7 of the Act, to comply with the same request on a previous occasion,
the Commissioner shall notify the requesting person of the data controller's address for the receipt of notices from data subjects exercising their rights under that section and of such other information as the Commissioner considers necessary to enable that person to exercise his rights under that section.

(3)   If the request indicates that a data protection principle has been contravened by a data controller the Commissioner shall either–
      (a) notify the requesting person of the rights of data subjects and the remedies available to them under Part II of the Act together with such particulars as are contained in the data controller's entry in the register as are necessary to enable the requesting person to avail himself of those remedies; or
      (b) if the Commissioner considers that notification in accordance with sub-paragraph (a) would not assist the requesting person or would, for any other reason, be inappropriate, treat the request as if it were a request for an assessment which falls to be dealt with under section 42 of the Act.

(4)   The Commissioner shall not be required, in response to any request referred to in paragraphs (2) and (3) above, to supply to the requesting person a duly certified copy in writing of the particulars contained in any entry made in the register other than on payment of such fee as is prescribed for the purposes of section 19(7) of the Act.

Persons resident in the United Kingdom

5(1)   Where a request for assistance in exercising any of the rights referred to in Article 8 of the Convention in a country or territory (other than the United Kingdom) specified in the request is made by a person resident in the United Kingdom and submitted through the Commissioner under Article 14(2) of the Convention, the Commissioner shall, if he is satisfied that the request contains all necessary particulars referred to in Article 14(3) of the Convention, send it to the foreign designated authority in the specified country or territory.

(2)   If the Commissioner decides that he is not required by paragraph (1) above to render assistance to the requesting person he shall, where practicable, notify that person of the reasons for his decision.

Restrictions on use of information

6   Where the Commissioner receives information from a foreign designated authority as a result of either–

(a) a request made by him under article 3(3) above; or

(b) a request received by him under articles 3(2) or 4 above,

the Commissioner shall use that information only for the purposes specified in the request.

Data Protection (Fees under section 19(7)) Regulations 2000 (SI 2000/187)

Made 31st January 2000
Laid before Parliament 7th February 2000
Coming into force 1st March 2000

The Secretary of State, in exercise of the powers conferred upon him by section 19(7) of the Data Protection Act 1998, having regard to the definition of "fees regulations" in section 16(2) of that Act, and after consultation with the Data Protection Commissioner in accordance with section 67(3) of the Act, hereby makes the following Regulations:

1   These Regulations may be cited as the Data Protection (Fees under section 19(7)) Regulations 2000 and shall come into force on 1st March 2000.

2   The fee payable by a member of the public for the supply by the Information Commissioner under section 19(7) of the Data Protection Act 1998 of a duly certified written copy of the particulars contained in any entry made in the register maintained under section 19(1) of that Act shall be £2.

Data Protection (Subject Access) (Fees and Miscellaneous Provisions) Regulations 2000 (SI 2000/191)

Made 31st January 2000
Laid before Parliament 7th February 2000
Coming into force 1st March 2000

The Secretary of State, in exercise of the powers conferred on him by sections 7(2), (7), (8) and (11) (having regard to the definitions of "prescribed", "the prescribed maximum" and "the prescribed period" in section 7(10)), 8(1) and 67(2) of the Data Protection Act 1998 and having consulted the Data Protection Commissioner in accordance with section 67(3) of that Act, hereby makes the following Regulations:

Citation, commencement and interpretation

1(1) These Regulations may be cited as the Data Protection (Subject Access) (Fees and Miscellaneous Provisions) Regulations 2000 and shall come into force on 1st March 2000.

(2) In these Regulations "the Act" means the Data Protection Act 1998.

Extent of subject access requests

2(1) A request for information under any provision of section 7(1)(a), (b) or (c) of the Act is to be treated as extending also to information under all other provisions of section 7(1)(a), (b) and (c).

(2) A request for information under any provision of section 7(1) of the Act is to be treated as extending to information under the provisions of section 7(1)(d) only where the request shows an express intention to that effect.

(3) A request for information under the provisions of section 7(1)(d) of the Act is to be treated as extending also to information under any other provision of section 7(1) only where the request shows an express intention to that effect.

Maximum subject access fee

3 Except as otherwise provided by regulations 4, 5 and 6 below, the maximum fee which may be required by a data controller under section 7(2)(b) of the Act is £10.4 Limited requests for subject access where data controller is credit reference agency

Limited requests for subject access where data controller is credit reference agency

4(1) In any case in which a request under section 7 of the Act has been made to a data controller who is a credit reference agency, and has been limited, or by virtue of section 9(2) of the Act is taken to have been limited, to personal data relevant to an individual's financial standing–

(a) the maximum fee which may be required by a data controller under section 7(2)(b) of the Act is £2, and

(b) the prescribed period for the purposes of section 7(8) of the Act is seven working days.

(2) In this regulation "working day" means any day other than–
(a) Saturday or Sunday,
(b) Christmas Day or Good Friday,
(c) a bank holiday, within the meaning of section 1 of the Banking and Financial Dealings Act 1971, in the part of the United Kingdom in which the data controller's address is situated.

(3) For the purposes of paragraph (2)(c) above–
(a) the address of a registered company is that of its registered office, and
(b) the address of a person (other than a registered company) carrying on a business is that of his principal place of business in the United Kingdom.

Subject access requests in respect of educational records

5(1) This regulation applies to any case in which a request made under section 7 of the Act relates wholly or partly to personal data forming part of an accessible record which is an educational record within the meaning of Schedule 11 to the Act.

(2) Except as provided by paragraph (3) below, a data controller may not require a fee under section 7(2)(b) of the Act in any case to which this regulation applies.

(3) Where, in a case to which this regulation applies, the obligation imposed by section 7(1)(c)(i) of the Act is to be complied with by supplying the data subject with a copy of information in permanent form, the maximum fee which may be required by a data controller under section 7(2)(b) of the Act is that applicable to the case under the Schedule to these Regulations.

(4) In any case to which this regulation applies, and in which the address of the data controller to whom the request is made is situated in England and Wales, the prescribed period for the purposes of section 7(8) of the Act is fifteen school days within the meaning of section 579(1) of the Education Act 1996.

Certain subject access requests in respect of health records

6(1) This regulation applies only to cases in which a request made under section 7 of the Act–
(a) relates wholly or partly to personal data forming part of an accessible record which is a health record within the meaning of section 68(2) of the Act, and
(b) does not relate exclusively to data within paragraphs (a) and (b) of the definition of "data" in section 1(1) of the Act.

(2) Where in a case to which this regulation applies, the obligation imposed by section 7(1)(c)(i) of the Act is to be complied with by supplying the data subject with a copy of

information in permanent form, the maximum fee which may be required by a data controller under section 7(2)(b) of the Act is £50.

(3)   Except in a case to which paragraph (2) above applies, a data controller may not require a fee under section 7(2)(b) of the Act where, in a case to which this regulation applies, the request relates solely to personal data which–

      (a) form part of an accessible record–

          (i)   which is a health record within the meaning of section 68(2) of the Act, and

          (ii) at least some of which was made after the beginning of the period of 40 days immediately preceding the date of the request; and

      (b) do not fall within paragraph (a) or (b) of the definition of "data" in section 1(1) of the Act.

(4)   For the purposes of paragraph (3) above, an individual making a request in any case to which this regulation applies may specify that his request is limited to personal data of the description set out in that paragraph.

SCHEDULE

MAXIMUM SUBJECT ACCESS FEES WHERE A COPY OF INFORMATION CONTAINED IN AN EDUCATIONAL RECORD IS SUPPLIED IN PERMANENT FORM

Regulation 5(3)

1   In any case in which the copy referred to in regulation 5(3) includes material in any form other than a record in writing on paper, the maximum fee applicable for the purposes of regulation 5(3) is £50.

2   In any case in which the copy referred to in regulation 5(3) consists solely of a record in writing on paper, the maximum fee applicable for the purposes of regulation 5(3) is set out in the table below.

TABLE

number of pages of information comprising the copy	maximum fee

fewer than 20	£1
20-29	£2
30-39	£3
40-49	£4
50-59	£5
60-69	£6
70-79	£7
80-89	£8
90-99	£9
100-149	£10
150-199	£15
200-249	£20
250-299	£25
300-349	£30
350-399	£35
400-449	£40
450-499	£45
500 or more	£50

Data Protection (Subject Access Modification) (Health) Order 2000 (SI 2000/413)

Made 17th February 2000

Coming into force 1st March 2000

Whereas a draft of this Order has been laid before and approved by a resolution of each House of Parliament:

Now, therefore, the Secretary of State, in exercise of the powers conferred on him by sections 30(1) and (4) and 67(2) of the Data Protection Act 1998 and after consultation with the Data Protection Commissioner in accordance with section 67(3) of that Act, hereby makes the following Order:

Citation and commencement

1   This Order may be cited as the Data Protection (Subject Access Modification) (Health) Order 2000 and shall come into force on 1st March 2000.

Interpretation

2   In this Order–

"the Act" means the Data Protection Act 1998;

"the appropriate health professional" means–

(a) the health professional who is currently or was most recently responsible for the clinical care of the data subject in connection with the matters to which the information which is the subject of the request relates; or

(b) where there is more than one such health professional, the health professional who is the most suitable to advise on the matters to which the information which is the subject of the request relates; or

(c) where–

(i) there is no health professional available falling within paragraph (a) or (b), or

(ii) the data controller is the Secretary of State and data to which this Order applies are processed in connection with the exercise of the functions conferred on him by or under the Child Support Act 1991 and the Child Support Act 1995 or his functions in relation to social security or war pensions,

a health professional who has the necessary experience and qualifications to advise on the matters to which the information which is the subject of the request relates;

"care" includes examination, investigation, diagnosis and treatment;

"request" means a request made under section 7;

"section 7" means section 7 of the Act; and

"war pension" has the same meaning as in section 25 of the Social Security Act 1989 (establishment and functions of war pensions committees).

Personal data to which Order applies

3(1)   Subject to paragraph (2), this Order applies to personal data consisting of information as to the physical or mental health or condition of the data subject.

(2)   This Order does not apply to any data which are exempted from section 7 by an order made under section 38(1) of the Act.

Exemption from the subject information provisions

4(1)   Personal data falling within paragraph (2) and to which this Order applies are exempt from the subject information provisions.

(2)   This paragraph applies to personal data processed by a court and consisting of information supplied in a report or other evidence given to the court by a local authority, Health and Social Services Board, Health and Social Services Trust, probation officer or other person in the course of any proceedings to which the Family Proceedings Courts (Children Act 1989) Rules 1991, the Magistrates' Courts (Children and Young Persons) Rules 1992, the Magistrates' Courts (Criminal Justice (Children)) Rules (Northern Ireland) 1999, the Act of Sederunt (Child Care and Maintenance Rules) 1997 or the Children's Hearings (Scotland) Rules 1996 apply where, in accordance with a provision of any of those Rules, the information may be withheld by the court in whole or in part from the data subject.

Exemptions from section 7

5(1)   Personal data to which this Order applies are exempt from section 7 in any case to the extent to which the application of that section would be likely to cause serious harm to the physical or mental health or condition of the data subject or any other person.

(2)   Subject to article 7(1), a data controller who is not a health professional shall not withhold information constituting data to which this Order applies on the ground that the exemption in paragraph (1) applies with respect to the information unless the data controller has first consulted the person who appears to the data controller to be the appropriate health professional on the question whether or not the exemption in paragraph (1) applies with respect to the information.

(3)   Where any person falling within paragraph (4) is enabled by or under any enactment or rule of law to make a request on behalf of a data subject and has made such a request, personal data to which this Order applies are exempt from section 7 in any case to the extent to which the application of that section would disclose information–

    (a) provided by the data subject in the expectation that it would not be disclosed to the person making the request;

    (b) obtained as a result of any examination or investigation to which the data subject consented in the expectation that the information would not be so disclosed; or

    (c) which the data subject has expressly indicated should not be so disclosed, provided that sub-paragraphs (a) and (b) shall not prevent disclosure where the data subject has expressly indicated that he no longer has the expectation referred to therein.

(4) A person falls within this paragraph if–
  (a) except in relation to Scotland, the data subject is a child, and that person has parental responsibility for that data subject;
  (b) in relation to Scotland, the data subject is a person under the age of sixteen, and that person has parental responsibilities for that data subject; or
  (c) the data subject is incapable of managing his own affairs and that person has been appointed by a court to manage those affairs.

Modification of section 7 relating to data controllers who are not health professionals

6(1) Subject to paragraph (2) and article 7(3), section 7 of the Act is modified so that a data controller who is not a health professional shall not communicate information constituting data to which this Order applies in response to a request unless the data controller has first consulted the person who appears to the data controller to be the appropriate health professional on the question whether or not the exemption in article 5(1) applies with respect to the information.

(2) Paragraph (1) shall not apply to the extent that the request relates to information which the data controller is satisfied has previously been seen by the data subject or is already within the knowledge of the data subject.

Additional provision relating to data controllers who are not health professionals

7(1) Subject to paragraph (2), article 5(2) shall not apply in relation to any request where the data controller has consulted the appropriate health professional prior to receiving the request and obtained in writing from that appropriate health professional an opinion that the exemption in article 5(1) applies with respect to all of the information which is the subject of the request.

(2) Paragraph (1) does not apply where the opinion either–
  (a) was obtained before the period beginning six months before the relevant day (as defined by section 7(10) of the Act) and ending on that relevant day, or
  (b) was obtained within that period and it is reasonable in all the circumstances to re-consult the appropriate health professional.

(3) Article 6(1) shall not apply in relation to any request where the data controller has consulted the appropriate health professional prior to receiving the request and obtained in writing from that appropriate health professional an opinion that the exemption in article 5(1) does not apply with respect to all of the information which is the subject of the request.

Further modifications of section 7

7   In relation to data to which this Order applies—

    (a) section 7(4) of the Act shall have effect as if there were inserted after paragraph (b) of that subsection "or, (c) the information is contained in a health record and the other individual is a health professional who has compiled or contributed to the health record or has been involved in the care of the data subject in his capacity as a health professional";

    (b) section 7(9) shall have effect as if—

        (i) there was substituted—

            "(9)   If a court is satisfied on the application of—

                (a) any person who has made a request under the foregoing provisions of this section, or

                (b) any other person to whom serious harm to his physical or mental health or condition would be likely to be caused by compliance with any such request in contravention of those provisions,

            that the data controller in question is about to comply with or has failed to comply with the request in contravention of those provisions, the court may order him not to comply or, as the case may be, to comply with the request."; and

        (ii) the reference therein to a contravention of the foregoing provisions of that section included a reference to a contravention of the provisions contained in this Order.

Data Protection (Subject Access Modification) (Education) Order 2000 (SI 2000/414)

Made 17th February 2000

Coming into force 1st March 2000

Whereas a draft of this Order has been laid before and approved by a resolution of each House of Parliament:

Now, therefore, the Secretary of State, in exercise of powers conferred upon him by sections 30(2) and (4) and 67(2) of the Data Protection Act 1998, and after consultation with the Data Protection Commissioner in accordance with section 67(3) of the Act, hereby makes the following Order:

Citation and commencement

1   This Order may be cited as the Data Protection (Subject Access Modification) (Education) Order 2000 and shall come into force on 1st March 2000.

Interpretation

2   In this Order–

"the Act" means the Data Protection Act 1998;

"education authority" in article 6 has the same meaning as in paragraph 6 of Schedule 11 to the Act;

"Principal Reporter" means the Principal Reporter appointed under section 127 of the Local Government etc (Scotland) Act 1994 or any officer of the Scottish Children's Reporter Administration to whom there is delegated under section 131(1) of that Act any function of the Principal Reporter;

"request" means a request made under section 7; and

"section 7" means section 7 of the Act.

Personal data to which the Order applies

3(1)   Subject to paragraph (2), this Order applies to personal data consisting of information constituting an educational record as defined in paragraph 1 of Schedule 11 to the Act.

(2)   This Order does not apply–

(a) to any data consisting of information as to the physical or mental health or condition of the data subject to which the Data Protection (Subject Access Modification) (Health) Order 2000 applies; or

(b) to any data which are exempted from section 7 by an order made under section 38(1) of the Act.

Exemption from the subject information provisions

4(1)   Personal data falling within paragraph (2) and to which this Order applies are exempt from the subject information provisions.

(2)   This paragraph applies to personal data processed by a court and consisting of information supplied in a report or other evidence given to the court in the course of proceedings to which the Magistrates' Courts (Children and Young Persons) Rules 1992, the Magistrates' Courts (Criminal Justice (Children)) Rules (Northern Ireland) 1999, the Act of Sederunt (Child Care and Maintenance Rules) 1997 or the Children's Hearings (Scotland) Rules 1996 apply where, in accordance with a provision of any of those Rules, the information may be withheld by the court in whole or in part from the data subject.

Exemptions from section 7

5(1)   Personal data to which this Order applies are exempt from section 7 in any case to the extent to which the application of that section would be likely to cause serious harm to the physical or mental health or condition of the data subject or any other person.

(2)   In circumstances where the exemption in paragraph (1) does not apply, where any person falling within paragraph (3) is enabled by or under any enactment or rule of law to make a request on behalf of a data subject and has made such a request, personal data consisting of information as to whether the data subject is or has been the subject of or may be at risk of child abuse are exempt from section 7 in any case to the extent to which the application of that section would not be in the best interests of that data subject.

(3)   A person falls within this paragraph if–
    (a) the data subject is a child, and that person has parental responsibility for that data subject; or
    (b) the data subject is incapable of managing his own affairs and that person has been appointed by a court to manage those affairs.

(4)   For the purposes of paragraph (2), "child abuse" includes physical injury (other than accidental injury) to, and physical and emotional neglect, ill-treatment and sexual abuse of, a child.

(5)   Paragraph (2) shall not apply in Scotland.

Modification of section 7 relating to Principal Reporter

6   Where in Scotland a data controller who is an education authority receives a request relating to information constituting data to which this Order applies and which the education authority believes to have originated from or to have been supplied by or on behalf of the Principal Reporter acting in pursuance of his statutory duties, other than information which the data subject is entitled to receive from the Principal Reporter, section 7 shall be modified so that–
(a)   the data controller shall, within fourteen days of the relevant day (as defined by section 7(10) of the Act), inform the Principal Reporter that a request has been made; and
    (b) the data controller shall not communicate information to the data subject pursuant to that section unless the Principal Reporter has informed that data

controller that, in his opinion, the exemption specified in article 5(1) does not apply with respect to the information.

Further modifications of section 7

7(1) In relation to data to which this Order applies–

(a) section 7(4) of the Act shall have effect as if there were inserted after paragraph (b) of that subsection "or (c) the other individual is a relevant person";

(b) section 7(9) shall have effect as if–

(i) there was substituted–

"(9) If a court is satisfied on the application of–

(a) any person who has made a request under the foregoing provisions of this section, or

(b) any person to whom serious harm to his physical or mental health or condition would be likely to be caused by compliance with any such request in contravention of those provisions,

that the data controller in question is about to comply with or has failed to comply with the request in contravention of those provisions, the court may order him not to comply or, as the case may be, to comply with the request."; and

(ii) the reference to a contravention of the foregoing provisions of that section included a reference to a contravention of the provisions contained in this Order.

(2) After section 7(ii) of the Act insert–

"(12) A person is a relevant person for the purposes of subsection (4)(c) if he–

(a) is a person referred to in paragraph 4(a) or (b) or paragraph 8(a) or (b) of Schedule 11;

(b) is employed by an education authority (within the meaning of paragraph 6 of Schedule 11) in pursuance of its functions relating to education and the information relates to him, or he supplied the information in his capacity as such an employee; or

(c) is the person making the request."

Data Protection (Subject Access Modification) (Social Work) Order 2000 (SI 2000/415)

Made 17th February 2000
Coming into force 1st March 2000

Whereas a draft of this Order has been laid before and approved by a resolution of each House of Parliament:

Whereas the Secretary of State considers that the application of the subject information provisions (or those provisions without modification) in the circumstances and to the extent specified in this Order would be likely to prejudice the carrying out of social work:

Now, therefore, the Secretary of State, in exercise of the powers conferred on him by sections 30(3) and (4) and 67(2) of the Data Protection Act 1998, and after consultation with the Data Protection Commissioner in accordance with section 67(3) of that Act, hereby makes the following Order:

Citation and commencement

1   This Order may be cited as the Data Protection (Subject Access Modification) (Social Work) Order 2000 and shall come into force on 1st March 2000.

Interpretation

(1)   In this Order–
"the Act" means the Data Protection Act 1998;
"compulsory school age" in paragraph 1(f) of the Schedule has the same meaning as in section 8 of the Education Act 1996, and in paragraph 1(g) of the Schedule has the same meaning as in Article 46 of the Education and Libraries (Northern Ireland) Order 1986;
"Health and Social Services Board" means a Health and Social Services Board established under Article 16 of the Health and Personal Social Services (Northern Ireland) Order 1972;
"Health and Social Services Trust" means a Health and Social Services Trust established under the Health and Personal Social Services (Northern Ireland) Order 1991;
"Principal Reporter" means the Principal Reporter appointed under section 127 of the Local Government etc (Scotland) Act 1994 or any officer of the Scottish Children's Reporter Administration to whom there is delegated under section 131(1) of that Act any function of the Principal Reporter;
"request" means a request made under section 7;
"school age" in paragraph 1(h) of the Schedule has the same meaning as in section 31 of the Education (Scotland) Act 1980;

"section 7" means section 7 of the Act; and

"social work authority" in article 6 means a local authority for the purposes of the Social Work (Scotland) Act 1968.

(2)   Any reference in this Order to a local authority in relation to data processed or formerly processed by it includes a reference to the Council of the Isles of Scilly in relation to data processed or formerly processed by the Council in connection with any functions mentioned in paragraph 1(a)(ii) of the Schedule which are or have been conferred upon the Council by or under any enactment.

Personal data to which Order applies

3(1)   Subject to paragraph (2), this Order applies to personal data falling within any of the descriptions set out in paragraphs 1 and 2 of the Schedule.

(2)   This Order does not apply–

(a) to any data consisting of information as to the physical or mental health or condition of the data subject to which the Data Protection (Subject Access Modification) (Health) Order 2000 or the Data Protection (Subject Access Modification) (Education) Order 2000 applies; or

(b) to any data which are exempted from section 7 by an order made under section 38(1) of the Act.

Exemption from subject information provisions

4   Personal data to which this Order applies by virtue of paragraph 2 of the Schedule are exempt from the subject information provisions.

Exemption from section 7

5(1)   Personal data to which this Order applies by virtue of paragraph 1 of the Schedule are exempt from the obligations in section 7(1)(b) to (d) of the Act in any case to the extent to which the application of those provisions would be likely to prejudice the carrying out of social work by reason of the fact that serious harm to the physical or mental health or condition of the data subject or any other person would be likely to be caused.

(2)   In paragraph (1) the "carrying out of social work" shall be construed as including–

(a) the exercise of any functions mentioned in paragraph 1(a)(i), (d), (f) to (j), (m), (o), (r), (s) or (t) of the Schedule;

(b) the provision of any service mentioned in paragraph 1(b), (c) or (k) of the Schedule; and

(c) the exercise of the functions of any body mentioned in paragraph 1(e) of the Schedule or any person mentioned in paragraph 1(p) or (q) of the Schedule.

(3)   Where any person falling within paragraph (4) is enabled by or under any enactment or rule of law to make a request on behalf of a data subject and has made such a

request, personal data to which this Order applies are exempt from section 7 in any case to the extent to which the application of that section would disclose information–

(a) provided by the data subject in the expectation that it would not be disclosed to the person making the request;

(b) obtained as a result of any examination or investigation to which the data subject consented in the expectation that the information would not be so disclosed; or

(c) which the data subject has expressly indicated should not be so disclosed,

provided that sub-paragraphs (a) and (b) shall not prevent disclosure where the data subject has expressly indicated that he no longer has the expectation referred to therein.

(4) A person falls within this paragraph if–

(a) except in relation to Scotland, the data subject is a child, and that person has parental responsibility for that data subject;

(b) in relation to Scotland, the data subject is a person under the age of sixteen, and that person has parental responsibilities for that data subject; or

(c) the data subject is incapable of managing his own affairs and that person has been appointed by a court to manage those affairs.

Modification of section 7 relating to Principal Reporter

6 Where in Scotland a data controller who is a social work authority receives a request relating to information constituting data to which this Order applies and which originated from or was supplied by the Principal Reporter acting in pursuance of his statutory duties, other than information which the data subject is entitled to receive from the Principal Reporter, section 7 shall be modified so that–

(a) the data controller shall, within fourteen days of the relevant day (within the meaning of section 7(10) of the Act), inform the Principal Reporter that a request has been made; and

(b) the data controller shall not communicate information to the data subject pursuant to that section unless the Principal Reporter has informed that data controller that, in his opinion, the exemption specified in article 5(1) does not apply with respect to the information.

Further modifications of section 7

7(1) In relation to data to which this Order applies by virtue of paragraph 1 of the Schedule–

(a) section 7(4) shall have effect as if there were inserted after paragraph (b) of that subsection "or, (c) the other individual is a relevant person";

(b) section 7(9) shall have effect as if–

(i) there was substituted–

"(9) If a court is satisfied on the application of–

(a) any person who has made a request under the foregoing provisions of this section, or

(b) any person to whom serious harm to his physical or mental health or condition would be likely to be caused by compliance with any such request in contravention of those provisions,that the data controller in question is about to comply with or has failed to comply with the request in contravention of those provisions, the court may order him not to comply or, as the case may be, to comply with the request.";
and

    (ii) the reference to a contravention of the foregoing provisions of that section included a reference to a contravention of the provisions contained in this Order.

(2)   In relation to data to which this Order applies by virtue of paragraph 1 of the Schedule, section 7 shall have effect as if after subsection (11) there were inserted–

"(12)   A person is a relevant person for the purposes of subsection (4)(c) if he–

(a) is a person referred to in paragraph 1(p), (q), (r), (s) or (t) of the Schedule to the Data Protection (Subject Access Modification) (Social Work) Order 2000; or

(b) is or has been employed by any person or body referred to in paragraph 1 of that Schedule in connection with functions which are or have been exercised in relation to the data consisting of the information; or

(c) has provided for reward a service similar to a service provided in the exercise of any functions specified in paragraph 1(a)(i), (b), (c) or (d) of that Schedule,

and the information relates to him or he supplied the information in his official capacity or, as the case may be, in connection with the provision of that service.".

SCHEDULE

Personal Data to which this Order Applies

Article 31

1.   This paragraph applies to personal data falling within any of the following descriptions–

    (a) data processed by a local authority–

        (i) in connection with its social services functions within the meaning of the Local Authority Social Services Act 1970 or any functions exercised by local authorities under the Social Work (Scotland) Act 1968 or referred to in section 5(1B) of that Act, or

        (ii) in the exercise of other functions but obtained or consisting of information obtained in connection with any of those functions;

    (b) data processed by a Health and Social Services Board in connection with the provision of personal social services within the meaning of the Health and Personal Social Services (Northern Ireland) Order 1972 or processed by the Health and Social Services Board in the exercise of other functions but obtained or consisting of information obtained in connection with the provision of those services;

(c) data processed by a Health and Social Services Trust in connection with the provision of personal social services within the meaning of the Health and Personal Social Services (Northern Ireland) Order 1972 on behalf of a Health and Social Services Board by virtue of an authorisation made under Article 3(1) of the Health and Personal Social Services (Northern Ireland) Order 1994 or processed by the Health and Social Services Trust in the exercise of other functions but obtained or consisting of information obtained in connection with the provision of those services;

(d) data processed by a council in the exercise of its functions under Part II of Schedule 9 to the Health and Social Services and Social Security Adjudications Act 1983;

(e) data processed by a probation committee established by section 3 of the Probation Service Act 1993 or the Probation Board for Northern Ireland established by the Probation Board (Northern Ireland) Order 1982;

(f) data processed by a local education authority in the exercise of its functions under section 36 of the Children Act 1989 or Chapter II of Part VI of the Education Act 1996 so far as those functions relate to ensuring that children of compulsory school age receive suitable education whether by attendance at school or otherwise;

(g) data processed by an education and library board in the exercise of its functions under article 55 of the Children (Northern Ireland) Order 1995 or article 45 of, and Schedule 13 to, the Education and Libraries (Northern Ireland) Order 1986 so far as those functions relate to ensuring that children of compulsory school age receive efficient full-time education suitable to their age, ability and aptitude and to any special educational needs they may have, either by regular attendance at school or otherwise;

(h) data processed by an education authority in the exercise of its functions under sections 35 to 42 of the Education (Scotland) Act 1980 so far as those functions relate to ensuring that children of school age receive efficient education suitable to their age, ability and aptitude, whether by attendance at school or otherwise;

(i) data relating to persons detained in a special hospital provided under section 4 of the National Health Service Act 1977 and processed by a special health authority established under section 11 of that Act in the exercise of any functions similar to any social services functions of a local authority;

(j) data relating to persons detained in special accommodation provided under article 110 of the Mental Health (Northern Ireland) Order 1986 and processed by a Health and Social Services Trust in the exercise of any functions similar to any social services functions of a local authority;

(k) data processed by the National Society for the Prevention of Cruelty to Children or by any other voluntary organisation or other body designated under this sub-paragraph by the Secretary of State or the Department of Health, Social Services and Public Safety and appearing to the Secretary of State or the Department, as the case may be, to be processed for the purposes of the provision of any service similar to a service provided in the exercise of any functions specified in sub-paragraphs (a)(i), (b), (c) or (d) above;

(l) data processed by–

(zi) a Strategic Health Authority established under section 8 of the National Health Service Act 1977;

(i) a Health Authority established under section 8 of the National Health Service Act 1977;

(ii) an NHS Trust established under section 5 of the National Health Service and Community Care Act 1990;

(iiza) an NHS foundation trust within the meaning of section 1(1) of the Health and Social Care (Community Health and Standards) Act 2003;

(iia) a Primary Care Trust established under section 16A of the National Health Service Act 1977; or

(iii) a Health Board established under section 2 of the National Health Service (Scotland) Act 1978,which were obtained or consisted of information which was obtained from any authority or body mentioned above or government department and which, whilst processed by that authority or body or government department, fell within any sub-paragraph of this paragraph;

(m) data processed by an NHS Trust as referred to in sub-paragraph (l)(ii) above in the exercise of any functions similar to any social services functions of a local authority;

(mm) data processed by an NHS foundation trust as referred to in sub-paragraph (l)(iiza) above in the exercise of any functions similar to any social services functions of a local authority;

(n) data processed by a government department and obtained or consisting of information obtained from any authority or body mentioned above and which, whilst processed by that authority or body, fell within any of the preceding sub-paragraphs of this paragraph;

(o) data processed for the purposes of the functions of the Secretary of State pursuant to section 82(5) of the Children Act 1989;

(p) data processed by any children's guardian appointed under rule 4.10 of the Family Proceedings Rules 1991 or rule 10 of the Family Proceedings Courts (Children Act 1989) Rules 1991, by any guardian ad litem appointed under Article 60 of the Children (Northern Ireland) Order 1995 or Article 66 of the Adoption (Northern Ireland) Order 1987 or by a safeguarder appointed under section 41 of the Children (Scotland) Act 1995;

(q) data processed by the Principal Reporter;

(r) data processed by any officer of the Children and Family Court Advisory and Support Service for the purpose of his functions under section 7 of the Children Act 1989, rules 4.11 and 4.11B of the Family Proceedings Rules 1991, and rules 11 and 11B of the Family Proceedings Courts (Children Act 1989) Rules 1991;

(s) data processed by any officer of the service appointed as guardian ad litem under rule 9.5(1) of the Family Proceedings Rules 1991;

(t) data processed by the Children and Family Court Advisory and Support Service for the purpose of its functions under section 12(1) and (2) and section 13(1), (2) and (4) of the Criminal Justice and Court Services Act 2000;

(u) data processed for the purposes of the functions of the appropriate Minister pursuant to section 12 of the Adoption and Children Act 2002 (independent review of determinations).

2   This paragraph applies to personal data processed by a court and consisting of information supplied in a report or other evidence given to the court by a local authority, Health and Social Services Board, Health and Social Services Trust, probation officer, officer of the Children and Family Court Advisory and Support Service or other person in the course of any proceedings to which the Family Proceedings Courts (Children Act 1989) Rules 1991, the Magistrates' Courts (Children and Young Persons) Rules 1992, the Magistrates' Courts (Criminal Justice (Children)) Rules (Northern Ireland) 1999, the Act of Sederunt (Child Care and Maintenance Rules) 1997, the Children's Hearings (Scotland) Rules 1996 or the Family Proceedings Rules 1991 apply where, in accordance with a provision of any of those Rules, the information may be withheld by the court in whole or in part from the data subject.

Data Protection (Crown Appointments) Order 2000
(SI 2000/416)

Made 17th February 2000
Coming into force 1st March 2000

Whereas a draft of this Order has been laid before and approved by a resolution of each House of Parliament:

Now, therefore, the Secretary of State, in exercise of the powers conferred upon him by paragraph 4 of Schedule 7 to the Data Protection Act 1998, and after consultation with the Data Protection Commissioner in accordance with section 67(3) of that Act, hereby makes the following Order:

1   This Order may be cited as the Data Protection (Crown Appointments) Order 2000 and shall come into force on 1st March 2000.

2   There shall be exempted from the subject information provisions of the Data Protection Act 1998 (as defined by section 27(2) of that Act) personal data processed for the purposes of assessing any person's suitability for any of the offices listed in the Schedule to this Order.

SCHEDULE

EXEMPTIONS FROM SUBJECT INFORMATION PROVISIONS

Article 2

Offices to which appointments are made by Her Majesty:–
- (a) Archbishops, diocesan and suffragan bishops in the Church of England
- (b) Deans of cathedrals of the Church of England
- (c) Deans and Canons of the two Royal Peculiars
- (d) The First and Second Church Estates Commissioners
- (e) Lord-Lieutenants
- (f) Masters of Trinity College and Churchill College, Cambridge
- (g) The Provost of Eton
- (h) The Poet Laureate
- (i) The Astronomer Royal

Data Protection (Processing of Sensitive Personal Data) Order 2000 (SI 2000/417)

Made 17th February 2000
Coming into force 1st March 2000

Whereas a draft of this Order has been laid before and approved by a resolution of each House of Parliament:

Now, therefore, the Secretary of State, in exercise of the powers conferred on him by section 67(2) of, and paragraph 10 of Schedule 3 to, the Data Protection Act 1998 and after consultation with the Data Protection Commissioner in accordance with section 67(3) of that Act, hereby makes the following Order:

1(1) This Order may be cited as the Data Protection (Processing of Sensitive Personal Data) Order 2000 and shall come into force on 1st March 2000.

(2) In this Order, "the Act" means the Data Protection Act 1998.

2 For the purposes of paragraph 10 of Schedule 3 to the Act, the circumstances specified in any of the paragraphs in the Schedule to this Order are circumstances in which sensitive personal data may be processed.

SCHEDULE

CIRCUMSTANCES IN WHICH SENSITIVE PERSONAL DATA MAY BE PROCESSED

Article 2

1(1) The processing–
    (a) is in the substantial public interest;
    (b) is necessary for the purposes of the prevention or detection of any unlawful act; and
    (c) must necessarily be carried out without the explicit consent of the data subject being sought so as not to prejudice those purposes.

(2) In this paragraph, "act" includes a failure to act.

2 The processing–
    (a) is in the substantial public interest;
    (b) is necessary for the discharge of any function which is designed for protecting members of the public against–
        (i) dishonesty, malpractice, or other seriously improper conduct by, or the unfitness or incompetence of, any person, or

(ii) mismanagement in the administration of, or failures in services provided by, any body or association; and

(c) must necessarily be carried out without the explicit consent of the data subject being sought so as not to prejudice the discharge of that function.

3(1)   The disclosure of personal data–
(a) is in the substantial public interest;
(b) is in connection with–
(i) the commission by any person of any unlawful act (whether alleged or established),
(ii) dishonesty, malpractice, or other seriously improper conduct by, or the unfitness or incompetence of, any person (whether alleged or established), or
(iii) mismanagement in the administration of, or failures in services provided by, any body or association (whether alleged or established);
(c) is for the special purposes as defined in section 3 of the Act; and
(d) is made with a view to the publication of those data by any person and the data controller reasonably believes that such publication would be in the public interest.

(2)   In this paragraph, "act" includes a failure to act.

4   The processing–
(a) is in the substantial public interest;
(b) is necessary for the discharge of any function which is designed for the provision of confidential counselling, advice, support or any other service; and
(c) is carried out without the explicit consent of the data subject because the processing–
(i) is necessary in a case where consent cannot be given by the data subject,
(ii) is necessary in a case where the data controller cannot reasonably be expected to obtain the explicit consent of the data subject, or
(iii) must necessarily be carried out without the explicit consent of the data subject being sought so as not to prejudice the provision of that counselling, advice, support or other service.

5(1)   The processing–
(a) is necessary for the purpose of–
(i) carrying on insurance business, or
(ii) making determinations in connection with eligibility for, and benefits payable under, an occupational pension scheme as defined in section 1 of the Pension Schemes Act 1993;
(b) is of sensitive personal data consisting of information falling within section 2(e) of the Act relating to a data subject who is the parent, grandparent, great grandparent or sibling of–

(i) in the case of paragraph (a)(i), the insured person, or

(ii) in the case of paragraph (a)(ii), the member of the scheme;

(c) is necessary in a case where the data controller cannot reasonably be expected to obtain the explicit consent of that data subject and the data controller is not aware of the data subject withholding his consent; and

(d) does not support measures or decisions with respect to that data subject.

(2) In this paragraph–

(a) insurance business" means business which consists of effecting or carrying out contracts of insurance of the following kind–

(i) life and annuity,

(ii) linked long term,

(iii) permanent health,

(iv) accident, or

(v) sickness; and

(b) "insured" and "member" includes an individual who is seeking to become an insured person or member of the scheme respectively.

(2A) The definition of "insurance business" in sub-paragraph (2) above must be read with–

(a) section 22 of the Financial Services and Markets Act 2000;

(b) any relevant order under that section; and

(c) Schedule 2 to that Act.

6 The processing–

(a) is of sensitive personal data in relation to any particular data subject that are subject to processing which was already under way immediately before the coming into force of this Order;

(b) is necessary for the purpose of–

(i) effecting or carrying out contracts of long-term insurance of the kind mentioned in sub-paragraph (2)(a)(i), (ii) or (iii) of paragraph 5 above;] or

(ii) establishing or administering an occupational pension scheme as defined in section 1 of the Pension Schemes Act 1993; and

(c) either–

(i) is necessary in a case where the data controller cannot reasonably be expected to obtain the explicit consent of the data subject and that data subject has not informed the data controller that he does not so consent, or

(ii) must necessarily be carried out even without the explicit consent of the data subject so as not to prejudice those purposes.

7(1) Subject to the provisions of sub-paragraph (2), the processing–

(a) is of sensitive personal data consisting of information falling within section 2(c) or (e) of the Act;

(b) is necessary for the purpose of identifying or keeping under review the existence or absence of equality of opportunity or treatment between persons–

(i) holding different beliefs as described in section 2(c) of the Act, or

      (ii) of different states of physical or mental health or different physical or mental conditions as described in section 2(e) of the Act,

with a view to enabling such equality to be promoted or maintained;

    (c) does not support measures or decisions with respect to any particular data subject otherwise than with the explicit consent of that data subject; and

    (d) does not cause, nor is likely to cause, substantial damage or substantial distress to the data subject or any other person.

(2)   Where any individual has given notice in writing to any data controller who is processing personal data under the provisions of sub-paragraph (1) requiring that data controller to cease processing personal data in respect of which that individual is the data subject at the end of such period as is reasonable in the circumstances, that data controller must have ceased processing those personal data at the end of that period.

8(1)   Subject to the provisions of sub-paragraph (2), the processing–

    (a) is of sensitive personal data consisting of information falling within section 2(b) of the Act;

    (b) is carried out by any person or organisation included in the register maintained pursuant to section 1 of the Registration of Political Parties Act 1998 in the course of his or its legitimate political activities; and

    (c) does not cause, nor is likely to cause, substantial damage or substantial distress to the data subject or any other person.

(2)   Where any individual has given notice in writing to any data controller who is processing personal data under the provisions of sub-paragraph (1) requiring that data controller to cease processing personal data in respect of which that individual is the data subject at the end of such period as is reasonable in the circumstances, that data controller must have ceased processing those personal data at the end of that period.

9   The processing–

    (a) is in the substantial public interest;

    (b) is necessary for research purposes (which expression shall have the same meaning as in section 33 of the Act);

    (c) does not support measures or decisions with respect to any particular data subject otherwise than with the explicit consent of that data subject; and

    (d) does not cause, nor is likely to cause, substantial damage or substantial distress to the data subject or any other person.

10   The processing is necessary for the exercise of any functions conferred on a constable by any rule of law.

Data Protection (Miscellaneous Subject Access Exemptions) Order 2000 (SI 2000/419)

Made 17th February 2000
Coming into force 1st March 2000

Whereas a draft of this Order has been laid before and approved by a resolution of each House of Parliament:

Whereas the Secretary of State considers it necessary for the safeguarding of the interests of data subjects or the rights and freedoms of other individuals that the prohibitions or restrictions on disclosure contained in the enactments and instruments listed in the Schedule to this Order ought to prevail over section 7 of the Data Protection Act 1998:

Now, therefore, the Secretary of State, in exercise of the powers conferred on him by sections 38(1) and 67(2) of the Data Protection Act 1998, and after consultation with the Data Protection Commissioner in accordance with section 67(3) of that Act, hereby makes the following Order:

1   This Order may be cited as the Data Protection (Miscellaneous Subject Access Exemptions) Order 2000 and shall come into force on 1st March 2000.

2   Personal data consisting of information the disclosure of which is prohibited or restricted by the enactments and instruments listed in the Schedule to this Order are exempt from section 7 of the Data Protection Act 1998.

SCHEDULE

EXEMPTIONS FROM SECTION 7

Article 2

PART 1

ENACTMENTS AND INSTRUMENTS EXTENDING TO THE UNITED KINGDOM

PART II

ENACTMENTS AND INSTRUMENTS EXTENDING TO ENGLAND AND WALES

(a)   *Adoption records and reports*
Sections 57 to 62, 77 and 79 of, and Schedule 2 to, the Adoption and Children Act 2002.
Regulation 14 of the Adoption Agencies Regulations 1983.
Regulation 41 of the Adoption Agencies Regulations 2005.
Regulation 42 of the Adoption Agencies (Wales) Regulations 2005.
Rules 5, 6, 9, 17, 18, 21, 22 and 53 of the Adoption Rules 1984.
Rules 5, 6, 9, 17, 18, 21, 22 and 32 of the Magistrates' Courts (Adoption) Rules 1984.

Rules 24, 29, 30, 65, 72, 73, 77, 78 and 83 of the Family Procedure (Adoption) Rules 2005.

(b)   *Statement of child's special educational needs*
Regulation 19 of the Education (Special Educational Needs) Regulations 1994.

(c)   *Parental order records and reports*
Sections 50 and 51 of the Adoption Act 1976 as modified by paragraphs 4(a) and (b) of Schedule 1 to the
    Parental Orders (Human Fertilisation and Embryology) Regulations 1994 in relation to parental
    orders made under section 30 of the Human Fertilisation and Embryology Act 1990.
Rules 4A.5 and 4A.9 of the Family Proceedings Rules 1991.
Rules 21E and 21I of the Family Proceedings Courts (Children Act 1989) Rules 1991.

PART III

ENACTMENTS AND INSTRUMENTS EXTENDING TO SCOTLAND

(a)   *Adoption records and reports*
Section 45 of the Adoption (Scotland) Act 1978.
Regulation 23 of the Adoption Agencies (Scotland) Regulations 1996.
Rule 67.3 of the Act of Sederunt (Rules of the Court of Session 1994) 1994.
Rules 2.12, 2.14, 2.30 and 2.33 of the Act of Sederunt (Child Care and Maintenance Rules) 1997.
Regulation 8 of the Adoption Allowance (Scotland) Regulations 1996.

(b)   *Information provided by principal reporter for children's hearing*
Rules 5 and 21 of the Children's Hearings (Scotland) Rules 1996.

(c)   *Record of child or young person's special educational needs*
Section 60(4) of the Education (Scotland) Act 1980.
Proviso (bb) to regulation 7(2) of the Education (Record of Needs) (Scotland) Regulations 1982.

(d)   *Parental order records and reports*
Section 45 of the Adoption (Scotland) Act 1978 as modified by paragraph 10 of Schedule 1 to the
    Parental Orders (Human Fertilisation and Embryology) (Scotland) Regulations 1994 in relation to
    parental orders made under section 30 of the Human Fertilisation and Embryology Act 1990.
Rules 2.47 and 2.59 of the Act of Sederunt (Child Care and Maintenance Rules) 1997.
Rules 81.3 and 81.18 of the Act of Sederunt (Rules of the Court of Session 1994) 1994.

PART IV

ENACTMENTS AND INSTRUMENTS EXTENDING TO NORTHERN IRELAND

(a)   *Adoption records and reports*
Articles 50 and 54 of the Adoption (Northern Ireland) Act 1987.
Rule 53 of Order 84 of the Rules of the Court of Judicature (Northern Ireland) 1980.
Rule 22 of the County Court (Adoption) Rules (Northern Ireland) 1980.
Rule 32 of Order 50 of the County Court Rules (Northern Ireland) 1981.

(b)   *Statement of child's special educational needs*

Regulation 17 of the Education (Special Educational Needs) Regulations (Northern Ireland) 1997.

(c)   *Parental order records and reports*

Articles 50 and 54 of the Adoption (Northern Ireland) Order 1987 as modified by paragraph 5(a) and (e) of Schedule 2 to the Parental Orders (Human Fertilisation and Embryology) Regulations 1994 in respect of parental orders made under section 30 of the Human Fertilisation and Embryology Act 1990.

Rules 4, 5 and 16 of Order 84A of the Rules of the Court of Judicature (Northern Ireland) 1980.

Rules 3, 4 and 15 of Order 50A of the County Court Rules (Northern Ireland) 1981.

Data Protection (Processing of Sensitive Personal Data) (Elected Representatives) Order 2002 (SI 2002/2905)

Made 19th November 2002
Coming into force 17th December 2002

Whereas a draft of this Order has been laid before and approved by a resolution of each House of Parliament:

Now, therefore, the Lord Chancellor, in exercise of the powers conferred upon him by section 67(2) of, and paragraph 10 of Schedule 3 to, the Data Protection Act 1998, and after consultation with the Information Commissioner in accordance with section 67(3) of that Act, hereby makes the following Order:

1   This Order may be cited as the Data Protection (Processing of Sensitive Personal Data) (Elected Representatives) Order 2002 and shall come into force on the twenty-eighth day after the day on which it is made.

2   For the purposes of paragraph 10 of Schedule 3 to the Data Protection Act 1998, the circumstances specified in any of paragraphs 3, 4, 5 or 6 in the Schedule to this Order are circumstances in which sensitive personal data may be processed.

SCHEDULE

CIRCUMSTANCES IN WHICH SENSITIVE PERSONAL DATA MAY BE PROCESSED

Interpretation

1   In this Schedule, "elected representative" means–

(a) a Member of the House of Commons, a Member of the National Assembly for Wales, a Member of the Scottish Parliament or a Member of the Northern Ireland Assembly;

(b) a Member of the European Parliament elected in the United Kingdom;

(c) an elected member of a local authority within the meaning of section 270(1) of the Local Government Act 1972, namely–

(i) in England, a county council, a district council, a London borough council or a parish council,

(ii) in Wales, a county council, a county borough council or a community council;

(d) an elected mayor of a local authority within the meaning of Part II of the Local Government Act 2000;

(e) the Mayor of London or an elected member of the London Assembly;

(f) an elected member of–

(i) the Common Council of the City of London, or

(ii) the Council of the Isles of Scilly;

(g) an elected member of a council constituted under section 2 of the Local Government etc (Scotland) Act 1994; or

(h) an elected member of a district council within the meaning of the Local Government Act (Northern Ireland) 1972.

2   For the purposes of paragraph 1 above–

    (a) a person who is–

        (i) a Member of the House of Commons immediately before Parliament is dissolved,

        (ii) a Member of the Scottish Parliament immediately before that Parliament is dissolved, or

        (iii) a Member of the Northern Ireland Assembly immediately before that Assembly is dissolved,

shall be treated as if he were such a member until the end of the fourth day after the day on which the subsequent general election in relation to that Parliament or Assembly is held;

    (b) a person who is a Member of the National Assembly for Wales and whose term of office comes to an end, in accordance with section 2(5)(b) of the Government of Wales Act 1998, at the end of the day preceding an ordinary election (within the meaning of section 2(4) of that Act), shall be treated as if he were such a member until the end of the fourth day after the day on which that ordinary election is held; and

    (c) a person who is an elected member of the Common Council of the City of London and whose term of office comes to an end at the end of the day preceding the annual Wardmotes shall be treated as if he were such a member until the end of the fourth day after the day on which those Wardmotes are held.

Processing by elected representatives

3   The processing–

    (a) is carried out by an elected representative or a person acting with his authority;

    (b) is in connection with the discharge of his functions as such a representative;

    (c) is carried out pursuant to a request made by the data subject to the elected representative to take action on behalf of the data subject or any other individual; and

    (d) is necessary for the purposes of, or in connection with, the action reasonably taken by the elected representative pursuant to that request.

4   The processing–

    (a) is carried out by an elected representative or a person acting with his authority;

    (b) is in connection with the discharge of his functions as such a representative;

(c) is carried out pursuant to a request made by an individual other than the data subject to the elected representative to take action on behalf of the data subject or any other individual;

(d) is necessary for the purposes of, or in connection with, the action reasonably taken by the elected representative pursuant to that request; and

(e) is carried out without the explicit consent of the data subject because the processing–

    (i) is necessary in a case where explicit consent cannot be given by the data subject,

    (ii) is necessary in a case where the elected representative cannot reasonably be expected to obtain the explicit consent of the data subject,

    (iii) must necessarily be carried out without the explicit consent of the data subject being sought so as not to prejudice the action taken by the elected representative, or

    (iv) is necessary in the interests of another individual in a case where the explicit consent of the data subject has been unreasonably withheld.

Processing limited to disclosures to elected representatives

5   The disclosure–

(a) is made to an elected representative or a person acting with his authority;

(b) is made in response to a communication to the data controller from the elected representative, or a person acting with his authority, acting pursuant to a request made by the data subject;

(c) is of sensitive personal data which are relevant to the subject matter of that communication; and

(d) is necessary for the purpose of responding to that communication.

6   The disclosure–

(a) is made to an elected representative or a person acting with his authority;

(b) is made in response to a communication to the data controller from the elected representative, or a person acting with his authority, acting pursuant to a request made by an individual other than the data subject;

(c) is of sensitive personal data which are relevant to the subject matter of that communication;

(d) is necessary for the purpose of responding to that communication; and

(e) is carried out without the explicit consent of the data subject because the disclosure–

    (i) is necessary in a case where explicit consent cannot be given by the data subject,

    (ii) is necessary in a case where the data controller cannot reasonably be expected to obtain the explicit consent of the data subject,

(iii) must necessarily be carried out without the explicit consent of the data subject being sought so as not to prejudice the action taken by the elected representative, or

(iv) is necessary in the interests of another individual in a case where the explicit consent of the data subject has been unreasonably withheld.

Data Protection (Processing of Sensitive Personal Data) Order 2006
(SI 2006/2068)

Made 25th July 2006
Coming into force in accordance with article 1(1)

The Secretary of State makes the following Order in exercise of the powers conferred by section 67(2) of and paragraph 10 of Schedule 3 to the Data Protection Act 1998;

In accordance with section 67(3), he has consulted the Information Commissioner;

In accordance with section 67(4) of that Act, a draft of this instrument was laid before Parliament and approved by a resolution of each House of Parliament.

Citation, commencement and interpretation

1(1) This Order may be cited as the Data Protection (Processing of Sensitive Personal Data) Order 2006 and shall come into force on the day after the day on which it is made.

(2) In this Order–
"the Act" means the Data Protection Act 1998;
"caution" means a caution given to any person in England and Wales or Northern Ireland in respect of an offence which, at the time when the caution is given, is admitted and includes a reprimand or warning to which section 65 of the Crime and Disorder Act 1998 applies;
"conviction" has the same meaning as in section 56 of the Act;
"payment card" includes a credit card, a charge card and a debit card;
"pseudo-photograph" includes an image, whether made by computer-graphics or otherwise howsoever, which appears to be a photograph.

Condition relevant for purposes of the First Principle: processing of sensitive personal data

2(1) For the purposes of paragraph 10 of Schedule 3 to the Act, the circumstances specified in paragraph (2) are circumstances in which sensitive personal data may be processed.

(2) The processing of information about a criminal conviction or caution for an offence listed in paragraph (3) relating to an indecent photograph or pseudo-photograph of a child is necessary for the purpose of administering an account relating to the payment card used in the commission of the offence or for cancelling that payment card.

(3) The offences listed are those under–
 (a) section 1 of the Protection of Children Act 1978,
 (b) section 160 of the Criminal Justice Act 1988,
 (c) article 15 of the Criminal Justice (Evidence etc) (Northern Ireland) Order 1988,
 (d) article 3 of the Protection of Children (Northern Ireland) Order 1978,

(e) section 52 of the Civic Government (Scotland) Act 1982, or

(f) incitement to commit any of the offences in sub-paragraphs (a)–(e).

Data Protection (Processing of Sensitive Personal Data) Order 2009
(SI 2009/1811)

Made 7th July 2009
Coming into force in accordance with article 1(1)

The Secretary of State, in exercise of the powers conferred by section 67(2) of and paragraph 10 of Schedule 3 to the Data Protection Act 1998, makes the following Order;

In accordance with section 67(3) of the Data Protection Act 1998, the Secretary of State has consulted the Information Commissioner;

In accordance with section 67(4) of the Data Protection Act 1998, a draft of this instrument was laid before Parliament and approved by a resolution of each House of Parliament;

Citation, commencement and interpretation

1(1)　This Order may be cited as the Data Protection (Processing of Sensitive Personal Data) Order 2009 and shall come into force on the day after the day on which it is made.

(2)　In this Order "prison" includes young offender institutions, remand centres and secure training centres and "prisoner" includes a person detained in a young offender institution, remand centre or secure training centre.

Condition relevant for purpose of the First Principle: processing of sensitive personal data

2(1)　For the purposes of paragraph 10 of Schedule 3 to the Data Protection Act 1998, the circumstance specified in paragraph (2) is a circumstance in which sensitive personal data may be processed.

(2)　The processing of information about a prisoner, including information relating to the prisoner's release from prison, for the purpose of informing a Member of Parliament about the prisoner and arrangements for the prisoner's release.

Tribunal Procedure (First-tier Tribunal) (General Regulatory Chamber) Rules 2009 (L 20) (SI 2009/1976)

Made 16th July 2009
Laid before Parliament 21st July 2009
Coming into force 1st September 2009

After consulting in accordance with paragraph 28(1) of Schedule 5 to the Tribunals, Courts and Enforcement Act 2007, the Tribunal Procedure Committee has made the following Rules in exercise of the power conferred by sections 9(3), 22 and 29(3) and (4) of, and Schedule 5 to, that Act.

The Lord Chancellor has allowed the Rules in accordance with paragraph 28(3) of Schedule 5 to the Tribunals, Courts and Enforcement Act 2007.

PART 1

INTRODUCTION

Citation, commencement, application and interpretation

1(1)   These Rules may be cited as the Tribunal Procedure (First-tier Tribunal) (General Regulatory Chamber) Rules 2009 and come into force on 1st September 2009.

(2)   These Rules apply to proceedings before the Tribunal which have been allocated to the General Regulatory Chamber by the First-tier Tribunal and Upper Tribunal (Chambers) Order 2008.

(3)   In these Rules–

"the 2007 Act" means the Tribunals, Courts and Enforcement Act 2007;

"appellant" means a person who–

(a) commences Tribunal proceedings, whether by making an appeal, an application, a claim, a complaint, a reference or otherwise; or

(b) is added or substituted as an appellant under rule 9 (addition, substitution and removal of parties);

"charities case" means an appeal or application in respect of a decision, order or direction of the Charity Commission, or a reference under Schedule 1D of the Charities Act 1993;

"document" means anything in which information is recorded in any form, and an obligation under these Rules or any practice direction or direction to provide or allow access to a document or a copy of a document for any purpose means, unless the Tribunal directs otherwise, an obligation to provide or allow access to such document or copy in a legible form or in a form which can be readily made into a legible form;

"General Regulatory Chamber" means the General Regulatory Chamber of the First-tier Tribunal established by the First-tier Tribunal and Upper Tribunal (Chambers) Order 2008;

"hearing" means an oral hearing and includes a hearing conducted in whole or in part by video link, telephone or other means of instantaneous two-way electronic communication;

"notice of appeal" means a document which starts proceedings;

"party" means–

(a) a person who is an appellant or a respondent;

(b) if the proceedings have been concluded, a person who was an appellant or a respondent when the Tribunal finally disposed of all issues in the proceedings;

"practice direction" means a direction given under section 23 of the 2007 Act;

"respondent" means–

(a) in proceedings appealing against or challenging a decision, direction or order, the person who made the decision, direction or order appealed against or challenged;

(b) a person against whom an appellant otherwise brings proceedings; or

(c) a person added or substituted as a respondent under rule 9 (addition, substitution and removal of parties);

"transport case" means proceedings under the Road Traffic Act 1988, the Road Traffic Offenders Act 1988, the Greater London Authority Act 1999, the Postal Services Act 2000, the Vehicle Drivers (Certificates of Professional Competence) Regulations 2007 and the European Communities (Recognition of Professional Qualifications) Regulations 2007;

"Tribunal" means the First-tier Tribunal.

Overriding objective and parties' obligation to co-operate with the tribunal

2(1) The overriding objective of these Rules is to enable the Tribunal to deal with cases fairly and justly.

(2) Dealing with a case fairly and justly includes–

(a) dealing with the case in ways which are proportionate to the importance of the case, the complexity of the issues, the anticipated costs and the resources of the parties;

(b) avoiding unnecessary formality and seeking flexibility in the proceedings;

(c) ensuring, so far as practicable, that the parties are able to participate fully in the proceedings;

(d) using any special expertise of the Tribunal effectively; and

(e) avoiding delay, so far as compatible with proper consideration of the issues.

(3) The Tribunal must seek to give effect to the overriding objective when it–

(a) exercises any power under these Rules; or

(b) interprets any rule or practice direction.

(4)   Parties must–
     (a) help the Tribunal to further the overriding objective; and
     (b) co-operate with the Tribunal generally.

Alternative dispute resolution and arbitration

3(1)   The Tribunal should seek, where appropriate–
     (a) to bring to the attention of the parties the availability of any appropriate alternative procedure for the resolution of the dispute; and
     (b) if the parties wish, and provided that it is compatible with the overriding objective, to facilitate the use of the procedure.

(2)   Part 1 of the Arbitration Act 1996 does not apply to proceedings before the Tribunal.

PART 2

GENERAL POWERS AND PROVISIONS

Delegation to staff

4(1)   Staff appointed under section 40(1) of the 2007 Act (tribunal staff and services) may, with the approval of the Senior President of Tribunals, carry out functions of a judicial nature permitted or required to be done by the Tribunal.

(2)   The approval referred to at paragraph (1) may apply generally to the carrying out of specified functions by members of staff of a specified description in specified circumstances.

(3)   Within 14 days after the date that the Tribunal sends notice of a decision made by a member of staff pursuant to an approval under paragraph (1) to a party, that party may apply in writing to the Tribunal for that decision to be considered afresh by a judge.

Case management powers

5(1)   Subject to the provisions of the 2007 Act and any other enactment, the Tribunal may regulate its own procedure.

(2)   The Tribunal may give a direction in relation to the conduct or disposal of proceedings at any time, including a direction amending, suspending or setting aside an earlier direction.

(3)   In particular, and without restricting the general powers in paragraphs (1) and (2), the Tribunal may–
     (a) extend or shorten the time for complying with any rule, practice direction or direction, unless such extension or shortening would conflict with a provision of another enactment containing a time limit;

(b) consolidate or hear together two or more sets of proceedings or parts of proceedings raising common issues, or treat a case as a lead case (whether under rule 18 or otherwise);

(c) permit or require a party to amend a document;

(d) permit or require a party or another person to provide documents, information or submissions to the Tribunal or a party;

(e) deal with an issue in the proceedings as a preliminary issue;

(f) hold a hearing to consider any matter, including a case management issue;

(g) decide the form of any hearing;

(h) adjourn or postpone a hearing;

(i) require a party to produce a bundle for a hearing;

(j) stay (or, in Scotland, sist) proceedings;

(k) transfer proceedings to another court or tribunal if that other court or tribunal has jurisdiction in relation to the proceedings and–

(i) because of a change of circumstances since the proceedings were started, the Tribunal no longer has jurisdiction in relation to the proceedings; or

(ii) the Tribunal considers that the other court or tribunal is a more appropriate forum for the determination of the case;

(l) suspend the effect of its own decision pending the determination by the Tribunal or the Upper Tribunal of an application for permission to appeal against, and any appeal or review of, that decision.

Procedure for applying for and giving directions

6(1) The Tribunal may give a direction on the application of one or more of the parties or on its own initiative.

(2) An application for a direction may be made–

(a) by sending or delivering a written application to the Tribunal; or

(b) orally during the course of a hearing.

(3) An application for a direction must include the reason for making that application.

(4) Unless the Tribunal considers that there is good reason not to do so, the Tribunal must send written notice of any direction to every party and to any other person affected by the direction.

(5) If a party or any other person sent notice of the direction under paragraph (4) wishes to challenge a direction which the Tribunal has given, they may do so by applying for another direction which amends, suspends or sets aside the first direction.

Failure to comply with rules, practice directions or tribunal directions

7(1) An irregularity resulting from a failure to comply with any provision of these Rules, a practice direction or a direction does not of itself render void the proceedings or any step taken in the proceedings.

(2) If a party has failed to comply with a requirement in these Rules, a practice direction or a direction, the Tribunal may take such action as the Tribunal considers just, which may include–

    (a) waiving the requirement;

    (b) requiring the failure to be remedied;

    (c) exercising its power under rule 8 (striking out a party's case);

    (d) exercising its power under paragraph (3); or

    (e) barring or restricting a party's participation in the proceedings.

(3) The Tribunal may refer to the Upper Tribunal, and ask the Upper Tribunal to exercise its power under section 25 of the 2007 Act in relation to, any failure by a person to comply with a requirement imposed by the Tribunal–

    (a) to attend at any place for the purpose of giving evidence;

    (b) otherwise to make themselves available to give evidence;

    (c) to swear an oath in connection with the giving of evidence;

    (d) to give evidence as a witness;

    (e) to produce a document; or

    (f) to facilitate the inspection of a document or any other thing (including any premises).

Striking out a party's case

8(1) The proceedings, or the appropriate part of them, will automatically be struck out if the appellant has failed to comply with a direction that stated that failure by the appellant to comply with the direction would lead to the striking out of the proceedings or that part of them.

(2) The Tribunal must strike out the whole or a part of the proceedings if the Tribunal–

    (a) does not have jurisdiction in relation to the proceedings or that part of them; and

    (b) does not exercise its power under rule 5(3)(k)(i) (transfer to another court or tribunal) in relation to the proceedings or that part of them.

(3) The Tribunal may strike out the whole or a part of the proceedings if–

    (a) the appellant has failed to comply with a direction which stated that failure by the appellant to comply with the direction could lead to the striking out of the proceedings or part of them;

    (b) the appellant has failed to co-operate with the Tribunal to such an extent that the Tribunal cannot deal with the proceedings fairly and justly; or

    (c) the Tribunal considers there is no reasonable prospect of the appellant's case, or part of it, succeeding.

(4) The Tribunal may not strike out the whole or a part of the proceedings under paragraph (2) or (3)(b) or (c) without first giving the appellant an opportunity to make representations in relation to the proposed striking out.

(5) If the proceedings, or part of them, have been struck out under paragraph (1) or (3)(a), the appellant may apply for the proceedings, or part of them, to be reinstated.

(6) An application under paragraph (5) must be made in writing and received by the Tribunal within 28 days after the date on which the Tribunal sent notification of the striking out to that party.

(7) This rule applies to a respondent as it applies to an appellant except that–
    (a) a reference to the striking out of the proceedings is to be read as a reference to the barring of the respondent from taking further part in the proceedings; and
    (b) a reference to an application for the reinstatement of proceedings which have been struck out is to be read as a reference to an application for the lifting of the bar on the respondent from taking further part in the proceedings.

(8) If a respondent has been barred from taking further part in proceedings under this rule and that bar has not been lifted, the Tribunal need not consider any response or other submission made by that respondent, and may summarily determine any or all issues against that respondent.

Addition, substitution and removal of parties

9(1) The Tribunal may give a direction adding, substituting or removing a party as an appellant or a respondent.

(2) If the Tribunal gives a direction under paragraph (1) it may give such consequential directions as it considers appropriate.

(3) Any person who is not a party may apply to the Tribunal to be added or substituted as a party.

(4) If a person who is entitled to be a party to proceedings by virtue of another enactment applies to be added as a party, and any conditions applicable to that entitlement have been satisfied, the Tribunal must give a direction adding that person as a respondent or, if appropriate, as an appellant.

Orders for costs

10(1) The Tribunal may make an order in respect of costs (or, in Scotland, expenses) only–
    (a) under section 29(4) of the 2007 Act (wasted costs);
    (b) if the Tribunal considers that a party has acted unreasonably in bringing, defending or conducting the proceedings; or
    (c) where the Charity Commission is the respondent and a decision, direction or order of the Charity Commission is the subject of the proceedings, if the Tribunal considers that the decision, direction or order was unreasonable.

(2) The Tribunal may make an order under paragraph (1) on an application or on its own initiative.

(3) A person making an application for an order under this rule must–

    (a) send or deliver a written application to the Tribunal and to the person against whom it is proposed that the order be made; and

    (b) send or deliver a schedule of the costs or expenses claimed with the application.

(4) An application for an order under paragraph (1) may be made at any time during the proceedings but may not be made later than 14 days after the date on which the Tribunal sends to the person making the application the decision notice recording the decision which finally disposes of all issues in the proceedings.

(5) The Tribunal may not make an order under paragraph (1) against a person ("the paying person") without first–

    (a) giving that person an opportunity to make representations; and

    (b) if the paying person is an individual, considering that person's financial means.

(6) The amount of costs or expenses to be paid under an order under paragraph (1) may be ascertained by–

    (a) summary assessment by the Tribunal;

    (b) agreement of a specified sum by the paying person and the person entitled to receive the costs or expenses ("the receiving person"); or

    (c) assessment of the whole or a specified part of the costs or expenses incurred by the receiving person, if not agreed.

(7) Following an order under paragraph (6)(c) a party may apply–

    (a) in England and Wales, to the county court for a detailed assessment of costs in accordance with the Civil Procedure Rules 1998 on the standard basis or, if specified in the order, on the indemnity basis;

    (b) in Scotland, to the Auditor of the Court of Session for the taxation of the expenses according to the fees payable in the Court of Session; or

    (c) in Northern Ireland, to the county court for the costs to be taxed.

Representatives

11(1) A party may appoint a representative (whether legally qualified or not) to represent that party in the proceedings.

(2) If a party appoints a representative, that party must send or deliver to the Tribunal and to each other party written notice of the representative's name and address.

(3) Anything permitted or required to be done by or provided to a party under these Rules, a practice direction or a direction may be done by or provided to the representative of that party except–

    (a) signing a witness statement; or

    (b) sending or delivering a notice under paragraph (2), if the representative is not an authorised advocate or authorised litigator as defined by section 119(1) of the Courts and Legal Services Act 1990, an advocate or solicitor in Scotland or a barrister or solicitor in Northern Ireland.

(4)   A person who receives due notice of the appointment of a representative–

    (a) must provide to the representative any document which is required to be sent to the represented party, and need not provide that document to the represented party; and

    (b) may assume that the representative is and remains authorised until receiving written notification to the contrary from the representative or the represented party.

(5)   At a hearing a party may be accompanied by another person whose name and address has not been notified under paragraph (2) but who, with the permission of the Tribunal, may act as a representative or otherwise assist in presenting the party's case at the hearing.

(6)   Paragraphs (2) to (4) do not apply to a person who accompanies a party under paragraph (5).

Calculating time

12(1)   An act required by these Rules, a practice direction or a direction to be done on or by a particular day must be done before 5pm on that day.

(2)   If the time specified by these Rules, a practice direction or a direction for doing any act ends on a day other than a working day, the act is done in time if it is done on the next working day.

(3)   In this rule "working day" means any day except a Saturday or Sunday, Christmas Day, Good Friday or a bank holiday under section 1 of the Banking and Financial Dealings Act 1971.

Sending and delivery of documents

13(1)   Any document to be provided to the Tribunal under these Rules, a practice direction or a direction must be–

    (a) sent by prepaid post or by document exchange, or delivered by hand to the address specified for the proceedings;

    (b) sent by fax to the number specified for the proceedings; or

    (c) sent or delivered by such other method as the Tribunal may permit or direct.

(2)   Subject to paragraph (3), if a party provides a fax number, email address or other details for the electronic transmission of documents to them, that party must accept delivery of documents by that method.

(3)   If a party informs the Tribunal and all other parties that a particular form of communication, other than pre-paid post or delivery by hand, should not be used to provide documents to that party, that form of communication must not be so used.

(4)   If the Tribunal or a party sends a document to a party or the Tribunal by email or any other electronic means of communication, the recipient may request that the sender provide a hard copy of the document to the recipient. The recipient must make such a request as soon as reasonably practicable after receiving the document electronically.

(5)   The Tribunal and each party may assume that the address provided by a party or its representative is and remains the address to which documents should be sent or delivered until receiving written notification to the contrary.

Prevention of disclosure or publication of documents and information

14(1)   The Tribunal may make an order prohibiting the disclosure or publication of–
            (a)   specified documents or information relating to the proceedings; or
            (b)   any matter likely to lead members of the public to identify any person whom the Tribunal considers should not be identified.

(2)   The Tribunal may give a direction prohibiting the disclosure of a document or information to a person if–
            (a)   the Tribunal is satisfied that such disclosure would be likely to cause that person or some other person serious harm; and
            (b)   the Tribunal is satisfied, having regard to the interests of justice, that it is proportionate to give such a direction.

(3)   If a party ("the first party") considers that the Tribunal should give a direction under paragraph (2) prohibiting the disclosure of a document or information to another party ("the second party"), the first party must–
            (a)   exclude the relevant document or information from any documents that will be provided to the second party; and
            (b)   provide to the Tribunal the excluded document or information, and the reason for its exclusion, so that the Tribunal may decide whether the document or information should be disclosed to the second party or should be the subject of a direction under paragraph (2).

(4)   If the Tribunal gives a direction under paragraph (2) which prevents disclosure to a party who has appointed a representative, the Tribunal may give a direction that the documents or information be disclosed to that representative if the Tribunal is satisfied that–
            (a)   disclosure to the representative would be in the interests of the party; and
            (b)   the representative will act in accordance with paragraph (5).

(5)   Documents or information disclosed to a representative in accordance with a direction under paragraph (4) must not be disclosed either directly or indirectly to any other person without the Tribunal's consent.

(6)   The Tribunal may give a direction that certain documents or information must or may be disclosed to the Tribunal on the basis that the Tribunal will not disclose such documents or information to other persons, or specified other persons.

(7)   A party making an application for a direction under paragraph (6) may withhold the relevant documents or information from other parties until the Tribunal has granted or refused the application.

(8)   Unless the Tribunal considers that there is good reason not to do so, the Tribunal must send notice that a party has made an application for a direction under paragraph (6) to each other party.

(9)   In a case involving matters relating to national security, the Tribunal must ensure that information is not disclosed contrary to the interests of national security.

(10)   The Tribunal must conduct proceedings and record its decision and reasons appropriately so as not to undermine the effect of an order made under paragraph (1), a direction given under paragraph (2) or (6) or the duty imposed by paragraph (9).

Disclosure, evidence and submissions

15(1)   Without restriction on the general powers in rule 5(1) and (2) (case management powers), the Tribunal may give directions as to–
   (a) the exchange between parties of lists of documents which are relevant to the appeal, or relevant to particular issues, and the inspection of such documents;
   (b) the provision by parties of statements of agreed matters;
   (c) issues on which it requires evidence or submissions;
   (d) the nature of the evidence or submissions it requires;
   (e) whether the parties are permitted or required to provide expert evidence, and if so whether the parties must jointly appoint a single expert to provide such evidence;
   (f) any limit on the number of witnesses whose evidence a party may put forward, whether in relation to a particular issue or generally;
   (g) the manner in which any evidence or submissions are to be provided, which may include a direction for them to be given–
       (i) orally at a hearing; or
       (ii) by written submissions or witness statement; and
   (h) the time at which any evidence or submissions are to be provided.

(2)   The Tribunal may–
   (a) admit evidence whether or not–
       (i) the evidence would be admissible in a civil trial in England and Wales; or
       (ii) the evidence was available to a previous decision maker; or
   (b) exclude evidence that would otherwise be admissible where–

(i) the evidence was not provided within the time allowed by a direction or a practice direction;

(ii) the evidence was otherwise provided in a manner that did not comply with a direction or a practice direction; or

(iii) it would otherwise be unfair to admit the evidence.

(3)   The Tribunal may consent to a witness giving, or require any witness to give, evidence on oath, and may administer an oath for that purpose.

Summoning or citation of witnesses and orders to answer questions or produce documents

16(1)   On the application of a party or on its own initiative, the Tribunal may–

(a) by summons (or, in Scotland, citation) require any person to attend as a witness at a hearing at the time and place specified in the summons or citation; or

(b) order any person to answer any questions or produce any documents in that person's possession or control which relate to any issue in the proceedings.

(2)   A summons or citation under paragraph (1)(a) must–

(a) give the person required to attend 14 days' notice of the hearing or such shorter period as the Tribunal may direct; and

(b) where the person is not a party, make provision for the person's necessary expenses of attendance to be paid, and state who is to pay them.

(3)   No person may be compelled to give any evidence or produce any document that the person could not be compelled to give or produce on a trial of an action in a court of law in the part of the United Kingdom where the proceedings are due to be determined.

(4)   A summons, citation or order under this rule must–

(a) state that the person on whom the requirement is imposed may apply to the Tribunal to vary or set aside the summons, citation or order, if they have not had an opportunity to object to it; and

(b) state the consequences of failure to comply with the summons, citation or order.

Withdrawal

17(1)   Subject to paragraph (2), a party may give notice of the withdrawal of its case, or any part of it–

(a) at any time before a hearing to consider the disposal of the proceedings (or, if the Tribunal disposes of the proceedings without a hearing, before that disposal), by sending or delivering to the Tribunal a written notice of withdrawal; or

(b) orally at a hearing.

(2)   Notice of withdrawal will not take effect unless the Tribunal consents to the withdrawal.

(3)   A party who has withdrawn their case may apply to the Tribunal for the case to be reinstated.

(4)   An application under paragraph (3) must be made in writing and be received by the Tribunal within 28 days after–
      (a) the date on which the Tribunal received the notice under paragraph (1)(a); or
      (b) the date of the hearing at which the case was withdrawn orally under paragraph (1)(b).

(5)   The Tribunal must notify each party in writing of a withdrawal under this rule.

Lead cases
18(1)   This rule applies if–
      (a) two or more cases have been started before the Tribunal;
      (b) in each such case the Tribunal has not made a decision disposing of the proceedings; and
      (c) the cases give rise to common or related issues of fact or law.

(2)   The Tribunal may give a direction–
      (a) specifying one or more cases falling under paragraph (1) as a lead case or lead cases; and
      (b) staying (or, in Scotland, sisting) the other cases falling under paragraph (1) ("the related cases").

(3)   When the Tribunal makes a decision in respect of the common or related issues–
      (a) the Tribunal must send a copy of that decision to each party in each of the related cases; and
      (b) subject to paragraph (4), that decision shall be binding on each of those parties.

(4)   Within 28 days after the date on which the Tribunal sent a copy of the decision to a party under paragraph (3)(a), that party may apply in writing for a direction that the decision does not apply to, and is not binding on the parties to, a particular related case.

(5)   The Tribunal must give directions in respect of cases which are stayed or sisted under paragraph (2)(b), providing for the disposal of or further directions in those cases.

(6)   If the lead case or cases lapse or are withdrawn before the Tribunal makes a decision in respect of the common or related issues, the Tribunal must give directions as to–
      (a) whether another case or other cases are to be specified as a lead case or lead cases; and
      (b) whether any direction affecting the related cases should be set aside or amended.

Transfer of charities cases to the Upper Tribunal

19(1)   This rule applies to charities cases.

(2)   The Tribunal may refer a case or a preliminary issue to the President of the General Regulatory Chamber with a request that the case or issue be considered for transfer to the Upper Tribunal.

(3)   If a case or issue has been referred by the Tribunal under paragraph (2), the President of the General Regulatory Chamber may, with the concurrence of the President of the appropriate Chamber of the Upper Tribunal, direct that the case or issue be transferred to and determined by the Upper Tribunal.

Procedure for applying for a stay of a decision pending an appeal

20(1)   This rule applies where another enactment provides in any terms for the Tribunal to stay or suspend, or to lift a stay or suspension of, a decision which is or may be the subject of an appeal to the Tribunal ("the substantive decision") pending such appeal, including an enactment which provides for–
    (a)   an appeal to the Tribunal against a decision not to stay the effect of the substantive decision pending an appeal; or
    (b)   an application to the Tribunal for an order that the substantive decision shall take effect immediately.

(2)   A person who wishes the Tribunal to decide whether the substantive decision should be stayed or suspended must make a written application to the Tribunal which must include–
    (a)   the name and address of the person making the application;
    (b)   the name and address of any representative of that person;
    (c)   the address to which documents for that person should be sent or delivered;
    (d)   the name and address of any person who will be a respondent to the appeal;
    (e)   details of the substantive decision and any decision as to when that decision is to take effect, and copies of any written record of, or reasons for, those decisions; and
    (f)   the grounds on which the person making the application relies.

(3)   In the case of an appeal against a refusal by the registrar to stay a decision to refuse an application for registration as a driving instructor, an application under paragraph (2) must be sent or delivered to the Tribunal so that it is received within 10 days after the date on which the registrar sent notice of the refusal to the person making the application.

(4)   If the Tribunal grants a stay or suspension following an application under this rule–
    (a)   the Tribunal may give directions as to the conduct of the appeal of the substantive decision; and
    (b)   the Tribunal may, where appropriate, grant the stay or suspension subject to conditions.

(5)   Unless the Tribunal considers that there is good reason not to do so, the Tribunal must send written notice of any decision made under this rule to each party.

PART 3

PROCEEDINGS BEFORE THE TRIBUNAL

CHAPTER 1

BEFORE THE HEARING—CASES OTHER THAN CHARITIES CASES

Application of this Chapter

21   This Chapter applies to cases other than charities cases.

The notice of appeal

22(1)   An appellant must start proceedings before the Tribunal by sending or delivering to the Tribunal a notice of appeal so that it is received–

(a) in an appeal against a refusal or revocation of a licence to give driving instruction, within 14 days of the date on which notice of the decision was sent to the appellant;

(b) otherwise, within 28 days of the date on which notice of the act or decision to which the proceedings relate was sent to the appellant.

(2)   The notice of appeal must include–

(a) the name and address of the appellant;

(b) the name and address of the appellant's representative (if any);

(c) an address where documents for the appellant may be sent or delivered;

(d) the name and address of any respondent;

(e) details of the decision or act, or failure to decide or act, to which the proceedings relate;

(f) the result the appellant is seeking;

(g) the grounds on which the appellant relies; and

(h) any further information or documents required by a practice direction.

(3)   If the proceedings challenge a decision, the appellant must provide with the notice of appeal a copy of any written record of that decision, and any statement of reasons for that decision that the appellant has or can reasonably obtain.

(4)   If the appellant provides the notice of appeal to the Tribunal later than the time required by paragraph (1) or by any extension of time under rule 5(3)(a) (power to extend time)–

(a) the notice of appeal must include a request for an extension of time and the reason why the notice of appeal was not provided in time; and

(b) unless the Tribunal extends time for the notice of appeal under rule 5(3)(a) (power to extend time) the Tribunal must not admit the notice of appeal.

(5)   When the Tribunal receives the notice of appeal it must send a copy of the notice of appeal and any accompanying documents to each respondent.

The response

23(1)   Each respondent must send or deliver to the Tribunal a response to the notice of appeal so that it is received–
  (a) in a transport case, within 14 days after the date on which the respondent received the notice of appeal;
  (b) otherwise, within 28 days after the date on which the respondent received the notice of appeal.

(2)   The response must include–
  (a) the name and address of the respondent;
  (b) the name and address of the respondent's representative (if any);
  (c) an address where documents for the respondent may be sent or delivered;
  (d) any further information or documents required by a practice direction or direction; and
  (e) whether the respondent would be content for the case to be dealt with without a hearing if the Tribunal considers it appropriate.

(3)   The response must include a statement as to whether the respondent opposes the appellant's case and, if so, any grounds for such opposition which are not contained in another document provided with the response.

(4)   If the proceedings challenge a decision, the respondent must provide with the response a copy of any written record of that decision, and any statement of reasons for that decision, that the appellant did not provide with the notice of appeal and the respondent has or can reasonably obtain.

(5)   If the respondent provides the response to the Tribunal later than the time required by paragraph (1) or by any extension of time under rule 5(3)(a) (power to extend time), the response must include a request for an extension of time and the reason why the response was not provided in time.

(6)   In a transport case, the Tribunal must send a copy of the response and any accompanying documents to each other party.

(7)   In any other case, the respondent must send or deliver a copy of the response and any accompanying documents to each other party at the same time as it provides the response to the Tribunal.

Appellant's reply

24(1)   The appellant may make a written submission and provide further documents in reply to a response.

(2)   Any reply and accompanying documents provided under paragraph (1) must be sent or delivered to the Tribunal within 14 days after the date on which the respondent or the Tribunal sent the response to the appellant.

(3)   If the appellant provides the reply to the Tribunal later than the time required by paragraph (2) or by any extension of time under rule 5(3)(a) (power to extend time) the reply must include a request for an extension of time and the reason why the reply was not provided in time.

(4)   In a transport case, the Tribunal must send a copy of any reply and any accompanying documents to each other party.

(5)   In any other case, the appellant must send or deliver a copy of any reply and any accompanying documents to each other party at the same time as it provides the reply to the Tribunal.

CHAPTER 2

BEFORE THE HEARING–CHARITIES CASES

Application of this Chapter

25   This Chapter applies to charities cases.

The notice of appeal

26(1)   An appellant must start proceedings before the Tribunal by sending or delivering to the Tribunal a notice of appeal so that it is received–

    (a) if the appellant was the subject of the decision to which the proceedings relate, within 42 days of the date on which notice of the decision was sent to the appellant; or

    (b) if the appellant was not the subject of the decision to which the proceedings relate, within 42 days of the date on which the decision was published.

(2)   The notice of appeal must include–

    (a) the name and address of the appellant;

    (b) the name and address of the appellant's representative (if any);

    (c) an address where documents for the appellant may be sent or delivered;

    (d) the basis on which the appellant has standing to start proceedings before the Tribunal;

    (e) the name and address of any respondent;

    (f) details of the decision or act, or failure to decide or act, to which the proceedings relate;

    (g) the result the appellant is seeking;

    (h) the grounds on which the appellant relies; and

    (i) any further information or documents required by a practice direction.

(3)   If the proceedings challenge a decision, the appellant must provide with the notice of appeal a copy of any written record of that decision, and any statement of reasons for that decision that the appellant has or can reasonably obtain.

(4)   If the notice of appeal relates to a reference under Schedule 1D of the Charities Act 1993–
      (a) if the appellant is the Charity Commission, it must send evidence of the Attorney General's consent to the reference with the notice of appeal; and
      (b) on receiving the notice of appeal the Tribunal must publish details of the reference and information as to how a person likely to be affected by the reference can apply to be added as a party to the proceedings.

(5)   If the appellant provides the notice of appeal to the Tribunal later than the time required by paragraph (1) or by any extension of time under rule 5(3)(a) (power to extend time)–
      (a) the notice of appeal must include a request for an extension of time and the reason why the notice of appeal was not provided in time; and
      (b) unless the Tribunal extends time for the notice of appeal under rule 5(3)(a) (power to extend time) the Tribunal must not admit the notice of appeal.

(6)   The appellant must send or deliver a copy of the notice of appeal and any accompanying documents to the respondent at the same time as it provides the notice of appeal to the Tribunal.

The response

27(1)   The respondent must send or deliver to the Tribunal a response to the notice of appeal so that it is received within 28 days after the date on which the respondent received the notice of appeal.

(2)   The response must include–
      (a) the name and address of the respondent;
      (b) the name and address of the respondent's representative (if any);
      (c) an address where documents for the respondent may be sent or delivered;
      (d) any further information or documents required by a practice direction or direction; and
      (e) whether the respondent would be content for the case to be dealt with without a hearing if the Tribunal considers it appropriate.

(3)   The response must include a statement as to whether the respondent opposes the appellant's case and, if so, any grounds for such opposition which are not contained in another document provided with the response.

(4)   If the proceedings challenge a decision, the respondent must provide with the response a copy of any written record of that decision, and any statement of reasons for that

decision, that the appellant did not provide with the notice of appeal and the respondent has or can reasonably obtain.

(5)   If the proceedings challenge a decision, the respondent must provide with the response a list of–

      (a) the documents relied upon by the respondent when reaching the decision; and

      (b) any other documents which the respondent considers could adversely affect its case or support the appellant's case.

(6)   If the respondent provides the response to the Tribunal later than the time required by paragraph (1) or by any extension of time under rule 5(3)(a) (power to extend time), the response must include a request for an extension of time and the reason why the response was not provided in time.

(7)   The respondent must send or deliver a copy of the response and any accompanying documents to each other party at the same time as it provides the response to the Tribunal.

Appellant's reply

28(1)   The appellant may send or deliver to the Tribunal a reply to the respondent's response and any additional documents relied upon by the appellant.

(2)   Any reply must be sent or delivered to the Tribunal so that it is received within 28 days after the date on which the respondent sent the response to the appellant.

(3)   If the appellant provides a reply to the Tribunal later than the time required by paragraph (2) or by any extension of time under rule 5(3)(a) (power to extend time) the reply must include a request for an extension of time and the reason why the reply was not provided in time.

(4)   The appellant may provide with the reply a list of documents on which the appellant relies in support of the appeal or application, and which–

      (a) the appellant did not provide with the notice of appeal; and

      (b) the respondent did not include in any list of documents provided under rule 27(5).

(5)   The appellant must send or deliver a copy of any reply and any accompanying documents to each respondent at the same time as it provides the reply to the Tribunal.

Secondary disclosure by the respondent

29(1)   If the appellant provides a reply under rule 28, the respondent must send or deliver to the Tribunal, so that it is received within 14 days after the date on which the respondent received the appellant's reply, a list of any further material which–

    (a) might reasonably be expected to assist that appellant's case as disclosed by that appellant's reply; and.

    (b) was not included in a list of documents provided by the respondent with the response.

(2) If the respondent provides the list to the Tribunal later than the time required by paragraph (1) or by any extension of time under rule 5(3)(a) (power to extend time), the response must include a request for an extension of time and the reason why the response was not provided in time.

(3) The respondent must send or deliver a copy of the list to each other party at the same time as it provides the response to the Tribunal.

Provision of copy documents

30(1) If a party has provided a list of documents under rule 27, 28 or 29, that party must within 7 days of receiving a request from another party–

    (a) provide that other party with a copy of any document specified in the list; or

    (b) make such document available to that party to read or copy.

Involvement of the Attorney General under section 2D of the Charities Act 1993

31(1) If the Tribunal directs that all the necessary papers in proceedings be sent to the Attorney General under section 2D(2) and (3) of the Charities Act 1993, the Attorney General must notify the Tribunal whether the Attorney General intends to intervene in the proceedings within 28 days of receiving the papers.

(2) The Attorney General may at any time notify the Tribunal that the Attorney General intends to intervene in the proceedings on the Attorney General's own initiative.

(3) If the Tribunal requests that the Attorney General argue a question in relation to the proceedings under section 2D(4)(b) of the Charities Act 1993, the Tribunal must provide to the Attorney General–

    (a) a statement of the question;

    (b) an account of the proceedings to date;

    (c) the reasons the Tribunal considers it necessary to have the question fully argued; and

    (d) copies of the documents the Tribunal considers necessary to enable the Attorney General to decide whether it is appropriate to argue the question.

(4) If the Attorney General notifies the Tribunal that the Attorney General intends to intervene in, or to argue a question in relation to, proceedings under section 2D(4) of the Charities Act 1993, the Tribunal must hold a case management hearing.

CHAPTER 3

HEARINGS

Decision with or without a hearing

32(1)   Subject to paragraphs (2) and (3), the Tribunal must hold a hearing before making a decision which disposes of proceedings unless–

    (a) each party has consented to the matter being determined without a hearing; and

    (b) the Tribunal is satisfied that it can properly determine the issues without a hearing.

(2)   This rule does not apply to a decision under Part 4 (correcting, setting aside, reviewing and appealing Tribunal decisions).

(3)   The Tribunal may in any event dispose of proceedings without a hearing under rule 8 (striking out a party's case).

(4)   Notwithstanding any other provision in these Rules, if the Tribunal holds a hearing to consider a preliminary issue, and following the disposal of that preliminary issue no further issue remains to be determined, the Tribunal may dispose of the proceedings without holding any further hearing.

Entitlement to attend and take part in a hearing

33(1)   Subject to rule 35(4) (exclusion of a person from a hearing) each party is entitled to–

    (a) attend any hearing that is held; and

    (b) send written representations to the Tribunal and each other party prior to the hearing.

(2)   The Tribunal may give a direction permitting or requesting any person to–

    (a) attend and take part in a hearing to such extent as the Tribunal considers proper; or

    (b) make written submissions in relation to a particular issue.

Notice of hearings

34(1)   The Tribunal must give each person entitled, permitted or requested to attend a hearing (including any adjourned or postponed hearing) reasonable notice of the time and place of the hearing and any changes to the time and place of the hearing.

(2)   The period of notice under paragraph (1) in relation to a hearing to consider disposal of the proceedings must be at least 14 days, except that the Tribunal may give shorter notice–

    (a) with the parties' consent; or

    (b) in urgent or exceptional circumstances.

Public and private hearings

35(1)   Subject to the following paragraphs, all hearings must be held in public.

(2)   The Tribunal may give a direction that a hearing, or part of it, is to be held in private.

(3)   Where a hearing, or part of it, is to be held in private, the Tribunal may determine who is permitted to attend the hearing or part of it.

(4)   The Tribunal may give a direction excluding from any hearing, or part of it–
   (a) any person whose conduct the Tribunal considers is disrupting or is likely to disrupt the hearing;
   (b) any person whose presence the Tribunal considers is likely to prevent another person from giving evidence or making submissions freely;
   (c) any person who the Tribunal considers should be excluded in order to give effect to the requirement at rule 14(10) (prevention of disclosure or publication of documents and information); or
   (d) any person where the purpose of the hearing would be defeated by the attendance of that person.

(5)   The Tribunal may give a direction excluding a witness from a hearing until that witness gives evidence.

Hearings in a party's absence

36   If a party fails to attend a hearing the Tribunal may proceed with the hearing if the Tribunal–
   (a) is satisfied that the party has been notified of the hearing or that reasonable steps have been taken to notify the party of the hearing; and
   (b) considers that it is in the interests of justice to proceed with the hearing.

CHAPTER 4

DECISIONS

Consent orders

37(1)   The Tribunal may, at the request of the parties but only if it considers it appropriate, make a consent order disposing of the proceedings and making such other appropriate provision as the parties have agreed.

(2)   Notwithstanding any other provision of these Rules, the Tribunal need not hold a hearing before making an order under paragraph (1), or provide reasons for the order.

Decisions

38(1)   The Tribunal may give a decision orally at a hearing.

(2)   Subject to rule 14(10) (prevention of disclosure or publication of documents and information), the Tribunal must provide to each party as soon as reasonably practicable after making a decision which finally disposes of all issues in the proceedings (except a decision under Part 4)–

(a) a decision notice stating the Tribunal's decision;

(b) written reasons for the decision; and

(c) notification of any right of appeal against the decision and the time within which, and manner in which, such right of appeal may be exercised.

(3)   The Tribunal may provide written reasons for any decision to which paragraph (2) does not apply.

PART 4

CORRECTING, SETTING ASIDE, REVIEWING AND APPEALING TRIBUNAL
DECISIONS

Interpretation

39   In this Part–

"appeal" means the exercise of a right of appeal on a point of law under section 11 of the 2007 Act; and

"review" means the review of a decision by the Tribunal under section 9 of the 2007 Act.

Clerical mistakes and accidental slips or omissions

40   The Tribunal may at any time correct any clerical mistake or other accidental slip or omission in a decision, direction or any document produced by it, by–

(a) sending notification of the amended decision or direction, or a copy of the amended document, to each party; and

(b) making any necessary amendment to any information published in relation to the decision, direction or document.

Setting aside a decision which disposes of proceedings

41(1)   The Tribunal may set aside a decision which disposes of proceedings, or part of such a decision, and re-make the decision or the relevant part of it, if–

(a) the Tribunal considers that it is in the interests of justice to do so; and

(b) one or more of the conditions in paragraph (2) are satisfied.

(2)   The conditions are–

(a) a document relating to the proceedings was not sent to, or was not received at an appropriate time by, a party or a party's representative;

(b) a document relating to the proceedings was not sent to the Tribunal at an appropriate time;

(c) a party, or a party's representative, was not present at a hearing related to the proceedings; or

(d) there has been some other procedural irregularity in the proceedings.

(3)   A party applying for a decision, or part of a decision, to be set aside under paragraph (1) must make a written application to the Tribunal so that it is received no later than 28 days after the date on which the Tribunal sent notice of the decision to the party.

Application for permission to appeal

42(1)   A person seeking permission to appeal must make a written application to the Tribunal for permission to appeal.

(2)   An application under paragraph (1) must be sent or delivered to the Tribunal so that it is received no later than 28 days after the latest of the dates that the Tribunal sends to the person making the application–

(a) written reasons for the decision;

(b) notification of amended reasons for, or correction of, the decision following a review; or

(c) notification that an application for the decision to be set aside has been unsuccessful.

(3)   The date in paragraph (2)(c) applies only if the application for the decision to be set aside was made within the time stipulated in rule 41 (setting aside a decision which disposes of proceedings) or any extension of that time granted by the Tribunal.

(4)   If the person seeking permission to appeal sends or delivers the application to the Tribunal later than the time required by paragraph (2) or by any extension of time under rule 5(3)(a) (power to extend time)–

(a) the application must include a request for an extension of time and the reason why the application was not provided in time; and

(b) unless the Tribunal extends time for the application under rule 5(3)(a) (power to extend time) the Tribunal must not admit the application.

(5)   An application under paragraph (1) must–

(a) identify the decision of the Tribunal to which it relates;

(b) identify the alleged error or errors of law in the decision; and

(c) state the result the party making the application is seeking.

Tribunal's consideration of application for permission to appeal

43(1)   On receiving an application for permission to appeal the Tribunal must first consider, taking into account the overriding objective in rule 2, whether to review the decision in accordance with rule 44 (review of a decision).

(2)   If the Tribunal decides not to review the decision, or reviews the decision and decides to take no action in relation to the decision, or part of it, the Tribunal must consider whether to give permission to appeal in relation to the decision or that part of it.

(3)   The Tribunal must send a record of its decision to the parties as soon as practicable.

(4)   If the Tribunal refuses permission to appeal it must send with the record of its decision–

    (a) a statement of its reasons for such refusal; and

    (b) notification of the right to make an application to the Upper Tribunal for permission to appeal and the time within which, and the method by which, such application must be made.

(5)   The Tribunal may give permission to appeal on limited grounds, but must comply with paragraph (4) in relation to any grounds on which it has refused permission.

Review of a decision

44(1)   The Tribunal may only undertake a review of a decision–

    (a) pursuant to rule 43(1) (review on an application for permission to appeal); and

    (b) if it is satisfied that there was an error of law in the decision.

(2)   The Tribunal must notify the parties in writing of the outcome of any review, and of any right of appeal in relation to the outcome.

(3)   If the Tribunal takes any action in relation to a decision following a review without first giving every party an opportunity to make representations, the notice under paragraph (2) must state that any party that did not have an opportunity to make representations may apply for such action to be set aside and for the decision to be reviewed again.

Power to treat an application as a different type of application

45   The Tribunal may treat an application for a decision to be corrected, set aside or reviewed, or for permission to appeal against a decision, as an application for any other one of those things.

Tribunal Procedure (Upper Tribunal) Rules 2008 (SI 2008/2698)

Made 9th October 2008
Laid before Parliament 15th October 2008
Coming into force 3rd November 2008

After consulting in accordance with paragraph 28(1) of Schedule 5 to, the Tribunals, Courts and Enforcement Act 2007 the Tribunal Procedure Committee has made the following Rules in exercise of the power conferred by sections 10(3), 16(9), 22 and 29(3) and (4) of, and Schedule 5 to, that Act.

The Lord Chancellor has allowed the Rules in accordance with paragraph 28(3) of Schedule 5 to the Tribunals, Courts and Enforcement Act 2007.

PART 1

INTRODUCTION

Citation, commencement, application and interpretation

1(1)   These Rules may be cited as the Tribunal Procedure (Upper Tribunal) Rules 2008 and come into force on 3rd November 2008.

(2)   These Rules apply to proceedings before the Upper Tribunal except proceedings in the Lands Chamber.

(3)   In these Rules–
"the 2007 Act" means the Tribunals, Courts and Enforcement Act 2007;
"appellant" means–
    (a) a person who makes an appeal, or applies for permission to appeal, to the Upper Tribunal;
    (b) in proceedings transferred or referred to the Upper Tribunal from the First-tier Tribunal, a person who started the proceedings in the First-tier Tribunal; or
    (c) a person substituted as an appellant under rule 9(1) (substitution and addition of parties);
"applicant" means a person who applies for permission to bring, or does bring, judicial review proceedings before the Upper Tribunal and, in judicial review proceedings transferred to the Upper Tribunal from a court, includes a person who was a claimant or petitioner in the proceedings immediately before they were transferred;
"appropriate national authority" means, in relation to an appeal, the Secretary of State, the Scottish Ministers or the Welsh Ministers, as the case may be;
"authorised person" means an examiner appointed by the Secretary of State under section 66A of the Road Traffic Act 1988, or a person acting under the direction of such an examiner, who has detained the vehicle to which an appeal relates;

"dispose of proceedings" includes, unless indicated otherwise, disposing of a part of the proceedings;

"document" means anything in which information is recorded in any form, and an obligation under these Rules or any practice direction or direction to provide or allow access to a document or a copy of a document for any purpose means, unless the Upper Tribunal directs otherwise, an obligation to provide or allow access to such document or copy in a legible form or in a form which can be readily made into a legible form;

"hearing" means an oral hearing and includes a hearing conducted in whole or in part by video link, telephone or other means of instantaneous two-way electronic communication;

"interested party" means–

(a) a person who is directly affected by the outcome sought in judicial review proceedings, and has been named as an interested party under rule 28 or 29 (judicial review), or has been substituted or added as an interested party under rule 9 (substitution and addition of parties); and

(b) in judicial review proceedings transferred to the Upper Tribunal under section 25A(2) or (3) of the Judicature (Northern Ireland) Act 1978 or section 31A(2) or (3) of the Supreme Court Act 1981, a person who was an interested party in the proceedings immediately before they were transferred to the Upper Tribunal;

"judicial review proceedings" means proceedings within the jurisdiction of the Upper Tribunal pursuant to section 15 or 21 of the 2007 Act, whether such proceedings are started in the Upper Tribunal or transferred to the Upper Tribunal;

"mental health case" means proceedings before the Upper Tribunal on appeal against a decision in proceedings under the Mental Health Act 1983 or paragraph 5(2) of the Schedule to the Repatriation of Prisoners Act 1984;

"party" means a person who is an appellant, an applicant, a respondent or an interested party in proceedings before the Upper Tribunal, a person who has referred a question to the Upper Tribunal or, if the proceedings have been concluded, a person who was an appellant, an applicant, a respondent or an interested party when the Tribunal finally disposed of all issues in the proceedings;

"permission" includes leave in cases arising under the law of Northern Ireland;

"practice direction" means a direction given under section 23 of the 2007 Act;

"respondent" means–

(a) in an appeal, or application for permission to appeal, against a decision of another tribunal, any person other than the appellant who–

(i) was a party before that other tribunal;

(iii) otherwise has a right of appeal against the decision of the other tribunal and has given notice to the Upper Tribunal that they wish to be a party to the appeal;

(b) in an appeal against any other decision except a decision of a traffic commissioner, the person who made the decision;

(c) in judicial review proceedings–
    (i) in proceedings started in the Upper Tribunal, the person named by the applicant as the respondent;
    (ii) in proceedings transferred to the Upper Tribunal under section 25A(2) or (3) of the Judicature (Northern Ireland) Act 1978 or section 31A(2) or (3) of the Supreme Court Act 1981, a person who was a defendant in the proceedings immediately before they were transferred;
    (iii) in proceedings transferred to the Upper Tribunal under section 20(1) of the 2007 Act, a person to whom intimation of the petition was made before the proceedings were transferred, or to whom the Upper Tribunal has required intimation to be made;

(ca) in proceedings transferred or referred to the Upper Tribunal from the First-tier Tribunal, a person who was a respondent in the proceedings in the First-tier Tribunal;

(d) in a reference under the Forfeiture Act 1982, the person whose eligibility for a benefit or advantage is in issue; or

(e) a person substituted or added as a respondent under rule 9 (substitution and addition of parties);

"tribunal" does not include a traffic commissioner;

"working day" means any day except a Saturday or Sunday, Christmas Day, Good Friday or a bank holiday under section 1 of the Banking and Financial Dealings Act 1971.

Overriding objective and parties' obligation to co-operate with the Upper Tribunal

2(1) The overriding objective of these Rules is to enable the Upper Tribunal to deal with cases fairly and justly.

(2) Dealing with a case fairly and justly includes–
    (a) dealing with the case in ways which are proportionate to the importance of the case, the complexity of the issues, the anticipated costs and the resources of the parties;
    (b) avoiding unnecessary formality and seeking flexibility in the proceedings;
    (c) ensuring, so far as practicable, that the parties are able to participate fully in the proceedings;
    (d) using any special expertise of the Upper Tribunal effectively; and
    (e) avoiding delay, so far as compatible with proper consideration of the issues.

(3) The Upper Tribunal must seek to give effect to the overriding objective when it–
    (a) exercises any power under these Rules; or
    (b) interprets any rule or practice direction.

(4) Parties must–
    (a) help the Upper Tribunal to further the overriding objective; and
    (b) co-operate with the Upper Tribunal generally.

Alternative dispute resolution and arbitration

3(1)   The Upper Tribunal should seek, where appropriate–

      (a) to bring to the attention of the parties the availability of any appropriate alternative procedure for the resolution of the dispute; and

      (b) if the parties wish and provided that it is compatible with the overriding objective, to facilitate the use of the procedure.

(2)   Part 1 of the Arbitration Act 1996 does not apply to proceedings before the Upper Tribunal.

PART 2

GENERAL POWERS AND PROVISIONS

Delegation to staff

4(1)   Staff appointed under section 40(1) of the 2007 Act (tribunal staff and services) may, with the approval of the Senior President of Tribunals, carry out functions of a judicial nature permitted or required to be done by the Upper Tribunal.

(2)   The approval referred to at paragraph (1) may apply generally to the carrying out of specified functions by members of staff of a specified description in specified circumstances.

(3)   Within 14 days after the date on which the Upper Tribunal sends notice of a decision made by a member of staff under paragraph (1) to a party, that party may apply in writing to the Upper Tribunal for that decision to be considered afresh by a judge.

Case management powers

5(1)   Subject to the provisions of the 2007 Act and any other enactment, the Upper Tribunal may regulate its own procedure.

(2)   The Upper Tribunal may give a direction in relation to the conduct or disposal of proceedings at any time, including a direction amending, suspending or setting aside an earlier direction.

(3)   In particular, and without restricting the general powers in paragraphs (1) and (2), the Upper Tribunal may–

      (a) extend or shorten the time for complying with any rule, practice direction or direction;

      (b) consolidate or hear together two or more sets of proceedings or parts of proceedings raising common issues, or treat a case as a lead case;

      (c) permit or require a party to amend a document;

      (d) permit or require a party or another person to provide documents, information, evidence or submissions to the Upper Tribunal or a party;

      (e) deal with an issue in the proceedings as a preliminary issue;

      (f) hold a hearing to consider any matter, including a case management issue;

(g) decide the form of any hearing;

(h) adjourn or postpone a hearing;

(i) require a party to produce a bundle for a hearing;

(j) stay (or, in Scotland, sist) proceedings;

(k) transfer proceedings to another court or tribunal if that other court or tribunal has jurisdiction in relation to the proceedings and–

    (i) because of a change of circumstances since the proceedings were started, the Upper Tribunal no longer has jurisdiction in relation to the proceedings; or

    (ii) the Upper Tribunal considers that the other court or tribunal is a more appropriate forum for the determination of the case;

(l) suspend the effect of its own decision pending an appeal or review of that decision;

(m) in an appeal, or an application for permission to appeal, against the decision of another tribunal, suspend the effect of that decision pending the determination of the application for permission to appeal, and any appeal;

(n) require any person, body or other tribunal whose decision is the subject of proceedings before the Upper Tribunal to provide reasons for the decision, or other information or documents in relation to the decision or any proceedings before that person, body or tribunal.

Procedure for applying for and giving directions

6(1) The Upper Tribunal may give a direction on the application of one or more of the parties or on its own initiative.

(2) An application for a direction may be made–

    (a) by sending or delivering a written application to the Upper Tribunal; or

    (b) orally during the course of a hearing.

(3) An application for a direction must include the reason for making that application.

(4) Unless the Upper Tribunal considers that there is good reason not to do so, the Upper Tribunal must send written notice of any direction to every party and to any other person affected by the direction.

(5) If a party or any other person sent notice of the direction under paragraph (4) wishes to challenge a direction which the Upper Tribunal has given, they may do so by applying for another direction which amends, suspends or sets aside the first direction.

Failure to comply with rules etc

7(1) An irregularity resulting from a failure to comply with any requirement in these Rules, a practice direction or a direction, does not of itself render void the proceedings or any step taken in the proceedings.

(2)   If a party has failed to comply with a requirement in these Rules, a practice direction
       or a direction, the Upper Tribunal may take such action as it considers just, which may
       include–
       (a) waiving the requirement;
       (b) requiring the failure to be remedied;
       (c) exercising its power under rule 8 (striking out a party's case); or
       (d) except in mental health cases, restricting a party's participation in the
            proceedings.

(3)   Paragraph (4) applies where the First-tier Tribunal has referred to the Upper Tribunal
       a failure by a person to comply with a requirement imposed by the First-tier Tribunal–
       (a) to attend at any place for the purpose of giving evidence;
       (b) otherwise to make themselves available to give evidence;
       (c) to swear an oath in connection with the giving of evidence;
       (d) to give evidence as a witness;
       (e) to produce a document; or
       (f) to facilitate the inspection of a document or any other thing (including any
            premises).

(4)   The Upper Tribunal may exercise its power under section 25 of the 2007 Act
       (supplementary powers of the Upper Tribunal) in relation to such non-compliance as
       if the requirement had been imposed by the Upper Tribunal.

Striking out a party's case

8(1)   The proceedings, or the appropriate part of them, will automatically be struck out if
       the appellant or applicant has failed to comply with a direction that stated that failure
       by the appellant or applicant to comply with the direction would lead to the striking
       out of the proceedings or that part of them.

(2)   The Upper Tribunal must strike out the whole or a part of the proceedings if the
       Upper Tribunal–
       (a) does not have jurisdiction in relation to the proceedings or that part of them;
            and
       (b) does not exercise its power under rule 5(3)(k)(i) (transfer to another court or
            tribunal) in relation to the proceedings or that part of them.

(3)   The Upper Tribunal may strike out the whole or a part of the proceedings if–
       (a) the appellant or applicant has failed to comply with a direction which stated
            that failure by the appellant or applicant to comply with the direction could
            lead to the striking out of the proceedings or part of them;
       (b) the appellant or applicant has failed to co-operate with the Upper Tribunal to
            such an extent that the Upper Tribunal cannot deal with the proceedings fairly
            and justly; or
       (c) in proceedings which are not an appeal from the decision of another tribunal
            or judicial review proceedings, the Upper Tribunal considers there is no

reasonable prospect of the appellant's or the applicant's case, or part of it, succeeding.

(4)   The Upper Tribunal may not strike out the whole or a part of the proceedings under paragraph (2) or (3)(b) or (c) without first giving the appellant or applicant an opportunity to make representations in relation to the proposed striking out.

(5)   If the proceedings have been struck out under paragraph (1) or (3)(a), the appellant or applicant may apply for the proceedings, or part of them, to be reinstated.

(6)   An application under paragraph (5) must be made in writing and received by the Upper Tribunal within 1 month after the date on which the Upper Tribunal sent notification of the striking out to the appellant or applicant.

(7)   This rule applies to a respondent or an interested party as it applies to an appellant or applicant except that–

(a)   a reference to the striking out of the proceedings is to be read as a reference to the barring of the respondent or interested party from taking further part in the proceedings; and

(b)   a reference to an application for the reinstatement of proceedings which have been struck out is to be read as a reference to an application for the lifting of the bar on the respondent or interested party taking further part in the proceedings.

(8)   If a respondent or an interested party has been barred from taking further part in proceedings under this rule and that bar has not been lifted, the Upper Tribunal need not consider any response or other submission made by that respondent or interested party, and may summarily determine any or all issues against that respondent or interested party.

Addition, substitution and removal of parties

9(1)   The Upper Tribunal may give a direction adding, substituting or removing a party as an appellant, a respondent or an interested party.

(2)   If the Upper Tribunal gives a direction under paragraph (1) it may give such consequential directions as it considers appropriate.

(3)   A person who is not a party may apply to the Upper Tribunal to be added or substituted as a party.

(4)   If a person who is entitled to be a party to proceedings by virtue of another enactment applies to be added as a party, and any conditions applicable to that entitlement have been satisfied, the Upper Tribunal must give a direction adding that person as a respondent or, if appropriate, as an appellant.

Orders for costs

10(1)   The Upper Tribunal may not make an order in respect of costs (or, in Scotland, expenses) in proceedings transferred or referred by, or on appeal from, another tribunal except–

(a)   in proceedings transferred by, or on appeal from, the Tax Chamber of the First-tier Tribunal; or

(b)   to the extent and in the circumstances that the other tribunal had the power to make an order in respect of costs (or, in Scotland, expenses).

(2)   The Upper Tribunal may not make an order in respect of costs or expenses under section 4 of the Forfeiture Act 1982.

(3)   In other proceedings, the Upper Tribunal may not make an order in respect of costs or expenses except–

(a)   in judicial review proceedings;

(c)   under section 29(4) of the 2007 Act (wasted costs); or

(d)   if the Upper Tribunal considers that a party or its representative has acted unreasonably in bringing, defending or conducting the proceedings.

(4)   The Upper Tribunal may make an order for costs (or, in Scotland, expenses) on an application or on its own initiative.

(5)   A person making an application for an order for costs or expenses must–

(a)   send or deliver a written application to the Upper Tribunal and to the person against whom it is proposed that the order be made; and

(b)   send or deliver with the application a schedule of the costs or expenses claimed sufficient to allow summary assessment of such costs or expenses by the Upper Tribunal.

(6)   An application for an order for costs or expenses may be made at any time during the proceedings but may not be made later than 1 month after the date on which the Upper Tribunal sends–

(a)   a decision notice recording the decision which finally disposes of all issues in the proceedings; or

(b)   notice of a withdrawal under rule 17 which ends the proceedings.

(7)   The Upper Tribunal may not make an order for costs or expenses against a person (the "paying person") without first–

(a)   giving that person an opportunity to make representations; and

(b)   if the paying person is an individual and the order is to be made under paragraph (3)(a), (b) or (d), considering that person's financial means.

(8)   The amount of costs or expenses to be paid under an order under this rule may be ascertained by–

(a)   summary assessment by the Upper Tribunal;

(b)   agreement of a specified sum by the paying person and the person entitled to receive the costs or expenses ("the receiving person"); or

(c) assessment of the whole or a specified part of the costs or expenses incurred by the receiving person, if not agreed.

(9) Following an order for assessment under paragraph (8)(c), the paying person or the receiving person may apply–

(a) in England and Wales, to the High Court or the Costs Office of the Supreme Court (as specified in the order) for a detailed assessment of the costs on the standard basis or, if specified in the order, on the indemnity basis; and the Civil Procedure Rules 1998 shall apply, with necessary modifications, to that application and assessment as if the proceedings in the tribunal had been proceedings in a court to which the Civil Procedure Rules 1998 apply;

(b) in Scotland, to the Auditor of the Court of Session for the taxation of the expenses according to the fees payable in that court; or

(c) in Northern Ireland, to the Taxing Office of the High Court of Northern Ireland for taxation on the standard basis or, if specified in the order, on the indemnity basis.

Representatives

11(1) A party may appoint a representative (whether a legal representative or not) to represent that party in the proceedings.

(2) If a party appoints a representative, that party (or the representative if the representative is a legal representative) must send or deliver to the Upper Tribunal . . . written notice of the representative's name and address.

(2A) If the Upper Tribunal receives notice that a party has appointed a representative under paragraph (2), it must send a copy of that notice to each other party.

(3) Anything permitted or required to be done by a party under these Rules, a practice direction or a direction may be done by the representative of that party, except signing a witness statement.

(4) A person who receives due notice of the appointment of a representative–

(a) must provide to the representative any document which is required to be provided to the represented party, and need not provide that document to the represented party; and

(b) may assume that the representative is and remains authorised as such until they receive written notification that this is not so from the representative or the represented party.

(5) At a hearing a party may be accompanied by another person whose name and address has not been notified under paragraph (2) but who, subject to paragraph (8) and with the permission of the Upper Tribunal, may act as a representative or otherwise assist in presenting the party's case at the hearing.

(6) Paragraphs (2) to (4) do not apply to a person who accompanies a party under paragraph (5).

(7)   In a mental health case if the patient has not appointed a representative the Upper Tribunal may appoint a legal representative for the patient where–

(a) the patient has stated that they do not wish to conduct their own case or that they wish to be represented; or

(b) the patient lacks the capacity to appoint a representative but the Upper Tribunal believes that it is in the patient's best interests for the patient to be represented.

(8)   In a mental health case a party may not appoint as a representative, or be represented or assisted at a hearing by–

(a) a person liable to be detained or subject to guardianship or after-care under supervision, or who is a community patient, under the Mental Health Act 1983; or

(b) a person receiving treatment for mental disorder at the same hospital home as the patient.

(9)   In this rule "legal representative" means an authorised advocate or authorised litigator as defined by section 119(1) of the Courts and Legal Services Act 1990, an advocate or solicitor in Scotland or a barrister or solicitor in Northern Ireland.

Calculating time

12(1)   An act required by these Rules, a practice direction or a direction to be done on or by a particular day must be done by 5pm on that day.

(2)   If the time specified by these Rules, a practice direction or a direction for doing any act ends on a day other than a working day, the act is done in time if it is done on the next working day.

(3)   In a special educational needs case or a disability discrimination in schools case, the following days must not be counted when calculating the time by which an act must be done–

(a) 25th December to 1st January inclusive; and

(b) any day in August.

(4)   Paragraph (3) does not apply where the Upper Tribunal directs that an act must be done by or on a specified date.

(5)   In this rule–

"disability discrimination in schools case" means proceedings concerning disability discrimination in the education of a child or related matters; and

"special educational needs case" means proceedings concerning the education of a child who has or may have special educational needs.

Sending and delivery of documents

13(1)   Any document to be provided to the Upper Tribunal under these Rules, a practice direction or a direction must be–

(a) sent by pre-paid post or by document exchange, or delivered by hand, to the address specified for the proceedings;

(b) sent by fax to the number specified for the proceedings; or

(c) sent or delivered by such other method as the Upper Tribunal may permit or direct.

(2) Subject to paragraph (3), if a party provides a fax number, email address or other details for the electronic transmission of documents to them, that party must accept delivery of documents by that method.

(3) If a party informs the Upper Tribunal and all other parties that a particular form of communication, other than pre-paid post or delivery by hand, should not be used to provide documents to that party, that form of communication must not be so used.

(4) If the Upper Tribunal or a party sends a document to a party or the Upper Tribunal by email or any other electronic means of communication, the recipient may request that the sender provide a hard copy of the document to the recipient. The recipient must make such a request as soon as reasonably practicable after receiving the document electronically.

(5) The Upper Tribunal and each party may assume that the address provided by a party or its representative is and remains the address to which documents should be sent or delivered until receiving written notification to the contrary.

Use of documents and information

14(1) The Upper Tribunal may make an order prohibiting the disclosure or publication of–

(a) specified documents or information relating to the proceedings; or

(b) any matter likely to lead members of the public to identify any person whom the Upper Tribunal considers should not be identified.

(2) The Upper Tribunal may give a direction prohibiting the disclosure of a document or information to a person if–

(a) the Upper Tribunal is satisfied that such disclosure would be likely to cause that person or some other person serious harm; and

(b) the Upper Tribunal is satisfied, having regard to the interests of justice, that it is proportionate to give such a direction.

(3) If a party ("the first party") considers that the Upper Tribunal should give a direction under paragraph (2) prohibiting the disclosure of a document or information to another party ("the second party"), the first party must–

(a) exclude the relevant document or information from any documents that will be provided to the second party; and

(b) provide to the Upper Tribunal the excluded document or information, and the reason for its exclusion, so that the Upper Tribunal may decide whether the document or information should be disclosed to the second party or should be the subject of a direction under paragraph (2).

(5)   If the Upper Tribunal gives a direction under paragraph (2) which prevents disclosure to a party who has appointed a representative, the Upper Tribunal may give a direction that the documents or information be disclosed to that representative if the Upper Tribunal is satisfied that—
    (a) disclosure to the representative would be in the interests of the party; and
    (b) the representative will act in accordance with paragraph (6).

(6)   Documents or information disclosed to a representative in accordance with a direction under paragraph (5) must not be disclosed either directly or indirectly to any other person without the Upper Tribunal's consent.

(7)   Unless the Upper Tribunal gives a direction to the contrary, information about mental health cases and the names of any persons concerned in such cases must not be made public.

(8)   The Upper Tribunal may, on its own initiative or on the application of a party, give a direction that certain documents or information must or may be disclosed to the Upper Tribunal on the basis that the Upper Tribunal will not disclose such documents or information to other persons, or specified other persons.

(9)   A party making an application for a direction under paragraph (8) may withhold the relevant documents or information from other parties until the Upper Tribunal has granted or refused the application.

(10)   In a case involving matters relating to national security, the Upper Tribunal must ensure that information is not disclosed contrary to the interests of national security.

(11)   The Upper Tribunal must conduct proceedings and record its decision and reasons appropriately so as not to undermine the effect of an order made under paragraph (1), a direction given under paragraph (2) or (8) or the duty imposed by paragraph (10).

Evidence and submissions

15(1)   Without restriction on the general powers in rule 5(1) and (2) (case management powers), the Upper Tribunal may give directions as to—
    (a) issues on which it requires evidence or submissions;
    (b) the nature of the evidence or submissions it requires;
    (c) whether the parties are permitted or required to provide expert evidence, and if so whether the parties must jointly appoint a single expert to provide such evidence;
    (d) any limit on the number of witnesses whose evidence a party may put forward, whether in relation to a particular issue or generally;
    (e) the manner in which any evidence or submissions are to be provided, which may include a direction for them to be given—
        (i) orally at a hearing; or
        (ii) by written submissions or witness statement; and
    (f) the time at which any evidence or submissions are to be provided.

(2) The Upper Tribunal may–
   (a) admit evidence whether or not–
      (i) the evidence would be admissible in a civil trial in the United Kingdom; or
      (ii) the evidence was available to a previous decision maker; or
   (b) exclude evidence that would otherwise be admissible where–
      (i) the evidence was not provided within the time allowed by a direction or a practice direction;
      (ii) the evidence was otherwise provided in a manner that did not comply with a direction or a practice direction; or
      (iii) it would otherwise be unfair to admit the evidence.

(3) The Upper Tribunal may consent to a witness giving, or require any witness to give, evidence on oath, and may administer an oath for that purpose.

Summoning or citation of witnesses and orders to answer questions or produce documents

16(1) On the application of a party or on its own initiative, the Upper Tribunal may–
   (a) by summons (or, in Scotland, citation) require any person to attend as a witness at a hearing at the time and place specified in the summons or citation; or
   (b) order any person to answer any questions or produce any documents in that person's possession or control which relate to any issue in the proceedings.

(2) A summons or citation under paragraph (1)(a) must–
   (a) give the person required to attend 14 days' notice of the hearing or such shorter period as the Upper Tribunal may direct; and
   (b) where the person is not a party, make provision for the person's necessary expenses of attendance to be paid, and state who is to pay them.

(3) No person may be compelled to give any evidence or produce any document that the person could not be compelled to give or produce on a trial of an action in a court of law in the part of the United Kingdom where the proceedings are due to be determined.

(4) A person who receives a summons, citation or order may apply to the Upper Tribunal for it to be varied or set aside if they did not have an opportunity to object to it before it was made or issued.

(5) A person making an application under paragraph (4) must do so as soon as reasonably practicable after receiving notice of the summons, citation or order.

(6) A summons, citation or order under this rule must–
   (a) state that the person on whom the requirement is imposed may apply to the Upper Tribunal to vary or set aside the summons, citation or order, if they did not have an opportunity to object to it before it was made or issued; and
   (b) state the consequences of failure to comply with the summons, citation or order.

Withdrawal

17(1)   Subject to paragraph (2), a party may give notice of the withdrawal of its case, or any part of it–

   (a) at any time before a hearing to consider the disposal of the proceedings (or, if the Upper Tribunal disposes of the proceedings without a hearing, before that disposal), by sending or delivering to the Upper Tribunal a written notice of withdrawal; or

   (b) orally at a hearing.

(2)   Notice of withdrawal will not take effect unless the Upper Tribunal consents to the withdrawal except in relation to an application for permission to appeal.

(3)   A party which has withdrawn its case may apply to the Upper Tribunal for the case to be reinstated.

(4)   An application under paragraph (3) must be made in writing and be received by the Upper Tribunal within 1 month after–

   (a) the date on which the Upper Tribunal received the notice under paragraph (1)(a); or

   (b) the date of the hearing at which the case was withdrawn orally under paragraph (1)(b).

(5)   The Upper Tribunal must notify each party in writing of a withdrawal under this rule.

Notice of funding of legal services

18   If a party is granted funding of legal services at any time, that party must as soon as practicable–

   (a) (i) if funding is granted by the Legal Services Commission or the Northern Ireland Legal Services Commission, send a copy of the funding notice to the Upper Tribunal; or

   (ii) if funding is granted by the Scottish Legal Aid Board, send a copy of the legal aid certificate to the Upper Tribunal; and

   (b) notify every other party in writing that funding has been granted.

Confidentiality in child support or child trust fund cases

19(1)   Paragraph (3) applies to an appeal against a decision of the First-tier Tribunal in proceedings under the Child Support Act 1991 in the circumstances described in paragraph (2), other than an appeal against a reduced benefit decision (as defined in section 46(10)(b) of the Child Support Act 1991, as that section had effect prior to the commencement of section 15(b) of the Child Maintenance and Other Payments Act 2008).

(2)   The circumstances referred to in paragraph (1) are that–

   (a) in the proceedings in the First-tier Tribunal in respect of which the appeal has been brought, there was an obligation to keep a person's address confidential; or

    (b) a person whose circumstances are relevant to the proceedings would like their address (or, in the case of the person with care of the child, the child's address) to be kept confidential and has given notice to that effect–

       (i) to the Upper Tribunal in an application for permission to appeal or notice of appeal;

       (ii) to the Upper Tribunal within 1 month after an enquiry by the Upper Tribunal; or

       (iii) to the Secretary of State, the Child Maintenance and Enforcement Commission or the Upper Tribunal when notifying a change of address after proceedings have been started.

(3) Where this paragraph applies, the Secretary of State, the Child Maintenance and Enforcement Commission and the Upper Tribunal must take appropriate steps to secure the confidentiality of the address, and of any information which could reasonably be expected to enable a person to identify the address, to the extent that the address or that information is not already known to each other party.

(4) Paragraph (6) applies to an appeal against a decision of the First-tier Tribunal in proceedings under the Child Trust Funds Act 2004 in the circumstances described in paragraph (5).

(5) The circumstances referred to in paragraph (4) are that–

    (a) in the proceedings in the First-tier Tribunal in respect of which the appeal has been brought, there was an obligation to keep a person's address confidential; or

    (b) a person whose circumstances are relevant to the proceedings would like their address (or, in the case of the person with care of the eligible child, the child's address) to be kept confidential and has given notice to that effect–

       (i) to the Upper Tribunal in an application for permission to appeal or notice of appeal;

       (ii) to the Upper Tribunal within 1 month after an enquiry by the Upper Tribunal; or

       (iii) to HMRC or the Upper Tribunal when notifying a change of address after proceedings have been started.

(6) Where this paragraph applies, HMRC and the Upper Tribunal must take appropriate steps to secure the confidentiality of the address, and of any information which could reasonably be expected to enable a person to identify the address, to the extent that the address or that information is not already known to each other party.

(7) In this rule–
"eligible child" has the meaning set out in section 2 of the Child Trust Funds Act 2004; and"HMRC" means Her Majesty's Revenue and Customs.

Power to pay expenses and allowances

20(1)   In proceedings brought under section 4 of the Safeguarding Vulnerable Groups Act 2006, the Secretary of State may pay such allowances for the purpose of or in connection with the attendance of persons at hearings as the Secretary of State may, with the consent of the Treasury, determine.

(2)   Paragraph (3) applies to proceedings on appeal from a decision of–
   (a) the First-tier Tribunal in proceedings under the Child Support Act 1991, section 12 of the Social Security Act 1998 or paragraph 6 of Schedule 7 to the Child Support, Pensions and Social Security Act 2000;
   (b) the First-tier Tribunal in a war pensions and armed forces case (as defined in the Tribunal Procedure (First-tier Tribunal) (War Pensions and Armed Forces Compensation Chamber) Rules 2008); or
   (c) a Pensions Appeal Tribunal for Scotland or Northern Ireland.

(3)   The Lord Chancellor (or, in Scotland, the Secretary of State) may pay to any person who attends any hearing such travelling and other allowances, including compensation for loss of remunerative time, as the Lord Chancellor (or, in Scotland, the Secretary of State) may determine.

Procedure for applying for a stay of a decision pending an appeal

20A(1)   This rule applies where another enactment provides in any terms for the Upper Tribunal to stay or suspend, or to lift a stay or suspension of, a decision which is or may be the subject of an appeal to the Upper Tribunal ("the substantive decision") pending such appeal.

(2)   A person who wishes the Upper Tribunal to decide whether the substantive decision should be stayed or suspended must make a written application to the Upper Tribunal which must include–
   (a) the name and address of the person making the application;
   (b) the name and address of any representative of that person;
   (c) the address to which documents for that person should be sent or delivered;
   (d) the name and address of any person who will be a respondent to the appeal;
   (e) details of the substantive decision and any decision as to when that decision is to take effect, and copies of any written record of, or reasons for, those decisions; and
   (f) the grounds on which the person making the application relies.

(3)   In the case of an application under paragraph (2) for a stay of a decision of a traffic commissioner–
   (a) the person making the application must notify the traffic commissioner when making the application;
   (b) within 7 days of receiving notification of the application the traffic commissioner must send or deliver written reasons for refusing or withdrawing the stay–
      (i) to the Upper Tribunal; and

(ii) to the person making the application, if the traffic commissioner has not already done so.

(4) If the Upper Tribunal grants a stay or suspension following an application under this rule–
   (a) the Upper Tribunal may give directions as to the conduct of the appeal of the substantive decision; and
   (b) the Upper Tribunal may, where appropriate, grant the stay or suspension subject to conditions.

(5) Unless the Upper Tribunal considers that there is good reason not to do so, the Upper Tribunal must send written notice of any decision made under this rule to each party.

PART 3

PROCEDURE FOR CASES IN THE UPPER TRIBUNAL

Application to the Upper Tribunal for permission to appeal

21(2) A person may apply to the Upper Tribunal for permission to appeal to the Upper Tribunal against a decision of another tribunal only if–
   (a) they have made an application for permission to appeal to the tribunal which made the decision challenged; and
   (b) that application has been refused or has not been admitted.

(3) An application for permission to appeal must be made in writing and received by the Upper Tribunal no later than–
   (a) in the case of an application under section 4 of the Safeguarding Vulnerable Groups Act 2006, 3 months after the date on which written notice of the decision being challenged was sent to the appellant; or
   (b) otherwise, a month after the date on which the tribunal that made the decision under challenge sent notice of its refusal of permission to appeal, or refusal to admit the application for permission to appeal, to the appellant.

(4) The application must state–
   (a) the name and address of the appellant;
   (b) the name and address of the representative (if any) of the appellant;
   (c) an address where documents for the appellant may be sent or delivered;
   (d) details (including the full reference) of the decision challenged;
   (e) the grounds on which the appellant relies; and
   (f) whether the appellant wants the application to be dealt with at a hearing.

(5) The appellant must provide with the application a copy of–
   (a) any written record of the decision being challenged;
   (b) any separate written statement of reasons for that decision; and
   (c) if the application is for permission to appeal against a decision of another tribunal, the notice of refusal of permission to appeal, or notice of refusal to admit the application for permission to appeal, from that other tribunal.

(6) If the appellant provides the application to the Upper Tribunal later than the time required by paragraph (3) or by an extension of time allowed under rule 5(3)(a) (power to extend time)–

    (a) the application must include a request for an extension of time and the reason why the application was not provided in time; and

    (b) unless the Upper Tribunal extends time for the application under rule 5(3)(a) (power to extend time) the Upper Tribunal must not admit the application.

(7) If the appellant makes an application to the Upper Tribunal for permission to appeal against the decision of another tribunal, and that other tribunal refused to admit the appellant's application for permission to appeal because the application for permission or for a written statement of reasons was not made in time–

    (a) the application to the Upper Tribunal for permission to appeal must include the reason why the application to the other tribunal for permission to appeal or for a written statement of reasons, as the case may be, was not made in time; and

    (b) the Upper Tribunal must only admit the application if the Upper Tribunal considers that it is in the interests of justice for it to do so.

(2) If the Upper Tribunal gives permission to appeal–

    (a) the Upper Tribunal must send written notice of the permission, and of the reasons for any limitations or conditions on such permission, to each party;

    (b) subject to any direction by the Upper Tribunal, the application for permission to appeal stands as the notice of appeal and the Upper Tribunal must send to each respondent a copy of the application for permission to appeal and any documents provided with it by the appellant; and

    (c) the Upper Tribunal may, with the consent of the appellant and each respondent, determine the appeal without obtaining any further response.

(3) Paragraph (4) applies where the Upper Tribunal, without a hearing, determines an application for permission to appeal–

    (a) against a decision of–

        (i) the Tax Chamber of the First-tier Tribunal;

        (ii) the Health, Education and Social Care Chamber of the First-tier Tribunal;

        (iia) the General Regulatory Chamber of the First-tier Tribunal;

        (iii) the Mental Health Review Tribunal for Wales; or

        (iv) the Special Educational Needs Tribunal for Wales; or

    (b) under section 4 of the Safeguarding Vulnerable Groups Act 2006.

(4) In the circumstances set out at paragraph (3) the appellant may apply for the decision to be reconsidered at a hearing if the Upper Tribunal–

    (a) refuses permission to appeal; or

    (b) gives permission to appeal on limited grounds or subject to conditions.

(5)   An application under paragraph (4) must be made in writing and received by the Upper Tribunal within 14 days after the date on which the Upper Tribunal sent written notice of its decision regarding the application to the appellant.

Notice of appeal

23(1)   This rule applies–
(a) to proceedings on appeal to the Upper Tribunal for which permission to appeal is not required, except proceedings to which rule 26A applies;
(b) if another tribunal has given permission for a party to appeal to the Upper Tribunal; or
(c) subject to any other direction by the Upper Tribunal, if the Upper Tribunal has given permission to appeal and has given a direction that the application for permission to appeal does not stand as the notice of appeal.

(2)   The appellant must provide a notice of appeal to the Upper Tribunal so that it is received within 1 month after–
(a) the date that the tribunal that gave permission to appeal sent notice of such permission to the appellant; or
(b) if permission to appeal is not required, the date on which notice of decision to which the appeal relates was sent to the appellant.

(3)   The notice of appeal must include the information listed in rule 21(4)(a) to (e) (content of the application for permission to appeal) and, where the Upper Tribunal has given permission to appeal, the Upper Tribunal's case reference.

(4)   If another tribunal has granted permission to appeal, the appellant must provide with the notice of appeal a copy of–
(a) any written record of the decision being challenged;
(b) any separate written statement of reasons for that decision; and
(c) the notice of permission to appeal.

(5)   If the appellant provides the notice of appeal to the Upper Tribunal later than the time required by paragraph (2) or by an extension of time allowed under rule 5(3)(a) (power to extend time)–
(a) the notice of appeal must include a request for an extension of time and the reason why the notice was not provided in time; and
(b) unless the Upper Tribunal extends time for the notice of appeal under rule 5(3)(a) (power to extend time) the Upper Tribunal must not admit the notice of appeal.

(6)   When the Upper Tribunal receives the notice of appeal it must send a copy of the notice and any accompanying documents–
(a) to each respondent; or
(b) in an appeal against the decision of a traffic commissioner, to–
(i) the traffic commissioner;

(ii) the appropriate national authority; and

(iii) in a case relating to the detention of a vehicle, the authorised person.

Response to the notice of appeal

24(1) This rule and rule 25 do not apply to an appeal against a decision of a traffic commissioner, in respect of which Schedule 1 makes alternative provision.

(1A) Subject to any direction given by the Upper Tribunal, a respondent may provide a response to a notice of appeal.

(2) Any response provided under paragraph (1) must be in writing and must be sent or delivered to the Upper Tribunal so that it is received–

(a) if an application for permission to appeal stands as the notice of appeal, no later than 1 month after the date on which the Upper Tribunal sent notice that it had granted permission to appeal to the respondent; or

(b) in any other case, no later than 1 month after the date on which the Upper Tribunal sent a copy of the notice of appeal to the respondent.

(3) The response must state–

(a) the name and address of the respondent;

(b) the name and address of the representative (if any) of the respondent;

(c) an address where documents for the respondent may be sent or delivered;

(d) whether the respondent opposes the appeal;

(e) the grounds on which the respondent relies, including (in the case of an appeal against the decision of another tribunal) any grounds on which the respondent was unsuccessful in the proceedings which are the subject of the appeal, but intends to rely in the appeal; and

(f) whether the respondent wants the case to be dealt with at a hearing.

(4) If the respondent provides the response to the Upper Tribunal later than the time required by paragraph (2) or by an extension of time allowed under rule 5(3)(a) (power to extend time), the response must include a request for an extension of time and the reason why the response was not provided in time.

(5) When the Upper Tribunal receives the response it must send a copy of the response and any accompanying documents to the appellant and each other party.

Appellant's reply

25(1) Subject to any direction given by the Upper Tribunal, the appellant may provide a reply to any response provided under rule 24 (response to the notice of appeal).

(2) Any reply provided under paragraph (1) must be in writing and must be sent or delivered to the Upper Tribunal so that it is received within one month after the date on which the Upper Tribunal sent a copy of the response to the appellant.

(3) When the Upper Tribunal receives the reply it must send a copy of the reply and any accompanying documents to each respondent.

References under the Forfeiture Act 1982

26(1)   If a question arises which is required to be determined by the Upper Tribunal under section 4 of the Forfeiture Act 1982, the person to whom the application for the relevant benefit or advantage has been made must refer the question to the Upper Tribunal.

(2)   The reference must be in writing and must include–
(a) a statement of the question for determination;
(b) a statement of the relevant facts;
(c) the grounds upon which the reference is made; and
(d) an address for sending documents to the person making the reference and each respondent.

(3)   When the Upper Tribunal receives the reference it must send a copy of the reference and any accompanying documents to each respondent.

(4)   Rules 24 (response to the notice of appeal) and 25 (appellant's reply) apply to a reference made under this rule as if it were a notice of appeal.

Cases transferred or referred to the Upper Tribunal, applications made directly to the Upper Tribunal and proceedings without notice to a respondent

26A(1)   Paragraphs (2) and (3) apply to–
(a) a case transferred or referred to the Upper Tribunal from the First-tier Tribunal; or
(b) a case, other than an appeal or a case to which rule 26 (references under the Forfeiture Act 1982) applies, which is started by an application made directly to the Upper Tribunal.

(2)   In a case to which this paragraph applies–
(a) the Upper Tribunal must give directions as to the procedure to be followed in the consideration and disposal of the proceedings; and
(b) the preceding rules in this Part will only apply to the proceedings to the extent provided for by such directions.

(3)   If a case or matter to which this paragraph applies is to be determined without notice to or the involvement of a respondent–
(a) any provision in these Rules requiring a document to be provided by or to a respondent; and
(b) any other provision in these Rules permitting a respondent to participate in the proceedings
does not apply to that case or matter.

PART 4

JUDICIAL REVIEW PROCEEDINGS IN THE UPPER TRIBUNAL

Application of this Part to judicial review proceedings transferred to the Upper Tribunal

27(1)   When a court transfers judicial review proceedings to the Upper Tribunal, the Upper Tribunal–

(a) must notify each party in writing that the proceedings have been transferred to the Upper Tribunal; and

(b) must give directions as to the future conduct of the proceedings.

(2)   The directions given under paragraph (1)(b) may modify or disapply for the purposes of the proceedings any of the provisions of the following rules in this Part.

(3)   In proceedings transferred from the Court of Session under section 20(1) of the 2007 Act, the directions given under paragraph (1)(b) must–

(a) if the Court of Session did not make a first order specifying the required intimation, service and advertisement of the petition, state the Upper Tribunal's requirements in relation to those matters;

(b) state whether the Upper Tribunal will consider summary dismissal of the proceedings; and

(c) where necessary, modify or disapply provisions relating to permission in the following rules in this Part.

Applications for permission to bring judicial review proceedings

28(1)   A person seeking permission to bring judicial review proceedings before the Upper Tribunal under section 16 of the 2007 Act must make a written application to the Upper Tribunal for such permission.

(2)   Subject to paragraph (3), an application under paragraph (1) must be made promptly and, unless any other enactment specifies a shorter time limit, must be sent or delivered to the Upper Tribunal so that it is received no later than 3 months after the date of the decision, action or omission to which the application relates.

(3)   An application for permission to bring judicial review proceedings challenging a decision of the First-tier Tribunal may be made later than the time required by paragraph (2) if it is made within 1 month after the date on which the First-tier Tribunal sent–

(a) written reasons for the decision; or

(b) notification that an application for the decision to be set aside has been unsuccessful, provided that that application was made in time.

(4)   The application must state–

(a) the name and address of the applicant, the respondent and any other person whom the applicant considers to be an interested party;

(b) the name and address of the applicant's representative (if any);

(c) an address where documents for the applicant may be sent or delivered;

(d) details of the decision challenged (including the date, the full reference and the identity of the decision maker);

(e) that the application is for permission to bring judicial review proceedings;

(f) the outcome that the applicant is seeking; and

(g) the facts and grounds on which the applicant relies.

(5) If the application relates to proceedings in a court or tribunal, the application must name as an interested party each party to those proceedings who is not the applicant or a respondent.

(6) The applicant must send with the application–

(a) a copy of any written record of the decision in the applicant's possession or control; and

(b) copies of any other documents in the applicant's possession or control on which the applicant intends to rely.

(7) If the applicant provides the application to the Upper Tribunal later than the time required by paragraph (2) or (3) or by an extension of time allowed under rule 5(3)(a) (power to extend time)–

(a) the application must include a request for an extension of time and the reason why the application was not provided in time; and

(b) unless the Upper Tribunal extends time for the application under rule 5(3)(a) (power to extend time) the Upper Tribunal must not admit the application.

(8) When the Upper Tribunal receives the application it must send a copy of the application and any accompanying documents to each person named in the application as a respondent or interested party.

Acknowledgment of service

29(1) A person who is sent a copy of an application for permission under rule 28(8) (application for permission to bring judicial review proceedings) and wishes to take part in the proceedings must send or deliver to the Upper Tribunal an acknowledgment of service so that it is received no later than 21 days after the date on which the Upper Tribunal sent a copy of the application to that person.

(2) An acknowledgment of service under paragraph (1) must be in writing and state–

(a) whether the person intends to support or oppose the application for permission;

(b) their grounds for any support or opposition under sub-paragraph (a), or any other submission or information which they consider may assist the Upper Tribunal; and

(c) the name and address of any other person not named in the application as a respondent or interested party whom the person providing the acknowledgment considers to be an interested party.

(3) A person who is sent a copy of an application for permission under rule 28(8) but does not provide an acknowledgment of service may not take part in the application for permission, but may take part in the subsequent proceedings if the application is successful.

Decision on permission or summary dismissal, and reconsideration of permission or summary dismissal at a hearing

30(1)   The Upper Tribunal must send to the applicant, each respondent and any other person who provided an acknowledgment of service to the Upper Tribunal, and may send to any other person who may have an interest in the proceedings, written notice of–

      (a) its decision in relation to the application for permission; and

      (b) the reasons for any refusal of the application, or any limitations or conditions on permission.

(2)   In proceedings transferred from the Court of Session under section 20(1) of the 2007 Act, where the Upper Tribunal has considered whether summarily to dismiss of the proceedings, the Upper Tribunal must send to the applicant and each respondent, and may send to any other person who may have an interest in the proceedings, written notice of–

      (a) its decision in relation to the summary dismissal of proceedings; and

      (b) the reasons for any decision summarily to dismiss part or all of the proceedings, or any limitations or conditions on the continuation of such proceedings.

(3)   Paragraph (4) applies where the Upper Tribunal, without a hearing–

      (a) determines an application for permission to bring judicial review proceedings and either refuses permission, or gives permission on limited grounds or subject to conditions; or

      (b) in proceedings transferred from the Court of Session, summarily dismisses part or all of the proceedings, or imposes any limitations or conditions on the continuation of such proceedings.

(4)   In the circumstances specified in paragraph (3) the applicant may apply for the decision to be reconsidered at a hearing.

(5)   An application under paragraph (4) must be made in writing and must be sent or delivered to the Upper Tribunal so that it is received within 14 days after the date on which the Upper Tribunal sent written notice of its decision regarding the application to the applicant.

Responses

31(1)   Any person to whom the Upper Tribunal has sent notice of the grant of permission under rule 30(1) (notification of decision on permission), and who wishes to contest the application or support it on additional grounds, must provide detailed grounds for contesting or supporting the application to the Upper Tribunal.

(2)   Any detailed grounds must be provided in writing and must be sent or delivered to the Upper Tribunal so that they are received not more than 35 days after the Upper Tribunal sent notice of the grant of permission under rule 30(1).

Applicant seeking to rely on additional grounds

32 The applicant may not rely on any grounds, other than those grounds on which the applicant obtained permission for the judicial review proceedings, without the consent of the Upper Tribunal.

Right to make representations

33 Each party and, with the permission of the Upper Tribunal, any other person, may–
    (a) submit evidence, except at the hearing of an application for permission;
    (b) make representations at any hearing which they are entitled to attend; and
    (c) make written representations in relation to a decision to be made without a hearing.

PART 5

HEARINGS

Decision with or without a hearing

34(1) Subject to paragraph (2), the Upper Tribunal may make any decision without a hearing.

(2) The Upper Tribunal must have regard to any view expressed by a party when deciding whether to hold a hearing to consider any matter, and the form of any such hearing.

Entitlement to attend a hearing

35 Subject to rule 37(4) (exclusion of a person from a hearing), each party is entitled to attend a hearing.

Notice of hearings

36(1) The Upper Tribunal must give each party entitled to attend a hearing reasonable notice of the time and place of the hearing (including any adjourned or postponed hearing) and any change to the time and place of the hearing.

(2) The period of notice under paragraph (1) must be at least 14 days except that–
    (a) in applications for permission to bring judicial review proceedings, the period of notice must be at least 2 working days; and
    (b) the Upper Tribunal may give shorter notice–
        (i) with the parties' consent; or
        (ii) in urgent or exceptional cases.

Public and private hearings

37(1) Subject to the following paragraphs, all hearings must be held in public.

(2) The Upper Tribunal may give a direction that a hearing, or part of it, is to be held in private.

(3)   Where a hearing, or part of it, is to be held in private, the Upper Tribunal may determine who is entitled to attend the hearing or part of it.

(4)   The Upper Tribunal may give a direction excluding from any hearing, or part of it–
        (a) any person whose conduct the Upper Tribunal considers is disrupting or is likely to disrupt the hearing;
        (b) any person whose presence the Upper Tribunal considers is likely to prevent another person from giving evidence or making submissions freely;
        (c) any person who the Upper Tribunal considers should be excluded in order to give effect to the requirement at rule 14(11) (prevention of disclosure or publication of documents and information);
        (d) any person where the purpose of the hearing would be defeated by the attendance of that person; or
        (e) a person under the age of eighteen years.

(5)   The Upper Tribunal may give a direction excluding a witness from a hearing until that witness gives evidence.

Hearings in a party's absence

38   If a party fails to attend a hearing, the Upper Tribunal may proceed with the hearing if the Upper Tribunal–
        (a) is satisfied that the party has been notified of the hearing or that reasonable steps have been taken to notify the party of the hearing; and
        (b) considers that it is in the interests of justice to proceed with the hearing.

PART 6

DECISIONS

Consent orders

39(1)   The Upper Tribunal may, at the request of the parties but only if it considers it appropriate, make a consent order disposing of the proceedings and making such other appropriate provision as the parties have agreed.

(2)   Notwithstanding any other provision of these Rules, the Tribunal need not hold a hearing before making an order under paragraph (1).

Decisions

40(1)   The Upper Tribunal may give a decision orally at a hearing.

(2)   The Upper Tribunal must provide to each party as soon as reasonably practicable after making a decision which finally disposes of all issues in the proceedings (except a decision under Part 7)–
        (a) a decision notice stating the Tribunal's decision; and

(b) notification of any rights of review or appeal against the decision and the time and manner in which such rights of review or appeal may be exercised.

(3) Subject to rule 14(11) (prevention of disclosure or publication of documents and information), the Upper Tribunal must provide written reasons for its decision with a decision notice provided under paragraph (2)(a) unless–
  (a) the decision was made with the consent of the parties; or
  (b) the parties have consented to the Upper Tribunal not giving written reasons.

(4) The Upper Tribunal may provide written reasons for any decision to which paragraph (2) does not apply.

PART 7

CORRECTING, SETTING ASIDE, REVIEWING AND APPEALING DECISIONS OF THE UPPER TRIBUNAL

Interpretation
41 In this Part–
  "appeal", except in rule 44(2) (application for permission to appeal), means the exercise of a right of appeal under section 13 of the 2007 Act; and
  "review" means the review of a decision by the Upper Tribunal under section 10 of the 2007 Act.

Clerical mistakes and accidental slips or omissions
42 The Upper Tribunal may at any time correct any clerical mistake or other accidental slip or omission in a decision or record of a decision by–
  (a) sending notification of the amended decision, or a copy of the amended record, to all parties; and
  (b) making any necessary amendment to any information published in relation to the decision or record.

Setting aside a decision which disposes of proceedings
43(1) The Upper Tribunal may set aside a decision which disposes of proceedings, or part of such a decision, and re-make the decision or the relevant part of it, if–
  (a) the Upper Tribunal considers that it is in the interests of justice to do so; and
  (b) one or more of the conditions in paragraph (2) are satisfied.

(2) The conditions are–
  (a) a document relating to the proceedings was not sent to, or was not received at an appropriate time by, a party or a party's representative;
  (b) a document relating to the proceedings was not sent to the Upper Tribunal at an appropriate time;
  (c) a party, or a party's representative, was not present at a hearing related to the proceedings; or

(d) there has been some other procedural irregularity in the proceedings.

(3) A party applying for a decision, or part of a decision, to be set aside under paragraph (1) must make a written application to the Upper Tribunal so that it is received no later than 1 month after the date on which the Tribunal sent notice of the decision to the party.

Application for permission to appeal

44(1) A person seeking permission to appeal must make a written application to the Upper Tribunal for permission to appeal.

(2) Paragraph (3) applies to an application under paragraph (1) in respect of a decision–
    (a) on an appeal against a decision in a social security and child support case (as defined in the Tribunal Procedure (First-tier Tribunal) (Social Entitlement Chamber) Rules 2008);
    (b) on an appeal against a decision in proceedings in the War Pensions and Armed Forces Compensation Chamber of the First-tier Tribunal;
    (ba) on an appeal against a decision of a Pensions Appeal Tribunal for Scotland or Northern Ireland; or
    (c) in proceedings under the Forfeiture Act 1982.

(3) Where this paragraph applies, the application must be sent or delivered to the Upper Tribunal so that it is received within 3 months after the date on which the Upper Tribunal sent to the person making the application–
    (a) written notice of the decision;
    (b) notification of amended reasons for, or correction of, the decision following a review; or
    (c) notification that an application for the decision to be set aside has been unsuccessful.

(4) Where paragraph (3) does not apply, an application under paragraph (1) must be sent or delivered to the Upper Tribunal so that it is received within 1 month after the latest of the dates on which the Upper Tribunal sent to the person making the application–
    (a) written reasons for the decision;
    (b) notification of amended reasons for, or correction of, the decision following a review; or
    (c) notification that an application for the decision to be set aside has been unsuccessful.

(5) The date in paragraph (3)(c) or (4)(c) applies only if the application for the decision to be set aside was made within the time stipulated in rule 43 (setting aside a decision which disposes of proceedings) or any extension of that time granted by the Upper Tribunal.

(6)   If the person seeking permission to appeal provides the application to the Upper
        Tribunal later than the time required by paragraph (3) or (4), or by any extension of
        time under rule 5(3)(a) (power to extend time)–
            (a) the application must include a request for an extension of time and the reason
                why the application notice was not provided in time; and
            (b) unless the Upper Tribunal extends time for the application under rule 5(3)(a)
                (power to extend time) the Upper Tribunal must refuse the application.

(7)   An application under paragraph (1) must–
            (a) identify the decision of the Tribunal to which it relates;
            (b) identify the alleged error or errors of law in the decision; and
            (c) state the result the party making the application is seeking.

Upper Tribunal's consideration of application for permission to appeal

45(1)   On receiving an application for permission to appeal the Upper Tribunal may review
        the decision in accordance with rule 46 (review of a decision), but may only do so if–
            (a) when making the decision the Upper Tribunal overlooked a legislative
                provision or binding authority which could have had a material effect on the
                decision; or
            (b) since the Upper Tribunal's decision, a court has made a decision which is
                binding on the Upper Tribunal and which, had it been made before the Upper
                Tribunal's decision, could have had a material effect on the decision.

(2)   If the Upper Tribunal decides not to review the decision, or reviews the decision and
        decides to take no action in relation to the decision or part of it, the Upper Tribunal
        must consider whether to give permission to appeal in relation to the decision or that
        part of it.

(3)   The Upper Tribunal must send a record of its decision to the parties as soon as
        practicable.

(4)   If the Upper Tribunal refuses permission to appeal it must send with the record of its
        decision–
            (a) a statement of its reasons for such refusal; and
            (b) notification of the right to make an application to the relevant appellate court
                for permission to appeal and the time within which, and the method by which,
                such application must be made.

(5)   The Upper Tribunal may give permission to appeal on limited grounds, but must
        comply with paragraph (4) in relation to any grounds on which it has refused
        permission.

Review of a decision

46(1)   The Upper Tribunal may only undertake a review of a decision–
            (a) pursuant to rule 45(1) (review on an application for permission to appeal); or

(b) pursuant to rule 47 (reviews of decisions in proceedings under the Forfeiture Act 1982).

(2) The Upper Tribunal must notify the parties in writing of the outcome of any review and of any rights of review or appeal in relation to the outcome.

(3) If the Upper Tribunal decides to take any action in relation to a decision following a review without first giving every party an opportunity to make representations, the notice under paragraph (2) must state that any party that did not have an opportunity to make representations may apply for such action to be set aside and for the decision to be reviewed again.

Review of a decision in proceedings under the Forfeiture Act 1982

47(1) A person who referred a question to the Upper Tribunal under rule 26 (references under the Forfeiture Act 1982) must refer the Upper Tribunal's previous decision in relation to the question to the Upper Tribunal if they–

(a) consider that the decision should be reviewed; or

(b) have received a written application for the decision to be reviewed from the person to whom the decision related.

(2) The Upper Tribunal may review the decision if–

(a) the decision was erroneous in point of law;

(b) the decision was made in ignorance of, or was based on a mistake as to, some material fact; or

(c) there has been a relevant change in circumstances since the decision was made.

(3) When a person makes the reference to the Upper Tribunal, they must also notify the person to whom the question relates that the reference has been made.

(4) The Upper Tribunal must notify the person who made the reference and the person who to whom the question relates of the outcome of the reference.

(5) If the Upper Tribunal decides to take any action in relation to a decision following a review under this rule without first giving the person who made the reference and the person to whom the question relates an opportunity to make representations, the notice under paragraph (4) must state that either of those persons who did not have an opportunity to make representations may apply for such action to be set aside and for the decision to be reviewed again.

SCHEDULE 1

PROCEDURE AFTER THE NOTICE OF APPEAL IN APPEALS AGAINST DECISIONS OF TRAFFIC COMMISSIONERS

1 This Schedule applies to an appeal against the decision of a traffic commissioner.

2   The only parties to the appeal are the appellant and any person added as a party under rule 9 (substitution and addition of parties).

3   On receipt of a copy of a notice of appeal under rule 23(6)(b), the traffic commissioner must send to the Upper Tribunal a copy (and, on request, further copies) of–
    (a) a written record of the decision appealed against and reasons for the decision;
    (b) all documents produced to the traffic commissioner in connection with the decision;
    (c) if a public inquiry was held, the transcript of the inquiry or, if no such transcript was produced, the traffic commissioner's note of the inquiry; and
    (d) in an appeal under section 50 of the Public Passenger Vehicles Act 1981 or section 37 of the Goods Vehicles (Licensing of Operators) Act 1995, a list of the names and addresses of objectors and representors.

4   On receipt of a list under paragraph 3(d) the Upper Tribunal must send a copy of the notice of appeal–
    (a) where the appellant had applied for, or for the variation of, an operator's licence, to each person who made an objection to the application;
    (b) where the appellant had made an objection to an application for, or (in the case of a goods vehicle operator's licence) for the variation of, an operator's licence, to the person who made the application and to every other person who made an objection to the application; and
    (c) in an appeal under section 37(5) of the Goods Vehicles (Licensing of Operators) Act 1995, each person who made representations under section 12(4) or 19(2) of that Act against the application for, or for the variation of, the operator's licence in question.

5   The appropriate national authority and any person to whom the Upper Tribunal has sent a copy of the notice of appeal under paragraph 4 may apply for a direction under rule 9(2) adding them as a respondent.

6   An application under paragraph 5 must be sent or delivered to the Upper Tribunal so that it is received within 14 days of the date that the Upper Tribunal sent a copy of the notice of appeal to the person making the application.

7   If a person specified in paragraph 8 makes an application in accordance with paragraphs 5 and 6, the Upper Tribunal must give a direction under rule 9(2) adding that person as a respondent.

8   The persons specified for the purposes of paragraph 7 are–
    (a) the appropriate national authority;
    (b) an objector who was sent a copy of the notice of appeal under paragraph 4(a) or (b); and
    (c) a person who made an application and was sent a copy of the notice of appeal under paragraph 4(b).

9   The Upper Tribunal must notify each other party of any application under paragraph 3 and the Upper Tribunal's decision in respect of each such application.

10   Any party may make a request to the Upper Tribunal for copies of specified documents provided by the traffic commissioner under paragraph 3.

11   On receiving a request under paragraph 9 the Upper Tribunal–

(a) must provide the requested copies unless it considers the request unreasonable; and

(b) if it considers the request unreasonable, give details of why it considers the request unreasonable.

First-tier Tribunal and Upper Tribunal (Composition of Tribunal) Order 2008 (SI 2008/2835)

Made 29th October 2008
Coming into force 3rd November 2008

The Lord Chancellor makes the following Order in exercise of the powers conferred by section 145(1) of, and paragraph 15 of Schedule 4 to, the Tribunals, Courts and Enforcement Act 2007.

In accordance with paragraph 15(8) of that Act the Lord Chancellor has consulted the Senior President of Tribunals.

In accordance with section 49(5) of that Act a draft of this instrument was laid before Parliament and approved by a resolution of each House of Parliament.

Citation and commencement

1   This Order may be cited as the First-tier Tribunal and Upper Tribunal (Composition of Tribunal) Order 2008 and comes into force on 3rd November 2008.

Number of members of the First-tier Tribunal

2(1)   The number of members of the tribunal who are to decide any matter that falls to be decided by the First-tier Tribunal must be determined by the Senior President of Tribunals in accordance with paragraph (2).

(2)   The Senior President of Tribunals must have regard to–

    (a) where the matter which falls to be decided by the tribunal fell to a tribunal in a list in Schedule 6 to the Tribunals, Courts and Enforcement Act 2007 before its functions were transferred by order under section 30(1) of that Act, any provision made by or under any enactment for determining the number of members of that tribunal; and

    (b) the need for members of tribunals to have particular expertise, skills or knowledge.

Number of members of the Upper Tribunal

3(1)   The number of members of the tribunal who are to decide any matter that falls to be decided by the Upper Tribunal is one unless determined otherwise under paragraph (2).

(2)   The tribunal may consist of two or three members if the Senior President of Tribunals so determines.

Tribunal consisting of single member

4(1)   Where a matter is to be decided by a single member of a tribunal, it must be decided by a judge of the tribunal unless paragraph (2) applies.

(2)   The matter may be decided by one of the other members of the tribunal if the Senior President of Tribunals so determines.

Tribunal consisting of two or more members

5   The following articles apply where a matter is to be decided by two or more members of a tribunal.

6   The number of members who are to be judges of the tribunal and the number of members who are to be other members of the tribunal must be determined by the Senior President of Tribunals.

7   The Senior President of Tribunals must select one of the members (the "presiding member") to chair the tribunal.

8   If the decision of the tribunal is not unanimous, the decision of the majority is the decision of the tribunal; and the presiding member has a casting vote if the votes are equally divided.

First-tier Tribunal and Upper Tribunal (Chambers) Order 2008 (SI 2008/2684)

Made 13th October 2008
Laid before Parliament 15th October 2008
Coming into force 3rd November 2008

The Lord Chancellor, with the concurrence of the Senior President of Tribunals, makes the following Order in exercise of the power conferred by section 7(1) and (9) of the Tribunals, Courts and Enforcement Act 2007.

Citation and commencement

1   This Order may be cited as the First-tier Tribunal and Upper Tribunal (Chambers) Order 2008 and shall come into force on 3rd November 2008.

First-tier Tribunal Chambers

2   The First-tier Tribunal shall be organised into the following chambers–
(a) the Social Entitlement Chamber;
(b) the War Pensions and Armed Forces Compensation Chamber; . . .
(c) the Health, Education and Social Care Chamber;
(d) the Tax Chamber;
(e) the General Regulatory Chamber;
(f) the Immigration and Asylum Chamber.

Functions of the Social Entitlement Chamber

3   To the Social Entitlement Chamber are assigned all functions relating to appeals–
(a) in cases regarding support for asylum seekers, failed asylum seekers, persons designated under section 130 of the Criminal Justice and Immigration Act 2008, or the dependants of any such persons;
(b) in criminal injuries compensation cases;
(c) regarding entitlement to, payments of, or recovery or recoupment of payments of, social security benefits, child support, vaccine damage payment, health in pregnancy grant, and tax credits, with the exception of–
(ai) appeals under section 11 of the Social Security Contributions (Transfer of Functions, etc) Act 1999 (appeals against decisions of Her Majesty's Revenue and Customs);
(i) appeals in respect of employer penalties or employer information penalties (as defined in section 63(11) and (12) of the Tax Credits Act 2002);
(ii) appeals under regulation 28(3) of the Child Trust Funds Regulations 2004;
(ca) regarding saving gateway accounts with the exception of appeals against requirements to account for an amount under regulations made under section 14 of the Saving Gateway Accounts Act 2009;

(cb) regarding child trust funds with the exception of appeals against requirements to account for an amount under regulations made under section 22(4) Child Trust Funds Act 2004 in relation to section 13 of that Act;

(d) regarding payments in consequence of diffuse mesothelioma;

(e) regarding a certificate or waiver decision in relation to NHS charges;

(f) regarding entitlement to be credited with earnings or contributions;

(g) against a decision as to whether an accident was an industrial accident.

Functions of the War Pensions and Armed Forces Compensation Chamber

4   To the War Pensions and Armed Forces Compensation Chamber are assigned all functions relating to appeals under the War Pensions (Administrative Provisions) Act 1919 and the Pensions Appeal Tribunals Act 1943.

Functions of the Health, Education and Social Care Chamber

5   To the Health Education and Social Care Chamber are assigned all functions relating to–

(a) an appeal against a decision related to children with special educational needs;

(b) a claim of disability discrimination in the education of a child;

(c) an application or an appeal against a decision or determination related to work with children or vulnerable adults;

(d) an appeal against a decision related to registration in respect of the provision of health or social care;

(dd) an application in respect of, or an appeal against a decision related to, the provision of health care or health services;

(e) an appeal against a decision related to registration in respect of social workers and social care workers;

(f) an appeal against a decision related to the provision of childcare;

(g) an appeal against a decision related to an independent school or other independent educational institution;

(h) applications and references by and in respect of patients under the provisions of the Mental Health Act 1983 or paragraph 5(2) of the Schedule to the Repatriation of Prisoners Act 1984.

Functions of the Tax Chamber

5A   To the Tax Chamber are assigned all functions, except those functions assigned to the Social Entitlement Chamber by article 3 or to the Finance and Tax Tax and Chancery Chamber by article 8, relating to–

(a) an appeal, application, reference or other proceeding in respect of a function of the Commissioners for Her Majesty's Revenue and Customs or an officer of Revenue and Customs;

(b) an appeal in respect of the exercise by the Serious Organised Crime Agency of general Revenue functions or Revenue inheritance tax functions (as defined in section 323 of the Proceeds of Crime Act 2002).

Functions of the General Regulatory Chamber

5B   To the General Regulatory Chamber are assigned all functions relating to–

(a) proceedings in respect of the decisions and actions of regulatory bodies which are not assigned to the Health, Education and Social Care Chamber by article 5;

(b) matters referred to the First-tier Tribunal under Schedule 1D to the Charities Act 1993; and

(c) the determination of remuneration for carrying mail-bags in a ship or aircraft.

Functions of the Immigration and Asylum Chamber of the First-tier Tribunal

5C   To the Immigration and Asylum Chamber of the First-tier Tribunal are assigned all functions relating to immigration and asylum matters, except for matters assigned to–

(a) the Social Entitlement Chamber by article 3(a); and

(b) the General Regulatory Chamber by article 5B(a).

Upper Tribunal Chambers

6   The Upper Tribunal shall be organised into the following chambers–

(a) the Administrative Appeals Chamber;

(b) the Tax and Chancery Chamber;

(c) the Lands Chamber;

(d) the Immigration and Asylum Chamber of the Upper Tribunal.

Functions of the Administrative Appeals Chamber

7   To the Administrative Appeals Chamber are assigned all functions relating to–

(a) an appeal–

(i) against a decision made by the First-tier Tribunal, except an appeal assigned to the Tax and Chancery Chamber by article 8(a) or the Immigration and Asylum Chamber of the Upper Tribunal by article 9A(a);

(ii) under section 5 of the Pensions Appeal Tribunals Act 1943 (assessment decision) against a decision of the Pensions Appeal Tribunal in Northern Ireland established under paragraph 1(2) of Schedule 1 to the Pensions Appeal Tribunals Act 1943;

(iii) against a decision of the Pensions Appeal Tribunal in Scotland established under paragraph 1(2) of Schedule 1 to the Pensions Appeal Tribunals Act 1943;

(iv) against a decision of the Mental Health Review Tribunal for Wales established under section 65 of the Mental Health Act 1983c;

(v) against a decision of the Special Educational Needs Tribunal for Wales;

(vi) under section 4 of the Safeguarding Vulnerable Groups Act 2006 (appeals);

(vii)   against a decision of the Information Commissioner transferred to the Upper Tribunal from the First-tier Tribunal under Tribunal Procedure Rules;

(viii) against a decision of a traffic commissioner;

(b) an application, except an application assigned to the Tax and Chancery Chamber by article 8(e), for the Upper Tribunal–
  (i) to grant the relief mentioned in section 15(1) of the Tribunal, Courts and Enforcement Act 2007 (Upper Tribunal's "judicial review" jurisdiction);
  (ii) to exercise the powers of review under section 21(2) of that Act (Upper Tribunal's "judicial review" jurisdiction: Scotland);
(c) a matter referred to the Upper Tribunal by the First-tier Tribunal under section 9(5)(b) of the Tribunals, Courts and Enforcement Act 2007, except where the reference is assigned to the Tax and Chancery Chamber by article 8(d) or the Immigration and Asylum Chamber of the Upper Tribunal by article 9A(b);
(d) a determination or decision under section 4 of the Forfeiture Act 1982.

Functions of the Tax and Chancery Chamber

8(1)   To the Tax and Chancery Chamber are assigned all functions relating to–
  (a) an appeal against a decision of the First-tier Tribunal made–
    (i) in the Tax Chamber; or
    (ii) in a charities case;
  (aa)   a reference or appeal in respect of–
    (i) a decision of the Financial Services Authority;
    (ii) a decision of the Bank of England; or
    (iii) a decision of a person relating to the assessment of any compensation or consideration under the Banking (Special Provisions) Act 2008;
  (ab)   a reference in respect of a decision of the Pensions Regulator;
  (b) an application under paragraph 50(1)(d) of Schedule 36 to the Finance Act 2008;
  (c) proceedings transferred to the Upper Tribunal under Tribunal Procedure Rules–
    (i) from the Tax Chamber of the First-tier Tribunal; or
    (ii) from the First-tier Tribunal in a charities case;
  (d) a matter referred to the Upper Tribunal under section 9(5)(b) of the Tribunals, Courts and Enforcement Act 2007–
    (i) by the Tax Chamber of the First-tier Tribunal; or
    (ii) by the First-tier Tribunal in a charities case;
  (e) an application for the Upper Tribunal to grant the relief mentioned in section 15(1) of the Tribunals, Courts and Enforcement Act 2007 (Upper Tribunal's "judicial review" jurisdiction), or to exercise the powers of review under section 21(2) of that Act (Upper Tribunal's "judicial review" jurisdiction: Scotland), which relates to–
    (i) a decision of the First-tier Tribunal mentioned in paragraph (a)(i) or (ii);
    (ii) a function of the Commissioners for Her Majesty's Revenue and Customs or an officer of Revenue and Customs, with the exception of any function in respect of which an appeal would be allocated to the Social Entitlement Chamber by article 3;

(iii) the exercise by the Serious Organised Crime Agency of general Revenue functions or Revenue inheritance tax functions (as defined in section 323 of the Proceeds of Crime Act 2002), with the exception of any function in relation to which an appeal would be allocated to the Social Entitlement Chamber by article 3;

(iv) a function of the Charity Commission, or one of the bodies mentioned in paragraph (aa) or (ab).

(2) In this article "a charities case" means an appeal or application in respect of a decision, order or direction of the Charity Commission, or a reference under Schedule 1D of the Charities Act 1993.

Functions of the Lands Chamber

9   To the Lands Chamber are assigned–

(a) all functions relating to–

(i) compensation and other remedies for measures taken which affect the ownership, value, enjoyment or use of land or water, or of rights over or property on land or water;

(ii) appeals from decisions of leasehold valuation tribunals, residential property tribunals and valuation tribunals;

(iii) appeals on questions of the value of land or interests in land arising in tax proceedings; and

(iv) proceedings in respect of restrictive covenants, blight notices or the obstruction of light;

(b) the Upper Tribunal's function as arbitrator under section 1(5) of the Lands Tribunal Act 1949; and

(c) any other functions transferred to the Upper Tribunal by the Transfer of Tribunal Functions (Lands Tribunal and Miscellaneous Amendments) Order 2009.

Functions of the Immigration and Asylum Chamber of the Upper Tribunal

9A   To the Immigration and Asylum Chamber of the Upper Tribunal are assigned all functions relating to–

(a) an appeal against a decision of the First-tier Tribunal made in the Immigration and Asylum Chamber of the First-tier Tribunal; and

(b) a matter referred to the Upper Tribunal under section 9(5)(b) of the Tribunals, Courts and Enforcement Act 2007 by the Immigration and Asylum Chamber of the First-tier Tribunal.

Resolution of doubt or dispute as to chamber

10   If there is any doubt or dispute as to the chamber in which a particular matter is to be dealt with, the Senior President of Tribunals may allocate that matter to the chamber which appears to the Senior President of Tribunals to be most appropriate.

Re-allocation of a case to another chamber

11(1)   Subject to paragraph (2), the Chamber President of the chamber to which a case has been assigned or allocated by or under this Order may allocate that case to another chamber within the same tribunal, by giving a direction to that effect.

(2)   A Chamber President may give a direction under paragraph (1) only if the Chamber President of the chamber to which the case is to be allocated has first consented to the giving of the direction.

(3)   A direction under paragraph (1) may be given at any point in the proceedings.

Qualifications for Appointment of Members to the First-tier Tribunal and Upper Tribunal Order 2008 (SI 2008/2692)

Made 15th October 2008
Laid before Parliament 15th October 2008
Coming into force 3rd November 2008

The Lord Chancellor, with the concurrence of the Senior President of Tribunals, makes the following Order in exercise of the powers conferred by paragraph 2(2) of Schedule 2 and paragraph 2(2) of Schedule 3 to the Tribunals, Courts and Enforcement Act 2007.

1(1)   This Order may be cited as the Qualifications for Appointment of Members to the First-tier Tribunal and Upper Tribunal Order 2008 and shall come into force on 3rd November 2008.

(2)   In this Order "registered medical practitioner" means a fully registered person within the meaning of the Medical Act 1983 whether or not they hold a licence to practise under that Act.

2(1)   A person is eligible for appointment as a member of the First-tier Tribunal or the Upper Tribunal who is not a judge of those tribunals if paragraph (2), (3) or (4) applies.

(2)   This paragraph applies to a person who is–
    (a) a registered medical practitioner;
    (b) a registered nurse;
    (c) a registered dentist;
    (ca) a registered optometrist;
    (d) a clinical psychologist;
    (e) an educational psychologist;
    (f) a pharmacologist;
    (g) a veterinary surgeon or a veterinary practitioner registered under the Veterinary Surgeons Act 1966;
    (h) a Member or Fellow of the Royal Institution of Chartered Surveyors; or
    (i) an accountant who is a member of–
        (i) the Institute of Chartered Accountants in England and Wales;
        (ii) the Institute of Chartered Accountants in Scotland;
        (iii) the Institute of Chartered Accountants in Ireland;
        (iv) the Institute of Certified Public Accountants in Ireland;
        (v) the Association of Chartered Certified Accountants;
        (vi) the Chartered Institute of Management Accountants; or
        (vii)   the Chartered Institute of Public Finance and Accountancy.

(3)   This paragraph applies to a person who is experienced in dealing with the physical or mental needs of disabled persons because they–
    (a) work with disabled persons in a professional or voluntary capacity; or
    (b) are themselves disabled.

(3A) A person is not eligible for appointment under paragraph (3) if they are a registered medical practitioner.

(4) This paragraph applies to a person who has substantial experience–

 (a) of service in Her Majesty's naval, military, or air forces;

 (b) of educational, child care, health, or social care matters;

 (c) of dealing with victims of violent crime;

 (d) in transport operations and its law and practice;

 (e) in the regulatory field;

 (f) in consumer affairs;

 (g) in an industry, trade or business sector and the matters that are likely to arise as issues in the course of disputes with regulators of such industries, trades or businesses;

 (h) in tax matters and related tax procedures;

 (i) in a business, trade, charity or not-for-profit organisation;

 (j) in immigration services or the law and procedure relating to immigration;

 (k) of data protection;

 (l) of freedom of information (including environmental information) rights;

 (m) of service as a Member or Senior Officer of a local authority in England.

Transfer of Tribunal Functions Order 2010
(SI 2010/22)

Made 6th January 2010
Coming into force in accordance with article 1

The Lord Chancellor makes the following Order in exercise of the powers conferred by sections 30(1) and (4), 31(1), (2) and (9) and 38 of, and paragraph 30 of Schedule 5 to, the Tribunals, Courts and Enforcement Act 2007.

The Welsh Ministers have consented to the making of this Order in so far as their consent is required by section 30(8) of that Act.

A draft of this Order was laid before Parliament and approved by a resolution of each House of Parliament in accordance with section 49(5) of that Act.

Citation, commencement and extent

1(1)   This Order may be cited as the Transfer of Tribunal Functions Order 2010 and, subject to paragraph (2), comes into force on 18th January 2010.

(2)   The following provisions of this Order come into force on 6th April 2010–
    (a) paragraph (5);
    (b) article 2(2), (3)(b) and (4);
    (c) article 3 in respect of the Financial Services and Markets Tribunal;
    (d) Schedule 1 in respect of the Financial Services and Markets Tribunal and the Pensions Regulator Tribunal;
    (e) in Schedule 2, paragraphs 3(c)(i), 4(c), 5 to 9, 12 to 14, 15(c), 17(b), 18(b), 20 to 23, 43 to 49, 74 to 89, 92(h) to (k) and 141 to 151;
    (f) in Schedule 3, paragraphs 16 to 38, 90 to 94, 140 to 142, 143(d), 144 to 146, 148 to 158, 176 to 189 and 191 to 200; and
    (g) Part 2 of Schedule 4.

(3)   Subject as follows, this Order extends to England and Wales, Scotland and Northern Ireland.

(4)   Except as provided by paragraph (5), an amendment, repeal or revocation of any enactment by any provision of Schedule 2, 3 or 4 extends to the part or parts of the United Kingdom to which the enactment extends.

(5)   The amendments, repeals and revocations made by the following provisions do not extend to Northern Ireland–
    (a) in Schedule 2, paragraphs 5(b), 9(b), 77 to 79, 83 to 85, 88, 142(b) and 143(b);
    (b) in Schedule 3, paragraphs 90 to 94;
    (c) in Part 2 of Schedule 4, the entries relating to–
        (i) the Tribunals, Courts and Enforcement Act 2007 in so far as it relates to paragraph 40 of Schedule 10;
        (ii) the Pensions Act 2008;

(iii) the Pensions Regulator Tribunal Rules 2005; and

(iv) the Lord Chancellor (Transfer of Functions and Supplementary Provisions) (No 2) Order 2006.

Transfer of functions of certain tribunals

2(1)   The functions of the following tribunals are transferred to the First-tier Tribunal–

(a) tribunals drawn from the Adjudication Panel for England;

(b) the Claims Management Services Tribunal;

(c) the Gambling Appeals Tribunal;

(d) the Immigration Services Tribunal; and

(e) the Family Health Services Appeal Authority.

(2)   The functions of the Financial Services and Markets Tribunal are transferred to the Upper Tribunal.

(3)   The functions of the following tribunals are transferred to the First-tier Tribunal and the Upper Tribunal with the question as to which one of them is to exercise the functions in a particular case being determined by, or under, Tribunal Procedure Rules–

(a) the Information Tribunal; and

(b) subject to paragraph (4), the Pensions Regulator Tribunal.

(4)   The functions of the Pensions Regulator Tribunal exercisable in relation to Northern Ireland are not transferred.

Abolition of tribunals

3   The tribunals mentioned in article 2(1), (2) and (3)(a) are abolished.

Persons becoming judges and other members of the First-tier Tribunal and the Upper Tribunal

4   A person who, immediately before this Order comes into force, holds an office listed in a part of Schedule 1, is to hold the office or offices set out in the corresponding entry in the table below.

Table not reproduced

Consequential, transitional and saving provisions

5(1)   Schedule 2 contains amendments to primary legislation as a consequence of the transfers effected by this Order.

(2)   Schedule 3 contains amendments to secondary legislation as a consequence of the transfers effected by this Order.

(3)   Schedule 4 contains repeals and revocations as a consequence of the amendments in Schedules 2 and 3.

(4)   Schedule 5 contains transitional and saving provisions.

SCHEDULE 1

Persons Becoming Judges and Members of the First-tier Tribunal and Upper Tribunal

Not reproduced

SCHEDULE 2

Consequential Amendments to Primary Legislation

Not reproduced

SCHEDULE 3

Consequential Amendments to Secondary Legislation

Not reproduced

SCHEDULE 4

Repeals and Revocations

Not reproduced

SCHEDULE 5

Transitional and Saving Provisions

Article 5(4)

Interpretation of Schedule 5

1   In this Schedule–

"old tribunal" means a tribunal, the functions of which are transferred by article 2, but does not include the Pensions Regulator Tribunal in respect of its functions exercisable in Northern Ireland;

"new tribunal" means–

(a) the Upper Tribunal, in respect of–

(i) the functions of the Financial Services and Markets Tribunal and the Pensions Regulator Tribunal;

(ii) the functions of the Information Tribunal of deciding appeals under section 28 of the Data Protection Act 1998 or section 60 of the Freedom of Information Act 2000 (including that section as applied and modified by regulation 18 of the Environmental Information Regulations 2004) (appeals in relation to national security certificates);

(b) the First-tier Tribunal, in respect of–

(i) the tribunal functions mentioned in article 2(1);

(ii) the functions of the Information Tribunal other than those mentioned in paragraph (a)(ii);

"transfer date" means the date on which the functions of an old tribunal are transferred to a new tribunal by article 2.

Transitional and saving provisions

2   Any proceedings before an old tribunal which are pending immediately before the transfer date shall continue on and after the transfer date as proceedings before the new tribunal.

3(1)   The following sub-paragraphs apply where proceedings are continued in a new tribunal by virtue of paragraph 2.

(2)   Where a hearing began before the transfer date but was not completed by that date, the new tribunal must be comprised for the continuation of that hearing of the person or persons who began it.

(3)   The new tribunal may give any direction to ensure that proceedings are dealt with fairly and, in particular, may–

    (a) apply any provision in procedural rules which applied to the proceedings before the transfer date; or

    (b) disapply provisions of Tribunal Procedure Rules.

(4)   In sub-paragraph (3) "procedural rules" means provision (whether called rules or not) regulating practice or procedure before a tribunal.

(5)   Any direction or order given or made in proceedings which is in force immediately before the transfer date remains in force on and after that date as if it were a direction or order of the new tribunal.

(6)   A time period which has started to run before the transfer date and which has not expired shall continue to apply.

(7)   An order for costs may only be made if, and to the extent that, an order for costs could have been made by the old tribunal before the transfer date.4Paragraph 5 applies where–

    (a) an appeal lies to a court from any decision made by an old tribunal before the transfer date;

    (b) that right of appeal has not been exercised; and

    (c) the time to exercise that right of appeal has not expired prior to the transfer date.

5   In the circumstances set out at paragraph 4, such of the following provisions as is appropriate shall apply as if the decision were a decision made on or after the transfer date by the new tribunal–

    (a) section 11 of the Tribunals, Courts and Enforcement Act 2007 (right to appeal to Upper Tribunal);

    (b) section 13 of the Tribunals, Courts and Enforcement Act 2007 (right to appeal to Court of Appeal);

(c) section 78(9A) to (9D) or section 78B(4) to (7) of the Local Government Act 2000 (as inserted or amended by Schedule 2 to this Order).

6   Any case to be remitted by a court on or after the transfer date and which, if it had been remitted before the transfer date, would have been remitted to an old tribunal, shall be remitted to the new tribunal.

7   Staff appointed to an old tribunal before the transfer date are to be treated on and after that date, for the purpose of any enactment, as if they had been appointed by the Lord Chancellor under section 40(1) of the Tribunals, Courts and Enforcement Act 2007 (tribunal staff and services).

8A   A decision made by an old tribunal before the transfer date is to be treated on or after the transfer date as a decision of the new tribunal.

Appeals from the Upper Tribunal
to the Court of Appeal Order 2008
(2008/2834)

Made 29th October 2008
Coming into force in accordance with article 1

The Lord Chancellor makes the following Order in exercise of the power conferred by section 13(6) of the Tribunals, Courts and Enforcement Act 2007.

A draft of this Order was laid before Parliament and approved by a resolution of each House of Parliament in accordance with section 49(5) of that Act.

1   This Order may be cited as the Appeals from the Upper Tribunal to the Court of Appeal Order 2008 and shall come into force on 3rd November 2008.

2   Permission to appeal to the Court of Appeal in England and Wales or leave to appeal to the Court of Appeal in Northern Ireland shall not be granted unless the Upper Tribunal or, where the Upper Tribunal refuses permission, the relevant appellate court, considers that–

    (a) the proposed appeal would raise some important point of principle or practice; or

    (b) there is some other compelling reason for the relevant appellate court to hear the appeal.

Practice Note

Protection of Confidential Information in Information Rights Appeals Before the First-tier Tribunal in the General Regulatory Tribunal on Or After 18 January 2010

1. This Practice Note sets out the arrangements for protecting confidential information in First-tier Tribunal (Information Rights) appeals and related matters. In this Practice Note references to Rules are references to the Tribunal Procedure (First-tier Tribunal) (General Regulatory Chamber) Rules 2009 as amended by the Tribunal Procedure (Amendment No 3) Rules 2010 (the Rules). Introduction

2. As with all courts and tribunals, it is of course essential that information which is relevant to proceedings is, as far as is possible, available to all parties to a case.

3. However, the nature of appeals to the First-tier Tribunal (Information Rights) under the Freedom of Information Act 2000 (FOIA) is such that the Tribunal will often require to see information which must be kept confidential from one or more of the other parties to the appeal. Amongst other things, this can mean that during the hearing the party requesting the information is asked to leave the room

4. For instance, there will be cases where a person who made a request for information under section 1(1) FOIA is a party to an appeal which examines the application of exemptions to the obligation to supply information. In many cases the Tribunal will need to see the information which has been withheld in order to reach its decision. However, in cases where disclosure has been refused, it would in most cases undermine the very object of the exemption if the information in question were to be disclosed, during the Tribunal proceedings, to the person who made the request. The Tribunal will need to ensure that that information is kept confidential. This is in accordance with the overriding objective under Rule 2 of dealing with cases fairly and justly.

5. Considerations of confidentiality can often also apply to other information which the Tribunal requires to see, such as written and oral evidence and submissions. For example, in considering whether exemptions have been applied correctly, the Tribunal may require evidence on why disclosure would result in prejudice. Such evidence will often also reveal something of the nature of the requested information in a way which would undermine the objectives of the exemption. Equally, it may reveal other information which the Tribunal requires in order to determine the case, but which would be exempt under FOIA, for example, commercially sensitive information that is revealed in documents recording a public authority s consultation with third parties under the Section 45 Code of Practice.

6. The legal basis for the Tribunal dealing with confidential information in proceedings was considered in the Ruling in Sugar v Information Commissioner and the BBC dated 12th May 2006. Although this Ruling was applied under the Information Tribunal (Enforcement Appeals) Rules 2005 as amended it is considered that the legal position is the same under the Rules.

7. This Practice Note covers:

      A. Confidentiality and Redaction
      B. Joinder
      C. Witnesses
      D. Documents
      E. Decisions

A. Confidentiality and Redaction

8.   Where a party to proceedings claims that an exemption under Part II of FOIA has been applied, or would apply to information (such as documentary or oral evidence and submissions) and the Tribunal requires to see the information in order to determine the appeal, the Judge should ensure action is taken to maintain appropriate confidentiality. This applies in particular when the Tribunal is making directions under Rule 5 as to the disclosure of documents, statements of facts and evidence and skeleton arguments.

9.   For example, on exchange between the parties of lists of relevant documents, the Judge should consider ensuring that directions provide, as necessary, for some entries to be kept confidential from one or more parties to the proceedings. This may require parties to prepare two versions of such documents one full version for the Tribunal, and one version to be exchanged with the other parties, which does not include information which needs to be kept confidential. See section D below.

10. Similar considerations apply to evidence and submissions which are prepared and put before the Tribunal. In order for the Tribunal to ensure that it has all the information that it requires, and that the parties provide it with as full oral evidence and submissions as possible, it may be necessary for some information to be kept confidential from one or more of the parties, or redacted if appropriate. See section C below.

11. For example, as the Notice of Appeal and replies to the Notice are required to be sent to all parties to the case, the Judge should consider whether the Tribunal requires further preliminary details of a party s case to be provided on a confidential basis.

12. Factors that should be considered when making directions, to ensure appropriate confidentiality include: The primary objective is to ensure that the Tribunal has all the information that it requires in order to make a just and fair decision in a case. The Judge will want to take necessary steps to ensure that the parties provide it with relevant documents and evidence, and that the parties are able to make full and frank submissions. Where a party claims that documents or evidence need to be kept confidential from one or more of the other parties to the case because they claim the documents or evidence are exempt under FOIA, or would be if a request were received, the Tribunal should consider ensuring appropriate confidentiality. Whether the hearing or part of the hearing should be held in private or a party excluded from part of the hearing as provided for under Rule 35. In relation to the latter the Tribunal must always consider the potential detrimental effect that an order to exclude may have on a party who may be denied the opportunities he would otherwise have in accordance with the overriding objective in particular as identified under Rule 2(2)(c) (ensuring, so far as practicable, that the parties are able to participate fully in the proceedings).

13. Parties should understand that at times the Judge may have to make directions during the hearing to hold part of it in private. This means that those who cannot see what is claimed to be confidential information, or hear evidence presented that needs to refer directly to its contents will be asked to leave the room for the minimum length of time necessary to examine such evidence. For the avoidance of doubt those excluded will be those from whom the information needs to be kept confidential, which normally will mean everyone other than those parties from whom the documents are requested and any related parties and those representing the Information Commissioner.

B. Joinder

14. It is essential that the Tribunal has before it all the information that it requires in order to take a decision on a case. In some cases, the Tribunal will require information from persons who are not automatically parties to an appeal.

15. For example, when the Information Commissioner issues a Decision Notice under section 50 FOIA he is seeking to resolve a complaint concerning a request for information that was made to a public authority. When a Decision Notice is appealed to the Tribunal, one of the parties to the original complaint (that is, the complainant or the public authority) will not automatically be a party to the appeal the parties will be the person bringing the appeal, and the Information Commissioner.

16. In particular where the public authority is not a party to the appeal, the Tribunal will very often require information from the public authority in order to determine a case. For example, if there is a dispute of fact over whether or not the public authority held information for the purposes of section 1(1) FOIA, the Tribunal may require evidence from the public authority on this point. In some cases, the Tribunal may need evidence from a public authority who is not the subject of the Information Commissioner s decision. For example, cases involving the National Archives and papers over 30 years old usually require input from the public authority that transferred files to the National Archives. Such considerations often apply if an appeal will potentially determine a person s liability under FOIA but that person is not an existing or original party. Third parties who have provided information to a public authority may also have an interest in an appeal.

17. While the requestor has an interest in the appeal, he or she may not be well placed to assist the Tribunal in its determination of the case.

18. The most straightforward options in this situation are for the Tribunal to invite that party to apply to be joined or for the Tribunal to order that the other person be joined as a party to the appeal. This will enable the Tribunal to give that person an opportunity to be heard or to ensure that the person provides it with all the information, evidence and submissions that it requires to determine the case. The Tribunal also has the power to receive evidence from people who are not parties. It is sometimes appropriate to receive letters from the requestor but not to join him/her as a party. Where the requestor is not a party, the arrangements to ensure confidentiality of documents are less complex and the hearing can be run more efficiently.

19. When making preliminary directions in a case, the Judge should consider whether it is advisable to invite a person to apply to be joined or to order that any person who has an interest in the proceedings, or can provide the Tribunal with information to enable it to determine the case, should be joined to the proceedings under Rule 9. This should be kept under review as the case proceeds.

20. Factors that a Judge might consider when deciding whether to invite to apply or make an order under Rule 9: The need to ensure that the Tribunal has before it all the information that it requires in order to determine the case and whether it can get that information without joining a party; Where it appears that an appeal may determine the rights or liabilities of a person who is not a party to an appeal, the desirability of that person having the opportunity to make representations; Any evidence or expertise which a person may be able to provide to the Tribunal, which would assist in the determination of the appeal; Whether the issues at stake in the appeal may be of significance beyond the facts of the particular case; Any representations made by a person who applies to be joined under Rule 9(3).

C. Witnesses

21. The parties can call witnesses to give evidence before the Tribunal, but these witnesses need to be relevant to the case see ruling in Keston Ramblers Association v The Information Commissioner (1) and London Borough of Bromley (2) dated 7th June 2006. The Tribunal usually requires such evidence to be set out in written witness statements which are served on the other parties and filed with the Tribunal before the hearing in accordance with any directions. Where the statement deals with confidential information, two versions of the statement may need to be prepared.

22. In the event that witness statements are to be filed, unless there is good reason, they should comply with the following requirements. Witness statements will not be rejected on the ground that they are not in a satisfactory form, but it is helpful for the Tribunal if the following requirements are adhered to:

    a. The witness statement should be headed with the title of the proceedings for example: Case Number EA 200X/XXXX A.B. Appellant Information Commissioner Respondent [name of additional parties of joined party, if any] [Joined Party/Additional Party]

    b. At the top right hand corner of the first page there should be clearly written:
        (i) the party on whose behalf the statement has been made, for example appellant or the name of the party, for example Mrs Smith ,
        (ii) if more than one statement has been filed, the number of the statement in relation to that witness, for example 2nd statement .

    c. The witness statement must, if possible, be in the intended witness's own words, the statement should be written in the first person and should also state:
        (i) the full name of the witness,

    (ii) their place of residence or, if they are making the statement in a professional, business or other occupational capacity, the address at which they work, the position they hold and the name of their firm or employer,

    (iii) their occupation or, they have none, their description, and

    (iv) the fact that they are a party to the proceedings or are employed by a party to the proceedings, if that is the case.

d. Where a witness refers to an exhibit or exhibits, he/she should state "I refer to the (description of exhibit) marked "..." or where there is a reference to another document that should include the page number in any bundle.

e. A witness statement should:

    (i) be produced in A4 format,

    (ii) be fully legible,

    (iii) have the pages numbered consecutively at the bottom of the page in the middle,

    (iv) be divided into numbered paragraphs.

f. A witness statement is the equivalent of the oral evidence which that witness would, if called, give in evidence. The Tribunal may or may not require the witness at any hearing to give evidence on oath but any witness statement must contain a statement from the witness confirming that he or she believes the contents of the statement to be true. Something like: "I believe that the facts stated in this witness statement are true" or Insofar as the matters to which I refer are within my own knowledge they are true; insofar as they are not within my own knowledge they are true to the best of my knowledge, information and belief.

g. Where the witness refers to confidential information then either two versions of the statement should be prepared, one with the confidential information and one without it, or there should be a separate closed statement containing only the confidential material. The open statement or version should be served on all parties and the closed statement or version only on those parties who are entitled to see the confidential information at this stage in the proceedings. Parties must be careful to ensure that a separate closed statement does not contain additional non-confidential evidence which the other party is entitled to see. h. Any alteration to a witness statement must be initialled by the person making the statement. The completed statement must be signed by the witness. i. Witness statements should be filed electronically with the Tribunal in MS Word format if possible as well as being provided as part of the hard copy bundle of documents dealt with in section D. below.

23. Depending on the directions, witnesses may be called to appear before the Tribunal at an oral hearing. Usually the witness will not be required to repeat the evidence in their witness statement but will be subject to questioning by the other parties and the Tribunal. The witness may be required to swear an oath to tell the truth on a holy book of the witness choosing or affirm before giving evidence.

24. After a hearing, or where the case is being decided on the papers, it may in rare cases be necessary for the Tribunal to seek further evidence from the parties. The Tribunal may then seek more information through an additional written witness statement.

D. Documents

25. Where the Tribunal has ordered that a bundle is filed for any hearing or determination on the papers under Rule 13, unless there is good reason, the bundle should include a copy of:
    (a) the Notice of Appeal,
    (b) the Reply or Replies, including those put in by Additional Parties,
    (c) the disputed [Decision] Notice,
    (d) the document requesting the information, the public authority s response (i.e. s. 17 letter) and any document from the applicant requesting an internal review of the decision and the public authority s response to that request,
    (e) copies of all orders and directions made by the Tribunal
    (f) any other necessary and relevant documents,
    (g) all witness statements to be relied on,
    (h) an agreed statement of facts, if applicable, and a chronology of events.

26. Parties should always aim to keep the bundle as relevant and compact as possible in order to minimise the size of bundles where possible.

27. The documents should be in the bundle in the sequence set out in paragraph 25 above and within (6) above any correspondence should be filed chronologically. It is not necessary or desirable for there to be more than one copy of any document in the bundle. For example, there is no need to include a copy of the Decision Notice separately if it has been annexed to the Notice of Appeal. However, any document which refers to another document (which if included in the bundle would otherwise be a duplicate) must be marked with a reference to where the copy of the document may be found within the bundle (for example see page XX of the bundle). The bundle should be paginated (continuously) throughout at the bottom right hand corner of the page, or else tabbed dividers should be used, with each section paginated. There should be an index with a description of each document and the page number. Dividers should be used for the different sections, particularly if there is more than one lever arch file of documents.

28. The bundle should normally be contained in a ring binder or lever arch file. Where more than one bundle is supplied, they should be clearly distinguishable, for example, by different colours, letters or numbers. If there are numerous bundles, a core bundle should be prepared containing the core documents essential to the proceedings, with references to the supplementary documents in the other bundles.

29. If a document to be included in the bundle is illegible, a typed copy should be included in the bundle next to it, suitably cross-referenced.

30. Any documents (such as the requested information that is the subject of the appeal) that have been ordered to be disclosed to the Tribunal but not to one or more of the parties (see

section A Confidentiality and Redaction) must be included in a separate bundle. This bundle should also contain any closed witness statement(s) or skeleton arguments which concern any confidential information (see section C. Witnesses). The document(s), witness statement(s), skeletons and bundle must be clearly marked as not to be disclosed to [name of relevant party] or to the public . This information should not be disclosed to any person except with the consent of the party who provided the information.

31. The Tribunal may wish to direct that the parties agree the final index to the bundle of documents after any witness statements have been submitted. Once written evidence has been submitted, the parties and the Tribunal are better placed to assess whether further documents are necessary to determine the issues on appeal.

E. Decisions

32. At the end of the hearing the Tribunal will give its decision or retire to consider its decision which will be given later, usually within 3 weeks of the hearing. The Tribunal will also provide any material findings of fact and reasons for the decision. The decision with reasons will be signed by the Judge and then sent to the parties and very soon afterwards will be published on the Tribunal s web site. Under Rule 38(2) the Tribunal must have regard to the desirability of safeguarding the privacy of data subjects, commercially sensitive information and any exempt information. As a result the decision may be part open and part closed. The closed part of a decision is usually contained in a confidential annex. The Tribunal should refer to the existence of a closed decision in its open decision, so that all parties are aware of the existence of a closed decision.

33. To help ensure that no confidential information is released through the Tribunal s decision, it is good practice to send a draft of the decision to the originator of the confidential information, which will usually be the public authority and the Information Commissioner if he has already had sight of the information. It will usually be sent to solicitors, lay clients and their advisors under an embargo1 so that that they have the opportunity to indicate if any confidential information is contained in the decision and at the same time ask them to check for any clerical mistakes or accidental slips or omissions. Usually only a short period of 3 to 5 days is given for the exercise. After having given those parties the opportunity to indicate whether any confidential information is contained in the open part of the decision, the Tribunal will often show the open part of the decision to the other parties for them to check for any clerical mistakes or accidental slips or omissions. Recipients must ensure that neither the draft decision nor its substance is disclosed more widely or used in the public domain before it is finalised and them promulgated (signed by the Judge and published).

34. An example of the wording of an embargoed decision is as follows: We enclose the draft decision in the above named appeal, embargoed in order to give counsel, solicitors, lay clients and their advisors only, the opportunity to indicate if any parts of the decision need to be part of a confidential annex and to point out to the Tribunal any clerical mistakes or other accidental slips or omissions by 12 noon on 27th April 2010. The draft decision must

under no circumstances be shown or the contents disclosed to others not covered by the embargo until promulgated. No extensions of time will be permitted.

35. In relation to the closed part of a decision if the public authority, which has provided the confidential information, desires to provide the closed part of 1 The CPR (see PD 40(e)) permits the draft decision to be shown to lay clients as well as solicitors. Lay clients are often best placed to check that the decision does not contain confidential information the person who gave oral evidence can often tell better than the solicitor whether a particular fact was given in open or closed session. the decision to a 3rd party, such as another public authority who was the source of the information, then the Tribunal is unlikely to object to such disclosure.

1 February 2010

General Regulatory Chamber First-tier Tribunal GRC Guidance Note 2 Permission to Appeal on or after 18 January 2010

1. The Tribunal Procedure (First-tier Tribunal) (General Regulatory Chamber) Rules 2009 as amended by the Tribunal Procedure (Amendment No 3) Rules 2010 (the Rules) provide for the correcting, setting aside, reviewing and appealing of First-tier Tribunal (FTT) decisions. When considering what should happen after a decision has been handed down the judge should bear in mind all of these various powers.

2. GRC jurisdictions will use a similar format for applications for permission to appeal to the Upper Tribunal (UT) with accompanying notes or their documentation must be approved by the President of the GRC. An example of the format and notes are contained in the annex to this Guidance Note.

3. Under paragraph 13 of the Senior President of Tribunals Practice Statement on the Composition of Tribunals dated 21st August 2009 (PS) where the Tribunal has given a decision that disposes of proceedings (the substantive decision), any matter decided under, or in accordance with, rule 5(3)(l) or Part 4 of the Tribunal Procedure (First-tier Tribunal) (General Regulatory Chamber) 2009 Rules as amended or section 9 of the Tribunals, Courts and Enforcement Act 2007 must be decided by one judge, unless the Chamber President considers it appropriate that it is decided either by:-

   a. the same members of the Tribunal as gave the substantive decision; or

   b. a Tribunal, constituted in accordance with paragraphs 4 to 12 [of the PS] comprised of different members of the Tribunal to that which gave the substantive decision.

4. In order for the Chamber President to consider whether it is appropriate for one judge to consider such an application under paragraph 13 of the PS all applications after the disposal of a case must be sent to the Principal Judge (PJ) of the jurisdiction in question. The PJ should then consider whether the matter should be referred to the Chamber President to exercise any of his powers under paragraph 13 a. and b. If there is no reason to think that it should be referred to the Chamber President then the PJ should decide whether an application should be dealt with by the judge who presided or the panel who heard the case, or some other judge including the PJ or new panel.

5. In order for the Chamber President to be aware of applications for permission which are granted or refused PJs are requested to notify the Chamber President of decisions to give or refuse permission to appeal to the UT by emailing him a copy of the decision together with a copy of the application for permission to appeal within 7 days of the decision at john.angel@judiciary.gsi.gov.uk.

John Angel Acting President General Regulatory Chamber

9 February 2010

Joint Office Note No. 2
General Regulatory Chamber of the First-tier Tribunal
Administrative Appeals Chamber of the Upper Tribunal
Discretionary Transfers of Information Rights Appeals on or after 18 January 2010

1.   Rules 19(1), (2) and (3) of the Tribunal Procedure (First-tier Tribunal) (General Regulatory Chamber) 2009 apply to an appeal under the Data Protection Act 1998 (DPA) or the Freedom of Information Act 2000 (FOIA), including DPA and FOIA as applied and modified by the Privacy and Electronic Communications Regulations 2003 and the Environmental Information Regulations 2004. They enable some or all of the questions arising in such appeals (IR Appeals) to be dealt with in the Upper Tribunal (UT) rather than the First-tier Tribunal (FTT).

2.   Rule 19(2) provides that the FTT may refer a case or preliminary issue to the President of the General Regulatory Chamber (GRC) with a request that the case or preliminary issue be considered for transfer to the UT. Under Rule 19(3) where such a request has been made the President of the GRC may, with the concurrence of the President of the appropriate chamber of the UT, direct that the case or issue be transferred to and determined by the UT. In IR Appeals the appropriate chamber of the UT will be the Administrative Appeals Chamber (AAC).

3.   Ordinarily IR Appeals will be dealt with in the GRC, and the AAC will not become involved at the first-level appeal stage. Cases or issues will only be suitable for transfer where some special feature merits this course. Examples may be where a case is of considerable public importance or involves complex, sensitive or unusual issues.

4.   Cases where no request for transfer is made by any party: If a GRC judge dealing with an IR appeal considers that that there is some special feature which may merit transfer, then that judge should advise the Principal Judge of the IR jurisdiction of the GRC and the President of the GRC. If the President of the GRC considers that transfer of the case or a preliminary issue may be appropriate, the next steps will involve the AAC as well as the GRC. First, the President of the GRC will advise the lead judge of the AAC s Information Rights judicial group (UT Judge Wikeley) (or, if he is unavailable, another judge of that Group) and the President of the AAC. Second, if the President of the AAC agrees that such transfer merits consideration then the GRC President will unless there is good reason to the contrary - invite observations from all actual or potential parties on the proposed transfer. Third, either the GRC president will, if thought appropriate and the AAC President concurs, make a direction that the case or issue be transferred to and determined by the AAC, or the parties will be advised that the proposed direction will not be made.

5. Cases where transfer is requested by one or more of the parties: Upon receipt of such a request the GRC judge dealing with the case should notify the Principal Judge of the IR jurisdiction of the GRC and the President of the GRC. Unless there is good reason to the contrary the President of the GRC should at this stage invite observations from all actual or potential parties. If in the light of those observations the President of the GRC considers that transfer of the case or a preliminary issue may be appropriate, the next steps will be as set out in the preceding paragraph, modified as appropriate.

Secretary of State for Constitutional Affairs' Code of Practice on the discharge of public authorities' functions under Part I of the Freedom of Information Act 2000

Issued under section 45 of the Act.

November 2004

Presented to Parliament by the Secretary of State for Constitutional Affairs pursuant to section 45(5) of the Freedom of Information Act 2000

Foreword

Code Of Practice

Foreword

INTRODUCTION

1. The Code of Practice, to which this is a foreword, fulfils the duty of the Secretary of State set out in section 45 of the Freedom of Information Act 2000, to provide guidance to public authorities as to the practice which it would, in his opinion, be desirable for them to follow in connection with the discharge of their functions under Part I of the Act. It is envisaged that Regulations to be made with respect to environmental information will make provision for the issue by the Secretary of State of a Code of Practice applying to the discharge of authorities' functions under those Regulations.

2. This foreword does not form part of the Code itself.

3. The Government is committed to greater openness in the public sector. The Freedom of Information Act will further this aim by helping to transform the culture of the public

sector to one of greater openness, enabling members of the public to better understand the decisions of public authorities, and ensuring that services provided by the public sector are seen to be efficiently and properly delivered. Conformity with the Code will assist this.

4. The aims of the Code are to:

- facilitate the disclosure of information under the Act by setting out good administrative practice that it is desirable for public authorities to follow when handling requests for information, including, where appropriate, the transfer of a request to a different authority;

- protect the interests of applicants by setting out standards for the provision of advice which it would be good practice to make available to them and to encourage the development of effective means of complaining about decisions taken under the Act;

- facilitate consideration by public authorities of the interests of third parties who may be affected by any decision to disclose information, by setting standards for consultation; and

- promote consideration by public authorities of the implications for Freedom of Information before agreeing to confidentiality provisions in contracts and accepting information in confidence from a third party more generally.

ROLE OF THE INFORMATION COMMISSIONER

5. The Information Commissioner has a duty under section 47 of the Act to promote the following of good practice by public authorities, and in particular to promote observance of the requirements of the Act and of the provisions of this Code of Practice. The Act confers a number of powers on him to enable him to carry out that duty specifically in relation to the Code.

Practice Recommendations

6. If it appears to the Commissioner that the practice of a public authority in relation to the exercise of its functions under the Act does not conform with that proposed in this Code of Practice, he may give to the authority a recommendation, under section 48 (known as a "practice recommendation"), specifying the steps which should, in his opinion, be taken for promoting such conformity.

7. A practice recommendation must be given in writing and must refer to the particular provisions of the Code of Practice with which, in the Commissioner's opinion, the public authority's practice does not conform. A practice recommendation is simply a recommendation and cannot be directly enforced by the Information Commissioner. However, a failure to comply with a practice recommendation may lead to a failure to comply with the Act. Further, a failure to take account of a practice recommendation may lead to an adverse comment in a report to Parliament by the Commissioner.

8.   It should be noted that because the provisions of the Act relating to the general right of access will not be brought into force until 1 January 2005, the Commissioner's powers to issue practice recommendations in relation to the handling of individual requests for information under the general rights of access will not take effect before that date.

Decision and Enforcement Notices

9.   The Commissioner may also refer to non-compliance with the Code in decision notices issued as a result of a complaint under s 50 of the Act and enforcement notices issued under s 52 of the Act where, irrespective of any complaints that may have been received, the Commissioner considers that a public authority has failed to comply with any requirement of Part 1 of the Act. Where relevant, the Commissioner will make reference to the specific provisions of the Code in specifying the steps to be taken to ensure compliance with the Act.

Information Notices

10.   If the Information Commissioner reasonably requires any information for the purpose of determining whether the practice of a public authority conforms to the Code, under section 51 of the Act he may serve an "information notice" on the authority, requiring it to provide specified information relating to its conformity with the Code.

Compliance with notices

11.   Under the provisions of section 54 of the Act, if a public authority fails to comply with a decisions, information or enforcement notice, the Commissioner may certify in writing to the court that the public authority has failed to comply with that notice. The court may then inquire into the matter and, after hearing any witnesses who may be produced against or on behalf of, the public authority, and after hearing any statement that may be offered in defence, deal with the authority as if it had committed a contempt of court.

PART I OF THE FREEDOM OF INFORMATION ACT

12.   The Code provides guidance on good practice for public authorities in connection with the discharge of their functions under Part I of the Act. The main features of Part I Freedom of Information Act 2000 are:

- general rights of access in relation to recorded information held by public authorities, subject to certain conditions and exemptions;

- in cases where access to information is refused in reliance on an exemption from disclosure, a duty on public authorities to give reasons for that refusal;

- a duty to provide reasonable advice and assistance to applicants approaching public authorities seeking information;

- a duty on every public authority to adopt and maintain a publication scheme, approved by the Commissioner, which relates to the publication of information by the authority, and to publish information in accordance with the scheme (an authority may adopt a model publication scheme approved by the Commissioner).

Duty to provide advice and assistance

13. Section 16 of the Act places a duty on public authorities to provide reasonable advice and assistance to applicants. A public authority is to be taken to have complied with this duty in any particular case if it has conformed with the provisions of this Code in relation to the provision of advice and assistance in that case. The duty to assist and advise is enforceable by the Information Commissioner. If a public authority fails in its statutory duty, the Commissioner may issue a decision notice under section 50 , or an enforcement notice under section 52

14. Public authorities should not forget that other Acts of Parliament may be relevant to the way in which authorities provide advice and assistance to applicants or potential applicants, e.g. the Disability Discrimination Act 1995 and the Race Relations Act 1976 (as amended by the Race Relations (Amendment) Act 2000)

PROCEDURES AND TRAINING

15. All communications in writing to a public authority, including those transmitted by electronic means, may contain or amount to requests for information within the meaning of the Act, and so must be dealt with in accordance with the provisions of the Act. While in many cases such requests will be dealt with in the course of normal business, it is essential that public authorities dealing with correspondence, or which otherwise may be required to provide information, have in place procedures for taking decisions at appropriate levels, and ensure that sufficient staff are familiar with the requirements of the Act and the Codes of Practice issued under its provisions. Staff dealing with correspondence should also take account of any relevant guidance on good practice issued by the Commissioner. Authorities should ensure that proper training is provided in this regard. Larger authorities should ensure that they have a central core of staff with particular expertise in Freedom of Information who can provide expert advice to other members of staff as needed.

16. In planning and delivering training authorities should be aware of other provisions affecting the disclosure of information such as Environmental Information Regulations and the Data Protection Act 1998.

FURTHER GUIDANCE

17. The DCA has produced a suite of guidance which provides advice for public authorities in order to help them fulfil their obligations under the Freedom of Information Act. Of

particular relevance to authorities will be the Guidance on Processing Requests, which provides detailed advice on handling requests for information. The suite of guidance also includes detailed guidance on the application of exemptions. This should be referred to for further guidance on the factors which should be taken into account when considering whether exemptions apply.

18. The Information Commissioner's Office have also issued "Awareness Guides" on its web-site. Again, these Awareness Guides provide detailed, practical guidance on best practice which should be followed by public authorities. The Commissioner will also publish the internal advice developed for use by complaint caseworkers and summaries of complaint cases considered by the Commissioner and the Tribunal.

19. More specialist advice on the Act is also available from representative bodies (for instance the Local Government Association and the Association of Chief Police Officers) and by Government Departments for small public authorities falling within their general policy areas (for instance the DfES for schools.)

Code of Practice

Having consulted the Information Commissioner, this Code of Practice is issued by the Secretary of State for Constitutional Affairs under section 45 of the Freedom of Information Act 2000 (c 36) on 25 November 2004. The Code provides guidance to public authorities, as defined in the Act, as to the practice which it would, in the Secretary of State's opinion, be desirable for them to follow in connection with the discharge of their functions under Part I of the Act.

Laid before Parliament on 25 November 2004 pursuant to section 45(5) of the Freedom of Information Act 2000.

I INTRODUCTION

1. This Code of Practice provides guidance to public authorities as to the practice which it would, in the opinion of the Secretary of State for Constitutional Affairs, be desirable for them to follow in connection with the discharge of their functions under Part I (Access to information held by public authorities) of the Freedom of Information Act 2000 ("the Act").

2. Words and expressions used in this Code have the same meaning as the same words and expressions used in the Act.

II THE PROVISION OF ADVICE AND ASSISTANCE TO PERSONS MAKING REQUESTS FOR INFORMATION

3. The following paragraphs of this Code apply in relation to the provision of advice and assistance to persons who propose to make, or have made, requests for information to public authorities. They are intended to provide guidance to public authorities as to the practice which it would be desirable for them to follow in the discharge of their duty under section 16 of the Act.

Advice and assistance to those proposing to make requests:

4. Public authorities should publish their procedures for dealing with requests for information. Consideration should be given to including in these procedures a statement of:

- what the public authority's usual procedure will be where it does not hold the information requested (see also III—"Transferring requests for information), and

- when the public authority may need to consult other public authorities and/or third parties in order to reach a decision on whether the requested information can be released (see also IV—"Consultation with third parties).

5. The procedures should include an address or addresses (including an e-mail address where possible) to which applicants may direct requests for information or for assistance. A telephone number should also be provided, where possible that of a named individual who can provide assistance. These procedures should be referred to in the authority's ublication scheme.

6. Staff working in public authorities in contact with the public should bear in mind that not everyone will be aware of the Act, or Regulations made under it, and they will need where appropriate to draw these to the attention of potential applicants who appear unaware of them.

7. Where a person is unable to frame his or her request in writing, the public authority should ensure that appropriate assistance is given to enable that person to make a request for information. Depending on the circumstances, consideration should be given to:

- advising the person that another person or agency (such as a Citizens Advice Bureau) may be able to assist them with the application, or make the application on their behalf;

- in exceptional circumstances, offering to take a note of the application over the telephone and then send the note to the applicant for confirmation (in which case the written note of the telephone request, once verified by the applicant and returned, would constitute a written request for information and the statutory time limit for reply would begin when the written confirmation was received).

This list is not exhaustive, and public authorities should be flexible in offering advice and assistance most appropriate to the circumstances of the applicant.

Clarifying the request:

8. A request for information must adequately specify and describe the information sought by the applicant. Public authorities are entitled to ask for more detail, if needed, to enable them to identify and locate the information sought. Authorities should, as far as reasonably practicable, provide assistance to the applicant to enable him or her to describe more clearly the information requested.

9. Authorities should be aware that the aim of providing assistance is to clarify the nature of the information sought, not to determine the aims or motivation of the applicant. Care should be taken not to give the applicant the impression that he or she is obliged to disclose the nature of his or her interest as a precondition to exercising the rights of access, or that he or she will be treated differently if he or she does (or does not). Public authorities should be prepared to explain to the applicant why they are asking for more information. It is important that the applicant is contacted as soon as possible, preferably by telephone, fax or e-mail, where more information is needed to clarify what is sought.

10. Appropriate assistance in this instance might include:

    - providing an outline of the different kinds of information which might meet the terms of the request;

    - providing access to detailed catalogues and indexes, where these are available, to help the applicant ascertain the nature and extent of the information held by the authority;

    - providing a general response to the request setting out options for further information which could be provided on request.

    This list is not exhaustive, and public authorities should be flexible in offering advice and assistance most appropriate to the circumstances of the applicant.

11. In seeking to clarify what is sought, public authorities should bear in mind that applicants cannot reasonably be expected to possess identifiers such as a file reference number, or a description of a particular record, unless this information is made available by the authority for the use of applicants.

Limits to advice and assistance

12. If, following the provision of such assistance, the applicant still fails to describe the information requested in a way which would enable the authority to identify and locate it, the authority is not expected to seek further clarification. The authority should disclose any information relating to the application which has been successfully identified and found for which it does not propose to claim an exemption. It should also explain to the applicant why it cannot take the request any further and provide details of the authority's

complaints procedure and the applicant's rights under section 50 of the Act (see "Complaints Procedure in section VI).

Advice and assistance and fees

13. Where the applicant indicates that he or she is not prepared to pay the fee notified in any fees notice given to the applicant, the authority should consider whether there is any information that may be of interest to the applicant that is available free of charge.

14. Where an authority is not obliged to comply with a request for information because, under section 12(1) and regulations made under section 12, the cost of complying would exceed the "appropriate limit" (i.e. cost threshold) the authority should consider providing an indication of what, if any, information could be provided within the cost ceiling. The authority should also consider advising the applicant that by reforming or re-focussing their request, information may be able to be supplied for a lower, or no, fee.

15. An authority is not expected to provide assistance to applicants whose requests are vexatious within the meaning of section 14 of the Act. Guidance on what constitutes a vexatious request can be found in the DCA Handbook – 'Guidance on Processing Requests'. The Information Commissioner has also issued advice on dealing with vexatious and repetitious requests.

III TRANSFERRING REQUESTS FOR INFORMATION

16. The following paragraphs apply in any case in which a public authority is not able to comply with a request (or to comply with it in full) because it does not hold the information requested, and proposes, in accordance with section 1(1)(a), to confirm that it does not hold that information.

17. If the authority has reason to believe that some or all of the information requested, but which it does not hold, is held by another public authority, the authority should consider what would be the most helpful way of assisting the applicant with his or her request.

18. In most cases this is likely to involve:

- contacting the applicant and informing him or her that the information requested may be held by another public authority;

- suggesting that the applicant re-applies to the authority which the original authority believes may hold the information; and

- providing him or her with contact details for that authority.

19. However, in some cases the authority to which the original request is made may consider it to be more appropriate to transfer the request to another authority in respect of the information which it does not hold. In such cases, the authority should consult the other authority with a view to ascertaining whether it does in fact hold the information and, if

so, whether it is obliged to confirm this under section 1(1) of the Act. If that is the case, the first authority should proceed to consider transferring the request. A request (or part of a request) should not be transferred without confirmation by the second authority that it holds the information, and will confirm as much to the applicant on receipt of a request.

20. Before transferring a request for information to another authority, the original authority should consider:

- whether a transfer is appropriate; and if so

- whether the applicant is likely to have any grounds to object to the transfer. If the authority reasonably concludes that the applicant is not likely to object, it may transfer the request without going back to the applicant, but should tell him or her it has done so.

21. Where there are reasonable grounds to believe an applicant is likely to object, the authority should only transfer the request to another authority with his or her consent. If the authority is in any doubt, it may prefer to advise the applicant to make a new request to the other authority, and to inform the applicant that the other authority has confirmed that it holds the information.

22. Where a request or part of a request is transferred from one public authority to another, the receiving authority should comply with its obligations under Part I of the Act in the same way as it would in the case of a request that is received direct from an applicant. The time for complying with such a request should be calculated by regarding the date of transfer as the date of receipt of the request.

23. All transfers of requests should take place as soon as is practicable, and the applicant must be informed as soon as possible once this has been done.

24. Where a public authority is unable either to advise the applicant which public authority holds, or may hold, the requested information or to facilitate the transfer of the request to another authority (or considers it inappropriate to do so) it should consider what advice, if any, it can provide to the applicant to enable him or her to pursue his or her request.

IV CONSULTATION WITH THIRD PARTIES

25. There are many circumstances in which:

- requests for information may relate to persons other than the applicant and the authority; or

- disclosure of information is likely to affect the interests of persons other than the applicant or the authority.

26. It is highly recommended that public authorities take appropriate steps to ensure that such third parties, and those who supply public authorities with information, are aware of the public authority's duty to comply with the Freedom of Information Act, and that therefore information will have to be disclosed upon request unless an exemption applies.

27. In some cases is will be necessary to consult, directly and individually, with such persons in order to determine whether or not an exemption applies to the information requested, or in order to reach a view on whether the obligations in section 1 of the Act arise in relation to that information. But in a range of other circumstances it will be good practice to do so; for example where a public authority proposes to disclose information relating to third parties, or information which is likely to affect their interests, reasonable steps should, where appropriate, be taken to give them advance notice, or failing that, to draw it to their attention afterwards.

28. In some cases, it may also be appropriate to consult such third parties about such matters as whether any further explanatory material or advice should be given to the applicant together with the information in question. Such advice may, for example, refer to any restrictions (including copyright restrictions) which may exist as to the subsequent use which may be made of such information.

29. No decision to release information which has been supplied by one government department to another should be taken without first notifying, and where appropriate consulting, the department from which the information originated.

30. Where information to be disclosed relates to a number of third parties, or the interests of a number of third parties may be affected by a disclosure, and those parties have a representative organisation which can express views on behalf of those parties, the authority may consider whether it would be sufficient to notify or consult with that representative organisation. If there is no representative organisation, the authority may consider that it would be sufficient to notify or consult with a representative sample of the third parties in question.

V FREEDOM OF INFORMATION AND CONFIDENTIALITY OBLIGATIONS

31. Public authorities should bear clearly in mind their obligations under the Freedom of Information Act when preparing to enter into contracts which may contain terms relating to the disclosure of information by them.

32. When entering into contracts with non-public authority contractors, public authorities may be asked to accept confidentiality clauses, for example to the effect that information relating to the terms of the contract, its value and performance will not be disclosed. Public authorities should carefully consider the compatibility of such terms with their obligations under the Act. It is important that both the public authority and the contractor are aware of the limits placed by the Act on the enforceability of such confidentiality clauses.

33. The Act does, however, recognise that there will be circumstances and respects in which the preservation of confidentiality between public authority and contractor is appropriate, and must be maintained, in the public interest.

34. Where there is good reason, as recognised by the terms of the exemption provisions of the Act, to include non-disclosure provisions in a contract, public authorities should consider the desirability where possible of making express provision in the contract identifying the

information which should not be disclosed and the reasons for confidentiality. Consideration may also be given to including provision in contracts as to when consultation with third parties will be necessary or appropriate before the information is disclosed.

35. Similar considerations will apply to the offering or acceptance of confidentiality obligations by public authorities in non-contractual circumstances. There will be circumstances in which such obligations will be an appropriate part of the acquisition of information from third parties and will be protected by the terms of the exemption provisions of the Act. But again, it will be important that both the public authority and the third party are aware of the limits placed by the Act on the enforceability of expectations of confidentiality, and for authorities to ensure that such expectations are created only where to do so is consistent with their obligations under the Act.

VI COMPLAINTS PROCEDURE

36. Each public authority should have a procedure in place for dealing with complaints both in relation to its handling of requests for information. The same procedure could also usefully handle complaints in relation to the authority's publication scheme. If the complaints cannot be dealt with swiftly and satisfactorily on an informal basis, the public authority should inform persons if approached by them of the details of its internal complaints procedure, and how to contact the Information Commissioner, if the complainant wishes to write to him about the matter.

37. When communicating any decision made to refusing a request, in reliance on an exemption provision, public authorities are obliged, under section 17(7) of the Act notify the applicant of particulars of the procedure provided by the public authority for dealing with complaints (or to state that it does not have one). In doing so, they should provide full details of their own complaints procedure, including how to make a complaint and inform the applicant of the right to complain to the Commissioner under section 50 if he or she is still dissatisfied following the authority's review.

38. Any written reply from the applicant (including one transmitted by electronic means) expressing dissatisfaction with an authority's response to a request for information should be treated as a complaint, as should any written communication from a person who considers that the authority is not complying with its publication scheme. These communications should be handled in accordance with the authority's complaints procedure, even if, in the case of a request for information under the general rights of access, the applicant does not expressly state his or her desire for the authority to review its decision or its handling of the application.

39. The complaints procedure should provide a fair and thorough review of handling issues and of decisions taken pursuant to the Act, including decisions taken about where the public interest lies in respect of exempt information. It should enable a fresh decision to be taken on a reconsideration of all the factors relevant to the issue. Complaints

procedures should be as clear and simple as possible. They should encourage a prompt determination of the complaint.

40. Where the complaint concerns a request for information under the general rights of access, the review should be undertaken by someone senior to the person who took the original decision, where this is reasonably practicable. The public authority should in any event undertake a full re-evaluation of the case, taking into account the matters raised by the investigation of the complaint.

41. In all cases, complaints should be acknowledged promptly and the complainant should be informed of the authority's target date for determining the complaint. Where it is apparent that determination of the complaint will take longer than the target time (for example because of the complexity of the particular case), the authority should inform the applicant and explain the reason for the delay. The complainant should always be informed of the outcome of his or her complaint.

42. Authorities should set their own target times for dealing with complaints; these should be reasonable, and subject to regular review. Each public authority should publish its target times for determining complaints and information as to how successful it is with meeting those targets.

43. Records should be kept of all complaints and of their outcome. Authorities should have procedures in place for monitoring complaints and for reviewing, and, if necessary, amending, procedures for dealing with requests for information where such action is indicated by more than occasional reversals of initial decisions.

44. Where the outcome of a complaint is a decision that information should be disclosed which was previously withheld, the information in question should be disclosed as soon as practicable and the applicant should be informed how soon this will be.

45. Where the outcome of a complaint is that the procedures within an authority have not been properly followed by the authority's staff, the authority should apologise to the applicant. The authority should also take appropriate steps to prevent similar errors occurring in future.

46. Where the outcome of a complaint is that an initial decision to withhold information is upheld, or is otherwise in the authority's favour, the applicant should be informed of his or her right to apply to the Commissioner, and be given details of how to make an application, for a decision on whether the request for information has been dealt with in accordance with the requirements of Part I of the Act.

Lord Chancellor's Code of Practice
on the management of records

Issued under section 46 of the Freedom of Information Act 2000

Presented to Parliament by the Lord Chancellor pursuant to
section 46(6) of the Freedom of Information Act 2000

Code of Practice

Foreword

Introduction

(i)   The Code of Practice ("the Code") which follows fulfils the duty of the Lord Chancellor set out in section 46 of the Freedom of Information Act 20001 (the Act). This foreword provides background but does not form part of the Code itself.

(ii)   The Code is in two parts. In Part 1, the Code provides guidance to all relevant authorities as to the practice which it would, in the opinion of the Lord Chancellor, be desirable for them to follow in connection with the keeping, management and destruction of their records. This applies not only to public authorities but also to other bodies that are subject to the Public Records Act 1958 or the Public Records Act (Northern Ireland) 1923. Collectively they are called relevant authorities.

(iii) The Code also describes, in Part 2, the procedure to be followed for timely and effective review and transfer of public records to The National Archives or to a place of deposit (as defined in section 4 of the Public Records Act 1958) or to the Public Record Office of Northern Ireland under the Public Records Act 1958 or the Public Records Act (Northern Ireland) 1923.

Importance of records management

(iv)   Freedom of information legislation is only as good as the quality of the records and other information to which it provides access. Access rights are of limited value if information cannot be found when requested or, when found, cannot be relied upon as authoritative. Good records and information management benefits those requesting information because it provides some assurance that the information provided will be complete and reliable. It benefits those holding the requested information because it enables them to locate and retrieve it easily within the statutory timescales or to explain why it is not held. It also supports control and delivery of information promised in an authority's Publication Scheme or required to be published by the Environmental Information Regulations 2004 (the EIR).

(v)   Records management is important for many other reasons. Records and information are the lifeblood of any organisation. They are the basis on which decisions are made, services provided and policies developed and communicated. Effective management of records and other information brings the following additional benefits:

- It supports an authority's business and discharge of its functions, promotes business efficiency and underpins service delivery by ensuring that authoritative information about past activities can be retrieved, used and relied upon in current business;

- It supports compliance with other legislation which requires records and information to be kept, controlled and accessible, such as the Data Protection Act 1998, employment legislation and health and safety legislation;

- It improves accountability, enabling compliance with legislation and other rules and requirements to be demonstrated to those with a right to audit or otherwise investigate the organisation and its actions;

- It enables protection of the rights and interests of an authority, its staff and its stakeholders;

- It increases efficiency and cost-effectiveness by ensuring that records are disposed of when no longer needed. This enables more effective use of resources, for example space within buildings and information systems, and saves staff time searching for information that may not be there;

- It provides institutional memory.

(vi) Poor records and information management create risks for the authority, such as:

- Poor decisions based on inaccurate or incomplete information; . Inconsistent or poor levels of service;

- Financial or legal loss if information required as evidence is not available or cannot be relied upon;

- Non-compliance with statutory or other regulatory requirements, or with standards that apply to the sector to which it belongs;

- Failure to handle confidential information with an appropriate level of security and the possibility of unauthorised access or disposal taking place;

- Failure to protect information that is vital to the continued functioning of the organisation, leading to inadequate business continuity planning;

- Unnecessary costs caused by storing records and other information for longer than they are needed;

- Staff time wasted searching for records;

- Staff time wasted considering issues that have previously been addressed and resolved;

- Loss of reputation as a result of all of the above, with damaging effects on public trust.

(vii) The Code is a supplement to the provisions in the Act and its adoption will help authorities comply with their duties under the Act. Consequently, all relevant authorities are strongly encouraged to pay heed to the guidance in the Code. The Code is complemented by the Code of Practice under section 45 of the Act and the Code of Practice under Regulation 16 of the EIR.

(viii) Authorities should note that if they fail to comply with the Code, they may also fail to comply with legislation relating to the creation, management, disposal, use and re-use of records and information, for example the Public Records Act 1958, the Data Protection Act 1998, and the of their statutory obligations.

Role of the Information Commissioner

(ix)　The Information Commissioner has a duty under section 47 of the Act to promote the following of good practice by public authorities and in particular to promote observance of the requirements of the Act and the provisions of this Code of Practice. In order to carry out that duty specifically in relation to the Code, the Act confers a number of powers on the Commissioner.

Practice recommendations

(x)　If it appears to the Information Commissioner that the practice of an authority in relation to the exercise of its functions under the Act does not conform to that set out in the Code, the Commissioner may issue a practice recommendation under section 48 of the Act. A practice recommendation will be in writing and will specify the provisions of the Code that have not been met and the steps that should, in the Commissioner's opinion, be taken to promote conformity with the Code. A practice recommendation cannot be directly enforced by the Information Commissioner. However, a failure to comply with a practice recommendation may lead to a failure to comply with the Act or could lead to an adverse comment in a report to Parliament by the Information Commissioner.

Information Notices

(xi)　If the Information Commissioner reasonably requires any information in order to determine whether the practice of an authority conforms with that recommended in the Code, he may serve on the authority a notice (known as an 'information notice') under section 51 of the Act. An information notice will be in writing and will require the authority to provide the Information Commissioner with specified information relating to conformity with the Code. It will also contain particulars of the rights of appeal conferred by section 57 of the Act.

Enforcement of information notices

(xii)　Under section 54 of the Act, if an authority fails to comply with an information notice, the Information Commissioner may certify in writing to the court that the authority has failed to comply. The court may then inquire into the matter and, after hearing any witnesses who may be produced against or on behalf of the authority, and after hearing any statement that may be offered in defence, deal with the authority as if it had committed a contempt of court.

Authorities subject to the Public Records Acts

(xiii) The Code should be read in the context of existing legislation affecting the management of records. In particular, the Public Records Act 1958 (as amended) gives duties to bodies subject to that Act in respect of the records they create or hold. It also requires the Chief Executive of The National Archives to supervise the discharge of those duties.

(xiv) The Public Records Act (Northern Ireland) 1923 sets out the duties of public record bodies in Northern Ireland in respect of the records they create and requires that records should be transferred to, and preserved by, the Public Record Office of Northern Ireland. The title 'Keeper of Public Records' is used in the Public Records Act 1958 and the Freedom of Information Act 2000. This is one of the titles of the Chief Executive of The National Archives. The title 'Chief Executive of The National Archives' is used in this Code in recognition of the fact that it is the title used for operational purposes.

(xv) The Information Commissioner will promote the observance of the Code in consultation with the Chief Executive of The National Archives when dealing with bodies which are subject to the Public Records Act 1958 and with the Deputy Keeper of the Records of Northern Ireland for bodies subject to the Public Records Act (Northern Ireland) 1923. Before issuing a practice recommendation under section 48 of the Act to a body subject to either of the Public Records Acts, the Information Commissioner will consult the Chief Executive of The National Archives or the Deputy Keeper of the Records of Northern Ireland as appropriate.

Role of the Lord Chancellor's Advisory Council on National Records and Archives and the Sensitivity Review Group in Northern Ireland

(xvi) The Advisory Council on National Records and Archives (hereafter 'the Advisory Council') has a statutory role to advise the Lord Chancellor on matters concerning public records in general and on the application of the Act to information in public records that are historical records. The Lord Chancellor, having received the advice of his Advisory Council, may prepare and issue guidance. The guidance may include advice on the review of public records and on the periods of time for which the Advisory Council considers it appropriate to withhold categories of sensitive records after they have become historical records.

(xvii) The National Archives provides support as appropriate to the Advisory Council in its consideration of applications from authorities relating to retention or access to public records and in its preparation of guidance for the Lord Chancellor to issue to authorities.

(xviii) In Northern Ireland the Sensitivity Review Group, consisting of representatives of Northern Ireland departments, provides advice on the release of public records. The Public Record Office of Northern Ireland provides support to the Group. Guidance may be issued by the Deputy Keeper of the Records of Northern Ireland following consultation with the Departments responsible for the records affected by the guidance. The legal entity to which this provision applies is the Advisory Council on Public Records. Since April 2003 the Council has functioned as The Advisory Council on National Records and Archives and so that name is used in this Code. 7In this context, the term 'public records' applies only to the records of bodies that are subject to the Public Records Act 1958. The term 'historical record' is defined at section 62 of the Act.

Code of Practice

The Lord Chancellor, having consulted the Information Commissioner and the appropriate Northern Ireland Minister, issues the following Code of Practice pursuant to section 46 of the Freedom of Information Act 2000.

Laid before Parliament on 16 July 2009 pursuant to section 46(6) of the Freedom of Information Act 2000.

INTRODUCTION

Aims of the Code

1.1 The aims of the Code are:

- To set out the practices which relevant authorities should follow in relation to the creation, keeping, management and destruction of their records (Part 1 of the Code); and

- To describe the arrangements which bodies responsible for public records should follow in reviewing public records and transferring them to The National Archives or to a place of deposit for public records, or to the Public Record Office of Northern Ireland (Part 2 of the Code).

1.2. Part 1 of the Code provides a framework for relevant authorities to manage their records. It sets out recommended good practice for the organisational arrangements, decisions and processes required for effective records and information management.

1.3 Part 2 provides a framework for the review and transfer of public records that have been selected for permanent preservation at The National Archives, a place of deposit for public records or the Public Record Office of Northern Ireland. It sets out the process by which records due for transfer are assessed to determine whether the information they contain can be designated as open information or, if this is not possible, to identify the exemptions that apply and indicate for how long they should apply. Relevant authorities is the collective term used in the Act for bodies that are public authorities under the Freedom of Information Act and bodies that are not subject to that Act but are subject to the Public Records Act 1958 or the Public Records Act (Northern Ireland) 1923. Public records are the records of bodies that are subject to the Public Records 1958 or the Public Records Act (Northern Ireland) 1923. For the avoidance of doubt, the term 'public records' includes Welsh public records as defined by section 148 of the Government of Wales Act 2006. The legal entity to which this provision applies is the Public Record Office. Since April 2003 the Public Record Office has functioned as part of The National Archives and is known by that name. For that reason the name 'The

National Archives' is used in this Code. In the Environmental Information Regulations 2004 (the EIR), exemptions are called exceptions. For simplicity the term exemption is used throughout the Code and should be taken to apply also to exceptions in the EIR.

Scope of the Code

2.	The Code applies to all records irrespective of the technology used to create and store them or the type of information they contain. It includes, therefore, not only paper files series and digital records management systems but also business and information systems (for example case management, finance and geographical information systems) and the contents of websites. The Code's focus is on records and the systems that contain them but the principles and recommended practice can be applied also to other information held by an authority.

Interpretation

3.	For the purposes of this Code, 'records' are defined as in the relevant British Standard13, namely 'information created, received, and maintained as evidence and information by an organization or person, in pursuance of legal obligations or in the transaction of business'. Some specific terms which are not defined in the Act have been included in the Glossary at Annex A. Other words and expressions used in this Code have the same meaning as the same words and expressions used in the Act.

Supplementary guidance

4.	More detailed guidance on both parts of the Code has been published separately. Standards and guidance which support the objectives of this Code most directly are listed at Annex B.

PART 1: RECORDS MANAGEMENT

Summary of recommended good practice in records management

5.1	Good practice in records management is made up of a number of key elements. The following list summarises the good practice recommended in Part 1 of the Code. Guidance on each element is given in sections 6-14 of this Part.

a)	Authorities should have in place organisational arrangements that support records management (see section 6);

b)	Authorities should have in place a records management policy, either as a separate policy or as part of a wider information or knowledge management policy (see section 7);

c)	Authorities should ensure they keep the records they will need for business, regulatory, legal and accountability purposes (see section 8);

d) Authorities should keep their records in systems that enable records to be stored and retrieved as necessary (see section 9);

e) Authorities should know what records they hold and where they are, and should ensure that they remain usable for as long as they are required (see section 10);

f) Authorities should ensure that records are stored securely and that access to them is controlled (see section 11);

g) Authorities should define how long they need to keep particular records, should dispose of them when they are no longer needed and should be able to explain why records are no longer held (see section 12);

h) Authorities should ensure that records shared with other bodies or held on their behalf by other bodies are managed in accordance with the Code (see section 13);

i) Authorities should monitor compliance with the Code and assess the overall effectiveness of the programme (see section 14).

Organisational arrangements to support records management

6. Authorities should have in place organisational arrangements that support records management.

6.1 These arrangements should include:

a) Recognition of records management as a core corporate function, either separately or as part of a wider information or knowledge management function. The function should cover records in all formats throughout their lifecycle, from planning and creation through to disposal and should include records managed on behalf of the authority by an external body such as a contractor;

b) Inclusion of records and information management in the corporate risk management framework. Information and records are a corporate asset and loss of the asset could cause disruption to business. The level of risk will vary according to the strategic and operational value of the asset to the authority and risk management should reflect the probable extent of disruption and resulting damage;

c) A governance framework that includes defined roles and lines of responsibility. This should include allocation of lead responsibility for the records and information management function to a designated member of staff at sufficiently senior level to act as a records management champion, for example a board member, and allocation of operational responsibility to a member of staff with the necessary knowledge and skills. In small authorities it may be more practicable to combine these roles. Ideally the same people will be responsible also for compliance with other information legislation, for example the Data Protection Act 1998 and the

Re-use of Public Sector Information Regulations 2005, or will work closely with those people;

d) Clearly defined instructions, applying to staff at all levels of the authority, to create, keep and manage records. In larger organisations the responsibilities of managers, and in particular heads of business units, could be differentiated from the responsibilities of other staff by making it clear that managers are responsible for ensuring that adequate records are kept of the activities for which they are accountable;

e) Identification of information and business systems that hold records and provision of the resources needed to maintain and protect the integrity of those systems and the information they contain;

f) Consideration of records management issues when planning or implementing ICT systems, when extending staff access to new technologies and during re-structuring or major changes to the authority;

g) Induction and other training to ensure that all staff are aware of the authority's records management policies, standards, procedures and guidelines and understand their personal responsibilities. This should be extended to temporary staff, contractors and consultants who are undertaking work that it has been decided should be documented in the authority's records. If the organisation is large enough to employ staff whose work is primarily about records and information management, they should be given opportunities for professional development;

h) An agreed programme for managing records in accordance with this part of the Code;

i) Provision of the financial and other resources required to achieve agreed objectives in the records management programme.

Records management policy

7. Authorities should have in place a records management policy, either as a separate policy or as part of a wider information or knowledge management policy.

7.1 The policy should be endorsed by senior management, for example at board level, and should be readily available to staff at all levels.

7.2 The policy provides a mandate for the records and information management function and a framework for supporting standards, procedures and guidelines. The precise contents will depend on the particular needs and culture of the authority but it should as a minimum:

a) Set out the authority's commitment to create, keep and manage records which document its principal activities;

b) Outline the role of records management and its relationship to the authority's overall business strategy;

c) Identify and make appropriate connections to related policies, such as those dealing with email, information security and data protection;

d) Define roles and responsibilities, including the responsibility of individuals to document their work in the authority's records to the extent that, and in the way that, the authority has decided their work should be documented, and to use those records appropriately;

e) Indicate how compliance with the policy and the supporting standards, procedures and guidelines will be monitored.

7.3 The policy should be kept up-to-date so that it reflects the current needs of the authority. One way of ensuring this is to review it at agreed intervals, for example every three or five years, and after major organisational or technological changes, in order to assess whether it needs amendment.

7.4 The authority should consider publishing the policy so that members of the public can see the basis on which it manages its records.

Keeping records to meet corporate requirements

8. Authorities should ensure they keep the records they will need for business, regulatory, legal and accountability purposes.

Deciding what records should be kept

8.1 Authorities should consider what records they are likely to need about their activities, and the risks of not having those records, taking into account the following factors:

a) The legislative and regulatory environment within which they operate. This will be a mixture of generally applicable legislation, such as health and safety legislation and the Data Protection Act 1998, and specific legislation applying to the sector or authority. For example, the Charity Commission is required by its legislation to keep an accurate and up-to-date register of charities. This factor also includes standards applying to the sector or authority or to particular functions such as finance;

b) The need to refer to authoritative information about past actions and decisions for current business purposes. For example, problems such as outbreaks of foot and mouth disease may recur and in order to deal with each new outbreak a local authority needs reliable information about what it did during previous outbreaks and who was responsible for specific measures, such as closing public footpaths;

c) The need to protect legal and other rights of the authority, its staff and its stakeholders. For example, a local authority needs to know what land and buildings it owns in order to ensure proper control of its assets and to protect itself if challenged;

d) The need to explain, and if necessary justify, past actions in the event of an audit, public inquiry or other investigation. For example, the Audit Commission will expect to find accurate records of expenditure of public funds. Or, if an applicant complains to the Information Commissioner's Office (ICO) about the handling or outcome of an FOI request, the ICO will expect the authority to provide details of how the request was handled and, if applicable, why it refused to provide the information.

8.2 Having considered these factors, authorities should set business rules identifying:

a) What records should be kept, for example which decisions or actions should be recorded;

b) By whom this should be done, for example, by the sender or recipient of an email or voicemail;

c) At what point in the process or transaction this should be done, for example when drafts of a document should be frozen and kept as a record;

d) What those records should contain;

e) Where and how they should be stored, for example in a case file.

8.3 As part of this process authorities should consider whether any of these records should be subject to particular controls so as to ensure their evidential value can demonstrated if required by showing them to:

a) Be authentic, that is, they are what they say they are;

b) Be reliable, that is, they can be trusted as a full and accurate record;

c) Have integrity, that is, they have not been altered since they were created or filed;

d) Be usable, that is, they can be retrieved, read and used.

Ensuring those records are kept

8.4 All staff should be aware of which records the authority has decided to keep and of their personal responsibility to follow the authority's business rules and keep accurate and complete records as part of their daily work. Managers of business units, programmes and projects should take responsibility for ensuring that the agreed records of the unit, programme or project's work are kept and are available for corporate use.

8.5 Authorities should ensure that staff creating or filing records are aware of the need to give those records titles that reflect their specific nature and contents so as to facilitate retrieval.

8.6   Staff should also be aware of the need to dispose of ephemeral material on a routine basis. For example, print-outs of electronic documents should not be kept after the meeting for which they were printed, trivial emails should be deleted after being read, and keeping multiple or personal copies of documents should be discouraged.

Records systems

9.   Authorities should keep their records in systems that enable records to be stored and retrieved as necessary.

Choosing, implementing and using records systems

9.1   Authorities should decide the format in which their records are to be stored. There is no requirement in this Code for records and information to be created and held electronically, but if the authority is operating electronically, for example using email for internal and external communications or creating documents through word processing software, it is good practice to hold the resulting records electronically. In addition, authorities should note that the EIR require them progressively to make environmental information available to the public by electronic means (Regulation 4).

9.2   Authorities are likely to hold records and other information in a number of different systems. These systems could include a dedicated electronic document and records management system, business systems such as a case management, finance or geographical information system, a website, shared workspaces, audio-visual material and sets of paper files with related registers. In some cases related records of the same business activities may be held in different formats, for example digital files and supporting paper material.

9.3   Records systems should be designed to meet the authority's operational needs and using them should be an integral part of business operations and processes. Records systems should have the following characteristics:

a)   They should be easy to understand and use so as to reduce the effort required of those who create and use the records within them. Ease of use is an important consideration when developing or selecting a system;

b)   They should enable quick and easy retrieval of information. With digital systems this should include the capacity to search for information requested under the Act;

c)   They should be set up in a way that enables routine records management processes to take place. For example, digital systems should be able to delete specified information in accordance with agreed disposal dates and leave the rest intact;

d)   They should enable the context of each record and its relationship to other records to be understood. In a records management system this can be achieved by classifying and indexing records within a file plan or business classification scheme to bring together related records and enable the sequence of actions and context of each document to be understood. This approach has the added benefit of enabling handling decisions, for example relating to access or disposal, to be applied to groups of records instead of to individual records;

e) They should contain both information and metadata. Metadata enables the system to be understood and operated efficiently, the records within the system to be managed and the information within the records to be interpreted;

f) They should protect records in digital systems from accidental or unauthorised alteration, copying, movement or deletion;

g) They should provide secure storage to the level of protection required by the nature, contents and value of the information in them. For digital systems this includes a capacity to control access to particular information if necessary, for example by limiting access to named individuals or by requiring passwords. With paper files this includes a capacity to lock storage cupboards or areas and to log access to them and any withdrawal of records from them;

h) They should enable an audit trail to be produced of occasions on which selected records have been seen, used, amended and deleted.

9.4   Records systems should be documented to facilitate staff training, maintenance of the system and its reconstruction in the event of an emergency.

Limiting the active life of records within record systems
9.5   Folders, files and similar record assemblies should not remain live indefinitely with a capacity for new records to be added to them. They should be closed, that is, have their contents frozen, at an appropriate time.

9.6   The trigger for closure will vary according to the nature and function of the records, the extent to which they reflect ongoing business and the technology used to store them. For example, completion of the annual accounting process could be a trigger for closing financial records, completion of a project could be a trigger for closing project records, and completion of formalities following the death of a patient could be a trigger for closing that person's health record. Size is a factor and a folder should not be too big to be handled or scrutinised easily. For digital records a trigger could be migration to a new system. Authorities should decide the appropriate trigger for each records system and put arrangements in place to apply the trigger.

9.7   New continuation or part files should be opened if necessary. It should be clear to anyone looking at a record where the story continues, if applicable.

Storage and maintenance of records
10.   Authorities should know what records they hold and where they are, and should ensure that they remain usable for as long as they are required.

Knowing what records are held
10.1   The effectiveness of records systems depends on knowledge of what records are held, what information they contain, in what form they are made accessible, what value they

have to the organisation and how they relate to organisational functions. Without this knowledge an authority will find it difficult to:

a) Locate and retrieve information required for business purposes or to respond to an information request;

b) Produce a Publication Scheme or a reliable list of information assets available for re-use;

c) Apply the controls required to manage risks associated with the records; d) Ensure records are disposed of when no longer needed.

10.2 Authorities should gather and maintain data on records and information assets. This can be done in various ways, for example through surveys or audits of the records and information held by the authority. It should be held in an accessible format and should be kept up to date.

10.3 Authorities should consider publishing details of the types of records they hold to help members of the public planning to make a request for information under the Act.

Storing records

10.4 Storage should provide protection to the level required by the nature, contents and value of the information in them. Records and information will vary in their strategic and operational value to the authority, and in their residual value for historical research, and storage and preservation arrangements reflecting their value should be put in place.

10.5 Authorities should be aware of any specific requirements for records storage that apply to them. For example, the Adoption National Minimum Standards issued by the Department of Health and the Welsh Assembly Government in 2003 require indexes and case files for children to be securely stored to minimise the risk of damage from fire or water.

10.6 Storage should follow accepted standards in respect of the storage environment, fire precautions, health and safety and, if applicable, physical organisation. It should allow easy and efficient retrieval of information but also minimise the risk of damage, loss or unauthorised access.

10.7 Records that are no longer required for frequent reference can be removed from current systems to off-line or near off-line (for digital media) or to off-site (for paper) storage where this is a more economical and efficient way to store them. They should continue to be subject to normal records management controls and procedures.

10.8 The whereabouts of records should be known at all times and movement of files and other physical records between storage areas and office areas should be logged.

Ensuring records remain usable

10.9 Records should remain usable for as long as they are required. This means that it should continue to be possible to retrieve, use and rely on them.

10.10 Records in digital systems will not remain usable unless precautions are taken. Authorities should put in place a strategy for their continued maintenance designed to ensure that information remains intact, reliable and usable for as long as it is required. The strategy should provide for updating of the storage media and migration of the software format within which the information and metadata are held, and for regular monitoring of integrity and usability.

10.11 Records in digital systems are particularly vulnerable to accidental or unauthorised alteration, copying, movement or deletion which can happen without trace. This puts at risk the reliability of the records which could damage the authority's interests. Authorities should assess these risks and put appropriate safeguards in place.

10.12 Back-up copies of records in digital systems should be kept and stored securely in a separate location. They should be checked regularly to ensure that the storage medium has not degraded and the information remains intact and capable of being restored to operational use. Back-ups should be managed in a way that enables disposal decisions to be applied securely without compromising the authority's capacity to recover from system failures and major disasters.

10.13 Physical records such as paper files may also require regular monitoring. For example, formats such as early photocopies may be at risk of fading, and regular checks should be made of any information in such formats that is of continuing value to the authority.

10.14 Metadata for records in any format should be kept in such a way that it remains reliable and accessible for as long as it is required, which will be at least for the life of the records.

Business continuity plans

10.15 Business continuity plans should identify and safeguard records considered vital to the organisation, that is:

a) Records that would be essential to the continued functioning or reconstitution of the organisation in the event of a disaster;

b) Records that are essential to ongoing protection of the organisation's legal and financial rights.

The plans should include actions to protect and recover these records in particular.

Security and access

11. Authorities should ensure that records are stored securely and that access to them is controlled.

11.1 Authorities should ensure that their storage arrangements, handling procedures and arrangements for transmission of records reflect accepted standards and good practice in information security. It is good practice to have an information security policy addressing these points.

11.2 Ease of internal access will depend on the nature and sensitivity of the records. Access restrictions should be applied when necessary to protect the information concerned and should be kept up to date. Particular care should be taken with personal information about living individuals in order to comply with the 7th data protection principle, which requires precautions against unauthorised or unlawful processing, damage, loss or destruction. Within central Government, particular care should be taken with information bearing a protective marking. Other information, such as information obtained on a confidential basis, may also require particular protection.

11.3 Transmission of records, especially outside the authority's premises, should require authorisation. The method of transmission should be subject to risk assessment before a decision is made.

11.4 External access should be provided in accordance with relevant legislation.

11.5 An audit trail should be kept of provision of access, especially to people outside the immediate work area.

Disposal of records

12. Authorities should define how long they need to keep particular records, should dispose of them when they are no longer needed and should be able to explain why records are no longer held.

12.1 For the purpose of this Code, disposal means the decision as to whether the record should be destroyed, transferred to an archives service for permanent preservation or presented, and the putting into effect of that decision.

General principle

12.2 As a general principle, records should be kept for as long as they are needed by the authority: for reference or accountability purposes, to comply with regulatory requirements or to protect legal and other rights and interests. Destruction at the end of this period ensures that office and server space are not used and costs are not incurred in maintaining records that are no longer required. For records containing personal information it also ensures compliance with the 5th data protection principle which requires that personal data is kept only for as long as it is needed.

12.3 Records should not be kept after they have ceased to be of use to the authority unless:

 a) They are known to be the subject of litigation or a request for information. If so, destruction should be delayed until the litigation is complete or, in the case of a request for information, all relevant complaint and appeal provisions have been exhausted;

 b) They have long-term value for historical or other research and have been or should be selected for permanent preservation. (Note that records containing personal information can be kept indefinitely for historical research purposes because they thereby become exempt from the 5th data protection principle.)

 c) They contain or relate to information recently released in response to a request under the Act. This may indicate historical value and destruction should be delayed while this is re-assessed.

Making disposal decisions

12.4 Disposal of records should be undertaken only in accordance with clearly established policies that:

    a) Reflect the authority's continuing need for access to the information or the potential value of the records for historical or other research;

    b) Are based on consultation between records management staff, staff of the relevant business unit and, where appropriate, others such as legal advisers, archivists or external experts;

    c) Have been formally adopted by the authority;

    d) Are applied by properly authorised staff;

    e) Take account of security and confidentiality needs.

12.5 The policies should take the form of:

    a) An overall policy, stating in broad terms the types of records likely to be selected for permanent preservation. The policy could be a separate policy, part of the records management policy or a preamble to a disposal schedule;

    b) Disposal schedules which identify and describe records to which a pre-defined disposal action can be applied, for example destroy x years after [trigger event]; review after y years, transfer to archives for permanent preservation after z years.

12.6 Disposal schedules should contain sufficient details about the records to enable the records to be easily identified and the disposal action applied to them on a routine and timely basis. The amount of detail in disposal schedules will depend on the authority's needs but they should at least:

    a) Describe the records, including any relevant reference numbers;

    b) Identify the function to which the records relate and the business unit for that function (if that is not clear);

    c) Specify the retention period, i.e. how long they are to be kept;

    d) Specify what is to happen to them at the end of that period, i.e. the disposal action;

    e) Note the legal, regulatory or other reason for the disposal period and action, for example a statutory provision.

Disposal schedules should be arranged in the way that best meets the authority's needs.

12.7 Disposal schedules should be kept up to date and should be amended if a relevant statutory provision changes. However, authorities should consider keeping information about previous provisions so that the basis on which records were previously destroyed can be explained.

12.8 If any records are not included in disposal schedules, special arrangements should be made to review them and decide whether they can be destroyed or should be selected for permanent preservation. Decisions of this nature should be documented and kept to provide evidence of which records have been identified for destruction, when the decision was made, and the reasons for the decision, where this is not apparent from the overall policy.

Implementing disposal decisions

12.9 Disposal schedules and disposal decisions should be implemented by properly authorised staff. Implementation arrangements should take account of variations caused by, for example, outstanding requests for information or litigation.

12.10 Records scheduled for destruction should be destroyed in as secure a manner as required by the level of confidentiality or security markings they bear. For example, records containing personal information about living individuals should be destroyed in a way that prevents unauthorised access (this is required to comply with the 7th data protection principle). With digital records it may be necessary to do more than overwrite the data to ensure the information is destroyed. Some authorities use the term 'retention schedules'. Because 'retention' has a specific meaning in Part 2 of the Code, the term disposal schedules is used throughout the Code.

12.11 When destruction is carried out by an external contractor, the contract should stipulate that the security and access arrangements established for the records will continue to be applied until destruction has taken place.

12.12 In some cases there will be more than one copy of a record. For example, there are likely to be back-up copies of digital records, or there may be digital copies of paper records. A record cannot be considered to have been completely destroyed until all copies, including back-up copies, have been destroyed, if there is a possibility that the data could be recovered.

Documenting the destruction of records

12.13 Details of destruction of records should be kept, either as part of the audit trail metadata or separately. Ideally, some evidence of destruction should be kept indefinitely because the previous existence of records may be relevant information. However, the level of detail and for how long it should be kept will depend on an assessment of the costs and the risks to the authority if detailed information cannot be produced on request.

12.14 At the very least it should be possible to provide evidence that as part of routine records management processes destruction of a specified type of record of a specified age range took place in accordance with a specified provision of the disposal schedule. Evidence of this nature will enable an authority and its staff to explain why records specified in a court order cannot be provided or to defend themselves against a charge under section

77 of the Act that records were destroyed in order to prevent their disclosure in response to a request for information.

Records for permanent preservation

12.15 Records selected for permanent preservation and no longer required by the authority should be transferred to an archives service that has adequate storage and public access facilities. Transfer should take place in an orderly manner and with a level of security appropriate to the confidentiality of the records.

12.16 Part 2 of the Code sets out the arrangements that apply to the review and transfer of public records. The approach set out in Part 2 may be relevant to the review and transfer of other types of records also.

Records created in the course of collaborative working or through out-sourcing

13. Authorities should ensure that records shared with other bodies or held on their behalf by other bodies are managed in accordance with the Code.

13.1 When authorities are working in partnership with other organisations, sharing information and contributing to a joint records system, they should ensure that all parties agree protocols that specify:

    a) What information should be contributed and kept, and by whom;

    b) What level of information security should be applied;

    c) Who should have access to the records;

    d) What disposal arrangements should be in place;

    e) Which body holds the information for the purposes of the Act.

13.2 Instructions and training should be provided to staff involved in such collaborative working.

13.3 Records management controls should be applied to information being shared with or passed to other bodies. Particular protection should be given to confidential or personal information. Protocols should specify when, and under what conditions, information will be shared or passed, and details should be kept of when this information has been shared or passed. Details should be kept also of how undertakings given to the original source of the information have been respected.

13.4 Some of an authority's records may be held on its behalf by another body, for example a body carrying out work for the authority under contract. The authority on whose behalf the records are held is responsible for ensuring that the provisions of the Code are applied to those records.

Monitoring and reporting on records and information management

14. Authorities should monitor compliance with the Code and assess the overall effectiveness of the programme.

14.1 Authorities should identify performance measures that reflect their information management needs and arrangements and the risks that non-compliance with the Code would present to the authority, including the impact on risks identified in the overall risk management framework.

14.2 The performance measures could be general in nature, for example that a policy has been issued, or could refer to processes, such as the application of disposal schedules to relevant records with due authorisation of destruction, or could use metrics such as retrieval times for paper records held off-site that have been requested under the Act.

14.3 Authorities should put in place the means by which performance can be measured. For example, if metrics are to be used, the data from which statistics will be generated must be kept. Qualitative indicators, for example whether guidance is being followed, can be measured by spot checks or by interviews.

14.4 Monitoring should be undertaken on a regular basis and the results reported to the person with lead responsibility for records management so that risks can be assessed and appropriate action taken.

14.5 Assessing whether the records management programme meets the needs of the organisation is a more complex task and requires consideration of what the programme is intended to achieve and how successful it is being. This requires consideration of business benefits in relation to corporate objectives as well as risks and should include consultation throughout the authority.

PART 2: REVIEW AND TRANSFER OF PUBLIC RECORDS

Purpose of Part 2

15.1 This part of the Code applies only to authorities which are subject to the Public Records Act 1958 or the Public Records Act (Northern Ireland) 1923. Under those Acts, authorities are required to identify records worthy of permanent preservation and transfer them to The National Archives, a place of deposit for public records or the Public Record Office of Northern Ireland as appropriate. This part of the Code sets out the arrangements which those authorities should follow to ensure the timely and effective review and transfer of public records. Arrangements should be established and operated under the supervision of The National Archives or, in Northern Ireland, in conjunction with the Public Record Office of Northern Ireland.

15.2 The general purpose of this part of the Code is to facilitate the performance by the authorities, The National Archives, the Public Record Office of Northern Ireland and places of deposit of their functions under the Act. In reviewing records for public access, authorities should ensure that public records become available at the earliest possible time in accordance with the Act and the EIR.

Selection of public records for permanent preservation

16.1 Section 12 of the Code describes the arrangements that authorities should follow for the disposal of records. In this context, disposal means the decision as to whether the record should be destroyed, transferred to an archives service for permanent preservation or presented and the putting into effect of that decision.

16.2 Authorities that have created or are otherwise responsible for public records should ensure that they operate effective arrangements to determine which records should be selected for permanent preservation in accordance with the guidance in section 12.

Retention or transfer of public records

Records subject to the Public Records Act 1958

17.1 Under the Public Records Act 1958, records selected for preservation must be transferred by the time they are 30 years old unless the Lord Chancellor gives authorisation for them to be retained in the department for a further period under section 3(4) of the Public Records Act 1958. Records may be transferred earlier by agreement between the parties involved.

17.2 Public records may be transferred either to The National Archives or to a place of deposit for public records appointed by the Lord Chancellor under section 4 of that Act. For guidance on which records may be transferred to which archives service, and on the transfer of UK public records relating to Northern Ireland, see Annex B. For the avoidance of doubt, Part 2 of the Code applies to all such transfers.

17.3 Authorities should submit applications to retain records for a further period to The National Archives for review and advice. The Lord Chancellor's Advisory Council will then consider the case in favour of retention for a further period. The Advisory Council will consider the case for retaining individual records, or coherent batches of records, on the basis of the guidance in chapter 9 of the White Paper Open Government (Cm 2290, 1993) or subsequent revisions of Government policy. Some categories of records are covered by a standard authorisation by the Lord Chancellor (known as 'blanket retentions') which are reviewed every 10 years.

Records subject to the Public Records Act (Northern Ireland) 1923

17.4 In Northern Ireland, transfer under the Public Records Act (Northern Ireland) 1923 to the Public Record Office of Northern Ireland takes place normally at 20 years. Under section 3 of that Act, records may be retained for a further period if the principal officer of the department, or a judge if court records are involved, certifies to the Minister responsible for Northern Ireland public records that they should be retained.

Determining the access status of public records before transfer

The access review

18.1 Authorities preparing public records for transfer to The National Archives, a place of deposit for public records or the Public Record Office of Northern Ireland should review the access status of those records. The purpose of this review is to:

    a) Consider which information must be available to the public on transfer because no exemptions under the Act or the EIR apply;

    b) Consider whether the information must be released in the public interest, notwithstanding the application of an exemption under the Act or the EIR;

    c) Consider which information must be available to the public at 30 years because relevant exemptions in the Act have ceased to apply;

    d) Consider which information should be withheld from public access through the application of an exemption under the Act or the EIR.

18.2 Those undertaking the review should ensure that adequate consultation takes place, both within the authority and with other authorities that might be affected by the decision, for example authorities that originally supplied the information. This is particularly advisable for records being transferred earlier than required.

Public records to be transferred as open

18.3 If the outcome of the review is that records are to be transferred as open, the transferring department should designate the records as open. There will be no formal review of this designation by The National Archives, places of deposit or the Public Record Office of Northern Ireland.

Public records to be transferred as subject to an exemption – general

18.4 If the outcome of the review is identification of specified information which the authority considers ought not to be released under the terms of the Act or the EIR, the authority should prepare a schedule that:

    a) Identifies the information precisely;

    b) Cites the relevant exemption(s);

    c) Explains why the information may not be released;

    d) Identifies a date at which either release would be appropriate or the case for release should be reconsidered.

18.5 Authorities should consider whether parts of records might be released if the sensitive information were redacted, i.e. rendered invisible or blanked out. Information that has been redacted should be stored securely and should be returned to the parent record when the exemption has ceased to apply.

Public records to be transferred as subject to an exemption – The National Archives

18.6 The schedule described above should be submitted to The National Archives for review and advice prior to transfer. If the outcome of the review is that some or all of the information in the records should be closed after it is 30 years old, the schedule will be considered by the Advisory Council. The Advisory Council may respond as follows

    a) By accepting that the information may be withheld for longer than 30 years and earmarking the records for release or re-review at the date identified by the authority;

    b) By accepting that the information may be withheld for longer than 30 years but asking the authority to reconsider the later date designated for release or re-review;

     c) By questioning the basis on which it is considered that the information may be withheld for longer than 30 years and asking the authority to reconsider the case;

18.7 If the Advisory Council accepts that the information should be withheld, the records will be transferred as closed (in whole or in part as appropriate) and the relevant closure period applied.

Public records to be transferred as subject to an exemption – the Public Record Office of Northern Ireland

18.8 The schedule described at paragraph 18.4 should be submitted to the Public Record Office of Northern Ireland for review and advice.

18.9 If the outcome of the review is that the records should be closed after transfer, the schedule will be considered by the Sensitivity Review Group. The Sensitivity Review Group may respond as follows:

     a) By accepting that the information should be withheld for longer than 30 years and earmarking the records for release or re-review at the date identified on the schedule;

     b) By questioning the basis on which it is considered that the information may be withheld for longer than 30 years and asking the responsible authority to reconsider the case.

18.10 If the Sensitivity Review Group accepts that the information should be withheld, the records will be transferred as closed (in whole or in part as appropriate) and the relevant closure period applied.

Public records to be transferred as subject to an exemption – places of deposit for public records

18.11 Places of deposit should be informed which records cannot be made publicly available on transfer, which exemptions apply to the information they contain and for what reason, and for how long those exemptions should be applied.

Transmission of public records

19.1 It is the responsibility of authorities transferring records to ensure that those records are adequately prepared and are transferred with the level of security appropriate to the confidentiality of the information they contain.

Access after transfer of public records

Freedom of Information requests after transfer

20.1 For the avoidance of doubt, none of the actions described in this Code affects the statutory rights of access established under the Act or the EIR. Requests for exempt information in public records transferred to The National Archives, a place of deposit for public records or the Public Record Office of Northern Ireland will be dealt with on a case by case basis in accordance with the provisions of the Act or the EIR.

Expiry of closure periods

20.2 When an exemption has ceased to apply under section 63 of the Act the records will become automatically available to members of the public at the date specified in the finalised schedule (i.e. the schedule after it has been reviewed by the Advisory Council or the Sensitivity Review Group as appropriate).

20.3 In other cases, if the authority concerned wishes to extend the period during which the information is to be withheld, it should submit a further schedule explaining the sensitivity of the information. This is to be done before the expiry of the period stated in the earlier schedule. The process outlined at paragraphs 18.6–18.10 will then be applied. In Northern Ireland, Ministerial agreement is required for any further extension of the closure period and referral to the Minister will be an additional stage in the process.

Annex A Glossary

Disposal – the decision as to whether the record should be destroyed, transferred to an archives service for permanent preservation or presented and the putting into effect of that decision.

Disposal schedules – schedules that identify types of records and specify for how long they will be kept before they are destroyed, designated for permanent preservation or subjected to a further review.

Keeping records – in the context of this Code, keeping records includes recording the authority's activities by creating documents and other types of records as well as handling material received.

Metadata – information about the context within which records were created, their structure and how they have been managed over time. Metadata can refer to records within digital systems, for example event log data. It can also refer to systems such as paper files that are controlled either from a digital system or by a register or card index, for example the title and location.

Place of deposit – an archives office appointed to receive, preserve and provide access to public records that have been selected for preservation but are not to be transferred to The National Archives. The power of appointment has been delegated by the Lord Chancellor to the Chief Executive of The National Archives or an officer of appropriate seniority.

Presentation – an arrangement under the Public Records Act 1958 whereby records that have not been selected for permanent preservation are presented to an appropriate body by The National Archives.

Public records – records that are subject to the Public Records Act 1958 or the Public Records Act (Northern Ireland) 1923. The records of government departments and their executive agencies, some non-departmental public bodies, the courts, the NHS and the armed forces are public records. Local government records are not public records in England and Wales but those in Northern Ireland are.

Records – information created, received, and maintained as evidence and information by an organization or person, in pursuance of legal obligations or in the transaction of business. 21

Retention – an arrangement under the Public Records Act 1958 whereby authorities are permitted to delay the transfer of specified public records for an agreed period and to retain them until the end of that period.

Records system – the term used for an information or process system that contains records and other information. It can be either a paper-based system or a digital system. Examples are correspondence file series, digital records management systems, case management systems, function-specific systems such as finance systems, etc.

Annex B Standards and guidance supporting the Code

Not reproduced

Code of Practice on the discharge of the obligations of public authorities under the Environmental Information Regulations 2004
SI 2004 No. 3391

laid before Parliament on 16 February 2005

Issued under Regulation 16 of the Regulations, February 2005

FOREWORD TO THE CODE OF PRACTICE

Introduction

1. The Code of Practice, to which this is a foreword, is prepared in accordance with Regulation 16 of the Environmental Information Regulations 2004 (EIR) and provides guidance to public authorities as to the practice that would be desirable for them to follow in connection with discharging their functions under the EIR. However, if public authorities do not follow the Code's recommendations it will be difficult for them to meet their obligations under the Regulations.

2. The definition of 'public authority' for the purposes of the EIR is wider than that under section 3(1) of the Freedom of Information Act 2000 (FOIA). Those bodies subject to both the FOIA and the EIR will need to consider the Code provisions relevant to the appropriate regime (this Code or the FOIA section 45 Code). Public authorities covered only by the EIR need only consider this Code of Practice on access to information.

Recommendations for EIR public authorities on record keeping, management and destruction are set out in the FOIA section 46 Code of Practice.

3. This Code applies where a request for environmental information is received, as defined in the EIR. Any request for other information should be handled in accordance with the FOIA and other access regimes such as the Data Protection Act as appropriate. Where a request relates to information, part of which is environmental and part of which is not, then each part of the request should be handled in accordance with the relevant legislation.

4. This foreword does not form part of the Code itself.

5. An access to environmental information regime has been in place since 1992, in the form of the Environmental Information Regulations 1992, as amended by the Environmental Information (Amendment) Regulations 1998, and also the Environmental Information Regulations (Northern Ireland) 1993 and 1998. The introduction of replacement Regulations in England, Wales and Northern Ireland (and of similar regulations in Scotland) enables compliance with the UK's commitments under the UNECE Convention on Access to Information, Public Participation in Decision-making, and Access to Justice in Environmental Matters (the "Aarhus" Convention), and with EU Directive 2003/4/EC. Increased public access to environmental information and the

dissemination of such information contribute to a greater awareness of environmental matters, a free exchange of views, more effective participation by the public in environmental decision- making and, eventually, to a better environment (Recital 1, Directive 2003/4/EC).

6. The Government is committed to greater openness in the public sector. FOIA and EIR will further this aim by helping to transform the culture of the public sector to one of greater openness, enabling members of the public to scrutinise the decisions of public authorities more closely and ensure that services provided by the public sector are more efficiently and properly delivered. Conformity with the Code will assist this.

7. The Code is a supplement to the provisions in the EIR. It is not a substitute for legislation. Public authorities should seek legal advice as considered necessary on general issues relating to the implementation of the EIR or its application to individual cases. They should also refer to the Government's Guidance on the EIR and to any guidance issued by the Information Commissioner.

8. The provisions of the EIR granting a general right of access came into force on 1st January 2005 and the Commissioner's powers to handle appeals and issue guidance will also took effect on 1st January 2005.

9. This code of practice outlines to public authorities the practice that it would, in the opinion of the Secretary of State, be desirable for them to follow in connection with the discharge of their duties under the Environmental Information Regulations 2004 (EIR).

10. The aims of the Code are to:

    – facilitate the disclosure of information under the EIR by setting out good administrative practice that it is desirable for public authorities to follow when handling requests for information including, where appropriate, the transfer of a request to a different authority;

    – to set out good practice in proactive dissemination of environmental information;

    – to protect the interests of applicants by setting out standards of advice and assistance that should be followed as a matter of good practice;

    – to ensure that third party rights are considered and that authorities consider the implications for access to environmental information before agreeing to confidentiality provisions in contracts and accepting information in confidence from a third party;

    – to encourage, as matter of good practice, the development of effective review and appeal procedures of decisions taken under the EIR.

11. Although there is a power under EIR for the Secretary of State to issue the Code, the provisions of the Code are not legislation. However, authorities are expected to abide by

the Code unless there are good reasons, capable of being justified to the Information Commissioner, why it would be inappropriate to do so.

12. The requirements for dealing with requests for environmental information are contained in the EIR and public authorities must comply with these provisions at all times. However, Regulation 16 applies section 47 of the FOIA, which places a duty on the Information Commissioner to promote good practice by public authorities ("good practice" includes compliance with the provisions of the Code), and section 48 of the FOIA which enables the Information Commissioner to issue a "practice recommendation" to a public authority if it appears to him that the practice of the authority does not conform with that proposed in the Code.

13. Public authorities and others are encouraged to contact the Information Commissioner's Office for advice and assistance about their duties under the Regulations. The Information Commissioner can provide valuable, detailed assistance to help organisations achieve compliance through the development of good practice. Further, Regulation 9 of the EIR places a duty on public authorities to provide advice and assistance to applicants and potential applicants. Authorities will have complied with this duty in any particular case if they have conformed with the Code in relation to the provision of advice or assistance in that case.

Main differences between requirements under the FOIA and EIR that must be reflected in this code

14. The main differences are:

    i. the range of bodies covered by the EIR is wider to allow for consistency with the EC Directive, and includes public utilities and certain public private partnerships and private companies, such as those in the water, waste, transport and energy sectors;

    ii. requests for environmental information need not be in writing;

    iii. the information held by a public authority includes holding information held on behalf of any other person;

    iv. the duty to provide advice and assistance requires a public authority to respond within 20 working days when requesting more particulars from the applicant;

    v. the time limits for responding to a request apply to ALL requests including those involving consideration of the public interest. Regulation 7 allows for an extension from 20 to 40 working days for complex and high volume requests;

    vi no exception is made for requests that will involve costs in excess of the 'appropriate limit' within the meaning of the Fees Regulations made under sections 9, 12 and 13 of the FOIA. Except in specified limited circumstances, ALL requests must be dealt with and any charges imposed must be reasonable;

vii there are differences in the exceptions available under EIR and the exemptions available under FOIA; viii the requirement for public authorities to have in place a complaints and reconsideration procedure to deal with representations alleging non-compliance with the EIR is mandatory. Each of these differences is explained in greater detail in the EIR Guidance that can be found at http://www.defra.gov.uk/environment/pubaccess/ . The Guidance also explains the scope of environmental information and provides further information on terminology, including "emissions" and "held by or for".

Duty to provide advice and assistance

15.   Regulation 9 of the EIR places a duty on public authorities to provide advice and assistance to applicants. A public authority is deemed to have complied with this duty in any particular case if it has conformed with this Code in relation to the provision of advice and assistance in that case. The duty to assist and advise is enforceable by the Information Commissioner. If a public authority fails in its statutory duty, the Commissioner may issue a decision notice under section 50, or an enforcement notice under section 52 of the FOIA.

16.   Public Authorities should not forget that other Acts of Parliament may be relevant to the way in which authorities provide advice and assistance to applicants or potential applicants, e.g. the Disability Discrimination Act 1995 and the Race Relations Act 1976 (as amended by the Race Relations (Amendment) Act 2000).

Copyright

17.   Public authorities should be aware that information that is disclosed under the EIR might be subject to copyright protection. If an applicant wishes to use any such information in a way that would infringe copyright, for example by making multiple copies, or issuing copies to the public, he or she would require a licence from the copyright holder. HMSO have issued guidance, which is available at http://www.hmso.gov.uk/copyright/managing_copyright.htm or by telephone on 01603 621000.

18   http://www.hmso.gov.uk/copyright/guidance/gn_19.htm explains more fully the distinction between the supply of information held by public authorities under Freedom of Information legislation and the re- use of that information and those circumstances where formal licensing is required.

19.   Reports on the environment may be commissioned by public authorities from outside organisations. In general, public authorities should seek to ensure that the copyright of any such reports rests with them. If not, it should be made clear to the outside organisation that under the terms of the EIR, the public authority will likely be making copies of their reports, or parts thereof, available to the public in response to EIR applications, and it may not be solely environmental information contained in reports that will be disclosed.

Practice recommendations

20. The Information Commissioner has a duty to enforce compliance and promote good practice. The following (described in paragraphs 21-24) are the principal tools at his disposal. The Information Commissioner (the Commissioner) is issuing guidance for public authorities on dealing with requests for environmental information, which may be helpful in setting out in more detail the Commissioner's enforcement powers.

21. In accordance with the powers provided in section 74 of the FOIA, Regulation 16(5) of EIR provides that the general functions of the Commissioner under sections 47-49 of the FOIA shall apply under EIR. Under section 47 of the FOIA, the Information Commissioner has a duty to promote the observance of this Code by public authorities. If it appears to the Commissioner that the practice of a public authority in the exercise of its functions under the EIR does not conform with that proposed in the Code of Practice, he may give to the authority a recommendation, under section 48 (known as a "practice recommendation"), specifying the steps which should, in his opinion, be taken to promote such conformity. Unless the public authority appeals against the decision of the Commissioner the public authority must comply with the recommendation of the Commissioner. There is no statutory time limit for this; it will depend on the circumstances of the case but the Commissioner can specify a particular time limit for compliance in the recommendation in question, and will take into consideration the measurements of Articles 9(1) and 9(4) of the Aarhus Convention in setting any time limit.

22. A practice recommendation must be given in writing and must refer to the particular provisions of the Code of Practice with which, in the Commissioner's opinion, the public authority's practice does not conform. A practice recommendation is simply a recommendation and cannot be directly enforced by the Commissioner. However, a failure to comply with a practice recommendation may lead to a failure to comply with the EIR. Further, a failure to take account of a practice recommendation may lead to an adverse comment in a report to Parliament by the Commissioner.

Information notices

23. Regulation 18 of the EIR applies the enforcement and appeal provisions of FOIA to environmental information. The Information Commissioner determines whether the practice of a public authority conforms to this Code. Where an application has been received under section 50 of the FOIA, under section 51 of the FOIA, he may serve an information notice on the authority requiring it to provide information relating to its conformity with the Code.

24. Under the provisions of section 54 of the FOIA, if a public authority fails to comply with an information notice the Commissioner may certify in writing to the court that the public authority has failed to comply with that notice. The court may then inquire into the matter and, after hearing any witnesses who may be produced against or on behalf of the public authority, and after hearing any statement that may be offered in defence, deal with the authority as if it had committed a contempt of court.

Code of Practice on the Discharge of the Obligations of Public Authorities Under the Environmental Information Regulations 2004 (SI 2004 No 3391)

The Secretary of State, after consulting the Information Commissioner, issues the following Code of Practice pursuant to Regulation 16 of the Environmental Information Regulations 2004. Laid before Parliament on 16 February 2005 pursuant to Regulation 16 of the Environmental Information Regulations.

I   TRAINING

1.   All communications to a public authority, including those not in writing and those transmitted by electronic means, potentially amount to a request for information within the meaning of the EIR, and if they do they must be dealt with in accordance with the provisions of the EIR. It is therefore essential that everyone working in a public authority who deals with correspondence, or who otherwise may be required to provide information, is familiar with the requirements of the EIR and this Code in addition to the FOIA and the other Codes of Practice issued under its provisions, and takes account of any relevant guidance on good practice issued by the Commissioner. Authorities should also ensure that proper training is provided.

2.   Requests for environmental information may come in the form of verbal requests which has specific implications for training provision.

3.   In planning and delivering training, authorities should be aware of other provisions affecting the disclosure of information such as the FOIA, the Data Protection Act 1998, and anti-discrimination legislation (such as the Disability Discrimination Act).

II   PROACTIVE DISSEMINATION OF INFORMATION

4.   Under Regulation 4, a public authority has a duty to progressively make the information available to the public by electronic means which are easily accessible, and to take reasonable steps to organize information relevant to its functions with a view to active and systematic dissemination.

5.   Consideration should be given to making web sites accessible to all and simple to use, so that information can be readily found, for example by enabling search functions and having an alphabetical directory as well as tree structures. Information should not be 'buried' on a site.

6.   Public authorities should consider how to publicise applicants' rights to information, for example as part of general information on services provided by the authority.

7.   When public authorities are considering what information to disseminate proactively, they should not restrict themselves to the minimum requirements as listed in the Directive. For example, consideration should be given to disseminating frequently requested information, which will reduce individual requests for such information in the future.

III   THE PROVISION OF ADVICE AND ASSISTANCE TO PERSONS MAKING REQUESTS FOR INFORMATION

8.   The provision of advice and assistance to persons making requests for environmental information differs from that provided to those making general requests for information under FOIA:

  – requests for environmental information need not be in writing;

  – EIR contains no equivalent to the 'appropriate limit' exemption under section 12 of the FOIA; and

  – the duty to provide advice and assistance under EIR requires the public authority to request that the applicant provide more particulars within 20 working days of the request where a request is formulated in too general a manner.

9.   Every public authority should be ready to provide advice and assistance, including but not necessarily limited to the steps set out below. This advice and assistance should be available to those who propose to make, or have made requests and help them to make good use of the Regulations. The duty on the public authority is to provide advice and assistance "so far as it would be reasonable to expect the authority to do so".

10.   Appropriate assistance might include:

  – providing an outline of the different kinds of information that might meet the terms of the request;

  – providing access to detailed catalogues and indexes, where these are available, to help the applicant ascertain the nature and extent of the information held by the authority; and

  – providing a general response to the request setting out options for further information that could be provided on request.

  – advising the person that another person or agency (such as a Citizens Advice Bureau) may be able to assist them with the application or make the application on their behalf.

11.   This list is not exhaustive and public authorities should be flexible in offering advice and assistance most appropriate to the circumstances of the applicant.

12.   Public authorities should publish their procedures for dealing with requests for information. These procedures may include what the public authority's usual procedure will be where it does not hold the information requested. (See also VI - "Transferring requests for information"). It may also alert potential applicants to the fact that the public authority may want to consult other public authorities and/or third parties in order to reach a decision on whether the requested information can be released. Potential applicants may wish to be notified before any transfer of request or consultation is made. If this is the case, the published procedure should therefore alert them to say so in their applications. (See also VII - "Consultation with third parties".) The procedures should include an address or addresses (including an e-mail address where possible) to which applicants may direct requests for information or for assistance. A telephone number should also be provided and where possible the name of an individual who can provide assistance. These procedures should be referred to in the authority's publication scheme where it has one.

13.   Public authorities may wish to consider publishing their procedures for reviewing refusals for requests. In addition, public authorities will also wish to consider providing information about other access regimes (where appropriate), provide guidance about frequently requested information, and provide information relating to previous disclosures.

14.   Staff in public authorities in contact with the public should bear in mind that not everyone will be aware of the EIR or the FOIA and they should draw the legislation to the attention of potential applicants who appear unaware of them. Any question which cannot be dealt with on the spot should be treated as a request for information.

15.   A request for information under the EIR can be in any form and need not be in writing. However, for a response to be made by the public authority it will need contact details to either provide the information or refuse the request. A request in writing includes a request transmitted by electronic means. Where a person finds it difficult to specify very clearly the nature of their request, the public authority should ensure that appropriate assistance is given to enable that person to make a request for information. For example, if a request is formulated in too general a manner the public authority shall, as soon as possible and not later than 20 working days after receipt of the request, ask the applicant to provide more particulars and shall assist them in doing so. However, Public Authorities should be aware of the dangers of over- bureaucratising procedures when responding to requests for routine information.

Clarifying the Request

16.   Where the applicant does not describe the information sought in a way which would enable the public authority to identify or locate it, or the request is ambiguous, the authority should, as far as practicable, provide assistance to the applicant to enable him or her to describe more clearly the information requested. Authorities should be aware

that the aim of providing assistance is to clarify the nature of the information sought, not to determine the aims or motivation of the applicant. Care should be taken not to give the applicant the impression that he or she is obliged to disclose the nature of his or her interest or that he or she will be treated differently if he or she does. It is important that the applicant is contacted as soon as possible, preferably by telephone, fax or e-mail, where more information is needed to clarify what is sought. Public authorities should also be prepared to explain why they are asking for additional information. The 20 day time limit stops running when a request for clarification is issued.

17. In seeking to clarify what is sought, public authorities should bear in mind that applicants cannot reasonably be expected to possess identifiers such as a file reference number, or a description of a particular record, unless this information is made available by the authority for the use of applicants.

18. If, following the provision of such assistance, the applicant is still unable to describe the information requested in a way that would enable the authority to identify and locate it, the authority is not expected to seek further clarification. The authority should disclose any information relating to the application that has been successfully identified and found that it can disclose. It should also explain to the applicant why it cannot take the request any further and provide details of the authority's complaints procedure and where applicable the applicant's rights under section 50 of the FOIA (see "Complaints Procedure" in section XII below).

19. Where the applicant indicates that he or she is not prepared to pay any charge requested, the authority should consider whether there is any information that may be of interest to the applicant that is available free of charge.

20. There is no EIR equivalent to the 'appropriate limit' under section 12 of the FOIA. A public authority is expected to deal with all requests for environmental information. However, cost may be relevant when considering whether to apply the exceptions relating to 'manifestly unreasonable' or 'too general'. . Where the applicant makes a request that is clear but which involves the provision of a very large volume of information, and specifies a cost ceiling, the authority should consider providing an indication of what information could be provided within the cost ceiling.

21. There are no special provisions for dealing with requests that appear to be part of an organised campaign. Such requests are to be expected and dealt with in the usual way. Repeatedly requested information may be best made available by means of a publication scheme. Being part of a campaign does not necessarily make a request 'manifestly unreasonable'.

Form and Format

22. Regulation 6 allows for the applicant to be given the information available in a particular form or format unless there is another reasonable approach to supplying the information. A public authority should be flexible, as far as is reasonable, with respect to form and format, taking into account the fact, for example, that some IT users may not be able to

read attachments in certain formats, and that some members of the public may prefer paper to electronic copies.

23. Although there is no specific reference in the Regulations to the provision of information in the form of a summary or digest, a request for environmental information may include a request for information to be provided in the form of a digest or summary. This should generally be provided so long as it is reasonably practical to do so, taking into account the cost. Many applicants will find a summary more useful than masses of data, and this should be taken into account when considering proactive dissemination.

IV TIMELINESS IN DEALING WITH REQUESTS FOR INFORMATION

24. Requests for information must be responded to within 20 working days. The 20 day time limit can be extended to 40 working days if the complexity and volume of the information requested means that the 20 working days deadline cannot be complied with. Unlike FOIA, there is no provision to further extend the time limit for cases where the public interest has to be balanced.

25. Public authorities are required to comply with all requests for information as soon as possible and they must not delay responding until the end of the 20 working day period under Regulation 5(2)(b) if the information could reasonably have been provided earlier.

26. Public authorities must aim to make all decisions as soon as possible and in any case within 20 working days, including in cases where a public authority needs to consider where the public interest lies. However, it is recognised there will be some instances where, because of the complexity and volume of the information requested it will not be possible to deal with an application within 20 working days. In such cases a public authority is expected to inform the applicant of this as soon as possible and within 20 working days, and should, be as specific as possible in their response to the applicant indicating when they will receive the information and the reasons for the delay. The 20 days will halt at the point that the authority issues a request for payment of an advance charge, and commences again at the point payment is received, Authorities must in any case comply with or refuse the request within 40 working days. Authorities may find it helpful to formulate a policy about how to apply the provision on making a time extension.

27. It is of critical importance for the body receiving a request to identify the request for environmental information in the first instance, and then to meet the timetable. Monitoring the timeliness of responses is easiest where requests for information are in writing. Where requests for environmental information are made otherwise than in writing (e.g. by telephone or in person) public authorities will need a system for recording the request. This may, for example, involve making a written note of the request and asking the applicant to confirm its accuracy.

V   CHARGES

28.   The EIR does not require charges to be made but public authorities have discretion to make a reasonable charge for environmental information. However, if they are providing access to a public register, or if the applicant examines the information at the offices of the public authority or in a drop in library or other place which the public authority makes available for that examination, access to the information shall be free of charge. When making a charge, whether for information that is proactively disseminated or provided on request, the charge must not exceed the cost of producing the information unless that public authority is one entitled to levy a market-based charge for the information, such as a trading fund.

29.   Where a public authority proposes to make a charge, a schedule of charges should be made available (including, e.g. a price list for publications, or the charge per unit of work which will be incurred to meet a request). When an advance payment is required, the applicant should be notified and the public authority should invite the applicant to say whether they wish to proceed with the request, or their request, or part of it, or whether the request may be met in some other way (for example, by visiting the offices of the public authority to inspect the information or by making use of more easily identifiable data). Where a requirement for advance payment has been notified, the period between the notification and the receipt of payment will be disregarded in determining the response times for meeting requests (Regulation 8(5)). The request will remain active for up to 60 working days from the date of notification. If no payment is received during this time the request lapses but the applicant may make a new application at any time. When a fee payment is received the public authority should release the information promptly and within the appropriate time limit.

30.   Public authorities should ensure that any charges they make are reasonable, and in accordance with the EIR and the guidance. http://www.defra.gov.uk/environment/pubaccess/

VI   TRANSFERRING REQUESTS FOR INFORMATION

31.   A request whether in writing or received in any other form can only be transferred where a public authority receives a request for environmental information that it does not itself hold and which is not held by any other person on its behalf. If a public authority in receipt of a request holds some of the information requested, a transfer can only be made in respect of the information it does not hold but is held by another public authority.

32.   Public authorities should bear in mind that "holding" environmental information under the EIR includes holding a copy of a record produced or supplied by another person or body and, unlike FOIA, it extends to holding a record on behalf of another person or body. Where information is held on behalf of another person or body it will be appropriate to consult on whether the environmental information requested should be supplied unless the outcome can be predicted with reasonable confidence. (See also VII

– Consultation with Third Parties). (Special provisions apply to the National Archives and other public record holding bodies under Regulation 17 including the Public Records Office Northern Ireland).

33.   The authority receiving the initial request must always deal with that request in accordance with the EIR. When the authority receiving the original request does not hold all the information requested it must still deal with the request for information it does hold. The authority must also advise the applicant that it does not hold part of the requested information, or all of it, whichever applies. However, before doing this, the authority must be certain as to the extent of information requested that it holds itself. If information is freely available via a third party's public register, an authority may point to that register as part of providing advice and assistance, but this does not alter the authority's responsibility to respond to the request, for example if the applicant requests the information in the format in which it is held by the authority.

34.   If the authority to whom the initial request was made believes that some or all of the information requested is held by another public authority, the authority should consider what would be the most helpful and expeditious way of assisting the applicant with his or her request. In most cases this is likely to involve:

- contacting the applicant and informing him or her that the information requested may be held by another public authority;

- suggesting that the applicant re-applies to the authority that is believed to hold the information;

- providing him or her with contact details for that authority;

- if the public authority receiving the request and the authority holding the information are publicly perceived as indelibly linked, explaining to the applicant the difference between the two authorities.

35.   However, in some cases the authority to whom the original request is made may consider it to be more appropriate to transfer the request for information that it does not itself hold to another authority. In such cases, the authority should always consult with the other authority with a view to ascertaining whether it does hold the information and, if so, whether it should transfer the request to it. A request (or part of a request) should not be transferred if there is any reason to doubt that the second authority holds the information. When consulting a second authority the identity of the person requesting the information should not be disclosed unless that person has consented.

36.   Before transferring a request for information to another authority, the authority should firstly consider whether a transfer is appropriate. If a transfer is appropriate the authority should first obtain the consent of the applicant who may have valid reasons for not wishing their request to be transferred to a third party. If consent is given the applicant should always be provided with sufficient details concerning the date and destination of transfer.

37. Where a request or part of a request is transferred from one public authority to another, the receiving authority must comply with its obligations under the EIR in the same way as it would for a request that is received direct from an applicant. The time for complying with such a request will be measured from the day that the receiving authority receives the request.

38. All transfers of requests should take place as soon as is practicable, and the applicant should be notified as soon as possible once this has been done by issuing a refusal letter under Regulation 14.

39. Where a public authority is unable either to advise the applicant which public authority holds, or may hold, the requested information or to facilitate the transfer of the request to another authority (or considers it inappropriate to do so) it should consider what advice, if any, it can provide to the applicant to enable him or her to pursue his or her request. In this event the public authority should also issue a refusal letter in accordance with Regulation 14. The refusal letter should explain that the public authority does not hold the information.

VII CONSULTATION WITH THIRD PARTIES

40. Public authorities must always remember that unless an exception is provided for in the EIR in relation to any particular information, they will be obliged to disclose that information in response to a request. Authorities are not obliged by the EIR to consult in respect of information which may be wholly or jointly owned by third parties, but may make a commitment to do so.

41. All EIR exceptions are subject to the public interest test; unlike FOIA, the EIR contains no 'absolute' exceptions. Moreover, lack of consent of a third party does not necessarily preclude disclosure, as in each case the public interest must be balanced. If the public interest in disclosing the information outweighs the public interest in withholding it, the information must be disclosed. (Information on emissions must be disclosed in accordance with Regulation 12 and personal data must be considered in accordance with DPA requirements).

42. A public authority may consider that consultation is not appropriate where the cost of consulting with third parties would be disproportionate because, for example, many third parties are involved or there has been earlier consultation on the status and sensitivity of the information. It should be noted that in this context 'third party' is specifically a person or body affected by the information that is the subject of the consultation. In such cases the authority should consider what is the most reasonable course of action for it to take in light of the requirements of the EIR, the potential effects of disclosure, and the public interest.

43. Where the consent of a number of third parties may be relevant and those parties have a representative organisation that can express views on behalf of those parties the authority may, if it considers consultation appropriate, consider that it would be sufficient

to consult that representative organisation. If there is no representative organisation, the authority may consider that it would be sufficient to consult a representative sample of the third parties in question.

44.   The fact that the third party has not responded to consultation does not relieve the authority of its duty to disclose information under the EIR, or its duty to reply within the time specified in the EIR.

45.   In all cases, it is for the public authority that received the request, not the third party (or representative of the third party) to weigh the public interest and to determine whether or not information should be disclosed under the EIR. A refusal to consent to disclosure by a third party does not in itself mean information should be withheld, although it may indicate interests involved. Note that in the case of public records transferred to a public record office there is a requirement to consult (see Regulation 17).

VIII ENVIRONMENTAL INFORMATION REGULATIONS AND PUBLIC SECTOR CONTRACTS

46.   When entering into contracts public authorities should refuse to include contractual terms that purport to restrict the disclosure of environmental information held by the authority and relating to the contract beyond the restrictions permitted by the EIR. Public authorities cannot "contract out" of their obligations under the Regulations. This means that they cannot sign a contract that gives an undertaking to a private firm (or anyone else) that they will not comply with their obligations under the Regulations. Unless an exception provided for under the EIR is applicable in relation to any particular information and the balancing of public interest favours refusal, a public authority will be obliged to disclose that information in response to a request, regardless of the terms of any contract. Where personal data is concerned this will be done in accordance with the requirements of Regulation 13 and the Data Protection Act 1998.

47.   When entering into contracts with non-public authority contractors, public authorities may be under pressure to accept confidentiality clauses so that information relating to the terms of the contract, its value and performance will be exempt from disclosure. Public authorities should reject such clauses wherever possible and explain the relevance of the public interest test. Where, exceptionally, it is necessary to include non-disclosure provisions in a contract, an option could be to agree with the contractor a schedule of the contract that clearly identifies information that should not be disclosed. But authorities will need to take care when drawing up any such schedule, and be aware that any restrictions on disclosure provided for could potentially be overridden by their obligations under the EIR, as described above.

48.   In any event, public authorities should not agree to hold information 'in confidence' which is not in fact confidential in nature. Authorities should be aware that certain exceptions including those for commercial confidentiality, and voluntarily supplied data,

are not available when the information requested is about emissions into the environment.

49. Any acceptance of confidentiality provisions must be for good reasons and capable of being justified to the Commissioner.

50. It is for the public authority to disclose information pursuant to the EIR, and not the non-public authority contractor, unless that contractor received the request and is, itself, a body subject to the EIR. However, a public authority may have concerns regarding contractual matters and not wish the contractor to release information without consulting them. In these cases, contracts or other working arrangements should be made to ensure appropriate consultation about the handling of requests for information exchanged between the parties. Any such constraints should be drawn as narrowly as possible and according to the individual circumstances of the case. Apart from such cases, public authorities should not impose terms of secrecy on contractors.

51. With contracts in existence prior to EIR 2004 being enacted, if an authority receives a request for information whose release would mean an actionable breach of confidence, the authority should refer to the guidance issued by the Information Commissioner. Public authorities in this position should seek their own legal advice as appropriate.

52. Under the EIR, some contractors, including public utilities that have been privatised, are subject to the requirements of the EIR.

IX ACCEPTING INFORMATION IN CONFIDENCE FROM THIRD PARTIES
53. A public authority should only accept information from third parties in confidence if it is essential to obtain that information in connection with the exercise of any of the authority's functions and it would not otherwise be provided. Even in these circumstances it will be necessary to explain the relevance of the public interest test and the fact that there could be circumstances in which the public interest in disclosure equals or outweighs the adverse effects of disclosure on a third party. In addition, public authorities should not agree to hold information received from third parties "in confidence" which is not confidential in nature (paragraph 47). Again, acceptance of any confidentiality provisions must be for good reasons, capable of being justified to the Commissioner. (Special provisions apply to archives (paragraph 32).

X CONSULTATION WITH DEVOLVED ADMINISTRATIONS
54. Public authorities should consult with the relevant devolved administration before disclosing information provided by or directly concerning that administration, except where:

- the views of the devolved administration can have no effect on the decision of the authority (for example where there is no applicable exception so the information must be disclosed under EIR); or

- where the outcome may be predicted with reasonable confidence and in the circumstances, consultation would be too costly or time consuming.

55. Similarly, the devolved administrations should consult with the relevant non-devolved public authority before disclosing information provided by or directly concerning that authority, except where the views of the public authority can have no effect on the decision whether to disclose, or where consultation would be disproportionate in the circumstances.

XI   REFUSAL OF REQUEST
Advice on withholding of information is covered in Chapter 7 of the Guidance.

56. Where a request for information is refused or partially refused in accordance with an exception, the EIR requires that the authority notify the applicant which exception has been claimed and why that exception applies. Public authorities should not unless the statement would involve the disclosure of information which would itself be withheld in accordance with the EIR merely paraphrase the wording of the exception. They should state clearly in the decision letter the reason why they have decided to apply that exception in the case in question. The EIR also requires authorities, when withholding information, to state the reasons for claiming that the public interest in maintaining the exception outweighs the public interest in disclosure. Public authorities should specify the public interest factors (for and against disclosure) that they have taken into account before reaching the decision (again, unless the statement would involve the disclosure of information which would itself be withheld in accordance with the EIR). They should also include details of the complaints procedure.

57. For monitoring purposes public authorities should keep a record of all applications where either all or part of the requested information is withheld, the basis on which it was withheld (including the exception or exceptions which were applied), and, where relevant, a full explanation of how the public interest test was applied and the factors which were considered. Public authorities should also keep copies of redacted information, together with a copy of the information that the applicant actually received in case of a subsequent complaint. Senior managers in each public authority will need this information to determine whether cases are being properly considered and whether the reasons for refusals are sound. The information will also be required if the applicant appeals against the refusal, or refers the case to the Information Commissioner. This could be done by requiring all staff that refuse a request for information to forward the details to a central point in the organisation for collation. Details of information on complaints about applications which have been refused (see XII – "Complaints procedure") could be collected at the same central point.

XII   REVIEW AND COMPLAINTS PROCEDURES
58. Each public authority must have a review procedure in place. This procedure may be used by any person who considers that their request has not been properly handled or who are otherwise dissatisfied with the outcome of the consideration of their request and

where the issue is such that it cannot be resolved informally in discussion with the official dealing with the request. Information relating to the complaints procedure should be included in an authority's publication scheme if it has one, or made readily available elsewhere. Under Regulation 18, the enforcement and appeal provisions of the FOIA will apply in respect of a complaint made after 1st January 2005.

59. Any decision made in relation to a request under the EIR that contains a refusal must be in writing and public authorities are obliged under Regulations 14 (5) to notify the applicant of his or her right of complaint. They should provide details of their own complaints procedure, including how to make a complaint and inform the applicant of the right to complain to the Commissioner under section 50 of the FOIA if he or she is still dissatisfied following the authority's review. However, as a matter of good practice authorities should provide details of their complaints procedure when responding to all requests. It is for the applicant to decide whether they are content with the response they receive; they may have concerns that they wish to pursue in circumstances where the public authority claims to have fully complied with their request.

60. Any written reply from the applicant (including one transmitted electronically) expressing dissatisfaction with an authority's response to a valid request for information should be treated as a complaint, as should any written communication from a person who perceives the authority is not complying with its publication scheme where it has one. These communications should be handled in accordance with the authority's review procedure pursuant to Regulation 11, even if the applicant does not state his or her desire for the authority to review their decision or the handling of their application.

61. The complaints procedure should be a fair and impartial means of dealing with handling problems and reviewing decisions taken pursuant to the EIR, including decisions taken about where the public interest lies. It should be possible to reverse or otherwise amend decisions previously taken. Complaints procedures should be clear and not unnecessarily bureaucratic. They should be capable of producing a prompt determination of the complaint.

62. In all cases, complaints should be acknowledged and the complainant should be informed of the authority's target date for determining the complaint. Where it is apparent that determination of the complaint will take longer than the target time (for example because of the complexity of the particular case), the authority should inform the applicant and explain the reason for the delay. The complainant should always be informed of the outcome of his or her complaint.

63. Authorities must consider each complaint, decide whether they have complied with their requirements under EIR and respond to the complainant within 40 working days from the time when the complaint was received.

64. Records should be kept of all complaints and of their outcome. Authorities should have procedures in place for monitoring complaints and for reviewing, and if necessary amending procedures for dealing with requests for information where such action is indicated by more than occasional reversals of initial decisions.

65.   Where the outcome of a complaint is that information should be disclosed which was previously withheld, the information in question should be disclosed with immediate effect.

66.   Where the outcome of a complaint is that the procedures within an authority have not been properly followed by the authority's staff, the authority should apologise to the applicant. The authority should also take appropriate steps to prevent similar errors occurring in future.

67.   Where the outcome of a complaint is that an initial decision to withhold information is upheld or is otherwise in the authority's favour, the applicant should be informed of his or her right to apply to the Commissioner and be given details of how to make an application for a decision on whether the request for information has been dealt with in accordance with the requirements of the EIR. As failure to deal with a complaint promptly may be grounds for complaint to the Information Commissioner, authorities should set out details of the timescale for dealing with complaints in their complaints procedure, which should be made readily available.

Directive 95/46/EC of the European Parliament and of the Council of 24 October 1995 on the protection of individuals with regard to the processing of personal data and on the free movement of such data

THE EUROPEAN PARLIAMENT AND THE COUNCIL OF THE EUROPEAN UNION,

Having regard to the Treaty establishing the European Community, and in particular Article 100a thereof,

Having regard to the proposal from the Commission,

Having regard to the opinion of the Economic and Social Committee,

Acting in accordance with the procedure referred to in Article 189b of the Treaty,

(1) Whereas the objectives of the Community, as laid down in the Treaty, as amended by the Treaty on European Union, include creating an ever closer union among the peoples of Europe, fostering closer relations between the States belonging to the Community, ensuring economic and social progress by common action to eliminate the barriers which divide Europe, encouraging the constant improvement of the living conditions of its peoples, preserving and strengthening peace and liberty and promoting democracy on the basis of the fundamental rights recognized in the constitution and laws of the Member States and in the European Convention for the Protection of Human Rights and Fundamental Freedoms;

(2) Whereas data-processing systems are designed to serve man; whereas they must, whatever the nationality or residence of natural persons, respect their fundamental rights and freedoms, notably the right to privacy, and contribute to economic and social progress, trade expansion and the well-being of individuals;

(3) Whereas the establishment and functioning of an internal market in which, in accordance with Article 7a of the Treaty, the free movement of goods, persons, services and capital is ensured require not only that personal data should be able to flow freely from one Member State to another, but also that the fundamental rights of individuals should be safeguarded;

(4) Whereas increasingly frequent recourse is being had in the Community to the processing of personal data in the various spheres of economic and social activity; whereas the progress made in information technology is making the processing and exchange of such data considerably easier;

(5) Whereas the economic and social integration resulting from the establishment and functioning of the internal market within the meaning of Article 7a of the Treaty will necessarily lead to a substantial increase in cross-border flows of personal data between all those involved in a private or public capacity in economic and social activity in the

Member States; whereas the exchange of personal data between undertakings in different Member States is set to increase; whereas the national authorities in the various Member States are being called upon by virtue of Community law to collaborate and exchange personal data so as to be able to perform their duties or carry out tasks on behalf of an authority in another Member State within the context of the area without internal frontiers as constituted by the internal market;

(6) Whereas, furthermore, the increase in scientific and technical cooperation and the coordinated introduction of new telecommunications networks in the Community necessitate and facilitate cross-border flows of personal data;

(7) Whereas the difference in levels of protection of the rights and freedoms of individuals, notably the right to privacy, with regard to the processing of personal data afforded in the Member States may prevent the transmission of such data from the territory of one Member State to that of another Member State; whereas this difference may therefore constitute an obstacle to the pursuit of a number of economic activities at Community level, distort competition and impede authorities in the discharge of their responsibilities under Community law; whereas this difference in levels of protection is due to the existence of a wide variety of national laws, regulations and administrative provisions;

(8) Whereas, in order to remove the obstacles to flows of personal data, the level of protection of the rights and freedoms of individuals with regard to the processing of such data must be equivalent in all Member States; whereas this objective is vital to the internal market but cannot be achieved by the Member States alone, especially in view of the scale of the divergences which currently exist between the relevant laws in the Member States and the need to coordinate the laws of the Member States so as to ensure that the cross-border flow of personal data is regulated in a consistent manner that is in keeping with the objective of the internal market as provided for in Article 7a of the Treaty; whereas Community action to approximate those laws is therefore needed;

(9) Whereas, given the equivalent protection resulting from the approximation of national laws, the Member States will no longer be able to inhibit the free movement between them of personal data on grounds relating to protection of the rights and freedoms of individuals, and in particular the right to privacy; whereas Member States will be left a margin for manoeuvre, which may, in the context of implementation of the Directive, also be exercised by the business and social partners; whereas Member States will therefore be able to specify in their national law the general conditions governing the lawfulness of data processing; whereas in doing so the Member States shall strive to improve the protection currently provided by their legislation; whereas, within the limits of this margin for manoeuvre and in accordance with Community law, disparities could arise in the implementation of the Directive, and this could have an effect on the movement of data within a Member State as well as within the Community;

(10) Whereas the object of the national laws on the processing of personal data is to protect fundamental rights and freedoms, notably the right to privacy, which is recognized both in Article 8 of the European Convention for the Protection of Human Rights and

Fundamental Freedoms and in the general principles of Community law; whereas, for that reason, the approximation of those laws must not result in any lessening of the protection they afford but must, on the contrary, seek to ensure a high level of protection in the Community;

(11) Whereas the principles of the protection of the rights and freedoms of individuals, notably the right to privacy, which are contained in this Directive, give substance to and amplify those contained in the Council of Europe Convention of 28 January 1981 for the Protection of Individuals with regard to Automatic Processing of Personal Data;

(12) Whereas the protection principles must apply to all processing of personal data by any person whose activities are governed by Community law; whereas there should be excluded the processing of data carried out by a natural person in the exercise of activities which are exclusively personal or domestic, such as correspondence and the holding of records of addresses;

(13) Whereas the activities referred to in Titles V and VI of the Treaty on European Union regarding public safety, defence, State security or the activities of the State in the area of criminal laws fall outside the scope of Community law, without prejudice to the obligations incumbent upon Member States under Article 56 (2), Article 57 or Article 100a of the Treaty establishing the European Community; whereas the processing of personal data that is necessary to safeguard the economic well-being of the State does not fall within the scope of this Directive where such processing relates to State security matters;

(14) Whereas, given the importance of the developments under way, in the framework of the information society, of the techniques used to capture, transmit, manipulate, record, store or communicate sound and image data relating to natural persons, this Directive should be applicable to processing involving such data;

(15) Whereas the processing of such data is covered by this Directive only if it is automated or if the data processed are contained or are intended to be contained in a filing system structured according to specific criteria relating to individuals, so as to permit easy access to the personal data in question;

(16) Whereas the processing of sound and image data, such as in cases of video surveillance, does not come within the scope of this Directive if it is carried out for the purposes of public security, defence, national security or in the course of State activities relating to the area of criminal law or of other activities which do not come within the scope of Community law;

(17) Whereas, as far as the processing of sound and image data carried out for purposes of journalism or the purposes of literary or artistic expression is concerned, in particular in the audiovisual field, the principles of the Directive are to apply in a restricted manner according to the provisions laid down in Article 9;

(18) Whereas, in order to ensure that individuals are not deprived of the protection to which they are entitled under this Directive, any processing of personal data in the Community

must be carried out in accordance with the law of one of the Member States; whereas, in this connection, processing carried out under the responsibility of a controller who is established in a Member State should be governed by the law of that State;

(19)   Whereas establishment on the territory of a Member State implies the effective and real exercise of activity through stable arrangements; whereas the legal form of such an establishment, whether simply branch or a subsidiary with a legal personality, is not the determining factor in this respect; whereas, when a single controller is established on the territory of several Member States, particularly by means of subsidiaries, he must ensure, in order to avoid any circumvention of national rules, that each of the establishments fulfils the obligations imposed by the national law applicable to its activities;

(20)   Whereas the fact that the processing of data is carried out by a person established in a third country must not stand in the way of the protection of individuals provided for in this Directive; whereas in these cases, the processing should be governed by the law of the Member State in which the means used are located, and there should be guarantees to ensure that the rights and obligations provided for in this Directive are respected in practice;

(21)   Whereas this Directive is without prejudice to the rules of territoriality applicable in criminal matters;

(22)   Whereas Member States shall more precisely define in the laws they enact or when bringing into force the measures taken under this Directive the general circumstances in which processing is lawful; whereas in particular Article 5, in conjunction with Articles 7 and 8, allows Member States, independently of general rules, to provide for special processing conditions for specific sectors and for the various categories of data covered by Article 8;

(23)   Whereas Member States are empowered to ensure the implementation of the protection of individuals both by means of a general law on the protection of individuals as regards the processing of personal data and by sectorial laws such as those relating, for example, to statistical institutes;

(24)   Whereas the legislation concerning the protection of legal persons with regard to the processing data which concerns them is not affected by this Directive;

(25)   Whereas the principles of protection must be reflected, on the one hand, in the obligations imposed on persons, public authorities, enterprises, agencies or other bodies responsible for processing, in particular regarding data quality, technical security, notification to the supervisory authority, and the circumstances under which processing can be carried out, and, on the other hand, in the right conferred on individuals, the data on whom are the subject of processing, to be informed that processing is taking place, to consult the data, to request corrections and even to object to processing in certain circumstances;

(26)   Whereas the principles of protection must apply to any information concerning an identified or identifiable person; whereas, to determine whether a person is identifiable,

account should be taken of all the means likely reasonably to be used either by the controller or by any other person to identify the said person; whereas the principles of protection shall not apply to data rendered anonymous in such a way that the data subject is no longer identifiable; whereas codes of conduct within the meaning of Article 27 may be a useful instrument for providing guidance as to the ways in which data may be rendered anonymous and retained in a form in which identification of the data subject is no longer possible;

(27) Whereas the protection of individuals must apply as much to automatic processing of data as to manual processing; whereas the scope of this protection must not in effect depend on the techniques used, otherwise this would create a serious risk of circumvention; whereas, nonetheless, as regards manual processing, this Directive covers only filing systems, not unstructured files; whereas, in particular, the content of a filing system must be structured according to specific criteria relating to individuals allowing easy access to the personal data; whereas, in line with the definition in Article 2 (c), the different criteria for determining the constituents of a structured set of personal data, and the different criteria governing access to such a set, may be laid down by each Member State; whereas files or sets of files as well as their cover pages, which are not structured according to specific criteria, shall under no circumstances fall within the scope of this Directive;

(28) Whereas any processing of personal data must be lawful and fair to the individuals concerned; whereas, in particular, the data must be adequate, relevant and not excessive in relation to the purposes for which they are processed; whereas such purposes must be explicit and legitimate and must be determined at the time of collection of the data; whereas the purposes of processing further to collection shall not be incompatible with the purposes as they were originally specified;

(29) Whereas the further processing of personal data for historical, statistical or scientific purposes is not generally to be considered incompatible with the purposes for which the data have previously been collected provided that Member States furnish suitable safeguards; whereas these safeguards must in particular rule out the use of the data in support of measures or decisions regarding any particular individual;

(30) Whereas, in order to be lawful, the processing of personal data must in addition be carried out with the consent of the data subject or be necessary for the conclusion or performance of a contract binding on the data subject, or as a legal requirement, or for the performance of a task carried out in the public interest or in the exercise of official authority, or in the legitimate interests of a natural or legal person, provided that the interests or the rights and freedoms of the data subject are not overriding; whereas, in particular, in order to maintain a balance between the interests involved while guaranteeing effective competition, Member States may determine the circumstances in which personal data may be used or disclosed to a third party in the context of the legitimate ordinary business activities of companies and other bodies; whereas Member States may similarly specify the conditions under which personal data may be disclosed to a third party for the purposes of marketing whether carried out commercially or by

a charitable organization or by any other association or foundation, of a political nature for example, subject to the provisions allowing a data subject to object to the processing of data regarding him, at no cost and without having to state his reasons;

(31) Whereas the processing of personal data must equally be regarded as lawful where it is carried out in order to protect an interest which is essential for the data subject's life;

(32) Whereas it is for national legislation to determine whether the controller performing a task carried out in the public interest or in the exercise of official authority should be a public administration or another natural or legal person governed by public law, or by private law such as a professional association;

(33) Whereas data which are capable by their nature of infringing fundamental freedoms or privacy should not be processed unless the data subject gives his explicit consent; whereas, however, derogations from this prohibition must be explicitly provided for in respect of specific needs, in particular where the processing of these data is carried out for certain health-related purposes by persons subject to a legal obligation of professional secrecy or in the course of legitimate activities by certain associations or foundations the purpose of which is to permit the exercise of fundamental freedoms;

(34) Whereas Member States must also be authorized, when justified by grounds of important public interest, to derogate from the prohibition on processing sensitive categories of data where important reasons of public interest so justify in areas such as public health and social protection - especially in order to ensure the quality and cost-effectiveness of the procedures used for settling claims for benefits and services in the health insurance system - scientific research and government statistics; whereas it is incumbent on them, however, to provide specific and suitable safeguards so as to protect the fundamental rights and the privacy of individuals;

(35) Whereas, moreover, the processing of personal data by official authorities for achieving aims, laid down in constitutional law or international public law, of officially recognized religious associations is carried out on important grounds of public interest;

(36) Whereas where, in the course of electoral activities, the operation of the democratic system requires in certain Member States that political parties compile data on people's political opinion, the processing of such data may be permitted for reasons of important public interest, provided that appropriate safeguards are established;

(37) Whereas the processing of personal data for purposes of journalism or for purposes of literary of artistic expression, in particular in the audiovisual field, should qualify for exemption from the requirements of certain provisions of this Directive in so far as this is necessary to reconcile the fundamental rights of individuals with freedom of information and notably the right to receive and impart information, as guaranteed in particular in Article 10 of the European Convention for the Protection of Human Rights and Fundamental Freedoms; whereas Member States should therefore lay down exemptions and derogations necessary for the purpose of balance between fundamental rights as regards general measures on the legitimacy of data processing, measures on the

transfer of data to third countries and the power of the supervisory authority; whereas this should not, however, lead Member States to lay down exemptions from the measures to ensure security of processing; whereas at least the supervisory authority responsible for this sector should also be provided with certain ex-post powers, e.g. to publish a regular report or to refer matters to the judicial authorities;

(38) Whereas, if the processing of data is to be fair, the data subject must be in a position to learn of the existence of a processing operation and, where data are collected from him, must be given accurate and full information, bearing in mind the circumstances of the collection;

(39) Whereas certain processing operations involve data which the controller has not collected directly from the data subject; whereas, furthermore, data can be legitimately disclosed to a third party, even if the disclosure was not anticipated at the time the data were collected from the data subject; whereas, in all these cases, the data subject should be informed when the data are recorded or at the latest when the data are first disclosed to a third party;

(40) Whereas, however, it is not necessary to impose this obligation of the data subject already has the information; whereas, moreover, there will be no such obligation if the recording or disclosure are expressly provided for by law or if the provision of information to the data subject proves impossible or would involve disproportionate efforts, which could be the case where processing is for historical, statistical or scientific purposes; whereas, in this regard, the number of data subjects, the age of the data, and any compensatory measures adopted may be taken into consideration;

(41) Whereas any person must be able to exercise the right of access to data relating to him which are being processed, in order to verify in particular the accuracy of the data and the lawfulness of the processing; whereas, for the same reasons, every data subject must also have the right to know the logic involved in the automatic processing of data concerning him, at least in the case of the automated decisions referred to in Article 15 (1); whereas this right must not adversely affect trade secrets or intellectual property and in particular the copyright protecting the software; whereas these considerations must not, however, result in the data subject being refused all information;

(42) Whereas Member States may, in the interest of the data subject or so as to protect the rights and freedoms of others, restrict rights of access and information; whereas they may, for example, specify that access to medical data may be obtained only through a health professional;

(43) Whereas restrictions on the rights of access and information and on certain obligations of the controller may similarly be imposed by Member States in so far as they are necessary to safeguard, for example, national security, defence, public safety, or important economic or financial interests of a Member State or the Union, as well as criminal investigations and prosecutions and action in respect of breaches of ethics in the regulated professions; whereas the list of exceptions and limitations should include the tasks of monitoring, inspection or regulation necessary in the three last-mentioned areas

concerning public security, economic or financial interests and crime prevention; whereas the listing of tasks in these three areas does not affect the legitimacy of exceptions or restrictions for reasons of State security or defence;

(44) Whereas Member States may also be led, by virtue of the provisions of Community law, to derogate from the provisions of this Directive concerning the right of access, the obligation to inform individuals, and the quality of data, in order to secure certain of the purposes referred to above;

(45) Whereas, in cases where data might lawfully be processed on grounds of public interest, official authority or the legitimate interests of a natural or legal person, any data subject should nevertheless be entitled, on legitimate and compelling grounds relating to his particular situation, to object to the processing of any data relating to himself; whereas Member States may nevertheless lay down national provisions to the contrary;

(46) Whereas the protection of the rights and freedoms of data subjects with regard to the processing of personal data requires that appropriate technical and organizational measures be taken, both at the time of the design of the processing system and at the time of the processing itself, particularly in order to maintain security and thereby to prevent any unauthorized processing; whereas it is incumbent on the Member States to ensure that controllers comply with these measures; whereas these measures must ensure an appropriate level of security, taking into account the state of the art and the costs of their implementation in relation to the risks inherent in the processing and the nature of the data to be protected;

(47) Whereas where a message containing personal data is transmitted by means of a telecommunications or electronic mail service, the sole purpose of which is the transmission of such messages, the controller in respect of the personal data contained in the message will normally be considered to be the person from whom the message originates, rather than the person offering the transmission services; whereas, nevertheless, those offering such services will normally be considered controllers in respect of the processing of the additional personal data necessary for the operation of the service;

(48) Whereas the procedures for notifying the supervisory authority are designed to ensure disclosure of the purposes and main features of any processing operation for the purpose of verification that the operation is in accordance with the national measures taken under this Directive;

(49) Whereas, in order to avoid unsuitable administrative formalities, exemptions from the obligation to notify and simplification of the notification required may be provided for by Member States in cases where processing is unlikely adversely to affect the rights and freedoms of data subjects, provided that it is in accordance with a measure taken by a Member State specifying its limits; whereas exemption or simplification may similarly be provided for by Member States where a person appointed by the controller ensures that the processing carried out is not likely adversely to affect the rights and freedoms of data

subjects; whereas such a data protection official, whether or not an employee of the controller, must be in a position to exercise his functions in complete independence;

(50) Whereas exemption or simplification could be provided for in cases of processing operations whose sole purpose is the keeping of a register intended, according to national law, to provide information to the public and open to consultation by the public or by any person demonstrating a legitimate interest;

(51) Whereas, nevertheless, simplification or exemption from the obligation to notify shall not release the controller from any of the other obligations resulting from this Directive;

(52) Whereas, in this context, ex post facto verification by the competent authorities must in general be considered a sufficient measure;

(53) Whereas, however, certain processing operation are likely to pose specific risks to the rights and freedoms of data subjects by virtue of their nature, their scope or their purposes, such as that of excluding individuals from a right, benefit or a contract, or by virtue of the specific use of new technologies; whereas it is for Member States, if they so wish, to specify such risks in their legislation;

(54) Whereas with regard to all the processing undertaken in society, the amount posing such specific risks should be very limited; whereas Member States must provide that the supervisory authority, or the data protection official in cooperation with the authority, check such processing prior to it being carried out; whereas following this prior check, the supervisory authority may, according to its national law, give an opinion or an authorization regarding the processing; whereas such checking may equally take place in the course of the preparation either of a measure of the national parliament or of a measure based on such a legislative measure, which defines the nature of the processing and lays down appropriate safeguards;

(55) Whereas, if the controller fails to respect the rights of data subjects, national legislation must provide for a judicial remedy; whereas any damage which a person may suffer as a result of unlawful processing must be compensated for by the controller, who may be exempted from liability if he proves that he is not responsible for the damage, in particular in cases where he establishes fault on the part of the data subject or in case of force majeure; whereas sanctions must be imposed on any person, whether governed by private of public law, who fails to comply with the national measures taken under this Directive;

(56) Whereas cross-border flows of personal data are necessary to the expansion of international trade; whereas the protection of individuals guaranteed in the Community by this Directive does not stand in the way of transfers of personal data to third countries which ensure an adequate level of protection; whereas the adequacy of the level of protection afforded by a third country must be assessed in the light of all the circumstances surrounding the transfer operation or set of transfer operations;

(57) Whereas, on the other hand, the transfer of personal data to a third country which does not ensure an adequate level of protection must be prohibited;

(58) Whereas provisions should be made for exemptions from this prohibition in certain circumstances where the data subject has given his consent, where the transfer is necessary in relation to a contract or a legal claim, where protection of an important public interest so requires, for example in cases of international transfers of data between tax or customs administrations or between services competent for social security matters, or where the transfer is made from a register established by law and intended for consultation by the public or persons having a legitimate interest; whereas in this case such a transfer should not involve the entirety of the data or entire categories of the data contained in the register and, when the register is intended for consultation by persons having a legitimate interest, the transfer should be made only at the request of those persons or if they are to be the recipients;

(59) Whereas particular measures may be taken to compensate for the lack of protection in a third country in cases where the controller offers appropriate safeguards; whereas, moreover, provision must be made for procedures for negotiations between the Community and such third countries;

(60) Whereas, in any event, transfers to third countries may be effected only in full compliance with the provisions adopted by the Member States pursuant to this Directive, and in particular Article 8 thereof;

(61) Whereas Member States and the Commission, in their respective spheres of competence, must encourage the trade associations and other representative organizations concerned to draw up codes of conduct so as to facilitate the application of this Directive, taking account of the specific characteristics of the processing carried out in certain sectors, and respecting the national provisions adopted for its implementation;

(62) Whereas the establishment in Member States of supervisory authorities, exercising their functions with complete independence, is an essential component of the protection of individuals with regard to the processing of personal data;

(63) Whereas such authorities must have the necessary means to perform their duties, including powers of investigation and intervention, particularly in cases of complaints from individuals, and powers to engage in legal proceedings; whereas such authorities must help to ensure transparency of processing in the Member States within whose jurisdiction they fall;

(64) Whereas the authorities in the different Member States will need to assist one another in performing their duties so as to ensure that the rules of protection are properly respected throughout the European Union;

(65) Whereas, at Community level, a Working Party on the Protection of Individuals with regard to the Processing of Personal Data must be set up and be completely independent in the performance of its functions; whereas, having regard to its specific nature, it must advise the Commission and, in particular, contribute to the uniform application of the national rules adopted pursuant to this Directive;

(66) Whereas, with regard to the transfer of data to third countries, the application of this Directive calls for the conferment of powers of implementation on the Commission and the establishment of a procedure as laid down in Council Decision 87/373/EEC (1);

(67) Whereas an agreement on a modus vivendi between the European Parliament, the Council and the Commission concerning the implementing measures for acts adopted in accordance with the procedure laid down in Article 189b of the EC Treaty was reached on 20 December 1994;

(68) Whereas the principles set out in this Directive regarding the protection of the rights and freedoms of individuals, notably their right to privacy, with regard to the processing of personal data may be supplemented or clarified, in particular as far as certain sectors are concerned, by specific rules based on those principles;

(69) Whereas Member States should be allowed a period of not more than three years from the entry into force of the national measures transposing this Directive in which to apply such new national rules progressively to all processing operations already under way; whereas, in order to facilitate their cost-effective implementation, a further period expiring 12 years after the date on which this Directive is adopted will be allowed to Member States to ensure the conformity of existing manual filing systems with certain of the Directive's provisions; whereas, where data contained in such filing systems are manually processed during this extended transition period, those systems must be brought into conformity with these provisions at the time of such processing;

(70) Whereas it is not necessary for the data subject to give his consent again so as to allow the controller to continue to process, after the national provisions taken pursuant to this Directive enter into force, any sensitive data necessary for the performance of a contract concluded on the basis of free and informed consent before the entry into force of these provisions;

(71) Whereas this Directive does not stand in the way of a Member State's regulating marketing activities aimed at consumers residing in territory in so far as such regulation does not concern the protection of individuals with regard to the processing of personal data;

(72) Whereas this Directive allows the principle of public access to official documents to be taken into account when implementing the principles set out in this Directive,

HAVE ADOPTED THIS DIRECTIVE:

CHAPTER I GENERAL PROVISIONS

Article 1 — Object of the Directive

1. In accordance with this Directive, Member States shall protect the fundamental rights and freedoms of natural persons, and in particular their right to privacy with respect to the processing of personal data.

2. Member States shall neither restrict nor prohibit the free flow of personal data between Member States for reasons connected with the protection afforded under paragraph 1.

Article 2 — Definitions

For the purposes of this Directive:

(a) 'personal data' shall mean any information relating to an identified or identifiable natural person ('data subject'); an identifiable person is one who can be identified, directly or indirectly, in particular by reference to an identification number or to one or more factors specific to his physical, physiological, mental, economic, cultural or social identity;

(b) 'processing of personal data' ('processing') shall mean any operation or set of operations which is performed upon personal data, whether or not by automatic means, such as collection, recording, organization, storage, adaptation or alteration, retrieval, consultation, use, disclosure by transmission, dissemination or otherwise making available, alignment or combination, blocking, erasure or destruction;

(c) 'personal data filing system' ('filing system') shall mean any structured set of personal data which are accessible according to specific criteria, whether centralized, decentralized or dispersed on a functional or geographical basis;

(d) 'controller' shall mean the natural or legal person, public authority, agency or any other body which alone or jointly with others determines the purposes and means of the processing of personal data; where the purposes and means of processing are determined by national or Community laws or regulations, the controller or the specific criteria for his nomination may be designated by national or Community law;

(e) 'processor' shall mean a natural or legal person, public authority, agency or any other body which processes personal data on behalf of the controller;

(f) 'third party' shall mean any natural or legal person, public authority, agency or any other body other than the data subject, the controller, the processor and the persons who, under the direct authority of the controller or the processor, are authorized to process the data;

(g)   'recipient' shall mean a natural or legal person, public authority, agency or any other body to whom data are disclosed, whether a third party or not; however, authorities which may receive data in the framework of a particular inquiry shall not be regarded as recipients;

(h)   'the data subject's consent' shall mean any freely given specific and informed indication of his wishes by which the data subject signifies his agreement to personal data relating to him being processed.

Article 3 — Scope

1.   This Directive shall apply to the processing of personal data wholly or partly by automatic means, and to the processing otherwise than by automatic means of personal data which form part of a filing system or are intended to form part of a filing system.

2. This Directive shall not apply to the processing of personal data:

–   in the course of an activity which falls outside the scope of Community law, such as those provided for by Titles V and VI of the Treaty on European Union and in any case to processing operations concerning public security, defence, State security (including the economic well-being of the State when the processing operation relates to State security matters) and the activities of the State in areas of criminal law,

–   by a natural person in the course of a purely personal or household activity.

Article 4 — National law applicable

1.   Each Member State shall apply the national provisions it adopts pursuant to this Directive to the processing of personal data where:

(a)   the processing is carried out in the context of the activities of an establishment of the controller on the territory of the Member State; when the same controller is established on the territory of several Member States, he must take the necessary measures to ensure that each of these establishments complies with the obligations laid down by the national law applicable;

(b)   the controller is not established on the Member State's territory, but in a place where its national law applies by virtue of international public law;

(c)   the controller is not established on Community territory and, for purposes of processing personal data makes use of equipment, automated or otherwise, situated on the territory of the said Member State, unless such equipment is used only for purposes of transit through the territory of the Community.

2.   In the circumstances referred to in paragraph 1 (c), the controller must designate a representative established in the territory of that Member State, without prejudice to legal actions which could be initiated against the controller himself.

CHAPTER II GENERAL RULES ON THE LAWFULNESS OF THE PROCESSING OF PERSONAL DATA

Article 5

Member States shall, within the limits of the provisions of this Chapter, determine more precisely the conditions under which the processing of personal data is lawful.

SECTION I

PRINCIPLES RELATING TO DATA QUALITY

Article 6

1.   Member States shall provide that personal data must be:

(a)   processed fairly and lawfully;

(b)   collected for specified, explicit and legitimate purposes and not further processed in a way incompatible with those purposes. Further processing of data for historical, statistical or scientific purposes shall not be considered as incompatible provided that Member States provide appropriate safeguards;

(c)   adequate, relevant and not excessive in relation to the purposes for which they are collected and/or further processed;

(d)   accurate and, where necessary, kept up to date; every reasonable step must be taken to ensure that data which are inaccurate or incomplete, having regard to the purposes for which they were collected or for which they are further processed, are erased or rectified;

(e)   kept in a form which permits identification of data subjects for no longer than is necessary for the purposes for which the data were collected or for which they are further processed. Member States shall lay down appropriate safeguards for personal data stored for longer periods for historical, statistical or scientific use.

2.   It shall be for the controller to ensure that paragraph 1 is complied with.

SECTION II

CRITERIA FOR MAKING DATA PROCESSING LEGITIMATE

Article 7

Member States shall provide that personal data may be processed only if:

(a)   the data subject has unambiguously given his consent; or

(b) processing is necessary for the performance of a contract to which the data subject is party or in order to take steps at the request of the data subject prior to entering into a contract; or

(c) processing is necessary for compliance with a legal obligation to which the controller is subject; or

(d) processing is necessary in order to protect the vital interests of the data subject; or

(e) processing is necessary for the performance of a task carried out in the public interest or in the exercise of official authority vested in the controller or in a third party to whom the data are disclosed; or

(f) processing is necessary for the purposes of the legitimate interests pursued by the controller or by the third party or parties to whom the data are disclosed, except where such interests are overridden by the interests for fundamental rights and freedoms of the data subject which require protection under Article 1 (1).

SECTION III

SPECIAL CATEGORIES OF PROCESSING

Article 8 — The processing of special categories of data

1. Member States shall prohibit the processing of personal data revealing racial or ethnic origin, political opinions, religious or philosophical beliefs, trade-union membership, and the processing of data concerning health or sex life.

2. Paragraph 1 shall not apply where:

(a) the data subject has given his explicit consent to the processing of those data, except where the laws of the Member State provide that the prohibition referred to in paragraph 1 may not be lifted by the data subject's giving his consent; or

(b) processing is necessary for the purposes of carrying out the obligations and specific rights of the controller in the field of employment law in so far as it is authorized by national law providing for adequate safeguards; or

(c) processing is necessary to protect the vital interests of the data subject or of another person where the data subject is physically or legally incapable of giving his consent; or

(d) processing is carried out in the course of its legitimate activities with appropriate guarantees by a foundation, association or any other non-profit-seeking body with a political, philosophical, religious or trade-union aim and on condition that the processing relates solely to the members of the body or to persons who have regular contact with it in connection with its purposes and that the data are not disclosed to a third party without the consent of the data subjects; or

(e)   the processing relates to data which are manifestly made public by the data subject or is necessary for the establishment, exercise or defence of legal claims.

3.   Paragraph 1 shall not apply where processing of the data is required for the purposes of preventive medicine, medical diagnosis, the provision of care or treatment or the management of health-care services, and where those data are processed by a health professional subject under national law or rules established by national competent bodies to the obligation of professional secrecy or by another person also subject to an equivalent obligation of secrecy.

4.   Subject to the provision of suitable safeguards, Member States may, for reasons of substantial public interest, lay down exemptions in addition to those laid down in paragraph 2 either by national law or by decision of the supervisory authority.

5.   Processing of data relating to offences, criminal convictions or security measures may be carried out only under the control of official authority, or if suitable specific safeguards are provided under national law, subject to derogations which may be granted by the Member State under national provisions providing suitable specific safeguards. However, a complete register of criminal convictions may be kept only under the control of official authority.

Member States may provide that data relating to administrative sanctions or judgements in civil cases shall also be processed under the control of official authority.

6.   Derogations from paragraph 1 provided for in paragraphs 4 and 5 shall be notified to the Commission.

7.   Member States shall determine the conditions under which a national identification number or any other identifier of general application may be processed.

Article 9 — Processing of personal data and freedom of expression

Member States shall provide for exemptions or derogations from the provisions of this Chapter, Chapter IV and Chapter VI for the processing of personal data carried out solely for journalistic purposes or the purpose of artistic or literary expression only if they are necessary to reconcile the right to privacy with the rules governing freedom of expression.

SECTION IV

INFORMATION TO BE GIVEN TO THE DATA SUBJECT

Article 10 — Information in cases of collection of data from the data subject

Member States shall provide that the controller or his representative must provide a data subject from whom data relating to himself are collected with at least the following information, except where he already has it:

(a)   the identity of the controller and of his representative, if any;

(b) the purposes of the processing for which the data are intended;

(c) any further information such as

  – the recipients or categories of recipients of the data,

  – whether replies to the questions are obligatory or voluntary, as well as the possible consequences of failure to reply,

  – the existence of the right of access to and the right to rectify the data concerning him

in so far as such further information is necessary, having regard to the specific circumstances in which the data are collected, to guarantee fair processing in respect of the data subject.

Article 11 — Information where the data have not been obtained from the data subject

1. Where the data have not been obtained from the data subject, Member States shall provide that the controller or his representative must at the time of undertaking the recording of personal data or if a disclosure to a third party is envisaged, no later than the time when the data are first disclosed provide the data subject with at least the following information, except where he already has it:

(a) the identity of the controller and of his representative, if any;

(b) the purposes of the processing;

(c) any further information such as

  – the categories of data concerned,

  – the recipients or categories of recipients,

  – the existence of the right of access to and the right to rectify the data concerning him

in so far as such further information is necessary, having regard to the specific circumstances in which the data are processed, to guarantee fair processing in respect of the data subject.

2. Paragraph 1 shall not apply where, in particular for processing for statistical purposes or for the purposes of historical or scientific research, the provision of such information proves impossible or would involve a disproportionate effort or if recording or disclosure is expressly laid down by law. In these cases Member States shall provide appropriate safeguards.

SECTION V

THE DATA SUBJECT'S RIGHT OF ACCESS TO DATA

Article 12 — Right of access

Member States shall guarantee every data subject the right to obtain from the controller:

(a) without constraint at reasonable intervals and without excessive delay or expense:

  – confirmation as to whether or not data relating to him are being processed and information at least as to the purposes of the processing, the categories of data concerned, and the recipients or categories of recipients to whom the data are disclosed,

  – communication to him in an intelligible form of the data undergoing processing and of any available information as to their source,

  – knowledge of the logic involved in any automatic processing of data concerning him at least in the case of the automated decisions referred to in Article 15 (1);

(b) as appropriate the rectification, erasure or blocking of data the processing of which does not comply with the provisions of this Directive, in particular because of the incomplete or inaccurate nature of the data;

(c) notification to third parties to whom the data have been disclosed of any rectification, erasure or blocking carried out in compliance with (b), unless this proves impossible or involves a disproportionate effort.

SECTION VI

EXEMPTIONS AND RESTRICTIONS

Article 13 — Exemptions and restrictions

1. Member States may adopt legislative measures to restrict the scope of the obligations and rights provided for in Articles 6 (1), 10, 11 (1), 12 and 21 when such a restriction constitutes a necessary measures to safeguard:

(a) national security;

(b) defence;

(c) public security;

(d) the prevention, investigation, detection and prosecution of criminal offences, or of breaches of ethics for regulated professions;

(e) an important economic or financial interest of a Member State or of the European Union, including monetary, budgetary and taxation matters;

(f)   a monitoring, inspection or regulatory function connected, even occasionally, with the exercise of official authority in cases referred to in (c), (d) and (e);

(g)   the protection of the data subject or of the rights and freedoms of others.

2.   Subject to adequate legal safeguards, in particular that the data are not used for taking measures or decisions regarding any particular individual, Member States may, where there is clearly no risk of breaching the privacy of the data subject, restrict by a legislative measure the rights provided for in Article 12 when data are processed solely for purposes of scientific research or are kept in personal form for a period which does not exceed the period necessary for the sole purpose of creating statistics.

SECTION VII

THE DATA SUBJECT'S RIGHT TO OBJECT

Article 14 — The data subject's right to object

Member States shall grant the data subject the right:

(a)   at least in the cases referred to in Article 7 (e) and (f), to object at any time on compelling legitimate grounds relating to his particular situation to the processing of data relating to him, save where otherwise provided by national legislation. Where there is a justified objection, the processing instigated by the controller may no longer involve those data;

(b)   to object, on request and free of charge, to the processing of personal data relating to him which the controller anticipates being processed for the purposes of direct marketing, or to be informed before personal data are disclosed for the first time to third parties or used on their behalf for the purposes of direct marketing, and to be expressly offered the right to object free of charge to such disclosures or uses.

Member States shall take the necessary measures to ensure that data subjects are aware of the existence of the right referred to in the first subparagraph of (b).

Article 15 — Automated individual decisions

1.   Member States shall grant the right to every person not to be subject to a decision which produces legal effects concerning him or significantly affects him and which is based solely on automated processing of data intended to evaluate certain personal aspects relating to him, such as his performance at work, creditworthiness, reliability, conduct, etc.

2.   Subject to the other Articles of this Directive, Member States shall provide that a person may be subjected to a decision of the kind referred to in paragraph 1 if that decision:

(a)   is taken in the course of the entering into or performance of a contract, provided the request for the entering into or the performance of the contract, lodged by the data subject, has been satisfied or that there are suitable measures to safeguard his legitimate interests, such as arrangements allowing him to put his point of view; or

(b)   is authorized by a law which also lays down measures to safeguard the data subject's legitimate interests.

SECTION VIII

CONFIDENTIALITY AND SECURITY OF PROCESSING

Article 16 — Confidentiality of processing

Any person acting under the authority of the controller or of the processor, including the processor himself, who has access to personal data must not process them except on instructions from the controller, unless he is required to do so by law.

Article 17 — Security of processing

1.   Member States shall provide that the controller must implement appropriate technical and organizational measures to protect personal data against accidental or unlawful destruction or accidental loss, alteration, unauthorized disclosure or access, in particular where the processing involves the transmission of data over a network, and against all other unlawful forms of processing.

Having regard to the state of the art and the cost of their implementation, such measures shall ensure a level of security appropriate to the risks represented by the processing and the nature of the data to be protected.

2.   The Member States shall provide that the controller must, where processing is carried out on his behalf, choose a processor providing sufficient guarantees in respect of the technical security measures and organizational measures governing the processing to be carried out, and must ensure compliance with those measures.

3.   The carrying out of processing by way of a processor must be governed by a contract or legal act binding the processor to the controller and stipulating in particular that:

–   the processor shall act only on instructions from the controller,

–   the obligations set out in paragraph 1, as defined by the law of the Member State in which the processor is established, shall also be incumbent on the processor.

4.   For the purposes of keeping proof, the parts of the contract or the legal act relating to data protection and the requirements relating to the measures referred to in paragraph 1 shall be in writing or in another equivalent form.

SECTION IX

NOTIFICATION

Article 18 — Obligation to notify the supervisory authority

1. Member States shall provide that the controller or his representative, if any, must notify the supervisory authority referred to in Article 28 before carrying out any wholly or partly automatic processing operation or set of such operations intended to serve a single purpose or several related purposes.

2. Member States may provide for the simplification of or exemption from notification only in the following cases and under the following conditions:

    —   where, for categories of processing operations which are unlikely, taking account of the data to be processed, to affect adversely the rights and freedoms of data subjects, they specify the purposes of the processing, the data or categories of data undergoing processing, the category or categories of data subject, the recipients or categories of recipient to whom the data are to be disclosed and the length of time the data are to be stored, and/or

    —   where the controller, in compliance with the national law which governs him, appoints a personal data protection official, responsible in particular:

    —   for ensuring in an independent manner the internal application of the national provisions taken pursuant to this Directive

    —   for keeping the register of processing operations carried out by the controller, containing the items of information referred to in Article 21 (2),

    thereby ensuring that the rights and freedoms of the data subjects are unlikely to be adversely affected by the processing operations.

3. Member States may provide that paragraph 1 does not apply to processing whose sole purpose is the keeping of a register which according to laws or regulations is intended to provide information to the public and which is open to consultation either by the public in general or by any person demonstrating a legitimate interest.

4. Member States may provide for an exemption from the obligation to notify or a simplification of the notification in the case of processing operations referred to in Article 8 (2) (d).

5. Member States may stipulate that certain or all non-automatic processing operations involving personal data shall be notified, or provide for these processing operations to be subject to simplified notification.

Article 19 — Contents of notification

1. Member States shall specify the information to be given in the notification. It shall include at least:

(a)   the name and address of the controller and of his representative, if any;

(b)   the purpose or purposes of the processing;

(c)   a description of the category or categories of data subject and of the data or categories of data relating to them;

(d)   the recipients or categories of recipient to whom the data might be disclosed;

(e)   proposed transfers of data to third countries;

(f)   a general description allowing a preliminary assessment to be made of the appropriateness of the measures taken pursuant to Article 17 to ensure security of processing.

2.   Member States shall specify the procedures under which any change affecting the information referred to in paragraph 1 must be notified to the supervisory authority.

Article 20 — Prior checking

1.   Member States shall determine the processing operations likely to present specific risks to the rights and freedoms of data subjects and shall check that these processing operations are examined prior to the start thereof.

2.   Such prior checks shall be carried out by the supervisory authority following receipt of a notification from the controller or by the data protection official, who, in cases of doubt, must consult the supervisory authority.

3.   Member States may also carry out such checks in the context of preparation either of a measure of the national parliament or of a measure based on such a legislative measure, which define the nature of the processing and lay down appropriate safeguards.

Article 21 — Publicizing of processing operations

1.   Member States shall take measures to ensure that processing operations are publicized.

2.   Member States shall provide that a register of processing operations notified in accordance with Article 18 shall be kept by the supervisory authority.

The register shall contain at least the information listed in Article 19 (1) (a) to (e).

The register may be inspected by any person.

3.   Member States shall provide, in relation to processing operations not subject to notification, that controllers or another body appointed by the Member States make available at least the information referred to in Article 19 (1) (a) to (e) in an appropriate form to any person on request.

Member States may provide that this provision does not apply to processing whose sole purpose is the keeping of a register which according to laws or regulations is intended to provide information to the public and which is open to consultation either by the public in general or by any person who can provide proof of a legitimate interest.

CHAPTER III

JUDICIAL REMEDIES, LIABILITY AND SANCTIONS

Article 22 — Remedies
Without prejudice to any administrative remedy for which provision may be made, inter alia before the supervisory authority referred to in Article 28, prior to referral to the judicial authority, Member States shall provide for the right of every person to a judicial remedy for any breach of the rights guaranteed him by the national law applicable to the processing in question.

Article 23 — Liability
1.   Member States shall provide that any person who has suffered damage as a result of an unlawful processing operation or of any act incompatible with the national provisions adopted pursuant to this Directive is entitled to receive compensation from the controller for the damage suffered.

2.   The controller may be exempted from this liability, in whole or in part, if he proves that he is not responsible for the event giving rise to the damage.

Article 24 — Sanctions
The Member States shall adopt suitable measures to ensure the full implementation of the provisions of this Directive and shall in particular lay down the sanctions to be imposed in case of infringement of the provisions adopted pursuant to this Directive.

CHAPTER IV

TRANSFER OF PERSONAL DATA TO THIRD COUNTRIES

Article 25 — Principles
1.   The Member States shall provide that the transfer to a third country of personal data which are undergoing processing or are intended for processing after transfer may take place only if, without prejudice to compliance with the national provisions adopted pursuant to the other provisions of this Directive, the third country in question ensures an adequate level of protection.

2.   The adequacy of the level of protection afforded by a third country shall be assessed in the light of all the circumstances surrounding a data transfer operation or set of data transfer operations; particular consideration shall be given to the nature of the data, the purpose and duration of the proposed processing operation or operations, the country of origin and country of final destination, the rules of law, both general and sectoral, in

force in the third country in question and the professional rules and security measures which are complied with in that country.

3. The Member States and the Commission shall inform each other of cases where they consider that a third country does not ensure an adequate level of protection within the meaning of paragraph 2.

4. Where the Commission finds, under the procedure provided for in Article 31 (2), that a third country does not ensure an adequate level of protection within the meaning of paragraph 2 of this Article, Member States shall take the measures necessary to prevent any transfer of data of the same type to the third country in question.

5. At the appropriate time, the Commission shall enter into negotiations with a view to remedying the situation resulting from the finding made pursuant to paragraph 4.

6. The Commission may find, in accordance with the procedure referred to in Article 31 (2), that a third country ensures an adequate level of protection within the meaning of paragraph 2 of this Article, by reason of its domestic law or of the international commitments it has entered into, particularly upon conclusion of the negotiations referred to in paragraph 5, for the protection of the private lives and basic freedoms and rights of individuals.

Member States shall take the measures necessary to comply with the Commission's decision.

Article 26 — Derogations

1. By way of derogation from Article 25 and save where otherwise provided by domestic law governing particular cases, Member States shall provide that a transfer or a set of transfers of personal data to a third country which does not ensure an adequate level of protection within the meaning of Article 25 (2) may take place on condition that:

(a) the data subject has given his consent unambiguously to the proposed transfer; or

(b) the transfer is necessary for the performance of a contract between the data subject and the controller or the implementation of precontractual measures taken in response to the data subject's request; or

(c) the transfer is necessary for the conclusion or performance of a contract concluded in the interest of the data subject between the controller and a third party; or

(d) the transfer is necessary or legally required on important public interest grounds, or for the establishment, exercise or defence of legal claims; or

(e) the transfer is necessary in order to protect the vital interests of the data subject; or

(f) the transfer is made from a register which according to laws or regulations is intended to provide information to the public and which is open to consultation either by the public in general or by any person who can demonstrate legitimate interest, to the extent that the conditions laid down in law for consultation are fulfilled in the particular case.

2.   Without prejudice to paragraph 1, a Member State may authorize a transfer or a set of transfers of personal data to a third country which does not ensure an adequate level of protection within the meaning of Article 25 (2), where the controller adduces adequate safeguards with respect to the protection of the privacy and fundamental rights and freedoms of individuals and as regards the exercise of the corresponding rights; such safeguards may in particular result from appropriate contractual clauses.

3.   The Member State shall inform the Commission and the other Member States of the authorizations it grants pursuant to paragraph 2.

If a Member State or the Commission objects on justified grounds involving the protection of the privacy and fundamental rights and freedoms of individuals, the Commission shall take appropriate measures in accordance with the procedure laid down in Article 31 (2).

Member States shall take the necessary measures to comply with the Commission's decision.

4.   Where the Commission decides, in accordance with the procedure referred to in Article 31 (2), that certain standard contractual clauses offer sufficient safeguards as required by paragraph 2, Member States shall take the necessary measures to comply with the Commission's decision.

CHAPTER V

CODES OF CONDUCT

Article 27

1.   The Member States and the Commission shall encourage the drawing up of codes of conduct intended to contribute to the proper implementation of the national provisions adopted by the Member States pursuant to this Directive, taking account of the specific features of the various sectors.

2.   Member States shall make provision for trade associations and other bodies representing other categories of controllers which have drawn up draft national codes or which have the intention of amending or extending existing national codes to be able to submit them to the opinion of the national authority.

Member States shall make provision for this authority to ascertain, among other things, whether the drafts submitted to it are in accordance with the national provisions adopted pursuant to this Directive. If it sees fit, the authority shall seek the views of data subjects or their representatives.

3.   Draft Community codes, and amendments or extensions to existing Community codes, may be submitted to the Working Party referred to in Article 29. This Working Party

shall determine, among other things, whether the drafts submitted to it are in accordance with the national provisions adopted pursuant to this Directive. If it sees fit, the authority shall seek the views of data subjects or their representatives. The Commission may ensure appropriate publicity for the codes which have been approved by the Working Party.

CHAPTER VI

SUPERVISORY AUTHORITY AND WORKING PARTY ON THE PROTECTION OF INDIVIDUALS WITH REGARD TO THE PROCESSING OF PERSONAL DATA

Article 28 — Supervisory authority

1. Each Member State shall provide that one or more public authorities are responsible for monitoring the application within its territory of the provisions adopted by the Member States pursuant to this Directive.

   These authorities shall act with complete independence in exercising the functions entrusted to them.

2. Each Member State shall provide that the supervisory authorities are consulted when drawing up administrative measures or regulations relating to the protection of individuals' rights and freedoms with regard to the processing of personal data.

3. Each authority shall in particular be endowed with:

   – investigative powers, such as powers of access to data forming the subject-matter of processing operations and powers to collect all the information necessary for the performance of its supervisory duties,

   – effective powers of intervention, such as, for example, that of delivering opinions before processing operations are carried out, in accordance with Article 20, and ensuring appropriate publication of such opinions, of ordering the blocking, erasure or destruction of data, of imposing a temporary or definitive ban on processing, of warning or admonishing the controller, or that of referring the matter to national parliaments or other political institutions,

   – the power to engage in legal proceedings where the national provisions adopted pursuant to this Directive have been violated or to bring these violations to the attention of the judicial authorities.

   Decisions by the supervisory authority which give rise to complaints may be appealed against through the courts.

4. Each supervisory authority shall hear claims lodged by any person, or by an association representing that person, concerning the protection of his rights and freedoms in regard to the processing of personal data. The person concerned shall be informed of the outcome of the claim.

Each supervisory authority shall, in particular, hear claims for checks on the lawfulness of data processing lodged by any person when the national provisions adopted pursuant to Article 13 of this Directive apply. The person shall at any rate be informed that a check has taken place.

5.   Each supervisory authority shall draw up a report on its activities at regular intervals. The report shall be made public.

6.   Each supervisory authority is competent, whatever the national law applicable to the processing in question, to exercise, on the territory of its own Member State, the powers conferred on it in accordance with paragraph 3. Each authority may be requested to exercise its powers by an authority of another Member State.

The supervisory authorities shall cooperate with one another to the extent necessary for the performance of their duties, in particular by exchanging all useful information.

7.   Member States shall provide that the members and staff of the supervisory authority, even after their employment has ended, are to be subject to a duty of professional secrecy with regard to confidential information to which they have access.

Article 29 — Working Party on the Protection of Individuals with regard to the Processing of Personal Data

1.   A Working Party on the Protection of Individuals with regard to the Processing of Personal Data, hereinafter referred to as 'the Working Party', is hereby set up.

It shall have advisory status and act independently.

2.   The Working Party shall be composed of a representative of the supervisory authority or authorities designated by each Member State and of a representative of the authority or authorities established for the Community institutions and bodies, and of a representative of the Commission.

Each member of the Working Party shall be designated by the institution, authority or authorities which he represents. Where a Member State has designated more than one supervisory authority, they shall nominate a joint representative. The same shall apply to the authorities established for Community institutions and bodies.

3.   The Working Party shall take decisions by a simple majority of the representatives of the supervisory authorities.

4.   The Working Party shall elect its chairman. The chairman's term of office shall be two years. His appointment shall be renewable.

5.   The Working Party's secretariat shall be provided by the Commission.

6.   The Working Party shall adopt its own rules of procedure.

7.   The Working Party shall consider items placed on its agenda by its chairman, either on his own initiative or at the request of a representative of the supervisory authorities or at the Commission's request.

Article 30

1.   The Working Party shall:

(a)   examine any question covering the application of the national measures adopted under this Directive in order to contribute to the uniform application of such measures;

(b)   give the Commission an opinion on the level of protection in the Community and in third countries;

(c)   advise the Commission on any proposed amendment of this Directive, on any additional or specific measures to safeguard the rights and freedoms of natural persons with regard to the processing of personal data and on any other proposed Community measures affecting such rights and freedoms;

(d)   give an opinion on codes of conduct drawn up at Community level.

2.   If the Working Party finds that divergences likely to affect the equivalence of protection for persons with regard to the processing of personal data in the Community are arising between the laws or practices of Member States, it shall inform the Commission accordingly.

3.   The Working Party may, on its own initiative, make recommendations on all matters relating to the protection of persons with regard to the processing of personal data in the Community.

4.   The Working Party's opinions and recommendations shall be forwarded to the Commission and to the committee referred to in Article 31.

5.   The Commission shall inform the Working Party of the action it has taken in response to its opinions and recommendations. It shall do so in a report which shall also be forwarded to the European Parliament and the Council. The report shall be made public.

6.   The Working Party shall draw up an annual report on the situation regarding the protection of natural persons with regard to the processing of personal data in the Community and in third countries, which it shall transmit to the Commission, the European Parliament and the Council. The report shall be made public.

CHAPTER VII

COMMUNITY IMPLEMENTING MEASURES

Article 31 — The Committee

1. The Commission shall be assisted by a committee composed of the representatives of the Member States and chaired by the representative of the Commission.

2. The representative of the Commission shall submit to the committee a draft of the measures to be taken. The committee shall deliver its opinion on the draft within a time limit which the chairman may lay down according to the urgency of the matter.

   The opinion shall be delivered by the majority laid down in Article 148 (2) of the Treaty. The votes of the representatives of the Member States within the committee shall be weighted in the manner set out in that Article. The chairman shall not vote.

   The Commission shall adopt measures which shall apply immediately. However, if these measures are not in accordance with the opinion of the committee, they shall be communicated by the Commission to the Council forthwith. It that event:

   — the Commission shall defer application of the measures which it has decided for a period of three months from the date of communication,

   — the Council, acting by a qualified majority, may take a different decision within the time limit referred to in the first indent.

FINAL PROVISIONS

Article 32

1. Member States shall bring into force the laws, regulations and administrative provisions necessary to comply with this Directive at the latest at the end of a period of three years from the date of its adoption.

   When Member States adopt these measures, they shall contain a reference to this Directive or be accompanied by such reference on the occasion of their official publication. The methods of making such reference shall be laid down by the Member States.

2. Member States shall ensure that processing already under way on the date the national provisions adopted pursuant to this Directive enter into force, is brought into conformity with these provisions within three years of this date.

   By way of derogation from the preceding subparagraph, Member States may provide that the processing of data already held in manual filing systems on the date of entry into force of the national provisions adopted in implementation of this Directive shall be brought into conformity with Articles 6, 7 and 8 of this Directive within 12 years of the date on which it is adopted. Member States shall, however, grant the data subject the right to obtain, at his request and in particular at the time of exercising his right of access, the rectification, erasure or blocking of data which are incomplete, inaccurate or stored in a way incompatible with the legitimate purposes pursued by the controller.

3.   By way of derogation from paragraph 2, Member States may provide, subject to suitable safeguards, that data kept for the sole purpose of historical research need not be brought into conformity with Articles 6, 7 and 8 of this Directive.

4.   Member States shall communicate to the Commission the text of the provisions of domestic law which they adopt in the field covered by this Directive.

Article 33

The Commission shall report to the Council and the European Parliament at regular intervals, starting not later than three years after the date referred to in Article 32 (1), on the implementation of this Directive, attaching to its report, if necessary, suitable proposals for amendments. The report shall be made public.

The Commission shall examine, in particular, the application of this Directive to the data processing of sound and image data relating to natural persons and shall submit any appropriate proposals which prove to be necessary, taking account of developments in information technology and in the light of the state of progress in the information society.

Article 34

This Directive is addressed to the Member States.

Done at Luxembourg, 24 October 1995.
For the European Parliament

Regulation (EC) No 1049/2001 of the European Parliament and of the Council of 30 May 2001 regarding public access to European Parliament, Council and Commission documents

THE EUROPEAN PARLIAMENT AND THE COUNCIL OF THE EUROPEAN UNION,

Having regard to the Treaty establishing the European Community, and in particular Article 255(2) thereof,

Having regard to the proposal from the Commission

Acting in accordance with the procedure referred to in Article 251 of the Treaty

Whereas:

(1) The second subparagraph of Article 1 of the Treaty on European Union enshrines the concept of openness, stating that the Treaty marks a new stage in the process of creating an ever closer union among the peoples of Europe, in which decisions are taken as openly as possible and as closely as possible to the citizen.

(2) Openness enables citizens to participate more closely in the decision-making process and guarantees that the administration enjoys greater legitimacy and is more effective and more accountable to the citizen in a democratic system. Openness contributes to strengthening the principles of democracy and respect for fundamental rights as laid down in Article 6 of the EU Treaty and in the Charter of Fundamental Rights of the European Union.

(3) The conclusions of the European Council meetings held at Birmingham, Edinburgh and Copenhagen stressed the need to introduce greater transparency into the work of the Union institutions. This Regulation consolidates the initiatives that the institutions have already taken with a view to improving the transparency of the decision-making process.

(4) The purpose of this Regulation is to give the fullest possible effect to the right of public access to documents and to lay down the general principles and limits on such access in accordance with Article 255(2) of the EC Treaty.

(5) Since the question of access to documents is not covered by provisions of the Treaty establishing the European Coal and Steel Community and the Treaty establishing the European Atomic Energy Community, the European Parliament, the Council and the Commission should, in accordance with Declaration No 41 attached to the Final Act of the Treaty of Amsterdam, draw guidance from this Regulation as regards documents concerning the activities covered by those two Treaties.

(6) Wider access should be granted to documents in cases where the institutions are acting in their legislative capacity, including under delegated powers, while at the same time

preserving the effectiveness of the institutions' decision-making process. Such documents should be made directly accessible to the greatest possible extent.

(7) In accordance with Articles 28(1) and 41(1) of the EU Treaty, the right of access also applies to documents relating to the common foreign and security policy and to police and judicial cooperation in criminal matters. Each institution should respect its security rules.

(8) In order to ensure the full application of this Regulation to all activities of the Union, all agencies established by the institutions should apply the principles laid down in this Regulation.

(9) On account of their highly sensitive content, certain documents should be given special treatment. Arrangements for informing the European Parliament of the content of such documents should be made through interinstitutional agreement.

(10) In order to bring about greater openness in the work of the institutions, access to documents should be granted by the European Parliament, the Council and the Commission not only to documents drawn up by the institutions, but also to documents received by them. In this context, it is recalled that Declaration No 35 attached to the Final Act of the Treaty of Amsterdam provides that a Member State may request the Commission or the Council not to communicate to third parties a document originating from that State without its prior agreement.

(11) In principle, all documents of the institutions should be accessible to the public. However, certain public and private interests should be protected by way of exceptions. The institutions should be entitled to protect their internal consultations and deliberations where necessary to safeguard their ability to carry out their tasks. In assessing the exceptions, the institutions should take account of the principles in Community legislation concerning the protection of personal data, in all areas of Union activities.

(12) All rules concerning access to documents of the institutions should be in conformity with this Regulation.

(13) In order to ensure that the right of access is fully respected, a two-stage administrative procedure should apply, with the additional possibility of court proceedings or complaints to the Ombudsman.

(14) Each institution should take the measures necessary to inform the public of the new provisions in force and to train its staff to assist citizens exercising their rights under this Regulation. In order to make it easier for citizens to exercise their rights, each institution should provide access to a register of documents.

(15) Even though it is neither the object nor the effect of this Regulation to amend national legislation on access to documents, it is nevertheless clear that, by virtue of the principle of loyal cooperation which governs relations between the institutions and the Member States, Member States should take care not to hamper the proper application of this Regulation and should respect the security rules of the institutions.

(16) This Regulation is without prejudice to existing rights of access to documents for Member States, judicial authorities or investigative bodies.

(17) In accordance with Article 255(3) of the EC Treaty, each institution lays down specific provisions regarding access to its documents in its rules of procedure. Council Decision 93/731/EC of 20 December 1993 on public access to Council documents, Commission Decision 94/90/ECSC, EC, Euratom of 8 February 1994 on public access to Commission documents, European Parliament Decision 97/632/EC, ECSC, Euratom of 10 July 1997 on public access to European Parliament documents, and the rules on confidentiality of Schengen documents should therefore, if necessary, be modified or be repealed,

HAVE ADOPTED THIS REGULATION:

Article 1 — Purpose

The purpose of this Regulation is:

(a) to define the principles, conditions and limits on grounds of public or private interest governing the right of access to European Parliament, Council and Commission (hereinafter referred to as 'the institutions') documents provided for in Article 255 of the EC Treaty in such a way as to ensure the widest possible access to documents,

(b) to establish rules ensuring the easiest possible exercise of this right, and

(c) to promote good administrative practice on access to documents.

Article 2 — Beneficiaries and scope

1. Any citizen of the Union, and any natural or legal person residing or having its registered office in a Member State, has a right of access to documents of the institutions, subject to the principles, conditions and limits defined in this Regulation.

2. The institutions may, subject to the same principles, conditions and limits, grant access to documents to any natural or legal person not residing or not having its registered office in a Member State.

3. This Regulation shall apply to all documents held by an institution, that is to say, documents drawn up or received by it and in its possession, in all areas of activity of the European Union.

4. Without prejudice to Articles 4 and 9, documents shall be made accessible to the public either following a written application or directly in electronic form or through a register. In particular, documents drawn up or received in the course of a legislative procedure shall be made directly accessible in accordance with Article 12.

5. Sensitive documents as defined in Article 9(1) shall be subject to special treatment in accordance with that Article.

6.   This Regulation shall be without prejudice to rights of public access to documents held by the institutions which might follow from instruments of international law or acts of the institutions implementing them.

Article 3 — Definitions

For the purpose of this Regulation:

(a)   'document' shall mean any content whatever its medium (written on paper or stored in electronic form or as a sound, visual or audiovisual recording) concerning a matter relating to the policies, activities and decisions falling within the institution's sphere of responsibility;

(b)   'third party' shall mean any natural or legal person, or any entity outside the institution concerned, including the Member States, other Community or non-Community institutions and bodies and third countries.

Article 4 — Exceptions

1.   The institutions shall refuse access to a document where disclosure would undermine the protection of:

(a)   the public interest as regards:

— public security,

— defence and military matters,

— international relations,

— the financial, monetary or economic policy of the Community or a Member State;

(b)   privacy and the integrity of the individual, in particular in accordance with Community legislation regarding the protection of personal data.

2.   The institutions shall refuse access to a document where disclosure would undermine the protection of:

— commercial interests of a natural or legal person, including intellectual property,

— court proceedings and legal advice,

— the purpose of inspections, investigations and audits,

unless there is an overriding public interest in disclosure.

3.   Access to a document, drawn up by an institution for internal use or received by an institution, which relates to a matter where the decision has not been taken by the institution, shall be refused if disclosure of the document would seriously undermine the institution's decision-making process, unless there is an overriding public interest in disclosure.

Access to a document containing opinions for internal use as part of deliberations and preliminary consultations within the institution concerned shall be refused even after the decision has been taken if disclosure of the document would seriously undermine the institution's decision-making process, unless there is an overriding public interest in disclosure.

4. As regards third-party documents, the institution shall consult the third party with a view to assessing whether an exception in paragraph 1 or 2 is applicable, unless it is clear that the document shall or shall not be disclosed.

5. A Member State may request the institution not to disclose a document originating from that Member State without its prior agreement.

6. If only parts of the requested document are covered by any of the exceptions, the remaining parts of the document shall be released.

7. The exceptions as laid down in paragraphs 1 to 3 shall only apply for the period during which protection is justified on the basis of the content of the document. The exceptions may apply for a maximum period of 30 years. In the case of documents covered by the exceptions relating to privacy or commercial interests and in the case of sensitive documents, the exceptions may, if necessary, continue to apply after this period.

Article 5 — Documents in the Member States

Where a Member State receives a request for a document in its possession, originating from an institution, unless it is clear that the document shall or shall not be disclosed, the Member State shall consult with the institution concerned in order to take a decision that does not jeopardise the attainment of the objectives of this Regulation.

The Member State may instead refer the request to the institution.

Article 6 — Applications

1. Applications for access to a document shall be made in any written form, including electronic form, in one of the languages referred to in Article 314 of the EC Treaty and in a sufficiently precise manner to enable the institution to identify the document. The applicant is not obliged to state reasons for the application.

2. If an application is not sufficiently precise, the institution shall ask the applicant to clarify the application and shall assist the applicant in doing so, for example, by providing information on the use of the public registers of documents.

3. In the event of an application relating to a very long document or to a very large number of documents, the institution concerned may confer with the applicant informally, with a view to finding a fair solution.

4. The institutions shall provide information and assistance to citizens on how and where applications for access to documents can be made.

Article 7 — Processing of initial applications

1. An application for access to a document shall be handled promptly. An acknowledgement of receipt shall be sent to the applicant. Within 15 working days from registration of the application, the institution shall either grant access to the document requested and provide access in accordance with Article 10 within that period or, in a written reply, state the reasons for the total or partial refusal and inform the applicant of his or her right to make a confirmatory application in accordance with paragraph 2 of this Article.

2. In the event of a total or partial refusal, the applicant may, within 15 working days of receiving the institution's reply, make a confirmatory application asking the institution to reconsider its position.

3. In exceptional cases, for example in the event of an application relating to a very long document or to a very large number of documents, the time-limit provided for in paragraph 1 may be extended by 15 working days, provided that the applicant is notified in advance and that detailed reasons are given.

4. Failure by the institution to reply within the prescribed time-limit shall entitle the applicant to make a confirmatory application.

Article 8 — Processing of confirmatory applications

1. A confirmatory application shall be handled promptly. Within 15 working days from registration of such an application, the institution shall either grant access to the document requested and provide access in accordance with Article 10 within that period or, in a written reply, state the reasons for the total or partial refusal. In the event of a total or partial refusal, the institution shall inform the applicant of the remedies open to him or her, namely instituting court proceedings against the institution and/or making a complaint to the Ombudsman, under the conditions laid down in Articles 230 and 195 of the EC Treaty, respectively.

2. In exceptional cases, for example in the event of an application relating to a very long document or to a very large number of documents, the time limit provided for in paragraph 1 may be extended by 15 working days, provided that the applicant is notified in advance and that detailed reasons are given.

3. Failure by the institution to reply within the prescribed time limit shall be considered as a negative reply and entitle the applicant to institute court proceedings against the institution and/or make a complaint to the Ombudsman, under the relevant provisions of the EC Treaty.

Article 9 — Treatment of sensitive documents

1. Sensitive documents are documents originating from the institutions or the agencies established by them, from Member States, third countries or International Organisations, classified as 'TRÈS SECRET/TOP SECRET', 'SECRET' or 'CONFIDENTIEL' in

accordance with the rules of the institution concerned, which protect essential interests of the European Union or of one or more of its Member States in the areas covered by Article 4(1)(a), notably public security, defence and military matters.

2. Applications for access to sensitive documents under the procedures laid down in Articles 7 and 8 shall be handled only by those persons who have a right to acquaint themselves with those documents. These persons shall also, without prejudice to Article 11(2), assess which references to sensitive documents could be made in the public register.

3. Sensitive documents shall be recorded in the register or released only with the consent of the originator.

4. An institution which decides to refuse access to a sensitive document shall give the reasons for its decision in a manner which does not harm the interests protected in Article 4.

5. Member States shall take appropriate measures to ensure that when handling applications for sensitive documents the principles in this Article and Article 4 are respected.

6. The rules of the institutions concerning sensitive documents shall be made public.

7. The Commission and the Council shall inform the European Parliament regarding sensitive documents in accordance with arrangements agreed between the institutions.

Article 10 — Access following an application

1. The applicant shall have access to documents either by consulting them on the spot or by receiving a copy, including, where available, an electronic copy, according to the applicant's preference. The cost of producing and sending copies may be charged to the applicant. This charge shall not exceed the real cost of producing and sending the copies. Consultation on the spot, copies of less than 20 A4 pages and direct access in electronic form or through the register shall be free of charge.

2. If a document has already been released by the institution concerned and is easily accessible to the applicant, the institution may fulfil its obligation of granting access to documents by informing the applicant how to obtain the requested document.

3. Documents shall be supplied in an existing version and format (including electronically or in an alternative format such as Braille, large print or tape) with full regard to the applicant's preference.

Article 11 — Registers

1. To make citizens' rights under this Regulation effective, each institution shall provide public access to a register of documents. Access to the register should be provided in electronic form. References to documents shall be recorded in the register without delay.

2.   For each document the register shall contain a reference number (including, where applicable, the interinstitutional reference), the subject matter and/or a short description of the content of the document and the date on which it was received or drawn up and recorded in the register. References shall be made in a manner which does not undermine protection of the interests in Article 4.

3.   The institutions shall immediately take the measures necessary to establish a register which shall be operational by 3 June 2002.

Article 12 — Direct access in electronic form or through a register

1.   The institutions shall as far as possible make documents directly accessible to the public in electronic form or through a register in accordance with the rules of the institution concerned.

2.   In particular, legislative documents, that is to say, documents drawn up or received in the course of procedures for the adoption of acts which are legally binding in or for the Member States, should, subject to Articles 4 and 9, be made directly accessible.

3.   Where possible, other documents, notably documents relating to the development of policy or strategy, should be made directly accessible.

4.   Where direct access is not given through the register, the register shall as far as possible indicate where the document is located.

Article 13 — Publication in the Official Journal

1.   In addition to the acts referred to in Article 254(1) and (2) of the EC Treaty and the first paragraph of Article 163 of the Euratom Treaty, the following documents shall, subject to Articles 4 and 9 of this Regulation, be published in the Official Journal:

   (a)   Commission proposals;

   (b)   common positions adopted by the Council in accordance with the procedures referred to in Articles 251 and 252 of the EC Treaty and the reasons underlying those common positions, as well as the European Parliament's positions in these procedures;

   (c)   framework decisions and decisions referred to in Article 34(2) of the EU Treaty;

   (d)   conventions established by the Council in accordance with Article 34(2) of the EU Treaty;

   (e)   conventions signed between Member States on the basis of Article 293 of the EC Treaty;

   (f)   international agreements concluded by the Community or in accordance with Article 24 of the EU Treaty.

2.   As far as possible, the following documents shall be published in the Official Journal:

(a) initiatives presented to the Council by a Member State pursuant to Article 67(1) of the EC Treaty or pursuant to Article 34(2) of the EU Treaty;

(b) common positions referred to in Article 34(2) of the EU Treaty;

(c) directives other than those referred to in Article 254(1) and (2) of the EC Treaty, decisions other than those referred to in Article 254(1) of the EC Treaty, recommendations and opinions.

3. Each institution may in its rules of procedure establish which further documents shall be published in the Official Journal.

Article 14 — Information
1. Each institution shall take the requisite measures to inform the public of the rights they enjoy under this Regulation.

2. The Member States shall cooperate with the institutions in providing information to the citizens.

Article 15 — Administrative practice in the institutions
1. The institutions shall develop good administrative practices in order to facilitate the exercise of the right of access guaranteed by this Regulation.

2. The institutions shall establish an interinstitutional committee to examine best practice, address possible conflicts and discuss future developments on public access to documents.

Article 16 — Reproduction of documents
This Regulation shall be without prejudice to any existing rules on copyright which may limit a third party's right to reproduce or exploit released documents.

Article 17 — Reports
1. Each institution shall publish annually a report for the preceding year including the number of cases in which the institution refused to grant access to documents, the reasons for such refusals and the number of sensitive documents not recorded in the register.

2. At the latest by 31 January 2004, the Commission shall publish a report on the implementation of the principles of this Regulation and shall make recommendations, including, if appropriate, proposals for the revision of this Regulation and an action programme of measures to be taken by the institutions.

Article 18 — Application measures
1. Each institution shall adapt its rules of procedure to the provisions of this Regulation. The adaptations shall take effect from 3 December 2001.

2.   Within six months of the entry into force of this Regulation, the Commission shall examine the conformity of Council Regulation (EEC, Euratom) No 354/83 of 1 February 1983 concerning the opening to the public of the historical archives of the European Economic Community and the European Atomic Energy Community with this Regulation in order to ensure the preservation and archiving of documents to the fullest extent possible.

3.   Within six months of the entry into force of this Regulation, the Commission shall examine the conformity of the existing rules on access to documents with this Regulation.

Article 19 — Entry into force

This Regulation shall enter into force on the third day following that of its publication in the *Official Journal of the European Communities*.

It shall be applicable from 3 December 2001.

This Regulation shall be binding in its entirety and directly applicable in all Member States.

Done at Brussels, 30 May 2001.

Directive 2003/4/EC of the European Parliament and of the Council

of 28 January 2003

on public access to environmental information
and repealing Council Directive 90/313/EEC

THE EUROPEAN PARLIAMENT AND THE COUNCIL OF THE EUROPEAN UNION,

Having regard to the Treaty establishing the European Community, and in particular Article 175(1) thereof,

Having regard to the proposal from the Commission,

Having regard to the opinion of the European Economic and Social Committee,

Having regard to the opinion of the Committee of the Regions,

Acting in accordance with the procedure laid down in Article 251 of the Treaty in the light of the joint text approved by the Conciliation Committee on 8 November 2002,

Whereas:

(1)   Increased public access to environmental information and the dissemination of such information contribute to a greater awareness of environmental matters, a free exchange of views, more effective participation by the public in environmental decision-making and, eventually, to a better environment.

(2)   Council Directive 90/313/EEC of 7 June 1990 on the freedom of access to information on the environment initiated a process of change in the manner in which public authorities approach the issue of openness and transparency, establishing measures for the exercise of the right of public access to environmental information which should be developed and continued. This Directive expands the existing access granted under Directive 90/313/EEC.

(3)   Article 8 of that Directive requires Member States to report to the Commission on the experience gained, in the light of which the Commission is required to make a report to the European Parliament and to the Council together with any proposal for revision of the Directive which it may consider appropriate.

(4)   The report produced under Article 8 of that Directive identifies concrete problems encountered in the practical application of the Directive.

(5)   On 25 June 1998 the European Community signed the UN/ECE Convention on Access to Information, Public Participation in Decision-Making and Access to Justice in Environmental Matters ('the Aarhus Convention'). Provisions of Community law must be consistent with that Convention with a view to its conclusion by the European Community.

(6)   It is appropriate in the interest of increased transparency to replace Directive 90/313/EEC rather than to amend it, so as to provide interested parties with a single, clear and coherent legislative text.

(7)   Disparities between the laws in force in the Member States concerning access to environmental information held by public authorities can create inequality within the Community as regards access to such information or as regards conditions of competition.

(8)   It is necessary to ensure that any natural and legal person has a right of access to environmental information held by or for public authorities without his having to state an interest.

(9)   It is also necessary that public authorities make available and disseminate environmental information to the general public to the widest extent possible, in particular by using information and communication technologies. The future development of these technologies should be taken into account in the reporting on, and reviewing of, this Directive.

(10)   The definition of environmental information should be clarified so as to encompass information in any form on the state of the environment, on factors, measures or activities affecting or likely to affect the environment or designed to protect it, on cost-benefit and economic analyses used within the framework of such measures or activities and also information on the state of human health and safety, including the contamination of the food chain, conditions of human life, cultural sites and built structures in as much as they are, or may be, affected by any of those matters.

(11)   To take account of the principle in Article 6 of the Treaty, that environmental protection requirements should be integrated into the definition and implementation of Community policies and activities, the definition of public authorities should be expanded so as to encompass government or other public administration at national, regional or local level whether or not they have specific responsibilities for the environment. The definition should likewise be expanded to include other persons or bodies performing public administrative functions in relation to the environment under national law, as well as other persons or bodies acting under their control and having public responsibilities or functions in relation to the environment.

(12)   Environmental information which is physically held by other bodies on behalf of public authorities should also fall within the scope of this Directive.

(13)   Environmental information should be made available to applicants as soon as possible and within a reasonable time and having regard to any timescale specified by the applicant.

(14)   Public authorities should make environmental information available in the form or format requested by an applicant unless it is already publicly available in another form or format or it is reasonable to make it available in another form or format. In addition, public authorities should be required to make all reasonable efforts to maintain the

environmental information held by or for them in forms or formats that are readily reproducible and accessible by electronic means.

(15) Member States should determine the practical arrangements under which such information is effectively made available. These arrangements shall guarantee that the information is effectively and easily accessible and progressively becomes available to the public through public telecommunications networks, including publicly accessible lists of public authorities and registers or lists of environmental information held by or for public authorities.

(16) The right to information means that the disclosure of information should be the general rule and that public authorities should be permitted to refuse a request for environmental information in specific and clearly defined cases. Grounds for refusal should be interpreted in a restrictive way, whereby the public interest served by disclosure should be weighed against the interest served by the refusal. The reasons for a refusal should be provided to the applicant within the time limit laid down in this Directive.

(17) Public authorities should make environmental information available in part where it is possible to separate out any information falling within the scope of the exceptions from the rest of the information requested.

(18) Public authorities should be able to make a charge for supplying environmental information but such a charge should be reasonable. This implies that, as a general rule, charges may not exceed actual costs of producing the material in question. Instances where advance payment will be required should be limited. In particular cases, where public authorities make available environmental information on a commercial basis, and where this is necessary in order to guarantee the continuation of collecting and publishing such information, a market-based charge is considered to be reasonable; an advance payment may be required. A schedule of charges should be published and made available to applicants together with information on the circumstances in which a charge may be levied or waived.

(19) Applicants should be able to seek an administrative or judicial review of the acts or omissions of a public authority in relation to a request.

(20) Public authorities should seek to guarantee that when environmental information is compiled by them or on their behalf, the information is comprehensible, accurate and comparable. As this is an important factor in assessing the quality of the information supplied the method used in compiling the information should also be disclosed upon request.

(21) In order to increase public awareness in environmental matters and to improve environmental protection, public authorities should, as appropriate, make available and disseminate information on the environment which is relevant to their functions, in particular by means of computer telecommunication and/or electronic technology, where available.

(22) This Directive should be evaluated every four years, after its entry into force, in the light of experience and after submission of the relevant reports by the Member States, and be subject to revision on that basis. The Commission should submit an evaluation report to the European Parliament and the Council.

(23) Since the objectives of the proposed Directive cannot be sufficiently achieved by the Member States and can therefore be better achieved at Community level, the Community may adopt measures, in accordance with the principle of subsidiarity as set out in Article 5 of the Treaty. In accordance with the principle of proportionality, as set out in that Article, this Directive does not go beyond what is necessary in order to achieve those objectives.

(24) The provisions of this Directive shall not affect the right of a Member State to maintain or introduce measures providing for broader access to information than required by this Directive,

HAVE ADOPTED THIS DIRECTIVE:

Article 1 — Objectives
The objectives of this Directive are:

(a) to guarantee the right of access to environmental information held by or for public authorities and to set out the basic terms and conditions of, and practical arrangements for, its exercise; and

(b) to ensure that, as a matter of course, environmental information is progressively made available and disseminated to the public in order to achieve the widest possible systematic availability and dissemination to the public of environmental information. To this end the use, in particular, of computer telecommunication and/or electronic technology, where available, shall be promoted.

Article 2 — Definitions
For the purposes of this Directive:

1. 'Environmental information' shall mean any information in written, visual, aural, electronic or any other material form on:

(a) the state of the elements of the environment, such as air and atmosphere, water, soil, land, landscape and natural sites including wetlands, coastal and marine areas, biological diversity and its components, including genetically modified organisms, and the interaction among these elements;

(b) factors, such as substances, energy, noise, radiation or waste, including radioactive waste, emissions, discharges and other releases into the environment, affecting or likely to affect the elements of the environment referred to in (a);

(c) measures (including administrative measures), such as policies, legislation, plans, programmes, environmental agreements, and activities affecting or likely to affect the elements and factors referred to in (a) and (b) as well as measures or activities designed to protect those elements;

(d) reports on the implementation of environmental legislation;

(e) cost-benefit and other economic analyses and assumptions used within the framework of the measures and activities referred to in (c); and

(f) the state of human health and safety, including the contamination of the food chain, where relevant, conditions of human life, cultural sites and built structures inasmuch as they are or may be affected by the state of the elements of the environment referred to in (a) or, through those elements, by any of the matters referred to in (b) and (c).

2. 'Public authority' shall mean:

(a) government or other public administration, including public advisory bodies, at national, regional or local level;

(b) any natural or legal person performing public administrative functions under national law, including specific duties, activities or services in relation to the environment; and

(c) any natural or legal person having public responsibilities or functions, or providing public services, relating to the environment under the control of a body or person falling within (a) or (b).

Member States may provide that this definition shall not include bodies or institutions when acting in a judicial or legislative capacity. If their constitutional provisions at the date of adoption of this Directive make no provision for a review procedure within the meaning of Article 6, Member States may exclude those bodies or institutions from that definition.

3. 'Information held by a public authority' shall mean environmental information in its possession which has been produced or received by that authority.

4 'Information held for a public authority' shall mean environmental information which is physically held by a natural or legal person on behalf of a public authority.

5. 'Applicant' shall mean any natural or legal person requesting environmental information.

6. 'Public' shall mean one or more natural or legal persons, and, in accordance with national legislation or practice, their associations, organisations or groups.

Article 3 — Access to environmental information upon request

1. Member States shall ensure that public authorities are required, in accordance with the provisions of this Directive, to make available environmental information held by or for them to any applicant at his request and without his having to state an interest.

2. Subject to Article 4 and having regard to any timescale specified by the applicant, environmental information shall be made available to an applicant:

    (a) as soon as possible or, at the latest, within one month after the receipt by the public authority referred to in paragraph 1 of the applicant's request; or

    (b) within two months after the receipt of the request by the public authority if the volume and the complexity of the information is such that the one-month period referred to in (a) cannot be complied with. In such cases, the applicant shall be informed as soon as possible, and in any case before the end of that one-month period, of any such extension and of the reasons for it.

3. If a request is formulated in too general a manner, the public authority shall as soon as possible, and at the latest within the timeframe laid down in paragraph 2(a), ask the applicant to specify the request and shall assist the applicant in doing so, e.g. by providing information on the use of the public registers referred to in paragraph 5(c). The public authorities may, where they deem it appropriate, refuse the request under Article 4(1)(c).

4. Where an applicant requests a public authority to make environmental information available in a specific form or format (including in the form of copies), the public authority shall make it so available unless:

    (a) it is already publicly available in another form or format, in particular under Article 7, which is easily accessible by applicants; or

    (b) it is reasonable for the public authority to make it available in another form or format, in which case reasons shall be given for making it available in that form or format.

    For the purposes of this paragraph, public authorities shall make all reasonable efforts to maintain environmental information held by or for them in forms or formats that are readily reproducible and accessible by computer telecommunications or by other electronic means.

    The reasons for a refusal to make information available, in full or in part, in the form or format requested shall be provided to the applicant within the time limit referred to in paragraph 2(a).

5. For the purposes of this Article, Member States shall ensure that:

    (a) officials are required to support the public in seeking access to information;

    (b) lists of public authorities are publicly accessible; and

    (c) the practical arrangements are defined for ensuring that the right of access to environmental information can be effectively exercised, such as:

— the designation of information officers;

— the establishment and maintenance of facilities for the examination of the information required,

— registers or lists of the environmental information held by public authorities or information points, with clear indications of where such information can be found.

Member States shall ensure that public authorities inform the public adequately of the rights they enjoy as a result of this Directive and to an appropriate extent provide information, guidance and advice to this end.

Article 4 — Exceptions

1. Member States may provide for a request for environmental information to be refused if:

(a) the information requested is not held by or for the public authority to which the request is addressed. In such a case, where that public authority is aware that the information is held by or for another public authority, it shall, as soon as possible, transfer the request to that other authority and inform the applicant accordingly or inform the applicant of the public authority to which it believes it is possible to apply for the information requested;

(b) the request is manifestly unreasonable;

(c) the request is formulated in too general a manner, taking into account Article 3(3);

(d) the request concerns material in the course of completion or unfinished documents or data;

(e) the request concerns internal communications, taking into account the public interest served by disclosure.

Where a request is refused on the basis that it concerns material in the course of completion, the public authority shall state the name of the authority preparing the material and the estimated time needed for completion.

2. Member States may provide for a request for environmental information to be refused if disclosure of the information would adversely affect:

(a) the confidentiality of the proceedings of public authorities, where such confidentiality is provided for by law;

(b) international relations, public security or national defence;

(c) the course of justice, the ability of any person to receive a fair trial or the ability of a public authority to conduct an enquiry of a criminal or disciplinary nature;

(d)   the confidentiality of commercial or industrial information where such confidentiality is provided for by national or Community law to protect a legitimate economic interest, including the public interest in maintaining statistical confidentiality and tax secrecy;

(e)   intellectual property rights;

(f)   the confidentiality of personal data and/or files relating to a natural person where that person has not consented to the disclosure of the information to the public, where such confidentiality is provided for by national or Community law;

(g)   the interests or protection of any person who supplied the information requested on a voluntary basis without being under, or capable of being put under, a legal obligation to do so, unless that person has consented to the release of the information concerned;

(h)   the protection of the environment to which such information relates, such as the location of rare species.

The grounds for refusal mentioned in paragraphs 1 and 2 shall be interpreted in a restrictive way, taking into account for the particular case the public interest served by disclosure. In every particular case, the public interest served by disclosure shall be weighed against the interest served by the refusal. Member States may not, by virtue of paragraph 2(a), (d), (f), (g) and (h), provide for a request to be refused where the request relates to information on emissions into the environment.

Within this framework, and for the purposes of the application of subparagraph (f), Member States shall ensure that the requirements of Directive 95/46/EC of the European Parliament and of the Council of 24 October 1995 on the protection of individuals with regard to the processing of personal data and on the free movement of such data are complied with.

3.   Where a Member State provides for exceptions, it may draw up a publicly accessible list of criteria on the basis of which the authority concerned may decide how to handle requests.

4.   Environmental information held by or for public authorities which has been requested by an applicant shall be made available in part where it is possible to separate out any information falling within the scope of paragraphs 1(d) and (e) or 2 from the rest of the information requested.

5.   A refusal to make available all or part of the information requested shall be notified to the applicant in writing or electronically, if the request was in writing or if the applicant so requests, within the time limits referred to in Article 3(2)(a) or, as the case may be, (b). The notification shall state the reasons for the refusal and include information on the review procedure provided for in accordance with Article 6.

Article 5 — Charges

1. Access to any public registers or lists established and maintained as mentioned in Article 3(5) and examination in situ of the information requested shall be free of charge.

2. Public authorities may make a charge for supplying any environmental information but such charge shall not exceed a reasonable amount.

3. Where charges are made, public authorities shall publish and make available to applicants a schedule of such charges as well as information on the circumstances in which a charge may be levied or waived.

Article 6 — Access to justice

1. Member States shall ensure that any applicant who considers that his request for information has been ignored, wrongfully refused (whether in full or in part), inadequately answered or otherwise not dealt with in accordance with the provisions of Articles 3, 4 or 5, has access to a procedure in which the acts or omissions of the public authority concerned can be reconsidered by that or another public authority or reviewed administratively by an independent and impartial body established by law. Any such procedure shall be expeditious and either free of charge or inexpensive.

2. In addition to the review procedure referred to in paragraph 1, Member States shall ensure that an applicant has access to a review procedure before a court of law or another independent and impartial body established by law, in which the acts or omissions of the public authority concerned can be reviewed and whose decisions may become final. Member States may furthermore provide that third parties incriminated by the disclosure of information may also have access to legal recourse.

3. Final decisions under paragraph 2 shall be binding on the public authority holding the information. Reasons shall be stated in writing, at least where access to information is refused under this Article.

Article 7 — Dissemination of environmental information

1. Member States shall take the necessary measures to ensure that public authorities organise the environmental information which is relevant to their functions and which is held by or for them, with a view to its active and systematic dissemination to the public, in particular by means of computer telecommunication and/or electronic technology, where available.

    The information made available by means of computer telecommunication and/or electronic technology need not include information collected before the entry into force of this Directive unless it is already available in electronic form.

    Member States shall ensure that environmental information progressively becomes available in electronic databases which are easily accessible to the public through public telecommunication networks.

2.   The information to be made available and disseminated shall be updated as appropriate and shall include at least:

(a)   texts of international treaties, conventions or agreements, and of Community, national, regional or local legislation, on the environment or relating to it;

(b)   policies, plans and programmes relating to the environment;

(c)   progress reports on the implementation of the items referred to in (a) and (b) when prepared or held in electronic form by public authorities;

(d)   the reports on the state of the environment referred to in paragraph 3;

(e)   data or summaries of data derived from the monitoring of activities affecting, or likely to affect, the environment;

(f)   authorisations with a significant impact on the environment and environmental agreements or a reference to the place where such information can be requested or found in the framework of Article 3;

(g)   environmental   impact studies and risk assessments concerning the environmental elements referred to in Article 2(1)(a) or a reference to the place where the information can be requested or found in the framework of Article 3.

3.   Without prejudice to any specific reporting obligations laid down by Community legislation, Member States shall take the necessary measures to ensure that national, and, where appropriate, regional or local reports on the state of the environment are published at regular intervals not exceeding four years; such reports shall include information on the quality of, and pressures on, the environment.

4.   Without prejudice to any specific obligation laid down by Community legislation, Member States shall take the necessary measures to ensure that, in the event of an imminent threat to human health or the environment, whether caused by human activities or due to natural causes, all information held by or for public authorities which could enable the public likely to be affected to take measures to prevent or mitigate harm arising from the threat is disseminated, immediately and without delay.

5.   The exceptions in Article 4(1) and (2) may apply in relation to the duties imposed by this Article.

6.   Member States may satisfy the requirements of this Article by creating links to Internet sites where the information can be found.

Article 8 — Quality of environmental information

1.   Member States shall, so far as is within their power, ensure that any information that is compiled by them or on their behalf is up to date, accurate and comparable.

2.   Upon request, public authorities shall reply to requests for information pursuant to Article 2(1)b, reporting to the applicant on the place where information, if available, can

be found on the measurement procedures, including methods of analysis, sampling, and pre-treatment of samples, used in compiling the information, or referring to a standardised procedure used.

Article 9 — Review procedure

1. Not later than 14 February 2009, Member States shall report on the experience gained in the application of this Directive.

   They shall communicate the report to the Commission not later than 14 August 2009.

   No later than 14 February 2004, the Commission shall forward to the Member States a guidance document setting out clearly the manner in which it wishes the Member States to report.

2. In the light of experience and taking into account developments in computer telecommunication and/or electronic technology, the Commission shall make a report to the European Parliament and to the Council together with any proposal for revision, which it may consider appropriate.

Article 10 — Implementation

Member States shall bring into force the laws, regulations and administrative provisions necessary to comply with this Directive by 14 February 2005. They shall forthwith inform the Commission thereof.

When Member States adopt these measures, they shall contain a reference to this Directive or shall be accompanied by such reference on the occasion of their official publication. The methods of making such reference shall be laid down by Member States.

Article 11 — Repeal

Directive 90/313/EEC is hereby repealed with effect from 14 February 2005.

References to the repealed Directive shall be construed as referring to this Directive and shall be read in accordance with the correlation table in the Annex.

Article 12 — Entry into force

This Directive shall enter into force on the day of its publication in the Official Journal of the European Union.

Article 13 — Addressees

This Directive is addressed to the Member States.

Done at Brussels, 28 January 2003.

Convention on Access to Information, Public Participation in Decision-making and Access to Justice in Environmental Matters done at Aarhus, Denmark, on 25 June 1998

The Parties to this Convention,

Recalling principle 1 of the Stockholm Declaration on the Human Environment,

Recalling also principle 10 of the Rio Declaration on Environment and Development,

Recalling further General Assembly resolutions 37/7 of 28 October 1982 on the World Charter for Nature and 45/94 of 14 December 1990 on the need to ensure a healthy environment for the well-being of individuals,

Recalling the European Charter on Environment and Health adopted at the First European Conference on Environment and Health of the World Health Organization in Frankfurt-am-Main, Germany, on 8 December 1989,

Affirming the need to protect, preserve and improve the state of the environment and to ensure sustainable and environmentally sound development,

Recognizing that adequate protection of the environment is essential to human well-being and the enjoyment of basic human rights, including the right to life itself,

Recognizing also that every person has the right to live in an environment adequate to his or her health and well-being, and the duty, both individually and in association with others, to protect and improve the environment for the benefit of present and future generations,

Considering that, to be able to assert this right and observe this duty, citizens must have access to information, be entitled to participate in decision-making and have access to justice in environmental matters, and acknowledging in this regard that citizens may need assistance in order to exercise their rights,

Recognizing that, in the field of the environment, improved access to information and public participation in decision-making enhance the quality and the implementation of decisions, contribute to public awareness of environmental issues, give the public the opportunity to express its concerns and enable public authorities to take due account of such concerns,

Aiming thereby to further the accountability of and transparency in decision-making and to strengthen public support for decisions on the environment,

Recognizing the desirability of transparency in all branches of government and inviting legislative bodies to implement the principles of this Convention in their proceedings,

Recognizing also that the public needs to be aware of the procedures for participation in environmental decision-making, have free access to them and know how to use them,

Recognizing further the importance of the respective roles that individual citizens, non-governmental organizations and the private sector can play in environmental protection,

Desiring to promote environmental education to further the understanding of the environment and sustainable development and to encourage widespread public awareness of, and participation in, decisions affecting the environment and sustainable development,

Noting, in this context, the importance of making use of the media and of electronic or other, future forms of communication,

Recognizing the importance of fully integrating environmental considerations in governmental decision-making and the consequent need for public authorities to be in possession of accurate, comprehensive and up-to- date environmental information,

Acknowledging that public authorities hold environmental information in the public interest,

Concerned that effective judicial mechanisms should be accessible to the public, including organizations, so that its legitimate interests are protected and the law is enforced,

Noting the importance of adequate product information being provided to consumers to enable them to make informed environmental choices,

Recognizing the concern of the public about the deliberate release of genetically modified organisms into the environment and the need for increased transparency and greater public participation in decision-making in this field,

Convinced that the implementation of this Convention will contribute to strengthening democracy in the region of the United Nations Economic
Commission for Europe (ECE),

Conscious of the role played in this respect by ECE and recalling, inter alia, the ECE Guidelines on Access to Environmental Information and Public Participation in Environmental Decision-making endorsed in the Ministerial Declaration adopted at the Third Ministerial Conference "Environment for Europe" in Sofia, Bulgaria, on 25 October 1995,

Bearing in mind the relevant provisions in the Convention on Environmental Impact Assessment in a Transboundary Context, done at Espoo, Finland, on 25 February 1991, and the Convention on the Transboundary Effects of Industrial Accidents and the Convention on the Protection and Use of Transboundary Watercourses and International Lakes, both done at Helsinki on 17 March 1992, and other regional conventions,

Conscious that the adoption of this Convention will have contributed to the further strengthening of the "Environment for Europe" process and to the results of the Fourth Ministerial Conference in Aarhus, Denmark, in June 1998,

Have agreed as follows:

Article 1 — Objective
In order to contribute to the protection of the right of every person of present and future generations to live in an environment adequate to his or her health and well-being, each Party

shall guarantee the rights of access to information, public participation in decision-making, and access to justice in environmental matters in accordance with the provisions of this Convention.

Article 2 — Definitions

For the purposes of this Convention,

1.   "Party" means, unless the text otherwise indicates, a Contracting Party to this Convention;

2.   "Public authority" means:

   (a)   Government at national, regional and other level;

   (b)   Natural or legal persons performing public administrative functions under national law, including specific duties, activities or services in relation to the environment;

   (c)   Any other natural or legal persons having public responsibilities or functions, or providing public services, in relation to the environment, under the control of a body or person falling within subparagraphs (a) or (b) above;

   (d)   The institutions of any regional economic integration organization referred to in article 17 which is a Party to this Convention.

   This definition does not include bodies or institutions acting in a judicial or legislative capacity;

3.   "Environmental information" means any information in written, visual, aural, electronic or any other material form on:

   (a)   The state of elements of the environment, such as air and atmosphere, water, soil, land, landscape and natural sites, biological diversity and its components, including genetically modified organisms, and the interaction among these elements;

   (b)   Factors, such as substances, energy, noise and radiation, and activities or measures, including administrative measures, environmental agreements, policies, legislation, plans and programmes, affecting or likely to affect the elements of the environment within the scope of subparagraph (a) above, and cost-benefit and other economic analyses and assumptions used in environmental decision-making;

   (c)   The state of human health and safety, conditions of human life, cultural sites and built structures, inasmuch as they are or may be affected by the state of the elements of the environment or, through these elements, by the factors, activities or measures referred to in subparagraph (b) above;

4.   "The public" means one or more natural or legal persons, and, in accordance with national legislation or practice, their associations, organizations or groups;

5.   "The public concerned" means the public affected or likely to be affected by, or having an interest in, the environmental decision-making; for the purposes of this definition, non-

governmental organizations promoting environmental protection and meeting any requirements under national law shall be deemed to have an interest.

Article 3 — General Provisions

1. Each Party shall take the necessary legislative, regulatory and other measures, including measures to achieve compatibility between the provisions implementing the information, public participation and access-to-justice provisions in this Convention, as well as proper enforcement measures, to establish and maintain a clear, transparent and consistent framework to implement the provisions of this Convention.

2. Each Party shall endeavour to ensure that officials and authorities assist and provide guidance to the public in seeking access to information, in facilitating participation in decision-making and in seeking access to justice in environmental matters.

3. Each Party shall promote environmental education and environmental awareness among the public, especially on how to obtain access to information, to participate in decision-making and to obtain access to justice in environmental matters.

4. Each Party shall provide for appropriate recognition of and support to associations, organizations or groups promoting environmental protection and ensure that its national legal system is consistent with this obligation.

5. The provisions of this Convention shall not affect the right of a Party to maintain or introduce measures providing for broader access to information, more extensive public participation in decision-making and wider access to justice in environmental matters than required by this Convention.

6. This Convention shall not require any derogation from existing rights of access to information, public participation in decision-making and access to justice in environmental matters.

7. Each Party shall promote the application of the principles of this Convention in international environmental decision-making processes and within the framework of international organizations in matters relating to the environment.

8. Each Party shall ensure that persons exercising their rights in conformity with the provisions of this Convention shall not be penalized, persecuted or harassed in any way for their involvement. This provision shall not affect the powers of national courts to award reasonable costs in judicial proceedings.

9. Within the scope of the relevant provisions of this Convention, the public shall have access to information, have the possibility to participate in decision-making and have access to justice in environmental matters without discrimination as to citizenship, nationality or domicile and, in the case of a legal person, without discrimination as to where it has its registered seat or an effective centre of its activities.

Article 4 — Access to Environmental Information

1. Each Party shall ensure that, subject to the following paragraphs of this article, public authorities, in response to a request for environmental information, make such information available to the public, within the framework of national legislation, including, where requested and subject to subparagraph (b) below, copies of the actual documentation containing or comprising such information:

   (a) Without an interest having to be stated;

   (b) In the form requested unless:

      (i) It is reasonable for the public authority to make it available in another form, in which case reasons shall be given for making it available in that form; or

      (ii) The information is already publicly available in another form.

2. The environmental information referred to in paragraph 1 above shall be made available as soon as possible and at the latest within one month after the request has been submitted, unless the volume and the complexity of the information justify an extension of this period up to two months after the request. The applicant shall be informed of any extension and of the reasons justifying it.

3. A request for environmental information may be refused if:

   (a) The public authority to which the request is addressed does not hold the environmental information requested;

   (b) The request is manifestly unreasonable or formulated in too general a manner; or

   (c) The request concerns material in the course of completion or concerns internal communications of public authorities where such an exemption is provided for in national law or customary practice, taking into account the public interest served by disclosure.

4. A request for environmental information may be refused if the disclosure would adversely affect:

   (a) The confidentiality of the proceedings of public authorities, where such confidentiality is provided for under national law;

   (b) International relations, national defence or public security;

   (c) The course of justice, the ability of a person to receive a fair trial or the ability of a public authority to conduct an enquiry of a criminal or disciplinary nature;

   (d) The confidentiality of commercial and industrial information, where such confidentiality is protected by law in order to protect a legitimate economic interest. Within this framework, information on emissions which is relevant for the protection of the environment shall be disclosed;

   (e) Intellectual property rights;

(f)   The confidentiality of personal data and/or files relating to a natural person where that person has not consented to the disclosure of the information to the public, where such confidentiality is provided for in national law;

(g)   The interests of a third party which has supplied the information requested without that party being under or capable of being put under a legal obligation to do so, and where that party does not consent to the release of the material; or

(h)   The environment to which the information relates, such as the breeding sites of rare species.

The aforementioned grounds for refusal shall be interpreted in a restrictive way, taking into account the public interest served by disclosure and taking into account whether the information requested relates to emissions into the environment.

5.   Where a public authority does not hold the environmental information requested, this public authority shall, as promptly as possible, inform the applicant of the public authority to which it believes it is possible to apply for the information requested or transfer the request to that authority and inform the applicant accordingly.

6.   Each Party shall ensure that, if information exempted from disclosure under paragraphs 3 (c) and 4 above can be separated out without prejudice to the confidentiality of the information exempted, public authorities make available the remainder of the environmental information that has been requested.

7.   A refusal of a request shall be in writing if the request was in writing or the applicant so requests. A refusal shall state the reasons for the refusal and give information on access to the review procedure provided for in accordance with article 9. The refusal shall be made as soon as possible and at the latest within one month, unless the complexity of the information justifies an extension of this period up to two months after the request. The applicant shall be informed of any extension and of the reasons justifying it.

8.   Each Party may allow its public authorities to make a charge for supplying information, but such charge shall not exceed a reasonable amount. Public authorities intending to make such a charge for supplying information shall make available to applicants a schedule of charges which may be levied, indicating the circumstances in which they may be levied or waived and when the supply of information is conditional on the advance payment of such a charge.

Article 5 — Collection and Dissemination of Environmental Information

1. Each Party shall ensure that:

(a)   Public authorities possess and update environmental information which is relevant to their functions;

(b)   Mandatory systems are established so that there is an adequate flow of information to public authorities about proposed and existing activities which may significantly affect the environment;

(c) In the event of any imminent threat to human health or the environment, whether caused by human activities or due to natural causes, all information which could enable the public to take measures to prevent or mitigate harm arising from the threat and is held by a public authority is disseminated immediately and without delay to members of the public who may be affected.

2. Each Party shall ensure that, within the framework of national legislation, the way in which public authorities make environmental information available to the public is transparent and that environmental information is effectively accessible, inter alia, by:

(a) Providing sufficient information to the public about the type and scope of environmental information held by the relevant public authorities, the basic terms and conditions under which such information is made available and accessible, and the process by which it can be obtained;

(b) Establishing and maintaining practical arrangements, such as:

(i) Publicly accessible lists, registers or files;

(ii) Requiring officials to support the public in seeking access to information under this Convention; and

(iii) The identification of points of contact; and

(c) Providing access to the environmental information contained in lists, registers or files as referred to in subparagraph (b) (i) above free of charge.

3. Each Party shall ensure that environmental information progressively becomes available in electronic databases which are easily accessible to the public through public telecommunications networks. Information accessible in this form should include:

(a) Reports on the state of the environment, as referred to in paragraph 4 below;

(b) Texts of legislation on or relating to the environment;

(c) As appropriate, policies, plans and programmes on or relating to the environment, and environmental agreements; and

(d) Other information, to the extent that the availability of such information in this form would facilitate the application of national law implementing this Convention,

provided that such information is already available in electronic form.

4. Each Party shall, at regular intervals not exceeding three or four years, publish and disseminate a national report on the state of the environment, including information on the quality of the environment and information on pressures on the environment.

5. Each Party shall take measures within the framework of its legislation for the purpose of disseminating, inter alia:

(a) Legislation and policy documents such as documents on strategies, policies, programmes and action plans relating to the environment, and progress reports on their implementation, prepared at various levels of government;

(b) International treaties, conventions and agreements on environmental issues; and

(c) Other significant international documents on environmental issues, as appropriate.

6. Each Party shall encourage operators whose activities have a significant impact on the environment to inform the public regularly of the environmental impact of their activities and products, where appropriate within the framework of voluntary eco-labelling or eco-auditing schemes or by other means.

7. Each Party shall:

(a) Publish the facts and analyses of facts which it considers relevant and important in framing major environmental policy proposals;

(b) Publish, or otherwise make accessible, available explanatory material on its dealings with the public in matters falling within the scope of this Convention; and

(c) Provide in an appropriate form information on the performance of public functions or the provision of public services relating to the environment by government at all levels.

8. Each Party shall develop mechanisms with a view to ensuring that sufficient product information is made available to the public in a manner which enables consumers to make informed environmental choices.

9. Each Party shall take steps to establish progressively, taking into account international processes where appropriate, a coherent, nationwide system of pollution inventories or registers on a structured, computerized and publicly accessible database compiled through standardized reporting. Such a system may include inputs, releases and transfers of a specified range of substances and products, including water, energy and resource use, from a specified range of activities to environmental media and to on-site and off-site treatment and disposal sites.

10. Nothing in this article may prejudice the right of Parties to refuse to disclose certain environmental information in accordance with article 4, paragraphs 3 and 4.

Article 6 — Public Participation in Decisions on Specific Activities

1. Each Party:

(a) Shall apply the provisions of this article with respect to decisions on whether to permit proposed activities listed in annex I;

(b) Shall, in accordance with its national law, also apply the provisions of this article to decisions on proposed activities not listed in annex I which may have a significant effect on the environment. To this end, Parties shall determine whether such a proposed activity is subject to these provisions; and

(c)   May decide, on a case-by-case basis if so provided under national law, not to apply the provisions of this article to proposed activities serving national defence purposes, if that Party deems that such application would have an adverse effect on these purposes.

2.   The public concerned shall be informed, either by public notice or individually as appropriate, early in an environmental decision-making procedure, and in an adequate, timely and effective manner, inter alia, of:

(a)   The proposed activity and the application on which a decision will be taken;

(b)   The nature of possible decisions or the draft decision;

(c)   The public authority responsible for making the decision;

(d)   The envisaged procedure, including, as and when this information can be provided:
(i) The commencement of the procedure;

(ii) The opportunities for the public to participate;

(iii) The time and venue of any envisaged public hearing;

(iv) An indication of the public authority from which relevant information can be obtained and where the relevant information has been deposited for examination by the public;

(v) An indication of the relevant public authority or any other official body to which comments or questions can be submitted and of the time schedule for transmittal of comments or questions; and

(vi) An indication of what environmental information relevant to the proposed activity is available; and

(e)   The fact that the activity is subject to a national or transboundary environmental impact assessment procedure.

3.   The public participation procedures shall include reasonable time-frames for the different phases, allowing sufficient time for informing the public in accordance with paragraph 2 above and for the public to prepare and participate effectively during the environmental decision-making.

4.   Each Party shall provide for early public participation, when all options are open and effective public participation can take place.

5.   Each Party should, where appropriate, encourage prospective applicants to identify the public concerned, to enter into discussions, and to provide information regarding the objectives of their application before applying for a permit.

6.   Each Party shall require the competent public authorities to give the public concerned access for examination, upon request where so required under national law, free of charge and as soon as it becomes available, to all information relevant to the decision-making referred to in this article that is available at the time of the public participation procedure, without prejudice to the right of Parties to refuse to disclose certain information in accordance with article 4, paragraphs 3 and 4. The relevant information shall include at least, and without prejudice to the provisions of article 4:

(a)   A description of the site and the physical and technical characteristics of the proposed activity, including an estimate of the expected residues and emissions;

(b)   A description of the significant effects of the proposed activity on the environment;

(c)   A description of the measures envisaged to prevent and/or reduce the effects, including emissions;

(d)   A non-technical summary of the above;

(e)   An outline of the main alternatives studied by the applicant; and

(f)   In accordance with national legislation, the main reports and advice issued to the public authority at the time when the public concerned shall be informed in accordance with paragraph 2 above.

7.   Procedures for public participation shall allow the public to submit, in writing or, as appropriate, at a public hearing or inquiry with the applicant, any comments, information, analyses or opinions that it considers relevant to the proposed activity.

8.   Each Party shall ensure that in the decision due account is taken of the outcome of the public participation.

9.   Each Party shall ensure that, when the decision has been taken by the public authority, the public is promptly informed of the decision in accordance with the appropriate procedures. Each Party shall make accessible to the public the text of the decision along with the reasons and considerations on which the decision is based.

10.   Each Party shall ensure that, when a public authority reconsiders or updates the operating conditions for an activity referred to in paragraph 1, the provisions of paragraphs 2 to 9 of this article are applied mutatis mutandis, and where appropriate.

11.   Each Party shall, within the framework of its national law, apply, to the extent feasible and appropriate, provisions of this article to decisions on whether to permit the deliberate release of genetically modified organisms into the environment.

Article 7 — Public Participation Concerning Plans, Programmes and Policies Relating to the Environment

Each Party shall make appropriate practical and/or other provisions for the public to participate during the preparation of plans and programmes relating to the environment, within a transparent and fair framework, having provided the necessary information to the public.

Within this framework, article 6, paragraphs 3, 4 and 8, shall be applied. The public which may participate shall be identified by the relevant public authority, taking into account the objectives of this Convention. To the extent appropriate, each Party shall endeavour to provide opportunities for public participation in the preparation of policies relating to the environment.

Article 8 — Public Participation During the Preparation of Executive Regulations And/or Generally Applicable Legally Binding Normative Instruments

Each Party shall strive to promote effective public participation at an appropriate stage, and while options are still open, during the preparation by public authorities of executive regulations and other generally applicable legally binding rules that may have a significant effect on the environment. To this end, the following steps should be taken:

(a) Time-frames sufficient for effective participation should be fixed;

(b) Draft rules should be published or otherwise made publicly available; and

(c) The public should be given the opportunity to comment, directly or through representative consultative bodies.

The result of the public participation shall be taken into account as far as possible.

Article 9 — Access to Justice

1. Each Party shall, within the framework of its national legislation, ensure that any person who considers that his or her request for information under article 4 has been ignored, wrongfully refused, whether in part or in full, inadequately answered, or otherwise not dealt with in accordance with the provisions of that article, has access to a review procedure before a court of law or another independent and impartial body established by law.

   In the circumstances where a Party provides for such a review by a court of law, it shall ensure that such a person also has access to an expeditious procedure established by law that is free of charge or inexpensive for reconsideration by a public authority or review by an independent and impartial body other than a court of law.

   Final decisions under this paragraph 1 shall be binding on the public authority holding the information. Reasons shall be stated in writing, at least where access to information is refused under this paragraph.

2. Each Party shall, within the framework of its national legislation, ensure that members of the public concerned

   (a) Having a sufficient interest

   or, alternatively,

   (b) Maintaining impairment of a right, where the administrative procedural law of a Party requires this as a precondition, have access to a review procedure before a court of law and/or another independent and impartial body established by law, to challenge the substantive and procedural legality of any decision, act or omission subject to the provisions of article 6 and, where so provided for under national law and without prejudice to paragraph 3 below, of other relevant provisions of this Convention.

What constitutes a sufficient interest and impairment of a right shall be determined in accordance with the requirements of national law and consistently with the objective of giving the public concerned wide access to justice within the scope of this Convention. To this end, the interest of any non-governmental organization meeting the requirements referred to in article 2, paragraph 5, shall be deemed sufficient for the purpose of subparagraph (a) above. Such organizations shall also be deemed to have rights capable of being impaired for the purpose of subparagraph (b) above.

The provisions of this paragraph 2 shall not exclude the possibility of a preliminary review procedure before an administrative authority and shall not affect the requirement of exhaustion of administrative review procedures prior to recourse to judicial review procedures, where such a requirement exists under national law.

3. In addition and without prejudice to the review procedures referred to in paragraphs 1 and 2 above, each Party shall ensure that, where they meet the criteria, if any, laid down in its national law, members of the public have access to administrative or judicial procedures to challenge acts and omissions by private persons and public authorities which contravene provisions of its national law relating to the environment.

4. In addition and without prejudice to paragraph 1 above, the procedures referred to in paragraphs 1, 2 and 3 above shall provide adequate and effective remedies, including injunctive relief as appropriate, and be fair, equitable, timely and not prohibitively expensive. Decisions under this article shall be given or recorded in writing. Decisions of courts, and whenever possible of other bodies, shall be publicly accessible.

5. In order to further the effectiveness of the provisions of this article, each Party shall ensure that information is provided to the public on access to administrative and judicial review procedures and shall consider the establishment of appropriate assistance mechanisms to remove or reduce financial and other barriers to access to justice.

Article 10 — Meeting of the Parties

1. The first meeting of the Parties shall be convened no later than one year after the date of the entry into force of this Convention. Thereafter, an ordinary meeting of the Parties shall be held at least once every two years, unless otherwise decided by the Parties, or at the written request of any Party, provided that, within six months of the request being communicated to all Parties by the Executive Secretary of the Economic Commission for Europe, the said request is supported by at least one third of the Parties.

2.   At their meetings, the Parties shall keep under continuous review the implementation of this Convention on the basis of regular reporting by the Parties, and, with this purpose in mind, shall:

(a)   Review the policies for and legal and methodological approaches to access to information, public participation in decision-making and access to justice in environmental matters, with a view to further improving them;

(b)   Exchange information regarding experience gained in concluding and implementing bilateral and multilateral agreements or other arrangements having relevance to the purposes of this Convention and to which one or more of the Parties are a party;

(c)   Seek, where appropriate, the services of relevant ECE bodies and other competent international bodies and specific committees in all aspects pertinent to the achievement of the purposes of this Convention;

(d)   Establish any subsidiary bodies as they deem necessary;

(e)   Prepare, where appropriate, protocols to this Convention;

(f)   Consider and adopt proposals for amendments to this Convention in accordance with the provisions of article 14;

(g)   Consider and undertake any additional action that may be required for the achievement of the purposes of this Convention;

(h)   At their first meeting, consider and by consensus adopt rules of procedure for their meetings and the meetings of subsidiary bodies;

(i)   At their first meeting, review their experience in implementing the provisions of article 5, paragraph 9, and consider what steps are necessary to develop further the system referred to in that paragraph, taking into account international processes and developments, including the elaboration of an appropriate instrument concerning pollution release and transfer registers or inventories which could be annexed to this Convention.

3.   The Meeting of the Parties may, as necessary, consider establishing financial arrangements on a consensus basis.

4.   The United Nations, its specialized agencies and the International Atomic Energy Agency, as well as any State or regional economic integration organization entitled under article 17 to sign this Convention but which is not a Party to this Convention, and any intergovernmental organization qualified in the fields to which this Convention relates, shall be entitled to participate as observers in the meetings of the Parties.

5.   Any non-governmental organization, qualified in the fields to which this Convention relates, which has informed the Executive Secretary of the Economic Commission for Europe of its wish to be represented at a meeting of the Parties shall be entitled to

participate as an observer unless at least one third of the Parties present in the meeting raise objections.

6.   For the purposes of paragraphs 4 and 5 above, the rules of procedure referred to in paragraph 2 (h) above shall provide for practical arrangements for the admittance procedure and other relevant terms.

Article 11 — Right to Vote

1.   Except as provided for in paragraph 2 below, each Party to this Convention shall have one vote.

2.   Regional economic integration organizations, in matters within their competence, shall exercise their right to vote with a number of votes equal to the number of their member States which are Parties to this Convention. Such organizations shall not exercise their right to vote if their member States exercise theirs, and vice versa.

Article 12 — Secretariat

The Executive Secretary of the Economic Commission for Europe shall carry out the following secretariat functions:

(a)   The convening and preparing of meetings of the Parties;

(b)   The transmission to the Parties of reports and other information received in accordance with the provisions of this Convention; and

(c)   Such other functions as may be determined by the Parties.

Article 13 — Annexes

The annexes to this Convention shall constitute an integral part thereof.

Article 14 — Amendments to the Convention

1.   Any Party may propose amendments to this Convention.

2.   The text of any proposed amendment to this Convention shall be submitted in writing to the Executive Secretary of the Economic Commission for Europe, who shall communicate it to all Parties at least ninety days before the meeting of the Parties at which it is proposed for adoption.

3.   The Parties shall make every effort to reach agreement on any proposed amendment to this Convention by consensus. If all efforts at consensus have been exhausted, and no agreement reached, the amendment shall as a last resort be adopted by a three-fourths majority vote of the Parties present and voting at the meeting.

4.   Amendments to this Convention adopted in accordance with paragraph 3 above shall be communicated by the Depositary to all Parties for ratification, approval or acceptance. Amendments to this Convention other than those to an annex shall enter into force for

Parties having ratified, approved or accepted them on the ninetieth day after the receipt by the Depositary of notification of their ratification, approval or acceptance by at least three fourths of these Parties. Thereafter they shall enter into force for any other Party on the ninetieth day after that Party deposits its instrument of ratification, approval or acceptance of the amendments.

5. Any Party that is unable to approve an amendment to an annex to this Convention shall so notify the Depositary in writing within twelve months from the date of the communication of the adoption. The Depositary shall without delay notify all Parties of any such notification received. A Party may at any time substitute an acceptance for its previous notification and, upon deposit of an instrument of acceptance with the Depositary, the amendments to such an annex shall become effective for that Party.

6. On the expiry of twelve months from the date of its communication by the Depositary as provided for in paragraph 4 above an amendment to an annex shall become effective for those Parties which have not submitted a notification to the Depositary in accordance with the provisions of paragraph 5 above, provided that not more than one third of the Parties have submitted such a notification.

7. For the purposes of this article, "Parties present and voting" means Parties present and casting an affirmative or negative vote.

Article 15 — Review of Compliance

The Meeting of the Parties shall establish, on a consensus basis, optional arrangements of a non-confrontational, non-judicial and consultative nature for reviewing compliance with the provisions of this Convention. These arrangements shall allow for appropriate public involvement and may include the option of considering communications from members of the public on matters related to this Convention.

Article 16 — Settlement of Disputes

1. If a dispute arises between two or more Parties about the interpretation or application of this Convention, they shall seek a solution by negotiation or by any other means of dispute settlement acceptable to the parties to the dispute.

2. When signing, ratifying, accepting, approving or acceding to this Convention, or at any time thereafter, a Party may declare in writing to the Depositary that, for a dispute not resolved in accordance with paragraph 1 above, it accepts one or both of the following means of dispute settlement as compulsory in relation to any Party accepting the same obligation:

    (a) Submission of the dispute to the International Court of Justice;

    (b) Arbitration in accordance with the procedure set out in annex II.

3.   If the parties to the dispute have accepted both means of dispute settlement referred to in paragraph 2 above, the dispute may be submitted only to the International Court of Justice, unless the parties agree otherwise.

Article 17 — Signature

This Convention shall be open for signature at Aarhus (Denmark) on 25 June 1998, and thereafter at United Nations Headquarters in New York until 21 December 1998, by States members of the Economic Commission for Europe as well as States having consultative status with the Economic Commission for Europe pursuant to paragraphs 8 and 11 of Economic and Social Council resolution 36 (IV) of 28 March 1947, and by regional economic integration organizations constituted by sovereign States members of the Economic Commission for Europe to which their member States have transferred competence over matters governed by this Convention, including the competence to enter into treaties in respect of these matters.

Article 18 — Depositary

The Secretary-General of the United Nations shall act as the Depositary of this Convention.

Article 19 — Ratification, Acceptance, Approval and Accession

1.   This Convention shall be subject to ratification, acceptance or approval by signatory States and regional economic integration organizations.

2.   This Convention shall be open for accession as from 22 December 1998 by the States and regional economic integration organizations referred to in article 17.

3.   Any other State, not referred to in paragraph 2 above, that is a Member of the United Nations may accede to the Convention upon approval by the Meeting of the Parties.

4.   Any organization referred to in article 17 which becomes a Party to this Convention without any of its member States being a Party shall be bound by all the obligations under this Convention. If one or more of such an organization's member States is a Party to this Convention, the organization and its member States shall decide on their respective responsibilities for the performance of their obligations under this Convention. In such cases, the organization and the member States shall not be entitled to exercise rights under this Convention concurrently.

5.   In their instruments of ratification, acceptance, approval or accession, the regional economic integration organizations referred to in article 17 shall declare the extent of their competence with respect to the matters governed by this Convention. These organizations shall also inform the Depositary of any substantial modification to the extent of their competence.

Article 20 — Entry Into Force

1. This Convention shall enter into force on the nineteenth day after the date of deposit of the sixteenth instrument of ratification, acceptance, approval or accession.

2. For the purposes of paragraph 1 above, any instrument deposited by a regional economic integration organization shall not be counted as additional to those deposited by States members of such an organization.

3. For each State or organization referred to in article 17 which ratifies, accepts or approves this Convention or accedes thereto after the deposit of the sixteenth instrument of ratification, acceptance, approval or accession, the Convention shall enter into force on the ninetieth day after the date of deposit by such State or organization of its instrument of ratification, acceptance, approval or accession.

Article 21 — Withdrawal
At any time after three years from the date on which this Convention has come into force with respect to a Party, that Party may withdraw from the Convention by giving written notification to the Depositary. Any such withdrawal shall take effect on the ninetieth day after the date of its receipt by the Depositary.

Article 22 — Authentic Texts
The original of this Convention, of which the English, French and Russian texts are equally authentic, shall be deposited with the Secretary-General of the United Nations.

IN WITNESS WHEREOF the undersigned, being duly authorized thereto, have signed this Convention.

DONE at Aarhus (Denmark), this twenty-fifth day of June, one thousand nine hundred and ninety-eight.

Annex I
LIST OF ACTIVITIES REFERRED TO IN ARTICLE 6, PARAGRAPH 1 (a)

1. Energy sector:
   – Mineral oil and gas refineries;

   – Installations for gasification and liquefaction;

   – Thermal power stations and other combustion installations with a heat input of 50 megawatts (MW) or more;

   – Coke ovens;

   – Nuclear power stations and other nuclear reactors including the dismantling or decommissioning of such power stations or reactors 1/ (except research installations for the production and conversion of fissionable and fertile materials whose maximum power does not exceed 1 kW continuous thermal load);

– Installations for the reprocessing of irradiated nuclear fuel;

– Installations designed:

  – For the production or enrichment of nuclear fuel;

  – For the processing of irradiated nuclear fuel or high–level radioactive waste;

  – For the final disposal of irradiated nuclear fuel;

  – Solely for the final disposal of radioactive waste;

  – Solely for the storage (planned for more than 10 years) of irradiated nuclear fuels or radioactive waste in a different site than the production site.

2. Production and processing of metals:

– Metal ore (including sulphide ore) roasting or sintering installations;

– Installations for the production of pig–iron or steel (primary or secondary fusion) including continuous casting, with a capacity exceeding 2.5 tons per hour;

– Installations for the processing of ferrous metals:

  (i) Hot–rolling mills with a capacity exceeding 20 tons of crude steel per hour;

  (ii) Smitheries with hammers the energy of which exceeds 50 kilojoules per hammer, where the calorific power used exceeds 20 MW;

  (iii) Application of protective fused metal coats with an input exceeding 2 tons of crude steel per hour;

– Ferrous metal foundries with a production capacity exceeding 20 tons per day;

– Installations:

  (i) For the production of non–ferrous crude metals from ore, concentrates or secondary raw materials by metallurgical, chemical or electrolytic processes;

  (ii) For the smelting, including the alloying, of non–ferrous metals, including recovered products (refining, foundry casting, etc.), with a melting capacity exceeding 4 tons per day for lead and cadmium or 20 tons per day for all other metals;

– Installations for surface treatment of metals and plastic materials using an electrolytic or chemical process where the volume of the treatment vats exceeds 30 m^3.

3. Mineral industry:

– Installations for the production of cement clinker in rotary kilns with a production capacity exceeding 500 tons per day or lime in rotary kilns with a production capacity exceeding 50 tons per day or in other furnaces with a production capacity exceeding 50 tons per day;

- Installations for the production of asbestos and the manufacture of asbestos–based products;

- Installations for the manufacture of glass including glass fibre with a melting capacity exceeding 20 tons per day;

- Installations for melting mineral substances including the production of mineral fibres with a melting capacity exceeding 20 tons per day;

- Installations for the manufacture of ceramic products by firing, in particular roofing tiles, bricks, refractory bricks, tiles, stoneware or porcelain, with a production capacity exceeding 75 tons per day, and/or with a kiln capacity exceeding 4 m^3 and with a setting density per kiln exceeding 300 kg/m^3.

4.   Chemical industry: Production within the meaning of the categories of activities contained in this paragraph means the production on an industrial scale by chemical processing of substances or groups of substances listed in subparagraphs (a) to (g):

(a)   Chemical installations for the production of basic organic chemicals, such as:

(i)   Simple hydrocarbons (linear or cyclic, saturated or unsaturated, aliphatic or aromatic);

(ii)   Oxygen–containing hydrocarbons such as alcohols, aldehydes, ketones, carboxylic acids, esters, acetates, ethers, peroxides, epoxy resins;

(iii) Sulphurous hydrocarbons;

(iv) Nitrogenous hydrocarbons such as amines, amides, nitrous compounds, nitro compounds or nitrate compounds, nitriles, cyanates, isocyanates;

(v)   Phosphorus–containing hydrocarbons;

(vi) Halogenic hydrocarbons;

(vii)   Organometallic compounds;

(viii)   Basic plastic materials (polymers, synthetic fibres and cellulose–based fibres);

(ix) Synthetic rubbers;

(x)   Dyes and pigments;

(xi) Surface–active agents and surfactants;

(b)   Chemical installations for the production of basic inorganic chemicals, such as:

(i)   Gases, such as ammonia, chlorine or hydrogen chloride, fluorine or hydrogen fluoride, carbon oxides, sulphur compounds, nitrogen oxides, hydrogen, sulphur dioxide, carbonyl chloride;

(ii) Acids, such as chromic acid, hydrofluoric acid, phosphoric acid, nitric acid, hydrochloric acid, sulphuric acid, oleum, sulphurous acids;

(iii) Bases, such as ammonium hydroxide, potassium hydroxide, sodium hydroxide;

(iv) Salts, such as ammonium chloride, potassium chlorate, potassium carbonate, sodium carbonate, perborate, silver nitrate;

(v) Non-metals, metal oxides or other inorganic compounds such as calcium carbide, silicon, silicon carbide;

(c) Chemical installations for the production of phosphorous–, nitrogen–or potassium–based fertilizers (simple or compound fertilizers);

(d) Chemical installations for the production of basic plant health products and of biocides;

(e) Installations using a chemical or biological process for the production of basic pharmaceutical products;

(f) Chemical installations for the production of explosives;

(g) Chemical installations in which chemical or biological processing is used for the production of protein feed additives, ferments and other protein substances.

5. Waste management:

–   Installations for the incineration, recovery, chemical treatment or landfill of hazardous waste;

–   Installations for the incineration of municipal waste with a capacity exceeding 3 tons per hour;

–   Installations for the disposal of non–hazardous waste with a capacity exceeding 50 tons per day;

–   Landfills receiving more than 10 tons per day or with a total capacity exceeding 25 000 tons, excluding landfills of inert waste.

6. Waste–water treatment plants with a capacity exceeding 150 000 population equivalent.

7. Industrial plants for the:

(a) Production of pulp from timber or similar fibrous materials;

(b) Production of paper and board with a production capacity exceeding 20 tons per day.

8. (a) Construction of lines for long–distance railway traffic and of airports 2/ with a basic runway length of 2 100 m or more;

(b) Construction of motorways and express roads; 3/

(c) Construction of a new road of four or more lanes, or realignment and/or widening of an existing road of two lanes or less so as to provide four or more lanes, where such new road, or realigned and/or widened section of road, would be 10 km or more in a continuous length.

9. (a) Inland waterways and ports for inland–waterway traffic which permit the passage of vessels of over 1 350 tons;

    (b) Trading ports, piers for loading and unloading connected to land and outside ports (excluding ferry piers) which can take vessels of over 1 350 tons.

10. Groundwater abstraction or artificial groundwater recharge schemes where the annual volume of water abstracted or recharged is equivalent to or exceeds 10 million cubic metres.

11. (a) Works for the transfer of water resources between river basins where this transfer aims at preventing possible shortages of water and where the amount of water transferred exceeds 100 million cubic metres/year;

    (b) In all other cases, works for the transfer of water resources between river basins where the multiannual average flow of the basin of abstraction exceeds 2 000 million cubic metres/year and where the amount of water transferred exceeds 5% of this flow.

    In both cases transfers of piped drinking water are excluded.

12. Extraction of petroleum and natural gas for commercial purposes where the amount extracted exceeds 500 tons/day in the case of petroleum and 500 000 cubic metres/day in the case of gas.

13. Dams and other installations designed for the holding back or permanent storage of water, where a new or additional amount of water held back or stored exceeds 10 million cubic metres.

14. Pipelines for the transport of gas, oil or chemicals with a diameter of more than 800 mm and a length of more than 40 km.

15. Installations for the intensive rearing of poultry or pigs with more than:

    (a) 40 000 places for poultry;

    (b) 2 000 places for production pigs (over 30 kg); or

    (c) 750 places for sows.

16. Quarries and opencast mining where the surface of the site exceeds 25 hectares, or peat extraction, where the surface of the site exceeds 150 hectares.

17. Construction of overhead electrical power lines with a voltage of 220 kV or more and a length of more than 15 km.

18. Installations for the storage of petroleum, petrochemical, or chemical products with a capacity of 200 000 tons or more.

19.   Other activities:

- Plants for the pretreatment (operations such as washing, bleaching, mercerization) or dyeing of fibres or textiles where the treatment capacity exceeds 10 tons per day;

- Plants for the tanning of hides and skins where the treatment capacity exceeds 12 tons of finished products per day;

    (a) Slaughterhouses with a carcass production capacity greater than 50 tons per day;

    (b) Treatment and processing intended for the production of food products from:

        (i) Animal raw materials (other than milk) with a finished product production capacity greater than 75 tons per day;

        (ii) Vegetable raw materials with a finished product production capacity greater than 300 tons per day (average value on a quarterly basis);

    (c) Treatment and processing of milk, the quantity of milk received being greater than 200 tons per day (average value on an annual basis);

- Installations for the disposal or recycling of animal carcasses and animal waste with a treatment capacity exceeding 10 tons per day;

- Installations for the surface treatment of substances, objects or products using organic solvents, in particular for dressing, printing, coating, degreasing, waterproofing, sizing, painting, cleaning or impregnating, with a consumption capacity of more than 150 kg per hour or more than 200 tons per year;

- Installations for the production of carbon (hard–burnt coal) or electrographite by means of incineration or graphitization.

20.   Any activity not covered by paragraphs 1–19 above where public participation is provided for under an environmental impact assessment procedure in accordance with national legislation.

21.   The provision of article 6, paragraph 1 (a) of this Convention, does not apply to any of the above projects undertaken exclusively or mainly for research, development and testing of new methods or products for less than two years unless they would be likely to cause a significant adverse effect on environment or health.

22.   Any change to or extension of activities, where such a change or extension in itself meets the criteria/thresholds set out in this annex, shall be subject to article 6, paragraph 1 (a) of this Convention. Any other change or extension of activities shall be subject to article 6, paragraph 1 (b) of this Convention.

Notes

1. Nuclear power stations and other nuclear reactors cease to be such an installation when all nuclear fuel and other radioactively contaminated elements have been removed permanently from the installation site.

2. For the purposes of this Convention, "airport" means an airport which complies with the definition in the 1944 Chicago Convention setting up the International Civil Aviation Organization (Annex 14).

3. For the purposes of this Convention, "express road" means a road which complies with the definition in the European Agreement on Main International Traffic Arteries of 15 November 1975.

Annex II
ARBITRATION

1. In the event of a dispute being submitted for arbitration pursuant to article 16, paragraph 2, of this Convention, a party or parties shall notify the secretariat of the subject matter of arbitration and indicate, in particular, the articles of this Convention whose interpretation or application is at issue. The secretariat shall forward the information received to all Parties to this Convention.

2. The arbitral tribunal shall consist of three members. Both the claimant party or parties and the other party or parties to the dispute shall appoint an arbitrator, and the two arbitrators so appointed shall designate by common agreement the third arbitrator, who shall be the president of the arbitral tribunal. The latter shall not be a national of one of the parties to the dispute, nor have his or her usual place of residence in the territory of one of these parties, nor be employed by any of them, nor have dealt with the case in any other capacity.

3. If the president of the arbitral tribunal has not been designated within two months of the appointment of the second arbitrator, the Executive Secretary of the Economic Commission for Europe shall, at the request of either party to the dispute, designate the president within a further two–month period.

4. If one of the parties to the dispute does not appoint an arbitrator within two months of the receipt of the request, the other party may so inform the Executive Secretary of the Economic Commission for Europe, who shall designate the president of the arbitral tribunal within a further two–month period. Upon designation, the president of the arbitral tribunal shall request the party which has not appointed an arbitrator to do so within two months. If it fails to do so within that period, the president shall so inform the Executive Secretary of the Economic Commission for Europe, who shall make this appointment within a further two–month period.

5. The arbitral tribunal shall render its decision in accordance with international law and the provisions of this Convention.

6. Any arbitral tribunal constituted under the provisions set out in this annex shall draw up its own rules of procedure.

7.   The decisions of the arbitral tribunal, both on procedure and on substance, shall be taken by majority vote of its members.

8.   The tribunal may take all appropriate measures to establish the facts.

9.   The parties to the dispute shall facilitate the work of the arbitral tribunal and, in particular, using all means at their disposal, shall:

(a)   Provide it with all relevant documents, facilities and information;

(b)   Enable it, where necessary, to call witnesses or experts and receive their evidence.

10. The parties and the arbitrators shall protect the confidentiality of any information that they receive in confidence during the proceedings of the arbitral tribunal.

11. The arbitral tribunal may, at the request of one of the parties, recommend interim measures of protection.

12. If one of the parties to the dispute does not appear before the arbitral tribunal or fails to defend its case, the other party may request the tribunal to continue the proceedings and to render its final decision. Absence of a party or failure of a party to defend its case shall not constitute a bar to the proceedings.

13. The arbitral tribunal may hear and determine counter–claims arising directly out of the subject matter of the dispute.

14. Unless the arbitral tribunal determines otherwise because of the particular circumstances of the case, the expenses of the tribunal, including the remuneration of its members, shall be borne by the parties to the dispute in equal shares. The tribunal shall keep a record of all its expenses, and shall furnish a final statement thereof to the parties.

15. Any Party to this Convention which has an interest of a legal nature in the subject matter of the dispute, and which may be affected by a decision in the case, may intervene in the proceedings with the consent of the tribunal.

16. The arbitral tribunal shall render its award within five months of the date on which it is established, unless it finds it necessary to extend the time limit for a period which should not exceed five months.

17. The award of the arbitral tribunal shall be accompanied by a statement of reasons. It shall be final and binding upon all parties to the dispute. The award will be transmitted by the arbitral tribunal to the parties to the dispute and to the secretariat. The secretariat will forward the information received to all Parties to this Convention.

18. Any dispute which may arise between the parties concerning the interpretation or execution of the award may be submitted by either party to the arbitral tribunal which made the award or, if the latter cannot be seized thereof, to another tribunal constituted for this purpose in the same manner as the first.

Precedents

Precedent 1
Simple request under the Freedom of Information Act

Request for information made under the *Freedom of Information Act 2000*

TO: Westminster City Council
Westminster City Hall
64 Victoria Street
London
SW1E 6QP

APPLICANT: John Citizen

ADDRESS FOR CORRESPONDENCE:
123 Birdcage Walk
London
SW1A 6BD
Tel: 020 - 7654 3210
Fax: 020 - 7654 3201
e-mail: jc@world.co.uk

DESCRIPTION OF THE INFORMATION REQUESTED:
All information taken into account in the decision to refuse my application made under the Building Control Regulations 2000 (dated 1 January 2010 and relating to works at 123 Birdcage Walk), that refusal being conveyed by letter to me dated 30 March 2010, including all representations received by the Council and all advice given and recommendations made by officers of the Council.

PREFERRED MEANS OF COMMUNICATION:
Provision of a copy of the information in printed form

DATE OF THIS REQUEST: Tuesday, 1 June 2010

SIGNED:..
John Citizen

Precedent 2
Request under the Freedom of Information Act 2000 where a qualified exemption is likely to be relied upon

Request for information made under the *Freedom of Information Act 2000*

TO: Information Rights Team
     Information Management Group
     Foreign and Commonwealth Office
     Old Admiralty Building
     London
     SW1A 2PA

APPLICANT: John Citizen

ADDRESS FOR CORRESPONDENCE:
     123 Birdcage Walk
     London
     SW1A 6BD
     Tel: 020 - 7654 3210
     Fax: 020 - 7654 3201
     e-mail: jc@world.co.uk

DESCRIPTION OF THE INFORMATION REQUESTED:
1.   All assessments (howsoever described) of the extent to which existing UK legislation (most notably the Prevention of Corruption Act 1906 as amended by Part 12 of the Anti-Terrorism, Crime and Security Act 2001) implements the OECD Convention on Combating Bribery of Foreign Public Officials in International Business Transactions.

2.   All communications (howsoever described) from a publicly-listed company in the United Kingdom (or a person, firm or organisation acting on its behalf) making representations (howsoever described) on or in relation to the implementation by the United Kingdom of the OECD Convention on Combating Bribery of Foreign Public Officials in International Business Transactions.

3.   All communications (howsoever described) from a foreign government (or a person, firm or organisation acting on its behalf) making representations (howsoever described) on or in relation to the implementation by the United Kingdom of the OECD Convention on Combating Bribery of Foreign Public Officials in International Business Transactions.

PREFERRED MEANS OF COMMUNICATION:
     Provision of a copy of the information in printed form

DATE OF THIS REQUEST:

Tuesday, 1 June 2010

FURTHER INFORMATION:
1. In the event that you believe that information or more information answering the terms of this request is held by another public authority, please advise by return but continue to process this request in relation to all information answering the terms of the request held by you.

2. This request is considered to be perfectly clear. In the event, however, that you require further information in order to identify and locate the information requested, please advise by return.

3. There is an overwhelming public interest in disclosing the information requested:

    (1) On 14 December 1988 the United Kingdom ratified the OECD Convention on Combating Bribery of Foreign Public Officials in International Business Transactions, with it entering into force on 15 February 1999.

    (2) Article 1(1)-(2) of the Convention provides that each party to the Convention must take such measures as may be necessary to establish that it is a criminal offence under its law for any person to engage in what it defines as bribery of a foreign public official.

    (3) In March 2005, the OECD approved and adopted its Phase 2 Report on the application by the United Kingdom of the OECD Convention on Combating Bribery of Foreign Public Officials in International Business Transactions, recording "the lead examiners' concerns about the level of implementation of the OECD Convention by the UK authorities." See in particular paras 181-188.

    (4) It is in the public interest to know whether the responsible Ministry itself holds information that supports the OECD's assessment.

    (5) The information will assist in informed discussion on an issue of fundamental public importance.

SIGNED:...
    John Citizen

Notes:
1. Although an applicant is not obliged to spell out the public interest in disclosure of the information requested, it is considered that where reliance upon a qualified exemption is predictable and it is possible to identify aspects of the public interest in disclosure, these should be included in order to maximise the prospects of success.

Precedent 3
Request under the Data Protection Act 1998 for personal information relating to the applicant

Request for data made under section 7 of the *Data Protection Act 1998*

TO: Westminster City Council
Attention: The Data Controller for the purposes of the *Data Protection Act 1998*
P.O. Box 240
Westminster City Hall
64 Victoria Street
London
SW1E 6QP

APPLICANT: John Citizen

ADDRESS FOR CORRESPONDENCE:
123 Birdcage Walk
London
SW1A 6BD
Tel: 020 - 7654 3210
Fax: 020 - 7654 3201
e-mail: jc@world.co.uk

REQUEST:
Pursuant to section 7 of the *Data Protection Act 1998*, you are hereby required:
- (1) to inform me whether personal data of which I am the data subject are being processed by or on behalf of you;
- (2) if "yes" to (1), to give me a description of:
  - (a) the personal data of which I am the data subject;
  - (b) the purposes for which those data are being or are to be processed; and
  - (c) the recipients or classes or recipients to whom those data are or may be disclosed;
- (3) to communicate to me in an intelligible form:
  - (a) the information constituting any personal data of which I am the data subject; and
  - (b) any information available to you as to the source of those data; and
- (4) to inform me of the logic involved in any decision-taking significantly affecting me.

PREFERRED MEANS OF RECEIPT OF INFORMATION:
Please provide the data in printed form

DATE OF THIS REQUEST:
Tuesday, 1 June 2010

CHEQUE ENCLOSED:
A cheque in the sum of £10 (ten pounds) made payable to Westminster City Council is enclosed.

FURTHER INFORMATION:

1. I have signed this document and enclosed a personal cheque as proof of my identity. Although I consider that these a perfectly adequate evidence of my identity, should you feel the need for further proof, please advise me by return.

2. This request is considered to be perfectly clear. In the event, however, that you require further information in order to locate the information requested, please advise by return.

3. To the extent that compliance with this request would disclose information relating to another individual and that individual can be identified from that information and that individual has not consented to the disclosure of the information to me, please redact just that part of the information from which that individual can be identified.

SIGNED:..
John Citizen

Precedent 4
Request under the Environmental Information Regulations 2004

Request for information made under the Request under the
Environmental Information Regulations 2004

TO: Environment Agency
      PO Box 544
      Rotherham,
      S60 1BY

APPLICANT: John Citizen

ADDRESS FOR CORRESPONDENCE:
      123 Birdcage Walk
      London
      SW1A 6BD
      Tel: 020 - 7654 3210
      Fax: 020 - 7654 3201
      e-mail: jc@world.co.uk

DESCRIPTION OF THE INFORMATION REQUESTED:
All assessments prepared or revised since 1 January 2005 identifying or relating to shortcomings
(howsoever described) in the flood defences in Sheffield, South Yorkshire.

PREFERRED MEANS OF COMMUNICATION:
Provision of a copy of the information in printed form

DATE OF THIS REQUEST:
      Tuesday, 1 June 2010

SIGNED:...
      John Citizen

Precedent 5
Composite request under the Freedom of Information Act 2000 and the Environmental Information Regulations 2004

Request for information made under the Freedom of Information Act
2000 and the Environmental Information Regulations 2004

TO: Department of Environment Food and Rural Affairs
      Attention: The Freedom of Information Unit or Officer
      Nobel House
      17 Smith Square
      London
      SW1P 3JR

APPLICANT: John Citizen

ADDRESS FOR CORRESPONDENCE:
      123 Birdcage Walk
      London
      SW1A 6BD
      Tel: 020 - 7654 3210
      Fax: 020 - 7654 3201
      e-mail: jc@world.co.uk

REQUEST:
I request the information described below. To the extent that the information described below
is "environmental information", this request is made pursuant to the *Environmental Information
Regulations 2004*. To the extent that the information described below is not "environmental
information", this request is made pursuant to the *Freedom of Information Act 2000*.

DESCRIPTION OF THE INFORMATION REQUESTED:
1.   All information taken into account by the Minister in making his decision on or about 1
      January 2010 under reg. 5(5)(a) of the *Control of Pesticides Regulations Act 1986* to suspend
      the authorisation of ABC Chemical UK Limited for one of its products (dichlorvos) ("**the
      Decision**").

2.   To the extent not covered by 1., all information taken into account by any person within
      the Department involved with advising (whether directly or indirectly) the Minister in
      relation to the Decision.

3. To the extent not covered by 1. or 2., all other information held by the Department relating to the authorisation of ABC Chemical UK Limited for dichlorvos.

4. This request excludes [*insert*]

PREFERRED MEANS OF COMMUNICATION:
Provision of a copy of the information in printed form

DATE OF THIS REQUEST:
Tuesday, 1 June 2010

FURTHER INFORMATION:
1. In the event that you believe that information or more information answering the terms of this request is held by another public authority, please advise by return but continue to process this request in relation to all information answering the terms of the request held by you.

2. This request is considered to be perfectly clear. In the event, however, that you require further information in order to identify and locate the information requested, please advise by return.

SIGNED:..
        John Citizen

Notes:
1. The applicant does not need to identify to which statutory regime the right of access belongs.

2. Useful addresses can be found at http://www.tagish.co.uk/links/

3. The request should nominate a body which is a public authority within the meaning of the Act. Identification of the most suitable public authority is important as the obligation is upon that public authority to disclose information that it (and not any other public authority) holds. A public authority may transfer the request if it relates to information that it does not hold but which it believes is held by another public authority.

4. It is not essential to include telephone or fax numbers nor an e-mail address. However, provision of these may speed up matters where the public authority claims that it requires further information from the Applicant in order to identify and locate the information requested.

5. The description of the information requested is very important. It must be as precise as possible. Although it has not been done in this example, it will often be sensible to limit the information by date in some way. Where various sorts of information is sought, it is prudent to enumerate the information in separate paragraphs, each as precise as possible,

as this will help to prevent the whole request being found vexatious and will facilitate severance of its parts in the event that the costs of compliance will involve exceeding the appropriate limit. If there is already certain information the applicant holds, it is desirable to expressly exclude that information from the request, so as to reduce expense and minimise the scope for refusal on the grounds of excessive effort.

6. It is not essential to specify the preferred means of communication, but if it is specified then the public authority must, so far as reasonably practicable, give effect to the preference. Section 11(1) sets out the three means of communication. It is permissible to select more than one means of communication.

7. The Further Information section is entirely optional. It is included in order to maximise the chances of a helpful response.

Precedent 6
Request for internal review (complaint)

Request for internal review (complaint)
Freedom of Information Act 2000 and
Environmental Information Regulations 2004

TO: *insert name and address of public authority*

FROM: *insert name, postal address and e-mail address of applicant*

1.   This is a complaint seeking internal review of a decision refusing me access to information sought under the Freedom of Information Act 2000.

2.   On 5 January 2010 I made a request for information under the Freedom of Information Act 2000, a copy of which is attached.

3.   By letter dated 1 February 2010, *insert name* advised that I would be given access to [none *or* only some] of the information falling within the terms of my request for information. I was informed that access to that information was being refused on the basis that it was exempt information under sections [*insert*] of the Freedom of Information Act 2000 [and regulations [*insert*] of the Environmental Information Regulations 2004] and that the public interest in maintaining the applicable exemptions outweighed the public interest in disclosure. A copy of that letter is attached.

4.   By this letter I seek a review of that decision. Please ensure that you adhere to paragraphs 36-46 of the section 45 Code of Practice. In particular, you should ensure that a full re-evaluation is undertaken by a person senior to *insert name.*

5.   Please acknowledge receipt of this request for review by return e-mail and at the same time let me know your target date for determination of this complaint.

6.   In relation to any item of information falling within the terms of my request for which you claim exemption, please set out each exemption relied upon, the precise basis upon which you rely on that exemption and, if it is a qualified exemption, identify precisely and comprehensively the public in interest in maintaining the exemption in relation to that information.

SIGNED: ....
         John Citizen

DATED: *insert date*

Precedent 7
Complaint to the Information Commissioner

Application under section 50(1) of the Freedom of Information Act 2000

TO: The Information Commissioner's Office
      FOI/EIR Complaints Resolution Team
      Wycliffe House
      Water Lane
      Wilmslow
      Cheshire   SK9 5AF.

MADE BY: John Citizen
           123 Birdcage Walk
           London
           SW1A 6BD

           Tel: 020 - 7654 3210 (daytime)
           Fax: 020 - 7654 3201
           e-mail: jc@world.co.uk

[*also insert, if applicable, name, address and contact details of solicitors*]

PUBLIC AUTHORITY TO WHICH THIS APPLICATION RELATES
Insert name and postal address of public authority
       Tel: *insert*
       Fax: *insert*
       e-mail: *insert*
       Ref: *insert*

SUMMARY OF COMPLAINT:

On *insert date* I sent *insert name of public authority* a request for information under the Freedom of Information Act 2000 [and the Environmental Information Regulations 2004]. A copy of that request is attached.

As at the date of this complaint, I have not received any response from *insert name of public authority*.

or   By letter [*or whatever*] dated *dd/mm/yyyy* the *insert name of public authority* gave me a fees notice stating that the amount of £nnnn would by charged by it for complying with its duties under the Act.. A copy of that letter is attached. For the reasons set out below, the *insert name of public authority* has charged me too much.

or   By letter [*or whatever*] dated *dd/mm/yyyy* the *insert name of public authority* supplied me with certain information, a copy of which is attached. The information I received is not what I requested and the *insert name of public authority* has not provided me with all or any of the information that falls within the terms of my request.

or   By letter [*or whatever*] dated *dd/mm/yyyy* the *insert name of public authority* advised me that it was refusing to give me access to any [*or some*] of the information held by it and falling within the terms of my request. A copy of the refusal letter is attached. For the reasons set out below and so far as I am able to tell, none of the information falling within the terms of my request falls within any provision in Part II of the Freedom of Information Act 2000. Further, even if some information does fall within a provision, to the extent that that provision is a qualified provision, for the reasons set out below, the public interest in maintaining that exemption does not outweigh the public interest in disclosing that information.

or   By letter [*or whatever*] dated *dd/mm/yyyy* the *insert name of public authority* advised me that it does not hold any information answering the terms of my request. A copy of that letter is attached. For the reasons set out below, it is unlikely that the *insert name of public authority* holds no information that falls within the terms of my request and it is therefore likely that the *insert name of public authority* has not complied with its duty to provide me with the information held by it answering the terms of my request.

SUBMISSIONS IN SUPPORT OF MY COMPLAINT

1.   [*insert submissions that support the complaint, including public interest considerations, material relevant to likely harm to a protected interest and so forth*]

In the case of a complaint against a refusal to disclose, conclude with:

n.   I would ask that the Information Commissioner, in dealing with my complaint, require the *insert name of public authority* to supply the Information Commissioner with a copy of all the information answering the terms of my request in order that the Information Commissioner can best determine for himself whether any of the exemptions relied upon by the *insert name of public authority* is properly applicable to the information for which it is claimed and whether the public interest in maintaining that exemption outweighs the public interest in disclosing that information.

....

John Citizen

DATED: *insert date*

Precedent 8
Appeal to the First-Tier Tribunal

First-tier Tribunal (Information Rights)

Notice of Appeal

This form is for making an appeal / application to the First-tier Tribunal (Information Rights) against a decision of the Information Commissioner. The First-tier Tribunal (Information Rights) is administered by the Tribunals Service, an executive agency of the Ministry of Justice, and is independent of the Information Commissioner Please read the guidance *Guide to completing the Notice of Appeal / Application* before completing this form.

First-tier Tribunal (Information Rights) Team
Tribunals Operational Support Centre
PO Box 9300,
Leicester LE1 8DJ

Tel: 0845 600 0877
Fax: 0116 249 4253

Please complete the form legibly, using black ink and capital letters. If you need more space on which to write, please include the name of the person making the appeal and any relevant reference numbers on the paper that you use.

1. About the Information Commissioner's Notice

Information Commissioner's Notice reference number:

Date of the Notice you are appealing:

Date you received the written notification of the Notice:

Please supply a copy of the Notice with this form and tick in the box to show it is attached

2. Disputed Notice

Please indicate the Act under which you are appealing (if you know)

The Data Protection Act 1998- section 48 ☐

The Freedom of Information Act 2000 – Section 57 ☐

The Environmental Information Regulations – Reg 18 ☐

The Freedom of Information Act 2000 – Section 60 or
Data Protection Act – Section 28 ☐
Please include a copy of the disputed certification
(For all notice of appeals under FOIA Section 60 and DPA Section 28, the appeal will be transferred to be heard in the Upper Tribunal)

Please give the details of the public authority to whom your original request for information was sent or the complainant who made the request whichever is applicable:

Name of correspondent: / Public Authority if applicable	

Address:	

Please attach:

(a) a copy of the original request for information, and

(b) a copy of the Information Commissioner's Notice against which you are appealing

Please tick the box to indicate that these documents are attached ☐

3. Time Limit for making an appeal / application

The appellant is required to lodge an appeal with the Tribunal within 28 days of the Information Commissioner's Notice.

The tribunal may accept a notice of appeal outside this time limit under certain circumstances.

The Tribunal will only grant leave to proceed outside of the time limit if you request an extension of time and provide the reason(s) why the notice was not provided in time. The Tribunal will then consider whether to grant you the right to bring your appeal.

Please tick this box if you would like the Tribunal to consider an out of time appeal (see Explanatory Notes) ☐

Please set out below the reasons that you would like the Tribunal to consider when assessing whether to accept your out of time appeal. You can use extra A4 sheets of paper if required.

4. Appellant's details

Name:

Address:

Postcode:

Landline:

Mobile:

Fax:

e-mail:

Organisation name:

Job title:

Preferred mode of communication:

email: post: fax:

Please indicate if you are willing
to accept service of notices and   yes: no:
other documents by e-mail:

5. Representative's details

Firm/organisation:

Address:

Postcode:

Landline:

Mobile:

Fax:

e-mail:

Reference:

Job title:

6. Grounds for Appeal / Application

Please provide full details about the grounds for your appeal. Please add additional pages if required

See attached Grounds for Appeal

7. Supporting Documents

Please list the documents that you wish the Tribunal to consider in support of your appeal.

You can use an extra A4 sheet of paper if required. Please attach the documents and tick the box to indicate that they have been attached ☐

8. Type of Hearing and Venue

Please note that the appeal will be dealt with by reference to all appropriate papers unless you inform the Tribunal you require an oral hearing.

Please indicate whether you wish for the appeal to be dealt with at an oral hearing or based on written submissions, by ticking the appropriate box below (please see explanatory notes before making a selection). Please note that whichever method is preferred a full Tribunal Panel (a legally qualified Judge and two non legal members) will consider the appeal. Oral hearings will usually take longer to arrange

Paper Hearing: ☐

Oral Hearing: ☐

Please note that oral hearings will usually take place in London unless the parties request a hearing elsewhere. Parties will be informed in writing by post or email as soon as hearing date has been set.

1411

9. About your requirements

Please state if you, your representative, or witness has a disability or other special needs that you wish to bring to the Tribunals attention in order to assist the hearing of your appeal. Please also state if an interpreter is required.

10. Signature

NB: The form must be signed and dated by the applicant or someone authorised to do so. If a non-legal representative is appointed, the applicant must file with this Notice of Appeal / Application for Review a written statement, signed by the applicant, that the representative is authorised to act on their behalf.

I am:–   The appellant: [ ]   The Representative of the appellant: [ ]

Name:

Signature:

Date:

Please send your completed form to:
  Information Rights, First-tier Tribunal
  General Regulatory Chamber
  Arnhem House Support Centre
  PO Box 9300
  Leicester LE1 8DJ
  Email: informationtribunal@tribunals.gsi.gov.uk

We can help if you need information in a different format (e.g. Braille, large print). We can also provide this form in Welsh if required. If you need any of these services please contact the Tribunal.

This form can also be downloaded from our website: www.informationtribunal.gov.uk

IN THE FIRST-TIER TRIBUNAL
GENERAL REGULATORY CHAMBER

B E T W E E N:

[Appellant's name]

Appellant

- and -

Information Commissioner

Respondent

GROUNDS FOR APPEAL

Factual background

1.   The Appellant is a journalist with Times Newspapers Ltd ("**the Times**").

2.   The Charity Commission is a public authority within the meaning of the *Freedom of Information Act 2000* ("**FOIA**").

3.   In 1998 George Galloway MP founded "The Mariam Appeal." The Mariam Appeal's namesake is Mariam Hamza. The core activity of the Mariam Appeal was to collect money so as to fund bringing Mariam Hamza, at the time four years old, living in Iraq and suffering from leukaemia, to the UK to receive treatment. Its object also included arranging for medical treatment for other Iraqi children also suffering from leukaemia.

4.   From its creation in 1998 until it ceased operation in early 2003, the known total income of the Mariam Appeal was just under £1,468,000.

5.   In response to a newspaper article written by the Appellant and published in *The Times*, on 24 April 2003 the Charity Commission opened an evaluation into the use of the Mariam Appeal's funds for non-charitable purposes. Following that evaluation, on 27 June 2003 the Charity Commission launched an inquiry under section 8 of the *Charities Act 1993* to investigate how the monies raised for the Appeal between March 1998 and April 1999 had been spent.

6.   At the same time, the Charity Commission continued to evaluate the use of funds in the later stages of the Mariam Appeal. On 13 November 2003 a second inquiry was opened to investigate how monies raised throughout the lifetime of the Mariam Appeal had been expended.

7.   The inquiries launched in April and November 2003 were closed on 17 March 2004.

8.   The Charity Commission concluded that the Mariam Appeal was charitable and should have been registered with the Charity Commission and placed on the Register of Charities: §8. The Charity Commission also concluded that while some of the payments

1413

made to Mr Galloway and the other trustees of the Mariam Appeal were made in breach of trust, because there was no bad faith the Charity Commission would not be pursuing recovery of those sums: §18.

9.   In December 2005, the Charity Commission opened a new inquiry into the Mariam Appeal as a result of allegations that the Mariam Appeal had received donations from contracts made under the UN Oil-for-Food Programme for Iraq.

10.   This inquiry closed in April 2007.

11.   Following this inquiry, the Charity Commission concluded that donations to the Mariam Appeal resulted from improper sources, namely contacts made under the Programme, and that the Mariam Appeal's trustees had failed to sufficiently inquire into the source of the donations: §§30, 33, 43. Accordingly, the Charity Commission concluded that the charity trustees did not properly discharge their duty of care as trustees to the Mariam Appeal in respect of these donations: §46.

Procedural background

12.   By e-mail dated 8 June 2007 the Appellant made a request for information under section 1 of the FOIA to the Charity Commission in the following terms:

> "Please would you let me know in writing if you hold information of the following description:
>
> > Information concerning:
> >
> > > The inquiry into the Mariam Appeal which took place between December 2005 and April 2007, the results published on June 8, 2007.
> >
> > If any part of the information requested is covered by one or more of the absolute exemptions in the Act please treat this request as a request for that part of the information which is not covered by the absolute exemption. If you need further details in order to identify the information requested or a fee is payable please let me know as soon as possible.
> >
> > If you are of the view that there may be further information of the kind requested but it is held by another public authority please let me know as soon as possible. Please continue with this application as soon as possible.
> >
> > I believe that the information requested is required in the public interest for the following reasons:
> >
> > 1. To uphold public confidence that the Charity Commission conducts its inquiries in a spirit of fairness to all parties;
> > 2. To provide assurance that the Charity Commission liaises fully with all relevant authorities so its inquiries are as thorough as possible;
> > 3. To ensure that the Charity Commission spends money correctly when making inquiries into charities and their trustees."

13.   By letter dated 4 July 2007 ("**the Initial Decision**"), the Charity Commission:

(1)   Informed the Appellant that it held information concerning the Inquiry into the Mariam Appeal which took place between December 2005 and April 2007.

(2)   Advised the Appellant that pursuant to its duty to assist applicants (s 16) it had re-cast his request for information into the following:

"Please would you provide me with information about:

The inquiry into the Mariam Appeal which took place between December 2005 and April 2007, its results published on June 8 2007.

Your request appears to encompass all information that the Commission holds regarding the Inquiry. " (**"the Request"**)

(3)   Advised the Appellant that it considered that s 31 of the FOIA was engaged "in respect of information relating to the Mariam Appeal."

(4)   So far as the s 2(2)(b) public interest test and s 31(1) were concerned, advised that it considered that:

"at this time, [the] balance of the public interest weighs more strongly with securing the Commission's ability to carry out its functions efficiently and therefore lies in withholding the information."

(5)   Advised that it also considered that the Appellant's request:

"engages the exemptions under s 27 (international relations), s 32 (information contained in court records and for the purposes of inquiries), section 40 (personal information), section 41 (information provided in confidence) and section 42 (legal professional privilege)."

14.   By letter dated 4 July 2007 the Appellant asked the Charity Commission to review the Initial Decision. By e-mail dated 16 July 2007 the Appellant explained the grounds on which he considered the Initial Decision to be incorrect. He challenged, in particular, the Charity Commission's analysis of the public interest balance.

15.   On 25 July 2007 the Charity Commission gave its written decision on the Appellant's review request. Under the heading "Decision" it wrote:

"3.   The Commission determined that the absolute exemption from disclosure created by section 32(2) of the Act, concerning information which is held pursuant to an inquiry, applies in this case. Although that determination resolved the question raised by the review, the Commission went on to consider whether any of the other exemptions in the Act applied. It concluded that the law enforcement exemption (relied upon in the original decision) in particular applied and, accordingly, also upheld the decision on that additional ground." (**"the Review Decision"**)

Accordingly, the Charity Commission supplied the Appellant with none of the information that it held answering the terms of the Request.

16.   In the course of the letter embodying the Review Decision, the Charity Commission:

(1)   Noted that the request:

"had been for information other than information which is absolutely exempt under the Act" (§14).

(2) "Decided that the absolute exemption from disclosure created by section 32(2) of the Act was applicable to the request" (§16) and:

> "concluded that application of that exemption to the requested information had the result that there was no information held by the Commission that was caught by the request...[and] that that was enough to dispose of the request and to resolve the question raised by the review" (§17).

(3) Having noted that the Initial Decision had relied primarily on other exemptions:

> "decided therefore to consider whether those exemptions would apply even if, contrary to the opinion that they had formed, section 32 had no application to the case" (§18).

(4) Concluded that:

> "a significant proportion of the information obtained during the course of the section 8 inquiry had the requisite quality of confidence"

> so as to engage s 41 of the FOIA (§§19-20).

(5) Noted that "some of the information subject to the request" would engage section 21 (§21).

(6) Noted "that information subject to the request would have included personal information" thereby engaging s 40 of the FOIA (§22).

(7) Without identifying which information falling within the terms of the Request was caught by s 31(1)(g) (§§23-24), proceeded to consider the s 2(2)(b) public interest test (§§25-33), concluding:

> "...that the critical factor weighing against disclosure was the fact that other regulatory bodies are actively considering (in the light of the Commission's findings and those of the Parliamentary Commissioner for Standards) whether they need to conduct investigations themselves." (§33)

(8) Stated their satisfaction that the exemptions provided by ss 27 and 42 of the FOIA "were engaged in this case", before stating that "they considered that it was not necessary to consider the application of those exemptions" (§34).

17. By e-mail dated 30 October 2007 and pursuant to s 50 of the Act, the Appellant applied to the Information Commissioner for a decision whether the Charity Commission had dealt with the Request in accordance with the requirements of Part I of the Act:

> "Please could you review a decision by the Charity Commission to withhold information concerning its inquiry into the Mariam Appeal." ("**the IC Appeal**")

18. By decision notice dated 9 September 2008, the Information Commissioner rejected the IC Appeal, stating:

> "The Commissioner has concluded that all of the requested information is exempt by virtue of the sections 32(2)(a) and 32(2)(b). However, in handling this request the Commissioner has also concluded that the public authority failed to provide a refusal notice compliant with sections 17(1)(b), 17(1)(c) and 17(3) of the Act." ("**the IC Decision**")

19. In the course of explaining the IC Decision, the Information Commissioner:

(1)   Recorded that the Charity Commission had advised him that it held approximately 20 lever arch files of information that fell within the terms of the Request (§10).

(2)   Recorded that the Charity Commission had advised him that it was satisfied:
      "that all of the information that it holds which is the subject of the this request is only held by virtue of being contained in documents acquired or created for the purposes of this particular inquiry." (§16)

(3)   Recorded his belief:
      "....that it is reasonable to conclude that this particular inquiry [*i.e.* the Mariam Inquiry] was one that was being conducted in line with the powers conferred on the public authority by section 8(1) of the Charities Act 1983." (§19)

(4)   Recorded his satisfaction:
      "...that the information held by the public authority in relation to the inquiry was either provided to it by a third party and therefore falls within the scope of section 32(2)(a), or was created by it for the purposes of the inquiry and therefore falls within the scope of section 32(2)(b). In the Commissioner's opinion the information held by the public authority could not fall outside the scope of either of these two sub-sections." (§20)

(5)   Recorded his satisfaction:
      "...that the information falling within the scope of the request is only held by virtue of being contained in the inquiry documents. That is to say, the information is not held by the public authority for any of other purpose." (§21)
      This conclusion was seemingly reached on the basis that as the Mariam Appeal had not been registered as a charity the Charity Commission would not have received or created any documents about it prior to the commencement of its inquiry (§§21-23).

(6)   Concluded that he was therefore satisfied:
      "...that all of the information falling within the scope of the request is exempt on the basis of sections 32(2)(a) and 32(2)(b). As section 32 is an absolute exemption, there is no need for the Commissioner to consider the public interest test as set out at section 2 of the Act." (§24)

(7)   On the basis of the conclusion at (6):
      "[did] not consider it necessary to reach a decision as to the applicability or otherwise of the other exemptions that the public authority also relied upon to withhold the requested information." (§25)

(8)   Decided that the Charity Commission had failed in its duty under section 17 of the FOIA by not explaining why it considered ss 27, 32, 40, 41 and 42 of the FOIA also applied to information falling within the terms of the request and by not explaining why it considered that the public interest test favoured withholding the information (§26).

Points of appeal

20. The Tribunal is asked to consider afresh which information held by the Charity Commission and falling within the terms of the Request is rendered exempt information by s 32 of the FOIA.

21. The Tribunal cannot properly determine this appeal without examining for itself the information held by the Charity Commission that falls within the terms of the Request.

Section 32(2)(a)

22. So far as this exemption is concerned, it will only apply to such information as has all the following attributes:
    (1)   The information must be contained in a document.
    (2)   The document must have been "placed in the custody" of the Charity Commission.
    (3)   The person must have placed the document of the Charity Commission for the purposes of its inquiry.

23. As to attribute (1), information that is recorded electronically (regardless of whether that information is also elsewhere contained in a document) does not satisfy this requirement.

24. As to attribute (2), a person can only be said to have placed a thing "in the custody" of another where that person retains property in that thing and is entitled to request and obtain the return of that thing. For example, person "A" does not "place a document in the custody" of person "B" where B has compelled A to give B the document. Nor, for example, is a document "placed in the custody" of B where B has itself gathered or obtained that document. Nor, for example, is a document "placed in the custody" of B where B is not obliged to return that document to the person from whom B obtained it.

25. As to attribute (3), where a person placed a document in the custody of the Charity Commission before the commencement of the Charity Commission's first inquiry under s 8 of the *Charities Act 1993* (*i.e.* before 27 June 2003) that will not have been for the purposes of the inquiry. Similarly, where a person placed a document in the custody of the Charity Commission after completion of the first inquiry (17 May 2004) and before the commencement of the second inquiry (December 2005) that will not have been for the purposes of the inquiry. And, again, where a person placed a document in the custody of the Charity Commission after completion of the second inquiry (April 2007) that will not have been for the purposes of the inquiry. Even within the dates concerned, a document will only have been placed in the custody of the Charity Commission for the purposes of its inquiry if the donor's purpose in giving it to the Charity Commission related to the particular object of the inquiry. The stated purpose of the first inquiry was "to investigate how the monies raised for the [Mariam] Appeal between March 1998 and April 1999 had been spent" (§5). Later that purpose was extended "to investigate how the monies raised throughout the lifetime of the Appeal had been expended" (§7). The stated purpose of the second inquiry was "to ascertain whether any funds resulting from contracts made under the [U.N. Oil-for-Food] Programme were donated to the Appeal; if so, to establish what was the legal status of those funds; and to examine the extent to

which the trustees of the Appeal properly discharged their duties and responsibilities in receiving those funds" (§15).

26. Further, even where a person placed a document in the custody of the Charity Commission for the purposes of one of its inquiries, both those inquiries having concluded at the time of the Request, no such document remained placed in the custody of the Charity Commission for the purpose of either inquiry.

27. Where the same information is held by the Charity Commission other than by it having been contained in a document satisfying attributes (2) and (3), both instances of the information will be outside s 32(2)(a): that is the effect of the words "only by virtue of." This is so regardless of which instance of the information was first held by the Charity Commission. Thus, information that the Charity Commission has copied over from a document satisfying attributes (2) and (3) will not fall within s 32(2)(a). That information may, however, fall within s 32(2)(b).

Section 32(2)(b)

28. So far as this exemption is concerned, it will only apply to such information as has all the following attributes:
    (1) The information must be contained in a document.
    (2) The document must have been created by the person within the Charity Commission conducting the section 8 inquiry.
    (3) The document must have been created by that person for the purposes of the Charity Commission's inquiry.

29. As to attribute 1, see §23 above.

30. As to attribute 2, the exemption will not cover a document created by someone other than the person within the Charity Commission conducting the section 8 inquiry. Thus, it will not cover a document, created by someone else, but then edited or otherwise modified by the person within the Charity Commission conducting the section 8 inquiry. Nor will it cover a document created by a member of staff of the Charity Commission not actually conducting the section 8 inquiry.

31. As to attribute 3, see §25 above *mutatis mutandis*.

32. The Appellant repeats §27 above.

Other exemptions

33. Neither the Information Commissioner nor the Charity Commission should be permitted in this appeal to rely on any exemption other than s 32(2) of the FOIA. If the Tribunal decides to exercise its discretion to allow the Information Commissioner and/or the Charity Commission (should it be joined), to rely on a further exemption, that should be confined to s 31(1)(g) of the FOIA, being the only provision substantively considered by Charity Commission in the Initial Decision and in the Review Decision.

34.   In the event that the Tribunal allows the Information Commissioner and/or the Charity
        Commission (should it be joined), to rely on an exemption other than s 32(2) of the FOIA,
        the Appellant will then set out his position in relation to those exemptions, including (if
        necessary) his position in relation to the s 2(2)(b) public interest balancing exercise.

DATED:

Precedent 9
 Joinder Notice

IN THE FIRST-TIER TRIBUNAL
GENERAL REGULATORY CHAMBER

B E T W E E N:

H.M. Treasury

Appellant

- and -

The Information Commissioner

Respondent

JOINDER NOTICE

Tribunal Procedure (First-tier Tribunal) (General Regulatory Chamber) Rules 2009, r. 9(3)

REQUEST TO BE ADDED AS A PARTY TO THE APPEAL

1.   By letter dated 1 March 2010 addressed to Joan Citizen, the Tribunal enquired whether Joan Citizen wished to be joined as a party to these proceedings.

2.   With that letter Joan Citizen received a copy of the Information Commissioner's Reply in this appeal, in which the Information Commissioner suggested that Ms Citizen be invited to apply to be joined as a party to this appeal: *Information Commissioner's Reply* §35.

3.   Joan Citizen, being a person that has an interest in the proceedings, hereby gives notice under rule 9(3) of the *Tribunal Procedure (First-tier Tribunal) (General Regulatory Chamber) Rules 2009* that she wishes to be joined to this appeal.

Joan Citizen's interest in this appeal
4.   [*Set out the request and the date it was made; the date of the request for internal review; the response; the date of complaint to the Information Commissioner and the outcome*].

5.   Ms Citizen was and remains acutely interested in receiving the requested information. [*Set out why*]

6.   The joinder of Ms Citizen will ensure that she is not deprived of the opportunity to make representations in an appeal that will determine her right to receive the requested information or any part of it.

7.   By being made a party to the appeal, Ms Citizen will also be able to assist in putting before the Tribunal a balanced account of the information and evidence that it requires in order to determine the appeal, including:

(1) the extent to which the subject matter of the requested information has a continuing and current impact;

(2) the extent of interest in the information sought, the sectors having an interest in the information sought and the nature of that interest;

(3) the extent to which like information has been previously disclosed and the effects of that disclosure;

(4) the extent to which other information relating to the same topic is already in the public domain such that disclosure of the requested information would not be likely to distort public understanding of the issue and/or would add to the account that is already in the public domain;

(5) the extent to which the information would assist in enabling informed public participation and debate upon the subject matter of the requested information; and

(6) generally, the public interest that would be served by the disclosure of the requested information.

8.   Joan Citizen is also anxious that the wider issues arising through the appeal are addressed, namely:

(1) [*set out any wider issues*]

Full name and address of the person seeking to be joined to the appeal
       Joan Citizen
       123 Birdcage Walk
       London
       SW1A 6BD

       Tel: 020 - 7654 3210
       Fax: 020 - 7654 3201
       e-mail: jc@world.co.uk

Name and address of appointed representatives
       Set out name, address, telephone, fax, DX and e-mail details of solicitors

All correspondence and notices concerning the appeal should be sent to the above-named representatives.

REPLY TO THE NOTICE OF APPEAL

Unless otherwise stated, all references to paragraphs are to paragraphs of the
Appellant's Grounds of Appeal, dated 15 January 2010

Introductory

9.   Ms Citizen notes paragraph 1.

10.   Ms Citizen puts in issue paragraph 2.

11.   As to paragraphs 3-9:

    (1) This does not constitute a full or balanced summary of the events.

    (2) In particular, the Appellant is put to proof that [*insert*].

    (3) Ms Citizen puts the Appellant to proof as to each of the assertions made in paragraph 6.

    (4) Ms Citizen puts the Appellant to proof of there being confidentiality in the documents described in paragraph 7.

    (5) Ms Citizen puts the Appellant to proof that disclosure of the requested information would have an adverse effect on [*insert*].

The exemptions relied upon by the Appellant

12.   As to paragraphs 10-18:

    (1) Ms Citizen notes:

        (a) that the Appellant identifies section 35(1)(a) of the *Freedom of Information Act 2000* as the "key" applicable exemption;

        (b) that the Appellant contends that none of the requested information is statistical information within the meaning of section 35(2) of the Act, but that if (contrary to the Appellant's primary position) it is, the Appellant relies on section 36(2)(b) of the Act as the applicable exemption; and

        (c) that the Appellant does not rely on any other exemption in Part II of the Act.

    (2) Ms Citizen puts the Appellant to proof that all or any of the requested information relates to the formulation or development of government policy.

    (3) Ms Citizen puts the Appellant to proof that none of the requested information constitutes statistical information within the meaning of section 35(2) of the Act.

    (4) Ms Citizen puts the Appellant to proof that disclosure of any statistical information within the requested information would or would be likely to inhibit the free and frank disclosure of advice.

(5) Ms Citizen puts the Appellant to proof that disclosure of any statistical information within the requested documents would or would be likely to inhibit the free and frank exchange of views for the purposes of deliberation.

The public interest

13. As to paragraphs 19-33:

(1) In relation to each and every item of requested information, Ms Citizen puts the Appellant to proof that in all the circumstances of the case, the public interest in maintaining the section 35(1)(a) exemption outweighs the public interest in disclosing that information.

(2) In relation to each and every item of requested information, Ms Citizen puts the Appellant to proof that that information does not constitute factual information that has been used, or that was intended to be used, to provide an informed background to decision-taking.

(3) To the extent that the requested information is statistical information within the meaning of section 35(2), Ms Citizen puts the Appellant to proof that in all the circumstances of the case, the public interest in maintaining the section 36(2)(b) exemption outweighs the public interest in disclosing that information.

14. Specifically:

(1) Ms Citizen puts in issue that all or any of the requested information constituted or formed part of a "wide-ranging discussion of sensitive policy issues" or "candid debate" or a "risk assessment."

(2) Ms Citizen puts the Appellant to proof that the requested information relates to government policy that is currently being developed or formulated. The requested information relates to government policy that was formulated, developed, settled and then implemented some 2 years ago.

(3) Ms Citizen puts the Appellant to proof that disclosure of any of the requested information (being information that is now over 2 years old) would in future inhibit a due consideration of the formulation or development of government policy on this or related topics.

(4) Ms Citizen puts the Appellant to proof that disclosure of any of the requested information (being information that is now over 2 years old) would weaken the decision-making process or confidence in that process.

(5) Ms Citizen puts the Appellant to proof that disclosure of all or any of the requested information (being information that is now over 2 years old) would or would be likely to have a detrimental effect on the quality of advice or of policy decision-making.

(6) Ms Citizen puts the Appellant to proof that the requested information would or would be likely to be taken out of context or misunderstood.

(7) Ms Citizen puts the Appellant to proof that disclosure of all or any of the requested information (being information that is now over 2 years old) would in future prejudice the provision of candid and frank advice to Ministers on such matters.

15. Further:

(1) None of the matters identified by the Appellant in its *Grounds of Appeal*, even if proven, would sufficiently support the public interest in maintaining the section 35 or 36 exemption in relation to the requested information.

(2) The section 35(1)(a) exemption is directed to the *formulation* or *development* of policy, and the public interest in maintaining that exemption is materially lessened once the policy has been developed and formulated.

(3) The public interest in maintaining the exemptions in sections 35 and 36 is highly time-sensitive.

(4) By placing into the public domain a considerable amount of information about [*insert*] the Appellant acknowledged the public interest in disclosure of official information relating to [*insert*].

(5) The Appellant has already released into the public domain policy discussion documents relating to [*insert*] (including those released as part of the internal review process). To the extent (if any) that release of policy discussion by officials would have a "chilling" effect on future policy advice, that effect will have already resulted from material already released into the public domain and by the prospect of further such material being thus released into the public domain. There is no objective evidence that release of the requested information will have an additional "chilling effect" sufficient for the public interest in maintaining the section 35(1)(a) exemption to outweigh the public interest in disclosing the requested information.

16. There is a compelling public interest in disclosing the information as:

(1) It relates to a decision that had and continues to have a significant impact on a significant proportion of the population.

(2) It would provide a fuller picture of the thinking behind the [*insert*], thereby making the decision-making process more transparent.

(3) It would facilitate a reasoned analysis of the basis for [*insert*].

(4) It would facilitate informed debate on [*insert*].

(5) It would foster understanding and appreciation of the reasons for [*insert*].

(6) It would reassure interested members of the public that all policy options were considered before the policy was selected and implemented.

(7) It would increase confidence in the policy-making process.

(8) It would enhance the openness and accountability of [*insert*].

(9) It would lessen unnecessary secrecy in Government.

(10)   It will assist in transforming the culture of Government to one of openness.

17.   To the extent that the requested information constitutes factual information that has been used to provide an informed background to decision-taking, there is a particular public interest in disclosure.

DATED: 1 June 2010

Procedural Guides for Dealing
with Requests for Information

Dealing with a Request for Information under the
Freedom of Information Act 2000

Time limits

1.   Step 1 to Step 5 (inclusive) must, as a general rule, be complied with promptly and in any event not later than the twentieth working-day following the "date of receipt" of the request. The time-limit will be deferred in certain circumstances.

2.   Step 6 to Step 9 (inclusive), if not already complied with at the same time as Step 5, must as a general rule thereafter be complied with within such time as is reasonable in the circumstances.

Step 1   Determining whether the request is a valid request.

1.   The recipient of the request must be a "public authority" to which the FOI Act applies.

2.   The request must:
    — be in writing;
    — state the name of the applicant;
    — state an address for correspondence; and
    — describe the information requested.
If there are formal details missing, the recipient public authority may have to help the applicant as part of its duty to advise and assist.

3.   The request must be adequately particularised in order to enable the recipient public authority to identify and locate the information. If it is not adequately particularised, the public authority is not obliged to provide the information nor otherwise to deal with the request. The public authority may be obliged to assist the applicant adequately particularise the request.

4.   The public authority should determine whether the cost of compliance with the request would be excessive. As to the form of the refusal notice if the cost of compliance is excessive. The public authority may be obliged to assist the applicant in these circumstances.

5.   The public authority should determine whether the request is vexatious. As to the form of the refusal notice if the request is vexatious.

6.   The public authority should determine whether the request is a repeat request. As to the form of the refusal notice if it is a repeat request. As to the cumulative cost of compliance.

7.   The identity and motive of the applicant are generally irrelevant to the validity of a request.

Step 2   Locating the information that answers the terms of the request.

1.   The recipient public authority must search for and locate the information held by it that answers the terms of the request. Determine if what is sought:

    —   is "information" for the purposes of the Act;

    —   is "held" by a public authority;

    —   information that may be altered by a public authority after receipt of a request but before answering it.

2.   The recipient public authority must identify which of the information located is "environmental information". Environmental information must be dealt with under the Environmental Information Regulations 2004 (see separate guide following).

3.   If the recipient public authority believes that another public authority holds the requested information, it may be necessary to transfer the request to that public authority.

4.   If the recipient public authority locates either no information or only some information answering the terms of the request, some explanation to the applicant may be required.

Step 3   Identifying any exempt information.

1.   Although information constitutes exempt information according to whether it falls within one or more of the provisions of Part II of the Act (ss 21–44), where more than one such provision applies to information, a public authority may, in refusing a request, choose the provision or provisions upon which it relies. For each provision relied upon, the public authority must bear in mind whether it is an absolute exemption or a qualified exemption: see paras 2-4 below.

2.   In relation to each item of information answering the terms of the request, determine whether that information is exempt by reason of a purely class-based, absolute exemption. That is to say, the public authority must determine whether that information:

    (1)   constitutes information that is reasonably accessible to the applicant otherwise than under the FOI Act;

    (2)   constitutes information held by the requested public authority that was directly or indirectly supplied to it by, or that relates to, any of the specified security bodies;

    (3)   constitutes information held by the requested public authority only by virtue of that information being contained in a formal document filed with a court or tribunal, in a formal document served for the purposes of court or tribunal proceedings, or in a formal document created by a court or by staff of a court;

    (4)   constitutes information held by the requested public authority only by virtue of it being contained in a document placed in the custody of a person conducting an inquiry or arbitration, or in a document created by a person conducting an inquiry or arbitration, for the purposes of the inquiry or arbitration;

    (5)   constitutes information for which exemption is required for the purpose of avoiding an infringement of the privileges of either House of Parliament;

    (6)   constitutes personal data of which the applicant is the data subject;

(7)   constitutes personal data of which the applicant is not the data subject, that is not manual data and the disclosure of which would contravene one of the data protection principles;

(8)   constitutes personal data of which the applicant is not the data subject and the disclosure of which would contravene one of the data protection principles (in the case of manual data, disregarding the exemptions from the data protection principles granted by s 33A of the Data Protection Act 1998);

(9)   constitutes information obtained by the public authority from any other person (including another public authority) the disclosure of which would constitute an actionable breach of confidence by the public authority; or

(10) constitutes information the disclosure of which is prohibited by or under an enactment, is incompatible with any Community obligation or would constitute a contempt of court.

3.   In relation to each item of information answering the terms of the request, determine whether that information is exempt by reason of a prejudice-based, absolute exemption. That is to say, the public authority must determine whether it constitutes information held by the House of Commons or the House of Lords that, in the reasonable opinion of the Speaker of the House of Commons or the Clerk of the Parliaments respectively, if disclosed under the FOI Act, would or would be likely to:

(i)   prejudice the convention of the collective responsibility of Ministers of the Crown etc;

(ii)   inhibit the free and frank provision of advice or exchange of views for the purposes of deliberation; or

(iii) otherwise prejudice the effective conduct of public affairs;

4.   In relation to each item of information answering the terms of the request, determine whether that information is exempt by reason of a purely class-based, qualified exemption. That is to say, the public authority must determine whether that information:

(1)   constitutes information intended for future publication;

(2)   constitutes confidential information obtained from a foreign state or from an international organisation or court;

(3)   constitutes information held by a public authority for the purposes of a criminal investigation or proceedings;

(4)   constitutes information relating to the formulation of government policy;

(5)   constitutes communications with Her Majesty or the Royal Household;

(6)   constitutes environmental information; or

(7)   constitutes information in respect of which a claim to legal professional privilege could be maintained.

5.   In relation to each item of information answering the terms of the request, determine whether that information is exempt by reason of a prejudice-based, qualified exemption. That is to say, the public authority must determine whether that information:

(1)   constitutes information whose exemption is required for the purpose of safeguarding national security;

1429

(2)   constitutes information whose disclosure would or would be likely to prejudice the defence of the British Islands or colonies or the armed forces;

(3)   constitutes information whose disclosure would or would be likely to prejudice relations between the United Kingdom and any other State or international organisation or to prejudice the interests of the United Kingdom abroad;

(4)   constitutes information whose disclosure would or would be likely to prejudice relations between administrations within the United Kingdom;

(5)   constitutes information the disclosure of which would or would be likely to prejudice the economic or financial interests of the United Kingdom or any part of it;

(6)   constitutes information the disclosure of which would or would be likely to prejudice the prevention or detection of crime, etc.;

(7)   constitutes information the disclosure of which would or would be likely to endanger the physical or mental health of an individual or endanger an individual's safety;

(8)   constitutes information that would or would be likely to prejudice an auditing body's audit functions;

(9)   constitutes information, other than that held by the House of Commons or the House of Lords that, in the reasonable opinion of a qualified person, if disclosed under the FOI Act, would or would be likely to:

    (i)   prejudice the convention of the collective responsibility of Ministers of the Crown, etc;

    (ii) inhibit the free and frank provision of advice or exchange of views for the purposes of deliberation; or

    (iii) otherwise prejudice the effective conduct of public affairs or

(10)   constitutes a trade secret or constitutes information the disclosure of which would or would be likely to prejudice the commercial interests of any person.

6.   Where:

(1)   either:

    (a) it appears to a public authority that information is not exempt information; or

    (b) although the information is exempt information, the public authority does not intend to rely on a particular provision in Part II (ss 21–44) of the Act, and

(2)   disclosure of the information, or of the existence of the information, will have implications for a third party,

then the public authority should, as a matter of good practice, give consideration to consulting with that third party before concluding Step 3.

Step 4   In relation to exempt information, determining whether under Part II of the FOI Act the existence duty does not arise.

1.   This Step need not be complied with in relation to exempt information that has been (or within the time-limit will be) communicated to the applicant in accordance with s 1(1)(b)

of the Act. In other words, it need not be complied with in relation to information rendered exempt information only by one or more qualified exemptions, where the public authority has, within the time-limit, reached a decision that, in all the circumstances of the case, the public interest in maintaining the exemption does not outweigh the public interest in disclosing the information and has communicated the information to the applicant

2. In relation to other exempt information, the public authority must determine if the duty on it to inform the applicant whether it holds information of the description specified in the request does not arise by reason of a provision in Pt II (ss 21–44) of the FOI Act. Subject to the public interest weighing exercise (Step 7), the duty to confirm or deny will not arise:

(1) Where the information sought:
    (a) has at any time been held for the purposes of a criminal investigation or is confidential information obtained for the purposes of the authority's functions relating to such an investigation;
    (b) has at any time been held as part of court or arbitral proceedings;
    (c) is held by a government department and relates to the formulation of policy or to Ministerial communications;
    (d) relates to communications with the Royal Family or the conferring of honours or dignities;
    (e) is required to be made available under the access to environmental information provisions; or
    (f) constitutes personal data of which the applicant is the data subject,
    then the public authority is excused from the duty to confirm or deny that such information is held.

(2) Where, or to the extent that, exclusion from confirmation or denial of a holding of the information sought is required:
    (a) to safeguard national security;
    (b) to avoid an infringement of the privileges of either House of Parliament;
    (c) to avoid an actionable breach of confidence;
    (d) to maintain the possibility of a claim of legal professional privilege; or
    (e) to avoid contravention of an enactment or of a community obligation, or to avoid a contempt of court,
    then the public authority is excused from the duty to confirm or deny that any information answering the request is held.

(3) Where the information sought:
    (a) is intended for future publication;
    (b) is supplied by, or relates to, bodies dealing with security matters; or
    (c) is confidential information obtained from the Government of any State other than the United Kingdom or from an international organisation or court,
    then the duty to confirm or deny does not arise if, or to the extent that, confirmation or denial that the requested public authority holds the information

sought would itself involve the disclosure of any information so exempted from disclosure.

(4) Where confirmation or denial that the public authority holds the information sought would, or would be likely to, prejudice:
   (a) the defence of the nation or the effectiveness of the armed forces;
   (b) relations between the United Kingdom and another state or an international organisation or the interests of the United Kingdom abroad;
   (c) governmental relations within the United Kingdom;
   (d) the economic interests of the United Kingdom or the financial interests of any administration within the United Kingdom;
   (e) the efficacy of law enforcement;
   (f) the exercise of an auditing body's functions;
   (g) Cabinet confidentiality, the frank provision of advice or the effective conduct of public affairs;
   (h) the physical or mental health or safety of an individual; or
   (i) the commercial interests of a person,
   then the duty to confirm or deny is, to that extent, disapplied.

(5) Where the information sought constitutes personal data of which the applicant is not the data subject and where confirmation or denial that the public authority holds the information requested would contravene one of the data protection principles or s 10 of the Data Protection Act 1998 or the information is exempt from s 7(1)(a) of that Act, then the duty to confirm or deny is, to that extent, disapplied.

3. In relation to:
   (1) information accessible to a applicant by other means; and
   (2) information that constitutes a trade secret,
   there is no disapplication of the duty to confirm or deny the existence of such information.

Step 5   The first part of the response.

1. Having carried out Step 1 to Step 4, the public authority must respond promptly and in any event within specified time-limits.

2. The public authority may decide to give the applicant a fees notice. If a fees notice is given, this will defer the date for compliance with Step 5 for the period during which the fees notice is unsatisfied. In relation to the fees that may be sought. If the public authority has not received the fee within 3 months of the fees notice having been given to the applicant, the public authority is thereafter not obliged to comply with the request.

The duty to communicate

3. Where information is required to be communicated to the applicant, the means by which the recipient public authority does so may need to be in accordance with a preference expressed by the applicant. By communicating the information, the public authority is excused from compliance with the duty to confirm or deny in relation to that information

and, so far as that information is concerned, that concludes the public authority's duties under s 1(1).

4. Where the public authority is not obliged to communicate information on the basis that it is exempted by an absolute exemption, the public authority must, within the required time, give a refusal notice that includes all the details required by s 17(1). The public authority may also be required to confirm or deny the existence of information (see paras 6-8 below).

5. Where the information is rendered exempt information by a qualified exemption, then:
    (1) If the public authority has, within the time specified in s 10(1), reached a decision that in all the circumstances of the case, the public interest in maintaining the exemption outweighs the public interest in disclosing the information, then the public authority must within the specified period give a notice that includes:
        — all the details required by s 17(1); and
        — a statement of the reasons for the claim that, in all the circumstances of the case, the public interest in maintaining the exemption outweighs the public interest in disclosing the information.
    (2) If the public authority has not, within the time specified in s 10(1), reached a decision that, in all the circumstances of the case, the public interest in maintaining the exemption outweighs the public interest in disclosing the information, then the public authority must within the specified period give a notice that includes:
        — all the details required by s 17(1);
        — an indication that no decision as to the application of s 2(2)(b) has yet been reached; and
        — an estimate of the date by which the public authority expects the public interest weighing decision to have been reached.
    The public authority will then have to deal with Step 6 and Step 8 (i.e. weighing the public interest and informing the applicant of the outcome of that process). In either case, the public authority may also be required to confirm or deny the existence of information (see paras 6–8 below).

The duty to confirm or deny
6. Where, or to the extent that, under Step 4, a public authority is not obliged to inform the applicant that it holds information of the description specified in the request on the basis that the duty to confirm or deny is excluded by an absolute exclusion, the public authority must, within the time-limit, give a refusal notice that includes all the details required by s 17(1). So far as that information is concerned, that concludes the public authority's duties under s 1(1) of the Act.

7. Where, or to the extent that, under Step 4, a public authority is not obliged to inform the applicant that it holds information of the description specified in the request on the basis that the duty to confirm or deny is excluded by a qualified exclusion and:
    (1) The public authority has, within the time specified in s 10(1), reached a decision that in all the circumstances of the case, the public interest in maintaining the

1433

exclusion of the duty to confirm or deny outweighs the public interest in disclosing whether the public authority holds the information, then the public authority must within the time-limit give a notice that includes:

— all the details required by s 17(1); and

— a statement of the reasons for the claim that, in all the circumstances of the case, the public interest in maintaining the exclusion outweighs the public interest in disclosing whether the public authority holds the information.

So far as that information is concerned, that concludes the public authority's duties under s 1(1) of the Act.

(2)   The public authority has not, within the time specified in s 10(1), reached a decision that, in all the circumstances of the case, the public interest in maintaining the exclusion of the duty to confirm or deny outweighs the public interest in disclosing whether the public authority holds the information, then the public authority must within the time-limit give a notice that includes:

— all the details required by s 17(1);

— an indication that no decision as to the application of s 2(1)(b) has yet been reached; and

— an estimate of the date by which the public authority expects the public interest weighing decision to have been reached.

So far as this information is concerned, the public authority will then have to deal with Step 7 and Step 8.

8.   Where, or to the extent that, under Step 4, a public authority is obliged to inform the applicant that it holds information of the description specified in the request but is not, under Step 3, obliged to communicate that information to the applicant, the public authority must inform the applicant in writing that it holds information of the description specified in the request. So far as that information is concerned, that concludes the public authority's duties under s 1(1) of the Act.

Step 6   In relation to each item of information to which para 5(2) in Step 5 applies, determining whether the public interest in maintaining the exemption outweighs the public interest in disclosing the information.

1.   As to the manner in which the public interest is to be weighed, see Ch 14.

2.   Where information relates to a third party, it may be prudent to consult the third party before making the public interest determination.

Step 7   Where para 7(2) in Step 5 applies, determining whether the public interest in maintaining the exclusion of the duty to confirm or deny outweighs the public interest in disclosing whether the public authority holds the information.

1.   As to the manner in which the public interest is to be weighed, see Ch 14.

Step 8   The second part of the response.

1.   The second part of the response is only required where the public authority, having to any extent relied upon a claim that s 2(1)(b) or 2(2)(b) applies (i.e. that the public interests weighed in favour of exemption/exclusion), did not in the first part of the response (Step 5) state that it was so relying on s 2 and state the reasons for that claim.

2.   The public authority must respond within such time as is reasonable in the circumstances.

The duty to communicate

3.   Where the public interest in maintaining the exemption outweighs the public interest in disclosing the information, the public authority must within the reasonable time, give a separate notice that states the reasons for the claim that, in all the circumstances of the case, the public interest in maintaining the exemption outweighs the public interest in disclosing the information.

4.   Where the public interest in maintaining the exemption does not outweigh the public interest in disclosing the information, the public authority must communicate the information to the applicant. So far as that information is concerned, that concludes the public authority's duties under s 1(1).

5.   Where information is required to be communicated to the applicant, the means by which the recipient public authority does so may need to be in accordance with a preference expressed by the applicant.

The duty to confirm or deny

6.   Where, or to the extent that, under Step 5, a public authority is not obliged to inform the applicant that it holds information of the description specified in the request on the basis that the public interest in maintaining the exclusion of the duty to confirm or deny outweighs the public interest in disclosing that the public authority holds the information, the public authority must, within the reasonable time, give a separate notice that states the reasons for the claim that, in all the circumstances of the case, the public interest in maintaining the exemption outweighs the public interest in disclosing the information. So far as that information is concerned, that concludes the public authority's duties under s 1(1) of the Act.

Step 9   Discretionary disclosure and assisting the applicant.

1.   Where, as a result of the exercise in Step 5 or Step 8, the information requested by the applicant is not required to be disclosed, the public authority may:

   (1)   Consider whether as a matter of discretion the information should be disclosed; and

   (2)   Otherwise offer the applicant assistance. In particular, where the applicant has another statutory means of access to some or all the information requested (e.g. under the Data Protection Act 1998), the public authority should so advise the applicant.

   (3)   Where a public authority has, in part or in whole, refused a request for information, it should, as a matter of good practice, advise the applicant of his rights of appeal.

Dealing with a Request for Information under the Environmental Information Regulations 2004

Time limits

1. Step 1 to Step 5 (inclusive) must, as a general rule, be complied with promptly and in any event not later than the twentieth working-day following the "date of receipt" of the request. The time-limit will be deferred in certain circumstances.

2. Step 6 to Step 9 (inclusive), if not already complied with at the same time as Step 5, must as a general rule thereafter be complied with within such time as is reasonable in the circumstances.

Step 1   Determining whether the request is a valid request.

1. The recipient of the request must be a "public authority" to which the EIR apply.

2. The request:
    — need not be in writing;
    — should state the name of the applicant; and
    — must describe the information requested.

    If there are formal details missing, the recipient public authority may have to help the applicant as part of its duty to advise and assist.

3. The request must be adequately particularised in order to enable the recipient public authority to identify and locate the information. If the request is vague, the public authority is not obliged to provide the information. The public authority may be obliged to assist the applicant adequately particularise the request.

4. The public authority should determine whether the request is manifestly unreasonable.

5. The identity and motive of the applicant are generally irrelevant to the validity of a request.

Step 2   Locating the information that answers the terms of the request.

1. The recipient public authority must search for and locate the information held by it that answers the terms of the request. Check if what is sought:
    — is "information" for the purposes of the Regulations;
    — is "held" by a public authority;
    — information that may be altered by a public authority after receipt of a request but before answering it.

2. If the recipient public authority believes that another public authority holds the requested information, it may be necessary to transfer the request to that public authority.

3. If the recipient public authority locates either no information or only some information answering the terms of the request, some explanation to the applicant may be required.

Step 3   Identifying any excepted information.

1.   Although information constitutes excepted information according to whether it falls within one or more of the provisions of Part 3 of the Regulations, where more than one such provision applies to information, a public authority may, in refusing a request, choose the provision or provisions upon which it relies. For each provision relied upon, the public authority must bear in mind whether it is an absolute exemption or a qualified exception.

2.   In relation to each item of information answering the terms of the request, determine whether that information is exempt by reason of a purely class-based, absolute exception. That is to say, the public authority must determine whether:

(1)   the public authority is acting in a judicial or legislative capacity;

(2)   the public authority is one of the Houses of Parliament and disclosure would constitute an infringement of the privileges of either House;

(3)   constitutes personal data of which the applicant is not the data subject, that is not manual data and the disclosure of which would contravene one of the data protection principles;

(4)   constitutes personal data of which the applicant is not the data subject and the disclosure of which would contravene one of the data protection principles (in the case of manual data, disregarding the exemptions from the data protection principles granted by s 33A of the Data Protection Act 1998); or

(5)   the information is already publicly available and easily accessible to the applicant in another form or format.

3.   In relation to each item of information answering the terms of the request, determine whether that information is excepted by reason of a purely class-based, qualified exception. That is to say, the public authority must determine whether the request involves the disclosure of internal communications.

4.   In relation to each item of information answering the terms of the request, determine whether that information is exempt by reason of a prejudice-based, qualified exception. That is to say, the public authority must determine whether disclosure of that information would adversely affect:

(1)   international relations, defence, national security or public safety;

(2)   the course of justice, the ability of a person to receive a fair trial or the ability of a public authority to conduct an inquiry of a criminal or disciplinary nature;

(3)   intellectual property rights;

(4)   the confidentiality of the proceedings of that or any other public authority where such confidentiality is provided by law;

(5)   the confidentiality of commercial or industrial information where such confidentiality is provided by law to protect a legitimate economic interest;

(6)   the interests of the person who provided that information, where that person:

(i)   was not under, and could not have been put under, any legal obligation to supply it to that or any other public authority,

(ii)   did not supply it in circumstances such that that or any other public authority is entitled apart from the regulations to disclose it, and

    (iii)   has not consented to its disclosure;
    (7)   the request relates to material that is still in the course of completion, to unfinished documents or to incomplete data; or
    (8)   the protection of the environment to which the information relates.

6.   Where:
    (1)   either:
        (a) it appears to a public authority that information is not excepted information; or
        (b) although the information is excepted information, the public authority does not intend to rely on a particular provision in Part 3 of the Regulations, and
    (2)   disclosure of the information, or of the existence of the information, will have implications for a third party,
    then the public authority should, as a matter of good practice, give consideration to consulting with that third party before concluding Step 3.

Step 4   **In relation to each item of information to which para 4 in Step 3 applies, determining whether the public interest in maintaining the exception outweighs the public interest in disclosing the information.**

1.   As to the manner in which the public interest is to be weighed, see Ch 15.

2.   Where information relates to a third party, it may be prudent to consult the third party before making the public interest determination.

Step 5   **In relation to excepted information falling within para 4(1) in Step 3, determining whether confirmation or denial that the public authority holds the information would adversely affect international relations, defence, national security or public safety.**

1.   This Step need not be complied with in relation to excepted information that has been (or within the time-limit will be) communicated to the applicant in accordance with the Regulations. In other words, it need not be complied with in relation to information rendered excepted information only by one or more qualified exceptions, where the public authority has, reached a decision that, in all the circumstances of the case, the public interest in maintaining the exceptions does not outweigh the public interest in disclosing the information and has communicated the information to the applicant.

2.   In relation to other excepted information falling within para 4(1) in Step 3, the public authority must inform the applicant whether it holds information of the description specified in the request unless to do so would adversely affect adversely affect international relations, defence, national security or public safety and to do so would not be in the public interest .

Step 6   **The response.**
1.   Having carried out Step 1 to Step 5, the public authority must respond promptly and in any event within specified time-limits.

2.   The public authority may decide to give the applicant a fees notice. If a fees notice is given, this will defer the date for compliance with Step 4 for the period during which the fees notice is unsatisfied. In relation to the fees that may be sought, see Ch 6.

3.   Where information is required to be communicated to the applicant, the means by which the recipient public authority does so may need to be in accordance with a preference expressed by the applicant.

4.   Where the public authority is not obliged to communicate information, the public authority must, within the required time, give a refusal notice that includes all the details required.

Step 7   Discretionary disclosure and assisting the applicant.
1.   Where, as a result of the exercise in Step 3 or Step 4, the information requested by the applicant is not required to be disclosed, the public authority may:
   (1)   Consider whether as a matter of discretion the information should be disclosed; and
   (2)   Otherwise offer the applicant assistance. In particular, where the applicant has another statutory means of access to some or all the information requested (e.g. under the Data Protection Act 1998), the public authority should so advise the applicant.
   (3)   Where a public authority has, in part or in whole, refused a request for information, it should, as a matter of good practice, advise the applicant of his rights of appeal.

Parliamentary History of the Freedom of Information Act 2000

House of Commons
First reading:
  18 November 1999: *Hansard*, vol 339, col 124

Second reading:
  7 December 1999: *Hansard*, vol 340, cols 714-798

Standing Committee B:
  1st Sitting, 21 December 1999;
  2nd Sitting, 11 January 2000 (morning);
  3rd Sitting, 11 January 2000 (afternoon);
  4th Sitting, 18 January 2000 (morning);
  5th Sitting, 18 January 2000 (afternoon);
  6th Sitting, 20 January 2000;
  7th Sitting, 25 January 2000 (morning);
  8th Sitting, 25 January 2000 (afternoon);
  9th Sitting, 27 January 2000;
  10th Sitting, 1 February 2000 (morning);
  11th Sitting, 1 February 2000 (afternoon);
  12th Sitting, 8 February 2000 (morning);
  13th Sitting, 8 February 2000 (afternoon);
  14th Sitting, 10 February 2000

Debate:
  4 April 2000: *Hansard*, vol 347, cols 830-935,
  5 April 2000: *Hansard*, vol 347, cols 981-1123

Third reading:
  5 April 2000: *Hansard*, vol 347, col 1123

Debate:
  27 November 2000: *Hansard*, vol 357, cols 663-781

House of Lords
First reading:
  6 April 2000: *Hansard*, vol 611, col 1490

Second reading:
  20 April 2000: *Hansard*, vol 612, col 823-893

Committee:
  17 October 2000: *Hansard*, vol 617, cols 883-954 and 971-1020
  19 October 2000: *Hansard*, vol 617, cols 1208-1300
  24 October 2000: *Hansard*, vol 618, cols 273-314
  25 October 2000: *Hansard*, vol 618, cols 407-476

Debate:
  14 November 2000: *Hansard*, vol 619, cols 134-158 and 173-266

Third reading:
  14 November 2000: *Hansard*, vol 619, col 817

Royal Assent
  30 November 2000

FOIA and FOI(S)A Comparative Table

FOIA section	Description	FOI(S)A section
21	Information available by other means	25
22	Information intended for future publication	27
23	Information supplied by or relating to national security bodies	-
24	National security	31
25	Certificates	-
26	Defence	31
27	International relations	32
28	Relations within the United Kingdom	28
29	The economy	33
30	Investigations and proceedings by public bodies	34
31	Law enforcement	35
32	Court records etc	37
33	Audit functions	40
34	Parliamentary privilege	-
35	Formulation of government policy	29
36	Prejudice to effective control of public affairs	30
37	Communications with Her Majesty etc and honours	41
38	Health and safety	39
39	Environmental information	39
40	Personal information	38
41	Information provided in confidence	36
42	Legal professional privilege	36
43	Commercial interests	33
44	Prohibitions on disclosure	26

Index

Introductory Note

References such as '178–9' indicate (not necessarily continuous) discussion of a topic across a range of pages. Wherever possible in the case of topics with many references, these have either been divided into sub-topics or only the most significant discussions of the topic are listed. Because the entire work is about 'information rights', the use of this term and certain others which occur constantly throughout the book as entry points has been minimized. Information will be found under the corresponding detailed topics.